Mexico & Central America

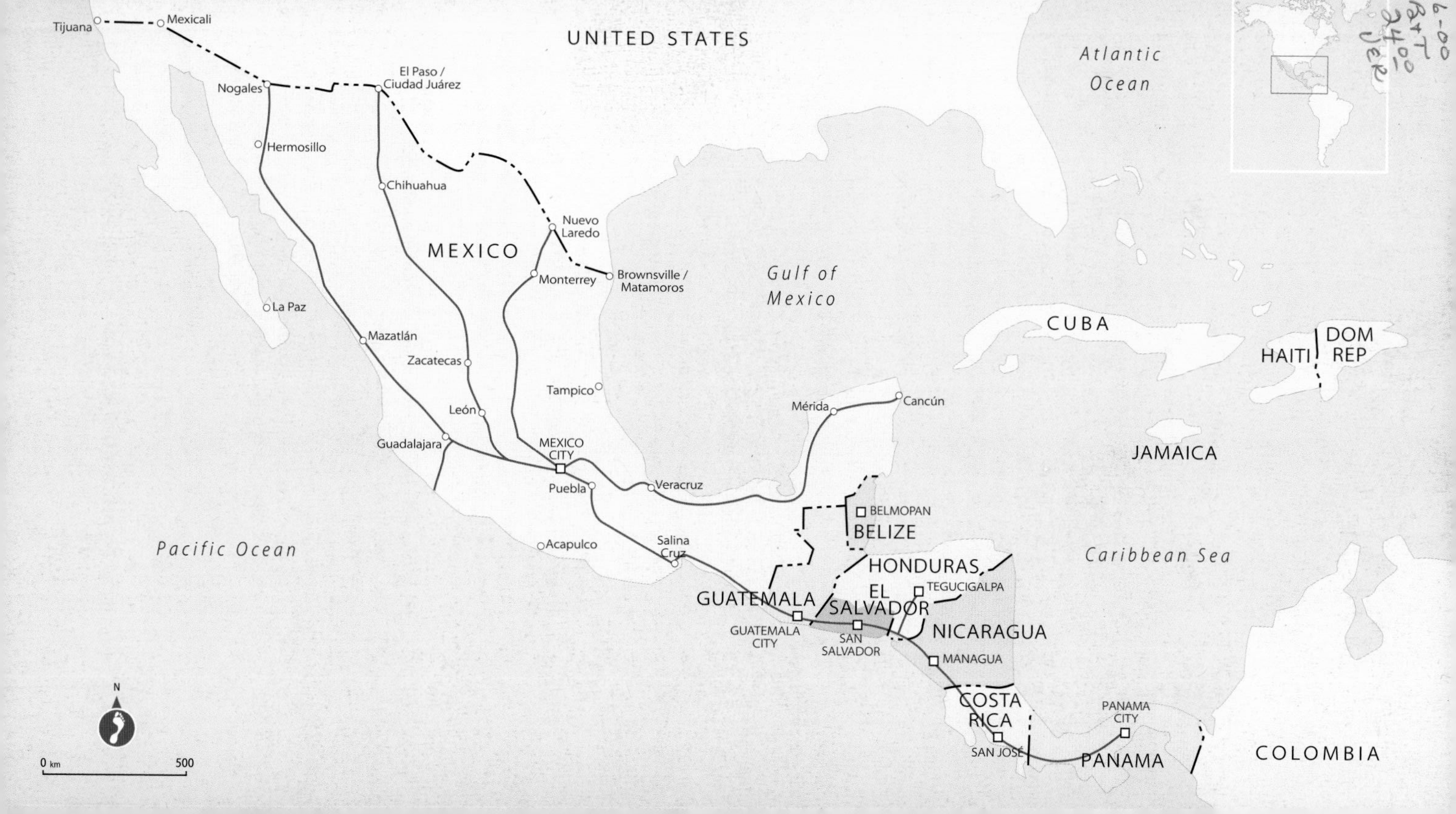

6-00
B+T
24⁰⁰
VER

ATLANTIC OCEAN

UNITED STATES

Tijuana
Mexicali
Nogales
Hermosillo
La Paz
El Paso / Ciudad Juárez
Chihuahua
Mazatlán
Zacatecas
León
Guadalajara
MEXICO
Nuevo Laredo
Monterrey
Tampico
Brownsville / Matamoros
MEXICO CITY
Puebla
Acapulco
Veracruz
Salina Cruz
Mérida
Cancún

Gulf of Mexico

CUBA
JAMAICA
HAITI
DOM REP
Caribbean Sea
COLOMBIA

BELIZE
BELMOPAN
GUATEMALA
GUATEMALA CITY
EL SALVADOR
SAN SALVADOR
HONDURAS
TEGUCIGALPA
NICARAGUA
MANAGUA
COSTA RICA
SAN JOSÉ
PANAMA
PANAMA CITY

Pacific Ocean

N

0 km   500

Mexico & Central America Handbook

Published by Footprint Handbooks
6 Riverside Court
Lower Bristol Road
Bath BA2 3DZ. England
T +44 (0)1225 469141
F +44 (0)1225 469461
Email discover@footprintbooks.com
Web www.footprintbooks.com

ISBN 1 900949 39 3
ISSN 0965-5492
CIP DATA: A catalogue record for this
book is available from the British Library

In USA, published by
Passport Books, a division of
NTC/Contemporary Publishing Group
4255 West Touhy Avenue, Lincolnwood
(Chicago), Illinois 60712-1975, USA
T 847 679 5500 F 847 679 24941
Email NTCPUB2@AOL.COM

ISBN 0-8442-4838-X
Library of Congress Catalog Card
Number: 99-74365

© Footprint Handbooks Ltd 1999
Tenth edition

Credits

Series editor
Patrick Dawson
Editorial
Senior editor: Sarah Thorowgood
Editor: Jo Williams
Maps: Sarah Sorensen
Production
Pre-press Manager: Jo Morgan
Typesetting: Emma Bryers, Bookcraft Ltd
and Ann Griffiths
Maps: Kevin Feeney, Richard Ponsford,
Robert Lunn, Claire Benison, Alasdair
Dawson and Simon Dennett
Proof reading: Tim Heybyrne and Howard
David

Design
Mytton Williams

Photography
Front cover: Tony Stone Images
Back cover: Pictor International
Colour section: South American Pictures;
La Belle Aurore; Still Pictures; James Davis
Travel Photography; M & P Fogden; The
Travel Library; Jamie Marshall; Ben Box;
Tony Stone Images; Robert Harding
Picture Library

Printed and bound
in Italy by LEGOPRINT

Mexico & Central America **Handbook**

Footprint

Sarah Cameron and Ben Box

*La gran alegría de la partida estriba cabalmente
en lo imprevisto.*
The great joy in setting out lies entirely in the
unexpected.

Mariano Azuela, *Los de abajo*

Contents

Left: *the Arch of Santa Catalina frames Agua volcano, Antigua Guatemala. Until an earthquake in 1773 forced the Spaniards to move their capital, Antigua was the finest colonial city in Central America. Today it is a major cultural centre.*

Introduction

Ever since Earth's continents settled into the pattern which we recognize today, the Central American isthmus has been the point where worlds meet. As a land bridge between North and South America it has tremendous importance in terms of biodiversity. Visitors can now enjoy a huge variety of national parks and other protected areas, some for particular species like the quetzal (the national bird of Guatemala) or for unique habitats (like dry tropical forests), others for the great wanderers of the planet (whales, marine turtles, the Monarch butterfly, migrating birds). Another aspect of movement in the region is its geological instability, with volcanoes lending a spectacular, if perilous beauty along a great spine from central Mexico to Panama. Earthquakes have also had a dramatic effect on many places, for instance Antigua Guatemala with its ruined colonial churches and, more recently, Mexico City and Managua.

Archaeological evidence shows how the cultures of Mesoamerica traded to the north and south and, while the magnificent cities of the prehispanic cultures now stand unadorned, there are countless museums which display the evidence of that interchange of goods and trophies. Having gained footholds in Panama and in Mexico early in the 16th century, the Spaniards moved north and south and, once Balboa had set eyes on the Pacific Ocean in 1513, a new east-west axis was added. Today in Panama the ruins of Panamá Viejo and Portobelo are all that remain of the royal road by which the wealth of South America was transported back to Europe, but they are just two examples out of many superb colonial buildings, a great proportion of which are still in use.

On 31 December 1999 the 12th-century manifestation of the transisthmian crossing, the Panama Canal, will finally come under the sole jurisdiction of Panama. The demands of international trade are such that the Canal is now regarded as inadequate for some modern vessels and expansion is underway. At the same time, alternatives are being studied: new waterways, so-called "dry canals" and combinations of river and land routes. Regardless of whether any of these options come to fruition, their very consideration highlights the importance of this crossroads between oceans and hemispheres.

For all the comings-and-goings, though, more settled elements can be found, as in the traditional aspects of annual festivals, weaving patterns and methods, or the spiritual life of diverse communities. There are also unique moments of peace, for instance the first sounds of the tropical dawn, looking out over the roof of the forest from the summit of a Maya pyramid, or watching the sunset from a Pacific beach.

The 10th edition of the *Mexico & Central American Handbook* appears in Footprint's new livery, with colour photography and colour printing, new map designs, wider margins and a return to single column layout. The format incorporates more space and greater ease of navigation through the intricacies of getting around the region. It aims to give you all the information you need to make an informed choice from a wide range of possibilities. It will give you the practical details to bring your plans to reality and the incentives to explore further on your own.

For all its new look, this edition is no different from its predecessors in that the book has been updated on the basis of the broadest network of sources. Correspondents in the region keep us up-to-date with new developments in tourism. The media and, increasingly, the internet help us to cover the constantly changing political, economic and social scene. Most important of all, the travellers who use the book point us in new directions and reconfirm the old favourites which have been the mainstay of any holiday in the region.

Landscapes

Left: yellow brittlebush flowers bloom at dawn, one of many desert vistas in the Baja California peninsula, Mexico.

Below: Playa Cacique on Isla Contadora, in the Pearl Islands group, in the Gulf of Panama.

Centre: volcanoes dominate the skyline in El Salvador, overlooking the capital, San Salvador, and Lake Ilopango. **Left**: maize (corn) is the staple crop of the entire region; here fields are irrigated near the Río Copán in Honduras.

Wildlife

Right: *red-eyed tree frog,* agalychnis callidryas, *resting on a purple stem in tropical forest in Belize, has become one of the symbols* of the drive to protect *Central America's biodiversity.* **Centre**: *the northern tamandua,* tamandua Mexicana, *an anteater of the rain forest of Costa Rica.*

Above: *violet sabrewing,* campylopterus hemileucurus, *one of the region's many hummingbirds, visiting an epiphytic bromeliad,* guzmania nicaraguensis, *in the Costa Rican cloud forest.* **Right:** *the jaguar,* panther onca, *is the elusive, revered hunter of the rain forests of Central and South America.*

Archaeology

Left: the prehispanic cultures of Mesoamerica shared the ability to create magnificent stone monuments, such as the so-called Pyramid of the Sorceror (El Adivino) at Uxmal, Yucatán, Mexico, a Classic-period Maya city (600-900AD).

Centre: Tula is the most important Toltec site in Mexico (950-1150AD). The Atlantes, warrior sculptures over six metres high, each carry a dart thrower and a sheaf of arrows; their breastplate is depicted in the shape of a butterfly.

Above: at Copán, Honduras, the work of the 4th-9th century AD Maya masons is among the best found anywhere in the region. **Left**: the Olmecs (BC1150-150) are regarded as the forerunners of the other cultures of the area; they left remarkable sculptures of animals and humans, among them huge stone heads, Villahermosa, Mexico.

Lifestyle

Right: markets are the hub of most rural communities, people gather from far and wide to exchange produce. Large cities also have markets, but also all the trappings of modern commerce, as in this busy street in the twin cities of Tegucigalpa and Comayagüela, Honduras.

Top left: mangoes on sale in the Central de Abastos (wholesale market), Mexico City.
Above: selling lillies, the national flower of Guatemala, in the market at Zunil in the west of the country.

Right: Indians meet in the main plaza of Chamula, Chiapas, Mexico. In the Maya regions of Mexico and Guatemala, beautiful textiles are a part of everyday life.

Art and handicrafts

Left: handicrafts may be utilitarian, such as pots for sale in the market at Sololá, Guatemala, held every Tuesday and Friday. **Below**: or they can be purely decorative. The town of Sarchí, in the Meseta Central of Costa Rica, concentrates on intricate designs and bright colours applied to oxcarts or furniture.

Centre: molas are handsewn appliqué work for blouse fronts, made by the Kuna Indians of Panama. **Left**: making Aztec-inspired designs on the pavement of the Zócalo, the main plaza in Mexico City.

Architecture

Right: 20th-century civic and religious architecture in Mexico City.

Top left: *La Merced church, León, Nicaragua, was built by the Spaniards in 1615. It is a city largely unaltered since colonial times. Volcán Telica stands in the background.* **Centre**: *the Mexican flag flies over the capital's Plaza de Constitución (or Zócalo). The Plaza is flanked by the Palacio Nacional, the Cathedral and the recently uncovered Templo Mayor of the Aztecs.* **Right**: *the façade of the Atlantic Railway Museum building in San José, Costa Rica. Sadly, the trains no longer run.*

Festivals

Left: Easter procession in Antigua, Guatemala where men carry floats supporting a statue of Christ over carpets of flowers and coloured sawdust.

Top right: sophisticated images are made in most Mexican towns and villages to celebrate the Feast of the Dead (2 November). This is a family occasion when forebears are honoured. **Left**: at a religious ceremony in Guatemala, participants dress as Biblical figures.

Centre: the feathers of the costumes at a fiesta in Puebla, Mexico, recall the high value placed on feathers by the Aztecs.
Next page: incense bearers on the Thursday of Semana Santa (Holy Week) in San Cristóbal de las Casas, Mexico.

Essentials

2

Essentials

Planning your trip

"Where to go" is perhaps the most frequently asked question about Mexico and Central America, particularly by the first time visitor. There is no shortage of images of Mexico and Central America in travel articles, on television holiday programmes and on the Internet. The main enticement is the scope for adventurous holidays, whether it be branching out from a resort like Puerto Vallarta or climbing a volcano, diving, white water rafting or looking for the elusive quetzal bird in Guatemalan or Panamanian forests. Equally visible are the pyramids and sculptures of the Aztecs, Maya and other cultures, the Spanish colonial heritage, from the grandest cathedral to the smallest village church, the flora and fauna of a vast array of habitats, Indian markets, or the mere prospect of lazing at some palm-shaded or hibiscus-covered hideaway. The countries themselves are by no means secret places, unseen by the camera lens or untouched by the sturdy shoe. We know from the correspondence we receive that the popularity of the region is already great and there are many more visitors than there are letter writers to the *Mexico & Central American Handbook*.

Detailed planning information is given for each country:
Belize, page 719
Costa Rica, page 1039
El Salvador, page 783
Guatemala, page 577
Honduras, page 847
Mexico, page 68
Nicaragua, page 967
Panama, page 1159

The question of which country to visit is not answered in this first section of the Handbook. Rather here, the practicalities of how to get to the region together with what generally to expect are covered. If you look at the first pages of each country chapter, you will find an overview to help you start planning what to see and when to go. You will also find important information pertinent to that destination. The suggestions are, of course, not definitive, as one of the fascinations of travelling is to be able to get away from the crowd and explore off the beaten track.

By the time this edition of the *Mexico & Central American Handbook* is in use, it will be a year or more since Hurricane Mitch deluged much of Central America with a year's rain in less than a week. Honduras was worst hit, with hardly any part of the country escaping damage. Neighbouring areas of Nicaragua, Guatemala, El Salvador and Belize were also affected and there was some flooding in Costa Rica. In terms of loss of life, homelessness, washed-out agricultural land, wrecked roads and bridges, the statistics were appalling. Equally disheartening is the size of the bill for reconstruction and restoring the progress which was at last beginning to materialize after decades of political and social upheaval. This is not the place to catalogue either what was destroyed or what is being done to rebuild. Those interested can contact official and non-governmental organizations, websites and other sources to find out the current situation. Suffice it to say, a tremendous will to overcome Mitch's worst efforts has emerged and tourism is one of the most immediate ways outsiders can help. By going there, you will be bringing in much needed foreign exchange and your presence will show solidarity with the people's desire to help themselves rise above the tragedy.

Not one of the major tourist destinations in any of the countries affected is now off limits. Travellers can move freely through the region, with a guarantee of finding lodging, food and all necessary services. If planning to go far from the beaten track, it is advisable to enquire if your presence would be an inconvenience to the local inhabitants, but the editors have yet to hear of anywhere where visitors have not been welcome. This applies even to the Mosquitia of Honduras, which suffered severely from floods and loss of productive land.

In Guatemala and Nicaragua particularly, the scale of tourist cancellations after Mitch was out of proportion to the area affected in each country. It is to be hoped that the reluctance of visitors to return to these countries, and to Honduras even though almost all its tourism infrastructure has reopened, will not be prolonged.

Natural forces have always been a part of this region's way of life, from the fertile soil on the slopes of the active volcano to the power of the sun, whose death the prehispanic civilizations so feared. Whether it is gentle or destructive, the environment is an integral part of any journey and will always add to the excitement.

Before you travel

Documents

Passports Latin Americans, especially officials, are very document-minded. You should always carry your passport in a safe place about your person, or if not going far, leave it in the hotel safe. If staying in a country for several weeks, it is worth while registering at your Embassy or Consulate. Then, if your passport is stolen, the process of replacing it is simplified and speeded up. Keeping photocopies of essential documents, including your flight ticket, and some additional passport-sized photographs, is recommended.

It is your responsibility to ensure that your passport is stamped in and out when you cross frontiers. The absence of entry and exit stamps can cause serious difficulties: seek out the proper immigration offices if the stamping process is not carried out as you cross. Also, do not lose your entry card; replacing one causes a lot of trouble, and possibly expense. Citizens of countries which oblige visitors to have a visa can expect more delays and problems at border crossings.

If planning to study in Latin America for a long period, make every effort to get a student visa in advance.

Identity and Membership Cards Membership cards of British, European and US motoring organizations can be useful for discounts off items such as hotel charges, car rentals, maps, and towing charges, etc. Student cards must carry a photograph if they are to be of any use in Latin America for discounts. Business people should carry a good supply of visiting cards, which are essential for good business relations in Latin America. Identity, membership or business cards in Spanish (or a translation) and an official letter of introduction in Spanish are also useful.

If you are in full-time education you will be entitled to an International Student Identity Card (ISIC), which is distributed by student travel offices and travel agencies in 77 countries. The ISIC gives you special prices on all forms of transport (air, sea, rail etc), and access to a variety of other concessions and services. If you need to find the location of your nearest ISIC office contact: The ISIC Association, Box 15857, 1001 NJ Amsterdam, Holland T+45-33939303.

Money

The three main ways of keeping in funds while travelling are with US dollars cash, US dollars travellers' cheques (TCs), or plastic.

Cash
See inside front cover for exchange rates

Sterling and other currencies are not recommended. Though the risk of loss is greater, the chief benefit of US dollar notes is that better rates and lower commissions can usually be obtained for them. In many countries, US dollar notes are only accepted if they are in excellent, if not perfect, condition (likewise, do not accept local currency notes in poor condition). Take and accept 'new style' US dollar bills (US$20, 50, 100) with centre thread microprinting and watermarks, as there are countless forged 'old style' notes in circulation. Low-value US dollar bills should be carried for changing into local currency if arriving in a country when banks or *casas de cambio* are closed (US$5 or US$10 bills). They are very useful for shopping: shopkeepers and exchange shops (*casas de cambio*) tend to give better exchange rates than hotels or banks (but see below). The better hotels will normally

Insurance tips

Insurance companies have tightened up considerably over recent years and it is now almost impossible to claim successfully if you have not followed procedures closely. The problem is that these often involve dealing with the country's red tape which can lead to some inconvenience at best and to serious delays at worst. There is no substitute for suitable precautions against petty crime.

The level of insurance that you carry is often dictated by the sums of medical insurance which you carry. It is inevitably the highest if you go through the USA. Also don't forget to obtain sports extensions if you are going to do sports such as diving, rafting and climbing. Most policies do not cover very high levels of baggage/cash. Don't forget to check whether you can claim on your household insurance. They often have worldwide all risks extensions. Most policies exclude manual work whilst away although working in bars or restaurants is usually alright.

Here are our tips: they apply to most types of policies but always check the details of your own policy before you leave.

1 Take the policy with you (a photocopy will do but make sure it is a complete one).

2 Do not travel against medical advice. It will invalidate your medical insurance cover.

3 There is a 24 hour medical emergency service helpline associated with your insurance. You need to contact them if you require in-patient hospital treatment or you need to return home early. The telephone number is printed on the policy. Make sure you note the time of the call, the person you were talking to and get a reference number. Even better get a receipt from the telephone company showing the number you called. Should you need to be airlifted home, this is always arranged through the insurance company's representative and the hospital authorities. Ironically this can lead to quite intense discussions which you will not be aware of: the local hospital is often quite keen to keep you!

4 If you have to cancel your trip for whatever reason, contact your travel agent, tour operator or airline without delay.

5 If your property is damage by an airline, report it immediately and always within three days and get a 'property irregularity report' from them.

6 Claims for baggage left unattended are very rarely settled unless they were left in a securely locked hotel room, apartment etc; locked in the boot of a car and there is evidence of a forced entry; cash is carried on your person or is in a locked safe or security box.

7 All loss must be reported to the police and/or hotel authorities within 24 hours of discovery and a written report obtained.

8 If medical attention is received for injury or sickness, a medical certificate showing its nature must be obtained, although some companies waive this if only out-patient treatment is required. Keep all receipts in a safe place as they will be needed to substantiate the claim.

9 There may be a date before which claims must be submitted. This is often within 30 days of returning home. It is now usual for companies to want your policy document, proof that you actually travelled (airline ticket or travel agent's confirmation of booking), receipts and written reports (in the event of loss). **NB** photocopies are not accepted.

---

change travellers' cheques for their guests (often at a rather poor rate), but if you are travelling on the cheap it is essential to keep in funds; watch weekends and public holidays carefully and never run out of local currency. Take plenty of local currency, in small denominations, when making trips into the interior.

These are convenient but they attract thieves (though refunds can of course be arranged) and you will find that they are more difficult than dollar bills to change in small towns (denominations of US$50 and US$100 are preferable, though one does need a few of US$20). American Express, Visa or Thomas Cook US$ TCs are recommended, but less commission is often charged on Citibank or Bank of America TCs, if they are cashed at Latin American branches of those banks. These TCs are always accepted by banks, even though they may not be as well known outside banks as those of American Express, Visa or Thomas Cook. It is a good idea to take two kinds of cheque: if large numbers of one kind have recently been forged or stolen, making people suspicious, it is unlikely to have happened simultaneously with the other kind.

Travellers' cheques
In Mexico, casas de cambio may be open longer hours than banks, but they do not offer better exchange rates.

Several banks charge a high fixed commission for changing TCs because they don't really want to be bothered. Exchange houses (*casas de cambio*) are usually much better for this service. Some establishments may ask to see the customer's record of purchase before accepting.

Plastic
See inside front cover for credit card company web addresses

It is straightfoward to obtain a cash advance against a credit card and, in the text, we give the names of banks that do this.

There are two international ATM (automatic telling machine) acceptance systems, Plus and Cirrus. Many issuers of debit and credit cards are linked to one, or both. Look for the relevant symbol on an ATM and draw cash using your PIN. Frequently, the rates of exchange on ATM withdrawals are the best available. Find out before you leave what ATM coverage there is in the countries you will visit and what international 'functionality' your card has. Check if your bank or credit card company imposes handling charges. Obviously you must ensure that the account to which your debit card refers contains sufficient funds. With a credit card, obtain a credit limit sufficient for your needs, or pay money in to put the account in credit. If travelling for a long time, consider a direct debit to clear your account regularly. Do not rely on one card, in case of loss. If you do lose a card, immediately contact the 24-hour helpline of the issuer in your home country (keep this number in a safe place). (With thanks to Nigel Baker, Debit Card Manager, Natwest Bank plc, London.)

For purchases, credit cards of the Visa and Mastercard (Eurocard, Access) groups, American Express (Amex), Carte Blanche and Diners Club can be used. Make sure you know the correct procedure if they are lost or stolen. Credit card transactions are normally at an officially recognized rate of exchange; they are often subject to tax. Many establishments in Latin America charge a fee of about five percent on credit card transactions; although forbidden by credit card company rules there is not a lot you can do about this, except get the charge itemized on the receipt and complain to the card company. For credit card security, insist that imprints are made in your presence and that any imprints incorrectly completed should be torn into tiny pieces. Also destroy the carbon papers after the form is completed (signatures can be copied from them).

NB In general terms, Mastercard ATMs are available throughout Mexico, but only in Central American capitals. The Mastercard/Cirrus connection is poorly represented in Guatemala; check with your card issuer before leaving home. Visa is of greater use in Central America than Mastercard. **NB** Also money can be transferred between banks. A recommended method is, before leaving, to find out which local bank is correspondent to your bank at home, then when you need funds, telex your own bank and ask them to telex the money to the local bank (confirming by fax). Give exact information to your bank of the routing number of the receiving bank. Cash in dollars, or local currency depending on the country, can be received within 48 banking hours.

Exchange
When departing by air, never forget that you have to pay airport departure tax; do not leave yourself short of money.

Before changing money on the street, check whether exchange rates are significantly better than in a bank or *casa de cambio*. If changing money on the street, do not do so alone. If unsure of the currency of the country you are about to enter, check rates with more than one changer at the border, or ask locals or any traveller who may be leaving that country.

Whenever you leave a country, sell any local currency before leaving, because the further away you get, the less the value of a country's money.

Americans should know that if they run out of funds they can usually expect no help from the US Embassy or Consul other than a referral to some welfare organization. Find out before you go precisely what services and assistance your embassy or consulate can provide if you find yourself in difficulties.

What to take
A good principle is to take half the clothes and twice the money, that you think you will need.

Everybody has his/her own list. Those items most often suggested include **air cushions** for slatted seats, **inflatable travel pillow** for neck support, **strong shoes** (and remember that footwear over nine and a half English size, or 42 European size, is difficult to obtain in Latin America except Argentina and Brazil); a **small first-aid kit** and handbook, **fully waterproof top clothing, waterproof treatment** for leather footwear, **wax earplugs** (which are impossible to find outside large cities) and **airline-type eye mask** to help you sleep in noisy and poorly curtained hotel rooms, **sandals** (rubber-thong Japanese-type, or other – can be worn in showers to avoid athlete's foot), a **polyethylene sheet** 2 x 1 metre to cover possibly infested beds and shelter your luggage, **polyethylene bags** of varying sizes (up to heavy duty rubbish bag size) with ties, a **toilet bag** you can tie round your waist, a **sheet sleeping-bag** and pillow-case or a separate pillow-case – in some countries they are not changed often in cheap hotels; a 1½-2 metre piece of **100% cotton** can be used instead of a towel (dries quicker, is lighter), as a bedsheet, beach towel, makeshift curtain and wrap; a **mosquito net** (or a hammock with a fitted net), a **straw hat** which can be rolled or flattened and reconstituted after 15 minutes soaking in water, a **clothes line**, a **nailbrush** (useful for scrubbing dirt off clothes as well as off oneself), a **vacuum flask**, a **water bottle**, a small **dual-voltage immersion heater**, a small dual-voltage (or battery-driven) **electric fan**, a light nylon waterproof **shopping bag**, a universal bath- and basin-**plug** of the flanged type that will fit any waste-pipe (or improvise one from a sheet of thick rubber), **string, velcro, electrical insulating tape**, large **penknife** preferably with tin and bottle openers, scissors and corkscrew – the famous Swiss Army range has been repeatedly recommended (for knife sharpening, go to a butcher's shop), **alarm clock** or watch, **candle, torch** (flashlight) – especially one that will clip on to a pocket or belt, **pocket mirror, pocket calculator**, an **adaptor** and **flex** to enable you to take power from an electric-light socket (the Edison screw type is the most commonly used), a **padlock** for the doors of the cheapest and most casual hotels (or for tent zip if camping), spare chain-lengths and padlock for securing luggage to bed or bus/train seat. Remember not to throw away spent batteries containing mercury or cadmium; take them home to be disposed of, or recycled properly.

Useful medicaments are given in the **Health** section (page 50); to these might be added some **lip salve with sun protection**, and **pre-moistened wipes** (such as 'Wet Ones'). Always carry **toilet paper. Natural fabric sticking plasters**, as well as being long-lasting, are much appreciated as gifts. **Dental floss** can be used for backpack repairs, in addition to its original purpose. Never carry firearms. Their possession could land you in serious trouble.

A note for **contact lens wearers**: the availability of products for the care of lenses varies from country to country (throughout Central America, but not Mexico, it is hard to find). In any country, lens solutions can be difficult to find outside major cities. Where available, it is expensive. Practice also varies as to whether it is stocked by chemists/pharmacies or opticians.

Be careful when asking directions. Women probably know more about the neighbourhood; men about more distant locations. Policemen are often helpful. However, many Latin Americans will give you the wrong answer rather than admit they do not know.

Travelling with children

People contemplating overland travel in Latin America with children should remember that a lot of time can be spent waiting for buses, trains, and especially for aeroplanes. On bus journeys, if the children are good at amusing themselves, or can readily sleep while travelling, the problems can be considerably lessened. If your child is of an early reading age, take reading material with you as it is difficult, and expensive, to find. A bag of, say 30 pieces, of Duplo or Lego can keep young children occupied for hours. Travel on trains, while not as fast or at times as comfortable as buses, allows more scope for moving about. Some trains provide tables between seats, so that games can be played. (Beware of doors left open for ventilation, especially if air-conditioning is not working – Ed.) For health matters, see page 50

Food can be a problem if the children are not adaptable. It is easier to take biscuits, drinks, bread etc with you on longer trips than to rely on meal stops where the food may not be to taste. Avocados are safe, easy to eat and nutritious; they can be fed to babies as young as six months and most older children like them. A small immersion heater and jug for making hot drinks is invaluable, but remember that electric current varies. Try and get a dual-voltage one (110v and 220v). **Food**

On all long-distance buses you pay for each seat, and there are no half-fares if the children **Fares** occupy a seat each. For shorter trips it is cheaper, if less comfortable, to seat small children on your knee. Often there are spare seats which children can occupy after tickets have been collected. In city and local excursion buses, small children generally do not pay a fare, but are not entitled to a seat when paying customers are standing. On sightseeing tours you should *always* bargain for a family rate – often children can go free. (In trains, reductions for children are general, but not universal.)

All civil airlines charge half for children under 12, but some military services don't have half-fares, or have younger age limits. Note that a child travelling free on a long excursion is not always covered by the operator's travel insurance; it is advisable to pay a small premium to arrange cover.

If hiring a car, check that it has rear seat belts.

Hotels In all hotels, try to negotiate family rates. If charges are per person, always insist that two children will occupy one bed only, therefore counting as one tariff. If rates are per bed, the same applies. In either case you can almost always get a reduced rate at cheaper hotels. Occasionally when travelling with a child you will be refused a room in a hotel that is 'unsuitable'. (In restaurants, you can normally buy children's helpings, or divide one full-size helping between two children.)

Nappies/diapers: buy them at every available opportunity in case of short supply later on.

Travel with children can bring you into closer contact with Latin American families, and generally, presents no special problems – in fact the path is often smoother for family groups. Officials tend to be more amenable where children are concerned and they are pleased if your child knows a little Spanish. Moreover, even thieves and pickpockets seem to have some of the traditional respect for families, and may leave you alone because of it! Always carry a copy of your child's birth certificate and passport-size photos.

Getting there

Some countries in Latin America officially require travellers who enter their territory to have an onward or return ticket. (Look under Essentials sections for the countries you intend to visit.) In 1998-99 this regulation was rarely enforced by any country. (It does not apply to travellers with their own vehicles.) In lieu of an onward ticket out of the country you are entering, any ticket out of another Latin American country may suffice, or proof that you have sufficient funds to buy a ticket (a credit card will do).

Air Details of all the main airlines flying to each country are given in the relevant **Essentials** sections. Weight allowances if going direct from Europe are 20 kilograms for economy and business class or 30 kilograms for first class. If you have special baggage requirements, check with an agency about anomalies which exist on different weight allowances one way, for example. Certain carriers (eg Iberia, Air France) offer a two piece allowance out of the UK only, each piece up to 32 kilograms. Many people travel to Mexico and Central America via the USA, and all carriers via the USA offer this allowance in both directions. However, weight limits for internal flights are often lower; best to enquire beforehand.

Prices & **1** Fares from Europe to Latin American destinations vary from airline to airline, destination discounts to destination and according to time of year. Check with an agency for the best deal for when you wish to travel. There is a wide range of offers to choose from in a highly competitive environment in the UK.

2 Most airlines offer discounted (cheaper than official) fares of one sort or another on scheduled flights. These are not offered by the airlines direct to the public, but through agencies who specialize in this type of fare. In UK, these include Journey Latin America, 12-13 Heathfield Terrace, Chiswick, London, W4 4JE (T0181-7478315) and 28-30 Barton Arcade, 51-63 Deansgate, Manchester, M3 2BH (T0161-8321441); Trailfinders, 194 Kensington High St, London, W8 7RG (T0171-9383939); Encounter Overland, 267 Old Brompton Rd, London, SW5

9JA (T0171-3706845); Hayes & Jarvis, 152 King St, London, W6 0QU (T0181-2227844); South American Experience, 47 Causton St, Pimlico, London, SW1P 4AT (T0171-9765511); STA Travel, Priory House, 85 Shaftesbury Avenue, WC1, for bookings and enquiries T0171-3616262, for a free copy of The Guide T0171-3616166; Trips Worldwide, Bristol T0117-9872626. In the USA, **eXito**, 5699 Miles Ave, Oakland, CA 94618, T1-800-655-4053, F510-655-4566, T worldwide 510-6552154, exito@wonderlink.com, www.wonderlink.com/exito. The very busy seasons are as follows: 7 December-15 January and July to mid-September. If you intend travelling during those times, book as far ahead as possible.

3   With the promotion of Cancún as a gateway from Europe, there has been an increase in the number of scheduled flights to Mexico, at the expense of charter flights from Britain (eg Iberia flies daily Madrid-Miami-Cancún; Air Europa Madrid to Cancún, twice a week; Air France/AeroMéxico twice weekly Paris-Cancún; Condor Flugdienst from Frankfurt to Cancún, Acapulco and Puerto Vallarta – also to San José, Costa Rica). British Airways operates a twice weekly flight from London Gatwick to Cancún and three scheduled services a week from London Heathrow to Mexico City. British Airways' flights link with AeroMéxico and, to a lesser extent, Mexicana for access to the rest of the country. If you do not stop over in Mexico City, low-cost add-ons are available to Mexican domestic destinations through British Airways' link with the main national airlines. Between February and June scheduled airfares from Europe to Mexico City can be very low, commensurate with some transatlantic fares (the same does not apply to holiday destinations like Cancún or Acapulco). It is therefore worth considering Mexico City as an entry/exit point for a Mexican trip. For the widest range of options and keenest prices Mexico City is best, but US carriers provide the bulk of access both to Cancún and to the other regional points which have no direct access from Europe (but through fares are available). If flexible on time, you can seek promotional fares on smaller Mexican carriers not represented in Europe when you arrive.

4   Other fares fall into three groups, and are all on scheduled services:

Essentials

A Excursion (return) fares: with restricted validity either 7-90 days, or 7-180 days (Mexico), depending on the airline; 7-90 days (Central America). These are fixed date tickets where the dates of travel cannot be changed after issue without incurring a penalty.

B Yearly fares: these may be bought on a one-way or return basis, and usually the returns can be issued with the return date left open. You must, however, fix the route.

C Student (or Under 26) fares (there is a wider range of these to Mexico than elsewhere): Some airlines are flexible on the age limit, others strict. One way and returns available, or 'Open Jaws' (see below). There is also a wider range of cheap one-way student fares originating in Latin America than can be bought outside the continent. **NB** There is less availability in the busy seasons (see above).

5   For people intending to travel a linear route and return from a different point from that which they entered, there are 'Open Jaw' fares, which are available on student, yearly, or excursion fares. Iberia and KLM are good for 'Open Jaw' fares within Mexico, or to Mexico and elsewhere. Continental and American have a wide range of 'Open Jaw' fares within Mexico, but not regionally.

6   Many of these fares require a change of plane at an intermediate point, and a stopover may be permitted, or even obligatory, depending on schedules. Simply because a flight stops at a given airport does not mean you can break your journey there – the airline must have traffic rights to pick up or set down passengers between points A and B before it will be permitted. This is where dealing with a specialized agency (like Journey Latin America!) will really pay dividends. On multi-stop itineraries, the specialized agencies can often save clients hundreds of pounds.

7   Although it's a little more complicated, it's possible to sell tickets in London for travel originating in Latin America at substantially cheaper fares than those available locally. This is useful for the traveller who doesn't know where he or she will end up, or who plans to travel for more than a year. But a one-way ticket from Latin America is more expensive than a one-way in the other direction, so it's always best to buy a return (but see Student fares, above).

8   Certain Central American countries impose local tax on flights originating there. Among these are Guatemala, Costa Rica and Mexico.

9   There are several cheap French charters to Mexico and Guatemala, but no-one in the UK sells them. There are a number of 'packages' that include flights from Mexico to Cuba which can be bought locally in Mexico, or in advance from London.

Travellers starting their journey in continental Europe should make local enquiries about charters and agencies offering the best deals.

10   If you buy discounted air tickets *always* check the reservation with the airline concerned to make sure the flight still exists. Also remember that IATA airlines' schedules change in March and October each year, so if you're going to be away a long time it's best to leave return flight coupons open. **NB** If you know that you will be returning at the very busy seasons (see paragraph 2, above), you should make a reservation.

Specialist tour companies

Austral Tours, 20 Upper Tachbrook St, London, SW1, T0171-2335384, F0171-2335385, www.latinamerica.co.uk

Campus Travel, 52 Grosvenor Gardens, London, 0870 240 1010, www.usitcampus.co.uk

Cox & Kings Travel, St James Court, 45 Buckingham Gate, London, T0171-8735001

Dragoman, Camp Green, Debenham, Suffolk, IP14 6LA T01728-861133, www.dragoman.co.uk

Encounter Overland, 267 Old Brompton Rd, London SW5 9JA, T0171-3706845

eXito, 5699 Miles Ave, Oakland, CA 94618, T1-800-6554053, T (worldwide) 510-6552154, www.wonderlink.com/exito.

GAP Adventures, 19 Duncan Street, Toronto, Ontario M5H 3H1, T1 800 465 5600, UK 01373 858956, www.gap.ca

Hayes & Jarvis, 152 King St, London W6 0QU, T0181-2227844

Journey Latin America, 12 and 13 Heathfield Terrace, Chiswick, London W4 4JE, T0181-7478315, F0181-7421312 and 28-30 Barton Arcade, 51-63 Deansgate, Manchester M3 2BH, T0161-8321441, F0161-8321551, sales@journeylatinamerica.co.uk

Maya Tours, 2608 North Ocean Boulevard, Suite 108, Pompano Beach, FL 33062, USA, T954 742 6262, F954 783 7414, www.mayatour.com

South American Experience, 47 Causton St, Pimlico, London SW1P 4AT, T0171-9765511, F0117 976 6908, www.sax.mcmail.com

South American Tours, Hanauer Landstrasse208-216, D-60314, Germany, T++49 69 40 58 97-0, F++49 69 44 04 32, sat.fre@t-online.de

STA Travel, Priory House, 6 Wrights Lane, London W8 6TA, T0171-3616166, www.statravel.co.uk

Trailfinders, 194 Kensington High St, London W8 7RG, T0171-9383939 and also Birmingham, T0121 2361234, Bristol T0117 9299000, Manchester, T0161 839 6969, Newcastle, T 0191 261 2345 and Dublin, T01-677 7888

Trips Worldwide, 9 Byron Place, Clifton, Bristol BS8 1J, T0117 987 2626, F0117 987 2627, www.tripsworldwide.co.uk

Veloso Tours, 33-34 Warple Way, London W3 0RG, T020 8762 0616, F020 8762 0716, www.veloso.com

Essentials

In addition, it is vital to check in advance whether you are entitled to any refund or re-issued ticket if you lose, or have stolen, a discounted air ticket.

Aviateca, Taca, Lacsa, and Nica operate a Visit Central America Pass (VICA), based on a flight into, and a flight out of Central America, plus as many flights as you wish to pay for within Central America. Fares are priced on a complex zoning system and range from US$337-US$1,373. Under IATA mileage fare principles, it is worth investigating the incorporation of stopovers into a linear route, say Guatemala City-Panama City, at no extra cost. Mexicana and AeroMéxico offer an airpass both within Mexico (minimum two flights) and international/domestic combined (minimum three flights); fares are set according to banding system. The pass is valid for up to 90 days. Details of AeroMéxico and Mexicana's Mexiplan are given in Mexico, Essentials. Aero California has an airpass which links Mexico City, northwest Mexico, Baja California and southwest USA; minimum two flights, valid 90 days, good basic tariffs. **Air passes**

If you buy internal airline tickets in Latin American countries you may find cash refunds difficult to get if you change your plans: it is better to change your ticket for a different one. Overbooking by Latin American airlines is very common (largely due to repeated block bookings by travel agents, which everyone knows will not be used), so always reconfirm the next stage of your flight within 72 hours of your intended departure. And it does no harm to reconfirm yet again in the last 24 hours, just to show them you mean it, and turn up for the flight in good time (at least two hours before departure). Also provide the airline with a contact phone number for the week prior to departure.

We advise people who travel the cheap way in Latin America to pay for all transport as they go along, and not in advance. This advice does not apply to people on a tight schedule:

paying as you go along may save money, but it is likely to waste your time somewhat. The one exception to this general principle is in transatlantic flights; here money is saved by booking as far as possible in one operation. International air tickets are very expensive if purchased in Latin America. If buying airline tickets routed through the USA, check that US taxes are included in the price.

The Amerbuspass covers the whole of Latin America, from Mexico City to Ushuaia, and entitles the holder to 15-20 percent discounts on tickets with participating operators; bookable in all Latin American capitals, Europe, Asia, Africa, Oceania, it is valid for 9,999 miles, up to 180 days. Unlimited stopovers, travel with either a confirmed or open itinerary. Contact TISA Internacional, B Irigoyen 1370, Oficina 25/26, 1138 Buenos Aires, Argentina, T43071956/46311108, F43078899, PO Box 40 Suc 1 (B), 1401 Buenos Aires.

Bus travel

Although visa requirements for British air travellers with round-trip tickets to the USA have been relaxed, it is advisable to have a visa to allow entry by land, or on airlines from South and Central America which are not 'participating carriers' on the Visa Waiver scheme. If you are thinking of travelling via the USA, or of visiting the USA after Latin America, you are strongly advised to get your visa and find out about any other requirements from a US Consulate in your own country, not while travelling.

Travel to the USA

The US Department of Agriculture places restrictions on agricultural items brought to the United States from foreign countries as well as those brought to the mainland from Hawaii, Puerto Rico, and the US Virgin Islands.

Travellers are required to list on the Customs' declaration form any meats, fruits, vegetables, plants, animals, and plant and animal products they are bringing into the country.

USDA inspectors will confiscate illegal items for destruction. Travellers who fail to declare

Essentials

items can be fined up to US$100 on the spot, and their exit from the airport will be delayed. Some items are permitted. Call 301-436-5908 for a copy of the helpful pamphlet, 'Travelers Tips'.

Sea There are few shipping services which carry passengers to Central America from Europe, the USA or elsewhere. The only regular service that does is Horn Line, sailing from Hamburg, Le Havre, via the French Antilles, Willemstad (Cura‡ao), Cartagena, Chiriquí Grande (Panama) and Moín in Costa Rica before returning to Antwerp and Hamburg: £1,500 one way, £2,405 round trip (35 days). There is a 42-day round-trip sailed by a German consortium from Liverpool, via Hamburg, Moerdijk and Bilbao, to Havana, Tampico and Veracruz, then back to Liverpool, for £2,965 (to Havana one way, 22 days, $1,490; to Veracruz 30 days, £1,980). A German consortium sails Hamburg, Bilbao, San Juan (Puerto Rico), Río Haina (Dominican Republic), Veracruz or Tampico, La Guaira (Venezuela), Río Haina, San Juan, Bilbao, Antwerp, Hamburg on a 55-day round trip, starting at £3,305 per person. Fyffes have a 28-day round trip from Portsmouth or Southampton, via Flushing to Big Creek (Belize) and Puerto Cortés (Honduras), calling at Waterford on the homeward leg. Polish Ocean Line has a very flexible service from Gdynia to La Guaira and Puerto Cabello (Venezuela), Cartagena (Colombia), Puerto Limón, Puerto Cort,s, Santo Tomás de Castilla, New Orleans, Houston, and back to Gdynia, 2½-3 months, £2,650 per person in a double cabin, £2,800 single. Various ships pass through the Panama Canal en route to the west coast of South America, eg Chilean Lines' New Orleans – Chile Voyage, Furness Withy's charter, *Cap Blanco*, sailing from Felixstowe to Chile, while the German *Cap Ortegal* stops in Puerto Limón on its round trip from Felixstow to a number of Caribbean ports. Another German vessel makes a 21-day round trip Houston, Altamira, Veracruz, Puerto Limón, Manzanillo (Panama), Cartagena, Baranquilla, Puerto Cabello, La Guaira, San Juan, Río Haina, New Orleans, Houston.

Our thanks are due to John Alton of Strand Voyages, Charing Cross Shopping Concourse, The Strand, London WC2N 4HZ, T0171-8366363, F0171-4970078, for the above information. Enquiries regarding passages should be made through agencies in your own country, or through Strand Voyages, who also have information on occasional one-way services to the Gulf of Mexico from Europe. Also in the UK, information can be obtained from Cargo Ship Voyages Ltd, Hemley, Woodbridge, Suffolk, IP12 4QF, T/F01473-736265, and The Cruise People, 88 York Street, London W1H 1DP, T0171-7232450 (reservations 0800-526313). In Europe, contact Wagner Frachtschiffreisen, Stadlerstrasse 48, CH-8404, Winterthur, Switzerland, T052-2421442, F2421487. In the USA, contact Freighter World Cruises, 180 South Lake Ave, Pasadena, CA 91101, T818-4493106, or Travltips Cruise and Freighter Travel Association, 163-07 Depot Rd, PO Box 188, Flushing, NY11358, T800-8728584.

Details on shipping cars are given in Motoring, below, and in the relevant country sections.

Touching down

Rules, customs
& etiquette

Appearance There is a natural prejudice in all countries against travellers who ignore personal hygiene and have a generally dirty and unkempt appearance. Most Latin Americans, if they can afford it, devote great care to their clothes and appearance; it is appreciated if visitors do likewise. How you dress is mostly how people will judge you. Buying clothing locally can help you look less like a tourist. It may be advantageous to carry a letter from someone in an official position testifying to one's good character, on official-looking notepaper.

Men wearing earrings are liable to be ridiculed in more 'macho' communities (for example in some rural areas). A medium weight shawl with some wool content is recommended for women: it can double as pillow, light blanket, bathrobe or sunscreen as required. For men, a smart jacket can be very useful.

Courtesy Remember that politeness – even a little ceremoniousness – is much appreciated. Men should always remove any headgear and say "con permiso" when entering offices, and be prepared to shake hands (this is much more common in Latin America than in Europe or North America); always say "Buenos días" before midday, or "Buenas tardes" and wait for a reply before proceeding further. Always remember that the traveller from abroad has enjoyed greater advantages in life than most Latin American minor officials, and should be friendly and courteous in consequence. Never be impatient; do not criticize situations in public: the officials may know more English than you think and they can certainly interpret gestures and facial expressions. Be judicious about discussing politics with strangers (especially in Guatemala, Honduras, Nicaragua and El Salvador). Politeness can be a liability, however, in some situations; most Latin Americans are disorderly queuers. In Mexico, though, orderly queuing is common. On the other hand, Mexicans rarely respect punctuality. In commercial transactions (such as buying a meal or goods in a shop) politeness should be accompanied by firmness, and always ask the price first.

Politeness should also be extended to street traders; saying "No, gracias" with a smile is better than an arrogant dismissal. Whether you give money to beggars is a personal matter, but your decision should be influenced by whether a person is begging out of need or trying to cash in on the tourist trail. In the former case, local people giving may provide an indication. Giving money to children is a separate issue, upon which most agree: don't do it. There are occasions where giving food in a restaurant may be appropriate, but first inform yourself of local practice.

Moira Chubb, from New Zealand, suggests that if you are a guest and are offered food that arouses your suspicions, the only courteous way out is to feign an allergy or a stomach ailment. If worried about the purity of ice for drinks, ask for a beer.

Photography Always ask permission before photographing people. Film prices vary but are not much different from Europe. Film can be bought cheaply in the USA or in the Colón Tax Free Zone (Panama). Slide film is difficult to find. Kodachrome is almost impossible to buy, and Fuji Film is less easy to find than Kodak in Central America. Some travellers (but not all) have advised against mailing exposed films home; either take them with you, or have them developed, but not printed, once you have checked the laboratory's quality. Note that postal authorities may use less sensitive equipment for X-ray screening than the airports do. Modern controlled X-ray machines are supposed to be safe for any speed of film, but it is worth trying to avoid X-ray as the doses are cumulative. Many airport officials will allow film to be passed outside X-ray arches; they may also hand-check a suitcase with a large quantity of film if asked politely. Western camera shops sell double lead-lined bags which will protect new and used film from X-rays.

Dan Buck and Anne Meadows write: A note on developing film in Latin America. Black and white is a problem. Often it is shoddily machine-processed and the negatives are ruined. Ask the store if you can see an example of their laboratory's work and if they hand-develop.

Jeremy Till and Sarah Wigglesworth suggest that exposed film can be protected in humid areas by putting it in a balloon and tying a knot. Similarly, keeping your camera in a plastic bag may reduce the effects of humidity.

Drugs Users of drugs, even of soft ones, without medical prescription should be particularly careful, as some countries impose heavy penalties – up to 10 years' imprisonment – for even the simple possession of such substances. In this connection, the planting of drugs on travellers, by traffickers or the police, is not unknown. If offered drugs on the street, make no response at all and keep walking. Note that people who roll their own cigarettes are often suspected of carrying drugs and subjected to intensive searches. Advisable to stick to commercial brands of cigarettes – but better still not to smoke at all.

Keeping safe Generally speaking, most places in Latin America are no more dangerous than any major city in Europe or North America. In provincial towns, main places of interest, on day time buses and in ordinary restaurants the visitor should be quite safe. Nevertheless, in large cities (particularly in crowded places such as markets and bus stations), crime exists, most of which is opportunistic. If you are aware of the dangers, act confidently and use your common sense you will lessen many of the risks. The following tips, all endorsed by travellers, are meant to forewarn, but not alarm, you. Keep all documents secure; hide your main cash supply in different places or under your clothes (extra pockets sewn inside shirts and trousers, pockets closed with a zip or safety pin, moneybelts – best worn below the waist rather than at it or around the neck, neck or leg pouches, and elasticated support bandages for keeping money and cheques above the elbow or below the knee have been repeatedly recommended – the last by John Hatt in *The Tropical Traveller*). Waist packs worn outside the clothes are not safe. Keep cameras in bags (preferably with a chain or wire in the strap to defeat the slasher) or briefcases; take spare spectacles (eyeglasses); don't wear wrist-watches or jewellery. If you wear a shoulder-bag in a market, carry it in front of you. Backpacks are vulnerable to slashers: a good idea is to cover the pack with a sack (a plastic one will also keep out rain and dust) with maybe a layer of wire netting between, or make an inner frame of chicken wire.

Ignore mustard smearers and paint or shampoo sprayers, and strangers' remarks like 'what's that on your shoulder?' or 'have you seen that dirt on your shoe?'. Furthermore, don't bend over to pick up money or other items in the street. These are all ruses intended to distract your attention and make you easy for an accomplice to steal from. If someone follows you when you're in the street, let him catch up with you and 'give him the eye'. While you should take local advice about being out at night, do not assume that daytime is safer than nighttime. If walking after dark, walk in the road, not on the pavement/sidewalk.

Be wary of 'plainclothes policemen'; insist on seeing identification and on going to the police station by main roads. Do not hand over your identification (or money – which he should not need to see anyway) until you are at the station. On no account take them directly back to your lodgings. Be even more suspicious if he seeks confirmation of his status from a passer-by. If someone tries to bribe you, insist on a receipt. If attacked, remember your assailants may well be armed, and try not to resist.

It is best, if you can trust your hotel, to leave any valuables you don't need in safe-deposit there, when sightseeing locally. Always keep an inventory of what you have deposited. If you don't trust the hotel, lock everything in your pack and secure that in your room (some people take eyelet-screws for padlocking cupboards or drawers). If you lose valuables, always report to the police and note details of the report – for insurance purposes.

When you have all your luggage with you at a bus or railway station, be especially careful: don't get into arguments with any locals if you can help it, and lock all the items together with a chain or cable if you are waiting for some time. Take a taxi between airport/bus station/railway station and hotel, if you can possibly afford it. Keep your bags with you in the taxi and pay only when you and your luggage are safely out of the vehicle. Make sure the taxi has inner door handles, in case a quick exit is needed. Avoid night buses; never arrive at night; and watch your belongings whether they are stowed inside or outside the cabin (rooftop luggage racks create extra problems, which are sometimes unavoidable – make sure your bag is waterproof). Major bus lines often issue a luggage ticket when bags are stored in the bus' hold, generally a safe system. When getting on a bus, keep your ticket handy; someone sitting in your seat may be a distraction for an accomplice to rob you while you are sorting out the problem. Finally, never accept food, drink, sweets or cigarettes from unknown fellow-travellers on buses or trains. They may be drugged, and you would wake up hours later without your belongings. In this connection, never accept a bar drink from an opened bottle (unless you can see that that bottle is in general use): always have it uncapped in front of you.

For specific local problems, see under the individual countries in the text.

Rape This can happen anywhere in the world. If you are the victim of a sexual assault, you are advised in the first instance to contact a doctor (this can be your home doctor if you prefer). You will need tests to determine whether you have contracted any sexually-transmitted diseases; you may also need advice on post-coital contraception. You should also contact your embassy, where consular staff are very willing to help in cases of assault.

Police Whereas in Europe and North America we are accustomed to law enforcement on a systematic basis, in general, enforcement in Latin America is achieved by periodic campaigns. The most typical is a round-up of criminals in the cities just before Christmas. In December, therefore, you may well be asked for identification at any time, and if you cannot produce it, you will be jailed. If a visitor is jailed his or her friends should provide food every day. This is especially important for people on a diet, such as diabetics. In the event of a vehicle accident in which anyone is injured, all drivers involved are automatically detained until blame has been established, and this does not usually take less than two weeks.

Never offer a bribe unless you are fully conversant with the customs of the country. Wait until the official makes the suggestion, or offer money in some form which is apparently not bribery, for example 'In our country we have a system of on-the-spot fines (*multas de inmediato*). Is there a similar system here?' Do not assume that officials who accept a bribe are prepared to do anything else that is illegal. You bribe them to persuade them to do their job, or to persuade them not to do it, or to do it more quickly, or more slowly. You do not bribe them to do something which is against the law. The mere suggestion would make them very upset. If an official suggests that a bribe must be paid before you can proceed on your way, be patient (assuming you have the time) and he may relent.

Travelling alone Many points of security, dress and language have been covered already. First time exposure to countries where sections of the population live in extreme poverty or squalor and may even be starving can cause distress to travellers. So can the exceptional curiosity extended to visitors, especially women. Simply be prepared for this and try not to over-react. These additional hints have mainly been supplied by women, but most apply to any single traveller. When you set out, err on the side of caution until your instincts have adjusted to the customs of a new culture. If, as a single woman, you can befriend a local woman, you will learn much more about the country you are visiting. Unless actively avoiding foreigners like yourself, don't go too far from the beaten track; there is a very definite 'gringo trail' which you can join, or follow, if seeking company. This can be helpful when seeking safe accommodation, especially if arriving after dark (which is best avoided). Remember that for a single woman a taxi at night can be as dangerous as wandering around on her own. At borders dress as smartly as possible. Travelling by train is a good way to meet locals, but buses are much easier for a person alone; on major routes your seat is often reserved and your luggage can usually be locked in the hold. It is easier for men to take the friendliness of locals at face value; women may be subject to much unwanted attention. To help minimize this, do not wear suggestive clothing and, advises Alex Rossi of Jawa Timur, Indonesia, do not flirt. By wearing a wedding ring, carrying a photograph of your 'husband' and 'children', and saying that your 'husband' is close at hand, you may dissuade an aspiring suitor. If politeness fails, and a man persists, specially mentioning sex or being obnoxious, do not feel bad about showing offence and departing. When accepting a social invitation, make sure that someone knows the address and the time you left. Ask if you can bring a friend (even if you do not intend to do so). A good rule is always to act with confidence, as though you know where you are going, even if you do not. Someone who looks lost is more likely to attract unwanted attention. Do not disclose to strangers where you are staying. (Much of this information was supplied by Alex Rossi, and by Deirdre Mortell of Carrigaline, Co Cork).

Where to stay

A cheap but not bad hotel might be US$7 a night upwards in Mexico, less in some, but not all of, the Central American countries. For those on a really tight budget, it is a good idea to ask for a boarding house – *casa de huéspedes, hospedaje, pensión, casa familial* or *residencial*, according to country – they are normally to be found in abundance near bus and railway stations and markets. Good value hotels can also be found near truckers' stops/service stations; they are usually secure. There are often great seasonal variations in hotel prices in resorts. In Mexico, couples should ask for a room with *cama matrimonial* (double bed), normally cheaper than a room with two beds. Note that in the text the term 'with bath' usually means 'with shower and toilet', not 'with bath tub'. Remember, cheaper hotels don't always supply soap, towels and toilet paper. Useful tips: book even cheap hotels in advance by registered mail, if you receive no reply, don't worry. In any class, hotel rooms facing the street may be noisy; always ask for the best, quietest room. To avoid price hikes for gringos, ask if there is a cheaper room.

Hotels
See inside front cover for our hotel grade price guide.

The electric showers used in innumerable hotels should be checked for obvious flaws in the wiring; try not to touch the rose while it is producing hot water.

Cockroaches These are ubiquitous and unpleasant, but not dangerous. Take some insecticide powder if staying in cheap hotels, trailer parks, etc; Baygon (Bayer) has been recommended. Stuff toilet paper in any holes in walls that you may suspect of being parts of cockroach runs.

Toilets   Many hotels, restaurants and bars have inadequate water supplies. **Almost without exception, used toilet paper should not be flushed down the pan, but placed in the receptacle provided.** This applies even in quite expensive hotels. Failing to observe this custom will block the pan or drain, a considerable health risk.

Camping   Organized campsites are referred to in the text immediately below hotel lists, under each town. If there is no organized site in town, a football pitch or gravel pit might serve. Obey the following rules for 'wild' camping: (1) arrive in daylight and pitch your tent as it gets dark; (2) ask permission to camp from the parish priest, or the fire chief, or the police, or a farmer regarding his own property; (3) never ask a group of people – especially young people; (4) never camp on a beach (because of sandflies and thieves). If you can't get information from anyone, camp in a spot where you can't be seen from the nearest inhabited place and make sure no one saw you go there.

    If taking a cooker, the most frequent recommendation is a multifuel stove (eg MSR International, Coleman Peak 1), which will burn unleaded petrol or, if that is not available, kerosene, benzina blanca, etc. Alcohol-burning stoves are simple, reliable, but slow and you have to carry a lot of fuel: for a methylated spirit-burning stove, the following fuels apply, *alcohol desnaturalizado, alcohol metílico, alcohol puro (de caña)* or *alcohol para quemar* (avoid this in Honduras as it does not burn). Ask for 95 percent, but 70 percent will suffice. In Mexico fuel is sold in supermarkets; in all countries it can be found in chemists/pharmacies. Gas cylinders and bottles are usually exchangeable, but if not can be recharged; specify whether you use butane or propane. Gas canisters are not always available. Camping supplies are usually only available in larger cities, so stock up when possible.

Hammocks   A hammock can be an invaluable piece of equipment, especially if travelling on the cheap. It will be of more use than a tent because many places have hammock-hooks, or you can sling a hammock between trees, etc. Bryan Crawford, of Beauly, Inverness-shire, Scotland, recommends carrying a 10 metre rope and some plastic sheeting. 'The rope gives a good choice of tree distances and the excess provides a hanging frame for the plastic sheeting to keep the rain off. Metal S-hooks can be very useful, especially under lorries'. Don't forget a mosquito net if travelling in insect-infected areas. Tips on buying a hammock are given in the Mérida (Yucatán) **Shopping** section. Good hammocks are also sold in Guatamala. If in any doubt about quality or size, seek advice before buying. And as Remo Bulgheroni of Killroergen (Switzerland) says: 'don't make a mess with your end strings because it makes your hammock useless and only the sellers can help you fast.'

Youth hostels   Organizations affiliated to the Youth Hostels movement exist in Mexico, Costa Rica and Guatemala. Further information in the country sections and from the IYHA.

Getting around

See above for details of air passes within the region.

Buses & trains   There is an extensive road system for with frequent bus services. Some bus services in Mexico and Central America are excellent. In mountainous country, however, do not expect buses to get to their destination, after long journeys, anywhere near on time. Do not turn up for a bus at the last minute; if it is full it may depart early. Tall travellers are advised to take aisle, not window seats on long journeys as this allows more leg room. When the journey takes more than three or four hours, meal stops at country inns or bars, good and bad, are the rule. Often no announcement is made on the duration of the stop: ask the driver and follow him, if he eats, eat. See what the locals are eating – and buy likewise, or make sure you're stocked up well on food and drink at the start. For drinks, stick to bottled water or soft drinks or coffee (black). The food sold by vendors at bus stops may be all right: watch if locals are buying, though unpeeled fruit is of course reliable. (See above on **Security** in buses.)

In the few countries where **trains** run, they are slower than buses. They tend to provide finer scenery and you can normally see much more wildlife than from the road – it is less disturbed by one or two trains a day than by the more frequent road traffic.

The machine What kind of motoring you do will depend on what kind of car you set out with. Four-wheel drive is not necessary, although it does give you greater flexibility in mountain and jungle territory. Wherever you travel you should expect from time to time to find roads that are badly maintained, damaged or closed during the wet season, and delays because of floods, landslides and huge potholes. Don't plan your schedules too tightly.

Diesel cars are much cheaper to run than petrol ones, and the fuel is easily available. Most towns can supply a mechanic of sorts, and probably parts for Bosch fuel injection equipment. Watch the mechanics like a hawk, since there's always a brisk market in spares, and some of yours may be highly desirable. That apart, they enjoy a challenge, and can fix most things, eventually.

The electronic ignition and fuel metering systems on modern emission controlled cars are allergic to humidity, heat and dust, and cannot be repaired by bush mechanics. Standard European and Japanese cars run on fuel with a higher octane rating than is commonly available in North, South or Central America. Unleaded fuel is now available nearly everywhere. Note that in some areas gas stations are few and far between. Fill up when you see one: the next one may be out of fuel. In Mexico don't rely on finding Premium grade at filling stations; carry on octane booster if necessary.

Security Spare no ingenuity in making your car secure. Your model should be the Brink's armoured van: anything less secure can be broken into by the determined and skilled thief. Use heavy chain and padlocks to chain doors shut, fit security catches on windows, remove interior window winders (so that a hand reaching in from a forced vent cannot open the window). All these will help, but none is foolproof. Anything on the outside – wing mirrors, spot lamps, motifs etc – is likely to be stolen too. So are wheels if not secured by locking nuts. Try never to leave the car unattended except in a locked garage or guarded parking space. Remove all belongings and leave the empty glove compartment open when the car is unattended. Also lock the clutch or accelerator to the steering wheel with a heavy, obvious chain or lock. Street children will generally protect your car fiercely in exchange for a tip. Don't wash your car: smart cars attract thieves. Be sure to note down key numbers and carry spares of the most important ones (but don't keep all spares inside the vehicle).

Documents A 'carnet de passage' is no longer accepted in any country. Land entry procedures for all countries are simple, though time-consuming, as the car has to be checked by customs, police and agriculture officials (see, however, Mexico, **Automobiles** in **Essentials**, on regulations). All you need is the registration document in the name of the driver, or, in the case of a car registered in someone else's name, a notarized letter of authorization. Note that Costa Rica does not recognize the International Driving Licence, which is otherwise useful. In Guatemala, Honduras and Costa Rica, the car's entry is stamped into the passport so you may not leave the country even temporarily without it. A written undertaking that the vehicle will be re-exported after temporary importation is useful and may be requested in Nicaragua, Costa Rica and Panama. Most countries give a limited period of stay, but allow an extension if requested in advance. Of course, do be very careful to keep **all** the papers you are given when you enter, to produce when you leave. (An army of 'helpers' loiters at each border crossing, waiting to guide motorists to each official in the correct order, for a tip. They can be very useful, but don't give them your papers.) Bringing a car in by sea or air is much more complicated and expensive: generally you will have to hire an agent to clear it through. Insurance for the vehicle against accident, damage or theft is best arranged in the country of origin: in Latin American countries it is very expensive to insure against accident and theft, especially as you should take into account the value of the car increased by duties

Motoring

Essentials

Essentials

calculated in real (ie non devaluing) terms. If the car is stolen or written off, you will be required to pay very high duty on its value. A few countries (eg Costa Rica) insist on compulsory third party insurance, to be bought at the border; in other countries it's technically required, but not checked up on (again, see Mexico, **Automobiles**, for details on Sanborns and other insurers, who will insure vehicles for driving in Mexico and Central America). Get the legally required minimum cover – not expensive – as soon as you can, because if you should be involved in an accident and are uninsured, your car could be confiscated. If anyone is hurt, do not pick them up (you become liable). Seek assistance from the nearest police station or hospital if you are able to do so. You may find yourself facing a hostile crowd, even if you are not to blame. Expect frequent road checks by police, military (especially Honduras, where there is a check point on entering and leaving every town), agricultural and forestry produce inspectors, and any other curious official who wants to know what a foreigner is doing driving around in his domain. Smiling simple-minded patience is the best tactic to avoid harassment.

Shipping a vehicle to and beyond Central America Two shipping lines recommended by the South American Explorers Club for shipping cars from the US to Panama are Wilhelmsen Lines, World Trade Center, 401E Pratt St, Suite 1400, Baltimore, MD 21202, T410-6597900, F410-6597994; A American Cargo Service Inc, 2305 Northwest 107 Ave, Box 122, Miami, FL 331720, T305-5928065, F305-4773936.

Shipping from Panama to mainland South America is expensive; you must shop around to find the cheapest way. The shipping lines and agents, and the prices for the services from Panama and elsewhere change frequently. Current details will be found in the Panama chapter under **Shipping a Vehicle,** page 1165.

Car Hire The main international car hire companies operate in all countries, but tend to be very expensive, reflecting the high costs and accident rates. Hotels and tourist agencies will tell you where to find cheaper rates, but you will need to check that you have such basics as spare wheel and toolkit and functioning lights etc. You'll probably have more fun if you drive yourself, although it's always possible to hire a car with driver. If you plan to do a lot of driving and will have time at the end to dispose of it, investigate the possibility of buying a second hand car locally: since hiring is so expensive it may well work out cheaper and will probably do you just as well. For visiting Mexico and beyond, investigate the cost of buying a vehicle in the USA and selling it there at the end of a round trip (do not try to sell a car illegally in Mexico or Central America).

Car Hire Insurance Check exactly what the hirer's insurance policy covers. In many cases it will only protect you against minor bumps and scrapes, not major accidents, nor 'natural' damage (eg flooding). Ask if extra cover is available. Also find out, if using a credit card, whether the card automatically includes insurance. Beware of being billed for scratches which were on the vehicle before you hired it.

NB For RV/motorhome users, a surge protector is recommended to prevent damage to electrical equipment. Ground your trailer with a rod and jumper cable/jump lead.

Motorcycling People are generally very friendly to motorcyclists and you can make many friends by returning friendship to those who show an interest in you.

The motorcycle should be off road capable: for example the BMW R80/100/GS for its rugged and simple design and reliable shaft drive, or the BMW F650 but a Kawasaki KLR 650s, Honda Transalp/Dominator, or the ubiquitous Yamaha XT600 Tenere would also be suitable. Buying a bike in the States and driving down works out cheaper than buying one in the UK. A road bike can go most places an off road bike can go at the cost of greater effort.

Get to know the bike before you go, ask the dealers in your country what goes wrong with it and arrange a link whereby you can get parts flown out to you. Get the book for international dealer coverage from your manufacturer, but don't rely on it. They frequently have few or no parts for modern, large machinery.

Security This is not a problem in most countries. Try not to leave a fully laden bike on its own. An Abus D or chain will keep the bike secure. A cheap alarm gives you peace of mind if you leave the bike outside a hotel at night. Most hotels will allow you to bring the bike inside. Look for hotels that have a courtyard or more secure parking and never leave luggage on the bike overnight or whilst unattended. Also take a cover for the bike.

Documents A passport, International Driving Licence, and bike registration document are necessary. In Mexico and Central America, a *carnet de passages* is not required.

Shipping Bikes may be sent from Panama to Colombia by cargo flight (eg CAC). You must drain the fuel and oil and remove the battery, but it is easier to disconnect and seal the overflow tube. Tape cardboard over fragile bits and insist on loading the bike yourself. The Darién Gap is impossible unless you carry the bike.

Border Crossings All borders in Central America seem to work out at about US$20 per vehicle. The exceptions to this are Mexico (see **Automobiles** in **Mexico** Essentials) and Panama (approximately US$4.50). All borders are free on exit, or should be on most occasions. Do not try to cross borders on a Sunday or a holiday anywhere as you are charged double the rate in Central American countries. It is sometimes very difficult to find out exactly what is being paid for. If in doubt ask to see the boss and/or the rule book.

Hitchhiking

This custom is quite common in Latin America, and travellers have reported success in virtually all countries. Neatness of appearance certainly helps. See Essentials sections for local conditions. If trying to hitchhike away from main roads and in sparsely-populated areas, however, allow plenty of time.

Hitchhiking in Latin America is reasonably safe and straightforward for males and couples, provided one speaks some Spanish. It is a most enjoyable mode of transport – a good way to meet the local people, to improve one's languages and to learn about the country. Truck drivers in particular are often well versed in things of interest one is passing, for example crops and industries. Some trucking companies, though, do not allow their drivers to take hitchhikers.

A few general hints: in remoter parts, make enquiries first about the volume of traffic on the road. On long journeys, set out at crack of dawn, which is when trucks usually leave. They tend to go longer distances than cars.

Cycling

Hallam Murray writes: Unless you are planning a journey almost exclusively on paved roads – when a high quality touring bike such as a Dawes Super Galaxy would probably suffice – a mountain bike is strongly recommended. The good quality ones (and the cast iron rule is never to skimp on quality) are incredibly tough and rugged, with low gear ratios for difficult terrain, wide tyres with plenty of tread for good road-holding, cantilever brakes, and a low centre of gravity for improved stability. Although touring bikes, and to a lesser extent mountain bikes, and spares are available in the larger Latin American cities, remember that in the developing world most indigenous manufactured goods are shoddy and rarely last. In some countries, such as Mexico, imported components can be found but they tend to be extremely expensive. (Shimano parts are generally the easiest to find.) Buy everything you possibly can before you leave home.

Richard's New Bicycle Book (Pan, £12.99) makes useful reading for even the most mechanically minded.

Useful tips Wind, not hills is the enemy of the cyclist. Try to make the best use of the times of day when there is little; mornings tend to be best but there is no steadfast rule. Take care to avoid dehydration, by drinking regularly. In hot, dry areas with limited supplies of water, be sure to carry an ample supply. For food, carry the staples (sugar, salt, dried milk, tea, coffee, porridge oats, raisins, dried soups, etc) and supplement these with whatever local foods can be found in the markets. Give your bicycle a thorough daily check for loose nuts or bolts or bearings. See that all parts run smoothly. A good chain should last 2,000 miles, 3,200

Essentials

kilometres or more but be sure to keep it as clean as possible – an old toothbrush is good for this – and to oil it lightly from time to time. Remember that thieves are attracted to towns and cities, so when sightseeing, try to leave your bicycle with someone such as a café owner or a priest. Country people tend to be more honest and are usually friendly and very inquisitive. However, don't take unnecessary risks; always see that your bicycle is secure (most hotels will allow bikes to be kept in rooms). In more remote regions dogs can be vicious; carry a stick or some small stones to frighten them off. Traffic on main roads can be a nightmare; it is usually far more rewarding to keep to the smaller roads or to paths if they exist. Most cyclists agree that the main danger comes from other traffic. A rear view mirror has frequently been recommended to forewarn you of trucks or cars which are too close behind. You also need to watch out for oncoming, overtaking vehicles, unstable loads on trucks, protruding loads, etc. Make yourself conspicuous by wearing bright clothing and a helmet; also, displaying a Mexican flag helps to keep the truckers patient and prompts encouragement. Most towns have a bicycle shop of some description, but it is best to do your own repairs and adjustments whenever possible. If undertaking maintenance of your own bike though, make sure you know how to do it, and research what tyres you will need, before you go.

Ryan Flegal of Los Angeles, California, says that, instead of taking your own expensive bicycle from home with the attendant need for specialized tools and high risks of loss, one can buy a bike in Latin America. 'Affix a sturdy rear rack, improvise securing luggage to the bicycle, and go. Carry only a patch kit and wrench to remove the wheel, and rely on the many bike mechanics in the area to do the rest'. Another cyclist, Andy Walter (Swindon UK), agrees that local mechanics, of whom there are plenty in Mexico (usually in every town), are competent and inventive. Paul Olai-Olssen of Oslo, Norway, recommends a steel frame, rather than aluminium, because it is more durable when heavily laden over long periods and can be welded if damaged (aluminium cannot).

Matthias Müller of Berlin 31 adds: From Guatemala to Panama, border officials ask for a document of ownership and a frame number for your bicycle. Without these you will have a lot of trouble crossing frontiers.

Recommended reading: *Latin America by Bike – A Complete Touring Guide,* Walter Sienko (The Mountaineers, 1993); *Bicycling Mexico,* Erick Weisbroth and Eric Ellman (Hunter Publishing Inc, 1990); *Bicycling Baja,* Bonnie Wong (Sunbelt Publications, 1988).

The Expedition Advisory Centre, administered by the Royal Geographical Society, 1, Kensington Gore, London SW7 2AR has published a useful monograph entitled *Bicycle Expeditions,* by Paul Vickers. Published in March 1990, it is available direct from the Centre, price £6.50 (postage extra if outside the UK). In the UK there is also the Cyclists' Touring Club, CTC, Cotterell House, 69 Meadow, Godalming, Surrey, GU7 3HS, T01483-417217, cycling@ctc.org.uk, for touring and technical information.

Hiking & trekking A network of paths and tracks covers much of Central America and is in constant use by the local people. In Guatemala, which has a large Indian population, you can walk just about anywhere, but in the more European countries, particularly Costa Rica you must usually limit yourself to the many excellent national parks with hiking trails. Most Central American countries have an Instituto Geográfico Militar which sells topographical maps, scale 1:100,000 or 1:50,000. The physical features shown on these are usually accurate; the trails and place names less so. National Parks offices also sell maps.

Hiking and backpacking should not be approached casually. Even if you only plan to be out a couple of hours you should have comfortable, safe footwear (which can cope with the wet) and a daypack to carry your sweater and waterproof (which must be more than showerproof – Ed). At high altitudes the difference in temperature between sun and shade is remarkable. The longer trips mentioned in this book require basic backpacking equipment. Essential items are: backpack with frame, sleeping bag, closed cell foam mat for insulation, stove, tent or tarpaulin, dried food (not tins), water bottle, compass, trowel for burying excreta (which can be done after burning toilet paper in the excavated hole – take care fire doesn't spread). Some but not all of these things are available locally.

Hikers have little to fear from the animal kingdom apart from insects (although it's best to avoid actually stepping on a snake), and robbery and assault are very rare. You are much more of a threat to the environment than vice versa. Leave no evidence of your passing; don't litter and don't give gratuitous presents of sweets or money to rural villagers. Respect their system of reciprocity; if they give you hospitality or food, then is the time to reciprocate with presents.

Maps and Guide Books Those from the Institutos Geográficos Militares in the capitals (see above) are often the only good maps available in Latin America. It is therefore wise to get as many as possible in your home country before leaving, especially if travelling by land. A good source of maps is Stanfords, UK, T0171-8361321, F0171-8360189, who have an international mail order service. A recommended series of general maps is that published by International Travel Maps (ITM), 345 West Broadway, Vancouver BC, V5Y 1P8, Canada, T604-87893621, F604-8794521, most compiled with historical notes by the late Kevin Healey. Available (among others) are South America South, North East and North West (1:4M), Ecuador (1:1M), Central America (1:1.8M), Panama (1:800,000), Guatemala and El Salvador (1:500,000), El Salvador (1:375,000), Nicaragua (1:750,000), Honduras (1:750,000), Costa Rica (1:500,000), Belize (1:350,000), Mexico (1:3.3M), the Yucatán (1:1M) and Baja California (1:1M). Another map series that has been mentioned is that of New World Edition, Bertelsmann, Neumarkter Strasse 18, 81673 München, Germany, *Mittelamerika, Südamerika Nord, Südamerika Sud, Brasilien* (all 1:4,000,000). For information on Bradt Publications' titles (eg on Belize, Cuba and several South American destinations) and imported maps and guides, contact 41 Nortoft Rd, Chalfont St Peter, Bucks, SL9 0LA, UK, T/F01494-873478. Worthy of mention here are *Backpacking in Mexico* and *Backpacking in Central America*, by Tim Burford.

A very useful book, highly recommended, aimed specifically at the budget traveller is *The Tropical Traveller*, by John Hatt (Penguin Books, 3rd edition, 1993).

The **South American Explorers' Club** is at Avenida Portugal 146 (Casilla 3714), Lima, Peru (T4250142), Jorge Washington y Leonidas Plaza, Apartado 17-21-431, Eloy Alfaro, Quito, Ecuador (T225228), and 126 Indian Creek Rd, Ithaca, NY 14850, USA T607-2770488, F607-2776122, explorer@samexplo.org, www.samexplo.org. Books, maps and travel planning services are available at the US office. The South American Explorers Club is represented in the UK by Bradt Publications.

The Latin American Travel Advisor: this complete travel information service offers the most up-to-date detailed and reliable information about 17 South and Central American countries. Public safety, health, weather and natural phenomena, travel costs, economics and politics are highlighted for each nation. You can subscribe to this comprehensive quarterly newsletter (a free sample is available), obtain country reports by email or fax and choose from a wide selection of Latin American maps. Orders may be placed by mail, fax, or through the Web; credit cards accepted. Individual travel planning assistance is available for all customers. Contact PO Box 17-17-908, Quito, Ecuador, international F593-2562566, USA and Canada toll free F1888-2159511, LATA@pi.pro.ec, www.amerispan. com/lata/.

See below, for *AmeriSpan*, in the USA and Guatemala, who can provide useful information.

Another website worth visiting for information, especially on ecotourism and language schools, is Ron Mader's *El Planeta Platica:* /www.planeta.com.

Keeping in touch

Language
*See inside back cover
for useful words and
phrases*

Without some knowledge of Spanish you will become very frustrated and feel helpless in many situations. English, or any other language, is absolutely useless off the beaten track (except in Belize). Some initial study, to get you up to a basic Spanish vocabulary of 500 words or so, and a pocket dictionary and phrase-book, are most strongly recommended: your pleasure will be doubled if you can talk to the locals. Not all the locals speak Spanish, of course; you will find that some Indians in the more remote highland parts of Guatemala speak only their indigenous languages, though there will usually be at least one person in each village who can speak Spanish.

Language classes are available at a number of centres in Mexico and Central America, for instance Cuernavaca, Antigua, Quezeltanango, San José, and others. See the Directory under individual towns for details, under Language Courses.

AmeriSpan, PO Box 40007, Philadelphia, PA 19106, T (worldwide) 215-7511100, (USA, Canada) 800-8796640, F215-7511986, offers Spanish immersion programmes, educational tours, volunteer and internship positions throughout Latin America. Language programmes are offered in Costa Rica (San José, Escazú, Alajuela, Heredia, Manuel Antonio, Monteverde), El Salvador, Guatemala (Antigua, Quetzaltenango), Honduras (Copán), Mexico (Cancún, Cuernavaca, Guanajuato, Oaxaca, Mérida, Morelia, San Miguel de Allende), Panama City as well as throughout South America, Puerto Rico and the Dominican Republic. The AmeriSpan Tourist Resource Center in Antigua, Guatemala, offers local services as well as the programmes etc listed above, T502-8320164, F8321896, amerispan@guate.net, 6 Av Norte 40A, Antigua, Guatemala. In Guatemala, Honduras and Costa Rica they offer a discount card for use in hotels, restaurants and shops. Contact AmeriSpan at above address, info@amerispan.com, or www.amerispan.com for details.

**Using your
limited Spanish
in Mexico &
Central America**

Whether you have been taught the 'Castillian' pronounciation (all *z's*, and *c's* followed by *i* or *e*, are pronunounced as the *th* in *think*) or the 'American' pronounciation (they are pronounced as *s*), you will encounter little difficulty in understanding either: Spanish pronunciation varies geographically much less than English. There are, of course, regional accents and usages; there are even a few variations in spelling – *Méjico* and *Tejas* are standard from Guatemala South – but the basic language is essentially the same everywhere.

Pronouns In the Americas, the plural, familar pronoun *vosotros* (with the verb endings – *áis*, – *éis*), though much used in Spain, is never heard. Two or more people, including small children, are always addressed as *Ustedes (Uds)*. The singular, familiar prounoun tú is replaced in many areas – though not in Mexico or Panama – by the pronoun vos; when it is, the accent on the verb tends to move toward the end: instead of *tú quieres*, one hears *vos querés* (though both will be understood).

Inappropriate use of the familiar forms (*tú, vos*) can sound imperious, condescending, infantile, or imply a presumption of intimacy that could annoy officials, one's elders, or, if coming from a man, women.

To avoid cultural complications if your Spanish is limited, stick to the polite forms: *Usted (Ud)* in the singular, *Ustedes* in the plural, and you will never give offense. Remember also that a person who addresses *you* as *tú*, does not necessarily expect to be *tuteada* (so addressed) in return.

You should, however, violate this rule when dealing with a small child, who might be intimidated by *Usted*: he/she is, after all, normally so addressed only in admonitions such as

Essentials

'¡No, Señor, Ud no tomará un helado antes del almuerzo!' 'No, Sir, you will not have ice cream before lunch!'

Expressions of time Many misunderstandings about engagements stem from terminology rather than tardiness. Note that in Mexico, *ahora* is often a synonym for *hoy*, 'today', not the 'now', in the dictionary; 'now' or 'soon' are *ahorita*; 'right now' is *ahora mismo* or *enseguida*. In Panamá, ahora means 'in a little while', 'in a bit', not 'now'.

In Central America, *en la tarde*, while it could conceivably mean at 1230 or 1300 in the afternoon, is more likely to mean 1500 or 1600, even 1730 or 1800. A polite way of pinning down a vague commitment is to ask, with a smile, *'¿Como para a qué hora más o menos?'.*

Note also that a Spanish speaker, calculating the number of days until some future event, will count *today*; an English speaker starts counting *tomorrow*, one day hence. If an immigration official tells you you must wait *'tres días'* for some approval, he may well mean only until 'the day after tomorrow' (three days *including* today), not three days counting *from* tomorrow; a three-day hotel stay in Latin America consists of three days and two nights, not three days and nights as in English. (When asked how long you plan to stay, say *'tres noches'* to be clear.)

Hence a British fortnight is a *quincena*, from *quince* (15), not catorce (14). *Del lunes en ocho* (8) means the following Monday, not Tuesday; *de hoy en cinco* (5) means four days hence, not five; an event that occurs on alternate Sundays is said to take place *cada quince (15) días*. To clarify, ask *'¿el lunes 11 o el martes 12?'* ('Monday the 11th or Tuesday the 12th?').

Money The word *peso* has many meanings. In some countries as in Costa Rica, where the *colón* is official, or Puerto Rico (the US$), the local currency is also called a peso. In conversation along the US-Mexico border, *diez pesos oro* means US$10, as opposed to diez pesos plata (MN$10, or 10 Mexican pesos; MN = *Moneda Nacional*). In Panama, a *peso* is the hefty half-dollar (US$0.50) coin, once a preferred form of wage payment or savings for country people because it 'feels' like 'serious money'. Menudo, tripe soup in Mexico, is 'small change' elsewhere.

Terms of address Almost anyone qualified by credentials or custom to a title more elevated than *Sr, Sra,* or *Srta,* uses it. A physician, dentist, or veterinarian is always addressed as *Doctor(a)*, as is any holder of a doctoral degree. Primary school teachers, often not university graduates, are always *Maestro(a)*, as are some skilled crafts people, builders, etc. Secondary school and all university teachers, are always addressed as *Profesor(a)*, or, informally by their students, as *Profe*. Lawyers and university graduates in any of the arts or social sciences are addressed as *Licenciado(a)*; graduate engineers, and holders of any degree in a technical field, use *Ingeniero(a)*, abbreviated *Ing*. Architects use *Arquitecto(a)*, abbreviated *Arq*. Protestant clergy are always *Reverendo(a)*, never just *Sr(a)*.

Address male strangers over the age of 20 or so as Señor, or, if substantially older than you, as *Don*. Younger men may be addressed as *Joven*. Address female strangers over the age of 20 or so, or younger women if they are obviously accompanied by (their own) children or a husband, as *Señora*. Younger women can safely be addressed as *Señorita*, or if younger than you, as *Joven*. Address middle-aged or older women as *Doña*.

Note that the terms *Señorita* and *Señora* have implications of virginity as well as marital status. An elderly woman who has no children and has never married may well correct you if addressed as Señora. So might a younger women whose escort is a friend, still a fiancé, or a relative. This is a grave matter for the women concerned, and the appropriate response is *'Disculpe, Señorita',* unaccompanied by a smile, which might be interpreted as a smirk.

Once you have learned a person's name young people among themselves, as everywhere, use given names or nicknames immediately. Whenever the person addressed is a few years older, however, use the form *Señora González*, or to imply respectful friendship, *Señor Juan*. Where the age difference is substantial, use *Doña Mercedes* or *Don Francisco*. Reply to officials' questions with *Sí, Señor* or *No, Señora*.

General hints Note that in Central America, the proper response to *¡Gracias!* is as often as not *¡A la orden!* ('Yours to command!') rather than the *'¡De nada!'* ("Tis nought!') taught in school.

Travellers whose names include *b's* and *v's* should learn to distinguish between them when spelling aloud as *be larga* and *ve corta* or *uve*. (Children often say *ve de vaca* and *be de burro* to distinguish between the two letters, pronounced interchangeably, either as *b* or *v*, in Spanish.)

Postal services vary in efficiency from country to country and prices are quite high; pilfering is **Postal services** frequent. All mail, especially packages, should be registered. Check before leaving home if your Embassy will hold mail, and for how long, in preference to the Poste Restante/General Delivery (Lista de Correos) department of a country's Post Office. (Cardholders can use American Express agencies.) If there seems to be no mail at the Lista under the initial letter of your surname, ask them to look under the initial of your forename or your middle name. Remember there is no W in Spanish, look for letters under V, or ask. For the smallest risk of misunderstanding, use title, initial and surname only.

AT&T's 'USA Direct', Sprint and MCI are all available for calls to the USA. It is much cheaper than **Telephone** operator-assisted calls. Other countries have similar systems, eg UK, Canada; obtain details **services** before leaving home. *See inside front cover*

Communicating by fax is a convenient way of sending messages home. Many places with *for telephone dialling* public fax machines (post offices, telephone companies or shops) will receive messages as *codes* well as send. Fax machines are often switched off; you may have to phone to confirm receipt.

Email is becoming more common and public access to the internet is fairly widespread with **Email &** cybercafés opening in both large and small towns. We list some cybercafés in the text. Three **internet** websites which give information on cybercaf,s are: www2.planeta.com/mader/ ecotravel/coffeeag/cybercafe.html, www.netcafeguide.com and www.latinworld.com (which also gives a directory of internet resources on Latin America and the Caribbean). The site www.spanishconnection.com offers a Latin American search engine directory, as well as email, e-commerce and translation services.

Latin America has more local and community radio stations than practically anywhere else in **World Band** the world; a shortwave (world band) radio offers a practical means to brush up on the **Radio** language, sample popular culture and absorb some of the richly varied regional music. International broadcasters such as the BBC World Service, the Voice of America, and Boston (Mass)-based Monitor Radio International (operated by *Christian Science Monitor*), in both English and Spanish.

Compact or miniature portables are recommended, with digital tuning and a full range of shortwave bands, as well as FM, long and medium wave. Detailed advice on radio models (£150 for a decent one) and wavelengths can be found in the annual publication, *Passport to World Band Radio* (Box 300, Penn's Park, PA 18943, USA £14.99). Details of local stations are listed in *World Radio and TV Handbook* (WRTH), PO Box 9027, 1006 AA Amsterdam, The Netherlands, £19.99. Both of these, free wavelength guides and selected radio sets, are available from the BBC World Service Bookshop, Bush House Arcade, Bush House, Strand, London WC2B 4PH, UK, T0171-5572576.

Literature This Handbook does not at present have space to contain sections on Latin **Media** American literature. Interested readers are recommended to see Jason Wilson, *Traveller's Literary Companion, South and Central America* (Brighton, UK: In Print, 1993), which has extracts from works by Latin American writers and by non-Latin Americans about the various countries and has very useful bibliographies.

Music of the region

Essentials

Mexico Mexican Music is particularly attractive and vibrant and a vigorous radio, film and recording industry has helped make it highly popular throughout Latin America. There can be no more representative an image of Mexico than the Mariachi musician and his *charro* costume. The Spanish *conquistadores* and the churchmen that followed them imposed European musical culture on the defeated natives with a heavy hand and it is this influence that remains predominant. Nobody knows what precolumbian music sounded like and even the music played today in the Indian communities is basically Spanish in origin. African slaves introduced a third ingredient, but there is no Afro-Mexican music as such and indeed there are few black Mexicans. The music brought from Europe has over the centuries acquired a highly distinctive sound and style of which every Mexican is justly proud, even if many of the young now prefer to listen to Anglo-American rock and pop, like their counterparts the world over.

There is a basic distinction between Indian and Mestizo music. The former is largely limited to the Indians' own festive rituals and dances, religious in nature and solemn in expression. The commonest instruments are flute and drum, with harp and violin also widely used. Some of the most spectacular dances are those of the Concheros (mainly urban), the Quetzales (from the Sierra de Puebla), the Voladores (flying pole – also Sierra de Puebla), the Tarascan dances from around Lake Pátzcuaro and the Yaqui deer dance (Sonora).

Mestizo music clearly has more mass appeal in what is an overwhelmingly mixed population. The basic form is the *son* (also called *huapango* in eastern areas), featuring a driving rhythm overlaid with dazzling instrumentals. Each region has its own style of *son*, such as the *son huasteco* (Northeast), *son calentano* (Michoacán/ Guerrero), *chilena* (Guerrero coast), *son mariachi* (Jalisco), *jarana* (Yucatán) and *son jarocho* (Veracruz). One *son jarocho* that has achieved world status is 'La Bamba'. Instrumental backing is provided in almost all these areas by a combination of large and small guitars, with the violin as virtuoso lead in the *huasteca* and the harp in Veracruz. The *chilena* of Guerrero was inspired by Chilean sailors performing their national dance, the *cueca*, during a naval visit to Acapulco in 1822, while Yucatán features a version of the Colombian *bambuco*. The *son* is a dance form for flirtation between couples, as befits a land of passionate men and women, and often involves spectacular heel-and-toe stamping by the man. Another widespread dance rhythm is the *jarabe*, including the patriotic 'Jarabe Tapatío', better known to the English-speaking world as the 'Mexican Hat Dance'. Certain regions are known for more sedate rhythms and a quite different choice of instruments. In the north, the Conjunto Norteño leads with an accordion and favours the polka as a rhythm. In Yucatán they prefer wind and brass instruments, while the Isthmus of Tehuantepec is the home of the *marimba* (xylophone), which it shares with neighbouring Guatemala.

For singing, as opposed to dancing, there are three extremely popular genres. First is the *corrido*, a narrative form derived from old Spanish ballads, which swept across the country with the armies of the Revolution and has remained a potent vehicle for popular expression ever since. A second is the *canción* (literally 'Song'), which gives full rein to the romantic, sentimental aspect of the Mexican character and is naturally slow and languid. 'Las Majojñanitas' is a celebrated song for serenading people on their birthdays. The third form is the *ranchera*, a sort of Mexican Country and Western, associated originally with the cattle-men of the Bajío region. Featured in a whole series of Mexican films of the 1930s and 1940s, *rancheras* became known all over the Spanish-speaking world as the typical Mexican music. The film and recording industry turned a number of Mexican artists into household names throughout Latin America. The 'immortals' are Pedro Infante, Jorge Negrete, Pedro Vargas, Miguel Aceves Meía and the Trio Los Panchos, with Agustín Lara as an equally celebrated and prolific songwriter and composer, particularly of romantic *boleros*. To all outsiders and most Mexicans however there is nothing more musically Mexican than *mariachi*, a word said to be derived from the French 'mariage', introduced at the time of Maximilian and Carlota.

Originating in the state of Jalisco, mariachi bands arrived in Mexico City in the 1920s and have never looked back. Trumpets now take the lead, backed by violins and guitars and the players all wear *charro* (cowboy) costume, including the characteristic hat. They play all the major musical forms and can be found almost every evening in Mexico City's Plaza Garibaldi, where they congregate to be seen, heard and, they hope, hired. This is the very soul of Mexico.

Finally, there are a number of distinguished 20th century composers who have produced symphonies and other orchestral works based on indigenous and folk themes. Carlos Chávez is the giant and his 'Sinfonía India' a particularly fine example. Other notable names are Silvestre Revueltas ('Sensemayá'), Pablo Moncayo ('Huapango'), Blas Galindo ('Sones de Mariachi') and Luis Sandi ('Yaqui Music').

Native music is at its most vigorous and flourishing at either end of the region, in Guatemala and Panama. In the intervening four republics its presence is more localized and indeed elusive. From Guatemala southwards a rich musical tradition based largely on the marimba (xylophone) as an instrument and the son as a song/dance genre fades fast but continues tenuously all the way down to Costa Rica, while Panama has its own very distinctive vein of traditional music, with a combination of Spanish and African elements. While the influence of Mexican music is all pervasive in the northern five republics, Panama is more closely linked with the Caribbean coasts of Colombia and Venezuela in its musical idioms.

Guatemala This is the heartland of the *marimba*, which it shares with parts of southern Mexico. How this came about has been much debated between adherents of a native precolumbian origin and those who believe the *marimba* came from Africa with colonial slavery. Whatever its origins, it is now regarded as the national instrument in Guatemala, belonging equally to Indian and *ladino*. Among the Indians the more rustic *marimba de tecomate* with gourds as resonators is still to be found, whereas most instruments now have the box resonator. The manufacture and playing of *marimbas* has developed to the point where a number of them are now combined to form an orchestra, as with the Pans of Trinidad. Among the best known *marimba* orchestras are the Marimba Tecún Umán, Marimba Antigua and highly sophisticated Marimba Nacional de Concierto. Every village has its *marimba* players and no wedding or other secular celebration would be complete without them. The music played is generally either a fast or slow *son*, but the modern repertoire is likely to include many Mexican numbers.

Although the *marimba* is basic to the Indians as well as to the *ladinos*, the former have other instruments for their religious rituals and processions, such as the *tun* (a precolumbian drum), *tzicolaj* (flute), *chirimía* (oboe) and violin. These are the instruments that accompany the colourful vernacular dances of the 'Culebra' (snake), 'Venado' (deer) and 'Palo Volador' (flying pole), as also the 'Baile de las Canastas' and 'Rabinal Achí', two precolombian historical dramas that have amazingly survived the conquest and colonial period and are still performed at Chajul and Rabinal (Alta Verapaz) respectively.

El Salvador and Honduras Two countries that tend to 'hide their light under a bushel' as regards native music. It is here above all that the Mexican music industry seems to exert an overwhelming cultural influence, while the virtual absence of an Indian population may also be partly responsible, since it is so often they who maintain traditions and hold to the past, as in Guatemala. Whatever the reason, the visitor who is seeking specifically Salvadorean or Honduran native music will find little to satisfy him or her. El Salvador is an extension of 'marimba country', but in both republics popular songs and dances are often accompanied by the guitar and seem to lack a rhythm or style that can be pinpointed as specifically local. An exception in El Salvador is the music played on the *pito de caña* and *tambor* which accompanies the traditional dances called 'Danza de los Historiantes', 'La Historia' or 'Los Moros y Cristianos'. Over 30 types of dance have been identified, mostly in the west and centre of the country, although there are a few in the east. The main theme is the conflict between christianized *indígenos* and 'heretic' *indígenos* and the dances are performed as a ritual on the local saint's day. Honduras shares with Belize and Guatemala the presence of Garifuna or Black Caribs on the Caribbean coast. These descendants of Carib Indians and escaped black slaves were deported to the area from St Vincent in the late 18th century and continue to maintain a very separate identity, including their own religious observances, music and dances, profoundly African in spirit and style.

Nicaragua Here we again find ourselves in 'marimba country' and here again the basic musical genre is the *son*, here called the 'Son Nica'. There are a number of popular dances for couples with the names of animals, like 'La Vaca' (cow), 'La Yeguita' (mare) and 'El Toro' (bull). The folklore capital of Nicaragua is the city of Masaya and the musical heart of Masaya is the Indian quarter of Monimbó. Here the *marimba* is king, but on increasingly rare occasions may be supported by the *chirimía* (oboe), *quijada de asno* (asses jaw) and *quijongo*, a single-string bow with gourd resonator. Some of the most traditional Sones are 'El Zañate', 'Los Novios' and 'La Perra Renca', while the more popular dances still to be found are 'Las Inditas', 'Las Negras', 'Los Diablitos' and 'El Torovenado', all involving masked characters. Diriamba is another centre of tradition, notable for the folk play known as 'El G eguense', accompanied by violin, fife and drum and the dance called 'Toro Guaco'. The Caribbean coast is a totally different cultural region, home to the Miskito Indians and English speaking black people of Jamaican origin concentrated around Bluefields. The latter have a maypole dance and their music is typically Afro-Caribbean, with banjos, accordeons, guitars and of course drums as the preferred instruments.

Costa Rica This is the southernmost in our string of 'marimba culture' countries. The guitar is also a popular instrument for accompanying folk dances, while the *chirimía* and *quijongo*, already encountered further north, have not yet totally died out in the Chorotega region of Guanacaste Province. This province is indeed the heartland of Costa Rican folklore and the 'Punto Guanacasteco', a heel-and-toe dance for couples, has been officially decreed to be the 'typical national dance', although it is not in fact traditional, but was composed at the turn of the century by Leandro Cabalceta Brau during a brief sojourn in gaol. There are other dances too, such as the 'Botijuela Tamborito' and 'Cambute', but it must honestly be said that they will not be found in the countryside as a tradition, but are performed on stage when outsiders need to be shown some native culture. Among the country's most popular native performers are the duet Los Talolingas, authors of 'La Guaria Morada', regarded as the 'second national anthem' and Lorenzo 'Lencho' Salazar, whose humorous songs in the vernacular style are considered quintessentially 'tico'.

Some of the republic's rapidly deculturizing Indian groups have dances of their own, like the 'Danza de los Diablitos' of the Borucas, the 'Danza del Sol' and 'Danza de la Luna' of the Chorotegas and the `Danza de los Huesos' of the Talamancas. A curious ocarina made of beeswax, the *dru mugata* is still played by the Guaymí Indians and is said to be the only truly precolumbian instrument still to be found. The drum and flute are traditional among various groups, but the guitar and accordeon are moving in to replace them. As in the case of Nicaragua, the Caribbean coast of Costa Rica, centred on Puerto Limón, is inhabited by black people who came originally from the English speaking islands and whose music reflects this origin. The *sinkit* seems to be a strictly local rhythm, but the *calypso* is popular and the *cuadrille*, square dance and maypole dance are also found. There is too a kind of popular hymn called the saki. Brass, percussion and string instruments are played, as also the accordeon.

Panama Panama is the crossroads of the Americas, where Central America meets South America and the Caribbean backs onto the Pacific. One of the smallest Latin American republics and the last to achieve independence, from Colombia, it nonetheless possesses an outstandingly rich and attractive musical culture. Albeit related to that of the Caribbean coast of Colombia and Venezuela, it is extremely distinctive. The classic Panamanian folk dances are the *tambor* or *tamborito*, *cumbia*, *punto* and *mejorana*, largely centred on the central provinces of Coclé, and Veraguas and those of Herrera and Los Santos on the Azuero Peninsula. Towns that are particularly noted for their musical traditions are Los Santos, Ocú, Las Tablas, Tonosí and Chorrera. The dances are for couples and groups of couples and the rhythms are lively and graceful, the man often dancing close to his partner without touching her, moving his hat in rhythmic imitation of fanning. The woman's *pollera* costume is arguably the most beautiful in Latin America and her handling of the voluminous skirt is an important element of the dance. The tamborito is considered to be Panama's national dance and is accompanied by three tall drums. The *cumbia*, which has a common origin with the better known Colombian dance of the same name, has a fast variant called the *atravesado*, while the punto is slower and more stately. The name *mejorana* is shared by a small native guitar, a dance, a song form and a specific tune. The commonest instruments to be found today are the tall drums that provide the basic beat, the violin, the guitar and the accordeon, with the last named rapidly becoming predominant. The *tuna* is a highly rhythmic musical procession with womens' chorus and massed hand-clapping.

Turning to song, there are two traditional forms, both of Spanish origin, the *copla*, sung by women and accompanying the *tamborito*, and the *mejorana*, which is a male solo preserve, with the lyrics in the form of *décimas*, a verse form used by the great Spanish poets of the Golden Age. It is accompanied by the ukulele-like guitar of the same name. Quite unique to Panama are the *salomas* and *gritos*, the former between two or more men. The yodelling and falsetto of the *salomas* are in fact carried over into the singing style and it is this element, more than any other, that gives Panamanian folk song its unique and instantly recognizable sound. There are other traditional masked street dances of a carnavalesque nature, such as the very African 'Congos', the 'Diablicos Sucios' (dirty little devils) and the 'Grandiablos' (big devils). In the area of the Canal there is a significant English speaking black population, similar to those in Nicaragua and Costa Rica, who also sing *calypso*, while the Guaymí (Ngöbe-Buglé) Indians in the west and the Kuna and Chocó (Emberá-Wunan) of the San Blas islands and Darién isthmus possess their own song, rituals and very attractive flute music.

David M Fishlow adds: when travelling in rural areas during working hours, listen for the distinctive yodelling call of Panamanian farm workers, who greet each other in the fields over long distances with the *saloma*, a cry that slides from a rumble in the throat to a falsetto and back into a rumble, usually rendered in Spanish as 'Ajuuúa'. Folk tradition says the custom was adopted from the Indians, who are certainly among its most expert and frequent practitioners. Psychologists say letting fly with such a yelp releases the fatigue and heat-induced tension built up by long hours swinging a machete to eliminate weeds from pastures, or to prepare fields for planting. Complex *saloma* based calls have heavily influenced Panamanian traditional song and the chanting that accompanies much dance. The 'Ajuuúa' can also be heard as an expression of approval at baseball games, football matches, and anywhere high spirits provide the occasion for whoops of delight.

Food

There is a paragraph on each nation's food under **Essentials**. Most restaurants serve a daily special meal, usually at lunchtime, which is cheaper than other dishes and good. Vegetarians should be able to list all the foods they cannot eat; saying 'Soy vegetariano/a' (I'm a vegetarian) or 'no como carne' (I don't eat meat) is often not enough.

Shopping

Remember that these can almost invariably be bought more cheaply away from the capital, though the choice may be less wide. Bargaining seems to be the general rule in most countries' street markets, but don't make a fool of yourself by bargaining over what, to you, is a small amount of money.

Souvenirs
You can also ship items home

If British travellers have no space in their luggage, they might like to remember Tumi, the Latin American Craft Centre, who specialize in Mexican and Andean products and who produce cultural and educational videos for schools: at 23/2A Chalk Farm Rd, London NW1 8AG (F0171-485 4152), 8/9 New Bond Street Place, Bath BA1 1BH (T01225 462367, F01225 444870), 1/2 Little Clarendon St, Oxford OX1 2HJ (T/F01865-512307), 82 Park St, Bristol BS1 5LA (T/F0117 929 0391). Tumi (Music) Ltd specializes in different rhythms of Latin America. See *Arts and Crafts of South America*, by Lucy Davies and Mo Fini, published by Tumi (1994), for a fine introduction to the subject. There are similar shops in the USA.

Responsible tourism

Much has been written about the adverse impacts of tourism on the environment and local communities. It is usually assumed that this only applies to the more excessive end of the travel industry such as the Spanish Costas and Bali. However it now seems that travellers can have an impact at almost any density and this is especially true in areas 'off the beaten track' where local people may not be used to western conventions and lifestyles, and natural environments may be very sensitive.

Of course, tourism can have a beneficial impact and this is something to which every traveller can contribute. Many national parks are part funded by receipts from people who travel to see exotic plants and animals, Barro Colorado (Panama) and the Cockscomb Jaguar Sanctuary (Belize) are good examples of such sites. Similarly, travellers can promote patronage and protection of valuable archaeological sites and heritages through their interest and entrance fees.

However, where visitor pressure is high and/or poorly regulated, damage can occur. This is especially so in parts of the Caribbean where some tour operators are expanding their activities with scant regard for the environment or local communities. It is also unfortunately true that many of the most popular destinations are in ecologically sensitive areas easily disturbed by extra human pressures. The desire to visit sites and communities that are off the beaten track is a driving force for many travellers. However, these are the areas that are often most sensitive to change as a result of increased pressure from visitors. Eventually the very features that tourists travel so far to see may become degraded and so we seek out new sites, discarding the old, and leaving someone else to deal with the plight of local communities and the damaged environment.

Fortunately, there are signs of a new awareness of the responsibilities that the travel industry and its clients need to endorse. For example, some tour operators fund local conservation projects and travellers are now more aware of the impact they may have on host cultures and environments. We can all contribute to the success of what is variously described as responsible, green or alternative tourism. All that is required is a little forethought and consideration. It would be impossible to identify all the possible impacts that might need to be addressed by travellers, but it is worthwhile noting the major areas in which we can all take a more responsible attitude in the countries we visit. These include, changes to natural ecosystems (air, water, land, ecology and wildlife), cultural values (beliefs and behaviour) and the built environment (sites of antiquity and archaeological significance). At an individual level, travellers can reduce their impact if greater consideration is given to their activities. Backpacking along the Maya trade routes makes for great stories, but how do local communities cope with the sudden invasive interest in their lives? Will the availability of easy tourist money and gauche behaviour affect them for the worse, possibly diluting the significance of culture and customs? Similarly, have the environmental implications of increased visitor pressure been considered? Litter and disturbance of wildlife might seem to be small issues and, on an individual scale they probably are, however multiplied several fold they become more serious (as the Inca Trail in Peru can attest).

Some of these impacts are caused by factors beyond the direct control of travellers, such as the management and operation of a hotel chain. Even here it is possible to voice concern about damaging activities and an increasing number of hotels and travel operators are taking 'green concerns' seriously, even if it is only to protect their share of the market.

Environmental legislation Legislation is increasingly being enacted to control damage to the environment, and in some cases this can have a bearing on travellers. The establishment of national parks may involve rules and guidelines for visitors and these should always be followed. In addition there may be local or national laws controlling behaviour and use of natural resources (especially wildlife) that are being increasingly enforced. If in doubt, ask. Finally, international legislation, principally the Convention on International Trade in Endangered Species of Wild Fauna and Flora (CITES), may affect travellers.

CITES aims to control the trade in live specimens of endangered plants and animals and also 'recognizable parts or derivatives' of protected species. Sale of Black Coral, Turtle Shells, Protected Orchids and other wildlife is strictly controlled by signatories of the convention. The full list of protected wildlife varies, so if you feel the need to purchase souvenirs and trinkets derived from wildlife, it would be prudent to check whether they are protected. Every country included in this Handbook is a signatory of CITES. In addition, most European countries, the USA and Canada are all signatories of CITES. Importation of CITES protected species into these countries can lead to heavy fines, confiscation of goods and even imprisonment. Information on the status of legislation and protective measures can be obtained from Traffic International, UK office, 219C Huntingdon Rd, Cambridge, CB3 0DL, T01223-277427, F01223-277237, traffic @wcmc.org.uk.

Green travel companies and information The increasing awareness of the environmental impact of travel and tourism has led to a range of advice and information services as well as spawning specialist travel companies who claim to provide 'responsible travel' for clients. This is an expanding field and the veracity of claims needs to be substantiated in some cases. The following organizations and publications can provide useful information for those with an interest in pursuing responsible travel opportunities.

Organizations GREEN GLOBE, a membership organization, advises anyone involved in the travel industry on environmental policy, T UK 01223-890250, F890258, 101453.3077@ compuserve.com; also on this number is Environmental Travel Solutions Ltd. **Tourism Concern** Aims to promote a greater understanding of the impact of tourism on host communities and environments; Southlands College, Wimbledon Parkside, London SW19 5NN, T UK-0181-9440464, tourconcern@gn.apc.org, www.gn.apc. org/ tourismconcern. **Rethinking Tourism Project**, PO Box 581938, Minneapolis, MN 55458-1938, USA, T612-5210098, RTProject@aol.com. **Centre for the Advancement of Responsive Travel** CART has a range of publications available as well as information on alternative holiday destinations, T UK-01732-352757.

Health

Staying healthy in Latin America is straightforward. With the following advice and precautions you should keep as healthy as you do at home. Most visitors return home having experienced no problems at all beyond an upset stomach. However, in Latin America the health risks, especially in the lowland tropical areas, are different from those encountered in Europe or the USA. It also depends on how you travel, and where. There are clear health differences in the various countries of Latin America and between the risks for the business traveller, who stays in international class hotels in large cities, the backpacker who is trekking from country to country and the tourist who heads for the beach. There are no hard and fast rules to follow: you will often have to make your own judgement on the healthiness or otherwise of your surroundings. There are English (or other foreign language) speaking doctors in most major cities who have particular experience in dealing with locally-occurring diseases. Your Embassy representative will often be able to give you the name of local reputable doctors and most of the better hotels have a doctor on standby. If you do fall ill and cannot find a recommended doctor, try the Outpatient Department of a hospital – private hospitals are usually less crowded and offer a more acceptable standard of care to foreigners. It is worth remembering that, apart from mosquitoes, the most dangerous animals are men, be they bandits or behind steering wheels. Think carefully about violent confrontations and wear a seat belt if you are lucky enough to have one available to you.

Before travelling

Take out medical insurance. Make sure it covers all eventualities especially evacuation to your home country by a medically equipped plane. You should have a dental check up, obtain a spare glasses prescription, a spare oral contraceptive prescription (or enough pills to last) and, if you suffer from a chronic illness (such as diabetes, high blood pressure, ear or sinus troubles, cardio-pulmonary disease or nervous disorder), you should arrange for a check up with your doctor. He will be able at the same time to provide you with a letter explaining the details of your disability in English and if possible Spanish. Check the current practice in countries you are visiting for malaria prophylaxis (prevention). If you are on regular medication, make sure you have enough to cover the period of your travel.

Children More preparation is probably necessary for babies and children than for an adult and perhaps a little more care should be taken when travelling to remote areas where health services are primitive. This is because children can be become more rapidly ill than adults (although, on the other hand, they often recover more quickly). Diarrhoea and vomiting are the most common problems, so take the usual precautions, but more intensively. Breastfeeding is best and most convenient for babies, but powdered milk is generally available and so are baby foods in most countries. Papaya, bananas and avocados are all nutritious and can be cleanly prepared. The treatment of diarrhoea is the same as it is for adults, except that it should start earlier and be continued with more persistence. Children get dehydrated very quickly in hot countries and can become drowsy and uncooperative unless cajoled to drink water or juice plus salts. Upper respiratory infections, such as colds, catarrh and middle ear infections are also common and if your child suffers from these normally, take some antibiotics against the possibility. Outer ear infections after swimming are also common and antibiotic eardrops will help. Wet wipes are always useful and sometimes difficult to find in Latin America, as, in some places, are disposable nappies.

Medicines & what to take There is very little control on the sale of drugs and medicines in Latin America. You may be able to buy any and every drug in pharmacies without a prescription. Be wary of this because pharmacists can be poorly trained and might sell you drugs that are unsuitable, dangerous or old. Many drugs and medicines are manufactured under licence from American or European companies, so the trade names may be familiar to you. This means you do not have to carry a whole chest of medicines with you, but remember that the shelf life of some items, especially vaccines and antibiotics, is markedly reduced in hot conditions. Buy your supplies at the better outlets where there are more refrigerators, even though they are more expensive, and check the expiry date of all preparations you buy. Immigration officials occasionally confiscate scheduled drugs (Lomotil is an example) if they are not accompanied by a doctor's prescription. Self-medication may be forced on you by circumstances so the following information contains the names of drugs and medicines which you may find useful in an emergency or in out-of-the-way places.

Medical Kit check list **Sunglasses**: a type designed for intense sunlight; **Earplugs**: for sleeping on aeroplanes and in noisy hotels; **Suntan cream**: with a high protection factor; **Insect repellent**: containing DET for preference; **Mosquito net**: lightweight, permethrin-impregnated; **Tablets**: for travel sickness; **Tampons**: can be expensive in some countries in Latin America; **Condoms**; **Contraceptives**; **Water sterilizing tablets**; **Antimalarial tablets**; **Anti-infective ointment**: eg Cetrimide; **Dusting powder for feet etc**: containing fungicide; **Antacid tablets**: for indigestion; **Sachets of rehydration salts plus anti-diarrhoea preparations**; **Painkillers**: such as paracetamol or aspirin; **Antibiotics**: for diarrhoea etc. **First Aid Kit**: Small pack containing a few sterile syringes and needles and disposable gloves. The risk of catching hepatitis etc from a dirty needle used for injection is now negligible in Latin America, but you may feel safer carrying your own supplies – available from camping shops and at airports.

Vaccination & immunisation Smallpox vaccination is no longer required anywhere in the world and cholera vaccination is no longer recognized as necessary or effective for international travel by the World Health Organisation. Nevertheless, some immigration officials are still demanding proof of vaccination against cholera in Latin America and in some countries outside Latin America, following the outbreak of the disease which originated in Peru in 1990-91 and subsequently affected most surrounding countries. Although it is very unlikely to affect visitors to Latin

Essentials

America, the cholera epidemic continues to make its greatest impact in poor areas where water supplies are polluted and food hygiene practices are insanitary.

Vaccination against the following diseases is recommended:

Yellow Fever This is a live vaccination not to be given to children under nine months or persons allergic to eggs. Immunity lasts for 10 years, an International Certificate of Yellow Fever Vaccination will be given and should be kept because it is sometimes asked for. Yellow fever is very rare in Latin America, but the vaccination is practically without side effects and almost totally protective.

Typhoid A number of new vaccines against this condition are now available; the older TAB and monovalent typhoid vaccines are being phased out. The newer, eg Typhim Vi, cause less side effects, but are more expensive. For those who do not like injections, there are now oral vaccines.

Poliomyelitis Despite its decline in the world this remains a serious disease if caught and is easy to protect against. There are live oral vaccines and in some countries injected vaccines. Whichever one you choose it is a good idea to have a booster every 3-5 years if visiting developing countries regularly.

Tetanus & other routine vaccinations One dose should be given with a booster at six weeks and another at six months and 10 yearly boosters thereafter are recommended. Children should already be properly protected against diphtheria, poliomyelitis and pertussis (whooping cough), measles and HIB all of which can be more serious infections in Latin America than at home. Measles, mumps and rubella vaccine is also given to children throughout the world, but those teenage girls who have not had rubella (German measles) should be tested and vaccinated. Hepatitis B vaccination for babies is now routine in some countries. Consult your doctor for advice on tuberculosis inoculation: the disease is still widespread in Latin America.

Infectious Hepatitis This is less of a problem for travellers than it used to be because of the development of two extremely effective vaccines against the A and B form of the disease. It remains common, however, in Latin America. A combined hepatitis A & B vaccine is now licensed and has been available since 1997 – one jab covers both diseases.

Other vaccinations These might be considered in the case of epidemics eg meningitis. There is an effective vaccination against rabies, which should be considered by all travellers, especially those going through remote areas or if there is a particular occupational risk, eg for zoologists or veterinarians.

Further information Further information on health risks abroad, vaccinations etc may be available from a local travel clinic. If you wish to take specific drugs with you such as antibiotics these are best prescribed by your own doctor. Be aware, however, that not all doctors are experts on the health problems of remote countries. More detailed or more up-to-date information than local doctors can provide is available from various sources. In the UK there are hospital departments specializing in tropical diseases in London, Liverpool, Birmingham and Glasgow and the Malaria Reference Laboratory at the London School of Hygiene and Tropical Medicine provides advice about malaria, T0891-600350. In the USA the local Public Health Services can give such information and information is available centrally from the Centres for Disease Control (CDC) in Atlanta, T404-3324559, www.cdc.gov. In Canada contact IAMAT, 40 Regal Rd, Guelph, Ontario, M6E 1B8.

There are in addition computerized databases which can be accessed for destination-specific, up-to-the-minute information. In the UK there is MASTA (Medical Advisory Service to Travellers Abroad), T0171-6314408, Tx8953473, F0171-4365389 and Travax (Glasgow, T0141-9467120 ext 247). Other information on medical problems overseas can be obtained from the book by Dr Richard Dawood (Editor) – *Travellers' Health, How to Stay*

Healthy Abroad (Oxford University Press 1992 £7.99). We strongly recommend the new, revised and updated edition (publication imminent), especially to the intrepid traveller heading for the more out of the way places. General advice is also available in the UK in Health Information for Overseas Travel (Department of Health) available from HMSO and International Travel and Health (WHO). Handbooks on First Aid are produced by the British & American Red Cross and by St John's Ambulance (UK).

On the way

For most travellers a trip to Latin America means a long air flight. If this crosses time zones then jetlag can be a problem. The main symptoms are tiredness and sleepiness at inconvenient times and, conversely, a tendency to wake up in the middle of the night feeling like you want your breakfast. Most find that the problem is worse when flying in an easterly direction. The best way to get over jetlag is to try to force yourself into the new time zone as strictly as possible. This may involve, on a westward flight, trying to stay awake until your normal bedtime and on an eastward flight, forgetting that you have lost some sleep on the way out and going to bed relatively early but near your normal time on the evening after you arrive. The symptoms of jetlag may be helped by keeping up your fluid intake on the journey, but not with alcohol. The hormone melatonin seems to reduce the symptoms of jetlag but is not presently licensed in most of Europe although it can be obtained from health food stores in the USA.

On long-haul flights it is also important to stretch your legs at least every hour to prevent slowing of the circulation and the possible development of blood clots. Drinking plenty of non-alcoholic fluids also helps.

If travelling by boat then sea sickness can be a problem – this is dealt with in the usual way by taking anti motion-sickness pills.

Staying healthy on arrival

The thought of catching a stomach bug worries visitors to Latin America but there have been great improvements in food hygiene and most such infections are preventable. Travellers' diarrhoea and vomiting is due, most of the time, to food poisoning, usually passed on by the insanitary habits of food handlers. As a general rule the cleaner your surroundings and the smarter the restaurant, the less likely you are to suffer.

Foods to avoid: uncooked, undercooked, partially cooked or reheated meat, fish, eggs, raw vegetables and salads, especially when they have been left out and exposed to flies. Stick to fresh food that has been cooked from raw just before eating and make sure you peel fruit yourself. Wash and dry your hands before eating – disposable wet-wipe tissues are useful for this.

Shellfish eaten raw are risky and at certain times of the year some fish and shellfish concentrate toxins from their environment and cause various kinds of food poisoning. The local authorities notify the public not to eat these foods. Do not ignore the warning. Heat treated milk (UHT) pasteurized or sterilized is becoming more available in Latin America as is pasteurized cheese. On the whole matured or processed cheeses are safer than the fresh varieties. Fresh unpasteurized milk can be a source of food poisoning germs, tuberculosis and brucellosis. This applies equally to ice-cream, yoghurt and cheese made from unpasteurized milk, so avoid these home-made products – the factory made ones are probably safer.

Tap water is rarely safe outside the major cities, especially in the rainy season. Stream water, if you are in the countryside, is often contaminated by communities living surprisingly high up in the mountains. Filtered or bottled water is usually available and safe, although you must make sure that somebody is not filling bottles from the tap and hammering on a new crown cap. If your hotel has a central hot water supply, this water is safe to drink after cooling. Ice for drinks should be made from boiled water, but it rarely is, so stand your glass on the ice cubes, rather than putting them in the drink. The better hotels have water-purifying systems.

(margin) Essentials

(margin) Intestinal upsets

Travellers' diarrhoea   This is usually caused by eating food which has been contaminated by food poisoning germs. Drinking water is rarely the culprit. Sea water or river water is more likely to be contaminated by sewage and so swimming in such dilute effluent can also be a cause.

Infection with various organisms can give rise to travellers' diarrhoea. They may be viruses, bacteria, eg Escherichia coli (probably the most common cause worldwide), protozoa (such as Amoeba and Giardia), Salmonella and cholera. The diarrhoea may come on suddenly or rather slowly. It may be accompanied by vomiting or by severe abdominal pain, and the passage of blood or mucus is a sign of dysentery.

Diagnosis and treatment   If you can time the onset of the diarrhoea to the minute ('acute') then it is probably due to a virus or a bacterium and/or the onset of dysentery. The treatment, in addition to rehydration, is an antibiotic such as ciprofloxacin 500 milograms every 12 hours; the drug is now widely available and there are many similar ones.

If the diarrhoea comes on slowly or intermittently ('sub-acute') then it is more likely to be protozoal, ie caused by an amoeba or Giardia. Antibiotics such as ciprofloxacin will have little effect. These cases are best treated by a doctor as is any outbreak of diarrhoea continuing for more than three days. Sometimes blood is passed in amoebic dysentery and for this you should certainly seek medical help. If this is not available then the best treatment is probably tinidazole (Fasigyn) one tablet four times a day for three days. If there are severe stomach cramps, the following drugs may help but are not very useful in the management of acute diarrhoea: loperamide (Imodium) and diphenoxylate with atropine (Lomotil). They should not be given to children.

Any kind of diarrhoea, whether or not accompanied by vomiting, responds well to the replacement of water and salts, taken as frequent sips of some kind of rehydration solution. There are proprietary preparations consisting of sachets of powder which you dissolve in boiled water, or you can make your own by adding half a teaspoonful of salt (3.5 grams) and four tablespoonful of sugar (40 grams) to a litre of boiled water.

Thus the linchpins of treatment for diarrhoea are rest, fluid and salt replacement, antibiotics such as ciprofloxacin for the bacterial types and special diagnostic tests and medical treatment for the Amoeba and Giardia infections. Salmonella infections and cholera, although rare, can be devastating diseases and it would be wise to get to a hospital as soon as possible if these are suspected.

Fasting, peculiar diets and the consumption of large quantities of yoghurt have not been found useful in calming travellers' diarrhoea or in rehabilitating inflamed bowels. Oral rehydration has on the other hand, especially in children, been a life saving technique and should always be practised, whatever other treatment you use. As there is some evidence that alcohol and milk might prolong diarrhoea they should be avoided during and immediately after an attack. So should chillies!

Diarrhoea occurring day after day for long periods of time (chronic diarrhoea) is notoriously resistant to amateur attempts at treatment and again warrants proper diagnostic tests (most towns with reasonable sized hospitals have laboratories for stool samples). There are ways of preventing travellers' diarrhoea for short periods of time by taking antibiotics, but this is not a foolproof technique and should not be used other than in exceptional circumstances. Doxycycline is possibly the best drug. Some preventatives such as Enterovioform can have serious side effects if taken for long periods.

Paradoxically constipation is also common, probably induced by dietary change, inadequate fluid intake in hot places and long bus journeys. Simple laxatives are useful in the short-term and bulky foods such as maize, beans and plenty of fruit are also useful.

Water purification   There are a number of ways of purifying water in order to make it safe to drink. Dirty water should first be strained through a filter bag (camping shops) and then boiled or treated. Bringing water to a rolling boil at sea level is sufficient to make the water safe for drinking, but at higher altitudes you have to boil the water for a few minutes longer to ensure that all the microbes are killed.

There are sterilizing methods that can be used and there are proprietary preparations containing chlorine (eg Puritabs) or iodine (eg Pota Aqua) compounds. Chlorine compounds generally do not kill protozoa (eg Giardia).

There are a number of water filters now on the market available in personal and expedition size. They work either on mechanical or chemical principles, or may do both. Make sure you take the spare parts or spare chemicals with you and do not believe everything the manufacturers say.

Spending time at high altitude in Latin America, especially in the tropics, is usually a pleasure – it is not so hot, there are no insects and the air is clear and spring-like. Travelling to high altitudes, however, can cause medical problems, all of which can be prevented if care is taken.

High altitude

On reaching heights above about 3,000 metres, heart pounding and shortness of breath, especially on exertion are a normal response to the lack of oxygen in the air. A condition called acute mountain sickness can also affect visitors. It is more likely to affect those who ascend rapidly. This takes a few hours or days to come on and its symptoms are: a bad headache; extreme tiredness; sometimes dizziness; loss of appetite and frequently nausea and vomiting. Insomnia is common and is often associated with a suffocating feeling when lying in bed. Keen observers may note that their breathing rate tends to wax and wane at night and that their face tends to be puffy in the mornings – this is all part of the syndrome. Anyone can get this condition and past experience is not always a good guide: the author, having spent years in Peru travelling constantly between sea level and very high altitude never suffered symptoms, then was severely affected whilst climbing Kilimanjaro in Tanzania.

The treatment of acute mountain sickness is simple – rest, painkillers (preferably not aspirin based) for the headache and anti sickness pills for vomiting. Oxygen is actually not much help, except at very high altitude. Various local panaceas – Coramina glucosada, Effortil, Micoren are popular in Latin America and mate de coca (an infusion of coca leaves widely available and perfectly legal) will alleviate some of the symptoms.

To prevent the condition: on arrival at places over 3,000 metres have a few hours rest in a chair and avoid alcohol, cigarettes and heavy food. If the symptoms are severe and prolonged, it is best to descend to a lower altitude and to reascend slowly or in stages. If this is impossible because of shortage of time, or if you are going so high that acute mountain sickness is very likely, then the drug acetazolamide (Diamox) can be used as a preventative and continued during the ascent. There is good evidence of the value of this drug in the prevention of soroche, but some people do experience peculiar side effects. The usual dose is 500 milograms of the slow release preparation each night, starting the night before ascending above 3,000 metres.

Watch out for sunburn at high altitude. The ultraviolet rays are extremely powerful. The air is also excessively dry at high altitude and you might find that you skin dries out and the inside of your nose becomes crusted. Use a moisturiser for the skin and some vaseline wiped into the nostrils. Some people find contact lenses irritate because of the dry air. It is unwise to ascend to high altitude if you are pregnant, especially in the first three months, or if you have a history of heart, lung or blood disease, including sickle cell.

A more unusual condition can affect mountaineers who ascend rapidly to high altitude – acute pulmonary oedema. Residents at altitude sometimes experience this when returning to the mountains from time spent at the coast. This condition is often preceded by acute mountain sickness and comes on quite rapidly with severe breathlessness, noisy breathing, cough, blueness of the lips and frothing at the mouth. Anybody who develops this must be brought down as soon as possible, given oxygen and taken to hospital.

A rapid descent from high places will make sinus problems and middle ear infections worse and might make your teeth ache. Lastly, don't fly to altitude within 24 hours of scuba diving. You might suffer from 'the bends'.

Full acclimatization to high temperatures takes about two weeks. During this period it is normal to feel a bit apathetic, especially if the relative humidity is high. Drink plenty of water (up to 15 litres a day are required when working physically hard in the tropics), use salt on your food and avoid extreme exertion. Tepid showers are more cooling than hot or cold ones. Large hats do not cool you down, but do prevent sunburn. Remember that, especially in the highlands, there can be a large and sudden drop in temperature between sun and shade and

Heat & cold

Essentials

between night and day, so dress accordingly. Warm jackets or woollens are essential after dark at high altitude. Loose cotton is still the best material when the weather is hot.

Air pollution Many large Latin American cities are notorious for their poor air quality. Expect sore throats and itchy eyes. Sufferers from asthma or bronchitis may have to increase their regular maintenance treatment.

Insects These are mostly more of a nuisance than a serious hazard and with a bit of preparation, you can prevent being bitten entirely. Some, such as mosquitoes are, of course, carriers of potentially serious diseases, so it is sensible to avoid being bitten as much as possible. Sleep off the ground and use a mosquito net or some kind of insecticide. Preparations containing pyrethrum or synthetic pyrethroids are safe. They are available as aerosols or pumps and the best way to use these is to spray the room thoroughly in all areas (follow the instructions rather than the insects) and then shut the door for a while, re-entering when the smell has dispersed. Mosquito coils release insecticide as they burn slowly. They are widely available and useful out of doors. Tablets of insecticide which are placed on a heated mat plugged into a wall socket are probably the most effective. They fill the room with insecticidal fumes in the same way as aerosols or coils.

You can also use insect repellents, most of which are effective against a wide range of pests. The most common and effective is diethyl metatoluamide (DET). DET liquid is best for arms and face (take care around eyes and with spectacles – DET dissolves plastic). Aerosol spray is good for clothes and ankles and liquid DET can be dissolved in water and used to impregnate cotton clothes and mosquito nets. Some repellents now contain DET and permethrin, an insecticide. Impregnated wrist and ankle bands can also be useful.

If you are bitten or stung, itching may be relieved by cool baths, antihistamine tablets (care with alcohol or driving) or mild corticosteriod creams, eg hydrocortisone (great care should be exercised: never use if there is any hint of infection). Careful scratching of all your bites once a day can be surprisingly effective. Calamine lotion and cream have limited effectiveness and antihistamine creams are not generally recommended – they can cause allergies themselves. Bites which become infected should be treated with a local antiseptic or antibiotic cream such as cetrimide, as should any infected sores or scratches.

When living rough, infestations of the skin with body lice (crabs) and scabies are easy to pick up. Use whatever local commercial preparation is recommended for lice and scabies. Crotamiton cream (Eurax) alleviates itching and also kills a number of skin parasites. Malathion lotion five percent (Prioderm) kills lice effectively, but avoid the use of the toxic agricultural preparation of malathion, more often used to commit suicide.

Ticks Ticks usually attach themselves to the lower parts of the body often after walking in areas where cattle have grazed. They take a while to attach themselves strongly, but swell up as they start to suck blood. The important thing is to remove them gently, so that they do not leave their head parts in your skin because this can cause a nasty allergic reaction some days later. Do not use petrol, vaseline, lighted cigarettes etc to remove the tick, but, with a pair of tweezers remove the beast gently by gripping it at the attached (head) end and rock it out in very much the same way that a tooth is extracted. Certain tropical flies which lay their eggs under the skin of sheep and cattle also occasionally do the same thing to humans with the unpleasant result that a maggot grows under the skin and pops up as a boil or pimple. The best way to remove these is to cover the boil with oil, vaseline or nail varnish so as to stop the maggot breathing, then to squeeze it out gently the next day.

Other animal bites & stings It is a very rare event indeed for travellers, but if you are unlucky (or careless) enough to be bitten by a venomous snake, spider, scorpion or sea creature, try to identify the creature, without putting yourself in further danger. Snake bites in particular are very frightening, but in fact rarely poisonous – even venomous snakes bite without injecting venom. What you might expect if bitten are: fright, swelling, pain and bruising around the bite and soreness of the regional lymph glands, perhaps nausea, vomiting and a fever. Signs of serious poisoning would be the following symptoms: numbness and tingling of the face, muscular spasms, convulsions, shortness of breath or a failure of the blood to clot, causing generalized bleeding. Victims should be taken to a hospital or a doctor without delay. Commercial snake bite and scorpion kits are available, but are usually only useful for the specific types of snake or scorpion. Most serum has to be given intravenously so it is not much good equipping yourself with it unless you are used to making injections into veins. It is best to rely on local practice in these cases, because the particular creatures will be known about locally and appropriate treatment can be given.

Reassure and comfort the victim frequently. Immobilize the limb by a bandage or a splint or by getting the person to lie still. Do not slash the bite area and try to suck out the poison because this sort of heroism does more harm than good. If you know how to use a tourniquet in these circumstances, you will not need this advice. If you are not experienced, do not apply a tourniquet. **Treatment of snake bite**

Avoid walking in snake territory in bare feet or sandals – wear proper shoes or boots. If you encounter a snake stay put until it slithers away, and do not investigate a wounded snake. Spiders and scorpions may be found in the more basic hotels, especially in the Andean countries. If stung, rest and take plenty of fluids and call a doctor. The best precaution is to keep beds away from the walls and look inside your shoes and under the toilet seat every morning. **Precautions**

Certain tropical sea fish when trodden upon inject venom into bathers' feet. This can be exceptionally painful. Wear plastic shoes when you go bathing if such creatures are reported. The pain can be relieved by immersing the foot in extremely hot water for as long as the pain persists. **Marine bites & stings**

The burning power of the tropical sun, especially at high altitude, is phenomenal. Always wear a wide brimmed hat and use some form of suncream or lotion on untanned skin. Normal temperate zone suntan lotions (protection factor up to seven) are not much good; you need to use the types designed specifically for the tropics or for mountaineers or skiers with protection factors up to 15 or above. These are often not available in Latin America. Glare from the sun can cause conjunctivitis, so wear sunglasses especially on tropical beaches, where high protection factor sunscreen should also be used. **Sunburn**

In Latin America AIDS is increasing and is not wholly confined to the well known high risk sections of the population, ie homosexual men, intravenous drug abusers and children of infected mothers. Heterosexual transmission is now the dominant mode and so the main risk to travellers is from casual sex. The same precautions should be taken as with any sexually transmitted disease. The AIDS virus (HIV) can be passed by unsterilized needles which have been previously used to inject an HIV positive patient, but the risk of this is negligible. It would, however, be sensible to check that needles have been properly sterilized or disposable needles have been used. If you wish to take your own disposable needles, be prepared to explain what they are for. The risk of receiving a blood transfusion with blood infected with the HIV virus is greater than from dirty needles because of the amount of fluid exchanged. Supplies of blood for transfusion should now be screened for HIV in all reputable hospitals, so again the risk is very small indeed. Catching the AIDS virus does not always produce an illness in itself (although it may do). The only way to be sure if you feel you have been put at risk is to have a blood test for HIV antibodies on your return to a place where there are reliable laboratory facilities. The test does not become positive for some weeks. **AIDS**

In South and Central America malaria is theoretically confined to coastal and jungle zones, but is now on the increase again. Mosquitoes do not thrive above 2,500 metres, so you are safe at altitude. There are different varieties of malaria, some resistant to the normal drugs. Make local enquiries if you intend to visit possibly infected zones and use a prophylactic regime. Start taking the tablets a few days before exposure and continue to take them for six weeks after leaving the malarial zone. Remember to give the drugs to babies and children **Malaria** also. Opinion varies on the precise drugs and dosage to be used for protection. All the drugs may have some side effects and it is important to balance the risk of catching the disease against the (albeit rare) side effects. The increasing complexity of the subject is such that as the malarial parasite becomes immune to the new generation of drugs it has made concentration on the physical prevention of being bitten by mosquitoes more important. This involves the use of long sleeved shirts or blouses and long trousers, repellents and nets. Clothes are now available impregnated with the insecticide permethrin or deltamethrin or it is possible to impregnate the clothes yourself. Wide meshed nets impregnated with permethrin are also available, are lighter to carry and less claustrophobic to sleep in.

Prophylaxis and treatment If your itinerary takes you into a malarial area, seek expert advice before you go on a suitable prophylactic regime. This is especially true for pregnant women who are particularly prone to catch malaria. You can still catch the disease even when sticking to a proper regime, although it is unlikely. If you do develop symptoms (high fever, shivering, headache, sometimes diarrhoea), seek medical advice immediately. If this is not possible and there is a great likelihood of malaria, the treatment is:

If the local strain is likely to be sensitive to it, then the treatment is Chloroquine, a single dose of four tablets (600 milograms) followed by two tablets (300 milograms) in six hours and 300 milograms each day following.

If it is falciparum malaria or the type is in doubt, take local advice. Various combinations of drugs are being used such as Quinine, Tetracycline or Halofantrine. If falciparum malaria is definitely diagnosed, it is wise to get to a good hospital as treatment can be complex and the illness very serious.

Infectious hepatitis (Jaundice) The main symptoms are pains in the stomach, lack of appetite, lassitude and yellowness of the eyes and skin. Medically speaking there are two main types. The less serious, but more common is hepatitis A for which the best protection is the careful preparation of food, the avoidance of contaminated drinking water and scrupulous attention to toilet hygiene. The other, more serious, version is hepatitis B which is acquired usually as a sexually transmitted disease or by blood transfusion. It is less commonly transmitted by injections with unclean needles and possibly by insect bites. The symptoms are the same as for hepatitis A. The incubation period is much longer (up to six months compared with six weeks) and there are more likely to be complications.

Hepatitis A can be protected against with gamma globulin. It should be obtained from a reputable source and is certainly useful for travellers who intend to live rough. You should have a shot before leaving and have it repeated every six months. The dose of gamma globulin depends on the concentration of the particular preparation used, so the manufacturer's advice should be taken. The injection should be given as close as possible to your departure and, as the dose depends on the time you are likely to spend in potentially affected areas, the manufacturer's instructions should be followed. Gamma globulin has really been superseded now by a proper vaccination against hepatitis A (Havrix), which gives immunity lasting up to 10 years. After that boosters are required. Havrix monodose is now widely available as is junior Havrix. The vaccination has negligible side effects and is extremely effective. Gamma globulin injection can be a bit painful, but it is cheaper than Havrix and may be more available in some places.

Hepatitis B can be effectively prevented by a specific vaccine (Engerix) – three shots over six months before travelling. If you have had jaundice in the past it would be worthwhile having a blood test to see if you are immune to either of these two types, because this might avoid the necessity and costs of vaccination or gamma globulin. There are other kinds of viral hepatitis (C, E, G etc) which are fairly similar to A and B, but vaccines are not available as yet.

Other afflictions

Athlete's Foot This and other fungal skin infections are best treated with tolnaftate or clotrimazole.

Chagas' Disease (South American trypanosomiasis) This is a chronic disease, very rarely caught by travellers and difficult to treat. It is transmitted by the simultaneous biting and excreting of the Reduvid bug, also known as the Vinchuca or Barbeiro. Somewhat resembling a small cockroach, this nocturnal bug lives in poor adobe houses with dirt floors often frequented by opossums. If you cannot avoid such accommodation, sleep off the floor with a candle lit, use a mosquito net, keep as much of your skin covered as possible, and use DET repellent or a spray insecticide. If you are bitten overnight (the bites are painless) do not scratch them, but wash thoroughly with soap and water.

Dengue Fever This is increasing worldwide, including in Mexico and Central American countries and the Caribbean. It can be completely prevented by avoiding mosquito bites in the same way as malaria. No vaccine is available. Dengue is an unpleasant and painful disease, presenting with a high temperature and body pains, but at least visitors are spared the more serious forms (haemorrhagic types) which are more of a problem for local people who have been exposed to the disease more than once. There is no specific treatment for dengue – just pain killers and rest.

Intestinal Worms These are common and the more serious ones, such as hookworm, can be contracted from walking barefoot on infested earth or beaches. Some cause an itchy rash on the feet "cutaneous larva migrans". Schistosomiasis (bilharzia) is also present in some lakes – take local advice before swimming in them.

Leptospirosis Various forms of leptospirosis occur throughout Latin America, transmitted by a bacterium which is excreted in rodent urine. Fresh water and moist soil harbour the organisms which enter the body through cuts and scratches. If you suffer from any form of prolonged fever consult a doctor.

Prickly heat A very common intensely itchy rash is avoided by frequent washing and by wearing loose clothing. It is cured by allowing skin to dry off (through use of powder and spending two nights in an air-conditioned hotel!).

Psychological Disorders First time exposure to countries where sections of the population live in extreme poverty or squalor can cause odd psychological reactions in visitors, or what is more commonly known as culture shock. So can the incessant pestering, especially of women, which is unfortunately common in some of these countries. Simply be prepared for this and try not to over-react.

Rabies Remember that rabies is endemic throughout Latin America, so avoid dogs that are behaving strangely and cover your toes at night from the vampire bats, which also carry the disease. If you are bitten by a domestic or wild animal, do not leave things to chance: scrub the wound with soap and water and/or disinfectant, try to have the animal captured (within limits) or at least determine its ownership, where possible, and seek medical assistance at once. The course of treatment depends on whether you have already been satisfactorily vaccinated against rabies. If you have (this is worthwhile if you are spending lengths of time in developing countries) then some further doses of vaccine are all that is required. Human diploid vaccine is the best, but expensive: other, older kinds of vaccine, such as that derived from duck embryos may be the only types available. These are effective, much cheaper and interchangeable generally with the human derived types. If not already vaccinated then anti rabies serum (immunoglobulin) may be required in addition. It is important to finish the course of treatment whether the animal survives or not.

Typhus This can still occur and is carried by ticks. There is usually a reaction at the site of the bite and a fever. Seek medical advice.

Other tropical diseases and problems found in jungle areas: These are usually transmitted by biting insects. They are often related to African diseases and were probably introduced by the slave labour trade. Onchocerciasis (river blindness) carried by blackflies is found in parts of Mexico. Leishmaniasis (Espundia) is carried by sandflies and causes a sore that will not heal or a severe nasal infection. Wearing long trousers and a long sleeved shirt in infected areas protects against these flies. DET is also effective. Epidemics of meningitis occur from time-to-time. Be careful about swimming in piranha or caribe infested rivers. It is a good idea not to swim naked: the Candiru fish can follow urine currents and become lodged in body orifices. Swimwear offers some protection.

When you return home

Remember to take your antimalarial tablets for six weeks after leaving the malarial area. If you have had attacks of diarrhoea it is worth having a stool specimen tested in case you have picked up amoebas. If you have been living rough, blood tests may be worthwhile to detect worms and other parasites. If you have been exposed to Bilharzia (schistosomiasis) by swimming in lakes etc, check by means of a blood test when you get home, but leave it for six weeks because the test is slow to become positive. Report any untoward symptoms to your doctor and tell him exactly where you have been and, if you know, what the likelihood is of having contracted the disease to which you were exposed.

The above information has been compiled for us by Dr. David Snashall, who is presently Senior Lecturer in Occupational Health at the United Medical Schools of Guy's & St Thomas' Hospitals in London and Chief Medical Advisor of the British Foreign and Commonwealth Office. He has travelled extensively in Central and South America and the Caribbean, worked in Peru and in East Africa and keeps in close touch with developments in preventative and tropical medicine.

The Mundo Maya

Integrated tourism and conservation

This ambitious project aims to tap the tourist potential of that region of southern Mexico and Central America once dominated by the Maya. It involves the cooperation of public and private tourist bodies of Mexico, Guatemala, Belize, El Salvador and Honduras. It is one of the regions of the world with the greatest variety of tourist attractions. As well as archaeological sites, the various countries share to a greater or lesser degree modern Maya culture, national parks, beaches, lakes, volcanoes and various types of forest. There is still a long way to go before the fully integrated tourist circuit envisaged in the late 1980s comes to fruition, but the whole idea is well established. Government representatives have been meeting since 1988 and the concept was given huge impetus by a feature in the *National Geographic magazine* of October 1989.

Many archaeological sites are already popular tourist attractions, with the accompanying infrastructure (Tikal, Guatemala for examle, page 646; Palenque, Chichén Itzá, Mexico page 443 and page 478; Copán, Honduras page 922). Others, while thoroughly excavated, are less well-known and yet others, still under excavation, are becoming part of the tourist route (eg Caracol, Belize page ; Calakmul, Mexico page 521; Joya del Cerén, El Salvador page 817). As present-day knowledge of the historical Maya grows, so efforts are being made to safeguard the traditions of the Maya peoples living now, traditions which are both centuries old and enmeshed with Catholicism. In the context of the Mundo Maya, such safeguards must include the avoidance of the worst aspects of voyeuristic tourism. Both people and their environment face economic and population pressures. The expansion of natural parks, for instance the enlargement by 55,000 hectares of the Montes Azules biological reserve in Lacandonia to include Bonampak and Yaxchilán (Mexico page 450), have been welcomed. Parks in existence cover rainforest and cloud forest, Belize's diverse environments, including marine, the Caribbean coast of Honduras, the *biotopos* in Guatemala and the waterbird sanctuaries in northern Yucatán, Mexico. Of the landscapes, one can mention the chain of volcanoes extending through Mexico, Guatemala and El Salvador, associated with which are some beautiful lakes, or, offshore, the cayes and reefs of Belize.

The Mundo Maya should prove beneficial in terms of road building, flight links, hotel construction and ease of access between neighbouring countries. One major question surrounds this development, though; is there a danger that the Mundo Maya will isolate this region as a tourist 'hot spot', to the detriment of the region itself (ie as an extension of what is generally accepted to be overdevelopment at Cancún, Mexico page 487), and to the detriment of other parts of Mexico and the rest of Central America through a lack of comparable funding? Mexican tourism projects are spread over many are as in the country, taking in a wide array of archaeological heritage, both pre-conquest and colonial. Beach developments, such as Huatulco (Mexico see page 388), are taking place concurrently with whatever progress is being made on the Mundo Maya. A colonial cities programme, covering 51 places, has been developed. For both Guatemala and Belize, the Mundo Maya will build on the attractions to which visitors are already drawn. While Copán, Honduras' main Maya connection may act as an enticement for people to travel to other parts of the country, El Salvador will expect the Mundo Maya to encourage the reemergence of a tourist industry as the country rebuilds after the civil war. Much depends upon how great a percentage of Mundo Maya tourism is concentrated in the package tour market.

Two different bodies have been promoting the Maya World, or Maya Route. In Mexico and Central America, the **Organizatión Mundo Maya** was established in 1990. It coordinates the activities of the five countries and its executive secretariat rotates among the member countries every 2 years. In the member states apply to the tourism secretariats or institute for information. The colour section appearing in the middle of the Handbook has been kindly sponsored by the Organizatión.

In the USA, the **Ruta Maya Foundation** was set up by Wilbur Garrett, the author of the above-mentioned article. He may be contacted at Ruta Maya Foundation, 209 Seneca Rd, Great Falls, VA 22066, USA, T(703) 450-4160, F450-4170, e-mail: billgarret@aol.com.

Essentials

Precolumbian civilizations

The Aztec Empire which Hernán Cortés encountered in 1519 and subsequently destroyed was the third major power to have dominated what is now known as Mexico. Before it, the empires of Teotihuacan and Tula each unified what had essentially been an area of separate Indian groups. All three, together with their neighbours such as the Maya (dealt with below) and their predecessors, belong to a more-or-less common culture called Mesoamerica.

Despite the wide variety of climates and terrains that fall within Mesoamerica's boundaries, from northern Mexico to El Salvador and Honduras, the civilizations that developed there were interdependent, sharing the same agriculture (based on maize, beans and squash) and many sociological features. These included an enormous pantheon, with the god of rain and the feathered serpent hero predominant; the offering of blood to the gods, from oneself and from sacrificial victims usually taken in war; pyramid-building; a game played with a rubber ball; trade in feathers, jade and other valuable objects, possibly from as far away as the Andean region of South America; hieroglyphic writing; astronomy; an elaborate calendar.

The Mesoamerican calendar was a combination of a 260-day almanac year and the 365-day solar year. A given day in one of the years would only coincide with that in the other every 52 years, a cycle called the Calendar Round. In order to give the Calendar Round a context within a larger timescale, a starting date for both years was devised; the date chosen by the Classic Maya was equivalent to 3113 BC in Christian time. Dates measured from this point are called Long Count dates.

Historians divide Mesoamerican civilizations into three periods, the Pre-classic, which lasted until about AD 300, the Classic, until AD 900, and the Post-classic, from 900 until the Spanish conquest. An alternative delineation is: Olmec, Teotihuacan and Aztec, named after the dominant civilizations within each of those periods.

Olmecs Who precisely the Olmecs were, where they came from and why they disappeared, is a matter of debate. It is known that they flourished from about 1400 to 400 BC, that they lived in the Mexican Gulf Coast region between Veracruz and Tabasco, and that all later civilizations have their roots ultimately in Olmec culture. They carved colossal heads, stelae (tall, flat monuments), jade figures and altars; they gave great importance to the jaguar and the serpent in their imagery; they built large ceremonial centres, such as San Lorenzo and La Venta. Possibly derived from the Olmecs and gaining importance in the first millenium BC was the centre in the Valley of Oaxaca at Monte Albán. This was a major city, with certain changes of influence, right through until the end of the Classic period. Also derived from the Olmecs was the Izapa civilization, on the Pacific border of present day Mexico and Guatemala. Here seems to have taken place the progression from the Olmec to the Maya civilization, with obvious connections in artistic style, calendar-use, ceremonial architecture and the transformation of the Izapa Long-lipped God into the Maya Long-nosed God.

Teotihuacan Almost as much mystery surrounds the origins of Teotihuacan as those of the Olmecs. Teotihuacan, 'the place where men become gods', was a great urban state, holding in its power most of the central highlands of Mexico. Its influence can be detected in the Maya area, Oaxaca and the civilizations on the Gulf Coast which succeeded the Olmecs. The monuments in the city itself are enormous, the planning precise; it is estimated that by the 7th century AD some 125,000 people were living in its immediate vicinity. Early evidence did not suggest that Teotihuacan's power was gained by force, but research now indicates both human sacrifice and sacred warfare. Again for reasons unknown, Teotihuacan's influence over its neighbours ended around 600 AD. Its glory coincided with that of the Classic Maya, but the latter's decline occurred some 300 years later, at which time a major change affected all Mesoamerica.

Toltecs The start of the Post-classic period, between the Teotihuacan and Aztec horizons, was marked by an upsurge in militarism. In the semi-deserts to the north of the settled societies of central Mexico and Veracruz lived groups of nomadic hunters. These people, who were given the general name of Chichimecs, began to invade the central region and were quick to adopt the urban characteristics of the groups they overthrew. The Toltecs of Tula were one such invading force, rapidly building up an empire stretching from the Gulf of Mexico to the Pacific in central Mexico. Infighting by factions within the Toltecs split the rulers and probably hastened the empire's demise sometime after 1150. The exiled leader Topíltzin Quetzalcóatl (Feathered Serpent) is possibly the founder of the Maya-Toltec rule in the Yucatán (the Maya spoke of a Mexican invader named Kukulcán – Feathered Serpent). He is certainly the mythical figure the Aztec ruler, Moctezuma II, took Cortés to be, returning by sea from the east.

Mixtecs

Another important culture which developed in the first millenium AD was the Mixtec, in western Oaxaca. They infiltrated all the territory held by the Zapotecs, who had ruled Monte Albán during the Classic period and had built many other sites in the Valley of Oaxaca, including Mitla. The Mixtecs, in alliance with the Zapotecs successfully withstood invasion by the Aztecs.

Aztecs

The process of transition from semi-nomadic hunter-gatherer to city and empire-builder continued with the Aztecs, who bludgeoned their way into the midst of rival city states in the vacuum left by the destruction of Tula. They rose from practically nothing to a power almost as great as Teotihuacan in about 200 years. From their base at Tenochtitlán in Lake Texcoco in the Valley of Mexico they extended through aggression their sphere of influence from the Tarascan Kingdom in the north to the Maya lands in the south. Not only did the conquered pay heavy tribute to their Aztec overlords, but they also supplied the constant flow of sacrificial victims needed to satisfy the deities, at whose head was Huitzilopochtli, the warrior god of the Sun. The speed with which the Aztecs adapted to a settled existence and fashioned a highly effective political state is remarkable. Their ability in sculpting stone, in pottery, in writing books, and in architecture (what we can gather from what the Spaniards did not destroy), was great. Surrounding all this activity was a strictly ritual existence, with ceremonies and feasts dictated by the two enmeshing calendars.

It is impossible to say whether the Aztec Empire would have gone the way of its predecessors had not the Spaniards arrived to precipitate its collapse. Undoubtedly, the Europeans received much assistance from people who had been oppressed by the Aztecs and who wished to be rid of them. Needless to say, Cortés, with his horses and an unknown array of military equipment in relatively few hands, brought to an end in two years an extraordinary culture.

Maya

The best known of the pre-Conquest Indian civilizations of the present Central American area was the Maya, which is thought to have evolved in a formative period in the Pacific highlands of Guatemala and El Salvador between 1500 BC and about AD 100. After 200 years of growth it entered what is known today as its Classic period when the civilization flourished in Guatemala, El Salvador, Belize and Honduras, and in Chiapas, Campeche and Yucatán (Mexico).

The Maya civilization was based on independent and antagonistic city states, including Tikal, Uaxactún, Kaminaljuyú, Iximch,, Zaculeu and Quirigu in Guatemala; Copán in Honduras; Altún Ha, Caracol, Lamanai in Belize; Tazumal and San Andrés in El Salvador; and Palenque, Bonampak (both in Chiapas), Uxmal, Mayapán, Tulum and the Puuc hill cities of Sayil, Labn and Kabah (all on the Yucatán peninsula) in Mexico. Recent research has revealed that these cities, far from being the peaceful ceremonial centres as once imagined, were warring adversaries, striving to capture victims for sacrifice. Furthermore, much of the cultural activity, controlled by a theocratic minority of priests and nobles, involved blood-letting, by even the highest members of society. Royal blood was the most precious offering that could be made to the gods. This change in perception of the Maya was the result of the discovery of defended cities and of a greater understanding of the Maya's hieroglyphic writing. Although John Lloyd Stephens' prophecy that 'a key surer than that of the Rosetta stone will be discovered' has not been fulfilled, the painstaking decipherment of the glyphs has uncovered

Essentials

many of the secrets of Maya society (see Breaking the Maya Code by Michael D Coe, Thames and Hudson).

Alongside the preoccupation with blood was an artistic tradition rich in ceremony, folklore and dance. They achieved paper codices and glyphic writing, which also appears on stone monuments and their fine ceramics; they were skilful weavers and traded over wide areas, though they did not use the wheel and had no beasts of burden. The cities were all meticulously dated. Mayan art is a mathematical art: each column, figure, face, animal, frieze, stairway and temple expresses a date or a time relationship. When, for example, an ornament on the ramp of the Hieroglyphic Stairway at Copán was repeated some 15 times, it was to express that number of elapsed 'leap' years. The 75 steps stand for the number of elapsed intercalary days. The Mayan calendar was a nearer approximation to sidereal time than either the Julian or the Gregorian calendars of Europe; it was only .000069 of a day out of true in a year. They used the zero centuries in advance of the Old World, plotted the movements of the sun, moon, Venus and other planets, and conceived a cycle of more than 1,800 million days.

Their tools and weapons were flint and hard stone, obsidian and fire-hardened wood, and yet with these they hewed out and transported great monoliths over miles of difficult country, and carved them over with intricate glyphs and figures which would be difficult enough with modern chisels. Also with those tools they grew lavish crops. To support urban populations now believed to number tens of thousands, and a population density of 150 per square kilometre (compared with less than 1 per square kilometre today), an agricultural system was developed of raised fields, fertilized by fish and vegetable matter from surrounding canals.

The height of the Classic period lasted until AD 900-1000, after which time the Maya concentrated into Yucatán after a successful invasion of their other lands by non-Maya people (this is only one theory: another is that they were forced to flee because of drought and a peasant rebellion). They then came under the influence of the Toltecs who invaded Yucatán; Chichén Itzá is considered to be an example of a Maya city which displays a great many Toltec features. From that time their culture declined. The Toltecs, who had firm control in Yucatán in the 10th century, gradually spread their empire as far as the southern borders of Guatemala. They in turn, however, were conquered by the Aztecs, who did not penetrate into Central America.

Mexico

3

Mexico

Cortes, asked what the country looked like, crushed a piece of parchment in his fist, released it and said: "That is the map of Mexico." This crumpled land is so splendid to the eye, and so exotic to the other senses, that millions visit it each year. Its coastlines reveal some of the best beaches in the world on the Pacific Ocean, the Gulf of California, the Gulf of Mexico and the Caribbean Sea, with a wide range of watersports on offer. Inland, archaeological treasures and colonial cities invite exploration and help explain the history of the diverse peoples who live here.

Mexico is the third largest country in Latin America and the most populous Spanish-speaking country anywhere. Its geography ranges from swamp to desert, from tropical lowland jungle to high alpine vegetation above the tree line, from thin arid soils to others so rich that they grow three crops a year. Over half the country is at an altitude of over 1,000 metres and much at over 2,000 metres; over half is arid and another 30 percent semi-arid. Only about 30 million hectares (16 percent of the total land area) can be cultivated.

Mexico

Essentials

Planning your trip

Where to go Mexico's size makes it impossible for anyone (unless you have unlimited time) to see it all in one go. Fortunately, with so many attractions, and with relatively good transport links, it is not difficult to select a worthwhile variety of options. The Pacific, the Gulf of Mexico and the Caribbean Sea provide thousands of miles of beaches on either side of the country. The bulk of the interior is made up of mountains and plateaus, in the north predominantly arid, but in the south, more densely forested and wet. Added to this are two extremities, the long arm of Baja California in the northwest, and the flat Yucatán peninsula in the southeast. Within this jumble of landscapes are some of the most important **archaeological** remains of the Americas, dating from a succession of cultures. When the **Spaniards** conquered the land, they built cities of great beauty, while **post-revolutionary** Mexico has seen some striking innovations in design and artwork. There are also many **national parks** with great opportunities for nature and adventure tourism.

In northern Mexico four major routes head from the US border to Mexico City, one on each coast, one through the industrial centre of Monterrey and the colonial cities of San Luis Potosí and Querétaro, and the fourth through Chihuahua, Durango and the colonial cities of Zacatecas and Aguascalientes. From Chihuahua a dramatic railway runs through the **Copper Canyon** to Los Mochis, a port on the Pacific Highway. This road runs through resorts such as Mazatlán to **Guadalajara**, the country's second city. From here you can either continue to the capital, or take time out at Pacific resorts like Puerto Vallarta or Manzanillo, or the smaller places in between. In this huge area there is no shortage of historical significance (such as connections with the Mexican Revolution), indigenous lifestyle, traditional customs and communities with strong links 'north of the border'.

For all its size and air pollution, **Mexico City** has some unmissable sites, such as the heart of the city around the Zócalo and the Alameda, the National Anthropological and Archaeological Museum and other art treasures, colonial Coyoacán and the few remaining waterways of the Aztecs' Tenochtitlán at Xochimilco. There are plenty of day excursions outside the city, such as Teotihuacan, Cuernavaca, Puebla and nearby volcanoes, but most can also be combined on journeys to the Gulf coast and the port city of Veracruz, or to the Pacific Coast and the famous resort of Acapulco, or south towards Guatemala.

As you head south, a worthwhile stopping place is **Oaxaca**, a delightful colonial city, handicraft and market centre with some fine festivals. Within a short distance are prehispanic cities, while the **beaches** of the state's coast, eg Puerto Escondido, Puerto Angel, Huatulco, are at varying stages of development to suit all tastes. Carrying on through the Isthmus of Tehuantepec, you reach a Mexico less influenced by either the Spaniards or the twentieth century. The mountains and forests of **Chiapas** have become part of the tourist phenomenon known as the Maya World, which includes the Yucatán, as well as neighbouring countries. This is not just the archaeological heritage of ruined cities like Palenque, Chichén Itzá or Uxmal, but also contemporary Maya society in which traditions are jealously guarded. The **Yucatán** is being heavily developed for beach tourism, Cancún being the prime example of the exploitation of natural resources to fit the developer's dream. If you prefer something quieter there are other resorts and villages to explore, on and offshore.

For yet another change of pace and environment, **Baja California** is just across the US border. Tourists are drawn by its deserts, cactii, beaches and lagoons where whales come to breed.

When to go The best season for a business visit is from late January to May, but for pleasure between October and early April, when it hardly ever rains in most of the country. August is not a good time because it is a holiday month throughout Central America and most internal flights and other transport are heavily booked (also see **Travel in Mexico**).

Special interest travel

Surfing Some of the world's most exhilarating surfing can be experienced along Mexico's Pacific coast. The highlights are perhaps the huge Hawaian size surf that pounds the Baja shoreline, the alleged longest break in the world at Bahía de Matanchén beside San Blas, and the reknowned Mexican Pipeline at Puerto Escondido. There are numerous possibilities, ranging from developed beaches to remote bays accessible only by four-wheel drive vehicles. Many are to be found at the bocas of rivers where sandbars are deposited and points are formed. It is impossible to name all the good beaches; this is a selection starting in the north.

Isla de Todos Santos in front of Ensenada has big swells. It is much frequented by American surfers and is best in winter. There are 20 good beaches around Playa San Miguel. Punta Mirador beside San José and the beach nearby, named only "Kilometre 28", receive some massive waves, particularly in summer. A wetsuit is usually neccessary when surfing in Baja.

Mazatlán is the point on the mainland where currents escape the shielding effects of the peninsula and surfing is possible. As the geographical centre point on Mexico's surfing coast it has been chosen as home to the Surfing Association (PO Box 310). In front of the town Isla de la Piedra is good as is El Caimanero and near Teacapan. San Blas is an excellent learning centre. The waves are normally not too big, and there are few rocks or dangerous currents. Best in the spring and summer, particularly between July and October which is when, about three times a year, conditions in the Bahía de Matanchén conform a break that links the points at Santa Cruz, Atacama and Isletas beaches. It then becomes possible to surf continuously for more than a mile! South of San Blas, still in Nayarit, are the Playas San Francisco and Sayulita and the Punta de Mita. Up to here only southern currents reach the coast. From Jalisco down northern currents also come into play.

The Colima coast offers good surfing at Boca de Pascuales near Tecomán and at Río Ticla. Before Zihuatanejo are Río Nexpa and Petacalco and, just outside Acapulco, Revolcadero beach is battered by surf to match its name. Puerto Escondido is, perhaps, the Mecca of Mexican surfing. Surfers come here to Zicatela beach to attempt the pipeline and are duly washed up on the shore.

Diving Diving is practised off most of Mexico's coastline but two regions, Quintana Roo and Baja California shine out. The first offers warm water reefs close in-shore and visibility of over 30 metres. Southern Baja is also a magnet for divers and offers adventurous diving in deep waters.

Cozumel, in Quintana Roo, has some of the best diving in the world and there is a marine park at Palancar Reef. Also excellent are Santa Rosa, San Francisco and Chankanaab. There is concern, however, over the damage to the reef inflicted by the new cruise ship pier, and more are planned. At Isla Mujeres the most dived sites include Los Manchores, Bandera and El Garafón. Elsewhere along this coast Punta Nizuc is accessible from Cancun while Akumal is famous for its wrecks. Banco Chinchorro is a magnificent biosphere reserve accessible from Majahual and Xcalak.

Southern Baja is warmer than the North but it is still advisable to wear a wetsuit, not least to protect from skin irritating hydroza oganisms. There are marine forests and a reef at Cabo Pulmo. The rock formations off Pichilingüe are worth seeing and there is a wreck off Isla Espíritu Santo. A fine underwater cavern lies off Isla Cerralvo and the Islas Gaviotas are also dived. If you feel experienced enough to brave the currents off Cabo San Lucas then there are impressive submarine sandfalls to a depth of 65 metres.

Other centres for diving away from the peninsula and the Caribbean include Puerto Vallarta; nearby are the Islas Marietas and the reef of the Los Arcos marine park. Puerto Escondido and the Bays of Huatulco offer clear waters which is more than can be said for the Gulf of Mexico although it too has its attractions. Here there is a reef off Veracruz. Best dive sites are at La Blanquilla, Antón Lizardo and there is a wreck at Isla Verde.

A full day's boat ride from Progreso, Yucatán, will bring you to the reef system of Arrecife Alacrán.

All Mexican Government tourist agencies are grouped in the Department of Tourism **Finding out**
building at Avenida Masaryk 172, near corner of Reforma. See under Mexico City for full **more**
details. A few cities run municipal tourist offices to help travellers. A calendar of *fiestas* is
published by *Mexico This Month*. *Travellers Guide to Mexico*, published annually by the
Secretaría de Turismo, lists resorts, attractions, hotels, sports, businesses, etc, US$17.

In a similar vein to the Ruta Maya (see the Introduction to this book), but purely Mexican, is
the Colonial Cities Schedule, which links 51 cities in eight circuits. Full details are available
from the Secretaría de Turismo, T/F52507414.

If you have any complaints about faulty goods or services, go to the ***Procuraduría Federal de
Protección del Consumidor*** of which there is a branch in every city (head office in Mexico
City, José Vasconcelos 208, CP 06720, México DF, T57613801/11). Major cities, like Acapulco,
also have a Procurador del Turista. The Tourist Office may also help with these, or criminal
matters, while the Agente del Ministro Público (Federal or State District Attorney) will also
deal with criminal complaints.

Tourist offices overseas **Canada**, 2 Bloor St West, Suite 1801, Toronto, Ontario, M4W 3EZ,
T416-9250704. **France**, 4 Rue Notre Dame des Victories, 75002 Paris, T331-40200734.
Germany, Welsenhuttenplatz 26, D600 Frankfurt am Main 1, T4969-253413. **Italy**, Via
Barberini 3, 00187 Rome, T396-4742986. **UK**, 60-61 Trafalgar Square, 3rd floor, London, WC2N
3DS, T0171-8393177. **USA**, 405 Park Avenue, Suite 1401, New York, NY 10022, T212-7557261.

There are telephone numbers that tourists can call to clarify problems. In USA, phone
Mexican Turismo, Miami, T1-800-4468277. In North America T1-800-44-MEXICO, for English
information for US and Canadian citizens (separate offices in USA and Canada), 24 hours a
day, seven days a week. There is a Houston number which anyone can call, T1-713-8808772
for information on surface tourism. In Mexico, tourists can call T91-800-00148 and in Mexico
City T56041240. The Secretaría de Turismo has an emergency hot line, open 24 hours a day:
T05-52500123/0151.

Before you travel

Documents A passport is necessary, but US and Canadian citizens need only show a birth **Getting in**
certificate (or for US, a naturalization certificate). Tourists need the free tourist card, which can
be obtained from any Mexican Consulate or Tourist Commission office, at the Mexican airport
on entry, from the offices or on the aircraft of airlines operating into Mexico, and at land
borders, ask for at least 30 days (maximum 180 days); if you say you are in transit you may be
charged US$8, with resulting paper work. **NB** Not all Mexican consuls in USA are aware of
exact entry requirements; it is best to confirm details with airlines which fly to Mexico. Tourist
cards are available for citizens of Western European countries (except Cyprus and Malta), the
USA, Canada, Australia, New Zealand, Hungary, Iceland, Japan, Singapore, South Korea,
Argentina, Bermuda, Chile, Costa Rica, Uruguay, Venezuela and Israel. The tourist card is also
available at border offices of the American Automobile Association (AAA), which offers this
service to members and non-members. There is a multiple entry card valid for all visits within
six months for US nationals. The normal validity for other nationals is 90 days, but sometimes
only 15-30 days are granted at border crossings; insist you want more if wishing to stay
longer. Although technically you are only supposed to stay 180 days a year on a tourist card
(also known as an FM-T), one correspondent lived in Mexico for five years on a tourist card,
making short visits to the USA three to four times a year, with no problems. Tourist cards are
not required for cities close to the US border, such as Tijuana, Mexicali, etc.

If you are travelling with a person under 18 years of age, you must go to a Mexican
Consulate to have two photographs stamped by the Consulate on the back of the person's
tourist card. If a person under 18 is travelling alone or with one parent, both parents' consent
is required, certified by a notary public or authorized by a Consulate. A divorced parent must
be able to show custody of a child. (These requirements are not always checked by
immigration authorities.) Exact details are available from any Mexican Consulate.

Renewal of entry cards or visas must be done at Servicios Migratorios, Homero 1832, Col

··

☞ **Mexico embassies & consulates**

Australia, 14 Perth Avenue, Yarralumia, 2600 A.C.T., Camberra, T (61-2) 6273-3963, F (61-2) 6273-1190

Austria, Türkenstrasse 15. 1090, Vienna, T (431) 310-7383, F(431) 310-7387

Belgium, Av Franklin Roosvelt 94, 1050 Bruxelles, T (322) 629-0777, F(322) 646-8768

Canada, 45 O´Connor Street, Suite 1500 K1P 1A4, Ottawa Ont., T (613) 233-8988, 233-9272, F(613) 235-9123

Denmark, Strandvejen 64E Hellerup, 2900, Copenhagen, T (45) 3961-0500, F(45) 3961-0512

Germany, Adenaueralle 100, 53113, Bonn, T(228) 914-860, F(228) 21-1113

Finland, Simonkatu 12 "A" 7th floor, 00100 Helsinki, T (3580) 694-9400, F(3580) 694-9411

France, 9, Rue de Longchamp, 75116 Paris, T (331) 5370-2770, F(331) 4755-6529

Ireland, 43 Ailesbury Road, Ballsbridge 4, Dublín, T(3531) 260-0699, F(3531) 260-0411

Israel, Trade Tower 25 Hemered St, 5th. Floor 68125. Tel-Aviv, T (9723) 516-3938, F(9723) 516-3711

Italy, Via Lazzaro Spallanzani 16, 00161.

Rome, T(39-6) 440-4400, F(39-6) 440-3876

Norway, Drammensveien 108-B, 0244. Oslo, T (47) 2243-1165, F(47) 2244-4352

New Zealand, 111-115 Customhouse Quay, 8th floor. Wellington, T (644) 472-5555, F(644) 472-5800

Holland, Nassauplein 17 2585 EB, The Hague, T (3170) 360-2900, F(3170) 356-0543

South Africa, PO Box 9077, Pretoria 0001, T(27-12) 342-5190, F(27-12) 342-5234

Spain, Carrera de San Jeronimo 46 28014 Madrid, T(341) 369-2814, F(341) 420-2292

Switzerland, Bernastrasse 57, 3005, Berne, T(4131) 351-1875, F(4131) 351-3492

UK, 42 Hertford Street, Mayfair, London W1Y 7TF, T (171) 499-8586, F(171) 495-4035

USA, 1911 Pennsylvania Ave. NW, 20006 Washington D.C., T(202) 728-1600, F(202) 728-1698

There are embassies/consulates in most other European countries, many US cities, throughout the Americas, and selected countries elsewhere. Addresses and email numbers can be found on www.sre.gob.mx/delegaciones/embajadas.ht

··

Morales, Mexico City, only 60 days given, expect to wait up to 10 days for a replacement tourist card, open Monday-Friday 0930-1400, take metro to Polanco then a taxi, or in Guadalajara, or at international airports (there is a helpful office at Room 78 in the International Airport). There are also immigration offices in cities such as Oaxaca or Acapulco who can renew tourist cards. To renew a tourist card by leaving the country, you must stay outside Mexico for at least 72 hours. Take travellers' cheques or credit card as proof of finance. The Oaxaca immigration office will renew your tourist card for only 15 days unless you have US$1,000 in cash for one month's stay, credit cards not accepted.

Travellers not carrying tourist cards need visas (South Africans and those nationalities not listed above need a visa), multiple entry not allowed, visa must be renewed before re-entry. Business visitors and technical personnel who want to study the Mexican market, appoint an agent, or enter the country for technical purposes should apply for the requisite visa and permit. Those entering Mexico to sell or plan investments should obtain form FM3 for the Mexican consulate in their home country; this costs about US$100 and is valid for a year. For a single visit of less than 30 days, use FMVC which costs nothing. Conducting business on a tourist visa can lead to several hours' detention and a heavy fine. (Since 1 April 1994, business visas for US and Canadian citizens are free.) For a *Visitante Rentista* visa (non-immigrant pensioner) for stays over six months (up to two years) the following are required: passport, proof of income from abroad of US$750 per month (or 400 days of the minimum wage), which is reduced by half if you own a house in Mexico, and your tourist card.

We would warn travellers that there have been several cases of tourist cards not being honoured, or a charge being imposed, or the validity being changed arbitrarily to 60 days or less. In this case, complaint should be made to the authorities in Mexico City. If, on leaving Mexico, your tourist card is not taken from you, post it to the Mexico City address above. **Very important**: Do not lose your tourist card. You have to surrender it when you leave the country. If you haven't got it, this will cost you time, worry and/or money (though some US borders crossings are very lax). If you lose it, contact the nearest immigration office ASAP; a replacement can take a week or more.

If you want to return to Mexico after leaving there to visit Belize or Guatemala, remember that you will need a new visa/tourist card if yours is not marked for multiple entry.

At the land frontiers with Belize and Guatemala, you may be refused entry into Mexico if you have less than US$200 (or US$350 for each month of intended stay, up to a maximum of 180 days). This restriction does not officially apply to North American and European travellers. If you are carrying more than US$10,000 in cash or travellers' cheques, you must declare it. In most cases entering Mexico from Belize and Guatemala only 30 days entry is given, possibly renewable for up to 60 days.

Customs The luggage of tourist-card holders is often passed unexamined. If flying into Mexico from South America, expect to be thoroughly searched (body and luggage) at the airport. US citizens can take in their own clothing and equipment without paying duty, but all valuable and non-US-made objects (diamonds, cameras, binoculars, typewriters, computers, etc), should be registered at the US Customs office or the port of exit so that duty will not be charged on returning. Radios and television sets must be registered and taken out when leaving. Anyone entering Mexico is allowed to bring in: clothing, footwear and personal cleaning items suitable for the length of stay; camera, or video recorder; books and magazines; one used article of sporting equipment; up to three litres of wine, beer or spirits; 20 packs of cigarettes, or 20 cigars, or 200 grammes of tobacco; medicines for personal use. Foreigners who reside legally outside Mexico are also allowed: a portable TV, stereo, 20 records or audio cassettes, a musical instrument, five used toys, fishing tackle, tennis racket, a pair of skis, a boat up to five metres without an engine, camping equipment, a tent. Those entering by trailer, private plane or yacht may also bring a videocassette recorder, bicycle, motorbike and kitchen utensils. Anything additional to this list with a value of over US$300, if entering by land, air or sea, is taxable and must be declared as such (for Mexicans returning the value is US$50). This stipulation is rarely invoked for those entering by motor home. Goods imported into Mexico with a value of more than US$1,000 (with the exception of computer equipment, where the limit is US$4,000) have to be handled by an officially appointed agent. One recommended agency is *Agencia Promoción y Servicio Aduanal*, Durango 111, Col Peñon de los Baños T57855769, F57857476, pysasa@aaadam.com.mx, who will arrange everything, including delivery to one's address. The export of goods is relatively simple, but this too is best effected through an accredited agency.

There are no restrictions on the import or export of money apart from gold but foreign gold coins are allowed into the USA only if they are clearly made into jewellery (perforated or otherwise worked on). On return to the USA a person may take from Mexico, free of duty, up to US$100 worth of merchandise for personal use or for personal gifts, every 31 days, if acquired merely as an incident of the trip. One litre of alcoholic drinks may be taken across the border from Mexico (beer is counted as an alcoholic drink); Texas will allow you to pay the small state tax, Arizona will not. All foreign citizens are subject to this law. Archaeological relics may not be taken out of Mexico. US tourists should remember that the US Endangered Species Act, 1973, prohibits importation into the States of products from endangered species, for example tortoise shell. The Department of the Interior issues a leaflet about this. Llama, alpaca, etc, items may be confiscated at the airport for fumigation and it will be necessary to return to the customs area on the Mexico City airport perimeter two to three days later to collect and pay for fumigation. Production of passport will be required and proof that goods are to be re-exported otherwise they may also be subject to import duties.

Money

Until 1 January 1993, the monetary unit was the Mexican peso (represented by an 'S' crossed with a vertical line), divided into 100 centavos. On that date three zeros were eliminated from the peso, so that 1,000 pesos now equals one new peso. The word 'new' has now been dropped and the currency is again referred to as the peso. There are notes for 10, 20, 50, 100, 200 and 500 pesos; coins for 5, 10, 20 and 50 centavos and for 1, 2, 5, 10, 20 and 50 pesos. The **Currency** one and two-peso coins and the 10 and 20 are similar in size, check the number on the coin. Old coins and notes are no longer legal tender.

Credit cards American Express, Mastercard and Visa are generally accepted in Mexico and cash is obtainable with these credit cards at certain banks. Automatic Teller Machines (ATM, *cajero automático*) of Banamex accept Visa, Mastercard and ATM cards of the US Plus and Cirrus ATM networks for withdrawals up to 1,500 pesos. ATM withdrawals on Visa can also be made at branches of Bancomer and Cajeros RED throughout the country. ATMs are now found even in small towns allowing you to travel without carrying large amounts of cash or travellers' cheques. Many banks are affiliated to Mastercard but locations of ATMs should be checked with Mastercard in advance. Visa is more commonly found. There have been repeated instances of Banamex ATMs stating that cash cannot be given, 'try again later', only for the card holder to find that his/her account has been debited anyway. If you get a receipt saying no cash dispensed, keep it. Emergency phone numbers for Mastercard, T001-800-3077309, and Visa, T95-800-8472911, toll free. **NB** An American Express card issued in Mexico states 'valid only in Mexico', and is used only for peso transactions. All other American Express cards are transacted in US dollars even for employees living in Mexico. Amex travellers' cheques are readily accepted and can easily be purchased with an Amex credit card. If you are enrolled in the Amex Express Cash programme you can withdraw cash with your Amex card from Banco Inverlat ATMs. There is a six percent tax on the use of credit cards. Before you travel, check that your credit cards have not been accidentally demagnetized.

Exchange In the border states such as Baja California Norte, the most-used currency is the US dollar, and the Mexican peso is often accepted by stores on the US side of the border. Travellers' cheques from any well-known bank can be cashed in most towns if drawn in US dollars; travellers' cheques in terms of European currencies are harder to cash, and certainly not worth trying to change outside the largest of cities. The free rate of exchange changes daily and varies from bank to bank and even from branch to branch (Banamex usually has the best rates). Until the new day's rate is posted, at any time between 1000 and 1100, yesterday's rate prevails. Many banks, including in Mexico City, only change foreign currency during a limited period (often between 1000 and 1200, but sometimes also 1600-1800 in Banamex), which should be remembered, especially on Friday. Many people pay in their wages on Friday, so longer queues can be expected. *Casas de cambio* are generally quicker than banks for exchange transactions, and stay open later, but their rates are not as good. Telegraphic transfer of funds *within* Mexico is not reliable. Beware of short-changing at all times. For information on Western Union services (for USA only), T1-800-3254045.

Student cards Only national, Mexican student cards permit free entry to archaeological sites, museums, etc, see **Setej** page 301. The surest way to get in free is to go on Sunday, when all such places have no entry charge, but are crowded in consequence.

Getting there

Air There are several international airports, the two busiest ones being Mexico City and Cancún, both of which receive frequent flights from Europe, North and South America and the Caribbean. For cities other than the capital, see text below for details.

From Europe Several airlines have regular direct flights from Europe to Mexico City. Air France and AeroMéxico from Paris; Iberia and AeroMéxico from Madrid; KLM from Amsterdam; British Airways from London (Gatwick); Lufthansa and Delta from Frankfurt, (LTU and Condor charter flights from Germany to Mexico City or Cancún) is City Bird from Brussels. Aeroflot fly to Mexico City from Moscow via Shannon on Wednesday. Most connecting flights in Europe are through Madrid or Gatwick.

From North America From the **USA** to Mexico City with a variety of airlines including American Airlines, AeroMéxico, Delta, Continental, United, Northwest, Taesa and Americawest, from Atlanta, Austin, Boston, Chicago, Dallas, Denver, Detroit, Houston, Laredo, Las Vegas, Los Angeles, McAllen, Miami, Oakland, Ontario (CA), Orlando, Philadelphia, Phoenix,

Portland, Salt Lake City, San Antonio (TX), San Diego, San Francisco, San José (CA) and Washington DC. From **Canada**, Japan Airlines fly from Vancouver, Canadian Airlines and Mexicana fly from Toronto and Mexicana flies from Montreal.

From the Far East Japan Airlines twice weekly flight from Tokyo stops at Vancouver.

From Latin America Flights from South and Central America: Lan Chile, AeroMéxico, Mexicana and Lacsa from Santiago, Chile (Lacsa via San José); Mexicana and Lan Chile from Buenos Aires; Lacsa, AeroMéxico, Mexicana from Lima, some flights via Panama City; Lloyd Aéreo Boliviano from Santa Cruz, Bolivia via Panama City; Mexicana from Caracas; Avianca and Mexicana from Bogotá; Varig from Rio and São Paulo; AeroMéxico also fly from São Paulo; Aviateca, KLM Taca, AeroCaribe, and Mexicana from Guatemala City; Copa from Guayaquil, Managua, Panama City, San Pedro Sula; also Lacsa, Aviateca and Mexicana from Panama; Lacsa, United, Aviateca and Mexicana from San José, Costa Rica; Taca from Tegucigalpa, who fly via San Salvador; Aviateca from Managua, San Salvador.

From the Caribbean Mexicana and Cubana fly from Havana; Air Jamaica and American Airlines have connecting flights from Kingston and Montego Bay via Miami.

From the USA There are many border crossings all along the frontier with the USA. Some **Road** are busier than others depending on the number of trucks which pass through. The main crossings are at Tijuana, Mexicali, Nogales, Cindad Juárez, Piedras Negras, Nuevo Laredo and Matamoros.

From Guatemala The principal border town is Tapachula, with a crossing over the Talismán Bridge or at Ciudad Hidalgo. A more interesting route is via Ciudad Cuauhtémoc. For road and river travel see the Yucatán Peninsula.

From Belize The border crossing at Santa Elena is near Chetumal, where public transport can be arranged. See Chetumal for details.

Touching down

When arriving in Mexico by air, make sure you fill in the immigration document before **Airport** joining the queue to have your passport checked. If you are not given one on the plane, find **information** one in the arrivals hall. Also at Mexico City airport you may be subject to a brief interview by the Federal District Health Service; this is in relation to the control of cholera, yellow fever and other diseases.

Airport departure tax US$17.30 on international flights (dollars or pesos accepted); US$10.50 on internal flights, may be included in ticket price.

NB VAT is payable on domestic plane tickets bought in Mexico. Domestic tax on Mexican flights is 15 percent, on international flights 3.75 percent.

Budget travellers should note that there is a definite tourist economy, with high prices and, on **Cost of living** occasion, unhelpful service. This can be avoided by seeking out those places used by locals; an understanding of Spanish is useful. The prices of accommodation and transport in this chapter can only be taken as representative. In hotels there are sometimes no single rooms, or they cost 80 percent of the price of doubles. As accommodation will probably be your main expense this should be built into your budget if travelling singly. You are advised to check all local prices before booking. VAT (IVA) is charged on all but some basic goods; it is generally 15 percent on almost all consumer goods, including hotel and restaurant bills, but 25 percent is charged on some luxury items. VAT is already included in the final price of the good or service.

Doctors and dentists provide good quality care at high prices (taking appropriate insurance is highly recommended). Film is reasonably cheap, but developing is expensive and of poor quality.

Gay travellers should be aware of 'public decency' laws which allow the police much **Rules, customs** latitude: for as little as holding hands on the beach you can be arrested, even in Acapulco **& etiquette** which has many attractions for gay visitors.

Touching down

Hours of business The hours of business in Mexico City are extremely variable. All banks are open from 0900 to 1330 from Monday to Friday, some stay open later, and (head offices only) 0900 to 1230 on Saturday. Business offices usually open at 0900 or 1000 and close at 1300 or 1400. They reopen at 1400 or 1500, but senior executives may not return until much later, although they may then stay until after 1900. Other businesses, especially those on the outskirts of the city, and many Government offices, work from 0800 to 1400 or 1500 and then close for the rest of the day. Business hours in other parts of the country vary considerably according to the climate and local custom.

IDD 52. Equal tones with long pauses mean it is ringing. Short equal tones with short pauses indicates it is engaged.

Official time US Central Standard Time, six hours behind GMT; Daylight Saving Time, from first Sunday in April to last Sunday in October, five hours behind GMT. In Sonora, Sinaloa, Nayarit and Baja California Sur, seven hours behind GMT; and in Baja California Norte (above 28th Parallel) eight hours behind GMT (but seven hours behind GMT between 1 April and end October).

Weights and measures The metric system is compulsory.

Clothing People are usually smartly dressed in Mexico City. There is little central heating, so warm clothing is needed in winter. Four musts are good walking shoes, sun hats, dark glasses, and flip-flops for the hot sandy beaches. Topless bathing is now accepted in parts of Baja California, but ask first, or do as others do. Men may need a jacket and tie in some restaurants. It is difficult to obtain shoes over US size nine and a half, but it is possible to have them made.

Identification It is becoming increasingly common when visiting offices or tourist sites within government buildings to have to present some form of identification (*identificación* or *credencial*, photocopied passport will usually do), to register one's name, and sometimes to leave the ID with the security guard in exchange for a pass. This can be irksome but remember that the people on the door are only doing their job.

Photography There is a charge of US$4-5 for the use of video cameras at historical sites. If you want to use professional equipment including use of a tripod, the fee is US$150 per day.

Tipping Tipping is more or less on a level of 10-15 percent; the equivalent of US$0.25 per bag for porters, the equivalent of US$0.20 for bell boys, theatre usherettes, and nothing for a taxi driver unless he gives some extra service. It is not necessary to tip the drivers of hired cars.

Prohibitions **Drugs** Note that anyone found in possession of narcotics, in however small a quantity, is liable to a minimum prison sentence of 10 years, with a possible one-year wait for a verdict. Narcotics include 'magic mushrooms'.

Smoking Smoking is not allowed on most forms of public transport, including intercity buses, the metro and *peseros*; there are generally non-smoking areas in the better restaurants. However, the attitude towards smoking is more relaxed than in the USA and some other countries. The price of a pack of cigarettes ranges from US$0.30-US$1.20, most pharmacies stock cigarettes. Mexican brands are available in airport duty free shops but only for US dollars and at a much higher equivalent price. Ordinary airport shops charge up to 30 percent more than standard shops.

Safety Mexico is generally a safe country to visit, although crime is on the increase and precautions over personal safety should be taken, especially in Mexico City. Never carry valuables visibly or in easily picked pockets. Leave passports, tickets and important documents in an hotel safety deposit, not in your room. Underground pedestrian crossings are hiding places for thieves, take extra care at night. Cars are a prime target for theft. There has also been a rapid rise in robbery by taxi drivers in Mexico City. The drivers most often pick up their victims on

Avenida Cuauhtémoc, Alvaro Obregón or Insurgentes after 2200, stop in poorly lit streets where accomplices get in the cab and assault the passenger. As with driving at night in the States of Guerrero and Oaxaca, avoid travelling by bus at night in these districts and Veracruz and Chiapas; if at all possible make journeys in day light. Also, beware of getting too friendly with young gringos who seem to be living in Mexico permanently, unless, of course, they have jobs. Many of them stay in Mexico for the cheap drugs, and are not above robbery and assault to finance their habit. Couples, and even more, women on their own, should avoid lonely beaches. Those on the west coast are gaining a reputation as drug landing points. Some women experience problems, whether accompanied or not; others encounter no difficulties at all. (In discos women are supposed to wait until asked to dance by a man.) The police service has an equivalent to the Green Angels (see above), the Silver Angels, who help victims of crime to file a report. US citizens should present this report to the nearest embassy or consulate.

Speaking Spanish is a great asset in avoiding rip-offs for gringos, especially short changing and overcharging (both rife), and to make the most of cheap *comedores* and market shopping.

Mexico

Where to stay

Hotel prices in the lower and middle categories are still very reasonable by US and European standards. Prices of top and luxury hotels have risen more steeply. Complaints about standards, etc, may be reported to the Department of Tourism, Presidente Masaryk 172, Colonia Polanco, Mexico City, T52501964 and 52508555. English is spoken at the best hotels. There is a hotel (or *hospedaje*) tax, ranging between one percent and four percent, according to the state. Generally levied only when a formal bill is issued.

Sleeping

Casas de huéspedes are usually the cheapest places to stay, although they are often dirty with poor plumbing. Usually a flat rate for a room is charged, so sharing works out cheaper. Sleeping out is possible anywhere, but is not advisable in urban areas. Choose a secluded, relatively invisible spot. Mosquito netting (*pabellón*) is available by the metre in textile shops and, sewn into a sheet sleeping bag, is ample protection against insects.

Beware of 'helpfuls' who try to find you a hotel, as prices quoted at the hotel desk rise to give them a commission. If backpacking, it is best for one of you to watch over luggage while the other goes to book a room and pay for it; some hotels are put off by backpacks. During peak season (November-April), it may be hard to find a room and clerks do not always check to see whether a room is vacant. Insist, or if desperate, provide a suitable tip. The week after Semana Santa is normally a holiday, so prices remain high, but resorts are not as crowded as the previous week. When using a lift, remember PB (*Planta Baja*) stands for ground floor. Discounts on hotel prices can often be arranged in the low season (May-October), but this is more difficult in Yucatán and Baja California. There is not a great price difference between single and double rooms. Rooms with double beds are usually cheaper than those with two singles. Check out time from hotels is commonly 1400. When checking into a hotel, always ask if the doors are locked at night, preventing guests from entering if no nightguard is posted. Always check the room before paying in advance. Also ask if there is 24-hour running water.

Motels and Auto-hotels, especially in central and south Mexico, are not usually places where guests stay the whole night (you can recognize them by curtains over the garage and red and green lights above the door to show if the room is free). If driving, and wishing to avoid a night on the road, they can be quite acceptable (clean, some have hot water, in the Yucatán they have a/c), and they tend to be cheaper than respectable establishments.

NB In the highlands, where it can be cold at night, especially in winter, many hotels do not have heating; be prepared. The cheaper hotels often provide only one blanket so you may need a sleeping bag. This applies in popular tourist centres such as San Cristóbal de Las Casas, Oaxaca, Pátzcuaro.

Experiment in International Living Ltd, 'Ostesaga', West Malvern Road, Malvern,

Mexico

Worcestershire, WR14 4EN, UK, T01684-562577, F562212, or Ubierstrasse 30, 5300 Bonn 2, Germany, T0228-957220, F0228-358282, with offices in 38 countries, can arrange stays with families in Mexico from one to four weeks. This has been recommended as an excellent way to meet people and learn the language.

21 *albergues* exist in Mexico, mostly in small towns; they are usually good value and clean. The **Youth hostels** hostels take YHA members and non-members, who have to pay more. You have to pay a deposit for sheets, pillow and towel; make sure that this is written in the ledger or else you may not get your deposit back. Hostels have lockers for valuables; take good care of your other possessions.

Most sites are called Trailer Parks, but tents are usually allowed. For camping and youth-hostel **Camping** accommodation, see page 286 for *Villas Deportivas Juveniles*. Beware of people stealing clothes, especially when you hang them up after washing. *Playas Públicas*, with a blue and white sign of a palm tree, are beaches where camping is allowed. They are usually cheap, sometimes free and some have shelters and basic amenities. You can often camp in or near National Parks, although you must speak first with the guards, and usually pay a small fee. Paraffin oil (kerosene) for stoves is called *petróleo para lámparas* in Mexico; it is not a very good quality (dirty) and costs about US$0.05 per litre. It is available from an *expendio*, or *despacho de petróleo*, or from a *tlapalería*, but not from gas stations. Methylated spirits is called *alcohol desnaturalizado* and is available from chemists. Calor gas is widely available, as it is throughout Central America. Gasolina Blanca may be bought in *ferreterías*, ironmongers or paint shops, prices vary widely, also ask for Coleman fuel. Alcohol for heating the burner can be obtained from supermarkets. Repairs to stoves at Servis-Coleman at Plaza de San Juan 5, Mexico City. Katadyn water-purifying filters can be bought in Mexico City at: Katadyn/Dispel, Distribuidores de Purificadores y Electrodomésticos, Fco Javier Olivárez Muñoz, Sinaloa 19 PB, Colonia Roma, CP 06700, Mexico DF, T55330600, F52077174, spare parts also available.

Getting around

Note that the majority of internal routes involve a change in Mexico City, for example there is **Air** no direct flight Acapulco-Cancún. Promotional packages for local tourism exist, with 30-40 percent discount, operated by hoteliers, restauranteurs, hauliers and AeroMéxico and Mexicana. These may be the best value if going from and returning to the same city. Their tickets are not interchangeable. Mexicana and AeroMéxico in combination offer MexiPlan tickets, which are for a minimum of two coupons covering five zones of the country; the pass is eligible only to those arriving on transatlantic flights, valid 3-90 days. Fares range from US$50-145 per coupon; extra coupons may be bought and reservations may be changed. There are several other airlines flying internal routes (a few with international flights as well), for example Aero California, Aeromar, Serolitoral, Taesa, Saro, Aviacsa and Aero Caribe (details are given in the text above).

Bus services have been upgraded in recent years and are generally organized, clean and **Bus** prompt. However, the ordinary traveller should not be beguiled into thinking that it is necessary to purchase an expensive ticket in order to travel comfortably. On many routes, the second, or 'normal', class has disappeared. First class is perfectly satisfactory, but there now exist three superior classes, usually called 'Primera Plus', 'Futura' and 'Ejecutiva', which offer various degrees of comfort and extra services. Companies offering these services include UNO (recommended) and ETN, as well as the major bus companies. The extras are reclining seats, toilets, drinks, videos, etc. ETN has exceptional buses with three seats in a row but prices about 35-40 percent (in some cases double) above regular first class. The superior classes are probably best for journeys over six hours, but take a warm garment at night because a/c can be very cold. On day time journeys consider whether you want to see the scenery or a video. If going on an overnight bus, book seats at the front as toilets get very smelly by morning. No standing (in theory), and you may have to wait for the next one (next day, perhaps) if all seats are taken. You *must* book in advance for buses travelling in the Yucatán Peninsula, especially around Christmas, but it is also advisable to book if going elsewhere. Some companies, for example ADO, are computerized in main cities, so advance reservations can be made. Bus seats are particularly hard to get during school holidays, August and the 15 days up to New Year when many public servants take holidays in all resorts; transport from Mexico City is booked up a long time in advance and hotels are filled, too. In the north especially, try to travel from the starting-point of a route; buses are often full at the mid-point of their routes. Beware of 'scalpers' who try to sell you a seat at a higher price, which you can usually get on a stand-by basis, when somebody doesn't turn up, at the regular price. Sometimes it helps to talk to the driver, who has two places to use at his discretion behind his seat (don't sit in these until invited). Lock your luggage to the rack with a cycle lock and chain. If protecting luggage with chicken wire it will set off metal detectors used by Cristóbal Colón bus line in southern Mexico. Stowing your luggage on the roof is not advisable on night buses since theft can occur. Luggage racks on both classes of long-distance bus are spacious and will take a rucksack with a little persuasion (either of the rucksack itself, or the bus driver). However well-organized a company (for example ADO), always check that your luggage is on your bus if you are putting it in the hold.

Second-class buses usually operate from a different terminal from first class buses and are often antiques (interesting, but frustrating when they break down) or may be brand new. They call at towns and villages and go up side roads the first-class buses never touch. They stop quite as often for meals and toilets as their superiors do and, unlike the first-class buses, people get on and off so often that you may be able to obtain a seat after all. Autobuses Unidos (AU) are usually a little cheaper than other services, but they stop more often, including at the roadside when flagged down. They will not stop on curves, walk until you find a straight stretch. It is not unusual to have to stand on these buses. Some second class seats are bookable (for example in Baja California), others are not, it depends on the company. In general, it is a good idea to take food and drink with you on a long bus ride, as stops may depend on the driver. When a bus stops for refreshment, remember who your driver is and follow him; also memorize your bus' number so you do not miss it when it leaves.

First class fares are usually 10 percent dearer than second class ones and the superior classes are even more, quite pricey. On a long journey you can save the price of a hotel room by travelling overnight, but in many areas this is dangerous and not recommended. Some companies give holders of an international student card a 50 percent discount on bus tickets, especially during summer holiday period; persistence may be required. Look out for special offers, including discounts at some hotel chains. If making a day trip by bus, do not lose your ticket; you will have to show the driver and operator proof that you have paid for the return. There seem always to be many buses leaving in the early morning. All classes of bus invariably leave on time. Buses are sometimes called *camiones*, hence *central camionero* for bus station. A monthly bus guide is available for US$1 (year's subscription) from Guía de Autotransportes de México, Apartado 8929, México 1, DF.

Motoring   **Permits**   Vehicles may be brought into Mexico on a Tourist Permit for 180 days each year. The necessary documents are: passport, birth certificate or naturalization papers; tourist card; vehicle registration (if you do not own the car, a notarized letter from the vehicle's owner, be it the bank, company, whoever, is necessary); a valid driver's licence. National or international driving licences are accepted. The original and two photocopies are required for each. It takes 10 days to extend a permit, so ask for more time than you expect to need. Don't overstay, driving without an extension gets a US$50 fine for the first five days and then rises abruptly to *half the value of the car!* US$12 is charged for the permit, payable only by credit card (Visa, Mastercard, American Express or Diners Club), not a debit card, in the name of the car owner, as recorded on the vehicle registration. The American Automobile Association (AAA) is permitted to issue Tourist Permits for 'credit card' entry, free to members, US$20 to non-members, but this service in California is available only to members. If you do not have a credit card, you have to buy a refundable bond in cash to the value of the vehicle according to its age (a set scale exists), which is repaid on leaving Mexico. The bond is divided into two parts, the bond itself and administration; the latter, accounting for about 43 percent of the total cost, is retained by the authorities; the bond is refunded. The bond is issued by Afianziadora Mexicana at US/Mexican border crossings, or by Sanborn's (see below). It may be waived if you are only going to the State of Sonora, under the Sonora Department of Tourism's 'Only Sonora' programme.

English versions of leaflets giving the rules on temporary importation of vehicles state that you must leave at the same crossing by which you entered. The Spanish versions do not say this and in practice it is not so. The temporary importation permit is multiple entry for 180 days; within that period you can enter and leave by whatever crossing, and as often as you like. Remember, though, that you must have a new tourist card or visa for each new entry.

On entry, go to Migración for your tourist card, on which you must state your means of transport. This is the only record of how you entered the country. At the Banjército desk sign an 'Importación Temporal de Vehículos' 'Promesa de retornar vehículo', which bears all vehicle and credit card details so that, if you sell your car illegally, your credit card account can be debited for the import duty. Next you purchase the 'Solicitud de importación temporal', which costs US$12; it bears a hologram which matches the dated sticker which must be displayed on the windscreen, or, on a motorcycle, on some safe surface. Then go to 'Copias' to photocopy all necessary documents and papers issued. The sticker and other entry documents must be surrendered on departure. They can only be surrendered at a Mexican border crossing, with date stickers cancelled by Banjército at Immigration. If you neglect to do this, and re-enter Mexico with an expired uncancelled sticker on you car, you will be fined heavily for each 15-day period that has elapsed since the date of expiry. If you intend to return to Mexico within the 180-day period, having surrendered your sticker and documents, keep safe the 'Importación Temporal de Vehículos' form, stamped 'Cancelado', as a receipt. If entry papers are lost there can be much delay and expense (including enforcement of the bond) in order to leave the country. Banjércitco (Banco del Ejército) offices at borders are open daily, for 24 hours, except at Naco (daily 0800-2400), Tecate (daily 0800-1600), Tijuana (Monday-Friday 0800-2200, Saturday 0800-1800, Sunday 1200-1600), Columbia, Texas (Monday-Friday 1000-1800), Ojinaga (Monday-Friday 0730-2100, Saturday 0730-1600, Sunday 0800-1600). Each vehicle must have a different licensed driver (that is, you cannot tow another vehicle into Mexico unless it has a separate driver).

On arrival, you have to find the place where car permits are issued; this may not be at the border. If driving into Mexico from California, Nogales is probably the easiest crossing, which means going first into Arizona. The main car documentation point here is Km 21, south of Nogales. Entering at Tijuana, it seems that car entry permits are given at Mexicali (which means taking the very busy Route 2 through Tecate), or, if you drive through Baja California, at the ferry offices in Santa Rosalía or La Paz. This does not apply if you are not going beyond Baja. In Nuevo Laredo permits are issued at a new complex in town, opposite the train station. If crossing from Brownsville to Matamoros and require longer than 10 days, send a fax with car details to immigration at the border three days before leaving the country. Before crossing the border, pick up the fax and show it at the US side of the border. Most visitors to Mexico at this border are just crossing for shopping and only need a 10 day visa.

Insurance According to latest official documents, insurance for foreign cars entering Mexico is not mandatory, but it is highly recommended to be insured. Arranging insurance when crossing from the USA is very easy as there are many offices at US border crossings. Policy prices vary enormously between companies, according to age and type of vehicle, etc. **NB** In Mexico foreign insurance will not be honoured; you must ensure that the company you insure with will settle accident claims outside Mexico.

Sanborn's Mexican Insurance Service, for example, with offices in every US border town, and many more, will provide insurance services (many comprehensive plans available, include full-year cover) within Mexico and other parts of Latin America, and provides free 'Travelogs' for Mexico and Central America with useful tips. Their head office is *Sanborn's Insurance*, Travco Services Inc. 2009 S 10th Street, McAllen, TX 78503, T 956-686 3601, F956-686 0732, Toll free 800-222-0158, info@sanbornsinsurance.com, www.sanbornsinsurance.com. Also, *Tepeyac,* with offices at most Mexican cities, towns and border crosings (including Tapachula), and in USA (eg in San Diego, Mexican American Insurance Agency, corner of 6th and A Sts, downtown, T2337767); *Aseguradora Mexicana SA (Asemex)*, with offices in Tijuana, T850301/04, 24 hours, Ensenada, Mexicali, La Paz, and adjusters throughout Baja California and that border zone; *International Gateway Insurance Brokers* (also offers insurance for Mexican residents visiting USA), PO Box 609, Bonita, CA 92002-0609, T619-4223022, F619-4222671; also 2981 North Grande Av, Nogales, T2819141, F2810430; 1155 Larry Mahan, Suite H, El Paso, T5956544, F5921293; Hidalgo 79F, Riberas del Pilar, Centro Comercial Máscaras, Chapala, T52559, F54316; Escuela Militar de Aviación 60, Chapultepec, Guadalajara, T152992, F341448; Misión de San Diego, No 1517 Despacho 1C, Tijuana, T341446, F341448; Revolución Morelos s/n, Cabo San Lucas, T31174, F30793; Blvd Costera Miguel de la Madrid, Km 10, Plaza Galerías local 3, Manzanillo. *Mex-Insur* in San Diego CA, T4252390, will issue a policy and refund each full 24 hours not used as long as you return over the Mexican/US border. *Points South Caravan Tours*, 11313 Edmonson Avenue, Moreno Valley, CA 92560-5232, T909-2471222 or toll free USA and Canada 1-800-4211394, offers Mexican insurance.

Entering Mexico from Guatemala presents few local insurance problems now that *Tepeyac* (see above), has an office in Tapachula, and *Seguros La Provincial*, of Avenida Gen Utrillo 10A, upstairs, San Cristóbal de Las Casas, have an office in Cuauhtémoc, Avenida Cuauhtémoc 1217 PB, Sr García Figueroa, T5-6040500. Otherwise, try in Tuxtla Gutiérrez (Segumex). In Mexico City, try *Grupo Nacional Provincial*, Río de la Plata 48, T52867732, who have offices in many towns.

British AA and Dutch ANWB members are reminded that there are ties with the AAA, which extends cover to the US and entitles AA members to free travel information including a very useful book and map on Mexico (note that some AAA offices are not open at weekends or on US holidays). Luggage is no longer inspected at the checkpoints along the road where tourist cards and/or car permits are examined.

Spare parts the only Japanese makes for which spare parts are sold in Mexico are Datsun and Nissan. Most other cars are US makes.

Gasoline is either unleaded, 90 octane, called *magna sin*, which costs about US$0.30 per litre and *nova*, leaded, 80 octane, US$0.30 per litre. *Magna sin* is sold from green pumps from green and white Pemex stations; *nova* from blue pumps and diesel from purple pumps. They are in the process of introducing diesel sin and withdrawing regular diesel. Unleaded petrol is now available in almost all stations, very few have only nova. Always fill up when you can and carry spare fuel. If your own vehicle is fitted with a catalytic converter you can remove it to use either leaded or unleaded fuel. (Mexican petrol is not very clean, so check spark plugs frequently; most mechanics will let you use their wire brushes free of charge.) There are dozens of minor swindles, including overcharging, practised at filling stations. Make sure you are given full value when you tank up, that the pump is set to zero before your tank is filled, that both they and you know what money you've proffered, that your change is correct, that the pump is correctly calibrated, and that your filler cap is put back on. There is no legal surcharge for service at night, nor additional taxes: two more games frequently tried.

The **Free Assistance Service of the Mexican Tourist Department's** green jeeps (*ángeles verdes*) patrol most of Mexico's main roads. Every state has an Angeles Verdes Hotline and it is advisable to find out the relevant number when entering each state. The drivers speak English, are trained to give first aid and to make minor auto repairs and deal with flat tyres. They carry gasoline and have radio connection. If you want your vehicle to be escorted through Mexico City, offer to pay about US$15, and the police will do it for you. All help is completely free. Gasoline at cost price. Parking: Multi-storey car parks are becoming more common but parking is often to be found right in city centres under the main square.

Further information A useful source of information and advice (whose help we acknowledge here) is the Recreation Vehicle Owner's Association of British Columbia, Box 2977, Vancouver, BC, V6B 3X4 (members receive *RV Times* publication; Mexican insurance arranged for members). RV tours including Mexico are available from RV Adventuretours, 305 West Nolana Loop #2, McAllen, Tx78505, USA. Another recommended source of information in Canada is *Mexi-Can Holidays Ltd*, 150-332 Water St, Vancouver, BC V6B 1B6, T604-6853375, F604-6853321. Motorists are referred to: *Clubmex*, PO Box 1646, Bonita, California 91908, USA, T619-5853033, F619-4208133, publishes a regular newsletter for its members (annual subscription US$35). The newsletter gives useful information and advice for drivers, specialist trips for sport fishing enthusiasts, and some interesting travel articles. *Clubmex* also arranges insurance for members. ***Mexico Travel Monthly Report***, Carolyn Files, Box 1498, Imperial Beach, CA 91933-1498, T/F619-4296566, has also been recommended. ***Winter in Mexico Caravans Inc*** (a member of *The Escapees Club*, which issues a bi-monthly newsletter), 101 Rainbow Drive, Livingston, Texas 77351, T303-7619829, offers advice on caravan trips to Mexico, runs tours for caravanners, including a birdwatching tour, and issues its own bulletin. *R Ving in Mexico, Central America and Panamá*, by John and Liz Plaxton (Travel 'N Write, Canada, 1996) has been recommended as full of useful information. Also *Aim*, on retirement and travel in Mexico, Apartado postal 31-70, Guadalajara 45050, Jalisco.

In Case of Accident Do not abandon your vehicle. Call your insurance company immediately to inform it of the accident. Do not leave Mexico without first filing a claim in Mexico. Do not sign any contract or agreement without a representative of the insurance company being present. Always carry with you, in the insured vehicle, your policy identification card and the names of the company's adjusters (these are the recommendations of Asemex). If, in an accident, bodily injury has occurred or the drivers involved cannot agree who is at fault, the vehicles may be impounded. Drivers will be required to stay in the vicinity in cases of serious accidents, the insured being confined to a hotel (or hospital) until the claim is settled (according to Sanborn's). Should parties to an accident be incarcerated, a bail bond will secure release. A helpline for road accidents is available by phoning 02 and asking the operator to connect you to Mexico City T56849715/56849761.

Warnings On all roads, when two vehicles converge from opposite directions, or when a vehicle is behind a slow cart, bicycle, etc, the driver who first flashes his lights has the right of way. This also applies when a bus or truck wishes to turn left across the opposing traffic: if the driver flashes his lights he is claiming right of way and the oncoming traffic must give way. At 'Alto' (Halt) signs, all traffic must come to a complete stop. At a crossroad, however, the first person to come to a complete halt then has precedence to cross. This requires a lot of attention to remember your place in the sequence (this is the same system as in the USA). Do not drive at night. If it is unavoidable don't drive fast; farm and wild animals roam freely. Night-time robberies on vehicles are on the increase especially in Guerrero and Oaxaca States. 'Sleeping policemen' or road bumps can be hazardous in towns and villages as often there are no warning signs; they are sometimes marked *'zona de topes'*, or incorrectly marked as *vibradores*. In most instances, their distinguishing paint has worn away.

Roadworks are usually well-marked. If your vehicle breaks down on the highway and you do not have a warning triangle or a piece of red cloth to act as a warning, cut branches from the roadside and lay them in the road in front of and behind your vehicle.

Foreigners may be searched for drugs on the west coast. The following precautions should help towards an incident-free passage of a drug search. Carry copies of all prescriptions for medicines (typed). Keep medicines in the original container. Carry a notice of all medical conditions that need a hypodermic syringe or emergency treatment. Never take packages for another person. Never take hitchers across a border. Always cross a border in your own vehicle. Check your vehicle carefully for suspicious packages secreted by someone other than yourself. If you have bodywork done in Mexico, supervise it yourself and keep records, even photos, of the workshop that did it. If you did have work done on your vehicle, call for a sniffer dog to cover yourself. Prior to inspections, open all doors, hatches, etc. Put away all money and valuables. Offer no drinks, cigarettes or gifts to the inspectors; accept none. When searched, cooperate with narcotics officers (who wear black and yellow, and have an identity number on a large fob attached to the belt); do not intrude, but watch the proceedings closely.

If you are stopped by police in town for an offence you have not committed and you know you are in the right, do not pay the 'fine' on the spot. Take the policeman's identity number, show him that you have his number and tell him that you will see his chief (*jefe*) at the tourist police headquarters instead. It is also advisable to go to the precinct station anyway whenever a fine is involved, to make sure it is genuine. There have been reports of drivers being subject to demands for bribes, especially on the Mexico City-Guadalajara route. If stopped in a remote area, it is not advisable to get into a dispute with a policeman; drugs may be planted in your vehicle or other problems may occur.

Note that cars must by law display a number/license plate front and back; as this is not the case in some US States, you may have to improvise.

Tourists' cars cannot, *by law*, be sold in Mexico. This is very strictly applied. You may not leave the country without the car you entered in, except with written government permission with the car (and trailer if you have one) in bond.

If your car breaks down and cannot be repaired, you must donate it to the Mexican people. This is done through the Secretaría de Hacienda. If you have to leave Mexico in a hurry and cannot take the car with you, you have to get permission from the Secretaría de Hacienda which will guard your car until you return.

Road Tolls (See also page 176.) A toll is called a 'cuota', as opposed to a non-toll road, which is a 'vía libre'. There are many toll charges, mostly of US$1 to 2, on roads and bridges. Some new freeways bypassing city centres charge US$4-12, or more for 50 kilometres. Because of the high cost of toll roads, they are often quite empty, which means that good progress can be made on them. With the privatization of many freeways, hefty tolls are charged to roadusers (double the car fee for trailers and trucks). Some can be avoided if you seek local, or motoring club (see above) advice on detours around toll gates (follow trucks). This may involve unpaved roads which should not be attempted in the wet. Two advantages of toll roads are that they are patrolled and safe, even at night, and drivers are insured against accident or breakdown.

Car hire Car rental is very expensive in Mexico and 15 percent VAT is added to rental costs. Rates will vary from city to city. It can be cheaper to arrange hire in the US or Europe, but rentals booked abroad cannot be guaranteed (though usually they are). Proceed with caution. At some tourist resorts, however, such as Cancún, you can pick up a VW beetle convertible for US$25 per day, which you will not be told about abroad. Renting a vehicle is nearly impossible without a credit card. It is twice as expensive to leave a car at a different point from the starting point than a round trip. Check the spare tyre, that the fuel gauge works and that you have been given a full tank, that the insurance is valid on unmade roads and that you know how the alarm (if fitted) turns off, the car will not go if the alarm is set off. A short length of strong chain and a padlock for securing the trunk are worthwhile for VW beetles (Mexican models are the cheapest cars available for hire but do not come with any frills, a/c, radio, etc).

Cycling Peter Cossins (of Bath) writes: 'Considering that it is a large country with many sparsely populated areas, Mexico offers plenty of enjoyable places for riding. The main problems facing cyclists are the heavy traffic which will be encountered on many main roads, the poor condition of the same main roads and the lack of specialized spare parts particularly for mountain bikes. It is possible to find most bike spares in the big cities, but outside these places it is only possible to find the basics: spokes, tyres, tubes etc. Traffic is particularly bad around Mexico City and on the road between Mazatlán and Guadalajara. The easiest region for cycling is the Gulf of Mexico coast, however the roads are dead flat, straight and generally boring. The mountains may appear intimidating, but gradients are not difficult as clapped-out buses and trucks have to be able to climb them. Consequently, much of the best riding is in the sierra. If cycling in Baja, avoid riding in mid-Summer, even during October temperatures can reach 45°C+ and water is very scarce all the time. Also beware of Mexican bike mechanics who will attempt to repair your bike rather than admit that they don't know what they are doing, particularly when it comes to mountain bikes.' Wolfgang Schroppel from Urbach and Friedemann Bar from Plüderhausen in Germany also advise that: 'for cyclists the toll roads are generally preferable to the ordinary highways. There is less traffic, more lanes and a wide paved shoulder. Some toll roads have 'no cyclists' signs but even the police pay no attention. If you walk your bicycle on the sidewalk through the toll station you don't have to pay (if using the toll roads, take lots of water, there are few facilities). Overland buses, especially on the Pacific Coast highway from Tijuana to Guadalajara, forced us off the road several times as there is no shoulder. They believe more in God than in their brakes. This is very dangerous for cyclists. It is useful to fit a rear view mirror, so you can jump off the road before you get hit'.

It is reported to be allowed to take bicycles on any bus in Mexico, free of charge, and airlines (AeroMéxico for one) should do the same, although they may need to be packed. Some bus drivers, however, will expect a tip when loading the luggage. If leaving Mexico City towards Veracruz, consider taking a bus as far as Texmelucan avoiding Chalco – not so much because of the traffic but from risk of robberies. There are about 20 bicycle shops in Mexico City, one next to the other, on the street that leads from the Mercado Merced towards the Zócalo, Merced metro station. Make sure you insist on quality, known brand parts, as some of the Mexican brands are made out of inferior/soft material. Most Mexican bicycles have 28 inch wheels, so this size of tyre is easy to find; good 26 inch tyres for road use can be found, but are rare.

Hitchhiking

Hitchhiking is usually possible for single hikers, but apparently less easy for couples. It is generally quick, but not universally safe (seek local advice). Do not, for example, try to hitch in those parts of Guerrero and Oaxaca States where even driving alone is not recommended. In more out of the way parts, short rides from village to village are usually the rule, so progress can be slow. Getting out of big cities is best done by taking a local bus out of town in the direction of the road you intend to take. Ask for the bus to the 'Salida' (exit) to the next city on that road. From Mexico City to the US border, the route via Tula, Ciudad Valles and Ciudad Victoria, the Sierra Madre Oriental, is scenic but slow through the mountains. The quicker route is via Querétaro, San Luis Potosí and Matehuala. Elsewhere, the most difficult stretches are reported to be Acapulco-Puerto Escondido, Santa Cruz-Salina Cruz and Tulum-Chetumal. It is very easy to hitch short distances, such as the last few kilometres to an archaeological site off the main road; offer to pay something, like US$0.50.

Motorbikes

Grant and Susan Johnson, of Horizons Unlimited, Vancouver, tell us that motor-cycling is good in Mexico as most main roads are in fairly good condition and hotels are usually willing to allow the bike to be parked in a courtyard or patio. This advice is confirmed by Francesca Pagnacco of Exeter, UK.

In the major tourist centres, such as Acapulco, Puerto Vallarta or Cancún, motorbike parts can be found as there are Honda dealers for bike and jet ski rentals. All Japanese parts are sold only by one shop in Mexico City at extortionate prices (but parts and accessories are easily available in Guatemala at reasonable prices for those travelling there). For BMW repairs and some parts, Ashley Rawlings recommends BMW Mexico City, Grupo Baviera SA de CV, Calzada de Tlalpan 4585, Apartado postal 22-217-CP 14330, T55734900.

Taxis

To avoid overcharging, the Government has taken control of taxi services from airports to cities and only those with government licences are allowed to carry passengers from the airport. Sometimes one does not pay the driver but purchases a ticket from a booth on leaving the airport. No further tipping is then required, except when the driver handles heavy luggage for you. The same system has been applied at bus stations but it is possible to pay the driver direct.

Train

Much of the passenger equipment in use dates from the forties or fifties, including a number of *autovías*. Some railways are being privatized and services may change. In 1999 there were still services Mexico City-Saltillo, Saltillo - Piedras Negras, Mexico City-Veracruz, Veracruz-Coatzacoalcos, Coatzacoalcos - Tapachula, Coatzacoalcos- Mérida, Ciudad Hidalgo-Tapachula, Mérida-Tizimín, Mérida-Valladolid, Mérida-Peto, Tampico-Ciudad Victoria, Aguascalientes-Torreón, Puebla-Oaxaca, Chihuahua-Los Mochis, www.ferrocarriles.com. The *primera preferente* services (see text for routes) provide reclining seats and heating in carpeted carriages. The railways claim that you can see more from a train than from any other form of transport; this may well be true, but trains are slower than the buses (they can, however, be very crowded); they sometimes have comfortable sleeper cars with *alcobas* (better berths) and *camarines* (small sleepers). Tickets are best booked at the stations: agencies tend to add a large commission and the tickets they issue sometimes turn out not to be valid. A condensed railway timetable is published monthly, see under Mexico City, **Trains**.

Walking

Do not walk at night on dark, deserted roads or streets.

Keeping in touch

Language **Learning Spanish** The National Registration Center for Study Abroad, 823 North 2nd St, PO Box 1393, Milwaukee, WI 53201, USA, T414-2780631, F414-2718884, Tx810-0071205, will advise on tuition within a worldwide consortium of language schools. It will also make all arrangements for study in Mexico. The catalogue costs US$3; phone for information and newsletter. Affiliated schools in Mexico are in San Miguel de Allende, Cuernavaca, Mazatlán, Mérida, Morelia, Guadalajara, Puebla, Acapulco, Mexico City, Aguascalientes, Toluca, Saltillo, Oaxaca. *AmeriSpan Unlimited*, PO Box 40513, Philadelphia, PA 19106-0513, (USA and Canada) T800-8796640, 215-8290996 (worldwide), F215-8290418, info@amerispan.com, has affiliated schools in eight Mexican cities and also provides many services and advice for travellers (see also under Antigua, Guatemala).

Postal services Rates are raised periodically in line with the peso's devaluation against the dollar but are reported to vary between towns. They are posted next to the windows where stamps are sold. Rates in pesos are: within Mexico, letters up to 20 grammes US$2.60, postcards US$1.80; to North and Central America and the Caribbean: letters US$3.90 (20 grammes), postcards US$2.90; South America and Europe US$4.90, postcards US$3.50; Asia and Australia US$5.50, postcards US$4.00. International service has improved and bright red mail-boxes, found in many parts of the city, are reliable. Weight limit two kilograms (five kilograms for books) from Mexico to the UK. About three months to Europe. Small parcel rate cheaper. Parcel counters often close earlier than other sections of the post office in Mexico. See below for the accelerated service, Mexpost. As for most of Latin America, send printed matter such as magazines registered. Many travellers have recommended that one should not use the post to send film or cherished objects as losses are frequent. Do not seal overseas parcels before visiting the Post Office, as they have to be inspected before sending. A permit is needed from the Bellas Artes office to send paintings or drawings out of Mexico. Not all these services are obtainable outside Mexico City; delivery times in/from the interior may well be longer than those given above. Poste restante ('general delivery' in the US, *lista de correos* in Mexico) functions quite reliably, but you may have to ask under each of your names; mail is sent back after 10 days (for an extension write to the Jefe de la Administración of the post office holding your mail, any other post office will help with this). Address *'favor de retener hasta llegada'* on envelope.

Within Mexico many businesses use first and second class passenger buses to deliver letters and parcels. Each piece is signed for and must be collected at the destination. The service is considered quick and reliable. Should it be necessary to send anything swiftly and safely (in Mexico and other countries), there are many courier firms; the post office's own EMS/Mexpost accelerated service, paid for by weight, is quick and reliable, otherwise the best known is DHL (Mexico City T52270299), but it is about twice the cost of Estrella Blanca (T53686577) or Federal Express (T52289904).

Telephone services Most public phones take phone cards only (Ladatel) costing 25.50 or 100 pesos from shops and news kiosks everywhere. AT&T's USA Direct service is available, for information in Mexico dial 412-5537458, ext 359. From LADA phones (see below), dial **01, similar for AT&T credit cards. To use calling cards to Canada T95-800-0101990. Commercially-run *casetas*, or booths (for example Computel), where you pay after phoning, are up to twice as expensive as private phones, and charges vary from place to place. Computel's main office is on the 27th floor of Torre Latinoamericana in Mexico City. They have offices countrywide with long opening hours (if using commercial booths to make credit-card calls, check in advance what charges are imposed). It is better to call collect from private phones, but better still to use the LADA system. Collect calls on LADA can be made from any blue public phone, silver phones for local and direct long distance calls, some take coins. Others take foreign credit cards (Visa, Mastercard, not Amex, 'a slot machine scenario', not all phones that say they take cards accept them, others that say they don't do).

NB You cannot make transatlantic calls on a 25-peso LADA phone card. LADA numbers are: **01** long distance within Mexico, add city code and number (half-price Sunday); **001** long distance to USA and Canada, add area code and number; **00** to rest of the world, add country code, city code and number; it is not possible to call collect to Germany, but it is possible to Israel. Cheap rates vary according to the country called. For information dial 07 or 611-1100. Foreign calls (through the operator, at least) cannot be made from 1230 on 24 December until the end of Christmas Day. The *Directorio Telefónico Nacional Turístico* is full of useful information, including LADA details, federal tourist offices, time zones, yellow pages for each state, Sights and maps.

Telecommunications Telégrafos Nacionales maintains the national and international telegraph systems, separate from the Post Office. There is a special office at Balderas 14-18, just near corner of Colón, in Mexico City to deal with international traffic (open 0800-2300, Metro Hidalgo, exit Calle Basilio Badillo). There are three types of telegraph service: *extra urgente*, *urgente* and *ordinario*; they can only be prepaid, not sent collect. There is a telegraph and telex service available at Mexico City airport. Fax is common in main post offices. **Email and internet:** A list of some(but not all) cybercafes in Mexico can be found at the website of the Asociación Mexicana de Cyber Cafes: www.amcc.org.mx.

Media

Newspapers The more important journals are in Mexico City. The most influential dailies are: *Excelsior, Novedades, El Día* (throughout Mexico), *Uno más Uno; The News,* in English, now available in all main cities (Groupo Novedades, which comprises *Novedades* and *The News* has a web site at www.novedades.com.mx); *The Mexico City Times* (in English, less US-oriented than *The News*); *El Universal* (*El Universal Gráfico*); *La Jornada* (more to the left), *La Prensa*, a popular tabloid, has the largest circulation. *El Nacional* is the mouthpiece of the Government; *El Heraldo*; *Uno más Uno* publishes a supplement, *Tiempo Libre*, on Thursday, listing the week's cultural activities. In Guadalajara, *El Occidental, El Informador* and *Siglo 21*. The *Guadalajara Reporter*, the weekly English-language newspaper, has a monthly on-line edition at www.guadalajara-reporter.com/. *Siglo 21* is on-line at mexplaza.udg.mx/Siglo 21, and *El Informador* at www.infored.com.mx. There are influential weekly magazines *Proceso*, and *Siempre; Epoca*, and *Quehacer Político* weekly also. The political satirical weekly is *Los Agachados*. The New York edition of the *Financial Times* is usually available on the day of issue (from about 1000) at various shops at Mexico City Airport, also from the *Casa del Libro*, Calle Florencia 37 (Zona Rosa), as well as from shops at Hamburgo 141 (Zona Rosa) and Homero (Polanco). Other British and European papers (two to three days old) are available from the same places.

Food and drink

Food

Usual meals are a light breakfast (although this can consist of several courses), and a heavy lunch between 1400 and 1500. Dinner, between 1800 and 2000, is light. Many restaurants give foreigners the menu without the *comida corrida* (set meals), and so forcing them to order *à la carte* at double the price; watch this! Try to avoid eating in restaurants which don't post a menu. Meals in modest establishments cost about US$1.50-2 for breakfast, US$2-3 for lunch (*comida corrida*, US$3-5.50 for a special *comida corrida*) and US$5-8 for dinner (generally no set menu). À la Carte meals at modest establishments cost about US$7; a very good meal can be had for US$11 at a middle level establishment. Much higher prices are charged by the classiest restaurants (for example, in Mexico City, US$15-22 medium class, US$30 first class, US$40 luxury). The best value is undoubtedly in small, family-run places. For those who are self-catering the cost of food in markets and supermarkets is not high. In resort areas the posh hotels include breakfast and dinner in many cases. Check bills and change, even if service is included waiters may deduct a further tip from the change, they will hand it back if challenged. In some restaurants, beer will not be served unless a meal is ordered.

Among the least appetizing places to eat in Mexico are fast food chain restaurants named after their American counterparts.

Local cuisine

Tamales, or meat wrapped in maize and then banana leaves and boiled. Turkey, chicken and pork with exotic sauces: *mole de guajolote* and *mole poblano* (*chile* and chocolate sauce with grated coconut) are famous. *Tacos* (without *chiles*) and *enchiladas* (with all too many of them)

Mexico

are meat or chicken and beans rolled in *tortillas* (maize pancakes) and fried in oil; they are delicious. Try also spring onions with salt and lime juice in *taquerías*. *Nopales* are opuntia leaves cooked with onions and spices, wrapped in tortilla, slimy but delicious. Indian food is found everywhere: for instance, *tostadas* (toasted fried tortillas with chicken, beans and lettuce), or *gorditas*, fried, extra-thick tortillas with sauce and cheese. Black kidney beans (*frijoles*) appear in various dishes. Try *crepas de cuitlacoche*, best during rainy season, this consists of a pancake stuffed with maize fungus, which has a delicate mushroomy taste, very moreish. In the Pátzcuaro area ask for *budín de cuitlacoche*, with tomato, cream and *chiles*. Red snapper (*huachinango*), Veracruz style, is a famous fish dish, sautéd with *pimientos* and spices. Another excellent fish is the sea bass (*róbalo*). Fruits include a vast assortment of tropical types: avocados, bananas, pineapples, *zapotes*, pomegranates, guavas, limes and *mangos de Manila*, which are delicious. Don't eat fruit unless you peel it yourself, and avoid raw vegetables. Travellers in northwest Mexico (Baja, Chihuahua, Sonora and Sinaloa) should note that there are restrictions on transporting fruits (sanitation permit required) in an effort to contain the spread of fruit fly. Try *higos rebanados* (delicious fresh sliced figs), *guacamole* (a mashed avocado seasoned with tomatoes, onions, coriander and *chiles*) and of course, *papaya*, or pawpaw. Mexico has various elaborate regional cuisines. Some Maya dishes are *sopa de lima* (chicken, rice, *tostada* and lime), *pok chuk* (pork in achiote sauce), *pibil* (a mild sauce on meat or chicken, cooked in banana leaves), *longanizo* sausage from Valladolid. Chinese restaurants, present in most towns, generally give clean and efficient service.

European continental breakfast is very hard to find. For those who like a light, sweet breakfast, try *avena*, a fairly liquid porridge prepared with milk or water, with liberal amounts of cinnamon. Mexican chocolate made with milk is quite filling. In markets, *arroz con leche* is rice boiled in milk until it starts to dissolve, flavoured with cinnamon and sugar. Milk is only safe when in sealed containers marked *pasteurizado*. Fried eggs are known as *huevos estrellados*. On 6 January, Epiphany, the traditional *rosca*, a ring-shaped sweet bread with dried fruit and little plastic baby Jesuses inside, is eaten. The person who finds a baby Jesus in his piece must make a crib and clothes for Him, and invite everyone present to a *fiesta* on 2 February, Candelaria.

Drink The beer is good: brands include Dos Equis-XX, Montejo, Bohemia, Sol and Superior. Negra Modelo is a dark beer, it has the same alcohol content as the other beers. Beer *suero* is with lime juice and a salt-rimmed glass, or *michelada* with chile sauce (both available in Oaxaca). Local wine is cheap and improving in quality; try Domecq, Casa Madero, Santo Tomás, etc; the white sold in oyster restaurants *ostionerías* is usually good. Cetto Reisling Fumé has been recommended. The native drinks are *pulque*, the fermented juice of the agave plant (those unaccustomed to it should not over indulge), *tequila*, made mostly in Jalisco, and *mescal* from Oaxaca; also distilled from agave plants. Mescal usually has a 'gusano de maguey' (worm) in the bottle, considered by Mexicans to be a particular speciality. Tequila and mescal rarely have an alcoholic content above 40-43 percent; tequila Heredura, Sauza and Cuervo have been recommended. Also available is the Spanish aniseed spirit, *anís*, which is made locally. Imported whiskies and brandies are expensive. Rum is cheap and good. *Puro de caña* (called *chingre* in Chinanteca and *posh* in Chamula) is distilled from sugar cane, stronger than mescal but with less taste; it is found in Oaxaca and Chiapas. There are always plenty of non-alcoholic soft drinks (*refrescos*), try the *paletas*, safe and refreshing (those of Michoacán are everywhere) and mineral water (bottled water is available throughout the country in small bottles or more economical large ones which are useful to refill small ones). Fresh juices (as long as not mixed with unpurified water) and milk shakes (*licuados*) are good and usually safe. If you don't like to drink out of a glass ask for a straw, *popote*. Herbal teas, for example camomile, are available. There are few outdoor drinking places in Mexico except in tourist spots.

Holidays and festivals

Sunday is a statutory holiday. Saturday is also observed as a holiday, except by the shops. There is no early-closing day. National holidays are as follows:

New Year (1 January), Constitution Day (5 February), Birthday of Benito Juárez (21 March),

Maundy Thursday, Good Friday and Easter Saturday, Labour Day (1 May), Battle of Puebla (5 May), President's Annual Message (1 September), Independence Day (16 September), Discovery of America (*Día de la raza*) (12 October), Day of the Revolution (20 November), Christmas Day (25 December).

Santos Reyes 6 January, Mother's Day 10 May, All Souls' Day 1-2 November and Our Lady of Guadalupe 12 December, are not national holidays, but are widely celebrated.

Health

The Social Security hospitals are restricted to members, but will take visitors in emergencies; they are more up to date than the Centros de Salud and Hospitales Civiles found in most centres, which are very cheap and open to everyone. There are many homeopathic physicians in all parts of Mexico. You are recommended to use bottled or mineral water for drinking, except in hotels which normally provide purified drinking water free. Ice is usually made from *agua purificada*. Coffee water is not necessarily boiled. Bottled water is available everywhere. Tehuacán mineral water is sold all over Mexico; both plain and flavoured are first class. Water-sterilizing tablets and water purification solution, Microdyn, can be bought at pharmacies. Raw salads and vegetables, and food sold on the streets and in cheap cafés, especially in Mexico City, may be dangerous. Women who are breast-feeding should avoid eating chile. Advisable to vaccinate against hepatitis, typhoid, paratyphoid and poliomyelitis if visiting the low-lying tropical zones, where there is also some risk of malaria; advice and malaria pills from sixth Floor, San Luis Potosí 199, Colonia Roma Nte, Mexico City, 0900-1400 (chloroquine is available cheaply in most large chemists/pharmacies under the brand name Aralen; mefloquire-Larium, is not available). Dengue fever is spreading in Mexico so seek advice on where the Aedes mosquito is present and protect yourself against being bitten. Note also that cholera is on the rise. Hepatitis is a problem in Mexico and, if you have not been vaccinated, gamma globulin is available at better pharamacies/chemists. Heavy eating and drinking of alcohol is unwise in the capital because of its altitude; so is overdoing it physically in the first few days. Some people experience nose-bleeds in Guadalajara and Mexico City because of pollution; they cease with fresh air. Locals recommend Imecol for 'Montezuma's Revenge' (the very common diarrhoea).

Further reading

Travellers wanting more information than we have space to provide, on archaeological sites for instance, would do well to use the widely available *Panorama* guides and the *Easy Guides* written by Richard Bloomgarden, with plans and good illustrations. Also available are Miniguides to archaeological and historical sites, published in various languages by INAH, US$0.75 each. You will appreciate archaeological sites much more if you do some research before visiting them. Do not expect to find leaflets or books at the sites, stock up before you visit. For ornithologists: *A Field Guide to Mexican Birds*, Peterson and Chalif, Houghton Mifflin, 1973, has been recommended; *Finding Birds in Mexico*, by Ernest P Edwards, Box AQ, Sweet Briar, Virginia 24595, USA, recommended as detailed and thorough. Two books by Rudi Robins: *One-day Car Trips from Mexico City*, and *Weekend trips to Cities near Mexico City*. Highly recommended, practical and entertaining is *The People's Guide to Mexico* by Carl Franz (John Muir Publications, Santa Fe, NM), now in its eighth edition, 1990; there is also a *People's Guide Travel Letter*. *Back Country Mexico, A Traveller's Guide and Phrase Book*, by Bob Burlison and David H Riskind (University of Texas Press, Box 7819, Austin, Texas, 78713-7819) has been recommended. *Mexico From The Driver's Seat*, by Mike Nelson, is published by Sanborn's (see **Motoring**, above). Also *Hidden Mexico* by Rebecca Brüns.

Recommended reading for the Maya archaeological area: *The Maya*, by MD Coe (Pelican Books, or large format edition, Thames and Hudson); C Bruce Hunter, *A Guide to Ancient Mayan Ruins* (University of Oklahoma Press, 1986); Joyce Kelly, *An Archaeological Guide to Mexico's Yucatán Peninsula* (the states of Yucatán, Quintana Roo and Campeche) (University of Oklahoma Press, Norman and London, 1993, with maps, photos, 364 pages, accessible, informative and very good). *More Maya Missions. Exploring Colonial Chiapas*, written and illustrated by Richard D Perry (Espadaña Press, PO Box 31067, Santa Barbara, CA 93130, USA) is the latest in a series; also published, *Maya Missions* (in Yucatán) and *Mexico's Fortress Monasteries* (Central Mexico and Oaxaca). For the Puuc region, *Guide to Puuc Region*, Prof Gualberto Zapata Alonzo (US$7.30), has been recommended. For a contemporary account of travel in the Maya region, see *Time among the Maya*, by Ronald Wright. Perhaps the most descriptive of travel in the region is John L Stephens, *Incidents of Travel in Central America, Chiapas and Yucatán*, with illustrations by Frederick Catherwood (several editions exist). *Western Mexico: A Traveller's Treasury*, by Tony Burton (Editorial Agata, Guadalajara), has also been suggested for further reading.

For a short guide to the people, politics, geography, history, economy and culture, *In Focus, Mexico* by John Ross is recommended as part of the In Focus series published by Latin America Bureau in 1996, ISBN 1 899365 05 2.

Maps The Mexican Government Tourist Highway map is available free of charge at tourist offices (when in stock). If driving from the USA you get a free map if you buy your insurance at Sanborn's in the border cities. The official map printers, Detenal, produce the only good large-scale maps of the country.

Guía Roji publish a wide range of regional maps, city plans and gazettes, available at most bookshops. The Dirección General de Oceanografía in Calle Medellín 10, near Insurgentes underground station, sells excellent maps of the entire coastline of Mexico. Good detailed maps of states of Mexico and the country itself from Dirección General de Geografía y Meteorología, Avenida Observatorio 192, México 18, DF, T55151527 (go to Observatorio underground station and up Calle Sur 114, then turn right a short distance down Avenida Observatorio). Best road maps of Mexican states, free, on polite written request, from Director General de Programación, Xola 1755, p 8°, México 12 DF. Building is on the corner of Xola with Avenida Universidad. Mapas Turísticos de México has Mexican (stocks Detenal maps) and world-maps, permanent exhibition at Río Rhin 29, Col Cuauhtémoc, Mexico 5, T5662177. Maps also available from Instituto Nacional de Estadística, Geografía e Informática (INEGI), which has branches in Mexico City (see page 301) and in state capitals (US$3 per sheet). Pemex road atlas, *Atlas de Carreteras y Ciudades Turísticas*, US$5 in bookshops (for example Sanborns), has 20 pages of city maps, almost every road one may need, contour lines, points of interest, service stations, etc (it is rarely on sale in Pemex stations), recommended. Similar, and good, is *The Green Guide*. As well as its maps of *Mexico City* and *Baja California*, ITM of Vancouver (PO Box 2290, Vancouver, BC, V6B 3W5, Canada) publish a map of *Mexico* (1:3,300,000, 1993-94), *Mexico: South* (1:1,000,000, 1992-93) and *Yucatán* (1:1,000,000, third edition, 1993-95). The Mexican Automobile Association (AMA) is at Orizaba 7, 06700 México DF, T52088329, F55116285; they sell an indispensable road guide, with good maps and very useful lists of hotels, with current prices. The ANA (Asociación Nacional Automobilística) sells similar but not such good material; offices in Insurgentes (Metro Glorieta) and Avenida Jalisco 27, México 18 DF. For road conditions consult the AMA, which is quite reliable. The AAA road map is fine for major roads, less good off the beaten track. Also recommended, maps published by HFET SA, Fresas 27, Col de Valles, Mexico DF, T55592310/ 55592320, Mexico City, Estado de México and Mapectual Road Atlas of whole country, US$6 (from Sanborns). The best road map obtainable outside the country is Berndtson & Berndtson *Yucatán* 1:1,000,000, plastic coated, but already outdated (as they all are) by ambitious road building programme undertaken by Pemex (rural roads) and the Federal government.

Laredo to Mexico City: the Gulf Route

*The first four sections describe the four great road routes from the US border towards Mexico City. First, the 1,226-kilometre Gulf Route from **Laredo** (by Pan-American Highway), which takes in the major industrial centre of **Monterrey** and the port of **Tampico**. The route passes through the coastal state of Tamaulipas before entering Huastec and Otomí Indian regions and then leads to the old silver-mining centre of Pachuca.*

Crossing into Mexico

The first route to be opened was the Gulf Route. Traffic from the central and eastern parts of the United States can enter northeast Mexico through four gateways along the Río Bravo; at **Matamoros** (see below), opposite Brownsville; at **Reynosa** opposite McAllen; at **Ciudad Miguel Alemán**, opposite Roma; and at **Nuevo Laredo**, opposite Laredo.

The roads from these places all converge upon Monterrey (a new toll road from Nuevo Laredo is the quickest route, US$12).

There are alternative roads from Reynosa and Matamoros which join the Nuevo Laredo-Mexico City highway at Montemorelos and Ciudad Victoria, respectively: the latter runs along the tropical Gulf coastal plain and then climbs sharply through the Sierra Madre Oriental to Ciudad Victoria, at 333 metres.

By **car**, the best way is by the **Colombia Bridge**: on Interstate 35, take the exit to Milo (the first exit north of the Tourist Bureau and is signed, take Farm Road 1472 west), little traffic and friendly staff, but it does involve a 40-kilometre detour (it is well signposted on the Mexican side). The toll on the international bridge is US$1.25/N$6). Once in Mexico you can either go back to Nuevo Laredo, or continue to Monterrey either on Route 85 or following the railway line via Ciudad Anáhuac and Lampazos.

The direct route is on San Bernardo parallel to I 35 on the west; turn west at Washington, south at Salinas, cross about 10 traffic lights and turn east to the **International bridge**. Do not be directed into the narrow columns: after verbal processing, go three kilometres to the full processing location at Av Cesar López de Lara 1200, opposite train station. This entails six steps, including photocopying of documents (keep copies), US$2-3, and the bureaucracy described under **Motoring** in Essentials.

If pressed for time, avoid 20 November and other national holidays as there are delays at customs owing to Mexicans visiting the USA in large numbers. Border formalities can take two hours or more.

The Nuevo Laredo **bus** station is not near the border; take a bus to the border, then walk across. It is not possible to get a bus from the Laredo Greyhound terminal to the Nuevo Laredo terminal unless you have a ticket to the interior. Connecting tickets from Houston via Laredo to Monterrey are available, 14 hours. Some buses to Laredo connect with Greyhound buses in the USA.

Crossing points

**Laredo, USA/
Nuevo Laredo,
Mexico**

*Population: 400,000
Phone code: 871
Colour map 2, grid B5*

This is the most important town of the border crossings. Nuevo Laredo is a bit of a tourist trap but it is fun to stroll through the souvenir shops.

Essentials (Laredo) 2 trailer parks, the better of the two is east side of Route I 35, Main Street exit, 10 minutes from border. **Banks** *UNB Convent* and *Matamoros* charges 1% commission on TCs, it charges pesos, open 0830-1600 Mon-Fri. *IBC*, no commission under US$500. **Communications** Fax: and to receive letter, TCR, Martin and Sandra Resendez, 820 Juárez, near post office, international service. **Embassies & consulates** *Mexican Consulate*, Farragut and Maine, 4th light on the right after leaving Interstate 35, open 0800-1400 Mon-Fri, helpful. **Useful addresses** Car insurance: *AAA* on San Bernardo Av (exit 4 on Interstate 35). *Sanborns* on Santa Ursula (exit 16 on Interstate 35), a bit more expensive, open 24 hours a day. *Johnson's Mexico Insurance*, Tepeyac Agent, Lafayette and Santa Ursula (59 and Interstate 35), US$2.60 per day, open 24 hours, recommended. Car tyres: Tire Center of Laredo Inc, 815 Park, at San Bernardo Av.

Essentials (Nuevo Laredo) **C** *Alameda*, on plaza. **C** *Dos Laredos*, Matamoros y 15 de Junio. **E** *Calderón*, with bath, hot water, fan, run down, friendly. Many **F** hotels, none of which have been recommended. **Motels**: **A** *Hacienda*, Prol Reforma 5530. **B** *Reforma*, Av Guerrero 822. **Shopping** *Centro Artesanal Nuevo Laredo*, Maclovio Herrera 3030, T26399. **Trains** To **Mexico City**, US$12 2nd class, US$22 *primera preferente*, daily at 1855, 24 hours, it can get cold at night, meals on train poor, take your own food, or buy at stations (leaves Mexico City for the border at 0900). Information: Av López César de Lara y Mina, Apdo Postal 248, Nuevo Laredo, Tamps, 88000 Mexico, T28097; or PO Box 595, Laredo, Tx78042. **Buses** To **Mexico City** with Estrella Blanca/Transportes del Norte 9 buses a day, 16½ hours, US$42. Buses for **Monterrey** (4 hours, US$10, departures every hour), **Guadalajara** (18 hours, US$46.50, 9 a day, Transportes del Norte or Estrella Blanca), to **San Luis Potosí**, US$38, **Tampico**, **Morelia** (17 hours, US$43).

Mexico north

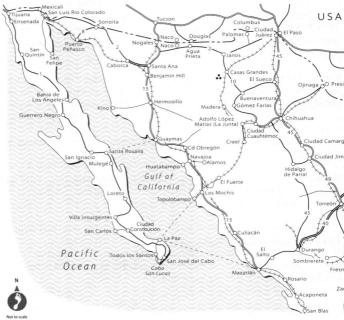

After 130 kilometres of grey-green desert, the road from Nuevo Laredo climbs the Mamulique Pass, which it crosses at 700 metres, and then descends to Monterrey. From Laredo to Monterrey there is a toll road ('cuota') and a non-toll road ('vía Libre'). The latter goes through Sabinas Hidalgo (hotels and museum). There is a toll bypass and a free truck route around Monterrey.

This is the border town, population 300,000, opposite McAllen.

Sleeping on the Zócalo D *San Carlos*, recommended, and **E** *Plaza*. In McAllen on the US side of the border. **E** *Arcade*, corner of Cedar and North 12th St, 2 blocks from Greyhound terminal, south from Valley Transit bus terminal.

McAllen (USA)/ Reynosa (Mexico)

Phone Code: 892

A town with a bright and unforbidding museum, designed to let a prospective tourist know what he can expect in Mexico. It is well worth a visit. Visas can be obtained in **Brownsville** on the US side of the border from the Mexican Consulate at 940, East Washington. Crossing the border by car here is quick and easy; permission is granted for six months (multiple entry) for passengers and vehicle, paperwork takes only about 10 minutes if everything is in order. The return journey is equally easy.

Brownsville (USA)/ Matamoros

Population: 400,000
Phone code: 891
Colour map 2, grid B6

Essentials C *Ritz*, Matamoros y Siete. There are 4 motels on the road to the beach, all **B/C**. **Shopping** *Centro Artesanal Matamoros*, C 5 Hurtado and Alvaro Obregón (T20384). **Transport Buses** Several lines run first-class buses to **Mexico City** in 14 hours for US$38. Transportes del Norte to **Ciudad Victoria** for US$10.75 (4 hours).

110 kilometres south of Matamoros is **San Fernando de Presas**, a convenient distance from the border, especially if driving to the USA. **B** *Hotel Las Palomas*, on highway, quite good; excellent pizza place, serving more than pizza, near the *Hotel América*.

Colour map 2, grid C6

Monterrey

Capital of Nuevo León state, third largest city in Mexico, 253 kilometres south of the border and 915 kilometres from Mexico City. The city is dominated by the Cerro de la Silla (saddle) from the east and the Cerro de las Mitras in the west. Evenings are cool. Its population is still growing in spite of its unattractive climate: too hot in summer, too cold in winter, dusty at most times and a shortage of water. It now turns out (using cheap gas from near the Texas border and increasingly from the new gas fields in the south), over 75 percent of Mexico's iron and steel, and many other products accompanied by an almost permanent industrial smog. Its people are highly skilled and educated, but its streets are congested, its layout seems unplanned and its architecture uninspiring except in the centre which has undergone renewal and remodelling in recent years. The city now has a modern and efficient Metro System. The centre

Population: 3,000,000
State Population: 1995
3,549,273
Altitude: 538m
Phone code: 83
Colour map 2, grid B5

lies just north of the Rio Santa Catarina. Plaza Zaragoza, Plaza 5 de Mayo, the Explanada de Los Héroes and Parque Hundido link with the Gran Plaza to the south to form what is claimed to be the biggest civic square in the world. It runs north-south and is nine blocks long by two blocks wide; its centrepiece is the Faro de Comercio (lighthouse of commerce). To the east of the Faro is the 18th century Cathedral badly damaged in the war against the USA in 1846-47, when it was used by Mexican troops as a powder magazine. Running along the west side of the northern part of the plaza are the Torre Latina, High Court and State Congress; opposite, on the east side are the Biblioteca and the Teatro de La Ciudad, all modern buildings. It is bordered at its southern end by the Municipal Palace, and at its northern limit is the Government Palace looking over the Explanada de Los Héroes. (There is a clean public convenience beneath the Plaza, on Matamoros between Avs Zua Zua and Zaragoza, near the Neptune Fountain). The older area to the east of the Cathedral is known as the Barrio Antiguo.

Museums C Morelos is a pedestrians-only shopping centre. Its famous **Instituto Tecnológico** (Av Garza Sada 2501) has valuable collections of books on 16th century Mexican history, of rare books printed in Indian tongues, and 2,000 editions of Don Quixote in all languages. The new **Mexican History Museum**, off north end of plaza, is an excellent interactive museum, good for children. ■ *T3424820. Opens 1000.*.

The **Monterrey Museum** is in the grounds of the Cuauhtémoc Brewery, Av Alfonso Reyes 2202 Nte (500 metres north of Metro Central). ■ *T3286060. Tuesday-Sunday 1100-2000, Wednesday 1000-2000 (beer – in small bottles – is handed out free in the gardens). Visits to brewery Monday-Friday 0930-1530, Saturday 0930-1300. The* **Mexican Baseball Hall of Fame** is in part of the museum, as is a

Monterrey centre

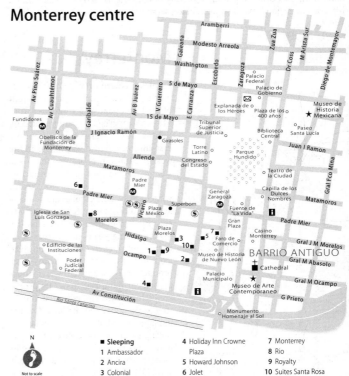

N

Not to scale

■ **Sleeping**	4 Holiday Inn Crowne	7 Monterrey
1 Ambassador	Plaza	8 Rio
2 Ancira	5 Howard Johnson	9 Royalty
3 Colonial	6 Jolet	10 Suites Santa Rosa

museum of Modern Art (temporary shows). ■ *T3285746. Tuesday-Friday 0930-1700, Saturday-Sunday 1030-1800.*.

Museum of Contemporary Art (Marco), Zua Zua y PR Jardon, T3424820, is one of the best modern art galleries in Mexico, temporary shows, good bookshop. ■ *Wednesday and Sunday 1100-2100, other days 1100-1900, closed Monday. US$2, free Wednesday*. Two other art galleries with temporary shows are the **Pinacoteca de Nuevo León**, Parque Niños Héroes, ■ *T3315462, Tuesday-Sunday 1000-1800*, and **Centro Cultural de Arte**, Belisario Domínguez 2140 Pte, Col Obispado, ■ *T3471128, Monday-Friday 0900-1300, 1500-1800.*

Museum of Glass, Zaragoza y Magallanes (Metro del Golfo). ■ *T3291000 x1219. 0900-1300, 1500-1800, closed Thursday.*

Museum of Popular Cultures, Abasolo 1024, Barrio Antiguo. ■ *T3456504, Tuesday-Sunday 1000-1800*. Also in the centre is **Metropolitan Museum of Monterrey** in the old Municipal Palace building, Zaragoza s/n between Corregidora y Hidalgo. ■ *T3441971, Monday-Sunday 0800-2000.*

The **Alfa Cultural Centre**, in the Garza García suburb, has a fine planetarium and an astronomy and physics section with do-it-yourself illustrations of mechanical principles, et cetera. In a separate building is a Rufino Tamayo stained-glass window. ■ *T3565696, Tuesday-Friday 1500-2100, Saturday 1400-2100, Sunday 1200-2100, closed Monday. Reached by special bus from west end of Alameda, hourly on the hour 1500-2000.* Another museum in this locality, with exhibits on Nuevo León, is the **Museo del Centenario**, Libertad 116, esq Morelos San Pedro, Garza García. ■ *T3383075, Monday-Sunday 0900-2000.*

The **Alameda Gardens**, between Avs Aramberri and Washington, on Av Pino Suárez, are a pleasant place to sit. ■ *1000-1700, closed Tuesday.* The Cerro del Obispado affords good views, smog permitting. **The Palace** (1787) is a regional museum. ■ *Sunday 1000-1700, Tuesday-Saturday 1000-1300, 1500-1800.* It served as HQ for both Pancho Villa and Gen Zachary Taylor. Take No 1 bus which stops at the foot of the hill.

Zoo

Parque La Pastora, Av Eloy Cavazos, east of centre.

Excursions

In the hills around are the bathing resort of **Topo Chico**, six and a half kilometres to the northwest; water from its hot springs is bottled and sold throughout Mexico. Reached by a road heading south (extension of Av Gómez Morín), is **Chipinque**, an ecological park in the Sierra Madre, with magnificent views of the Monterrey area. It is popular for hiking, mountain biking and climbing, with peaks reaching 2,200 metres.

West of Monterrey, off the Saltillo road are the **García Caves** (about 10 kilometres from Villa García, which is 40 kilometres from Monterrey). The entrance is 800 metres up, by cable car, and inside are beautiful stalagmites and stalactites. At the foot of the cable car are a pool and recreational centre. A tour of the caves takes one and a half hours, and it is compulsory to go in a group with a guide. You can take a bus to Villa García, but it is a dusty walk to the caves. On Sunday Transportes Saltillo-Monterrey run a bus to the caves at 0900, 1000 and 1100. Otherwise, take an agency tour, for example Osetur (details from Infotur); book at *Hotel Ancira* (on Tuesday, US$3.50).

Hidalgo is a small town 38 kilometres northwest of Monterrey on the Monclava road. Dominating the area are the massive limestone cliffs of **Potrero Chico** (four kilometres west of town, take road leading on from Calle Francisco Villa). There is a noisy Recreational Park at the foot of the cliffs with balneario and restaurants. Passing through the short canyon between 610-metre cliffs you come to a peaceful enclosed valley with excellent walking. The cliffs are a magnet for big-wall climbers, particularly during the US winter, and have some of the hardest pitches in the world (up to 5.12d) including the 650-metre long 'Sendero Luminoso' route on the central pillar of 'El Toro'. A sheet guide describing 80 of the best climbs and places to camp by Jeff Jackson is available at the store on the left before you reach the *balneario*.

Mexico

Accommodation **F** at *rancho*. Autobuses Mina leave at hourly intervals from Monterrey bus station to Hidalgo (bus station on plaza).

Another excellent rock climbing area is at the **Cañón de la Huasteca**, near Santa Catarina, 20 kilometres west of Monterrey along route 40, in the northern part of the Cumbres de Monterrey National Park, where there are prehistoric glyphs.

Sleeping
It is difficult to obtain accommodation because of the constant movement of people travelling north/south.

■ *on map, page 94*
Price codes: see inside front cover

There are many new hotels in the luxury category in the centre and on radial routes coming into the city (not all listed). Most of the cheap hotels are situated in the area around the bus station (Metros Central and Cuauhtémoc).

L *Crowne Plaza*, Av Constitución 300 Ote, near Plaza Zaragoza, best, T3196005. **L** *Holiday Inn*, Av Alfonso Reyes 101 Nte, T3766555, also at Av Eugenio Garza Sada 3680 Sur, T3296000, and at Av San Jerónimo 1082, T3896020. **L** *Monterrey*, Morelos 574 Ote, T3454988.

A *Ambassador*, Hidalgo 310 Ote y Galeana, T3406390. **A** *Jolet*, Padre Mier 201 Pte, T3405505. **A** *Río*, Padre Mier 194 Pte, T3432090. **A** *Royal Courts* (Best Western), Av Alfonso Reyes 314, T3762292. **A** *Suites Santa Rosa*, Escobedo 930 Sur, T3424200. **C** *Yamallel*, Zaragoza 912, Nte Madero, T753400, good.

D *Del Norte*, Juan Méndez y Democracia 260 Pte (north of Av Colón, near bus station) T3752140, TV, a/c. **D** *Posada*, Amado Nervo 1138 Nte, T3722467, with bath, clean, recommended. Further down same street at Juan Méndez 1518 Nte y Aquiles Serdán is

Monterrey metro system & main streets

Related map
A Monterrey centre, page 94

Not to scale

To
Alfa cultural centre

D *Monterrey La Silla*, T/F3727579, TV, and opposite at 1515, **E** *La Silla*, its sister hotel, clean, friendly, recommended.

E *Estación*, Guadalupe Victoria Pte 1450, T3750755, opposite train station, bath, a/c. **E** *Nuevo León*, Amado Nervo 1007 Nte con Av Madero, with bath (hot water), dark, seedy, poor value, close to bus station. Many hotels between Colón and Reforma, 2 blocks from the bus station, nothing below US$15. **D** *Victoria*, Bernardo Reyes 1205 Nte, with bath, parking, a bit noisy.

Motels A *El Paso Autel*, Zaragoza y Martínez. **D** *Motel/Trailerpark Nueva Castilla*, on Highway 85 before Saltillo bypass, 12 spaces for RVs with hook-up, pool, hot showers, reasonable restaurant, clean but drab, US$17 for vehicle and 2 people; several on Nuevo Laredo highway.

Youth hostel Av Madero Ote s/n, Parque Fundidora, CP64000.

23 eating places around the 'Zona Rosa' and Plaza Zaragoza in the heart of town.   **Eating**

Vegetarian *Los Girasoles*, Juan Ignacio Ramón 200 Ote (Esquina Guerrero, 1 block from Juárez), possibly best, good value. *Superbom*, Padre Mier, upstairs, good menú.

Adventure sports: *Asociación de Excursionismo y Montañismo*, Washington Pte 2222-B,   **Sports**
Col María Luisa, T3271929 or 3562715 (for Sr Angel Medina). **Baseball**: at *Estadio de Baseball Monterrey*, Parque Niños Héroes, T3518022. **Bullfighting**: at *Plaza de Toros*, M Barragán y Alfonso Reyes, north of bus station, T3740505. **Football**: at *Estadio Tecnológico*, off Av Garza Sada, southeast of centre, T358200; *Estadio Universitario*, Parque Niños Héroes, north of centre, T3762238.

Local There are 2 **metro** lines and exten-   **Transport**
sions planned. The blue line, the longer, runs south from the suburb of San Bernabé and then makes a right angle turn traversing the city eastwards passing by the bus and train stations. It connects with the green line (at Cuauhtémoc near the bus station) which runs south into the centre. Tickets bought from machines (2 pesos a ticket, less for more than one). **Car rental**: Monterrey, Serafín Peña 740-A Sur, T3446510. **National**, Escobedo Sur 1011 Local 8, T3446363.

Air Gen Mariano Escobedo airport (MTY), 24 kilometres from centre. Daily flights from Mexico City take 1 hour 20 minutes. Many flights to USA (Atlanta, Charlotte, Chicago, Dallas, Dayton, Houston, Huntsville, Las Vegas, Los Angeles, Louisville, Pensacola, San Antonio), to Havana, Cuba, Toronto, Canada and Mexican cities: Acapulco, Aguascalientes, Cancún, Chihuahua, Ciudad Juárez, Cuernavaca, Culiacán, Durango, Guadalajara, Hermosillo, La Paz, León, Los Cabos, Mazatlán, Mérida, Monclova, Morelia, Piedras Negras, Puebla, Puerto Vallarta, Querétaro, Saltillo, San Luis Potosí, Tampico, Tijuana, Torreón, Veracruz, Villahermosa.

López Mateos

Cam A Apodaca

Av Félix Galván

Av Las Américas

Av Ruiz Cortínez

Av Miguel Alemán

Av Benito Juárez

Palacio Federal

Lerdo de Tejada

Exposición

Av Chapultepec

Mexico

Trains Station on Miguel Nieto Nte (Metro Central) T3510532. Check locally to see if any trains are running.

Buses Terminal on Av Colón, between Calzada B Reyes and Av Pino Suárez (Metro Cuauhtémoc), T3183737. Monterrey-**Mexico City**, US$36, 12½ hours. A more scenic trip is from Mexico City (northern bus terminal) to **Ciudad Valles**, 10 hours, from where there are many connecting buses to Monterrey. To **San Luis Potosí**, US$18. To **Nuevo Laredo**, departures every hour, 4 hours, US$12. To **Matamoros**, Transportes del Norte, 4 hours, US$12. To **Chihuahua** with Transportes del Norte, 8 a day, 12 hours, US$33. Frequent buses to **Saltillo**, but long queues for tickets. To **Guadalajara**, US$38. To **Tampico**, US$18, 7-8 hours. To **Torreón**, US$14. To Santiago for Cola de Caballo falls, US$1.65.

NB Motorists: if driving Monterrey-Saltillo, there is nothing to indicate you are on the toll-road until it is too late. The toll is US$7. Look for the old road.

Directory **Airline offices** AeroMéxico, T435560. American Airlines, T403031.Aviacsa, T364400. Mexicana, T800-7150220. Taesa, T597775. Continental, T95-800-5379222. **Banks** If stuck without pesos on Sun, the red hotel/restaurant just opposite the bus station changes TCs if you buy something in the restaurant. **Communications** Post Office: Palacio Federal, Av 5 de Mayo y Zaragoza (behind Government Palace), T3424003. **Embassies & consulates** British (Honorary) Mr Edward Lawrence, Privada de Tamazunchale 104, Colonia del Valle, Garza García, T3337598. Canadian, T3443200. US, T3452120. German, T3385223. French, T3364498. Guatemalan, T3728648. Netherlands, T3425055. Israeli, T3361325. Swedish, T3463090. Swiss, T3383675. **Hospitals & medical services** Hospital General de IMSS, Pino Suárez y Jl Ramón, T3455355. Angeles Verdes, T3402113. **Red Cross**: T3751212. **Tourist offices** State Tourist Office is in the Kalos Building west of Municipal Palace, Zaragoza 1300 Sur, level A-1, T3401080, 3444343. An easier to find office is at Padre Mier y Dr Coss on the east side of the plaza, open Tuesday-Sunday 1000-1700, sometimes closes at lunchtime. **Official Tour Service (Osetur)** run tours around the city and Nuevo León, T3471614, 3471533. Large city maps available, free at the Edif Kalos office. Office by an airport on highway from Nuevo Laredo, helpful.

Monterrey to Ciudad Victoria

Leaving Monterrey, the road threads the narrow and lovely Huajuco canyon; from Santiago village a road runs to within two kilometres of the Cola de Caballo, or Horsetail, Falls, in the **Cumbres de Monterrey** national park, the largest in Mexico. (First-class hotel on the way, and you can get a colectivo, US$1.65, from the bus stop to the falls, and a horse, US$1.65, to take you to the top of the falls, entrance US$2.40; cost of guide US$5.) Deeper into the park are other waterfalls, the 75-metre Cascada El Chipitín and Cascada Lagunillas. There is a two-day circuit, 'Recorrido de Matacanes', starting at Las Adjuntas, taking in both these falls and involving river canyoning, abseiling and swimming through tunnels. Ask at Asociación de Excursionismo y Montañismo in Monterrey. The road drops gradually into lower and warmer regions, passing through a succession of subtropical valleys with orange groves, banana plantations and vegetable gardens.

At **Montemorelos**, just off the highway, 79 kilometres south of Monterrey, a branch road from the Matamoros-Monterrey highway comes in. On 53 kilometres is **Linares** (Population: 100,000), a fast-expanding town. **B** Escondido Court, motel, clean, a/c, pool and restaurant, recommended, 1½ kilometres north of Linares on Route 855. **B** Hotel Guidi, near the plaza. Buses fromLinares to **San Luis Potosí**, US$16.

A most picturesque 96-kilometre highway runs west from Linares up the lovely Santa Rosa canyon, up and over the Sierra Madre. After Iturbide, turn south on top of the Sierra Madre and continue on a good road through the unspoilt Sierra via La Escondida and Dr Arroyo. Alternatively, stay on the main road for San Roberto, north of Matehuala (see page 109) and join the Highway 57 route from Eagle Pass to Mexico City.

Ciudad Victoria

Capital of Tamaulipas state, a quiet, clean, unhurried city with a shaded plaza. Here Route 85 from Monterrey and Route 101 from Matamoros meet. It is often used as a stop-over.

Km 706
Population: 300,000
State Population: 1995
2,526,387
Altitude: 336m
Phone book 131
Colour map 2, grid C6

The **Parque Siglo 21** is the same end of town as the bus station. The centrepiece is a planetarium which looks like a huge red ball that landed on the banks of the Río San Marcos. Good view of the sierra from behind the planetarium where there is a large Rosa de los Vientos. Across the river is the Government Plaza, a 12-storey glass tower, the tallest thing in town. Also the state library in a green, tiled, Aztec-style building. The **Centro Cultural Tamaulipas**, 15 y Hidalgo, opposite the Palacio del Gobierno is a functional, modern building with a library and various cultural functions. The **Museo de la Universidad Autónoma de Tamaulipas** on the plaza has a good section on the Huasteca culture. On top of a hill is a tiny church: the temple of Nuestra Señora de Guadalupe, the patron saint of Mexico. (With thanks to Dan Golopentia, Seattle.)

The north-south streets (parallel to the Sierra) have names and numbers, the east-west streets have only names.

Mexico

Excursions

Tamatán, a suburb (plenty of colectivos), has a large park with a zoo and a small lake, popular with Mexicans at leisure. Take a colectivo to Ejido Libertad for the **Parque Ecológico Los Troncones**, where you can walk along the river and in the hills; good swimming holes.

Northeast of Ciudad Victoria is Nueva Ciudad Padilla; nearby is Viejo Padilla, where Agustín de Iturbide was shot in 1824. Also nearby is Presa Vicente Guerrero, a large lake with good fishing and many tourist facilities.

East of Ciudad Victoria sits the quiet town of **Soto La Marina**, with several places to stay including the new **D** *Hotel María Cristina*, which is good if you want to avoid the large city of Ciudad Victoria. Southwest of Ciudad Victoria, 20 kilometres along Route 101 (direction Jamuave) is a sign to the Zona Arqueológica **El Balcón de Moctezuma**. The site consists of circular buildings and staircases, showing Huastec influence. It is similar to Chicomostoc, La Quemada and Casas Grandes and was a commercial centre with contacts with tribes in present day USA. Ask for the guide Don Gabino, who took part in the excavations completed in June 1990. From the signpost to the Zona Arqueológica it's a four-kilometre walk, then 100 metres uphill (a high clearance vehicle can get within 100 metres and you can park at Altas Cumbres near the site). We are grateful to Helmut Zettl, Ebergassing, for this information.

Sleeping

A *Santorín* (Best Western), Cristóbal Colón Nte 349, T128938, F128342, a/c, TV, parking, restaurant. **B** *Sierra Gorda*, Hidalgo 990 Ote, T32280, garage US$0.70 a night. Several **E** hotels by bus station and in the centre. **Motels** **B** *Panorámica*, Lomas de Santuario, T25506. **D** *Los Monteros*, Plaza Hidalgo, T20300, downtown. **Trailer Park** *Victoria RV Trailer Park*, Libramiento 101-85, T/F24824, follow signs, good service, electricity, hot showers; owner (Rosie) has travel information, US$10 for 2 plus vehicle.

Eating

Chavos, C 12, Hidalgo y Juárez, all you can eat buffet. *Daddy's* on the plaza, sort of a *Denny's*, with a Mexican touch for the homesick American. Locals congregate at *Café Cantón*, half a block from the plaza on C 9.

Transport

Train To Tampico, Tuesday, Thursday, Saturday, 1440 arrives 1930, returns 0750, arrives 1240. Check locally all rail services available. **Buses** Terminal is on the outskirts. Omnibuses Blancos to Ciudad Valles (see below) for US$8.50. Bus Ciudad Victoria-Mexico City 10 hours, US$26.65.

Directory

Tourist office C 16 y Rosales near Parque Alameda.

Ciudad Mante

Colour map 2, grid C6 After crossing the Tropic of Cancer the road enters the solid green jungle of the tropical lowlands. 137 kilometres south of Ciudad Victoria is **Ciudad Mante** (Route 85, Km 570), which is almost exactly the mid-way point between Matamoros and Mexico City and makes a convenient stop-over place. The city is, however, dirty. It has a

Ciudad Victoria

Mexico

Museo de Antropología e Historia, with objects from the Huastec culture.

Excursions

45 kilometres north of Ciudad Mante is the village of **Gómez Farias**, an important centre for ornithological research: the highlands above the village represent the northernmost extent of several tropical vegetation formations. Many tropical bird species reach the northern limit of their range. Gómez Farias is reached by turning off the main highway, 14 kilometres over a paved road to the town plaza. From there, an easy two-kilometre walk provides excellent views of bird habitats. (Jim Turner, Oak Grove, Missouri). A one-hour drive, plus five hours' walk, leads to **El Cielo Biosphere Reserve** which has four different ecosystems at various altitudes, including tropical jungle and cloud forest (about 200 metres to 2,500 metres). In the reserve is Canindo Research Station.

South of Ciudad Mante at Km 548 is Antiguo Morelos. A road turns off west to San Luis Potosí (see page 111) 314 kilometres, and Guadalajara (see page 211).

Sleeping

Best hotel is probably the **B** *Mante*, Guerrero 500 Nte, T20990, shaded grounds at north edge of business sector. **D** *Monterrey*, Av Juárez 503, Ote, T21512, in old section, with bath, hot water, a/c, cable TV, helpful manager speaks English, safe parking, recommended, new annex at back, restaurant not so good; several hotels a few blocks south of Zócalo.

Tampico

Monterrey trains run via Ciudad Victoria to the Caribbean port of **Tampico**, definitely not a tourist attraction, reached by a fine road from Ciudad Mante, in a rich sugar-growing area, a deviation of 156 kilometres. Tampico, founded in 1522 by Gonzalo de Sandoval but sacked by pirates in the 17th century and refounded in 1823, has the faded grandeur of a once prosperous river port and is situated on the northern bank of the Río Pánuco, not far from a large oilfield: there are storage tanks and refineries for miles along the southern bank. The summer heat, rarely above 35°C, is tempered by sea breezes, but June and July are trying. Cold northerlies blow now and again during the winter. There are two pleasant plazas, Plaza de Armas at Colón y Carranza, with

Population: 560,000
Phone code: 121
Colour map 2, grid C6

squirrels in the trees, and Plaza de la Libertad, Madero y Juárez. There are two interesting buildings on the Plaza de Armas: the **Catedral Santa Iglesia** has an international flavour: a clock from England, an altar from Carrara in Italy and swastikas inlaid into the aisle floor. The former **Palacio Municipal** on the northwest corner (now DIF building), is an art nouveau construction. Huge, interesting market, but watch your possessions carefully. Fishing (both sea and river) is excellent.

Excursions The **Playa de Miramar**, a beach resort, is a tram or bus-ride from the city, but is reported dirty. If walking there, go along the breakwater (Escollera Norte) on north side of Río Pánuco, for views of the shipping and to see the monument to Mexican merchant seamen killed in the Second World War. Laguna del Carpintero, just north of the centre is popular for watersports.

The **Museo de la Cultura Huasteca** in **Ciudad Madero**, an adjacent town, is worth visiting (Instituto Tecnológico, Av 1 de Mayo y Sor Juana Inés de la Cruz – in poor condition); take a colectivo, 'Madero', from the centre of Tampico to the Zócalo in Ciudad Madero, then another to the Instituto; small but select collection ■ *1000-1500, except Monday*. Ciudad Madero claims to be Mexico's petroleum capital, with a huge oil refinery.

Sleeping **AL** *Camino Real*, Av Hidalgo 2000, T38811. **AL** *Impala*, Mirón 220 Pte, T20990. **AL** *Inglaterra*, Mirón y Olmos, T92857. **AL** *Mansión Real*, T91515, Colón 104 (near Plaza de Armas). **B** *Imperial*, López de Lara Sur 201, T25678, clean, shower, fan, but noisy. **B** *Nuevo León*, Aduana N 107, T24370, a/c, shower, clean. **B** *Tampico*, Carranza 513, T90057. **C** *Ritz*, on Miramar beach (see above), deserted at night.

Several cheap hotels near Plaza de la Libertad: **E** *América*, T23478, near market on Olmos, dirty but safe and friendly. **E** *Hawaii*, Héroes de Cañonero 609 (2 blocks east of Plaza

Tampico

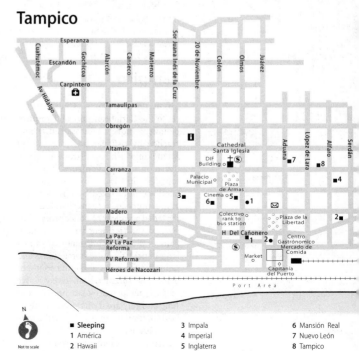

■ Sleeping	3 Impala	6 Mansión Real
1 América	4 Imperial	7 Nuevo León
2 Hawaii	5 Inglaterra	8 Tampico

Not to scale

Libertad), T41887, dark rooms,clean, and others on this street. **E** *Rex*, dirty, no hot water. All hotels downtown near market should be treated with discretion; many have a rapid turnover. RVs can stay in the parking lot of the airport, which has rest rooms, US$15 per vehicle, noisy from traffic.

Emir, FA Olmos between Díaz Mirón y Madero, good for breakfast, *El Selecto*, opposite market. There are many cheap restaurants in the Centro Gastronómico Mercado de Comida east of the market. **Eating**

April to August is the **Deep Sea Fishing** competition season. The main competitions are the 'Torneo Internacional de Róbalo' (April); 'Torneo Internacional de Marlin' (June) and 'Torneo Internacional del Sabalo' (July and August). **Sports**

(Re)Founders day, beginning of **April**. **Festivals**

Air The Gen F Javier Mina airport (TAM), T280571/72 is 8 kilometres from the centre. **Transport** Mexicana has daily flights to Mexico City and Aeroliteral flies to San Antonio (Texas), Ciudad del Carmen, Monclova, Monterrey, Piedras Negras, Poza Rica, San Luís Potosí, Torreón, Veracruz and Villahermosa. Aero California flies to Los Angeles via Mexico City, Tepic and Tijuana. Continental Express flies to Dallas and Houston. **Train** Train station is beside Capitanía del Puerto. Trains Tuesday, Thursday, Saturday to Ciudad Victoria 0750, arrives 1240, returns 1440, arrives 1930. **Bus**: station is several kilometres from the centre on Av Ejército Mexicano on the far side of Laguna del Carpintero. Colectivos to bus station leave from C Olmos between market and plaza. To **Monterrey**, US$19.50, 7-8 hours; to **Ciudad Valles**, US$5.70; to **Mexico City**, US$18, 9 hours; to **San Luis Potosí**, US$16, 7 hours.

Airline offices *Aero California,* T138400. *AeroMéxico,* T170939. *Mexicana,* T139600. **Directory** **Communications** Post Office: on Madero 309 Ote, T121927. **Embassies & consulates** German *Consul*, 2 de Enero, 102 Sur-A, Hon Consul Dieter Schulze. Postal Address: Apdo 775, T129784/129817. Also deals with British affairs. **Hospitals & medical services** Red Cross: T21313. **Tourist office** 20 de Nov 218, helpful.

A second 145-kilometre paved road west from Tampico through the oil camp of **Ebano** joins the Nuevo Laredo-México highway further south at Ciudad Valles. There are direct buses to Brownsville (Texas). A splendid new bridge was opened in 1988 to replace the ferry to **Villa Cuauhtémoc**, south of Tampico. Further south, the coast road, Route 180, enters Veracruz state, leading to Tuxpan, Poza Rica and Veracruz. **Routes**

Ciudad Valles

Ciudad Valles is on a winding river and a popular stop-over with many hotels. **Museo Regional Huasteco**, centre of archaeological and ethnographic research for the Huastec region. ■ *C Rotarios y C Artes (or Peñaloza), 1000-1200, 1400-1800, Monday-Friday.* Visit the market, which is very busy. There are many cheap places to eat tacos.

Km 476
Population: 320,000
Colour map 2, grid C6

Héroes de Chapultepec
2 de Enero
Zaragoza
Iturbide
Río Pánuco

● **Eating**
1 Emir
2 Selecto

Mexico

Sleeping **A** *Valles*, T20050, with trailer park, full hook-up, hot shower, a bit run-down, US$10 for 2 in car, on Carretera México-Laredo. **B** *San Fernando*, T20184, on main highway, clean, large rooms, a/c, TV, parking. **D** *Condesa*, Av Juárez 109, T20015, clean, basic, fan, friendly, OK. 11 kilometres south of town is campground *El Banito*, warm sulphur pools, good restaurant, a bit run down.

Transport **Buses** Omnibús Ote to San Luis Potosí for US$7 (4 hours); Mexico City 10 hours.

Tamazunchale

Km 370
Population: 150,000
Altitude: 206 m
Colour map 3, grid B4

Tamazunchale, with riotous tropical vegetation, is perhaps the most popular of all the overnight stops. (**B** *Mirador*, good, but passing traffic by night is noisy. **E** *Hotel OK*, cheapest but not recommended.) The potholed road south of here begins a spectacular climb to the highland, winding over the rugged terrain cut by the Río Moctezuma and its tributaries. The highest point on the road is 2,502 metres. From (Km 279) **Jacala** (two very basic hotels, erratic water supply) there is a dizzying view into a chasm. **Zimapán** (*Posada del Rey*, fascinating but very run down, out on the highway), with a charming market place and a small old church in the plaza, is as good a place as any to stay the night. From (Km 178) **Portezuelo** a paved road runs west to Querétaro (see page 114), 140 kilometres.

Ixmiquilpan

In an area of 23,300 square kilometres north and south of (Km 169) **Ixmiquilpan**, just off the highway, 65,000 Otomí Indians 'live the bitterest and saddest life'. The beautifully worked Otomí belts and bags may sometimes be bought at the Monday market, and also in the Artesanía shop in the main street almost opposite the government aid offices.

See early Indian frescoes in the main church, which is one of the 16th century battlemented Augustinian monastery-churches; the monastery is open to the public. John Streather writes: "At sunset each day white egrets come to roost in the trees outside the church; it's worth going up on to the battlements to see them swoop down. The church of El Carmen is worth a visit too, lovely west façade and gilded altars inside. There is also a 16th century bridge over the river; beautiful walk along the ahuehuete-lined banks."

Excursions Near Ixmiquilpan are several warm swimming pools, both natural and manmade: San Antonio, Dios Padre, Las Humedades, and near Tephé (the only warm-water bath, clean, entry US$0.40) and Tzindejé (this is about 20 minutes from town). The Otomí villages of La Lagunita, La Pechuga and La Bonanza, in a beautiful valley, have no modern conveniences.

The **Barranca de Tolantongo**, 37 kilometres northeast of Ixmiquilpan, is about 1,500 metres deep with a waterfall and thermal spring; at weekends there is a small eating place. Entry US$2, car parking US$2 at entrance to recreational area; camping permitted. To get there take the road towards El Cardonal, then an unpaved turn-off about three kilometres before El Cardonal (there is a bus from Pachuca).

Sleeping **C** *Hotel Diana*, rear buildings slightly dearer rooms but much cleaner, recommended, safe parking. **E** *Hotel/Restaurant Los Portales*, 1 block from main square, clean, safe parking, mediocre food.

Actopán to Tula

Actopán (Km 119) has another fine 16th century Augustinian church and convent (**B** *Hotel Rira*). From Actopán a 56-kilometre branch road runs to one of Mexico's great archaeological sites: Tula, capital of the Toltecs (see page 313).

On the way to Tula there is an interesting cooperative village, **Cruz Azul**. Free concerts on Sunday mornings at 1000 in front of main market. At (Km 85) Colonia, a road runs left for eight kilometres to Pachuca.

Pachuca

This is one of the oldest silver-mining centres in Mexico and capital of Hidalgo state. The Aztecs mined here before the Spaniards came and the hills are honeycombed with old workings and terraced with tailings.

Although the centre is largely modern, there are a number of colonial buildings among its narrow, steep and crooked streets. These include the treasury for the royal tribute, **Las Cajas Reales (1670)**, Venustiano Carranza 106, now used as offices; **Las Casas Coloradas** (1785), on Plaza Pedro María Anaya, now the Tribunal Superior Justicia; and a former **Franciscan convent** (1596) on Arista y Hidalgo next to Parque Hidalgo. **Casa de las Artesanías** for Hidalgo state is at the junction of Av Revolución y Av Juárez. In the Plaza Independencia is a huge clock with four Carrara marble figures. The modern buildings include a notable **theatre**, the **Palacio de Gobierno** (which has a mural depicting ex-President Echeverría's dream of becoming Secretary-General of the UN), and the **Banco de Hidalgo**. The town centre is partly pedestrianized. Colectivos run from Julián Carrillo (very frequent, US$0.40) to the large silver-mining camp of Real (or Mineral) del Monte, picturesque and with steep streetspachuca

Population: 320,000; State Population: 1995 2,111,782; Altitude: 2,445m Colour map 3, grid B4

Mexico

The **Museo de la Minería** at Mina 110 has an excellent display of the history of mining in Pachuca. ■ *Tuesday-Sunday 1000-1400, 1500-1800. Free entry.* An outstanding **photographic museum** is in the large cloister on the far side of the convent. ■ *Tuesday-Sunday 1000-1800. Free.* The **Museo Regional de Hidalgo**, displaying chronological exhibits of the state's history, is known as the Centro Cultural Hidalgo. ■ *Tuesday-Sunday, 0900-1800 – may close early on Sunday pm.* In the complex there is a souvenir shop with reproductions of ceramic and metal anthropological items and recordings of indigenous music, a library and exhibition hall.

Museums

Cornish miners settled at **Real del Monte** in the 19th century; their blue-eyed descendants may be seen among the local inhabitants. Note also the Flemish-style gable roofs. At each entry to the town is a mural commemorating the first strike in the Americas, by silver miners in 1776. The Panteón Inglés (English cemetery) is on a wooded hill opposite the town (ask the caretaker for the key). Mineral del Chico is a beautiful little town 30 kilometres from Pachuca in **El Chico National Park**. The Park has many campsites (mostly dirty with no facilities). There is no information/maps at the Park headquarters. The town is full of weekend homes for the wealthy of Mexico City. There are huge rock formations covered in pine forests; splendid walks. Bus from Pachuca.

Excursions

B *Ciro's* Independencia, recommended. **C** *El Dorado*, Guerrero 721, T42831, clean, friendly. **C** *Motel San Antonio*, 6 kilometres from Pachuca on road to Mexico City (ask repeatedly for directions), spacious rooms, good value, clean, quiet, restaurant. **D** *De los Baños*, on Plaza Independencia, rooms not up to standard of entrance, good, friendly and helpful, recommended. **D** *Grenfell*, Plaza Independencia 116, T50277, with bath, clean, friendly, pleasant, good value (cheaper without bath, but communal toilets are filthy), bus from bus station passes the door. **D** *Hidalgo*, Matamoros 503, recommended. **D** *Juárez*, Barreda 107, with bath, some rooms without windows, just before Real del Monte, in superb wooded surroundings. **F** *Colonial*, Guerrero 505, central.

Sleeping

Casino Español, Everardo Márquez, old-time favourite. *La Blanca*, next to *Hotel de los Baños*, local dishes, recommended. *El Buen Gusto*, Arista y Viaducto Nuevo Hidalgo, clean, good value *comida corrida*. *Palacio*, Av Juárez 200D, excellent breakfast, central. *El Rinconcito*, on

Eating

Juárez, good cheap food. 'Paste' is the local survivor from Cornish miners' days; a good approximation of the real pasty, but a bit peppery! Pastes Pachuqueños, Arista 1023, recommended.

Transport **Buses** Terminal is outside town; take any bus marked 'Central'.

Directory **Tourist office** In clock tower, Plaza Independencia, opposite *Hotel Grenfell*.

North and east of Pachuca

North of Pachuca via Atotonilco el Grande, where there are a chapel and convent half-way down a beautiful canyon, is the impressive **Barranca de Metztitlán** which has a wealth of different varieties of cacti, including the 'hairy old man' cactus, and a huge 17th century monastery. Farther north (difficult road) is Molango, where there is a restored convent, Nuestra Señora de Loreto. 34 kilometres northeast of Pachuca is **San Miguel Regla**, a mid-18th century *hacienda* built by the Conde de Regla, and now run as a resort, fine atmosphere, excellent service; pool, lush gardens, tennis, horse-riding, log fires, highly recommended: T91-771-54311, or 56800448/ 56516369 (Mexico City) for reservations (**A1** full board). A road continues to **Tulancingo**, on the Pachuca-Poza Rica road, Route 130. 17 kilometres from Pachuca, and a further four kilometres off Route 130 to the right is **Epazoyucan**, a village with an interesting convent of San Andrés. After Tulancingo, Route 119 branches off to the right to **Zacatlán**, famous for its apple orchards, plums, pears and cider. Its alpine surroundings include an impressive national park, **Valle de las Piedras Encimadas** (stacked rocks), camping possible. Nearby is AL *Posada Campestre al Final de la Senda*, a ranch with weekend accommodation, horse riding, walks, T Puebla 413821 for reservations. Some 16 kilometres south of Zacatlán is **Chignahuapan** (about one and a half hours from Puebla), a leading producer of *sarapes*, surrounded by several curative spas.

30 kilometres from Tulancingo on Route 130 is *La Cabaña* restaurant, of log-cabin construction; thereafter, the road descends with many bends and slow lorries, and in winter there may be fog. At **Huachinango**, an annual flower fair is held in March; 22 kilometres from here is **Xicotepec de Juárez** (**B** *Mi Ranchito*, one of the nicest small hotels in Mexico; **D** *Italia*, near main square). Along the route are the villages of **Pahuatlan** and **San Pablito**, where sequined headbands are made, and paintings are done on flattened *amate* bark. The entire route from desert to jungle is 190 kilometres, five hours.

Pachuca to Mexico City

A four-lane highway now runs from Pachuca to Mexico City via (Km 27) Venta de Carpio, from which a road runs east to Acolman, 12 kilometres, and Teotihuacan, another 10 kilometres. Neither of these places should be missed (see page 310); buses are available from Pachuca; get them at the tollbooth on the highway to Mexico City.

At Santa Clara, 13 kilometres short of the Capital, the road forks. The right-hand fork (easy driving) goes direct to the City; the left fork goes through Villa Madero, where you can see the shrine of Guadalupe.

Eagle Pass: Piedras Negras to Mexico City

A popular route which goes through various mining centres (for silver and gemstones): Real de Catorce is now a ghost town; San Luis Potosí has many historical features, as does Querétaro, now an industrial city retaining a well-kept colonial centre. This route, 1,328 kilometres (825 miles), is 102 kilometres longer than the Laredo route, but is very wide, very fast and much easier to drive.

Crossing into Mexico

Piedras Negras, is across the Río Bravo from Eagle Pass, Texas. Beyond Hermanas (137 kilometres) the highway begins to climb gradually up to the plateau country.

Eagle Pass (USA)/ Piedras Negras
Population: 150,000
Altitude: 220m
Colour map 2, grid A6

Essentials Shopping: Artesanía shop – Centro Artesanal Piedras Negras, Edif la Estrella, Puerta México, T21087. **Trains**: Train to Saltillo Tuesday, Thursday, Saturday, 0730 arrives 1630, returns Monday, Wednesday, Friday, 0815, arrives Piedras Negras 1715. Check locally, all services in a state of flux in 1999.

Monclova (243 kilometres from border) has one of the largest steel mills in Mexico, and 250,000 people. Take in enough gasoline at Monclova to cover the 205 kilometres to Saltillo. Hotel, restaurant and camping prices have risen rapidly.

Monclova
Colour map 2, grid B5

Saltillo

The capital of Coahuila state is a cool, dry popular resort noted for the excellence of its *sarapes*. Its 18th century cathedral, a mixture of romanesque, churrigueresque, baroque and plateresque styles, is the best in northern Mexico and it has a grand market. Good golf, tennis, swimming. College students from the USA attend the popular Summer School (T149541, F149544).

Km 448;
Population: 650,000
State Population: 1995 2,172,136
Altitude: 1,600m
Phone code: 841
Colour map 2, grid B5

Museo de los Aves (the Bird Museum), on Hidalgo y Bolívar 151 (a few blocks north of Sarape factory) contains hundreds of stuffed birds, café. ■ *Small admission charge, open Tuesday-Saturday 1000-1800, Sunday 1100-1800, T140167, guides available.* On Boulevard Nazario Ortiz Garza, the house of the artist Juan Antonio Villarreal Ríos (Casa 1, Manzana 1, Colonia Saltillo 400, T152707/151206 – home) has an exhibition in every room of Dali-esque work, entry is free and visitors are welcome, phone first. Good views from El Cerro del Pueblo overlooking city. An 87-kilometre road runs east to Monterrey, both toll (US$7) and *vía libre*. You turn right for Mexico City.

A short bus ride away is the quaint village of **Arteaga**, shady parks and beautiful stream. Three restaurants at entrance to village. Many buses from Saltillo.

Several hotels a short distance from the plaza at the intersection of Allende and Aldama, the main streets. Saltillo is a conference centre and has many hotels in the luxury range, several on north end of Boulevard V Carranza north of Boulevard Echeverría Nte eg: *Holiday Inn Eurotel*, No 4100, T151000; *Imperial del Norte,* No 3800, T150011; *Posada San José Inn*, Carranza y Nogal, T152303, cheaper; *Motel El Paso*, No 3101, T151035; *Huizache*, No 1746, T161000. **AL** *San Jorge*, Manuel Acuña Nte 240, T22222, F29400, in the centre. **B** *Rancho El Marillo*, Prol Obregón Sur y Echeverría, T174078, converted hacienda, excellent value, meals

Sleeping

available. **B** *Saade*, Aldama 397 Pte, T129120. **B** *Urdiñola*, Victoria 211, T40940, reasonable. **C** *Jardín*, Padre Flores 211, T125916, basic, cold water, safe motorcycle parking.

D *Hidalgo*, Padre Flores 217, T149853, without bath, not worth paying for bath in room, cold water only (hot baths open to public and guests for small fee). **E** *Brico*, Ramos Arizpe (Pte) 552, T125146, cheap, noisy, clean, tepid water. **E** *El Conde*, Pérez Treviño y Acuña T120136. Several hotels in front of the bus station, eg **D** *Saltillo*, T170237. **E** *Central*, T170004, with bath, ample safe parking, clean, comfy. **F** *Bristol Aldama*, near *Hotel San Jorge*, recommended.

Several good motels **L** *Camino Real*, Blvd Los Fundadores 2000, T300000, F53813. **A** *La Fuente*, Blvd Los Fundadores, T301599.

Trailer park Turn right on road into town from Monterrey between *Hotel del Norte* and *Kentucky Fried Chicken*, hook-ups, toilets, basic.

Eating *El Tupanco*, Allende 225 Sur, expensive. *Victoria*, Padre Flores 221, by *Hotel Hidalgo* has reasonable *comida*. *Café Plaza*, off Plaza de Armas, good breakfasts. *Sta Torta*, Hidalgo Sur, 1 block from plaza. *Arcasa*, Victoria, for local food. *Urdiñola*, next door, good breakfast. *El Campanario Saloon and Grill*, Ocampo, open noon-midnight, recommended. Excellent *licuados* (milkshakes) upstairs in the market. Many restaurants and bars in front of the bus station. Drinks and night-time view can be had at the *Rodeway Inn* on the north side of town.

Festivals Local *feria* in first half of **August**; cheap accommodation impossible to find at this time. Indian dances during **30 May and 30 August**; picturesque ceremonies and bullfights during **October** *fiestas*. *Pastorelas*, the story of the Nativity, are performed in the neighbourhood in Christmas week.

Transport **Air** The airport (SLW) is 16 kilometres from town. Flights to Mexico City daily with Mexicana. Aeroliteral flies to Guadalajara and Monterrey.

Trains To Mexico City Tuesday, Thursday, Saturday 0235, arrives 1900. To Piedras Negras

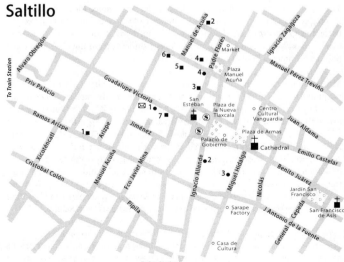

Saltillo

Monday, Wednesday, Friday 0815, arrives 1715.

Buses Terminal is on Boulevard Echeverría, 3 kilometres south of centre (from centre yellow bus marked 'Periférico' from Allende y Lerdo de Tejada); minibuses to Pérez Treviño y Allende (for centre) will take luggage. Bus to **Mexico City**, 1st class, US$32, 11 hours. To **Ciudad Acuña**, 2nd class, US$15, 8 hours. To **San Luis Potosí**, US$14. To **Parral**, US$22, 9 hours; to **Monterrey** and **Nuevo Laredo** with Transportes del Norte. For **Torreón**, US$10.50, 3 hours, all buses originate in Monterrey and tickets only sold when bus arrives; be prepared to stand.

Banks *Bancomer*, Allende y Victoria. *Banamex*, Allende y Ocampo. **Communications** Telephones: long-distance calls from *Café Victoria*, Padre Flores 221, near market. **Tourist office** Blvd Echeverría (ring road) 1560, Edificio Torre Saltillo, p 11, T151714. Recommended tour guide for Saltillo is *Salvador R Medina*, T174255, F174093. — **Directory**

Chris and Miyuki Kerfoot write: From Saltillo to Matehuala by second class bus, Estrella Blanca, one and a half hours, US$3.75 to San Roberto, which is no more than a road junction (a 96-kilometres road runs east over the Sierra Madre to Linares, on the Gulf Route (see page 98) with a Pemex petrol station, hitch to the junction of Highways 58 and 68 and catch a bus (Transportes Tamaulipas) to Matehuala (US$5, four and a half hours). From these junctions near Caleana to La Soledad the scenery is worthwhile, as the road winds its way up and down through wooded valleys. The final section to Matehuala passes through undulating scrub country. — **Saltillo to Matehuala**

There are three Pemex stations between Saltillo and Matehuala, the most northerly one being also a police checkpoint for traffic heading north. Between Matehuala and San Luis Potosí there are frequent Pemex stations. The 'vía libre' from Saltillo to San Luis Potosí is good all the way; the turn-off to the 'custa' road is well signposted.

Matehuala is an important road junction. *Fiesta*, 6-20 January.

A *Motel Trailerpark Las Palmas*, on the north edge of town (Km 617), T20001, clean, English spoken and paperbacks sold, bowling alley and miniature golf, tours to Real de Catorce (see below) arranged. *El Dorado* nearby, T20174, cheaper, recommended. *E Alamo*, C Guerrero 116, T20017, hot showers, clean and very pleasant rooms, safe motorcycle parking, friendly, recommended. *Restaurant La Fontella* in the centre, good regional food. — **Sleeping**

Buses To **Real de Catorce**, US$2. **San Luis Potosí**, with Estrella Blanca, 2½ hours, US$6.25. **Mexico City** (US$22), **Monterrey** and **Querétaro**. — **Transport**

Real de Catorce

56 kilometres west of Matehuala is one of Mexico's most interesting old mining towns, Real de Catorce, founded in 1772. This remarkable city, clustering around the sides of a valley, used to be so quiet that you could hear the river in the canyon, 1,000 metres below. It is becoming increasingly popular as a tourist destination, with new hotels being built. — *Altitude: 2,765m* / *Colour map 2, grid B5*

To get there, turn left along the Zacatecas road through Cedral. After 27 kilometres turn left off the paved road, on to a cobblestone one. The road passes through Potrero, a big centre for nopal cactus. Some people live in the old mine workings and old buildings. Huichol Indians are seen here occasionally. A silver mine is still being worked at Santana.

Real de Catorce is approached through Ogarrio, an old mine gallery widened (only just) to allow trucks through (US$1.65 toll to drive through). It is two and a half kilometres long, and very eerie, with the odd tunnel leading off into the gloom on either side. There is an overtaking bay half way through. A small chapel to the Virgen de los Dolores is by the entrance. The tunnel opens out abruptly into the old city, originally called Real d'Alamos de la Purísima Concepción de los Catorce. Legend has it that 14 bandits hid in nearby caves until the silver was discovered and the town founded. Engineers came from Ireland, Germany and France.

Sights   The first church was the **Virgen del Guadalupe** (1779), a little way out of town (beautiful ceiling paintings remain, as well as the black coffin used for the Mass of the Cuerpo Presente). Many of the images from this church were moved to the **Church of San Francisco** (1817), which is believed to be miraculous. The floor of the church is made of wooden panels, which can be lifted up to see the catacombs below. In a room to one side of the main altar are *retablos*, touchingly simple paintings on tin, as votive offerings to the Saint for his intercession. Next to the church is a small museum (■ *US$0.10*) showing mining equipment, et cetera, worth a visit. In the early 19th century, when the population was about 40,000, Real minted its own coins, which circulated only within the city limits (they are now collectors' items). After the Second World War the population fell dramatically to about 400, but it has risen now to about 1,200, since silver is being worked again and tourism is growing. Guided tours are available from the **Casa de la Moneda**, in front of the Cathedral; they include the **Palenque**, an eight-sided amphitheatre built in 1863, which seated 500-600 people (this is otherwise closed to the public). In the Casa de la Moneda you can see silversmiths at work.

There are good hikes in the surrounding mountains. Very peaceful. Take good footwear, sun protection and a jumper. A 30-minute walk takes you to the ghost town 'pueblo fantasmo' from where there are fine views over the town.

Sleeping   One in the main street, very comfortable with restaurant and bar, expensive, another, **D** *Hotel Real*, in a side street, clean, nice atmosphere, friendly Italian owner, good restaurant, recommended. **D** *La Posada del Sol*, on way to cemetery from main square, with bath, TV, beautiful views, poor restaurant, recommended. **E** *Providencia*, on main street, hot water, clean, restaurant. Several other hotels, and various restaurants. Accommodation is easy to find: boys greet new arrivals and will guide motorists through the peculiar one-way system (or face a police fine).

Eating   *El Eucalyptus*, on way to Bócalo, Italian-Swiss run, excellent homemade pasta, vegetarian food, cakes, pricey but recommended. Many cheap restaurants on main street and stalls selling tacos and hot drinks.

Festivals   There is a pilgrimage here for San Francisco (whose day is 4 October), on foot from Matehuala, overnight on **3 October** (take local bus from Matehuala to La Paz and join the groups of pilgrims who set out from early evening onwards; walk takes about seven hours, be prepared for rain). It is possible to walk from Matehuala to Real de Catorce, other than on the San Francisco pilgrimage, with the aid of the 1:50,000 map from INEGI (see **Essentials**, page 90). On Good Friday, thousands of visitors gather to watch a lively passion play 'with almost real Roman soldiers and very colourful Jews and apostles'.

Transport   **Trains**   Real de Catorce can also be reached from Saltillo or San Luis Potosí by train, but schedules are awkward and trains are often cancelled. Station, called Catorce, is 13 kilometres away. There is one hotel and you can stay in private homes. Jeeps collect passengers from the station (US$16.50 per jeep) and follow a more spectacular route than the minibuses.

No fuel on sale in Real de Catorce; the Pemex Station before Cedral does not have *magna sin*, the one before Matehuala does.

Buses   Many buses a day to Matehuala with Transportes Tamaulipas, from the corner of C del Guerrero and Mendiz, US$2 one-way. A taxi can be hired nearby for US$25, economic for 4 people; local buses from office 1 block north of the Zócalo.

Huizache (785 kilometres from Eagle Pass) is the junction with the Guadalajara-Antiguo Morelos-Tampico highway. At 901 kilometres you come to San Luis Potosí.

San Luis Potosí

423 kilometres from Mexico City, the capital of its state is the centre of a rich mining and agricultural area, which has expanded industrially in recent years. Glazed, many-coloured tiles are a feature of the city: one of its shopping streets, the main plaza, and the domes of many of its churches are covered with them. It became an important centre after the discovery of the famous San Pedro silver mine in the 16th century, and a city in 1658.

Population: 850,000
State Population: 1995
2,191,712
Altitude: 1,880m
Phone code: 48
Colour map 2, grid C5

Sights

The **Cathedral** is on **Plaza Hidalgo**. See the churches of **San Francisco**, with its white and blue tiled dome and suspended glass boat in the transept (try and get into the magnificent sacristy); **El Carmen**, in **Plaza Morelos**, with a grand tiled dome, an intricate façade, and a fine pulpit and altar inside (the **Teatro de la Paz** is next door); the baroque **Capilla de Aránzazu**, behind San Francisco inside the regional museum (see below); the **Capilla de Loreto** with a baroque façade; **Iglesia de San Miguelito**, in the oldest part of the city; **San Agustín**, with its ornate baroque tower; and the startling modern **Templo de la Santa Cruz**, in the Industria Aviación district, designed by Enrique de la Mora. The **Palacio de Gobierno**, begun 1770, contains oil-paintings of past governors, and the colonial treasury, **Antigua Real Caja**, built 1767. ■ *Some rooms may be visited Monday-Friday 0930-1330.*

Other points of interest are the pedestrian precinct in C Hidalgo and the **Caja del Agua** fountain (1835) in Av Juárez. **Plaza de San Francisco** is very pleasant. The modern railway station has frescoes by Fernando Leal. The **Teatro Alarcón** is by Tresguerras (see under Celaya, page 165). Locally made *rebozos* (the best are from Santa María del Río) are for sale in the markets. The **University** was founded in 1804. A scenic road leads to Aguascalientes airport.

Museums

Museo Regional de Arte Popular, next to San Francisco church. ■ *Tuesday-Saturday 1000-1345, 1600-1745; Sunday 1000-1400, Monday 1000-1500.* Nearby is **Museo Regional Potosino**, archaeological, and a collection of wrought iron work, Capilla Aránzazu on second floor. ■ *Tuesday-Friday 1000-1300, 1500-1800, Saturday 1000-1200, Sunday 1000-1300.* **La Casa de la Cultura** on Av Carranza, halfway between the centre and university, is a converted mansion with frequent art displays and musical recitals. ■ *Tuesday-Friday, 1000-1400, 1600-1800, Saturday 1000-1400, 1800-2100.* **Museo Nacional de la Máscara**, in Palacio Federal, has an excellent collection of masks. ■ *Tuesday-Friday 1000-1400, 1600-1800, Saturday-Sunday 1000-1400, entry US$0.20 plus US$0.20 for use of camera.* In Parque Tangamanga (still under development south of city) is **Museo Tangamanga** in an old hacienda, also a Planetarium, observatory and open air theatre (open 0600-1800). In Plaza España, next to the Plaza de Toros, is a **Museo Taurino**, east of Alameda on Universidad y Triana. ■ *Tuesday-Saturday 1100-1330, 1730-1930.* **Casa Othon**, Manuel José Othon 225, is the birthplace and home of the poet. ■ *Tuesday-Friday 0800-1900, Saturday and Sunday 1000-1300.*

Excursions

Hot springs at Ojocaliente, Balneario de Lourdes and Gogorrón. **Balneario de Lourdes** (B hotel, clean, nice atmosphere, small pool) is south of San Luis Potosí. **Gogorrón** is clean and relaxing, with pools, hot tubs, picnic grounds and campsites. There is a restaurant. A day trip or overnight camp-out is recommended in the lightly wooded hills and meadows near the microwave station (at 2,600 metres) 40 kilometres east of San Luis Potosí: go 35 kilometres along the Tampico highway and continue up five kilometres of cobblestone road to the station. Good views and flora.

Sleeping
Many hotels between the railway station and the cathedral.

NB For motorists driving into the centre, parking is very difficult. There is an *estacionamiento* near the police station on Eje Vial, US$1 for first hour, US$0.65 for each subsequent hour.

AL *Panorama*, Av Venustiano Carranza 315, T121777, F124591. **A** *María Cristina*, Juan Sarabia 110, Altos, T129408, F186417, with swimming pool on roof, modern, clean, with

Mexico

restaurant, good value. **C** *Nápoles*, Juan Sarabia 120, T128418, F142104, good restaurant attached, recommended.

D *Nacional*, Manuel José Othon, on the Alameda, 1 block from train station, cheaper without bath, basic. **D** *Progreso*, Aldama 415, T120366, dark, rather seedy. **D** *Universidad*, Universidad 1435, between train and bus station, clean, friendly, hot showers. **D-E** *Jardín*, Los Bravo 530, T123152, good, hot water, restaurant recommended. **E** *El Principal*, Juan Sarabia opposite *María Cristina*, with bath, OK, loud TV in hall. **E** *Gran*, Bravo 235, **F** without bath, hot water, friendly but basic, dirty.

Youth hostel Diagonal Sur, on the southwest side of the Glorieta Juárez, 5 minutes' walk from central bus station, CP 78000, T181617.

Motels All along Highway 57: **L** *Hostal del Quijote*, Km 420, T181312, F185105, 5-star, convention facilities, 6 kilometres south on the San Luis Potosí-Mexico City highway, one of the best in Mexico. **A** *Cactus*, T121871. **A** *Santa Fe*, T125109; all with pools. Also **AL** *Tuna* (Best Western), Highway 80, near exit to Guadalajara, T131207, F111415, parking, pool, restaurant and bar, near University campus. **C** *Mansión Los Arcos*, a few kilometres south of San Luis Potosí, signposted, with restaurant and safe parking.

Eating *Los Molinos*, in *Hostal del Quijote*, excellent well-served food; *Tokio*, Los Bravo 510, excellent *comida*. *El Girasol*, Guerrero 345, vegetarian; good cafetería at bus station. *Café Florida*, Juan Sarabia 230; many other reasonably-priced eating places at western end of Alameda Juan Sarabia. *Café Progreso*, Aldama, next to hotel of same name, good coffee, cheap food, clean toilets.

San Luis Potosí

■ Sleeping		▲ Other
1 Jardín	4 Nápoles	1 Caja de Agua
2 María Cristina	5 Panorama	2 Casa de la Cultura
3 Nacional	6 Progreso	3 Mercado Hidalgo

N

Not to scale

In the second half of **August**.

Local sweets and craftwork at Plaza del Carmen 325, Los Bravo 546 and Escobedo 1030. The famous local painter, Vicente Guerrero, lives in a modest neighbourhood at Plata 407, Colonia Morales (T138057) where he also has his studio. **Markets** Head north on Hidalgo and you come to Mercado Hidalgo, then Mercado República, and Mercado 16 de Septiembre. 3-storey hypermarket, *Chalita*, on Jardín San Juan de Dios between Av Alavaro Obregón and Los Bravo. **Health food store** 5 de Mayo 325, fairly limited.

Air The airport (SLP) is nearly 6 kilometres from the centre. Flights to Chicago, San Antonio in Texas. Many daily to Mexico City, also flights to Aguascalientes, Guadalajara, Monterrey, Tampico.

    Trains On the Mexico City-Saltillo line, trains 3 days a week (if running) in either direction.

    Buses Bus station on outskirts of town 1½ kilometres from centre. Bus to centre US$0.20. To bus station from Manuel José Othon or Sarabia. To **Guanajuato** with Flecha Amarilla, 5 hours, several stops, US$8. They also go to **Querétaro**, US$7, 2 hours, US$13.25 (ETN luxury service) (88 kilometres of 4-lane highway have been built north of Querétaro, about half the way, and 40 kilometres have also been completed to the south of San Luis Potosí); to **San Miguel de Allende**, 2nd class, daily, with Flecha Amarilla; to **Nuevo Laredo**, US$42. To **Linares**, US$14.80. To **Matehuala**, 2½ hours, US$6.25, with Estrella Blanca. To **Monterrey**, US$18. To **Mexico City**, US$10, 5 hours non-stop, US$28 with ETN.

Airline offices *Aeromar*, T177936. *AeroMéxico*, T018-00-0214010. *Mexicana*, T178836. *United*, T901-800-0030777 (English), 800-4265561 (Spanish). **Communications Post Office:** Morelos y González Ortega. **Email:** Café Cibernético, Av Carranza 416. **Tourist offices** *Dirección Estatal de Turismo*, Carranza 325. *Coordinación Regional de Turismo*, Jardín Guerrero 14 (Plaza San Francisco), both helpful.

(1,021 kilometres from border) **San Luis de la Paz**, the junction with Route 110 leading west to three of the most attractive towns in Mexico: Dolores Hidalgo, Guanajuato, and San Miguel de Allende. (see pages 159-170). No one who yields to the temptation of this detour can expect to get back to the main route for three or four days.

Near San Luis de la Paz is another of Mexico's mining ghost-towns, Pozos, once one of the most important mining centres of Mexico. First you come to the ruins. It's very silent and a complete contrast to Real de Catorce. Many of the mining shafts still remain pristine and very deep. Drive on and you reach the town, where several workshops have prehispanic musical instruments and artefacts for show and sale, all handmade mostly in Pozos; Camino de Piedra on Plaza Zaragozo also sells CDs, T-shirts and souvenirs. Particularly

Pozos
Altitude: 2,305m
Colour map 3, grid B3

Orientation

4 Museo 16 de Septiembre
5 Museo República
6 Museo Tangamanga
7 Museo Taurino
8 San Miguelito
9 Templo de Santa Cruz

Mexico

helpful is the lady at *Calmecac* (■ *near the square, Monday-Saturday 1000-1900*), who demonstrates how many of the not-so-obvious instruments work. There is a Museo Cultural (■ *1000-1600*) with a modest display and workshop.

Pozos was founded in 1576 when silver was discovered. Last century the population reached 80,000 but following the Revolution most of the foreign (French and Spanish) owners left and the workforce migrated to the capital. After the 1985 earthquake there, people who had lost their homes drifted back. The men now work in Querétaro and the women work at home making clothes to sell in local markets. The population has slowly risen to 2,000. The town is very quiet and the whole area was decreed a historical monument in 1982. (Francesca Pagnacco, Exeter, Devon.) There are no rooms to let. Pozos can be reached by bus from San Miguel de Allende (change at San Luis de la Paz) or San José de Iturbe.

Querétaro

Population: 550,000
State Population: 1995
1,248,844
Altitude: 1,865m
Colour map 3, grid B3

Route 57 from San Luis Potosí to Querétaro is divided dual carriageway. Querétaro is 215 kilometres from the capital and 1,105 kilometres from Eagle Pass. Because of the altitude it can be quite cold at night. The city was founded in 1531 and the name means 'Place of Rocks' in Tarascan. It is now an important industrial centre and capital of Querétaro state, an old and beautiful city, dotted with attractive squares. (No buses in the centre.) Hidalgo's rising in 1810 was plotted here, and it was also here that Emperor Maximilian surrendered after defeat, was tried, and was shot, on 19 June 1867, on the Cerro de las Campanas (the Hill of Bells), outside the city.

La Corregidora (Doña Josefa Ortiz de Domínguez, wife of the Corregidor, or Mayor), a member of the group of plotters for independence masquerading as a society for the study of the fine arts, was able, in 1810, to get word to Father Hidalgo that their plans for revolt had been discovered. Hidalgo immediately gave the cry

Querétaro

(*grito*) for independence. Today, the Corregidor gives the Grito from the balcony of the **Palacio Municipal** (on Plaza Independencia) every 15 September at 1100 (it is echoed on every civic balcony thoughout Mexico on this date). La Corregidora's home may be visited.

Sights

The **Santa Rosa de Viterbo** church and monastery, remodelled by Francisco **Sights** Tresguerras (tours in English); his reconstruction of **Santa Clara**, one of the loveliest churches in Mexico, and that is saying much; the church and monastery of **Santa Cruz**, which served as the HQ of Maximilian and his forces (view from the bell tower); the church of **San Felipe**, now being restored for use as the Cathedral; the splendid **Palacio Federal**, once an Augustinian convent with exceptionally fine cloisters, now restored with an art gallery containing some beautiful works; the **Teatro de la República**, where Maximilian and his generals were tried, and where the Constitution of 1917 (still in force) was drafted; the **aqueduct**, built in 1726 and very impressive. Several *andadores* (pedestrian walkways) have been developed, greatly adding to the amenities of the city. The *andadores* replace particular roads in places, for example Av 16 de Septiembre becomes Andador de la Corregidora in the centre, and then reverts to its original name. ■ *Walking tours can be arranged through the Tourist Office, daily at 1030 and 1800, two and a half hours, in Spanish but you can ask if an English-speaking guide is available, US$1.80, recommended. City tour plus execution site and Juárez monument, excellent value, from J Guadalupe Velásquez 5, Jardines de Oro, Santa Cruz, T21298, daily at 1130, US$12. On Sunday, family excursions leave the Plaza de Armas at 1000.*

The important and elegant **Museo Regional** is on the main plaza, known as the **Museums** Plaza de Armas or as Plaza Obregón (not all its galleries are always open). It contains much material on the revolution of 1810 and the 1864-67 period (entry free).

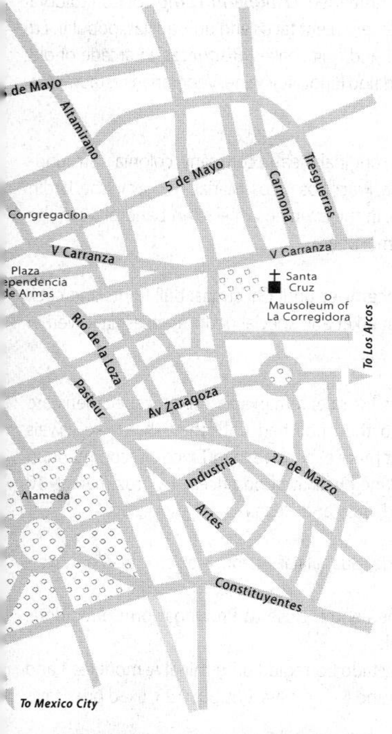

L-A *Mesón de la Merced*, 16 de Septiembre **Sleeping** Ote 95, Centro, T141498, F145198 (in Mexico ■ *on maps* City T55142728/52075666), small, elegant, *Price codes:* restaurant with Mexican cuisine. **AL** *Holiday* *see inside front cover* *Inn*, Av 5 de Febrero y Pino Suárez, on Highway 57, T160202, F168902, 5-star, restaurant, bars; also 5-star, *Antigua Hacienda Galindo*, Km 5 on road to Amealco, Apdo Postal 16, T120050, F120100. **AL** *Mirabel*, Constituyentes 2, T143585, good, garage, restaurant. **AL** *Mesón de Santa Rosa*, Pasteur Sur 17, Centro, T145623/5781, F125522 (in Mexico City 55142728), small-300-year old inn, tastefully modernized, good restaurant with international and Mexican cuisine. *Casa Blanca*, 4-star, Constituyentes 69 Pte, T160102, F160100. *Real de Minas*, Constituyentes 124, T160444/160257, 4-star. **B** *Del Marqués*, Juárez Nte 104, T120414, clean.

D *El Cid*, Prolongación Corregidora, T123518, more of a motel, clean, good value. **D** *Plaza*, Plaza Obregón, T121138, with bath, good location, airy, lovely inner patio, modernized, safe, clean, comfortable, recommended. **D** *San Agustín*, Pino Suárez 12, T123919, small.

(Map labels:) de Mayo · Altamirano · 5 de Mayo · Tresguerras · Carmona · Congregación · V Carranza · V Carranza · Plaza Independencia de Armas · Santa Cruz · Mausoleum of La Corregidora · Río de la Loza · To Los Arcos · Pasteur · Av Zaragoza · Industria · 21 de Marzo · Alameda · Artes · Constituyentes · To Mexico City

E *Corregidora*, Corregidora 138, T140406, reasonable but noisy. **E** *Posada La Academia*, Pino Suárez 3, just off Plaza Constitución with bath and TV. **E** *Posada La Colonial*, Juárez 19 Sur, T120239, good value. **E** *San Francisco*, Corregidora 144 Sur, T120858, with bath. **E** *Hidalgo*, near Zócalo, Madero 11 Pte, T120081, with bath, quiet, friendly, excellent value for 2 or more, not so for singles (English owner, Adrian Leece). On the whole, it is difficult to find good, cheap accommodation in Querétaro. **F** *Posada Teresa*, Reforma 51 Ote, T126180, basic.. **F** *Posada Familiar*, Independencia 22, T120584, basic but OK courtyard.

Youth hostel **E** Av del Ejército Republicano, ex-Convento de la Cruz, **E**, running water am only, T143050.

Motels *Posada Campestre*, Madero y Circunvalación, T162728. **AL** *Jurica*, edge of town on road to San Luis Potosí, former *hacienda*, with gardens, squash, golf-course, opulent, T121081. **AL** *La Mansión*, 6½ kilometres south of town, excellent dining facilities, gorgeous grounds. **A** *Azteca*, 15 kilometres north on road to San Luis Potosí, T122060. **A** *Flamingo*, on Constituyentes Pte 138, T162093, comfortable.

Eating
● *on maps*

Mesón Santa Rosa, Pasteur 17, in hotel of same name, good but expensive, restored colonial building. *Fonda del Refugio*, Jardín Corregidora, pretty but food is poor; *La Corregidora*, on the other side of the street, is reported as greatly superior. *Lonergan's*, Plaza de Armas, pleasant café with small art gallery, magazines in English, French and German. *Don Juan*, Jardín Corregidora, recommended (*Pizza Piazza* at same location is not recommended). *Flor de Querétaro*, on Plaza Obregón, Juárez Nte 5, good but pricey. On same square, *Manolo*, good *paella*. *La Cocina Mexicana*, Pino Suárez 17, opposite *Hotel San Agustín*, cheap and good but rather dark, à la carte better value than *comida corrida*. *Los Tacos de mi General*, Av Reforma y Manuel G Najera, cheap and good 4-course *comida corrida*.

Arcangel, Plaza Chica, pleasant setting, good food. *Café de Regio*, Pino Suárez 24A, good coffee and cakes. *La Buena Fortuna*, Independencia 28, bookshop, friendly café. *Le Bon Vivant*, Pino Suárez, cheap, good value, recommended. *Ostionería Tampico*, Corregidora Nte 3, good cheap fish. *Leo's*, at La Cruz market, excellent tacos and quesadillas, popular. *La Mariposa*, A Peralta 7, excellent coffee, *tortas* and fruit shakes. *Bisquetes*, in arcade of old *Gran Hotel* on Zócalo, good value. Try local Hidalgo Pinot Noir wine. Vegetarian restaurant at Independencia 5, just off Plaza Constitución.

Entertainment *Corral de Comedias*, Carranza 39, T120765, an original theatre company, colonial surroundings and suppers. *JBJ Disco*, Blvd Zona Dorada, Fracc Los Arcos. Mariachis play in the Jardín Corregidora, 16 de Septiembre y Corregidora, in the evenings. The town band plays in the Jardín Obregón on Sunday evening, lovely atmosphere.

Festivals There is a *feria agrícola* from 2nd week of **December** until Christmas; bull fights and cock fights. On **New Year's Eve** there is a special market and special performances are given in the main street.

Shopping There are local opals, amethysts and topazes for sale; remarkable mineral specimens are shaped into spheres, eggs, mushrooms, and then polished until they shine like jewels (US$10-30, cheaper than San Juan del Río, but more expensive than Taxco). Recommended is Joyería Villalón, Andador Libertad 24a, for fine opals at good prices. La Cruz market, 10 minutes' walk from centre is very well stocked, busy and clean.

Transport **Air** There are flights from Chihuahua, Durango, Guadalajara, Leon, Mexico City, Monterrey, Morelia, Puerto Vallarta and Torreón.

Trains The station is not far north of the centre, close to Prolongación Corregidora. Check locally for services, trains are not reliable.

Buses Bus station southeast of city, near Estado Corregidora, Terminal A, modules 1 and 2, 1st class and plus, Terminal B, modules 3, 4 and 5, 2nd class. Bus US$0.25, fixed price taxis

The missions of Querétaro

A little-known feature of Querétaro is the existence of 18th century missions in the far northeast of the state. They were founded by Fray Junípero de la Serra, who later went on to establish missions in California with names like Nuestra Señora de Los Angeles and San Francisco de Asís. He is also said to have planted a miraculous tree in the convent of the Santa Cruz in Querétaro by thrusting his staff into the ground. The tree is apparently the only one of its kind in the world to have cruciform thorns.

All five missions have been restored, and two of them have hotels nearby. The journey itself requires something of a head for heights in that there are said to be 700 curves en route. There is a slightly shorter way, but that has over 1,000 …

Tim Connell

Mexico

to centre, about US$1.25. To **Mexico City**, frequent 1st and 2nd class buses, 2½ hours, US$7.15, several companies, US$15.50 ETN; 9 buses a day to Mexico City airport with Primera Plus; to **Nuevo Laredo**, US$51, to **San Miguel de Allende**, 1 hour, hourly with Flecha Amarilla, US$2.20. To **Guadalajara**, US$12 (US$22 ETN). To **San Juan del Río**, US$2, 30 minutes, frequent. To **Tula** US$5. To **Guanajuato**, US$5.75, 2½ hours (Flecha Amarilla), 1030, 1230, 1430; to **San Luis Potosí**, Flecha Amarilla, US$7, ETN, US$13.25, 2 hours; to **Pachuca**, US$4.50, 4½ hours (Estrella Blanca, poor buses).

Airline offices *Aeromar*, T206936. **Communications** Post Office: Arteaga Pte 5 (inadequate). *DHL*, International courier service, Blvd Zona Dorada 37, Fracc Los Arcos, T142526 or 145256, open Mon-Fri 0900-1800, Sat 0900-1200. **Tourist offices** *State office*, Pasteur Nte 4, on Plaza Independencia at junction with Libertad, T121412, F121094; Federal office, Av Constituyentes Ote 102 (away from centre T138483/138511). **Directory**

Excursions from Querétaro

The road to the **Missions of Querétaro** goes through the small market town of **Ezequiel Montes** (*Population:* 5,000), reached either by a road turning northeast from the main highway 21 kilometres from Querétaro, or by Route 120 from San Juan del Río (see below). Two places of interest off the first-mentioned road are the town of Colón (14 kilometres off the road, with 17th century Templo de Nuestra Señora de los Dolores de Soriana) and **Bernal**, 75 kilometres from Querétaro, a centre for clothing, blankets, wall hangings and carpets made by cottage industry. Near Bernal is the remarkable **Peñón de Bernal**, a massive rocky outcrop 350 metres high. On the night before and the day of the Spring equinox (21 April) there is a festival held here. Local indigenous people believe the mountain is an energy point, because of its distinctive shape, and come to get energy for the coming year from the first sun of the year.

48 kilometres from Querétaro is San Juan del Río, near where the best fighting bulls are raised; the town is a centre for handicrafts, and also for polishing gemstones: opals and amethysts. There is one friendly and reasonable shop: La Guadalupana, 16 de Septiembre 5; others are expensive and less friendly. Several *balnearios* in San Juan (try *Venecia*, cold water, very quiet mid-week, US$1.30). **San Juan del Río** *Colour map 3, grid B3*

Sleeping AL *Hotel Mansión Galindo*, T20050, restored hacienda; apparently given by Cortés to his mistress Malinche, beautiful building. **D** *Hotel Layseca*, Av Juárez 9 Ote, colonial building, large rooms, nice furniture, excellent, car parking, no restaurant; several picturesque hotels, **D. E** *Estancia*, good, enclosed parking.

A branch road runs northeast from San Juan to the picturesque town of Tequisquiapán, with thermal baths, fine climate, watersports, weekend residences, **Tequisquiapán** *Colour map 3, grid B3* expensive, good hotels, *Artesanías Bugambilia*, on the main square, recommended. Note that town is deserted from Monday to Thursday and big reductions in hotel prices can be found. On the other hand, there is nothing other than the resort: a good cheap Mexican meal is hard to find. The dam near the town is worth a visit. There is a geyser, at Tecozautla, one and a quarter hours from Tequisquiapán. Between San Juan del Río and Tequisquiapán, a small track leads off the main road four kilometres to the village of La Trinidad, near which lie some of the opal mines which are still in operation.

Sleeping and eating A *El Relox*, Morelos 8, T30066, spa pool open to non-residents. *Maridelphi*, similar price. *Las Cavas*, Paseo Media Luna 8, T30804, F30671. Restaurant *La Chiapaneca*, Carrizal 19, centre, opposite craft market, is very good, reasonably-priced, clean.

Buses San Juan del Río-Tequisquiapán US$1, 20 minutes.

Beyond Tequisquiapán is **Cadereyta** (Km 75), colonial in style, with two noteworthy churches in the main square, one dedicated to St Peter, the other St Paul. The latter houses an important collection of colonial religious art. Nearby is the Casa de los Alemanes, which houses an enormous collection of cacti. There is a petrol station at Cadereyta and another at Vizarrón, a local centre for marble.

San Joaquín
Colour map 3, grid B3

Tarantulas abound. The roads to both ruins are steep and the ruins are often swathed in mist.

East of Route 120, there are ruins at San Joaquín (Km 138): **Ranas** and **Toluquilla** which have both been only partially excavated. The former receives about 200 visitors a month, the latter only 40 visitors a month. You must register upon arriving. A donation is requested. The sites have been attributed to the Toltecs and the Chichimecs. Ranas is a 30-minute walk from the village and has stupendous views from a series of terraced platforms and pyramids (entry US$1); Toluquilla lies 10 kilometres from the village (poorly marked road). Although there were only, at most, 200 inhabitants, there are six ball courts! Fifteen minutes' walk from San Joaquín is a beautiful cave (Las Grutas). San Joaquín is famous for the annual Huapango dance festival on 15 April. The village itself is picturesque and has hotels.

Sleeping E *Victoria*, halfway up hill, Av Insurgentes, basic. E *Mesón de Joaquín*, T25315, next to bus park, good value rooms for four and a campground with shelters and barbecue stands on the outskirts above the town.

Transport San Joaquín can be reached in three hours by car or bus on a windy road going through desert and then misty pine forests. Flecha Amarilla six a day, earliest from Querétaro 0620, last 1620, US$4; Flecha Azul who also run buses San Joaquín-San Juan del Rio.

The bends really start after Vizarrón. Much of the journey from here on is through rather arid and yet dramatic terrain with gorges and panoramic views. The high point (aptly enough) is called la Puerta del Cielo, as you can actually look down on the clouds. As the road begins to descend so the vegetation becomes more tropical and the weather gets much warmer. (Jalpan is at only 700 metres above sea level, Concá 500). There is a petrol station at Ahuacatlán (Km 166), before Jalpan.

Jalpan
Colour map 3, grid B4

Jalpan, the first of the missions, becomes visible way below in a broad lush valley. It is the largest of the missions, which are located in valleys that spread out from here. Jalpan was the first to be founded in 1774 and has cloisters as well as the main church. The town itself is picturesque without being spoilt. It makes a good base for day trips to the other missions. Also there are pleasant walks along tree-lined river banks. There is a nice museum in town, worth a visit, open 1000-1500, 5 pesos. All the churches are distinguished by the profusion of baroque carving, their superb location and the care with which they have been conserved. They are all different and all worth the trip: **Landa de Matamoros**, 18 kilometres east of Jalpan, **Tilaco**, 25 kilometres beyond Landa to the east, and **Tancoyol**, 37 kilometres to the north of Landa. (The roads are good apart from the last 15 kilometres into Tilaco).

Sleeping **D** *Posada Fray Junípero*, Ezequiel Montes 124, T121241, opposite church, with bath and TV, clean, friendly, credit cards, colonial style, pool, restaurant, good value but noisy because of bus station. **E** *Posada Aurora*, with bath, hot water, fan, clean, friendly, recommended.

Eating *Las Cazuelas*, to right of church, delicious tacos, very clean. *Las Jacarandas*, next to bus station, good *comida corrida*, reasonably priced, clean. Shrimp cocktails at stalls on plaza.

Buses 3 direct from Mexico City, US$11, 6 hours, beautiful trip. Hourly from Jalpan to Landa de Matamoros, US$0.50, 20 minutes. To Tilaco and Tancoyol 40-minute bus journey to La Lagunita, hourly, then combis (on market day, Saturday) or hitchhike. To Querétaro every hour, 5 hours, US$3.50, 2nd class, Flecha Amarilla. To Ciudad del Valle, frequent, via Matamoros and Xilitla, 2nd class, Transp Vencedor.

38 kilometres north northwest of Jalpan is Concá. *Acamaya*, freshwater crayfish, is a local speciality. At the bridge of Concá a hot water river flows into one with cold water. The church is built on a ridge, creating a dramatic skyline when viewed from below. The village is very small. Two restaurants and a general store. Hourly bus to Concá from Jalpan, US$1.30. There is a large hotel in its own grounds a few kilometres from the village and mission, again in colonial style with a pool fed by warm spring water.

    It is possible to drive from Concá to San Luis Potosí, which is about three hours further on. The journey to Jalpan from Querétaro takes about six hours. At least three days should be allowed to see everything properly.

Concá
Colour map 3, grid B3

Querétaro and the Missions

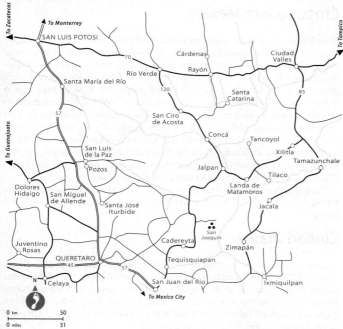

Mexico

Mexico

Xilitla
Colour map 3, grid B4

Between Jalpan and Ciudad Valles is the charming village of Xilitla, overlooking a lush tropical valley. Famous for the house (*El Castillo*) and garden (Las Pozas) of the late Edward James, born 1907, millionaire heir to the Phelps Dodge copper fortune, with connections to the British royal family. Las Pozas is 30 minutes' walk from Xilitla and is fascinating with extravagant concrete structures intertwined with exuberant vegetation, waterfalls, birds and butterflies. Accommodation at **A-B** *El Castillo*, includes breakfast, pool, fine views, run by Avery and Leonore Danzinger, T52136, 50038, F50055. Several smaller hotels too. At *Restaurant Los Cayos* (good view), try *enchiladas huastecas* and local coffee. Buses from Jalpan every hour, US$2.30, two and a half hours.

Querétaro to Mexico City

There is a four-lane motorway (US$3 a car) from Irapuato past Querétaro to Mexico City. The Mexico City motorway passes close to Tula and Tepozotlán (see page 312). There are various country clubs along the road. In the state park of El Ocotal is a Swiss-chalet style hotel, **B**, with excellent restaurant.

Mexico City

Ciudad Juárez to Mexico City

A route of much historical interest: **Chihuahua** *has strong links with the revolutionary and independence movements, besides being the starting point for a magnificent rail journey to the Pacific, through Tarahumara Indian country:* **Zacatecas** *is a mining centre.* **Aguascalientes** *is colonial, but of far greater colonial significance are* **Guanajuato** *and* **San Miguel de Allende**, *while* **Dolores Hidalgo** *is the birthplace of Mexican independence.*

Crossing into Mexico

El Paso (USA)/ Ciudad Juárez

From El Paso you can get on a bus outside Gate 9 of the Greyhound terminal and pay the driver (US$5); as you cross the border he should stop and wait for your documents to be processed. On entry you are automatically given 30 days to stay in Mexico, unless you ask for longer. Trolley buses cross the border for short trips. Alternatively you can walk across (US$0.35 toll per person). Walking from Mexico to the USA costs US$0.55 (toll for cars leaving Mexico US$2.05). Border formalities are minimal, although you are likely to have your bags searched on entering the USA on foot because most pedestrians do not carry luggage. If you cross into the USA with a view to leaving the USA by plane, as a non-US citizen you must ask for an immigration card for when you do leave; you may have problems without one. Remember, also, to have your US visa if you require one. The US Embassy charges US$20 to make an enquiry so make sure you have everything you need.

There is a new border crossing at Santa Teresa, New Mexico, just west of El Paso. For trucks and southbound travellers by car, this will avoid the congestion of Ciudad Juárez.

Ciudad Juárez

Population: 1,100,000
Altitude: 1,150m
Phone code: 16
Colour map 2, grid A2

Opposite El Paso, Texas; to Mexico City: 1,866 kilometres. Juárez and El Paso have over 1.1 million people each; the cross border industry has made Ciudad Juárez the largest *maquiladora* city in the world. Twin plant assembly and manufacturing operations now supersede tourism and agriculture in the city. **NB** El Paso is on Mountain Standard Time, which is one hour behind Central Standard Time and General Mexican Time.

The Spanish conquistador Cabeza de Vaca discovered the Paso del Norte on the Camino Real. The name was retained until 1888 when Porfirio Díaz renamed the city after Benito Juárez. Today four bridges link the two cities: Santa Fe, for pedestrians and cars leaving Mexico; Stanton Street, for pedestrians and cars leaving USA; Cordova bridge (two-way traffic); and the new Zaragosa toll bridge to the east. The Río Bravo/Grande, which divides the cities and forms the border, has been canalized and is used for irrigation upstream, so often it has little or no water.

In Ciudad Juárez, the **Nuestra Señora de Guadalupe de El Paso del Norte** mission **Sights** was the first established in the region; the building was completed in 1668. It, and the nearby **Cathedral**, are two blocks west of Av Juárez on 16 de Septiembre. At the junction of Av Juárez and 16 de Septiembre is the Aduana, the former customs building, now the **Museo Histórico**. In Parque Chamizal, just across the Cordova bridge, are the **Museo de Arte Prehispánica** with exhibits from each Mexican state, **Botanic Gardens** and a memorial to Benito Juárez. Continuing south down Av Lincoln, you come to the Pronaf area with the **Museo de Arte Historia**. The University Cultural Centre and the **Fonart** artizan centre, which acts as a Mexican 'shop window' is well worth it for the uninitiated tourist. There are a number of markets, the racetrack is very popular (with dog races in spring and summer), the **Plaza Monumental de Toros** (López Mateos y Triunfo de la República) holds bullfights between April and August, and *charreadas* (rodeos) are held at various locations. The main street is Av Juárez, on or near which are most of the souvenir shops, hotels, cheap and expensive restaurants, clubs and bars. The bars and other nightlife cater mostly for El Paso high school students who can drink at 18 in Mexico, but not till 21 in El Paso.

Ciudad Juárez / El Paso detail

Not to scale

To the east of **El Paso**, the **Ysleta Mission** is the oldest in Texas (1680), built by Franciscan monks and Tigua Indians, who have a 'reservation' (more like a suburb) nearby; the Socorro mission (1681) and San Elizario Presidio (1789, rebuilt 1877-87) are in the same direction. There are a number of museums, including the **Americana Museum** in the Civic Centre (which also houses a performing arts centre, convention centre and tourist office), the **Museum of Art** at 1211 Montana and The **Fort Bliss Air Defence Museum** of the nearby Air Base. Conducted tours of El Paso (US$10 – same price for Juárez) usually take in Fort Bliss, the University, the Scenic Drive and the Tigua Reservation. Very few services are open at weekends in El Paso.

■ **Sleeping**
1 Gardner
2 Paso del Norte

▲ **Other**
1 Americana Museum
2 City Hall

3 Civic Centre
4 Cleveland Square
5 Performing Arts Centre
6 Public Library
7 San Jacinto Square

AL *Calinda Quality Inn*, Calz Hermanos **Sleeping** Escobar 3515, T137250. *Holiday Inn Express*, Paseo Triunfo de la República 8745, T296000, F296020. **B** *Impala*, Lerdo Nte 670, T91160431/0491, clean, OK. **C** *Continental*,

Mexico

Lerdo Sur 112 (downtown), T150084, clean, TV, noisy, friendly, restaurant good. **C** *Parador Juárez*, Miguel Ahumada 615 Sur, T159184; and many others in the upper price ranges. **D** *Correo*, Lerdo Sur 250, just across 16 de Septiembre. **F** *San Luis*, Mcal y Morelos, 1 block south of, and behind, Cathedral, cheapest but filthy and insecure.

In **El Paso** there are many places to stay, including *Westin Paso del Norte Hotel*, with its Tiffany glass dome, black and pink marble lobby and European chandeliers (the most expensive), T5343000; **A** *Ramada*, on Oregon, recommended, T5443300. Also on Oregon, **B** *International Hotel*, a/c, TV, clean, recommended. **E** *Juárez*, Lerdo Nte 143, close to Stanton St bridge, comfortable, hot water, good value. **D** *Gardner*, 311 East Franklin Av, T5323661, hot water, shared bath, TV and phone in room, rooms with bath available, also serves as **Youth Hostel**. Many motels.

Eating *Many eating places either side of the border.*	In Juárez, *Taco Cabaña* on C de la Peña, next to *Hotel Continental*, and *El Gordo No 2*, Francisco Madero, ½ block from 16 de Septiembre, are good for tacos and burritos (about US$2-3). *Plaza Lerdo Café*, Lerdo Sur 285 at Galeana, good breakfasts. *El Saucito*, Lerdo Sur 263, popular, good breakfasts. *Florida*, Juárez 301, 2 blocks from *Hotel Impala*, clean, good food and service; plenty of Chinese restaurants.
Festivals	2-5 May, *Festival de la Raza*; music, dance, cultural events. **5 May** celebrations on Av Juárez. **15 September**, Independence. **June-July**, *Feria Juárez* in Parque Chamizal.
Shopping	Tourist market on Av 16 de Septiembre, 3 blocks past *Hotel Continental* (on opposite side) away from Juárez.
Transport	**Local Taxis**: in Juárez, charge by zone, from US$2.75 to US$7.25. **Air** Ciudad Juárez's airport, Abraham González (CJS), is 19 kilometres south of the city (T190734/164363); flights with AeroMéxico, Aerolitoral, Taesa and/or Aero California to

Ciudad Juárez / El Paso

*Related map
A Ciudad Juárez/El Paso detail,
page 121*

Mexico City, Chihuahua, Ciudad Obregón, Culiacán, Durango, Guadalajara, Hermosillo, Ixtapa, Léon, Los Cabos, Mazatlán, Monterrey,Torreón, Tijuana and Zacatecas. El Paso's airport (ELP) is near Fort Bliss and Biggs Field military airbase with flights by American, Delta, America West Airlines and Southwest Airlines to all parts of the USA. There are also flights to El Paso from Chihuahua and Guadalajara. Colectivo Ciudad Juárez airport to El Paso, or El Paso airport, US$15.50.

Trains Station in Ciudad Juárez is at Eje Vial Juan Gabriel e Insurgentes, a couple of blocks south of junction of Av Juárez and 16 de Septiembre. Information: T122557 149717 (Nacionales de México) or 5452247 (Amtrak in El Paso).

Road Sanborns, for insurance and information, 440 Raynolds, El Paso, T915-7793538, F7721795, open Monday-Friday 0830-1700. AAA office: 916 Mesa Av, El Paso. **Buses** Terminal is at Boulevard Oscar Flores 4010, T132083, south of the centre. There is a taxi information booth which can give you estimated fares before you approach a driver. From the terminal to centre or Santa Fe bridge, taxi fare is about US$8. If you walk from the terminal to the highway, take any bus going to the right marked *centro* for US$0.30. Shuttle bus to **El Paso** US$5, hourly, to Greyhound Terminal. From Ciudad Juárez, several bus companies run to **Chihuahua** (4 hours, US$17.50) and on to **Mexico City** (26 hours, eg Omnibús de México, US$66, good service), via all the major cities en route, eg **Torreón** (US$30), **Zacatecas** (US$45), **Aguascalientes** (US$50, Turistar Ejecutivo US$84) or **San Luis Potosí** (US$50), **Querétaro** (US$60). Services also to **Monterrey** (US$45), eg Trans del Norte, 8 a day, **Hermosillo** (US$30) and **Tijuana** (US$44 1st class, Caballero Azteca), **Guadalajara** (US$50), **Mazatlán** (US$53), and other Pacific coast destinations. **Express Limousine service**: El Paso-Los Angeles, US$40, El Paso-Albuquerque US$27; the El Paso office is just across the Juárez bridge at 6th and Oregon. Greyhound, El Paso, T5322365. **Turismos Rápidos**, 828 South El Paso, off Santa Fe Bridge, to many US destinations.

Directory

Airline offices *Aero California*, T183399. *AeroMéxico*, T138719. *Taesa*, T292370. **Banks** In Ciudad Juárez most *cambios* are on Av Juárez and Av de las Américas; there is also a *cambio* at the bus terminal. Rates vary very little, some places charge commission on TCs; some are safer than others. The best and most convenient exchange houses are in El Paso: *Valuta Corp*, 301 Paisano Drive, buys and sells all foreign currencies but poor rates, wires money transfers, open 24 hrs including holidays, commission charged on all TCs except Amex. *Melek Corp*, 306 Paisano Drive, not open 24 hrs, otherwise offers most of the same services as Valuta but only dollars and pesos. *Loren Inc*, 1611 Paisano Drive, much the same, but rates slightly worse (if coming from US immigration, when you reach Paisano Drive/Highway 62, turn east for these places). In El Paso, banks are closed on Sat. **Communications** Post Office: on corner of Lerdo Sur and C Ignacio de la Pena. **Embassies & consulates** *US*, López Mateos 924, Cd Juárez, T134048. *British* (Honorary) Mr CR Maingot, C Fresno 185, Campestre Juárez, T75791. *Mexican*, 910, E San Antonio, El Paso, T5334082. **Tourist offices** In Ciudad Juárez, on ground floor of the Presidencia (City Hall, at Malecón y Francisco Villa), on left as you cross Santa Fe bridge, T152301/140837; in El Paso T5340536. El Paso Tourist Office in Civic Centre Plaza, T5340686; also at airport.

Ciudad Juárez to Chihuahua

The road is wide, mostly flat, easy to drive, and not as interesting as the Gulf and Pacific routes. From Ciudad Juárez, for some 50 kilometres along the Río Bravo, there is an oasis which grows cotton of an exceptionally high grade. The next 160 kilometres of the road to Mexico City are through desert; towns en route are Salamayuca (restaurant), at Km 58; **Villa Ahumada** (Km 131, *Hotel Cactus*, T42250. **D** *Casa Blanca*, with bath and hot water, room heater, clean, opposite train depot on main street, half a block south of bus terminal). At Km 180 is Moctezuma (restaurant). The road leads into grazing lands and the valley of Chihuahua. The road Chihuahua-Ciudad Juárez is being made into an *autopista*; toll 30 kilometres north of Chihuahua, US$6.30 for cars or pick-ups (the alternative is a long two-sides-of-a-triangle detour to avoid the toll).

Mexico

Crossing into Mexico: Palomas and Agua Prieta

Columbus (USA)/ Palomas
Colour map 2, grid A2

Mexico Route 2 runs west from Ciudad Juárez, roughly parallel with the Mexico-US border. Between Juárez and Janos, at the northern end of lateral Mexico 24, is the dusty border town of Palomas, Chihuahua, opposite Columbus, New Mexico. The modern border facilities are open 24 hours. Palomas itself has few attractions apart from limited duty-free shopping for liquor and pharmaceuticals, but Columbus was the site of Pancho Villa's 1916 incursion into New Mexico, which led to reprisals by the forces of American Gen John J Pershing. **The Columbus Historical Museum** (■ *daily from 1000 to 1600*), three miles north of the border, offers exhibits on Villa's sacking and burning of Columbus.

Essentials Reasonable accommodation at **D** *Hotel Restaurant San Francisco*, also *Motel Santa Cruz Hotel Regis*. On the Columbus side, **A3** *Martha's Place* (T5312467), an attractive bed and breakfast, and **C** *Motel Columbus*. **Camping** Excellent, well-maintained sites at Pancho Villa State Park, opposite the Columbus Historical Museum, for US$7 per night, additional charge for electrical hook-up. There is no public transport on the US side, but hourly buses connect Palomas with Tres Caminos, where travellers can board buses from Juárez to Nuevo Casas Grandes (see below).

Janos
Colour map 2, grid A2

At the intersection of Mexico Route 2 and Chihuahua Route 10 to Nuevo Casas Grandes is **Janos** (*Restaurant Durango*, de facto bus station at the intersection, has good inexpensive food; several others at junction, plus **D** *Hotel Restaurant La Fuente*). The landscape between Ciudad Juárez and Nuevo Casas Grandes is quite barren and, in the winter months, it can be cold.

Near Janos are the northernmost **Mennonite colonies** in Mexico; numerous vendors sell Mennonite cheese, which also has a market in upscale restaurants across the border in New Mexico. The German-speaking Mennonites are very conspicuous, the men in starched overalls and the women in long dresses and leggings, their heads covered with scarves.

Douglas (USA)/ Agua Prieta
Population: 80,000
Colour map 2, grid A2

Northwest of Janos, via the border route of Mexico 2, are the border crossings of **Agua Prieta** (opposite Douglas, Arizona) and **Naco** (adjacent to its Arizona namesake and a short distance south of the historic, picturesque copper mining town of Bisbee). Agua Prieta is growing rapidly with the proliferation of *maquiladoras* on both sides of the border. If possible, avoid crossing in late afternoon, when traffic across the border can be very congested as Mexican labourers return home from Douglas.

Agua Prieta is 162 kilometres from Janos via Route 2, which crosses the scenic Sierra San Luís, covered by dense oak-juniper woodland, to the continental divide (elevation 1,820 metres) at Puerto San Luís, the border between the states of Sonora and Chihuahua. There are outstanding views of the sprawling rangelands to the west. Southbound motorists from the USA must present their papers to Mexican customs at La Joya, a lonely outpost 70 kilometres northwest of Janos.

Sleeping Unusually for Mexican cities, Agua Prieta lacks true budget accommodation in the centre and near the border; the main alternatives are **B** *Motel La Hacienda*, 2 blocks from the border. **B** *Hotel El Greco*; **B** *Motel Ruiz*. In Naco, the only formal accommodation is **D** *Motel Colonial*, which is often full, but the manager may tolerate a night's auto camping within the motel compound. Accommodation is cheaper in Douglas, on the Arizona side: **C** *Border Motel*. The venerable **B** *Gadsden Hotel*, a registered historical landmark, has been used as a location for Western films. **C** *Motel 6*. Rates are higher in Bisbee, a very popular tourist destination, but the town offers good value for money. **Camping**: RV parks on the Arizona side charge about US$10 per night for vehicle, US$5 for tent camping: *Double Adobe Trailer Park* off Highway 80, *Copper Horse Shoe R V Park* on Highway 666.

Eating In Agua Prieta, *El Pollo Loco*, near the plaza, for roasted chicken; in Naco, *Restaurant Juárez*. On the Douglas side, restaurant at *Hotel Gadsden* is good and reasonable, but the best selection in the area is at Bisbee, 10 miles north of Naco.

Buses From Agua Prieta, Tres Estrellas and Transportes Norte de Sonora offer service to **Ciudad Juárez** (4 daily, US$13.25), **Chihuahua** (9 daily, US$20), **Nogales** (4 daily, US$8.25), **Tijuana** (6 daily, US$33), **Hermosillo** (8 daily, US$13.25), **Guaymas** (4 daily, US$18), **Navojoa** (3 daily, US$24.75), **Los Mochis** (4 daily, US$30), and **Mexico City** (daily, US$82.50). Bridgewater Transport (T3642233) connects Douglas with Tucson twice daily (US$30), with connections to Los Angeles (US$92, but more expensive if purchased in California).

Useful services On the Douglas side, the Chamber of Commerce (T3642477) at 1125 Pan American has good information on Mexico as well as Arizona, with a wealth of maps (including Agua Prieta) and brochures. Librolandia del Centro, a bookstore, has a good selection of material on local and regional history.

Crossing the border Both the Agua Prieta and Naco ports of entry are open 24 hours. There is no public transport other than taxi to Naco, Arizona, but there are buses from Naco, Sonora, to Agua Prieta and Nogales. Mexican automobile insurance is not available in Naco, Sonora, but readily obtained at Douglas. Mexican consulate in Douglas, helpful.

Warning Drug smuggling, auto theft, and other illegal activities are common knowledge along the southeastern Arizona border. Watch your belongings and money closely even during 'routine' searches by US Customs officials, whose reputation has been sullied by reports of corruption in recent years. Moreover, the police in Agua Prieta have a bad reputation for stopping drivers for no good reason and trying to extract bribes on the threat of jail.

Casas Grandes

The archaeological site of Casas Grandes, or Paquimé, can be reached from Chihuahua, Ciudad Juárez or Agua Prieta. Nuevo Casas Grandes is a town built around the railway; it is very dusty when dry, the wind blowing clouds of dust down the streets, and when wet the main street becomes a river. There is not much to do, but there are cinemas which show US and Mexican films (don't be put off by people standing at the back, there are usually seats free).

Colour map 2, grid A2

Casas Grandes/Paquimé was probably a trading centre, which reached its peak between 1210 and 1261 AD. The city was destroyed by fire in 1340. Its commercial influence is said to have reached as far as Colorado in the north and into southern Mexico. At its height, it had multi-storeyed buildings; the niches that held the beams for the upper floors are still visible in some buildings. A water system, also visible, carried hot water from thermal springs to the north, and acted as drainage. Most of the buildings are of a type of adobe, but some are faced with stone. You can see a ball court and various plazas among the buildings. The site is well-tended. Significant archaeological reconstruction is under way at Casas Grandes. About two hours is sufficient to see it all. ■ *Open 1000-1700, entry US$3.50.* To get there take a yellow bus from outside the furniture shop at 16 de Septiembre y Constitución Pte in Nuevo Casas Grandes, US$0.20, 15 minutes. From the square in Casas Grandes village either take C Constitución south out of the square past the school, walk to the end of the road, cross a gulley, then straight on for a bit, turn right and you will see the site, or take Av Juárez west out of the square and turn left at the sign to Paquimé, one kilometre.

Paquimé ceramics, copying the original patterns, either black on black, or beige with intricate red and grey designs, are made in the village of Mata Ortiz, 21 kilometres from Nuevo Casas Grandes. Either take a bus from C Jesus Urueta, west of the railway track, at 1630 (return at 0800), US$2.40, take the train which is supposed to pass through Nuevo Casas Grandes on Tuesday, Thursday and Saturday at 1300, arriving 1400 (return Monday, Wednesday, Friday 1225), or hitch.

Sleeping

Sleeping can only be found in Nuevo Casas Grandes

B *Motel Hacienda*, Av Juárez 2603, T41046/7/8/9/50, the best, sometimes has Paquimé ceramics on sale. **C** *California*, Constitución Pte 209, reasonable, takes credit cards, hot water takes a while to come through. **C** *Motel Piñón*, Juárez 605, T41066, helpful. **C** *Paquimé*, with fan and a/c, clean, large, pleasant, recommended. **C** *Parque*, Av Juárez, just past main square heading north, with TV and phone. **D** *Juárez*, A Obregón 110, between bus companies, supposedly hot water, some English spoken, friendly, safe parking, basic bathroom (take your key with you when you go out); *Suites Victoria*, Guadalupe Victoria, 1 block west of Constitución Pte, off 5 de Mayo.

Eating

Café de la Esquina, 5 de Mayo y A Obregón, near bus offices, cheap, clean, friendly, popular. *Tacos El Brasero*, Obregón opposite *Hotel Juárez*, open 24 hours. *Dinno's Pizza*, Minerva y Constitución Ote, fair, takes credit cards, opposite Ciné Variedades. *Alameda*, next to *Hotel California*, for breakfast and *comida corrida*, average. *Denni's*, Juárez y Jesús Urueta, mostly steaks, quite good, good service.

Transport

Trains The station, between Constitución Pte and Ote (as is the railway), is at 1,454 metres.

Buses All bus offices are on Alvaro Obregón. Several daily to **Ciudad Juárez**, 3 companies, 4 hours, US$10.60; 3 companies to **Chihuahua**, 5 hours, US$12.10; Omnibús de México to **Mexico City** once a day via El Sueco, once via Cuauhtémoc, also to **Monterrey**; Chihuahua Madera to **Cuauhtémoc** and **Madera**; Caballero Azteca to **Agua Prieta** (3 a day), **Hermosillo**, **Tijuana** and **Nogales** (once each).

Directory

Banks Banks on 5 de Mayo and Constitución Ote; *Casa de Cambio California* next to hotel of that name. **Communications** Long-distance telephone: at Rivera bus office, on Alvaro Obregón.

From Chihuahua, the turn-off from the road to Ciudad Juárez is near El Sueco (157 kilometres from Chihuahua, 219 from Ciudad Juárez); from here State Highway 10 to Nuevo Casas Grandes (198 kilometres) passes through Constitución (bus stop), Flores Magón (hotel) and Buenaventura (114 kilometres, a pleasant-looking place). About 100 kilometres from El Sueco a brief section of 'camino sinuoso' affords views of the plains you have just crossed; from Buenaventura the road passes through different valleys, of varying degrees of fertility, the most productive being Buenaventura itself and Lagunillas. Buses from Chihuahua to Nuevo Casas Grandes go either via El Sueco or via Ciudad Cuauhtémoc (see below) and Madera (the Sierra route, see also below), which has some pleasant landscapes (if heading south from the USA, via Casas Grandes, you can continue on the Sierra route to Creel on the Chihuahua-Los Mochis railway).

Madera

Population: 13,000
Altitude: 2,100m
Colour map 2, grid A2

Madera is in the Sierra Madre, surrounded by rugged mountain scenery. It is high enough to receive snow in winter (rainy season September-March, best time to visit May-August). The region around Madera has ample scope for tourism: archaeological sites, birdwatching, hunting, fine landscapes and good infrastructure. It can be reached by second class train from Nuevo Casas Grandes. By road from the north is via Buenaventura and Gómez Farías. From Chihuahua either turn off Ruta 16 at La Junta (see below) and take Ruta 37 via Guerrero (*Posada Alicia*; Pemex magna sin), or turn off at Ciudad Cuauhtémoc onto Ruta 65 via Alvaro Obregón (restaurants, Pemex magna sin), Bachiniva (restaurants, Pemex) and Soto Maynes (Pemex magna sin). Before Gómez Farías, turn west onto Ruta 180; this takes you through Bavícora, site of George Hearst's ranch (Pemex, nova only) and on to Madera.

Madera's prosperous past

During the Porfirio Díaz era, two US financiers were granted rights to exploit the area: George Hearst (of the famous newspaper family), who farmed cattle between Madera and Gómez Farias, and William Green. In exchange for building the railway, which now runs between Chihuahua, Nuevo Casas Grandes and Ciudad Juárez, Green was allowed to extract timber from the forests. He wished to extend the railway to Cananea (northern Sonora), to take lumber to the mine he owned there, but this section was never built. In 1904 the first saw mills were in operation. The town developed, with a 66-room hotel, a casino and the largest wooden box-making factory in the world at the time. Green went bankrupt in 1908. During the Revolution, the factories casting iron for the railway turned to making cannon; Pancho Villa ordered two and also permitted the workers to take over management of the factories since the US managers had left. Eventually the North Americans returned following the workers' lack of success.

Francesca Pagnacco

Sleeping **A** *Motel Real del Bosque*, Carretera Chihuahua, Barrio Americano, on main road into town, T157-20066, F20538, 3-star, clean, friendly, parking, bar, disco, restaurant, English spoken, director Angel Leal Estrada is also president of local Comité Pro Turismo, very enthusiastic, tours organized from the hotel (see Excursions below); he is planning to build a backpackers' hostel. **C** *Parador de la Sierra*, C 3 y Independencia, T20277, clean, heating, discount for more than 1 night, off-street parking, restaurant. **C** *María*, C 5 y 5 de Mayo, cheaper rooms available, heating, clean, limited parking, restaurant open 24 hours, good. **C** *Mirmay*, C 3 y Guerrero, T20944, next to *Café Los Lobos*, not too clean. **F** *Motel Maras*, C5 (one block south of *Mirmay*), hot water, noisy, clean apart from dusty rooms.

Eating Several restaurants in town.

Transport **Local** Madera has an **airstrip**; call *Motel Real del Bosque* to arrange a landing (Unicom 122.8 and ADF 1300 service). Estrella Blanca **bus** (T20431) to/from Chihuahua every hour, takes 5 hours, bus stop on C 5.

Directory **Banks** *Banamex*, only place for Visa and Mastercard advances, *Bancomer* and *Banrural* will change dollars (possibly TCs).

Excursions Madera is on an important waterfowl migratory route, with white-fronted, blue and snow geese, mallard, pintail, teal, widgeon and redhead duck, and sandhill crane passing through. This does mean that it has become a popular centre for shooting (season mid-November-February), but birdwatching expeditions can be arranged at *Motel Real del Bosque*.

Taking C 3 in a northerly direction out of town, the road soon becomes dirt (stony, potholed, good suspension advisable). It parallels the railway to Casas Grandes, passing through pine forest and cultivated fields and heads into the plateau of the Sierra Madre. 12 kilometres from town, after a signpost to Nuevo Madera, is a lake and dam, **Presa Penitentes**, to the right. At the water's edge, the clockwise track takes you to the far side where you can fish for rainbow trout. Anticlockwise takes you to a picnic area with restaurant and toilets, children's play area and volley ball pitch. Camping possible; the restaurant is always staffed. Behind the dammed part of the lake is a rainbow trout farm, open 0900-1700 every day, fish can be bought. Waterskiing on the lake (four hours' tour from *Motel Real del Bosque*, US$30, minimum four people, alternatively hitchhiking is possible). Another trout farm and trailer park is under construction near Nuevo Madera.

Back on the main road, you come to a signed turning right to Las Varas, which leads to Casas Grandes (there is another, unsigned turning to Las Varas further on). Straight on is **El Salto**, a 35-metre waterfall, best seen after the spring thaw (March-April). The fall is along a track to the left; to see it you have to walk round the

Mexico

rim of a little canyon. It is possible to hike down to the river below (about one hour). Ask at the house on the track to the fall if you want to camp (no facilities).

Four kilometres from the turn-off to El Salto is the entrance to **Cuarenta (40) Casas**, with a visitors' hut (one hour 15 minutes from Madera). 40 Casas is a series of cave dwellings, inhabited originally by Indians of the Paquimé culture. Some of the houses have the palet-shaped windows/doorways also seen at Casas Grandes (called here La Cueva de las Ventanas); some are of two storeys. There is a good view of the cave houses from the visitors' hut. A trail descends to the river before climbing steeply to the cave, 45 minutes-one hour one way. ■ *40 Casas is open 0900-1600 every day (except 16 September), entry free. Camping is possible only when personnel are staying the night, no facilities other than water. (Tour from Motel Real del Bosque, six hours, US$65, minimum four people, alternatively hitchhiking is possible.)*

South of Madera is the **Misión Tres Ojitos**, where the Spanish priest, Padre Espronceda, makes ham. Fiesta 7 October, Virgen del Rosario, with rodeos and other activities. Take the road to La Junta from Madera and at the signpost, turn off right. On the dirt road, take the left fork through the village. Go past the church and on the right the Mission is signed (10 kilometres from Madera).

In Madera there is a sign indicating **Zona Arqueológica Huapoca**, going west on Independencia. At Km 13 on this good dirt road is **Lago Campo 3**, shallow and marshy, with wildlife. Camping and picnicing possible. (The lake's name comes from a logging camp.) At 18 kilometres from town you reach 2,500 metres, with stunning views of the Sierra Madre. Plenty of birdlife can be seen from the road. The Huapoca Ranch, a US-owned experimental horse-breeding centre at Km 30, does not take visitors. At Km 41 is the entrance to the **Zona Arqueológica Anasazi**, which contains the **Nido del Aguila** cave dwellings and the **Cueva del Serpiente**. The two-kilometre road to the site is terrible; about 300 metres are impassable (you have to find somewhere to park before the 'estacionamiento'). There is no path to the Nido del Aguila, but if you keep to the left slope from the 'car park', you reach first a mirador, then the cave around a big bluff. There is another mirador further on. A guide is necessary. On the righthand hillcrest from the 'car park' is the **Cueva del Serpiente**: a path leads to a sign on a tree, behind which to the left is a crevasse. 10 minutes into the crevasse (steep in places) is a set of three chambers and the remains of two others. Follow round on a narrow ledge to 11 more complete chambers and three ruins. All the rooms (covered in graffiti, unfortunately) can be entered; the rows of rooms interconnect and have the typical palet-shaped windows. A strong torch is useful for locating the inner rooms. If you jump up and down, the ground sounds hollow, suggesting that there are more rooms below. The views are magnificent.

At Km 44 is a brightly-painted house where, in November-December, they sell cheese. The beautiful valley of the Río Huapoca becomes visible at Km 51. A sign to Aguas Termales at Km 53 leads on to another terrible track, to hot springs with a small pool under a waterfall and a cooler section nearer the river (two toilets). The main road then crosses the Puente Huapoca suspension bridge, built in 1950 (a tour this far, including lunch, fishing, and swimming in the rapids, from *Motel Real del Bosque*, 10 hours, costs US$65). **NB** In this area, close any gates that you go through; farmers graze cows and horses on the land, which is private.

58 kilometres from Madera is the turn-off to **Cueva Grande**. A clear trail leads in 15 minutes to a waterfall, behind which is the 50-metre cave with two complete two-storey houses and some ruins. Visitors can climb to the upper storey and in the ruins see exactly how the constructions were made. Behind the house on the right is a circular trough which was used to store grain. The cave was inhabited from 1060 AD. There are rock pools for swimming by the fall (best March-April) and it is possible, but difficult, to climb to the head of the fall. At the car park you can camp or have a barbecue (but remember if lighting a fire to encircle it with stones; forest fires are a real danger).

Crossing into Mexico: Ojinaga to Chihuahua

Chihuahua may also be reached from the border at **Ojinaga**: this route is recommended not only for the ease of crossing (it is used only by cattle ranchers, no hassles), but also for the spectacular scenery either side of the border.

From Interstate 10 (San Antonio-El Paso), turn southwest after Fort Stockton on Highway 67. This goes to Alpine, 107 kilometres, no gas en route, where there are eight motels, most on Highway 90. From Alpine it is 42 kilometres to Marfa, where the film 'Giant' was made in 1955 with James Dean, Elizabeth Taylor, Rock Hudson. In *Motel El Paisano* there are signed photos of the film crew on display, T915-7293145; two other motels. 14 kilometres east of Marfa on Highway 90 is a viewing point for the Marfa 'Ghost Lights', an unexplained natural phenomenon. At Marfa Highway 67 head south 96 kilometres to **Presidio**. On the way, look out for two bizarre rock formations, a kneeling elephant with its back to the road, and a profile of Abraham Lincoln. 32 kilometres from Marfa, Shafter is passed, a silver mining ghost town; no gas on this stretch. In Presidio (*Population:* 3,500) is C *Motel Siesta*, clean, TV, pool; **B** *Three Palms Inn*, with bath, a/c, clean, friendly, takes credit cards, pool, open 0700-2200; *Rose's Café*, opposite, has good meals for US$6, open 0600-2130, try the 'hot chocolage', good breakfasts; two other restaurants. Also bank, post office (*Presidio Information Center* next door, T915-2294478, 0900-1800), fuel, shops. Southeast of Presidio is Big Bend National Park; to the northwest is Pinto Canyon.

Presidio (USA)/ Ojinga
Colour map 2, grid A3

Crossing the border Follow signs to Ojinaga; pass US immigration on left (if you need to, surrender US visa waiver form here). On the Mexican side, a guard will check your passport. Those with vehicles then park before doing paperwork. Boys selling chiclets will look after your car/bike, but you can see it through the office windows. There are separate desks for personal and vehicle papers. Photocopying can be done for US$1. Get insurance before Presidio, no one sells it there, but you could ask Stella McKeel Agency, T915-2293221/5. Full details of entry requirement for drivers is given in **Essentials**, page 80. The border is open 24 hours.

Leaving Mexico, note that the bus station is two kilometres from the border. Make sure all your papers are stamped correctly.

Essentials In Ojinaga 5 hotels, including **D** *Armendariz*, Zaragoza near Zócalo, T31198/32241, clean, safe parking. *Casa de Huéspedes*. Cheaper to stay in Ojinaga than Presidio. Cheap meals at *Lonchería Avenida* opposite bus station. **Festivals**: 1-4 June. Daily buses to/from Chihuahua, US$6; also daily train service. *Bancomer* on Zócalo, changes TCs, no commission; opposite is *Casa de Cambio Allende*, cash only, poorer rates.

.42 kilometres from Ojinaga on Route 16 towards Chihuahua is **El Peguis**, overlooking an extraordinary canyon. Also here is *garita*, where vehicle papers are checked (in the middle of nowhere). A further 46 kilometres is **Coyame**, a village with caves one kilometre away; ask for a guide (tourist complex, thermal springs, *balneario*, no hotel). Pemex with magna sin in Coyame. The road continues in good condition southwest, with no fuel stations until **Aldama**, 26 kilometres from Chihuahua. This pleasant town has tree-lined avenues, a shady central square and a church (1876) of pink sandstone (hotels, two motels on road to Chihuahua, restaurant *Campestre* opposite the motels, clean, friendly). After Aldama the traffic increases on the way to the state capital.

Mexico

Chihuahua

Population: 800,000
State Population: 1995
2,792,989
Altitude: 1,420m
Phone Code: 14
Colour map 2, grid B2

Capital of Chihuahua state; centre of a mining and cattle area (375 kilometres from the border, 1,479 kilometres from the capital). It is mostly a modern and rather rundown industrial city, but has strong historical connections, especially with the Mexican Revolution. Pancho Villa operated in the country around, and once captured the city by disguising his men as peasants going to market. Summer temperatures often reach 40°C but be prepared for ice at night as late as November. Rain falls from July to September. The local hairless small dog has a constant body temperature of 40°C (104°F), the world's only authentic 'hot dog'.

Sights There are also associations with the last days of Padre Hidalgo: the old tower of the **Capilla Real** in which he awaited his execution is now in the **Palacio Federal** (Libertad y Guerrero). The dungeon (calabozo) is quite unremarkable and the Palacio itself is very neglected. The **Palacio de Gobierno**, on the other hand, is in fine condition, with a dramatic set of murals by Aaron Piña Morales depicting Chihuahua's history. There are a number of old mansions (see Museums below) and the Paseo Bolívar area is pleasant. Calle Libertad is for pedestrians only from Plaza Constitución to the Palacios de Gobierno and Federal. Calle Cuarta (4a) and streets that cross it northwest of Juárez are bustling with market stalls and restaurants. Worth looking at is the **Cathedral** on Plaza Constitución, begun 1717, finished 1789; its Baroque façade dates from 1738, the interior is mostly unadorned, with square columns, glass chandeliers and a carved altar piece. In the southeast of the town near C Zarco are ancient aqueducts. Walk north along Ocampo and over the river for fine views of the city at sunset.

Museums The **Quinta Luz** (1914), C 10 No 3014, where Pancho Villa lived, is now the **Museo de la Revolución**, with many old photographs, the car in which Pancho Villa was assasinated ("looking like a Swiss cheese from all the bullet holes"), Villa's death mask and postcards of the assassinated leader, well worth a visit. ■ *Open 0900-1300 and 1500-1900, US$1.* The **Museo Regional**, in the former mansion Quinta Gameros at Bolívar 401, with interesting exhibits and extremely fine Art-Nouveau rooms: the dining room, child's room features Little Red Riding Hood scenes; bathroom, frogs playing among reeds, et cetera, exhibition of Paquimé ceramics, and temporary exhibitions. ■ *Open Tuesday-Sunday 0900-1300, 1600-1900, US$0.70.* **Museo de Arte e Industria Populares**, Av Reforma 5 (Tarahumara art and lifestyle; shops). ■ *Open Tuesday – Saturday 0900-1300, 1600-1900, free.* **Museo de Casa Juárez**, C Juárez y Quinta, house and office of Benito Juárez. ■ *Monday-Friday 0900-1500, 1600-1800.* **Museo de Arte Sacro**, Libertad y Segunda. ■ *Monday-Friday 1400-1800.*

Excursions For **Santa Eulalia** silver mine, take a blue and white bus from near the old bus station. Bus is marked *Chihuahua Postillo* and leaves hourly. After visiting the mine (fine views) walk down to Santa Eulalia town where there is a mining museum.

Sleeping
■ *on maps*
Price codes:
see inside front cover

AL *Palacio del Sol*, Independencia 500 y Niños Héroes, T166000, F159947, smart, with Torres del Sol travel agency and Número Uno car rental. **AL** *San Francisco*, Victoria 409, T167770, *Degá* restaurant good for steaks. **B** *El Campanario*, Blvd Díaz Ordaz 1405, 2 blocks southwest of Cathedral, T154545, good rooms, clean, TV, recommended. **C** *Balflo*, Niños Héroes 702, T160300, modern, poor value. **C** *El Cobre*, C 10A y Progreso T151730, with bathroom, hot water, TV, very comfortable, *Bejarano* restaurant good, reasonable laundry.

D *Plaza*, behind cathedral, C 4, No 206, T155833, noisy, quite clean, cold shower, fair, run down. **D-E** *Reforma*, C Victoria 809, T106848, also colonial (including rooms, some floors look unsafe), friendly, clean, fan, hot water, restaurant, TV in reception, safe, parking next door for cars (US$0.25) or motorbikes in courtyard, recommended. **D-E** *Cortez*, Gómez Farías

Mexico

6 (near Plaza Constitución, T100471, clean, quiet, big courtyard, pleasant. **D** *Del Carmen*, C 10 No 4, T157096, with hot water, a/c, OK. **E** *San Juan*, Victoria 823, T100035, in old colonial house, but rooms (repairs needed, a bit sombre) are in another part, reasonable food, water sometimes scarce, friendly. **E** *Roma*, Libertad 1015, T102363, with hot water, run down (taxi drivers on commission bring tourists here), neither has restaurant. **E-F** *Posada Aida*, C 10 y Av Juárez, with bath and hot water, friendly, helpful, 3 yappy chihuahua dogs!, night porter will watch cars parked outside, recommended (*Cabral* on C 10 is not recommended, rooms

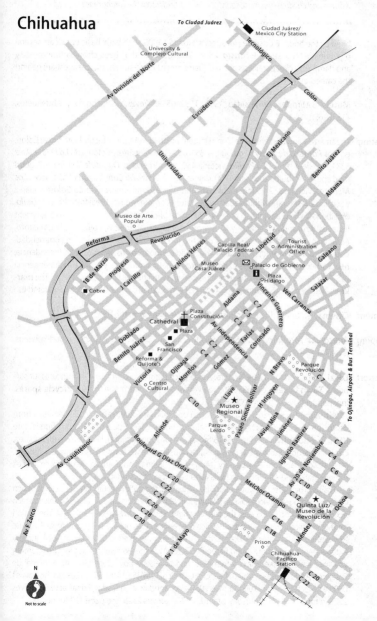

Chihuahua

Not to scale

Tarahumara Indians

This is the country of the long-haired, fleet-footed Tarahumara Indians, able, it is said, to outstrip a galloping horse and to run down birds. A few Indians can be seen in Chihuahua and Nuevo Casas Grandes, mostly women and children and most, sadly, begging. Tarahumara can be seen in much less unfortunate conditions and in greater numbers in Creel and beyond, but note that the Indians are shy, living in remote ranchos rather than the towns. 12 December is a festival for the Tarahumara.

hired by the hour). **E** *Casa de Huéspedes*, Libertad 1405, with bath, basic but clean, several others in the same street. **E** *Turista*, Juárez 817, with bath, dirty beds, clean bathroom, noisy and damp. The cheaper hotels are in C Juárez and its cross-streets; the cheapest are behind the cathedral.

Motels B *Mirador*, Universidad 1309, T132205. **C** *Nieves*, Tecnológico y Ahuehuetes, T132516.

Eating
● *on maps*
The smartest and best are in the 'Zona Dorada', northeast of the centre on Juárez, near Colón, eg: **Los Parados de Tomy Vega**, Juárez 3316, **La Calesa**, Juárez y Colón, and **La Olla**, Juárez 3331, excellent steaks. **La Parilla**, Victoria 450, recommended. **Quijote's**, Victoria 807, good food and value, buffet meals till 1700, dinner also, friendly. **Mi Café**, Victoria 1000, good. **Los Milagros**, Victoria 812, young people's meeting place, good atmosphere. **La Galatea**, Juárez y Segunda, restaurant within department store, recommended for breakfast, cheap. **El Gallo**, on Libertad, good and cheap breakfasts; **Flor de Michoacán**, on Libertad, serves excellent licuados. **Armando's**, Aldama y V Guerrero, for snacks, refrescos, coffee. **Café Calicanto**, Aldama 411, good coffee shop. **Café Merino**, Av Juárez y Ocampo, recommended. **Ostionería de la Monja**, near main Plaza, good seafood. **Tortas México**, on Independencia, near cathedral, good breakfasts. **Kosmovita** for natural products (shop), at Independencia 725. Corn (maize) is sold on the streets, excellent with cheese, lime, salt and chile. The **market** is between C 2 y 6, southeast of Av Niños Héroes, small but good for fruit and vegetables.

Entertainment **Cinema** On Universidad near Post Office, shows films from the USA.

Shopping *Artesanías Tarahumaras*, C5 y Doblado 312, T130627, crafts, baskets, wood carvings, jewellery.

Transport **Local Taxi**: work on a zone system. Agree price before boarding, to avoid unpleasant surprises. **Town buses**: cost US$0.20, go everywhere, ask which one to take. **Bicycle spares**: Independencia 807, open 0900-2000.

Air Airport Gen Fierro Villalobos (CUU) on Boulevard Juan Pablo II, 18 kilometres from centre on road to Ojinaga, T200676, airport buses collect passengers from hotels, fare US$1.10. Also minibuses. Taxi US$16 (no other transport at night). Flights to Ciudad Juárez, Ciudad Obregón, Culiacán, Guadalajara, Hermosillo, La Paz, Loreto, Los Cabos, Los Mochis, Manzanillo, Mazatlán, Mexico City, Monterrey, Tijuana and Torreón. Aeroméxico to Los Angeles daily, and Aerolitoral to Dallas and El Paso in the USA.

Trains There are 2 railway stations in Chihuahua: the station for Ciudad Juárez and Mexico City (no passenger services 1999) is 3 kilometres along Av Niños Héroes, left at Av Colón, which becomes Av Tecnológico, past the river and right along Av División Nte, T130714. The station for the 631 kilometres Chihuahua-Pacífico railway is 1 block behind the prison (near Av 20 de Noviembre and Boulevard Díaz Ordaz – take bus marked C Rosario, or walk up Av Independencia, then right along Paseo Bolívar or Av 20 de Noviembre); in the early morning you may have to take a taxi. Information and tickets by post: Departamento Regional de Pasajeros, Apdo Postal 46, Chihuahua, CHIH, Mexico, T157756, F109059. To Los Mochis daily at 0700, arrives 1950, returns 0600 arrives 2050, also Monday, Wednesday, Friday at 0800, arrives 2225, returns Tuesday, Thursday, Staurday 0700, arrives 2325 (see page 133 for details)

Buses Bus terminal on Boulevard Juan Pablo II, 8 kilometres from centre on way to airport, southeast of town, T202286, 20 minutes by bus to centre (US$0.30), or taxi US$4 (fixed price). Buses from centre at Niños Héroes between Ocampo and C 10. There is an exchange office (beware shortchanging), cafetería and left luggage. To **Mexico City** and intermediate destinations, frequent services with several companies: **Mexico City**, 20 hours, US$57; **Querétaro**, US$45.50; **San Luis Potosí**, US$36.50; **Aguascalientes**, US$33.50; **Zacatecas**, US$33, 12 hours; **Durango**, US$32; **Torreón**, US$16.50. 2nd class bus, to **Hidalgo del Parral**, US$7, 1st class US$10.50, 2½ hours. To **Mazatlán**, 2 companies, US$38, 19 hours, heart-stopping view. To **Creel**, US$11.50, 4-5 hours, 9 a day 0700-1730, paved all the way; to **Nuevo Casas Grandes**, see above (note that Chihuahua-Madera buses go either via El Sueco, or via the Sierra). At busy times allow several hours to buy tickets for buses going north, often full as they start elsewhere: to **Ciudad Juárez**, many buses, US$17.50. To other border points: Caballero Azteca to **Tijuana**, US$55, 3 a day, or with Tres Estrellas de Oro at 2400, 1st class express, US$50, and to **Agua Prieta**, US$20, 4 a day; also to **Hermosillo**, US$31, twice. Trans del Norte to **Nuevo Laredo** at 2030, US$36; also to **Monterrey**, US$33, and **Saltillo**, US$25 (other companies also to Monterrey). To **Guadalajara**, several, US$41, including Estrella Blanca which also goes to **Acapulco**, US$63, and **Puerto Vallarta**, US$58.

Airline offices *AeroMéxico*, T156303. **Banks** *Bancomer* on Plaza Constitución offers better rates than *Multibanco Comermex* on same square. *Casa de Cambio Rachasa*, Independencia y Guadelupe Victoria, on Plaza, poorer rates, no commission on cash, 2% on TCs, open Mon-Sat 0900-2100 (also at Aldama 711). *Hernández*, Aldama 410, T162399, Mon-Fri 0900-1400, 1600-1900, Sat 0900-1500. Exchange is available in the bus terminal, but rates are slightly better downtown. **Communications** Calle Libertad in the Palacio Federal. Also in Central Camionera. Credit card phone outside AeroMéxico office on Guadalupe Victoria, ½ block from Plaza Constitución (towards Carranza). Main phone office on Av Universidad. **Email:** *Cyber Café Canaco*, Chamber of Commerce, Av Cuauhtémoc 1800, 2nd floor, US$3.75 per hr. **Laundry** Ocampo 1412. Julián Carrillo 402. **Tour companies & travel agents** *Guillermo Bechman*, T30253, arranges stays at cabins above Bahuichivo, near Copper Canyon. *Viajes Flamingo*, *Santa Anita Hotel*, T91 (681) 21613, F83393, will book train tickets in advance, no commission charged, English spoken. *Turismo Al Mar*, T165950, accommodation and rail packages to Copper Canyon, 5 nights and some meals, US$500 for 2 people. *Turismo Espectacular*, T266460, Elena Flores, speaks English, very helpful. **Tourist offices** Palacio de Gobierno T151526, F160032, for general information, maps, pamphlets, etc, open Mon-Fri 0900-1900, Sat-Sun 0900-1400. Administration office at Departamento de Comercio y Turismo, Libertad 1300 y C 13, 10th floor, Mon-Fri 0900-1500, T162436.

Directory

Chihuahua to Los Mochis

The train journey to **Los Mochis** is very spectacular and exciting on the descent to the coast beyond Creel: book seats in advance. Sit on left hand side of carriage going to Los Mochis. The *primera especial* leaves daily at 0700, supposedly arriving at Creel at about 1125, Divisadero at 1245 (20 minute stop), Bahuichivo at 1430, and Los Mochis at 2050, local time, but delays are common (land slides and accidents may cause delays of two days and more). Reserved seat US$49, bring your own drinking water and toilet paper; fare to Creel US$22; double check all details as they are subject to frequent change. Do not take large amounts of cash or jewellery, there are security problems on the railway. There is food at two or three stations along the way including Divisadero. An ordinary train ('mixto') to Los Mochis leaves Monday, Wednesday, Friday at 0800, but often late, tickets are not sold until the first class train has left (second class only, carriages are good, a/c and comfortable, most windows do not open, mixed reports on cleanliness, US$10; fare to Creel US$4.50, arrives 1400), reaching Divisadero at 1530 and Los Mochis at 2225. As the most interesting part of the journey is between Creel and Los Mochis it is better to travel from Los Mochis; that section of the line is described under Los Mochis. If wishing to see the best scenery, there is little point in taking the train Chihuahua- Creel- Chihuahua (on this stretch, the cheaper train is just as good as the *primera especial*). If planning to spend a few days in Creel, there are frequent buses Chihuahua-Creel.

Delays are possible in the rainy season.

A US company, DRC Rail Tours (PO Box 671107, Houston, Tx772-671107, T713-6597602, or 800-6597602) sells deluxe rail trips on The South Orient Express, a private train running through the Copper Canyon, using restored vintage carriages. From three to nine day tours, fares from US$995 per person, double occupancy, to US$2,299; service does not operate beginning January to mid-February, nor end-April to end-September.

West of Chihuahua are high plains, windy and sparsely populated. This is a large apple-growing zone; diesel stoves next to the trunks of some varieties provide the fruit with sufficient heat to ripen. From Chihuahua, the railway and road (Route 16, *cuota* and *libre* after Km 45, latter good) cross the Sierra of the Tarahumara Indians, who call themselves the Raramuri ('those who run fast'). They were originally cave-dwellers and nomads, but now work as day-labourers in the logging stations and have settled around the mission churches built by the Spanish in the 17th century. Soon after La Junta/López Matías, where the railway divides to Nuevo Casas Grandes and to Creel, a road branches south while Route 16 continues to Hermosillo. The southerly road goes through beautiful scenery to Creel, 90 kilometres from the turning.

Creel

Population: 5,000
Altitude: 2,356m
Colour map 2, grid B2

Creel (very cold in winter) is the commercial centre of the Tarahumara region, important for its timber and as a tourist centre. Creel is easily reached by car from El Paso or Arizona. The town is named after Enrique Creel (1854-1931), economist and entrepreneur, governor of Chihuahua state in 1907, who built the railway and planned to improve the Tarahumara's lives by establishing a colony here. His statue stands in the central square, just below the railway. Around the square are two churches (one of which broadcasts classical music in the evening), the Presidencia

Chihuahua environs

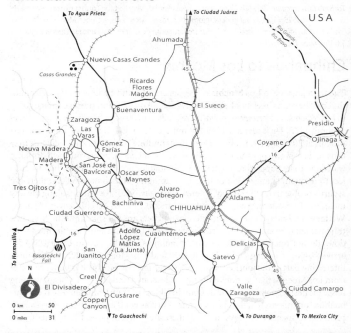

Municipal containing the post office (second door inside on right), the Banco Serfín and the Misión Tarahumara, which sells maps of the region (US$5 for topographical sheets, US$2.50 for simpler ones), description of the train ride and other good buys (such as excellent photographs of Indians, wood carvings, baskets, books). The Misión acts as a quasi-tourist office; open Monday-Saturday 0900-1300. There are several souvenir shops selling Tarahumara weavings, musical instruments, pine-needle baskets, et cetera. Also on sale are books such as *The National Parks of Northwest Mexico* (also obtainable from R Fisher, PO Box 40092, Tucson, Arizona 85717). Look also for *Tarahumara of the Sierra Madre* by John Kennedy (published by AHM, ISBN 0-88295-614-0).

A *Motel Parador La Montaña*, Av López Mateos 44, T145-60075 F60085 (full board available), will exchange foreign currency at reasonable rates, TV, clean, quiet, restaurant, bar, organizes excursions, safe parking. **A** *Motel Cascada Inn*, López Mateos 49, T60253, F60151 (L3 for full board), clean, parking, restaurant; *Parador* and *Cascada* have live music most evenings. **A** *Pension Creel*, Av López Mateos 61, about 1 kilometre from the plaza and railway station, T145-60071, F145-60200, breakfast included, shared bath, kitchen and living room, cabins with kitchen for rent (same price), very nice, dormitory annex at edge of town (**E** per person), tourist information, mountain bikes for hire and tours organized.

 B *Margarita's Plaza Mexicana* , Elfido Batista Caro, T60245, including dinner and

Sleeping
Make hotel reservations in advance as not many rooms are available

Mexico

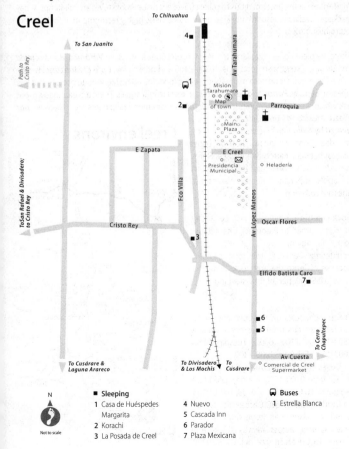

Creel

Key to map:

N
Not to scale

breakfast, bar. **B** *Nuevo*, other side of railway from station, T60022, F60043, meals over-priced, but nice and clean, some inside rooms dark. **C** *Korachi*, in cabin, **E** in room, not help-ful. **C-E** *Cabañas Berti's*, Av López Mateos 31, T60086, heating, soap and towels, parking, one kitchenette, excursions, friendly owner Sr Sergio Arnoldo Rascón plays guitar in local clubs. **D** *Posada de Creel*, 1½ blocks south of station on opposite side of the tracks, T/F145-60142, Apdo Postal 7, remodelled building, gas fires in rooms, very clean, **F** per per-son without bath in dormitory, hot water, helpful, English-speaking managers, coffee served from 0630, recommended.

F per person *Casa de Huéspedes Margarita*, López Mateos 11, T60045, between the two churches on corner of square, cheapest in dormitory (packed high season with mattresses on floor) rising to **D**, double with bath, breakfast and dinner included, good communal meals, very popular meeting place (book in advance in high season), Margarita's reps meet arriving passengers, quite pushy, organizes tours (see below), horses can be hired (US$2.50 per hour with guide, lazy horses), highly recommended (if full, Margarita's sister will put you up for **E** with dinner and breakfast, enjoyable).

A few kilometres out of town, 40 minutes drive from station set in high grassland near Cusárare waterfall, is **L** per person *Copper Canyon Sierra Lodge,* (Apdo 3, 33200 Creel, Chi-huahua, full board, US reservation, 2741 Paldan St, Auburn Hills, MI48326, T800-7763942, or T810-3407230, F810-3407212, minimum stay 3 days, closed in June, reservations cannot be made direct at the hotel, minibus to collect travellers, rustic woodstoves and oil-lamps, 8-day packages available; Jesús Manuel is a guide based here, highly recommended for excellent burro hiking trips.

Eating There are plenty of eating places in the town, on López Mateos, eg **Verónica**, good *comida corrida*, and **Estela**, also good, open 0800-2100 and on Sunday. *Café El Manzano*, beside railway line, good food. Also many shops selling food (including Mennonite cheese), but few open on Sunday. *Panadería* next to *Estela* will sell to individuals. There are bars in town, but ask which are the better ones (many are for Mexican men only); beers are expensive. *Bar Plaza Mexicana*, on Elfido Batista Caro, owned by *Margarita's* (see hotels), is recom-mended. Good ice cream shop on López Mateos between Parroquía and Oscar Flores. Next door is *Mi Café*, good food, cheap, try the apple empanadas, friendly. Water short-ages are common.

Sport **Rock climbing:** *Umarike*, US$50 per ½ day, at Humira (road to Batopilas), Chapultepec rock (in town) abseil at Basaseachi, bouldering. Generally top rope climbing because of loose volcanic rock. Rents out tents (US$6.50 per night), sleeping bags, stoves.

Transport **Trains** Schedules given above and under Los Mochis: station office is open Monday 0800-1000, 1100-1600; Tuesday-Friday 1000-1600, Saturday 1000-1300.

Buses To **Chihuahua** with Estrella Blanca from 0700-1730, 6 a day, US$11.50, 4-5 hours. To **Guachochi**, 0700, 1600, US$3. To **Ciudad Juárez** 0800. Buses also to sur-rounding villages. All leave from outside *Hotel Korachi*, across railway track from square. To **Cusárare** (see below), at 0700,

Creel environs

US$1.75, or lift in *Margarita's* transport US$4.50, or hitchhike.

NB There is a time change (though generally not recognised) locally between Creel (GMT – 6 hours) and Los Mochis (GMT – 7 hours).

Banks *Banco Serfín*, on the square, very friendly, open 0900-1300, changes dollars cash no commission, but commission charged on TCs (US$1 per cheque), TCs must be authorized by manager, Visa and Mastercard advances, no commission; on Sat and Sun exchange at shops, but at poor rates; some places accept dollars, also at poor rates. **Communications** Post Office: on west side of main square, Presidencia Municipal, no sign. Long-distance phone office in *Hotel Nuevo*. **Laundry** Pink house opposite side of tracks from square, US$3 per load, 2 hrs, good, Mon-Sat 0900-2000, restricted hrs on Sun. General stores also on López Mateos. **Tour companies & travel agents** Tours and rentals: many people hang around the square offering tours in a variety of vehicles, or other means of transport. Roberto Venegas, T60049, recommended, has van. **Horses:** for rent at several locations, eg Rarajipa 18 (near *Expediciones Umarike*), US$4 per hour to Christ statue above town, US$3.20 per hour for 4-5 hour ride to waterfalls. **Bicycle hire:** *Expediciones Umarike*, Av Ferrocarril s/n, north of tracks west of plaza, PO Box 61, T/F4560212, run by Arturo Gutiérrez and his Welsh wife Audrey, very friendly, open every day, cosy offices with literature and real coffee, US$6.50 for ½ day, US$10.50 whole day, provide map, good bikes, must deposit ID; longer guided tours available on bike or in 4WD eg to **Tararecua Canyon**. Also bikes from *Complejo Turístico Arareko*, López Mateos, opposite *Berlis*, US$2 per hour, US$11 per day, poor bikes. Map of town on the wall between Banco Serfín and Misión Tarahumara.

Directory

Creel is an excellent centre for trekking and horse riding. It is also a good centre for reaching several deep canyons, including that of the Río Urique, known as the **Barranca del Urique**, or **del Cobre** (the Urique, or Copper Canyon – see below).

Excursions

From the town footpaths lead to the Cristo Rey statue, to a viewpoint on Cerro Chapultepec and into the hills around. To see inhabited Tarahumara caves, turn right off the main road south out of town, about five minutes (by car) after the turn off signed to San Rafael. The woman and her daughters welcome visitors. Further to the south, walk to San Ignacio mission, passing the Valle de Hongos (mushrooms), entry fee charged by local community US$3.25; continue to **Laguna Arareco** (eight kilometres from Creel), around which one can walk (the lake is just off the Creel-Guachochi/Batopilas road), entry fee US$1.30. 20 kilometres away, on the same road, is **Cusárare** ('place of the eagles'), with a Jesuit church (1767) painted by Indians and a 30-metre waterfall, entry fee US$1. To get to the falls: 100 metres after the junction to Cusárare there is a hotel sign on the right; turn right, pass the hotel and then the bridge, at the junction turn right, about 45 minutes walk; it is not well-signposted. There is very good hiking around Cusárare, but as the Misión in Creel does not stock the Creel/Cusárare topographical map, a guide may be necessary. Sr Reyes Ramírez and his son have been recommended for tours to the canyon, US$20 per day for two people, including guide and two pack donkeys. Allow four days to see the canyon properly, tough hiking. The canyon is hot by day and cold by night. Accommodation is extra. The American Cristóbal, at *Margarita's* has also been recommended.

Just past Laguna Arareco is an unsigned right turn onto a bumpy track which leads, in one and a half hours in a hardy vehicle, to the top of the **Recohauta canyon**. A clear path descends in an hour or so to first a dry river, then the Río Tararécua. Follow the path along the river to where hot springs come out of the canyon's side. A pool has been made. In heavy rain many paths are flooded. The climb back up to the top also takes about an hour (loose scree on the path), or you can continue to other hot springs, several hours' walk, camping equipment essential (look out for the green arrows). Backpacking in the canyon is beautiful and, with a topographical map, original walks are easy to do. There are more trails than shown on maps: if the one you are on leads to a river or house it is not too difficult to find another, but many are vague and some lead to cliff edges. Do not add to the litter in the canyon.

At Cusárare, the road bifurcates. One branch heads southeast to **Norogachi**, 75 kilometres from Cusárare, with Tarahumara school and authentic costumes worn on Sunday, typical fiestas. This road continues to join the more usual route to Guachochi, which is the southern fork out of Cusárare.

Guachochi
Colour map 2, grid B2

156 kilometres from Creel Guachochi has a wild west appearance. There is a bank. From Guachochi you can walk four hours to the impressive **Barranca de Sinforosa**. Outside the town take road to the left of a wooden hut, after six kilometres take another left turn just after crossing a viaduct, carry on until you come to a gate on the left side of the road before it veers off to the right. Beyond the gate there is an orchard with a tower in the middle. It seems that you have to cross several sets of barbed wire to get to the canyon. The canyon is not visible until you reach the edge of it. Marlen Wolf and Markus Tobler of Switzerland write: "You will reach a point several hundred metres above the Río Verde where you can see an unforgettable extended system of immense canyons, grander than you can see from El Divisadero or on crossing the Barranca del Cobre. You can descend to the river on a path". This is not advisable for women alone.

Sleeping C *Melina*, Belisario Domínguez 14, T30255, clean, hot water, bar. **D** *Chaparre*, T30001, overpriced but good restaurant, bath, TV, hot water; **E** *Orpimel*, in same building as bus station.

Buses To Creel twice daily 0730 and 1330, US$3 (check at *Korachi Hotel* for schedule from Creel); also reached from Hidalgo del Parral, bus leaves for Parral at 0800 and 1200, now paved, but not spectacular.

The road south out of Cusárare leads eventually to Batópilas, passing a turn-off to El Tejabán above the *Barranca del Urique/Cobre* (this is claimed to be the 'real' copper canyon); **Basíhuare** ('Sash') village, surrounded by pink and white rock formations (40 kilometres from Creel); Puente del Río Urique, spanning the Urique canyon, ideal camping climate. At the T junction Creel-Guachochi-Bufa is a small restaurant/hotel, **F** *La Casita*, very primitive and romantic. The road is paved as far as the junction but is bumpy from then on. Just after the junction, three kilometres down into the valley is **Samachique**, where the *rari-pame* race, kicking a wooden ball for 241 kilometres without rest, often takes two to three days and nights in September. Stranded travellers can find a room and food at the bus stop (no more than a shack) in Samachique, which is one kilometre off the main route to Batópilas (1330 bus from Guachochi arrives at 1500 after Creel bus has gone through). If wishing to hitch to Batópilas (two and a half hour drive) take the right fork as you walk back out of Samachique, it rejoins the route at a junction where you can wait for traffic both coming through and by-passing the village. **Quírare**, 65 kilometres from Creel offers sights of Batópilas canyon, of great beauty. After Quírare there is an awesome 14 kilometres descent to La Bufa in Batópilas Canyon, and on to Batópilas, possibly the most scenic road in northern Mexico.

Batópilas
Colour map 2, grid B2

Batópilas, 120 kilometres from Creel, is a little town of 1,100 inhabitants, quiet, palm-fringed, subtropical, delightful and hot, hemmed in by the swirling river and the cactus-studded canyon walls. There are good parties in the Plaza at Christmas and New Year. It is a good centre for walking – the Urique canyon can be reached (see box). Horses, pigs, goats and chickens wander freely along the cobblestone streets. Mangoes and other citrus fruits are grown. Europeans arrived here in 1690. The Mina de Guadalupe was discovered in 1780 by Pedro de la Cruz. Batópilas became a thriving silver-mining centre, with mines owned by the Shepard family. Their mansion (near the bridge), abandoned during Pancho Villa's campaign, must be one of the most elaborate adobe houses anywhere, but it is now overgrown and dilapidated. Shepard, whose big strike was the La Bufa mine, built houses, bridges and canals around the town. Apparently, Batópilas was the second place in Mexico, after the capital, to receive electricity (Joe Bowbeer, Rio Rancho, NM). The town

Batopilas to Urique

A three-day hike goes from the Batópilas Canyon to Urique (once known as the Royal Way), from where you can get a ride to Bahuichivo for a train to Creel or Las Mochis.

Routes *Batópilas-Cerro Colorado-Piedra Redonda-Cerro El Manzano-La Estación-Los Alisos-Urique. You climb from 500 metres, reaching 2,200 metres before descending to Urique at 600 metres. It can be very hot in the canyons: drink at least four litres of water a day (you can fill up at settlements along the way) and take plenty of sunblock. There are many junctions of paths and so if you are without a guide it is vital to check that you are on the correct route as often as possible (try not to wander into marijuana plantations).*

One recommendation if you are using the 'Batópilas' survey map (1:50,000 sheet G13A41, covering the entire route, available from the Misión Tarahumara in Creel US$5) is that you take the ridge path (not marked on the 1979 edition) after Cerro El Manzano to La Estación, both for the views and directness.

Horseriding *A recommended guide (not cheap) is Librado Balderrama Contreras who will guide you to Urique or to surrounding attractions such as Mesa Quimoba, Mesa de San José and Monerachi. Mules can be hired, from several places in town, with a handler, for carrying gear.*

only has electricity from 1800 to midnight, although a new generator is expected. Manuel Gómez Morín, founder of the PAN, lived in Batópilas. His house (now a store) on the main street has a plaque proclaiming the place where he first 'saw the light'. There are two plazas, the second, the tiny, shady Plaza Constitución is at the end of town, above the main plaza. Notable houses from are the 18th century: Casa Barfusson, Casa Morales and the early 19th century Casa Bigleer.

Sleeping The owners of the *Copper Canyon Sierra Lodge* (Creel) have opened the **LL** *Copper Canyon Riverside Lodge* (US reservations, T800-7763942, F810-3407212), same prices for full board, closed in June, renovated 19th century hacienda, with gardens, luxurious. **C** *Mari*, reservations as for *Parador de la Montaña* in Creel. **E** *Batópilas*, clean, also *Parador Batópilas*, more expensive, but not too much. **E** *Chulavista*, on way into town, owned by Don Mario, near bridge at entrance to village, clean, hot water. Basic rooms also at **F** *Restaurant Clarita* (basic accommodation) and Sra Monsé, **E-F** – ask prices first – at plaza (she sells Tarahumara violins), rooms with gas lamps. She can give information in English (which she likes to practice on tourists). *Carmen's Youth Hostel*, basic accommodation, good food, friendly.

Eating *Restaurant El Puente Colgante*, new, pleasant and friendly, bit pricey. Meals at the private house of Sra Enedina Caraveo de Hernández on the Plaza Constitución are good and cheap, large portions. *Restaurant Carolina*, between bridge and centre, friendly owner, good selection, planning to move to Plaza Constitución. In the village there are only basic supplies in shops. The store on the plaza, *Tienda Grande* (Casa Morales), can change travellers' cheques at a poor rate. Bring insect repellent against locally-nicknamed 'assassin bug' or bloodsucking insect.

Transport Buses from Creel, Tuesday, Thursday, and Saturday at 0700, 5-6 hours (paved as far as Samachique turn-off) depending on weather, US$9.50, buy ticket the day before, very crowded. Tickets are sold from *Restaurant La Herradura* in the main street; the best time to try is when the bus (white with 'Batópilas' in blue on the side) stands outside from about 1225 having just arrived on its return to Creel, Monday, Wednesday, and Friday, leaves Batópilas at 0500 (have a torch handy as it is very dark). Supply lorry leaves for Chihuahua Tuesday, Thursday, Saturday at 0600, takes passengers.

Directory Communications Telephone office on corner of plaza, open 0900-1300, 1500-1900. **Tour companies & travel agents** Several people in Creel offer trips to

Batópilas. A recommended guide is Pedro Estrada Pérez (limited English but patient), T560079. An overnight trip for 4 (minimum) costs US$60 per person, plus lodging and meals, including trip to Jesuit mission at Satevo (see below). Many hotels arrange tours to some of the places mentioned in this section: prices vary from hotel to hotel, some require a minimum number of people, some provide lunch. Some examples, to Cusárare (US$12-15), mission and falls, and Basíhuare; Recohauta hot springs (US$8 plus US$1.50 entrance); San Ignacio, Valle de Hongos and Laguna Arareco; to Basaseachi (US$58 includes lunch, minimum 4 from *Parador La Montaña*); Batópilas; Divisadero (US$20, minimum 5, from *Margarita's*). These tours are pricey, but good fun and may involve more walking or climbing than advertised. Recommended for guided tours deep into the Urique Canyon is Adventure Specialists, Inc (president Gary Ziegler), Bear Basin Ranch, Westcliffe, CO 81252 (303/7832519, 800/6218385, ext 648), US$700-800 for 11-day tours from El Paso, vigorous, knowledgeable.

The **Porfirio Díaz Mine** above the bridge into town can be explored to about three kilometres into the mountain (take torch); as you get into the mine there is the sickly, sweet smell of bat droppings, after about one kilometre the air is thick with disturbed bats. **Satevo**, a seven-kilometre walk from Batópilas along the river, a poor place with 15 houses, two of which sell drinks, has a 350-year-old Jesuit Mission whose dome has been repainted and whose interior is under repair. The family next door has the key (US$ donation appreciated). The route to Satevo can be driven on a rough jeep track. The surrounding area, but not the town, is inhabited by the Tarahumaras known as Gentiles (women don't look at, or talk to, men). If you go 'off road' here, beware of drug cultivation areas. It is possible to walk in the other direction to **Cerro Colorado** and back in a day (eight kilometres, three hours each way, along road that departs from north side of bridge). In this tiny village some people still mine for gold, carrying the ore down to the river by donkey where it is ground up in water-powered stone mills. Like Batópilas it has interesting industrial archaeology, drainage ditches, tunnels, canals and bridges. You can camp in the schoolyard, or on a small beach 15 minutes before the town. With luck you can hitch to Cerro Colorado, then walk two hours to Munérachi, a remote village, to meet Tarahumara Indians (best to arrange a local guide through Sra Monsé on the plaza in Batópilas as drug cultivation in this part of the canyon means some areas are unsafe). At **Cerro Yerbanis** there are amazing views of Batópilas Canyon.

Divisadero
Colour map 2, grid B2

The Barranca del Urique/del Cobre is a long way from Creel. Apart from the access from Batópilas (see box, page 139), or from Bahuichivo (see rail description from Los Mochis), the simplest way to see the canyon is to go to Divisadero or *Posada Barrancas* by rough road, paved halfway from Creel (hitch, no public transport), or by train. The *primera especial* leaves Creel at 1225, US$5, the ordinary train at 1320, US$1, one and a half hours, *Posada Barrancas* is five minutes further on, same fare. To hitch, walk along López Mateos out of Creel to the paved main road; continue for one kilometre to the turning to San Rafael and wait for a lift there. Single women should only accept a ride if other women are in the vehicle and ask the women how far they are going. Return to Creel on the slow train at 1700 (or by hitching back); alternatively nip out for 10-15 minutes and continue to Los Mochis, or stay overnight.

Sleeping at Divisadero A *Hotel Divisadero Barrancas*, PO Box 661, 31238 Chihuahua, T103330, F156575, full board and includes 2 tours (to Balancing Rock, see below, and San Luis de Majuachic). 2-3 kilometres by road, 5 minutes by train from Divisadero is **A** *Posada Barrancas Mirador*, across the tracks from the old *Posada Barrancas*, new hotel has views from every room, full board, free lemonade on arrival and free margarita later, recommended, book through *Hotel Santa Anita*, Los Mochis, T681-57046, F681-20046, tours arranged, including hike or horseback trip to a Tarahumara village. A *Hotel Mansión Tarahumara* (reservations, Av Juárez 1602-A, Chihuahua, T154721, F165444), reached from

Posada Barrancas station, full board, good food, lovely rooms, clean, friendly. Reservations are advisable. If you want the train to stop at *Posada Barrancas*, tell a railway official. To stay more cheaply at Divisadero.

C *Casa de Huéspedes Díaz*, rooms with 2 double beds, hot water on request, prepares meals. **E** *Cabañas* and bed and breakfast near church, 2 food shops, or, walk 1½ kilometres down the road, past the 'camping' sign to a hamlet of 3 houses. First house on left has a rustic room with earth floor and lantern with a double and a single bed, **F**. Breakfast and dinner available with the friendly Gutiérrez family. To hike into canyon, take path at the back of their house to a stone wall and stream that leads down into the canyon. Follow trails down to Tarahumara Indian dwellings and interesting mushroom-shaped rocks. Ask locals for *'piedras como hongos'*. From the canyon rim, best views are in the late afternoon.

The Balancing Rock is at the edge of the canyon; it wobbles in a stomach-churning way as you stand on it. Reached by *camioneta* from *Hotel Divisadero Barrancas*, or walk one to two kilometres from Divisadero (away from Creel) and on the left you will see the wooden entrance gate. From there it is 45 minutes to the rock with stops at the canyon viewing points. Guides available at hotel. Car drivers can park outside the entrance, or ask at the hotel for the key to open the gate. Also here is a marked trail for mountain bikes.

Excursions

From *Posada Barrancas Mirador* you can hike down five minutes to a Tarahumara cave dwelling, souvenirs sometimes on sale. You can also hike around the rim to the village.

The canyon can also be reached on foot from Divisadero or *Posada Barrancas*; from the former it is six kilometres (walk or hitch) along the dirt road that runs beside the railway to the house of Florencio Manzinas (at the first group of houses you come to). He will hire out donkeys, give directions to the canyon (for a small tip), or will accompany you as guide (more expensive). He also provides food and accommodation in his house, or may let you camp free. From there it's a day's hike along narrow, slippery, often steep and sometimes overgrown trails into the canyon, descending from cool pine forest into gradually more subtropical vegetation as you approach the river and the canyon floor. At this point there are mango, orange and banana trees. Take plenty of water for the hike as, after descending the first section following a stream, you have to go over another hill before getting down to the river, which means several hours without access to water.

30 kilometres northeast of Creel is San Juanito, a little larger than Creel, with cobblestone streets which are less dusty than other towns in the region. It has an annual *fiesta* on 20-24 June (**C** *Motel Cobre*, very nice rooms). It is on the main road to Chihuahua, which continues to La Junta, a road and rail junction between Chihuahua and Madera, on one of the routes to Nuevo Casas Grandes and Ciudad Juárez.

San Juanito
Colour map 2, grid B2

East of La Junta, some 105 kilometres west of Chihuahua, is Ciudad Cuauhtémoc, a town surrounded by 20 or so Mennonite villages (*campos*), self-sufficient agricultural communities. The Mexican Mennonites, originally from Belgium, Holland and Germany, arrived from Canada early in the 20th century. Many are blond, blue-eyed and speak old German; they can be seen in town (also in Chihuahua and Nuevo Casas Grandes) selling cheese and vegetables and buying supplies.

Ciudad Cuauhtémoc
Colour map 2, grid B2

Sleeping **A** *Motel Tarahumara Inn*, corner of Allende and C 5, T22801/24865, comfortable, plenty of hot water, good restaurant, travel agency, safe parking, popular, worth booking ahead, recommended. **E** *Hotel del Norte*, C Reforma, basic, sometimes no hot water).

Buses Bus from Chihuahua US$3.80 every 30 minutes after 0700 (hourly 0500-0700); also from Creel. Toll between Ciudad Cuauhtémoc and Chihuahua, US$5.50.

Basaseachi falls
Colour map 2, grid B2

A very rough road northwest from San Juanito goes 75 kilometres to the Basaseachi falls, the highest single-jump waterfall in North America, 311 metres. Low-bodied cars would be wise to take the longer route via La Junta, on the Cuauhtémoc road; the San Juanito road is dangerous because there are long straight stretches encouraging speed, but very little traction; via La Junta it is further (195 kilometres from Creel, compared with 125 kilometres from Creel via San Juanito), takes marginally longer at just over three hours, but it is a very good paved road; both scenic routes. The falls are at their best in July-September. The top of the falls are three kilometres from town (two kilometres by dirt road, one kilometre by signed trail). A paved road leads to a car park (with taco stalls) and mirador one and a half kilometres above the falls. From here a path leads to the top of the falls and continues steeply to the pool at the bottom (best to swim in the morning when the sun still strikes the pool). Two thirds of the way to the bottom is the *Mirador Ventana* offering the best viewpoint of the falls. Hitching is difficult here, better to take a tour (US$16). The road goes on through beautiful mountains and forest to **Yepachic**, winding its way though Maicova, Yécora and **San Nicolás** into Sonora. From San Nicolás the road continues to the Pacific highway at Ciudad Obregón (it is paved from San Juanito to Hermosillo, but watch out for rock and mud slides in the rainy season on the older section in the mountains, it is heavily potholed from San Nicolás to Ciudad Obregón). The scenery is beautiful, the services in the villages limited, but you will probably not meet another tourist.

   NB Unleaded fuel is not available for 320 kilometres until one and a half kilometres before *Hotel Alma Rosa* (coming from Hermosillo), and the next is at La Junta, 80 kilometres from *Alma Rosa*, on the Cd Cuauhtémoc road. It is available in Anáhuac, on Route 16 libre, near Cd Cuauhtémoc. There is also *magna sin* in Creel.

Sleeping Free camping at trailhead, no water, and near the lookout on the other side of the canyon. Hotels: **C** *Alma Rosa*, 1 kilometre towards Hermosillo, some new rooms with fire places and oil lamps, TV, electricity 0800-2000, hot water. **E** *Nena*, 'downtown', bathroom in room, but no door, no electricity after dark, provides oil lamps; *Deny* also 'downtown', has own generator.

South from Chihuahua

Ciudad Delicias
Colour map 2, grid B3

The first major town is on Route 45; it is the centre of a major agricultural area. There is a Museo de Paleontología, with fossils from the Zona de Silencio (see below) and from the inland sea that covered the area 80 million years ago (Av Río Chuvíscar Norte y Círculo de la Plaza de la República). At the same address is a cultural centre, open 0900-2000, Monday-Saturday, T28513.

Sleeping *Casa Grande*, Av 6 Ote 601, T40404, 5-star. *del Norte*, Av Agricultura Nte 5, T20200, 4-star. *Baeza*, C 2 Nte 309, T21000, 3-star. *Delicias*, near market, several others of similar quality nearby.

Markets *Mercado Juárez*, Av del Parque y 3 Nte, local produce and handicrafts, Monday-Saturday 0900-2000, Sunday 0900-1500. *Mercado Morelos*, C 4 Sur 600.

Transport Train Station: Av 7 Ote, T20834. **Buses** To/from Chihuahua hourly, US$3; Omnibus de México, Av 6 y C 2 Nte, T21020; Estrella Blanca, Av 6 Nte 300, T21509; Rápidos Delicias, Av 5 Nte 301, T21030.

Ciudad Camargo
Colour map 2, grid B3

(Km 1,332), a small cattle town in a green valley, quiet except for its eight days of *fiesta* for Santa Rosalía beginning on 4 September, when there are cockfights, horse racing and dancing. Black bass fishing at the dam lake, and warm sulphur springs five kilometres away.**B** *Siesta Inn*, south edge of town on highway. **Motel**: **D** *Victoria*, Comonfort y Jiménez, clean and cheap.

From **Ciudad Jiménez** (1,263 kilometres from Mexico City. **B** *Motel Florido*, hot water) there are two routes to Fresnillo and Zacatecas: the Central Highway through Durango or a more direct route via Torreón (237 kilometres from Ciudad Jiménez), passing Escalón (restaurant), **Ceballos** (**E** *Hotel San José*, basic), Yermo (restaurants) and Bermejillo (restaurant), on Route 49.

Between Escalón and Ceballos is the Zona del Silencio (the Silent Zone), a highly magnetic area where, it is claimed, electrical appliances fall silent, aircraft radar goes haywire, and so on. It inspires much interest and research but as yet no proof.

Torreón

Torreón is the principal industrial city of La Laguna cotton and wheat district. It is reported hot, polluted, without colonial atmosphere. Here is the Bolsón de Mayrán, an oasis of about 28,500 square kilometres which might be irrigated, but only about 2,000 square kilometres have been developed and much of that is stricken with drought. On the opposite side of the mostly dry Nazas River are the two towns of **Gómez Palacio** (*feria* first half of August) and Lerdo.

Population: 700,000
Altitude: 1,137m
Phone code: 17
Colour map 2, grid B4

Mexico

In Torreón A *Palacio Real*, Morelos 1280, T60000. A *Paraíso del Desierto*, Independencia y Jiménez, T61122, resort. A *Río Nazas*, highrise, very good, on Av Morelos y Treviño. **A-D** *Posada de Sol*, Bulevar Revolucionario, opposite La Unidad de Deportes sports complex, modern motel, secure parking, small restaurant, bar, hot showers, rooms range from basic, windowless, clean *cabañas* to large, North American-style rooms with TV, good value. **D** *Galicia*, Cepeda 273, good. **D** *Laguna*, Carrillo 333. **D** *Princesa*, Av Morelos near Parque Central. Few decent places to eat in the centre.

Sleeping

In Gómez Palacio **C** *Motel La Siesta*, Av Madero 320 Nte, T140291/142840, clean, hot water, safe parking, good. **D** *Motel La Cabaña*, hot water. **E** *Colonial*, 3 blocks south of train station, hot water, bath, only internal locks on doors, basic.

Air Torreón airport is 14.5 kilometres from the centre. Services to Chihuahua, Ciudad Juárez, Culiacán, Durango, Guadalajara, Hermosillo, Ixtapa, La Paz, Los Angeles (California), Mazatlán, Mexico City, Monterrey, Piedras Negras, San Antonio (Texas) and Tijuana. **Buses** Local buses on Bulevar Revolucionario go to all parts of the city. The new Torreón bus station is 5 kilometres south of the city; if coming from the north, drivers allow you to leave the bus in the centre. There is a shuttle service between the centre and the bus station; taxis to centre operate a fixed-fare system. To **Chihuahua**, 6 hours, US$16.50; to **Tepic**, US$30; to **Ciudad Juárez**, US$30; about 6 a day to **Durango**, 4½ hours 2nd class. There is also an airport. Note that Gómez Palacio has its own bus station, without a shuttle to the centre. City buses outside have frequent services to all three city centres, US$0.33. When leaving either bus terminal, make sure that your bus does not stop at the other terminal; this can cause long delays. **Train** There is a daily service Torreón-Aguascalientos, 0900, arrives 1945, returns 1010, arrives 1930.

Transport

Between Gómez Palacio and Zacatecas are **Cuencamé** (**D** *Motel la Posta*, hot water, north of town; hotel south of town, **D**, not recommended, damp, dirty, but has parking; just north of Cuencamé, as you turn off Ruta 49 onto Ruta 40 to Durango is *Menudo El Zancas*, 100 metres on left, a truckers' meal stop open 24 hours, which is excellent, set meal US$3.45), **Río Grande** (**D** *Hotel Río*) and **Fresnillo**, birthplace of the artist Francisco Goitia and musician Manuel M Ponce, with many old buildings and a museum. (**C** *Motel La Fortuna*, comfortable, hot water; **D** *Hotel Cuauhtémoc*, basic.)

Hidalgo del Parral

Colour map 2, grid B3

From Ciudad Jiménez it is 77 kilometres to (Km 1,138) Hidalgo del Parral (usually just called Parral), an old mining town of 100,000 people with narrow streets. The city's history is split between its mining heritage and the fact that Pancho Villa was assassinated here. In 1629, Juan Rangel de Viezma discovered 'La Negrita' the first mine in the area. Now known as 'La Prieta', it overlooks the city from the top of Cerro la Prieta. Rangel founded the town in 1631 under the name of San Juan del Parral; it was renamed Hidalgo in honour of the father of the Revolution in 1833. When Parral was founded, the population consisted of Spaniards, mestizos, black slaves from Cuba and Africa, and Indians (who became the workforce for the mining industry). The mine owners were generous benefactors to the city, leaving many beautiful buildings which still stand. On 8 September 1944, severe damage was caused by a flood. The decrease in population, either through drowning or flight, led to a recession.

Hidalgo del Parral is now a pleasant, safe, affluent city. It has a compact centre with a string of shaded plazas, many bridges over the sinuous, and often dry, Río del Parral and several churches. A one-way system operates in the centre, with pedestrian crossings marked with faded yellow lines; drivers should proceed with extreme caution and be wary of obscurely placed traffic lights.

Sights On the Plaza Principal is the **Parroquia/Templo de San José**, with a beautiful interior. **Plaza G Baca** has a statue to El Buscador de Ilusiones, a naked man panning for

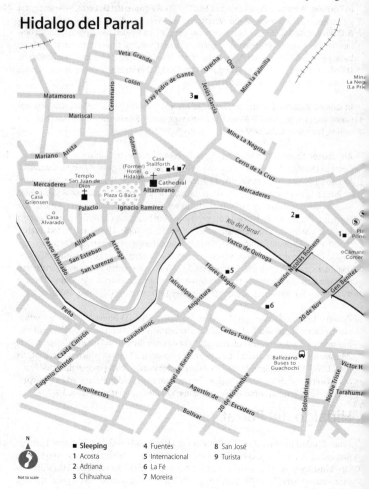

Hidalgo del Parral

■ Sleeping	4 Fuentes	8 San José
1 Acosta	5 Internacional	9 Turista
2 Adriana	6 La Fé	
3 Chihuahua	7 Moreira	

N
Not to scale

gold. The **cathedral** is on this square and, on the opposite side, is the **Templo San Juan de Dios** with an exuberant altar piece, painted gold. Across the road from the cathedral is the former *Hotel Hidalgo* (not in use), built in 1905 by mine owner Pedro Alvarado and given to Pancho Villa in the 1920s. Next door is **Casa Stallforth** (1908), the shop and house of a German family who supplied everything imaginable to the city. It is still a shop, with the original interior. Continuing on Mercaderes, before the bridge, is **Casa Griensen**, now the Colegio Angloamericano Isaac Newton. Griensen, another German, married Alvarado's sister. Behind this house is **Casa Alvarado**, still a private residence, only for viewing from the outside. Crossing the bridge at the end of Mercaderes, you come to the site of Villa's death, on the corner of Plaza Juárez. Also worth seeing is the façade of the **Teatro Hidalgo** on Plazuela Independencia. Just off Av Independencia is the **Templo de la Virgen del Rayo** (the Virgin of the Lightning).

Excursions

21 kilometres north of Parral on Route 45 is the turning for Talamantes, which is a further 11 kilometres down a dirt road in good condition. Turn right at the square and continue three kilometres out of town to the **Ojo de Talamantes**, a warm, natural pool of clear spring water, two metres deep. ■ *daily, 0900-1800, US$1)*. There is also a manmade swimming pool, picnic areas, changing rooms and toilets. Boats, in poor shape, can be rented, US$6 per hour. Bring your own food, not much on sale. The village itself is virtually a ghost town, with the remains of what must have been great estates. No public transport runs to Talamantes.

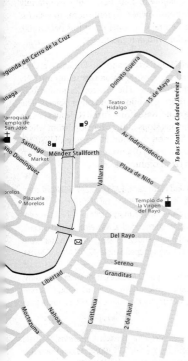

26 kilometres east of Parral on the Jiménez road, a well-signed road leads five kilometres south to **Valle de Allende** (*Population*: 4,000). Originally called Valle de San Bartolomé, it was the site of the first Franciscan mission in Chihuahua, founded in the late 16th century by Fray Agustín Rodríguez. The original monastery building still stands on the main square, but it is unused (it has also been used as a *refrigeradora* to store apples). Also on the square is the Parroquia de San Bartolomé and an unsightly Pepsi plant (no longer in production), which replaced the building in which the heads of the Independence leaders Hidalgo, Allende, Aldama and Jiménez were deposited for a night on their parade around the country after their execution. The town was renamed after Allende in 1825. Valle de Allende is a beautiful little town with a shaded central square, many colonial-style houses and a number of orchards which produce fruit and walnuts. During Semana Santa there is a reenactment of Christ carrying the Cross to Calvary; all the villagers take part. The painter of the murals in the Palacio de Gobierno,

Mexico

The assassination of Pancho Villa

The infamous assassination of Pancho Villa took place in the town centre on 20 July 1923. Villa owned a house on Calle Zaragoza (now a shop called Almacenes Real de Villa, painted bright pink) and was making his way from there to the Hotel Hidalgo, which he also owned, when he was ambushed on Av Juárez. The house chosen by the assassins is now the Museo Pancho Villa (open Monday-Friday 0900-2000, Saturday 0900-1300). 12 of the 100 bullets fired hit Villa, who was taken immediately to the Hotel Hidalgo. The death mask taken there can be seen in the museum and also in the museum in Chihuahua. His funeral took place the next day and he was buried in the Panteón Municipal; his tomb is still there even though the body has been transferred to Mexico City.

Chihuahua, lives here and is setting up an art school and ceramics workshop.

Outside town is the ruined Hacienda San Gregorio, dating from the 19th century. Among the visible features is the Rebote court, in which a type of squash/rackets was played, using a hard leather bat and a stone ball wrapped in metal (there were a lot of injuries; a gentler form of Rebote is played in town using a tennis ball and bare hands). The Balneario El Trébol is open April-September: swimming pools for adults and children, toilets, changing rooms, entry US$1; picnic areas. Behind the Balneario you can swim or fish in the Río Allende.

Rooms to let at *Almacén La Norteña*, C Cuauhtémoc 40, basic but clean, family atmosphere. There is a scheme for private house owners to rent rooms to visitors. *Getting there:* From Parral leave from the Central Camionera, last bus back 1800, US$1.30, 30 minutes. There is a Pemex station with *magna sin*.

Southwest of Parral are the mining towns of Santa Bárbara and San Francisco el Oro. **Santa Bárbara** was founded in 1567 and a Franciscan mission was set up in 1571. The church on the town square dates from this time. The Museo Comunitario El Minero, C Allende (free), has many items relating to mining and other objects. The town is quite pretty and you can walk to the mine. Buses from Parral (C Jesús García) take 30 minutes, US$0.50, half hourly. The bus stops at the Mercado, from where buses go to **San Francisco el Oro** (every hour on the hour, 20 minutes, US$0.30, also to Parral). The mine dominates the town; it was discovered in 1658. The town has little to offer the visitor and the church (20th century) is ugly.

Sleeping **B** *Adriana*, Colegio 2, between Plaza Principal and Plaza Baca, T22570, F24770, a/c, restaurant, bar, parking. **C** *Acosta*, Agustín Barbachano 3, T20221, F29555, off Plaza Principal, quiet, parking for car or motorbike, rooftop terrace with fine view, laundry facilities, very clean, central, friendly, helpful, hot water, excellent value, recommended. **C** *Moreira*, Jesús García 2, near cathedral, unwelcoming. **C** *San José*, Santiago Méndez 5, near Plaza Principal, with bath, safe parking, clean, central. **C** *Turista*, Plazuela Independencia 12, T24489, F24784, clean, nice.

D *Chihuahua*, Colón 1, off Jesús García, clean, simple. **D** *Fuentes*, near Plaza Baca, dirty, dour rooms, restaurant has cheap *comida corrida*. **E** *Margarita*, near bus station, recommended. **F** *Internacional*, Flores Magón, basic, friendly, parking, dirty. **F** *La Fe*, Flores Magón 57, shared bath, dirty.

Eating *La Parroquia* in *Hotel San José*, good value meals, including breakfast. *Morelos*, Plazuela Morelos 22, off Plaza Principal, clean, rather expensive, open 0700-2300, Friday and Saturday open 24 hours. On Independencia: *Café Corales*, Flores Magón opposite Buses Ballezano, good beef sandwiches. *Nutripan*, No 221, cakes, pastries and bread, including brown; sliced brown bread at *La Patita*, No 60; wide choice of bread and cakes at *El Parralense*, off Independencia on C Los Ojitos.

Mercado Hidalgo on the corner of Plaza Principal, *comedores*, fruit, vegetables, shoes, etc. Boutiques on Independencia. **Centro Naturista El Vergel**, in front of Casa Alvarado, massage, physiotherapy, natural medicines, herbs and vitamins for sale, etc. **Homeopathic pharmacy**, 20 de November 90. **Shopping**

Buses The bus station is outside the town; 20 minutes' walk, on Av Independencia, east of centre, taxi about US$2. To **Durango**, Transportes Chihuahuenses US$18, 6 hours. To **Zacatecas**, Omnibús de México, US$30, 9 hours. To **Chihuahua**, frequent departures, 2½ hours, US$7 2nd class, US$10.50 1st. Also to **Guachochi** (see page 138). Few bus lines start here so it is difficult to reserve seats. Buses Ballezano to Guachochi leave from office on Carlos Fuero y Flores Magón at 0800, 1230, 1545, US$4. **Transport**

Banks *Banco Unión*, in *Hotel Adriana* complex, exchange until 1200, poor rates, similarly at *Banamex* opposite. Good rates at *Bancomer*, Plaza Principal until 1200. Opposite is *Cambios de Oro*, no commission, good rates, open Mon-Fri 0900-1900, Sat until 1400. *Cambios Palmilla*, Maclovio Herrera 97, Plaza Baca, good rates, open daily 0900-2100. Also at Gasolinera Palmilla on road to Santa Bárbara, 3 kilometres out of town. **Communications** Post Office: on Del Rayo, just over bridge from centre, open 0800-1500. **Tourist office** There is no tourist office but advice may be had from the Cámara de Comercio, Colegio 28, T20018. **Directory**

An alternative route to Parral from Chihuahua is by Ruta 24, which turns south from Ruta 16, 38 kilometres west of Chihuahua. It is a lonely road, if shorter than the major road, and in good condition. After 50 kilometres there is a restaurant and Pemex station with magna sin at the turning to Satevó. At Km 110 is *Centro Trailer El Chamuco*, restaurant, rooms to let (**C**), clean, hot water. A few kilometres further is Valle Zaragoza, lots of *comedores*, Pemex magna sin. Then nothing until Parral. **Routes**

Parral to Durango

Ruta 45, south of Parral, is in good condition all the way to Durango. Pemex magna sin is available at Villa de Nieve, just before Caunutillo. Here, three kilometres down a winding road, well signed, is Pancho Villa's hacienda, with an excellent museum (give a donation to the man who opens the door). Villa was given the hacienda in exchange for promising to lay down his arms and retire to private life (28 July 1920). After Revolución the road becomes dead straight for many kilometres. Pemex magna sin (and a federal document check) at the big cross roads for Torreón. Between Rodeo and Durango, is the 'Western landscape' beloved of Hollywood film-makers. Cinema enthusiasts can

Durango environs

visit the Western sets of Villa del Oriente (nine kilometres from Durango) and Chupaderos (10.5 kilometres), both decaying (especially the latter) but smelling authentically of horse (Cía San Juan del Río buses go there or take a taxi, US$14, which takes you to both sets with a 15-minute stay at each). Also after Rodeo there are some beautiful villages along the river. Four kilometres off the road, at San Juan del Río, is a Pemex station with magna sin. Half-way down the side road to San Juan is a signed road to Coyotada, off which is a four-kilometre road to Pancho Villa's birthplace and museum (modest, a few artefacts and photos, free, donation welcome). For extensive new information on this region we are grateful to Francesca Pagnacco (Exeter, UK).

Durango

Population: 600,000
State Population: 1995
1,430,964
Altitude: 1,924m
Phone code: 18
Colour map 2, grid C3

Victoria de Durango, capital of Durango state: founded in 1563 (Km 926 – some 260 kilometres southwest of Torreón). It is a pleasant city, with parks, many beautiful old buildings (see the Casa de los Condes de Suchill, now Bancomer, on 5 de Febrero), a Cathedral (1695) and a famous iron-water spring. The main street is Av 20 de Noviembre. Parque Guadiana at west edge of town, with huge eucalyptus trees, is a nice place to relax. Good views of the city from Cerro de Los Remedios: many flights of steps up to a chapel.

Excursions   Presa Victoria can be reached by bus from Durango; one can swim in the lake enclosed by the dam. Balneario La Florida on the outskirts is pleasant (take green 'Potreros' bus on C Pasteur). Take a bus from Plaza Boca Ortiz to the big *hacienda* in Ferreria, a seven-kilometre walk along mostly deserted roads leads to the Mirador la Ventana with great views.

Santiago Papasquiaro is three hours north on Ruta 23 (on the way, in Canatlán, are Mennonite colonies), **D** *Hotel División del Norte*, Madero 35, T186-20013, in a former convent; the owner's husband was in Pancho Villa's División del Norte. *Restaurant Mirador*, across from the market, good food. There are a number of hot springs in the area, Hervideros is the most popular, take the bus to Herreras, then 30 minutes' walk. **Tepehuanes**, one hour further on, is a small pleasant town with two hotels. Walk to Purísima and then to a small, spectacular canyon. A dirt road continues to **Guanacevi**, a mining town in the Sierra.

Durango is on the Coast-to-Coast Highway from Mazatlán to Matamoros. The 320-kilometre stretch of road from Durango west to Mazatlán is through splendid mountain scenery. 60 kilometres from Durango is El Tecuán Parque Recreativo, nice forest location, no facilities but camping free. For a day trip, go as far as **El Salto** (96 kilometres), seven buses a day, but go early to get ticket. The town is dirty and

Durango

■ Sleeping
1 Campo México Courts
2 Casa Blanca
3 Posada Durán
4 Posada San Jorge
5 Roma

Not to scale

uninviting, but the people are very friendly (**E** *Hotel Diamante*, Fco 1 Madero, T60700, clean, basic, friendly, no running water in room, recommended).

Between Durango and Zacatecas is **Sombrerete**, a small, lively and pretty colonial silver mining town, which at the height of its prosperity at the end of the 17th Century rivalled Zacatecas, and has 10 good churches and the superb, partially restored Franciscan convent **San Mateo**, 1567. Next door to it is the elliptical **Chapel of the Third Order**. (Hotels: **D** *Avenida Real*, clean, restaurant. **E** *Real de Minas*, T493-50340, clean, comfortable, enclosed parking. **E** *Villa de Llerena*, T493-0077, on main plaza, clean but dark rooms; *La Calera* restaurant, good). Seven kilometres north of the Durango road 12 kilometres before Sombrerete is the Sierra de los Organos or Valley of the Giants, now a national park, where John Wayne made several of his westerns. It is named after the organ-like basaltic columns which are supposed to resemble organ pipes. Good hiking possibilities.

A *Fiesta Mexicana*, 20 de Noviembre y Independencia, T121050, F121511, very pleasant, lots of plants. **A** *Motel Los Arcos*, T87777, near bus station, Heróica Colegio/ Militar 2204, T172216, good restaurant. **B** *Campo México Courts*, 20 de Noviembre extremo Ote, T187744, F183015, good but restaurant service poor. **B** *Casa Blanca*, 20 de Noviembre 811 Pte, T13599, F14704, nice, big old hotel in the centre, unguarded parking lot. **B** *Posada San Jorge*, Constitución 102 Sur, T13526, F16040, old colonial building, patio, large rooms, friendly, parking, recommended. **C** *Reyes*, 20 de Noviembre 220, clean. **C** *Roma*, 20 de Noviembre 705 Pte, T/F120122, clean, comfortable.

D *Gallo*, 5 de Febrero 117, with bath, clean, motorcycle parking, recommended. **D** *Reforma*, 5 de Febrero y Madero, T131622, authentic 60s lobby, clean, comfortable rooms, free indoor parking, good restaurant, recommended. **D** *Karla*, P Juárez opposite bus station, T16348, small, clean, friendly but noisy. **D** *Pancho Villa*, P Juárez 206, opposite bus station, T187311, across roundabout from bus station, clean, pleasant, TV. **D** *Plaza Catedral*, Constitución 216 Sur, T132480, well-appointed. **D-E** *Posada Durán*, 20 de Noviembre 506 Pte, T12412, colonial inn on Plaza de Armas, recommended by AAA, good atmosphere, helpful staff. **E** *Oasis*, Zarco between 20 de Noviembre y 5 de Febrero, with bath, hot water, rooms on the top floor have a good view. **E** *Buenos Aires*, Constitución 126 Nte, T123128, fairly clean.

Youth hostel Villa Deportiva Juvenil, Av Heróico Colegio Militar with 20 de Noviembre, dormitory, gym, pool.

Good breakfasts at *Café Salum*, 5 de Febrero y Progreso, nice. *Mariscos Ramírez*, in front of the market, good seafood. *La Peña*, Hidalgo 120 north, Friday night is fiesta night with local music and singing, very popular. There is a good food store on the first block of Progreso where local foodstuffs are displayed in bulk. *El Zocabón*, on 5 de Febrero, off main plaza , recommended. *Gorditas Gabino*, Constitución 112 Nte, very cheap, good. Also recommended is *La Unica* on 20 de Noviembre y Pasteur. *Gardy*, F de Urdiñola 239, Calle Nueva Viscaya, T187162, vegetarian.

Feria first half of **July**.

Sleeping
■ *on maps*
Price codes:
see inside front cover

Eating
● *on maps*

Festivals

To Ciudad Juárez & Chihuahua

Av Felipe Pescador

To Mexico City & Zacatecas

Voladores

Cuauhtémoc

Porras

Lázaro Cardena

1 ■

Mexico

Transport **Air** Guadalupe Victoria Airport (DGO) is 5 kilometres from centre. There are international flights from Chicago (Mexicana), Los Angeles (Aero California) and Tucson (Aerolitoral), and domestic flights from Chihuahua, Ciudad Obregón, Culiacán, Guadalajara, Hermosillo, Ixtapa, Mazatlán, Mexico City, Monterrey, Tijuana and Torreón.

Buses Bus station out of town: minibus No 2 to centre, US$0.25. Several buses a day cross the Sierra Madre Occidental to **Mazatlán** (Transportes Chihuahuenses, 1st class, 7 hours, US$14.80), 0400 and 1000. This is recommended if you cannot do the Los Mochis-Chihuahua journey, sit on left side. 2nd class buses for camera buffs stop more frequently. **Guadalajara**, US$22.25; **Chihuahua**, US$32, 10 hours. 2nd class bus to **Hidalgo del Parral**, 7 hours, US$18 with Transportes Chihuahuenses. **Zacatecas**, Omnibús de México, 4½ hours, US$7.75. Town buses stop running early in evening, so try to arrive before dark if you wish to avoid a long walk or taxi ride to centre.

Directory **Airline offices** *Mexicana*, T136299, *Aero California*, T177177, 0800-1900. *AeroMéxico*, next to Cathedral, T178828, 0900-1900. **Banks** *Bancomer*, near Villa Deportiva Juvenil. **Communications** Post Office: Av 20 de Noviembre 500 B Ote. **Email:** at 5 de Febrero 203, US$2.50 hour. **Tourist office** On large roundabout at edge of city centre, helpful.

Zacatecas

Founded 1548, capital of Zacatecas state (Km 636 from capital). This picturesque up-and-down mining city is built in a ravine, pink stone houses towering above one

Zacatecas

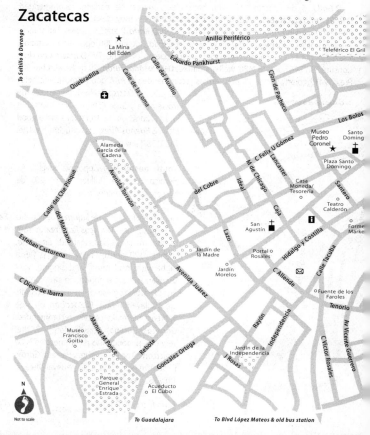

To Saltillo & Durango

Anillo Periférico

Teleférico El Gril

★ La Mina del Edén

Eduardo Pankhurst

Quebradilla

Calle del Auxilio

Calle de la Loma

Cjon de Pacheco

Los Bolos

Museo Pedro Coronel ★

Santo Doming ✝

Alameda García de la Cadena

C Felix U Gómez

M de Chicago

C Félix U Gómez

Plaza Santo Domingo

Avenida Torreón

del Cobre

Ideal

Casa Moneda/ Tesorería

Santero

Teatro Calderón

Calle del Che Pinque

del Manzano

Caja

San Agustín ✝

Forme Marke

Esteban Castorena

Lazo

Jardín de la Madre

Portal Rosales

Hidalgo y Costilla

Calle Tacuba

C Diego de Ibarra

Jardín Morelos

Avenida Juárez

C Allende

✉

Fuente de los Faroles

Tenorio

Museo Francisco Goitia

Manuel M Ponce

Rebote

Rayón

Independencia

Av Vicente Guerrero

González Ortega

Jardín de la Independencia

C Víctor Rosales

J Rosas

N

Parque General Enrique Estrada

Acueducto El Cubo

Not to scale

To Guadalajara

To Blvd López Mateos & old bus station

another and scattered over the hills. The largest silver mine in the world, processing 10,000 tonnes of ore a day or 220 tonnes of silver, is at **Real de Angeles**.

The **Cathedral** (1730-52) with fine Churrigueresque façade; the **San Agustín** church, with interior carvings now being restored; the Jesuit church of **Santo Domingo** and the little houses behind it (in the church, ask the sacristan to turn the lights on so you can see the frescoes in the sacristy by Francisco Antonio Vallejo). **Plaza Hidalgo** and its statues; the **Casa Moneda** (better known as the Tesorería, **founded 1810**); the **Teatro Calderón**, and the chapel of **Los Remedios** (1728). The **Mina del Edén**, Av Torreón y Quebradilla, is worth a visit, the old mine has a short section of mine railway in operation (not a proper train), tour lasts about one hour, commentary in fast Spanish, admission US$2 (see below); there is also a disco in the mine, entry US$10, buy ticket before 2030, varied music. On the way to the mine note the interesting façade (1738) brought from the hacienda of Los Condes de San Mateo, which now adorns the main offices of the local cattle-breeding association.

Zacatecas is famous for its *sarapes* and has two delicacies: the local cheese, and *queso de tuna*, a candy made from the fruit of the nopal cactus (do not eat too much, it has laxative properties). Visit the small *tortilla* factories near the station, on the main road. Several good silverware shops around the Cathedral area. Zacatecas is reckoned by many travellers to be the most pleasant town in this part of Mexico.

The **Museo Pedro Coronel** on Plaza Santo Domingo.   Houses an excellent

Sights

Population: 150,000
State Population: 1995
1,336,348
Altitude: 2,495m
Phone code: 492
Colour map 2, grid C4

Mexico

Museums

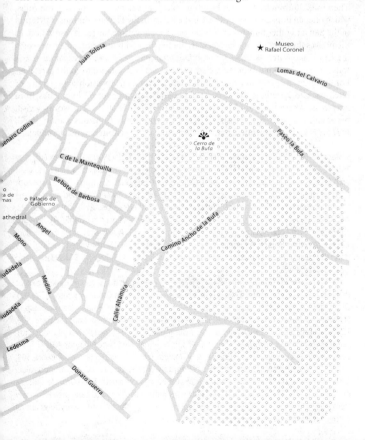

collection of European and modern art (including Goya, Hogarth, Miró, Tapié) as well as folk art from Mexico and around the world (take a guide to make the most of the collections). ■ *1000-1400, 1600-1900; closed Thursday, US$4.35*. The **Rafael Coronel Museum**, housed in the ex-Convento de San Francisco, has a vast collection of masks and puppets, primarily Mexican, nice garden. ■ *US$4.35, students US$1.75, closed Wednesday*. The **Cerro de La Bufa**. Recommended for the views which dominate the city, best light in early mornings, nice walk, crowded Sunday, contains the **Museo de la Toma de Zacatecas**, commemorating Pancho Villa's victory over Huerta's forces in 1914 (■ *US$0.60*). There is also a statue of Villa, an observatory, and the Mausoleo de Los Hombres Ilustres, on the hill. ■ *Cablecar, US$0.80 one way, starts at 1000, finishes 1800 (cancelled when windy)*. The **Museo Francisco Goitia**, housed in what was once the governor's mansion, is by the Parque General on Enrique Estrada, Col Sierra de Alicia near the old **Acueducto del Cubo**, with modern paintings by Zacatecans. ■ *US$0.80*.

Excursions   Beyond Zacatecas to the east lies the Convento de Guadalupe, a national monument, with a fine church and convent, which now houses a museum of colonial religious art. ■ *US$3.45, Tuesday-Sunday 1000-1700*. Next door is Museo Regional de Historia, under development. Frequent buses, No 13, from López Mateos y Salazar, near old terminal, US$0.15, 20 minutes. Visit also the **Chicomostoc** ruins (also known as **La Quemada**) 56 kilometres south by taking the 0800 or 1100 Línea Verde bus from main terminal to Adjuntas (about 45 minutes, US$0.60), on the Villanueva road. Then walk 30 minutes through beautiful, silent, nopal-cactus scenery to the ruins, which offer an impressive view. There is the Palace of the Eleven Columns, a pyramid of the Sun and other remains on a rocky outcrop, in various stages of restoration. In themselves the ruins are not spectacular, but together with the setting they are worth the trip. Take water. ■ *US$3.35; no information on site, so ask for explanations*. A museum is being built. Women are advised to keep at a distance from the caretaker. For the return from the junction at Adjuntas wait for a bus (possibly a long wait), or hitch back to Zacatecas. **Jerez** is an old colonial town about 65 kilometres from Zacatecas, where the wide brimmed *sombrero charro* is still worn, worth a visit, becoming popular with tourists; C *Hotel Leo*, short walk from bus station, good; D *Hotel Félix*, recommended; frequent buses to Zacatecas from new bus terminal.

Sleeping   L *Mesón de Jobito*, Jardín Juárez 143, Centro, T/F43500 (in Mexico City
■ *on maps*   T55142728/52075666), in heart of Centro Histórico, small, select hotel, attractive restaurant
Price codes: with international and Mexican cuisine. L *Quinta Real*, Av González Ortega, T29104, beauti-
see inside front cover   ful, built around old bull ring (said to be the 2nd oldest in Latin America), aqueduct goes past the front door. **AL** *Continental Plaza*, opposite Cathedral, on Av Hidalgo, T26183. **AL** *Galería*, López Mateos s/n, T23311, near old bus station, very comfortable. **AL** *Howard Johnson's*, Blvd López Mateos y Callejón del Barrio, T23311. **A** *Aristos*, Lomas de Soledad, T21788. **A** *María Bonita*, Av López Velarde 319, T24545, F26645, hot water, heating, very good. **B** *Posada de La Moneda*, near Cathedral, Av Hidalgo 413, T20881, F23693, nice and clean, but a bit noisy.

   D *Posada de los Condes*, Juárez 107, T21093, F21650, a bit noisy, rooms darkish except those at front with balconies. **D** *Condesa*, opposite *Posada de los Condes*, Av Juárez, T21160, OK, helpful, some rooms quiet with good views of Cerro de la Bufa, cheap restaurant. **D** *Colón*, Av López Velarde 508, T20464, clean, showers. **D** *Gami*, Av López Mateos 309, T28005, rooms with TV, OK. **D** *Insurgentes*, Insurgentes 114, off Plaza del Vivar, without bath, hot showers extra. **E** *Barranca*, opposite old bus terminal, Blvd López Mateos 401, T21494, poor value, and noisy traffic. **E** *Conde de Villarreal* (was *Zamora*), Plaza de Zamora 303, T21200, with bath, central, very basic. **E** *Del Parque*, González Ortega 302, clean, good value. **E** *Morelos*, Morelos 825, T22505, economical, very basic, shared bath. **E** *Río Grande*, Calzada de la Paz 217, T25349, with bath (**F** without), ask for quiet room on the patio, beautiful view from one side, clean, friendly, hot water, good value; the cheap hotels (very few) are all within 5 minutes' walk of the old bus station, towards Av Hidalgo.

Motels **B-C** *Hacienda Del Bosque*, T20747, Fortín de la Peña, close to centre so may be noisy, attractive rooms, good food, has camping facilities and hook-ups, showers and toilets, only for small cars and vans. **C** *Parador Zacatecas*, excellent, Pan-American Highway.

Youth hostel Parque del Encantado 103, T21151/21891, CP 98000, on bus route to centre from bus station, no singles. Also Av de los Deportes beside Estadio Fco Villa, CP 98064, T29377.

Trailer park at Morelos junction, about 20 minutes northwest of the city, where Route 54 Saltillo-Guadalajara crosses Route 49. Hook-ups, basic, US$8, behind Pemex.

Eating
● *on maps*

La Cuija, in old Centro Comercial on Av Tacuba, good food, music, atmosphere. *El Jacalito*, Juárez 18, excellent *comida corrida* and breakfast. *La Cabana*, Jardín de la Independencia, cheap, excellent set meals. *Burgerlandia*, beside Teatro Calderón, good. *El Carnerito*, Av Juárez 110, cheap. *Pizzería Fugazetta*, Av Guerrero 136, charming, good pizzas. *Mr Laberinto*, Av Hidalgo 342344, luxury atmosphere, 1970s décor, quite cheap, good breakfast and dinners, recommended. *Nueva Galicia*, Plazuela Goitia 102, wide range Mexican food. *El Paraíso*, Av Hidalgo y P Goitia, corner of market, bar/restaurant, nice atmosphere, closed Sunday; opposite is *Nueva España*, bar with loud music, closed Sunday. *Chapa Rosa*, Plaza Genaro Codina 112, good, moderate prices. *La Unica*, Aldana 243, good food, cheap. *La Cantera Musical*, Av Tacuba, Mexican, good atmosphere, poor a/c, good food but drinks limited after 2000. Good cafés include: *Cafetería La Terazza*, in market on a balcony, very pleasant, good *malteadas*. *Café Arús*, Centro Comercial, Av Hidalgo y Costilla, serves breakfast. *Los Comales*, Hidalgo 611, good value. *Acrópolis*, opposite Cathedral, 50-year-old café and diner, good breakfast, slow service. *Café Zaz*, Av Hidalgo y Costillo 201. Several cheap restaurants along Av Independencia. *El Quixote* (at *María Bonita Hotel*), Av López Velarde, good breakfasts. *Helder*, near old bus station, excellent breakfasts. Plenty of good coffee shops selling real *expresso* coffee. Many good *tamales* sold on the streets.

Health food Store at Rayón 413, excellent food at reasonable prices.

Festivals

Spreads over most of **September**, a rainy month here. There are bullfights on Sunday.

Shopping

Interesting shops on Independencia selling hats, riding equipment, fruit and other produce, not touristy. Cheap postcards for sale in the toy shop and stationers on Hidalgo on the right if coming from the Cathedral. Between Hidalgo and Tacuba the elegant 19th century market building has been converted into a pleasant shopping centre (popular café on balcony, reasonable). The market is now dispersed in various locations a few blocks to the southwest.

Transport

Air La Calera airport (ZCL) 27 kilometres north of city (taxi US$20), flights daily to Mexico City, Tijuana, Guadalajara, Ciudad Juárez, Morelia, Aguascalientes. Direct flights to several US cities: Chicago, Denver, Los Angeles, Oakland, California.

Trains Zacatecas is on the line Mexico City-Querétaro-Chihuahua. Check locally whether there are trains running.

Buses New terminal 4 kilometres north of town; taxi US$1.20; red No 8 buses from Plaza Independencia (US$0.15) or white camionetas from Av González Artegú (old bus station on Boulevard A López Mateos only serves local destinations). To **Durango** with Estrella Blanca, 5 hours, US$8 (if continuing to Mazatlán, stay the night in Durango in order not to miss the views on the way to the coast). To **Chihuahua** via Torreón, 12 hours, 1st class US$33; **Jiménez**, US$27; to **Hidalgo del Parral** with Chihuahuenses and Omnibús de México, US$30, 10 hours; **San Luis Potosí** with Estrella Blanca or Trans Chihuahuenses, 3½ hours, US$6. **Ciudad Juárez** 1st class with Omnibús de México at 1930, 11 hours, US$45; to **Guadalajara**, 6½ hours, several companies, US$15, but shop around for different journey times (road windy and in poor condition in parts). **Aguascalientes**, every 30 minutes, 2½ hours, US$3, or US$6 1st class. To **León**, 4½ hours, US$10. To **Mexico City**, 8 hours, US$25. Apart from buses to Mexico City, Chihuahua and a few other major towns, most routes do not have bookable seats. As the majority of buses pass through Zacatecas and don't start their journey there, long waits are probable.

Directory   **Airline offices** *Mexicana*, T23248. *Taesa*, T20050. **Banks** *Banamex* recommended. *Bancomer* has a Visa cash dispenser and gives cash (pesos) on Visa cards. Both on Av Hidalgo. **Communications** Fax: service at *Telégrafos*, Av Hidalgo y Juárez. Email: *Café @rroba*, Félix U Gómez 520 B, 0900-2200, daily, US$2 per hr, chmnet@gauss.logicnet.com.mx. **Post Office**: C Allende 111. **Cultural centres** *Alianza Francesa*, Callejón del Santero 111, T40348, French film every Tues at 1900 (free). **Hospitals & medical services** *Santa Elena Clinic*, Av Guerrero, many specialists, consultation, US$15. **Language school** *Fénix Language Institute*, T21643. **Laundry** *Lavandería El Indio Triste*, Juan Tolosa 828, US$.80 per kg. **Tour companies & travel agents** *Cantera Tours*, Centro Comercial El Mercado, Av Ramón López Velarde 602-6, Local A-21T29065. *Viajes Masoco*, Enlace 115, Col Sierra de Alca, T25559, tours to Chicomostoc and Jerez, US$15.50. **Tourist offices** *Prolongación González Ortega s/n*, Centro, T40393, friendly, helpful, free maps, good hotel information, including cheaper hotels. Ask here about language classes at the University.

Aguascalientes

Founded in 1575, capital of its state, the name comes from its hot mineral springs. An oddity is that the city is built over a network of tunnels dug out by a forgotten people. It has pretty parks, a pleasant climate, delicious fruits, and specializes in drawn linen threadwork, pottery, and leather goods.

Sights
Km 508
Population: 750,000
State Population: 1995
862,335
Altitude: 1,987m
Phone code: 491
Colour map 3, grid B2

Palacio de Gobierno (once the castle home, started in 1665, of the Marqués de Guadalupe: splendid courtyard, with decorated arches on two levels; the grand staircase in the centre, built in the 1940s, blends in magnificently with the earlier structure; also colourful murals), and the Palacio Municipal (good town plan from entrance booth). Among the churches **San Antonio**, on Zaragoza, should not be missed, neither should the **Carmelite Temple of San Marcos**, baroque façade, built 1655-1765 on the site of a chapel which had existed since the mid-16th century, in the barrio of San Marcos. Beyond the church of San Marcos is an enormous concrete commercial and leisure complex known as Expo-Plaza which includes the *Fiesta Americana* hotel and new bull-ring. There is much industrial development on the outskirts.

Teatro Morelos next to the Cathedral; T50097. The **University** is 30 minutes from the city centre. Its administrative offices are in the ex-Convento de San Diego, by the attractive Jardín del Estudiante, and the Parián, a shopping centre.

South of the centre on Boulevard J M Chávez is an aviary, with 50 species of bird, in the **Parque Héroes Mexicanos**. The market is not far away. There is carp fishing at El Jocoqui and Abelardo Rodríguez. The bull ring is on Av López Mateos.

Museums   **Museo de Aguascalientes**, C Zaragoza 505, is by the Church of San Antonio; it has a collection of contemporary art, including fine paintings by Saturnino Herrán, and works by Orozco, Angel, Montenegro and others. ■ *Daily from 1030, except Sunday and Monday*. The **José Guadalupe Posada** museum is in a gallery, by the Templo del Cristo Negro, close to a pleasant garden – Díaz de León (known locally as the Jardín del Encino); it has a remarkable collection of prints by the lithographer Posada, best known for his *calaveras*, macabre skeletal figures illustrating and satirizing the Revolution and events leading up to it. Cultural events in the courtyard on Saturday and Sunday. ■ *Tuesday-Sunday 1000-1400, 1700-2100, shut Monday. US$1.*

Museo de Arte Contemporaneo, C Juan de Montoro, just east of Plaza. The **Casa de las Artesanías** is also near the main square. The **Casa de la Cultura**, on Venustiano Carranza and Galeana Norte, is a fine colonial building. It holds a display of *artesanía* during the *feria*. Nearby, on Carranza is the **Museo Regional de Historia**.

Hacienda de San Blas, 34 kilometres away, contains the **Museo de la Insurgencia**, with murals by Alfredo Zermeño.

Thermal Baths Balneario Ojo Caliente, east end of town beyond train station, at end of Calzada Revolución (Alameda), claims to have been founded in 1808, some private baths (US$3.50 per hour) and two public pools (closed 1998), take bus marked 'Alameda'; saunas, squash and tennis courts on the site. At end of Alameda fork right to Deportivo Ojocaliente, a large complex with several pools, US$0.65. 20 kilometres north is a thermal swimming pool at Valladolid (camping is permitted in the grounds, secure, night watchman in attendance).

Encarnación de Díaz (**C** *Hotel Casa Blanca*, Anguiano 107 on the plaza, hot water, secure parking nearby, reasonable restaurant) is halfway to **Lagos de Moreno** (Km 425), a charming old town with fine baroque churches; the entry over the bridge, with domes and towers visible on the other side, is particularly impressive. See the ex-convent of the Capuchins and the Teatro Rosas Moreno. *Feria* last week of July and first of August. Lagos de Moreno has several hotels (on main plaza: **C** *La Traje*; **D** *París*; **D** *Plaza*, best rooms facing the front, small and dark at the back; just off the plaza is **C** *Colonial*. **C** *Victoria*, two blocks away, near river) and restaurants (recommended is *La Rinconada*, colonial building, old photos, on plaza two blocks behind Municipalidad, which is on main plaza, good *enchiladas*). A road (Route 80) turns off right to Guadalajara, 197 kilometres away; the same road leads, left, to Antiguo Morelos via San Luis Potosí. 42 kilometres southwest on Route 80 is the colonial town of **San Juan de los Lagos**, a major pilgrimage centre, crowded during Mexican holidays, famous for glazed fruit; many hotels. There is also a fine view on entering this town: as the road descends you see the twin-towered church with its red, blue and yellow tiled dome.

Excursions

Mexico

LL *Elizabeth*, Av de La Convención de 1914 (inner ring road) 107 Sur, T782926, F782036. **LL** *Fiesta Americana*, on Expo-Plaza, Col Flores, T186010, F186118. **L** *Gran Hotel Hacienda de la Noria*, Av Héroe de Nacozari Sur 1315, Col La Salud, T184343, F185259 (in Mexico City T55142728/52075666), very comfortable, jacuzzi in all rooms, Mexican, Japanese and international cuisine, gardens, swimming pool. **AL** *De Andrea Alameda*, Alameda esq Av Tecnológico, T184417, F183759, old hacienda, large rooms, good restaurant. **B** *Hotel Suites Alamo*, Alameda 129, T56885, pool. **D** *Imperial*, Moctezuma y 5 de Mayo, on plaza, large sparse rooms. **D** *Praga*, with TV, Zaragoza 214, T52357, OK.

On main plaza D *Señorial*, Colón 104, T52179, rooms with phone, helpful lady speaks English. **D-E** *Don Jesús*, Juárez 427, T55598, hot water 3 hours morning and evening, good value. **D** *San José*, Hidalgo 207, T51431, friendly. At Rep de Brasil 403, **E** *Casa de Huéspedes*, near main plaza, and at No 602, **D** *Gómez*, T70409. Cheap hotels around Juárez market (Av Guadalupe y C Guadalupe Victoria), eg **E** *Brasil*, Guadalupe 110, T51106, with bath, quiet, and **D** *Bahía*, No 144, with bath.

E *Casa de Oro*, on Hidalgo 205, next to San José, good. **E** *Maser*, Montoro 303, T53562, 3 blocks from Cathedral on Montaro, *comedor* for breakfast. **E** *México*, no bath or hot water. **E** *Casa Belén*, López Mateos y Galeana, T158593, central, hot water, clean, friendly. **E** *Reforma*, Nieta y Galleana, 1 block west of main plaza, colonial style, large courtyard, rooms bit dark, friendly, clean.

Motel A *El Medrano*, Chávez 904, T55500, F68076. **B** *La Cascada*, Chávez 1501, T61411.

Youth hostel Av de la Convención y Jaime Nuno s/n, CP 20190, T700873.

Sleeping
■ *on maps*
Price codes:
see inside front cover

Try the area around 5 de Mayo for *pollo rostizado*. Good *comida corrida* at *Sanfer*, Guadalupe Victoria 204, also at *Woolworth* restaurant 1 block away. *Jacalito*, López Mateos, also near Plaza Crystal, cheap *tortas*, clean. *Mexicali Rose*, López Mateos, US$10 *comida corrida*. Also *Freeday* video bar and restaurant, near Benito Juárez statue, lively at weekends. *Café*

Eating
Lack of conventional facilities, except in some of the more expensive hotels

Mexico

Parroquia on Hidalgo, 1 block west off Madero, good, cheap. *Jugos Acapulcos*, Allende 106, good *comida corrida*.

Festivals The area is famous for viticulture; the local wine is called after San Marcos, and the *feria* in his honour lasts for 3 weeks, starting in the middle of **April**, with processions, cockfights (in Mexico's largest *palenque*, seating 4,000), bullfights, agricultural shows etc. The Plaza de Armas is lavishly decorated. The *feria*, covered by national TV networks, is said to be the biggest in Mexico. Accommodation can be very difficult and prices double during the *feria*. Bullfight also on New Year's day.

Shopping Many shops selling boots made to order, eg at *Zapatería Cervantes*, Guerrero 101 Sur y Nieto, T151943. **Bookshop** *Librería Universal*, Madero 427. **Market** Main one at 5 de Mayo y Unión, large and clean, with toilet on upper floor.

Transport **Air** The airport (AGU) is 21 kilometres from the town centre. Domestic flights to Culiacán, Mexico City, Monclova, Monterrey, Puerto Vallarta, Reynosa, San Luis Potosí, Tijuana and Zacatecas with a variety of airlines. US flights to Los Angeles with AeroMéxico.

Trains Train station at east end of Av Madero (T153858). Bus 17 goes there from C Hornedo, 1 block behind *Hotel Reforma*. To Torreón daily 1010, arrives 1930, returns 0900, arrives 1945.

Buses Bus station about 1 kilometre south of centre on Av Circunvalación Sur with post office and pharmacy. To **Guadalajara**, 5 hours, US$8.25 1st, US$15.50 ETN, 5 a day (2 hours direct with Estrella Blanca). To **Guanajuato** US$4.50 with Flecha Amarilla, 3½ hours. To **Zacatecas**: US$3, every 30 minutes, 1st class US$6, 2½ hours. To **Ciudad Juárez**, US$46.25. ETN (luxury service) to **Mexico City** US$34, 9 a day, 7 hours, ordinary fare US$14. Some 170 kilometres to the east is San Luis Potosí (see page 110). To **Tijuana**, Elite, 1530, 2100, US$108; to **Monterrey**, Turistar Ejecutivo US$35 also to **Nuevo Laredo**, US$52, Cd Juárez, US$84, Chihuahua, US$62; to **Morelia**, Primera Plus, 4 a day, US$17; **León**, 21 a day, US$7; **Puerto Vallarta** at 2230, US$31; **Querétaro**, 8 a day US$15.50; to **San Luis Potosí**, Futura, 16 a day between 0600-2300, US$9.

Directory **Airline offices** *Aero California*, T72310. *AeroMéxico*, T70252. *Taesa*, T82698. **Banks** On Plaza Inverlat, *ATM* takes Amex. *Banamex*, ATM. **Communications** Post Office: Hospitalidad, near El Porián shopping centre. **Email:** *Café @rroba*, A Obregón 450 d2, US$2 per hr. **Cultural centres** *El Centro Cultural Los Arquitos*, Narcozari y Alameda, T170023, formerly a 19th Century bathhouse, restored 1993, museum, bookshop, café. **Hospitals & medical services** Red Cross: T152055. **Tourist offices** Federal tourist office in Palacio de Gobierno, T60123. Tourism Development office at Av de La Convención Pte 1626, T125585, F122357.

León

Population: 1,200,000
Altitude: 1,885m
Phone code: 47
Colour map 3, grid B2

León

After about 1,600 kilometres of desert or semi-arid country, we now enter, surprisingly, the basin of Guanajuato, known as the Bajío, greener, more fertile, higher (on average over 1,800 metres), and wetter, though the rainfall is still not more than 635 to 740 millimetres a year. The Bajío is the granary of central Mexico, growing maize, wheat, and fruit. The towns we pass through, León, Irapuato, and Celaya, have grown enormously in population and importance. 50 kilometres before Léon there are some impressive buttes (isolated, steep hills).

(Km 382) León (de los Aldamas), in the fertile plain of the Gómez River, is now said to be Mexico's fifth city. Nuño de Guzmán reached the area that is now León on 2 December 1530. Local farms and estates were granted to the Spaniards until eventually Don Martín Enríquez de Almanza decreed on 12 December 1575 that a city, called León, would be founded if 100 volunteers could be persuaded to live there for 10 years, or a town if only 50 could be found. On 20 January 1576 a town was founded by Dr Juan Bautista de Orozco but León did not become a city until 1830. The business centre is the delightful **Plaza de Constitución**.

There is a striking **Palacio Municipal**, a cathedral, many shaded plazas and gardens. **Sights** The Palacio Municipal is said to have been built as a result of a winning lottery ticket bought by a local doctor! The small **cathedral** was started by Jesuits in 1744, but they were expelled from Mexico in 1767 by Carlos III. It was eventually finished in 1837 and consecrated in 1866. The **Templo Expiatorio** has been under construction for most of this century, catacombs open 1000-1200 (closed Wednesday), well worth seeing. The **Teatro Doblado** on Av Hermanos Aldama stages opera, ballet, classical concerts, contemporary theatre and houses art exhibitions. The **Casa de Cultura** also houses exhibitions and is 'buzzing' at night. Also worth seeing is the **Casa de Las Monas** on 5 de Mayo 127/9 where Pancho Villa issued the Agrarian Reform law on 24 May 1915, and the beautiful **Santuario de Guadalupe**. A new tourist attraction, the **Parque Metropolitano** on Prolongación Morelos, Camino a la Presa, opened in 1995. León is the main shoe centre of the country (high quality shoes in the Plaza del Zapato shopping mall, Hilario Medina, and cheaper ones in places round the bus station), and is noted for its leather work (buy in the Plaza Piel shopping mall opposite the Plaza del Zapato, and along Belisario Domínguez), fine silver-trimmed saddles, and *rebozos*.

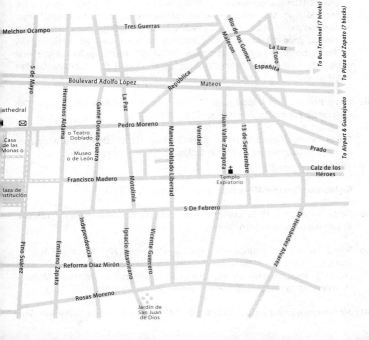

Museums The **Museo de León** on Hermanos Aldama has art exhibitions. ■ *Tuesday-Saturday, 1000-1400 and 1630-1930, Sunday 1000-1400.* The **Museum of Anthropology and History** on Justo Sierra is a beautiful building; the **Explora Science Museum** is on Boulevard Fco Villa 202, T116711.

Excursions Between León and **Silao** (bus from León US$0.70), left off Highway 45 at Km 387 (going south) are the famous swimming pools of Comanjilla fed by hot sulphurous springs. There is a luxurious, hacienda-style hotel (**AL**) with restaurant. From Silao take micro to León Centro and change at Los Sauces for Comanjilla turn-off, well signposted. 11 kilometres beyond Silao, at Los Infantes, a short side road through the picturesque Marfil canyon leads to Guanajuato.

Sleeping **AL** *Fiesta Americana*, Blvd A López Mateos 1102 Ote, T136040, F135380. **A** *Camino Real*, Blvd A López Mateos 1311 Ote, T163939, F163940. **B** *Real de Minas*, A López Mateos 2211, T710660, F712400, recommended. **B** *Estancia*, A López Mateos 1317 Pte, T/F169900, restaurant recommended. **B** *Condesa*, on Plaza, Portal Bravo 14, T131120, F148210, 3-star, restaurant recommended. **B** *León*, Madero 113, T141050, F132262, 3-star. **B** *Robert*, Blvd L Mateos Ote 1503, T167213. **B** *Roma*, Nuevo Vallarta 202, T/F161500, 3-star. **B** *Señorial*, near Plaza, Juárez 221, T145959. **C** *Fénix*, Comonfort 338, 2-star. *Colón*, 20 de Enero 131, 1-star. **D** *Fundadores*, J Ortiz de Domínguez 218, T161727, F166612, better than similarly-priced hotels in centre. **D** *Posada de Fátima*, Belisario Domínguez 205, clean, central. **D** *Rex*, 5 de Febrero 104, near Plaza, recommended. **D** *Monte Carlo*, Justo Sierra 432, clean, friendly, central. **D** *Tepeyac*, Av Obregón 727, 1-star, OK, rooms a bit dark. Also several cheaper ones near market.

At **Silao** (for airport) **B** *Villa Victoria*, Alvaro Obregón 245, T21831, F22422; *San Javier*, C Coecillo y Libramiento de Silao, T20642.

Eating Several in Colonia Jardines del Moral area in centre, including: *El Jardín de Ling Choy*, Blvd A López Mateos 2105 Pte, T177507, also *La Pagoda de Ling Choy*, López Mateos 1501 Ote, T149026, both Chinese. *Kamakura*, Rocío 114, T184383, Japanese. *Lupillos*, Blvd A López Mateos 2003 Ote, opposite stadium, T711868, pasta and pizza; also several branches of the US fast food chains. Many restaurants in the Gran Plaza complex next to Macdonalds. Vegetarian snacks at *GFU*, on López Mateos, near IMSS building. *Cadillac*, $\frac{1}{2}$ block from cathedral on Hidalgo, good *comida corrida* US$5. *Panteón Taurino*, Calzado de Los Héroes 408, T134969, expensive but worth visiting to see the incredible decor. Look for listings in local guides, lots of places offering seafood, pizzas, Spanish, Oriental, Arab, Argentine, Brazilian and Mexican food.

Nightlife Lots of **bars** including *JJ Sport*, Rocío 115-A, Jardines del Moral. *Pepe's Pub*, Madero 120, Zona Centro. *Fut-bol Bar*, Blvd Hidalgo 923-B, T178020.

Discos Including *Domus*, Blvd López Mateos 2611 Ote, T116614. *Ossy's*, Salida a Lagos por Av Paseo de los Insurgentes, T176880. *La Iguana*, C Comercial Insurgentes Local 4 y 5B, T181416.

Nightclubs *Piano Bar Maya*, Prolongación Calzada 112, T169734.

Festivals *Fiesta*: San Sebastián, **19-24 January**, very crowded, good fun (if staying outside León, take an early bus out of town when leaving).

Shopping Several shopping centres: *La Gran Plaza*, Blvd López Mateos 1902 Pte. *Plaza Mayor*, Av de las Torres, Esq Prolongación Morelos. *Plaza León*, Blvd López Mateos 1102 Ote. *Centro Comercial Insurgentes*, Blvd López Mateos y Alud, Jardines del Moral. *Plaza del Zapato*, Hilario Medina y Blvd López Mateos, T146442. *Plaza Piel*, Hilario Medina y López Mateos.

Transport **Air** New international airport, del Bajío (BJX), 18 kilometres from León, 6 kilometres from

Silao: American Airlines to Dallas and Memphis; Mexicana to Chicago; Continental (T185254) to Houston and Orlando; AeroMéxico and Mexicana to Los Angeles; Taesa to Oakland, California; Mexicana to San José, California. Several airlines fly to Mexico City (with connections to external and Mexican destinations), Ciudad Juárez, Durango, San Luís Potosí, Torreón, Puebla, Puerto Vallarta, Querétaro, Tijuana, Monterrey, Chihuahua, Zacatecas, Guadalajara, Morelia. Taxis are expensive to León; either take one to Silao, US$10, and then take a bus to León or Guanajuato, or walk 1½ kilometres to the main road and take a bus from there.

Buses Terminal has post office, long distance phones, restaurant and shops (street plan on sale, US$2.75). Plenty of buses to **Mexico City**, US$14 (US$28 ETN, T131410), **Querétaro**, US$6. Irapuato and Celaya. Frequent services to **Guanajuato**, 40 minutes, US$3 ETN. To **Zacatecas**, 4½ hours, US$10. To **Poza Rica**, Omnibús de México, T135798, US$21. Same company to **Monterrey**, US$25, and **Guadalajara**, every 30 minutes, first at 0600, 4 hours, US$8, US$16 ETN. Many buses run to **Ciudad Juárez**, US$50, passing through the cities mentioned above (eg Durango US$16.50, Chihuahua, US$38.50). Primera Plus, T146000; Elite, T169879; Futura, T145451; Turistar Ejecutivo, T145451; Turistar Plus y Estrella Blanca, T145451, 133216; Tres Estrellas de Oro, T169879, 169932.

The highway from León to Mexico City is dual carriageway all the way.

Airline offices *AeroMéxico*, Madero 410, T166226, 149667. *Mexicana*, Blvd A López Mateos 401 Ote, T149500, 134550. *Taesa*, Pedro Moreno 510 Centro, T143660, 161940. *Continental*, Blvd A López Mateos 2307 Pte, T135199, 143937, 91-80090050. **Banks** *Bancomer*, Belisario Domínguez 322, and *Banco Internacional* on the plaza. **Communications** Post Office: on Obregón y 5 de Mayo, open Mon-Fri 0800-1900. **Tour companies & travel agents** *Viajes Sindy de León*, 20 de enero 319, T131224, F165080, recommended. *Jovi de León*, Madero 319 Centro, T145094, F166217, recommended. **Tourist office** In Edif Cielo 501 on López Mateos Pte y M Alemán. Helpful but limited information (good city map available free at Palacio Municipal).

Directory

Guanajuato

The beautiful capital of Guanajuato state and a university city, now declared a national monument and Unesco World Heritage Zone, has been important for its silver since 1548. Its name derives from the Tarascan Quanax-Huato, place of frogs. It stands in a narrow gorge amid wild and striking scenery; the Guanajuato River cutting through it has been covered over and several underground streets opened – an unusual, though often confusing system. Some, like Padre Belaunzarán, are not entirely enclosed; others, such as Hidalgo, are, so they fill with traffic fumes (as does much of the city). The Túnel Los Angeles leads from the old subterranean streets to the modern roadway which connects with the Carretera Panorámica and the monument to Pipila (see below). Taking traffic underground has not relieved the congestion of the surface streets, which are steep, twisted and narrow, following the contours of the hills. Some are steps cut into the rock: one, the **Callejón del Beso** (Street of the Kiss), is so narrow that kisses can be – and are – exchanged from opposite balconies. Parking for hotels is often at a distance away. Over the city looms the shoulder of La Bufa mountain (you can hike to the summit up a trail which takes one hour: from the Pipila monument (see below), follow the main road for about one kilometre to the hospital. Walk past the hospital to a power station where the main trail starts; if you pass the quarry, note the quality of the stone masonry on the mason's shelter).

Population: 150,000
State Population: 1995
4,393,160
Altitude: 2,010m
Phone code: 473
Colour map 3, grid B3

Guanajuato contains a series of fine museums (see below) as well as the most elegant marble-lined public lavatories in Mexico. The best of many colonial churches are **La Compañía** (Jesuit, 1765, note the brick ceiling, by the University); **San Diego** (1663) on the Jardín de la Unión; the **Parroquia del Inmaculado Corazón de María**, on Juárez, opposite Mercado Hidalgo, has interesting statues on the altar; the **Basílica** (Cathedral, 1693, on Plaza de la Paz), **San Roque** (1726) on a small park

Sights

Mexico

between Juárez and Pocitos, and **San Francisco** (1671).

When Father Hidalgo took the city in 1810, the Alhóndiga was the last place to surrender, and there was a wanton slaughter of Spanish soldiers and royalist prisoners. When Hidalgo was himself caught and executed, along with three other leaders, at Chihuahua, their heads, in revenge, were fixed at the four corners of the Alhóndiga. There is a fine view from the **monument to Pipila**, the man who fired the door of the Alhóndiga so that the patriots could take it, which crowns the high hill of Hormiguera. Look for the 'Al Pipila' sign. Local buses go from *Hotel Central*, on the hour, to the Pipila, otherwise it's a steep but short climb up (about 15 minutes); a number of cobbled stairways through picturesque terraces go up (or down) for example Callejón del Calvario, leading off Sopeña. Take a camera for fine panoramic views of the city. The Carretera Panorámica which encircles the city passes the Pipila monument. At its eastern end the Panorámica goes by the **Presa de la Olla**, a favourite picnic spot; good cheap meals available from roadside stalls. From the dam, Paseo de la Olla runs to the city centre, passing mansions of the wealthy silver barons and the **Palacio de Gobierno** (note the use of local stone). Also on the east side of the Panorámica is Casa de las Leyendas, with entertainment for children. Local pottery can be bought in the **Mercado Hidalgo** (1910), in the centre; there is also a Casa de Artesanías behind the **Teatro Juárez** (see Entertainment below).

Museums A most interesting building is the massive **Alhóndiga de Granadita**, built as a granary, turned into a fortress, and now a museum with artefacts from the pre-Colombian and colonial periods. ■ *US$1.80.* An unusual sight shown to visitors is of mummified bodies in the small **Museo de las Momias** in the Panteón Municipal, above the city off Tepetapa; buses go there ('Momias', signposted Panteón Municipal, US$0.10, 10 minutes, along Av Juárez), but you can walk. It's a gruesome and disturbing spectacle, glass cases of naturally mummified bodies, their mouths gaping from skin contraction, some bodies with shoes and socks on, and, it is claimed, the smallest mummy in the world. ■ *US$2, US$0.75 to take photos, tip the Spanish-speaking guide, open 0900-1800, large queues on Sunday.* The **Museo**

Guanajuato

Iconográfico del Quijote, opened in 1987 at Manuel Doblado 1, is highly recommended: paintings, drawings, sculptures of the Don, entry free (see **Festivals** below for Festival Cervantino). The painter **Diego Rivera** was born in C de Pocitos, No 47; visit the museum there with permanent collection of his work on various floors showing his changing styles; on the ground floor are his bed and other household objects; temporary exhibitions also held. ■ *US$1 opens 1000*. Also on Pocitos No 7, just across from the University is the **Museo del Pueblo** in a beautiful 17th century mansion; it has one room of work by the muralist José Chávez Morado, a room of selected items of all Mexican art forms and temporary exhibitions. ■ *Tuesday-Sunday, 0900-1900, US$1*. In the University is the **Museo Alfredo Dugues**, of natural history. ■ *Monday-Friday, 0900-1400, 1630-1900*. The University was founded in 1732; its façade of coloured stone, above a broad staircase, glows richly at sunset. Also in the University is the **Sala Hermenegildo Bustos**, which holds art exhibitions. The School of Mining has a **Museo de Minería** on the Carretera Panorámica, north of the city. ■ *Monday-Friday 0900-1300, 1630-1900*.

Excursions

Tours of the city and outskirts by minibus cost US$6.15, rising to US$18 for tours out of town and US$40 to the south of the state; if you want a guide in English, prices multiply. The splendid church of **La Valenciana**, one of the most impressive in Mexico, is five kilometres out of town on the Dolores Hidalgo road; it was built for the workers of the Valenciana silver mine, once the richest in the world. The church, dedicated to San Cayetano, has three huge, gilt altars, a wooden pulpit of sinuous design, large paintings and a cupola. The style is churrigueresque, done in grey-green and pink stone; the façade is also impressive.

The **Valenciana mine** (1548) is surrounded by a wall with triangular projections on top, said to symbolize the crown of the King of Spain. The huge stone walls on the hillside, supported by enormous buttresses, created an artificial level surface from earth excavated higher up the slope. With care you can walk freely in the whole area. Guides are available to take you round (about 30 minutes), interesting. ■ *0900-1700, US$1*. A local 'Valenciana' bus starts in front of *Hotel Mineral de Rayas*, Alhóndiga 7, leaving every 30 minutes during the day, US$0.10, 10 minutes ride; 10 minutes walk between church and mine pit-head; don't believe anyone who tells you a taxi is necessary, but don't walk to it along the highway, it is narrow and dangerous. At the mine is a gift shop with a reasonable selection of silver. Also well worth a visit is the Casa de Conde de la Valenciana, formerly the mining company's head office, now an attractive craft shop with pleasant café. If you stay on the 'Valenciana' bus to the end of the line, a church brightly-painted and turned into a restaurant, you will see a dirt road to the left which leads to a recreation area with reservoir and picnic area, also several walks into the hills.

At the former *Hacienda de San Gabriel de Barrera* (now a four-star hotel, AL, T23980, F27460), at Marfil on the Irapuato road, there are 15 patios and gardens, a chapel, museum and colonial furniture (take bus marked 'Marfil' from outside *Hotel Central*, 10 minutes). 30 kilometres west of

Guanajuato is **Cerro Cubilete**, with a statue of Christ the King, spectacular view of the Bajío, local buses take one and a half hours, US$1.15, 0700, 0900, 1100, 1400, 1600 from Guanajuato (also from Silao for US$0.75). Dormitory at the site (US$1.50) food available, but best to take your own, plus drink (and toilet paper); last bus up leaves at 1600 from Silao and Guanajuato. See also the three local silver mines of Rayas, the city's first mine, La Valenciana (see above) and La Cata. All are to the north of the city, reached from the Carretera Panorámica. It is possible to visit the separating plant at **La Cata**, but visitors are not admitted to mines. At the old site of La Cata mine (local bus near market), is a church with a magnificent baroque façade and the shrine of El Señor de Villa Seca (the patron of adulterers) with *retablos* and crude drawings of miraculous escapes from harm, mostly due to poor shooting by husbands.

Presa de Insurgentes, a few kilometres up the mountain highway, has a parking area and a couple of tables for picnics; it is a nursery for plants to be planted around the countryside. Four kilometres up a narrow road from **Presa de la Olla** is **Panifiel**, a village with an old church. Children will take visitors into the mission whose doors are held shut against stray animals by a large, round stone just inside the doors (a child's arm is small enough to fit beneath to move the stone). Take lunch.

Sleeping
■ *on maps*
Price codes:
see inside front cover

At the bus station you will probably be met by a tour guide who will suggest a hotel, perhaps arrange a discount, and then try to persuade you to buy a tour of the city. The guides have a hotel price list, which is higher than the official price list, which in turn differs from what hoteliers actually charge, but not by much. Most hotels charge in advance. Some also try to insist on a room with two beds, which is more expensive than with a double bed. Hotel rooms can be hard to find after 1400. Book ahead during holidays and weekends. There are frequent water shortages, so that hotels with no reservoirs of their own have no water on certain days; when there is water, do not drink it.

On Dolores Hidalgo road exit **AL** *Castillo de Santa Cecilia*, tourist-bus haven, T20485, F20153. **AL** *Parador San Javier*, Plaza Aldama 92, opposite side of Dolores road, T20626, F23114, genuine hacienda style; and Motels given below. On exit to Irapuato, **AL** *Real de Minas*, Nejayote 17 at city entrance, T21460, F21508; on the Panorámica, not far from Pipila, **AL** *Paseo de la Presa*, T23761, F23224, quiet, good value, fantastic views, small pool, tennis courts. On Jardín de la Unión, **AL** *Posada Santa Fe*, No 12, T20084, F24653, good restaurant on open terrace with excellent service, and **B** *San Diego*, No 1, T21321, F25626, good bar and restaurant but slow, colonial style, very pleasant. **AL** *La Casa de Los Espíritus Alegres*, ex-Hacienda La Trinidad No 1, Marfil, 3 kilometres from Guanajuato, T/F473-31013, 18th century hacienda house now owned by US artists, bed and breakfast, library, parking, bus stop close by, no children, pets or smoking, in USA contact Joan Summers, 2817 Smith Grade, Santa Cruz, CA 95060, T408-4230181. **B** *Hostería del Frayle*, Sopeña 3, next door to Teatro Juárez, T21179, rooms next to the Teatro are noisy, nice adjoining *Café Veloce*. **B** *La Abadía*, San Matías 50, T/F22464.

On Insurgents are **D** *Alhóndiga*, No 49, T20525, good, clean, quiet, restaurant *La Estancia*; **C** *del Conde*, No 1, T21465, with excellent and reasonable restaurant *Mesa de los Reyes*, and **D** *Murillo Plaza*, No 9, T21884, hot water. **D** *Posada La Condesa*, Plaza de La Paz, small, basic rooms, clean, hot water, drinking water available. **D** *El Minero*, Alhóndiga 12A, T25251, restaurant. **D** *Mineral de Rayas*, Alhóndiga 7, T21967, with bath, clean linen, pool, garage, restaurant, bar and *Danny's Bar*. **D** *Molino del Rey*, Campañero 15, T22223, simple and quaint. **D-F** *Casa Kloster*, Alonso 32, T20088, book ahead, good location, very friendly, rooms for 4, a few with private bath, some without windows, clean, very good value, repeatedly recommended, often full, gardens, no parking (touts in town will say it is shut, but it is not).

On Juárez **C-D** *Central*, No 111, T20080, near Cine Reforma, friendly, good restaurant but noisy for rooms beside it. **C** *El Insurgente*, No 226, T22294, pleasant, clean, avoid rooms on 4th floor where there is a disco, good breakfasts. **D** *Granaditos*, No 109, with bath, hot showers, clean, friendly, run down. **D-E** *Posada del Carmen*, No 111A, T29330, recommended, bath, TV. **D** *Posada San Francisco*, Av Juárez y Gavira, T22084, on Zócalo, good value but noisy on outside rooms, no hot water, lovely inner patio. **D** *Reforma*, No 113, T20469, with bath, overpriced, little hot water. **E** *Posada Juárez*, T22559, recommended; and **E** *del Comercio*, T22065. Other hotels are mostly in our C range. Accommodation in private home, **F** per person *Marilú Ordaz*, Barranca 34, T24705, friendly, 5 minutes' walk from market.

Motels Many on Dolores Hidalgo road exit: **A** *Villa de Plata*, T21173. Trailer Park 1 kilometre north of *Mineral de Rayas*, there is a sign on the Ruta Panorámica, hot showers. **B** *De Los Embajadores*, Paseo Embajadores, T20081, Mexican décor, restaurant, famous Sunday lunch. **B** *El Carruaje*, T22140, F21179. **B** *Guanajuato*, T20689, good pool and food, quiet, recommended. **B** *Valenciana*, T20799.

Tourists are given the à la carte menu; ask for the *menú de día* or *comida corrida* (but they stop serving them early). Reasonable food, *comida corrida* very good value, at *El Retiro*, Sopeña 12, near Jardín de la Unión; also on Sopeña, *Pizzería Mamma Fan* and *La Colmena*. *Pizza Piazza*, Plaza San Fernando and several other locations, cheap and good. *Cuatro Ranas*, in *Hotel San Diego*, Jardín Unión 1, good location but loud US music and overpriced, reasonable *menú del dia*, US$3. *Valadez* on Jardín de la Unión y Sopeña, excellent *menú del día*; also on Jardín de la Unión, *Bar Luna* and *El Gallo*, popular with travellers, good. *La Lonja*, on the corner of the Jardín opposite *Hotel San Diego*, is a pleasant and lively bar, beers come with complimentary dish of tacos with salsa; meals at *Casino de Guanajuato* on Jardín de la Unión. *La Bohemia*, C Alonso, opposite *Casa Kloster*, overpriced and uninspiring. *Mesón de Marco*, Juárez 25, 'rare' Mexican food, flights in balloon offered at US$100, T27040. *La Carreta*, mostly chicken, fair, on Av Juárez about 200 metres up from Mercado Hidalgo; also on Juárez, *Tasca de los Santos*, on Plaza de la Paz, smart. *Diva's*, Plaza de la Paz 62B, smart, highly recommended. *El Zaguán*, Plaza de la Paz No 48, very good and cheap food, entertainment inside courtyard. *Café Truco 7*, Callejón Truco, off Plaza de la Paz, menu of the day US$2-3, relaxed family atmosphere, recommended, theatre in back room Friday and Saturday pm. *La Flor Alegre* (*casa de pan pizza*), Plazuela de San Fernando 37, good, clean and cheap. *El Mexicano*, Juárez 214, good *comida corrida* with dessert and drink. *El Granero*, Juárez 25, good *comida*, until 1700. *La Mancha*, C Galarza 7, recommended for *comida corrida*, reasonable price. *Cafetería Neverria*, opposite University, good, inexpensive. *Vegetariano*, Callejón Calixto 20, inexpensive, sells wholewheat bread. *Jelly Shot Bar*, below *Hostería del Frayle*, lovely atmosphere, cheap drinks, recommended. *El Unicornio Azul* on Plaza Baratillo is a good health food shop, *pan integral*, also sells cosmetic products. Also on Plaza Baratillo is *Café Las Musas*, good value breakfast. You can eat well and cheaply in the market (eg *bolillos* – sandwiches, fresh fruit juices) and in the *locales* behind Mercado Hidalgo (some open till 2200; better value on 1st floor; the ladies have been forbidden by their rivals in the covered market to shout the merits of their menus, but their mime is just as engaging). Good *panaderías* also, eg *Panadería Internacional*, Contarranas y Sopena, sells wholewheat bread. Dairy products are safe, all coming from the pasteurizing plant at Silao. Also from Silao come strawberries in December.

Eating
● *on maps*

Sketches from classical authors out of doors in lovely old plazas from April to August. Teatro Juárez on Sopeña (a magnificent French-type Second empire building, US$0.50 to view, US$0.35 to take photos), shows art films and has symphony concerts, US$1.50. A band plays in Jardín de la Unión (next to the theatre) 3 times a week. The Teatro Principal is on Cantarranas, by Plaza Mexiamora. 2 nightclubs have been recommended: *Disco El Grill* on Alonso (100 metres from *Casa Kloster*) and *Disco Los Comerciales* on C Juan Valle.

Entertainment

Arts festival, the *Festival Cervantino de Guanajuato* (in honour of Cervantes), is an important cultural event in the Spanish-speaking world, encompassing theatre, song and dance. There is a mixture of free, open-air events, and paying events. Internationally famous artists from around the world perform. The festival lasts 2 weeks, is highly recommended and is

Festivals

Mexico

very crowded; accommodation must be booked in advance (usually held the last 2 weeks in October, check dates). For information telephone Guanajuato 47320959, or Mexico City 55334121, The International Cervantino Festival, Alvaro Obregón 273, 4th Floor, Colonia Roma, 06700 México DF. *Viernes de las Flores* is held on the Friday before Good Friday, starting with the Dance of the Flowers on Thursday night at about 2200 right through the night, adjourning at Jardín de la Unión to exchange flowers. Very colourful and crowded. During the Christmas period, students dress up in traditional costumes and wander the streets singing carols and playing music. Groups leave from in front of the theatre at 2030.

Shopping Fonart shop opposite La Valenciana church (see above). Excellent selection of handicrafts. High prices but superb quality.

Transport **Trains** Station is off Tepetapa (continuation of Juárez), west of centre. Passenger service no longer runs, although a high speed trainline linking the whole State of Guanajuato is under construction.

Buses A clean, new bus terminal has opened on the road to Silao, near toll gate, 20 minutes from centre by bus, US$0.30, pick up from outside Mercado Hidalgo. Taxi to centre, US$1.50. Some buses go through the centre en route to the bus station, and you can get off here. At the terminal is a tourist office (reported permanently closed but with notice board listing hotels, addresses and phone numbers, when open has free town map), post office, long-distance phone (not international; 0700-2200), restaurant, left-luggage and shops. To **Mexico City**, US$11, 5 hours, about 7 companies, each with 3-4 buses daily, ETN US$25, 3 Estrellas de Oro at 0700 and 1500 via Dolores Hidalgo (US$2.25), San Miguel Allende (US$3.30 – also Flecha Amarilla, $1\frac{1}{2}$ hours) and Querétaro, $3\frac{1}{2}$ hours (US$5.75); super express at 1700; also Omnibús de México (T27702/20438), Estrella Blanca and Chihuahuenses (book in advance). Bus Guanajuato-Dolores Hidalgo, Flecha Amarilla, US$2, 1 hour 25 minutes (of which the first 20 minutes is from bus station back into Guanajuato, so catch bus outside *Hotel Mineral de Rayas* – same applies to buses for San Miguel de Allende).

To **Guadalajara** 5 hours, US$10.15, several companies, via Léon and Lagos de Moreno. To **Zacatecas**, with Omnibús de México 1st class, at 2100, US$10, $5\frac{1}{2}$ hours. Half hourly service to **Morelia** Flecha Amarilla, 2nd class, 4-5 hours, US$6). To **San Luis Potosí**, US$8 en route to Tampico (US$20 with Omnibús de México). Buses also to Monterrey, Ciudad Juárez and Nuevo Laredo, but some involve a change in León. In fact, to many destinations it is better to go to León and pick up the more frequent services that go from there (buses every 10 minutes Guanajuato-León, US$1.30). Flecha Amarilla have more buses, to more destinations, than other companies in this area; it is not the most reliable company and buses tend to leave when full. Set fare for city buses, US$0.25.

Directory **Banks** *Bancomer, Banca Serfín, Banamex*, 0900-1100. **Communications** Post Office: corner of Subida San José, by La Compañía church. **Telephone:** international phone calls from phone booths with coins, or collect. Long-distance offices in Miscelánea Unión shop, by Teatro Principal and on Pocitos, opposite Alhóndiga de Granaditas. **Email:** on Alonso 70B, 0900-1800, Mon-Sat, US$5 hour. **Language**

schools **Spanish courses:** for foreigners at the University and at *Instituto Falcón*, Presa 80, T7311084, F7310745, www.infonet.com.mx/falcon, good quality instruction. Also at the University are many US exchange students so you can usually find someone who speaks English. See also **Learning Spanish** in Essentials. **Laundry** *Lavandería Internacional*, Alhóndiga 35A, self or service wash (US$3.45). *La Burbuja Express*, Plazuela Baratillo. *Lavandería Automática Internacional*, Manuel Doblado 28, US$3.50; *Lavandería del Centro*, Sopeña 26, US$3.60. **Tourist offices** Plaza de la Paz; they have all hotel rates (except the cheapest) and give away folders. Map on sale US$1.35, compared with US$2.70 for state map with town plans at bus station. Federal representative office, Juárez 250 (opposite old bus station).

Irapuato is noted for delicious strawberries, which should on no account be eaten unwashed. It is a prosperous industrial and agricultural town and an important distribution centre.

Irapuato
Route 45, Km 315
Population: 475,000
Colour map 3, grid B3

In the town centre, around the **Plaza de los Fundadores** and the **Jardín Hidalgo**, there is a cluster of historic buildings. The **Templo del Hospital** built around 1550, rebuilt 1617, façade completed 1733, said to have the country's largest chandelier. Outside, the **Cruz Monolítica** commemorates the visit of San Sebastian of Aparicio. The façade of the **Templo de San Francisco**, also known as El Convento (1799), is a mixture of baroque and neo-classical. The huge **Parroquia** (parish church) was rebuilt mid-18th century. The **Presidencia Municipal**, 19th century, incorporates a former 18th century school, the **Colegio de Enseñanza para Niños**. The fountain, **Fuente de los Delfines** was given to the town by Emperor Maximilian.

Unfortunately, the centre has been invaded by unsightly and incongruous modern buildings. Just off the centre is the 16th century church of **San José**, with fine examples of American indigenous art. Also the **Templo of Nuestra Señora de Guadalupe** (1890), with its striking late neo-classical gold-leaf-decorated interior.

Sleeping and eating *Hotel Real de Minas*, T62380, overpriced, with equally overpriced restaurant, on Portal Carrillo Puerto, quiet rooms on church side. *Restaurant El Gaucho*, Díaz Ordaz y Lago.

Celaya

Celaya is famous for its confectionery, especially a caramel spread called *cajeta*, and its churches, built by Mexico's great architect Francisco Eduardo Tresguerras (1759-1833), a native of the town. His best is considered to be El Carmen, with a fine tower and dome. He also built a fine bridge over the Río de la Laja. On 12 October 1570 the royal cedula was granted to found a town, the Villa de la Purísima Concepción de Zalaya, close to an Otomí settlement known as Nat Tah Hi. Zalaya, or Celaya, was in fact founded on 1 January 1571, but both dates are celebrated locally. Its status was elevated to that of city on 20 October 1655 by King Felipe IV of Spain. The city was located in a productive agricultural region and soon became important as a supply centre for the mines, thereby boosting commerce and making it prosperous. It was an important trading post on the route to Guanajuato, Zacatecas and Guadalajara as well as the transport of metals to the capital. The 17th and 18th centuries saw the construction of many great houses and religious buildings and in 1725 a university was founded. Don Miguel Hidalgo y Costilla arrived in Celaya with 40,000 men on 21 September 1810 in his quest for independence. He lodged in the Mesón de Guadalupe (now the *Hotel Guadalupe*) and received the support of the city, being proclaimed Captain General of the rebel army. He left with 50,000 fighters. Industrialization dates from 1836, when the first factory was built to produce thread and cloth. The railway arrived in 1878, the same year in which the first *cajeta* factory was started. Nowadays industrial enterprises include food processing, mechanical engineering, chemical products and others.

Km 265
Population: 420,000
Altitude: 1,800m
Phone code: 461
Colour map 3, grid B3

Templo del Carmen, built by Tresguerras in 1802-1807, the interior and exterior are neoclassical with a simple elegance, you can see Tresguerras' own paintings inside.

Sights

Mexico

Convento de San Francisco, one of the largest in the country, the interior is 17th century baroque. The façade of the cloisters was rebuilt by Tresguerras. **Templo de San Francisco** was rebuilt in 1683 after the original chapel was demolished. The façade is neoclassical and was rebuilt, together with the altars, by Tresguerras between 1810-1820. **Claustro Agustino** dates from the beginning of the 17th century and was the municipal prison until 1961. It is currently the Casa de la Cultura and often has art exhibitions. **Templo de San Agustín** was built in 1609 in the plateresque style. **Templo de la Tercera Orden** is another of Tresguerras' neoclassical works, built in 1820 with marvellous altars. **Columna de la Independencia** was built by Tresguerras and was the first monument in the country to celebrate Mexico's freedom in 1828. **Torre Hidráulica**, also known as the **bola de agua** (ball of water), has been adopted as the symbol of the city; it was inaugurated on the centenary of independence and holds one million litres of water. **Casa del Diezmo**, built at the end of the 17th century, now houses the tourist office. The **Presidencia Municipal** has impressive murals up the stairways in the entrance off the main square, a metamorphosis of people and events in Mexico's history, created in 1980 by Octavio Ocampo González, a local artist of international fame. Another of his murals, showing the evolution of man, is in the library of the **Instituto Tecnológico de Celaya**, on C Irrigación. The **Mausoleo de Tresguerras**, is a baroque chapel where the famous architect is buried.

Sleeping

There are some 30 hotels of different prices and standards; many of the better hotels are outside the centre.

AL *Celaya Plaza*, Blvd López Mateos y Carretera Panamericana, T46260, F46889, 143 rooms, tennis, spa, meeting rooms. **B** *Plaza Bajío Inn*, Libertad 133, T38603, F37353, 80 rooms, central, restaurant, disco, convention facilities, parking, medical service, laundry. **C** *Isabel*, Hidalgo 207, T22096, F33449, restaurant, bar, laundry, parking. **E** *Guadalupe*, Portal Guadalupe 108, T21839, F29514, very old hotel with historical connections, central, cheaper rooms without bath.

Eating

Many restaurants serving steak and others specializing in seafood. *El Caserío*, Blvd López Mateos 1302 Pte, T55608, Spanish cuisine. *La Mansión del Marisco*, Blvd López Mateos 1000, esq Fco Juárez, T55262, fish and seafood, live music at weekends. *El Mezquital*, Blvd A

Celaya

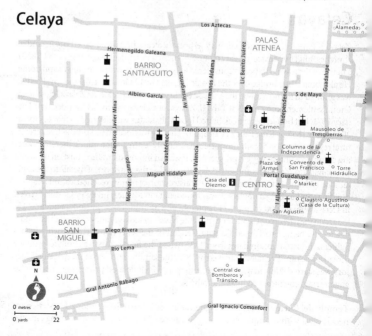

López Mateos 1113 Ote, meat and traditional barbeque. *Mamma O'Fan*, 3 restaurants, at Benito León 203, Blvd A López Mateos 1008 Ote, and Plaza Juárez 127, in Apaseo el Grande, Italian food, pizza, pasta, etc.

10-20 January is the fiesta of the appearance of the Virgin of Guadalupe in the Tierrasnegras barrio, one of the oldest districts of Celaya. There is drama, dancing, fireworks and eating a typical *antojito*, 'gorditas de Tierrasnegras'. **Easter** is marked by visiting several *balnearios*: Balnearios Los Arcos y Aguacaliente and others in the area, Cortázar, Villagrán, Juventino Rosas, Apaseo el Grande and Apaseo el Alto. There are processions through the streets, much eating of local delicacies, and on **Easter Sunday** Judas is burned in many places in the city. The Virgen del Carmen is celebrated **16 July**. The anniversary of the founding of the city is celebrated in **October**. The Day of the Dead is a movable feast, celebrated in the week leading up to the 2nd Monday in **November**, unlike the rest of the country. Since 1844 a Christmas regional fair has been held in the 2nd half of **December** with exhibitions of farming, livestock, crafts and cultural and sporting events.

Festivals

Six buses a day to Mexico City airport with Primera Plus. There is a 24-hour pharmacy at the bus station. Bus companies serving Celaya: ETN, T28664; Omnibús de México, T23614; Elite, T20533; Tres Estrellas de Oro, T23776; Flecha Amarilla, T22489; Tucán, T36543; Turismos de Celaya, T34280.

Transport

Tourist office *Casa del Diezmo*, Juárez 204, T/F34313, helpful.

Directory

From Celaya to Querétaro, to join the route from Eagle Pass (see page 114), there is a 56-kilometre limited-access toll motorway (US$4.35 a car), or the old road through Apaseo el Alto.

From Guanajuato, Celaya can be reached via the historic towns of Dolores Hidalgo, Atotonilco and San Miguel Allende. 15 kilometres from Guanajuato on the road to Dolores is **Santa Rosa**; in a story book setting in the forest is **D** *Hotel El Crag*, clean; *Restaurant La Sierra* next door (the Flecha Amarilla bus stops here on the way to Dolores Hidalgo). There are two or three other places, including *Rancho de Enmiedo*, good dried meat specialities and beautiful scenery. The road corkscrews up in spectacular fashion before winding down through impressive rocky outcrops and ravines to the plain on which Dolores Hidalgo stands. The last 10 kilometres or so are very arid.

Dolores Hidalgo

The home of Father Hidalgo, is 54 kilometres from Guanajuato, a most attractive, tranquil small town; celebrations are held on 15 and 16 September. The main square, or Jardín, is lovely, dominated by a statue of Hidalgo. On one side is the church of **Nuestra Señora de los Dolores** (1712-1778) in which Hidalgo gave the Grito; the façade is impressive, and the churrigueresque side altar pieces, one of gold leaf, one of wood are more ornate than the main altar. It is not always open. In an arcade beside the

Population: 135,000
Colour 3, grid B3

Mexico

church is the tourist office (limited). Also on the Jardín are many restaurants and cafés, and banks.

Sights **La Asunción**, Puebla y Sonora, has a large tower at one end, a dome at the other, with large murals and a tiled floor inside. Two blocks away, at Puebla y Jalisco, is Plaza de los Compositores Dolorenses with a bandstand. Between these two sites on Puebla is the post and telegraph office. Visit Hidalgo's house, **Casa Hidalgo**, Morelos y Hidalgo, a beautiful building with a courtyard and wells, many memorabilia and one room almost a shrine to the Father of Independence. ■ *Tuesday-Saturday 1000-1800, Sunday 1000-1700, US$4.35.* The **Museo de la Independencia**, on Zacatecas was formerly a jail, now has displays of striking paintings of the path of Independence. Traditional Talavera tiles still made here and ceramics can be seen all over the town. ■ *US$0.70.*

Excursions About five kilometres southeast of town on a dirt track (walk or hitch) are the ruins

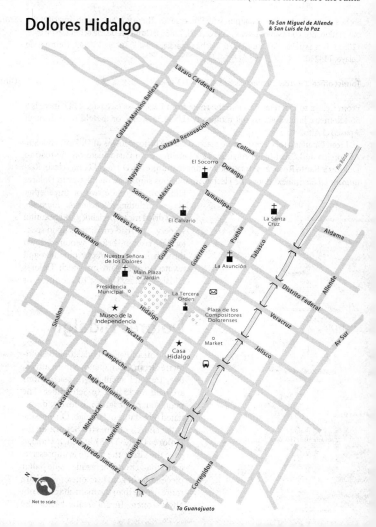

Dolores Hidalgo

To San Miguel de Allende & San Luis de la Paz

To Guanajuato

Not to scale

of the **Hacienda de la Erre**, Padre Hidalgo's first stop on the independence route after leaving Dolores (free entrance to the untended ruins and grounds). The standing walls are only three to four metres high; there are about four rooms with ceilings; the patio, with a lot of litter is overgrown, but the chapel has been rebuilt. Outside is the huge mezquite tree under which Hidalgo is supposed to have said mass for his insurgent troops.

The walk (one and a half to two hours) starts from the plaza, then take C Guerrero to the east, take Tamaulipas to the main road. Turn left for one kilometre to a gravel road on the left on a long curve. Follow this to the Hacienda in a fertile area with plenty of trees; in May there is much colour with the cacti in flower.

Sleeping *Hotel María Dolores*, Av de los Héroes 13, T20517, 2-star. **C** *Posada Las Campanas*, Guerrero 15, T20427. **D** *Caudillo*, Querétaro 8, just off plaza, opposite Cathedral, T20198, clean, good value. **D** *Posada Hidalgo*, Hidalgo 15, T/F20477, clean, dark rooms, TV. **D** *Posada Cocomacan*, on the plaza, T20018, pleasant colonial house where Juárez stayed, comfortable, good value, good food, parking, recommended. **E** *Posada Dolores*, on Yucatán, with bath, clean, OK, small room.

Eating *Caballo Blanco*, on Jardín by corner of Hidalgo and Guerrero, good value. Excellent ice cream at *Helado Torres*, southwest corner of Jardín. *Fruti-Yoghurt*, Hidalgo y Guerrero, just off Jardín, delicious yoghurt, wholefood cakes and biscuits, also sells homeopathic medicines, etc. **Market** On Tabasco, south side, between Jalisco and Hidalgo. Another market, near *Posada Dolores*, on Yucatán.

Transport Bus station is at Hidalgo y Chiapas, 5 minutes from main square; has restaurant, toilets, left luggage, local phones. Frequent buses to Guanajuato, Querétaro (US$3.80), León (US$3.65), Mexico City (US$10.50), San Luis Potosí (US$5) and San Luis de la Paz (US$2). To Aguascalientes, US$6.50, 2nd class, via San Felipe.

Directory **Tourist offices** On the Zócalo. They can direct you to places making the traditional talavera tiles which can be bought at very good prices.

Atotonilco About 20 kilometres further on is the small town of Atotonilco, where there is a church built around 1740 whose inside walls and ceiling are covered with frescoes done in black, red and grey earth: unrivalled anywhere for sheer native exuberance. It was from Atotonilco's church that Padre Hidalgo took the banner of the Virgen de Guadalupe to act as his battle standard.

Sleeping **A** *Parador El Cortijo*, Apdo Postal 585, San Miguel de Allende, T91-46521700, very good, pool open to non-residents US$3.30, below the hotel on Querétaro-Dolores Hidalgo road are Las Grutas thermal baths, which belong to the hotel. Take Dolores Hidalgo bus from San Miguel de Allende bus station, or 'Santuario' hourly bus from covered market off Plaza Allende near top of San Miguel: either passes the door.

Thermal Baths Across the river from Atotonilco is the tiny village of San Miguelito. A short distance beyond, natural thermal waters rise from the river bed; local women construct hot tubs, called *arenas*, by piling sand around the springs in which to wash clothes and themselves. There is a spa, the **Balneario Taboada** (admission US$2, open Wednesday-Sunday), between Atotonilco and San Miguel (about 20 minutes bus ride direct from San Miguel market; it is a long walk from the main road, better to go by car or taxi). The Spa has a small hot pool, a fine swimming pool and good fishing in a nearby lake – very popular (café open only Saturday and Sunday). Near the Spa is *Hacienda Taboada* hotel (five-star, large thermal pool, swimming pool, prior booking necessary – open only to guests). Another spa is close by, **Santa Verónica**, with huge clean pool, open 0900-1800, US$2.50, bus stops outside, recommended. From San Miguel de Allende, for either spa, catch bus from Mesones by the market.

San Miguel de Allende

Population: 150,000
Altitude: 1,850m
Phone code: 415
Colour map 3, grid B3

A charming old town on a steep hillside facing the broad sweep of the Río Laja and the distant blue of the Guanajuato mountains, is 50 kilometres north of Querétaro by paved road, 90 kilometres from Guanajuato. The city was founded as San Miguel in 1542, and Allende added in honour of the independence patriot born there. Its twisting cobbled streets rise in terraces to the mineral spring of El Chorro, from which the blue and yellow tiled cupolas of some 20 churches can be seen. It has been declared a national monument and all changes in the town are strictly controlled. The area around Parque Juárez and El Chorro is very picturesque with steep alleyways and women washing clothes in the springs. In recent years there has been a large influx of American residents (now numbering over 1,000) and tourists, with a consequent rise in prices.

Sights

Social life revolves around the market and the Jardín, or central plaza, an open-air living room for the whole town. Around it are the colonial **Palacio Municipal**, several hotels, and the **Iglesia Parroquial** (parish church), adorned by an Indian mastermason in the late 19th century, Zeferino Gutiérrez, who provided the austere Franciscan front with a beautiful façade and a Gothic tower; see also the mural in the chapel. The church of **San Felipe Neri**, with its fine baroque façade, is at the southwest end of the market. Notable among the baroque façades and doors rich in churrigueresque details is the **Casa del Mayorazgo de Canal**, and **San Francisco** church, designed by Tresguerras. The convent of **La Concepción**, built in 1734, now houses an art school, the **Centro Cultural Nigromonte**, locally known as Bellas Artes (good cafetería in its courtyard), one of the rooms off the courtyard contains a large mural by Siqueiros, locked up because of vandalism, but you can get the key from the secretary at the entrance; the summer residence of the Condes del Canal, on San Antonio, contains an art school and a language school, the Instituto Allende, started in the 1940s by Stirling Dickinson (which has an English-language library and runs Spanish courses, usually without accommodation, but some rooms can be rented – for others, see below). Tours of old houses and gardens start from the public library, Sunday 1215, four hours (US$8). A magnificent view of the city can be gained from the mirador on the Querétaro road (the views are also good before you get to the Mirador).

Excursions

A good all-day hike can be made to the **Palo Huérfano** mountain on the south side of town. Take the road to just before the radio pylon then take the trails to the summit, where there are oaks and pines. Between San Miguel de Allende and Celaya is **Comonfort** (25 kilometres); from there go three kilometres north to Rancho Arias: on a hilltop to the west are precolumbian pyramids. Cross the river north of the church and climb to ruins via goat-tracks. **El Charco del Ingenio** Botanical Gardens (reached by taking a bus to El Gigante shopping centre, turn left and continue for 15 minutes, or go up C Homobono, a more interesting and attractive route) cover an area of 64 hectares with lovely views, a deep canyon, an artificial lake and cacti. ■ *US$1 (free on Wednesday).*

Sleeping

Many weekend visitors from Mexico City: book ahead if you can

■ on maps
Price codes:
see inside front cover

A good source of information on inexpensive accommodation is the English language paper published weekly by the Anglo-Mexican Library on Insurgentes.

AL *Mansión del Bosque*, Aldama 65, T20277, half-board. **AL** *Villa Jacarandá*, Aldama 53, T21015, central, a couple of blocks behind cathedral, very good restaurant. **AL** *Casa Luna B&B*, Pila Seca 11, T/F21117, casaluna@unisono.net.mx, American-run, excellent breakfast included, beautiful themed rooms, no smoking inside, highly recommended. **AL** *Misión de los Angeles*, de luxe, 2 kilometres out on Celaya road, T21026, colonial style, swimming pool, convenient facilities. **A** *Posada de San Francisco*, main square, T20072, pleasant restaurant. **A** *Posada La Aldea*, C Ancha de San Antonio, T21022, colonial style, clean, quiet, swimming pool, gardens. **B** *Parador San Miguel Aristos*, at Instituto Allende, Ancha de San Antonio 30, T20149, students given priority, large rooms, some with a fireplace and kitchen, parking US$2. **B** *Rancho-Hotel El Atascadero*, T20206, on road to Querétaro, in an old colonial hacienda, very satisfactory. **B** *Vista Hermosa Taboada*, Allende 11, very popular, nice old colonial building, some ground floor rooms dark and noisy.

Near Jardín, on C Vinaron, **C** *Posada La Fuente*, has a few rooms, good food (by arrangement), Ancha de San Antonio 95, T20629. **C** *Posada de las Monjas*, Canal 37, T20171, with shower, excellent set meals in restaurant, clean and attractive, very good value, a converted convent, also has a few D rooms at back if you ask. **C** *Mesón San Antonio*, Mesones 80, T20580, renovated mansion, clean, friendly, quiet. **C** *Monteverdi*, T21814, clean, hot water; **C** *Posada Carmina*, Cuña de Allende 7, T20485, colonial building, courtyard for meals, recommended. **C-D** *Quinta Loreto*, Loreto 13, T22380, TV, clean, quiet, swimming pool, pleasant garden, next to Mercado de Artesanías, hot water problems, good, cheap food, restaurant closed in evening (but beware of mosquitoes). **D** *Casa de Huéspedes*, Mesones 27, T21378, family atmosphere, clean, hot water, popular, roof garden, nice location, good value. **D** *Sautto*, Dr Macías 59, T20072, for room with fridge, fireplace and bath, new rooms best, rustic, garden, hot water, parking, recommended. **D** *Hidalgo*, Hidalgo 22, hot water (but not all day), rooms not always cleaned and vary in quality. **D** *San Sebastián*, Mesones 7, T20707, near market, recommended, with bath, charming, large rooms with fireplace, clean, car park, noisy at front (most rooms at the back), courtyard. **E** unnamed *Casa de Huéspedes* on C Mesones, 150 metres east of Plaza Allende, clean, quiet, hot shower. **E** *Vianey*, del Fecolo; another cheap *Casa de Huéspedes* on Animas, just past the market building. **E-F** *La Huerta*, bath, clean, well-furnished, quiet, at the bottom of a dead-end street 4 blocks from the market in woodland, dark and unpleasant at night for lone females walking back, free parking, but watch your valuables, no phone. **F** per person *El Nuevo Hostal*, Jaime Nuno 28, T20674, shared bath, friendly, cosy, clean, kitchen and laundry facilities available.

Motels AL *Villa del Molino*, on road to Mexico City. **B** *Siesta*, on road to Guanajuato, with trailer park, gardens; *KAO campgrounds* further out on same road, quiet, grassy site, all facilities, pleasant, Dutch owner.

Mesón de San José, Mesones 38, Mexican and international cuisine, vegetarian dishes, excellent breakfasts, nice setting, German/Mexican owners, open 0800-2200, live music Sunday, gift shop, recommended. *Mama Mía*, C Umaran west of main square, main meals good but not cheap, free live folk music or films in pm, excellent cheap breakfasts. *Café de la Parroquia*, Jesus 11, good, French owner speaks English. *Andale Pizza*, Hidalgo 17, good and economical pizzas, salad and *comida corrida*, recommended. *Casa Mexas*, Canal 15, good American food, clean, popular with gringos, English TV. *Matador*, Hernández Maciás 76, clean, excellent food, not too expensive, recommended. *Italia*, hotel/restaurant, on Dr Hernández, pasta, nice; nearby on C Codo is *Harem*, Lebanese food, occasionally music, friendly. *Rincón Español*, opposite Correos, good *comida corrida*, recommended, flamenco at weekends. *El Jardín*, C San Francisco, close to Plaza, friendly service, good food, also vegetarian, violinist plays upstairs at weekends for price of a drink. *Flamingos*, Juárez, good set lunch US$4.50. *La Princesa*, Recreo 5, set menu 1300-2000, including glass of wine, live music from 2100, cosy cellar atmosphere. *La Guarida del Zorro*, Recreo 16 entre Correo y Hospicio, excellent steaks and *parrillada*, good value, pleasant atmosphere. *La Vianda*, Zacateros 56, good for cheap *comida corrida* at lunchtime. *La Vendimie*, C Hidalgo, English proprietor, poetry readings Monday pm (must book), occasional fish and chips. *La Pirata*, Jesús, excellent, cheap, popular with Mexicans and tourists in the know. *Doña Anita*, Mesones 23, good. *El Infierno*, Mesones, just below Plaza Allende, excellent *sopa azteca*, good value, *menú del día*, US$2.50. *El Tomate*, vegetarian restaurant on Mesones, attractive, spotless, excellent food, generous helpings, not cheap. *Tentenpié*, C Allende, pleasant café/taquería. Good cheap chicken restaurant on C San Francisco between Juárez and Reloj (roast chicken in windows). *Eclipse*, Hidalgo 15, recommended vegetarian, menu del dia US$4. *Tío Lucas*, Mesones, opposite Teatro Angeles Peralta, very good, recommended.

Eating
● *on maps*

Mexico

Entertainment English language films at *Villa Jacarandá* hotel video bar. US$5 including alcoholic drink and popcorn.

Festivals **End-July to mid-August**, classical chamber music festival, information from Bellas Artes. Main ones are Independence Day (**15-16 September**); *Fiesta of San Miguel* (**28 September-1 October**, with Conchero dancers from many places); *Day of the Dead* (**2 November**); the *Christmas Posadas*, celebrated in the traditional colonial manner (**16-24 December**); the *pre-Lenten carnival*, Easter Week, and *Corpus Christi* (**June**). There is a Christmas season musical celebration, started in 1987, which attracts musicians of international level, T20025.

Shopping **Bookshop** *El Colibrí*, Díez de Sollano 30, good selection of French and English books. The English-language *The News* is sold on the Jardín.

Handicrafts Pottery, cotton cloth and brasswork. In the Mercado de Artesanías the merchandise tends to be souvenirs rather than real handicrafts; prices are high and the selection

San Miguel de Allende

To Dolores Hidaigo & Atotonilco

To Celaya & Guanajato

N
Not to scale

■ Sleeping	3 Posada la Aldea	6 Sautto
1 La Huerta	4 Quinta Loreto	7 Vista Hermosa
2 Posada Carmina	5 San Sebastián	Taboada

poor. Tuesday is the best day for bargains. The shops on Canal have a good selection and quality is high, but so are the prices; bargaining is next to impossible. It may be better to try elsewhere for genuine handicrafts (eg the Ciudadela handicraft market in the capital). *La Casa del Vidrio*, Correo 11, offers an excellent selection of brown-glass items at fair prices (sale prices in the summer, 40 percent off). *Joyería Rubí*, Correo 7, good value, jewellery made to order, recommended.

Trans The railway station is a long way from the centre, beyond the bus terminal. Both are **Transport** served by bus.

Buses The bus station is on the outskirts, regular bus to the centre US$0.25, returns from the market or outside *Posada San Francisco* on the Jardín. Frequent buses to **Guanajuato** (2 hours) with Flecha Amarilla and Estrella Blanca, via Dolores Hidalgo, US$3.30. To **Dolores Hidalgo**, US$1.50. Buses to **Mexico City** via Querétaro (US$2.20) 4 a day before 1200, US$12, 2nd class with Flecha Amarilla, crowded but interesting. Bus at 0530 to Mexico City airport with Primera Plus. Buses to **Morelia** until 2040 daily, 4 hours, US$6.25, 2nd class. Bus to **Atotonilco** US$1, plus short walk. **NB** There are 2 routes between San Miguel de Allende and Guanajuato: the southerly route is faster than the northerly route through Dolores Hidalgo.

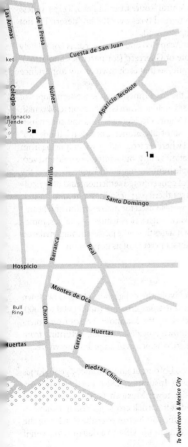

Banks *Casa de Cambio Deal* on Correo, **Directory** opposite Post Office, and on Juárez. **Embassies & consulates** Consulate: *US Consular Agent*, Plaza Colondrinas arcade, C Hernandes Macías, T22357, emergencies 20068/20980, Mon and Wed 0900-1300, 1600-1900, Tues and Thur 1600-1900. **Email** *Red Com*, Boulevard Rosales y Madero, US$3 per hr; another cybercafé at Recreo 11. **Language schools** Many of the schools demand payment in US dollars (technically illegal) and you may prefer to arrange private tuition for US$3-4 per hr. *Academia Hispanoamericana*, recommended for language lessons and sessions on Mexican history, folklore, literature, singing and dancing; very helpful; accommodation with families. The *Academia América-Española* offers full time Spanish courses; *Casa de la Luna* teaches Spanish less formally. *Inter/Idiomas*, 20 de Enero Sur 42, Col San Antonio 37750, T24115, F20135, small classes, 2-4 hrs a day of classes, fees from US$10 per day, accommodation list available, also Mexican history and cookery classes, recommended. *Card Game Spanish*, Pilancón 19, T21758, F20135, intensive courses for beginners or intermediate, run by Warren Hardy, the inventor of the Card Game method. See also **Learning Spanish** in Essentials. The library arranges 'amigo' sessions where Mexicans and foreigners can practice English and Spanish for free. Many activities arranged here. **Laundry** On Pasaje de Allende, US$3 wash and dry, same day service; unnamed laundry at Correo 42, good. **Libraries** English language library on Insurgentes has an excellent selection on Mexico; very extensive bilingual library, with computer

To Querétaro & Mexico City

centre and English-speaking staff. **Tour companies & travel agents** *Viajes Vertiz*, on Hidalgo, American Express agent, mail collection and cheque cashing available. Excursions organized by the friends of the local school for handicapped children are US$10 per person, interesting destinations to local ranch or artesans or houses not normally open to the public. **Tourist office** On Plaza next to the church, helpful with finding hotels, English spoken, US$2 for city map. **Useful addresses Immigration:** for tourist card extensions, etc, at Shopping Centre *Gigante* above the town. Take 2 copies of passport, tourist card and credit card or Tcs.

Nogales to Guadalajara: the Pacific Highway

*The road along the Pacific Coast gives access to several resorts (for example **Guaymas**, **Mazatlán**, Puerto Vallarta), to ferry terminals for Baja California, and to the Los Mochis end of the railway to **Chihuahua**. It heads inland, through **Tepic**, towards **Guadalajara**.*

In summer, west coast drivers prefer the Central Route from El Paso, Texas, unless they love heat. It is dangerous to drive on retread tyres over the hot desert. Do not drive at night and never park or sleep along the road.

The Pacific Highway down the coast to Acapulco and Salina Cruz is completely paved but has military searches in the State of Guerrero (for narcotics and arms). There are many motels along the whole route, so that each town of any importance has one or more nearby.

From Nogales to Guaymas on the Gulf, the road runs along the western slopes of the Sierra Madre, whose summits rise to 3,000 metres. From Guaymas on to Mazatlán it threads along the lowland, with the Sierra Madre Occidental's bold and commanding escarpment to the east. Like the west coasts of all continents between latitudes 20° and 30°, the whole area is desert, but fruitful wherever irrigated by water flowing from the mountains. Summers are very hot, sometimes rainy, but winters are mild and very dry. Within the Sierra Madre nomadic people hunt the many wild animals; along the coasts available water determines the spots of concentrated settlement and of agriculture. Mexico gets most of its wheat from the southern part of Sonora state, and the irrigated valley bottoms (around Hermosillo) are also used for maize, cotton and beans. Farther south, in frost-free Sinaloa and Nayarit, sugar, rice, winter vegetables, tomatoes, and tobacco are grown. The three coastal states the route passes through make up 21 percent of Mexico's area, but include only six percent of its population

Crossing into Mexico

Nogales (USA)/ Nogales The Nogales crossing is open 24 hours. To avoid the congestion of the downtown route, motorists are generally advised to use the truck crossing (open 0600 to 2000, currency exchange available), which is reached by the Mariposa Av exit from Interstate 19, two and a half miles north of downtown Nogales, Arizona. Returning from Mexico to the US, follow the sign to the 'Periférico' which avoids the downtown area.

Ideally get a tourist card before crossing the border, at an insurance agent (Jones Associates, linked to International Gateway Insurance, 2981 north Grand Av, Nogales, T602-2819141, F2810430), border town Mexican consulate or tourist office. Try to get your tourist card validated at the truck crossing. You may have to hassle for a tourist card at the immigration office 50 metres over the border on the right. Explain that you are not simply returning to the USA in a day or two, even if you are!

Motor vehicle documents can be obtained at the Mexican Customs post 21 kilometres south of Nogales, on the highway to Santa Ana, along with US insurance (which may also be obtained at the border proper). There is a tourist office and a cambio here. Two photocopies of vehicle registration, driver's licence, insurance papers, credit card and visitor's permit (approved), are required; a photocopy machine is available. Drivers leaving Mexico are advised by a large sign to surrender papers here; this involves crossing the southbound traffic and joining the queues of drivers entering Mexico. It can be chaotic. The post is greatly improved, but has few officers who speak English; high vehicles should avoid the low inspection shed. Those whose destination lies within Sonora State may find these entry procedures are not needed. Check locally.

Bus passengers should seek out the tourist office at the border to obtain a tourist card. Customs agents at the bus station will turn a blind eye if you get on a bus without a tourist card, but if the bus is stopped for routine checks (frequent) you may get sent back to the border.

Nogales

Nogales lies astride a mountain pass at 1,120 metres across from Nogales, Arizona. Population estimates range from 180,000 to 240,000, with another 20,000 on the Arizona side. Nogales is the largest town in the Pimería Alta, the area of southern Arizona and northern Sonora occupied by the Pima Indians at the arrival of the Spaniards. The Pimería Alta Historical Society, a block from the border in Nogales, Arizona, is open weekdays 0900 to 1700, Saturday 1000 to 1600, and Sunday from 1300 to 1600; no admission charge. It has excellent exhibits on the history of the region, a valuable library and archives, and also organizes tours to the Sonoran missions. The staff are a good source of information on the Mexican side. The city's commercial centre is squeezed into a few narrow blocks centred on Av Obregón.

Km 2,403
Phone code: 631
Colour map 1, grid A3

The northwest border: Mexicali - Nogales

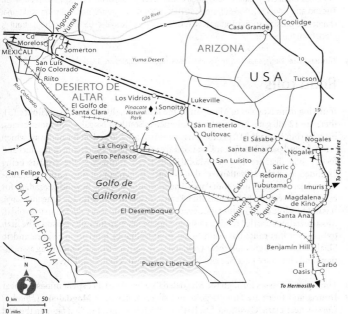

The town is a mining area and a busy trans-shipment point for fruit and vegetables destined for US supermarkets; walnut groves (*nogales*) and cattle ranches surround it, and the bordertown flavour is that of a miniature Tijuana: liquor stores, glass, silver and leather goods, cheap bars and colourful markets.

Sleeping   **B** *Fray Marcos de Niza*, Campillo 91, gaudy but none too good. **C** *Granada*, López Mateos y González, T22911. **C** *Olivia*, Obregón, 125, T22200, a/c, TV, reasonable. **D** *Motel Miami*, Campillo and Ingenieros, friendly, good restaurant, recommended; there is a wide selection of cheaper hotels on Juárez, a 1-block extension of Av López Mateos between Campillo and the border, 2 blocks from the Mexican port of entry.

Eating   *El Greco*, upstairs at Obregón and Pierson, has attractive, reasonably priced international menu. Other recommended restaurants on or near Obregón, including *El Cid* (No 124, good but dear), *Olivia*, *Casa de María*, *El Toro Steakhouse*. *Café Olga*, Juárez 37 next to bus station, open all hours.

Festivals   *Cinco de Mayo festival*, lasting 4 days, celebrates the defeat of the French army at Puebla on 5 May 1862.

Transport   **Trains**   There are no passenger services on the Pacific Railway from Nagales to Guadalajara any more but this may change with privatization. Check locally for information.

   Buses   Nogales' new bus terminal is 8 kilometres south of the city centre, along the highway to Magdalena and Hermosillo; parking US$1 per hour. Taxis at the border ask US$5 to take you to the bus station, but on the return journey the booth selling taxi vouchers charges less than US$4. A local bus, 1 peso, leaves 1 block from the border. Bus 46 from Juárez goes to the terminal (US$.25). To **Mexico City**, 42 hours with Transportes de Pacífico, daily at 2030, or twice daily with Norte de Sonora, US$88. To **Guadalajara**, 1st class, US$60, 4 daily with Transportes de Pacífico. Other destinations include **Hermosillo** (US$10), **Guaymas** (US$10), **Los Mochis** (Elite US$20), **Mazatlán** (US$43), **Tepic** (US$53), **Agua Prieta** (US$9), **Tecate** (US$25), **Tijuana** (US$25), and **Chihuahua** (US$28). On the Arizona side 1 block from the port of entry, Citizen Auto Stage Company (T2875628) runs 10 buses daily between **Tucson** and Nogales (US$6.50); stops at Tucson airport en route. Stopovers (no additional charge) are possible to visit Tumacacori mission, north of Nogales. US Greyhound is about $\frac{1}{4}$ block from the border.

Directory   **Tourist office**   None; small brochures and a basic map of Nogales are available.

Road tolls

If driving from Nogales to Mazatlán by the four-lane, divided toll road (Route 15), there are 12 toll gates, The first is 88 kilometres south of Nogales. No motorcycles, bicycles (but see page 84), pedestrians or animals are allowed on the highway, which is fenced and patrolled. The toll stations are well lit, have good bathrooms, fuel and food. Total distance Nogales-Mazatlán is 1,118 kilometres; the road is being extended beyond Mazatlán so that about 70 percent of the entire Nogales-Guadalajara route is now four-lane. The *autopista* sections beyond Mazatlán, for example the sections before and after Tepic, are worth taking for the time they save. It is not possible to list in this guide every toll location and every deviation to avoid it. Most deviations are dirt roads and should not be taken in the rainy season. The high toll cost on this route has contributed to a decline in tourism in Sonora and in Sinaloa. On toll routes and their avoidance, seek advice from US motoring associations and clubs (see page 82) as costs and conditions change rapidly.

Magdalena Valley   The highway passes through the Magdalena Valley. The Cocóspera mines are near **Imuris** and there are famous gold and silver mines near **Magdalena** (*Hotel El Cuervo*, near plaza, C without TV, B with) which has a great Indian *fiesta* in the first

The Kino missions

Padre Eusebio Francisco Kino was the foremost pioneer missionary of northwest Mexico and Baja California. He attempted the first major settlement of the Baja peninsula (San Bruno, 1683); after its failure he was assigned to the mainland, where he blazed a ruta de misiones as far as present-day Tucson. Kino was a versatile and hardy Jesuit of Italian origin – astronomer, cartographer, farmer, physician, navigator, explorer and a

man of unlimited faith. Most of his adobe mission buildings were later replaced by substantial Franciscan churches, such as at Pitiquito, Oquitoa and at Magdalena, where his grave was discovered in 1966; the remains are enclosed in glass in situ and the site is a colonial monument. The church of San Ignacio, between Magdalena and Imuris (see below) is in excellent repair, with a wooden spiral staircase of mesquité.

Mexico

week of October. On the Magdalena bypass is a toll, US$5, avoidable by driving through town (at north of town heading south, 95 kilometres south of Nogales, keep left to avoid the backstreets). The free road south to Hermosillo becomes 'speed bump alley'. See also page 177. Beyond, the cactus-strewn desert begins. At 120 kilometres from Nogales is Santa Ana, where the road from Tijuana and Mexicali comes in.

From Imuris, a major highway junction with numerous inexpensive restaurants, Mexico 2 heads east (to Naco and Agua Prieta) through the scenic Sierra de Pintos to the historic and still important copper mining centre of **Cananea**, where a 1906 miners' strike against the American-owned Cananea Consolidated Copper Company was one of the critical events in the last years of the Porfirio Díaz dictatorship. Hundreds of Arizona Rangers crossed the border to join the Sonora militia in putting down the strike, which is commemorated at the Museo de La Lucha Obrera, the former city jail, on Av Juárez. There are several motels along the highway.

The northwest border

From Baja California Route 2 from Tijuana (see page 529) runs close to the border, going through Mexicali (see page 524), San Luís Río Colorado, Sonoita, and Caborca to Santa Ana, where it joins the West Coast Highway (Route 15) to Mexico City. Route 15 is a divided four-lane motorway from Nogales to Guaymas. East of Mexicali the fast four-lane highway crosses the fertile Mexicali valley to a toll bridge over the diminished Colorado River, and continues to San Luís Río Colorado, a cheerfully tourist-oriented border town in the 'free zone' and serving cotton country: summer bullfights, small nightlife district like those of the Old West, including a so-called 'zona de tolerancia'. Americans cross the border to purchase eyeglasses, prescription pharmaceuticals and have dental work done at much lower prices than in the USA. The port of entry is open 24 hours, but there is no public transport from Yuma. **AL** *Hotel San Angel. El Reuy* and others on Av Obregón, en route to Sonoita. Budget hotel: *Capra*.

San Luís Río Colorado
Population: 134,000
Colour map 2, grid A2

North of San Luís (35 kilometres) is Baja's last international border crossing point, the farming town of Algodones. Border open 0600-2000, but motor vehicle documents are processed weekdays only, 0800-1500. The road north from San Luís skirts the Algodones dunes, the longest in North America. Algodones has one hotel, the rather misnamed **E** *Motel Olímpico*, dozens of souvenir stands, and several decent restaurants. Mexican car insurance is readily available, and there are several *casas de cambio*.

At Andrade, on the California side, the Quechan Indians operate an RV park and campground (US$12 per site with electricity, US$8 without; including hot showers, access to laundry room). Winter is the peak season, as the town is nearly deserted during the unbearably hot summer. From the west bank of the river, notice the abandoned Hanlon headgate for the Alamo Canal, which burst in 1905 and poured water into California's Imperial Valley for eight months, creating the enormous 'Salton Sea'.

Algodones
Population: 12,000
Colour map 1, grid A2

There is public transportation hourly between Algodones and Mexicali but, other than taxi, there is none from Yuma, Arizona, to Andrade (although the road has recently been paved and the number of visitors is rapidly increasing). Most visitors park at the lot operated by Quechan Indians from the nearby Fort Yuma Reservation (US$1, but there is plenty of free parking with easy distance of the border, except on the busiest days).

Pozos Nine kilometres south of San Luís is Pozos, which 40 years ago had 60,000 inhabitants, now only 2,500. It has ruins of large buildings, churches, but no hotels. State highway 40 runs south to Riíto (gas and a few stores) then follows the railway across the edge of the barren Gran Desierto to **El Golfo de Santa Clara**, a good-sized fishing town which has a fish-processing plant, supermarket, general store, church and a couple of eating places. The tidal range at the head of the Gulf is wide but there are good sandy beaches nearby at high tide. Public camping area (no facilities) at the end of a three-kilometre sandy track past the town. The highway is paved, a round-trip from San Luís of 230 kilometres.

Desierto de After leaving San Luís Río Colorado, Highway 2 crosses the sandy wastes of the
Altar Desierto de Altar – Mexico's own mini-Sahara. The road is very narrow in places, watch out for overloaded Mexican trucks. For 150 kilometres there are no facilities (gas at Los Vidrios), only three houses and an enveloping landscape of sand dunes, cinder cones and a dark lava flow from the Cerro del Pinacate, so extensive that it stands out vividly on photographs from space. All the area around the central range is protected by the **Pinacate Natural Park**; a gravel road 10 kilometres east of Los Vidrios gives access to the northern sector of the park, which contains much wildlife: for example puma, deer, antelope, wild boar, Gila monster, wild sheep, quail, red-tailed eagle. Several volcanic craters, the treacherous lava fields and an interesting cinder mine may also be visited (the area was used to train US astronauts during the Moon missions). Visitors must register at the entrance and are restricted to the Cerro Colorado and Elegante Crater area.

Lukeville After a hot and monotonous 200 kilometres from San Luís, Route 2 reaches the
(USA)/ sun-bleached bordertown of **Sonoita**, a short distance from Lukeville, Arizona. (**NB**
Sonoita If coming from Lukeville to San Luís Río Colorado, make sure you turn right (west) at Sonoita and not left (south) to San Luisito; they are both on Highway 2 but 320 kilometres apart in opposite directions!). Sonoita has little of interest itself, but there are several American-style accommodations: **C** *Motel Sol de Desierto*, a/c but no heat in some rooms (request extra blankets). **B-C** *Motel San Antonio*. **B** *Motel Excelsior*. Restaurants are few and mediocre at best – the coffee shop at Lukeville is a better alternative. Transportes Norte de Sonora and Tres Estrellas de Oro both run first-class bus services. Water and snacks should be carried anywhere in this very arid region, and, if driving your own vehicle, the tank should be kept full and replenished wherever possible. Arizona's picturesque Organ Pipe Cactus National Monument is just across the border from Sonoita.

The border crossing between Lukeville and Sonoita is open from 0800 to 2400. Camping is possible at developed sites near visitor centre at Organ Pipe National Monument for US$8 (US$3 visitor permit is valid for 15 days).

Highway 8 goes southwest from Sonoita through 100 kilometres of sand dunes; a sign, 'Dunas – 10 kilometres', at Km 80, points to a sandy road to dramatic, desolate inland dunes through mountain-rimmed black lava fields, four-wheel drive recommended.

Puerto One of the most important shrimping ports on the Gulf; the huge shrimp are too
Peñasco expensive for the US market and are mostly exported to Japan. It is very popular
Population: 60,000 with Arizona and California RV drivers for fishing, surfing and the beach. It lies on
Colour map 1, grid A2 the Mexicali railway and also has a regular air service. On the north side of the bay, 12

kilometres, is La Choya, largely a gringo place, sandy streets, full of trailers and beach cottages, and several fine beaches. Fishing tournaments are held in the Bahía La Choya; Playa de Oro has good surf but Playa Hermosa now suffers from pollution. South of the town is the elite community of Las Conchas, security gate, US-owned beach chalets, self-contained. Souvenirs are the mirrors, necklaces and figurines locally made from coral, seashells and snail shells.

Sleeping **C** *Viña del Mar*, C 1 de Junio y Blvd Malecón Kino, T33600, modern resort, cliffside jacuzzi, video-disco, etc, attractive rooms, good value. **D** *Motel Mar y Sol*, Km 94 on Sonoita Rd, pleasant gardens, restaurant, a/c, friendly. **D** *Motel Señorial*, T32065, C Tercera 81, 1 block from main beach, good restaurant, dearer upstairs rooms are a/c. **E** *Motel Davis*, Emiliano Zapata 100, T34314, pleasant.

Camping *Playa de Oro Trailer Resort*, Matamoros 36, T32668, 2 kilometres east, laundry, boat ramp, 200 sites, US$12 for 2. *Playa Bonita RV Park*, on lovely Playa Bonita, T32596, 245 spaces, restaurant, shop, laundry. *Playa Miramar*, C Matamoros y Final Av Campeche, T32351, 105 spaces, laundry, boat ramp, satellite hook-ups. *Pitahaya Trailer Park*, beachfront at *Hotel Villa Granada*, east of town, 25 spaces, full hook-ups, toilets, no showers. Nominal camping fee at La Choya, showers.

Eating *Costa Brava Restaurant*, Kino y 1 de Junio, best in town, modest prices, exotic menu, pleasant. *Café La Cita*, 1 de Junio near the gas station, authentic Mexican, budget. *La Curva*, Kino y C Comonfort, T33470, Americanized menu, popular, budget prices, little atmosphere. *La Gaviota* coffee shop at *Hotel Viña del Mar*, good breakfasts and views.

Festivals Navy Day is held in Puerto Peñasco, **29 May-1 June**, with a colourful parade, dancing and a widely-attended sporting contest.

Shopping *Jim-Bur Shopping Center*, Benito Juárez near railway crossing, is the main commercial hub. Try *El Vaquero* or *El Gift Shop* for souvenirs and camping supplies. Fresh fish from open-air fish market on the Malecón (old town). **Laundry** Laundromat Liz, C Altamirano y C Simón Morua.

Transport **Air** Great Lakes Aviation flies from Albuquerque via Tucson and from Phoenix several times a week.

Directory **Banks** 2 banks. **Tourist Office** In Jim-Bur Shopping Centre.

Recently-paved state highway 37 continues on south and east, roughly following the rail line to Caborca (180 kilometres) – an alternative to the inland Highway 2 route.

Route 2 continues from Sonoita to Caborca (150 kilometres), passing through a number of small towns (San Emeterio, San Luisito) and a more mountainous but still arid land. Customs and Immigration station near Quitovac (28 kilometres south of Sonoita), where tourist cards and vehicle papers are validated as you enter the Mexican 'mainland'.

Caborca
Population: 38,000
Altitude: 286m
Colour map 1, grid A3

Caborca lies on the Mexicali-Benjamín Hill railway in the midst of a gently sloping plain. A 'Grape Fair' is held 21-26 June, with wine exhibitions and industrial and agricultural show. Caborca's restored Church of Nuestra Señora de la Concepción was one of the 25 missions founded by Padre Kino in Sonora and Arizona between 1687 and 1711. (It was also used in 1857 as a fortress during a raid by US renegades under self-styled 'General' Crabb; their defeat is still commemorated by a fair held each 6 April.) Caborca is the best base for exploring the Kino missions.

Sleeping *Motel Posada San Cristóbal*. **A** *Motel El Camino*. **C** *Motel San Carlos*. **D** *Hotel San Francisco*. **D** *Hotel Yaqui*, clean, a/c, TV; service station and general facilities.

Altar to Arizona border

Highway 2 continues east through **Altar** (café, gas station) to join Highway 15 at Santa Ana (*Population:* 12,500; *Altitude:* 690 metres), a small town of little note. The Fiesta of Santa Ana is held 17-26 July: horse racing, fireworks, etc. **B** *Motel San Francisco*, a/c, shower baths, restaurant; motel across the road not so nice, also **B**. There is a Canadian-Mexican trailer park south of town, on the right going south, space for nine to 10 trailers, rustic, useful overnight stop. Two kilometres west is San Francisco, with another Kino mission.

From Altar, there is a little-travelled alternative route to El Sásabe, Sonora/Arizona, 68 miles southwest of Tucson via Arizona Routes 86 and 286, perhaps the most isolated, forlorn and least frequented legal border crossing between the United States and Mexico. The 98-kilometres dirt road from Altar, which passes west of the Sierra del Carrizal and Sierra de San Juan, is passable for any ordinary vehicle except after the heaviest rains (**NB** Mexican maps for Sonora tend to be inaccurate in this area). From Altar, drive three kilometres northeast toward Saric and bear left at the clearly signed junction; do not continue on the more inviting paved route unless you wish to visit the Kino mission sites and churches at Oquitoa and Tubutama – although maps show an equivalent dirt road beyond Saric to El Sásabe, there are numerous closed gates, some of them locked, over *ejido* (community) lands. Keep an eye out for semi-wild longhorn cattle along the road to El Sásabe.

Sonora (USA)/ El Sásabe

The border at El Sásabe is open from 0800 to 2000, but there is no public transportation on either side, nor is there any Mexican automobile insurance agency. For information as to road conditions, phone US Customs (T602-8234231); although they appear not to encourage traffic over this route, they will tell you whether vehicles have entered recently from Mexico and what drivers have said about the road.

42 kilometres south the Pacific Highway reaches **Benjamín Hill**, where the Mexicali railway joins the main Nogales-Guadalajara track; brightening up this forgettable junction is the Children's Park, with an amusement park, lake, zoo, and a delightful scaled-down children's railway (motel, cheaper than those in Santa Ana, but only 10 minutes away if not preferable). For northbound drivers there is a drug search at Benjamín Hill.

There is little of note on the straight run south to Hermosillo through semi-arid farming and rangeland, apart from the little towns of El Oasis and nearby Carbó (on the rail line) – both have gasoline supplies. 158 kilometres from Santa Ana the land becomes greener and the irrigated fields and citrus groves begin to enclose.

Hermosillo

Population: 698,300
State Population:
1995 2,083,630
Altitude: 237m
Phone code: 62
Colour map 1, grid B3

Capital of Sonora state, Hermosillo is a modern city, resort town and centre of a rich orchard area. Just east, the Rodríguez Dam captures the fickle flow of the Río Sonora, producing a rich strip of cotton fields, vegetables, melons, oranges and grapes. The local farmers are also big exporters of turkey and beef. Hermosillo's expanding industries draw many people from the hinterland, especially the new Ford assembly plant (manufacturing cars for the US market) as well as electronics and clothing manufacturers.

Sights

Reminders of an illustrious colonial past can be found around the central Plaza Zaragoza (invaded by noisy blackbirds at sunset): the imposing **Catedral de La Asunción** (1779, neoclassical, baroque dome, three naves) and the **Palacio de Gobierno**, with its intricately-carved pillars and pediment, historical murals and grandiose statues amid landscaped gardens. Highway 15 sweeps into Hermosillo from the north as a wide boulevard, vibrant in summer with orange-flowering trees, becoming Búlevar Rosales through the commercial centre before exiting south across the ring road (Periférico) for Guaymas (toll at Hermosillo US$5.35). The old traditional quarter is to the east of it, a few blocks southeast of Plaza Zaragoza, where delightful houses and narrow streets wind around the base of Cerro de la Campana (fine views). On the eastern slope is the **Museo de Sonora**. ■ *Wednesday-Saturday 1000-1730, Sunday 1000-1530, free.*

Not far north of downtown (Rosales y Transversal) is **University City**, with its modern buildings of Mexican architecture blended tastefully with Moorish and Mission influences. The main building contains a large library auditorium and interesting museum, open daily 0900-1300, closed holidays. There is an active fine arts and cultural life, with many events throughout the year open to visitors (check at Tourist Office for details). Two kilometres south of Plaza Zaragoza, near the Periférico Sur, is the wonderful **Centro Ecológico de Sonora**, a botanical garden and zoo displaying Sonoran and other desert flora and fauna in well-cared-for surroundings.

Generally poor standard of hotels, although there are **AL** *Señorial*, Blvd E Kino y Guillermo Carpena, T155155, F155093, a/c, pool, parking, restaurant, bar. **AL** *Holiday Inn* on Blvd Eusebio Kino 368 (northeast entry highway), T151112, with restaurant, bars, entertainment, etc.**C** *San Alberto*, Serdán y Rosales, T121800, with breakfast, a/c, cable TV, pool, good value. **C-D** *Kino*, Pino Suárez 151, Sur (base of Campana hill), T124599, popular business hotel, a/c, TV, fridge.**D** *Guaymas Inn*, 5½ kilometres north, a/c rooms with shower. **D** *Monte Carlo*, Juárez y Sonora, T123354, a/c, old, clean, very popular, as is adjoining restaurant. **D** *Washington*, Dr Noriega Pte 68, T131183, clean, a/c, basic rooms off narrow courts, with bath, best budget hotel, parking for motorbikes.**E** *Casa de los Amigos*, contact the Asociación Sonorense de los Amigos, Felipe Salido 32, Col Centro Hermosillo, T/F170142, dormitories, living room, library, garden, laundry and kitchen. **E** *Royal*, in centre, a/c but grubby. A/c is desirable in summer; check that it works before taking room. Cheap hotels and *casas de huéspedes* can be found around Plaza Zaragoza and along Sonora near Matamoros (red-light activity, choose carefully).

Sleeping

Motels **C** *Bugambilia*, Padre Kino 712, T145050. **C** *Motel El Encanto*, Blvd E Kino 901, a/c, phone, TV, comfortable. Too close to railway station.

Jardín Xochimilco, Obregón 51, Villa de Seris, very good beef, not cheap. *Mariscos Los Arcos de Hermosillo*, Michel y Ocampo (4 blocks south of Plaza), fresh seafood, attractive and expensive. *Henry's Restaurant*, across the road from *Motel Encanto*, Blvd Kino Nte, nice old house, good. *La Huerta*, San Luis Potosí 109, seafood, *René's Café*, Rosales y Moreno, good value lunches, pleasant. *El Rodeo Rosticería*, Dr Noriega Pte 92, recommended. *San César*, P Elias C 71 Pnte, excellent chop sueys, seafood and expensive 'gringo' food. Mexican specialities better value, open for breakfast.

Eating

Air The Gen Pesquira/García airport (HMO) is 12 kilometres from town. Daily to Mexico City, AeroMéxico, Mexicana, Aero California and Taesa. Other domestic flights to Chihuahua, Ciudad Juárez, Ciudad Obregón, Cuernavaca, Culiacán, Durango, Guadalajara, Guerrero Negro, La Paz, Los Cabos, Los Mochis, Mazatlán, Mexicali, Monterrey, Tijuana and Torreón. International flights to Los Angeles, Tucson and Phoenix.

Trains Station just off Highway 15, 2½ kilometres north of downtown.

Buses Bus station on Búlevar Transversal 400, north of University; to **Nogales** US$10, 4 hours, hourly 0230-1830 (Tres Estrellas de Oro, 1st class); to **Agua Prieta**, 7 hours, US$14, 6 a day (2nd class); **Guaymas**, hourly round the clock, US$6, 2½ hours; to **Los Mochis**, 1st class, US$22, 7½ hours through scrubland and wheat fields. Bus to **Tijuana**, US$35 1st class, 11 hours, there can be long queues, especially near Christmas. Bus to **Mazatlán** 10-12 hours, US$30. To **Kino**, US$3.35, 4 a day, 2 hours (2nd class).

Transport

Airline offices AeroMéxico, T168206. *Mexicana*, T171103. *Great Lakes*, T91-80000307. *Taesa*, T173606. **Embassies & consulates** US Consulate, T172375 for appointment, Mon-Fri 0900-1700. **Tourist office** Palacio de Gobierno, ground floor, T172964.

Directory

Bahía Kino
Phone code: 624
Colour map 1, grid B3

A paved 118-kilometre road runs west past the airport to Bahía Kino, divided into the old, somnolent and somewhat down-at-heel fishing village, and the new **Kino Nuevo**, a 'winter gringoland' of condos, trailer parks and a couple of expensive hotels. Although the public beaches are good, most American visitors come for the sportfishing. The Seri Indians, who used to live across El Canal del Infiernillo (Little Hell Strait) from the port on the mountainous Isla del Tiburón (Shark Island), have been displaced by the navy to the mainland, down a dirt road from Bahía Kino in a settlement at Punta Chueca (no east access). They come into Kino on Saturday and Sunday to sell their ironwood animal sculptures (non-traditional) and traditional basketware (not cheap). They may usually be found at the *Posada del Mar Hotel*. A fine **Museo Regional de Arte Seri** has opened on Mar de Cortez, the main boulevard.

Sleeping A *The Anchor House*, beautiful bed and breakfast house on the beach, American-run, PO Box 80-83340, T20141. *Hotel Posada del Mar*, T181205, F181237, quality declining; *Hotel Saro*, 5 rooms, on beach.

Camping On the beaches is possible with or without tent. Camping at one of the trailer parks costs about US$12 a night (eg *Kino Bay RV Park*, Av Mar de Cortez, PO Box 857, Hermosillo, T624-20216/621-53197). *Islandia Marina Trailer Park*, Puerto Peñasco y Guaymas, US$10, English spoken, hospitable. June Ellen Hayna runs an RV Park, PO Box 50, T20615, also cabins, **B**.

Eating Reasonably-priced meals are available in old Kino at *La Palapa* and *Marlin* restaurants (latter next to *Islandia Marina Trailer Park*), extremely fresh seafood and snacks. *El Pargo Rojo*, really good seafood, recommended.

Directory There is no bank in the area. The nearest is in Miguel Alemán, between Kino and Hermosillo, 48 kilometres away (Bancomer).

Guaymas and Bahia San Carlos

Guaymas
Population: 200,000
Colour map 1, grid B3

At Km 1,867 (from Mexico City) the road reaches the Gulf at the port of Guaymas , on a lovely bay backed by desert mountains; excellent deep-sea fishing, and seafood for the gourmet. Miramar beach, on Bocachibampo bay with its blue sea sprinkled with green islets, is the resort section. Watersports on 10 May. The climate is ideal in winter but unpleasant in summer. The 18th century church of San Fernando is worth a visit; so also, outside the town, is the 17th century church of San José de Guaymas. Excursions to the cactus forests.

Sleeping B *Ana*, C 25 No 135, T20593, near cathedral, a/c. **B** *Santa Rita*, Serdán and C 9, with bath, a/c, clean, good. **E** *América*, Alemán (C 20) y Av 18, T21120, a/c, dirty, noisy. **F** *Casa de Huéspedes Martha*, C13, with bath, fan, hot water, clean, garden, recommended. **Motels**: **B** *Flamingos*, Carretera Internacional, T20960. **C** *Malibu*, T22244, Carretera Internacional N. **At Miramar Beach**: **AL** *Playa de Cortés*, T11224, F10135, also has excellent RV park (US$18.50 per day), hot showers, clean, hotel has private beach, pool, restaurant and bar, etc. **A** *Leo's Inn*, at opposite end of the beach, T29490, PO Box 430, Guaymas.

Eating *Todos Comen*, on Serdán, good food at reasonable prices.

Transport The Gen José M Yanez airport (GYM) is 5 kilometres from Guaymas on the way to San Carlos. AeroMéxico (T622-20123) has flights to La Paz, Mexico City and Phoenix. Mesa Airlines also fly to Phoenix.

San Carlos 15 kilometres north of Guaymas (or 12 kilometres from Highway 15) is the **Bahía San Carlos**, very Americanized and touristy, where 'Catch 22' was filmed; above the bay a twin peaked hill, the Tetas de Cabra, is a significant landmark; good fishing with an international tournament each July. North of San Carlos further development is taking place on Sonora Bay. Both Miramar and San Carlos beaches are easily reached by bus. The free beaches are dirty.

Sleeping *Condominio Pilar*, check office for rentals, good camp area. **A-B** *Hotel Fiesta San Carlos*, T60229, PO Box 828, clean, good food (US$10-15), pool. **AL** *Tetakawi Hotel, Suites and RV Park* (Best Western), T60220, F60248, PO Box 71, San Carlos, Guaymas, by beach, swimming pool, bar, snack bar, disco, a/c, cable TV, trailer park rates US$14 per day. Next, after 10 kilometres, is **B-C** *Creston Motel*, beach side, clean, good value. *The Country Club*, with hotel and tennis, is extensive. **A2-B** *La Posada de San Carlos*, on the beach, very nice. After 10 kilometres from the Highway a road branches to **C** *Dorada Rental Units*, T60307, PO Box 48, on beach, pleasant, and **C** *Ferrer Apartments*, cooking facilities, hot water, pleasant patio, good value. At Km 13 the road forks: left 1 kilometre to 2 secluded bays with limited trailer camping, and right to the new Marina Real, the *Howard Johnson Hotel* (trailer park next door), *Club Mediterranée*, T622-60176, F60070, all on Sonora Bay, and beyond a beach with open camping.

Eating *Cantón*, Serdán between 20 and 21, Guaymas, good Chinese. *Piccolo*, good pasta, salads, good value. Just over 1 kilometre up a dirt track is *Restaurant Norsa*, good limited menu, no alcohol.Generally, restaurants are overpriced.

Transport Buses 1st class bus to **Hermosillo** (2½ hours, US$6); **Mazatlán**, frequent, 12 hours, US$30; **Tijuana**, 18 hours, US$47. To **Culiacán**, 9 hours, US$16.50. Buses from Empalme to Los Mochis/Sufragio with Autotransportes Tufesa, US$9.50, 5½ hours, T32770. **Ferry** Sematur sail from Guaymas to **Santa Rosalía**, Baja California, 7-hour trip, see schedule, page 552 for details.

Directory Tourist office Av Serdán, lots of pamphlets. 7 kilometres from the Highway, behind the shops, are the post office and police station; the beer depository will sell by the half case. After 10 kilometres are the gas station and bank opposite the phone and fax centre.

From Guaymas to Mazatlán is 784 kilometres. There is a toll eight kilometres west of Empalme, US$5; this is on the toll road which skirts Guaymas completely. An alternative route goes into Guaymas, but forks to avoid the centre from both north and south. A third route goes into the centre of Guaymas which should be avoided unless you have business there. Toll at Esperanza, US$5. First comes Ciudad Obregón, mainly important as the centre of an agricultural region. It is a good place for buying leather goods, such as western boots and saddles.

Ciudad Obregón
Population: 180,000
Colour map 2, grid B1

Sleeping **A** *Motel Valle Grande*, M Alemán y Tetabiate, T40940. **A** *Costa de Oro*, M Alemán 210, T41765, well-kept and pleasant. **C** *Dora*, California 1016 Sur. **C** *San Jorge*, M Alemán 929 Nte, T6414 9514, F6414 4353, a/c, TV, restaurant, bar, pool, safe parking, clean, friendly, with colonial Spanish decor; also 2 hotels on street of main bus station (turn right on leaving), 1 block to **D** *La Aduana*, dirty, cold water, and further down, *Gema*. **Youth hostel**: Laguna de Nainari s/n, CP 85000, ask for bus to Seguro Social – state hospital – and walk round lake to hostal from there Villas Deportivas Juveniles campsite, T64141359.

Eating Expensive but good local food at *Café Bibi*, behind cathedral.

Transport The airport (CEN) is 16 kilometres from town. Flights to Chihuahua, Culiacán, Durango, Guadalajara, Hermosillo, La Paz, Loreto, Los Cabos, Los Mochis and Mexico City. Flights to US cities: Los Angeles and Tucson.

Directory Airlines: *AeroMéxico*, T64132190; *Great Lakes*, T91-800-00307; *Taesa*, T64139525.

Navojoa

Population: 200,000
Colour map 2, grid B1

From Ciudad Obregón to Navojoa is a four-lane highway in poor condition (toll at Navojoa, US$7). Navojoa has the *Motel El Rancho* (T20004) and *Motel del Río* (T20331) and a trailer park in the north of town on Route 15 (run down, shaded, US$10 for full hook-up, US$5 for car or small jeep, dollars preferred to pesos). West of Navojoa, on Huatabampo bay, are the survivors of the Mayo Indians; their festivals are in May.

Alamos

Colour map 2, grid B1

52 kilometres into the hills is the delightful old colonial town of Alamos, now declared a national monument. It is set in a once famous mining area fascinating for rock enthusiasts. Although the area was explored by the Spanish in the 1530s, development did not begin for another 100 years when the Jesuits built a mission nearby. In 1683 silver mines were discovered near the village of **Aduana** and the population began to rise. By the 1780s there were over 30,000 people and the town had provided emigrants to settle new towns such as San Francisco and Los Angeles. At the end of the 18th century silver production was at its peak and Alamos was the world's greatest producer. Political recognition followed and in 1827 it was made capital of Occidente (Sonora and Sinaloa). However, the mining industry declined in the 19th century and by 1909 most of the mines had closed because of rising costs and revolutions. In 1933 the railroad was abandoned and the population declined to only 1,000 inhabitants. This has since recovered to about 6,200, largely because of US immigration, attracted by the sunny climate, attractive architecture and surroundings, and the proximity of the US border. You can visit the very photogenic old mine site of Aduana, near the village of Minas Nuevas on the road between Navojoa and Alamos, bus US$0.25. There is a good, unnamed restaurant there, American-run, reservations essential, ask in Alamos. Several walking tours of Alamos are offered by the local US community, including a tour of the historical colonial town, and one of the homes and gardens, proceeds are reported to support school children's scholarships. The **Museo Costumbrista** has good explanations of the history of Alamos. The Alamos Music Festival is an annual event held for seven days at the end of January.

Sleeping **L-AL** *Casa Encantada*, Juárez 20, T64280482, F64280221, in USA F714-7522331, courtyard rooms to luxury suites, bed and breakfast, charming, small pool, will find rooms elsewhere if town is 'full'. **AL-A** *Mansión de la Condesa Magdalena*, same ownership, beautifully renovated, clean, quiet, relaxing, colonial rooms, beautiful gardens, excellent food, recommended; also *Posada La Hacienda*, on edge of town. **B** *Los Portales Hotel*, T80111, with beautiful frescoes, on plaza. **D** *Somar*, on the road into Alamos, T80125, Madero 110. *El Caracol Trailer Park*, US$8.50, rustic, good pool, not always open; 2 other trailer parks, *Real de los Alamos*, US$10, with pool (too far to walk from town) and *Dolisa*, C Madero 72, T642-80131, US$12, also **B-C** motel, small rooms, a/c, fireplace, with bath, TV.

Transport **Air** There is a paved, 1,190-metre landing strip but no scheduled services. **Buses** Navojoa-Alamos every hour on the half hour from 0630, US$2, until 1830, 1 hour, good road. Bus station for Alamos is about 8 blocks from main bus station, but you must ask directions because it is a confusing route. **NB** For drivers heading north, there is a fruit and vegetable checkpoint on entering Sonora state. Toll at Sinaloa border US$5.35. Further toll and drug search 16 kilometres north of Los Mochis, US$3.35.

Los Mochis

Population: 200,000
Phone code: 68
Colour map 2, grid B1

Los Mochis, in a sugar cane area, is a fishing resort 25 kilometres from the sea with a US colony. The name is derived either from a local word meaning 'hill like a turtle', or possibly, from 'mocho', meaning one-armed, perhaps after a cowboy thus mutilated. The city was founded in 1904 around a sugar mill built by the American, Benjamin Johnson. His wife built the Sagrado Corazón church. The family lost everything in the Revolution. There are plenty of night spots and bars visited by roaming mariachis, who play excellent music. A stairway leads up the hillside behind La Pérgola, a pleasant public park near the city reservoir, for an excellent view of Los Mochis. Toll at Los Mochis US$3.65.

Mexico

AL *Santa Anita*, Leyva y Hidalgo, T187046, F120046, comfortable, clean dining room (good), **Sleeping** noisy a/c, stores luggage, mixed reports about *Flamingo* travel agency attached (T121613, F183393), has own bus service to station, safe garage to leave car while visiting Copper Canyon, US$4 per day; it is usually possible to change dollars. Under same ownership is *Plaza Inn*, on Leyva, the main street; also on this street, **B** *El Dorado*, 20 minutes from centre, a/c, pool, friendly, very good, and *Florida*. **C** *Beltrán*, Hidalgo 281 Pte, T120688, F120710, noisy a/c, TV, recommended, has all travel timetables and will make reservations.

D *América*, Allende Sur 655, T121355, F125983, no hot water in early am, noisy, a/c, has restaurant with good, cheap sandwiches, enclosed parking. **D** *Fénix*, A Flores 365 Sur, T122623, F158948, safe, clean, wake up call, very good. **D** *del Valle*, Guillermo Prieto y Independencia, T120105, a/c, bath, OK but pricey. **D** *El Parque*, Obregón 600 Pte, across from Parque Sinaloa, T120260, fan, US$2 more for a/c. **D** *Hidalgo*, opposite *Beltrán* at No 260 Pte, T123456, cheap cafetería, friendly, sometimes no hot water. **D** *Lorena*, Prieto y Obregón 186 Pte, T120239, F120958, with bath, TV, gloomy, poor value, but good cafetería. **D** *Montecarlo*, Independencia y A Flores 322 Sur, T121818, clean, a/c, TV, restaurant, parking. **F** *Los Arcos*, Allende, T123253, without bath, clean but dingy, fills up quickly, some rooms noisy, more expensive with a/c.

Motel **D** *Santa Rosa*, López Mateos 1051 north, modest.

Trailer Park *Río Fuerte Trailer Resort*, 16 kilometres north of Los Mochis on Route 15, good, heated swimming pool, recommended, US$10 per car and 2 people, US$14.50 motor

Los Mochis

■ Sleeping		● Eating
1 América	6 Fénix	1 El Delfín
2 Balderrama	7 Hidalgo	2 El Farellón
3 Beltrán	8 Lorena	3 España
4 Del Valle	9 Los Arcos	4 Mi Cabaña Tacos
5 El Parque	10 Montecarlo	

home, offers hunting, shooting, fishing expeditions. **NB** The Pemex Station 1.5 kilometres south of here has a very bad reputation and bad pumps. Ask at *Río Fuerte* which service stations are best, eg the one 16 kilometres south on the right. There is another *Hotel Resort y Trailer Park* on Highway 15 at the turn-off to Topolobampo, sophisticated, with disco.

Eating *El Farellón*, Flores and Obregón, good seafood and service, reasonably priced; opposite, on Obregón, is *España*, very good. *Café León*, Obregón 419, good meals, including breakfast, cakes, inexpensive. *El Vaquero* in *Hotel Montecarlo*, recommended. *El Delfín*, on Allende Sur near Obregón, restaurant and bar, nice atmosphere (owner's husband is a mariachi musician). *El Taquito*, Leyva, 1 block from Santa Anita, is open 24 hours. *Tay-Pak*, near Independencia, Chinese, good clean, reasonably priced. *Chispa*, Leyva Sur 117, near Morelos, art deco design, clean, good. *Mi Cabaña Tacos*, corner of Obregón y Allende, popular with locals, friendly, recommended. *Las Palmeras*, excellent, reasonably priced; good seafood at *El Bucanero*. *Birria* is a local beef dish; many places to eat are referred to as a *birriería*.

Transport **Air** Airport Federal (LMM) is 6½ kilometres from town. Flights to Chihuahua, Ciudad Obregón, Culiacán, Guadalajara, Hermosillo, La Paz, Los Cabos, Mazatlán, Mexico City, Monterrey and Tijuana with a variety of airlines. Flights to Los Angeles, Phoenix and Tucson with AeroMéxico and/or Aero California.

Trains For **Creel and Chihuahua**, see below. **NB** If coming from Chihuahua and you don't want to stay in Los Mochis, assuming the train is not overdelayed, you can take a night bus to Mazatlán at 2200, arriving 0630. Los Mochis station has toilets and local phones; ticket office is open 1 hour before train leaves. The station is 8 kilometres from town; do not walk there or back in the dark. There is a bus service from 0500, US$0.15 from corner of hotels *Hidalgo* and *Beltrán*, otherwise take the 0500 bus from *Hotel Santa Anita*, US$3.50 (for house guests only), or taxi, of which there is any number going into town after the arrival of the Chihuahua train. Taxis in the centre go from Hidalgo y Leyva; fare to station US$5 per car, bargaining not possible, make sure price quoted is not per person, rip-offs are common. Bus to town from corner of 1st junction from station from 0530.

If driving and looking for secure parking while taking the train, ask for Sr Carlos at the station ticket office, he will guard the car at his home for a modest fee. There is more expensive parking downtown.

Buses Unlike most cities in Mexico, each bus company has its own terminal in Los Mochis. **Mexico City**, US$60, 25 hours. **Guadalajara**, frequent, Tres Estrellas de Oro, 1st class, US$31. **Ciudad Obregón**, US$16.50. **Tijuana**, US$53, several daily up to 24 hours. **Mazatlán**, 5½ hours, US$16.50, 1st class, Tres Estrellas de Oro or Transportes Norte de Sonora, hourly, also Estrella Blanca. **Nogales**, US$22, 9 hours. Elite buses leave every hour until 2200. No reservations can be made for buses north or south at the terminal of Tres Estrellas de Oro and it is difficult to get on buses. Try instead Transportes de Pacífico, 3 blocks away and next to TNS terminal. First class bus to **Guaymas** 5½ hours, US$9.50 with Tufesa. To **Tepic**, US$32, 13 hours. Local buses to destinations around Sinaloa eg Topolobampo, Guasave, San Blas (Sufragio) and Culiacán leave from Autotransportes del Norte de Sinaloa Terminal near Post Office and Mercado Cuauhtémoc.

Directory **Airline offices** *Aero California*, T181616. **Banks** *Casa de Cambio Rocha*, T125500, opposite *Hotel Beltrán*; others, and banks, on Leyva. American Express at *Viajes Krystal*, Av Obregón, all services. **Communications** **Post Office:** Ordóñez Pte, between Prieto y Zaragoza Sur, south of centre, open Mon-Fri 0900-1400,1600-1800. **Hospitals & medical services** Hospital: *Fátima*, Loaizo 606 Pte, T155703/123312, private, English spoken, maybe a good place to start in an emergency. **Laundry** *Lavamatic*, Allende 218; another laundry at Juárez 225.

Topolobampo
Colour map 2, grid B1 A side road, running southwest from Los Mochis crosses the salt flats to Topolobampo (20 kilometres, 30 minutes). The town is built on a number of hills facing the beautiful bay-and-lagoon-indented coast. In the bay, which has many outlets, there are a number of islands; sunsets here are lovely. Boats can be hired, and fishing trips are available from the jetty. It is difficult to find a beach unless one pays for a

private launch. Pemex has a storage facility here and Topolobampo is being developed as a deep-water port. This is as a consequence of the full operation of the Ojinaga (see page 129) – Pacific railway (of which the Los Mochis-Creel-Chihuahua route forms part). Originally conceived in 1872 as an outlet for US goods from Kansas and the south to Japan, the line across the Mexican Sierra was not completed until 1961.

Sleeping **B** *Yacht Hotel*, 3-4 kilometres south of town, modern, a/c, clean and good food, quiet, good views, but seems to close for the winter. **E** *Estilo Europeo Poama*, at the ferry terminal, 10 minutes walk from Los Mochis bus; for other accommodation go to Los Mochis.

Ferry Topolobampo-La Paz, Baja California Sur. For schedule and fares, see page 552. No reservations, buy ticket in Los Mochis (office T183986) or on day of travel at Muelle Topolobampa office, opens 3 hours prior to departure (be there at least 2 hours before sailing) T686-20141, F20035. Travel agency *Viajes Paotán*, Rendón y Angel Flores, can book tickets for you on day of departure. See also page 551.

To Creel and Chihuahua by train

The journey (see page 134) shows the spectacular scenery of the Sierra Madre and the Barranca del Urique/Cobre (Urique, or Copper Canyon). The *servicio estrella* train should leave daily at 0600 (but often at 0700), US$27 to Creel (about nine hours), US$49 to Chihuahua (about 14 hours, but expect delays). Bring your own toilet paper, food and drinking water. Tickets must be bought in advance, not on the train, either on morning of departure or, in high season (July-August, New Year, Holy Week) a day or more before. Return tickets are valid for 30 days. Tickets can be bought at Flamingo Travel (mixed reports) in *Hotel Santa Anita*, but they will try to persuade you to book into their preferred (expensive) hotels. It may be worth buying tickets from them to avoid long queues at the station. Buy return tickets as it is impossible to reserve seats from Creel back to Los Mochis. A local bus (US$0.10) leaves from the crossroads near *Hotel Beltrán* for train station. Departs 0530, arriving 0555.

The ordinary train, *Tarahumara*, leaves at 0700, Tuesday, Thursday, Saturday, US$5.50 to Creel, 13 hours, US$10 to Chihuahua, not possible to reserve seats. Second class is reasonably comfortable and it is possible to open the windows, many stops. On either train, sit on the right for the best views, except when approaching Temoris, then return to the right until the first tunnel after Temoris; thereafter good views can be seen on either side. On the *primera especial* the windows do not open so, to take photos, stand between the carriages. Motorists taking the train to Creel have been advised to park in front of the station as there are lights and people at all times.

To begin with the journey is through flat country; Sufragio is reached after 40 minutes, **El Fuerte** after one and a half hours. This town has recently been renovated and has interesting colonial architecture in the centre (it was founded in 1564). The station is 10 kilometres from the town; taxis US$4 per person. *Posada del Hidalgo* in historical mansion, details from *Hotel Santa Anita* in Los Mochis. **D** *Hotel Oasis*, half a block from C Benito Juárez in centre, not very clean, some rooms better than others, a/c expensive restaurant. **D** *Hotel San Francisco*, good value. Good restaurants, nice plaza.

El Fuerte
Population: 120,000
Colour map 2, grid B1

The high, long bridge over the Río Fuerte heralds the beginning of more interesting scenery (this is the first of 37 major bridges); three hours from Los Mochis the first, and longest, of the 86 tunnels is passed, then, 10 minutes later the Chinapas bridge (this is approximately the Sinaloa/ Chihuahua border, where clocks go forward an hour). Before Temoris (four hours) the track loops round to the left, goes through Temoris, then enters a tunnel in which the railway turns through 180°.

Temoris, an attractive town 11 kilometres above the station, in the mining and cattle country of the lower western Sierra Madre, is a good base for visiting working

Temoris

ranches, Tarahumara villages, waterfalls and swimming holes, on foot, horseback or mountainbike. Colectivos make the trip or you may be able to hitch with local merchants. There are three hotels in the area and several cheap restaurants. *Campamento Adame* (T60750/60612, best to phone in advance), a good choice for backpackers, has cabañas, dormitories and tent sites with shower and cooking facilities. Gilberto Adame is friendly and helpful and can arrange trips by whatever mode into the mountains. He also has a bus for local touring. There is a fiesta for San Miguel in the last week of September.

Bahuichivo Bahuichivo (five hours) has a simple hotel, **E** *Viajero*, restaurant next door, and a few shops; if you don't want to go all the way you can return from here (Bahuichivo-Creel, 1st class, US$4, three hours).

Urique From Bahuichivo, bus and pick-ups make the five-hour journey to Urique, in the heart of the Barranca del Urique. Before the canyon is the town of Cerocahui, on a meander in the river, with a solid red stone church (one hotel – **LL** *Mission*, full board, book in Flamingo agency in Los Mochis). At the lip of the canyon is a mirador offering fine views. The road into the canyon is spectacular, only rivalled by the road to Batópilas.

Urique has a hot, subtropical climate, houses sprawl along the river interspersed with citrus groves. One and a half hour's walk (seven kilometres) upstream from Urique (crossing to other side by hanging bridge) is the Mission church of Guadalupe Coronal in a small village. Downstream is the village of Guapalayna (four and a half kilometres) with another old small church. Two simple hotels, the one on the main street, **F** *Cañón de Urique*, south of centre, is good value. *Restaurant Plaza*, across main street from plaza, garden at back, friendly. No private phones, telephone office on plaza, open 0800-1300, 1400-1900, Monday-Saturday, 0800-1200 Sunday. Bus leaves from Urique to return to Bahuichivo at 0800, US$5.50, on arrival and before departure it goes up and down the main street.

Cuiteco (five and a half hours) has the **B** *Hotel Cuiteco*, delightful, with a patio which has an unimpeded view of the mountains, quiet, oil lamps, gas stove in courtyard; **San Rafael** (20 minutes later), where there is a 10-minute stop, is just after the La Laja bridge and tunnel; in a further 25 minutes *Hotel Posada Barrancas* is reached, followed in five minutes by **El Divisadero**, where there is an all-too-brief, 10-minute stop to view the Barranca del Urique, buy souvenirs from the Tarahumara women, and let the down train pass. 17 kilometres beyond Pitorreal (seven hours) is the Lazo loop, in which the track does a 360° turn; soon afterwards the highest point, Los Ojitos, is passed. Creel is reached in eight hours, see page 134.

Culiacán

Km 1,429
Population: 950,000
State Population: 1995
2,424,745
Phone code: 67
Colour map 2, grid C2

Some 210 kilometres beyond Los Mochis Culiacán is the capital of Sinaloa state, founded 1531 by Beltrán de Guzmán, chief centre for winter vegetables. No longer a colonial city, but attractive and prosperous; it has a university.

The highway is widened and divided for 90 kilometres south of Los Mochis to Guamúchil, where the old freeway continues to Culiacán. North of the city, the north and southbound carriageways are on different levels with no divide (very dangerous). A new toll section of freeway heads nearer to the coast, past Navolata, bypasses Culiacán and rejoins Highway 15 a few kilometres south of that city. Note, though that this is a very isolated stretch of road and there have been robberies on it at times. Do not drive at night. The area around Culiacán is also a drugs-growing region.

Excursions The safe beaches of **Altata** are 30 minutes by paved road. 18 kilometres west of

Altata on gravel, then sand (passable) is Tambor Beach, wind and waves, and fewer people than Altata. **Imala**, 25 kilometres northeast by a poor road has thermal baths reaching 40°C.

A *Executivo*, Madero y Obregón, T139370. **C** *Del Valle*, Solano 180, T139026, noisy, not rec- **Sleeping** ommended. **D** *San Francisco*, Hidalgo 227, with bath, clean, friendly, free parking. **E** *Louisiana*.

Motels **A** *Los Tres Ríos*, 1 kilometre north of town on highway 15, trailer park, US$10, pool, resort style, good restaurant. *Pizzería Tivoli*, good, friendly. **C** *Los Caminos*, Carretera Internacional y Blvd Leyva Solano, T153300, a/c, phone, satellite TV, restaurant, pool, nightclub, safe parking, clean rooms.

Air Airport Federal de Bachigualato (CUL) 10 kilometres from centre. Airlines: Aero Califor- **Transport** nia, T160250; AeroMéxico, T153772; Taesa, T168899. Flights to Acapulco, Aguascalientes, Chihuahua, Ciudad Obregón, Cuernavaca, Durango, Guadalajara, Hermosillo, La Paz, Los Angeles (California), Los Cabos, Los Mochis, Mexico City, Monterrey, Reynosa, Tijuana, Torreón, Tucson (Arizona) and Uruapán.

Buses To Tepic, 8¼ hours, US$12; to Guaymas, 9 hours, US$16.50.

Two thirds of the way between Culiacán and Mazatlán, at the Cruce de Coyotitán, there are **Routes** two possible side trips off Highway 15: right to the mouth of the Río Piaxtla on the coast where at Estación Dimas there are petroglyphs, and left up into the cordillera to San Ignacio, reaching eventually the village of Tepehuaje with hiking possibilities in Los Picachos Los Frailes (2,511 metres). Some 28 kilometres after Coyotitán along Highway 15 (good condition) you come to a roadside monument marking the Tropic of Cancer. Toll 27 kilometres north of Mazatlán, US$11.35.

Mazatlán

Beyond the Tropic of Cancer, 13 kilometres is (Km 1,089) Mazatlán, spread along a *Population: 800,000* peninsula at the foot of the Sierra Madre. It is the largest Mexican port on the Pacific *Phone book: 678* Ocean and the main industrial and commercial centre in the west. The beauty of its *Colour map 2, grid C2* setting and its warm winters have made it a popular resort, but unfortunately with expansion it has lost some of its attraction. It overlooks Olas Altas (High Waves) bay, which has a very strong current.

Tourism is now concentrated in the Zona Dorada, which includes the beaches of **Beaches** Gaviotas, Los Sabalos, Escondida, Delfín, Cerritos, Cangrejo and Brujas (north of **Playa Brujas** is a rocky area which is good for snorkelling); the area is built up and accommodation is expensive. From Olas Altas the promenade, lined by hotels with a long beach at its foot, curves around the bay, first as Paseo Claussen, then Av del Mar which leads to Av Camarón Sabalo in the Zona Dorada. The sunsets are superb seen from this side of the peninsula; at this time of day high divers can be watched and the fishermen return to the north beach. There are many good beach bars from which to view the setting sun. Buses from C Arriba go to Zona Dorada for US$0.50.

On the other side of the peninsula the Av del Puerto promenade overlooks a number of islands. From the ferry terminal at the southern end of Av del Puerto, a boat can be taken to **Isla de los Chivos** for US$1; there you can stroll along the beaches and eat at the beach bars. There are more islands in the nearby lagoons, which teem with wild life. The best beaches, three to five kilometres from the city, are easily reached by taxi. The lighthouse, on El Faro island, is 157 metres above sea-level.

Music Firmly rooted and extremely popular in the State of Sinaloa is a type of orchestra known as the Banda Sinaloense or Tamborera, which can be seen and heard playing 'Chaparral' at almost any time of day or night in restaurants, dance halls, bars, at family parties or on the street. It usually has from 14 to 16 musicians: four saxophones, four trumpets, clarinets, tuba, three to four men on drums and other percussion instruments, including *maracas*, *guiro*, and loud, strong voices. It is unabashed, brutal music, loud and lively. One such Banda plays every afternoon at the *Chaparral* bar, opposite the Conasupo market near the bus station.

Sights The old part of town is located around **Plaza Machado**, which is on C Carnival. Half a block from the plaza is the **Teatro Peralta**, the 17th century opera house, which has been restored and reopened to the public. **Aquarium** Av de los Deportes III, just off the beach, behind *Hotel Las Arenas*, interesting, includes sharks and blindfish. ■ *Opens 0900, adults US$3, children US$1.50.*

Museum **Museo Arqueológico de Mazatlán**, Sixto Osuna 115, half a block from *Hotel Freeman*, small, covering state of Sinaloa, recommended. ■ *US$1, free gallery in same building.*

Excursions To **Isla de la Piedra**, 30 kilometres of now littered beach. Take a small boat from south side of town from Armada (naval station near brewery), regular service, US$1,

Mazatlán

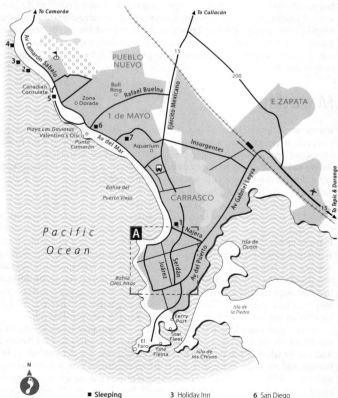

*Related map
A Mazatlán centre,
page 191*

■ Sleeping	3 Holiday Inn	6 San Diego
1 Aguamarina	4 Oceano Palace	7 Sands
2 El Cid	5 Playa Mazatlán	

Mexico

walk across island (10 minutes) to a clean beach where there is good surfing. Local *comedores* on beach provide primitive accommodation, or ask for permission to camp on the beach. Try smoked fish sold on a stick. Beware of sandflies. Star Fleet boats may be rented at the sports fishing docks for a cruise round the Dos Hermanos rocks, where boobies and many other birds can be seen. A boat excursion on the *Yate Fiesta* cruises out at 1000 or 2000 (with dancing), from second last bus stop in the direction of Playa del Sur. Refreshments included, and you can see the wildlife in the day time.

Four kilometres south of Mazatlán at El Verde is a sea turtle reserve in an area of mangroves.

At the foot of the Sierra Madre, 30 minutes from Mazatlán is **LL** *Rancho Las Moras*, a converted tequila ranch, now with six hotel rooms and five villas, tennis courts, pool, laundry service, children's summer camp, restaurant and riding for all abilities (daytime activities for non-residents available), reservations T69-165044, F165045, highly recommended (address of office Av Camarón Sabalo 204, Suite 6, Zona Dorada 82110, Mazatlán, or 9297 Siempre Viva Road, Suite 15-474, San Diego, CA 92173, USA), from Route 15, take the road towards La Noria for nine kilometres, then turn left up dirt road at sign.

Along the northern beach, Av Camarón Sabalo or just off it, are: **LL-L** *Los Sábalos*, RT Loaiza 100, T835333, Health Club facilities. **LL-AL** *Playa Mazatlán*, same street, T134455, good atmosphere. *El Cid*, resort, 4 hotels, Camarón Sabalo, with *El Caracol* nightclub and *Club 21*, T133333. *Camino Real* (T131111). *Luna Palace*, T146006, F146106. *Royal Villas*, T166161. *Balboa Towers*, T137784. *Costa de Oro*, T132005. *Fiesta Inn*, T890100. *Double Tree Club Resort*, T130200. *Pueblo Bonito*, T143700. *El Quijote Inn*, T141134. *Oceano Palace* (Best Western), T130666, F139666. *Holiday Inn*, Camarón Sabalo 696, T132222, F841287, resort facilities), all in our **LL-AL** ranges. **L-A** *Las Flores*, RT Loaiza 212, T135100, F143400. **A** *Las Palmas*, Camarón Sabalo 305, Zona Dorada, PO Box 135, T165664, F165666, good value, recommended. **A-C** *Tropicana*, RT Loaiza 27, T838000, F835361, a/c, shower, large rooms,

Sleeping
The expensive hotels are in the area known as the Zona Dorada; budget hotels can be found around Cerro de la Nevería and on C Angel Flores, C Aquiles Serdán and C José Azueta. Ask taxi drivers for the cheaper places.

Mazatlán centre

balconies, filters on taps/faucets for drinking water, recommended; **B** *Azteca Inn*, Camarón Sabalo, T134477, F137476, pool.

Along Av del Mar, across the road from the beach (front rooms in all are likely to be noisy), are: **AL** *De Cima*, T827300. **AL** *Hacienda*, T827000. **AL** *Don Pelayo/Days Inn*, Av del Mar I, III, T831888, F840799, TV, a/c, pool, parking off street, bar (may be noisy late at night). **AL-A** *Aguamarina*, No 110, T817080, F824624. **B-C** *The Sands (Las Arenas)*, pool, a/c, TV, fridge, garden, good restaurant, recommended, on beach. **C** *Amigos Plaza*, Av del Mar 900, T830333, F837282, before *Las Brisas*, some rooms a/c, noisy at weekends, otherwise OK. **C-E** *San Diego*, Av del Mar s/n y Rafael Buelna, T835703; *Las Jacarandas*, Av del Mar 2,500, just before Zona Dorada, T841177, F841077, pool, garden, good value.

Along Olas Altas beach are: **D** *Belmar*, No 166 Sur, T851112, F813428, modernized but old, a bit run down, pool. **C-D** *La Siesta*, No 11 Sur, T812640, F137476, a/c, clean, friendly, safe, very good, nice patio, restaurant: *Shrimp Bucket*.

On Paseo Centenario is: **C** *Olas Altas*, T813192, with fan, efficiently run and clean, good views, restaurant. Most of the others are in the downtown area away from the beach front: **C** *Villa del Mar*, Aquiles Serdán 1506, next door at 1510 is a business with fax and email service. **D** *Del Centro*, JM Canizales 705 Pte, T821673, behind main church. **D** *Económico*, with bath and fan, noisy, dark but very clean, next to bus station, 500 metres from main beach. **D** *Milán*, JM Canizales 717. **D** *Posada Familiar Sarita*, Mariano Escobedo, colonial, near beach. **D-E** *Vialta*, Azueta 2006, 3 blocks from market, with bath and fan, nice central patio, friendly, helpful, comfortable. **E** *San Fernando*, 21 de Marzo 926, T815980, with bath, hot water eventually, very basic, very friendly, recommended, car park outside. **E** *Casa de Huéspedes El Castillo*, José Azueta 1612, 2 blocks from market, clean, family atmosphere, big rooms. **E** *Lerma*, Simón Bolívar 5, near beach, with fan and hot showers, friendly, clean, simple, but quiet and cool, highly recommended. **E** *Roma*, Av Juan Carrasco 127, T823685, 2 blocks from beach, with bath but some rooms noisy, clean. **E** *Zaragoza*, Zaragoza 18, old and pretty, with bath, cheap cold drinks, free drinking water, parking for motorbikes.

North of the city there are undeveloped beaches with free overnight camping; some have camped alone, but it is safer in a group (take bus to Sabalos and get out where it turns round). At least 10 trailer parks on Playa del Norte/Zona Dorada and on towards the north, including **D** *Casa Blanca Disco*, cheapest, on beach side, dirty. Big hotels rapidly expanding all along north beach seashore to Mármol.

Motels Strung all along the ocean front. On RT Loaiza: **A** *Los Arcos*, No 214, T/F135066, on beach. **A** *Marley/Suites Lindamar*, No 222, T/F135533, recommended, reservations necessary. **AL** *La Casa Contenta*, No 224, T134976, F139986, apartments. **C** *Del Sol*, Av del Mar 200, T814712, big rooms, with a/c and TV, clean, bright, nice pool, English spoken, motorcyclists allowed to park in front of room, close to aquarium, also have some apartments with kitchen. **C** *Papagayo*, Papagayo 712, T816489. *La Posta Trailer Park* (turn inland at *Valentino's Disco* from northern beach road), busy, hook-ups at most sites, ½ block off beach, with swimming pool and tent space, lots of shade. **D** *Mar Rosa Trailer Park*, Camarón Sabalo 702 2½ kilometres north of *La Posta*, T136187, hot water, safe, own beach, recommended. 3 blocks up the road opposite is *San Fernando*, clean, good, little shade. 4 kilometres north of *Mar Rosa* is **D** *Playa Escondida*, Av Sábalo-Cerritos 999, T880077, laid back, 236 spaces for RV park, not all have water and electricity, OK (**B-D** in bungalows), pool, volleyball, TV. Beware of theft from trailer parks. If driving to trailer parks north of the city, pass airport on Route 15, avoid left fork 'Centro y Playas'; follow route signed 'Culiacán' but do not go onto the toll road to Culiacán which starts at the Carta Blanca agency. Keep left and 10 kilometres further turn left at sign 'Playa Cerritos', at beach road turn left again. This leads to **E** *Maravilla Trailer Park*, next to Edif DIF, PO Box 1470, Mazatlán, T40400, 35 spaces, hot showers, clean, quiet; *Holliday*, opposite beach, and *Canoa*, private club, nice, expensive. If coming to Mazatlán from the north turn right at 'Playas Mazatlán Nte' sign on Highway 15; after about 14 kilometres you reach the junction with the Av Camarón Sabalo.

Eating *Mamucas*, Bolívar 404, seafood expensive. *Shrimp Bucket* and *Señor Frog*, Olas Altas 11 and Av del Mar, same owners, very famous, popular, good. *La Cumbre*, Benito Juárez and Hidalgo, few seats, very busy, not many tourists, open 1100-1500, recommended. *Beach Boys Club*, on Malecón near fisherman's monument, good value meals, US-owned. *El Paraíso*, on beach in Zona Dorada is recommended. *Balneario Playa Norte*, Av del Mar, near monument, friendly, reasonable prices, recommended; also on Av del Mar, Playa Norte, *Bella Mar*, good, comparatively cheap. Many restaurants along Camaron Sabalo, eg *Villa Italia*, good varied menu; *Señor Pepper*, elegant décor, good service, food reasonable; *Doney's*, good home cooking, expensive, recommended. *Lobster Trap*, Camarón Sabalo 307, good chicken(!). *Mariscos El Camichín*, Paseo Claussen 97, excellent seafood parillada, good value, recommended. *Joncol's*, Flores 608 Pte, a/c, downtown, popular. *Los Comales*, Angel Flores, 2 blocks from Correo, good. Best value fish meals, US$4, above the markets near Plaza de la República (bring beer with you from supermarket opposite – not sold in cheap restaurants). Try mixed fish dish, US$15 for 2, very good. *Bar Pacífico*, on main plaza, excellent guacamole and chicken wings, pleasant atmosphere; *Las Cazuelas*, Canizales 273, good cheap *comedor*, friendly. *Cenaduria el Tunel*, Carnaval 1207, opposite theatre, excellent chicken *enchiladas*. *Pastelería y Cafetería Panamá*, several branches for reasonable meals, pastries, coffee, the one behind the cathedral on C Juárez is recommended. *Casa del Naturista*, Zaragoza 809, sells good wholegrain bread. US fast food places, eg *McDonald's*, *Pizza Hut*, are more expensive than in North America.

Entertainment *Joe's Oyster Bar*, very good disco behind *Hotel Los Sabalos*, open-air, US$10 cover charge and open bar.

Festivals The local Shrovetide carnival is almost as good as at Veracruz.

Sports **Fishing** is the main sport (sailfish, tarpon, marlin, etc). Its famous fishing tournament follows Acapulco's and precedes the one at Guaymas. In the mangrove swamps are egrets, flamingos, pelicans, cranes, herons, and duck. Nearby at Camarones there is **parasailing**, drawn by motorboats. The northern beach tourist strip offers boat trips to nearby deserted islands, snorkel hire and paragliding. **Bungee jumping** is done at junction Camarón Sabalo y Rafael Buelna opposite *McDonalds*, US$26. Always check with the locals whether **swimming** is safe, since there are strong rip currents in the Pacific which run out to sea and are extremely dangerous. There is a free Red Cross treatment station 9 blocks along the avenue opposite the Beach Man on the right. There are **bull-fights** at Mazatlán, good view from general seats in the shade (*sombra*), although you can pay much more to get seats in the first 7 rows – Sunday at 1600, very touristy.

Transport **Local** Green and white express buses on the 'Sabalo centro' route run from Playa Cerritos to the city centre along the seafront road, US$0.35. Taxis charge an average US$3.50-5 between Zona Dorada and city centre. From Bahía del Puerto Viejo to centre, taxi US$1, bus US$0.20. **Car hire**: all on Camarón Sabalo: **Budget**, No 402, T132000, F143611. **National**, No 7000, T136000, F139087, US$280 per week. **AGA**, No 316, T144405.

Air Airport Gen Rafael Buelna (MZT) 19 kilometres from centre. Taxi, fixed fare US$24 airport-Mazatlán; micro bus US$6 per person. Flights to Mexico City, Guadalajara, La Paz, Durango, Ciudad Juárez, Hermosillo, Los Cabos, Los Mochis, Monterrey, Puerto Vallarta, Querétaro, Tijuana and Torreón. US destinations: Los Angeles, San Francisco, Denver, Seattle, Tucson, San Antonio and Phoenix.

Trains Take 'Insurgentes' bus out to Morelos railway station.

Buses Terminal at Chachalaco y Ferrusquilla s/n, T812335/815381; take 'Insurgentes' bus from terminal to Av Ejército Mexicano for the centre, via market at C Serdán; if you cross the boulevard and take bus in the other direction it goes to the railway station (US$0.60); alternatively take a *pulmonía*, a taxi which looks like a golf cart, which costs US$3 to Zona Dorada. Computel outlet open 24 hours daily at bus station with fax and long distance phone services. Bus fare to **Mexico City** about US$55, 18 hours (Tres Estrellas de Oro, T813680, 1st class, express at 2100 a little more expensive; Transportes del Pacífico hourly 1st class slightly cheaper but over 20 hours, via Irapuato and Querétaro). **Mexicali** US$50,

Mexico

Pullman, 21 hours. **Guadalajara**, several companies, several times a day, US$19.25 (10 hours). To **Chihuahua**, US$38 1st class, 19 hours. To crossroads for **San Blas**, US$8; **Tepic** US$8 (5¼ hours; Tepic is the best place to make connections to Puerto Vallarta); bus (frequent) to **Los Mochis** (5½ hours), US$18 with Transportes Norte de Sonora, Estrella Blanca or Autotransportes del Pacífico, tickets available only 45 minutes before departure. Autotransportes del Pacífico buses go hourly to Culiacán (US$11) and Los Mochis 0800-2030 via the expressway. To **Navojoa**, US$11 1st class; 2 daily 1st class buses to **Durango**, Futura at 0930, Transportes Chihuahuaenses at 1400, 7 hours, US$15, several 2nd class buses, take an am bus to see the scenery; **Guaymas**, 12 hours, US$30. Elite (own waiting room) to **Puerto Vallarta**, 1600, US$20, **Guadalajara**, 7 daily, US$26, **Mexico City**, 1100, 1400, 1945, 2100, US$58, **Tijuana** 1345, US$80, **Nogales**, 2115, US$58. Ejecutivo (luxury) bus to **Guadalajara** at 2200, US$38. Bus to **Rosario** US$1.65, can then with difficulty catch bus to Caimanero beach, nearly deserted. Terminal Alamos, Av Ote Guerrero 402, 2 blocks from market, buses to **Alamos** every hour on the half hour.

Tolls: Mazatlán to Culiacán US$65. **Cycling**: beware, the road Mazatlán-Tepic-Guadalajara has been described as 'the most dangerous in the world for cyclists'.

Ferry La Paz (Baja California Sur), see schedule, page 552, for other information see under La Paz, Baja California section. Allow plenty of time for booking and customs procedure. Tickets from Hotel Aguamarina, Av del Mar 110, with 10 percent commission, also from travel agents. Ferry terminal is at the southern end of Av del Puerto, quite a way from centre (take bus marked 'Playa Sur', which will also go from street corner opposite ferry terminal to Av Ejército Méxicano near bus station). **NB** Ticket office for La Paz ferry opens 0830-1300 only, on day of departure, arrive before 0800, unclaimed reservations on sale at 1100. Don't expect to get vehicle space for same-day departure.

Directory **Airline offices** *Aero California*, T69-132042. *AeroMéxico*, T69-841111. *Alaska Airlines*, T95-800-4260333. *Mexicana*, T69-827722. *United*, T91-800-0030700. **Banks** *Banamex*, Benito Juárez and Angel Flores, also Av Camarón Sabalo 434, 0900-1330, 1530-1730. *Casas de Cambio* on same avenida, Nos 109, 1009 and at junction with Rodolfo T Loaiza; also at R T Loaiza 309. **Communications** Post Office: Benito Juárez y 21 de Marzo, opposite Government Palace, T812121. DHL is a couple of doors from *Mail Boxes etc* (see below), 0900-1330, 1500-1800 Mon-Fri, 0830-1330 Sat. **Telephones:** 1 block from American Express; also 21 de Marzo y B Juárez. Computel phone and fax service, Aquiles Serdán 1512, T69-850109, F850108. Phone rental, Accetel, Camarón Sabalo 310-4, T165056. There are public phones taking international credit cards all along Camarón Sabalo and Rodolfo T Loaiza in the Zona Dorada for long distance calls. **Internet:** *Mail Boxes Etc*, Camarón Sabalo 310, T164009, F164011, mail boxes, courier service, fax service, US$3.50 per 15 mins, mailboxes@ red2000.com.mx; across the street at Centro Comercial Lomas, local 9 is another internet outlet, US$5 per 1 hr, T140008. *Red 2000*, Plaza Las Américas, email, internet. **Embassies & consulates** Consulates: *Canada*, *Hotel Playa Mazatlán*, Rodolfo T Loaiza 202, T137320/F146655. *US* Consulate, T134455 ext 285. *France*, Jacarandas 6, T828552. *Netherlands*, Av Sabalo Cerritos, T135155. *Germany*, Jacarandas 10, T822809. *Italy*, Av Olas Altas 66-105, T814855. *Norway*, F Alcalde 4, T813237. *US*, RT Loaiza, opposite *Hotel Playa Mazatlán*, Mon-Fri 0930-1300, T/F165889. **Hospitals** *Hospital General*, Av Ferrocarril, T840262. *Cruz Roja Mexicana*, Alvaro Obregón 73, T813690. **Laundry** On Av del Mar, between bus station and *Hotel Aguamarina*, also on Benito Suárez near *Hotel Lerma*. **Tour companies & travel agents** Travel agents: *Explora Tours*, Centro Comercial Lomas, Av Camarón Sabalo 204-L-10, T139020, F161322, very helpful, recommended. *Zafari Tours*, Paseo Claussen 25, ferry bookings, helpful. *Hudson Tours*, T131764, for mountain biking. **Tourist offices** *Camarón Sabalo*, past the main part of the Zona Dorada, in Banrural building, 4th floor, opposite *Mar Rosa* trailer park and *Holiday Inn*, a long way to go to get information easily obtained at any travel agency or hotel information desk. Information from www.mazcity.com.mx/homepage.htm; tourist news, www.pacificpearl.com. **Useful telephone numbers** Emergency: call T06; Red Cross T813690; Ambulance T851451; Police T821867.

Mazatlán to Durango

24 kilometres beyond Mazatlán, the Coast-to-Coast Highway to Durango (a spectacular stretch in good condition), Torreón, Monterrey and Matamoros turns off left at Villa Unión. Heading east, the road reaches **Concordia**, a delightful colonial town with a well-kept plaza and a splendid church (2 **F** hotels, one at each end of town on the main road), then climbs the mountains past **Copalá**, another mining ghost-town (basic hotel); *Daniel's Restaurant*, open 0900-1700. Copalá can be reached by tour bus from Mazatlán or by Auriga pick-up truck from Concordia. On this road, 40 kilometres from Concordia, three kilometres before **Santa Lucía**, at La Capilla del Taxte, 1,240 metres, there is a good German hotel and restaurant, **D**, *Villa Blanca*, T21628. Before reaching **La Ciudad** (one very basic hotel) and the plains the road goes through a spectacular section, winding through many vertical-sided canyons with partly forested slopes. The road is a phenomenal feat of engineering, as it is cut into the cliff side with steep drops below. At one point, called *El Espinozo del Diablo*, (Devil's Spine) the road is a narrow bridge (approximately 50 metres long) with vertical drops either side and superb views to the south and north. After reaching the high plateau, the road passes through heavily logged pine forests to Durango. **NB** Cyclists will find this road hard work in this direction, as there are many bends and steep hills. Trucks are frequent but travel at very reduced speeds.

Route to Tepic

The road to Tepic continues south from Villa Unión. At **Rosario**, 68 kilometres south of Mazatlán, an old mining town riddled with underground workings, the church is worth a visit (**D** *Hotel Los Morales*, with a/c, **E** with fan, on main highway opposite Pemex, clean, quiet, good bathrooms; there is a very good *palapa* and hilltop restaurant with limited access, 360° view). South of Rosario is **Escuinapa** (several kilometres north of Escuinapa is **B** *Motel Virginia*, Carretera Internacional Km 1107-1108, T69-532755, good clean, *palapa* restaurant next door, possible trailer parking). There is a good seafood restaurant on the left at the entrance of Escuinapa coming from Mazatlán.

In Escuinapa a good road turns off 30 kilometres to the coast at Teacapán. The Boca de Teacapán, an inlet from the sea opening into lagoons and the mangrove swamps, is the border between Sinaloa and Nayarit. The area has palm trees, much bird and animal life, cattle ranches, and is an exporter of shrimp and mangoes. The fishing is excellent and you can buy fresh fish directly from the fishermen on Teacapán beach. There are fine beaches such as Las Cabras, La Tambora and Los Angeles. Dolphins can be seen at certain times of year. Buses from Escuinapa; tours from Mazatlán US$45 (eg Marlin Tours, T135301/142690, F164616).

Teacapán
Colour map 2, grid C3

Sleeping **B** *Rancho Los Angeles*, Teacapán Ecológico (Las Palmas 1-B, Col Los Pinos, Mazatlán, T/F817867), former home of a drug baron (deceased), 16 kilometres south from Teacapán towards Escuinapa, on beach, good value, swimming pool, trailer park, US$12; **D** *Hotel Denisse*, on square, T/F69545266, José Morales and Carol Snobel, clean, next to phone office, noisy, local trips arranged; you can also rent houses with kitchen facilities a few kilometres before Teacapán on the road at Hacienda Los Angeles; three trailer parks (*Oregon*, US$8, no signs, on beach in town, run down but one of better places to stay, new Mexican hotel next door; *Las Lupitas*, US$8, rustic, run down; another on bay, take road next to *Las Lupitas*, US$3, primitive, pretty setting). **SR** *Wayne's Restaurant*, on beach behind *Palmeras Hotel*, recommended.

Quaint little towns just off the highway between Mazatlán and Tepic: **Acaponeta** (turnoff for El Novillero beach, large waves and many sandflies), Rosamorada, Tuxpan and Santiago Ixcuintla, all with colonial religious buildings and archaeological museums.

Mexico

Mexcaltitán From Highway 15, the island of **Mexcaltitán** can be reached. Turn off to Sentispac, from where a dirt road leads to La Batanga on Laguna Mexcaltitán; from Tepic take bus to Santiago Ixcuintla and then colectivo to La Batanga (30 minutes). Boats go to the small island (20-minute ride through mangroves), which is only about 350 metres in diameter, now a fishing village, but reputed to be one of the stopping places, around end 11th century, on the Aztecs' search for a home and subsequent migration to the central Valley of Mexico. The name means 'place of the temple of the moon'. There is a museum. The town's streets are sometimes flooded during the rainy season and the entire village takes to boats. Its *fiesta*, St Peter and St Paul, is on 28-29 June.

San Blas

Colour map 3, grid B3   The resort is 69 kilometres from Tepic and is overcrowded during US and Mexican summer holidays. Founded in 1768, little is left of the old Spanish fortress, **Basilio**, but there are various colonial ruins. Above the town are **La Contaduría**, the Spanish counting (1773) house, and **La Marinera**, a ruined church. In town near the harbour is the old customs house (1781-85) and a stone and adobe church on the plaza (1808-78). Up to the mid-19th Century San Blas was a thriving port and still has a naval base and a (smelly) harbour. In August it becomes very hot and there are many mosquitoes, but not on the beach two kilometres from the village (but there are other biting insects, so take repellent anyway); few tourists at this time or early in the year. The best beach is **Playa de las Islitas** (the one in town is dirty). Seven kilometres from San Blas (bus, taxi US$3 per car) is the beach of **Matanchén**, good swimming but many mosquitoes. Good homemade fruit cakes and bread sold here. Surfing can be done at these beaches, but rarely at any one time is the surf up at all of them. Check at Juan Bananas (see below, **Surfing**). About three times a year it is possible to surf non stop for over a mile, from town towards Las Islitas, relaying on a series of point breaks. 16 kilometres south from San Blas is the beautiful Los Cocos beach (see below). The beach is empty except at weekends. **NB** Don't wander too far from public beach; tourists have warned against attacks and robberies.

Excursions   Four-hour boat trips to see whales and dolphins are available. Ask at the Tourist Office. Armando is a good guide, charges US$52 for three people.

It is possible to take a three-hour jungle trip in a boat (bus to *embarcadero* on Matenchen road) to **La Tovara**, a small resort with fresh-water swimming hole, brimming with turtles and catfish restaurant, and not much else, or walking, to do. Tour buses leave from the bridge one kilometre out of town and cost US$30 for canoe with six passengers but cheaper to arrange trip at *embarcadero* US$22. Official prices are posted but it still seems possible to shop around. Away from the swimming hole there are coatis, raccoons, iguanas, turtles, boat-billed herons, egrets and parrots. Avoid fast motorized boats as the motor noise will scare any animals. Tours on foot are better. Crocodiles are kept in caves along the route. You have to pay US$2 to see the poor, shabby creatures, not recommended. Twilight tours enable naturalists to see pottos and, if very lucky, an ocelot. La Tovara is crowded at midday during the summer. A cheaper one and a half to two hours' cruise is also possible from the *embarcadero*, US$14.50 for boat which simply goes to the swimming hole (20 minutes away, first part through tunnel of mangroves). When arranging your trip make sure you are told the length of journey and route in advance. You can take a bus from San Blas towards Santa Cruz (see below under Tepic) and get off at Matanchén beach (see above). From here, a boat for half-day hire includes the best part of the jungle cruise from San Blas.

Sleeping   **A1** *Marino Inn*, Bataillon, T50340, a/c, friendly, pool, fair food. **A1** *Garza-Canela*, Cuauhtémoc Sur 106, T50112, very clean, highly recommended, excellent restaurant, small pool, nice garden. **B** *Bucanero*, Juárez Pte 75, T50101, with bath and fan, frequented by

Americans, food good, pool, lizards abound, noisy discos 3 times a week and bar is open till 0100 with loud music. **B** *Posada del Rey*, very clean, swimming pool, excellent value, on Campeche, T50123; *Posada de Morales* also has a swimming pool, more expensive, ½ block from *Posada del Rey*, T50023. **C** *San Blas Motel*, near Zócalo, patio, fans, good value, swimming pool, safe parking. **D** *Flamingos*, Juárez Pte 105, huge rooms, ceiling fans, colonial, clean, friendly. **D** *Posada Azul*, 4 blocks from plaza towards beach, 3-bedded rooms with fan and hot water, **F** for simple 2-bedded rooms without bath, cooking facilities. **D-E** *El Tesoro de San Blas*, 50 metres south of dock, 5 minutes from centre, rooms and villas, hot water, satellite TV, US owners. **E** *María's*, fairly clean with cooking, washing and fridge facilities, without bath, **D** with bath and fan, a bit noisy, no single rooms, friendly, recommended. No camping or sleeping permitted on beaches but several pay campsites available. **Trailer park** at town beach; all trailer parks in the centre are plagued by mosquitoes. The best trailer park is on Los Cocos beach: *Playa Amor*, good beach, on a narrow strip of land between road to Santa Cruz and cliff, good, popular, 16 kilometres south of town, US$7-10. Next south is **E** *Hotel Delfín*, with bath, balcony, good view, good value; then *Raffles Restaurant* with trailer and camping area attached (no facilities). Last on Los Cocos beach is *Hotel y Restaurante Casa Mañana*, T324-80610 or Tepic T/F321-33565, Austrian run, good food. Many apartments for rent.

Amparo, on main plaza, cheap and good; *Tumba de Yako*, on way to beach, yoghurt and **Eating** health foods, and the original version of *pan de plátano* that is advertised all over town. Also sells banana bread at Las Islitas, recommended. *MacDonald* just off Zócalo, good breakfast. Plenty of seafood restaurants on the beach; eg *Las Olas*, good and cheap. On Sunday women prepare delicious pots of stew for eating al fresco on the plaza.

Surfing: *Tumba de Yako* (see above, **Eating**) rents out boards, US$1.80 per hour, US$6.50 **Sports** per day, owner, Juan Bananas, was Mexican surfing champion, gives lessons.

Bus station on corner of plaza; to **Tepic**, frequent US$3, 1½ hours. To **Guadalajara**, US$10, 8 **Transport** ½ hours.

Banks *Banamex* just off Zócalo, exchange 0830-1000 only. *Comercial de San Blas* on the main **Directory** square will change money, plus commission. **Tourist office** On road to old ruined customs house, 1 block from plaza, T50021, info in English on history of San Blas plus town map.

Before reaching Tepic both road and railway begin the long climb from the lowland level over the Sierra Madre to the basin of Jalisco, 1,500 metres above sea-level. The Mirador El Aguila is on Highway 15, 11 kilometres after the junction to San Blas; it overlooks a canyon where many birds can be seen in the morning and the late afternoon.

Tepic

Capital of Nayarit state, Tepic was founded in 1531 at the foot of the extinct volcano of Sangagüey. It is a slightly scruffy town with much rebuilding going on but clean. There are many little squares, all filled with trees and flowers.

Km 807
Population: 200,000
State Population: 1995
895,975
Altitude: 900
Phone code: 32
Colour map 3, grid B1

The landscape around Tepic is wild and mountainous; access is very difficult. Here live the Huichol and Cora Indians. Their dress is very picturesque; their craftwork – bags (carried only by men), scarves woven in colourful designs and necklaces (*chaquira*) of tiny beads and wall-hangings of brightly coloured wool – is available from souvenir shops (these handicrafts are reported to be cheaper in Guadalajara, at the Casa de Artesanías). You may see some in Tepic but it is best to let Indians approach you when they come to town if you want to purchase any items.

The **Cathedral** (1891), with two fine Gothic towers, in Plaza Principal, has been **Sights** restored; it is painted primrose yellow, adorned with gold. Worth seeing are the

Palacio Municipal, painted pink; the **Casa de Amado Nervo** (the poet and diplomat), Zacatecas Nte 281 (■ *Monday-Friday 1000-1400, Saturday 1000-1300*); the **Museo Regional de Antropología e Historia (Museo de Nayarit)**, Av México 91 Nte (open 0900-1900, Monday-Friday, 0900-1500 Saturday); **Museo de Los Cuatro Pueblos** (Tepehuanos, Huicholes, Cora, Nahuatl), Hidalgo y Zacateca, ■ *Monday-Friday 0900-1400, 1600-1900, Saturday-Sunday 0900-1400*; **Emilia Ortez Museum of Art**, C Lerdo 192 Pte (■ *Monday-Saturday 0900-1400);* **Museo de Arte Visual 'Aramara'**, Allende 329 Pte (■ *Monday-Friday 0900-1400 and 1600-2000, Saturday 0900-1400);* **Plaza de los Constituyentes** (México y Juárez) with, on one side, the **Palacio de Gobierno**; and the **ExConvento de la Cruz**, on the summit of a hill close to the centre. The tombs in the cemetery are worth seeing.

Sleeping **B** *Real de Don Juan*, Av México 105 Sur, on Plaza de Los Constituyentes, T/F161888, parking. **B-C** *Bugam Villas*, Av Insurgentes y Libramiento Pte, T180225, F180225, very comfy rooms with a/c, TV, pool, garden, restaurant with great food and good wine list. **C** *Fray Junipero Serra*, Lerdo Pte 23, T122525, main square, comfortable, big rooms, clean, a/c, good restaurant, friendly, good service, recommended. **C** *Ibarra*, Durango 297 A Nte, T123870, luxurious rooms, with bath and fan (some rooms noisy), and slightly spartan, cheaper rooms without bath, very clean, DHL collection point. **C** *San Jorge*, Lerdo 124, T121324, very comfortable, good value. **C** *Villa de las Rosas*, Insurgentes 100, T131800, fans, friendly, noisy in front, good food, but not clean.

D *Altamirano*, Mina 19 Ote, T127131, near Palacio del Gobierno, parking, noisy but good value. **D** *Santa Fe*, Calzada de la Cruz 85, near La Loma park, a few minutes from centre, with TV, clean, comfortable, good restaurant. **D** *Sierra de Alicia*, Av México 180 Nte, T120322, F121309, with fan, tiled stairways, friendly. **E** *Las Américas*, Puebla 317 Nte, T163285. **E** *México*, México 116 Nte, T122354. **E** *Nayarit*, E Zapata 190 Pte, T122183. **E** *Sarita*, Bravo

Tepic

112 Pte, T121333, clean, TV, restaurant, parking, good. **E** *Tepic*, Dr Martínez 438, T131377, near bus station outside town, with bath, clean, friendly but noisy. **F** *Pensión Morales*, Insurgentes y Sánchez, 4 blocks from bus station, clean and friendly, hotel is now closed but family still put up backpackers in what is now private house. **F** *Camarena*, 4 blocks from Zócalo, San Luis Nte 63, without bath, clean, friendly.

Motels **B** *La Loma*, Paseo la Loma 301 (swimming pool), T132222, run down. *Bungalows and Trailer Park Koala*, La Laguna, Santa María del Oro, has bungalows at US$20, each accommodating up to 4, several trailer sites (US$10) and a large campground. Good cheap meals available. Fishing and waterskiing on nearby lagoon.

El Apacho, opposite *Hotel Ibarra*, good *sopes*, cheap. *El Tripol*, in mall, near plaza, excellent **Eating** vegetarian. *Danny O* ice cream shop next door. *Café Farolito*, Zacatecas 129, for *comida corrida*. *Roberto's* and *Chante Clair*, both good food and near La Loma Park, closed Sunday. *La Terraza*, Mexican and American food, pies, cakes; good vegetarian restaurant at Veracruz 16 Nte, try the granola yoghurts. *Tiki Room*, San Luís Nte opposite *Hotel Camarena*, restaurant, art gallery, video bar, fun. Restaurant in bus terminal, overpriced. Lots of fish stalls by market on Puebla Nte. The local *huevos rancheros* are extremely picante.

Air Airport Amado Nervo (TPQ) with flights to Los Angeles, Mexico City, Tampico and **Transport** Tijuana daily with Aero California, T161636 or AeroMéxico, T139047.

Trains Station at Prolongación Allende y Jesús García, T134861.

Buses Bus station is a fairly short walk into town, T136747; bus from centre to terminal from Puebla Nte by market. At bus station there are phones, including credit card, post office, left luggage and tourist information (not always open). Bus to **San Blas** from main bus terminal and from local bus station on park at Av Victoria y México, from 0615 every hour US$3. To **Guadalajara**, US$12.50, 3 hours frequent departures, several companies; **Mazatlán**, 4½ hours, US$8; to **Los Mochis**, US$32; to **Puerto Vallarta**, 3 hours, US$6; **Mexico City**, US$30.25.

Banks *Casas de cambio* at México 91 and 140 Nte, Mon-Sat 0900-1400, 1600-2000. **Directory** **Communications** Telephones: credit card phone at Veracruz Nte y Zapata Pte. **Tour companies & travel agents** *Viajes Regina*, tours to San Blas, 8 hrs, US$22.50; Playas de Ensueño, Fri, 8 hrs, US$15.50; Tepic city tour, Mon and Sat, 3 hrs, US$7. *Tovara*, Ignacio Allende 30. **Tourist offices** México 178 Nte, 1 block from cathedral, T121905, officially open daily, 0900-2000 (in reality not so), English spoken, helpful. *Municipal Tourist Office*, Puebla y Amado Nervo, T165661, F126033, also very helpful. Also offices at Convento de la Cruz, Airport and bus station.

One can visit **Cora** villages only by air, as there are no real roads, and it takes at least **Huaynamota** two days. However, it is possible to visit Huichol villages from the small town of **Huaynamota** in the mountains northeast of Tepic which has become much easier to reach with the opening of the Aguamilpa Dam. Boats leave from the west end of the dam at 0900 and 1400 (US$7, one and a half hours, return at 0700, 1030), stopping at *embarcaderos* for villages along the way. The valley, despite being flooded, is still beautiful, particularly at the narrower parts of the dam where huge boulders hang precariously on clifftops. The *embarcadero* for Huaynamota is at the end of the dam where the Río Atengo feeds in. A community truck meets the launch (US$1.30). It is eight kilometres up a dirt road to the town which is half populated by Huichol, some of whose traditional houses can be seen on its fringes. There are no hotels. Ask at church or at store (basic supplies) on long south side of plaza for possible lodging. A good view over the river valley may be had from the large boulder beside the road at the edge of town. From Huaynamota ask around for guides to Huichol villages four or more hours away. *Semana Santa* week is famous, many people from surrounding communities converge on Huaynamota at this time. *Getting there:* Kombis leave Tepic from terminal on Av México just below Zaragoza when full, US$2, 1½ hours. Kombis leave for the dam from Av Mexico just down from Zaragoza, US$2, 1½ hours.

Lagoons About 50 kilometres from Tepic, off the Guadalajara road, is an attractive area of volcanic lagoons, take the bus to **Santa María del Oro** for the lagoon of the same name. On the south side of the toll road is the Laguna Tepetiltic and near Chapalilla is another lake at San Pedro Lagunillas.

Santa Cruz To various beaches along the coast, some of them off the Nogales highway, for

Tepic environs

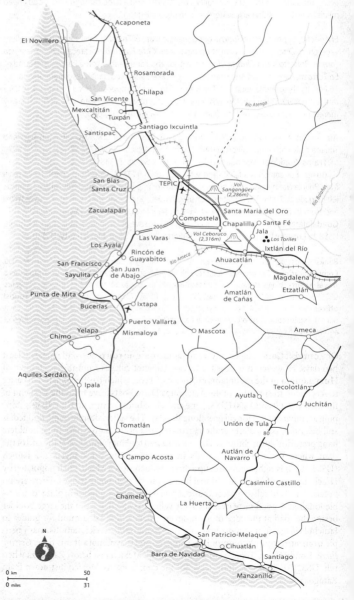

example, **Santa Cruz**, about 37 kilometres from Tepic (rocky beach). No hotels, but there are rental apartments, a camping area and accommodation at *Peter's Shop*, E, basic but pleasant and friendly. Simple food available, *Restaurant Belmar*, fish and rice, all reminiscent of the South Seas. There is a shrimp farm nearby. (two buses a day from San Blas to Santa Cruz, US$1.10, or two and a half hours ride by open-sided lorry, US$0.75.)

A road runs south from Tepic through **Compostela** (**F** *Hotel Naryt*, with bath, basic but clean) a pleasant small town with an old church, El Señor de la Misericordia, built 1539. From Compostela one can catch an old bus to **Zacualapán**, one and a half hours over a paved road, to visit a small enclosed park with sculptures that have been found in the area, two blocks from main square. Gate to the park must be unlocked by caretaker: inside there is a small museum. Zacualapán is a pleasant village, knock on a door to ask for the caretaker.

A road from Compostela reaches the coast at **Las Varas** (**E** *Hotel Contreras*, with fan and bath, clean, small rooms). Las Varas is connected also by good road to San Blas, north up the coast. Beaches on the coast road south to Puerto Vallarta include **Chacala**, nice free beach lined with coconut palms, good swimming, cold showers (restaurant *Delfín*, delicious smoked fish) and reached by an unsurfaced road through jungle. **Rincón de Guayabitos** is being developed as a tourist resort with hotels, holiday village and trailer park (**C** *Coca*, among several hotels and restaurants on a rocky peninsula to the south of the beach). Then come Los Ayala, Lo de Marcos and **San Francisco** (*Costa Azul Resort*, on beach, delightful, pool, apartments, restaurant). **Sayulita** is a beach resort with accommodation and restaurants but the beach is littered (*Trailer Park* highly recommended, on beautiful beach, German owner, very friendly, US$10 per day, also has bungalows, Apdo 5-585, CP 06500, Mexico DF, Mexico City T55721335, F53902750, turn off Route 200 at Km 123, two and a half kilometres; *Tía Adriana's* Bed and breakfast, T/F32751092, November-June, good, central, good value). **Punta de Mita**, a fishing village and beach resort at the tip of a peninsula with fish restaurants, miles of beach, abundant bird life (nearby **A3** *Hotel and Trailer Park Piedras Blancas*, good, also camping, US$10, hook-ups US$12-14, restaurants; excellent restaurant at Playa Desileteros not cheap but delicious food, Medina or Pacífico bus from Puerto Vallarta every 15 minutes). There are boat trips to the nearby **Islas Marietas**, where there are caves and birds. Camping is possible on the beach. Simple accommodation available or stay at the attractive **C** *Quinta del Sol*. **Los Veneros**, between Bucerías and Punta de Mita is a pretty cove with fairly safe sea bathing where there is a private beach club reached down a seven-kilometre private road through woods to the beach. Entry US$8 including a margarita or non-alcoholic infusion of 'Jamaica' made from hibiscus petals, beautifully designed, clean, two restaurants, bar, gardens, café, terraced towards beach, food excellent, no extra charge for sunbeds/umbrellas, further development likely according to environmental priorities, horse riding, mountain bikes, watersports, archaeological trail, guided tour, botanical garden in preparation. Open daily 1000-1800, T10088/10158, you can take a shuttle bus from Los Veneros bus station. Cruz de Huanacaxtle, **Bucerías** (*Hotel Playa de Bucerías*, Km 154, and **B** *Marlyn*), **Peñita de Jaltemba** (**C** bungalows at north end of town, with clean rooms and kitchen; **C-D** *Hotel Mar Azul*) and others.

Coast road to Puerto Vallarta

Mexico

Puerto Vallarta

The road south from Tepic, through Compostela, enters Jalisco state just before **Puerto Vallarta**. This is the second largest resort in Mexico, Greater Puerto Vallarta is drawn-out along some 25 kilometres of the west-facing curve of the deeply-incised Banderas Bay. For ease of reference, it can be split into five sections: **North central**, the oldest, with the main plaza, cathedral and seafront Malecón as well as an uninviting strip of pebble/sand beach; **South central**, across the Rio

Population: 100,000
Phone book 322
Colour map 3, grid B1

Puerto Vallarta

Mexico

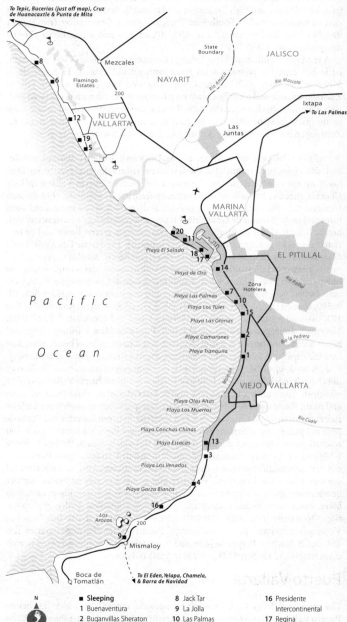

To Tepic, Bucerías (just off map), Cruz de Huanacaxtle & Punta de Mita

Mezcales

Flamingo Estates

NAYARIT

NUEVO VALLARTA

State Boundary

JALISCO

Rio Ameca

Rio Mascota

Ixtapa
To Las Palmas

Las Juntas

MARINA VALLARTA

P a c i f i c

O c e a n

EL PITILLAL

Rio Pitillal

20

11
18
17

Playa El Salado

14

Playa de Oro

7

Zona Hotelera

Playa Las Palmas

10

Playa Los Tules

15

Playa Las Glorias

Playa Camarones

2

Rio la Pedrera

Playa Tranquila

1

Malecón

VIEJO VALLARTA

Playa Olas Altas
Playa Los Muertos

Rio Cuale

Playa Conchas Chinas

Playa Estacas

13

3

Playa Los Venados

Playa Garza Blanca

4

16

Los Arocos

9 Mismaloy

Boca de Tomatlán

To El Eden, Yelapa, Chamela, & Barra de Navidad

N

0 km 10
0 miles 6.3

Related map
A Puerto Vallarta
centre, page 205

■ **Sleeping**
1 Buenaventura
2 Buganvillas Sheraton
3 Camino Real
4 Casa Grande
5 Diamond
6 Diamond Sunset
7 Fiesta Americana

8 Jack Tar
9 La Jolla
10 Las Palmas
11 Marriott
12 Oasis Marival
13 Playa Conchas Chinas
14 Playa de Oro
15 Plaza Vallarta

16 Presidente
Intercontinental
17 Regina
18 Royal Mazua
19 Sierra
20 Velas Vallarta

Cuale, is newer but similarly packed with shops and restaurants and bordered by the fine, deep sand of Playa de los Muertos; **South shore**, where the mountains come to the sea, several cove beaches and a scattering of big hotels; **North hotel zone**, a long stretch from town towards the cruise ship terminal and the airport, with mediocre beaches, many big hotels, several commercial centres; **Marina Vallarta**, further north, with a dazzling array of craft, a golf course, smart hotels and poor quality beach, you can't walk far because of condominiums built around the marina; **Nuevo Vallarta**, 18 kilometres north of centre, with golf course and marina, in the neighbouring state of Nayarit (time difference), modern, all-inclusive hotels are strung along miles of white sand beach, far from amenities.

A highly commercialized sun-and-sand holiday resort marred by congestion and widespread condominium developments, Puerto Vallarta also has its advantages. The stepped and cobbled streets of the old centre are picturesque, accommodations and restaurants are varied enough to suit everybody, there is much good hiking in the surrounding hills and watersports and diving are easily accessible. Increasingly it has become a base for excursions and for special interest trips including ornithology and whale watching.

Most travellers will find the central area the most convenient to stay in; its two halves are divided by the Rio Cuale and a narrow island where souvenir shops, cafés and the museum are located. The most dramatic beach in the centre is Playa de los Muertos, apparently named after the murderous activities of pirates in the late 16th century, although the 'dead' tag could apply equally to the fierce undertow or possibly to the pollution which affects this corner of the bay. The authorities are trying to get people to use a sunnier sobriquet: 'Playa del Sol'. Conchas Chinas is probably the best beach close to town, being quiet and clean (at any holiday time, though, every beach is packed); a cobblestone road leads to Conchas Chinas from route 200, just after *Club Alexandra*.

NB Those confined to wheelchairs are warned that parts of Puerto Vallarta are bad, with high kerbs, steps and cobblestone streets. North Central and south Central are both difficult, but the northern area and the Marina are flatter and more accessible.

During the rainy season, June-September, some trips are not possible. From November-April, humpback whale watching is organized. A recommended trip including snorkelling is with John Pegueros, who owns the schooner *Elias Mann*. Contact him at Lázaro Cárdenas 27, Apdo Postal 73, Bucerías, Nayarit, CP63732, T329-80060, F80061. Tickets from Marina Vallarta, US$60 includes some meals, starts 0800. See also **Tour companies and travel agents** below.

40 kilometres northeast of Puerto Vallarta is the inland village of **Las Palmas**, a typical though unremarkable *pueblo* (buses every 30 minutes, one hour 10 minutes). On the way is the workers' *pueblo* of **Ixtapa**, established by the Montgomery Fruit Co in 1925. Near here are postclassic stone mounds scattered over a wide area.

10 kilometres south of Puerto Vallarta, along the coast road is **Mismaloya**, where John Huston made *Night of the Iguana* with Richard Burton. A lovely beach backed by a steep subtropical valley, even though the *La Jolla Mismaloya* hotel looms over the sands. The beach is clean and you can hire umbrellas and chairs for the day, US$1; beware of undertow at low tide. The film set has been developed as 'Iguana Park'. There are many condominiums on the north side. You can go horse riding up the valley with Victor, of Rancho Manolo, beside the road bridge, T80018. **Boca de Tomatlán**, four kilometres further south, is a quaint and rather down at heel fishing village at the river estuary. There are apartments to rent, simple restaurants, a dirty beach and a footbridge across the river. To **Yelapa**, an Indian village with a waterfall, now commercialized with entertainment ranging from live music to rodeo. Tourist water taxi from pier (Los Muertos) US$12 return, leaves 1030, 1100. From fisherman's quay on Malecón (by *Hotel Rosita*, opposite *McDonald's*) US$5 one way, leaves 1130. From Boca de Tomatlán (bus, US$0.30) water taxi is US$3.50 one way, from beach, leaves 1030. Organized tours may be better value for anyone wanting to

Excursions

Mexico

combine such activities as snorkelling at Los Arcos en route. **B** *Lagunitas*, cabina hotel with pool. *Tino's Oasis* is an excellent place to stay, American owned, cheap. Alternatively stay with Mateo and Elenita, **C**, including breakfast, visit their waterfall. Camping available 30 minutes' walk up valley, US$4 per person, in beautiful setting, owners Beto and Felicidad (ask for Felicidad's home-made tortillas "the best in Mexico").

Walk or mountain bike up valley of Río Cuale, through magnificent hills with dense subtropical vegetation, some bathing pools, many birds, a few *ranchitos* and *pueblecitos*. To begin, walk to eastern extremity of Lázaro Cárdenas, cross wide bridge and turn sharp right; walk along cobbled street with river on right. Pass *colonia* of Buenos Aires and water purification plant; later cross suspension footbridge and continue up rough track with river on left. Two kilometres later, recross the now crystalline Río Cuale via stepping stones. Go as far as you like. 54 kilometres onward is the ex-mining (silver, gold) village of **Cuale**; cobbled streets, rustic.

Sleeping

■ *on maps, page 202 & 205*
Price codes:
see inside front cover

North Central **L** *Casa Kimberley*, Zaragoza 445, T21336, former home of Richard Burton and Elizabeth Taylor, 10 rooms full of memorabilia of the actors, breakfast included, much cheaper in low season. **AL** *Casa Del Puente*, by bridge opposite market, T20749, suites with kitchen in a private villa suspended above river, delightful, book months ahead. **B** *Cuatro Vientos*, Matamoros 520, T20161, up steep cobbled street from church, lots of steps, great views, restaurant, plunge pool, breakfast included. **C** *Rosita*, Paseo Díaz Ordaz 901, at north end of Malecón, T32000, F32142, resort's original holiday hotel (est 1948) with pool, on town beach, excellent value and location, recommended.

D *Hotel Escuela*, Hidalgo 300, corner Guerrero, T24910, F30294, is where they teach trainee hotel personnel, a bit clinical, with street noise, but said to be good value. **E** unmarked *hospedaje* at Allende 257, esq Guadalupe, T20986, US owner, Isabel Jordan also has rooms and *cabañas* in Yelapa, more expensive.

South Central **L** *Meza Del Mar*, Amapas 380, T24888, F22308, perched high above Los Muertos beach with slow lifts, balconies remain in shade, small pool, all-inclusive packages. **L** *Playa Los Arcos*, Olas Altas 380, T20583, F22418, good location for restaurants, undersized pool terrace overflows to Los Muertos beach. **AL** *Buenaventura*, Mexico 1301, T23737, F23546, on shore, fringe of centre, lively holiday hotel. **AL** *Molina de Agua*, Ignacio L Vallarta 130, T21957, F26056, cabins in pleasant wooded glade on bank of river, a/c, good service, 2 pools, recommended. **AL** *San Marino Plaza* (formerly the *Oro Verde*, Rodolfo Gómez 111, T20350, F22431, a/c, pleasant, friendly, standard holiday package, compact pool terrace adjoins los Muertos beach. **A** *Casa Corazón*, Amapas 326, T/F21371, hard to find US-owned hideaway on steep slope down to Los Muertos beach, overpriced but 3 big rooms on top terrace with spectacular views worth the premium, including big breakfast. **B** *Eloisa*, Lázaro Cárdenas 179, T26465, F20286, on square by Playa de los Muertos, a holiday hotel with small pool, most rooms face dim hallways. **B** *Gaviotas*, behind *Eloisa*, Madero 154, Parque Lázaro Cárdenas, T21500, F25516, faintly colonial, balcony access, glimpses of sea. **B** *Posada de Roger*, Basilio Badillo 237, T20639, F30482, courtyard arrangement, neat rooms off narrow access balconies, tiny and overpriced, splash pool. **B** *Posada Río Cuale*, Aquiles Serdán 242, near new bridge, T/F20450, small pool in front garden, not very private, nice, colonial-style rooms. **C** *Gloria del Mar*, Amapas 115, T25143, by Playa de los Muertos, charmless but clean, convenient holiday base, small rooms.

D *Belmar*, Insurgentes 161, T/F20572, spartan, ill-lit but friendly, on main road near buses. **D** *Yasmín*, B Badillo 168, T20087, a claustrophobic courtyard arrangement behind *Café Olla*, good value, noisy till at least 2300. There are several cheaper hotels grouped in C Francisco y Madero, west of Insurgentes: **E** *Azteca*, No 473, T22750, probably best of this group. **E** *Villa del Mar*, No 440, T20785, also satisfactory. **E-F**, and within a few doors are: *Cartagena*, No 428, *Lina*, No 376, T21661, with bath, no hot water, run down, rooms on street noisy, *Analiz* and *Bernal*, No 423, T23605, friendly, large rooms, fan, good showers, recommended, all convenient for restaurants, a few blocks from long distance buses.

North Hotel Zone LL *Fiesta Americana*, T42010, F42108, maintains high service standards in Disneyesque jungly theme. **LL** *Krystal Vallarta*, T40202, F40150, has suites, apartments, flanking cobbled lanes in Mexican *pueblo* style, amid greenery, fountains, wrought iron streetlights. **LL** *Sheraton Bouganvilias*, T30404, F20500, dated block on good patch of beach close to downtown, vast but unexciting expanse of grounds. **LL** *Continental Plaza*, Playa Las Glorias, T40123, F45236, in overly-cute 'Old Mexico' style. **LL** *Holiday Inn*, T61700, F45683, unmissable deep mustard edifice shares undersized pool with hulking condominium next door. **LL** *Moranda Casa Grande*, T30916, F24601, all-inclusive, tasteless. **LL** *Qualton Spa*, T44446, F44445, blocky atrium hotel with crowded pool area extending to beach. **L** *Las Palmas*, Blvd Medina Ascencio, Km 2.5, T40650, F40543, castaway-on-a-desert-island theme, all rooms with sea view. **AL** *Hacienda Buenaventura*, Paseo de la Marina, T46667, F46242, modern, with colonial influence, pleasant pool, is nicest in zone but 100 metres to beach and on main road, discounts out of season. **AL** *Los*

Puerto Vallarta centre

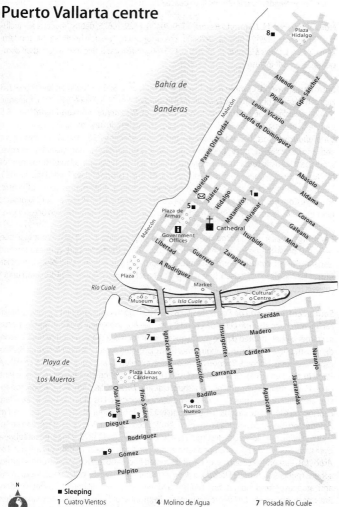

N

Not to scale

■ **Sleeping**

1 Cuatro Vientos	4 Molino de Agua	7 Posada Río Cuale
2 Eloisa	5 Paraíso	8 Rosita
3 Fontana del Mar	6 Playa Los Arcos	9 San Marino Plaza

Pélicanos, T41010, F41111, small-scale, rooms enclose central quadrangle with pool, 100 metres to beach. **AL** *Plaza Las Glorias*, T44444, F46559, attractive white low-rise, breezy beachfront location. **AL** *Suites del Sol*, Francia y Liverpool, T42541, F42213, above offices at busy junction on wrong side of road for beach, jumbled open-plan public rooms, tiny pool, large rooms; *Vista Club Playa de Oro*, Av Las Garzas, T46868, F40348, near cruise ship terminal, a predictable all-inclusive with much manufactured fun, many activities. Cheap hotels are scarce here: **C** *Motel Costa del Sol*, 300 metres north of *Sheraton*, opposite side, T22055.

Marina Vallarta LL *Marriott Casa Magna*, T10004, F10760, grandiose interiors, superb pool, upmarket restaurants. **LL** *Westin Regina*, T11100, F11141, vibrant colours, imaginative lighting, much cascading water, lush gardens. **LL** *Royal Maeva*, T10200, big, brassy all-inclusive packages. **LL** *Velas Vallarta*, T10751, F10755, Moorish touches to big, part timeshare hotel with verdant gardens. **AL** *Plaza Iguana*, T10880, F10889, small pool adjoins marina promenade, 10 minutes walk to beach.

Nuevo Vallarta LL *Diamond Resort*, T329-70400, F329-70626, gaudy, raucous all- inclusive. **LL** *Sierra*, T329-71300, F329-70800, colourful building-block hotel, smart, modern, all-inclusive. **L** *Oasis Marival*, T329-70100, F70160, more established and sedate than competitors here, all-inclusive.

Southern shore LL *Camino Real*, Playa de las Estacas, T15000, F16000 on lovely beach 3 kilometres south of centre. **LL** *La Jolla de Mismaloya*, Km 11.5, T80660, F80500, romantic though overdeveloped setting on filmset beach. **LL** *Presidente Intercontinental*, Km 8.5 Carretera a Barra de Navidad, T80507, F80116, stylish luxury on quiet sandy cove. **L** *Majahuitas Resort*, between Quimixto and Yelapa beaches, T322-15808, run by Margot and Lirio González, including breakfast and dinner, 3 guesthouses, more planned, on cove, sandy beach, rustic furniture, solar energy, riding and snorkelling available, 30 percent of profits go to indigenous community of Chacala. **AL** *Casa Grande*, Playa Palo María, T21023, hulking twin towers of all-inclusive fun on crummy beach, 4 kilometres south of centre. **AL** *Playa Conchas Chinas*, Km 2.5 Carretera a Barra de Navidad, T/F15770, about 1 kilometre before *Camino Real*, on west side of road, spacious rooms with kitchenettes and ocean views.

Camping 2 trailer parks: *Tacho*, on road to Pipala, opposite Marina, 60 spaces but spacious, US$14.50 (treat the police at the traffic lights/turn off to the trailer park with caution and respect). *Puerto Vallarta*, north of centre, just north of bypass then east 2 blocks, popular. Also at fishing village of Yelapa, best reached by boat from *Hotel Rosita* at 1130: camp under shelters (*palapas*), about US$4 per person.

Eating **South Centre** *Posada de Roger*, Basilio Badillo 237, good courtyard dining, mainly Mexi-
● *on maps* can menu, cheapish. *Café Olla*, lower end Basilio Badillo, good value Mexican and barbecue in cramped open-fronted dining room, queues wait for more than an hour in high season, demonstrating a lack of imagination rather than discerning palate. *Puerto Nuevo*, on Badillo, expensive but good food. *Buengusto*, Rodríguez, excellent home cooked Mexican meals. *A Page in the Sun* (café), Olas Altas opposite *Los Arcos* hotel on corner, coffee is excellent, cakes home-made, second-hand bookshop. *Daiquiri Dick's*, Olas Altas 314, T20566, restaurant and bar open for breakfast, lunch and dinner, opposite Los Muertos beach, excellent cooking, classical harp and guitar music Sunday 1300-1500, about US$18-20 per person. *Las Palopas*, on the beach near Playa de Los Muertos, good food, service, value, décor and atmosphere. *Felipe's*, Prolongación Insurgentes 466, Col Alta Vista, T23820, 21434, beautiful view over town from large balcony, good food and service, can share 1 portion between 2. *Los Arbolitos*, east end of Lazaro Cardenas, 3 balconied floors above river, Mexican, good atmosphere, moderate prices. *El Dorado*, palapa restaurant on Playa de los Muertos, inexpensive and attractive surroundings but touristy and besieged by belligerent chiclet vendors, 3rd-rate musicians etc. *La Fuente del Puente*, riverfront at old bridge, opposite market, Mexican, colourful, good music, good value meals but drinks expensive. *Jazz Café/Le Bistro*, by the bridge on Insurgentes, garden, bamboo, beside river, pleasant for coffee and classical

music (piano or harp) in morning, crowded and expensive in evening, many vegetarian dishes, clean. *Café Maximilian*, Olas Altas 380-B, rear part of *Playa Los Arcos*, open 1600-2300, closed Sunday, huge Austrian owner, food recommended, about US$22 per person meal with wine, clean, efficient, busy, some tables on pavement.

North Centre *Pepe's Tacos*, on Honduras, opposite Pemex at northern end of downtown, cheap, ethnic and delicious in spartan pink/white dining room, open all night. *Juanita's*, Av México 1067, attracts locals as well as value-seeking gringos, good. *Gaby*, C Mina, small, family-run, eat in garden, excellent food, cheap and clean. *Las Margaritas*, Juárez 512, forget the queues at the popular gringo restaurants, this one is excellent, moderately-priced, cosmopolitan and curiously under-patronized, colonial-style courtyard, recommended. *Café Amadeus*, Miramar 271, up steps from Guerrero, classical music, books, board games in delightful whitewashed rooms or balcony perched above old town, coffee, delectable cakes, recommended. *La Dolce Vita*, midway along Malecón, is hugely popular (queues) Italian and pizza place favoured by package tourists. *Rico Mac Taco*, Av México, corner Uruguay, busy, cheap and widely popular eatery.

Nightlife *Carlos O'Brian's*, Malecón and *Andale*, Olas Altas, attract a motley crowd of revellers and start hopping after 2200. Martini types head for *Christine*, at *Hotel Krystal*, for spectacular light show, disco, expensive drinks and cover. Many clubs and late bars throughout central area.

Shopping Endless opportunities, including armies of non-aggressive beach vendors. The flea market is grossly overpriced; the many shops often better value, but not to any great degree. Guadalajara is cheaper for practically everything. The market is by the bridge at the end of Insurgentes, sells silver, clothes, souvenirs as well as meat and fish. Large, well-stocked supermarket nearby. Jewellery at *Olas de Plata*, Francisco Rodríguez 132. Plaza Malecón has 28 curio shops, restaurant, music etc. *GR* supermarket, Constitución 136, reasonable for basics. Second-hand books, English and some in German, at *Rosas Expresso*, Olas Altas 399.

Transport **Local Buses**: Mismaloya to Marina, US$0.24, but complicated routing. The main southbound artery through town is México-Morelos-Vallarta, the main northbound is Juárez-Insurgentes. Plaza Lázaro Cárdenas is the main terminal in south of town and starting point for Mismaloya-Boca buses going south. Buses marked 'Olas Altas' go to south Central, those marked 'Hoteles' or 'Aeropuerto' to north hotel zone and beyond. Buses are also marked for 'Marina' and 'Mismaloya/Boca' (Boca de Tomatlán). The ones marked 'Centro' go through town, those with 'Tunel' take the bypass. Buses to outlying villages with Medina bus line, terminal at Brasil, between Brasilia and Guatemala, regular (15-20 minutes) service to Nuevo Vallarta, San José, San Juan, Bucerías, L Manzanilla, Punta de Mita and others. Fares from US$0.75-US$1.50. **Car hire**: widely available. **Scooter hire**: opposite *Sheraton*, T21765.

    Air International Ordaz airport (PVR) 6 kilometres from centre, T11325. If you walk 100 metres to the highway and catch a local bus to town, it will cost far less than the US$10 taxi fare. International flights from Anchorage (Alaska), Austin (Texas), Boston (MA), Burbank (California), Chicago, Dallas, Denver (Colorado), Frankfurt (Germany), Houston, Los Angeles, New York, Phoenix (Arizona), Portland (Oregon), San Diego (California), San Fransisco, Seattle and Tampa. Mexican destinations served include Mexico City, Guadalajara, Acapulco, Chihuahua, Ciudad Juárez, Morelia, Queretaro, Tijuna, Aguascalientes, León, Los Cabos, Mazatlán and Monterrey.

    Buses All buses leave from a central bus station almost opposite the airport. Taxis from the airport to the bus station charge inflated prices, but there are buses. Frequent service to Guadalajara, ETN 8 a day, US$21.25, Transportes del Pacífico, 1st class, US$16.25. Elite runs to Guadalajara, Mexico City, Tijuana, Mazatlán, Cd Juárez, Monterrey, Zihuatanejo, Acapulco, Aguascalientes, Tecoman. Primera Plus to Guadalajara, León, Querétaro, Metaque, Manzanillo (US$9.50, dep 0300, $4\frac{1}{2}$ hours), Cd Guzmán, Colima, and Barra de Navidad, 4 hours, 0800 and 1300.

Directory **Airline offices** *AeroMéxico*, T42777. *Alaska Airlines*, T95-800-4260333, or 11350. *American Airlines*,

Mexico

T91-800-90460, or 11799. *America West*, T800-2359292, 800-5336862, or 11333. *Continental*, T91-800-90050, or 11025. *Delta*, T91-800-90221, or 11032. *Taesa*, T50899. *Mexicana*, T48900. *United*, T911-800-00307, 800-4265561. **Banks** *Cambios* on nearly every street in tourist areas. Rates inferior to Guadalajara. Check *Bancomer's cambio* at Juárez 450, for best rates. Like most, it is open every day until late. Numerous banks offer slightly better rates (but slower service) and ATMs for Visa, Mastercard. **Communications Post Office:** Mina between Juárez and Morelos. Long distance **phone** (*casetas*) and **fax** at Lázaro Cárdenas 267, open daily to 2300, also in lobby of *Hotel Eloisa*, both US$3 per minute to Europe. Many shops bear *Larga distancia* sign, check tariffs. **Internet:** *Net House CyberCafé*, Ignacio L Vallarta 232, T26953, open 24 hours. **Embassies & consulates Consulates:** *Canada*, Edif Vallarta Plaza, Zaragoza 160, 1st floor, interior 10, T25398, F23517, open 1000-1400. *USA*, T20069/30074. **Hospitals & medical services** Doctor: *Dra Irma Gittelson*, Juárez 479, speaks French and English, very helpful. **Emergency:** T915-7247900. **Laundry** Practically one on every block in south central; numerous throughout resort. **Tour companies & travel agents** *American Express*, Morelos 660, esq Abasolo, T32955, F32926, town guide available. **Open Air Expeditions**, Guerrero 339, T23310, openair@vivamexico.com, Oscar and Isabel run hiking trips (mountain or waterfall), whale watching (winter), kayaking, birdwatching and other trips from US$40, knowledgeable guides. *Vallarta Adventure*, Edif Marina Golf, local 13-C, Marina Vallarta, T/F10657, boat trips, whale watching, Las Marietas (US$50), Sierra Madre expedition (US$60), jeep safari (US$60), dolphin encounter (US$60), Las Caletas by night or by day (US$50), also scuba diving, PADI certification, a 2-tank dive to Las Marietas, or Las Caletas, with lunch costs US$80, 0900-1630. *Mountain Bike Adventures*, Guerrero 361, T31834, offer trips for cyclists of varying grades of competence, from local environs up to 3-4 days in old silver towns of Sierra Madre, all equipment provided including good, front-suspension bikes, from US$36. *Sierra Madre*, facing the Malecón near Domínguez, are agents for many tours and some of their own, including a long, all-day truck safari to Sierra Madre mountains. *Rancho El Charro*, T40114, horseback expeditions to jungle villages, Sierra Madre silver towns. Independent horse riding guides and horses congregate at lower end of Basilio Badillo; also occasionally at fisherman's wharf, by *Hotel Rosital*, for short beach and mountain trips, agree price beforehand. Many agents and hotel tour desks offer boat trips, car hire and tours at big discounts if you accept a timeshare presentation. Worthwhile savings are to be made for those prepared to brazen out the sales pitch, and many do. **Tourist office** *Morelos* 28-A; in the government building on the main square, very helpful; T30744/20242. Tourist news, tribuna@pnet.puerto.net.mx. **Useful addresses Immigration:** Morelos 600, T11380.

South of Puerto Vallarta

South of Puerto Vallarta paved Route 200 continues down the coast to Melaque, Barra de Navidad and Manzanillo. Beaches and hotels on this route: 103 kilometres south of Puerto Vallarta and 12 kilometres inland, at the town of **Tomatlán** (not to be confused with Boca de Tomatlán, on the coast), are a few modest hotels (eg **E** *Posada Carmelita*, with bath, clean); at **Chamela**, Perula village at north end of Chamela beach. **C** *Hotel Punta Perula*, T333-70190, on beach, Mexican style; *Villa Polonesia Trailer Park*, US$12 for car and two people, recommended, full hook-ups, hot showers, on lovely beach (follow signs from Route 200 on unmade road); restaurant on road to trailer park, clean, good food. Pemex at Chamela is closed, no other for miles. Two hours south of Puerto Vallarta is the luxury resort **LL** *Las Alamandas*, T328-55500, beautiful beach, health club, horse riding, tennis etc. The resort is one kilometre south of Puente San Nicolás on Route 200, turn right towards coast at sign to Quemaro. Owned by Isobel Goldsmith, it is very exclusive, has been featured in several magazines for the clientèle it attracts and reservations should be made in advance. In the UK 0171-3731762. The excellent **AL** *Hotel Careyes* is en route, and several others, **A-B** *El Tecuán*, Carretera 200, Km 32.5, T333-70132 (lovely hotel, gorgeous beach, mediocre bar/restaurant, pool, highly recommended), and, eight kilometres further south, **A** *Hotel Tenacatita* near the village of the same name (see page 239). The road continues to Zihuatanejo and Acapulco, and finally to Salina Cruz. The road from 40 kilometres south of Chamela to Melaque is very poor.

Tepic to Guadalajara

Route 15 leaves Tepic for Guadalajara. At Chapalilla is a turn-off to Compostela and Puerto Vallarta. At **Ahuacatlán**, 75 kilometres from Tepic, the 17th century ex-convent of San Juan Evangelista stands on the Plaza Principal; handicrafts on sale here. Nearby, the village of **Jala** has a festival mid-August. **E** *Hotel Cambero*. From here the **Ceboruco** volcano can be reached in a day. On the main road a lava flow from Ceboruco is visible (*El Ceboruco, parador turístico*, with restaurant, information, toilets and shop; buses do not stop here). 84 kilometres (one and a quarter hours by bus) from Tepic is **Ixtlán del Río** (**D** *Hotel Colonial*, Hidalgo 45 Pte, very friendly, recommended; *Motel Colón*; cheaper hotels round the Zócalo are *Roma* and *Turista*). Two kilometres out of town along this road are the ruins of **Los Toriles**, a Toltec ceremonial centre on a warm, wind-swept plain. The main structure is the Temple of Quetzalcoatl, noted for its cruciform windows and circular shape. The ruins have been largely restored, admission US$2.35, some explanatory notes posted around the site. There is a caretaker but no real facilities. The journey from Tepic to Guadalajara cannot easily be broken at Ixtlán for sightseeing since buses passing through in either direction tend to be full; bus on to Guadalajara three hours, US$4.25. There are a few souvenir shops, a Museo Arqueológico in the Palacio Municipal, a *casa de cambio* and a railway station. Harvest (maize) festival mid-September. Two kilometres beyond the Los Toriles site is *Motel Hacienda*, with pool. The road climbs out of the valley through uncultivated land, trees intermixed with prickly pear and chaparral cactus. Jalisco state is entered (see below) and 19 kilometres before Tequila is Magdalena (hotel, *Restaurant Magdalena*), congested with traffic, small lake nearby. As the bus approaches Tequila there may be opportunities to buy the drink of the same name on board. The blue agave, from which it is distilled, can be seen growing in the pleasant, hilly countryside.

Tequila

Tequila, 58 kilometres from Guadalajara, is the main place where the famous Mexican drink is distilled. Tours of the distilleries are available (see box) and stores will let you sample different tequilas before you buy. Often around 20 bottles are open for tasting. The town is attractive and a mix of colonial and more modern architecture. It is a pleasant place to stay but there is not much to do other than tour the distilleries and there is little in the way of nightlife. A day trip from Guadalajara is possible. Coming into town from Guadalajara, the road forks at the Pemex station, the right fork is the main highway and the left fork continues into town as C Sixto Gorjón, the main commercial street. Buses will let you off here, from where it is five to seven blocks to the main plaza. Along C Sixto Gorjón there are several liquor stores selling tequila, restaurants where you can eat for under US$5, pharmacies, doctors, dentists and the Rojo de los Altos bus ticket office at No 126A. There are two plazas next to each other. On one is the **Templo de Santiago Apóstol**, a large, pretty old stone building, with a 1930s municipal market next to it. Behind the church is the *Elypsis* discotheque, open at weekends. Also on this plaza is the Post Office and Banamex. About a block behind Banamex where Sixto Gorjón ends, is the entrance to the Cuervo tequila distillery. On the other square is the **Sauza Museo de Tequila** at C Albino Rojas 22, open until 1400, and the **Presidencia Municipal** with tourist office.

Population: 33,000
Altitude: 1,300m
Phone code: 374
Colour map 3, grid B2

Sleeping

D *Motel Delicias*, Carretera Internacional 595, on the highway from Guadalajara about 1 kilometre before Tequila, best available, TV, off-street parking. **E** *Abasolo*, Abasolo 80, parts under construction, rooms have TV. **F** *Colonial*, Morelos 52, corner of Sixto Gorjón, characterless, but central, clean and not run down, some rooms with private bath. **F** *Morelos*, corner of Morelos and Veracruz, a few blocks from the plaza, above a billiard hall, basic, ask in bar downstairs if there is no one at the hotel desk. Half-way between Tequila and Guadalajara, in

Mexico

 "A field of upright swords" – the making of tequila

The quote from Paul Theroux's The Old Patagonian Express *describes the swathes of blue agave grown in the dry highlands of the state of Jalisco and a few neighbouring areas. Agave is the raw material for the firewater, tequila, and although there are some 400 varieties of agave, only one, the blue agave is suitable. The spiky leaves are hacked off and the central core, weighing around 45 kilograms, is crushed and roasted to give the characteristic smell and flavour to the drink. The syrup extracted is then mixed with liquid sugar, fermented for 30-32 hours and then distilled twice. White tequila is the product of a further four months in wooden or stainless steel vats. It can be drunk neat, with a pinch of salt on the back of your hand, followed by a suck on a wedge of lime, or mixed into cocktails such as the famous Margarita. Gold tequila is a blend of white tequila and tequila which has been aged in wooden casks. Añejo, or aged, tequila, is a golden brown from spending at least two years in oak casks. As it ages it becomes smoother and is drunk like a fine brandy or aged rum. Special premium tequila has no sugar added, it is pure agave*

aged in wooden casks.

In pre-conquest times, the Indians used the agave sap to brew a mildly alcoholic drink, pulque, which is still drunk today. The Spaniards, however, wanted something more refined and stronger. They developed mescal and set up distilleries to produce what later became tequila. The first of these was established in 1795 by royal decree of King Charles IV of Spain. It is still in existence today: La Rojena, the distillery of José Cuervo, known by its black crow logo, is the biggest in the country. Around the town of Tequila there are 12 distilleries, of which 10 produce 75 percent of the country's tequila. Tours of the distilleries can be arranged with free samples and of course shopping opportunities. Tequila Cuervo, T6344170, F6348893, in Guadalajara, or T20076 in Tequila (contact Srta Clara Martínez for tours). Tequila Sauza, T6790600, F6790690, dating from 1873, see the famous fresco illustrating the joys of drinking tequila. Herradura, T6149657, 6584717, F6140175, in Amatitlán, 8 kilometres from Tequila in an old hacienda outside the village, which has adobe walls and cobblestone streets, worth a visit.

the mountains, is the British-run **LL** *Rancho Río Caliente*, 8 kilometres from the highway, a vegetarian thermal resort (room rates vary accordingly to location), riding and hiking excursions, massages and other personal services extra, taxi from Guadalajara 1 hour, US$25, for reservations in USA, Spa Vacations, PO Box 897, Millbrae, CA 94030, T650-6159543, F650-6150601.

Eating *El Callejón*, C Sixto Gorjón 105, rustic Mexican decor, main courses for under US$5, *antojitos* for less than US$3, hamburgers also available. *El Marinero*, C Albino Rojas 16B, nice seafood restaurant with strolling musicians. *El Sauza*, Juárez 45, beside Banamex, restaurant/bar, Mexican atmosphere.

Transport **Buses** 2nd class from the old terminal, Sala B, in Guadalajara, Rojo de los Altos, up to 2 hours, US$2. Return from outside Rojo de los Altos ticket office, C Sixto Gorjón, 126A, every 20 minutes, 0500-1600, then every 30 minutes until 2000. **Taxi**: to Guadalajara US$19, plus US$7 in tolls if you take the expressway.

Directory **Banks** *Banamex*, corner of Sixto Gorjón and Juárez, 24-hr ATM accepts Visa, Mastercard, and cards from the Cirrus and Plus networks. *Casa de cambio*, C Sixto Gorjón 73, open 0900-1400, 1600-2000, change cash and TCs.

NB There is a time change between Nayarit and Jalisco; the latter is six hours behind GMT, the former, as with all the Pacific coast north of Jalisco, seven hours behind.

Guadalajara to Mexico City

Mexico City

From the second city, Guadalajara, with its fine historical centre, to the capital, an area rich in crafts and traditions, especially the music and dance of Jalisco and Michoacán. There are lakes to visit (Chapala and Pátzcuaro), volcanoes (Colima, Paricutín, Toluca), the colonial city of Morelia, and worthwhile detours to the Pacific coast and to the towns south of Toluca.

The cultural life of Jalisco state has been helped by an economy based on crafts, agriculture, and livestock, with fewer pockets of abject poverty than elsewhere in Mexico. Many villages have traditional skills such as pottery, blown glass, shoemaking, and a curious and beautiful form of filigree weaving in which miniature flower baskets, fruit and religious images are shaped from chilte (chicle, the raw substance from which chewing-gum is made). The state is the original home of Mexico's mariachis: roving musical groups dressed in the gala suits and sombreros of early 19th century rural gentry.

Mexico

Guadalajara

Guadalajara, Mexico's second city founded on 14 February 1542 and capital of Jalisco state, 573 kilometres from Mexico City, and warmer than the capital. Graceful colonial arcades, or *portales*, flank scores of old plazas and shaded parks. The government is doing its best (within a limited budget) to preserve the colonial atmosphere and restore noteworthy buildings. It is illegal to modify the façades of colonial buildings in the centre. During the past 25 years the city has developed to the west of Av Chapultepec, where the best shops and residential neighbourhoods are now located. The climate is mild, dry and clear all through the year, although in summer it can be thundery at night. Pollution from vehicles can be bad downtown and the winter is the worst time for smog. However, afternoons are usually clear and sunny and during the rainy summer season smog is no problem.

Population: 5,000,000 in metropolitan area
State Population: 1995 5,990,054
Altitude: 1,650m
Phone code: 03
Colour map 3, grid B2

The heart of the city is the Plaza de Armas. On its north side is the **Cathedral**, begun in 1561, finished in 1618, in rather a medley of styles; its two spires are covered in blue and yellow tiles. There is a reputed Murillo Virgin inside (painted 1650), and the famous La Virgen del Carmen, painted by Miguel de Cabrera, a Zapotec Indian from Oaxaca. In the dome are frescoes of the four gospel writers and in the Capilla del Santísimo are more frescoes and paintings of the Last Supper. From outside you can see the sunset's rays streaming through the dome's stained glass. The Cathedral's west façade is on Plaza de los Laureles, on the north side of which is the **Palacio Municipal** (1952), which contains murals by Gabriel Flores of the founding of the city.

Also on the Plaza de Armas is the **Palacio de Gobierno** (1643) where in 1810 Hidalgo issued his first proclamation abolishing slavery (plaque). **José Clemente Orozco's** great murals can be seen on the central staircase; they depict social struggle, dominated by Hidalgo, with the church on the left, fascism on the right and the suffering peasants in the middle. More of Orozco's work can be seen in the **Congreso**, an integral part of the Palacio de Gobierno (entrance free), and in the main **University of Guadalajara** building in the Museo de Arte (small fee, good café), on Avs Juárez y Tolsá (re-named Enrique Díaz de León), in the dome of which is portrayed man asleep, man meditating, and man creating: lie on your back or look in a mirror. Other works by this artist can be seen at the University's main Library, at Glorieta Normal, and at the massive Cabañas Orphanage near the Mercado de la Libertad, now known as **Instituto Cultural Cabañas**. The Orphanage is a beautiful building with 22 patios, which is floodlit at night. ■ *Tuesday-Saturday 1015-1800, Sunday 1015-1445, entry US$1, US$15 to take photos.* The contents of the former Orozco museum in Mexico City have been transferred here. Look for 'Man of Fire' painted in the dome. Also in the Instituto Cabañas, exhibitions of Mexican art are

Sights

Guadalajara is generally a safe city. The centre is not deserted at night and people wander the streets in sociable groups. Normal precautions required against pickpockets but little more. Much safer than many US cities.

Mexico

The founding of a city

Nuno Beltrán de Guzmán, the founder of the city, named it after his birthplace in Spain, but was less certain about where he wanted it built. Its first location was at Nochistlán, but Guzmán ordered it moved to Tlacotlán and then in 1533 to what is now Tonalá. Still dissatisfied, in 1535 he moved it back to Tlacotlán, but it suffered repeated attacks from the Cazcanes, Tecuejes and Zapoteco Indians. After a particularly bloody massacre, the 26 survivors abandoned what was left of their village and moved to the site of present day Guadalajara.

shown and other events are held, listed under Entertainment below.

Going east from the Cathedral is the Plaza de la Liberación, with a statue of Hidalgo, where the national flag is raised and lowered daily (with much ceremony). On the north side are the **Museo Regional** (see **Museums** below) and the **Palacio Legislativo** (neo-classical, remodelled in 1982 ■ *open to the public 0900 to 1800*); it has a list of the names of all the Constituyentes, from Hidalgo to Otero (1824-57 and 1917). At the eastern end of this plaza is the enormous and fantastically decorated **Teatro Degollado** (1866, see **Entertainment** below), well worth seeing even if you do not go to a performance. ■ *1000-1400*.

A pedestrian mall, **Plaza Tapatía**, has been installed between the Teatro Degollado and the Instituto Cultural Cabañas, crossing the Calzada Independencia, covering 16 square blocks. It has beautiful plants, fountains, statuary, a tourist office, and is designed in colonial style. Facing Cabañas, on Morelos, is a sculpture by Rafael Zamarripa of Jalisco's symbol: two lions (in bronze) supporting a tree. The **Mercado Libertad** (San Juan de Dios, see **Shopping**), is south of Plaza Tapatía and between the market and Cabañas is a park, with a fine modern sculpture 'The Stampede', by Jorge de la Peña (1982).

Churches | **Churches** include **Santa Mónica** (1718), Santa Mónica y Reforma, small, but very elaborate with impressive arches full of gold under a clear atrium and a richly carved façade; **La Merced**, Hidalgo y Pedro Loza, beautiful interior with a remarkable number of confessional booths; **El Carmen**, Av Juárez 638, with a main altar surrounded by gilded Corinthian columns; **San José**, Alcalde y Reforma, a 19th century church with a fine gilded rococo pulpit, eight pillars in a semicircle around the altar, painted deep red and ochre behind, give an unusual effect, the overall light blue gives an airy feel; in the plaza outside is a statue of Núñez, defender of the Reforma, who was killed in 1858; **San Miguel de Belén**, Hospital 290, enclosed in the Hospital Civil Viejo which contains three fine late 18th century *retablos*; behind the hospital is the **Panteón de Belén**, a beautiful old cemetery closed to new burials for many years, entrance at C Belén 684 at corner of C Eulogio Parra, open until 1500; **San Agustín**, Morelos y Degollado (16th century), quite plain, with carved stones, musical school next door; and **San Francisco** (1550) with a three-tiered altar with columns, a feature repeated on the façade. To the north of this last church is the **Jardín San Francisco** (pleasantly shaded, starting point for horse-drawn carriages), and to the west the old church of **Nuestra Señora de Aránzazu**, with three fantastic churrigueresque altarpieces; equally impressive are the coloured ceilings and the finely carved dado, the only light comes from high-up windows and from the open east door. In the shadow of San Francisco is a modern statue to teachers. **María de Gracia**, V Carranza y Hidalgo, is beautiful. The **Santuario de Guadalupe**, on the corner of Av Alcalde and Juan Alvarez, is lovely inside; outside, in the Jardín del Santuario, fireworks are let off on 12 December, the day of the Virgin of Guadalupe, with musicians, vendors, games and people celebrating in the plaza.

Other sights worth seeing are the **Parque Alcalde**, Jesús García y Av de los Maestros, to the north of the centre; the **Plaza de Los Mariachis**, Obregón and Leonardo Vicario, near Mercado Libertad; and the **Templo Expiatorio**, Av Enrique Díaz de

León y Madero, with fine stained glass and intricate ceiling, gothic style, still unfinished after most of a century. There is a large park, zoological garden with plenty of Central American animals and aviaries in a delightful atmosphere (■ *US$1*) and planetarium just past the bullring going out on Calzada Independencia Nte. **Selva Mágica** amusement park is inside the zoo; it has a dolphin and seal show three to four times a day.

On Calzada Independencia Sur, at the intersection of Constituyentes and González Gallo is **Parque Agua Azul**. ■ *0800-1900, Tuesday to Sunday, US$0.20.* A

Guadalajara

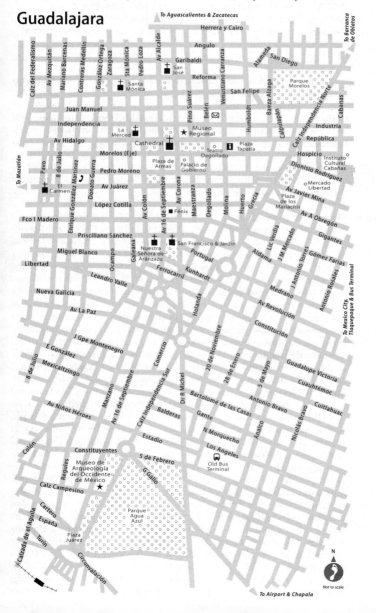

Mexico

☞ *The Cristero War*

The 1917 Constitution contained many provisions to curtail the political and economic power of the Catholic Church and the governments of the 1920s were decidedly anti-clerical in their efforts to implement it. Many, including President Plutarco Elías Calles (1924-28), who consolidated the Sonoran Dynasty in power for 15 years after the Revolution, sought to extirpate the Church. Catholic resistance turned to civil war (1926-29), which was most virulent in west-central parts of the country where many clergy and others lost their lives. The war cry of the Catholic rebels was 'Viva Cristo Rey' (long live Christ the King), which became shortened to Cristero as a nickname for the rebels and their war. The rebels were eventually betrayed by the Vatican and the bishops, who reached a compromise peace settlement with the Government.

park with a good aviary, trees, flowers and fountains, it contains the **Auditorio González Cano**, an outdoor concert bowl with portraits of famous Jalisco musicians, the **Teatro Experimental** and the **Casa de las Artesanías de Jalisco** (see **Crafts** below). On the other side of Calzada Independencia Sur is **Plaza Juárez** with an impressive monument ringed by the flags of other Latin American countries (take bus 52 or 54 up Av 16 de Septiembre or 60 or 62 up Calzada Independencia back to centre).

There are three universities (visit architectural faculty near Parque Mirador, 20 minutes by car from centre, or take bus (see local **Transport** below), overlooking Barranca de Oblatos, a huge canyon).

Museums **Museo de Arqueología del Occidente de México**, Calzada Independencia Sur y Calzada del Campesino (Plaza Juárez). Objects from Jalisco, Colima and Nayarit, pottery, ornaments, weapons, figures, illustrations of tombs, very comprehensive, small booklet in English. ■ *Monday-Friday 1000-1400, 1600-1800, Saturday-Sunday 1100-1430, 2 pesos.* **Museo Regional de Guadalajara**, Liceo 60, between Hidalgo y C Independencia (northeast of Cathedral). ■ *T6142227.* In an old seminary (1710) with a good prehistoric section (including the complete skeleton of a mammoth found in Jalisco), an interesting display of shaft tombs, excellent display of Colima, Nayarit, and Jalisco terracotta figures (but less extensive than Museo Arqueológico), possibly the finest display of 17th-18th century colonial art in Mexico outside the Museo Virreinal in Mexico City, musical instruments, Indian art and one room devoted to the history of Jalisco from the Conquistadores to Iturbide (highly recommended). ■ *Monday-Friday 0900-1900, Saturday 0900-1800, Sunday 0900-1500, US$2, free Sunday and holidays, over 60s and students with ID.* **Museo de Periodismo y Artes Gráficas**, Av Alcalde 225, between San Felipe and Reforma, T6139285/6, restored and opened 1994, the building is known as the Casa de los Perros because of two large dog statues on the roof. The first printing shop in Guadalajara was here and the first '*periódico insurgente*' in the Americas, *El Despertador Americano* was published here in 1810. The museum contains old printing presses, newspapers, etc. When Av Alcalde was widened in 1950, the building's façade was moved back nine metres. ■ *Tuesday-Saturday 1000-1800, Sunday 1100-1500, entrance 5 pesos, students with ID half price, over 60s free, Sunday free.* **Museo de la Ciudad**, C Independencia 684, in pretty colonial building with two columned patios, with information on the city from its founding to the present day, including maps and population statistics. ■ *Wednesday-Saturday 1000-1730, Sunday 1000-1430, 3 pesos, free Sunday and for over 60s.* **Albarrán Hunting Museum**, Paseo de los Parques 3530, Colinas de San Javier, with a collection of rare animals from all over the world. ■ *Saturday and Sunday 1000-1400.* **Casa Museo López Portillo**, C Liceo 177, T6132411/2435, formerly the family home of the ex-President, restored 1982 when he was in office. It is a colonial house with a large tiled courtyard, and surrounding rooms furnished with 18th and 19th century

Tapatío

The word 'tapatío' is used to describe the people of Guadalajara and sometimes of the State of Jalisco but it is believed to derive from the Indian word 'tlapatiotl', used in the valley of Atemajac to describe a monetary and commercial unit, equivalent to 'three'. In Guadalajara everything was sold in groups of three. The first known reference to the word 'tlapatiotl' was in the work of Fray Francisco Jiménez, Cuatro libros de la naturaleza y virtudes medicinales de las plantas y animales de la Nueva España, published in 1615, where the word referred to a commercial unit.

Italian and French furniture. It is also used as a cultural centre with classes in music, dance, literature, children's literature, chess, Indian culture and languages. Across the street at Liceo 166 in another nice colonial building are the offices of the **Instituto Nacional de Antropología e Historia** (INAH), where there is a library with books on Guadalajara. ■ *1000-1600.* **Casa José Clemente Orozco**, Aurelio Aceves 29, pedestrian street half a block from Los Arcos, built in 1940s and donated to the state of Jalisco by the family on his death in 1951. ■ *1000-1600.* Two other museums are the **Museo de Cera**, Libertad 1872 entre Colonias y Hemerson and the **Museo del Juguete**, Hidalgo 1291, esq General Coronado. The **Casa de la Cultura**, Av 16 de Septiembre y Constituyentes, holds contemporary art exhibitions and lectures.

In a northwest suburb of Guadalajara are the Basílica de **Zapopán**, completed 1690, with a miraculous image of Nuestra Señora, known as La 'Generala' on the main altar, given to the Indians in 1542, and, next door, a museum of Huichol Indian art. ■ *Monday-Friday 1000-1400, Saturday-Sunday 1000-1300.* At one end of the pedestrian street, Paseo Teopitzintli, leading to the plaza and Basílica is the colonial style Arco de Ingreso. Tourist office is in the Casa de La Cultura, two blocks behind

Excursions

Zapopán

the Basílica on Guerrero. ■ *T633 0571, open Monday-Friday 0900-2100, Saturday 0900-1300.* Zapopán is reached by bus 275 along Av Alcalde, or take line 1 of the metro to Avila Camacho stop and pick up bus 175 to Zapopán. (**NB** There are several different 175s, check with driver that bus goes all the way to Zapapán.) Agricultural fair in November.

Eight kilometres (northeast) to the canyon of **Barranca de Oblatos**, 600 metres deep, reached by bus 42 and others from the market to end of line (admission US$0.10), with the Río Grande de Santiago cascading at the bottom (except in dry season). Guides to the bottom. Once described as a stupendous site; now spoilt by littering and sewage. See especially the Cola de Caballo waterfall and the Parque Mirador Dr Atl. The park is crowded on Sunday; Balneario Los Comachos, a large swimming pool with diving boards set on one side of the Barranca de Oblatos, has many terraces with tables and chairs and barbecue pits under mango trees; drinks and snacks on sale; now described as dirty. ■ *US$1.50.*

You can also visit the **Barranca de Huentitán**, access via the Mirador de Huentitán at the end of Calzada Independencia Norte, interesting flora, tremendous natural site, view better than at Oblatos. One hour to the bottom (no guide needed) and the river which is straddled by the historic bridge of Huentitán. Buses to Huentitán: 60, 62A, 'Jonilla Centro' from city centre; 44 'Sevilo C Médico', stops 100 metres short. All buses cost US$0.25.

En route for Tepic is the Bosque de Primavera, reached by town buses. Pine forests ideal for picnics, although increasingly littered; US$0.50 for a swim. Good restaurant, *Los Pioneros*, Carretera a Tesistán 2005, esq Av Hospital Angel Leaño, with bar, live music, attractions and US 'Wild West' atmosphere.

Four hours north of Guadalajara on the road from Zapopán through San Cristóbal de la Barranca is the small town of **Totatiche** near the Río Tlatenango, founded by the Caxcan Indians but taken over by the Spaniards between 1592-1600. Both Totatiche and neighbouring Temastián were evangelized by Franciscans and the church is in the classical Franciscan style, with a three-tiered tower. In the church is the urn containing the remains of the recently beatified Father Cristóbal Magallanes, who was killed in the Cristero War (see box). Next to the church is the Museo Cristero containing personal effects and furniture. At **Temastián**, 12 kilometres away, the Basílica houses an image of Christ venerated for escaping a lightening bolt which destroyed the cross it was on, known as 'el Señor de los Rayos'. Its fiesta is 11 January and is celebrated with dancing, parades and rodeos.

Tonalá 15 kilometres southwest of Guadalajara on the road to Mexico City is **Tonalá**, noted for its Sunday and Thursday markets, where you can pick up bargains in pottery and ceramics. The market is held on the central avenue, where all the buses from Guadalajara stop. Calle Benito Juárez intersects this avenue and is a main shopping street. It runs to the main plaza (where it intersects with C Madero, the other main shopping street in the centre) and on another block to the Parroquia Santiago de Tonalá, a very beautiful church built in the mid-17th century. On the plaza is the cream coloured Iglesia Sagrado Corazón. The walls are lined with crucifixion paintings. Also on the plaza are the Presidencia Municipal, a pastel blue-green colonial style building, and the municipal market (food and crafts). On Juárez: Aldana Luna, at No 194, sells wrought iron furniture (T6830302); Plaza Juárez is a large building at No 141 with several craft shops in it; Artesanías Nuño (T6830011), at No 59, sells brightly painted wooden animals. On Madero: there is a *casa de cambio* at No 122; *Restaurant Jalapeños* at No 23 serves pizza, beer and regular meals; **D** *Hotel Tonalá*, opposite, at No 22, is plain but in good shape, some rooms with TV. Another attractive restaurant is *El Rincón del Sol*, at 16 de Septiembre 61, serving steaks and Mexican food.

Many in our price ranges **A** and up, including: **LL** *Quinta Real*, Av México 2727 y López Mateos, T6150000, F3001797, designed as colonial manor, convenient location, good, 78 large, well-furnished rooms, but original art work, good restaurant. **LL** *Continental Plaza*, in the Expo Guadalajara Convention Centre, 20 minutes from airport, 5 minutes from Plaza del Sol, Av de las Rosas 2933, Rinconada del Bosque, T6780505, F6780511, 466 rooms, 22 storeys high, luxury, impressive, including breakfast. **LL** *Fiesta Americana*, López Mateos at Minerva circle, T8253434, 91 (800) 50450, F6303725, rooms not as grand as the price might suggest, but excellent views from upper floors, and impressive towering hallway. **L** *Camino Real*, Vallarta 5005, T1218000, F1218070, 5 pools, tennis, putting green, children's playground, 3 restaurants, bars, conference facilities, some way from the centre. **L** *Holiday Inn*, Guadalajara-Airport, Av Providencia 2848, T6789000, F6789002. **L-AL** *Holiday Inn Crowne Plaza*, Av López Mateos 2500 Sur, opposite Plaza del Sol, shopping centre, T6341034, 91 (800) 36555, F6319393, restaurant, nightclub, etc, and also opposite Plaza del Sol, is **LL** *Presidente Intercontinental*, López Mateos Sur and Av Moctezuma, T6781237, F6781222, some deluxe suites with private patio, high rise tower with built-in shopping centre, cavernous lobby.

AL *Plaza Génova* (Best Western), Juárez 123, T6137500, F6148253, including continental breakfast and welcome cocktail, clean, good service, good restaurant, recommended. **AL** *El Tapatío*, Blvd Aeropuerto 4275, T6356050, F6356664, in Tlaquepaque, nearest hotel to airport, fine view of city, extensive grounds, very attractive and comfortable rooms. **AL-A** *Aranzazú*, Av Revolución 110 Pte, T6133232, F6133232 ext 1369, central, very good. **AL-A** *Calinda Roma*, Juárez 170, T6148650, F6142629. **AL-A** *La Villa del Ensueño*, Florida 305, Tlaquepaque, in USA F8185970637, aldez@soca.com, 8 rooms, 2 suites, pool, including breakfast, no smoking, English and Spanish spoken. **AL-A** *Fénix*, Av Corona 160, just off López Cotilla, T6145714, F6134005, high rise block, roof garden with drinks, good restaurant. **AL-B** *de Mendoza*, Venustiano Carranza 16, T6134646, 91 (800) 36126, F6137310, just off Plaza Tapatía, pleasant, small rooms but pretty colonial-style lobby and restaurant, small pool, recommended. **A** *Santiago de Compostela Plaza*, Colón 272, near Plaza San Francisco, T6138880, F6581925, colonial style.; **A-B** *Plaza Diana*, Av Circunvalación Agustín Yañez 2760, T6155510, F6303685, 126 rooms, many refurbished 1995, a/c, TV, restaurant with low-cal menu. **A-C** *Francés*, Maestranza 35, T6130917, F6582831, colonial building with central patio, oldest hotel in the city, built in 1610, have a drink there at 'happy hour' 1800-1900, to enjoy the bygone atmosphere, disco and bar music noisy at night, some rooms small but very good value penthouse suite for 4, with 2 very large bedrooms, living room and kitchen, expensive parking underneath adjoining Plaza de la Liberación.

B *del Parque*, Av Juárez 845, T8252800, clean, friendly, courteous, near Parque Revolución, *tren ligero*, University administration. **B** *Internacional*, Pedro Moreno 570, T6130330, F6132866, clean, comfortable, safe, recommended; **B** *Nueva Galicia*, Av Corona 610, T6148780, F6133892, older style. **B** *Posada del Sol*, López Mateos Sur 4205, T6315205, F6315731. **B-C** *Rotonda*, Liceo 130, T6141017, central, near Cathedral, remodelled 19th century building, attractive, dining area in courtyard, cheap set lunches, nice public areas, rooms OK, with TV, phones, covered parking. **B-C** *San Francisco Plaza*, Degollado 267, T6138954/8971, F6133257, threadbare, many rooms face inwards, street rooms noisy, several patios, hot water, TV, pleasant.

C *El Parador* at new bus terminal, T6000910, F6000015, overpriced because of location (does not take Amex), spartan rooms with TV, expensive laundry, clean, noisy, pool, 24-hour café *El Jardín*. **C** *Hotel Plaza Los Arcos*, Av Vallarta 2456, T6163816, F6163817, 1-bedroom suites, huge hard bed, sitting room, kitchen, good bathroom, very clean, 2-weekly and monthly rates available.

D-E *Estación*, Calzada Independencia Sur 1297, T6190051, across the main boulevard beside train station, quiet, clean, safe, luggage store, hot water, recommended, small, limited restaurant, station porters will carry luggage there US$0.50-1. **E** *Sevilla*, Prisciliano Sánchez 413, T6149037, good, clean (4 blocks south of cathedral), owner speaks English, good restaurant (not always open).

There are cheap hotels along Calzada Independencia (very noisy), on 5 de Febrero and in the 2 blocks north of the old bus station, C 28 de Enero and C 20 de Noviembre (where there is a small market, good for breakfasts) and the side streets (although rooms can sometimes

Sleeping
■ *on maps*
Price codes:
see inside front cover

Mexico

be filthy, so check); they include **D** *Nueva York*, Independencia Sur 43; T6173398, with bath, hot water. **D-E** *Canadá*, Estadio, T6192798, ½ block from old bus station, all rooms with bath, hot water, some with TV, clean, good value. **E** *Casa de Huéspedes Norteña*, basic. **E** *Lincoln*, good, clean, helpful. **E** *Royal*, C Los Angeles, near old bus terminal, clean. **F** *León*, Calz Independencia Sur 557, bath, towel, hot water, clean, staff friendly and helpful; on 5 de Febrero, **D-E** *San José* (No 116), T6191153, *Emperador* (No 530), T6192246, remodelled, adequate, all rooms have TV and phone, enclosed parking, good public areas, and *Monaco* (No 152); on 20 de Noviembre, *San Carlos* (No 728B), *Praga Central* (No 733A) and *Madrid* (No 775), all **D-E**, good , but rooms on street are noisy.

Cheaper hotels in the centre, and near Mercado Libertad: several on Javier Mina, eg **D** *Ana Isabel*, Javier Mina 184, T6177920, central, TV, clean, tiny rooms but very good value, tell them when you are checking out or room may be relet before you have gone. **D** *Azteca*, 1½ blocks from Mercado Libertad, clean, parking around the corner (ask at the desk). **D** *Continental*, on C Corona, recommended. **E** *González*, behind Mercado Corona, 4 blocks west of cathedral, González Ortega 77, basic, often full, very friendly, not clean. **D-E** *Posada Tapatía*, López Cotilla 619, T6149146, colonial style house, 2-3 blocks from Federalismo, one of the better budget places, traffic can be a problem. **D** *Maya*, López Cotilla 39, T6144654, with private bath, blankets, pleasant atmosphere. **D-E** *México 70*, Javier Mina, opposite Mercado Libertad, with bath, clean, TV available. **D** *Imperio*, next door, clean and popular, noisy; other hotels on Corona of similar quality but cheaper. **D** *Posada San Pablo*, Madero 218, shared bath, hot water, family run. **D** *Janeiro*, Obregón 93, by market, very clean, good value, cheap laundry service, noisy from Mariachi music in nearby square. **E** *Hamilton*, Madero 381, with bath, clean, friendly, good value. **F** *del Maestro*, Herrera y Cayro No 666, between Mariano Barcenas and Contreras Medallín, buses from Cathedral 52, 54, 231, from bus station 275), no sign, not very clean, friendly, OK. **F** *Lisboa*, on corner of Grecia and Juárez in precinct, noisy, shared bath, but cheap.

Motels   AL *Las Américas*, López Mateos Sur 2400, T6314256, F6314415, opposite Plaza del Sol shopping centre, a/c, pool, good. **B** *Del Bosque*, L Mateos Sur 265, T1214700, F1221955, TV and phone in all rooms. **C** *Isabel*, Montenegro 1572, sector Hidalgo, T8262630, pleasant, pool. There are additional ones at the end of Vallarta; and along López Mateos near the edge of town, before the *periférico* road.

Trailer Parks *La Hacienda*, Circunvalación Pte 66, 16 kilometres out of town, in Col Cd Granja, off Av Vallarta on left before you reach periférico and head to Tepic, T6271724, F6271724 ext 117, US$10 for 2, US$14 for 4, shaded, pool, clubhouse, hook-ups. Also *San José del Tajo*, 25 kilometres from city on Route 15/80 towards Manzanillo, about 1 kilometre from city boundary, full hook-up, hot showers, pool, laundry facilities, US$13.35 for vehicle and 2 people, reported in need of repair.

Youth hostel At Prolongación Alcalde 1360, Sector Hidalgo, T8530033, away from centre in a complex of state government buildings and run by the state, entrance gate at intersection of Alcalde and Tamaulipas on east side of Alcalde, office open until 2000, women's and men's dormitories, bunk beds and lockers which can be padlocked, pillow and blanket, fairly clean, many mosquitoes. Buses 52 and 54 along Av Alcalde from the centre pass the hostel, or bus 275 goes as far as La Normal traffic circle, from where it is about 2 blocks north, buses stop between 2200-2300, a taxi from down town costs US$2-3 but many people walk, about 30 minutes. Also *Villa Juvenil Guadalajara II* at Prolongación Federalismo y Lázaro Cárdenas, Unidad Deportiva, CP 44940, T8115628, ask for Arq Abel Buenrostro, sleeps 90, take line 1 of *tren ligero* south from centre and get off at Unidad Deportiva.

Eating
● *on maps*

As can be expected in a city of this size there is a wide variety of restaurants on offer, look in local tourist literature for the latest in International, Mexican, Spanish, Italian, Argentine, Arab, Chinese, Japanese or German cooking. There are also fast food outlets, pizzerías and Mexican cafeterías and bars. *Carnes Asadas Tolsa*, Enrique Díaz de León 540 and Chapultepec, T8256875, recommended. *Piaf*, Marsella 126, excellent, French cuisine, live music, friendly, closed Sunday. *Búfalo*, Calderón de la Barca y Av Vallarta, tacos and cheap *comida corrida*, very friendly. *La Banderillas*, Av Alcalde 831, excellent food at reasonable prices. *El Mexicano*, Plaza Tapatía, Morelos 81, rustic Mexican decor, recommended. *Madrid*, Juárez 264 y Corona, good breakfast, excellent coffee and fruit salad, very smoky (from cigarettes). *La Catedral del Antojito*, Pedro Moreno 130, a pedestrian street, colonial style house, restaurant upstairs above bridal gown shops, serves tacos, tortas, etc, good meal for under US$2. *Café Madoka*, Enrique González, Martínez 78, T6133134, just south of Hidalgo, excellent very early breakfasts, well known for the men who play dominoes there. Many cheap restaurants in the streets near the old bus station, especially in C de Los Angeles, and upstairs in the large Mercado Libertad (San Juan de Dios) in centre, but not very hygienic here. *La Trattoria*, Niños Héroes 3051, very good, reasonably priced Italian, very popular (queues form for lunch from 1400). Delicious *carne en su jugo* (beef stew with potatoes, beans, bacon, sausage, onion and avocado, garnished with salsa, onion and coriander) from *Carnes Asadas El Tapatío* in Libertad market (there are 3), or *Carnes Asadas Rigo's*, C Independencia 584A, popular. Goat is a speciality, roasted each day and served with radish, onion and chilli. *Karne Garibaldi*, Garibaldi 1306, esq J Clemente Orozco, Col Sta Teresita, nice place, serves *carne en su jugo*. For those so inclined, *Lido*, Colón 294 y Miguel Blanco (Plaza San Francisco), serves *criadillas*, bull's testicles. *Cortijo La Venta*, Federación 725, T6171675, open daily 1300-0100, invites customers to fight small bulls (calves) after their meal (the animals are not harmed, guests might be), restaurant serves meat, soups, salads. *El Ganadero*, on Av Américas, excellent beef, reasonable prices. *Café Pablo Picasso*, Av Américas 1939, T6361996/6141, breakfast, lunch, dinner and tapas, galería, boutique, smart clientèle, pricey, decorated with photos of Picasso and his work. *Café D'Osio*, around the corner from *Hotel Hamilton*, on corner of Prisciliano Sánchez and Ocampo, excellent breakfast and vast delicious tortas, especially the roast pork, not expensive, open 0900-1800. *El Asadero*, opposite the basilica in Zapopán suburb (see **Excursions** above), is very good. *La Calle*, Autlán 2, near Galería de Calzado and bus terminal, expensive but good, with garden. Good *Lonchería* at Morelos 99 y Gerardo Juárez, by Tourist Office, try *tortas de lomo doble carne con aguacate*. *La Bombilla*, López Cotilla y Penitenciaría, very good for *churros* and hot chocolate. In the cloister of La Merced is a fast food place, popular with young people. *La Chata*, Francisco Zarco 2277, and *Gemma*, López Mateos Sur 1800, 2 chains serving Mexican food, are usually quite good (*Gemma* has 8 branches in the city and does Guadalajaran 'lonches', *tortas ahogadas*). *La Pianola*, Av México 3220 and several locations, good, reasonable prices, serves *chiles en nogada*, excellent. A good place for fish is *El Delfín Sonriente*, Niños Héroes 2293, T6160216/7441, nice, attractive; a good Mexican restaurant is *La Gorda*, C Juan Alvarez 1336, esq Gral Coronado, Col Sta Teresita. *La Rinconada*, Morelos 86 on Plaza Tapatía, is in a beautiful colonial building, columned courtyard, carved wood doors, entrées at US$4-8 range, open until 2130, separate bar. Plenty of US fast food places: *Pizza Hut*, *McDonald's*, *Burger King*, *Carl's Junior*, with several outlets.

In **Tlaquepaque** (see Shopping below), *Restaurante Sin Nombre*, Madero 80, in colonial house, seating in courtyard, tropical plants and birds, including peacocks. Nearby, same owner, is *El Portico*, also in colonial house on corner of Obregón and Independencia. Other attractive restaurants in colonial houses are *El Patio*, Independencia 186, and *Casa Fuerte*, Independencia 224.

La Fuente, Pino Suárez 78, very popular, mixed clientèle, live music, lots of atmosphere. Many bars serve snacks, *botanas*, with drinks between 1300 and 1500, free. Most of these bars are for men only, though. **NB** The bars in the centre are popular with the city's gay population, eg *Botanero el Ciervo* is a gay bar, 20 de Noviembre 797, corner of C Los Angeles, opposite old bus station. | **Bars & nightclubs**

Discos   2 gay discos are *SOS*, Av La Paz 1413, and *Monica's* in Sector Libertad, to the east of the centre, both well known locally.

Cinema   Average cost of a ticket is US$2. Good quality films, some in English, are shown in the evenings at 1600, 1800, 2000, US$1.25 at the ciné-teatro in the *Instituto Cultural Cabañas* (see **Sights** above), which also has a good cafetería. | **Entertainment**

Music   Concerts and theatre in the ex-Convento del Carmen. A band plays every

Thursday at 1800 in the Plaza de Armas, in front of the Palacio de Gobierno, free. Organ recitals in the Cathedral. *Peña Curicacalli*, Av Niños Héroes almost at corner of Av Chapultepec, T8254690, opens 2000, US$5 cover charge, food and drink available, fills up fast; local groups perform variety of music including Latin American folk music Friday, Saturday.

Theatre *Ballet Folklórico de la Universidad de Guadalajara*, every Sunday at 1000 in the Degollado Theatre, superb, highly recommended, prehispanic and Mexican-wide dances, and other cultural shows, US$2-10, T6583812, 6144773 (check before you go, if there is another function in the theatre they may perform elsewhere). The *Grupo Folklórico Ciudad de Guadalajara* performs here every Thursday at 2000. The *Ballet Folklórico del Instituto Cultural Cabañas* performs Wednesday 2030 at the Instituto Cultural Cabañas, US$3. The Instituto is also an art school, with classes in photography, sculpture, ceramics, literature, music, theatre and dance.

Festivals **21 March** commemorates Benito Juárez' birthday and everything is closed for the day. Ceremonies around his monument at the Agua Azul park. In **June** the Virgin of Zapopán (see **Excursions** above), leaves her home to spend each night in a different church where fireworks are let off. The virgin has a new car each year but the engine is not started, men pull it through the streets with ropes, the streets are decorated. The climax is 12 October when the virgin leaves the Cathedral for home, there are great crowds along the route. Throughout the month of **October** there is a great *fiesta* with concerts, bullfights, sports and exhibitions of handicrafts from all over Mexico. **28 October-20 December**, *fiesta* in honour of the Virgin of Guadalupe; Av Alcalde has stalls, music, fair etc. In December there is one at Parque Morelos and hand-made toys are a special feature.

Shopping The best shops are no longer in the centre, although a couple of department stores have branches there. The best stores are in the shopping centres, of which there are many, small and large, mainly on the west side. The newest and biggest is La Gran Plaza, 3 floors, Sears, Salinas and Roche, 12-screen cinema, many smaller shops, between Av Lázaro Cárdenas and Av Vallarta, near where they merge. Plaza México is another large centre, and nearby, with smaller boutiques, Plaza Bonito. The Plaza del Sol shopping centre, with over 100 shops, is located beyond Chapalita in the south of the city, while the equally modern Plaza Patria, with as many shops, is at the north end near the Zapopán suburb. There are many other shopping malls such as the Galeriá del Calzado (on Av México, several blocks west of Av López Mateos), selling, as the name implies, only shoes. *El Toro Loco*, and *Botas Los Potrillos*, on Morelos by Plaza Tapatía, sell good boots.

The markets, in particular the Libertad (San Juan de Dios) which has colourful items for souvenirs with lots of Michoacán crafts including Paracho guitars and Sahuayo hats, leather jackets, and delicious food upstairs on the 1st level (particularly goat meat, *birria*, also *cocada*), fruit juices and other soft drinks; the *tianguis* (Indian market) on Av Guadalupe, Colonia Chapalita, on Friday is of little interest to foreigners, bus 50 gets you there; the *tianguis* near the University Sports Centre on Calzada Tlaquepaque on Sunday.

Bookshops English books available at a reasonable mark up, at *Sanborns*, Av Vallarta 1600 y Gen San Martín, Juárez y 16 de Septiembre, Plaza Bonita and López Mateos Sur 2718 (near Plaza de Sol), also English language magazines in all stores, pharmacy section, mid-priced restaurants with good food. German journals at *Sanborns*, Av Vallarta branch. *Librería Británica*, Av Hidalgo 1796-B, Sector Hidalgo, 6155807, F6150935. *Sandi's*, Av Tepeyac 718, Colonia Chapalita, T1210863, F6474600, has a good selection of English-language books, including medical textbooks and cards. *Librería México* in Plaza del Sol, local 14, area D, on Av López Mateos side, T1210114, has US magazines and newspapers. *El Libro Antiguo*, Pino Suárez 86, open 1000-2000, mostly Spanish but large selection of English paperbacks. *Librería La Fuente*, C Medellín 140, near C Juan Manuel in the centre, T6135238, sells used books and magazines in English and Spanish, interesting to browse in, some items quite old, from 1940s and 1950s. Bookshops can be found on López Cotilla, from González Martínez towards 16 de Septiembre.

The Guadalajara International Book Fair

Guadalajara is one of the true music capitals of Mexico, famous for its Mariachi Square and street musicians. You frequently find some of the best popular music in town being played by live musicians on street corners or on the move, on the public buses. The graphic arts are also well served here, Guadalajara being the home of many fine examples of Mexican mural art, by José Clemente Orozco, David Siqueiros and others.

What is not so well known is that this city is also the site of the third largest book fair in the world, held every year in late November/early December. It takes place in the new Gran Salón de Exposiciones in Guadalajara and, except for the book fairs in Frankfurt and Buenos Aires, there is none more important anywhere. Those others are somewhat stuffy affairs, though, that are unfriendly to the general public and intended mostly for the trade. In Guadalajara everyone is invited, and the book fair festivities go on inside and outside the convention hall. Inside, in 1997, 800 publishers from 25 countries were represented, and writers, agents, publicists, designers and film people of every sort were seen walking up and down the aisles between exhibits. The general public is welcome (250,000 people attended the fair in 1997) and you can run into the likes of Isabel Allende and Carlos Fuentes, while visiting with all manner of commercial, university and avant-garde presses. Outside the hall, there are round the clock readings of poetry and fiction, music, celebrations of children's literature, games, food and drink. You can find impromptu street theatre, comedy, improvization, dance, jugglers, fire-eaters, clowns ... anything you wish.

For information, write (in English or Spanish) to FIL Guadalajara, Francia 1747, Col Moderna, Guadalajara, Jalisco 44190, Mexico, T523-8100331, F523-8100379, fil@udgserv.cencar.udg.mx. Or write to FIL New York, c/o David Unger, Division of Humanities NAC 6/293, The City College of New York, New York, NY 10031, USA, T212-6507925, F212-6507912, daucc@cunyvm.cuny.edu.
Terence Clarke

Mexico

Crafts 2 glass factories at **Tlaquepaque** where the blue, green, amber and amethyst blown-glass articles are made (bus 275 from the centre goes through Tlaquepaque en route to bus station). Calle Independencia is the main shopping street and closed to traffic. The **Museo Regional de la Cerámica** is at Independencia 237. For beautiful, expensive furniture go to *Antigua de Mexico*, No 255, lovely building, used to be a convent, the family has branches in Nogales and Tucson so furniture can be shipped to their shops there. *La Casa Canela*, opposite, sells furniture and crafts, don't miss the colonial kitchen at the back of the house. *Adobe Diseño*, also in a colonial house, sells expensive leather furniture. Visit the shop of *Sergio Bustamante*, who sells his own work (good modern jewellery): expensive but well worth a look, a stream runs through this house with a colonial façade on C Independencia 236. Some way from the main shopping area is the *Casa de los Telares* (C de Hidalgo 1378), where Indian textiles are woven on hand looms. Potters can be watched at work both in Guadalajara and at Tlaquepaque; you may find better bargains at **Tonalá** (pottery and ceramics, some glass), see **Excursions**, above, on market days Thursday and Sunday; take bus 275 (see local **Transport** below), bumpy 45 minutes journey. Overall, Tlaquepaque is the cheapest and most varied source of the local crafts, with attractive shops set in old colonial villas; best buys: glass, papier mâché goods, leather (cheapest in Mexico), and ceramics. See also the *Tienda Tlaquepaque*, at Av Juárez 267-B, in Tlaquepaque, T6355663. *Casa de Artesanías de Jalisco*, González Gallo 20, T6194664, open 1000-1900 (1400 Sunday), free, in Parque Agua Azul: high quality display (and sale) of handicrafts, ceramics, paintings, handblown glass, dresses, etc (state-subsidized to preserve local culture, reasonably priced but not cheap – a percentage goes to the artisan). There is another shop-cum-exhibition at the *Instituto de Artesanía Jaliscense, Casa de Las Artesanías Normal*, Av Alcalde 1221, T6244624. Calle Independencia runs from Boulevard Tlaquepaque (the main avenue into Guadalajara) to the main plaza (where you can see the restored Parroquia de San Pedro Tlaquepaque and the Basílica La Teranensis) and then to the *Parián*, another plaza on the southeast corner. The Parián is a very large, square building occupying most of the plaza, with bars (pretty woodwork and tiling) and kitchens around the perimeter. The rest is an open courtyard with tables and mariachis, who play Friday, Saturday, Sunday, 1530 and 2130, also roving mariachis play on demand for a fee.

Sports **Bullfights**: October to March; football throughout year; *charreadas* (cowboy shows) are held in mid-September at Unión de San Antonio; *charreada* near Agua Azul Park at Aceves Calindo Lienzo, Sunday at 1200. Baseball, April-September. **Golf**: at Santa Anita, 16 kilometres out on Morelia road, championship course; Rancho Contento, 10 kilometres out on Nogales road; San Isidro, 10 kilometres out on Saltillo road, noted for water hazards; Areas, 8 kilometres out on Chapala road (US$13 during the week, US$20 at weekends is the average price for a round). The *Guadalajara Country Club*, has a beautiful clubhouse and golf course in the middle of the city, near the Plaza Patria shopping centre, Mar Caribe 260, T8173502, phone ahead for start time and to check green fee. **Hiking**: club *Collí*, bulletin board Av Juárez 460, details from *Café Madrid*, Juárez 264 or T6233318, 6179248.

Transport **Local** Horse-drawn carriages US$5 for a short ride or US$7.50 per hour from the Museo Regional de Guadalajara at the corner of Liceo and Hidalgo. Tourist Office in Plaza Tapatía has a full list of local buses. If in doubt ask bus driver. Regular buses cost US$0.20, Línea Azul 'luxury' bus US$0.45. Some useful lines: No 275, from Zapopán-Plaza Patria-Glorieta Normal-Av Alcalde-Av 16 de Septiembre-Av Revolución-Tlaquepaque-new bus station-Tonalá (there are different 275s, from A to F, most follow this route, check with driver); route 707 also goes to Tonalá (silver-blue bus with Tur on the side); bus 60 goes along Calzada Independencia from zoo, passing Estadio Jalisco, Plaza de Toros, Mercado Libertad and Parque Agua Azul to the old bus terminal and the railway station (note, if you are going to Parque Mirador, take bus 62 northbound, otherwise 62 has the same route as 60); there is also a new trolley bus that runs along the Calzada to the north terminus of the Calzada at the entrance to the Mirador, better than 60 or 62; to train station take 60 or 62 south along Calz Independencia or 52 or 54 south along Av Alcalde/16 de Septiembre; to the old bus station, minibus 174 south along Calz Independencia from Mercado Libertad, or bus 110 south along Av Alcalde; bus 102 runs from the new bus terminal along Av Revolución, 16 de Septiembre and Prisciliano Sánchez to Mercado Libertad; No 258 or 258A from San Felipe (north of Cathedral) or 258D along Madero to Plaza del Sol; No 371 from Tonalá to Plaza del Sol. A shuttle bus runs between the 2 bus stations. The Metro, or *Tren Ligero*, has Línea 1 running under Federalismo from Periférico Sur to Periférico Nte. Línea 2, runs from Juárez station westbound and passes Mercado Libertad. Fare US$0.40, one-peso coins needed to buy tokens. **Car rental**: Quick, T6142247, VW Sedan US$40 per day, including tax, insurance, 400 kilometres per day; **Budget**, T6130027, Nissan Tsuru, a/c, US$70 per day, unlimited mileage; **National**, T6147175, VW Sedan, US$50 per day, including 300 kilometres per day; **Avis**, T91 (800) 70777, VW Sedan US$40, plus US$18 insurance and 15 percent tax, unlimited mileage; **Hertz**, T6146162, VW Sedan US$15 per day, including 300 kilometres per day. Others scattered throughout city. **Taxis**: no meters used. A typical ride in town costs US$1.50-2.50. From the centre to the new bus station is about US$4 and to the airport US$8-10.

Air Miguel Hidalgo (GDL), 20 kilometres from town; fixed rate for 3 city zones and 3 classes of taxi: *especial, semi-especial* and colectivo, no tip necessary. Bus No 176 'San José del 15', leaves from intersection of Corona and Calz Independencia every 20 minutes, US$0.25, grey bus. Autotransportes Guadalajara-Chapala runs 2nd class buses from old bus terminal every 15 minutes, 0655-2125, US$0.35, stop at airport on way to/from Chapala. Many flights daily to and from Mexico City, 65 minutes. Connections by air with nearly all domestic airports. US cities served include Chicago, Cincinnati, Dallas, Houston, Jacksonville, Los Angeles, Miami, New York, Oakland, Phoenix, Salt Lake City, San Diego, San Francisco, San José (California).

Trains Ferrocarriles Nacionales de México, T6500826; Ferrocarril del Pacífico, T6500570 at the station, or office, Av Libertad 1875, T6265665, 6263102. There are currently no passenger services from Guadalajara; check locally for information.

Warning Do not accept cups of coffee at the station however friendly or insistent the offer is, they may be drugged. If possible avoid arriving at night.

Buses New bus station near the El Alamo cloverleaf, 10 kilometres from centre; buses 102 and 275 go to the centre, US$0.25, frequent service (see **Local Transport** above), journey takes at least 30 minutes. There is a new luxury bus service (Linea Azul) running from Zapopán, along Avila Camacho, past Plaza Patria shopping centre to the glorieta La Normal, south down Av Alcalde, through Tlaquepaque, to the new bus station and ending in Tonalá, seats guaranteed, US$0.45. Another luxury bus service to the centre is Línea Cardenal. No buses after 2230. Official taxi fares from the bus station to various zones of the city are posted on the booths for buying taxi tickets located in each of the 7 modules of the terminal, to the centre US$3 day time, US$4 night time. Bus tickets are sold at 2 offices on Calzada Independencia underneath the big fountain on Plaza Tapatía, open 0900-1400, 1600-1900. Because of the distance from the centre of town, it is worth getting your departure information before you go into town. Shop around. It helps to know which company you wish to travel with as their offices are spread over a large area, in 7 modules. All modules have phones, but only Nos 1 and 2 long distance, all have left luggage, toilets, taxi booths, tourist information booths (not always manned), restaurants and shops; outside No 5 is a map of urban bus routes. A number of bus companies change dollars at rates marginally worse than *cambios*.

    Module 1: Bus company: **Cienaga**, T6000363, to Ocotlán every 30 minutes 0615-2115, US$2.50, 1 hour, to La Barca every 30 minutes 0630-2100, US$3.50, to Zamora, US$5.50, 2nd class, they serve sodas on board. **La Alteña**, T6000770, 2nd class to Tepatitlán, US$2.50, Arandas US$4, Mexico City US$20, León US$8.50, Lagos de Moreno US$6.25, Querétaro US$12.50, Atotonilco US$3.50, Dolores Hidalgo US$12.25, Guanajuato US$10. **Costalegre**, T6000270, 2nd class to Barra de Navidad, US$10. **Primera Plus** (a 'plus' level service), T6000398/0014/0654/0142, same numbers for **Flecha Amarilla** (2nd class service), and **Servicios Coordinados** (1st class service), all part of the same group, Primera Plus to Colima US$9, Manzanillo US$12, León US$10.50, Guanajuato US$12.50, Aguascalientes US$6.50, San Miguel de Allende US$16.50, Querétaro US$13.50, Morelia US$12.25, Mexico City US$24.25 (7 hours), also a bus that leaves at 0020 that takes the new toll road for the same price and takes 6 hours. **Servicios Coordinados** (buses have toilets) to Morelia US$10.50, León US$9.50, Lagos de Moreno US$7.25, Colima US$8, Manzanillo US$10.50, Querétaro US$12.50. **ETN** has a ticket booth in module 1 (no credit cards) but their main ticket booth is in module 2 and all their buses leave from there. Module 1 has remodelled bathrooms, US$0.25, and smaller free bathrooms, a magazine/snack shop (also beer), torta stand, cafetería, fruit juice stand, and phone office for long-distance and fax. There are also LADA (long-distance) phones outside the terminal entrance that take debit cards available at the snack shop inside, and other LADA phones next to them that take coins.

    Module 2: Bus company: **ETN**, T6000477/0858/0605/0778 (luxury service), American Express cards, round-trip tickets sold at a slight discount, own waiting room with bathrooms, snack bar, and gift shop, to Aguascalientes US$12.50, Colima US$12, Manzanillo US$15.50, Guanajuato US$15.50 (3 a day), León US$13.25 (8 a day), Morelia US$16.25 by non-toll roads (2 a day) and US$20 by the new toll road (7 a day), Querétaro US$17.50, Puerta Vallarta US$21.25 (8 a day, takes toll road to Tepíc part of the way), Toluca via toll road US$27.50 (3 a day), Uruapan US$12.50 (some take toll road, others don't, same price), Mexico City northern bus terminal US$31.25 (7 hours, mostly uses old toll road via Querétaro, not the new one), Mexico City Observatorio bus terminal US$31.25 (some take the new freeway, 6 hours), San Luis Potosí US$17. La Línea (1st class and 'plus' service), T6001221, to Manzanillo US$8 (plus) and US$10.50 (1st class), Colima US$9 (plus) and US$8 (1st class), Cd Guzmán US$5.50 (1st class), Morelia US$12 (plus) and US$10.50 (1st class), some take new toll road, Uruapan US$10 (plus) and US$8.75 (1st class), some take new toll road, Pátzcuaro US$9.50 (1st class), Mexico City US$22.50 at 2300 by new toll road with one stop in Toluca. **Omnibús de México**, T6000814, 1st class, with toilets, video, a/c, main ticket counter is in module 6, buses leave from module 6 and stop by module 2 to pick up passengers before going on to their destination. **Autobuses de Occidente**, T6000055, "plus", 1st and 2nd class service, to La Barca US$3 (2nd class), Zamora US$5 (2nd class), US$5.50 (1st class), US$6 (plus), Morelia

US$9 (2nd class), US$10.50 (1st class), US$12.25 (plus), Toluca US$16 (2nd class), US$17.50 (1st class), Mexico City US$19.75 (2nd class), US$22.50 (1st class), Uruapan US$8 (2nd class), US$9 (1st class), US$10 (plus), Colima US$8 (1st class), US$9 (plus), Manzanillo US$10.50 (1st class), US$12 (plus), Lázaro Cárdenas US$18.25 (1st class), US$21 (plus). **Autotransportes del Sur**, T6000346, 2nd class with assigned seats if you get on at the beginning of the trip in Guadalajara, to Cd Guzmán US$5, Colima US$7, Cuyatlán US$8.75, Manzanillo US$9.50, Sayula US$3.25, Lázaro Cárdenas US$16.25. **Autotransportes Mazamitla**, T6000733, 2nd class, 0600-1830 hourly to Mazamitla, 3 hours. Module 2 has video games, coin operated LADA phones by entrance to bathrooms, a dulcería, juice bar, torta stand, self-service restaurant, and a Computel outlet for making long-distance and fax calls that takes Visa, Mastercard, and American Express.

Module 3: Bus company: **Elite** (1st class but more like plus service, recommended), T6790462, to Tijuana US$84, Mexicali US$67, Nogales US$62.50, Los Mochis US$36.50, Mazatlán US$26, Tepíc US$10. **Norte de Sonora** (1st class), T6000285, ticket counter here but buses leave from module 4. **Transportes del Pacífico**, T6000339, buses that leave after 2100 leave from module 4, Greyhound passes for US$85 good for 3 consecutive days of travel anywhere in the USA, to Tepíc US$10 (1st class) and US$9 (2nd class), Mazatlán US$19.25 (1st class) and US$16.75 (2nd class), Nogales US$85 (1st class) and US$54.25 (2nd class), Tijuana US$71 (1st class) and US$62 (2nd class), Puerta Vallarta US$22 (1st class). **Futura** (plus service), T6790404, all buses except those to Mexico City, US$22.50, and Tepic leave from module 7. **Autocamiones Cihuatlán** (plus service), T6000598, to Melaque US$12.60, to Barra de Navidad US$12.75, to Manzanillo US$15.40. **Autotransportes Guadalajara, Talpa, Mascota (ATM)**, T6000098, Talpa US$5 (2nd class), Ameca US$2.50 (2nd class), 1st class service weekends US$6.25 to Talpa via Ameca. Module 3 has a self-service restaurant, magazine/snack shop, shoe shine and 2 coin operated LADA phones by the entrance to the bathrooms.

Module 4: Bus company: **Transportes del Pacífico**, T6000339, buses that leave after 2100 leave from here (see above, module 3). **Norte de Sonora** (1st class with bathrooms, video, a/c), T6000778, to Tijuana US$61.50, Nogales US$54.25, Mazatlán US$16.75, Tepíc US$9.40, San Blas US$10.25. **Elite** (have ticket counter here but buses leave from module 3, see above). **ATM** (see module 3), buses leave from both modules 3 and 4 for the same destinations. **Autocamiones Cihuatlán** (2nd class service, 'plus' service from module 3, serves same destinations,see module 3). Module 4 has shoe shine, snack/magazine shop, self-service restaurant, 2 LADA coin phones by bathrooms.

Module 5: Bus company: **Rojo de los Altos** (2nd class), T6790454/0455/0434, to Arandas US$4, Torreón US$22.40, Durango US$19.75, Zacatecas US$11. **Omnibus de Oriente/Linea Azul**, T6000231, to Mexico City US$22.50 (1st class) and US$19.75 (2nd class), Lagos de Moreno US$7.25 (1st class) and US$6 (2nd class), Querétaro US$12 (2nd class), Matamoras US$35.40 (1st class) and US$30.25 (2nd class), San Luis Potosí US$12.40 (1st class) and US$10.75 (2nd class), Reynosa US$33.50 (1st class) and US$29.75 (2nd class), Cd Victoria US$23.60 (1st class) and US$20.20 (2nd class). Tepatitlán (2nd class), T6000665, to Tepatitlán every 30 minutes 0600-2030, US$2.75, to Zapotlanejo every 20 minutes 0600-2100, also goes to the *penal* at Puente Grande for US$0.40, if you're in the mood to visit the prison where some of the worst criminals are kept. Module 5 has a gift/snack shop, torta stand, self-service restaurant, and 24-hour phone/fax booth.

Module 6: Bus company: **Omnibús de México** (1st class to plus service, all with bathrooms, video, a/c), T6000068, they have the entire module except for a small ETN ticket counter (ETN buses leave from module 2), to Mexico City US$22.50, Monterrey US$27.20, Durango US$23, Torreón US$26, Tampico US$25.50, San Luis Potosí US$12.40, Cd Juárez US$54, Reynosa US$33.50, Matamoras US$35.40, Nuevo Laredo US$36.20, Zacatecas US$12.50. Module 6 has a self-service restaurant, gift/snack shop, shoe shine, 2 LADA coin operated phones by bathrooms.

Module 7: **Futura** (plus service), T6790404, buses to Mexico City and Tepíc leave from here and stop at module 3 to pick up more passengers, for all other destinations the buses leave from module 7 only, to Cd Juárez US$54 (dep 1800), Chihuahua US$41.25 (dep 1800), Nuevo Laredo US$36.20 (dep 1930), Torreón US$26 (dep 2200). **Turistar Ejecutivo** (luxury service, like ETN), to Cd Juárez US$70.25 (dep 1600), Chihuahua US$54 (dep 1600), Nuevo Laredo US$47 (dep 1730 and 2100), Monterrey US$36.50 (4 buses 1730-2130), Mexico City US$30.25 (dep 2300), Saltillo US$30.25 (dep 1900 and 2230), Aguascalientes US$12.50 (dep 1600). **Transportes del Norte** and **Transportes Chihuahuenses** are affiliated with the above 2 companies, their ticket booths mainly sell tickets for the other two. Module 7 has a gift/snack shop, remodelled bathrooms for 2 pesos (also free bathrooms), shoe shine, a *Burger Bus* and *Viva Pollo*, an office for making long distance calls, and 2 LADA coin operated phones by bathrooms.

The old central bus station, Los Angeles y 28 Enero serves towns within 100 kilometres. You have to pay 20 centavos to enter the terminal (open 0545-2215). It has 2 *salas* (wings): A and B, and is shaped like a U. The flat bottom of the U fronts Dr R Michel, where the main entrances are. There is a side entrance to Sala A from C Los Angeles and to both A and B from C 15 de Febrero via a tunnel. Taxi stands on both sides of the terminal of C Los Angeles and 15 de Febrero. By the entrances to the salas is a Computel outlet with long-distance and fax service. A fax to the USA costs US$2 per minute, to Europe US$2.50. There are lots of Ladatel phones for long distance and local calls outside the main entrance, some take coins and others debit cards. There is also a magazine stand selling maps of the city and a shoe shine service in front of the terminal. The shuttle buses to the new bus station leave from here, 2 pesos. In Sala A there are 2nd class buses to Tepatitlán and Zapotlanejo and *la penal* (the prison), with Oriente. 1st class buses to the same destinations leave from the new bus terminal. Buses to Chapala (every 30 minutes, 0600-2140, US$1.60) and Ajijic (every 30 minutes, 0700-2100, US$1.80) leave from here with Autotransportes Guadalajara-Chapala. Round trip package to the balneario at San Juan Cosalá, US$5.25 including admission to the baths. In Sala B, Omnibus de Rivera sells tickets to the same balneario for US$1.50 and at La Alteña booth for the balnearios Agua Caliente and Chimulco. A Primera Plus/Servicios Coordinados booth sells tickets to places served by the new bus terminal. There is a Computel outlet with phone service, no fax, a luggage store and a magazine stand. Both salas have several food stands serving tortas, etc, and there are bathrooms.

Airline offices *Mexicana*, reservations T6787676, arrival and departure information T6885775, ticket **Directory** offices: Av Mariano Otero 2353, by Plaza del Sol, T1120011, Av 16 de Septiembre 495, T6148195, Plaza Patria, local 8H, T6415352, López Cotilla 1552, T6153099/3480, between Av Chapultepec and Américas. *AeroMéxico*, reservations T6690202, airport information T6885098, ticket offices, Av Corona 196 and Plaza del Sol, local 30, Zona A. *Delta*, López Cotilla 1701, T6303530. *Aero California*, López Cotilla 1423, T8268850. On Av Vallarta: *Air France*, No 1540-103 T6303707), *American*, No 2440 (T6164090 for reservations, T6885518 at airport), *KLM*, No 1390-1005 T8253261; *Continental*, ticket office Astral Plaza, Galerías del *Hotel Presidente Intercontinental*, locales 8-9, T6474251 reservations, T6885141 airport. *Saro*, Av 16 de Septiembre 334, T91-800-83224. *Taesa*, López Cotilla 1531B, just past Av Chapultepec, reservations T91 (800) 90463. *United*, Plaza Los Arcos, Av Vallarta 2440, local A13, T6169489.

Banks There are many *casas de cambio* on López Cotilla between Independencia and 16 de Septiembre and one in Plaza del Sol. Despite what they say, *casas de cambio* close 1400 or 1500 till 1600, not continuously open 0900-1900. *American Express*, Plaza los Arcos, Local 1-A, Av Vallarta 2440, esq Fco García de Quevedo, about 5 blocks east of Minerva roundabout, T6300200, F6157665, open 0900-1800 for the travel agency and 0900-1430, 1600-1800 to change money. Across Prisciliano Sánchez from the Jardín San Francisco is a *Banco Inverlat* with a 24-hr ATM which gives cash on American Express cards if you are enrolled in their Express Cash programme.

Communications Post Office: V Carranza, just behind Hall of Justice, open Mon-Fri 0800-1900, Sat 0900-1300. There are also branches at the Mercado Libertad and at the old bus station, convenient for the cheap hotels. To send parcels abroad go to Aduana Postal in same building as main post office, open Mon-Fri 0800-1300, T6149002. Federal Express has 3 outlets: Av Américas 1395, Plaza del Sol locales 51 and 55, Av Washington 1129, next to Bolerana 2000, T8172502, F8172374. United Parcel Service at Av Américas 981, local 19, T91-80090292. **Telecommunications:** international collect calls can be made from any coin-box phone kiosk and direct dial calls can be made from LADA pay phones, of which there are many all over the city. You can also make long-distance calls and send faxes from *Computel* outlets: one in front of old bus station, one on Corona y Madero, opposite *Hotel Fénix*. Another chain, *Copyroyal*, charges 3 times as much for a fax to USA. *Mayahuel*, Paseo Degollado 55 has long distance service, fax, sells Ladatel cards, postcards and maps. There is a credit card phone at Ramón Corona y Av Juárez, by Cathedral. 2 USA Direct phones, one within and one beyond the customs barrier at the airport. **Email:** Cyber café with Internet access at López Cotilla 773203, primer piso, southwest corner of Parque Revolución, T8263771, 8263286, F826 5610, www.internet-café.com.mx, or www.i-set.com.mx/cybercafé. They charge US$2.50 per hr for Internet access and give free course in its use; 1 peso per page to print; they receive your email, US$0.60 per page to print out; will notify you when any messages come in; also serve pizza, snacks, beer and soft drinks. Another cyber café is *Arrobba*, Av Lázaro Cárdenas 3286, just west of intersection with López Mateos, open Mon-Sat 1000-2200, Internet access US$3.10 per hr, printouts US$0.25, www.arrobba.com.mx, drinks, snacks, salads.

Cultural centres *Goethe Institute*, Morelos 2080 y Calderón de la Barca, T6156147, 6160495, F6159717, library, nice garden, newspapers. *Alliance Française*, López Cotilla 1199, Sector Juárez, T8252140, 8255595. *The Instituto Cultural Mexicano-Norteamericano de Jalisco* (see below, **Language schools**). *US* at Enrique Díaz de León 300.

Embassies & consulates *Australia*, López Cotilla 2030, T6157418, F6303479, open 0800-1330, 1500-1800. *Austria*, Montevideo 2695, Col Providencia, T6411834, open 0900-1330. *Belgium*, Metalúrgica 2818, Parque Industrial El Alamo, T6704825, F6700346, open Mon-Fri 0900-1400. *Brazil*, Cincinati 130, esq Nueva Orleans, Col La Aurora, next to train station, T6192102, open 0900-1700. *Canada*, Hotel Fiesta Americana, local 31, T6156215, open 0830-1700. *Denmark*, Calz Lázaro Cárdenas 601, p 6°, T6695515, F6785997, open 0900-1300, 1600-1800. *Dominican Republic*, Colón 632, T6135478, F6145019, open 0900-1400, 1600-1900. *Ecuador*, C Morelos 685, esq Pavo, T6131666, F6131729, open 1700-2000. *El Salvador*, C Fermín Riestra 1628, entre Bélgica y Argentina, Col Moderna, T8101061, hours for visas 1230-1400, normally visas will be received the same day. *Finland*, Justo Sierra 2562, p5°, T6163623, F6161501, open 0830-1330. *France*, López Mateos Nte 484 entre Herrera y Cairo y Manuel Acuña, T6165516, open 0930-1400. *Germany*, Corona 202, T6139623, F6132609, open 1130-1400. *Great Britain*, Eulogio Parra 2539, T6160629/7616021, F6150197, 0900-1500, 1700-2000. *Guatemala*, Mango 1440, Col del Fresno, T8111503, open 1000-1400. *Honduras*, Ottawa 1139, Col Providencia, T8174998, F8175007, open 1000-1400, 1700-1900. *Israel*, Av Vallarta 2482 Altos SJ, T6164554, open 0930-1500. *Italy*, López Mateos Nte 790-1, T6161700, F6162092, open 1100-1400, Tues-Fri. *Netherlands*, Calz Lázaro Cárdenas 601, p6°, Zona Industrial, T8112641, F8115386, open 0900-1400, 1630-1900. *Nicaragua*, Eje Central 1024, esq Toreros, Col Guadalupe Jardín, behind Club Atlas Chapalita, T6282919, open 1600-1800. *Norway*, Km 5 Antigua Carretera a Chapala 2801, Col La Nogalera, T8121411, F8121074, in the building Aceite El Gallo, open 0900-1800. *Perú*, Bogotá 2923, entre Terranova y Alberta, Col Providencia, T6423009, open 0800-1600. *Spain*, Av Vallarta 2185 SJ, T6300450, F6160396, open 0830-1330. *Portugal*, Colimán 277 Cd del Sol, T1217714, F6843925. *Sweden*, J Gpe Montenegro 1691, T8256767, F8255559, open 0900-1400, 1600-1900. *Switzerland*, Av Revolucion 707, Sector Reforma, T6175900, F6173208, open 0800-1400, 1600-1900. *USA*, Progreso 175, T8252700, F6266549.

Hospitals & medical services Dentist: *Dr Abraham Waxtein*, Av México 2309, T6151041, speaks English. **Doctor:** *Dr Daniel Gil Sánchez*, Pablo Neruda 3265, p2°, T6420213, speaks English. **Hospitals:** good private hospitals are *Hospital del Carmen*, Tarascos 3435, Fracc Monraz (behind Plaza México, a shopping centre), T8130042 (take credit cards). *Hospital San Javier*, Pablo Casals 640 (on the corner of Eulogio Parra and Aquaducto), Colonia Providencia, T6690222 (take credit cards). *Hospital Angel Leaño*, off the road to Tesistán, T8343434, affiliated with the University (UAG). A less well-equipped but good hospital near the centre that is also affiliated with the UAG is the *Hospital Ramón Garibay*, Enrique Díaz de León 238, across the street from the Templo Expiatorio, T8255313, 8255159, 8255115, 8255050, inexpensive out-patient clinic with various specialists. Probably the best private laboratory is the *Unidad de Patología*, Av México 2341, T6165410, takes credit cards. For those who cannot afford anything else there are the *Hospital Civil*, T6145501, and the *Nuevo Hospital Civil*, F6177177; *Antirrábico* (rabies), T6431917, you have to go to Clinic 3 of the Sector Salud to receive the vaccine, T8233262, at the corner of Circunvalación Division del Nte and Calzada Federalismo, across the street from a Telmex office, near the División Nte Station, Line 1, *tren ligero*, you can also get an AIDS blood test here. *Sidatel* (AIDS), T6137546. **Infectologist:** *Dr J Manuel Ramírez R*, Dom Ermita 103126, Col Chapalita, by the intersection of Lázaro Cárdenas and López Mateos, T6477161. **Ophthalmologist:** *Dr Virginia Rivera*, Eulogia Parra 2432, near López Mateos, T6166637, 6164046, English speaking. **Pharmacies:** 3 big chains of pharmacies are *Farmacias Guadalajara*, *Benavides* and *ABC*. The *Farmacia Guadalajara* at Av Américas and Morelos has vaccines and harder to find drugs, T6155094. Other good pharmacies for hard to find drugs are the *Farmacia Especializada*, Av Américas 124, just south of Av México, T6169388, and *Farmacia Géminis*, across the street from the *Hospital del Carmen*, T8132874.

Language schools *Centro de Estudios para Extranjeros de la Universidad de Guadalajara*, Tomás de Gómez 125, between Justo Sierra and Av México, T6164399, 6164382, registration US$85 pa, US$585 for 5 weeks of 4 hours per day instruction, US$490 for 5 weeks living with a Mexican family with

3 meals a day. *The Universidad Autónoma de Guadalajara (UAG)*, a private university, offers Spanish classes through their Centro Internacional de Idiomas, T6417051, ext 32251, 0800-1800, at Edif Humanidades (p1º), on the main campus on Av Patria 1201, Col Lomas del Valle 3a sección, US$350 for 4 weeks of 4 hours per day instruction, 5 days a week, 7 levels of instruction, each lasting 4 weeks, US$13 per day accommodation and 3 meals with Mexican family. *The Instituto Cultural Mexicano-Norteamericano de Jalisco*, at Enrique Díaz de León 300, T8255838, 8252666, US$440 for 6 weeks of 3 hours per day plus 30 minutes conversation, 5 days a week, 5 levels of instruction, cultural lectures on Fri, US$18 per day to live with Mexican family with 3 meals. *Spanish Language School AC*, Ermita 1443 entre 12 de Diciembre y Av Las Rosas, Col Chapalita, Apdo Postal 5-959, T/F1214774. *Vancouver Language Centre*, Av Vallarta 1151, Col América, T8260944, F8252051 (T1-604-6871600-Vancouver), US$150 for one week intensive programme. For German and French lessons see **Cultural centres**, above. See also National Registration Center for Study Abroad under **Learning Spanish** in **Essentials**.

Laundry Aldama 125, US$3.30 per 3 kg load (walk along Independencia towards train station, turn left into Aldama). **Tour companies & travel agents** *Expediciones México Verde*, José María Vigil 2406, Col Italia Providencia, T/F6415598, rafting specialists (Ríos Actopán, Jatate, Santa María, Antigua-Pescados, Filo Bobos, Usumacinta). **Tourist offices** Federal tourist office (*Sectur*), Morelos 102, Plaza Tapatía, T6148686 (Mon-Fri 0900-2000), has information in German and English including good walking tour map of the historic centre, helpful but often understaffed; Jalisco state offices at Paseo Degollado 105/Morelos 102, Plaza Tapatía, T6148686, open Mon-Sat 0900-2000, and a booth in capitol building. There are several booths staffed by Tourist Police near many of the main attractions. Municipal office at Pedro Moreno 1590, just west of Av Chapultépec and Los Arcos, over Av Vallarta, T6163332. *Siglo 21* newspaper has a good entertainments section, *Tentaciones* on Fri, every day it has good music, film and art listings. *Instituto Nacional de Estadística*, Geografía e Informática, 16 de Septiembre 670, T6149461, F6583969, new, fully computerized office, for maps and information, open 0800-2000.

Useful services Immigration: Mexican tourist cards can be renewed at the immigration office (primer piso) in the Palacio Federal on Av Alcalde between Calles Juan Alvarez and Hospital, across the avenue from the Santuario de Guadalupe. The Palacio Federal also contains a post and telegraph office and fax service.

"From Guadalajara to Irapuato: via **Tepatitlán** (79 kilometres, on the León road), a small market town with a *charro* centre, in an impressive setting with steep hills all around; **Arandas** has a curious neo-gothic church and a pleasant square with a white wrought-iron bandstand; the road then winds tightly up over a range of hills and then down into a long and heavily cultivated valley. 5-hour journey." writes Tim Connell.

Routes

San Miguel El Alto (*Population:* 50,000), northeast of Tapatitlán, off Route 80, is an old town, typical of the Jalisco area, where the tradition of the *serenata* is still practiced. On Sunday at 2000, men with confetti and roses line the square while the women promenade. The men signal their interest by throwing confetti on a girl's head; next time around he will offer her a rose. If she is interested she will walk with him round the plaza. At 2200 the police send everyone home and fortunate suitors may be allowed to walk their girlfriends home.

Chapala

Chapala town , 64 kilometres to the southeast on the northern shore of **Laguna de Chapala** (113 kilometres long, 24 to 32 wide), has thermal springs, several good and pricey hotels, three golf courses, and is a popular resort particularly with retired North Americans and Mexican day-trippers. Watch women and children play a picture-card game called *Anachuac*.

Phone code: 376
Colour map 4, grid B2

The divided highway from Guadalajara becomes Av Francisco Madero in town, with a grassy middle and large trees, Laurel de la India, giving shade. The avenue ends at the lake. The street that runs along the lakefront is Paseo Ramón Corona and is closed to traffic west of Av Madero. The other main street in town is Av Hidalgo, one block in from the lake, parallel to Ramón Corona. Av Hidalgo going west becomes the road to Ajijic and beyond. Uphill from the *Villa Montecarlo* hotel on C Lourdes (cobblestone) is La Iglesia de Lourdes, a small pastel pink church with a bell

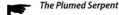

The Plumed Serpent

In May-July 1923, D H Lawrence lived in Chapala, renting a house called Los Cuentales. The house still stands at Zaragoza 307, although a second floor and some modernization have been added. The church that figures in the last pages of The Plumed Serpent *is on the waterfront, its humble façade and interior now covered by a handsome veneer of carved stone. Lawrence's novel published in 1926 explored Mexican society in the light of the revolution and there are descriptions of the countryside around Lake Sayula (in reality Lake Chapala) and its 'sperm' coloured, shallow water: "It was a place with a strange atmosphere: stony, hard, broken with round, cruel hills and the many and fluted bunches of the organ-cactus behind the old house, and an ancient road trailing past, deep in ancient dust."*

tower, facing down the street to the lake. Open during masses on Thursday and noon on Sunday.

The lake is set in beautiful scenery. There are boats of all kinds for hire, some go to the Isla de Alacranes (restaurant), water-fowl shooting in autumn and winter. Most fish in the lake have been killed by pollution, but the five centimetres 'XYZ' fish, called *charales*, are a delicacy. Lake water must be boiled. The water level is low because of irrigation demand and it is getting smelly and overgrown at the edges. Beside the lake, four blocks east of Av Madero along Paseo Ramón Corona, Parque de la Cristinia is worth a visit, popular with families at weekends, swimming pool. Horses for hire on the beach by the Parque, bargain. There is a market on the east side of the Zócalo with stalls selling handicrafts, places to eat, dirty public restrooms, one peso, entrance on street behind the market. Pemex sells magna sin.

Sleeping **B-C** *Villa Montecarlo*, west edge of town on Av Hidalgo at C Lourdes, family rooms or suites available, beautiful grounds with palms and mangoes, all rooms have phone, bath tub, balcony overlooking lake, pool, tennis, good restaurant, tables outside under massive laurel de la India tree. **D** *Chapala Haciendas*, Km 40, Chapala-Guadalajara highway, T52720, live music Wednesday and Saturday, unheated pool. **D** *Nido*, Av Madero 202, close to lake, T52116, brick building, old photos in reception hall, clean, cheaper without TV, accept Visa and MC, clean, good restaurant, swimming pool, parking for motorcycles beside pool. **E** *Casa de Huéspedes Palmitas*, C Juárez 531, behind market, TV, hot water, bath, but run down, noisy, cockroaches.

Furnished apartments for rent at Hidalgo 269, information at 274-A, also at Paseo Ramón Corona and C Juárez on the lake, 1 block east of Av Madero. Next door at Paseo Ramón Corona 16 is a pretty house with large lawn and gardens where rooms are rented by the week or month including morning coffee. Lots of real estate offices on Hidalgo, west of Madero, with house or apartment rentals. Chapala Realty, Hidalgo 223, helpful, T53676, F53528.

Trailer Park 1 kilometre from the lake between Chapala and Ajijic: *PAL*, Apdo Postal 1-1470, Guadalajara, T53764 or Chapala 60040, US$13 daily, 1st class, pool, good.

Eating *La Leña*, Madero 236, open air, serves *antojitos* and steaks, bamboo roof; next door is *Che Mary*, also attractive, outdoor seating. *Café Paris*, Madero 421, sidewalk tables, popular, *comida corrida* US$3, also breakfast, sandwiches; also on Madero are *El Patio*, good, cheap, and next door at 405A, *Los Equipales*. Where Madero reaches the lake is a restaurant/bar, *Beer Garden*, live amplified Mexican music, dancing, tables on the beach. *Bing's* ice cream parlour next door. *Cazadores*, on lake, old red brick house, mariachis sometimes, credit cards accepted. *La Langosta Loca*, Ramón Corona, seafood; 1 block further is the bar *Centro Botanero Los Caballos Locos*, and 2 doors down is the *Scotland Café*, in part of a colonial house with tables on the front porch and on the back lawn, as well as inside at the bar, open until 0200-0300. Several seafood places close by: *El Guayabo*, *El Guayabo Green*, *Cozumel*, *Huichos*, *Acapulquito*, *La Terraza Lupita*. Grocery store on southeast corner of Hidalgo and Madero and another one at Madero 423 next to the plaza.

On the *Fiesta de Francisco de Asís* (**2-3 October**) fireworks are displayed and excellent food **Festivals** served in the streets.

Local Bus: bus station on Av Madero at corner of Miguel Martínez. Buses from Guadalajara **Transport** every 30 minutes, 0515-2030, 1 hour. 2 blocks south of bus station, minibuses leave every 20 minutes for Ajijic, 2 pesos, and San Juan Cosalá, 3 pesos. **Taxi**: stand on Zócalo and at bus station.

Banks *Casa de cambio* on Av Madero near *Beer Garden*, open 0830-1700, Mon-Sat. *Banco Bital*, **Directory** Madero 208, next to *Hotel Nido*, 24-hr ATM taking Visa, MC, and cards of Cirrus and Plus networks. Nearby is a Banamex with 24-hr ATMs. *Casa de cambio* at Hidalgo 204 esq Madero, has phone on St for international calls that takes Visa, MC and Amex. *Bancomer* at Hidalgo 212 near Madero, 24-hr ATM taking Visa; across the St is a *Banco Serfín*, 24-hr ATM accepting Visa, MC, Diner's Club, Cirrus and Plus networks. *Lloyds*, Madero 232, is a real estate office, *casa de cambio*, travel agency and *sociedad de inversión*, many Americans keep their money here. **Communications** Postal services: *Mail Box, etc,* C Chapala-Jocotepec 155, opposite *PAL* Trailer Park, T60747, F60775. Shipping office at Hidalgo 236 uses Federal Express and DHL. Just west of it is the Post Office. At Hidalgo 223 is a UPS office. **Telephones:** Computel on the plaza, long distance and fax, accept Amex, MC, AT&T. Also pay phones for long distance calls on Zócalo and outside bus station. **Hospitals & medical services** Clinic: *IMSS* clinic on Niños Héroes between Zaragoza and Cinco de Mayo. Centro de salud at Flavio Romero de V and Guerrero. **Red Cross:** in Parque de la Cristinia. **Laundry** Zaragoza y Morelos. Dry cleaners at Hidalgo 235A, also repair shoes and other leather items. **Tourist offices** Regional office at Aquiles Serdán 26, T53141.

Seven kilometres to the west, a smaller, once Indian village, has an arty-crafty Amer- **Ajijic** ican colony with many retired North Americans. The village is pleasant, with cobbled streets, a pretty little plaza and many single storey villas. One block east of the plaza at the end of C Parroquia is the very pretty church of San Andrés, started in 1749. There is also a pretty stone church on the northwest corner of the plaza. On Colón in the two blocks north of the plaza are several restaurants, boutiques and galleries. Going south from the plaza, Colón becomes Morelos, crossing C

Mexico west central

Constitución and continues some five blocks to the lake with lots of restaurants, galleries and shops. The lake shore has receded about 200 metres from the original shore line and it is a bit smelly. The Way of the Cross and a Passion Play are given at Easter in a chapel high above the town. House and garden tours, Thursday 1030, two and a half hours, US$10, in aid of Lakeside School for the Deaf, T61881 for reservation. Bus from Chapala or taxi US$3.20.

Sleeping **B** *Hotel Danza del Sol*, T376-60220/61080, or Guadalajara 6218878, Av Lázaro Cárdenas 3260, Planta Baja, large complex, nice units and gardens, pool; under same management as **AL** *Real de Chapala*, Paseo del Prado 20, T60007, F60025, delightful, pleasant gardens. **A** *La Nueva Posada*, Donato Guerra 9, Apdo 30, T61444, F61344, breakfast included, vast rooms, Canadian management, horseriding, golf, tennis, theatre, gardens, swimming pool, restaurant (large, clean, pretentious, attractive outdoor seating in garden overlooking lake), colonial décor, delightful. **B** *Los Artistas Bed & Breakfast*, Constitución 105, T61027, F60066, artistas@acnet.net, 6 rooms, fireplaces, pool, living room, no credit cards, English and Spanish spoken. **C** *Laguna Bed 'n' Brunch*, Zaragoza 29, T61174, F61188, good value, clean, comfortable, with bath, parking. **D** *Mariana*, Guadalupe Victoria 10, T62221, 54813, breakfast available, weekly and monthly rates, all rooms have cable TV. **D** *Las Casitas*, motel-type with kitchen units, pool (just outside Ajijic, at Carretera Puente 20); similar is *las Calandrias* next door, furnished apartments, swimming pool, T52819. *Mama Chuy Club*, and *Villa Chello*, on hillside, T376-30013 for both, good, pools, spacious, monthly rentals, good value.

Eating *Los Telares* on main street, nice, courtyard garden; clean *lonchería* on plaza, good simple meals, cheap, grilled chicken, used by locals and Americans. *Ajijic*, pavement café on corner of plaza, cheap drinks, Mexican snacks, hearty *parrillada* Saturday, Sunday. *Los Girasoles*, 16 de Septiembre 18, moderately priced, Mexican food in walled courtyard. *Posada Ajijic*, Morelos, opposite pier, T60744, bar and restaurant, accept credit cards; pier here with fish restaurant at the end, indoor and outdoor seating and bar, used to be over water but stilts are now over dry land. *Bruno's*, on main street, excellent steaks. Fresh fish shop on plaza and other small food shops.

Directory **Hospitals & medical services** Clinics: *Clínica Ajijic*, Carretera Ote 33, T60662/60500, with 24-hr ambulance service, Dr Alfredo Rodríguez Quintana (home T61499). 2 dentists' offices on Colón, just south of plaza. **Useful services** Post Office: 1 block south of plaza, corner of Colón and Constitución; artisan clothes shops; newspaper shop near plaza sells *Mexico City Times*; small art gallery but few cultural events advertised. On the northwest corner of the plaza is a Computel booth for long distance phone and fax, open daily, 0800-2100. About ½ block north at Colón 24A is a *lavandería*, US$2 to wash and dry a load. Taxi stand on west side of plaza, next to it is a large map of Ajijic on one side and Chapala on the other, showing businesses and tourist sites. Opposite taxi stand at Colón 29 is a *casa de cambio*. On southwest corner of plaza is Banco Promex with 2 ATMs open 24 hours, accept Cirrus, Plus, Visa, MC, Diner's Club. **Immigration:** Castellanos 4, T62042. Ajijic Real Estate at Morelos 4, T62077, is an authorized UPS outlet. *El Ojo del Lago* is a free English newspaper, available at hotels and chapala@infosel.net.mx.

Beyond Ajijic on the lake is the Indian town of **Jocotepec**, a sizeable agricultural centre (*Population:* 18,000, recently invaded by more cosmopolitan types, little budget accommodation: **D** *Posada del Pescador*, *cabañas* on outskirts with bedroom, living room, kitchen and bathroom, set in a lovely garden; one other small hotel in town, **E**, bath, not clean); there is a local *fiesta* on 11-18 January. Jocotepec can be reached from Ajijic or from the Mexico-Guadalajara highway. Bus Chapala-Jocotepec US$2, every hour in each direction. The Indians make famous black-and-white *sarapes*.

Between Ajijic and Jocotepec lies the small town of **San Juan Cosalá**, less prosperous than Ajijic but pleasant, with cobblestone streets and fewer gringos. There are thermal springs (varied temperatures, crowded and noisy at weekends, five pools of different sizes) at *Hotel Balneario San Juan Cosalá* (Apdo Postal 181,

Chapala, T376-10302, F10222), which has private rooms for bathing with large tiled baths. Sunbathing in private rooms also possible. Bed and breakfast in clinical modern quarters with bar/restaurant. Rooms to let at **D** *Balneario Paraíso*. Bus service from Chapala. Fish restaurants are squeezed between the carretera and the lake at **Barrenada**, one kilometre east of town.

NB Route 80 from Laguna de Chapala to the Pacific Coast at Barra de Navidad is in very poor condition. Route 15 on the southern shore of Laguna de Chapala, which leads to Pátzcuaro (six hours) is in good condition, if slow and winding through the hills.

40 kilometres due south of Lake Chapala is the colonial town of **Mazamitla** (2,200 metres), a pleasant place on the side of a range of mountains, cold at night. It has a charming zócalo. Hotels, **D** *Posada Alpina*, on square; **E** *Fiesta de Mazamitla*, with bath, clean, recommended. *La Llorono County Club*, in Sierra del Tigre Woods, T6821186, has cabins, spa-club house and driving range. About four kilometres out of town is Zona Monteverde with pine forests, small *casitas* for rent, two good restaurants at entrance, T161826; steep hills, access only by car or taxi.

About 130 kilometres south of Guadalajara off the road (Jal 54) to Sayula and Ciudad Guzmán is Tapalpa, very pretty indeed. Three and a half hours drive from Guadalajara. The bus has several detours into the hills to stop at small places such as Zacoalco (Sunday market) and Amacueca. The road up to Tapalpa is winding and climbs sharply; the air becomes noticeably cooler and the place is becoming increasingly popular as a place for weekend homes. The town itself, with only 11,000 inhabitants, shows ample signs of this influx of prosperity. There are two churches (one with a curious atrium) and an imposing flight of stone steps between them, laid out with fountains and ornamental lamps. Tapalpa is in cattle country; the rodeo is a popular sport at weekends.

Tapalpa
Colour map 3, grid B2

The main street is lined with stalls, selling *sarapes* and other tourist goods on Sunday and fresh food the other days of the week. The only local speciality is *ponche*, an improbable blend of tamarind and mescal which is sold in gallon jars and recommended only for the curious or foolhardy. If you are planning a day trip get your return ticket as soon as you arrive as the last bus back to Guadalajara (1800 on Sunday) is likely to be full.

Sleeping and eating The more expensive restaurants have tables on balconies overlooking the square – the *Restaurante Posada Hacienda* (which has a US$1 cover charge) is well placed. Others are the *Buena Vista* (which also has rooms) and *La Cabaña*, and all are visited by the mariachis. Less grand is the **D** *Hotel Tapalpa*, with huge holes in the floor, but clean and fairly cheap. Some rooms are for hire (*Bungalows Rosita*, *Posada Hacienda* has nice bungalows with fireplace and small kitchen).

Jalisco Route 54 continues through Ciudad Guzmán (formerly Zapotlán) to join Route 110, which heads southwest from Zamora to Colima. Ciudad Guzmán is a clean, modern town with wide streets and a relaxed atmosphere. It is a good base for climbing the volcanoes, see below, **Colima**.

Ciudad Guzmán
Colour map 3, grid B2

Sleeping **AL** *Hacienda Nuera*, Hidalgo 177; **AL** *Real*, Colón. **B** *Posada San José*, M Chávez Madrueño 135. **C** *Reforma*, Javier Mina 33. **C-E** *Zaplotán*, on main plaza, reasonable, stores luggage. **C** *Posada San José*, M Chávez Madrueño 135, T20756, phone, TV. **D** *Tlayolan*, J Mina 33, T23317, clean, quiet. **D** *Hotel Flamingo*, near main square, excellent value, very modern, very clean, and quiet, recommended. **E** *Morelos*, Refugio B de Toscana 12.

Eating *Juanito*, on main square, steak dishes, good service. *Bon Appetit*, upstairs on main square, views of town, excellent chef called Blas Flores, large servings, Japanese, Greek and Continental food, recommended. *La Flor de Loto*, vegetarian on José Rodón 37C, cheap soya burgers; *Pilón Burgers* next to *Hotel Flamingo*, tiny, traditional. On C Priciliano Sánchez there are stalls selling juices, yoghurts and cereals. Good cheap meals in the market (upstairs).

Festivals There is a fair for 2 weeks in **October**. On one Sunday in October the festival of San José is celebrated. Farmers march to the church to give presents to San José, who they believe will bring rain to help their crops grow. In 1996, a bull ran through the streets on the first Saturday in October, which became an annual event. Famous Mexican singers perform at the local theatre throughout the month.

Transport Buses: To Colima 2 hours, US$3 (Flecha Amarilla); to Uruapan and Morelia involves changes in Tamazula and Zamora.

Directory Laundry:*José Rodón*, opposite *La Flor de Loto*, cheap.

Colima

Population: 150,000
State Population: 1995
487,324
Altitude: 494m
Phone code: 331
Colour map 3, grid B2

The capital of Colima state is a most charming and hospitable town with a 19th century Moorish style **arcade** on the main square and a strange rebuilt gothic ruin on the road beyond the **Cathedral** (late 19th century). Also on the east side of the main square is the **Palacio de Gobierno** (with interesting murals of the history of Mexico). Both are attractive buildings. Behind them is the Jardín Torres Quintero, another pretty but smaller plaza. Andador Constitución is a pedestrian street, with people selling paintings on the street, several small, attractive restaurants and a state run artisan's shop at the north end on the corner of Zaragoza. Crossing Zaragoza, Constitución is open to traffic, and one block north on the corner with Vicente Guerrero is the church of **San Felipe de Jesús** (early 18th century plateresque façade) where Miguel Hidalgo was at one time parish priest. Public swimming pool in Parque Regional Metropolitano on C Degollado about five to six blocks from southwest corner of the main plaza. **Teatro Hidalgo** on the corner of Degollado and Morelos, has a pink colonial façade and large carved wooden doors (only open during functions). Parque Núñez, five blocks east of the plaza is also pretty and twice the size of the plaza. South of Parque Núñez, about seven blocks, is Parque Hidalgo, a very large park with tall coconut palms. Young men can be seen climbing the palms to collect coconuts.

Museums **Museo de las Culturas de Occidente María Ahumada**, Calzada Pedro Galván, in Casa de Cultura complex. ■ *Tuesday-Sunday 0900-1300, 1600-1800*. **Museo de la Máscara, la Danza y el Arte Popular del Occidente**, C 27 de Septiembre y Manuel Gallardo, folklore and handicrafts (items for sale – in the University Institute of Fine Arts); **Museo de la Historia de Colima**, on the Zócalo.

Excursions **El Chanal** An archaeological site, about 15 kilometres to the north of Colima, with a small pyramid with 36 sculptured figures, discovered in 1944.
El Hervidero, 22 kilometres southeast of Colima, is a spa in a natural lake of hot springs which reach 25°C.
Comalá A pretty colonial town with whitewashed adobe buildings near Colima, worth a few hours' visit, bus US$0.25, 20 minutes every 30 minutes. The climate is somewhat cooler and more comfortable than Colima. The surrounding vegetation is lush with coffee plantations. In the town are two popular restaurants with *mariachis* and local specialities, *Los Portales* and *Comalá* on Plaza Mayor; they are open until 1800. Outside the town on the Colima road is the *Botanero Bucaramanga*, a bar with *botanas* (snacks) and *mariachis*. Eight kilometres northeast is the Escuela de Artesanía where handmade furniture, painted with fabulous bird designs, and other crafts are manufactured to order. **Suchitlán** (Sunday market) has *Los Portales de Suchitlán*, a good restaurant selling local specialities at Galeanas 10, T33954452. The people here are very small (*chaparrito*) and it is reflected in the size of the

Climbing the volcanoes at Colima

Colima volcano (3,842 metres), one of the most exciting climbs in Mexico, which erupted with great loss of life in 1941, and **El Nevado** (4,339 metres) are in the vicinity of Colima. They can be climbed by going to Ciudad Guzmán, and taking a bus to the village of Fresnito. Register with the police here before climbing. For El Nevado: from Fresnito it is 20 kilometres to the first (more comfortable) hut at 3,500 metres (beds, take water). A second hut is a bit further on (take the right fork in the road after the first hut). At weekends it may be possible to hitch. From the huts it is a strenuous three to four hour hike to the top. From the TV relay station descend to the obvious, sandy track that leads over the saddle towards Pico Nevado. Take the higher track to the stoney ridge. Stick to the right of the watercourse/rockfall, reaching the ridge which leads up towards the peak.

Sr Agustín Ibarra (T33628, ext 103) organizes day trips to within a two-hour climb of the summit (recommended), US$50 for 10 people to the huts, or three and a half hour horse ride to the refuge with a three-hour climb, US$10 per person. Sr Ibarra's dog Laika is also a great companion! It may be possible to hitch a lift down the next day with the TV maintenance crew who work at the top. The weather in this region is very unpredictable, beware of sudden heavy rains. Sr Ibarra provides homely accommodation in the village; otherwise ask where to camp. There are a couple of shops but only limited supplies. Hotels in Ciudad Guzmán, see text.

doorways. Further down the road at Km 18, Comala-San Antonio, is a beautiful, large, open-air restaurant, *Jacal de San Antonio*, on top of a hill overlooking a lush valley with the Volcán de Colima in the distance. About 18 kilometres beyond Comalá (look out for signposts), is the magnificent 18th century *estancia* of **San Antonio**; set in a green valley with an impressive roman-style aqueduct leading water down from a mountain spring. The road continues up and over a mountain stream; about a kilometre further on are **Las Marías**, a private mountain lake used as a picnic site, admission US$0.65.

B-C *Hotel América*, Morelos 162, T20366, a/c, cable TV, phone, largest rooms in new section, pretty interior gardens, travel agency, steam baths, good restaurant, central, friendly. **C-D** *Ceballos*, Torres Quintero 16, T21354, main square, fine building with attractive *portales*, some huge rooms with a/c, clean, good food in restaurant (pricey), secure indoor parking, very good value, highly recommended. **D-E** *Flamingos*, ex-*Gran Hotel*, pleasant small rooms with fan, Av Rey Colimán 18, T22526, near Jardín Núñez, with bath, simple, clean, breakfast expensive, disco below goes on till 0300 on Saturday and Sunday. **D-E** *La Merced*, Hidalgo 188, T26969, pretty colonial house with rooms around patio filled with plants, passageway to newer section, entrance at Juárez 82 with reception, all rooms same price, 2 beds cost more than one, TV, bath, highly recommended for budget travellers. **E** *Galeana*, Medellín 142, near bus terminal, basic. **E** *Núñez*, Juárez 80 at Jardín Núñez, basic, dark, with bath. **E** *San Cristóbal*, Reforma 98, T20515, near centre, run down. Many *casas de huéspedes* near Jardín Núñez. **D** *Rey de Colimán*, on continuation of Medellín on outskirts, large rooms. *Motel Costeño* on outskirts going to Manzanillo, T21925, is recommended. 3 motels coming in from Guadalajara: *María Isabel*, T26262; *Los Candiles*, T23212. *Villa del Rey*, T22917.

Sleeping

Several restaurants on the Zócalo serve inexpensive meals. *El Trébol* probably the best, on southwest corner; opposite on Degollado 67, is nice open-air restaurant on 2nd floor on south side of plaza, overlooking it. *Café de la Plaza*, Portal Medellín 20, beside *Hotel Ceballos*, comida corrida about US$4. *Los Naranjos*, Gabino Barreda 34, ½ block north of Jardín Torres Quintero, going since 1955, nice, well-known. *Samadhi*, Filomeno Medina 125, vegetarian, good, T32498, meal about US$3, opposite *La Sangre de Cristo*, church, good yoghurt and fruit drinks, attractive, large garden with iguanas. *Café Dali* is in the Casa de Cultura complex. *Café Colima* in Parque Corregidora. *Giovannis*, Constitución 58 El Nte, good pizzas and takeaway. Good yoghurt and wholemeal bread at *Centro de Nutrición Lakshmi*, Av Madero

Eating

265, run by Hari Krishnas. *La Troje*, T22680, on southeast of town heading to Manzanillo, good, mariachis, very Mexican. Try the local sweet *cocada y miel* (coconut and honey in blocks), sold in *dulcerías*.

Festivals *Feria* The annual fair of the region (agriculture, cattle and industry, with much additional festivity) runs from the last Saturday of **October** until the first Sunday of November. Traditional local potions (all the year round) include *Jacalote* (from black maize and pumpkin seeds), *bate* (*chía* and honey), *tuba* (palm tree sap) and *tecuino* (ground, germinated maize).

Transport **Air** Airport (CLQ) 19 kilometres from centre, T44160, 49817. Flights to Mexico City and Tijuana available. **Buses** Bus station on the outskirts; buses and *combis* run to centre, US$0.50, or taxi about US$1. Bus companies: ETN, T25899, La Línea, T20508, 48179; Primera Plus T48067; Omnibús de México, T47190; Sur de Jalisco, T20316; Elite, T28499. If going to **Uruapan** it is best to go to **Zamora** (7-8 hours, although officially 4) and change there. ETN bus to Guadalajara US$12, 2½-3 hours by autopista; plus service US$9, regular 1st class US$8, 2nd class US$7, all take autopista, non-stop; Colima-**Manzanillo** US$7. ETN to **Mexico City** US$51.65.

Directory **Airline offices** *Aero California*, T44850. *AeroMéxico*, T31340. *Aeromar*, T31340. **Banks** *Banco Inverlat* at Juárez 32 on west side of Jardín Núñez, ATM takes Amex, Visa, Diner's Club. *Casa de cambio* at Morelos and Juárez on southwest corner of same park. *Bancomer* at Madero and Ocampo 3 blocks east of plaza, ATM takes Visa and Plus. *Casa de cambio* across the street. *Banamex* a block south down Ocampo at Hidalgo has an ATM. **Communications** Post Office: Av Fco I Madero y Gral Núñez, northeast corner of Jardín Núñez. Telecommunication: Computel at Morelos 234 on south side for long distance phone and fax, and at bus station, open 0700-2200, accepts Visa, MC, Amex and AT&T cards. Fax not always in use. **Hospitals & medical services** Hospital: *Hospital Civil*, T20227. Pharmacy: *Farmacia Guadalupana* on northeast corner of Jardín Torres Quintero behind cathedral. Another pharmacy on northeast corner of Zócalo. **Red Cross:** T21451. **Laundry** *Lavandería Shell*, 27 de Septiembre 134, open 0900-2000, inexpensive, quick. **Tourist office** On the west side of the Zócalo, opposite the Cathedral, T24360, F28360, good, but no information on climbing local volcanoes.

Manzanillo

Population: 150,000
Phone code: 333
Colour map 3, grid B1

A beautiful, three-hour hilly route runs from Colima to Manzanillo, which has become an important port on the Pacific, since a spectacular 257-kilometre railway has been driven down the sharp slopes of the Sierra Madre through Colima. A new toll road has been opened between Guadalajara and Manzanillo, good, double-laned in some sections, driving time about four hours, but total cost US$17 in tolls. The tolls from Mexico City to Manzanillo total US$55. Occupations for tourists at Manzanillo, which is not a touristy town, include deep-sea fishing (US$250 to hire a boat for a day, including beer, *refrescos* and *ceviche*), bathing, and walking in the hills. There is a good snorkelling trip starting at the beach of *Club Las Hadas* (see below), US$40 includes soft drinks and equipment. The water is clear and warm, with lots to see. Trips two to three times daily, last one at 1230. There is a bullring on the outskirts on the road to Colima. The best beach is the lovely crescent of Santiago, eight kilometres north, but there are three others, all of which are clean, with good swimming.

Sleeping
■ *on maps*
Price codes:
see inside front cover

LL *Club Las Hadas*, Península de Santiago, T42000, a Moorish fantasy ("architecture crowned by perhaps the most flamboyantly and unabashedly phallic tower ever erected, and the palpable smell of money; should on no account be missed"). **AL** *La Posada*, Calz L Cárdenas 201, near the end of Las Brisas peninsula, T31899, US manager, beautifully designed rooms carved into the living rock of an outcrop; *Club Maeva*, Km 12.5 Carretera Santiago-Miramar, T50595, picturesque, opposite beach, clean rooms with bath and kitchen, meals included in price, several good restaurants. **AL** *Roca del Mar*, Playa Azul, T20302, vacation centre. **B** *Las Brisas Vacation Club*, Av L Cárdenas 207, T31747/32075, some a/c, good restaurant.

At **Santiago beach** AL *Playa de Santiago*, T30055, good but food expensive. **C** *Anita*, T30161, built in 1940, has a certain funky charm and it is clean and on the beach. **C** *Parador Marbella*, Blvd M de la Madrid Km 10, T31103, meals extra. *Marlyn*, T30107, 3rd floor rooms with balcony overlooking the beach, a bargain, recommended.

At the port **C** *Colonial*, good restaurant, México 100, T21080, friendly, avoid rooms above the record shop (very loud music). **D** *Casa de Huéspedes Posada Jardín*, Cuauhtémoc, reasonable. **D** *Emperador*, Davalos 69, T22374, good value, good, cheap restaurant. **D** *Flamingos*, 10 de Mayo y Madero, T21037, with bath, quite good. **E** *Casa de Huéspedes Central*, behind bus station, with bath, fan, OK. Visitors can also rent apartments in private condominiums, eg *Villas del Palmar* at Las Hadas, or *Club Santiago*, T50414 (contact Héctor Sandóval at Hectours for information).

México

Manzanillo centre

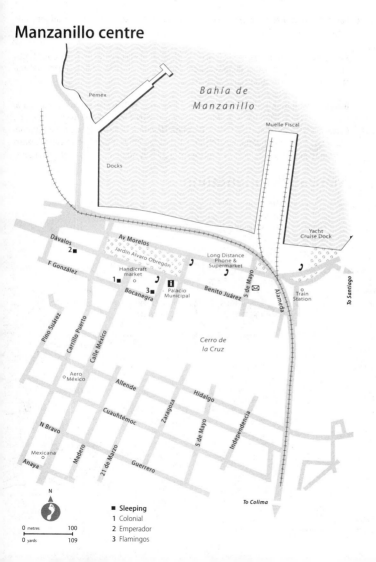

■ **Sleeping**
1 Colonial
2 Emperador
3 Flamingos

Camping At Miramar and Santiago beaches. 4.5 kilometres north of Manzanillo is *Trailer Park El Palmar*, T35533, with a large swimming pool, run down, very friendly, coconut palms, US$13 for 2 in camper-van. *La Marmota* trailer park, at junction of Highways 200 and 98, cold showers, bathrooms, pool, laundry facilities, US$8 per car and 2 people.

Eating
● *on maps*

Willy's Seafood Restaurant, Playa Azul, on the beach, French owner, primarily seafood, some meat, very good, 3-courses with wine US$15 per person. *Portofino's*, Blvd M de la Madrid, Km 13, Italian, very good pizza; next door is *Plaza de la Perlita*, good food, live music; also Italian, *Bugatti's*, Crucero Las Brisas. *Carlos and Charlie's*, Blvd M de la Madrid Km 6.9, on the beach, seafood and ribs, great atmosphere. Good but not cheap food at the 2 *Huerta* restaurants, the original near the centre, and *Huerta II* near the Las Hadas junction. *Johanna*, opposite bus station entrance, good food, cheap.

Transport

Local Car rental: National, Km 9.5 Carreterra Manzanillo-Santiago, T30611. **Budget**, same road, T31445.

Air Frequent flights from airport (ZLO) (T31119, 32525) 19 kilometres from town, to Mexico City and Guadalajara. Other domestic destinations: Chihuahua, Monterrey, Puerto Vallarta and Saltillo. US destinations: Los Angeles.

Buses To **Miramar**, US$0.50, leaves from J J Alcaraz, 'El Tajo'. Several to **Guadalajara**, US$11, or US$23 ENT, 6 hours. To **Mexico City** with ETN, luxury, US$62, with Autobus de Occidente, 19 hours, 1st class, US$25. **Barra de Navidad**, US$2.50, 1½ hours; to **Colima**, US$4, US$7 ENT; to **Tijuana**, bus US$80, 1st class, 36 hours. Down the coast to **Lázaro Cárdenas** and crossroads for Playa Azul (see page 244) by Autobus de Occidente or Galeana,

Manzanillo orientation

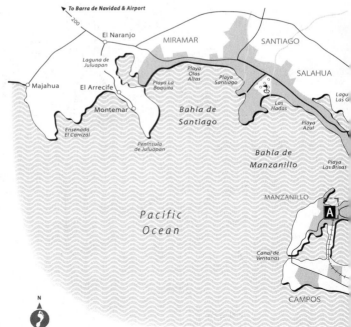

*Related map
A Manzanillo
centre, page 235*

7 hours. To **Acapulco**, US$8.50. To **Puerto Vallarta**, 1st class with Trans Cihuatlán at 0800 and 1200, 4½ hours, recommended. Bus terminal in Av Hidalgo outside centre, local buses go there. Taxi to centre US$1.50.

Hospitals & medical services *Hospital Civil*, T24161. Red Cross: T65770. **Tourist offices** Blvd Miguel de la Madrid 4960, T32277, F31426, halfway along Playa Azul. Tourist helpline (Angeles Verdes) T66600. **Airlines** *Aeromar* T30151; *Aerolitoral* T32424; *Mexicana* T21972; *AeroCalifornia* (Boulevard Miguel de La Madrid Km 13.5) T41414.

Directory

Southeast of Manzanillo is **Tecomán** (*Population:* 68,000) with delightful atmosphere. **B-C** *Gran Fénix*, larger rooms have a/c, smaller rooms are noisier but hotel is recommended; unnamed *pensión* on the corner of the Zócalo, if you face the church it is on your left, east. Try the local deep-fried *tortillas* filled with cheese. To the west of Tecomán is the small coastal resort of **Cuyutlán**, on the fast highway between Colima and Manzanillo. It has a pleasant, black-sand beach and **D** *Hotel Bucanero*, near the north end of the front, clean rooms, good restaurant, games room and souvenir shop. Swimming here is excellent and umbrellas and wooden walkways protect feet against the hot sun and sand. The coast road continues southeast to the unspoilt fishing village of **Boca de Apiza** (no hotels but some seafood restaurants). Abundant bird life at mouth of river. Halfway between Tecomán and Playa Azul is another uncrowded beach, **Maruata**, where you can ask the restaurant owner if you can camp or sling a hammock. The road continues to Playa Azul, Lázaro Cárdenas, Zihuatanejo and Acapulco: for 80 kilometres beyond Manzanillo it is good, then Route 200 in some parts is in poor condition and for long stretches you cannot see the ocean. In other places there are interesting coastal spots. About one hour south of Tecomán is the small village of **San Juan de Lima**, on a small beach; two or three hotels, the farthest south along the beach is very basic, **D**. There are a couple of restaurants, one unnamed, about 200 metres from the hotels, serving excellent red snapper and shrimp dishes. The road to Playa Azul is paved, in good condition.

NB Local police warn against camping in the wild in this area; it is not safe.

Another Route to Manzanillo Route 80 goes from Guadalajara to the coast, passing the outskirts of several pleasant towns with cobbled streets. The road is fairly trafficked as it plummets from the Sierra Madre to the coast. **Tecolotlán**, 200 kilometres north of Melaque, is a small town whose zócalo is one kilometre from the highway along rough cobbles. It has a few hotels, eg **D** *Albatros*, one block east of Zócalo, modern, clean, with bath, TV, highly recommended. **Autlán de Navarro**, 115 kilometres from Melaque, is a clean, modern, mid-sized town, with public phones in the zócalo and several hotels (eg **D** *Palermo*, pleasant, clean, with bath). 74 kilometres from Melaque is

Mexico

Casimiro Castillo, a small town with three hotels, including **E** *Costa Azul*, with bath, clean.

Melaque
Phone code: 335
Colour map 3, grid B1

The bay is one of the most beautiful on the Pacific coast, but is very commercialized and crowded at holiday times. An earthquake in 1994 has left a few, modern, buildings in ruins. A row of hotels along the beach has been made into holiday apartments. The beach is long, shelving and sandy with a rocky coast at each end and pelicans diving for fish. The waves are not so big at San Patricio beach.

Sleeping and eating **L-B** *Villas Camino del Mar*, Apdo Postal 6, San Patricio, T55207, F55498, rooms or villas on beach, 2 pools, discounts for long stays, up to 50 percent for a month, including tax, many US visitors stay all winter. **B** *Bungalows Azteca*, 23 kilometres from Manzanillo airport, for 4 at C Avante, San Patricio, T333-70150, with kitchenette, pool, parking. *Club Náutico El Dorado*, Gómez Farías 1A, T70230, very pleasant, good value, small swimming pool. **C** *Flamingo*, Vallarta 19, clean with fan, balconies, water coolers on each floor. Opposite is **D** *Santa María*, T70338, friendly, recommended. **D** *Posada Pablo de Tarso*, Gómez Farías 408, T70117, facing beach, pretty, galleried building, tiled stairs, antique-style furniture. **D** *San Nicolás*, Gómez Farías 54, T70066, beside Estrella Blanca bus station, noisy but clean. Off season, very pleasant, eg **D** *Monterrey*, Gómez Farías 27, T70004, on beach, clean, fan, bath, parking, superb view. *Trailer Park La Playa*, San Patricio, T70065, in the village, on beach, US$13 for car and 2 people, full hook-up, toilets, cold showers. If you follow the 'Melaque' signs, at the end of the main road is a free camping place on the beach at the bay, very good, easily accessible for RVs, popular for vehicles and tents. *Restaurant Los Pelícanos*, overpriced, on beach. Many restaurants on beach but most close at 1900. *Koala's at the Beach*, Alvaro Obregón 52, San Patricio, 2 blocks from *Camino del Mar*, small, good, great food in walled garden compound off dusty street, Canadian/Australian run.

Barra de Navidad
Phone code: 333
Colour map 3, grid B1

The village of Barra de Navidad is commercial but still pleasant, where there is a monument to the Spanish ships which set out in 1548 to conquer the Philippines. Barra is one and a half hours from Manzanillo; the beach is beautiful, very good for swimming, but at holiday times it is very crowded and a lot less pleasant. Pemex station at Route 200/Route 80 junction, has unleaded fuel. To change money, go to Cihuatlán from Barra, buses every 30 minutes; no tourist office. Bus to Manzanillo, US$2.50, one and a half hours.

Sleeping **B** *Tropical*, López de Legaspi 96, T70020, on beach, seedy but pleasant. **C** *Delfín*, Morelos 23, T70068, very clean, pool, hot water, highly recommended. Opposite is **C** *Sand's*, Morelos 24, T162859 (Guadalajara) or 70018 (Barra), bar, clean, some kitchen units, good value, pool. **C** *Hotel Barra de Navidad*, López de Legaspi 250, T70122, with balcony on beach, or bungalows where you can cook, pool, very good value. **D** *Hotel Jalisco*, Av Jalisco 91, hot water, safe but not very clean and noisy, nightclub next door with music till 0300. **D** *Marquez*, T55304, recommended. *San Lorenzo*, Av Sinaloa 87, T70139, is same price and much better, clean, hot water, good restaurant opposite. **E** *Posada Pacífico*, Mazatlán 136, one street behind bus terminal, clean, fan, friendly, good restaurant opposite. Ask about **camping** on beach.

Eating Fish restaurants eg *Antonio* on beach; many good restaurants on the Pacific side, a couple of good restaurants on the lagoon side, *Velero's*, delicious snapper and good views. *Amber*, Veracruz 101, half of menu vegetarian, real coffee, good breakfast and crêpes, highly recommended, closed lunchtime. *Pacífico*, very good barbecued shrimp, and good breakfasts.

Pretty seaside villages near Barra de Navidad include **La Manzanilla**, 14 kilometres north of Routes 200/80 junction (**D** *Posada de Manzanilla*, nice, recommended; *Posada del Cazador*, T70330); camping possible. South of village at end of Los Cocos beach is the **B** hotel and RV trailer park, *Paraíso Miramar*, T321-60434, pool, gardens, palm huts, restaurant, bar. three kilometres north of beach is Boca de Iguanas with two trailer parks: *Boca de Iguanas*, US$7 per person, vehicle free, hook-ups, cold showers, toilets, laundry facilities, clean, pleasant location, and *Tenacatita* (US$9d with hook-ups, US$7 without, cold showers, toilet, laundry facilities, restaurant). For both places take the unpaved road from Highway 200 to the abandoned *Hotel Bahía de Tenacatita*; at the T junction, turn right, pass the hotel, and the campsites are about 500 metres further on the left. This place is nothing to do with the village of **Tenacatita**. This has a perfect beach complete with palm huts, tropical fish among rocks (two sections of beach, the bay and oceanside). **D** *Hotel* (no name) in village near beach, or you can sleep on the beach under a palm shelter, but beware mosquitoes. Several kilometres north of Tenacatita is **AL** per person all inclusive *Blue Bay*, ex-*Fiesta Americana* resort, Km 20 Carretera Federal 200, T335-15020/15100, F15050, tennis, watersports, horseriding, disco, pool, gym, credit cards.

Michoacán

The State of Michoacán, where the Tarascan Indians live, is a country of deep woods, fine rivers and great lakes. Fruit, game, and fish are abundant. It has some of the most attractive towns and villages in the country. Visitors are attracted by the Tarascan customs, folklore, ways of life, craft skills (pottery, lacquer), music and dance. The dance is of first importance to them; it is usually performed to the music of wooden drum, flute and occasionally, a fiddle. Masks are often worn and the dance is part of a traditional ritual. The dances which most impress outsiders are the dance of Los Viejitos (Old Men; at Janitzio, 1 January); Los Sembradores (The Sowers; 2 February); Los Moros (The Moors; Lake Pátzcuaro region, *fiestas* and carnival); Los Negritos (Black Men; *fiestas* at Tzintzuntzán); Los Apaches (4 February, at the churches); Las Canacuas (the crown dance; Uruapan, on Corpus Christi). At the weddings of fisherfolk the couple dance inside a fish net. In the local *fandango* the woman has fruits in her hand, the man has a glass of *aguardiente* balanced on his head, and a sword.

South of Laguna de Chapala, you come to **Jiquilpan** (on Route 110 to Colima). There are frescoes by Orozco in the library, which was formerly a church. At least five hotels. **D** *Posada Palmira*, on main street, pleasant, clean, good restaurant. **E** *Imperial*, on main street, good value. **E** *Colonial Mendoza*, Route 15 in the centre, with bath, clean, good value, but noisy. Good, cheap, street foodstalls in the town.

Zamora (58 kilometres east of Jiquilpan) is an agricultural centre founded in 1540. There is a large, interesting gothic-style church in the centre, Catedral Inconclusa, started in 1898, work suspended during the Revolution, now with a projected completion date of 2000, several other, fine churches, and a market on C Corregidora. Nearby is tiny Laguna de Camecuaro, with boats for hire, restaurants and wandering musicians; popular at holiday times.

Zamora
Population: 135,000
Colour map 3, grid B2

Sleeping C *Fénix*, Madero Sur 401, T20266, clean, swimming pool, poor ventilation, pleasant balconies. **D** *Amalia*, Hidalgo 194, T21327, pleasant, some rooms noisy, restaurant OK. **D-E** *Posada Fénix*, Esquina Morelos y Corregidora, 1 block from zócalo, rooms of varying quality, nice owner, good laundry service. **E** *Posada Marena*, simple, clean; other cheap *hospedajes* near market, none very clean. **E** *Jasmín*, 2 kilometres on road to Morelia, opposite Pemex, with bath, clean, noisy. **Motel: A3** *Jérico*, Km 3 on La Barca road just north of town, T25252, swimming pool, restaurant.

Eating *El Campanario*, Nervo 22, off main square, recommended.

Transport Bus station at north edge of town, local bus to centre US$0.25, taxi US$3.50. Bus to Mexico City, 1st *plus*, US$16.50, 1st US$14.20. To **Guadalajara**, US$11, and US$10 to **Morelia**. To **Pátzcuaro**, 2½ hours, with Vía 2000.

Directory Tourist office Morelos Sur 76, T24015.

On 40 kilometres is **Carapán** (**E** *Motel La Hacienda*, friendly, clean, cold water, good restaurant), a crossroads at which a road goes north to **La Piedad de Cabadas**, a pleasant stopping place on the toll road between Guadalajara and Mexico City (**D** *Hotel Mansión Imperial*, parking. **E** *San Sebastián*, central, hot water, old but nice, parking across the street. **E** *Gran Hotel*, on main street, OK. *Restaurant El Patio*, near church, very good, dish of the day good value).

Paracho At Carapán a branch road runs 32 kilometres south through pine woods to Paracho, a quaint, very traditional Indian village of small wooden houses; in every other one craftsmen make guitars, *violins* and *mandolines* worth from US$15 to US$1,500 according to the wood used. A recommended workshop is that of Ramiro Castillo B, Av Independencia 259, Galeana 38, good value, friendly. Bargaining possible in all workshops. On the main plaza is the *Casa para el arte y la cultura Purhepecha* with information, library, shops etc. There is a guitar museum and concert hall, main venue for a famous week-long guitar festival in the second week of August (free concerts).

Sleeping D *Hermelinda*, in centre. **E** hotel on main road south of town, hot water morning only.

Eating *La Casona*, on main Plaza, quiet; *Café D'Gribet*, on main street, cheap and good snacks. Try local pancakes.

Transport Buses to/from Uruapan US$.80, 45 minutes. Also to Morelia via Pátzcuaro.

Uruapan

Population: 250,000
Altitude: 1,610m
Phone code: 452
Colour map 3, grid B2

This road continues south to Uruapan, the 'place where flowers are plentiful'. The most attractive of its three plazas is the **Zócalo** which has the **Jardín de los Mártires** at its west end. Opposite the Jardín is part of the former Collegiate church of San Francisco (17th century with later additions such as an interesting 1960s modern art interior) which houses the attractive **Casa de la Cultura** (small museum upstairs, free, with excellent display of the history of Uruapan). In the *portales* or at the market can be bought the local lacquered bowls and trays, or the delicate woodwork of the Paracho craftsmen, Patamban green pottery and Capácuaro embroideries. At the east end of the Zócalo is the restored hospital, built by Fray Juan de San Miguel in the 16th century; now a ceramics museum, the **Museo La Huatapería**. Adjoining it is a 16th century chapel now converted into a craft shop. Behind the chapel and museum is the Mercado de Antojitos and, beyond it, the clothes and goods market permanently occupying several streets. The food market has now moved out of the centre.

On M Trevino, between A Isaac and Amado Nervo, there is a house which is just one and a half metres wide and several stories high, possibly the narrowest structure in Mexico. The town suffers badly from traffic fumes.

The town is set among streams, orchards and waterfalls in the **Parque Nacional Eduardo Ruiz**, cool at night, well worth a visit. Local foods are sold in the Parque and there is a government-operated trout breeding facility. One kilometre from the centre is the entrance to the Parque, on the corner of Independencia and Colver City, with a good handicraft shop selling wooden boxes and bracelets (■ *US$0.35*). Walk there or catch a bus one block south of the Zócalo marked 'El Parque'.

Excursions Through coffee groves and orchards along the Cupatitzio (meaning Singing River) to the **Tzararacua Falls** (10 kilometres, entry US$0.25); restaurants at bus stop where you can hire a horse to the falls (US$4 per person). It is not advisable to walk to the falls alone. To extend the trip beyond the falls, cross the stone bridge to the

Mexico

other side of the stream. Take a path to the right which then switches back and heads up the other side of the gorge. After a while you will reach a plateau at the top of the mountain, with good views all around. A well-worn path/stream leads down the other side of the mountain to a more secluded waterfall, from the top of which are many paths down to the river and lake into which the stream flows (a great spot for a swim). Good camping some 300 metres below the village under the shelter on the top of a rim, with a view down into the valley to the waterfall (one kilometre away) and a small lake. A bus (marked Tzararacua, or Zupomita, but ask if it goes all the way) will take you from the Zócalo at Uruapan to Tzararacua, US$1 (15-25 minutes), weekends and public holidays only. Alternatively, try to buy a ticket to Tzararacua on the bus to Apatzinguán (which passes the falls) and ask the driver to let you off. If on a tight schedule, take a taxi.

Parque Cholinde, one and a half kilometres out of town (all uphill – take a bus), swimming pool, US$1.30; Colibrí Nurseries nearby. Balneario Caracha (frequent buses), alight at cross roads by sign, then walk one kilometre on road to pools, a delightful place, open daily (US$2) with restaurant, hotel, several pools and beautiful gardens. **Tingambato** ruins are half way along road to Pátzcuaro, about two kilometres downhill from Tingambato town (pyramid and ball court).

Sleeping

A *Victoria*, Cupatitzio 13, T36700, good, quiet, restaurant and garage. **B** *Concordia* on main plaza has nice restaurant, T30500. **B** *El Tarasco*, Independencia 2, T41500, pool, lovely, good restaurant, moderate prices. **B** *Plaza Uruapan*, Ocampo 64, T30333, good, clean, large rooms. **B** *Villa de Flores*, Emilio Carranza 15, T21650, quiet, pleasantly furnished, lovely flowers, recommended.

C *Atzimbal*, Calle Francisco Villa, T44325 (street where the mariachis are waiting), modern, recommended; on main plaza, **C** *Nueva Hotel Alameda*, Av 5 de Febrero, with bath, clean, TV, good value. **C** *del Parque*, Av Independencia 124, with bath, very nice, by entrance to national park, clean, quiet, enclosed parking, recommended. **D** *Acosta*, opposite bus station; nearby is **E** *Sandy*, with bath, TV, basic and **E** per person *Betty's*, with bath. **D** *Capri*, Portal Santos Degollado, by market, friendly. **D** *Los Tres Caballeros*, Constitución 50, T47170, walk out front door into market. **D** *Mi Solar*, Juan Delgado 10, T20912, good value, hot water, clean, recommended. **E** *Moderno*, main plaza, lovely building, with bath, water spasmodic, friendly, very basic. **E** *Oseguera*, main plaza, dirty but good hot shower.

Motels A *Mansión del Cupatitzio*, on the road to Guadalajara, T32100, pool, patio,

Uruapan

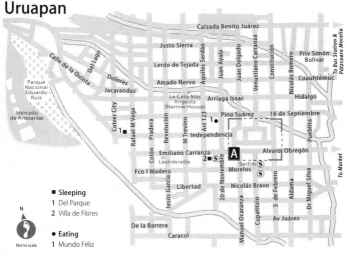

Sleeping
1 Del Parque
2 Villa de Flores

Eating
1 Mundo Féliz

N
Not to scale

Related map
A Uruapan
centre,
page 242

restaurant, good souvenir shop, outstanding. **B** *Paricutín*, Juárez 295, T20303, well-maintained. **B** *Pie de la Sierra*, Km 4 Carretera a Carapán, on north outskirts, T42510, good moderately-priced restaurant. **B** *Las Cabañas*, Km 1 Carretera a México, near the bus terminal, T34777, clean, local bus until 2200. One trailer park which takes small units only.

Eating *La Pergola*, on plaza, good breakfasts and coffee, recommended. *Café Tradicional de Uruapan*, just off Plaza, on same side as *Hotel Villa de Flores*, freshly-ground coffee, home-made chocolates, light meals, recommended. *Calypso*, Alvaro Obregón 2A, excellent cakes and hamburgers, ask for local speciality: *rumpope agua fresca*. Locals eat at open-air food stalls under one roof at back of church, very picturesque. *Café Sol y La Luna*, Independencia between Zócalo and Parque, arty/student bar, sometimes live music at weekends. *Monarca*, Cupatitzio opposite Banco Mexicano, cheap food and yoghurt; good icecream at *Bing*, Obregón on plaza. *La Puesta del Sol*, supermarket, Juan Ayala, has good meals. Local speciality, dried meat, *cecina*. Cheap meals from *comedors* in the *Mercado de Antojitos*.

Festivals In the first week of **April** the Zócalo is filled with pottery and Indians from all the surrounding villages. Around **16 September**, in nearby village of San Juan, to celebrate the saving of an image of Christ from the San Juan church at the time of the Paricutín eruption. The 2 weeks either side of **15 September** are *feria* in Uruapan, too.

Transport **Air** Daily flights from Mexico City, some via Morelia. Also flights from Culiacán, Guadalajara and Tijuana.

Buses Bus station on the northeast edge of town, necessary to get a city bus (US$0.25) into town, finishing at about 2100, or a taxi to the Plaza, US$3. Left luggage, US$0.35 per item for 7 hours. To **Mexico City**, 9¼ hours, Flecha Amarilla via Toluca leaves 0845 and then every hour, US$16.25, many stops; others less frequent but quicker, US$18.75. ETN has a deluxe service, US$28, 6 hours, several a day, hot and cold drinks, clean, good drivers. Omnibús de México has night buses and Tres Estrellas morning departures. To **Morelia**, 2nd class (Flecha Amarilla) US$4.60 (2½ hours), nice ride. Parhikuni, T38754, 1st class and plus with computerized reservations to Morelia, Apatzingan and Lázaro Cárdenas US$10.60. To **Colima** with Flecha Amarilla US$13.50, 6 hours, and to **Los Reyes**, US$2.20, 1¼ hours with same company. To **Zihuatanejo** (Galeana not recommended, or Occidente) 1st or 2nd class, several a day, 6½ hours, US$9 (2nd) along winding, intermittently paved road via Nueva Italia and Arteaga, which turns off just before Playa Azul at La Mira and on to Lázaro Cárdenas on the Río Balsas. From there, frequent

Uruapan centre

■ Sleeping	5 Mi Solar	9 Plaza Uruapan	● Eating
1 Capri	6 Moderno	(& tourist office)	1 Café Tradicional
2 Concordia	7 Nuevo Hotel	10 Regis	2 Café Zirahuen
3 El Tarasco	Alameda	11 Victoria	3 Calypso
4 Los Tres Caballeros	8 Oseguera		4 Pergola

Not to scale

buses to Zihuatanejo (see page 377). Bus to **Guadalajara**, several companies, US$10, 4$\frac{1}{2}$ hours, ETN US$17.75. Bus to **Pátzcuaro**, frequent, US$2, 1 hour.

Airlines *Aeromar*, T35050; *Taeso*, T70540. **Banks** *Banamex*, Cupatitzio y Morelos, visa agent. **Directory** *Bancomer*, East Carranza y 20 de Noviembre. *Serfín*, Cupatitzio. **Communications** Post Office: Reforma 13. **Telephone & fax:** Computel, Ocampo, on plaza, open every day 0700-2200. **Hospitals & medical services** Red Cross: T40300. **Laundry** Emilio Carranza 47, open Mon-Sat 0900-1400 and 1600-2000, US$3.20 service wash. *Mujer Santayo Lavandería*, Michoacán 14, T30876. **Tourist office** Ocampo 64, below *Hotel Plaza Uruapan* on east side of Zócalo, T36172. Open Mon-Sat 0900-1400 and 1600-2000, Sun 1000-1400.

Paricutín

Mexico

The volcano of Paricutín can be visited from Uruapan; it started erupting in the field of a startled peasant on 20 February 1943, became fiery and violent and rose to a height of 1,300 metres above the 2,200 metres-high region, and then died down after several years into a quiet grey mountain (460 metres) surrounded by a sea of cold lava. The church spires of San Juan, a buried Indian village, thrusting up through cold lava is a fantastic sight. If not taking an organized tour (with horses and guides), Paricutín is best reached by taking a 'Los Reyes' bus on a paved road to Angahuán, 34 kilometres, US$0.85, one hour, nine a day each way (hourly from 0500 to 1900) with Galeana, then hire a horse or mule or walk (one hour). Sres Juan Rivera, Francisco Lázaro (tour is a bit hurried, he lives in the second house on the right, coming from the *albergue*, see below), Atanacio Lázaro and his horse 'Conejo', and Lino Gómez are recommended, but there are a host of other guides at the bus stop (it is definitely worthwhile to have a guide – essential for the volcano – even though they are very persistent, best if you can speak Spanish, but it is expensive if you are on your own as you have to pay for the guide's mule too). A full day's excursion with mules to the area costs about US$8-12 per mule, with US$3-4 tip for the guide (six to seven hours); shorter journeys cost less. To go on foot with a guide costs US$8. Distance Angahuán-San Juan ruins, three kilometres, an easy walk: as you stand in the village square with the church in front but a bit to the left, turn right and take the first left after you leave the square and follow this cobbled street with telegraph poles on the left hand side for ¾ kilometre to a stone pillared gateway and a sight of the ruins. At the gate turn right down a dirt path/track which zig-zags downhill, past a plantation to a three forked junction. Take the centre path which winds through the lava field to the church. Alternatively start at the new hostel from where you can also see the church. Guide on foot to church US$5 per group.

To the peak of the volcano is 10 kilometres, a long, tough walk (also a long day on horseback for the unaccustomed, especially if you get a wooden saddle). Walk westwards round the lava field, through an avocado plantation. Wear good walking shoes with thick soles as the lava is very rough and as sharp as glass (some cannot make the last stretch over the tennis-ball size rocks); bear in mind the altitude too, as the return is uphill. One can continue on to the volcano itself; it takes seven to nine hours there and back. The cone itself is rather small and to reach it, there is a stiff 30-minute climb from the base. A path goes around the tip of the crater, where activity has ceased. Take something to drink because it is pretty hot and dusty out on the plains. If going in one day, leave Uruapan by 0800 so that you don't have to rush. Go even earlier in the rainy season as clouds usually build up by midday. Take sweater for the evening and for the summit where it can be windy and cold after a hot climb. Last bus back to Uruapan at 1900 (but don't rely on it).

Much better, though, is to stay the night in Angahuán, where there is an *albergue*, **Angahuán** **B** *cabañas*, sleep 6, with a log fire, or **E** per person in dormitory with bunk beds (dormitories closed in low season, both have hot showers), meals US$5, restaurant closes 1900 in low season, basic facilities, but clean and peaceful, warm and recommended but service poorer when few people are staying. It can be crowded and noisy at weekends. The *albergue* is a 30-minute walk from the bus stop on the main road: walk into the village, then right at the plaza from where there are signs. Go straight on until the road forks at an expensive-looking house with a satellite TV aerial. Take the left fork. From here, the *albergue* is about 10-15 minutes walk at the end of the road. It is possible to drive to the *albergue* where they try to charge US$1.60 for the free car park. There is a panoramic view from the *albergue* of the volcano, San Juan ruins and surrounding pine forest. The ruins are a further 30-minute walk. Camping possible near the hostel. Some families rent out rooms, for example that of Francisco Lázaro, near Zócalo, whose son, José, will guide you up the volcano. In the village are shops selling food and drink and a good local restaurant in the street behind the church. To reasonable restaurants on the road to the *albergue*. There is a water tap near the church; follow the signs. Just outside the village, on the dirt road to the main road, is the cemetery, which is interesting. The local Tarascan Indians still preserve their dialects. Angahuán is a Purépecha Indian village and in the evening the local radio station broadcasts in Puripeche over a public tannoy system in the plaza until 2200.

Los Reyes Past Angahuán and Peribán, after the volcano, over a paved road is the little town of Los Reyes; good swim above the electricity generating plant in clear streams (take care not to get sucked down the feed pipe!).

Sleeping C *Arias* behind Cathedral, T20792, best, clean, friendly. D *Fénix*, clean, between bus station and plaza, T20807. D *Oasis*, Av Morelos 229, C for a suite, with bath, hot water, clean, pleasant. D *Plaza*, not as good as *Arias* but nice, clean, on street facing Cathedral, T20666. E *Casa de Huéspedes*, clean, basic, lovely courtyard, a little further along the same road is E *Villa Rica*, often no water.

Eating *La Fogata*, in main square.

Buses From Uruapan to **Los Reyes** (Galeana, US$2.20) go via Angahuán (US$0.80) (so same frequency), depart from Uruapan bus station, not from the plaza as the tourist office says. Check that you are only charged to Angahuán if not continuing to Los Reyes. Bus from Los Reyes, on Av 5 de Mayo, to **Angahuán**, 1½-2 hours. Angahuán to Uruapan as above or local bus (US$.75) but it does not go to bus station. Bus to Los Reyes from Guadalajara with Ciénaga de Chapala 4 a day, 4 hours, US$8.25 1st class.

The Pacific coast of Michoacán

Playa Azul
Colour map 3, grid B2

Beware of the large waves at Playa Azul and of dangerous currents; always check with locals if particular beaches are safe.

The Pacific coast of Michoacán is only just coming under development. From Uruapan Route 37 goes to Playa Azul, 350 kilometres northwest of Acapulco (bus US$9, 10½ hours minimum) and 122 kilometres from Zihuatanejo (see page 377), a coconut-and-hammock resort (reported dirty and dilapidated) frequented much more by Mexicans than foreigners, with a few large hotels. The city of La Mira, on the main road, is larger than Playa Azul. 40 kilometres of excellent deserted beaches north of Playa Azul. At night there is much beautiful phosphorescence at the water's edge.

Sleeping D *El Delfín*, Venustiano Carranza s/n, T60007, no a/c, clean, pleasant, swimming pool. D *Hotel del Pacífico*, opposite beach, with bath, fan, clean, hammocks on roof, friendly, a bit run-down but recommended. E *Costa de Oro*, Francisco I Madero s/n, T60982, clean, with fan, recommended, safe parking; *Hotel Playa Azul*, Venustiano Carranza s/n, T60024/88, F60090, has a trailer park with 20 spaces, full hook-up, bathrooms, cold shower, 2 pools, bar and restaurant, US$13 for car and 2 people. Many small fish restaurants along beach, but most close early; *Martita*, highly recommended. Tap and shower water seems to smell of petrol.

Buses Buses ply up and down the coast road, stopping at the road junction 4 kilometres from Plaza Azul. Colectivos take you between town and junction. If driving north it is 5 hours to Tecomán (where the road from Colima comes down to the coast); there is nothing along this road.

Lázaro Cárdenas is the connecting point for buses from Uruapan, Manzanillo and Zihuatanejo. There is a Tourist Office at Nicolás Bravo 475, T21547, in the *Hotel Casablanca* building.

Lázaro Cárdenas
Colour map 3, grid B2

Sleeping C *Hotel de la Curva*, Vicente Guerrero esq Nicolás Bravo, T736569, F23237. **D** *Sol del Pacífico*, Fco Javier Mina 178, T20660, F70490. **E** *Viña del Mar*, Javier Mina 352, T/F20415. Avoid **E** *Hotel Sam Sam*, near terminal; go to *Capri*, Juan Alvarez 237, T20551, or *Costa Azul*, 5 de Mayo 276, T20780, both **E** with bath, or **E** *Verónica*, Javier Mina 47, T20254, 2 blocks left as you leave bus station, friendly, pleasant, noisy, restaurant in front part of hotel has nice atmosphere but indifferent food; several eating places in streets near bus terminal.

Buses Galeana to Manzanillo 7¾ hours, US$10; to Uruapan, US$10.75, 6½ hours; to Guadalajara, US$21.50 with La Línea; to Mexico City from 2nd US$17, 1st US$36.65 to 43.35, luxury; Flecha Roja to Zihuatanejo, 2 hours, US$3.65). If possible, book tickets in advance at the bus terminal for all journeys.

Buses continue along the coast road to La Mira, then another a short distance to **Caleta de Campos**, 76 kilometres northwest up the coast from Playa Azul. In this poor village perched above a beautiful bay, there is little food other than seafood. **D** *Hotel Yuritzi*, with bath, a/c, TV, **E** without, clean, no hot water, good views from front, changes travellers' cheques at reasonable rates. **E** *Los Arcos*, with bath, good views from most rooms; *cabañas* with hammock space at US$1 per person, northwest of village, where Río Nexpa reaches the coast. At beach here, five minutes from the village, popular with surfers, there are bars and restaurants. Be careful swimming, there are strong currents. *Fiesta*: 10-13 December; at 0200 on the 13th El Torito, a bull mask and sculpture loaded with fireworks appears. There are other elaborate, if dangerous fireworks.

86 kilometres further up the coast, to the northwest, is **Maruata**, unspoilt and beautiful. This is a turtle conservation area. There are floods in the rainy season and the river has washed away some of the beach. There are *cabañas* for rent (**F**) and *palapas* under which you can camp. For southbound traffic seeking Maruata, road signs are inadequate.

Quiroga

Back on the road **from Guadalajara to Morelia** via Zamora, at **Zacapu** (Km 400), see the Franciscan church (1548). At **Quiroga** (Km 357), a road turns off right for Pátzcuaro, heart of the Tarascan Indian country. The town is named after Bishop Vasco de Quiroga, who was responsible for most of the Spanish building in the area and for teaching the Indians the various crafts they still practise: work in wool, leather, copper, ceramics and canework; many Indians, few tourists. Fair and craft exhibitions in December. Good place to buy cheap leather jackets – most shops in town sell them. The night-time entertainment seems to be driving through town in a pick-up with blaring speakers in the back.

Colour map 3, grid B3

C *Misión don Vasco*, Av L Cárdenas y Gpe Victoria. 3 hotels on main street (Vasco de Quiroga): **E** *Tarasco*, colonial style, courtyard, clean, hot water, pleasant but front rooms noisy. **D** per person *Quiroga* and **D** *Tarisco* (was *San Diego*), cheapest in town, last two both modern with parking. *Cabañas Tzintzuntzan*, Km 6 Quiroga-Pátzcuaro road (Ojo de Agua), swimming pool, own pier, fully-furnished (contact *Hotel Casino*, Morelia, T31003). Trailer

Sleeping

Mexico

park 3 kilometres north of town. Old summer residence of a former Mexican president, apparently, wonderful view over Lake Pátzcuaro.

Buses from Pátzcuaro bus station every 15 minutes. Bus Quiroga-Mexico City, US$11, 1st *plus*.

Tzintzuntzan
Colour map 3, grid B3

pronounced rapidly as
sin-sun-san

Tzintzuntzan, () was the pre-conquest Tarascan capital; the ruins are just behind the village; a Purépecha ceremonial centre, with five pyramids, are across the road and up the hill (10 minutes walk) from the monastery. ■ *daily 0900-1700, US$2, Sunday free*. The monastry, C Magdalena, was built in 1533 but closed over 250 years ago. It has been restored, but its frescoes have deteriorated badly. The bells of its church date from the 16th century; a guard will show you round. In the grounds are some very old olive trees which are still bearing fruit, said to have been planted by Vasco de Quiroga. Fortuitously they were missed in a Spanish edict to destroy all Mexican olive trees when it was thought that Mexican olive oil would compete with Spain's. A most interesting Passion play is given at Tzintzuntzan and *fiestas* are very colourful. Beautiful and extensive display of hand-painted pottery, very cheap but also brittle. (It is available in other markets in Mexico.) Other handicrafts on sale include woodcarving, leather and basketwoven Christmas tree ornaments. Good bargaining opportunities.

Transport Bus from Pátzcuaro bus station every 15 minutes, US$0.50, same bus as for Quiroga, which is eight kilometres further on. **NB** If taking the route Uruapan-Pátzcuaro -Morelia, Tzintzuntzan and Quiroga come after Pátzcuaro.

Pátzcuaro

Population: 65,000
Altitude: 2,110m
Phone code: 434
Colour map 3, grid B2

23 kilometres from Quiroga (cold in the evenings), Pátzcuaro is one of the most picturesque towns in Mexico, with narrow cobbled streets and deep overhanging eaves. The houses are painted white and brown. It is built near Lago de Pátzcuaro, about 50 kilometres in circumference, with Tarascan Indian villages on its shores and many islands. The Indians used to come by huge dugout canoes (but now seem to prefer the ferry) for the market, held in the main plaza, shaded by great trees. It is a steep 3-kilometre walk uphill from the lake shore to the plaza, *colectivos* run every few minutes to the plaza chica.

Sights
There are several interesting buildings: the unfinished **La Colegiata** (1603), known locally as La Basílica, with its much venerated Virgin fashioned by an Indian from a paste made with cornstalk pith and said to have been found floating in a canoe. Behind the Basílica there are remains of the precolumbian town and of a pyramid in the precincts of the Museo de Artes Populares; the restored Jesuit church of **La Compañía** (and, almost opposite, the early 17th century church of the **Sagrario**) at the top of C Portugal. Behind this street are two more ecclesiastical buildings: the **Colegio Teresiano** and the restored **Templo del Santuario**; on C Lerín is the old monastery, with a series of small patios. (Murals by Juan O'Gorman in the Library, formerly San Agustín.) On C Allende is the residence of the first Governor. On C Terán is the church of **San Francisco**; nearby is **San Juan de Dios**, on the corner of C Romero. Visit also the **Plaza Vasco de Quiroga**. 15 minutes' walk outside the town is the chapel of **El Calvario**, on the summit of Cerro del Calvario, a hill giving wide views; views also from the old chapel of the **Humilladero**, above the cemetery on the old road to Morelia. This chapel is said to have been built on the spot where the last Tarascan emperor knelt in submission to the Spanish Conquistador, Cristóbal de Olid. Do not hike there alone, it is rather isolated.

The very well arranged **Museo de Artes Populares** is in the former Colegio de San Nicolás (1540). ■ *US$2*. Excellent for seeing regional ceramics, weaving, woodcarving and basketware. ■ *0900-1900 Monday-Saturday, 0900-1430 Sunday* (free), English speaking, friendly guide. Ask there for the Casa de los Once Patios, which contains boutiques selling handicrafts; you can see weavers and painters of lacquerwork in action. An 'International Hippy Crafts Market' is held every every Satur- day and Sunday on the north side of the Plaza Grande. See also the attractive Jardín de la Revolución (F Tena y Ponce de León) and, nearby, the old church of the Hospitalito. Excellent Friday and also Saturday markets, often much cheaper than shops; good copperware on sale. Woodcarving is another local speciality. Good crafts by intersection of Benigno Serrato and Lerín near the Basílica. Some stalls open daily on the main square, selling handicrafts, and there is a friendly handicraft shop on the road down to the lake, *Vicky's*, with interesting toys.

The best-known island is **Janitzio**, which has been spoilt by the souvenir shops, chil- dren wearing their saddest faces asking for pesos and the tourists (visit during the week if possible). It is 45 minutes by motorboat, leaves when full from 0800 onwards, US$2.50 return from Muelle General (30-minute walk from centre, cheaper from Muelle San Pedrito, 500 metres further on), tickets from office at dock, last boat back (return by any boat) at 1800. There is an unfortunate monument to Morelos, with mural inside, crowning a hill, US$0.30, which nevertheless affords magnificent views, and a circular path around the island. There are lots of good res- taurants on the island, those on the waterfront charge more than those on the hill,

Excursions

Mexico

Pátzcuaro

To Railway Station, Lake Pátzcuaro, Morelia & Uruapan

■ Sleeping	4 Mesón del Gallo	8 Posada La Basílica
1 El Artillero	5 Misíon San Manuel	9 Posada San Rafael
2 Gran	6 Posada de la Rosa	10 Los Escudos
3 Mansión Iturbe	7 Posada de la Salud	

N

Not to scale

same quality. Winter is the best time for fishing in the somewhat fish-depleted lake, where Indians traditionally threw nets shaped like dragonflies, now a rather rare event. The Government is planning to improve the lake's water quality, but there are still plenty of places selling white fish on the island, at about a quarter of the price in Pátzcuaro.

Another island to visit is **Yunen**, boat from Muelle General. The island is clean and quiet. There is a cabaña (**B**) on the hill with a good restaurant. During the week there are few *lanchas*, so be sure to arrange return trip unless you want to spend the night. Bring provisions. On a lakeside estate (formerly the country house of Gen Lázaro Cárdenas) is the Educational Centre for Community Development in Latin America, better known as Crefal (free films every Wednesday at 1930). For a truly spectacular view of the lake, the islands and the surrounding countryside, walk to Cerro del Estribo; an ideal site for a quiet picnic. It is a one and a half hour walk to the top from the centre of Pátzcuaro. Follow the cobbled road beyond El Calvario, don't take the dirt tracks off to the left. Cars go up in the afternoon, the best time for walking. No buses, 417 steps to the peak. The areas round Pátzcuaro are recommended for bird watching. If intending to drive around the lake, a high-clearance vehicle is necessary.

From Pátzcuaro one can also visit Tzintzuntzan and Quiroga by regular bus service. 30 minutes by local bus from Plaza Chica is **Ihuátzio**, on a peninsula 12 kilometres north of Pátzcuaro, eight kilometres from Tzintzuntzan. This was the second most important Tarascan city; two pyramids are well-preserved and afford good views of the lake. ■ *US$1.10, leaflets in Spanish or English, US$0.40.* The road to the pyramids is very bad, one kilometre from village, signposted. To get to Tzintzuntzan from Ihuátzio, take bus or hitch back to main road and wait for Pátzcuaro-Quiroga bus.

An excursion can be made into the hills to **Santa Clara del Cobre**, a sleepy village with red tiles and overhanging eaves, an attractive square with copper pots filled with flowers along each arcade, and a fine old church. Hand-wrought copper vessels are made here and there is a Museo del Cobre (■ *closed Monday, free*) with some excellent examples; it's half a block from the main square. There is a Banco Serfín which changes dollars cash and cheques between 1000 and 1200. *(Fiesta:* 12-15 August.) Take a bus to Pátzcuaro bus station, then another to Ario de Rosales (every 15 minutes), which passes Santa Clara, fare US$0.50 each way. Taxi from Pátzcuaro, US$10.50 return with one-hour wait. **C** *Camino Real*, Av Morelos Pte 213, T30281. **D** *Real del Cobre*, Portal Hidalgo 19, T30205. **D** *Oasis*, Portal Allende 144, T30040, both on main square.

Nearby is the pretty **Lago Zirahuen**, where you can take boat trips, eat at lakeside restaurants and visit the huge adobe church. **C** *Motel Zirahuen*, T23600, attractive, clean, garden restaurant, horse riding. Flecha Amarilla buses leave Pátzcuaro between 0930-1400, 30 minutes direct, last bus back at 1800. Past Santa Clara, on the La Huacana road, after Ario de Rosales, the road descends into the tropics; fine views all the way, which ends at Churumuco. Pátzcuaro-Ario de Rosales-Nueva Italia-Uruapan- Pátzcuaro takes about six hours, beautiful tropical countryside.

Sleeping

Rooms in some hotels are reserved 4 weeks prior to Día de los Muertos, other hotels do not take reservations, so it is pot luck at this time.

A *Posada de don Vasco*, Av Lázaro Cárdenas 450, T23971, F20262, 103 rooms, attractive, colonial-style hotel (halfway between lake and town), breakfast good, other meals poor, presents the Dance of the Old Men on Wednesday and Saturday at 2100, no charge, non-residents welcome but drinks very expensive to compensate, also mariachi band. **A** *Fiesta Plaza*, on Plaza Chica, beautiful interior patio, good. **B** *Las Redes*, Av de las Américas 6, T/F21275, near lake, 13 rooms, popular restaurant. **B** *Mesón del Cortijo*, Obregón, just off Américas, T21295, recommended, but often fully booked at weekends. **C** *Apo-Pau*, between lake and town (closest to town of the non-central hotels), pleasant, friendly.

In the centre **AL-B** *Mansión Iturbe*, Portal Morelos 59, T20368, www.mexconline.com/iturbe.htm, 14 rooms, English, French and German spoken, restored beautiful 1790 mansion on main plaza, breakfast included, nice décor, satellite TV, cold at night, expensive restaurant,

El Gaucho Viejo, Argentine *churrasco*, open 1800-2400, Wednesday-Sunday, folk music, 2 other restaurants, recommended. **A** *Mesón del Gallo*, Dr Coss 20, T21474, F21511, 25 rooms, good value, flower garden, tasteful furnishings. **B** *Misión San Manuel*, Portal Aldama 12 on main plaza, T21313, restaurant, highly recommended. **B** *Posada La Basílica*, Arciga 6, T21108, F20659, 12 rooms, nice restaurant with good views, central. **B** *Posada San Rafael*, Plaza Vasco de Quiroga, T20770, safe, average restaurant, parking in courtyard. **C** *Los Escudos*, Portal Hidalgo 73, T/F21290, 17th century building ('Baile de los Viejitos' every Saturday at 2000), recommended, ask for room with fireplace, good food.

D *Casa de Huéspedes Pátzcuaro*, Ramos 9, without bath. **D** *Concordia*, next to *Posada de la Rosa*, with bath and hot water, cheaper without (which means use of toilet, but no bath whatsoever), in poor shape, rooms on plaza noisy. **D** *El Artillero*, Ibarra 22, T21331, hot water, with bath, gloomy, noisy, not too clean or secure, no drinking water, near Zócalo (discounts for long stays paid in advance). **D** *Gran Hotel*, Portal Regules 6, on Plaza Bocanegra, T20443, small rooms, clean, friendly, pleasant, good food. **D** *Imperial*, Obregón 21, large clean rooms; these are all central. **D** *Hostal de la Salud*, Benigno Serrato 9, T20058, clean, quiet, pleasant, nice garden, excellent value, no hot water during middle of day, some rooms with individual fireplaces, recommended. **E** *Laguna*, Titere, with bath, cheaper rooms also with bath but no water, buckets outside!; **E** *Posada de la Rosa*, Portal Juárez 29 (Plaza Chica), with bath, **F** without, parking, colonial style, clean. **E** *Posada La Terraza*, Benito Juárez 46, T21027, central, gardens, hot water, kind señora. Also on Plaza Chica is **E** *Posada San Agustín*, very good value, clean, hot water.

There are many *hospedajes* and hotels near the bus station. Public baths, US$0.50.

Motels **B** *Chalamu*, Pátzcuaro Rd Km 20, T20948. **B** *Hostería de San Felipe*, Av Lázaro Cárdenas 321, T/F21298, friendly, clean, fireplaces in rooms, good restaurant (closes 2030), highly recommended. **B** *San Carlos*, Muelle Col Morelos, T21359. *Villa Pátzcuaro*, Av Lázaro Cárdenas 506, T20767, F22984 (Apdo Postal 206), 1 kilometre from centre, hot water, gardens, lots of birds, tennis, pleasant, also camping and caravan site. *Trailer Park El Pozo*, on lakeside, opposite *Chalamu*, T20937, hot showers am, large, delightful, well-equipped, US$10, owner speaks English, also camping (take water for drinking from the entrance rather than taps on the trailer pads).

Camping See **Motels** above.

Several lakeside restaurants serve fish dishes, but it is advisable to avoid locally caught fish. Many places close before 2000. Make sure you don't get overcharged in restaurants, some display menus outside which bear no resemblance to the prices inside. *Comida corrida* at restaurants around Plaza Grande and Plaza Chica costs about US$4 and is usually the same each day. *Los Escudos* restaurant, Plaza Quiroga, open till 2200, popular with tourists, try *sopa tarasca* (a flavoursome soup made with toasted tortillas, cream and cheese), good value and coffee. *San Agustín*, Plaza Bocanegra, friendly, good doughnuts on sale outside in pm. *Taquería Los Equipales*, Portal Allende 57, Plaza Vasco de Quiroga (under *Hotel Mansión Iturbe*), very good *tacos*, open from mid-afternoon into the night. *Mery Lerín*, Benigno Serrato (opposite Museo de Artes Populares) cheap local dishes. *Gran Hotel*, filling *comida corrida*, excellent *café con leche*. *Mandala*, Lerín 14, vegetarian, good value, also has rooms (**E** including breakfast); good chicken with vegetables and *enchiladas* over the market (budget restaurants here, usually open in evening). *Cafetería Dany's*, Benito Mendoza 30, T24412, between the 2 plazas, touristy, good snacks, fish, open 1200-2000, closed Monday. *Don Rafe*, Benito Mendoza, opens 0800, good. *Cafetería El Buho*, Tejerías 8, meals, drinks, slow but very good food, good value, stylish, friendly, recommended. *Cafetería Fumeiro*, below *Hotel Misión San Manuel*, good coffee house. *El Cazo de los Quesos*, Lloreda 27, T20512, fondue, pasta, open 1300-2200 Thursday-Sunday. *Camino Real*, next to Pemex, 100 metres from *El Pozo Trailer Park*, very good *comida corrida*, quick service. *Tortisam*, Benito Mendoza 12, *good tortas*. Excellent *paletería* and ice cream parlour at Codallos 24, also sells frozen yoghurt. Fruit and yoghurt for breakfast at *El Patio*, Plaza Vasco de Quiroga 19,

Eating
Local speciality is pescado blanco (white fish), but it is disappearing from menus as a result of overfishing and pollution.

Mexico

T20484, open 0800-2200, also serves good meals, good service, recommended. Breakfast available from small stands in the market, usually 0600-0700 (*licuados, arroz con leche*, etc). At the Plaza in Erongaricuaro, 17 kilometres clockwise around the lake, is a Hindu vegetarian restaurant at the weekends; also a local crafts fair (take ADO bus from bus or rail station, US$0.65).

Festivals 1-2 November: *Día de los Muertos* (All Souls' Day), ceremony at midnight, 1 November, at almost every village around the lake; if you are in the region at this time it is well worth experiencing. The ceremony is most touristy on Janitzio island and at Tzintzuntzan, but at villages such as Ihuátzio, Jarácuaro and Uranden it is more intimate. The tourist office has leaflets listing all the festivities. **6-9 December**, *Virgen de la Salud*, when authentic Tarascan dances are performed in front of the *basílica*. There is an interesting *fiesta* on **12 December** for the Virgin of Guadalupe; on **12 October**, when Columbus reached America, there is also a procession with the Virgin and lots of fireworks. Carnival in February when the Dance of the Moors is done.

Massage *Shiatsu Massage*, Stephen Ritter del Castillo, in Tocuaro, 15 minutes by bus or taxi clockwise around the lake about halfway to Erongaricuaro, T431-80309, Monday-Friday 0900-1700, excellent, English/Spanish bilingual.

Transport **Buses** New bus station (called Central) out of town, with left luggage office, colectivo to centre US$0.30, taxi US$1.70. Bus US$0.20 from Plaza Bocanegra. You can pick up buses from large roundabout 1 kilometre north of centre. Taxi US$1.45. To **Mexico City**, Tres Estrellas de Oro, Herradura de Plata (via Morelia – recommended US$15), Pegaso Plus (via Morelia – recommended US$16), Flecha Amarilla to Terminal Norte US$17, 7½ hrs and Autobuses de Occidente 1st (US$13.60) 5 hours, and 2nd class buses (US$12.20), 6 hours. Regular bus service to **Morelia**, 1 hour, US$2.10 with ADO, Herradura de Plata, Galeana and Flecha Amarilla (departs every 30 minutes). Buses to **Guadalajara** go through Zamora, US$10 (Flecha Amarilla), 6 hours; to **Lázaro Cárdenas**, for connections to Zihuatanejo, Acapulco, etc, hourly from 0600, US$12.50, 8 hours, long but spectacular ride through mountains and lakes (police checks likely); to **Uruapan**, US$2.50 (1 hour); to **Toluca**, 1st class US$17.50, from 0915, 5 hours. It is cheaper to get to Toluca by taking a bus to Morelia and then changing onto a PD bus for US$9. Local buses from corner of market in town to lakeside (colectivo to lakeside US$0.25).

A road bypassing the town is under construction: will be a toll road when open.

Directory **Banks** *Banamex*, Portal Juárez 32, T23846. *Promex*, Portal Regules 9, T20397. *Serfín*, Portal Allende 54, T21000. *Bancomer*, Zaragoza 23, T20334; *cambio* at Benito Mendoza 7, T20240. 4 ATMs in the centre. **Hospitals & medical services** **Dentist:** Dr Antonio Molina, T23032. Dr Augusto Tena Mora, T22232. **Doctor:** Dr Jorge Asencio Medina, T24038. Dr Javier Hernández and Dra Guadalupe Murillo, T21209. **Pharmacy:** *Gems*, Benito Mendoza 21, T20332, open 0900-2100 daily. **Laundry** *Lavandería 'San Francisco'*, Terán 16, T23939, Mon-Sat 0900-2000. **Tourist office** North side of Plaza Grande next to Banco Serfin, friendly, good information, Spanish only.

Morelia

Km 314
Population: 759,000
State Population: 1995
3,869,133
Altitude: 1,882m
Phone code: 43
Colour map 3, grid B3

Morelia, capital of Michoacán state, is a rose-tinted city with attractive colonial buildings (their courtyards are their main feature), rather quiet, founded in 1541. The narrow streets suffer from vehicle pollution. Thursday and Sunday are market days: specialities are pottery, lacquer, woodcarving, jewellery, blankets, leather sandals; in this connection see the **Casa de Artesanías de Michoacán**, in the ex-Convento de San Francisco, next to the church of the same name; it is full of fine regional products for sale, not cheap. Shops close early. Free weekly concerts are held in the municipal theatre. At the east edge of the downtown area, on the road to Mexico City, are the 224 arches of a ruined **aqueduct**, built in 1788 (walk 11 blocks east from Cathedral along Av Madero). Both Banamex and Bancomer have their offices in magnificent old houses; the patio of the former is especially fine. Many good language schools.

The **Cathedral** (1640), is set between the two main plazas, with graceful towers and a fine façade, in what is called 'sober baroque'; there are paintings by Juárez in the sacristy. The **Virgen de Guadalupe** (also known as San Diego), east of the aqueduct, has an ornate interior of terracotta garlands and buds, painted in pastels, like being inside a giant wedding cake. There are four huge oil paintings of the missionaries Christianizing the Indians. Other important churches are the modernized **Iglesia de la Cruz**, and the 18th century **Iglesia de las Rosas** in the delightful plaza of the same name (its ex-Convento now houses the Conservatorio de Música). The oldest of Morelia's churches is the **San Francisco** of the Spanish Renaissance period, but lacking many of the decorative features of that style.

Even more interesting than the colonial churches are the many fine colonial secular buildings still standing. The revolutionary José María Morelos, Melchor Ocampo, and the two unfortunate Emperors of Mexico (Agustín de Iturbide and the Archduke Maximilian of Austria) are commemorated by plaques on their houses. Morelos' birthplace, at Corregidora 113, is open to visitors, admission free. The **Colegio de San Nicolás** (1540) is the oldest surviving institution of higher education in Latin America. (It has a summer school for foreign students.) Opposite is the Centro Cultural Universitario, with many free events. The fine former Jesuit college, now called the **Palacio Clavijero**, contains government offices, with a helpful tourist office on the ground floor (corner of Madero Pte y Nigromante). Nearby on Av Madero is a library with carved wooden balconies and many historical volumes. Also notable are the **Law School**, in the former monastery of **San Diego**, next to the Guadalupe church; the **Palacio de Gobierno** (1732-70), facing the Cathedral; the **Palacio Municipal**; and the **Palacio Federal**. Visit also the churches of **La Merced**, with its lovely tower and strange, bulging *estípites* (inverted pyramidal supports), **Capuchinas** (Ortega y Montaño), which has some Churrigueresque *retablos*, and **Santa María**, on a hilltop south of the city.

Next to the Plaza de Morelos is the Alameda de Calzones, a shady pedestrianized walkway with restored mansions leading three blocks to the fountain of the Tarascans (three bare-chested women holding up a giant basket of fruit).

Museo de Michoacán (archaeological remains), C Allende. ■ *0900-1900 daily, closed Monday, 0900-1400 Sunday, US$4.35.* The **Casa de la Cultura**, Av Morelos Norte, housed in the ex-Convento del Carmen, which has a good collection of masks from various regions, crucifixes. ■ *daily, free.* Also workshops (nominal fee of US$1.55 for 12 weeks). The **Museo de Estado**, in the house of Iturbide's wife (Casa de la Emperatriz), southeast corner of Jardín de las Rosas, is well worth a visit. ■ *Open daily.* Most of the ground floor is dedicated to Tarascan history and culture, lots of information about Michoacán, and, at the front, an old pharmacy with all its bottles, cabinets, scales, et cetera, intact. The **Museo de Morelos**, on Morelos Sur, about three blocks south of the Cathedral, is a history museum (described by one correspondent as 'intensely nationalistic'). ■ *US$4.35.*

Sights

Museums

Fairly good zoo in Parque Juárez, south of the centre (25 minutes' walk south along Galeana). Planetarium.

Parks & zoos

AL *Calinda Quality Inn*, Av Acueducto, T145969, colonial-style, modern. **AL** *Alameda*, Av Madero Pte 313 y C de Jazmines, T122023, F138727, 'flashy'. **AL** *Virrey de Mendoza*, Portal Matamoros, T120633, superb old-style building, poor restaurant, service could be better, could be cleaner, poor ventilation, ask for room at front with balcony. **B** *Casino*, Portal Hidalgo 229, main square, T131003, clean, hot water, private bath, good restaurant. Off the Plaza de Armas and much quieter is the **B** *Posada de la Soledad*, Zaragoza 90 and Ocampo, T121888, F122111, fine courtyards, converted chapel as dining room, TV and fireplaces in rooms, parking opposite (free between 2000 and 0900, otherwise US$1 per hour), good value, María Luisa speaks English. **B** *Plaza Morelos*, Glorieta Morelos 31, T124499, large, cool, pleasant. **C** *Catedral*, Zaragoza 37, T130783, F130467, close to Plaza, spacious, nice bar,

Sleeping
Some of the cheaper hotels may have water only in the morning; check.

restaurant closes quite early, recommended. **C** *Florida*, Morelos Sur 165, T121819, clean, good value.

D *del Matador*, E Ruiz 531, opposite bus station, T124649, simple, with bath; another **D** hotel at E Ruiz 673, good value, but small rooms, overlooks the Casa de la Cultura, hot water. **D** *Don Vasco*, Vasco de Quiroga 232, T121484, with shower and hot water, clean, safe, some rooms dingy, recommended. **D** *Valladolid*, Portal Hidalgo 241, on main square, T120027, with bath, good value for its location but a bit drab. **E** *Carmen*, E Ruiz 63, T121725. **E** *Mintzicini*, Vasco de Quiroga (opposite *Don Vasco*), clean, small rooms, hot shower, TV, parking, helpful tourist office.

Cheap hotels on **Morelos Norte**: **D** *Concordia*, Gómez Farías 328, T123052, round corner from bus station. **E** *Colonial*, corner with 20 de Noviembre 15, T121897, pleasant, lots of hot water, good value. On Madero Pte: **D** *San Jorge*, No 719, T124610, with hot shower, clean; at No 670 is **E** *Vallarta*, T124095, fair; at No 537 is **E** *Fénix*, with bath, noisy, clean, cheap. **E** *Posada Lourdes*, No 340, basic, clean, quiet, hot water. **E-F** *Señorial*, Santiago Tapiá 543, 1 block south from bus terminal, basic, with bath. Cheap *posadas* and *casas de huéspedes* tend to be uninviting, although the half-dozen around the bus station are reported clean and cheap.

On **Santa María hill**, south of the city, with glorious views, are hotels *Villa Montaña*, T140231, F151423, each room a house on its own, run by French aristocrats, very expensive but value for money, superb restaurant, *Vista Bella* (T120248) and **C** *Villa San José* next door and much cheaper, reached only by car.

Motels **B** *Villa Centurión*, Morelos Rd, T132272, good antiques, pool, TV. **C** *El Parador*,

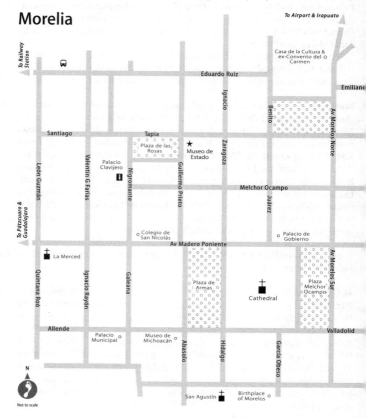

Morelia

Highway 45, with trailer park. **C** *Las Palmas*, Guadalajara Rd, also trailer park. 2 good trailer parks on Route 126 between Morelia and the capital: *Balneario Las Ajuntas*, after Queréndaro, and *Balneario Atzimba*, hot springs at Zinapécuaro.

Youth hostel At corner of Oaxaca and Chiapas No 180, T133177, 1 kilometre southwest of bus station (walk west to C Cuautla, then south along Cuautla to Oaxaca) **F** per person. Camping possible in a forest about 4 kilometres south of centre on unnumbered Pátzcuaro-signposted road.

Café de Conservatorio, on Plaza de Las Rosas (opposite music academy), not cheap but nice **Eating** atmosphere and tasty cakes. *Quinta Sol*, Aquiles Serdán 729, 5 blocks east of Morelos, also vegetarian, good *comida corrida*, US$4, served from 1400; both close daily at 1700 and both closed Sunday. *Comidas corridas* at *El Viejo Paral*, Madero Ote and Quiroga, and in an unnamed restaurant on Gómez Farias, on right hand side heading away from bus station, US$1.50. *La Flor de las Mercedes*, León Guzmán, colonial-style house, beautiful decor, moderate prices. *Las Palmas*, Melchor Ocampo 215, friendly and tasty. Try stewed kid, best in cheaper restaurants. *Pizza Tony's*, Madero Ote 698. *Pollo-Coa*, Madero Ote 890, near aqueduct, good food. *Viandas de San José*, Alvarado Obregón 263 (y E Zapata), good cheap *comida corrida*, excellent service, recommended. *Los Pioneros*, Aquiles Serdán y Av Morelos Nte, cheap, good local food. *La Bodega de la Iguana*, Av Camelinsa 3636, T144204, very good traditional cuisine, highly recommended. *Café Pindaro*, Morelos Nte 150, good breakfasts. On Gómez Farías, *Boca de Río*, at No 185, good fish. *Café del Olmo*, Benito Juárez 95, in a nice colonial building. There is a good café in *Casa de la Cultura*, with delicious home-made cakes. *Café Colón*, Ardiles Serdán 265, good coffee. The Mercado de Dulces, on Gómez Farías at west end of the Palacio Clavijero, is famous for fruit jams (*ates*), candies and *rompope* (a milk and egg nog).

Air Many flights daily to and from Mexico **Transport** City, 50 minutes, also to other Mexican destinations: Guadalajara, León, Monterrey, Puerto Vallarta, Tepic,, Tijuana, Uruapán and Zacatecas. To USA: Mexicana and Taesa to Chicago; Mexicana to Los Angeles, San Francisco and San José (California); Taesa to Oakland. No public transport to airport, 26 kilometres from city. Dollar and Budget car rental offices. Taxi to centre US$18.

Buses The terminal is on Eduardo Ruiz between León Guzmán and Gómez Farias, an easy walk to the town centre. Tourist Kiosk, though not always open, restaurants and left luggage. Many buses to **Guanajuato**, $4\frac{1}{2}$ hours, US$4.50. **Guadalajara**, US$16.25, also luxury service by ETN, US$20, T37440. To **Nuevo Laredo**, 17 hours, US$43. **Uruapan**, US$4.60 2nd class; **Irapuato**, US$4.55 2nd class, rough ride. Several direct daily to **Querétaro**, $3\frac{1}{2}$ hours. **Mexico City**, 2nd class $6\frac{1}{2}$ hours, $4\frac{1}{2}$ by 1st *plus*, US$10.50, every 90 minutes from 0600 to 2000, ETN luxury service US$15 to west terminal (see also diversion, below). Bus to **Acapulco** US$36.50, 15 hours. To

Mexico

Map labels:
arismo
Plan de Ayala
pata
20 de Noviembre
Alvaro
Belisario
Aquiles Serdán
Obregón
Domínguez
Templo de las Monjas
Palacio Federal
v Madero Oriente
F Juan D'Sn M
F Alonso
Navarrete
Bartolomé de las Casas
Vasco de Quiroga
San Francisco & Casa de Artesanías
V Santa María
Humboldt
Beau Mon
Corregidora
To Aqueduct, Toluca & Mexico City

Zitácuaro, US$4.60, 3 hours. Bus to **Pátzcuaro** every 30 minutes with Ruta Paraíso, Flecha Amarilla, Herradura de Plata and Parikhuni, 1 hour, US$2.10. Also about 15 a day to Zihuatanejo on the coast, US$14. For **Toluca** buses, many a day with ETN, 3 hours, US$14.80.

Directory **Airlines** Aeromar, T128545; **Taeso**, T134105. **Banks** *Bancomer*, Av Madero Oriente, just of main plaza, VISA, ATM. **Communications** Post Office: in Palacio Federal, is said to charge different rates from the rest of Mexico. **Hospitals & medical services** Dentist: *Dr Leopoldo Arroyo Contreras*, Abraham Gonzáles 35, T120751, near Cathedral, recommended. **Language schools** *Centro Mexicano de Idiomas*, Calz Fray Antonio de San Miguel 173, intensive weekly classes (US$280 for first week, other courses available include handicrafts, accommodation with families). *Baden-Powell Institute*, Antonio Alzate 565, T124070, from US$6.50 per hour to US$8.50 per hour, depending on length of course, lodging US$12 per day, including 3 meals, courses for all levels, plus cultural, social science and extracurricular courses, highly recommended. (See **Learning Spanish** in **Essentials**.) **Laundry** *Lavandería Chapultepec*, C J Ceballos 881. *Lavandería* on Santiago Tapiá towards bus station. **Tourist offices** Inside Palacio Clavijero (south end), has local hotel information list and map, English spoken, open 0900-2000, T128081 (closed Sun). Also kiosk at bus terminal, but not always open. Good city map available from *Casa de Cambio Troca Mex*, Melchor Ocampo y I Zaragoza.

North of Morelia

Just after Morelia there is a good road north to two lakeside villages. At **Cuitzeo**, the first one (hotel, *Restaurant Esteban*, by post office), there is a fine Augustinian church and convent (begun in 1550), a cloister, a huge open chapel, and good choir stalls in the sacristy. The church houses a good collection of Mexican graphic art, spanning four centuries, in a gallery in the basement. **Laguna de Cuitzeo**, on which it stands, is the second largest lake in Mexico; the road crosses it on a causeway. Ecological damage in the past has caused the lake to dry up on occasion. From here one can go to **Valle de Santiago** (**D** *Hotel Posada de la Parroquia*), attractive mountain scenery. The second village, 33 kilometres to the north, **Yuriria**, has a large-scale Indian version of the splendid church and convent at Actopán (see page 104). It is on Laguna de Yuriria, which looks like a grassy swamp. (Before Yuriria is Moreleón, the clothing distribution centre of Mexico – buses empty here.) The road continues to **Salamanca** (hotel, appalling traffic), where one turns left for Irapuato or right for Celaya and Querétaro. Mexico City-Morelia buses from the Central del Norte take the freeway to Celaya and then head south through Yuriria and Cuitzeo.

The road soon climbs through 50 kilometres of splendid mountain scenery: forests, waterfalls, and gorges, to the highest point at (Km 253), Puerto Gartan, and **Mil Cumbres** (2,886 metres), with a magnificent view over mountain and valley, and then descends into a tropical valley. A new, four-lane highway avoids the Mil Cumbres pass.

Another alternative to the Mil Cumbres pass is to take Route 126 from Morelia to **Queréndaro** (**E** *Hotel Imperial*, near church, pleasant rooms and courtyard, hot water, good value. Good *tacos* on main square), where the pavements are covered in *chiles* drying in the blazing sun, and all the shops are filled with large bags of *chiles* in the season, then at a junction 10 kilometres short of Zinapécuaro, turn right to join Route 15 (to Toluca and Mexico City) at Huajumbaro. If, instead of turning right you carry straight on, the road climbs and descends to **Maravatío** (hotel) and then climbs steeply, towards **Tlalpujahua**, an old mining town with a museum, several churches, and cobblestoned streets, very picturesque among forests and hills (*Casa de Huéspedes*). From Maravatío Route 122 goes south to join Route 15 just east of Ciudad Hidalgo. Also from Maravatío, Route 126 to Toluca has been upgraded to a toll road, renamed 15D and is one hour quicker than the route over the mountains on Route 15.

Northwest of Maravatío, on the Río Lerma (18th century bridge), lies the town of **Acámbaro**, founded 1526. It has a Franciscan church of the same date and monastery (finished 1532), with the Capilla de Santa Gracia (mid-16th century) and its ornate fountain. It was the point from which the irrigation system for the whole area was laid out when the town was founded. Acámbaro continues to thrive as an agricultural centre and an important railway junction. It is also on the main highway from Celaya to Toluca.

East of Morelia

Worth a glance are the façade of the 16th century church at **Ciudad Hidalgo** (Km 212; *Population:* 100,000). **D** *Hotel Fuente*, Morelos 37, T40518, some rooms have no keys, clean, showers, no water in the afternoon; **E** *Florida*, damp rooms, garage US$0.50 a night; *Restaurant Manolo*, inexpensive, good; *Restaurant Lupita's*, excellent, family run. Also see the old colonial bridge and church at **Tuxpan (Michoacán)** Km 193; **F** *Mara*, on main square, dirty, hot water, wood stove; *Tuxpan*, Miguel Cabrera, T50058, noisy. At Km 183 a side road runs, right, to the spa of **San José Purúa** at 1,800 metres, in a wild setting of mountain and gorge and woods. The radioactive thermal waters are strong. First-class hotel, beautiful spot, good restaurant, reservations in Mexico City, T55101538/4949. Trailers can park outside the guarded gate (24 hours, tip the guard for security), small charge for entry to grounds. Alternatively, drive down the steep hill to the river, just over the bridge on right is Agua Amarilla, a spa where you can camp for a small fee, friendly. Smaller, cheaper hotels lie on the road past the spa and in the town of Jungapeo. If driving with a trailer, do not take the downward hill to the village, your brakes may not hold.

Then comes Zitácuaro, with a pleasant plaza and a good covered market.

Zitácuaro

Sleeping A *Villa Monarca Inn*, T35346, F35350, on Morelia road, pool. **B** *Rancho San Cayetano*, 3 kilometres out on Huetamo road, T31926, chalets, friendly, clean, highly recommended. **B** *Rosales del Valle*, Revolución Sur 56, T31293, fair, some rooms hired for very

Ciudad Hidalgo to Toluca

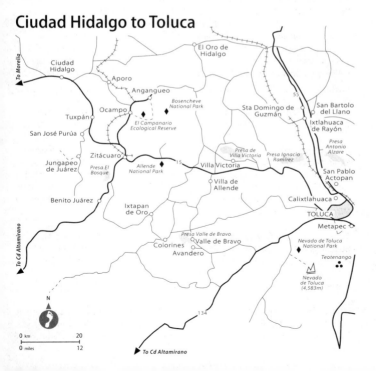

Mexico

Mexico

 Monarch butterflies

A turning off the main road at Angangueo brings you to a unique site, the wintering grounds of the Monarch butterfly in El Campanario Ecological Reserve, above the village of El Rosario. There are several trails to see the millions of large orange butterflies, which migrate every year to southeast Canada and northeast USA. They leave in March, after which there is nothing to see until the following November/December. Chris Sharp writes: "Huge clusters of the butterflies hang from branches and on warm days they take to the air in swirling masses of red clouds. The most impressive component of this is the sound of their wings, like a strong breeze blowing through the trees." Entry to the reserve, 0900-1700, is US$2, plus a tip for your guide (only Spanish spoken), try to form a small group to go round the reserve. There is a small visitors' centre and food kiosks near the entrance. **NB** The reserve is at a high altitude and you need to walk a few kilometres (30 minutes) to see the butterflies. Bring warm clothes. Very busy at weekends, when all the accommodation will be full; best to arrive at the sanctuary when it opens at 0900 to avoid the rush of tourists

The best base for visiting the reserve is the village of **Angangueo**. In December-March much of the village caters for the influx of butterfly watchers. It is very cold at night. **C** Albergue Don Bruno, Morelia 92, T60026,

good but a little overpriced, nice setting, restaurant. **D** Parakata 2, Matamoros 7, T80191. **D** La Margarita, Morelia, very clean, highly recommended, owner does tours to butterfly sanctuary. **E** Juárez, Nacional s/n, T80023, friendly, some rooms damp; **E** Paso de la Monarca, Nacional 20, T80187, large comfortable rooms, hot water, friendly, meals, highly recommended. There are several cafés and restaurants near the plaza, wholesome food, but not gourmet.

Half-hourly local bus (marked Angangueo) from Zitácuaro (Av Santos Degollado Ote, or from bus station on outskirts of town) to Ocampo, 1 hour, US$0.75, and from Ocampo another local bus (2 a day from corner 2 blocks east of plaza, 1000 and 1200, last one back at 1600, 1¼ hours, US$0.85, 12 kilometres on a mountainous dirt road) to El Rosario, from where it is a 40-minute walk to the Reserve. A truck from Ocampo to the butterfly refuge costs US$17, this can be shared, especially at weekends. All hotels will arrange transport to the Reserve, about US$20 per vehicle, 1 hour. Alternatively, walk, about 2½ hours (first hour steeply uphill), pleasant countryside. Aguila Tours, Amsterdam 291-C, Col Hipódromo Condesa, run tours from Mexico City from early December. Day trips cost around US$100-120. 4 direct buses to Mexico City, US$6. To Guadalajara, 3 a day, US$13, 8 hours.

short stays. **B** Salvador, Hidalgo Pte 7, T31107, clean and pleasant. **C** Lorenz, Av Hidalgo Ote 14, T30991, quiet, clean, TV, friendly, 9 blocks from bus station.

D México, Revolución Sur 22, T32811, clean, large rooms with cable TV, parking, restaurant, recommended. **D** Florida, with bath, clean, garage US$0.50 a night. **D** Hotel Colón, reasonable, fan, not very quiet, friendly management, can store luggage. **E** América, Av Revolución Sur, 1st block, TV, pleasant, clean, recommended. **E** Mary, on main street, hot shower, TV, clean; one block from Mary on same street is unnamed hotel, **F**, clean, TV, basic. **E** Posada Michoacán, main square, TV, clean, friendly, luggage store.

Buses To **Mexico City**, 3 hours, US$6; to Morelia, hourly, US$4.60, 3½ hours; to **Guadalajara**, 11 hours, US$14.80, 409 kilometres (bus station at end of Av Cuauhtémoc, next to market, taxi to centre, US$1).

Tourist office Km 4 Zitácuaro-Toluca, T30675.

Ixtapan del Oro
Population: 20,000
Colour map 3, grid B4

Ixtapan del Oro is a pleasant town in a valley, 70 kilometres southeast of Zitácuaro. It has a few hotels (eg **E** Posada Familiar Portal Moreno, with bath, clean). A road, mostly dirt, runs between Ixtapan del Oro and Valle de Bravo southeast of Zitácuaro.

(Km 86) A branch road, right, goes to the mountain resort of Valle de Bravo, a **Valle de Bravo** charming old town on the edge of an attractive artificial lake, with another Monarch butterfly wintering area nearby. This area gets the weekend crowd from Mexico City. (Two direct buses a day Zitácuaro-Valle de Bravo, one and a half hours, US$3.30; hourly buses to Toluca and Mexico City; 1st class bus to Toluca, US$3.50.)

Sleeping *Loto Azul Resort*, Av Toluca, T20157, F22747, 4-star. *Centro Vacacional ISSEMYM*, central, pool, restaurant, satisfactory, Independencia 404. **B** *Los Arcos*, good, is several kilometres beyond, in pine woods, excellent restaurant. **C** *Refugio del Salto*, Fontana Brava. **D** *Blanquita's*, opposite church off main plaza, basic, fairly clean, OK. **D** *Mary*, main plaza, hot showers. **D** *Casa Vieja*, Juárez 101, central. A few cheap *posadas familiares* around the plaza, ask.

Trailer Park Av del Carmen 26, T91726-21972 (or Toluca 91721-21580), familia Otero, English spoken, 5 hook-ups, 7 dry camping, 3 rentals, small private grounds, English spoken, recommended. **NB** Drivers with trailers must approach Avándaro from the Toluca end, no other way is safe because of the hills, narrow streets and town centre.

Eating *Alma Edith*, on Zócalo, good *comida corrida*. Good, cheap food in the *mercado*. Restaurants on pier are expensive.

Toluca Volcano

(Km 75) A road branches off the road to Toluca to the volcano of Toluca (**Nevado de Toluca**, or Xinantécatl; 4,558 metres, the fourth highest mountain in Mexico) and climbs to the deep blue lakes of the Sun and the Moon in its two craters, at about 4,270 metres, from which there is a wide and awe-inspiring view. It is 27 kilometres from the turning off the main road to the heart of the craters. During winter it is possible to ski on the slopes; two kilometres from the entrance is an *albergue* with food and cooking facilities. From here it is 10 kilometres to the entrance to the crater, where there is a smaller *albergue* (cooking facilities, food sold at weekends only, no bathroom or water, dirty), and then a further six kilometres to the lakes. A short cut from the small *albergue* takes 20 minutes to the crater (not possible to drive). At the third refuge (21 kilometres from the turn-off) is an attendant. Trips to the volcano are very popular at weekends. You can stay overnight at any of the refuges (F), although they are sometimes closed during the week, and there is a restaurant, but the trip can be done in one day from Toluca. If walking remember the entrance to the crater is on the far left side of the volcano.

To reach the Toluca volcano take the first bus to Sultepec from Toluca at about 0700, every two hours thereafter. Leave the bus where the road to the radio station branches off, just after Raices village (US$1), from there it is about 20 kilometres to the crater, hitching fairly easy, especially at weekends. Aim to get to the crater by midday, otherwise clouds will cover everything. Visitors must leave by 1700.

Toluca

Toluca, about 4½ hours from Morelia by bus, is the capital of the state of México. It is known mostly for its huge Friday market where Indians sell colourful woven baskets, *sarapes*, *rebozos*, pottery and embroidered goods (beware of pickpockets and handbag slashers). The new market is at Paseo Tollocan e Isidro Fabela, spreading over a number of streets, open daily. As well as for textiles, the city is famous for confectionery, *chorizos* (sausages) and for an orange liqueur known as *moscos*. It is also a centre of chemical industries which cause pollution.

Km 64
Population: 600,000
State Population: 1995
11,704,934
Altitude: 2,639m
Phone code: 721
Colour map 3, grid B4

The centre of the city is the **Plaza de los Mártires**, a very open space. On its south **Sights** side is the **Cathedral**, begun in 1870, but not completed until 1978 (incorporated in its interior is the baroque façade of the 18th century church of the Tercera Orden). Also on the south side is the **Church of Veracruz**, which houses a black Christ; its interior is very attractive. On three sides of the block which contains these two churches are **Los Portales** (C Bravo, C Hidalgo and C Constitución), arcaded shops and restaurants. Northeast of Plaza de los Mártires is a park, Plaza Angel María Garibay, with trees and fountains, on which is the **Museo de Bellas Artes**, formerly the Convento del Carmen, with seven halls of paintings (from Colonial Baroque – 18th century – to 20th century) and temporary exhibitions. A tunnel is said to run from the ex-Convento to all the central churches. ■ *Museum open Tuesday-Sunday 1000-1800, US$0.25, students half price, booklet US$1.35.* Next door is the **Templo del Carmen**, a neoclassical church with a gold and white interior. Next to the Carmen is Plaza España. At the eastern end of Plaza Garibay is the **Cosmovitral** and **Jardín Botánico** ■ *Tuesday-Sunday 0900-1700, US$0.60.* From 1933-1975 the building was the 16 de Septiembre market; in 1980 it was opened in its new form, a formal garden in honour of the Japanese Eizi Matuda, who set up the herbarium of Mexico State, with fountains and exhibitions, all bathed in the blues, oranges and reds of the vast stained glass work of Leopoldo Flores Valdez, a unique sight. One block west of Plaza Garibay is the **Palacio de Gobierno**. Four blocks west of Los Portales is the **Alameda**, a large park with a statue of Cuauhtémoc and many tall trees; on Sunday morning it is very popular with families strolling among the many stallholders. The entrance is at the junction of Hidalgo and Ocampo. At Ocampo y Morelos is the **Templo de la Merced**. The **Casa de las Artesanías** (Casart), with an excellent display of local artistic products for sale, is at Paseo Tollocan 700 (■ *daily 0930-1850*), more expensive than Mexico City. 10 kilometres south of the city is a good zoo, Zacango.

Toluca

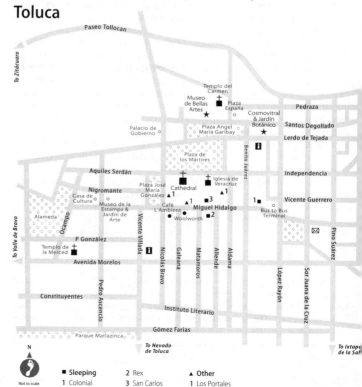

■ Sleeping	2 Rex	▲ Other
1 Colonial	3 San Carlos	1 Los Portales

From Toluca take a bus to the pyramids and Aztec seminary of **Calixtlahuaca**, two kilometres off the road to Ixtlahuaca; pyramids are to Quetzalcoatl (circular) and to Tlaloc; they are situated just behind the village, 10 minutes walk from the final bus-stop. ■ *US$4.35.*

Excursions

45 minutes north by car, near the town of Temoaya, is the Centro Ceremonial Otomí, a modern site for cultural events in a beautiful landscape.

See above for trips to Toluca volcano.

Along Route 55 south of Toluca, or reached from it, are a number of most interesting 'art and craft' producing villages, all with old churches. The first village is **Metepec**, the pottery-making centre of the valley, one and a half kilometres off the road to Tenango. The clay figurines made here, painted bright fuchsia, purple, green and gold, are unique. This is the source of the 'trees of life and death', the gaudily-painted pottery sold in Mexico. Craft workshops are very spread out. Market is on Monday. A recommended place to eat is *Las Cazuelitas*, near main church. Try the handmade tortillas. Interesting convent (bus Toluca-Metepec US$0.65). A detour east off Route 55 (or south from Route 15, the Toluca-Mexico City highway) goes to the town of **Santiago Tianguistenco** (*Population:* 38,000). Good *cazuelas*, *metates*, baskets and *sarapes*. Between July and early November displays of wild mushrooms for sale. Try *gordas* or *tlacoyos*, blue corn stuffed with a broad bean paste. If you are brave try *atepocates*; embryo frogs with tomato and chiles, boiled in maize leaves. Try restaurant *Mesón del Cid*, good regional food, go to kitchen to see choice. Try *sopa de hongos*, mushroom soup. Market day is Wednesday. The town is crowded at weekends.

San Mateo Atenco (*Population:* 65,000; *Altitude:* 2,570 metres), is situated south of the Toluca-Lerma 'corridor'. Settled in ancient times, it has featured in several important historical moments by virtue of occupying a bridge-head between lagoons: Axayácatl, Hernán Cortés and Hidalgo all passed this way. There is a Franciscan church and monastery, the earliest parts of which date from 1550. The town is famous for its shoes, and leather goods of all descriptions. Excellent bargains to be had. Market Friday and Saturday. On 25 October St Crispin, patron saint of shoemakers, is honoured in the open chapel of the church in the presence of the local bishop.

Holiday Inn, Carretera a México Km 57.5, T164666, F164099, restaurant, bar, parking. **C** *San Carlos*, Madero 210, T49422. **C** *Colonial*, Hidalgo Ote 103, T47066, pleasant courtyard with stained glass, with bath, clean, TV, cheap food (good restaurant, closed Sunday), recommended (bus from Terminal de Autobuses to Centro passes in front). **D** *Rex*, Matamoros Sur 101, T59300, with bath, hot water, no restaurant.

On Hidalgo Pte C *La Mansión*, No 408, T56578, with hot water, clean, garage, TV, no

Sleeping
■ *on maps*
Price codes:
see inside front cover

Mexico

Valle de Toluca, ancient and modern

The southern section of the Valle de Toluca used to contain within its boundaries the lake and headwaters of the River Lerma. The availability of water, and fertile land, led to the area being settled from the earliest times: there is evidence of human presence in this area dating from 10,000 BC. It was later to become the regional centre of one of the main Otomi groups, the Matlazincas.

In recent times the nature of the terrain and therefore the predominant economic activity of the population have changed. This has come about with the introduction of large-scale industry in and around Toluca, particularly along the Toluca-Lerma 'corridor'. The former lake and marshlands are now dry; commercial fishing has all but disappeared, and much of the agriculture is now of the intensive variety.

However, in several of the towns in this area, traditional products continue to flourish, aided in some cases by modern technology, for example leather goods in San Mateo Atenco, pottery in Metepec, textiles in Santiago Tianguistenco.

restaurant. **E** *Maya*, No 413, no check-in before 2000, shared bath, hot water, clean, small rooms without doorlocks, towels extra. All the above are in the centre, not many cheap hotels. **D** *Terminal*, adjoining bus terminal, T57960 (prices vary according to floor), restaurant next door.

Motels AL *Del Rey Inn*, T122122, F122567, Km 63, Mexico City road entrance (5-star), resort facilities; on same exit road, *Paseo*, T65730 (4-star) and *Castel Plaza Las Fuentes*, Km 57.5, T164666, F164798 (5-star).

Eating
● *on maps*

Ostionería Escamilla, Rayón Nte 404, good fish. *San Francisco*, Villada 108. *Café L'Ambient*, Hidalgo 231 Pte, snacks, meals, quite simple; next door are *Son Jei* and *Panadería Libertad* (good pizza takeaway), oriental; opposite, in Los Portales, is *Impala* for *comida corrida*, coffee. *Woolworth* restaurant, Hidalgo Pte casi Matamoros, is open Sunday from 0930 for good set breakfasts. *Fonda Rosita* in Los Portales central avenue going through to Plaza de los Mártires, is also open Sunday am, pleasant, Mexican. *Las Ramblas*, on Constitución side of Los Portales, Mexican food, average.

Transport
Bus station is some distance from the centre; inside, information is difficult to gather and all is confusion outside – look for a bus marked 'Centro', US$0.15; from centre to terminal buses go from, among other places Ignacio Rayón Nte e Hidalgo Ote, look for 'Terminal' on window (yellow or orange bus). To Mexico City, US$2.85, 1 hour. Bus to **Pátzcuaro**, 6 hours, US$17.50, several daily; to **Taxco**, 4 buses a day, book in advance, 3 hours, US$6 with Frontera, a spectacular journey. To **Morelia**, several buses daily with Herrachura de Plata, 4 hours, US$8.25, ETN US$14.80. Many buses to **Tenango de Arista** (US$0.65, 30 minutes), **Tenancingo** (US$2.25); also regular buses to **Calixtlahuaca** US$2.50 (1 hour) from platform 7.

Directory
Tourist offices Lerdo de Tejada Pte 101, Edif Plaza Toluca, 1° p, T50131, has a free *Atlas Turístico* of the state of México, including street maps of all towns of interest; Federal office at Villada 123, T48961.

From Toluca to the coast at Ixtapa (Route 134, see page 380), via Tejupilco (**C** *Hotel Juárez*), Ciudad Altamirano and La Salitrera: the road is paved (deteriorating in parts), traffic is sparse and the landscape hilly and pleasant.

South to Tenancingo

Route 55 descends gradually to **Tenango de Arista**, two hotels with car park alongside main road (Toluca-Tenango bus, US$0.65), where one can walk (20 minutes) to the ruins of **Teotenango** (Matlazinca culture, reminiscent of La Ciudadela at Teotihuacán, with five plazas, 10 structures, and one ball court). There is an interesting museum by the ruins of Teotenango; to enter go to the end of town on the right hand side. ■ *Eentry to museum and ruins US$1*. If you ask the guard, you can pitch a tent at the museum inside the gate. 48 kilometres from Toluca the road descends abruptly through gorges to **Tenancingo**, still at 1,830 metres, but with a soft, warm all-the-year-round climate. Half an hour by bus to the south (road unpaved) is the magnificent 18th century Carmelite convent of El Santo Desierto, where they make beautiful *rebozos*. The townspeople themselves weave fine *rebozos* and the fruit wines are delicious and cheap. Overlooking this busy commercial town is a statue of Christ on a hill. The daily market area is two blocks from the bus terminal (continue one block, turn left for two further blocks to the main square); market day is on Sunday (excellent local cheese).

Sleeping Recommended hotels at Tenancingo are **D** *Lazo*, Guadalupe Victoria 100, T20083 (1½ blocks straight on from market, away from bus terminal), with clean rooms in annex with shower, leafy courtyard, *El Arbol de la Vida* restaurant. **D** *María Isabel*, clean,

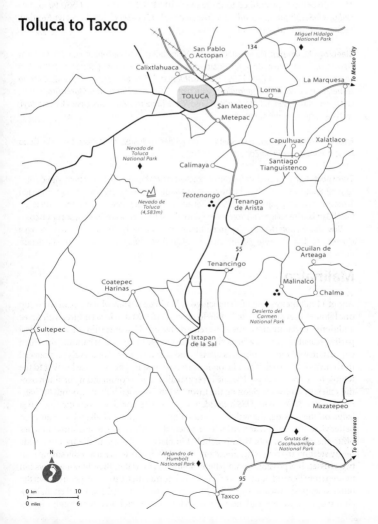

Toluca to Taxco

Mexico

well-lit. **E** *Hotel Jardín*, on main plaza, T20108, with bath, big, airy rooms, restaurant, good value. Good bakery in private house at Guillermo Prieto 302.

Buses Frequent buses to Toluca, US$2.25 with Tres Estrellas del Centro, 1 hour; also to Ixtapan de la Sal US$1 (change here for Taxco US$2.25), Malinalco, US$1.50, and Chalma.

Ixtapan de la Sal
Colour map 3, grid B4

On 32 kilometres from Tenancingo, on Route 55, is Ixtapan de la Sal, a pleasant forest-surrounded leisure resort with medicinal hot springs. In the centre of this quiet whitewashed town is the municipal spa. ■ *Adult admission US$1.60. The municipal spa's hours are 0700-1800, it is not always open.* At the edge of town is Parque Los Trece Lagos. 'The Thirteen Lake Park' is privately run and has a train running around; there are numerous picnic spots. Private baths charge US$6 for admission only; everything else is extra. For the hedonist there are private 'Roman' baths, for the stiff-limbed a medicinal hot-water pool, mud baths for the vain, an Olympic pool for swimmers, rowing boats and a water slide for the adventurous. The latter is 150 metres long (prohibited to those over 40). ■ *US$1.55 entry, US$0.90 for two slides, US$2.20 for slides all day, free midweek 1200-1400.* Market day: Sunday. Fiesta: second Friday in Lent.

Sleeping **AL** *Ixtapan*, Nuevo Ixtapan, T30304, including food and entertainment. **AL** *Vista Hermosa*, T30092, next door, full board only, good, friendly. **A** *Kiss* (*Villa Vergel*), Blvd San Román y Av Juárez, T30349, F30842. **B** *Casablanca*, Juárez 615, T30241, F30842. **C** *María Isabel*, T30122, good. **D** *Guadalajara*, with bath. **D** *Casa de Huéspedes Margarita*, Juárez, clean, recommended; **E** *Casa Guille*, C José María Morelos, with bath, clean. **E** *Casa Yuyi*, with bath, clean, good; many others.

Eating Plenty of reasonable restaurants on Av Benito Juárez, most close by 1900. Good value is *Fonda Jardín* on Zócalo.

Transport **Car**: Ixtapan de la Sal can be reached in two hours or so by car from Mexico City: turn off Route 15, the Toluca highway, at La Marquesa (see below), go through Santiago Tianguistenco and join Route 55 at Tenango. The road goes on to the Grutas de Cacahuamilpa (see page 364) from where you can continue either to Cuernavaca or Taxco.
Bus Bus to/from Mexico City three hours, US$5.35, every 30 minutes from Terminal Oriente; to Toluca every 30 minutes, US$4.20, two hours. Also to Taxco, Coatepec, Cuernavaca.

Malinalco

About 11 kilometres east of Tenancingo is Malinalco, from which a path winds up one kilometre, 20 minutes, to Malinalco ruins (1188, Matlazinca culture, with Aztec additions), certainly one of the most remarkable pre-Hispanic ruins in Mexico, now partly excavated. Here is a fantastic rock-cut temple in the side of a mountain which conceals in its interior sculptures of eagle and jaguar effigies. Apparently you can feel movement in the rock if you lie on it or lean against it. The staircase leading to the temple has over 430 steps. The site is very small, but in a commanding position over the valley, and now overlooking the town and the wooded hills all around. ■ *Tuesday-Sunday 1000-1630, US$2, Sunday free.* The site is visible from the town as a ledge on the hillside; the walk up passes a tiny, blue colonial chapel. For an even better view of the ruins carry straight on where the path leading to the ruins branches off to the right. This old road is cobbled in places and rises up the mountainside pretty steeply, arriving (after about one and a half hours walk) at a small shrine with two crosses. It is possible to camp here but there is no water. Breathtaking views can be seen from here off both sides of the ridge. The trail then carries on gently down the other side, past avocado trees, for 20 minutes, to the paved road to Tenancingo, almost opposite a new brick house with arches. It is possible to catch a bus back over the mountains to Malinalco. It would also be much quicker and easier (downhill walk mostly) to do this whole hike in reverse; catch the bus out (ask for the old road) and walk back.

You should not fail to visit also the Augustinian **Templo y Exconvento del Divino Salvador** (1552), in the centre of town, the nave of which has a patterned ceiling, while the two-storey cloisters are painted with elaborate, early frescoes. Just below the main square in front of the convent is the market (market day Wednesday).

You can also get to Malinalco from Toluca, or Mexico City, by taking a second class bus to **Chalma**. This is a popular pilgrimage spot, and when you get off the bus you will be offered (for sale) a corona of flowers. From the bus lot, walk up hill, past the market stalls, to the crossroads where blue colectivos leave for Malinalco until 2000 (10 kilometres, 20 minutes, US$1).

Sleeping

E *Hotel Santa Mónica*, Hidalgo 109, with bath, pretty courtyard, good value. E *Posada Familiar*; cabins for families at north edge of town; camping and trailer park *El Paraíso* opposite the small blue chapel (not well named: "no more than a parking lot with one dirty toilet").

Eating

La Playa on road to ruins, just off square, with garden, nice place; opposite is *La Salamandra*, good value; trout farm and fishery has a restaurant, superb, bring own supplies of beverages, bread, salad (trout costs US$5-6); also *El Rincón del Convento*, behind the convent on road to square.

Festivals

There is a *fiesta* in Malinalco on **6 August**.

Transport

A direct road runs from Tenancingo to Malinalco, paved to the summit of a range of hills, poor at the summit, then graded to the junction with the Malinalco-San Pedro Zictepec road; pick-up truck or buses run on this direct road hourly, 40 minutes, US$2.25 (in Malinalco bus leaves from corner of Av Progreso and the square). From Toluca you can go to Malinalco by leaving the Toluca-Tenancingo road after San Pedro Zictepec, some 12 kilometres north of Tenancingo, which is paved and 28 kilometres long. Terminal in Mexico City, Central del Pte, opposite Observatorio, at least 2 companies go there. Buses to Chalma from Mexico City leave frequently from Central del Pte, 2 hours, US$3.60 direct. This is also where you make connections if coming from Cuernavaca (take a Cuernavaca-Toluca bus to Santa Marta, then wait for a Mexico City or Toluca-Chalma bus).

Toluca to Mexico City

The basin of Toluca, the highest in the central region, is the first of a series of basins drained by the Río Lerma into the Pacific. To reach Mexico City from Toluca, 64 kilometres by dual carriageway, it is necessary to climb over the intervening mountain range. The centre of the basin is swampy. (Km 50) Lerma is on the edge of the swamp, the source of the Lerma River. The road climbs, with backward views of the snow-capped Toluca volcano, to the summit at Las Cruces (Km 32; 3,035 metres). At this point is the **Parque Nacional Miguel Hidalgo**, or **La Marquesa**, which has many facilities for weekend recreation (lakes with watersports, hiking, running, picnics et cetera). Here also is the turn-off for Chalma and Santiago Tianguistenco from Route 15. There are occasional great panoramic views of the city and the Valley of México during the descent (smog-permitting).

Mexico City

Mexico City, the capital, founded by the Spaniards in 1521, was built upon the remains of Tenochtitlan, the Aztec capital, covering some 200 square kilometres. The Valley of México, the intermont basin in which it lies, is about 110 kilometres long by 30 kilometres wide. Rimming this valley is a sentinel-like chain of peaks of the Sierra Nevada mountains. Towards the southeast tower two tall volcanoes, named for the warrior Popocatépetl and his beloved Ixtaccíhuatl (see page 316). Both are permanently snow-capped, but they are often not visible because of the smog. To the south the crest of the Cordillera is capped by the wooded volcano of Ajusco.

Population 20m
Altitude: 2,240m
Phone code: 5
Colour map 3, grid B4

About one in four of the total population live in this city, which has over half the country's manufacturing employment, and much of the nation's industrial smog (the worst months being December to February). Measures such as closing the huge Pemex refinery have reduced lead and sulphur dioxide emissions to acceptable levels, but the ozone level is occasionally dangerous. Common ailments are a burning sensation in the eyes (contact-lens wearers take note) and nose and a sore throat. Citizens are advised by the local authorities not to smoke and not to take outdoor exercise. The English-language dailies, *The News*, and the *Mexico City Times* give analysis of the air quality, with warnings and advice.

The city suffers from a fever of demolition and rebuilding, especially since the heavy damage caused by the September 1985 earthquake. This was concentrated along the Paseo de la Reforma, Av Juárez, the Alameda, and various suburbs and residential districts. About 20,000 people are believed to have lost their lives, largely in multi-storey housing and government-controlled buildings, including Juárez hospital in which there were about 3,000 fatalities.

Mexico City has long burst its ancient boundaries and spread; some of the new residential suburbs are most imaginatively planned, though there are many appalling shanty-towns. Like all big centres it is faced with a fearsome traffic problem, despite the building of inner and outer ring roads (the Circuito Interior and the Periférico). Nine metro lines now operate, plus the *tren ligero* in the south and the *tren férreo* in the east. There is a large traffic-free area east of the Zócalo.

Ins and outs

Getting there   Mexico City is well served by air and road, less well connected by rail. The airport is about 6 kilometres from the city centre. For details of international scheduled flights see **Essentials**, page 74, and for airport information see page 295. Domestic flights go out like spokes of a wheel to and from the capital to all major towns in Mexico. Long distance buses come in to four terminals, north, south, east and west, acording to where they have come from. The railway station is fairly central but services are unreliable. Passenger services from Saltillo in the north and Vera Cruz on the east coast.

Getting around   Traffic is congested and you are not recommended to try and drive round Mexico City. The metro is the most convenient form of public transport, see page 293, and is easy and cheap to use. It is also less polluted than the alternatives, such as buses and taxis. Most sites of interest are within easy walking distance of a metro station. Take care in the centre at quiet times (for example Sunday pm) and in Chapultepec (where Sunday is the safest day). At night you are advised to phone for a taxi.

Climate   Because of the altitude the climate is mild and exhilarating save for a few days in mid-winter. The normal annual rainfall is 660 millimetres, and most of it falls-usually in the late afternoon-between May and October. Even in summer the temperature at night is rarely above 13°C, and in winter there can be sharp frosts. Despite this, central heating is not common.

north of Chapultepec, a luxury residential area with many interesting art galleries and shops. It does not suffer from the tourists that crowd the Zona Rosa and other chic areas. Many old houses have carved stone façades, tiled roofs, gardens, especially on C Horacio, a pretty street lined with trees and parks. The Secretaría de Turismo Offices are on Av Presidente Masaryk at the corner of Hegel.

Historical centre

The great main square, or Plaza Mayor, centre of the oldest part, is always alive with people, and often vivid with official ceremonies and celebrations. The flag in the centre of the square is raised at 0600 (0500 in winter) and taken down, with ceremony, at 1800 each day (1700 in winter). On the north side, on the site of the Great Teocalli or temple of the Aztecs, is the cathedral. Wheeled traffic is restricted Monday-Friday 1000-1700. **The Zócalo**

The largest and oldest cathedral in Latin America, first built 1525; rebuilding began 1573; consecrated 1667; finished 1813. Singularly harmonious, considering the many architects employed and time taken to build it. Restoration work on the **The Cathedral**

Mexico

exterior has been completed; work continues inside. The Cathedral has been subject to subsidence over many years and a lengthy programme of work is under way to build new foundations (work currently suspended – nobody knows how to solve the problem!). Meanwhile, the weight of much of the building is being supported by massive scaffolding inside the Cathedral. A plumb line hanging from the cupola and a notice board by the west entrance give some idea of the extent of the problem. There is an underground crypt reached by stairs in the west wing of the main part of the building (closed for restoration since 1993). Next to the Cathedral is the **Sagrario Metropolitano**, 1769, with fine churrigueresque façade. Unlike the cathedral it was built on the remains of an Aztec pyramid and is more stable than the former.

To the side of the Cathedral are the Aztec ruins of the **Templo Mayor** or *Teocalli*, which were found in 1978 when public works were being carried out. They make a very worthwhile visit, especially since the Aztecs built a new temple every 52 years, and seven have been identified on top of each other. A **Museum (Museo Arqueológico del Sitio)** was opened in 1987 behind the temple, to house various sculptures found in the main pyramid of Tenochtitlán and six others, including the huge, circular monolith representing the dismembered body of Coyolxauhqui, who was killed by her brother Huitzilopochtli, the Aztec tutelary god, and many other

Zócalo and Alameda Central

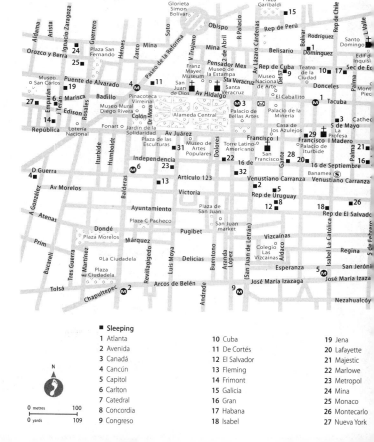

■ Sleeping

1 Atlanta	10 Cuba	19 Jena
2 Avenida	11 De Cortés	20 Lafayette
3 Canadá	12 El Salvador	21 Majestic
4 Cancún	13 Fleming	22 Marlowe
5 Capitol	14 Frimont	23 Metropol
6 Carlton	15 Galicia	24 Mina
7 Catedral	16 Gran	25 Monaco
8 Concordia	17 Habana	26 Montecarlo
9 Congreso	18 Isabel	27 Nueva York

objects. The Templo Mayor and museum are at Seminario 4 y Guatemala, entrance in the corner of the Zócalo. There is a café, bookshop and left luggage office, and TV displays in the halls with English subtitles. ■ *0900-1730 daily except Monday, last tickets at 1700, entry to museum and temple US$5, free Sunday, US$1.75 to take photos, US$3.45 to use video camera; guided tours in Spanish Tuesday-Friday 0930-1800, Saturday 0930-1300, in English Tuesday-Saturday 1000 and 1200, US$0.85 per person (sometimes cancelled at short notice).*

On C Maestro Justo Sierra, north of Cathedral (between C Guatemala and C San Ildefonso – see map) is the **Mexican Geographical Society** (No 19), in whose courtyard is a bust of Humboldt and a statue of Benito Juárez, plus a display of documents and maps (ask at the door to be shown in); opposite are the **Anfiteatro Simón Bolívar**, with murals of his life in the lobby and an attractive theatre, and the **Colegio San Ildefonso**. ■ *Open Monday-Sunday 1100-1800, except Wednesday 1100-2100, US$2, Sunday US$1.30.*

On the west side of the Zócalo are the Portales de los Mercaderes (Arcades of the Merchants), very busy since 1524. North of them, opposite the Cathedral, is: the **Monte de Piedad** (National Pawnshop) established in the 18th century and housed in a 16th century building. Prices are government controlled and bargains are often found. Auctions are held each Friday at 1000 (first, second and third Friday for jewellery and watches, fourth for everything else), US dollars accepted.

The Palacio Nacional

The National Palace takes up the whole eastern side of the Zócalo. Built on the site of the Palace of Moctezuma and rebuilt in 1692 in colonial baroque, with its exterior faced in the red volcanic stone called *tezontle*; the top floor was added by President Calles in the 1920s. It houses various government departments and the Juárez museum. ■ *Monday-Friday, 1000-1800, ID needed, free.* Over the central door hangs the Liberty Bell, rung at 2300 on 15 September by the President, who gives the multitude the *Grito* – '¡Viva México!'. The thronged frescoes around the staircase and court are by Diego Rivera (*The History of Mexico and Precolumbian Civilizations*). ■ *Open daily.* Guides: ask them for the US$2 booklet on the frescoes. In the C Moneda and adjoining the back of the Palace is the **Museo de las Culturas**, with interesting international archaeological and historical exhibits. ■ *0930-1800; closed Sunday, you have to show your passport at the entrance.* Also in Moneda are the site of the first university (building now dilapidated), the Palacio del Arzobispado, and the site of the first printing press.

Ex-Palacio Arzobispal, on the corner of Moneda and Licenciado Verdad. The Archbishop's palace until 1861 (foundations laid 1521, subject to flood and earthquake damage, major

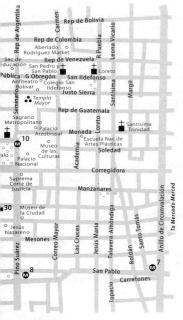

To Dirección General de Aduanas

Mexico

reconstruction in late 18th century), now owned by the Finance Ministry, it was restored and opened to the public in 1994. ■ *1000-1700 (closed Monday), US$1.15 (Sunday free).*

Museo de Artes e Industrias Populares de México, Av Juárez 44, was closed in 1996. The building was originally the church of the Corpus Christi convent, built between 1720-24. Since 1867, the church has been used variously as a warehouse, a Protestant church, a museum of hygiene and, from 1951, by the Instituto Nacional Indigenista (INI). The area in which it stands was badly affected by the 1985 earthquake and is scheduled for redevelopment.

Suprema Corte de Justicia de la Nación, opposite Palacio Nacional, on southeast corner of the Zócalo, see frescoes by Orozco ('*National Riches*' and '*Proletarian Struggle*'). Closes at 1400.

Palacio de Bellas Artes The Palacio was refurbished, inside and out, in 1994 to celebrate its diamond jubilee; the garden in front of the marble apron has been laid out as originally designed. A large, showy building, interesting for Art Deco lovers (see the fabulous stained glass skylight in the roof), houses a museum and a theatre, and a *cafetería* at mezzanine level (light, average continental food at moderate prices), and an excellent bookshop on the arts. The museum has old and contemporary paintings, prints, sculptures, and handicraft articles. The fresco by Rivera is a copy of the one rubbed out in disapproval at Radio City, New York, and there are spirited Riveras in the room of oils and water-colours. Other frescoes are by Orozco, Tamayo and Siqueiros. ■ *Daily, 1000-1730; Sunday, 1000-1330, US$2, free with ISIC.* There are also prestigious temporary fine art exhibitions (no extra charge). On the top floor is a museum of architecture (temporarary shows and history of the construction of the building). The most remarkable thing about the theatre is its glass curtain designed by Tiffany. It is solemnly raised and lowered before each performance of the Ballet Folclórico de México. The Palacio is listing badly, for it has sunk four metres since it was built. Operas are performed; there are orchestral concerts and performances by the Ballet Folclórico de México on Sunday, 0930 and 2100, Wednesday at 2100 (check press for details), you must book in advance. Tickets US$12 on the balcony, US$20 and US$25 (cheap balcony seats are not recommended because you see only a third of the stage set, although you can see the performers). Tickets on sale from 1100; hotels, agencies et cetera only sell the most expensive, cheaper tickets only at the theatre. Cheap concerts at 1200 on Sunday, and also at Teatro Hidalgo, behind Bellas Artes on Hidalgo, at the same time, book in advance. 50% concessions for students and teachers (show documents at counter on right before going to box office).

The Alameda Across the road is **Torre Latinoamericana**; on the 44th floor is a viewing platform with telescopes, ■ *0900-2300, US$3.50 to go up.* (The cafetería is poor, but try the Coca Cola with lemon ice-cream.) This great glass tower dominates the gardens of the **Alameda Central**, once the Aztec market and later the place of execution for the Spanish Inquisition. Beneath the broken shade of eucalyptus, cypress and ragged palms, wide paths link fountains and heroic statues. The park is illuminated at night. (Much rebuilding going on in this area.)

On the northern side of the Alameda, on Av Hidalgo, is the Jardín Morelos, flanked by two old churches: Santa Veracruz (1730) to the right and **San Juan de Dios** to the left. The latter has a richly carved baroque exterior; its image of San Antonio de Padua is visited by those who are broken-hearted for love. The **Franz Mayer** museum is located next to this church, in the former Hospital de San Juan de Dios, which was built in the 17th century. Recently rebuilt and exquisitely restored, it houses an important decorative arts collection (ceramics, glass, silver, time-pieces, furniture and textiles, as well as Mexican and European paintings from the 16th-20th centuries) and a library. Its cloister, with a pleasant cafetería, is an oasis of peace in the heart of the city. ■ *1000-1700 except Monday; admission US$1.15 (US$0.30 if only visiting the cloister).* On the same side of Hidalgo, next to the Franz Mayer, is the **Museo de la Estampa** (Museum of Engraving). ■ *1000-1700 (closed Monday), US$1.50.*

Escuela Nacional Preparatoria, north of Zócalo at Justo Sierra 27 (the street parallel to, and between, Guatemala and San Ildefonso), built 1749 as the Jesuit School of San Ildefonso in splendid baroque. There are important frescoes by Orozco (including '*Revolutionary Trinity*' and the '*Trench*') and, in the Anfiteatro Bolívar, frescoes by Diego Rivera ('*Creation*') and Fernando Leal, all of which are in excellent condition. There is another Leal mural, '*Lord of Chalma*', in the stairwell separating the two floors of Orozco works as well as Jean Charlot's '*Massacre in the Templo Mayor*', and in a stairwell of the Colegio Chico experimental murals by Siqueiros. The whole interior has been magnificiently restored. Occasional grand exhibitions.

Secretaría de Educación Pública, on Argentina 28, three blocks from Zócalo, built 1922, contains frescoes by a number of painters. Here are some of Diego Rivera's masterpieces, painted between 1923 and 1930, illustrating the lives and sufferings of the common people. ■ *Open daily, 1000-1800, free entry.* A long passageway connects the Secretaría with the older Ex-Aduana de Santo Domingo where there is a dynamic Siqueiros mural '*Patriots and Parricides*'.

Plaza Santo Domingo, two blocks north of the Cathedral, an intimate little plaza surrounded by fine colonial buildings: (a) the Antigua Aduana (former customs house); (b) on the west side, the Portales de Santo Domingo, where public scribes and owners of small hand-operated printing presses still carry on their business; (c) on the north side, the church of Santo Domingo, in Mexican baroque, 1737 – note the carving on the doors and façade; (d) the old Edificio de la Inquisición, where the tribunals of the Inquisition were held (by standing on tiptoe in the men's room one can see – if tall enough – through the window into the prison cells of the Inquisition, which are not yet open to the public). It became the Escuela Nacional de la Medicina and is now the **Museo de la Medicina Mexicana**(Brasil 33). There is a remarkable staircase in the patio; it also has a theatre. The nearby streets contain some fine examples of colonial architecture.

Two blocks east of Santo Domingo are the church and convent of **San Pedro y San Pablo** (1603), both massively built and now turned over to secular use. A block north is the public market of Abelardo L Rodríguez, with striking mural decorations.

Church of Loreto, built 1816 and now tilting badly, but being restored, is on a square of the same name, surrounded by colonial buildings. Its façade is a remarkable example of 'primitive' or 'radical' neoclassicism.

La Santísima Trinidad (1677, remodelled 1755), to be seen for its fine towers and the rich carvings on its façade.

The Mercado Merced (metro Merced), said to be the largest market in all the Americas, dating back over 400 years. Its activities spread over several blocks and it is well worth a visit. In the northern quarter of this market are the ruins of La Merced monastery; the fine 18th century patio is almost all that survives; the courtyard, on Av Uruguay, between C Talavera and C Jesús María, opposite No 171, is nearly restored.

The oldest hospital in continental America, **Jesús Nazareno**, 20 de Noviembre 82, founded 1526 by Cortés, was remodelled in 1928, save for the patio and staircase. Cortés' bones have been kept since 1794 in the adjoining church, on the corner of Pino Suárez and República de El Salvador, diagonally opposite the Museo de la Ciudad.

Avenida Madero leads from the Zócalo west to the Alameda. On it is **La Profesa** church, late 16th century, with a fine high altar and a leaning tower. The 18th century **Palacio de Iturbide**, Av Madero 17, once the home of Emperor Agustín (1821-23), has been restored and has a clear plastic roof. Wander around, it is now a bank head office.

From the Zócalo to the Alameda

The **Casa de los Azulejos** (House of Tiles) near the Alameda between 5 de Mayo. It was built in the 16th century, and is brilliantly faced with blue and white Puebla tiles (18th century). Occupied by the Zapatista army during the Revolution, it is now home to *Sanborn's Restaurant*. The staircase walls are covered with an Orozco fresco '*Omniscience*' (1925). (There are more Orozco frescoes at Biblioteca Iberoamericana on Cuba between 5 de Febrero and Argentina.) Over the way is the **Church of San Francisco**, founded in 1525 by the 'Apostles of Mexico', the first 12 Franciscans to reach the country. It was by far the most important church in colonial days. Cortés' body rested here for some time, as did Iturbide's; the Viceroys attended the church.

Beyond San Francisco church, Eje Lázaro Cárdenas, formerly C San Juan de Letrán, leads south towards **Las Vizcaínas**, at Plaza Las Vizcaínas, one block east, built in 1734 as a school for girls; some of it is still so used, but some of it has become slum tenements. In spite of neglect, it is still the best example of colonial secular baroque in the city. ■ *Not open to the public; permission to visit sometimes given.*

Museo San Carlos, Puente de Alvarado 50 (metro Revolución), a 19th century palace, has fine Mexican colonial painting and a first-class collection of European paintings. It is the former home of Señora Calderón de la Barca who wrote *Life in Mexico* while living there. ■ *Open to visitors 1000 to 1700, closed Monday.* The **Escuela Nacional de Artes Plásticas** at the corner of Academía and C Moneda, houses about 50 modern Mexican paintings. There is another picture gallery housing a collection of colonial paintings (16th-18th century), the **Pinacoteca Virreinal**, in the former church of San Diego in C Dr Mora, at the west end of the Alameda, opens at 0900, interesting. (Cheap concerts on Thursday at 2000.)

Moving eastwards along Av Hidalgo, before the Palace of Fine Arts, on the right is the **Post Office**, built 1904. The postal museum on the first floor is well worth a visit: exhibits from mid-18th century. ■ *Monday-Friday 0900-1800, Saturday 1000-1400, free.*

Plaza Santiago de Tlaltelolco North from the west side of the Post Office leads to the C Santa María la Redonda, at the end of which is **Plaza Santiago de Tlaltelolco**, next oldest Plaza to the Zócalo, heavily damaged in the 1985 earthquake. Here was the main market of the Aztecs, and on it, in 1524, the Franciscans built a huge church and convent. This is now the **Plaza de las Tres Culturas** (Aztec, colonial and modern): (a) the Aztec ruins have been restored; (b) the magnificent Franciscan church of Santiago Tlaltelolco (completed 1609) is now the focus of (c) the massive, multi-storey Nonoalco-Tlatelolco housing scheme, a garden city within a city, with pedestrian and wheeled traffic entirely separate. In October 1968, the Plaza de las Tres Culturas was the scene of serious distubances between the authorities and students, in which a large number of students were killed (see *The Other Mexico* by Octavio Paz, or *La Noche de Tlatelolco* by Elena Poniatowska, Biblioteca Era, 1971 – *Massacre in Mexico* in English, and the very readable, and startling, *68* by Paco Ignacio Taibo II, 1991, in Spanish).

Plaza Garibaldi About four blocks north of the Post Office off Eje Lázaro Cárdenas is **Plaza Garibaldi**, a must, especially on Friday and Saturday night, when up to 200 *mariachis* in their traditional costume of huge sombrero, tight silver-embroidered trousers, pistol and *sarape*, will play your favourite Mexican serenade for US$5 (for a bad one) to 10 (for a good one). If you arrive by taxi you will be besieged. The whole square throbs with life and the packed bars are cheerful, though there is some danger from thieves and pickpockets, particularly after dark. The Lagunilla market is held about four blocks northeast of the plaza, a hive of activity all week. On one side of Plaza Garibaldi is a gigantic eating hall, different stalls sell different courses, very entertaining.

Palacio de Minería, C Tacuba 9 (1797), is a fine old building, now restored, and once more level on its foundations. From 1910 to 1954 it was the Escuela Nacional de Ingeniería; there is a permanent exhibition of meteorites found all over Mexico (up to 14 tonnes). Free. (Cheap concerts on Sunday at 1700, upstairs.) Moved from the Plaza de la Reforma to Plaza Manuel Tolsá opposite the Palacio is the great equestrian statue, 'El Caballito', of King Charles IV cast in 1802; it weighs 26 tons and is the second-largest bronze casting in the world.

Museo Nacional de Arte, Tacuba 8, opposite Palacio de Minería, near main Post Office. ■ *Tuesday-Sunday, 1000-1730. US$2.00, Sundays free.* Built in 1904, designed by the Italian architect, Silvio Contri, as the Palacio de Comunicaciones. The building has magnificent staircases made by the Florentine firm Pignone. It houses a large collection of Mexican paintings, drawings, sculptures and ceramics dating from the 16th century to 1950. It has the largest number of paintings (more than 100) by José María Velasco in Mexico City, as well as works by Miguel Cabrera, Gerardo Murillo, Rivera, Orozco, Siqueiros, Tamayo and Anguiano. Giftshop.

Along the south side of the Alameda, running east, is Av Juárez, a fine street with a mixture of old and new buildings. Diego Rivera's huge (15 metres by 4.80 metres) and fascinating mural, the 'Sueño de una tarde dominical en la Alameda Central', was removed from the earthquake-damaged *Hotel del Prado* and now occupies its own purpose-built museum, the highly recommended **Museo Mural Diego Rivera**, on the north side of the Parque de la Solidaridad at Colón y Balderas. ■ *Tuesday-Sunday 1000-1800, US$1, free for students with ISIC card.* A stroll down C Dolores, a busy and fascinating street, leads to the market of San Juan. The colonial church of Corpus Christi, on Av Juárez, is now used to display and sell folk arts and crafts. The avenue ends at the small Plaza de la Reforma. At the corner of Juárez and Reforma is the Lotería Nacional building. Drawings are held three times a week, at 2000: an interesting scene, open to the public. Also at this site is a large yellow sculpture known as El Caballito after the original equestrian statue that has been moved to the front of the Palacio de Minería. Beyond Plaza de la Reforma is the **Monumento a la Revolución**: a great copper dome, soaring above supporting columns set on the largest triumphal arches in the world. Beneath the monument is the **Museo Nacional de la Revolución**, dealing with the period 1867-1917, very interesting, lots of exhibits, videos. ■ *Tuesday-Sunday, 1000-1700, US$0.60.*

South of this area, on Plaza Ciudadela, is a large colonial building, **La Ciudadela**, dating from 1700. It has been used for all kinds of purposes but is now a library.

The wide and handsome Paseo de la Reforma, three kilometres long, continues to the Bosque de Chapultepec: shops, offices, hotels, restaurants all the way. Along it are monuments to Columbus; to Cuauhtémoc and a 45-metre marble column to Independence, topped by the golden-winged figure of a woman, 'El Angelito' to the Mexicans. Just before entering the park is the Salubridad (Health) Building. Rivera's frescoes in this building cannot be seen by the public, who can view only the stained-glass windows on the staircases.

The Park at the end of Paseo de la Reforma, with its thousands of ahuehuete trees, is beautiful and is now being kept litter-free and well policed (park closes at 1700). The best day to visit is Sunday when it is all much more colourful. It is divided into three sections: the first, the easternmost, was a wood inhabited by the Toltecs and Aztecs; the second section, west of Boulevard Manuel Avila Camacho, was added in 1964, and the third in 1974. The first section contains a maze of pathways, a large and a small lake, a Plaza del Quijote and Monumento a los Niños Héroes, shaded lawns and a **zoo** with giant pandas and other animals from around the world, cages spacious, most animals seem content, well laid out. ■ *Free, closed Monday, shuts 1630.* At the top of a hill in the park (a long climb; train to the top US$0.20) is the Castillo de Chapultepec, with a view over Mexico Valley from its beautiful balconies. It has now become the **Museo Nacional de Historia**. ■ *0900-1700 (long queues on Sunday, closed Monday.* Its rooms were used by the Emperor Maximilian and the Empress Carlota during their brief reign. There is an impressive mural by Siqueiros, '*From the Dictatorship of Porfirio Díaz to the Revolution*' (in Sala XIII, near the

Bosque de Chapultepec

Mexico

entrance) and a notable mural by O'Gorman on the theme of independence as well as several by Camarena. Classical music concerts, free, are given on Sunday at 1200 by the Bellas Artes Chamber Orchestra; arrive early for a seat. ■ *Entrance US$4.35, free on Sunday.* Halfway down the hill is the new **Galería de Historia**, which has dioramas, with tape-recorded explanations of Mexican history, and photographs of the 1910 Revolution. Just below the castle are the remains of the famous Arbol de Moctezuma, known locally as 'El Sargento'. This immense tree, which has a circumference of 14 metres and was about 60 metres high, has been cut off at a height of about 10 metres.

Museo Nacional de Antropología
The crowning wonder of the park was built by architect Pedro Ramírez Vásquez to house a vast collection illustrating pre-conquest Mexican culture. It has a 350-metre façade and an immense patio shaded by a gigantic concrete mushroom, 4,200 square metres – the world's largest concrete and steel expanse supported by a single pillar. The largest exhibit (eight and a half metres high, weighing 167 tons) is the image of Tláloc the rain god, removed (accompanied by protesting cloud bursts) from near the town of Texcoco to the museum. Upstairs is a display of folk costumes, which may be closed Sunday. Attractions include *voladores* and Maya musicians. ■ *Tuesday-Saturday, 0900-1900 and Sunday, 1000-1800. Only Mexican student cards accepted. Entrance is US$2.50 except Sunday (free, and very crowded).*

Bosque de Chapultepec and Polanco

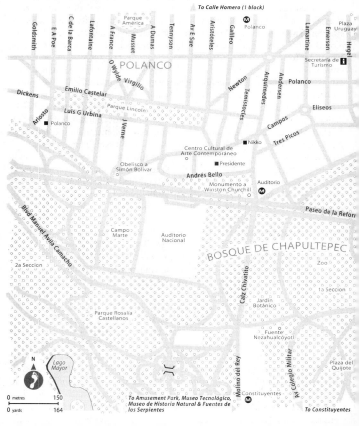

No written explanations in English. Guided tours in English or Spanish free with a minimum of five people. Ask for the parts you want to see as each tour only visits two of 23 halls. Excellent audio-visual introduction free (lasts one hour, includes 3D models). If you want to see everything, you need two days. Permission to photograph (no tripod or flash allowed) US$1.50, US$5 for video camera. On sale are English and Spanish books and a few in French and German, and guides to Mexican ruins, including maps. Guide books of the museum itself cost US$10-12. Cafetería on site is good, recommended, particularly for the soup, but pricey with long queues at times. The nearest metro is Auditorio.

Also in the first section of the Bosque de Chapultepec is the **Museo de Arte Moderno**, which shows Mexican art only in two buildings, pleasantly set among trees with some sculptures in the grounds. The smaller building shows temporary exhibitions. The delightfully light architecture of the larger building is spoilt by a heavy, vulgar marble staircase, with a curious acoustic effect on the central landing under a translucent dome, which must have been unplanned. ■ *1100-1800 daily except Monday(US$2, free with ISIC card)*. The **Museo Rufino Tamayo** (on the other side of Reforma, cross near the Museo de Arte Moderno, on the way to the Anthropological Museum) has a fine collection of works by Rufino Tamayo and shows contemporary Mexican and other painters. The interior space of the museum is unusual in that it is difficult to know which floor one is on. ■ *1000-1700 (closed*

Mexico

Monday), US$2, free to students with international card.

The second section of the Bosque de Chapultepec has a large amusement park. ■ *Wednesday, Friday and weekends, 1030-2000, US$1.*There is a wonderful section for children and another for adults and huge roller-coasters including the *Montaña Rusa*, one of the world's largest, on Saturday and Sunday only, US$0.40, bridle paths and polo grounds. Diego Rivera's famous fountain, the Fuente de Tláloc, is near the children's amusement park. Close by are the Fuentes de las Serpientes (Snake Fountains). There are two museums in this section: the **Museo de Tecnología** is free; it is operated by the Federal Electricity Commission, has touchable exhibits which demonstrate electrical and energy principles. It is located beside the roller-coasters. The **Museo de Historia Natural** is beside the Lago Menor of the second section. ■ *1000-1700, Tuesday to Sunday.* Both the Lago Menor and Lago Mayor are popular for boating; on the shore of each is a restaurant.

Centro Cultural de Arte Contemporáneo, Campos Elíseos y Jorge Eliot, Polanco (near *Hotel Presidente*, metro Polanco), has permanent and temporary exhibitions of painting, photography, installations (mostly Mexican), small entrance fee, highly recommended.

Modern buildings On Av Insurgentes Sur (at the corner of Mercaderes) is a remarkable building by Alejandro Prieto: the Teatro de Los Insurgentes, a theatre and opera house seating 1,300 people. The main frontage consists of a high curved wall without windows. This wall is entirely covered with mosaic decoration, the work of Diego Rivera: appropriate figures, scenes, and portraits composed round the central motif of a gigantic pair of hands holding a mask, worth going a distance to see.

The most successful religious architecture in Mexico today is to be found in the churches put up by Enrique de la Mora and Félix Candela; a good example is the chapel they built in 1957 for the Missionaries of the Holy Spirit, in a garden behind high walls at Av Universidad 1700. (An excellent Candela church, and easy to see, is the Church of La Medalla Milagrosa, just to the east of Av Universidad at the junction of Av División Norte, metro station División del Norte.) 'All the churches and chapels built by this team have such lightness and balance that they seem scarcely to rest on their foundations.' One of the seminal works of one of Mexico's greatest modern architects, Luís Barragán, is at Los Clubes, Las Arboledas bus from Chapultepec bus station. See also the *objet trouvé* mural at the Diana cinema in the centre of the city, and Orozco's great thundercloud of composition, the 'Apocalypse', at the Church of Jesús Nazareno. Both the *Camino Real Hotel* and the IBM technical centre were designed by Ricardo Legorreto; very well worth seeing. Consult Max Cetto's book on modern Mexican architecture. In this connection, University City (see page 304) is also well worth a look.

An example of modern hospital architecture is the huge Centro Médico Benito Juárez on Av Cuauhtémoc (corner with Morones Prieto), built after the 1985 earthquake. It contains a small shopping centre, theatre and art exhibition complex (Siglo XXI); entrance from metro station Centro Médico.

Museums and churches

For details of other museums, far from the centre, see under Suburbs, page 302, and Teotihuacan, page 310. **Museo de la Ciudad**, on Av Pino Suárez and República de El Salvador, shows the geology of the city and has life size figures in period costumes showing the history of different peoples before Cortés. It also has a photographic exhibition of the construction of the metro system. Permanent display sometimes inaccessible during temporary shows. In the attic above the museum is the studio of Joaquín Clausell, with walls covered with impressionist miniatures. ■ *Tuesday to Thursday. Free admittance.* Two blocks south of this museum at Mesones 139 is the **Anglican (Episcopal) Cathedral**, called the Cathedral of San José de Gracia. Built in 1642 as a Roman Catholic church, it was given by the Benito Juárez government to the Episcopal Mission in Mexico. Juárez himself often attended services in it.

Museo José-Luis Cuevas, Academia 13, in a large colonial building. It houses a permanent collection of paintings, drawings and sculptures (one is two-storeys high) by the controversial, contemporary Cuevas (**NB** the Sala Erótica), and temporary exhibitions. ■ *Tuesday-Friday 1000-1830, Saturday-Sunday 1000-1730, US$1.*

Museo Legislativo, inside Palacio Legislativo, Av Congreso de la Unión 66, entrance in Sidar y Rivorosa, metro Candelaria. ■ *1000-1800, closed Monday, free.* Shows development of the legislative processes in Mexico from pre-Hispanic times to the 20th century.

Museo Nacional de las Culturas, Moneda 13. ■ *0930-1800, closed Sunday, free.* Exhibits of countries from all over the world and some historical information.

The **Casa del Presidente Venustiano Carranza**, Lerma y Amazonas, is a museum.

Museo de la Charrería, on Isabel la Católica, esq José María Izazago, close to metro Isabel a Católica. Small, with interesting artefacts and history of the Charrea. Information labels in Spanish, English and some in French. ■ *Free.*

Museo de Arte Carrillo Gil, Av Revolución esq Los Leones, near San Angel; another museum of striking modern features, inside and out; paintings by Orozco, Rivera (**NB** some of his Cubist works), Siqueiros and others; ■ *US$3.35 entry*; good bookshop and cafetería.

Museo de Cera de la Ciudad de México (Wax Museum) in a remarkable house at Londres 6. ■ *1100-1900 daily.*

Museo de la Caricatura, C de Doncellas 97. ■ *Free.*

Instituto Nacional Indigenista, Av Revolución 1297.

Museo Universitario del Chopo, E G Martínez 10, between metro San Cosme and Insurgentes, near Insurgentes Norte. Contemporary international exhibitions (photography, art) in a church-like building designed by Eiffel. ■ *Wednesday-Sunday 1000-1400, 1600-1900.*

Casasola Archive, Praga 16, in Zona Rosa, T5649214, amazing photos of the revolutionary period, reproduction for sale.

The **Siqueiros Polyforum**, on Insurgentes Sur, includes a handicraft shop and a museum of art, with huge frescoes by Siqueiros, one of the largest in the world, inside the ovoid dome. ■ *Entrance to the frescoes US$0.40; open 1000-1900, closed for lunch.* Next door is the former *Hotel de México* skyscraper, which is to become Mexico's World Trade Centre.

The Plaza México is the largest bull ring in the world, with a capacity of some 55,000 **Bull Ring** spectators. It is situated in the Ciudad de los Deportes, just off Insurgentes Sur (Metro San Antonio or *pesero* to junction of Insurgentes Sur with Eje 5). With the

Mexico

Los Tres Grandes

The story of muralism in Mexico has largely been that of 'Los Tres Grandes', Diego Rivera, Jose Clemente Orozco and David Alfaro Siqueiros, although there were many other artists involved from the start. In 1914 Orozco and Siqueiros were to be found in the Carranza stronghold of Orizaba fomenting social and artistic revolution through the mouthpiece of the pamphlet 'La Vanguardia'. Seven years later, out of the turmoil and divisiveness of the Revolution, emerged a need for a visual expression of Mexican identity (Mexicanidad) and unity and in 1921 Orozco and Siqueiros answered the call of the Minister of Education, José Vasconcelos, to provide a visual analogue to a rapidly changing Mexico. Rivera was brought onto the team which in buildings like the National Preparatory School and the Ministry of Education attempted to produce a distinctly Mexican form of modernism, on a monumental scale, accessible to the people. These were ideas forged in Orizaba and later clarified in Europe (where Rivera and Siqueiros saw Italian frescoes) but which derived their popular form from paintings on the walls of pulquerías and in the satirical broadsheet engravings of José Guadalupe Posada. Themes were to include

Precolumbian society, modern agriculture and medicine and a didactic Mexican history pointing to a mechanized future for the benefit of all. Siqueiros in particular was keen to transform the working practice of artists who would henceforth work as members of cooperatives.

The 'movement' fell apart almost from its inception. There were riots objecting to the communist content of murals and the beginnings of a long ideological and artistic disagreement between Siqueiros and Rivera which would culminate on 28 August 1935 at the Palacio Bellas Artes with Rivera, brandishing a pistol, storming into a Siqueiros lecture and demanding a debate on what the Mexican Mural Renaissance had all been about! The debate ensued over several days before they agreed to disagree.

Despite the failings of the 'movement' many outstanding murals were painted over a long period. With Siqueiros frequently off the scene, in jail or in exile, 'Los Tres Grandes' became the big two; Rivera carving up much of Mexico City as his territory and Orozco taking on Guadalajara. However, Siqueiros outlasted both of them and carried the torch of muralism and revolution into the early 1970s.

apprentice season (*temporada chica*), running from May-October, and the *temporada grande,* from November-April, there are bull fights at 1600 or 1630 nearly every Sunday of the year. Alongside Madrid and Seville, the 'Mexico' is one of the world's three most important bull fighting venues. As virtually every great matador comes to fight in Mexico in the winter months, the chances of seeing an important event are high.

Admission charges range from US$1-18 in the cheaper *sol* (sun) half of the Plaza (binoculars almost essential in the upper rows and recommended in any case); seats in the *sombra* (shade) are more expensive, up to US$35 in the *barreras*. Best to buy tickets, especially for important fights, early on Saturday morning (from the *taquillas* at the Plaza). Details of what's on from the Plaza T5631659, or in the newspaper *'Ovaciones'*. Useful introductory reading to bull fighting includes Hemingway's *'Death in the Afternoon'*; Lapierre and Collins *'I'll Dress you in Mourning'*; and *'Matador'* magazine.

(A little to the west of where Los Insurgentes crosses Chapultepec, and on Av Chapultepec itself between C Praga and C Varsovia, are the remains of the old aqueduct built in 1779.) Besides the Bull Ring, the Sports City contains a football stadium holding 50,000 people, a boxing ring, a cinema, a *frontón* court for *jai-alai*, a swimming pool, restaurants, hotels, etc.

Mural sites

Aside from the main centres of mural painting already listed geographically in the text above (Palacio Nacional, Suprema Corte de Justicia, Palacio de Bellas Artes, Museo Mural Diego Rivera, Escuela Nacional Preparatoria-Ildefonso, Secretaría de Educación, Castillo de Chapultepec, Siqueiros Polyforum) there are other sites well worth visiting. They all lie within walking distance or short metro ride from the centre.

Tact should be shown when visiting these functioning workplaces – ask permission before heading off into labyrinthine buildings and always check about photo restrictions (invariably flash is prohibited).

Mercado Abelardo Rodríguez, on Venezuela, four blocks northeast of zócalo, with main entrance on Rodríguez Puebla, is fascinating as one of the only examples of a concerted attempt by a cooperative of artists of varying abilities, under the direction of Diego Rivera, to teach and record the *'workers revolution'* in an actual workers' environment. Today the work of this food market goes on, but the murals, at all the entrances, are largely ignored by traders and tourists alike. Perhaps the most emblematic is *'The Markets'* by Miguel Tzab on the ceiling above the stairs at the northwest entrance whilst Ramón Alva Guadarrama's *'The Labours of the Field'*, at the southeast corner reflects the market's agricultural base. Most elaborate are the murals of the American Greenwood sisters, Marion and Grace, showing *'Industrialization of the countryside'* and the *'Mine'*, on the stairs either side of the main entrance. Opposite, upstairs, is a relief mural by Isamu Noguchi. Permission to take photos must be gained from the market office behind the restaurant at the southwest entrance.

You can obtain a location plan of the murals at the tourist agency at No 72 on Venezuela beside the Teatro del Pueblo attached to the market. In the foyer of the theatre is Antonio Pujol's *'Problems of the Worker'*, much praised at time of completion in 1936. In the cloisters of the confusingly named Patio Diego Rivera, behind the ticket office, is Pablo O'Higgins' tirade against international fascism *'The Fight of the Workers against the Monopolies'*.

Next to the Museo Nacional de Arte is the **Cámara de Senadores**, Hipotenca Beride entre Donceles y Tacuba (Metro Allende or Bellas Artes), which has a violent mural (1957) by Jorge González Camarena, on the history of Mexico starting with the Pre-Cortesian battles between eagle and jaguar warriors.

The **Sindicato Nacional de Electricistas**, Antonio Caso 45 (west of Cristóbal Colón monument on Reforma), has one of Siqueiros' most important murals *'Portrait of the Bourgeoisie'* (1939-40), located up the second floor stairwell to the left of the entrance. It depicts the revolutionary struggle against international fascism and is considered a seminal work for its use of cinematic montage techniques and viewing points. Before taking photos ask permission in the *secretaría* office on the right at the end of the corridor on the second floor. 15-minute walk away at 118 Altamirano, Col San Rafael, is the **Teatro Jorge Negrete**, in the foyer of which is a later Siqueiros mural *'Theatrical Art in the Social Life of Mexico'* (1957), precursor in its expression of movement to his mural in Chapultepec Castle. Ask permission to see it in the office at No 128. No photos (nearest metro San Cosme).

At the **Hospital de La Raza** in what was once an outer entrance hall (but is now at the centre of the building) is Rivera's *'History of Medicine'* (1953) and to the left of the main entrance, in a naturally lit theatre foyer (usually locked but you can see it through the large frontal windows if there is nobody about with keys), is Siqueiros' *'For the Complete Safety of All Mexicans at Work'* (1952-54). Ask a security guard or at main reception for directions to the murals. (Metro La Raza – from station head south along right side of Insurgentes Norte, cross railway, straight ahead and then cross freeway by footbridge to the hospital). For permission to take photos here and at other medical centres you must ask permission at the Sede IMSS, Hidalgo 230 (Metro Bellas Artes).

Another hospital with a relevant themed mural is the **Centro Médico Nacional**, Av Cuauhtémoc, where Siqueiros' '*Apology for the Future Victory of Medicine over Cancer* (1958) has been restored following damage in the 1985 earthquake. Since 1996 it has been on display in the waiting area of the oncology building beyond the main entrance building on the right. At the entrance, as you come up the metro stairs, is a mural by Chávez Morado commemorating the rebuilding of the hospital in which many died during the earthquake (Metro Centro Médico).

Santa María La Ribera and San Cosme

These are two colonias (north of metro San Cosme) which became fashionable residential areas in the late 19th century, and many elegant, if neglected façades are to be seen. On the corner of Ribera de San Cosme and Naranjo (next to San Cosme metro) note the **Casa de los Mascarones**. Built in 1766, this was the Casa de Campo of the Conde del Valle de Orizaba, later the Escuela Nacional de Música. Recently restored, it now houses a UNAM computer centre. In the pleasant Alameda de Santa María, between Pino and Torres Bodet, stands an extraordinary Moorish pavilion designed by Mexicans for the Paris Exhibition in 1889. On its return to Mexico, the *kiosko* was placed in the Alameda Central, before being transferred to its present site in 1910. On the west side of this square, on Torres Bodet, is the **Museo del Instituto Geológico** of UNAM; apart from its collection of fossils and minerals (and magnificent early 20th century showcases), the building itself (1904) is worth a visit: swirling wrought-iron staircases and unusual stained-glass windows of mining scenes by Zettler (Munich and Mexico). ■ *Tuesday-Sunday 1000-1700, free.*

Sullivan Park (popularly known as Colonia Park or Jardín del Arte) is reached by going up Paseo de la Reforma to the intersection with Los Insurgentes, and then west two blocks between C Sullivan and C Villalongín. Here, each Sunday afternoon, there is a display of paintings, engravings and sculptures near the monument to La Madre, packed with sightseers and buyers; everything is for sale (beware of thieves).

   Reino Aventura, south of the city near the Mall del Sur, amusement park for children along Disneyland lines, clean, orderly, popular with families.

Basilica of Guadalupe The Basílica de Guadalupe, in the Gustavo A Madero district, often called La Villa de Guadalupe, in the outer suburbs to the northeast, is the most venerated shrine in Mexico, for it was here, in December 1531, that the Virgin appeared three times, in the guise of an Indian princess, to the Indian Juan Diego and imprinted her portrait on his cloak. The cloak is preserved, set in gold, but was moved into the new basilica next door in 1992, as a massive crack has appeared down the side of the old building. Visitors stand on a moving platform behind the altar to view the cloak. The huge, modern basilica is impressive and holds over 20,000 people (very crowded on Sunday). The original basilica has been converted into a museum, admission US$3. It still houses the original magnificent altar, but otherwise mostly representations of the image on the cloak, plus interesting painted tin plates offering thanks for cures, et cetera, from about 1860s. A chapel stands over the well which gushed at the spot where the Virgin appeared. The great day here is 12 December, the great night the night before: Indian dance groups provide entertainment in front of the Basilica. There are, in fact, about seven churches in the immediate neighbourhood, including one on the hill above (Iglesia del Cerrito – excellent view of the city, especially at night, free access); most of them are at crazy angles to each other and to the ground, because of subsidence; the subsoil is very soft. The **Templo de los Capuchinos** has been the subject of a remarkable feat of engineering in which one end has been raised 3,375 metres so that the building is now horizontal. There is a little platform from which to view this work. Buses marked La Villa go close to the site, or you can go by metro to La Villa (Line 6). The Virgin even has her own home page on the Internet, visit her on line at Interlupe. http://spin. com.mx/~msalazar.

Revolución, San Cosme, Santa María La Ribera

Mexico

Essentials
Sleeping

■ *on maps*
Price codes:
see inside front cover

Prices of the more expensive hotels do not normally include 15 percent tax; service is some-times included. Always check in advance. Reductions are often available; breakfast is rarely included in the room price. There are fair hotel reservation services at the railway station and at the airport; also services for more expensive hotels at bus stations.

Take care in the centre at quiet times (for example Sunday pm) and in Chapultepec (where Sunday is the safest day).

LL *Camino Real*, Mariano Escobedo 700, T52032121, F52506897. **LL** *Clarion Reforma Suites*, Paseo de la Reforma 373, T52078944, F52082719, new. **LL** *Four Seasons Mexico*, Paseo de la Reforma 500, T52301818, F52301817, new (1994), beautiful, excellent restaurant. **LL** *María Isabel Sheraton*, Paseo de la Reforma 325, T52073933, F52070684, opposite Angel of Independence, 'old-fashioned', all facilities, but restaurant overpriced. **LL** *Nikko*, Campos Eliseos 204, T52801111, F52809191. **LL** *Presidente*, Campos Eliseos 218, T53277700, F53277737, good location, exercise room. **LL** *Westin Galería Plaza*, Hamburgo 195, T52110014, F52075867, 3 restaurants, rooftop pool and gym. **LL** *Century*, Liverpool 152, T57269911, F55257475 (Golden Tulip hotel). **LL** *Fiesta Americana*, Paseo de la Reforma 80, T57051515, F57051313, with restaurants, bars, nightclubs, superior business facilities. **LL** *Imperial*, Reforma 64, T55664879, very good, restaurant, café, bar, 24-hour service, business facilities, etc. **LL** *Krystal*, Liverpool 155, T52289928, F55113490. A recommended hotel is the **LL** *Marco Polo*, Amberes 27, T52070299, F55333727, in the Zona Rosa, small, select

Zona Rosa & Colonia Cuauhtemoc

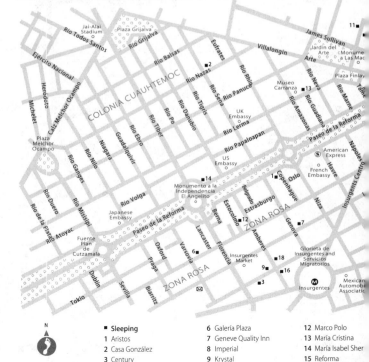

■ **Sleeping**	6 Galería Plaza	12 Marco Polo
1 Aristos	7 Geneve Quality Inn	13 María Cristina
2 Casa González	8 Imperial	14 María Isabel Sher
3 Century	9 Krystal	15 Reforma
4 Crowne Plaza	10 Madrid	16 Royal
5 Ejecutivo	11 Mallorca	17 Sevilla

0 metres 200
0 yards 219

hotel, price reductions at weekends, Mexican, Italian and international cuisine. **LL** *Marquis*, Paseo de la Reforma 465, Col Cuauhtémoc, T52113600, F52115561, new, all facilities, recommended as very fine. **LL** *Flamingos Plaza*, Av Revolución 333, T56270220, F55154850. **LL** *Royal Zona Rosa*, Amberes 78, T52289918, F55143330, good. **LL** *Howard Johnson Gran Hotel de México*, 16 de Septiembre 82 (Zócalo), T55104040, F55122085, has an incredible foyer, 30's style, 4th floor restaurant and balcony good for Zócalo-watching, especially on Sunday am (breakfast buffet US$10). *Crowne Plaza*, Paseo de la Reforma 1, T51285000, F51285050.

AL *Aristos*, Paseo de la Reforma 276, T52110112, F55256783. **AL** *Calinda Genève*, Londres 130, T52110071, F52087422, pleasant dining area. **AL** *Casa Blanca*, Lafragua 7 (1 block from Reforma and Revolución monument), T57051300, F57054197, modern. **AL** *Plaza Madrid*, Madrid 15, T57050836, F57050961. **AL** *Majestic* (Best Western), Madero 73 on Zócalo, T55218609, F55126262, interesting rooms, lots of tiles, carved wooden beams, large beds, quiet rooms overlook courtyard, magnificent breakfast in 7th floor restaurant with excellent views of centre. **AL** *Ritz* (Best Western), Madero 30, T55181340, F55183466. **AL** *Cortés* (Best Western), Av Hidalgo 85, T55182184, F55121863, is the only baroque-style hotel in Mexico City, a former pilgrims' guest house, with a pleasant patio, TV, good bathroom, no a/c or pool, quiet, good yet touristy floor show, good food. **AL** *María Cristina*, Lerma 31, T55669688, F55923447, attractive colonial style, comfortable, helpful, safe parking, recommended (book well in advance). **A** *Del Angel*, Río Lerma 154, T55331032. **A** *Ejecutivo*, Viena 8, T55666422, staff helpful, recommended. **A** *Metropol*, Luis Moya 39, T51086601, F55121273, good, clean, safe, touristy, average restaurant, good value, recommended. **A** *Regente*, París 9, T55668933, clean, friendly, noisy at front, restaurant. **A** *Royal Plaza*, Parroquia 1056, corner with Cuauhtémoc, T56058943 (**B** at weekends). **A** *Viena*, Marsella 28 (close to Juárez market and Cuauhtémoc metro), T55660700, quiet, Swiss decor, garage, dining room, recommended.

Hotels at or near the airport LL *Continental Plaza Aeropuerto*, Fundidora Monterrey 89, T52300505, entrance between sections B and C in airport, all facilities. **LL-L** *Ramada Ciudad de México*, Blvd Puerto Aéreo 502, T57858522, F57629934, free transport to/from airport. A short walk from the airport: **AL** *JR Plaza*, Blvd Puerto Aéreo 390, T57855200, F57843221, free transport to/from airport, expensive restaurant, quiet, good rooms with solid furniture, close to metro; next door is **A** *Aeropuerto*, Blvd Aeropuerto 380 (300 metres from airport over other side of highway) T57855318, noisy but OK, functional, expensive restaurant, good breakfast.

B *Brasilia*, excellent modern hotel, near Central del Nte bus station, on Av Cien Metros 48-25, T55878577, F53682714, king size bed, TV, 24-hour traffic jam in front. **B** *Cancún*, Donato Guerra 24, T55666083, F55666488, restaurant, safe, noisy, recommended. **B** *Catedral*, Donceles 95,

Jardin Pasteur

Monumento a Cristóbal Colón

Monumento Cuauhtémoc

Av Morelos

Atenas

Gral Prim

Lucerna

Viena

Milán

Lisboa

Versalles

Roma

amburgo

Berlin

Museo de Cera

Bruselas

Barcelona

Dinamarca

Bucareli

A González

Liverpool

Turín

Juárez Market

Marsella

Av Chapultepec

Plaza Morelia

Cuauhtemoc

Merida

Puebla

Morelia

Frontera

20

10

8

4

15

5

21

22

18 Suites Amberes
19 Suites Havre
20 Uxmal
21 Vasco de Quiroga
22 Viena

Mexico

T55182532, F55124344, behind Cathedral, clean, spacious, good service, recommended. **B** *Fleming*, Revillagigedo 35, T55104530, good value, central. **B** *Jena*, Jesús Terán 12, new, central, recommended (but not the travel agency on the premises). **B** *Lepanto*, Guerrero 90, TV, phone, modern, attractive, good restaurant. **B** *Mallorca*, Serapio Rendón 119, T55664833, clean, reasonable. **B** *Mayaland*, Maestro Antonio Caso 23, T55666066, with bath, good value, recommended, good restaurant. **B** *Palace*, Ignacio Ramírez 7, T55662400, very friendly, good restaurant. **B** *Polanco*, Edgar Poe 8, T52808082, near Chapultepec, dark, quiet, good restaurant. **B** *Premier*, Atenas 72, T55662701, good location, clean, front rooms noisy, will store bags. **B** *Prim*, Versalles 46, T55924600, F55924835, clean, good in all respects. **B** *Del Principado*, Londres 42, Zona Rosa (near Metro Insurgentes), T55332944, clean, rooms at back better, good restaurant. **B** *San Francisco*, Luis Moya 11, T55218960, F55108831, just off Alameda, great views, friendly, excellent value, takes credit cards, good set meals. **B** *Sevilla*, Serapio Rendón 126 and Sullivan, T55910522, restaurant, garage, reasonable (not to be confused with **AL** *Sevilla Palace*, Reforma 105, T55668877, which is smart). **B** *Vasco de Quiroga*, Londres 15 y Berlín, 3 minutes walk from Zona Rosa, T55462614, F55352257, clean, friendly, very good (ask for room away from the generator), restaurant downstairs.

C *Astor*, Antonio Caso 83, near Sullivan Park, new, clean, restaurant, recommended. **C** *Canadá*, Av 5 de Mayo 47, T55182106, F55211233, closest metro station Allende, with bath, hot water, TV, collect calls can be made for US$1, good value, friendly, helpful, no restaurant. **C** *Capitol*, Uruguay 12, T55181750, F55211149, attractive lobby, recently remodelled, TV, bath, clean, friendly, don't miss the restaurant in the same building: *El Malecón*. **C** *Casa González*, Lerma y Sena 69 (near British Embassy), T55143302, full board available, shower, English spoken by Sr González, clean, quiet and friendly, no credit cards, recommended. **C** *Congreso*, with bath, hot water, good, central, clean, quiet, TV, garage, at Allende 18, T55109888. **C** *Galicia*, Honduras 11, T55297791, good. **C** *Gilbert*, Amado Nervo 37, Col Buenavista, Mex 4DF, T55479260, good location but a bit spooky at night. **C** *Gillow*, 5 de Mayo e Isabel la Católica 17, T55181440, F55122078, central, large, clean, best rooms on 6th floor, many services, attractive, hospitable, good value, poor restaurant. **C** *La Villa de los Quijotes*, Moctezuma 20, near Basílica Guadalupe (metro La Villa), T55771088, modern, quiet, clean, expensive restaurant. **C** *Marlowe*, Independencia 17, T55219540, clean, but poor restaurant (tourist office at airport refers many travellers here – if this one is too expensive, the cheaper *Concordia*, see below, is round the corner). **C** *New York*, Edison 45, large, clean rooms, expensive restaurants. **C** *Parador Washington*, Dinamarca 42 y Londres, with bath, clean, safe area, café next door. **C** *Pisa*, Insurgentes Nte 58, recommended. **C** *Uxmal*, Madrid 13, quite close to Zona Rosa, clean rooms, same owner as more expensive *Madrid*, next door, No 15, T57050836, F57050961, with access to their better facilities, recommended.

The best of the cheaper hotels are in the old part of town between the Zócalo and the Alameda.

Near Allende metro **D** *Antillas*, B Domínguez 34, T55265674, with bath and TV, friendly, stores luggage. **D** *Atlanta*, corner of B Domínguez and Allende, T55181201, good, clean, quiet if you ask for a room away from street, friendly, luggage store. **D** *Avenidas*, Lázaro Cárdenas 38 (Bellas Artes metro), T55181007, with bath, central, friendly, will store luggage, good value, cheapest hotel that can be booked at airport. **D-E** *Cuba*, on Cuba 69, T55181380, with bath, TV, good beds but sheets too small, noisy. **D** *Florida*, Belisario Domínguez 57, TV, shower, clean, recommended. **D** *Lafayette*, Motolinia 40 and 16 de Septiembre, with bath, and TV, good, clean, quiet (pedestrian precinct), but check rooms, there's a variety of sizes. **D** *Principal*, C Bolívar 29, with bath, central, OK, friendly owner. **D** *San Antonio*, 2nd Callejón, 5 de Mayo 29, T55129906, clean, pleasant, popular, friendly, TV in room, recommended. **D** *Toledo*, López 22 (Bellas Artes Metro), T55213249, with bath, TV, warmly recommended. **D-E** *Habana*, República de Cuba 77 (near metro Allende), spacious rooms, huge beds, renovated, very clean, phone, TV, friendly and helpful staff, highly recommended. **D-E** *Isabel la Católica* on street of the same name, No 63, T55181213, F55211233, is pleasant, popular, clean, helpful, safe (taxi drivers must register at desk before taking passengers), roof terrace, large shabby rooms with bath and hot water (some without windows), central, a bit noisy, fax service, quite good restaurant, luggage held, rooms on top floor with shared bathroom are cheaper, recommended. **F** *Princess*, Cuba 55, with bath, good value, TV, fairly secure, front rooms noisy. **F** *Republica*, Cuba 57, T55129517, with bath, hot water, rooms upstairs quieter, 3 blocks from Bellas Artes, recommended. **E** *La Marina*, Allende 30 y B Domínguez, clean, comfortable, safe, friendly, TV, hot water, will store luggage, recommended. **F** per person (4-bed dormitories) *Pension del Centro*, Cuba 74, apt203 y Chile, Centro Histórico, T55120832, paic@data.net.mx, laundry, luggage store, email service. **E** *Rioja*, Av 5 de Mayo 45, T55218333, shared or private baths, reliable hot water, clean, popular, luggage store, well placed, recommended, next door to *Canadá*, see above; opposite are **E** *Juárez*, in small alley on 5 de Mayo 17, 1 minute walk from Zócalo, T55126929, ask for room with window, safe, clean, with bath, phone, radio, TV, recommended, and **F** *Zamora*, No 50, clean, cheap, hot water, some find it OK, others say it is falling apart, good *Café El Popular* next door. **D-E** *Washington*, Av 5 de Mayo 54, clean, small rooms, cable TV. **D** *Buenos Aires*, Av 5 de Mayo, safe, friendly, TV, stores luggage, hot water.

North of the Zócalo **E** *Tuxpán*, on Colombia, near Brasil, modern, clean, TV, hot shower. **F** *Rio de Janeiro*, on Brasil, near Colombia, dirty, noisy. **E** *Azores*, Brasil 25, T55215220, large rooms, TV, a/c.

North of Hildago metro **D** *Managua*, on Plaza de la Iglesia de San Fernando, with bath, phone, TV, good location, car park, very friendly, run down. **D** *Mina*, Jose T Salgado 18, esq Mina, T57031682, modern, clean, TV, large beds. **D** *Monaco* opposite, Guerrero 12, T55668333, comfortable, TV, modern, good service. almost behind is *La Fuente*, Orozco y Berra 10, T55669122, bath, TV, garage, bar (noisy bar opposite). **D** *Detroit*, Zaragoza 55, T55911088, hot shower, central, clean, has parking. **D** *Savoy*, Zaragoza 10, T55664611, near Hidalgo metro, convenient for Zócalo, with bath and hot water, clean, phone, TV, modernized, good value.

North of the Plaza de la República **C** *Oxford*, Ignacio Mariscal 67, T55660500, very clean, radio and satellite TV, helpful, but short stay. **C** *Texas*, Ignacio Mariscal 129, T55644626, with bath, clean, hot water, small rooms, good breakfasts. **D** *América*, Buena Vista 4 (near Revolución metro), with bath, hot water, TV, good service, recommended. **D** *Royalty*, Jesús Terán 21, opposite *Hotel Jena*, with bath, TV, clean, very quiet, near Hidalgo metro. **E** *Carlton*, Ignacio Mariscal 32-bis, T55662911, getting rough around the edges, small rooms but some with fine views, rooms at front noisy, recommended, good restaurant. **E** *Pennsylvania*, Ignacio Mariscal 15, T55350070, with bath, clean, TV. **E-F** *Casa de los Amigos*, Ignacio Mariscal 132 (T57050521/0646), near train and bus station (metro Revolución), in dormitory, **D-E** in double room, pay 2 nights in advance, use of kitchen, recommended, maximum 15-day stay, separation of sexes, run by Quakers for Quakers, or development-work related travellers, other travellers taken only if space is available, good information on volunteer work, travel and language schools, breakfast US$2.50 (weekdays only) and laundry facilities on roof, safe-keeping for luggage, English library, references or advance booking recommended. **E** *El Paraíso*, Ignacio Mariscal 99, T55668077, hot water, clean, private bath, TV, phone, recently renovated, friendly. **D** *Frimont*, Jesús Terán 35, T57054169, clean, central.

Near the railway station **D** *Pontevedra*, Insurgentes Nte opposite railway station, bath, hot water, TV, clean, helpful, will store luggage. **D** *Santander*, Arista 22, not far from railway station, with bath, good value and service, clean. **D** *Nueva Estación*, Zaragoza opposite Buenavista station, with bath, clean, quiet, friendly, colour TV. **D** *Yale*, Mosqueta 200, 5 minutes walk from Buenavista station, showers, toilet, large room with TV and phone, very good value, recommended. **D** *Encino*, Av Insurgentes, 1 block from the railway station, clean, private bath. **E** *Atoyac*, Eje de Guerrero 161, Col Guerrero, 200 metres from metro, clean, friendly, safe.

South of the Zócalo **D** *Concordia*, Uruguay 13, clean, hot water, friendly, some rooms airless, lift, phone, noisy. **D** *El Roble*, Uruguay y Pino Suárez, bath, TV, restaurant closes early, recommended. **D** *El Salvador*, Rep de El Salvador 16, T55211247, near Zócalo, modern, clean, laundry, safe, parking, good value. **D** *Monte Carlo*, Uruguay 69, T55181418/ 55212559/55219363 (D H Lawrence's hotel), elegant, clean, friendly owner (also suites), with bath, hot water, good about storing luggage, safe car park inside the hotel premises, US$3.45, rooms in front noisy, even rooms at the back vibrate with noise from disco 2230-0300 Wednesday-Saturday, can make collect calls abroad from room. **F** *San Pedro*, Mesones 126 and Pino Suárez, with bath, TV, tiny rooms, clean (but the occasional cock-roach) and friendly, good value.

South of the Alameda **D** *Danky*, Donato Guerra 10, with bath, central, hot water, phone, clean, easy parking (T55469960/61), recommended. **E** *Fornos*, Revillagigedo 92, near Balderas metro, 10 minutes walk to Alameda, extremely clean, bathroom, TV, radio, smarter bigger rooms for **D**, restaurant, large, indoor car park, friendly staff, Dutch-speaking, Spanish owner, very good value, highly recommended. **E** *Meave*, C Meave 6, esq Lázaro Cárdenas, T55216712, bath, TV, clean, quiet, very friendly, ground floor rooms rented by hour, but very discreet, recommended.

For longer stays, **B** *Suites Quinta Palo Verde*, Cerro del Otate 20, Col Romero de Terreros (Mexico 21 DF) T55543575, pleasant, diplomatic residence turned guest house, near the University; run by a veterinary surgeon, Miguel Angel, very friendly, speaks English and German, but the dogs are sometimes noisy. *Suites Amberes*, Amberes 64, Zona Rosa, T55331306, F52071509, kitchenette, good value, recommended. *Suites Havre*, Havre 74, T55335670, near Zona Rosa, recommended for longer stays, 56 suites with kitchen, phone and service. *Club Med* head office for Club Med and *Villas Arqueológicas* reservations, C Masaryk 183, Col Polanco, México 11570, T52033086/3833, Tx1763346.

Campsites Campo Escuela Nacional de Tantoco, Km 29.5 on road Mexico-City to Toluca, T55122279, cabins and campsite. The Dirección de Villas Deportivas Juveniles, address below (Condep), has details of campsites throughout the country; site in the capital, T56655027. They have either camping, or camping and dormitory accommodation on sites with additional facilities, including luggage lockers; ask in advance what documentation is required. The nearest trailer park is *Pepe's* in Tepotzotlán (see **Excursions** below), 43 kilo-metres north of the capital (address: Eva Sámano de López Mateos 62, T58760515/0616, in Mexico City, *Mallorca Travel Service,* Paseo de la Reforma 105, T57052424, F57052673); it costs about US$12 a night, 55 pads with full hook-ups, very friendly, clean, hot showers, Canadian run, recommended (owner has a hotel in Mexico City it you want to leave your trailer here and stay in the capital). If you want to bring your car into the city, find a cheap hotel where you can park and leave it, while you explore the city by bus, metro or on foot. Or try camping in the parking lot of the Museum of Anthropology.

Youth hostels Asociación Mexicana de Albergues de la Juventud, Madero 6, Of 314, México 1, D F. Write for information. There is a similar organization, Comisión Nacional del Deporte (Condep), which runs the Villas Deportivas Juveniles (see above); information office at Glorieta del Metro Insurgentes, local C-11, T55252916/55331291. Condep will make reser-vations for groups of 10 or more; to qualify you must be between 8 and 65 and have a 'tarjeta plan verde' membership card, US$6, valid 2 years, obtainable within 24 hours from office at Tlalpan 583, esq Soria, metro Xola, or a IYHF card. See also Setej, below, for information on hotels and other establishments offering lodging for students.

Eating

All the best hotels have good restaurants. The number and variety of restaurants throughout the city is vast; the following is a small selection.

Mexican food Note the *Hotel Majestic's* Mexican breakfast, Saturday and Sunday till 1200, excellent, go to terrace on 7th floor, otherwise food mediocre, live music. *San Angel Inn*, Las Palmas 50, in San Angel, is excellent and very popular, so book well in advance (San Angel can be reached by metro to Barranca del Muerto and bus 5 along Revolución). *Hostelería Santo Domingo*, Belisario Domínguez, 2 blocks west of Plaza Santo Domingo, good food and service, excellent music, the oldest restaurant in the city. *La Plancha Azteca*, Río Lerma

54, good tacos and tortas, moderate prices. *La Puerta del Angel*, Varsovia y Londres, local food and specializing in American cuts, very good. *Fonda del Recuerdo* for excellent *mole poblano,* Bahía de las Palmas 39A, 17DF, with music. *Club de Periodistas de México*, F Mata 8, near 5 de Mayo, open to public, OK. *Opera Bar*, 5 de Mayo near Bellas Artes, good atmosphere, expensive, see Pancho Villa's bullet-hole in ceiling (cocktails made with foreign spirits are 3 times as expensive as tequila). *Cardenal*, C Palma 23, food, service and music (from 1530) is outstanding, 1930s ambience. *Casa Zavala*, Bolívar y Uruguay, cheap, large selection of dishes. *El Huequito*, Bolívar 58, casual, friendly, cheap meals for US$2. *Focolare*, Hamburgo 87 (swank and high priced). *Taquería Lobo Bobo*, Insurgentes Sur 2117, excellent food, quite cheap, very friendly. *Nadja*, Mesones 65, near Pino Suárez, typical food, set menu for US$1.30, large portions, friendly, recommended. A very old restaurant with stunning tile décor and not touristy is the *Café Tacuba*, Tacuba 28, it specializes in Mexican food, very good enchiladas, tamales and fruit desserts, good service, live music, recommended. *México Viejo*, Tacuba 86 (near Zócalo), excellent breakfast, not touristy, pricey. *El Refugio*, Liverpool 166, tourist-oriented, good desserts, check bill carefully. *Doneraky*, Nuevo León y Laredo (Col Condesa), good tacos, recommended. *Don Albis*, Tomás Edison 100, delicious large cheap meals, popular with office workers. *La Luna*, Oslo y Copenhague, Zona Rosa, mostly Mexican, good breakfasts. *Casa Neri*, Bélgica 211, Col Portales, excellent authentic cooking, Oaxacan specialities, huge *comida corrida* for US$4. *La Lupe*, C Industria, metro: Coyoacán, leafy patio, good and cheap, open till 1800. Almost everywhere are American-style restaurant chains, eg *Vips, Toks, El Portón, Lyni's* and *Sanborns*, offering Mexican and international food, clean and reliable, but by no means cheap by local standards (breakfast US$3.50, lunch US$7).

International *Delmonico's*, Londres 87 and 16 de Septiembre 82, elegant *Jena*, Morelos 110 (deservedly famous, à la carte, expensive). *La Cava*, Insurgentes Sur 2465 (excellent food and steaks, lavishly decorated as an old French tavern, moderate). *Andreson's*, Reforma 400, very good atmosphere, excellent local menu, not cheap. *Keops*, Hamburgo 146, near Amberes in Zona Rosa, T55256706, reasonable food, good live music. also in Zona Rosa are *La Calesa de Londres*, Londres 102, good meat. and *Carousel Internacional*, Hamburgo and Niza, very popular drinking-hole for smartly-dressed Mexicans, resident Mariachi, food not gourmet but fun atmosphere, about US$15 per person. *Trevi*, Dr Mora y Colón (west end of Alameda), Italian/US/Mexican, reasonable prices. *Milomita*, Mesones 87, Centro, 0800-2000, specializes in American cuts of meat.

US and other Latin American *Sanborn's*, 36 locations (known as the foreigners' home-from-home) soda fountain, drugstore, restaurant, English, German and Spanish language magazines, handicrafts, chocolates, etc, try their restaurant in the famous 16th century *Casa de los Azulejos*, the 'house of tiles' at Av Madero 17, poor service, but many delicious local dishes in beautiful high-ceilinged room, about US$15-20 per person without wine (also has handicraft shops in basement and 1st floor). *New York Deli and Bagel*, Av Revolución 1321, just south of metro Barranca del Muerto, 0800-0100, good coffee and full meals available. Many US chain fast-food restaurants (eg *Burger Boy* for good value breakfasts, *McDonalds* and *Dunkin Donuts* on Madero). *Rincón Gaucho*, Insurgentes Sur 1162, Argentine food. Also Argenine, *Esquina La Pibe*, two locations just off Madero, OK. *El Patio del Gaucho*, Uruguay, moderate prices, attentive service, good *asado*, recommended.

Spanish *del Cid*, Humboldt 61, Castilian with medieval menu. *El Faro*, Belgrado y Reforma, Zona Rosa, very good, US$25-30 per head, closed in evenings except Thursday and Friday, closed Saturday. *Mesón del Castellano*, Bolívar y Uruguay, T518 6080, good atmosphere, plentiful and not too dear, excellent steaks, highly recommended. *Centro Catalán*, Bolívar 31, open 1100-1700 only, excellent paella and other Spanish cuisine (2nd floor). *Centro Castellano*, on Uruguay, excellent, cheap, try the steaks. *Vasco*, Madero 6, 1st Floor. *Mesón del Perro Andaluz*, Copenhague 26, and Luis P Ogazón 89, very pleasant.

Other European French cuisine at *Le Gourmet*, Dakota 155, said to be most expensive restaurant in Mexico, and also said to be worth it! *Ambassadeurs*, Paseo de la Reforma 12, swank and high priced. *Les Moustaches*, Río Sena 88 (second most expensive in town, probably). *Bellinghausen*, Londres y Niza, excellent food, lunch only, another branch *Casa Bell*, Praga 14, T5115733, smaller, identical menu, old house, elegant, recommended. *Chalet Suizo*, Niza 37, very popular with tourists, specializes in Swiss and German food, moderate. *Grotto Ticino*, Florencion 33, Swiss food, recommended. *Rivoli*, Hamburgo 123, a gourmet's delight, high priced. *Café Konditori*, Génova 61, Danish open sandwiches. *La Gondola*, Genova, great pasta. *La Casserole*, Insurgentes Sur 1880, near Núcleo Radio Mil building, French. *Sir Winston Churchill*, Avila Camacho 67, serves British food, expensive, smart, popular.

Oriental *Mr Lee*, Independencia 19-B, Chinese, seafood, good food, value and service. *Chen Wan*, Bolívar 104, large portions, set meal US$2-3.

Seafood *La Costa Azul*, López 127, y Delicias, Centro, good, cold lighting, reasonable prices. *Marisquito*, near Congress on Doncelo 12, very good.

Vegetarian *Restaurante Vegetariano*, Filomeno Mata 13, open until 2000, Sunday 0900-1900, good *menú del día* US$3. *Chalet Vegetariano*, near Dr Río de la Loza. *El Bosque*, Hamburgo 15 between Berlín and Dinamarca, recommended. Vegetarian restaurant at Motolinia 31, near Madero, is open Monday-Saturday 1300-1800, reasonably priced. *Karl*, on Amberes near junction Londres, excellent buffet lunch and dinner. *Saks*, Insurgentes Sur 1641, close to Teatro Insurgentes, very good. *Yug*, Varsovia 3, cheap vegetarian, 4-course set lunch US$3.50 (not very special). *Super Soya*, Tacuba, metro Allende, good juices and fruit salads, health food shop.

The best place to buy natural products is in the San Juan market (see **Markets** below), including tofu (*Queso de Soja*). Health food shop, *Alimentos Naturales*, close to metro Revolución, on P Arriagal. Health food shops in other metro stations.

A selection of restaurants in Polanco (in the lower price ranges): *La Parrilla Suiza*, Arquimedes y Pres Masaryk, for grilled meats, *alambres, sopa de tortilla* and other meat-and-cheese dishes, very popular, especially 1400-1600, service fair, moderately priced. *The City Bistro*, Lope de Vega 341, north of Horacio, serves finest English and international cuisine, also stunningly inventive dishes, moderately priced. *Zeco*, Sudermann 336, T55315211, Mexican-Italian, very good, middle price range, wines expensive. *Addetto*, Av Revolución 1382, Col Guadalupe Inn, T5625434, same ownership. *El Buen Comer Marcelín*, Edgar Allan Poe 50, T52035337, mainly French, very good. *Cambalache*, Arquimedes north of Pres Masaryk, Argentine steakhouse, good steaks, wide selection of wines, cosy atmosphere, not as expensive as *El Rincón Argentino*, Pres Masaryk 181, which is very expensive. For *tacos* and other tortilla-based dishes: *Los Tacos*, Newton just south of Horacio, inexpensive. *Chilango's*, Molière between Ejército Nacional and Homero, good value and service, MTV videos, recommended. *El Tizoncito*, south of Ejército Nacional just west of Pabellón Polanco mall, very popular at lunchtime. *El Jarrocho*, Homero between Emerson and Hegel, informal, eat-at-counter place, in expensive. *Embers*, Seneca y Ejército Nacional, 43 types of excellent hamburger, good French fries, recommended.

Cafés etc Many economical restaurants on 5 de Mayo, eg *Café La Blanca* at No 40, popular and busy atmosphere, good expresso coffee, recommended, open for Sunday breakfast and early on weekdays. *Torta Brava*, near Zócalo, good *comida*, friendly. *París*, No 10, good breakfast and dinner. *Popular*, No 52 between Alameda and Zócalo, on corner of alley to *Hotel Juárez*, cheap, rushed, 24 hours, meeting place. *Gili's Pollo*, opposite *Hotel Rioja*, excellent chicken, eat in or takeaway. *El 20 de Bolívar*, Bolívar 20, excellent service and highly recommended for breakfasts. *Comida Económica Verónica*, República de Cuba, 2 doors from *Hotel Habana* (No 77), recommended for tasty breakfasts and set *comida corrida*, very hot *chilaquiles*, good value and delightful staff. *La Rosita*, 2a C de Allende 14-C, cheap and good.

El Reloj, 5 de Febrero 50, good *comida* and à la carte. *Rex*, 5 de Febrero 40, near Zócalo, good café con leche and cheap *comidas*. *Shakey's*, Monte de Piedad (at the Zócalo), self-service, large helpings of pizza and chicken. *Pastelería Madrid*, 5 de Febrero 25, 1 block from *Hotel Isabel La Católica*, good pastries and breakfasts. *Bamerette*, Av Juárez 52 (*Hotel Bamer*), excellent breakfast. Good small restaurants in Uruguay, near *Monte Carlo Hotel*. the **Maple**, next to *Hotel Roble* at No 109, has been recommended for its *comida*, and *Pancho* (No 84), for its breakfasts, cheap meals and service. *Flor*, San Jerónimo 100, near *Hotel Ambar*, recommended for breakfast, non-touristy atmosphere, cheap. *Tic Tac*, Av Balderas, very good *comida corrida*. *La Habana*, Bucareli y Morelos, not cheap but good food and excellent coffee. Another centre for small restaurants is Pasaje Jacarandas, off Génova 44: *Llave de Oro* and many others. *La Casa del Pavo*, Motolinia near 16 de Septiembre, clean, courteous, excellent *comida corrida*. also C Motilinia between 5 de Mayo y Tacuba. Cheap cafeterías in C Belisario Domínguez. *Gaby's*, Liverpool y Napolés, excellent italian-style coffee, décor of old coffee machines etc. *Duca d'Este*, Av Florencia y Hamburgo, good coffee and pastries. *Il Mangiare*, opposite Siqueiros Polyforum (see above), very good sandwiches. *El Núcleo*, Lerma y Marne, excellent fruit salads, breakfasts and lunches, closes 1800 and all day Sunday. *Zenón*, corner of Madero 65 and Palma, trendy decor, average Mexican food, *comida corrida* US$1.50-3.50. *Enanos de Tapanco y Café*, Orizaba 161, between Querétaro and San Luis Potosí, great coffee, warm friendly atmosphere. Good breakfasts can be had at *Woolworth*, 16 de Septiembre. *Dulcería de Celaya*, 5 de Mayo 39, good candy store and lovely old premises. Good bakeries on 16 de Noviembre, near Zócalo. also *Panadería La Vasconia*, Tacuba 73, good, also sells cheap chicken and fries. *Jugos California* on Guerrero by Hidalgo metro, good juices. *Roxy*, Montes de Ocay Mazatlán (Col Condesa), good ice cream. Good juices and sandwiches at the *Juguería* on 5 de Mayo, next to *Hotel Rioja*. *El Sol*, Gómez Farías 67, Col San Rafael, frequented by journalists, superb Mexican cuisine, *comida corrida* US$2. See page 298, Internet for cybercafés.

Bar Jardín, in the *Hotel Reforma*. *El Morroco*, Conjunto Marrakesh, C Florencia 36. *Casino*, Isabel La Católica, near *Sanborn's*, superb painted glass doors and lavish interior, also has Spanish restaurant. *Abundio*, Zaragoza y Mosqueta, very friendly, free food. *Yuppies Sports Bar*, Genova, expensive but good atmosphere. Many safe gay bars in the Zona Rosa in the area between Niza and Florencia, north of Londres. | **Bars**

Entertainment, festivals and shopping

Cabarets and nightclubs Every large hotel has one. *El Patio*, Atenas 9. *Passepartout*, C Hamburgo. *La Madelon*, Florencia 36. *Brasileirinho*, León 160. *Guadalupana*, near Plaza Hidalgo, Coyoacán. There are many discotheques in the better hotels and scattered throughout town.

Cinemas A number show non-Hollywood films in original language (Spanish subtitles); check *Tiempo Libre* magazine, or *Mexico City News* for details. Some recommended cinemas are: *Cineteca Nacional*, metro Coyoacán (excellent bookshop on the cinema and related topics, library). *Cinematógrafo del Chopo*, C Dr Atl, non-commercial films daily 1700 and 1930, US$1; good cinema in Ciudad Universitaria; *Cine Latino*, Av Reforma between the statue of Cuauhtémoc and El Angel. *Cine Versalles*, Versalles (side street off Av Reforma, near statue of Cuauhtémoc). *Cine Electra*, Río Guadalquivir (near El Angel). *Cine Diana*, Av Reforma, at the end where Parque Chapultepec starts. *Cine Palacio Chino*, in the Chinese *barrio* south of Av Juárez (also interesting for restaurants). The sound is often very low on subtitled films, only option is to sit near speakers at front. Most cinemas, except *Cineteca Nacional*, charge half-price on Wednesday.

Folk music A fine place for light refreshments and music is the *Hostería del Bohemio*, formerly the San Hipólito monastery, near Reforma on Av Hidalgo 107, metro Hidalgo: poetry and music every night from 1700 to 2200, light snacks and refreshments US$4 minimum, expensive but no cover charge.

Entertainment

For all cultural events, consult Tiempo Libre, every Thursday from news stands, US$1, or monthly programme pamphlets from Bellas Artes bookshop.

Mexico

Theatres *Palacio de Bellas Artes* (for ballet, songs, dances, also concerts 2-3 times a week, see page 270), *Fábregas*, *Lírico*, *Iris*, *Sullivan*, *Alarcón*, *Hidalgo*, *Urueta*, *San Rafael* and *Insurgentes* in town and a cluster of theatres around the Auditorio Nacional in Chapultepec Park (check at Tourist Office for details of cheap programmes). Spectaculars (eg presidential inauguration) are often staged in the Auditorio Nacional itself. Also in Chapultepec Park is the Audiorama (behind the Castle on the Constituyentes side) where one may listen to recorded classical music in a small open ampitheatre in a charming wooded glade. A request book is provided, for the following day. There may be a free performance of a play in one of the parks by the Teatro Trashumante (Nomadic Theatre). Variety show nightly with singers, dancers, comedians, magicians and ventriloquists, very popular with locals, at *Teatro la Blanquita*, on Av Lazaro Cárdenas Sur near Plaza Garibaldi. The *Teatro de la Ciudad*, Donceles 36 (T55102197 and 55102942) has the Ballet Folklórico Nacional Aztlán, US$3-15 for tickets, very good shows Sunday am and Wednesday. On Sunday there is afternoon bull-fighting in a vast ring (see page 277). The balloon sellers are everywhere.

Festivals The largest is the Independence celebration on **15 September**, when the President gives the *grito*: 'Viva México' from the Palacio Nacional on the Zócalo at 2300, and rings the Liberty Bell (now, sadly, electronic!). This is followed by fireworks, and on **16 September** (0900-1400) there are military and traditional regional parades in the Zócalo and surrounding streets – great atmosphere.

Shopping Mexican jewellery and hand-made silver can be bought everywhere. Among the good silver shops are *Sanborn's*, *Calpini*, *Prieto*, and *Vendome*. Joyería Sobre Diseño (local 159) at the Ciudadela Market is helpful and will produce personalized jewellery cheaply. There are also good buys in perfumes, quality leather, and suede articles. *De Sol* on 16 de Septiembre, and on Periférico Sur, T58068427, for cheap food, drinks, clothes, domestic goods, etc. With the extension of the ring roads around the city, hypermarkets are being set up: there are 2, *Perisur* in the south of the city (with Liverpool, Sears, Sanborn's and Palacio de Hierro), open Tuesday-Friday 1100-2000, Saturday 1100-2100; and *Plaza Satélite* in the north (with Sumesa, Sears and Liverpool), open on Sunday. There is an ISSSTE supermarket in Tres Guerras, 2 blocks from metro Balderas and 1 block from Bucaveli. Luggage repairs (moderate prices) at Rinconada de Jesús 15-G, opposite Museo de la Ciudad de México on Pino Suárez, but opening times can be unreliable; better try the shop in Callejón del Parque del Conde off Pino Suárez opposite Hospital de Jesús church. At Pino Suárez metro station are several shops selling *charro* clothing and equipment (leggings, boots, spurs, bags, saddles, etc), eg *Casa Iturriaga*, recommended. Many small tailors are found in and around República de Brasil; suits made to measure in a week or less at a fraction of European prices. Guatemalan Refugee shop, Yosemite 45, Col Nápoles, off Insurgentes Sur, T5232114.

Art supplies *Casa Bernstein*, Rep de El Salvador 66.

Bookshops Many good ones in the city centre, especially along Av Juárez, Madero and Donceles, also along Miguel Angel de Quevedo (Coyoacán/San Angel – metro M A de Quevedo). Good literary and art bookshops belonging to *Educal* in the Palacio de Bellas Artes, the airport (area D), the Centro Nacional de Las Artes, the Cineteca Nacional, Coyoacán (Av Hidalgo), Museo del Carmen (San Angel) and the Museo Nacional de las Culturas (Moneda 13, Centro). Several shops belonging to the *Gandhi* chain (large selection, keen prices), main branch on Miguel Angel de Quevedo (good coffee upstairs), another opposite Palacio de Bellas Artes. One of the most famous bookshops is *El Parnaso*, Jardín Centenario, Coyoacán (its coffee is equally well known). Others include *Librería Británica*, Serapio Rendón 125 (near Parque Sullivan, west of Monumento Cuauhtémoc on Reforma), also Madero 30-A (limited range of titles in English). The *American Bookstore* (Madero 25, also on Revolución – 5-minute bus ride south from metro Barranca del Muerte) is much better in this and other respects – large stocks of Penguins and Pelicans, low mark up. For inexpensive editions in Spanish look out for branches of the *Librería del Sótano* (Av Juárez, Antonio Caso, M A de Quevedo), and of the *Fondo de Cultura Económico* (M A de Quevedo).

Librería Madero, Madero 12, good, also stocks antiquarian books. *Libros, Libros, Libros*, Monte Ararat 220, Lomas Barrilaco, T55404778, hundreds of hardback and paperback English titles; the shop at the entrance to the Templo Mayor has a good selection of travel books and guides in many languages. *Nueva Librería Francesa*, Hamburgo 172, T55251173/1213. *Librería Italiana*, Plaza Río de Janeiro 53, Col Roma, T55116180. The *Sanborn* chain has the largest selection of English-language magazines in the country, also stocks some best-selling paperbacks in English. *Casa Libros*, Monte Athos 355 (Lomas), large stock of second-hand English books, the shop is staffed by volunteers, gifts of books welcome, all proceeds to the American Benevolent Society. *Libros y Discos*, Madero 1. Plenty of Spanish bookshops on C Argentina and many open-shelf bookstores in the underpass between metros Zócalo and Pino Suárez. *UNAM* bookshop has a comprehensive range. Second-hand book market on Independencia just past junction with Eje Lázaro Cárdenas has some English books; also Puente de Alvarado, 100 metres from Hidalgo metro, and Dr Bernard 42, metro Niños Héroes. Second-hand Spanish and antiquarian booksellers on Donceles between Palma and República de Brasil, about 1½ blocks from Zócalo. *La Torre de Papel*, Filomeno Mata 6-A, in Club de Periodistas, sells newspapers from all over Mexico and USA. See also section on newspapers (**Essentials**).

Cycle shops *Tecno-Bicí*, Av Manuel Acuna 27 (Camarones metro station, line 7), stocks almost all cycle spares, parts, highly recommended; *Benolto*, near Polanco metro, stocks almost all cycle spares. Another good shop is between San Antonio and Mixcoac metro stations. The Escuela Médico Militar, near Pino Suárez metro station, has a very good shop, stocking all the best known international makes for spare parts. For excellent cycle repairs, see under Coyoacán, page 309.

Handicrafts *Fonart*, Fondo Nacional para el Fomento de las Artesanías, a state organization founded in 1974 in order to rescue, promote and diffuse the traditional crafts of Mexico. Main showroom at Av Patriotismo 691 (metro Mixcoac), T55981666, branches at Av Juárez 89 (metro Hidalgo), Londres 136 (Zona Rosa) and Coyoacán (Presidente Carranza 115). Competitive prices, quality superb. *The Mercado de Artesanías Finas Indios Verdes* is at Galería Reforma Nte SA, FG Bocanegro 44 (corner of Reforma Nte, near Statue of Cuitláhuac, Tlatelolco); good prices and quality but no bargaining. For onyx, *Müllers*, Londres y Florencia, near Insurgentes metro, good chess sets. For Talavera pottery from Puebla: *Uriarte*, Emilio Castelar 95-E, Polanco, T52822699, and Pabellón Altavista, Calz Desierto de Los Leones 52 D-6, San Angel, T56163119, www. talavera.com. There is an annual *national craft fair* in Mexico City, first week in December.

Markets *San Juan market*, C Ayuntamiento and Arandas, near Salto del Agua metro, good prices for handicrafts, especially leather goods and silver (also cheap fruit and health food); open Monday-Saturday 0900-1900, Sunday 0900-1600 (but don't go before 1000). The *Plaza Ciudadela* market (Mercado Central de Artesanías, open 1100-1800 weekdays, Sunday 1100-1400), beside Balderas 95 between Ayuntamiento y Plaza Morelos, government-sponsored, fixed prices, good selection, reasonable and uncrowded, is cheaper than San Juan, but not for leather; craftsmen from all Mexico have set up workshops here (best for papier maché, lacquer, pottery and Guatemalan goods) but prices are still cheaper in places of origin. *Mercado Lagunilla* near Glorieta Cuitláhuac (take *pesero* bus from metro Hidalgo) is a flea market where antique and collectable bargains are sometimes to be found, also a lot of rubbish (open daily but Sunday best day). The market, which covers several blocks, now has all sorts of merchandise, including a wider range of non-silver jewellery; good atmosphere. Market (Insurgentes) in C Londres (Zona Rosa) good for silver, but other things expensive, stallholders pester visitors, only place where they do so. There is a market in every district selling pottery, glassware, textiles, *sarapes* and jewellery. Try also *San Angel* market, although with little choice and expensive, many items are exclusive to it; good leather belts, crafts and silver; open Saturday only from about 1100. Mexican tinware and lacquer are found everywhere. Vast fruit and veg market, *Mercado Merced* (see page 271), metro Merced. A few blocks away on Fray Servando Teresa de Mier (nearest metro Fray Servando)

Mexico

lies the fascinating *Mercado Sonora*: secret potions and remedies, animals and birds as well as *artesanías*. *Buena Vista craft market*, Aldama 187 y Degollado (nearest metro Guerrero), excellent quality (open 0900-1800, Sunday 0900-1400). Also on Aldama, No 211, between Sol and Luna, the *Tianguis del Chopo* is held on Saturday, 1000-1600, selling clothes, records, etc, frequented by hippies, punks, rockers, and police. You can bargain in the markets and smaller shops. *Jamaica* market, Jamaica metro, line 4, huge variety of fruits and vegetables, also flowers, pottery, and canaries, parrots, geese, and ducks, indoor and outdoor halls.

Photography   Kodak film (Ektachrome, not Kodachrome) is produced in Mexico and is not expensive. Imported film is also available (eg Agfa slide film US$6). Cheapest film reported to be on Av Madero, eg 36 Slide Kodak Ektachrome costs US$4.50, but shop around. The price for slide film does not include processing. Small shops around República de Chile and Tacuba are cheaper than larger ones south of Av 5 de Mayo, but it may be worth paying more for good quality prints. Special offers abound, quality is good, prints normally ready in 45 minutes (no express charge), slides up to 48 hours. *Labo Mexicano del Imagen*, Carlos B, Zetina 34, Col Hipodromo Condesa, T5155540, excellent quality, fast service, normal prices. Several shops sell slide and print film (Fuji and Kodak) on Donteles, near Zócalo

Sports

Charreadas: (Cowboy displays), Rancho Grande de La Villa, at very top of Insurgentes Nte (nearest metro Indios Verdes, then walk north beyond bus station and keep asking), Sunday 1100-1500, US$1.30. **Football**: Sunday midday, Aztec and Olympic stadia (former has a great atmosphere at football matches, latter has a Rivera mural of the history of Mexican sport); also Thursday (2100) and Saturday (1700). Tickets from US$3.35 at Olympic Stadium. To Aztec Stadium take metro to Taxqueña terminus, then tram en route to Xochimilco to Estadio station; about 75 minutes from Zócalo. To Olympic Stadium take metro to Universidad terminus, then local bus (US$0.35) or taxi (US$1), leave Zócalo at 1045 for 1200 kick-off. **Golf**: at Chapultepec Golf Club and Churubusco Country Club. These are private clubs, open to visitors only if accompanied by a member. Green fees are US$20 upwards. **Horse races**: Hipódromo de las Américas, west of Boulevard Manuel Avila Camacho, off Av Conscriptos. Beautiful track with infield lagoons and flamingos, and plenty of atmosphere. Was in financial difficulties. Best to check whether it is open with Tourist Office, T52500123. **Hiking**: every weekend with the Alpino and Everest clubs. Club de Exploraciones de México, Juan A Mateos 146, Col Obrero (metro Chabacano), DF 06800, T55785730, 1930-2400 Wednesday or Friday organizes several walks in and around the city on Saturdays and Sundays, cheap equipment hire, slideshow Wednesday. Club Alpino Mexicano, Córdoba 234, Col Roma (metro Hospital General), T/F55749683, open Monday-Friday 1000-2000, Saturday 1000-1500, small shop (if club door is closed ask here for access). José María Aguayo Estrada, club president, very helpful; also arrange (free) mountain hiking at weekends, run ice climbing courses. **Equipment Suppliers**: *Vertimania*, Federico T de La Chica No 12, Plaza Versailles, Local 11-B, Col Satélite, T/F53935287. More central is: *Deportes Rubens*, Venustiano Carranza 17, T55185636, F55128312. **Stove repair**: *Serviso Coleman*, Marqués Sterling 23. **Climbing Wall**: *Rocadromo*, Lindavista, T7525674. Further reading: *'Ixtaccíhuatl'* and *'Toluca, Tolima'* by Alfredo Careaga Pardave; *'Mexico's Volcanoes'* by R Secord. **Ice-skating**: *Pista de Hielo San Jerónimo*, Av Contreras 300, Col San Jerónimo, metro B Muerto then bus to arena, T6831625, full-sized rink, crowded, closed Monday, US$3.50. *Pista de Hielo de Galerías Reforma*, Carr Mexico-Toluca 1725, Lomas Palo Alto, T2593543, US$3.50, small rink, not crowded. **Jai-Alai**: events with the foremost players in the world every day except Friday at the Frontón México across from Monumento a la Revolución, from 2000 (1900 Sunday) till 2400 (closed Monday), entry US$7, drinks expensive. It seats 4,000. Jackets and ties are needed for admission. Restaurant *El Rincón Pampero*. The people in the red caps are the *corredores*, who place the bets. Pari-mutuel betting. Also Frontón Metropolitano, on Bahía de Todos los Santos, near junction of Gutemberg and Calz Melchor Ocampo. **Swimming**: Agua Caliente, Las Termas, Elba, Centro Deportivo Chapultepec and others.

Transport

Budget Rent Auto, Reforma 60; **Hertz**, Revillagigedo 2; **Avis**, Medellín 14; **VW**, Av **Car hire** Chapultepec 284-6; **National Car Rental**, Insurgentes Sur 1883; **Auto Rent**, Reforma Nte 604; quick service at Av Chapultepec 168, T55335335 (57629892 airport); **Pamara**, Hamburgo 135, T55255572, 200 kilometres free mileage; **Odin**, Balderas 24-A; and many local firms, which tend to be cheaper. It is generally cheaper to hire in the US or Europe. **NB** When driving in the capital you must check which 'día sin auto' 'hoy no circula' applies to your vehicle's number plate; if your car is on the street when its number is prohibited, you could be fined US$80. This should not apply to foreign-licensed cars. The regulation covers the state of México besides the Distrito Federal. The ban applies to the last digit of your number plate: Monday 5,6; Tuesday 7,8; Wednesday 3,4; Thursday 1,2; Friday 9,0; Saturday, all even numbers and 0; Sunday, all odd numbers (emergency only at weekends). You can drive freely in 'greater' Mexico City on Saturday, Sunday and between 2200 and 0500.

Buses have been coordinated into one system: odd numbers run north-south, evens **City buses** east-west. Fares on large buses, which display routes on the windscreen are US$0.15, exact fare only. There are 60 direct routes and 48 feeder (SARO) routes. Thieves and pickpockets haunt the buses plying along Reforma and Juárez. A most useful route for tourists (and well-known to thieves, so don't take anything you don't require immediately) is No 76 which runs from C Uruguay (about the level of the Juárez Monument at Parque Alameda) along Paseo de la Reforma, beside Chapultepec Park. A *Peribus* service goes round the entire Anillo Periférico (see Traffic System.) Trolley buses also charge US$0.15. *Peseros* run on fixed routes, often between metro stations and other known landmarks; destination and route displayed on the windscreen. Avoid the smaller, white VW Kombis which do not have catalytic converters and which can be unpleasant. *Peseros* can be hailed almost anywhere and stop anywhere (press the button or say 'bajan'); this can make long journeys slow. If a bus runs on the same route, it is preferable as it has fixed stops. Fares are US$0.20 up to 5 kilometres, US$0.25 up to 10 kilometres and US$0.35 beyond.

There is a metro information service at Insurgentes station on Pink Line which dispenses **Metro** maps and most interchange stations have information kiosks. The *Atlas de Carreras*, US$1.65 *Beware of* has a map of Mexico City, its centre and the metro lines marked. *Pronto's* map of the metro- *pickpocketing at any* politan area displays the metro clearly. Good metro and bus maps at the Anthropology *time on the metro,* Museum, US$1.25. *Guía práctica del Metro*, US$9, explains all the station symbols; also *Guía* *many reports; the* *cultural del Metro*, US$3, both for sale at Zócalo station. All the stations have a symbol, eg the *police are not as* grasshopper signifying Chapultepec. *helpful as the*

There are 9 lines in service. **1** from Observatorio (by Chapultepec Park) to Pantitlán in the *vigilancias.* eastern suburbs (violet). It goes under Av Chapultepec and not far from the lower half of Paseo de la Reforma, the Mercado Merced, and 3 kilometres from the airport. **2**, from Cuatro *See colour map* Caminos in the northwest to the Zócalo and then south above ground to Taxqueña (blue); **3**, *section for metro map* from Indios Verdes south to the University City (olive) (free bus service to Insurgentes); **4**, from Santa Anita on the southeast side to Martín Carrera in the northeast (turquoise); **5**, from Pantitlán, via Terminal Aérea (which is within walking distance of gate A of the airport, but some distance from the international gates – opens 0600), crossing Line 3 at La Raza, up to Politécnico (yellow) (if using La Raza to connect with Line 5, note that there is a long walk between Lines 5 and 3, through the Tunnel of Knowledge); **6**, from El Rosario in the northwest to Martín Carrera in the northeast (red); **7**, from El Rosario in the northwest to Barranca del Muerto in the southwest (orange); **9** parallels 1 to the south, running from Tacubaya (where there are interesting paintings in the station) in the west to Pantitlán in the east (brown). Line **8**, the newest, runs from Garibaldi (north of Bellas Artes, Line 2), through Chabacano (Line 9), Santa Anita (Line 4), to Constitución de 1917 in the southeast (green). In addition to the numbered lines: running southeast from Pantitlán, Line A, the *metro férreo* goes as far as La Paz, 10 stations in all. From Taxqueña the *tren ligero* goes as far as Xochimilco, a very convenient way to this popular destination. Line B is to be built from Buenavista to Ciudad Azteca in Ecatepec, north of the city. Music is played quietly at the stations. Tickets 1.50 pesos, buy several to avoid queuing, check train direction before entering turn-stile or you may have to pay again.

An efficient, modern system (virtually impossible to get lost), and the best method of getting around the city, especially when the pollution is bad. Trains are fast, frequent, clean and quiet although overcrowded at certain times (eg early morning, 1400-1500 and 1830-2000). Pino Suárez, Hidalgo and Terminal Central del Norte are particularly infamous for thieves. Between 1800 and 2100 men are separated from women and children at Pino Suárez and certain other stations. 2 pieces of medium-sized luggage are permitted. At the Zócalo metro station there is a permanent exhibit about the city, interesting. At Pino Suárez, station has been built around a small restored Aztec temple. Art in the metro: Line 1, Pino Suárez and Tacubaya; Line 2, Bellas Artes and Panteones; Line 3, La Raza, scientific display in the Tunnel of Knowledge, and south of Coyoacán; Line 4, Santa Anita; Line 5, Terminal Aérea; Line 6, all stations, Line 7, Barranca del Muerto; Line 9, Mixuca. **NB** Lines 1, 2, 3 and A open 0500-0030 Monday-Friday, 0600-0130 Saturday and 0700-0030 Sunday and holidays; the other lines open 1 hour later on weekdays (same hours on weekends and holidays). Do not take photos or make sound-recordings in the metro without obtaining a permit and a uniformed escort from metro police, or you could be arrested. For lost property enquire at Oficina de Objetos Extraviados at Chabacano (intersection of lines 2, 8 and 9), open Monday-Friday only.

Taxi There are 3 types: 1) 'turismo' taxis which operate from first class hotels, the Museo Nacional de Antropología, etc – the most expensive. 2) Taxis from 'sitios'(fixed) ranks, from bus terminals, railway station and other locations; no meters, you pay a fixed sum in advance. About double the normal price but safer. Usually US$8-10 for destinations in the city, for which you pay in advance at a booth (check your change); they charge on a zone basis, US$4.60 for up to 4 kilometres, rising to US$22 for up to 22 kilometres (the same system applies at the airport – see below). 3) Taxis on unfixed routes are green (lead-free petrol) and can be flagged down anywhere; tariffs US$0.35 plus 5 cents for each 250 metres or 45 seconds, between 2200 and 0600 they charge 20 percent extra. They have meters (check they are working properly and set at zero); if you do not bargain before getting in, or if the driver does not know the route well, the meter will be switched on, which usually works out *cheaper* than negotiating a price. Some drivers refuse to use their meter after 1800. Note that radio-telephone taxis, and those with catalytic converters have a basic fee of 2.50 pesos. Drivers often do not know where the street you want is; try to give the name of the intersection between two streets rather than a number, because the city's numbering can be erratic. A tip is not normally expected, except when special help has been given. For information, or complaints, T56055520/6727/ 5388/ 6894; if complaining make sure you take the taxi's ID No. A fourth type of taxi travel, by tricycle, is now being encouraged to counter exhaust pollution; good way to see the architecture of the centre.

Warning Lone travellers, especially female, are advised to take only official taxis from hotels or ordered by phone. If you have to hail a taxi in the street, choose one with a licence plate beginning with S, not L. Reports of rapes, muggings, robbery etc, particularly at night. Tourist Police advise that you make note of registration and taxi numbers before getting in.

Traffic system
Eje Lázaro Cárdenas used to be called C San Juan de Letrán.

The city has two ring roads, the Anillo Periférico through what were the city outskirts when first built, and the Circuito Interior running within its circumference. You can cross the city via Viaducto and Periférico but only with a *small* motorhome or car. In the centre, there is a system of Ejes Viales. It consists of a series of freeways laid out in a grid pattern, spreading from the Eje Central; the latter serves as a focal point for numbering (Eje 2 Pte, Eje I Ote etc). Norte, Sur, Oriente, Poniente refer to the roads' position in relation to the Eje Central. The system is remarkably clear in its signposting with special symbols for telephones, information points, tram stops, etc. Beware of the tram lines – trams, buses, emergency services and folk in a hurry come down at high speed; and as often as not this lane goes against the normal flow of traffic! Bicycles are permitted to go the wrong way on all roads, which also 'adds to the spice of life'. Traffic wardens at most corners direct the flow of traffic (some visitors find city driving a nightmare). Traffic can be extremely heavy and, at certain times, very slow moving. You must, however, have a good map (see above).

Mexico

The airport terminal is divided into sections, each designated by a letter. A row of shops and **Airport** offices outside each section contains various services. Section **A**: national arrivals; post office, city of Mexico tourist office, exit to taxis and metro, INAH shop, telecommunications office. Between **A** and **B**: AeroMéxico; Bancomer ATM. Outside **B**: Banamex. Between **B** and **C**: entrance to *Continental Plaza* hotel, *casa de cambio*. **C** Mexicana; map shop. Ladatel phones just after C (Ladatel cards are sold at many outlets in the airport). Between **C** and **D**: Exposición Diego Rivera exhibition hall. **C-D**: Other national airline offices; bookshop. **D**: national and international departures; *cambio* opposite. By D are more national airline desks and long distance phones. Also by D is a bar and restaurant. From D you have to leave the building to get to **E**: international arrivals; car hire offices, exchange (Banamex), 24-hour luggage lockers (US$2.50 per day). **F**: international check-in; banks. Upstairs at E-F are shops, fast food restaurants (mostly US-style), exchange and phones. Pesos may be bought at any of the bank branches liberally spread from A to F. Most foreign currencies or travellers' cheques accepted, also most credit cards. The rate can vary considerably, so shop around. When buying dollars (and other 'hard' currency, when available, **Coberturas Mexicanas** almost always offers the best rates (Local 1, section D and local 8/9, section E). Only US$500 may be changed back into dollars after passing through immigration and customs when leaving. Exchange facilities in E or F (particularly on the upper floor) are less crowded. Banks and *casas de cambio* between them provide a 24-hour service. Phone calls from the airport may be made at many locations, but you have to keep trying all the phones to find one in operation that will accept the method of payment you wish to use. Look for the Lada 'multitarjeta' phones. There is a phone office at the far end of F, which accepts Amex and, in theory, Visa, Mastercard and other cards. It is very expensive though.

Fixed-price taxis by zone, buy tickets from booths at exits by A, E and F; you can buy tickets before passing customs but they are cheaper outside the duty free area; rates range from US$5 upwards, according to distance (per vehicle, not per person), drivers may not know, or may be unwilling to go to, cheaper hotels. For losses or complaints about airport taxis, T55713600 Ext 2299; for reservations 55719344/57848642, 0800-0200. The fixed price taxi system is efficient and safe. A cheaper alternative (about 50 percent) if one doesn't have too much luggage is to cross the Boulevard Puerto Aéreo by the metro Terminal Aérea and flag down an ordinary taxi outside the *Ramada* hotel. Journey about 20 minutes from town centre if there are no traffic jams. There are regular buses to the airport (eg No 20, along north side of Alameda) but the drawback is that you have to take one to Calzada Ignacio Zaragoza and transfer to trolley bus at the Boulevard Puerto Aéreo (ie at metro station Aeropuerto). Buses to airport may be caught every 45 minutes until 0100 from outside *De Carlo Hotel*, Plaza República 35. It takes an hour from downtown and in the rush hour, most of the day, it is jam-packed. But you can take baggage if you can squeeze it in. To get to the airport cheaply, take metro to Terminal Aérea and walk, or take metro to Boulevard Pto Aéreo and then a *pesero* marked 'Oceanía', which will leave you at the Terminal metro station. Avoid rush hours especially if you have luggage. There are airport information kiosks at A, D, E and F. There is an hotel desk before passing through customs. The tourist office at A has phones for calling hotels, no charge, helpful, but Spanish only. The travel agency at east exit will book hotels or reconfirm flights, charges 5 pesos. For air freight contact the Agencia Aduanales, Plazuela Hermanos, Colima 114, Monday-Friday 0900-1700, US$5.75 per kilo.

The Buenavista central station (a spacious building) is on Insurgentes Nte, junction Alzate **Trains** with Mosqueta, nearest metro Revolución or Guerrero. Left luggage for US$1 per piece per day, open 0630-2130. *Cafetería* reasonable. At the station there are long distance phone and fax services and an information desk. In 1999 the only passenger services to Saltillo in the north on Monday, Wednesday, Friday at 0900, arriving 2355, returning Tuesday, Thursday, Saturday, 0235-1900, and to Veracruz daily at 0845 and 2015 (arriving 1915 and 0600), returning 0820 and 2200 (arriving 1940 and 0800). A monthly timetable, *Rutas Ferroviarias*, is available from the station (Departamento de Tráfico de Pasajeros) and from ticket offices. Reservations T5976177, 5 lines; information T55471084/1097. If planning a train journey, find out in advance whether the service is actually running, the departure time, which floor the ticket will be sold on and when, and arrive 1 hour in advance. In general, 1st class tickets

Mexico

can be bought in advance, 2nd class are only available on the day. **NB** Lost or stolen tickets will not be replaced.

Long-distance buses

for details of bus services, see destinations in text

At all bus stations there are many counters for the bus companies, not all are manned and it is essential to ask which is selling tickets for the destination you want (don't take notice boards at face value). On the whole, the bus stations are clean and well organized. Book ahead where possible. Buses to destinations in north Mexico, include US borders, leave from **Central del Norte**, Av Cien Metros 4907, which has a *casa de cambio*, 24-hour cafés, left luggage, pharmacy, bakery and phone offices for long distance calls (often closed and poorly informed, very high charges). The bus station is on metro line 5 at Autobuses del Norte. City buses marked Cien Metros or Central del Norte go directly there. **Central del Sur**, at corner of Tlalpan 2205 across from metro Taxqueña (line 2), serves Cuernavaca, Acapulco, Zihuatanejo areas. Direct buses to centre (Donceles) from Central del Sur, and an express bus connects the Sur and Norte terminals. It is difficult to get tickets to the south, book as soon as possible; the terminal for the south is chaotic. The **Central del Poniente** is situated opposite the Observatorio station of line 1 of the metro, to serve the west of Mexico. You can go to the centre by bus from the 'urbano' terminal outside the Poniente terminal (US$0.10). The **Central del Oriente**, known as TAPO, Calzada Ignacio Zaragoza (metro San Lazaro, Line 1), for buses to Veracruz, Yucatán and southeast, including Oaxaca (it has a tourist information office open from 0900; luggage lockers, US$2.65 per day, key is left with guard; post office, *farmacia* changes travellers' cheques). To Guatemala, from TAPO, take a bus to Tapachula, Comitán or Ciudad Cuauhtémoc, pesos only accepted. There are also buses departing from Mexico City airport (outside Sala D), to Puebla, Toluca, Cuernavaca and Querétaro, very convenient. Buy ticket from driver.

All bus terminals operate taxis with voucher system and there are long queues (check change carefully at the taxi office). It is much easier to pay the driver, although beware of extra charges. Easier still is to flag down a VW taxi on the street outside the terminal. In the confusion at the terminals some drivers move each other's cabs to get out of the line faster and may take your voucher and disappear. Fares are given under **Taxis** above. The terminals are connected by metro, but this is not a good option at rush hours, or if carrying too much luggage. Advance booking is recommended for all trips, and very early reservation if going to *fiestas* during Holy Week, etc. At Christmas, many Central American students return home via Tapachula and buses from Mexico City are booked solid for 2 weeks before, except for those lines which do not make reservations. You must go and queue at the bus stations; this can involve some long waits, sometimes 2-2½ hours. Even if you are travelling, you may sometimes be required to buy a *boleto de andén* (platform ticket) at many bus stations. Note that many bus companies require luggage to be checked in 30 minutes in advance of departure.

Bus companies: (tickets and bookings) **Going North**: Transportes del Norte, at Av Insurgentes Centro 137, near Reforma (T55875511/5400); dep from Central Norte. Omnibús de México, Insurgentes Nte 42, at Héroes Ferrocarrileros (T55676756 and 55675858). Greyhound bus, Reforma 27, T55352618/4200, F55353544, closed 1400-1500 and all day Sunday; information at Central Norte from Transportes del Norte (Chihuahuenses) or Tres Estrellas bus counters, prices only, no schedules. **Going to Central States**: Autobuses Anáhuac, Bernal Díaz 6 (T55910533); Central Norte departures. **Going Northwest**: ETN, Central México Norte, T55673773, or Central del Poniente T52730251; Tres Estrellas de Oro, Calzada Vallejo 1268 Nte (Col Santa Rosa), T53911139/3021, Central Norte. **Going northeast**: ADO, Av Cien Metros 4907 (T55678455/5322). Beware of ADO selling tickets for buses and then not running the service. Although the ticket will be valid for a later bus, there are then problems with overbooking (your seat number won't be valid). **Going South** (including Guatemala): Cristóbal Colón, Boulevard Gral Ignacio Zaragoza 200, T55427263 to 66; from Central del Oriente; also ADO, Buenavista 9 (T55923600 or 55427192 at terminal). **Going Southwest**: Estrella de Oro, Calzada de Tlalpan 2205 (T55498520 to 29).

Warning Beware of con men at bus terminals or airport. Reports of one, Bernardo Kan, who claims to have been robbed and unable to get his flight. He pledges to return your borrowed money in Palenque where his mother lives, but this is fictitious.

Directory

The majority are on Paseo de la Reforma: No 325, *Avensa* (T52084998/3018). *Delta*, No 381, T55254840, **Airline offices**
52021608, airport T57623588. *American Airlines*, No 314, T52086396/53999222/ 55713219 (airport).
Avianca, No 195, T55668588/55463059. *Iberia*, No 24, T55664011/55922988/ 57625844 (airport). *Aero
California*, No 332, T52071392. *Alitalia*, No 390-1003, T55335590/1240/1243. *Japan Airlines*, No 295,
T55336883/5515, 55718742 (airport). *Canadian Airlines*, No 390, T52076611/3318. On C Hamburgo:
Swissair, No 66, T55336363. *SAS*, No 61, T55330098/0177, 55119872 (airport). *Air Canada*, No 108, p5º,
T55112004, 55142516. *Alaska Airlines*, No 213-1004, T55331747/6. *Ecuatoriana de Aviación*, No 213,
T55334569, 55141274, 57625199 (airport). *Air France*, Edgar Allan Poe 90, T56276000, airport 55716150.
Mexicana, Xola 535, Col del Valle, T56604433/4444, 57624011 (airport). *KLM*, Paseo de las Palmas 735,
T52024444. *Lufthansa*, Paseo de las Palmas 239, T52028866. *Cubana*, Temístocles 246, Polanco,
T52550646/0835. *Continental*, Andrés Bello 45, T55469503, 55357603, 55713661 (airport). *Aeromar*,
Sevilla 4, T52076666, 55749211. *Aeroflot*, Insurgentes Sur 569, T55237139. *United Airlines*, Leibnitz 100,
loc 23-24, T52501657, 55455147. *AeroMéxico*, Insurgentes Sur 724, T52076311/8233. *British Airways*,
Jaime Balmes 8,Los Morales, T53870300. *El Al Israel Airlines*, Paseo de las Palmas, T57351105, 52022243.
Icelandic Airlines, Durango 103, T55140159, 55116155/8461. *Lacsa*, Río Nazas 135, T555110640,
55250025. *Northwest Airlines*, Reforma y Ambares 312, T55113579, Reforma 300, T55257090. *Pan
American Airways*, Plaza Comermex 1-702, T53950022/0077. *Taca*, Morelos 108, Col Juárez,
T55468807/8835.

Banks 0930-1700 Mon-Fri, 0900-1300 Sat, although some branches open earlier and close later. Always **Banks**
see if there is a special counter where currency transactions can be effected, to avoid standing in queues
which can be long, particularly on Fri. It often happens when you are queueing up that bank employees
ask you what you are wishing to do (¿Qué operación quiere hacer?). This is not a nosey inquiry, but rather
a desire to be of assistance. Branches of all major Mexican banks proliferate in most parts of the city. Cash
advances on credit cards is easy, and good rates. TCs in most major currencies can be cashed at any
branch of Bancomer or Banco Serfín without undue delay. Banks do not charge commission for changing
TCs. The exchange of foreign currency notes, other than dollars, can be difficult apart from at the airport
and main bank branches in the city centre. There are 2 *casas de cambio* at the airport which specialize in
obscure currencies. Before buying or selling currency, check the day's exchange rate from a newspaper
and then shop around. There is often a great disparity between different banks and *casas de cambio*
particularly in times of volatile currency markets. In general, banks are better for buying pesos and casas
de cambio for buying 'hard' currency. Hotels usually offer very poor rates. *Banco de Comercio* (Bancomer,
Visa agent), head office at Av Universidad 1200, also Venustiano Carranza y Bolívar, good quick cambio,
same rate for cash and TCs. *Banco Nacional de México (Banamex)*, C Palmas (Banamex's offices nearby,
at Av Isabel la Católica 44, are in a converted baroque palace, ask the porter for a quick look into the
magnificent patio. Another worthwhile building is the bank's branch in the Casa Iturbide, where Agustín
de Iturbide lived as emperor, at Madero 17 with Gante). *Banco Internacional* recommended, they deal
with Mastercard (Carnet) and Visa (usually quicker than Bancomer or Banamex for cash advances against
credit card), also *Banco Serfín*, corner of 16 de Septiembre y Bolívar, or Madero 32, near Bolívar. *Citibank*,
Paseo de la Reforma 390, for Citicorp TCs, they also give cash advances against credit cards with no
commission. *American Express* emergency number, T53262626, platinum, T53262929; also office at
Reforma 234 esq Havre, T5330380, will change cheques on Sats, 0930-1330, also open Mon-Fri until 1800
(there are 5 other AmEx offices in Mexico City, including Campos Eliseos 204, local 5, Polanco; Centro
Comercial Perisur). For more details on Visa and Master Card, see **Essentials** under **Credit cards**, page
74. There are many *casas de cambio*, especially on Reforma, Madero and in the centre. Their hrs may be
more convenient, but their rates can be poor. *Central de Cambios* (Suiza), Madero 58, west of Zócalo and
Casa de Cambio Plus, Av Juárez, have been recommended for rates. The Perisur shopping centre,
Insurgentes and Periférico Sur, has a *casa de cambio* (T56063698) which is usually open until 1900, with a
better exchange rate in the morning. See also **Airport** above.

Post Office: Tacuba y Lázaro Cárdenas, opposite Palacio de Bellas Artes, open for letters 0800-2400 **Communications**
Mon-Fri, 0800-2000 Sat, and 0900-1600 Sun. For parcels open 0900-1500 Mon-Fri only; parcels up to 2
kg (5 kg for books) may be sent. It is an interesting historic building with a stunning interior, worth a
visit. Philatelic sales at windows 9 to 12. Mail kept for only 10 days at poste restante window 3,
recommended, but closed Sat and Sun (see page 86). If they can't find your mail under the initial of
your surname, ask under the initials of any other names you may happen to have. EMS Mexpost,
accelerated national and international postage is available at the central post office, the airport, Zona

Rosa, Coyoacán and 13 other post offices in the city; payable by weight. Other post offices (open 0800-1900 Mon-Fri, 0800-1300 Sat) which travellers may find useful: Centre, Nezahualcóyotl 184 and Academia 4; P Arriaga y Ignacio Mariscal, 2 blocks north of Monumento a la Revolución; Zona Rosa, Londres 208; Tlatelolco, Flores Magón 90; San Rafael, Schultz 102; Polanco, Polanco 79A; Lomas de Chapultepec, Prado Nte 525; Buenavista, Aldama 216; San Angel, Dr Gálvez 16; Coyoacán, Higuera 23; Iztapalapa, Calzada Ermita Iztapalapa 1033; Xochimilco, Prolongación Pino 10; also at the airport and bus terminals. In all there are 155 branches in the federal capital, so there is no need to go to the Palacio de Correos.

Telephones: see **Essentials** for details of the LADA phone system. Finding a phone box that works can be a problem. Most public phones take phone cards (Ladatel), costing 20-50 pesos, from shops and news kiosks everywhere. Calls abroad can be made from phone booths with credit cards (via LADA system). International calls can easily be made from the phone office in the Central del Oriente bus terminal. There are several places, including some shops, all officially listed, with long-distance phones. For information dial 07.

Internet: *Novanet*, Nuevo León 104 y Michoacán, Col Hipódromo (Metro Chilpancingo), T55537503. *Café Java Chat*, Genova 44 K, Zona Rosa(Metro Insurgentes), US$4 per hour, free coffee and soft drinks. *Cyberpuerto*, Alfonso Reyes 238, Col Hipódromo, T52860869. *Café Pedregal*, Av San Jerónimo 630, Col Jardines del Pedregal T56816672. *Internet Station*, Arquímedes 130, local 20 (Metro Polanco) T52806091. *Internet Café* in Plaza Computacion at Cárdenas end of Uruguay, US$3.25 per hour, free coffee, soft drinks US$0.60. *Ragnatel*, Centro Comercial Santa Fé, local 472, Col Antigua Mina la Totolapa T52580782. *Interlomas*, Paseo de la Herradura 5, Col Fernando la Herradura, Huixquilucan T52450330. *Cafe@Rock Shop*, Belisario Domínguez 17, Coyoacán, T55543699. *Tarea*, Presidente Carranza esq Tres Cruces, Coyoacán, T56592420. Most of the above open Mon-Sat 1000-2200, but check. Rates US$3-3.30 hour. **NB** The symbol @ is called arroba in Spanish.

Cultural centres *American Community School of Mexico*, complete US curriculum to age of 12, Observatorio and C Sur 136, T5166720. *American Chamber of Commerce*, Lucerna 78. *Benjamin Franklin Library*, Londres 116 (has *New York Times* 2 days after publication). *Anglo-Mexican Cultural Institute* (with British Council Library), Maestro Antonio Caso 127, T55666144. *British Council*, Lope de Vega 316, Polanco, T52631900, F52631910. *Instituto Italiano*, Francisco Sosa 77, Coyoacán, T55540044/53, has 3-week intensive and painless courses in Spanish, 3 hrs a day. *Goethe-Institut*, Tonalá 43 (metro Insurgentes), 0900-1300, 1600-1930. *Colegio Alemán*, Alexander V Humboldt, Col Huichapan, Del Xochimilco (CP 16030, México DF). *Instituto Francés de la América Latina*, Nazas 43, free films every Thur at 2030.

Embassies & consulates Check location of embassies and consulates; they tend to move frequently. Most take 24 hrs for visas; check to make sure you have a visa and not just a receipt stamp. *Guatemalan Embassy*, Explanada 1025, Lomas de Chapultepec, 11000 México DF, T55407520/55209249, F52021142, am only (take No 47 bus from Observatorio to Virreyes, then walk up hill, or No 76 'Km 15.5 por Reforma', or 'por Palmas', or taxi); to visit Guatemala some nationalities need a compulsory visa costing US$10 in US$ cash only (eg Australians and New Zealanders), others need either a free visa (take a passport photo) or a tourist card (issued at the border), the current regulations are given in Guatemala: **Essentials**, open 0900-1300 for visas. *Belizean Embassy*, Bernardo de Gálvez 215, Lomas Virreyes, México DF, T55201346, F55318115, open 0900-1300 Mon-Fri, visa US$10, takes a day. *Honduran Consulate*, Alfonso Reyes 220, T55156689/52115425 (metro Chilpancingo), visas issued on the spot (no waiting) valid up to 1 year from date of issue, cost varies per nationality, up to US$20 for Australians. *Salvadorean Embassy*, Monte Altai 320, T52028250, 55200856, metro Auditorio. *Nicaraguan Consulate*, Payo de Rivera 120, Col Virreyes, Lomas de Chapultepec, T55204421 (bus 13 along Reforma, get out at Monte Altai and walk south on Monte Athos), visas for 30 days from date of issue, 1 photograph, US$25, plus US$5 if you want it 'on the spot'. *Costa Rican Embassy*, Río Póo 113, Col Cuauhtémoc, T55257764 (metro Insurgentes). *Panamanian Embassy*, Campos Eliseos 111-1, T52504259/4229, near Auditorio metro (visa US$20 for Australians). *Colombian Consulate*, Reforma 195, p3º, will request visa from Bogotá by telegram (which you must pay for) and permission can take up to a month to come through. *Ecuador*, Tennyson 217, T55453141. *USA Embassy*, Reforma 305, Col Cuauhtémoc, T52110042, F55119980, open Mon-Fri 0830-1730, if requiring a visa for the States, it is best to get it in your home country. *Canadian Embassy*, Schiller 529 (corner Tres Picos), near Anthropological Museum, T57247900, www.canada.org.mx. *Australian Embassy*, Plaza Polanco Torre B, Jaime Balmes 11, p10º, Colonia Los Morales, T53959988. *New Zealand Embassy*, JL Lagrange 103, p10º, Polanco, T52815486, F52815212. *British Embassy*, C Río Lerma 71, T52072593/2449 (Apdo 96 bis, Mexico 5), open Mon and Thur 0900-1400 and 1500-1800, Tues, Wed, Fri, 0900-1500. Consular

Section at C Usumacinta 30, immediately behind main Embassy Building. reading room in main building; poste restante for 1 month, please address to Consular section, this is not an official service, just a valuable courtesy. **British Chamber of Commerce**, Río de la Plata 30, Col Cuauhtémoc, T52560901. **Hon Irish Consulate**, Sylvia Moronadi, San Gerónimo 790a, metro Miguel Angel, T55953333, open Mon-Fri 0900-1700. **German Embassy**, Byron 737, Colonia Rincón del Bosque, T52805534, 55456655, open 0900-1200. **French Embassy**, Havre 15, near the Cuauhtémoc Monument, T55331360. **Netherlands Embassy**, Monte Urales 635-203 (near Fuente de Petróleos), T52028267, F52026148. **Swedish Embassy**, Paseo de las Palmas 1375. **Danish Embassy**, Tres Picos 43, Colonia Polanco, Apdo Postal 105-105, 11580 México DF, T52553405/4145/3339, open Mon-Fri 0900-1300 (nearest metro Auditorio). **Finnish Embassy**, Monte Pelvoux 111, p4º, 11000, Mexico, DF, T55406036. **Swiss Embassy**, Edificio Torre Optima, Paseo de las Palmas 405, p11º, Col Lomas de Chapultepec, T55208535, open 0900-1200 Mon-Fri. **Italian Embassy**, Paseo de las Palmas 1994, Col Lomas de Chapultepec, T55963655. **Polish Embassy**, Cracovia 40, CP 01000, T55504700. **Greek Consulate**, Paseo de las Palmas 2060, Col Lomas Reforma, T55966333/6936. **Israeli Embassy**, PO Box 25389, T55406340, F52844825. Sierra Madre 215 (nearest metro Auditorio), open Mon-Fri 0900-1200. **Japanese Embassy**, Apdo Postal 5101, Paseo de la Reforma 395, Colonia Cuauhtémoc, T52110028.

Hospital: **American British Cowdray Hospital**, (also known as El Hospital Inglés, or ABC), on Observatorio past C Sur 136. T52775000 (emergency: 55158359); very helpful. **Medical services:** Dr César Calva Pellicer (who speaks English, French and German), Copenhague 24, p3º, T55142529. Dr Smythe, Campos Elíseos 81, T5457861, recommended by US and Canadian Embassies. For any medical services you can also go to the Clínica Prensa, US$1.20 for consultation, subsidized medicines. Hospital de Jesús Nazareno, 20 de Noviembre 82, Spanish-speaking, friendly, drugs prescribed cheaply. It is a historical monument (see page 271). Most embassies have a list of recommended doctors and dentists who speak languages other than Spanish. Good dentist in south of city: Dr Ricardo Rosas Maldonado, Calzada de Tlalpan 1320 (metro Portales), T55399608. **Pharmacies:** **Farmacia Homeopática**, C Mesones 111-B. Farmacia Nosarco, corner of 5 de Febrero and República del Salvador, stocks wide range of drugs for stomach bugs and tropical diseases, may give 21 percent discount. Sanborn's chain and El Fénix discount pharmacies are the largest chains with the most complete selection (the Sanborn's behind the Post Office stocks gamma globulin). Many supermarkets have good pharmacies. **Vaccination centre:** Benjamín Hill 14, near metro Juanacatlán (Line 1). Open Mon-Fri 0830-1430, 1530-2030, avoid last 30 mins, also open on Sat from 0830-1430; typhoid free (this is free all over Mexico), cholera and yellow fever (Tues and Fri only) US$2; will give a prescription for gamma globulin. For hepatitis shots you have to buy gamma globulin in a pharmacy (make sure it's been refrigerated) and then an injection there (cheap but not always clean), or at a doctor's surgery or the ABC Hospital (see above). Gamma globulin is hard to find (see **pharmacies** above); try Hospital Santa Elena, Querétaro 58, Col Roma, T55747711, about US$50 for a vaccination. Malaria prophylaxis and advice free from San Luis Potosí 199, p6º, Colonia Roma Nte, 0900-1400, or from the Centro de Salud near metro Chabacano, opposite Supermercado Comercial Mexicano – no typhoid vaccinations here (ask at Centro de Salud Benjamín Hill, which does not supply malaria pills). It seems that paludrine is not available in Mexico, only chloroquine.

Hospitals & medical services

The UNAM has excellent classes of Spanish tuition and Mexican culture: Centro de Enseñanza para Extranjeros, US$200 for 6 weeks, 5 different levels, free additional courses in culture, free use of medical service, swimming pool, library, a student card from here allows free entry to all national monuments and museums and half price on many bus lines (eg ADO during summer vacations). See also **Learning Spanish** in **Essentials** page 86 and **Cultural centres** above.

Language schools

Laundry on Río Danubio, between Lerma and Panuco and at Chapultepec and Toledo, near Sevilla metro, expensive. **Lavandería** at Chapultepec y Toledo. **Lavandería Automática** at Edison 91 (nearest metro Revolución) has automatic machines, US$1.50 per 3 kg, US$1.50 drying. Also at Parque España 14 and Antonio Caso 82, near British Council, US$4 for 3kg, quick service. Dry cleaning shops (tintorerías or lavado en seco) are plentiful. Typical charges: jacket or skirt US$1.10, suit US$2.20, can take up to 48 hrs.

Laundry

English-speaking: Roman Catholic, St Patrick's, C Bondijito 248, Tacubaya, T55151993; Evangelical Union, Reforma 1870, Lomas de Chapultepec, T55200436; Baptist, Capital City Baptist Church, C Sur 138 y Bondijito, T55161862; Lutheran, Church of the Good Shepherd, Paseo de Palmas 1910, T55961034; Anglican, Mexican Anglican Cathedral, Mesones 139 (see page 276) has services in Spanish, for services in English, Christ Church, Monte Escandinavos 405, Lomas de Chapultepec, T52020949 (services at 0800 and 1000, sung Eucharist, take bus Reforma Km 15 or Km 16 to Monte Alti, then down hill off opposite

Places of worship

Mexico

Mexico

side of the road); First Church of Christ Scientist, 21 Dante, Col Anzures. Jewish, Beth Israel, Virreyes 1140, Lomas Virreyes, Nidche Israel (Orthodox), Acapulco 70, near Chapultepec metro.

Tour companies & travel agents

It is important to shop around as prices vary considerably. It is rare to find deals such as are available in Europe or the US.

Use a travel agent that has been recommended to you (if possible), as not all are efficient or reliable. One of the most reliable is: *Cultours*, Guanajuato 72 (Col Roma), T52640854/1004/1076, F52640919, highly recommended, good for flights to Europe, Central and South America and for changing flight dates, English spoken, ask for Icarus Monk. *Thomas Cook*, Campos Eliseos 345, Col Polanco, TCs agency only. *Wagons-Lits*, Av Juárez 88, T55181180, also Av De Las Palmas 731, T55400579, very helpful and knowledgeable. *Uniclam* agent in Mexico City is Srta Rosa O'Hara, Río Pánuco 146, Apto 702, Col Cuauhtémoc, T55255393. *Grey Line Tours*, Londres 166, T52081163, reasonably priced tours, car hire, produces *This is Mexico* book (free). *American Express*, Reforma 234 y Havre, T55330380, open Mon-Fri 0900-1800, Sat 0900-1300, charges US$3-4 for poste restante if you do not have their TCs and US$1 if no card or cheques are held for other services, service slow but helpful. *Mundo Joven Travel Shop*, Insurgentes Sur 1510 (on the corner of Río Churubusco), T56628244, F56631556, issues ISIC card, agents for International Youth Hostel Federation, hostellingmexico@remaj.com. *Corresponsales de Hoteles*, Blvd Centro 224-4, T53603356, for hotel reservations (upmarket). *Hadad Viajes*, Torres Adalid 205, of 602, Col de Valle, T56870488. *Asatej*, Insurgentes Sur 421, Local B.10, Col Hipódromo Condesa, Deleg, Cuauhtemoc, T55740899, F55743462, ve@ve.com.mx. *Humboldt Tours*, José María Velasco 34, San José Insurgentes, T56609152/6650, F56600735, one of Mexico's leading tour operators, good for individual tours as well as groups, multilingual staff. *Viajes Tirol*, José Ma Rico 212, Depto 503, T55345582/3323/1765, English and German spoken, recommended. *Turisjoven*, Tuxpan 54-903 (metro Chilpancingo). For cheap tickets to Cuba, ask round agencies around Hamburgo. *W Tours and Travel*, T56821718/1607, are also recommended. Finding a cheap flight to Europe is difficult. Try *Vacation Planning*, Copenhague 21-203, Zona Rosa, T55111604. *Beltravel*, Londres 51, Zona Rosa; *Viajes de Alba*, Villalongín 20-2, Col Cuauhtémoc, T57054180.

Specialists in adventure tourism

The Asociación Mexicana de Turismo de Aventura y Ecoturismo (AMTAVE) regulates and promotes many of the agencies listed below.Not all areas of adventure sport come under their umbrella, for instance specialist diving agencies (it being mainly a regional activity), remain unattached to any Mexico City-based organization. *Río y Montaña*, Prado Norte

450-T, Lomas de Chapultepec, T/F55202041, sea kayaking, rafting (Ríos Pescados-Antigua stretch, Filo Bobos, Usumacinta, Santa María, Río Grande, Jatate); climbing expertise – Alfonso de La Parra, one of the guides, has climbed Everest. *Al Aire Libre*, Centro Comercial Interlomas, Local 2122, Lomas Anahuac Huixquilucan, T2919217, rafting (Ríos Pescados-Antigua, Santa María, Amacuzac), climbing, caving (Chontalcuatlán, Zacacoltla, La Joya), ballooning, parapenting. *Intercontinental Adventures*, Homero 526-801, Col Polanco, T52254400, F52554465, run by Agustín Arroyo who is president of AMTAVE, operates mainly in Veracruz, historical tours, rafting and sea kayaking, represents *México Verde* agency (see under Guadalajara tour companies) in Mexico City. *Ecogrupos de México*, Centro Comercial Plaza Inn, Insurgentes Sur 1971251, T56619121, F56627354, nature tours eg butterfly habitats.

Tourist offices

The *Mexican Secretariat of Tourism* (Secretaría de Turismo) is at C Masaryk 172, p5º, between Hegel and Emerson, Colonia Polanco (reached by bus No 32), T52508555, ext 116, F52542636, emergency hot line 52500123/0151. The amount and quality of printed information available varies enormously, although it is possible to book hotels in other parts of the country. The tourist office produces a telephone directory in English and French. Better information is available at tourist information centres operated by the Mexico City Government at the following points: *Mexico City airport*, Sala B; *Amberes* 54, Zona Rosa. *Terminal de Autobuses del Norte*, main entrance. *TAPO* bus station, at the end of tunnel 1; in the Delegación Coyoacán, Plaza Hidalgo, Coyoacán; in the *Casa de la Cultura de San Angel*, corner of Revolución and Francisco I Madero, San Angel; *Embarcadero Nativiltas*, Xochimilco; opposite monument to Juárez, Alameda Central. You may refer complaints here, or to the tourist police, in blue uniforms, who are reported to be very friendly. Articles from the various craft displays can be bought. Free maps not always available, but try Cámara de Comercio de la Ciudad de México, Información Turística, open Mon-Fri 0900-1400, 1500-1800, at Reforma 42, which provides maps and brochures of the city (apparently for government employees only); may otherwise be got from Department of Public Works; or buy in bookshops. Bus and metro maps available. Information bureau outside Insurgentes metro station and on Juárez, just east of Paseo de la Reforma (closed Sun). Tourist information can be dialled between 0800 and 2000 (bilingual operator) on 55259380. For problems, eg theft, fraud, abuse of power by officials, T55160490, Protectur. Also try the *Agencia Especializada en Asuntos de Turista*, C Florencia 20, Col Juárez, English spoken, very helpful. The attorney-general's office for crimes against tourists: T56258761 (Zona Rosa)/56258763 (airport). A weekly magazine, *The Gazer/El Mirón* gives basic information and tips for Mexico City and elsewhere in Mexico. Also *Mexico City Daily Bulletin*, free from most hotels, good listings, exchange rate information unreliable. The magazine *Donde* (US$2) gives general information, details on hotels, restaurants, crafts and entertainment. *Concierge* is a monthly tourist guide in English and Spanish with information on Mexico City.

Useful addresses

Customs: Dirección General de Aduanas, 20 de Noviembre 195, T57092900. **Delegation building:** Av Central, the Ministry of Public Works is the place to report a theft; take a long book. **Immigration:** Servicios Migratorios, of the Secretaría de Gobernación, Homero 1832, Colonia Morales, Mon-Fri 0930-1400, get there early, long queues, no English spoken. The office is not easy to get to (it's one block before you get to the Periférico, on the left along Homero); the best way from most directions is to go to metro Polanco and take a taxi (US$1). There is a pesero which leaves Metro Chapultepec which also passes Polanco metro station, get off at the terminus and walk one block north to Homero y Gobernación; return pesero from outside the building. Here you can extend tourist cards for stays over 90 days or replace lost cards. New card will be given in 10 days; you may be given 10 days to leave the country. **Maps:** *Instituto Nacional de Estadística Geografía e Informática (INEGI)* sells maps and has information, branches in each state capital and in the Distrito Federal in the arcade below the traffic roundabout at Insurgentes (where the metro station is), open 0800-1600, all maps available, but only one index for consultation. The Automobile Club's (AMA) street map is good, but hard to find. Good maps of the city from HFET (see **Maps** in **Essentials**), *Guía Roji* (an excellent A to Z, US$14), *Ciudad de Mexico, mapa turístico* (Quimera Editores, 1999, 1:10,000, US$8.75) and *Trillas Tourist Guide* (US$6.50, recommended). Street vendors on Zócalo and in kiosks sell a large city map for US$3. Good large postcard/maps of Coyoacán, La Alameda Central and San Angel, available at many museums and bookshops. **Setej** (Mexican Students' Union): Hamburgo 301, Zona Rosa, metro Sevilla, issues student card, which is required to buy a hostel card, T52110743 or 52116636, deals with ISIS insurance. To obtain national student card you need 3 photos, passport, confirmation of student status and US$7. Open Mon-Fri 0900-1800, Sat 0900-1400.

Mexico

Suburbs of Mexico City

Churubusco Churubusco, 10 kilometres southeast, reached from the Zócalo by Coyoacán or Tlalpan bus, or from General Anaya metro station, to see the picturesque and partly ruined convent (1762) at Gen Anaya y 20 de Agosto, now become the **Museo Nacional de las Intervenciones**. ■ *0900-1800, closed Monday, US$3.35, free Sunday and holidays.* 17 rooms filled with mementoes, documents, proclamations and pictures recounting foreign invasions, incursions and occupations since independence (also has temporary exhibitions). The site of the museum was chosen because it was the scene of a battle when the US Army marched into Mexico City in 1847. Adjoining the ex-convento is the church of San Diego (16th century, with 17th and 18th century additions). Near the church, on the other side of Calzada Gen Anaya is the delightful Parque de Churubusco. One block from Tlalpan along Héroes del 47, to the left, is the 18th century church of San Mateo. There is a golf course at the Churubusco Country Club. Churubusco was for many years the home of Mexico's most important film studios; a smaller-scale operation now exists, devoted to post-production. The new Olympic swimming pool is here. Near enough to Coyoacán (see page 306) to walk there.

Tlalpan Tlalpan, six and a half kilometres further out, or direct from Villa Obregón (see page 305) a suburb with colonial houses, gardens, and near the main square, Plaza de la Constitución, an early 16th century church (San Agustín) with a fine altar and paintings by Cabrera. Reached by bus or trolley bus from the Taxqueña metro station. Two and a half kilometres west is the suburb of **Peña Pobre**, near which, to the northeast, is the Pyramid of **Cuicuilco**, believed to be the oldest in Mexico (archaeological museum on site, Insurgentes Sur Km 16, intersection with Periférico, open 0800-1800, closed Monday). The pyramid dates from the fifth or sixth century BC; it is over 100 metres in diameter but only 25 metres high.

Ajusco Another excursion can be made to Ajusco, about 20 kilometres southwest of Mexico City. Catch a bus from Estadio Azteca on Calzada Tlalpan direct to Ajusco. From the summit of the extinct **Volcán Ajusco** (3,929 metres), there are excellent views on a clear day. The way up is 10 kilometres west of the village, 400 metres west of where the road branches to Xalatlaco (there is a hut south of the road where the path goes to the mountain). Foothills are also pleasant.

Xochimilco

To Metro Taxqueña & Calzada de Tlalpan

Periférico

Tepepan

10 de Septiembre

5 de Mayo

Santa María Tepepan

Hidalgo

La Noria

Museo Dolores Olmedo

Prol División del Norte

Guada

Av M

Xoch

Santiago Tepalcatlalpan

Constit

A Serdán

N

0 metres 250
0 yards 273

▲ Landings
1 Belem
2 Caltonga

Xochimilco

Some 20 kilometres to the southeast of the city centre, Xochimilco has many attractions, not least the fact that it lies in an unpolluted area. Easiest access is by bus, pesero or metro to Metro Tasqueña, then (about 20 minutes) *tren ligero*. Get off at terminal (misleadingly named 'Embarcadero', as there are several *embarcaderos*, see map and below).

Meaning 'The place where flowers are grown', it was an advanced settlement long before the arrival of the Spaniards. Built on a lake, it developed a form of agriculture using 'chinampas', or 'floating gardens'; the area is still a major supplier of fruit and vegetables to Mexico City. The Spaniards recognized the importance of the region and the need to convert the indigenous population: evidence of this is the considerable number of 16th and 17th century religious buildings in Xochimilco itself and in the other 13 pueblos which make up the present-day Delegación, or municipality.

Xochimilco is famous for its canals and colourful punt-like boats, or *trajineras*, which bear girls' names. There are seven landing-stages, or *embarcaderos*, in the town, the largest of which are Fernando Celada and Nuevo Nativitas (the latter is where most coach-loads of tourists are set down, large craft-market). All are busy at weekends, especially Sunday afternoon. Official tariffs operate, although prices are

Mexico

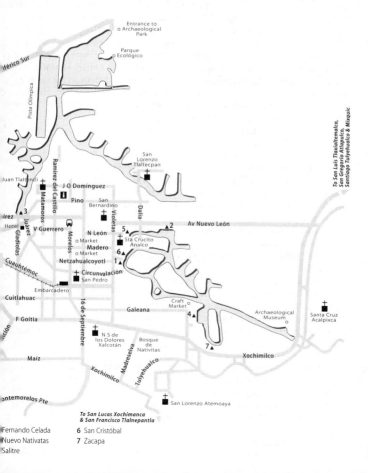

Fernando Celada   6 San Cristóbal
Nuevo Nativitas   7 Zacapa
Salitre

sometimes negotiable: a boat taking six passengers costs US$5.75 per hour (a trip of at least one and a half hours is desirable); floating mariachi bands will charge US$3.50 per song, marimba groups US$1.50. Reasonably priced tourist menus (lunch US$2) from passing boats; good, clean and cheap restaurants opposite Fernando Celada (for example *Beto's*, US$2 for lunch); more expensive restaurants opposite Nuevo Nativitas.

The indisputable architectural jewel of Xochimilco is the church of **San Bernardino de Siena** (begun in 1535, completed 1595; magnificent Renaissance style retable, 1580-90) and its convent (circa 1585). The oldest Spanish-built religious edifice is the tiny chapel of **San Pedro** (1530). Also worthy of mention are **Nuestra Señora de los Dolores de Xaltocán** (17th century façade, 18th century retable), Santa Crucita Analco and San Juan Tlatentli. All are within walking distance of the centre of town.

For those who have an interest in church architecture there is a rich range in the villages to the west, south and east of Xochimilco; the main constraining factor for most travellers will be time (and the pronunciation of some of the names). **Santa María Tepepan** (1612-21), unique decorated earthenware font dated 1599; *tren ligero* Tepepan, walk up 5 de Mayo; **Santiago Tepatcatlalpan** (1770); **San Lucas Xochimanca** (16th century); **San Francisco Tlanepantla** (small 17th century chapel), village right in the country, superb views; **San Lorenzo Atemoaya** (16th century). After **Santa Cruz Acalpixca** (16th century with 17th century façade), near a mediocre Archaeological Museum, are the imposing **San Gregorio Atlapulco** (17th century; 16th century font), the tiny chapel of **San Luis Tlaxiatemalco** (1633) and the enormous **Santiago Tulyehualco** (late 18th century). Finally, beyond the boundary of the Xochimilco Delegación, is the church of **San Andrés Míxquic** (second quarter of 16th century; façade 1620; many alterations), built on the site of an earlier temple, using some of the original blocks which bear traces of pre-Hispanic designs; much-frequented around Día de los Muertos. All of these villages may be reached by pesero from the centre of Xochimilco, and there is also a bus to Tulyehualco (30 minutes). Eating places are generally limited to stalls with rolls, tacos and occasional spit-roasted chicken.

To the north of the town is the **Parque Ecológico** (■ *daily, 1000-1800, 1000-1700 winter months, US$1.50, children free, over-60s US$0.75*), an extensive area of grassland, lagoons and canals. Not much shade, but lots of birdlife. One can walk beyond the asphalt paths along the canal banks. There is also a punt-station. Access from Mexico City: bus, pesero or tren ligero to the Periférico, then pesero to Cuemanco; from Xochimilco, bus or pesero to Periférico, then likewise.

Museo Dolores Olmedo Patiño (Av México 5843, Xochimilco, on corner with Antiguo Camino a Xochimilco, one block southwest from La Noria *tren ligero* station, T55551016), set in eight acres of beautiful garden and grassland on site of an old estate, probably dating from 16th century. Rare Mexican hairless dogs and peacocks parade. Houses 137 works by Diego Rivera, 25 by Frida Kahlo, and an important collection of drawings by Angelina Beloff. There are also pre-Hispanic artefacts, 19th century antiques and Mexican folk art. Highly recommended. ■ *1000-1800, Tuesday-Sunday, US$1.50, students US$0.75*. Very pleasant open and covered café. **D** *Hotel Plaza El Mesón*, Av México 64, T56764163, mixed reports, noisy. Tourist office at Pino 36, open 0800-2100.

Ixtapalapa At the foot of the Cerro de Estrella, whose top is reached by a paved road or a path for some ruins, it has a small museum, a good view of volcanoes and two good churches: the Santuario del Calvario (1856), and San Lucas (1664), original roof timbers restored in 19th century, main door embodies Aztec motifs, fine interior. One of the most spectacular of Mexican passion-plays begins at Ixtapalapa on Holy Thursday.

Ciudad Universitaria (University City), world-famous, founded in 1551, is 18 kilometres via Insurgentes Sur on the Cuernavaca highway. Perhaps the most notable building is the 10-storey library tower, by Juan O'Gorman, its outside walls iridescent with mosaics telling the story of scientific knowledge, from Aztec astronomy to molecular theory.

The **Rectoría** has a vast, mosaic-covered and semi-sculptured mural by Siqueiros. Across the highway is the **Olympic Stadium**, with seats for 80,000, in shape, colour, and situation a world's wonder, but now closed, and run down. Diego Rivera has a sculpture-painting telling the story of Mexican sport. A new complex has been completed beyond the Ciudad Universitaria, including the newspaper library (the **Hemeroteca Nacional**), **Teatro Juan Ruiz de Alarcón**, **Sala Nezahuacoyotl** (concerts et cetera), bookshop and post office; also the **Museo Universitario Contemporáneo de Arte** and the **Espacio Escultórico** (sculptures – a large circular area of volcanic rock within a circle of cement – monoliths; on the opposite side of the road is another large area with many huge sculptures; stick to the path as it is possible to get lost in the vegetation). In the University museum there is an exhibition of traditional masks from all over Mexico. Beyond the Olympic Stadium is also the **Jardín Botánico Exterior** which shows all the cactus species in Mexico (■ *ask directions, it's a 30-minute walk, open 0700-1630*).

The University offers six-week courses (US$200, plus US$35 if you enroll late, good, student card useful).

Transport Bus (marked CU, one passes along Eje Lázaro Cárdenas; also bus 17, marked Tlalpan, which runs the length of Insurgentes) gets you there, about 1 hour journey. Another way to the university is on metro line 3 to Copilco station (20 minutes walk to University) or to Universidad station (30 minutes walk). At the University City there is a free bus going round the campus.

Further east is **Anahuacalli** (usually called the **Diego Rivera Museum**), ■ *Tuesday-Sunday 1000-1400, 1500-1800, closed Holy Week, US$1.70, free Sunday.* Here is a very fine collection of precolumbian sculpture and pottery, effectively displayed in a pseudo-Mayan tomb built for it by Diego Rivera. Reached by Kombi 29 bus from the Taxqueña metro station to Estadio Azteca, or take the bus marked División del Norte from outside Salto del Agua metro. Calle Museo branches off División del Norte. There is a big display here for the Day of the Dead at the beginning of November.

Villa Obregón

(Popularly known as **San Angel**) 13 kilometres southwest, has narrow, cobble-stone streets, many old homes, huge trees, and the charm of an era now largely past. Most of the distinguished architecture is of the 19th century. See the triple domes of its church, covered with coloured tiles, of the former Convento del Carmen, now the **Museo Colonial del Carmen**, which houses 17th and 18th century furniture and paintings. ■ *1000-1700.* See also the beautifully furnished and preserved old house, **Casa del Risco** , near the Bazar del Sábado, on Callejón de la Amargura; ■ *photographic ID required for entry, open Tuesday-Sunday 1000-1700, free;* also the church of San Jacinto, once belonging to a Dominican convent (1566). The **Museo de Arte Carrillo Gil**, Av Revolución 1608, has excellent changing exhibits and a permanent collection including several Diego Rivera Cubist works; the **Museo Estudio Diego Rivera** (Av Altavista y C Diego Rivera, opposite Antigua Hacienda de Goicochea – now *San Angel Inn*); is where Rivera and Frida Karlo lived and worked. Contains several works by Rivera, as well as belongings and memorabilia. The building was designed by Juan O'Gorman. **The Bazar del Sábado** is a splendid Saturday folk art and curiosity market. Reach San Angel by bus from Chapultepec Park or by metro line 3 to MA Quevedo. There is a YWCA (ACF) at San Angel, but it is expensive with hot water for two hours in the morning only, and use of kitchen 1800-2200. Excellent restaurants: the *San Angel Inn* is first class; good *panadería* by post office (which is no good for letters abroad). Between Villa

Mexico

Villa Obregón/San Angel

To City Centre

Obregón and Coyoacán is the monument to Obregón on the spot where he was assassinated in 1928 (by the junction of Av Insurgentes Sur and Arenal) ▪ *0900-1400*. Desierto de los Leones (see below) is reached from Villa Obregón by a scenic road. The **Centro Cultural San Angel** (on Revolución opposite Museo del Carmen) stages exhibitions, concerts, lectures et cetera; **La Carpa Geodésica**, Insurgentes Sur 2135 has theatre of all types from works for children to very avant-garde; the **Centro Cultural Helénico** (Insurgentes 1500, metro Barranca del Muerto) always has a lively and diversified programme of drama, music and dance.

Magdalena Contreras has many characteristics of the old Spanish village. Up in the hills in the southwest of the city, it can be reached by *pesero* or bus from San Angel (or by bus direct from Taxqueña), about 30-45 minutes. There is an attractive main square and an 18th century church on the site of an earlier structure. *Artesanías* and multiple *taquerías*, et cetera; good *comida corrida* at *Restaurante del Camino* and *Local 29* in the main square. From the village take another bus (bus station behind church), or *pesero*, up to **Los Dinamos** (three and a half kilometres), site of former pumping stations, now a National Park with picnic areas, waterfalls, horseriding, breathtaking scenery and, above all, clean air. There are *pulquerías* invitingly placed at intervals. If walking, bear in mind that you are quite a lot higher than in the city.

Coyoacán

The oldest part of Mexico City, Coyoacán is the place from which Cortés launched his attack on Tenochtitlán. It is also one of the most beautiful and best-preserved parts of the city, with hundreds of fine buildings from the 16th-19th centuries, elegant tree-lined avenues and carefully tended parks and, in the Jardín Centenario and the Plaza Hidalgo, two very attractive squares. There are no supermarkets, no high-rise buildings, no hotels, no metro stations (see below). It is an area that is best explored on foot. (An excellent postcard-cum-pedestrian map of the Centro Histórico of Coyoacán to be found in local book and gift shops.)

It is culturally one of the most lively parts of Mexico City, and with its attractive cafés and good shops it is much frequented by the inhabitants of the capital, particularly at weekends. From Villa Obregón, one can reach Coyoacán via a delightful walk through Chimalistac, across Universidad and down Av Francisco Sosa; or one can take a bus or *pesero* marked 'Tasqueña' as far as Caballocalco.

From the city centre, it is easiest to take the metro to Viveros, or General Anaya. **Sights** Alternatively, metro to Coyoacán then *pesero* for Villa Coapa, which drops you in the historic centre. If coming from metro Viveros (a large park in which trees are grown for other city parks), it is worth making a slight detour in order to walk the length of **Francisco Sosa**, said to be the first urban street laid down in Spanish America. At the beginning of this elegant avenue is the church of **San Antonio Panzacola** (18th century), by the side of Río Churubusco; nearby, on Universidad, is the remarkable, beautiful (and modern) chapel of **Nuestra Señora de la Soledad**, built in the grounds of the 19th century ex-hacienda El Altillo. A little way down, in Salvador Novo, is the **Museo de la Acuarela**. ■ *Free admission; open Tuesday-Sunday.* The terra-cotta fronted residence at No 383 is said to have been built by Alvarado. ■ *Courtyard and garden may be visited 0900-1600 Monday-Friday, no charge, enquire at entrance.* Many fine houses follow, mostly built in the 19th century. **Santa Catarina**, in the square of the same name, is a fine 18th century church; on Sunday, at about one o'clock, people assemble under the trees to tell stories (all are welcome to attend or participate). In the same square, the **Casa de la Cultura Jesús Reyes Heroles** should not be missed, with its delightful leafy gardens. Just before arriving at the **Jardín Centenario**, with its 16th century arches, is the **Casa de Diego Ordaz**. From metro General Anaya, there is a pleasant walk along Héroes del 47 (one block along on the left, 16th century church of **San Lucas**, across División del Norte and down Hidalgo (one block along on the left, and two blocks down San Lucas is the 18th century church of **San Mateo**). The **Museo Nacional de Culturas Populares** is on Av Hidalgo, just off Plaza Hidalgo, and should be seen. ■ *Tuesday-Sunday 1000-1600, free.* Permanent and temporary exhibitions, cinema-cum-auditorio; good bookshop on Mexican culture and folklore.

Coyoacán

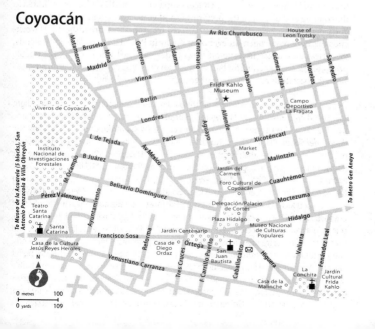

Mexico

The centre of Coyoacán is dominated by the church of **San Juan Bautista** (16th century with later additions; magnificent interior); also 16th century Franciscan monastery. Centenario is 16th century. The building which now houses the **Delegación** (Plaza Hidalgo) was built 244 years after the Conquest, on the site of the Palacio de Cortés. The beautiful 18th century church of **La Conchita** (in square of the same name) is reached by taking Higuera from Plaza Hidalgo; the interior, especially the altarpiece, is magnificent, but the church is normally open only on Friday evenings and Sunday mornings. On the corner of Higuera and Vallarta is what is reputed to be the house of La Malinche, Cortés' mistress. Admirers of Frida Kahlo will want to visit the **Museo Frida Kahlo**, Allende and Londres 247. Two rooms are preserved as lived in by Frida Kahlo and Diego Rivera, and the rest contain drawings and paintings by both; ■ *Open Tuesday-Sunday 1000-1700, admission US$1.50, no photos*. In the **Jardín Cultural Frida Kahlo**, near Plaza de La Conchita, there is a striking bronze statue of Frida by the contemporary Mexican sculptor Gabriel Ponzanelli.

Trotsky's house is at Río Churubusco 410, between Gómez Farías and Morelos. ■ *Tuesday-Sunday 1000-1700 (entry US$1.50, half-price with ISIC card, US$1.50 to take photos)*. **NB** Also the **Museo del Retrato Hablado** (Universidad 1330-C), the **Museo Geles Cabrera**, sculpture; Xicoténcatl 181; prior appointment, T56883016 and the **Museo del Automóvil** (División del Norte 3752).

Coyoacán has several **theatres**, medium and small, and similar establishments, for example the *Coyoacán* and *Usigli* theatres (Eleuterio Méndez, five blocks from metro Anaya), the *Foro Cultural de Coyoacán* (Allende; most events free of charge), the Museo de Culturas Populares (Hidalgo), the *Foro Cultural Ana-María Hernández* (Pacífico 181), the *Teatro Santa Catarina* (Plaza Sta Catarina), the *Rafael Solana* theatre on Miguel Angel de Quevedo (nearly opposite Caballocalco), the *Casa del Teatro*, Vallarta 31 and *Foro de la Conchita*, Vallarta 33. Also note *El Hábito* (Madrid) and *El hijo del cuervo* (Jardín Centenario) for avant-garde drama and cabaret, *Los talleres de Coyoacán* (Francisco Sosa) for dance and ballet, *Cadac* (Centenario) for traditional and experimental drama. On the edge of the Coyoacán Delegación (southeast corner of Churubusco and Tlalpan, Metro General Anaya) is the *Central Nacional de las Artes*, a huge complex of futuristic buildings dedicated to the training and display of the performing and visual arts. Good bookshop, library and cafeterías. Details to be found in *Tiempo Libre* and local broadsheets. At weekends there are many open-air events especially in Plaza Hidalgo. Also at weekends, the Artesanía market, in a site off Plaza Hidalgo, is well worth a visit; reasonable prices, and lots of potential for bargaining; as at most places where bargaining is possible, the best deals are to be had either early or late in the day.

Eating There are several pleasant *cafeterías* in the Jardín Centenario, some of which serve light snacks and *antojitos*; the best known is *El Parnaso*, adjacent to the bookshop of the same name. 2 of the best-known *cantinas* in Mexico are *La Guadalupana* (Higuera) and the *Puerta del Sol* on Plaza Hidalgo. No shortage of restaurants with *comida corrida*, though prices tend to be higher than in other parts of the city (US$1.75-2.50). Very good value are: *Rams*, Hidalgo, almost opposite Museo de Culturas Populares, excellent fish, US$1.75; *Fabio's*, overlooking Plaza Hidalgo and the Delegación, credit cards accepted; *Rincón Oaxaqueño*, Carrillo Puerto 12, US$1.75. Good value, too in the *Mercado*, between Malintzin and Xichoténcatl, US$1.15, possibly the most exquisite *quesadillas* in the whole of Coyoacán are found at local 31 (outside, opposite Jardín del Carmen, closed Wednesdays); stall holders are very friendly and fruit and veg sellers are ready to explain the names and uses of their goods; frequent musical entertainment particularly lunchtime and weekends. The *Restaurante Vegetariano*, Carranza y Caballocalco, offers an excellent US$5 buffet lunch; *El Morral*, Allende No 2, set lunch US$3, double at weekends, no credit cards, highly recommended, quieter upstairs, palatial lavatories. The *Caballocalco*, on Plaza Hidalgo, is expensive, but very good, especially for breakfast. There is a *Sanborn's* on Jardín Centenario, near to *El hijo del cuervo*. *Hacienda de Cortés*, Fernández Leal 74, behind Plaza de la

Conchita, exceptionally pleasant surroundings, large, shaded, outdoor dining area, excellent breakfast, good value, *comida corrida* US$5, try the *sábana de res con chilaquiles verdes*. *Pacífico*, Av Pacífico, in restored 19th century residence, specialities include pre-Hispanic dishes, not cheap but good value. Excellent *comida corrida* at **Villa Cristal**, Allende; elegant restaurant **La Doña**, Héroes del 47 No 141, good value.

Shopping

Many gift shops in the area, good taste and prices at **Etra**, on corner of Francisco Sosa opposite Jardín Centenario. **Mayolih**, Aldama with Berlín, 2 blocks from Museo Frida Kahlo; **La Casita** on Higuera. Also on Higuera are **La Rosa de los Vientos** (maps of all parts of the country) and the Post Office with Mexpost service. **Foto Coyoacán**, Fco Sosa 1, opposite the Arches, excellent, rapid developing, printing, English, French, German spoken. The best cycle repair in Mexico City is **Hambling González Muller**, Ezequiel Ordóñez 46-1, Col Copilco el Alto, T/F56585591, builds wheels and frames for Mexican racers, reasonable prices, highly recommended. **Sakurafoto**, Plaza Hidalgo, excellent service, English, German spoken. Good range of CDs and tapes at **Gandhi Discos**, Carrillo Puerto 6, excellent prices.

Transport

The *pesero* from metro Anaya to the centre of Coyoacán is marked 'Santo Domingo', alight at Abasolo or at the Jardín Centenario; it also goes past the Mercado (Malintzin). Alternatively, get off the metro at Ermita and get the *pesero* (Santo Domingo) from C Pirineos, on the west side of Tlalpan just north of the metro station. The *pesero* passes in front of the Frida Kahlo museum.

The **Huayamilpas Ecological Park** can be reached by *pesero* from the centre of Coyoacán. The lake and surrounding area are protected by local inhabitants.

Tenayuca

The pyramid of Tenayuca, 10 kilometres to the northwest, is about 15 metres high and the best-preserved in Mexico. The Aztecs rebuilt this temple every 52 years; this one was last reconstructed about 1507; well worth seeing, for it is surrounded with serpents in masonry. The easiest way to get there by car from Mexico City centre is to go to Vallejo, 11 kilometres north of the intersection of Insurgentes Norte and Río Consulado. ■ *Admission US$1.50, open 1000-1645.* By metro, take the line to the Central de Autobuses del Norte (see page 296), La Raza, and catch the bus there. By bus from Tlatelolco; ask driver and passengers to advise you on arrival as site is not easily visible. An excursion to Tula may go via Tenayuca. It is not far from the old town of **Tlalnepantla**: see the ancient convent (ask for the *catedral*) on the Plaza Gustavo Paz and the church (1583), which contains the first image, a Christ of Mercy, brought to the New World. Two and a half kilometres to the north is the smaller pyramid of **Santa Cecilia Acatitlán**, (difficult to find: head for church tower visible from footbridge over highway), interesting for its restored sanctuary. ■ *US$1.50.*

Los Remedios, a small town 13 kilometres northwest of Mexico City, has in its famous church an image, a foot high, adorned with jewels. See the old aqueduct, with a winding stair leading to the top of two towers. It can be reached by car or by taking the Los Remedios bus at Tacuba metro. Fiesta: 1 September to the climax 8 September.

At **Naucalpan**, northwest of the city (just outside the city boundary on Boulevard Toluca), pre-classic Olmec-influenced figurines can be seen in the **Museo de la Cultura de Tlatilco** (closed Monday), opposite the *Hotel Naucalpan* on Vía Gustavo Baz. This is said to be the oldest settlement in the Cuenca de México.

Excursions from Mexico City

Desierto de los Leones This beautiful forest of pines and broad-leaved trees, made into a national park, can be reached from Mexico City (24 kilometres) by a fine scenic road through Villa Obregón. In the woods is an old Carmelite monastery (begun 1602, finished 1611, abandoned because of cold and damp in 1780); around are numerous hermitages, inside are several subterranean passages and a secret hall with curious acoustic properties. Take a torch.

Take an hour's bus ride from Observatorio metro to La Venta and ask bus-driver where to get off for the path to the monastery (about four kilometres walk). One can either get there via the paved road or via the beautiful conifer-forest path, but the latter splits frequently so stick to what looks like the main path; or take the fire-break road below the row of shops and cheap restaurants near the main road. Food stalls abound, particularly at weekends when it is crowded. Do not leave valuables in your car. Many birds may be seen in the valley reached from the picnic area six kilometres south of La Venta on Route 15.

Acolman has the formidable fortress-like convent and church of San Agustín, dating from 1539-60, with much delicate detail on the façade and some interesting murals inside. Note the fine portal and the carved stone cross at the entrance to the atrium. Reached by bus from Indios Verdes metro station, or from the Zócalo. It is 35 kilometres northeast of the city and can be visited on the way to/from Teotihuacan.

Teotihuacan

Colour map 3, grid B4 Forty nine kilometres from Mexico City, with some of the most remarkable relics in the world of an ancient civilization. Thought to date from around 300 BC, the builders of this site remain a mystery. Where they came from and why the civilization disappeared is pure conjecture. It seems that the city may have housed 250,000 who were peace-loving but whose influence spread as far as Guatemala. So completely was it abandoned that it was left to the Aztecs to give names to its most important features.

Sights There are three main areas: the **Ciudadela**, the **Pyramid of the Sun** and the **Pyramid of the Moon**. The whole is connected by the nearly four kilometre-long Street of the Dead which runs almost due north. To the west lie the sites of Tetitla, Atetelco, Zacuala and Yayahuala (see below). To the northeast lies Tepantitla, with fine frescoes on a palace. The old city is traceable over an area of three and a half by six and a half kilometres. Reckon on about five to eight hours to see the site properly, arrive early before the vast numbers of the *ambulantes* (wandering sales people with obsidian, flutes, silver bangles and, in Plaza of the Sun, straw hats) and the big tourist groups at 1100. There is a perimeter road with a number of car parking places – go anticlockwise. The small pebbles embedded in mortar indicate reconstruction (most of the site apparently!).

Capable of holding 60,000 people, the citadel's main feature is the **Temple of Quetzalcoatl** (the Plumed Serpent, Lord of Air and Wind). Go to the east side of the one kilometre square. Behind the largest of the temples (take the right hand path) lies an earlier pyramid which has been partially restored. Lining the staircase are huge carved heads of the feathered serpents.

Follow the Street of the Dead to the **Plaza of the Sun**. You will pass small grassy mounds which are unexcavated temples. The Plaza contains many buildings, probably for the priests, but is dominated by the massive **Pyramid of the Sun** (64 metres high, 213 metres square at the base) and covering almost the same space as the Great Pyramid of Cheops in Egypt. The sides are terraced, and wide stairs lead to the summit. The original four metre covering of stone and stucco was removed by mistake in 1910. The view from the top gives a good impression of the whole site. But beware, it is a steep climb particularly between the third and fourth terrace.

The car park to the north leads to Tepantitla. The murals here depict the rain god Tláloc. There are many questions still to be answered about Teotihuacan culture; a recent discovery in 1997 of 50 clay figurines is one more piece in the jigsaw. The museum (admission included in price of ticket) now lies south of Pyramid of the Sun. It is well laid out and contains a large model of Teotihuacan in its heyday as well as many beautiful artefacts, recommended. There is an expensive restaurant at the museum, indifferent service, not always open.

The **Pyramid of the Moon** is about one kilometre further north and on your right a tin roof covers a wall mural of a large, brightly coloured jaguar (the **Jaguar Temple**). The plaza contains the 'A' altars – 11 in a peculiar geometric pattern. The

Teotihuacan

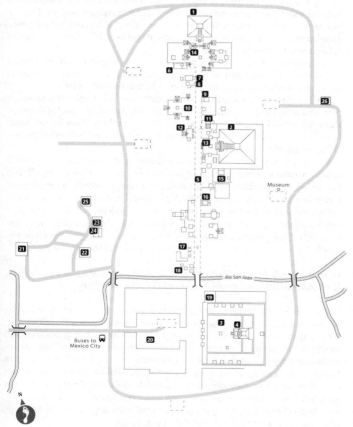

Mexico

Not to scale

1 Pyramid of the Moon	**10** Plaza of the Columns	**19** Plaza Two
2 Pyramid of the Sun	**11** Palace of the Sun	**20** Great Compound
3 Ciudadela	**12** Patio of the Four Little Temples	**21** Palace of Atetelco
4 Temple of Quetzalcoatl	**13** Plaza of the Sun	**22** Palace of Tetitla
5 Street of the Dead	**14** Plaza of the Moon	**23** Palace of Zacuala
6 Palaces of Quetzalpapalotl,	**15** House of the Priest	**24** Patio of Zacuala
Jaguars & Feathered Shells	**16** Viking Group	**25** Palace of Yayahuala
7 Temple of Agriculture	**17** Street of the Dead complex with	**26** Palace of Tepantitla
8 Mural of the Mythological Animals	'Superimposed Buildings' group	
9 Jaguar Temple & Mural	**18** Northwest Cluster	

Pyramid is only half the size of the Pyramid of the Sun. There are excellent views looking south down the Street of the Dead.

To the west of the Plaza of the Moon lies the **Palace of Quetzalpapalotl** (quetzalmariposa, or quetzalbutterfly), where the priests serving the sanctuaries of the Moon lived, it has been restored together with its patio. Note the obsidian inlet into the highly decorated carved pillars. There is a sign here forbidding high heels. Follow the path left under the Palace through the Jaguars' Palace with catlike murals protected from the sun by green canvas curtains to the **Temple of the Feathered Shells**. The base of the simple altar is decorated with shells, flowers and eagles.

You will pass several more temples on the west side of the Street of the Dead. If you want to visit Atetelco, go through the car park opposite the Pyramid of the Sun, turn right past *Restaurant Pirámides Charlies* (reputed to be the best on the site) and turn right along a small track. Alternatively to get to them from the museum, exit west and walk right up to main road, turning left after crossing the stream. They are well worth a visit; **Tetitla** a walled complex with beautiful frescoes and paintings, **Atetelco** with its three tiny temples and excellent murals and the abandoned sites of **Zacuala** and **Yayahuala**.

At the spring equinox, 21 March, the sun is perfectly aligned with the west face of the Pyramid of the Sun; many ad hoc sun worshippers hold unofficial ceremonies to mark the occasion (this is also Benito Juárez's birthday so entry is free).

NB If short of time, try to get lift from a tourist bus to the Pyramid of the Moon car park. This is the most interesting area. Also take food and water – most of the shops are on the west side and you may be some distance from them. There is a handicraft centre with weavings, obsidian carvings and explanations (and tastings) of the production of tequila and mescal.

■ *Site open daily 0800-1700. (If the entrance near the bus stop is not open when it says it is, at 0800, try entrance near the Pyramid of the Moon.) Entrance, US$2.50, cars free, free on Sunday (extra charge for videos, tripods not permitted). The outside sites may be closed on Monday. Son et lumière display, costs US$4 per person (good lumière, not so good son); lasts 45 minutes, 1900 in Spanish, 2015 in English (October-June only); take blanket or rent one. Official guidebook on sale, US$1, gives a useful route to follow. The Bloomgarden guide contains a useful map, good description and is recommended. At weekends, students give free guided tours, ask at the entrance.*

Sleeping **AL** *Villas Arqueológicas*, pool (Apdo Postal 44 55800, San Juan Teotihuacan, Edo de México, T60909/60244, F60928; in Mexico City, reservations at Club Med office).

Transport **Buses** From Terminal del Norte, Gate 8, platform 6 (Autobuses del Norte metro), Mexico City, which takes at least 45 minutes, US$2 one way (Pirámides buses are white with a yellow stripe). Bus returns from Door 1 (some others from 2 and 3) at Teotihuacan site, supposedly every 30 minutes. Some return buses to the capital terminate in the outskirts in rush hour without warning. You can also get a bus from Indios Verdes metro station. If driving, the toll on the Autopista Ecatepec-Pirámides is US$3. You can ride back to town with one of the tourist buses for about US$3. Note that the site is more generally known as 'Pirámides' than as 'Teotihuacan'. You can also take the metro to Indios Verdes (last stop on line 3), then a public bus (US$1) to the pyramids. Tours to Teotihuacan, picking you up at your hotel and usually including the Basílica de Guadalupe, normally cost US$30-35, with little time at the site.

The village of **San Juan Teotihuacan** is well worth a visit, if time permits (*pesero* from the road running round the site of the pyramids, US$0.20). It has a magnificent 16th century church (a few blocks down Cuauhtémoc from the square). Good, clean restaurant, *Los Pinos*, in Guadalupe Victoria, one block from the square, *comida corrida* US$1.65. Bus back to Mexico City (Terminal del Norte, or Metro Indios Verdes, US$1.25).

Tepotzotlan About 43 kilometres northwest of Mexico City just off the route to Querétaro, with a splendid Jesuit church of San Francisco Javier in churrigueresque style. There are fine colonial paintings in the convent corridors. The old Jesuit monastery has been converted into the **Museo Nacional del Virreinato**, a comprehensive and well- displayed collection covering all aspects of life under Spanish rule. ■ *1000-1700, closed Monday, US$4.35, Sunday free.* It is also a tourist centre with restaurants. There is a big market on Wednesday and Sunday when the town gets very congested; good selection of handicrafts and jewellery, as well as meat, cheese, and other foods. 28 kilometres north west is the 18th century Acueducto del Sitio, 61 metres at its highest, 438 metres long.

Sleeping and eating AL *Hotel Tepotzotlán*, C Industrias, about 3 blocks from centre, TV, restaurant, swimming pool, good views, secure parking, highly recommended; *Hotel San José*, Zócalo, nice rooms, poor service and value. The *Hostería del Monasterio* has very good Mexican food and a band on Sunday; try their coffee with cinnamon. *Restaurant Artesanías*, opposite church, recommended, cheap. Also good food at *Brookwell's Posada*.

Buses From near El Rosario metro station, US$1.50, 1 hour ride. Many Querétaro or Guanajuato buses from Terminal del Norte pass the turn-off at 'Caseta Tepotzotlán' from where one can take a local bus or walk (30 minutes) to the town. (Do not confuse Tepotzotlán with Tepoztlán, which is south of Mexico City, near Cuernavaca).

In the third week of December, *pastorelas*, or morality plays based on the temptation and salvation of Mexican pilgrims voyaging to Bethlehem, are held. Tickets are about US$10 and include a warming punch, the play, a procession and litanies, finishing with a meal, fireworks and music. Tickets from Viajes Roca, Neva 30, Col Cuauhtémoc, Mexico City.

Another half-day excursion is to Tula, some 65 kilometres, thought to be the most important Toltec site in Mexico; two ball courts, pyramids, a frieze in colour, and remarkable sculptures over six metres high have been uncovered. There are four huge warriors in black basalt on a pyramid, the great Atlantes anthropomorphic pillars. The museum is well worth visiting and there is a massive fortress-style church, dating from 1553, near the market. ■ *Admission to site and museum, US$2 weekdays, reduction with ISIC card, free Sunday and holidays. The small restaurant is not always open. Multilingual guidebooks at entrance, fizzy drinks on sale. Site is open Tuesday-Sunday 0930-1630 (museum open Wednesday-Sunday till 1630).* **Warning**: Assaults have been reported in the ballcourt; be alert at all times, especially in deserted areas of the site. There are no security guards. The town itself is pleasant, clean and friendly. If driving from Mexico City, take the turn for Actopán before entering Tula, then look for the Parque Nacional sign (and the great statues) on your left.

Tula
Colour map 3, grid B4

Sleeping and eating C *Hotel Catedral*, clean, pleasant, TV. *Restaurant la Cabaña*, on main square, local dishes, also *Nevería*, with good soup.

Transport 1½ hours by train from Buenavista station; at 0700 and 0900, returns at 1744 and 1955, US$1.20 (excellent breakfast for US$0.65), but can be several hours late; it follows the line of the channel cut by Alvarado to drain the lakes of Mexico Valley, visible as a deep canyon (from station walk along track 30 minutes to site). One can take bus back, which leaves earlier. It can also be reached by 1st class bus, 'Valle de Mesquital', from Terminal del Norte, Av de los Cien Metros, goes to Tula bus terminal in 2-2½ hours; US$3.20 each way, every 40 minutes 0600-2100; Tula bus terminal is 3 kilometres from the site, take a 'Chapantago' bus (every 20 minutes) to the entrance, 5 minutes (badly signposted), or a taxi, US$2, or walk, turning right out of the bus station. At the main road, cut diagonally left across road and take first right, which will take you to a bridge over an evil smelling river. Carry on to the main highway, then turn left. Also bus or car from Actopán, on the Pan-American Highway (see page 104). Tula-Pachuca US$3.30; safe to leave belongings at bus station. Grey Line excursions from Mexico City have been recommended.

Mexico

Mexico

Mexico City - Veracruz - Mexico City

A round tour by way of Tlaxcala, Cholula, Puebla, Tehuacán, Orizaba, Córdoba, Veracruz, and Xalapa. The route encompasses volcanoes, remains of the Tlaxcalan, Olmec and Totonac cultures, many fine colonial buildings in cities and villages and leads to the distinct Caribbean culture of Veracruz. A major detour goes to the Papaloapan region, in the south of Veracruz state, often neglected by visitors.

By road, the principal route is paved all the way (no Pemex service station on road between Puebla and Orizaba, a distance of about 150 kilometres); total distance: 924 kilometres, or 577 miles. A new toll *autopista* (motorway) now runs all the way from Mexico City to Veracruz (four tolls which range from US$4.35 to US$9). If wishing to avoid the toll route, note that the Vía Libre is very congested initially, and, at Ixtapulaca, just out of Mexico City, there is a series of *topes* (speed bumps) so high that they are a danger to ordinary saloon cars.

Our description is a trip along the old road, which goes east along the Puebla road, past the airport and swimming pools, and some spectacular shanty-towns. At

Mexico City environs

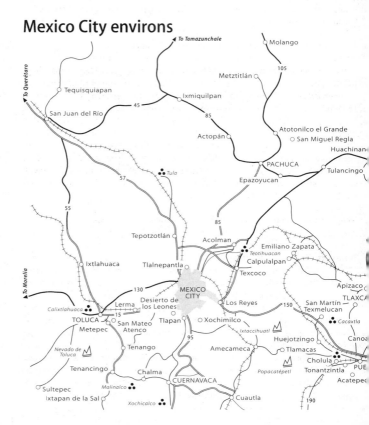

(Km 19) Los Reyes, a road runs left into a valley containing the now almost completely drained Lake Texcoco, a valley early settled by the *conquistadores*. Along it we come to **Chapingo**, where there is a famous agricultural college with particularly fine frescoes by Rivera in the chapel, *pesero* from Gen Anaya y San Ciprián or bus from TAPO-Autotransportes Mexico-Texcoco, US$0.70. ■ *Monday-Friday 0900-1800*. Next comes **Texcoco**, a good centre for visiting villages in the area. Bus from Mexico City, from Emiliano Zapata 92, near Candelaria metro station or TAPO. Near Chapingo a road runs right to the village of **Huexotla** (see the Aztec wall, with ruined fortifications and pyramid, and the 16th century Franciscan convent of San Luis Obispo). Another road from Texcoco runs through the public park of Molino de las Flores. From the old *hacienda* buildings, now in ruins, a road (right) runs up the hill of Tetzcotzingo, near the top of which are the Baños de Netzahualcoyotl, the poet-prince. (San Miguel de) **Chiconcuac** (road to San Andrés and left at its church), four kilometres away, is where Texcoco *sarapes* are woven. Tuesday is market day and there is a rousing *fiesta* in honour of their patron saint on 29 September.

Popocatépetl and Ixtaccíhuatl

At Km 29 is **Ixtapaluca** where a road on the right (south) leads to the small town of Amecameca, the starting point for Popocatépetl and Ixtaccíhuatl. where there is a youth hostel and Spanish countryside school: open all year, it caters for all abilities, small library, tourist information, economical tours. US$100 per week, five hours of

Colour map 3, grid B4

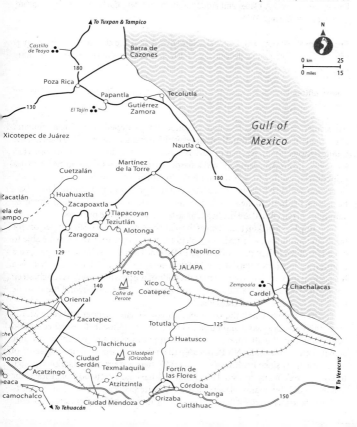

classes daily, Monday-Friday, three meals a day. Youth hostel services US$3 per day, meals extra. From Mexico City, take metro to Pantitlán, then a bus or *pesero* to Ixtapaluca. Behind the Mercado Municipal take another *pesero* on the 'Avila Camacho' route and get off at La Vereda (transportation from 0600-2100 daily). For information F55125992. On the way to Amecameca, see the restored 16th century convent and church at **Chalco**, and the fine church, convent and open-air chapel of the same period at **Tlalmanalco**.

Amecameca
Population: 57,000
Altitude: 2,315m
Colour map 3, grid B4

Amecameca is 60 kilometres from Mexico City. The Zócalo is pleasant, with good taco stands; the post office is also on the Zócalo. A road reaches the sanctuary of El Sacromonte, 90 metres above the town (magnificent views), a small and very beautiful church built round a cave in which once lived Fray Martín de Valencia, a *conquistador* who came to Mexico in 1524. It is, next to the shrine of Guadalupe, the most sacred place in Mexico and has a much venerated full-sized image of Santo Entierro weighing one and a half kilograms only. From the Zócalo, take the exit under the arch and head for the first white station of the cross; the stations lead to the top. Market day is Saturday, and an excellent non-touristy market on Sunday.

Sleeping Three hotels, **E**, close to Amecameca's main plaza (*Ameque*, clean, with bath), and rooms at the *San Carlos* restaurant on the main plaza, **F** with bath, noisy, good, modern, hot water. **Camping** Permitted at the railway station, ask the man in the office (leaving town, it's after the road to Tlamacas, on the right, 1-2 kilometres away).

Eating Several eating places and a good food market. *San Carlos*, on the main square, good food, set lunch US$1.75.

Buses from Mexico City with Cristóbal Colón. Los Volcanos 2nd class bus 1-1½ hours' journey, US$2, from the Central del Oriente; if hitching, take the Calzada Zaragoza, very dusty road.

Tourist offices Near plaza. Open 0900-1500. They can provide information and guides for Ixtaccíhuatl.

Popocatépetl

Amecameca is at the foot of the twin volcanoes **Popocatépetl** ('smoking mountain', 5,452 metres) and **Ixtaccíhuatl** (Eestaseewatl, 'sleeping woman', 5,286 metres); the saddle between them, reached by car via a paved road up to the Paso de Cortés (25 kilometres from Amecameca), gives particularly fine views. Legend has it that a princess was waiting for her warrior lover to return when news came of his death. Overcome with grief, she poisoned herself and when the warrior returned from battle he took her body to the top of Ixtaccíhuatl and jumped into its crater. The three summits of Iztaccíhuatl are the head, breasts and knees of the princess.

On Saturdays a pickup truck leaves the plaza at Amecameca, US$2 per person, for far up the mountain; also taxis for US$15 for two people (but you may be able to negotiate down to half this), offer trips to Paso de Cortés. Just before the pass, cars (but not pedestrians or taxis) pay US$0.10 entry to the national park. There is a hostal, **E**, at the pass. The road on the other side of the pass to Cholula is rough, steep and sandy (but scenic), a sturdy vehicle is needed. The road beyond the Paso de Cortés to Tlamacas is currently closed.

The best time to climb the volcanoes is between late October and early March when there are clear skies and no rain. From May to October the weather is good before noon; in the afternoons it is bad. Get permission and ask about volcanic activity before you climb. **NB Popocatépetl** has been closed to climbers because of volcanic activity since 1994. Twice during 1997 there were eruptions serious enough to cover Mexico City in ash. The authorities have an evacuation plan for some 300,000 people but many villagers on the slopes are suspicious that it is an excuse to take over lands. We suggest that readers seek local advice before planning an ascent.

From Paso de Cortés a road goes left (north) along another dirt road which leads *Ixtaccíhuatl* past a TV station for eight kilometres to the nearest parking to the summit of Ixtaccíhuatl at La Joya. Near the antennae is a *refugio* called Atzomani (safest place to park) and there is a box (*buzón*) for notifying potential rescue groups of your intended route. From there you find various routes to the summit (12-15 hours return) and three to four refuges to overnight (no furniture, bare floors, dirty). Ixtaccíhuatl has been described as "an exhilarating rollercoaster of successive summits." To climb **Ixtaccíhuatl** take a taxi to La Joya, from there follow the tracks up the grassy hill on the right, four to six hours to first huts. The first two huts are at 4,750 metres (places for 30 people), the third at 4,850 metres (10-15 people), and the last hut is at 5,010 metres (in poor condition, 10-12 people); the Luís Menéndez hut is the most salubrious. From the last hut it is two and a half to three hours to the top, set off at 0400, over two glaciers, some rock climbing required, crampons and ice-picks are necessary, can be hired in Amecameca.

A more technical route starts at the *buzón* and at first descends left into the valley. Walk three to four hours from La Joya to the Ayoloco glacier before which is a refugio for eight to 10 people at 4,800 metres, three to four hours to summit from here. Guides are available in Amecameca (Rigoberto Mendoza has been recommended). Cost is about US$110 and worth it, as walking on glaciers without knowing the conditions is hazardous.

Beyond Ixtapaluca the road climbs through pine forests to reach 3,196 metres about 63 kilometres from Mexico City, and then descends in a series of sharp bends to the town of San Martín **Texmelucan**, Km 91. The old Franciscan convent here has a beautifully decorated interior, and a former *hacienda* displays weaving and old machinery. The Zócalo is beautiful, with beaches covered in ceramic tiles and a central gazebo. Market day is Tuesday (**D-E** *Hotel San José*, with bath, variety of rooms, parking inside, recommended, at Pte 115; opposite is **E** *La Granja*, with bath, parking, recommended).

Tlaxcala

From Texmelucan a sideroad leads northeast for 24 kilometres to the once quaint old Indian town of Tlaxcala, with its pleasant centre of simple buildings washed in ochre, pink and yellow, and its vast suburbs. It is the capital of small Tlaxcala state whose wealthy ranchers breed fighting bulls, but whose landless peasantry is still poor.

Population: 36,000
State population 1995: 883,630
Altitude: 2,240m
Colour map 3, grid B4

The Church of **San Francisco**, is the oldest in Mexico (1521), from whose pulpit the **Sights** first Christian sermon was preached in New Spain (Mexico). Its severe façade conceals a most sumptuous interior (note the cedar and gold, star-spangled ceiling, and the 'No Photos' sign at the door); almost next door is the **Museo del Estado de Tlaxcala**, two floors of historical and artistic exhibits, interesting; also the extremely colourful murals (1966, still incomplete) depicting the indigenous story of Tlaxcala, the history of Mexico (■ *0900-1700, US$1*) and of mankind in the **Palacio de Gobierno**. Huge market every Saturday. **Casa de las Artesanías de Tlaxcala**, a 'living museum' where Otomi indians demonstrate traditional arts and customs including the sweatbath, cooking, embroidery, weaving and pulque-making, highly recommended. *La Fonda del Museo* is attached restaurant (see below).

A remarkable series of precolumbian frescoes are to be seen at the ruins of **Cacaxtla** **Excursions** near San Miguel del Milagro, between Texmelucan and Tlaxcala. The colours are still sharp and some of the figures are larger than life size. One wall, in turquoise, depicts a battle between an army dressed as jaguars and another dressed as eagles. Also depicted are two princes, the jaguar (the native prince), and the eagle, representing the invading Huaxtecas. The jaguar also represents Venus, the night, the rainy season, north, death, while the eagle is the sun, day, the dry season, south and life (Helmut Zettl, Ebergassing, who quotes the theories of Prof Michel Graulich of the Free University of Brussels). To protect the paintings from the sun and rain, a huge roof has been constructed. The site is open all day and an easily accessible visitors' centre has been opened (closed Monday). There is disappointingly little published information on the site, however. In theory there is a 'per picture' charge for photography, but this is not assiduously collected although flash and tripod are strictly prohibited.

From Puebla take a Flecha Azul bus marked 'Nativitas' from C 10 Pte y C 11 Nte to just beyond that town where a sign on the right points to San Miguel del Milagro and Cacaxtla (US$1). Walk up the hill (or colectivo US$0.20) to a large sign with its back to you, turn left here for the ruins.

The ruined pyramid of **Xicohténcatl** at San Esteban de **Tizatlán**, five kilometres outside the town, has two sacrificial altars with original colour frescoes preserved under glass. The pictures tell the story of the wars with Aztecs and Chichimecs. Amid the archaeological digs at Tizatlán are a splendid 19th century church and a 16th century chapel of San Esteban. Colectivo to Tizatlán from 1 de Mayo y 20 de Noviembre, Tlaxcala, at main square, you get out when you see a yellow church dome on the left.

The **Sanctuary of Ocotlán** (1541), on a hill in the outskirts of Tlaxcala (a stiff 20-minute climb from Juárez via Guribi and Alcocer, but worth it) commands a view of valley and volcano. It was described by Sacheverell Sitwell as 'the most delicious building in the world', but others have been less impressed. Nevertheless, its façade of lozenge-shaped vermilion bricks framing the white stucco portal and surmounted by two white towers 'with fretted cornices and salomonic pillars' is beautiful. The golden interior was worked on for 25 years by the Indian Francisco Miguel.

La Malinche Volcano, 4,461 metres, can be reached from Tlaxcala or Puebla (buses from the market beside the old railway station, one and a half hours, US$1, one at 0800 and others, return 1800). You go to La Malintzi Centro de Vacaciones at the base of the volcano, now closed to the public. The hike to the summit takes four hours, the descent one and a half (take an ice-axe, altitude is a problem). Alternatively, stay at nearby town of Apizaco. Reasonable hotel and restaurant next to the roundabout with a locomotive in the centre, safe parking. It is a good day trip from Puebla. Another route is via Canoa (bus from Puebla, US$0.50). Long hike to top, 10 hours return at a good pace, take warm clothes.

Sleeping **A** *Posada San Francisco* (Club Med), Plaza de la Constitución 17, T26022, F26818, lavishly decorated in colonial style. **C** *Alifer*, Morelos 11, uphill from plaza, T25678, safe parking. Several in **D** category near centre. **E** *Hotel-Mansión Xichoténcatl*, on Juárez, back rooms quieter.

Eating *Los Portales*, main square. *Restaurante del Quijote*, Plaza Felipe Xochiténcatl. *La Fonda del Museo* (see above), serves excellent 4-course traditional meals in a lovely setting, set lunch US$8. *Oscar's*, Av Juárez, near corner of Zitlalpopocatl, excellent sandwiches and juices. *La Arboleda*, Lira y Ortega, near square, good.

Entertainment *The Cine American*, on Boulevard G Valle (continuation of Av Juárez) has 2 for the price of 1 on Wednesday.

Festivals The annual fair is held **29 October-15 November** each year.

Transport Frequent Flecha Azul buses from Puebla, central bus station (platform 81/82) between 0600 and 2130, 45 minutes, US$1.20. Tlaxcala's bus station is about a 10-minute walk to the centre. To Cacaxtla US$0.40.

Laundry *Servi-Klim*, Av Juárez, 1½ blocks from plaza, good. **Tourist offices** Tourist office at Juárez y Landizábal, many maps and leaflets, very helpful, no English spoken.

(Km 106) **Huejotzingo** has the second-oldest church and monastery in Mexico, built 1529; now a museum. Market: Saturday, Tuesday. Dramatic carnival on Shrove Tuesday, portraying the story of Agustín Lorenzo, a famous local bandit. **D** *Hotel Colonial*, secure but poor value.

Cholula

A small somnolent town (with the Universidad de las Américas), but one of the strangest-looking in all Mexico. When Cortés arrived, this was a holy centre with 100,000 inhabitants and 400 shrines, or *teocallis*, grouped round the great pyramid of Quetzalcoatl. In its day it was as influential as Teotihuacan. There used to be a series of pyramids built one atop another. When razing them, Cortés vowed to build a chapel for each of the *teocallis* destroyed, but in fact there are no more than about 70.

Km 122
Population 20,000

Mexico

Sights The excavated pyramid, has eight kilometres of tunnels and some recently discovered frescoes inside, but only one kilometre of tunnel is open to the public, which gives an idea of superimposition (the frescoes are not open to the public). Museum near tunnel entrance has a copy of the frescos. ■ *1000-1700, admission US$2 on weekdays, free on Sunday and holidays, Guides charge US$6.50, recommended as there are no signs inside (some guides claim to speak English, but their command of the language is poor).* The entrance is on the main road into Cholula. From Zócalo follow Av Morelos crossing railway. The 16th century chapel of **Los Remedios** on top of it gives a fine view. The Franciscan fortress church of **San Gabriel** (1552) is in the plaza; ■ *open 0600-1200, 1600-1900, Sundays 0600-1900;* and next to it, the **Capilla Real**, which has 49 domes. ■ *Open 1000-1200, 1530-1800, Sundays 0900-1800.*

Excursions See the Indian statuary and stucco work of the 16th century church of Santa María de **Tonantzintla**, outside the town; the church is one of the most beautiful in Mexico (■ *open 1000-1800 daily*), and may also be reached by paved road from San Francisco **Acatepec**, which also has a beautiful, less ornate 16th century church (recently damaged by fire, although the façade of tiles is still intact. ■ *Supposedly open 0900-1800 daily, but not always so – key is held by José Ascac, ask for his shop.* They are off Highway 190 from Puebla to Izúcar de Matamoros. Both these places are easily reached from Cholula or Puebla. Best light for photography after 1500. Photography *inside* both churches is frowned upon. John Hemming says these two churches "should on no account be missed; they are resplendent with Poblano tiles and their interiors are a riot of Indian stucco-work and carving." Both churches, though exquisite, are tiny. Some visitors note that regular visiting hours are not strictly observed at Cholula, Acatepec, Tonantzintla and Huejotzingo.

One can visit Tonantzintla and Acatepec from Cholula main square with a 'peso-taxi'. Or one can take a kombi from Cholula to Acatepec or to Tonantzintla (marked Chilipo or Chipanco, ask which kombi goes to the church you want) for US$0.55 from junction of Avenue 5 and Avenue Miguel Alemán. This is two blocks from Zócalo, which is three blocks from tourist office. You can walk the one kilometre to the other church, and then take a bus or kombi back to Cholula or Puebla. Acatepec from CAPU in Puebla, US$0.45, 30 minutes, bus stops outside the church.

Sleeping **B** *Villas Arqueológicas*, 2 Pte 501, T471966, F471508, behind pyramid, affiliated to *Club Med*, heated pool, pleasant garden, tennis, French restaurant, rooms have heating, TV, phone, English and French spoken. **C** *Cali Quetzalcoatl*, on Zócalo, Portal Guerrero 11, T474199, clean, good restaurant. **C** *Posada Real*, 5 de Mayo 1400, at end of highway from Puebla, 3 blocks from pyramid, T476677. **C-D** *Campestre Los Sauces*, Km 122, Carretera Federal Puebla-Cholula, T471011, pool, tennis, restaurant/bar, gardens, TV and phone in rooms.

D *Reforma*, near main square. **D** *Super Motel* on the road from Puebla as you enter town, each room with private garage, very secure. **E** *Hotel de las Américas*, 14 Ote 6, T470991, near pyramid, actually a motel, modern with rooms off galleries round paved courtyard (car park), small restaurant, clean, good value. **E** *Trailer Park Las Américas*, 30 Ote 602, hot showers, secure, as are the furnished apartments. *Motel de la Herradura*, Carr Federal, T470100, will not quote rates by phone, close to *Los Sauces*, satellite TV, phones, hot water.

Eating *Restaurant Choloyan*, also handicrafts, Av Morelos, good, clean, friendly. *Pasta e Pizza*, Portal Guerrero 9B, centre. Try *licuados* at market stalls, fruit and milk and 1 or 2 eggs as you wish; *mixiote* is a local dish of lamb or goat barbecued in a bag. Pure drinking water sold behind the public baths, cheaper to fill own receptacle, funnel needed.

Transport **Buses** Frequent 2nd class Estrella Roja buses from **Puebla** to Cholula US$0.35 from 6 Pte y 13 Nte, 9 kilometres on a new road, 20 minutes, also 1st and 2nd class Estrella Roja buses from CAPU bus terminal hourly (be ready to get out, only a quick stop in Cholula); from Cholula take a 'Pueblo Centro' bus to the city centre, or a 'Puebla-CAPU' bus for the terminal; colectivos to Cholula, US$0.40. From **Mexico City**, leave for Cholula from Terminal del Oriente with Estrella Roja, every 30 minutes, US$3, 2½-3 hours, 2nd class every 20 minutes, a very scenic route through steep wooded hills. Good views of volcanoes.

Directory **Useful services** There is a *casa de cambio* on the corner of the main plaza, and a **travel agency** in the Los Portales complex on the plaza.

Just before Puebla one comes to the superb church of **Tlaxcalantzingo**, with an extravagantly tiled façade, domes and tower. It is worth climbing up on the roof for photographs.

Puebla

Km 134
Population: 1,222,177
State population 1995:
4,624,239
Altitude: 2,060m
Phone code: 22
Colour map 3, grid B4

'The City of the Angels', Puebla (de los Angeles) is one of Mexico's oldest and most famous cities and the capital of Puebla state. It was founded in 1531 by Fray Julián Garcés who saw angels in a dream indicating where the city should be built, hence its name. This also explains why Puebla wasn't built over Indian ruins like many other colonial cities. Talavera tiles are an outstanding feature of Puebla's architecture and their extensive use on colonial buildings distinguishes it from other colonial cities. Puebla is a charming city, pleasant and friendly and always popular with travellers. The centre, though still beautifully colonial, is cursed with traffic jams and pollution, except in those shopping streets reserved for pedestrians.

Sights The **Congreso del Estado** in C 5 Pte 128, formerly the Consejo de Justicia, near the post office, is a converted 19th century Moorish style town house. The tiled entrance and courtyard are very attractive, it had a theatre inside (shown to visitors on request), and is now the seat of the state government. The **Patio de los Azulejos** should also be visited; it has fabulous tiled façades on the former almshouses for old retired priests of the order of San Felipe Neri; the colours and designs are beautiful; it is at 11 Pte 110, with a tiny entrance on 16 de Septiembre, which is hard to find. Ring the bell on the top right and you may get a guided tour. Worth visiting is also the library of Bishop Palafox, in the Casa de la Cultura, 5 Ote No 5, opposite the Cathedral; it has 46,000 antique volumes, open at 1000. Known as the **Biblioteca Palafoxiana**, it is in a colonial building with a large courtyard which also houses paintings and art exhibitions. Next door at 5 Ote 9 is another attractive building, the Tribunal Superior de Justicia, built in 1762; you may go in the courtyard.

The Plaza y Mercado Parián is between Av 2 y 4 Ote and Av C 6 y 8 Nte. On C 8 Nte between Av 6 Ote and Av 4 Ote there are many small shops selling paintings. The area is also notable for onyx souvenir shops. Onyx figures and chess sets are attractive and cheaper than elsewhere, but the *poblanos* are hard bargainers; another attractive buy are the very tiny glass animal figures. In the adjoining Barrio del Artista the artists' studios are near to *Hotel Latino*. Live music and refreshments at small *Café del Artista*, C 8 Nte y Av 6 Ote. Just south at C 8 Nte 408 is the *Café Galería Amparo*, which serves light food. The University Arts Centre offers folk dances at various times, look for posters or enquire direct, free admission.

Also worth seeing are the church and monastery of **El Carmen**, with its strange façade and beautiful tile work; the **Teatro Principal** (1550), Av 8 Ote y C 6 Nte, possibly the oldest in the Americas; the grand staircase of the 17th century **Academia de las Bellas Artes** and its exhibition of Mexican colonial painting; and the Jesuit church of **La Compañía** (Av Don Juan de Palafox y Mendoza y 4 Sur), where a plaque in the sacristy shows where China Poblana lies buried. This mythical figure, a Chinese princess captured by pirates and abducted to Mexico, is said to have taken to Christianity and good works and evolved a penitential dress for herself which has now become the regional costume; positively dazzling with flowered reds and greens and worn with a strong sparkle of bright beads. Also worth visiting is the house of **Aquiles Serdán** (6 Ote 206), a leader of the Revolution, preserved as it was during his lifetime (■ *1000-1630, entrance 10 pesos*). It also houses the **Museo Regional de la Revolución Mexicana**. The tiled façade of the **Casa de los Muñecos**, 2 Nte No 1 (corner of the main square) is famous for its caricatures in tiles of the enemies of the 17th century builder (■ *entrance 8 pesos*); some rooms contain old physics instruments, old seismographs, cameras, telescopes, another has stuffed animals, but most rooms contain religious paintings from the 17th and 18th centuries. Avenida Reforma has many fine buildings, for example No 141 (*Hotel Alameda*), which is tiled inside and out. The **Palacio Municipal** is on the north side of the Zócalo. To the right of the entrance is the **Biblioteca del Palacio** (opened 1996) with some tourist information and books on the city. To the left is the **Teatro de la Ciudad** (opened 1995) where music and drama are performed. There is also an art gallery in the same building.

Puebla

*Related map
A Puebla centre,
page 324*

The **Casa de Dean**, 16 de Septiembre y 7 Pte, was built in 1580. The walls of the two remaining rooms are covered with 400-year-old murals in vegetable and mineral dyes, which were discovered in 1953 under layers of wallpaper and paint. After Pres Miguel de la Madrid visited in 1984 the house was taken over by the government (it was used as a cinema) and opened to the public. The murals were inspired by the poems of the Italian poet and humanist, Petrarca, and are believed to have been painted by Indians under the direction of the Dean, Don Tomás de la Plaza, whose house it was. The murals contain a mixture of classical Greek, pagan (Indian) and Christian themes. About 40 percent have been restored. ■ *US$1 plus tip for the guide if wanted.*

Churches On the central arcaded plaza is a fine **Cathedral**, one of the most beautiful and interesting anywhere, notable for its marble floors, onyx and marble statuary and gold leaf decoration. ■*Closed 1230-1600 and at 2000.* There are statues flanking the altar which are said to be of an English king and a Scottish queen. The bell tower gives a grand view of the city and snow-capped volcanoes. ■ *1130-1200 only, 10 pesos.* There are 60 churches in all, many of their domes shining with the glazed tiles for which the city is famous.

In the Rosario chapel of the Church of **Santo Domingo** (1596-1659), 5 de Mayo 407, the baroque displays a beauty of style and prodigality of form which served as an exemplar and inspiration for all later baroque in Mexico. The chapel has very detailed gold leaf all over it inside. The altar of the main church is also decorated with gold leaf with four levels (from floor to ceiling) of life size statues of religious figures. There is a strong Indian flavour in Puebla's baroque; this can be seen in the churches of Tonantzintla and Acatepec (see above); it is not so evident, but it is still there, in the opulent decorative work in the Cathedral. Beyond the church, up towards the Fuerte Loreto (see below), there is a spectacular view of volcanoes.

Other places well worth visiting are the churches of **San Cristóbal** (1687), 4 Nte y 6 Ote, with modern churrigueresque towers and Tonantzintla-like plasterwork inside; **San José** (18th century), 2 Nte y 18 Ote, with attractive tiled façade and decorated walls around the main doors, as well as beautiful altar pieces inside. One of the most famous and oldest local churches is **San Francisco** (14 Ote 1009), with a glorious tiled façade and a mummified saint in its side chapel; see also the pearl divers' chapel, given by the poor divers of Veracruz, the church thought it too great a sacrifice but the divers insisted. Since then they believe diving has not claimed a life. The **Capilla de Dolores**, the other side of Boulevard 5 de Mayo from San Francisco, is small but elaborately decorated. **Santa Catalina**, 3 Nte with 2 Pte, has beautiful altarpieces; **Nuestra Señora de la Luz**, 14 Nte and 2 Ote, has a good tiled façade and so has **San Marcos** at Av Reforma and 9 Nte. The Maronite church of **Belén** on 7 Nte and 4 Pte has a lovely old tiled façade and a beautifully tiled interior.

The church **La Puerta del Cielo** at the top of the Cerro de San Juan in Col La Paz, is modern but in classical style, with over 80 figures of angels inside.

Museums The **Museo de Artesanías del Estado** in ex-Convento de Santa Rosa (3 Nte 1203) has a priceless collection of 16th century Talavera tiles on its walls and ceilings, well worth a visit. ■ *1000-1630.*

The fragile-looking and extravagantly ornamented **Casa del Alfeñique** (Sugar Candy House), Av 4 Ote 418, a few blocks from the Cathedral is worth seeing, now the **Museo Regional del Estado**. ■ *US$0.40.*

The **Cinco de Mayo** civic centre, with a stark statue of Benito Juárez, is, among other things, a regional centre of arts, crafts and folklore and has a **Museo Regional de Puebla**, with magnificent collections but little information, ■ *1000-1700,* **Museo de Historia Natural**, auditorium, planetarium, fairgrounds and an open air theatre all nearby. In the same area, the forts of **Guadalupe** and **Loreto** were the scene of the Battle of Puebla, in which 2,000 Mexican troops defeated Maximilian's 6,000 European troops on 5 May 1862 (although the French returned victorious 10 days later). Inside the **Fuerte Loreto** (views of the city – and of its pollution) is a small museum, **Museo de la No Intervención**, depicting the battle of 1862. ■ *1000-1700, closed Monday, entry US$1.30.* 5 May is a holiday in Mexico.

Museo de Bello, the house of the collector and connoisseur Bello who died in 1938, has good displays of Chinese porcelain and Talavera pottery, Av 3 Pte 302; the building is beautifully furnished. ■ *US$1.10, free Tuesday and Sunday, guided tours, closed Monday.* **Museo de Santa Mónica** (convent) at 18 Pte 103, ■ *1000-1800, closed Monday*; generations of nuns hid there after the reform laws of 1857 made the convent illegal. **Museo Amparo**, 2 Sur 708, esq 9 Ote, has a good anthropological exhibition, modern, audiovisual explanations in Spanish, English, French and Japanese (take your own headphones, or hire them). ■ *1000-1800, closed Tuesday, free guided tour 1200 Sunday, admission US$2, students half-price, recommended.*

For railway enthusiasts there is an outdoor museum displaying old engines and wagons at 11 Nte, between 10 y 14 Pte, **El Museo Nacional de los Ferrocarriles Mexicanos**, in the old Puebla railway station known as El Mexicano.

Excursions

On the Prolongación Av 11 Sur is **Balneario Agua Azul**, in the suburbs, a complex with sulphur springs, playing fields, amusement park etc, popular with families ■ *T431330. Open daily 0600-1800. US$3.25, children US$2.25.* Bus from centre, route 1 on 11 Sur. 15 kilometres south of Puebla lies **Lago Valsequillo**, with *Africam*, a zoo of free-roaming African animals whose enclosures are nevertheless a bit cramped and uncomfortable. ■ *T358932. Open daily 1000-1700. US$4.50, children US$4.* Several daily Estrella Roja buses from bus station, US$2.40, round trip. Information from 11 Ote, T460888. A good, one day excursion is a round trip Puebla-Cacaxtla-Tlaxcala-Tizatlán-Puebla: details are given on page 317. There is a Volkswagen factory a few kilometres from town (buses leave from terminal marked VW). ■ *Open from 1100, book ahead for guided tours.*

Sleeping
■ *on maps*
Price codes:
see inside front cover

L *Camino Real*, 7 Pte 105, T290909, 91-800-90123, F328993, in ex-Convento de la Concepción, built 1593, beautifully restored, all rooms are different, quiet, bar, restaurant, room service, boutiques, dry cleaning. **AL** *Del Alba*, Blvd Hermanos Serdán 141, T486055, pool, gardens, Spanish restaurant. **AL** *Mesón del Molino*, Calz del Bosque 10, Col San José del Puente, T305331, 91-800-22612, F305519, rooms with 2 double beds, some have bath tubs, cable TV, restaurant/bar, small covered pool, chapel with mass 1300 Sunday. **AL** *Real de Puebla* (Best Western), 5 Pte 2522, T489600, F489850, helpful staff, restaurant open until 2300. **AL-A** *Condado Plaza*, Privada 6B Sur 3106, esq 31 Ote, Zona Dorada, T372733, 91-800-22456, F379305, cable TV, rooms have modems for computer hookup, convention halls for 40-300 people. **A** *Del Portal*, Portal Morelos 205, T460211, F323194, very good, but ask for room away from Zócalo side (noisy), restored colonial, plain rooms, TV, phone, parking across the street. **A** *Lastra*, Calz de Los Fuertes 2633, T359755, restaurant, pool, games room. **A** *Palacio San Leonardo*, 2 Ote No 211, T460555, F421176, modern rooms but wonderful colonial entrance hall with adjoining bar/restaurant. **A-C** *Aristos*, Av Reforma 533, esq 7 Sur, T320565, 320529, good facilities in rooms and bathrooms, gym with sauna, pool, attractive public areas, restaurant, piano bar, cheaper rates at weekends.

B *Posada San Pedro*, 2 Pte 202, T465077, 91-800-22808, F465376, attractive restaurant, parking. **B-C** *Royalty*, Portal Hidalgo 8, T424740, F424740 ext 113, pleasant, central, quiet, restaurant good but expensive and service slow, tables outside under the portales where a marimba band sometimes plays. **C** *Cabrera*, 10 Ote 6, T425099, 328525, with shower and phone, clean, quiet in interior rooms, don't be put off by outward appearance of hardware store, no restaurant. **C** *Colonial*, 4 Sur 105, T464199, across pedestrian street from La Compañía church, old-fashioned and charming, very friendly, colonial style, restaurant, accepts American Express cards, ask for back room, with bath, TV and phone. **C** *Gilfer*, 2 Ote No 11, T460611, F423485, attractive, modern building, large rooms, reasonable restaurant, excellent service; next door is **B-C** *Palace*, 2 Ote No 13, T322430, F425599, price depends on number and size of beds, attractive, modern lobby, cafetería, satellite TV, phones, 60 rooms.

C *Granada*, Blvd de la Pedrera 2303, T320966, F320424, very close to bus terminal, bus to centre leaves from front door, quiet, comfortable, restaurant, room service, TV in rooms. **C** *Imperial*, 4 Ote 212, T463825, good sized plain rooms with TV and phones, shower, clean, some rooms noisy, laundry, restaurant, gym, parking, 30 percent discount offered to *Handbook* owners, good value.

D *Alameda*, Reforma 141, close to the Zócalo, T420882, most rooms windowless, parking, TV, phone, bath, very clean, friendly, good value. **D** *Ritz*, 2 Nte 207 y 4 Ote, T324457, 2 blocks from Zócalo, reasonable, drab front rooms with balcony quieter, hot water. **D** *San Miguel*, 3 Pte 721, T424860, carpeted rooms, TV, phone. **D** *Virrey de Mendoza*, Reforma 538, T423903, old colonial house, plain, fairly basic rooms, high ceilings, TV, bath, beautiful wooden staircase. **D-E** *Santander*, 5 Pte 111, T463175, F425792, near Cathedral, colonial façade, recently renovated, hot showers, clean, simple, big bright rooms towards street, TV, enclosed parking, recommended. **D-E** *Teresita*, 3 Pte 309, T327072, small modern rooms, with bath ('comedy showers'), hot water, friendly. **E** *Casa de Huéspedes Los Angeles*, C 4 Nte 9, basic, communal bathrooms, irregular hot water, *comedor*, central. **E** *Embajadores*, 5 de Mayo 603, T322637, 2 blocks from Zócalo, without bath but limited water and insalubrious. Other cheap places on pedestrian mall on this street **E** *Latino*, C 6 Nte 8, T322325, next to Barrio del Artista, basic. **E** *Victoria*, near Zócalo, 3 Pte 306, T328992, clean, quiet, hot showers, recommended. **E-F** *Avenida*, 5 Pte 336 between 5 and 3 Sur, 2 blocks from Zócalo, price depends on number of beds and shared or private bathroom, airy rooms (except those without windows), quiet, friendly, clean, hot water am and evening, drinking water, recommended.Several basic *casas de huéspedes*, near markets, very cheap hotel (**F**), 2 blocks south of train station, *20 de Noviembre*, big rooms, no water 2000 to 0700, clean, bus to town.

Camping Possible on the extensive university grounds about 8 kilometres south of centre.

Motels **LL-AL** *Mesón del Angel* (Swiss run), Hermanos Serdán 807, T243000, F242227, near 1st Puebla interchange on Mexico-Puebla motorway, possibly best in town, but far from the centre, 192 rooms, a/c, cable TV, conference and banqueting facilities, 2 restaurants, bar, 2 pools, tennis. **B-D** *Panamerican*, Reforma 2114, T485466, restaurant, no bar, parking. recommended.

Eating **Local specialities** *Mole poblano* (meat or chicken with sauce of chiles, chocolate and

Puebla centre

coconut); best at *La Poblanita*, 10 Nte 1404-B, and *Fonda Santa Clara, 3 Pte 307, good for local specialities*. *Mixiote* is *borrego* (lamb) with chile wrapped in paper with hot sauce. *Chiles en Nogada* are *chiles poblanos* stuffed with fruit and topped with a sweet cream sauce made with ground nuts, then topped with pomegranate seeds, best in July-September, delicious. *Camotes* (candied sweet potatoes) and *dulces* (sweets). Also *nieves*: drinks of alcohol, fruit and milk, worth trying and excellent *empanadas*. Also noted are *quesadillas*: fried tortillas with cheese and herbs inside.

El Vasco, Portal Benito Juárez 105, on Zócalo, slow, most dishes US$3, US$6 for *plato mexicano*. Several others to choose from on Zócalo, eg *La Princesa*, Portal Juárez 101, good variety and good prices, breakfast US$2-3, *comida corrida* US$3. *Mac's*, US-style diner, good variety, cheap *comidas* at *Hermilo Nevados*, 2 Ote 408, good value. recommended. Also *Munich*, 3 Pte y 5 Sur. Many cheap places near main square with menus prominently displayed. *Cafetería La Vaca Negra*, Reforma 106, just off Zócalo, modern, attractive, part of a chain, meals US$2-7. *Hotel Royalty*, Portal Hidalgo 8, nice restaurant with meals around US$6-7, *platillos poblanos*, tables under the portales, marimba band plays sometimes. *Woolworth's*, corner of 2 Pte and 5 de Playo, 1½ blocks from northwest corner of Plaza Mayor, 0800-2200, good range of cheap, reasonable meals and some expensive dishes. *El Vegetariano*, 3 Pte 525, good (near *Hotel San Agustín*), serves breakfast, recommended. *Super-Soya*, 5 de Mayo, good for fruit salads and juices. Several other good places for *comidas corridas* on 5 de Mayo. *Librería Cafetería Teorema*, Reforma 540, esq 7 Nte, café, books and art, live music at night, good coffee and snacks, pastries, *platillos mexicanos*, recommended. *Cafetería Tres Gallos*, 4 Pte 110, good coffee and pastries. *Café Britannia*, Reforma 528, cheap, recommended. *Jugos y Licuados*, 3 Nte No 412, recommended. *Tony's Tacos*, 3 Nte and Reforma, quick and very cheap. *La Super Torta de Puebla*, on 3 Pte, good sandwich bar. *Tepoznieves*, 3 Pte 150 esq 3 Sur, rustic Mexican décor, serves all varieties of tropical fruit ice cream and sherbet. *La Pasita*, 5 Ote between 2 y 4 Sur, in front of Plaza de los Sapos, the oldest bar in Puebla, sells a drink by the same name, a local speciality, recommended. *Al Kalifa*, 2 Sur between 15 y 17 Ote, cheap tacos, very good Taco Arabe, recommended.

Feria in **mid-April** for 2 weeks. The *Fiesta Palafoxiano* starts on the last Friday in September until mid-November for 9 weekends of dancing, music, theatre, exhibitions etc, some free performances. **Festivals**

5 de Mayo is a pedestrian street closed to traffic from the Zócalo to Avenida 10. The entire **Shopping** block containing the Capilla del Rosario/Templo de Santo Domingo in the southeast corner has been made into a shopping mall (opened 1994), called the Centro Comercial La Victoria after the old La Victoria market. The old market building still exists. Built in 1913, it is a long, narrow building on the 3 Nte side of the mall and on its 2nd floor are many places to eat. The mall is a metal structure, painted green with glass panes. It houses department stores, boutiques and restaurants. Craft shop sponsored by the authorities: *Tienda Convento Santa Rosa*, C 3 Nte 1203, T28904. The famous Puebla Talavera tiles may be purchased from factories outside Puebla, or from *Uriarte*, Av 4 Pte 911 (spectacular building, tours Monday-Friday 1000-1200, 1700, Saturday 1000-1300, am best), recommended; *Talavera de la Reyna*, Camino a la Carcaña 2413, Recta a Cholula, T/F845821, also recommended (also in *Hotel Mesón del Angel*); *Centro de Talavera*, C 6 Ote 11; *D Aguilar*, 40 Pte 106, opposite Convent of Santa Mónica, and *Casa Rugerio*, 18 Pte 111; *Margarita Guevara*, 20 Pte 30. Mercado Venustiano Carranza, on 11 Nte y 5 Nte, good for *mole*. **Bookshop**: *Librería Británica*, C 25 Pte 1705-B, T408549, 374705.

Bicycle shops   There are several shops in 7 Nte, north of 4 Pte, international spare parts.

Las Termas, C 5 de Mayo 2810, T329562, gay bath house, entry US$2.50, steambaths, sauna, **Sports** gym; *Lidromasaje*, beer and soft drinks.

Mexico

Transport **Local** **Taxi**: radio taxi service, *Radio Omega*, T406299, 406369, 406371, new Chevrolet cars, 24-hour service, will deliver packages or pick up food or medicine and deliver it to your hotel.

Air Hermanos Serdán airport (PBC) has flights to Guadalajara, León, Mexico City, Monterrey and Tijuana.

Trains T201664 for information. Station is a long way from centre, very run down, in questionable neighbourhood. Micro bus No 1 on Sur 9 goes to station, US$0.35. Trains to **Oaxaca** (2nd class), leave Puebla 0640, 12 hours, no advance booking, returns from Oaxaca at 0720, superb scenery, crowded, highly recommended. The line weaves through cactus laden gorges recalling the Wild West. On clear days one gets a good view of Popocatépetl. There are many food sellers on train.

Buses **Terminal**: new, huge CAPU bus terminal for all buses north of city. From the centre to the terminal, take any form of transport marked 'CAPU', many colectivos and buses (route 12) on Av 9 Nte, fare US$1.50 per person flat rate. To the centre from the terminal take Kombi No 14, US$0.30, which stops at 11 Nte and Reforma at Paseo de Bravo (make sure it's a No 14 'directo', there is a No 14 which goes to the suburbs). The departure terminal has a *casa de cambio* (open 0900-1830), a Banco Serfín (Monday-Friday) with a 24-hour ATM compatible with Cirrus and Plus networks, *dulcería*, gift and craft shop, newsagent, 24-hour pharmacy, *pastelería*, cafetería, *caseta* for long distance phone calls, tourist information booth, booth selling taxi tickets (US$1.75 to the centre), next to it is a chart showing local bus routes, bathrooms (2 pesos), luggage store (1 peso per hour per bag), open 0700-2230. The arrivals terminal has some shops including small grocery, free bathrooms, long distance pay phones and taxi ticket booth (but you have to take ramp to the departure terminal to get the taxi). **Companies**: Autobuses de Oriente (ADO), T497144, Mercedes Benz buses, 1st class and 'GL' plus service; **Oro**, T497775, 497177, *gran turismo* or 1st class service; **UNO**, T304014, luxury service, accept American Express; **Estrella Roja**, T497099, 2nd class, 1st class and plus service; **Cristóbal Colón**, T497144 ext 2860, plus service; **Estrella Blanca**, T497561, 497433, 1st class, plus service and Elite; **Autobuses Unidos (AU)**, T497366, 497405, 497967, all 2nd class without toilets.

To **Mexico City**, ADO to TAPO (eastern) terminal at 0445, 0530, then every 20 minutes from 0600 to 2145, US$5; to Central del Sur terminal every hour from 0635 to 2135, US$5; to Central del Norte terminal every 20-40 minutes from 0520-2150, US$5, Estrella Roja to Mexico City airport every hour from 0300 to 2000, US$7, 2 hours. To Mexico City 2nd class every 10 minutes, US$4, 3 stops, 1st class, several a day US$5, plus service US$5.50; AU, every 12 minutes from 0510 to 2300. To **Tehuacán** direct ADO every 30-45 minutes from 0600-2100, US$4. To **Oaxaca**, all take new autopista, 4 hours; ADO 'GL' plus service, 2 daily, US$28.25, 1st class, 5 daily, US$12; UNO at 1800, US$18; AU, 2nd class. To **Jalapa**, ADO 'GL' plus service at 0805 and 1700, US$7, 1st class, 8 a day, US$6, 4 hours; AU, 2nd class. To **Villahermosa**, ADO 'GL' plus service via autopista, 2200, US$30, 1st class, 1900, 2145, US$25.50; UNO at 2100, US$41.25, 8 hours. To **Reynosa**, ADO at 1155, US$31.60. To **Chetumal**, ADO, 1145, US$42. To **Mérida**, ADO, 2105, US$44. To **Tuxtla Gutiérrez**, ADO, 2010, US$30; UNO, 2215, US$46, 14 hours. To **Tapachula**, UNO, 1830, US$53, 16 hours; Cristóbal Colón, plus service, 2115, US$37.50. To **San Cristóbal de las Casas**, Cristóbal Colón, plus service, 1715, 1845, 2215, US$36. To **Cuernavaca**, Oro, *gran turismo* service, 0700, 1100, 1500, 1900, US$5, 1st class hourly 0600-2000, US$4, 2 stops. To **Nuevo Laredo**, Estrella Blanca, 1st class, 1000, US$43. To **Monterrey**, Estrella Blanca, 1st class, 1030, US$34.50. To **Matamoros**, Estrella Blanca, 1st class, 1330, US$25. To **Ciudad Victoria**, Estrella Blanca, 1st class, 1030, US$25. To **Acapulco**, Estrella Blanca, plus service, 2200, US$23.25, 1st class, 1030, 1230, 2130, 2230, 2300, US$20.75. To **Tijuana**, Estrella Blanca Elite service, 1400, bypassing Mexico City, goes via Guadalajara (US$31), Tepic, Mazatlán, Nogales (US$85.75) and Tijuana (US$87.25).

Directory **Airline offices** *Aero California*, Blvd Atlixco 2703, locales B y C, Col Nueva Antequera, T304855; *AeroMéxico*, T91-800-90999, 320013/4, Av Juárez 1514, Col La Paz, flight connections at Monterrey; *Aeromar*, at airport, T329633, 329644, 91 (800) 70429; *Mexicana*, Av Juárez 2312, entre C 23 Sur y 25 Sur, T91-800-50220, 485600; *Lufthansa* and *LanChile*, at Av Juárez 2916, Col La Paz, T484400, 301109. **Banks** *Bancomer*, 3 Pte 116, changes TCs 0930-1300, good rates. On the Zócalo are *Banco Santander Mexicano*; *Banco Inverlat* at Portal Benito Juárez 109, changes money 0900-1400; and a *casa de* cambio at Portal Hidalgo 6 next to *Hotel Royalty*. On Av Reforma are: *Banamex*, No 135, ATMs accept Cirrus network cards; *Bancomer*, No 113, ATMs accept Visa and Plus network cards; *Banco Bital*, across the street, ATMs accept Plus and Cirrus network cards. All available 24 hrs. **Communications** Post Office: 5 Ote between 16 de Septiembre and 2 Sur, open Mon-Fri, 0800-2000, colonial building with red/orange bricks and blue and white tiles, also has email service for US$3 per half hour; at the *Escuela Sandoval*, on 5 Oriente, you can email for US$2 hour. *Soluciones Alternativas*, C 4 Nte 7, 101, first floor, no sign, email service US$2 hour. At the *BUAP University*, Av San Claudio esq 22 Sur, T444404, open Mon-Fri 0700-2100, Sat, Sun 0800-1800, 48PCs, but slow, US$2.50 hour. **Hospitals & medical services** Dentist: *Dr A Bustos*, Clínica de Especialidades Dentales, 2 Pte 105-8, T324412, excellent service, recommended. **Doctors:** *Dr Miguel Benítez Cortázar*, 11 Pte 1314, T420556, US$15 per consultation. *Dr Cuauhtémoc Romero López*, same address and phone. Hospitals: *Beneficiencia Española*, 19 Nte 1001, T320500. *Betania*, 11 Ote 1826, T358655. *UPAEP*, 5 Pte 715, T466099, F325921, outpatients T328913, 323641. The cheapest is *Universitario de Puebla*, 25 Pte y 13 Sur, T431377, where an outpatient consultation is US$5. **Laundry** In large commercial centre on Av 21 Pte y C 5 Sur, US$4 wash and dry, 3 hrs. Another on 9 Nte, entre 2 y 4 Pte, US$2.80 for good service wash. **Tour companies & travel agents** *American Express*, Centro Comercial Plaza Dorada 2, Héroes 5 de Mayo, locales 21 y 22, T375558, F374221, open Mon-Fri 0900-1800, Sat 0900-1300. **Tourist offices** 5 Ote 3, Av Juárez behind the Cathedral, next to the Post Office, T460928, closed Sat and Sun. Also at 5 Pte, next to Casa de la Cultura, closed Sat, Sun. Administrator of Museums, T327699.

An interesting day-trip from Puebla is to Cuetzalán market (via Tetela-Huahuaztla) **Cuetzalán** which is held on Sunday in the Zócalo (three hours' walk up). In first week of October each year dancers from local villages gather and *voladores* 'fly' from the top of their pole. Nahua Indians sell cradles (*huacal*) for children; machetes and embroidered garments. Women decorate their hair with skeins of wool. The Día de los Muertos (2 November) is interesting here. Big clay dogs are made locally, unique stoves which hold big flat clay plates on which *tortillas* are baked and stews are cooked in big pots. Also available in nearby Huitzitlán. You can also go via Zaragoza, Zacapoaxtla and Apulco, where you can walk along a path, left of the road, to the fine 35-metre waterfall of La Gloria. It can be very foggy at Cuetzalán, even when it is fine in Puebla. Tourist information, C Hidalgo y Bravo, helpful, good map.

From Cuetzalán it is a one-and-a-half-hour walk to the well-preserved, niched pyramids of **Yohualichan** (Totonac culture); there are five excavated pyramids, two of them equivalent to that at El Tajín, and three still uncovered. There has been earthquake damage, though. Take a bus from C Miguel Alvarado Avila y C Abosolo, more frequent in morning and market days to San Antonio and get off at the sign Pirámides Yohualichan (30 minutes, bad road), then walk two kilometres to the site. ■ *Closed Monday and Tuesday, entry US$2.* In the Cuetzalán area are 32 kilometres of caverns with lakes, rivers and wonderful waterfalls. These include **Tziculan** (follow C Emiliano Zapata, east of town) and **Atepolihuit** (follow Carretera Antigua up to the Campo Deportivo, west of town). Children offer to guide visitors to the ruins and the caves. (Claudio Rivero, Buenos Aires.)

Sleeping & eating Several cheap, quite clean hotels, eg **E** *Hotel Rivello*, G Victoria 3, T91-23310139, 1 block from Zócalo, with bath, **F** without, basic, friendly, clean. **E** *Posada Jackelin*, upper end of plaza, near market, behind church, pleasant. **E** *Posada Vicky*, on G Victoria. *Posada Quetzal*, C Zaragoza. Good, cheap restaurant: *Yokoxochitl*, 2 de Abril, good for breakfasts, huge juices. *Casa Elvira Mora*, Hidalgo 54, recommended. *Villacaiba* for seafood, Francisco Madero 6. *Café-Bazar Galería* in centre, good sandwiches and tea, nice garden, English magazines, recommended.

Transport Direct buses from Puebla (Tezuitecos line only) 5 a day from 0500 to 1530, US$6.50; quite a few return buses, but if none direct go to Zaragoza and change buses there. There are many buses to Zacapoaxtla with frequent connections for Cuetzalán.

(Km 151) **Amozoc**, where tooled leather goods and silver decorations on steel are made, both mostly as outfits for the *charros*, or Mexican cattlemen. Beyond Amozoc lies **Tepeaca** with its late 16th century monastery, well worth a visit; its weekly market is very extensive. On the main square is Casa de Cortés, where Hernán Cortés signed the second of five *cartas de Relación* in 1520 (open 1000-1700). An old Spanish tower or *rollo* (1580) stands between Tepeaca's main square and the Parroquia. Beyond Tepeaca, 57½ kilometres from Puebla, lies **Tecamachalco**: vast 16th century Franciscan monastery church with beautiful murals on the choir vault, in late medieval Flemish style, by a local Indian. **Language school**: Escuela de Español en Tecamachalco, run by Patricia O Martínez, C 29 Sur 303, Barrio de San Sebastián, Tecamachalco, CP 75480, Apdo Postal 13, T91-242-21121, very good; US$70 for one week, four hours a day, possible to live with families. There is a good seafood restaurant; enquire at José Colorado's *tienda* near the school.

Mexico

Tehuacán
Population: 190,000
Altitude: 1,676m
Phone code: 238
Colour map 3, grid C5

Beyond, the road leads to Tehuacán, a charming town with a pleasant, sometimes cool, climate. It has some old churches. Water from the mineral springs is bottled and sent all over the country by Garci Crespo, San Lorenzo and Peñafiel. From the small dam at Malpaso on the Río Grande an annual race is held for craft without motors as far as the village of Quiotepec. The central plaza is pleasant and shaded; the nights are cool. From Tehuacán there are two paved roads to Oaxaca: one, very scenic, through Teotitlán del Camino (US$1.65 by 2nd class bus), and the other, longer but easier to drive, through Huajuapan (see page 391). Railway junction for Oaxaca and Veracruz; no passenger trains on line to Esperanza. Wild maize was first identified by an archaeologist at Coxcatlán Cave nearby. There is an airport.

The Ayuntamiento on the Zócalo is decorated inside and out with murals and tiles. **Museo de Mineralogía Romero**, 7 Nte 356, one room with good collection of minerals from all over the world, ■ *0900-1200, 1600-1800, am only on Saturday, free.* A

Southern Mexico

short bus ride beyond Peñafiel Spa is the spa of **San Lorenzo** with spring-fed pools surrounded by trees, US$2 entry.

Sleeping *México*, Reforma Nte and Independencia Pte, 1 block from Zócalo, T20019, garage, TV, restaurant, renovated colonial building, pool, quiet. **B-C** *Bogh Suites*, 1 Nte 102, northwest side of Zócalo, T23006, new, businessman's hotel, safe parking. **D** *Iberia*, Independencia Ote 217, T31500, with bath, clean, airy, recommended, pleasant restaurant, noisy weekends, public parking nearby at reduced fee with voucher from hotel. **D** *Inter*, above restaurant of same name, close to bus station (ask there), hot shower, clean, modern. **E** *Madrid*, 3 Sur 105, T20272, opposite Municipal Library, comfortable, pleasant courtyard, cheaper without bath, recommended. Several *casas de huéspedes* along C 3 (Nte and Sur) but low standards.

Eating Many eating places on Zócalo with reasonable prices (eg on same corner as Cathedral, good breakfast). The main meal is served at midday in Tehuacán. Try *Restaurant Santander*, good but pricey. *Cafetería California*, Independencia Ote 108, excellent juices and *licuados*. *Pizzería Richards*, Reforma Nte 250, quite good pizzas, good fresh salads; excellent taco stands.

Transport ADO bus station on Av Independencia (Pte). Bus direct to **Mexico City**, 5 hours, US$10; to **Puebla**, 2½ hours, US$4; to **Oaxaca** (US$10.75, 5½ hours, AU at 1430, coming from Mexico City, may be full), **Veracruz**, US$7.75, and the Gulf: Autobuses Unidos, 2nd class on C 2 Ote with several buses daily to Mexico City and Oaxaca. Local bus to **Huajuapan** 3 hours, US$5; from there, frequent buses to Oaxaca.

Teotitlán del Camino, en route to Oaxaca, is a glaringly bright town with a military

base. Vehicles are stopped occasionally; make sure, if driving, that your papers are in order. From Teotitlán it is possible to drive into the hills, to the Indian town of **Huautla de Jiménez**, where the local Mazatec Indians consume the hallucinogenic 'magic' mushrooms made famous by Dr Timothy Leary. Huautla has 'all four seasons of the year in each day; springlike mornings; wet, foggy afternoons; fresh, autumn evenings; and freezing nights.' Hiking in the mountains here is worthwhile. (Hotel: **E** *Olímpico*, above market, no sign, clean, simple, small rooms, bath, friendly.) You cannot buy food in the town after 2000. Several daily buses to/from Mexico City and Oaxaca (US$6.50), children meet buses offering lodging in their homes. There are many police and military. Drivers may be waved down by people in the road up to Huautla; do not stop for them, they may be robbers.

The road from Tehuacán to the coast soon begins to climb into the mountains. At Cumbres we reach 2,300 metres and a wide view: the silvered peak of **Citlaltépetl** (or Orizaba – see page 331) volcano to the east, the green valley of

Orizaba below. In 10 kilometres we drop down, through steep curves, sometimes rather misty, to Acultzingo 830 metres below. The road joins the main toll road from Puebla to Orizaba at Ciudad Mendoza, where it has emerged from the descent through the Cumbres de Maltrata, which are usually misty and need to be driven with care and patience. (The expensive toll road Puebla-Orizaba is a much safer drive than the route we have described; it, too, is scenic.)

Orizaba
Km 317
Population: 115,000
Altitude: 1,283m
Colour map 3, grid B5

The favourite resort of the Emperor Maximilian, lost much of its charm in the 1973 earthquake, when the bullring, many houses and other buildings were lost, and is now heavily industrialized. The setting, however, is lovely. In the distance is the majestic volcanic cone of Orizaba. The town developed because of the natural springs in the valley, some of which are used by the textile and paper industries and others are dammed to form small pools for bathing beside picnic areas; Nogales (restaurant) is the most popular, Ojo de Agua is another. The Cerro del Borrego, the hill above the Alameda park, is a favourite early-morning climb. On the north side of the Zócalo is the market, with a wide variety of local produce and local women in traditional dress, and the many-domed San Miguel church (1690-1729). There are several other quite good churches, and there is an Orozco mural in the Centro Educativo Obrero on Av Colón. The Palacio Municipal is the actual cast-iron Belgian pavilion brought piece by piece from France after the famous 19th century Paris Exhibition, an odd sight.

Sleeping **B** *Aries*, Ote 6 No 265, T51116 (nightclub on top floor). **B** *Trueba*, Ote 6 and Sur 11, T42744, resort facilities. **D** *De France*, Ote 6 No 186, T52311, US$0.25 for parking in court-yard, charming building, clean, comfortable, shower, friendly, reasonable if uninspiring restaurant. **E** *Vallejo*, Madero Nte 242, dirty, smelly. **F** *América*, on the main street no 269, very friendly and good value.

Eating *Romanchu* and *Paso Real*, on the main street, have excellent cuisine. Hare Krishna vegetarian restaurant, *Radha's*, on Sur 4 between Ote 1 and 3, excellent. The Indian vegetarian restaurant on Sur 5, has an excellent *comida corrida*, highly recommended. *Crazy Foods*, opposite *Hotel De France*, good and cheap, nice sandwiches. In the market, try the local morning snack, *memelita picadita*.

Transport Bus to **Merida**, 1 a day (ADO), US$35, 1st class. To **Veracruz**, many buses, US$3.50, 1st class.

Directory **Tourist offices** Pte 2, across river from Zócalo, open mornings only.

A road leaves Orizaba southwards, up into the mountains of **Zongolica**, a dry, poor and isolated region, cold and inhospitable, inhabited by various groups of Indians who speak Nahuatl, the language of the Aztecs. Zongolica village is a good place to buy *sarapes*; take early bus from Orizaba (ask for direct one) to get clear views of the mountains.

Beyond Orizaba the scenery is magnificent. The road descends to coffee and sugar-cane country and a tropical riot of flowers. It is very pleasant except when a northerly blows, or in the intolerable heat and mugginess of the wet season (one cyclist, en route to Córdoba, warned that "this is where the real sweating starts").

Fortín de las Flores
Km 331
Colour map 3, grid B5

A small town devoted to growing flowers and exporting them. Sometimes Indian women sell choice blossoms in small baskets made of banana-tree bark. Near Fortín there is a viewpoint looking out over a dramatic gorge (entry free). The *autopista* from Orizaba to Córdoba passes over this deep valley on a concrete bridge.

Sleeping **B** *Posada la Loma*, Km 333 Carretera Nte 150, T30658, very attractive, tropical garden with butterflies, distant view of snow-capped volcano in early morning, moderately expensive. There are others, slightly cheaper, which also offer tropical gardens for relaxation. Note that Veracruz-Mexico City night trains sound their horns when passing Fortín which can be disturbing.

Pico de Orizaba

*Also known as Citlaltépetl, the highest mountain in Mexico (5,760 metres), it is not too difficult to climb, although acclimatization to altitude is advised and there are some crevasses to be negotiated. About four people a year ski on the glacier, but the surface is unpredictable. From Acatzingo one can go via a paved road to Tlachichuca (35 kilometres, or you can take a bus, every 30 minutes, from Puebla to Tlachichuca). Guides and transport can be arranged: Sr Reyes (F24515019), arranges trips in a four-wheel drive up an appalling road to two huts on the mountain, about US$50, including one night at his house, a former soap factory – very clean (**D** full board), his truck leaves at 1200, three-hour journey, and he picks you up at about 1600, Sr Reyes is well-equipped and keen to give ground support to climbers; Sr Canchola Limón, 3 Poniente 3, Tlachichuca, T15082, charges US$30 for transport to the mountain and pick up, registers your climbing intentions, has equipment, and can provide somebody to guard your equipment at the refugio (two days) for US$13; Sr Espinosa Coba, T15103, is another transporter. Alternatively, stay at **E** Hotel Panchita, Av Benito Juárez 5, T15035, hot water, bath, restaurant, friendly. **E** Hotel Gerar, 20 de Noviembre 200, with bath; or **E** Hotel Margarita, no sign, then, early in the morning hitch hike to the last village, Villa Hidalgo at 3,000 metres (about 15 kilometres) or take a taxi, US$10. From there it's about 10 kilometres (two hours) to the huts. The huts, one small (sleeps six, water nearby), one larger (sleeps 80, start of north route – normal – or Jamapa glacier route) and colder, are at 4,200 metres. There is no hut custodian; it's usually fairly empty, except on Saturday night. No food or light, or wood; provide your own. Take a good sleeping bag and warm clothes. Water close at hand, but no cooking facilities. Start from the hut at about 0500, first to reach the glacier at 4,700 metres, and then a little left to the rim. There is a hazardous section before you get to the Jamapa glacier where several icy slopes spill down from its lip and have become a bowling alley for dislodged rocks. Be vigilant. From the rim the summit, marked with a cross, is 100 metres further on and 40 metres higher up. Be very careful walking round the rim to the summit. It's about seven to eight hours to the top; the ice is not too steep (about 35-40°), take crampons, if not for the ascent then for the descent which takes only two and a half hours. At the weekend you're more likely to get a lift back to Tlachichuca. 1:50,000 maps are available from INEGI information and sales office, for example in Puebla (Av 15 de Mayo 2929), Veracruz or Mexico City.*

Volker Huss of Karlsruhe (Germany) informs us of an alternative route up the volcano; this is easier, because there is no glacier and therefore no crevasses, but is best done in the rainy season (April to October), when there is enough snow to cover the loose stone on the final stage. Crampons and ice-axe are necessary. The route is on the south face of the volcano. Stay in Orizaba and take a very early bus to Ciudad Serdán (depart 0530), or stay in Ciudad Serdán. At Serdán bus station take a bus, US$1.50, to San Antonio Atzitzintla, and then taxi US$4 to Texmalaquila; the driver will know the way. Five hours from Texmalaquila is the Fausto González hut at 4,760 metres (take own food and water). Miguel Quintero in Texmalaquila has mules for luggage transport to the shelter (US$5 per bag). Spend the night there and climb the final 1,000 metres early in the morning, about five hours. From the top are fine views, with luck even to Veracruz and Mexico City. In the rainy season the summit is usually free of cloud until midday. The entire descent takes six hours and can be done the same day. A recommended guide is Raimund Alvaro Torres, in Orizaba, C Sur 10 574, T27261940. An adventure travel shop on Pte 3 entre Sur 2 y 4, hires equipment and guides but their equipment is old and the guides not very knowledgeable.

Eight kilometres on in the rich valley of the Río Seco, an old colonial city, Córdoba is also crazy with flowers. Its Zócalo is spacious, leafy and elegant; three sides are arcaded; two of them are lined with tables. On the fourth is an imposing church with a chiming clock. There are several hotels in the Zócalo, which is alive and relaxed at night. In one of them, the *Hotel Zevallos*, Gen Iturbide signed the Treaty of Córdoba in 1821, which was instrumental in freeing Mexico from Spanish colonial rule.

Córdoba
Population: 126,000
Altitude: 923m
Colour map 3, grid B5

There is a local museum at C 3, No 303, open 1000-1300 and 1600-2000. Córdoba has the highest rainfall in Mexico, but at predictable times. The area grows coffee.

Sleeping **B** *Mansur*, Av 1 y C 3, T26600, on square, smart. **C** *Hostal de Borreña*, C 11 308, T20777, modern, clean, really hot water, some traffic noise but good value. Near the ADO terminal is **C** *Palacio*, Av 3 y C 2, T22186. **C** *Marina*, T22600. **D** *Iberia*, T21301, **D** *Trescado*, T22366 and *Casa de Huéspedes Regis* are all on Av 2. **E** *Las Carretas*, Av 4 No 512, with bath, clean, noisy, short stay, not recommended, can wash clothes. *Casa de Huéspedes La Sin Rival* and **E** *La Nueva Querétana* are at 511 and 508 of Av 4, respectively (latter is basic but cheap). **F** *Los Reyes*, C 3, recommended, shower, hot water, street rooms double-glazed, street parking OK.

Eating *Cantábrico*, C 3 No 9, T27646, 1 block from Zócalo, excellent meat and fish dishes, fine wines and good service, 'worth a trip from Mexico City!', highly recommended. *Brujes*, Av 2 No 306, good *comida corriente*.

Transport **Trains**: From Mexico City at 0815, continuing to Veracruz. There may be a 2nd class train for Tierra Blanca (US$1), Medias Aguas (US$3), Coatzacoalcos (US$4), Teapa (US$6.50), Palenque (US$8), Campeche (US$12) and Mérida (US$14), check locally. **Buses**: Bus station is at the end of Av 6. Direct services to **Veracruz**, 2 hours, US$4; **Puebla**, 3 hours, US$7.70; **Mexico City**, hourly, 5 hours, US$10; to **Coatzacoalcos**, US$13; **Oaxaca** and many others.

Directory **Banks** *Casa de Cambio* on Av 3 opposite *Bancomer*, recommended. **Car service**: Nissan, Chevrolet and Dodge dealers, mechanics all on C 11.

The direct road from Córdoba to Veracruz is lined, in season, by stalls selling fruit and local honey between **Yanga** and Cuitláhuac. Yanga is a small village named after the leader of a group of escaped black slaves in colonial times. A slightly longer but far more attractive road goes from Fortín de las Flores northwards through Huatusco and Totutla, then swings east to Veracruz. For cyclists, the 125 kilometres from Córdoba to Veracruz has no accommodation en route, but is mostly flat, so could be done in one day.

Veracruz

Km 476
Population: 1 m
Phone code 29
Colour map 3, grid B5

The principal port of entry for Mexico lies on a low alluvial plain bordering the Gulf coast. Cortés landed near here at Isla de Sacrificios, on 17 April 1519. The first settlement was called Villa Rica de la Vera Cruz; its location was changed various times, including to La Antigua, now a pleasant little colonial town with the ruins of Cortés' house. The present site was established in 1599.

NB If planning to visit Veracruz or the hills inland (for example Xalapa) between July and September, check the weather forecast because many tropical storms blow themselves out in this region, bringing heavy rain. From October to January the weather tends to be changeable, with cold, damp winds from the north. At this time the beaches and Malecón are empty and many resorts close, except over Christmas and New Year when the tourists flood in and all road transport is booked up five days in advance. Otherwise it is generally hot.

Veracruz is a mixture of the very old and the new; there are still many picturesque white-walled buildings and winding side-streets. It has become a great holiday resort, and can be touristy and noisy. The heart of the city is **Plaza Constitución** (Zócalo). The square is white-paved, with attractive cast iron lampstands and benches, and surrounded by the cathedral, with an unusual cross, depicted with hands, the governor's palace and colonial-style hotels. The plaza comes alive in the evening at weekends: an impressive combination of the crush of people, colour and marimba music in the flood-lit setting. From 15 July to the end of August there is jazz in the Zócalo from 1900.

Culturally, Veracruz is a Caribbean city, home to the *jarocho* costume (predominantly white), dance and music which features harps and guitars. The most famous dances, accompanied by the Conjunto Jarocho, are the *bamba* and *zapateado*, with much stamping and lashing of feet related to flamenco of Andalucía. Mexico's version of the Cuban *danzón* music and the indigenous *música tropical* add to the cultural richness. Many cultural events can be seen at the Instituto Veracruzano de Cultura, a few blocks from the Zócalo with a good, new café and library; a nice place to relax and mingle with students. At night the Malecón is very lively, noisy and sometimes fire-eaters and other performers entertain the public.

The food is good, the fishing not bad, and the people lively, noisy and welcoming. The local craft is tortoise shell jewellery adorned with silver, but remember that the import of tortoise shell into the USA and many other countries is prohibited.

Sights

There are two buildings of great interest: the very fine 17th century **Palacio Municipal** (1627), on Plaza Constitución, with a splendid façade and courtyard, and the castle of **San Juan de Ulúa** (1565), on Gallega Island, now joined by road to the mainland; take bus marked Ulúa from Malecón Av República. It failed to deter the buccaneers and later became a political prison. Mexico's 'Robin Hood', Chucho el Roto, was imprisoned there, and escaped three times. In 1915 Venustiano Carranza converted it into a presidential palace. ■ *It is not advisable to walk there, 0900-1700 Tuesday-Sunday, entry to the castle US$1.80.* The **Baluarte de Santiago**, a small fort which once formed part of the city walls, is at Francisco Canal y Gómez Farias. ■ *1000-1630, Tuesday-Sunday, US$4.35.* The **aquarium** has moved from the harbour breakwater to a new building at Villa del Mar; large underwater viewing tank, watch sharks and other exotic species. ■ *1000-1900 Monday-Friday, 0900-1900 Saturday and Sunday, US$4.35.* **Plazuela de la Campana**, by Serdán and Zaragoza, is an attractive small square.

There is a **city historical museum** with a good collection of photographs, well

Veracruz centre

N
Not to scale

■ **Sleeping**

1 Amparo	3 Colonial	5 Mar y Tierra
2 Baluarte	4 Emporio	6 Oriente

Mexico

displayed; it traces history from the Conquest to 1910; it is at Zaragoza 397. ■ *0900-1500 Monday-Saturday, US$0.35, English booklet available.* The **Carranza museum** on the Malecón, has photos of the revolution, the life of Carranza and his battles against the Huerta Regime (the last room shows a picture of Carranza's skeleton and the trajectory of the bullet that killed him). ■ *Tuesday-Sunday 0900-1700, entry free.*

On the way to Mocambo beach where the Boulevard Avila Camacho meets Boulevard Ruiz Cortines, is the **Museo Agustín Lara** ('La Casita Blanca', a must for anyone interested in modern Mexican popular music, the home of the greatest 20th century Mexican song-writer, Agustín Lara, who wrote more than 700 songs ('Solamente una vez', 'Veracruz', 'Granada', and 'María Bonita' among the most famous) many of which reverberate around the streets and squares of Veracruz. A pianist plays and sings Tuesday-Saturday 1100-1400, 1600-1900, and at other times visitors are welcome to play Lara's piano. ■ *US$2, free on Sunday.*

Beaches   The beach along the waterfront, and the sea, are filthy. There is much pollution from the heavy shipping. Amber from Simojordis is sold on the town beach. A short bus ride from the fish market takes you to **Mocambo** beach, which has a superb, 50 metres swimming bath (with restaurant and bar, admission US$3.30), beach restaurants, Caribbean-style beach huts and dirty sand; the water is quite a bit cleaner though still rather uninviting in colour. There are crabs and mosquitoes and much pestering by sellers. The Gulf is even warmer than the Caribbean. The beach is crowded. At holiday time cars race up and down, there are loud radios, etc. To Mocambo take a bus marked 'Boca del Río' on Av Zaragoza. There is little shade

Veracruz

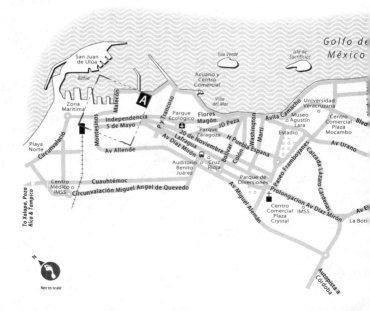

Not to scale

near the beach. There is a fine beach at Chachalacas, 50 kilometres north, not crowded (see page 347).

Excursions

Harbour trips from the Malecón US$4 per person for 35 minutes if 15 people turn up. On Sunday, to Mandinga for cheap fresh seafood (big prawns), and local entertainment.

La Antigua, the site of Cortés's house (see above), is one and a half kilometres off the road to Cradel, some 30 kilometres north of Veracruz. Take a Cardel bus from the second class part of the bus station (US$0.40) and get off at La Antigua Caseta, the first toll booth the bus comes to. Easy walk from there, 10-15 minutes. The house is worth the visit just to see the large ceiba roots growing all over the walls. A small boy at the site gives an excellent tour in Spanish. Boats can be hired on the river. **D** *Hotel Malinche*, quiet, laid back, peaceful.

Sleeping
Because of the liveliness of the Zócalo at night, hotels on the square can be noisy

AL *Calinda* (formerly *Veracruz*, Av Independencia esq Lerdo, near Zócalo, probably the best in the centre. **AL** *Emporio*, Paseo del Malecón, Insurgentes Veracruzanos y Xicoténcatl, T320020, F312261, very good, with bath, swimming pool, inexpensive *comida corrida* and superb buffet breakfast (US$5) Saturday-Sunday, rather old-fashioned. **AL** *Mocambo*, T371661, 8 kilometres out on Mocambo beach, 1930s palace, good service and food, highly recommended. **AL** *Puerto Bello* (aka *Howard Johnson's*), Avila Camacho 1263, T310011, F310867, good, clean, friendly, most rooms have sea-view, recommended. **B** *Baluarte*, opposite the small fort of Baluarte, Canal 265, T360844, good, clean, recommended. **B** *Colonial*, on Zócalo, T320193, swimming pool, indoor parking, recommended. **B** *Hawaii*, Malecón, T38088, F325524, 'funky' architecture, comfortable, quiet. **B** *Hostal de Cortés*, 3-star, Avila Camacho y de las Casas, T320065, F315744, convenient for clean beaches, helpful, recommended. **B** *Oriente*, M Lerdo 105, T312440, secure parking, clean, friendly, balconies (noisy from street), good fans, some a/c, recommended. **C** *Central*, Mirón 1612, T372222, next to ADO bus terminal, clean, fair, noisy, erratic hot water, friendly, get room at back, especially on 5th floor, laundry facilities. **C** *Cristóbal Colón*, Avila Camacho 681, T823844, small, quiet, some rooms with sea-view balconies, clean. **C** *Ruiz Milán*, Malecón y Gómez Farias, T361877, F361339, good.

■ *on maps
Price codes:
see inside front cover*

D *Casa de Huéspedes*, on Morelia, near Zócalo, with bath, hot water, quiet, clean, use of mosquito net needed, economical restaurant next door. **D** *Concha Dorada*, on Zócalo, very pleasant. **D** *Impala*, Orizaba 650, T370169, with bath, cold water, mosquitoes but clean, near bus station. **C** *Mar y Tierra*, Figueroa y Malecón, T313866, cheaper in low season, some rooms with balconies overlooking the harbour, restaurant serving good breakfast. **D** *Príncipe*, Collado 195, some distance from centre, very clean with hot shower and toilet. **D** *Royalty*, Abasolo 34, T361041, average, near beach, 20 minutes' walk from Zócalo, recommended, but noisy as it caters mainly

To Tinaja & Córdoba
*To San Andrés
Tuxtla & Coatzacoalcos*

to student groups. **D** *Santander*, Landero y Coss 123, T324529, with bath and TV, very clean. **E** *Amparo*, Serdán 482, T322738, with fan, insect screens, clean, hot water, good value, recommended. Opposite is **D** *Santo Domingo*, with bath, fan, OK, noisy, bakery attached. Nearby on Serdán is **C** *Mallorca*, with bath and fan, radio, newly furnished, very clean, highly recommended. **E** *Casa de Huéspedes La Tabasqueña*, Av Morelos 325, fan, new bathrooms, upper rooms less good, front rooms noisy, many others without windows, cheap, clean, safe, helpful. **E** *Faro*, near *Hotel Emporio*. Good value. **E** *Marsol de Veracruz*, Av Díaz Mirón 1242, T325399, right from ADO bus station 4 blocks, quiet, with bath, highly recommended, clean and helpful. **E** *Hatzin*, Reforma 6 and Avista, friendly, recommended. **E** *Paloma*, E Morales y Reforma, clean, basic, fan, friendly, good value. **E** *Sevilla*, Av Morelos 359, with fan and TV, negotiate. **F** *Las Nievas*, C Tenoya, off Plaza Zamora, with bath, fan, dark rooms. Many others in port area, reached by bus from the bus terminal.

Trailer Park The only trailer park is behind *Hotel Mocambo* (see above), dry camping, showers and bathrooms dirty, swimming pools empty, US$6.50 for vehicle and 2 people.

Youth hostel Paso Doña Juana, Municipio de Ursulo Galván, T320878, 2 hours by bus from town, US$2.30 a night; for information on Villas Deportivas Juveniles, see under Mexico City **Campsites**.

Eating
● *on maps*

Torros are the local drinks made of eggs, milk, fruit and alcohol, delicious and potent. *La Nueva Parroquia* on Malecón (not to be confused with original *Parroquia Café* – now *Gran Café del Portal*) 2 coffee houses in same block, very popular, excellent coffee and capuccino. In the main market, H Cortés y Madero, there are inexpensive restaurants in the mezzanine, overlooking the interior (watch out for extras that you did not order). In the fish market for excellent fish and shrimp cocktails, and opposite are *La Garlopa* and *Doña Paz/Normita*, good seafood. Excellent fresh fish at *Tano's* just off the Malecón, Mario Molina 20, highly recommended. There is a good local fish restaurant, *Olympica*, Zaragoza 250, near the fish market, 2 blocks from the Zócalo. *El Pescador*, for fish, Zaragoza 335 y Morales (not evenings) good cheap *comida corrida*; and the steakhouse *Submarino Amarillo*, Malecón 472. *Karen*, Arista 574 between Landero y Coss and Zaragoza, good fish restaurant. *Café de la Catedral*, Ocampo y Parque Zamora, large, local, few tourists, try fish stuffed with shrimps. *El Azteca de Cayetano*, Mario Molina 94. *Mondongos de fruta* (a selection of all the fruits in season, plus fruit-flavoured ice) are prepared on 1 plate; also *Mondongo de Fruta*, M Molina 88, not cheap but delicious for fruits, juices and ices. An interesting place is *Tiburón*, Av Landero y Coss 167, esquina A Serdán, 2 blocks from Zócalo, run by 'Tiburón' González, the 'Rey de la Alegría', or 'Rey Feo' of carnival; the walls are covered in pictures of him and his *comparsas*, dating back to at least 1945, has inexpensive, good food too. *La Paella*, Plaza Constitución, No 138, has its name written into the concrete of the entrance floor as well as a sign, good *comida corrida*. *Pizza Palace*, Zamora, buffet 1200-1700, US$5. *Emir Cafetería*, Independencia 1520, near F Canal, good breakfast. *La Quinta del Son*, on paved side street off Serdán, bar and restaurant, food nothing special but excellent Cuban-style *trova* band in pm. *Gran Café del Portal*, opposite Cathedral, traditional (marimba all day) but not cheap. *La Puerta del Sol*, on Molina, 1 block south of the Zócalo, friendly pub, cheap beer. For good value unpretentious food (not just fish) *El Tranvía*, General Prim esq Rayón, opposite Parque Zamora. *Le Blé*, coffee house, on road parallel to Blvd M Avila Camacho, between F Canal and Rayón. Good decor, fine variety of coffees. *Nevería y Refresquería Aparito*, A Serdán y Landero y Coss, near fish market, good for fruit and juices, try *mondongo de frutas*.

Festivals The *Shrovetide carnival* 7 weeks before Easter is said to be Mexico's finest, rivalling those of New Orleans, Brazil and Trinidad. The carnival starts a week before Shrove Tuesday and ends on Ash Wednesday; Saturday-Tuesday are the main days with parades. At this time it is very difficult to find higher-priced accommodation (especially on the Saturday), or tickets for transportation.

Transport **Air** At Las Bajadas (VER), 12 kilometres from the centre, to the capital several flights daily and flights up and down the coast: Monterrey, Tampico, Villahermosa, Ciudad del Carmen, Mérida, Cancún, Tapachula and Tuxtla Gutiérrez. Flights also to Houston, San Antonio and Havana.

Trains Rail to **Mexico City**: 2nd class train leaves Mexico City 0845 via Fortín and Córdoba, arr Veracruz, 1950, returns 0820 arr 1940. Another train from Mexico City via Xalapa leaves at 2015, arrives 0600, returns 2200, arrives 0800. There is also a train Veracruz to Coatzacoalcos 0920, arrives 1840 to connect with the 1910 service Coatzacoalcos- Tapachula.

Buses The majority of buses are booked solid for 3 days in advance throughout summer; at all times queues of up to 2 hours possible at Mexico City booking offices of bus companies (best company: ADO). Book outward journeys on arrival in Veracruz, as the bus station is some way out of town and there are often long queues. Referred to as ADO, it is divided into first and second class; the first class part, mostly ADO company, is on the main street, Díaz Mirón y Jalapa, T376790; Autobuses Unidos, Lafragua y Jalapa (2 blocks from ADO), T372376. For local buses, get accurate information from the tourist office. Buses to the main bus station along Av 5 de Mayo; marked ADO; and from the station to the centre, blue and white or red and white buses marked Díaz Mirón; pass 1 block from the Zócalo, US$0.35, or colectivos, also US$0.35. Taxi to ADO terminal from centre US$1.50. Bus to **Mexico City**, ADO, US$17.00, US$20.35 *primera plus* (5 hours), via Xalapa, non-stop, or stops only at Perote, misses out Orizaba, Fortín and Córdoba; to **Villahermosa** US$36 *primera plus* (7$\frac{1}{2}$ hours); to **Puebla**, US$9; to **Oaxaca**, ADO, 7-8 hours, 0715 and 2200, US$17, US$21.50 plus service; to **Mérida** US$43 (16 hours). To **Xalapa**, frequent departures, 2 hours, US$4. To **Zempoala** (see page 347), 2nd class buses from ADO terminal 30 minutes to Cardel then micro, US$0.40.

Connections with Guatemala: there are no through buses to Guatemala, but there are connecting services. The 'directo' train leaves Veracruz 2100 daily for Ixtepec and Tapachula (US$13.25 *primera preferente*); scheduled to take almost 24 hours, more like 38; not recommended, foul toilets, no lighting so high likelihood of robbery. Take your own toiletries and food, although there is a restaurant car, food is available at every stop. No sleeping accommodation. Local bus services run Tapachula-border and border-Guatemala City; quicker than the much more mountainous route further north. Bus Veracruz-Tapachula 14 hours, 1$\frac{1}{2}$-hour meal stop (at 0230), 4 10-minute station stops, US$30.75, *plus* service US$50, 1900 every night, 13 hours, video, reclining seats. Alternatively, take ADO bus to Oaxaca, then carry on to Tapachula (12 hours) by bus. This allows you to stop at intermediate points of your choice, has few 'comfort' stops. Buy bus tickets out of Veracruz in advance.

Directory

Airline offices *AeroMéxico*, García Auly 231, T350142. *Mexicana*, Av 5 de Mayo y A Serdán, T322242. **Banks** *Bancomer*, Independencia y Juárez has its own *casa de cambio* for dollars and TCs, good rates, open Monday-Friday 0930-1730, Saturday-Sunday 1100-1400, also branches at Prim esq Rayón, Blvd Avila Camacho e Iturbide, Centro Comercial Plaza Cristal, Centro Comercial Las Américas, Blvd Ruiz Cortines esq Fracc Costa de Oro. *Banco Serfín*, Díaz Mirón, 2 blocks from bus station, changes US$ cash and TCs; *Banamex* is at Independencia esq Juárez with branches at 5 de Mayo esq Emparán, Mario Molino casi esq 5 de Mayo, Centro Comercial Las Américas, Plaza Hotel Continental. American Express agency is *Viajes Olymar*, Blvd M Avila Camacho 2221, T313406. 2 *casas de cambio*: *La Amistad*, Juárez 112 (behind the hotels on the Zócalo), rates not as good as the banks but much quicker; *Hotel Veracruz* changes money at similar rates. **Communications** Post Offices: main post office by bridge to San Juan de Ulúa fortress, a fine building inaugurated in 1902 by Porfirio Díaz, open 0900-1200 Mon-Fri; also at Palacio Federal, 5 de Mayo y Rayón, 0800-1900. **Embassies & consulates** US Consular Agency: C Víctimas del 25 de Junio 388, in centre. **Laundry** Madero 616, US$2 per 3 kg, open 0730-2300. **Tourist offices** Palacio Municipal on the Zócalo, T329942, helpful but no hotel price list; Federal office, T321613.

Boca del Río

Some six kilometres to the south of Veracruz (colectivo from Av Zaragoza) is Boca del Río, beyond Mocambo, on the left bank of the mouth of Río Jamapa. In 1518 the Spaniard Grijalva, gave the already existing settlement the name of Río de Banderas as the inhabitants carried small flags in order to transmit messages. Despite commercial and residential development steadily filling up the space between Veracruz and Boca, the latter guards its own identity, and still has the atmosphere of a small village. Worthy of a visit is the church of Santa Ana (1716). Modern buildings of interest include the Palacio Municipal, Teatro del Pueblo, and the Casa de La Cultura.

Mexico

A 10-minute bus ride from Boca del Río to the other side of the river is **El Conchal**, a small residential development overlooking picturesque lagoons with a number of attractive restaurants. The bus continues along a low sandy spit to **Punta Antón Lizardo** where there is a small village with a few beach restaurants and good sand and bathing.

Sleeping **C** *Zamora*, comfortable rooms with a/c. **D** *Boulevard*. More expensive hotels are on the coast road (Blvd Avila Camacho and Blvd Miguel Alemán) where the best beaches are (not great-muddy sand).

Eating *Boulevard*, Blvd I Zaragoza esq Zamora, expensive. Excellent cheaper restaurants nearby serving large variety of fresh fish. In **El Conchal** *Restaurant El Payán*.

Routes The road is very winding from Orizaba so take travel sickness tablets if necessary. Philippe Martin, of the Touring Club Suisse, writes: 'The road from Veracruz to Oaxaca is spectacular but tiresome to drive and will take about a day. The road from Veracruz to La Tinaja and Tierra Blanca is good and fast although there are many lorries. From there to Miguel Alemán the road is bad, speed reasonable, still many lorries. The Tuxtepec area has lovely lowland, jungle areas, charming villages, and the traffic is sparser between Tuxtepec and Oaxaca, while there are no more gasoline stations. The road is very bad and winding and the fog only lifts after you leave the pines at 2,650 metres above sea-level. After a descent and another pass at 2,600 metres you enter the bare mountainous zone of Oaxaca. Very few eating places between Tuxtepec and Oaxaca.'

The Papaloapan Region

Puerto Alvarado is a modern, fishing port one and a half hours south from Veracruz by bus, none too pleasant for women on their own, many bars and drunks. **D** *Hotel Lety*, reasonable but for grim plumbing system; **D** *Hotel del Pastor*, avoid

Veracruz coast

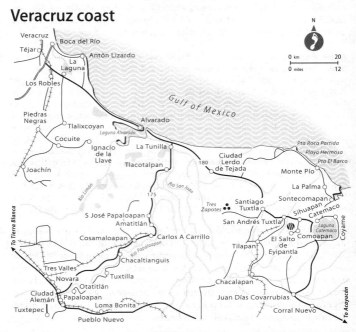

next-door restaurant; **D** *María Isela*, quiet, clean with fan, recommended. Beware of small boys with pea-shooters in the plaza. Exchange services 1000-1200. Fair/carnival 31 March-5 April. Cross the Río Papaloapan (Butterfly River) by a toll bridge (US$1.70) and go along Route 180 into the sugar-cane area around Lerdo de Tejada and Angel R Cavada. At El Trópico shop a dirt road turns left to some quiet beaches such as Salinas and Roca Partida. Only at Easter are the beaches crowded: they are normally the preserve of fishermen using hand nets from small boats. In the dry season (December-May) the road is passable around the coast to Huatusco.

At Tula, a little further along the main road, is a spectacular waterfall, **El Salto de Tula**; a restaurant is set beside the falls. The road then climbs up into the mountainous volcanic area of Los Tuxtlas, known as the Switzerland of Mexico for its mountains and perennial greenness.

A pleasant town of colonial origin, set on a river. In the main square is the largest known Olmec head, carved in solid stone, and also a museum containing examples of local tools, photos, items used in witchcraft (*brujería*), and the first sugar-cane press used in Mexico and another Olmec head. There is dancing to *jarana* bands in the Christmas fortnight. ■ *Museum open 0900-1500, Saturday-Sunday 0900-1200 and 1500-1800.*

Santiago Tuxtla
Colour map 3, grid B6

The archaeological site of **Tres Zapotes** lies to the west; it is reached by leaving the paved road south towards Villa Isla and taking either the dirt road at Tres Caminos (signposted) in the dry season (a quagmire from May-December), or in the wet season access can be slowly achieved by turning right at about Km 40, called Tibenal, and following the dirt road north to the site of the Museum. ■ *0900-1700, US$1.65. (If it is closed, the lady in the nearby shop has a key.)* A bus from Santiago Tuxtla goes at 1200 to the village of Tres Zapotes, the site is one kilometre walk (the bus cannot reach Tres Zapotes if rain has swollen the river that the road has to cross). Travellers with little time to spare may find the trip to Tres Zapotes not worth the effort. There is an Olmec head, also the largest carved stela ever found and stela fragments bearing the New World's oldest Long Count Date, equal to 31 BC. Not far from Tres Zapotes are three other Olmec sites: Cerro de las Mesas, Laguna de los Cerros, and San Lorenzo Tenochtitlán.

Sleeping **C** *Hotel Castellanos*, on Plaza, hot shower, clean, swimming pool (US$1 for non-residents), recommended. **D** *Caballeros*, small pool. **D** *Morelos*, family run, quiet, nicely furnished.

Eating *Chazaro*, near bridge over stream, small, good seafood especially *sopa de mariscos* and *chucumite* (fish), cheap.

Transport AU bus from Veracruz, 2nd class, 3 hours, US$2.

Banks Exchange at *Banco Comermex* on Plaza, TCs 0900-1330.

15 kilometres beyond lies San Andrés Tuxtla, the largest town of the area, with narrow winding streets, by-passed by a ring road. This town is also colonial in style and has a well-stocked market with Oaxacan foods such as *totopos, carne enchilada*, and *tamales de elote* (hard tortillas, spicy meat, and cakes of maize-flour steamed on leaves). It is the centre of the cigar trade. One factory beside the main road permits visitors to watch the process and will produce special orders of cigars (*puros*) marked with an individual's name in 30 minutes.

San Andrés Tuxtla
Population: 112,000
Colour map 3, grid B6

Sleeping **D** *Hotel Pasada San José*, Belisario Domínguez 10, T22020, close to plaza, run by nice family and staff, restaurant, pick-up truck for excursions, 2nd hotel at Monte Pío. **D** *Catedral*, near Cathedral, very nice. **D** *Figueroa*, Pino Suárez 10. **D** *Colonial*, Pino Suárez opposite *Figueroa*, with bath, hot water, clean. **D** *del Parque*, Madero 5, a/c, very clean, good

Mexico

restaurant. **D** *Zamfer*, ½ block from Zócalo. **E** *Casa de Huéspedes la Orizabana*, in the centre of town, without bath, clean, hot water, friendly. **E** *Juárez*, 400 metres down street from ADO terminal (No 417, T20974), clean, friendly. **E** *Ponce de León*, primitive, pleasant patio.

Eating Near the the town centre is the restaurant *La Flor de Guadalajara*, it appears small from the outside but is large and pleasant inside. Well recommended. Sells *tepachue*, a drink made from pineapple, similar in flavour to cider, and *agua de Jamaica*.

Transport Bus San Andrés Tuxtla-Villahermosa US$11, 6 hours; to Mexico City, 1st class, 9 hours, US$22.

Catemaco

Mexico

Population: 31,000
Colour map 3, grid B6

A pleasant town with large colonial church and picturesque situation on lake, 13 kilometres from San Andrés Tuxtla (bus service irregular, taxi US$5). There are stalls selling handicrafts from Oaxaca, and boat trips out on the lakes to see the shrine where the Virgin appeared, the spa at Coyame and the Isla de Changos, and to make a necklace of lilies, are always available (boat owners charge US$30-35 per boat). The town is noted for its *brujos* (sorcerers), although this is becoming more of a tourist attraction than a reality, and the Monte del Cerro Blanco to the north is the site of their annual reunion.

Excursions At Sihuapan, five kilometres from Catemaco, is a turning south on to a paved road which leads to the impressive waterfall of **Salto de Eyipantla** (well worth a visit, especially early am); there are lots of butterflies. There is a stairway down to the base and a path winding through a small village to the top. Small boys at the restaurant near the falls offer their services as guides. Take 2nd class AU bus Catemaco-Sihuapan; from 1030 buses leave every 30 minutes from Sihuapan to Eyipantla, otherwise it's a 20-minute walk to Comoapan, then take a taxi for US$2. There are also buses from the plaza in San Andrés Tuxtla.

Sleeping **A** *La Finca*, just outside town, T30430, pool, attractive grounds, beautiful setting beside lake,

A number of hotels are situated at the lakeside.

full at weekends, a/c, comfortable rooms, but poor food and service. **B** *Motel Playa Azul*, 2 kilometres on road to Sontecomapan, T30042, modern, a/c; in a nice setting, comfortable and shady, with water-skiing on lake, will allow trailers and use of showers. **C** *Posada Komiapan* (swimming-pool and restaurant), T30063, very comfortable. **C** *Catemaco*, T30203, excellent food and swimming pool, and **Berthangel**, T30411, a/c, satellite TV, similar prices; both on main square.

D *Del Cid*, 1 block from ADO bus terminal, with fan and bath, OK. **D** *Los Arcos*, T30003, clean, fan, good value. **D** *del Brujo*, Ocampo y Malecón, fan, a/c, shower, nice clean rooms, balcony overlooking the lake, recommended. **E** *Posada Viki*, on Zaragoza, next to *Gallardo*. **E** *San Francisco*, Matamoros 26, with bath, basic, but good and clean.

Trailer park At Solotepec, on the lakeside on the road to Playa Azul. US$6.50 per vehicle, very clean, hook-ups, bathrooms, recommended. Also *La Ceiba*, restaurant and trailer park, Av Malecón, 6 blocks west of Zócalo, by lakeshore, camping and hook-ups, bathrooms with hot water, restaurant and lakeside patio.

Eating On the promenade are a number of good restaurants: *María José*, best. *7 Brujas*, wooden restaurant open till 2400, good, try *mojarra* (local fish). *La Julita*, also lets rooms, **E**, with bath, pleasant, recommended. Opposite Cathedral are *La Pescada*, good fish, US$5 and *Melmar*, popular. *La Ola*, built almost entirely by the owner in the local natural materials, and *La Luna*, among others. At the rear of the market, diagonally from the back of *La Luna*, are some inexpensive, good restaurants serving *comida corrida* for US$2-2.50, *La Campesina* is recommended. Restaurant on 1st floor opposite Cathedral, nice atmosphere. Best value are those not directly on the lake, eg *Los Sauces*, which serves *mojarra*. *Bar El Moreno*, 2 de

Abril, at the beach, 'not too fancy' but good cuba libres and live synthesizer music.

Catemaco can be reached by direct AU 2nd class bus from Veracruz, every 10 minutes, many **Transport** stops, 4 hours, US$5, also ADO 1st class; buses also from Santiago Tuxtla, 2nd class. It is about 120 kilometres northwest of Minatitlán (see page 438); buses also from/to Villahermosa, 6 hours, US$10 (ADO). To Tuxtepec, change in San Andrés Tuxtla.

Banks *Bancomer*, opposite Cathedral, open Mon, Wed, Fri 0900-1400.   **Directory**

Sontecomapan and Gulf Coast

The Gulf Coast may be reached from Catemaco along a dirt road (which can be washed out in winter). It is about 18 kilometres to Sontecomapan, crossing over the pass at Buena Vista and looking down to the Laguna where, it is said, Francis Drake sought refuge. The village of **Sontecomapan** (*Population*: 1,465) (*Hotel Sontecomapan*), lies on an entry to the Laguna and boats may be hired for the 20 minutes' ride out to the bar where the Laguna meets the sea (US$10 return). A large part of the Laguna is surrounded by mangrove swamp, and the sandy beaches, edged by cliffs, are almost deserted except for local fishermen and groups of pelicans. Two good restaurants in Sontecomapan. Beaches are accessible to those who enjoy isolation, such as **Jicacal** and **Playa Hermosa**. Jicacal can be reached by going straight on from the Catemaco-Sontecomapan road for nine kilometres on a good dirt road to La Palma where there is a small bridge which is avoided by heavy vehicles; immediately after this take left fork (poor dirt road, there is a bus) for **Monte Pío**, a pretty location at the mouth of the river (**D** *Hotel Posada San José Montepío*, Playas Montepío, T21010, recommended, family-run, also basic rooms to let, **E**, and a restaurant), and watch out for a very small sign marked Playa Hermosa; road impassable when wet, about two kilometres, and then continuing for about four kilometres from there. Playa Jicacal is long and open, the first you see as you near the water. The track reaches a T-junction, on the right Jicacal, to the left to Playa Hermosa, *Hotel*, **E** and restaurant. It is not recommended to sleep on the beaches (assaults and robberies) although at Easter time many people from the nearby towns camp on the beaches. The place is busy at weekends.

Crossing the Isthmus

Acayucán is a pleasant town with several cinemas (**D** *Hotel Joalicia*, Zaragoza 4. **D** *Hotel Ritz*, Av Hidalgo 7, T50024, shower, fan, noisy, parking. **D** *Los Angeles*, cheaper without TV, clean, fans, friendly, pool, owners speak some English, space for car inside. **E** *San Miguel*, with bath, hot water and fan, not very attractive, but OK. **E** *Iglesias*), 267 kilometres from Veracruz on toll road (first class buses 'de paso', very hard to get on, four hours to Veracruz, second class five and a half hours). Turn right for Route 185 if you want to go across the Isthmus to Tehuantepec, Tuxtla Gutiérrez and Central America, but continue on Route 180 for Minatitlán, Coatzacoalcos and Villahermosa (Tabasco). The road across the Isthmus is straight but is not always fast to drive because of high winds (changing air systems from Pacific to Atlantic). Gasoline and food on sale at the half-way point, **Palomares**, where there is a paved road to Tuxtepec (see page 344), two and a half hours' drive. A few kilometres south of Palomares a gravelled road enters on the eastern side; this passes under an imposing gateway 'La Puerta de Uxpanapa' where some 24,500 families are being settled on land reclaimed from the jungle. There is a good hotel at **Matías Romero**, *Real del Istmo*, a/c, by the road, safe parking, good restaurant. The road crosses the watershed and passes across the flat coastal plain to Juchitán (see page 410).

Mexico

Alvarado to Papaloapan

Tlacotalpan
Colour map 3, grid B5

About 15 kilometres from Alvarado a new bridge replaces the old ferry-crossing at Buenavista over the Río Papaloapan and the 175 road heads southwards to the fishing village of Tlacotalpan where the Papaloapan and San Juan rivers meet. This town, regarded as the centre of Jarocho culture (an amalgam of Spanish, mainly from Seville, African and Indian cultures), has many picturesque streets with one-storey houses all fronted by stuccoed columns and arches painted in various bright pastel colours. Two churches in the Zócalo, and a Casa de las Artesanías on Chazaro, one and a half blocks from the Zócalo. The **Museo Salvador Ferrando** contains interesting local paintings and artefacts. ■ *US$0.50.* There is a famous *fiesta* there on 31 January which is very much for locals rather than tourists (accommodation is impossible to find during *fiesta*).

Sleeping and eating The **D** *Viajero* and *Reforma* hotels are good; so is the **C** *Posada Doña Lala*, Carranza II, T42580, F42111, with a/c and TV, good restaurant. **E** *Jarocho*, seedy, excellent *sopa de mariscos* and *jaiba a la tlacotalpina* (crab) at the *Restaurant La Flecha*.

Transport Buses go to Veracruz via Alvarado (US$2, 45 minutes), to San Andrés Tuxtla, Santiago Tuxtla (US$2.50, 1½ hours) and Villahermosa.

Cosamaloapan
Population: 103,000
Colour map 3, grid B6

Cosamaloapan, some 40 kilometres beyond Tlacotalpan on Route 175, is the local market centre with a number of hotels, and the staging point for most bus lines from Veracruz, Orizaba and Oaxaca. One of the largest sugar mills in Mexico is situated just outside the town – Ingenio San Cristóbal – and there is a local airstrip. From Cosamaloapan to Papaloapan the banks on either side of the river are lined with fruit trees. Chacaltianguis, on the east bank of the river, reached by car ferry, has houses fronted by columns.

40 kilometres beyond Cosamaloapan is a ferry to **Otatitlán**, also on the east bank of the river (it leaves whenever there are sufficient passengers, US$0.25 the ride). The town, also known as El Sanctuario, dates back to early colonial times, its houses with tiled roofs supported by columns, but most interesting is the church. The padre maintains that the gold-patterned dome is the largest unsupported structure of its kind in Mexico, measuring 20 metres wide and 40 high. El Sanctuario has one of the three black wooden statues of Christ brought over from Spain for the son of Hernán Cortés. During the anti-clerical violence of the 1930s attempts to burn it failed, although the original head was cut off and now stands in a glass case. The first weekend in May is the saint's day and fair, for which pilgrims flock in from the *sierra* and from the Tuxtlas, many in local dress. (*Restaurant-Bar Pepe* serves delicious but unusual local food. *Restaurant-Bar Ipiranga III* also offers excellent cooking; both by embarkation point.)

At **Papaloapan** on the eastern bank of the river, the main road from Orizaba to Rodríguez Clara (145) crosses the main road from Alvarado to Oaxaca (175); the railway station has services to Yucatán and Chiapas, and to Orizaba or Veracruz. On the west bank is the bus terminal of Santa Cruz (almost under the railway bridge) where all second class buses stop. A passenger ferry may be taken from here to Papaloapan (US$0.50). Although Papaloapan is the route centre for the area the most convenient centre is Tuxtepec, nine kilometres further south (see below).

Presa Miguel Aleman

The river basin drained by the Papaloapan and its tributaries covers some 47,000 square kilometres, about twice the size of the Netherlands, and is subject to a programme of regional development by the Comisión del Papaloapan, which includes the construction of two large dams to control the sometimes severe flooding of the lower basin. The lake formed behind Presidente Alemán dam at Temascal is scenically very attractive and boats may be hired to go to Mazatec Indian settlements on the islands or on the other side. There is also a daily ferry passing round the lake. **Soyaltepec** is the closest settlement, situated high above the water on an island, the peak crowned by a church. **Ixcatlan** lies on a peninsula jutting into the lake on the south side; it has one hotel and one restaurant, as well as a large beer repository. Ixcatlan may also be reached by dirt road from Tuxtepec, but it is less nerve-racking to take a ferry.

Temascal (Sunday is the most active day) may be reached by taking Route 145 from Papaloapan through Gabino Barreda, Ciudad Alemán (no facilities, centre of the Papaloapan Commission), Novara (petrol and three restaurants of varying prices, one air-conditioned), as far as La Granja where the turn to Temascal is clearly marked. (In Temascal there is a woman who offers very basic accommodation.)

Route 145 continues paved and straight past Tres Valles (cheap, good regional food; annual fair mid-November), and on to **Tierra Blanca**, a railway junction on the

Papaloapan to La Tinaja

Mexico

Papaloapan environs

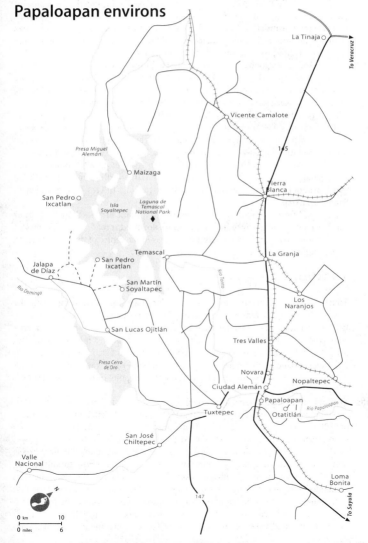

Tapachula-Veracruz and Mérida-Córdoba-Mexico City lines (Hotels: **D** *Principal*, own shower and fan, clean, just above bus station, noisy. **E** *Balun Canán*, cheap, hot. *Bimbis* restaurant by ADO bus station, good; shopping centre, market, car repairs, eg Volkswagen agent). Route 145 passes under a sign saying 'La Puerta del Papaloapan', to join the main Orizaba-Veracruz road (Route 150) at **La Tinaja**, a second class bus junction, also gasoline, and restaurants (one air-conditioned at service station). Papaloapan to La Tinaja takes about one hour, the road often has a lot of lorries and in the cane-cutting season great care should be taken at night for carts travelling on the road without lights. There are three railway crossings on the road, also poorly marked, two near La Granja and one near Tierra Blanca. The tarmac is often damaged in the wet season (June-December).

Papaloapan to Sayula From Papaloapan a paved road runs eastwards to Rodríguez Clara and on to Sayula de Alemán on the Trans-Isthmian road. This road passes through the main pineapple-producing region of Mexico, which has encouraged the development of towns such as **Loma Bonita** (local airstrip, hotels, restaurants and gasoline) and **Villa Isla** (Hotels: *La Choca* restaurant good, railway station, ADO bus terminal, and centre for the rich cattle-producing area that surrounds it).

From Villa Isla a good dirt road runs south to **Playa Vicente** (*Population*: 6,974), another ranching town, located beside a wide river (**F** *Hotel Ros Bal*, clean, safe, fan, good); excellent crayfish may be eaten at the *Restaurant La Candileja*, while the café on the central plaza serves tender steaks. Another dirt road leaves the Villa Isla-Playa Vicente road for **Abasolo del Valle** (*Population*: 2,000), but only reaches to within seven kilometres. The last few kilometres can be impassable by vehicle in the wet season. The town is set beside a lagoon and the houses are surrounded by fruit trees (no hotels or restaurants). Gasoline can be bought – ask at a shop who has some to sell.

At the cross-roads of the Papaloapan-Sayula road about 80 kilometres from Papaloapan, where the south turn is to Villa Isla, the north turn is a paved road which in about 30 minutes will take you past two turnings to Tres Zapotes and up to Santiago Tuxtla.

The road from Papaloapan continues east to a point just north of **Rodríguez Clara**, which is reached by branching off south down a dirt road. This is a compact, thriving town. There are two hotels, the better is in the centre of the town, **D** *Hotel Roa*; *Restaurant Mexicana* recommended.

Tuxtepec

Colour map 3, grid C5 Tuxtepec is the natural centre for a stay in the Papaloapan area. It is a large city in the state of Oaxaca, some nine kilometres south of Papaloapan (toll for Caracol bridge, US$0.40). There is a fascinating mixture of the music and exuberance of Veracruz with the food and handicrafts of Oaxaca. The town is built on a meander of the Río Santo Domingo and a good view can be had from the rear balcony of the market on Av Independencia; there are other viewpoints beyond the main shops. A hand-pulled ferry crosses the river from below the viewpoint next to *Hotel Mirador*.

Near the river watch out for gnats (rodadores), which bite sensitive skins leaving itchy welts.

Excursions To Temascal to see the dam (see above); also a visit to the Indian villages of **Ojitlán** and **Jalapa de Díaz** (bus Tuxtepec-Jalapa de Díaz, one and a half hours from the end of C 20 de Noviembre, US$5; hotel, **E** and food stores, good and cheaper *huipiles* from private houses) is well worth the ride; easily reached by car along semi-paved road. The Chinantec Indians' handicrafts may be bought on enquiry; hotels non-existent and eating facilities limited but some superb scenery, luxuriant vegetation and little-visited area. Ojitlán is best visited on Sunday, market day, when the Chinanteca *huipiles* worn by the women are most likely to be seen (bus Jalapa de Díaz-Ojitlán, one and a half hours). Part of the area will be flooded when the Cerro de Oro dam is finished and the lake will join that of Temascal. Heavily armed checkpoint on the road from Tuxtepec to Tierra Blanca (bus one and a half hours,

US$1.50), non-uniformed men, very officious, do not get caught with any suspicious goods.

El Rancho, Avila Camacho 850, T50641, restaurant, bar, evening entertainment, most expensive, accepts travellers' cheques as payment, recommended. **C** *María de Lourdes*, Av 5 de Mayo 1380, T91-28750410, hot water, clean, excellent car park, recommended. *Tuxtepec*, Matamoros 2, T50944, good value. **D** *Catedral*, C Guerrero, near Zócalo, very friendly, fan and shower. **D** *Robles*, Av 5 de Mayo, clean, basic, enclosed parking. **D** *Mirador*, Av Independencia, hot showers, fairly safe car park, with view of filthy river, good.

Nearby on same Av, **E** *Posada Guadelupana*, and **E** *Posada Real*. **E** *Sacre*, C Libertad, good, quiet. Nearby is **E** *Casa de Huéspedes Ocampo*, with bath, clean, friendly, room 10 is the best. Very good value is the **E** *Avenida* in Independencia round the corner from ADO bus station, with bath and fan, basic, clean but restaurant below not very good value. **E** *Posada del Sol*, basic and noisy, opposite Fletes y Pasajes bus station.

Sleeping
Many street names and numbers are not marked

El Estero, in a side street opposite market on Av Independencia (fish dishes and local cuisine excellent), *El Mino* (near Fletes y Pasajes bus terminal), *Mandinga*, Av 20 de Noviembre, for fish dishes, *Avenida*, next to hotel of same name. *Pata Pata*, around corner, on side street, half way down the block. *Ronda*, C Independencia, cheap and good. *La Mascota de Oro*, 20 de Noviembre 891, very friendly, cheap. *Las Palmas*, Riva Palacios, palm-thatched, excellent local food, friendly, heartily recommended. Beer from the barrel can be bought from the bar next to the Palacio Municipal, and the best ices are found in *La Morida*.

Eating

There are 4 bus terminals in town, clear street signs for each one. ADO bus services to **Mexico City** (Thursday, US$16.50), **Veracruz** and regular daily minibus (taking 5-6 hours) to **Oaxaca** leaving at 2230. AU (Autobuses Unidos, on Matamoros, $\frac{1}{2}$ block from Libertad) daily to wide variety of destinations. AU to Oaxaca, US$10 2nd class, 8 hours, slow, Buses Cuenca del Papaloapan, direct route, every 2 hours in am and pm, US$8.25, ADO at 2230, 10 hours, US$16.50. Also Transportes Chinantecos. Bus to **Acayucán**, ADO, 4 hours, US$3.30.

Transport

The Tuxtepec-Palomares road provides a short cut to the Transístmica; it passes through many newly cleared jungle areas. Armed robberies are said to be a danger on this road; the route via Sayula is 20 kilometres longer, but safer as well as quicker. The route from Tuxtepec to Minatitlan is being made into a toll road. The 'vía libre' remains in good condition, through Sayula and Acayucan.

Routes

The road to Tuxtepec north from Oaxaca (Route 175) is in bad repair but is a spectacular, steep and winding route, cars need good brakes and it is reported to be difficult for caravans (also very tough for cyclists, with few services and no accommodation en route – advised to take a bus!). "The road is good from Oaxaca as far as the national shrine at Juárez's birthplace at Ixtlán. North from there to the crestline of the mountain range is pretty dreadful – potholed and rutted with a scrubby pine forest cutting off any views for almost the whole route. It gets much better coming down the other side, however. The surface is smooth, the curves are well-engineered and the descent from alpine evergreen down into tropical rainforest is fascinating and exhilarating. Valle Nacional, at the bottom of the descent, is notable for what are surely the highest and most diabolically-shaped *topes* in the Mexican republic: at any speed, at any angle of approach, it was almost impossible to keep a VW from bottoming out on them." (Eric Mankin, California, USA.)

It takes about five hours to drive this journey in reverse, up **Valle Nacional**. This valley, despite its horrific reputation as the 'Valle de los Miserables' in the era of Porfirio Díaz, for political imprisonment and virtual slavery from which there was no escape, is astoundingly beautiful. The road follows the valley floor, on which are cattle pastures, fruit trees and a chain of small villages such as Chiltepec (very good bathing in the river), Jacatepec (reached by ferry over the river, produces rich honey and abounds in all varieties of fruit), Monte Flor (where swimming and picnicking

Mexico

are possible beside natural springs, but *very* cold water, and an archaeological site) and finally Valle Nacional. (Bus to Valle Nacional from Tuxtepec, one and a half hours, basic hotel, restaurants, stores, and gasoline available; river swimming.) The road climbs up into the Sierra, getting cooler, and slopes more heavily covered with tropical forest, and there are panoramic views.

San Pedro Yolox lies some 20 minutes' drive west of this route down a dirt road; it is a peaceful Chinantec village clustered on the side of the mountain, while Llano de Flores is a huge grassy clearing in the pine forest with grazing animals and cool, scented air. Wood from these forests is cut for the paper factory in Tuxtepec. Ixtlán de Juárez has gasoline. While houses in the lowlands are made of wood with palm roofs, here the houses are of adobe or brick.

Veracruz to Mexico City

By the road followed to Veracruz, the driving time from Mexico City is about nine hours. One can return to the capital by a shorter route through Xalapa which takes six hours; this was the old colonial route to the port, and is the route followed by the railway.

Xalapa

Population: approx 300,000
State population 1995: 6,734,545
Altitude: 1,425m
Colour map 3, grid B5

(Also spelt Jalapa) Capital of Veracruz state since 1885, 132 kilometres from the port, Xalapa is in the *tierra templada* and is a lively town in keeping with its climate. A settlement called Xallac (the place of the sandy waters) is known to have existed here in the 12th century. It has always been a good place to break the journey from the coast to the highlands and in the 18th century development was helped by the creation of a huge annual trading fair. There was a passion for building and renovation in the flamboyant gothic style during the first part of the 19th century. It is yet another 'City of Flowers', with walled gardens, stone-built houses, wide avenues in the newer town and steep cobbled crooked streets in the old. It is a hilly city and the numerous telephone and power lines give it a spaghetti effect.

Sights The 18th century **cathedral**, with its sloping floor, has been recently restored. Just outside Xalapa, on the road to Mexico City, is an excellent, modern **Archaeological Museum** (opened 1986) showing treasures of the Olmec, Totonac and Huastec coastal cultures. The colossal heads displayed in the grounds of the museum are Olmec; the museum has the best collection of Olmec monumental stone sculptures in Mexico. ■ *Tuesday-Sunday, 1000-1800, US$1, Tuesday free, half price for students with ID, guided tours included in fee. To get there take the Tesoría Avila Camacho bus which stops in front of the museum.* **Pinacoteca Diego Rivera,** Herrera 5 (Zócalo), small permanent collection of Rivera's paintings as well as temporary exhibitions. ■ *Tuesday-Sunday 1000-1800, free.* Xalapa has a University; you can take a pleasant stroll round the grounds, known as El Dique. Pico de Orizaba is visible from hotel roofs or Parque Juárez very early in the morning, before the haze develops. Two and a half kilometres along the Coatepec road are lush **botanical gardens** with a small museum. Take bus from the terminal marked Coatepec Briones, 10 minutes, ■ *US$0.20.*

Excursions **Hacienda Casa de Santa Ana**, was taken over in the revolution and is now a museum, **Museo Lencero**, with the original furniture. ■ *Entrance free, no bags allowed inside.* By bus from the centre, take Circunvalación bus to Plaza Cristal shopping centre, cross the road and catch bus to Miradores, ask to be put down near the museum. From the stop (by pedestrian bridge) it is a 7-minute walk to the museum.

Palo Gacho falls are worth a visit. Take the route 40 from Xalapa, towards Cardel, to Palo Gacho. The waterfalls can be reached on a dirt road next to the church, four kilometres steep descent. Avoid weekends.

To ruins of **Zempoala**, 40 kilometres north of Veracruz (hotel, *Chachalaca*, near sea, spotless, recommended), the coastal city which was conquered by Cortés and whose inhabitants became his allies. The ruins are interesting because of the round stones uniquely used in construction. ■ *US$1.40, small museum on site.* Sundays can be very crowded. It is pleasant site and setting and voladores are often in attendance. Take a picnic. Take 2nd class bus to Cardel, and then a micro to Zempoala.

Chachalacas is a beach with a swimming pool and changing facilities in an expensive hotel of the same name, US$1 adults. Thatched huts; local delicacies sold on beach, including *robalito* fish. It is worth asking the restaurants on the beach to let you hang up your hammock, most have showers and toilets. They charge US$2 if you agree to eat at their restaurant.

To **Texolo** waterfalls, some 15 kilometres southwest of Xalapa and five kilometres from the village of Jico (or Xico), just beyond the neighbouring town of Coatepec; there is a deep ravine and an old bridge, as well as a good, cheap restaurant at the falls. The old bridge is still visible but a new bridge across the ravine has been built. It is a pleasant place for a cold swim, birdwatching and walking, crowded at weekends. The film *Romancing the Stone* used Texolo as one of its locations. Jico village itself is pretty, US$0.60 by bus from Xalapa every 30 minutes. **Coatepec**, famous for its ice-cream, is a pleasant town and an important centre for the surrounding coffee haciendas. A *Hotel Posada de Coatepec*, very good with excellent restaurant, good value. Several good cafés and restaurants around the main plaza. Direct Coatepec bus from Xalapa bus terminal every few minutes, US$0.40, 10 minutes.

Naolinco is 30 minutes' ride, 40 kilometres northeast of Xalapa up a winding hilly road, *Restaurant La Fuente* serves local food and has nice garden. Las Cascadas, with a *mirador* to admire them from, are on the way into the town: two waterfalls, with various pools, tumble several thousand feet over steep wooded slopes. Flocks of *zopilotes* (buzzards) collect late in the afternoon, soaring high up into the thermals.

Two hours from Xalapa is the archaeological site of **Filobobos**. It includes El Cuajilote, a 400 metre wide ceremonial centre and Vega de la Peña, an area of basalt rocks decorated with bas-reliefs, a ball court and several pyramids by the river banks. Abundant wildlife here including toucans, parrots and otters. At the end of the Veracruz mountain range is the spectacular Encanto waterfall. Four-wheel drive is recommended for this journey by car: on the outskirts of Tlapacoyan, take the road marked Plan de Arroyas. After half an hour (many bends and hills) you'll see the sign for Filobobus on the left. This is a three-mile dirt track to a refreshment cabin, from where you can walk for 25 minutes to the ruins; follow signs for El Cuajilote. ■ *US$2.*

Mexico

Sleeping

Cheaper hotels are up the hill from the market, which itself is uphill from Parque Juárez (there is no Zócalo). Town centre hotels are generally noisy.

LL *Xalapa*, Victoria y Bustamante, T82222, good restaurant, excellent bookshop, changes travellers' cheques. **AL** *María Victoria*, Zaragoza 6, T80268, good. **AL** *Posada Coatepec*, Hidalgo 9, Centro, T160544, F160040 (in Mexico City T5142728/2075666), tastefully modernized colonial house, highly recommended. Reserve in advance, restaurant with Mexican and international cuisine. *Hostal del Tejar*, 20 de Noviembre Ote 552 esq Av del Tejar, T72459, F83691, 3-star, a/c, pool, parking. **B-C** *Hotel/Restaurant Mesón del Alférez*, Zaragoza y Sebastián Camacho, T/F186351, charming, small rooms, free parking opposite, good food, highly recommended. **C** *Hotel Suites Araucarias*, Avila Camacho 160, T73433, with large window, balcony and view (**D** without), TV, fridge, good cheap restaurant. **C** *México*, Lucio 4, T75030, clean, with shower, will change dollars.

D *Salmones*, Zaragoza 24, T75435, restaurant, excellent view of Orizaba from the roof, good restaurant, recommended. **D** *Principal*, Zaragoza 28, good if a bit shabby, safe parking nearby. **E** *Amoro*, near market, no shower but public baths opposite, very clean. **E** *Plaza*, Enríquez, T173310, all rooms with private bath and TV, some rooms airless., clean, safe, friendly, will store luggage, good view of Orizaba from the roof, recommended. **E** *Limón*, 100 metres up street on left side of cathedral on right hand side, with bath, TV. **F** *El Greco*, Av Revolución (opposite church), with bath, hot water, clean.

Eating The famous Xalapeño chilli comes from this region. *La Parroquia*, next door, and another one on Av Camacho, here same menu and prices as restaurant of same name in Veracruz, same chain. *La Casona del Beaterío*, Zaragoza 20, good atmosphere, tastefully restored house with patio and bubbling fountain, good breakfast. *Quinto Reyno*, Juárez 67 close to Zócalo, lunches only, excellent vegetarian with health-food shop, very good service. *La Champion*, Allende, going towards the Terminal, vegetation, nice atmosphere, good value *comida corrida* Monday-Saturday. *Café Linda*, Prime Verdad, good service and good value *comida corrida* every day, often live music in the evenings. *Estancia*, opposite Barranquilla, good food. *Aladino*, Juárez, up from ADO, excellent Mexican food. *Pizzaría*, Ursulo Galván. *La Sopa*, on Diamante, an alleyway just off Enríquez, great tapas, cheap. Several other small restaurants on Diamante including *La Fonda*, very pleasant upstairs and *El Diamante*. *Fruitlandia* on Abasolo (uphill from Cathedral), wonderful fresh juices. Health food shops, Ursulo Galván, near Juárez, good bread and yoghurt, another opposite the post office on Zamora. Several good cafés on Carrillo Puerto for good value *comida corrida*

Entertainment *Centro de Recreación Xalapeño* has exhibitions; live music and exhibitions in Ayora, underneath Parque Juárez; 10 pin bowling, Plaza Cristal, next to cinema.

    Cinemas There are 2 cinemas next to *Hotel Xalapa*, off Camacho; 3-screen cinema in Plaza Cristal; cinemas in the centre tend to show soft porn and gore.

    Theatre *Teatro del Estado*, Av Avila Camacho; good Ballet Folklórico Veracruzano and fair symphony orchestra.

    Nightclubs *La Tasca*, a club, good music, recommended. Another club is *La Cumbre* (rock).

Festivals *Feria de Primavera*, mid-April.

Shopping *Artesanía* shop on Alfaro, more on Barcenas, turn off Enríquez into Madero, right again at the top, the owner of *El Tazín* on the corner speaks English. **Books** *Instituto de Antropología*, Benito Juárez, has books in English and Spanish, student ID helps.

Transport **Local Bus** Many of the urban creamy yellow busses are for seated passengers only, so they will not stop for you if all the seats are full. **Car hire**: *Automóviles Sánchez*, Av Ignacio de la Llave 14, T79011, recommended. **Moped hire**: in Camacho US$4-6 per hour, Visa accepted.

    Air Airport 15 kilometres southeast, on Veracruz road.

    Trains Railway station on outskirts, buses from near market to get there. Trains **Mexico City-Veracruz stop here.**

    Buses A new 1st and 2nd class bus station has been built called CAXA; taxi from centre US$1.75. Taxi ticket office outside terminal on lower level. 5 hours from **Mexico City** by AU or ADO, from the Central de Oriente (TAPO). Frequent ADO service Xalapa-**Veracruz**, US$4, every 20 minutes 0700-2000. To **Puebla**, ADO, 'GL' Plus service, US$7, 1st class US$6, 4 hours, scenic route; also AU 2nd class. To **Coalzacoalcos**, 8 a day, US$17, up to 8 hours although you will be told 5 hours. To **Villahermosa**, ADO, 3 a day, 10 hours. To **Poza Rica**, US$11-14.50, 5 hours, about every 2 hours, the coast road is faster, while the impressive route via Teziutlán requires a strong stomach for mountain curves. For local second class destinations, e.g. Texolo, Coatepec, Jico, there is a Terminal at a roundabout.

Directory **Banks** *Banco Serfín* on Enríquez will change Tcs in dollars and other major currencies, *Santander* on Carrillo Puerto changes dollar TCs, *Bancomer* will not. Banks are slow, rates offered are rarely those advertised in the window and money transferred from abroad comes via Mexico City. *American Express* at Viajes Xalapa, Carrillo Puerto 24, T76535, in centre, sells cheques against Amex card but does not change them. *Casa de Cambio*, on right side of Zamora going down hill, English spoken. The liquor shop in Plaza Cristal will change dollars.Rates vary enormously, so shop around. Quick service and good rates at *Dollar Exchange*, Gutiérrez Zamora 36. **Communications** Post Office: letters can be sent to the Lista de Correos in C Diego Leño, friendly post office, and another at the bottom of Zamora. There is a telegraph office next door with Lista de Correos. **Telephone**: radio-telephone available opposite *Hotel María Victoria*; long distance phone in shop on Zaragoza, with a sign outside, others behind the government palace also in Zaragoza. **Email**: *Serviexpress*, Zaragoza 14B. *Café Chat* on

Camacho opposite Parque Bicentenial, another in shopping arcade off Enríquez. Most charge US$3 per hour. **Hospitals & medical services** Dentists: there are 2 dentists on Ursulo Galván. **Hospitals:** *Nicolás Bravo*, entrance in St on right. **Laundry** Several on Allende and Ursulo Galván, all charge by weight, usually US$3 per 3kg, some offer same day service, others up to 3 days. **Tour companies & travel agents** Travel agents: there are 4 on Camacho, the one nearest Parque Juárez is very helpful. **Tourist offices** Av Camacho, a long walk or short taxi ride. Look out for *Toma Nota*, free sheet advertising what is on, available from shop in front of *Hotel Salmones*.

The 140 road towards the capital continues to climb to **Perote**, 53 kilometres from Xalapa **E** *Hotel Central*, near plaza, quiet, friendly, with bath, TV. **F** *Gran Hotel*, on plaza, basic, limited water. The San Carlos fort here, now a military prison, was built in 1770-77; there is a good view of Cofre de Perote volcano. A road branches north to **Teziutlán** (**D** *Hotel Valdéz*, hot water, car park), with a Friday market, where good *sarapes* are sold, a local fair, *La Entrega de Inanacatl*, is held in the 3rd week in June. The old convent at **Acatzingo**, 93 kilometres beyond Perote on route 140, is worth seeing. Another 10 kilometres and you join the road to Puebla and Mexico City.

North from Veracruz

The 180 coast road from Veracruz heads to **Nautla** (one hotel, **E**, recommended, on main street; pleasant town, but nothing to see or do) three kilometres after which Route 131 branches inland to Teziutlán (see above). 42 kilometres up the coast from Nautla is **Tecolutla**, a very popular resort on the river of that name, toll bridge US$2.50. A fiesta takes place two days before the carnival in Veracruz, recommended.

Nautla & Tecolutla
Colour map 3, grid B5

Sleeping **B** *Villas de Palmar*. **D** *Playa*, good. **D** *Tecolutla*, best, and *Marsol* (run down) are all on the beach. **E** *Posada Guadalupe* and **E** *Casa de Huéspedes Malena* (pleasant rooms, clean) are on Av Carlos Prieto, near river landing stage. Other hotels, **D**, on road to Nautla. *Torre Molina* trailer park, 16 kilometres before Nautla on coastal Route 180 (coming from Veracruz), electricity, water and sewage disposal, hot showers, bathrooms, swimming pool, on beach, US$10 per vehicle with 2 people, recommended. *Restaurant Paquita*, next to *Hotel Playa*. recommended.

El Pital (15 kilometres in from the Gulf along the Nautla River, 80 kilometres south-east of Papantla and named after a nearby village), was identified early in 1994 as the site of an important, sprawling precolumbian seaport (approximately AD 100-600), which lay hidden for centuries under thick rainforest. Now planted over with bananas and oranges, the 100 or more pyramid mounds (some reaching 40 metres in height) were assumed by plantation workers to be natural hills. Little excavation or clearing has yet been done, but both Teotihuacan-style and local-style ceramics and figurines have been found, and archaeologists believe El Pital may mark the principal end point of an ancient cultural corridor that linked the north central Gulf Coast with the powerful urban centres of Central Mexico. As at nearby El Tajín, ball courts have been discovered, along with stone fragments depicting what may be sacrificed ball players.

El Pital

Papantla

Some 40 kilometres inland from Tecolutla is Papantla, built on the top of a hill over-looking the lush plains of northern Veracruz. It was the stronghold of a Totonac rebellion in 1836. Traditional Totonac dress is still seen: the men in baggy white trousers and sailor shirts and the women in lacy white skirts and shawls over embroidered blouses. Papantla is also the centre of one of the world's largest vanilla-producing zones, and the distinctive odour sometimes lingers over the town. Small animal figures, baskets and other fragrant items woven from vanilla

Population: 280,000
Colour map 3, grid B5

bean pods are sold at booths along Highway 180, as well as the essence; packaged in tin boxes, these sachets are widely used to freshen cupboards and drawers. The vanilla is processed in **Gutiérrez Zamora**, a small town about 30 kilometres east (close to Tecolutla), and a 'cream of vanilla' liqueur is also produced.

Sights The Zócalo, formally known as **Plaza Téllez**, is bordered by Enríquez on its down-hill north edge; on the south uphill side is the Cathedral of **Señora de la Asunción** (1700) with a remarkable 50 metre-long mural in its northern wall called *Homenaje a la Cultura Totonaca*, by Teodoro Cano García (1979), with the plumed serpent Quetzalcoatl along its entire length. *Voladores* perform each Sunday at 1100 in the church courtyard and as many as three times daily during the colourful 10 days of Corpus Christi (late May or early June), along with games, fireworks, artistic exhibitions, dances and cockfights. For a sweeping view of the area walk up Reforma to the top of the hill where the giant **Monumento al Volador** was erected in 1988. Murals and mosaic benches in the Zócalo also commemorate Totonac history and their

Papantla

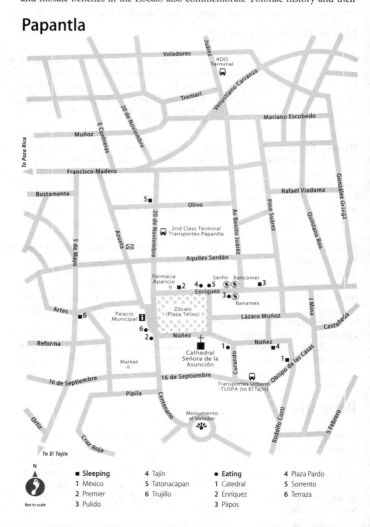

México

conception of creation. Beside the main plaza is the **Mercado Juárez** (poultry and vegetables); more interesting is **Mercado Hidalgo**, 20 de Noviembre off the north-west corner of the Zócalo (■ *daily 0600-2000*), where traditional handmade clothing is sold amid fresh produce and livestock.

About 12 kilometres away, in the forest, is **El Tajín**, the ruins of the capital of the Totonac culture (6th to 10th century AD, the name means 'hurricane'). ■ *0800-1800, except mid-August 0800-1900. US$2.80, free on Sunday. Guidebook US$1.25, available in Museo de Antropología, Mexico City, rarely available on site.* At the centre of this vast complex is the Pyramid of El Tajín (Pyramid of the Niches), whose 365 squared openings make it look like a vast beehive. There is a small modern museum, a cafetería and souvenir shops. In the wet season beware of a large, poisonous creature like a centipede. El Tajín can be visited either from Papantla or from Poza Rica, the oil town, see below.

Excursions

Mexico

El Tajín

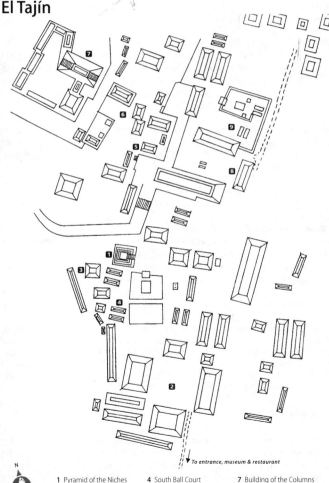

To entrance, museum & restaurant

N

Not to scale

1 Pyramid of the Niches
2 Plaza de Arroyo Group
3 Building 12
4 South Ball Court
5 Building I
6 Tajín Chico Group
7 Building of the Columns
8 Great Fret
9 Great Xicalcoliuhqui

Mexico

The voladores of El Tajín

Traditionally, on Corpus Christi, Totonac rain dancers erect a 30-metre mast with a rotating structure at the top of the Pyramid of El Tajín. Four voladores (flyers) and a musician climb to the surmounting platform. There the musician dances to his own pipe and drum music, whilst the roped voladores throw themselves into space to make a dizzy spiral descent, sometimes head up, sometimes head down, to the ground. Voladores are now in attendance every day (during high season, other times just weekends), most of the day, and fly if they think there are enough tourists, donations expected.

Four kilometres along a road east of the Río Tecolutla bridge (Puente de Remolino), near Paso de Correo (35 kilometres southeast of Papantla, past Chote), are the Totonac ruins of **Cuyuxquihui**, probably founded around AD 1250, shortly after El Tajín's demise, and later taken over by the Aztecs as a garrison. There is a large pyramid, platforms, altars and a ball court. From Papantla take bus marked 'Joloapan' (every hour, on hour) from 2nd class bus station.

Sleeping **B** *Premier*, on Zócalo, T21645, F21062, clean, a/c, TV, fax service, free car wash. **C** *Tajín*, C Dr Núñez 104, T20121, F21062, restaurant with good value breakfast and bar, fairly clean, parking, reasonable. **D-E** *Totonocapan*, 20 de Noviembre y Olivo, T21224, F21218, TV, a/c, hot water, bar/restaurant, good value. **E** *México*, Obispo de Las Casas y Núñez (beyond *Hotel Tajín*, opposite Cine Tajín), T20086, basic, cheapest in town. **E** *Pulido*, Enríquez 205, modern, T20036, noisy, with bath, parking. **E** *Trujillo*, C 5 de Mayo 401, rooms with basin, friendly.

Eating *Las Brisas del Golfo*, C Dr Núñez, reasonable and very good. *Sorrente*, Zócalo, covered in
Most open 0700-2400 decorative tiles, good, cheap, recommended. *Enríquez*, on Zócalo, popular, pleasant, not cheap. *Piipos*, Enríquez 100, speciality paella. *Catedral*, Núñez y Curado, behind Cathedral, plain, clean, cheap breakfasts and good 'fast' meals, 0630-2100.

Festivals The *Fiesta de la Vainilla* is held throughout the area in **early June**.

Transport **Local Taxi rank**: on Enríquez between 5 de Mayo and Zócalo and on Juárez.
Buses ADO terminal, Juárez 207, 5 blocks from centre (T20218). To **Mexico City**, 4 a day, 5 hours via Poza Rica, US$7; **Poza Rica**, 8 daily, 30 minutes, US$0.50; to **Xalapa**, 8 daily, 6 hours, US$6.25; 4 hours to **Veracruz**, US$14. 2nd class terminal (Transportes Papantla), 20 de Noviembre 200, many services to local destinations, including **El Tajín**, buses leave when full. Occasional minibus to El Tajín from southwest corner of Zócalo, US$2, unreliable schedule about every 1-1½ hours. Other buses (Transportes Urbano-TUSPA) for El Tajín leave from office on 16 de Septiembre near Obispo de las Casas (US$0.50).

Directory **Banks** *Bancomer* and *Banamex*, on Zócalo, 0900-1300, change cash and TCs till 1200. *Serfín*, between the 2, does not change TCs. **Communications** Post Office: Azueta 198, 2nd Flr, Mon-Fri 0900-1300, 1500-1800, Sat 0900-1200. **Hospitals & medical services** *Farmacia Aparicio*, Enríquez 103, daily 0700-2200. *Hospital Civil*, Madero 518, T20094. **Red Cross**: T20126. **Tourist offices** On 1st Flr of Palacio Municipal, on the Zócalo, T20026 ext 730, F20176, helpful, good local information and maps, bus schedules, English spoken, Mon-Fri 0900-1400 and 1800-2100.

Poza Rica

Population: 210,000 21 kilometres northwest of Papantla is Poza Rica, an ugly oil city, formed out of four
Colour map 3, grid B4 old *rancherías*, which happened to lie on top of the then 2nd largest oil strike in the world. It has an old cramped wooden market and a simple mural by O'Higgins ('From Primitive Pre-Hispanic Agricultural Works to the Present Day Oil Industry Development', 1959) on the outside of the *Palacio Municipal*, but little else to recommend it, apart from an inordinate number of dentists. The streets are busy, there

are several comfortable hotels and bus connections are very good. Flaring gas burn offs light up the night sky.

B *Poza Rica Inn*, Carretera a Papantla, Km 4, 'Holiday Inn look-a-like', T31922, F35888, poor restaurant. **B** *Robert Prince*, Av 6 Nte, 10 Ote, T25455, Col Obrera. **B** *Poza Rica*, 2 Nte, T20134, a Best Western hotel and experienced for what it offers, friendly, credit cards accepted, fairly comfortable, good *comida corrida* in restaurant, if arriving by taxi make sure the driver does not confuse it with the *Poza Rica Inn* outside town. **C** *Nuevo León*, Av Colegio Militar, T20528, opposite market, rooms quite spacious, fairly clean and quiet, recommended. **C** *Salinas*, Blvd Ruiz Cortines, 1905, on Cazones road, T20238, F33525, good, a/c, TV, restaurant, pool, secure parking. **D** *Berlím*, 2 Ote y 6 Nte, T20055, TV, fan. **E** *Aurora*, Bolívar 4, basic but quiet and fairly clean. **E** *Fénix*, 6 Nte (near Av Central Ote) basic, but one of

Sleeping

Mexico

Poza Rica

N
Not to scale

■ Sleeping	4 Fénix	8 Rossi	● Eating
1 Aurora	5 Nuevo León	9 San Antonio	1 Café Manolo
2 Berlim	6 Poza Rica	10 San Román	2 Loncheria El Petrolero
3 Casablanca	7 Robert Prince		

the better cheap places, opposite town centre ADO ticket office in an express mail company office. **E** *San Román*, 8 Nte 5. **E** *San Antonio*, Prolongación 20 de Noviembre (near Plaza), T33784, with bath, fan, friendly. Opposite is **E** *Rossi*, and next door **E** *Casa Blanca*, bath and TV, cheaper without. **F** *Cárdenas*, Bermúdez y Zaragoza, T26610, basic, not central. Cheap hotels are often frequented by short stay guests.

Eating *Lonchería El Petrolero*, Plaza Cívica 18 de Marzo y Av Central Ote, excellent bread baked on premises, popular with locals. *Café Manolo*, 10 Ote 60 y 6 Nte, good breakfast, moderate prices.

Transport **Air** Airport El Tajín, 3 kilometres south, T22119; several flights daily to Mexico City, **Buses** All buses leave from new terminal referred to as ADO, about 1½ kilometres from centre, take white bus from centre, or taxi, US$1.50. Terminal is divided into ADO (T20085, also office in centre, 6 Nte opposite Hotel Fénix, open daily, hours vary) and all others, good facilities, tourist office. ADO 1st class to **Mexico City** and **Tampico**, 21 daily each, 5 hours, US$14. Estrella Blanca 2nd class to Mexico City, 23 daily, US$7.25. To **Monterrey**, 4 a day, US$11. To **Veracruz**, 4 hours, US$11.50. To Xalapa, US$11-14.50, up to 5½ hours, frequent. To **Pachuca**, Estrella Blanca, 4½ hours, US$6, change in Tulancingo. To **Tecolutla** (see below), US$2.20, 1¼ hours. To **Barra de Cazones**, Trans Papantla or Autotrans Cazones, 1 hour, US$1.20 (often waits 30 minutes in Cazones on way back until bus fills). It is not always necessary to go to bus station to catch your bus: buses to Barra de Cazones leave the terminal but can be picked up as they pass through the centre along Boulevard Cortines. To **Papantla** bus may be caught on Av Central Ote by Plaza Cívico 18 de Marzo. To **El Tajín**, buses leave every 20-30 minutes 0700-2000 from behind Monumento de la Madre statue, marked Chote or Chote Tajín. Ask driver for fare to Las Ruinas, US$0.50, 20-25 minutes, most go to the entrance.

Directory **Airline offices** *Aero México*, Edif Géminis, Parque Juárez, T26142/28877. Aeromar, T43001.**Banks** *Bancomer*, opposite *Hotel Poza Rica*. *Serfín*, 4 Nte y 2 Ote. **Cultural centres** *Casa de la Cultura*, Guatemala 502, T23185. **Hospitals & medical services** Red Cross: Blvd Lázaro Cárdenas 106, T36871. **Laundry** *Yee del Centro*, Prolongación 20 de Noviembre, US$2.50 per 3 kg. **Tourist office** At back of *Palacio Municipal* on ground floor, T21390 ext 129, 21338.

From Poza Rica you can head north to visit the **Castillo de Teayo**, a pyramid with the original sanctuary and interesting carvings on top, buses every 30 minutes, change halfway. 25 kilometres along Route 8 is **Barra de Cazones** (not to be confused with Cazones, the town you pass on the way) with a dirty beach and a less developed, cleaner one on the north side of the river (ferry US$0.25). **B** *Mariner Costa*, on hill above river, pool, good view over boca. **D** *Estrella del Mar*, north end of south beach. Many restaurants.

Tuxpán

Colour map 3, grid B5 On the north bank of the wide Río Tuxpán, 55 kilometres from Poza Rica, 189 kilometres south of Tampico is Tuxpán (Veracruz), tropical and humid, 12 kilometres from the sea. Essentially a fishing town (shrimps a speciality), it is now decaying from what must have been a beautiful heyday. Interesting covered market, but beware of the bitter, over-ripe avocados; fruit sold on the quay. Beach about 12 kilometres east of town, reached by taxi or bus from Boulevard Reyes Heroles (marked 'Playa' US$0.50), at least 10 kilometres long. Few people weekdays, no hasslers, some sandflies; hire deckchairs under banana-leaf shelters for the day (US$2). Many restaurants line the beach (eg *El Arca*, friendly), with showers for the use of bathers (US$0.35), it is worth asking to hang up a hammock for US$2 per night.

Sleeping **B** *Hotel Florida*, Av Juárez 23, T40650, clean, hot water. **C** *Plaza Palmas*, on edge of town along bypass route, a/c, tennis, pool, secure parking, clean, boat launch to river, TV, good restaurant, fenced all round compound, recommended. **C-D** *Riviera*, Blvd Jesús Reyes Heroles 17a, T45349, on waterfront, parking, rooms vary in size so check first. **D** *California*, Arteaga 16, T40810, clean, hot water, good breakfast. **D** *Parroquia*, Berriozábal 4, beside Cathedral, T41630, clean, friendly, hot water, fan, noisy. **E** *Posada San Ignacio*, Melchor Ocampo 29, 1 block north of plaza, T42905, clean, with bath, fan, friendly, recommended. **E** *Tuxpán*, T44110, OK.

Cafetería El Mante, Juárez beside market, popular with locals, good *comida corrida*. Also *Bremen*, a/c, food good and cheap.

Eating

Nightlife *Hotel Teján*, over the river, south side, then about 1 kilometre towards the sea, very plush, good singers but US$6.50 cover charge; *Acropolis* disco, dull, no beer. **Cinema** Just off Boulevard Reyes Heroles, 1 block east of plaza.

Entertainment

Watersports: *Aquasport*, 7 kilometres along road to beach, T70259.

Sports

Buses ADO Terminal, east of market, near north end of bridge. Buses to Mexico City (Terminal del Nte), US$14.80, 6½ hours via Poza Rica.

Transport

Banks *Bancomer*, Juárez y Zapata; opposite is Serfín. **Tourist office** Av Juárez 20, T40177 ext 117.

Directory

Tuxpán (Veracruz)

N

Not to scale

■ **Sleeping**	3 Riviera	● **Eating**
1 Florida	4 San Ignacio	1 Cafetería El
2 Parroquia	5 Tuxpán	Mante

Mexico

Mexico City-Cuernavaca-Taxco-Acapulco

From the capital to the Pacific, with long-established resorts such as Acapulco, newer developments (Puerto Escondido, Huatulco) and the only-recently discovered (Zipolite). The route passes through Cuernavaca, the country seat of Aztecs and Spaniards, now a major tourist town, and the silver city of Taxco.

A 406-kilometre four-lane toll motorway connects Mexico City with Acapulco. (Total toll for the route at eight booths is US$89.) Driving time is about three and a half hours. The highest point, La Cima, 3,016 metres, is reached at Km 42. The road then spirals down through precipitous forests to Cuernavaca (Km 75).

Cuernavaca

Population: 1,000,000
State population 1995:
1,442,587
Altitude: 1,542m
Phone code: 73
Colour map 3, grid B4

Capital of Morelos state (originally Tlahuica Indian territory) 724 metres lower than Mexico City. The temperature never exceeds 27°C nor falls below 10°C, and there is almost daily sunshine even during the rainy season. The city has always attracted visitors from the more rigorous highlands and can be overcrowded. The Spaniards captured it in 1521 and Cortés himself, following the custom of the Aztec nobility, lived there. The outskirts are dotted with ultra-modern walled homes and most of its charm has been swamped by the city's rapid growth and a new industrial area to the south.

The centre of the city has two adjacent squares, the larger **Zócalo** and the smaller **Alameda**. At the western end of the Zócalo is the Palacio de Gobierno; north of the Zócalo, east of the Alameda is the Centro Las Plazas shopping mall. Heading north from the Alameda, C Vicente Guerrero is lined with shops in arcades. Calle Degollado leads down to the main market in a labyrinth of shops and alleys.

Sights The palace Cortés built in 1531 for his second wife stands at the eastern end of the tree-shaded Alameda; on the rear balcony is a Diego Rivera mural depicting the conquest of Mexico. It was the seat of the State Legislature until 1967, when the new legislative building opposite was completed; it has now become the **Museo Regional de Historia Cuauhnáhuac**, showing everything from mammoth remains to contemporary Indian culture, explanations are none-too-logical and most are in Spanish. ■ *1000-1700, closed Monday, US$1.80.* West of the centre, C Hidalgo leads to one of the main areas of historical interest in the city.

The **Cathedral** (entrance on Hidalgo, near Morelos), finished in 1552, known as Iglesia de la Asunción, stands at one end of an enclosed garden. 17th century murals were discovered during restoration; they depict the martyrdom of the Mexican saint San Felipe de Jesús on his journey to Japan. The scenes show monks in open boats, and mass crucifixions. The interior is bathed in different colours from the modern stained-glass windows. At the west end is a stone font full of water; the east end painted gold, contains the modern altar. In the entrance to the chapel of the Reserva de la Eucarista is a black and white fresco of the crucifixion. There are also two-storey cloisters with painted friezes and a fragment of massed ranks of monks and nuns. The Sunday morning masses at 1100 are accompanied by a special *mariachi* band. *Mariachis* also perform on Sunday and Wednesday evenings in the Cathedral. By the entrance to it stands the charming small church of the **Tercera Orden** (1529), whose quaint façade carved by Indian craftsmen contains a small figure suspected to be one of the only two known statues of Cortés in Mexico. (The other is a mounted statue near the entrance of the *Casino de la Selva* hotel.) Beside the cathedral, in the Casa de la Torre, is the **Museo Robert Brady**, housing a collection of paintings by, among others, Diego Rivera, Frida Kahlo, Paul Klee and

Francisco Toledo. It also has colonial furniture, textiles, prehispanic objects and African art and ceramics. ■ *1000 to 1800, closed Monday, US$1.30, café and shop.* The 18th century **Jardín Borda**, on C Morelos, was a favourite resort of Maximilian and Carlota; it has been restored and is in fine condition; (open-air concerts, exhibition rooms, café, good bookshop, museum). ■ *1000-1730, closed Monday, US$0.80.* Boats can be rented on the small lake, US$1-3 depending on duration. Next to the Jardín Borda is the church of Nuestra Señora de Guadalupe (neoclassical). Two kilometres on the right up Morelos (pesero), side by side are the churches of San José Tlaltenango (1521-23) and Nuestra Señora de la Natividad (early 19th century); bazaar on Sunday, second-hand English books.

The weekend retreat of the ill-fated imperial couple, in the Acapantzingo district, is now the **Herbolario y Jardín Botánico**, with a museum, Matamoros 200, Col Acapatzingo, peaceful, interesting, free. ■ *Open daily 0900-1700.* To get there take a bus from the centre to Acapantzingo and ask the driver for the Museo del

Mexico

Cuernavaca orientation

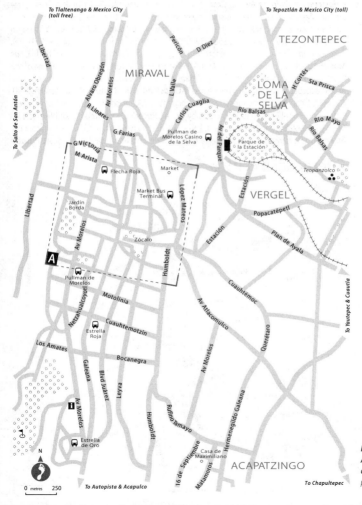

Related map
A Cuernavaca orientation, page 358

Herbolario, or, more easily, take a taxi US$1.75. Acapantzingo is a pleasant district. The house of David Alfaro Siqueiros, the painter, is now a museum (**Taller Siqueiros**) at C Venus 7 (a long way east of the centre) and contains lithographs and personal photographs. The very unusual **Teopanzolco** pyramid is to be found just east of the railway station. ■ *1000-1630, entry US$1.50.* At the pyramid's summit, remains of the temple can be seen. Also in the complex are various structures including a circular building, probably dedicated to Quetzalcoatl.

Excursions To the **Chapultepec Park**, southeast of the city centre, with boating facilities, small zoo, water gardens, small admission charge. Also east of the centre is a zoo and recreation centre at **Jungla Mágica**, built around a series of natural springs. To the potters' village of **San Antón**, perched above a waterfall, a little west of the town, where divers perform Sunday for small donations. In the vicinity of Cuernavaca are many spas, such as Xochitepec, Atotonilco, Oaxtepec, Temixco, Las Huertas and Los Manantiales at Xicatlocatla.

Sleeping **L** *Hostería Las Quintas*, Av Díaz Ordáz No 9 Col Cantarranas, T183949, F183895, built in tra-
Good value, cheap ditional Mexican style, owner has splendid collection of bonsai trees, restaurant, 2 pools, spa,
hotels are hard to find. outdoor jacuzzi, magnificent setting, fine reputation. **L** *Misión del Sol*, Av Gral Diego González 31, Col Parres 62550, T210999, F211195 (Toll-free 01-800-999-91-00), misolmex@mail.giga.com, spa resort with good sports facilities, recommended. **L** *Las Mañanitas*, Ricardo Linares 107, T141466/124646, F183672, reyl@infosel.net.mx (one of the best in Mexico), Mexican colonial style, many birds in lovely gardens, excellent food, only Amex accepted, reservation necessary. **AL** *Hacienda de Cortés*, Plaza Kennedy 90, T160867/158844, 16th century sugar *hacienda*, magnificent colonial architecture, garden, suites, pool, excellent restaurant, access by car. **AL** *Posada Jacarandas*, Cuauhtémoc 133, T157777, F157888, garden, restaurant, sports, laundry, safety box, conference hall, parking. **AL** *Posada San Angelo*, Privada la Selva 100, T141499, restaurant, gardens, pool. **AL** *Posada*

Cuernavaca centre

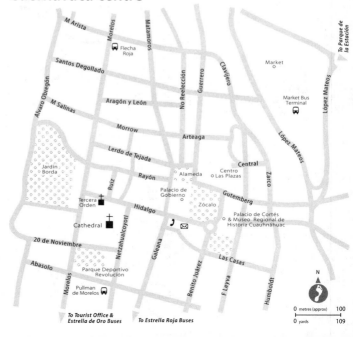

Maria Cristina, Francisco Leyva 200, T185767, near Zócalo, restaurant, pool, garden. **A2** ***Suites Paraíso***, Av Domingo Díaz 1100, T133365, family accommodation. On same avenue, ***Villa Bejar***, No 2350, T175000, F174953, Gran Turismo class, all facilities. **A** ***Posada Quinta Las Flores***, Tlaquepaque 210, Colonia Las Palmas, T141244/125769, 2 minutes' walk from Estrella de Oro bus station, 30 minutes from centre on foot, includes breakfast, no TV, helpful, pool, gardens, restaurant (set evening meal), small parking space, very pleasant, highly recommended. **B** ***Papagayo***, Motolinia 13, T141711, 5 blocks from Zócalo, 1 block from Estrella Roja bus station, on Friday-Saturday rooms are available only if one takes 2 meals a day, on other days price is **C**, room only, pool, gardens, convenient, good value, suitable for families, parking. **C** ***Bajo el Volcán***, Humboldt 117, T124873, 187537, pool, restaurant, fair. **C** ***Las Hortensias***, Hidalgo 22, T185265, takes Visa, pretty courtyard, central, long-distance phone service.

D ***Colonial***, Aragón y León 104, T186414, friendly, pleasant courtyard, clean airy rooms, English spoken, recommended. **D-E** ***Roma***, Matamoros 405, T120787, with hot water, am and evening, noisy. Several cheaper hotels in C Aragón y León between Morelos and Matamoros: eg **E** ***América***, No 111, safe, good value but noisy, clean, basic; some rent rooms by the hour.

Motels **A** ***Posada Cuernavaca***, Paseo del Conquistador, T130800, view, restaurant, grounds. **B** ***El Verano***, Zapata 602, T170652. **E** ***Royal***, Matamoros 19, hot water 0700-2300, central, clean, recommended. ***Suites OK Motel*** with ***Restaurant Las Margaritas***, Zapata 71, T131270, special student and long-term rates, apartments, trailer park, swimming pool and squash courts.

Eating

Hacienda de Cortés (see above); ***Las Mañanitas***, Ricardo Linares 107, beautiful but expensive, only Amex accepted; also beautiful is ***La India Bonita***, Morrow 20, excellent Mexican food but expensive. On the Zócalo and Alameda: ***Villa Roma, Café/Pastelería Viena*** (expensive); ***La Parroquia, La Universal*** (on corner of Zócalo and Alameda). Next to *La Universal* on the Alameda is *McDonalds*. Also for fast food, ***Subway*** (on Alameda) and others in Centro Las Plazas. ***Parrots***, next to the Museo Regional, opposite which, at Hidalgo y Juárez, are ***La Adelita*** and ***Flash Taco***. ***Marco Polo***, opposite Cathedral, good, Italian, good pizzas, popular meeting place. ***Vivaldi***, Pericon 102, restaurant and pastelería, very reasonable, popular with locals. There are other *cafés* opposite the cathedral. Near the Glorieta Niña in Col Las Palmas, ***Los Vikingos***, restaurant and *pastelería*, good. There is also a large *panadería pastelería* on this roundabout. Generally, it is not easy to find good, authentic Mexican cooking at reasonable prices. A major exception is ***La Pasadita***, Morelos esq Abasolo, where there is usually an amazingly wide choice at very good prices, quieter upstairs.

Pollo y Más, Juárez, decent, cheap *comida corrida*. ***Malvias***, Matamoros, next to *Motel Royal*, friendly, good value *comida corrida*. ***Jugos Hawai*** in Centro Las Plazas, fruit juices are sold from stalls beneath the bandstand on the Zócalo.

Shopping

Bookshop Second-hand English books at Guild House, C Tuxtla Gutiérrez, Col Chipitlán, T125197. **Handicrafts market** Behind Cortés' palace, moderately priced and interesting silver, textiles and souvenirs. When the tour buses arrive there are lots of handicraft sellers outside the cathedral gates.

Transport

Air Flights from Tijuana, Acapulco, Culiacán, Monterrey, Hermosillo and Guadalajara with Aerolíneas Internacionales.

Buses Each bus company has its own terminal; **Estrella de Oro** (B5), Morelos Sur 900, Col Las Palmas, T123055, 1st class buses to Mexico City, Taxco (0915, 2100), Ixtapa (2145), Lázaro Cárdenas (2015), Chipalcingo (0900, 1100, 1345, 1630), Aguascalientes (2200), Acapulco (7 daily 0715-2230) and Zihuatanejo (2015); this bus station is a US$3.25 taxi ride, or 25 minutes' walk from the centre. Local buses from the bus station up Morelos, marked Centro, or Buena Vista, all go to the Cathedral. From the centre take bus on Galeana marked Palmas. **Pullman de Morelos** has 2 termini: (B1) at Abasolo 106 y Netzahualcoyotl in the centre, T180907, for Mexico City (*ejecutivo dorado*) every 30 minutes from 0530, and some local departures to Alpuyeca, Tehuixtla, Zacatepec, Jojutla, Grutas de Cacahuamilpa, and (B4) at 'Casino de la Selva', Plan de Ayala 102, opposite Parque de la Estación, T189205, for *ejecutivo dorado* to Mexico City and 10 daily buses to Mexico airport (book 24 hours in advance at either terminal, US$6). **Flecha Roja** (B1) on Morelos Nte 503 y Arista, T125797, 2nd class to Mexico City (0530-2100), Taxco (0805-2035), Iguala, Tijuana (via Guadalajara, Mazatlán, Hermosillo, 1815, 2200), Querétaro (1400), San Luis Potosí (1701), Nuevo Laredo (via Saltillo, Monterrey, 1615), Acapulco (several daily) and Grutas de Cacahuamilpa (left luggage open 0700 to 2100 daily, US$0.25 per hour per item). **Estrella Roja** (B6), Galeana y Cuauhtemotzín, south of the centre, for Cuautla (every 15 minutes) via Yautepec, Matamoros and Puebla (via Izúcar de Matamoros, hourly 0500-1900). Many minibuses and 2nd class buses leave from a terminal by the market (B3).

To **Mexico City** 1½ hours, fares US$3.65 ordinary to US$4.25 *ejecutivo dorado*: Pullman de Morelos is said to be the most comfortable and fastest, from Southern Bus Terminus, Mexico City every 30 minutes.

To **Acapulco**, 4 hours, Estrella de Oro, US$14.75 (US$19.50 *plus*). For advance tickets for Acapulco or other points on the Pacific Coast, be at Estrella de Oro office between 1645 and 1700, 2-3 days before you want to travel, this is when seats are released in Mexico City and full fare from Mexico City to the coast must be paid. To **Zihuatanejo**, Estrella de Oro, 1 a day, US$23. To **Taxco**, Flecha Roja, 2nd-class buses, hourly on the ½-hour, or Estrella de Oro, 1st class, US$4.25; to **Puebla**, Estrella de Oro, *gran turismo* service, US$5, 1st class hourly, US$4, 2 stops; **Cuautla** (page 390) either Estrella Roja every 20 minutes, US$1.85, or 2nd class or minibus from market terminal, via Yautepec every hour, 1 hour, interesting trip; go there for long-distance buses going south (Puebla buses do not stop at Cuautla).

Warning: Theft of luggage from waiting buses in Cuernavaca is rife; don't ever leave belongings unattended. Robberies have been reported on the non-toll mountain road to Taxco and on the road to Mexico City.

NB to Drivers Cuernavaca to points west of Mexico City: on the toll road, north from Cuernavaca is a sign at Las Tres Marías to Toluca. Do not be tempted to take this route; it is well-surfaced but narrow over the pass before leading to the lakes at Zempoala, but thereafter it is almost impossible to navigate the backroads and villages to Toluca. Among the problems are livestock on the road, unsigned intersections, signposts to villages not marked on the Pemex atlas, heavy truck traffic, potholes, *topes* and congested village plazas. (Eric Mankin, Venice, CA.)

Directory **Banks** *Cambio Gesta*, Dwight D Morrow 9, T183750, open 0900-1800. *Divisas de Cuernavaca*, Morrow 12; many banks in the vicinity of the Zócalo. **Communications** Post Office: on Hidalgo, just off the Alameda. **Telephone:** Telmex on Hidalgo, just off the Alameda, LADA phones are outside, almost opposite junction of Netzahualcoyotl. There is a telephone office at *Parrots* restaurant and bar on the Alameda, next to the Museo Regional. **Internet:** *Axon Cyber Café*, Av Cuauhtémoc 129-B.

Language schools Spanish courses start from US$100 per week, plus US$60 registration at the *Centro de Lengua, Arte e Historia para Extranjeros* at the Universidad Autónoma del Estado de Morelos, Río Panuco 20, Col Lomas del Mirador, T161626 (accommodation with families can be arranged). Private schools charge

Cuernavaca
Language
School
MEXICO

The Place to Learn to Speak Spanish

★ Classes Start Every Monday
★ Four Students per Class Maximum
★ Cultural Sessions Included
★ Weekend Field Trips
★ Accomodations with Host Families

Tel: (52-7) 317-5151
Fax: (52-7) 316-3546
E-mail: cls@infosel.net.mx
http://cuernavaca.infosel.com.mx/cls

International Office:
P.O. Box 4133
Windham, New Hampshire 03087-4133
Tel: (603) 437-9714
Fax: (603) 437-6412
E-mail:roberto-alm@worldnet.att.net

US$100-150 a week, 5-6 hrs a day and some schools also have a US$75-125 registration fee. The peak time for tuition is summer: at other times it may be possible to arrive and negotiate a reduction of up to 25%. There is a co-operative language centre, *Cuaunhuac*, Morelos Sur 123, T123673/189275, F182693, inform@cuauhnahuac.edu.mx, intensive Spanish 6 hrs a day and flexible private classes, registration US$70, US$200 per week or US$650 per month high season, US$170 per week, US$560 per month low season, family stays US$18 per day shared room with meals or US$25 single room with meals, efficient, helpful. *Center for Bilingual Multicultural Studies*, Apdo Postal 1520, T171087/172488, F170533 or Los Angeles, LA, 213-851-3403. *Spanish Language Institute* (SLI), Pradera 208, Col Pradera, T110063 F175294, sli@infosel.net.mx, open 5 days a week, minimum 6 hrs per day, classes start every Monday. *Instituto Fénix*, Salto Chico 3, Col Tlaltenango, T131743, which also has excursions and minor courses in politics, art and music. *Cetlalic*, Madero 721, Col Miraval,

Mexico

Cuernavaca, T170850, F132637, cetlalic@mail.giga.com, a non-profit organization teaching the Spanish language, themed courses, plus Mexican and Central American history and culture, recommended. *Cemanahuac*, C San Juan 4, Las Palmas, T186407, F125418, 74052.2570@compuserve.com, claims high academic standards, field study, also weaving classes. *Experiencia*, C Leyva, Colonia Las Palmas, T126579, F185209, experiencia@infosel.net.mx, open 5 days a week, free 'intercambios' (Spanish-English practice sessions) Tuesday and Wednesday pm. *Centro de Artes y Lenguas*, Nueva Tabachín 22-A, T173126/130603, F137352, scale@infosel.net.mx, 5 hrs a day, registration US$100, 1 week minimum, classes US$160, US$300 a week accommodation with families including meals. *Cuernavaca Language School*, T175151, F163546, cls@infosel.net.mx, or PO Box 4133, Windham, New Hampshire, T(603) 437-9714, F(603) 437-6412. *Mexican Immersion Centre*, Piñanonas 26, Col Jacarandas, CP 62420, T221083, F157953, mic@axon.com.mx. *Encuentros*, Morelos 36, Col Acapantzingo, CP 62440, T125088, F129800, encuent@infosel.net.mx. *Universal*, JH Preciado 332, Col San Antón, T124902 (Apdo Postal 1-1826), 3 levels of language course, tutorials and mini courses on culture; and *Idel*, Apdo 1271-1, Calz de los Actores 112, Col Atzingo, T/F130157, 5 levels of course. Staying with a local family will be arranged by a school and costs US$12-20 a day including meals; check with individual schools, as this difference in price may apply even if you stay with the same family. See also **Learning Spanish** in **Essentials**.

Laundry In Las Palmas: *Oaxaca* behind Confía buildings, almost opposite *Restaurante Vikingos*, good. *Euro Klin*, Morelos Sur 700 block, a short way from Glorieta Niña towards centre. There is a good laundry behind the Cathedral. **Tour companies & travel agents** *Marín*, Centro Las Plazas, local 13, Amex agent, changes Amex TCs but poorer rate than *casas de cambio*, charges US$1 to reconfirm flights. Also in Centro Las Plazas, *Pegaso*, French, Italian, German, English spoken (the sign says), charges US$2 to reconfirm. *Viajes Adelina*, Pasaje Bella Vista, on Zócalo. **Tourist offices** Tourist kiosk on Vicente Guerrero outside *Posada San Angelo*. For cultural activities, go for information to the university building behind the Cathedral on Morelos Sur.

Cuernavaca environs

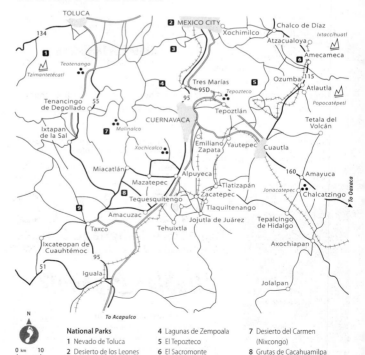

National Parks
1 Nevado de Toluca
2 Desierto de los Leones
3 Cumbres del Ajusco
4 Lagunas de Zempoala
5 El Tepozteco
6 El Sacromonte
7 Desierto del Carmen (Nixcongo)
8 Grutas de Cacahuamilpa
9 Alejandro de Humboldt

Tepoztlan

Tepoztlán is 24 kilometres northeast of Cuernavaca at the foot of the spectacular **El** *Population: 4,000*
Tepozteco national park, with the small Tepozteco pyramid high up in the moun-
tains. ■ *open anytime between 0900 and 1030, officially 1000-1630, US$3, free with*
student card. The only way into the park is on foot. It takes 40 minutes-one hour to
climb from the car park at the end of Avenida de Tepozteco to the pyramid. It is two
kilometres uphill, strenuous, climb up before the sun is too high, although most of
the climb is through trees. The trip is well worth it. The altitude at the top of the pyramid is 2,100 metres; the view from the top is expansive. Signs remind you on the way
that you must pay at the top; five minutes before the entrance a steel ladder has to be
scaled. Cold drinks are sold at the entrance for US$1.

The town has picturesque steep cobbled streets, an outdoor market and a remark- **Sights**
able 16th century church and convent (María de la Natividad): the Virgin and Child
stand upon a crescent moon above the elaborate plateresque portal, no tripod or
flash allowed. A mural by Juan Ortega (1887) covers the eastern end of the church.
There is a small archaeological museum with objects from all over Mexico behind
the church. ■ *Tuesday-Sunday 1000-1800, US$0.75.* There is a Saturday/Sunday
arts and crafts market on the plaza with a good selection of handicrafts from Mexico,
Guatemala and East Asia, expensive. Every November, first week, there is an arts festival with films and concerts (open air and in the main church's cloister). This was
the village studied by Robert Redfield and later by Oscar Lewis. In 1997 the main
road to the town was blocked by a wall of stones as a protest against a planned golf
links by a foreign investment group. There have been demonstrations by villagers.

A *Posada del Tepozteco*, T50010, F50323, a very good inn, quiet, old fashioned, with swim- **Sleeping**
ming pool, excellent atmosphere and view, highly recommended. **A** *Hotel Tepoztlán*, largest hotel, towering over the village, grand pool, popular, crowded at weekends, as they all
are. *Hotel Restaurant Anatlán de Quetzalcoatl*, T91739/51880, F51952, pool, children's
park, gardens. **A** *Posada Ali*, Netzahualcóyotl 2 'C', off Av del Tepozteco, T51971, 4 rooms, 2
family suites (AL) breakfast, pool, fine view. **A** *Casa Iccemanyan*, Familia Berlanga, C del
Olvido 26, 62520, Tepoztlán, T91-73950096/99 with 3 meals, **B** without meals, monthly rates
available, 4 cabañas, swimming pool, clothes washing facilities, use of kitchen, laundry, restaurant, English, French and German spoken, beautiful garden. **D** *Mesón del Indio*, Av
Revolución 44, no sign, Sr Lara. Basic.

Los Colorines, Av de Tepozteco 13-B. Good, Mexican vegetarian. Next door is *El Chinelo*, **Eating**
Mexican. *El Jardín del Tepozteco*, Italian, Wednesday-Sunday 1300-2200. *Axitla*, at beginning off path up to Tepozteco, open Friday, Saturday, Sunday and holidays. *La Costa de San
Juan*, by plaza on opposite side of street, meat and seafood. *Tapatía*, Av Revolución 1910
(just across street from church wall), good food and pleasant view from 1st floor, takes credit
cards. *El Ciruelo*, Zaragoza 17, quiet, nice décor, popular with wealthy Mexicans.

Local bus (Autobus Verde) from Cuernavaca market terminal, takes 1 hour, US$1 (bus returns **Transport**
to Cuernavaca from the top of the Zócalo); bus to Mexico City, US$3.35 1st class, US$3.65
primera plus, hourly. There are buses from Tepoztlán to Yautepec.

South of Cuernavaca

(Km 100) **Alpuyeca**, whose church has good Indian murals. A road to the left runs
to **Lago Tequesquitengo** (*Paraíso Ski Club*) and the lagoon and sulphur baths of
Tehuixtla. Near the lake a popular resort, with swimming, boating, water skiing and
fishing, is **AL** *Hacienda Vista Hermosa*, Hernán Cortés' original *ingenio* (sugar
mill), and several lakeside hotels. East of the lake is **Jojutla** (**D** *Hotel del Sur*, central,
clean, simple; and others). Near Jojutla is the old Franciscan convent of

Mexico (side tab)

Mexico

Tlaquiltenango (1540), frequent bus service from Cuernavaca, US$1.75, Pullman de Morelos. The route through Jojutla can be used if coming from the coast heading for Cuautla and wishing to avoid Cuernavaca. Enquire locally of road conditions off the major highways.

Cacahuamilpa From Alpuyeca also a road runs west for 50 kilometres to the Cacahuamilpa caverns (known locally as 'Las Grutas'); some of the largest caves in North America, well worth a visit; strange stalactite and stalagmite formations; steps lead down from near the entrance to the caverns to the double opening in the mountainside far below, from which an underground river emerges. ■ *Open 1000 to 1700 (take a torch), US$2.50, children US$1.50, including 2¼ hours guided tour in Spanish, every hour on the hour up to 1600 – crowded after 1100 and at weekends.* Guided tours take you two kilometres inside; some excursions have gone six kilometres; the estimated maximum depth is 16 kilometres. It is worth going with a guided tour as the caves are then lit properly (Spanish only). Don't miss the descent to the river exits at the base of the cliff, called Dos Bocas, tranquil and less-frequently visited.

Warning The disease *histoblastose* is present in the bat droppings in the cave (if you breathe in the tiny fungus it can cause a tumour on the lungs); to avoid it you can buy a dentist's face mask (US$0.20) (*cobre boca/protección de dentista*) at a pharmacy, eg try one opposite bus station.

Transport There are direct Pullman de Morelos buses from Cuernavaca at 1030 and 1200, returning 1700 and 1830, 1 hour, US$2; also Flecha Roja; they are usually overcrowded at weekends; enquire about schedules for local buses or buses from Taxco to Toluca, which stop there (from Taxco, 30 kilometres, 40 minutes).

Xochicalco At 15 kilometres on the westerly road from Alpuyeca is the right-hand turn to the Xochicalco ruins (36 kilometres southwest of Cuernavaca), topped by a pyramid on the peak of a rocky hill, dedicated to the Plumed Serpent whose coils enfold the whole building and enclose fine carvings which represent priests. The site is large: needs two to three hours to see it properly. There is a new museum which is well laid out and well explained and a cafetería. ■ *1000-1700.*

Xochicalco was at its height between 650 and 900 AD. It is one of the oldest known fortresses in Middle America and a religious centre as well as an important trading point. The name means 'place of flowers' although now the hilltops are barren. It was also the meeting place of northern and southern cultures and, it is believed, both calendar systems were correlated here. The sides of the Pyramid of the Plumed Serpent are faced with andesite slabs, fitted invisibly without mortar. After the building was finished, reliefs three to four inches deep were carried into the stone as a frieze. There are interesting underground tunnels (open 1100-1400); one has a shaft to the sky and the centre of the cave. There are also ball courts, an avenue 18.5 metres wide and 46 metres long, remains of 20 large circular altars and of a palace and dwellings. Xochicalco is well worth the four-kilometre walk from the bus stop; take a torch for the underground part. ■ *US$2, free with ISIC card.* Tickets must be bought at the museum about 500 metres from ruins. This new and striking edifice incorporates many ecological principles and houses some magnificent items from the ruins.

Transport To get to Xochicalco, take a Pullman de Morelos bus from Cuernavaca en route to El Rodeo (every 30 minutes), Coatlán or Las Grutas; alight from any of these buses at the turn-off, 4 kilometres from the site, then take a colectivo taxi, US$0.35-US$1.20 per person, or walk up the hill. From Taxco, take bus to Alpuyeca (US$1.60, 1 hour 40 minute) and pick up bus from Cuernavaca to turn off, or, taxi from junction at Alpuyeca directly to ruins (12 kilometres, US$2.50).

Taxco

Shortly after Amacuzac (Km 121) a further branch autopista scales mountainsides (with breathtaking views) taking you right to the outskirts of Taxco, a colonial gem, with steep, twisting, cobbled streets and many picturesque buildings, now wholly dedicated to tourism. The first silver shipped to Spain came from the mines of Taxco. José de la Borda made and spent three fortunes here in the 18th century; he founded the present town and built the magnificent twin-towered, rose-coloured parish church of **Santa Prisca** which soars above everything but the mountains. Large paintings about Mexican history at the Post Office. The roof of every building is of red tile, every nook or corner in the place is a picture, and even the cobblestone road surfaces have patterns woven in them. It is now a national monument and all modern building is forbidden. Gas stations are outside the city limits. The plaza is 1,700 metres above sea-level. A good view is had from the **Iglesia de Guadalupe**. There are superb views also from the *Teleférico* to Monte Taxco, US$1.50 return, you can return by bus. The *Teleférico* is reached by microbus along the main street from Santa Prisca. The climate is ideal, never any high winds (for it is protected by huge mountains immediately to the north); never cold and never hot, but sometimes foggy. The processions during Holy Week are spectacular. The main central area is full of shops and shopping tourists; the district between the four-storey Mercado and the Carretera Nacional is quieter and free of tourists. Also quieter are those parts up from the main street where the taxis can't go. Wear flat rubber-soled shoes to avoid slithering over the cobbles.

Population: 120,000
Colour map 3, grid C4

Mexico

Sights

One of the most interesting of Mexican stone-age cultures, the Mezcala or Chontal, is based on the State of Guerrero in which Taxco lies. Its remarkable artefacts, of which there are many imitations, are almost surrealist. The culture remained virtually intact into historic times. **Museum of the Viceroyalty** (formerly Casa Humboldt), where Baron von Humboldt once stayed, recently renovated with beautiful religious art exhibits, many from Santa Prisca. ■ *Tuesday-Saturday 1000-1700, Sunday 0900-1500, US$2.00, students US$1.00.* The **Casa Figueroa**, the 'House of Tears', so called because the colonial judge who owned it forced Indian labourers to work on it to pay their fines, is now a private house. **Museo Guillermo Spratling**, behind Santa Prisca, is a museum of prehispanic artefacts bought by William Spratling, a North American architect who came to Taxco in the 1920s. His designs in silver helped bring the city to world recognition and revived a dwindling industry. On his death bed Spratling donated his collection to the state. ■ *Tuesday-Sunday 1000-1700, US$1.80.* The **Museo de la Platería** is a new museum devoted to modern silverworking, on Plaza Borda 1; at the **Platería La Mina** on Av de los Plateros you can see mining techniques.

Excursions

Visit *Posada Don Carlos*, Bermeja 6, also Ventana de Taxco in *Hacienda del Solar* for view. 'Combi' to Panorámica every 30 minutes from Plaza San Juan, US$0.20, or you can walk up the steep hill from Plaza San Juan for views of the hills and volcanoes. About 20 kilometres out of Taxco a rodeo is held on some Suns at El Cedrito, costs about US$4-5, tickets in advance from Veterinario Figueroa on C Nueva near Flecha Roja terminal.

21 kilometres from Taxco to **Acuitlapán** waterfalls, with colectivo or Flecha Roja bus (US$1.20); four-kilometre narrow path from nearest village (snakes) to large clear pools for swimming. Taxis about US$7.50 per hour.

To **Cacahuamilpa** for caverns, 40 minutes, see page 364. Buses from 0820 but service erratic, US$1.65, colectivo van marked No 1, or take a long white taxi marked 'Grutas' from corner of the bus station, US$3.50. Take an Ixtapan bus from opposite the Flecha Roja bus terminal, US$1.50, one hour, which passes the turn off to the site, one kilometre downhill; Ixtapan-Taxco buses go to the site car park. Alternatively, to return, take bus coming from Toluca at junction, 500 metres from the caves.

Visit the villages where *amate* pictures are painted (on display at Museum of the Viceroyalty/Casa Humboldt and in the market). **Xalitla** is the most convenient as it is on the road to Acapulco, take 2nd class bus there. Villages near Taxco worth a visit include **Taxco el Viejo** (home of many individual jewellery makers), Tecapulco (enormous copper domed church) and **Tehuilotepec** (or '*Tehui*' – ancient church, fine hillside views; chicken *roticería* in main square). These villages are delightfully quiet after Taxco. Colectivos from near Estrella Blanca bus station. Other villages:

Taxco

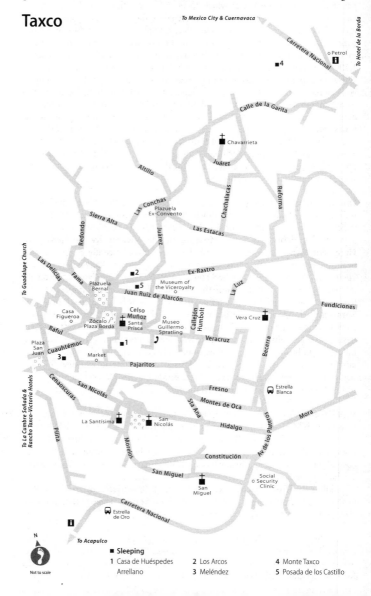

■ Sleeping

| 1 Casa de Huéspedes Arrellano | 2 Los Arcos | 4 Monte Taxco |
| 3 Meléndez | 5 Posada de los Castillo |

Maxela, Ahuelicán, Ahuehuepán and San Juan, past Iguala and before the Río Balsa.

33 kilometres from Taxco, at Km 55 on the road to Cuernavaca, is Zoofari, a private safari park with many animals roaming free (entrance US$5), well worth a visit, T/F Cuernavaca 209794.

Ixcateopán de Cuauhtémoc (Cuauhtémoc's birthplace), is a beautiful and peaceful village, where most of the buildings, and even the cobblestones, are made of marble. A statue honouring Cuauhtémoc stands at the entrance to the village. To get there, take a *pesero* from the road out of Taxco towards Acapulco. 22-23 February is the anniversary of Cuauhtémoc's death, called Día de la Mexicanidad. Runners come from Mexico City to Ixcateopán via Taxco, carrying a torch representing the identity of the Mexican people. Aztec dancers (in traditional dress and colourful plumed head-dresses) come from all over Mexico to dance all night and most of the following day.

Mexico

Sleeping
■ *on maps*
Price codes:
see inside front cover

AL *De la Borda*, on left as you enter Taxco, largest, all facilities, great views, T20225, dearest and best. **AL** *La Cumbre Soñada*, 1.5 kilometres or so towards Acapulco on a mountain top. Colonial, exquisite. **AL** *La Hacienda del Solar*, Acapulco exit of town, T20323, best restaurant in Taxco (*La Ventana*). **AL** *Rancho Taxco-Victoria*, Soto la Marina 15, walk to centre, fantastic view, good restaurant, recommended. **AL** *Monte Taxco*, on right entering Taxco, T21300, F21428, special prices sometimes available from Mexico City offices, T5259193, F5330314, spectacular hilltop setting, pool, riding, golf course, beware mosquitoes. **A** *Posada de la Misión*, Cerro de la Misión 32 (Mexico City – Cuernavaca buses stop outside), T20063, F22198, Juan O'Gorman mural, restaurant, good, pool, no a/c, quiet, recommended. **B** *Posada Don Carlos*, Cerro de Bermeja 6, converted old mansion, restaurant, good view. **B-C** *Agua Escondida*, near Zócalo at C Guillermo Spratling 4, T20726, with bath, nice view, rooftop bar, parking, pool. **C** *Posada San Javier*, down a small street opposite Municipalidad, clean, lovely garden, pool (sometimes dirty), excellent value, no restaurant. **C** *Meléndez*, near Zócalo, T20006, best rooms Nos 1 and 19, superb views, visited by jewellery vendors, if booking reconfirm before arrival. **C-D** *Los Arcos*, Juan Ruiz de Alarcón 2, T21836, reconstructed 17th century ex-convent, delightful rooftop garden, breakfast available, best rooms for views are 18 and 19, rooms overlooking street are noisy, otherwise recommended. **C-D** *Posada de los Castillos*, Alarcón 7, T23471, off main square, Mexican style, friendly, excellent value.

D-F *Casa de Huéspedes Arellano*, Pajaritas 23, below Santa Prisca and Plaza Borda, terrace, quiet at night, with bath, basic, old beds, hot water. **E** *Casa Grande*, Plazuela San Juan 7, T21108, pleasant, well furnished, rooms at the top are better, takes credit cards, good value. **E** *El Jumil*, Reforma 6, near Tourist Office North, without bath, hot water, basic, friendly, but noisy. **E** *Posada Santa Anita*, Av de los Plateros 106, T20752, close to Flecha Roja buses, with hot shower and toilet, cheaper without, very clean, basic, overpriced, noisy at night, friendly, secure parking; the cheapest hotels are in this area. **F** *Central*, round the left hand corner of *Casa de Huéspedes Arellano*, shared bath, quite clean, some rooms without windows.

Eating
● *on maps*

Restaurants tend to be pricey. There are many places on the Zócalo: *Alarcón*, overlooking Zócalo, very good. *Sr Costilla*, next to church on main square, good drinks and grilled ribs. *Papa's Bar*, on Zócalo, a discotheque and a small pizza place in an arcade. *Bora-Bora*, overlooks Zócalo, Guadalupe y Plaza Borda, good pizzas. *Pizzería Mario*, Plaza Borda, beautiful view over city, excellent pizzas, the 1st pizzeria in town, opened 30 years ago, highly recommended. *La Parroquia*, Plaza Borda 5, terrace with excellent views, good food and service. *La Hacienda*, Plaza Borda 4 (entrance is off the square), excellent, fair prices, exquisite *quesadillas* in the *nevería* on top of the silver shop Perlita looking on to the Plaza Borda. *Mi Taverna* next to the Post Office, excellent Italian food, friendly. *Concha Nuestra*, Plazuela San Juan (beneath *Hotel Casa Grande*), food and live Latin American music excellent, cheap for breakfasts, other meals pricey. *La Hamburguesa*, off Plaza San Juan, excellent *comida corrida*, US$1.80, home-cooked food, despite name. *De Cruz*, C Veracruz, good Mexican food at low prices. *Armando*, Av Plateros 205, opposite Flecha Roja bus station, excellent tacos.

Mexico

Shopping for silver

Silverwork is a speciality and there are important lead and zinc mines. Vendors will bargain and cheap silver items can often be found. Beware of mistaking the cheapish pretty jewellery, alpaca, an alloy of copper, zinc and nickel, for the real stuff. By law, real silver, defined as 0.925 pure, must be stamped somewhere on the item with the number 925. The downtown shops in general give better value than those on the highway, but the best value is among the booth-holders in the Pasaje de Santa Prisca (from the Zócalo). Prices usually drop in the low season. On the

second Sunday in December there is a national silversmiths' competition. The colourful labyrinthine produce and general market beneath the Zócalo is spectacular among Mexican markets; reasonable meals in the many fondas.

___NB___ All silver jewellers must be government-registered. Remember to look for the 925 stamp and, if the piece is large enough, it will also be stamped with the crest of an eagle, and initials of the jeweller. Where the small size of the item does not permit this, a certificate will be provided instead.

Pozolería Betty, Mora 20 (below bus station), good food includes the local beetle (jumil) sauce. Many small restaurants just near *Hotel Meléndez*. Excellent *comida corrida* (US$6) at **Santa Fe**, opposite *Hotel Santa Prisca* but disappointing *enchiladas*. Cheap *comida corrida* in market and good cheap restaurants on San Nicolás.

Festivals There is much festivity in **Semana Santa** (Holy Week); at this time the price of accommodation rises steeply. At any time it is best to book a room in advance because hoteliers tend to quote inflated prices to those without reservations.

Transport Book onward bus tickets to Mexico City on arrival. (Taxis meet all buses and take you to any hotel, approximately US$2.) Taxco is reached from **Mexico City** from the Central del Sur, Estrella de Oro, luxury US$10.65, *plus* US$8.65, non-stop, with video, 3 a day, 1st class US$7.65, quick, no overcrowding, 3 a day (2½ hours); back to Mexico City at 0700, 0900, 1200, but computerized booking allows seat selection in the capital; also Estrella Blanca, many a day, on the hour US$7.50, up to 5 hours. Buses to **Cuernavaca**; 1st class buses at 0900, 1600, 1800 and 2000 (Estrella de Oro), 2nd class about 5 a day, 1½ hours (Estrella Blanca), US$3, but can be erratic and crowded (watch out for pickpockets); buses en route to Mexico City drop passengers on the main highway, away from centre of Cuernavaca. Little 24-seaters, 'Los Burritos' (now called 'Combis'), take you up the hill from the bus terminal on main road, US$0.35, same fare anywhere in town. Spectacular journey to **Toluca**, missing out Mexico City, 2nd class buses only, from Estrella Blanca Terminal, US$6, 3 hours, change at Toluca for Morelia. To **Acapulco**, Estrella de Oro, or Estrella Blanca, US$11, 5 hours. Other destinations from Estrella Blanca Terminal include Iguala, Chilpancingo, Iztapan de la Sal and Cuernavaca by old road (via Puente de Isstla and Alpuleya).

Directory **Banks** Good rates at *Cambio de Divisar Argentu* on Plazuela San Juan 5. *Bancomer*, between Plazuela San Juan and Plaza Principal is OK. **Communications** Post Office: on Carretera Nacional about 100 metres east of Estrella de Oro bus terminal. Email: *Bar Azul*, San Nicolás, 1 peso per minute. **Laundry** *Lavandería La Cascada*, Delicias 4. **Tourist office** Av de los Plateros 1, T22274, open 0900-1400 and 1600-2000 every day. City tours from Tourist Office North, US$35 for up to 5 people.

36 kilometres south of Taxco join the Ruta 95 at **Iguala** (**E** *Hotel Central*, basic. **E** *Pasajero*. **E** *Mary*, OK, enclosed parking. Bus to Taxco US$1, to Cuernavaca US$4.25, to Mexico City from US$9.35 to US$15.35).

Chilpancingo

Beyond the Mexcala river, the road passes for some 30 kilometres through the dramatic canyon of Zopilote to reach the university city of Chilpancingo, capital of Guerrero state at Km 302. There is a small but grandly conceived plaza with solid neo-classical buildings and monumental public sculptures commemorating the workers' struggle: *'El Hombre hacia el Futuro'* and *'El Canto al Trabajo'* by Victor Manuel Contreras. In the Government Palace there is a museum and murals. The colourful reed bags from the village of Chilapa (see below) are sold in the market. The Casa de las Artesanías for Guerrero is on the right-hand side of the old main highway Mexico City – Acapulco. It has a particularly wide selection of lacquerware from Olinalá.

Population: 120,000
State population 1995:
2,915,497
Altitude: 1,250m
Colour map 3, grid C4

Not far from Chilpancingo are Oxtotitlán and Juxtlahuaca, where Olmec cave paintings can be seen.

Excursions

To reach the **Grutas de Juxtlahuaca** caves, drive to Petaquillas on the non-toll road then take a side road (paved, but poor in parts) through several villages to Colotlipa (colectivo from Chilpancingo – see below – US$1.50, one and a half hours). Ask at the restaurant on the corner of the Zócalo for a guide to the caves. They can only be visited with a guide (three hours' tour US$25, popular at weekends

Chilpancingo to Acapulco

Mexico

for groups; if on your own, try for a discount). The limestone cavern is in pristine condition; it has an intricate network of large halls and tunnels, stalagmites and stalactites, a huge underground lake, cave drawings from about 500 AD, a skeleton and artefacts. Take a torch, food and drink and a sweater if going a long way in.

Chilapa, east of Chilpancingo, is accessible by several local buses and is worth a visit (about one hour journey US$2). On Sunday there is an excellent craft market that covers all of the large plaza and surrounding streets, selling especially good quality and well-priced Olinalá lacquer boxes as well as wood carvings, textiles, leather goods, etc, worth a visit even if you don't buy anything. The Grutas de Oxtotitlán are about 18 kilometres north of Chilapa. *Hotel Camino Real* on plaza. *Restaurant Casa Pilla* on other side of plaza, local dishes, recommended.

Mexico

Sleeping *La Posada Meléndez*, large rooms, helpful, swimming pool, cheap *comida corrida* in restaurant, recommended. **D** *María Isabel* and *Cardeña*, both on same street. **D** *El Portal* on corner of plaza, T50135. **F** *Chilpancingo*, 50 metres from Zócalo, clean, shower.

Eating Small café at back of *Tienda Naturista*, Hidalgo, 2 blocks from plaza. Good yoghurt.

Festivals *Fiesta* starts on **December 16** and lasts a fortnight.

Transport **Buses** Cuernavaca-Chilpancingo, Estrella de Oro, US$8.30, or *plus* US$11 (9 a day). Buses Mexico City-Chilpancingo from US$11 to US$23.35 super luxury. To Acapulco with Futura US$3.80; To Taxco with Estrella de Oro US$4.50.

Olinalá This small town is known to most Mexicans for the beautiful lacquered wooden
Altitude: 1,350m objects made here (boxes, chests, screens, trays etc), but is visited by few. Situated in the east of the State of Guerrero, it lies in an area of mountains, rivers and ravines, which make access difficult. Most of the population is involved in the production and selling of the lacquer work, which is available from the artesans direct as well as from the more expensive shops on the square. The wood chiefly used is *linálloe*, which gives the objects a gentle fragrance. The lacquering techniques include both the scraping away of layers and applying new ones. Other villages in the area similarly devote themselves almost exclusively to their own *artesanías*. The church on the square is decorated inside with lacquer work. A chapel dedicated to Nuestra Señora de Guadalupe crowns a hill just outside the town, offering striking views. The hill is pyramid-shaped and there are said to be tunnels, but to date no archaeological investigations have been carried out. There are three **F** hotels around the square and a restaurant (no name displayed), above furniture shop on main square, exquisite Mexican cooking.

Transport **Buses**: Direct from Mexico City via Chilpancingo (Terminal Sur); also via Izúcar de Matamoros to Tlapa, then local bus. Local bus also from Chilapa. By **car**, there is 1 paved road (1 hour) from the Chilpancingo-Tlapa road to the south, the turning to Olinalá is between the villages of Tlatlauquitepec and Chiepetepec, about 40 kilometres west of Tlapa. There is an unpaved road (4 hours) from Chiautla to the north, but you have to cross rivers whose bridges are often washed away in the rainy season. A better unpaved road (2½ hours) from Santa Cruz to the east, near Huamuxtitlán on the route 92, fords the river Tlapaneco, which is feasible for most vehicles except in the rainy season. The scenery is spectacular, with huge bluffs and river valleys, but filling stations are infrequent. If Pemex in Olinalá has no fuel, local shops may sell it. Fill up when you can.

The new section of four-lane toll freeway runs from Iguala west of the old highway as far as Tierra Colorada, where it joins the existing four-lane section to Acapulco. Chilpancingo is bypassed, but there is an exit. This is the third improvement: the first motor road was pushed over the ancient mule trail in 1927, giving Acapulco its first new lease of life in 100 years; when the road was paved and widened in 1954, Acapulco began to boom.

About 20 kilometres from the coast, a branch road goes to the northwest of Acapulco; this is a preferable route for car drivers because it avoids the city chaos. It goes to a point between Pie de la Cuesta and Coyuca, is signed, and has a drugs control point at the junction.

Warning Do not travel by car at night in Guerrero, even on the Mexico City-Acapulco highway and coastal highway. Always set out early to ensure that you reach your destination in daylight. Many military checkpoints on highway. *Guerrilleros* have been active in recent years, and there are also problems with highway robbers and stray animals.

Acapulco

Acapulco is the most popular resort in Mexico, particularly in winter and spring. During Holy Week there is a flight from the capital every three minutes. It does not fit everyone's idea of a tropical beach resort. The town stretches for 16 kilometres in a series of bays and cliff coves and is invading the hills. The hotels, of which there are 250, are mostly perched high to catch the breeze, for between 1130 and 1630 the heat is sizzling; they are filled to overflowing in January and February. It has all the paraphernalia of a booming resort: smart shops, nightclubs, red light district, golf club, touts and street vendors and now also air pollution. The famous beaches and expensive hotels are a different world from the streets, hotels and crowded shops and buses of the city centre, which is only two minutes' walk away. The Zócalo is lively in the evenings, but the surrounding streets are grimy.

Population: 1 million
Phone code: 74
Colour map 3, grid C3

Acapulco in colonial times was the terminal for the Manila convoy. Its main defence, **Fuerte de San Diego**, where the last battle for Mexican independence was fought, is in the middle of the city and is worth a visit. ■ *1000-1800, Tuesday and Sunday only, free admission.*

Beaches

A campaign to tidy up the whole city and its beaches is in process. Acapulco was badly hit by storms in 1997; Hurricane Pauline left more than 111 dead along the coast, dozens missing and 8,000 homeless after mudslides swept away poor areas of the city. Now, however, there is almost no evidence of the damage. There are some 20 beaches, all with fine, golden sand; deckchairs on all beaches, US$0.50; parachute skiing in front of the larger hotels at US$12 for five minutes. Every evening, except Monday, there is a water skiing display opposite Fuerte de San Diego. The two most popular beaches are the sickle-curved and shielded **Caleta**, with its smooth but dirty water yet clean sands, and the surf-pounded straight beach of **Los Hornos**. Swimmers should look out for motor boats close in shore. At **Revolcadero** beach, development is continuing, with new luxury hotels, new roads and landscaping; it is being called Acapulco Diamante. Take local bus to **Pie de la Cuesta**, 12 kilometres, now preferred by many budget travellers to Acapulco itself, but also commercialized. There are several bungalow-hotels and trailer parks (see below), lagoon (six hours' boat trip US$10), now used for laundry, and long, clean, sandy beaches. At Pie de la Cuesta you drink *coco loco*, fortified coconut milk, and watch the sunset from a hammock. You can swim, and fish, the year round. Best free map of Acapulco can be obtained from the desk clerk at *Tortuga Hotel*.

The surf is dangerous on the beach west of the road and the beaches are unsafe at night

Excursions

Daily, amazing 40-metre dives into shallow (polluted) water by boys can be watched from the **Quebrada** (US$1.20, at 1915, 2015, 2115 and 2215).

The **lagoons** can be explored by motor boats; one, **Coyuca Lagoon** (also known as **La Barra**), is over 10 kilometres long (38 kilometres northwest of Acapulco); strange birds, water hyacinths, tropical flowers.

At **Playa Icacos** there is a marineland amusement park *Ci-Ci*, with a waterslide, pool with wave-machine and arena with performing dolphins and sea-lions (

Mexico (side tab)

nothing special). ■ *US$5.70 for whole day, 1000-1800.* Pleasant boat trip across beach to **Puerto Marqués**, US$2 return (or 30 minutes by bus); one can hire small sailing boats there, US$12 per hour. Bay cruises, two and a half hours, from Muelle Yates, US$9, including free bar, at 1100, 1630 and 2230. *Yate Bonanza* has been recommended, stops 30 minutes for swim in bay. Visit the island of **La Roqueta**, in a glass-bottomed boat; tours leave at 1100 and 1300 from Fuerte San Diego and return at 1500 and 1700, US$4; once on the island follow the path which goes over the hill towards the other side of the island (towards the right) where there is a small, secluded and usually empty bay (about 15 minutes' walk). Take food and drink with you as it is expensive on the island. Parachute sailing (towed by motor boats), US$12 for a few minutes, several operators. There is an **Aqua Marine museum** on a little island (Yerbabuena) off Caleta beach, with sharks, piranhas, eels, stingrays in an aquarium, swimming pool with water-chute, and breezy bar above. ■ *US$7.*

Sleeping　Hotels can cost up to US$200 a night double; cheaper for longer stays, but this also means less expensive hotels insist on a double rate even for 1 person and for a minimum period. In the off-season (May-November) you can negotiate lower prices even for a single for 1 night. For hotels in our C range and above in Acapulco you can make reservations at the bus terminal in Mexico City, helpful; similarly, at the 1st class bus station in Acapulco you can arrange hotel packages, eg 3 nights in 4-star accommodation for US$60. Hotel recommendations, and reservations, made at the bus terminal, often turn out to be dingy downtown hotels. If seeking a hotel in the D or C range, go to the *Doral Playa*, on Hornos beach, and use it as a base for exploring the hotels in surrounding streets.

Acapulco Bay

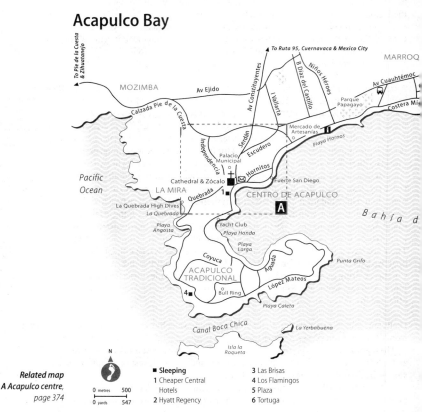

Related map
A Acapulco centre,
page 374

■ Sleeping	
1 Cheaper Central Hotels	3 Las Brisas
2 Hyatt Regency	4 Los Flamingos
	5 Plaza
	6 Tortuga

LL *Elcano*, Costera near golf club, T841950, many rooms with terrace, pool. **LL** *Villa Vera Raquet Club*, luxurious celebrity spot, T840333. The fabulous **LL** *Club Residencial de las Brisas*, T841733, a hotel where the services match the astronomical price, it begins at sea-level and reaches up the mountain slope in a series of detached villas and public rooms to a point 300 metres above sea-level, each room has own or shared swimming pool, guests use pink jeeps to travel to the dining-room and recreation areas. **LL** *Camino Real Diamante*, T812010, on edge of Diamante development at Revolcadero beach, luxury resort. **LL-AL** *Acapulco Plaza*, Costera 123, T859050, 3 towers, 2 pools, 5 bars, 4 restaurants, a city in itself. *Hyatt Regency*, next to naval base, Av Costera M Alemán 1, T842888, F843087. **L** *Acapulco Tortuga*, T848889, good discounts in low season; and **L** *Caleta*, Playa Caleta, T39940, remodelled. **L** *Romano Days*, T845332, on Costera, many groups.

AL *Fiesta Americana Condesa del Mar*, Costera at Condesa beach, T842828, all facilities. **AL** *Maris*, Alemán y Magallanes, T858440, very good. **AL** *Acapulco Imperial*, Costera 251, T851918. **A** per person *El Cid*, Hornos beach, T851312, clean, pool, recommended. **A** *Los Flamingos*, López Mateos, T820690/2, F839806, one of the finest locations in Acapulco, glorious cliff-top views, in the 1950s it was a retreat for John Wayne, Johnny Weissmuller et al, and the present owner preserves the atmosphere of those days, gardens, pool, restaurant, highly recommended, breakfast included. The *Acapulco Princess Country Club*, part of the *Acapulco Princess*, T843100, 20 kilometres away on Revolcadero beach, highly fashionable, delightful resort, all facilities, taxi to town US$10. **A** *Maralisa*, C Alemania s/n, T856677, smallish and elegant, Arab style, private beach, recommended.

B *Casa Blanca Tropical*, Cerro de la Pinzona, T821212, with swimming pool, recommended. **B** *do Brasil*, Costera Miguel Alemán on Hornos beach, T854364, shower, TV, all rooms with sea-view balcony, pool, restaurant, bar, travel agency, friendly, recommended. **B** *Club Majestic*, near Yacht Club and above city (a little hard to find), T834710, quiet, reasonable, good views. **B** *Playa Suites*, Costera Miguel Alemán, on beach, suites sleeping up to 6, good value. **B** *Real del Monte*, clean, friendly, on the beach, pool, good food, Playa del Coco opposite new convention centre, T841010. *Boca Chica*, Playa Caletillo, T836741, on promontory opposite island, pool, clean, direct access to bathing, free drinking water on each floor.

C *Doral Playa*, Hornos beach, T850103, a/c, pool, ask for front upper floors with balcony, good value. **C** *Embassy*, Costera Miguel Alemán, T840273, clean, a/c, pool.

D *Los Pericos*, Costera Miguel Alemán near Playa Honda, T824078, fan, clean, friendly, pool, recommended. **D** *Olivieda*, Costera Miguel Alemán, 1 block from cathedral, clean, fan, hot water, great views from top floor rooms. **D** *El Tropicano*, Costera Miguel Alemán 150, on Playa Icacos, a/c, clean, big garden, 2 pools, bars, restaurant, very friendly and helpful, recommended. **D** *San Francisco*, Costera 219, T820045, old part of town, friendly, good value, noisy in front.

Most cheaper hotels are grouped around the Zócalo, especially C La Paz and C Juárez.

To Ruta 95, Cuernavaca & Mexico City

LAS CUMBRES

Paseo del Farallón

Diana

ACAPULCO MODERNO

COSTA AZUL

Zona Hotelera

Alemán

Playa Condesa

Convention Centre

Zona Hotelera

La Redonda

ACAPULCO MODERNO

Playa Icacos

Ci Ci Recreation Centre

acapulco

COLONIA ICACOS

Naval Base

Punta del Guitarrón

PLAYA GUITARRON

Carretera Escénica

To Puerto Márquez & Airport

C *Acuario*, Azueta 11, T821784, popular. **C** *Fiesta*, clean and nice, with bath, fan, 2 blocks northwest from Zócalo, Azueta 16, T820019. **C** *Misión*, Felipe Valle 12, T823643, very clean, colonial, close to Zócalo, recommended. **C** *Añorve*, Juárez 17, T822093, 2 blocks off Zócalo, clean, with bath, front rooms better than back (but can be noisy from street in mornings). Opposite *Añorve* is **D** *Mama Helène*, who owns 2 hotels in same price range, and offers laundry service, homemade lemonade. **D-E** *California*, La Paz 12, T822893, 1½ blocks west of Zócalo, good value, fan, hot water, pleasant rooms and patio. **D** *Colimense*, JM Iglesias II, off Zócalo, T822890, pleasant, limited parking. **D** *Isabel*, La Paz y Valle, T822191, with fan, recommended, near Zócalo. **D** *Sacramento*, East Carranza y Valle, with bath and fan, no towel, soap or loo paper, friendly, noisy, OK, purified water, T820821. **D** *Santa Cecilia*, Francisco Madero 7, off Zócalo, with bath and fan, noisy, but otherwise fine. **D** *Santa Lucía*, López Mateos 33, T820441, family-owned, will negotiate if not full, good value. **D** *Hospedaje Bienvenidos*, behind Estrella de Oro bus terminal, clean, safe, sometimes noisy.

E *Aca-Plus*, Azueta 11, T831405, with bath and fan, clean, safe. **E** *La Posada*, Azueta 8, near Zócalo, with bath, more expensive in high season. **E-F** *Chamizal*, López Mateos 32, close to Zócalo, shower, OK. **E** *Paola*, Teniente Azueta, Centro, T826243, 2 blocks from Zocalo, hot shower, fan, roof terrace with pool, free coffee, highly recommended.

Many cheap hotels on La Quebrada, basic but clean with fan and bathroom, including **D** *El Faro*, No 63, T821365, clean. **D** *Casa de Huéspedes Aries*, No 30, with bath, nice. **D** *Asturia*, No 45, with bath, no single rooms, clean, friendly, pool, a few cockroaches on lower floor, otherwise recommended. **D** *Coral*, No 56, T820756, good value, friendly, reasonably quiet, small pool.

Acapulco centre

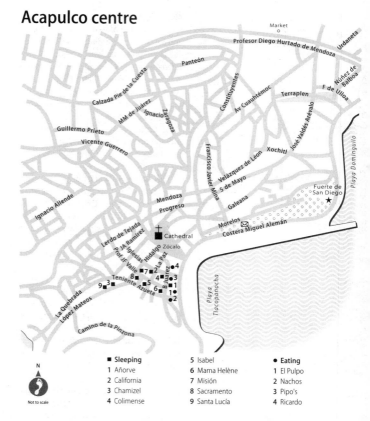

■ Sleeping	5 Isabel	● Eating
1 Añorve	6 Mama Helène	1 El Pulpo
2 California	7 Misión	2 Nachos
3 Chamizel	8 Sacramento	3 Pipo's
4 Colimense	9 Santa Lucía	4 Ricardo

N
Not to scale

E *Sagamar*, No 51, with bath, basic, friendly, some English spoken, safe, clean, use mosquito coil. **E** *Beatriz*, 3 blocks from Flecha Roja terminal, 2 from beach, for more than 1 night, central, fan, shower, pool.

D *Betty*, Belisario Domínguez 4, T835092, 5 minutes from bus station, with bath, fan, short stay, dirty. Not recommended. Just around corner on same street is **E** *Alberto*, much better. Turn left at *Betty* for several cheap *casas de huéspedes*.

Several nice places at Pie de la Cuesta, **D**, in clean rooms with shower: **C** *Villa Nirvana*, Pie de la Cuesta. Canadian/Mexican owners (depending on season) with kitchen, clean, pool, good value, recommended. **D** *Casa Blanca*, rooms for 3, management nice, food good. *Puesta del Sol*, expensive places for hammocks. **D** *Quinta Dora Trailer Park*, for hammock, managed by American, helpful. The student organization Setej offers dormitory accommodation, **D**, if one has a valid international student card, at Centro Vacacional, Pie de la Cuesta, 0700-2400.

For longer (1 month plus) stays, try **Amueblados Etel**, Av la Pinzona 92 (near Quebrada) for self-catering apartments, cheap off-season (before November), short stays possible in rooms (**C**), a/c, fan, hot shower, sundeck, large pool, recommended. **C** *Apartamentos Maraback*, Costera M Alemán. **D** *Amueblos Caletilla Diamante*, López Mateos 28, Las Playas, T827975, apartments with kitchen, pool, close to beach and market, safe parking.

Camping *Trailer Park El Coloso*, in La Sabana, small swimming pool. *Trailer Park La Roca* on road from Puerto Márquez to La Sabana. Both secure. *Estacionamiento Juanita* and *Quinta Dora* at Pie de la Cuesta (latter is 13 kilometres up the coast on Highway 200, *palapas*, bathrooms, cold showers, hook-ups, US$12 for 2 plus car, US$4 just to sling hammock). *Quinta Carla*, *Casa Blanca*, *U Kae Kim*, all US$50 a week upwards, but negotiable. *Acapulco West KDA*, on Barra de Coyuca, opened 1996, beachfront, security patrol, pool, restaurant, hot showers, laundry, store, volleyball, basketball, Spanish classes, telephones.

Motels **B** *Impala*, T840337. *Bali-Hai*, T857045. *Mónaco*, T856415, all along the Costera. **B** *Victoria*, Cristóbal Colón, 1 block behind Costera.

Eating
Fish dishes are a speciality of Acapulco

One of the oldest established and best restaurants is *Pipo's*, Almirante Breton 3 (off Costera near Zócalo) highly recommended, 2 other branches: Costera esq Plaza Canadá; and C Majahua, Puerto Márquez. There are a number of variously-priced restaurants along and opposite Condesa beach, including *Embarcadero* on the Costera, Thai/Mexican/US food, extraordinary décor with waterfalls, bridges, bamboo huts and 'a hall of mirrors on the way to the loo', expensive but worth it for the atmosphere. Many cheap restaurants in the blocks surrounding the Zócalo, especially along Juárez: for example, *El Amigo Miguel*, *Ricardo* (popular), Juárez 9 (near Zócalo), fixed menu lunch, good. *Nachos*, on Azueta, at corner of Juárez, popular, excellent prawns. *El Pulpo*, Miguel Alemán 183, $1\frac{1}{2}$ blocks from Zócalo, good filling breakfasts, friendly. By La Diana roundabout is *Pizza Hut*, reliable, with 'blissful a/c'. *Italianissimo*, nearby, decent pizza and garlic bread, average price for area. *Parroquia*, on Zócalo, excellent. *El Zorrito*, opposite *Ritz Hotel*, excellent local food with live music, average prices, reputedly popular with Julio Iglesias when he is in town. The *cafetería* at the southeast corner of the Zócalo serves good coffee. Another group of restaurants along the Caleta beach walkway; better value on Caleta beach itself is *La Cabaña*, good food, delightful setting. Yet another group with mixed prices on the Costera opposite the *Acapulco Plaza Hotel*. 250 or so to select from. *El Mayab*, Av Costera Miguel Aleman 151, good value, set meal, recommended.

Bars & nightclubs

There are dozens of discos including *Discoteca Safari*, Av Costera, free entry, 1 drink obligatory, good ambience; *Disco Beach*, Costera Miguel Alemán, between the *Diana* and *Hotel Fiesta Americana Condesa*, by beach, informal dress, open till 0500, good; every major hotel has at least 1 disco plus bars. Superb varied night-life always.

Mexico

Margin: Mexico

Transport **Local** Taxis US$9 an hour; sample fare: Zócalo to Condesa Beach US$3.65. Taxis more expensive from bus terminal, walk half a block round corner and catch one on the street. Several bus routes, with one running the full length of Costera Miguel Alemán linking the older part of town to the latest hotels, marked 'Caleta-Zócalo-Base', US$0.50, another operating to Caleta beach. Buses to Pie de la Cuesta, 12 kilometres, 1.50 pesos. Bus stops on the main thoroughfare are numbered, so find out which one you need. Many buses along the beach front may turn off at right angles; read the destination boards carefully.

Air Airport Alvarez Intl (ACA) 23 kilometres from Acapulco. Direct connections with New York, Miami, Chicago, Dallas, Houston, Los Angeles, Las Vegas, Memphis, San Fransisco, Tampa and Phoenix by Mexican and US carriers. Condor has a weekly scheduled flight from Frankfurt. Also many charter flights from Europe and North America. Mexico City, 50 minutes, also domestic services to Cuernavaca, Culiacán, Guadalajara, Mérida, Monterrey, Oaxaca, Puerto Vallarta and Tijuana. AeroMéxico T847009. Flights to Mexico City are worth booking at least a week in advance, especially in high season. Transportaciónes de Pasajeros Aeropuerto taxi service charge return trip (*viaje redondo*) when you buy a ticket, so keep it and call 24 hours in advance for a taxi, US$11. Airport bus takes 1 hour, US$3.35 and *does* exist (ticket office outside terminal).

Buses Bus terminal is on Av Ejido, reached by bus from Costera Miguel Alemán, allow at least 45 minutes during peak time. There is a left luggage office. Estrella de Oro buses leave from the bus station on Av Cuauhtémoc. **Mexico City**, 406 kilometres, 4-5 (1st class or above) – 8 hours; de luxe air-conditioned express buses (*futura*, highly recommended), US$28.35 and super luxury US$36.65; ordinary bus, US$21.65 1st and US$25.65 *plus*, all-day services from Estación Central de Autobuses del Sur by the Taxqueña metro station, Mexico City, with Estrella de Oro (10 a day, 1 stop) or Flecha Roja (part of Líneas Unidas del Sur, hourly). Taxi to Zócalo, US$5.50; bus, US$0.50. To **Manzanillo**, direct bus US$8.50. Several 1st class buses, Estrella de Oro, 5 hours, and Flecha Roja buses a day to **Taxco** US$11. To **Cuernavaca**, with Estrella de Oro, 6 hours, US$14.75-19.50. To **Oaxaca**, no direct bus, change at Puerto Escondido or Pachutla, waiting room and luggage deposit at Pochutla; also via Pinotepa Nacional (1 bus at 2100) but worse road. Bus to **Puerto Escondido** every hour on the half hour from 0430-1630, plus 2300, 2400, 0200, US$10.50, and *directo* at 1330 and 2300, US$20, seats bookable, advisable to do so the day before, $7\frac{1}{2}$ hours, many check-points, bad road; Flecha Roja, Transportes Gacela (US$15.65). To **Tapachula**: take Impala 1st class bus to Huatulco, arriving 1930; from there Cristóbal Colón at 2030 to Salina Cruz, arriving about midnight, then take 1st or 2nd class bus.

Directory **Airline offices** AeroMéxico and Mexicana offices in Torre Acapulco, Miguel Alemán 1252, Mexicana T841215. *American*, T669248. *Delta*, T800-9022100. *Taesa*, T852488. Condor, T800-5246975. **Communications** Post Office: Costera, 2 blocks south of Zócalo. **Telephones:** public offices will not take collect calls; try from a big hotel (ask around, there will be a surcharge). **Embassies & consulates** British Consul (Honorary) Mr DB Gore, MBE, *Hotel Las Brisas*, T846605. *Canadian*, Hotel Club del Sol, Costera Miguel Alemán, T856621. *Dutch*, El Presidente Hotel, T837148. *Finnish*, Costera Miguel Alemán 500, T847641. *French*, Av Costa Grande 235, T823394. *German*, Antón de Alaminos 46, T847437. *Norwegian*, Maralisa Hotel, T843525. *Spanish*, Av Cuauhtémoc y Universidad 2, T857205. *Swedish*, Av Insurgentes 2, T852935. *US*, Club del Sol Hotel, T856600. **Laundry** *Tintorería Bik*, 5 de Mayo. *Lavadín*, José María Iglesias 11a, T822890, next to *Hotel Colimense*, recommended. **Tourist offices** Costera Miguel Alemán at Hornos beach, T840599/7621, helpful, but double-check details; useful free magazines, *Aca-Sun* and *Acapulco guide*. Also at 'Flechas' bus station, very helpful, will make hotel bookings, but not in cheapest range. **Useful addresses** Immigration: Juan Sebastian el Cuno 1, Costa Azul el Lado, T849021, open 0800-1400, take a Hornos Base bus from Miguel Alemán, US$0.20, 30 minutes, visa extensions possible.

Coast northwest of Acapulco

The coastal road, Route 200, has many potholed stretches, so take care if driving. Between Acapulco and Zihuatanejo is **Coyuca de Benítez**, 38 kilometres from Acapulco, near the Laguna Coyuca (see above, Acapulco **Excursions**), a lagoon with little islands: Coyuca is a market town selling exotic fruit, cheap hats and shoes. There is no bank but shops will change US dollars. Pelicans fly by the lagoons, there are passing dolphins and plentiful sardines, and young boys seek turtle eggs. Take combi from town to La Barra on the lagoon. **D** *Parador de los Reyes*, clean, pool. **E** *Imperial*, off the main square. There is a *jai-alai* palace.

One and a half kilometres beyond Coyuca is a turn-off to El Carrizal (seven and a half kilometres), a delightful village of some 2,000 people, a short distance from a beautiful beach (many pelicans) with a steep drop-off (unsafe for children), dangerous waves and sharks behind them; good for spotting dolphins and, if you are lucky, whales. **El Carrizal**

Sleeping and eating Good restaurant (opposite *Hotel-Bungalows El Carrizal*) which has 6 rooms with bath and toilet, **E**, closes early (1800 for food), poor food, not very clean; more basic; **E** *Aída*, friendly, recommended, but little privacy, more expensive rooms more secure and mosquito-proof, all rooms with bath and fan, Mexican food (good fish), go all the way through the village to the hotel, which is on the sea.

Transport Frequent VW minibuses from Acapulco or Pie de la Cuesta, US$0.55.

A couple of kilometres southeast of El Carrizal is El Morro on an unpaved road between the ocean and the lagoon: the waves on the ocean side are very strong, while swimming in the lagoon is excellent. El Morro is a small fishing village (carp) reminiscent of African townships as it is constructed entirely of *palapa* (palm-leaf and wood). Every other house is a 'fish-restaurant', the best are one kilometre left along the beach to La Ramada; ask for bungalow rental (**F**), no running water but there is a toilet, mosquito nets on request; *El Mirador* (Jesús and Maty), rooms, canoe hire. One shop sells basic provisions; fruit and vegetables from Coyuca may be available. At El Morro you can rent a canoe for US$2 per hour and sail down river, past El Carrizal; you can also go up river to the lagoon, an all day trip, very beautiful with plenty of birdlife (beware, strong winds blow around midday off the sea). Minibuses run Coyuca-El Carrizal-El Morro. **El Morro**

San Jerónimo, 83 kilometres from Acapulco, has an 18th century parish church, you can make canoe trips up river to restaurants; **Técpan de Galeana**, 108 kilometres from Acapulco, is a fishing village. 10 kilometres north of Técpan is a turn-off to another El Carrizal, which is seven kilometres from the Pacific Highway. There is some public transport from Técpan, but plenty of cars go there (the road is rough). Very little accommodation, but plenty of hammock space; there is a beautiful beach and lagoon and the place is very friendly. At **Cavaquito** where a series of small rivers join the ocean and there is a large variety of birds and dense vegetation; three restaurants offer fish dishes, there is a reasonable modern hotel, *Club Papánoa*, with lovely views and a camping site; a cheaper, nameless hotel with restaurant on the beach, **E**; and one can also visit the lovely bay of Papanóa. **Técpan de Galeana & Cavaquito**

Zihuatanejo

A beautiful fishing port and expensive, commercialized tourist resort 237 kilometres northwest of Acapulco by the paved Route 200, which continues via Barra de Navidad along the Pacific coast to Puerto Vallarta (see page 201). This road goes through coconut plantations where you can buy *tuba*, a drink made from coconut milk fermented on the tree, only slightly alcoholic.

Population: 22,000
Colour map 3, grid C3

Sights   Despite being spruced up, 'Zihua', as it is called locally, still retains much of its Mexican village charm. There is an Indian handicraft market by the church, some beachside cafés and a small **Museo Arqueológico**, in the old Customs and Immigration building on Av 5 de Mayo. ■ *US$0.70*. At sunset thousands of swallows meet in the air above the local cinema in the centre of town and settle for the night within one minute on the telephone poles. The *plaza de toros* is at the town entrance with seasonal *corridas*.

Beaches   There are 5 beaches in the bay, including Playa de la Madera, near town and a bit dirty; better is Playa de la Ropa, 20 minutes' walk from centre, with the *Sotavento* and other hotels, and some beach restaurants. Also good is Las Gatas beach, secluded, a haven for aquatic sports which can be reached by boat from the centre (US$2 return) or a 20-minute walk from La Ropa beach over fishermen-frequented rocks (the boat is much safer, muggings on the path have occurred). Watch out for coconuts falling off the trees! Off the coast there are rock formations, to which divers go, and Isla Ixtapa, a nature reserve with numerous restaurants. Playa Linda is a beautiful beach (no hotels) easily reached by collectivo (30 minutes). The yacht, *Fandango Zihua*, takes bay cruises from the municipal pier.

Sleeping   **LL** *Villa del Sol*, Playa La Ropa, T42239, F4758, Apdo 84, no children under 12 in high season, *Difficult to find accommodation in March, and around Christmas/New Year.* very expensive but highly regarded. *Fiesta Mexicana*, Playa La Ropa, T43776, F43738, a/c, satellite TV, fine views, pool, restaurant, bar. **AL** *Catalina* and *Sotavento*, Playa de la Ropa, T42032, F42975, 105 steps to hotel, same facilities. **AL** *Irma*, Playa la Madera, T42025, F43738, good hotel but not best location. **B** *Bungalows Pacíficos*, T42112, highly recommended, advance reservation necessary, huge terrace, good views. **B** *Las Uraccas*, Playa La Ropa, T42049, cooking facilities, good value; **B** *Palacios*, T42055, good, on Playa de la Madera.

Several other hotels along Playa de la Madera, try **AL** *Villas Miramar*, T42106, F42149, suites, pool, lovely gardens, recommended. Central hotels: **A** *Avila*, Juan N Alvarez 8, T42010, a/c, phone. **A** *Zihuatanejo Centro*, Agustín Ramírez 2, T42669, bright rooms, a/c, recommended. **C** *Posada Citlali*, Vicente Guerrero 3, T42043. **D** *Las Tres Marías*, C La Noria 4, T42191, cross the wooden footbridge, very pleasant with large communal balconies overlooking town and harbour, clean but sparely decorated, tiny baths, nice plants, hotel has an annex on C Juan Alvarez 52, part of restaurant, similar rooms and tariffs, best on 2nd floor,

Zihuatanejo orientatation

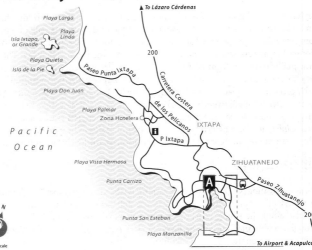

Related map
A Zihuatanejo centre, page 379

Not to scale

note that price doubles during Christmas holidays. **E** *Rosimar*, Ejido, T42140, quiet, hot water, some rooms TV. **E** *Casa Elvira* hotel-restaurant, on Juan N Alvarez, T42061, in older part of town on waterfront, very basic but clean, fan, with bath, the restaurant is on the beach front (the place to watch the world go by), good and reasonable. **D** *Casa Aurora*, N Bravo 27, clean with bath and fan, not all rooms have hot water, and **D** *Casa Bravo*, T42528. **D-E** *Casa La Playa*, on Juan N Alvarez, similar to *Elvira*, but not as good. **C** *Imelda*, Catalina González 11, T43199, clean, recommended, no restaurant.

Youth hostel Av Paseo de las Salinas s/n, CP 40880, T44662.

Zihuatanejo centre

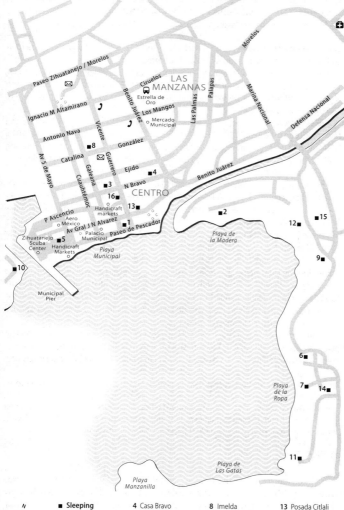

■ **Sleeping**	4 Casa Bravo	8 Imelda	13 Posada Citlali
1 Avila	5 Casa Elvira	9 Irma	14 Villa del Sol
2 Bungalows Pacíficos	6 Catalina & Sotavento	10 Las Tres Marías	15 Villas Miramar
3 Casa Aurora	7 Fiesta Mexicana	11 Las Uraccas	16 Zihuatanejo Centro
		12 Palacios	

Mexico

Mexico

Eating **On Playa la Ropa** *La Perla,* very popular, good food, slow service. *Elvira,* by *Hotel Sotavento,* small, attentive service, good value. *Rossy,* good, live music at weekends.

In Zihuatanejo Many including *El Patio,* excellent food and atmosphere, beautiful patio/garden, live music occasionally. *Il Piccolo,* restaurant and video bar, excellent value, good pizzas. *Gitano's. Coconuts,* good atmosphere, pricey, dinner only, recommended. *La Marina,* popular, recommended. *Puntarenas,* close to *Hotel Las Tres Marías,* excellent cooking, friendly, not expensive, popular, slow service. *Stall 27* at marketplace is very popular, cheap and good, try local lobster for about US$10; most meals cost US$6 or over.

Sports **Scuba diving**: hire of all equipment and guide from Zihuatanejo Scuba Center, T42147, English spoken. Off Playa de las Gatas is an underwater wall built, according to legend, by the Tarascan king Calzonzin, to keep the sharks away while he bathed; the wall is fairly massive and can be seen clearly while scuba diving. Many fish too. US$3 a day for mask, snorkel and fins.

Transport **Local** **Car hire**: Hertz, N Bravo and airport, T43050 or F42255; also with offices at the airport and in Ixtapa hotels: **Avis, Budget, Dollar, Economy.**

Air Ixtapa/Zihuatanejo international airport (ZIH), 20 kilometres from town, T42070/42100. Many flights from Mexico City and others from Guadalajara, Mazatlán and Monterrey, and, in the USA, Detroit, Houston, Los Angeles, Phoenix and San Francisco. Other destinations via Mexico City.

Buses Estrella de Oro operates its own terminal on Paseo Palmar, serving Acapulco and **Mexico City**; to the capital 0830, 1130, 1930 (with stops), US$24.20, direct (no stops) at 2000; 'Diamante' (wider seats, movie, stewardesses serving free drinks) non-stop 2100, arriving 0600, US$50; *plus* (wider seats, non-stop) 2200 arriving 0700, US$33. To **Lázaro Cárdenas** at 0600, 1500 and 1900, US$3.65, 2 hours. Direct to **Acapulco** 0600, US$8, *plus* at 1630.

The Central de Autobuses is on the Zihuatanejo-Acapulco highway opposite Pemex station (bus from centre US$0.20); 3 lines operate from here, all using good, 32-seater buses. The terminal is clean, with several snackbars. Estrella Blanca: to Mexico City almost hourly from 0600-2130, US$24.20; to Lázaro Cárdenas daily, for connections further north and to the interior, US$4; to **Manzanillo**, US$15, 9 hours; to **Acapulco**, US$6 hourly; to **Laredo** at 1730, 30 hours, US$65. Blancas Fronteras to Mexico City 2100 or 2200, US$33 (direct); to Acapulco 0100, 0900 and 1700, US$10.65; to Lázaro Cárdenas 4 a day, US$4.75; to **Puerto Escondido** and **Huatulco**, 2130, US$34. Cuauhtémoc serves all towns between Zihuatanejo and Acapulco almost half-hourly from 0400 to 2000. To **Acapulco**, Líneas Unidas del Sur, US$8, leave hourly, recommended. The old Central de Autobuses is half a block from the new; old buses use it, with erratic service to Mexico City via the less-used dangerous road through Altamirano (to be avoided if possible, robberies).

By **car** from Mexico City via the Toluca-Zihuatanejo highway (430 kilometres) or via the Acapulco-Zihuatanejo highway (405 kilometres). To Acapulco can be done in $3\frac{1}{2}$ hours, but sometimes takes 6 hours. To Lázaro Cárdenas, 103 kilometres, takes $3\frac{1}{2}$ hours, the road is very bad.

Directory **Airlines** AeroMéxico, T42018/32208/09; Delta (airport), T43386/686; Mexicana, *Hotel Dorado Pacífico,* Ixtapa, T3220810.. **Banks** *Banca Serfín* will change TCs at lower commission than in banks in hotel district. *Banamex. Bancomer.* Several *casas de cambio.* **Tourist offices** Tourist Office and Complaints, see under Ixtapa, below. **Useful telephone numbers** Customs at airport: T43262. **Immigration:** T42795. **Ministerio Público:** (to report a crime), T42900. **Police:** T42040. **Red Cross:** (ambulances), T42009.

Ixtapa

Population: 32,000
Colour map 3, grid C3

There are crocodiles in the beautiful lagoons at the end of the beach.

From Zihuatanejo one can drive seven kilometres or take a bus (US$0.30 from Paseo Zihuatanejo/Morelos) or taxi (US$5, colectivo, US$1) to **Ixtapa**, 'where there are salt lakes'. The resort, developed on a large scale, boasts 14 beaches: La Hermosa, Del Palmar, Don Juan de Dios, Don Juan, Don Rodrigo, Cuata, Quieta, Oliveiro, Linda, Larga, Carey, Pequeña, Cuachalate and Varadero. There are turtles, many species of shellfish and fish, and pelicans at El Morro de los Pericos, which can be seen by launch. There is an island a few metres off Quietas beach; boats go over at a cost of US$5. Ixtapa has 10 large luxury hotels and a *Club Méditerranée* (all obtain food-supplies from Mexico City making food more expensive, as local supplies aren't guaranteed); a shopping complex, golf course, water-ski/parachute skiing and tennis courts. There is a yacht marina and an 18-hole golf club, Palma Real. Isla Grande has been developed as a nature park and leisure resort. **NB** The beach can be dangerous with a strong undertow; small children should not be allowed in the sea unaccompanied.

All in LL-A range *Westin Resort Ixtapa*, T32121, F31091, spectacular, in a small jungle. **Krystal**, highly recommended, book in advance, T30333, F30216. *Dorado Pacífico*, T32025, F30126. **Sheraton**, Blvd Ixtapa, T31858, F32438, with panoramic lift, reductions for AAA members, recommended. *Stouffer Presidente*, T753-30018, F32312. *Aristos*, T31505, the first to open in Ixtapa. **Best Western Posada Real**, next to *Carlos and Charlie's Restaurant*, T31745, F31805. **Fontan Ixtapa**, T30003. **Holiday Inn SunSpree Resort**, Blvd Ixtapa, T800-09346, F31991. *Club Med*, Playa Quieta, T743-30742, F743-30393, taxi between centre and main hotels, US$3.

Sleeping

Camping *Playa Linda Trailer Park*, on Carretera Playa Linda at *Playa Linda Hotel*, just north of Ixtapa, 50 spaces, full hook-ups, restaurant, recreation hall, baby sitters, on beach, US$14 for 2, comfortable.

Besides those in every hotel, there are many others, including *Villa de la Selva*, recommended for food and views, book in advance, T30362. *El Sombrero*, Mexican, very good. *Montmartre* (French), *Onyx*, *Bogart's* (opposite *Hotel Krystal*), *Gran Tapa*, all more costly than in Zihuatanejo.

Eating

Every hotel without exception has at least 1 nightclub/disco and 2 bars.

Bars & nightlife

NB for motorists: although paved Highway 134 leads directly from Mexico City and Toluca to Ixtapa, there is no fuel or other supplies after **Ciudad Altamirano** (188 kilometres, pleasant motel on southwest edge of city, C with a/c). This road also runs through remote country, prone to landslides, and there is occasional bandit activity, with unpredictable army check-points (looking for guns and drugs). It is not recommended for non-Spanish speaking, or lone motorists.

Transport

Tourist office In Ixtapa Shopping Plaza, T31967/68.

Directory

The coastal route continues northwest to Lázaro Cárdenas and Playa Azul in Michoacán (see page 244). 20 kilometres north of Ixtapa is the pleasant little beach town of **Troncones**, with several restaurants and **AL** *Eden*, (evandjim@aol.com) American-run hotel in secluded cove, all rooms with balconies overlooking sea, price includes breakfast, and there is a restaurant serving gourmet Mexican food.

Coast east of Acapulco

Highway 200, E from Acapulco along the coast, is paved all the way to Puerto Escondido; this stretch is known as the Costa Chica. There is a bridge missing about 55 kilometres from Acapulco, near Playa Barra Vieja on the road past the airport along the coast. It is better to take the parallel inland road to **San Marcos** (**D** *Hotel San Marcos*, clean, restaurant, pool). This road, which is windy, hilly and with few services and little traffic, has been reported dangerous due to bandit hold ups of lone cars, check locally before driving this route.

Further along the coast is **Copala** (**F** *Casa de Huéspedes*, not recommended), 123 kilometres from Acapulco. Another 19 kilometres brings you to **Marquelia**, with excellent beaches about three kilometres from town (transport well nigh impossible,

Mexico

taxi US$6); there are no hotels, but you can spend the night in a hammock in one of the little restaurants on the beach (US$3 per night). The restaurant owners will look after luggage, but keep an eye on it anyway. Very good seafood, about US$5 per meal. Bus to Puerto Escondido US$7.35, five to six hours, very full coming from Acapulco. Another 65 kilometres brings you to **Cuajinicuilapa** (**F** *Hotel Marin*, clean, restaurant, recommended), from where it is an hour's *colectivo* ride to **Faro**, US$1.50. Last one leaves at about 1800. Faro (on Punta Maldonado) is a beautiful beach, unspoilt and clean. Simple hotel (**F**) right on beach, authentic fishing village, several huts serving food (check prices before ordering).

Pinotepa Nacional

Colour map 3, grid C4

From Cuajinicuilapa it is 51 kilometres to **Santiago Pinotepa Nacional**. "From Pinotepa Nacional you can visit the Mixtec Indian village of **Pinotepa de Don Luis** by *camioneta* (US$1, 50 minutes). These leave from beside the Centro de Salud in Pinotepa Nacional, taking paved road, via Tlacamana, to Don Luis (last one back to Pinotepa Nacional at 1300, or wait till next morning, nowhere to stay). The women there weave beautiful and increasingly rare sarong-like skirts (*chay-ay*), some of which are dyed from the purple of sea snails. Also, half-gourds incised with various designs and used both as caps and cups can be found. The *ferias* of Don Luis (20 January) and nearby San Juan Colorado (29-30 November) are worth attending for the dancing and availability of handicrafts." (Dale Bricker, Seattle.) Another village, **Huazolotitlan**, is known for mask making, take *camioneta* from near *Hotel Las Palomas*, three blocks from plaza, 40 minutes. Fiesta, first Friday in February with masked dancers.

Sleeping **D** *Hotel Carmona*, restaurant, good value but poor laundry service, helpful advice on visiting surrounding villages, parking. **E** *Marisa*, near Zócalo, with bath, more expensive with a/c. **E** *Tropical*, fan, clean, large rooms, quiet, parking.

Puerto Escondido

Population: 25,000
Phone code: 958
Colour map 3, grid C5

Puerto Escondido, 144 kilometres southeast of Pinotepa Nacional, is on a beautiful bay almost due south of Oaxaca, very touristy for much of the year, good surfing. Palm trees line the beach, which is not too clean. The expansion of the southeast end of town, 'to make it the next Acapulco' (in the words of one developer) is well-advanced. Many visitors are disappointed by the high costs and the commercialization in the main part of the town. There are, however, a number of beaches to visit and villages close by. 15 minutes by taxi or bus to the west is Manialtepec, with a lagoon, wild birds (Canadian ornithologist Michael Malone recommended for guided tours, US$35 approximately), and watersports such as water skiing; the village has rivers and hot springs. Villages inland include San Pedro and San Gabriel Mixtepec on the direct road to Oaxaca and, just-off this road, Santa Catarina Juquila, with a sanctuary. A trip to **Lagunas de Chacahua** is recommended. The excursion goes through mangroves and there are many birds to watch. Available through travel agencies in town. Recommended guide is Ana Márquez, located in Cooperative boating office, Av Marinero Principal, tours from US$15 a day.

Beaches Next to the Bahía Principal is Playa Marinero, with small bars, restaurants and handicrafts market. Further southeast is Zicatela, good for surfing, becoming more developed with an esplanade, hotels on the hill (though not high-rise) and a few restaurants on the beach. Two kilometres west of the centre is Puerto Angelito, recommended by locals as a safe and clean beach. Launches take passengers from the bay in Puerto Escondido, US$3.50 per person for maximum 10, or taxi US$2. At Manzanillo, with a small creek, is a coral reef and tropical fish; access to the beach on foot only. Beyond Puerto Angelito is Playa Carrizalillo (with trailer park behind) and then Playa Bacocho (two club/restaurants with pools).

NB There can be dangerous waves, and the cross-currents are always dangerous;

non-swimmers should not bathe except in the bay on which the town stands. Also, a breeze off the sea makes the sun seem less strong than it is, be careful. Do not stray too far along the beach; armed robbery by groups of three to five (or rape) is becoming more and more frequent, even in daylight, take as little cash and valuables as possible, US$ sought after. Also at La Barra beach 10 kilometres away. Be alert for dogs.

Sleeping

Very crowded during Holy Week, can be very difficult to find accommodation; prices rise on 1 November because of the local Fiesta de Noviembre, but are lower May/June. Most hotels are on the beach, little air-conditioning.

Many cheaper hotels have no hot water and cheap cabañas are often full of mosquitoes.

At Bacocho Beach LL-AL *Best Western Posada Real* (ex-*Bugambilias*), Blvd Benito Juárez II, T20237, F20192, about 2½ kilometres from town, off road to Acapulco, very pleasant, lovely gardens, pool, path to beach, attentive, a/c, good service, food included (à la carte, also lobster). **AL-A** *Villa Sol*, T20038, courtyard with 2 pools, small garden. **A** *Aldea de Bazar*, T20580, moorish style, huge garden with many palms, large pool, large rooms, good restaurant, recommended. **B** *Fiesta Mexicana*, T20150, bit run-down. **C** *Casa del Mar*. **A** *Paraíso Escondido*, Unión 1, T20444, noisy a/c, not on beach (up the hill almost all the way to the Crucero) but with own swimming pool, recommended, clean, colonial style, in summer when not full bar and restaurant open according to demand. **B** *Barlovento*, very comfortable, pool, recommended, but a little way out of town and away from beach – not advisable to walk there at night. **B** *Cabañas Zikatela*, on Zicatela beach, large clean rooms with fan and mini-fridge, swimming pool, bar service, small restaurant serving breakfast and cheese burgers. **B** *El Rincón del Pacífico*, Pérez Gasca 900, T20056, very popular, always full, on beach, with restaurant, hot water. **B** *Loren*, Pérez Gasca 507, T20448, clean, friendly, safe, recommended. **B** *Hotel Santa Fe*, Carretera Costera, on beach at north end of bay, noisy a/c, restaurant expensive but very good food. **C** *Casa Blanca*, Pérez Gasca, middle of beach, with fan and hot water, clean and well-furnished, balconies, pool. **C** *Margot's*, 30 metres south of the pedestrian zone in the centre, nice big rooms, good, cheap food. **C** *Nayar*, Pérez Gasca 407, T20113, big rooms, views, pool, TV, some with bath and fan, more expensive with a/c, hot water, restaurant, safe parking. **C** *Rocamar*, Pérez Gasca 601, T20339, by beach, upper rooms a/c and balconies, fans, hot water, restaurant, recommended.

D *Alderete*, opposite bus station, with private bath. **D** *Art and Harry's*, on ocean-front, free board use, great barbecues, good food. **D** *Bungalows Villa Marinero*, on Marinero beach, can also be reached from the main road to Zicatela, own cooking possible, friendly, kitchen/eating area, pool. **D** *Cabañas San Diego*, down a sand road just before bridge on road to Puerto Angel, safe, nice grounds but few facilities. **D** *Central*, 2 minutes uphill from bus terminal, clean, friendly. **D** *La Posada Económica*, 1 big dormitory, attached to restaurant, but also runs hotel across the road, ask for a room opposite the flat, good *huachinango*. **D** *Ribera del Mar*, behind Iglesia de la Soledad, uphill, fan, quiet, no hot water, laundry facilities, cheaper for longer stays, recommended. **D** *San Juan*, downhill from bus station, some rooms with seaview, English spoken, fair, small, enclosed car park, 2-3 cars. **D-E** *Castillo del Rey*, Av Pérez Gasca, T20442, near beach, clean, nice rooms, hot water, quiet, good beds, friendly, good value, highly recommended. **E** *Alojamiento Las Cabañas* has dormitories with bunks, on main road (south side), friendly, very nice, food is good, you will be charged for all beds regardless of whether they are occupied, unless you share the cabin. *Cabañas Cocoa Beach*, in the town near the church. US$4.50 per cabin (6 or 7 available), mosquito nets, cold shower, family-run. **E** *Cabañas Cortés*, for small, basic huts or large, basic huts, in all cases, take mosquito nets. **E** *Casa de Huéspedes Las Dos Costas*, fairly clean, acceptable for budget travellers. Lots of bungalows and *cabañas* at south end of the beach. **E** *Real del Mar*, near bus station (cheaper for longer stays), bath, no hot water, clean, nice view. **E** *Cabañas Villa*, María del Mar, end of Zicatela beach, pool, friendly. Also on Zicatela, **D-F** *Acuario*, shared bath, some with bath more expensive, pool, gym, scuba diving centre, recommended. **F** *Mayflower*, just off Pérez Gasca (pedestrian street) on Andador Libertad, T20367, F20422, shared rooms with fans, communal bathrooms, some more expensive rooms. They will let you sleep on the roof - very hot. **D-F** *Comedor Económico*, Av Oaxaca

Mexico

201, just above junction with Acapulco road, clean rooms with bath, run by Sra María del Carmen Silva Ruiz, good restaurant, garden, friendly.

Apartments *La Maison*, Andador Puerto Juárez C, Lomas de Puerto, Box 243, Puerto Escondido, Oax 71980, F958-20612 'para entregar a Pierre', 1 room (shared kitchen and patio), 3 apartments for 2, 3 and 5 people, with kitchen, all with bath, hot water, rates from US$180 for 2 to US$480 for 5 per week, high season (Christmas/New Year, Easter and 15 July to 31 August), low season US$130-370, reductions for long stays.

Camping   If camping, beware of clothes being stolen. *Carrizalillo Trailer Park*, near old airport on west side of town (follow signs from Tourist Office), on cliff top with path leading down to secluded beach, bathroom, cold showers, laundry facilities, swimming pool and bar, very pleasant, prices from US$8 to US$20 for 2 plus car depending on location and whether you have hook-up. *Neptuno* campsite for vehicles, tents and hammocks on water front in centre of town, vehicles and tents accepted, swimming pool, electricity, cold showers, US$10 per car with 2 people, rather rundown and noisy; next door is *Las Palmas* (better), about US$10 for 2 plus car, US$5 for tent, clean bathrooms, shade, recommended. *Hotel Playa Azul* has a con-stricted trailer park (not very convenient for large vehicles), access from a side road, has a good swimming pool.

Eating   Many restaurants on main street, Pérez Gasca, eg: *Lolys*, cheap and good, try *pescado a la parrilla*, with sweet onion sauce, and lemon pie after. *San Angel* for fish. *La Galería*, Italian, good pizzas but pricey. *Extacea*, good cheap meals and live music. *7 Regiones*, good for very late night tacos and frijoles. *La Estancia*, good, warm service, but expensive. *La Sardina de Plata*, popular. *Hermann's*, main street, good, cheap. South end of main street is *Mario's Pizzaland*, excellent pizzas at reasonable prices, friendly. *Lisa's Restaurant*, nice location on beach (just off Carretera Costera) good food, also has rooms to let, **D** off season, with fan, very clean, safe deposit, highly recommended. *Los Crotos*, also on the beach, good and varied food at reasonable prices, good service, recommended. *El Tiburón*, on beach, corner of Felipe Merbelín, lots of good food for US$2-3. *Super Café Puro* off top of flight of stairs

Puerto Escondido environs

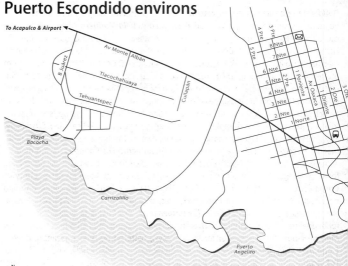

N

Not to scale

(shortcut up to main road) from opposite tourist kiosk on Pérez Gasca with pleasant terrace. Good place for breakfast. *Cappuccino*, Pérez Gasca, good coffee, fruit salads, some dishes pricey. Good *licuados* at *Bambú Loco*, also fish. *Las Palapas*, good, it is just over the stream (sewer) on the right. *Carmen's*, on a path from beach to main road to Zicatela, great pastries baked on the premises, also second-hand books and magazines. *Pepe's*, great sandwiches. *Alicia*, in town, best value but be careful with seafood, food is good quality, but very expensive near the beach. *El Cafecito*, next door to *Acuario cabañas* on Zicatela beach, excellent breakfasts, *pain au chocolat* made with Swiss chocolate, highly recommended, and next along is *Bruno's*, with 'starving surfer' meals of rice, frijoles, and tortillas for US$2, popular place for watching sunsets.

Bars & nightclubs Discos *Tubo*, on the beach. *El Son y La Rumba*, opposite, live salsa daily. *Tequila Bum-Bum* (pronounced Boom-Boom), downtown, international crowd, varied music, open air. *Bacocho*, popular with locals, Mexican pop, indoors.

Video bar *Bartly*, regular screenings of films and videos, upstairs area with hammocks, candle-lit, gives out wax crayons to encourage budding artists to doodle on the paper table cloths.

Shopping Small selection of foreign language books at *Papi's*, souvenir shop 3 doors from Mercado de Artesanías, buy or swap. Local crafts best not bought from vendors on the beach, but in the non-gringo part of town up the hill near where the buses stop.

Transport **Air** Airport (PXM) 3km, 10 minutes' drive from town, orange juice and coffee sold. Daily to Mexico City. Also flights to Huatulco and Oaxaca. Taxis to centre in VW combis, US$2.25 per person, Colectivos Combi, T20030.

Road The best route between Puerto Escondido and Oaxaca is via San Pedro Pochutla, using the coast road 200 and Route 175 inland. Bus drivers on the paved route have a radio for checking road conditions. The direct highway to Oaxaca is being upgraded. Don't take a stopping bus to Oaxaca on the direct road as robberies have been reported.

Buses To **Oaxaca**, 3 a day (including overnight), US$11.50 1st class, US$18.75 *plus* with Trans Oaxaca-Pacífico (direct), advertised as 7-hour trip, but can take up to 17 hours; also Estrella del Valle (1st class, from 2nd class terminal); Auto Transportes Oaxaca-Pacífico, via Pochutla, 10-18 hours (depending on roadworks), leaves at 0700, US$7 2nd class, 2300 1st class; all have bookable seats. Puerto Escondido-**Pochutla**, for Puerto Angel, several hourly from 0500 to 2000, about 1 hour, US$2, and on to **Salina Cruz**, Oaxaca-Pacífico company recommended. The road to Salina Cruz is now paved (bus US$9.75, about 7 a day, 10 hours). Bus to **Acapulco**, 2nd class US$10.50, Estrella Blanca, 3 a day; US$15.65, Flecha Roja (near La Solteca terminal), at least 7½ hours, not exciting. The 1030 bus stops for 2 hours' lunch at Pinotepa, book tickets at least 1 day in advance. First bus to Acapulco at 0400, hourly up to mid afternoon. Transportes Gacela run 3 direct buses a day to Acapulco at 1030, 1330 and 2300, only 2 short stops. The road is in bad condition. To/from **Mexico City** US$38.35 1st class, US$40.35 *plus*. To **Tehuantepec**, go to Salina Cruz and change there; 2 direct buses a day to **San Cristóbal de las Casas**, US$21.

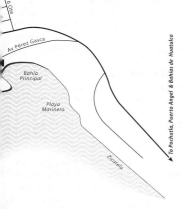

Mexico

Mexico

Directory **Airlines** Mexicana (T20098). **Banks** *Bancomer*, Pérez Gasca, open 0900-1200, slow service, no commission. *Banamex*, open 0900-1330. *Casa de cambio*, on Pérez Gasca, open till 2000, poor rates. **Hospitals & medical services** *Dr Francisco Serrano Severiano*, opposite Banpeco, speaks English, 0900-1300, 1700-2000. *Farmacia La Moderna*, Av Pérez Gasca 203, T20214, open 24 hrs. **Red Cross:** T20155. **Laundry** Pérez Gasca, beside *Hotel Nayar*, US$1.50 per kg. **Tourist office** T20175, 20846, kiosk on Av Pérez Gasca at bottom of hill.

Pochutla
Colour map 3, grid C5

San Pedro Pochutla is the crossroads of Route 175 from Oaxaca, Route 200 from Acapulco to Salina Cruz and a 10-kilometre road to Puerto Angel and the beaches. It is therefore important for bus connections. At Pochutla there is a prison; you can buy black coral necklaces made by prisoners very cheaply (but remember that black coral is an endangered species); they make and sell other handicrafts. Take vitamins or other useful small items to trade or give away. Leave documents and valuables outside (an 'interesting, eye-opening, if noisy, shopping trip').

Sleeping **A** *Costa del Sol*, on main street near the market, with a/c, **C** with ceiling fan, credit cards, bar, restaurant. **D** *Hotel Izala*, on main street (Lázaro Cárdenas) near plaza. Shower, fan, clean comfortable. **D** *San Juan*, with bath, good view, pleasant. **E** *Pochutla*, on Plaza, entrance on side street. **E** *Posada Sta Cruz*, opposite bus stop to Oaxaca, OK for 1 night. *Fla Tropical*, on La Constitución, by prison, basic, excellent ice-cream factory.

Transport Hourly bus to **Salina Cruz**, US$5, 4 hours, road occasionally closed by landslides. Pochutla-**Puerto Angel**, same regular service as for **Zipolite**, below; alternatively take a colectivo, or taxi, US$2.50, 30 minutes. Pochutla-**Oaxaca**, from 0500-2300, 5-9 hours, US$8 (Estrella del Valle, 1st class), 1st class not always available, 2nd class US$6, (Oaxaca-Pacífico); San José del Pacífico is a pleasant stop on the way, with good restaurant; alternatively via Salina Cruz, US$13.25, 8 hours (2nd class US$6). The bus service between Pochutla and **Puerto Escondido** (US$1.20, several every hour from 0500 to 2000, 1¼ hours) links with the bus to Puerto Angel. Bus Pochutla-**San Cristóbal de las Casas** at 1000 and 2200, 12-15 hours, 1st class (Cristóbal Colón, US$23, bus starts at Puerto Escondido so very few seats available in Pochutla, book in advance if possible), goes via **Huatulco**, **Salina Cruz**, **Tehuantepec** and **Tuxtla Gutiérrez**; to **Acapulco** at 2200 direct, 1st class, 12 hours, US$20. Estrella Blanca run an hourly bus to **Acapulco**, US$17, 8 hours.

Directory Banks: *Bancomer*, only 0930-1100, exchanges AmEx and Visa TCs but only US$100 per person a day. *Banamex* handles AmEx and Mastercard. Banks here sometimes run out of money, so best not to rely on them. **Hospitals & medical services**: There is a hospital outside Pochutla, US$2 for a consultation, medicines free.

Puerto Angel
Puerto Angel is a coffee port on the Pacific with a good, popular beach, 69 kilometres from Puerto Escondido, 240 kilometres from Oaxaca, with road connection but no direct buses; all services involve change at Pochutla. Just before Puerto Angel, a dirt road leads left to some small bays which have no people, are good for snorkelling, but can have dangerous waves. Playa del Panteón has been recommended as a relaxing place to stay with good restaurants.

In Puerto Angel take care of your belongings, but, more important, take extra care in the sea, the currents are very dangerous. The sea water is said to be polluted from animals on the beach, 'immediate stomach problems' reported. Lots of dogs everywhere. Scuba diving is possible with *Hotel La Cabaña* on Playa del Panteón. Experienced PADI instructors, up-to-date equipment, English spoken, T958-43116.

Sleeping On a hill away from the beach, **B** *Angel del Mar*, fan, dirty, run down, good view. **C** *Buena Vista*, nice rooms up hill, clean, relaxing but not very friendly. **D** *El Rincón Sabroso*, beautiful views, clean, quiet, friendly, no hot water. **D** *La Cabaña*, near the *Cañón de Vata*, fan, free coffee in morning, clean, friendly owner, no restaurant, recommended. **D** *Casa Penelope's*, Cerrada de la Luna s/n (Apdo postal 49, Puerto Angel CP 70902) T43073, comfortable, quiet rooms with ceiling fan, mosquito screens and Pacific views, parking, laundry, restaurant. **D-E** *Hotel Soraya*, fan, bath, very clean (changes dollars and travellers' cheques), unfriendly. **E** *Capis*, clean rooms, cold water, fan, excellent food, recommended. **E** *Anahi*, on road to *Angel del Mar*. With fan, Indonesian-style wash basins. **E** *Casa de Huéspedes Gladys*, just above *Soraya*, balcony, fine views, clean, recommended, owner can prepare food, no hot water. **F** *Casa de Huéspedes Leal*, shared bath, washing facilities, friendly, recommended. **F** *Familiar*, clean, friendly, fan. **E** *Casa de Huéspedes Gundi y Tomás* (Gundi and Tomás López), without bath, clean, or hammocks (**F**), popular with travellers, will store luggage, good value, snacks and breakfast (US1.50-3), sells food and beverages, often recommended. Gundi also runs **Pensión El Almendro**, with café (good ice-cream) and library. Similar is the **D** *Pensión Puesta del Sol*, run by Harald and Maria Faerber (suite more expensive), very friendly, English and German spoken, excellent restaurant, on road to Playa Panteón, clean, recommended. 50 metres along is **E** *Casa de Huéspedes Copy*, great rooms. **D** *Posada Cañón de Vata*, on Playa Panteón, Apdo Postal 74, Pochutla 70900, clean but dark, lovely setting, booked continuously, popular with Americans, quite good restaurant, mainly vegetarian. Possible to sleep on beach away from the naval base and soldiers who will move you on. **Estacahuite**, a beautiful, clean beach, 1 kilometre from town, 20 minutes' walk, has cabins (beware of jelly fish on the beach). There is a hut at the beach selling beer and fries, and it lends snorkelling gear.

Camping There is a campsite half way between Puerto Angel and Pochutla, very friendly, driveway is too steep for large vehicles, US$8.50 for 2 in camper van, recommended.

Eating An excellent restaurant at *Villa Valencia* hotel. Charming place, good food if a bit pricey, good restaurant *Capis* (has 10 rooms above). *Beto's* restaurant, just up hill on road to Zipolite, 5 minutes' walk from centre, good fish (fresh tuna) and cheap beer. *Mar y Sol*, cheap, good seafood. *Sirenita*, popular for breakfasts, and bar, friendly. *Cangrejito*, by Naval base gate, popular bar, also good breakfasts and excellent tacos. Many fish restaurants along the main street. 2 restaurants by fishing harbour used by locals, cheap.

Festivals 1 October.

Directory Communications: Post Office: for post office, go to Customs office; for other services go to Pochutla (eg exchange). **Telephone:** long distance phone next to *Soraya* at **Telmex**, open 0800-2200. **Medical Services**: There is a private doctor in Puerto Angel, but he charges US$17 minimum for a consultation, and it is hard to find him home.

Four kilometres west (30 minutes' walk) is the lovely but dangerous Zipolite beach. It is dangerous for bathing if you swim behind the waves or when the tide changes. It may be the last nude beach in Mexico (only at the far end), but do not walk to the beach at night, packs of dogs have attacked people. As far as personal safety goes, the eastern end is safer than the western end, it is also quieter. It has much less of a Mexican atmosphere than Puerto Angel, but is very popular with travellers.

Zipolite
name means 'the killing beach', according to legend; several drownings a month

Sleeping and eating Places to stay are usually either basic or overpriced. Every hut on the beach is a fish restaurant with cold drinks and hammock space, but lots of mosquitoes. Hammock rental is US$1-3. Hammock spot and vegetarian restaurant *Shambhala* run by Gloria, an American woman (30 minutes' walk to far west end coming from Puerto Angel), wonderful views, basic, rustic, but no longer receiving the good reports it used to get. *Lo Cósmico*, just before *Shambhala*, *cabañas* and very good crêpes, open all year; hammocks for rent from Philippe at 'Gloria end' of the beach; also at 'Gloria end', *Cristóbal Cabañas*, family run, clean, good meals, **E** for room, **E** basic *cabaña*, hammock hire, shared bathrooms. **E** *Roca Blanca*, friendly, helpful, hammock space, good and cheap food, good service. **E** *Cabañas El Tao*, 'rooms with a view', clean, friendly, shared bath, expensive breakfast; **F** *Lyoban's*, basic rooms, hammock space on 1st floor terrace, filling dishes served by family, table tennis.

Mexico

Cabañas Montebello, next to *La Puesta* bar, with hammocks, quiet and very clean, run by Luis and María. *Hamacas La Choza*, on way to *Shambhala*, with cheap restaurant but poor service, family atmosphere, hammocks to rent, luggage store. **E-F** *Cabañas Palapa del Pescador*, hammock, or a *palapa*, fresh fish available, English and French spoken, use of kitchen, safe luggage store, next door is *Restaurant Genesis*, 3rd on beach, ask for rooms, **E**, clean, charming, helpful, good meals (ask for house on the hill). There is a campsite suitable for tents only, water and bathroom: follow paved road, then unpaved road for 1 kilometre, then small road to the left. RVs can stay overnight in the parking lot, but no facilities. At the east end of the beach is *Lola's*, great views along beach, excellent food, also rooms (**E**) without bath, fan, basic, clean; good pizzas at *Gemini Pizzas*; there is a good *Panadería* on the road behind the beach, through the green gate. There are a couple of informal discos.

Transport Bus service from Pochutla to Zipolite every 20 minutes from 0600 to 1830, last bus back from Zipolite to Pochutla at 1900, US$0.70; fare to Puerto Angel US$0.35. Buses stop on the paved road behind the beach just after the 'Zipolite/Playa de los Muertos' sign. Taxi Puerto Angel-Zipolite, US$3.50 per person for any amount of passengers; to Pochutla US$5 (add US$3.50 to be taken to your *cabaña* door).

Several kilometres further up the coast is **San Agustín** beach, accessible by a path behind Shambhala (ask directions), beautiful, safe for swimming, with an extraordinary cave in the cliffs. Accommodation is now available (**F** for a room with shared toilet and shower, basic, dirty, but friendly: restaurant next to bus stop; hammock rental US$5).

Beyond is **Mazunte** beach, with accommodation, **E-F**, camping site and restaurant. There is also the **Museo de la Tortuga**. ■ *US$1.25, closed Monday.* From here you can walk along the shore to more empty beaches. About 15 kilometres from Zipolite on a dirt road is a sign to **Ventanilla** beach; follow the rough track until you find a thatched ranch and ask for Hilario Reyes. The beach is long and empty and there are two lagoons with fresh water. There are no cabins: you need your own tent (or hammock/mosquito net). Ventanilla beach is also dangerous for bathing. About 20 minutes' walk from Puerto Angel is **Playa de Mina**. Head towards Pochutla, turn right at the soccer pitch to the coast; it is 'a serene beach, paradise'.

Huatulco

Phone code: 958
Colour map 3, grid C5

East of Puerto Angel (50 kilometres, one hour) and 112 kilometres west of Salina Cruz, on the coast road, is the new resort of Huatulco being built on about 34,000 hectares around nine bays. Some estimate that it will surpass Cancún by the year 2000. Santa María Huatulco, near the airport, is now the town for the construction workers, while Santa Cruz Huatulco, the original village, is destined to become an 'authentic Mexican village' for the tourists. There are three separate areas of development: Zona Hotelera on Tangolunda Bay, with four luxury hotels, Santa Cruz Bay with a hotel, three banks, a tourist market and boats for hire, and Crucecita, downtown, with five hotels, all C, all within one block west of Plaza Principal. There are also a number of shopping centres around Plaza La Crucecita, with *artesanías* and boutiques. *Colectivos*, US$0.20, and taxis connect the three areas. Great care is to be taken to blend the resort into the landscape: about 80 percent of the total area is to be set aside as a nature reserve.

Beaches The nearest beach to Crucecita is Chahue Bay, about three kilometres, dangerous undertow, better to go to the Zona Hotelera, about six kilometres, which has a good beach. Other beaches are accessible by car or boat. *Lanchas* can be hired from Cooperativa Tangolunda for exploring the coves, US$10 per day. Guided tours of the Bahías de Huatulco from the major hotels or from Agencia de Viajes García Rendón, Av Alfonso Pérez Gasca, Puerto Escondido, T20114.

Huatulco's legendary cross

The name Huatulco means 'place of the wood', which refers to a cross planted on the beach, legend tells, by Quetzalcoatl. After resisting efforts to pull it down, it was found to be only a few feet deep when dug up; small crosses were made from it. A more likely history of the cross is told by Michael Turner in his research into Francis Drake's voyages. Until the establishment of Acapulco as the departure point for the Spanish Pacific fleet, Huatulco (Guatulco) was the main port on the Pacific, its heyday being from about 1537 to 1574. Drake sacked the port on his voyage around the world (1577-80) and Thomas Cavendish raided it in 1587. Cavendish burnt the church to the ground, but the crucifix (La Santa Cruz) survived, thereafter being incorporated into the village's name. The Spanish viceroy ordered Huatulco's abandonment in 1616. Huatulco's legendary cross

Mexico

Sleeping & eating *Sheraton*, T10055, F10335; *Royal Maeva*; *Holiday Inn Crowne Plaza*, Blvd Benito Juárez 8, T10044, F10221 and the *Club Méditerranée* (5-star, T10033, F10101. Reservations are cheaper when made at head office in C Masaryk, Mexico City. *Suites Bugambilias*, T70018, clean, recommended). **D** *Grifer*, good accommodation, friendly. There are 18 restaurants, some overpriced, and many *comedores*.

Camping There is a trailer park at Chahue (bathrooms, snackbar, but sites are quite stark).

Transport **Air** The airport, Bahías de Huatulco (HUX), is 17 kilometres from town, off the road to Pochutla, with direct flights from Mérida, Mexico City, Oaxaca, Palenque, Puerto Escondido and Tuxtla Gutiérrez..

Buses 3 bus companies; Gacela has direct buses to Acapulco at 0815 and 1315, and to Puerto Escondido at 1015. Several buses to Salina Cruz.

Directory **Airlines** *Aeroméxico*, T10336. *Mexicana*, T70243. *United*, T91-800-00307 or (Spanish) 800-426-5561. **Tourist office** On Av Guamuchl.

Mexico City to Guatemala

Mexico City

Out of a number of routes, we describe that through Oaxaca, a popular tourist town with many fine colonial buildings, markets, Indian traditions and, close by, several magnificent archaeological sites (Monte Albán, Mitla, and others). From Oaxaca, there is a coastal route to Guatemala and the more interesting Chiapas highland route. The main town of interest on the latter is San Cristóbal de Las Casas, which gives access to Maya villages, archaeological sites and lakes.

The National Railway runs daily from Mexico City to Tapachula, the border town. Taxi to Talismán, on the Guatemalan border, for bus to Guatemala City (also accessible from Puebla). There is a new bridge which links Ciudad Hidalgo with Tecún-Umán (formerly Ayutla) in Guatemala. Cristóbal Colón bus Mexico City-Guatemala City takes 23 hours, with a change at the border to Rutas Lima. Mexico City-Tapachula, 20 hours.

NB Motorists who know the area well advise that anyone driving from Mexico City to Tehuantepec should go via Orizaba - La Tinaja - Papaloapan - Tuxtepec - Palomares. This route is better than Veracruz-Acayucán and, if drivers are in a hurry, far preferable to the route which follows, via Izúcar de Matamoros and Oaxaca. Between Oaxaca and Tehuantepec the road, although paved throughout and in good condition, serpentines unendingly over the Sierras and is quite beautiful. But as the Oaxaca route is far more interesting and spectacular we describe it below. For the alternative journey through the Papaloapan region, see page 338.

Tolls Total road toll Mexico City – Oaxaca, US$8.35.

This road through southern Mexico is 1,355 kilometres long. It can be done in three or four days' driving time. There are bus services from Mexico City along the route through Oaxaca to Tehuantepec and on to the Guatemalan frontier through San Cristóbal de Las Casas to Ciudad Cuauhtémoc or through Arriaga to Tapachula. A road now runs (still rough in places) from Paso Hondo near Ciudad Cuauhtémoc via Comalapa and Porvenir to Huixtla on the south road, and from Porvenir to Revolución Mexicana.

Cuernavaca to Oaxaca

Cuautla
Population: 94,000
Colour map 3, grid B4

Take Route 160 via Yautepec to the semi-tropical town of Cuautla, with a popular sulphur spring (known as *aguas hediondas* or stinking waters) and bath, a crowded weekend resort for the capital. Tourist Cuautla is divided from locals' Cuautla by a wide river, and the locals have the best bargain: it is worth crossing the stream. The plaza is pleasant, traffic-free and well maintained. There is a market in the narrow streets and alleyways around 5 de Mayo. The tourist office is opposite *Hotel Cuautla*, on Av Obregón, satisfactory. The **Casa de la Cultura**, three blocks north of Zócalo offers useful information and maps. There is a museum/ex-convent next door.

Sleeping C *Jardín de Cuautla*, Dos de Mayo 94, opposite Colón bus station, modern, clean, but bad traffic noise, pool. 1 block from *Jardín de Cuautla* is **C** *Colonial*, modern, pool. **D** *Hotel Colón* in Cuautla is on the main square, good, clean; *Hotel-restaurante Valencia*, 4 blocks north of Cristóbal Colón terminal. **E** *Hotel España*, Dos de Mayo 22, 3 blocks from bus station, very good, clean, recommended. **D** *Hotel Madrid*, Los Bravos 27, 11 kilometres from Cuautla. On road to Cuernavaca is the **AL** *Hacienda de Cocoyoc*, an old converted *hacienda* with several swimming pools backed by the mill aqueduct, glorious gardens, 18-hole golf-course, tennis and riding, but isolated, Visa accepted but not Amex, reservations (essential in season) at Centro Comercial El Relox, Local 44, Insurgentes Sur 2374, México 01000 DF, T55507331.

Youth Hostel Unidad Deportiva, T20218, CP 60040.

Eating Try the delicious *lacroyas* and *gorditas*, tortillas filled with beans and cheese. 4 good restaurants in main square, all serving cheap *comidas*, try the one in the *Hotel Colón*; good restaurant at *Hotel Granada*, Defensa de Aguas 34.

Transport Buses from Mexico City to **Cuautla** from Central del Ote (Volcanes terminal), 2nd class US$1. Buses from Cuautla at Cristóbal Colón terminal, 5 de Mayo and Zavala, to **Mexico City** hourly US$3.65 1st class, US$4.65 *plus*; Estrella Roja 1st class, 2nd class buses or minibuses to **Cuernavaca** at least hourly, 1 hour, US$1.85; to **Oaxaca**, US$14.80, 2 Cristóbal Colón buses per day (2nd class 1430 and 1st class 2330), 7-8 hours, also ADO, most overnight and en route from Mexico City so book ahead, also try Fletes y Pasajes 2nd class buses, or change twice, at Izúcar de Matamoros and Huajuapan. Cristóbal Colón terminal will store luggage until they close at 2200. The 115 road leads to Amecameca (page 316).

Chalcatzingo

From Cuautla, this interesting Olmec sanctuary can be reached. It has an altar, a pyramid and rock carvings, one of which depicts a procession of warriors led by a prisoner with a beard and horned helmet (a Viking, some say), others depict battles between jaguars and men. To get there take Route 160 southeast, direction Izúcar de Matamoros; at Amayuca turn right towards Tepalcingo. Two kilometres down this road turn left towards Jonacatepec and it's five kilometres to the village of

Chalcatzingo (take a guide). There are buses from Puebla to Amayuca. A taxi from Amayuca costs US$5. Near Jonacatepec are the ruins of Las Pilas. Some seven kilometres further down the road to Tepalcingo is Atotonilco where there is a *balneario* for swimming (bus from Cuautla). (We are grateful to Helmut Zettl of Ebergassing for much of this information.)

After Cuautla take Route 160 with long descent and then ascent to Izúcar de Matamoros, famous for its clay handicrafts, 16th century convent of Santo Domingo, and two nearby spas, Los Amatitlanes (about six kilometres away) and Ojo de Carbón.

Izúcar de Matamoros
Population: 58,000
Colour map 3, grid C4

Sleeping **C** *Premier*, on Zócalo. **D** *Hotel Ocampo*, next to bus station. **E** *Las Fuentes*, bath and hot water, clean, quiet, TV, courtyard, recommended. **F** *La Paz*, off Zócalo, friendly, clean, basic rooms, hot water.

A road leads southwest from Izúcar to **Axochiapan** (Morelos state; **E** *Hotel Primavera*, bath, hot water, clean, tiny room), leading to a paved road to the village of **Jolalpan** with the baroque church of Santa María (1553). Very few restaurants in Jolalpan; ask where meals are to be had. Bus from Axochiapan stops in front of the church in Jolalpan. The road (and bus) continues to Atenango del Río in Guerrero state, the last 20-30 kilometres unpaved.

Route 190 heads north from Izúcar to Puebla (side road to Huaquechula: 16th century renaissance-cum-plateresque chapel) via **Atlixco** ('the place lying on the water'), with interesting baroque examples in the Capilla de la Tercera Orden de San Agustín and San Juan de Dios (**C** *Mansión Atlixco*, T50691, highly recommended). There is an annual festival, the Atlixcayotl, on San Miguel hill (**B** *Molina de Herrera*, Km 40 of carretera Puebla-Izúcar de Matamoros, 15 minutes from Atlixco, T448171, 50 a/c rooms with satellite TV, pool, restaurant, bar, convention hall for 300 people. **E** *Hotel Colonial* behind parish church, shared bath; *Restaurant La Taquería*, Av Libertad, one block from Plaza, highly recommended). Nearby, 20 minutes, are the curative springs of Axocopán. Thence to Acatepec (page 319) and, 30 kilometres, Puebla.

From Izúcar de Matamoros, Route 190 south switchbacks to Tehuitzingo. Then fairly flat landscape to **Acatlán** (**E** *Plaza*, clean, hot showers, TV, new, good restaurant, recommended. **E** *México*, 'grungy', cockroaches, try elsewhere; *Lux*; *Romano*, both **E**) a friendly village where black and red clay figures, and palm and flower hats are made. Carry on to Petalcingo (restaurant), then ascend to **Huajuapan de León**, with *Hotel García Peral*, on the Zócalo, good restaurant; *Hotel Casablanca*, Amatista 1, Col Vista Hermosa, also good restaurant (just outside Huajuapan on the road to Oaxaca); **C-D** *Plaza de Angel*, Central, nice, clean. **D** *Playa*, El Centro, hot water, clean, big windows, good value; and **D** *Hotel Bella Vista*; and **D** *Colón*, very good. 2nd class bus from Oaxaca to Huajuapan, four a day, US$3.50. The next town on Route 190 is **Tamazulapan** (Hotels **D** *Gilda*, one block south of Highway 190, central, new, large clean rooms, safe parking. **D** *México*, on highway, modern, clean, has lush courtyard, balconies, good restaurant with *comida corrida*. **D** *Santiago*, without sign on Zócalo. **E** *Hidalgo*, behind church; restaurant *Coquiz*, on Highway 190, good). 72 kilometres northwest of Oaxaca on Route 190 is **Yanhuitlán**, with a beautiful 400-year-old church, part of a monastery (Santo Domingo). Yanhuitlán is in the Sierra Mixteca, where Dominican friars began evangelizing in 1526. Two other important centres were San Juan Bautista at Coixtlahuaca and the open chapel at Teposcolula. The scenery and the altars, the huge convents in such a remote area, are a worthwhile day trip from Oaxaca. The new highway from **Nochixtlán** (**D** *Mixli*, outskirts at intersection with new highway, large beds, TV, parking, recommended but 20 minutes' walk from town. **E** *Hotel Sarita*, around corner is **E** *Elazcan*, clean, OK) to Oaxaca (103 kilometres) has been recommended for cyclists: wide hard shoulders and easy gradients.

México

The major route from Mexico City first runs generally eastwards to Puebla, where it turns south to wind through wooded mountains at altitudes of between 1,500 and 1,800 metres, emerging at last into the warm, red earth Oaxaca valley.

Oaxaca

Population: 300,000
State population 1995:
3,224,270
Altitude: 1,546m
Phone code: 951
Colour map 3, grid C5

Mexico

Oaxaca, 413 kilometres from Puebla, 531 kilometres from Mexico City, is a charming Indian town, of airy patios with graceful arcades, famous for its colourful market, its *sarapes*, crafts, dances and feast days.

The Zócalo with its arcades is the heart of the town; its bandstand has a few food stalls underneath. Since the streets surrounding the sides of the Zócalo and the adjacent Alameda de León have been closed to traffic it has become very pleasant to sit there or stroll. It is always active. Free music and dance events are often held in the evenings. In the daytime vendors sell food, in the evening their tourist wares and gardenias in the square. It is especially colourful on Saturday and Sunday nights when Indian women weave and sell their wares. Their weavings can also be seen during the week, on the Plazuela del Carmen, up Alcalá, one block beyond Santo Domingo.

Sights
Worth visiting is the state-government, **Palacio de Gobierno**, on the south side of the Zócalo; it has beautiful murals and entry is free. There are often political meetings or protests outside. Visit also the **Arcos Xochimilco** on García Vigil, starting at Cosipoji, some 10 blocks north of the Zócalo. This picturesque area is the remains of an aqueduct, with narrow, cobbled passageways under the arches, flowers and shops. There is a grand view from the amphitheatre on the **Cerro de Fortín**. The monument to Juárez is in the valley below. The house of the Maza family, for whom Bénito Juárez worked and whose daughter he married, still stands at Independencia 1306 (a plaque marks it). Similarly, a plaque marks the birthplace of Porfirio Díaz at the other end of Independencia, in a building which is now a kindergarten, near La Soledad. DH Lawrence wrote parts of *Mornings in Mexico* here, and revised *The Plumed Serpent*; the house he rented is on Pino Suárez. There is an **observatory and planetarium** on the hill northwest of the town. ■ *Shows on Wednesday, Friday, Saturday and Sunday at 1900, US$2, best to take a taxi (about US$3.50) the walk is dark and deserted.*

Churches
On the Zócalo is the 17th century **cathedral** with a fine baroque façade (watch the raising and lowering of the Mexican flag daily at 0800 and 1800 beside the cathedral), but the best sight, about four blocks from the square up the pedestrianized C Macedonio Alcalá, is the church of **Santo Domingo** with its adjoining monastery, now the Regional Museum (see below). The church's gold leaf has to be seen to be believed. The ceilings and walls, sculptured and painted white and gold, are beautiful. There is an extraordinary vaulted decoration under the raised choir, right on the reverse of the façade wall: a number of crowned heads appear on the branches of the genealogical tree of the family of Santo Domingo de Guzmán (died 1221), whose lineage was indirectly related to the royal houses of Castilla and Portugal. The entire ceiling of the central nave is painted. By making a donation (say US$1) to the church you can get the lady at the bookstall to light up the various features after 1800. The Capilla del Rosario in the church is fully restored; no flash pictures are allowed.

The massive 17th century church of **La Soledad** (between Morelos and Independencia, west of Unión) has fine colonial ironwork and sculpture (including an exquisite Virgen de la Soledad). Its interior is predominantly fawn and gold; the plaques on the walls are painted like cross-sections of polished stone. The chandeliers at the sides are supported by angels. The fine façade is made up of stone of different colours, pinks and greens. The church was built on the site of the hermitage to San Sebastian; begun in 1582, it was recommenced in 1682 because of earthquakes. It was consecrated in 1690 and the convent was finished in 1697. The **Museo Religiosa de la Soledad** on Independencia 107 has a display of religious artefacts; it is at the back of the church. In the small plaza outside the encircling wall,

Zapotec Indians

The Zapotec language is used by over 300,000 people in the State as a first or second language (about 20 percent of Oaxaca State population speaks only an Indian language). The Zapotec Indians, who weave fantastic toys of grass, have a dance, the Jarabe Tlacolula Zandunga danced by barefoot girls splendid in most becoming coifs, short, brightly coloured skirts and ribbons and long lace petticoats, while the men, all in white with gay handkerchiefs, dance opposite them with their hands behind their backs. Only women, from Tehuantepec or Juchitán, dance the slow and stately Zandunga, costumes gorgeously embroidered on velvet blouse, full skirts with white pleated and starched lace ruffles and huipil.

refreshments and offerings are sold. ■ *0900-1400 Monday-Sunday, US$0.30 donation requested.* There are elaborate altars at the church of **San Felipe Neri** (Av Independencia y García). There is an Indian version in paint of the Conquistadores arrival in Oaxaca and of an anti-Catholic uprising in 1700 at **San Juan de Dios** (20 de Noviembre y Aldama). On the ceiling are paintings of the life of Christ. This was the first church in Oaxaca, originally dedicated to Santa Catalina Mártir. The church of **San Agustín** (Armenta y López at Guerrero) has a fine façade, with bas-relief of St Augustine holding the City of God above adoring monks (apparently modelled on that of San Agustín in Mexico City, now the National Library).

Museums The **Museo Regional de Antropología e Historia** on M Alcalá, next to Santo Domingo has fine displays of pottery, glass, alabaster, jewellery and other treasures from Monte Albán, whose jewellery is copied with great skill in several workshops near Oaxaca. The **Instituto de Artes Gráficas de Oaxaca** (IAGO) is almost opposite the Museo Regional at Alcalá 507; it has interesting exhibition rooms, a good reference library and beautifully kept courtyards filled with flowers. ■ *Monday-Sunday 0900-2000, closed Tuesday, free, but donation appreciated.*

At Alcalá 202 is **Museo de Arte Contemporáneo**, good exhibition with library and café, *Amigos del Museo*, also free but donation appreciated. ■ *1030-2000 daily, except Tuesday US$1.50.* **Museo Rufino Tamayo**, Av Morelos 503, has an outstanding display of precolumbian artefacts dating from 1250 BC to AD 1100. ■ *1000-1400, 1600-1900, Sunday 1000-1500, closed Tuesday; entry US$1.50.* **Teatro Macedonio Alcalá**, 5 de Mayo with Independencia, beautiful theatre from Porfirio Díaz' time. The **Museo Casa de Juárez** at García Vigil 609, is where Juárez lived. The theatre and the house were closed for remodelling, ask at tourist office if they have reopened.

Market On Saturday Indians of the Zapotec and Mixtec groups come to the **Mercado de Abastos** near the 2nd class bus station on the outskirts of town, which starts before 0800; prices are rising because of the city's great popularity with tourists.

Excursions For good hikes, take local bus to San Felipe (north of the city); at the end of the line follow the dirt road to the left along the valley, cross the bridge and turn right (uphill) after the bridge, trails go into the mountains and to a waterfall (ask for La Cascada).

Sleeping
■ *on maps*
Price codes:
see inside front cover

L *Camino Real*, 5 de Mayo 300, T60611, beautifully converted convent, very elegant, good pool. **L** *Victoria*, colonial house turned into hotel, bedrooms with showers built round the garden, good value, swimming pool, TV (with 2 US satellite channels), discount for elderly couples who book directly, up to 30 percent, many tour groups, but out of town (around 15 minutes' walk) at Km 545 on Pan-American Highway (noisy), T52633, F52411.

AL *Hacienda La Noria*, Periférico con La Costa, T67555, F65347, motel-type, pool, good and convenient. Best Western also has **AL** *Hostal de la Noria*, Hidalgo 918, T147844, F163992, 2 blocks from Zócalo, new colonial style. **AL** *Misión de Los Angeles*, Calzada Porfirio Díaz 102, T51500, F51680, motel-style, 2 kilometres from centre, quiet and most attractive, with swimming pool. **AL** *Misión Oaxaca*, San Felipe del Agua, some way out, attractive. **A** *Calesa Real*, García Vigil 306, T65544, F67232, modern colonial but many small dark rooms, good but expensive, *Los Arcos* restaurant, parking, central, slow service. **A** *Gala*, Guerrero y Bustamante 103, southeast corner of Zócalo, also suites, cable TV, with a/c, very nice (no elevator).

B *Mesón del Rey*, Trujano 212, T60033, 1 block from Zócalo, clean, modern, fan, quiet except for street-facing rooms, good value, restaurant and travel agency, no credit cards. **B** *Monte Albán*, Alameda de León 1, T62777, friendly, colonial style, opposite Cathedral, regular folk dance performances are given here at 2030, US$3.50, photography permitted.

Oaxaca

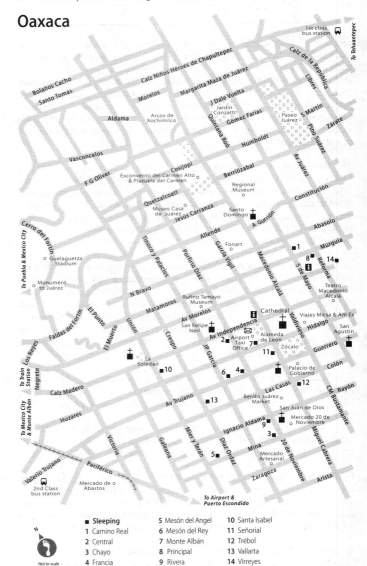

■ Sleeping		
1 Camino Real	5 Mesón del Angel	10 Santa Isabel
2 Central	6 Mesón del Rey	11 Señorial
3 Chayo	7 Monte Albán	12 Trébol
4 Francia	8 Principal	13 Vallarta
	9 Rivera	14 Virreyes

Not to scale

B *Santa Rosa*, Trujano y 20 de Noviembre, T46714, TV, phone, restaurant/bar, hot water, laundry, central, recommended. **B-C** *Mesón del Angel*, Mina, near Díaz Ordaz, clean, large rooms, good services, with pool, tours to ruins (see below), recommended. **B-C** *Villa de Campo*, Macedonia Alcalá 910, T59652, rooms and 4 suites, new, clean, quiet, tiled floors, safe, friendly, parking, pool, restaurant.

C *Antonio's*, Independencia 601, T67227, F63672, 1 block from Zócalo, colonial patio, with bath, hot water, spotless, good restaurant, closed in evening. **C** *Anturius*, Privada Emilio Carranza, new, clean, friendly, cafetería, recommended. **C** *California*, Chapultepec 822, T53628, near 1st class bus station, with bath, friendly, pleasant, restaurant. **C** *Del Arbol*, Calzada Madero 131, T64887, modern, comfortable, bath. **C** *Del Bosque*, exit road to Mitla, T52122, modern, restaurant. **C** *La Casa de la Tía*, 5 de Mayo 108, T68201, reductions for longer stays, has triples and a suite, restaurant and bar. **C** *Las Golondrinas*, Tinoco y Palacios 411, T68726, F42126, uphill from centre, 3 courtyards, cash only, pleasant. **C** *Plazuela*, La Bastida 115, pleasant, friendly. **C** *Posada de Chencho*, 4a Privada de la Noria 115, T40043, with shower, hot water, quiet, breakfast included, hospitable, enclosed parking, warmly recommended. **C** *Primavera*, Madero 438, T64508, opposite railway station, with bath, warm water, clean, friendly, good value, front rooms noisy. 2 blocks from the Zócalo at 5 de Mayo 208 is **C** *Principal*, T62535, colonial house, very clean, private shower with hot and cold water, rooms overlooking street are a bit noisy, English spoken, heavily booked. **C** *Rivera*, 20 de Noviembre 502, esq Aldama, T63804, and in 600 block). **C** *Las Rosas*, Trujano 112, old charm, nice patio, clean, excellent, quiet, friendly, good view from roof. **C** *Francia*, 20 de Noviembre 212, T64811, around enclosed courtyard, popular, some rooms scruffy without windows, friendly and helpful, recommended but noisy. **C** *Santa Clara*, Morelos 1004, T67144, clean, hot showers, friendly, quiet, no English spoken, very nice, recommended (same owner as *Reforma*, below). **C** *Señorial*, Portal de Flores 6 (on Zócalo), T63933, will store luggage, suites or rooms, with bath, swimming pool, on main square, good restaurant, no personal cheques or credit cards, cockroaches, recommended. **C-D** *Posada San Pablo*, M Fiallo 102, T64914, with bath, hot water, kitchen, large rooms in old convent, quiet, safe, clean, must stay more than 2 nights, highly recommended. **C-D** *Trébol*, Av Las Casas y Cabrera, T61256, F40342, pleasant, clean, with bath, breakfast available, friendly, good value, transport to Monte Albán, Mitla, Puerto Escondido. **C-D** *Veracruz*, Chapultepec 1020, T50511, next to ADO bus station, spotless, welcoming, comfortable, good if you arrive late at night by bus, expensive restaurant.

D *Aurora*, Bustamante 212, T64145, no private bath, 2 blocks from Zócalo. **D** *Casa Conzatti*, opening 1999, Gómez Farías 218, T38500, 50 rooms in colonial house. **D** *Chayo*, 20 de Noviembre 508, T64112, bath but no fan, water not always hot, clean, no singles, large courtyard used as car park (several others in same block). **D** *La Cabaña*, Mina 203, M Cabrera, with bath, cheaper without, safe, clean but noisy, hot water 0700-1000, 1700-2100. **D** *Vallarta*, Díaz Ordaz 309, T64967, clean, good value, enclosed parking, street rooms noisy, good set lunch. **D** *Yagul*, Mina 103 near market and Zócalo, family atmosphere, no hot water, use of kitchen on request. **D-E** *Villa Alta*, Cabrera 303, T62444, 4 blocks from Zócalo, friendly service, clean, stores luggage, recommended. Many cheap hotels in the block Mina, Zaragoza, Díaz Ordaz y García (not a safe area at night). **E** *del Valle*, Díaz Ordaz 105, with bath, hot water, friendly, a bit noisy, poor breakfast, next door to tourist bus to Monte Albán. **D-E** *Central*, 20 de Noviembre 104, T65971, private bathroom, hot water, good value but very noisy, fills up early. **D-E** *Chayo*, C 20 de Noviembre 508, clean, friendly, synthetic bed sheets. **D-E** *Virreyes*, Morelos 1001 y Reforma, problems with water, quiet, a bit tatty, rooms on street a bit noisy and unfriendly front desk, otherwise recommended. **E** *Arnel*, Aldama 404, T52856, homely, pleasant patio, good for meeting people, parking, not central, organize good tours, reservations not always honoured, not even after confirmation and arrival. **E** *Pasaje*, Mina 302, near market, with bathrooms, parakeets in patio, hot water but you have to ask, clean, provides good town plan. **E** *Posada Margarita*, La Bastida 115, with shower, clean, quiet, basic, near Santo Domingo. **E** *Reforma*, Av Reforma 102 between Independencia and Morelos, T60939, back rooms quieter, upper floors have good views, terrace on roof,friendly, but theft from rooms has been reported. At Díaz Ordaz 316 is **E-F** *Díaz Ordaz*, basic, water problems; and 2 doors along is **E** *Lupita*, large, pleasant rooms, upstairs rooms are bright and have mountain views, recommended. **E** *Posada El Palmar*, C JP García 504 and Aldama (2 blocks from the market), cheaper rooms without bathroom, convenient, friendly, family-run, hot water am, only 1 shower upstairs, electricity late pm only, safe motorcycle parking. **E** *Pombo*, Morelos 601 y 20 de Noviembre, near Zócalo, rooms vary so check first, hot shower, clothes washing not allowed, good value. **E** *Regional de Antequera*, Las Casas 901, 5 minutes' walk from 2nd class bus station, pleasant, clean, good value. **E** *San José*, Trujano 412, basic, dirty, cheap, lively, friendly. **E** *Posada Las Casas*, Las Casas y Díaz Ordáz, clean, recommended.

F *Hostal Santa Isabel*, Mier y Terán 103, T42865, (4 blocks from Zócalo), friendly, kitchen, luggage store, bicycle rental, recommended. **F** *Posada Halcún*, on 20 de Noviembre near *Hotel Rivera*, without bath, recommend. Many other cheap hotels in 400 block of Trujano.

There is also accommodation in private houses which rent rooms (*casas de huéspedes*). **E** per person *La Casa de María*, B Domínguez 205, Col Reforma, T/F40303, B&B, courtyard garden. **E** per person Mariana Arroyo runs a B&B from her home, Reforma 402, restaurant *La Olla*, also offers traditional Aztec massage from her cottage in San Felipe de Agua, north of town. **F** *Bengali*, C de Las Casas 508, more expensive with bath, basic, friendly, quiet, clean.

Villa María, Arteaga 410A, T65056, F42562, 5 blocks from the Zócalo, pleasant modern well furnished apts from US$180 per month with 24-hour security, maid service if required, recommended. On the road to Tehuantepec (Km 9.8): **C** *Hotel Posada Los Arcos*, Spanish-style motel at San Sebastián Totla. *Tourist Yu'u*, T60123, F60984, several tourist houses (**F** per person) in Oaxaca environs, each house has room with 4 beds, kitchen, bathroom.

Camping Oaxaca Trailer Park north of town off the road to Mitla at a sign marked 'Infonavit' (corner of C Pinos and C Violetas), US$4.50 for a tent, US$6 for a camper van, secure, clothes washing facilities not always available, try the delicious tamales across the road in the green restaurant; bus 'Carmen-Infonavit' from downtown.

Youth hostel *El Pasador*, Fiallo 305, T61287, **F** per person in dormitories, full of tourists, friendly, kitchen and laundry facilities, water supply problems, seldom any hot water, stores luggage, purified water, good place to meet travellers. New American/Danish owners promise many improvements. If full you can sling hammock on roof but same price. **Villa Deportiva Juvenil**, office at Belisario Domínguez 920, Col Reforma, bus from Las Casas y JP García in centre, 5 minutes, US$0.15, cold water, dormitories, clean, friendly, sheets and blankets provided.

Eating
● *on maps*

Most restaurants on the main square cater for tourists, and are therefore pricey (efficiency and standards depend a bit on how busy they are, but generally they are good): on the west side are *El Jardín*, a nice place to sit and watch all the activity (music, parades, aerobics, etc) in the Zócalo; upstairs is *Asador Vasco*, live Mexican music, good food and service; *La Primavera*, good value meals, good expresso coffee, slow; *La Casa de la Abuela*, upstairs on corner of Zócalo and Alameda de León. On the north side are *El Marqués*, very slow service, and *Pizza, Pasta y Más*, popular. On the east side, *Café El Portal*, Portal Benito Juárez, good food, quick service, *de Antequera*, *Café Amarantos* and *Mario's Terranova Restaurant*, excellent food, friendly and efficient service, pricey. *Flor de Oaxaca*, Armenta y López 311, pricey but excellent meals and delicious hot chocolate. *Los Arcos*, García Vigil 306 under *Calesa Real* hotel, good food in pretty setting and friendly service. *La Fuente de la Catedral*, corner of Gral García Vigil and Morelos, 1 block from cathedral, good for international and local specialities, steaks, good *tamales*, classical music, excellent buffet for US$7. *La Casita*, near main Post Office, Av Hidalgo 612, p1º, good food, reasonable prices, live music. *La Gran Torta*, on Independencia opposite Post Office, small, simple, family-run, cheap, good *pozole* and *tortas*. *Alameda*, JP García between Trujano and Hidalgo, excellent regional food, crowded Sunday, closes 1800. *Flami*, on Trujano near Zócalo, good food. *El Naranjo*, Trujano 203, in courtyard of 17th century house, traditional Oaxaca fare, not cheap. *Hostería Alcalá*, C Macedonio Alcalá 307, 5 minutes from Zócalo, not cheap but excellent food and quiet atmosphere, good service. At No 303 is *Plaza Garibaldi* and at No 706B *María Bonita*, typical

Oaxaca food. *La Quebrada*, Armenta y López, excellent fish, open only to 1800. *Guitarra, Pan Y Vino*, Morelos 511, regional food, music *soirées*. *Quince Letras*, Abasolo opposite *Hotel Santo Tomás*, excellent food, friendly service. *Santa Fe*, 103 Cinco de Mayo St, open 0800-2300, good, not cheap. *Santa Clara*, beside *Hotel Reforma*, good breakfast, set meal.

Vegetarian *Café Fuente y Señor de Salud*, Juárez just north of Morelos, pleasant, reasonable food. *Arco*, dearer, opposite ADO bus station, Niños Héroes de Chapultepec, loud music. *Manantial Vegetariano*, Tinoco y Palacios 303, excellent cheap meals, buffet US$4, pleasant patio, recommended. *Girasoles*, 20 de Noviembre 102, small but good food, recommended. *Flor de Loto*, Morelos 509, good value, clean, vegetarian and Mexican.

El Sagrario, 120 Valdivieso, T/F40303, live music, no cover charge, open 0800-0200, recommended. *Alfredo's Pizzería*, Alcalá, about 4 blocks north of the Zócalo, expensive wine by the glass. *Pizza Rústica Angelo y Domenico*, Allende y Alcalá, opposite Santo Domingo, very good, reasonable prices, recommended. *El Sol y la Luna*, on N Bravo, good although not cheap, live music some nights, open evenings only. *Las Chalotes*, Fiallo 116, French food, friendly service, expensive. The best Oaxacan food is found in the *comedores familiares* such as *Clemente, Los Almendros, La Juchita*, but they are way out of town and could be difficult to get to, or in *comedores populares* in the market. *El Bicho Pobre II*, Calzada de la República, lunch only, very popular, highly recommended. *La Verde Antequera*, Matamoros 3 blocks north of Zócalo, good daily lunch specials, best *comida corrida* in town for US$1. *Los Olmos*, Morelos 403, regional specialities, popular, friendly. *El Mesón*, buffets 0800-1830, good at US$2.50, breakfast, *comida corrida* 1200-1630 poor value at US$2, good tacos, clean, quick service, on Hidalgo at northeast corner of Zócalo. Almost opposite is *La Piñata*, good chicken in *mole* lunches. *El Laurel*, N Bravo 210, tasty home-style cooking, try the *mole*, open to 1800 Tuesday-Thursday, and to 2200 on Friday and Saturday; also close to Zócalo. *Bamby*, García Vigil 205, cheaper beer than elsewhere, good breakfast. *Pan Bamby*, García Vigil y Morelos, excellent bakery, recommended. *El Paisaje*, 20 de Noviembre, good, cheap chicken dishes. *Arte y Tradición*, García Vigil 406, craft centre with courtyard café, excellent service and food, open Monday-Saturday 1100-2200. *Los Canarios*, 20 de Noviembre, near *Hotel Chayo*, good *comida corrida*. *María Cristina's* in Mercado 20 de Noviembre, excellent *caldos* and *comidas*. The bar *El Favorito*, on 20 de Noviembre, a couple of blocks south of the Zócalo, is supposedly the original that inspired Malcolm Laury's bar in *Under the Volcano*. *Café Pitapé*, García Vigil 403 y N Bravo, friendly, good value. *Fiesta*, Las Casas 303, good for breakfast or *comida corrida*. *El Shaddai*, Av Hidalgo 121 y Galeano, family-run, good and cheap. *Gala*, Bustamante, just off Zócalo, opens 0730 for good breakfast, not cheap. *Trece Cielos*, Matamoros 101, good, cheap daily *menú*. *French Pastry Shop*, Trujano, 1 block west of Zócalo, good coffee, pastries, desserts. *Cafetería Alex*, Díaz Ordaz y Trujano, good *comida corrida*, coffee and breakfasts, delicious pancakes with fruit, good value, recommended. *Café y Arte Geono*, Alcalá 412, nice garden, good coffee and cakes. *Café Plaza*, 5 de Mayo near Santo Domingo, courtyard, good coffee. *TLC*, corner of Aldama y García, excellent tacos, tortas and juices in a calm patio setting. *Tito's*, Garcia Vigil No 116, good food at very reasonable prices. *Tartamiel*, Valerio Trujano, ½ block east of Zócalo, good bakery and cake shop. As is *La Luna*, Independencia 1105, 5 blocks east of cathedral. Several good places for cheap *menú del dia* on Porfirio Díaz, such as *Guidos*, popular, with cheap pasta and coffee, good restaurant opposite 1st class bus station, good value, one of the only sit-down places among taco stands. Good *dulcería* (sweet shop) in the 2nd class bus station. On C Mina y 20 de Noviembre, opposite the market are several mills where they grind cacao beans, almond, sugar and cinnamon into a paste for making delicious hot chocolate, eg *Mayordomo*, 20 de Noviembre y Mina, and *Guelaguetza*, next to *Hotel Galaxia*. Also at Mina y 20 de Noviembre is *La Casa de Dulce* sweet shop. In the Mercado 20 de Noviembre there are *comedores* and lots of stalls selling breads and chocolate. A local bread called *pan de yema*, is made, with egg-yolk, at the Mercado de Abastos (the Hermanas Jiménez bakery is most recommended). In the Oaxaca area you can find *chapulinas*, grasshoppers roasted with garlic, lemon and lots of salt, often sold on trains.

Mexico

Mexico

Entertainment   Folk dancing at the *Hotel Señorial* most nights of the week, advance booking recommended. *Eclipse* nightclub on P Diaz, free on Thursday. *Snob*, Niños Héroes Chapultepec, free Wednesday. Live salsa at *Rojo Caliente* on P Diaz. *Casa de Mezcal*, in front of the market, popular drinking hole.

     Cinemas *Ariel 2000*, Juárez y Berriózabal, subtitled films for US$2, half price Monday. *Cine Versalles*, Av Melchor Ocampo, north of Hidalgo (3 blocks east, ½ block north of Zócalo). *Cine Oaxaca*, Morelos near Alcalá; another cinema on Trujano, 1 block west of Zócalo.

Festivals   *Los Lunes del Cerro*, on the first two Mondays after 16 **July**. The first is the more spontaneous, when Indian groups come to a hill outside the city to present the seven regional dances of the State in a great festival, also known as La Guelaguetza. Main performance 1000-1300. Upper seats (rings C and D) free, arrive by 0700, ring B US$46, ring A US$62, be there one and a half hours in advance to get a good seat, tickets from Tourist Office. After each dance the dancers exchange presents and throw gifts to the audience in ring A. Hotels get booked early for the Guelaguetza and for the Day of the Dead, as does transport to Oaxaca on the days beforehand. *El Señor del Rayo*, a 9-day event in the third week of **October**, including excellent fireworks. **2 November**, the Day of the Dead, is a mixture of festivity and solemn commemoration, best appreciated at the Panteón General; the decoration of family altars is carried to competitive extremes (competition in C 5 de Mayo between Santo Domingo and the Zócalo on 1 November); traditional wares and foods, representing skulls, skeletons, coffins etc are sold in the market. Also celebrated more traditionally, in the outlying villages, especially in the cemetery of Acotlán. Ask before photographing. **8 to 18 December** with fine processions centred around the Church of Soledad and throughout the city, and 23 (Rábanos) with huge radishes carved in grotesque shapes sold for fake money; *buñuelos* are sold and eaten in the streets on this night, and the dishes ceremonially smashed after serving. **Night of 24 December**, a parade of floats (best seen from balcony of *Merendero El Tule* on the Zócalo; go for supper and get a window table). *Posadas* in San Felipe (5 kilometres north) and at Xoxo, to the south, the week before Christmas. Bands play in the Zócalo every evening except Saturday, and there are regional folk dances twice a week.

Shopping   *Aripo*, on García Vigil 809, T69211, government run, cheaper and better than most, service good, with very good small market nearby on junction of García Vigil and Jesus Carranza, for beautiful coloured belts and clothes. Superior craft shops at *Arte y Tradición*, García Vigil 406, good prices. *Sedetur* (see under **Tourist offices**), now run a shop selling crafts and all profits go to the artisans, good prices, recommended. *Casa Breno*, near Santo Domingo church, has unusual textiles and spindles for sale, happy to show visitors around the looms. *Fonart*, north Bravo 116, wide range of Mexican crafts, excellent quality, but pricey. *Lo Mexicano*, García Vigil, at end furthest from centre, excellent selection of high quality crafts at reasonable prices, run by young Frenchman. *Pepe*, Av Hidalgo, for jewellery, cheap local crafts. *Yalalag*, Alcalá 104, has good selection of jewellery, rugs and pottery, somewhat overpriced. *El Palacio de Gemas*, next door, is recommended for gemstones, good selection at reasonable prices, cheapest and largest selection of pottery plus a variety of fabrics and sandals at *Productos Típicos de Oaxaca*, Av Dr B Domínguez 602; city bus near ADO depot goes there. *Casa Aragón*, JP García 503, famous for knives and *machetes*; a large **Mercado Artesanal** also at JP García y Zaragoza. Fine cream and purple-black pottery (Zapotec and Mixtec designs) available at *Alfarería Jiménez*, Zaragoza 402. Other potteries at Las Casas 614, makers of the Oaxacan daisy design, and Trujano 508, bold flower designs. The nearby village of Atzompa (northwest of the city, buses from 2nd class terminal) is worth a visit for its interesting ceramics; local potters are very friendly. There are several Mezcal factories on the Mitla road which show the process of making Mezcal and sell it in black pottery bottles.

There are endless shopping temptations such as green and black pottery, baskets and bags made from cane and rushes, embroidered shirts, skirts, and blankets; Saturday is the best day for buying woollen sarapes cheaply. Unfortunately some of the woven products are of a different quality from the traditional product – more garish dyes and synthetic yarns are replacing some of the originals; but you can still find these if you shop around.

Bookshops *Librería Universitaria*, Guerrero 104, buys and sells books including English and a few German books. *Códice*, Alcalá 403; *Proveedora*, Independencia y Reforma, large, cheaper.

Hairdressers *Salón de Belleza Londres*, Morelos y Reforma, shampoo and set US$9.25, recommended.

Markets The *Mercado Juárez*, just southwest of the Zócalo in the block bounded by 20 de Noviembre, Las Casas, Cabrera and Aldama, sells fruit, vegetables, meat, cheeses, household goods, flowers, hats and some handicrafts (good leather bags are sold in and around this market). Immediately south of Mercado Juárez is *Mercado 20 de Noviembre*, for baked goods, with lots of good *comedores*. Look for the sautéd chilli insects sold on the streets. The *Mercado de Abastos* (referred to also as the Tianguis), open daily, which sells just about everything including baskets and pottery, is close to the 2nd class bus station. There is a large and interesting straw section here. Gilberto Segura T, 2 Galería de Artesanías, puesto 140, Mercado de Abastos, makes hammocks to your own design and specification, price depends on size, about US$20 for a single. Sr Leonardo Ruíz of Teotitlán del Valle, has an excellent carpet stall here. Market stallholders drive very hard bargains and often claim 'no change'; it may be possible to barter rather than bargain. Those disappointed with it should go to the Sunday market at *Tlacolula*.

Specialities Black earthenware, tooled leather, blankets, ponchos, shawls, embroidered blouses, the drink *mescal*. The best *mescal* in the region is El Minero. *Mescal* sours are good at the bar of *Misión Los Angeles*. The poor man's drink is *pulque*. Local *sarapes* are more varied and cheaper than in Mexico City.

Transport

Local Bus: local town minibuses, mostly US$0.30. To the bus station, buses marked 'VW' go from Av Juárez. To airport US$1.45. **Car hire**: phone ahead to book, a week before if possible. **Car park**: safe parking at *Estacionamiento La Brisa*, Av Zaragoza y Cabrera, US$3.50 per night, closed Sunday.

Air The Xoxocotlan (OAX) airport is about 9 kilometres south, direction Ocotepec. The airport taxis (*colectivos*) cost US$3 per person. Book at Transportaciones Aeropuerto Oaxaca on Alameda de León No 1-6, opposite the Cathedral in the Zócalo (T64350) for collection at your hotel to be taken to airport, office open Monday-Saturday 0900-1400, 1700-2000. From Mexico City several flights daily in less than an hour. Direct flights also from Cancún, Huatulco, Mérida, Palenque, Puerto Escondido, Tijuana, Tuxtla Gutiérrez and Villahermosa. International destinations include Havana and Los Angeles. Most domestic flights are in small, modern planes, spectacular. Be very careful when booking flights to Puerto Escondido on a small airline, they tend to be very erratic.

Trains Station on Calzada Madero at junction with Periférico, 15 minutes' walk from Zócalo. To Puebla daily 0720, arrives 1840, returns 0650 arriving 1810.

Buses 1st class terminal is northeast of Zócalo on Calzada de Niños Héroes (no luggage office, taxi from centre US$1.40). Note that many 2nd class buses leave from here too, especially towards the Guatemalan border; 2nd class, Autobuses Unidos (AU), is west of Zócalo on Calz Trujano (referred to as 'Central'), has left-luggage office, open until 2100. 1st class terminal is the only one for Villahermosa and the Yucatán. ADO and Cristóbal Colón have a ticket sales office in the centre at 20 de Noviembre 204-A, open Monday-Saturday 0900-1400, 1800-1900. Beware of double-booking and short-changing, especially when obtaining tickets from drivers if you have not booked in advance; beware also of thieves at both bus terminals, but especially on arrival of *plus* services. Cristóbal Colón to **Mexico City**, 6 hours, about 8 a day, mostly evenings; 2nd class by Fletes y Pasajes, comfortable, frequent departures with UNO; about 10 a day with ADO, 6 hours, robberies have been reported on these buses. Fares to the capital: 2nd class US$10.50, 1st class US$12.50, US$20 *plus*. Buses now travel via the new highway, through spectacular scenery. If buses to the capital are fully booked travel via Puebla. It is difficult to get tickets for buses from the capital to Oaxaca on Friday pm without booking in advance (you can book in advance and pay on day of travel); bus companies require 2 hours checking-in time in Mexico City on this route. 1st class to **Cuautla**, US$14.80 with ADO, 7 hours (change there for Cuernavaca and Taxco); **Puebla** (1st class, 4 hours, US$12, several companies, 2nd class, daytime bus 0730, local people, few tourists, cheap, superb scenery); to **Tuxtepec**, 1st class, 6 hours, US$16.50 with ADO, from same terminal,

Cuenca goes by a more direct, but still beautiful route 1st class US$8.25 (police have reported robberies on this route). To **Veracruz**, ADO, 2 a day from 1st class bus station, via Huajuapan, Tehuacán and Orizaba, 11 hours, US$21.50 *plus*, book early, or change as above, allow 16 hours. Cristóbal Colón to **Villahermosa**, US$22.70, book well ahead, 14 hours, daily at 1700 and 2100.

San Cristóbal de Las Casas, US$20, at 1930, 2000 and 2015, 12 hours, the 1st 2 hours are on very windy roads, don't eat just before travelling, book 1-2 days in advance with C Colón, there are daytime buses if you go 2nd class. **Tapachula**, 11 hours, US$24, 1st class, Cristóbal Cólon, also Fipsa, from 1st and 2nd class terminals. Book well in advance as buses often come almost full from Mexico City. To **Tuxtla Gutiérrez**, C Colón or ADO, 4 a day, 10 hours, *especial* at 2230, US$16, 2nd class US$10, daytime buses if you go 2nd class. To **Tehuantepec**, scenic, 5 a day, 2nd class US$6.50, Cristóbal Colón US$8, 7½ hours. To **Ciudad Cuauhtémoc**, US$33, 12 hours. To **Arriaga** US$7, 6 hours, 5 a day. To **Puerto Escondido**, 0900, 2130 1st class, US$20.25, gruelling 13 hours journey (can be longer) 3 a day, partly along dirt roads, interesting scenery. Night bus 5 hours faster. Probably better to go Oaxaca-**Pochutla** on new road with spectacular scenery, especially the cloud forest and 2 hours descent into Pochutla, 6½-10 hours, US$6 2nd class, US$8 1st-class, Estrella del Valle buses at 0800 and 2200, then change for Puerto Angel/Puerto Escondido; 1st class Cristóbal Colón bus 0930, 1030, US$13, 9 hours to Pochutla via Salina Cruz and Huatulco, much further but nice scenery. Oaxaca-Pacífico has good 2nd class buses (5 a day to Pochutla, 1 a day to Puerto Angel, US$5, at 1730 arrives in middle of the night). 1st class buses from 2nd class terminal to Pochutla via Salina Cruz and Huatulco, 7 hours, several daily. Buses to most local villages go from this terminal, too.

Directory **Airline offices** *Líneas Aéreas Oaxaqueñas* office at Av Hidalgo 503, T65362, airport 61280. There is a *Mexicana* office at Fiallo 102 y Av Independencia, T68414 (airport T62337). *AeroMéxico*, Av Hidalgo 513 Centro, T67101 (airport T64055). *Aviacsa*, agency on Zócalo, T31809/51500/45304 (airport T62332). *Aero Caribe*, at *Hotel Misión de los Angeles*, T56373 (airport T62247).

Banks Get to banks before they open, long queues form. *Bancomer*, on García Vigil, 1 block from Zócalo, exchanges TCs in own Casa de Cambio, 0900-1600, and has cash dispenser for Visa card. *Banpais* at corner of Zócalo has a better service. For Thomas Cook cheques, *Banco Internacional*. *Amex* office *Viajes Micsa*, at Valdivieso 2, T62700, just off Zócalo, very helpful, but lots of paperwork (no travel reservations). *Interdisa*, Valdivieso near Zócalo, Mon-Sat 0800-2000, Sun 0900-1700, cash, TCs, sells quetzales and exchanges many Western currencies, also changes TCs into dollars cash. *Comermer*, on Periférico near Abastos Market, best rates. *Casa de Cambio*, Abasolo 105, 0800-2000 changes TCs. *Casa de Cambio* at Armenta y López, near corner with Hidalgo, 0800-2000 Mon-Sat, shorter hrs on Sun. No problem to change TCs at weekends, many *casas de cambio* around the Zócalo.

Communications DHL, Amado Nervo 104D, esq Héroes de Chapal Fepec, open Mon-Fri 0900-1800, Sat 0900-1400, no credit card payments. **Post Office**: on Alameda de León, Independencia y 20 de Noviembre. **Telephone**: shop around. Self-service, long-distance phone at pharmacies at 20 de Noviembre y Hidalgo, Porfirio Díaz y Av Morelos, and at C Rayón 504. Caseta Larga Distancia Mesón del Rey, Trujano 212, open till 2200, F61434, night rate 2000-2200 and Sun till 1700; Computel which is almost next door, for long distance calls and fax, evening discounts, Trujano, 2 blocks west of Zócalo. Phone service to USA, collect or with credit card, in lobby of *Hotel Marqués del Valle*. **Internet**: *Makedonia*, Trujano 22, US$1.50 to send and US$1 to receive; *Multitel*, Alcalá 100, internet, fax, long distance phone; *Multimedia y Sistemas*, Morelos 600 altos, T/F68292, terran@antequera.com.

Embassies & consulates US Consular Agency, Alcalá 201, suite 204, T43054. *Canadian Honorary Consul*, Dr Liceaga 119-8, T33777. Combined *Honorary British* and *German* consul, address available at Federal Tourist Office.

Hospitals & medical services Pharmacy: 20 de Noviembre y Ignacio Aldama, open till 2300. Dentist: *Dra Marta Fernández del Campo*, Armenta y López 215, English-speaking, very friendly, recommended. **Doctor:** *Dr Víctor Tenorio*, Clínica de Carmen, Abasolo 215, T62612, close to centre (very good English). *Dr Marco Antonio Callejo* (English-speaking), Belisario Domínguez 115, T53492, surgery 0900-1300, 1700-2000.

Language schools There are many in the city; the following have been recently recommended: *Vinigulaza*, Abasolo 209, T/F46426, vinigulaza@infosel.net.mx, small groups, good place to talk with Mexican students, US$3.50 per hour. *Instituto Johann Goethe*, JP García 502, T/F43516, wide variety of courses, eg 4 weeks, 2 hrs a day US$160. *Instituto de Comunicación y Cultura*, M Alcalá 307-12, p2º, T63443, US$75 per week; accommodation can be arranged. *Centro de Idiomas*, Universidad Autónoma Benito Juárez, C de Burgoa, 5 blocks south of Zócalo, weekly or monthly classes (US$200 per month), or private tuition, very professional and good value for money, recommended. *Becari*, M Bravo 210, Plaza San Cristóbal, T/F46076, becari@antequera.com, or www.mexonline.com /becari.htm, 4 blocks north of Zocalo, US$75 per 15-hr week, fully-qualified teachers, courses including culture, history, literature and politics, with workshops on dancing, cooking or art, flexible programmes, recommended. See also **Learning Spanish** in **Essentials**. In addition to Spanish classes, local crafts (including cooking, weaving and pottery) are taught at the *Instituto Cultural Oaxaca*, Av Juárez 909, T53404/51323, F53728, inscuoax@antequera.com, http://antequera.com/inscuoax, more time spent on cultural classes than learning Spanish.

Laundry *ELA, Super Lavandería Automática*, Antonio Roldán 114, Col Olímpica, washes and irons. *Lavandería Azteca*, on Hidalgo between Díaz Ordaz y J P García, 0800-2000, 1000-1400 on Sun, quick service, delivers to nearby hotels, 1½ kg US$3.30. Another laundry at Hidalgo y J P García, 3½ kg, US$3.

Libraries English lending library with very good English books, a few French and Spanish, also English newspapers (*The News* from Mexico City), used books and magazines for sale, at Macedonio Alcalá 305, looks like an apartment block on the pedestrian street, a few blocks north of Zócalo (open Mon-Fri, 1000-1300, 1600-1900, Sat 1000-1300), US$13 per year plus US$13 returnable deposit. *The News* is also sold round the Zócalo by newsboys, from mid-morning, or from street vendor at Las Casas y 20 de Noviembre. The local library at Alcalá 200 (no sign) has a lovely courtyard and a reading room with Mexican newspapers and magazines. Next door is the library of the Museo de Arte Contemporáneo.

Public baths *Baños Reforma*, C Reforma 407, open 0700-1800, US$4 for steam-bath for 2, sauna for 1, US$3. *Baños San Rafael*, Tinoco y Palacios 514, Monday-Saturday 0600-1800, Sunday 0600-1530, hot water.

Tour companies & travel agents There are many in town. Most run the same tours, eg daily to Monte Albán; El Tule, Mitla and, sometimes, another village on this route; city tour; Fri to Coyotepec, Jalietza and Octotlan; Thur to Cuilapan and Zaachila; Sun to Tlacolula, Mitla and El Tule. Basically, the tours tie in with local markets. Try *Turismo El Convento de Oaxaca*, 5 de Mayo300, T61806, F40372, convento@antequera.com. Judith Reyes at *Arte y Tradición*, García Vigil 406, runs good tours to outlying villages in her VW van, US$8 per hour.

Tourist offices 5 de Mayo y Av Morelos, open 0900-2000 every day, excellent free map of city and surroundings. Sedetur tourist office at Independencia y García Vigil (Mon-Fri 0830-2000, Sat-Sun 0900-1500), has maps, posters, postcards, information; ask here about the *Tourist Yu'u* programme (T60123, F60984) in local communities. Tourist Police on Zócalo near cathedral, friendly and helpful. Instituto Nacional de Estadística, Geografía e Informática, Calz Porfirio Díaz 241A, for maps. There is a monthly tourist newspaper called *Oaxaca*, in Spanish, English and French; also *Oaxaca Times* in English.

Useful addresses Immigration: Periférico 2724, p2º, at Rayón, open Mon-Fri 0900-1400. **Luggage storage:** Servicio Turístico de Guarda Equipaje y Paquetería, Av Tinoco y Palacios 312, Centro, T40432, open 24 hrs.

Archaeological excursions from Oaxaca
Monte Albán

Monte Albán about 10 kilometres (20 minutes drive) uphill from Oaxaca, to see the pyramids, walls, terraces, tombs, staircases and sculptures of the ancient capital of the Zapotec culture. The place is radiantly colourful during some sunsets, but permission is needed to stay that late (take a torch/flashlight).

To the right, before getting to the ruins, is Tomb 7, where a fabulous treasure trove was found in 1932 (take a torch); most items are in the Museo Regional in the convent of Santo Domingo and the entrance is closed off by a locked gate. Tomb 172 has been left exactly as it was found, with skeleton and urns still in place. Tomb 104 (closes at lunchtime) contains an interesting statue of the rain god, Tlaloc. The remarkable rectangular plaza, 300 by 200 metres, is rimmed by big ceremonial platforms: the Ball Court, and possibly a palace to the east, stairs rising to an unexcavated platform to the south, several platforms and temples to the west and one, known as Templo de los Danzantes but in reality, probably a hospital, with bas-reliefs, glyphs and calendar signs (probably 5th century BC). A wide stairway leads to a platform on the north side. Most of the ruins visible are early 10th century AD, when the city was abandoned and became a burial place. Informative literature is available at the site. Explanations are in English and Spanish. (Recommended literature is the Bloomgarden *Easy Guide* to Monte Albán or *Easy Guide* to Oaxaca covering the city and all the ruins in the valley, with maps. In major hotels or the bookshop at Guerrero 108, and all the ruins.) ■ *The ruins are open 0830-1700. Entrance to ruins US$2, free on Sunday and public holidays (and for Mexican students). A charge of US$4 is made to use video cameras; guides charge US$15. Most people go in the morning, so it may be easier to catch the afternoon bus. There is a museum at the entrance. There is a drinks and snack bar and a handicrafts shop.*

Oaxaca environs

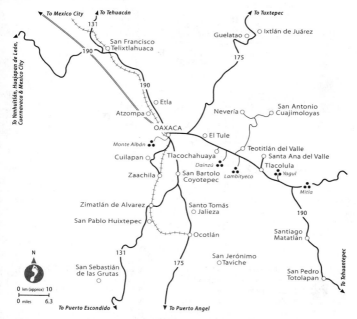

MEXICO

Transport **To Monte Albán**: Autobuses Turísticos depart from behind *Hotel Mesón del Angel*, Mina near Díaz Ordaz (bus tickets available from hotel lobby) hourly on the $\frac{1}{2}$-hour from 0830 to 1530 fare US$1.50 return, last bus back at 1730; 2 hours at the site, allowing not enough time to visit ruins before returning (you are permitted to come back on another tour on 1 ticket for an extra US$1 but you will not, of course, have a reserved seat for your return). Several buses from *Hotel Trébol*, 1 block south of Zócalo, US$1.30, 0930, 1030, returning 1330, 1400. Local buses also run from outside *Hotel Mesón del Angel*, which leaves you to walk or hitch the

Monte Albán

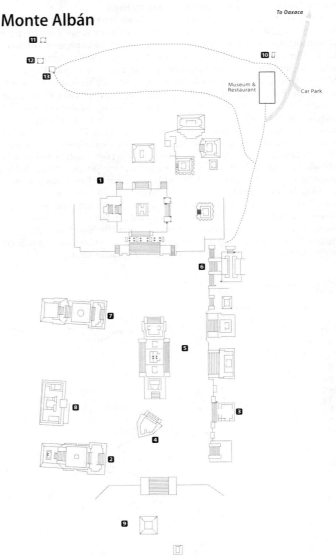

To Oaxaca

Museum & Restaurant

Car Park

1 North Platform and Sunken Patio	**4** Building I	**8** Building of the Dancers	**11** Tomb 172
2 South Platform	**5** Chapel	**9** Complex M	**12** Tomb 103
3 Palace	**6** Ball Court	**10** Tomb 7	**13** Tomb 104
	7 Complex IV		

N

Not to scale

remaining 3 kilometres (uphill) to the site. Taxis charge about US$5 per hour to go to any site. To give yourself enough time (3 hours is adequate at the site), you can walk 4 kilometres downhill from the ruins to Colonia Monte Albán and get a city bus back from there. Some prefer to walk up and take the bus back.

Route to Mitla

It is 42 kilometres from Oaxaca to Mitla, paved road (Route 190), but with many potholes and occasional flooding. On the way you pass **El Tule** (12 kilometres from Oaxaca) which has what is reputed the world's largest tree, a savino (*Taxodium mucronatum*), estimated at 2,000 years old, 40 metres high, 42 metres round at base, weighing an estimated 550 tons, fed water by an elaborate pipe system, in churchyard, ■ *US$0.25 entry* (bus from Oaxaca, 2nd class bus station, every 30 minutes, US$0.25, buy ticket on bus, sit on the left to see the Tule tree; alternatively colectivos for surrounding villages leave from near the 2nd class bus station, bus El Tule-Mitla US$0.40). El Tule has a good market with good food on sale and *La Sonora* restaurant on eastern edge of town has quite tasty food.

Tlacochahuaya, 16th century church, vivid Indian murals, carpets and blouses sold in market nearby, admission US$0.45 to church, visit cloisters at back and see decorated organ upstairs. Bus from Oaxaca 2nd class terminal, US$0.30.

A paved road leads off Route 190 to **Teotitlán del Valle**, where Oaxaca *sarapes* and *tapetes* (rugs) are woven, which is now becoming rather touristy. If you knock at any door down the street, you will get them only a little cheaper than at the market, but there is greater variety. The best prices are to be had at the stores along the road as you come into town, but may be even cheaper in Oaxaca where competition is stronger. (Make sure whether you are getting all-wool or mixture and check the quality. A well-made rug will not ripple when unfolded on the floor.) Buses leave every one to one and a half hours from 0800 from 2nd class bus terminal (US$0.60); the 3rd class bus may provide all the contacts you need to buy all the weavings you want! *Juvenal Mendoza*, Buenavista 9, will make any design any size into a rug to order (daily at 1100). Recommended for rugs is Pedro Gutiérrez, Cuauhtémoc 29.

Just before the turning for Teotitlán, turn right at Km 23.5 for **Dainzu**, one kilometre off the road, an important ruin recently excavated. ■ *Open daily 1000-1700, US$1, Sunday free.* At the base of the most prominent structure (called Cluster A) are bas reliefs of ball players and priests, similar to the Monte Albán dancers. The nearby site of **Lambityeco** is also well worth visiting, to see several fine and well-preserved stucco heads. ■ *1000-1700, US$1, Sunday free.* 2nd class bus Oaxaca-Lambityeco $0.80, bus goes on to Dainzu and back to Oaxaca.

Tlacolula (**D** *Hotel Guish-Bac*, Zaragoza 3, T20080, clean), has a most interesting Sunday market (beware pickpockets) and the renowned Capilla del Santo Cristo in the church. The chapel is similar in style to Santo Domingo in Oaxaca, with intricate white and gold stucco, lots of mirrors, silver altar rails and sculptures of martyrs in gruesome detail. Two beheaded saints guard the door to the main nave (fiesta 9 October). There is a pleasant walled garden in front of the church. A band plays every evening in the plaza, take a sweater, cold wind most evenings, starts at 1930. The square is colonnaded. On the main street is a *casa de cambio*. Tlacolula can be reached by bus from Oaxaca, from the 2nd class bus station every 30 minutes, but every 15 minutes on Sunday, US$0.60. Taxis and *peseros* stop by the church, except on Sunday when they gather on a street behind the church; ask directions. Tlacolula's bus station is just off the main highway, several blocks from the centre.

Tlacolula
Colour map 3, grid C5

Quality weavings can be found at **Santa Ana del Valle** (three kilometres from Tlacolula). Sr Alberto Sánchez García, Sor Juana I de la Cruz No 1 sells excellent wool with natural dyes. Turn right just after the school and left at the T-junction at the top of hill. Sr Sánchez's home is several compounds along on the right with a faded blue metallic gate door. Good prices. The village is peaceful and friendly with a

Mexico

small museum. Ask any villager for the keyholder. Cheap guesthouse. There are two *fiestas*, each lasting three days. One takes place the 2nd week of August, the other at the end of January. Buses leave from Tlacolula every 30 minutes.

Yagul The ruins of **Yagul** (on the way to Mitla), are an outstandingly picturesque site where the ball courts and quarters of the priests are set in a landscape punctuated by candelabra cactus and agave. Yagul was a large Zapotec and Mixtec religious centre; the ball courts are perhaps the most perfect discovered to date; also fine tombs (take the path from behind the ruins, the last part is steep) and temples. There is a superb view from the hill behind the ruins. ■ *Entrance to ruins daily 0800-1700, US$1.40. Guided tours in English on Tuesday, US$10, from Oaxaca travel agencies. Fletes y Pasajes buses and taxis from Oaxaca (allow at least US$8.50 per hour). Ask to be put down at paved turn off to Yagul (5 minutes after Tlacolula terminal). You will have to walk 1 kilometre from the bus stop to the site (overpriced Restaurant El Centotl half way, open 1100-1900, stock up on water, none at site) and you can return the same way or walk 3 kilometres to Tlacolula to catch a bus (signposted). Bus to Mitla US$0.40, to El Tule US$0.20. Car park US$0.20.*

Mitla
Colour map 3, grid C5

From the main road a turn left leads four kilometres to Mitla (whose name means 'place of the dead') where there are ruins of four great palaces among minor ones. Some of the archaeology, outside the fenced-in site, can be seen within the present-day town.

Magnificent bas-reliefs, the sculptured designs in the Hall of Mosaics, the Hall of the Columns, and in the depths of a palace, La Columna de la Muerte (Column of Death), which people embrace and measure what they can't reach with their fingers to know how many years they have left to live (rather hard on long-armed people). The museum just west of the Zócalo in the village is interesting (US$2). There is a soberly decorated colonial church with three cupolas (no access from church to ruins, or vice versa). Beautiful traditional Indian clothes and other goods may be bought at the new permanent market behind the church, bargaining possible. On the cobbled road from the town to the church and ruins are many *artesanía* shops and others selling good *mescal*. Sellers of carved wooden animals and figures congregate near the site entrance. A car and bus park is located behind the church also. ■ *Entry US$1.40 (Sunday free, students with ID free, use of video US$4.50), open 0800-1700 daily, literature available on site.*

Sleeping and eating C *Hotel y Restaurante Mitla*, on town square, clean, local food. C *Hotel y Restaurante La Zapoteca*, before bridge on road to ruins, newer and better than *Mitla*, cheaper food, good. The University of the Americas has a small guest-house, and runs the small Frissell museum in the Zócalo at Mitla, with very good and clean restaurant, *La Sorpresa*, good, cheap food, in a patio. Restaurant opposite site, *Santa María*. *María Elena* restaurant 100 metres from site towards village, good *comida corriente*. The local technical college provides accommodation, showers and a bathroom; it is also possible to arrange rooms with families.

Transport Taxi costs US$10 each to Mitla for 4 sharing, with time to take photographs at Tule and Mitla and to buy souvenirs at ruins. Tours (1000 till 1300, rather rushed) to Tule, Mitla and Tlacolula from Oaxaca agencies, cost US$7.50, not including entry fees. Fletes y Pasajes bus from Oaxaca, 2nd class bus station, every 20 minutes to Mitla, 1 hour, US$1; the ruins are 10 minutes' walk across the village (from the bus stop on the main road, 2 blocks from the square). Minibuses from Oaxaca leave a shorter walk to the ruins than regular buses.

From Mitla take a bus to San Lorenzo (one hour, US$1). Three kilometres from there is the village of **Hierve El Agua**. There are also two second class buses a day to Hieve El Agua at 0700 and 1400, returning 0900 and 1600. A cliff over which water from pools flows has created a stalactite, which looks like a petrified waterfall. You can swim in the mineral pools. There is no water in the dry season. There is a village-run hotel, **E** *Tourist-Yu'u*, T951-60123, rooms for six people with kitchen, hot water, discounts for students, good restaurant, recommended. Also several excellent foodstalls (quesadillas etc) above the car park.

From Mitla the road is paved as far as Ayutla, but an unpaved single track runs from then on to Playa Vicente (four-wheel drive recommended). Beautiful mountain scenery and cloud forest. No accommodation between Ayutla and Playa Vicente.

Excursions south of Oaxaca

Saturday trips from Oaxaca to market at **San Antonio Ocotlán** on the road to Puerto Angel, with good prices for locally woven rugs and baskets, also excellent fruit and veg (stallholders prefer not to be photographed); buses leave every 30 minutes for Ocotlán (not to be confused with another village called San Antonio) from the microbus station southeast of the Mercado Artesanal on Armenta y López (30 minutes' journey, US$0.35). Outside the Mercado de Abastos a steady stream of colectivos leave for US$0.70. Stop in **San Bártolo Coyotepec** to see black pottery (Doña Rosa's, she's been dead for years but her name survives, is a target for tours, but other families are just as good) and don't try to bargain (also red and green ceramics in the village), and in **Santo Tomás Jalieza**, where cotton textiles are made.

Cuilapan

17 kilometres southwest of Oaxaca is Cuilapan, where there is a vast unfinished 16th century convent, now in ruins, with a famous nave and columns, and an 'open chapel', whose roof collapsed in an earthquake. "At the back of the unfinished chapel is a board on which the Zapotec and Mixtec calendars had been correlated. On the left side is the date 1555 in Arabic numerals; the two calendars differed by 13 years, Zapotec 1555, Mixtec 1568. The last Zapotec princess, Donaji, daughter of the last ruler Cosijoeza, married a Mixtec prince at Tilantengo and was buried at Cuilapan. On the grave is an inscription with their Christian names, Mariana Cortez and Diego Aguilar." (Helmut Zettl, Ebergassing.) Reached by bus from Oaxaca from 2nd class bus station, on C Bustamante, near de Arista (US$0.50), take bus to Zaachila (US$0.60) which leaves every 30 minutes, then walk to unexcavated ruins in valley. **Zaachila** is a poor town, but there are ruins, with two Mixtec tombs, with owls in stucco work in the outer chamber and carved human figures with skulls for heads inside. ■ *US$1.50*. No restrictions on flash photography. There is an Indian market on Thursday. 80 kilometres south on Route 131 is **San Sebastián** (about 10 kilometres off the road) where there are caves. ■ *Ask for a guide at the Agencia Municipal next to the church; guide obligatory, US$1.50.* Take bus 175 from Oaxaca, terminal at C Bustamante, US$0.25.

Excursions northeast of Oaxaca

To San Pablo de **Guelatao** (65 kilometres from Oaxaca), the birthplace of Benito Juárez. The town is located in the mountains and can be reached by bus (US$1.50, three hours) along a paved but tortuously winding road. There are a memorial and a museum to Juárez on the hillside within the village (entry, US$0.20), and a pleasant lake with a symbolic statue of a shepherd and his lambs. The area is beautiful although the town is rather neglected.

Isthmus of Tehuantepec

We are approaching a more traditional part of Mexico; Tehuantepec isthmus and the mountains of Chiapas beyond, a land inhabited by Indians less influenced than elsewhere by the Spanish conquest. Only about 210 kilometres separate the Atlantic and the Pacific at the hot, heavily-jungled Isthmus of Tehuantepec, where the land does not rise more than 250 metres. There are a railway (to be renewed) and a Trans-Isthmian Highway between Coatzacoalcos and Salina Cruz, the terminal cities on the two oceans. Winds are very strong on and near the isthmus, because of the intermingling of Pacific and Caribbean weather systems. Drivers of high-sided vehicles must take great care.

NB In southern Mexico the word 'Zócalo' is not often used for the main square of a town: 'Plaza (Mayor)' is much more common.

Route 190 heads southeast from Oaxaca towards the Golfo de Tehuantepec and the Pacific. At Km 116, in **San José de Gracia**, is the hotel and restaurant *El Mirador*, **D**, clean, very friendly, noisy from passing trucks, overlooking a beautiful valley, parking in front. At Km 134 in the village of **El Camarón** is **E** *Hotel Santa Elena*, new, clean, friendly, fan and TV. There are some basic restaurants in the village.

Tehuantepec

Km 804
Population: 45,000
Altitude: 150m
Colour map 3, grid C6

Santo Domingo Tehuantepec is 257 kilometres from Oaxaca. A colourful place, it is on the bend of a river around which most of its activities take place and which makes it very humid. Tehuantepec is probably a better place to break the journey to Tapachula than Salina Cruz, but some find it a smelly, rundown city, others find it friendly nonetheless. Architecturally the town is dominated by the 16th Century Exconvento Rey Cosijopi. The plaza has arcades down one side, a market on the other, and many stands selling *agua fresca*, an iced fruit drink. At dusk the trees of the square are filled with black birds roosting and making an incredible noise. There is more noise from the music played through loud speakers at high volume. Houses are low, in white or pastel shades. The Indians are mostly Zapotecs whose social organization was once matriarchal: the women are high-pressure saleswomen, with some Spanish blood; their hair is sometimes still braided and brightly ribboned and at times they wear embroidered costumes. The men for the most part work in the fields, or as potters or weavers, or at the nearby oil refinery. Hammocks made in this area are of the best quality.

Tehuantepec

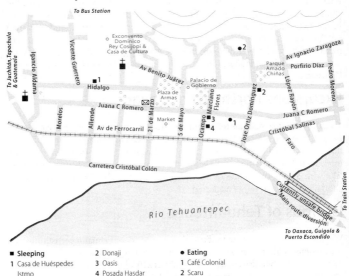

■ Sleeping	2 Donaji	● Eating
1 Casa de Huéspedes Istmo	3 Oasis	1 Café Colonial
	4 Posada Hasdar	2 Scaru

To neighbouring villages for *fiestas*. Near the town are the ruins of **Guingola**, 'the Mexican Machu Picchu', so called because of its lonely location on a mountain. It has walls up to three metres high, running, it is said, for 40 kilometres; there are the remains of two pyramids and a ball court. This last fortress of the Zapotecs was never conquered; Alvarado and his forces marched past it in 1522. Take the 0500 bus Tehuantepec towards Oaxaca and alight at Km 141, at the bridge (eight kilometres from Tehuantepec). Take the turn at the signpost 'Ruinas Guingola 7 kilometres'. Walk five kilometres then turn left, uphill, to the car park. From here it is one and a half hours to the ruins. Try to return before 0900 because it gets very hot; take plenty of water. Alternatively, take a taxi to the car park and ask the driver to return for you three hours later, or drive there. (With thanks to Helmut Zettl of Ebergassing.)

Excursions
Guingola, 'the Mexican Machu Picchu'

D *Donaji*, Juárez 10, a/c, near market, clean, friendly, recommended. **D** *Oasis*, on Av Juana C Romero, 1 block from plaza, good atmosphere, with bath and a/c, simple, safe parking, owner Julín Contreras is head of local Casa de Cultura and is looking for volunteers to help restore convent, good information on local history and traditions. **E** *Casa de Huéspedes Istmo*, Hidalgo 31, 1½ blocks before the main plaza, quiet, basic, with lovely patio. **E** *Posada de Hasdar*, next to *Oasis*, basic.

Sleeping
Mostly overpriced and basic.

Camping *Santa Teresa* Trailer Park, east side of town, 8 kilometres off Route 190 (take side road at *Hotel Calli* and follow signs), US$6.50 for car and 2 people, cold showers, restrooms, drinking water, restaurant, lovely mango grove, very friendly owner.

Cheap food on top floor of market. *Colonial*, good *comida corrida*. *Mariscos Silvia*, ½ block off route 190 on main road into town, excellent shrimp, moderate. *Colonial*, around corner from *Hotel Donaji*, good food, clean, friendly. *Scaru*, on Leona Vicario, good food, reasonable, nice courtyard. *Jugos Hawaii*, Av Juárez, on plaza, freshly squeezed juices, snacks, ice-cream, friendly. The local *quesadillas* made of maize and cheese are delicious; sold at bus stops. Tehuantepec is noted for its mangoes.

Eating

The town is divided into 15 wards, and each holds a *fiesta*, the main one at the end of **Holy Week**, when the women wear their finest costumes and jewellery. A large fair takes place the week leading up to Easter. There is another splendid *fiesta* in honour of St John the Baptist on **22-25 June**. **January** and **February** are good months for the ward *fiestas*.

Festivals

Road The highway between Tehuantepec and Tapachula is being made into a dual carriageway; the construction work may cause delays to road transport.

Transport

Buses 3-wheeled rickshaws take locals around town, you have to stand and hold on to the railing. There are several bus companies at north end of town, taxi to Zócalo US$1, or 15 minutes' walk. 1 bus a day to **San Cristóbal** at 1230, it may be full, standing is not allowed but the driver may accept a present and let you on (7½ hours, US$14.80). To **Coatzacoalcos** at 0730, 9-10 hours, US$8 2nd class. Bus to **Arriaga** at 0600, 0800, 1800 to connect to Tonalá. To **Tuxtla Gutiérrez**, 2130, 2200, 0030, 0400, 4½ hours, 2nd class at 0130, and Tapachula, US$14.80 (Cristóbal Colón). Bus to **Tonalá** (Cristóbal Colón) at 0030 and 0130. To **Oaxaca**, US$6.50, 5 hours, with Istmo, US$8 Cristóbal Colón, US$7 2nd class; to **Salina Cruz**, US$0.25 with Istmeños; to **Pochutla**, and **Puerto Escondido**, with Cristóbal Colón at 1445, US$9; to **Villahermosa**, Cristóbal Colón 1st class, US$14, 8 hours, 2nd class US$10.50. (**NB** Some buses from Salina Cruz do not stop at Tehuantepec.)

21 kilometres from Tehuantepec, a booming and evil-smelling port with a naval base, extensive oil-storage installations and an oil refinery. Bathing is dangerous because of the heavy swell from Pacific breakers and also sharks. Beware of overcharging in the marketplace. Car drivers should not park close to the beach in windy weather unless they want their vehicle sandblasted.

Salina Cruz
Population: 43,000
Colour map 3, grid C6

Sleeping C *Costa Real*, Progreso, near Manuel A Camacho, with parking. *Fuente*, bath, basic. *Río*, reasonable, near Cristóbal Colón bus station. **E** *Magda*, on 5 de Mayo, ½ block from Zócalo. *Parador*, on road to Juchitán, a/c, pool, recommended. **Eating** *Costa del Pacífico*, hires shower cabin, stores luggage. *El Lugar*, corner of Acapulco y 5 de Mayo on 1st floor.

Transport Buses: Two daily buses from Salina Cruz to **San Cristóbal** come from Oaxaca and are very often full (2nd class, US$14); take instead a 2nd class bus to **Juchitán**, then to Arriaga and from there to Tuxtla and San Cristóbal; a long route. To **Coatzacoalcos**, US$12.15, 6 hours. Salina Cruz-**Pochutla**, US$5, 4 hours; 2nd class to **Puerto Escondido**, 6 hours, slow, US$9.75. Frequent buses to **Tehuantepec**, 30 minutes, US$0.75. To **Tapachula** by Cristóbal Colón 2nd class, along the coast, 9-10 hours, 0740 and 2030, US$14.50, 1st class bus at 2000. No luggage storage at bus station. Cristóbal Colón terminal is on Av 5 de Mayo, ½ block from Zócalo. Istmeños are on Av Tampico at Progreso, new comfortable buses, recommended.

10 kilometres to the southeast is a picturesque fishing village with **La Ventosa** beach which, as the name says, is windy. Buses go to the beach every 30 minutes from a corner of the main square. **Sleeping D** *La Posada de Rustrian*, overlooking the sea, with bath in new block, half in old block, poor value; unnamed *pensión*, **E**, on right of road before asphalt ends. Friendly family at the top of the dirt road coming from Salina Cruz (on the right) and 200 metres after the first path that leads down to the beach, rents hammocks, US$1 a night, fried fish US$1. *Champas*, or hammocks under thatch shelters by the beach, US$1 a night. The owners serve drinks and food (fish, shrimps, crabs just caught) from early morning on. Prices often high. At the end of the road which crosses the village is a good restaurant under a high palm roof, excellent fish.

Warning It is not safe to wander too far off along the beach alone, nor to sleep on the beach or in your car.

Juchitán
Colour map 3, grid C6

Twenty seven kilometres beyond Tehuantepec on the road to Tuxtla Gutiérrez is **Juchitán de Zaragoza**. The town is very old, Indian, with an extensive market, many *fiestas* and a special one on 19 June. The women wear Zapotec dress as everyday costume. *El Palacio de Gemas*, next to *Hotel Don Alex*, is recommended for gemstones, good selection at reasonable prices.

Sleeping and eating E *Hotel Don Alex*, clean, cheapest. **D** *Hotel Casa Río*, has an Indian name, *Coty*, not posted, next to Casa Río shop, near market, clean. (Be prepared to bargain in cheap hotels). The Casa de Cultura can help if you want to stay with local people and learn about their culture, eg with Florinda Luis Orozco, Callejón de los Leones 18, entre Hidalgo y Aldana. Good restaurant in the **Casa Grande**, a beautifully restored colonial house on the main square. *Café Colón*, close to the bus station, good.

Transport 2nd class bus Oaxaca-Juchitán, at least twice a day, US$8.25, 6 hours, frequent Juchitán-Tuxtla, 1st class, 4 hours, US$7.15. Connect here with train from Veracruz to Tapachula, 18 hours, US$6, but Juchitán station is very dangerous (at night you are strongly advised to wait for the train in Ixtepec).

A road runs northwest to **Ixtepec** (airport), railway junction on the lines Veracruz-Tapachula and Salina Cruz- Medias Aguas (**E** *Casa de Huéspedes San Gerónimo*, close to train station and market. Clean, good. **E** *Panamericano*, noisy from railway station. **E** *San Juan*, bath, acceptable). Natural and man-made pools are fed by springs rising in Santiago Laollaga, free bathing, popular with Mexicans and well worth a trip.

Juchitán to Tapachula

Routes 190 and 200 merge to cross the isthmus from west to east. Accommodation is available at **Zanatepec** (Motel: **C-D** *Posada San Rafael*, very comfortable, safe parking); and at **Tapanatepec** (**D** *Motel La Misión* on Highway 190 on northern outskirts, T91971-70140, fan, hot water, clean, TV, hammock outside each room, affiliated restaurant, very good), where Highway 190 heads northeast to Tuxtla Gutiérrez and Highway 200 continues southeast to the Guatemalan border.

Arriaga (is a good stopping place; many banks around Zócalo for exchange. The road from Arriaga to Tapachula is a four-lane divided freeway.

Arriaga
Population: 12,000
Colour map 4, grid B1

Sleeping and eating **C** *Ik-Lumaal*, near Zócalo, a/c, clean, quiet, good restaurant. *El Parador*, Km 47 on road to Tonalá, T20199, clean with swimming pool. **D** *Colonial*, Callejón Ferrocarril, next to bus station, clean, friendly, quiet, limited free parking. **E** *Arbolitos*, fan, basic, clean, off main road. *Restaurant Xochimilco*, near bus stations.

Buses To many destinations, mostly 1st class, to Mexico City, US$26.50, 12-13 hours, at 1645. To Tuxtla with Fletes y Pasajes at 1400 and 1600, 4 hours, US$7. To Oaxaca, 6 hours, US$7.

The 200 road then goes to Tonalá, formerly a very quiet town but now noisy and dirty, with a small museum; good market (bus Tonalá-Tapachula, three hours, US$6.75; also buses to Tuxtla). Beyond Tonalá the road is mostly straight and in perfect condition. This is by far the most direct road for travellers seeking the quickest way from Mexico City to Guatemala.

Tonalá
Colour map 4, grid B1

Sleeping **B** *Galilea*, Av Hidalgo y Callejón Ote, T6230239, with bath, air-conditioned, good, basic cheap rooms on 1st floor, balconies, on main square, with good restaurants. **D** *Tonalá*, Hidalgo 172, T6230480, opposite museum. **E** *Casa de Huéspedes El Viajero*, Av Matamoros, near market, with bath, rough but OK. **E** *Faro*, 16 de Septiembre 24, near Plaza.

Eating *Santa Elena*, at the south end of town, near Cristóbal Colón bus station on outskirts. Good. On the Plaza, *Nora*. Numerous Chinese-named restaurants; good breakfast at restaurants on Zócalo.

Along the coast from Tonalá to Tapachula there are several fine-looking and undeveloped beaches (although waves and/or currents are dangerous). **Puerto Arista** (17 kilometres south of Tonalá) is now being built up, but it is still a relatively peaceful area with 32 kilometres of clean beach to relax on with no sales people; bus/colectivo from Tonalá every hour, 45 minutes, US$0.60, taxi US$2; plenty of buses to Arriaga, US$0.75. Many hotels, motels and restaurants on the beach; hot and in the wet season, sandflies. **B** *Arista Bougainvilla*, with private beach, a/c, pools, restaurant. Some restaurants (closed by 2000) have rooms to rent, eg *Turquesa*, small hotel/restaurant 3 blocks down on the right from where the road reaches the beach coming from Tonalá and turns right, next to bakery, no fan, basic, **F**. **Camping** **E-F** *José's Camping Cabañas*, (ask colectivo from Tonalá to take you there, US$0.60 extra), at east edge of town, follow signs, Canadian run, well organized, clean, laundry, restaurant (including vegetarian), library.

Excursions from Tonalá

Buses also from Tonalá to Boca del Cielo further down the coast, which is good for bathing and has *cabañas* with hammocks, and similarly Cabeza del Toro. **Paredón**, on the huge lagoon Mar Muerto, 14 kilometres west of Tonalá, has excellent seafood and one very basic guest house. You can take a local fishing boat out into the lagoon to swim; the shore stinks because fishermen clean fish on the beach among dogs and pigs. Served by frequent buses.

MEXICO

En route for Tapachula one passes through **Pijijiapan** where there is the *Hotel Pijijilton*(!) next to the Cristóbal Colón bus station; also **C** *Hotel El Estraneo*, very nice, parking in courtyard and **E** *Sabrina*, nice, clean and quiet, safe parking; many on Ruta México 200, eg *El Navegante Los Reyes*, **E** per bed, doubles only. Also **Huixtla**, which has a good market, no tourists (**E** *Casa de Huéspedes Regis*, Independencia Nte 23). From Huixtla, a good, scenic road winds off into the mountains parallel to the border, towards Ciudad Cuauhtémoc and Comitán. En route is the small, modern town of **Motozintla de Mendoza** with an attractive zócalo and three hotels: one on the plaza, another, *Rendón*, at Central Nte 415, friendly, parking, limited hot water, noisy; also, cheaper, **D** *Alberto*, Central Nte 305, quiet.

Tapachula

Population: 144,000
Phone code: 9
Colour map 4, grid C2

Tapachula is a pleasant, neat, but expensive, hot commercial town (airport; cinemas in centre). Avenidas runs north-south, Calles east-west (Oriente-Poniente). Odd-numbered Calles are north of Calle Central, odd Avenidas are east of Av Central. It is the road and rail junction for Guatemala (road crossings at the Talismán bridge, or at Ciudad Hidalgo).

Sleeping **A** *Motel Loma Real*, Carretera Costera No 200, Km 244, T6261440, 1 kilometre north of city, operates as a 1st class hotel, use of swimming pool, cold showers. **C** *Don Miguel*, 1 C Pte No 18, T6261143. **C** *San Francisco*, Av Central Sur 94, T6261454, F6252114, 15 minutes from centre, good, a/c, large rooms, hot water, TV, restaurant, safe parking. **C** *Posada Michel*, 5 C Pte No 23, T6252640, a/c. **C** *Santa Julia*, next to Cristóbal Colón terminal, bath, phone, TV, a/c, clean, good. In centre within 1 block of Plaza Central. **D** *Fénix*, 4 Av Nte 19, T6250755. **D** *Tabasco*, with shower, close to 1st-class bus station, poor value but friendly. **E** *Cinco de Mayo*, 5 C Pte y 12 Av Nte, with bath (cheaper without), not very clean, convenient for Talismán colectivos which leave ½ block away. **E** *Colonial*, 4 Av Nte 31, attractive courtyard, about 1 block from central square, good value, clean, safe. **E** *El Retorno*, opposite, on 5 C Pte, is unhelpful and noisy. **E** *Plaza Guizar*, 2 Av Nte, old, pleasant, clean, hot water, rooms differ so ask to see more than one. **E** *Rex*, 8 Av Nte 43, T6250376, similar *Hospedaje Carballo*, 6 Av Nte 18, T64370. **E** *San Román*, 9 C Pte entre 10 y 12 Av Nte, shower, fan, safe motorcycle parking, clean, quiet, friendly, drinks for sale.

On 11 C Poniente **D** *Alfa*, No 53, T6265442, clean, fan, cold shower, similar *Posada de Calu*, No 34, T6265659. **E** *Hospedaje Santa Cruz*, No 36, clean, fan, bath, no windows in some rooms; all a long way from Cristóbal Colón 2nd class terminal (15-20 blocks). Many hotels along Avenidas 4, 6, 8 (near Plaza). **E** *Pensión Mary*, Av 4 Nte No 28, T6263400, has cheap *comidas*. **E** *Atlántida*, 6 Av Nte, C 11/13 Pte, T6262136, helpful, clean, cheaper without window, fans, noisy, safe parking for 2. **E** *Hospedaje Madrid*, 8 Av Nte, No 43, T6263018, shared bath.

Eating Good restaurant next to Cristóbal Colón terminal and on main square. *Snoopy*, 4 Av 19, friendly, excellent tortas, breakfasts. *Viva Pizza*, Av Central, good pizza, reasonable price. Good, cheap chicken on Central Nte. *Heladas Irma*, C 13 Pte between Av 4 y 6, good ice-cream.

Shopping *Rialfer*, supermarket, Blvd Díaz, 2 doors from Banamex.

Transport **Air** Flights from Merida, Mexico City, Tuxtla Gutierrez, Veracruz daily. Kombis to airport from 2 C Sur 40, T6251287. From airport to border, minibuses charge US$26 for whole vehicle, so share with others, otherwise take colectivo to 2nd class bus terminal and then a bus to Ciudad Hidalgo.

Trains To Coatzacoalcos at 1300, arrives 0900 to connect with service to Veracruz. To get a seat, board the train hours in advance. Train also to Cd Hidalgo at 1315, arr 1435, return 0830-0950.

Buses Buses (Cristóbal Colón 1st class, Av 3 Nte y 17 Ote, T6262880; 2nd class

Prolongación 9 Pte s/n, T6261161) to/from Tapachula to **Mexico City**, US$40, 5 a day, all pm, 18 hours in theory (frequent stops for toilets and food, also frequent police checks, no toilet or a/c on bus), much better to take 'plus' service, 1915, US$58. Buses from Mexico City all leave pm also; the 1545 and 1945 go on to Talismán. Bus to **Oaxaca**, Cristóbal Colón and Fipsa (9 C Ote, T6267603) has luggage store, US$19, 14 hours, many passport checks (Fipsa has 4 a day, continuing to Puebla and Córdoba, take 1830 to see sunrise over the Sierra Madre; also has 2 a day to Mexico City). Cristóbal Colón, plus service to **Puebla**, US$37.50; UNO, US$53, 16 hours. To Tehuantepec and Salina Cruz 0915, 8 hours, US$14.80; to San Cristóbal de las Casas and Tuxtla Gutiérrez at 1100. The 2nd-class bus station is at 3 Av Nte, 9 C Ote. To **Oaxaca**, 10 hours, US$14.

Airlines Aviacsa, C Central Nte 52-B, T6263147, T/F6263159. AeroMéxico, 2 Av Nte 6, T6263921. Taesa, T6263702. **Banks** Avoid the crowds of streetwise little boys at the border; exchange is rather better in the town, bus station gives a good rate (cash only). *Banamex*, Blvd Díaz Ordaz, open 0830-1230, 1400-1600, disagreement over whether TCs are changed. *Bital* is the only bank open Sat, changes TCs. *Casa de cambio Tapachula*, 4 Av Nte y 3 C Pte, changes dollars, TCs, pesos, quetzales,

Directory

Mexico

Tapachula

To Tonalá & Tuxtla Gutiérrez

Migración
17 C Pte
14 Norte
12 Av Norte
8 Av Norte
6 Av Norte
4 Av Norte
2 Av Norte
1 Norte
3 Norte
7 Norte
9 Norte
17 C Ote
Cristóbal Colón
To Talismán
Colectivos to Talismán
9 C Pte
Av 5 Norte
15 C Ote
5 C Pte
13 C Ote
11 C Ote
Iglesia San Agustín
Parque Hidalgo
Mary
Colonial
Av Central Norte
9 C Ote
Fénix
C Central Pte
5 C Ote
2 C Pte
3 C Ote
4 C Pte
Templo de Buena Esperanza
C Central Oriente
1 C Ote
8 C Pte
Guatemalan Consul
C 6 Ote
Av 4 Sur
Av 2 Sur
Av Central Sur
C 8 Ote
Av 3 Sur
Av 5 Sur
Av 7 Sur
Av 9 Sur
To Airport & Puerto Madero

N
Not to scale

Mexico

lempiras and colones (open late Mon-Sat), but not recommended, poor rates, very difficult to change money on Sun. Try the supermarket. **Communications** Telephone: several long-distance phone offices, eg *Esther*, 5 Av Nte 46; *La Central*, Av Central Sur No 95; *Monaco*, 1 C Pte 18. **Embassies & consulates** *Guatemalan Consulate*, 2 C Ote 33 and 7 Av South, T6261252, taxi from Colón terminal, US$1. Open Mon-Fri 0800-1600; visa US$10, friendly and quick, take photocopy of passport, photocopier 2 blocks away, the consul may give a visa on Sat if you are willing to pay extra. **Laundry** There is a laundry, at Av Central Nte 99 between 13 y 15 C Ote, US$3 wash and dry, 1 hr service, about 2 blocks from Cristóbal Colón bus station, open Sun. Also on Central Nte between Central Ote y 1 C, opens 0800, closed Sun. **Tour companies & travel agents** *Viajes Tacaná*, operated by Sr Adolfo Guerrero Chávez, 4 Av Nte 6, T6263502/6263501/6263245; trips to Izapa ruins, to mountains, beaches and can gain entry to museum when closed. **Tourist offices** 4 Nte 35, Edif del Gobierno del Estado, p3º, between 3 and 5 Pte, T6265470, F6265522, Mon-Fri, 0900-1500, 1800-2000, helpful. **Useful addresses** Migración/Gobernación: 14 Av Nte 57, T6261263.

Frontier with Guatemala-Talismán

It is eight kilometres from Tapachula to the frontier at the Talismán bridge (open 24 hours a day).

Immigration The Mexican customs post is 200 metres from the Guatemalan one. Exit tax US$0.45. Lots of pushy children offer to help you through border formalities; pay US$2-3 for 1, which keeps the others away. **NB** The toilet at immigration at the crossing is dangerous, hold-ups have been reported day or night.

Guatemalan consulate In Tapachula, above.

Crossing by private vehicle Crossing into Guatemala by car can take several hours. If you don't want your car sprayed inside it may cost you a couple of dollars. Do not park in the car park at the control post, it is very expensive. **Driving into Mexico** See **Essentials, Motoring**, on the temporary importation of vehicles, page 80. Car papers are issued at the Garita de Aduana on Ruta 200 out of Tapachula. There is no other road, you can't miss it. Photocopies of documents must be made in town; no facilities at the Garita.

Sleeping There is a *hospedaje* at the border.

Exchange Exchange in town rather than with men standing around customs on the Guatemalan side (check rates before dealing with them, and haggle; there is no bank on the Guatemalan side).

Transport Kombi vans run from near the Unión y Progreso bus station, about US$1; *colectivo* from outside *Posada de Calu* to Talismán, US$0.60, also from C 5 Pte between Avs 12 y 14 Nte. Taxi Tapachula-Talismán, negotiate fare to about US$2. There are few buses between the Talismán bridge and Oaxaca or Mexico City (though they do exist); advisable therefore to travel to Tapachula for connection, delays can occur there at peak times. A taxi from Guatemala to Mexican Immigration will cost US$2, but it may be worth it if you are in a hurry to catch an onward bus. Hitchhikers should note that there is little through international traffic at Talismán bridge.

Frontier with Guatemala-Ciudad Hidalgo

There is another crossing south of Tapachula, at **Ciudad Hidalgo**, opposite Tecún Umán (you cannot change travellers' cheques here); there are road connections to Coatepeque, Mazatenango and Retalhuleu.

Immigration A few blocks from the town plaza is Mexican immigration, at the foot of the kilometre-long bridge across the Río Suchiate; cycle taxis cross the bridge for about US$1, pedestrians pay US$0.15.

Transport From C 7 Pte between Av 2 Nte and Av Central Nte, Tapachula, buses go to 'Hidalgo', US$1.25.

Excursions from Tapachula

The coastal town of **Puerto Madero**, 18 kilometres from Tapachula (bus US$1.80), is worse than Puerto Arista, because it is more built up and the beaches stink from rubbish being burned. Intense heat in summer. (**E** *Hotel Pegado*, run down, not recommended, better is unnamed *hospedaje*, also **E**. **F** *Hotel Puerto Madero*, accommodation in what are really remains of cement block room.) Water defences are being built, but the graveyard is under threat of being washed into the sea (watch out for skulls, etc). Many fish restaurants on beach.

Visit the ruins of **Izapa** (proto-classic stelae, small museum) just off the road to Talismán; the part of the site on the north is easily visible but a larger portion is on the south side of the highway, about one kilometre away, ask caretaker for guidance. These buildings influenced Kaminal Juyú near Guatemala City and are considered archaeologically important as a Proto-Mayan site. Some findings from the ruins are displayed in the **Museo Regional del Soconusco** on the west side of the Zócalo in Tapachula. To reach Izapa take kombi from Unión Progreso bus station. 45 kilometres northeast of Tapachula, beyond the turning to Talismán is **Unión Juárez** (**E** *Hotel Alijoat*, hot shower, reasonable restaurant. **E** *Hotel Colonial*; *Restaurant Carmelita* on the square is modest with fair prices). In Unión Juárez one can have one's papers stamped and proceed on foot via Talquián to the Guatemalan border at Sibinal. Take a guide.

A worthwhile hike can be made up the **Tacaná volcano** (4,150 metres), which takes two to three days from Unión Juárez. Ask for the road to Chiquihuete, no cars. The Tapachula tourist office can help; in Unión Juárez ask for Sr Umberto Ríos at *Restaurante Montaña*, he will put you in touch with guide Moises Hernández, who charges US$15 a day. It is possible to stay overnight in Don Emilio Velásquez' barn half way up, US$2; he offers coffee and tortillas. At the top are some *cabañas* in which you sleep for free, sleeping bag essential.

Chiapas Heartland

Beyond Las Cruces (near the Oaxaca-Chiapas border) we enter the mountainous Chiapas state, mostly peopled by Maya Indians whose extreme isolation has now been ended by air services and the two main highways. Chiapas ranks first in cacao production, second in coffee, bananas and mangoes, and cattle-grazing is important. Hardwoods are floated out down the rivers which flow into the Gulf.

NB Following the EZLN uprising in early 1994, check on political conditions in Chiapas state before travelling in the area. At the time of going to press, there was no fighting between the EZLN and the Mexican army.

From Las Cruces to Tuxtla Gutiérrez, Route 190 carries on to **Cintalapa** (**D** *Hotel Leos*, recommended and restaurant. **E** hotel on main street, clean, with bath and fan) whence there is a steep climb up an escarpment. Mike Shawcross writes: Anyone with a vehicle who has time to visit or is looking for a place to spend the night would find it well worth while to make a four-kilometre detour. 30 kilometres beyond Cintalapa a gravel road leads north (last section very rough, only accessible with four-wheel drive with high clearance) to the beautiful waterfall in **El Aguacero National Park** (small sign), which falls several hundred feet down the side of the Río La Venta canyon. There is a small car-park at the lip of the canyon. 798 steps lead down to the river and the base of the waterfall. Good camping but no facilities.

Carry on to **Ocozocoautla** (airport for Tuxtla. **D** *Posada San Pedro*, noisy, not recommended), make a long ascent followed by descent to (Km 1,085) **Tuxtla Gutiérrez**.

Tuxtla Gutiérrez

Population: 240,000
State population 1995:
3,606,828
Altitude: 522m
Phone code: 9
Colour map 4, grid B1

Capital of Chiapas, 301 kilometres from Tehuantepec. It is a hot, modern city with greatest interest to the tourist during the fair of Guadalupe.

The street system here is as follows: Avenidas run from east to west, Calles from north to south. The Avenidas are named according to whether they are north (Norte) or south (Sur) of the Avenida Central and change their names if they are east (Oriente) or west (Poniente) of the Calle Central. The number before Avenida or Calle means the distance from the 'Central' measured in blocks. Drivers should note that there are very few road signs.

Sights In the Parque Madero at the east end of town (Calzada de los Hombres Ilustres) is the **Museo Regional de Chiapas** with a fine collection of Mayan artefacts; ■ *open daily (US$1.25);* nearby is the **botanical garden**. ■ *Tuesday-Sunday, 0900-1600, free.* Also in this park is the **Teatro de la Ciudad**. There is a superb **zoo** some three kilometres south of town up a long hill, which contains only animals and birds from Chiapas, wild and in captivity ("monkeys and hundreds of agoutis wandering around"). It is said to be the best zoo in Mexico, if not Latin America, good for bird-watchers too, *quetzales* may be seen, aviary, nocturnal wildlife house, reptiles, insects, everything well explained. ■ *Tuesday-Sunday, 0830-1730; in Spanish only, free, but voluntary donation to ecological work recommended, shirts and posters for*

Tuxtla Gutiérrez centre & orientation

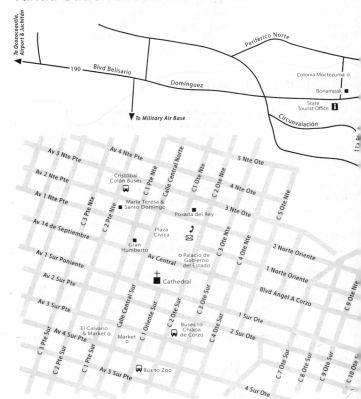

sale; the colectivos 'Zoológico' and 'Cerro Hueco' from Mercado, C 1a Ote Sur y 7 Sur Ote, pass the entrance every 20 minutes; taxi US$2.50 from centre. Town buses charge US$0.20. When returning catch the bus from the same side you were dropped off as it continues up the hill to the end of the line where it fills up.

Excursions

Two vast artificial lakes made by dams are worth visiting: the **Presa Netzahualcoyotl**, or Mal Paso, 77 kilometres northwest of Tuxtla, and **La Angostura**, southeast of the city. Information from the tourist office. Mal Paso can also be visited from Cárdenas (see page 439).

Sleeping

AL *Bonampak* (Best Western), Blvd Belisario Domínguez 180, T6132050, F6122737, west end of town, the social centre, clean, noisy at night, expensive restaurant. *Flamboyant*, Blvd Belisario Domínguez 1081, T6150888, F6191961, comfortable, good swimming pool. **B** *Gran Hotel Humberto*, Av Central Pte 180, T6122080, central, a/c, noisy disco. **B-C** *Palace Inn*, Blvd Belisario Domínguez Km 1081, 4 kilometres from centre, T6150574, F6151042, generally recommended, lovely garden, pool, noisy videobar. **C** *La Mansión*, 1 Pte Nte 221, T6122151, a/c, bath, safe, clean, but street-facing rooms are noisy and affected by traffic fumes; all centrally located. **C** *Posada del Rey*, 2 Av Nte Ote 310, T6122911, a/c, but damp. **C** *Regional San Marcos*, 1 Sur y 2 Ote No 176, T6131940, cheaper without TV, close to Zócalo, bath, fan or a/c, clean.

D *Mar-Inn*, pleasant, clean, 2 Av Nte Ote 347, T6122715. **D** *Posada de Chiapas*, 2 Sur Pte

MEXICO

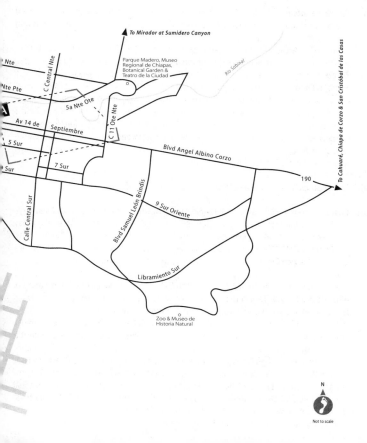

To Mirador at Sumidero Canyon

Parque Madero, Museo Regional de Chiapas, Botanical Garden & Teatro de la Ciudad

Río Sabinal

Nte

C Central Nte

5a Nte Ote

C 11 Ote Nte

Av 14 de Septiembre

5 Sur

7 Sur

Blvd Angel Albino Corzo

Calle Central Sur

Blvd Samuel León Brindis

9 Sur Oriente

190

To Cahuaré, Chiapa de Corzo & San Cristóbal de las Casas

Libramiento Sur

Zoo & Museo de Historia Natural

N

Not to scale

243, T6123354, small rooms with bath, TV, friendly. Opposite Cristóbal Colón bus station are **D** *María Teresa* (2 Nte Pte 259-B, T6130102), and **E** *Santo Domingo*, with shower, good if you arrive late, but noisy and very basic. **E** *Estrella*, 2 Ote Nte 322, T6123827, with bath, friendly, clean, quiet, comfy, a bit run-down but safe, free drinking water, recommended. **E** *La Posada*, 1 Av Sur Ote y 5 C Ote Sur, with or without bath, laundry facilities, friendly. **E** *Plaza Chiapas*, 2 Av Nte Ote y 2 C Ote Nte, T6138365, clean, with fan and hot shower, good value, enclosed car park, recommended. **F** *Posada Maya*, 4 Pte Sur 322, fan, clean. *Posada Muñiz*, 2 Sur Ote 245, near 2nd class bus station, not recommended but useful for early departures. **F** *Santa Elena*, Ote Sur 346. basic. **F** *Posada del Sol*, C 3 Nte Pte, 1 block from Cristóbal Colón buses, with hot shower and fan, good service, good value, basic, highly recommended.

Youth hostel Calz Angel Albino Corzo 1800, CP 29070, T6133405, run down, meals available.

Motels **C** *Costa Azul*, Libramiento Sur Ote No 3722, T6113364/6113452, comfy, clean, but everything designed for short-stay couples. **C** *El Sumidero*, Panamericana Km 1093, on left as you enter town from east, a/c, comfortable, but much passing trade. **C** *La Hacienda*, trailer-park-hotel, Belisario Domínguez 1197 (west end of town on Route 190), T6150849, camping US$7-8 per tent, 4 spaces with hook-up, hot showers, restaurant, minipool, US$13.50 for car and 2 people, a bit noisy and not easily accessible for RVs over 6 metres, owner speaks English.

Eating *Parrilla La Cabaña*, 2 Ote Nte 250, excellent *tacos*, very clean. *Los Arcos*, Central Pte 806, good international food. *Las Pichanchas*, pretty courtyard, typical food, dancing from Chiapas with *marimba* music between 1400-1700 and 2000-2300, on Av Central Ote 857, worth trying. *Mina*, Av Central Ote 525, near bus station, good cheap *comida*. *Café Mesón Manolo*, Av Central Pte 238, good value, reasonably priced. *Alemeda*, A1 Nte 133, near plazza, good breakfast. *Tuxtla*, Av 2 Nte Pte y Central, near plaza, good *comida corrida* and fruit salad, recommended. Nearby is *Canarios*, good value *almuerzos*. *La Parcela*, 2C Ote, near *Hotel Plaza Chiapas*, good, cheap, good breakfasts, recommended. *Los Gallos*, 2 Av Nte Pte, 20 metres from Cristóbal Colón terminal, open 0700-2400, good and cheap. *Las Delicias*, 2 Pte between Central and 1 Nte, close to Cristóbal Colón terminal, good breakfasts and snacks. *Super Cocina Uno*, on 1 Nte Ote between 2 and 3 Nte Ote, good cheap *comida corrida*. *Pizzería San Marco*, behind Cathedral, good. *Bing*, 1 Sur Pte 1480, excellent ice-cream; many others. Coffee shop below *Hotel Avenida*, Av Central Pte 224, serves excellent coffee.

Festivals *Fair of Guadalupe* on 12 December.

Transport **Buses** Cristóbal Colón 1st class bus terminal is at 2 Av Nte Pte 268 (opposite UNO and Maya de Oro) to **Villahermosa** at 1500, 2300, 8½ hours, US$10.30, Altos de Chiapas 6 a day between 0700 and 2345; to **Oaxaca** 1130, 1915, 10 hours, US$18 1st class, US$14 2nd class; to **Puebla**, ADO US$35, departs 1900, Cristóbal Colón 4 a day pm, UNO US$46, 14 hours; 4 a day pm to **Mexico City**, US$42. Frequent buses 0500-2300 to **San Cristóbal de Las Casas**, 2 hours, US$3 (2nd class US$2 superb mountain journey); colectivos from near Av 2 Sur Ote y C 2 Sur Ote do the journey for US$2. To **Comitán** 0500 then each hour to 1900 and 1 at 2300, Altos, US$5.80. Tuxtla-**Tapachula**, US$14, 16 a day; there are more 1st class than 2nd class to the Talismán bridge (1st class is less crowded). To **Ciudad Cuauhtémoc**, 7 a day, 0500-2230, US$7.75, including Altos. Oaxaca Pacífico buses to Salina Cruz, from 1st class bus terminal. Take travel sickness tablets for Tuxtla-Oaxaca road if you suffer from queasiness. To **Pochutla** at 0935 and 2015, 10 hours, US$18. To **Palenque**, Altos, 6 a day, 0500-2300, US$9, 7 hours, other buses pass through Palenque. To **Mérida** change at Villahermosa if no direct service at 1530 (Altos), US$26. The scenery between Tuxtla and Mérida is very fine, and the road provides the best route between Chiapas and Yucatán. To **Córdoba** ADO, 1725, 1900, Cristóbal Colón 2130, US$28.50. To **Tulum** 1230, US$37.50. To **Cancún** 1230, US$39. To **Tonalá** 1615, US$10 (UNO). To **Veracruz** 1930, US$27. To **Chetumal** 1430, US$32.

Left luggage at *Juguería* opposite bus station, will guard bag for US$0.50.

Air The new airport (Llano San Juan, TGZ) for Tuxtla is way out at the next town of Ocozocoautla, a long drive to a mountain top (taxi US$10.50). It is often shrouded in cloud and has crosswinds: there are times when aircraft do not leave for days or flights are switched to the other airport. There are VW taxis at the bus station and opposite *Hotel Humberto*, but they will not drive to the airport unless they have a full passenger load and may tout hotels before going there. Journey takes 45-50 minutes. Good facilities, including restaurant. There is also Terán airport, souvenir shop, cafetería, 10 minutes by taxi from the centre, US$3.00. Direct taxi to San Cristóbal from Terán airport for US$45. Flights to Hualtulco, Mérida, Mexico City, Oaxaca, Palenque, San Cristóbal de las Casas, Tapachula, Veracruz and Villahermosa.

Airlines Aviacsa, Av Central Pte 1144, T6126880/6128081, F6127086, new jets, 40 minutes. Aerocaribe, Av Central Pte 206, T6120020. **Banks** *Bancomer*Av Central Pte y 2 Pte Nte, for Visa and Tcs, open 0900-1500. *Banco Bital*, opens 0800, good rates and service. For cheques and cash at 1 Sur Pte 350, near Zócalo. **Communications** Post Office: on main square. **Telephone:** international phone calls can be made from 1 Nte, 2 Ote, directly behind post office, 0800-1500, 1700-2100 (1700-2000 Sun). **Internet:** free at Library of Universidad Autónoma de Chiapas, Route 190, 6 km from centre. E-mail from 675 Av 1 Nte Pte and C 6 Nte Pte, p1º, US$2 per hour. **Tour companies & travel agents** *Carolina Tours*, Sr José Narváez Valencia (manager), Av Central Pte 1138, T6124281; reliable, recommended; also coffee shop at Av Central Pte 230. **Tourist offices** For Chiapas Av Central Pte 1500 block (on left-hand side going up), Col Moctezuma, next to Bancomer building, in a complex with *artesanía* shop and cheap, a/c café, open 0900-1900 every day, has information on all Chiapas, including very useful state and other maps, English spoken, free; another office at 2 Nte Ote y C Central Nte; also in Zoo, am only. **Useful addresses** Immigration Office 1 Ote Nte.

Directory

Mexico

By excellent paved road through spectacular scenery, to the rim of the tremendous Canyon, over 1,000 metres deep. Indian warriors unable to endure the Spanish conquest hurled themselves into the canyon rather than submit. The canyon is in a national park, open 0600-1800, camping permitted outside the gate (bus US$3; taxi fare US$25 return; try to get a group together and negotiate with a *kombi* driver to visit the viewpoints on the road into the canyon, US$15 per vehicle, leave from 1 Nte Ote). To get to the first viewpoint only, take colectivo marked 'Km 4', get out at the end and walk about three kilometres up the road. With your own car, you can drive up to the last mirador (restaurant), two to three hours' trip, 20 kilometres west of the city. At Cahuaré, 10 kilometres in the direction of Chiapa de Corzo, it is possible to park by the river. If going by bus, US$1.50 each way, get out just past the large bridge on the Chiapa de Corzo road. Boat tours start from below this bridge, where there is lso a car park and restaurant serving good seafood. Boat trip into the Sumidero Canyon costs US$6.50 per person for the boat for one and a half to two hours; boats leave when full. US$65 to hire boat for private group. Take a sweater, the boats go very fast.

Sumidero Canyon
especially recommended at sunset

Tour from San Cristóbal including boat trip costs around US$33 with numerous travel agencies. It is easier to find people to make up numbers in Chiapa de Corzo than in Cahuaré, as the former is a livelier place with more restaurants, launches and other facilities. Good birdlife but sadly hundreds of plastic water bottles pollute the river. It is not recommended for swimming, besides, there are crocodiles.

15 kilometres on, a colonial town on a bluff overlooking the Grijalva River, is more interesting than Tuxtla: see a fine 16th century crown-shaped fountain, the 16th century church of Santo Domingo whose engraved altar is of solid silver, and famous craftsmen in gold and jewellery and lacquer work who travel the fairs. Painted and lacquered vessels made of pumpkins are a local speciality. There is a small lacquer museum. Chiapa de Corzo was a preclassic and proto-classic Maya site and shares features with early Maya sites in Guatemala; the ruins are behind the Nestlé plant, and some restored mounds are on private property in a field near modern houses. There are one and a half and two-hour boat trips along the river to spot crocodiles, turtles, monkeys and hummingbirds, cost US$50 or US$60 for 12 passengers, wait by water's edge, boats soon fill up, recommended.

Chiapa de Corzo
Population: 35,000
Colour map 4, grid B1

☞ *Hardship for Chiapas' Indians*

For the visitor to Chiapas, the state's wonders are many: lush tropical jungle, quaint colonial villages, or the modern, prosperous capital, Tuxtla Gutiérrez. However, the peacefulness masks the troubles of the state's indigenous peoples. Their plight was splashed across the world's press with the Zapatista uprising of January 1994 and has remained a photogenic story ever since (see **Recent Politics**, page 562).

Chiapas, the southernmost state and one of Mexico's poorest, appears much like its neighbour, Guatemala, and shares many of the same problems. Subsistence has been a way of life for centuries, illiteracy and infant mortality are high, particularly among those who have retained their languages and traditions, shunning the Spanish culture. The Chiapas government estimates that nearly one million Indians live in the state, descendants of the great Maya civilization of 250-900 AD. The Chiapas Indians of today are not a monolith; they are spread out across the state, they do not speak the same language, nor dress alike, have the same customs nor the same types of tribal government.

The Tzotziles and Tzeltales total about 626,000 and live mainly on the plateau and the slopes of the high altitude zones. The Choles number 110,000 and live in the towns of Tila, Tumbalá, Salto de Agua, Sabanilla and Yajalón. The 87,000 Zoques live near the volatile Chichonal volcano. The 66,000 Tojolabales live in Margaritas, Comitán, La Independencia, La Trinitaria and part of Altamirano. On the high mountains and slopes of the Sierra Madre are the 23,000 Mames and the 12,000 Mochós and Kakchikeles. The Lacandones, named after the rain forest they occupy, number only 500 today. Along the border with Guatemala are 21,500 Chujes, Kanjobales and Jacaltecos, although that number includes some refugees still there from the Guatemalan conflict, which ended in a negotiated peace in late 1996.

A minority of the Indians speak Spanish, particularly in the Sierra Madre region and among the Zoques. Many have dropped their típica clothing. Customary positions of authority along with stewardships and standard bearers have been dropped from tribal governance, but medicine men continue to practice. They still celebrate their festivals in ways unique to them and they think about their ancestors as they have for centuries. Many now live in the large cities, some even working for the government, but those who remain in el campo are for the most part, poor. They get by, eating tortillas with salt, some vegetables and occasionally beans. Many who leave for the city end up as domestic servants, labourers or street peddlers. The scarcity of land for the indigenous has been a political issue for many decades and limited land reform merely postponed the crisis which eventually erupted in the 1990s.

Larry Lee

Sleeping **D** *Hotel Los Angeles*, on Plaza, often full, warm shower, fan, beautiful rooms. **C** *La Ceiba*, T6160773, with fan, a/c extra, bath, restaurant, pool, recommended.

Eating *Jardín Turístico* on main plaza, good restaurant, open until 2000 (*plato jardín* is a selection of different regional dishes). Good seafood restaurants by the riverside. Along the pier there are many restaurants, including the *Verónica*, good food, cheap, slow service.

Bars Plaza filled with bars playing jukeboxes.

Festivals The *fiestas* here are outstanding: they reach their climax on **20-23 January** (in honour of San Sebastián) with a pageant on the river, but there are daylight *fiestas*, *Los Parachicos*, on **15**, **17** and **20 January**, and the *Chunta fiestas*, at night, from **9-23 January**. The *musical parade* is on **19 January**. There is another *fiesta* in early February and *San Marcos festival* on **25 April**, with various *espectáculos*.

Transport Buses from Tuxtla Gutiérrez, 380 C 3C Ote Sur, US$0.50, frequent; several buses a day (1 hour) to San Cristóbal de Las Casas, 2nd class, US$3.50. Cristóbal Colón to Mexico City, 1815, US$36.50.

Mike Shawcross tells us: The waterfall at the **Cueva de El Chorreadero** is well worth a detour of one kilometre (one restaurant here, recommended). The road to the cave is 10 kilometres past Chiapa de Corzo, a few kilometres after you start the climb up into the mountains to get to San Cristóbal. Camping possible but no facilities; take a torch to the cave.

35 kilometres east of Tuxtla, just past Chiapa de Corzo, a road runs north, 294 kilometres, to **Routes** Villahermosa via Pichucalco (see page 442), paved all the way. If driving to Villahermosa, allow at least 5 hours for the endless curves and hairpins down from the mountains, a very scenic route, nevertheless.

San Cristóbal de las Casas

San Cristóbal de Las Casas, 85 kilometres beyond Tuxtla Gutiérrez, founded in 1528 by Diego de Mazariegos and the colonial capital of the region stands in a high mountain valley. It was named after Bishop Las Casas, protector of the Indians. There is a plaque to him in the plaza. San Cristóbal was at the centre of the Zapatista uprising in 1994, see **History** for details.

Km 1,170
Population: 90,000
Altitude: 2,110m
Phone code: 9
Colour map 4, grid B2

Mexico

There are many old churches; two of them cap the two hills which overlook the town. **Santo Domingo**, built in 1547, has a baroque façade, a gilt rococo interior and a famous carved wooden pulpit (see below). Museum in the **Convent of Santo Domingo**, gives a very good history of San Cristóbal, and has a display of local costumes upstairs, with English explanations. ■ *1000-1700 closed Monday, US$2, free Sunday and holidays.* At the back of the building is a small library with books on Chiapas. Other churches include **San Nicolás**, with an interesting façade, **El Carmen**, **La Merced**, and **La Caridad** (1715). From the **Temple of Guadalupe** there is a good view of the city and surrounding wooded hills (from the north side of the Zócalo, go east along C Real de Guadalupe).

Sights
It is cold at night, in winter extremely so (eg September), bring warm clothing and night clothes.

At the opposite side of the city, behind the **Iglesia de San Cristóbal** is Cerrito San Cristóbal with good view over city (reached via Hermanos Domínguez at Ignacio Allende); parking area with stone benches, popular with picnickers. Churches are closed Sunday pm. 25 July is *fiesta* day, when vehicles are taken uphill to be blessed by the Bishop. **Museo Etnográfico**, Casa de la Artesanía, Av Hidalgo/Niños Héroes. ■ *0900-1400, 1700-2000 Tuesday-Sunday, free.* **Centro de Desarrollo de la Medicina Maya**, Av Salomón González Blanco 10 (walk up Utrilla, past main market and continue for one kilometre) has a museum on traditional lifestyle of Altos de Chiapas and Mayan healing techniques, herb garden. ■ *Tuesday-Friday 1000-1400, Saturday-Sunday 1000-1600, entry US$1.20.*

Various kinds of craftwork are sold in the new market, open daily, and in the Sunday markets of the local Indian villages. Most Indian tribes here are members of the Tzotzil and Tzeltal groups. The Tenejapans wear black knee-length tunics; the Chamulans white wool tunics; and the Zinacantecos multicoloured outfits, with the ribbons on their hats signifying how many children they have. The Chamula and Tenejapa women's costumes are more colourful, and more often seen in town, than the men's.

NB Check on the situation before you visit the surrounding villages. Travellers are strongly warned not to wander around on their own, especially in the hills surrounding the town where churches are situated, as they could risk assault. Warnings can be seen in some places frequented by tourists. Heed the warning on photographing, casual clothing and courtesy (see page 431).

Caves (**Las Grutas de San Cristóbal**) 10 kilometres southeast of the town contain **Excursions** huge stalagmites and are 2,445 metres long but only lit for 750 metres. ■ *US$0.30.* Refreshments available. Horses can be hired at Las Grutas for US$13 for a five-hour

Mexico

ride, guide extra, for rides on beautiful trails in the surrounding forest. Some of these are best followed on foot. Yellow diamonds on trees and stones mark the way to beautiful meadows. Stay on the trail to minimize erosion. **NB** Parts of the forest are a military zone. The land next to the caves is taken up by an army football pitch, but once past this, it is possible to walk most of the way back to San Cristóbal through woods and fields. Las Grutas are reached by Autotransportes de Pasaje/31 de Marzo colectivos every 15 minutes (0600-1900 US$0.60) from Av Benito Juárez 37B, across the Pan-American Highway just south of Cristóbal Colón bus terminal (or take *camioneta* from Pan-American opposite San Diego church 500 metres east of Cristóbal Colón). Colectivos are marked 'San Cristóbal, Teopisca, Ciudad Militar, Villa Las Rosas', or ask for minibus to 'Rancho Nuevo'. To the bus stop take 'San

San Cristóbal de Las Casas

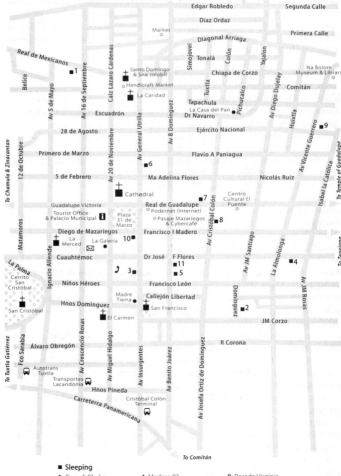

■ Sleeping

1 Casa di Gladys	4 Madero 83	8 Posada Virginia
2 Casa de Huéspedes Chamula	5 Palacio de Moctezuma	9 Rincón del Arco
3 Fray Bartolomé de las Casas	6 Posada Diego de Mazariegos	10 Santa Clara
	7 Posada Margarita	11 Villa Real

N
Not to scale

Diego' colectivo one block east of Zócalo to end of Benito Juárez. When you get to Las Grutas, ask the driver to let you out at Km 94, caves are poorly signed.

A *Casa Mexicana*, 28 de Agosto 1, T6780698, F6782627, cable TV, telephone, indoor patio with fountain, very plush and comfy, same owner as *La Galeria* restaurant, highly recommended. **A** *Casa Vieja*, María A Flores 27, T6782598, F6786268, elegant converted colonial house, relaxing, TV, good restaurant hot water, will heat rooms on request if weather cold, parking, laundry service. **A** *Catedral*, Guadalupe Victoria 21, T6785356, F6781363, pool, solarium, live music. **A** *Flamboyant Español*, 1 de Marzo 16, T6780045, hot water morning and evening, clean, beautiful coutryard, restaurant, gym, some rooms noisy. **A** *Mansión del Valle*, C Diego de Mazariegos 39, T6782582/3, F6782581, chic, classic colonial building, safe parking. **A** *Parador Ciudad Real*, Diagonal Centenario 32, T6781886, F6782853, west edge of city. **A** *Posada Diego de Mazariegos*, María A Flores 2, T6781825, F6780827, 1 block north of Plaza, recommended, comfortable, quiet, reception at 5 de Febrero, restaurant, live music regularly in the evening in bar *El Jaguar*. **B** *Bonampak* (Best Western), Calzado México 5, T6781621, F6781622, pool, restaurant, bar and excellent travel agency run by Pilar. **B** *Na Bolom*, Vicente Guerrero 33, beautiful 12-room guesthouse in cultural centre (see below), bath, fireplace, 3 meals available, lunch and dinner US$5 each with 3 hours notice, recommended. **B** *Ciudad Real*, Plaza 31 de Marzo 10, T6780187, F6780469, clean, good value, TV in rooms, good restaurant, attractive rooms, but noisy parrot talks a lot. **B** *Rincón del Arco*, 8 blocks from centre, friendly, Ejército Nacional 66, T6781313, F6781568, bar, restaurant, discotheque. Warmly recommended. **B** *Hotel Mónica*, Insurgentes 33, T6780732, F6782940, nice patio, restaurant, bar, recommended, and smaller at 5 de Febrero 18, T6781367. **B** *Parador Mexicano*, Av 5 de Mayo 38, T6781515, F6780055, tennis court, quiet and pleasant. **B** *Posada de los Angeles*, Madero 17, T6781173, F6782581, very good value, hot water, with bath and TV. **B** *Posada El Paraíso*, Av 5 de Febrero 19, T/F6780085, Mexican-Swiss owned, impeccable rooms varying in size, many open onto pretty patio, excellent restaurant, nearby parking beneath cathedral, highly recommended. **B** *Santa Clara*, Insurgentes 1, on Plaza, T6781140, F6781041, colonial style, clean, some rooms noisy, good restaurant, pool bar, pool, highly recommended. **B-C** *Arrecife de Coral*, Crescencio Rosas 29, T6782125/6782098, modern, clean, TV, hot water, garden, off-street parking, friendly owners.

C *Don Quijote*, Av Cristóbal Colón 7, T6780920, F6780346, bath, 24-hour hot water, garage, no credit cards. **C** *Molino de La Alborada*, Periférico Sur Km 4, south of airstrip, T6780935, modern ranch-house and bungalows. **C** *Palacio de Moctezuma*, Juárez 16, T6780352, F6781533, colonial style, good Mexican food, highly recommended. **C** *Plaza Santa Domingo*, Av Gen Utrilla 35, T6781927, F6786514. **D** *Capri*, Insurgentes 54, T6783018, F6780015, near Cristóbal Colón bus terminal, clean, helpful, recommended. **D** *Fray Bartolomé de Las Casas*, Insurgentes and Niños Héroes, nice courtyard, T6780932, F6783510, with bath, nice rooms (some dark) and patio with *Café Kate*, can be noisy, extra blankets available, safe parking. **D** *Maya Quetzal*, on Pan-American Highway, Km 1171, T6781181, F6780984, adjoining restaurant. **D** *Posada del Barón*, Belisario Domínguez 2, clean and comfortable, good value. **D** *Posada Los Morales*, Ignacio Allende 17, T6781472, cottages with open fires (wood US$0.80), kitchen (no pots or pans) and hot showers, beautiful gardens overlook city, parking possible (some cottages are very basic, with no water), beautiful bar/restaurant with live music. **D** *Posada San Cristóbal*, Insurgentes 3 near Plaza, T6786881, with bath, colonial style, renovated, pleasant. **C** *Real del Valle*, Av Real de Guadalupe 14, T6780680, F6783955, next to Plaza, with breakfast, very clean, friendly, avoid noisy room next to kitchen, hot water, laundry, credit cards accepted, parking. **D** *San Martín*, Real de Guadalupe 16, T6780533, near Plaza. Clean, hot water, left-luggage, highly recommended. **D** *Villa Real*, Av Benito Juárez 8, T6782930, clean, hot water, luggage deposit, safe, recommended. **D-E** *Posada El Cerillo*, Av B Domínguez 27, T6781283, hot showers, laundry facilities, no electricity 1300-1700, reports vary. **D** *Posada Vallarta*, Hermanos Pineda, near Cristóbal Colón bus terminal, cheaper if you pay for several nights in advance, clean, quiet, hot water, car parking, recommended.

Sleeping
■ *on maps*
Price codes:
see inside front cover

Mexico

E *Casa di Gladys* (Privates Gästelhaüs Casa Degli Ospiti), Diego de Mazariegos 65, Caja Postal 29240, 2 blocks from Santo Domingo, or **F** per person in dormitory, patio, hot showers, clean bathrooms, comfortable, breakfast available, Gladys meets Cristóbal Colón buses, highly recommended. laundry facilities, horseriding arranged, luggage store. **E** *Hotel de Silvia*, Cuauhtémoc 12, with bath and hot water, small, parking, recommended. **E** *Posada Casa Blanca*, Insurgentes 6-B, 50 metres south of Zócalo, with shower, hot water, friendly owner. **E** *Posada Insurgente*, Av Insurgentes 73, T6782435, clean, refurbished, good bathrooms with hot water, cold rooms, 1 block from Cristóbal Colón station. **E** *Posada Isabel*, Francisco León 54, T6782554, near Av JM Santiago, with hot shower, clean, quiet, good value, parking, recommended. **E** *Posada Lucella*, Av Insurgentes 55, T6780956, opposite Iglesia Santa Lucía (noisy bells!), some rooms with bath, hot water, others shared, good value, clean, safe, quiet rooms around patio, large beds, recommended. **E** *Posada Lupita Patrick*, Benito Juárez 12, T6781421, beds like hammocks, small, enclosed car park, strict controls of hot water and *No II* (**F**) at Insurgentes 46, T6781019. **E** *Posada Margarita*, Real de Guadalupe 34, T6780957, in private room without bath, spotless, communal sleeping **F**, washing and toilets, friendly, hot water, recommended, popular with backpackers, often full, attractive restaurant serves good breakfast and dinner (not cheap), wholefood, live music in evenings. **E** *Posada San Agustín*, large rooms, shared bath, family run, friendly, recommended. **E** *Posada Santiago*, No 32, T6780024, with private bath, clean, hot water, good cafetería, recommended. **E** *Posada Tepeyac*, Real de Guadalupe 40, 1 block from *Margarita*, with bath, friendly, clean, hot shower, avoid ground floor rooms, dark and gloomy, otherwise recommended. **E** *Posada Virginia*, Cristóbal Colón y Guadalupe, for 4 in room with bath, hot water, clean, recommended. **E** *Santo Domingo*, 28 de Agosto 3, 3 blocks from Zócalo, with bath, **F** without, hot showers, very friendly. **E** *Villa Betania*, Madero 87, T6784467, not central, airy rooms with bath and fireplace (US$4 extra if you want to light a fire), hot water in morning, clean, recommended. **E-F** *Jovel*, C Flavio Paniagua 28, T6781734, villa style, roof terrace, clean, quiet, limited hot water, extra blankets available, will store luggage, restaurant, horses for hire, laundry facilities, recommended. **E-F** *Posada Memetik*, on Dr José Flores 34, clean, pretty patio, including breakfast, recommended. **E** *Posada Doña Rosita*, Ejército Nacional 16, 3 blocks from main plaza, **F** in dormitory, fleas, kitchen and laundry facilities, breakfast US$1, Doña Rosita is very knowledgeable about local affairs and herbal medicine, but you may be moved around to fit in other guests.

F *Baños Mercederos*, C 1 de Marzo 55, shared quarters, good cheap meals, steam baths (highly recommended, US$2 extra). **F** *Casa de Huéspedes Chamula*, 18 C Julio M Corzo, clean, hot showers, washing facilities, friendly, parking, noisy, with shared bath, some rooms without windows, recommended. **F** *Casa de Huéspedes Santa Lucía*, Clemente Robles 21, T6780315, shared bath, ask for hot water, refurbished, 1 of the cheapest, recommended. **F** per person *Ma Adelina Flores 24*, address as name, including lunch or dinner. **F** *Madero 83 Hospedaje Bed and Breakfast*, Madero, 10 minutes from Zócalo, clean, small breakfast, popular with backpackers. **F** *Posada Casa Real*, Real de Guadalupe 51, communal bath, clean, friendly. **F** *Posada del Candil*, Mexicanos 7, T6782755, hot shower, parking, clean, laundry facilities, good value. **F** *Posada Chilan Balam*, Niños Héroes 9, family-run, hot water, very pleasant. **E** *Posada Maya*, Av Crescencio Rosas 11, hot water in shared showers, cheap café next door, recommended. Look on the bulletin board outside the tourist office for guesthouses advertising cheap bed and breakfast. **F** *Posadita*, Flavio Paniagua 30, with bath, clean, laundry facilities, recommended. **F** *Trivoli*, 20 de Noviembre near market, with bath, hot water, large rooms, good value, or dormitory; and, unnamed house at Real de Guadalupe 28, no breakfast but use of kitchen, ask owners at their café opposite. **F** *Globetrotters Bed & Breakfast*, Real de Guadalupe, rear Av Vicente Guerrero, shared bath, hot water, laundry, clean, quiet, friendly, recommended.

Camping *Rancho San Nicolás*, T6780057, at end of C Francisco León, 1½ kilometres east of centre, beautiful, quiet location, is a trailer park, but do take warm blankets or clothing as the temperature drops greatly at night, hot showers, US$7 for room in cabaña, US$5 to camp, US$12 for camper van with 2 people (electricity hook-up), children free, laundry facilities, recommended. Trailer Park *Bonampak* on Route 190 at west end of town, 22 spaces with full hook-up, hot shower, heated pool in season, restaurant, US$10 per vehicle, US$5 per person. 'White gas' available at small store on corner across from northeast corner of main market (Chiwit).

Eating
● *on maps*

La Parrilla, Av Belisario Domínguez 32, closed Saturday, not cheap but excellent grilled meats and cheese, open fire, cowboy decor with saddles as bar stools, recommended. *La Margarita*, Real de Guadalupe 34, concerts, good tacos. *Los Balcones*, Real de Guadalupe, friendly, good atmosphere, bit expensive. *La Galería*, Hidalgo 3, a few doors from Zócalo, popular with tourists, best coffee, good breakfast, good pasta, international (many German) newspapers, art gallery, videos at night, pool table, live music at weekends. *El Unicornio*, Av Insurgentes 33a, good. *Capri*, Insurgentes 16, good food, set meals at reasonable prices. *Tuluc*, Insurgentes 5, open 0630-2200, good value especially breakfasts, near Plaza, popular, classical music, art for sale and toys on display (SODAM, see below), recommended. *Kukulcán*, Insurgentes Sur 3, Mexican food. *El Pavo Real*, Insurgentes 60, near Cristóbal Colón terminal, regional food. *Sherlock's*, Insurgentes 57, international food, very good value, recommended. *Merendero*, JM Corzo y Insurgentes, OK, cheap. *El Teatro*, 1 de Marzo 8. French and Italian, café, bar, restaurant. *Oasis*, also 1 de Marzo 6 C, excellent milk shakes. *París-México*, Madero 20, smart, French cuisine, excellent cheap breakfasts, reasonably-priced *comida corrida*, good value for all dishes, classical music, highly recommended. *Faisán*, Madero, near Plaza, good breakfasts, excellent food and service. *Los Arcos*, Madero 6, varied menu, family run, inexpensive, good *comida corrida*, excellent service, closes 2100. Several other cheap, local places on F Madero east of Plaza 31 de Marzo. *Fulano*, on Madero 12, near Plaza, excellent set meal at reasonable price. *La Langosta* opposite, Madero 9, good *comida corrida*, cheap breakfast. *Flamingo*, Madero 14, nice décor, reasonable food (good paella). Next door is *El Mirador II*, good local and international food, excellent *comida corrida* US$3, recommended. *El Manantial*, 1 de Marzo 11, good licuados and juices. *El Tapanco*, Guadalupe 24B, good crépes, friendly. *Los Latinos*, Diego de Mazariegos 19, live music, popular with Mexicans. *Pierre's*, Real de Guadalupe 73, good quality French cuisine, will prepare custom dishes given notice. *Shanghai*, 20 de Noviembre 7B, Chinese. *Doña Lolita*, Insurgentes 7, excellent, cheap, good for breakfast and lunch. *El Gato Gordo*, Fco I Madero 28, on Plaza de la Calle Real, good, cheap, large portions, closed Tuesday. *Caxcan*, Av Insurgentes, cheap, good value breakfast, friendly.

Taco restaurants *Emiliano's Moustache*, Av Cresencio Rosa 7, popular with Mexicans, recommended. *La Salsa Verde*, 2 on 20 de Noviembre. *El Ambar*, Almolonga 43, friendly, cheap, recommended. *El Patorcito de Los Altos*, esq Allende y Clemente Robles, cheap. *El Pastor Coleto*, Panamericana y Hidalgo, near Pastorcito, popular with locals.

The town is a 'health food and vegetarian paradise'; shop around. *Madre Tierra*, Insurgentes 19 (opposite Franciscan church), Anglo-Mexican owned, European dishes, vegetarian specialities, good breakfasts, wholemeal breads from bakery (also takeaway), pies, brownies, chocolate cheese cake, classical music, popular with travellers, not cheap, good nightlife. *Las Estrellas*, Escuatirón 201, good cheap food, including vegetarian, good brown bread, try the *caldo Tlapeño*, nice atmosphere, Mexican/Dutch owned, recommended. *Café San Cristóbal* on Cuauhtémoc, good coffee sold in bulk too, chess hangout. *Café Altura*, 20 de Noviembre 4, vegetarian, organic coffee, music every night also has information on eco-tours to the Rancho El Roble, and to the Huitepec nature reserve, ask for Roland Lehmann. *La Selva Café*, Crescencio Rosas y Cuauhtémoc, selection of organic coffees, owned by growers collective, art gallery, lively in evenings, recommended. *Café Latté*, Real de Guadalupe 24D. *La Paz Dorada Café*, next to Guadalupe church halfway up stairs on right, friendly, good views. *Café Centro*, is Real de Guadalupe, popular for breakfast, good *comida*. *La Casa del Pan*, on B Domínguez and Dr Navarro, excellent wholemeal bread, breakfasts, live music, closed Monday, highly recommended but not cheap. *Tortas Tortugas*, Guadalupe Victoria, near corner of Av 20 de Noviembre, excellent sandwiches. *Pastelería Italiana*, 38A 20 de Noviembre, very good pastries and coffee. San Cristóbal is not lively in the evenings: main meeting place is around *ponche* stall on Plaza.

Entertainment Videos shown at *Centro Bilingüe*, on C Real de Guadalupe 55, 2 films a night except Sunday US$1.25 and *La Galería*, Av Miguel Hidalgo 3, US$1. *Cine Santa Clara*, Av 16 de Septiembre. International film festival 2nd half February. Film schedules are posted around town.

Festivals There is also a popular spring festival on Easter Sunday and the week after.

Shopping Part of the ex-convent of Santo Domingo has been converted into a cooperative, *Sna Jolobil*, selling handicrafts from many Indian villages especially textiles (best quality and expensive; also concerts by local groups). *Taller Lenateros*, Flavio A Paniagua 54, T6785174, paper and prints made from natural materials, offers workshops US$6.50 per day. *Weavers Co-op J'pas Joloviletic*, Utrilla 43. *SODAM* (Mutual Aid Society) with their shop at Casa Utrilla, Av Gral Utrilla 33, is a co-operative of Indian craftspeople selling beautiful wooden dolls and toys. Sales go towards a training fund for Chamula Indians, with a workshop based at Yaalboc, a community near San Cristóbal. For local goods try *Miscelánea Betty*, Gen Utrilla 45, good value. Souvenir markets on Gral Utrilla between Real de Guadalupe and Dr A Navarro. Amber museum in Plaza Sivan shop, Gen Utrilla 10, T6783507. Many shops on Av Real de Guadalupe for amber and jade plus other *artesanía*. The market north of Santo Domingo is worth seeing as well. Pasaje Mazariegos (in the block bounded by Real de Guadalupe, Av B Dominguez, Madero and Plaza 31 de Marzo) has luxury clothes and book-shops, restaurants and travel agents. *Casa de Artesanías*, Niños Héroes and Hidalgo.

Bookshops *Soluna*, Real de Guadalupe 13B, has a few English guidebooks, a wide range of Spanish titles and postcards. *Librería Chilam Balam*, Casa Utrilla, Av Gral Utrilla 33, good range of books, mostly in Spanish, also cassettes of regional music. *La Pared*, C Hidalgo 2, next to La Galería, bookshop which also hires books by the day, deposit required, excellent quality new and used books, also fax service. *La Quimera*, Real de Guadalupe 24.

Sports **Horse hire**: Carlos, T6781873/6781339. Horses can be hired from *Casa de Huéspedes Margarita*, prices US$16-20 for horse and guide, to Chamula, 5 hours, US$8, reserve the day before; or from Sr José Hernández, C Elias C 10 (1 block from Av Huixtla and C Chiapa de Corzo, not far from Na Bolom), US$10 for half a day, plus guide US$11.50; Real de Guadalupe 51A, to Chamula US$6.50, also to Rancho Nuevo and San José; Francisco Ochon, T6785911, goes to Chamula, US$6.50. The tourist office also has a list of other stables which hire out horses. Check the saddles; those made of wood are uncomfortable for long rides if you are not used to them.

Transport **Local Taxi**: US$1 anywhere in city, colectivo US$0.25. **Bike hire**: *Los Pingüinos* on Av 5 de Mayo 10B, T6780202, open 0915-1430, 1600-1900, rents mountain bikes for US$2 per hour or US$8.50 per day, US$10.50 for 24 hours. Guided biking tours half or full days, English, German spoken, guide Joel recommended, prices from US$7 to US$12.50, beautiful countryside and knowledgeable guides, highly recommended. *Rodada 28*, on María Adelina Flores, opposite *Casa Vieja Hotel*, open Monday-Saturday 0900-1330, 1600-2000, US$1.30 per hour, US$6.50 per day. Bike shops: *Bicipartes*, on Alvaro Obregón and 2 shops on Utrilla between Navarro and Primero de Marzo have a good selection of bike parts. **Car hire**: Budget, Mazariegos 36, T6781871.

Air San Cristóbal has a new airport (SZT) about 15 kilometres from town, Aerocaribe flies to Tuxtla Gutiérrez. There are also charter flights to see Lacanjá, Bonampak and Yaxchilán on the Río Usumacinta, 7 hours in all (US$100 per person if plane is full, more if not). All with Aerochiapas at airport.

Buses Beware of highly proficient pickpockets at bus stations. Some restaurants on Insurgentes near bus stations display signs saying they store luggage. Cristóbal Colón has its own bus station on Insurgentes, 1st class; to **Villahermosa**, 6 hours, US$11 (direct at 1415); to **Arriaga**, at 1200 via Tuxtla Gutiérrez, 235 kilometres, US$6; to **Coatzacoalcos** at 0630, 576 kilometres, US$14.80; to **Chiapa de Corzo**, 64 kilometres, several daily at 0800, 0830, 1100, 1400, 2 hours, US$3.35; *servicio plus* to Campeche 2100; direct to **Mérida** at 1730, US$23; 1st class bus to **Oaxaca**, about 12 hours, at 1700, US$21.50, 1900, US$21, daily, book well in advance, monotonous trip, 622 kilometres, robberies have been reported on these buses. Buses are regularly stopped and passengers questioned along this route. To do the trip in daytime, you need to change at Tuxtla Gutiérrez (0745 Cristóbal Colón to Tuxtla, then 1100 on to Oaxaca), Cristóbal Colón has hourly buses to Tuxtla between 0630 and 2030, US$2.50; to Comitán, 1000, US$3, 2 hours; to **Tehuantepec**, US$12, 0730,1815; to **Mexico City**, via Tuxtepec, about 18 hours, 1,169 kilometres, many buses daily, US$39; with Altos, to **Puerto Escondido** with Cristóbal Colón, 1st class, 0745,1815, US$22 (US$23 to **Pochutla**); to **Tapachula**, 9 hours, 5 a day, 0030-1645, US$14.80, 483 kilometres; to **Puebla** at 1530 and 1730, US$36, 1,034 kilometres; to **Veracruz**, 1840, US$39; to **Cd Cuauhtémoc**, US$5.50; to **Cancún**, US$30; **Playa del Carmen**, US$28; **Tulum**, US$26; **Chetumal** US$20. To **Cárdenas**, ADO US$12. Book tickets as far in advance as possible, during Christmas and Holy Week buses are sometimes fully booked for 10 days or more.

There is a new 210-kilometre paved road with fine views to **Palenque** (avoid night tie journeys because of armed robberies); Lacandonia 2nd class bus to Palenque from 2nd class bus station on C Allende (where the 1st class bus station is also), 7 a day between 0100 and 2015, 4-5 hours, US$5.50 (via Agua Azul, US$5.50); Cristóbal Colón, 1st class service, up to 4 times daily (including at least 1 *servicio plus*) US$7.50, bookings 5 days in advance; Maya de Oro, from Cristóbal Colón terminal, 3 times daily, a/c, videos, non-stop; Rodolfo Figueroa, 5 times a day, US$4.50, a/c. Other buses leave you at **Ocosingo**; Lacandonia, 2nd class to Ocosingo, 3 hours, US$2.75, Altos at 1725,1825. Refunds of fares to Palenque when reaching Ocosingo are not rare, and you then have to make your own way. Autotransportes Na-Bolom to **Tuxtla Gutiérrez**, Comitán and Palenque from just east of 1st class bus terminal (across the bridge): to Tuxtla 13 departures (1600 *servicio plus*), US$3 (2nd class US$1.50), 2 hours, to Palenque 0700 and 1300, US$6.50, to **Comitán**, 1100 and 1500, US$3.75, 2 hours. Autotrans Tuxtla, F Sarabia entre Carretera Panamericana y Alvaro Obregón 2nd class to Palenque, reserved seats, US$5. Minibuses to Tuxtla Gutiérrez leave from in front of 1st class bus station, when full, US$1.65.

Buses to Guatemala: Cristóbal Colón, south end of Av Insurgentes (left luggage facilities open 0600-2000 exc Sunday and holidays), clean station, direct 1st class buses to the Guatemalan border at Ciudad Cuauhtémoc, 170 kilometres, several daily from 0700, 3 hours, US$3.50 (leave bus at border, not its final destination). 1 ADO bus a day to the border at 1900, book in advance. Altos to Cuidad Cuautémoc/border, 3 a day, US$5. Cristóbal Colón to Comitán (if you can't get a bus to the border, take one to Comitán and get a pick-up there, US$0.50), hourly from 0700. 87 kilometres (a beautiful, steep route). Colectivos also leave for Comitán from outside the Cristóbal Colón bus station, US$2.

2nd class to border with Autotrans Tuxtla, US$2.75 (do not take 1430 ACL 2nd class, next to Trans Lacandonia, on Carretera Panamericana, it arrives too late for onward transport). For details on crossing the border at La Mesilla see page 434.

Airlines Aviacsa, in *Xanav* agency, Pasaje Mazariegos, local 2, Real de Guadalupe, T6784441, F6784384. **Banks** *Casa Margarita* will change dollars and TCs. Banks are usually open for exchange between 0900 and 1100 only, check times; this leads to queues. *Bancomer* charges commission, cash advance on Visa, American Express or Citicorp TCs, good rates and service. *Banco Internacional*, Diego de Mazariegos, good rates for cash and TCs (US$ only), fast, efficient, cash advance on Mastercard. *Banamex* changes cheques without commission, 0900-1100. *Banco Serfin* on the Zócalo, changes Euro, Amex, Mastercard TCs. *Casa de Cambio Lacantún*, Real Guadalupe 12, open daily 0900-1400, 1600-1900, Saturday/Sunday 0900-1300 (supposedly, may close early), no commission, at least US$50 must be changed. Quetzales can be obtained for pesos or dollars in the *cambio* but better rates are paid at the border.

Communications Post Office: Cuauhtémoc 13, between Rosas and Hidalgo, Mon-Fri 0800-1900, Sat 0900-1300. **Telephone:** *Computel*, Insurgentes 64B, fax, guards luggage; Telmex, Niños Héroes y Hidalgo. *La Llamada*, Real de Guadalupe, friendly and helpful. Long distance phone calls can be made from the *Boutique Santo Domingo* on Utrilla, esquina

Directory

Mexico

 Na Bolom

Na Bolom, Vicente Guerrero 33, the house of the archaeologists Frans (died 1963) and Trudi Blom (died 1993, aged 92), and a beautiful guest house (see above), with good library (open Monday-Friday 0930-1330, 1630-1900). At 1130 (Spanish) and 1630 (English) sharp, guides take you round display, rooms of beautiful old house, and garden (1½ hours), US$2.50 including video, a US PBS TV programme, at 1800, recommended. You cannot see the museum on your own. It is well worth visiting: beautifully displayed artefacts, pictures of Lacandón Indians, with information about their history and present way of life (in English).

Also only easily-obtainable map of Lacandón jungle. Na Bolom is closed Monday for tours. They also organize tours to villages, leaving at 1000, returning at 1430, US$9 per person, and special request tours for study programmes for groups. Pepe, a Tzeltal Indian, guides tours to Chamula and Zinacantán, US49, return 1500, recommended.

For further information, T6781418, F6785586. Na Bolom is non-profit making, all money goes towards helping the Lacandón Indians. The volunteer programme has been tentatively reinstated, contact Suzanna Paisley.

Paniagua, takes credit cards, collect possible; and at shops at Av 16 de Septiembre 22, Madero 75 and Av Insurgentes 60. Phone and fax services available at the Tourist Office in the Plaza. Cheap international calls from 2nd class bus station, no waiting. No operator-assisted phone calls are possible on Sun after 2000 in Chiapas. **Internet**: Podernet, Real de Guadalupe at Plaza 31 de Marzo, 1 block from plaza and DACSA at No 3; *Cybercafé*, Pasaje de Mazariegos. *Zecor*, Av 5 de Mayo 4-bis, T88208, US$3.50 per hour. Free half hour on the internet at the Telmex office, very slow, poor service, must have identification.

Cultural centres The *Casa de Cultura*, opposite El Carmen church on junction of Hnos Domínguez and Hidalgo, has a busy range of activities on offer: concerts, films, lectures, art exhibitions and conferences. *Centro Cultural El Puente*, Real de Guadalupe 55, T6782250, has excellent café, bookshop, information centre, workshops, eg photography, salsa, Mexican cooking, travel agency and gallery, closed Sun (see **Language schools**). *Casa/Museo de Sergio Castro*, Guadalupe Victoria 47 (6 blocks from plaza), T6784289, excellent collection of indigenous garments, talks (in English, French or Spanish) and slide shows about customs and problems of the indigenous population, open from 1800-2000, best to make appointment, entry free but donations welcome.

Hospitals & medical services *Dra Carmen Ramos*, Av Insurgentes 28, T6781680, or make an appointment through Tourist Office. **Red Cross:** T6780772.

Language schools *Centro Cultural El Puente*, Real de Guadalupe 55, Caja Postal 29230, T/F6783723 (Spanish programme), rates range from US$6 per hour to US$8.50 per hour depending on number in class and length of course, home stay programmes available from US$180 per week, registration fee US$100. *Universidad Autónoma de Chiapas*, Av Hidalgo 1, Dpto de Lenguas, offers classes in English, French and Tzotzil. *Instituto Jovel*, María Adelina Flores 21, Apdo Postal 62, T/F6784069, one-to-one (US$6.50 per hour) but can arrange group classes and handicraft workshops, tours offered, accommodation with families, US$285 for 2 weeks, US$130 each subsequent week, homestay US$140 per week, deposit US$13, recommended for good tuition and accommodation.

Laundry *Superklin*, C Crescencio Rosas 48, T6783275, US$1.30 per kg, for collection after 5 hrs. *Lavorama* at Guadalupe Victoria 20A; *Lavasor*, Real de Guadalupe 26, US$1.30 per kg, Mon-Sat 0800-2030. *Tinto Clean*, Guadalupe Victoria 20A. Clothes washed and mended by Isaiah and friendly staff, 8 Av B Domínguez, near corner of Real de Guadalupe.

Tour companies & travel agents *Mercedes Hernández Gómez*, leads tours of local villages, starting at 0900 from Kiosk on the Plaza 31 de Mayo, returns about 1500, about US$8 per person, repeatedly recommended. Mercedes is very informative and can be recognized by her long skirts and flowery umbrella. Many others take tours for same price. *Raúl and Alejandro* (T6783741) who leave from in front of the cathedral at 0930, returning at 1400, in blue VW minibus, US$7, good; *Víctor and Verónica* run 4-day camping trips to Lacandón communities, US$192, ask for them at Na Bolom, recommended. **Chincultic**, at *Posada Margarita* (address above), T/F6780957, runs tours to local sites and organizes horse riding tours to San Juan Chamula. **Hector Mejía**, T6780545, takes a walking tour (Tues and Thur, 0900, from outside Santo Domingo, US$9, 4 hrs) around cottage industries eg candymaker, dollmaker, toymaker. Longer tours such as to Bonampak and Yaxchilán can be booked by tour operators in San Cristóbal de Las Casas eg **Yaxchilán Tours**, Guadalupe 26D but they are much cheaper if booked in Palenque..

Tourist offices Helpful, at the Palacio Municipal, T6780414, west side of main Plaza, some English spoken. Ask here for accommodation in private house. Infomation on eco tours to Huitepec nature reserve. Good free map of town and surroundings. Another office at Hidalgo 2, a few paces from Zócalo. Maps of San Cristóbal US$0.35, also on sale at **Kramsky**, Diego de Mazariegos y 16 de Septiembre, behind Palacio Municipal (1-way traffic shown for Av 16 de Septiembre and Av Ignacio Allende actually goes in the opposite direction).

Useful addresses Immigration: on Carretera Pan Americana and Diagonal Centenario, opposite *Hotel Bonampak*. From Zócalo take Diego de Mazariegos towards west, after crossing bridge take Diagonal on the left towards Highway, 30-minute walk. Only 15-day extensions given.

Villages near San Cristóbal

You are recommended to call at Na Bolom (see box) before visiting the villages, to get information on their cultures and seek advice on the reception you are likely to get. Photography is resisted by some Indians (see below) because they believe the camera steals their souls, and photographing their church is stealing the soul of God, but also it is seen as invasive and sometimes profiteering. Many Indians do not speak Spanish. You can visit the villages of San Juan Chamula, Zinacantán and Tenejapa. While this is a popular excursion, especially when led by a guide (see above), several visitors have felt ashamed at going to look at the villagers as if they were in a zoo; there were many children begging and offering to look after private vehicles in return for not damaging them.

Zinacantán

Zinacantán is reached by VW bus from market, US$0.75, 30 minutes' journey, sometimes frequent stops while conductor lights rockets at roadside shrines, taxi US$4. The men wear pink/red jackets with embroidery and tassels, the women a vivid pale blue shawl and navy skirts. Annual festival days here are 6 and 19-22 January, 8-10 August, visitors welcome. At midday every day the women prepare a communal meal which the men eat in shifts. Main gathering place around church; the roof was destroyed by fire (US$0.40 charged for entering church, official ticket from tourist office next door; photography inside is strictly prohibited). There are two museums but both have recently closed because the community felt that they only benefited those most involved in them. Check before planning a visit. **Ik'al Ojov**, off C 5 de Febrero, five blocks down Av Cristóbal Colón from San Lorenzo church, and one block to the left; includes two traditional *palapas* or huts that people used to live in. Small collection of regional costumes. It occasionally holds shows and annual festival on 17 February. Tiny gift shop. Donation requested. The second museum is the **Museo Comunitario Autzetik ta jteklum**, run by women from Zinacantán, One block from San Lorenzo church, also exhibits local culture.

Chamula
The men wear grey, black or light pink tunics, the women bright blue blouses with colourful braid and navy or bright blue shawls.

You can catch a VW bus ride from the market every 20 minutes, last at 1700, last one back at 1900, US$0.70 per person (or taxi, US$4) and visit the local church; another popular excursion. A permit (US$1) is needed from the village tourist office and photographing inside the church is absolutely forbidden. There are no pews but family groups sit or kneel on the floor, chanting, with rows of candles lit in front of them, each representing a member of the family and certain significance attached to the colours of the candles. The religion is centred on the 'talking stones', and three idols and certain Christian saints. Pagan rituals held in small huts at the end of

August. Pre-Lent festival ends with celebrants running through blazing harvest chaff. Just after Easter prayers are held, before the sowing season starts. Festivals in Chamula should *not* be photographed, if you wish to take other shots ask permission, people are not unpleasant, even if they refuse (although children may pester you to take their picture for a small fee).

There are many handicraft stalls on the way up the small hill southwest of the village. This has a good viewpoint of the village and valley: take the road from southwest corner of square, turn left towards ruined church then up flight of steps on left.

Interesting walk from San Cristóbal to Chamula along the main road to a point one kilometre past the crossroads with the Periférico ring road (about two and a half kilometres from town centre); turn on to an old dirt road to the right, not sign-posted but first fork you come to between some farmhouses. Then back via the road through the village of Milpoleta, some eight kilometres downhill, five hours for the journey round trip (allow one hour for Chamula). Best not done in hot weather. Also, you can hike from Chamula to Zinacantán in one and a half hours: when leaving Chamula, take track straight ahead instead of turning left onto San Cristóbal road; turn left on small hill where school is (after 30 minutes) and follow a smaller trail through light forest. After an hour you reach the main road 200 metres before Zinacantán.

NB Signs in Chamula warn that it is dangerous to walk in the area, robberies have occurred between Chamula and both San Cristóbal and Zinacantán. Also seek full advice on any travel outside San Cristóbal de las Casas in the wake of events in early 1998 (see above).

Just past the three km sign from San Cristóbal, on the road to Chamula, is the **Huitepec** nature reserve. ■ *US$1.25*. Two and a half kilometres trail administered by Pronatura-Chiapas. The 135-hectare reserve contains grassland, oakwood forest, rising to cloud forest at 2,400 metres. As well as a wide diversity of plants, there are many birds, including some 50 migratory species and snakes. ■ *0900-1600, Tuesday-Sunday (take combi heading for Chamula from behind market). Guided tours restricted to Tuesday, Thursday, Saturday 0930-1100. Colectivos go there, US$0.50. Tours can be organized two to three days in advance at Pronatura office at María Adelina Flores 21, T6784069.*

Tenejapa
Drunkenness is quite open and at times forms part of the rituals. Best not to take umbrage if accosted.

The Thursday market is traditionally fruit and vegetables, but there are a growing number of music cassette and shooting gallery stalls. Excellent woven items can be purchased from the weavers' cooperative near the church. They also have a fine collection of old textiles in their regional ethnographic museum adjoining the handicraft shop. The cooperative can also arrange weaving classes. The village is very friendly and many men wear local costume. Few tourists (**F** *Hotel Molina*, simple

San Cristóbal de Las Casas environs

but clean; several *comedores* around the market). Buses leave from San Cristóbal market at 0700 and 1100 (one and a half hours' journey), and colectivos every hour, US$1. Ask permission to take pictures and expect to pay. Market thins out by noon.

Two other excursions can be made, by car or local bus, from San Cristóbal south on the Pan-American Highway (30 minutes by car) to **Amatenango del Valle**, a Tzeltal village where the women make and fire pottery in their yards, and then southeast (15 minutes by car) to **Aguacatenango**, picturesque village at the foot of a mountain. Continue one hour along road past Villa las Rosas (hotel) to **Venustiano Carranza**, women with fine costumes, extremely good view of the entire valley. There is a good road from Las Rosas to Comitán as an alternative to the Pan-American highway. Frequent buses.

NB Remember that locals are particularly sensitive to proper dress (that is neither men nor women should wear shorts, or revealing clothes) and manners; persistent begging should be countered with courteous, firm replies. It is best not to take cameras to villages: there are good postcards and photographs on sale.

Transport Get to outlying villages by bus or communal VW bus (both very packed); buses leave very early, and often don't return until next day, so you have to stay overnight; lorries are more frequent. To Zinacantán catch also VW bus from market. Buses and combis (US$1.50) from the market area to San Andrés Larrainzar (bus at 1000, 1100, 1400, with return same day, US$0.80 1-way) and Tenejapa. Transportes Fray Bartolomé de Las Casas has buses to Chanal, Chenalhó (US$15 with taxi, return, 1 hour stay), Pantelhó, Yajalón and villages en route to Ocosingo. Transportes Lacandonia on Av Crescencio Rosas also go to the villages of Huistán, Oxchuc, Yajalón, on the way to Palenque, Pujiltic, La Mesilla and Venustiano Carranza. If you are in San Cristóbal for a limited period of time it is best to rent a car to see the villages.

Ocosingo
Population: 70,000
Colour map 4, grid B2

Palenque (see page 443) can be reached by paved road from San Cristóbal de Las Casas, a beautiful ride via Ocosingo, which has a local airport, a colourful market and several hotels (**D** *Central* on Plaza. shower, clean, verandah. **E** *Bodas de Plata*, 1 Av Sur, clean, hot water. **E** *San Jacinto*, just off lower side of plaza, with bath, hot water, clean, friendly. *Aqua Azul*, simple rooms around courtyard, parking; *Posada Morales*) and clean restaurants, including *La Montura*, on the plaza, good. It was one of the centres of fighting in the Ejército Zapatista de Liberación Nacional uprising in January 1994. Many buses and colectivos to Palenque, two and a half hours, US$3.30 and San Cristóbal de Las Casas.

Toniná

Road to ruins, 12 kilometres away, is unpaved but marked with signs once you leave Ocosingo (possible in ordinary car, taxi US$6); a tour from San Cristóbal costs US$15. To walk from Ocosingo, start in front of the church on the plaza and follow the signs, or take the 0900 bus from the market to the jungle and get off where the road forks (ask). There is a short cut through the fields: after walking for two hours you come to an official sign with a pyramid on it: don't follow the arrow but take the left fork for about 15 minutes and go through a wooden gate on your right; follow the path for two to three kilometres (across a little stream and two more gates, ask farmers when in doubt). You end up in the middle of one of the last classic sites, with the palace high on a hill to your left. It is well worth visiting the ruins, which were excavated by a French government team (open 0900-1600). Temples are in the Palenque style with internal sanctuaries in the back room, but influences from many different Maya styles of various periods have been found. The huge pyramid complex, seven stone platforms making a man-made hill, is 10 metres higher than the Temple of the Sun at Teotihuacan and is the tallest pyramidal structure in the Mayan world. Stelae are in very diverse forms, as are wall panels, and some are in styles and in subject unknown at any other Maya site. A beautiful stucco mural was discovered in December 1990. Ask the guardian to show you the second unrestored ballcourt and the sculpture kept at his house. He will show you round the whole site; there is also a

Mexico

small museum. Entry US$1.30. (Drinks available at the site; also toilets and parking.) Beside the Ocosingo-Toniná road is a marsh, frequented by thousands of swallows in January.

10 minute walk from Toniná is **C** *Rancho Esmeralda*, owned by an American couple, cabañas, good meals, home-made bread, horse riding.

Some 15 kilometres from Ocosingo on the road to San Cristóbal de las Casas is a beautiful cave with stalagmites and stalactites and bats. It is visible from the road on the left (coming from Ocosingo), close to the road, but look carefully for it. Take a torch/flashlight and walk 15 metres to a 10 metres diameter chamber at the end of the cave (don't touch the geological formations as many stalactites have already been damaged).

Route to Guatemala

Comitán
Km 85
Population: 87,000
Altitude: 1,580m
Colour map 4, grid 2

For Guatemala, follow the 170-kilometre paved road via **Teopisca** (*pensión*, **E**, comfortable; *La Amistad* trailer park, run down, one dirty shower and bathroom, no electricity, not recommended), past **Comitán de Domínguez** , a lively, attractive town with a large, shady plaza.

Sleeping Accommodation inferior in quality and almost twice the price of San Cristóbal. **B** *Internacional*, Av Domínguez 22, T6720112, near Plaza, good, decent restaurant. **B** *Los Lagos de Montebello*, T6721092, on Pan-American Highway, Km 1,257, noisy but good. **B** *Real Balún Canán*, 1 Av Pte Sur 5, T6721094, restaurant. **E** *Delfín*, Av Domínguez 19-A, T6720013, small rooms but hot water, helpful and clean. **F** *Hospedaje Primavera*, C Central B Juárez 42, ½ block off Plaza, room without bath. **E** *Posada Panamericana*, 1 Av Pte Nte 2, T6720763, dirty. 1 block away is **E** *Hospedaje Montebello*, clean, sunny courtyard, laundry, fax service, friendly, recommended.

Eating *Helen's Enrique*, on Plaza opposite church, good food in pleasant surroundings. *Nevelandia*, Central Nte 1, clean, recommended. *Café Casa de La Cultura*, on the Plaza, sandwiches only. Live music daily at 2030 at *Buffalo Café*, near Plaza, Av Central y C Nte. Several small *comedores* on the Plaza and at market (cheap).

Transport Buses from San Cristóbal de las Casas with Cristóbal Colón, frequent between 0730 and 2030, US$3.75, 2 hours, last bus back at 1930. One Cristóbal Colón bus goes on to Tuxtla (via San Cristóbal), US$3.50, 4 hours. Minibuses from Comitán to Tuxtla leave from by the Cristóbal Colón bus station. Buses, kombis and pick-up trucks from Comitán run to the border at Ciudad Cuauhtémoc. Unleaded petrol is available in Comitán, in centre of town on east side of Pan-American Highway, and another 2 kilometres south of town, open 24 hours.

Directory Airline offices *Aviacsa*, 3 C Sur Pte, 12a, T6723519, F6720824, helpful, recommended. **Banks** *Bancomer*, on plaza will exchange Amex TCs; 2 others on plaza, none changes dollars after 1200; also a *casa de cambio*. **Embassies & consulates** *Guatemalan Consulate*, open Mon-Fri 0800-1200, 1400-1700, Sat 0800-1400 at 1a C Sur Pte 26 y 2 Av Pte Sur, T6722669; visa (if required) US$10 (even for those for whom it should be free), valid 1 year, multiple entry: tourist cards available at border. **Tourist office** On main square, in Palacio Municipal, ground floor, open Mon-Fri 1000-1400, 1700-2000.

Lagunas de Montebello and Chinkultic

Six kilometres south of Comitán take a right turn for the Mayan ruins of **Tenan Puente** (5 kilometres) situated in forest (more restored buildings than Chinkultic, see below), shortcut on foot. In 1996 the tomb of a Maya nobleman (1000 AD) was discovered here. A road branches off the Pan-American Highway, 16 kilometres further on, to a very beautiful region of vari-coloured lakes and caves, the **Lagunas de Montebello** (a national park). On no account visit the Lagunas alone because of rapes and robberies at gunpoint. Off the road to Montebello, 30 kilometres from the Pan-American Highway, lie the ruins of **Chinkultic**, with temples, ballcourt, carved stone stelae and *cenote* (deep round lake, good swimming) in beautiful surroundings; from the signpost they are about three kilometres along a dirt road and they close at 1600 (entry US$3). Watch and ask for the very small sign and gate where road to ruins starts (about one kilometre back along the main road, towards Comitán, from Doña María's, see below, don't attempt any short cuts), worth visiting when passing. Colectivo from Comitán US$1.

Kombi vans or buses marked Tziscao or Lagos to the Lagunas de Montebello (60 kilometres from Comitán, US$1.30 about one hour), via the Lagunas de Siete Colores (so-called because the oxides in the water give varieties of colours) leave frequently from 2 Av Pte Sur y 3 C Sur Pte, four blocks from Plaza in Comitán; buses go as far as Laguna Bosque Azul, one hour journey. For those with their own transport there are several dirt roads from Comitán to the Lagunas, a recommended route is the one via La Independencia, Buena Vista, La Patria and El Triunfo (beautiful views) eventually joining the road west of Chinkultic ruins.

Tziscao is nine kilometres along the road leading right from the park entrance, which is three kilometres before Bosque Azul; five buses a day Comitán-Tziscao; the last bus and colectivo back connecting with the 1900 bus to San Cristóbal is at 1600. The last combi to Comitán at 1700. A trip to the Lagunas de Siete Colores from Comitán can be done in a day (note that the less accessible lakes are hard to get to even if staying in the vicinity). It is also possible to hire a Kombi, which takes 12 people, to go to the Lakes and Chinkultic for US$15 per hour. A day trip to Chinkultic and the lakes from San Cristóbal de Las Casas is also possible, if exhausting (take passport and tourist card with you). The Bosque Azul area is now a reserve. The area is noted for its orchids and birdlife, including the famous *quetzal*; very crowded at weekends and holidays. Horse hire US$4 per hour, if you take a guide you pay for an extra horse.

Tziscao

Sleeping Before planning to spend the night in the area check with the Tourist Office. In 1999 rapes and robberies at gunpoint brought official advice to travellers not to stay the night. There are, as well as picnic areas, an *Albergue Turístico* on the shores of Lake Tziscao (10 kilometres, **F** per person, rooms for 4-6, toilet, blankets available, no hot water, reasonable kitchen facilities and bathrooms, excellent, reasonably-priced meals, camping including use of hotel facilities; boats for hire, friendly owners, one of whom, Leo, speaks good English and has an intimate knowledge of the region), a small, family-run restaurant at Laguna Bosque Azul with a wooden hut for sleeping, **F**, bring sleeping bag, 2 very basic food shops in the village (best to bring your own food from Comitán market), and there are small caves. Young boys are good guides, take powerful torch. *Posada Las Orquídeas* (better known as 'Doña María'), Km 31, on the road to Montebello near Hidalgo and the ruins of Chinkultic, dormitory or cabin, **F** per person, family-run, very basic (no washing facilities, often no water, 2 toilets, urn in a shack) but friendly, small restaurant serving plentiful Mexican food. Next door are cabañas/restaurant *El Pino Felíz*. **Youth Hostel**: Las Margaritas. *Hotel Bosque Bello*, 34 kilometres, reservations in Tuxtla, T6110966, or Comitán T6721702.

NB Mexican maps show a road running along the Guatemalan border from Montebello to Bonampak and on to Palenque; this road is not complete and no public transport or other traffic makes the trip.

From Hidalgo you can get to Comitán by pick-up or paying hitchhike for US$1 (not recommended for women); to the Guatemalan border go from Hidalgo to La Trinitaria and catch a bus or pick-up there.

Frontier with Guatemala – Ciudad Cuauhtémoc From Comitán the road winds down to the Guatemalan border at **Ciudad Cuauhtémoc** via La Trinitaria (near the turn-off to Lagunas de Montebello, restaurant but no hotel). In Ciudad Cuauhtémoc, not a town, despite its name; just a few buildings; the Cristóbal Colón bus station is opposite Immigration, with an overpriced restaurant and an excellent **E/F** *Hotel Camino Real*, extremely clean and quiet, changes dollars to pesos, highly recommended. Be sure to surrender your tourist card and get your exit stamp at Mexican immigration in Ciudad Cuauhtémoc before boarding a pick-up for Guatemalan immigration; you will only have to go back if you don't. A pick-up to the Guatemalan border, four kilometres, costs US$0.65 per person. Walk 100 metres to immigration and customs, open until 2100. Beyond the Guatemalan post at La Mesilla, El Tapón section, a beautiful stretch, leads to Huehuetenango, 85 kilometres. This route is far more interesting than the one through Tapachula; the border crossing at Ciudad Cuauhtémoc is also reported as easier than that at Talismán. Remember that Mexico is one hour ahead of Guatemala.

Entering Mexico from Guatemala 1) Tourist cards and visas are available at the border, recent reports say only 15 days are being given, but extensions are possible in Oaxaca or Mexico City; 2) it is forbidden to bring in fruit and vegetables; rigorous checking at 2 checkpoints to avoid the spread of Mediterranean mosquito.

Crossing by private vehicle Drivers entering Mexico: at the border crossing your vehicle is fumigated, US$7.25, get receipt (if re-entering Mexico, with documents from a previous entry, papers are checked here). Proceed 4 kilometres to Migración to obtain tourist card or visa, or have existing visa checked. Then go to Banjército to obtain the necessary papers and windscreen sticker or, if re-entering Mexico, to have existing papers checked (open Monday-Friday 0800-1600, Saturday-Sunday 0900-1400).

Exchange Don't change money with the Guatemalan customs officials: the rates they offer are worse than those given by bus drivers or in banks (and these are below the rates inside the country). There is nowhere to change travellers' cheques at the border and bus companies will not accept cheques in payment for fares. 300 metres after the border, however, you can get good rates for TCs at the Banco de café. The briefcase and dark glasses brigade changes cash on the Guatemalan side only, but you must know in advance what quetzal rates are.

Transport Buses are 'de paso' from San Cristóbal so no advance booking is possible. The Cristóbal Colón bus leaves Comitán 0800, 1100 (coming from San Cristóbal) and in pm for the border at Ciudad Cuauhtémoc, fare US$2.75. Autotransportes Tuxtla leave from Comitán (on the main highway at approximately 2 Av Sur) at regular intervals for the border, 1½ hours. There are at least 8 buses to Comitán 0800-1930 from Ciudad Cuauhtémoc, with 2nd class buses during the evening. Pick-ups charge US$1.55 per person Comitán-border; beware short-changing. From here take a taxi, US$1.65, or colectivo, to the Guatemalan side (4 kilometres uphill, minimum 3 people) and get your passport stamped. Cristóbal Colón (terminal near the Pan-American Highway, Comitán) has 1st class buses to **Mexico City** at 0900, 1100 and 1600 (which leave the border 2½ hours earlier), fare US$40.75 (from Mexico City to Comitán at 1415 and 2040, fully booked 2 hours in advance); to **Oaxaca** at 0700 and 1900, US$33; to **Tuxtla Gutiérrez** at 0600 and 1600, US$8, and to **Tapachula** (via Arriaga) at 1200 and 2000, US$20. Entering Mexico from Guatemala, to San Cristóbal, direct buses US$3.50, or take a minibus to Comitán, US$1.55; these connect with Kombis at the Autotransportes Tuxtla terminal for San Cristóbal de Las Casas.

Yucatán Peninsula

Mexico City

The states of Yucatán, Campeche and Quintana Roo, sold to tourists as the land of Maya archaeology and beach and island resorts (Cancún, Cozumel, etc). It pays to explore beyond the main itineraries, for lesser-known Maya sites, caves, lagoons, flamingo feeding grounds and villages with old churches. There are two road and river routes into Guatemala, and the main road access to Belize.

The peninsula of Yucatán is a flat land of tangled scrub in the drier northwest, merging into exuberant jungle and tall trees in the wetter southeast. There are no surface streams. The underlying geological foundation is a horizontal bed of limestone in which rainwater has dissolved enormous caverns. Here and there their roofs have collapsed, disclosing deep holes or cenotes in the ground, filled with water. Today this water is raised to surface-level by wind-pumps: a typical feature of the landscape. It is hot during the day but cool after sunset. Humidity is often high. All round the peninsula are splendid beaches fringed with palm groves and forests of coconut palms. The best time for a visit is from October to March.

In Yucatán and Quintana Roo, the economy has long been dependent on the export of henequén (sisal), and chicle, but both are facing heavy competition from substitutes and tourism is becoming ever more important.

History

The early history and accomplishments of the Maya when they lived in Guatemala and Honduras before their mysterious trek northwards is given in the introduction to the book. They arrived in Yucatán about 1200 BC, started building monumental stone structures during the centuries leading up to the end of the Pre-Classic period (250AD) and later rebuilt their cities, but along different lines, probably because of the arrival of Toltecs in the ninth and 10th centuries. Each city was autonomous, and in rivalry with other cities. Before the Spaniards arrived the Maya had developed a writing in which the hieroglyphic was somewhere between the pictograph and the letter. Fray Diego de Landa collected their books, wrote a very poor summary, the *Relación de las Cosas de Yucatán*, and with Christian but unscholarlike zeal burnt most of the codices which he never really understood.

In 1511 some Spanish adventurers were shipwrecked on the coast. Two survived. One of them, Juan de Aguilar, taught a nahuatl-speaking girl Spanish. She became interpreter for Cortés after he had landed in 1519. The Spaniards found little to please them: no gold, no concentration of natives, but Mérida was founded in 1542 and the few natives handed over to the conquerors in *encomiendas*. The Spaniards found them difficult to exploit: even as late as 1847 there was a major revolt, fuelled by the inhuman conditions in the *henequén* plantations, and the discrimination against the Maya in the towns, but it was the expropriation of the Maya communal lands that was the main source of discontent. In July 1847 a conspiracy against the Blancos, or ruling classes from Mexico, was uncovered in Valladolid and one of its leaders, Manuel Antonio Ay, was shot. This precipitated a bloody war, known as the Guerra de Castas (Caste War) between the Maya and the Blancos. The first act was the massacre of all the non-Maya inhabitants of Tepich, south of Valladolid. The Maya took control of much of the Yucatán, laying siege to Mérida, only to abandon it to sow their crops in 1849. This allowed the governor of Yucatán to counter-attack, driving the Maya by ruthless means into southern Quintana Roo. In Chan Santa Cruz, now called Felipe Carrillo Puerto, one of the Maya leaders, José María Barrera, accompanied by Manuel Nahuat, a ventriloquist, invented the 'talking cross', a cult that attracted thousands of followers. The sect, called Cruzob, established itself and renewed the resistance against the government from Mexico City. It was not until 1901 that the Mexican army retook the Cruzob's domain.

Mexico

People

The people are divided into two groups: the Maya Indians, the minority, and the *mestizos*. The Maya women wear *huipiles*, or white cotton tunics (silk for *fiestas*) which may reach the ankles and are embroidered round the square neck and bottom hem. Ornaments are mostly gold. A few of the men still wear straight white cotton (occasionally silk) jackets and pants, often with gold or silver buttons, and when working protect this dress with aprons. Carnival is the year's most joyous occasion, with concerts, dances, processions. Yucatán's folk dance is the Jarana, the man dancing with his hands behind his back, the woman raising her skirts a little, and with interludes when they pretend to be bullfighting. During pauses in the music the man, in a high falsetto voice, sings *bambas* (compliments) to the woman.

The Maya are a courteous, gentle, strictly honest and scrupulously clean people. They drink little, except on feast days, speak Mayan, and profess Christianity laced with a more ancient nature worship.

Access to sites and resorts

Many tourists come to Yucatán, mostly to see the ancient Maya sites and to stay at the new coastal resorts. A good paved road runs from Coatzacoalcos through Villahermosa, Campeche and Mérida (Route 180). Most of the great archaeological sites except Palenque are on or just off this road and its continuation beyond Mérida. An inland road from Villahermosa to Campeche gives easy access to Palenque. If time

Yucatán Peninsula

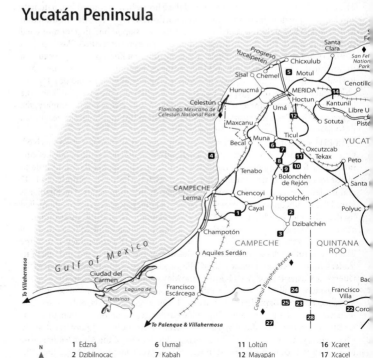

1 Edzná	6 Uxmal	11 Loltún	16 Xcaret
2 Dzibilnocac	7 Kabah	12 Mayapán	17 Xcacel
3 Hochob	8 Sayil	13 Chichén Itzá	18 Tulum
4 Jainu	9 Xlapac	14 Izamal	19 Chumyaxche
5 Dzibilchaltún	10 Labná	15 San Gervasio	20 Tancáh

N
Not to scale

is limited, take a bus from Villahermosa to Chetumal via Escárcega, which can be done overnight as the journey is not very interesting (unless you want to see the Mayan ruins off this road, see page 520). From Chetumal travel up the coast to Cancún, then across to Mérida. A train from Mexico City to Mérida goes through Palenque; Pullman passengers can make the whole trip without leaving the car in two nights. Route 307 from Puerto Juárez and Cancún to Chetumal is all paved and in very good condition. Air services from the USA and Mexico City are given under Villahermosa, Mérida, Cancún and Cozumel. Details of the road route between Guatemala and Yucatán are given on pages 448 and 471. The state of Quintana Roo is on the eastern side of the Yucatán Peninsula and has recently become the largest tourist area in Mexico with the development of the resort of Cancún, and the parallel growth of Isla Mujeres, Cozumel and the 100-kilometre corridor south of Cancún to Tulum. Growth has been such, in both Yucatán and Quintana Roo, that there are insufficient buses at peak times, old second class buses may be provided for first class tickets and second class buses take far too many standing passengers. There is a lack of information services. Where beaches are unspoilt they often lack all amenities. Many cheaper hotels are spartan. *Warning*: So many of the tourists coming to the coastal resorts know no Spanish that price hikes and short-changing have become very common there, making those places very expensive if one is not careful. In the peak, winter season, prices are increased anyway, by about 50 percent.

NB The use of tripods for photography at sites is subject to an extra fee of US$3.50, but for using video cameras the fee is US$7.50. Since the major archaeological sites get very crowded, it is best to visit them just before closing time. Note also that in spring and summer temperatures can be very high; take plenty of drinking water and adequate protection against the sun if walking for any length of time (for example around a large Maya site). See page 89 for recommended reading.

The Caribbean Coast

Quintana Roo (and especially Cozumel) is the main area for Diving and Watersports in the Yucatán Peninsula. More dive sites are found off the Belize Cayes. The text below gives information on some of the options available, with addresses of dive shops, etc. A recommended book is *The Dive Sites of Cozumel and the Yucatán* by Lawson Wood (published by New Holland Ltd, 1997, ISBN 1-85368-938-6), which also covers snorkelling and *cenote* diving. It should be noted that watersports in Quintana Roo are expensive and touristy, but operators are generally helpful; snorkelling is often organized for large groups. On the more accessible reefs the coral is dying and there are no small coral fishes as a necessary part of the coral life cycle. Further from the shore, though, there is still much reef life to enjoy.

Coatzacoalcos

Population: 186,000
Colour map 4, grid B1

The Gulf Coast gateway for Yucatán, one and a half kilometres from the mouth of its wide river. Pemex has a huge oil tanker loading port here. It is hot, humid and lacking in culture, and there is not much to do save watch the river traffic. River is too polluted for fishing and swimming, less than salubrious discos on the equally polluted beach by the pier at the river mouth; beach is dangerous at nights, do not sleep there or loiter. 39 kilometres up river is **Minatitlán**, the oil and petrochemical centre (*Population*: 145,000; airport), whose huge oil refinery sends its products by pipeline to Salina Cruz on the Pacific. The road between the two towns carries very heavy industrial traffic. The offshore oil rigs are serviced from Coatzacoalcos. Sulphur is exported from the mines, 69 kilmetres away. Both cities are often under a pall of smog and the air is constantly scented with petrochemical fumes and sometimes ammonia and sulphur compounds. There is a high incidence of lung disease. Not many foreigners visit either town

Sleeping

Very difficult as all hotels are used by oil workers. Don't spend the night on the street if you can't find lodging. Prices double those of hotels elsewhere.

In Coatzacoalcos A *Enríquez*, Ignacio de La Llave, good. **C** *Alex*, JJ Spark 223, T24137, with bath, fan, clean, safe parking. **D** *Oliden*, Hidalgo 100, with fan, clean, noisy (other similar hotels in this area). **E** *San Antonio*, Malpica 205, near market, with shower. Several others nearby. *Motel Colima* at Km 5, Carretera Ayucan-Coatzacoalcos, may have rooms if none in Coatzacoalcos; it is clean, in a quiet position, but does have a lot of red-light activity. **In Minatitlán B** *César*; **C** *Palazzo* on main street, a/c, credit cards accepted; **B** *Plaza*; **C** *Tropical*, with bath, no hot water. **D** *Hotel Nacional*, opposite *Palazzo*, Hidalgo 16, T37639, luggage store, friendly, with bath, fan, hot water, clean, recommended.

Eating

In Coatzacoalcos *Los Lopitos*, Hidalgo 615, good *tamales* and *tostadas*. *Mr Kabubu's* bar and restaurant, near *Hotel Alex*, good food and drinks. Cheap restaurants on the top floor of the indoor market near the bus terminal. *Cafetería de los Portales*, near main plaza, very good food and service. By the river here are several cafés, beware of overcharging. **In Minatitlan** *El Marino*, behind the colourful church on main plaza, opens relatively early, very good, clean and friendly service.

Transport

Air Minatitlán airport (MTT), 30 minutes from Coatzacoalcos, 10 minutes from Minatitlán. Mexicana to Mexico City and Monterrey. **Trains** Railway station is 5 kilometres from town at Cuatro at end of Puerto Libre bus route and on Playa Palma Sola route, smelly and dingy; irregular bus services. Better walk about 500 metres to the main road and get a bus there, US$0.25. Train to **Mérida**, via Palenque and Campeche at 2320, arrives 1325, but check whether it is running, service unreliable in 1999. Another station, in the city centre, serves Tapachula, 1910, 16-17 hrs, and Veracruz, 1000, 10½ hrs. **Buses** From Coatzacoalcos to **Mexico City**, US$26.50; to **Mérida** US$31; to **Córdoba**, US$13; to **Veracruz** (312 kilometres), US$12, 7¼ hours; to Xalapa, 8 hrs, US$17 or less, depending on number of stops; to **Ciudad del Carmen**, US$16.50; to **Salina Cruz**, US$12.15; to **Villahermosa**, US$7. The ADO and interurban bus terminal is some way from city centre. Taxi fare about US$1.50 but they will charge more. **Buses from Minatitlán**, two terminals, 1st class (ADO) near town centre, 2 blocks from Hidalgo, clean toilets, left luggage. ADO to many destinations. Cristóbal Colón buses leave from Sur, not ADO terminal, in Minatitlán. Taxi between the two, US$1.60. All buses originate in Coatzacoalcos and seat availability is assigned to each destination en route. Buses between the two town centres are marked *directo*, 40 mins, US$0.60. Those marked *Cantices* go via the airport, 200m walk from bus stop to terminal, much cheaper than US$15 taxis.

Directory

Communications **Post Office:** Carranza y Lerdo, Coatzacoalcos. Stamps and postage upstairs at Post Office on Hidalgo, Minatitlán.

39 kilometres east of Coatzacoalcos, on a side road off Route 180 is **Agua Dulce**, where there is a campground, *Rancho Hermanos Graham*, nice location, full hook-up, cold showers, only one bathroom for whole site, US$6.50 for car and two people.

On the Gulf Coast, further east (turn off Route 180 at Las Piedras, 70 kilometres from Coatzacoalcos, signposted), is **Sánchez Magallanes**, a pleasant, friendly town. You can camp safely on the beach.

Cárdenas, 116 kilometres from Coatzacoalcos and 48 kilometres from Villahermosa by dual carriageway, is the headquarters of the Comisión del Grijalva, which is encouraging regional development. It is very hard to find accommodation in Cárdenas, **D** *Hotel Yax-ol*, cheapest, with bath, a/c, parking, clean, on main plaza. **Cárdenas**

20 kilometres south of Cárdenas is the hot and dirty town of **Huimanguillo** (basic hotel *El Carmen*). Continuing up into the Sierra de Huimanguillo the road reaches Malpasito (taxi US$33 from Huimanguillo) where there is a lodge, *El Pava* (reservations at *Hotel El Carmen*). Beyond are the Raudales de Malpaso (cataracts) on Presa Netzahualcoyotl (accommodation, **E**, at ADO bus station, bus service once a day from Huimanguillo). There is a reguular launch across the dam (0600, 0700, 0900, 1100, 1300, 1500) to Apic-Pac where you can take a pick-up (two and a half hours, bumpy road) to Ocozocuautla and on to Tuxtla Gutiérrez (see map, page 416). **South of Cárdenas**

Villahermosa

Capital of Tabasco state, Villahermosa is on the Río Grijalva, navigable to the sea. It used to be a dirty town, but is now improving, though it is very hot and rainy. Between Cárdenas and Villahermosa are many stalls selling all varieties of bananas, a speciality of the area, and the road passes through the Samaria oilfield.

Population: 275,000
State population 1995: 1,748,664
Phone code: 931
Colour map 4, grid B1

The **cathedral**, ruined in 1973, has been rebuilt, its twin steeples beautifully lit at night; it is not in the centre. There is a warren of modern colonial-style pedestrian malls throughout the central area. The **Centro de Investigaciones de las Culturas Olmecas** (CICOM) is set in a new modern complex with a large public library, expensive restaurant, airline offices and souvenir shops, a few minutes' walk south out of town along the river bank.

Sights
Villahermosa can be difficult for lone women: local men's aggressive behaviour said to be due to the effect of eating iguanas.

The **Museo Regional de Antropología Carlos Pellicer Cámara** on three floors, has well laid out displays of Maya and Olmec artefacts, with an excellent bookshop. ■ *0900-2000, closed Monday, US$1.*

Museo de Cultura Popular, Zaragoza 810. ■ *Open daily 0900-2000.* **Museo de Historia de Tabasco**, Avenida 27 de Febrero esq Juárez, same hours.

At the northwest side of town (west of the downtown area) is Tabasco 2000, a futuristic mall/hotel/office area with an original statue of fishermen.

In 1925 an expedition discovered huge sculptured human and animal figures, urns and altars in almost impenetrable forest at La Venta, 120 kilometres from Villahermosa. Nothing to see there now: about 1950 the monuments were threatened with destruction by the discovery of oil nearby. The poet Carlos Pellicer got them hauled all the way to a woodland area near Villahermosa, now the **Parque Nacional de La Venta**, Boulevard Adolfo Ruíz Cortines, with scattered lakes, next to a children's playground and almost opposite the old airport entrance (west of downtown). There they are dispersed in various small clearings. The huge heads, one of them weighs 20 tons, are Olmec, a culture which flourished about 1150-150 BC; this is an experience which should not be missed. ■ *It takes up to two hours to do it justice, excellent guides, speak Spanish and English (US$6.65 for one hour 10 minutes).* There is also an excellent zoo with creatures from the Tabasco jungle: monkeys, alligators, deer, wild pigs and birds. ■ *0800-1600, closed Monday, US$1.50, recommended.* Outside the park, on the lakeside is an observation tower, Mirador de las Aguas, with excellent views. Entry free but only for the fit as there are lots of stairs.

Be sure to take insect repellent for the visit. Take a bus marked 'Gracitol' from ADO bus terminal US$0.30 (don't take a bus going to 'La Venta', if in doubt, ask), or, to walk from ADO, left at front entrance, left again at the overpass and straight ahead. Bus Circuito No 1 from outside second class bus terminal goes past Parque La Venta (taxi to La Venta park US$2). From Parque Juárez in the city, take a 'Fracc Carrizal' bus and ask to be let off at Parque Tomás Garrido, of which La Venta is a part.

Villahermosa is heaving under pressure from the oil boom, which is why it is now such an expensive place. Buses to Mexico City are often booked up well in advance, as are hotel rooms, especially during the holiday season (May onwards). Overnight free parking (no facilities) in the Campo de Deportes. It is hard to find swimming facilities in Villahermosa: Ciudad Deportiva pool for cardholders only. There is a bull ring.

Excursions Northwest of Villahermosa are the Maya ruins of **Comalcalco**, reached by bus (two a day by ADO, 1230 and 1800, US$2.50, or local Souvellera bus, US$2, one and a half hours over paved roads, Souvellera bus leaves from near the bridge where Avenida Universidad crosses Ruiz Cortines, four to five blocks north of Central Camionera in Villahermosa), then taxi to the ruins US$4.50 or to the entrance, US$0.35, and walk one kilometre, or walk the full three kilometres. The ruins are unique in Mexico because the palaces and pyramids are built of bricks, long and narrow like ancient Roman bricks, and not of stone. ■ *open daily 1000-1600, US$1.60.* From Comalcalco go to **Paraíso** near the coast, frequent buses from town to the beach eight kilometres away. Interesting covered market, good cocoa. **D** *Centro Turístico* beach hotel, clean, no hot water, food and drink expensive. Also **E** *Hotel Hidalgo*, in centre, clean.

Sleeping Tourists are often wiser to go directly to Palenque for accommodation; cheaper and no com-
The price difference petition from business travellers.
between a reasonable   Best is **LL** *Exalaris Hyatt*, Juárez 106, T34444, F55808, all services. **AL** *Holiday Inn*
and a basic hotel can ***Villahermosa Plaza***, Paseo Tabasco 1407, T64400, F64569, 4 kilometres from centre, restau-
be negligible, so one rant, bar, entertainment. **AL** *Cencali*, Juárez y Paseo Tabasco, T151999, F156600, excellent
might as well go for breakfast, highly recommended. **A** *Maya-Tabasco* (Best Western), Blvd Ruíz Cortines 907,
the former. T21111, F21133, all services, ask for special offers, sometimes as cheap as **D**. **B** *Don Carlos*,
Madero 418, T22493, F24622, central, clean, helpful, good restaurant (accepts American Express card), nearby parking. **B** *Plaza Independencia*, Independencia 123, T21299, F44724. **C** *Chocos*, Merino 100, T129444, F129649, friendly, clean, a/c, near ADO terminal. **C** *María Dolores*, Aldama 104, a/c, hot showers, excellent restaurant (closed Sunday). **C** *Palma de Mallorca*, Madero 516, T20144. **C** *Ritz*, Madero 1009, T121611, safe parking. Many other hotels along Madero (eg **D** *La Paz*, central).

Villahermosa

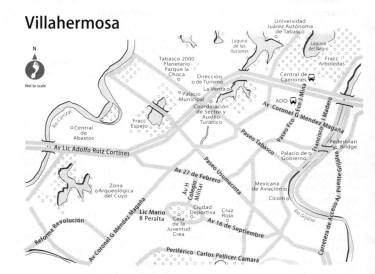

D *Oviedo*, Lerdo 303, good. **D** *Sofía*, Zaragoza 408, T26055, central, tolerable but overpriced, a/c. **E** *Madero*, Madero 301, T20516, damp, good value, some rooms for 4 are cheaper. **E** *Oriente*, Madero 425, clean, hot shower, fan, good restaurant, recommended. **E** *San Miguel*, Lerdo 315, T21500, good value, quiet, clean, shower, fan, very friendly, run down. **E** *Tabasco*, Lerdo 317, T20077, not too clean, cold water, mosquitoes. Several others on Lerdo. Cheap hotels, from **E** per person, on Calle Constitución (come out of main entrance of bus terminal, turn right then 1st left and continue for 5 blocks, but it's the red-light district).

Youth hostel The youth hostel at the back of the Ciudad Deportiva doesn't accept travellers arriving in the evening (4 kilometres southwest of the bus station), CP 80180, T56241.

A good restaurant at *Hotel Madan*, Madero 408, good breakfast, inexpensive fish dishes, a/c, newspapers, a good and quiet place to escape from the heat. *VIPs*, next door, reliable and moderately priced. *Cafetería La Terraza*, Reforma 304, in *Hotel Miraflores*, good breakfast. *Café Casino*, Suárez 530, good coffee. *Bruno's*, Lerdo y 5 de Mayo, cheap, good, noisy, good atmosphere. *Café La Barra*, Lerdo, near *Bruno's*, good coffee, quiet, pleasant. *El Torito Valenzuela*, next to *Hotel Madero*, Mexican specialities, excellent and inexpensive, highly recommended. *El Fogón*, Av Carlos Pellicer 304A, good value. *Blanca Mariposa*, near entrance to Parque La Venta, recommended. *Aquarius*, Fco Javier Mina 309, near Av Méndez, vegetarian food, juice bar and health food store. Avoid the bad and expensive tourist eating places on and near the river front. **Eating**

Ash Wednesday is celebrated from 1500 to dusk by the throwing of water in balloon bombs and buckets at anyone who happens to be on the street. **Festivals**

Local Taxis run mainly on a fixed route colectivo system (US$1.50 per stop), which can be a problem if you want to go somewhere else. You may have to wait a long time before a driver without fares agrees to take you. **Car hire**: Hertz car rental is available from the airport. **Agrisa**, M Ocampo esq Paseo Tabasco y Malecon, T129184, good prices, eg US$40 per day including taxes and insurance, but it is expensive to return the car to another city. **Transport**

    Air Airport Carlos R Pérez (VSA), 8 kilometres from town. Flights to Cancún, Ciudad del Carmen, Havana (Cuba), Houston (Texas), Mérida, Mexico City, Monterrey, Oaxaca, San Antonio (Texas), Tampico, Tuxtla Gutiérrez and Veracruz. VW bus to town US$3 per person, taxi US$9.50 for 2.

    Buses 1st class, ADO bus terminal is on Javier Mina between Méndez and Lino Merino, 12 blocks north of centre, computerized booking system, staff unhelpful. A taxi to the ADO terminal costs US$6, expensive but hard to avoid. Left luggage at ADO terminal, 0700-2300, US$0.30 per piece per hour, often closed. Alternatively, go to Sra Ana in minute restaurant/shop at Pedro Fuentes 817, 100 metres from ADO, reliable, open till 2000, small charge made, or, upstairs at 203 Javier Mina, opposite ADO, US$0.10 per piece per hour. Other private luggage depositories by the bus station also make a small charge. The Central Camionera 2nd class bus station is on Avenida Ruíz Cortines, near roundabout with fisherman statue, 1 block east of Javier Mina, opposite Castillo, 4 blocks north of ADO (ie 16 from centre); usually in disarray and it is difficult to get a ticket. Mind your belongings. Several buses (1st class) to **Mexico City**, US$30, 12 hours, direct bus leaves 1815 (Cristóbal Colón) or 1650 (ADO) then frequent through the night, expect to wait a few hours for Mexico City buses and at least 30 minutes in the ticket queue. To **Jalapa** with ADO, 3 a day, 10 hours; to **Campeche**, US$16.50 (6 hours), reservation required; to **Coatzacoalcos**, US$7; to **Tapachula**, US$20, 14 hours. Many buses a day to **Mérida** 8-10 hours, with ADO, US$19.50, 11 a day, or Cristóbal Colón at 1030 and 2230, US$22; if coming from Oaxaca to make a connection for Mérida, be prepared for long queues as most buses pass through en route from México City. To **San Andrés Tuxtla**, 6 hours, US$12.50. To **San Cristóbal**, US$9, 6 hours; also 2nd class bus with 1 change at Tuxtla, leaves 0800, arrives 2100, fine scenery but treacherous road. To **Puebla**, ADO 'GL' plus service via autopista, US$30, 1st class US$25.50; Cristóbal Colón from ADO terminal to **Oaxaca** via Coatzacoalcos and Tehuantepec at 1930 and 2130, 1st class, stops at about 7 places, US$27.50. Bus to **Veracruz**, many a day with ADO, 7 hours,

US$36 *primera plus*; to **Chetumal**, US$16, 10 hours, but the road is now in a very bad state and it can take much longer, 4 buses, erratic service. To **Catazajá**, US$4, 1½ hours. To **Palenque**, from ADO terminal, US$4.60, 1st class, US$2.50, 2nd class, 2½ hours, 8 a day in all from 0430 (difficult to get on a bus on Sunday). Circuito Maya, US$5.60, ADO; 1st class 1000 (buy ticket day before) and 1700, 1½ hours. To Emiliano Zapata and Tenosique (for Río San Pedro crossing into Guatemala, see page 448), buses 0700, 0800, 1330, 3-4 hours.

Directory   **Airline offices** *AeroMéxico* office, Periférico Carlos Pellicer 511, T26991 (airport 41675). *Mexicana*, Av Madero 109, or Desarrollo Urbano Tabasco 2000, T163785/560101 (airport 21164). *Aerocaribe*, Fco Javier Mina 301-A, T43202 (airport 44695). *Aviacsa*, T65736. **Banks** *Banco Internacional*, Suárez y Lerdo, changes TCs at good rates. *Banamex*, Madero y Reforma. *American Express*, Turismo Nieves, Sarlat 202, T41818. **Communications** **Postal services:** Post office on Ignacio in the centre. DHL, parcel courier service, Paseo Tabasco. **Tour companies & travel agents** *Viajes Villahermosa*, 27 de Febrero 207. **Tourist offices** In the 1st class bus station (English spoken) and another not far from La Venta park, in Edif Administrativo Tabasco 2000, at Paseo Grijalva and Paseo Tabasco (T163633, F163632), both good, closed 1300-1600. Many *papelerías* sell a city map for US$0.10.

South of Villahermosa

Teapa   This is a nice, clean little town with several hotels and beautiful surroundings. The
Colour map 4, grid B1   square is pleasant, and you can swim in the river or in the sulphur pool, El Azufre and cavern of Cocona. From Teapa, Tapijulapa on the Chiapas border can be visited, beautiful views.

Sleeping and eating   **C** *Quintero*, Eduardo R Bastar 108, T20045, behind Zócalo, a/c, fan, clean, friendly, enthusiastic restaurant. **D** Simple hotel in grounds of El Azufre, entry to pool included, no restaurant. **D** *Jardín*, at the top of the square, friendly, recommended. Good restaurant on main square, *El Mirador*. *Familiar*, main street 125, friendly, not cheap but filling, recommended.

Buses   There are buses between Teapa and Villahermosa on a paved road, 50 kilometres, 1 hour, US$1.65. Bus to Chiapa de Corzo at 0730, 7 hours, US$10, lovely, mountainous landscape (see page 419).

Pichucalco   80 kilometres southwest of Villahermosa on Route 195 is Pichucalco, an affluent
Colour map 4, grid B1   town with no beggars and a lively and safe atmosphere. The Zócalo is thronged in the evening with people on after-dinner *paseo*.

Sleeping and eating   There are many good restaurants and bars. **D** *Hotel La Loma*, Francisco Contreras 51, T30052, bath, a/c, or fan, ample parking, clean (opposite is a cheaper *posada* with resident monkey). **E** *Hotel México*, on left turn from bus station, with bath, fan, clean but musty. *Vila*, on Plaza. **D** *Jardín*, noisy. **D** *La Selva*.

Transport   Buses almost every hour to Villahermosa, US$4.

South of Pichucalco on Highway 195 on the way to Tuxtla Gutiérrez, is **Bochil**, an idyllic stopover (**D** *Hotel/Restaurant María Isabel*, 1 Av Sur Pte 44, basic but nice, delicious simple food).

Villahermosa to Guatemala

By car: 1) via Palenque to San Cristóbal de Las Casas (see below); 2) by Route 195 and 190 to Ciudad Cuauhtémoc via San Cristóbal de Las Casas (Highway 195 is fully paved, but narrow and winding with landslides and washouts in the rainy season, high altitudes, beautiful scenery). If this route is impassable, travel back by Route 180 to Acayucan, to 190, via 185 and go to Ciudad Cuauhtémoc or by Route 200 to Tapachula.

Villahermosa to Palenque

Palenque is reached by turning off the inland Highway, 186, at **Playas de Catazajá**, 117 kilometres from Villahermosa. No petrol stations until Catazajá where unleaded Magna-sin is available; if you look like running out, turn left for **Macuspana**, where there is one. Hotel in Macuspana: **D** *América*, basic, clean, comfortable, safe parking. Macuspana municipal *fiesta* 15-16 August. Palenque is 26 kilometres away on a good paved but winding road (minibus US$1.15, 30 minutes, taxi US$10). Coming from Campeche it is five hours' drive on a good road, apart from one rough stretch about one hour from Palenque; toll bridge US$0.60.

Palenque

The town of Palenque is nothing special but visitors come for the archaeological site eight kilometres from the town (143 kilometres from Villahermosa), a splendid experience, with its series of Maya hilltop temples in remarkably good condition. It is best to visit the ruins just before they close to avoid the crowds, but to avoid the heat arrive early. On the road to the ruins there are several waterfalls, one is just 250 metres from the entrance on the right (two minutes' walk from road).

Phone code: 934
Colour map 4, grid B2

The site is in a hot jungle clearing on a steep green hill overlooking the plain and crossed by a clear cascading brook. Interesting wildlife, mainly birds, also includes howler monkeys and mosquitoes. The ruins are impressive indeed, particularly the Templo de las Inscripciones, easy to climb from the back, in the heart of which was discovered an intact funerary crypt with the Sarcophagus of Lord Pacal, Palenque's greatest ruler, buried in AD 683 (you walk from the top of the pyramid into a staircase, descending to ground level, very humid; usually illuminated when the site is

Sights

Palenque

■ Sleeping	6 Regional	2 2nd Class Buses
1 Avenida	7 Vaca Vieja	3 2nd & Other 1st Class
2 Kashlan		Buses
3 La Cañada	🚌 Buses	
4 Maya Tulipanes	1 ADO & Cristóbal	
5 Misol-Há	Colón Bus Terminal	

N

Not to scale

open, but check). The temples around, with fantastic comb-like decorations on their intact roofs, and the sculptured wall panels, are undoubtedly the most exquisite achievement of the Maya. Groups of buildings and several tombs have been discovered in the last few years. Explanations in three languages on each temple are now legible (pamphlet with brief explanations in English available at the ticket office, US$1.30). You can also wander around in the jungle, many unexcavated ruins, take a torch and look out for spiders and snakes.

There is a five-hour hike starting to the left side of the Templo de las Inscripciones, follow the path uphill for one and a half hours until you reach a fence. Walk along several fields until you reach the village at the bottom of the valley (one hour). Coconut milk is available here. Turn right and follow the track uphill to a pass with fine views. Walking on through farmland you arrive back on the road by the museum at the ruins. Start early.

An excellent **museum**, with restaurant and gift shop, about one kilometre outside the ruins has some fine Maya carvings – stuccos, jade pieces, funerary urns, pottery and other artefacts excavated at the site. ■ *Open 1000, more like 1100, to 1700, closed Monday). Entry to ruins, US$2 (Sunday free), charge for car parking. The site opens at 0800 and closes at 1700 (guide, up to 10 people).* Beware of thieves at all times. A restaurant by the cascades serves a limited range of food, basic but friendly (stores luggage for US$0.25); shops quick to overcharge and souvenirs are dearer than elsewhere. A path runs from the museum to the main road via waterfalls with good swimming.

Hail a colectivo on the road, US$0.80 to town. The climate is hot and dry March-April, the coolest months are October to February. *Warning*: The area can have many mosquitoes; make sure you're up-to-date with your tablets (December-April usually few mosquitoes).

Palenque archaeological site

N

Not to scale

1 Temple of Inscriptions
2 Palace
3 Temple of the Sun
4 Temple of the Cross
5 Temple of the Foliated Cross
6 Temple of the Beautiful Relief
7 Ball Court
8 Temple of the Count
9 North Group

Palace plan

Sleeping

It is convenient to stay at hotels near the Pemex service station, as they are also nearer the ruins and the bus stations. (Prices treble around fiesta time.)

A *Misión Palenque*, far end of town in countryside, T50241, F50499, complete resort, noisy a/c, although poor service in restaurant reported, has a minibus service from Villahermosa airport for about US$20 return (2 hours' journey, avoids backtracking from airport into Villahermosa for transport to Palenque), has courtesy bus to ruins and to airfield for trips to Bonampak and Yaxchilán.
AL-C *Plaza Palenque* (Best Western), Km 27, Carretera Catazajá-Palenque, T50555, F50395, free transport Monday-Saturday

0800-1700, a/c, pool, relaxing, disco, 1½ kilometres from centre, 8 kilometres from ruins. **AL** *Maya Toucan*, on road into town, T50290, pool, a/c, bar, restaurant, lovely views from rooms. **AL** *Motel Chan-Kah Inn*, at Km 3 Carretera Ruinas, T51100, F50820, closest to ruins, cool bungalows, swimming pool fed from river, beautiful gardens, perfectly clean, recommended. Poor restaurant, with marimba music Friday-Sunday, and affiliated to **B** *Chan Kah Centro*, corner of Juárez and Independencia, T50318, F50489, a/c, restaurant, terrace bar with happy hour. **B** *Hotel Maya Tulipanes*, C Cañada 6, T50201, F51004, a/c, cable TV, rooms vary in size, price and quality, garage, pool, bar/restaurant next door, recommended. **B-C** *Motel Los Leones*, Km 2.5, about 5 kilometres before ruins on main road, T50201, F50033, hot water, a/c, TV, quiet, large restaurant, gringo food. **B-C** *Kashlan*, 5 de Mayo 105, T50297, F50309, with bath, fan or a/c, hot water, quiet, clean, will store luggage, video each pm, mosquito nets, helpful owner Ada Luz Navarro, tours to Agua Azul and Misol-Ha falls, US$8 per person, laundry opposite, restaurant with vegetarian food in same building, bus and boat tours to Flores offered, recommended.

C *Hotel La Cañada*, T50102, F50446, very rustic but very clean, with fan, good value, lovely garden, expensive restaurant, the owner, Sr Morales, is an expert on the ruins. **C** *Casa de Pakal*, Juárez 8, T50042, 1 block from Plaza, a/c, good but poor plumbing and not very friendly; next door is **E** *Misol-Há*, at Juárez 12, T50092, fan, with bath, hot water, clean, owner Susana Cuevas speaks English. **C** *Palenque*, 5 de Mayo 15, off Plaza, T50188, F50030, with bath, a/c restaurant, vast, rambling menage, 'going downhill fast', pool.

D *Lacroix*, Hidalgo 30, T50014, next to church, with bath, fan, no hot water, some cheaper rooms, pleasant place. **D** *Posada Mallorca*, on highway, T50838, small rooms, comfortable. **D** *Regional*, Av Juárez 79, T50183, 3 blocks from Plaza, hot showers (US$1.50 extra), lights located behind fans ensure constant flickering lights, noisy. **D** *Xibalba*, Merle Green 9, T50411, F50392, spacious rooms, clean, hot water, a/c, fan, recommended. **D** *La Posada*, at La Cañada, T50437, hot water, fans, basic, a little run down but OK, 'designed for young travellers, international ambience', peaceful, luggage store.

E *Naj K'in*, Hidalgo 72, with bath and fan, hot water 24 hours, noisy disco nearby, purified water in room and cooler in hallway, safe parking, excellent value. **E** *Avenida*, Juárez 216, T50116, with restaurant, clean, large rooms with fan, parking, but does not display price in rooms so ask for government list to check, no hot showers, some rooms with balcony. **E** *Casa de Huéspedes León*, Hidalgo (s/n) near junction with Abasolo, T50038, with bath, only cold water, some mosquitoes. **E** *La Selva*, Av Reforma 69, clean, hot water extra. **E** *Posada Alicia*, Av Manuel Velasco Suárez 59, T50322, between new market and C Novelos, with fan (ask for one), cold water, no towels, cheap, grubby, rooms on left as you enter are cooler, ask for rooms with communal bathroom. **E** *Posada San Francisco*, Hidalgo 113 and Allende, with bath, clean, quiet, no curtains, basic. **E** *Posada Shalom*, Av Juárez 156, T50944, new, friendly, clean, noisy, stores luggage, recommended. **E** *Santa Elena*, C Jorge de la Vega, behind ADO/Cristóbal Colón terminal but still fairly quiet, with bath, good value, clean, simple, fan, safe parking. **E** *Vaca Vieja*, 5 de Mayo 42, T50388, 3 blocks from Plaza, with bath, popular with gringos, good restaurant. **E** *Los Angeles*, next to ADO terminal, new, hot water, fan, comfortable, recommended. **E-F** *Posada San Juan*, T50616 (from ADO go up the hill and first right, it's on the 4th block on the left), with bath, cheaper without, cold water, and fan, clean, quiet, firm beds, secure locks, nice courtyard, very good for budget accommodation, safe parking available (also near buses, *Santo Domingo*, 20 de Noviembre 19, T50146, stores luggage). **E** *Posada Kin*, Abasolo s/n, 20 de Noviembre y 5 de Mayo T51714, very near Zócalo, clean doubles with bathroom, fan, tours available, safe and luggage store. **E-F** *Yun-Kax*, Av Corregidora 87 (behind *Santo Domingo*), T50146, quiet, clean, large rooms, hot water, recommended.

F *Joanna*, 20 de Noviembre y Allende, large, clean, airless rooms with fan and bath. **F** per person *Posada Charito*, Av 20 de Noviembre 15B, T50121, clean, friendly, family run, very good value, basic, some rooms very airless, ground floor best, laundry service. opposite is **E-G** *Posada Canek*, 20 de Noviembre, dearer rooms have bath, all with fan and toilet, very clean, ground floor dormitory near reception noisy, helpful staff, prices are per person and sharing is often required (regardless of sex), fills up early, arrive before 1000 check-out time. Nearby on 20 de Noviembre is **F** *Chacamax*, small rooms with bath, fan.

Camping *Trailer Park Mayabel*, on road to ruins 2 kilometres before entrance (bus from town US$0.30), for caravans and tents, US$8 per vehicle with 2 people. US$2.35 for tent or to sling hammock (an *ambulante* sells hammocks once a day, or you can hire them for an additional US$2.50), palmleaf huts, bathrooms, hot showers, good restaurant but not cheap, nice setting, popular so can be noisy, the place is not to everyone's taste; many mosquitoes and many ticks in long grass (we're told they avoid people who eat lots of garlic!). Watch your belongings; management sometimes stores luggage during the day (reluctant to store valuables). At night, around 0100, you can often hear the howler monkeys screaming in the jungle; quite eerie. The path between the campground and the ruins is not open; do not attempt to use this path. *Panchan Camping*, on road to ruins, cabins (**E**), rent a hammock for US$3 or camp for US$2, hot showers, clean, small pool, vegetarian meals, library, owner is archaeologist and is friendly and informative. *Trailer Park María del Mar*, 5 kilometres from Palenque, along road to ruins, T50533, US$12 for 2 in camper van with hook-up, camping US$5, restaurant and swimming pool, cold showers, clean, pretty setting (check that water is turned on). Good swimming at *Calinda Nututún* (entry US$1), 3.5 kilometres along Palenque-Ocosingo road, T50100, US$3.30 per person, vehicle free, US$2 per camping site per night, rather run down, no tent rentals, rooms (**B**) are neglected, toilets and bath; and beautiful lake and waterfall open to the public for a small fee. Misol-Ha, 2 kilometres off same road at Km 19, see below.

Eating Some restaurants accept dollars, but at less than the current rate. *Montes Azules*, Av Juárez, very tasty food in generous portions and at low prices, friendly and helpful owner, live marimba music Friday, Saturday, Sunday nights. *La Quebrada*, Av Juárez 120, breakfast and reasonably-priced meals, fast service, recommended. *Merolec*, down street from *La Posada*, new, good atmosphere and service, reasonable prices. *Lakan-Ha*, Juárez 20, fast, cheap, efficient; also on Av Juárez, *La Jícara Pícara*, Allende junction, very good value and very friendly, specializes in *pozole*, a maize stew. *El Rodeo*, Juárez 120, near Plaza, does inexpensive breakfasts and meat dishes, popular with travellers, good source of information, recommended. *La Ceiba* (Hnos Cabrera) on Juárez, good café for breakfast. *Los Aluxes*, Juárez 189, roof terrace, very good food and value, popular with backpackers, good breakfasts, slow service. *Francesa*, Juárez, 2 doors down from ADO bus office, nothing French but reasonable steak and chips. *Pizzería Palenque*, Juárez, T50332, good pizzas and prices. *Mara*, on 5 de Mayo by the Zócalo, excellent food, very welcoming. *Mariscos and Pescados*, off Juárez, opposite large *artesanía* market. *Las Tinajas*, 20 de Noviembre 41 y Abasolo, good, family run, excellent food, huge portions but not cheap. *Los Portales*, Av 20 de Noviembre e Independencia, cheap, good, recommended. *Artemio*, Av Hidalgo, near Plaza, reasonably-priced food, recommended. *Chan Kah*, on Plaza, good value, accepts credit cards. At Km 0.5 on Hidalgo (road to ruins) is *La Selva*, expensive, but excellent, smart dress preferred, live music at weekends. *Yunuen*, at *Hotel Vaca Vieja*, generous portions at reasonable prices, good steaks, popular with local ranchers. *La Palapa de Apo-Hel*, Av 5 de Mayo, s/n, between Independencia and Abasolo, a delightful little bamboo shack specializing in seafood, recommended. *California*, Av 5 de Mayo, opposite *Avenida*, near 2nd class buses, good value, Mexican specialities. Opposite *Hotel Kashlan*, *Café de los Altos*, good coffee. *El Rinconcito*, Allende, across from *Kashlan*, good, economical. *El Fogón de Pakal*, C Merle Green, La Cañada, delightful, good and varied menu. Good *pollo rostizado* in restaurant inside ADO office. Good *tacos* at food stalls east of Parque Central. Try the ice-cream at *Holanda* on Av Juárez, s/n, 4 doors west of Banamex, in the centre.

Festivals *Santo Domingo*, first week in August.

NB Visitors should respect the local customs and dress so as not to offend – footwear and shirts should always be worn.

Shopping Cotton, nylon and sisal hammocks can be bought along Avenida Juárez. Bargain.

Sports **Horse riding**: tours can be booked at the Clínica Dental Zepeda, Avenida Juárez s/n. The dentist is the owner of the horses.

Air Aerocaribe flies 3 times a week to Palenque from Cancún via Flores, Guatemala. There **Transport**
are also flights from Huatulco, Mérida, Oaxaca and Tuxtla Gutiérrez. For flights to Bonampak
and Yaxchilán, see below.

Trains Railway station for Palenque is 10 kilometres outside town (bus goes from in front
of *Posada Alicia* at 2000; from station to town, irregular service, be patient). Much better is a
taxi colectivo to/from railway station and Pemex service station US$1.50 for 2. Latest timeta-
bles show trains to Palenque starting at Coatzacoalcos at 2320, and continuing to
Campeche and **Mérida**, arriving there at 1325, from Mérida the train leaves at 0605, arriving
Coatzacoalcos at about 2000; keep your luggage with you (only 1 car, no sleeper) no light,
take a torch and insect repellent. Tickets on sale 1 hour before train arrives. The train may be
crowded so it may be necessary to stand all the way. The trains are unreliable with delays of
up to 11 hours. The station is not a pleasant place to wait in the dark. Do not rely on timetables, check all times in person before travel. **NB** If returning from Palenque to Mérida by train,
bear in mind that in December and January it is nearly impossible to make reservations.

Buses Micro buses run back and forth along the main street, passing the bus station
area, to and from the ruins, every 10 minutes, US$0.50 (taxi US$5). All bus companies have
terminals close to each other at west end of Avenida Juárez with 20 de Noviembre. **Taxis**
charge a flat rate of US$1 within the town.

Cristóbal Colón and ADO share a terminal. Buy ticket to leave on arrival, ADO 1st class on
sale the day before, buses are often full, very heavy ticket sales on 1 and 15 of each month
when salaries are paid.

ADO: 1st class bus to/from **Mexico City**, at 1800, 13 hours, 1,006 kilometres, US$43; to
Villahermosa, 6 a day between 0700 and 1900, $2\frac{1}{2}$ hours, US$5. 2nd class bus to
Villahermosa at 0800 and 1200, US$2.50. To Veracruz, only via Villahermosa, from there $7\frac{1}{2}$
hours with ADO, many a day, US$14.80. ADO buses, 7 a day, to **Ciudad del Carmen**,
US$13.25. Direct bus to **Campeche** from Palenque at 1700, 2nd class (Transportes del Sur),
US$10.65, or 2 with ADO, 0800 and 2100, US$ 12, 5-7 hours, change here for Mérida (a further
$2\frac{1}{2}$ hours). Daily ADO 1st class bus direct to **Mérida** at 0800, US$23, book in advance, 8 hours,
luxury service at 0100 daily, Cristóbal Cólon (US$25). 2nd class to Mérida US$17, dep 1700
and 2300, 9hrs. Alternatively, go for connections to Campeche or Mérida at Emiliano Zapata,
bus from Palenque at 0700, 0900, 1400, and 2000 (from ADO terminal) bus to Palenque at
0600 and 1230 (taxi Emiliano Zapata-Palenque US$28). See page 452. Another possiblity is to
take a bus to Catazajá (see page 442), where the 1500 Cristóbal Colón bus
Villahermosa-Campeche bus stops. To **Chetumal** with ADO, daily at 2030, with a/c, toilets,
stops at Escárcega for a meal, 8-10 hours; Maya de Oro 1st class, US$23; Cristóbal Colón at
2100, 7-8 hours; also 2nd class with Lacandonia at 0100, US$14.80. Note that ADO and
Cristóbal Colón buses arrive between 0400 and 0500, a bad time to look for a hotel or find a
bus to Belize. To **San Cristóbal de Las Casas**, good road throughout, 4 hours' journey,
Rodolfo Figueroa, a/c, TV, toilet, 3-4 a day, US$4.50 (beware travel sickness, many bends);
luxury service with Cristóbal Colón, a/c, video, 0230 and 2300 daily, also goes on to Tuxtla
Gutiérrez. ADO leaves at 0930, US$5. Autotransportes Tuxtla 5 expresses a day, US$7, also 1st
class US$5.25 and 2nd class US$4.30. ALTOS at 1230 and 1500, US$6. **Tuxtla Gutiérrez**, 5 a
day, 377 kilometres, US$11, $3\frac{1}{2}$ hours, 2nd class, via San Cristóbal de Las Casas. **NB** There are
military checks between Palenque and San Cristóbal de Las Casas; buses and cars are
stopped. If stopped at night in a private car, switch off engine and lights, and switch on the
inside light. Always have your passport handy.

Banks Exchange rate only comes through at 1000, then banks open until 1200. *Bancomer*, changes **Directory**
TCs, good rates. *Yax-Ha Cambio* on Juárez, open 0700-2000 daily, changes US$ cash and TCs. Next
door at No 28, is *Banamex*, open Mon-Fri 0930-1400, quick. *Restaurante El Rodeo* also changes TCs at
bank rate. At weekends TCs can be changed at many travel agencies and other shops on Av Juárez;
also, the owner at Farmacia Central will change US$ at a reasonable rate. ATMs at Bancomer and
Banamex, but with long queues.

Communications Post Office: Independencia, next to Palacio Municipal, helpful. **Telephone:**
long-distance telephones at ADO bus terminal, cheaper than many other telephone offices; at
Mercería bookshop in Aldama near Juárez, and a shop by *Hotel Palenque* in Zócalo. **Internet:** on
Independencia y Av 20 de Noviembre.

Laundry Opposite *Hotel Kashlan*, US$2 per 3 kg, mixed reports, open 0800-1930. At the end of Juárez is a laundry, US$3 per 3 kg. **Tour companies & travel agents** *Tonina*, Juárez 105, T50384, or small office on Juárez ½ block from plaza, mixed reports, clarify prices before tour, tours to Bonampak and Yaxchilán, 2 days, US$55 per person. *STS*, near Post Office, good prices for group tours, but prices do not include entry to sites, also watch out for hidden extras like cold drinks at lunch. *Kim Travel*, 3 days to Flores, Guatemala via Yaxchilán, Bonampak and a Lacondón village, US$ 80pp. *Yax-Ha*, Av Juárez 123, T50798, F50787, English spoken, recommended. *Shivalva* (Marco A Morales), Merle Green 1, La Cañada, T50411, F50392, tours of Palenque, Yaxchilán, Bonampak, Tikal, Guatemala City, Belize, Copán (also offers hotel booking for San Cristóbal de las Casas, but it's best to make your own choice). **Tourist offices** On Av Juárez y Abasolo, while office on Plaza, Jiménez y 5 de Mayo, is being renovated, open 0900-2100, useful map with hotel and restaurant listings, helpful and informative staff. Delegación de Turismo, T50356.

Road and river travel to Guatemala

Tenosique & Río San Pedro route The Río San Pedro route starts at Tenosique, a friendly place (money exchange at clothing shop Ortiz y Alvarez at Calle 28, Número 404, good rates for dollars to quetzales, poor for dollars to pesos) on the Palenque-Mérida railway line. From here you go by road to La Palma, boat to El Naranjo, Guatemala, and road to Flores.

Sleeping **D** *Rome*, C 28, No 400, T20151, clean, will change dollars for residents, bath, not bad. **E** *Azulejos*, C 26 No 416, with bath, fan, clean, hot water, friendly, helpful owner speaks some English, opposite church. **E** *Casa de Huéspedes La Valle*, C 19, with bath, clean, good, and others. Excellent and cheap *Taquería Pipirrín*, C 26, 512, near *Hotel Azulejos*.

Transport You can get to Tenosique from Villahermosa by ADO bus (0430, 0700, 0800, 1330), 4 hours, from Emiliano Zapata by frequent 1st or 2nd class bus, US$2, or on the México-Mérida railway line, 1 hour east by train from Palenque, US$0.75. From Palenque by road minibuses Libertad leave from 20 de Noviembre y Allende from 0700 to Emiliano Zapata, 1 hour, US$2.50 (take 0700 to be sure of making the boat at La Palma); and from there to Tenosique at 0800 or 0900, 90 minutes, US$2. ADO have a direct bus to Tenosique from Palenque at 0430, 2 hours, US$3.25. Many travel agents in Palenque organize colectivos direct to La Palma at 1000, US$14 per person to connect with the boat to El Naranjo (4 passengers minimum). Alternatively, take a colectivo before 0645 to Playas de Catazajá from the stop just up from ADO (US$1, 30 minutes); alight at the El Crucero de la Playa crossroads on the Villahermosa – Tenosique road and wait for the bus to pass at 0730 (2 hours to Tenosique, US$2). Similarly, from Tenosique to Palenque, take the Villahermosa bus (every hour or so during the day) as far as El Crucero de La Playa, and then take one of the regular minibuses running to Palenque. Bus also from Mexico City, ADO, 16½ hours, arrives 0700, US$45.50.

Tour companies & travel agents For planes to Bonampak contact Sr Quintero, T20099. *Hotel Kashlan* offers 2 and 3 day trips to Flores via Yaxchilán and Bonampak, reliable and recommended. *Kim Tours*, Av Juárez 27, T51499, do similar trips "strenuous but great", US$100 per person, recommended. Travel agencies in Palenque do the trip to Flores via La Palma and El Naranjo, US$35-55 per person, three passengers minimum (agencies will make up the numbers), departs 0500, arrive Flores 1900; via Corozal/Bethel, US$35 per person, via Yaxchilán and Bonampak, see below, minimum five people. It may take several days before you can join an organized trip in low season.

From Tenosique to **La Palma** on the Río San Pedro, orange *colectivos*, starting at 0600 from in front of the market, one hour, US$1, two hours by bus (from Tenosique bus station, which is outside town, take taxi, US$1.70 or colectivo to 'Centro', or walk 20 minutes). Taxi to La Palma US$7, shared by all passengers. From La Palma boats leave to El Naranjo (Guatemala) at 0800 (or when they have enough passengers) but timings are very irregular (they wait for a minimum of five passengers before leaving), at least four and a half hours, US$22 (to check boat times, T30811 Rural at the Río San Pedro). Be at boat one hour early, it sometimes leaves ahead of schedule; if this happens ask around for someone to chase it, US$3-4 per person for three people. If there are fewer than five passengers, the boat may be cancelled, in which case you must either wait for the next one, or hire a *rápido* (US$125, maximum four people). You may be able to arrange a slower boat for up to six people for US$100.

It is a beautiful boat trip, through mangroves with flocks of white herons and the occasional alligator, dropping people off at homesteads. There is a stop at the border post two hours into the journey to sign out of Mexico, a lovely spot with a lake and lilies. In the rain, luggage will get wet; take a raincoat and a torch. There is a pier at El Naranjo. In La Palma, two restaurants are poor value; one restaurant will change money at weekends at a reasonable rate. There are no officials on arrival at the jetty in El Naranjo; immigration is a short way uphill on the right (entry will cost US$5 in quetzales or dollars; beware extra unofficial charges at customs); bus tickets to Flores sold here.

At **El Naranjo** there are hotels (basic) and restaurants (you can wait in a restaurant till the 0100 bus departs, but electricity is turned off at 2200). The grocery store opposite immigration will change dollars into quetzales at a poor rate. From El Naranjo there is a dirt road through the jungle to Flores; buses leave at 0200, 0400, 0600, 1100, 1400 for Flores (minimum four to five rough, crowded hours, US$3) or hitchhiking apparently possible.

The Río Usumacinta route by road to Benemérito, boat to Sayaxché, Guatemala and road to Flores: Autotransportes Comitán Lagos de Montebello buses (Avenida Manuel Velasco Suárez, Palenque, three blocks from food market) run daily at 0330, 0530, 0800 to **Benemérito**, on the Mexican side of the Usumacinta, seven to 12 hours but will be quicker when the new paved road is completed, basic buses, dreadful road, crowded (it's about half the time in a *camioneta* if you can hitch a ride in one). You must visit immigration, about three kilometres from Benemérito, to sign out of Mexico (the bus will wait).

Río Usumacinta route

Once in Benemérito where there is a 2100 curfew (two basic *pensiones*), hope for a boat to Guatemala; this may take a couple of days. The boat goes to Sayaxché and should stop at Pipiles for immigration formalities. A trading boat takes two days, US$4-5; a motorized canoe eight hours, US$5-10. From Sayaxché, buses run to Flores.

Alternatively, take the bus Palenque-Frontera Echeverría, now more often known as Puerto Corozal, 1000, four hours by good road, US$5.50; or minibuses at 0730, 1100, 1400 from 5 de Mayo by *Restaurante El Caimito*, US$4.50 (many travel agencies in Palenque run minibuses on this route, leaving at 0600, to connect with the boat to Bethel, 35 minutes, and on to Flores as below). From Echeverría/Corozal there is a five-minute launch ride to La Técnica, then 20 minutes by bus to Bethel in Guatemala, from where a regular bus service goes to Flores at 1200, five hours (see Guatemala chapter, **El Petén**, page 638). Alternatively launches go directly to Bethel, US$40-45 per boat. At Echeverría/Corozal there is an immigration office; **F** *Posada XX*, nearby, and **F** *Posada Tumbalá*, better of the two; near the *embarcadero* are **C** *cabañas* with two double beds, built by the river boat company (Cooperativa Escudo Jaguar de Corozal) and two cheap *comedores*. Coming from Guatemala you may well get stuck at the border as the 0500 Santa Elena-Bethel bus does not connect with buses to Palenque (you may be able to get a lift with a pickup, or one of the tour buses which start arriving around 1200, bargain hard). Passengers have to wait until 0400 next day. Bus from Frontera Echeverría to Palenque, 0500, US$3 and at 1230, US$5. Many military checkpoints.

Palenque to Bonampak and Yaxchilán

Bonampak
Colour map 4, gid B2

Yaxchilán is a major Classic Maya centre built along a terrace and hills above the Río Usumacinta. The temples are ornately decorated with stucco and stone and the stone lintels are carved with scenes of ceremonies and conquests. There are more howler monkeys than people in Yaxchilán. ■ *0800-1600, US$2.* **Bonampak** was under the political domination of Yaxchilán, built in the late Classic period on the Río Lacanjá, a tributary of the Usumacinta. It is famous for its murals, dated at after AD 800, which relate the story of a battle and the bloody aftermath with the sacrificial torture and execution of prisoners. An article in *National Geographic*, February 1995, reproduces some of the murals with computer enhancement to show their original colours and most of the details. ■ *0800-1600, free.* Do not visit ruins at night, it is forbidden.

At **Lacanjá** (nine kilometres from Bonampak) there is a community of Lacandón Indians. They have curly hair, rare in Mexico, and wear white gowns. For more details ask at Na-Bolom in San Cristóbal de Las Casas. There are four campsites here where you can sling a hammock, *Kin Bor, Vicente K'in, Carlos Chan Bor* and *Manuel Chan Bor* (best to bring food and mosquito net). Local guides can be hired for hikes in the jungle and to the ruins of Bonampak. Lucas Chambor at the Casa de Cultura is a good source of advice. There have been some reports of hostility towards tourists. Transport Lacanjá-Bonampak with locals US$6.50-9. The walk through the jungle is beautiful and crosses several streams. Another walk in the area is to the Cascadas de Moctuniha (one hour each way US$6.50 with guide).

Transport A new road has been built to **Bonampak**: 2 lanes, paved. Autotransportes Comitán Lagos de Montebello (Manuel Velasco 48, 2 blocks west of plaza, Palenque) buses at 0300, 0430, 0630, 0900 and 2000 all pass the turn off to Bonampak, US$5.50, check details in advance. Last colectivo returning from Echeverría to Palenque passing crossroads for Bonampak at 1500. Buses from Palenque from Chancala bus terminal every 3 hours or so, from 0730 to **San Javier**, 3 hours; colectivos US$4. From San Javier a jungle trail leads to Bonampak, easy to follow but several hours walk with nowhere to stay en route. Take your own tent, hammock, sleeping bag as it gets cold at night, food and drink. **Yaxchilán** is reached by 1-hour boat journey from Echeverría, you must register at the immigration office here if you are continuing on to Guatemala. US$67 for up to 4 people, US$92 for more than 5, to hire a motorboat for the round trip, no problem finding a boat (max 10 people, cost includes boatman staying overnight), but try to be there before 0900 to give you time to meet other travellers wanting to share launch, you may be able to share with tour parties who arrive from 0900 onwards. It is a beautiful ride, and rewarding ruins at the end of it. The custodian of the ruins is very helpful. Camping is restricted to the INAH site on the Usumacinta.

Air Flights from Palenque to **Bonampak** and **Yaxchilán**, in light plane for five, about US$600 per plane, to both places, whole trip six hours. Prices set, list available; Viajes Misol-Ha run charter flights to Bonampak and Yaxchilán for US$150 per person return, minimum four passengers. ATC Travel Agency, agents for Aviacsa, at Avenida Benito Juárez and Allende, open 0800-1800 daily except Sunday, to Bonampak; book at airport, may be cheaper from Tenosique, best to visit in May – the driest month. **Road** Bonampak is over 30 kilometres from Frontera Echeverría/Corozal and can be reached from the crossroads to Lacanjá on the road to Echeverría/Corozal.

Tour Companies & Travel Agents From Palenque, a two-day road and river trip to Bonampak and Yaxchilán is sold by travel agencies, US$55 per person, all transport and food included; or one day trip to Yaxchilán, US$35; entrance to sites included in cost. Strenuous, but good value: the usual schedule is four-hours bus ride to Echeverría/Corozal (mostly tarmac), one hour boat to Yaxchilán, next day boat to Echeverría, one hour bus to Bonampak turn-off, walk to Bonampak and back, three to four hours bus to Palenque (arriving 2200). Colectivos Chambala at Hidalgo y Allende, Palenque, also run two-day trips, slightly cheaper, again all inclusive, minimum six passengers. Taxis charge US$20 per person for the return trip to Bonampak. Lacandón Indians running an ecotourism project take passengers in three-wheelers to the ruins (or to Lacanjá Chansayab community), US$7. However you go, take suitable footwear and rain protection for jungle walking, drinking water, insect repellent and passport (there are many military checkpoints). Beware of sandflies, black flies which cause river blindness, and mosquitoes; there is basic accommodation at the site, take hammock and mosquito net. The workers are not to be trusted, thieving has been reported.

Agua Azul and Misol-Ha

A series of beautiful waterfalls aptly named for the blue water swirling over natural tufa dams on seven kilometres of fast-flowing river, Agua Azul is a popular camping spot reached by a four-kilometre paved road from the junction with the paved road to San Cristóbal, 65 kilometres from Palenque. Best visited in dry season as in the rainy season it is hard to swim because of the current (don't visit if it was raining the day before). Three kilometres upstream is the Balcón Ahuau waterfall, good beach for sunbathing. It is extremely popular at holiday time (visit in the morning, less crowded). ■ *Entrance fee to this ejidal park US$0.65 on foot, US$2.50 for cars.*

The Liquidizer 🖜

One of the falls is called 'The Liquidizer', an area of white water in which bathing is extremely dangerous. On no account should you enter this stretch of water; many drownings have occurred. Obey the notice posted in an adjacent tree. If you walk some way up the lefthand side of the river you come to uncrowded areas where the river is wider and safer for swimming but do seek local advice about pools away from the main swimming area. Note also that violent robberies have been reported and the river bridge is a particularly risky spot. Never go alone, groups of at least four are best.

It is possible to walk upriver to the rainforest; follow the river till you come to a rickety bridge across a stream, cross this and continue through a meadow until you rejoin the river; carry on to a lovely beach with trees and the river thundering through a gorge. Further progress is difficult. Beware of ticks when camping in long grass, use kerosene to remove them (or eat raw garlic to repel them!). Flies abound during the rainy season (June-November). The river near the campsite is often badly polluted with soap and detergents. Horses can be rented for riding downstream where there are also uncrowded pools for swimming. Eight kilometres downstream on the Rio Xumulha is **Agua Clara**, a reserve, with small zoo, white beaches, horseriding and kayaking. One hotel and restaurant (ask for details at Tourist Delegation in Palenque).

Between Palenque and Agua Azul are the **Misol-Ha** waterfalls. ■ *Entry US$0.65, US$2.50 for a car.* There is an interesting cave to the right of the big falls, about 25 metres deep, with a pool inside and another waterfall; take a torch and beware of bats! It is also worth going behind the waterfall.

There are a few restaurants and many food stalls (if on a tight budget, bring your own). There are 2 places with *cabañas* for hammocks (hammock rental US$1.50 and up, US$3.50 per person in beds in dormitory); if staying, be very careful of your belongings; thefts have been reported. *Camping Agua Azul* is popular and reliable, opposite the parking lot; camping costs US$1.75, US$3.30 for 2 in camper van, and US$0.15 for use of toilets (100 metres further on are free public toilets), no other facilities. RVs can stay overnight at Agua Azul, using the facilities, without paying extra (as long as you do not leave the park). Plenty of food stalls, 2 restaurants. Follow the path up the falls to a second site, cheaper, less crowded. There are also more *cabañas* and nice places to sling a hammock further upstream, all cheaper and less touristy than lower down. *Hamacas Casa Blanca* next to *Comedor El Bosque*, 2 kilometres upstream, big room with mosquito-netted windows, accommodates 10, shared toilet, US$2 per person (US$1.70 with own hammock), free locked luggage store. 750 metres upstream from *Casa Blanca* is the last house on this path. Here you can sling a hammock for US$1

Sleeping & eating

(US$0.50 with own hammock), friendly family atmosphere, good views, store luggage, basic but good dinner, recommended. *Restaurant Económico* will rent out a small hut with hammocks, friendly, helpful, excellent food, safe luggage store. At Misol-Ha: **D** cabañas are for rent and a restaurant.

Transport Coop Chambalum, Calle Allende, and Viajes Aventura Maya, Avenida Juárez 123, Palenque run tours to Agua Azul and Misol-Ha for US$15, leaving 1000 returning 1630, and 1200 returning 1900 (30 minutes at Misol-Ha, 4 hours at Agua Azul, take swimsuit). Other minibuses from minibus terminal (near 4 Esquinas): they leave 0930-1000 from Palenque, 2 hours at Agua Azul, arriving back in Palenque at 1500, stopping for 15 minutes at Misol-Ha, US$6.65-8 ($\frac{1}{2}$ price 1-way). Colectivos from Hidalgo y Allende, Palenque, for Agua Azul and Misol-Ha, 2 a day, US$9; colectivos can also be organized between Misol-Ha and Agua Azul, in either direction. Taxi US$45 with 2 hours at Agua Azul, or to both falls US$65. Several buses from Palenque daily (direction San Cristóbal de Las Casas or Ocosingo), to crossroads leading to the waterfall, US$3.35, 2nd class, 1$\frac{1}{2}$ hours. From the crossroads walk the 4 kilometres downhill to the falls (or hitch a ride on a minibus for US$0.20). Back from the junction 1400-1600 with Transportes Maya buses. There are buses between San Cristóbal de Las Casas and Palenque (to 2nd class bus station, Transportes Maya) which will stop there, but on a number of others you must change at Temo, over 20 kilometres away, north of Ocosingo, which may require a fair wait.

Villahermosa to Campeche

Emiliano Zapata
Population: 13,000
Colour map 4, grid B2

There are two highways: inland Highway 186, via Escárcega, with two toll bridges (cost US$4.25), and the slightly longer coastal route through Ciudad del Carmen, Highway 180; both converge at Champotón, 66 kilometres south of Campeche. Highway 186 passes Villahermosa's modern international airport and runs fast and smooth in a sweeping curve 115 kilometres east to the Palenque turnoff at Playas del Catazajá; beyond, off the highway, is Emiliano Zapata (*Fiesta*: 26 October), a busy cattle centre, with Pemex station.

Sleeping D *Ramos*, opposite bus station, with a/c, **E** with fan, reasonable restaurant, friendly; *Bernat Colonial*, all basic. There is a mediocre hotel here, painted blue, on a quiet plaza by the river, 200 metres from main road. On the main road is restaurant *La Selva*, good food.

Transport From Emiliano Zapata, all ADO: to **Tenosique**, frequent, first at 0700, 0830, 0900, last at 2000, 2100, US$2, 90 minutes (plus 2, 2nd class companies); to **Villahermosa**, 17 departures between 0600 and 2000, US$6; to **Mérida**, 5 a day between 0800 and 2100, US$21; to **Escárcega**, 5 between 0630 and 2100, US$5.50; to **Chetumal**, 2130, US$14.

The river town of **Balancán** is a further 60 kilometres northeast and has a small archaeological museum in its Casa de Cultura (**E** *Hotel Delicias*); *fiesta* 14 December. In 10 kilometres the main highway has crossed the narrow waist of Tabasco state and entered Campeche, a popular destination for hunters and fishermen.

Escárcega
Population: 20,300
Colour map 4, grid B2

Route 186 is paved for the 140 kilometre run to Escárcega (officially Francisco Escárcega). The condition of this route is good up to Escárcega, but poor around the town itself, good around Champotón (see below), and paved right up to Campeche. Escárcega is a hot, straggling town which relies heavily on the many buses passing through. Service stations (fill up here if going east to Chetumal), a few overpriced hotels and cafés and the ADO first class bus station cluster near the junction of Highways 186 and 261. The rest of town spreads two kilometres east along the Chetumal highway (186), also called Calle Justo Sierra to the second class Autobuses del Sur terminal just east of the railway crossing. The oil boom has expanded the town's services considerably in recent years.

Sleeping **C** *Motel Akim Pech*, on Villahermosa highway, a/c or fans and bath, reasonable rooms, restaurant in motel, another across the street, also Pemex station opposite (sells unleaded *magna sin*). **D** *Berta Leticia*, C 29 No 28, with bath, fairly clean. **D** *Casa de Huéspedes Lolita* on Chetumal highway at east end of town, pleasant. **D** *María Isabel*, Justo Sierra 127, T40045, a/c, restaurant, comfortable, back rooms noisy from highway. **D-E** *Escárcega*, Justo Sierra 86, T40186, bath, parking, hot water, noisy, grubby, overpriced, good restaurant, small garden, about 500 metres east of ADO, on the road Chetumal-Villahermosa. **D-E** *El Yucateco*, C 50 No 42-A, T40065, with or without a/c, central, tidy, fair value. **E** *Las Gemelas*, behind Pemex on Highway 186 west of intersection and ADO, noisy, decrepit, overpriced. **E** *San Luís*, C 28 facing the Zócalo, simple and lazily-maintained.

Eating *La Choza*, on Chetumal highway by railway line, local atmosphere, good, inexpensive; budget prices and *típico* fare also at *Juanita*, same building as *Akim-Pech*; nearby is *Mi Ranchito*, grilled meal or chicken, popular; plenty of food in the town market (begins at Calle 31 on the corner of the plaza).

Transport Escárcega is an important transport hub and buses run regularly from the 2nd class bus station to Palenque beginning at 0430 (US$7, 3 hours); for other connections to Palenque, go to Emiliano Zapata, not all Villahermosa buses stop there, though. 1st class services on to Campeche (US$2), Mérida and Villahermosa depart from the ADO terminal; buses plying beautifully-surfaced Highway 186 east to Chetumal are ADO, 4 a day, and Autobuses del Sur, 3 at night, US$8.50 and US$7.25 respectively, 4 hours. Buses to Xpujil leave from central terminal, 3 hours, US$4.

Directory **Banks** *Bancomer*, C 31 No 26 with limited currency exchange facilities. **Communications** Post Office: on C 28.

Off this road are many interesting ruins (see page 521), such as **Balamku** (105 kilometres, discovered only in 1990), **Chicanná** (145 kilometres), **Becán** (watch for very small sign) and **Xpujil** (153 kilometres); little excavation has yet been undertaken in this region, but these ruins do give a good idea of how such sites look when stumbled upon by archaeologists.

Highway 261 runs 86 kilometres due north from Escárcega through dense forest to the Gulf of Mexico, where it joins the coastal route at Champotón, a relaxed but run down fishing and shrimping port spread along the banks of the Río Champotón. In prehispanic times it was an important trading link between Guatemala and Central Mexico; Toltec and Maya mingled here, followed by the Spaniards (where blood was shed when Francisco Hernández de Córdoba was fatally wounded in a skirmish with the inhabitants in 1517). On the south side of town can be seen the remnants of a 1719 fort built as a defence against the pirates who frequently raided this coast. The Feast of the Immaculate Conception (8 December) is celebrated with a joyous festival lasting several days.

Champotón
Population: 18,000
Colour map 4, grid A2

Sleeping **C** *Snook Inn*, C 30 No 1, T80088, a/c, fan, pool, owner speaks English, favourite with fishing enthusiasts and bird hunters; for larger game (plentiful in the surrounding jungle) there are 3 primitive but comfortable jungle camps to the south; recommended guide is José Sansores (*Hotel Castelmar*, Campeche). *Gemenis*, C 30 No 10; *D'Venicia*, C 38. *Imperial*, C 28 No 38, all **E**, simple, with fans, river views, regular food.

Eating A few unpretentious restaurants, usually seafood menus but venison (*venedo*) and *pato* plentiful in season: *La Palapa*, on the seafront, covered terrace, speciality fish stuffed with shrimp, "very fresh and tasty, splendid place".

Directory **Banks** Try the *Banco del Atlántico* for currency transactions, open Mon-Fri 0900-1230.

Villahermosa to Campeche via the coast

Although Highway 180 is narrow, crumbling into the sea in places and usually ignored by tourists intent on visiting Palenque, this journey is a beautiful one and more interesting than the fast toll road inland to Campeche. The road threads its way from Villahermosa 78 kilometres north through marshland and rich cacao, banana and coconut plantations, passing turnoffs to several tiny coastal villages with palm-lined but otherwise mediocre beaches, to the river port of **Frontera** (*Population*: 28,650), from where Graham Greene began the research journey in 1938 that led to the publication of *The Lawless Roads* and later to the *The Power and the Glory*. The Feria Guadalupana is held from 3-13 December, agricultural show, bullfights, *charreadas*, regional dances.**D** *Chichén Itzá*, on Plaza, not very clean, fan, shower, hot water. **E** *San Agustín*, very basic, fan, no mosquito net. *Restaurant Conquistador*, beside church, very good.

The road briefly touches the coast at the Tabasco/Campeche state border before running east beside a series of lakes (superb bird watching) to the fishing village of **Zacatal** (93 kilometres), at the entrance to the tarpon-filled **Laguna de Términos** (named for the first Spanish expedition which thought it had reached the end of the 'island' of Yucatán). Just before Zacatal is the lighthouse of **Xicalango**, an important precolumbian trading centre near where Cortés landed in 1519 on his way to Veracruz and was given 20 female slaves, including 'La Malinche', the Indian princess baptized as Doña Marina who, as the Spaniards' interpreter, was to play an important rôle in the Conquest. A bridge crosses the lake's mouth to Ciudad del Carmen.

Ciudad del Carmen

Population: 151,400
Phone code: 938
Colour map 4, grid B2

This is the hot, bursting-at-the-seams principal oil port of the region and is being developed into one of the biggest and most modern on the Gulf. Its important shrimping and prawning fleets are also expanding (good photo possibilities along the trawler-filled docks east of the ferry landing) and much ship building is undertaken. The site was originally established in 1588 by a pirate named McGregor as a lair from which to raid Spanish shipping; it was infamous until the pirates were wiped out by Alfonso Felipe de Andrade in 1717, who then named the town after its patroness, the Virgen del Carmen.

Carmen is situated on a narrow, largely forested (coconut palm) island, little more than a sandspit, 151 square kilometres and 38 kilometres long. It is joined to the mainland at either end by bridges which are among the longest in the Americas. One, on the east end of the island at Puerto Real, called La Unidad, 3,222 metres, built in 1922 (US$1.85 toll) links with Isla Aguada, and the other, 3,865 metres, between Zacatal (mainland) and La Puntilla, was completed in 1994. The town is principally concentrated at the west end of the island and shows few signs of the ugliness often associated with oil-boom centres (the rigs are mainly way off-shore). It is not, as yet, visited by many tourists, but is well worth a detour en route to, or from, the Yucatán, and is a good place for those curious to see something of the development of the Mexican fishing and oil industries.

Most streets in the centre are numbered; even numbers generally run west-east, and odd south-north. Calle 20 is the seafront malecón and the road to the airport and University is Calle 31.

Sights The attractive, cream-coloured **Cathedral** (Parroquia de la Virgen del Carmen, begun 1856, notable for its stained glass), along with the **Palacio Municipal** and Library, stands on the **Plaza Principal**, or Plaza Zaragoza, a lush square laid out in 1854, near the waterfront, with wooden gazebo (free band concerts Thursday and

Sunday evenings), Spanish lanterns, brick walkways and elegant wrought-iron railings from Belgium. There is a modest **Archaeological Museum** in the Liceo Carmelita showing locally-excavated items. ■ *US$0.25 admission.* **La Iglesia de Jesús** (1820) opposite Parque Juárez is surrounded by elegant older houses. Nearby is the Barrio del Guanal, the oldest residential quarter, with the church of **Virgen de la Asunción** (1815) and houses with spacious balconies and tiles brought from Marseilles. Close by is the **Casa de la Cultura** in a French style building (1860s) with library and temporary exhibitions and concerts.

There are several good beaches with restaurants and watersports, notably scenic Playa Caracol (southeast of the centre) and the Playa Norte (extensive white sand, safe bathing). Near the latter is a small zoo with some 50 native species and family recreation area. 16 kilometres along the road to Puerto Real on the Playa Bahamita which runs the rest of the way along the north coast as far as the Unidad bridge, is a balneario of the same name (pool and restaurants) from where you can take a boat trip to Laguna de Términos. Beaches are composed of a gritty sand mixed with sea shells and are generally clean, but oil processing does periodically have a bad effect. Campers are warned about the biting chiggers and sharp shells are hard on tents.

Living costs in Carmen tend to be higher than the norm, partly on account of the spending power of the oil workers but also because most commodities have to be brought in. However there are hotels and restaurants in the budget range.

A *EuroHotel*, C 22 No 208, T31030, large and modern, 2 restaurants, pool, a/c, disco, built to accommodate the flow of Pemex traffic. **B** *Hotel del Parque*, C 33 No 1. **B** *Isla del Carmen*, C 20 No 9, T22350, a/c, restaurant, bar, parking. **B** *Lli-Re*, C 32 y 29, T20588, commercial hotel with large sparsely-furnished a/c rooms, TV, servibars, oddly old-fashioned but comfortable, restaurant with good but not cheap fish dishes. **B** *Technotel*, Av Camarón. **B** *Los Sandes*, Av Periférica. **C** *Aquario*, C 51 No 60, T22547, a/c, comfortable. **C** *Lino's*, C 31 No 132, T20738, a/c, pool, restaurant, also has 10 RV spaces with electricity hook-ups.

Sleeping
■ *on maps*
Price codes:
see inside front cover

Ciudad del Carmen

■ Sleeping
1 El Ancla
2 Euro
3 Lli-Re
4 Los Sandes
5 Technotel

▲ Other
1 Palacio Municipal
2 Parque Zaragoza
3 Parque Zoológico
4 Parroquia de la Virgen del Carmen

D *Zacarías*, C 24 No 58, T20121, modern, some cheaper rooms with fans, brighter a/c rooms are better value, recommended. **E** *Internacional*, C 20 No 21, T21344, uninspiring outside but clean and friendly, 1 block from Plaza, some a/c. **E** *Roma*, on C 22, fan, cold showers, good value; other budget class places nearby are *Casa de Huéspedes Carmen*, C 20 No 142, *Villa del Mar*, C 20 y 33. There are several **E** range hotels near the ADO bus station on Avenida Periférica eg *El Ancla*, simple rooms, TV, a/c, good restaurant in spectacular waterside setting.

Eating
• *on maps*

The better hotels have good restaurants (the shrimp and prawns are especially tasty); others recommended are ***Pepe's***, C 27 No 15, a/c, attractive seafood dishes; ***Vía Veneto***, in the *EuroHotel*, reasonable prices, good breakfasts; ***El Kiosco***, in *Hotel del Parque* with view of Zócalo, modest prices, eggs, chicken, seafood and Mexican dishes, but not clean, poor service; *La Mesita*, outdoor stand across from ferry landing, well-prepared shrimp, seafood cocktails, extremely popular all day; *La Fuente*, C 20, 24-hour snack bar with view of the Laguna; for 'best coffee in town' try ***Café Vadillo*** or other tiny cafés along pedestrian walkway (C 33) near the Zócalo; inexpensive snacks also in the thriving Central Market (C 20 y 37, not far northwest of Zócalo), many bakeries and supermarkets throughout the city, eg *Conasuper*, C 20 y 37.

Festivals

The town's patroness is honoured with a cheerful fiesta each 15-30 June, bullfights, cultural events, fireworks, etc.

Transport

Local Car hire (not cheap): **Auto-Rentas del Carmen**, C 33 No 121 (T22376); **Fast** (T22306), and **Auto Panamericana**, C 22 (T22326).

Air Carmen's efficient airport (Avenida Aviación, only 5 kilometres east of the Plaza) has also benefited from the oil traffic with flights daily to Mérida, Mexico City, Poza Rica, Tampico, Veracruz and Villahermosa.

Buses ADO bus terminal some distance from centre. Take bus or colectivo marked 'Renovación' or 'ADO', they leave from around the Zócalo. At least 8 ADO services daily to **Campeche** (3 hours) and **Mérida** (9 hours, US$14.80), includes 3 departures between 2100 and 2200 (worth considering if stuck for accommodation); hourly bus to **Villahermosa** via the coast, 3 hours. A connection can be made to **Palenque** at 2330 or 0400, a slow but worthwhile trip. Buses also travel via **Escárcega**, where connections can be made for Chetumal and Belize.

Directory

Airlines Mexicana, C 22 y 37, T21171. **Banks** *Banco del Atlántico* or *Banamex*, both at C 24 y 31. **Communications** Post Office: at C 29 y 20, 1 block from the Plaza. **Tourist office** On C 20 near C 23 has little to promote in this non-tourist town, emphasis is on fishing excursions, basic street map available. **Fishing excursions** can be arranged through the *Club de Pesca Nelo Manjárrez* (T20073) at C 40 and C 61, coastal lagoons are rich in tarpon (*sábalo*) and bonefish.

Isla Aguada
Colour map 4, grid B2

11 kilometres beyond Carmen is the *Rancho El Fénix*, with an interesting iguana (*lagarto*) hatchery. Highway 180 runs northeast along the Isla del Carmen and crosses the bridge to Isla Aguada (**C** *Hotel Tarpon Tropical*, **D** *Motel La Cabaña* and Trailer Park at former boatlanding just after the toll bridge, full hook-up, hot showers, laundry facilities, quiet, US$12 for vehicle and two people), actually a narrow peninsula with more deserted shell-littered beaches on the Gulf shore, and undulates its way northeast through tiny fishing villages towards Campeche; there are many offshore oil rigs to be seen. At Sabancuy (85 kilometres from Carmen) a paved road (57 kilometres) crosses to the Villahermosa-Escárcega highway. 63 bumpy kilometres later, Highway 180 reaches Champotón (see above).

Sihoplaya & Seybaplaya

Continuing north, Highways 180 and 261 are combined for 17 kilometres until the latter darts off east on its way to Edzná and Hopelchen (bypassing Campeche, should this be desired). A 66-kilometres toll *autopista*, paralleling Highway 180, just inland from the southern outskirts of Champotón to Campeche, is much quicker than the old highway. Champotón and Seybaplaya are bypassed. We describe the places reached from Highway 180, narrow and slow (beware many speed bumps), which runs on a little further to the resort of **Sihoplaya**. Here is the widely-known **C** *Hotel Siho Playa* (T62989), a former sugar hacienda with a beautiful setting and beach facilities, pool, disco/bar, breezy rooms, etc, but, despite remodelling in the past, it has seen better days; camping possible, US$5; restaurant is overpriced and poor but nowhere else to eat nearby; very popular, nonetheless, with *campechano* families and good views from the iguana-covered jetty of pelicans diving for their supper. Regular buses from Campeche US$1. A short distance further north is the larger resort of **Seybaplaya**, an attractive place where fishermen mend nets and pelicans dry their wings on posts along the beach. On the Highway is the open-air *Restaurant Veracruz*, serving delicious red snapper (fresh fish at the seafront Public Market is also good value), but in general there is little to explore; only the *Balneario Payucán* at the north end of the bay makes a special trip worthwhile; this is probably the closest decent beach to Campeche (33 kilometres) although a little isolated, since the water and sand get filthier as one nears the state capital.

Campeche

Highway 180 enters the city as the divided Avenida Resurgimiento, which passes either side of the huge **Monumento al Resurgimiento**, a stone torso holding aloft the torch of Democracy. The city, capital of Campeche state, is beautifully set on a small bay on the western coast of Yucatán, 252 kilometres from Mérida and 444 kilometres from Villahermosa. Originally the trading village of Ah Kim Pech, it was here that the Spaniards, under Francisco Hernández de Córdoba, first disembarked on Mexican soil (20 March 1517) and thus began mestizo Mexico. The city was founded by Francisco de Montejo in 1540; export of local dyewoods, chiclé, timber and other valuable cargoes soon attracted the attention of most of the famous buccaneers, who constantly raided the port from their bases on Isla del Carmen, then known as the Isla de Tris. Combining their fleets for one momentous swoop, they fell upon Campeche on 9 February 1663, wiped out the city and slaughtered its inhabitants. Five years later the Crown began fortifying the site, the first Spanish colonial settlement to be completely walled. Formidable bulwarks, three metres thick and 'a ship's height', and eight fortress/bastions (*baluartes*) were built in the next 36 years. All these precautions soon defeated pirate attacks and Campeche prospered until Mexican independence (only Campeche and Veracruz had the privilege of conducting international trade), after which it declined into an obscure fishing and logging town. Only with the arrival of a road from the 'mainland' in the 1950s and the oil boom of the 1970s has Campeche begun to see visitors in any numbers, attracted by its historical monuments and relaxed atmosphere (*campechano* has come to mean an easy-going, pleasant person).

Like many of the Yucatán's towns, Campeche's streets in the Old Town are numbered rather than named. Even-numbers run north/south beginning at Calle 8 (no-one knows why) near the Malecón, east to Calle 18 inside the walls; odd-numbers run east (inland) from Calle 51 in the north to Calle 65 in the south. Most of the points of interest are within this compact area. The full circuit of the walls is a long walk; buses marked 'Circuito Baluartes' provide a regular service around the perimeter. Running in from the northeast is Avenida Gobernadores, on which are situated the bus and railway stations.

Of the original walls, only seven of the *baluartes* and an ancient fort (now rather **Sights** dwarfed by two big white hotels on the seafront) near the cathedral remain. Some house museums: (see below).

The heart of Campeche is its **Plaza Principal** or Zócalo, bounded by Calle 8, Calle 10, Calle 55 y 57 and filled with a strange mixture of colonial past and ultramodern; an atmosphere of small-town Spain gives it a delightful ambience during the evening *paseo*. The old houses within the walls are warmly coloured but often in a bad state of

Population: 151,000
State population 1995:
642,082
Phone code: 981
Colour map 4, grid A1

Mexico

Mexico

repair; efforts are now being made to spruce the place up. The best way to see the Old City is to walk its narrow streets; the shady **Alameda** (bottom of Calle 57 opposite the Baluarte San Francisco) offers respite from the sun and contains the unusual **Puente de los Perros** (Bridge of the Dogs), a colonial bridge guarded by carved stone dogs honouring the Dominican missionaries called the 'Hounds of God' for their zealous pursuit of converts. You can also take a tour by tram (*tranvía*), US$1, 45 minutes, to many of the sites east and west of the Zócalo.

Representative of the city's increasing modernity are big white luxury hotels on the seafront, and the square glass **Palacio de Gobierno** (colourful murals) and adjoining concrete **Congreso**; although both were designed to blend in with the native architecture, conservative Campechanos dismiss them as 'The Jukebox' and 'The Flying Saucer' respectively. The futuristic Ciudad Universitaria almost rivals that of Mexico City. Other interesting sights include: the **Fuerte José El Alto**, some distance northeast on Calle 7 beyond the railway ('San José El Alto' bus from the market), with excellent views, and adjacent refurbished church and Jesuit college (1756), now a museum and cultural centre with frequently changing exhibits, gift shop; incorporated into the church is Yucatán's first lighthouse (1864).

Churches Remnants of the **Convento de San Francisco** (1546), lie 20 minutes' walk northeast along the seafront, where Cortés' grandson, Jerónimo, was baptized (1563) in the font, which is still in use; close by is **Pozo de la Conquista**, the spring from which Hernández de Córdoba's men filled their casks in 1517. The somewhat dull and crumbling Franciscan **Cathedral** (1540-1705), facing the Plaza, has an elaborately carved façade and the Santo Entierro (Holy Burial), a sculpture of Christ in a mahogany sarcophagus with silver trim. There are, however, several better 16th and 17th century churches. The most interesting are **San Francisquito** (16th century with wooden altars painted in vermilion and white), Jesús, San Juan de Dios, Guadalupe and Cristo Negro de San Román.

Museums **Baluarte La Soledad**, just west of the Central Plaza, is the largest of the seaward defences. There are three rooms of Maya stelae and sculpture, first class. ■ *Tuesday-Saturday, 0900-1400, 1600-2000; Sunday 0900-1300, US$0.50.* **Baluarte San Carlos**, near the Palacio de Gobierno, houses the city's museum, there are also interesting scale models of the 18th century defences and a collection of colonial arms and seafaring equipment, small library, a fine view from the cannon-studded roof, dungeons and a government-sponsored handicrafts market; for a few pesos, guides will conduct you through underground passageways which once provided escape routes from many of the town's houses (most have now been bricked up), ■ *Open 0800-2000, US$0.40.* **Baluarte San Pedro**, Calle 18 y 51, five blocks south of the Plaza, has a permanent *artesanía* exhibition. ■ *Monday-Friday, 0900-1300, 1700-2000, free.* **Baluarte Santiago**, one block north of the Plaza, with the Xmuch Haltun Botanical Gardens: 250 species of Yucatecan plants exhibited in a courtyard of fountains, a delightful spot to relax. ■ *Tuesday-Saturday, 0800-2000; Sunday 0900-1400, free.*

The **Fuerte de San Miguel**, on the Malecón four kilometres southwest, is the most atmospheric of the forts (complete with drawbridge and a moat said to have once contained either crocodiles or skin-burning lime, take your pick!); it houses the **Museo Arqueológico**, with a well-documented display of precolumbian exhibits including a display of jade masks and black funeral pottery from Calakmul and recent finds from Jaina. ■ *Tuesday-Saturday, 0900-2000, Sunday 0900-1300, admission US$1, recommended.*

Excursions **Lerma** is virtually a small industrial suburb of Campeche, with large shipyards and fish processing plants; the afternoon return of the shrimping fleet is a colourful sight; *Fiesta de Polk Kekén* held on 6 January, traditional dances. Close by is **Playa Bonita**, touted as a wonderful place to go (and hordes of Yucatecanos do during the *temporada* season); the beach has lockers, showers, *palapas* and dressing sheds but the water is now polluted and the sand hopelessly littered. Oil storage tanks nearby do little to improve the view, but the *malecón* is useful for car parking. Rickety buses marked 'Lerma' or 'Playa Bonita' run from Campeche, crowded, US$1, eight kilometres. A short distance to the south is the slightly better but less accessible San Lorenzo beach, rocky and peaceful but littered with cans and bottletops nonetheless.

AL *Ramada Inn*, Av Ruíz Cortines 51, T62233, F11618 (5-stars), on the waterfront. **AL** *Alhambra*, Av Resurgimiento 85, T66822, F66132, 4-star, south end of town, a/c, disco, pool, satellite TV, quiet but popular with Mexican families in summer. **B** *Baluartes*, Av Ruíz Cortines, T63911, nice, bit run down, parking for campers, who can use the hotel washrooms, very good restaurant, pool. Several on Calle 10 including **D** *América-Plaza*, No 252, T64588, hot water, friendly, no safe deposit, clean, fans but hot, safe parking, with night watchman, at the back of the *Ramada Inn*; **E** *Posada Del Angel*, C 10 No 307, T67718 (opposite cathedral), a/c, attractive, some rooms without windows, clean, recommended. **E** *Roma*, C 10 No 254, T63897, run down, dirty, dark, difficult parking, not safe (often full). **D** *Autel El Viajero*, López Mateos 177, overcharges, but often only one left with space in the afternoon, T65133. **D** *Central*, on Gobernadores opposite ADO bus station, misleadingly named, a/c, hot water, clean, friendly, noisy. **D** *Colonial*, C 14 No 122, T62222, clean, good, several blocks from Zócalo. **D** *López*, C 12 No 189, T63344, interesting art deco design, clean if a bit musty, with bath, uncomfortable beds, a/c. **E** *Campeche*, C 57 No 1, across from the park at the end of C 57, T65183, fan, cold water, washing facilities. **E** *Reforma*, C 8 No 257, T64464, dirty, run down, upper floor rooms best, basic. **F** *Hospedaje Teresita*, C 53 No 31, 3 blocks northeast of Plaza, quiet, welcoming, very basic rooms with fans, no hot water.

Sleeping
In general, prices are high. Beware of overcharging and, if driving, find a secure car park.

Camping *Trailer Park Campeche*, on Agustín Melgar and C 19, 5 kilometres south of centre, close to the Bay in uninviting suburb of Samulá (signposted), 25 spaces and tent area, full hook-ups, good amenities, cold showers, pleasant site, owners speak some English, US$3.25 per person, US$6.50 for car with 2 people, 'Samulá' bus from market (US$0.15) or a 'Lerma' bus down coast road, alight at Melgar and walk. Tourist Office often gives permission to pitch tents in their grounds, as will the Youth Hostel. There is a trailer park near the tourist office, open evenings only, until 2000, no tent or hammock facilities.

Youth hostel Avenida Agustín Melgar s/n, Col Buenavista, CP 24020, T61802/67718, in the south suburbs, near University, Fuerte San Miguel and Trailer Park, take Samulá or ISSSTE bus from market US$0.15 (ISSSTE bus also from bus station), segregated dormitories with 4 bunk beds in each room (US$1.50 per person), lovely grounds, pool, cafetería (breakfast 0730-0930, lunch 1400-1600, dinner 1930-2130, about US$1.50), clean and friendly, towels provided.

La Perla, C 10 No 345, good fish, busy and popular, venison, squid, locals' haunt, sometimes erratic service, off Plaza. *Mirador*, C8 y 61, good fish, moderate prices. *Lonchería Puga*, C 8 y C 53, open 0700, recommended. *Del Parque*, on Zócalo, good, US$5 meal and drink. *Marganza*, C 8, upmarket, good breakfast and meals, excellent service. *Heladería Bing*, C 12 y 59, good ice-cream. *Av Fénix*, on Juárez where the street bends towards the terminal, generous breakfasts. Good food in the market, but don't drink the tap water. It is hard to find reasonably-priced food before 1800; try the restaurant at the ADO terminal, or *La Parroquia*, C 55 No 9, open 24 hours, good local atmosphere, friendly and clean, recommended. Opposite is *Los Portales*, authentic local atmosphere, try the *sopa de lima*. *Disco Bar Bali Hai*, on Malecón south of town, good drinks and *tapas*, moderately priced. *Bar El Portón*, C 18 entre 61 y 63, near walls, courtyard, friendly.

Eating

Campeche is widely-known for its seafood, especially large shrimps (*camarones*), black snapper (*esmedregal*) and *pan de cazón*: baby hammerhead shark sandwiched between corn tortillas with black beans. Food stands in the Market serve *típico tortas*, *tortillas*, *panuchos* and *tamales* but hygiene standards vary widely; barbecued venison is also a marketplace speciality. Fruit is cheap and in great variety; perhaps best to resist the bags of sliced mangoes and peel all fruit yourself. (The word 'cocktail' is said to have originated in Campeche, where 17th century English pirates enjoyed drinks adorned with palm fronds resembling cock's tails.)

Festivals *Feria de San Román*, second 2 weeks of **September**. *Fiesta de San Francisco*, **4-13 October**. Good *Carnival* in **February/March**. 7 August is a *state holiday*.

Shopping Excellent cheap Panama hats *(jipis)*, finely and tightly woven so that they retain their shape even when crushed into your luggage; cheaper at the source in Becal (see under **From Campeche to Mérida**). Handicrafts are generally cheaper than in Mérida. The attractive new market, from which most local buses depart, is beside Alameda Park at the south end of Calle 57 and is worth a visit. Plenty of bargains here, especially Mexican and Maya clothes, hats and shoes, fruit and vegetables; try ice-cream, though preferably from a shop rather than a barrow. *Super 10* supermarket behind the post office has an excellent cheap bakery inside. There are souvenir shops along Calle 8, such as *Artesanía Típica Naval* (No 259) with exotic bottled fruit like *nance* and *maranón*, or *El Coral* (No 255) with a large variety of Maya figurines; many high-quality craft items are available from the *Exposición* in the Baluarte San Pedro; *Artesanías Campechanos*, C 55 No 25, recommended. Camping and general supplies, and laundrette, at *Superdíaz* supermarket in Akim-Pech shopping area at Av Miguel Alemán y Av Madero, some distance north of the Zócalo (open 0800-2100).

Transport **Local Car hire**: next to *Hotel Ramada Inn*, Av Ruíz Cortines 51, T62233. **Hertz** and **Autorent** car rentals at airport (good for neighbourhood excursions).

Air Modern and efficient airport (CPE) on Porfilio, 10 kilometres northeast. AeroMéxico direct daily to Mexico City (T65678). If on a budget, walk 100 metres down service road (Avenida Aviación) to Avenida Nacozari, turn right (west) and wait for 'China-Campeche' bus to Zócalo.

Trains Railway station is at Gobernadores y Avenida Héroes de Nacozari (3 kilometres), plenty of 'Centro' buses; some banditry in this region, trains from Campeche not really recommended. Campeche is on the Merida-Coatzacoalcos line via Palenque, which is supposed to run daily, but may not run at all.

Buses ADO bus terminal at Gobernadores 289, esq Chile, on way to train station ('Gobernadores' or 'Centro' buses to the Plaza Principal, taxis about US$2, or 30 minutes' walk). First class buses to Merida, 8 a day ADO, $2\frac{1}{2}$ hours, US$6, 2nd class US$4. First class buses go by the Vía Corta, which does *not* pass through Uxmal, Kabah, etc. Check bus times. Campeche-Uxmal, US$4.50, 2nd class, 3 hours, 0600 and 1200. To **Escárcega**, hourly from 0600 to 1700, 2 hours, US$2. Buses along inland road to **Villahermosa**, take posted times with a pinch of salt, 2nd class, 5 a day, US$14.25, 1st class US$16.50, $6\frac{1}{2}$ hours, 2300 bus comes from Mérida but empties during the night. Bus via Emiliano Zapata (US$7.75, 2 hours before Villahermosa) to **Palenque**, change at Emiliano Zapata, or direct, 1 daily, 2nd class (Transportes del Sur), US$10.65,2 with ADO, US$ 12, 5-7 hours, check if it is direct even if it says non-stop, see page 447. ADO bus to **Mexico City**, US$56.

Directory **Banks** *Banamex*, C 10 No 15. *Bancomer*, opposite the Baluarte de la Soledad. *Banco del Atlántico*, C 50 No 406; open 0900-1300 Mon-Fri; all change TCs and give good service. *American Express* (T11010), C 59 in Edif Belmar, oficina 5, helpful for lost cheques, etc. Plenty of places to get cash on credit cards and ATMs. **Communications** Post Office: Av 16 de Septiembre (Malecón) y C 53 in the Edif Federal (go to the right upon entry for telegraph service); open Mon-Fri 0800-2000, Sat 0900-1300 for *Lista de Correos*, registered mail, money orders and stamps.**Internet:** *Cybercafé Campeche*, C 61 between C 10 and 12, open 0900-1300, US$4 per hour; *Telmex*, C 8 between C 51 y 53, free; Calle 51 No 45, between 12 and 14. **Cultural centres** *Centro Manik*, C 59 No 22 entre 12 y 14, T/F62448, opened 1997 in restored house in centre, vegetarian restaurant, bookshop, handicrafts, art gallery, music lessons, conferences, concentrates on ecology, environmentalism and health, also developing ecotourism in southern Campeche. **Laundry** C 55 entre 12 y 14, US$0.60 per kg. **Tourist offices** C 12 No 153, T66068/66767. Tourist information is also available at Baluarte San Carlos y Santiago and Baluarte Santa Rosa, C 14, T67364, open 0900-1600, 1800-2000, library. **Useful addresses** The *Oficina de Migración* at the Palacio Federal will extend Mexican visas. Take copies of your passport.

Maya sites in Campeche state

A number of city remains (mostly in the unfussy Chenes architectural style) are scattered throughout the rainforest and scrub to the east of Campeche; little excavation work has been done and most receive few visitors. Getting to them by the occasional bus service is possible in many cases, but return trips can be tricky. The alternatives are one of the tours run by some luxury hotels and travel agencies in Campeche (see below) or renting a vehicle (preferably with high clearance) in Campeche or Mérida. Whichever way one travels, carrying plenty of drinking water is strongly advised.

The closest site to the state capital is Edzná ('House of Grimaces'), reached by the highway east to Cayal, then right turn onto Highway 261 (the road to Uxmal, see page 462), a total distance of 61 kilometres. A paved short cut southeast through China and Poxyaxum (good road) cuts off 11 kilometres; follow Avenida Nacozari out along the railway track. Gracefully situated in a lovely, tranquil valley with thick vegetation on either side, Edzná was a huge ceremonial centre, occupied from about 600 BC to AD 200, built in the simple Chenes style mixed with Puuc, Classical and other influences. Centrepiece is the magnificent, 30 metre-tall, 60 square metre **Temple of the Five Storeys**, a stepped pyramid consisting of four levels of living quarters for the priests and a shrine and altar at the top; 65 steep stairs ascend it from the Central Plaza. Opposite is the recently-restored **Paal U'na**, Temple of the Moon. Excavations are being carried out on the scores of lesser temples by Guatemalan refugees under the direction of Mexican archaeologists, but most of Edzná's original sprawl remains hidden away under thick vegetation; imagination is still needed to picture the extensive network of irrigation canals and holding basins built by the Maya along the below-sea-level valley. Some of the site's stelae remain in position (two large stone faces with grotesquely squinting eyes are covered by a thatched shelter); others can be seen in various Campeche museums. There is also a good example of a *sacbe* (white road). Edzná is well worth a visit especially in July (date varies) when a Maya ceremony to Chac is held, either to encourage or to celebrate the arrival of the rains. ■ *Edzná is open Tuesday-Sunday 0800-1700, US$2; small comedor at the entrance. Local guides available. There is a tourist bus which leaves from the town wall at 0900, US$10 per person. At weekends take a bus towards Pich from Campeche market place at 0700, 1000 and 1030 (1 hour trip) but may leave hours late, return buses pass the site (5 minutes' walk from the Highway) at 0930, 1230 and 1300. In the week, the Pich bus leaves Campeche at 1400, which is only of any use if you are prepared to sleep rough as there is nowhere to stay in the vicinity; hitching back is difficult, but you may get a ride to El Cayal on the road to Uxmal.*

Edzná
Colour map 4, grid A3

MEXICO

Tour Companies & Travel Agents *Viajes Programados*, C 59, Edif Belmar, in Campeche offers daily 2-hour tours at 1000; tours from the *Baluartes Hotel*. *Picazh Servicios Turísticos*, C 16 No 348 entre 357 y 359, T64426, run transport to ruins, with or without guide, recommended; the Tourist Office can also recommend reliable guides for regional tours, eg Sr Antonio Romero. Evaristo Perezque, T66860, recommended guide. Maestro Zavala (from Puerto de Tierra) offers personal and friendly service. Prices range from US$10-21 depending on the number of people and whether you have a guide, entry to site usually not included.

Of the remoter and even less-visited sites beyond Edzná, Hochob and Dzibilnocac are the best choices for the non-specialist. **Hochob** is reached by turning right at **Hopelchén** on Highway 261, 85 kilometres east of Campeche. This quiet town has an impressive fortified 16th century church but only one hotel, **D** *Los Arcos*. A traditional honey and corn festival is held on 13-17 April, another *fiesta* takes place each 3 May on the Día de la Santa Cruz. From here a narrow paved road leads 41 kilometres south to the village of **Dzibalchén**; no hotels but hammock hooks and toilet facilities upon request at the Palacio Municipal, there are some small eating places around the Zócalo. Don Willem Chan will guide tourists to Hochob (he also rents bikes for

Hochob

US$3.50 per day), helpful, speaks English. Directions can be obtained from the church here (run by Americans); essentially you need to travel 18 kilometres south-west on a good dirt road (no public transport, hopeless quagmire in the rainy season) to the village of Chenko, where locals will show the way (four kilometres through the jungle). Remember to bear left when the road forks; it ends at a small *palapa*, from which the ruins are a kilometre's walk up a hill with magnificent view over the surrounding forest. Hochob covered a large area but, as at Edzná, only the hilltop ceremonial centre (the usual Plaza surrounded by elaborately decorated temple buildings) has been properly excavated; although many of these are mounds of rubble, the site is perfect for contemplating deserted yet accessible Maya ruins in solitude and silence. The one-room temple to the right (north) of the plaza is the most famous structure: deep-relief patterns of stylized snakes moulded in stucco across its façade were designed to resemble a mask of the ferocious rain god Chac. A door serves as the mouth. Some concentration is needed to see this due to erosion of the carvings. A fine reconstruction of the building is on display at the Museo de Antropología in Mexico City. ■ *Open daily 0800-1700, US$4.35. Early-morning 2nd class buses serve Dzibalchén, but, as always, returning to Campeche later in the day is often a matter of luck.*

Dzibilnocac 20 kilometres northeast of Dzibalchén at Iturbide, this site is one of the largest in Chenes territory. Only three temples have been excavated here (many pyramidal mounds in the forest and roadside *milpas*); the first two are in a bad state of preservation, but the third is worth the visit: a unique narrow edifice with rounded corners and remains of a stucco façade, primitive reliefs and another grim mask of Chac on the top level. Much of the stonework from the extensive site is used by local farmers for huts and fences, keep an eye out in the vegetation for thorns and snakes. Other sites in the region would require four-wheel drive transport and be likely to appeal only to professional archaeologists. ■ *Open daily 0800-1700, US$4.35.* A bus leaves Campeche at 0800, 3 hours, return 1245, 1345 and 1600, US$3.35. If driving your own vehicle, well-marked 'km' signs parallel the rocky road to Iturbide (no accommodation); bear right around the tiny Zócalo and its attendant yellow church and continue on (better to walk in the wet season) for 50 metres, where the right branch of a fork leads to the ruins.

Jaina Two small limestone islands, Jaina and Piedra, lie just off the coast 40 kilometres and 55 kilometres north of Campeche. Discovered by Morley in 1943, excavations on Jaina have revealed the most extensive Maya burial grounds ever found, over 1,000 interments dating back to AD 652. The bodies of religious and political leaders were carried long distances from all over the Yucatán and Guatemala to be buried beneath the extremely steep **Pyramids of Zacpol** and **Sayasol** on Jaina. The corpses were interred in jars in crouching positions, clutching statues in their folded arms, some with jade stones in their mouths; food, weapons, tools and jewellery accompanied the owner into the afterlife. Terracotta burial offerings (including figurines with movable arms and legs) have provided a revealing picture of Maya customs, dress and living habits; many of these are now on display in Campeche or in the museum at Hecelchakán (see below). Although a vehicular track from Hecelchakán on Highway 180 leads west to the beach opposite Jaina, the islands are Federal property, are guarded and were closed to visitors in May 1999. Major restoration and excavation is in progress and the island will reopen in a few years as an accessible tourist attraction.

Campeche to Merida

There are two **routes**: the so-called 'Camino Real', Vía Corta or Short Route (173 kilometres via the shortcut along the railway line to Tenabó), using Highway 180 through Calkiní, Becal and Umán (taken by all first class and *directo* buses), and the 'Ruta Maya' or Long Route (254 kilometres), Highway 261 through Hopelchén and

Muná, which gives access to many of the peninsula's best-known archaeological sites, especially Uxmal.

On the direct route, State Highway 24 provides a convenient link from Campeche to Highway 180 at **Tenabó** (36 kilometres against 58 kilometres), from where the well-paved road runs on through rising ground and sleepy villages, each with its traditional *Zócalo*, solid church and stone houses often made from the materials of nearby Maya ruins, to **Hecelchakán** (18 kilometres, large service station on the bypass), with a 1620 Franciscan church and the rustic Museo Arqueológico del Camino Real on the Zócalo. Although dusty, the museum's five rooms give an informative overview of Mayan cultural development with the help of maps, stelae, a diorama and many Jaina burial artefacts. ■ *Tuesday-Saturday 0900-1400, US$1.85.*

The highway bypasses **Calkiní** (**E** *Posada del Viajero*, not recommended, in a state of decay; service station) and after 33 kilometres arrives at **Becal** (*Population*: 4,000), the centre for weaving Panama hats, here called *jipis* (pronounced 'hippies') and ubiquitous throughout the Yucatán. Many of the town's families have workshops in cool, moist backyard underground caves, necessary for keeping moist and pliable the shredded leaves of the *jipijapa* palm of which the hats are made; most vendors are happy to give the visitor a tour of their workshop, but are quite zealous in their sales pitches. Prices better for *jipis* and other locally-woven items (cigarette cases, shoes, belts, etc) in the *Centro Artesanal, Artesanías de Becaleña* (Calle 30 Número 210), than in the shops near the Plaza, where the hat is honoured by a hefty sculpture of three concrete sombreros! More celebrations of homage take place each 20 May during the *Feria del Jipi*.

Just beyond Becal, the Highway passes under a 19th century stone arch which is supposed to mark the Campeche/Yucatán border (although nobody seems totally sure of where the line is) and runs 26 kilometres to **Maxcanu**. Here the road to Muná and Ticul branches right (see page 477); a short way down it (right) is the recently-restored Maya site of **Oxkintoc**. The Pyramid of the Labyrinth can be entered (take a torch) and there are other ruins, some with figures. ■ *Entrance US$3, ask for a guide at Calcehtoc which is four kilometres from the ruins and from the Grutas de Oxkintoc (no bus service).* These, however, cannot compare with the caves at Loltún or Balancanché. Highway 180 continues north towards Mérida through a region of numerous *cenotes*, soon passing a turnoff to the turn-of-the-century Moorish-style *henequén* (sisal) hacienda at **San Bernardo**, one of a number in the state which can be visited (another to the east at Yaxcopoil on Highway 261, gigantic machinery, in operation until 1985; ■ *US$1.30*); an interesting colonial museum chronicling the old Yucatán Peninsula tramway system is located in its lush and spacious grounds. Running beside the railway, the highway continues 47 kilometres to its junction with the inland route at **Umán**, a *henequén* processing town of 7,000 with another large 17th century church and convent dedicated to St Francis of Assisi; there are many *cenotes* in the flat surrounding limestone plain. Highway 180/261 is a divided four-lane motorway for the final 18 kilometre stretch into Mérida. There is a ring road around the city.

Mérida

Capital of Yucatán state, Mérida was founded in 1542 on the site of the Mayan city of Tihoo.

Calle 65 is the main shopping street and the Plaza Mayor is between Calle 61/63 y 60/62. Odd-number streets run east and west, even numbers north and south. In colonial times, painted or sculpted men or animals placed at intersections were used as symbols for the street: some still exist in the small towns of Yucatán. All streets are one-way. The houses are mostly of Spanish-Moorish type, painted in soft pastel tones, thick walls, flat roofs, massive doors, grilled windows, flowery patios. Redevelopment is rapid; many of the old houses are being pulled down. The city suffers from pollution caused by heavy traffic, narrow streets and climatic conditions

Population: 525,000
State population 1995: 1,555,733
Phone code: 99
Colour map 4, grid A3

favouring smog-formation. Mérida is a safe city in general (though be careful on Calle 58 and near the market), but the large influx of visitors in recent years is creating 'mostly quiet hostility' towards them. Begging and much molestation from car-washers, shoe-shiners, souvenir-peddlers and others wishing to 'help you find the right hammock, just to practise English'.

Sights

Check that the address you need is in the centre; there are many fraccionamientos (estates) around the town.

Its centre is the Plaza Mayor, green and shady; its arcades have more than a touch of the Moorish style. It is surrounded by the severe twin-towered 16th century **Cathedral**, the **Palacio Municipal**, the **Palacio de Gobierno**, and the **Casa Montejo**, originally built in 1549 by the *conquistador* of the region, Francisco de Montejo, rebuilt around 1850 and now a branch of the Banco Nacional de México (Banamex). In Paseo de Montejo, together with many shops and restaurants, there are a few grand late 19th century houses and a notable independence monument at one end. The **Casa de los Gobernadores**, or Palacio Cantón, on Paseo de Montejo at Calle 43 is an impressive building in the turn-of-the-century French style of the Porfirio Díaz era. It now houses the **Museo de Antropología e Historia** which is very good on Maya history. ■ *Closed on Monday (open 0800-1400 Sunday, 0800-2000 all other days, US$1.60, photography permitted).* The **Museo de Arte Popular** (Museum of Peninsular Culture, Calle 59, between 50 and 48, run by the Instituto Nacional Indigenista (INI), a contemporary crafts museum, is well worth visiting (inexpensive gift shop, small stock). ■ *Open Tuesday-Saturday 0800-2000, Sunday 0900-1400, closed Monday.* The **Museo de la Ciudad** is on Calle 61 entre Calle 58 y 60. ■ *Open Tuesday-Saturday 0800-2000, Sunday 0800-1400, closed Monday, entry free.*

There are several 16th and 17th century churches dotted about the city: **La Mejorada**, behind the Museum of Peninsular Culture (Calle 59 between 48 and 50), **Tercera Orden**, **San Francisco** and **San Cristóbal** (beautiful, in the centre). The **Ermita**, an 18th century chapel with beautiful grounds, is a lonely, deserted place 10-15 minutes from the centre.

Along the narrow streets ply horse-drawn cabs of a curious local design. In all the city's parks you will find *confidenciales*, S-shaped stone seats in which people can sit side by side facing each other.

In the **Palacio de Gobierno**, on the Plaza Mayor, there is a series of symbolic and historical paintings, finished 1978, by a local artist, Fernando Castro Pacheco. The Palacio is open evenings and well lit to display the paintings.

In **Parque El Centenario** is a zoo; a popular place for family outings on Sunday. In the **Parque de las Américas** is an open-air theatre giving plays and concerts, and bands play in various plazas in the evenings. Enquire at hotels about the house and garden tours run by the local society women for tourists to raise money for charity.

Every Thursday evening there is free local music, dancing and poetry at 2100 in the **Plaza Santa Lucía**, two blocks from the Plaza Mayor (Calle 55 y 60), chairs provided, Sunday mornings there is a small flea market. Every Sunday (from 0900 to 2100) all the roads in the centre are closed to motor traffic: everyone takes to the streets to stroll, chat, cycle around or ride in a horse-drawn open carriage ('the best time to be in the city'). There is a weekly programme of events organized by the Municipality (every night except Saturday), including regional dancing and folk guitar concerts. The Tourist Office has details. The **Casa de Cultura** (Calle 63 y 64) has several rooms; an open-air theatre, concert hall, art gallery and display of regional handicrafts. There are monuments to Felipe Carrillo Puerto, an agrarian labour leader prominent in the 1910 revolution.

Excursions

West of Mérida (29 kilometres) is **Hunucmá**, an oasis in the dry Yucatán, about 30 minutes from the Central Camionera bus station, US$0.50.

The road divides here, one branch continuing 63 kilometres west to Celestún, the other running 24 kilometres northwest to the coast at **Sisal**, a languid, faded resort which served as Mérida's port from its earliest days until replaced by Progreso last

MÉXICO

century; the old Customs House still retains some colonial flavour, snapper and bass fishing from the small wharf is rewarding; the windy beach is acceptable but not in the same league as Celestún's. Sisal's impressive lighthouse, painted in traditional red-and-white, is a private residence and permission must be sought to visit the tower, the expansive view is worth the corkscrew climb. Frequent buses (0500-1700) from Mérida, Calle 50 between Calle 65 y 67, two hours, US$1.50. *Sisal del Mar Hotel Resort*, luxury accommodation, in USA T800-4510891 or 305-3419173. More modest are **E** *Club Felicidades*, a 5-minute walk east of the pier, bathrooms not too clean; **E** *Club de Patos*, similar but a slight improvement; **E** *Los Balnearios*, with shower (cold water) and fan, prickly mattresses; **E** *Yahaira* (**F** low season), large clean rooms. *Restaurant Juanita*, reasonable.

Mérida

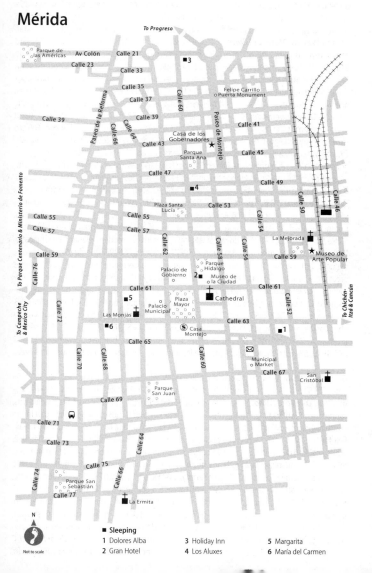

■ **Sleeping**

1 Dolores Alba   3 Holiday Inn   5 Margarita

2 Gran Hotel   4 Los Aluxes   6 María del Carmen

Not to scale

Sleeping

Cheaper hotels tend to be south of the main Plaza (odd streets numbered 63 and higher), near the market and especially the bus station (Calle 69 y 68). More expensive hotels are on the north side of the city and near the Paseo Montejo. Sometimes there are special deals at the more expensive hotels, offers available through counter at ADO terminal.

L *Hyatt Regency*, C 60 No 344 x Colón, T256722, F257002, luxury hotel with boutiques, car hire, money exchange, tennis, gym, *Peregrina* restaurant; opposite is a *Fiesta Americana*. **L-AL** *Holiday Inn*, Av Colón No 489 x Montejo, T256877, F247755 (connected with LADA International direct dialling), all facilities, elegant but a long way from the centre. **AL** *Calinda Panamericana*, C 59, No 455 x 52, T239111, F248090, good, expensive, with elaborate courtyard in the Porfirian style, very spacious and airy, ordinary rooms in new building behind, good buffet breakfast, with swimming pool, 5 blocks from centre. **AL** *Casa del Balam*, C 60, No 488 x 57, T248844, F245011 (Mayaland Resort, in USA T305-3446547/800-4518891), a/c, close to centre, noisy at front, restaurant, bar, pool, neocolonial style, facilities rather below 5-star. **AL** *Best Western María del Carmen*, C 63, No 550 x 68, T239133, F239290, pool in courtyard with 300-yr old Ceiba tree, a/c, new wing better than old, good value. **AL** *Castellano*, C 57, No 513 x 62, T230100, modern, clean but a bit run-down, friendly, pool. **AL** *El Conquistador*, Paseo del Montejo 458 x 35, T262155, modern, specializing in package tours, unhelpful, poor value for independent travellers, good buffet breakfast. **AL** *Los Aluxes*, C 60 No 444, T242199, delightful, pool, restaurants, very convenient, first class, 2 large new wings away from traffic noise. **A-C** *Del Gobernador*, C 59, No 533 x 66, T237133, F281590, a/c, bar, restaurant, good pool, excellent value, highly recommended; and others in our A range and above. **B** *Gran Hotel*, Parque Hidalgo, C 60 No 496, T247730, F247622, does not accept Amex card, with a/c, TV, hot water, phone, clean, helpful, owner speaks English, Fidel Castro has stayed here frequently, as have other politicians, film and stage stars, expensive restaurant attached, free parking nearby on C 61 x 56 y 54 (opposite Banco BCH, ask front desk to stamp the parking receipt). **B** *Maya Yucatán*, C 58 No 483 x 57, T235395, F234642, with bath, a/c, clean, swimming pool, TV, good restaurant. **B** *Reforma*, C 59, No 508 x 62, T247922, swimming pool (open to non-residents US$1), refurbished, nice. **B** *Aragón*, C 57 No 474 x 52 y 54, T240242, F260699, a/c, clean, restaurant, good breakfast offering free coffee all day, good value. **B** *Caribe*, Parque Hidalgo, C 59 No 500, T249022, F248733, tiny pool, a/c, cheaper with fan, modern, elegant, tasteful patio, helpful. **C** *Casa San Juan*, C 62, No 545A x 69 y 71, T236823, F862937,c.sanjuan@sureste.com, restored 19th century house with pleasant courtyard, large rooms with bath, a/c, includes breakfast. **C** *Colón*, C 62, No 483, T234355, rooms old and shabby, pool, dirty, not recommended. **C** *Del Parque*, C 60 No 495 x 59, T17840, with bath and a/c, clean, friendly, recommended. **C** *México*, C 60, No 525 x 67, T219255, good restaurant, attractive. **C** *Peninsular*, C 58, No 519 x 65 y 67, T236996, 1 block from post office and market, small pool, a/c, clean, comfortable, convenient, friendly. **C** *Posada Toledo*, C 58, No 487 x 57, T231690, good value, central, a/c extra, in charming old house, lots of plants, has paperback exchange. **C** *Sevilla*, C 62, No 511 x 65, T215258, near Zócalo, private bath, clean, quiet, fan, but rooms without proper windows.

D *América*, simple, private shower and toilet, noisy, will look after luggage, C 67, No 500, x 58 y 60, T215133, about 10 minutes from bus station and near centre, good value, recommended. **D** *Dolores Alba*, C 63, No 464 x 54, T285650, F283163, does not take credit cards, rooms with bath and a/c (have to pay extra), quiet, friendly, safe parking in courtyard, pool, cool on 1st floor, have to pay for children under 10, good value, good breakfast for US$2.40 0700-1000, will make reservations for sister establishment at Chichén Itzá, when checked out, will not permit you or your luggage in hotel beyond 2000. **D** *Flamingo*, C 58 y 59, T217740, near Plaza, with private shower, swimming pool, noisy, so get room at the back, clean, helpful, laundry. **D** *María Teresa*, C 64 No 529 x 65 y 67, T211039, friendly, safe, central, with bath and fan, a bit noisy. Some rooms **E** recommended. **D** *Montejo*, C 57 No 507 x 62 y 64, T280277, noisy a/c, fan, clean, comfortable, convenient, safe, recommended. **D** *Mucuy*, C 57, No 481 x 56 y 58, T211037, good, but 1st floor rooms very hot, with shower, use of fridge, washing facilities, efficient, nice gardens, highly recommended (although owner can be irritable, his wife is nice), but long way from bus station. **D** *Posada del Angel*, C 67, No 535, x 66 y 68, T232754, clean, with shower and fan. **D** *Príncipe Maya Airport Inn*,

T214050, some rooms noisy from nightclub, convenient for airport. **D** *San Jorge*, across from ADO bus terminal, T219054, with fan and bath, stores luggage, clean, but take interior room as the street is noisy. **D** *Hospedaje San Juan*, 1 block north of arch by Iglesia San Juan, clean rooms with fan and bath. **D** *Santa Lucía*, C 55 No 508, almost opposite Plaza Santa Lucía, T282662, parking, small pool, TV, a/c, very clean, very good value, recommended. **D-E** *Pantera Negra*, C 67 No 547B x 68 y 70, T240251, including lavish breakfast, beautiful old Mexican house, with cool quiet patio, well-stocked bookshelves, clean, communal bath, very friendly English owner, recommended. **D-E** *Trinidad Galería*, C 60, esq 51, T232463, F232419, pool, hot water, fan, nice atmosphere and arty décor, a bit run down, laundry service, mixed reports. **D-E** *Nacional*, C 61 x 54 y 56 (3 blocks from Plaza Mayor), friendly, pool, café, large clean rooms with fan, a/c. **D** *Hotel del Prado*, C50 y 67; **E** with fan, safe parking, pool, a/c, recommended. **E** *Casa Becil*, C 67 No 550-C, x 66 y 68, convenient for bus station, fan, bath, hot water, clean, safe, popular, breakfast, owner speaks English, quiet, friendly, make you feel at home, recommended. **E** *Casa Bowen*, restored colonial house (inside better than out), corner of C 66, No 521-B, x 65, near ADO bus station, often full at weekends, rooms on the main street noisy, bath, hot water but irregular supply, exchanges dollars, cheap laundry service, stores luggage, clean, mosquitoes, some rooms with kitchen (but no utensils), good. **E** *Casa de Huéspedes*, C 62, No 507 x 63 y 65, shared Victorian showers and toilets, very poor water supply but drinking water available, run down, will keep luggage for small fee, mosquitoes, so take coils or net, pleasant and quiet except at front, laundry expensive. **E** *Centenario*, with bath, friendly, clean, safe on C 84 x 59 y 59A, T232532. **E** *Del Mayab*, C 50, No 536A x 65 y 67, T285174, with bath, clean, friendly, tiny swimming pool and car park. **E** *Meridano*, C 54 No 478 x 55 y 57, T232614, nice courtyard, clean, hot water. **E** per person *Latino*, C 66, No 505 x 63, T213841, with fan and shower (water supply problems), friendly and clean, parking outside. **E** per person *Lol-be* C 69 x 66 y 68, with bath, fan, friendly. **E** *Las Monjas*, C 63 y 66, clean, quiet, luggage store, recommended. **E** *Margarita*, C 66, No 506 x 63, T237226, with shower, clean, good, rooms a bit dark, downstairs near desk noisy, cheaper rooms for 5 (3 beds), friendly. **E** *Oviedo*, C 62, next to *Sevilla*, near main Plaza, with bath, friendly, clean, luggage deposit, quieter rooms at the back. **E** *Rodríguez*, C 69, C 54 y 56, T236299, huge rooms, with bath, central, clean, safe. **E** *San Luis*, C 61, No 534 x 68, T217580, with fan and shower (and US$2.25 for noisy a/c), basic, friendly, patio pool, restaurant. **E** *Trinidad*, C 62, No 464 x 55, T213029, old house, cheaper rooms with shared bath, hot water, clean bathrooms, tranquil, courtyard, sun roof, lovely garden, can use pool at the other hotel, lots of rules and regulations, recommended. **E** *Posada Central*, C68 x C65 y C67, with bath, clean, good beds, new rooms, parking, luggage store, recommended.

F *Centenario II*, C 69, No 563 x 68 y 70, opposite ADO bus station, fan, small rooms, friendly. **F** *San José*, west of Plaza on C 63, No 503, bath, hot water, basic, clean, friendly, rooms on top floor are baked by the sun, one of the cheapest, popular with locals, will store luggage, good cheap meals available, local speciality Poc Chuc recommended.

Camping *Trailer Park Rainbow*, Km 8, on the road to Progreso, is preferable, US$5 for 1 or 2, hot showers. *Oasis Campground*, 3 kilometres from Mérida on Highway 180 to Cancún, F432160, with hook-ups, hot showers, laundry, rundown, US manager, US$7 for car and 2 people.

On main plaza: *Louvre* (northwest corner), good, cheap, quick friendly service; *Lido*, C 62 y 61, good value meals and breakfast; *Pizza Bella*, good meeting spot, pizzas US$4-7, excellent cappuchino; *La Choza*, Av Reforma y C 23, near Plaza de Toros, bands play there daily except Monday, from 1300-2100; *Los Almendros*, C 50A, No 493 x 59, in high-vaulted, white-washed thatched barn, for Yucatán specialities, first rate, expensive, mind the peppers, especially the green sauce and avoid both the leathery poc chuc and the watery ice-cream, sometimes live music played, popular. *Pórtico del Peregrino*, C 57, x 60 y 62, dining indoors or in an attractive leafy courtyard, excellent food but not cheap; next door is *Pop*, a/c, excellent snacks, popular with foreigners, very charming; *El Tuche*, C60 near University, good local dishes and occasional live music; *Patio de las Fajitas*, C 60 No 482 x 53, 7 blocks from Zócalo,

Eating
Try Xtabentun, the liqueur made from sweet anise and honey since ancient Mayan times.

not cheap but pleasant open air setting; meat served on a hot griddle at the table; also in the same building is *La Casona*, Italian dishes, quite smart. The *Patio Español*, inside the *Gran Hotel*, well cooked and abundant food, local and Spanish specialities, breakfasts, moderate prices. A good hotel restaurant for value and cooking is *El Rincón* in *Hotel Caribe*. *Alberto's Continental*, C64 No 482 x C57, local, international and Lebanese food, colonial mansion, recommended. *La Prosperidad*, C 53 y 56, good Yucateca food, live entertainment at lunchtime; *El Escorpión*, just off plaza on C 61, good cheap local food; *Tianos*, C 59 No 498, x C 60 (outdoor seating), friendly, touristy, good food, pricey, check your change, sometimes live music; next door, on Parque Hidalgo, is *El Mesón*, pleasant with tables on the square; *El Faisán y El Venado*, C 59 No 617 x 80 y 82, expensive, regional food, Mayan dance show, near zoo; *Pizzería Vita Corleone*, C 59 No 508, near Plaza, good; the café at the *Gran Chopur* dept store serves good food, large portions, a/c. *Amaro*, C 59 No 507, x 60 y 62 with open courtyard and covered patio, good food, esp vegetarian, try *chaya* drink from the leaf of the *chaya* tree, their curry, avocado pizza and home-made bread, are also very good, open 1200-2200, closed on Sunday. *Santa Lucía* C60, x 55 y 57 (near plaza of same name), moderate prices, good fish dishes, music Friday, Saturday. *Cafe Continental*, C 60 x 55 y 53, open 0630-1400, cheap buffet breakfast, nice setting, classical music, recommended. *Marys*, C 63 No 486, x C 63 y 58, very cheap, mainly Mexican customers, recommended. *Alameda*, excellent value Lebanese food, some vegetarian, can ask for half portions, recommended. *Mily's*, C 59 x 64 y 66, *comida corrida* for under US$3; *La Pérgola* (both drive-in and tables), at corner C 56 y C 43, good veal dishes. Warmly recommended. Also in Colonia Alemán at C 24 No 289A. *Los Cardenales*, C 69 No 550-A x 68, close to bus station, good food at reasonable prices, good value, open for breakfast, lunch and dinner; *El Ardillo* and *El Viajero*, both near bus station, offer good cheap, local meals. Cold sliced cooked venison (venado) is to be had in the Municipal Market; *Café Restaurante Express*, on C 60, at Parque Hidalgo, breakfast, good cheap *comida,* traditional coffeehouse where locals meet, coffee variable but try the 'horchata', slow service; *Taco Le*, Pasaje Picheta, next to Palacio Gobierno, generous portions, good value; *Mil Tortas*, good cheap sandwiches, not very cheap, C 62 y 65 x 67; *El Trapiche*, C 62 No 491, excellent fruit salads and licuados, highly recommended. *Tortacos*, C 62 y 65, good, cheap Mexican food; many other *torta* places on Calle 62, but check them carefully for best value and quality; *Govinda*, C 55 No 496, x 60 y 58, open until 1600, a good range of vegetarian dishes, fruit juices, at reasonable prices, pleasant atmosphere, also makes wholemeal bread and pastries to take away; *Kuki's*, C 61 x 62, opposite taxi stand, very good coffee, snacks, expresso, cookies by the kilo, highly recommended. *Naturalmente*, C 20 No 104, x C 23, Colonia Chuburrá, not in centre, vegetarian, recommended. *El Cielo*, C62 x 45 y 47, vegetarian, set meal only, open Monday-Saturday midday-late afternoon, recommended banana bread and wholemeal rolls at *Pronat* health shop on C 59, No 506, x C 62 (but don't have breakfast there); *Jugos California*, good fruit salads, C 60, in C 65, at the main bus station and many other branches all over city. *Bing*, Paseo Montejo 56A y C 37, 13 blocks from centre, about 30 different flavours of good ice-cream. Good *panadería* at C 65 y 60, banana bread, orange cake. Another good bakery at C 62 y 61. Good cheap street fare at Parque Santa Ana, closed middle of day.

Bars & nightclubs **Nightlife** Most bars open 1000-2300, but a few expensive discos remain open until 0300. Two recommended spots: *El Tuche*, C 60 No 482 x 55 y 57, just north of Plaza, cabaret with live music and dance, salsa, local bands, good food at reasonable prices, very popular with locals; *Trovador Bohemia*, Parque Santa Lucía, guitar trios (*trova*) nightly at 2100, entrance US$3. 7 good cinemas regularly show films in English, US$2, try the *Cine Plaza Internacional*, C 58, x 62 y 64 and the cinema at Parque Hidalgo, C 60.

Entertainment **Theatre** *Teatro Peón Contreras*, C 60 with 57. Shows start at 2100, US$4, ballet etc. The University puts on many theatre and dance productions.
Cinema *Cine 59*, C 59 x 68 y 70.

Festivals **Carnival** during the week before Ash Wednesday (best on Saturday). Floats, dancers in regional costume, music and dancing around the Plaza and children dressed in animal suits. On **6 January** Mérida celebrates its birthday.

Know your hammock

Different materials are available for hammocks. Some you might find are: sisal, very strong, light, hard-wearing but rather scratchy and uncomfortable, identified by its distinctive smell; cotton, soft, flexible, comfortable, not as hard-wearing but good for four to five years of everyday use with care. It is not possible to weave cotton and sisal together although you may be told otherwise, so mixtures are unavailable. Cotton/silk mixtures are offered, but will probably be an artificial silk. Nylon, very strong, light but hot in hot weather and cold in cold weather. Never buy your first hammock from a street vendor and never bargain then accept a packaged hammock without checking the size and

quality. The surest way to judge a good hammock is by weight: 1,500 grams (3.3 lbs) is a fine item, under one kilogram (2.2 lbs) is junk (advises Alan Handleman, a US expert). Also, the finer and thinner the strands of material, the more strands there will be, and the more comfortable the hammock. The best hammocks are the so-called 3-ply, but they are difficult to find. There are three sizes: single (sometimes called doble), matrimonial and family (buy a matrimonial at least for comfort). If judging by end-strings, 50 would be sufficient for a child, 150 would suit a medium-sized adult, 250 a couple. Prices vary considerably so shop around and bargain hard.

Markets All the markets, and there are several, are interesting in the early morning. One can **Shopping** buy traditional crafts: a basket or *sombrero* of sisal, a filigree necklace, also a good selection of Maya replicas. Tortoiseshell articles are also sold, but cannot be imported into most countries, as sea turtles are protected by international convention. The Mérida market is also particularly good for made-to-measure sandals of deerskin and tyre-soles, panama hats, and hammocks of all sizes and qualities. Some of the most typical products are the *guayabera*, a pleated and/or embroidered shirt worn universally, its equivalent for women, the *guayablusa*, and beautiful Mayan blouses and *huipiles*. The **Mercado de Artesanías** has many nice things, but prices are high and the salespeople pushy. Good postcards for sale, though. There are several frequently recommended shops for hammocks (there is little agreement about their respective merits, best to compare them all and let them know you are comparing, shops employing touts do not give very good service or prices): *El Hamaquero*, C 58 No 572, x 69 y 71, popular, but beware the very hard sell. *El Campesino*, the market, Eustaquio Canul Cahum and family, will let you watch the weaving. *El Mayab*, C 58, No 553 y 71, friendly, limited choice but good deals available; and *La Poblana*, C 65, x 58 y 60, will bargain, especially for sales of more than 1, huge stock, a bit curt if not buying there and then; also *Jorge Razu*, C 56 No 516B, x 63A y 63, very convincing salesman, changes Travellers' cheques at good rates, recommended. *El Aguacate*, C 58 No 604, corner of C 73, good hammocks, patronized by locals, another branch on C62 opposite *El Trapiche*, helpful, bargaining possible if buying several items. *Rada*, C 60 No 527, x 65 y 67, T241208, F234718, good. *Santiago*, C 70 No 505, x 61 y 63, very good value. To mail a hammock abroad can be arranged through some shops, try *La Poblana*, or *El Aguacate* for help with the forms and method of parcelling and addressing. In the market prices are cheaper but quality is lower and sizes smaller. There are licensed vendors on the streets and in the main plaza; they will bargain and may show you how hammocks are made; some are very persistent. Good silver shops and several antique shops on Calle 60, x 51 y 53. *Bacho Arte Mexicano*, C 60 No 466, x C 53 y 55, also sells other jewellery and ornaments; *La Canasta*, No 500, good range of handicrafts, reasonable prices. Good panama hats at *El Becaliño*, C 65 No 483, esq 56A, diagonally opposite Post Office. *Paty*, C 64 No 549, x C 67 y 69, stocks reputable 'Kary' brand guayaberas, also sells hammocks. Calle 62, between Calle 57 y 61, is lined with *guayabera* shops, all of a similar price and quality. Embroidered *huipil* blouses cost about US$25. Clothes shopping is good along Calle 65 and in the García Rejón Bazaar, Calle 65 y 60. Good leather sandals with soles made from old car tyres, robust and comfortable, from the market, US$10. Excellent cowboy boots for men and women, maximum size 10, can be bought around the market for US$46. *Casa de las Artesanías*, C 63, x 64 y 66, good. There is a big supermarket, *San Francisco de Assisi*, on C 67 y 52, well stocked; also *San Francisco de Assisi* at C 65, x Av 50 y 52.

Bookshop *Librerías Dante*, C 59, No 498 x 58 y 60. C61 x 62 y 64 (near Lavandería La Fe) used books.

Cameras and film Repairs on Calle 53 y 62. Mericolor, C 67 y 58, recommended for service and printing; also Kodak on Parque Hidalgo. Many processors around crossing of Calle 59 y 60. Prices are high by international standards.

Camera repairs *Fotolandia*, C 62 No 479G y 57, T248223.

Backpack repair *Industria de Petaquera del STE*, C 64 no 499, T283175. *Macay*, Pasaje Revolución, beside Cathedral, run by University.

Transport **Local Car hire**: car reservations should be booked well in advance wherever possible; there is a tendency to hand out cars which are in poor condition once the main stock has gone, so check locks, etc, on cheaper models before you leave town. All car hire firms charge around US$40-45 a day although bargains can be found in low season. Cheapest in 1999 was **World Rent a Car**, C60 No 486A, x 55 y 57, T240587, US$40, very fair when car was damaged. **Avis**, C 57 No 507A x 62, T236191. **Hertz**, C 55, No 479, x 54, T242834. **Budget**, Prol Paseo Montejo 49, T272708. **Panam**, *Hotel Montejo Palace*, T234097, or C 56A No 483 x 43, T231392. **Ximbal**, C 44, No 500, Col Jesús Carranza (owner Roger de Jesús García Pech), English spoken, VW Beetles in good condition, accepts Amex. **Easy Way** (Turismo Planeta), C 59, No 501 x 60, T281560, competitive prices, new cars. Most car hire agencies have an office at the airport and, as all share the same counter, negotiating usually takes place. Many agencies also on Calle 60 (eg **Executive**, down from *Gran Hotel*, good value, **Mexico-Rent-a-Car**, cheap, and **Veloz Rent a Car**, No 488, in lobby of *Hotel Casa del Balam*, good). VW Beetles from **Agencia de Viajes América** have been recommended, can be very cheap, friendly. All agencies allow vehicles to be returned to Cancún at an extra charge. Be careful where you park in Mérida, yellow lines mean no parking.

Car service: *Servicillos de Mérida Goodyear*, very helpful and competent, owner speaks English, serves good coffee while you wait for your vehicle. Honest car servicing or quick oil change on Calle 59, near corner of Avenida 68.

Taxi: we are warned that taxi drivers are particularly prone to overcharge by taking a long route, so always establish the journey and fare in advance. There are a dozen taxi stands in the city, eg beside the Cathedral (T212136), at Calle 57A y 60 (T212133), at Calle 59 y 60 (T212500), and at the airport (T230391). Stands display fixed charges. Taxi from centre to bus terminal, US$4.50, to airport US$15. Taxis are hard to find on Sunday pm. **Toll road**: there is a toll road from Kantunil, 68 kilometres east of Mérida, to Xcan, whereafter it is a divided free way to Cancún; the toll is about US$15, which has to be paid in full however little of the road you use. The only exits from the toll road are at Chichén-Itzá and Valladolid. The toll road, Route 180D, is free of traffic, has a speed limit of 110 kph and takes under 3 hours, boring but fast. The old road, Route 180, is free and goes through lots of villages with speed bumps (*topes*), about 5 hours.

Air Airport Rejón (MID), 8 kilometres from town. From Calle 67, 69 and 60 bus 79 goes to the airport, marked Aviación, US$0.20, roughly every 20 minutes. Taxi US$8, voucher available from airport, you don't pay driver direct; colectivo US$2.50. There is a tourist office with a hotel list. No left luggage facilities. Lots of flights to Mexico City daily, 1¾ hours. Other internal flights to Acapulco, Cancún, Chetumal, Ciudad del Carmen, Guadalajara, Huatulco, Monterrey, Oaxaca, Palenque, Tapachula, Tijuana, Tuxtla Gutiérrez, Veracruz and Villahermosa. International flights from Belize City, Houston, Miami and Havana. Package tours Mérida-Havana-Mérida are available (be sure to have a confirmed return flight). For return to Mexico ask for details at Secretaría de Migración, Calle 60, Número 285. Food and drinks at the airport are very expensive.

Trains Station at Calle 48 y 55. Services were so bad in 1999 that delays of days were common and many services were completely cancelled. The Tourist Office advises you to find an alternative means of transport. Timetables show a daily service to *Coatzacoalcos* at 0605, arriving 2000, returning 2320, arriving 1325; also *Tizimín* at 0600, arrives 1025, returns 1240, arrives 1700; to *Valladolid* at 1605, arrives 2000, returns 0350, arrives 0800; to *Peto* via Ticul and Oxkutzcab at 1430, arrives 1915, returns 0410, arrives 0840.

Buses Almost all buses except those to Progreso, or Tizimín etc (see below) leave from the 1st class terminal on Calle 70, Número 555, entre Calle 69 y 71 (it is called CAME). The station has lockers; it is open 24 hours a day. About 20 minutes' walk to centre, taxi US$2. Most companies have computer booking. Schedules change frequently. ADO terminal has nowhere to store luggage. To **Mexico City**, US$42, 24-28 hours, about 6 rest stops (eg ADO, 5 a day); direct Pullman bus Mexico City 2200. 14 hours to **Coatzacoalcos**, US$31. Bus to **Veracruz**, ADO 1430 and 2100, US$43, 16 hours; to **Chetumal**, see **Road to Belize** below. To **Ciudad del Carmen** 8 a day, 1st class, ADO, US$14.80, 9 hours. Buses to **Tulum**, via Chichén Itzá, Valladolid, Cancún and Playa del Carmen, several daily, from main terminal, 6 hours, US$7, 2nd class, drops you off about 1 kilometre from the ruins. For buses to Uxmal and Chichén Itzá see under those places. Regular 2nd class buses to **Campeche**, with ATS (US$4, 3½ hours) also pass Uxmal, 6 a day between 0630 and 1900; 1st class fare (not via Uxmal), ADO, US$6, 8 daily, 2½ hours. Buses to **Puerto Juárez** and **Cancún** (Autobuses de Oriente), every hour 0600 to 2400, US$8 2nd class, US$14 1st class, US$20 *plus*, 4½ hours. Buses to and from Cancún stop at Calle 50, x Calle 65 y 67. If going to Isla Mujeres, make sure the driver knows you want Puerto Juárez, the bus does not always go there, especially at night. Buses to **Progreso** (US$1.65) with Auto Progreso, leave from the bus station on Calle 62, x Calle 65 y 67 every 15 minutes from 0500-2100. To **Valladolid**, US$4.50 2nd class, US$6, 1st express (10 a day). Many buses daily to **Villahermosa**, US$22, 1st class (several from 1030 to 2330) better than 2nd class, 11 hours, US$19.50; 1 direct bus daily at 1330 via Villahermosa and Campeche to **Tuxtla Gutiérrez**, arrives 0630 next day, US$35 with Autotransportes del Sureste de Yucatán. Buses to **Palenque** 0800, 2200 (US$23) and 2330 (US$17) from ADO terminal, 8-9 hours, Cristóbal Colón luxury service US$25; Alternatively take Villahermosa bus to Playas de Catazajá (see page 443), US$16.50, 8½ hours, then minibus to Palenque, or go to Emiliano Zapata, 5 buses a day US$21, and local bus (see page 447). To **Tenosique** at 2115, US$23.35. To **San Cristóbal de las Casas**, at 1800, US$21 (arr 0800-0900), and another at 0700 (Autotransportes del Sureste de Yucatán) also 2 a day with Cristóbal Colón, 1915 and 2345. Buses to Celestún and Sisal from terminal on Calle 71, x Calle 64 y 66. To **Celestún**, 1st class, US$2.50, 2 hours, 2nd class, US$2, 2½ hours, from bus station on Calle 71, entre 64 y 66, frequent departures. To **Tizimín**, **Cenotillo** and **Izamal** buses leave from Calle 50 x Calle 65 y 67. Route 261, Mérida-Escárcega, paved and in very good condition.

To **Guatemala**: take a bus from Mérida to San Cristóbal and change there for Comitán, or to Tenosique for the routes to Flores. A more expensive alternative would be to take the bus from Mérida direct to Tuxtla Gutiérrez (times given above), then direct either Tuxtla-Ciudad Cuauhtémoc or to Tapachula.

To Belize: road paved all the way to Chetumal. Bus Mérida-Chetumal US$18.50 luxury, US$16.50, first class, takes 7 hours (Autotransportes del Caribe, Autotransporte Peninsular), US$13 second class.

Directory

Airline offices *Mexicana* office at C 58 No 500 x 61, T246633, and Paseo Montejo 493, T247421 (airport T461332). *AeroMéxico*, Paseo Montejo 460, T279000, airport T461400. *Taesa*, T202077. *Aviacsa*, T269193/263253. *AeroCaribe*, Paseo Montejo 500B, T286790, airport T461361. *Aviateca*, T243605.

Banks *Banamex* (passport necessary), at C 56 y 59 (Mon-Fri 0900-1300, 1600-1700), ATM cash machine, quick service, good rates. *Banco Atlántico*, C 61 y 62, quick, good rates. Many banks on C 65, off the Plaza. Most have ATM cash machines, open 24 hours, giving cash on Visa or Mastercard with PIN-code. Reliable ATM machine (no queues) at *Inverlat Red Servicaja*, C 62 No 513, x 65 y 67. Cash advance on credit cards possible only between 1000 and 1300. *Centro Cambiario*, C 61 x C 54 y 52. *Casa de Cambio*, C 56 No 491 x 57 y 59, open 0900-1700 Mon-Sun.

NB Banks closed Monday following carnival.

Communications Post Office: C 65 y 56, will accept parcels for surface mail to USA only, but don't seal parcels destined overseas: they have to be inspected. For surface mail to Europe try Belize, or mail package to USA, *poste restante*, for collection later if you are heading that way. An air mail parcel to Europe costs US$15 for 5 kg. Also branches at airport (for quick delivery) or on C 58. DHL on Av Colón offers good service, prices comparable to Post Office prices for air mail packages over 1 kg. **Telephone:** international telephones possible from central bus station, airport, the shop on the corner of C 59 y 64, or public telephones, but not from the main telephone exchange. Many phone card and credit card phone booths on squares along C 60, but many are out of order. Collect calls can be made on Sat or Sun from the *caseta* opposite central bus station, but beware overcharging (max US$2). Telegrams and faxes from C 56, x 65 y 65A (same building as Post Office, entrance at the back), open 0700-1900, Sat 0900-1300. *Tel World* offer long distance fax service from offices on C 60 No 486, x 55 y 57. **Internet:** *Cybernet*, C 62 x59 y 57, US$5 per hour; free internet service at *Telmex*, esq C 59 y 61, Mon-Fri only, arrive early, it gets busy; also *Cybercafé*, at C 59 y 58, US$3 hour; C53 No 498 x 58 y 60; and in Callejón del Congreso, C57A No 8, x 58 y 60.

Cultural centres *Alliance Française*, C 56 No 476, x C 55 y 57, has a busy programme of events, films (Thur 1900), a library and a cafetería open all day.

Embassies & consulates *British Vice Consul*, also *Belize*, Major A Dutton (retd), MBE, C 58-53 No 450, T286152, 0900-1600. Postal address Apdo 89. *USA*, Paseo Montejo 453 y Av Colón (T255011). *Canada*, Av Colón, No 309-D, 19 x 62, T256419. *Cuba*, C 1-C No 277A, x 38 y 40, T444215.

Hospitals & medical services Doctor: *Dr A H Puga Navarrete* (speaks English and French), C 13 No 210, x C 26 y 28, Colonia García Gineres, T250709, open 1600-2000. **Hospital:** *IDEM*, C 66, x 67 y 65, open 24 hrs, specializes in dermatology.

Language schools *Instituto de Español*, C 29, Col Mexico, T271683, 4merida@modernspanish.com. See also **Learning Spanish** in Mexico essentials.

Laundry C 59, x C 72 y 74, at least 24 hrs. *Lavandería* on C 69, No 541, 2 blocks from bus station, about US$3 a load, 3-hr service. *La Fé*, C 61 No 518, x C 62 y 64, US$3.30 for 3 kg, highly recommended. (Shoe repair next door). Self-service hard to find.

Tour companies & travel agents *Wagon-Lits (Cooks)*, helpful, Av Colón 501 (Plaza Colón), T55411.

American Express, Paseo Montejo 494, x 43 y 45, Col Centro, T284222, F244257. *Yucatán Trails*, C 62, No 482, is very helpful, run by Canadian, Denis Lafoy. *Viajes Colonial*, in lobby of *Hotel Colonial*, C 62 No 476, T236444, F283961, trips to Cuba, very helpful, recommended. *Viajes T'Ho*, lobby of *Hotel Reforma*, C 59, No 508 y 62, T236612/247922, for tours in private cars, also for flights to Havana and to Palenque. *Ecoturismo Yucatán*, C 3 No 235, x 32-A y 34, Col Pensiones, T252187, F259047, Alfonso Escobedo. *Bon Voyage*, C 59, x 60 y 62, T232258, very helpful, speak English. *Ceiba Tours*, C 60 No 459, T244477, efficient and friendly staff. *Cultur Servicios*, C 86, No 499-C, T249495/249677, F249781, cultur@finred.com.mx.

Tourist offices C 57 esq 60, opposite Iglesia de Jesús, also has exchange facilities. Also tourist office at the airport, which has maps. Instituto Nacional de Estadística, Geografía e Informática (INEGI), C 40 x 39 y 41, for maps and information.

Useful addresses Immigration Office: C 60, No 448, entre 51 y 49, Dpto 234, p1º, T214824/211714, Pasaje Camino Real, extension of stay easy and quick, open 0830-1300, Mon-Fri. Also helpful in the case of lost tourist cards.

A small, dusty fishing resort much frequented in summer by Mexicans, standing on the spit of land separating the Río Esperanza estuary from the ocean. The long beach is relatively clean except near the town proper (litter, the morning's fishing rejects, insects, weeds that stick to feet, etc), with clear water ideal for swimming, although rising afternoon winds usually churn up silt, little shade; along the beach are many fishing boats bristling with *jimbas* (cane poles), used for catching local octopus. There are beach restaurants with showers. A plain Zócalo watched over by a simple stucco church is the centre for what little happens in town. Cafés (some with hammock space for rent) spill onto the sand, from which parents watch offspring splash in the surf. Even the unmarked post office operating Monday-Friday, 0900-1300, is a private residence the rest of the week.

Celestún
Colour map 4, grid A2

Facilities

15 roomy and comfortably furnished cabins, all with a beautiful view of the emerald green Gulf of Mexico. Surrounded by a coconut grove, at the border of one of the most fascinating Mexican biological reserves, in the middle of our 3 mile virgin beach, the hotel is fully oriented towards environment protection.

Freshwater swimming pool, spectacular white sand beach covered with thousands of seashells and spacious gardens with exotic coastal dune flora.

ECO PARAISO
CELESTÚN YUCATÁN MÉXICO

Km 10 de la Antigua
Carretera a Sisal
Municipio de Celestún
Yucatán, México

Tel: 52 (991) 621 00/620 60
Fax: 52 (991) 621 11
E-mail: buger@mail.internet.com.mx

The immediate region is a National Park, created to protect the thousands of migratory waterfowl (especially flamingos and pelicans) who inhabit the lagoons; fish, crabs and shrimp also spawn here, and manatees, toucans and crocodiles may sometimes be glimpsed in the quieter waterways. Boat trips to view the wildlife can be arranged with owners at the river bridge one kilometre back along the Mérida road (US$30 for one large enough for six to eight, one and a half hours, bargaining possible). Trips also arranged at *Restaurant Avila*, US$25 per boat, two to three hours, and from the beach in front of *Hotel María del Carmen*, US$42 per boat, three hours (but much time is spent on the open sea). Ensure in advance that the boatman will cut his motor frequently so as not to scare the birds; morning is the best viewing time as later on flamingos move deeper into the park. January-March is best time to see them. Also ask to be taken to the freshwater swimming hole. It is often possible to see flamingos from the bridge early in the morning and the road to it may be alive with egrets, herons and pelicans. Important to wear a hat and use sun-screen. Hourly buses to Mérida 0530-2030, one hour, US$3.

Sleeping LL *Eco Paraiso*, Km 10 de la Antiqua Carretera a Sisal, T62100, F62111, burger@mail.internet.com.mx, in coconut grove on edge of reserve, pool, tours to surrounding area including flamingos, turtle nesting etc. **D** *Gutiérrez*, C 12 (the *malecón*) No 22, large beds, fans, views, clean. **D** *María del Carmen*, new, spacious and clean, recommended. **E** *San Julio*, C 12 No 92, also large bright rooms and clean bathrooms, owner knowledgeable about the area.

Eating Many beachside restaurants along Calle 12, but be careful of food in the cheaper ones; recommended is *La Playita*, for fried fish, seafood cocktails; bigger menu and more expensive is *Chemas*, for shrimp, oysters and octopus; *Avila* also safe for fried fish. Food stalls along Calle 11 beside the bus station should be approached with caution.

Dzibilchaltún Halfway to Progreso turn right for the Maya ruins of Dzibilchaltún. This unique city, according to carbon dating, was founded as early as 1000 BC. The site is in two halves, connected by a sacbé (white road). The most important building is the Templo de las Siete Muñecas (Seven Dolls, partly restored and on display in the museum) at the east end. At the west end is the ceremonial centre with temples, houses and large plaza in which there is a ruined colonial church. At its edge is the *Cenote Xlaca* containing very clear water and 44 metres deep (you can swim in it, take mask and snorkel as it is full of interesting fish); very interesting nature trail starting half way between temple and cenote; rejoins the sacbé half way along. ■ *0800-1700, US$4.50, free with ISIC card. Museum at entrance by ticket office (site map available), where you can buy drinks. VW combis leave from Parque San Juan, corner of Calle 62 y 67A, every 1 or 2 hours between 0500 and 1900, stopping at the ruins en route to Chablekal, a small village further along the same road. There are also 5 direct buses a day on weekdays, from Parque San Juan, marked 'Tour/Ruta Polígono'; bus returns from site entrance on the hour, passing the junction 15 minutes later, taking 45 minutes from junction to Mérida (US$0.60).*

Progreso A port 39 kilometres away from Mérida, 45 minutes by road; temperatures range
Population: 14,000 from 27° to 35°C. Main export: *henequén*. It claims to have the longest stone-bridge
Colour map 4, grid A3 pier in the world (it is being extended to six kilometres, unfortunately not open to the general public). The beach has no shade but there is always a breeze and plenty of new hotels and houses have been built. The shallow waters are good for swimming. Most of the palm trees along the front are dying from a virus (*amarrillamiento letal*). It is very popular with Mexican tourists at weekends and holiday times (July-August), but is quiet otherwise.

Sleeping on beach C *Progreso*, clean, friendly, traffic noise. **C** *Tropical Suites* (more with kitchen), clean, recommended. **E** *San Miguel*, C 78 No 148, hot shower, fan, clean. **E** *Playa*

Linda, by beach, with shower, kitchen and fan, cockroaches, quiet. **E** *Hostal*, clean, big rooms. Police permit free beach camping; huts for hammocks. Many homes, owned by Mexico City residents, available for rent, services included.

Eating Good restaurants are *Capitán Marisco*, and *Charlie's* expensive but good; *Soberanis*, for seafood tacos; *El Cordobés*, good service, recommended. *La Terraza*, variable results, expensive; *Pelícanos*, corner of C 21 y 20 on sea front, good and friendly, recommended. *La Conkaleña* is a good deli (Dutch owner). Many good restaurants along the beach. Good local market with lowest food prices in Yucatán, especially seafood. You can buy fresh shrimps cheaply in the mornings on the beach. The beach front by the pier is devoted to cafés with seafood cocktails as their speciality. They also have little groups performing every weekend afternoon in summer; and the noise can be both spirited and deafening.

Entertainment 2 cinemas.

Transport **Buses** Progreso-Mérida US$1.15 every 15 minutes. The bus and train stations are close together, 3 blocks inland, 5 minutes' walk east of the pier. **Boats** Can be hired to visit the reef of Los Alacranes where many ancient wrecks are visible in clear water.

A short bus journey (four kilometres) west from Progreso are **Puerto Yucalpetén** and **Chelem**, a dusty resort. Balneario Yucalpetén has a beach with lovely shells, but also a large naval base with further construction in progress. **AL** *Fiesta Inn* on the beach and *Mayaland Club* (Mayaland Resorts, in USA T800-45108891/305-3419173), villa complex. Yacht marina, changing cabins, beach with gardens and swimming pool. Between the Balneario and Chelem there is a nice hotel with some small bungalows, *Hotel Villanueva* (two kilometres from village, hot rooms), and also *Costa Maya*, on C 29 y Carretera Costera, with restaurant. In Chelem itself is a new hotel, **B** *Las Garzas*, C 17 No 742, T244735, a/c, cable TV, bar, good restaurant, private beach club, pool, pleasant. Fish restaurants in Chelem, *Las Palmas* and *El Cocalito*, reasonable, also other small restaurants. Five kilometres east of Progreso is another resort, **Chicxulub**; it has a narrow beach, quiet and peaceful, on which are many boats and much seaweed. Small restaurants sell fried fish by the *ración*, or kilo, served with tortillas, mild chilli and *cebolla curtida* (pickled onion). Chicxulub is reputed to be the site of the crater made by a meteorite crash 65 million years ago which caused the extinction of the dinosaurs. The beaches on this coast are often deserted and, between December and February, 'El Norte' wind blows in every 10 days or so, making the water turbid and bringing in cold, rainy weather.

Uxmal

(Pronounced Ooshmál) is 74 kilometres from Mérida, 177 kilometres from Campeche, by a good paved road. If going by car, there is a new circular road round Mérida: follow the signs to Campeche, then Campeche via *ruinas*, then to Muná via Yaxcopoil (long stretch of road with no signposting). Muná-Yaxcopoil about 34 kilometres. The Uxmal ruins are quite unlike those of Chichén Itzá (see below), and cover comparatively little ground. Uxmal, the home of the Xiu tribe, was built during the Classic Period (AD600-900). Its finest buildings seem to have been built much later. See El Adivino (the Sorcerer, a 30-metre high pyramid, topped by two temples with a splendid view); the Casa de las Monjas (Nunnery), a quadrangle with 88 rooms much adorned on their façades; the Casa del Gobernador (House of the Governor), on three terraces, with well preserved fine sculptures; the Casa de las Tortugas (House of the Turtles) with seven rooms; the Casa de las Palomas (House of the Doves), probably the oldest; and the so called 'Cemetery Group'.

There are caves which go in for about 100 metres near the main entrance (rather dull). Many iguanas (harmless) wandering about, watch out for occasional scorpions and snakes, and beware of biting insects in the long grass. ■ *Ruins open at 0800,*

Colour map 4, grid B3

close at 1700, entrance US$5 weekdays, free on Sunday (students with Mexican ID, US$1.75), US$3 to use video camera. A new visitors' centre at the entrance to the ruins houses a museum, souvenir shops and a restaurant (no refreshments sold in the ruins); also a good selection of guide books here. A free film is shown in English alternating with Spanish showings. Guided tours cost US$20. Luggage can be left at the visitors' centre. There is a car park, US$1.50. There is a son et lumière display at the ruins nightly, English version (US$5) at 2100, Spanish version (US$3.20) 2000 (check for times), recommended (special bus for Spanish version only leaves at 1730 from terminal at Calle 69, between 68 and 70, returning 2100, US$4.10 return). 2nd class bus from Mérida to Campeche ('Via Ruinas') passes Uxmal, can buy tickets on bus, 2 hours' journey, 4 hours just enough to see ruins. From Mérida at least 6 2nd-class buses a day from 0600, 1½ hours, US$1.50, 1st class bus (Autotransportes del Sur) at 0800, returns 1430 (can be overcrowded). Advance seat booking is strongly recommended. ATS buses stop outside main entrance to site to drop off and pick up passengers, including those going on to Campeche. After the Spanish show it may be possible for those without tour bus tickets to get a ride to Muná from where the last bus to Mérida leaves at 2200. Colectivo to Muná US$1, colectivo Muná-Mérida US$1.50. There is, however, a bus to Campeche at 2315 (can be crowded). Good service with Yucatán Trails, informative but hurried (see page 473). For best photographs early morning or late afternoon arrival is essential.

Sleeping & eating **AL** *Misión Park Uxmal*, T/F247308, Km 78, 1-2 kilometres from ruins on Mérida road, rooms a bit dark. **A** *Hacienda Uxmal*, T280840, 300-400 metres from ruins, is good, efficient and relaxing (3 restaurants open 0800-2200), a/c, gardens, swimming pool (the pottery that decorates the rooms is made by Miguel Zum, Calle 32, Ticul); also owns **L** *Lodge Uxmal*, T232202, at entrance, comfortable, a/c, bath, TV, fair restaurant – in Mérida: Mayaland Resorts, Av Colón 502, T252122, F257022.

A *Club Méditerranée Villa Arqueológica*, T47030, beautiful, close to ruins, good and expensive restaurant, excellent service, swimming pool, recommended. For cheap accommodation, go to Ticul, 28 kilometres away (see below). Restaurant at ruins, good but expensive. Restaurant of **D** *Rancho Uxmal*, about 4 kilometres north of ruins, T20277, comfortable rooms, hot and cold water, camping for US$5, pool, reasonable food but not cheap (no taxis to get there). **NB** There is no village at Uxmal, just the hotels.

Camping No camping allowed, but there is a campsite, *Sacbe*, at Santa Elena, about 15 kilometres south, between Uxmal and Kabah, on Route 261, Km 127 at south exit of village. Postal address: Portillo, Apdo 5, CP 97860, Ticul, Yuc. (2nd class buses Mérida-Campeche pass by, ask to be let out at the Campo de Baseball.) 9 electric hook-ups (US$7-10 for motor home according to size), big area for tents (US$2.75 per person with tent), palapas for hammocks (US$2.65 per person), cars pay US$1, showers, toilets, clothes washing facilities also 3 bungalows with ceiling fan (**E**), breakfast, vegetarian lunch and dinner available

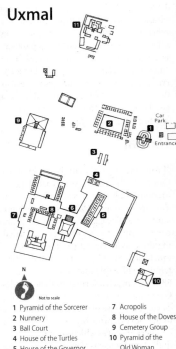

Uxmal

N

Not to scale

1 Pyramid of the Sorcerer
2 Nunnery
3 Ball Court
4 House of the Turtles
5 House of the Governor
6 Great Pyramid
7 Acropolis
8 House of the Doves
9 Cemetery Group
10 Pyramid of the Old Woman
11 North Group

(US$2.65 each), French and Mexican owners, a beautifully landscaped park, fastidiously clean, and impeccably managed, highly recommended.

On the road from Uxmal to Mérida is **Muná** (15 kilometres from Uxmal, 62 from Mérida); delightful square and old church, no hotel, but ask in *Restaurant Katty*, just on plaza, whose owner has two rooms with two double beds at his home, **E**, clean, friendly, hot showers, recommended (restaurant has good, cheap *enchiladas en mole*). Also ask in shops by bus stop in town centre for accommodation in private homes. There is a new direct road (Highway 293) from Muná to Bacalar, Quintana Roo, just north of Chetumal.

On either side of the main road, 37 kilometres south of Uxmal and often included in tours of the latter, are the ruins of Kabah; on one side there is a fascinating Palace of Masks (or *Codz-Poop*), whose façade bears the image of Chac, mesmerically repeated 260 times, the number of days in the Almanac Year, each mask made up of 30 units of mosaic stone: even the central chamber is entered via a huge Chac mask whose curling snout forms the doorstep. On the other side of this wall, beneath the figure of the ruler, Kabal, are impressive carvings on the door arches which depict a man about to be killed, pleading for mercy, and of two men duelling. This side of the road is mostly reconstructed; across the road the outstanding feature is a reconstructed arch marking the start of the sacbe (sacred road), which leads all the way to Uxmal, and several stabilized, but unclimbable mounds of collapsed buildings. The style is classic Puuc. Watch out for snakes and spiders. ■ *Admission, US$1.75, free on Sunday.*

Kabah

Further south of Uxmal, about half-way between Mérida and Campeche, a paved road branches off to the left to the **Sayil** ruins (five kilometres), **Xlapak** (about 11 kilometres) and **Labná** (about 14 kilometres). Both Sayil and Labná are in low, shrubby bush country. Sayil has several fine structures scattered over a wide area, including the massive Gran Palacio with a colonnaded façade; walks of several hundred metres are involved, but do not stray from the marked paths as many mapping trails merely lead off into the forest. Xlapak has one, well-reconstructed palace and two partially reconstructed buildings. Labná has an astonishing arch, two palace structures and a pyramid all within a 200 metres radius, quiet, lovely setting among trees. These sites can each be explored in one to two hours. ■ *Entrance to each site US$1.75, all are free on Sunday.* Refreshments and water are available, at the sites. From Labná, continue to immense galleries and caves of **Bolonchen** which are now illuminated (bus from Mérida).

Sayil, Xlapak & Labná

Transport Autotransportes del Sur run a 'Ruta Puuc' bus at 0800 from terminal at C69 x 68 y 70 in Mérida, which passes Uxmal at 0930 before leaving passengers for about 30 minutes each at Labná, Sayil, Kabah and Xlapak, returning to Uxmal and waiting 2-2½ hours before returning to Mérida at 1430; cost is US$ 5.50 (entry to ruins extra) strongly recommended to book the day before. The only disadvantage is that you get to Uxmal in the midday heat when the crowds are there. If visiting Sayil, Xlapak and Labná only, you can take a taxi from the village of Santa Elena at the turn-off (see camping *Sacbe*, above), costing US$22 for 1-3 persons. By hire-car one can continue to Oxcutzcab (see below). Buses (infrequent) going through Santa Elena en route to Mérida do not return to main road as they continue on backroads, so it is best to go into Santa Elena for bus after visiting Kabah rather than waiting at the roadside.

The road from Mérida (and also from Uxmal) to Chetumal is through Muná, Ticul (where pottery, hats and shoes are made; quite a good base for visiting Uxmal and Loltún), and Felipe Carrillo Puerto.

Ticul
Colour map 4, grid A3

Sleeping and eating **C** *Motel Bougambileas*, C 23, clean but overpriced. **D** *Plaza*, on Zócalo, with bath, clean, a/c. **D-E** *Sierra Sosa*, shower, fan, cheapest rooms dungeon-like but clean, helpful, friendly. **E** *Cerro Motor Inn*, run down. **E** *San Miguel*, C 28 near Plaza, fan, quiet, good value, parking, recommended. Next door is a good little *pizzería*; next door again is *Los Almendros* restaurant, opposite Cinema Ideal. *Los Delfines*, C27 No 216, x 28 y 30, recommended.

Oxkutzcab
Colour map 4, grid A3

16 kilometres after Ticul is Oxkutzcab, a good centre for catching buses to Chetumal, Muná, Mayapán and Mérida (US$2.20). It is a friendly place with a large market on the side of the Plaza and a church with a 'two-dimensional' façade on the other side of the square.

Sleeping and eating D *Tucanes*, with a/c, E with fan, not very clean, by Pemex station. E *Casa de Huéspedes*, near bus terminal, large rooms with bath, TV, fan, friendly, recommended. *Bermejo*, C 51, No 143. E *Trujeque*, just south of main plaza, a/c, TV, clean, good value, discount for stays over a week. Hammocks provided in some private houses, usually full, fluent Spanish needed to find them. *Su Cabaña Suiza*, C54 No101, good, cheap set lunch, family-run, recommended. (No money exchange facilities; go to Banco Atlántico in Tekax, 25 minutes away by bus.)

Loltún

Nearby, to the south, are the caverns and precolumbian vestiges at **Loltún** (supposedly extending for eight kilometres). ■ *Caves are open Tuesday-Sunday, admission at 0930, 1100, 1230 and 1400 (US$3 with obligatory guide, one hour 20 minutes), recommended. Caretaker may admit tours on Monday, but no lighting.* Take pickup (US$0.30) or truck from the market going to Cooperativa (an agricultural town). For return, flag down a passing truck. Alternatively, take a taxi, US$10 (can be visited from Labná on a tour from Mérida). The area around Ticul and Oxcutzcab is intensively farmed with citrus fruits, papayas and mangos. After Oxkutzcab on Route 184 is **Tekax** with restaurant *La Ermita* serving excellent Yucateca dishes at reasonable prices. From Tekax a paved road leads to the ruins of **Chacmultun**. From the top you have a beautiful view. There is a caretaker. All the towns between Muná and Peto, 14 kilometres northeast of Tzucacab off the Route 184, have large old churches. Beyond the Peto turn-off the scenery is scrub and swamp as far as the Belizean frontier.

Mayapán

Route 18 leads southeast from Mérida to join Route 184 at Ticul. It passes first through **Kanasin**, to which there are frequent buses. The restaurant, *La Susana*, is known especially for local delicacies like *sopa de lima*, *salbutes* and *panuchos*. Clean, excellent service and abundant helpings at reasonable prices. There are two large pyramids in village of **Acanceh** en route. Between Acanceh and Mayapán is Tecóh, with the caverns of **Dzab-Náh**; you must take a guide as there are treacherous drops into *cenotes*. Mayapán is a large, peaceful late Maya site easily visited by bus from Mérida (every 30 minutes from terminal at Calle 50 y 67 behind the municipal market, one hour, US$1 to Telchquillo). It can also be reached from Oxcutzcab. Beware of snakes at site (entrance US$4.35).

Chichén Itzá

Colour map 4, grid A3

120 kilometres by a paved road (Route 180) running southeast from Mérida. The scrub forest has been cleared from over five square kilometres of ruins. The city was built by the Maya in late Classic times (AD 600-900). By the end of the 10th century, the city was more-or-less abandoned. It was reestablished in the 11th-12th centuries, but much debate surrounds by whom. Whoever the people were, they were heavily influenced by the Toltecs of Central Mexico.

The major buildings in the north half display a Toltec influence. Dominating them is El Castillo, its top decorated by the symbol of Quetzalcoatl, and the balustrade of the 91 stairs up each of the four sides is decorated at its base by the head of a plumed, open-mouthed serpent. There is also an interior ascent of 61 steep and narrow steps to a chamber lit by electricity where the red-painted jaguar which probably served as the throne of the high priest burns bright, its eyes of jade, its fangs of flint (see below for entry times). There is a ball court with grandstand and towering walls each set with a projecting ring of stone high up; at eye-level is a relief showing the decapitation of the winning captain (sacrifice was an honour; some theories, however, maintain that the losing captain was killed). El Castillo stands at the centre of

Chichén Itzá

N

Not to scale

1 Castillo	7 Well of Sacrifice	12 House of the Deer
2 Ball Court	8 Temple of the Warriors	13 Red House
3 Temple of the Jaguar	& Chacmool Temple	14 El Caracol (Observatory)
4 Platform of the Skulls	9 Group of Thousand	15 Nunnery
(Tzompantli)	Columns	16 'Church'
5 Platform of Eagles	10 Market	17 Akabdzilo
6 Platform of Venus	11 Tomb of the High Priest	

the northern half of the site, and almost at right-angles to its northern face runs the sacred way to the Cenote Sagrado, the Well of Sacrifice. Into the Cenote Sagrado were thrown valuable propitiatory objects of all kinds, animals and human sacrifices. The well was first dredged by Edward H Thompson, the US Consul in Mérida, between 1904 and 1907; he accumulated a vast quantity of objects in pottery, jade, copper and gold. In 1962 the well was explored again by an expedition sponsored by the National Geographic Society and some 4,000 further artefacts were recovered, including beads, polished jade, lumps of copal resin, small bells, a statuette of rubber latex, another of wood, and a quantity of animal and human bones. Another *cenote*, the Xtoloc Well, was probably used as a water supply. To the east of El Castillo is the Temple of the Warriors with its famous reclining Chac-mool statue. This pyramidal platform has now been closed off to avoid erosion.

Old Chichén, where the Maya buildings of the earlier city are found, lies about 500 metres by path from the main clearing. The famous El Caracol, or observatory is included in this group as is the Casa de las Monjas, or Nunnery. A footpath to the right of Las Monjas takes one to the Templo de los Tres Dinteles (the Three Lintels) after 30 minutes' walking. It requires at least one day to see the many pyramids, temples, ballcourts and palaces, all of them adorned with astonishing sculptures, and excavation and renovation is still going on. Interesting birdlife and iguanas can be seen around the ruins. ■ *Entry to Chichén Itzá, 0800-1700, US$5 free Sunday and holidays, when it is incredibly crowded, students with Mexican ID US$1.75); you may leave and re-enter as often as you like on day of issue. Check at entrance for opening times of the various buildings. Best to arrive before 1030 when the mass of tourists arrives.* **Son et lumière** *(US$5 in English, US$1.35 in Spanish) at Chichén every evening, in Spanish at 1900, and then in English at 2000; nothing like as good as at Uxmal. A tourist centre has been built at the entrance to the ruins with a restaurant, free cinema (short film in English at 1200 and 1600), a small museum, books and souvenir shops (if buying slides, check the quality), with exchange facilities at the latter; luggage deposit free, open 0800-1700. Car park US$1.50. Entry to see the jaguar in the substructure of El Castillo along an inside staircase at 1100-1500, closed Sunday (but entry time does vary). Try to be among the first in as it is stuffy inside and queues form at busy times. Drinks and snacks available at entrance (expensive) and at Cenote, also guidebooks, clean toilets at former. Also toilets on the way to old Chichén, and a drinks terrace with film supplies. The site is hot, take a hat, sun cream, sun glasses, shoes with good grip and drinking water. The* **Easy Guide** *by Richard Bloomgarden is interesting though brief, available in several languages.* **Panorama** *is the best. José Díaz Bolio's book, although in black and white and therefore cheaper) is good for background information, but not as a guide to take you round the ruins. Guides charge US$4-6 per person for a 1½-hour tour (they are persistent and go too fast). Recommended guide from Mérida: Miguel Angel Vergara, Centro de Estudios Maya Haltun-Ha, T271172, F267707, PO Box 97148.*

There are tours daily to the **Balankanché** caves, three kilometres east, just off the highway; ■ *Caretaker turns lights on and off, answers questions in Spanish, every hour on the hour, minimum six, maximum 20 persons; open 0900-1700, US$3.45, free Sunday (allow about 45 minutes for the 300 metre descent), closed Saturday and Sunday afternoons. There are archaeological objects, including offerings of pots and metates in a unique setting, except for the unavoidable, 'awful' son et lumière show (five a day in Spanish; 1100, 1300 and 1500 in English; 1000 in French; it is very damp and hot, so dress accordingly). Bus Chichén Itzá or Pisté – Balankanché hourly at a quarter past, US$0.50, taxi US$15.*

An interesting detour off the Chichén – Mérida highway is to turn in the direction of Yaxcaba at Libre Unión, after three kilometres turn on to a dirt road, singposted to cenote **Xtojil**, a beautiful cenote with a Maya platform, which has well-preserved carvings and paintings.

The 3 hotels closest to the ruins are **AL** *Hacienda Chichén*, once owned by Edward Thompson with charming bungalows. **AL** *Mayaland Hotel*, including breakfast and dinner, pool, but sometimes no water in it, no a/c, just noisy ceiling fans, but good service and friendly (in USA T800-4518891/305-3419173). **AL** *Villas Arqueológicas*, T985-62830, Apdo Postal 495, Mérida, pool, tennis, restaurant (expensive and poor). Both are on the other side of the fenced-off ruins from the bus stop; you cannot walk through ruins, either walk all the way round, or take taxi (US$1-1.50).

Sleeping
All are expensive for what they offer.

Further away **A** *Lapalapa Chichén*, with breakfast and dinner, a few kilometres from the ruins, excellent restaurant, modern, park with animals. **B** *Sunset Club*, 10 minutes' walk from Pisté village, 30 minutes from Chichén Itzá, takes credit cards, room with bath, hot water, fan, TV, swimming pool, recommended. Nearby is **C** *Pirámide Inn*, 1½ kilometres from ruins, at the Chichén end of Pisté, clean but run down, with good food, swimming pool, friendly English-speaking owner, Trailer Park and camping US$6.50 for 2 plus car in front of hotel, US$4.50 in campground (owned by *Stardust*, see below, but still check in at hotel reception, cold showers). **D** *Dolores Alba*, small hotel (same family as in Mérida, where you can make advance reservations, advisable in view of long walk from ruins), 2½ kilometres on the road to Puerto Juárez (bus passes it), in need of renovation, with shower and fan, clean, has swimming pool and serves good, expensive meals, English spoken, RVs can park in front for US$5, with use of restroom, shower and pool, free transport to the ruins (be careful if walking along the road from the ruins after dark, there are many trucks speeding by, carry a flashlight/torch).

Other hotels at **Pisté** about 2 kilometres before the ruins if coming from Mérida (taxi to ruins US$2.50): no accommodation under US$10. **B-C** *Stardust Posada Annex*, good value, especially if you don't want TV or a/c (fans available), swimming pool, popular with German tour groups, average restaurant. **D** *Maya Inn*, on main road to Chichén Itzá, with bath, **E** without, also hammock space, clean. **D** *Posada Chac Mool*, fan, bath, clean, laundry service, safe parking, a bit noisy but recommended. **D** *Posada Olalde*, quiet, 100 metres from main road at end of C 6. **D** *Posada Novelo*, near *Pirámide Inn*, run by José Novelo who speaks English, good cheap restaurant, guest access to pool at nearby *Stardust Inn*. **D** *Posada el Paso*, on main road into village from Chichén, with shower, good value, very friendly, safe parking, nice restaurant. **D** *Posada el Paso*, on main road into village from Chichén, with shower, good value, very friendly, safe parking, nice restaurant. A lot of traffic passes through at night, try to get a room at the back.

There is a small pyramid in the village opposite the **A** *Hotel Misión Chichén Itzá*, a/c, pool (disappointing, gloomy, poor restaurant), not easily seen from the road; it has staircases with plumed serpents and a big statue facing north on top; close by is a huge plumed serpent, part coloured, almost forming a circle at least 20 metres long. Unfortunately the serpent has been largely destroyed to make way for the *Posada Chac Mool*. There is no sign or public path, climb over gate into scrubland, the serpent will be to right, pyramid to left. The whole construction is an unabashedly modern folly made 25 yrs ago by a local stone-mason who used to work on the archaeological expeditions.

Mostly poor and overpriced in Chichén itself (cafés inside the ruins are cheaper than the restaurant at the entrance to the ruins, but they are still expensive). *Hotel Restaurant Carrousel* (rooms **D**); *Las Redes*; *Nicte-Ha* opposite is cheaper and has chocolate milk shakes; *Fiesta* in Pisté, Calle Principal, Yucatecan specialities, touristy but good. Next door is a place serving good *comida corrida* for US$5.35; *Poxil*, Mérida end of town, for breakfast; *El Paso* in Pisté, good meals but doesn't open for breakfast as early as it claims. *Sayil* in Pisté has good *pollo pibil* for US$2.60. Restaurants in Pisté close 2100-2200.

Eating

Hammocks are sold by *Mario Díaz* (a most interesting character), excellent quality, huge, at his house 500 metres up the road forking to the left at the centre of the village. 35 kilometres from Chichén is Ebtún, on the road to Valladolid. A sign says 'Hammock sales and repairs': it is actually a small prison which turns out 1st class cotton or nylon hammocks; haggle with

Shopping

Mexico

wardens and prisoners; there are no real bargains, but good quality. Silver at orange coloured shops opposite *Posada Novelo*.

Transport **Road** If driving from Mérida, follow Calle 63 (off the Plaza) out as far as the dirt section, where you turn left, then right and right again at the main road, follow until hypermarket on left and make a left turn at the sign for Chichén Itzá. Hitchhiking to Mérida is usually no problem.

Buses Chichén Itzá is easily reached (but less easily during holiday periods) from Mérida by (ADO) 2nd class, 2½ hours, US$3 from 0500, bus station on C 71 x 64 y 66. 1st class bus, US$4.50. Return tickets from the gift shop near entrance to site. Buses drop off and pick up passengers until 1700 at the top of the coach park opposite entrance to *artesanía* market (thereafter take a taxi to Pisté or colectivo to Valladolid for buses). Monday am 2nd class buses may be full with workers from Mérida returning to Cancún. Many buses a day between 0430 and 2300 go to **Cancún** and **Puerto Juárez**, US$6.20. The first bus from Pisté to Puerto Juárez is at 0730, 3 hours. ADO bus office in Pisté is between *Stardust* and *Pirámide Inn*. Budget travellers going on from Mérida to Isla Mujeres or Cozumel should visit Chichén from Valladolid (see below) although if you plan to go through in a day you can store luggage at the visitors' centre. Buses from **Valladolid** go every hour to the site, the 0715 bus reaches the ruins at 0800 when they open, and you can return by standing on the main road 1 kilometre from the entrance to the ruins and flagging down any bus going straight through. Colectivo entrance-Valladolid, US$1.65. Bus Pisté-Valladolid US$1.50; Pisté-**Tulum**, 1 bus only at 1300, US$4. Chichén Itzá-Tulum, bus at 1330 and 1445, 4 hours, very crowded.

Directory **Banks** Bank in Pisté, *Banamex*, open 0900-1300. **Communications** Telephone: international calls may be placed from *Teléfonos de México*, opposite *Hotel Xaybe*.

Izamal
Population: 15,385
Colour map 4, grid A3

On the way back, turn to the right at Kantunil (68 kilometres from Mérida) for a short excursion to the charming, friendly little city of **Izamal**. (It can be reached by direct bus either from Mérida or Valladolid, a good day excursion.) Once a major Classic Maya religious site (founded by the priest Itzamná), Izamal became one of the centres of the Spanish attempt to Christianize the Maya.

Fray Diego de Landa, the historian of the Spanish conquest of Mérida (of whom there is a statue in the town), founded the huge convent and church which now face the main Plaza de la Constitución. This building, constructed on top of a Maya pyramid, was begun in 1549 and has the second largest atrium in the world. There is a throne built for the Pope's visit in 1993. The image of the Inmaculada Virgen de la Concepción in the magnificent church was made the Reina de Yucatán in 1949 and the patron saint of the state in 1970. Just two and a half blocks away, visible from the convent across a second square and signposted, are the ruins of a great mausoleum known as Kinich-Kakmo pyramid. ■ *The entrance is next to the tortilla factory (0800-1700, free).* You climb the first set of stairs to a broad, tree-covered platform, at the end of which is a further pyramid (still under reconstruction). From the top there is an excellent view of the town and surrounding *henequén* and citrus plantations. Kinich-Kakmo is 195 metres long, 173 wide and 36 high, the fifth highest in Mexico. In all, 20 Maya structures have been identified in Izamal, several on Calle 27. Another startling feature about the town is that the entire colonial centre, including the convent, the arcaded government offices on Plaza de la Constitución and the arcaded second square, is painted a rich yellow ochre, giving it the nickname of the 'golden city'.

Four blocks up Calle 27, at the junction with Calle 34 is a small church on a square. The front door may be locked, but a little door outside leads to a spiral staircase to the interior gallery (note the wooden poles in the ceilings) and to the roof. The treads on the stairs are very narrow.

Sleeping and eating On Plaza de la Constitución, **D** *Kabul*, poor value, cell-like rooms. **E** *Canto*, basic, room 1 is best, friendly. Several restaurants on Plaza de la Constitución. *Gaby* just off the square on C 31. *El Norteño* at bus station, good, cheap; *Wayane*, near statue of Diego de Landa, friendly, clean.

Entertainment Activity in town in the evening gets going after 2030.

Shopping Market: Calle 31, on Plaza de la Constitución, opposite convent, closes soon after lunch.

Transport Bus station is on Calle 32 behind government offices, can leave bags. 2nd class to **Mérida**, every 45 minutes, 1½ hours, US$1.50, lovely countryside. Bus station in Mérida, Calle 50 entre Calle 65 y 67. 6 a day to/from **Valladolid** (96 kilometres), about 2 hours, US$2.30-3.

Directory Banks: Bank on square with statue to Fray Diego de Landa, south side of convent. **Communications**: Post Office: on opposite side of square to convent.

From Izamal one can go by bus to **Cenotillo**, where there are several fine *cenotes* within easy walking distance from the town (avoid the one *in* town), especially Ucil, excellent for swimming, and La Unión. From Mérida, take 0600 train to Tunkas, and then bus to Cenotillo (direct bus from Mérida, same service as to Izamal), the train continues from Tunkas to Tizimín, arr 1140. Lovely train ride, two and a half hours, US$1.50. Past Cenotillo is Espita and then a road forks left to Tizimín (see below).

The cemetery of **Hoctun**, on the Mérida-Chichén road, is also worth visiting, impossible to miss, there is an 'Empire State Building' on the site. Take a bus from Mérida (last bus back 1700) to see extensive ruins at **Aké**, a unique structure. Public transport in Mérida is difficult: from an unsigned stop on the corner of Calle 53 y 50, some buses to Tixcocob and Ekmul continue to Aké; ask the driver.

Valladolid

East of Chichén Itzá, and easily reached from Mérida is Valladolid, a pleasant Yucatecan town bypassed by the paved road between Mérida and Puerto Juárez/Cancún. Here also is a large Franciscan church, situated on the pleasant plaza, in the middle of which is a fountain with a statue of a woman wearing a *huipil*, pouring water from a jar. Good nightlife in the plaza where at dusk there is a cacophony of birdsong. In the western outskirts, in the Barrio del Convento de Sisal, is the former convent of San Bernardino de Siena; built in 1552, it is one of the oldest churches in the Yucatán, worth a visit, guide US$1 (closed Monday). See **History** for a description of the Caste War, which took place around Valladolid. Indigenous people were prohibited to enter the plaza or walk in the adjoining streets.

Population: 19,300
Colour map 4, grid A3

A lovely deep *cenote*, Zací, with a thatched-roof restaurant and lighted promenades, is on Calle 36 between Calle 37 y 39, sometimes you cannot swim in it because of the algae. ■ *Admission US$1 (children half-price), open 0800-1800.* Road turns left from Cancún road a couple of blocks from main plaza.

You can swim in the electrically-lit *cenote* of Xkeken at **Dzit-Nup**, a huge cave with blue water: wonderful swimming with stalactites and flying bats overhead. Go early to avoid tour groups and take a torch for exploring. ■ *open until 1800, US$1, taxi US$2 one way from Valladolid seven kilometres away.* Colectivos leave several times a day from in front of *Hotel María Guadalupe*, or take Valladolid-Mérida bus and alight at Dzit-Nup junction, US$0.80, then hitch or walk the last couple of kilometres, or it's 30 minutes by bicycle (take Calle 39 towards Mérida; leaving town you reach a fork in the road, go left, unsigned for Mérida and after 10 minutes or so in a car you'll see the sign for Dzit-Nup; turn left and the cenote is on the left).

Excursions

B *Mesón del Marqués*, north side of Plaza Principal, T91985, F622680, Amex, only credit card, cash payment in advance, a/c, with bath, on square, with good but pricey restaurant and shop (helpful for information), cable TV, swimming pool, excellent value, recommended. **C** *María de la Luz*, C 42 No 193-C, Plaza Principal, T62071, takes Visa, good, a/c, swimming pool (non-residents, US$0.50), excellent restaurant, buffet breakfast US$3.50,

Sleeping

comida corrida US$5, closes at 2230. **D** *Posada Osorio*, C 40 x 35 y 33, clean, quiet. **D** *San Clemente*, C 42 No 206, T62208, with a/c, spacious, quiet, clean, has car park, TV, small swimming pool, restaurant, opposite cathedral, in centre of town, recommended. **D** *Zací*, C 44 No 191, a/c, cheaper with fan, TV, good pool with café beside it, clean, quiet. **D** *María Guadalupe*, C 44 No 198, T62068, quiet, fan, clean and good value, hot water, washing facilities, parking. **D-E** *Maya*, C 41 No 231, x 48 y 50, T62069, fan or a/c, clean, quiet, good value, laundry service, also runs good restaurant 2 doors away. **E** *Lily*, C 44, with hot shower, cheaper with shared bath, fan, basic, not too clean, good location, laundry facilities, motorcycle parking US$3, friendly. **E-F** *Mendoza*, C 39 No 204C x C 44 y 46, T62002, good, clean, hot water, noisy, safe parking, cheaper with shared bath, communal toilets dirty. **F** per person *Sr Silva* (see **Transport: bike hire**), rents large, airy rooms with fan and bathroom, recommended.

Eating *Los Portales* on southeast corner of main square, very good and cheap. *La Sirenita*, C 41 No 168-A, a few blocks east of main square, highly recommended for seafood, popular, only open to 1800, closed Sunday. Next to *Hotel Lily* are **Panadería La Central** and **Taquería La Principal**. Marginally cheaper food at the **cocinas familiares**, Yucatecan food, pizzas, burgers, etc, northeast corner of Plaza Principal, next to *Mesón del Marqués*, try the **Janet**, half way back. Cheap meals in the market, Calle 37, 2 blocks east of the cenote Zací. There is a well-stocked supermarket on the road between the centre and bus station.

Shopping Quality cheap leather goods from *Mercado de Artesanías*, Calle 39 x 42 y 44.

Transport **Local Bike hire**: Sr Silva, Calle 44, x Calle 39 y 41, US$1 per hour. Antonio, in front of *Hotel María Guadalupe*, US$0.50 per hour.

Trains Station at the south end of Calle 42. There is 1 train every day to Mérida at 0350, great views.

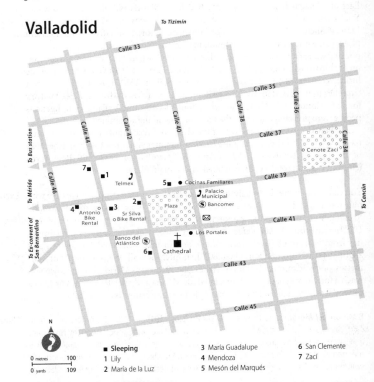

Valladolid

■ **Sleeping**	3 María Guadalupe	6 San Clemente
1 Lily	4 Mendoza	7 Zací
2 María de la Luz	5 Mesón del Marqués	

Buses New bus station is at Calle 54 y 37, 6 blocks west of plaza, taxi US$0.80. Old terminal is at Calle 46 y 39, 4 blocks west of plaza, for 2nd class buses. Some 1st class buses drop at the La Isleta terminal 8 kilometres from town, but then connect with a bus to either the Zócalo or new bus station. Check all bus times at bus terminal. To **Chichén Itzá**, take Mérida bus (make sure it takes you to the stop opposite the Unidad de Servicios), 2nd class, US$1.50, frequent, from 0600-2400, 1 hour ride, also to Balankanché caves; many buses go to **Mérida**, first at 0600, US$6, 2nd class US$4.50 (3 hours); and to **Cancún** from 0400 to 2100, US$5.50, 2 hours, US$5 2nd class (can take $3\frac{1}{2}$ hours but scenic ride through local villages), from 0700. To **Playa del Carmen** at 0430 (reservations available) and 1300 via Cobá (US$2.50) and the crossroads 1 kilometre from Tulum, US$8.50, 2nd class ($3\frac{1}{2}$ hours), more frequently via Cancún from 0130 to 1400, US$8 1st class, US$6 2nd class (4 hours); to **Tulum**, daily at 1400, 2nd class via Cobá, 3 hours. To **Coba** 0800 daily. To **Tizimín**, hourly 2nd class, 1 hour, US$1; to **Río Lagartos** (via Tizimín), US$2; **Felipe Carrillo Puerto**, at 0600 and 0930 and others for **Chetumal** (most 'de paso', buy tickets on the bus, only 2 direct, at 0630 and 1330), 2nd class, US$8, 5 hours.

Directory

Banks *Bancomer* on east side of square, changes TCs between 0900 and 1330. *Banco del Atlántico*, corner of C 41 y 42, quick service for TCs, from 1000. **Communications Post Office:** on east side of Plaza, 0800-1500 (does not accept parcels from abroad). **Telephones:** Telmex phone office on C 42, just north of square; expensive Computel offices at bus station and next to *Hotel San Clemente*; Ladatel phonecards can be bought from *farmacias* for use in phone booths. **Internet:** C42 No 206, next to *San Clemente Hotel*; also at C50 y 39. **Laundry** *Teresita*, C 33 between 40 and 42, US$6 for $5\frac{1}{2}$ kg.

Tizimín

Population: 30,000
Colour map 4, grid A3

A paved road heads north from Valladolid to Tizimín, a pleasant, busy town with an austere 16th century church and a convent (both may be closed), open squares and streets with low houses. It has a famous New Year *fiesta*. There is also a local *cenote*, Kikib, and the Maya ruins of **Kulubá** are one hour, 50 kilometres away (taxi US$18.50). 15 kilometres north of Temozón, on the road from Valladolid to Tizimín, are the interesting Maya ruins of **Ek Balam** (US$1.50). A colectivo leaves from La Candelaria park, Wednesday-Sunday only.

Sleeping There are several hotels, eg **D** *San Jorge*, on main plaza, a/c, good value. **D** *San Carlos*, 2 blocks from main square, with bath, fan, clean, good. **D** *Tizimín*, on main square. **D** *Posada* next to church.

Eating There is a good but expensive restaurant, *Tres Reyes*, also *Los Portales* on main square, and others, including many serving cheap *menú del día* around the plaza.

Entertainment On the edge of town is a vast pink disco, popular with Meridanos.

Transport Trains: To Mérida 1240, 5 hours, US$2. **Buses**: From Mérida from Calle 50 entre Calle 65 y 67, 1st class, 3 hours, US$6. In Tizimín there are 2 bus terminals side-by-side: Expreso del Oriente for Valladolid, Mérida, Cancún (3 hours, US$6), and Playa del Carmen, and Pullman Ejecutivo Noreste for Mérida (3 *ejecutivo* and at least 7 1st class), Río Lagartos (3 1st class and 11 2nd class between 0515 and 1900, US$1), San Felipe (2 1st, 5 2nd class), Chiquilá, Valladolid (5 a day, US$1), and Felipe Carrillo Puerto, Bacalar and Chetumal (0530 and 1430).

Communications Telephone: long-distance phone at C 50 No 410, just off plaza.

Río Lagartos

The road continues north over the flat landscape to Río Lagartos, itself on a lagoon, where the Maya extracted salt. Río Lagartos has been declared a nature reserve to protect waterfowl habitat (local and migratory) and turtle nesting beaches. The town however, is filthy. Swimming from the island opposite Río Lagartos, where boats are moored; access to beach by boat only.

Bus from Río Lagartos to **San Felipe** (13 kilometres), where you can bathe in the sea, access to beach here, too, only by boat; basic accommodation in the old cinema, **F**, ask in the shop *Floresita*; also houses for rent; Miguel arranges boat trips to the beach (US$3), he lives next door to the old cinema; good cheap seafood at *El Payaso* restaurant; on the waterfront is *La Playa* restaurant, recommended; on a small island with ruins of a Maya pyramid, beware of rattlesnakes. One can also go from Río Lagartos to **Los Colorados** (15 kilometres) to swim and see the salt deposits with red, lilac and pink water (no shade, beware of sunburn). Early morning boat trips can be arranged in Río Lagartos to see the flamingos (US$35, in eight to nine seater, two and a half to four hours, cheaper in five-seater, but no shade, fix the price before embarking; in mid-week few people go so there is no chance of negotiating, but boat owners are more flexible on where they go; at weekends it is very busy, so it may be easier to get a party together and reduce costs). There are often only a few pairs of birds feeding in the lagoons east of Los Colorados; ask for Adriano who is a good guide and bird expert, or for Manuel at the Río Lagartos bus stop. Make sure you are taken to the furthest breeding grounds, to see most flamingos, and pelicans. There is also a road around the main congregating area. Check before going whether the flamingos are there, they usually nest here during May-June and stay through July-August. Salt mining is disturbing their habitat.) Not a lot else here, certainly no accommodation, but if you are stuck for food, eat inexpensively at the *Casino* (ask locals).

Sleeping and eating E *Hotel Nefertiti*, run down, fish restaurant. E *Cabañas* at Tere and Miguel's house, with 2 double beds, mosquito nets and bath, near harbour. *Cueva Macumba* restaurant near harbour, good Mexican food, friendly, will arrange breakfast if requested in advance. *Isla Contoy*, C 19 No 134, friendly, recommended, fresh seafood and other dishes, good. Restaurant at seashore, good, well decorated, evening only; *lonchería*, opposite hotel, open for lunch. There are a number of small eating-places.

Festivals *Fiesta*, 12 December, La Virgen de Guadalupe.

Transport There are frequent buses from Tizimín (see above), and it is possible to get to Río Lagartos and back in a day from Valladolid, if you leave on the 0630 or 0730 bus (taxi Tizimín-Río Lagartos US$25, driver may negotiate) and last bus back from Río Lagartos at 1730.

El Cuyo
Colour map 4, grid A4

The road goes east along the coast on to El Cuyo, rough and sandy, but passable. El Cuyo has a shark-fishing harbour. Fishermen cannot sell (co-op) but can barter fish. Fry your shark steak with garlic, onions and lime juice. El Cuyo is a very quiet, friendly place with a beach where swimming is safe (there is less seaweed in the water the further from town you go towards the Caribbean). *La Conchita* restaurant (good value meals) has *cabañas* with bath, double bed and hammock (**D**). Opposite *La Conchita* bread is sold after 1700. From Tizimín there are kombis (US$2.70, one and a half hours) and buses (slower, four times a day) to El Cuyo, or take a kombi to Colonia and hitch from there (Sheila Wilson, Stoke Poges, UK).

Holbox Island
Colour map 4, grid A4

Also north of Valladolid, turning off the road to Puerto Juárez after Nuevo Xcan, is Holbox Island. Buses to **Chiquilá** for boats, three times a day, also direct from Tizimín at 1130, connecting with the ferry, US$2.20. The ferry leaves for Holbox 0600 and 1430, one hour, US$1, returning to Chiquilá at 0500 and 1300. A bus to Mérida connects with the 0500 ferry. If you miss the ferry a fisherman will probably take you (for about US$14). You can leave your car in the care of the harbour master for a small charge; his house is east of the dock. Take water with you if possible. The beach is at the opposite end of the island to the ferry, 10 minutes' walk. During 'El Norte' season, the water is turbid and the beach is littered with seaweed.

Sleeping E *Hotel Holbox* at dock, clean, quiet, cold water, friendly; house with 3 doors, ½ block from plaza, rooms, some beds, mostly for hammocks, very basic, very cheap, outdoor toilet, no shower, noisy, meals available which are recommended; rooms at pink house off plaza, **D**, clean, with bath. *Cabañas*, **D**, usually occupied; take blankets and hammock (ask at fishermen's houses where you can put up), and lots of mosquito repellent. **Camping** Best camping on beach east of village (north side of island).

Eating *Lonchería*, on plaza. Restaurant on main road open for dinner. All bars close 1900. Bakery with fresh bread daily, good. Fish is generally expensive.

Entertainment Disco Opens 2230, admission US$2.75.

There are five more uninhabited islands beyond Holbox. Beware of sharks and barracuda, though few nasty occurrences have been reported. Off the rough and mostly unpopulated bulge of the Yucatán coastline are several islands, once notorious for contraband. Beware of mosquitoes in the area.

At the border between Yucatán and Quintana Roo states, Nuevo Xcan (see page 514), police searches are made for those leaving Quintana Roo for items which may transmit plant and other diseases.

Cancún

This famous resort near the northeastern tip of the Yucatán peninsula, is a thriving holiday resort and town. The town is on the mainland; the resort, usually known simply as the Zona Hotelera (Hotel Zone), is on an island shaped like the number seven, encompassing the Laguna Nichupté. The population is almost all dedicated to servicing the tourist industry. A bridge at each end of the island links the hotel zone with the mainland in a seamless ribbon, not yet developed along its entire length, but not far off. Beaches stretch all along the seaward side of the Zona Hotelera; both sand and sea are clean and beautiful. Watersports take place on the Caribbean and on the Laguna, but when bathing, watch out for the warning flags at intervals along the shore.

Population: 30,000
Phone code: 98
Colour map 4, grid A4

Ins and outs

Cancún is the second busiest international airport in Mexico and receives flights, both scheduled and chartered, from Europe, North, South and Central America and the Caribbean, while Los Angeles provides connecting flights from the Far East. There are good connections with many Mexican cities, see **Air** below for details. Being stuck out at the extreme east of the Yucatan Peninsula it takes a long while to get to Cancún overland from anywhere in Mexico, but there is a good road along the east coast from Belize.

Getting there

Buses, marked 'Hoteles', run every five minutes from the southern end of the Zona Hotelera to the town and back. At busy times they are packed with holidaymakers trying to locate where they should get off. There are also lots of buses to other resorts and beaches along the coast and for excursions inland to the towns and archaeological sites. Car hire is reasonably priced if you want to explore on your own.

Getting around

Its scale is huge, with skyscraper hotels and sprawling resorts between the beach and Bulevar Kukulkán, which runs the length of the island. At the northern end are shopping malls and an archaeological museum with local finds, next to the old Convention Centre (a new Convention Centre has been constructed opposite the *Fiesta Americana Coral Beach*.) There are vestiges of Maya occupation here, San Miguelito and El Rey towards the south of the island and a small temple in the grounds of the *Sheraton*, but they are virtually lost in the midst of the modern concrete and the architectural fantasies. Near El Rey (open 0800-1630), land is being reclaimed for the construction of a golf course, marina, hotel and commercial centre. Prices are

Zona Hotelera

Mexico

Mexico

higher on Cancún than elsewhere in Mexico because everything is brought in from miles outside.

It is about four kilometres from the Zona Hotelera to the town, which is full of tourist shops, restaurants and a variety of hotels which are cheaper than on the island. The town is divided into 'supermanzanas', indicated by SM in addresses, each block being divided further by streets and avenues. The two main avenues are Tulum and Yaxchilán, the former having most of the shops, exchange facilities, many restaurants and hotels. Its busiest sector runs from the roundabout at the junction with Bulevar Kukulkán to the roundabout by the bus station.

Sleeping
■ on maps
Price codes:
see inside front cover

Hotels fall roughly into 2 categories: those in the Zona Hotelera, which are expensive and tend to cater for package tours, but which have all the facilities associated with a beach holiday; those in the town are less pricey and more functional. The list below gives more detail on the latter.

In the Zona Hotelera LL *Camino Real*, T830100, F831730. **LL** *Sheraton Cancún Resort and Towers*, PO Box 834, Cancún, T831988, F850202. **L** *Hyatt Cancún Caribe*, T830044, F831514, and *Hyatt Regency*, T830966, F831349. *Stouffer Presidente*, T830200, F832515. *Miramar Misión Park Plaza*, T831755, F831136. *Playa Blanca*, Av Kukulkán Km 3.5,

Cancún environs

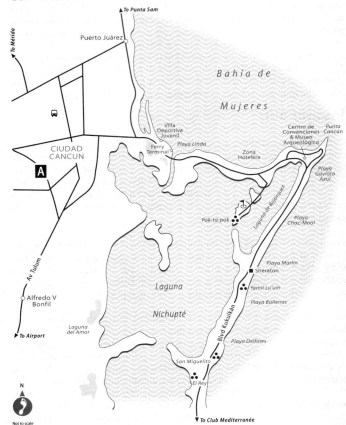

T830071, F830904, resort facilities; and *Krystal*, T831133, F831790. *Oasis Cancún*, T850867, F850131, huge hotel but well separated to give intimate feel, nice pool, helpful staff, about 15 kilometres from centre. Slightly less expensive: *Aristos*, T830011, F830078, *Calinda Quality Cancún Beach*, T830800, F831857, and *Calinda Viva*, same phone, F832087. *Club Lagoon Marina*, T831101, F831326. Also represented are 3 hotels in the *Fiesta Americana* chain, *Days Inn*, *Holiday Inn* (2, 1 in the *Zona Hotelera*, 1 in the centre), *Marriott*, *Meliá* (2), *Radisson* (also 2), and many more hotels, suites and villas. At the southern end of the island is the *Club Méditerranée* with its customary facilities (T842409, F842090); **B** *Laguna Verde Suites Hotel*, on Pok-ta-pok island, nicely furnished suites sleeping up to 4, kitchens, pool, shuttle to beach, good value.

Hotels in Cancún town   Most are to be found on Avenida Tulum and Avenida Yaxchilán and the streets off them. In Cancún town you will be lucky to find a double under US$20; many do not serve meals. **AL** *Best Western Plaza Caribe*, Av Tulum y Uxmal, T841377, F846352, opposite bus terminal. **AL** *Plaza del Sol*, Yaxchilán y Gladiolas, T843888, F844393, modern, comfortable. **A** *Caribe Internacional*, at the junction of Yaxchilán and Sunyaxchén, T843499, F841993. **A-B** *El Rey del Caribe*, Av Uxmal y Náder, T842028, F849857, a/c, kitchenettes, pool, garden with hammocks, parking, older style, friendly, recommended.

In our B range   *Antillano*, Av Tulum y Claveles, T841532, F841132, a/c, TV, phone, pool. *Cancún Rosa*, Margaritas 2, local 10, T842873, F840623, close to bus terminal, a/c, TV, phone, comfortable rooms. *El Alux*, Av Uxmal 21, T840662, turn left and first right from bus station,

Cancún centre

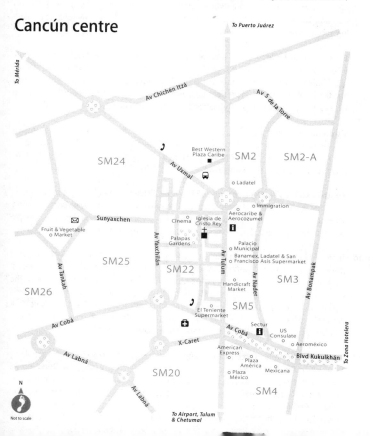

Mexico

a/c with bath, clean, TV, some rooms cheaper, good value, recommended. *Hacienda*, Sunyaxchén 38-40, a/c, TV. *Margarita*, Yaxchilán y Jazmines, T849333, F849209. *María de Lourdes*, Av Yaxchilán SM 22, T844744, F841242. *Batab*, Av Chichén 52 SM23, Apdo Postal 555, T843821, 843720, hotel-batab@ mail.interacces.com.mx, a/c, TV, clean, hot water, phone, OK.

In our C range *Coral*, Sunyaxchén 30 (towards post office), T842901. *Cotty*, Av Uxmal 44, T840550, near bus station, a/c, TV, clean. *Lucy*, Gladiolas 25, between Tulum and Yaxchilán, T844165, a/c, kitchenettes, takes credit cards. *Novotel*, Av Tulum y Azucenas, T842999, F843162, close to bus station, rooms start at under US$30 with fan, but rise to **B** range with a/c, popular, noisy on Avenida Tulum side. *Parador*, Av Tulum 26, T841310, F849712, close to bus terminal, some rooms noisy, inefficient, a/c, TV, phone, pool, restaurant attached, clean. *Rivemar*, Av Tulum 49-51 y Crisantemas, T841708, a/c, phone, TV. *Villa Maya Cancún*, Uxmal 20 y Rubia, T842829, F841762, a/c, pool, *La Francesa* bakery next door. *Villa Rossana*, Yaxchilán, opposite *Plaza del Sol*.

D *Azteca*, Av López Portillo, hot water, good, cheap restaurant next door. **D** *Colonial*, Tulipanes 22 y Av Tulum, T841535, a/c, with bath, cheaper with fan, quiet, TV, phone, poor service, not too clean. **D** *Jardín*, SM64, Mza 14, Lote 20, No 37, T848704, clean, friendly, a bit noisy. **D** *María Isabel*, Palmera 59, T849015, near bus station and Av Tulum, fan and a/c, hot water, TV, small and clean, friendly, helpful, avoid rooms backing onto noisy air shaft. **D** *Tankah*, **C** with a/c, TV, recommended. 10 minutes walk north of bus station (3 blocks right of Plaza 2000 mall) are **D-E** *Pina Hermanos*, friendly, hot water, strong box facility and next door **D** *Mar y Tierra*, similar. **D** *Guadalupe*, Av Cortéz Portillo near Av Tulum, safe parking, recommended.

E per person *De Valle*, Av Uxmal (near Av Chichén Itzá), noisy club next door but clean, OK. **E** *San Carlos*, Cedro 14, T840786, west side of Av Tulum, 300 metres north of bus station, with shower, fan, quiet, recommended. **E** *Tropical Caribe*, Cedro 10 SM 23, T411442, bath and fan, quiet, secure, run down, not too clean (walk north up Avenida Tulum from junction with Uxmal for about 5 blocks, turn left at *Suites Dokamar* and hotel is on the right).

Camping Not permitted in Cancún town except at the Villa Deportiva youth hostel. There is a trailer park, *Rainbow*, just south of the airport. *El Meco Loco*, campground, 2 kilometres north of passenger ferry to Isla Mujeres, full hook ups for RVs, good showers, small store, access to small beach, buses into town.

Youth hostel **E** *Villa Deportiva Juvenil*, is at Km 3.2 Blvd Kukulkán, T831337, on the beach, 5 minutes' walk from the bridge towards Cancún town, next to *Club Verano Beat*, dormitory style, price per person, US$10 deposit, 10 percent discount with membership card, 8 people per room, friendly, basic, dirty, plumbing unreliable, sketchy locker facilities, camping US$5.

Eating
● *on maps*

There is a huge variety of restaurants, ranging from hamburger stands to 5-star, gourmet places. Just about every type of cuisine can be found. The best buys are on the side streets of Cancún town, while the largest selection can be found on Avs Tulum and Yaxchilán. The ones on the island are of slightly higher price and quality and are scattered along Avenida Kukulkán, with a high concentration in the shopping centres (of which there are about 10). If you are in no hurry to eat, look at what the restaurants are offering in the way of dishes, prices and drinks specials, then decide, if you can resist the pressurized selling.

The best is said to be *100% Natural*, opposite *Hotel Caribe Internacional* on Yaxchilán y Sunyaxchén freshly-prepared food, friendly staff, 'invigorating eating'. *La Doña*, on Av Yaxchilán between Av Uxmal and Av Sunyaxchén, good cheap breakfast, and lunch, clean, a/c, friendly. *Rincón Yucateca*, Av Uxmal 24, opposite *Hotel Cotty*, good Mexican breakfasts, popular. *Pericos*, Av Yaxchilán 71, Mexican seafood and steaks, live Mexican music, not cheap. *Los Huaraches*, on Uxmal opposite Yaxchilán, fast food, cheap *empanada* specials after 1300; many others on Av Uxmal, not too expensive. *Los Almendros*, Av Bonanpak y Sayil, Lote 60, 61 and 62, in front of bull ring, good local food. *El Pescador*, Tulipanes 28, good seafood but expensive. *Pop*, next to *Hotel Parador*, for quicker-type food, good value. *Torta y Torta*, Av Tulum (opposite *McDonalds*), good juices, cheap. *Bing*, Av Tulum y Uxmal, close to Banpais bank, best ice-cream. *Jaguari*, Zona Hotelera, Brazilian, opens 1700, set price, has been recommended. *Piemonte Pizzería*, Av Yaxchilán 52, good food and value, appetizing aperitifs on the house, recommended. *Las Tejas*, Av Uxmal, just before C Laurel, good food at reasonable prices. On Av Tulum, *Olé Olé*, good meat, friendly. *Tacolote*, Av Cobá 19, good food and excellent value, cheerful, popular; taco stands can be found each evening on and around the squares between Avs Tulum and Yaxchilán, good family atmosphere. *Comida Casera*, Av Uxmal opposite bus terminal, good coffee. *La Chiquita del Caribe*, Av Xel-Há at Mercado 28, great seafood, good value, recommended. The native Mexican restaurants in the workers' colonies are cheapest. Best bet is to buy food and beer in a store such as *chedravi* on Avenida Tulum y Cobá.

Entertainment Ballet Folclórico de México, nightly dinner shows at 1900 at *Continental Villas Plaza Hotel*, Zona Hotelera, T851444, ext 5706. *La Boom* disco, almost opposite Playa Linda dock, near the youth hostel, US$7 for all you can drink. Salsa club *Batachá* in *Miramar Misión* hotel, US$5 entry charge, popular with locals, good music. Crococun crocodile ranch, 30 kilometres on road to Playa del Carmen. Good cinema at Kulkulcán Plaza showing English language films.

Sports **Bungee jumping**: from a crane hoist. **Parasailing**: from beaches on Zona Hotelera.

Shopping The market, at Avenida Tulum 23, is basically a handicrafts market, with jewellery, clothing, hats, etc. Downtown there are several supermarkets, big and small, for food and drink, eg *Comercial Mexicana*, near Ladatel. *San Francisco de Asís*. Next to *Hotel Caribe Internacional*, on Yaxchilán, are 2 24-hour *farmacias*.

Bookshop *Fama*, Av Tulum 105, international books and magazines, English, French, German.

Transport **Local Car hire**: Budget Rent-a-Car in Cancún has been recommended for good service. A 4-door Nissan Sentra, a/c, can be hired for US$24 per day from Budget at the airport, insurance US$15. **Avis**, Plaza Caracol, cheapest but still expensive. There are many car hire agencies, with offices on Avenida Tulum, in the Zona Hotelera and at the airport; look out for special deals, but check vehicles carefully. Beware of overcharging and read any documents you sign carefully. Rates vary enormously, from US$40 to US$80 a day for a VW Golf (VW Beetles are cheaper), larger cars and jeeps available. **Car parking**: do not leave cars parked in side streets; there is a high risk of theft. Use the parking lot on Avenida Uxmal.

Air Cancún airport (CUN) is 16 kilometres south of the town (very expensive shops and restaurant, exchange facilities, double check your money, especially at busy times, poor rates too, 2 hotel reservation agencies, no rooms under US$45). 2 terminals, Main and South (or 'FBO' building), white shuttle minibuses between them. From Cancún domestic destinations include Chetumal, Chichén Itzá, Cozumel, Guadalajara, Mérida, Mexico City, Monterrey, Oaxaca, Palenque, Tijuana, Tuxtla Gutiérrez, Veracruz and Villahermosa. International flights: Albany (US Air), Amsterdam (Martinair); Atlanta (AeroMéxico); Barcelona (Iberia); Belize City (Aero Caribe); Buenos Aires (Mexicana, Acrotineas Argentinas); Charlotte (US Air); Cologne/Bonn (Condor); Dallas (American Airlines, AeroMéxico); Dusseldorf (LTU); Flores, Guatemala (Aero Caribe, Mayan World Airlines, Aviateca); Frankfurt (LTU, Condor); Guatemala City (Aviateca, Mayan World Airlines; Havana (Aero Caribe, Cubana); Houston (Continental, AeroMéxico); Indianapolis (American Trans Air); Lima (Mexicana); London (British Airways); Los Angeles (AeroMéxico, Mexicana, Northwest Airlines); Madrid (Iberia); Memphis (Northwest); Miami (American Airlines, Mexicana, AeroMéxico, Iberia); Munich (Condor); New Orleans (Acroméxico, Lacsa); New York (AeroMéxico, Continental, US Air); Panama City (Lloyd Aéreo Boliviano); Philadelphia (American Airlines, US Air); Rio de Janeiro (Varig); St

Louis, Missouri (TWA); San Antonio (Continental); San Francisco (Mexicana); San José (Lacsa); Santa Cruz, Bolivia (LAB); Santiago (Lan Chile); São Paulo (Varig); Tampa (Northwest); Vienna (Lauda Air); Washington DC (Continental). Many charters from Europe and North America. Reconfirm flights at a travel agent, they charge, but it is easier than phoning.

On arrival at Cancún, make sure you fill in documents correctly, or else you will be sent back to the end of the long, slow queue. At customs, press a button for random bag search. Colectivo taxi buses run from the airport to Avenida Tulum via the Zona Hotelera, US$6-8; taxis on the same route charge US$25.35. Buses leave from various points on Avenida Tulum every 15 minutes (stops marked with airport symbol), US$0.50, buses have Aeropuerto on the windscreen. Taxi drivers will tell you that only they go to the airport, US$10 from bus terminal, elsewhere US$15 minimum, usually US$14 (beware of overcharging; even if you take a 'Hoteles' bus to the last hotel, the taxi fare remains the same for the rest of the journey to the airport). At Cancún airport, official ticket for taxi to Playa del Carmen costs US$50, paid in advance. Colectivo for 8-10 people US$10 per person. If you leave the airport area on foot, walk along main road to Cancún, about 500 metres outside the area is a control booth; behind it taxis are allowed to pick you up for Playa del Carmen for about US$20 after bargaining. From the airport to the main road is 4 kilometres; you can hitch on the main road.

Taxis Fares are fixed and cheap, US$1 to anywhere in central Cancún, US$3 to hotel zone from the centre.

Buses Local bus ('Hoteles' Route), US$0.40 (taxis cost about US$15); to Puerto Juárez from Avenida Tulum, marked 'Puerto Juárez or 'Colonia Lombardo', US$0.70. Cancún bus terminal, at the junction of Avs Tulum and Uxmal, is the hub for routes west to Mérida and south to Tulum and Chetumal, open 24 hours, left luggage US$0.60 for 24 hours. Many services to **Mérida**, 4 hours, ranging from *plus* with TV, a/c, etc, US$20, to 1st class US$14, to 2nd class US$8; all services call at **Valladolid**, US$5.50 1st class, US$5 2nd class; to **Chichén Itzá**, many buses, starting at 0630, Expreso de Oriente 1st class to Mérida, US$6.20, 2½ hours. Expreso de Oriente also has services to **Tizimín** (3 hours, US$6), Izamal, Cenotillo and Chiquilá. Caribe Express (T74173/4) has a 1330 service to **Campeche** via Mérida, US$38. Caribe Inter 3 times a day to Mérida via Francisco Carrillo Puerto, calling at Polyuc, Peto, Tekax, Oxkutzcab, Tikul, Muná and Uman. To **San Cristóbal**, 3 a day, US$30, 18 hours. To **Villahermosa**, US$60. Autotransportes del Oriente to **Playa del Carmen** have been recommended, 2nd class, US$2.25. Inter Playa Express every 30 minutes to **Puerto Morelos**, US$1, **Playa del Carmen**, US$2.25 and **Xcaret**, US$2.25; 3 times daily to **Puerto Aventuras**, US$2.50, **Akumal**, US$3, **Xel-Há**, US$3.30 and **Tulum**, US$4.25. Other services to Playa del Carmen and Tulum are more expensive, eg 1st class Caribe Inter to Playa del Carmen US$3, 2nd class US$2.35, and US$4.75 to Tulum. Last bus to Playa del Carmen 2000, first bus to Tulum 0430. These services are en route to **Chetumal** (US$17 luxury, US$13.50 1st class, US$10 2nd, 5 hours). Several other services to Chetumal, include Caribe Express, deluxe service with a/c.

Boat The Playa Linda boat dock is at the mainland side of the bridge across Canal Nichupté, about 4 kilometres from centre, opposite the *Calinda Quality Cancún Beach*. It has shops, agencies for boat trips, a snack bar and Computel. Trips to Isla Mujeres, with snorkelling, bar, shopping, start at US$27.50, or US$35 with meal; ferry to Isla Mujeres 0900, 1100, 1330, returning 1600 and 2000, about 45 minutes. Cheaper ferries go from Puerto Juárez, see below. *M/V Aqua II* has all inclusive day cruises to Isla Mujeres starting from US$44 (sometimes discounts for user of the *Handbook*), T871909. **Boat trips**: *Nautibus*, a vessel with seats below the waterline, makes trips to the reefs, 1½ hours, a good way to see fish, Playa Linda dock, T833552. There are a number of other cruises on offer. Atlantis submarines offer trips in a 48-passenger vessel to explore natural and man-made reefs off Cancún. For more information contact Robert Theofel in Cancún on T834963.

Directory   **Airline offices** *AeroMéxico*, Av Cobá 80, T841186. *Mexicana*, Av Cobá 13, T844444. *Aerocaribe* and *Aerocozumel*, Av Tulum 29, T842000. *American Airlines*, Aeropuerto, T860055. *Continental*, Aeropuerto, T860040. *NW*, Aeropuerto, T860044. *Aviacsa*, Av Cobá 55, T874214. *Aviateca*, Plaza de Las

Américas between Cobá y Bonampak, T843938. *Lacsa*, Av Bonampak y Av Cobá, T860008. *Cubana*, T860192, outside the departure terminal at the airport, or down town, Yaxchilán 23, T/F877373.

Banks Many Mexican banks, best rates. Many small *casas de cambio*, which change cash and TCs (latter at poorer rates) until 2100 and give cash against credit cards (Visa, Mastercard and some others); recommended is *Cunex*, Av Tulum 13, half way round the roundabout, close to Av Cobá. *American Express*, Av Tulum, for money transfers in cash or TCs, plus flight service. Rates are better in town than at the airport. It is possible to change dollar TCs into dollars cash, but not 1-for-1.

Communications Post Office: at end of Av Sunyaxchen, a short distance from Av Yaxchilán. Telephones: *Telmex* caseta just off Av Cobá on Alcatraces; another *caseta* on Av Uxmal next to *Los Huaraches* restaurant. *Ladatel* phones in Plaza América, at San Francisco de Asís shopping centre and opposite the bus station on the end wall of a supermarket at Tulum y Uxmal. *Computel* phone and fax, more expensive, at Yaxchilán 49 and other locations. **Fax:** at Post Office, Mon-Sat, and at San Francisco de Asís shopping, Mon-Sat until 2200. **Internet:** Av Tulum 219, T875675, US$4.50 per hour.

Embassies & consulates Consulates: downtown, unless stated otherwise, most open am only: *Costa Rica*, C Mandinga, manzana 11, SM 30, T844869. *Canada*, Plaza México 312, p2º, T843716, 1100-1300. *France*, Instituto Internacional de Idiomas, Av Xel-Há 113, SM 25, T846078, 0800-1100, 1700-1900. *Germany*, Punta Conoco 36, SM 24, T841898. *Italy*, La Mansión Costa Blanca Shopping Center, Zona Hotelera, T832184. *Spain*, Cielo 17, Depto 14, SM 4, T841895. *Sweden*, Av Náder 34, SM 2-A, T847271, 0800-1300, 1700-2000. *USA*, Av Náder 40, T842411, 0900-1400, 1500-1800.

Language school *El Bosque del Caribe*, C Piña 1, SM25, T841038, F845888, bearibe@mail.cancun-language.com.mx.

Tour companies & travel agents *American Express*, Av Tulum 208, esq Agua, Super Manzana 4, T845441, F846942.

Mexico

Tourist offices *State Tourist Office*, Av Tulum, between Comermex and city hall. *Sectur Federal Tourist Office*, corner of Av Cobá and Av Náder, closed weekends, but kiosk on Av Tulum at Tulipanes is open sometimes at weekends. There are kiosks in the Zona Hotelera, too, eg at Mayfair Plaza. Downtown and in the Zona Hotelera closest to downtown most street corners have a map. See free publication, *Cancún Tips*, issued twice a year, and *Cancún Tips Magazine*, quarterly, from Av Tulum 29, Cancún, QR 77500, Mexico.

Puerto Juárez   About three kilometres north of Cancún. It is the dock for the cheaper ferry services to Isla Mujeres; there is also a bus terminal, but services are more frequent from Cancún. There are many buses between Cancún and Puerto Juárez, for example No 8 opposite bus terminal (US$0.70), but when the ferries arrive from Isla Mujeres there are many more taxis than buses (taxi fare should be no more than US$2, beware overcharging).

Sleeping and eating A *Hotel Caribel*, resort complex, with bath and fan; in the same price range is *San Marcos*. Other hotels include **D** *Kan Che*, first hotel on right coming from Cancún, fan, clean, swimming pool on beach, good value. *Posada Hermanos Sánchez*, 100 metres from bus terminal, on road to Cancún. **D** *Fuente Azul* opposite the dock. *Restaurants Natz Ti Ha* and *Mandinga* by the ferry dock, serve breakfast. **E** *Pina Hermanos*, SM 68, Manzana 6, Lote 14, Col Puerto Juárez, T842150, 10 minutes from Cancún by depot, excellent value, friendly, clean, secure. *Cabañas Punta Sam*, clean, comfortable, on the beach, **D** with bath (**C** in high season). Possible to camp, with permission, on the beach near the restaurant next door. A big trailer park has been built opposite *Punta Sam*, 150 spaces, camping **F** per person, shop selling basic commodities. Irregular bus service there, or hitchhike from Puerto Juárez. Check to see if restaurant is open evenings. Take mosquito repellent.

Transport Buses On the whole it is better to catch outgoing buses in Cancún rather than in Puerto Juárez: there are more of them. **Ferry** Passenger ferry to Isla Mujeres leaves from the jetty opposite the bus terminal at Puerto Juárez 16 times a day between 0600 and 2100, returning 0500-1930; sometimes leaves early, last boats back may not sail at all (US$2.20 for fast ferry, eg *Caribbean Queen*, 20 minutes, US$1 for slower boat, 40 minutes; both types leave at $\frac{1}{2}$ hour intervals). There are also small water taxis, but these are much more expensive (US$6 at least to the town or El Garrafón). At the jetty is a luggage store (0800-1800) and a tourist information desk. Car ferry from Punta Sam to Isla Mujeres (about 75 cars carried), 5 kilometres by bus from Cancún via Puerto Juárez (facilities to store luggage), US$1.50 per person and US$6-7 per car; 6 times a day between 0830 and 2200, returning between 0715 and 2200 (45-minute journey).

Isla Mujeres

Bathing on the Caribbean side of the island can be unsafe because of strong undertows and cross-currents.

Colour map 4, grid A4

The island (which got its name from the large number of female idols first found by the Spaniards) has long silver beaches (beware sandflies), palm trees and clean blue water at the north end (although the large *Del Prado* hotel dominates the view there). There is pollution near the town, and a naval airstrip to the southwest of it. There are limestone (coral) cliffs and a rocky coast at the south end. The southeast cliffs are good for walking and swimming and fish observation is good just south and west of the lighthouse. A lagoon on the west side is now fouled up. The island has suffered from competition from Cancún and although it is touristy, it is worth a visit. A disease destroyed practically all the palms which used to shade the houses and beach, but new, disease-resistant varieties have been planted and are growing to maturity.

The town is at the northwest end of the island; at the end of the north-south streets is the northern beach (Playa Coco), the widest area of dazzling white sand on the island (watersports equipment is rented at very high prices, also umbrellas and chairs). The island is best visited April to November, off-season (although one can holiday here the year round).

The main activity in the evening takes place in the square near the church, where there are also a supermarket and a cinema. The Civil Guard patrols the beaches at night.

At El Garrafón, seven kilometres, there is a tropical fish reserve (fishing forbidden) **El Garrafón** on a small coral reef. With a snorkel you can swim among a variety of multicoloured tropical fish. They aren't at all shy, but the coral is dead and not colourful. ■ *Entry US$3, and the same for a locker with an extra US$3.35 key deposit, rental US$4 a day for mask and snorkel, same again for fins, US$5 for underwater camera, plus deposit of US$30, passport, driver's licence, credit card or hotel key, from shops in the park. Reef trips by boat cost US$11.65 without equipment hire, US$15 with hire.* El Garrafón is a very popular excursion on the island and from Cancún; the water is usually full of snorkellers between 1100 and 1400. It is open 0800-1630; there are showers, toilets, expensive restaurants and bars, reasonable snack bar, shops and a small museum-cum-aquarium.

Taxi from the town to El Garrafón costs US$2, fixed rate. There is a bus which goes half-way to El Garrafón, the end of the line being at the bend in the road by the entrances to Casa Mundaca and Playa Paraíso (bus fare US$0.85). You can walk from El Garrafón to Playa Paraíso in 30 minutes. Near Playa Paraíso is a turtle farm

Isla Mujeres & Yucatán northeast coast

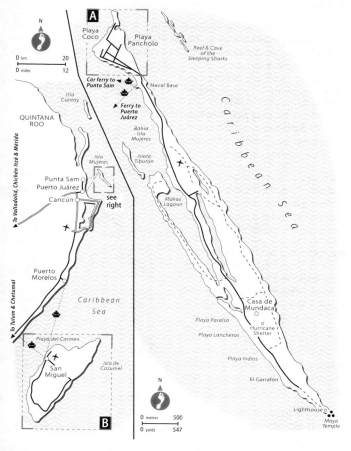

Related maps
A Isla Mujeres town, page 496
B Isla de Cozumel, page 503

Mexico

for presentation of the species (signposted), well worth a visit. This beach, and its neighbour, Lancheros, is quite clean, with palms, restaurants and toilets. The area of sand is quite small. Sadly, there are pens at the shore containing nurse sharks, which swim up and down their cages like big cats in a zoo. If so moved, you can join them in the water. Playa Indios, south of Lancheros, towards El Garrafón, has similar facilities and 'entertainment'.

The curious remains of a pirate's domain, called **Casa de Mundaca**, is in the centre of the island; a big, new arch gate marks its entrance. Paths have been laid out among the large trees, but all that remains of the estate (called Vista Alegre) are one small building and a circular garden with raised beds, a well and a gateway. Fermín Mundaca, more of a slave-trader than a buccaneer, built Vista Alegre for the teenage girl he loved. She rejected him and he died, broken-hearted, in Mérida. His epitaph there reads 'Como eres, yo fui; como soy, tu serás' (what you are I was; what I am you shall be). See the poignant little carving on the garden side of the gate, 'La entrada de La Trigueña' (the girl's nickname).

At the southern tip is a small, ruined Mayan lighthouse or shrine of Ixtel, just beyond a modern lighthouse. The lighthouse keeper sells coca-cola for US$1, hammocks and conch shells. The view from the Maya shrine is beautiful, with a pale turquoise channel running away from the island to the mainland, deep blue water surrounding it, and the high-rise hotels of Cancún in the distance. Looking north from the temple you see both coasts of the island stretching away from you.

Isla Contoy   Trips to Isla Contoy (bird and wildlife sanctuary), while suspended from Cancún, are still possible from Isla Mujeres, US$40, nine hours, with excellent lunch, two hours of fishing, snorkelling (equipment hire extra, US$2.50) and relaxing. Boats from the cooperative at the town pier may not leave until full, their trips are warmly recommended and include an excellent fish lunch and two hours snorkelling. From the same point boat trips go to the lighthouse at the entrance to the harbour, Isla Tiburón, El Garrafón and Playa Lancheros for lunch, three to four hours, US$16.65 per person. You will be approached by boatmen on the boat from Puerto Juárez, and on arrival.

There is public transport on Isla Mujeres, that is taxis at fixed prices, and the bus service mentioned above. You can walk from one end of the island to the other in two and a half hours. At the top of the rise before El Garrafón, by the speed humps and the houses for rent, is a point where you can see both sides of the island. A track leads from the road to the Caribbean coast, a couple of minutes stroll. You can then walk down the east coast to the southern tip.

Sleeping   The island has several costly hotels and others, mainly in the **D** category, and food, especially fresh fruit, is generally expensive.

At Christmas hotel prices are increased steeply and the island can heave with tourists, especially in January.

Reasonable hotels to stay at on Isla Mujeres are **AL** *Posada del Mar*, Alte Rueda 15, T20212 (including meals), has pleasant

Isla Mujeres town

0 metres   150
0 yards   164   ➤ *To Puerto Juárez*

■ **Sleeping**
1 Belmar & Pizzería Rolandi
2 Benly
3 Caracol
4 Osorio
5 Perlas del Caribe
6 Poc-Na
7 Posada del Mar
8 Rocas del Caribe

drinks terrace but expensive drinks, restaurant for residents only. **A** *Belmar*, Av Hidalgo 110 x Madero y Abasolo, T70430, F70429, a/c, TV, restaurant *Pizza Rolandi* downstairs. **A** *El Mesón del Bucanero*, Hidalgo 11, T20210, F20126, all rooms with fan. **A** *Las Perlas del Caribe*, Caribbean side of town, clean, a/c, pool, recommended. **B** *Cabinas María del Mar*, over-looks Coco beach, a/c, lovely beach bar with hammocks and rocking chairs for 2. **C** *Berny*, Juárez y Abasolo, T20025, with bath and fan, basic, problems with water supply, swimming pool, long-distance calls possible, residents only, but does not even honour confirmed reser-vations if a deposit for 1 night's stay has not been made. **C** *Caracol*, Matamoros 5, T70150, F70547, cheaper with fan, hot water, terrace balcony, stoves for guests' use, bar, coffee shop, laundry, central, clean, good value. **C** *El Paso*, Morelos 13, p2º, with bath, clean, facing the pier. **C** *Isla Mujeres*, next to church, with bath, renovated, run by pleasant Englishman. **C** *Rocas del Caribe*, Madero 2, 100 metres from ocean, cool rooms, big balcony, clean, good service. **C** *Vistalmar*, on promenade about 300 metres left from ferry dock (**D** for longer stays), ask for rooms on top floor, bath, balcony, fan, insect screens, good value.

D *Caribe Maya*, Madero 9, central, modern, a/c, cheaper with fan, very clean and comfy. **D** *Carmelina*, Guerrero 4, T70006, central with bath and a/c, clean, safe, but no toilet paper, soap, blankets or hot water, unfriendly family, rents bikes and snorkelling gear, advance pay-ment for room required daily. **D** *Isleñas* Madero and Guerrero, with bath, cheaper without, very clean, helpful. **D** *Las Palmas*, central, Guerrero 20, 2 blocks from north beach, good, clean. **D** *María José*, Madero 25, T20130, clean, fans, friendly, scooter hire. **D** *Xul-Ha*, on Hidalgo towards north beach, with fan. **E** *Osorio*, Madero, 1 block from waterfront, clean, fan, with bath and hot water, friendly, reception closes at 2100, recommended. *La Reina* bak-ery nearby. **F** *Poc-Na Hostal*, T70090, price per person, is cheapest, dormitories or 3 rooms, try for central section where there are fans, clean, everything works, no bedding, linen extra, gringo hang-out, good and cheap café, book exchange, video, take insect repellent, book in advance, but get receipt if paying in advance (San Jorge laundry is just 1 block away, US$2 per kilogram).

Camping There is a trailer park on the island, with a restaurant. At Playa Indios is *Camping Los Indios* where you can put up your hammock. **NB** If you arrive late, book into any hotel the first night and set out to find what you want by 0700-0800, when the first ferries leave the next morning.

Eating

Many beach restaurants close just before sunset.

El Limbo at *Roca Mar Hotel* (Nicolás Bravo y Guerrero), excellent seafood, good view, rea-sonable prices. *Miriti*, opposite ferry, quite good value. *Miramar*, on Rueda Medina, next to ferry, fine seafood. *Pizza Rolandi*, see above, good breakfast, popular. *Gomar*, Madero y Hidalgo, expensive, possible to eat outside on verandah or in the colonial-style interior, pop-ular. *Chen Huayo*, Hidalgo, near basketball courts, excellent Mexican food, cheap. *Arriba*, Hidalgo, popular, lively, delicious food, good value. *Las Gemelas*, also on Hidalgo, US-owned, vegetarian options, good value. *Mano de Dios*, near the beach, cheap, quite good. *Eric's*, very good inexpensive Mexican snacks. *Tropicana*, 1 block from pier, simple, popular, cheap. *Cielito Lindo*, waterfront, open air, good service; good fish restaurant 50 metres to left of jetty. *La Peña*, overlooks beach, good pizzas, happy hour, nice atmosphere. *La Langosta*, good Mexican dishes, lovely view. *Bucanero*, downtown, steak, seafood, prime rib, classy for Islas Mujeres. *Red Eye Café*, breakfast and lunch only, closed Monday, excellent buffet, good coffee, friendly. *Robert's* on square, cheap and good. *Giltri*, in town, good value. *Café Cito* on B Juárez, 1 block west of *Tequila*, best breakfast, small portions, good health food, recommended. *Lomita*, Benito Juárez Sur, blue house, excellent Mexican food, cheap, friendly. *Ciro's* lobster house, not too good but *Napolito's*, opposite, is excel-lent. Small restaurants round market are good value. Daily fish barbecue at El Paraíso beach. At Garrafón Beach: *El Garrafón*, *El Garrafón de Castilla*, catering for tour boats from Cancún; between Playa Indios and El Garrafón, *María's Kankin Hotel and Restaurant*, French cuisine.

Disco-bars *Tequila*, on Hidalgo, video bar and restaurant. *Bad Bones* has live rock-and-roll. **Night life**

Festivals Between **1-12 December** there is a *fiesta* for the Virgin of Guadalupe, fireworks, dances until 0400 in the Plaza. In **October** there is a festival of music, with groups from Mexico and the USA performing in the main square.

Sports **Watersports**: you can rent skin and scuba diving equipment, together with guide, on the waterfront north of the public pier, a boat and equipment costs about US$50 per person for ½ day, check how many tanks of air are included and shop around. They can set up group excursions to the Cave of the Sleeping Sharks; English spoken. It is no cheaper to hire snorkel gear in town than on the beach. Deep sea fishing for 10 in a boat from *Aguamundo*. Diving is not in the class of Cozumel.

Shopping Opposite the restaurant *Gomar* are several souvenir shops, selling good stone Maya carvings (copies), macramé hangings and colourful wax crayon 'Maya' prints. *El Paso Boutique*, opposite ferry, trades a small selection of English novels.

Transport **Bike hire**: worth hiring a bicycle, US$5 a day (about US$7 deposit eg *Sport Bike*, Av Juárez y Morelos), or a moped (US$5 per hour, US$15-20 all day, shop around, credit card, passport or money deposit, helmet not required), to explore the island in about 2 hours. Do check if there is any damage to the bicycle *before* you hire. Bicycles for hire from several hotels. Try Ciro's Motorrentor by *Hotel Caribe* for good motorbikes.

Directory **Banks** *Banco del Atlántico*, Av Juárez 5, 1% commission, but better on mainland. **Communications Telephone:** Ladatel cards are sold at *Artesanía Yamily*, Hidalgo, just north of the square. **Internet:** Compulsla on Abosolo, open daily 0900-1400, 1600-2200, subject to variation. **Laundry** *Tim Pho*, on corner of Juárez and Abosolo, fast and cheap, US$2 for big load. **Tourist office** On square, opposite the basketball pitch.

South of Cancún

Ruta 307 runs southwest from Cancún along the coast to Playa del Carmen and Tulum, where it runs inland, skirting the wetlands along the shore via Felipe Carrillo Puerto to Chetumal and the border with Belize.

Puerto Morelos, a slowly developing charming fishing village not far south of Cancún (bus US$1), has three hotels. **A** *Ranco Libertad*, 1 kilometre south of village, just after ferry terminal, US-run, friendly, new-age therapies available, recommended; **C** *Inglaterra*, spacious rooms with fan, bath, quiet, recommended. **D** *Amor*, near bus stop, quiet, clean, safe motorcycle parking, good restaurant; also free camping. Hotels close in the low season, but one of the restaurants in town has good value rooms. **Eating** *Los Pelícanos* nice setting next to beach, very good seafood, recommended. Puerto Morelos is popular with scuba divers and snorkellers, but beware of sharks.

Playa del Carmen

Colour map 4, grid A4 A fast growing beach centre, with many new hotels and restaurants. In Maya times it was a departure point for boats to Cozumel; modern services have resumed with the development of Playa del Carmen as a satellite resort to Cancún. 'Playa', as it is usually known, has several kilometres of white sand beaches, which are relatively clean; those to the north of town are the most pleasant. There are sandflies though, and, from time to time, certain plankton in the water cause an itchy rash that the locals call *Agua Mala*. Pharmacists stock cream and pills to treat it. Avenida Juárez runs from Highway 307 to the park which fronts the sea. One block south of the park is the ferry terminal. All along Avenida 5, the street which parallels the beach, are restaurants and shops, with hotels on the streets running back from the beach. Playa is conveniently placed between Cancún and Tulum, giving easy access to these and other tourist sites on the coast and inland.

Outside town are At Km 297/8, north of Playa del Carmen, **AL** *Cabañas Capitán Lafitte*, very good, pool, excellent cheap restaurant on barren beach; under same ownership is **AL** *Shangri-Lá Caribe*, T22888, 7 kilometres south, closer to town (at north end of the bay north of Playa), cabins, equally good, excellent beach with diving (Cyan-Ha, PADI) and snorkelling, sailing, easy birdwatching beside hotel; beside *Shangri-Lá* is **L** *Las Palapas*, breakfast

Sleeping
*Hotels fill up early;
cheaper rooms are
hard to find in January.*

Playa del Carmen

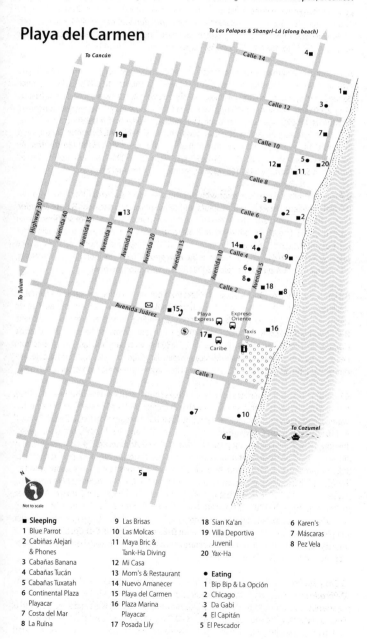

■ Sleeping
1 Blue Parrot
2 Cabiñas Alejari
  & Phones
3 Cabañas Banana
4 Cabañas Tucán
5 Cabañas Tuxatah
6 Continental Plaza
  Playacar
7 Costa del Mar
8 La Ruina

9 Las Brisas
10 Las Molcas
11 Maya Bric &
  Tank-Ha Diving
12 Mi Casa
13 Mom's & Restaurant
14 Nuevo Amanecer
15 Playa del Carmen
16 Plaza Marina
  Playacar
17 Posada Lily

18 Sian Ka'an
19 Villa Deportiva
  Juvenil
20 Yax-Ha

● Eating
1 Bip Bip & La Opción
2 Chicago
3 Da Gabi
4 El Capitán
5 El Pescador

6 Karen's
7 Máscaras
8 Pez Vela

and dinner included, cabins with hammocks outside, good, T22977, F41668 (Mexico City F53798641); at Km 296, **A** *El Marlín Azul*, swimming pool, good food.

Most luxurious is **L** *Continental Plaza Playacar*, T30100, F30105, a huge new development just south of the ferry terminal, excellent in every respect, non-residents can use swimming pool, no charge; in the same development as this 5-star hotel is the 5-star *Diamond Resort*, Apdo Postal 149, T30340, F30348 and the 4-star *Caribbean Villages*, T30434, F30437, both all-inclusive club operations, the latter in the middle of the golf course; there are also villas for rent from US$65 to US$280, PO Box 139, Playa del Carmen, T/F30148.

At the north end of town, on a popular stretch of beach between Calle 12 y 14, is **AL-B** *Blue Parrot*, T30083, F44564 (reservations in USA 904-7756660, toll free 800-6343547), price depends on type of room and facilities, has bungalows, no a/c, with excellent bar (Happy Hour 2200) and café, volley ball court, deep sea fishing expeditions, highly recommended. **AL** *Molcas*, T30070, near ferry pier, pool, a bit shabby, friendly staff, interesting architecture, it's open-air restaurant across street is good and reasonable. **AL** *Cabañas Tucan*, Av 5 beyond C 14, clean, good, mosquito net, highly recommended. **A** *Hotel Maranatha*, Av Juárez between Avs 30 and 35, T30143, F30038 (US Res T1-800-3298388), luxury with all facilities. **A** *San Juan*, Av 5 No 165, T30647, including continental breakfast.

B *Azul Profundo*, next to *Blue Parrot*, with bath and balcony. **B** *Costa del Mar*, T30058, on little road between C 10 y 12, clean, restaurant (disappointing) and bar, pool. **B** *Rosa Mirador*, behind the *Blue Parrot*, **AL** in high season, hot showers, fan, best views from 3rd floor, owner Alberto speaks English, recommended. **B** *Marasol*, C 6, clean, balconies overlooking sea. **B-F** *Cabañas Alejari*, C 6 going down to beach, T30374, very nice, shop has long distance phones. Next to *Alejari* on the beach is **AL** *Pelícano*, T30997, including good breakfast, impersonal, and **A** *Albatrós Royale*, T30001, clean, very good, no pool.

B *Mom's*, Av 30 y C 4, T30315, about 5 blocks from bus station or beach, clean, comfortable, small pool, good restaurant with Chinese home cooking and plenty of vegetables, *Yax-Ha* cabins, on the beach, via Av 5 by C 10 (price depending on size and season), excellent. **B-C** *Cabañas Banana*, Av 5 entre C 6 y 8, T30036, cabins and rooms, kitchenettes. **B-C** *Casa de Gopala*, C 2 Nte and Av 10 Nte (PO Box 154), T/F30054, with bath and fan, 150 metres from beach, quiet and central, American/Mexican owned, large rooms, quiet and comfortable, recommended. **B-C** *El Acuario*, Av 25 Nte x 2 y 4 Nte, large rooms some with kitchen, a/c, pool.

C *Cabañas Tuxatah*, 2 minutes from sea, 2 blocks south from Av Juárez (Apdo 45, T30025), German owner, Maria Weltin speaks English and French, with bath, clean, comfortable, hot water, laundry service, beautiful gardens, breakfast US$4, recommended. **C** *Delfín*, Av 5 y C 6, T30176, with bath. **C** *Maya Bric*, Av 5, between C 8 and 10, T30011, hot water, clean, friendly, pool, Tank-Ha dive shop (see below). **C** *Nuevo Amanecer*, C 4 west of Av 5, very attractive, fans, hot water, hammocks, mosquito nets, clean, laundry area, pool room, helpful, recommended. **C** *Sian Ka'an*, Av 5 y C 2, T30203, 100 metres from bus station, modern rooms with balcony, clean, recommended. Others in the **C** range include *El Elefante*, C 10 entre Av 10 x 15, T30262, with bath, modern but basic, and *Playa del Carmen*, Av Juárez, between C 10 y 15, T30293, opposite bank. **C** *Posada Freud*, Av 5 entre C 8 y 10 Nte, T/F30601, with bath, fan, some with kitchenette, Palapa-style, quiet, clean, Austrian owner, simpler rooms without bath available priced at **D-E**, recommended. **C-D** *Castillo Verde*, C 26 x Av 5 y 10, T/F30990, 10 minutes from centre at north end of town, with bath, hot water, garden, free coffee, Swiss-German owned.

D *Casa Tucan*, C 4 Nte, x 10 y 15 Av Nte, T/F30283, nice patio, small but clean rooms. **D** *Posada Lily*, with shower, fan, safe, clean, but noisy in am and cell-like rooms, Av Juárez at Caribe bus stop; under same ownership *Dos Hermanos*, 3 blocks west and 2 blocks north of *Posada Lily*, clean, hot showers, fan, quiet. **C-D** *Posada Papagaio*, Av 15 x C 4 y 6, with fan and bath, mosquito net, very nicely furnished rooms, friendly, highly recommended.

D *Posada Marixchel*, C 30 con 1 Sur, T20823, with shower, safe, fan, clean, recommended.
D *Posada Mar Caribe*, Av 15, small, friendly, recommended.

E *Posada Fernández*, Av 10 opposite C 1, with bath, hot water and fan, friendly, recommended. **E-F** *Cabañas La Ruina*, at the beach end of C 2, popular, crowded, noisy, clean, lots of options and prices, from 2 to 3-bedded cabins, hammock space under *palapa*, with or without security locker, hammock in open air, camping US$3, space for vehicles and camper vans, linen rental, bath extra, cooking facilities. **E-F** *Mi Casa* (painted red), Av 5 opposite *Maya Bric*, also apartments (**E**) with kitchenette, patchy mosquito net, fan, well-furnished, bath, cold water, owner speaks German, English, and Spanish, nice garden, recommended. Lots of new places going up, none under US$10 a night. Small apartments on Avenida 5, esq Calle 6, approximately US$200 per month, with kitchen; also rooms near basketball court, US$100 per month.

Youth Hostel *Villa Deportiva Juvenil*, from US$2 camping, US$5 in dormitory ("hot with only 2 fans and a lot of beds"), to US$20 for up to 4 in cabin with fan and private shower, comfortable, with basketball court, clean, recommended, but difficult to find, especially after dark, but it is signposted: it's 5 blocks up from Avenida 5, on Calle 8 Nte (T5252548).

Camping See above under *La Ruina*; also *Camping Las Brisas* at the beach end of Calle 4. *Punta Bete*, 10 kilometres north, the right-hand one of 3 at the end of a 5-kilometre road, on beach, US$3 for tent, also 2 restaurants and cabañas. *Outback*, small trailer park on beach at end of C 6, US$10 for car and 2 people.

Máscaras, on square, highly recommended. Also on the square, *El Tacolote*, tacos, etc, and *Las* **Eating** *Piñatas*; *Da Gabi*, just up C 12 from *Blue Parrot*, good pastas, Mexican dishes, "best pizzas in town", breakfast buffet, also has rooms in C range. Next to *Cabañas Yax-Ha* is *El Pescador*, fish, has a variety of beers. *El Tarraio*, on seafront, cheap seafood, closes 2100. On or near Avenida 5: *Pez Vela*, Av 5 y C 2, good atmosphere, food, drinks and music (closed 1500-1700). *Pollo Caribe*, near bus station between C 2 and Juárez, set chicken menu for US$2, good, closes early when chicken runs out. *Nuestra Señora del Carmen*, Av 5 y C 2, family-run, cheap, generous portions, recommended. *La Parrilla*, Av 5 y C8, large portions good service, reasonably priced, live music every night, popular. *Playa Caribe*, 1 block up Av 5 from plaza, fish and seafood specialities, good breakfast, nice atmosphere, cheap, and popular with budget minded travellers, drinks for US$1 but small. *Karen's Pizza*, Av 5 entre C 2 y 4, pizzas, Mexican dishes, cable TV, popular. *El Capitán*, C 4 just off Av 5, good meals and music, popular. Next door is *Sabor* for sandwiches, juices, breakfast, English-spoken, recommended. *Los Almendros*, C 8, excellent Mexican food, cheap, friendly. *Lonchería Maquech*, C 1 entre Av 5 y 10, vegetarian lunch daily, cheap, friendly, recommended. *Limones*, Av 5 y C 6, good food, popular, reasonable prices; across C 6, still on Av 5 is *Flippers*, good atmosphere, good food especially fish, moderately priced. *Bip Bip*, Av 5 between C 4 and 6, best pizza in town. *La Hueva del Coronado*, same block, seafood and local dishes, reasonable. *Calypso House* also in same block. *La Lunada*, Av 5 entre C 6 y 8. *El Correo*, just beyond *Posada Fernández*, Mexican, cheap, excellent *menú del día* and *pollo pibil*, recommended. *Marinelly*, Av 10 No 110, clean, good food and prices, not touristy. *La Choza*, 5 Av entre Juárez y C 2, great food, cheap set menus. *Sophie's*, C 2 (opposite *Cabañas La Ruina*), good food, videos shown. *Media Luna*, Av 5 y C 15, good atmosphere, delicious poached eggs for breakfast, and Italian food. *El Chino*, C 4 Nte entre C 10 y 15, popular with Mexicans, seafood, Yucatán specialities, good breakfast, inexpensive, friendly. *Panadería del Caribe*, Av 5 entre C 4 y 2, for breads and cakes. *Panificadora del Carmen*, Av 30, just before Youth Hostel, excellent, open until 2300, has a café/restaurant at the side called *La Concha*. *Zermat Bakery* at extreme end of pedestrian C Nte, 5 blocks from bus station, recommended for pastries. Various places serve breakfast close to Post Office. Many places have 'happy hour', times vary, shop around.

La Opción, Av 5 beside *Bip Bip*, upstairs, shows video films, usually 2 a night. *Ziggy's Bar and* **Night life** *Disco* on the square, very busy Friday/Saturday night, expensive drinks; live music in a number of places at night, look for notices. *Pez Vela* has live music at about 2000 followed by

Happy Hour. *Blue Parrot*, C 12, live music and shows most evenings, happy hour 1700-2000, and 2300-0200, very popular. *Señor Frags* (Carlos 'n Charlie's chain), by the pier, "a sure sign that this small town is developing fast".

Sports **Diving**: Tank-Ha Dive Center, at *Maya Bric Hotel*, resort course US$60 (diving lesson in the hotel pool before first dive), 1-tank dive US$35, 2-tank US$50, packages from US$90-395, PDIC certification course US$350. Dive shop at *Yax-Ha Cabañas*. Also El Oasis Dive Shop, Calle 4 entre Av 5 y 10; Albatros Watersports; Costa del Mar Dive Shop, beside *Blue Parrot*; and others. Cavern diving with Yucatech Expeditions has been recommended; 2 tank day trip costs US$100 all inclusive. Check Dive shops carefully, there have been reports of drunken dive masters. **Snorkelling**: *Seafari*, Av 5, for snorkelling.

Shopping Hypermarket on edge of town, Calle 20.

Transport **Local Car hire**: Continental Car Rental, Av Juárez; **Playa**, at Plaza Marina Playacar; **National** at *Hotel Molcas*.

　　Air Aero Caribe has daily flights to Chichen Itzá.

　　Buses To/from **Cancún**, 1 hour 15 minutes, Playa Express (Avenida Juárez, entre Av 5 y 10) goes every 30 minutes, US$2.25; also Caribe (Avenida Juárez, by *Posada Lily*) to Cancún luxury bus at 1215, 1st class 3 times a day. To Cancún international airport, take a 2nd class bus to the crossroads (US$2.50) and walk, or take a taxi (US$1.65) the 4 kilometres to the terminal. *Tierra Maya* (see tour companies) also arrange shared transport from hotel to airport, book 2 days in advance. Caribe luxury buses to **Mérida**, US$25.30, **Campeche** US$42, and **Chetumal** US$13.50, also 1st (US$10) and 2nd class (US$7) to Chetumal, Felipe Carrillo Puerto; 2nd class calls at **Tulum**, US$1.40. Expreso Oriente (Av Juárez y Av 5) has luxury, 1st and 2nd class buses to Mérida via Cancún, many a day, US$17.50, US$14.30 and US$12 respectively; also to **Valladolid** 1st class US$8.50, US$6 2nd, 4 hours; **Tizimín**, US$9, and 2nd class Tulum (US$1.20), **Cobá** (US$3.30), Valladolid (US$8.50) at 0500, 1000 and 1700, 2nd class US$6. In all, several buses a day to Tulum between 0530 and 1845, 1 hour. To **Puebla**, ADO at 1800, 20 hours, US$40; to **Mexico City**, ADO at 0700, 1200, 1800, 24 hours, US$35; to **San Cristóbal de Las Casas**, different classes, US$22-30, 3 a day, can book only 1 day in advance, Maya de Oro 1st class at 1845.

　　Taxis to Cancún airport cost US$25. Beware of those who charge only US$5 as they are likely to charge an extra US$20 for luggage. Tours to Tulum and Xel-Há from kiosk by boat dock US$30; taxi tours to Tulum, Xel-Há and Xcaret, 5-6 hours, US$60; taxi to Xcaret US$6.65. Taxis congregate on the Avenida Juárez side of the square (Sindicato Lázaro Cárdenas del Río, T30032/30414).

　　Ferry For **Cozumel**, *Mexico I, II* and *III* waterjets, US$5 1-way, minimum 30 minutes' journey (schedules change frequently). **NB** Waterjets are like floating buses and you have to sit inside.

Directory **Banks** Banks open 0900-1300, get there early to avoid crowds. *Banco del Atlántico* on Av Juárez y Av 10, 2 blocks up from plaza. *Bancomer*, Av Juárez, 5 blocks west of Av 5, No banks currently giving cash advances on credit cards, *casa de cambio* on Av 5 opposite tourist information booth, reasonable rates for US$ cash, no commission. **Communications** Post Office: Av Juárez y Av 15, open 0800-1700 Mon-Fri, 0900-1300 Sat. Telephones: Computel next to bus station on Av Juárez. Long distance phones at shop at *Cabañas Alejari*. International fax service at Turquoise Reef Realty, in same block as *Hotel Playa del Carmen*, cost of phone call plus US$3.65 for first sheet, US$1.65 for second. **Internet**: *Cybersol Sistemas* (known as *Internet Playa*), Av 5 Nte x 12 y 14, T/F31210, clients@pya.com.mx. *Maya Com* Av 30 y C4; *Ciberia* C 4 y Av 16. **Hospitals & medical services** Doctor: *Dr Víctor Macías*, Av 35 x C2 y 4, T30493, Emergency and tourist medicine, English-speaking, ambulance. Dentist: *Perla de Rocha Torres*, Av 20 Nte s/n entre 4 y 6, T30021, speaks English, recommended. **Laundry** Av Juárez, 2 blocks from bus station; another on Av 5. **Tour companies & travel agents** *Tierra Maya Tours*, north end Av 5, T47918, F30537, Box 24, professional and nice. **Tourist office** Tourist kiosk on square, with information and leaflets, books, guided tours to Tulum and Cobá, US$30 includes transport, entry to site, and English-speaking guide, Mon and Fri, 0930. *Destination Playa del Carmen* bulletin gives details of many of the services in town, plus map.

Cozumel

The island is not only a marvellous place for snorkelling and scuba diving, but is *Colour map 4, grid A4* described as a "jewel of nature, possessing much endemic wildlife including pygmy species of coati and raccoon; the birdlife has a distinctly Caribbean aspect and many endemic forms also" – Jeffrey L White, Tucson, Arizona. A brief visit does not afford much opportunity to see the flora and fauna on land; the forested centre of the island is not easy to visit, except at the Maya ruins of San Gervasio (see below), and there are few vantage points. On the other hand, the island has a great deal to offer the tourist. The name derives from the Maya 'Cuzamil', land of swallows.

Maya pilgrims hoped to visit once in their lifetime the shrine to Ix-Chel (goddess of the moon, pregnancy, childbirth, all things feminine, but also floods, tides and destructive waters), which was located on the island. By the 14th century AD, Cozumel had also become an important trading centre. The Spaniards first set foot on the island on 1 May 1518 when Juan de Grijalva arrived with a fleet from Cuba. Spanish dominance came in 1520. By the 18th century, the island was deserted.

Cozumel

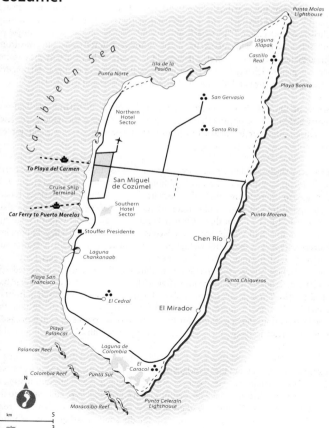

Sights In all, there are some 32 archaeological sites on Cozumel, those on the east coast mostly single buildings (lookouts, navigational aids?). The easiest to see are the restored ruins of the Maya-Toltec period at **San Gervasio** in the north (seven kilometres from Cozumel town, then six kilometres to the left up a paved road, toll US$1). ■ *Entry to the site is US$4.35, open 0800-1600; guides are on hand, or you can buy a self-guiding booklet at the librería on the square in San Miguel, or at the **Flea Market**, for US$1.* It is an interesting site, quite spread out, with *sacbes* (Maya roads) between the groups of buildings. There are no large structures, but a nice plaza, an arch, and pigment can be seen in places. It is also a pleasant place to listen to birdsong, see butterflies, animals (if lucky), lizards and landcrabs (and insects). **Castillo Real** is one of many sites on the northeastern coast, but the road to this part of the island is in very bad condition and the ruins themselves are very small. **El Cedral** in the southwest (three kilometres from the main island road) is a two-room temple, overgrown with trees, in the centre of the village of the same name. Behind it is a ruin, and next to it a modern church with a green and white façade (an incongruous pairing). In the village are large, permanent shelters for agricultural shows, rug sellers, and locals who pose with *iguanas doradas*. **El Caracol**, where the sun, in the form of a shell, was worshipped is one kilometre from the southernmost Punta Celarain. At Punta Celarain is an old lighthouse.

San Miguel de Cozumel
Phone code 987
Colour map 4, grid A4

This is the main town on the sheltered west coast. Here the ferries from the mainland and the cruise ships dock. The town is particularly touristy and expensive during Christmas and Easter. The waterfront, Avenida Rafael Melgar, and a couple of streets behind it are dedicated to the shoppers and restaurant-goers, but away from this area the atmosphere is quite Mexican. Fishermen sell their catch by the passenger ferry pier, which is in the centre of town. It is a friendly town, with a good range of hotels (both in town and in zones to the north and south) and eating places.

Museum On waterfront between Calle 4 y 6, history of the island, well laid-out (entry US$3). Bookshop, art gallery, rooftop restaurant has excellent food and views of sunset, good for breakfast, too from 0700 ('The Quick' is excellent value), recommended.

Beaches The best public beaches are some way from San Miguel town: in the north of the island they are sandy and wide, although those at the Zona Hotel Norte were damaged in 1989 and are smaller than they used to be. At the end of the paved road, walk up the unmade road until it becomes 'dual carriageway'; turn left for the narrow beach, which is a bit dirty. Cleaner beaches are accessible only through the hotels. South of San Miguel, **San Francisco** is good if narrow (clean, very popular, lockers at *Pancho's*, expensive restaurants), but others are generally narrower still and rockier. All the main hotels are on the sheltered west coast. The east, Caribbean coast is rockier, but very picturesque; swimming and diving on the unprotected side is very dangerous owing to ocean underflows. The only safe place is at a sheltered bay at **Chen Río**. Three good (and free) places for snorkelling are the beach in front of *Hotel Las Glorias*, 15 minutes' walk south from ferry, you can walk through the hotel's reception; **Playa Corona**, further south, too far to walk, so hitch or take a taxi, small restaurant and pier; **Xul-Ha**, further south, with a bar and comfortable beach chairs.

Excursions A circuit of the island on paved roads can easily be done in a day (see *Local Transport* below). Head due east out of San Miguel (take the continuation of Avenida Benito Juárez). Make the detour to San Gervasio before continuing to the Caribbean coast at *Mescalito's* restaurant. Here, turn left for the northern tip (road unsuitable for ordinary vehicles), or right for the south, passing Punta Moreno, Chen Río, Punta Chiqueros (restaurant, bathing), El Mirador (a low viewpoint with sea-worn rocks, look out for holes) and Paradise Cove. At this point, the paved road heads west while an unpaved road continues south to Punta Celarain. On the road west, opposite the turnoff to El Cedral, is a sign to *Restaurante Mac y Cía*, an excellent fish restaurant on a lovely beach, popular with dive groups for lunch. Next is Playa San Francisco (see above). A few more kilometres lead to the former *Holiday Inn*, the last big hotel south of San Miguel. Just after this is **Parque Chankanab**,

San Miguel de Cozumel

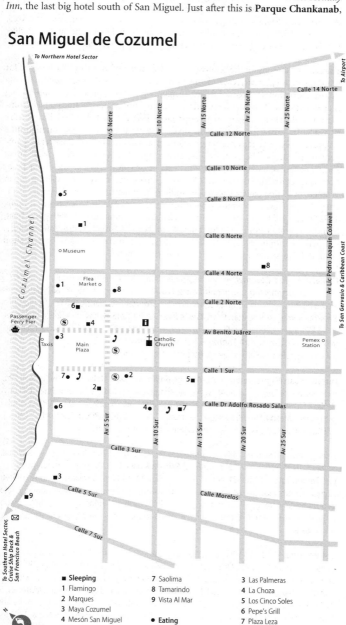

■ Sleeping	7 Saolima	3 Las Palmeras
1 Flamingo	8 Tamarindo	4 La Choza
2 Marques	9 Vista Al Mar	5 Los Cinco Soles
3 Maya Cozumel		6 Pepe's Grill
4 Mesón San Miguel	● Eating	7 Plaza Leza
5 Pepita's	1 Carlos 'n Charlie's	8 The Sports Page
6 Plaza Cozumel	2 Casa Deni's	

Not to scale

which used to be an idyllic lagoon behind the beach (nine kilometres from San Miguel). After it became totally spoilt, it was restored as a National Park, with the lagoon, crystal clear again, a botanical garden with local and imported plants, a 'Maya Area' (rather artificial), swimming (ideal for families with young children), snorkelling, dive shops, souvenirs, expensive but good restaurants and lockers (US$2). ■ *Entry costs US$4, snorkelling mask and fins US$5, use of underwater camera US$25, open 0800-1600.* Soon the road enters the southern hotel zone at the *Stouffer Presidente*, coming to the cruise ship dock and car ferry port on the outskirts of town.

Diving The island is famous for the beauty of its underwater environment. The best reef for scuba diving is Palancar, reached only by boat. Also highly recommended are Santa Rosa and Colombia. There are at least 20 major dive sites. Almost all Cozumel diving is drift diving, so if you are not used to a current choose an operator you feel comfortable with. There are over 20 dive operators. PADI, NAUI or SSI certification are all available; most trips are two-tank dives, US$40-50, but one-tank and nighttime dives are easily arranged. The better establishments have more dive masters accompanying reef trips. There are two hyperbaric chambers on the island, which treat about one tourist a week. Don't let the next one be you and follow safe diving practices with a concerned dive master. A resort course costs on average US$60, an Open Water certification course US$350, including equipment. Lots of packages are available. The following operators have been recommended: *Chino's Scuba Shop*, T/F24487, *Caribbean Diver's*, T21080, F21426, two-tank dive US$50, good boat, friendly; *Ecotour Caraibe*, C 1 Sur entre Avenida 5 y 10, small groups, safe, friendly, inexpensive; *Studio Blue*, C Dr Salas, safe diving; there are many others, shop around. It is also possible to go cavern diving in Cenotes.

Sleeping **LL** *Meliá Mayan Cozumel*, in northern hotel zone, 5 kilometres from airport, T20072,
Prices rise 50 percent F21599. *El Cozumeleño*, also in north zone, T20149, F20381, good, but like all hotels in this
around Christmas. area, a bit inconvenient. South of San Miguel are *Stouffer Presidente*, T20322, F21360, first class, but some distance from town. *Fiesta Inn*, T22900, F21301, linked to beach by tunnel, and 5 kilometres south, new *Fiesta Cozumel*, 4-star. *La Ceiba*, T20844, F20065, and others (all in the **LL-AL** range). **A** *Tontan*, 3 kilometres north of town (taxi US$1) on waterfront, pool, clean, safe, snorkelling, cheap restaurant, recommended.

Hotels in San Miguel town In **AL-A** range *Bahía*, Av Rafael Melgar y C 3 Sur (above *Kentucky Fried Chicken*), a/c, phone, cable TV, fridge, even-numbered rooms have balcony, T20209, F21387, recommended. *Barracuda*, Av Rafael Melgar 628, T20002, F20884, popular with divers. *Mesón San Miguel*, on the plaza, T20233, F21820. *Plaza Cozumel*, C 2 Nte 3, T22711, F20066, a/c, TV, phone, pool, restaurant, car hire, laundry.

B range hotels include *Maya Cozumel*, C 5 Sur 4, T20011, F20781, a/c, pool, good value. *Safari*, T20101, F20661, a/c. *Soberanis*, Av Rafael Melgar 471, T20246, a/c, restaurant terrace bar. *Tamarindo*, C 4 Nte 421, entre 20 y 25, T/F23614, bed and breakfast, 3 rooms, shared kitchen, hammocks, dive gear storage and rinse tank, purified drinking water, laundry, safe deposit box, TV, run by Eliane and Jorge, Spanish, English and French spoken, child care on request. *Vista del Mar*, Av R Melgar 45, T20545, near ferry deck, pool, a/c, restaurant, parking, good value.

C *Al Marestal*, C 10 y 25 Av Nte, T20822, spacious, clean rooms, fan or a/c, cool showers, swimming pool, very good. *Elizabeth*, Adolfo Rosado Salas 44, T20330, a/c, suites with fridge and stove, also has villas at C 3 Sur y Av 25 Sur. 2 doors away is *Flores*, a/c, cheaper with fan. *López*, on plaza, C Sur 7-A, T20108, hot showers, clean, main square, no meals. *Marqués*, 5 Av Sur entre 1 Sur y A R Salas, T20677, a/c, cheaper with fan, recommended. Close by are *Mary Carmen* and *El Pirata*, both cheaper with fan. *Posada Cozumel*, C 4 Nte 3, T20314, pool, showers, a/c, cheaper with fan, clean.

D *Blanquita*, 10 Nte, T21190, comfortable, clean, friendly, owner speaks English, rents snorkelling gear and motor-scooters, recommended. *José de León*, Av Pedro J Coldwell y 17 C Sur, fairly clean, showers. *Posada del Charro*, 1 block east of *José de León*, same owner, same facilities. *Flamingo*, C 6 Nte 81, T21264, showers, fan, clean, family-run, good value, recommended. *Kary*, 25 Av Sur y A R Salas, T22011, a/c, showers, pool, clean. *Paraíso Caribe*, 15 Av Nte y C 10, fan, showers, clean. *Pepita's*, 15 Av Sur 120, T20098, a/c, fan, fridge, owner, Eduardo Ruiz, speaks English, Spanish, French, Italian, German and Mayan, clean, recommended.

E *Posada Letty*, C 1 Sur y Av 15 Sur, clean, hot water, good value, recommended. *Saolima*, A R Salas 260, T20886, clean, fan, showers, hot water, recommended.

Camping Not permitted although there are 2 suitable sites on the south shore. Try asking for permission at the army base.

Very few hotels in town have restaurants since there are so many other places to eat. *Las Palmeras*, at the pier (people-watching spot), very popular for breakfast, opens 0700, always busy, recommended. *Morgans*, main square, elegant, expensive, good. *Plaza Leza*, main square, excellent and reasonable. *La Choza*, A R Salas 198, expensive, Mexico City food, recommended. *Prima*, AR Salas 109, Italian food, run by New Yorker, speaks some Hebrew. *Miss Dollar*, AR Salas y Av 20, good Mexican food, US$2 *comidas*, very friendly. *Karen's Pizza and Grill*, Av 5 Nte entre Av B Juárez y C 2 Nte, pizza cheap, good. *Western Grill*, Av 5, near Zócalo, excellent breakfasts. *Gatto Pardo*, 10 Av Sur 121, good pizzas and try their 'tequila slammers'. *Café del Puerto*, 2nd floor by pier, South Seas style. *El Moro*, 75 Bis Nte 124, entre 4 y 2, good, closed Thursday. *Santiago's Grill*, 15 Av Sur y A R Salas, excellent, medium price-range, popular with divers; also popular with divers is *Las Tortugas*, 10 Av Nte, just north of square, good in the evening. *El Capi Navegante*, 2 locations: by market for lunch, and C 3 y 10 Av Sur, more up market, seafood at each. *Alfalfa*, C 5 Sur, between RE Melgar and 5 Av, mostly vegetarian meals but owner Dawne Detraz expanding with more fish and chicken and health food shop, daily hot special US$3 with salad and drink, excellent coffee, friendly, highly recommended. *La Yucatequita*, 9 C Sur y 10 Av Sur, genuine Mayan food, closes at 2130, best to go day before and discuss menu. *La Misión*, Av Benito Juárez y 10 Av Nte, good food, friendly atmosphere. *Pepe's Grill*, waterfront, 2 blocks south of pier, expensive and excellent. *Acuario*, on beach 6 blocks south of pier, famous for seafood, aquarium in restaurant (ask to see the tanks at the back). *Carlos and Charlie's* restaurant/bar, popular, 2nd floor on waterfront 2 blocks north of pier. *Pancho's Backyard*, Rafael Melgar 27, in *Los Cinco Soles* shopping complex, Mexican food and wine elegantly served, good food. *Mi Chabalita*, 10 Av Sur entre C 1 Sur y C Salas, friendly, cheap and good Mexican food. *Pepe Pelícano*, 2 houses left of *Saolima Hotel*, cheap and clean. *Casa Deni's*, C 1 Sur 164, close to Plaza, open air restaurant, very good, moderate prices. *The Sports Page*, C 2 Nte y Av 5, US-style, breakfasts, burgers, steaks, lobster, satellite TV, money exchange, phones for USA; US-style breakfasts also at *Los Cocos*, next to ProDive on A R Salas. *Diamond Bakery*, 15 Av y 1 Av Sur, inconspicuous sign, good bread and pastries, also have a café on the waterfront. *Zermatt*, Av 5 y C 4 Nte, good bakery.

Naked Turtle, on east side (has basic rooms to let). *Mescalito's*, see above, another place, like *The Sports Page,* to write a message on your T-shirt and leave it on the ceiling; several other bar restaurants on the east side.

Eating
In general, it is much cheaper to eat in town than at the resort hotels to the north or south.

Nightclubs *Joman's* (very seedy), *Scaramouche* (the best, Av R Melgar y C A R Salas), *Neptuno* (Av R Melgar y C 11, south of centre, these 2 are state-of-the-art discos), as well as hotel nightclubs.

Night life

Film 2 shops develop film, both quite expensive (about US$20 for 36 prints). Best to wait till you get home.

Shopping

Local Bus: the main road around Cozumel is paved, but public buses serve only the

Transport

expensive hotels north of town. **Bike hire**: it is best to hire a bicycle (quiet) when touring around the island so you can see wildlife: iguanas, turtles, birds. Rental charges are US$5 for 12 hours, US$8 for 24 hours, eg from *Splash*, on Calle 6 Nte, T20502, 0800-2000. **Taxi**: all carry an official price list. Downtown fare US$1.15; to north or south hotel zones US$2.35; San Francisco beach US$10; Maya ruins US$30; island tour includes San Gervasio US$50. **Vehicle rental**: many agencies for cars, jeeps and mopeds, eg Avis, Budget, Hertz, National, and local companies. Car hire ranges from about US$55 a day for a VW Beetle to US$70 minimum for a jeep. Discounted vehicle hire plus free breakfast at a 5-star hotel in return for listening for 1 hour about an offer to buy holiday units, no commitments, "a great deal for the budget traveller". Ask at information desks around town. Scooter rental is US$27 a day high season, US$22 low. One Pemex filling station, at Avenida Juárez y Avenida 30; beware overcharging. If taking a moped be aware of traffic laws, helmets must be worn, illegal parking is subject to fines, etc (single women should not ride alone on the eastern side of the island).

Air Cozumel-Mexico City direct with Mexicana, or via Cancún; Continental to Houston; Aero Caribe to Cancún and Chichén Itzá.

Ferry See under Playa del Carmen for passenger ferries. Car ferry goes from Puerto Morelos twice a day (including 1200): US$27 for a car, US$3 per passenger; the entrance to the car ferry on Cozumel is just past the cruise ship dock. Because of the treatment cars receive on the ferry, it may be better to leave your car on the mainland and do without it on the island.

Directory **Banks** 4 banks on the main square, all exchange money in morning only, but not at same hours: Bital; on Juárez (all with ATM machines), *Bancomer*, *Banamex*, *Atlántico*. Casas de cambio on Av 5 Nte and around square, 3.5% commission, open longer hours. **Communications Post Office:** Av Rafael Melgar y C 7 Sur. **Telephone:** Ladatel phones on main square at corner of Av Juárez y Av 5, or on A R Salas, just up from Av 5 Sur, opposite *Roberto's Black Coral Studio* (if working). For calls to the USA go to *The Sports Page*. Telmex phone offices on the main square next to *Restaurant Plaza Leza*, open 0800-2300, and on A R Salas entre Avs 10 y 15. There are also expensive Computel offices in town, eg at the cruise ship dock. **Laundry** On A R Salas entre Avs 5 y 10, coin op or service wash. Cheap laundry opposite *Posada Letty*. **Tour companies & travel agent** *Aviomar*, Av 5 No 8a, x 2 y 4 Nte, T24622, F21728. **Tourist office** *Sectur* tourist office in Plaza Cozumel on Av Juárez, entre 5 Av y 10 Av, p1º, English-speaking service in am, opens 1800 in pm. On arrival, cross the road from the pier to the square where lots of information kiosks give maps, tour information, etc. A good map (*The Brown Map*), includes reef locations, is available from stores and shops. *The Blue Guide*, free, has maps and practical details, available everywhere. Booklets on archaeological sites and the region, and Mexico City newspapers are available at the *papelería* on the east side of the square.

Playa del Carmen to Tulum

Xcaret There are some Maya ruins on the mainland at Xcaret, a turnoff left on Route 307 to Tulum, after Playa del Carmen. The Maya site, an ancient port called Pole, was the departure point for voyages to Cozumel. It has now been redesigned as a daytrip from Cancún. The ruins and three linked *cenotes* and sea water lagoons form part of a clean, well-tended park, catering exclusively for day-trippers, which costs US$18.50 (children under five years free) to enter. This entitles you to visit the small ruins, the aviary, the beach, lagoon and inlet, to take an underground river trip (life vest included) and to use all chairs, hammocks and *palapas*. Everything else is extra: food and drink (none may be brought in), snorkel rental (US$7), snorkel lessons, reef trips (US$10), diving, horse riding (US$30) and lockers (for which you have to pay US$1 each time you lock the door). There are also dolphins in pens with which you may swim for US$50. No sun tan lotion may be worn in the sea, but there is a film of oils in the sea nonetheless. Buses from Playa del Carmen leave you at the turn-off (US$0.65), by a roadside restaurant which is very clean (accepts Visa). This is a one kilometre walk from the entrance to Xcaret. The alternative is to take a taxi, or a tour from Playa del Carmen or Cancún (in a multicoloured bus). You can also walk along the beach from Playa del Carmen, three hours.

Cenote diving

There are over 50 cenotes in this area, accessible from Ruta 307 and often well signposted, and cave diving has become very popular. However, it is a specialized sport and unless you have a cave diving qualification, you must be accompanied by a qualified dive master. A cave diving course involves over 12 hours of lectures and a minimum of 14 cave dives using double tanks, costing around US$600. Specialist dive centres offering courses are Mike Madden's CEDAM Dive Centres, PO Box 1, Puerto Aventuras, T/F98735129; Aquatech, Villas De Rosa, PO Box 25, Aventuras Akumal No 35, Tulum, T/F41271. The Akumal Dive Centre, PO Box 1, Akumal, Playa del Carmen, T41259, F98873164. These three have a 100 percent safety record. Other operators include Yax-Há Dive Centre, T22888; Akumal Explorers, T22453; Dos Ojos (Divers of the Hidden World), T44081. Some of the best cenotes are 'Carwash', on the Cobá road, good even for beginners, with excellent visibility; 'Dos Ojos', just off Ruta 307 south of Aventuras, the second largest underground cave system in the world, with a possible link to the Nohoch Nah Chich, the most famous

Paamul, just south of Playa del Carmen and about 92 kilometres south of Cancún, is a fine beach on a bay, planned for development, with chalets (**C** with bath, fan, terrace for hammocks, comfortable, pretty, clean, recommended) and campsites (recommended). Snorkelling and diving; reef a few metres off shore. Second-class buses from Cancún and Playa del Carmen pass.

Akumal
Colour map 4, grid A4

A luxury resort, 102 kilometres south Cancún, 20 kilometres north of Tulum, is reached easily by bus from there or from Playa del Carmen (30 minutes). **L** *Hotel Club Akumal Caribe*, is one of many luxury hotels, villas and condos which can be booked in the US through Caribbean Fantasy, PO Box 7606, Loveland, Colorado 80537-0606, caribbfan@aol.com, accommodation is all **LL-AL** *Akmal Caribe* has a restaurant (there is a small supermarket nearby at *Villas Mayas*), poor service, overpriced, no entertainment, excellent beach, with coral reef only 100 metres offshore. Eat at restaurant marked *Comidas Económicas* outside the gate. **LL** *Club Aventuras Akumal*, T98722887, all inclusive resort owned by Oasis group, small pool, on pleasant beach. **AL** *Villas Mayas*, bungalows, with bath, comfortable, some with kitchens, on beach, snorkelling equipment for hire, US$6 per day, restaurant with poor service, recommended as base for excursions to Xelhá, Tulum and Cobá. There is a small lagoon three kilometres north of Akumal, good snorkelling.

Playa Aventuras is a huge beach resort south of Akumal. **LL** *Club Puerto Aventuras*, another Oasis hotel, sandwiched between the sea and marina, all inclusive with 309 rooms. Two ferries run daily to Cozumel. Also just south of Akumal are **Chemuyil** (*palapas*, thatched shelters for hammocks, US$4, free shower, expensive restaurant, laundry facilities) and **Xcacel** (campground has water, bathrooms, cold showers and restaurant, very clean, US$2 per person, vehicles free, snorkel hire US$5 a day, beautiful swimming in the bay). Ask guards if you can go on turtle protection patrol at night (May-July).

Laguna Xelhá

13 kilometres north of Tulum, 122 kilometres from Cancún (bus from Playa del Carmen, 45 minutes), this beautiful clear lagoon, is full of fish, but no fishing allowed as it is a national park (open 0800-1630), entry US$10. Snorkelling gear can be rented at US$7 for a day, but it is often in poor repair; better to rent from your hotel. Lockers cost US$1. Arrive as early as possible to see fish as the lagoon is full of tourists throughout most of the day. Snorkelling areas are limited by fencing (you need to dive down about a metre because above that level the water is cold and fresh with few fish; below it is the warm, fish-filled salt water). Bungalows, first-class hotels, fast food restaurants being built. Very expensive food and drink. There is a marvellous jungle path to one of the lagoon bays. Xelhá ruins (known also as Los Basadres) are located across the road from the beach of the same name. Entry

US$3.35, few tourists but not much to see. You may have to jump the fence to visit; there is a beautiful cenote at the end of the ruins where you can have a lovely swim. Small ruins of **Ak** are near Xelhá. Closer to Tulum, at **Tancáh**, are newly-discovered bright post-classical Maya murals but they are sometimes closed to the public.

Tulum

Colour map 4, grid A4 The Tulum ruins, Maya-Toltec, are 131 kilometres south of Cancún, one kilometre off the main road. They are 12th century, with city walls of white stone atop coastal cliffs. The temples were dedicated to the worship of the Falling God, or the Setting Sun, represented as a falling character over nearly all the west-facing doors (Cozumel was the home of the Rising Sun). The same idea is reflected in the buildings, which are wider at the top than at the bottom.

The main structure is the Castillo, which commands a view of both the sea and the forested Quintana Roo lowlands stretching westwards. All the Castillo's openings face west, as do most, but not all, of the doorways at Tulum. Look for the alignment of the Falling God on the temple of that name (to the left of the Castillo) with the pillar and the back door in the House of the Chultún (the nearest building in the centre group to the entrance). The majority of the main structures are roped off so that you cannot climb the Castillo, nor get close to the surviving frescoes, especially on the Temple of the Frescoes. In 1993 the government began a major improvement and conservation programme to improve facilities at the site.

Tulum is these days crowded with tourists (best time to visit is between 0800 and 0900). Take towel and swimsuit if you wish to scramble down from the ruins to one of the two beaches for a swim (the larger of the two is less easy to get to). The reef is from 600 to 1,000 metres from the shore, so if you wish to snorkel you must either be a strong swimmer, or take a boat trip.

■ *The site is open 0800-1700, about 2 hours needed to view at leisure (entry US$2, parking US$1.50, students with Mexican ID free, Sunday free). There is a tourist complex at the entrance to the ruins. Guide books can be bought in the shops; Panorama guide book is interesting, others available. Local guides can also be hired. The parking area is near Highway 307, and a handicraft market. A small train takes you from the parking area to the ruins for US$1, or it is an easy 500-metre walk. The paved road continues down the coast to Bocapaila and beyond, access by car to this road from the car park is now forbidden. To reach the road south of the ruins, access is possible 1 kilometre from Tulum village.*

Public buses drop passengers at El Crucero, a crossroads 500 metres north of the car park for Tulum Ruinas (an easy walk) where there is an ADO bus terminal which opens for a few hours at 0800; at the crossroads are some hotels, a shop (will exchange travellers' cheques), on the opposite side of the

Tulum

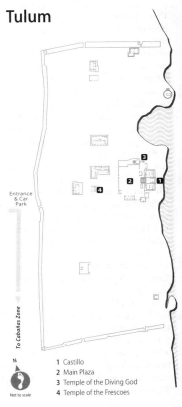

1 Castillo
2 Main Plaza
3 Temple of the Diving God
4 Temple of the Frescoes

Entrance & Car Park

To Cabañas Zone

Not to scale

road a naval base and airstrip, and a little way down Highway 307 a Pemex station. The village of **Tulum** is four kilometres south of El Crucero. A taxi from the village to the ruins costs US$2.50. It is not very large and has a bus station, a post office but no bank; there are five to six grocery shops, two *panaderías*, a hotel and restaurants.

At El Crucero C *El Faisán y El Venado*, TV, a/c, OK, restaurant serving pizzas, Mexican dishes and very expensive drinks; across the road is **E** *Hotel El Crucero de Tulum*, much more basic, damp, dirty, but a/c, hot water, staff unhelpful, good restaurant with shop attached. Almost opposite bus stop is a new hotel, **C**, large, clean, a/c, parking, with restaurant (24 hours), good food and service; and *Chilam-Balam*, across the road, also serves good food.

At Tulum village D-E *Hotel Maya*, a/c or fan, shower, reasonable, restaurant with slow service, near bus stop, small shop, parking in front. Several chicken restaurants and *Leonor's* for fish and Mexican food, good but pricey.

To reach the following accommodation it is better to get off the bus in town and take a taxi (US$3-5 depending on season), otherwise $\frac{1}{2}$ hour walk from the site. Accommodation is generally expensive for the facilities offered, and in high season *cabañas* are difficult to get. Establishments are listed according to proximity to the ruins (in all these places, beware theft); **E-F** *Cabañas El Mirador*, small, quiet, cabins (won't rent to singles), hammocks available, camping, 2 showers, use of restaurant toilets (clean), expensive bar and restaurant, slow service, 10 minutes' walk from ruins; next is **E-F** *Santa Fe*, about 1 kilometre from the ruins (a path leads along the beach and then through forest to the ruins, 10 minutes), basic *cabañas*, new toilets and showers, US$1 extra for mosquito net, hammocks or tents, water problems, reported insecure (free camping possible further up the beach), has a restaurant, good breakfasts and fish dinners, reggae music, English, French and Italian spoken, basic toilets; next, with good restaurant, are **C-E** *Cabañas Don Armando*, T43856/44539/44437, *cabañas* for up to 4, no singles, prices variable, the best, very popular, most (but not all) staff are friendly and helpful, mixed reports on atmosphere, good restaurant but bottled water expensive, bar with noisy disco till 0200, certain bus tickets available. Next along is the Fishing Association, rents out *cabañas*, friendly.

C-D *Cabañas Diamante K*, on the beach, nice bar and restaurant, recommended. **E** *Cabañas Mar Caribe*, 15 minutes from ruins. **B** *Bungalows Paraíso*, 3 kilometres from ruins, price varies according to who is on desk, nice cabins with fan, hot shower, clean, electricity 1800-2200, poor restaurant.

Next comes a resort complex: **AL** *Sian Ka'an/Osho Oasis* (owned by Sanyasins), for reservations phone US office T/F707-7781320, in Mexico T98712094, 5 kilometres south from ruins by beautiful secluded beach, wooden huts, well-equipped, electricity, mosquito net, good showers, washing facilities, clean, full board option for US$18, excellent vegetarian food, meditation and yoga groups, relaxed, highly recommended, credit cards not accepted; on same road, 500 metres north is *Zamas Cabañas*, simple restaurant on beach, highly recommended. **D-F** *La Perla*, 5 kilometres south of Tulum, *cabañas*, camping and restaurant, comfortable, good food, family atmosphere, near beach, recommended (Monica Koestinger, Lista de Correos, Tulum, Quintana Roo); next to *La Perla* is **D** *Nosho Tunich*, 1 hour walk from ruins, clean *cabañas*, good food; near the cabaña resort are exchange facilities, dive shop and 2 bike rental shops.

B *Hotel Posada Tulum*, 8 kilometres south of the ruins on the beach, has an expensive restaurant, hot water (cheaper with cold water), electricity am and 1800-2300, changes dollars, no credit cards. **A-B** *Anna y José* restaurant, 6 kilometres south of ruins, recommended, which also has *cabañas* and rooms, some are right on the beach, very clean, comfortable, very hospitable. **E** *Tita Tulum*, eco hotel, with bath; taxi to Tulum, US$3-5. For places to stay in Sian Ka'an Biosphere Reserve, see below.

Diving: Several dive shops all along the Tulum corridor. See page 509 for cave diving

See page 509 for cave diving

Sleeping

When arriving by bus, alight at El Crucero for the ruins and nearby accommodation. A new hotel is under construction at the site.

Sports

operators and specialist courses. Many untrained snorkelling and diving outfits, take care. AKTUN next to *Hotel El Mesón*, 1 kilometre out of Tulum on main road, gunnar.wagner@aktundive.com, German/Mexican-run, experienced NACD and IANTD instructor, very friendly, speaks English, French & Dutch.

Transport **Buses** Bus station but few buses start here. 2nd class buses on the Cancún-Playa del Carmen-Felipe Carrillo Puerto-Chetumal route stop at Tulum; also 3 Inter Playa buses a day from Cancún, US$4.25. To **Felipe Carrillo Puerto**, several between 0600-1200 and 1600-2200, 1 hour, US$2, continuing to **Chetumal**, 2nd class, US$7, 1st class US$8.50, 4 hours. To **Cobá**: the Playa del Carmen-Tulum-Cobá-Valladolid bus passes El Crucero at 0600, 1100 and 1800 (in the other direction buses pass Tulum at 0715 and 1545, all times approximate, may leave 15 minutes early). Fare Tulum-Cobá US$1.35, 45 minutes. To **Mérida**, several daily, US$7, 2nd class, 6 hours. To **Tizimín** daily at 1400, via Cancún and Valladolid. To **Escárcega** and **Córdoba** 0800; to Palenque US$25. To San Cristóbal 1845, often late, US$32; to Villahermosa 1630, 2100, US$28; to Mexico City, 0815, 1315, 2100 US$62; to **Veracruz** 1630. Autobuses del Caribe offices are next door to *Hotel Maya*. Buy tickets here rather than wait for buses at the crossroads, but this still does not ensure getting a seat. It may be better to go to Playa del Carmen (US$1.40) for more connections to nearby destinations. If travelling far, take a bus to Felipe Carrillo Puerto and transfer to ADO there. **Taxis**: Tulum town to ruins US$3.50; to the *cabañas* US$3-5; to Cobá about US$25. **Bicycles**: can be hired in the village at US$1 per hour, a good way to visit local centres (Cristal and Escondido are recommended as much cheaper, US$2, and less commercialized than Xcaret).

Directory **Banks** 4 money exchange booths near bus station in Tulum village. TCs can be changed at the offices of the GOPI Construction Company, though not at a very good rate. **Communications** Telephone: long-distance phones in ADO terminal in town; also fax office, F98712009, also offer bike rental.

About 20 kilometres south of Tulum is the site of **Muyil** (entry US$1), with one pyramid undergoing reconstruction and two other relatively untouched buildings. Very quiet, with interesting birdlife.

Sian Ka'an Biosphere Reserve

The Reserve covers 1.3 million acres of the Quintana Roo coast. About one third is covered in tropical forest, one third is savannas and mangrove and one third coastal and marine habitats, including 110 kilometres of barrier reef. Mammals include jaguar, puma, ocelot and other cats, monkeys, tapir, peccaries, manatee and deer; turtles nest on the beaches; there are crocodiles and a wide variety of land and aquatic birds. For all information, go to the office of Los Amigos de Sian Ka'an, Plaza América, Avenida Cobá 5, third floor, suites 48-50, Cancún (Apdo Postal 770, 77500 Cancún, T849583), open 0900-1500, 1800-2000, very helpful. Do not try to get there independently without a car. Ecocolors, Cancún, T/F849580, in collaboration with Los Amigos, run tours to the Reserve, US$115 for a full day, starting at 0700, pick up at hotel, everything included: in winter the tour goes through a canal, in summer it goes birdwatching, in both cases a visit to a Maya ruin, a cenote, snorkelling, all equipment, breakfast and evening meal are included. two-day camping trips can be arranged. Two-hour boat trips through the Biosphere can be taken for US$50. Trips can also be arranged through *Cabañas Ana y José*, near Tulum, US$50, daily except Sunday. It is possible to drive into the Reserve from Tulum village as far as Punta Allen (58 kilometres; the road is opposite the turning to Cobá; it is not clearly marked, and the final section is badly potholed); beyond that you need a launch. From the south it is possible to drive to Punta Herrero (unmade road, see **Majahual**, below). No explanations are available for those going independently.

Sleeping At **Punta Allen** is a small fishing village with houses for rent (cooking facilities), and a good, non-touristy restaurant, *La Cantina* (US$3-4 for fish). There are also 2 comfortable *cabañas* at a place called **A** *Rancho Sol Caribe*, with bath, restaurant, recommended. Reservations to:

Diane and Michael Sovereign, Apdo Postal 67, Tulum, CP 77780, T12091/F12092. **Punta Herrero** is 6 hours from Chetumal, 10 from Cancún; *rancheros* are very hospitable, camping is possible but take all food and plenty of insect repellent. In the Reserve, 8 kilometres south of Tulum, are the quiet, pleasant **AL** *Cabañas Los Arrecifes*, with smart chalets on the beach and others behind, cheaper, with good fish restaurant shaped like a ship (no electricity), limited menu. 100 metres away are **D** *Cabañas de Tulum*, also with good restaurant, clean

Tulum to Chetumal

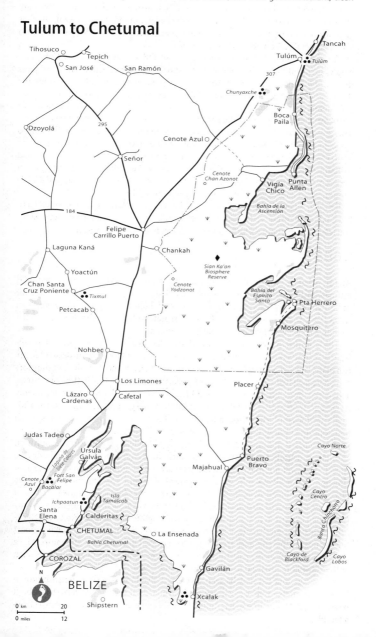

cabins with shower, electricity 1730-2100; interesting fish in the cenote opposite, take taxi there (US$5-6 from ruins car park), empty white beaches. *Pez Maya* and *Boca Paila* are expensive fishing lodges. *Casa Blanca* is an exclusive hotel reached only by small plane. *Rancho Retiro*, camping US$2, food and beer served, very relaxed atmosphere.

The ruins of **Chumyaxche**, three pyramids (partly overgrown), are on the left-hand side of the road to Felipe Carrillo Puerto, 18 kilometres south of Tulum (they are mosquito-infested). Entry US$4. Beyond the last pyramid is Laguna Azul, which is good for swimming and snorkelling in blue, clean water (you do not have to pay to visit the pool if you do not visit the pyramids).

The road linking Tulum with the large but little-excavated city of Cobá (see below) turns off the main Highway 307 just before Tulum Pueblo. This road joins the *vía libre* Valladolid-Cancún road at **Nuevo Xcan**, thus greatly shortening the distance between Chichén Itzá and Tulum (do not take the *cuota* road which no longer exits at Nuevo Xcan). The Cobá-Valladolid bus passes Nuevo Xcan (no hotel but the owner of the shop where the road branches off to Cobá may offer you a room). There is an *aduana* post in Nuevo Xcan. If going from Valladolid or Cancún to Cobá, look for the *Villas Arqueológicas* sign at Nuevo Xcan. Note, many maps show a road from Cobá to Chemax, west of Xcan. This road does not exist; the only road from the north to Cobá is from Nuevo Xcan. For drivers, there is no Pemex station between Cancún and Valladolid, or Cancún-Cobá-Tulúm, or Valladolid-Cobá-Tulúm, all are journeys of 150 kilometres without a fill-up.

Between Nuevo Xcan and Cobá is the tiny village of **Punta Laguna**, which has a lake and forest, preserved through the efforts of ecotourists. Ask for Serapio to show you round; he does not speak English, and depends mainly on tourists for his income.

Cobá

An important Maya city in the eighth and ninth centuries AD, whose population is estimated to have been between 40,000 and 50,000, but which was abandoned for unknown reasons, is 47 kilometres inland from Tulum. The present day village of Cobá lies on either side of Lago Cobá, surrounded by dense jungle. It is a quiet friendly village, with few tourists staying overnight.

The entrance to the ruins is at the end of the lake between the two parts of the village. A second lake, Lago Macanxoc, is within the site. There are turtles and many fish in the lakes. It is a good birdwatching area. Both lakes and their surrounding forest can be seen from the summit of the Iglesia, the tallest structure in the Cobá group. There are three other groups of buildings to visit: the Macanxoc group, mainly stelae, about one and a half kilometres from the Cobá group; Las Pinturas, one kilometre northeast of Macanxoc, a temple and the remains of other buildings which had columns in their construction; the Nohoch Mul group, at least another kilometre from Las Pinturas. Nohoch Mul has the tallest pyramid in the northern Yucatán, a magnificent structure, from which the views of the jungle on all sides are superb. You will not find at Cobá the great array of buildings which can be seen at Chichén Itzá or Uxmal, nor the compactness of Tulum. Instead, the delight of the place is the architecture in the jungle, with birds, butterflies, spiders and lizards, and the many uncovered structures which hint at the vastness of the city in its heyday (the urban extension of Cobá is put at some 70 square kilometres). An unusual feature is the network of ancient roads, known as *sacbes* (white roads), which connect the groups in the site and are known to have extended across the entire Maya Yucatán. Over 40 *sacbes* pass through Cobá, some local, some of great length, such as the 100-kilometre road to Yaxuná in Yucatán state.

At the lake toucans may be seen very early; also look out for greenish-blue and brown mot-mots in the early morning. The guards at the site are very strict about opening and closing time so it is difficult to gain entry to see the dawn or sunset from a temple.

The paved road into Cobá ends at Lago Cobá; to the left are the ruins, to the right *Villas Arqueológicas*. The roads around Cobá are badly potholed. ■ *Cobá is becoming more popular as a destination for tourist buses, which come in at 1030; arrive before that to avoid the crowds and the heat (ie on the 0430 bus from Valladolid, if not staying in Cobá). Take insect repellent. The site is open 0800-1700, entry US$2.50, free on Sunday. Guide books: Bloomgarten's Tulum and Cobá, and Descriptive Guide book to Cobá by Prof Gualberto Zapata Alonzo, which is a little unclear about dates and details, but is still useful and has maps. Free map from Hotel Restaurant Bocadito.*

B *Villas Arqueológicas* (Club Méditerranée), about 2 kilometres from site on lake shore, open to non members, excellent, clean and quiet, a/c, swimming pool, good restaurant with moderate prices, but expensive beer. Do not arrive without a reservation, especially at weekends; on the other hand, making a reservation by phone seems to be practically impossible. In the village, on the street leading to the main road, is **E** *Hotel Restaurant Bocadito*, run down, spartan rooms with fan, intermittent water supply, poor security, good but expensive restaurant (which is popular with tour groups), books and handicrafts for sale, recommended.

Sleeping

There are plenty of restaurants in the village, on the road to *Villas Arqueológicas* and on the road to the ruins, they are all quite pricey, also a grocery store by *El Bocadito* and souvenir shops. *Nicte-Ha*, good and friendly. *Pirámides*, on corner of track leading to *Villas Arqueológicas*, highly recommended.

Eating

Local Buses into the village turn round at the road end. There are 3 a day to Valladolid, coming from Playa del Carmen and Tulum, passing through at 0630, 1130 and 1830, 2 hours to Valladolid, US$2.50; 2 buses a day to Tulum and Playa at 0630 and 1500, US$1 to Tulum. A taxi to Tulum costs around US$25. If you miss the bus there is a taxi to be found at *El Bocadito*.

Transport

Banks *Sterling Store*, opposite entrance to ruins.

Directory

The cult of the 'talking cross' was founded here (see page 435). The Santuario de la Cruz Parlante is five blocks west of the Pemex station on Highway 307. The beautiful main square is dominated by the Catholic church, built by the Cruzob in the 19th century. Legend has it that the unfinished bell tower will only be completed when the descendants of those who heard the talking cross reassert control of the region. In the plaza is lots of playground equipment for children. (With thanks to Suzanne Elise Tourville, St Louis, Missouri.)

Felipe Carrillo Puerto
Colour map 4, grid A3

Sleeping & eating *Hotel Carrillo Puerto* has been recommended. **C** *El Faisán y El Venado*, 2 blocks northeast of main square, mixed reports on cleanliness, but hot water and good value restaurant, popular with locals. **D** *Tulum*, with better restaurant. **E** *Chan Santa Cruz*, just off the plaza, good, basic, clean and friendly (*Restaurante 24 Horas* is open 24 hours, OK). **E** *Hotel Esquivel*, just off Plaza, fair, noisy. **D** *San Ignacio*, near Pemex, good value, a/c, bath, towels, TV, secure car park; next door is restaurant *Danburger Maya*, good food, reasonable prices, helpful. **F** *María Isabel*, on same road, clean, friendly, laundry service, quiet, safe parking. *Restaurant Addy*, on main road, south of town, good, simple. There are a few food shops in the village selling sweet breads, and mineral water.

Transport Bus station opposite Pemex. Autotransportes del Caribe (Playa Express) to Cancún daily from 0600, 1st and 2nd class to Tulum, US$2, and Playa del Carmen en route. Bus Felipe Carrillo Puerto-Mérida, via Muná, US$10, 4½ hours; to Valladolid, 2nd class, 2 hours, US$3.75; to Chetumal, 1st class, 2 hours, US$3.35.

Chetumal

Population: 120,000
State population 1995:
703,442
Phone code: 99
Colour map 4, grid B4

Capital of the state of Quintana Roo, Chetumal is now being developed for tourism (albeit slowly). It is a free port with clean wide streets, and a pleasant waterfront with walks, parks and trees from where you can see Belize. It is 240 kilometres south of Tulum. The Chetumal Bay has been designated a Natural Protected Area for manatees, which includes a manatee sanctuary.

Sights

The 'paseo' near the waterfront on Sunday night is worth seeing. The State Congress building has a mural showing the history of Quintana Roo. Avenida Héroes is the main shopping street. Good for foreign foodstuffs – cheaper at the covered market in the outskirts than in the centre. A new commercial centre is being built at the site of the old bus station.

Museo de la Cultura Maya is on Avenida Héroes de Chapultepec by the market, good models of sites and touchscreen computers explaining Mayan calendar and glyphs, although few original Maya pieces, some explanations in English, excellent overview, guided tours available, good bookshop with English magazines. ■ *Tuesday-Thursday, 0900-1900, Friday and Saturday 0900-2000, Sunday 0900-1400, US$1.75, cold a/c, highly recommended.*

Sleeping
Accommodation may be a problem during the holiday season.

AL *Los Cocos*, Héroes de Chapultepec 138, T20544, reductions for AAA members, a/c, pool, restaurant, breakfast recommended. **A** *Continental Caribe/Holiday Inn*, Av Héroes 171, T21100, F21676. **A** *El Marqués*, Av Lázaro Cárdenas 121, T22998, 5 blocks from centre, fan, a/c, hot water, restaurant, recommended. *Marlon*, Av Benito Juárez, new, no details as yet. **C** *Real Azteca*, Belice 186, T20720, cheerful, friendly, but no hot shower (2nd floor rooms best, but still not too good). **D** *Caribe Princess*, Av A Obregón 168, T20520, a/c, TV, good, very clean, no restaurant, recommended. **D-E** *Jacaranda*, Av Obregón 201, T21455, clean, good, bath, safe parking. **D-E** *Luz María*, Carmen de Merino 204, T20202, friendly but not very clean, owner speaks English. **D-E** *El Dorado*, Av 5 de Mayo 42, T20315, hot water, a/c, very friendly, quiet, recommended. **E** *Big Ben*, Héroes 48-A, T20965, clean, shabby, safe, cheaper rooms for 4, with bath. **E** *Motel Casablanca*, Alvaro Obregón 312, clean, quiet, very good value, recommended. **E** *Crystal*, Colón y Av Belice, fan, bath, parking. **E** *María Dolores*, Alvaro Obregón 206, T20508, bath, hot water, fan, clean, windows don't open, noisy, restaurant *Solsimar* downstairs good and popular. **E** *Tulum*, Héroes 2, T20518, above market, noise starts 0530, but clean, with bath and fan, friendly, large rooms. **E** *Ucum*, Gandhi 4, T20711 (no singles) with fan and bath, clean, pleasant, quiet (rooms away from street), expensive laundry, enclosed car park, good value, restaurant next door recommended for ceviche. **E-F** *Boston*, Belice 290, between bus station and centre, a/c, not very good. **E-F** *Cuartos Margot*, 5 de Mayo 30, some with bath, clean, charming. **F** *Ejidal*, Av Independencia entre Obregón y P Blanco, bath, clean, recommended. Plenty more.

Camping *Sunrise of the Caribbean*, Trailer Park on the road to Calderitas, US$15 for car and 2 people, cold showers, electricity, laundry facilities, *palapas*, boat ramp.

Youth hostel Calzada Veracruz y Alvaro Obregón, referred to as CREA, T23465, CP 77050, hot water, clean, run down, friendly, good breakfast, camping US$2, recommended.

Eating

Cheap snacks at *Lonchería Ivette* on Mahatma Gandhi 154. *Pandoja*, Gandhi y 16 de Septiembre, good food. *Chicho's Lobster House*, Blvd Bahía esq Vicente Guerrero, T27249, expensive but good seafood, friendly. *Bambino Pizzas*, P Blanco 215, good. *Maria's*, 5 de Mayo y Obregón, delicious local food, good and inexpensive fish. *Sergio Pizza*, Obregón 182, pizzas, fish, and expensive steak meals, a/c, good drinks, excellent service. *Mar Caribe*, 22 de Enero entre F Madero y Independencia, snacks only. Good breakfasts at the *Hotel Los Cocos*, US$5. Several 1 block west of intersection of Héroes y Obregón, eg *Bienvenidos*, good. *Solsimar*, Obregón 206 (closed Sunday), popular, reasonable prices. *El Vaticano*, popular with locals, good atmosphere, cheap. *Arcada*, Héroes y Zaragoza, open 24 hours, with mini-market at the back. Another area with many restaurants is about 4 blocks north of market, then 3 blocks west, eg *Barracuda*, good seafood. *Pacho Tec*, small lunch room next to electricity plant, try the chicken broth. Delicious yoghurt ice in shop opposite market. Try *Safari* roadhouse in Calderitas suburb for enterprising nightlife. Good juices at *Jugos Xamach*, corner of Salvador y Quintana Roo, friendly local spot.

Shopping Shops are open from 0800-1300 and 1800-2000. *Super San Francisco* supermarket, near bus station, is better than the one behind *Arcada* restaurant.

Transport **Local Taxis**: no city buses; taxis operate on fixed price routes, US$0.50 on average. Cars with light-green licence plates are a form of taxi. **Fuel**: *Magna Sin* (unleaded fuel) is sold at the petrol station just outside Chetumal on the road north at the beginning of the road to Escárcega, also at Xpujil (see page 521). **Garage**: Talleres Barrera, helpful, on Primo de Verdad; turn east off Héroes, then past the electrical plant.

Air Airport (CTM) 2½km from town. Flights to Cancún, Merida, Belize City (Aero Caribe), Mexico City, Monterrey and Tijuana (Aviacsa, T27765).

Buses The main bus station is 2-3 kilometres out of town at the intersection of Insurgentes y Belice, clean facilities, reasonable café; left luggage in the shop, US$0.75 per day; all passengers have to go through the customs *semáforo* (red/green light) on entry. Taxi from town US$2. Colectivo taxi from town US$0.80, bus to town from Avenida Belice. Many

Chetumal

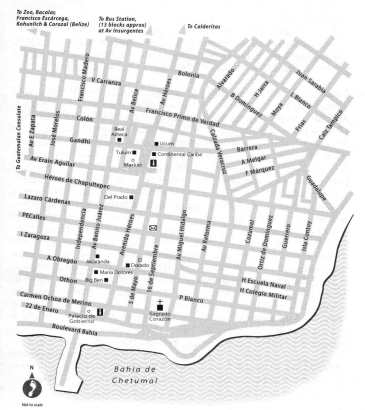

To Zoo, Bacalar, Francisco Escárcega, Kohunlich & Corozal (Belize)
To Bus Station, (13 blocks approx) at Av Insurgentes
To Calderitas

To Guatemalan Consulate

Francisco Madero
V Carranza
Av Belice
Av Héroes
Bolonia
Alvarado
H Jara
B Domínguez
Juan Sarabia
L Blanco
Moya
Fritas
Calz Tampico
Av E Zapata
José Morelos
Colón
Real Azteca
Francisco Primo de Verdad
Gandhi
Ucum
Tulum
Continental Caribe
Calzada Veracruz
Barrera
A Melgar
F Márquez
Av Eraín Aguilar
Market
Héroes de Chapultepec
Guadalupe
Lazaro Cárdenas
Del Prado
PECalles
Independencia
Av Benito Juárez
Avenida Héroes
Av Miguel Hidalgo
Av Reforma
Cozumel
Ortiz de Domínguez
Guerrero
Isla Contoy
I Zaragoza
A Obregón
Jacaranda
El Dorado
María Dolores
Othon
Big Ben
5 de Mayo
16 de Septiembre
H Escuela Naval
H Colegio Militar
Carmen Ochoa de Merino
22 de Enero
Palacio de Gobierno
Sagrado Corazón
P Blanco
Boulevard Bahía

Bahía de Chetumal

N

Not to scale

MEXICO

buses going to the border, US$0.30; taxi from Chetumal to border, 20 minutes, US$6 for two. Buses are often all booked a day ahead especially long distance journeys, so avoid unbooked connections. Expect passport checks on buses leaving for Mexican destinations. Autobuses del Caribe to **Mexico City**, 22 hours, US$40, once a day via **Villahermosa** at 0800 (US$16, 8 hours, the road is bad and it can take longer); also 2 ADO buses to Mexico City, and 3 ADO to Villahermosa; to **Puebla**, US$40; bus to **Escárcega**, 4 between 1300 and 2100, $3\frac{1}{2}$ hours, US$7.25, 2nd class; from Chetumal to **Palenque**, ADO 1st class at 2215, Maya de Oro 1st class at 2200, US$23, 9 hours (2 stops), 2nd class at 2130, US$14.80, otherwise a change is necessary at Emiliano Zapata (bus to there at 0900, 1300, US$11.50), then change again at Catazajá, or Catazajá itself (then take a colectivo), or Escárcega. Lacandonia has 2nd class bus to **San Cristóbal** via Palenque at 2130, US$19. Bus to **Mérida**, luxury US$18.30, US$16.50 1st class (Caribe Express and Autobuses del Caribe), about 7 hours, 2nd class US$13. To **Felipe Carrillo Puerto**, US$3.35, $1\frac{1}{2}$ hours, many, on excellent road. To **Cancún**, 6 hours, boring road, several daily, between 0700 and 2400 (luxury US$17, 1st class US$13.50, 2nd class US$10). To **Tulum**, several 2nd class from 0630, US$7, 1st class from 0700, 4 hours, US$8.50. To **Playa del Carmen**, 1st class US$10, 2nd class US$7. To **Minatitlán**, 12 hours, US$22.50. There are also buses to Veracruz, Campeche, Villahermosa, Córdoba, Xpujil and Puerto Juárez. Green *colectivos* at Francisco Primo de Verdad y Avenida Hidalgo go along the coast to Cancún.

To **Belize**, Batty Bus from ADO to **Belize City**, 5 a day, schedules change frequently, taking $3\frac{1}{2}$-5 hours on paved road, US$8.50, in pesos, US dollars or Belize dollars. Money changers in the bus terminal offer marginally poorer rates than those at the border. Venus Bus to Belize City leaves from the square by Mercado Nuevo on Calzada Veracruz y 2° Circuito Periférico, 3 blocks from main terminal (US$1 taxi ride), morning departures, again frequent schedule changes, first bus leaves at 0600. Be there in good time; they sometimes leave early if full. If intending to stay in Belize City, do not take a bus which arrives at night as it is not recommended to look for a hotel in the dark. Bus Chetumal-**Orange Walk**, $2\frac{1}{2}$ hours, US$4.50. **San Juan Travel** at the main bus station has a direct daily service to Flores (US$30) and Tikal (US$33) in **Guatemala**, at 1430 from ADO terminal, 8 hours to Flores, 6 hours to Tikal.

Directory **Banks** For exchange, *Banamex*, Obregón y Juárez, changes TCs. *Banco Mexicano*, Juárez and Cárdenas, TCs or US$ cash, quick and courteous service. Several on, or near, *Héroes* with ATMs. Banks do not change quetzales into pesos. Good rates at *Bodegas Blanco* supermarket beside bus terminal; will change US dollars and Belize dollars (only if you spend at least 15% of the total on their groceries!). Batty Bus ticket counter will change pesos into Belizean dollars. Try also *Casa Medina*, L Cárdenas. Pemex stations will accept US and Belizean dollars, but at poor rates for the latter. *San Francisco de Assisi* supermarket changes TCs, next to bus station. **Embassies & consulates** *Guatemala* Av Héroes de Chapultepec 354, T26565, open for visas, Mon-Fri 0900-1700. There is a Guatemalan consul in Belize, where **visas to Guatemala** may be obtained, see Guatemala **Information for travellers** for requirements and fees, usually takes 15 minutes, 30 days only available, passport photo and photocopy of passport required. *Belize* Hon Consul, Lic Francisco Lechón Rosas, Av Alvaro Obregón 232-1, T20100; visas usually given in 10 minutes (US$25). **NB** A list of nationalities who do *NOT* need a visa for Belize is given in the Belize **Information for travellers** section. All others **must** have a visa in advance. The surest place to get one is in Mexico City at the Belize Embassy, or in Mérida. **Hospitals & medical services** Malaria prophylaxis available from Centro de Salud, opposite hospital (request tablets for 'paludismo'). **Laundry** *Lavandería Automática* 'Lava facil', corner of Héroes and Confederación Nacional Campesina. **Tour companies & travel agents** *Turismo Maya* at *Hotel Continental Caribe* will arrange flights to and within Belize, T20555. For a trip to Belize, the Cayes, or Guatemala, contact Moisés Vega Beall at the 24-hour restaurant *Arcada*, speaks good English, helpful in finding something to suit your budget and in dealing with paper work, eg immigration. **Tourist offices** *Secretaría Estatal de Turismo*, Av Miguel Hidalgo 22, p1°, esq Carmen Ochoa de Merino. Office on Blvd Bahía and 5 de Mayo, useful city booklet and map of Quintana Roo; also a kiosk in the small plaza on Héroes and Aguilar (closed Sunday).

Mexican customs Mexican customs procedure can be slow particularly at peak holiday times when Belizeans come on charter buses for cheap shopping; over the bridge is Belizean passport control. Visitors who have been to South America recently should check whether they require a health certificate, available from the Centro de Salud at the border. Note that fresh fruit cannot be imported into Belize.

Frontier with Belize

Entering Mexico Tourist cards are available at the border. It has been reported that only 15 days are given but you can get an additional 30 days at the Servicios Migratorios in Chetumal.

Crossing by private vehicle Leaving Mexico by car: go to the Mexican immigration office to register your exit and surrender your vehicle permit and tourist card: very straightforward, no charges. Go to the office to obtain compulsory Belizean insurance (also money changing facilities here). Entering Belize, your car will be registered in your passport.

Exchange Money checked on entering Belize. Excess Mexican pesos are easily changed into Belizean dollars with men waiting just beyond customs on the Belize side, but they are not there to meet the early bus. You can change US for Belizean dollar bills in the shops at the border, but this is not necessary as US$ are accepted in Belize. If you can get a good rate (dollars to pesos) in the bank, it is sometimes better to buy Belizean dollars with pesos in *casas de cambio* than to wait until you enter Belize where the dollar/Belize dollar rate is fixed at 1:2.

Transport It is difficult to hitch to the Belizean border. To hitch once inside Belize, it is best to take the *colectivo* from in front of the hospital (1 block from the bus station, ask) marked 'Chetumal-Santa Elena', US$1. For buses to Belize, see above.

North of Chetumal

Six kilometres north are the stony beaches of **Calderitas**, bus every 30 minutes from Colón, between Belice and Héroes, US$1.80 or taxi, US$5, many fish restaurants. Camping at Calderitas, signposted, OK, US$2.75. 16 kilometres north **Laguna de los Milagros**, a beautiful lagoon for swimming, and 34 kilometres north of Chetumal, on the road to Tulum (page 510), is **Cenote Azul**, over 70 metres deep, with a waterside restaurant serving inexpensive and good seafood and regional food (but awful coffee) until 1800 and a trailer park (Apartado 88, Chetumal, relaxing place to camp; other *cenotes* in area). Both are deserted in the week. About three kilometres north of Cenote Azul is the village of **Bacalar** (nice, but not special) on the Laguna de Siete Colores; swimming and skin-diving; colectivos from terminal (Suchaa) in Chetumal, corner of Miguel Hidalgo y Primo de Verdad, from 0700-1900 every 30 minutes, US$1.60, return from plaza when full, also buses from Chetumal bus station every two hours or so, US$1.60. There is a Spanish fort there overlooking a beautiful shallow, clear, fresh water lagoon; abundant birdlife on the lakeshore. This is the fort of **San Felipe** (■ *entrance US$0.70, small museum*), said to have been built around 1729 by the Spanish to defend the area from the English pirates and smugglers of logwood (there is a plaque praying for protection from the British). The British ships roamed the islands and reefs, looting Spanish galleons laden with gold, on their way from Peru to Cuba. There are many old shipwrecks on the reef and around the Chinchorro Banks, 50 kilometres out in the Caribbean (information kindly provided by Coral Pitkin of the *Rancho Encantado*, see below).

Sleeping and eating Hotel and good restaurants on the Laguna. At Bacalar is *Restaurant La Esperanza*, 1 block north from plaza, thatched barn, good seafood, not expensive. 1 cheap place on the plaza, *Punta y Coma. Orizaba*, 3 blocks from Zócalo, cheap, large menu including vegetarian, recommended. Several lakeside bars also serve meals, mostly fish: *Ojitos*, *Los 6 Hermanos*, *Sian Kaan*, *El Pez de Oro*, *El Fuerte*, but no details on any of these. Camping possible at the end of the road 100 metres from the lagoon, toilets and shower, US$0.10, but lagoon perfect for washing and swimming. *Balneario Ejidal*, with changing facilities and restaurant (good fried fish), recommended; gasoline is sold in a side-street. About 2 kilometres south of Bacalar (on left-hand side of the road going towards the village) is **D** *Hotel Las Lagunas*, very good, wonderful views, helpful, clean, comfortable, hot water, swimming pool and opposite a sweet-water lake; restaurant is poor and overpriced. 3 kilometres north of Bacalar is the resort hotel **AL** *Rancho Encantado*, on the west shore of the lagoon, half-board also available, Apdo 233, Chetumal, T/F98380427 (USA res: T800-7481756 or F505-7510972, PO Box 1644, Taos, New Mexico), with private dock, tour boat, canoes and windsurf boards for rent, private cabins with fridge and hammock, very good. North of Bacalar a direct road (Route 293) runs to Muná, on the road between Mérida and Uxmal.

North of Chetumal are also the unexcavated archaeological sites of **Ichpaatun** (13 kilometres), Oxtancah (14) and Nohochmul (20).

Just after the turn off to Muná, at Cafetal, is an unpaved road east to **Majahual** on the coast (56 kilometres from Cafetal), a peaceful, unspoilt place with clear water and beautiful beaches. Kombi from the bus terminal next to *Hotel Ucum* in Chetumal at 0600, returns 1300. Accommodation at *Restaurant Los Piratas del Caribe*, owned by a French family, simple rooms without bath, excellent restaurant, inexpensive. Excursion possible to Banco Chinchorro offshore, where there is a coral bank and a white sandy beach.

About two kilometres before Majahual a paved road to the left goes to Puerto Bravo and on to Placer and Punta Herrero (in the Sian Ka'an Biosphere Reserve, see above). Three and a half kilometres along this road a right turn goes to the *Sol y Mar* restaurant, with rooms to rent, bathrooms and spaces for RVs, also coconut palms and beach. 10½ kilometres along the Punta Herrero road, again on the right, is *Camidas Trailer Park*, with palm trees, *palapas*, restaurant and restrooms, space for four RVs, US$5 per person, car free.

East of Chetumal

Xcalak
Population: 250
Colour map 4, grid B4

Across the bay from Chetumal, at the very tip of Quintana Roo is Xcalak, which may be reached from Chetumal by private launch (two hours), or by the unpaved road from Cafetal to Majahual, then turning south for 55 kilometres (186 kilometres from Chetumal, suitable for passenger cars but needs skilled driver). Daily colectivos from 0700-1900, from 16 de Septiembre 183 y Mahatma Ghandi (T27701), check return times. Bus runs Friday 1600 and Sunday 0600, returning Saturday morning and Sunday afternoon (details from Chetumal tourist office). Xcalak is a fishing village with a few shops with beer and basic supplies and one small restaurant serving Mexican food. A few kilometres north of Xcalak are two hotels, *Costa de Cocos* and *Villa Caracol*, both American run, latter is good, comfortable *cabañas*, expensive. From, here trips can be arranged to the Banco Chinchorro or to San Pedro, Belize. *Villa Caracol* has sport fishing and diving facilities. In the village you may be able to rent a boat to explore Chetumal Bay and the unspoiled islands of Banco Chinchorro. Do *not* try to walk from Xcalak along the coast to San Pedro, Belize; the route is virtually impassable.

West of Chetumal

Kohunlich
Colour map 4, grid B3

From Chetumal you can visit the fascinating Mayan ruins that lie on the way (route 186) to Escárcega. There are few tourists in this area and few facilities. Take plenty of drinking water. About 25 kilometres from Chetumal at Ucum (fuel), you can turn off five kilometres south to visit **Palmara**, located along the Río Hondo, which borders Belize, swimming holes and restaurant. Just before Francisco Villa (61 kilometres from Chetumal) lie the ruins of **Kohunlich**, 8.4 kilometres south of the main road, one and a half hours' walk, take plenty of water (hitching difficult), where there are fabulous masks (early classic, AD 250-500) set on the side of the main pyramid, still bearing red colouring; they are unique of their kind (allow an hour for the site). 200 metres west of the turning is a *migración* office and a stall selling beer; wait here for buses, which have to stop, but first class will not pick up passengers. Colectivos 'Nicolás Bravo' from Chetumal, or bus marked Zoh Laguna from bus station pass the turning.

Xpujil (119 kilometres from Chetumal, leaded and unleaded fuel is available), has one large pyramid, eighth century AD, recently restored and worth a visit, about one kilometre west of bus terminal/junction. ■ *Open daily 0800-1700, US$2, Sunday free.* If stuck overnight there is accommodation in Xpujil in *cabañas* (**D**) at *Hotel El Mirador Maya*, a bit run-down but has a good restaurant. *Restaurant Calakmul* has *cabañas* (**D**), T/F29162, PO Box 24640, with mosquito nets and fan, some with bath, basic, restaurant good, recommended.

Xpujil
Colour map 4, grid B3

Seven kilometres beyond Xpujil lies the large Maya site of Becán shielded by the forest with wild animals still wandering among the ruins, surrounded by a water-less moat and a low wall, now collapsed, with vast temples and plazas and a decayed ball court (site is visible from the road, RVs may be parked at the ruins, no facilities). ■ *0800-1700 every day, US$2, Sunday free, lots of mosquitoes.*

Becán

Two kilometres further on and 10 minutes down a paved road lies Chicanná, with a superb late classic Maya temple with an ornate central door which has been formed in the shape of the open-fanged jaws of the plumed serpent. A 10-minute path leads from the first site to a second, which has a pyramid with lovely Chac masks (about one hour is enough to see both sites). At Chicanná there is **AL** *Ramada Chicanná Eco Village*, in Mexico City T57053996, F55352966, in Campeche T98162233, 100 rooms in thatched cabins, restaurant, bar, pool, jacuzzi, solar heating, rainwater showers etc, most waste recycled. No camping permitted at either site.

Chicanná
Colour map 4, grid B2

Two sites, a bit further away, accessible from Xpujil village are **Hormiguero** (Hill of the Ants), and **Río Bec**. Helmut Zettl (Ebergassing) writes: "The latter was discovered in 1912 by an American, but was lost for almost 60 years. It was rediscovered in 1973 by an American couple who were researching a documentary on the Maya and were shown the overgrown temple by a *chiclero*. Try to find a driver and guide in Xpujil to make the six to seven hours' expedition, well worth it, but only possible in the dry season (December-March)." Recommended is Serge 'Checo' Rion, Avenida Insurgentes 1033, Col La Unidad, 77000, Chetumal, F(983)24514, US$200 for five to six people in four-wheel drive, full day's trip.

On either side of the Chetumal-Francisco Escárcega road at this point stretches the **Calakmul Biosphere Reserve** (south it reaches to the Guatemala border). 180 species of birds have been registered here, including the endangered king vulture, two species of eagle, and others. At Km 98 on the Escárcega road is a paved turn off (65 kilometres, one and a quarter hours) to the ruins of **Calakmul**, which are undergoing restoration. The government is now suggesting that Calakmul was the largest of all Mayan sites with about 1,500 structures. There are some 116 carved monuments studied so far but most of the inscriptions have been eroded. One theory is that Calakmul, or Oxte'tun, which was its old name, was an important centre, maybe the capital of the Serpent's Head Kingdom. There is evidence that the kingdom attacked Palenque in 599 and 611 AD and Tikal, another superpower, in 657. In 695 the king, Pata de Jaguar, attacked Tikal again but was defeated, and from this time the influence of Calakmul declined, with a loss of power and prestige. ■ *Entrance US$3 per car, US$1.50 per person.*

Calakmul
Colour map 4, grid B2

Transport Buses leave from Chetumal bus terminal along the road to Francisco Villa and Xpujil, passing the entrance to Becán. Many taxis and colectivos in Xpujil for the ruins (US$8 for taxi includes waiting time). 2nd class buses from Chetumal to Xpujil at 0630, 1200, 1400, 1930 (confirm all prices with bus station) and others later, stopping service, 4 hours; 1st class (direct), US$3.30, 0900,1130, 1230, 1300 and others; 2nd class fare Chetumal-Francisco Villa US$1.65, 1 hour 10 minutes, Francisco Villa-Xpujil US$2.20, 2 hours 20 minutes. Last bus from

Xpujil to Chetumal at 1700 (1st class ADO); similarly, last bus back from Becán is just before 1700. Taxi from Xpujil to Chicanná costs US$5, 30 minutes. Bus from Cancún (goes on to Villahermosa), leaves at 1700, US$13.50, 6 hours, returns Cancún 0700 (ADO). Colectivos, a bit more expensive, leave from east of the electricity plant in Chetumal. Xpujil, Becán and Chicanná are in Campeche state and, at the state border, passports and tourist cards must be shown.

Maps of roads in Quintana Roo are obtainable in Chetumal at Junta Local de Caminos, Secretaría de Obras Públicas.

Mexico City

Baja California

A land of hot, parched deserts, but deserts of infinite variety and everchanging land-scapes, clothed in a fascinating array of hardy vegetation. Most visitors find Baja a magical place of blue skies, fresh air, solitude and refuge from the rat race north of the border.

The land

Baja California (Lower California) is that long narrow arm which dangles south-wards from the US border between the Pacific and the Gulf of California for 1,300 kilometres. It is divided administratively into the states of Baja California and Baja California Sur, with a one hour time change at the state line. The average width is only 80 kilometres. Rugged and almost uninhabited mountains split its tapering length. Only the southern tip gets enough rain: the northern half gets its small quota during the winter, the southern half during the summer. Not only the north-ern regions near the USA, but also the southern Cape zone are attracting increas-ing numbers of tourists. The US dollar is preferred in most places north of La Paz.

Stretching 1,704 kilometres from Tijuana to Cabo San Lucas, Highway 1 is gen-erally in good repair, although slightly narrow and lacking hard shoulders. Roads in the north are more potholed than those in Baja California Sur. Service stations are placed at adequate intervals along it, but motorists should fill their tanks at every opportunity and carry spare fuel, particularly if venturing off the main roads. Stations in small towns may not have fuel, or may sell from barrels at inflated prices. The same conditions apply for Highways 5 (Mexicali-San Felipe), 3 (Tecate-Ensenada-San Felipe road) and 2 (Tijuana 196 Mexicali-San Luís-Sonoita). Hitchhiking is difficult, and there is very little public transport off the main highway.

The costs of food and accommodation are more expensive than the rest of Mex-ico, but less than in the USA. Tijuana, Ensenada and La Paz all have a good range of duty-free shopping. Stove fuel is impossible to find in Baja California Sur. Beware of overcharging on buses and make a note of departure times of buses in Tijuana or Ensenada when travelling south: between Ensenada and Santa Rosalía it is very difficult to obtain bus timetable information, even at bus stations. Don't ask for English menus if you can help it, prices often differ from the Spanish version. Always check change, overcharging is rife. Note also that hotels have widely diver-gent winter and summer rates; between June and November tariffs are normally lower than those given in the text below (especially in expensive places).

Border crossing There is no immigration check on the Mexican side of the border. The buffer zone for about 120 kilometres south of the frontier allows US citizens to travel without a tourist card. Some have reported travelling in Baja Cali-fornia Sur without a tourist card. If you are bringing in a vehicle you should try to get a tourist card/vehicle permit in Tijuana (see page 528); if you are travelling beyond Baja California, with or without a vehicle, getting a tourist card in Tijuana will save a lot of trouble later. Immigration authorities are also encountered at Mexicali, at Ensenada, at Quitovac, 28 kilometres south of Sonoita (Sonora) on Highway 2, and when boarding the ferries to cross the Gulf. Ferries ply from Pichilingüe (north of La Paz) and Santa Rosalía to various places on the mainland (see text). As a car needs an import permit, make sure you get to the ferry with lots of time and preferably with a reservation if going on the Pichilingüe-Mazatlán ferry. (See under La Paz below.)

Insurance and Medical Services Insurance covering bodily injury is not available locally. Motorcycle insurance costs about US$3 a day. If you require X-ray facilities after an accident it appears that the only place between Tijuana and Los Cabos with X-ray equipment and an on-call technician is Ciudad Constitución.

Maps There are only two really comprehensive maps: the road map published by the ACSC, which gives highly detailed road distances (but in miles) and conditions, and which is available only to AAA members (the AAA also publishes a *Guide to Baja California* for members only); and International Travel Map (ITM) Production's *Baja California 1:1,000,000* (second edition 1992-93), which includes extra geographical and recreational detail on a topographic base. Many specialist maps and guides are available in book stores in Southern California. Both guidebooks and maps are sadly rare in Baja itself.

History

Cortés attempted to settle at La Paz in 1534 after one of his expeditions had brought the first Europeans to set foot in Baja, but the land's sterile beauty disguised a chronic lack of food and water; this and sporadic Indian hostility forced the abandonment of most early attempts at settlement. Jesuit missionary fathers arrived at Loreto in 1697 and founded the first of their 20 missions. The Franciscans and then Dominicans took over when the Jesuits were expelled in 1767. The fathers were devoted and untiring in their efforts to convert the peninsula's three ethnic groups, but diseases introduced unknowingly by them and by ships calling along the coasts soon tragically decimated Indian numbers; some Indians remain today, but without tribal organization. Scattered about the Sierras are the remains of 30 of these well-meaning but lethal missions, some beautifully restored, others only eroded adobe foundations. Most are within easy reach from Highway 1, although four-wheel drive is necessary for remoter sites such as San Pedro Mártir and Dolores del Sur.

Today's population of about 2.8 million has increased by two-thirds in the past decade through migration from Mexico's interior and Central Pacific coast.

Economy

The development of agriculture, tourism, industry, migrant labour from California, and the opening of the Transpeninsular Highway has caused an upsurge of economic growth and consequently of prices, especially in areas favoured by tourists.

The Morelos dam on the upper reaches of the Colorado River has turned the Mexicali valley into a major agricultural area: 400,000 acres under irrigation to grow cotton and olives. The San Quintín Valley and the Magdalena Plain are other successful areas where crops have been wrenched from the desert. Industries are encouraged in all border regions by investment incentives; called *maquiladoras*, they are foreign-owned enterprises which import raw materials without duty, manufacture in Mexico and ship the products back to the United States.

Crossing into Mexico

Celexico (USA)/ Mexicali The border is open 24 hours a day for all formalities. Day visitors may prefer to park on the California side, since the extremely congested Avenida Cristóbal Colón, which parallels the frontier fence, is the only access to the US port of entry; entering Mexico, follow the diagonal Calzada López Mateos, which leads to the tourist office and train and bus stations. Mexican automobile insurance is readily available on both sides of the border.

Pedestrians travelling from Mexicali to Calexico should take the underpass beneath Calzada López Mateos, which passes through the utterly indifferent Mexican immigration office before continuing to the US side.

Highway 2 runs east from Mexicali through San Luis Río Colorado, Sonoita and Caborca to join the Pacific Highway at Santa Ana; see page 180.

Mexicali

Population: 850,000
State population 1995: 2,108,118
Phone code: 65
Colour map 1, grid A1

Capital of Baja California, Mexicali is not as geared to tourism as Tijuana and thus retains its busy, business-like border town flavour. It is a good place to stock up on supplies, cheap clothing and footware, and souvenirs.

The new **Centro Cívico-Comercial**, Calzada López Mateos, is an ambitious urban development comprising government offices, medical school, hospitals, bull-ring, bus station, cinemas, etc.

Sights The **City Park**, in the southwest sector, contains a zoo, picnic area and **natural history museum**. ■ *Tuesday-Friday 0900-1700; weekend 0900-1800).* University of Baja California's **Regional Museum**, Avenida Reforma y Calle L, has interesting exhibits illustrating Baja's archaeology, ethnography and missions. ■ *Tuesday-Friday 0900-1800, weekend 1000-1500, admission free.* **Galería de la Ciudad**, Avenida Obregón 1209, between Calle D y E, former state governor's residence, features work of Mexican painters, sculptors and photographers. ■ *Monday-Friday 0900-2000.* There are *charreadas* (rodeos), held on Sunday during the April-October season, at two separate *charro* grounds on eastern and western outskirts of Mexicali. Mexicali has numerous Chinese restaurants, the legacy of immigration which began in Sonora in the late 19th century.

Calexico, the much smaller city on the California side of the border, is so thoroughly Mexicanized that it can be difficult to find a newspaper from San Diego or Los Angeles. Mexican shoppers flock here for clothing bargains.

Sleeping **AL** *Crowne Plaza*, Blvd López Mateos y Av de los Héroes 201, T573600, F570555. **AL** *Holiday Inn*, Blvd Benito Juárez 2220, T65661300, F664901, a/c, best in town. Also **A** *Castel Calafía*, Calzada Justo Sierra 1495, T682841, a/c, plain but comfortable, dining room. **A** *Lucerna*, Blvd Juárez 2151, T541000, a/c, meeting rooms, bar, nightclub. **B** *Del Norte*, C Melgar y Av Francisco Madero, T540575, some a/c and TV, across from border crossing, pleasant but a little noisy, has free parking for guests and offers discount coupons for breakfast and dinner in its own restaurant. **C** *La Siesta*, Justo Sierra 899, T541100, reasonable, coffee shop. **D** *Rivera*, near the railway station, a/c, best of the cheaper hotels. *Fortín de las Flores*, Av Cristóbal Colón 612, T524522, and **D** *Las Fuentes*, Blvd López Mateos 1655, T571525, both with a/c and TV but noisy, tolerable if on a tight budget.

Motels **B-C** *Azteca de Oro*, C Industria 600, T571433, opposite the train station and only a few blocks from the bus terminal, a/c, TV, a bit scruffy but convenient. Others around town and in Calexico just across the border around east 4th St. **B-C** *Hotel De Anza*, on the Calexico side, excellent value for money.

Youth hostel Avenida Salina Cruz y Coahuila 2050, CP 21050, T551230.

Many good nightclubs on Avenida Justo Sierra, and on your left as you cross border, several **Night life**
blocks away.

Air Airport (MXL) 25 kilometres east, Boulevard Aviación; flights to Mexico City, Guadalajara, **Transport**
Hermosillo, La Paz, Mazatlán, Monterrey, and San Antonio (Texas). Charter services.

   Trains The railway station to the south is about 3½ kilometres from the tourist area on
the border and Calle 3 bus connects it with the nearby bus terminal. There were no services
in 1999. Internet: refer to URLs www.trainweb.com/travel/mexico.html; mexican.railspot.
com/; www.celorio.com/ferro/mexlist/mexlist.html.

   Buses Tijuana, 3 hours, US$16.50 luxury liner, US$6.50 1st class, US$5 2nd class, sit on
right for views at the Cantú Grade; **San Felipe**, 3 hours, 4 a day, US$7, **Guadalajara**, US$77.
Mazatlán, US$50. **Hermosillo**, 10 hours, US$22. **Mexico City**, US$96. **Ensenada**, US$9.
Santa Rosalía, US$33. **La Paz**, daily 1630, 24 hours, US$60.50. All trips leave from the new
central bus station (Camionera Central) on Avenida Independencia; 4 major bus companies
have their offices here. Autotransportes Tres Estrellas de Oro serves both Baja and the mainland. Golden State buses from Mexicali to Los Angeles (US$40) tickets available at
trailer/kiosk across from *Hotel del Norte*. Greyhound from Los Angeles to Calexico (901 Imperial Avenue), US$33, 6 hours. San Diego to Calexico via El Centro, US$20, 3 to 4 hours. The
1200 bus from San Diego connects with the Pullman bus to Mazatlán, US$40, 21 hours. Local
buses are cheap, about US$0.55. 'Central Camionera' bus to Civic Centre and bus station.

Airline offices *Mexicana*, T535402. *Taesa*, T663921. *AeroMéxico*, T91-800-90999. **Banks** All major **Directory**
banks: currency exchange is only from 0900-1330. *Casas de cambio* in Calexico give a slightly better
rate. Several *cambios* on López Mateos. **Tourist offices** *State Tourism Office*, C Comercio, between
Reforma and Obregón ('Centro Cívico' bus); better is *Tourist and Convention Bureau*, Calzada López
Mateos y C Camelias, helpful, English spoken, open Monday-Friday 0800-1900, Saturday 0900-1300.
The Procuraduría de Protección al Turista, which provides legal assistance for visitors, is in the same
building as the State Tourism office.

San Felipe

Paved Highway 5 heads south from Mexicali 196 kilometres to San Felipe, passing at *Population: 13,000*
about Km 34 the Cerro Prieto geothermal field. After passing the Río Hardy (one of *Colour map 1, grid A2*
the peninsula's few permanent rivers) and the **Laguna Salada** (Km 72), a vast dry
alkali flat unless turned into a muddy morass by rare falls of rain, the road continues
straight across sandy desert until entering San Felipe around a tall, white, dou-
ble-arched monument. Floods can cut the road across the Laguna Salada; when it is
closed, motorists have to use Highway 3 from Ensenada to get to San Felipe.

   San Felipe is a pleasant, tranquil fishing and shrimping port on the Gulf of California with a population of about 13,000, with about 3,000 North American RV temporary residents and a further 3,000 on winter weekends. Long a destination for devoted
sportfishermen and a weekend retreat for North Americans, San Felipe is now experiencing a second discovery, with new trailer parks and the paving of many of the town's
sandy streets. A public library is planned, recycling plant, artificial breakwater reef and
two golf courses are under construction. Even the *Las Macetas* hotel (the 'grey ghost')
may see completion in the near future. There is an airport eight kilometres south. San
Felipe is protected from desert winds by the coastal mountains and is unbearably hot
during the summer; in winter the climate is unsurpassed, and on weekends it can
become overcrowded and noisy. A good view of the wide sandy beach can be had from
the Virgin of Guadalupe shrine near the lighthouse.

AL *Aquamarina Condohotel and Villas*, 4 kilometres south on Punta Estrella Rd, cheaper **Sleeping**
Sunday-Thursday, on beach, pool, attractive rooms, a/c. **AL** *Castel*, Av Misión de Loreto 148,
T71282, a/c, 2 pools, tennis etc, best in town. **B** *La Trucha Vagabunda*, Mar Báltico, near *El
Cortés Motel*, T71333, also a few RV spaces and *Restaurant Alfredo* (Italian), seafood, interna-
tional cuisine. **B** *Vagabond Inn*, on same street, 3 kilometres south of town, a/c, pool and

beach. **B** *Villa del Mar*, pool, volley ball court, restaurant. **C** *Fiesta San Felipe*, 9 kilometres south on the airport road, isolated, every room has Gulf view, tennis, pool, restaurant, VAT (IVA) not included in bill. **C** *Riviera*, 1 kilometre south on coastal bluff, T71185, a/c, pool, spa, restaurant.

Motels **B** *Chapala*, some a/c, free coffee, clean but pricey, on beachfront, T71240. **B** *El Capitán*, Mar de Cortés 298, T71303, a/c, some balconies, pool, lovely rancho-style building, hard beds but otherwise OK. **B** *El Cortés*, on Av Mar de Cortés, T71055, beachside esplanade, a/c, pool, palapas on beach, launching ramp, disco, restaurant. **C** *El Pescador*, T71044, Mar de Cortés and Calzada Chetumal, a/c, modest but comfortable.

Camping Many trailer parks and campgrounds in town and on coast to north and south, including **D** *El Faro Beach and Trailer Park*, on the bay 18 kilometres south. **E** *Ruben's, Playa Bonita, La Jolla, Playa de Laura, Mar del Sol*, and the more primitive *Campo Peewee* and *Pete's Camp*, both about 10 kilometres north.

Eating *Green House*, Av Mar de Cortés 132 y Calzada Chetumal, good food, beef or chicken *fajitas* a speciality, friendly service, cheap breakfasts, 'fish filet for a fiver'! 0730-0300 daily. *Clam Man's Restaurant*, Calzada Chetumal, 2 blocks west of Pemex station, used to belong to the late, famous Pasqual 'The Clam Man', oddly decorated, but excellent clams, steamed, fried, barbecued, at budget prices. *Los Misiones* in *Mar del Sol* RV park, small menu, moderately-priced, seafood crêpes a speciality, popular with families, good service. *Las Redes*, Mar de Cortés Sur. *Ruben's Place*, Junípero Serra, both favourites for seafood. *El Toro II*, Chetumal, Mexican and American food, popular for breakfasts; other pleasant places on Av Mar de Cortés: *Corona*, No 348; *El Nido*, grilled fish and steaks (closed Wednesday), No 358; *Puerto Padre*, Cuban; *George's*, No 336, steaks, seafood, live music, pleasant, friendly, popular with US residents, recommended.

Festivals *Navy Day* is celebrated on **1 June** with a carnival, street dancing and boat races.

Transport Transportes ABC and TNS buses to **Ensenada**, direct, over the mountains, at 0800 and 1800, 3½ hours, US$9. Bus to **Mexicali** US$8, 4 a day from 0730, 2 hours. Hitching to Mexicali is not difficult (much traffic), but beware the desert sun. Bus station is on Mar Báltico near corner of Calzada Chetumal, in town centre.

Directory **Tourist office** *Mar de Cortés y Manzanillo*, opposite *El Capitán Motel*, helpful, little handout material, open Tues-Sun 0900-1400 and 1600-1800.

Coastal route south of San Felipe

Puertecitos
Colour map 1, grid A2
The road south has been paved as far as Puertecitos, a straggling settlement mainly of North American holiday homes. There is an airstrip, a simple grocery store, a Pemex station and **Campo Los Chinos**, US$7 per tent, basic toilets, intermittent water. Nice beach. Fishing is good outside the shallow bay and there are several tidal hot springs at the southeast point. The road continues south along the coast (well graded with improvements continuing, acceptable for standard vehicles), leading to the tranquil **Bahía San Luís Gonzaga**, on which are the basic resorts of Papa Fernández and Alfonsinas (hotel, **D**, hot water, good but expensive restaurant); the beach here is pure sand and empty. From here, the 'new' road heads west over hills to meet Highway 1 near Laguna Chapala, 53 kilometres south of Cataviña, opening up a circular route through northern Baja California. Between the bay and Highway 1 is *Coco's Corner*, a friendly pit stop, offering meals and, if stranded, basic accommodation.

Coastal route west of Mexicali

The road from Mexicali west to Tijuana is fast and well surfaced, it runs across barren desert flats, below sea level and with organ-pipe cacti in abundance, until reaching the eastern escarpment of the peninsula's spine; it winds its way up the Cantú Grade to **La Rumorosa**, giving expansive, dramatic vistas of desert and mountain. The numerous wrecked trucks and cars which litter the canyons along the Cantú Grade, together with countless crosses, emphasize the need for careful driving and better than adequate brakes. If pulling off the highway for the view, do so only on wide shoulders with good visibility in both directions. La Rumorosa, sited high enough on a boulder-strewn plateau to receive a sprinkling of snow in winter, has a service station. There are three more Pemex stations along the highway before it reaches Tecate after 144 kilometres.

Crossing into Mexico

Tecate

The border crossing is open from 0700-2400. To get to border immigration facilities, go north three blocks, uphill, from the west side of the Parque. You will pass the theatre. Mexican offices are on the left, US on the right. The orderly and friendly Mexican immigration and customs officers will only process vehicle papers between 0800 and 1600; at other hours, continue to Mexicali or Sonoita. All documents obtainable at the border. Tourist cards may also be obtained at the bus terminal; services to the interior resemble those from Tijuana (Tres Estrellas de Oro to Mexico City, US$93.50).

Tecate
Population: 40,000
Colour map 1, grid A1

Visitors will find that placid Tecate more resembles a Mexican city of the interior rather than a gaudy border town, perhaps because there is no population centre on the US side. It is a pleasant place to break the journey, especially around the shady Parque Hidalgo, where families promenade on weekends.

Brewing is the most important local industry; the landmark Tecate Brewery, which produces Tecate and Carta Blanca beers, offers tours on the first three Saturdays of the month between 0800 and 1200. There are many *maquiladora* industries.

Northern Baja California

USA

Tijuana
Rosarito Tecate
2 Calexico
3 La Rumorosa MEXICALI
Laguna
Salada
Ensenada San Luis Río
Colorado
Parque
Nacional
Maneadero Constitución
de 1857
Santo Tomás Golfo de
Santa
San Clara
Vicente Crucero la
Trinidad
Parque
Colonet Nacional
Sierra San
Pedro-Martir
Pacific Picacho San Felipe
Ocean del Diablo
San Quintín

El Rosario Puertecitos

Punta
N Baja

Cataviña *Bahía
San Luis
Gonzaga*

0 km 50
0 miles 31

To Sonoita

Sleeping A *Motel El Dorado*, Juárez 1100, T41102, a/c, central, comfortable. C *Hotel Hacienda*, Juárez 861, T41250, a/c, clean. C *Hotel Paraíso*, Aldrete 83, T41716. 10 kilometres south of Tecate, on the road to Ensenada, is A *Rancho Tecate*, T40011. Budget-minded travellers may try E *Hotel México*, Juárez 230, gloomy rooms with or without bath, rumoured to be a staging post for unauthorized border crossings. D *Hotel Frontera*, Callejón Madero 131, T41342, basic but clean and friendly, is probably a step up in quality (Antonio Moller Ponce, who resides here, is knowledgeable on the area's history and ethnohistory).

Eating Excellent Mexican and Italian specialities at *El Passetto*, Libertad 200 near Parque Hidalgo. Many other good ones.

Directory Tourist office The Baja California Secretary of Tourism, opposite the park at Libertad 1305, provides a useful map of the town and other information. English spoken.

The highway continues west past the Rancho La Puerta, a spa and physical fitness resort, strictly for the rich, vegetarian meals, petrol station. Leaving the Rodríguez Reservoir behind, Highway 2 enters the industrial suburb of La Mesa and continues into Tijuana as a four-lane boulevard, eventually to become Avenida Revolución, one of the city's main shopping streets.

A new alternative to Route 2 is the only completed segment of the four-lane Tijuana-Mexicali motorway, between Tecate and Otay Mesa, Tijuana. It is very fast, but carries almost no traffic because of the US$4 toll.

Crossing into Mexico

San Diego (USA)/ Tijuana

There is no passport check at the border, although US freeways funnelling 12 lanes of traffic into three on the Mexican side means great congestion, particularly at weekends. A quieter recommended alternative is the **Otay Mesa** crossing (open 0600-2200) eight kilometres east of Tijuana, reached from the US side by SR-117. Traffic is less frantic and parking much easier but car insurance and vehicle permit facilities are no longer available here. From the Mexican side it is harder to find: continue on the bypass from Highway 1-D to near the airport to 'Garita de Otay' sign.

If travelling on into Mexico, don't follow the crowds who cross without visiting immigration: try to deal with US exit formalities and get an entry stamp at the border as it will avoid serious problems later on. Be sure to get an entry stamp on your tourist card as well as your passport. The Migración office is difficult to find: try the right hand lane marked 'Customs'. When entering with a vehicle or motorcycle you should be able to obtain your tourist card/vehicle permit at this office, then you are supposed to get a stamp from a vehicle registry office about 100 metres south. The officials will ask for copies of your documents, including the vehicle permit. As they have no photocopier you can look for the copy shop opposite, above a liquor store, or return to the USA, go two blocks north and look for the mail box rental company opposite the *Jack-in-the-Box*. There is an immigration office for tourist cards and vehicle documents on the righthand side of Highway 1 as it enters Ensenada. Alternatively, you can forget the stamp and hope you won't be asked for it later (do not do this if going beyond Baja California). If entering by bicycle, go to 'secondary', the immigration area to the right, where an official will process your tourist card to travel beyond Ensenada. Cyclists are not allowed on highway 1-D (the toll road), so head for Highway 1 (libre) to Ensenada. Going into the USA, be prepared for tough immigration procedures.

If entering without a vehicle, you can get a tourist card from Tijuana airport or at the bus terminal; there is no passport check at the border but there is a small immigration office for entry stamps. Money changers operate in the shopping centre 200 metres from the border and opposite this is the bus stop for the bus terminal. A tourist office at the border gives out maps of the border area explaining money changing, buses, etc. When leaving the USA without a vehicle, you can ask a security guard at the footbridge to take your US entry card to the US immigration office, as there is no passport check on the US side. You can send your card to a US Consulate.

Immigration officials are reluctant to grant visa extensions; you need to get one at your next port of call.

Those visiting Tijuana for the day often find it easier to park on the San Ysidro side and walk across the footbridge to the city centre. (Parking fees near the border range from US$5 to US$7 per 24 hours.) Alternatively, the 'San Diego Trolley' is an entertaining way to reach the border, taking visitors from downtown San Diego to 'la línea' from US$1-3; departures every 15 minutes between 0500 and 0100 (tickets sold from machines at stops). There is a visitor information kiosk at the Trolley's southern terminus.

Tijuana

On the Pacific, where 35 million people annually cross the border, fuelling the city's claim to be 'the world's most visited city'. It came to prominence with Prohibition in the United States in the 1920s when Hollywood stars and thirsty Americans flocked to the sleazy bars and enterprising nightlife of Tijuana and Mexicali. Today, tourism is the major industry; although countless bars and nightclubs still vie for the visitor's dollar, it is duty-free bargains, horse racing and inexpensive English-speaking dentists which attract many visitors. This area is much more expensive than further south, especially at weekends. Modern Tijuana is Mexico's fourth-largest city and one of the most prosperous.

Population: 1.5m
Phone code: 66
Colour map 1, grid A1

The **Centro Cultural**, Paseo de los Héroes y Avenida Independencia contains a museum, excellent book *Las Californias*, handicraft shops, restaurant, concert hall, and the ultra-modern spherical Omnimax cinema, where three films are shown on a 180° screen, best to sit at the back/top so you don't have to lean too far back: English performance at 1400 daily, US$4.50, Spanish version at 1900 costs US$3.75. The **Casa de la Cultura** is a multi-arts cultural centre with a 600-seat theatre. The Cathedral of **Nuestra Señora de Guadalupe** is at Calle 2. The **Jai-Alai Palace** (Palacio Frontón) is at Avenida Revolución y Calle 7; games begin at 2000 nightly except Wednesday, spectators may bet on each game. Tijuana has two bullrings, the **Plaza de Toros Monumental** at Playas de Tijuana (the only one in the world built on the sea shore). A few metres away is an obelisk built into the border chain-link fence commemorating the Treaty of Guadalupe Hidalgo, 1848, which fixed the frontier between Mexico and the USA. **El Toreo** bullring is three kilometres east of downtown on Búlevard **Agua Caliente**; *corridas* alternate between the two venues between May and September; Sunday at 1600 sharp. Tickets from US$4.50 (*sol*) to US$16 (sombra). Horse and dog racing is held at the Agua Caliente track, near the Tijuana Country Club; horse racing Saturday and Sunday from 1200; greyhound meetings Wednesday-Monday at 1945, Monday, Wednesday, Friday at 1430. Admission US$0.50, reserved seats US$1. *Charreadas* take place each Sunday from May to September at one of four grounds, free. Tourism office will give up-to-date information. A walk along the barrio beside the border (don't go alone) to see the breached fence will demonstrate the difference between the first and third worlds.

Sights
If entering from the USA: it is easier to sightsee in Tijuana without luggage, so stay in San Diego and make a day excursion before travelling on.

LL *Fiesta Americana Tijuana*, Blvd Agua Caliente 4500, T817000, heated pool, suites, etc, first rate. **AL-A** *Country Club*, Blvd Agua Caliente y Tapachula 1, T817733, F817066. *Hacienda de Río*, Blvd Sánchez Taboada 10606, T848644, F848620. *La Mesa Inn*, Blvd Díaz Ordaz 50 y Gardenia, T816522, F812871. *Centenario Plaza*, Blvd Agua Caliente 22400, T818183. *Lucerna*, Héroes y Av Rodríguez in new Río Tijuana development, T841000, a/c, pool, piano bar, popular with business travellers. *Paraíso-Radisson*, Blvd Agua Caliente 1 at the Country Club, T817200, pool, sauna, bar, a/c, etc. **A-B** *El Conquistador*, Blvd Agua Caliente 700, T817955, colonial style, a/c, pool, sauna, disco. **B** *Calinda Tijuana*, near the Paraíso-Radisson, a/c, pool, disco, convention centre. **B** *Palacio Azteca*, Highway 1 South, T865301, a/c, modern, cocktail bar, extensively remodelled, in older, congested part of city. **B-C** *Hotel Caesar*, C 5 y Av Revolución, T851606, a/c, restaurant, decorated with bullfight posters, unique character, good. **C** *La Villa de Zaragoza*, behind the Jai-Alai *frontón*, a/c, comfortable. **C** *Nelson*, Av Revolución 502, T854302, central, simple clean rooms, coffee shop.

Sleeping
■ *on maps*
Price codes:
see inside front cover

D *Adelita*, hot showers, cockroaches, basic, C 4 2017. **D** *Hotel del Pardo*, C 5 y Niños Héroes, acceptable, noisy in parts. **D** *París*, C 5 1939, adequate, value-for-money budget hotel. **D** *Rey*, C 4 2021, central, old but comfortable. **D** *St Francis*, Benito Juárez 2, more with bath, central, recommended. **E** *Hotel del Mar*, C 1 1448, opposite *Nelson*, central but in a poor section, communal bathroom, good budget hotel. Recommended along Calle Baja California are **E** *Hotel Virrey* and **E** *Pensión Noche Buena*, irregular water supply; nearby and as good are **D** *Rivas*, on Constitución, friendly, clean, a little noisy; **E** *Fénix*, Miguel Martínez 355;

E *Machado*, restaurant, basic, reasonable, C 1 No 1724; **E** *San Jorge*, Av Constitución 506, old but clean, basic.

Motels **B-C** *León*, C 7 1939, T856320. **C-D** *La Misión*, in Playas de Tijuana near the bullring, T806612, modern, a/c, restaurant, pool, popular with businessmen. **D** *Golf*, T862021, opposite each other on Blvd Agua Caliente, next to *Tijuana Country Club*, both OK, and **D** *Padre Kino*, T864208, an older-type motel.

Youth hostel T832680/822760, far from centre, Vía Ote y Puente Cuauhtémoc, Zona del Río, dirty, not recommended, inexpensive cafetería on premises, open 0700-2300.

Eating *Tijuana Tilly's*, excellent meal, reasonably priced. *La Leña*, downtown on Av Revolución between C 4 y 5, excellent food and service, beef and Mexican specialities; countless others, including new complex near border crossing. *Casa del Taco*, Revolución y Hidalgo, has taco buffet.

Night life **Nightclubs** Recommended: *Flamingos*, south on old Ensenada Rd. *Chantecler*.

Shopping The Plaza Río Tijuana Shopping Centre, Paseo de Los Héroes, is a new retail development; opposite are the Plaza Fiesta and Plaza del Zapato malls, the latter specializing in footware. Nearby is the colourful public market. Downtown shopping area is Avs Revolución and Constitución. Bargaining is expected at smaller shops, and everyone except bus drivers is happy to accept US currency.

Transport **Air** Rodríguez airport (TIJ), 17 kilometres, 20 minutes from San Diego, CA; cheaper flights

Tijuana

than from the US. Prices vary considerably so shop around. Lots of flights to Mexico City, also to Acapulco, Aguascalientes, Cancún, Chihuahua, Ciudad Juárez, Colima, Cuernavaca, Culiacán, Durango, Guadalajara, Hermosillo, La Paz, León, Los Mochis, Mazatlán, Mérida, Monterrey, Morelia, Oaxaca, Puebla, Puerto Vallarta, Reynosa, San Luís Potosí, Tampico, Tepic, Torreón, Uruapan and Zacatecas . Also Los Angeles in the USA. Taxi between airport and centre is quoted at US$15 (bargaining may be possible from centre to airport); colectivo from airport to border, 'La Línea', US$3.20. Mexicoach run from San Diego to Tijuana airport for US$15, combination bus to Plaza La Jolla and taxi to airport.

Buses Local buses about US$0.30, taxis ask US$10 (but shouldn't be that much), 'Central Camionera' or 'Buena Vista' buses to bus station, downtown buses to border depart from Calle 2 near Avenida Revolución. Local buses also go to the border from the bus station, every 30 minutes up to 2300, marked 'La Línea/Centro', US$0.50. New bus station is 5 kilometres southeast of centre on the airport road at the end of Vía Ote (at La Mesa). It is very crowded and inefficient; take advantage of toilet facilities as long distance buses are usually so full of luggage and goods that getting to the toilet at the back is impossible. There is a bank which changes travellers' cheques. Parking at bus terminal US$1 per hour. To **Mexico City** (every couple of hours) 1st class (Tres Estrellas de Oro, T869515/869060), normal about 38-45 hours, US$100, express US$110, poor, expensive food at stops, *plus* service US$115, or special (with video and more comfort), US$132, 38 hours. (Transportes del Pacífico, similar fares, express only). 2nd class (Transportes del Norte de Sonora), US$86. Other 1st class routes: **Guadalajara**, 36 hours, US$82.50; **Hermosillo**, 12 hours, US$35; **Los Mochis**, 22 hours, US$53, Tres Estrellas de Oro; **Mazatlán**, 29 hours, US$62.75; Sonoita US$16.50, Culiacán US$54; Querétaro US$99. By ABC line: **Ensenada**, about hourly 0500-2400, 1$\frac{1}{2}$ hours, US$2.90, bus leaves from behind Centro Comercial at border; **Mexicali**, hourly from 0500-2200, US$6.50 first class; **San Quintín**, 7 a day, US$7.15; **Santa Rosalía**, 1600, direct, US$37; La Paz, 0800, US$60.50, packed full; Autobuses Aragón to La Paz, cheaper, 4 a day, 24 hours. There are also many services east and south from the old bus station at Avenida Madero and Calle 1 (Comercio). From Tijuana bus terminal Greyhound has buses every 2 hours to San Diego via the Otay Mesa crossing, except after 2200, when it uses the Tijuana crossing; coming from San Diego stay on the bus to the main Tijuana terminal, entry stamp given at border (ask driver to get it for you), or at bus station. Long queues for immigration at lunchtime. Fare San Diego-Tijuana US$12.50, 2 hours. Walk across 'La Línea' border and catch a Golden State bus to downtown Los Angeles, US$13 (buy ticket inside *McDonalds* restaurant), 12 a day, or take trolley to downtown San Diego and there get Greyhound, US$20, or Amtrak train, US$25, to Los Angeles. Golden State is the cheapest and fastest; its terminal is about 1 kilometre from Greyhound terminal in downtown LA, but stops first at Santa Ana and elsewhere if requested. If travelling beyond Los Angeles, ask about layovers in LA before buying a through ticket. Tijuana is a major transportation centre and schedules are complex and extensive.

Directory

Airline offices *Aero California*, T842100. *AeroMéxico*, T854401. *Mexicana*, T832851. *Taesa*, T848484. **Banks** Many banks, all dealing in foreign exchange. For Visa TCs, go to *Bancomer*. Better rate than *cambios* but less convenient. Countless *casas de cambio* throughout Tijuana open day and night. Some *cambios* collect a commission (up to 5%), even for cash dollars; ask before changing. **Communications** Telephones: Computel, C 7 y Av Negrete, metered phones, fax, computer facilities. **Embassies & consulates** *Canadian Consul*, C Germán Gedovis 5-201, T840461. *Mexican Consulate-General*, in San Diego, CA, 549 India St, Mon-Fri 0900-1400, for visas and tourist information. *US Consulate*, C Tapachula 96, between Agua Caliente racetrack and the Country Club, Mon-Fri 0800-1630, T6817400. **Tourist offices** *State Tourism Secretariat*, main office on Plaza Patria, Blvd Agua Caliente, Mon-Fri 1000-1900. Branch offices at airport, first tollgate on Highway 1-D to Ensenada, and at the Chamber of Commerce, C 1 and Av Revolución, English-speaking staff, helpful, Mon-Fri 0900-1400, 1600-1900; Sat 0900-1300. Brochures and schematic maps available; no hotel lists. Chamber of Commerce also offers rest rooms and first aid facilities to visitors. *Procuraduría de Protección al Turista* is in the Government Centre in the Río Tijuana development; 0800-1900. **Useful telephone numbers** Emergency: Fire: 135. Police: 134. Red Cross: 132; valid for Tijuana, Rosarito, Ensenada, Tecate, Mexicali and San Luís Río Colorado.

South of Tijuana

A dramatic 106-kilometre toll road (Highway 1-D) leads along cliffs overhanging the Pacific to Ensenada; the toll is in three sections of US$2 each. There are emergency phones approximately every two kilometres on the toll road. This is the safest route between the two cities and 16 exit points allow access to a number of seaside developments and villages along the coast.

Rosarito
Population: 50,000
Colour map 1, grid A1

Largest is Rosarito , variously described as a drab resort strung out along the old highway, or 'a breath of fresh air after Tijuana', with numerous seafood restaurants, curio shops, etc. There is a fine swimming beach; horseriding on north and south Rosarito beaches. In March and April accommodation is hard to find as college students in great numbers take their holiday here.

Sleeping Many hotels and motels, including **A-B** *Festival Plaza*, Blvd Benito Juárez, T20842, F20224, deluxe, pool, shopping, 1 block from beach. **A-B** *Quinta del Mar Resort Hotel*, pool, sauna, tennis, also condos and townhouses with kitchens (T21145), *Beachcomber Bar*, good food, relatively cheap, good for watching the sunset; best is the **A-B** *Rosarito Beach Hotel*, T21106 (US toll free 1-800-3438582), Benito Juárez 31, which was one of the casinos which opened during Prohibition; its architecture and decoration are worth a look. Several motels in **D** range, including *René's Motel*, T21020, plain but comfortable.

Directory **Tourist offices** Quinta Plaza Mall, Benito Juárez 96, 0900-1600 daily.

The coast as far as Puerto Nuevo and nearby **Cantamar** (Km 26 and 28) is lightly built-up (toll between Cantamar and Highway 1 US$2.30, none heading towards Cantamar); there are several trailer parks and an amazing number of restaurants specializing in lobster and seafood (impressive is *Jatay*, built on four levels, Puerto Nuevo). There is fine surfing to the north and 'hassle-free' hang-gliding areas south of Cantamar. 11 kilometres south is an archaeological garden (Plaza del Mar) with an exhibition of precolumbian stone art, open to visitors. At **Punta Salsipuedes**, 51 kilometres south of Tijuana by the tollway, a *mirador* affords sweeping views of the rugged Pacific coast and the offshore Todos Santos Islands. The section of Highway 1-D for several kilometres beyond this point is subject to landslides.

Ensenada

Population: 255,700
Colour map 1, grid A1

Baja's third city and leading seaport. It is a delightful city on the northern shore of the Bahía de Todos Santos, whose blue waters sport many dolphins and underline the austere character of a landscape reduced to water, sky and scorched brown earth. Sport and commercial fishing, canning, wineries, olive groves and agriculture are the chief activities. The port is rather unattractive and the beach is dirty.

Tourist activity concentrates along Avenida López Mateos, where most of the **Sights** hotels, restaurants and shops are located. The twin white towers of **Nuestra Señora de Guadalupe**, Calle 6, are a prominent landmark; on the seafront boulevard is the new **Plaza Cívica**, a landscaped court containing large busts of Juárez, Hidalgo and Carranza. A splendid view over city and bay can be had from the road circling the Chapultepec Hills on the western edge of the business district. Steep but paved access is via the west extension of Calle 2, two blocks from the bus station. The **Bodegas de Santo Tomás** is Mexico's premier winery, Avenida Miramar 666, between Calle 6 y 7. ■ *T82509; daily tours at 1100, 1300, 1500, US$2. Charreadas* are held on summer weekends at the *charro* ground at Blancarte y Calle 2. A weekend street market is held from 0700-1700 at Avenida Riversoll y Calle 7; the fish market at the bottom of Avenida Macheros specializes in 'fish tacos' (a fish finger wrapped in a taco!). *Ensenada Clipper Fleet* runs daily fishing trips (■ *0700-1500*) from the sportfishing terminal. Also seasonal whale-watching trips and bay and coastal excursions.

LL *Las Rosas Hotel and Spa*, on Highway 1, 7 kilometres west of town, suites, spectacular **Sleeping** ocean views, pool, sauna, restaurant. **LL** *Punta Morro Hotel Suites*, on coast 3 kilometres west of town, rooms have kitchens and fridges, 2 and 3-bedroom apartments available, pool. **LL** *San Nicolás Resort Hotel*, López Mateos y Av Guadalupe, T61901, a/c, suites, dining room, disco. In the ranges **AL-A**: *Villa Marina*, Av López Mateos y Blancarte, T83321, heated pool, coffee shop. *La Pinta*, Av Floresta y Blvd Bucaneros (on Friday-Saturday, **B** Sunday-Thursday), TV, pool, restaurant. *Punta Morro*, 3 kilometres north on Highway 1, rooms and suites, a/c, pool, kitchens, etc. *Quintas Papagayo*, 1½ kilometres north on Highway 1, T44575, landscaped beach resort complex with all facilities, Hussong's *Pelícano* restaurant attached, seafood and local specialities, 0800-2300, best value for an Ensenada 'splurge'. **B** *Bahía*, López Mateos, T82101, balconies, suites, fridges, quiet, clean, parking, a/c, good value, popular. **B** *Misión Santa Isabel*, López Mateos and Castillo, T83616, pool, suites, Spanish Mission-style, attractive. **D** *América*, López Mateos opposite State Tourist Office, T61333, basic, hard beds, kitchenettes, good. **D** *Plaza*, López Mateos 540, central, plain but clean, rooms facing street noisy. **D** *Ritz*, Av Ruíz y C 4, No 381, T40573, central, a/c, TV, phone, coffee shop, parking. **D** *Royal*, Av Castelum, bath, parking.

Several cheaper hotels around Miramar and C 3, eg **C-D** *Perla del Pacífico*, Av Miramar 229, quite clean, hot water. **E** *Río*, Av Miramar and C 2, basic, noisy until 0300 when local bars shut. **E** *Pacífico No 1*, Av Gastelum 235, communal bath. Note that some of the larger hotels have different rates for summer and winter; cheaper tariffs are given above, check first! All hotels are filled in Ensenada on weekends, get in early.

Motels In our **AL-A** ranges: *Ensenada Travelodge*, Av Blancarte 130, T81601, a/c, heated pool, whirlpool, family rates available, restaurant. *Cortés*, López Mateos 1089 y Castillo, T82307, F83904. *Casa del Sol* (Best Western), López Mateos 101, T81570, F82025, a/c, TV, pool, comfortable. *El Cid*, on Friday-Saturday, **B** on Sunday-Thursday, Av López Mateos 993, T82401, Spanish-style building, a/c, fridges, suites available, dining room, lounge, disco. **C** *Balboa*, Guerrero 172 y Cortés, T61077, modern, comfortable, some way east of downtown. **C** *Villa Fontana*, López Mateos y C Blancarte, T83434, good location, old but large clean rooms, cheerful, English spoken. **D** *Costa Mar*, Av Veracruz 319 at Playa Hermosa (1 kilometre south), ½ block from beach, T66425, TV, phones, etc, agreeable. **E** *Pancho*, Av Alvarado 211, shabby but clean rooms, opposite the *charro* ground, cheapest habitable motel in town.

Trailer parks A great many good trailer parks eg *Campo Playa RV Park*, Blvd Costero y C Agustín Sangines, south of town, US$8-10 per person.

El Rey Sol, López Mateos 1000 y Blancarte, French/Mexican, elegant, reasonable prices. *La* **Eating** *Góndola*, López Mateos between Miramar and Macheros, clean, Mexican dishes and pizzas, including lobster. **Mesón de Don Fernando**, López Mateos, good breakfasts, tacos and sea-food, good value. **Taco Factory**, López Mateos y Av Gastelum, good tacos, many varieties. **Cantina Hussong's**, Av Ruíz 113, an institution in both the Californias, 1000-1400. **Cha-Cha Burgers**, Blvd Costero 609, 'American style burgers', fish, chicken, fast food 1000-2200. **Pancho's Place** (don't confuse with *Motel Pancho*), Ejército Nacional (Highway 1) y San Marcos, well-run, wide menu, pleasant. **Restaurant Muylam**, Ejército Nacional y Diamante, seafood and Chinese cuisine, 1200-2400. **China Land**, Riveroll 1149 between C 11 y 12, Sichuan, Mandarin and Cantonese cuisine, authentic, not cheap, 1200-2300. **El Pollo**, Macheros y C 2, grilled chicken 'Sinaola style', fast food 1000-2200 every day of year. **Las Brasas**, López Mateos 486, between Ruíz and Gastelum barbecue chicken and fish, Mexican specialities, attractive patio dining, 1100-2200, closed Tuesday. **Mandarin**, López Mateos 2127, between Soto and Balboa (Chinese), elegant surroundings, good food, expensive, considered to be the best *chifa* in Ensenada. **Domico's**, Av Ruíz 283, also Chinese restaurants in same avenue. **Lonchería la Terminal**, opposite bus station, cheap and filling *comida*, good but basic.

Transport **Air** Airport 8 kilometres south. No scheduled services. **Buses** To **Tijuana**, US$2.90, 1½ hours.

Directory **Tourist offices** Av López Mateos y Espinoza, part of the Fonartartesan centre, Mon-Sat 0900-1900, accommodation literature; the Procuraduría is next door, same hours plus Sun 0900-1600. *Tourist and Convention Bureau*, Lázaro Cárdenas y Miramar, Mon-Sat 0900-1900, Sun 0900-1400, helpful; free copies of *Ensenada News and Views*, monthly English-language paper with information and adverts on northern Baja, Tijuana and Ensenada. **Useful addresses** Immigration: *Oficina de Migratorios*, beside the shipyard, for tourist entry permits.

Southeast to San Felipe

Highway 3 east to San Felipe leaves Ensenada at the Benito Juárez *glorieta* monument as the Calzada Cortés. 26 kilometres out of Ensenada, an eight-kilometre dirt road branches south for a steep descent to the basic resort of **Agua Caliente** (**C** *Hotel Agua Caliente*, restaurant, bar, closed in winter; adjoining is a campground and large concrete pool heated to 38° by nearby hot springs; access road should not be attempted in wet weather). Free camping at the end of the road three kilometres beyond Agua Caliente, no facilities but good hiking in the area.

At Km 39, a paved road leads off three kilometres to Ojos Negros, continuing east (graded, dry weather) into scrub-covered foothills. It soon climbs into the ponderosa pine forests of the Sierra de Juárez. 37 kilometres from Ojos Negros, the road enters the **Parque Nacional Constitución de 1857**. The jewel of the park is the small Laguna Hanson, a sparkling shallow lake surrounded by Jeffery pines; camping here is delightful, but note that the lake is reduced to a boggy marsh in dry seasons and that the area receives snow in mid-winter. A high-clearance vehicle is necessary for the continuation north out of the park to Highway 2 at El Cóndor 15 kilometres east of La Rumorosa.

At Km 92½, Ejido Héroes de la Independencia, a graded dirt road runs eight kilometres east to the ruins of Mission Santa Catarina, founded in 1797 and abandoned after a raid by the Yuman Indians in 1840; the Paipái women in the village often have attractive pottery for sale.

Highway 3 descends along the edge of a green valley to the rapidly developing town of Valle de Trinidad. A reasonable dirt road runs south into the **Parque Nacional Sierra San Pedro Mártir** and *Mike's Sky Rancho* (35 kilometres), a working ranch which offers motel-style accommodation, a pool, camping and guided trips into the surrounding mountains; rooms **E**, good meals.

After leaving the valley, the highway follows a canyon covered in dense stands of barrel cacti to the San Matías Pass between the Sierras Juárez and San Pedro Mártir which leads onto the desolate Valle de San Felipe. The highway turns east and emerges onto open desert hemmed in by arid mountains. 198½ kilometres from

Ensenada it joins Highway 5 at the La Trinidad T-junction, 148 kilometres from
Mexicali and 50 kilometres from San Felipe.

South from Ensenada

Highway 1 south from Ensenada passes turn-offs to several beach resorts. Just
before the agricultural town of **Maneadero**, a paved highway runs 23 kilometres
west onto the Punta Banda pensinsula, where you can see **La Bufadora** blowhole,
one of the most powerful on the Pacific. Air sucked from a sea-level cave is expelled
as high as 16 metres through a cleft in the cliffs. Concrete steps and viewing platform
give easy access. Tourist stalls line the approach road and boys try to charge US$1 for
parking (restaurants *Los Panchos* and *La Bufadora*, Mesquite-grilled seafood,
palapa dining, both 0900 to around sunset). This is one of the easiest side trips off
the length of Highway 1.

NB Tourist cards and vehicle documents of those travelling south of Maneadero
are supposed to be validated at the immigration checkpoint on the southern outskirts of the town; the roadside office, however, is not always in operation. If you are
not stopped, just keep going.

Chaparal-clad slopes begin to close in on the highway as it winds it's way south, passing through the small towns of Santo Tomás (**D** *El Palomar Motel*, adequate but
overpriced rooms, restaurant, bar, general store and gas station, RV park with full
hook-ups, campsite with swimming pool, clean, refurbished, US$10, nearby ruins
of the Dominican Mission of 1791, local Santo Tomás wine, cheaper out of town)
and **San Vicente** (**E** *Motel El Cammo*, Highway 1, south of town, without bath,
friendly, OK restaurant; two Pemex stations, cafés, tyre repairs, several stores),
before reaching **Colonet**. This is a supply centre for surrounding ranches; several
services. A dry weather dirt road runs 12 kilometres west to **San Antonio del Mar**:
many camping spots amid high dunes fronting a beautiful beach renowned for surf
fishing and clam-digging.

Santo Tomás
Colour map 1, grid A1

14 kilometres south of Colonet a reasonable graded road branches to San Telmo
and climbs into the mountains. At 50 kilometres it reaches the *Meling Ranch* (also
called San José), which offers resort accommodation for about 12 guests. 15 kilometres beyond San José the road enters the **Parque Nacional Sierra San Pedro
Mártir** and climbs through forests (four-wheel drive recommended) to three astronomical observatories perched on the dramatic eastern escarpment of the central
range. The view from here is one of the most extensive in North America: east to the
Gulf, west to the Pacific, and southeast to the overwhelming granite mass of the
Picacho del Diablo (3,096 metres), Baja's highest peak. The higher reaches of the
park receive snow in winter. The observatories are not open to visitors.

179 kilometres from Ensenada, San Quintín is a thriving market city almost joined
to Lázaro Cárdenas five kilometres south. There are service stations in both centres
and San Quintín provides all services. Rising out of the peninsula west of San
Quintín bay is a line of volcanic cinder cones, visible for many kilometres along the
highway; the beaches to the south near Santa María are hugely popular with fishermen, campers and beachcombers.

San Quintín
Population: 15,000
Colour map 1, grid A1

Sleeping AL *La Pinta*, isolated beachfront location 18 kilometres south of San Quintín then
5 kilometres west on paved road, a/c, TV, balconies, tennis, nearby airstrip, reasonably priced
breakfasts, even for non-residents. **E** *Hada's Rooms*, just north of Benito Juárez army camp
in Lázaro Cárdenas, cheapest in town, shabby, basic, sometimes closed when water and
electricity are cut off.

Motels A-C *Molino Viejo/The Old Mill*, on site of old English mill, part of an early agricultural scheme, upgraded by new American owners, new wing, new bar and dining room
with good food and drink, on bay 6 kilometres west of highway and south of Lázaro

Cárdenas, rough access road, some kitchenettes, also one 6-bed dormitory, 15 RV spaces with full hook-up (US$15), camping (US$10), electricity 0800-0900, 1800-2200, various sizes of boat for rent, recommended as 'delightfully well-run and cosy' (in USA, representative is The Baja Outfitter, 223 Via de San Ysidro, Ste 76, San Ysidro, CA 92173, T619-4282779, F619-4286269, or T800-4797962). **C** *Cielito Lindo*, 2 kilometres beyond the *La Pinta Hotel* on south shore of bay, restaurant, cafetería, lounge (dancing Saturday nights), electricity Monday-Saturday 0700-1100, 1500-2400, Sunday 0700-2400, modest but pleasant, US$5 for vehicles to camp overnight (use of showers), last kilometre of access road unpaved, messy after rain. **C** *San Carlos*, by *Muelle Viejo* restaurant, large rooms, friendly, good value. **D** *Ernesto's*, next door, rustic, overpriced, popular with fishermen, electricity 0700-2100. **D** *Muelle Viejo*, between *Ernesto's* and the old English cemetery, restaurant, bad access road, hot showers, bay views. **E** *Chávez*, on highway north of Lázaro Cárdenas, family-style, clean rooms, TV, plain but good value. **E** *Romo*, about 200 metres from post office, clean, OK, convenient if arriving late. **E** *Sánchez*, a few kilometres before town in Col Guerrero, large rooms, clean. **E** *Uruapan*, very clean and friendly.

Camping *Pabellón RV Campground*, 15 kilometres south and 2 kilometres west on coast, 200 spaces, no electricity, disposal station, toilets, showers, beach access, US$5 per vehicle, great area for clam-digging. *Posada Don Diego*, off Highway in Colonia Guerrero (south of town, Km 174), wide range of facilities, laundry, restaurant, etc, 100 spaces, US$7; at south end of Colonia Guerrero is *Mesón de Don Pepe RV Park*, smaller and more modest, full hook-ups, restaurant with view of campground so you can watch your tent, US$5. *Campo Lorenzo* is just north of Molino Viejo, 20 spaces, full hook-ups but mostly permanent residents. Trailer park attached to *Cielito Lindo Motel*, comfortable.

Eating *El Alteño*, on highway next to the cinema, bare but clean roadhouse, fresh seafood and Mexican dishes, Mariachi music, moderate prices, closed July-September. *Tres Estrellas de Oro*, where the bus company stops for lunch, reasonably priced and sized meals. *Muelle Viejo*, next to motel, overlooks old pier, reasonably-priced seafood, modest decor. *Mi Lien* on Highway 1, north end of town, very good Chinese food.

Festivals 20 November *Day of the Revolution*, street parades with school children, bands and the military.

El Rosario
Colour map 1, grid A1

After leaving the San Quintín valley, bypassing Santa María (fuel), the Transpeninsular Highway (officially the Carretera Transpeninsular Benito Juárez) runs near the Pacific before darting inland at El Consuelo Ranch. It climbs over a barren spur from which there are fine views, then drops in a succession of tight curves into **El Rosario**, 58 kilometres from San Quintín. This small, agricultural community has a Pemex station, small supermarket, a basic museum, and meals, including Espinosa's famous lobster *burritos* (expensive and not particularly good) and omelettes, also a good *taco* stand outside the grocery store at night. Three kilometres south is a ruined Dominican Mission, founded 1774 upstream, then moved to its present site in 1882; take the graded dirt road to Punta Baja, a bold headland on the coast, where there is a solar-powered lighthouse and fishing village.

Sleeping **D** *Motel Rosario*, small, basic; new motel at south end of town. **D** *Sinai*, comfortable, very clean, small RV park, friendly owner makes good meals, but beware of overcharging.

Central desert of Baja California

Highway 1 makes a sharp 90° turn at El Rosario and begins to climb continuously into the central plateau; gusty winds increase and astonishingly beautiful desertscapes gradually become populated with many varieties of cacti. Prominent are the stately *cardones*: most intriguing are the strange, twisted *cirios* growing to heights of six to 10 metres. They are unique to this portion of Baja California as far south as the Vizcaino Desert, and to a small area of Sonora state on the mainland. At Km 62 a five-kilometre track branches south to the adobe remains of **Misión San Fernando Velicatá**, the only Franciscan mission in Baja, founded by Padre Serra in 1769. Five kilometres further on, Rancho El Progreso offers expensive meals and refreshments (possible to camp behind Rancho, and RV park, fill up with water if

Southern Baja California

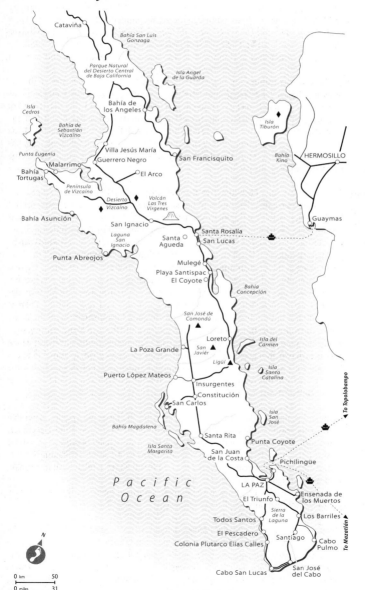

Cataviña

Bahía San Luis
Gonzaga

Parque Natural
del Desierto Central
de Baja California

Isla Angel
de la Guarda

Bahía de
los Angeles

Isla
Cedros

Bahía de
Sebastián
Vizcaíno

Isla
Tiburón

Bahía
Kino

HERMOSILLO

Punta Eugenia

Villa Jesús María

San Francisquito

Malarrimo

Guerrero Negro

Bahía
Tortugas

El Arco

Península
de Vizcaíno

Desierto
Vizcaíno

Volcán
Las Tres
Vírgenes

Bahía Asunción

San Ignacio

Santa Rosalía

Guaymas

Laguna
San
Ignacio

Santa
Agueda

San Lucas

Punta Abreojos

Mulegé

Playa Santispac
El Coyote

Bahía
Concepción

San José de
Comondú

Loreto

Isla del
Carmen

La Poza Grande

San
Javíer

Ligüí

Isla
Santa
Catalina

Puerto López Mateos

Insurgentes

Constitución

Isla
San
José

San Carlos

Bahía Magdalena

Santa Rita

Punta Coyote

Isla Santa
Margarita

San Juan
de la Costa

Pichilingüe

*Pacific
Ocean*

LA PAZ

El Triunfo

Ensenada de
los Muertos

Sierra
de la
Laguna

Los Barriles

Todos Santos

El Pescadero

Santiago

Cabo
Pulmo

Colonia Plutarco Elías Calles

Cabo San Lucas

San José
del Cabo

To Topolobampo

To Mazatlán

N

0 km   50
0 miles   31

possible). The highway is now in the **Parque Natural Desierto Central de Baja California** (as yet not officially recognized). About 26 kilometres north of Cataviña a strange region of huge boulders begins, some as big as houses; interspersed by cacti and crouching elephant trees, this area is one of the most picturesque on the peninsula.

Cataviña is only a dozen buildings, with a small grocery store/*Café La Enramada*, the only Pemex station on the 227-kilometre stretch from El Rosario to the Bahía de Los Angeles junction (there are in fact two fuel stations, but do not rely on either having supplies), and the attractive **A** *La Pinta Hotel*, a/c, pool, bar, electricity 1800-2400, good restaurant, tennis, 28 rooms, recommended. Attached to *La Pinta* is the *Parque Natural Desierto Central de Baja California Trailer Park*, flush toilets, showers, restaurant, bar, US$3 per site. Two kilometres south of Cataviña is *Rancho Santa Inés*, which has dormitory-style accommodation (**E**), meals and a paved airstrip.

Highway 1 continues southeast through an arid world of boulder-strewn mountains and dry salt lakes. At 53 kilometres the new graded road to the Bahía San Luís Gonzaga (see under San Felipe) branches off to the east. After skirting the dry bed of Laguna Chapala (natural landing strip at southern end when lake is totally dry), the Transpeninsular Highway arrives at the junction with the paved road east to Bahía de Los Angeles; **C** *Parador Punta Prieta*, fair, 20 RV spaces with full hook-ups, few facilities; gas station at junction, fuel supply sometimes unreliable, small store at the junkyard opposite the gas station.

Bahía de los Angeles
Population: 1,245
Colour map 1, grid B2

The side road runs 68 kilometres through *cirios* and *datilillo* cactus-scapes and crosses the Sierra de la Asamblea to Bahía de Los Angeles (no public transport but hitchhiking possible), a popular fishing town which, despite a lack of vegetation, is one of Baja's best-known beauty spots. The bay, sheltered by the forbidding slopes of Isla Angel de la Guarda (Baja's largest island), is a haven for boating (winds can be tricky for kayaks and small craft). The series of tiny beaches at the foot of the Díaz *cabañas* are good for swimming, but watch out for stingrays when wading. There is good clamming and oysters. Facilities in town include: gas station, bakery, grocery stores, two trailer parks and four restaurants, paved airstrip; water supply is inadequate, a water truck visits weekly, electricity is cut off about 2200 nightly. There is also a modest but interesting museum in town, good for information on the many mines and mining techniques used in the region around the turn of the century, such as the San Juan Mine high in the mountains 24 kilometres south-southwest which had its own two-foot guage railway and wire rope tramway down to a smelter at Las Flores as early as 1895; the relic steam locomotive and mine car on display beside the airstrip are from this remarkable mine (which returned US$2mn in gold and silver before closing down in 1910).

Lynn and Walt Sutherland from Vancouver write: "Bahía de los Angeles is worth a visit for its sea life. There are thousands of dolphins in the bay June-December. Some stay all year. In July and August you can hear the whales breathe as you stand on shore. There are large colonies of seals and many exotic seabirds. Fishing is excellent. A boat and guide can be rented for US$40 a day; try Raúl, a local fisherman, who speaks English." Camping free and safe on beach.

La Gringa is a beautiful beach 13 kilometres north of town, many camping sites, pit toilets, rubbish bins, small fee.

Sleeping and eating C *Villa Vita Motel*, modern, a/c, pool, jacuzzi, boat launch, trailer park, electricity 0700-1400, 1700-2000, bar, dining room. **D** *Casa de Díaz*, 15 rooms, restaurant, grocery store, campground, boat rentals, clean but cockroaches, well-run, popular. *Guillermo's Trailer Park*, flush toilets, showers, restaurant, gift shop, boat ramp and rentals. *Guillermo's* also has a restaurant in a white building on main street, above the gift shop, well-prepared Mexican food, attractive, reservations advised at weekends. *La Playa RV Park*,

Whale watching

Whale watching is the main attraction on **Laguna Ojo de Liebre**, *usually known as* **Scammon's Lagoon** *after the whaling captain who entered in 1857. California Grey Whales mate and give birth between end-December and February, in several warm-water lagoons on central Baja's Pacific coast. Most leave by the beginning of April, but some not departing until as late as May or June. They can be seen cavorting and sounding from the old salt wharf 10 kilometres northwest of Guerrero Negro on the Estero San José, or from a designated 'whale watching area' with observation tower on the shore of Scammon's Lagoon 37 kilometres south of town. The access road branches off Highway 1, eight kilometres east of the junction (if going by public transport, leave bus at the turn off and hitch). US$3 is charged to enter the park. Local personnel may collect a small fee for camping at the watching area, this pays to keep it clean. The shores of Scammon's Lagoon are part of the* **Parque Natural de Ballena Gris**. *Watch between 0700 and 0900 and again at 1700. The authorities in Guerrero Negro say that boats are not allowed on to the lagoon to watch whales, but pangas are available for hire (US$10 per person). There are also daily tours including one and a half hours boat trip, sandwiches and transport to the lagoon, US$30 per person.*

The road to the park has little whale signs at regular intervals. It is sandy in places, so drive with care.

on beach, similar facilities and tariff (US$4 per site). **Sal y Mauro** campsite, first gravel road on left before entering town, friendly, recommended. **Restaurant Las Hamacas**, on north edge of town, budget café with bay view, slow service, popular for breakfast.

State border

The highway now runs due south. Three kilometres from the highway is **San Ignacio** (**D-E** *Hotel La Posada*; grocery stores). There is a small and interesting museum on the edge of the square about nearby cave paintings. Trips to the caves are available. Before you enter Baja California Sur you pass Punta Prieta (three stores) and Rosarito (one store and one restaurant) and go through **Villa Jesús María** (gas station, store, cafés) to the 28th parallel, the state border between Baja California and Baja California Sur (soaring stylized eagle monument and **A** *Hotel La Pinta*, a/c, pool, dining room, bar, trailer park attached, 60 spaces, full hook-ups, US$5, laundry and gasoline at hotel).

NB Advance clocks one hour to Mountain time when entering Baja California Sur, but note that Northern Baja observes Pacific Daylight Saving Time from first Sunday in April to last Sunday in October; time in both states and California is thus identical during the summer.

Three kilometres beyond the state line and four kilometres west of the highway; 714 kilometres south of Tijuana, 414 from San Quintín, Guerrero Negro is the halfway point between the US border and La Paz. There are two gas stations, bank (Banamex, does not change travellers' cheques), hospital, cafés, stores, an airport with scheduled services (just north of the Eagle monument), and the headquarters of Exportadora de Sal, the world's largest salt-producing firm. Seawater is evaporated by the sun from thousands of salt ponds south of town; the salt is loaded at the works 11 kilometres southwest of town and barged to a deepwater port on Cedros Island. From there ore carriers take it to the USA, Canada and Japan, guided tour possible.

Guerrero Negro
Population: 9,000
Colour map 1, grid B2

Sleeping *San Ignacio*, on road into town from highway, new, clean, good but exact prices unknown. **D** *San José*, opposite bus terminal, clean, will help to organize whale-watching tours. **E** *Cuartos de Sánchez-Smith*, C Barrera, west end of town, basic rooms, some with showers, cheapest in town. **Camping**: *Malarrimo Trailer Park*, on highway at east end of town, flush toilets, showers, bar, US$10 per vehicle, whale watching tours arranged. **Motels**: **C** *Cabañas Don Miguel* (same owner and location as *Malarrimo Restaurant*), east end of town, very clean, TV, fan, quiet, recommended. **D** *El Morro*, on road into town from highway, modest, clean. **E** *Las Dunas*, few doors from *El Morro*, friendly, modest, clean, recommended. **E** *Gámez*, very basic, near city hall.

Eating   Good restaurant at bus station. *Malarrimo Restaurant-Bar*, fishing decor, good fish and steak menu, moderate prices, music, open for breakfast, runs whale-watching tours, US$30 per person, including transport to boats and lunch. *El Figón*, next to *Las Dunas*, good breakfast. *Mario's Restaurant-Bar*, next to *El Morro*, modest surroundings and fare, disco. Excellent taco stall a few blocks towards town from *El Morro*. Good bakery on main street.

Transport Air   Airport (GUB), 3km from town, receives scheduled services only from Hermosillo. There regular flights to Cedros Island and Bahía Tortugas; information from airfield downtown. **Bus**   To Tijuana, 0830, 1830.

After Guerrero Negro the highway enters the grim Vizcaíno Desert. A paved but badly potholed road leads due east (42 kilometres) to El Arco, other abandoned mining areas and crossing to **San Francisquito** on its beautiful bay on the Gulf (77 kilometres), and to Santa Gertrudis Mission (1752), some of whose stone ruins have been restored; the chapel is still in use. It should be stressed that these minor Bajan roads require high-clearance, preferably 4x4, vehicles carrying adequate equipment and supplies, water and fuel. A new gravel road from Bahía de Los Angeles (135 kilometres) gives easier road access than from El Arco and opens up untouched stretches of the Gulf coast.

Vizcaíno Peninsula   Vizcaíno Peninsula which thrusts into the Pacific south of Guerrero Negro is one of the remotest parts of Baja. Although part of the Vizcaíno Desert, the scenery of the peninsula is varied and interesting; isolated fishcamps dot the silent coast of

Vizcaíno Peninsula

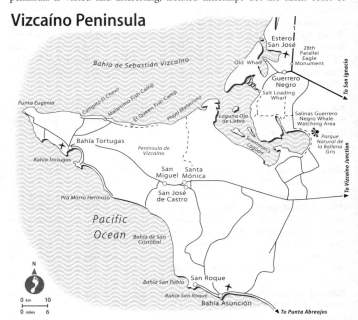

beautiful coves and untrodden beaches. Until recently only the most hardy ventured into the region; now an improved dry-weather road cuts west through the peninsula to Bahía Tortugas and the rugged headland of Punta Eugenia. It leaves Highway 1 at Vizcaíno Junction (also called Fundolegal, Pemex station, café, market, pharmacy and auto parts store; **D** *Motel Olivia* at Vizcaíno, small rooms with TV, private bath, hot water; nearby is small shop with reasonably priced telephone service), 70 kilometres beyond Guerrero Negro is paved for eight kilometres to Ejido Díaz Ordaz. The new road passes Rancho San José (116 kilometres) and the easily-missed turn-off to Malarrimo Beach (where beachcombing is unparalleled). After another bumpy 50 kilometres is **Bahía Tortugas**, a surprisingly large place (*Population*: 3,200) considering its remoteness. Many facilities including eating places, health clinic, gas station, airport with services to Cedros Island and Ensenada, and the small **D-E** *Vera Cruz Motel*, restaurant, bar, very modest but the only accommodation on the peninsula apart from a trailer park at Campo René, 15 kilometres from Punta Abreojos. Two roads leave the Vizcaíno-Bahía Tortuga road for **Bahía Asunción** (*Population*: 1,600), which has the peninsula's only other gas station, then following the coast to Punta Prieta, La Bocana and Punta Abreojos (93 kilometres). A lonely road runs for 85 kilometres back to Highway 1, skirting the Sierra Santa Clara before crossing the salt marshes north of Laguna San Ignacio and reaching the main road 26 kilometres before San Ignacio.

San Ignacio

Population: 2,200
Colour map 1, grid B2

The Highway continues southeast on a new alignment still not shown on most maps and, 20 kilometres from Vizcaíno Junction, reaches the first of 23 microwave relay towers which follow Highway 1 almost to the Cape. They are closed to the public but make excellent landmarks and, in some cases, offer excellent views. 143 kilometres from Guerrero Negro is the turnoff for San Ignacio. Here the Jesuits built a mission in 1728 and planted the ancestors of the town's date palm groves. On the square is the beautifully-preserved mission church, completed by the Dominicans in 1786. Near the mission is a good museum. The town is very attractive, with thatched-roof dwellings and pastel-coloured commercial buildings; there is limited shopping but several restaurants, service station, mechanical assistance.

Sleeping **A** *La Pinta*, on road leading into town, a/c, pool, all facilities, built in mission style, attractive but overpriced. **E** *Cuartos Glenda*, with shower, basic but cheapest in town, on highway east. **Motel** **D** *La Posada*, on rise 2 blocks from zócalo (difficult to find), well-maintained, fans, shower, best value in town, worth bargaining (owner can arrange trips to the cave paintings for US$25 per person).

Camping *San Ignacio Transpeninsula Trailer Park*, Government-run, on Highway 1 behind Pemex station at the junction, full hook-ups, toilets, showers, US$4 per site, cheap restaurant nearby; basic campground on left of road into San Ignacio, grass, run down, helpful owner, Martín, cheap dates in season. *El Padrino RV Park*, on same road on the right, basic, cold water showers, sites on sand, decent restaurant.

Eating *Lonchería Chalita*, on Zócalo, excellent value. *Restaurant Tota* has received poor reports.

Laguna San Ignacio

A 70-kilometre road from San Ignacio leads to Laguna San Ignacio, one of the best whale viewing sites; mothers and calves often swim up to nuzzle boats and allow their noses to be stroked. In 1997 a plan to build the world's largest sea salt plant near the whale breeding grounds sparked controversy worldwide. Diesel engines to pump 6,000 gallons of water per second out of the lagoon to create salt flats and a one and a half kilometre pier to transport salt to cargo ships were forecast to disrupt the whales' migration and reproduction. The company, Essa, 51 percent owned by the Mexican government and 49 percent owned by Mitsubishi, already operates in the Laguna Ojo de Liebre. The Cooperativa Laguna de San Ignacio, Calle Juárez 23, off the Zócalo in San Ignacio, takes fishermen to the lagoon every day and can some-times accommodate visitors. The road is rough and requires a high clearance vehicle.

There are many cave painting sites around San Ignacio; colourful human and ani-mal designs left by Baja's original inhabitants still defy reliable dating, or full under-standing. To reach most requires a trek by mule over tortuous trails; Oscar Fischer, owner of the *La Posada Motel*, arranges excursions into the sierras (about US$10 per person to Santa Teresa cave). The cave at the **Cuesta del Palmarito**, five kilometres east of Rancho Santa Marta (50 northwest of San Ignacio), is filled with designs of humans with uplifted arms, in brown and black; a jeep and guide (if one can be found) are required. A better road leads east from the first microwave station past Vizcaíno Junction up to **San Francisco de la Sierra**, where there are other paintings and petroglyphs in the vicinity (US$120 per person for trip with own car).

Highway 1 leaves the green *arroyo* of San Ignacio and re-emerges into the arid central desert. To the north, the triple volcanic cones of **Las Tres Vírgenes** come into view, one of the most dramatic mountain scenes along this route. Dark brown lava flows on the flanks are evidence of relatively recent activity (eruption in 1746, smoke emission in 1857). The highest peak is 2,149 metres above the Gulf of California; the sole vegetation on the lunar-like landscape is the thick-skinned elephant trees.

Two and a half million hectares of the Vizcaíno Desert are now protected by the **Reserva de la Biósfera El Vizcaíno**, supposedly the largest in Latin America. It was decreed in November 1988 and has absorbed the Parque Nacional Ballena Gris. It runs south from the state border to the road from San Ignacio to Laguna San Ignacio and Highway 1 near Santa Rosalía; it stretches from the Pacific to the Gulf. Encom-passed by the reserve are the desert, the Vizcaína Peninsula, Scammon's Lagoon, Las Tres Vírgenes volcano, the Laguna San Ignacio and several offshore islands.

Santa Rosalía
Population: 14,500
Colour map 1, grid B3

72 kilometres from San Ignacio is Santa Rosalía. It was built by the French El Boleo Copper Company in the 1880s, laid out in neat rows of wood frame houses, many with broad verandahs, which today give Santa Rosalía its distinctly un-Mexican appear-ance. Most of the mining ceased in 1953; the smelter, several smokestacks above the town and much of the original mining operation can be seen on the north of town.

Sights There is a small museum off Calle Francisco next to the Impecsa warehouse, historic exhibits of mining and smelting. The port was one of the last used in the age of sail. The church of Santa Bárbara (Avenida Revolución y Calle C, a block north of the main plaza), built of prefabricated galvanized iron for the 1889 Paris Worlds' Fair from a design by Eiffel, was shipped around the Horn to Baja. A car ferry leaves for Guaymas, from the small harbour, seven hours (T20014, fares are the same as for the La Paz-Topolobampo ferry, see schedule, page 552; tickets sold on day of departure).

Drivers should note that Santa Rosalía's streets are narrow and congested; larger vehicles should park along the highway or in the ferry dock parking lot. The Pemex station is conveniently located on the highway, unlike at Mulegé (see below), so larger RVs and rigs should fill up here.

Sleeping D *El Morro*, on Highway 2 kilometres south of town, T20414, on bluff with Gulf views, modern, Spanish-style, a/c, bar, restaurant (good food, generous portions, reasonable prices). **D** *Francés*, Av 11 de Julio on the north Mesa, T20829, a/c, restaurant, bar, pool not always filled, historic 2-storey wooden French colonial building overlooking smelter and Gulf, photos of sailing vessels on walls, charming, lukewarm water. **D** *Olvera*, on main plaza, 2nd floor, a/c, showers, clean, good value. **D** *Playa*, Av La Playa between C B y Plaza, central, fans, bathrooms, good budget hotel. **D** *Real*, Av Manuel Montoya near C A, similar to *Olvera*, recommended. **E** *Blanca y Negra*, basic but clean, Av Libertad at end of C 3. **E** *Central*, Av Obregón, large rooms, shared bath.

Camping Possible on the beach under *palapas*, access via an unmarked road 500 metres south of *El Morro*, free, no facilities, a beautiful spot. Also trailer park *El Palmar*, 3 kilometres south of town, US$5 for 2, showers, laundry, good value.

Eating *Balneario Selene*, T20685, on Highway opposite Pemex. *Palapa Mauna Loa*, T21187, on Highway below copper smelter, good spaghetti and pizzas, popular. *Panadería El Boleo*, widely noted for its delicious French breads.

Transport Tres Estrellas de Oro bus station (T220150) near tourist office and Pemex station 2 kilometres south of ferry terminal; stop for most Tijuana-La Paz buses, several per day. To **La Paz**, 1100, US$24. Autobus Aguila, C 3 y Constitución, T20374.

Directory Communications: Post Office: only from here and La Paz can parcels be sent abroad; customs check necessary first, at boat dock. **Laundry**: Opposite *Hotel Central*, wash and dry US$2.50 per load.

Painted cave sites can be visited from the farming town of **Santa Agueda**, turnoff eight kilometres south of Santa Rosalía then rough dirt road for 12 kilometres. (four-wheel drive necessary, guide can be arranged at the Delegado Municipal, Calle Madero, Mulegé.) The caves are in the San Borjita and La Trinidad deserts; the drawings depict animals, children and, some claim, female sexual organs. The fishing village of **San Lucas**, on a palm-fringed cove, is 14 kilometres south of Santa Rosalía; camping is good and popular on the beaches to north and south. *San Lucas RV Park*, on beach, no hook-ups, flush toilets, boat ramp, ice, restaurant, US$5 per vehicle, 35 spaces, recommended. Offshore lies Isla San Marcos, with a gypsum mine at the south end.

Just beyond **San Bruno** is a reasonable dirt road to **San José de Magdalena** (15 kilometres), a picturesque farming village dating back to colonial days; ruined Dominican chapel, attractive thatched palm houses, flower gardens. An awful road leads on for 17 kilometres to Rancho San Isidro, from where the ruined Guadalupe Mission can be reached on horseback. At San Bruno, *Costa Serena* beach camping, no hook-ups, one shower, clean beach with good fishing and shrimping. Similar is *Camp Punta Chivato*, just before Mulegé, no hook-ups but clean toilets and shower, beautiful location.

61 kilometres south of Santa Rosalía, is another oasis community whose river enters the gulf as a lushly-vegetated tidal lake. There are lovely beaches, good diving, snorkelling and boating in the Bahía Concepción. The old Federal territorial prison (La Cananea) is being converted into a museum. There is a good cheap fish restaurant 40 minutes' walk along the river; the lighthouse, 10 minutes further on provides tremendous views and the sunsets are unforgettable. South of the bridge which carries the highway over the river is the restored Mission of Santa Rosalía de Mulegé, founded by the Jesuits in 1705; good lookout point above the mission over the town and its sea of palm trees. Locals swim at an excellent spot about 500 metres inland from the bridge and to the right of the track to the Mission. The bank will only change a minimum of US$100. **NB** One Pemex station is in the centre; not convenient for large vehicles, and a one-way system to contend with, but there is another Pemex station four and a half kilometres south of the bridge, on the road out of town towards Loreto, with restaurant and mini-market.

Mulegé
Population: 5,000
Colour map 1, grid B3

Sleeping **B** *Baja Hacienda*, C Madero 3, lovely courtyard, pool, rooms refurbished, bar, trips to cave paintings and kayaking offered (US$25 per person), recommended. **B** *Serenidad*, 4 kilometres south of town near the river mouth on beachside road, may be closed because of long-running dispute with members of a local *ejido* who claim the land and have occupied the resort developed and run for many years by the Johnsons, T20111. **B** *Vista Hermosa*, opposite the *Serenidad*, a/c, pool, excellent restaurant, bar with satellite

US TV. **C** *Las Casitas*, Callejón de los Estudiantes y Av Madero, central, a/c, showers, restaurant next door, shady garden patio, fishing trips arranged, pleasant older hotel, well-run. **D** *Suites Rosita*, Av Madero near main plaza, a/c, kitchenettes, clean and pleasant, hot water, a bit run down but good value. **D** *Terraza Motel*, C Zaragoza y Moctezuma, in business district, 35 rooms, rooftop bar, TV, parking, clean. Several **E-F** *Casas de Huéspedes*, eg *Manuelita*, *Nachita*, *Canett*, all basic but reasonably clean.

Camping *The Orchard (Huerta Saucedo) RV Park*, on river south of town, partly shaded, off Highway 1, pool, free coffee, book exchange, boat ramp, fishing, up to US$10.50 for 2, discount with AAA/AA membership, recommended. *Villa María Isabel RV Park*, on river and Highway east of *Orchid*, pool, recreation area, disposal station, American-style bakery. *Jorge's del Río Trailer Park*, grassy, on river at east end of Highway bridge by unpaved road, hot water, clean, plenty of shade but watch belongings at night. *Pancho's RV Park*, next to *María Isabel*, off Highway 1, little shade. *Oasis Río Baja RV Park*, on same stretch as those above, reasonable. All the foregoing have full hook-ups, flush toilets, showers, etc. From here on down the Bahía Concepción coast and beyond are many *playas públicas* (*PP*); some have basic facilities, most are simple, natural camping spots on beautiful beaches where someone may or may not collect a fee. At Mulegé is the Playa Sombrerito at the hat-shaped hill (site of Mexican victory over US forces in 1847), restaurant and store nearby. White gas is sold at the *ferretería* 'on the far side of town from the main entrance' in large cans only. Bicycle repairs near *Doney's Tacos*.

Eating *Patio El Candil*, C Zaragoza, simple outdoor dining. *Azteca* and *Vista Hermosa* at *Hotel Terraza*, good food, budget prices. *Paco y Rosy's*, signed turnoff from Highway 2 kilometres south, rustic, friendly, Chinese, open from 1800. *Tandil* and *Las Casitas*, romantic and quiet atmosphere, good. *Equipales*, C Zaragoza, p2º, recommended for good local cooking and for breakfasts. *Baja Burger*, between *Las Casitas* and *Hotel Baja Hacienda*, traditional burgers and *quesadillas*, ice-cream. *Doney's Tacos*, Fco Madero, end farthest from centre, good food and clean. Good pizza place under the bridge, on the river between *Jorge's Trailer Park* and town, reasonable prices, English book exchange. Good fish restaurant on the beach near the lighthouse. In the plaza next to the *Hacienda* is a good *taco* stand in am and vendors selling chips and *churros* in pm. Next to *Doney's* on Madero is a Corona beer store, selling ice-cold beer with plastic bags of ice supplied.

Sports Dive shop: Calle Madero 45, rents equipment and runs trips around Bahía Concepción.

Transport Buses to the south do not leave at scheduled times. Allow plenty of time to complete your journey.

Directory Communications: Telephone and fax abroad at mini-supermarket *Padilla*, 1 block from Pemex station. **Laundry**: *Lavamática*, C Doblado, opposite Tres Estrellas bus station.

South of Mulegé

Beyond Mulegé the Highway climbs over a saddle and then runs along the shores of the bay for 50 kilometres. This stretch is the most heavily-used camping and boating area on the Peninsula; the water is beautiful, swimming safe, camping excellent, varied marine life. Bahía Concepción and **Playa Santispac**, 23 kilometres south of Mulegé, are recommended, many small restaurants (for example *Ana's*, which sells water, none other available, food good value) and *palapas* (shelters) for hire (day or overnight, US$2.50). You can get to Santispac from Mulegé on the La Paz bus. Beyond Santispac is Playa Burro and, beyond that, an unnamed beach. Further south from El Coyote is **Playa Buenaventura**, which has *palapas* and three *cabañas* for rent (US$20), and an expensive restaurant serving wine, burgers and spaghetti.

From the entrance to the beach at Requesón, veer to the left for Playa La Perla, which is small and secluded. In summer this area is extremely hot and humid, the sea is too salty to be refreshing and there can be midges.

A new graded dirt road branches off Highway 1 to climb over the towering **Sierra Giganta**, whose desert vistas of flat-topped mesas and *cardón* cacti are straight out of the Wild West; it begins to deteriorate after the junction (20 kilometres) to San José de Comondú and limps another 37 kilometres into San Isidro after a spectacular drop into the La Purísima Valley. San Isidro has a population of 1,000 but little for the visitor; five kilometres down the valley is the more attractive oasis village of La Purísima (*Population*: 800). The road leads on southwards to Pozo Grande (52 kilometres) and Ciudad Insurgentes (85 kilometres), it is now beautifully paved and is probably the fastest stretch of road in Baja. Two side roads off the San Isidro road lead down to the twin towns of San Miguel de Comondú and San José de Comondú (high-clearance vehicles are necessary); both oasis villages of 500 people each. One stone building remains of the mission moved to San José in 1737; the original bells are still at the church. A new graded road leads on to Pozo Grande and Ciudad Insurgentes.

1,125 kilometres from Tijuana, Loreto is one of the most historic places in Baja. Here settlement of the Peninsula began with Father Juan María Salvatierra's founding of the Mission of Nuestra Señora de Loreto on 25 October 1697. Nestled between the slopes of the Sierra Giganta and the offshore Isla del Carmen, Loreto has experienced a tourist revival; fishing in the Gulf here is some of the best in Baja California.

Loreto
Population: 7,500
Phone code: 113
Colour map 1, grid C3

The Mission is on the Zócalo, the largest structure in town and perhaps the best-restored of all the Baja California mission buildings. It has a gilded altar. The museum beside the church is worth a visit: there are educational displays about the missions, Bajan history and historic horse and ranching equipment, book shop. ■ *Open Tuesday-Saturday 0900-1700.* Inscription over the main door of the mission announces: 'Mother of all the Missions of Lower and Upper California'.

Sleeping **LL** *Diamond Eden*, all-inclusive, luxury, beachfront, 10 minutes from airport, 224 rooms, a/c, 2 pools, fitness centre, 2 restaurants, 6 bars, golf, John McEnroe Tennis Centre, mostly package holiday business. **A** *Oasis*, C de la Playa y Baja California, T30112, on bay at south end of Loreto in palm grove, large rooms, pool, tennis, restaurant, bar, skiffs (pangas) for hire, fishing cruises arranged, pleasant and quiet, a/c. **A-B** *La Pinta*, on Sea of Cortés 2 kilometres north of Zócalo, a/c, showers, pool, tennis, restaurant, bar, considered by many the best of the original 'Presidente' paradores, 30 rooms, fishing boat hire, recommended. **C** *La Siesta Bungalows*, small, manager owns the dive shop and can offer combined accommodation and diving trips. **C** *Misión de Loreto*, C de la Playa y Juárez, T30048, colonial-style with patio garden, a/c, pool, dining rooms, bar, fishing trips arranged, very comfortable, but poor service, check for discounts. **D** *Villa del Mar*, Colina Zaragoza, near sports centre, OK, restaurant, bar, pool, bargain rates, on beach. **Motel** **E** *Salvatierra*, C Salvatierra, on south approach to town, a/c, hot showers, clean, good value. **E** *Casa de huéspedes San Martín*, Benito Juárez, 200 metres from beach, with shower, good.

Camping *Ejido Loreto RV Park*, on beach 1 kilometre south of town, full hook-ups, toilets, showers, free coffee, laundry, fishing and boat trips arranged, US$5 per person. Butter clams are plentiful in the sand.

Eating On Calle de la Playa, *Embarcadero*, owner offers fishing trips, average prices for food. *El Nido* and *El Buey*, both good (latter barbecues); several *taco* stands on Calle Salvatierra. *Playa Blanca*, Hidalgo y Madero, rustic, American meals, reasonable prices. *César's*, Emiliano Zapata y Benito Juárez, good food and service, candelit, moderate prices. *Café Olé*, Madero 14, Mexican and fast food, palapa-style, open-air breakfasts, budget rates.

Diving Scuba and snorkelling information and equipment booth on municipal beach near the fishing pier; the beach itself stretches for 8 kilometres, but is dusty and rocky. Beware of stingrays on the beach.

Transport Air International, 4 kilometres south; Aero California (T50500) daily to Los Angeles; Aerolitoral to Chihuahua, Ciudad, Obregón, La Paz and other destinations in high season. Charter flights to Canada.

Buses Bus station at Calle Salvatierra opposite intersection of Zapata; to **La Paz** 6 a day, from 0700, US$10.75; to **Tijuana** 1500, 1800, 2100, 2300, US$30, 17 hours.

Route south of Loreto

Just south of Loreto a rough road runs 37 kilometres through impressive canyon scenery to the village of **San Javier**, tucked in the bottom of a steep-walled valley; the settlement has only one store but the Mission of San Javier is one of the best-preserved in North America; it was founded by the Jesuits in 1699 and took 59 years to complete. The thick volcanic walls, Moorish ornamentation and bell tower are most impressive in so rugged and remote a location. Near San Javier is Piedras Pintas, 16 kilometres from the main road, close to Rancho Las Parras; there are eight prehistoric figures painted here in red, yellow and black. The road to San Javier Mission is in poor shape, sturdy vehicle required. In San Javier, you can stay in hostal and restaurant *Palapa*, close to the church, or in a **E** two-bed house with kitchen rented by Ramón Bastida in a beautiful, quiet garden, five minutes' walk along the path behind the church.

The highway south of Loreto passes a picturesque stretch of coast. Fonatur, the government tourist development agency, is building a resort complex at **Nopoló** (eight kilometres), which it was hoped would one day rival its other resort developments at Cancún, Ixtapa and Huatulco. An international airport, streets and electricity were laid out, then things slowed down; today there is the 15-storey **LL** *El Presidente Hotel*, T30700; international class, self-contained, on its own imported-sand beach; nearby lighted Loreto Tennis Center, half-finished foundations, weeds and an absence of people. 16 kilometres further on is **Puerto Escondido**, with a new yacht harbour and marina; although the boat landing and anchoring facilities are operating, the complex is still far from complete, slowed by the same diversion of funds to other projects as Nopoló. There is, however, the *Tripui Trailer Park*, claimed to be the best in Mexico (PO Box 100, Loreto), landscaped grounds, paved roads, coin laundry, groceries, restaurant and pool, lighted tennis court, playground; 116 spaces (most rented by the year), US$17 for two, extra person US$5 (T706-8330413). There are three lovely *PP*s between Loreto and Puerto Escondido (none has drinking water); Notrí, Juncalito and Ligüí: palm-lined coves, which are a far cry from the bustle of the new resort developments nearby. Beyond Ligüí (36 kilometres south of Loreto) Highway 1 ascends the eastern escarpment of the Sierra Giganta (one of the most fascinating legs of Highway 1) before leaving the Gulf to strike out southwest across the Peninsula again to Ciudad Constitución.

Ciudad Constitución
Colour map 1, grid C3

The highway passes by **Ciudad Insurgentes**, a busy agricultural town of 13,000 with two service stations, banks, auto repairs, shops and cafés (no hotels/motels), then runs dead straight for 26 kilometres to **Ciudad Constitución**, which is the marketing centre for the Magdalena Plain agricultural development and has the largest population between Ensenada and La Paz (50,000). Although not a tourist town, it has extensive services of use to the visitor: department stores, restaurants, banks, public market, service stations, laundries, car repairs, hospital (see introduction to this section, **Insurance and Medical Services**) and airport (near Ciudad Insurgentes). Many businesses line Highway 1, which is divided and doubles as the palm-lined main street, with the first traffic lights since Ensenada, 1,158 kilometres away.

Sleeping D *Casino*, a block east of the *Maribel* on same street, T20754, quieter, 37 clean rooms, restaurant, bar. **D** *Maribel*, Guadalupe Victoria y Highway 1, T20155, 2 blocks south of San Carlos road junction, a/c, TV, restaurant, bar, suites available, clean, fine for overnight stop. **E-F** *El Arbolito*, basic, clean, central.

Camping *Campestre La Pila*, 2½ kilometres south on unpaved road off Highway 1, farmland setting, full hook-ups, toilets, showers, pool, laundry, groceries, tennis courts, ice, restaurant, bar, no hot water, US$10-13 for 4. *RV Park Manfred*, on left of main road going north into town, very clean, friendly and helpful, Austrian owner (serves Austrian food).

Eating *Dragón de Oro*, Zapata y Highway 1, Chinese. *Panadería Superpan*, north of market hall, excellent pastries.

Excursions Deep artesian wells have made the desert of the Llano de Magdalena bloom with citrus groves and a chequerboard of neat farms growing cotton, wheat and vegetables; this produce is shipped out through the port of **San Carlos**, 58 kilometres to the west on **Bahía Magdalena**, 40 minutes by bus from Ciudad Constitución. Known to boaters as 'Mag Bay', it is considered the finest natural harbour between San Francisco and Acapulco. Protected by mountains and sand spits, it provides the best boating on Baja's Pacific coast. Small craft can explore kilometres of mangrove-fringed inlets and view the grey whales who come here in the winter season. The best time to whale-watch is January-March, US$25 per hour for a boat for up to six persons. **C** *Hotel Alcatraz*. **E** *Las Palmas*, on same street as bus station, clean, fan, hot water. **E** *Motel Las Brisas*, 1 block behind bus station, clean, friendly, quiet.

On the narrow south end of Magdalena Island is Puerto Magdalena, a lobstering village of 400. Seven kilometres away is a deepwater port at Punta Belcher.

Whales can be seen at Puerto López Mateos further north (access from Cd Insurgentes or Cd Constitución); no hotel, but ask for house of María del Rosario González who rents rooms (**E**) or take a tent and camp at the small harbour near the fish plant. Alternatively, stay in Ciudad Constitución, several daily buses. On **Santa Margarita Island** are Puertos Alcatraz (a fish-canning community of 300) and Cortés (important naval base); neither is shown on the ACSC map.

Highway 1 continues its arrow-straight course south of Ciudad Constitución across the flat plain to the village of Santa Rita. 28 kilometres beyond Santa Rita, it makes a 45° turn east, where a road of dubious quality runs to the remote missions of San Luís Gonzaga (64 kilometres) and La Pasión (49 kilometres); it is planned to extend it to the ruins of Dolores del Sur (85 kilometres) on the Gulf of California, one of Baja's most inaccessible mission sites. There is a service station at the village of El Cien; meals and refreshments are available at the Rancho San Agustín, 24 kilometres beyond.

La Paz

Capital of Baja California Sur, La Paz is a relaxed modern city, nestled at the southern end of La Paz Bay (where Europeans first set foot in Baja in 1533). Sunsets can be spectacular. Prices have risen as more tourists arrive to enjoy its winter climate, but free port status ensures that there are plenty of bargains (although some goods, like certain makes of camera, are cheaper to buy in the USA). Oyster beds attracted many settlers in the 17th century, but few survived long. The Jesuit mission, founded here in 1720, was abandoned 29 years later. La Paz became the territorial capital in 1830 after Loreto was wiped out by a hurricane. Although bursting with new construction, there are still many touches of colonial grace, arched doorways and flower-filled patios. The early afternoon *siesta* is still observed by many businesses, especially during summer.

Population: 168,000, 1991
State population 1995: 375,450
Phone code: 112
Colour map 2, grid C1

Sights Heart of La Paz is the **Plaza Constitución**, facing which are the Government Buildings and the graceful **Cathedral of Nuestra Señora de la Paz**, built in 1861-65 on or
near the site of the original mission. The Post Office is a block northeast at
Revolución de 1910 y Constitución. The street grid is rectangular; westerly streets
run into the Paseo Alvaro Obregón, the waterfront **Malecón**, where the commercial
and tourist wharves back onto a tangle of streets just west of the main plaza; here are
the banks, City Hall, Chinatown and many of the cheaper *pensiones*. The more
expensive hotels are further southwest. A must is the **Museo Antropológico de
Baja California Sur**, Ignacio Altamirano y 5 de Mayo (four blocks east of the Plaza),
with an admirable display of peninsula anthropology, history and pre-history, folklore and geology. The bookshop has a wide selection on Mexico and Baja. ■ *Tuesday-Saturday 0900-1800; free.* A carved mural depicting the history of Mexico can
be seen at the **Palacio de Gobierno** on Isabel La Católica, corner of Bravo.

Excursions There are boat tours from the Tourist Wharf on the Malecón around the bay and to
nearby islands like Espíritu Santo. Travel agencies offer a daily boat tour to **Los
Lobos Islands** ranging from US$40 (basic) to US$80; the tour should include lunch
and snorkelling, six hours, you can see pelicans, sealions and dolphins, with luck
whales, too. 17 kilometres west of La Paz a paved road branches northwest off Highway 1 around the bay leading to the mining village of **San Juan de la Costa**, allowing
a closer look at the rugged coastal section of the Sierra de la Giganta. Pavement ends
after 25 kilometres, the road becomes wide, rolling, regularly graded; OK for large

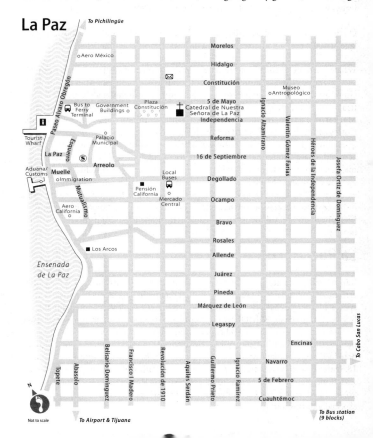

La Paz

RVs to San Juan, which is a company town of neat-rowed houses; phosphorus is mined and loaded by conveyor and deep-water dock, to be shipped to processing plants for fertilizer production. After San Juan (45 kilometres), the road is passable for medium-size vehicles to Punta Coyote (90 kilometres), closely following the narrow space between mountains and coast; wonderful untouched camping spots. From Coyote to **San Evaristo** (27 kilometres) the track is poor, rugged vehicle recommended, travel time from Highway 1 about four and a half hours; San Evaristo is a sleepy fishing village on a delightful cove sheltered on the east by the Isla San José. Ideal boating area but as yet undiscovered. Visit the salt-drying operations near San Evaristo or on San José. This is a rewarding excursion for those with smaller, high-clearance vehicles (vans and pick-ups) for the steep final 20 mile stretch.

State Highway 286 leads southeast out of La Paz 45 kilometres to **San Juan de Los Planes** (*Population*: 1,350), a friendly town in a rich farming region. A fair road continues another 15 kilometres to the beautiful **Ensenada del los Muertos**, good fishing, swimming and 'wild' camping. A further 11 kilometres is the headland of **Punta Arena de la Ventana**, with a magnificent view of the sterile slopes of Isla Cerralvo. (**LL** *Hotel Las Arenas*, resort overlooking Ventana Bay). Six kilometres before Los Planes, a graded road leads to the Bahía de la Ventana and the small fishing villages of La Ventana and El Sargento; lovely beaches facing Cerralvo Island.

Beaches Many, most popular on the Pichilingüe Peninsula, most have restaurants (good seafood restaurant under *palapa* at Pichilingüe). Going north from La Paz to ferry terminal on Highway 11; Palmira, Coromuel (popular with paceños), El Caimancito (admission fee), Tesoro. Wind surfing and catamaran trips can be arranged. Pichilingüe (bus from 1000-1400 and 1600-1800, US$1.30 from station at Paseo Alvaro Obregón y Independencia), 100 metres north of ferry terminal is a *playa pública*. Balandra (rubbish bins, *palapas*, US$2) and Tecolote (same but camping free under *palapas*) are reached by the road beyond the ferry terminal (paved for some distance beyond this point), which ends at a gravel pit at Playa Cachimba (good surf fishing), 13 kilometres northeast of Pichilingüe; beaches facing north are attractive but can be windy, some sandflies. El Coyote (no water or facilities) is on the east coast and reached by a road/track from La Paz running inland along the middle of the peninsula. El Comitán and El Mogote, are to the southwest of La Paz on the bay, tranquil, no surf. In October (at least) and after rain, beware of stinging jelly fish in the water.

Sleeping
■ *on maps*
Price codes:
see inside front cover

AL *Los Arcos*, Paseo Alvaro Obregón 498 at Allende, T22744, a/c, pool, restaurant, coffee shop, across the Malecón from the beach, walking distance of centre, fishing trips arranged, excellent value. **AL** *Cabañas de los Arcos*, opposite with shared facilities, a/c, pool, slightly cheaper, T22297. **AL** *Gran Hotel Baja*, 'the only high-rise structure south of Ensenada', so easy to find, T23844, restaurant, bar, pool, disco, etc, on beach, trailer park adjacent. **AL** *La Posada*, on bay 3½ kilometres southwest of centre, 5 blocks off Highway 1 on Colima, T20653, a/c, pool, tennis, bar, restaurant, quiet and relaxing, recommended but away from the centre. **AL** *El Morro*, 3½ kilometres northeast on Palmira Beach, Moorish-style, a/c, TV, fridges, apartments with kitchenettes, pool, restaurant, bar. **AL** *El Presidente Sur*, 6½ kilometres northeast at Caimancito Beach, T26544, good location but furthest from town, a/c, pool, restaurant, bar, next door to Governor's mansion. **AL** *Misiones de La Paz*, on El Mogote sandspit, isolated, accessible by launch from *Hotel La Posada*, T24021, a/c, showers, pool, restaurant, cocktail bar, quiet. **AL** *Palmira*, T24000, 3½ kilometres northeast of Pichilingüe Rd, a/c, pool, tennis, restaurant, disco, convention facilities, fishing trips arranged, popular with families. **A** *La Perla*, on the water front, T20777, clean, a/c, friendly, restaurant expensive, locked garage.

C *María Dolores Gardenias*, Aquíles Serdán y Vicente Guerrero, a/c, pool, restaurant (good), excellent, value. **C** *Mediterráneo*, Allende 36, T51195 (**D** low season) a/c, beautiful setting, has outstanding restaurant.

D *Hospedaje Marelí*, Aquíles Serdán 283 y Bravo, a/c, clean, 10 minutes' walk to Plaza

Constitución, pleasant, recommended. **D** *Lorimar* on Bravo, hot showers, clean, very helpful, run by a Mexican/American couple, popular, good place to meet fellow travellers, good value restaurant, free ferry booking service. **D** *Veneka*, Madero 1520, T54688, nice, clean and friendly, safe parking, excellent *margaritas*, good restaurant, specials are recommended, chained monkey in courtyard, not recommended for animal lovers.

E *Cuartos Jalisco*, Belisario Domínguez 251, very basic. **E** *Pensión California*, C Degollado 209 near Madero, basic, fan, shower, garden patio, noisy, friendly, weekly deals, basic and not too clean. **E** *Posada San Miguel*, C Belisario Domínguez Nte 45, near plaza, colonial-style, bathroom, clean, hot water (limited), quiet, recommended. **F** *San Carlos*, 16 de Septiembre y Revolución, clean but noisy, laundry upstairs. **E-F** *Hostería del Convento*, C Madero 85, basic, fans, clean, shower, tepid water between 0700 and 0900, beautiful patio. **F** *Miriam*, Av 16 de Septiembre, price per person.

Camping *El Cardón Trailer Park*, 4 kilometres southwest on Highway 1, partly-shaded area away from beach, full facilities, US$11 for 2. *Aquamarina RV Park*, 3½ kilometres southwest, 400 metres off Highway 1 at C Nayarit, on bay, nicely landscaped, all facilities, marina, boat ramp, fishing, scuba trips arranged, US$17 for 2. *La Paz Trailer Park*, 1½ kilometres south of town off Highway 1, access via C Colima, deluxe, nearest RV Park to La Paz, very comfortable, US$12 for 2. The *ferretería* across from the main city bus terminal sells white gas stove fuel (*gasolina blanca*). *La Perla de la Paz* department store, C Arreola y 21 de Agosto, sells general camping supplies. CCC Supermarket, opposite Palacio de Gobierno, is good for supplies.

Youth hostel On Carretera al Sur (Highway 1), Blvd Forjadores de Sudcalifornia Km 3, CP 23040, T24615, dormitory bunk, open 0600-2300, good value, '8 de Octubre' bus from market.

Eating *Palapa Adriana*, on beachfront, open air, excellent service but beware overcharging.
● *on maps* *Antojitos*, next to *Pirámide* on 16 de Septiembre de 1810, friendly, good value. *Rossy*, Av 16 de Septiembre, good for breakfast, fish, cheap. *Café Chanate*, behind tourist office, open evening only, good atmosphere, jazz music, sometimes live. *La Caleta* on the waterfront, recommended. *La Tavola Pizza*, good value. *La Revolución*, Revolución, between Reforma and Independencia, cheap breakfast and lunch. Vegetarian restaurant *El Quinto*, Independencia y B Domínguez, expensive (whole wheat bread is half the price at the *panadería* in the market place). Excellent and cheap tacos at a restaurant with no name on Av 16 de Septiembre, near the bus station. Good *lonchería* and juice bars in the market.

Festivals *Pre-Lenten Mardi Gras* (carnival) in **February or March**, inaugurated in 1989, is becoming one of Mexico's finest. The Malecón is converted into a swirling mass of dancing, games, restaurants and stalls, and the street parade is happy and colourful. Well worth a visit, but book accommodation far in advance.

Shopping A duty-free port (but see above). *Casa de las Artesanías de BCS*, Paseo Alvaro Obregón at Mijares, just north of *Hotel Los Arcos*, for souvenirs from all over Mexico. *Centro de Arte Regional*, Chiapas y Encinas (5 blocks east of Isabel La Católica), pottery workshop, reasonable prices. *Fortunato Silva*, Highway 1 (Abasolo) y Jalisco at south end of town, good quality woollen and hand-woven cotton garments and articles. *Bazar del Sol*, Obregón 1665, for quality ceramics and good Aztec art reproductions. *Solco's*, Obregón y 16 de Septiembre, large selection of Taxco silver, leather, onyx chess sets. The Mercado Central, Revolución y Degollado, and another at Bravo y Prieto, have a wide range of goods (clothes, sandals, guitars, etc), plus fruit and vegetables. Tourist shops are concentrated along the Malecón between the Tourist and Commercial Wharves.

Sports **Diving**: *Baja Diving and Service*, Obregón 1680, hires equipment and takes diving trips (US$320 for 4-day PADI course); snorkelling day trip about US$35, very good. *La Paz BCS Dive Centre*, Esquerro 1560, T/F57048.

Local Rentals: *Viajes Palmira* rents cycles and mopeds, Av Obregón, opposite *Hotel los* **Transport** *Arcos*, T24030. **Budget**, **Avis**, **Hertz**, **Auto Renta Sol** and **Auto Servitur** booths at airport.

Air Gen Manuel Márquez de León International Airport (LAP), 11 kilometres southwest on paved road off Highway 1. Taxi fare US$6, supposedly fixed, but bargain. Flights within Mexico to Chihuahua, Cuidad Juárez, Ciudad Obregón, Culiacán, Guadalajara, Guaymas, Hermosillo, Loreto, Los Cabos, Los Mochis, Mazatlán, Mexico City, Monterrey, Tijuana. US destinations include Los Angeles, Phoenix, San Antonio, Seattle and Spokane.

Buses Local buses about US$0.50, depot at Revolución de 1910 y Degollado by the Public Market. Central Bus Station (Central Camionera): Jalisco y Héroes de la Independencia, about 16 blocks from centre (taxi US$2), terminal for Tres Estrellas de Oro and Autotransportes Aguila (a/c buses, video, toilet); Autotransportes de La Paz leave from Public Market. **Ciudad Constitución**, 13 departures a day, US$7.70; **Loreto**, 3 per day, US$11.50; **Guerrero Negro**, 6 per day, US$24; **Ensenada**, US$43; **Tijuana**, US$60.50, **Mexicali**, US$55. To the Cape: **San Antonio**, US$1.75, **Miraflores** US$5, **San José del Cabo**, US$6.60, **Cabo San Lucas**, US$8 (all 10 departures per day). **Todos Santos**, 6 per day, US$4.40; Cabo San Lucas via west loop US$7.70.

Ferry For schedule to Mazatlán and Topolobampo, see page 552. Modern ferry terminal at Pichilingüe, 21 kilometres north on paved highway. Tickets for the same day are sold at the terminal itself. In advance, tickets may be bought at Sematur, 5 de Mayo y Guillermo Prieto, between Reforma and Independencia, T53833/54666, open 0700-1200.) Travel agents sell ferry tickets, eg *Turismo Express*, Esplanada Alvaro Obregón y 16 de Septiembre, 23000 La Paz, T56310-3, F56310. Tourist cards must be valid, allow 2 hours as there are long queues, trucks have loading priority. It should be noted that many motorists have had difficulty getting reservations or having them honoured. Try to book at least 2 weeks ahead (6 weeks at Christmas, Easter, July and August). If you have left it to the last minute, get to the ticket office at 0400 and you may be able to get a cancellation. **NB** Vehicles must have car permits, obtainable at ferry terminal and at Sematur, or at Registro Federal de Vehículos in Tijuana; automobile clubs will provide information. Conditions on the ferry are reported to have improved from the former 'cockroach haven'. The deck gets wet during the night, but the top deck is very refreshing in summer (OK to sleep on deck); toilets quickly get blocked and are then locked up, so make an early call and bring your own toilet paper. Restaurants on board are reasonably priced and food OK. To get a tourist cabin, insist that you will share with strangers, a friendly chat may help. At busy periods, the queue for seats starts at 0630. Book cars 4 weeks in advance. On arrival, buses to Mazatlán may be full, ask about rides on the ferry. Bus to ferry terminal from Medrita Travel Agency, Paseo Alvaro Obregón y Calle 5 de Mayo, frequent departures; from terminal, Calle Ejido (first on the left after leaving the ferry). Reasonable facilities at terminal but crowded; large parking lots, officials may permit RVs to stay overnight while awaiting ferry departures. **NB** On all ferry crossings, delays can occur from September if there is bad weather, which could hold you up for 3 days; fog at the entrance to Topolobampo harbour is often a problem; mechanical breakdowns are not unknown! Keep a flexible schedule if travelling to the mainland.

Airline offices *Aero California*, city office at Malecón y C Bravo, T51023. *AeroMéxico*, T20091. **Directory** **Banks** Banks will not exchange TCs after 1100. *Banamex*, C Arreola y Esquerro. 2 *casas de cambio* on 5 de Mayo off Obregón, 0800-2000, better rates than banks. **Laundry** *Laundromat Yoli*, C 5 de Mayo y Rubio. **Tour companies & travel agents** Sea kayaking and whale watching tours starting in La Paz, are offered by OARS, PO Box 67, Angels Camp CA 95222, T209-7364677, European office: 67 Verney Ave, High Wycombe, Bucks HP12 3ND, England, T01494-448901. **Tourist office** On Tourist Wharf at bottom of 16 de Septiembre, helpful, English spoken, open Mon-Fri 0800-1500, Sat 0900-1300, 1400-1500, open till 1900 high season, will make hotel reservations, some literature and town maps. Fax facilities here (send and receive worldwide), also noticeboard for rides offered, crew wanted etc. **Useful addresses** **Immigration:** Second floor of large building on Paseo Alvaro Obregón, opposite the pier, reported to be very helpful, possible to extend visa here.

Sematur ferry schedule

Route	La Paz - Mazatlán	Mazatlán - La Paz	La Paz - Topolobampo	Topolobampo - La Paz	Sta Rosalia - Guaymas	Guaymas - Sta Rosalia
Frequency and Class	Sun - Fri	Fri - Wed	Wed, Thur	Wed, Thur	Tues, Fri	Tues, Fri
	Salón US$21 Turista US$42 Cabina US$62 Especial US$83	Salón US$21 Turista US$42 Cabina US$62 Especial US$83	Salón US$14 Turista US$28 Cabina US$42 Especial US$55	Salón US$14 Turista US$28 Cabina US$42 Especial US$55	Salón US$14 Turista US$28	Salón US$14 Turista US$28
	Wed	Thur	Fri - Tues	Fri - Tues		
	Load Ferry	Load Ferry	Load Ferry	Load Ferry		
	Salón US$21	Salón US$21	Salón US$14	Salón US$14		
Departure	1500	1500	2200	2200	2300	0900
Arrival	0900	0900	0800	0800	0800	1500

Fare pp sharing accommodation

Children under 12 ½ price

Children under 2 free

No pregnant women allowed on board

SALON – General seating

TURISTA - Cabin with bunkbeds & washbasin

CABINA - Cabin with bunkbeds & bathroom

ESPECIAL - Cabin with living room, bedroom, bathroom & closet

Routes on request for cars, motor homes, trailers, motorcycles etc

SEMATUR OFFICES:

Central reservation T 01-800-6969600

Terminal Pichilingüe, La Paz T (112) 25005, F 55717

Terminal de Transbordadores, Mazatlán T (69) 817020/21, F 817023, www.ferrysematur.com.mx/sematur.htm

Muelle Fiscal, Topolobampo T (686) 20141, F 20035

Muelle Fiscal, Sta Rosalia T (115) 20014/13

Muelle Fiscal, Guaymas T (622) 23390, F 23393

Festival Tours, Texas 36, Col Nápoles, México DF, CP 03810 T 56827043, 56826213, F 56827378;1 Allende Sur 655, Bajos del Hotel América, Los Mochis, T 183986; Ignacio Ramírez 2215 esq Benito Juárez, La Paz, T 53833, 54666

La Paz to Santiago

South of La Paz and its plain, the central mountain spine rises again into the wooded heights of the Sierra de la Laguna and bulges out into the 'Cape Region', Baja's most touristically-developed area. The highway winds up to El Triunfo, a picturesque village (almost a ghost town); silver was discovered at El Triunfo in 1862. The town exploded with a population of 10,000 and was for a while the largest town in Baja. The mines closed in 1926 but small-scale mining has resumed in places. There is a craft shop at the village entrance where young people make palm-leaf objects.

El Triunfo
Present-day miners are using arsenic in the old mine tailings; these areas are fenced and signed.

Eight kilometres further on is the lovely mountain town and farming centre of **San Antonio** (gasoline, groceries, meals), which was founded in 1756 and served briefly as Baja's capital (1828-30) when Loreto was destroyed. Eight kilometres south of San Antonio was the site of Santa Ana, where silver was first discovered in 1748. It was from this vanished village that the Viceroy and Padre Junípero Serra planned the expedition to establish the chain of Franciscan missions in Alta California.

San Antonio

Highway 1 climbs sharply from the canyon and winds past a number of ancient mines, through the peaceful orchard-farming town of San Bartolo (groceries and meals) and down to the coastal flats around Los Barriles, a small town with fuel, meals and limited supplies. A number of resort hotels are situated near here along the beautiful Bahía de Palmas and at nearby Buena Vista; none is in the 'budget' class but all are popular (**AL** *Hotel Palmas de Cortéz*, nice beach location; *Víctor's* campground is clean, well-organized with all facilities; nearby is *Tío Pancho's* restaurant, mediocre food but good atmosphere.

Los Barriles

The Highway turns inland after Los Barriles (106 kilometres from La Paz). An 'East Cape Loop' turns east off the Highway through La Rivera (**E** *La Rivera RV Park* in palm grove next to beach, excellent swimming, hot showers, laundry, friendly, recommended), where a new spur leads towards **Cabo Pulmo**; it is being paved at a rapid rate and will eventually take a slightly inland route paralleling the coast to San José del Cabo. Off Cabo Pulmo, a beautiful headland, is the Northern Pacific's only living coral reef; fishing, diving and snorkelling are excellent (56 kilometres from Los Barriles). There are many camping spots along the beautiful beaches of this coast.

Santiago is a pleasant, historic little town three kilometres off Highway 1. On the tree-lined main street are a Pemex station, café and stores grouped around the town plaza. One kilometre further west is the Parque Zoológico, the Cape's only zoo, modest but informative, free admission. The Jesuits built their 10th mission in Santiago in 1723 after transferring it from Los Barriles. The town was one of the sites of the Pericué Indian uprising of 1734. **D** *Palomar*, a/c, hot showers, restaurant, bar, on main street, modest, good meals).

Santiago
Population: 2,000
Colour map 2, grid C1

Three and a half kilometres south of the Santiago turnoff Highway 1 crosses the Tropic of Cancer, marked by a large concrete sphere, and runs south down the fertile valley between the lofty Sierra de la Laguna (West) and the Sierra Santa Clara (East), to Los Cabos International Airport. San José del Cabo is 14 kilometres further south.

San José del Cabo

The largest town south of La Paz founded in 1730, it is now essentially a modern town divided into two districts: the resort sectors and new Fonatur development on the beach, and the downtown zone to the north, with the government offices and many businesses grouped near the tranquil Parque Mijares, and numerous shops and restaurants along Calle Zaragoza and Doblado. The north end of Boulevard Antonio Mijares has been turned into a "mini-gringoland ... which could have been

Population: 10,000
Phone code: 114
Colour map 2, grid C1

transplanted from the Main Street of Disneyland" (Scott Wayne). San José also has two service stations, hospital, auto parts and mechanical repairs. The attractive church on the Plaza Mijares was built in 1940 on the final site of the mission of 1730; a tile mosaic over the entrance depicts the murder of Padre Tamaral by rebellious Indians in 1734. Most of the top hotels are located west of San José along the beaches or nearby estero; the Fonatur development blocks access to much of the beach near town; best are Playas Nuevo Sol and California, about three kilometres from downtown. Unofficial camping is possible on those few not fronted by resort hotels.

Sleeping **LL** *Palmilla*, one of the top resorts in Baja, 8 kilometres west at Punta Palmilla (outstanding surfing nearby), some a/c, showers, pool, beach, tennis, narrow access road, restaurant, bar, skin diving, fishing cruisers and skiffs for hire (daily happy hour allows mere mortals to partake of margarita and appetizers for US$3 and see how royalty and film stars live!) **LL** *Stouffer Presidente Los Cabos*, Blvd Mijares s/n, T20038, F20232, on lagoon south of town, a/c, all facilities, boat rentals, centrepiece of the Fonatur development at San José del Cabo. **L-AL** *Posada Real Cabo* (Best Western), next door, T20155, F20460, a/c, colour TV, showers, pool, tennis, restaurant, bar, gift shop, fishing charters. **AL** *Calinda Aquamarina-Comfort Inn*, next to *Posada Real Cabo*, T20077, US Comfort Inn chain, a/c, beach, pool, restaurant, bar, fishing, clean and comfortable. *Aston Cabo Regis Resort and Beach Club*, in hotel zone on Blvd Finisterra, a/c, colour TV, showers, kitchenettes, private balconies, pool, tennis, golf course, restaurant. **AL** *Castel Cabo*, on beach off Paseo San José south of town, T20155, a/c, another Fonatur hotel. **C** *Nuevo Sol*, on beach south of intersection of Paseo San José and Highway 1, pool, restaurant, sports facilities, nicely-landscaped, acceptable and good beachside value. **C** *San José Inn*, on last paved street north of beach, clean, quiet, cool, comfortable, ceiling fans, good value. **D** *Collí*, in town on Hidalgo above Budget Rent-a-Car, T20052, fans, hot showers, 12 clean and adequate rooms. **D** *Pagamar*, Obregón between Degollado y Guerrero 3½ blocks from plaza, fans, café, hot showers, clean, good value. **E** *Ceci*, Zaragoza 22, 1 block west of plaza, T20051, fans, hot showers (usually), basic but clean, excellent value, central.

Motel **D** *Brisa del Mar*, on Highway 1, 3 kilometres southwest of town near Hotel Nuevo Sol, 10 rooms, restaurant, bar, pool, modest but comfortable, at rear of trailer park on outstanding beach.

Camping *Brisa Del Mar Trailer Park*, 100 RV sites in fenced area by great beach, full hook-ups, flush toilets, showers, pool, laundry, restaurant, bar, fishing trips arranged, popular, good location ('unofficial' free camping possible under *palapas* on beach), recommended.

Transport **Air** To Los Cabos International Airport (SJD), 14 kilometres, take a local bus, US$3, which drops you at the entrance road to the airport, leaving a 2-kilometre walk, otherwise take a taxi. Airport to San Jose del Cabo in colectivo US$7. Flights to the USA: Anchorage, Burbank, Dallas, Denver, Fort Lauderdale, Houston, Los Angeles, New York, Orange County, Phoenix, Portland, San Diego, San Francisco, Seattle, Spokane, Tucson. Domestic flights: Chihuahua, Ciudad Obregón, Culiacán, Guadalajara, Hermosillo, Los Mochis, Mazatlán, Mexico City, Monterrey, Puerto Vallarta.

Bus Bus station on Calle Manuel Doblado opposite hospital, about 7 blocks west of plaza. To **Cabo San Lucas** (Tres Estrellas) daily from 0700, US$1.25, 30 minutes; to **La Paz** daily from 0630, US$9, 3 hours.

Directory **Airlines** *Aerocalifornia*, T33700. *Mexicana*, T222722. *Alaska Airlines*, T95800-4260333. **Laundry** Self-service at Playa de California.

All the beaches and coastal areas between San José del Cabo and Cabo San Lucas have become public after protests by local inhabitants against private developments.

These include: *Hotel Cabo San Lucas, Twin Dolphin* (T30140), and *Calinda Cabo Baja-Quality Inn* (T30045), part of Cabo Bello residential development (all **LL**). At Km 25, just after the *Twin Dolphin*, a dirt road leads off to Shipwreck Beach, where a large ship rots on the shore. Five kilometres before Cabo a small concrete marker beside the highway heralds an excellent view of the famous Cape. The Highway enters Cabo San Lucas past a Pemex station and continues as Boulevard Lázaro Cárdenas to the Zócalo (Guerrero y Madero) and the Kilómetro 0 marker.

Cabo San Lucas

Grown rapidly in recent years from a sleepy fishing village of 1,500 inhabitants in 1970. It is now a bustling, expensive international resort with a permanent population of 8,500. There are trailer parks, many cafés and restaurants, condominiums, gift shops, discos and a marina to cater for the increasing flood of North Americans who come for the world-famous sportfishing or to find a retirement paradise. Everything is quoted in US dollars and food is more American than Mexican. The town fronts a small harbour facing the rocky peninsula that forms the 'Land's End' of Baja California. Francisco de Ulloa first rounded and named the Cape in 1539. The sheltered bay became a watering point for the treasure ships from the Orient; pirates sheltered here too. Now it is on the cruise ship itinerary. A popular attraction is the government-sponsored regional arts centre, located at the cruise liner dock.

Colour map 2, grid C1

Sleeping In our **L** range *Finisterra*, perched on promontory near Land's End, T30000, a/c, TV, shower, pool, steps to beach, poolside bar with unsurpassed view, restaurant, entertainment, sportfishing cruisers. *Giggling Marlin Inn*, central on Blvd Marina y Matamoros, a/c, TV, showers, kitchenettes, jacuzzi, restaurant, bar, fishing trips arranged, lively drinking in attached cocktail bar. *Hacienda Beach Resort*, at north entrance to harbour, some a/c, showers, pool, tennis, yacht anchorage, various watersports, hunting, horseriding, restaurant, etc, claims the only beach safe from strong Pacific swells. *Marina Sol Condominiums*, high season 16 October-30 June, on 16 de Septiembre, between Highway 1 and Bay, full service hotel in 3 and 7-storey buildings. *Solmar*, T30022, the southernmost development in Baja California, a/c, showers, ocean view, pool, tennis, diving, restaurant, poolside bar, fishing cruisers, beach with heavy ocean surf. **B** *Mar de Cortéz*, on Highway 1 at Guerrero in town centre, T30032, a/c, showers, helpful, pool, outdoor bar/restaurant, good value. **C** *Casablanca*, C Revolución between Morelos y Leona Vicario, central, ceiling fan (**D** in rooms with floor fan), hot shower, clean, but basic in cheaper rooms, quiet and friendly. **C** *Marina*, Blvd Marina y Guerrero, T30030, central, a/c, restaurant, bar, can be noisy, pricey. **D** *Dos Mares*, Hidalgo, a/c, TV, clean, small pool, parking space, recommended.

Youth hostel **D** Av de la Juventud s/n, T30148, private bath, **F** per person in dormitory, not very central, but quite smart and clean.

Motel **C** *Los Cabos Inn*, Abasolo y 16 de Septiembre, central, 1 block from bus station, fans, showers, central, modest, good value. **D** *El Dorado*, Morelos (4 blocks from bus terminal), clean, fan, hot water, private bath.

Camping *El Arco Trailer Park*, 4 kilometres east on Highway 1, restaurant. *El Faro Viejo Trailer Park*, 1½ kilometres northwest at Matamoros y Morales, shade, laundry, ice, restaurant, bar, clean, out-of-town but good. *Vagabundos del Mar*, 3½ kilometres east on Highway 1, pool, snack bar, laundry, good, US$15 for 2. *Cabo Cielo RV Park*, 3 kilometres east on Highway 1. *San Vicente Trailer Park*, 3 kilometres east on Highway 1, same as Cabo Cielo plus pool, both reasonably basic, rates unknown. All have full hook-ups, toilets and showers.

Eating As alternatives to expensive restaurants, try the 2 pizza places just beyond *Mar de Cortéz*, one next to the telephone office, the other in the block where the street ends; also *Flor Guadalajara*, C Lázaro Cárdenas, on the way out of town a few blocks beyond 'Skid Row', good local dishes. Half a block uphill from *Hotel Dos Mares*, is **San Lucas**, Hidalgo s/n, good food at very reasonable prices, highly recommended. *Edith's*, 1 block from Medeno beach, evenings only, great views. *Mi Casa*, behind Plaza. *The Office Restaurant*, on Medeno beach, good food, moderate prices, live dance show every Thursday, recommended. There is a good bakery in front of the large modern supermarket in the centre of town. The supermarket is stocked with a full range of US foodstuffs.

Transport   **NB** There are no **ferries** from Cabo San Lucas to Puerto Vallarta. **Buses** Bus station at 16 de Septiembre y Zaragoza, central, few facilities. To **San José del Cabo**, 8 departures a day, US$1.25. To **La Paz** 6 a day from 0630, US$8; **Tijuana** US$44, 1600 and 1800 daily via La Paz.

Directory   **Communications** Post Office: is at Morelos y Niños Héroes. **Tourist offices** Next to ferry landing, town maps, Fonatur office.

Beaches   Ringed by pounding surf, columns of fluted rock enclose Lover's Beach (be careful if walking along the beach, huge waves sweep away several visitors each year), a romantic sandy cove with views out to the seal colonies on offshore islets. At the very tip of the Cabo is the distinctive natural arch ('el arco'); boats can be hired to see it close-up, but care is required because of the strong rips. At the harbour entrance is a pinnacle of rock, Pelican Rock, which is home to vast shoals of tropical fish; it is an ideal place for snorkelling and scuba diving or glass-bottomed boats may be rented at the harbourside. (45-minute harbour cruise in glass-bottomed boat to 'el arco', Lover's Beach, etc US$5 per person; most hotels can arrange hire of skiffs to enable visits to the Arch and Land's End, about US$5-10 per hour.)

Many firms rent aquatic equipment and arrange boating excursions, etc; the beaches east of Cabo San Lucas offer endless opportunities for swimming, scuba diving and snorkelling: Cabo Real, five kilometres, has showers and restrooms, modest fee; Barco Barrado (Shipwreck Beach), 10 kilometres, is a lovely beach.

West coast beaches

Todos Santos   Highway 19, the western loop of the Cape Region, was not paved until 1985 and the
Population: 4,000   superb beaches of the west coast have yet to suffer the development and crowding of
Colour map 2, grid C1   the east. The highway branches off Highway 1 just after San Pedro, 32 kilometres south of La Paz, and runs due south through a cactus-covered plain to Todos Santos, a quiet farming town just north of the Tropic of Cancer. There has been a recent influx of expats from the USA and there is a community of artists and craftspeople. There is a Pemex station, cinema, stores, cafés, a bank, clinic and market, a museum: the Casa de la Cultura (Calle Topete y Pilar). Todos Santos was founded as a Jesuit mission in 1734; a church replacing the abandoned structure, built in 1840, stands opposite the Civic Plaza on Calle Juárez. The ruins of several old sugar mills can be seen around the town in the fertile valley. Fishing is also important. *El Tecolote*, on Juárez, has a selection of books in English, some on the region, and the US owner is helpful with Essentials such as access to the Sierra de la Laguna.

Sleeping B *Hotel California*, formerly the *Misión de Todos Santos Inn*, historic brick building near town centre, Calle Juárez, a block north of Highway 19, fans, showers, pool, a/c, dining room; opposite is **D** *Motel Guluarte*, fan, fridge, shower, pool, good value; **D-E** *Misión de Pilar*, clean, good value. **E** *Miramar*, south end of village, new, with bath, hot water, fan, pool, clean, safe, parking, recommended. **Camping** *El Molino Trailer Park*, off Highway at south end of town, 30 minutes from beach, full hook-ups, flush toilets, showers, laundry, American owner, very helpful, US$8 for 4. No camping here but apparently OK to use the beach (clean – but look out for dogs – see below). Several kilometres south is *Trailer Park San Pedrito* (see below), on the beach, closed to camping, new hotel being built, full hook-ups, flush toilets, showers, pool, laundry, restaurant, bar, US$12 for RVs.

Eating On main plaza is *Café Santa Fe*, gourmet Italian food, pricey but very highly rated restaurant.

Two kilometres away is the Pacific coast with some of the most beautiful beaches of **Beaches** the entire Peninsula. Nearest is **Playa Punta Lobos**, a popular picnic spot, but too much rubbish and unfriendly dogs for wild camping; better is the sandy cove at **Playa San Pedrito** (four kilometres southeast). Backed by groves of Washingtonia fan palms and coconut palms, this is one of the loveliest wild camping spots anywhere. Opposite the access road junction is the **Campo Experimental Forestal**, a Botanical Garden with a well-labelled array of desert plants from all regions of Baja; staff are very informative. Here too is the *San Pedrito RV Park* (see above), an open area on the beach, one of the most beautifully-sited RV parks in Baja. 11 kilometres south of Todos Santos is **El Pescadero**, a fast-growing farming town with few facilities for visitors.

   Seven kilometres south of El Pescadero is *Los Cerritos RV Park* on a wide sandy beach, 50 RV or tent sites but no hook-ups, flush toilets, US$3 per vehicle. Playa Los Cerritos is a *playa pública*; there are several camping areas but no facilities, US$2 per vehicle. The succession of rocky coves and empty beaches continues to Colonia Plutarco Elías Calles, a tiny farming village in the midst of a patchwork of orchards. The highway parallels the coast to Rancho El Migriño, then continues south along the coastal plain; there are no more camping spots as far as Cabo San Lucas. Many now prefer the west Loop to the main highway; it is 140 kilometres from the junction at San Pedro, thus cutting off about 50 kilometres and up to an hour's driving time from the Transpeninsular Highway route.

In the rugged interior east of Todos Santos is the **Parque Nacional Sierra de la** **Parque** **Laguna** (under threat and not officially recognized). Its crowning peak is the **Nacional Sierra** Picacho La Laguna (2,163 metres), beginning to attract a trickle of hikers to its 'lost **de la Laguna** world' of pine and oak trees, doves and woodpeckers, grassy meadows and luxuriant flowers; there is nothing else like it in Baja. The trail is steep but straight forward; the panoramic view takes in La Paz and both the Gulf and Pacific. Cold at night. It can be reached from Todos Santos by making local enquiries; three-day guided pack trips are also offered by the *Todos Santos Inn*, US$325 per person. Alternatively, take a taxi from Todos Santos to La Burrera, from where it is eight hours walk along the littered path to the Laguna.

Background

The land

Mexico has an area equal to about a quarter of the United States, with which it has a frontier of 2,400 kilometres. The southern frontier of 885 kilometres is with Guatemala and Belize. It has a coast line of 2,780 kilometres on the Gulf of Mexico and the Caribbean, and of 7,360 kilometres on the Pacific and the Gulf of California.

The structure of the land mass is extremely complicated, but may be simplified (with large reservations) as a plateau flanked by ranges of mountains roughly paralleling the coasts. The northern part of the plateau is low, arid and thinly populated; it takes up 40 percent of the total area of Mexico but holds only 19 percent of its people. From the Bolsón de Mayrán as far south as the Balsas valley, the level rises considerably; this southern section of the central plateau is crossed by a volcanic range of mountains in which the intermont basins are high and separated. The basin of Guadalajara is at 1,500 metres, the basin of México at 2,300 metres, and the basin of Toluca, west of Mexico City, is at 2,600 metres. Above the lakes and valley bottoms of this contorted middle-land rise the magnificent volcano cones of Orizaba (5,700 metres), Popocatépetl (5,452 metres), Ixtaccíhuatl (5,286 metres), Nevado de Toluca (4,583 metres), Matlalcueyetl or La Malinche (4,461 metres), and Cofre de Perote (4,282 metres). This mountainous southern end of the plateau, the heart of Mexico, has ample rainfall. Though only 14 percent of the area of Mexico, it holds nearly half of the country's people. Its centre, in a small high intermont basin measuring only 50 square kilometres, is Mexico City, with 20 or so million inhabitants.

The two high ranges of mountains which rise east and west of the plateau, between it and the sea, are great barriers against communications: there are far easier routes north along the floor of the plateau to the United States than there are to either the east coast or the west. In the west there are transport links across the Sierra Madre Occidental from Guadalajara to the Pacific at the port of Mazatlán, continuing northward through a coastal desert to Nogales. The Sierra Madre Oriental is more kindly; in its mountain ramparts a pass inland from Tampico gives access to Monterrey, a great industrial centre, and the highland basins; and another from Veracruz leads by a fair gradient to the Valley of México.

South of the seven intermont basins in the south-central region the mountainland is still rugged but a little lower (between 1,800 and 2,400 metres), with much less rainfall. After some 560 kilometres it falls away into the low-lying Isthmus of Tehuantepec. Population is sparse in these southern mountains and is settled on the few flat places where commercial crops can be grown. Subsistence crops are sown on incredibly steep slopes. The Pacific coast here is forbidding and its few ports of little use, though there is massive development of tourism in such places as Acapulco, Zihuatanejo, Puerto Escondido and Huatulco. Very different are the Gulf Coast and Yucatán; half this area is classed as flat, and much of it gets enough rain the year round, leading to its becoming one of the most important agricultural and cattle raising areas in the country. The Gulf Coast also provides most of Mexico's oil and sulphur. Geographically, North America may be said to come to an end in the Isthmus of Tehuantepec. South of the Isthmus the land rises again into the thinly populated highlands of Chiapas.

Climate Climate and vegetation depend upon altitude. The *tierra caliente* takes in the coastlands and plateau lands below 750 metres. The *tierra templada*, or temperate zone is at 750 to 2,000 metres. The *tierra fría*, or cold zone, is from 2,000 metres upwards. Above the tree line at 4,000 metres are high moorlands (*páramos*).

The climate of the inland highlands is mostly mild, but with sharp changes of temperature between day and night, sunshine and shade. Generally, winter is the dry season and summer the wet season. There are only two areas where rain falls the year round: south of Tampico along the lower slopes of the Sierra Madre Oriental and across the

Isthmus of Tehuantepec into Tabasco state; and along the Pacific coast of the state of Chiapas. Both areas together cover only 12 percent of Mexico. These wetter parts get most of their rain between June and September, when the skies are so full of clouds that the temperature is lowered: May is a hotter month than July. Apart from these favoured regions, the rest of the country suffers from a climate in which the rainy season hardly lives up to its name and the dry season almost always does.

National parks

Mexico is the world's third most biologically diverse country, behind only Brazil and Colombia. It boasts between 21,600 and 33,000 of the 250,000-odd known species of higher plants (including 150 conifers, and around 1,000 each of ferns, orchids, and cacti), 693-717 reptiles (more than any other country), 436-455 mammals (second only to Indonesia), 283-289 amphibians (fourth in the world), 1,018 birds, 2,000 fish, and hundreds of thousands of insect species. Five Mexican vertebrates (all birds) have become extinct in the 20th century, and about 35 species are now only found in other countries; 1,066 of around 2,370 vertebrates are listed as threatened.

This is of course an immense country, with an immense range of habitats and wildlife; the far south is in the Neotropical kingdom, with a wealth of tropical forest species, while the far north is very much part of the Nearctic kingdom, with typically North American species, and huge expanses of desert with unique ecosystems. The greater part of the country is a transition zone between the two kingdoms, with many strange juxtapositions of species that provide invaluable information to scientists, as well as many endemic species. Many of these sites are now protected, but are often of little interest except to specialists; what's more Mexico's National Parks per se were set up a long time ago primarily to provide green recreation areas for city dwellers; they are generally small and often now planted with imported species such as eucalyptus, and thus of no biological value. However the country does also have a good number of Biosphere Reserves, which are both of great biological value and suitable for tourism.

Starting in the far south, in Chiapas, **El Triunfo Biosphere Reserve** protects Mexico's only cloud forest, on the mountains (up to 2,750 metres) above the Pacific coast; the main hiking route runs from Jaltenango (reached by bus from Tuxtla) to Mapastepec on the coastal highway. Groups need to book in advance through the state's Institute of Natural History, on Calzada de Hombres de la Revolución, by the botanical garden and Regional Museum (Apdo 391, Tuxtla 29000; T23663, F29943, ihnreservas@laneta.apc.org).

From Jaltenango you need to hike or hitch a ride about 29 kilometres to Finca Prusia and then follow a good muletrack for three hours to the El Triunfo campamento (1,650 metres). There are endemic species here, including the very rare azure-rumped tanager; the horned guan is found only here and across the border in the adjacent mountains of Guatemala. Other wildlife includes the quetzal, harpy eagles, jaguars, tapirs, and white-lipped peccary.

Turn left in the clearing for the route down to Tres de Mayo, 25 kilometres away; this is an easy descent of five hours to a pedestrian suspension bridge on the dirt road to Loma Bonita. From here you should take a pick-up to Mapastepec, 25 kilometres away.

Also in Chiapas is the immense **Lacandón Forest**, supposedly protected by the **Azules Biosphere Reserve** but in reality still being eaten away by colonization and logging. New plant species and even families are still being discovered in this rainforest, best visited either from the Bonampak and Yaxchilán ruins, or by the road/boat route via Pico de Oro and Flor de Café to Montebello.

In the Yucatán the **Sian Ka'an Biosphere Reserve** is one of the most visited in Mexico, being just south of Cancún; it's a mixture of forest, savanna and mangrove swamp, best visited on a day-trip run by Los Amigos de Sian Ka'an at Av Cobá 5, third floor, offices 48-50, Apdo 770, Cancún (T849583, F873080, sian@cancun.rce.com.mx). It is also well worth visiting the **Río Lagartos** and **Río Celestún** reserves on the north and west coasts of Yucatán, well known for their flamingos. The **Calakmul Biosphere Reserve** is important mainly for its Mayan ruins, seeming to the layman more like scrub than forest.

Across the country's centre is the Transversal Volcanic Belt, one of the main barriers to Nearctic and Neotropic species; it's easiest to head for the **Ixta-Popo National Park** (from

Amecameca), the **Zoquiapan National Park** (on the main road to Puebla) or the **El Tepozteco National Park** (on the main road to Cuernavaca), and naturally the volcanoes themselves are well worth climbing.

Only small areas of the northern deserts and sierras are formally protected. The most accessible areas are in Durango state, including **La Michilía Biosphere Reserve**, with pine, oak and red-trunked Arbutus and Arctostaphylus trees typical of the Sierra Madre Occidental. A daily bus runs to San Juan de Michis, and you should get off at a T-junction two kilometres before the village and walk west, first getting permission from the Jefe de Unidad Administrativo, Instituto de Ecología, Apdo 632, 34000 Durango (T121483); their offices are at Km 5 on the Mazatlán highway. The **Mapimí Biosphere Reserve** covers an area of desert matorral (scrub) which receives just 200 millimetres of rain a year; it lies to the east of Ceballos, on the Gómez Palacio-Ciudad Jiménez highway. In addition to many highly specialized bushes and cacti, this is home to giant turtles, now in enclosures at the Laboratory of the Desert.

There is a great variety of protected areas in Baja California, all of considerable biological value: the highest point (3,000 metres) is the **Sierra de San Pedro Mártir**, in the north, which receives plenty of precipitation and has largely Californian fauna and flora. A dirt road starts at the Puente San Telmo, on the main road down the west coast, and leads almost 100 kilometres to an astronomical observatory. Desert environments are, of course, unavoidable here, with 80 endemic cacti: the **Gran Desierto del Altar** is a dry lunar landscape, best seen from the main road along the US border, while the **El Vizcaíno Biosphere Reserve** protects a huge area of central Baja, characterized by agaves and drought-resistant scrub. However the main reason for stopping here is to see the migration of the grey whale to its breeding grounds. In the far south, the **Sierra de La Laguna** boasts a unique type of cloud forest, with several endemic species; to get here you have to cross about 20 kilometres of desert from just south of Todos Santos to La Burrera, and then follow a trail for 11 kilometres to a rangers' campamento at about 1,750 metres.

Limited information on National Parks and Biosphere Reserves can be had from SEDESOL (Ministry of Social Development), Av Revolución 1425, Mexico DF (Barranca del Muerto metro), where you'll also find the National Institute of Ecology (INE), for more general information on conservation; their publications are stocked by the Librería Bonilla, nearby at Francia 17.

Non-governmental conservation organizations include Naturalia (Apdo Postal 21541, 04021 México DF; T6746678, F6745294), and Pronatura (Asociación Mexicano por la Conservación de la Naturaleza, Av Nuevo León 144, Col Hipódromo Condesa, México DF, T2869642).

History

Pre-conquest   Of the many Indian nations in the vast territory of Mexico, the two most important before the Conquest were the Aztecs of Tenochtitlán (now Mexico City) and the Maya of Yucatán. The Aztecs, a militarist, theocratic culture, had obtained absolute control over the whole Valley of México and a loose control of some other regions. The Maya were already in decline by the time the Spaniards arrived. A brief history of these and other pre-Conquest, Mexican people is given in **Precolumbian civilizations**, page 62.

Spanish rule   The 34-year-old **Hernán Cortés** disembarked near the present Veracruz with about 500 men, some horses and cannon, on 21 April 1519. They marched into the interior; their passage was not contested; they arrived at Tenochtitlán in November and were admitted into the city as guests of the reigning monarch, Moctezuma. There they remained until June of the next year, when Pedro de Alvarado, in the absence of Cortés, murdered hundreds of Indians to quell his own fear of a rising. At this treacherous act the Indians did in fact rise, and it was only by good luck that the Spanish troops, with heavy losses, were able to fight their way out of the city on the Noche Triste (the Night of Sorrows) of 30 June. Next year Cortés came back with reinforcements and besieged the city. It fell on 30 August 1521, and was utterly razed. Cortés then turned to the conquest of the rest of the country. One of the main factors in his success was his alliance with the Tlaxcalans, old rivals of the

Aztecs. The fight was ruthless, and the Aztecs were soon mastered.

There followed 300 years of Spanish rule. In the early years all the main sources of gold and silver were discovered. Spanish grandees stepped into the shoes of dead Aztec lords and inherited their great estates and their wealth of savable souls with little disturbance, for Aztec and Spanish ways of holding land were not unlike: the *ejido* (or agrarian community holding lands in common), the *rancho*, or small private property worked by the owner; and that usually huge area which paid tribute to its master, the Spanish *encomienda*, soon to be converted into the *hacienda*, with its absolute title to the land and its almost feudal way of life. Within the first 50 years all the Indians in the populous southern valleys of the plateau had been christianized and harnessed to Spanish wealth-getting from mine and soil. The more scattered and less profitable Indians of the north and south had to await the coming of the missionizing Jesuits in 1571, a year behind the Inquisition. Too often, alas, the crowded Jesuit missions proved as fruitful a source of smallpox or measles as of salvation, with the unhappy result that large numbers of Indians died; their deserted communal lands were promptly filched by some neighbouring *encomendero*: a thieving of public lands by private interests which continued for 400 years.

By the end of the 16th century the Spaniards had founded most of the towns which are still important, tapped great wealth in mining, stock raising and sugar-growing, and firmly imposed their way of life and belief. Government was by a Spanish-born upper class, based on the subordination of the Indian and *mestizo* populations and a strict dependence on Spain for all things. As throughout all Hispanic America, Spain built up resistance to itself by excluding from government both Spaniards born in Mexico and the small body of educated *mestizos*.

Revolution & civil war

The standard of revolt was raised in 1810 by the curate of Dolores, **Miguel Hidalgo**. The Grito de Dolores: "Perish the Spaniards" ("*Mueran los gachupines*"), collected 80,000 armed supporters, and had it not been for Hidalgo's loss of nerve and failure to engage the Spaniards, the capital might have been captured in the first month and a government created not differing much from the royal Spanish government. But 11 years of fighting created bitter differences.

A loyalist general, **Agustín de Iturbide**, joined the rebels and proclaimed an independent Mexico in 1821. His Plan of Iguala proposed an independent monarchy with a ruler from the Spanish royal family, but on second thoughts Iturbide proclaimed himself Emperor in 1822: a fantasy which lasted a year. A federal republic was created on 4 October 1824, with General Guadalupe Victoria as President. Conservatives stood for a highly centralized government; Liberals favoured federated sovereign states. The tussle of interests expressed itself in endemic civil war. In 1836, Texas, whose cotton-growers and cattle-ranchers had been infuriated by the abolition of slavery in 1829, rebelled against the dictator, Santa Ana, and declared its independence. It was annexed by the United States in 1845. War broke out and US troops occupied Mexico City in 1847. Next year, under the terms of the treaty of Guadalupe Hidalgo, the US acquired half Mexico's territory: all the land from Texas to California and from the Río Grande to Oregon.

Benito Juárez

A period of reform dominated by independent Mexico's great hero, the Zapotec Indian, Benito Juárez, began in 1857. The church, in alliance with the conservatives, hotly contested by civil war his liberal programme of popular education, freedom of the press and of speech, civil marriage and the separation of church and state. Juárez won, but the constant civil strife wrecked the economy, and Juárez was forced to suspend payment on the national debt. Promptly, Spain, France and Britain landed a joint force at Veracruz to protect their financial rights. The British and the Spanish soon withdrew, but the French force pushed inland and occupied Mexico City in 1863. Juárez took to guerrilla warfare against the invaders.

The **Archduke Maximilian of Austria** became Emperor of Mexico with Napoleon III's help, but United States insistence and the gathering strength of Prussia led to the withdrawal of the French troops in 1867. Maximilian, betrayed and deserted, was captured by the Juaristas at Querétaro, tried, and shot on 19 June. Juárez resumed control and died in July 1872. He was the first Mexican leader of any note who had died naturally since 1810.

General Porfirio Díaz Sebastián Lerdo de Tejada, the distinguished scholar who followed Juárez, was soon tricked out of office by Gen Porfirio Díaz, who ruled Mexico from 1876 to 1910. Díaz's paternal, though often ruthless, central authority did introduce a period of 35 years of peace. A superficial prosperity followed upon peace; a civil service was created, finances put on a sound basis, banditry put down, industries started, railways built, international relations improved, and foreign capital protected. But the main mass of peasants had never been so wretched; their lands were stolen from them, their personal liberties curtailed, and many were sold into forced labour on tobacco and henequen plantations from which death was the only release. It was this open contradiction between dazzling prosperity and hideous distress which led to the upheaval of November 1910 and to Porfirio Díaz's self-exile in Paris.

A new leader, **Francisco Madero**, who came from a landowning family in Coahuila, championed a programme of political and social reform, including the restoration of stolen lands.

Madero was initially supported by revolutionary leaders such as **Emiliano Zapata** in Morelos, **Pascual Orozco** in Chihuahua and **Pancho Villa** in the north. During his presidency (1911-13), Madero neither satisfied his revolutionary supporters, nor pacified his reactionary enemies. After a coup in February 1913, led by Gen Victoriano Huerta, Madero was brutally murdered, but the great new cry, *Tierra y Libertad* (Land and Liberty) was not to be quieted until the revolution was made safe by the election of Alvaro Obregón to the Presidency in 1920. Before then, Mexico was in a state of civil war, leading first to the exile of Huerta in 1914, then the dominance of Venustiano Carranza's revolutionary faction over that of Zapata (assassinated in 1919) and Villa.

Later, **President Lázaro Cárdenas** fulfilled some of the more important economic objectives of the revolution; it was his regime (1934-40) that brought about the division of the great estates into *ejidos* (or communal lands), irrigation, the raising of wages, the spread of education, the beginnings of industrialization, the nationalization of the oil wells and the railways. Later presidents nationalized electric power, the main airlines and parts of industry, but at the same time encouraged both Mexican and foreign (mainly US) entrepreneurs to develop the private sector. All presidents have pursued an independent and non-aligned foreign policy.

Recent politics In 1946, the official party assumed the name **Partido Revolucionario Institucional (PRI)**, since when it held a virtual monopoly over all political activity. Having comfortably won all elections against small opposition parties, in the 1980s electoral majorities were cut as opposition to dictatorship by the Party grew. Corruption and fraud were claimed to be keeping the PRI in power. The PRI candidate in 1988, **Carlos Salinas de Gortari**, saw his majority dramatically reduced when **Cuauhtémoc Cárdenas** (son of the former president), at the head of a breakaway PRI faction, stood in opposition to him. The disaffected PRI members and others subsequently formed the **Partido de la Revolución Democrática (PRD)**, which rapidly gained support as liberalization of many of the PRI's long-held political and economic traditions became inevitable. In 1989, for the first time, a state governorship was conceded by the PRI, to the right wing party, **Partido de Acción Nacional (PAN)**.

On New Year's Day of the election year, 1994, at the moment when the North American Free Trade Agreement (NAFTA – Mexico, USA and Canada) came into force, a guerrilla group briefly took control of several towns in Chiapas. The **Ejército Zapatista de Liberación Nacional (EZLN)** demanded social justice, indigenous people's rights, democracy at all levels of Mexican politics, an end to government corruption, and land reform for the peasantry. Peace talks were overshadowed by the assassination in Tijuana on 23 March of the PRI's appointed presidential candidate, Luis Donaldo Colosio. Further disquiet was caused by the murder of the Tijuana police chief and the kidnapping of several prominent businessmen and other linked killings in subsequent months. To replace Colosio, President Salinas nominated **Ernesto Zedillo Ponce de León**, a US-trained economist and former education minister. Despite continued unrest in Chiapas, Zedillo won a comfortable majority in the August elections, as did the PRI in Congress. Zedillo's opponents, Cuauhtémoc Cárdenas of PRD and Diego Fernández Cevallos of PAN claimed fraud, to no effect.

On 28 September, the PRI general secretary, José Francisco Ruiz Massieu, was shot dead. In November, his brother Mario, deputy attorney general and chief investigator into the murder, resigned, claiming a high-level cover-up by PRI officials. The ensuing row within the PRI overshadowed Zedillo's inauguration on 1 December. Zedillo appointed a reformist cabinet and announced a judicial review. However, the Chiapas state governorship elections had been won dubiously by the PRI candidate and the governorship of Tabasco was also disputed.

On 20 December, Zedillo devalued the peso, claiming that political unrest was causing capital outflows and putting pressure on the currency. In fact, devaluation was necessary for a variety of economic reasons, but Zedillo linked the economic necessity with the political situation in the South. On 22 December, however, a precipitate decision to allow the peso to float against the dollar caused an immediate crisis of confidence and investors in Mexico lost billions of dollars as the peso's value plummeted.

The 1994 devaluation

Economic problems mounted in the first half of 1995 and Mexicans were hard hit by the recession. The PRI was heavily defeated by the PAN in state elections in Jalisco (February) and in Guanajuato (May). In the same month, a narrow PRI victory in Yucatán was hotly disputed. In August the PAN retained the state governorship of Baja California Norte, first won in 1989. In Chiapas, Zedillo suspended the controversial PRI governor, but the tension between EZLN and the army continued. A 72-hour campaign to apprehend the EZLN leader, Subcomandante Marcos, was a failure. Talks recommenced in April, with the EZLN calling a ceasefire but the first peace accord was not signed until February 1996.

Zedillo appointed as attorney general Antonio Lozano of PAN, who uncovered PRI involvement in Colosio's murder and ordered the arrest of Raúl Salinas, brother of ex-president Carlos Salinas, for masterminding the murder of Ruiz Massieu. This broke the convention granted former presidents and their families of immunity from criticism or prosecution. Carlos Salinas acrimoniously left Mexico. Meanwhile, scandal within the PRI continued: Mario Ruiz Massieu was arrested in the USA on suspicion of covering up Raúl Salinas' involvement in the Ruiz Massieu murder and of receiving money from drugs cartels when he was in charge of anti-narcotics operations. Raul Salinas was also investigated for alleged money laundering and illicit enrichment after his wife was arrested in Switzerland trying to withdraw US$84mn from an account opened in a false name. Stories of his massive fortune in land and investment filled the Mexican newspapers.

Intrigue & corruption

Political reform advanced in 1996. Despite a boycott of talks by the PAN, the other major parties agreed to introduce direct elections for the mayoralty of Mexico City; abolish government control of the Federal Electoral Institute, which will become independent; introduce constitutional reforms to allow referenda and guarantee fairer access to the media for party broadcasts during elections. The President's campaign to clean up government was strengthened when he sacked the governor of Guerrero for his alleged involvement in a peasant massacre.

Political reform

In 1997, Manuel Camacho, a PRI outcast, founded a new party, Partido del Centro Democrático, to contest the presidential elections. A former Foreign Minister, Mayor of Mexico City and peace negotiator in Chiapas, Camacho was expelled from the PRI after he complained at not being chosen as the presidential candidate for the PRI in the 1994 elections.

Mid-term congressional elections were held in July 1997 for six state governorships, the entire 500-seat Congress and one third of the Senate, as well as the mayoralty of Mexico City. The PRI suffered a huge blow at the polls, and for the first time ever it lost control of Congress, winning only 239 seats. The PRD surged to become the second largest party in the lower house, with 125 deputies, while the PAN won 122. The PRD also gained the mayoralty of Mexico City (Cuauhtémoc Cárdenas took office in December having won almost twice as many votes as his PRI rival) and the Speaker of the legislature (Porfirio Muñoz Ledo, unanimously elected by the new, four-party opposition bloc).

The Chiapas massacre In 1997 the EZLN renewed its protests at the slow pace of change after a year of no negotiations, accusing the government of trying to change the terms of the agreed legal framework for indigenous rights. The low-intensity war continued in Chiapas, where 60,000 troops heavily outnumbered the EZLN fighters hiding in the Lacandón forest. In December 1997, 45 people were massacred in Acteal, Chenalhó, near San Cristóbal de las Casas, by paramilitaries linked to the PRI. The victims, refugees from communities previously attacked by paramilitaries, were mostly women and children. Human rights groups and church leaders blamed the government for failing to disarm paramilitary groups and not negotiating a solution to the Chiapas conflict. The local mayor was implicated and arrested with 39 others, charged with taking part in the massacre. There were calls for more senior government officials to be removed. Early in 1998 the Interior Minister resigned, followed by the State Governor. The army increased its pressure on the EZLN and its civilian supporters in its search for weapons in defiance of the 1995 Law of Dialogue, which forbade persecution of Zapatistas unless peace talks were abandoned. Meanwhile, foreign observers were deported for violating their tourist visas and engaging in 'political activity' in Chiapas.

Presidential elections 2000 During 1999 the political parties manoeuvred and schemed prior to chosing their presidential candidates. President Zedillo relinquished his traditional role in choosing his successor and the PRI will have a US-style primary election to select a candidate. A nationwide, secret ballot will be held on November 1999 in which any member of the electorate can vote. Several high ranking PRI officials left office by mid-year to campaign for their election. The PRD and the PAN discussed ways of writing to keep the PRI from government in 2000, but their ideological differences prevented them from agreeing on an alliance.

Culture

People About nine percent are considered white and about 30 percent Indian; about 60 percent are *mestizos*, a mixture in varying proportions of Spanish and Indian; a small percentage (mostly in the coastal zones of Veracruz, Guerrero and Chiapas) are a mixture of black and white or black and Indian or *mestizo*. Mexico also has infusions of other European peoples, Arab and Chinese. There is a national cultural prejudice in favour of the Indian rather than the Spanish element, though this does not prevent Indians from being looked down on by the more hispanic elements. There is hardly a single statue of Cortés in the whole of Mexico, but he does figure, pejoratively, in the frescoes of Diego Rivera and his contemporaries. On the other hand the two last Aztec emperors, Moctezuma and Cuauhtémoc, are national heroes.

Indians Among the estimated 24 million Indians there are 54 groups or sub-divisions, each with its own language. The Indians are far from evenly distributed; 36 percent live on the Central Plateau (mostly Hidalgo, and México); 35 percent are along the southern Pacific coast (Oaxaca, Chiapas, Guerrero), and 23 percent along the Gulf coast (mostly Yucatán and Veracruz): 94 percent of them, that is, live in these three regions. There are also sizable concentrations in Nayarit and Durango, Michoacán, and Chihuahua, Sinoloa and Sonora. The main groups are: Pápago (Sonora); Yaqui (Sonora); Mayo (Sonora and Sinaloa); Tarahumara (Chihuahua); Huastec and Otomí in San Luis Potosí; Cora and Huichol (Nayarit); Purépecha/Tarasco (Michoacán); scattered groups of Nahua in Michoacán, Guerrero, Jalisco, Veracruz and other central states; Totonac (Veracruz); Tiapaneco (Guerrero); in Oaxaca state, Mixtec, Mixe and Zapotec; in Chiapas, Lacandón, Tzoltzil, Tzeltal, Chol and others; Maya in Campeche, Yucatán and Quintano Roo.

Land ownership The issue of access to the land has always been the country's fundamental problem, and it was a despairing landless peasantry that rose in the Revolution of 1910 and swept away Porfirio Díaz and the old system of huge estates. The accomplishments of successive PRI governments have been mixed. Life for the peasant is still hard. The minimum wage barely allows a simple diet of beans, rice, and *tortillas*. The home is still, possibly, a shack with no windows, no water, no sanitation, and the peasant may still not be able to read or write, but something was done to redistribute the land in the so-called *ejido* system, which gave either communal or personal control of the land. The peasant was freed from the landowner, and his family received some basic health and educational facilities from the state. In 1992 new legislation was approved which radically overhauled the outdated agricultural sector with far-reaching political and economic consequences. Farmers now have the right to become private property owners, if two-thirds of the *ejido* votes in favour; to form joint ventures with private businessmen; and to use their land as collateral for loans. Private property owners may form joint stock companies, thereby avoiding the constitutional limits on the size of farms and helping them to raise capital. The failure of any agricultural reforms to benefit the peasants of Chiapas was one of the roots of the EZLN uprising in early 1994.

Religion

Roman Catholicism is the principal religion, but the State is determinedly secular. Because of its identification firstly with Spain, then with the Emperor Maximilian and finally with Porfirio Díaz, the Church has been severely persecuted in the past by reform-minded administrations, and priests are still not supposed to wear ecclesiastical dress (see *The Lawless Roads* and *The Power and the Glory*, by Graham Greene). Rapprochement between State and Church was sought in the early 1990s.

The Economy

Structure of production

Mexico has been an oil producer since the 1880s and was the world's leading producer in 1921, but by 1971 had become a net importer. This position was reversed in the mid-1970s with the discovery in 1972 of major new oil reserves. Mexico is the world's sixth largest producer at 2.9 million barrels a day of crude petroleum, 65 percent of this coming from offshore wells in the Gulf of Campeche, and 28 percent from onshore fields in the Chiapas-Tabasco area in the southeast. Mexico depends on fossil fuels to generate 100 percent of its electricity and exports of crude oil, oil products and natural gas account for about a third of exports and about 40 percent of government revenues.

Mexico's mineral resources are legendary. Precious metals make up about 36 percent of non-oil mineral output. The country is the world's leading producer of silver (although low prices have forced the closure of hundreds of mines), fluorite and arsenic, and is among the world's major producers of strontium, graphite, copper, iron ore, sulphur, mercury, lead and zinc. Mexico also produces gold, molybdenum, antimony, bismuth, cadmium, selenium, tungsten, magnesium, common salt, celestite, fuller's earth and gypsum. It is estimated that although 60 percent of Mexico's land mass has mineral potential, only 25 percent is known, and only five percent explored in detail.

Agriculture has been losing importance since the beginning of the 1970s and now contributes only 5.8 percent of gdp. About 13 percent of the land surface is under cultivation, of which only about one-quarter is irrigated. Over half of the developed cropland lies in the interior highlands. Mexico's agricultural success is almost always related to rainfall and available water for irrigation. On average, four out of every 10 years are good, while four are drought years.

Manufacturing, including oil refining and petrochemicals, contributes 17.6 percent of gdp. Mexico City used to be the focal point for manufacturing activity but the government now offers tax incentives to companies relocating away from Mexico City and the other major industrial centres of Guadalajara and Monterrey; target cities are Tampico, Coatzacoalcos, Salina Cruz and Lázaro Cárdenas, while much of the manufacturing export activity takes place in the in-bond centres along the border with the USA. There are now over 3,000 *maquiladoras* (in-bond), in northern Mexico and manufacturing and *maquila* exports tripled in 1991-98 to around US$100m. Several large industrial plants have been ordered closed to control pollution in Mexico City.

Tourism is a large source of foreign exchange and the largest employer, with about a third of the workforce. About 6.7 million tourists visit Mexico every year, of whom about 85 percent come from the USA. The Government is actively encouraging new investment in tourism and foreign investment is being welcomed in hotel construction projects.

Recent trends During 1978-81 the current account of the balance of payments registered increasing deficits because of domestic expansion and world recession. Mounting public sector deficits were covered by foreign borrowing of increasingly shorter terms until a bunching of short term maturities and a loss of foreign exchange reserves caused Mexico to declare its inability to service its debts in August 1982, thus triggering what became known as the international debt crisis. Under the guidance of an IMF programme and helped by commercial bank debt rescheduling agreements, Mexico was able to improve its position largely because of a 40 percent drop in imports in both 1982 and 1983. In 1986, however, the country was hit by the sharp fall in oil prices, which reduced export revenues by 28 percent, despite a rapid growth of 37 percent in non-oil exports through vigorous promotion and exchange rate depreciation policies. Several debt rescheduling and new money agreements were negotiated during the 1980s with the IMF, the World Bank and the commercial banks. Mexico managed to secure progressively easier terms, helped by the US administration's concern for geopolitical reasons, and debt growth was contained. Prepayment of private debt and debt/equity conversions even reduced the overall level of foreign debt. In 1989, Mexico negotiated the first debt reduction package with commercial banks, which was designed to cut debt servicing and restructure debt over a 30-year period supported by collateral from multinational creditors and governments. As a result of this agreement and higher oil prices during the Gulf crisis, foreign exchange reserves rose sharply and the Government was able to curb the rate of currency depreciation and reduce interest rates. Large capital inflows financed a growing trade and current account deficit caused by strong demand for imports as the economy picked up.

The economic improvement allowed President Salinas to open negotiations with the USA on a free trade agreement which, including Canada, would open up the whole of North America (NAFTA). Major economic reforms were introduced to encourage private investment, including the privatization of many state-owned industries, banks and basic public services, such as telephones, motorways, water treatment, electricity generation, railways and ports. New legislation made it easier to invest in mining (except uranium) and foreign investment was permitted in several previously restricted areas. The Government's tight fiscal and monetary policies led to low inflation and a budget surplus, but at the cost of high real interest rates to attract capital from overseas to finance the massive current account deficit.

The political unrest in the first half of 1994 threatened the stability of the peso against the dollar, so interest rates remained high to protect the currency. Rising US interest rates further increased the cost of financing the current account deficit (US$29.5bn in 1994), dampened confidence and jeopardized a rapid return to economic growth, already depressed by the high cost to the private sector of restructuring to compete within NAFTA. Partly for political reasons, the Salinas government refused to devalue the peso and increased domestic credit, despite the dangerous accumulation of public and private short term debt and an excess supply of pesos. Poor debt management led to a bunching of maturities at the end of the year of the dollar-linked *tesobonos* issued by the Government. Soon after Zedillo had succeeded Salinas, the peso was devalued and then floated (see above, **History**) after US$4bn of reserves were lost in two days.

The subsequent financial crisis had severe repercussions on other Latin American economies (the 'Tequila effect'). Its swiftness, and the scale of capital flight, prompted large-scale international emergency funding to help the country honour its short term debts. The IMF pledged US$17.8bn, while a US$20bn credit line was offered by President Clinton. On 9 March 1995 an austerity programme was imposed despite opposition from Mexican industry and the middle classes. It cut government spending by 10 percent, reduced subsidies on basic items such as tortillas, raised VAT from 10 to 15 percent and increased tariffs on electricity, petrol and telephone calls by up to 35 percent. Real incomes were forecast to fall by 50 percent; many businesses faced bankruptcy as they could not service bank loans. This in turn led to a banking crisis; bank deposits fell by 18.5 percent while non-performing loans trebled to 18 percent of banks' total loan portfolio. Of the 18 banks privatized in 1992, seven collapsed. They and others had to be taken over by foreigners. Emergency schemes to keep banks solvent and provide interest relief for small debtors cost the Government about US$70bn by 1998.

Inflation soared to 52 percent in 1995 (compared with eight percent in 1994), while gdp fell by 6.9 percent. While imports fell, exports grew significantly to turn a trade deficit throughout 1994 into a surplus of US$7.4bn in 1995. Moreover, international reserves began to recover. Interest rates started to fall and the stock market showed signs of recovery, but the middle and lower classes felt betrayed. The recession continued to threaten jobs and real wages, with pay settlements averaging only half the rate of inflation. The trade union movement split in 1996 with the traditional faction supporting the government and a rebel wing seeking an independent labour movement, which contributed to the erosion of the traditionally close ties between the government, labour and employers.

By the end of 1996 economic improvement was apparent and inflation was halved. At the beginning of 1997 Mexico was able to settle its debts with the USA, paying off the emergency loan, and confidence surged. Growth reached seven percent in 1997, led by manufacturing for export, which increased its output by 9.8 percent, followed by transport and communications with 9.5 percent because of large investments in the liberalized telecommunications sector. Exports grew by 15 percent to US$110bn. Private savings were encouraged with the launch of private pension funds in 1997, attracting some 10 million investors.

Although the floating peso allowed Mexico to weather the storm caused by the collapse of the Asian economies, the country cam under renewed pressure when Brazil devalued. Mexico withstood the crisis better than many Latin American countries because of an austere budget, but the stock market tumbled in January 1999 and the peso weakened for a few months. Higher oil prices, increased taxation and spending cuts were expected to benefit the fiscal accounts, but gdp growth was forecast to slow. In mid-1999 the Institute for the Protection of Bank Savings (IPAB) was created to handle the legacy of the post-1994 banking crisis. The autonomous body will lower deposit insurance, raise capital, increase reserves against overdue loans and improve loan portfolios by 2005. Foreign banks are expected to increase their presence in Mexico and contribute to restoring the financial health of the banking system. In its final year before presidential elections in 2000, the government negotiated an international financial support package of US$23.7bn (including a US$4.2bn IMF standby agreement) to help Mexico in any future attack on its currency.

Government

Under the 1917 Constitution Mexico is a federal republic of 31 states and a Federal District containing the capital, Mexico City. The President, who appoints the Ministers, is elected for six years and can never be re-elected. Congress consists of the 128-seat Senate, half elected every three years on a rotational basis, and the 500-seat Chamber of Deputies, elected every three years. There is universal suffrage.

The States enjoy local autonomy and can levy their own taxes, and each State has its Governor, legislature and judicature. The President has traditionally appointed the Chief of the Federal District but direct elections were held in 1997 for the first time.

Local administration

Central America

Central America

Central America comprises the seven small countries of Guatemala, Belize (formerly British Honduras), El Salvador, Honduras, Nicaragua, Costa Rica and Panama. Together they occupy 544,700 square kilometres, which is less than the size of Texas. The total population of Central America in 1997 was about 33.7 million and it is increasing by two and a half percent each year.

The degree of development in these countries differs sharply. Costa Rica and Panama have the highest per capita income, with two of the highest rates of literacy in all Latin America. At the other end of the scale, Honduras and Nicaragua have the lowest standards of living. In all cases, the distribution of income is very unequal.

Geographically, these countries have much in common, but there are sharp differences in the racial composition and traditions of their peoples. Costa Ricans are mostly white, Guatemalans are largely Amerindian or mestizo; Hondurans, Nicaraguans and Salvadoreans are almost entirely mestizo. Panama has perhaps the most racially varied population, with a large white group. Most of these countries also have a black element, the largest being found in Panama, Nicaragua and Belize.

NB In the chapters below, information is given on border crossings and entry and exit taxes. Travellers should note that official policy may be disregarded by officials who prefer to set their own, more arbitrary regulations. This may be for a variety of reasons (including the wish to supplement low pay). If you want to debate the issue at the border, find out from a consulate what the regulations are in advance.

History

Early, post-conquest history

At the time of the coming of the Spaniards there were several isolated groups of Indians dotted over the Central American area: they were mostly shifting cultivators or nomadic hunters and fishermen. A few places only were occupied by sedentary agriculturists: what remained of the Maya (see **Precolumbian Civilizations**) in the highlands of Guatemala; a group on the southwestern shores of Lakes Managua and Nicaragua; and another in the highlands of Costa Rica. The Spanish conquerors were attracted by precious metals, or native sedentary farmers who could be christianized and exploited. There were few of either, and comparatively few Spaniards settled in Central America.

It was only during his fourth voyage, in 1502, that Columbus reached the mainland of Central America; he landed in Panama, which he called Veragua, and founded the town of Santa María de Belén. In 1508 Alonso de Ojeda received a grant of land on the Pearl Coast east of Panama, and in 1509 he founded the town of San Sebastián, later moved to a new site called Santa María la Antigua del Darién (now in Colombia). In 1513 the governor of the colony at Darién was Vasco Núñez de Balboa. Taking 190 men he crossed the isthmus in 18 days and caught the first glimpse of the Pacific; he claimed it and all neighbouring lands in the name of the King of Spain. But from the following year, when Pedrarias de Avila replaced him as Governor, Balboa fell on evil days, and he was executed by Pedrarias in 1519. That same year Pedrarias crossed the isthmus and founded the town of Panamá on the Pacific side. It was in April 1519, too, that Cortés began his conquest of Mexico.

Central America was explored from these two nodal points of Panama and Mexico. Cortés' lieutenant, Pedro de Alvarado, had conquered as far south as San Salvador by 1525. Meanwhile Pedrarias was sending forces into Panama and Costa Rica: the latter was abandoned, for the natives were hostile, but was finally colonized from Mexico City when the rest of Central America had been taken. In 1522-24 Andrés Niño and Gil Gonzales Dávila invaded Nicaragua and Honduras. Many towns were founded by these forces from Panama: León, Granada, Trujillo and others. Spanish forces from the north and south sometimes met and fought bitterly. The gentle Bartolomé de Las Casas, the 'apostle of the Indies', was active as a Dominican missionary in Central America in the 1530s.

Settlement

The groups of Spanish settlers were few and widely scattered, and this is the fundamental reason for the political fragmentation of Central America today. Panama was ruled from Bogotá, but the rest of Central America was subordinate to the Viceroyalty at Mexico City, with Antigua Guatemala as an Audiencia for the area until 1773, thereafter Guatemala City. Panama was of paramount importance for colonial Spanish America for its strategic position, and for the trade passing across the isthmus to and from the southern colonies. The other provinces were of comparatively little value.

The small number of Spaniards intermarried freely with the local Indians, accounting for the predominance of *mestizos* in present-day Central America. In Guatemala, where there were the most Indians, intermarriage affected fewer of the natives, and over half the population today is pure Indian. On the Meseta Central of Costa Rica, the Indians were all but wiped out by disease; as a consequence of this great disaster, there is a buoyant community of over two million whites, with little Indian admixture, in the highlands. Blacks predominate all along the Caribbean coasts of Central America; they were not brought in by the colonists as slaves, but by the railway builders and banana planters of the 19th century and the canal cutters of the 20th, as cheap labour.

Independence and Federation

On 5 November 1811, José Matías Delgado, a priest and jurist born in San Salvador, organized a revolt in conjunction with another priest, Manuel José Arce. They proclaimed the independence of El Salvador, but the Audiencia at Guatemala City quickly suppressed the revolt and took Delgado prisoner.

It was the revolution of 1820 in Spain itself that precipitated the independence of

Central America. When on 24 February 1821, the Mexican general Agustín de Iturbide announced his Plan of Iguala for an independent Mexico, the Central American *criollos* decided to follow his example, and a declaration of independence, drafted by José Cecilio del Valle, was announced in Guatemala City on 15 September 1821. Iturbide invited the provinces of Central America to join with him, and on 5 January 1822, Central America was declared annexed to Mexico. Delgado refused to accept this decree, and Iturbide, who had now assumed the title of Emperor Agustín the First, sent an army south under Vicente Filísola to enforce it in the regions under Delgado's influence. Filísola had completed his task when he heard of Iturbide's abdication, and at once convened a general congress of the Central American provinces. It met on 24 June 1823, and established the Provincias Unidas del Centro de América. The Mexican republic acknowledged their independence on 1 August 1824, and Filísola's soldiers were withdrawn.

The congress, presided over by Delgado, appointed a provisional governing *junta* which promulgated a constitution modelled on that of the United States on 22 November 1824. The Province of Chiapas was not included in the Federation, for it had already adhered to Mexico in 1821. No federal capital was chosen, but Guatemala City, by force of tradition, soon became the seat of government.

Breakdown of federation

The first President under the new constitution was Manuel José Arce, a liberal. One of his first acts was to abolish slavery. El Salvador, protesting that he had exceeded his powers, rose in December 1826. Honduras, Nicaragua, and Costa Rica joined the revolt, and in 1828 Gen Francisco Morazán, in charge of the army of Honduras, defeated the federal forces, entered San Salvador and marched against Guatemala City. He captured the city on 13 April 1829, and established that contradiction in terms: a liberal dictatorship. Many conservative leaders were expelled and church and monastic properties confiscated. Morazán himself became president of the Federation in 1830. He was a man of considerable ability; he ruled with a strong hand, encouraged education, fostered trade and industry, opened the country to immigrants, and reorganized the administration. In 1835 the capital was moved to San Salvador.

These reforms antagonized the conservatives and there were several risings. The most serious revolt was among the Indians of Guatemala, led by Rafael Carrera, an illiterate *mestizo* conservative and a born leader. Years of continuous warfare followed, during the course of which the Federation withered away. As a result, the federal congress passed an act which allowed each province to assume what government it chose, but the idea of a federation was not quite dead. As a result, Morazán became President of El Salvador. Carrera, who was by then in control of Guatemala, defeated Morazán in battle and forced him to leave the country. But in 1842, Morazán overthrew Braulio Carrillo, then dictator of Costa Rica, and became president himself. At once he set about rebuilding the Federation, but was defeated by the united forces of the other states, and shot on 15 September 1842. With him perished any practical hope of Central American political union.

The separate states

Costa Rica, with its mainly white population, is a country apart, and Panama was Colombian territory until 1903. The history of the four remaining republics since the breakdown of federation has been tempestuous in the extreme. In each the ruling class was divided into pro-clerical conservatives and anti-clerical liberals, with constant changes of power. Each was weak, and tried repeatedly to buttress its weakness by alliances with others, which invariably broke up because one of the allies sought a position of mastery. The wars were rarely over boundaries; they were mainly ideological wars between conservatives and liberals, or wars motivated by inflamed nationalism. Nicaragua, for instance, was riven internally for most of the period by the mutual hatreds of the Conservatives of Granada and the Liberals of León, and there were repeated conflicts between the Caribbean and interior parts of Honduras.

Of the four republics, Guatemala was certainly the strongest and in some ways the most stable. While the other states were skittling their presidents like so many ninepins, Guatemala was ruled by a succession of strong dictators: Rafael Carrera (1844-65), Justo Rufino Barrios (1873-85), Manuel Cabrera (1898-1920), and Jorge Ubico (1931-44). These were separated by intervals of constitutional government, anarchy, or attempts at dictatorship which failed. Few presidents handed over power voluntarily to their successors; most of them were forcibly removed or assassinated.

Despite the permutations and combinations of external and civil war there has been a recurrent desire to reestablish some form of *la gran patria centroamericana*. Throughout the 19th century, and far into the 20th, there have been ambitious projects for political federation, usually involving El Salvador, Honduras and Nicaragua; none of them lasted more than a few years. There have also been unsuccessful attempts to reestablish union by force, such as those of Barrios of Guatemala in 1885 and Zelaya of Nicaragua in 1907.

During colonial times the area suffered from great poverty; trade with the mother country was confined to small amounts of silver and gold, cacao and sugar, cochineal and indigo. During the present century the great banana plantations of the Caribbean, the coffee and cotton trade and industrialization have brought some prosperity, but its benefits have, except in Costa Rica and Panama, been garnered mostly by a relatively small landowning class and the middle classes of the cities. Nicaragua is now a case apart; extensive and radical reforms were carried out by a left-leaning revolutionary government, but protracted warfare and mistakes in economic management have left the country still extremely poor.

Regional integration Poverty, the fate of the great majority, has brought about closer economic cooperation between the five republics, and in 1960 they established the Central American Common Market (CACM). Surprisingly, the Common Market appeared to be a great success until 1968, when integration fostered national antagonisms, and there was a growing conviction in Honduras and Nicaragua, which were doing least well out of integration, that they were being exploited by the others. In 1969 the 'Football War' broke out between El Salvador and Honduras, basically because of a dispute about illicit emigration by Salvadoreans into Honduras, and relations between the two were not normalized until 1980. Despite the handicaps to economic and political integration imposed by nationalist feeling and ideological differences, hopes for improvement were revived in 1987 when the Central American Peace Plan, drawn up by President Oscar Arias Sánchez of Costa Rica, was signed by the Presidents of Guatemala, El Salvador, Honduras, Nicaragua and Costa Rica. The plan proposed formulae to end the civil strife in individual countries, achieving this aim first in Nicaragua (1989), then in El Salvador (1991). In Guatemala, a ceasefire after 36 years of war led to the signing of a peace accord at the end of 1996. After the signing of the peace accords, emphasis has shifted to regional economic and environmental integration. National and international bodies insist that to maintain peace the gulf between rich and poor must be eradicated, including in those countries not previously affected by civil war. Moreover, the indigenous peoples, who are usually at the lowest end of the social scale must be given greater assistance.

In October 1993, the presidents of Guatemala, El Salvador, Honduras, Nicaragua and Costa Rica signed a new Central American Integration Treaty Protocol, to replace that of 1960 and set up new mechanisms for regional integration. The Treaty was the culmination of a series of annual presidential summits since 1986 which, besides aiming for peace and economic integration, has established a Central American Parliament and a Central American Court of Justice.

Although intraregional trade grew to US$1.6bn in 1996 (compared with US$413mn in 1986), economic circumstances since 1994 have forced each government to pursue independent policies. For example, Costa Rica signed a bilateral agreement with Mexico, contrary to the region's aim of negotiation as a group with the North American Free Trade Agreement. Subsequently, however, Guatemala, El Salvador and Honduras have been negotiating a trade agreement with Mexico, with a view to Nicaragua joining later. The issue of a regional import tariff structure has been undermined by national interests in both Guatemala and El Salvador who have at various times set their own rates in contravention of regional accords. In addition, Nicaragua and Costa Rica were in dispute over the illegal immigration of Nicaraguan workers into Costa Rican agricultural jobs. Despite these disputes, all the governments are anxious to consolidate integration in order to make Central America a competitive trading bloc.

Guatemala

4

Guatemala

Essentials

Planning your trip

Guatemala is the most popular of the Central American republics and the only one which is **Where to go** largely Indian in language and culture. Two-thirds of it is mountainous and about the same proportion forested. Its Pacific coastline is 240 kilometres long and its Caribbean coast 110 kilometres.

The capital, **Guatemala City**, is modern, polluted and commercial. Although it is the main entry point for air travellers, few stay there long, preferring to go 45 kilometres west to the capital it replaced, **Antigua**. This city, built by the Spanish Conquistadores, was destroyed by earthquakes, but the ruins of the colonial architecture and its location, at the foot of three volcanoes, make Antigua one of the prime tourist destinations in the country. It is also a major centre for learning Spanish.

Heading northeast from Guatemala City towards the Caribbean, it is an easy detour to the Verapaz region of the highlands. **Cobán** is the main focus, giving access to traditional villages, the caves at Lanquín, the natural bridge of Semuc Champey and, at Purulhá, the reserve which protects the quetzal, the national bird. From Cobán you can either return to the main Caribbean highway, or take the backroads to Lago de Izabal (see below). Just off the highway is one of the country's main Maya archaeological sites, **Quiriguá**. Also from this route is the road to the famous basilica at Esquipulas and one access to Copán in Honduras. On Guatemala's short **Caribbean** shore is Lívingston, which is popular with young travellers. From here or the nearby port of Puerto Barrios boats go to Belize. Behind the coast, on the Río Dulce, are two lakes, Lago de Izabal and El Golfete, on whose shores is the Biotopo Chocón-Machacas, a manatee reserve.

In the forests of the northern lowlands of **El Petén** are most of Guatemala's archaeological sites. The majestic **Tikal** is the most developed for tourism. Others include Uaxactún and El Ceibal; a number of adventurous trips can be made to outlying Maya cities. The chief centre for exploring El Petén is **Flores**, a town built on an island in lake Petén Itzá. There are routes from here to Belize and Mexico.

The highlands west of Guatemala City are also the Maya Indian areas, full of colour on market days and during fiestas, with communities characterized by their costumes and industries. There are many villages around the spectacularly beautiful **Lago Atitlán**, which is overlooked by volcanoes. The main town is **Panajachel**, which used to be the typical gringo hangout, but that distinction has been taken over by San Pedro La Laguna. A little over an hour north of Atitlán is the most famous market of **Chichicastenango**, a town where the indigenous people cling firmly to their traditions, despite the weekly influx of tourists. The market must be experienced, but there are many other markets and many other districts which have their own unique customs, for instance the Quiché region or the Ixil triangle.

Towards Mexico are towns such as Huehuetenango, Quetzaltenango and Retalhuleu which provide good opportunities for discovering western Guatemala. Near Huehuetenango are the Cuchumatanes mountains, in the heart of which **Todos Santos Cuchumatán** is becoming increasingly popular as a place to learn about the Mam way of life. Spanish schools in Todos Santos, Huehuetenango and Quetzaltenango offer more than just language classes, with weaving or volunteer work as optional extras. As in other parts of Guatemala, volcanoes dominate the landscape, but there are also hot springs, hiking possibilities and some magnificent scenery on roads which descend from highlands to the Pacific lowlands.

The majority of visitors spend most of their time in the highlands, where the dry season lasts **When to go** from November to April. Some places enjoy a respite from the rains (the *canicula*) in July and August. Days are warm and nights are cool, so it is advisable to take some warm clothing, especially for the higher altitudes. On the Pacific and Caribbean coasts you can expect rain all year round, heaviest on the Pacific in June and September with a dry spell in between, but with no dry season on the Caribbean. In the lowlands of El Petén, the wet season is roughly the same as the highlands, May to October, and this is also the time when the mosquitoes are most active. December to February are cooler months, while March to April are hot and dry.

Finding out more Instituto Guatemalteco de Turismo (Inguat), 7 Av 1-17, Zona 4, Centro Cívico, Apartado Postal 1020-A, Guatemala City, T3311333 to 3311347, F3318893, 3314416, inguat@guate.net, www.travel-guatemala.org.gt. Free information 1-801-4648281 (local), 1-888-4648281 (USA). Inguat provides bus timetables, hotel and camping lists and road maps. Tourist information is provided at the Mexican border for those entering Guatemala. Maps include Belize as Guatemalan territory. Roads marked in the Petén are inaccurate.

Tourist offices overseas Inguat: *USA*, 299 Alhambra Circle, Suite 510, Coral Gables, Florida 33134, T305-4420651/4420412, F4421013, 1-800-742-4529. *Mexico*, Río Nilo 55, Mezzanine 1, Col Cuauhtémoc, CP 06500, DF, T/F525-2081991. *Dominican Republic*, Pedro Henríquez Ureña, 136-A, Apdo 235, Santo Domingo, T809-5631792, F809-5670115. *Germany*, Am Burghof 11, D66625, Nohfelden, T6852-900588. *Italy*, Viale Prassilla 152, 00124, Rome, T396-50912740, F5053406. *Spain*, Calle Rafael Salgado 3, 4th Izquierda, 28036 Madrid, T/F341-3441559. *Canada*, 72 McGill St, Toronto, Ontario, M4B 1H2, T/F416-3488597.

In the UK, information on Guatemala and the Maya of Guatemala, Mexico, Belize and Honduras can be found at The Guatemalan Indian Centre, 94A Wandsworth Bridge Rd, London SW6 2TF, T/F0171-3715291, library, video archive and textile collection (annual membership £5). Open Tuesday and Thursday, 1400-1800, Saturday 1000-1800. Closed January and August, and two weeks around Easter.

Maps The *Instituto Geográfico Nacional* (IGN) produces detailed maps, see under Guatemala City. The best map of the country is the International Travel Map No 642 Third Edition 1998, 1:500,000 published by ITMB, 345 West Broadway, Vancouver BC, Canada V5Y 1PB, about US$11.

Getting in

Documents Only a valid passport is required for citizens of: all Western European countries; USA, Canada, Mexico and all Central American countries; Panama, Brazil, Chile, Paraguay, Uruguay and Venezuela; Australia, Israel, Japan and New Zealand. Visas (US$10) or Tourist Cards (US$5) are required by citizens of Bahrain, Kuwait, Saudi Arabia, Czech Republic, Slovakia, Poland, Philippines, Iceland and South Africa. All others must have a visa, which may require prior reference to immigration authorities in Guatemala which takes three to four weeks. Visas, tourist cards and passport stamps are normally valid for 30 days (but may be granted for longer if you ask). Tourist cards may be given to you at land frontiers and should be free if not otherwise required. However, regulations change frequently, best to check in advance with consulates in your home country before leaving. Children under 13 do not require a tourist card provided they are included on their parents' document.

Tourist cards must be renewed in Guatemala City after 30 days (visas also after 30 days or on expiry) at the immigration office: *Dirección General de Migración*, 41 C, 17-36, Zona 8, T4751390, open weekdays 0800-1600. This office extends visas and renews tourist cards on application (before noon) for 30 days at a time (up to 90 days maximum), this takes at least one day, usually two (but you will have to insist in any event), costs US$10, fingerprints and photograph required, and you may not be given the full 90 days. To stay more than six months, seek permission at the Immigration Department in Guatemala City. You may need stamped paper (*papel sellado*). Avoid Friday, get there early. Diplomatic passport holders go to the Ministerio de Relaciones Exteriores in the National Palace, Zona 1. Multiple entry visas for tourist purposes only are free for US citizens and are valid for three or five years (very useful if travelling back and forth between neighbouring countries). Business visas cost US$10. Two photographs and a letter from the company (in duplicate) required. If experiencing obstruction in renewing a visa, it is easier to leave the country for three days and then come back.

Although not officially required, some airlines may not allow you to board a flight to

Guatemala embassies and consulates

Argentina, Avenida Santa Fe No 830, 5th Floor, CP 1059, Buenos Aires, T(1)3139180, F3139181 (also covers **Paraguay**).

Austria, Salesianergasse 25/5, A-1030, Vienna, T1-7143570, F7143569 (also covers **Hungary** and **Romania**).

Barbados, 2nd Floor, Trident House, Broad Street, Bridgetown, T4352542, F4352638.

Belgium, Avenue Winston Churchill, 185, 1180, Brussels, T2-3456992, F3446499 (also covers **Holland** and **Luxembourg**).

Belize, 1 St John St, Belize City, T2-33314, F35140.

Brazil, Shis QL. 08, Conjunto 05, Casa 11, Brasília, CEP 70460, T61-2483164, F2484383.

Canada, 130 Albert St, Suite 1010, Ottawa, Ontario, KIP 5G4, T613-2337237, F2330135.

Chile, Casilla No 36, Correo 10, Las Condes, Santiago, T2-3414012, F2253630.

China (Taiwan), 12, Lane 88 Chien Kuo, North Road, Section 1, Taipei, T25077043, F5060577.

Colombia, Transversal 29 A, No 139A-41, Bogotá, T1-2580746, F2745365. **Costa Rica**, De la Pizza Hut en Plaza del Sol, Curridabat, 50 metres east, 100 metres north, 50 metres east, Casa No 3, San José, T2245721, F2832556.

Dominican Republic, Pedro Henríquez Ureña, No 136-A, Ensanche La Esperilla, Santo Domingo, T5670110, F5670115 (also covers **Haiti**).

Ecuador, Avenida República No 192, y Diego de Almagro, Edif Casa Blanca, 4th Floor B, Quito, T2-545714, F501927.

Egypt, Mohamed Fahmi El Mohdar St, No 8, Madinet Nasr, Cairo, T2-2611114, F2611814 (also covers **Turkey**).

El Salvador, 15 Avenida Norte, No 135, San Salvador, T2712225, F2213019.

France, 73 Rue de Courcelles, 75008 Paris, T1-42277863, F47540206 (also covers **Portugal** and **Switzerland**).

Germany, Zietenstrasse 16, 53173, Bonn, T228-351579, F354940.

Honduras, Calle Principal, Colonia Loma Linda Norte, Tegucigalpa, T325018, F315655.

Israel, 74 Hey Be'lyar St, Apt 6, Kikar Hamedina, 62198, Tel Aviv, T3-5467372, F5467317 (also covers **Greece**).

Italy, Via Dei Colli della Farnesina 128, 00194, Rome, T6-36303750, F3291639.

Japan, Nr 38 Kowa Bldg, Room 905, Nishi-Azabu, Minato-Ku, Tokyo 106, T3-38001830, F34001820 (also covers **Australia**, **Bangladesh**, **India**, **Iraq**, **Philippines** and **Thailand**).

Korea (South), 602 Garden Tower Building, 98-78 Wooni-Dong, Chongro-Ku, Seoul, 110-350, T2-7653265, F7636010.

Mexico, Avenida Explanada No 1025, Lomas de Chapultepec, 11000 México, DF, T5-5407520, F2021142.

Nicaragua, Km 11½ de la carretera a Masaya, Managua, T2-799609, F799610.

Norway, Oscars Gate 59, 0258, Oslo, T22-556004, F556047 (also covers **Denmark**).

Panama, Calle Abel Bravo y Calle 57, Bella Vista, Edif Torre Cancún, Apt 14-A, Panama City, T2693475, F2231922.

Peru, Inca Ricap No 309, Lima 11, T/F14-635885 (also covers **Bolivia**).

Poland, Ul Genewska 37, 03-940 Warsaw, T22-6178342 (also covers **Ukraine**).

Russia, Karoby Val No 7, Apt 92, 117049, Moscow, T095-2382214, F9566270.

Spain, Calle Rafael Salgado No 3, 4th Izquierda, 28036, Madrid, T1-3441417, F4587894 (also covers **Morocco**).

Sweden, Wittstockgaten 30, S 115, 27 Stockholm, T8-6805229, F6604229 (also covers **Finland**).

United Kingdom, 13 Fawcett Street, London SW10 9HN, T0171-3513042, F0171-3765708.

Uruguay, Rambla República del Perú 757, Apt 602, Montevideo, T2-719497, F704366.

USA, 2220 R St NW, Washington DC, 20008, T202-7454952, F7451908.

Venezuela, Avenida Francisco Miranda, Torre Dozsa, Primer Nivel, Urb El Rosal, Caracas, T2-9521166, F9521992.

Guatemala without an outward ticket (eg SAM in Colombia).

Apart from the visa or tourist card charge, there should be no other entry fees if you are travelling by public transport; see note on **Taxes** below. For cars, see under **Road Travel**. If entering overland it is most advisable to have obtained a visa in advance (fewer hassles).

Identification must always be carried while you are in Guatemala for police and military checks.

Customs   You are allowed to take in, free of duty, personal effects and articles for your own use, two bottles of spirit and 80 cigarettes or 100 grammes of tobacco. Once every six months you can take in, free, dutiable items worth US$100. Temporary visitors can take in any amount in quetzales or foreign currencies; they may not, however, take out more than they brought in. The local equivalent of US$100 per person may be reconverted into US dollars on departure at the airport, provided a ticket for immediate departure is shown.

Money

Currency   The unit is the *quetzal*, divided into 100 centavos. There are coins of 25, 10, 5 and 1 centavos. The paper currency is for 50 centavos and 1, 5, 10, 20, 50, 100 and 500 quetzales. If you have money sent to Guatemala, you can opt to take it in US$ or quetzales. Miami airport is sometimes a good place to buy quetzales at favourable rates.

   Warning   Torn notes are not always accepted, so avoid accepting them yourself if possible. There is often a shortage of small change, but when you arrive in Guatemala and change money, especially at weekends, insist on being given some small notes to pay hotel bills, transport, et cetera.

Exchange   When changing travellers' cheques, ensure that your two signatures are a perfect match. Amex cheques are less easy to change outside the main cities than citibank and visa. Passport and purchase receipt is normally required, especially in the capital, but other identification with a photo may be enough. Banks usually charge upto two percent per transaction to advance quetzales on Visa card or other, and you will probably get a less favourable rate of exchange. Visa is the most widely recognized card. ATMs for the withdrawal of cash are available for Visa at Banco Industrial, and Mastercard/Cirrus sometimes at Banco Granai y Townson (G y T). Visa ATMs are much more common than Mastercard. Visa assistance, T9990115. Mastercard T9991480. Amex cards are not widely accepted. For Western Union, T3312841.

Credit cards   Some establishments make a charge for use of credit cards. Check before you sign.

Getting there

Air   **From Canada**   Connections are made through San Salvador, Los Angeles or Miami.

From the Caribbean   Copa from Santo Domingo and San Juan; Copa from Kingston and Montego Bay, Jamaica, and Port au Prince via Panama.

From Central America   From San Salvador: Taca, Aviateca, Copa. From Tegucigalpa: Taca. From San Pedro Sula: Taca and Copa. From Mexico City: Aviateca, Mexicana, KLM. From Cancún: Aviateca and Mayan World Airlines. From Belize: Taca (see under Flores for flights from Belize and Mexico to the Petén). From Managua: Copa, Aviateca. From San José: Aviateca, Lacsa, United Airlines, Copa, Mexicana. From Panama: Copa, Taca (via San Salvador), Lacsa (via San José). See **Introduction and Hints**, page 27, for regional airpasses.

From Europe   KLM flies from Amsterdam via Mexico City, Iberia flies from Barcelona and Madrid via Miami, with connecting flights from other European cities. Alternatively, fly to Miami, Atlanta or Houston and connect with daily flights to Guatemala City.

From South America   SAM/Lacsa from Bogotá via San José, Copa via Panama. **NB** You will have to have an outward ticket from Colombia to be allowed a visa (though worth checking with Colombian embassy first); round trip tickets Guatemala-Colombia are stamped 'Refundable only in Guatemala', but it is possible either to sell the return part on San Andrés island – at a discount – or to change it to an alternative destination. Lacsa from Santiago (Chile) and Lima with a stopover in San José, otherwise Copa via Panama.

Touching down

Official time Guatemalan time is 6 hours behind GMT.

Hours of business Business and commercial offices are open from 0800-1200, and 1400-1800 except Saturday. Shops: 0900-1300, 1500-1900, but many mornings only on Saturday. Banks in Guatemala City: 0900-1500. In the interior banks tend to open earlier in the morning, close for lunch and stay open later. In the main cities some banks are introducing later hours, up to 2000, while in the main tourist towns, some banks are open 7 days a week. Government offices open 0700-1530.

IDD 502. Long equal tones with long pauses mean it is ringing. Short equal tones with short pauses indicate engaged.

Voltage Generally 110 volts AC, 60 cycles, but for variations see under individual towns. Electricity is generally reliable in the towns but can be a problem in the remoter areas, eg Petén. Take a torch to be on the safe side.

Weights and measures The metric system is obligatory on all Customs documents: specific duties are levied on the basis of weight, usually gross kilograms. United States measures are widely used in commerce; most foodstuffs are sold by the pound. The metric tonne of 1,000 kilograms is generally used; so is the US gallon. Old Spanish measures are often used; eg vara (32.9 inches), caballería (111.51 acres), manzana (1.727 acres), arroba (25 pounds), and quintal (101.43 pounds). Altitudes of towns are usually

From the USA American (Atlanta; Miami), Continental (Chicago; Houston; New York; San Francisco), Aviateca (Dallas), Delta (Atlanta), United (Los Angeles; San Francisco), Lacsa (Los Angeles; San Francisco), Taca (Dallas; Los Angeles; Miami; New York; San Francisco; Washington DC).

Round-trips Miami-Guatemala are good value, and useful if one does not want to visit other Central American countries. MCOs are not sold in Guatemala.

For international flights to **Flores** see page 644.

Touching down

There is a 17 percent ticket tax, single or return, on all international tickets sold in Guatemala. A stamp tax of two percent is payable on single, return, baggage tickets and exchange vouchers issued in Guatemala and paid for in or out of the country. Hence it is usually cheaper to buy air tickets outside the country. A US$5 tourism tax is levied on all tickets sold in Guatemala to Guatemalan residents for travel abroad. There is also a US$20 or quetzal equivalent, airport and departure tax, and a Q5/US$1 (officially) tourist tax at all borders, charged on leaving overland (borders may not be open 24 hours). These taxes vary from one border crossing to another, and from one official to another, and may be charged on entry as well as departure. Bribery is rife at border crossings, whether you are entering with a car or on foot. Always ask for a receipt and, if you have time and the language ability, do not give in to corrupt officials. Report any complaint to an Inguat representative. **Airline ticket & departure taxes**

Entry tax There is no entry tax, officially, except for those nationalities which need a tourist card. See Documents, above. See also Airline ticket and departure taxes, above.

Remember that most of the tourist areas you are likely to visit in Guatemala are over 1,500 metres and it will be cold in the evening and at night. Bad weather may bring noticeable drops in temperature. In many tropical areas where mosquitoes and other biting insects are common, take long trousers and long-sleeved shirts for after dusk. The sun is strong everywhere at midday, you may need a hat. **Clothing**

Hotel staff: bell boys, US$0.25 for light luggage, US$0.50 for heavy. Chamber maids at discretion. Restaurants: 10 percent in the better places (see if a service charge has already been added to the bill). Taxi drivers: none. Airport porters: US$0.25 per piece of luggage. Cloakroom attendants are not tipped. **Tipping**

Guatemalan children are becoming persistent in asking for money in some tourist areas. If you give in to one, another dozen will immediately appear. It may be better to pass on items like soap, shampoo, sewing kits picked up from hotels.

Safety Following the 1996 ceasefire between government and URNG forces, travellers should not encounter difficulties, but if going to very isolated areas it may be wise to check conditions prior to travelling. In some parts of the country you may be subject to military or police checks. Local people are reluctant to discuss politics with strangers; it is best not to raise the subject. Do not necessarily be alarmed by 'gunfire' which is much more likely to be fireworks etc, a national pastime, especially early in the morning.

Robberies and assaults on tourists are becoming more common. Single women should be especially careful, but tourist groups are not immune and some excursion companies take necessary precautions. Bus hijacks are becoming more frequent; if possible travel by day, especially on the road between the capital and El Petén. Specific warnings are given in the text, but visitors are advised to seek up-to-date local advice on places to avoid at the earliest opportunity. National police T110; tourist police in Antigua, T832-0532/3 ext 35.

Volunteer work If you would like to volunteer to help in local children's homes, write to: *Casa Guatemala*, 14 C, 10-63, Zona 1, Guatemala City, or Casa Alianza, Apartado Postal 400, Antigua, Guatemala. Also contact *Ak'tenamit*, AP 2675, 09001 Guatemala City, T2541560; they are based at Clínica Lámpara, near Lívingston, supported by the British Commonwealth Association and run health, education and sanitation projects. Teachers of English, nurses, engineers, builders and fundraisers needed. Several language schools in Quetzaltenango and Huehuetenango fund community development projects and seek volunteers from among their students. Also, *Asociación de Rescate y Conservación de Vida Silvestre* (ARCAS), which returns wild animals to their natural habitat, takes volunteer workers; contact ARCAS, Flores, Petén, Guatemala, T/F9260566 or their Guatemala City office, 11 C 6-66, Zona 1, T/F2535329. Their centre is 15 kilometres from Flores towards Tikal. An *orphanage* in El Naranjo takes volunteers, see page 653. *Fundación Solar*, Ivan Azurdia (speaks English), T/F3322548/3601172, funsolar@guate.net, works on environmental and social community projects. It needs environmental specialists, biologists, engineers and social workers/anthropologists specializing in developing countries. *Quezaltrekkers*, c/o Casa Argentina, Diagonal 12 8-37, Zona 1, Quetzaltenango, T7612740, runs hiking trips in the highlands. Funds raised support street children; volunteer guides welcome. Information on work opportunities with local organizations can be obtained from *Central Index of Appointments Overseas* (CIAO), 39 Adair Rd, Eastney, Portsmouth, Hants, PO4 9PH T/F01705-431840, contactus@ciao-directory.org, www.ciao-directory.org.

Where to stay

Hotels The tourist institute Inguat publishes a list of maximum prices for single, double and triple occupancy of almost 300 hotels throughout the country in all price ranges, though the list is thin on the budget hotels. They will deal with complaints about overcharging if you can produce bills etc. Room rates should be posted in all registered hotels. Rooms in the more expensive hotels are subject to 10 percent sales tax and 10 percent tourism tax. Ask if taxes (*impuestos*) are included when you are given the room rate. Most budget hotels do not supply toilet paper, soap or towels. Busiest seasons, when hotels in main tourist centres are heavily booked, are Easter, December and the European summer holiday (July-August).

Getting around

Air A new internal air service using Cessna Grand Caravan aircraft commenced in November 1998 by Inter, part of the Taca group, linking Guatemala City with Puerto Barrios (some call at Río Dulce), Quetzaltenango, Retalhuleu, Cobán, Playa Grande and Huehuetenango, T3612144/3615784/3326034 (Guatemala). See under Flores/Santa Elena for services to Tikal, and under the other destinations for details.

The railways were closed down in 1995 though the track mostly remains. There is yet another **Train** initiative to revive the route Guatemala City to Puerto Barrios in 1999.

There is an extensive network of bus routes throughout the country. The buses are mostly in a **Bus** poor state of repair and overloaded (simply because the driver and his assistant keep the excess over the rental and running costs, and legal safety restrictions are not applied). Some routes have better Pullman services, faster and more reliable. The correct fare should be posted up. We receive complaints that bus drivers charge tourists more than locals. This is becoming more widespread. One way to keep your bus fares down, ask the locals, then tender the exact fare on the bus. Many long distance buses leave very early in the morning. Try to arrange your passage the previous day and arrive in good time to get a seat. Make sure you can get out of your hotel/*pensión*. For long trips, take snacks and water. For international bus journeys make sure you have small denomination local currency or US dollar bills for border taxes. In the smaller towns, you will probably be woken up by the horns of arriving and departing buses. At Easter there are few buses on Good Friday or the Saturday but they run again on Easter Sunday.

On several popular tourist routes, for example airport-Antigua, Antigua-Panajachel, there are minibuses, comfortable, overpriced, not as much fun as regular buses but convenient. They can be booked through hotels and travel agencies and will usually pick you up from your hotel. Also check carefully that the bus is going all the way to your destination. In the country, travellers frequently say it is great to travel on the roof of the bus. However, you should know that it is illegal and, of course, can be dangerous.

NB Many long names on bus destination boards are abbreviated: Guate = Guatemala City, Chichi = Chichicastenango, Xela = Xelajú = Quetzaltenango, Toto = Totonicapán, etc. Buses in the west and north are called *camionetas*. Regarding pronunciation, 'X' is pronounced 'sh' in Guatemala, as in Yucatán.

Bringing a vehicle into Guatemala requires the following procedure: visit immigration and **Car** pay Q5 for an entry stamp; visit *cuarantena agropecuaria* (Ministry of Agriculture quarantine); at Aduana (Customs), pay US$20 for all forms, tourist permit and a sticker for your vehicle. All stamps are put on a strip of paper. When entering the country, ask the officials to add any important accessories you have to the paper, for example spare wheels, radio, a/c unit etc. If border officials try to charge you more than the above, demand a written receipt or resist if one is not given. Always double check 'Ingreso' papers before leaving the border. The tourist permit for a vehicle is valid for 30 days, even though driver and passengers may be given 90 days. The tourist vehicle permit is renewable at the Aduana, 10 C, 13-92, Zona 1, after completion of forms at 12th Floor of Edif Financiero, 8 Av y 21 C, Zona 1, Centro Cívico. The process costs around US$7 and can take several days. Your passport must contain a visa for the period requested. It is rumoured that you can apply for a new vehicle permit at immigration and customs at a border post. On leaving by car, four stamps on a strip of paper are required: exit stamp from Migración (Q5, or Q10 at weekends, or for any other excuse); surrender of vehicle permit at Aduana; *cuarantena agropecuaria* (quarantine); vehicle inspection (not always carried out). You are then supposed to surrender your stamped strip of paper. Motorcycle entry permit costs the same as a car, better to pay in quetzales if you can. The description of your vehicle on the registration document must match your vehicle's appearance exactly. Spare tyres for cars and motorcycles must be listed in the vehicle entry permit, otherwise they are liable to confiscation. It is better not to import and sell foreign cars in Guatemala as import taxes are very high. We understand you can air freight a motorcycle and maybe a car to Colombia from Guatemala without too much hassle. Check with SAM office in Guatemala City.

The paved roads have vastly improved in the past two years and now are of a high standard, making road travel faster and safer. Even cycle tracks (*ciclovías*) are beginning to appear on new roads, eg near Puerto San José. However, a new driving hazard in the highlands is the deep gully (for rainwater or falling stones) alongside the road. Road work was continuing in 1999 and may cause significant delays here and there. High clearance is essential on many roads in remoter areas and four-wheel drive vehicle useful.

Identification should be carried at all times. Police cars are now frequently seen on main highways, especially near borders. Stopping is compulsory: if driving your own vehicle, watch out for the 'ALTO' sign. For a minor traffic offence, you should only be given a citation by the police. Police officers are not allowed, officially, to retain your personal or vehicle documents. If they insist on doing so, ask to go to the nearest police station. Also, officially, you should not give any money to traffic police. Experience shows, however, that police may impound your licence if you are stopped for an infraction, which can take some time to redeem. To avoid this if your papers are in order, a tip of say US$3.50-9, depending on circumstances, will help. If your papers are not in order, a larger tip may be necessary. Another suggestion is to take one or more International Driving Licences as well as your national licence. Tourists involved in traffic accidents will have to pay whether the guilty party or not. After an accident, do not move your vehicle. If someone is injured or killed, the foreigner will have to pay all damages. Car insurance can be arranged at *Seguros G & T*, 7 Av, 1-82, Zona 4, Guatemala City, T3341361 and at their offices in Coatepeque, Mazatenango, Zacapa, Jalapa and Huehuetenango, depending on length of stay, etc. Also La Ceiba SA, 13 C 3-40, Zona 10, Edif. Atlantis Of. 1001, T3661606/1616, F3661658/9. Sanborns in the USA (see **Automobiles**, Mexico **Essentials**), provides insurance for Guatemala only if you buy Mexico cover through them.

Gasoline costs US$1.60 'normal', US$1.70 'premium' for the US gallon. Unleaded is available in major cities, at Melchor de Mencos (Belize border) and along the Pan-American Highway but not in the countryside. Diesel costs US$1.20 a gallon. If coming in from Mexico fill up before you enter. Just about all motorbike parts and accessories are available at decent prices in Guatemala City at *Canella*, 7 Av, 8-65, Zona 4, T3348051/55, open Monday-Friday 0830-1730, closed for lunch, Saturday 0830-1230; opposite is *FPK*, 7 Av, 8-08, Zona 4, T3319777/81, F3316012; better availability than anywhere else in Central America. Excellent BMW bike mechanic, Johann Ferber, Autofix, Av Petapa 11-00, Zona 12, Guatemala City, T714189.

Border crossings from Mexico to Western Guatemala: *Tecún Umán/Ciudad Hidalgo* is the main truckers' crossing. It is very busy and should be avoided at all costs by car (hitch hikers, on the other hand, are sure to find a long-distance lift here). *Talismán* is more geared to private cars; there are the usual hordes of helpers to guide you through the procedures, for a fee. *La Mesilla* is the simplest for private cars and you can do your own paperwork with ease. All necessary documents can be obtained here. Any of the three crossings is straightforward going from Guatemala to Mexico (with thanks to Francesca Pagnacco, Exeter).

Car hire Hired cars may not always be taken into neighbouring countries (none is allowed into Mexico); rental companies that do allow their vehicles to cross borders charge US$7-10 for the permits and paperwork. Credit cards or cash are accepted for car rental.

Cycling Shirley Hudson (Mosier, Oregon) writes: The scenery is gorgeous, the people friendly and colourful. The hills are steep, steep, steep and sometimes long. The Pan-American Highway is OK from Guatemala City west; it has a shoulder and traffic is not very heavy. Cycling is hard, but enjoyable. Buses are frequent and easy to load a bicycle on the roof; many buses do so, charging about two thirds of the passenger fare. On the road, buses are a hazard for cyclists, Guatemala City is particularly dangerous. Look out for the cycle tracks (*ciclovías*) on a few main roads.

Hitchhiking Hitchhiking is comparatively easy, but increasingly risky, especially for single women, also beware of theft of luggage, especially in trucks. The best place to try for a lift is at a bridge or on a road out of town; be there no later than 0600, but 0500 is better as it is when truck drivers start their journey. Trucks usually charge US$1-1.50 upwards for a lift/day. It may be worth asking around the trucks the night before if anyone is going your way. Recently, travellers suggest it can be cheaper by bus. The only way to retrieve 'lost' luggage is by telling the police the vehicle registration number. In remote areas, lifts in the back of a pick-up are usually available: very crowded, but convenient when bus services are few and far between, or stop early in the day.

Keeping in touch

Postal services

The Post Office has been privatized and the service much improved. Airmail to Europe takes 10-14 days (letters cost US$0.60 for first 20 grammes, US$1.90 for 20-50 grammes and pro-rata to maximum weight, two kilograms). Airmail letters to US and Canada cost US$0.45. Airmail parcel service to the US is reliable (four to 14 days): 500 grammes US$14, one kilogram US$17.50, up to two kilograms US$35, correspondingly more expensive to other overseas destinations, and may be a little more from provincial cities. Note, that parcels over two kilograms may only be sent abroad from Guatemala City. This procedure is detailed on page 599. (See in the text for alternative services to the Post Office for sending packets abroad.) **NB** The Lista de Correos charges US$0.03 per letter received. Correos y Telégrafos, 7 Av y 12 C, Zona 1; Telgua next door. Also, no letters may be included in parcels: they will be removed. All Post Offices are normally closed Saturday and Sunday. Local telegrams cost US$0.50 for 20 words. Urgent telegrams are charged double the ordinary rate but are generally reliable within the country.

Telephone services

NB All telephone numbers in the country are seven figure basis (since 1996). No prefixes (eg 0 for numbers outside Guatemala City) are necessary. For directory enquiries, dial 1524.

Telephone calls to other countries can be made at any time; to Europe, these are slightly cheaper between 1900 and 0700. The cost of overseas calls is: USA/Canada direct dialled US$1 per minute; Europe US$3.50, less to Spain; Australia/New Zealand US$5. Operator calls are more expensive, usually minimum three minutes. For Sprint, dial 195; for MCI dial 189; UK (BT-9999 044). Collect calls may be made from public phones in Guatemala City, Antigua, Quetzaltenango (possibly elsewhere) only to Central America, Mexico, USA (including Alaska), dial 196 for the operator. For direct calls, dial USA (190), Spain (191), Canada (198), Italy (193). For other countries, enquire. Collect calls cannot be made to the UK; from a private phone you can call for one minute and ask the person at the other end to phone back (at Telgua you have to pay for a minimum of three minutes). All telephone services and the international cable service are in the hands of Telgua which is still settling down as a privatized service. Check the latest dialling and charging details from the current phone book available in all hotels. Remember there are very few public telephones outside the main towns.

Fax: US$3.50 (US$2 per additional minute) to the US; US$5 (US$4 per additional minute) to Europe; and US$5.50 (US$4.50 per additional minute) to other countries. However, check around, there are wide variations in fax charges made, some by the page, some by time. Rates available in Antigua and Quetzaltenango are cheaper than elsewhere; Guatemala City prices are high.

Email is now widely used. Ask around in the cities for the best rates.

Media

Newspapers The main newspapers are *Prensa Libre* and *El Gráfico* in the morning. *La Hora* in the afternoon (best). *Siglo Veintuno* is a good newspaper, started in 1989. *El Regional*, excellent weekly paper (Antigua). *Tinamit* is a left-wing weekly, on Thursday. Weekly magazine *La Crónica* is worth reading. Recommended. There are several free booklets and newsletters aimed at the tourist: *The Revue*, produced in Antigua bi-weekly, carries advertisements, lodgings, tours and excursions, covering Antigua, Panajachel, Xela, Río Dulce and Guatemala City. *Guía Turística* covers Antigua, Atitlán, Tikal and Copán. *Guatemala News* and *Guatemala Weekly* are English language newspapers, free and widely available in Guatemala City, Antigua and Panajachel.

Food and drink

Food

Traditional Central American/Mexican food such as tortillas, tamales, tostadas, etc are found everywhere. Tacos are less spicy than in Mexico. *Chiles rellenos* are a speciality in Guatemala, chiles stuffed with meat and vegetables which may be *picante* (spicy) or *no picante*. *Churrasco*, charcoal-grilled steak, is often accompanied by *chirmol*, a sauce of tomato, onion and mint. *Guacamole* (avocado mashed with onion and spices) is also excellent. Local dishes include *pepián* (thick meat stew with vegetables) in Antigua, *patín* (tomato-based sauce served with *pescaditos*, ie small fish from Lake Atitlán, wrapped in leaves), *sesina* (beef marinated in lemon and bitter orange) from the same region. On All Saints Day (1 November) *fiambre* is widely prepared for families and friends who gather on this holiday. It consists of all kinds of meat, fish, chicken, vegetables, eggs, cheese served as a salad with rice, beans etc.

Desserts include *mole* (plantain and chocolate), *torrejas* (sweet bread soaked in egg and panela or honey) and *buñuelos* (similar to profiteroles) served with hot cinnamon syrup.

For breakfast try *mosh* (oats cooked with milk and cinnamon), fried plantain with cream, black beans in various forms. *Pan dulce* (sweet bread), in fact bread in general, and local cheese are recommended. Try *borracho* (cake soaked in rum).

Drink Local beers are good (Monte Carlo, Cabra, Gallo and Moza, a dark beer); bottled, carbonated soft drinks (*gaseosas*) are safest. Milk should be pasteurized. Cold, freshly made *refrescos* and ice creams are delicious made of many varieties of local fruits, *licuados* are fruit juices with milk or water, but the standard of hygiene varies, take care. Water should be filtered or bottled. Various brands are available almost everywhere. If you are planning to spend some time travelling in Guatemala, take an orange squeezer with you. Oranges are plentiful and cheap but a glass in a café or hotel, not necessarily fresh, will cost up to US$1.

Shopping

Woven goods are normally cheapest bought in the town of origin. Try to avoid middlemen and buy direct from the weaver. You won't do better anywhere else in Central America. Guatemalan coffee is highly recommended, although the best is exported; that sold locally is not vacuum-packed.

Kerosene is called 'Gas corriente', and is good quality, US$0.80 per US gallon; sold only in gas stations.

Film for transparencies is hard to find; it is available at 9 C, 6-88, Zona 1, Guatemala City, also in large cities like Antigua, Xela and Cobán.

Holidays and festivals

1 January; Holy Week (four days); 1 May: Labour Day; 30 June; 15 August: (Guatemala City only); 15 September: Independence Day; 12 October: Discovery of America; 20 October: Revolution Day; 1 November: All Saints; 24 December: Christmas Eve: from noon; 25 December: Christmas Day; 31 December (from noon).

12 October and Christmas Eve are not business holidays. During Holy Week, bus fares may be doubled.

Although specific dates are given for *fiestas* there is often about a week of jollification beforehand.

Health

Guatemala is healthy enough if precautions are taken about drinking-water, milk, uncooked vegetables and peeled fruits; carelessness on this point is likely to lead to amoebic dysentery, which is endemic. In Guatemala City three good hospitals are: *Bella Aurora*, 10 Calle A Zona 14, *Centro Médico*, 6 Av 3-47, Zona 10, T3323555, and *Herrera Llerandi*, 6 Av/9 C, Zona 10, T3345959, but you must have full medical insurance or sufficient funds to obtain treatment. English and other languages are spoken. Most small towns have clinics. At the public hospitals, which are seriously underfunded and care for serious problems is not good, you may have an examination for a nominal fee, but drugs are expensive. There is an immunization centre at Centro de Salud No 1, 9 C, 2-64, Zona 1, Guatemala City (no yellow fever vaccinations). In the high places avoid excessive exertion. If going to the Maya sites, jungle areas and coastal regions, prophylaxis against malaria is strongly advised; there may also be a yellow fever risk. Cholera has been reported since 1991 and you should be particularly careful buying uncooked food in market *comedores* where good hygiene may be doubtful. You may pick up parasites if you swim in lakes.

Further reading

Guatemala for You by Barbara Balchin de Koose (Piedra Santa, Guatemala City). *I, Rigoberta Menchú*, by Rigoberta Menchú; *Sweet Waist of America: Journeys around Guatemala*, by Anthony Daniels (London: Hutchinson, 1990). The novels of Miguel Angel Asturias, notably *Hombres de Maíz, Mulata de tal* and *El señor presidente*. Mario Payeras' *Los días de la selva* is a first-hand account of the guerrilla movement in the 1970s.

Guatemala
City ☐

Guatemala City and Antigua

The present capital, commercial and administrative centre of the country, smog-bound and crowded, and the former capital, now one of Latin America's most popular places for learning Spanish. Antigua has many major ruins, evidence of the earthquakes that have bedevilled its history. Both cities are overlooked by volcanoes active and dormant.

Population: 1,150,452
Altitude: 1,500m
Colour map 4, grid C3

Guatemala City was founded by decree of Charles III of Spain in 1776 to serve as capital after earthquake damage to the earlier capital, Antigua, in 1773. The city lies on a plateau in the Sierra Madre. The lofty ranges of these green mountains almost overhang the capital. To the south looms a group of volcanoes.

The city was almost completely destroyed by earthquakes in 1917-18 and rebuilt in modern fashion or in copied colonial; it was further damaged by earthquake in 1976, but most of the affected buildings have been restored.

Ins and outs

Getting there The airport is in the south part of the City at La Aurora, 4 kilometres from the Plaza Central. The Zona 4 bus terminal (2nd class service only, not recommended for tourists, poor and unsafe) between 1-4 Av and 7-9 C serves the Occidente (west), the Costa Sur (Pacific coastal plain) and El Salvador. The area of 19 C, 8-9 Av, Zona 1, next to the Plaza Barrios market, contains many bus offices and is the departure point for the Oriente (East), the Caribbean zone, Pacific coast area towards the Mexican border and the north, to Flores and Tikal. First class buses often depart from company offices in the south-central section of Zona 1.

Getting around Guatemala City is large. Any address not in Zona 1 – and it is absolutely essential to quote Zone numbers in addresses – is probably some way from the centre. Addresses themselves, being purely numerical, are usually easy to find. 19 C, 4-83 is on 19 C between 4 Av and 5 Av. **NB** All addresses in the text are Zona 1 unless stated otherwise. (C = Calle, Av = Avenida.)

Climate The *climate* is temperate, with little variation around the year. The average annual temperature is about 18°C, with a monthly average high of 20° in May and a low of 16° in December-January. Daily temperatures range from a low of 7°C at night to a high of about 29° at midday. The rainy seasons are from late April to June (light), September to October, with an Indian summer (*canicula*) in July and August; the rain is heaviest in early September. It averages about 1,270 millimetres a year, and sunshine is plentiful. The city has a serious smog problem, mainly brought about by vehicle emissions. (See **Traffic**, page 598.)

Sights

Centre   At the city's heart lies the **Parque Central**: it is intersected by the north-south running 6 Av, the main shopping street. The eastern half has a floodlit fountain; on the west side is **Parque Centenario**, with an acoustic shell in cement used for open-air concerts and public meetings. The Parque Central is popular on Sunday with many *indígenas* selling textiles. To the east of the plaza is the Cathedral; to the west are the Biblioteca Nacional and the Banco del Ejército; to the north the large Palacio Nacional. Behind the **Palacio Nacional**, built of light green stone, is the Presidential Mansion. The old centre of the city is Zona 1. It is still a busy shopping and commercial area, with several good hotels and restaurants, and many of the cheaper places to stay. However, the main activity of the city has been moving south for some years, first to Zona 4, now to Zonas 9, 10 and 14. With the move have gone companies, commerce, banks, embassies, museums and the best hotels and restaurants. Industry is mostly to the north and southwest. The best residential areas are in the hills to the east, southeast and west.

In the centre, the most notable public buildings built 1920-44 after the 1917 earthquake are the **Palacio Nacional** (the guards have keys and may show you

Guatemala City

City centre

0 metres 150
0 yards 164

Presidential Residence
Palacio Nacional
5 Calle
7 Avenida
8 Avenida
6 Avenida
Parque Centenario
Parque Central
Market
6 Calle
7 Calle
Cathedral
8 Calle
Biblioteca Nacional
4 Avenida
5 Avenida
Panamericana
9 Calle
Pensión Meza
1 Calle
La Merced
12 Av
5 Calle
A
6 Calle
8 Calle
9 Calle
10 Calle
Ritz Continental & Taca
Carmen El Bajo
Museo Nacional de Arte Popular e Industria
9 Avenida
10 Avenida
11 Avenida
5 Av
6 Av
7 Av
10 Av
10 Calle
11 Calle
12 Calle
San Francisco
13 Calle
12 Calle
13 Calle
14 Calle
Posada Belén
Chalet Suizo
15 Calle
ZONA 1
18 Calle
19 Calle
ZONA 3
Av Elena
Av Centroamérica
Teatro Nacional
Diagonal 2
Centro Cívico
Banco de Guatemala
Ciudad Olímpica
24 Calle
26 Calle
28 Calle
Santuario Expiatorio
Ruta 2
ZONA 4
Conquistador Ramada
Ruta 5
Diagonal 6
12 Av
ZONA 5
Campo de Marte
Av Bolívar
ZONA 8
Ruta 7
Yurrita Chapel
10 Av
1 Calle
2 Calle
Cortijo Reforma
Popol Vuh Museum
Ixchel Museum
To Antigua & the West
El Trébol
Av La Castellana
4 Av
5 Av
6 Av
7 Av
5 Calle
6 Calle
8 Calle
Parque Centroamérica
ZONA 10
Av La Reforma
10 Calle
ZONA 9
11 Calle
12 Calle
12 Calle
Blvd Liberación
Parque Aurora
14 Calle
14 Calle
Camino Real
To El Salvador
N
Museo Nacional de Antropología y Etnografía
Museo de Arte Moderno
Museo Nacional de Historia Natural
Handicrafts
20 Calle
ZONA 13
ZONA 14
0 metres 300
0 yards 327

Guatemala

round the rooms of state), the Police Headquarters, the Chamber of Deputies and the Post Office. In the northern part (Zona 2) is the fine **Parque Minerva**, where there is a huge relief map of the country made in 1905 to a horizontal scale of 1 in 10,000 and a vertical scale of 1 in 2,000 (■ *0800-1700, US$0.25*). Buses 1 (from Av 5, Zona 1) and 18 run to the park, where there are basketball and baseball courts, swimming pool, bar and restaurant and a children's playground (it is unsafe at night). The modern Centro Cívico, which links Zona 1 with Zona 4, includes the Municipalidad, the Palacio de Justicia, the Ministerio de Finanzas Públicas, the Banco de Guatemala, the mortgage bank, the social-security commission and the tourist board.

South of the centre: Av La Reforma

The **Teatro Nacional** dominates the hilltop of the west side of the Civic Centre. There is an excellent view of the city and surrounding mountains from the roof. An old Spanish fortress provides a backdrop to the Open Air Theatre adjoining the blue and white mosaic-covered Teatro Nacional; open Monday-Friday (unaccompanied tours not permitted in the grounds).

The railway station is in the southern part of Zona 1, at 10 Av, 18C, facing the Plaza named for Justo Rufino Barrios, to whom there is a fine bronze statue on Av Las Américas, Zona 13, in the southern part of the city. To see the finest residential district go south down 7 Av to Ruta 6, which runs diagonally in front of Edif El Triángulo, past the Yurrita chapel (Zona 4), into the wide tree-lined **Av La Reforma**. At the beginning of the avenue are the Botanical Gardens; at its southern end is **Parque El Obelisco** (also known as Próceres or Independencia) with the obelisk to Guatemalan independence. La Aurora international airport, the Zoo, the Observatory, the Archaeological and the Modern Art Museums and racetrack are in **Parque Aurora**, Zona 13, in the southern part of the city. There is a magnificent view all the way to Lake Amatitlán from **Parque de Berlín** at the south end of Av Las Américas, the continuation of Av La Reforma, though some recent poor quality building has spoilt the foreground.

Kaminal Juyú

On the west outskirts in Zona 7 are the Mayan ruins of Kaminal Juyú (Valley of Death). About 200 mounds have been examined by the Archaeological Museum and the Carnegie Institute. The area is mainly unexcavated, but there are three excavated areas open to the public, and a sculpture shed. ■ *0900-1600, free*. Approach from C de San Juan Sacatepéquez, then turn right along Av 30; the park is at the far end.

Churches

Most of the churches worth visiting are in Zona 1. The **Cathedral** was begun 1782 and finished 1815 in classical style with notable blue cupolas and dome. Inside are paintings and statues from ruined Antigua. Solid silver and sacramental reliquary in the east side chapel of Sagrario. Next to the Cathedral is the colonial mansion of the Archbishop.

Cerro del Carmen, in the top corner of Zona 1, 11 Av y 1 Calle A, was built as a copy of a hermitage destroyed in 1917-18, containing a famous image of the Virgen del Carmen, situated on a hill with views of the city, was severely damaged in 1976 and remains in poor shape.

La Merced (11 Av y 5 C), dedicated in 1813, which has beautiful altars, organ and pulpit from Antigua as well as jewellery, art treasures and fine statues.

Santo Domingo (12 Av y 10 C), 1782-1807, is a striking yellow colour, reconstructed after 1917, image of Nuestra Señora del Rosario and sculptures.

Santuario Expiatorio (26 C y 2 Av) holds 3,000 people; colourful, exciting modern architecture by a young Salvadorean architect who had not qualified when he built it. Part of the complex (church, school and auditorium) is in the shape of a fish.

Las Capuchinas (10 Av y 10 C) has a very fine St Anthony altarpiece, and other pieces from Antigua.

Santa Rosa (10 Av y 8 C) was used for 26 years as the cathedral until the present building was ready. Altarpieces again from Antigua (except above the main altar).

San Francisco (6 Av y 13 C), a large yellow and white church which shows earthquake damage (1976) outside, has a sculpture of the Sacred Head, originally from Extremadura (Spain). Interesting museum with paintings at the back, though in poor condition.

Capilla de Yurrita (Ruta 6 y Vía 8, Zona 4), built in 1928 on the lines of a Russian Orthodox church as a private chapel. It has been described as an example of "opulent 19th century bizarreness and over-ripe extravagance." There are many wood carvings, slender white pillars, brown/gold ornamentation and an unusual blue sky window over the altar.

Carmen El Bajo (8 Av y 10 C) built in the late 18th century; the façade was severely damaged in 1976.

Museums

Museo Nacional de Antropología y Etnología, Salón 5, Parque Aurora, Zona 13, T4720489, contains stelae from Piedras Negras and typical Guatemalan costumes, and good models of Tikal, Quiriguá and Zaculeu, and other Maya items. Contains sculpture, murals, ceramics, textiles, a collection of masks and an excellent jade collection. ■ *0900-1600, Tuesday-Friday; admission US$0.40.* **Museo de Arte Moderno**, Salón 6, Parque Aurora, Zona 13, T4720467, 'modest, enjoyable collection'. ■ *Tuesday-Friday, 0900-1600, US$0.12.* **Museo Nacional de Historia Natural**, collection of national fauna: stuffed birds, animals, butterflies, geological specimens etc, in Parque Aurora, 7 Av, 6-81, Zona 13. T4720468. ■ *Tuesday-Friday, 0900-1600, Saturday-Sunday, 0900-1200, 1400-1600, US$0.20.* **Museum of Natural History** of the University of San Carlos, C Mcal Cruz 1-56, Zona 10. T3346065. Botanical garden and stuffed animals. ■ *Monday-Friday, 0900-1200, 1400-1800, closed 1 December-15 January, Holy Week and holidays. Entrance free.* **Museo Nacional de Arte Popular e Industrias**, 10 Av, 10-72, Zona 1, T2380334. Small exhibition of popular ceramics, textiles, silversmiths' work etc. ■ *Tuesday-Friday 0900-1600, Saturday and Sunday 0900-1200, 1400-1600 (US$0.12).* **Museo Ixchel del Traje Indígena**, in the Campus of Universidad Francisco Marroquín, 6 C Final, Zona 10, T3313739/3638, has a collection of Indian costumes. In addition to costumes there are photos from early 20th century, paintings and very interesting videos. Has a shop selling textiles not usually available on the tourist market, prices are fixed. ■ *Monday-Friday, 0800-1745, Saturday 0900-1245, entrance US$2.15, students US$0.85, children US$0.60.* **Museo Popol Vuh de Arqueología**, also at 6 C Final, Zona 10, T3612301. Extensive collection of pre-Columbian and colonial artefacts. Has a replica of the Dresden Codex, one of the only Maya parchment manuscripts in existence. ■ *Monday-Friday, 0900-1700, Saturday, 0900-1300. Entrance US$2 (students US$0.80, children US$0.50). US$5 charge to take photographs.* **Museo Nacional de Historia**, 9 C, 9-70, T2536149. Historical documents, and objects from independence onward; and colonial furniture and arms (several rooms are closed for renovations 1998). ■ *Monday-Friday 0830-1600.* **Museo Fray Francisco Vásquez**, 13 C, 6-34, 18th century paintings. ■ *Monday-Friday 0900-1200.* **Museo Puiz de Arte Contemporaneo**, 7 Av, 8-35, Zona 9 ■ *Tuesday-Saturday 0900-1700, Sunday 0900-1400.* **Cedim**, 5 C 'A', 20-12, Zona 11, Colonia El Mirador I, new centre of docmentation and investigation of Mayan culture.

Each museum has a sign in 4 languages to the effect that 'The Constitution and Laws of Guatemala prohibit the exportation from the country of any antique object, either precolumbian or colonial'. The USA in fact prohibits the import of such items and penalties are severe

Gardens and zoos

Botanical Gardens, 1 C in Zona 10, off Av La Reforma ■ *Monday-Friday, 0800-1200, 1400-1800, Saturday 0830-1230, opened in 1922 and there are over 700 species of plants; most of them labelled. Admission free.*

The **Parque Zoológico La Aurora** is in La Aurora park; ■ US$1, newer areas show greater concern for the animals' well-being.

Essentials

Sleeping

■ *on maps*
Price codes:
see inside front cover

NB Prices at more expensive hotels are subject to 10% VAT (IVA) and 10% service. Thefts from hotel rooms and baggage stores have been reported; do not leave valuables unsecured. Better prices in the more expensive hotels may be obtained by booking corporate rates through a reputable travel agent or simply asking at the desk if any lower prices are available. The water supply in hotels tends to be spasmodic: ask when you arrive if there are any difficulties. Hotels are often full at holiday times, eg Easter, Christmas, when visitors from other countries and the interior come to shop. At the cheaper hotels it is not always possible to get single rooms. There are many cheap *pensiones* near bus and railway stations and market; those between C 14 and C 18 are not very salubrious.

The following list gives hotels by Zone; hotels are listed according to category.

Zona 1 **AL** *Ritz Continental*, 6 Av A, 10-13, T2381671, F2381527, breakfast included, clean, TV, a/c, pool, restaurant, recently refurbished, recommended. **AL** *Pan American*, 9 C, 5-63, T2326807, F2518749, central, quiet and comfortable, TV and baths with plugs, try to avoid rooms on the main road side, restaurant with good and reasonably-priced food (lunch recommended, served by staff in typical costumes), parking. **A** *Del Centro*, 13 C, 4-55, T2381281, F2300208, large comfortable rooms, cable TV, good restaurant (but expensive wines), live entertainment in bar, excellent service, recommended.

B-C *Posada Belén*, 13 C, 'A' 10-30, T2329226, T/F2513478, with bath in a colonial-style house, quiet, good laundry service, friendly, Francesca and René Sanchinelli speak English, often full, will store luggage safely, good dining room, avoid rather noisy room next to front door. No children under 5. Recommended but not to everyone's taste. **B** *Sevilla*, 9 Av, 12-29, T2382226, F2328431, with bath, cheaper without, nice restaurant, bar, hot water, cable TV, Turkish bath, laundry, accepts major credit cards, parking, good value.

C *Centenario*, 6 C, 5-33, T2380381, clean, clothes washing facilities on top floor. **C** *Chalet Suizo*, 14 C, 6-82, T2513786, with or without shower (triples available), popular, often crowded, locked luggage US$0.50 per day, safe, clean. Recommended but noisy rooms on street (avoid rooms 9 to 12, noisy pump will disturb sleep and 19-21 very thin walls), nice new extension, big rooms, constant hot water. *Café Suizo* next door, good breakfast (with muesli) and snacks. **C** *Colonial*, 7 Av, 14-19, T2326722, F2328671, reasonable restaurant for breakfast, quiet. Recommended, although ground floor rooms are small and poorly ventilated, ask for 2nd Floor. **C** *Continental*, 12 C, 6-10, T2305814, F2518265, 2 floors up, some cheaper rooms, seen better days, central, huge comfortable rooms, with bath, very clean, hot water. **C** *Excel*, 9 Av 15-12, T2532709, clean, cable TV, courtyard parking. **C** *Lito*, 10 C, 1-35, T2325565, popular with Swiss travellers, with bath, quiet, clean. **C** *Spring*, 8 Av 12-65, T2302858, F2320107, with shower and hot water, cheaper without, quaint, lovely patio gardens, good breakfasts, guarded parking lot nearby, popular. Recommended. **C-D** *Monteleone*, 18 C, 4-63, T2382600, F2382509, in front of Antigua terminal, good clean rooms, secure, friendly.

D *Capri*, 9 Av 15-63, T2328191, F2300496, with shower, **F** without, some rooms noisy, clean, helpful, good restaurant, hot water, cable TV. **D** *Maya Excelsior*, 7 Av, 12-46, T2382761, F2501917, faded glory, crowded, noisy and commercial but comfortable rooms, good service and recommended restaurant.

E *Ajau*, 8 Av, 15-62, T2320488, clean, cable TV, quiet, good, close to El Petén buses. **E** *Lessing House*, 12 C, 4-35, T2513891, small, clean, friendly, often full. **E** *Hernani*, 15 C, 6-56, T2322839, no restaurant, friendly, safe to leave luggage while travelling, Spanish owner. **E** *Costa del Sol*, 17 C, 8-35, T2321916, bath, hot water, noisy, adjoining *cafetería* poor value. **E** *La Fuente*, 16 C, 3-46, T2539924, quiet, will store luggage. **E** *Maya Quiché*, 7 Av y 11 C, very friendly, many families use it, good restaurant attached. **E** *San Diego*, 15 C, 7-14, T2322958, run down, uncomfortable beds, no bag storage facilities, annex opposite (7-37), **F**, good value, full

Land of
Discoveries

MAYA WORLD

Where Man, Nature and Time are One

MUNDO MAYA®

BELIZE   EL SALVADOR   GUATEMALA   HONDURAS   MEXICO

The Maya World

MUNDO MAYA

The Maya World awaits discovery. More than 2000 years ago the Maya civilization built magnificent cities of pyramids, temples and observatories where sages scanned the heavens, predicted solar eclipses, and invented a calendar even more precise than the one we use today. They were also artists – evident in carvings, pottery and murals.

Their temples now lie silent but their descendants still inhabit the area continuing the customs and rituals of their ancestors into the next millennium.

The Maya consider themselves to be at one with nature, and it is easy to see why. Breathtaking landscapes crowd the 500,000 square kilometre Maya World, labeled one of the most geographically varied areas in the world.

A mask found at Calakmul, Mexico

Union of five countries

Since 1988 government representatives from Belize, El Salvador, Guatemala, Honduras and Mexico have met to discuss a regional tourism program which, in 1990, officially became 'Mundo Maya' (Maya World).

Maya World seeks to improve the lot of local communities though development projects and also protects the environment and culture for the benefit of future generations.

Various strategies for new projects are frequently discussed by the five countries involved, as well as the importance of training programmes and international promotion.

Within Maya World tourism and conservation no longer mean a contradiction in terms, rather the protection of natural resources and an improvement in the lives of entire communities.

A colourful procession in Guatemala

An encounter with time and nature

Maya World has something for everyone's interests, including: archaeology, ecotourism, history, adventure, traditional cultures, sun and sand, and of course, many more.

For those in search of nature and contact with different cultures, Maya World offers a range of more than memorable experiences.

The opportunities are endless.

Red hot lava adds colour to the moonlit sky

MUNDO MAYA

Belize

Belize is a colorful mix of Caribbean, European and Maya influences - a cultural melting pot with a spectacular natural and historical heritage.

The Belize Barrier Reef stretches the length of this exotic country: 185 miles of continuous coral, second only to the Great Barrier Reef in Australia. Here, divers can explore the Hol Chan Marine Reserve, the world famous Blue Hole, a deep blue well far out to sea, and the Lighthouse Reef atoll.

Over 200 cayes or tropical islands lie in the shadow of the reef, making Belize an island hopper's dream. Travel experiences range from the tropical luxury of the lively Caribbean resort of San Pedro Ambergris Caye, to a hammock on a deserted island.

Hidden deep in the rainforest, Caracol remains shrouded in mystery

Back on the mainland, this exotic nation boasts some of the most spectacular jungle scenery and variety wildlife in the Maya World. The northern coastal lagoons are a haven for rare birds while Cockscomb Basin sits proudly as the only jaguar sanctuary in the world. In central Belize, Mountain Pine Ridge is a 288-square-mile reserve featuring mountains, waterfalls, caves and areas of dense tropical forest. Jungle lodges abound and travellers can take their pick from canoeing, caving, hiking, horseriding and wildlife watching.

Evidence shows that Belize was settled around 2000 BC and the ruins of countless ancient cities still dot the landscape. The oldest site in the Maya World is located here: Cuello, dates to approximately 1000 BC and the largest single sculptured jade piece – the famous Jade Head – recovered to date was found at Altun Ha. Among the most famous sites found in Belize are Caracol, Xunantunich and Cahal Pech.

Belize City is the nation's largest city (Belmopan is the capital). The spirit of the Maya World is in the faces of the Garifuna and Creole children as they help prepare a daily meal in their villages; in women dressed in traditional colourful garb as they celebrate the Deer Dance, a nine-day Maya cultural celebration; in women with their daughters, waist-deep in creeks, washing the family's clothes; or in the many professional guides who will gladly explain the mystical Maya culture at any one of the hundreds of Maya sites within Belize. While deeply immersed in the traditions of the Maya, Belize is interestingly the only English-speaking country in the Maya World.

Jade head found at Altun Ha

El Salvador

MUNDO MAYÁ

Before the Spanish Conquest, El Salvador was known as Cuzcatlán, meaning "land of precious things."

The smallest country in the Maya World, El Salvador boasts 25 volcanoes rising above jagged mountains. San Miguel, Santa Ana, Quetzaltepeque and Izalco can be scaled and offer spectacular views. The crater lakes of Coatepeque, Ilopango and Güija are major tourist attractions. Waterfalls and rivers abound and the Pacific coast is famous for beaches of golden and black sand such as Costa del Sol, Zunzal, El Tamarindo and Barra de Santiago. Nature buffs can visit the reserves of Cerro Verde, El Imposible and Montecristo for a look at the flora and fauna of the upland pine and cloud forests.

There are 25 Volcanoes in El Salvador. Shown here is Izalco

The ancient Maya were one of many preHispanic civilizations to pass through El Salvador.

The most important archaeological sites in the country are Tazumal, Quelapa, San Andrés and Joya de Cerén, a VII century village buried under a thick layer of ash when a nearby volcano erupted. Hailed as the "New World Pompeii", the site is important because it is yielding information on Maya farmers, a group about which little is known.

San Salvador, the nation's capital, was founded in 1525 and still possesses some colonial and XIX century buildings, not to mention several interesting museums.

The towns of Santa Ana, San Miguel, Panchimalco, Metapán, Chalchuapa and Izalco have colonial churches with fine examples of religious art.

Salvadoreans welcome visitors to their country, sharing with them their delicious cuisine, fiestas and colourful handicrafts of straw, wicker, wood and pottery, made in the traditional villages of Ilobasco (miniature clay figures called sorpresas), La Palma and Nahuizalco.

Pre-hispanic vase from El Salvador's Museum of Culture

MUNDO MAYA

Honduras

The landscapes in Honduras are varied and the wildlife diverse. Mountain ranges covered in pine and cloud forest give way to vast tracts of lowland jungle traversed by broad rivers like the Río Plátano and Patuca. There are lakes and coastal lagoons, caves and waterfalls. The Caribbean coast is 547 miles of unspoilt beach, secluded bays and wetlands teeming with birdlife. Offshore lie the Bay Islands which were once a refuge for pirates and now welcome divers and sun worshippers alike. The reefs fringing the largest islands - Roatán, Guanaja and Utilá - are some of the finest in the Caribbean.

Fortunately, large tracts of Honduras have been declared national parks and ecotourism is being promoted in reserves such as Río Plátano, Pico Bonito, Cusuco, Cuero y Salado and Celaque.

The ancient Maya inhabited the western reaches of Honduras and their city of Copán was one of the most important centres in the Maya World.

The Spanish heritage is manifest in the capital, Tegucigalpa, second city Comayagua, and the XVII century silver towns of Santa Lucía and Valle de Angeles. On the Caribbean coast lie the ports of Omoa and Trujillo with their imposing fortresses built to protect the area from pirates. Also on the coast Tela and La Ceiba boast XIX century Caribbean-style plantation houses.

Replica of the Rosalila temple, Museum of Mayan Sculpture, Copán

México

The Mexican Maya World encompasses the states of Campeche, Chiapas, Quintana Roo, Tabasco and Yucatán, each possessing its own charm, abundant natural and cultural attractions.

A trip through the Mexican Maya World might take in the ancient cities of Palenque (Chiapas); Comalcalco (Tabasco); Edzná (Campeche); Uxmal and mighty Chichén Itzá (Yucatán); and Tulum (Quintana Roo), among other sites.

Nature lovers can take a boat trip through the magnificent El Sumidero Canyon in Chiapas, explore the Coconá Caves in Tabasco or trek along jungle paths in Campeche. In the Yucatán, they can watch flamingoes at Río Lagartos national park or swim in a cenote (sinkhole). In Quintana Roo, the endless white beach of Cancún, Isla Mujeres and the stretch of coastline known as the Cancún-Tulum Corridor are paradise for sun worshippers and nearby Cozumel is one of the top dive destinations in the world.

The legacy of the Mexican Maya World also includes gracious cities and convents built by the Spaniards as part of their drive to colonize the area.

Spanish fortifications at Campeche

Nowadays, visitors can take a carriage ride through the streets of Mérida, Yucatán; explore the forts built to protect Campeche from pirate attacks; or enter an ornate church in San Cristóbal de las Casas, Chiapas.

The rural communities of the Maya dot the landscape.

Culture buffs can meet Maya weavers in Chiapas while in the Yucatán, they can attend a bustling market or join a pilgrimage.

MUNDO MAYA

Guatemala

A land of contrasts and colour at the heart of the Maya World, Guatemala combines the majesty of the ancient Maya with all the passion of their descendants, who account for over half the country's population of 9,000,000.

Writers and painters alike have been inspired by Guatemalan landscapes. Girdled by three volcanoes, Atitlán has been hailed as the most beautiful lake in the world. Home to the majority of the Maya groups, the upland plateau called the Altiplano possesses endless pinewoods and rolling meadows. Further north, El Petén is a refuge for wildlife such as the jaguar, howler monkey, tapir and macaw. The Caribbean coast boasts sites of interest such as Lake Izabal and Río Dulce.

Market day, Chchicastenango

The legacy of the ancient Maya is headed by the magnificent World Heritage Site of Tikal, famous for its temple pyramids. Other sites in El Petén are Uaxactún, Ceibal, El Mirador and Dos Pilas. Mixco Viejo, Zaculeu and Quiriguá, with its immense stelae, lie further south.

The Spaniards also left their mark on the Guatemalan landscape. La Antigua Guatemala, capital of a colonial empire until 1773, boasts gracious churches, convents and mansions, many of which have been restored. In the south, the lovely white cathedral at Esquipulas is the shrine of the Black Christ; Guatemala City and Quetzaltenango also possess colonial monuments.

Tikal, legendary city of the Maya

The Guatemalan Maya are divided into 23 groups, each speaking their own language, reenacting preHispanic rituals and wearing the traditional dress of their community. Visitors should pay a visit to Chichicastenango, a town that comes alive with the vibrant colours of native traditional dress on market day; the Lake Atitlán villages and the craft center of Totonicapán.

ORGANIZACION MUNDO MAYA

Direccion Ejecutiva, Plaza Building, Bliss Parade, Belmopan, Belize, Central America
Tel. (501) 8-23783, Fax (501) 8-22976, E-mail: mundomaya@btl.net

BELIZE

Ministry of Tourism, Constitution Drive, Belmopan, Belize, Central America
Tel. (501) 8-23393, Fax (501) 8-23815, E-mail: tourismdpt@btl.net

EL SALVADOR

Corporación Salvadoreña de Turismo (CORSATUR), Boulevard de Hipódromo 508, Col. San Benito, San
Salvador, República del Salvador
Tel. (503) 243-78-35, Fax (503) 243-04-27, E-mail: corsatur@salnet.net

GUATEMALA

Instituto Guatemalteco de Turismo (INGUAT), 7a. Avenida 1-17, Zona 4, Centro Civico, Ciudad de Guatemala, República de Guatemala
Tel. (502) 331-20-59, Fax (502) 331-88-93

HONDURAS

Instituto Hondureño de Turismo (IHT), Edificio Europa 5o. Nivel, Col. San Carlos, A.P. 3261, Tegucigalpa,
República de Honduras
Tel. (504) 222-40-02, Fax (504) 238-21-02, E-mail: ihturism@hondutel.hn

MEXICO

Secretaría de Turismo de México (SECTUR), Av. Presidente Mazaryk, No. 172, 6o. Piso, Col. Chapultepec
Morales, C.P. 11587, México, D.F.
Tel. (525) 545-41-31, Fax (525) 250-44-06

MAYA WORLD

Where Man, Nature and Time are One

MUNDO MAYA®

BELIZE   EL SALVADOR   GUATEMALA   HONDURAS   MEXICO

by 1000. **E** *CentroAmérica*, 9 Av, 16-38, T2326917, with 3 meals, US$1 extra with bath, safe deposit, cheap restaurant, staff very helpful, bright, hot water, iced drinking water, peaceful.

F *Bilbao*, 15 C 8-45, some English spoken, shared showers but some rooms with private bath, good toilets. Also **E** *Bilbao II*, 13 Av 12-51, T2323140, fairly clean, functional, safe. **F** *Bristol*, 15 C, 7-36, T2381401, shared bath, pleasant, back rooms are brighter, friendly, will store luggage, but noisy and not too clean. **F** *Fénix*, 7 Av, 15-81, T2516625, nice old building, some rooms with bath, hot water, clean, safe, very helpful, corner rooms noisy, good meals, breakfast available. **F** *San Martín*, 16 C, 7-59, round the corner from the *Fénix*, same management, with or without bath, modern, clean, helpful, a bit noisy. **F** *Pensión Meza*, 10 C, 10-17, T2323177, beds in dormitories **F**, other rooms **E**, popular, helpful staff, English spoken, hot electric showers, noisy, dirty, damp, inhabited mainly by young travellers, motorcycle parking, good place to arrange travel with others, basic, beware of petty theft, good restaurant next door. **F** *El Virrey*, 7 Av, 15-46, T2328513, OK. If the popular tourist hotels are full try 1 of 3 *Hoteles Metropolitanos* at: 17 C, 1-69 (**E**), 19 C, 1-53 (**E**) and 8 C, 0-40 (**F**).

AL *Conquistador Ramada*, Vía 5, 4-68, T3312222, F3347245, luxurious, but mixed reports. **Zona 4**
AL *Plaza*, Vía 7, 6-16, T3316173, F3316824, outdoor pool, squash court, lovely garden, good restaurant but suffering from location.
    E *Venecia*, 4 Av A, 6-90, T3316991, with bath, comfortable, meals poor but cheap.

L *El Dorado*, 7 Av, 15-45, T3317777, F3321877, standard luxury hotel. **L** *Princess Reforma*, **Zona 9**
13 C 7-65, T3344545, F3344546, attractive, comfortable, a/c, excellent service, cable TV, phone, pool. Recommended. Hertz, travel agency.
    AL *Cortijo Reforma*, Av La Reforma 2-18, T3320712, F3318876, attractive rooms, suites, good restaurant, comfortable. **AL** *Apartotel Alamo*, 10 C, 5-60, T3324942, large rooms, bare walls and under airport flight path. **A** *Villa Española*, 2 C, 7-51, T3322515, motel style, reasonably clean and modern, restaurant, bar, reasonable prices, parking, colonial atmosphere, good security. Recommended. **AL** *Residencia El Sol*, 3 C, 6-42, T3604823, F3604793, with bath, convenient, clean, kitchenettes, suitable for longer stays.
    D *Aguilar*, 4 Av, 1-51, T3347164, modern, good cheap food, a bit noisy, handy if you are going on to El Salvador by bus. **D** *Apartamentos Los Pinos*, 5 Av, 6-65, T3310321, F3394329, suitable for longer stays, dining area, cooking facilities. **D** *Istmo*, 3 Av, 1-38, T3324389, good restaurant, good value.

LL *Camino Real*, Av La Reforma 14-01, T3334633, F3374313, a Westin hotel, been the best **Zona 10**
hotel in the city for a long time, no airport transfers, good restaurant. **LL** *Radisson Suites Villa Magna*, 1 Av, 12-46, T3329797, F3329772, large, luxurious suites with kitchenette, a/c, laundry, garage, credit cards accepted, no restaurant but many nearby, good for long rental. **LL** *Clarion Suites*, 14 C 3-08, T3633333, F3633303, full service suites, buffet breakfast, comfortable. **L** *Holiday Inn*, 1 Av, 13-22, T3322555, F3322584, with breakfast, full service business hotel, gym, pool.
    AL *Posada de Los Próceres*, 16 C, 2-40, T3681405, friendly staff, free transport from airport, secure. **AL** *Residencial Reforma La Casa Grande*, Av La Reforma 7-67, T/F3320914, near US Embassy, small restaurant, garage. **AL** *Stofella*, 2 Av 12-28, T3346191, F3310823, elegant hotel, with breakfast, good. **AL** *Mansion San Carlos*, Av La Reforma 7-89, T3629076/7, F3316411, small charming hotel, opened 1997. Recommended.
    C *Mr Toni*, 4 C, 4-27, T/F3348416, hot showers, big rooms, TV, clean, parking, credit cards accepted, quiet, English spoken, pricey, hard to find at night.

LL *Hyatt Regency*, Calzada Roosevelt, 22 Av, T4401237, F4401234, large convention hotel, **Zona 11**
centrepiece of new commercial zone 'Tikal Futura', all services but isolated from the city.

L *Meliá Guatemala*, Av Las Américas, 9-08, T3390666, F3390690, good, new pool, suites **Zona 13**
available. *Apartotel Casa Blanca*, Av Las Américas 5-30, US$920 a month, pleasant, a bit noisy from highway and airport. *Aeropuerto Guest House*, 15 Calle A, 7-32, see under **Airport** below.

B *Hincapié Guest House,* Av Hincapié 18-77, T3327771/3140, on far side of airport runway, near old terminal building, call for free transport from airport, cable TV.

Zona 15   **LL** *Quinta Real*, Blvd Los Próceres, Km 9, T3655050, F3655051, a summit hotel, on road to El Salvador, restaurant pool, luxury services.

Eating

● *on maps*   In the capital, the visitor can easily find everything from the simple national cuisine (black beans, rice, meat, chicken, soup, avocado, cooked bananas – *plátanos* – and tortillas with everything) to French, Chinese, Italian and German food (and pastries). There are fast food restaurants (very popular) and traditional *comedores* in all commercial zones of the city where you will get good value for money; a reasonable set meal will cost no more than US$2.50. The cheapest places to eat are in street stalls and the various markets, but take normal precautions if you eat there.

The best restaurants are now in the south of the city, notably Zona 10. Below we list good value restaurants of all types in Zonas 1, 9 and 10. Some have branches elsewhere in the city.

Zona 1   The best lunchtime menu is at the *Hotel Pan American*, 9C, 5-63 (see **Sleeping**). There are many modest but good places to eat in the area covered by the Centre Detail Map: *Altuna*, 5 Av, 12-31, good Spanish, recommended. *Arriu Cuan*, 5 Av, 3-27, food from Cobán, good atmosphere, live music. *El Gran Pavo*, 13 C, 4-41, Mexican, comfortable. *Canton*, 6 Av, 14-20, good Chinese, good value. *Lido*, 11 C between 7 and 8 Av, good set lunch about US$3. *Señor Sol*, 5C, 11-32, vegetarian. *El Vegetariano*, 14C, 6-74, next to *Chalet Suizo*, varied menu. *Mezón de Don Quijote*, 11C, 12-31, good budget lunch. *Jensen*, 14C, 0-53, good coffee and refreshments. *Piccadilly*, 6 Av y 11 C, good Italian and other dishes, modest prices, also at 7 Av, 12-00, Zona 9.

Zona 9   *El Rodeo*, 7 Av, 14-84, excellent steaks, marimba, recommended. *Teppanyaki*, 7 Av, 10-65, good value Japanese, recommended. *Los Gauchos*, 7 Av, 10-65, steakhouse in same complex, good. *Mediterráneo*, 7 Av, 3-31, Italian/Spanish, nice garden, good food. *La Calle Ocho*, 8C, 6-01, good steaks, modest prices. *Lai Lai*, 7 Av, 13-27, Chinese, popular, good value, recommended. *Los Antojitos*, Av La Reforma 15-02, typical menus, good, other branches in the city. *Young Bin Guan*, 6C, 1-57, good Korean and Japanese. *El Parador*, 4 Av y 12C, excellent *platos típicos*, very reasonable value.

Zona 10   Most of the best restaurants are in the 'Zona Viva', within 4 blocks of the Av La Reforma, between 6C and 16C. The main dish at a top restaurant will cost around US$15. Drinks, particularly wines, are expensive.

Steakhouses *Hacienda de Los Sánchez*, 12C, 2-25, good steaks and local dishes. *Hacienda Real*, 13C, 1-10, excellent steak selection, recommended. *A Fuego Lento*, 16C, 6-17, expensive but first class. *Montano*, 12C, 3-28, colonial décor, family run, live music. *Jakes*, 17C, 10-40, very good food, run by Jake Denburg, New York owner and chef (you cannot miss him or his cigar). Recommended. *Los Ranchos*, 2 Av y 12 C, Nicaraguan owner, fine steaks.

Italian *Fabios*, 1 Av, 15-54, first class. *Il Boccaccio*, 14C, 5-08, very good, recommended. *Tre Fratelli*, 2 Av, 13-25, mainly Italian, Californian chef. *Romanello*, 1 Av, 12-70, excellent pasta.

Seafood *Mar Abierta*, 3 Av, 12-38, pleasant garden setting, excellent seafood. *Puerto Barrios*, 7 Av, 10-65, Peruvian owner, very good.

French *Jean François*, Diag 6 (Calle Real de Guadalupe), 13-63, in an elegant shopping complex, fine food, recommended. *Estro Armónico*, 15C, 1-11, European dishes, classical music background, also at Vía 4, 4-36, Zona 4.

Swiss/Austrian *Grishun*, 14 Av, 15-36, friendly atmosphere, good Swiss dishes. *Los*

Alpes, 10C, 1-09, good light meals, excellent cakes and chocolates. *Café Wien*, next to *Camino Real*, probably the best for coffee and cakes.

Guatemalan *Kacao*, 2 Av, 13-44, local dishes attractively prepared, typical décor. *La Escudilla del Tecolate*, 14C, 4-73, good local dishes from around the country, live music at weekends.

Spanish *Mario's*, 1 Av, 12-98, good menu, reasonably priced. *Oh Madrid*, 13C, 3-43, with tapas bar.

Mexican *Los Cebollines*, 1 Av, 13-42, authentic Mexican, live music Wednesday-Saturday, good, several branches in the city.

There are bars with good music, often live, in many of the better hotels, eg *Camino Real*, *Hyatt*, *Holiday Inn*, *Meliá*, *El Dorado*, *Conquistador Ramada* and *Cortijo Reforma*. Generally, bars tend to close around midnight.
Bars & discotheques

Bars with music: *La Bodeguita del Centro*, 12C, 3-55, Zona 1, live music most evenings, talks, plays, films, exhibitions upstairs, lively. *El Establo*, Av La Reforma, 10-31, Zona 10, excellent music 1900-0100. *Pandora's Box*, Ruta 3-38, Zona 4, popular.

Other bars: *Las Cien Puertas*, Pasaje Aycinea, 9 C between 6 and 7 Av, just off Parque Central, wonderful atmosphere, excellent food, outdoor seating, friendly, if gates of the passage are locked, knock on them to be let in. *Shakespeare's Pub*, 13C, 1-51, Zona 10, English style bar, good atmosphere, live music at weekends. *Bar Europa*, 11C, 5-16, Zona 1, popular peace-corps/travellers hangout, will change US dollars and travellers' cheques. *Cavi*, 17C between 7 and 8 Av, Zona 1, Spanish bar. *Sports Grill and Bar*, 2 Av, 13-37, Zona 10, also snacks and non-stop TV sport.

Discotheques: *Kahlúa*, 1 Av 15-06 Zona 10; *Casbah* 14C 1-42, live music most evenings; *Plush*, 1 Av 11-31, Zona 10; *The Barn*, Km 15 Carretera al Salvador, Zona 15; *Carlos y Charles*, 3 Av 12-38, Zona 10. All open late, weekends to 0300.

Entertainment, Shopping and sport

Cinemas Cinemas are numerous and often show films in English with Spanish subtitles. Prices are US$1.50-2.50.
Entertainment

Concerts Concerts of the Philharmonic Orchestra take place in the *Teatro Nacional*, Centro Cívico, 24 C, Zona 1. During the rainy season at the *Conservatorio Nacional*, 5 C, y 3 Av, Zona 1, and occasionally in the Banco de Guatemala.

Music Guatemala (with southern Mexico) is the home of marimba music (see **Music of the region**, page 44). There is an interesting exhibition room in the Museo Universitario de San Carlos, 9 Av, 9-79, showing the history of the instrument and many examples. Marimba is often played at fiestas, in up market restaurants and hotels as well as occasional formal concerts.

Theatres *Teatro Nacional*. *Teatro Gadem*, 8 Av, 12-15, Zona 1. *Antiguo Paraninfo de la Universidad*, 2 Av, 12-30, Zona 1. *Teatro Universidad Popular*, 10 C, 10-32, Zona 1. *Teatro Artistas Unidos*, 3 Av, 18-57, Zona 1. *La Cúpula*, 7 Av y 13 C, contemporary plays, concerts and classic cinema, details in press. Occasional plays in English, and many other cultural events, at *Instituto Guatemalteco Americano* (IGA), address under *Cultural Centres*, below. List of current offerings outside *Teatro del Puente*, 7 Av, 0-40, Zona 4, and in local English-language publications and city newspapers.

7 December, *Devil's Day*, hundreds of street fires are lit, any old rubbish is burnt so the smell is awful, but it's spectacular.
Festivals

Large shopping centres have been opened in the last few years, very popular locally and good for a wide selection of local crafts, art works and the local scene. Don't miss the *dulces*, candied fruits and confectionery. The best centres are *Centro Comercial Montúfar*, 12 C y 1 Av, Zona 9, *Centro Comercial Los Próceres*, 18 C y 3 Av, Zona 10, and *Centro Comercial La Pradera*,
Shopping

Carretera Roosevelt y 26 Av, Zona 10.

The **Central Market** operates behind the Cathedral, from 7 to 9 Av, 8 C, Zona 1; one floor is dedicated to native textiles and crafts, and there is a large, cheap basketware section on the lower floor. Apart from the **Mercado Terminal** in Zona 4 (large, watch your belongings), there is the **Mercado del Sur**, 6 Av, 19-21, Zona 1, primarily a food market though it has a section for popular handicrafts. There is also an *artesanía* market in Parque Aurora, near the airport, where marimba music is played, and which is strictly for tourists. Silverware is cheaper at the market than elsewhere in Guatemala City. The market is, however, recommended for all local products. Bargaining is necessary at all markets in Guatemala. Also, *4 Ahau*, 11 C, 4-53, Zona 1, very good for *huipiles*, other textiles, and crafts and antiques, run by *Dr Italo Morales* who has a great knowledge of local cultures. Hand-woven textiles from *Miranda* factory, 8 Av, 30-90, Zona 8. *El Patio*, 12 C, 3-57, Zona 1. *Rodas Antiques*, 5 Av, 8-42, Zona 1 and **Barrientos Antigüedades**, 10 C, 4-64, Zona 1, have high priced silver and antiques. *Maya Exports*, 7 Av, 10-55, Zona 1, credit cards accepted. **Sombol**, Av Reforma y C 14, Zona 9, long established, good for handicrafts, dresses and blouses. *La Momosteca* has a stall in Plaza Barrios and a shop at 7 Av, 14-48, Zona 1, and sells both textiles and silver. *Pasaje Rubio*, 9 C near 6 Av, Zona 1, good for antique silver charms and coins. Shop hours 0900-1300, 1500-1900 weekdays; may open all day on Saturday.

Bookshops *Géminis*, 6 Av, 7-24, Zona 9, T3310064 (good selection), has English books, also at 3 Av, 17-05, Zona 14, T3661031. *La Plazuela*, 12 C, 6-14, Zona 9, US magazines, English and Spanish books, large selection of second-hand books. *Vista Hermosa* 2 C, 18-50, Zona 15, T/F3691003 (English, German, Spanish). *Don Quijote*, Av Reforma y 14 C, Zona 10 (in Galería), good selection in Spanish. *Museo Popol Vuh* bookshop has a good selection of books on pre-Columbian art, crafts and natural history; also bookshop of *Camino Real* hotel which has US newspapers. Bookshops also at *Conquistador-Ramada*, Museo Ixchel, and the airport. *Librería del Pensativo*, La Cupola, Av 7, 13-01, Zona 9. *Librería Artemis*, 12C, 10-55, Zona 1, T2203645/9, or 5 Av, 12-11, Zona 1, T2533532, good selection. *Instituto Guatemalteco Americano* (IGA), Ruta 1 y Vía 4, Zona 4 (also library). *Luna y Sol*, 12 C, 3-55, Zona 1, next to *Bodeguita del Centro*, good selection of books, cassettes etc. *Eximia*, 12 C, 0-85, Zona 9, Local 5, Plaza Lorenzo, T3317073, a good place to browse, stocks English and Spanish books on ecology, mysticism, psychology, also posters, cards, crystal, quartz and gemstones. *Piedra Santa*, 11 C, 6-50, Zona 1, 5a C, 8-61 Zona 1, 6a C, 9-68, Zona 1, 12 C, 1-25, Zona 10 (Edif Géminis 10, L 202 y 203) and Calzada Roosevelt 22-50 Zona 7 (Edif Econocentro, L20). *VRISA Bookshop*, 15 Av, 3-64, Zona 1, T7613237, good selection of second-hand books in English, also café.

Camera repairs *Fototécnica*, Av Centro América 15-62, efficient, good stock. Batteries for cameras hard to come by but try *Celcomer* in Centro Comercial Montufar on 12 C in Zona 9. Kodak's main local distributor is near the zoo for a wide supply of camera products. Film is easy to find; slide film, Ektachrome 36 exp 100 ASA costs around US$10, shop at 9C, 6-88. Other film shops are being opened by Kodak, Fuji, etc, in shopping centres and commercial areas.

Maps Maps can be bought from the *Instituto Geográfico Nacional* (IGN), Av Las Américas 5-76, Zona 13, T3322611, F3313548, open 0900-1715 Monday to Friday, closed Saturday and Sunday. The whole country is covered by about 200 1:50,000 maps either available in colour or photocopies of out of print sections. Topographical detail is good but they have not been updated since 1982. There is, however, an excellent 1996 1:15,000 map of Guatemala City in 4 sheets. A general *Mapa Turístico* of the country is available here, also at Inguat and elsewhere. All map sheets cost US$6.

Sports   **Bowling**: ten-pin variety and billiards at Bolerama, Ruta 3, 0-61, Zona 4, 2 blocks from *Conquistador-Ramada* hotel. **Golf**: there is an 18-hole golf course at the *Guatemala Country Club*, 8 kilometres from the city, and a 9-hole course at the *Mayan Club*. You must be invited by a member (enquire at *Shakespeare Pub*). **Hang gliding**: *Asociación de Vuelo Libre*, 12 C, 1-25, Zona 10, Oficina 1601, Edif Géminis 10, T3353215. Flying over Lakes Atitlán and Amatitlán, best time November to May. **Swimming pools**: apart from those at the Parque Minerva (page 590) there are pools at *Ciudad Olímpica*, 7 C y 12 Av, Zona 5 (monthly membership only, US$2.50 a month – photograph required; you may be allowed in for a single swim); *Piscina Ciudad Vieja*, Zona 15; *Baños del Sur*, 13 C 'A', 7-34, Zona 1, has hot baths for US$0.50, saunas for US$1.50. Try also the hotels and the campsites near Amatitlán. The *Camino Real* sells tickets for its pool to non-guests. **Tennis**: *Guatemala Lawn Tennis Club* and the *Mayan Club* are the chief centres for tennis.

Transport

Local Bus: in town, US$0.14 per journey on regular buses, US$0.18 on new red express buses. Not many before 0600 or after 2000, but fixed route taxis (*ruteleros*), cost about US$0.36 and run on certain routes 24 hours. **Taxis**: white/yellow cost from US$1 for a short run to US$5-9 for longer runs inside the city (for example US$6 Zona 9 to centre). Hourly rates are from US$5. Prices double at night. Large black taxis are more expensive. Taxis of the *Amarillo Express*, *Azules*, *Concordia* and *Palace* companies recommended. *Taxis Circulante Rojo*, T2894415 also recommended, otherwise service is generally bad, partly because traffic in the city is dreadful and getting worse. No meters, so agree fares in advance and make arrangements to share before you approach the taxi or you will pay double. Taxis always available in Parque Central and Parque Concordia (6 Av and 15 C, Zona 1) and at the Trébol (the main crossroads outside city if coming from Pacific or Highlands by bus, convenient for airport).

Local

Car Insurance: Granai y Townson, 7 Av, 1-82, Zona 4.

Car rental: Hertz, 7 Av, 14-76, Zona 9, T3315374, F3317924. **Avis**, 12 C, 2-73, Zona 9, T3312750, F3321263. **Budget**, Av La Reforma y 15 C, Zona 9, T3316546, F3312807, airport T3310273. **National**, 12 C, 7-69, Zona 9, T3324702, F3370221, airport T3318218. **Dollar**, 6 Av 'A', 10-13, Zona 1, T2323446 (at *Hotel Ritz*), airport T3317185. **Tikal**, 2 C, 6-56, Zona 10, T3324721. **Quetzal**, Aeropuerto La Aurora, Zona 13, of 15, T3316693, F3321011. **Tabarini**, 2 C, 'A', 7-30, Zona 10, T3316108, airport T3314755 (have Toyota Land Cruisers). **Rental**, 12 C, 2-62, Zona 10, T3610672, F3342739, good rates, also motorbikes. **Tally**, 7 Av, 14-60, Zona 1, T2320421, F2531749 (have Nissan and Mitsubishi pick-ups), very competitive. Recommended. **Ahorrent**, Boulevard Liberación, 4-83, Zona 9, T3615661, and at airport, good service, hotel delivery.

Check carefully the state of the car when you hire. You may be charged for damage already there. Average rates are US$50-60 per day all inclusive (US$60-80 Hertz, or Avis). Local cars are usually cheaper than those at international companies; if you book ahead from abroad with the latter, take care that they do not offer you a vehicle which is not available. If you wish to drive to Copán, you must check that this is permissible; Tabarini and Hertz do allow their cars to cross the border. Insurance rate (extra) varies from US$4-6 a day, check carefully what excess will be charged (could be as high as US$500 but travel insurance should cover this in the event of an accident).

Car repairs: *Christian Kindel*, 47 C, 16-02, Zona 12. Chevrolet *Automecánica Cidea*, 10 Av, 30-57, Zona 5, T3325437/8 (good supply of parts). Honda, *Frank Autos*, 7 Av, 10-01, Zona 9, T3319287. For muffler service (or to remove a catalytic converter if you are heading into countries without lead-free petrol), *Leonardo's*, Av Castellana 40-76, Zona 8. General Motors (Cofiño Stahl), 10 Av, 31-71, Zona 5, T3347143/5. Isuzu/Renault (Canella S.A) T3383260.

Motorbike rental: *Moto-Rent*, 11 C, between 2 and 3 Av, Zona 9. Good Hondas for rent at reasonable prices, about US$15 per day for a Honda XL 185. Bikes can also be rented at the airport, a Jawa 180 cc for US$15, primitive but it works. Recommend to take jacket and gloves, particularly when touring the countryside. Avoid riding a bike in Guatemala City, it is very polluted. *VRISA Bike Rental*, 15 Av, 0-67, Zona 1, T7613862, mountain bikes from US$2.50 per day, also town bikes and good maps

Motorcycle repairs: Mike and Andy Young, 27 C, 13-73, Zona 5, T3319263, open 0700-1530. Excellent mechanics for all vehicles, extremely helpful. Honda **motorcycle** parts from *FA Honda*, Vía 8, 5-34, Zona 4, T4715232. General manager and chief mechanic are

German, former speaks English. Car and motorcycle parts from *FPK*, 7 Av, 8-08, Zona 4, T3319777.

Traffic: some traffic lights operate at rush hours; at dangerous junctions they operate 24 hours. Avenidas have priority over Calles (except in Zona 10, where this rule varies). City traffic has been getting worse for some time. Various reversible systems, not well signed, operate in weekday rush hours. Main routes are clogged with traffic from 0630 to 2000 with a little respite in the middle of the day.

Air Tourist information desk is facing you as you come through immigration, open 0600-2100, T3314256, has maps and general information. No left luggage facilities. The better eating places are in the departures section, near Gate 8. All prices are marked up in airport shops.

There are banks in the arrival and departure areas offering reasonable rates. The *Banco del Quetzal* office is open 7 days a week, weekdays 0800-2100, Saturday, Sunday and holidays 0800-1100, 1500-1800, sometimes open earlier or may stay open for late flights (only place to change foreign banknotes). When shut, try airport police or porters who may be able/willing to change US$ cash for quetzales.

Taxi to town, US$4.50-6, bargaining difficult. Beware of rogue taxis (*taxis fantasmas*) that operate as part of a robbery network. Buses nos 5 (in black not red), 6, 20 and 83 from 8 Av, Zona 1, and the Zona 4, 4 Av, 1 C, bus terminal, run the 30-minute journey between airport and centre (US$0.20). (Bus 20 runs from Centro Cívico to Aeropuerto Local.) There is also a bus to 7 Av, 18 C (price increases at night). From airport, buses leave just outside the upper level every 5-10 minutes, until 1930. For transport to Antigua, ask at the *Ramada* desk when their shuttle is leaving, US$7-10 per person (last shuttle around 1600-1730).

Some domestic flights (check!) to Flores (see page 641) leave from a separate terminal at La Aurora. This is located on the opposite side of the runway and reached via Av Hincapié, in Zona 13. Any chartered flights will leave from this terminal. It is 150m to Av Américas and buses to town. For scheduled flights to other domestic airfields in Guatemala, see under **Getting around** page 582.

NB The airport is officially closed from 2100-0400, so you cannot stay the night there, but there is **C** *Aeropuerto Guest House*, 5 minutes' walk from the airport at 15 C A, 7-32, Zona 13, T3323086, with free transport to and from the airport, shared baths, clean, safe, will order take-away food from nearby.

Trains No passenger trains at present.

Buses The principal companies operating from Guatemala City are: **Transportes Unidos**, 15 C, 3-4 Av, Zona 1, T2324949, 2536929 (Antigua). **Delta y Tropical**, 1C y 2 Av, Zona 4 (Escuintla and Taxisco). **Escobar y Monja Blanca**, 8 Av, 15-16, Zona 1, T2511878, 2381409 (Biotopo del Quetzal and Cobán). **Veloz Quichelense** (Chichicastenango), **Chatia Gomerana** (La Democracia), **Transportes Cubanita** (Reserva Natural de Monterrico) all at Zona 4 terminal. **Galgos**, 7 Av, 19-44, Zona 1, T2323661, 2534868 (Quetzaltenango and Mexican border). **Rutas Orientales**, 19C, 8-18, Zona 1, T2537282/2512160 (Chiquimula, Esquipulars and Honduran border). **Los Halcones**, 7 Av, 15-27, Zona 1, T2381929 (Huehuetenango). **Transportes Velásquez**, 20C, 2 Av, Zona 1 (Mexican border). **Transportes Rebuli**, 21C, 1-34, Zona 1, T2302748/4741539 (Panajachel). **Transportes Litegua**, 15C, 10-42, Zona 1, T2538169 (Puerto Barrios). **Transportes Esmeralda**, Trébol, Zona 12 (Pacific coast). **Fuentes del Norte**, 17C, 8-46, Zona 1, T2513817 (Río Dulce and Santa Elena for Tikal). **Línea Máxima del Petén**, 9 Av, 17-28, Zona 1 (Santa Elena). **Melva Internacional**, 3 Av, 1-38, Zona 9, T3310874 (El Salvador border). **Transportes Poaquileña**, 20C, Av Bolívar, Zona 1 (Tecpán). **Transportes Fortaleza**, 19C, 8-70, Zona 1, T2323643 (Tecún Umán). See under destinations for schedules and fares.

Information on interior bus services is available at Inguat, see Tourist Information above.

International buses: to San Salvador. Quality Pullmantur, 1 Av, 13-22, Zona 10 (Holiday Inn), T3329785/6, buses leave 0700, 1300, 1500 Monday-Saturday, 0800, 1500 Sunday, US$27.50 one way, US$49.50 return, booking advisable though space usually available on early buses. Tickets from all travel agencies in Guatemala City and Antigua. Ticabus (11 C 2-72, Zona 9, T2224808/3314279) at 1230 daily, to San Salvador (US$9) with connections to

Tegucigalpa (US$25), Managua (US$47), San José (US$64) and Panama (US$91). All other San Salvador buses leave from 3 Av, 1-38, Zona 9, T3310874, all companies are part of a cooperative and buses leave between 0400 and 1630, around US$8. Companies include: Transportes Centroamérica, 7 Av, 15-59, Zona 1, T2384985, Melva and Pezzarossi.

Reserve the day before if you can (all except Pezzarossi go also to Santa Ana). Taking a bus from Guatemala City as far as, say, San José is tiring and tiresome (the bus company's bureaucracy and the hassle from border officials all take their toll).

To **Honduras** avoiding El Salvador, take bus to Esquipulas, then minibus to border.

To **Mexico**: Fortaleza has buses to Tecún Umán, US$4 (see above); Galgos have several buses daily to Talismán, US$6.50, connections with Cristóbal Colón bus line – rebookings at the border may be necessary, they also have a luxury service at 0630 to Tapachula, US$16. Velásquez have 0830 bus daily to La Mesilla, connections with Cristóbal Colón.

Directory

Local airlines: *Taca Group* (includes Aviateca, Lacsa, Nica, Inter and Taca), 10 C, 6-39, Zona 1, T2381415, and at airport, T3347722 (for Inter domestic services, see page 582, **Getting around**). *Aerovías* T3327470/3615703, for Flores and Belize City, *Tapsa*, T3319180, F3345572, for Flores: these 2 have offices at Av Hincapié and 18 C, Zona 13 at the national part of the airport. *Jungle Flying*, Av Hincapié, 18 C, Zona 13, T3604917, 3604920.

International airlines: *Aero México*, 13 C, 8-44, Zona 10, T3336001. *Aerolíneas Argentinas*, 10 C 3-17, Zona 10, T3311567, **Air France**, Av Reforma 9-00, Edif Panamericana, Zona 9, T3340043, F3311918. *Avianca* and *SAM*, Av La Reforma 13-89, Zona 10, T/F3346797. *British Airways*, 1 Av, 10-81, Zona 10, T3327402, F3327401. *Copa*, 1 Av 10-17, Zona 10, T3611567, airport, T3318790. *Continental*, 18C, 5-56, Zona 10, T3669985. *Delta*, 15C, 3-20, Zona 10, T3370642, F3370588. *Iberia*, Edif Galerías Reforma 204, Av La Reforma 8-60, Zona 9, T3320911, F3343817. *JAL and American*, 7 Av 15-45, Zona 9, T (JAL) 3318531, T (American) 3347379. *KLM* 6 Av 20-25, Zona 10, open 0900-1700, T3370222). *Lufthansa*, Diagonal 6 10-01, Zona 10, T3365526, F3392995. *Mexicana*,13 C 8-44, Zona 10, T3336048. *United*, Edif El Reformador, Av La Reforma 1-50, Zona 9, T3322995, F3323903.

Banks change US dollars into quetzales at the free rate, but actual rates and commission charges vary; if you have time, shop around. *Banco de Guatemala*, 7 Av and 22 C, Zona 1, open Mon-Thur 0830-1400, Fri 0830-1430. There are several banks on 7 Av, open from 0830. Try the *Banco Industrial* (with Visa ATM), Av 7, near Central Post Office, will only change TCs with proof of purchase, *Multibanco*, 12 C, between 6-7 Av, good exchange rates. *Banco Internacional*, or *Bandesa*, 9 C between 9 and 10 Avs, Zona 1. *Lloyds* Bank plc, 6 Av, 9-51, Edif Gran Vía, Zona 9, T3327580, F3327641, agencies at Av Roosevelt, Zona 10, La Parroquía and Petapa, open weekdays, 0900-1500. *Bancafé*, Av La Reforma 9-30, Zona 9, T3311311, open Mon-Fri, to 2000. *Citibank*, Av Reforma 15-45, Zona 10, T3336574, open Mon-Fri 0900-1500. *American Express*, Edif Plaza Panamericana, Av La Reforma, 9-00 (Bancafé building) planta baja, Zona 9, T3340040/3347463, F3311418 (bus 101 from Av 10). Open Mon-Fri 0900-1630, will hold mail, Apartado Postal 720-A, for all services, agencies throughout the country. Quetzales may be bought with Visa or Mastercard at *Credomatic*, minimum withdrawal US$100, in the basement of *Banco del Quetzal* 7 Av, 6-22, Zona 9 (open until 2000, Mon-Fri, 0800-1300 Saturday), T3318333, also 7 Av 6-26, Zona 9, T3317436, and at 11 C, 5-6 Av, Zona 1 (next to *Bar Europa*). You can also draw quetzales on Diners Club card, not less than US$125 or more than US$1,000 equivalent, once every 2 weeks maximum, 12 C, 4-74, Zona 9, Edif Quinta Montúfar, p 4, T3316075/3329615. Other places to use Mastercard are: *Shell/Circle K*, Av Las Américas, 18C, Zona 14, and *Banco Agrícola Mercantil*, 7 Av, 7 C Zona 9. Visa: *Construbanco*, also 7 Av, 7C Zona 9, *Hotel Radisson* and *Hotel Camino Real* both in Zona 10. Thomas Cook TCs are not easy to cash, but try Banamex on Av La Reforma, Zona 10. See under **Air** for airport exchange.

Central Post Office: 7 Av, 12 C, Zona 1, T2326101/6107. Open Mon-Fri 0900-1730. Ground floor for overseas parcel service (airmail only; allow plenty of time). Watch your belongings when standing in queues here. This is the only post office in the country from which parcels over 2 kg can be sent abroad. You have to show your goods, which will be weighed, make a customs list before packing (cardboard box or flour sack, staff will lend a needle and give instructions), all in an office at the back of the building (No 119). See page 585 for postage rates. Poste restante keeps mail for 2 months (US$0.03 per letter). See also Amex under **Banks** above. If you are awaiting an incoming parcel, the Post Office will inform you at a private address that the item has arrived. You must then clear customs, Aduana de Fardos Postales, 10 C, 13-92, Zona 1, and pay the charges, which may be high. At customs, there are lists of parcels received, which you can ask to see. There may also be information in rooms 110 and 233 in the main post office. **Telecommunications: NB** See **Telephone services** in Essentials, page 585. Empresa Guatemalteca de Telecomunicaciones (Telgua), 7 Av, 12-39, Zona 1 or 4 Av, 6-54 for international calls. Open 0700-2400, 7 days a week, national and international telephone service. Local telegrams from central post office. Calls within Guatemala are surprisingly cheap on Sunday, Q1 will get you a brief call anywhere in the country. **Email and internet:** *Café Internet*, 16 C/5 Av, Zona 10, 18 workstations, good coffee, and many other places.

Cultural centres
Goethe Institut, 11 C between 3 and 4 Av, German newspapers. *Alianza Francesa*, 4 Av, 12-39, Zona 1, free film shows on Mon, Wed and Sat evenings, other activities on other evenings, recommended. *Sociedad Dante Alighieri* (Italian cultural centre), 4 Av, 12-47, T2325724. *American Society*, Diagonal 6 at 13 C, Zona 10, p 4, Edif Rodríguez, T/F3371416, Mon-Fri 1300-1800. *Instituto Guatemalteco Americano* (IGA), Ruta 1 y Vía 4, Zona 4, T3310022, offers 6-week Spanish courses, 2 hrs a day, for US$60, also houses US Embassy commercial library. Several other schools in the city.

Embassies & consulates
Addresses change frequently. *USA*, Av La Reforma 7-01, Zona 10 (T3311541/55). Mon-Fri 0800-1200, 1300-1700. *Canada*, 13 C 8-44, Zona 10, T3336102/3634348. Mon-Fri 0830-1100. *Mexico*, Embassy, 15C, 3-20, Zona 10, T3337254, Consulate, 13 C, 7-30, Zona 9, T3318165/3325249. Open 0815-1530 for tourist card applications and issues cards at 1500 that afternoon, those with straightforward applications, for example US, can get them at the border and avoid queues. *El Salvador*, 4 Av, 13-60, Zona 10, T3666147. Mon-Fri, 0800-1400. *Honduras*, 9 Av, 16-34. Open 0900-1400, visas cost US$15, T3374344 (take 24 hrs, quicker in Esquipulas). *Belize*, Casa El Reformador, Av La Reforma 1-50, Zona 9, p 8. Open 0800-1130, T3345531. *Nicaragua*, 10 Av, 14-72, Zona 10. Open Mon-Fri 0900-1300, English spoken, T3680785. *Costa Rica*, Edificio Galerías Reforma Oficina 320, Av La Reforma, 8-60, Zona 9, T3320531. *Panama*, 5 Av, 15-45, Centro Empresarial, Zona 10, T3337182. 0830-1300 Mon-Fri, visa given on the spot, US$10, valid for 3 months for a 30-day stay, English spoken.

Argentina, 2 Av, 11-04, Zona 10, T3314969. *Bolivia*, 7 Av, 15-13, Zona 1, T2326156. *Brazil*, 18 C, 2-22, Zona 14, T3370949. *Colombia*, Edificio Géminis 10, 12 C 1-25, Zona 10, T3353604. *Chile*, 14 C, 15-21, Zona 13, T3321149. *Ecuador*, 4 Av 12-04, Zona 14, T3372902. *Peru*, 2 Av, 9-67, Zona 9, T3318558. *Uruguay*, 6 Av 20-25, Zona 10, T3370229. *Venezuela*, 8 C, 0-56, Zona 9 T3316505.

Israel, 13 Av 14-07, Zona 10, T3336951. *Japan*, Ruta 6, 8-19, Zona 4, T3319666. *South Africa*, 10 Av, 30-57, Zona 5, T3326890.

Austria, 6 Av, 20-25, Zona 10, T3682324. Mon to Fri 1100 to 1300. *Belgium*, 15 C A 14-44, Zona 10, T3681150. *Denmark*, 7 Av 20-36 (Apartment 1, p 2), Zona 1, T2381091. *Finland*, 2 C, 18-37, Zona 15, T3659270. *France*, 16 C, 4-53, Zona 10, T3373639/3372207. *Germany*, 20 C, 6-20, Zona 10, T3336903, open 0900-1200. *Netherlands*, Consulate General, 12 C, 7-56, Edif La Curaçao, Zona 9, p 4, T3313505 (open 0900-1200). *Norway*, 14 C, 3-51, Zona 10, T3665908. *Italy*, 5 Av, 8-59, Zona 14, T3374558. Mon, Wed, Fri 0800-1430, Tues, Thur 0800-1330, 1500-1800. *Portugal*, 5 Av, 12-60, Zona 9, T3341054. *Spain*, 6 C, 6-48, Zona 9, T3343757. *Sweden*, 8 Av, 15-07, Zona 10, T3336536. *Switzerland*, Edif Seguros Universales, 4 C, 7-73, Zona 9, T3340743. Mon-Fri 0900-1130. *British Embassy*, Ed Centro Financiero, Torre 2, p 7, 7 Av 5-10, Zona 4 (T3321601/02/04/06). Mon-Thur 0900-1200, 1400-1600, Fri 0800-1100, passports normally replaced in 5 working days or less, helpful, report all attacks/thefts (Australian/New Zealand citizens should report loss or theft of passports here).

Hospitals & medical services
For hospitals see **Health**, page 586. Dentists: *Dr Freddy Lewin*, Centro Médico, 6 Av 3-69, Zona 10, T3325153 (German, English). *Dr Bernal Herrera*, 6 C, 1-50, Zona 1, T2518249 (English, Japanese). *Amicelco*, 5 Av, 4-12, Zona 1, sells drugs to pharmacies but will also supply gamma globulin etc to the public at reasonable prices. Doctors: *Dr Mariano A Guerrero*, 5 Av, 3-09, Zona 1, German-speaking, understands English (US$10 for treatment). *Dr Manuel Cáceres*, 6 Av, 8-92, Zona 9, 1600-1800, speaks English and German. *Dr Boris Castillo Camino*, 6 Av, 7-55, Zona 10, office 17, T3345932, recommended. Also *Dr Román Ferrate Felice* at 5 Av, 2-63, Zona 1, recommended for consultation (US$6). Opticians: *Optico Popular*, 11 Av 13-15, Zona 1, T2383143, excellent service for repairs. **Emergency:** T3345955/3323555 for hospitals, T128 for ambulance, T125 for Red Cross (Cruz Roja).

Laundry
Lava-Centro Servimatic, Ruta 6, 7-53, Zona 4 (opposite Edif El Triángulo), sometimes has hot water. *Lavomatic*, 8 Av, 17/18 C, Zona 1. *Lavandería Super Wash*, Av 12, 12-28, Zona 1, T2329362, US$1.50 per load, US$1.80 per dryer. *Express* (dry cleaners), 7 Av, 3-49, Zona 4. *El Siglo* (dry cleaners), 7 Av, 3-50,

Zona 4, 11 Av, 16-35, Zona 1, 4 Av, just up from 13 C, Zona 1 and 12 C, 1-55, Zona 9. Dry cleaner also at Vía 2, 4-04, Zona 4, open Mon-Fri, 0730-1830.

Non-Catholic Churches: *Episcopalian Church of St James*, Av Castellana, 40-08, Zona 8, and the *Union Church of Guatemala* (Plazuela España, Zona 9). Sun morning service in English at the first: 0930; at the second: 1100. **Synagogue:** 7 Av, 13-51, Zona 9. Service at 0930 Sat.

Places of worship

Thieves and handbag snatchers operate throughout the centre of Zona 1, especially between 4 Av and 8 Av from the Cathedral to 18 C. Some operate in pairs on motorbikes. Take extra care walking at night; it is best to take a taxi. Do not park on the street, either day or night, or your car may well be broken into. There are plenty of lock-up garages and parking lots (*estacionamientos*). If you are robbed, report the incident to the Policía Nacional, 6 Av, 13-71, Zona 1. Obtaining the Police report may take a couple of days.

Security

Archaeological tours: *Turismo Kim'Arrin*, Edif Maya, Office No 103, Vía 5, 4-50, Zona 4, and *Panamundo Guatemala Travel Service* also arrange tours to Maya sites.

    Travel agents: *Clark Tours*, Diagonal 6, 10-01, Zona 10, T3392877, F3392909, and several other locations in Zonas 9, 10 and 13, long established, very helpful, tours to Copán, Quiriguá, etc. For address of **American Express**, see under **Banks** above. *Setsa Travel*, 8 Av, 14-11, very helpful, tours arranged to Tikal, Copán, car hire. *Aire, Mar y Tierra*, Plaza Marítima, y 6 Av, Zona 10, T3370149, and Edif Herrera, 5 Av y 12 C, Zona 1, and *Tourama*, Av La Reforma 15-25, Zona 10, both recommended, German and English spoken. *Izabal Tours*, Alfredo Toriello, 7a Av 14-44, Zona 9, Local 14, T3340323, F3320372, highly recommended for special interest and educational tours, very knowledgeable. *Servicios Turísticos del Petén*, 2 Av, 7-78, Zona 10, T3341813, trips to Flores and Tikal (owns *Hotel Maya Internacional*, Flores). *Maya Expeditions*, 15 C, 1-91, Zona 10, T3634955, F3634965, mayaexp@guate.net, very experienced, varied selection of short and longer river/hiking tours, white-water rafting, bungee jumping, cultural tours, official guides to Piedras Negras archaeological excavations. *Salga Travel*, 14 C 0-61, Zona 10, La Casona in front of *Hotel Camino Real*, T/F3337445, very helpful. *Interconti Travel*, Av Reforma 6-46, Zona 9, T3390990, F3391001, English and German. *Nancy's*, 11 C, 5-16, Zona 1, T2533271, very helpful. *Aventuras Naturales*, Av La Reforma, 1-50, Zona 9, Edif El Reformador, T/F3345222, aventuras@centramerica.com, specialized trips in Guatemala including guided birding tours. *Viajes de Guatemala*, 15 C, 7-75, Zona 10, T/F3682252, arranges helicopter flights from Flores to Uaxactún, Río Azul and Mirador, and helicopter rental. *Jungle Flying*, Av Hincapié and 18 C, Zona 13, T3604917/4920 at airport, tours to Copán, Honduras, US$180 including flight, entry to site, guide and lunch. *Mersans*, 43 Av, 0-44, Zona 11, T/F5910789, good for bus excursions, German spoken. *Mayapan*, 6 Av 7-10, Zona 2, T2518840, F2321866. *Viajes Internacionales*, 6 Av 9-62, Zona 1, T3319392, helpful, English spoken. *Destinos Turísticos*, SA, 12 C 1-25, Zona 10, Edif Géminis 10, Torre Norte, Oficina 1102, T/F3352819/2821, destinos@guate.net, UK Agent: Penelope Kellie, Winchester 01962-779317, F01962-779458. *Four Directions*, 18 Av, 6-03, Colonia Miraflores, Zona 11, T3605604, F3605614, specializing in small guided groups.

Tour companies & travel agents

Inguat, 7 Av, 1-17, Zona 4 (Centro Cívico), T3311333/47, F3318893/3314416, inguat@guate.net, very friendly, English and some German, Italian and Japanese spoken, provides medium and higher priced hotel list, has general information on buses, market days, museums, etc, open Mon-Fri 0800-1600, accurate map of city, other maps, information, major tourist attractions. For information on the Biotopos (Nature reserves) contact **CECON**, Av La Reforma 0-63 Zona 10, T3310904, cecon@usac.edu.gt, who can also advise on voluntary work opportunities.

Tourist offices

Fire service: T122. **Immigration office:** *Dirección General de Migración*, 41 C, 17-36, Zona 8, T4751420, F4751281, for extensions of visas, take photo to 'Inspectoría'. If you need new entry stamps in a replacement passport (ie if one was stolen), go to room 201, police report required, plus a photocopy and a photocopy of your passport. They need to know date and port of entry to check their records. Whole process takes only about 30 minutes. Take bus 71 'Terminal' from 10 Av. For voluntary work permits or residency queries, ask for Sra Betty López. See Documents under Essentials, page 578. **Police:** T120 or 137 or 138.

Useful addresses

Guatemala City to Antigua

The shortest route to **Antigua** is 45 kilometres via San Lucas Sacatepéquez (see page 617) by paved double-lane highway (Calzada Roosevelt/Calzada Internacional) passing (25 kilometres out) El Mirador (1,830 metres), with a fine view of the capital. The road then rises to 2,130 metres and gradually drops to 1,520 metres at Antigua. The main road between Guatemala City and Antigua suffers from heavy traffic at weekends.

Antigua

Population: 43,000
Altitude: 1,520m
Colour map 4, grid C2

Antigua was the capital city until it was heavily damaged by earthquake in 1773. Founded in 1543, after destruction of a still earlier capital, Ciudad Vieja, it grew to be the finest city in Central America, with a population of around 50,000, numerous great churches, a University (1676), a printing press (founded 1660), and famous sculptors, painters, writers and craftsmen.

Antigua is a city constantly being damaged by earthquakes. Even when it was the capital, buildings were frequently destroyed and again rebuilt, usually in a grander style, until the final cataclysm in 1773. For many years after that it was abandoned and many of the accumulated treasures were removed to Guatemala City. Although it became slowly repopulated in the 19th century, little was done to prevent further collapse of the main buildings until late in the 20th century when the inestimable value of the remaining monuments was finally appreciated. Since 1972 efforts to preserve what was left have gained momentum. The major earthquake of 1976 was a further setback, but now you will see many sites busy with restoration, preservation or simple clearing.

Agua volcano is due south of the city and the market is to the west. Avenidas are numbered upwards running from east (Oriente) to west (Poniente), and Calles upwards from Norte to Sur. Avenidas are Norte or Sur and Calles Oriente or Poniente in relation to where 5 C and 4 Av cross on the corner of the Parque Central; however, unlike Guatemala City, house numbers do not give one any clue about how far from the Parque Central a place is.

Ins & outs Despite its air of tranquility, Antigua is not without unpleasant incidents. Take care and take advice (for example from Casa Andinista or the Tourist Office) on where not to go. The situation has improved with the arrival of the Tourist Police (green uniforms) who are helpful and conspicuous; office 4 Av Norte in the side of the Municipal Palace. If you wish to go to Cerro de la Cruz, check with them. Antigua is generally safe at night, but best to keep to the well lighted area near the centre. Report incidents to police, tourist office and Casa Andinista. Firemen (*bomberos*) can also be helpful.

Sights ■ *Entry fees in 1998 were Q10 for most ruins and museums for foreigners, Q2 for Guatemalans.* There is a fine exhibition with photographs and drawings of restoration plans in La Compañía de Jesús, 3 C Poniente y 6 Av Norte, ■ *0900-1700, free.*

Colonial architecture Centre of the city is the **Parque Central**, the old Plaza Real, where bullfights and markets were held in the early days. The present park was constructed in the 20th century though the fountain is original 18th century. The **Cathedral**, to the east, dates from 1680 (first cathedral was demolished 1669). Much has been destroyed since then and only two of the many original chapels are now in use. The remainder can be visited. The **Palace of the Captains-General** is to the south, 1764 – the original building, begun 1543 was destroyed in 1773 but part has been restored in the 20th century and now houses police and government offices. The **Municipal Palace** (Cabildo – see **Museums** below) is to the north and an arcade of shops to the west.

From archaeological site to cultural centre

The Hotel Casa Santo Domingo (3 C Oriente 28) purchased most of the old Dominican church and monastery property to create a Cultural Centre with a theatre for performing arts, contemporary art gallery, colonial art museum for the hotel's fine collection and an open air theatre-chapel. In 1997 the Cultural Centre was opened and activities included historical national cinema, music, dance, theatre and more. In progress is a projection room for school children's cultural heritage programmes, coordinated by Elizabeth Bell. Recent archaeological excavations have turned up some startling finds at the site. Prehispanic burials and ceramics have confirmed that there was never a formal Maya settlement under the colonial capital. Isolated Maya burials date from 1300 AD while other remains pre-date this time. Quite unexpectedly, when cleaning out a burial vault in September 1996, the greatest find in Antigua's history was unearthed. The vault had been filled with rubble but care was taken in placing stones a few feet away from the painted surface. The painting, from 1683, is in pristine colours of natural red and blue. A Guatemalan specialist, Margarita Estrada, was called in to prevent climatic changes and preserve the 'Calvary' scene under the chapel of Nuestra Señora del Socorro. While opening a vent to resolve a humidity problem in 1997, human remains were found. These were 'feeding' the lichens on the mural. Now open to the public on a limited basis, you can see other archaeological findings on display in a burial vault nearby and in a new archaeological museum being set up in 1999. Entry to the museums and the church, US$1.40, free if hotel guest. The site is also included in Elizabeth Bell's walking tour of Antigua (see **Tour companies**).

The other most important monuments are the following:

The cloisters of the convent of **Las Capuchinas**, 2 Av Norte y 2 C Oriente (1736), look 12th century with immensely thick, round pillars. The church and monastery of **San Francisco**, 1 Av Sur y 7 C Oriente, the church has been restored and is in use. Do not miss the tomb of Hermano Pedro, much revered by all the local communities who hope for his canonization in due course. There is a small museum in the south transept. The convent of **Santa Clara**, 6 C Oriente y 2 Av Sur, was founded about 1700 and became one of the biggest in Antigua, but did not survive the 1773 earthquake. The adjoining garden is an oasis of peace. **El Carmen**, 3 C Oriente y 3 Av Norte, has a beautiful façade with strikingly ornate columns, tastefully illuminated at night, but the rest of the complex is in ruins. Likewise **San Agustín**, 5 C Poniente y 7 Av Norte, was a fine building, but only survived intact from 1761 to 1773 and earthquake destruction continued until the final portion of the vault collapsed in 1976, leaving an impressive ruin. **La Compañía de Jesús**, 3 C Poniente y 6 Av Norte, at one time covered the whole block. The church is now being protected from further deterioration with the help of the Spanish government. Do not miss the exhibition in the entrance. The church and cloisters of **Escuela de Cristo**, C de Pasos y C de la Cruz, a small independent monastery, have survived and were restored between 1940 and 1960. It is a refreshing, simple church with some interesting original art. **La Recolección**, C de la Recolección, although started late (1700) became one of the biggest and finest of Antigua's religious institutions. It is now the most awe-inspiring ruin of the city. **San Jerónimo**, C de la Recolección, was at first a school for La Merced, three blocks away, but later became the local customs house (Real Aduana). There is an impressive fountain in the courtyard. **La Merced**, 1 C Poniente y 6 Av Norte, is a fine complex, its white and yellow façade dominates the plaza. The church and cloisters were built with earthquakes in mind and survived better than most. The church remains in use and the cloisters are being further restored. Antigua's finest fountain is in the courtyard. **Santa Teresa**, 4 Av Norte, was a modest convent, but the church walls and the lovely west front have fortunately survived.

Other ruins including **Santa Isabel**, **Santa Cruz**, **La Candelaria**, **San José El**

Viejo and **San Sebastián** are round the edges of the city and there is an interesting set of the Stations of the Cross, each a small chapel, from San Francisco to **El Calvario** church, which was where Pedro de Betancur (Hermano Pedro) planted an esquisuchil tree and worked as a gardener. He was also the founder of the **Belén Hospital** in 1661 which was destroyed in 1773. However, some years later, his name was given to **San Pedro Hospital** which is one block south of the Parque Central. Also, not to be missed, is **Santo Domingo**, 3 C Oriente 28, now a hotel (see Box).

Apart from the ruins, Antigua is a very attractive place. It is the cultural centre of Guatemala, arts flourish here and indigenous music can be heard everywhere. The Marimba Antigua even plays Bach and Mozart. Indian women sit in their colourful costumes amid the ruins and in the Parque Central. In the late afternoon light, buildings such as Las Capuchinas are very attractive and in the evening the Cathedral is beautifully illuminated as if by candlelight. There are good views from the **Cerro de la Cruz**, 15 minutes walk from the northern end of town.

Museums   **Colonial Art museum**, C 5 Oriente, half block from Parque Central, in the building where the San Carlos University was first housed, now has mostly 17-18th century religious art, well-laid out in large airy rooms round a colonial patio. **Museo de Santiago** in municipal offices to north of Plaza (also known as Museo de Armas); **Museo del Libro Antiguo** (same location), contains a replica of a 1660 printing press (original is in Guatemala City), old documents, collection of 16th-18th century books (1500 volumes in library). ■ *Both open daily 0900-1600.* The Casa Popenoe (1632), 1 Av Sur, between 5 and 6 C Oriente, is a restored colonial house containing many old objects from Spain and Guatemala ■ *1400-1600, Monday to Saturday (it's still a private house), US$1.* There is also a small museum in **Convento de Capuchinas**. **Museum of Indian Music**, K'ojom, 5 C Poniente a la final (by Alameda Santa Lucía), good collection of traditional musical instruments, slide shows on music and culture with free coffee, ■ *0930-1600 Monday-Saturday, US$0.85.*

Sleeping   **LL** *Casa Santo Domingo*, 3 C Oriente No 28, T8320140, F8320102, including breakfast, *In the better hotels,* beautifully designed in ruins of 17th century convent with prehispanic archaeological finds, *advance reservations* good service, beautiful gardens, good restaurant, worth seeing even if you don't stay there *are advised for* (see box). **L** *Antigua*, 5 Av Sur and 8 C (4 blocks south of Parque), T8320331, F8320807, beau-*weekends and* tiful gardens, pool (see **Swimming** below), buffet Sunday breakfast US$6, lunch US$13.50. *Dec-Apr. During Holy* **L** *Radisson Antigua*, 9 C Poniente and Carretera Ciudad Vieja, T8320011, F8320237, 2 pools *Week hotel prices are* (see below), lunch buffet Saturday and Sunday, tennis courts, discotheque, gymnasium, *generally double, or* sauna, free airport transfers.
more, and in the   **AL** *Posada del Angel*, 4 Av Sur 24 A, T/F8320260, elangel@IBM.net, **AL** in May, September *Jul-Aug period, find* and October, **LL** in Christmas week, price including taxes and breakfast, colonial style, wood *your accommodation* fires, beautifully furnished, attention to detail, USA T/F6179340065 (A-006, P O Box 669004, *early in the day* Miami Springs, FL 33266). **AL** *Posada de Don Rodrigo*, 5 Av Norte 17, T8320291, very agree-able if a little worn, good food, buffet breakfast recommended, in colonial house (Casa de los ■ *on maps* Leones), marimba music weekends and evenings. **AL** *Quinta de las Flores*, C del Hermano *Price codes:* Pedro 6, T8323721, F8323725, well-equipped apartments, pool, beautiful garden, good *see inside front cover* value. Recommended. **AL** *Casa Azul*, 4 Av Norte 5, T8320961, F8320944, www.infoguate.com/casazul, pool, sauna, cable TV, comfortable, full breakfast included. **A** *El Carmen*, 3 Av Norte 9, T8323850, F8323847, with breakfast, price negotiable midweek, roof garden, credit cards accepted. **A** *Aurora*, 4 C Oriente 16, T/F8320217, good breakfast available, the oldest hotel in the city, old plumbing but it works, clean, English spoken, quieter rooms face the patio, beautiful gardens, parking, good value. **A** *El Mesón Panza Verde*, 5 Av Sur 19, T/F8322925, small number of comfortable rooms, upstairs has good views of volcanoes. **A** *Posada del Hermano Pedro*, 3 C Oriente 3, T8323926, F8322090, converted colonial house.

     B *Convento Santa Catalina*, 5 Av Norte 28, T8323080, F8323079, under the arch, nice atmosphere but some rooms dark. **B** *Centro Colonial*, 4 C Poniente, 22, T/F8320657, with bath, cable TV, bijou colonial around a tiny courtyard. Recommended. **B** *Posada del Farol*, C

Los Nazarenos No 17, T/F8323735, 7 rooms with bathroom, hot water, fridge, cable TV, laundry, friendly, clean. Recommended. **B** *Unicornio*, 4 C Poniente 22A, T/F8323229, very nice.
B *Posada Santiago de los Caballeros*, 7 Av Norte No 67, T8320465, near Parque San
Sebastián. **B** *Camino de Santiago*, Carretera salida a Guatemala, 100 metres outside the city,
T8321420, large traditionally furnished rooms, with bath, hot water, nice patio and garden,
friendly owner former diplomat. **B** *Residencial El Capuchino*, 1 Av Norte 5A, T8323919, hot
water, family rooms carpeted, cable TV, refrigerator, with 2 other hotels around same court-
yard; **B** *La Cúpula Antigua*, 1 Av Norte 5 C, T8324605 and **B** *Panchoy*, 1 Av Norte 5B,
T8320937, F8323919, near town exit with similar facilities. **B** *El Caserón*, 3 Av Norte 9,

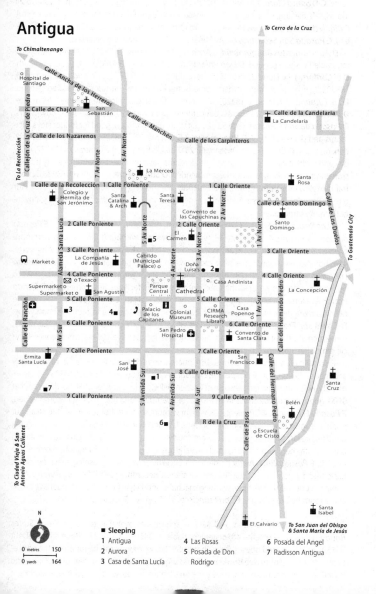

Antigua

Sleeping
1 Antigua
2 Aurora
3 Casa de Santa Lucía
4 Las Rosas
5 Posada de Don Rodrigo
6 Posada del Angel
7 Radisson Antigua

T8324406, small but friendly and comfortable, enter through *Café Los Penitentes*. **B** *Posada de la Escuela de Cristo*, 9 C Oriente 19, T/F8323255, with breakfast, charming colonial house and gardens. **B** *Posada San Sebastián II*, 3 Av Norte No 4, T8322621, breakfast, laundry, English-speaking owner, use of kitchen, good.

C *Posada de Doña Marta*, 7 Av Norte 100, T8320261, clean, attractive, good value. **C** *El Descanso*, 5 Av Norte 9, T8320442, 4 rooms on 2nd Floor, with private bath, clean, pleasant, family atmosphere. **C** *Posada Asjemenou*, 5 Av Norte 31, near La Merced, T8322670, nice gardens, friendly, laundry, popular with tour groups and with Dutch tourists. **C** *San Jorge*, 4 Av Sur 13, T/F8323132, with continental breakfast, parking, room service, fireplace, good value. **C-D** *Santa Clara*, 2 Av Sur 20, T8320342. 8 rooms, 4 with private bath, hot water, dark rooms, safe parking, breakfast and bar service, Doña María Panedes, the owner, very helpful. **C** *Rigoletto*, C Ancha de los Herreros 27 (road to Jocotenango), T8322732, restaurant (Italian). **C** *Posada San Sebastián I*, 2 Av Sur 36, T/F8323282, bed and breakfast.

D *Apartamentos Bougambilia*, C Ancha de Los Herreros 27, T8322732, with bath, parking, cable TV, kitchen, good. **D** *Don Valentino*, 5 C Poniente 28, T8320384, clean, with bath. **D** *El Confort*, 1 Av Norte 2, T8320566, beautiful gardens. **D** *El Rosario Lodge*, 5 Av Sur 36, T8320336, very quiet, with garden, some bungalow rooms with fireplace, good parking. **D** *La Tatuana*, 7 Av Sur 3, T8320537, rooms rather small, colourful, friendly, clean, safe. **D** *Plaza Real*, 5 Av S 8, T8320581, basic, friendly, hot water, cheap restaurant downstairs. **D** *Posada de San Luquitas*, C de San Luquitas 30, near *Radisson*, good for longer stays, nice rooms and patio, cable TV. **D** *Bugambilia*, 3 C Oriente 19, T/F8325780, bed and breakfast, parking, quiet. **D** *Cristal*, C del Desengaño 25, 7 blocks from Parque Central, T8324177, noisy day and night, clean, friendly, good, not all rooms have hot water, beautiful courtyard, will store luggage, cooking facilities. Recommended. **D** *San Vicente*, 6 Av Sur 6, T8323311, central, nice view from upper rooms, clean, friendly, hot showers, safe parking, storage, cycles for hire. **D** *Posada Doña Luisa*, 7 Av Norte 4, next to Ruina San Agustín, clean, friendly, private bath, family atmosphere.

E *Las Rosas*, 6 Av Sur 8, T8320644, clean, quiet, hot water, family atmosphere. **E** *Posada de Doña Angelina*, 4 C Poniente 33, with hot shower, **F** without (rooms in new part more expensive, but good), noisy, near market and bus station. **E** *Posada La Merced*, 7 Av Norte, 43A, hot shower, clean, some new rooms without bath, popular with groups. **E** *Posada Landivar*, 5 C Poniente 23, T8322962, no singles, cheaper without bath, good beds, close to bus station, safe, hot water all the time, clothes washing facilities. Recommended. **E** *Tienda Pati*, 8 Av Norte 23, private guesthouse, very friendly, clean. **E-F** *Primavera*, 3 C Poniente near Alameda de Santa Lucía and bus station, hot water, clean and friendly, good value. **D-E** *Villa San Francisco*, 1 Av Sur 15, T/F8323383, with bath, cheaper without or dormitory, some rooms without window, clean, quiet, friendly, inexpensive T/F and email service, bicycle rental. Recommended.

F *Angélica Jiménez*, 1 C Poniente 14A, offers accommodation for more than a week only and meals, cheap, clean. **F** *Hospedaje El Pasaje*, Alameda de Santa Lucía 3, T8323145, clean, friendly, noisy, washing facilities, use of kitchen, will store luggage for US$0.50, doors shut at 0100, good view of volcanoes from roof, avoid damp ground floor rooms. Recommended. **F** *Posada El Refugio*, 4 C Poniente 28, with or without showers, hot water, not too clean but popular, some cooking and laundry facilities, lots of comings and goings (not very secure), good for breakfast, parking Q5 in adjacent courtyard (pay at end of stay), close to bus station but don't stay here if you have to catch an early bus, the gate is locked and nobody around to open it. **F** *Posada Ruiz*, Alameda de Santa Lucía 17, hot water, washing machine, noisy, basic, friendly, good café opposite, near bus station. Recommended. **F** *Posada Ruiz No 2*, 2 C Poniente, hot water, safe, busy, washing machine, good view from veranda, but have a look at the room before taking it. **F** *San Francisco*, 3 C Oriente 19, clean, under US$3.

For longer stays, ask around. Full service apartments available for example at **Suites Bouganvillas**, 9 C Poniente 48, price negotiable, T3346078, F3346075. Rooms from about US$50 per month, and houses, from about US$150 per month, can be found on the noticeboard at *Casa Andinista* (see **Bookshops**) and sometimes advertised in the Tourist Office and in *Doña Luisa's* café. You do not have to be on a language course to stay with local families, it is cheap and convenient, about US$40-60 a week including meals, and a good way of meeting local people. Look on noticeboards for recommended families or ask in shops outside central area of town. Elfego and Naty Valenzuela, C Hermano Pedro 20, very nice house with patio and roof terrace, good hot showers, US$40 per week with board. Martha, 2 Av Sur 53, US$48 for 2, including meals, for a week. Estela López, 1 C Poniente No 41A, US$35 per week for room and 3 meals per day, clean, friendly. Doña Alicia Reyes, Colonia Candelaria 62, spotless, 4 rooms, roof patio, excellent meals, recommended, US$50 per week. Familia Cuellar de Toledo, 8 Av Norte, No 23, friendly, family rents rooms, clean. Private house, C de la Recolección 53, nice double garden, friendly, clean good. Good accommodation in Jocotenango, 15 minutes walk, 5 minutes in kombi (on road to Chimaltenango), Doña Marina's, 13 C 1-69, Colonia los Llanos; Carmen Urrutia, 12 C 1-69, Colonia Los Llanos, Jocotenango, T8322216, excellent house and food.

Camping: Campervan parking, try the Texaco station by the *Radisson Antigua*, otherwise camping around Antigua is not advisable.

In several of the more expensive hotels. *El Sereno*, 4 Av Sur 9, T8323593, expensive, popular at weekends. *Welten*, 4 C Oriente 21, not cheap but very good, interesting food in a delightful garden setting, reservations T8320630, closed Tuesday, also shows films most evenings. *Asados de la Calle del Arco*, 5 Av, 4 C Poniente, charming, good food, not very expensive. *Doña Luisa*, 4 C Oriente 12, 1½ blocks east of the Plaza, a popular meeting place with an excellent bulletin board, serves pies and bread, breakfasts, ice cream, good coffee, good burgers, extensive menu. *La Fuente*, next to Doña Luisa, good pasta and light meals, tables set around fountain, relaxing, *huipil* market held in courtyard Saturday 0900-1400. *La Cenicienta*, 5 Av Norte 7, decidedly has the best cakes and cookies, for example cinnamon roll, etc. *Café Flor*, 4 Av Sur, good, helpful owners, Thai food, shows videos, and *La Estancia*, steakhouse, 4 C Poniente. *Bianchi*, 4 C, between Av 5 and 6, consistently good food, pizzas, not cheap. *El Mesón Panza Verde*, 5 Av Sur 19, quite expensive but one of the best in town (see also **Sleeping**). *Fonda de la Calle Real*, 5 Av Norte No 5, also at 3 C Poniente 7, speciality is *queso fundido*, live music Friday, Saturday and Sunday evenings, good. *Quesos y Vino*, 5 Av Norte 31A, good Italian food, open late, another branch at 2 C Oriente 22 up from Capuchinas. *El Capuchino*, 6 Av, between C 4 and 5, good Italian food, especially pizzas, and salads, try the garlic spaghetti, friendly English-speaking owner from Philadelphia, has US cable TV. *Café Opera*, 6 Av Norte y 2 C Poniente, Italian owned, good music, good food and atmosphere but expensive. *Caffé Mediterraneo*, 6 C Poniente 6 A, 1 block south of Parque Central, very good Italian and pasta. Recommended. *Fridas*, 5 Av Norte 29, near arch, good Mexican. *Barcelona Viva*, 4 C Oriente 3 G, good Spanish, closed Monday. *Café Los Penitentes*, 3 C Oriente 8, good coffee and snacks (see **Sleeping**, *El Caserón*). *Café Jardín*, on west side of main plaza, good value, nice atmosphere. *Hamburguesa Gigante* on main plaza, cheap. *Panchoy*, 6 Av Norte 1-B, good beef and fondue, very good choice and quality. *Comedor Veracruz* in the market, fair, *Veracruz II* next door. *Asjemenou*, 5 C Poniente 4, serves Italian dishes, good food, excellent expresso and best *cappuchino* outside Italy(?), very small, therefore always full, good breakfast, excellent bread, slow service, but recommended. *Café Bistro*, 5 Av Sur 14, pleasant atmosphere, also shows videos. *Lina*, near market on Alameda de Santa Lucía, serves good, cheap meals. *Da Vinci*, 7 Av Norte 18 B, Guatemalan food and pasta, good atmosphere, lunch specials. On Alameda Santa Lucía *Jugocentro*, *Peroleto*, for fruits and yoghurt. *Wienercafé*, Alameda de Santa Lucía, good breakfasts, set lunch, cakes and pies, good Austrian menu, popular with students. *Tostaduria Antigua*, 6 Av Sur No 12A, good coffee roasted and brewed, many say best coffee in town, cheap, friendly American owner. *Rainbow Room*, 7 Av Sur, between 6-7 C Poniente (open 0700-2200), bookshop with vegetarian food, good breakfasts, but note the 10% service charge added to bill, popular with travellers, recommended for word-of-mouth information, also poetry evenings, see under **Bookshops**. *Café Condesa*, 5 Av Norte 4, west side of main plaza, popular, capuccino, breakfast, desserts, Sunday brunch 1000-1400, US$6, friendly. Recommended. *Crepería Papillón*, 7 Av Norte 13B, open 1700-2300, excellent crêpes. *Pastelería Okrassa*, 6 Av, C, 1-2, for meat and fruit pies. *Punto Internacional*, 5 Av 35, very

Eating
● *on maps*

Guatemala

clean, good food. *La Casa de las Mixtas*, 3 Poniente 29a, good cheap traditional breakfasts. *El Salvador*, 2 C Oriente between 4-3 Av, friendly, delicious Salvadorean/French cuisine. *Cerveceria*, 2 C Oriente between 5-6 Avenidas, open Friday-Saturday night only, excellent fondue, good cheap wine. *La Bodegona*, 5 C Poniente, international food and drink. Recommended. *El Pedregal*, C 4 Poniente 16, between 5 and 6 Av, good cheap breakfast and lunch. *La Escudilla*, 4 Av Norte 4, for good breakfast and lunch, nice courtyard, German spoken. *Las 5 Puertas*, 6 Av Norte 59B, good value, English spoken. *Cafetería Charlotte*, C de los Nazarenos 9 C, between 6 and 7 Av Norte, good breakfasts, light meals, cakes, good coffee, German books and newspapers. *Gatorgrill*, 7 Av Norte 13 B, light meals, open 1000-2300. *Deliciosa*, delicatessen, 3 C Poniente 2, good snacks and other items. **Chinese**: *Suk Mei*, 7 Av Norte 18, good value. Recommended. *Su-Chow*, 5 Av Norte, near La Merced, good, inexpensive. *Gran Muralla*, 4C Poniente 18, reasonable. *La India Misteriosa*, 3 Av Sur No 4, Indian, including vegetarian, new.

Bars & nightlife *Bar Picasso*, 7 Av Norte, entre 2 y 3 C, popular, loud music, closed some Sundays. *Latinos*, 7 Av Norte, entre 3 y 4 C, live music occasionally, good dance floor, also *Abstracto* next door, loud music. *Moscas y Miel*, 2 blocks from Parque Central, open late. *Jazz Gruta*, Calzada Santa Lucía 17, live music at weekends, cover charge US$1.25-3.50, food, happy hour Monday-Thursday 1900-2200. *Bar Chimenea*, 7 Av Norte y 2 C Poniente, large dance floor, cheap drinks, popular with gringos. *Casbah*, 5 Av Norte 30 just past the arch, good dance floor, techno, night club atmosphere, open 1900-0100. *Macondo*, 5 Av Norte 28, 'English-style pub', good Western and local music, Swiss owned. *La Canoa*, 5 C Poniente, near Plaza, good mix, salsa, crowded. *Campanas*, 3 Av Norte, 1 block east of Plaza. *Rikis Bar*, 4 Av Norte 4, usually full, popular with students and visitors. *Mojito*, 4 Av Norte 16, interesting décor, Cuban music. *Panelinos*, 6 Av y 1C, play your own guitar. Most bars have a happy hour betrween 1800-2100.

Entertainment **Cinemas** *Cinemaya*, 6A C Poniente 7, Antigua Coneplex, with wide film choice. *Ciné Sin Ventura*, 7 C Poniente 7. *Cine Bistro*, 5 Av Sur, nice atmosphere, food available. *Tecún Umán*, 6 C Poniente near *Rainbow Room*, 5 films a day. All show films or videos in English, or with subtitles, none is a large theatre.

Dance lessons *Escuela de Danza*, 5 Av Norte 25. *Ritmo Latino Dance Academy*, 3 Av Sur 4, merengue, salsa, punta, US$4 per hour, open 1600-1900. *Nahual*, 6 Av Norte 9 (Spanish school), similar programme and cost.

Workshops *Art Workshops in La Antigua*, 4 C Oriente/Colonia El Virrey 13, PO Box 14, T/F8323584. US contact: 4758 Lyndale Ave South, Minneapolis, MN 55409-2304, T612-8250747, F8256637, USA, info@artguat.org. A wide variety of courses offering instruction in all forms of expression (weaving, painting, photography, writing, etc), November-April, all-inclusive packages available, tuition costs about US$350.

Festivals *Holy Week*. The most important and colourful processions are those leaving La Merced on Palm Sunday and Good Friday, and Escuela de Cristo and the Church of San Felipe de Jesús (in the suburbs) on Good Friday. Bright carpets, made of dyed sawdust and flowers, are laid on the route. The litter bearers wear purple until 1500 on Good Friday afternoon, and black afterwards. Only the litter bearing Christ and His Cross passes over the carpets, which are thereby destroyed. Reserve accommodation at least 6 months in advance during Holy Week or stay in Guatemala City. Also **21-26 July** and **31 October-2 November** (All Saints and All Souls, in and around Antigua). On **7 December**, the citizens celebrate the *Burning of the Devils* by lighting fires in front of their houses thereby starting the Christmas festivities.

Shopping *Mercado de Artesanías* At 7 Av between 4 C and 3 C (in La Compañía de Jesús ruins, touristy but good bargains possible). Main market is by the bus terminal. *Casa de Artes* for traditional textiles and handicrafts, antiques, jewellery, etc, 4 Av Sur. *Casa de los Gigantes* for textiles and handicrafts opposite San Francisco Church. *Fábrica de Tejidos Maya*, 1 Av Norte, C, 1-2, makes and sells good cheap textiles, tablecloths, etc. *Armario*, 5 Av Sur y 6 C Poniente, modern design, traditional weaving, nice patio with café. The *Utatlán* cooperative on 5 Av Norte specializes in good handicrafts and antiques (expensive). There are many other stores selling textiles, handicrafts, antiques, silver and jade on 5 Av Norte and 4 C Oriente (*Ixchel* on 4 C Oriente sells blankets from Momostenango. *Kashlan P'ot*, in Galería La Fuente, 4 C Oriente 14, T8322369). *Nim P'ot*, 5 Av Norte 2a, traditional textiles. *Galería de Arte Estipite*, 4 C Oriente 7 (also *Restaurante Patio de las Delicias*), Wednesday-Sunday 1200-1530, 1830-2200, Central American artists, will ship works of art abroad. A number of jade-carving factories may be visited, for example *Jades, SA*, 4 C Oriente 34 (branches on same street Nos 1 and 12), open daily 0900-2100 (also coffee shop), *La Casa del Jade*, 4 C Oriente 3 (open daily 0900-1800) or *JC Hernández*, 2 Av Sur 77. *San José*, Calzada Santa Lucía Norte, No 23 A. Jade is sold on the Parque Central on Saturday more cheaply. Painted ceramics can be obtained from private houses in Av del Chajón 1 (C San Sebastián) near C Ancha, and glazed pottery from the *Fábrica Montiel*, north of C Ancha on the old road to San Felipe. Near San Felipe is the silver factory where many of the silver ornaments sold in Antigua and Guatemala City are made. Various local handicrafts at *Hecht House* in the same area. *Colibrí*, 4 C Oriente 3B, sells quality weavings. Ceramic birds at handicrafts shop in the *Posada de Don Rodrigo* (see under **Sleeping** above). *Calzado Fase*, 6 Av Norte 61, makes made-to-measure leather boots. *El Unicornio*, 4 C Poniente 38A, entre 7 Av y Calzada, near market. Tobacco shop, owned by JM Cunningham (British), open 0700-1800 daily. For local sweets/candies: *Doña María Gordillo's*, 4 C Oriente 11, is famous throughout the country. *Zapote*, 6 Av Sur between 5 and 6 C Poniente, top quality fruit, vegetables, herbs, spices, imported cheese etc, Canadian run, good. *Dulces Típicos y Artesanías*, 7C Poniente 17, good value candies, candles, etc. *La Casa Dulces Típicos*, 7 C Oriente 20 A, near San Francisco, quality candies. *La Bodegona* is a discount supermarket on 4 C Poniente between Alameda Santa Lucía and 7 Av Sur, dingy but well-stocked.

Bookshops *Casa Andinista*, 4 C Oriente 5A, sells books in Spanish and English (including the *Mexico and Central America* and the *South American Handbooks*), photographs, posters, rubbings, maps, large selection of postcards, cards, camping gear for rent (opposite *Doña Luisa's*, which sells *Time* and *Newsweek*), good information on reputable language schools. Repeatedly recommended. *Un Poco de Todo*, on west side of Plaza, sells (and buys) English, French and German language books, postcards, maps, good value. *Casa del Conde*, 5 Av Norte 4, sells books in English and Spanish and guides to Guatemalan sites, good for books on Central America. *Librería Pensativo*, 5 Av Norte 29, good for books in Spanish about Central America. *Rainbow Reading Room*, 7 Av Sur 18, campfire in evenings with musicians, nice atmosphere, secondhand books, see also **Tour companies**. *Hamlin y White*, 4 C Oriente 12 A (through Jades, SA), good selection of magazines including *Time*, *Newsweek*, *National Geographic*, etc, books and maps.

Film developing *Unifoto Fuji Antigua*, 4 C Oriente near plaza, open Sunday, 1 hour service. *Rapi Revelado*, next to *Café Condesa* on square, closed Sunday, 1 hour service. *Foto Juárez Gonzáles*, 4 C Poniente 32, closed Sunday, good, all day service. *Foto Solís*, 5 Av Norte 13, open Sunday, 1 hour service, US$8.75 for 24 exposures, US$12.30 for 36.

Hairdressers For men, all over town. For women, 6 C Poniente 29A, around corner from *Rainbow Café*, US$3.50 for cut and blow dry, good.

Market There is an extensive daily market, particularly on Monday, Thursday and Saturday (best) next to the bus terminal at end of 4 C Poniente, west of Alameda Santa Lucía. Good handmade textiles, pottery and silver. A wider selection of *típicas* can be found at the market at the northwest corner of 6 Av Norte y 4 C Poniente. Several women sell *típicas* in front of Convento Santa Clara, on 4 C Oriente between 2 Av Sur y 3 Av Sur alongside the picturesque communal washing place.

Karate school: Bie Sensei (Danish), 3rd degree black belt gives hour-long lessons. For more information ask at Tourist Office. **Riding**: for horse riding English style, see San Juan del Obispo, page 614. **Swimming**: non-residents may use the pool at the *Hotel Antigua* for a charge of US$4.50 Monday-Friday, US$7 Saturday-Sunday (US$78 per month), also at *Radisson Antigua* for US$4 per day or US$60 per month. Both hotels have special Sunday prices for buffet lunch, swimming and marimba band (the *Radisson* also has children's shows). *Antigua Spa Resort*, T311456, swimming pool, steam baths, sauna, gymnasium, **Sports**

Guatemala

jacuzzi, beauty salon. Also *Casa Solmor*, Av San Sebastián, near Parque San Sebastián. Warm mineral springs (public pool and private cubicles, less than US$1) at San Lorenzo El Tejar: Chimaltenango bus to San Luis Las Carretas (about 8 km) then 2 km walk to 'Balneario', or direct bus to San Lorenzo and a 5 minutes walk, popular with local families on Sunday, good day trip by motorbike. The last part of the road is not very safe for pedestrians on their own. At Jocotenango, *Fraternidad Naturista Antigua*, C Real 30, T8322443, with public saunas US$2, massage US$5.20, health foods, medicinal herbs, dietary advice, open Sunday-Thursday 0700-1800, Friday 0700-1300, closed Saturday, 2 km northwest of Antigua. Pool *El Pilar* 30 minutes walk on road to San Juan del Obispo, US$0.60 entrance.

Transport **Local Bike hire**: *Mayan Bike Tours* offer guided tours around Antigua, Lake Atitlán and other areas, 1 Av Sur 15, T/F8326506, Spanish, English, German, French, Italian spoken, recommended. *Old Town Outfitters*, 6 C Poniente No 7, T8324243, trvlnlite@hotmail.com, mountain bike tours, outdoor equipment on sale, maps, information, mechanic. **Car rental**: **Avis**, 5 Av Norte between the square and the arch. *Tabarini*, 2 C Poniente 19 A, T8323091. Also at *Turansa* (see **Travel agents** above). **Motorcycle hire**: Jopa, 6 Av Norte 3, T8320794, Yamaha 175, and Kawasaki 125, ask for Juan Pablo, who is very knowledgeable about what excursions to make; US$109 and US$115 per week respectively, also 4-hourly, 1, 2 and 3-day rates, all with free kilometres. Good bikes, locks, tools and helmets (in poor shape, but better than nothing) available.

Buses From **Guatemala City**, buses leave when full between 0500 and 1900, US$0.50, 45 minutes, from several locations: Av Bolívar, 32 C, Zona 3, 2 Av 19-62, Zona 1, 15C between Avs 3 y 4, Zona 1 and 18C, Av 4-5 (at least 10 bus lines, ask your hotel in the capital which is nearest). Buses to Guatemala City leave from Alameda Santa Lucía near the market, with the same frequency as buses in Antigua. To **Chimaltenango**, on the Pan-American Highway, half-hourly, US$0.35, for connections to Los Encuentros (for Lake Atitlán and Chichicastenango), Cuatro Caminos (for Quetzaltenango) and Huehuetenango (for the Mexican border). It is possible to get to Chichicastenango and back by bus in a day, especially on Thursday and Sunday for the market. Direct Transpopeye bus to **Panajachel** at 0700, from 4 C Poniente opposite gas station, a few doors east of Alameda Santa Lucía, US$4 (pay on board), 2½ hours. To **Escuintla**, Grenadiña and Ruta América, at 0600, 0630 and 1300, 2 hours, US$0.60. Buses and minibuses also to nearby villages.

Hotels and travel agents run frequent shuttle services to Guatemala City and airport (1 hour) from 0400-1830 return 0630-2000 daily, US$7 to US$10 depending on time of day, details from *Atitrans*, 6 Av Sur 8, T8323371. There are also shuttles to Chichicastenango, US$12, Panajachel, US$12, Quetzaltenango, US$25, and other destinations, but check for prices and days available. Taxi to Guatemala City US$25.

Directory **Banks** *Lloyds* Bank plc, 4 C Oriente 2 on northeast corner of Plaza, Mon-Fri 0900-1500, changes Amex TCs at Q10 commission, also changes TCs into US$ cash at 2% plus Q10. *G&T Bank*, 5 Av Norte about 4 doors north of junction with 5 C Poniente, also changes Amex TCs, any amount between 1000-1200 Mon-Fri, US$100 only 1200-1800 and 1000-1400 on Sat. *Banco del Quetzal* on Plaza, good rates, no commision. *Banco del Agro*, north side of Plaza, open Mon-Fri until 2000. *Banco Industrial*, 5 Av Sur 4, near Plaza, gives cash on Visa ATM (24 hr) and Visa credit card at normal rates, no commission. Branch of *Banco del Agro*, Alameda Santa Lucía y 5 C, near Post Office, open 0900-1800, Mon-Sat, US dollars not obtainable, may exchange personal cheques for quetzales. *Banco del Occidente*, 4 C Poniente y 5 Av Norte, open to 1900, Mon-Fri, and Sat morning. *Banco Continental*, 5 Av Sur 20 A, good rates, open Sat morning. Cash advances on Mastercard at *Jades, SA* (see Shopping). **NB** Check around for rates (including commission) for the best deal of the day. No banks change money in the week between Christmas and New Year. At this time, at weekends, etc, *Hotels Don Rodrigo* and *Villa San Francisco* will change money.

Communications Post Office at Alameda Santa Lucía and 4 C, near market (local cables from here), open 0800-1600 Mon-Fri; *lista de correos* keeps letters for a month. Boxes of books up to 2 kg can be sent from the post office, but other packages weighing more than 2 kg must be posted from

Guatemala City (do not seal parcels before going to the capital). There are strict rules on how to wrap parcels, see instructions at counter 3. **Courier services:** *Quick Shipping*, 6 C Poniente 27. *DHL*, 6 C Poniente y 6 Av Sur. *Aéreo Systems*, 6 Av Norte. *UPS*, 6 C Poniente No 15, T8320614. **Telephones:** *Telgua*, 5 Av Sur on corner of plaza for international calls and cables. However, ask around for cheaper rates. You can make collect calls from a public phone to some countries (see **Essentials**, page 585). Some hotels and restaurants will also let you use their fax machines to send and receive messages, for example *Sueños del Quetzal* restaurant. For a small charge you can phone abroad, leave the number and be called back. **Email:** *Enlaces*, Av 6 Norte, Calle 4 y 5, US$1.50 per hour. *Cybermania*, 5 Av Norte 25B T8326556, US$1 per hour, open Mon-Sat 0900-2100, Sun till 1900. *Visión Servicios Turísticos*, 3 Av Norte 3, T8323293, F8321955, vision@GUATEMALAinfo.com, www.GUATEMALAinfo.com, Guatemalan/American run, cheap phone calls, faxes, also luggage store, book exchange, recommended. *Conexión* is an electronic mail service, fax, telex, email, telegrams, send and receive, message service, translations, word processing, computers available for customers' use, 4 C Oriente No 14, T8323768, F8320082, users@conexion.com, cost: sending to arrive before 1800 US$5, after 1800 US$4, receiving US$1. *Tecnicámaras Antigua*, 3 C Poniente 21, garlo@tikal.net.gl. US$2 to send 40 lines, US$1 to receive 1 page, also repair cameras, good service. *Intertel*, 5 Av Norte 30, T/F8322640, Mon-Fri 0700-2200, Sat-Sun 0800-1800, to Europe 1 min US$3.50, 1 page fax US$7.50, USA US$1.75 and US$4.50, Canada US$2.25 and US$5.50 respectively. *C@fenet Antigua*, 6 Av Norte No 14, T8322651, good rates. Check bulletin board in *Doña Luisa's* for cheap ways to telephone overseas and email/internet.

Cultural centres *The Alianza Francesa*, 3 C Oriente 19, has French music on Fri between 1600 and 2000. Regular talks and slide shows, films (information from Casa Andinista or *Doña Luisa's*), also French newspapers. *Proyecto Cultural El Sitio*, 5 C Poniente 15, has concerts and other cultural activities, and a very good library including books in English, coffee shop. Tues-Sun 1100-1900. Concerts also at *Hotel Posada Don Rodrigo* (marimba 1900-2100, Grupo Folklórico Hunapú in bar 2000-2100). Cultural Centre at the **Casa Santo Domingo**, 3 C Oriente 28, with cinema, music, dance, theatre and art galleries (see tinted box).

Hospitals & medical services Doctor: *Dr Julio R Aceituno*, 2 C Poniente, No 7, T320512, speaks English. *Dr José del Valle Monge*, 8 C Oriente 5, good English and German, US$4 for consultation. *Dr Joel Alvarado*, 4 C Poniente 21, keeps regular hours and a quick cure for dysentery. *Dr Sergio Castañeda*, 6 Av Norte 52, recommended by Alianza Francesa. *Centro de Especialidades*, Alameda Santa Lucía 35, several specialists, will check for parasites as will *Hospital Privado Hermano Pedro*, Av El Desengaño 12A. **Hospital emergency:** T832030. **Dentist:** *Dr Asturias*, a few doors up from *Doña Luisa's*. **Public toilets:** 4 C Oriente, near central plaza, 35 centavos per person, dirty.

Language schools There are about 60 Spanish schools, consequently Antigua is full of foreigners learning the language, 300-600 at any one time. Not all schools are officially authorized by the Ministry of Education and Inguat. Rates depend on how many hours tuition you have a week and vary from school to school. As a rough guide the average fee for 4 hrs a day, 5 days a week is US$85 (US$125 for 8 hrs a day), at a reputable school, though many are cheaper. You will benefit more from the classes if you have done some study before you arrive. There are guides who take students around the schools and charge a high commission (make sure this is not added to your account). They may tackle tourists on the bus from the capital. Before making any commitment, find somewhere to stay and shop around at your leisure. Mary Cano at Alianza Lingüística 'Cano' (see address below) is recommended. She is honest, helpful, speaks English and knows the budget hotels. Also check in *The Revue*. Some points to bear in mind: accommodation with families is often linked to a particular school so be sure about one before you pay a week in advance for the other. Average accommodation rates with a family with 3 meals a day are US$40-60 per week. In some cases lodging is group accommodation, run by the schools; if you prefer single accommodation, ask for it. All schools offer one-to-one tuition; if you can meet the teachers in advance, so much the better, but don't let the director's waffle distract you from asking pertinent questions. Paying more does not mean you get better teaching and the standard of teachers varies within schools as well as between schools. Some schools are cheaper in the afternoons than in the mornings. Beware of 'hidden extras' and be clear on arrangements for study books. Some schools have an inscription fee. Several schools use a portion of their income to fund social projects.

Latest indications are that learning Spanish in Quetzaltenango or Huehuetenango is preferable to Antigua if you want to avoid Antigua's international atmosphere. Some, eg Francisco Marroquín, also offer Indian language tuition

We list only those schools of which we have received favourable reports from students: *Proyecto Lingüístico Francisco Marroquín*, 7 C Poniente 31 T8323777. *Sevilla Academia de Español*, Apartado Postal 380, 1a Av Sur 8, T/F8320442, sevilla@guatenet.net.gt. *CSA (Academia Cristiana de Español)*, 6 Av Norte No 15, Apartado Postal 320, T/F8320367. *Centro Lingüístico Maya*, 5 C Poniente 20,

T/F8320656. *Tecún Umán*, 6 C Poniente 34, T/F8322792. *Quiché*, 3 Av Sur No 15A, T8320575, F8322893. *Academía de Español Guatemala*, 3 Av Sur 15, Apartado Postal 405, T/F8320344. *Español Dinámico*, 6 Av Norte 63, T8322440. *Jiménez*, near La Merced, 1 C Poniente 41. *Don Pedro de Alvarado*, 1 C Poniente 24, T8324180. *Instituto Antigüeño de Español*, 1 C Poniente No 33, T8322682. *Centro Lingüístico Atabal*, 1 Av Norte 6, T8320791. *Popol Vuh Professional Language School*, 7 Av Norte No 82, PO Box 230, Roberto King and Lesvia Arana Gallardo (directors). *La Enseñanza*, C El Portal 1, T8320692, run by Aura and Paty Miranda. *Hombres de Maíz*, Callejón Camposeco 5, 2 blocks from La Merced, run by Rosa and Nery Méndez. *Latinoamérica Spanish Academy*, José Sánchez Corado, 3 C Poniente, F8322657. *Alianza Lingüística 'Cano'*, 2 Av del Chajón No 8A, PO Box 366. Recommended private teachers: Julia Solís, 5 C Poniente 36. Sandra Rosales, 7 C Oriente 21. Amalia Jarquín, Av El Desengaño No 11, T8322377. Julio César Pérez, 1 C Poniente 10. Leticia Isgueredo, 5a Av Norte #33A, T8321222, recommended. Also recommended is *Proyecto Bibliotecas Guatemala*, 6 Av Norte 41B, T8323768, 25% of profits go towards founding and maintaining public libraries in rural towns. See also *AmeriSpan*, page 40. Also check advertisements in *Doña Luisa's* and the Tourist Office (Director helpful) for private lessons (about US$2 per hour).

Laundry All charge about US$0.75 per kilogram and close Sun and half-day Sat. *Lavandería Gilda*, 5 C Poniente entre 6 y 7 Av, very good. *Central*, 5 C Poniente 7 B. There are many others around the centre of town.

Libraries Research: *The Centro de Investigaciones Regionales de Mesoamérica (Cirma)*, 5 C Oriente 5, offers good facilities for graduate students and professional scholars of Middle American history, anthropology and archaeology. Open Mon-Fri 0800-1800, Sat 0900-1300. **Public Library:** *The Granai y Townson library*, just north of the Plaza on 4 C Oriente, is open to the public, Mon-Fri 0900-1200, 1300-1700.

Shop around for tours **Tour companies & travel agents** *Connection Travel*, at *Radisson Antigua*, recommended. *Tivoli Travel*, 4 C Oriente 10, T8324274, highly recommended, helpful with any travel problem, speak English, French, Spanish, German, Italian, reconfirm tickets, good value tours, manager Kathy Töpke's husband, Sr Núñez, is recommended as good car mechanic (he owns *taller* at Km 41). *Club de Viajeros*, 5 C Poniente 7, and 1 C Poniente 14 'C', T8323408/4175, offers a variety of excursions and flights. *Sin Fronteras*, 3a C Poniente 12, T8321226, F8322674, sinfronteras@guate.net, local tours, rafting, horseriding, bicycle tours, national and international air tickets including discounts with ISIC and GO25 cards. *Adventure Travel Center-Viareal*, 5 Av Norte 25B, T8320162, daily trips to Guatemalan destinations (including Río Dulce sailing, river and volcano trips), El Salvador, Honduras; typical costs: to Guatemala, US$7-10 depending on the time of day, Panajachel US$12, Rio Dulce US$37 either deluxe minibus or taxi, and reports of a minibus to Copán (Honduras) at US$30. *Centro de Viajes*, 5 Av Norte 15, T/F8322728, on-line airline ticketing. *Space*, 1 C Poniente No 6 B, T8324182, F8320938, and *Total Petén*, 6 C Poniente No 6, T8320478, good service to El Petén. *Turansa*, in *Hotel Radisson Antigua*, T8324692, good for flights, for example to Tikal. *Antigua Tours*, Casa Santo Domingo, 3 C Oriente 28, T8320140 ext 341, T/F8320228, elizbell@guate.net, run by Elizabeth Bell, author of *Antigua Guatemala: An Illustrated History of the City and its Monuments* (11th ed, 1995, also in Spanish and Italian), *Lent and Easter Week in Antigua* (1st ed, 1995) and *Antigua Guatemala: the city and its heritage* (1999), offers walking tours of the city (US$15 per person), book in advance, Mon 1400-1630, Tues-Wed, Fri-Sat 0930-1200, T8320228, T/F8323660, and 45 mins slide lecture at Christian Spanish Academy, 6 Av Norte 15, Tues 1800, US$3 per person (in USA 7907 NW 53rd St, Suite 409 L570, Miami, FL33166). Highly recommended. *Area Verde Expeditions*, 4 Av Sur 8, T8323132, T/F in USA 719-5397102, recommended for whitewater rafting and kayaking, US$160 for 3 day trip, birdwatching and historical tours including trips to Honduras and Belize. *Eco-Tour Chejo's*, 3 C Poniente 24, T8325464, well guarded walks up volcanoes, to Pacaya with police armed escort on the road and 6 armed security guards going up the volcano. Interesting tours are also available to coffee fincas, flower plantations and a macademia nut plantation etc. Ask the tour companies for ideas.

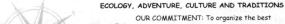

Guatemala

Aventuras Vacacionales, 1a Av Sur 11B, T/F8323352, sailing trips on *Las Sirenas* with Capt John Clark (see under Río Dulce page 636). *Rainbow Travel*, 7 Av Sur 8, T/F8324206, myers@gua.gbm.net, full local travel service, specialists in bargain international flights, recommended. *Vision Travel*, 3a Av Norte 3, T8323293, F8321955, www.guatemalinfo.com. Located behind the cathedral, they offer a wide range of tours. English spoken.

A bi-weekly magazine, *The Revue* (4 C Oriente No 23, T/F8320767, Revue@conexion.com), has information, articles and advertisements in English, free. For independent advice, ask Mike Shawcross at *Casa Andinista*, 4 C Oriente 5 A.

Tourist offices *Inguat* office at 4 C Oriente No 12A, very helpful, lots of maps and information, English and a little German spoken. Open 0800-1800, normally daily, T8320763. The tourist office can arrange guides for visits to monuments for between US$3 and US$6 per day.

Useful addresses Tourism police: T8320532/3, ext 35.

Excursions from Guatemala City and Antigua

Whether you are staying in Guatemala City or Antigua, the places in this section can be conveniently visited on a day or overnight basis.

Ciudad Vieja Ciudad Vieja is five and a half kilometres southwest of Antigua at the foot of Agua volcano. In 1527, Alvarado moved his capital, known as Santiago de Los Caballeros, from Iximché to this site, actually to what is now San Miguel Escobar, a suburb of Cuidad Vieja. On 11 September 1541, after days of torrential rain, an immense mud-slide came down the mountain and overwhelmed the city. Alvarado's widow, Doña Beatriz de la Cueva, newly elected Governor after his death, was among the drowned. There are few ruins to be seen, those in the north of the village are believed to be part of a small monastery. Today Cuidad Vieja is a mere village (*Hospedaje Shigualita*, cheap, at south end of village), but with a handsome church, founded 1534, one of the oldest in Central America. Larrys Macadamia factory, two blocks down from the market, is worth a visit. *Fiesta*: December 5-9. Bus US$0.10. At **San Juan del Obispo**, five kilometres south of Antigua, is the restored palace of Francisco Marroquín, first bishop of Guatemala, now a convent. The parish church has some fine 16th century images. For horse riding, English style, Fred and Paula Haywood offer instruction and scenic rides from their stables at 2 Av Sur 3, 1 block from the Palacio and bus terminal.

Santa María de Jesús Beyond San Juan del Obispo, on the side of Agua volcano, is the charming village of Santa María de Jesús, with a beautiful view of Antigua. In the early morning, there are good views of all three volcanoes two kilometres back down the road towards Antigua. Beautiful *huipiles* are worn, made and sold from a couple of stalls, or ask at the shops on the plaza. Frequent buses to and from Antigua on main market days, US$0.20 (Monday, Thursday, Saturday) otherwise 0700 only; last bus returns at 1700. *Fiesta* on 10 January. Sleeping at *Municipalidad* F; E *Hospedaje y Comedor El Oasis* on road to Antigua has clean, pleasant rooms. The road, very steep in places, high clearance vehicle necessary, continues on to the main road to Escuintla at Palín. Excellent views of Pacaya Volcano.

San Antonio Aguas Calientes About three kilometres northwest of Ciudad Vieja is San Antonio Aguas Calientes. The hot springs unfortunately disappeared with recent earthquakes. The village has many small shops selling locally made textiles; *Carolina's Textiles* is recommended for a fine selection, while just down the road *Alida* has a shop almost as large. You can watch the weavers in their homes by the roadside. Carmelo and Zoila Guarán give weaving lessons for US$1 per hour, as do Rafaela Godínez, very experienced, and Felipa López Zamora, on the way to the church, 30 metres from bus station (bring your own food and she will cook it with you), US$2 daily. Sra María Natividad Hernández is also recommended. You will need some time (say several afternoons) to make some progress. There is a market most days in the centre. Anacleta has a fine collection of textiles. Telephones were being installed in early 1999. *Fiestas*: 16-21 January; Corpus Christi, 1 November. Frequent buses from Antigua.

A good off-road route to Lake Atitlán can be made by suitable car or motorbike: just past Ciudad Vieja, take the unmade road west to the villages of San Miguel Dueñas and Acatenango, then take the unmade road north to Patzicía (see page 668). This route can be incorporated in a one day round trip Antigua-Atitlán-Antigua. Another good trip is north from Antigua to Chimaltenango, see page 665.

Volcanoes

The three nearby volcanoes provide incomparable views of the surrounding countryside and are best climbed on a clear night with a full moon or with a very early morning start. Altitude takes its toll and plenty of time should be allowed for the ascents. Plenty of water must be carried and the summits are cold. Ankle boots, preferably full climbing boots recommended, especially on Fuego to cope with the cinders. Descents take from a third to a half of the ascent time. Tourist Office in Antigua helpful. Enquire there about conditions (both human and natural) before setting out. There is a volcano-climbing club: *Club de Andinismo*, Chigag, Volcano Tours, Daniel Ramírez Ríos (helpful), 6 Av Norte, No 34, Antigua, T/F8323343, who is a guide certified by the Guatemalan Tourist Commission (he has a guest house, *Albergue Andinista*, with use of kitchen). Recommended for volcano tours are *ICO's Expeditions*, C del Desengaño 2, and *Gran Jaguar* at 4 C Poniente 30, T8322712. **Warning** Robberies and rapes have occurred even where large parties are climbing these volcanoes. No incidents have been reported since February 1997, but you should make full enquiries before setting out. Any attack should be reported to your embassy.

The easiest of the three (or the least difficult as one traveller described it), is climbed from Santa María de Jesús (directions to start of ascent in village). The crater has a small shelter (dirty), which is/was a shrine, and about 10 antennae. Fine views (though not guaranteed) of Volcán de Fuego; three to five hours climb if you are fit, at least two hours down. Make sure you get good directions; there are several old avalanches you have to cross and regain the trail, if you do not you may get lost. To get the best views before the clouds cover the summit, it is best to stay at the radio station at the top. Climbing at night is recommended by torchlight/moon with help from fireflies, Saturday-Sunday is recommended for the ascent. A bus from Antigua to Santa María de Jesús around 0600 (irregular) allows you to climb the volcano and return to Antigua in one day. Most organized tours are during the day and cost about US$20 per person with guide and security, less if there is a larger party. They normally leave Antigua about 0500, returning in the evening.

Agua Volcano
3,760m

Agua can also be climbed from **Alotenango**, a village between Agua and Fuego volcanoes (*fiesta* 18-20 January), south of Ciudad Vieja, nine kilometres from Antigua. Looking at the market building, take the left route up; turn left at the T junction, then first right and up. Only two decision points: take the right fork, then the left. It is not advisable to descend Agua towards Palín (southeast – see page 660) as there is precipitous forest, steep bluffs, dry watercourses which tend to drop away vertically and a route is hard to plot.

The best trail (west of the one shown on the 1:50,000 topographic map) heads south at La Soledad, 2,300 metres (15 kilometres west of Ciudad Vieja on Route 10) 300 metres before the road (Route 5) turns right to Acatenango (good *pensión*, **F**, with good cheap meals). A small plateau, La Meseta on maps, known locally as El Conejón, provides a good camping site two-thirds of the way up (three to four hours). From here it is a further three to four hours harder going to the top. There is a shelter, holding up to 15 people, on the lower of the two summits. Though dirty and

Acatenango Volcano
3,976m

in poor condition, this is the best place to sleep. The climb to the higher peak takes about 45 minutes. Excellent views of the nearby (lower) active crater of Fuego and you can watch the activity of Pacaya at night. To reach La Soledad, take a bus heading for Yepocapa or Acatenango (village) and get off at La Soledad, or from Antigua to San Miguel Dueñas, and then hitch to La Soledad. Alternatively, take an early bus to Ciudad Vieja from where you can hitch to Finca Concepción Calderas (bus Ciudad Vieja-Calderas 0645 Saturday only), then one hour walk to La Soledad. Be sure to take the correct track going down (no water on the way). A recommended guide is Martin Sis who lives by the main junction at Soledad.

Fuego Volcano
3,763m
For experienced hikers only

This can be climbed via Volcán de Acatenango, sleeping on the col between the two volcanoes where there is a primitive shelter, then a further four hours of tiring loose ash to the crater. Harder is the long climb from Alotenango. For the first hour or so, until the trees, take a guide, or go down from Alotenango market place, over river, and at the concrete gateway turn right, up the main track. Ignoring the initial left fork, plantation/orchard entrances and all 90° turnoffs, take the next three left forks and then the next two right forks. Do not underestimate water needed for the climb. It is seven hours ascent with an elevation gain of 2,400 metres. A very hard walk, both up and down, and easy to lose the trail. Steep, loose cinder slopes, very tedious in many places. It is possible to camp about three quarters of the way up in a clearing. Fuego has had frequent dangerous eruptions in recent years though generally not without warning. Check in Antigua before attempting to climb.

Pacaya Volcano

Another popular excursion is to the still active Pacaya volcano (last major eruption January 1987, a minor 'blow' in 1996 but still steaming early 1999). Tours are available for US$8 per person upwards, depending on the number in the party, with *Eco-Tour Chejo's, Ceprotur, Tivoli, Gran Jaguar* and other Antigua tour agencies. Take independent advice on which tour company guides to employ (eg Inguat or Mike Shawcross). The popular time for organized trips is to leave Antigua at 1300 and return 2200. Security officers and often police escorts go with the trips, but take torch, refreshments and water with you. Tour agencies can arrange camping with guide and guard, at around US$70, negotiable, including transport. The volcano can be reached by private vehicle, the road from Antigua is partly paved. Alternatively take a bus from the central bus station in Zona 4 to **San Vicente de Pacaya**, 0700 and 1530 (US$0.35); then walk to **San Francisco** (one and a half hours); or Guatemala City-Palín bus to turn-off to San Vicente, wait for bus to San Vicente and San Francisco, last at 1800 (buses from San Francisco to junction on Guatemala City-Escuintla road 0500, 0900, 1200 and 1500). There are guides available in both San Vicente and San Francisco, about US$2.50. The road to San Francisco is not easy to drive, even in four-wheel drives. Part of the crater has collapsed and the route has had to be changed. The last part up the cone is steep and takes about 30 minutes. Check the situation in advance in San Francisco for both climbing and camping (if safe, take torch, warm clothing and a handkerchief to filter dust and fumes). It is recommended to go up overnight with a good camera, tent and sleeping bag, camp at a respectful distance from the cone or at a local home, all arranged by a guide from *ICO's Expeditions* or *Gran Jaguar* (see above). To get good night-time photographs, a tripod or similar is required for exposure eight seconds at f2.8 on 100 ASA film. Beware cold and cloud; however, you can warm your hands on the lava blocks, or keep warm overnight if you camp near the hot ash. Sunrise comes with awesome views over the desolate black lava field to the distant Pacific (airborne dust permitting) and the peaks of Fuego, Acatenango and Agua. People do scramble up from the 40 metre view-point to watch the venting in the crater below ("scary but unmissable"). Be warned, though, that this can be very dangerous. Enquire if the volcano is active before going – much more exciting trip if it is.

If you miss the last bus back to Palín or San Vicente, you can stay overnight with Luis the Mexican in San Francisco (a good guide), or you can sleep in the porch at the school in El Cedro, the village below San Francisco, or in a house at the entrance to San Vicente (US$1), or with other locals. Another recommended guide is Salvador, whose house is near the bus stop for Guatemala.

At the village of **San Felipe** (US$0.05 by bus, or 15 minutes walk from Antigua) is a figure of Christ which people from all over Latin America come to see. *Restaurant El Prado* is recommended. There is a small silver workshop which is worth visiting.

North of Guatemala City

Two Indian villages north of Guatemala City can be reached by bus though the service is sometimes erratic. At **Chinautla** (nine and a half kilometres), the village women turn out hand-made pottery. Eight kilometers beyond is another small village, **San Antonio las Flores**: good walking to a small lake (70 minutes) for bathing.

At **San Lucas Sacatepéquez**, the Fábrica de Alfombras Típicas Kakchikel at Km 29½, Carretera Roosevelt (usually known as the Pan-American Highway), will make rugs for you. Restaurants: *La Parrilla, La Cabaña, Nim-Guaa, La Diligencia*, and *El Ganadero*, all good for steaks; *Delicias del Mar* for seafood. Five kilometres beyond San Lucas is **Santiago Sacatepéquez**, whose *fiesta* on 1 November, Día de los Muertos (All Souls Day), is characterized by colourful kite-flying; also 25 July. Market Wednesday and Friday.

A most interesting short trip by car or bus from the capital is to **San Pedro Sacatepéquez**, 22½ kilometres northwest. Good view over Guatemala valley and mountains to the north. Its inhabitants, having rebuilt their village after the 1976 earthquake, are returning to the weaving for which the village was renowned before the disaster. Bus from Guatemala City, Zona 4 bus terminal, US$0.20, one hour. *Fiestas*: Carnival before Lent; 28-30 June (rather rough, much drinking) and great ceremony on 15 March when passing the Image of Christ from one officeholder to the next, and in honour of the same image in May. About 10 kilometres west of San Pedro is **Santo Domingo Xenacoj**, reached by bus from the Zona 4 terminal, Guatemala City. It has a fine old church and produces good *huipiles*.

Six and a half kilometres north of San Pedro, through a flower-growing area, is **San Juan Sacatepéquez**, where textiles are also made.

28 kilometres north of San Juan Sacatepéquez is **Mixco Viejo**, the excavated site of a post-classic Mayan fortress, which spans 14 hilltops, including 12 groups of pyramids. Despite earthquake damage it is worth a visit, recommended. It was the 16th century capital of the Pokomam Maya; there are a few buses a day from the Zona 4 bus terminal in Guatemala City, ask about departure times. The bus goes to Pachalum; ask to be dropped at the entrance. A new bridge now enables you to drive to the site where you can buy refreshments.

The road, Ruta 5, continues another 70 kilometres north into Baja Verapaz, to the village of **Rabinal** which was founded in 1537 by Las Casas as the first of his 'peaceful conquest' demonstrations to Emperor Charles V. It has a handsome 16th century church, Sunday market interesting; brightly lacquered gourds, beautiful *huipiles* and embroidered napkins, all very cheap. The local pottery is exceptional.

Rabinal

Sleeping & eating F *Hospedaje Caballero*, 1 C, 4-02, without bath. F *Pensión Motagua*, friendly, has bar attached, not recommended for women travelling alone. F *Posada San Pablo*, clean, friendly, will do laundry, hard beds, no hot water. *Restaurant El Cevichazo* has good food. *Los Gauchos*, simple meal with beer US$3.

Festivals On **17-25 January** with masked dancers.

Buses From Guatemala City 5½ hours, a beautiful, occasionally heart-stopping ride. Buses go north through Rabinal to Cobán (see page 621).

Guatemala

Salamá This is the capital of Baja Verapaz and is normally reached from the capital through El Rancho on the Atlantic Highway, paved all the way. Alternatively, it can be reached from San Juan Sacatepéquez and Rabinal through San Miguel Chicaj along another road which offers stunning views (bus Rabinal-Salamá US$0.50, takes 1-1½ hours; Salamá-Guatemala, US$1.60). Its church contains carved gilt altarpieces. Market day is Monday; worth a visit. Exchange at Banco de Guatemala, 5 Av, 6-21.

Sleeping **D** *Tezulutlán*, Ruta 4, 4-99, Zona 1, T9400141, just off plaza, best, with bath, cheaper without, restaurant, some rooms have hot water, clean, quiet. **F** pp *Pensión Verapaz*, 3 C, 8-26 and **F** pp *Hospedaje Juárez*, 10 Av, 8-98, both with bath, cheaper without, latter has laundry facilities, good. **F** *San Ignacio*, 4 C 'A' 7-09, T/F9400186, with bath, cheaper without, clean, friendly.

Eating *Restaurante Las Tejas*, opposite Shell station as you enter town from the east, good, specialty is *caldo de chunto* (turkey soup). *El Ganadero*, good steaks. *Giorgio's Hamburger Gallery*, on small street opposite *La Carreta* on 6 C, good for breakfast. *Pollo To Go*, Parque Central, good. *Happy Ranch*, 7 Av, Zona 1, good for drinks in evening. *Deli-Donus*, good coffee and fresh orange juice.

Caribbean region

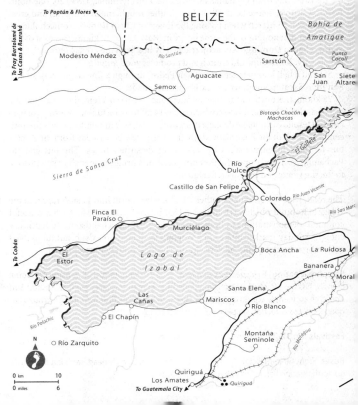

Guatemala City to the Caribbean

The Atlantic Highway is the main road to Guatemala's Caribbean coast with its two main ports. From Puerto Barrios there is access by the Jungle Trail to Honduras and to Lake Izabal. The Biotopo of the national quetzal bird is found just off an alternative route to Lake Izabal, through Alta Verapaz (via Cobán: nearby are natural rock formations at Lanquín and Semuc Champey). Easier routes to Honduras go through Chiquimula, either to Esquipulas, or to the Maya site at Copán across the border.

The Atlantic Highway from Guatemala City to the Caribbean port of Puerto Barrios (Route CA9) is fully paved, very busy with heavy vehicles and with dramatic scenery as it winds down to the Motagua Valley which gives access to the Honduran border, Cobán and the Petén. **NB** The distances between filling stations are greater than in other parts of the country. Along the way is **Sanarate** (**C** *Hotel Las Vegas*, 1 Av 1-21, T9252197), **El Progreso** (also known as Guastatoya – **B** *Casa Guastatoya*,

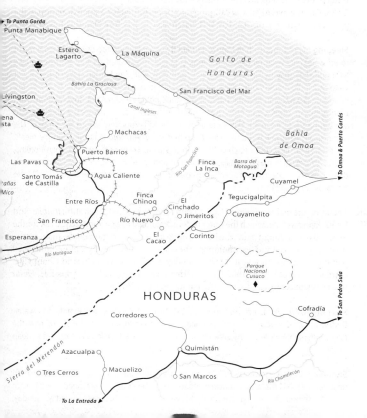

T9451589, bath, swimming pool, good restaurant, relaxed, friendly, do not confuse with *Central Guastatoya*, which should be avoided) and **El Rancho**.

Route to Alta Verapaz

El Rancho
Colour map 4, grid C3

The branch road to Cobán is at **El Rancho**, Km 85, plenty of *comedores* at the junction. This is better than the route through Rabinal and Salamá (see page 617). North of El Rancho is San Agustín, an entrance for the **Sierra de las Minas** National Park, which is one of Guatemala's largest conservation areas. To visit, get a *permiso* in Salamá at the Oficina Defensores Naturales.

Biotopo del Quetzal

Between Cobán and Guatemala City at Km 160.5, four kilometres south of Purulhá and 53 kilometres from Cobán, is the **Biotopo del Quetzal**, a reserve established by Mario Dary Rivera, a biologist of San Carlos university, for the preservation of the quetzal bird and its cloud-forest habitat.

A series of trails, taking up to three hours to cover on foot, lead more than 300 metres up the mountainside. The reserve is in two parts. The lower part has two trails (one hour and two and a half hours), the other is inaccessible except with permission. Most animals have naturally retreated from tourists. Nevertheless, there are now reported to be increasing numbers of quetzales in the Biotopo, but still very elusive (some are tagged electronically and the wardens can tell if they are in the vicinity). They feed on the fruit of the aguacatillo and guaramo trees early in the morning or early evening. Ask for advice from the rangers. There are two cold water swimming pools. Camping possible, toilets and showers. ■ *Open 0700 to 1600 every day, US$5.* Parking overnight and camping may be permitted for a small donation to the park, check with Cecon, T3310904 (Guatemala City), before planning to visit.

Sleeping At Km 156 is the hotel and restaurant **B** *Posada Montaña del Quetzal*, bungalows or room, café, bar, swimming pool, gardens (T3351805 in Guatemala City for reservations although they may get lost by inefficient front desk staff, book in advance, especially at weekends). 100 metres north of the entrance to the Biotopo is the **E** *Hospedaje Los Ranchitos*, in 3-room, 10-bed cabins, fairly basic, also 2 stone houses each with 4 double rooms with bathrooms, spacious, clean, hot water, limited restaurant. The *Hospedaje* is a good place to see the bird (not frequent, but more likely in the early morning July to November). The *farmacia* at **Purulhá** has rooms to let, **F**. *Comedor San Antonio* in Purulhá, simple meals. Electricity is a problem, a torch is handy in this area. **Transport Buses** Cobán-Purulhá, US$0.50; from Guatemala City, take a Cobán bus and ask to be let out at the Biotopo; more difficult to get a bus back to the capital, last one at 1600; bus El Rancho-Biotopo, US$1.25, 1½ hours; Biotopo-Cobán, US$0.75.

Tactic
Colour map 4, grid C3

Tactic, on the main Guatemala City-Cobán road, is famous for beautiful *huipiles* and for its 'living well', in which the water becomes agitated as one approaches, ask for the Pozo Vivo; it is along a path which starts opposite the Esso station on the main road – now reported dirty and disappointing. The colonial church has Byzantine-influenced paintings, well worth a visit. Market Sunday and Thursday. Balneario Cham Che, entrance free, cold water from natural springs, take picnic, barbecues possible. *Fiesta* third week in August and a colourful parade on Good Friday.

Sleeping C *Chi' Ixim*, Km 183 just beyond Tactic, T9539198, restaurant, hot water. **D** *Mansión La Cañada*, 2 C 11-08, hot water. **D** *Villa Linda*, 4 C 6-25, T9539216, near the plaza, with bath. **F** *Hotel Sulmy*, nice, clean, meals, US$0.75. **F** *Pensión Central*, clean, cheap meals.

Shopping Doña Rogelia sells *huipiles* made in the surrounding area, and the silversmith near her shop will make silver buttons etc to order. The Cooperativa Origen Maya Pocom 'Ixoq Aj Kemool', is an association of 60 weavers, open Tuesday, Thursday, Sunday,

0900-1700 for sales, orders and to watch the women weaving (contact Rosalía Asig locally for more information).

Santa Cruz Verapaz is 15 kilometres northwest of Tactic at the junction with the road to Uspantán (see page 684) which has a fine 16th century church and a festival 1-4 May. A *Hotel Park*, on main road near the junction, Km 196.5, T9504539/9513388, 60 rooms, some bungalows, restaurant, bar, excellent gardens small zoo, Italian owner, recommended. Six kilometres west towards Uspantán is **San Cristóbal Verapaz**, which has a large colonial church with interesting altar silver and statue of San Joaquín (**F** *Hospedaje Oly*, quiet, friendly, nice patio/garden, good value; restaurant: *Viajeros*, OK). The lake is popular for fishing and swimming. Market: Sunday; festival 21-26 July.

Santa Cruz Verapaz
Colour map 4, grid C3

Cobán

Cobán, capital of Alta Verapaz Department, is the centre of a rich district producing coffee and cardamom, of which Guatemala is the world's largest exporter. The plant is tall, reed-like, with coarse leaves and white spiky flowers. It is 130 kilometres by road south to El Rancho and the highway to Guatemala City. Cobán was founded by Apostle of the Indies, Las Casas, in 1544. See the church of El Calvario (1559), now completely renovated, original façade still intact. Daily market. Cobán is a good place for finding textiles.

Population: 59,310
Altitude: 1,320m
Climate: semi-tropical
Colour map 4, grid C3

Near Cobán is the old colonial church of **San Juan Chamelco**, well worth a visit. One hour walk from San Juan Chamelco is Aldea Chajaneb, where there is **B** *Don Jerónimo's*, sbrizuel@c.net.gt, www.goosemail.com/jeronimo, bungalows to rent, with full board including vegetarian meals, hiking, swimming and tubing, massage, great for relaxation. From Cobán take a taxi to *Jerónimo's*, 40 minutes, about US$6. Or take a bus from Cobán to Chamelco, then bus or pick-up to Chamil (no schedule) and ask to be put down at *Don Jerónimo's*. Beyond Chamil to the southeast are cloud forests up to heights of 2,650 metres. 10 kilometres' walk into the mountains is the Indian community of Chicacnab, and an ecological project, Proyecto Ecológico Quetzal, office: 2 C 14-36, Cobán, T9521047, bidaspeq@guate.net. Adventurous travellers are invited to visit the project which is supervised by two US Peace Corps volunteers.

Excursions

San Pedro Carchá (five kilometres east of Cobán, bus US$0.10, 15 minutes, frequent; buses from the capital as for Cobán; **F** *Hotel La Reforma*, 4 C, 8-45 A, T9521448, basic, motorcycle parking). Local speciality *kackic*, a turkey broth. It used to be famous for its pottery, textiles, wooden masks, and silver, but only the pottery and silver are available. A small local museum displays examples of local crafts. Balneario Las Islas is on a small river popular with the locals for bathing, barbecue facilities. Also visit Vivero Verapaz, the orchid farm of Otto Mittelstaedt (two and a half kilometres southwest, entry US$1), more than 23,000 specimens, which mostly flower from October-February, the best time to go. Truck northwest to Sebol (see page 656), seven hours, US$1.20.

B *La Posada*, 1 C, 4-12, T9521495, attractive colonial hotel with well-kept gardens, full board available, reasonable, no credit cards, see **Eating**. **B** *Hostal Doña Victoria*, 3 C, 2-38, Zona 3, T9522213, F9522214, in 400-year-old convent, colonnaded gallery, attractive gardens, good restaurant, excursions arranged, for example Lanquín etc, US$20 per person. Recommended.

D *El Recreo*, 10 Av, 5-01, Zona 3, T9522160, F9522333, clean, good breakfast. **D** *Oxib Peck*, 1 C, 12-11, T9521039, with bath, restaurant, TV. **D** *Posada de Don Antonio*, 5 Av 1-51, Zona 4, T9522287, with bath, comfortable rooms, TV, garden, car park. **D** *Central*, 1 C, 1-79, T9521442, check you are not overcharged, very clean, with hot shower, good restaurant entered through *Café San Jorge*.

Sleeping
■ *on maps*
Price codes:
see inside front cover

Guatemala

E pp *Hostal Casa D'Acuña*, 4 C, 3-11, Zona 2, T9521547, F9521268, excellent meals, owner's wife is from USA, clean, family runs Tourist Office (see below), pleasant courtyard, hot water, good restaurant, laundry. Recommended. E *La Colonia*, 2 C, 10-88, Zona 4, T9522029, clean, hot water sometimes, restaurant, family-owned, friendly, car parking. E *Perla María*, 4 Av 1-25, Zona 4, T9521988, hot water, with bath, TV, car park. E *Posada de Carlos V*, 1 Av, 3-44, Zona 4, T/F9521780, restaurant, car park. E *Posada la Hermita*, on the edge of town, 2 km towards Chisec, same owner as *El Recreo*, who can arrange transport, very clean, restaurant, superb view.

F *El Chino*, 14 C at the end of 4 Av, good. F *Hospedaje Maya*, opposite Ciné Norte, cold showers, friendly. Recommended. F *La Paz*, 6 Av, 2-19, T9521358, with extension which is recommended, hot water, safe parking, pleasant, comfortable beds, laundry facilities, restaurant, garden (popular, but one report of theft, 1998). F *Monterrey*, 6 Av, 1-12, T9521131, clean, big rooms, good value. Recommended. F *Pensión Familiar*, Diagonal 4, 3-36, Zona 2, 1 block north of Parque Central, hot water in morning, clean, basic, 3 pet toucans, airless rooms in basement. F *Santo Domingo*, Col Chichochoc, Zona 5, T9521569, on road to Caribbean Highway, cheaper without bath, clean, OK, restaurant. F *Villa Imelda*, 2 C, 2 Av, Zona 3, near Monja Blanca bus station, OK. Accommodation is hard to find in August and even at other times of the year in the town centre. At no time be tempted to spend the night in the covered market, very dangerous.

Eating
● *on maps*

La Posada (address above), good soups, good lunch menu US$6. Recommended. *El Bistro*, in *Hostal Casa Acuña*, excellent menu, often crowded. Recommended. *Kam Mun*, 1 C, Zona 2, 100m from main plaza, inexpensive Chinese and local food, good. *El Refugio*, 2 Av, 2 C, Zona 3, good steaks. *Café Santa Rita*, on main plaza, good *típico* menu, open 0700-2100, good breakfasts, friendly, popular, good value. *Café El Tirol*, 1 C 3-13, on main plaza, good meals, 33 different coffees, also homemade wholemeal bread, good cakes, nice garden, slow service. *Sociedad de Beneficencia*, 2 C 6-16, Zona 2, very good value. *El Chino*, 4 C, 3 Av, small, good typical dishes. *Cantonés*, Diag 4-24, just off main plaza, good menu, quality food, good value, friendly. Recommended. *Renée Yoghourt y Helados*, 1 C, behind church, delicious fresh fruit yogurt, good ice creams. Recommended. *Convite Café*, 1 C, 3-28, K'ekchí specialities, good, cheap.

Festivals

Holy Week (which is said to be fascinating), *Rabín Ahau*, in *July*, meeting of cultural groups from the whole country and election of a 'reina indigenista', and **3 August** (procession of saints with brass bands, pagan deer dancers and people enjoying themselves), followed by a folklore festival, **22-28 August**.

Transport

Local Car rental: *Ochoch Pec*, at entrance to town, T9513474, about US$60 per day including insurance.

Long distance Air To Guatemala City, 3 a week, U$30 one way plus tax, service extended to Playa Grande.

Buses From **Guatemala City**: US$4.50. Transportes Escobar-Monja Blanca (hourly from 0400 till 1700, 4 hours, arrive early in the morning and book a seat on the first available bus, or book in advance). Also Transportes Expreso Verapaz, 16 C, 8 Av, deluxe service daily at 1315, US$3.50. To **El Estor**, 2 a day, 8 hours, US$2. The trip from the capital via Rabinal, along an old dirt road, takes about 12 hours (change buses in Salamá). To **Uspantán**, 1015, 5 hours, scenic, US$1.40. To **Sacapulas**, daily, 1000. Cobán can also be reached from **Quiché** (page 682) and from **Huehuetenango** (page 689). There are also buses from **Flores** via Sayaxché and Sebol. To **Salamá**, minibus, US$1.75, 2¼ hours.

Directory

Banks Most banks around the main plaza will change money. Mastercard accepted at *G & T Bank* (also has ATM). Visa ATM at *Banco Industrial*. **Communications** Telephones: you can make international calls from Telgua. Cheaper from *Hostal Acuña* or *Hostal Doña Victoria*. *Internet Café* in same building as *CaféTirol*. **Hospitals & medical services** Doctor: *Dr Juan José Guerrero P*, 6 Av,

4-49, Zona 3, T9521186. Recommended. **Tour companies & travel agents** *Epiphyte Adventures*, Apartado Postal 94 A, 2 Av, 2 C, T/F512169, for off the beaten track tours. **Tourist offices** Tourist office on main plaza, run by knowledgeable Acuña family from *Hostal Acuña*, who also run day trips to the caves of Lanquín and Semuc Champey, from US$30, highly recommended, stop several times on the way to look at plants and taste fruits, T9521547, English spoken.

To the west of Cobán is Nebaj which can be reached by taking a truck from Cobán to **Routes** Sacapulas and travelling on from there, or by bus from Huehuetenango. See page 684 and 692 for places en route to Sacapulas, Nebaj and Huehuetenango.

There are two roads from Cobán to the Petén. One goes 66 kilometres due north from Cobán through Chisec and is described on page 657. The better road north goes through San Pedro Carchá (see above) and continues unpaved 40 kilometres to Pajal, thence to Sebol on the road between Raxruhá and Modesto Méndez.

About 20 kilometres along the road to Chisec, near Finca Sonté, there is an even more dreadful road northwest to **Playa Grande**, from where there is a track to the **Laguna Lachua National Park**. The lake, at 170 metres, is surrounded by dense jungle and is virtually unspoilt. You can camp, or sling a hammock and there is water laid on (though it needs to be purified before drinking). There is a friendly caretaker who will rent canoes and may allow you to stay the night in his cabin. Bring your own food. There are buses and pick-ups from Cobán which take 12-15 hours, presumably only in the dry season. This area of Alta Verapaz is quite close to the Mexican border (Chiapas). Enquire carefully about the safety of the zone before visiting. There is an airfield at Playa Grande and Inter run a service to Guatemala City three times a week, US$50.

Lanquín and Semuc Champey

At Pajal there is a turning right and a bad 10 kilometres to **Lanquín** cave, in which *Colour map 4, grid B3* the Río Lanquín rises. The road is very rough, and particularly bad for the last 12 kilometres (it can take two and a half hours). The views are superb, though. You can camp at the cave. Caves are normally open 0800-1200, 1330-1700, US$2, check at the Municipalidad. The sight of the bats flying out at dusk is impressive. The cave is very slippery and the ladders and handrails are poor, so wear appropriate shoes. The caretaker will leave the lights on for one hour only so take a torch for additional lighting or in case of a power failure. It may take you up to one and a half hours to go to the end of the caves and back. Outside the cave you can swim in the deep, wide river, and camp (free) or sling a hammock under a large shelter.

In Lanquín church, there are fine images and some lovely silver. Lanquín *fiesta* 22-28 August.

From Lanquín one can visit the natural bridge of **Semuc Champey** stretching 60 metres across the Cahabón gorge, 10 kilometres walk to the south, or two to three hours along a new road which runs to the footbridge over the Río Cahabón, 20 minutes from Semuc Champey. At the end of the road, which is very steep in places, is a car park (occasional cars for a hitch, and pickups from Lanquín will take you for US$0.55). A steep track heads down to the new bridge half-way along the road (the route is not signposted so ask frequently for the shortest route). US$1 is charged to cross the new bridge. The natural bridge has water on top of it as well as below, and the point where the Río Cahabón goes underground is spectacular, though very dangerous, about 10 minutes unsigned walk upstream. One can swim in the pools on top of the bridge. At Semuc Champey are places where you can camp. Insect repellent and a mosquito net are essential. If planning to return to Lanquín the same day, start early to avoid the midday heat. There are a couple of places en route where you can get a drink. Camping is possible at Semuc Champey, US$1.45, resin cedar wood from local market useful for starting fires.

You can hike from Cobán or San Pedro Carchá to Lanquín via Semuc Champey in five or six days camping beside rivers, visiting caves and canyons in this limestone region. There are coffee, cardamom and banana plantations on the way. Unless you speak K'ekchí, conversation is difficult with the people in the countryside, few of whom speak Spanish. For information and guide possibilities enquire at *Hostal Acuña* in Cobán.

24 kilometres east of Lanquín is **Cahabón** village, from where it is possible to cross the mountains to Senahú (see below). The hike takes a full day (if setting out from Sehahú, it may be possible to hitch a lift to Finca Volcán, then it's only six hours; either way it is quicker than by road).

Sleeping   **C** *El Recreo*, T9522160 (through hotel of same name in Cobán) at entrance to **Lanquín** village, clean, good meals, friendly, pool. Recommended.
    F (all under US$3) *El Hogar del Turista*, clean, helpful, very friendly, good pancakes in *comedor* downstairs, limited water and electricity, noisy, basic. **F** *Hospedaje La Divina Providencia*, hot water and a good (for Lanquín), cheap restaurant, small dark rooms, friendly. **F** *Hospedaje El Centro* (no sign), close to church, friendly, good simple dinner, basic. There is another *comedor* in town, which is good. There is accommodation, **F**, in **Cahabón**.

Transport   **Buses** From Cobán 0545, 1300, 1330, 1500, 3 hours, US$1.60, continue to Cahabón. Return from Cahabón, similar service, eg 0700 Lanquín-Cobán, very crowded (you can try hitching from San Pedro Carchá, from the fumigation post, where all trucks stop, to the turn-off to Lanquín, then 12 km walk – very little traffic). From Lanquín to Flores: take the 0730 or 0800 Cobán bus to Pajal, 1 hour, US$0.30, the 0930 Pajal to Sebol, 5½ hours, US$1 (page 657), pick-up, hitch or bus to Flores. The road is beautiful and quiet, but not recommended for women alone. Pajal is just a shop. Pick-up Lanquín-Sebol, US$1. Petrol/gas station in Lanquín by the church.

Cobán and Tactic to El Estor

From Tactic, a reasonable and very beautiful road runs down the Polochic valley to El Estor (see page 637). This road is served by the Cobán-El Estor buses and is quite easy to hitch. **Tamahú** (12 kilometres) and **Tucurú** (28 kilometres, two hotels) produce pretty *huipiles*; main market days are Sunday and Thursday and there are interesting images in the Tucurú church. *Fiesta* in Tamahú 23-25 January.
    47 kilometres beyond Tucurú is a turnoff to **Senahú**, where there is magnificent walking in the area. Climb to the cemetery for good views. *Fiesta* in Senahú 9-13 June.

Sleeping   **Pensiones at Senahú** (all under US$3): *Senahú*, same group as *El Recreo* in Cobán. **F** *González*, good meals for US$0.60, at entrance to village, no sign, old finca, romantic exterior. **F** *Edilson*, good for information on hikes. *Pensión Oly*, in centre, not recommended. **F** *Gladys*, near main square, meals for US$0.55.

Transport   **Buses** From Cobán, 8 hours, Autotransportes Valenciano and Brenda, departures from Cobán 2 direct a day, but check, US$1.25, particularly crowded on Sunday.

Beyond the turn-off to Senahú, the road continues to **Telemán** (bus from Senahú at 0300 and 1030), **Panzós** (pick-up from Telemán; guest house; bus to El Estor evening) and Cahaboncito (six kilometres from Panzós). Here you can either carry on to El Estor, or take the road to Cahabón and Lanquín. Coming from El Estor, alight at the Senahú turn off, hitch or wait for bus from Cobán which should pass on its way to Senahú around 1200 and 1600. Trucks take this road, passing the turning at about 0800, on Friday and Sunday, and possibly Thursday, otherwise little traffic (the alternative is to go back to Cobán and go from there to Lanquín). Work was underway in 1999 to connect El Estor with Río Dulce along Lago de Izabal.

Continuing on the Atlantic Highway

From El Rancho at Km 85, the Atlantic Highway continues down the wide Río Motagua valley with much evidence of the heavy water flow associated with Hurricane Mitch in late 1998. At Km 120 is **Teculután** (**D** *Turicentro Teculután*, on the main road, T9347227, mainly for day visitors, pool, restaurant; **E** *Casa Grande*, 5 C 5-91, T9347270, restaurant; **F** *Paty*, friendly, clean) followed at Km 126 by the **B** *Longarone*, T9347269, with bungalows and a/c, good service, good food, pool, in a delightful setting, good place for trips to Quiriguá and Copán. Nearby is **B** *Atlántico*, T9347160, also good, quiet, with good value restaurant. **D** *Pasabien*, T9347201, smaller than the others but similar facilities, pool, restaurant. **D** *Santa Cruz*, bath, fan, no a/c, clean, good value. The Pasabien waterfall and swimming hole is a few kilometres north at the bottom of the Sierra de las Minas at the end of a dirt road, pleasant. Geologists will be interested in the Motagua fault near Santa Cruz. At **Río Hondo**, 138 kilometres from Guatemala City there is **E** *Hawaii*, helpful, rather individual idea of door locks, clean except for resident cockroaches. Also *Posada del Río*, Km 137. At weekends excellent fruit can be bought along the roadside here.

Routes to Honduras

Before the entry to Río Hondo, a paved road, poorly signed, runs south five kilometres to **Estanzuela**, a small town with a natural history museum including fossil remains of a prehistoric giant sloth (Eremotherium) found in Guatemala City Zona 6, and some mammoth bones, together with more recent finds and present day species. There is also a local archaeological section, good. ■ *0800-1200, 1300-1700, entrance free*. Shortly before Estanzuela you pass a monument commemorating the 1976 earthquake which activated a faultline that cuts across the road and can be seen in the fields on either side of the road, relating to the Motagua fault. The epicentre of this massive 7.5 earthquake which killed 23,000 people was at Los Amates, 65 kilometres down the valley towards Puerto Barrios. Minibus to Zacapa, US$0.40.

Zacapa

Eight kilometres further on is Zacapa. Sulphur springs for rheumatic sufferers at Baños de Agua Caliente, well worth a visit (closed on Monday: two baths, one private, US$3, good value, the other state-owned, semi-abandoned and usually closed; camping possible nearby; no bus). It is a busy but unattractive town, 148 kilometres from Guatemala City. To add to the natural disasters of the area, the Río Grande which flows past the town to join the Motagua at Río Hondo did considerable local damage during the 1998 hurricane. The road bridge at the entrance was damaged and the railway bridge alongside destroyed. Zacapa is known for its sharp cheese and *quesadilla*, a Madeira-type cheesecake sold throughout the country.

Population: 15,000
Altitude: 187m
Climate: hot and dry
Colour map 4, grid C3

D *Miramundo*, 17 Av 5-41, T9412674, restaurant, pool, a/c, TV. **E** *Wong*, 6 C, 12-53, cold showers, friendly, secure, will store luggage, noisy parrot (Arturo). **F** *De León*, at entrance to town, cheaper without bath, clean, good value but make sure your room is securely locked. **F** *Posada Doña María*, east of Zacapa at Km 181 on road to Puerto Barrios, with bath. Recommended. **F** *Central*, opposite market, clean, friendly, noisy parrots, very good, delightful setting.

Sleeping

Chow Mein, Chinese food, varying reports. *Comedor Lee*, 50 metres from *Pensión Central*, good rice, friendly Chinese owners. *Po Wing*, just north of plaza, Chinese. *Tío Juan*, at crossroads near *Hotel Wong*, good value.

Eating

4-9 December, 30 April-1 May, small local ceremony.

Festivals

Guatemala

Transport **Buses** From Guatemala City to **Zacapa**, US$2.25 with Rutas Orientales, 0500-1830, every 30 minutes, 3 hours. To **Esquipulas** same service, US$1, 1½ hours. To **Puerto Barrios**, US$2, 3¼ hours.

Directory **Banks** All around the central plaza, will change TCs.

Chiquimula

21 km from Zacapa
Population: 42,000
Colour map 4, grid C3

From Zacapa the paved road runs south to Chiquimula and Esquipulas. Chiquimula, capital of its Department and a pleasant town, has a number of interesting churches including the Templo Santuario facing the plaza, with a colonnaded vault, dome and fine stained glass windows. On the outskirts is the Iglesia Vieja, a church ruined by 1765 earthquake. Daily market. The town has an attractive central plaza surrounded by a circle of ceiba trees and fenced green areas. A road, 203 kilometres, runs west through splendid scenery to the capital (see page 629). There is a lively daily market, biggest on Sunday mornings.

Sleeping **D** *Posada Don Adán*, 8 Av 4-30, T9420549, a/c, telephone, TV, good. **E** *Chiquimulja*, 3 C, 6-51, on the central plaza, T9420387, with bath, good quality, fan, clean, inside parking, good value. **E** *Posada Perla del Oriente*, 12 Av 2-30, T9420014, restaurant, quiet. Recommended. **E** *Hernández*, 3 C 7-41, T9420708, with bath, hot water, pool, TV, parking. **E** *Central*, 3 C 8-30, T9420118, small but convenient. **E** *Victoria*, 2 C, 9-99, T9422238, next to bus station so ask for rooms away from street, all rooms with bath, cold water, fan, cable TV, towels, soap, shampoo, drinking water all provided, good restaurant, good value, will store luggage. Recommended. **F** *Cabrera*, green building to right of bus terminal, market outside, shower, fan, clean, friendly. **F** *Dario*, 8 Av, 4-40, 1½ blocks from main plaza, with or without bath, friendly, English spoken. Recommended. **F** *Hospedaje Martínez*, round the corner from the bus station, clean, safe, cold showers but noisy morning with buses.

Eating *El Tesoro*, 7 Av, 4-40, south side of plaza, extensive menu, good typical dishes, main dishes US$4-7. Recommended. *El Chino*, 8 Av, 2-3 C, 1½ blocks from plaza, Chinese, very large helpings. *Deli Pizza*, 8 Av, 3 C, above Esso, good pizza selection. *Cafetería Rancho Típico*, 3 C, 9 Av, good local lunch. *Holanda Helados*, next to *El Chino*, ice creams and milk shakes. *Cherry Helados*, 8 Av, 3 C, opposite Shell, cheese, yogurt, ice cream, fruit juices. *Guayacán*, 3 C, 7 Av, buffet style lunch 1100-1500. *La Bandeja*, 7 Av, 5 C, open wood fired *parrillada*, open air seating. *Ranchen Chileno*, 8 Av, 5 C, *churrascos*, seafood, grills, not cheap. *Pastelería Las Violetas*, 2 C, 8, 9 Av, near *Hotel Victoria* is a good bakery as is *Superpanadería Las Violetas*, 7 Av, 4, 5 C. Many small *comedores* between 3 C and 4 C with good *liquados* and *batidos* for example *Via Lactea, Albrita, Jumena María*, all good.

Festivals 11-18 August, *Virgen del Tránsito*.

Transport **Buses** From **Guatemala City**, Transportes Guerra and Rutas Orientales, on the hour every hour, US$3, 3½ hours; from **Zacapa** US$0.30, from **Quiriguá**, US$1, from **Puerto Barrios** US$3, 4 hours, several companies, and from **Cobán** via El Rancho (where a change must be made) US$1.65. Buses to El Florido (Honduras border), see below. To **Esquipulas** US$1.65, 1 hour, every 30 minutes.

Directory **Banks** *Banco de Comercio*, 3 C, 5-91, Zona 1, corner of main plaza. Mon-Fri 0830-1400. *Banco del Agro* will change Amex cheques, helpful. *Bancafé* is agent for Amex. *Banco Granai y Townson*. All have extended opening hours mostly to 2000. Also *Almacén Nuevo Cantón*, on the plaza, will change quetzales into dollars.

Southwest of Chiquimula, an interesting excursion can be made to the Volcán de **Ipala** (1,650 metres). Take an 0830 bus to Ipala (basic *pensión*), arrives 1000, stay on the bus and ask the driver to let you off at Aldea El Chaparroncito (10 minutes after

Ipala). From here it's one and a half hours ascent, red arrows every now and then, two small villages on the way (drinks available), hot, dusty path. The crater lake is good for swimming, cool. One hour hike down. Last bus Ipala – Chiquimula 1700. Another ascent goes via Muncipio Agua Blanca and Aldea Monterrico, but there is less transport to the start of the trail.

Route to Copán (Honduras)

At **Vado Hondo** (10 kilometres from Chiquimula) on the road to Esquipulas, a smooth dirt road branches east to the Honduran border (48 kilometres) and on (11 kilometres) to the great Mayan ruins of Copán (see Honduras section, **Copán and Western Honduras**, page 919). It goes through the small town of **Jocotán** (**F** *Pensión Ramírez*, showers, pleasant, very friendly, good local food from *comedor*. **F** *Pensión Sagastume*, very friendly, garden, safe parking for motorcycles, bus will stop outside, good meals on request. Meals also at the bakery; exchange at *farmacia*, with 10 percent commission). Good place to buy cheap hammocks in the market. *Fiesta* 25 July. Hot springs four kilometres from town. The road goes on to the border at **El Florido** and to Copán (paved on the steep parts, dirt on the flat road). If driving, note that in wet weather there may be several fords to cross on the Guatemalan side.

Guatemalan immigration Border open 0700-1800. If you need a visa for Guatemala, you must get one in advance. Tourist cards are available at the border. If going to Copán for a short visit, the Guatemalan official will give you a 72-hour pass, stapled into the passport. You must return through this frontier within the period, but you will not require a new visa.

Crossing by private vehicle Crossing by car normally takes ½-1 hour, you need 11 stamps, 5 in Guatemala and 6 in Honduras and you will have to pay for almost every one. Ask for receipts and try bargaining. The vehicle will be sprayed: make sure none of the disinfectant gets inside.

Honduran consulate In the lobby of the *Hotel Payaquí*, Esquipulas, very helpful. Quicker to get your Honduran visa here than in the capital. Cost is US$5, though latest reports indicate that there may be no one there empowered to issue visas.

Transport There are buses from Chiquimula to the border at El Florido at 0600, 0645, 0830, 1030-1530 hourly. Transportes Vilma, US$1.35, booking the day before can help, it is often chaotic in the morning. Hang on to your bags at all times. At 1400 and 1730 there are buses as far as Jocotán, bus Jocotán to the border US$0.50, taxi US$5. Taxi Chiquimula – border US$10 (there may be colectivos for US$3). Chiquimula-Copán and back same day US$25. Bus (Vilma) from Zacapa-El Florido at 0530 which will allow you 2-3 hours in Copán and return same day. It is impossible to visit Copán from Guatemala City by bus and return the same day. However travel agents do a 1-day trip for about US$35 per person.

If you have any undue difficulties at this border, ask to see the *delegado*. You can leave your car at the border and go on to Copán by public transport thus saving the costs of crossing with a vehicle.

For a better road to Honduras from Chiquimula, see below – Agua Caliente.

Frontier with Honduras – El Florido

The border is 1 kilometre past the village.

To visit Río Dulce, the Puerto Barrios area or the Mayan ruins of El Petén, take a bus from Chiquimula to Río Hondo (US$0.35, one hour), or a bus to Bananera (Morales) and change there.

Esquipulas

The main road continues south from Vado Hondo through interesting forested scenery and steep mountains to San Jacinto and **Quezaltepeque** (no hotel, but a

Population: 7,500
Altitude: 940m

comedor one kilometre towards Esquipulas has rooms). Thence to Padre Miguel where you turn east to Esquipulas. If possible, stop at the mirador, one kilometre from the town for a spectacular view. It is a typical market town in semi-highland and pleasantly cool. At the end of its one and a half kilometre main avenue is a magnificent white basilica, one of the finest colonial churches in the Americas. In it is a black Christ carved by Quirio Catano in 1594 which draws pilgrims from all Central America, especially on 1-15 January, during Lent and Holy Week and 21-27 July. It attracted 1.2 million visitors in 1995, and a visit from Pope John Paul II in February 1996. The image was first placed in a local church in 1595, but was moved to the basilica, built to house it, in 1758. The old quarter near the Municipal Building is worth a visit.

The Benedictine monks who look after the shrine are from Louisiana and therefore speak English. They show visitors over their lovely garden and their extensive library. If you wish to see this, go midweek. On Saturday and Sunday the town is very busy with pilgrims and the dark nave of the basilica is transformed by hundreds of candles, and there are long queues to pass by the Black Christ behind the altar. Surrounding the church are the inevitable sellers of relics and mementoes.

Esquipulas was host to the Peace Congress in 1986 that helped to settle the civil wars in Nicaragua and El Salvador.

Sleeping Plenty of hotels, *pensiones* and *comedores* all over town. When quiet mid-week, bargain for lower room prices.

AL *Gran Chorti*, at Km 222 on the highway to Chiquimula, T9431148, F9431551, all you would expect from a luxury hotel. **A** *Legendario*, 3 Av/8 C, T9431824, F9431022, built round garden, 2 pools, restaurant, cable TV, comfortable. **D** *Posada del Cristo Negro*, 2 km south on road to Honduras at Km 224, T9431482, motel style, swimming pool, restaurant, good. **B** *Internacional*, 10 C 0-85, T9431167, 2 blocks from basilica, clean, hot showers, TV, restaurant, parking.

B *Payaquí*, **D** in annex, 2 Av 11-26, T9431143, F9431371, hot water and drinking water, swimming pool, protected car parking, restaurant, bar, credit cards, lempiras and colones accepted. **C** *Los Angeles*, 2 Av 11-94, T9431254, with bath, **D** without, restaurant, parking. Recommended. **E** *El Angel*, 2 Av/11 C, T9431372, with bath, cold water. **E** *Pensión Casa Norman*, 3 Av 9-20, T9431503, nice rooms with bath, hot water but run down. **F** pp *Santa Rosa*, 10 C/1 Av, T9432908, hot water, noisy, poor service. **F** *París*, 2 Av, 10-48, T9431276, pretty basic.

Eating Plenty of restaurants, but prices are high for Guatemala eg: *La Hacienda*, 2 Av 10-20, steaks; *La Rotunda*, 11 C/1 Av, standard menu; *Quan Lee*, 11 C 1-37, Chinese; *Victoria*, facing church on 3 Av.

Transport Buses from the capital every 30 minutes 0400-1800, US$4 (4-5 hours), Rutas Orientales 1 Av/11 C, T9431366/0576, and Rutas Guatesqui (unreliable).

Directory **Banks** *Bancafé* and *Banco Granai y Townson*, latter changes TCs. *Banca Real* has Visa ATM. No bank will exchange lempiras, but plenty of money changers in the centre. Better rates than at the borders. **Communications** Post Office at end of Av 5.

Frontier with Honduras – Agua Caliente

The Honduran frontier is 10 kilometres beyond Esquipulas.

Guatemalan immigration Open 0700-1200, 1400-1800.

Honduran consulate In the lobby of the *Hotel Payaquí*, Esquipulas, very helpful. Quicker to get your Honduran visa here than in the capital. Cost is US$5, though latest reports indicate that there may be no one there empowered to issue visas.

Crossing by private vehicle Paperwork is reported as a tedious experience here, insisting on receipts will keep costs down.

Transport Minibuses run from Esquipulas to the border US$0.60 and then continue to

Nueva Ocotepeque.

They like to overcharge in order to 'help you to use up left over quetzales'.

We have received complaints about this border crossing reflecting badly on both sides, but differences seem to depend on the individual officials. Standard tariffs should apply.

Part of the Department of Chiquimula falls within the International Biosphere **Montecristo-Trifinio**, a reserve of cloud forest and its surroundings in the Montecristo range. The reserve is administered jointly by Guatemala, Honduras and El Salvador.

35 kilometres south of Chiquimula at the Padre Miguel junction, turn right on highway CA12 for El Salvador, or from Esquipulas, take the road to Concepción Las Minas and then join the same road to **Anguiatú**.

19 kilometres from Padre Miguel. **Guatemalan immigration** Open 0700-1800. Colectivos to/from Padre Miguel junction (US$1.10, 45 minutes) connecting with buses to Chiquimula and Esquipulas.

Frontier with El Salvador – Anguiatú

From the southeast corner of Guatemala City (Zona 10) the Pan-American Highway leads out toward the Salvadorean border. After a few kilometres a turning to **San José Pinula** (F *Hotel San Francisco*, large rooms, no running water, but they will fill a tub for you; most people don't stay the whole night; one other hotel, poorer; *fiesta* 16-20 March). Finca Santa Inés, nearby, is set up as *Fundación de Voluntarios de Centro América de la Paz*, coordinating volunteer work. Enquire: Av Simeón Cañas 9-49, Zona 2, Guatemala City, T/F6343212/6347212. After San José, the road leads to an unpaved winding branch road, 203 kilometres long through fine scenery to **Mataquescuintla** (F *Pensión Olimpia*, small rooms, clean, cold showers, good value), Jalapa, San Pedro Pinula, San Luis Jilotepeque, and Ipala to Chiquimula (see page 626). This road is impassable in the wet; buses San José Pinula to Mataquescuintla at 1130, and Mataquescuintla-Jalapa, several. It was the route to the great shrine at Esquipulas, but visitors now use the Atlantic Highway to Río Hondo and the new road to Honduras past Zacapa (see page 625) and Chiquimula.

Alternative route to Chiquimula and Esquipulas

Capital of Jalapa Department, 114 kilometres from Guatemala City, Jalapa is set in an attractive valley at 1,380 metres. The road from the Atlantic Highway (Sanarate) to Jalapa was being paved in 1999. *Fiesta* 2-5 May.

Jalapa
Population: 42,000
Colour map 4, grid C3

Sleeping **D** *Villa del Río*, Av Chilichapa 2-66, T9225581, friendly, restaurant, parking. **F** *Méndez*, 1 Calle A, 1-27, Zona 2, T9224835, 1 block from market, hot water, towels. Recommended. *Pensión Casa del Viajero*, 1 Av 0-70, T9224086, clean, bath, warm water. At least 2 other *hospedajes*.

Eating *Casa Real*, 1 block from market. Reasonable prices, pleasant.

Transport **Buses** To Esquipulas 0900, 7½ hours, US$1.60; to Chiquimula, 8 hours. To Guatemala via Jutiapa, hourly, 4½ hours. For the road Jalapa to Jutiapa, Cuilapa and the capital see page 658.

Atlantic highway to Puerto Barrios

Back on the Atlantic Highway, 11 kilometres from Río Hondo at Km 149 is **A** *Valle Dorado*, T9412542, F9412543, a family resort popular at weekends with many recreational facilities, a/c, cable TV, three restaurants.

Quiriguá

Open 0800-1700,
entry US$3,
locals US$0.30

Quiriguá is about half way between Zacapa and Puerto Barrios on the Atlantic Highway and about four kilometres from some remarkable Maya late classic period remains: temple, carved stelae, etc. It is believed that Quiriguá was an important trading post between Tikal and Copán, rose to prominence in its own right in the middle of the eighth century but was abandoned at the end of the ninth at about the same time as Tikal. The Kings of Quiriguá were involved in the rivalries and wars and shifting alliances between Tikal, Copán and Calakmul. One of the stelae tells of the decapitation of the Copán king in the plaza here as a sacrifice after a battle in 738 AD. In 1975 a stone sun-god statue was unearthed here. The tallest stone is over eight metres high with another three metres or so buried. Some stelae have been carved in the shapes of animals, some mythical, all of symbolic importance to the Maya. Many of the stelae are now in a beautiful park (but all have shelters which makes photography difficult). It is most distressing to hear that graffiti is reported on some stones. Take insect-repellent. The best reference book is SG Morley's *Guide Book to Ruins of Quiriguá*, which should be obtained before going to the ruins. The site, which is close to the Río Motagua, was inundated during Hurricane Mitch, but has been satisfactorily restored.

Sleeping **E** *Eden*, safe, helpful, nice rooms, shared bath, clean. **F** *Royal*, with bath, clean, mosquito netting on all windows, unfriendly, poor value, but social centre for locals who come for a drink with their horses, good restaurant. **F** *Pensión San Martín*, near train station, under US$3. **Camping**: in car park of the ruins, US$0.50.

Transport From the main highway to the ruins, about 3 km, there is an occasional bus, US$0.20; alternatively ride on the back of a motorbike, US$0.50, walk or take a taxi. From *Hotel Royal* walk past church towards train station, follow tracks branching off to right through banana plantation for about 45 minutes to the ruins. Reached by road from Guatemala City to Los Amates, then a 3½-km dirt road (ask to be put down at the 'ruinas de Quiriguá', 5 km after Los Amates), Velázquez bus at 0700, US$1.25, 3½ hours. If driving the road branches off the Atlantic Highway at Km 205 which is where the bus stops (free overnight vehicle parking at ruins, check with warden).

**Bananera/
Morales**
Colour map 4, grid B3

13 kilometres from Quiriguá is the turn off for Mariscos and the shores of Lago de Izabal (see page 636). A further 28 kilometres are the twin towns of **Bananera/Morales**. As its name suggests, it is the most important town in the banana growing area which goes down the Motagua Valley to the Caribbean. This was the area most affected by the 1998 hurricane when virtually all the plantations were destroyed. However, it has been comparatively easy to clear the area and replanting was well under way by mid-1999. There are several banks in Morales including a new agency of Lloyds Bank, Av Bolívar, Centro Comercial El Portal. Fiesta 15-21 March.

Sleeping **E** *Harris*, with bath. **F** *Hospedaje Liberia*, basic, but OK. **F** *Pensión Montalvo*, T9478226, next to station, basic but clean, friendly, quiet. Best place to eat cheaply, *Carnita Kelly*, good meat, homemade tortillas. One decent restaurant in Morales, *Nineth*.

Transport From Bananera there are buses to the Río Dulce crossing (road paved, 30 km, US$1 in minibus), Puerto Barrios and the Petén (US$4, 10 hours to Flores); return buses from Río Dulce to Bananera start at 0600. Morales is a short distance off the main road, check carefully where the bus you want will stop.

Jungle trail to Honduras

Over the past few years a route between Guatemala and Honduras has been pioneered, mainly by back-packers, through the plantations and jungles of the lower Río Motagua. It follows routes taken by local people but remains only a semi-official crossing. There are two recognized overland routes from Puerto Barrios to Puerto Cortés. For both, take an early bus from the market in Puerto Barrios through Entre Ríos to the banana plantations. There are buses from 0500, approximately hourly.

The first crossing starts near Finca Chinoq (to which there is a plantation railway from Entre Ríos on which you may be able to hitch a ride), where you ask for the river crossing at El Cinchado. A few families live here and can change your quetzales, sell you warm sodas and very local food. Ask for the path to Corinto, which is about 3 hours walk and can be very hot and/or very wet. Look for tree trunks that act as bridges over the canals and ask frequently for the trail. You should pass Jumeritos in about 1 hour where drinks and fruit are available. You will pass through jungle, farms and plantations and see the mountains of Honduras to the E and S, Corinto is at their base. Look out for snakes and be prepared for swarms of mosquitoes. You can pay someone to guide you through this section. From Corinto, you can get a bus to Puerto Cortés. This is the route which a new road follows with a concrete bridge over the river leading to Corinto. We have heard, however, that completion was delayed by the storms of 1998.

For the second route, now well frequented, take a canoe downstream from El Cinchado or

stay on the bus to Punto Cuatro or La Inca (US$1) where you can find a boat to take you to the border (minimum 5 people, US$2, about 30 minutes). From there, find another canoe to take you up the narrow waterways into Honduras (US$2, 45 minutes) and leave you with a walk or possibly a pickup truck to Cuyamelito, which is on the road from Corinto to Puerto Cortés. The pickup passes the immigration office for entry stamps. Other boats make the longer trip towards Tegucigalpita closer still to Puerto Cortés, but this can depend on the water level and is not recommended. This trip can leave you with a 2-hour walk to the road. Make sure you know where you are when you leave the boat. From Tegucigalpita there are buses to Omoa and Puerto Cortés.

Check carefully on conditions before you leave dry land. You will be crossing the Río Motagua flood plain and rain here or upstream can cause difficulties. We have received several accounts from travellers who have been caught by rising water levels. Heavy rain may also close the road from Corinto to Omoa in Honduras. Take food and water with you and make sure you are at least on the road by dark. It is useful to have both quetzales and lempiras with you. An average time from Entre Ríos to the road in Honduras is 7 hours, but much depends on how long you have to wait for transport.

Boats can be hired in either Lívingston or Puerto Barrios to take you directly to Puerto Cortés or Omoa, which may be worth it if there is a group of you. The fare is about US$200 for 4 people, about 3 hours, weather permitting.

Puerto Barrios

Puerto Barrios, on the Caribbean, 297 kilometres from the capital by the Atlantic Highway, has now been largely superseded as a port by Santo Tomás. It is the capital of the Department of Izabal. The beach of Escobar on the northern peninsula is recommended, access by car or taxi, toll, US$0.25. The launch to Lívingston leaves from here, and one can take a boat to Puerto Modesto Méndez, on the Río Sarstún. Fiesta 12-22 July.

Population: 37,800
Colour map 4, grid B3

L *Amatique Bay*, on coast near airport, T3633333 (Guatemala City) resort and marina complex with private 300-m beach, open but construction continues, excellent restaurant. **C** *El Reformador*, 16 C y 7 Av, T9480533, rooms on 2 levels around a green courtyard, some with a/c, restaurant, clean, quiet, accepts credit cards. Recommended. **C** *Del Norte*, 7 C y 1 Av, T9480087, 'rickety old wooden structure' on sea front, most rooms with bath, cheaper

Sleeping

without, a timeless classic, but with a/c in a concrete newer part, pool, will change US$ cash at good rate, expensive restaurant but worth it for atmosphere, no credit cards. **C** *Internacional*, 7 Av/16 C, cheaper without a/c, TV, pool, restaurant.

D *Caribe*, 7 C, 6 y 7 Av, T9480494, a/c, TV, parking, cold shower, clean, boat trips. **D** *Europa*, 8 Av, 8 and 9 C, T9480127, clean, with bath, but water problems, good restaurant, car parking outside hotel.

E *Español*, 13 C between 5 and 6 Av, T9480738, with bath, clean, comfortable, good value.

F *Caribeña*, 4 Av, between 10 and 11 C, T9480860, close to boat and bus terminals, has popular restaurant. Recommended. **F** *El Dorado*, 13 C between 6 and 7 Av, with bath, noisy, friendly. **F** *Pensión Xelajú*, 8 Av, between 9 and 10 C, T9480482, quiet, clean. There are other cheap hotels on 7 and 8 C between 6 Av and 8 Av (for example **F** *Canadá*, 6 C, between 6 and 7 Av). Cockroaches, unfriendly, otherwise reasonable, and on and near 9 C towards the sea.

Eating Most hotels. *Cafesama*, 7 C y 6 Av, open 24 hours, reasonable. *Ranchón La Bahía*, 7 C y 6 Av, good seafood, snacks and sandwiches, reasonable prices but watch the bill. *Safari*, north end of 5 Av, overlooking bay, good seafood. *Al Mar Caribe*, on the waterfront, has open air section where you can sit and watch the cargo boats loading. *Pizzería Pastelería Salinas*, 7 C y 7 Av, clean, pleasant, cheap. *Caribeña*, 4 Av entre 10 y 11 C, good value breakfast and lunch. *El Triángulo*, at crossroads near bus terminal, clean, busy, good. *Copos* and *Frosty* ice-cream parlours, 8 C between 6 and 7 Av, both good and clean. *Frutiland*, good juices, sandwiches. Numerous others, undistinguished, in centre and several good places on streets facing the market. Avoid *Quick Burger*. Nightlife is aimed at visiting seamen, with lots of nightclubs and prostitutes.

Entertainment **Cinemas** *Palacio Del Cine*, 7 Av y 7 C, historic building. Also cinema next to the Banco Granai y Townson. Both show US movies.

Shopping **Market** In block bounded by 8 and 9 C and 6 and 7 Av. Footwear is cheap.

Transport **Air** Two daily Inter flights to Guatemala City at 0720 and 1720, US$50 one way.

Buses To **Guatemala City**, Litegua, hourly 0500-1700, US$5. Also specials with a/c US$6.20, 4 daily, first at 0630, 5 hours, address in Puerto Barrios 6 Av entre 9 y 10 C. Fuentes del Norte runs a regular service; also Unión Pacífica y Las Patojas (9 Av, 18-38, Zona 1, Guatemala City). Bus to **El Rancho** (turn-off) for Biotopo del Quetzal and Cobán, US$2.40, 4 hours. To **Chiquimula**, first at 0500 operated by Carmencita, 4 hours, US$3. Bus station is in the centre, by the railway.

Directory **Banks** *Lloyds* Bank, 15 C/7 Av, open 0900-1500, Mon-Fri, also handles Mastercard. *Banco de Guatemala* on seafront (9 C Final), opens and closes 30 mins earlier. *Bancafé*, 13 C y 7 Av, open Mon to Fri until 2000 and on Sat 1000-1400. *Banco G & T*, 7 C y 6 Av, also opens late. *Construbanco*, 7 C y 7 Av, does visa advances, and changes TCs, open till 1900. *Banco del Comercio*, *Banco Industrial*, 7 Av/7 C, Visa ATM. *Quinto* store in the market place changes money. **Communications** Post Office: 3 Av y 7 C, behind Bandegua building. Cables/Telephones: *Telgua*, 10 C y 8 Av.

Frontier with Belize – Puerto Barrios & Lívingston/ Punta Gorda **Guatemalan immigration** There are immigration offices in Puerto Barrios (C 7, 100m from the sea front) and Lívingston (C 9, near landing). Best to get your exit and entry stamps in Puerto Barrios. At Puerto Barrios, the boat is met by immigration officials who collect passenger's passports. Passports with entry stamp are returned in the immigration building.

Transport **Boats to Belize**: there is no regular ferry from either Puerto Barrios or Lívingston to **Punta Gorda**, Belize. There are several charter boats which charge US$10-12.50, about 1 hour. You must have your exit stamp before you can buy a ticket. Be warned also that your luggage will get wet and the boats do not handle well in rough weather (see also the corresponding comments under Belize).

Guatemalan immigration Best to get your exit stamp in Puerto Barrios before leaving. If **Frontier with** you are going by land (see Box: Jungle trail), there is an immigration office in Entre Ríos and at **Honduras** the El Cinchado river crossing but they are not always attended. Coming into Guatemala, see if you can use these facilities.

Honduran consulate If you need a visa, you must obtain it in Guatemala City.

Santo Tomás de Castilla

A few kilometres south of Puerto Barrios on Santo Tomás bay, this is now the coun-   *Colour map 4, grid B3* try's largest and most efficient port on the Caribbean. It was formerly known as Matías de Gálvez and now handles 77 percent of the country's exports and half the imports as well as 20 percent of El Salvador's imports and 10 percent of its exports. Cruise ships put into Santo Tomás. Apart from *Hotel Puerto Libre* (see below), no good hotel or eating place as yet, and no shops. There is sea bathing, but the sea and beach are none too clean. There is fresh water bathing past the port and the garrison. A free permit to visit and view ships can be obtained from the Secretaría Guarda Portuaria office, 200 metres from the port entrance.

B *Puerto Libre*, 25 rooms, at highway fork for Santo Tomás and Puerto Barrios, T9483065,   **Sleeping** F9483513, a/c and bath, TV, phone for international calls, restaurant and bar, swimming pool.

Buses To Guatemala City one has either to take a local bus to Puerto Barrios or the highway   **Transport** fork by the *Hotel Puerto Libre* to catch the Pullman bus. **Sea Shipping**: it is possible to ship a car to New Orleans: the cost depends on size of car.

Banks *Bancafé*, *Banoro*, *Banco del Quetzal*.   **Directory**

Above Santo Tomás, to the southwest, is the Cerro San Gil which rises to 1,300 metres and is classified as 'super humid rainforest'. This is being conserved as a wildlife refuge. A good place from which to visit the area is **Las Pavas**, eight kilometres northwest of Santo Tomás; **L** *Cayos del Diablo*, T9482361, F9482364, reservations T3334633 (Guatemala City), with full board, Best Western, rustic bungalows, bird watching, a/c, restaurant. Behind the hotel you can walk to the waterfalls on the Río Las Escobas, a beautiful spot, but best in the rainy season.

Lívingston

Lívingston, mostly Garifuna blacks, a few English-speaking) is very quiet, now there   *Population: 5,000* is little trade save some export of famous Verapaz coffee from Cobán, and bananas.   *Colour map 4, grid B5* It is the centre of fishing and shrimping in the Bay of Amatique. Many young travel-   *The beach is rather* lers congregate here for the Caribbean atmosphere. Beach discotheques at the week-   *dirty and dangerous* end are popular.

Northwest along the coast towards the Río Sarstún, which is the border with Belize,   **Excursions** is Río Blanco beach followed by **Playa Quehueche** (also spelt Keueche), where there is *Hotel El Chiringuito*, thatched roof, good music, relaxing atmosphere and good food, with six bungalows available – a good place to stop for a few days. Guided jungle trips arranged. Five minutes before *El Chiringuito* is **E** *Hotel Seaguilan*, bungalows with bath, comfortable, clean, shop nearby, good and cheap breakfast and dinner. Recommended.

10 minutes walk beyond Quehueche, about six kilometres (two hours) from Lívingston, is **Los Siete Altares**, beautiful waterfalls and pools, at their best during the rainy season (well recommended). Early Tarzan movies were filmed here. There are several places on the way where you will have to wade. Best to have sandals or equivalent for this. See **Security**, below. Also paddle up the Río Dulce gorge.

Guatemala

Biotopo Chocón-Machacas

The Lake Izabal area is a habitat for the manatee (sea cow). A reserve has been set up halfway between Fronteras and Lívingston on the northern shore of El Golfete, where the Río Dulce broadens into a lake 5 kilometres across. The reserve has been set up to protect the mangrove swamps and the local wildlife including jaguars and tapirs as well as the endangered manatee. It covers 135 square kilometres, with both a land and an aquatic *trail. The Park, like the Biotopo del Quetzal, is run by Centro de Estudios Conservacionistas (Cecon) and Inguat; entry US$5. Ask for booklet at the visitor centre. There is a good campsite in the Biotopo, 400 metres from the entrance US$1 per night, toilets but no food. The likeliest way to see manatees is to hire a rowing boat and allow plenty of time; the animals are allergic to the noise of motor boats. Better, stay overnight.*

Cayucos can be hired near Texaco station, US$5 per day. Tours by boat from Lívingston US$7, four hours. Inland near Tatín, up river and before reaching the Biotopo Chocón Machacas (see below), are hot springs for a relaxing swim.

Boats can be hired in Lívingston to visit beaches along the coast towards San Juan and the Río Sarstún, or to cross Amatique Bay to the north to the tip of the long finger of land beyond Puerto Barrios. At **Estero Lagarto**, near Punta Manabique, there was a laid-back resort called *Pirate's Point*, now closed, but you can still visit the miles of white sand, good snorkelling, fishing and birdwatching. A boat for the day costs about US$25-30 shared between several passengers, 45-60 minutes crossing. Transport may also be arranged through the Empresa Portuaria in Puerto Barrios or with one of the fishermen whose boats leave from the house of Doña Licha, near *African Place*. At the 'neck' of the peninsula there is a channel (Canal Ingleses) which connects the bay with the Caribbean. You can take a boat through the channel but look out for leaking or overloaded boats in this area.

Sleeping
■ *on maps*
Price codes:
see inside front cover

AL *Tucán Dugú* (Friday-Sunday, less in week – all rooms with bath), to book T9481572/588, or Guatemala City 3321259, sea view, swimming pool, restaurant, bars , laundry service, mini aquatic zoo. **C** *Hospedaje Doña Alida*, 200m beyond *Tucán Dugú*, on right, T9481567, clean, tepid water, in bungalows or rooms, with or without bath, pleasant, quiet, charming owner. **C** *Pensión Adila*, opposite *Hotel Berrisford*, family run, welcoming, clean. **D** *Flamingo*, turn right near *African Place* then left along the beach, with garden, own water supply and generator, German owner, run down. **C** *Henry Berrisford*, T9481568, near *Casa Rosada*, 28 rooms, cheaper without a/c, restaurant, run down. **E** *African Place*, looks like a cross between a mosque and a castle, main street, with bath, **F** without, clean, Spanish owners, huge rooms, pleasant, restaurant (overpriced), breakfast served, left on paved road at top of hill. **E** *Casa Rosada*, on the water, 80m first left from dock, thatched cabins for 2-3 persons each, attractively decorated, handpainted furniture, good meals set for the day, watch out for electrical fittings, swimming and trips can be arranged, peaceful. Recommended. Often full, call Telgua in Lívingston for reservations, hotel will call back. **E** *Garífuna*, T481091, first paved road to the right on the way to the *African Place*, halfway to the beach, 10 rooms some with private bath, comfortable, laundry. Recommended. **E** *The Bungalows*, on the beach towards Siete Altares, mosquito nets, ask at *Bahía Azul* restaurant (owners), free transport from Lívingston. **F** *Caribe*, T9480494, 100m first left from dock, same road as *Casa Rosada* and *Henry Berrisford*, with bath, cheaper rooms without, noisy but good. **F** *El Viajero*, from port turn left, clean, friendly. Recommended. **F** *Minerva*, left off road to *African Place*, near *Restaurant Margoth*, basic but clean. **F** *Río Dulce*, 300m from dock on the main street, basic, clean. **E** *Lívingston Seagull Bungalows*, owned by Manuel García de la Peña, T3313908/3318449, F3310784, 5 minutes by boat from Lívingston. **F** pp *La Marina*, on Río Dulce, with good breakfast, peaceful. Camping is said to be good around Lívingston, but check on security and use hammock to avoid rats. Beware of theft from hotel rooms; rats can be a problem in run down and cheaper hotels. Across the river from Lívingston is the **D** *Sierramar*, simple accommodation, good restaurant.

El Tiburón, restaurant of the *Tucán Dugú*, very good but expensive. *El Malecón*, 50m from dock, on left, reasonable. *Margoth*, don't be put off by the building, the food is good and reasonably priced. *La Cabaña Garífuna*, down from *African Place*, relaxed, good but a little pricey. Recommended. *Dante's*, on the street going to the *Garífuna* and *African Place* hotels, grilled fish and seafood, fresh fruit and vegetables, try jumbo shrimp wrapped in bacon and marinated in tequila, large portions, competitive prices, clean kitchen, nicely decorated, book exchange, friendly, helpful, good information, highly recommended, live music most nights, bar. Opposite *Dante's* is **Ubouhu Garífuna**, which does nice Garífuna food. *El Jaguar*, main street, Caribbean style, Garífuna background music, fish and seafood, good. *La Cueva*, opposite Catholic church, nice decoration, music, extensive menu. *Cafetería Coni*, clean, good, cheap. *Café McTropic*, opposite *Hotel Río Dulce*, great breakfasts, 2 menus lunch and dinner. *Café Lily*, cheap, friendly, food OK. **Happy Fish**, good. *Piel Canela*, 200m from *African Place*, good, small Garífuna bar. *Bahía Azul*, excellent breakfasts with huge pancakes, good fruit and home-made yoghurt, has tourist information, will arrange trips to beaches and Río Dulce and to Omoa in Honduras, US$25. *Bala Bala*, near the ferry dock, international food, good. Fresh fish is available everywhere, ask for *tapado* in fish restaurants, a rich soup with various types of seafood, banana and coconut. Women sell *pan de coco* on the streets. You can buy cold, whole coconuts, US$0.20, from the orange crush stand on the main street, which they split for you with a machete.

Eating
● *on maps*

24-31 December, *Garifuna fiesta*, 26 November.

Festivals

Ferries   A ferry **from Puerto Barrios to Lívingston** (22½ km), at the mouth of the Río Dulce, leaves daily, 0500, 1000 and 1700 (schedules change frequently) taking 1½ hours; arrive at least 1 hour in advance to ensure a seat, cost US$1.20. Tickets on the boat, or from the ALM shipping office, 1 Av, between 11 C and 12 C, who will advise if there are other sailings and details of excursions. Launch returns to Puerto Barrios 0500 and 1400 daily (to connect theoretically with the last bus to Guatemala City). Buy ticket previous afternoon, office in front of *Tucán Dugú*. Private launches taking 10-12 people also ply this route, 30-40 minutes, US$3, much better, leave when full, about once an hour. **From Puerto Barrios-Lívingston to Río Dulce**, with stops at Aguas Calientes and Biotopo, cost US$14 one way, easy to arrange, enquire at the ALM office in Puerto Barrios. One can get the mail boat from Lívingston up to the new bridge at Río Dulce (from where you can catch the bus to Tikal) at 0600, Tuesday and Friday (1300 in the other direction), but schedules subject to change. Other boats will also do the trip to Río Dulce, cost about US$8 one-way, US$12.50 return, leaving out the Biotopo. Take food and drink with you, though there are some places for refreshments on the way. *Cayucos* are cheaper than *lanchas*, and if you want to share, get a group together; fare about US$10 per person for a group of 6. Taking a boat is the best way to reach Lívingston, travelling through beautiful scenery. Ask for Carlos at the *Cafetería Coni* who can arrange trips and act as guide (Spanish). Recommended boats: Nery's boat *Yertzy*; Mariel or Cambell with *Lidia II* (speak good English). **To Omoa or Puerto Cortés in Honduras**, boats go Tuesday, Friday sometimes, more often Saturday, return Tuesday, Friday, 1000, US$25, plus a US$ exit fee, payable at immigration, also see *Bahía Azul* restaurant, above. **To Punta Gorda in Belize**, there is no regular ferry service from Lívingston. Most days fast motor boats make the trip to Punta Gorda, enquire at the jetty and negotiate a fare, US$25 per person minimum for 3 or more. Anyone who says they will take you must have a manifest with passengers names stamped and signed at Immigration Office. Boats can be hired to go to southern Belize cayes, US$14 per day, maximum 6 passengers. Recommended.

Transport
The ferry from Puerto Barrios to Lívingston has been referred to as the 'barfy barque', there is much pitching and heaving.

Banks *Banco de Comercio* will change TCs. Some hotels will change TCs, as will the Chinese shop, *Café McTropic* and *El Malecón*. **Communications** *Telgua* next to the *Túcan Dugú*, open 0700-2100. Opposite is a store/gift shop whose French owner has email services and will allow you to use his satellite telephone at good rates. **Security**   Don't stroll on the beach after dark, or in daylight at the Siete Altares end as there is a serious risk of robbery. People are frequently robbed on their way to Siete Altares. Women should not go alone. Do not leave belongings unattended. Never drink from unsealed liquor bottles; they may be drugged as a prelude to robbery. Also there are many stray dogs that get aggressive at night.

Directory

Lago de Izabal

Fronteras, commonly known as **Río Dulce**, is 23 kilometres upstream from Lívingston at the entrance to **Lago de Izabal** (site of new bridge, toll US$1).

There are yachting facilities at Río Dulce. *Once Around Suzanna Laguna Marina* is reached by two minutes shuttle boat from northeast corner of the bridge across the Río Dulce; good, inexpensive food and drinks at the Marina. Swimming in Lago de Izabal near the hotels is not advisable.

There are many agents offering trips on the river, on Lago de Izabal, on other rivers (some fast flowing), in the neighbourhood, canoe hire, jungle walks, and so on.

Unfortunately, Río Dulce has become something of a tourist trap. Standards of hotels and river attractions are high, but prices are now out of line. If you want value for money in the local context, best to arrange a group and bargain for a reasonable price.

Sleeping & eating   A *Turicentro Marimonte*, Km 275, 500m to right at Shell station, bungalows, T9478585, for reservations F3344964, restaurant, pool, no real camp site but you can park a camper van overnight, US$2 per car, US$6 per person, use of showers and pool. The US-owned **A** *Catamaran*, T9478361, F3671633, thatched bungalows, pool, friendly and helpful, expensive restaurant but good food, is reached by outboard canoe (US$1.50 from Río Dulce, 2 km or 10 minutes downstream, T3611937, Guatemala City, for reservations). **A** *Del Río*, a few kilometres downstream, including 3 meals, **F** without meals, has seen better days (Guatemala City T3310016 for reservations). **B** *Viñas del Lago*, on the lake, pool, clean, attractive, friendly service, restaurant slow and overpriced. **D** *Río Dulce*, beside bridge, with bath, cheaper without, fan, clean but damp and basic. **E** *Café Sol*, 500m north of bridge, friendly, clean, own boat dock. **F** *Hospedaje Riverside*, cold water, shared bath, fan, friendly, good (no water in late evening), about 200m on left bank on the right after the bridge going northeast is not recommended, overcharges, unfriendly). **F** *Marilú*, El Relleno on north side, with bath, but rooms are sheds full of holes, uncertain water supply, no electricity late evening, beware of overcharging. **F** *Backpackers Inn*, by the bridge on the south bank of the river, ferry service from the town, cheaper with hammock, profits to Casa Guatemala (see below). Recommended. *Comedor El Quetzal*, near the bridge at Río Dulce, has excellent sea food. At Punta Bacadilla, 30 minutes downstream, there is a bar, restaurant and a place to sling your hammock for US$1 per night, tent sites and hammock rentals available, mosquitoes abound however, and not all reports are favourable. *Hacienda Tijax* near the bridge at Río Dulce, has 4 jungle lodges, **A-E**, depending on season, beautiful jungle trail on property.

Entertainment   Sports Sailing: Captain John Clark offers sailing trips from Brunos – under the north end of the bridge on his 46-ft Polynesian catamaran, *Las Sirenas*, highly recommended. One 3-day sail is to Río Dulce canyon, Lívingston, Lago Izabal, hot waterfalls, Castillo de San Felipe, US$145 per person double occupancy. The other 6 day sail is to Río Dulce, Lívingston and the Belize Cayes, US$350 per person double occupancy, including food, taxes, snorkelling and fishing gear, windsurf boards. Trips leave on Friday, credit cards accepted (with 6% commission). Also offered are swimming, kayaks, canoes, sailing, windsurfing and accommodation (**E** in rooms, **F** in tents, cheaper in hammocks, **F** in a Chinese junk); restaurant and bar. For information contact *Aventuras Vacacionales SA*, 1 Av Sur, 11 B, Antigua, T/F8323352 or *Tivoli Travel*, Antigua T8323401; also shorter trips. A boat from the bridge to Lívingston costs US$60 for 2 people, a day trip with a stopover at the Biotopo, Aguas Calientes, hot springs where you can bathe, and some lagoons. Highly recommended. It is probably cheaper to hire a boat here than in Lívingston for this trip. All prices, tours and numbers of passengers negotiable.

Transport   Air   To Guatemala City, Inter 4 flights a week, US$50 one way. **Buses**   To Guatemala City and Flores: through buses stop at Río Dulce. Both destinations 6-7 hours, about US$6. Litegua buses go to Guatemala in 5 hours, leaves 0745 and 1200, direct.

At the entrance to Lake Izabal, two kilometres upstream, is the old Spanish fort of **Castillo de San Felipe** with a pleasant park, restaurant and swimming pool. ■ *0800-1700, US$0.75*. The fortification was first built about 1600, was rebuilt and expanded in 1688 and restored as a national monument in 1955-56.

Castillo de San Felipe

Sleeping **AL** *Banana Palms*, T9478115, cheaper family rooms, full service, marina, restaurant poor service. **AL** *Viñas del Lago*, T9027505, on lakeside, beach, restaurant, pool. **E** *Don Humberto*, good value.

Transport Boat from El Relleno (Río Dulce) below the new bridge, US$2.50 return for 1, US$0.50 per person in groups; it is a 5 km walk (practically impossible after rain) or take a camioneta from 2 blocks up the road to Tikal US$0.25.

On the northwest shore of Lago Izabal the name, El Estor, dates back to the days when the British living in the Atlantic area got their provisions from a store situated at this spot. Nickel-mining began here in 1978 but was suspended after the oil crisis of 1982 because the process depended on cheap sources of energy. The mine is still closed, but there is oil prospecting. It is a good place to relax, quiet, cheap and in a beautiful setting. You can hire a boat from Río Dulce to El Estor for about US$60, passing near the hot waterfall inland at Finca El Paraíso, which can be reached by a good trail in about 40 minutes, or by tractor from the shore. You can sit under the hot waterfall and swim in the cooler pools below; entrance US$1.

El Estor is now reached by a new road on the northern shore of Lago de Izabal: from Río Dulce it is 45 kilometres (dusty). The ferry from Mariscos no longer runs. For the routes from El Estor to Cobán via either Panzós and Tactic, or Cahabón and Lanquín, see page 624.

El Estor
Colour map 4, grid B4

Sleeping & eating **D** *Vista al Lago*, 6 Av, 1-13, T9497205, owned by Oscar Paz who will take you fishing, clean, friendly. **E** *Los Almendros*, T9487182, away from the lake, pleasant, clean, safe. Recommended. **F** *Santa Clara*, 5 Av 2-11, friendly, basic, clean, warm shower, others at similar prices. **F** *Villela*, 6 Av 2-06, T7497214, big rooms with bath, nice, clean, friendly, patio. Recommended. Also restaurants: *Hugo's*, good. *Rancho Mari*, fish and beer only, big helpings, delicious. *Marisabella*, 8 Av/1 C, good spaghetti, also has rooms, **C**. *Dorita*, at ferry point for Mariscos friendly, very good meals, good value; a *comedor* 1 block from *Hotel Vista al Lago* on waterfront is good and cheap, eggs, beans and coffee for US$0.50.

Transport **Bus** Río Dulce-El Estor, 1½ hours, US$1.45. To **Cobán**, Transportes Valenciana, 0800 (in theory), 7 hours, US$2. All buses leave El Estor in the morning. To **Río Dulce** US$8 by private *lancha*.

Directory **Banks** *Corpobanco* accepts TCs and Mastercard.

On the shore of Lago de Izabal is *Casa Guatemala*, a children's orphanage, run by a lady called Angie, where you can work in exchange for basic accommodation and food. There are about 200 children. Ask for information in Fronteras.

Mariscos is on the southern shore of Lago de Izabal. It used to be the dock for the ferry to El Estor, now replaced by the road from Río Dulce. Many Guatemalans have holiday homes on Lago de Izabal, particularly around Mariscos. From Mariscos there are buses to the twin town of **Bananera/Morales**, US$0.60 and Puerto Barrios, US$1.

Mariscos

Sleeping **F** *Hospedaje Karilinda*, scruffy rooms, run down, good food, right on the lake. **F** *Marinita*, next door, restaurant. **F** *Cafetería/Hospedaje Los Almendros*, basic, poor value. Good *comedor* at minibus terminal. *Cauca* (dory) trips can be arranged to Lívingston, via San Felipe, from Mariscos, 5 hours, US$18 for 3 people.

□Guatemala
City

El Petén: the Maya Centres and the Jungle

Mostly deep in the jungle and reached only in the dry season, or, as with the majestic Tikal, full-blown tourist sites, ancient Maya cities are the main attraction of El Petén. Flores on Lake Petén Itzá is the chief starting point; another, but less developed and less-easily accessible is Sayaxché. From both there are tough road and river routes into Mexico; from Flores is the principal road route to Belize.

El Petén Department in the far north was so impenetrable that its inhabitants, the Itzáes, were not conquered by the Spaniards until 1697. It is now reached by road either from Km 245, opposite Morales, on the Atlantic Highway, or from Cobán, through Sebol and Sayaxché, or by air. The local products are chicle and timber (the tropical forest south of Flores is being rapidly destroyed) and mosquitoes in the rainy season; take plenty of repellent, and reapply frequently.

In 1990 16,000 square kilometres of the north of Petén was declared the Maya Biosphere Reserve, the largest protected tropical forest area in Central America.

Maya Biosphere Reserve

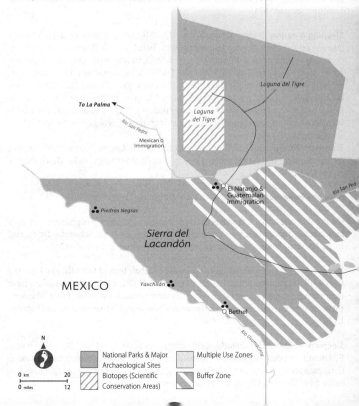

Within the Reserve are several of the most important Mayan sites including Tikal (in its own National Park), Uaxactún, El Mirador, El Zotz and Río Azul. It is a sparsely inhabited area and, apart from Tikal, contains none of the standard tourist attractions though the route from Flores to Mexico via El Naranjo more or less follows the Reserve's southern border.

From either Guatemala City or Puerto Barrios, the road from the Atlantic Highway is paved to **Modesto Méndez** (no accommodation, but you can borrow a hammock). A new bridge has been built here over the Río Sarstún, the entrance to Petén Department, then 215 kilometres on a road which is narrow and winding in stretches, otherwise broad, dusty and potholed. Despite the first paved 45 kilometres to San Luis, it takes seven hours to drive in a private car. There are plans to pave the road to Flores and work began in 1999. Take advice before you drive or cycle this route, especially if you are alone or may be travelling at night.

Those who wish to break the journey could get off the bus and spend a night in Morales, **San Luis** (F *Pensión San Antonio*, nice; *Comedor Oriente*, cheap, good), Río Dulce or Poptún.

Poptún is 100 kilometres before Flores. At certain times of the year delicious mangoes are on sale in this area. Good view of the town from Cerro de la Cruz, a 15 minutes' walk from the market. *Fiesta* 26-30 April. **Sleeping F** *Pensión Isabelita*, clean, recommended but no electricity at night. **F** *Pensión Gabriel*, cheaper. **Transport Buses** 5 minibuses a day from Flores, US$3 or take Fuentes del Norte bus, US$1.15, 4 hours. Bus

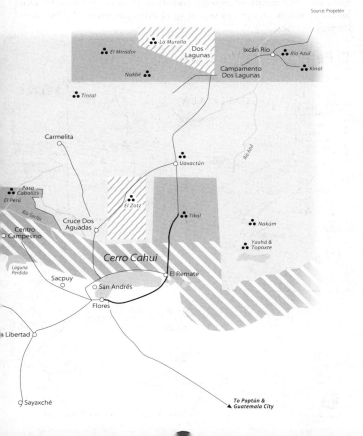

Source: Propetén

Poptún-Guatemala City at 0900 and 2400 (en route from Flores), 11 hours, US$6, long and bumpy; take this bus also for Cobán, alight at the turn-off to Sebol, 5 kilometres before Modesto Méndez, hitch to Fray Bartolomé de las Casas (see page 657), then take 0500 bus to Cobán. Alternatively, take bus (4 daily, 2½ hours, US$1) to Sayaxché and to Cobán via Chisec with pick up truck or hitch, a long ride, need a day to recover from bruises (see page 657). La Pinita has a service from Flores to Poptún and Sayaxché, see below. Bus Poptún-Río Dulce US$5.

Three kilometres south of Poptún is *Finca Ixobel*, T/F9277363, a working farm owned by Carole DeVine, widowed after the assassination of her husband in 1990. This highly acclaimed 'paradise' has become the victim of its own reputation and is frequently crowded, not helped by the tourist buses which stop for coffee and cake. However, one may still camp peacefully for US$2 per person. There are shelters, tree houses, hot showers, free firewood, one unforgettable parrot, swimming, riding, rafting, many short and longer treks in the jungle, farm produce for sale; excellent family-style meals available, and there is a small guest house, **E, F** in dormitory, travellers cheques exchanged. Beware of the thief (Toni, the spider monkey and his friend). This is a popular stop for backpackers. They have a restaurant-bar (also called *Ixobel*, excellent too, and *hospedaje* next door) in the centre of Poptún where the regular buses stop. Ask there for transport to the *Finca*. Expeditions are organized; the one day River Cave Trip (where you can jump into a cave river in complete darkness!) is recommended, US$3.50. Three day jungle expeditions are also organized. Héctor Gómez also offers jungle treks of four days visiting caves and forest on his own property with groups of four to 12 people, recommended (organized through the Finca).

El Petén & Alta Verapaz

Maya Biosphere Reserve

Created by congressional decree in 1990, the 16,000 square kilometres **Maya Biosphere Reserve** is (at least in theory) by far the largest protected area in Guatemala, covering the northern third of El Petén. Following UNESCO's model, biosphere reserves aim to link conservation of biodiversity with sustainable human development by having several zones of protection and use. In the Maya Biosphere Reserve, strictly protected **core areas**, the National Parks and biotopos (areas set aside for scientific study by the University of San Carlos) are bordered by a **multiple use zone**, where some non-destructive extractive use is permitted. To the south of these protected zones a 15 kilometre-wide **buffer zone** is designed to inhibit further encroachment into the reserve proper.

A number of major international conservation organizations work with Guatemalan government agencies in developing sustainable economic alternatives for villagers in the reserve. These include extraction of traditional forest products, primarily pimienta (allspice), chicle (tree sap used in chewing gum), xate (pronounced shatay, small palm fronds used in flower arrangements) and lesser quantities of ornamental and medicinal plants. The main threats to the integrity of the reserve are illegal logging and waves of settlers from Guatemala's impoverished southeastern departments. The rate of forest clearance has begun to slow down over the last year as the reserve management programmes take effect, but real protection is marginal and fragile. While the extractive use is sustainable, the income generated is insufficient to halt the threat to the forest. Much of the hope for the future of the forest is pinned on sustainable tourism. With a wealth of neotropical wildlife and hundreds of remote Maya sites, there is much to see. On a low-key, small-scale expedition with a good guide, you could expect to encounter some of the following: jaguars, pumas, monkeys, tapirs, peccaries, crocodiles, turtles and some of the 500 bird species in the reserve.

Peter Eltringham

---

35 kilometres east of Poptún are the caves of **Naj-tunich**, discovered in 1980, with Mayan cave paintings dating from around 750 AD with hieroglyphs referring to Popul-Vuh. The Mayans believed that caves were the entrance to the underworld.

Seven kilometres north of Poptún is **Machaquilá, B** *Hotel Ecológico Villa de Los Castellanos*, T9277222, F9277365, mailing address 13C 'B' 32-69, Zona 7, Tikal III, Guatemala City, 01007 Guatemala: an ecotourist project and hotel on the Río Machaquilá, international, local and vegetarian food, hot water, laundry, phone and fax, money exchange, excursions to archaeological sites, caves, jungle trails, recommended. Also on the Río Machaquilá, 15 minutes' walk (follow signs) from bridge, *Cocay Camping*, hammocks available US$2, or dormitory US$3 with breakfast, good food, trips arranged, also rooms nearby.

24 kilometres north of Poptún, eight kilometres northeast of Dolores, is the small Maya site of **Ixcún**, unexcavated, with a number of monuments (some carved), and a natural hill topped by the remains of ancient structures. The access road is impassable in the rainy season.

Flores/Santa Elena

NB Since Tikal is a 'must' on the visitor's itinerary, there are many tourists at Flores and the ruins. Demand has outstripped supply, prices are therefore high and quality of service often poor. If you have several days available, consider staying in Flores/Santa Elena and making the easy trip to the ruins each day, though this will involve paying daily to enter the Park. Sadly theft is common, and watch out for rip-offs. Tikal, however, will not disappoint you.

Colour map 4, grid B3

The Department's capital, **Flores** (*population*: 5,000), lies in the heart of the Petén, and is built on an island in Lake Petén Itzá. There is a small cathedral on the highest point of the island (which was the site of a Mayan temple) overlooking the central plaza. It is linked by a causeway with **Santa Elena** (airport) and **San Benito**, to the west. There have been heavier than average rains in the past few years and the level of the lake, which has no surface outlet, has been rising, giving problems to some lakeside properties and making the causeway difficult. From Flores the ruins of Tikal and other Maya cities can be reached. Many hotels have inclusive daily trips to Tikal. (For a description of Maya culture, see the section on **Precolumbian civilizations** at the beginning to this book).

Lake excursions

Swimming in the lake is not rec anywhere. There are various nasties in the water inc fungi and bacteria. Ear infections are common

Dugouts or fibreglass one or two-seaters can be hired to paddle yourself around the lake (US$2 per hour). Check dugouts for lake-worthiness. 'Radio Petén' island, the small island which used to have a radio mast on it, is US$0.12 by boat. Petencito (La Guitarra) island in the lake is being developed for tourism (known as 'Paraíso Escondido'); there is a small **zoo** of local animals (including spider monkeys, collared peccaries, pumas and jaguars), birds (parrots, toucans, and macaws etc), and reptiles, entry US$1.70. The zoo conditions are not good and you need to take insect repellent. There are two water toboggan slides, and plant-lined walks, good but popular at weekends, entry US$2. Dugout to island, US$3 per person. Boat tours of the whole lake cost about US$10 per boat, calling at these islands, a lookout on a Maya ruin and *Gringo Perdido* (see page 646); whatever you may request, the zoo will almost certainly be included in the itinerary. **San Benito**, a US$0.05 (US$0.10 after 1800) ride across the lake (or walk from Santa Elena), has some small restaurants (for example *Santa Teresita*), which are cheaper but less inviting than those in Flores. A dirty village, but good football matches at weekends. *Fiesta* 1-9 May. Regular launch service from San Benito across the lake to San Andrés (US$0.12) and San José (US$0.15) on northwest shore.

San Andrés, about 16 kilometres by road from Santa Elena is a quiet, pleasant village on a hillside with a Spanish language school, Eco-Escuela, T/F9268106, office in Flores, founded by Eco-Escuela (Conservation International), 1015 18th St NW, Suite 1000, Washington DC 20036, USA, T202-9732264, F202-8875188, sister@conservation.org, with normally about 15 pupils in residence with local families. Courses cost about US$120 per week for 25 hours study and accommodation and meals with a family. This is a good starting point for visiting El Mirador as the bus from Santa Elena stops outside *Comedor Angelita* at the junction of the road to Carmelita. Local accommodation including: **F** *Hospedaje El Reposo Maya*, clean, good. Two kilometres from the village on the Santa Elena road is **AL** *Hotel Nitún*, T/F9260494 in Flores, luxury cabañas on wooded hillside above lake, run by friendly couple Bernie and Lauren, who cook fantastic meals and organize expeditions to remote sites. Bus to Santa Elena at 1330 daily, but most people go by boat, every hour from 0500 to 1100 and on demand (20 people) until late.

Two kilometres further northeast on the lake is **San José**, a traditional Maya Itzá village, where efforts are being made to preserve the Itzá language. Most buses come this far (lakeside bungalows, **E**, check at *El Tucán* restaurant in Flores). Four kilometres beyond the village a signed track leads to the Classic period site of **Motul**, with several plazas, tall pyramids and some stelae depicting Maya kings.

Three kilometres south by road or 45 minutes walking from Santa Elena are the **Aktun Kan caves**, a fascinating labyrinth of tunnels, entry US$1.20.

SSleeping

■ *on maps*
Price codes: see inside front cover

In Flores: **B** *Sabana*, T/F9261248, including breakfast and evening meal, huge rather spartan rooms, good service, clean, pleasant, good view, caters for European package tours. **B** *La Casona de las Isla*, on the lake, T9260523, F9260593, elegant rooms, fans, clean, friendly, good restaurant, bar, garden, takes major credit cards, also caters for tour groups; also owns **B** *Casazul*, 4 blocks away on lake shore, with bath, cable TV, no pool or restaurant, clean. Recommended. **C** *La Mesa de los Mayas*, T9261240, charming, clean, friendly, good bathrooms. Recommended. **C** *Petén*, T9260692, F9260662, with hot water, lake view, clean, pool, take care with the electrics, breakfast a little extra, helpful travel agency (will change travellers' cheques), recommended minibus service to Tikal, may give free ride to airport, very obliging, will store luggage, ask for the new rooms at the front. **C** *Yum Kax*, T9260686, with bath and a/c. **C** *Villa del Lago* next door, T9260629, smart, very clean, hot water, cheaper with shared bath, balcony over lake, breakfast on terrace overlooking the lake, cool drinks, friendly. Recommended. **D** *Santa Rita*, with bath, clean, excellent service. Recommended. **E** *El Itzá*, T9260686, basic, no hot water, dangerous fixtures, but friendly. **E** *El Itzá II*, nice rooms, shower, but watch your belongings. **E** *El Tucán*, T9260677, on the lakeside, 4 rooms only, fan, comfortable, good restaurant in garden with collection of birds, friendly, nice view over lake. **E** *La Canoa*, near the causeway to Flores, with bath, small restaurant, OK. **E** *La Jungla*, F9260634, good beds, helpful, bath, fan, hot water, clean. Recommended. Travel agent, restaurant behind, see below. **E** *Tayazal*, T9260568, rooms with 2 double beds, can sleep 4, clean sheets, fan, hot showers downstairs, roof terrace, drinking water available, very accommodating, can arrange Tikal trip. **F** *El Tucán II*, near *El Tucán*, fan, clean, unreliable water, nice common room on 2nd floor, basic. **F** *Doña Goya*, behind tourist office, clean, friendly family, breakfast available.

In Santa Elena: **L** *Petén Espléndido*, T9260880, F9260886, restaurant, rooms with balcony, pool, also conference centre. **AL** *Del Patio Tikal*, T9260104, clean, hot water, a/c, modern, colour TV, expensive restaurant, best booked as part of package. **AL** *Maya Internacional*, T9261276, tax extra, beautifully situated on the lake front, subject to flooding, restaurant not recommended. **A** *Tziqui Na Ha*, near airport, T9260175, a/c pool, overpriced. **A** *Del Trópico*, T9260728, new commercial hotel at top end of main road. **C** *Costa del Sol*, T9261336, 1 block from bus station, pool, friendly. **D** *Posada Santander*, opposite Banco Industrial, T9260574, free airport transfer. **D** *Sac Nicte*, by lake below road to Flores, rooms with balcony upstairs, electric shower, fan, some trouble with water and electricity, not very clean, friendly, minibus to Tikal. **D** *San Juan I*, close to the Catholic Church, T9260562, F9260041, bus stop outside (hence you will probably be woken at 0400 whether you are travelling or not), travel agency inside acts as Aviateca office, tours arranged, pleasant, full of budget travellers, luxurious remodelled rooms (**C** with a/c, TV, hot water) and older (seedy) rooms, **F** with shared bath, credit cards accepted, also cash advances on credit cards and travellers' cheques exchange, clean, safe, public phone, parking, take care with the electric heaters (restaurant not recommended). **E** *Alonzo*, 6 Av, 4-99, T9260105, with bath, **F** without, fan, popular, minibus to Tikal, they sell Tikal Jet air tickets, quiet except on Friday when the Evangelical church next door has an all night vigil. **E** *Coral Pek*, T9260073, clean, friendly. **E** *Continental*, next to *Alonzo*, pleasant large rooms with bath, cheaper without, with fan, good beds, mosquito nets, friendly, clean, hot water. **F** *Jade*, very simple, intermittent electricity, helpful, just by the causeway to Flores, will store luggage, laundry facilities, try to choose your room. **F** *San Juan II*, close to the lake, cheaper without bath, front rooms noisy, staff helpful and friendly, luggage store, money exchange.

In San Benito: **F** *Hotel Miraflores*, good, private showers. **F** *Calle Real*, clean, comfortable, friendly. **F** *Hotel Rey*, friendly, untidy, noisy. **F** *San Juan*, clean (last 3 under US$3).

Between Santa Elena and El Remate: **AL** *Villa Maya*, on Lake Peténchel, 8 km from Santa Elena airport on road to Tikal, T9260086, bungalows, nice setting beside lake, helpful, pool. Recommended. Only drawback is set menu, if you do not like it you are a long way from an alternative restaurant.

In Flores: *El Jacal*, on road to left of causeway, good regional dishes, good fish, animal skins on walls, reasonable prices. *Gran Jaguar*, pleasant, very good. Recommended (relocated to other side of lake because of flooding). *La Jungla*, pleasant, reasonably priced, good portions, avoid spaghetti bolognese. *El Faisán*, reasonable prices, good food. *El Tucán*, see **Sleeping**, the best place at sunset but slow service. *La Mesa de los Mayas*, cheap set lunch, clean, toucan in cage, mixed reports. *Pizzería Picasso*, good Italian food, normal prices, try their spaghetti con pesto, also Mexican dishes. *La Canoa*, very friendly, good breakfasts (try the pancakes), dinners start at US$1.50. *El Koben*, open patio, friendly, expensive but good value.

Eating
• *on maps*

Guatemala

In Santa Elena: *El Rodeo*, 2 C y 5 Av, excellent, reasonable prices but slow service, classical music. Opposite is **Doña Amintas**, good value café/restaurant, fresh homemade pasta, friendly. *Jennifers*, on road to causeway, good sandwiches, none too clean but cheap, popular. *La Parranda* on the lake. *Petenchel*, next to *El Rodeo*, vegetarian and other food, music, reasonable prices. **Leo Fu Ho**, by the causeway, good Chinese.

Santa Elena market, well-stocked, 2 blocks from **Hotel San Juan**, just off Telgua road. Several ice cream shops (*Gémini* 'artificial').

NB In restaurants, do not order **tepescuintle**, a rabbit-sized jungle rodent that is endangered. Imported goods, especially soft drinks, are expensive in Flores.

Festivals   12-15 January.

Transport   **Local Car hire**: at airport, mostly Suzuki jeeps, cost about US$65-80 per day; *Jade* agency is recommended; also ask at **Hotel San Juan I**. Petrol is sold in Santa Elena.

Air   Several companies fly from Guatemala City to Flores (airport actually in Santa Elena) including Aviateca, Mayan World Airlines, Tapsa (recommended) and Tikal Jet – check carefully which terminal in Guatemala. Aviateca charges more than the others, but enquire about special offers: for example Aviateca may offer reduction if you buy an international ticket from them. The cost of a one-way flight in March 1999 was between US$25-30, shop around in Guatemala City and Antigua. The schedules appear to change frequently, but all fly daily at 0700 or 0800; flights back leave between 1600 and 1700, but check.

Aviateca, Mexicana, Aero Caribe and Mayan World Airlines fly to and from Cancún (Mexico) usually daily. 3 days a week AeroCaribe fly to Palenque. Tropic Air, Taca and Maya Airways fly to Belize City, daily. Be early for flights, overbooking is common and reconfirming is no help. Banco del Quetzal, 0800-1200, 1400-1700, and a cambio booth. Taxi to Flores, US$2. You must have passport (or identity documents) to pass through Santa Elena airport. *Inguat Tourist Office* at Santa Elena airport, T9260533, open 0730-1000, 1500-1800 daily.

Buses   The Flores bus terminal is in Santa Elena, a 10-minute walk from Flores (urban bus US$0.10, taxi whatever you can bargain). Services from **Guatemala City** are run by La Petenera, T9260070 (early morning and late afternoon each way) US$10, 15 hours; Fuentes del Norte, throughout the day including express buses, US$12-15 depending on time of day, and ordinary buses, US$9, 12-15 hours with refreshment stops, take food anyway and your passport in case of army checks, very crowded (try riding on roof for breathing space); and Guatemala City-Santa Elena, Línea Máxima del Petén overnight, leaving at 1600, 1900 and 2000, US$13; all these buses leave Guatemala City from 17 C between 8-10 Avs, Zona 1. There is another service, Línea Dorada from 16 C y 10 Av, leaving at 1900, US$18 including sandwich, pillow and blanket, reservation advised. Recommended. If you are going only to Poptún or Fronteras/Río Dulce make sure you do not pay the full fare to Guatemala City: in practice, this means you will probably have to take a 2nd class bus, Fuentes del Norte. Route is via Morales and Modesto Méndez; from Flores "the first 6 hours are terrifying, a virtual rollercoaster: book early if you want a front seat!". Also minibus, more expensive, faster but beware owner saying nothing else is available. Bus Flores to **Río Dulce**, US$6, Fuentes del Norte, 8 hours. Bus between Flores and **Quiriguá** (see page 630), US$5, 11 hours. In the rainy season the trip can take as much as 28 hours, and in all weathers it is very uncomfortable and crowded (flights warmly recommended). To **Sayaxché** from behind the market, 0600, 1300. Buses run around the lake to San Andrés, with one at 1200 continuing to Cruce dos Aguadas and Carmelita for access to El Mirador. For transport to **Belize City**, see page 652, below.

NB There were several hold-ups of buses between Santa Elena and Modesto Méndez in 1997 and 1998.

To travel overland to **Copán**, take a bus from Flores to Río Hondo, then from Río Hondo to Chiquimula, then from Chiquimula to El Florido (see page 627) and finally from there to Copán.

Directory   **Banks** Flores: *Banco de Guatemala*, C 30 de Junio between 1 and 2 Av, open Mon-Thur, 0830-1400,

Decline and fall of the Tikal Empire

Dr Patrick Culbert, University of Arizona, found two different kinds of skeletons in Tikal: those who died well fed and others who suffered from malnutrition and lack of iron. He concluded that the normal dead must have been priests, who fed on the sacrifices of food and drinks given by the peasants to the gods to ward off a poor harvest. The farmers must have died from starvation when the harvest failed. This theory has been confirmed by findings in Belize of Dr David Pendergast, University of Toronto, where peasants looted the tombs of dead priests, but dared not threaten the living. The Tikal astronomer priests who prophesied good harvests erred in 790, after which there was drought, failed harvests and soil erosion, accompanied by malnourishment, starvation and death among the peasants. There was rebellion among the peasants, while frustration and disillusionment followed within the

priesthood. Their subsequent lack of interest in astronomy is reflected in the decline in the number of calendar stela: 20 were dated 790 AD, 12 of them 810, only 3 dated 830 and the last one 889 AD. Competition between the Maya cities and the decline of the peasantry, leaving them outnumbered by the priesthood, led to the abandonment of Tikal around this time. Further research by scholars from the University of Florida who conducted chemical analyses of lime and burned grass and roots of the Lake Chichancanab in the Yucatán has shown that the lake was at its driest between 800-900 AD. Similar effects on other lakes in Costa Rica, Mexico and wood fires in Costa Rica, point to a massive drought in the area at that time, leading to the collapse of the Maya Empire.

Helmut Zettl

Fri 0830-1430, changes Amex TCs. **Banco Hipotecario** also for Amex TCs. **Santa Elena:** *Banco del Café*, best rates for Amex TCs. *Banco Granai y Townson. Banco Industrial*, visa ATM. *Carpobanco*, near bus station, good exchange rates for cash and TCs. Also *Banco del Quetzal* (see airport). The major hotels and travel agents change cash and TCs. Others near bus terminal. For cash advances, see *Hotel San Juan I*.

Communications Post Office: Flores: near the church. **Santa Elena:** close to *Hotel San Juan I*, on opposite side of street. **Fax:** *Cahui-Intertel*, T/F9260494, Flores, near where the boats leave for San Benito. **Telephone:** Telgua in Santa Elena. **Email:** *Internet Café* and one other.

Hospitals & medical services *Centro Médico Maya*, Santa Elena, Dra Sonia de Baldizón, speaks some English. Recommended.

Laundry *Lavandería Fénix* with dryer, US$2 wash and dry (in Flores).

Tour companies & travel agents Flores: *Petén Travel Agency*, can arrange trips in Tikal, Sayaxché and region and to other Maya sites. *Total Petén*, T9260662/0692, F9260662/1258. **Santa Elena:** *San Juan Travel Agency*, T/F9260041/2, reliable transport to Tikal (see **Access**, page 648 below), US$30 including tour, also excursions to Ceibal US$30, and Uaxactún US$20, with non-bilingual guide. Excellent service to Belize, US$20, 0500, arrives 1100, wake up call if you stay at *San Juan* hotel, otherwise collect from your hotel, bus links with Chocolate's boat to Caye Caulker, ticket US$8 from *San Juan* but US$6 in Belize; also to Chetumal at 0500, US$30, arrives 1300. *Transportes Inter-Petén*, 10 C, 10-32, Zona 1, San Benito, T9260574, for transport to archaeological sites, Belize, etc.

Tourist offices ProPetén, Calle Central, T/F9260495/0370, associated with Conservation International (see above under San Andrés, Eco-Escuela), part of *Cincap* (ecological, cultural and craft information centre for El Petén, on the plaza); also has free maps of Tikal and other local information includes details of the Scarlet Macaw Trail, a 5-day hike through the Maya Biosphere Reserve. Open 0800-1700. Always check with Propetén before setting out to any sites, to see whether they have vehicles going, for example to El Mirador. Tourist information office on the main plaza.

Volunteer work Check with Arcas office in Flores for local work with wild animal rehabilitation, minimum 2 weeks, food and accommodation cost about US$17 per week (see page 582).

31 kilometres from Santa Elena is El Cruce/Puente Ixlú where the main road turns right for Melchor de Mecos and Belize (see page 652). A paved road continues north to Tikal passing **El Remate** in a short distance, on the end of Lago Petén Itzá. Beyond El Remate is the **Biotopo Cerro Cahuí**, 700 hectares, which was opened in 1989. **El Remate & Cerro Cahuí**

This is a lowland jungle area where one can see three species of monkeys, deer, jaguar, peccary, ocellated wild turkey and some 450 species of birds; run by Cecon and Inguat. There are several trails through hilly country with good views of the lake, entry US$5. Interesting though some say that you will see more in the jungle around Tikal.

Sleeping About 1.8 km from the entrance to the Cerro Cahuí Park is **L** *Camino Real*, on shore of lake, T9260204, F9260222, all rooms have views, free minibus from airport, good restaurant, a/c, free use of boats on the lake, cable TV etc. 1 km closer to the park is **C** *El Gringo Perdido Parador Ecológico* (T Guatemala City 2325811, F2538761, Viajes Mundial, 5 Av, 12-44, Zona 1), with a restaurant, cabin (**D** without food), camping (US$3 a night) and good swimming in the lake though some parts muddy, good meals, owner keen on triathlon. Good walking. It is about 4 kilometres from El Cruce on the Tikal road, turning off to the left along the north shore of the lake. To get there walk 3 km from El Remate, or ask for a boat in *El Gringo Perdido* store, El Remate. The road from El Remate to *El Gringo Perdido* is sometimes flooded.

Up the hill overlooking **El Remate**: **AL** *La Mansión del Pájaro Serpiente*, overlooking the lake, suites in secluded hillside, attractive garden. **E** *La Casa de Don David*, about 2 km from the main road, clean, friendly owner, good meals, good value. **In El Remate: F** *John's Lodge*, friendly, good food, hammocks and beds. **F** *El Mirador del Duende*, 'eco-camping', community phone 9260269, F Telgua 9260397, run by Manuel Soto Villafuente and his family, overlooks lake Petén Itzá, camping US$2.50 or cabins US$4, vegetarian food, jungle trips, US$25 per day. Canoes (US$4 per day), boat trips, mountain bikes, horses and guides are available. No electricity, take flashlight (mixed reports 1998, also check source of drinking water).

Shopping In El Remate is a handicraft shop selling carvings in tropical hardwood made by a group of local farmers; items cost from US$6 to US$60. Recommended. Tourist and minibuses stop here. 20 minutes walk northeast of El Cruce.

El Perú   A visit to El Perú is included in the *Scarlet Macaw Trail*, a five day trip into the Laguna del Tigre National Park (see page 653), through the main breeding area of the scarlet macaw. The trip begins by road to Centro Campesino, served by daily bus from Santa Elena (in wet conditions the road is only passable as far as Sacpuy), then on horseback to the Río Sacluc, where you pick up the boat to El Perú. The site is large though little excavated, but contains some carved stelae; the attraction is the wild setting. Upstream the route continues to the campsite at the 150 metres Buena Vista cliffs and on to the road at Cruce dos Aguadas, between San Andrés and Carmelita. The tour is run by *Epiphite Adventures* (contact at ProPetén, Flores), the cost depends on the level of support required. Doing it on your own is possible, though you may have to wait for connections and you will need a guide, about US$20 per day. El Perú can be reached by hiring a boat to go upstream on the Río San Pedro from El Naranjo.

Tikal

Colour map 4, grid B3   The road from Flores/Santa Elena to Tikal is the only paved road in El Petén, although it can still be closed in wet weather. The great Maya ruins of vast temples and public buildings are reached by bus from Santa Elena (see below).

The ruins   The site of Tikal was first occupied around 300 BC and became an important Mayan centre from AD 300 onwards. The oldest stela found has been dated as AD 292. The main structures which cover two and a half square kilometres were constructed from AD 600 to AD 800 and at its height, the total 'urban' area was over 100 square kilometres. From this time, Tikal declined and the last stela recorded date is AD 889. The site was finally abandoned in the 10th century.

An overall impression of the ruins (a national park) may be gained in four to five

Bat bite advice

There are increasing numbers of bats in Tikal, and anyone bitten must seek medical aid right away. This means an immediate return to Guatemala City and a visit to the Centro de Salud, 9 C between Av 2 and 3 for treatment, including tetanus shots if necessary. The treatment is free.

hours, but you need at least two days to see it properly. A nature trail, with signs in Spanish labelling trees and plants, leads eventually to the ruins (turn left at the first and second roads you meet). All the pyramids can be climbed except Temple I; Temple IV, the highest, especially recommended. A network of tunnels linking some of the temples has recently been discovered near El Mundo Perdido, but these are now closed owing to vandalism. **NB** Take care on the pyramids, every year there are fatal accidents often involving children. Take water and snacks with you, it is likely to be hot, and you will walk several kilometres. There is officially nowhere to store luggage at Tikal while you are visiting the ruins but you may be able to persuade the Inspectoría to help, or try *Comedor Tikal*.

Entrance You can enter Tikal National Park from 0600-1730 daily. A charge of US$7 (Q 50) per day is payable at the entrance, 18 kilometres from the ruins. If you enter after 1500, your ticket is valid the following day. Extended passes to see the ruins at sunrise/sunset (until 2100) may be possible from the Inspectoría office on the slope by the path to the ruins (especially good for seeing animals, for example around Temple III between sunrise and 0800) but enquire about this when you enter the Park. It is best to visit the ruins after 1400, or before 0900 (fewer tourists). A photocopied plan of the site is available at the entrance gate for US$1. It rains here most days for a while between April and December. It is busiest November to January, during the Easter and Northern Hemisphere summer holidays, and most weekends.

Museums The new museum (on same side of the road as *Jungle Lodge*) is worth a visit; a good collection of Maya ceramics and a reproduction of the tomb of the ruler Chac. ■ *Monday-Friday 0900-1700, Saturday and Sunday 0900-1600, US$1.50*; restaurant and gift shop in same building. There is also a stelae museum in the Visitor Centre, entrance free.

Wildlife It is a marvellous place for seeing animal and bird life of the jungle. Take binoculars. There is a secluded part, called 'El Mundo Perdido', in which wildlife can be seen, particularly birds early in the morning. *Birds of Tikal*, by Frank B Smithe, is available at the museum, but for the serious bird watcher, Peterson's *Field Guide to Mexican Birds* is recommended (covers most Central American birds also) and a quality guide to North American birds is helpful if visiting Tikal in the early months of the year. Ask for Normandy Bonilla González if you would like a local expert. Wildlife includes spider monkeys, howler monkeys (re-established after being hit by disease), three species of toucan (most prominent being the 'Banana Bill'), deer, foxes and many other birds and insects. Pumas have been seen on quieter paths and coatimundis (*pizotes*) in large family groups, sometimes rummaging through the bins. Mosquitoes can be a real problem even during the day if straying away from open spaces.

Guides The guide book (Spanish or English), *Tikal*, by W R Coe, has an essential map (updated 1988) price US$13 at Tikal, slightly more in Antigua; some visitors find the text difficult to connect with what is seen. A good free map available in Chetumal bus station and travel agents. Without a guide book, a guide, US$10-20, is essential as outlying structures can otherwise easily be missed – and there are many kilometres of trails (Maximiliano has been recommended, he will meet you at 0500, US$20, speaks Spanish; another is Yolanda Quintana,

T Flores 9260265; guides who speak English charge US$40). Guides are available by the hotels, at the Rangers' Office (Inspectoría), or where the buses park.

Access To visit Tikal you can take package tours from Guatemala City or Antigua: prices for the most basic 1-day excursion start at about US$72 return (including flights and transfers), prices rise if guide, lunch and accommodation are added, up to US$250 for 3 days/2 nights. If you are in a party of say 6 to 10 it may be worth investigating a private plane, cost similar to the US$250 per person quoted, and more time flexibility at Tikal. Servicios Turísticos del Petén, 2 Av 7-78, Zona 10, Guatemala, T3341813/3346236. Highly recommended. Check in Belize for air tour packages, with for example Tropic Air, 3 days for around US$400, day return US$120.

From Santa Elena, it is possible to visit Tikal in a day. San Juan Travel Agency minibuses leave hourly between 0400 and 1000, return 1230, 1400, 1500, 1600, 1700, 1 hour, US$6 return, US$3.50 one way. Several other companies and hotels also run minibuses at the same price although out of season you can bargain. If you have not bought a return ticket you can often get a discounted seat on a returning bus if it is not full. The 0400 bus should get you to Tikal in time to see the sunrise, but do not rely on it. However, you will have the whole complex to yourself for several hours, a memorable experience. Minibuses meet Guatemala City-Flores flights to take visitors to Tikal, but check arrangements with your airline or hotel and ask around for the best price. They tend to leave when full, so you might miss your return flight. Taxi to Tikal costs US$30 per vehicle, or US$45 waiting for return. Mario Grijalba, T9260624, has been recommended.

Sleeping It is advisable to book hotel rooms or camping space as soon as you arrive, in high seasons, book in advance. The telephone numbers given are in Flores, Tikal has no phones.

Tikal

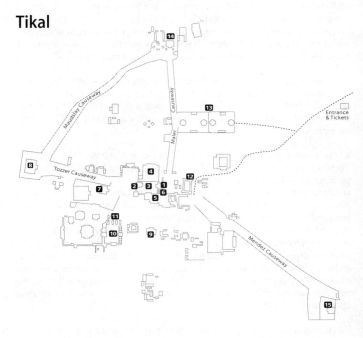

N

Not to scale

1 Temple I (Jaguar Temple)	6 Ball Court	12 Market
2 Temple II	7 Temple III	13 Twin Pyramid Plazas
3 Great Plaza	8 Temple IV	14 North Group
4 North Acropolis	9 Temple V	15 Temple of Inscriptions
5 Palace Complex	10 Seven Temples Group	
(Central Acropolis)	11 Triple Ball Court	

AL *Jungle Lodge*, reservations direct T9261519/0634, or may be made at 29 C, 18-01, Zona 12, Guatemala City, T4768775. New, spacious bungalows, with bath, hot water and fan (electricity 1800-2230 maximum), **C** without bath, it is cheaper to pay in quetzales than dollars at the lodge, they will cash travellers' cheques, full board available (food fair, but service slow and portions small), *Jungle Lodge's* Tikal tours (US$5) have been recommended. **AL** *Tikal Inn*, T9260065, in room (1 to 4 people) and **B** for up to 4 in a lodge. Cheap accommodation without electricity also available, guests only restaurant, breakfast and dinner included in room price, pool, helpful, they have a pet ocelot who is very cute but its teeth are sharp.

A *Jaguar Inn*, full board, less without food, will provide picnic lunch at US$1.30, its electricity supply is the most reliable (1800-2200), will store luggage, you may share your room with bugs and lizards. Tents can be hired at about US$10, to use in their campground, includes mattress and sheets, sleep 2-3; if you have your own tent, you pay about US$3 per person. Wife of proprietor, Patricia (English), is very knowledgeable on local wildlife.

Camping: there is 1 campsite (US$6 for tent or hammock space), by the old airstrip (which is closed except for emergencies for ecological reasons), rents tents US$10 per person, a few small hammocks with mosquito netting for US$3, best to bring your own, very popular. Take your own water as the supply is very variable, sometimes rationed, sometimes unlimited, depending on season. Bathing is possible in a pond at the far end of the airstrip (check first). Beware of chiggers in the grass. Same charge for vehicle overnight parking.

Wear light cotton clothes, a broad-brimmed hat and take plenty of insect repellent. The nights can be cold; warm garments advisable

Comedor Tikal, good food and reasonably priced, will store luggage for small fee. *Imperio Maya* (opens 0530), good food and lots of it at reasonable prices, friendly, has a store selling basic items. *Restaurant del Parque*, annex to the stelae museum, consistently poor reports. Other *comedores*. Sometimes the restaurants only have chicken on the menu.

Eating

Economical travellers are best advised to bring their own food (you can pay US$2 for a candy bar), and especially drink. Soft drinks are available near every major temple or pyramid (at least US$0.75) but you will need plenty of water so bring some with you. No banking services available, and exchange rates locally in hotels, etc are poor. Bring enough quetzales with you. If staying the night, take a torch: electricity at Tikal is only available 1800-2200 and then is intermittent.

Other Maya sites in the area

25 kilometres north of Tikal is Uaxactún (pronounced Wash-ak-tún), which has a stuccoed temple with serpent head decoration. Uaxactún is one of the longest-occupied Maya sites and contains the oldest complete Mayan astronomical complex. It was researched by the Carnegie Institution between 1926 and 1937. The ruins lie either side of the village, the main group to the north and a smaller group with observatory to the south. Beneath lies the oldest building yet found in Petén. At the moment there is no charge and you can wander freely through the tranquil site, usually accompanied by a group of children selling handmade corn husk dolls. The road from Tikal is in good condition and takes less than one hour in any vehicle. The village is little more than a row of houses either side of a disused airstrip. At the *Hotel El Chiclero* there is a museum of the life and work of the *chicleros*, which also includes objects, especially vases, discovered in the excavations here and nearby. These mainly date from the late pre-classical period 250 BC-300 AD. Entry free. At the west end of the airstrip a dirt road, passable by vehicles, leads 30 kilometres southwest to **El Zotz**. The road is hardly ever used by trucks except to go specifically to El Zotz, but it is easy to walk, camping halfway at an *aguada* for water. The site is in a *biotopo* and, as always, there is some basic infrastructure for the guards, and you can camp. The temples are two kilometres from the camp and completely unrestored but tragically slashed by looters. The tallest group, El Diablo, is a little further on and you are advised to take a guide from the *biotopo*. Each evening the sky is darkened by the fantastic spectacle of tens of thousands of bats flying out of a cave next to the camp. 'Zotz' means 'bat' in Mayan. You can continue on the dirt road for four to five hours

Uaxactún
Colour map 4, grid B3

Exploring El Petén

to reach Cruce dos Aguadas, where you can pick up a bus or truck, or, if time and supplies permit, head north to Carmelita and El Mirador.

Sleeping E *El Chiclero* is the best accommodation in the village, neat and clean, hammocks and rooms in a garden, also best food and the owners, Antonio and Neria Baldizón, have the best information and will help to organize an expedition.

F pp *El Tecomate*, cabins and hammocks at the village entrance, run by Manuel Soto.

F *Ecocampamento*, a campsite 150m from the ruins with toilets, showers (but no running water) and guard service, but reported not well run. There is a village laundry service and *comedores*.

Transport A daily Pinita bus leaves Santa Elena at 1300 via Tikal, 1530, arriving with luck at about 1630, returning next day at 0600, US$2. Tours from Tikal (arranged by hotels), US$12 per person; ask in the parking lot by the airstrip for transport.

Tour companies & travel agents Contact the *Association of Eco-Cultural Guides of Uaxactún* for tours and expeditions to Xultún, Río Azul, El Zotz, Nakbé and El Mirador. A guided tour of the ruins is US$15 for 2 people, US$20 for 3 or more. Jungle treks including food, mules, guides etc are US$30 per person per day for 8-10 days. Antonio and Neria Baldizón have high clearance pick-ups, used to supply the *chicle* and *xate* camps, and have plenty of experience in organizing both vehicle and mule trips to any site. Manuel Soto or the village guides can take you on foot, with more chance of seeing wildlife.

Río Azul & Kinal From Uaxactún a dirt road leads north to the *campamento* of **Dos Lagunas**, where the guards of the *biotopo* live by the side of a small, tranquil lake. It is a lovely place to camp, with few mosquitoes, but swimming will certainly attract crocodiles. The guards' camp at **Ixcán Río**, on the far bank of the Río Azul can be reached in one long day's walk, crossing by canoe if the water is high. If low enough to cross by vehicle you can drive to the **Río Azul** archaeological site, a further six kilometres on a wide, shady, track. It is also possible to continue into Mexico if your paperwork is OK. A barely passable side track to the east from the camp leads to the ruins of **Kinal**. The big attraction at Río Azul are the famous painted tombs, technically off limits to visitors without special permission, though the guards may show you one or two for a tip. The early classic standing architecture includes a 47 metre pyramid, under investigation each dry season. It is a difficult climb up it, but the view from the top reveals the forest canopy (you will almost certainly see monkeys) over to the Calakmul Biosphere Reserve to the west and the Río Bravo Conservation Area to the east.

Tours The cost can be surprisingly reasonable if you get a small group together with your own food and camping equipment. Hire a truck and driver, about US$120 per day, from Uaxactún. A guide can be hired in either Uaxactún or Dos Lagunas, and he will be essential to help clear the road. The best place to pick up information beforehand is to visit David Kuhn at the *Casa de Don David* in El Remate. He can contact Antonio at *El Chiclero* and arrange a guide from the nearby *Biotopo Cerro Cahuí*.

El Mirador

The largest Maya site in the country is at **El Mirador**, just short of the northern border with Mexico, 36 kilometres direct from **Carmelita**, which is itself 64 kilometres north of Flores. So far there has been only minimal clearing and excavation. No permission is needed to visit the site because there are permanent guards there to check you are not removing any souvenirs. If you are uncertain, check with the Archaeology Dept behind the Gobernación in Flores. There are paintings and treasures; guards will show you around if no one else is on hand. The larger of the two huge pyramids, called La Danta, is 70 metres high. The other is called El Tigre and is a wonderful place to be on top of at night, with a view of endless jungle and other sites, including Calakmul, in Mexico.

El Tintal, a day's hike from El Mirador, is said to be the second largest site in Petén, connected by a causeway to El Mirador, with great views from the top of the pyramids. **Nakbé**, about 10 kilometres southeast of El Mirador, is the earliest known lowland Maya site (1000 BC-400 BC), with the earliest examples of carved monuments. It is currently being excavated by Richard Hansen, who leads trips to the site, recommended, organized by *Far Horizons*, PO Box 91900, Albuquerque, New Mexico, T505-3439400, journey@ farhorizon.com.

Sleeping In Carmelita ask around for space to sling your hammock or camp. Simple accommodation and meals at **F** *Campamento Nakbé*. Brigido, who has worked with archaeologists at El Mirador and Nakbé may offer you hospitality for the night, **F**. There is a basic *comedor*. Local *tiendas* are notoriously understocked, bring sufficient food and water purification tablets for onward journeys from Flores.

Transport Drive or hitchhike to Carmelita beyond San Andrés on Lake Petén Itzá, 1 bus daily. Also usually 1 truck a day, San Andrés to Carmelita. Ask at ProPetén in Flores to see whether they have any vehicles going. You are unlikely to get to El Mirador in the rainy season, September-January.

Directory **Tour companies & travel agents** Ask in Carmelita for guides with mules to go to El Mirador and/or other sites. Carlos Catalán is highly recommended, you can contact him through the ProPetén office, T9260495. Sebastián Hernández and Rudy are also recommended, but Chepe, who lives next door to the doctor, is not, he doesn't have mules and may not be able to obtain them. A guide with a mule costs about US$25-30 per day but a full 5-day trip for 4 people with guide, mules, horses for riding, hammocks and nets will cost around US$300. Take water, food, tents and torches. Allow 2 days each way, unless you want a forced march. It is about 25 km to El Tintal, a camp where you can sling a hammock, or another 10 km to El Arroyo, where there is a little river for a swim near a *chiclero* camp and fewer mosquitoes than at El Tintal. It takes another day to El Mirador or longer if you detour via Nakbé. You will pass *chiclero* camps on the way, who are very hospitable, but very poor. Gifts in return for staying with them are much appreciated: food, batteries for torches (used to guard against nocturnal snakes). At El Mirador you can camp near the guards' camp; they may let you use their kitchen if you are polite (they also appreciate gifts, for example a giant can of peaches). Watch out for scorpions.

Yaxhá The road from Flores to the Belize border passes through **El Cruce/Puente Ixlú**, where the road to Tikal heads north. There is a *campamento*, information and the ruins of **Ixlú**. About 65 kilometres from Flores, on the same road, is a turning left, a dry weather road which brings you in eight kilometres to Lake Yaxhá. On the northern shore is the site of **Yaxhá**, the third-largest known classic Maya site in the country, accessible by causeway. It is in the early stages of excavation but recent work has restored some of the main temples. In the lake is the site of **Topoxte**. (The island is accessible by boat.) The site is unique since it flourished between the 12th and 14th centuries, long after the abandonment of all other classic centres.

Sleeping On the south shore, **B** *El Sombrero*, T9265229, F9265198, with bath, cheaper without, comfortable cabins and rooms in a beautiful setting, restaurant. The owner,

Gabriela Moretti, organizes riding trips to Yaxhá and Nakúm, and has a boat to take you to Topoxte. Inguat have constructed a campsite with thatched shelters (free at the moment) on the north shore, just below the ruins, a wonderful place to stay.

Nakum 20 kilometres further north lies Nakum, with standing Maya buildings. The road is bad and subject to flooding, but work is taking place here as well so more facilities may be available soon. A number of other sites are being opened up to promote tourism. At the moment the only one easily visited is **El Pilar**, the largest site in the Belize River valley and straddling the border, set in an international archaeological park. Best reached from San Ignacio, Belize. Plenty of mosquitoes.

Melchor de Mencos Since the establishment of formal diplomatic relations between Guatemala and Belize in September 1991. **Melchor de Mencos** has become a busy border town for travellers and trade between Guatemala and Mexico as well as Belize. Fiesta 15-22 May.

Sleeping & services E *Mayab*, clean, comfortable, fan, **F** with shared showers and toilets, cold water, no nets on windows, take own mosquito net, safe parking. **F** *Zacaleu*, T9265163, clean, good value, shared toilets/showers. *La Chinita*, 1 block from *Mayab*, good dinner under US$2. *El Hilton*, good meals, reasonable prices. *Ribera*, at the border, good, pleasant view. Also at the border the new **D** *Hotel Palace Frontera*, T9265196, with restaurant, hot water, car rental services, on the banks of the Río Mopan, T9265196. Tienda Unica will change travellers' cheques, but at a poor rate.

Frontier with Belize – Melchor de Mencos/ Benque Viejo **Belizean and Mexican consulates** If you need a visa for either of these countries, obtain them in Guatemala City. However, 72-hour transit visas are available at the border which will cover you to the Mexican border at Chetumal but not into Mexico. If you intend to stay in Belize, you may be able to get a visa at the border but there could be extra charges when you leave the country.

Crossing by private vehicle There is unleaded fuel at the Melchor de Mencos petrol station but none in Belize.

Exchange There are good rates for quetzales, Belize dollars and Mexican pesos on the street, but better at the Banco de Guatemala office at the border, open 0800-1400, Monday-Thursday, to 1430 Friday. Street changers accept travellers' cheque when the bank is closed.

Transport There are several buses from Santa Elena to Melchor de Mencos, starting at 0500, about 2½-3 hours including breakfast stop, US$2.65. Bus from Melchor de Mencos to Flores include Autobuses de Rosita, on main street near *Hotel Mayab* or better at the market. These buses call at El Cruce/Puente Ixlú (the turn off for Tikal). Bus El Cruce to Tikal US$1.80, El Cruce to Melchor de Mencos, US$2. Connecting buses for San Ignacio, Belmopan and Belize City wait at Melchor de Mencos (if you catch the 0500 bus from Santa Elena you can be in Belize City by noon). In addition, there is a non-stop minibus service at 0500 from Santa Elena to Belize City, reserve previous day with travel agents, cost US$20. This service terminates at the A&R Station in Belize from where boats to the Cayes leave. Note that all buses stop at the border, there is no need to take a taxi or walk to the bus station in Melchor de Mencos.

To Mexico through Belize There is a bus at 0500 direct to Chetumal, Mexico, arriving 1300 (Mexican time), US$30, plus US$3.50 to leave Belize. If you don't take this direct bus, from Flores or Tikal to Chetumal in a day is possible if the 0500 bus from Flores to Melchor de Mencos, or 0630 from Tikal (change at El Cruce) connects with a bus at 0920 from the border to Belize City, from where you can take an afternoon bus to Chetumal. Total cost about US$12, 12 hours. You may be able to lower the price by taking slower, cheaper transport at the risk of not getting to Mexico the same day.

To Mexico through El Petén

A rough, unpaved road runs 160 kilometres west from Flores to **El Naranjo** on the Río San Pedro, a centre for oil exploration, unfriendly, near the Mexican border. There is a big army base there. At *Posada San Pedro* (see below – under same ownership as *Maya Internacional* in Santa Elena) there is information, group travel, guides, and arrangements for travel as far as Palenque. Electricity is turned off at 2200. An orphanage, run by an American and his Guatemalan wife, advertises for volunteers in *Doña Luisa's*, Antigua (they have a clinic, school, garden, etc).

Guatemalan immigration Immigration office near the landing stage in the same building as the hotel.

Frontier with Mexico – El Naranjo/ La Palma

Sleeping & eating F *Quetzal*, by the dock, basic, poor service, overpriced restaurant, bathe in river. Several even more basic *hospedajes* in town, but across the river, upstream from the ferry. **D** *Posada San Pedro* has neat, simple *cabañas* with mosquito nets, T9261276 in Flores, T3341823 in Guatemala City. The restaurant by the dugouts is expensive, others in town better value.

Exchange You can change money at the grocery store opposite immigration, which will give you a better US$/Q rate than the Mexican side of the border. Even so, rates here are poor. Better to buy pesos in Flores.

Transport Pinita buses leave Santa Elena from *Hotel San Juan* for El Naranjo, daily at 0500, 1000, 1200, 1400, 4 hours, US$3. To be sure of a seat you are better off heading to the marketplace where you can pick up Del Rosío buses until 1600. The bus drops you at the side of the ruins (adorned with machine gun posts) by the dock. Several travellers have said that there is no point in getting the 0500 bus if going to Mexico because the boat almost always waits for the arrival of the next bus. Boat is supposed to leave for Mexico at around 1300, but often goes about 1400. Probably what happens is that the boat leaves when full, so if there are many travellers leaving Santa Elena, better get the earlier bus. There are buses back to Santa Elena at 0200, 0400, 0600, 1100 and 1400.

From El Naranjo, daily boats leave at 0600 and sometime around 1300, for La Palma in Mexico, US$22, cheaper to pay in quetzales, 4-5 hours including Mexican border crossing, from where buses go to Tenosique and on to Palenque. **NB** The 1300 boat will often get you to La Palma just in time to miss the last bus to Tenosique, be prepared to stay the night. If there are fewer than 5 passengers for the boat, it may be cancelled and your alternatives are to wait for the next boat, or hire a *rápido*, maximum 6 persons US$125. Return from La Palma to El Naranjo at 0800, 1400. Bus La Palma-Tenosique at 1700, and one other, also *colectivos*; it is not possible to go to Palenque the same day unless you hire a taxi in La Palma. Mexican tourist cards can be obtained at the border. Beautiful trip, but take waterproofs, a torch and some food with you. Beware mosquitoes. Expect thorough searches on both sides of the border. Depending on the level of the water, this can be an exciting trip through the narrower, rocky stretches. Look for the border marked by a straight line cleared up to a distant white obelisk.

The **Laguna del Tigre National Park and Biotopo** is a vast area of jungle and wetlands north of El Naranjo. The best place to stay is the Cecon camp, the headquarters of the *biotopo*, across the river below the ferry; a boy will paddle you over in a canoe. This is where the guards live and they will let you stay in the bunk house and use their kitchen. Getting into the reserve is not easy and you will need to be equipped for a week or more, but a few people (occasionally scientists) go up the Río Escondido. The lagoons abound in wildlife, including enormous crocodiles and spectacular birdlife. There is a cluster of ruins near the border, extremely difficult to reach.

Laguna del Tigre

Frontier with Further south, another route leads into the Mexican state of Chiapas. There are two
Mexico – Río points on the Río Usumacinta which you can reach by launch and continue by bus
Usumacinta into Mexico. They are Benemérito de las Américas (frontier post upstream at
Pipiles) and Frontera Echeverría (immigration office near the wharf). You are
advised, however, to get your exit stamp in Flores and your visa or free Mexican
tourist card in advance.

For the first option, take a bus from Santa Elena via La Libertad to **Bethel** (regular
Pinita bus service, 0500, 1100, five hours, US$4); ask the driver to drop you at immi-
gration while he drives around the village, then collect you for the 20-minutes ride to
La Técnica village (an extra US$1.10) though this road was closed (poor state) in
early 1998 and the boat trip started at Bethel. From here it is a five minute ferry ride
to **Frontera Echeverría/Corozal** on the Río Usumacinta. Immigration at Bethel
charges US$3/Q15 exit tax. In Bethel there is lodging at the **E** *Posada Maya*, just over
one kilometre outside the village run by the village co-op as part of an eco-tourism
project, the only place to stay but a bit inconvenient, superb setting, open-sided
thatched shelters with tents or hammocks and mosquito nets, all with clean sheets,
built in plaza of a Maya site overlooking the river, *cabañas*, mainly used by passing
tour groups. If you need to stay in the village you can borrow a hammock from a
comedor or camp by the riverbank. There are guides with horses to take you to
nearby attractions, including a lovely *cenote*; further afield are more ruins in the jungle. Bethel itself has sizeable ruins. Bus leaves Bethel for Flores at 1200. You get your
Mexican immigration stamp at Corozal. A dirt road leads up 18 kilometres to the
Frontier Highway (35 kilometres to the San Javier junction for Lacanjá and
Bonampak). From Frontera Echeverría it is six to eight hours by bus to Palenque,
US$5. **NB** The 0500 bus from Santa Elena does not get you to Bethel for an onward
connection to Palenque. You have to wait until the 0400 direct bus from Frontera
Echeverría next morning. However, there are often pickups and the main road has
buses day and night; also try tour buses.

Alternatively, go from Santa Elena to Sayaxché, 61 kilometres (see below), then
take a boat down the Río de la Pasión to the military post at **Pipiles** (exit stamps must
be given here) and on to the town of **Benemérito** on the Río Usumacinta (trading
boat twice a week US$4-5, two days; motorized cargo canoe US$5-10, eight hours;
private launch US$100, four hours). The trading boats (maize) give a good insight
into riverside life, stopping frequently at hamlets to drop and pick up passengers.
Grapefruit are in such plentiful supply that no one bothers to sell them (still, it is
polite to ask before picking them up off the ground). If stuck at Pipiles, a farmer who
lives 800 metres upstream may take you to Benemérito in his launch. If there is more
than one maize boat at Pipiles move up to the first one because they often wait up to
three days to get a better price. At Benemérito, a shop near the river lets out rooms at
the back, no electricity, water from well. From Benemérito, buses go at 0600, 0700,
0800 and 1300 to immigration just past the Río Lacantún (or hitch in a truck); buses
wait here before continuing to Palenque. Unpaved road, seven to 12 hours by bus
Benemérito-Palenque (more in the wet). There are also boats from Sayaxché to
Frontera Echeverría/Corozal, but they charge from US$275 for a 20-seater. Get
Mexican tourist card in advance to avoid offering bribes at border, and get your exit
visa in Flores. Take also hammock, mosquito net, food and insect repellent; the only
accommodation between Sayaxché and Palenque is a basic room in Benemérito,
and dollars cannot be exchanged. Yaxchilán and Bonampak in Mexico can be visited from the road Benemérito-Palenque.

Sayaxché Sayaxché is a good centre for visiting the Petén, whether your interest is in the wild-
Colour map 4, grid B3 life or the Maya ruins. To cross the ferry near the village costs US$2 for a car (free for
motorcycles); foot passengers US$0.10. Fiesta 5-13 June.

Sleeping & eating All places are pretty grim. **E** *Guayacán*, known locally as *Hotel de
Godoy* after the owner Julio Godoy, T928-6111, is a good source of information on the area,

on south bank of river, close to ferry, 2 rooms with bathrooms, new rooms built, but pretty basic.

F *Mayapán*, friendly, clean, basic, rents bicycles to visit El Ceibal US$5 per day. **F** *Yaxkín*, with fan, cheaper without, good food, friendly, cheap, owner speaks English, very informative.

F (under US$3) *Casa de Huéspedes Carmen Kilkan*, near the football field, very friendly, no running water or electricity, rats, otherwise OK!, camping permitted, US$0.75 pp, ask there for Juanita (American), knowledgeable, will arrange trips and accompany you. **F** *Hotel Sayaxché*, basic, dirty, food not bad. *Restaurant Montaña*, Julián Mariona Morán, T/F9266114, will give you information, he also owns **A** *Posada Caribe* at Laguna Petexbatún (see below). If travelling south, stock up with fruit in the market and, if driving, fuel at the service station.

Transport Buses: There are buses to and from Guatemala City via Sebol from 0700 when conditions allow. You can also catch pickup trucks to Sebol from 0630 or earlier, 7½ hours, terrible road, police checks, reported great fun (especially on an off-road bike)! Also buses to and from Santa Elena, Flores, 0600, 1300 (US$0.80, 3 hours); La Pinita has a bus to Flores, US$2 (intermittent transport south in the rainy season), but note that Pinita has a policy of charging foreign tourists double the normal fare. If hitching to Flores, try for a ride on an oil truck at the river crossing in Sayaxché to La Libertad (oil refinery), then truck or bus to Flores.

River *Viajes Don Pedro* runs launches to El Ceibal, Petexbatún and Aguateca, 4 hours, and 2-day trips to Yaxchilán (in Mexico). Although Don Pedro organizes interesting jungle tours, his son, the guide, tends to change the plans and alter the length of the trip once you have started. *Viajes Turísticos La Montaña* (Julián Mariona Morán, see above); good guide Antonio Chiquín Cocul, at *Hotel Guayacán*, good tours to Maya sites, US$7 per person.

Driving Flores-Cobán: take the road from Santa Elena to Sayaxché, unpaved, lots of potholes, dusty (don't follow a truck), many oil transporters, especially near the La Libertad intersection to Bethel. In Sayaxché the road to Cobán is signed (200 km): go left for Cobán. After a few kilometres is an intersection to El Ceibal. The road improves up to the first mountain ridge. Keep asking for the road to Sebol, which is better than the direct route to Cobán via Chisec. At all times, ask directions. Do not drive at night, there is a real danger of getting lost and of hitting cattle. Petrol/gasoline is available in La Libertad and Sayaxché.

Directory Banks You can change US$ bills at various places in town and TCs at the bank. Pesos can be bought in the store *La Moderna* or *Hotel Guayacán*.

Up the Río de la Pasión from Sayaxché is El Ceibal (also known as Seibal in the **El Ceibal** archaeological literature), where the ruins were excavated by Peabody Museum and Harvard. The ceremonial site is about one and a half kilometres from the left bank of Río de la Pasión and extends for one and a half square kilometres. One of the main structures to be seen is the 30 metres temple, partially restored, with four staircases, linked by a sacbé (causeway) to an unusual circular pyramid, believed to be unique in the Petén. Some of the best preserved *stelae* in Guatemala are found in a jungle park setting. Only about two percent of the site has been reconstructed. There is now a difficult road linking Sayaxché with El Ceibal – impassable in the wet (leave bus at El Paraíso on the main road – local pick-up from Sayaxché US$0.20 – then walk to the ruins, a further seven kilometres, one and a half hours) so the trip can be made either by road or by river (launch hire US$35 round trip four passengers, two hours each way – *pensión* **F**). You can sling a hammock at El Ceibal and use the guard's fire for making coffee if you ask politely – a mosquito net is advisable, and take repellent for walking in the jungle surroundings. If you leave belongings at El Ceibal, make sure they are in reliable care, theft is not uncommon. Tours can be arranged in Flores for a day visit to Sayaxché and El Ceibal but there is limited time to see the site (US$30-40 per person).

From Sayaxché the ruins of the **Altar de Sacrificios** at the confluence of the Ríos de la Pasión and Usumacinta can also be reached. Also within reach of Sayaxché is **Itzán**, discovered in 1968. Further down the Río Usumacinta is Yaxchilán, just over the border in Mexico (temples still standing, with sculptures and carved lintels – see Mexico, page 450, **Yucatán Peninsula**). You can sometimes talk your way onto one of the boats leaving Corozal (see above) with a tour group aboard to visit Yaxchilán. Best to have good Spanish, but you will pay less than the tour party.

Piedras Negras Still further down the Río Usumacinta in the west of Petén is Piedras Negras, a huge Classic period site. It has been saved from the major looting which afflicted most other sites in Petén by its role as a base for guerrillas during Guatemala's protracted insurgency. With the signing of the peace treaty, a five year research project, undertaken by Prof Stephen Houston of Brigham Young University and Dr Héctor Escobedo of San Carlos University, has recently begun. In the 1930s Tatiana Proskouriakoff first recognized that the periods of time inscribed on stelae here coincided with human life spans or reigns, and so began the task of deciphering the meaning of Maya glyphs. Until 1997 no research had taken place at Piedras Negras since 1939. The site on a cliff high above the river is today one of the best places to observe how modern archaeological techniques interpret the Maya world. If plans to construct hydroelectric dams on the Usumacinta go ahead, this and many other sites will be inundated.

Advance arrangements are necessary with a rafting company to reach Piedras Negras. Maya Expeditions in Guatemala City (address on page 601), is the official tour operator for the project; they run two week expeditions, taking in a number of sites, including Piedras Negras, where they provide logistic support for the current archaeological research. Each participant contributes US$200 towards the project's expenses, an amount matched by Maya Expeditions. The archaeologists give special tours and presentations and visitors are given full details of the latest research. This trip is a real adventure. The riverbanks are covered in the best remaining tropical forest in Guatemala, inhabited by elusive wildlife and hiding more ruins. Once you've rafted down to Piedras Negras, you have to raft out. Though most of the river is fairly placid, there are the 30 metres Busilhá Falls, where a crystal clear tributary cascades over limestone terraces, and two deep canyons, with impressive rapids to negotiate, before reaching the take-out two days later.

Laguna Petexbatún The Río de la Pasión is a good route to visit other, more recently discovered Maya ruins. From Laguna Petexbatún (16 kilometres), a fisherman's paradise, which can be reached by outboard canoe from Sayaxché (US$10 or more for six people and luggage) excursions can be made to unexcavated ruins: these include **Arroyo de la Piedra** (a small site with a number of mounds and stelae, between Sayaxché and Dos Pilas), **Dos Pilas** itself (many well-preserved stelae, important tomb find of a King here in 1991), **Aguateca**, where the ruins are so far little excavated, giving a feeling of authenticity, and where an excursion can be made over the only known Maya bridge and down into a huge chasm. Lagoon fishing includes 150-lb tarpon, snoek and local varieties. Many interesting birds, including toucan and *guacamayo*.

Sleeping Highly recommended is **A** *Posada Caribe*, run by Julián Mariona Morán, T9260436, T/F9286114, including 3 meals, comfortable *cabañas* with bathroom and shower, excursion to Aguateca by launch and a guide for jungle excursions where you can see lots of animals and birds. The only other hotel, **AL** *Posada Mateos*, with bath, hot water, electricity, in bungalows, T9260505, or can be booked in advance by tour agencies. Jungle guides can be hired for US$1.50-2.50 per day. Camping is possible at Escobado, on the lakeside, occasional public launches from Sayaxché. Take water and food.

Sebol
Colour map 4, grid B3
100 kilometres northeast of Cobán, 50 kilometres north of Lanquín is Sebol from where roads go north into the Petén and east to Izabal. There is nowhere to stay in Sebol but, if you get stuck there, ask at the control station (the big house) if you may

sleep on the floor. The Río Sebol (part of the Río de la Pasión system) offers good bathing a short distance to the north (follow the signs to La Playa). Two hours north at Balneario Las Islas there is also good swimming and walks, well signposted, crowded at weekends, good camping, good *comedor* (US$3 by boat, one and a half to two hours). On 24 August, all-night mass is celebrated in Sebol (free food at 0100) with games played on the church lawn in the daylight hours.

10 kilometres from Sebol is **Fray Bartolomé de Las Casas** (**F** *Hospedaje Ralíos*, shared bath, OK. **F** *Damelito*, on main plaza, own generator, clean friendly, good breakfast. **F** *Evelyne*, main street, no meals, restaurants), a pleasant village which has a *fiesta* from 30 April-4 May with a parade and rodeo on 1 May. No bus service to Fray Bartolomé from 16 January to end of wet season, bargain with pick-up drivers to/from Sebol. There is an airstrip nearby, charters possible. A rough dirt road links Sebol with Sayaxché via **Raxrujá**, 'a hole', with strong military presence. Most of this 120-kilometres road is in poor condition, particularly the section from Raxrujá to (Cruce) El Pato. Thereafter going north, the road improves though it can be very difficult in the wet season (coming south it is often not possible to travel Sayaxché-Sebol in one day and you get stuck overnight in Raxrujá, from where transport only leaves in the morning). Hitching with oil tankers is possible. Near Raxrujá is an extensive river cave. In the wet season there is occasional boat transport Sebol-El Pato-Sayaxché.

Sleeping All under US$3 **In Raxrujá**: **F** *Pensión Aguas Verdes*, basic, pleasant. **F** *Pensión La Reina*, rough, no water, dirty, bad. Good *pensión* near bridge, **F** pp, no bath (except the river!) *comedor* opposite. Many *comedores*, for example *El Piloto*, good, meal US$1. *El Ganadero*, quite good. In **El Pato**: 2 *hospedajes*, first at the port, dirty, monkey in garden; second at **F** *Farmacia Margarita/Hospedaje El Amigo*, better, basic, mosquito net necessary, owner's son has pick-up transport. Good *comedor*, **Tonito**, behind soccer field.

Transport Local transport connects most of these towns, but do not travel at night and always ask about security. From Sayaxché there are buses at 0600, 0730 and 1430 to within 20 km of Raxrujá, at which point you have to change to a pick-up because buses cannot cope with the road; there are also pick-ups all the way, check times, several a day, 6 hours, US$2.60; after about 2½ hours is a road junction with a *comedor*, at least 2 buses a day from here to Sayaxché (1 at midday), 3½ hours. There are many more roads in this area than maps show, there are also military camps, so expect occasional checks by the army. El Pato-Raxrujá, minibus 0500 daily; Raxrujá-Sebol, occasional bus, US$0.40, pick-up from 0700 more common, US$0.75 (very bad road, 2 hours for 25 km) or El Pato-Sebol. Fray B de Las Casas-Cobán, 0500, 9 hours, US$1.50 (Cobán-Sebol at 0530). You can also go from Lanquín to Sayaxché via Pajal, Las Casas, Sebol and Raxrujá (see page 624), not recommended as a 1-day journey, better to rest in Raxrujá. The road from Raxrujá via Chisec to Cobán is very steep and rocky. Part, over the Sierra de Chamá, is known as the staircase! It is passable in the dry season with high clearance vehicle (not advisable for a standard car). In the wet even four-wheel drives cannot manage this road. Recommended for spectacular scenery but you need lots of time. Even well after the wet season, ie mid-January, a bus may not be able to get all the way from Sayaxché to Cobán, even though tickets may be sold. Pick-ups will do the trip via Chisec, 11-12 hours, US$4, a terrible squash, but ask as many people as possible before embarking if a bus is running via Sebol. **Chisec** to Cobán takes five hours driving in normal conditions.There is a petrol station in Chisec (on the right heading for Cobán). The owner of *Pinchazo* workshop also owns *Costa Sur* hotel and restaurant, on right entering from Sayaxché; meals US$1, car park outside, friendly, good advice on road conditions. From Sebol, there is an 0300 bus to Poptún (see page 639), via Fray Bartolomé de Las Casas and San Luis (on the Morales-Río Dulce-Poptún-Flores road). This route is impassable in the rainy season. From San Luis there is an 0630 bus to Flores, stopping at Poptún (4½ hours). It is easy to get a ride on one of the many trucks which run on all these routes. You can also go from Sebol to Modesto Méndez on the Morales-Flores road but it is extremely slow going because of potholes, winding narrow roads and big rocks (very difficult in the wet).

Guatemala
City

Southern Guatemala

*From Guatemala City to San Salvador, and to the Pacific ports of San José and Puerto
Quetzal: some of the busiest roads in the country passing through major agricultural
areas. Several beach resorts, and bird and turtle reserves near Monterrico.*

Routes to El Salvador

There are three routes through Southern Guatemala to El Salvador. Much of it is
delightful coffee country with pine-dominated forests on the many old volcanoes.
The southern route runs along the inland side of the coastal plain which has many
sugar plantations and cattle ranches. Inland some lower land is noticeably dry. The
main towns are busy but scruffy with little to attract the visitor.

Route 1: The first route is the paved Pan-American Highway through Barberena (with many
Pan-American flowering trees along the road and fruit stalls near the villages) and Cuilapa which
Highway keeps to the crest of the ridges most of the way to the border, 166 kilometres.

65 kilometres along the Highway is **Cuilapa**, capital of Santa Rosa Department.
There is a busy market at the top end of the town. **E** *Hospedaje Posada K-Luy*, 4 C,
1-166, T8865372, clean, comfortable, parking, friendly owner, cable TV. Opposite
is the family grocery store as clean and smart as the *hospedaje*. A few kilometres
beyond Cuilapa the Highway crosses the Río de los Esclavos by a bridge first built in
the 16th century. At **Los Esclavos** is **C** *Turicentro Los Esclavos*, T8865139,
F8865158, pool, hot water, good restaurant, a/c. It overlooks a deep river gorge
which has been dammed on the other side of the road, making an attractive tourist
spot. The Turicentro is popular at weekends.

50 kilometres on is **Jutiapa** (*population*: 9,200), a pleasant, lively town with a big
food market in Zona 3; at least 6 hotels/*hospedajes* nearby, for example **B** *Linda
Vista*, 4 Av, 3-55, Zona 3, T8444312, F8441115, a/c, parking. **C** *Del Sol*, Km 117
Carretera Panamericana, T8441507, hot water, restaurant. **E** *Ordóñez*, 4 C, 8-33,
Zona 3, T8441273, a/c, restaurant, parking. **D** *Posada del Peregrino*, C 15 de
Septiembre 0-30, Zona 3, T8441770. **E** *Posada Belén*, T8442946. Beyond, it goes
through the villages of El Progreso, dominated by the imposing Volcán Suchitán,
2042 metres (**E** *Najarro*, 2 C/7 Av), and Asunción Mita, where another road runs left
to Lago de Güija. Between Jutiapa and El Progreso is the *Centro Turístico Guantepec*,
swimming pool and restaurant, camping permitted (free). Before reaching the border at San Cristóbal it dips and skirts the shores (right) of **Lago Atescatempa**, an
irregular sheet of water with several islands and set in heavy forest. Most of this section of the Pan-American was resurfaced in 1998/9 and is in excellent condition.
From the border to San Salvador is 100 kilometres.

Frontier with El As the Pan-American Highway, this is the principal crossing between the two coun-
Salvador – San tries. Heavy transport and international buses favour this route.
Cristóbal

Tourist offices There is a tourist office (Inguat) by the border, who will advise you on
accommodation and travel.

Guatemalan immigration Open 0600-2000 but it is usually possible to cross outside
these hours with additional charges.

Transport Local services on the Guatemalan side are poor but hitchhikers should have no problem.

At El Progreso, a good paved road goes north 43 km to Jalapa (see page 629) through open, mostly dry country, with volcanoes always in view. There are several interesting crater lakes eg Laguna del Hoyo near Monjas, well worth a visit. The higher ground is forested, the air is transparent, it is a pleasant area off the beaten track.

A right turn after Cuilapa (just before Los Esclavos) towards Chiquimulilla (road No 16, with old trees on either side, some with orchids in them) leads after 20 kilometres to a sign to Ixpaco. A two to three-kilometre steep, narrow, dirt road goes to the **Laguna de Ixpaco**, an impressive, greenish-yellow lake, boiling in some places, emitting sulphurous fumes, set in dense forest. There is a bus service. Continue south along this winding road to Chiquimulilla, a delightful trip through coffee fincas and farmland.

Route 2: via Jalpatagua

The second, quicker way of getting to San Salvador is to take a paved highway which cuts off right from the first route at Molino, about seven kilometres beyond the Esclavos bridge. This cut-off goes through El Oratorio and **Jalpatagua** (**E** *Posada de Don Meme*, 4 Av 2-40, T8419180, restaurant; **F** *El Centenario*, clean, a/c, pool) to the border, continuing then to Ahuachapán and San Salvador.

Frontier with El Salvador – Valle Nuevo/ Chinamas

Since the construction of the Santa Ana bypass, this has become a popular route for lighter traffic between the two countries.

Guatemalan immigration We have heard that bargaining with officials can reduce the costs of transit.

Sleeping F *Motel Martha*, 15 kilometres into Guatemala, pool, excellent breakfast.

Directory Tourist offices There is a helpful tourist office on the Salvadorean side.

Route 3: the coastal route to El Salvador

The third route goes southwest from Guatemala City past Amatitlán to Escuintla where it joins the Pacific Highway. East from Escuintla the road is paved through Guazacapán to the border bridge over the Río Paz at La Hachadura (El Salvador), then through the coastal plain to Sonsonate and on to San Salvador, 290 kilometres in all; this road gives excellent views of the volcanoes. It takes two hours from Escuintla to the border.

30 kilometres east of Escuintla is the **Parque Auto Safari Chapín**, an improbable wildlife park, well patronized at weekends and holidays. 18 kilometres beyond is **Taxisco**, just off the road, a busy place which has an interesting white church with a curious hearts and holly design on the façade. Several banks on the Plaza Central, food and lodging very basic. Nearby, however, at Km 114 is **D** *Baru*, pool, a/c, restaurant nearby. To the east is Guazacapán which merges into **Chiquimulilla**, three kilometres to the north, the most important town of the area. There are good quality leather goods available (**E** *San Carlos*, Barrio Santiago, T/F8850187, 24 rooms, restaurant).

30 kilometres beyond at **Pedro de Alvarado** (formerly Pijije) on the border there are several *hospedajes* (all under US\$3, basic).

Frontier with El Salvador – Pedro de Alvarado/ La Hachadura

This is becoming a busier crossing as roads on both sides have improved. Transit is normally straightforward. There is basic accommodation on both sides and food at the service station restaurant. However, it is not recommended that you plan to stay here. The last bus for Sonsonate in El Salvador leaves at 1800.

See **Getting around** in **Essentials** for entry and exit procedures with a vehicle. It is possible to leave Guatemala without the aid of the 'helpers' who hang around this border.

Guatemala City to the Pacific Coast

The first part of this route to Escuintla is one of the busiest roads in the country, paved throughout, much of it a divided highway. It connects the capital with all the Pacific ports and with the most important agricultural area of the country. During the past few years, this route has been substantially improved, by passing Villa Nueva and Amatitlán. For the main descent from Palín to west of Escuintla there is a new *autopista* (motorway toll for cars, US$1). There is an impressive panorama of the coastal plain on the way down and fabulous views of Fuego, Agua and Pacaya volcanoes on the way up.

The old road can still be used below Villa Nueva, the turn off is about two kilometres south. In a short distance, straight ahead is the United Nations Park, entry US$0.30, children US$0.20, sadly neglected, but still a good place for a picnic and with a grand view over Lago Amatitlán towards Pacaya. There is a *teleférico* (cable car) to the Park from the town, built in 1978, still operating Saturday-Sunday, 1000-1700. From the Park, the road drops steeply down to:

Amatitlán
Population: 12,225
Altitude: 1,240m
Colour map 4, grid C3

The town is 27 kilometres by road southwest of the capital, on Lake Amatitlán, 12 by four kilometres (but diminishing in size as a result of sedimentation in the Río Villalobos which drains into it – caused by deforestation). Fishing and boating; bathing is not advisable, as the water has become seriously contaminated. Sunday boat trips cost US$1, or less, for 30 minutes; beware of people offering boat trips which last no more than 10 minutes. Very popular and colourful at weekends. The thermal springs on the lake side, with groves of trees and coffee plantations, feed pools which *are* safe to bathe in. The lake is surrounded by picturesque chalets with lawns to the water's edge. A mostly dirt road goes round the lake; a branch runs to the slopes of Pacaya volcano, US$0.15 by bus (see page 616). The town has two famous ceiba trees; one is in Parque Morazán. Bank changes dollars cash but not travellers' cheques. Buses from Guatemala City (every 30 minutes, US$0.20) go right to the lakeside. **Fiestas** *Santa Cruz*, 1-7 May.

Sleeping D *Blanquita*, on the road to Guatemala City, with bath. E *Amatitlán*, 3 blocks from *Karla*, parking inside, dirty bathrooms, overpriced, friendly but noisy. D *Los Arcos y Anexo Rocareña*, T6330337, a weird concrete building set against the hillside by the outlet of the lake, comfortable rooms, cheaper without view, with bath, pool, a/c, parking, restaurant. E *Motel Seul*, Km 27.5. F *Hospedaje Don Leonel*, 8 C, 3-25, shared bath, clean, secure. F *Hospedaje y Comedor Kati*, clean, pleasant dining room. F *Pensión Karla*, clean, friendly, family-run.

Eating Many restaurants are near the lake, beware of local fish because of water pollution.

Palín

Palín, 14½ kilometres from Amatitlán, has a Sunday Indian market in a plaza under an enormous ceiba tree. Grand views to east, of Pacaya, to northwest, of Agua volcano, to west, of Pacific lowland. Power plant at Michatoya falls below town. An unpaved road runs northwest to Antigua through Santa María de Jesús (see page 614). See the old Franciscan church (1560). *Fiestas*: 25-30 July, and movable feasts of Holy Trinity and Sacred Heart. Textiles here are exceptional, but are becoming hard to find. F *Pensión Señorial*, basic. F *Napolitana*, also basic. F *Miramonte*, C Central, friendly.

Escuintla, 18 kilometres from Palín on the road to San José, is a large, rather ugly provincial centre in a rich tropical valley. There is a large market on Sunday, and a daily market over two blocks. Near the market is the police HQ, fortress-like, painted sky blue. Marimbas frequently play in the central plaza. The local banana bread is worth trying and *basitas*, real fruit ice-lollies. The town is now circled on three sides by new highways relieving the centre of much traffic though it is still very busy, with lots of streetlife, eating places, bars (many with prostitutes from San Salvador) and, at weekends, much drunkenness. Agua volcano looms to the north. Road north to Antigua. There is a meat packing and several industrial plants.

Escuintla
Population: 62,500
Altitude: 335m
Colour map 4, grid C2

Sleeping A *Sarita*, Av Centroamérica 15-32, Zona 3, T8880482, F8881959, pool (day use US$3), a/c, good restaurant, popular with passing travellers. **C** *Texas*, Av Centroamérica, 15-04, T8880183, more modest version of nearby *Sarita*.

D *Costa Sur*, 12 C, 4-13, Zona 1, T8881819, a/c, TV, clean, friendly owner, speaks English, good value.

E *Istcuintlan*, 4 Av, 6-30, next to Bancafé, with bath, fan, clean, sparsely furnished, courteous owner speaks English. **E** *Rosario*, 4 Av, 11-46, looks OK. **E** *Las Rosas*, 4 Av, 11-21, about 400m from bus terminal heading into town, for a clean, basic room, better rooms also.

Eating *Pizzería Al Macarone*, 4 Av, 6-103, modern, smart, excellent pizzas and pastas, Italian ice cream, set lunch US$2, good value. *Los Camarones*, 4 Av, 10-90, seafood at reasonable prices, spacious dining area, off street parking. *Cevichería El Delfín*, 1 C, 3-87, clean, good *caldo de mariscos*. Recommended. *Chungking*, 4 Av 4-41, Chinese, good, inexpensive, also operates adjoining well stocked supermarket. *Chop Suey*, 4 Av, 11-16, good oriental. *La Fuente*, 4 Av, 3-10, also Chinese, pleasant modern setting. *Pastelería Diveli*, 3 Av, just off central plaza. *Martita*, Av Centroaméricán, 6-01, Zona 3, good café open for breakfast. Earliest for breakfast is *Campero*, 4 Av, 5-21, open at 0700. Several other sandwich places with good milk shakes.

Festivals 6 (holiday) to 15 December.

Transport Many buses to the capital (US$0.50) also direct to Antigua at 0700, US$0.60 (poor road).

Directory Banks Banco G&T, 4 Av, 2 C. Others on 4 Av. *Banco Industrial, Banco del Agro, Banco Occidente, Banco Continental*. Most change TCs and service Visa/Mastercard. **Embassies & consulates** Consulate: *El Salvador*, 16 C, 3-20, near the Esso Station, will issue visas. *Honduras*, 6 Av, 8-24.

The Pacific Highway goes west to the Mexican border at Tecún Umán (200 kilometres). As a route to Mexico, it is shorter, faster and easier to drive, but hotter and much less picturesque than the El Tapón route to the north. The road is a fine four lane divided highway to Siquinalá (to be extended), and a good, fast, recently improved trunk road thereafter to the border. Although busy, apart from completion of some bridges and maintenance, this is an excellent road. If driving, take care in towns that have not yet been bypassed and be wary of the large, decrepit tractor-trailers carrying sugar cane to the several large mills in the season.

Puerto San José to Monterrico

South of Esquintla, the road and a new highway built in 1991 continue south to **San José** (*population*: 8,000), 52 kilometres beyond Escuintla, 109 kilometres by road from the capital. The new highway, which leads directly to Puerto Quetzal, was being widened to four lanes in 1999.

San José used to be the country's second largest port. The climate is hot, the streets and most of the beaches dirty and at weekends the town fills up with people from the

San José
Colour map 4, grid C2

capital. Fishing, swimming, though beware the strong undercurrent. San José has the big disadvantage of requiring most ships to anchor offshore and discharge by lighter. A new harbour, **Puerto Quetzal**, to take all shipping alongside, has been completed, three kilometres to the east, although the oil terminal remains at San José. Restaurants near the entrance to Puerto Quetzal: *Cafetería Sol y Mar*, seafood specialities; *Taberna Tarro Dorado*, Km 115, open air deck, seafood etc.

Sleeping AL *Turicentro Agua Azul*, Km 106, T/F8811667, 4 different swimming pools, food reasonable, 32 rooms. **A** *Posada Quetzal*, Av 30 de Junio, 1 Av, T8811892, F8811601, pool, restaurant. **A** *Posada Quetzal II*, Barrio Miramar No 26, same T and F as above, 500m from the mole. Recommended. **A** *Eden Pacific*, Barrio El Laberinto, T8811605, pools, beach cabins, guarded parking. **A** *Turicentro Martita*, 5 C, Av del Comercio, Lote No 26, T/F8811504, hot water, pool, restaurant. **B** *Real Toledo*, Barrio Peñate, T8811405, hot water, pool, restaurant. **B** *Perla del Mar*, Av del Comercio 8-38, 100m from beach, T8811011, a/c, garage. **D** *Casa San José*, Av del Comercio, 9 C, T7765587, beside the railway bridge, with bath, fan, cable TV, restaurant, try their *caldo de mariscos*, bar, parking. **D** *Papillon*, Barrio Miramar, T8811064, on the beach, with bath, fan, bar, restaurant. **E** *Viñas del Mar*, on the beach, with bath, run down, friendly. **F** *Veracruz*, on the main street, very basic, dark but friendly. No accommodation at present in Puerto Quetzal.

Eating Best food is in the hotels for example *Papillon*, on the beach, serves *cacerolas* (fish and shrimp soup). Plenty of other places on the beach.

Festivals 16-22 March, when town is crowded and hotel accommodation difficult to get.

Transport Buses San José-**Guatemala City** (Transportes Unidas), half hourly from 0530, US$1.50, 2 hours; from **Iztapa** to San José US$0.12. To **Escuintla**, US$0.50.

Five kilometres to the west of San José is **Chulamar**, a popular beach at weekends, good bathing. **LL** *Radisson Villas del Pacífico*, on the beach at the west end of town, T8813131, full board, cheaper midweek, private beach, beautiful gardens, many facilities. **B** *Santa María del Mar*, T8811283, chalets and rooms, a/c, pools, restaurant, private beach with changing facilities (US$6 for day ticket). Many new houses are being built. It is lifeless during the week with nowhere but expensive resorts to stay.

13 kilometres to the east of San José is the smart resort of **Likin**, which fronts on both the Chiquimulilla canal and the Pacific. The construction of Puerto Quetzal has altered the configuration of the coast and the outer beach, with bungalows and restaurant, is being severely eroded by tides and sand, further damaged by the 1998 hurricane. Likin and the adjacent resort of San Marino are not open to the public, only by owners' invitation.

Iztapa An interesting trip can be taken through Chiquimulilla canal by launch from the old Spanish port of Iztapa, now a bathing resort a short distance to the east. At Iztapa you can camp on the beach (take great care if bathing, waves are particularly dangerous along this coast) and rent launches. Buy food before crossing. Much damage to the canal banks was done by the 1998 hurricane, with buildings collapsing into the water. Flood damage in the town had not been cleared six months later. It is a bleak place to visit at present. If going further east by road along the coast, you need to cross the canal by ferry which takes cars.

Sleeping L *Fins 'n' Feathers Inn*, Aldea Buena Vista, T8811832, pool, restaurant, parking etc. **D** *Sol y Playa*, 1 C, 5-48, on canal, with swimming pool, friendly staff, rooms OK, good food, interesting view from roof. **F** *Pollo Andra*, owned by Tex Mex (from Tennessee), nice beds, overhead fans, attached restaurant, good fish, good value. **E** *Brasilia*, 1C, 4-27, Zona 1, basic. Some local people may put you up. Cabins along the beach for hire but few have water and they are very rustic.

Eating *Marina del Capitán*, good *ceviches*, packed lunches for fishing trips. *Playa Grande* is similar.

It is possible to cross the inlet at Iztapa (US$0.30 for foot passengers, US$3 for a car) **Monterrico** and take the dirt/sand road to Monterrico, about 25 kilometres east. This road is impassible when waterlogged and equally when the sand is too dry, but you may be lucky – there is a bus route. The best approach to **Monterrico** is from Taxisco on the main lowland route to El Salvador and thence to La Avellana, 19 kilometres. It is a small black sand resort (beach shoes advisable), a few shops and *comedores*. Its popularity is growing fast but mainly as a weekend and holiday resort. Bird and turtle reserves in the mangrove swamps nearby combine estuarine and coastal ecosystems with a great variety of waterbirds and aquatic plants. Turtles normally visit October-December. The reserve is operated by the Conservation Department of the Public University (USAC) and Inguat. Free, but donations welcome. Take insect repellent, guides available. Well worth taking a boat trip at sunrise or sunset, negotiate the price. This reserve is also on the migratory routes of North and South American birds.

To get to the beach, take the motor boats from **La Avellana** (see **Transport**) through mangrove swamps, with plenty of wildlife to watch. The landing stage at Monterrico is 10-15 minutes' walk from the ocean front along which are the main restaurants and places to stay. There are private chalets for some distance along the coast, four wheel drive essential, all roads are unconsolidated sand. 'Taxis' (trucks) will help you with luggage. If you drive to La Avellana, arrange for safe parking there, about US$3 per day. It will cost you the same in Monterrico unless you can reach your hotel.

There are no direct telephones, though it may be possible to phone out with a credit card. Numbers shown are mobiles or in Guatemala City. Apart from *San Gregorio*, all hotels are small, simple, with minimal services, busy at weekends and holidays, but peaceful otherwise. There is little shade on the beach. The 'main street' leads to the beach. Places to stay are mostly along the beach to the left.

Sleeping **B** *San Gregorio*, behind *Kaiman*, T/F2384690, nice modern rooms with bath, shaded pool, tienda, friendly, quiet, good value. **D** *Johnny's Place*, first along the beach, cabins for 4, refrigerator, stove for rent, fan, nets on windows. **D** *Baule Beach*, beyond *Kaiman*, with bath, mosquito nets, run by ex Peace Corps volunteer, Nancy, seafood restaurant. **D** *Kaiman*, next to *Johnny's Place*, Italian run, with bath, fan, mosquito nets, pool, good value restaurant. **D** *Pez de Oro*, at the end of strip, fan, good restaurant. **F** *Sagastume* and **F** *La Sirena*, both to the right on beach, basic. **Camping** possible at east end of beach, US$3, take drinking water with you.

Eating *Neptuno*, alongside *San Gregorio*, Swiss owned, very good food. *El Divino Maestro*, good shrimps and shark, but order in morning for evening. *Pig Pen*, on beach, run by 2 Australians, also bar and surfboard rental. Look for a good plate of shrimps at *comedores* on the main street. *Comedor Susy* is good.

Transport **Buses** To San José nominally at 0500 and 1100 US$0.40, but check (see above). Best to take a boat from Monterrico 'inland' through the canals to **La Avellana**, about 25 minutes, foot passengers US$0.40, cars US$6, last boats at 1800, and then by bus to Taxisco, 10 a day. Buses run by Cubanita from Guatemala City, Terminal Zone 4, to La Avellana via Taxisco at 1030, 1230 and 1430, 5 hours, US$3.

South and west of Escuintla

West of Escuintla at Siquinalá (**E** *El Recreo*, 9 Av 4-51, T8802086, in the centre, good, and a branch of *Savilá* (Escuintla) restaurant chain at Km 82, T8802044, very good) is a turn off south to **La Democracia** (seven kilometres), where sculptures found on the Monte Alto and Costa Brava estates (*fincas*) are displayed in the main plaza. These remarkable stones are believed to date from 400 BC or earlier. Visit the Museo del Pueblo on the main plaza (closed Monday). This road continues 40 kilometres to **Sipacate** on the coast (see below) with a half hourly bus service through La Democracia to Guatemala City.

At **Santa Lucía Cotzumalguapa**, a friendly town, is the ninth century site of **Bilbao** (or **Cotzumalguapa**), which shows Teotihuacan and Veracruz influences, from which classic Mayan culture developed. Three large statues in sugar cane fields can be reached on foot from the tracks leading from Av 4, just beyond the town. Ask locals for guidance to 'Las Piedras'. **El Baúl**, a pre-classic monument (stelae) which dates back to the Izapa civilization (see the **Precolumbian civilizations** section, page 62), is six kilometres north of Santa Lucía. To reach the El Baúl site, go along 1 Av to the end and into the countryside north of the town. Four kilometres from the Pacific Highway, the road turns sharply to cross a bridge, immediately after which the road forks. Bear right marked to Los Tarros sugar refinery, and look after one kilometre to the left where a dirt track leads 250 metres through cane fields to a low hill with a prominent tree on top. You can drive close to the hill. On top are two impressive stones, both used still by locals for religious rites. One is against the tree and has many Olmec style glyphs. The other is a very impressive half buried head with oriental type features.

The left fork on the road leads to El Baúl refinery, and inside the compound, beside the factory, is a 'museo', actually a small field area with dozens of stones, many well preserved, found on the finca. New stones found as they work the land are added to the collection. By contrast, there are three ancient steam engines previously used on the farm, two of them built by Koppel (Berlin) in the 1920s. On the Las Ilusiones and Finca Pantaleón estates are ruined temples, pyramids and sculptures, and there are other stelae to be found in the area, though most items have now been transferred to museums in Guatemala City.

Sleeping   At Santa Lucía: **B** *Santiaguito*, on the main road at Km 90, T8825435, swimming pool, good restaurant. Recommended. **D** *El Camino*, opposite *Santiaguito*, T8825316, bath, hot water, fan, some with a/c, TV, run down, restaurant *Bonanza* next door. **At La Democracia**: **F** *Pensión San Marcos*, 2 blocks from central plaza, very basic. Good restaurant on main road near Shell station, *La Casa de los Olmecas*, palm thatched building, simple menu.

Transport   Buses   From the Zona 4 terminal in the capital buses run to both places.

Sipacate   The Chiquimulilla Canal runs along much of this coast separating the mainland from the narrow black sand beach. To get to the beach here, take a canoe across the canal where there is the pleasant *Rancho Carrillo* (see below). Good swimming in the ocean provided there are calm conditions (the dangers of bathing along this coast must not be underestimated). There is a good beach east towards San José as far as Buena Vista in the Sipacate-Naranjo National Park, mainly a bird and turtle sanctuary. There are also mangrove wetlands in this area. At Buena Vista the Río Acamé reaches the sea. You can reach the Park (no facilities) by pick-up from Sipacate along the mainland side of the lagoon, or by motorized canoe.

Sleeping   E *La Costa*, pleasant rooms round a fine grass lawn, peaceful, owner speaks English, good value. Warmly recommended. **E** *Hospedaje La Bendición*, noisy, overpriced. **Across the canal**: **E** *Rancho Carrillo*. Take the canoe from their private wharf, rustic wooden cabins, running water, electricity, bar, excellent seafood in the restaurant, private launch for fishing or sightseeing, packed lunches arranged.

23 kilometres beyond Santa Lucía Cotzumalguapa is **Cocales**, where a road north leads to Patulul and in 30 kilometres to Lake Atitlán at San Lucas Tolimán. This is a

good surfaced road which climbs up from the Pacific plains to the coffee region dominated by volcanoes, Agua and Fuego to the right and Atitlán in front. Excellent cheese, ice cream and other dairy products at Lacteos Parma, 16 kilometres short of San Lucas. Bus from Panajachel to Cocales, two and a half hours, US$1.05, five a day between 0600 and 1400.

60 kilometres south of Cocales on a good paved road is the coastal resort of **Tecojate**, popular with Guatemalans specially at holiday times. The road stops at the *estero* (tidal lagoon) and motor launches cross to the excellent black sand beach, five minutes, US$0.25 per person, or you can paddle across at low tide. Private, rustic beach houses, but no formal public accommodation. Beachside places to eat. Buses from Guatemala City and other closer centres mostly passing though Cocales. Parking for the day US$1, more at holiday times. Do not bathe in the *estero*.

Tecojate

The Pacific Highway continues through San Antonio Suchitepéquez to Mazatenango, see the **Western Guatemala** section.

West from Guatemala City

There is some beautiful scenery west of the capital, with interesting markets and colourful Indian costumes in the towns and villages. Lake Atitlán, in the shadow of three volcanoes, is a jewel of the region, the villages around it having acquired varying degrees of tourist consciousness. In the highlands is the famous market of Chichicastenango. North of here are the Quiché and Ixil regions, very traditional , but which suffered heavily in Guatemala's bloody recent past.

Guatemala City to Lake Atitlán

The Pacific Highway goes west from Guatemala City to Tapachula in Mexico. The Pan-American Highway (fully paved) cuts off northwest at San Cristóbal Totonicapán and goes into Chiapas by El Tapón, or Selegua, canyon. This is a far more interesting route, with fine scenery.

About 12 kilometres west of the capital a road (right) leads to San Pedro Sacatepéquez (see page 617) and Cobán (see page 621). Our road twists upwards steeply, giving grand views, with a branch to **Mixco** (16½ kilometres from Guatemala City, but now fast being absorbed as another suburb). Here, local priests will provide tourists lodging at **E** *Casa Sacerdotal*, 12 C Final, Colonia El Rosario, Zona 3, behind the seminary. Call Gladys Montes de Rubio, T5954684, for reservations. At Km 18.5, *Restaurante Los Tilos*, open 1000-1900, good lunches, pies a speciality. Recommended. About 14 kilometres beyond, at San Lucas Sacatepéquez, is the exit to Antigua. **Sumpango**, which is a little over 19 kilometres beyond this turn-off, has a daily market, best on Sunday, and *huipiles* can be bought from private houses; they are of all colours but predominantly red, as it is believed to ward off the evil eye. Good font in church. *Fiesta* 27-29 August.

At Chimaltenango, another road runs left, 20 kilometres, to Antigua. This tree-lined road leads to Parramos where it turns sharp left. Straight on through the village, in 1½ kilometres, is **B** *Posada de Mi Abuelo*, Carretera a Yepocapa, T8391842, F4762870, a delightful inn formerly a coffee farm and still in the family, country atmosphere, nice gardens, horseriding, good restaurant. The main road continues through picturesque mountains to Pastores, Jocotenango to Antigua. This road is served by a shuttle-bus (US$0.35 or US$0.45 in minibus, US$8-9 in taxi), so Antigua

Chimaltenango

can be included in the Guatemala-Chichicastenango circuit.

Chimaltenango is the capital of its Department. Excellent views at 1,790 metres, from which water flows one side to the Atlantic, the other side to the Pacific. Thermal swimming pool at San Lorenzo El Tejar, which can be reached by bus from Chimaltenango. Market: Wednesday. *Fiesta:* 22-27 July. At Km 56 is a gallery, *Comalapa*, open 0800-1800 daily, prices lower than Antigua and Guatemala City, worth a trip. Bus to Panajachel, US$1.70.

Sleeping C *La Villa*, Km 50, Carretera Panamericana, T8391130, hot water, good restaurant. **E** *San Angel*, 1 C, 4-37, T8391423, restaurant, pleasant. **F** *Pensión Los Alamos*, 2 Av 2-32, T8391324, pleasant rooms, shared toilets/showers, cold water, clean, helpful. **F** *Pensión Río*, OK. Good restaurants nearby: *La Marylena* and *La Casa de las Leyendas* at Km 56 on the main road. Many *comedores* among the vehicle service establishments on the highway.

Directory Banks *Lloyds Bank*, 1 C 5-45. *Banco Continental, BAM* and *Bancor*.

Buses to Antigua pass the park of **Los Aposentos**, three kilometres (lake and swimming pool). At **San Andrés Itzapa** (six kilometres south of Chimaltenango) there is a very interesting chapel to Maximón (San Simón) which is well worth a visit. Open till 1800 daily. Shops by the chapel sell prayer pamphlets and pre-packaged offerings.

A side-road runs 21 kilometres north to San Martín **Jilotepeque** over deep *barrancas*; markets on Sunday, Thursday. Bus from Chimaltenango, US$0.50. *Fiesta:* 7-12 November (main day 11). Fine weaving. Striking *huipiles* worn by the women. 10 kilometres beyond Chimaltenango is Zaragoza, a former Spanish penal settlement, and beyond that (right) a road (13 kilometres) leads north to the interesting village of **Comalapa** (**D** *Pixcayá*, 0 Av 1-82, T4712069, hot water, parking; also *pensión*, under US$3): markets 1000-1430, Monday-Tuesday, bright with Indian costumes. Fine old church of San Juan Bautista (1564). *Fiestas:* 22-26 June.

There are several local artists working in Comalapa; no studios, so best to ask where you can see their work.

Six kilometres beyond Zaragoza the road divides. The southern branch, the old Pan-American Highway, goes through Patzicía and Patzún to Lake Atitlán (see below), then north to Los Encuentros. The northern branch, the new Pan-American Highway, much faster, goes past Tecpán and over the Chichoy pass, also to Los Encuentros. From Los Encuentros there is only the one road west to San Cristóbal Totonicapán, where the new road swings northwest through El Tapón and La Mesilla to Ciudad Cuauhtémoc, the Mexican border settlement; and the old route goes west through Quetzaltenango and San Marcos to Tapachula, in Mexico.

Tecpán The northern road to Los Encuentros: from the fork the Pan-American Highway runs 19 kilometres to near **Tecpán**, which is slightly off the road at 2,287 metres. It has a particularly fine church: silver altars, carved wooden pillars, odd images, a wonderful ceiling which was severely damaged by the 1976 earthquake. The church is being slowly restored: the ceiling is missing and much of its adornment is either not in evidence, or moved to a church next door. The women wear most striking costumes. Market: Thursday and Sunday.

Near Tecpán are the very important Mayan ruins of **Iximché**, once capital and court of the Cakchiqueles, five kilometres of paved road south of Tecpán (nice walk), ■ *0800-1700, US$3.60, nationals US$0.30*. The first capital of Guatemala after its conquest by the Spaniards was founded near Iximché; followed in turn by Ciudad Vieja, Antigua and Guatemala City. The ruins are well-presented with three plazas, a palace, and two ballcourts on a promontory surrounded on three sides by steep slopes. There is a museum at the site.

Sleeping & eating C *Hotel Iximché*, T8391656. F *El Sucro*, basic, water only at night. F *Posada de Doña Ester*, clean, hot water. *Casa de Don Pedro*, good *churrasco*. *Restaurant de la Montaña*, 1 km after the road to Tecpán. The owner of *Zapatería La Mejor* has a guest house, **F**. Also *Restaurante Katok*, on the highway, good grills, *chorizos*, cheeses and hot chocolate, but expensive. Better value at *El Pedregal*, just off the main road at Km 90, toward Xetzac, 2 km after junction to Tecpán, look for a bright yellow sign just after a narrow bridge. Run by a German family, open 0730-1030 and 1200-1500, excellent breakfasts for US$2.30 and lunches US$3.50, fresh homemade dishes, often full at weekends.

Festivals 25 September-5 October.

Transport Buses From Guatemala City (Zona 4 terminal), 2¼ hours, every hour; easy day trip from Panajachel.

Beyond Tecpán the road climbs up a spectacular 400 metres to the summit of the Chichoy pass. The pass is often covered in fog or rain but on clear days there are striking views. 58 kilometres from the fork is Los Encuentros (and the road to Chichicastenango) and three kilometres further on is the direct road Sololá and Panajachel. 12 kilometres before Los Encuentros is Las Trampas intersection with the new paved road to Godínez and Lake Atitlán (not signed). This is a good road, especially now that the road from Godínez down to Panajachel is paved. Buses run along it, and it's worth taking if in a car.

Sololá

Sololá, 11 kilometres from the junction, has superb views across Lake Atitlán. Fine modern white church with brightly coloured stained glass windows and an attractive clock tower dated 1914 on the west side of the plaza. Good Tuesday and even better Friday markets, to which many of the Indians go (mornings only, go early, Friday market gets underway on Thursday). Good selection of used *huipiles*. Note costumes of men. Great *fiesta* 11-17 August. Hot shower 500 metres from market on Panajachel road, behind Texaco station, US$0.18.

Tightly woven woollen bags are sold here: far superior to the usual type of tourist bags. Prices are high because of nearness of tourist centres of Panajachel and Chichicastenango.

Population: 40,785
Altitude: 2,113m
Colour map 4, grid C2

Sleeping E *Del Viajero*, 7 Av, 10-45, T7623683, on Parque Central, no windows, one room with bath, remainder shared, spacious, clean and friendly, good food. E *Belén*, 10 C 4-36, T7623105, hot water, restaurant. F *El Paisaje*, 9 C, 5-6 Av 2 blocks from Parque Central, pleasant colonial courtyard, shared baths and toilets, clean, hot water, restaurant, good breakfast, family run, laundry facilities. F *Santa Ana*, 6 Av, 8 C, opposite large supermarket, basic, clean, friendly, rooms around a lawn, shared facilities, good value.

Eating *El Cafetín*, Parque Central, delicious lake fish, *mojarra*. *Cafetería Karol* and *Café Favy*, open all day for cheap meals and snacks, but coffee expensive. *Helados Topsy* for ice cream, all within a block of Parque Central.

Transport Buses To **Chichicastenango** US$0.35, 1½ hours. Bus to **Panajachel**, US$0.25, or 1½-2 hours' walk; to **Chimaltenango**, US$1; to **Quetzaltenango** at 1200, US$1.50. Colectivo to **Los Encuentros**, US$0.15; to **Guatemala City** (Rebuli) direct US$1.50, 3 hours.

Directory Banks *Banco G y T*, 7 Av y 9C, Zona 2, 0900-1800.

From Sololá the old Pan-American Highway (all newly paved) drops 550 metres in eight kilometres to Panajachel: grand views on the way. Take the bus up (US$0.25, they stop early in the evening). It is quite easy to walk down direct by the road (the views are superb, particularly early in the morning), you also miss the unnerving bus ride down! It is a two hour walk. A longer, but rewarding walk is along the road west from Sololá to San José Chacayá, then down to the lake through the Finca María Linda. About four to five hours to Santa Cruz La Laguna on the lake and another three hours along, below San Jorge to Panajachel. You may have to strike up the hill to avoid fenced off private land in the section near the tower blocks.

The southern road from Zaragoza to Lake Atitlán is much more difficult than the northern, with several steep hills and many hairpin bends. This was the original Pan American highway but several sections were severely damaged by the 1976 earthquake and some sections were not repaired and the route diverts on to other roads. Parts were repaved in 1995 but others are in a poor state. Nevertheless, if you have the time and a sturdy vehicle, it is a rewarding trip. The route goes through **Patzicía**, a small Indian village founded 1545 (no accommodation). Market on Wednesday and Saturday. *Fiesta* for the patron, Santiago, on 22-27 July. The famous church, which had a fine altar and beautiful silver, was destroyed by the 1976 earthquake; some of the silver is now in the temporary church. 14 kilometres beyond (road in good condition, with one steep hill) is the small town of **Patzún**; its famous church, dating from 1570, was severely damaged; it is still standing, but is not open to the public. Sunday market, which is famous for the silk (and wool) embroidered napkins worn by the women to church, and for woven *fajas* and striped red cotton cloth; other markets Tuesday and Friday. *Fiesta*: 17-21 May (San Bernardino). Lodgings at the tobacco shop, **F**, or near market in unnamed *pensión*.

The road now leaves Patzún at its east entrance, goes south to Xepatán and back to meet the main road after a 17-kilometre detour, five kilometres short of **Godínez**. Here there is a good place for meals and five buses a day to Panajachel, US$0.35. There is no bus Patzún-Godínez, and very little motor traffic of any sort. From Godínez, a good paved road turns off south to the village of San Lucas Tolimán and continues to Santiago Atitlán; the latter can be reached by a lake boat from Panajachel.

The main road continues straight on for Panajachel; it is very steep but was paved in 1999. The high plateau, with vast wheat and maize fields, now breaks off suddenly as though pared by a knife. From a viewpoint here, there is an incomparable view of Lake Atitlán, 600 metres below; beyond it rise three 3,000 metres-high volcano cones, Tolimán, Atitlán and San Pedro, to the west. The very picturesque village of San Antonio Palopó is right underneath you, on slopes leading to the water. It is about 12 kilometres from the viewpoint to Panajachel. For the first six kilometres you are close to the rim of the old crater and at the point where the road plunges down to the lakeside is **San Andrés Semetabaj** with a beautiful ruined early 17th century church. Market on Tuesday. Bus to Panajachel, US$0.20.

Panajachel

Colour map 4, grid C2
Take care while walking in the lake area, preferably do not go alone. Keep your belongings under control, theft is common, especially in Panajachel and in village markets

Visitors to Lake Atitlán tend to stay at or near **Panajachel**, which extends one kilometre up from the lake. Six hotels are actually on the lakeshore: *Atitlán, Visión Azul, Monterrey, Del Lago, Playa Linda* and *Tzanjuyu*. The main attraction is the scenery. The town itself has suffered from the tourist invasion and is inhabited by many *gringos* ('Gringotenango'). Facilities are now good, though, and it is recommended as a centre from which to visit this part of the Guatemalan highlands. The main tourist season is the second half of November to February. There is water-skiing (at weekends), private boating (kayaks for hire) and swimming, but be warned, there are parasites in the water, as in many lakes.

Sights   The old town is away from the lake and dominated by the church, originally built in 1567, but frequently damaged and restored subsequently, including after the 1976 earthquake. It has a fine decorated wooden roof and a mixture of catholic statues and Maya paintings in the nave. The municipality building is on one side and an

Guatemala

Lake Atitlán

Lake Atitlán is 147 kilometres from the capital via the northern road and Los Encuentros, 133 kilometres via the southern road and Patzún, and 148 kilometres via Escuintla and Cocales to San Lucas Tolimán (see page 664). It is a further 31 kilometres from San Lucas to Panajachel. The lake, 1,562 metres above sea-level, about 7-10 kilometres across and 18 kilometres long, is one of the most beautiful and colourful lakes in the world. It changes colour constantly – lapis lazuli, emerald, azure – and is shut in by purple mountains and olive green hills. Over a dozen villages on its shores, some named after the Apostles, house 3 tribes with distinct languages, costumes and cultures. The lake was the only place in the world where the poc, a large flightless water grebe, could be seen. The poc is now extinct because of loss of habitat, increased human population, pollution and the introduction of non-native fish. The British Royal Society for the Protection of Birds also cites replacement by, or hybridization with, the pied-billed grebe, which it closely resembled. There is no surface outlet now, though at some time in the past it presumably drained through the gap south of San Lucas, at present 30 metres above the water surface. The water level varies, but has been falling slowly for several years.

interesting bell tower on the other. Behind, up the hill, is the market, worth a visit on Sunday mornings especially for embroideries. In contrast, the modern town, alsmost entirely devoted to tourism, spreads out towards the lake. Calle Santander is the principal street, leading directly to the short but attractive promenade and boat piers. There are hotels everywhere, the best on the lake shore, unfortunately disfigured recently by a monstrous tower block built near the *Atitlán* hotel. For this area, and the San Buenaventura Nature Reserve, see page 679. Visit La Galería (near *Rancho Grande Hotel*), where Nan Cuz, an Indian painter, sells her pictures which evoke the spirit of village life.

L *Atitlán*, 1 km west of centre on lake, T7621441/1429 (3608405, F3340640 Guatemala City for reservations), excellent rooms and service, beautiful gardens. **L** *Barceló Del Lago*, on lakeshore, T7622047/1555, includes free board, pool (non-residents US$2). Recommended. **AL** *Posada de Don Rodrigo*, Final C Santander, T7622322, attractive colonial atmosphere. **B** *Tzanjuyu*, T7621317/18, on the lake, balconies and private beach, seen better days. **A** *Cacique Inn* (full board available), C del Embarcadero, T/F7621205, large comfortable rooms, no credit cards, swimming pool, magnificent house and garden, English spoken, good food. Recommended. **B** *Monterrey*, T7621126, discounts for longer stays, clean, friendly, good food, restaurant, great garden. **A** *Playa Linda*, above public beach, T7621159, rooms sleep up to 6, fireplace, beautiful view, slow service in restaurant. **A** *Visión Azul*, near *Hotel Atitlán*, T7621426, friendly staff, good meals but grubby pool, hot water in evenings.

B *Dos Mundos*, C Santander 4-72, T/F7622078, pool, cable TV, fireplaces, good mid-level place to stay. **B** *El Aguacatal*, also near *Hotel del Lago*, T7621482, has bungalows, for 4-6, good value. **B** *Rancho Grande*, on C Rancho Grande, T7621554, cottages in charming setting, 4 blocks from beach, popular for long stay, good, simple food, including breakfast. Recommended. **B** *Müllers Guest House*, C Rancho Grande, 1-81, T7622442, comfortable, quiet, good breakfast. Recommended. **B** *Regis*, C Santander, T7621149, well-kept house, rooms or apartments, garden, friendly, good service but breakfast expensive. **B** *Turicentro Los Geranios*, near *Hotel del Lago*, T7622185, has fully-equipped new bungalows which sleep 6, this price on Saturday and Sunday, **C**, on other days, outdoor pool.

C *Bungalows El Rosario*, about half block south of *Hotel del Lago*, T7621491, safe, clean, run by Indian family, hot water. **C** *Bungalows Guayacán*, T7621479, beautifully located among coffee bushes 700m from centre on road to Santa Catarina Palopó. **C** *Fonda del Sol*, C Real, T7621162, with bath, occasional hot water, or **E** without, comfortable, garden, good restaurant. **C** *Mini Motel Riva Bella*, C Real, T/F7621353, bungalows, with bath, good, clean, nice garden. Recommended. **C** *Paradise Inn*, C del Río, T7621021, on the lake, clean, friendly, showers in rooms, hot water, sauna. **C** *Montana*, Callejón Don Tino, near Belltower in the Old

Sleeping
■ *on maps*
Price codes:
see inside front cover

Town, T7620326, comfortable, TV, hot water, parking. **C** *Gran*, C Real, T7622940, near buses, good. **C** *Posada Ixchel*, C del Río near public beach, T7622375, with breakfast, pool, cable TV.

D *El Centro*, next to Texaco station, T7622167, nice rooms, hot water, parking, washing facilities. **D** *Galindo*, C Real, T/F7621168, with bath, hot water, thin walls, nice garden and good set meal, US$3.50, but smelly and noisy. **D** *Hospedaje Santa Isabel*, T7621462, near the jetty, new rooms built in an orchard, private bath, safe. **D** *Mayan Palace*, C Real, T7621028, with shower, hot water, clean, friendly, but a bit small and noisy. **D** *Posada de los Volcanes*, C Santander 5-51, T7622367, with bath, hot water, clean, comfortable, quiet, friendly owners, Julio and Janet Parajón. **D** *Primavera*, C Santander, T7621427, clean, expensive restaurant serves German food, washing machine, friendly. Recommended. **D** *Utz-Jay*, C 15 de Febrero, T/F7621358, 2 blocks from the lake, nice large garden, very clean and quiet, friendly owners. Recommended. **D** *Cristinita*, C El Frutal 1-79, T7621184, breakfast extra, with bath, hot water, attractive gardens. **D** *Miralrío*, C El Amate, T7620348, opposite the stadium, opened 1998, hot water, free coffee.

E *Casa Linda*, on C Santander between *Mayan Palace* and tourist office, hot shower, nice garden, friendly, central, quiet. **E** *Del Camino*, next to Texaco, with bath (private bathrooms separate from bedrooms), clean, comfortable. **E** *Hospedaje Mi Chosita*, just beyond *Last Resort*, clean, friendly, family atmosphere, warm water, but very small cabins. **E** *Hospedaje Ramos*, close to public beach, run by an Indian family, friendly, safe, loud music from nearby cafés, clean, good value. **E** *Mario's Rooms*, Av Santander, T7621313, with garden, clean,

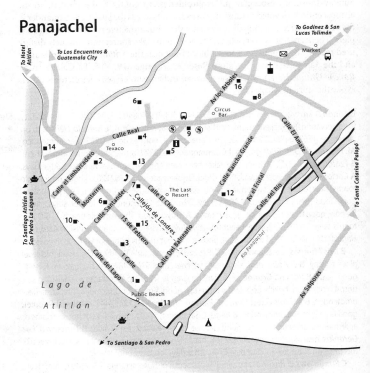

Panajachel

To Godinez & San Lucas Tolimán

To Los Encuentros & Guatemala City

To Hotel Atitlán

Market

Av los Árboles

Circus Bar

Calle El Amate

Calle Real

Texaco

Calle Rancho Grande

Calle el Embarcadero

Calle Monterrey

The Last Resort

Calle El Chali

Av el Frutal

Calle del Río

To Santiago Atitlán & San Pedro La Laguna

Calle Santander

Callejón de Londres

Calle Del Balneario

Río Panajachel

To Santa Catarina Palopó

15 de Febrero

1 Calle

Calle del Lago

Lago de Atitlán

Public Beach

Av Salpores

To Santiago & San Pedro

■ Sleeping
1 Barceló del Lago
2 Cacique Inn
3 El Aguacatal
4 Fonda del Sol
5 Hospedaje Santander

6 Hospedaje Santa Elena & Annex
7 Mario's
8 Maya Kanek
9 Mayan Palace
10 Monterrey

11 Playa Linda
12 Rancho Grande
13 Regis
14 Tzanjuyu
15 Utz-Jay
16 Zanahoria

N

Not to scale

laundry, hot showers US$0.35, good breakfast. **D** *Maya Kanek*, T7621104, C Real near church, good, with bath, hot water, garden, clean, friendly, good value. **E** *Posada La Casita*, with bath, hot shower, basic, friendly, next to police station and market, buses stop outside but quiet at night. **E** *La Zanahoria Chic*, 3 Av 0-46, T7621249, above restaurant *La Zanahoria*, friendly, hot water, good value. **E** *Montufar*, next door to *Casa Linda*, family owned, friendly, hot shower, safe. **E** *Hospedaje El Viajero*, final C Santander, with bath, comfortable large rooms, hot water, friendly, laundry facilities.

F *Cabaña Country Club*, C del Balneario, cheaper rooms, hot showers, clean, sheets 100% nylon, parking for 2 cars. **E** *Hospedaje García*, C El Chali, shared shower, hot water extra, mixed reports. **F** *Hospedaje Eddy*, C Chinimaya, off C Rancho Grande, T7622466, basic, friendly, quiet. **F** *Hospedaje Pana*, on side street opposite *Restaurant Zanahoria*, clean, friendly, hot water, coffee, fruit juice and beer available, luggage store, gymnasium. **F** *Hospedaje Sánchez*, C Santander y C El Chali, clean, friendly, cold water, family run, quiet, comfortable. Recommended. **F** *Hospedaje Santa Ana*, off Av Los Arboles, without bath, simple, adequate. **F** *Hospedaje Santa Elena* C Monterrey off C Real, with bedding, cheaper without, all facilities charged extra, friendly, safe parking for motorcycles; has annex, also **F**, hot showers US$0.40, clean, family atmosphere. **F** *Hospedaje Zulema*, C del Balneario y 5 C, near *Hotel del Lago*, upstairs rooms best, clean, hot showers, good place to wash clothes. Recommended. **F** *Posada de Doña Carmen*, C del Balneario, new, hot water, garden, quiet, very friendly, good value, motor cycle parking. **F** *Salvavidas*, without bath, hot shower US$0.50, cold free, nice family, lovely gardens, very popular, arrive before 1000. **F** *Santander*, C Santander, friendly, nice rooms, lovely garden. Recommended. **F** *Santo Domingo*, 30m from *Vista Hermosa*, shared bath, pleasant. **F** *Villa Martita*, C Santander, close to lake, friendly. Recommended. **F** *Vista Hermosa*, C Monterrey, basic, hot showers, pleasant family.

F *Hospedaje Buena Vista*, with bath, cheaper without, hot showers extra, basic but clean and secure. **F** *Hospedaje Eli's*, opposite *Hospedaje Pana*, basic, cold water, good. **F** *Londres*, Callejón Londres off C Santander, good atmosphere, very basic, under US$3.

For long stay, ask around for houses to rent; available at all prices from US$125 a month for a basic place, to US$200, but almost impossible to find in November and December. Domingo Can, whose office is in the same building as Gallery Bookstore, rents pretty houses with fireplaces, electric showers, private yards. *Apartamentos Boheme* at Callejón Chinimaya rent furnished bungalows. Break-ins and robberies of tourist houses are not uncommon. The water supply is variable, with water sometimes only available 0630-1100.

Camping: possible in the grounds of *Hotel Visión Azul*, US$3.50 per person with facilities. There is also a site on the road to Santa Catarina Palopó near the bridge. However, there was flood damage after Hurricane Mitch in 1998 (also to the bridge), ask if it is reopened. There is free camping beyond the river south of the public beach, but not recommended.

Many of the higher priced hotels have restaurants open to the public, as does *Fonda del Sol* (large varied menu, reasonable prices, recommended). *Casa Blanca*, C Real, very expensive, but good, German owned. Opposite is *La Laguna*, excellent cooking, nice garden, log fire indoors. *The Last Resort*, C El Chali, 'gringo bar', all-you-can-eat breakfast, reasonable prices, bar, table tennis, good information. *El Patio*, C Santander, good food, very good breakfast, quiet atmosphere. *El Cisne*, opposite *Hotel del Lago*, attractive, clean, good cheap set meals. *Brisas del Lago*, good meals at reasonable prices, on lake shore. A number of others on beach front, for example *El Pescador* for fish (good bass), about US$4. Next door *Los Pumpos*, good fish dishes, but overpriced. There are a number of vegetarian restaurants: *Comedor Hsieh*, Av Los Arboles, friendly, good quality, fair prices. Recommended. *Casa de Pays*, Av Los Arboles (pie shop, also known as *La Zanahoria*, or *The Carrot*), good food, good value, clean, also has rooms (shows English language videos in evening US$1). *Taverna del Dragón*, C Santander, vegetarian, Eastern and international dishes, uses only purified water, good, meeting place for German-speaking and other international tourists. *Bella Vista*, C Santander, large servings, good set menu US$3. *Bombay*, Av Los Arboles, 0-42, good Indian food, vegetarian recipes from several countries, German beer, pleasant patio,

Eating
● *on maps*

good food, set lunch less than US$2, good service, operates as the *East/West* restaurant during the day. *Las Chinitas*, C Santander, Chinese, cooked in front of you, inexpensive, friendly, good. *Hamburguesa Gigante*, C Santander, good honest burgers. *Papagayo*, C Santander, German run, good food, a bit expensive. *Las Palmeras*, C Santander, cheap. *Guajimbo's*, C Santander, good atmosphere, excellent food, fast service, live music some evenings, recommended. *Rancho Los Gauchos*, C Santander, Uruguayan steakhouse. *El Patio*, C Santander, good food. *El Bistro*, at end of Santander, dinner only, homemade dishes, great salads, pasta and chocolate mousse, expensive but recommended. *Deli 2* at end of C Santander, recommended for all meals. Go for the *pastel del día*. *Tocoyal*, on beach near *Hotel del Lago*, good for breakfast, good value. *Bar y Restaurant Las Gaviotas*, 2 Av del Balneario, very good, national and international food, service not up to same standard. *Pana Pan* has excellent wholemeal breads and pastries, banana bread comes out of the oven at 0930, wonderful, cinnamon rolls also recommended. *Pizza Hot* at Flyin' Mayan Yacht Club, on corner of C Real 00-54 and Los Arboles, US run, excellent pizzas and banana pie, coffee, newspapers to read. Pizzas also at *Yax Che*, C Real 1-04, opposite *Maya Kanek*, which caters for vegetarians. *Circus Bar*, has pizzas, good coffee, German/French owners, popular. *Ranchón Típico*, C Santander. *Chisme*, Av Los Arboles, good food, try eggs McChisme for breakfast, good fresh pasta, excellent banana cake, good atmosphere, popular, a bit pricey, open 0700-2200 daily except Wednesday, English and occasionally German magazines. The yoghurt dishes at *Mario's* restaurant are good, his crêpes filled with yoghurt and fruit are recommended. *Connections*, Av Santander, good value. *Don Cokey* on Av Los Arboles near *Circus Bar*, open 1200-0100, typical cuisine, popular. *Cafetería Panajachel*, C Real, good breakfasts, *comidas* US$3, cable TV. *Cafetería Vía Linda*, C 15 de Febrero, good cheap food, excellent breakfast. *Amigos*, Av Los Arboles, attractive, popular, good. Recommended. *La Típica*, C Real 50m from church, good *comida corriente*, good value.

Festivals 1-7 October.

Entertainment *Chapiteau*, discotheque, open 2000 to early morning Tuesday to Saturday, US$1-1.50 cover charge, opposite *Hotel del Lago*. *Circus Bar*, good live music at weekends, open 1700-0100 daily. *Grapevine Video Bar*, C Santander, 2 screens, about 10 films a day, US$1.15, good coffee and brownies, also snacks and sandwiches, open 1500-0100. *Nuan's Bar*, in small shopping arcade just down road from *Circus Bar*, happy hour 2200-2300, small dance floor. A number of other video bars.

Shopping *Tinamit Maya Shopping Centre*, C Santander, many stalls for typical items, bargain for good
Many small stores prices. *The Chocolate Factory* (*Casa de Pájaros*) sells books as well as chocolate. Another
selling local chocolate shop is on the other side of the main street, near the bank, good, but expensive.
handicrafts Also on road to San Andrés Semetabaj is the *Idol's House*, an antique shop where you must bargain. Indians sell their wares cheaply on the lakeside; varied selection, bargaining easy/expected. You can buy daily Guatemalan and (sometimes) international newspapers at *Almacén Rosales*, C Real 0-32. *Chalo's Tienda*, on C Real, is the town's 'mini-supermarket'. *Tienda Las Golondrinas*, C Real, good value store. *Tienda Típica Luxito*, C El Chali, typical products at sensible prices.

Transport **Local Bicycle hire**: US$1 per hour or US$5 for 8 hours. Several places to hire eg C Santander next to *Hotel El Viajero*, or ask at Inguat. **Car rental**: 2 doors down from post office, cheapest US$40 a day with unlimited mileage. **Kayak hire**: US$2 per hour, good Kayaks. **Motorcycle rental**: about US$6 per hour, plus fuel and US$100 deposit. Shop near the Church, another at the junction of C Real and C Santander, and 2 places near *Circus Bar*. Bikes generally poor, no locks or helmets provided. Motorcycle parts from *David's Store*, opposite *Hotel Maya Kanek*, good prices, also does repairs and rents bikes. **Ultralight flights**: US$26 for 15 minutes, thrilling and nerve-racking first time up, but a good way to see the lake. Ask Inguat for current opportunities.

Buses Rebuli to **Guatemala City**, 3 hours, US$1.75, crowded, 9 a day between 0500 and 1430; from Guatemala City either Transportes Rebuli or alternatively and probably faster,

Galgos bus for Quetzaltenango as far as Los Encuentros, and a local bus (up to 1830) to Panajachel. Direct bus to **Quetzaltenango** 8 a day between 0530 and 1415, US$2, 2½ hours (from there to Mexico, bus to Tecún Umán via Coatepeque). There are direct buses to **Los Encuentros** on the Pan-American Highway (US$0.50, the junction for routes to the capital, Quetzaltenango and Chichicastenango and the cheapest way to travel, but at busy times the buses may be already full). To **Chichicastenango** direct, 11 a day between 0645 and 1700, US$1, 1½ hours, a minibus tour can cost US$6.50. There are direct buses to **Cuatro Caminos**, US$0.50 (see page 687) from 0530, for connections to Totonicapán, Quetzaltenango, Huehuetenango, etc. Bus to **Chimaltenango** (for Antigua), US$1.40, change there for **Antigua**. There is also a direct bus (Transpopeye) 1100, US$3.60, which leaves from opposite the bank. Bus to **Sololá**, US$0.25, every 30 minutes. Best to wait for buses by the market on C Real.

The fastest way to **Mexico** is probably by bus south to Cocales, 2½ hours, 5 buses between 0600 and 1400, then many buses along the Pacific highway to Tapachula on the border. There are tourist minibuses to the Mexican border US$40, enquire at hotels and travel agents.

Directory

Banks *Banco Inmobilario* on Av Los Arboles, open Mon-Fri 0900-1700, Sat 0900-1300 will change TCs. Also *Banco Industrial*, C Santander (TCs and Visa ATM), and *Banco Agrícola Mercantil*, C Real, also changes TCs. There is a *cambio* on the street near *Mayan Palace* for US dollars cash and TCs, good rate. The barber's shop near the bank will change TCs. The Kodak Camera Club near the Tourist Office offers slightly better rates.

Communications Post Office: near the church. It is difficult but not impossible to send parcels of up to 1 kg abroad as long as packing requirements are met. *Get Guated Out*, Centro Comercial, Av Los Arboles, T/F7622015, good and inexpensive service to send larger parcels, they use the postal system but pack and deal with formalities for you. Next to *Restaurant Chisme*, a parcel service in the handicrafts shop claims economy rates to USA cheaper than post office (more expensive to Europe); can send over 2 kg. Central America Link sends parcels to USA, US$18.50 plus US$4.10 per kilogram, and to Europe US$24.50 plus about US$10 per kilogram, 6 days to Miami. If you can collect your parcel in Miami and mail it from there to Europe it is cheaper (7790 NW 64th St, Miami, FL 33166, T305-5925219). *DHL*, Edif Rincón Sai, C Santander. **Telephones:** *Telgua*, 2nd Floor Edif Los Pinos, C Santander. *Maya Communications* office is in new shopping centre on C Santander, next to Inguat, T/F502-9622194, interlinked with Antigua and Quetzaltenango, also email. Many internet and email services in centre, shop around for best prices.

Hospitals & medical services Health: Centro de Salud on C Real, just downhill from the road to San Antonio Palopó. *Dr Hernández Soto*, office near Texaco station, US$5 for a short consultation. There are good clinics at Santiago Atitlán and San Lucas Tolimán, which specialize in treating dysentery. Outbreaks of cholera have been reported in the lake area since 1991. Enquire locally about the safety of water, lake fish, etc. Amoebic dysentery and hepatitis are less common than in the past. Treatment free, so a donation is appropriate. Fleas are endemic. Take care to treat bites in case of infection. 1 litre plastic bags and larger plastic containers of water are sold in Panajachel.

Language schools *Pana Atitlán Language School*, C de la Navidad 0-40. Recommended. See also *AmeriSpan* see page 40.

Tour companies & travel agents *Turísticos San Nicolás*, C Santander, T7622078, ask for Gregorio, one of the few agencies prepared to negotiate private taxi services to towns and villages in the area. Other agencies operate fixed schedules at expensive rates. *Servicios Turísticos Atitlán*, C Santander next to *Hotel Regis*, T7622075.

Tourist offices Inguat is in Edif Rincón Sai, C Santander near C Real, T7621392. Open daily 0800-1700; has maps, ask about local email services. Bus and boat timetables posted on door when closed. The staff are very helpful and speak English and Italian. They can also help booking internal flights, sometimes with discounts. Check with Inguat whether it is safe to climb the volcanoes.

Around the lake

Cost of boat trips and schedules change all the time. Best to go down to the lake, find out what is available and plan ahead. There are two piers (see map). You can go from either pier to Santiago Atitlán or San Pedro La Laguna, but the best services are from the end of C Rancho Grande. Typical fares: Panajachel-Santiago US$1.50, Panajachel-San Pedro US$1.50, Santiago-San Pedro US$1.70. You can also hire boats for trips, cost depending on the number of people and size of boat. Virtually all the dozen or so communities round the lake have piers, so you can negotiate the best deal. The only reliable services back to Panajachel are from Santiago or San Pedro up to about 1600. Buy tickets on the boat or on the dockside. The Tourist Office has the latest information on boats, there are usually tours available Panajachel-San Pedro-San Antonio Palopó. This takes a full day eg 0930-1500, with stops of one hour or so at each, US$6. San Pedro and Santiago and back, US$5. It takes one hour 15 minutes from Panajachel to Santiago. At almost any time of year, but especially in January-March, strong winds occasionally blow up quickly across the lake (El Xocomil). This can be dangerous in small boats.

The lake is some 50 kilometres in circumference and you can walk on or near the shore for most of it. Here and there the cliffs are too steep to allow for easy walking and private properties elsewhere force you to move up 'inland'.

Santa Catarina Palopó The town is within walking distance of Panajachel, about four kilometres, the road hugs the side of the hill with a continous view of the lake. It has an attractive adobe church. Reed mats are made here, and you can buy *huipiles* (beautiful, green, blue and yellow) and men's shirts. Watch weaving at *Artesanías Carolina* on way out towards San Antonio. Bargaining is normal. From Santa Catarina you can walk to the Mirador of Godínez for views, but the path is very steeply uphill for quite a while.

Sleeping AL *Villa Catarina*, T7621291, nice setting, modern, traditional style. Also **A** *Bella Vista*, T7621566, on road to San Antonio Palopó, overlooking lake, quiet. Look for the art gallery 'El Dzunum'. Houses can be rented here.

Festivals 25 November.

Transport Truck from Panajachel US$0.12, bus at 0915 US$0.20, also minibuses and ask about boat services.

San Antonio Palopó Six kilometres beyond Santa Catarina San Antonio Palopó has another splendid 16th century church; it lies in an amphitheatre formed by the mountains behind. Up above there are hot springs and a cave in the rocks used for local ceremonies. The village is noted for the costumes and headdresses of the men, and *huipiles* and shirts are cheaper than in Santa Catarina. Note that although the road was being improved in 1999, it was incomplete between Santa Catarina and San Antonio. A good hike is to take the bus from Panajachel to Godínez, take the path toward the lake 500 metres south along the road to Cocales, walk on down from there to San Antonio Palopó (one hour) and then along the new road back to Panajachel via Santa Catarina Palopó (three hours). You can walk on round the lake from San Antonio, but you must eventually climb steeply up to the road at Agua Escondida.

Sleeping **B** *Hotel Terrazas del Lago*, T7620157, F7620037 or T2326741 (Guatemala City), on the lake with view, bath, clean, restaurant, Polish born owner Feliks Stopowski speaks German and English. He has built the hotel over the past 27 years, a unique structure. You can stay in private houses (ask around) or rent rooms (take sleeping bag).

Festivals 12-14 June.

Transport The only bus from Panajachel to San Antonio is at 0915, US$0.35, but there are pick-ups, US$0.55. Enquire about boats.

Panaranjo One and a half kilometres further south along the top main road is Panaranjo from where a track leads towards the lake and down to Finca Tzanpetey, 30-40 minutes. From there it is possible to walk to San Lucas Tolimán but the path is narrow and delicate in places where it climbs up 50-100 metres to negotiate the steepest drops to the lake. After one kilometre you reach the north end of the San Lucas lake shore and it is an easy walk. Less strenuous is to walk on from Panaranjo to San Gabriel, ask for the 'extravio para San Lucas' which is behind the school to the right, then bear left, for a delightful route through fields of corn, tomato, potatoes, chillies, beans and coffee, then following a deep dry water course to a spectacular view of the lake and volcanoes. A traverse follows to a band of cypress where the path descends using the roots of trees to help you, alpine-style, down to San Lucas. Good footwear essential.

San Lucas Tolimán is at the southeastern tip of the lake. *Fiestas* include Holy Week with processions, arches and carpets on the Thursday and Friday, and 15-20 October. Many Indians in their finest clothes take part. There is a market on Tuesday, Friday and Sunday. Two banks in town, open 0830-1700, change travellers' cheques.

Sleeping & eating D *Villa Real Internacional*, T7220102, with bath, hot water, restaurant, parking. **D** *Brisas del Lago*, prominent position overlooking the lake, 10 rooms at present, restaurant, bar. Camping possible near the lake but ask, and check for safety. **Restaurants**: *Comedor Victoria*, Guatemalan food. *Café Tolimán*, on the lakeside, home made yoghurt and local dishes. *La Fonda*, ½ block north of plaza, clean, good local food.

Transport Boats There are usually boats to and from Panajachel on market days, but enquire. Boats can be hired for specific trips or for the day. **Buses** Bus to Guatemala City via Panajachel at 0700 and several others. To Guatemala City via Cocales and Carretera del Pacífico, 10 a day from 0400, US$2, 3½ hours. To Santiago, hourly between 0900 and 1800, 1 hour, returning hourly between 0300 and 1300. Bus San Lucas to Quetzaltenango, US$1.50, 0430 and 0600.

From San Lucas the cones of **Atitlán**, 3,535 metres, and **Tolimán**, 3,158 metres, can be climbed. The route leaves from the south end of the town and makes for the saddle (known as Los Planes, or Chanán) between the two volcanoes. From there it is south to Atitlán and north to the double cone and crater of Tolimán. Though straightforward, each climb is complicated by many working paths and thick cover above 2,600 metres. If you are fit, either can be climbed in eight hours, five hours down. Ask at the Municipalidad for information and for available guides. Though formal permission is not required, they will give you a note to indicate your excursion is registered, which could be useful. Maps are not available locally.

Cloud on the tops is common, least likely November-March

Santiago Atitlán

From San Lucas, a new surfaced road goes 16 kilometres through coffee fincas to **Santiago Atitlán**. On the right is the hill, **Cerro de Oro**, with a small village of that name on the lake. The fine church at Santiago was founded in 1547. It has a wide nave with colourful statues. The original roof was lost to earthquakes. The women wear fine costumes and the men wear striped, half-length embroidered trousers. There is a daily market, best on Friday. A coooperative, *Asociación Q'Na'Wnaq* sells local textile and leather products and supports widows and orphans.

B *Posada de Santiago*, overlooking the Bahía de Santiago, 1½ km south of town, T/F7217167, comfortable cabins, with breakfast, run by David Glanville from USA, interesting atmosphere, good restaurant, canoeing, mountain biking, riding arranged, recommended. **E** *Tzutuhil*, T7217174, above *Ferretería La Esquina*, with bath, clean, comfortable, restaurant, great views, good. **E** *Hospedaje Chi-Nim-Ya*, good (good café opposite, cheap, large helpings). **F** *Pensión Rosita*, near the church, friendly, safe, basic, restaurant. Houses can be rented, but check for scorpions and poisonous spiders in the wooden frames. *Santa Rita* restaurant, brightly decorated, good and cheap. The *Galería Nim Pot* is worth a visit, near the school.

Sleeping

Sports *Aventura en Atitlán*, Jim and Nancy Matison, Finca San Santiago, 10 km outside Santiago Atitlán. Offer riding and hiking tours from their property, half day and full day trips,

Entertainment

convenient for those staying elsewhere around Lago de Atitlán, for information, T2015527 (Guatemala City).

Festivals **5 June** and **23-27 July** (main day 25). The celebrations of *Holy Week* are worth seeing, but it may be hard to find a room. The celebrations include the display of Maximón, whose idol is housed in the town.

Transport **Buses** To Guatemala City, US$2.15 (5 a day, first at 0300). Buses to Panajachel at 0600, 2 hours, or take any bus and change on the main road just south of San Lucas. **Boats** At least 7 a day to and from Panajachel, 1 hour 15 minutes, US$1.50.

From Santiago Atitlán, a rough road goes south towards the Pacific coast, passing through Chicacao (where the road becomes paved). The road passes through little villages and coffee plantations.

Parque Nacional Atitlán Five kilometres north of Santiago Atitlán had a small reserve for the *poc*, the Atitlán grebe, now extinct, see box, page 669. Also in the reserve is the *pavo del cacho* (a big black bird with a red horn on its head), though there is some doubt if any are now left. To get there, go by canoe from Santiago (US$0.65), with the reserve workers, or on foot, about 30 minutes on the San Lucas Tolimán road, but ask directions. Safe camping, take food and water; the guards may put you up in one of their cabins.

Seven kilometres south of Santiago Atitlán is a mirador and *refugio* called **Quetzal Reserve** where a path winds up and down through rain forest. Follow the path past the *Posada de Santiago*, then go left at the fork and stay on the road until you come to the reserve and viewpoint, both on the left.

Lake Atitlán

To Los Encuentros, Chichicastenango & Guatemala City

Sololá
Santa Lucía Utatlán
San José Chacayá
San Jorge la Laguna
San Andrés Semetabaj
Santa Cruz la Laguna
Panajachel
Santa Catarina Palopó
Tzununá
San Marcos la Laguna
To Patzún
San Pablo la Laguna
Godínez
Santa Clara la Laguna
San Antonio Palopó
Lago de Atitlán
San Juan la Laguna
San Pedro la Laguna
Agua Escondida
Cerro de Oro
Volcán San Pedro
San Gabriel
Santiago Atitlán
San Lucas Tolimán
Volcán Tolimán
To Chicacao
To Volcán Atitlán
To Pacific Coast

N
Not to scale

Distances
Sololá - Panajachel 8 km
Panajachel - Santa Catarina 4 km
Santa Catarina - San Antonio 6 km

San Andrés Sem - Godínez 10 km
San Lucas - Santiago 16 km
San Marcos - Tzununá 3 km
Tzununá - Santa Cruz 5 km

San Pedro La Laguna

San Pedro has taken over as the young people's laid back haven that was Panajachel 10 years ago. It is a small, poor village but living costs are low and it is known as a good place to hang out for a short or longer period. Some of these semi- permanent inhabitants now run bars and cafés or sell home made jewellery.

San Pedro is at the foot of the **San Pedro volcano** (3,020 metres), which can be climbed in four to five hours, three hours down, not difficult except for route finding through the coffee plantations and heavy cover. A guide is therefore advisable unless you walk part of the way the day before to make sure you know where you are going. The route starts one and a half kilometres along the road to Santiago, and where the road takes a sharp turn to the right, go left through coffee plantations to the west flank of the volcano; after one hour there is only one path and you cannot get lost. A recommended guide is Ventura Matzar González, C Principal, Cantón Chuacante, San Pedro, T7621140. Go early (0530) for the view, because after 1000 the top is usually smothered in cloud; also you will be in the shade all the way up and part of the way down.

The abysmal road around the volcano to Santiago Atitlán (20 kilometres) can be cycled (boats charge half fare for a bike from Panajachel – beware overcharging); it is a tough three to four hours ride requiring some experience and good brakes. If hiring a bike in Panajachel, check the machine carefully. Set out early and allow enough time to catch the last boat back. Motorcyclists (except expert off-roaders) also find this stretch very demanding.

Canoes are made here (hire, US$3.20 for two hours) and a visit to the rug-making cooperative on the beach is of interest. Backstrap weaving is taught at some places, about US$0.50 per day. Try Rosa Cruz, past the 'Colonel's Place', turn right up the hill. Local people in San Pedro speak Tzutuhil. Market days Thursday and Sunday (better). Horse hire in San Pedro from two houses next to each other on path closest to beach, US$6.50 for three hours with guide to neighbouring villages (rather primitive saddles leave you bow-legged). You can also walk from San Pedro to San Juan along the lake and up to **Santa María Visitación**, an attractive village with spectacular views.

There are two landing piers at San Pedro. From Panajachel you arrive at the *muelle* (pier), boats to and from Santiago stop at the *playa* (beach) about 500 metres southeast round the shore. From both cobbled streets climb up the hill to meet in the centre of the town.

Fiesta 27-30 June with traditional dances.

Sleeping **F** *Pensión Chuazanahi* (known as the Colonel's Place and Villa Sol), up from the *playa*, shared bath, reasonable meals, good banana pancakes, friendly staff, nice rooms. Up the hill are *Hotel* and **F** *Hospedaje San Francisco*, rooms with lake view, expanding 1999, garden, cooking facilities, cold water, helpful owner, washing facilities, good value. Nearby is **F** *Hospedaje Peneleu*, hot water, kitchen. Recommended. **F** *Hospedaje Chuacanté*, in front of church, clean, family run, hot water. **F** *San Pedro*, near *Chuazanahi*, bargain for a decent price, cold drinks available, laundry and hot shower if you stay more than 1 night, nice balcony, noisy with a lot of people coming and going, not recommended for single women, clean. Rooms also at **F** *Blue House* down road beside *Chuazanahi*. **F** *Tikaaj*, good, wooden cabins a few metres from *playa*, popular with backpackers, lovely garden, but very basic, restaurant opposite, good and cheap. Houses can be rented from US$5 a week to US$50 a month. **F** *Familia Penelón*, 200m along path opposite the green *farmacia*, friendly, clean, meals available, basic. **F** *Casa Elena*, along path behind *Nick's Place*, shared bath, clean. 100m to the right of the *Muelle* is **F** *Valle Azul*, good value, nice view, good restaurant, but very run down. **F** *Hospedaje Xocomil*, up the hill behind *Casa Elena*, clean, basic, cold water, washing facilities, helpful. **F** *Casa Rosario*, nice garden.

Eating Good food is available at **Chez Michel**, turn right from *playa* along beach road, past Pensión

Chuazanahi, friendly (some French spoken), steaks US$1.50, interesting dishes at weekends. *Sascha*, run by Dutch woman, on right side of first pier you come to by boat, good lasagne, cakes, popular. Good food but slow service at **Comedor Ranchón**, opposite *Chuazanahi*, good fish, possibly the best food in town. *Pachanay*, 150m from *Chuazanahi*, lunch and dinner, good, cheap, good rice dishes, reggae music, 'hippy'-type atmosphere. *Otty's* also has good, cheap food. Buy banana bread from the **Panadería El Buen Gusto**, near centre of town. **Comedor la Ultima Cena**, opposite the Municipalidad, good pizzas, pancakes, very popular, service for food can be very slow but beer comes quickly. *El Mesón*, clean, good food, near landing stage. *El Fondeadero*, next to *El Mesón*, good food, lovely terraced gardens, reasonable prices. *Nick's Place*, on the left up from the *muelle*, cheap, popular, comfy sofas, free films every night. *Rosalinda*, near centre of village, for breakfast (eg *mosh*), local fish and for banana and chocolate cakes. *El Tambor*, good bakery also serves pizzas. *Jocabed*, tofu burgers and other soya dishes. **Comedor Amigos Viajeros**, good cooks, nice view. *Aladan*, pizzas, run by a French couple. **Café Arte**, uphill from *Hotel San Pedro*, good value, art gallery. *La Arboleda*, by *playa* pier, good. *Pinocchio*, Italian, good, reasonable prices, closed Sunday. *Johanna*, best place in the evening, music, dancing. **Thermal Bath** along the shore from the *playa*, good vegetarian food, good coffee, expensive. *Tulipán* has wide variety and vegetarian dishes. *Viajero*, good food, loud music, good value. *Maharishi*, run by Antonio from USA, somewhat eccentric but good vegetarian and other dishes, everything fresh.

Be careful of drinking water in San Pedro, both cholera and dysentry exist here. Centro Médico opposite Educación Básica school, good doctor who does not speak English.

Transport Up to 10 *lanchas* a day leave from Panajachel for **San Pedro**. The boat fare is about US$1.50 (US$5 to take motorcycle in boat). There is a launch from Santiago to San Pedro which leaves when full (45 minutes, US$1.70). There are daily buses San Pedro-Quetzaltenango, 0430, 0530, 3½ hours, cold, US$2.

From San Pedro, you can walk to Panajachel (at least seven hours) through San Juan (look for Los Artesanos de San Juan, T7621150, and another image of Maximón displayed in the house opposite the Municipalidad), San Pablo, San Marcos and finally Santa Cruz (a difficult track – you have to climb and traverse the steep slopes going down to the lake). You can get beautiful views of the lake and volcanoes in the early morning light. Sisal bags and hammocks are made at **San Pablo La Laguna** (**F** *Hospedaje Bisente*, under US$3, nice patio, the family makes meals).

Two kilometres further round a bay is **San Marcos La Laguna**, backed by mountains which go up to 2,900 metres. Here is Las Pirámides Centre, which runs yoga and meditation courses and has some basic accommodation. **D** *Posada Schuman*, T2022216 (cellular), modern, nice bungalows close to the shore, clean, sauna, friendly. **D** *Casa La Paz*, 3 bungalows, vegetarian restaurant. **E** *Paco Real*, chalets, hot water, friendly. **F** *Unicornio*, close to the lake, wooden cabins, hot water, log fires, shared kitchen, massage and sauna, boat tours.

Santa Cruz La Laguna From San Marcos, there is a path of sorts through Tzununá and around the lake to Santa Cruz La Laguna and Panajachel. It is possible to go 'inland' at Tzununá, climb up to the rim, and follow it to San José and Sololá with great views of the lake most of the way. A good day's walk, take plenty of water.

Along the lake it is a tough eight kilometres to Santa Cruz with some climbing up and down the mountain sides. In Santa Cruz there is an interesting 16th century church with many curious wooden statues.

Sleeping **Santa Cruz**: **E** *Arca de Noé*, on the lakeside, bungalow accommodation, restaurant. **E** *Posada Abaj*, nearby, bungalows and rooms, home made meals, beautiful garden, German spoken. **E** *La Iguana Perdida*, next to *Arca de Noé*, F7621196, also cheaper dormitory, 3 meals a day, 3-course dinner at 1930 round large table, vegetarian options, home-baked bread, no electricity, dive school (see below). **F** *Hospedaje Rosa García*, a short distance along the lake, comfortable rooms, good food. **F** *Hospedaje Hernández*, in the village, clean, friendly, cold water only. *Flor del Lago* restaurant serves good chicken, the owner speaks only Cakchiquel, but her daughter speaks Spanish.

Diving *La Iguana Perdida* offers diving in the lake, which is quite different from diving in the sea. There are spectacular walls that drop off, rock formations you can swim through, trees underwater, and because of its volcanic nature, hot spots. Prices: US$25 single tank, US$45 2-tank dives, US$150 PADI Open Water Course, US$150 PADI Advanced Course, PADI Rescue and Dive Master also available.

From Santa Cruz to Panajachel along the coast is difficult, steep and unconsolidated, with few definitive paths. If you do get to the delta of the Río Quiscab, you may find private land is barred. The alternatives are either to go up to Sololá, about six kilometres and 800 metres up, or get a boat. Just before Panajachel, behind the tower blocks, is the **Finca San Buenaventura**, which has been transformed into an interesting **Nature Reserve**. This was one of the largest coffee plantations in the area and includes some 100 hectares of forest. There is now a Visitor Centre, a Butterfly Reserve, a Bird Refuge, an Orchid Garden and several nature trails. It is associated with the *Hotel Atitlán* (see under Panajachel). The Reserve is open 0800-1700, US$4, students US$2. For further information T7622059, Felipe Marín.

The old and new Pan-American Highways rejoin 11 kilometres from Sololá. Three kilometres east is Los Encuentros, the junction of the Pan-American Highway and the paved road 18 kilometres northeast to Chichicastenango. *Altitude*: 2,579 metres. (Very poor accommodation available, under US$3, if you miss a bus connection, easy to do as they are often full.) Buses for Panajachel stop outside the green police office, about 250 metres from where the bus stops en route between the border and capital.

Los Encuentros

Chichicastenango

(Often called 'Chichi' and also known as Santo Tomás) Chichicastenango (*Altitude*: 2,071 metres) is the hub of the Maya-Quiché highlands, and is very popular with tourists. Nights are cold. About 1,000 *ladinos* live in the town, but 20,000 Indians live in the hills nearby and flood the town, almost empty on other days, for the Thursday and Sunday markets.

Derivation of town's name: *chichicaste*, a prickly purple plant like a nettle, which grows profusely, and *tenango*, place of. The town itself is charming: winding streets of white houses roofed with bright red tiles wandering over a little knoll in the centre of a cup-shaped valley surrounded by high mountains. Fine views from every street corner. The costumes are particularly splendid: the men's is a short-waisted embroidered jacket and knee breeches of black cloth, a gay woven sash and an embroidered kerchief round the head. The cost of this outfit, over US$200, means that fewer and fewer men are in fact wearing it. Women wear *huipiles* with red embroidery against black or brown and skirts with dark blue stripes. The Sunday market is much the same as the one on Thursday: but it certainly becomes very touristy after the buses arrive from Guatemala City (bargains may be had after 1530 when the tourist buses depart). Articles from all over the Guatemalan highlands may be bought including rugs, carpets and bedspreads. In fact the markets begin on the previous afternoon. You must bargain hard, although reductions may be limited owing to the non-bargaining of package tourists. Good value handicrafts can be bought at the shop next door to Cooperativo Santo Tomás, opposite *Mayan Inn* on market place; also from *Popol Vuh*, opposite *Pensión Girón*, which has a good range of clothing in modern designs, good value. However, prices are generally cheaper in Panajachel.

The town is built around a large square plaza, with two churches facing one another: **Santo Tomás** parish church and **Calvario**. Santo Tomás is open to visitors, although

Sights

Guatemala

photography is not allowed, and visitors are asked to be discreet and enter by a side door. There is a fine, carved dark wood altar reredos and six others, with saints in niches, along the aisles. Groups burn incense and light candles on the steps and platform before entering. Inside, from door to high altar, stretch rows of glimmering candles, Indians kneeling beside them. Later they offer copal candles and flower-petals to the 'Idolo', a black image of Pascual Abaj, a Maya god, on a hilltop one and a half kilometres southwest of the plaza. Next to Santo Tomás are the cloisters of the Dominican monastery (1542) where the famous Popol Vuh manuscript of Maya mythology was found and translated into Spanish in 1690. Father Rossbach's jade collection can be seen in the **municipal museum** on the main plaza ■ *0800-1200, 1400-1600, closed Tuesday*. To reach the idol, go along 5 Av, turn right on 9 C, down the hill, cross the stream and take the second track from the left going steepest up hill. Pass through a farm now belonging to a mask maker who you can visit and buy masks. Follow the path to the top of the hill where you may well see an Indian ceremony in progress. About half an hour's walk. You can also visit the 'mask factory' one block from the plaza, and buy them from Manuel Mejía Guarcas, 6 Av 9-36.

Sleeping

You won't find accommodation easily on Sat evening, when prices are increased

AL *Mayan Inn*, T7561176, F7561212, classic, colonial style courtyard hotel, huge rooms, simple, antique furniture, fireplaces, friendly staff, bar, marimba music, laundry service, expensive restaurant. **B** *Villa Grande*, just south of town, T7561053, single storey units set along a hillside, charmless conference venue, huge sunken bathtubs, pool, quiet. **AL** *Santo Tomás*, 7 Av, 5-32, T7561316, F7561306, very attractive building with beautiful colonial furnishings (a museum in itself), often full at weekends, very good, friendly service, helpful owner (Sr Magermans), pool, sauna, good restaurant (set meals US$6) and bar, marimba music in evening, same day laundry, two nice garden patios with fountains.

D *Chalet House*, 3 C, 7-44, T/F7561360, with bath, clean, small, family atmosphere, don't be put off by dingy street, good. **C** *Maya Lodge*, 6 C, 4-08, T7561177, with bath, with breakfast, overlooking market, dark overpriced. **B** *Chugüilá*, 5 Av, 5-24, T/F7561134, clean, good **D** without bath (some rooms have fireplaces, wood costs US$0.90 a day extra), marimba on Saturday, restaurant, indoor parking, front rooms noisy otherwise recommended.

D *Pensión Girón* (cheaper without bath), on 6 C, 4-52, Edif Girón, T7561156, good, hot water, helpful, clean, ample parking. **D** *Posada El Arco*, 4 C, 4-36, helpful, clean, very pretty, small, friendly, garden, washing facilities, negotiate lower rates for stays longer than 1 night, some large rooms, good view, English spoken, cold water, garage. **D** *Bella Vista*, 4a Av 2-18, T2041097, comfortable, nice views.

E *El Salvador*, 10 C, 4-47, 2 blocks from main plaza, 50 large rooms with bath and fireplace (wood available in market), good views, **F** in small rooms without bath, good value. **E** *Posada Belén*, 12 C, 5-55, T7561244, with bath, less expensive without, hot water, check electrics, balcony, clean, friendly, will do laundry, fine views.

F *Posada Santa Marta*, 5 Av, 3-27, with cold water, bath and sheets (cheaper without either). Local boys will show you other cheap lodgings for a fee. Try the fire station (Los Bomberos) at weekends.

Camping: free overnight vehicle parking at Shell station next to the *Hotel Santo Tomás*.

Eating

The best food is in the top hotels, but is expensive

There are several good restaurants in the Centro Comercial Santo Tomás on the north side of the plaza (market). The best is *Las Brasas Steak House*, upstairs, nice atmosphere, wide steak menu, good food, accepts credit cards. Also upstairs *La Fonda de Tzijolaj*, good meals, good service, reasonable prices (ask the owner for an interesting English-Spanish-Quiché phrase book). *Buenaventura*, good value, friendly owner Manuel Ventura. *La Villa de los Cofrades*, café downstairs good for breakfasts, snacks, restaurant upstairs, good value, and across the street above the Pharmacy.

Nearby are *Katokok*, 6 C 6-45, upstairs, good budget food. *Tziguan Tinamit*, on the corner of 6 C/5 Av, some local dishes, steaks, tasty pizzas, breakfasts, good. *Tapena*, 5 Av 5-21, opposite *Chugüilá*, clean, good. Also suggested are *Antojitos Tzocomá*, 5 Av near *Posada Santa Marta*, good food, cheap, friendly, a locals' place. *Cafetería Tuttos*, near *Posada Belén*, good breakfasts, pizzas, reasonable prices. There are plenty of cheap small *comedores* round the plaza, eg *Tu Café*, 5 Av 6-44, family run, good breakfast, simple *almuerzo*. On market days there are plenty of good food stalls in the centre of the plaza.

Santo Tomás, **18-21 December**: processions, dances, marimba music (well worth a visit – very crowded); New Year's Eve; Holy Week; 1 November; 20 January; 19 March; 24 June (shepherds). There is also a *fiesta* at the end of May. **Festivals**

Most buses run through Chichicastenango to and from Santa Cruz del Quiché. A few start from 7 Av/8 C by the old telephone office (where there is still a row of phones). Buses passing through all stop at 5 Av/6 C by the *Hotel Chugüilá* where there are always police and bus personnel to give information. **Transport**

To **Guatemala City**, every 30 minutes from 0300 to 1700, 3 hours, US$1.70, also Pullman, 0700 and 1300, US$2.15 (**NB** sometimes more than one vehicle will cover a particular service). To **Sololá**, 0930 hourly to 1330, 45 minutes, US$0.60, same buses continue to **Panajachel**, 60 minutes, US$0.80. To **Antigua** take any Guatemala City bus and change at Chimaltenango. To **Quetzaltenango**, 0630, 0800 and 1200, 2½ hours, US$1.45. To

Chichicastenango

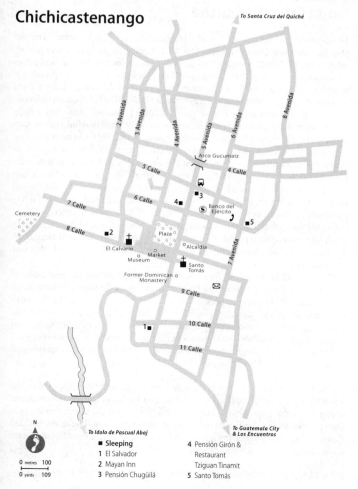

To Santa Cruz del Quiché

2 Avenida
3 Avenida
4 Avenida
5 Avenida
6 Avenida
8 Avenida

Arco Gucumatz

5 Calle
4 Calle
6 Calle
7 Calle
Cemetery
8 Calle

Banco del Ejército

El Calvario
Plaza
Alcaldía
Market
Museum
Santo Tomás
Former Dominican Monastery
7 Avenida

9 Calle

10 Calle

11 Calle

N

0 metres 100
0 yards 109

To Idolo de Pascual Abaj

To Guatemala City & Los Encuentros

■ **Sleeping**
1 El Salvador
2 Mayan Inn
3 Pensión Chugüilá

4 Pensión Girón & Restaurant Tziguan Tinamit
5 Santo Tomás

Mazatenango, 0630, 5 hours, US$2.30. Otherwise, to these places, Mexico and all points west, take any bus to Los Encuentros and change.

To **Santa Cruz del Quiché**, at least every half hour, 30 minutes, US$0.35. To **Nebaj** direct, 4 a day from 1000. For other northern destinations, change at Santa Cruz.

Check the price before travelling and tender the exact fare if possible. There are additional buses to local villages especially on market days.

Directory **Banks** *Banco del Ejército*, open Tues-Sun. *Banco Industrial*, opposite, both on 6 C between 5/6 Av. *G&T*, 5 Av 6-15. *Bancafé*, corner 5 Av/6 C, is open every day. All change US$ cash and TCs. *Mayan Inn* will exchange cash, *Santo Tomás* TCs and cash at holiday times. **Communications** Post Office: 7 Av 8-47. **Telephones**: Telgua, 6 C half a block from *Hotel Santo Tomás*. **Shipping Service**: *Cropa Panalpina*, 7 Av opposite Post Office, will pack and ship your purchases back home by air cargo, eg minimum 5.5 kg to North America US$112, Europe US$134, all inclusive. **Courier service**: *DHL*, 5 Av, 1 block north of Plaza.

Quiché and the Ixil Triangle

Santa Cruz del Quiché

Population: 7,750
Altitude: 2,000m
Colour map 4, grid C2

19 kilometres north by paved road from Chichicastenango is **Santa Cruz del Quiché**, commonly known simply as Quiché, a quaint, friendly town, with a colourful daily market, which covers several blocks. There are few tourists here and prices are consequently reasonable. Good selection of local cloth. Quiché's speciality is palm hats, which are made and worn in the area. Three kilometres away are the remains of temples and other structures of former Quiché capital, **Gumarcaj**, sometimes spelt **K'umarkaaj** and now generally called **Utatlán**. This was largely destroyed by the Spaniards, but the stonework of the original buildings can be seen in the ruins, in a very attractive, well-maintained setting. They can be reached on foot: from the bus station, walk west along 10 C to a lane marked to K'umarkaaj, on the right which winds upward for the last 150 metres. The walk takes about 40 minutes. ■ *0700-1800, entry US$1.45, nationals US$0.30.* There are two subterranean burial chambers (take a torch, or you can hire one for Q 2, there are unexpected drops) still used by the Indians for worship and chicken sacrifices; small but interesting museum at the entrance with a scale model of Utatlán, which should be visited before the site. Ask at the site for a good guide, Leopoldo. The site is huge and only a small part is open to the public, although much of it belongs to the local municipality. The seven plazas, many temples, ball court, gladiator's archway and other features are marked.

On the road northwest to San Antonio Ilotenango are the thermal baths of Balneario Pachitac, in a delightful location about four kilometres from Quiché. There is a fine tiled swimming pool, and a smaller one for children, fed from a warm underground spring, clean and refreshing. Free entry, changing rooms and picnic area. Bring your own food but cold drinks available. It is a pleasant walk from Quiché along the road bordered by massive clumps of sunflowers, go west along 2 C from the centre and straight on for four kilometres. Hitching possible, probably an occasional bus to and from San Antonio.

Sights The large Parque Central has a military garrison on the east side with a jail on the lower floor and a sinister military museum with reminders of recent conflicts above. Alongside is the large, white church, substantially restored, atmospheric organ music before masses, and arum lillies (*cartuchos*) everywhere. The municipalidad façade is chocolate and banana. There is a fine statue of Tecún Umán in the centre and a colourful mural at the north end.

Sleeping **D** *Rey K'iché*, 8 C, 0-9, 2 blocks from bus terminal, built 1997, clean, comfortable, hot water, parking, restaurant, TV. **D** *Maya Quiché*, 3 Av 4-19, T7551667, with bath, hot water, restaurants. **E** *San Pascual*, 7 C, 0-43, T5555107, with bath, **F** without, occasional hot water in morning, clean, quiet, locked parking. Recommended.

F *Posada Monte Bello*, 4 Av, 9-20, clean, peaceful, nice garden, off street parking. **F** *Posada Calle Real*, 2 Av, 7-36, 25 very small rooms, parking, hot shower, clean, friendly, good value. **F** *Hospedaje San Francisco*, past church uphill, clean, good value. **F** *La Cascada*, 10 Av, 10 C, friendly, clean. **F** *Tropical*, 1 Av, 9 C, Zona 5, basic accommodation near bus terminal.

Eating

El Torito Steak House, 4 C, ½ block west of Parque Central, good meat and chicken dishes. *Pic Nic*, 2 Av, 0-45, reasonable prices. *Video 2000*, 3 C, 1 Av, inexpensive menu, *churrascos*, pizzas, hamburgers etc. *La Casona*, 2 C, 4-05, old colonial house, good selection, also vegetarian, good quality. Recommended. *Las Rosas*, 1 Av 1-28, opens for good breakfasts at 0700, good *almuerzos*. *Comedor Fliper*, 1 Av 7-31, 2 blocks from plaza, good cheap, clean. *Cafetería Mary*, 5 Av, 1 block from plaza, good. *Café Kail* on main plaza, good ice cream, cakes, also main dishes, popular with foreign visitors. *Musicafé*, 1 Av 1-16, good food, reasonable. *La Cabañita Café*, 1 Av 1-13, charming small café with pinewood furniture, home made pies and cakes, great vanilla shakes, excellent breakfasts (waffles, cereals, etc), great snacks for example *sincronizadas*, evenings only. Recommended. *Celajes*, on main plaza, good food. Good *comedor* 2 blocks north of northeast corner of main plaza, clean, cheap, friendly, pretty wooden tables. *Comedor Los Viajeros*, 1 Av, 8 C, near bus terminal, clean, good, simple meals. *La Esquina*, in the bus terminal, good for snacks while waiting for bus.

Try sincronizadas (hot tortillas baked with cubed ham, spiced chicken and cheese)

Festivals

About **14-20 August** (but varies around Assumption).

Transport

Bus terminal at 10 C y 1 Av, Zona 5, Reina de Utatlán from **Guatemala City**, Zona 4 bus terminal, 0600-1600, 3½ hours (US$1.60), via Los Encuentros and Chichicastenango (US$0.30, from *Pensión Chugüilá*). To **Nebaj** and **Cotzal**, 5 a day, US$1.40, 4-5 hours; a rough but breathtaking trip, arrive in good time to get a window seat (may leave early if full). To **Uspantán**, via **Sacapulas**, 3 a day, 5 hours, US$1.80, ride on top for good view (for continuation to **Cobán** and **San Pedro Carchá**, see below). To **Joyabaj**, several daily, via Chiché and Zacualpa, US$0.50, 1½ hours.

It is possible to get to **Huehuetenango** in a day via Sacapulas (0930 bus), then truck from bridge to Aguacatán, bus from there 1430 to Huehuetenango. There are also daily buses to **Quetzaltenango** and **San Marcos**, and to **Panajachel**.

Directory

Banks *Banco Industrial*, 3 C y 2 Av, top corner of Parque Central; *Banco G & T*, 6 C y 2 Av, open 0900-1900 Mon-Fri, 1000-1400 Sat, Visa and Mastercard, does not cash TCs. **Communications Post Office:** on 3 C between 1 Av and 0 Av, Zona 5. *Telgua*, on 1 Av/2 C, Zona 5.

There is a paved road east from Quiché to (eight kilometres) **Santo Tomás Chiché**, normally known simply as **Chiché**, a picturesque village with a fine rarely-visited Indian Saturday market (*fiesta*, 25-28 December). Buses and vans (US$0.25) run from Quiché. There is also a road to this village from Chichicastenango. Although it is a short-cut, it is rough and now virtually impassable in any vehicle. It makes a good three to four hours walk however.

45 kilometres further east from Chiché is **Zacualpa**, where beautiful woollen bags are woven. There is an unnamed *pensión* near the plaza; on the plaza itself is a private house which has cheap rooms and meals. (Mosquito coils are a must.) Market: Sunday, Thursday. Church with remarkably fine façade. Two shops opposite each other on the road into town sell weavings, good prices.

Joyabaj

On another 11 kilometres is **Joyabaj**, where women weave fascinating *huipiles*, with a colourful Sunday market, followed by a procession at about noon from the church led by the elders with drums and pipes. This was a stopping place on the old route from Mexico to Antigua. There is good walking in the wooded hills around, for example north to Chorraxaj (two hours), or across the Río Cocol south to Piedras

Blancas to see blankets being woven (ask for Santos López). Ask at the Conalfa office in Joyabaj for information or a guide. The Centro Xoy, C de la Hospital, arranges tours (for the benefit of community development) and offers Spanish and Quiché lessons. During *fiesta* week (9-15 August) Joyabaj has a *palo volador*, two men dangle from a 20 metre pole while the ropes they are attached to unravel to the ground. The villages of San Pedro and San Juan Sacatepéquez (see page 617) can be reached from Joyabaj by a dry-season road suitable only for strong vehicles and thence to Guatemala City. The scenery en route is spectacular.

Sleeping F *Pensión Mejía*, near the church, basic but clean. If staying for several days, ask at Centro Xoy for families to stay with. There is a restaurant next to the Esso station on the Santa Cruz end of the plaza with a bank opposite (will change US$ cash).

Transport Buses Joyita bus, Guatemala City 3-4 Av, 7-9 C, Zona 4, to Joyabaj. 10 a day between 0200 and 1600, 5 hours, US$1.50.

San Andrés Sajcabaja 35 kilometres northeast of Quiché is **San Andrés Sajcabaja**, an Indian village on the Río Xoljá, in a terraced landscape, wooded above, semi arid lower down. **D** *Posada San Rafael*, T7551834, including full board, traditional adobe rooms, ecotourism project run by Guatemalan/French family, horseriding, hiking, visits to local Maya sites. Bus from Quiché, US$2.

Sacapulas
Altitude: 1,220m
Colour map 4, grid C2

A poor road goes north from Quiché, 48 kilometres, to Sacapulas, a quiet, friendly town at the foot of the Cuchumatanes mountains. Here there are the remains of a bridge over Río Negro, built by Las Casas. Primitive salt extraction. Market under two large ceiba trees on Thursday and Sunday (larger, selling local wares, baskets, some traditional clothing). The colonial church has surprising treasures inside, built 1554. There are hot springs along the south bank of the river a few hundred metres east of the bridge, which are recommended for a hot bath. They are shallow, dug out depressions along the bank and a small bucket (a *guacal* or a *palangana*) is recommended to assist in bathing.

Sleeping & eating F *Restaurante Río Negro (Gloris)*, 20 rooms, basic, friendly, cold communal showers, but hot springs opposite, clean, good meals well-prepared, excellent milkshakes. *Elvi's*, on edge of town towards Chichi, good breakfast and evening meals. *Panadería Karla*, near plaza, good *chocobananos* with nuts. *Comedor Central* near the market. Small *tiendas* near the plaza and women near the bridge sell *enchiladas*, *tamales*, etc.

Transport Buses The ride from Quiché to Sacapulas is recommended, fabulous views on switchback road. All buses from Quiché to Uspantán and Aguacatán go through Sacapulas, US$1, 3 hours. Try to persuade them to let you ride on the roof. Return buses, Sacapulas-Quiché appear all to be in the early hours. Bus to Huehuetenango via Aguacatán (see below), at 0300 and 0530, basically for those taking local produce to market, 4½ hours; this road is beautiful, but can be closed in rainy season (it's a tough road to drive at any time).

The road east to Cobán

There have been reports of robberies on the road between Uspantán and Cobán as recently as late 1998

The road east from Sacapulas is one of the most beautiful, and roughest, mountain roads in all Guatemala, with magnificent scenery in the narrow valleys. Truck to Cobán, several daily morning, US$1.25, seven hours, if lucky, usually much longer. There is no direct bus to Cobán; instead, take one of the three Quiché-Uspantán buses (passing Sacapulas at about 1230, 1400, 1600), or a truck, to **Uspantán**, *fiesta* 6-10 May. Stay the night at the **F** *Hospedaje El Viajero*, two blocks east of Plaza, then two blocks south, basic, clean, pleasant, informative about the area, or **F** *Galindo*, four blocks east of Parque Central, clean, friendly, recommended. There are several places to eat, *Cafetería Kevin* is good, serves vegetables, or *Cafetería Los Pericos*, on the road to Quiché, good food, good value. Then take the early morning bus at 0300 to Cobán; you may be able to spend the night on the bus before it leaves. Truck to Cobán 0800-0900. Hitchhiking to Cobán is also possible. (Truck Uspantán-San Cristóbal Verapaz, US$1.25.) Buses to Quiché at 0300, 2200.

Between Sacapulas and Uspantán is **Cunén** (*fiesta* several days around the beginning of February, with parades of Eskimos, parrots, bears, Arabs etc, who gather at the Church and make their way round the town, especially interesting at night; one *pensión*, **F** across the road from the yellow *tienda* with the satellite dish, friendly, clean, cold shower. *Tienda y Comedor Rech Kanah María*, next to church, good; no food after 2000 anywhere). The road is not suitable for road motorcycles; off-road bikes and high-clearance vehicles OK. Fuel is sold at Uspantán, Chicamán (10 kilometres beyond) and San Cristóbal Verapaz, but supply is unreliable.

It is a five hour walk from Uspantán south to **Chimul**, the birthplace of Rigoberta Menchú, the Nobel Peace Prize winner in 1992. The village was virtually erased during the 1980s, but settlement is coming to life again. You can get a lift on market day in the afternoon, but not all the way.

The Ixil Triangle

13 kilometres north of Sacapulas, five kilometres before Cunén, is a spectacular road to the village of Nebaj (see below). It is easy enough to get by truck to Nebaj (US$0.50) and there are buses from Quiché. It is not so easy to get to the other two villages of the Ixil Triangle, **Chajul** and **San Juan Cotzal** (a new road is being completed between the two), but the 0500 bus from Quiché and Sacapulas to Nebaj on Sunday seems to continue to both. Chajul has a *pensión*, basic, **F** (under US$3); also a small *comedor*. Chajul's main festival is the second Friday in Lent. Cotzal also has a *pensión*. The village's fiesta is 21-24 June, culminating in the day of St John the Baptist on 24 June. There is a conquistador dance and it is very colourful. The local women's headwear has huge pom poms. Nebaj to Cotzal is a pleasant four hour walk. There are no formal lodging or restaurant facilities in other small villages and it is very difficult to specify what transport facilities are available in this area as trucks and the occasional pick-up or commercial van (probably the best bet – ask, especially in *Las Tres Hermanas*, Nebaj) are affected by road and weather conditions. For this reason, be prepared to have to spend the night in villages. Chajul has a pilgrimage to Christ of Golgotha on the second Friday in Lent, beginning the Wednesday before (the image is escorted by 'Romans' in blue police uniforms!) Chajul has its market Tuesday and Friday. In Cotzal the market is on Saturday. Look out for the attractive local *huipiles*.

Nebaj

On the main plaza of **Nebaj** are two weaving cooperatives selling *cortes* (skirts), *huipiles* and handicrafts from the town and the surrounding area, bargaining possible. *Huipiles* may be bought from María Santiago Chel (central market) or Juana Marcos Solís who can be found in the parque central on market days or at home (see under **Eating**) who gives weaving lessons from one day to six months. The local costume is colourful and very beautiful; the *corte* is bright red and the *huipil* is of a geometric design in red, purple, green and yellow. The women also wear a headdress with pompoms on it. Visitors are asked by young women to visit their homes to see (and buy) 'típicas', weavings (prices are usually better than in the market, but the sellers are very persistent and there is much rivalry between them); boys meet all incoming buses and will guide you to a *hospedaje*. This village has very good Sunday and Thursday markets. Nebaj has a *fiesta* on 12-15 August. There are magnificent walks from Nebaj along the river or in the surrounding hills. The views of the Cuchumatanes mountains are spectacular.

Colour map 4, grid C2

Excursions To a waterfall take the road to Chajul and after 20 minutes take the left fork to follow the river; another 40 minutes brings you to a pretty waterfall; lovely scenery. A guide is Jacinto (has a notebook of testimonials); he charges US$2 for a morning's walking.

There is good walking west of Nebaj, and the roads are better in this direction than to Chajul and Cotzal since there are a number of 'model villages' resettled by the government. These include **Acul**, follow 5 C out of town, downhill, over the bridge then, 50 metres further, the main path veers left, but go straight on; from here the route is self-evident, any forks come back together. By road leave town on Av 4, the Shell station road, at the first fork after the 'turret', follow the main road left and at the next fork take the small, unsigned track to the left. There is a good cheese farm one kilometre west of the village, whose late Italian owner was making Swiss cheese for 50 years (the cheese is for sale, US$3.50 for about 500 grammes). **Tzalbal**, two and a half hours walking; **Salquil Grande**, 26 kilometres northwest of Nebaj (several hours walk); **La Pista**, where the airstrip is. None has accommodation or restaurants. Apart from the rare bus, there is no public transport, only pick-ups; ask for advice at *Las Tres Hermanas*. **Las Violetas**, 15 minutes walk from the centre of Nebaj, is a squatters' village where people who have come down from the mountains live when they arrive in Nebaj.

Sleeping **F** *Ilebal Tenau*, Av Salida Chajul, no sign, hot water, shared bath, very clean, friendly, parking inside. **F** *Ixil*, 5 Av, 10 C, in a colonial house, pretty central patio with fountain, clean, pleasant and comfortable, big rooms. Recommended. *Posada Don Pablo*, tiny rooms but very clean, soap, towels, even a plug in the basin, good.

Under US$3: **F** *Hospedaje Esperanza*, 6 Av, 2-36, very friendly, clean, hot shower extra, noisy from evangelical church, owner's daughter gives weaving lessons, US$7 per day. **F** *Las Clavellinas*, nice, basic, without bath. Recommended. **F** *Las Tres Hermanas*, 5 Av y 4 C, no sign, 2 blocks from plaza, friendly, full of character, popular with foreigners, wood-fired hot water, not too clean (considerable wildlife), dark, basic, some beds very hard, good food available for about US$1.

Eating *Comedor Irene*, 5 C close to plaza, painted blue-green, good food, plenty of vegetables, full of character. Recommended. *Comedor Las Delicias*, good *comida corriente*. *Maya Inca*, 1 block from plaza, excellent food and coffee, try chocolate pancakes for breakfast, run by Peruvians hence the name. *Los Boxboles* a *comedor* at the home of the weaver Juana Marcos Solís (see above) in Cantón Simacol, head towards Chajul from the plaza on Av 15 de Septiembre, turn right up 0 Av at the pila on Salida Chajul, take first left and her house is last on the left. Excellent *tamalitos*, *boxboles* (squash leaves with *masa* and chopped meat or chicken spread on them, rolled tightly, boiled and served with *salsa* and fresh orange juice) and other local dishes, but food only prepared with several hours notice. Recommended. Juana also has a sauna, US$1.75 for 2 or more, US$2.65 for 1, 2 hours notice required.

Transport Buses to **Quiché** (US$1.60) and **Guatemala City** all leave early morning or late at night. From Nebaj, bus to **Sacapulas** and Quiché 0100, 0400, 0500 (coming from Cotzal), and on Sunday 0800, 2½ hours to Sacapulas (US$0.60), a further 1½ to Quiché (service times unreliable). Direct buses daily to **Huehuetenango**, Rutas Garcías, 5-6 hours, at 0100 and 2330. You can travel to Cobán in a day by getting a truck or pick-up from outside the village or earliest bus to Sacapulas, get off at junction to Cunén and hitch or catch a bus from there. There is a Shell station, but supply is unreliable and prices are high.

Directory **Banks** *Bancafé* changes Amex Tcs.

Western Guatemala

Yet more market towns and villages, with characteristic weaving or other crafts, can be found on the routes through western Guatemala. The volcanic chain is also still in evidence. In the cool highlands, Quetzaltenango is a good centre for reaching Indian villages, or for heading to Mexico, including a descent to the Pacific lowlands. Another good centre is Huehuetenango, on the highland route to Mexico. Also from Huehuetenango you can go to the Indian village and weaving centre of Todos Santos Cuchumatán, or head east to Aguacatán and the scenic road to Quiché.

Totonicapán to la Mesilla

The stretch of Pan-American Highway between Los Encuentros and San Cristóbal Totonicapán (60 kilometres) runs past **Nahualá** (*population*: 1,370; *altitude*: 2,470 metres), an Indian village where *metates*, or stones on which maize is ground to make *tortillas*, are made. The inhabitants wear distinctive costumes, and are considered by other Indians to be somewhat hostile. Good church. Market on Thursay and Sunday (this is the time to visit), at which finely embroidered cuffs and collars are sold, also very popular *huipiles*, but check the colours, many run. No accommodation except perhaps with Indian families at a small cost. *Fiesta* (Santa Catalina) on 23-26 November (main day 25). Remember the Indians do not like to be photographed.

There is another unpaved all-weather road a little to the north and 16 kilometres longer, from Los Encuentros through Totonicapán (40 kilometres) to San Cristóbal. The route from Chichicastenango to Quiché, Xecajá and Totonicapán takes a day by car or motorcycle, but is well worth taking and recommended by cyclists. No buses.

14½ kilometres east of Cuatro Caminos (see below), is the capital of its Department. There are sulphur baths, but they are dirty and crowded. Market (mind out for pickpockets) considered by Guatemalans to be one of the cheapest, and certainly very colourful, on Tuesday (small), and Saturday (the main market noted for ceramics and cloth); annual fair 24-30 September with main *fiesta* on 29 September. *Casa de Cultura*, 3 C, displays collection of fiesta masks and stuffed animals, well worth a visit. *Chuimekená* cooperative is at 9 Av between C 1 and 2, Zona Palín, fine variety of handicrafts and woven cloth.

Totonicapán
Population: 52,000, almost all Indian
Altitude: 2,500m
Colour map 4, grid C2

Sleeping E *Hospedaje San Miguel*, 3 C, 7-49, Zona 1, T7661452, clean, comfortable, hot water, prices treble on market day. F *Pensión Blanquita*, 13 Av, 4 C, hot showers, good. F *El Centro*, 7 C, 7-33, Zona 4.

Eating *Centro Siam*, 2 blocks from church, Thai and Chinese dishes. *Comedor Lety*, opposite *Hospedaje San Miguel*, excellent. *Comedor Brenda*, 8 Av, 6 y 7 C, also good.

Transport Buses Frequent buses to **Quetzaltenango** along a paved road (fine scenery), US$0.35. Bus to **Los Encuentros**, US$1.50.

Directory Banks *Banco G&T*, 2 C, 1-95, Zona 1.

San Cristóbal Totonicapán, one kilometre from the **Cuatro Caminos** road junction (Pan-American Highway, with the roads to Quetzaltenango, Totonicapán, Los Encuentros and Huehuetenango), has a huge church, built by Franciscan friars, of which the roof has recently been renovated. The silver-plated altars and screens, all hand-hammered, are worth seeing. Noted for textiles (and *huipiles* in particular) sold all over Guatemala. Also well known for ceramics. Market, Sunday, on the other

San Cristóbal Totonicapán
Population: 3,168
Altitude: 2,340m

side of the river from the church (only two blocks away), spreading along many streets. The town is notably clean and quiet on non-market days. Unhappily there is plenty of garbage down by the river. Frequent bus service to Quetzaltenango. **Festivals** 22-27 July.

Sleeping **D** *Nuevo Hotel Reforma*, T7661051, with bath, hot water, a/c, parking. **E** *Pensión Reforma*, T7661438, a/c, parking, restaurant, in Barrio La Reforma, T/F7661438. **F** *Hospedaje Amigo*.

San Francisco El Alto Two kilometres along the Quetzaltenango road from Cuatro Caminos junction a newly paved road runs north to San Francisco El Alto (three kilometres) and Momostenango (19 kilometres). **San Francisco** (*Altitude*: 2,640 metres) stands in the mountain cold, above the great valley in which lie Totonicapán, San Cristóbal and Quetzaltenango. Church of metropolitan magnificence, notice the double-headed, Hapsburg eagle. Visit the roof on market days for a fine view of activities and surroundings (US$0.20). The white west front of the church complements the bright colours of the rest of the plaza, especially the vivid green and pink of the Municipalidad. The Post Office is by the church. Crammed market on Friday, with Indians buying woollen blankets for resale throughout country; do not miss the fascinating cattle market at the entrance to town. An excellent place for buying woven and embroidered textiles of good quality, but beware of pickpockets. Go early, the market begins to close about 1030. On non-market days many of the textile shops (there are dozens) are open for business, though most are selling standard, rather than Maya textiles. Colourful New Year's Day celebrations. It is a pleasant walk from San Francisco down to the valley floor, then along the river to San Cristóbal. Frequent buses to Quetzaltenango and Totonicapán, about one hour to either. Close by in the mountains to the west is San Andrés Xecul, see under Quetzaltenango **Excursions**.

Sleeping & eating **F** *Vista Hermosa*, 3 Av, 2-22, T7661030, no showers, fleas. **F** *Galaxia*, 2 Av, 2-63, with bath, spacious rooms, check for water problems. **F** *Hospedaje Central San Francisco de Asís* on main street near market. *Real*, 1 Av 4-67, Chinese and other dishes, good value.

Directory Banks Several, *G & T*, open 0900-1500; *Banco de Comercio*, 2 C 2-64, cashes TCs.

Momostenango

At 2,220 metres this is the chief blanket-weaving centre. Indians can be seen beating the blankets on stones to shrink them. The Feast of the Uajxaquip Vats (pronounced 'washakip') is celebrated by 30,000 Indians every 260 days by the ancient Mayan calendar. Frequent masked dances also. Momostenango means 'place of the altars', and there are many on the outskirts but they are not worth looking for; there is, however, a hilltop image of a Mayan god, similar to the one outside Chichicastenango. There are said to be 300 medicine-men practising in the town; their insignia of office is a little bag containing beans and quartz crystals. The town centre is dominated by the huge church, which has a dark interior lined with saints in glass cases. There is a heavy, dark reredos with six white columns and beaten silver on the altar. The Christ figure is strikingly lit from behind. The municipal building is finally being rebuilt in 1999; it was heavily damaged by the 1976 earthquake and remained untouched in the interim. Outside town are three sets of *riscos*: eroded columns of sandstone with embedded quartz particles, which are worth visiting. The most dramatic are the least accessible, in the hills to the north of the town. The town is quiet except on Wednesday and Sunday, the market days (the latter being larger, and interesting for weaving; also try *Tienda Manuel del Jesús Agancel*, 1 Av, 1-50, Zona 4 for good bargains, especially blankets and carpets; on non-market days, ask for weavers' houses). It has a spring-fed swimming pool; also sulphur baths (five in all) at Pala Grande, four kilometres northwest of Momostenango (take the road first towards Santa Ana); the water is black, but worth experiencing, take soap. Bus service from Cuatro Caminos (US$0.35) and Quetzaltenango, US$0.55.

Sleeping **F** *Ixcel*, on main street, one block from plaza, with bath, cheaper without, clean. **F** *Hospedaje Paclom*, on same street, pretty inner courtyard, water mornings only, no showers, friendly but watch out for overcharging, cheap meals. **F** *Galaxia*, ½ block south of market, clean cold water, shower. **F** *Hospedaje Roxane*, bad, avoid. *Comedor Tonia*, friendly, cheap. *Flipper*, 1 C y 2 Av 'A', good *liquados*.

At San Cristóbal the old and the new routes of the Pan-American Highway, which joined at Los Encuentros, part again. The new route to the Mexican border at Ciudad Cuauhtémoc goes northwest. It climbs for several kilometres before dropping down past the *ladino* town of Malacatancito (48 kilometres) and swinging northwest, bypassing Huehuetenango before entering the **Selegua (El Tapón) gap** to Mexico. The road is in good condition.

Huehuetenango

Population: 39,000
Altitude: 1,905m
Colour map 4, grid C2

A six and a half kilometre spur from this road leads to **Huehuetenango**, a mining centre in farming country, with Indians from remote mountain fastnesses coming in for the daily market, and particularly Wednesday. Huehuetenango (colloquially known as Huehue) is the last town before the La Mesilla border post, on the Pan-American Highway into Mexico. It is also an appropriate town for the serious Spanish language student: there is very little English spoken here, and the language schools are good.

The city has a very attractive central plaza extending for two blocks between 2 C and 4 C, pretty sculptured gardens, a relief map of the Department, an ancient bougainvillea, statues and fountains, overlooked by a fine neoclassical cathedral and public buildings. A delightful place to stroll or sit during the day or evening. Within three or four blocks to the north and west of the plaza are a number of good value hotels and restaurants, with a busy daily market to the east. At the north end of 1 C is El Calvario church, with park and children's playground. The skyline to the north of the city is dominated by the Cuchumatanes Mountains, the largest area over 3,000 metres in Central America.

The ruins of **Zaculeu**, the old capital of the Mam tribe, are five kilometres west on top of a rise with steep drops on three sides. Half a dozen structures have been restored by covering the surfaces in concrete. The visual effect is unsatisfactory though the size and shape of the pyramids and other buildings are probably structurally correct. There has been minimal disturbance to the rest of the large site, which is a haven of quiet with wide views of the Cuchumatanes mountains behind and the plains below. The museum has many exhibits from the site from 400 AD to 1524 AD. Notable are some remarkable *incensarios* and early sewing instruments, foreshadowing the great Maya textile culture. Admission is US$3.50, nationals US$0.30, open 0800-1800, but the museum is closed for lunch. There are food and drink stalls at the entrance. A bus leaves Salvador Osorio School, final C 2, Huehuetenango, every half hour, US$0.15, last return at 1830. To walk, about one hour, either take 6 Av north, cross the river and follow the road round to the left, through Zaculeu modern village to the ruins, or go past the school and turn right beyond the river. There are signs but they are barely visible. A taxi costs about US$5.

Chiantla, five kilometres north of Huehuetenango, has a great pilgrimage to the silver Virgin of La Candelaria on 28 January to 2 February. The statue is set behind glass, upstairs; ask the priest's permission to take photos. Another *fiesta* on 8 September and interesting processions in Holy Week. The pink and white church is well

Excursions

Guatemala

worth a visit. There is a splendid roof and an impressive see-through altar with an ambulatory to the *camarín*, where the virgin and child, virtually encased in silver, can be visited. Beside the church, the parochial school is set in a nice garden. Good walking in the neighbourhood. Daily market, largest on Sunday. **F** *Hospedaje Cuchumatanes*, 7 C, one block from plaza, friendly, clean, big rooms, communal shower. Buses leave regularly from 1 Av and 1 C. 15 kilometres north of Chiantla is a *mirador*, which has magnificent views over mountain and valley (see page 693).

Sleeping
■ *on maps*
Price codes:
see inside front cover

Out of town: **A** *Los Cuchumatanes*, about 3 km out of town, Zona 7, T7641951, F7642816, good restaurant, clean swimming pool (known as Brasilia), good value. **C** *Centro Turístico Pino Montano*, at Km 259 on the Pan-American Highway, 2 km past the fork to Huehuetenango on the way to La Mesilla, a bit run down, pool, a/c, restaurant, parking, T7641637. **C** *El Prado*, Cantón San José, Zona 5, just beyond the new bus terminal, T/F7642150/51, clean. **C** *Cascata*, Lote 4, 4-42, Colonia Alvarado, Zona 5, T7641188, new, rooms on top floor best, clean, hot showers, restaurant disappointing. **E** *Trinitaria*, opposite bus station, with bath, **F** without, hot water extra, convenient but untidy.

In town: **C** *Casa Blanca*, 7 Av 3-41, T7690777, F7642586, comfortable, 2 good restaurants, 1 in pleasant garden, good value. **C** *Zaculeu*, 5 Av, 1-14, T7641086, attractive hotel, with charming lounge, cable TV, restaurant (varying reports but good breakfasts). **E** *Gran Hotel Shinula*, 4 C 2-40, T7641225, clean, bath, restaurant. **E** *Mary*, 2 C, 3-52, T/F7641228/1618, with bath, cheaper without, good beds, hot water, parking, clean, safe, good value. **E** *Todos Santos Inn*, 2 C, 6-74, T7641241, shared bath, hot water, TV, helpful, clean, luggage stored, parking locally Q 8 per night. Recommended. **E** *Vásquez*, 2 C, 6-67, T7641338, with bath cheaper without, TV lounge, parking, clean. **E** *La Sexta*, 6 Av 4-29, T7646612, with bath, cheaper without, under new management 1998, restaurant, good for breakfast, clean, good value. **E** *Lerri Colonial*, 2 C 5-49, T7641526, with bath, cheaper without, hot water, restaurant, parking. **F** *Hospedaje Huehueteco*, 2 C, 1-40, close to market, basic but clean, small single rooms, larger doubles with bath, no electricity 0700-1800. **E** *Gobernador*, 4 Av, 1-45,

Huehuetenango

T7641197, with bath, cheaper without, clean, shower, cafetería serves breakfast, limited parking. Recommended. **F** *Maya*, 3 Av, 3-55, with bath, tepid water, safe, basic. **F** *Central*, 5 Av, 1-33, communal baths, hot water, basic, laundry facilities, cheap, nice roof to sit on, parking, good breakfast, lunch and dinner. **F** *El Viajero*, 2 C 5-36, clean but very basic. There are a number of basic *pensiones* on 1 Av and near the market area. These are not recommended for single women.

Camping: camping at Zaculeu ruins, or further on the same road at the riverside, unofficial, no facilities.

All hotel restaurants are open to the public. *Las Bouganvillas*, 5 Av near 4 C, on the Plaza, large, unusual 4-storey building most of which is a popular restaurant, very good breakfasts, *almuerzos*, sandwiches, recommended. *Las Brasas*, 4 Av, corner of 2 C, steakhouse and Chinese dishes, good quality. Recommended. *La Fonda de Don Juan*, 2 C, 5-35, Italian (try the *cavatini*), excellent sandwiches, big choice of desserts, *licuados*, good pizzas, reasonable prices. *La Cabaña del Café*, 2 C 6-50, delightful place for coffee and cakes or light meal, rustic décor, very clean, good service, recommended. *Mi Tierra Internet Café*, 4 C 6-46, good drinks and light meals, nice setting, popular, recommended. *Los Pollos*, 3 C, 5 y 6 Av, full chicken meal US$3, also takeaway, open 24 hours. *Los Amigos*, behind the cathedral, good, low prices. *Bon Apetit*, 5 Av, reasonable prices. There are numerous cheap *comedores* near the market, but check for hygiene. *El Edén*, 2 km down road to Chiantla, good food. *El Jardín*, 6 Av y 4 C, Zona 1, meat dishes, good pancakes and milkshakes, local dishes. Recommended. *Pizza Hogareña*, 6 Av between 4 and 5 C, recommended, popular, always full. *Rico Mac Pollo*, 3 Av, for chicken. *Le Kaf*, 6 C, 6-40, western-style, varied menu, live music every evening, good travel information. Recommended. *Doña Estercita's*, 2 C entre 6 y 7 Av, coffee, *licuados* and pastries. Recommended. *Pan Deli's*, 2 C entre 3 y 4 Av, next to *Hotel Mary*, good breakfasts. *Restaurante Los Alpes*, 2 C/5 Av. *Rinconcito Huehueteco*, near bus station in Zona 4, good. Good *taco* stand on corner opposite bus station.

Eating

● *on maps*

Fiesta **12-17 July** and festivities **7 December** for the *quemando del Diablo* (burning the Devil) with fireworks etc.

Festivals

Artesanías y Antigüedades Ixquil, 5 Av, 1-56. Good selection of *huipiles* from local villages, reasonable prices. Recommended.

Shopping

Air   To Guatemala City, daily at 0945 (except Sunday) US$35 (plus tax). The airport is southwest of the city.

Transport

There is a new **bus** terminal on southwest outskirts of town about 2 km from the centre. Yellow urban buses shuttle between 'Terminal' and 'Centro', ruta 11, US$0.08. To **Guatemala City** (about 5 hours): US$3.75, Los Halcones, 7 Av, 3-62, Zona 1, 0700, 1400 in each direction, reliable. Rápidos Zaculeu, 3 Av, 5-25, 0600 and 1500, good service. Transportes Velásquez, 10 a day 0215-1600, US$4, recommended. El Cóndor, 5 a day. To **La Mesilla**: frequent buses, US$2, 2½ hours. To **Quetzaltenango**, US$1.65, 2½ hours. To **Cuatro Caminos**, US$1, 2 hours; to **Los Encuentros**, for Lake Atitlán and Chichicastenango, US$2.50; also, direct to **Chichicastenango**, Rutas Garcías, 0300 and 1100, US$3.20, via Sacapulas and Santa Cruz del Quiché, others includes Rutas Zaculeu to **Sacapulas**, US$0.75; to **Nebaj** 1130 daily, 5-6 hours, direct, Rutas Garcías, US$2, 3-4 hours (bus stops in Aguacatán); to **Cobán**, take 1100 bus to Sacapulas and continue by truck; to **Nentón**, **Cuilco** and other outlying villages, enquire at the new bus station. Several bus companies go to **Todos Santos Cuchumatán** between 1100-1300, 3-4 hours, US$1.25, note that the first to leave is not necessarily the first to arrive. Travellers arriving from the Mexican border should check the posted timetables for onward buses. Also, buy your tickets to where the bus takes you, eg Cuatro Caminos, Los Encuentros, not to your final destination if a change of buses is involved.

Banks   Many local banks, some open Sat morning. The bigger banks change TCs. Good rates at *Banco*

Directory

G&T, 2 C y 5 Av. Visa advances from **Construbanco**. To change Mexican pesos by Zoila Martínez just inside market at 2 Av/4 C, or ask at the *Farmacia del Cid*. **Multibanco**, on C 4, has a Visa ATM. **Communications** *Telgua*, Edif El Triángulo, 9 Av 6-142, on main road out of town, Mon-Fri 0800-2000, Sat 0800-1800, Sun 0800-1200. Telephones also next to Post Office. **Internet:** several places around the centre, eg *Mi Tierra Internet Café* charges Q 20 per ½ hr, address myearth@quetzal.net. **Post Office:** on 2 C 3-54, across the street from *Hotel Mary*. **Embassies & consulates** *The Honorary Mexican Consul*, Lic Tomás Del Cid Fernández, T7641366, at the *Farmacia del Cid* (5 Av y 4 C) will provide you with a Mexican visa or tourist card for US$1. Open Mon-Fri 0800-1200, 1500-1700, T7641366, F7641353. Helpful, has latest information. **Language schools** Spanish: some operate in the summer months only (see general notes on schools in Antigua and Quetzaltenango). *Casa Xelajú*, Apdo Postal 302, 6 C, 7-42, Zona 1. *Fundación XXIII*, 6 Av, 6-126, Zona 1, T7641478. *Instituto El Portal*, 1 C, 1-64, Zona 3. *Rodrigo Morales* (at *Sastrería La Elegancia*), 9 Av, 6-55, Zona 1, private classes. Recommended. *Instituto Zaculeu de España*, 4 C, 9-25, Zona 1. *Spanish Academy Xinabajul*, 6 Av, 0-69, Zona 1, T7641518, director María Eugenia Domínguez. Private teacher, Abesaida Guevara de López, 10 C A, 10-20, Zona 1, T7642917, US$125 per week includes room and board, recommended. Information on schools is posted in several restaurants: *Pizza Hogareña*, *El Jardín*, *La Fonda* and at the Post Office. **Useful adddresses** Car insurance: for Mexico and Guatemala can be arranged at *Banco G & T* (see above).

Aguacatán

Altitude: 1,670m
Colour map 4, grid C2

The views are fine on the road which runs between Huehuetenango and Sacapulas. Aguacatán is 26 kilometres east of Huehuetenango, 36 kilometres from Sacapulas (**F** *Nuevo Amanecer*, clean, quiet, friendly, meals. **F** *Pensión La Paz*. **F** *Hospedaje Aguacatán*, two blocks east of market and two north, noisy, above arcade – all under US$3). Aguacatán has an interesting market on Sunday (beginning Saturday night) and Thursday (excellent peanuts). The women wear beautiful costumes and head-dresses. *Fiesta* 40 days after Holy Week, Virgen de la Encarnación.

The source of the Río San Juan is about two kilometres down the C Principal north of the centre of Aguacatán, then three kilometres down a signposted turnoff. There is a two-kilometre walking route, turn left up a dirt road by the evangelist Templo Buenas Nuevas, and straight to the 'fuente'. There is a US$0.20 admission charge to the park, which is a delightful place for a freezing cold swim. It is surrounded by onion and garlic fields. Take a picnic, only soft drinks available nearby. Camping is permitted.

Transport Buses Los Verdes, 1 Av, 2-34, Huehuetenango, has buses to Aguacatán at 1300 (last return bus at 1500), US$0.50, and buses for **Sacapulas**, Quiché, Nebaj and Cobán pass through the village. There are jeeps, Huehuetenango-Aguacatán. Taxi Huehuetenango-Aguacatán US$15 for a 3-hour trip including source of Río San Juan. Zaculeu, 1 Av, 2-53, to Sacapulas, 1400, 2 hours, US$1 (truck at 1630, arrives 2000, US$1), and from the same place Alegres Mañanitas has a bus to Quiché at 0415. Bus to Chichicastenango from Aguacatán 0400, very crowded, or take a truck. The Campo Alegre company has buses to Nebaj from the *Hospedaje San José*, 1 Av and 4 Calle A, and buses for Cobán leave from the same area.

San Mateo Ixtatán
Colour map 4, grid B2

The road runs north 117 kilometres to **San Mateo Ixtatán**, at 2,530 metres, in the Cuchumatanes mountains. The *huipiles* made there are unique and are much cheaper than in Huehuetenango. Market, Sunday and Thursday. The road passes through San Juan Ixcoy, **Soloma** (watch out for young pickpockets in plaza and market; *Mansión Kathy*, run down. **F** *Hospedaje San Ignacio*, basic, fleas, noisy. **F** *Hospedaje San Juan*, charges for hot shower, secure parking), and **Santa Eulalia** (**F** *Hospedaje El Cisne*). San Mateo itself (**F** *Pensión El Aguilar*, very basic, under US$3, no showers, bring own sheets or sleeping bag) is a colourful town, with an interesting old church and black salt mines nearby. There are some impressive ruins on the outskirts of the town. The European Community has an office here.

After San Mateo the road runs 27 kilometres east to **Barillas** (several cheap *pensiones* including **F** *Terraza*, friendly, clean; **F** *Montecristo*, on main road, basic, irregular water, clean, good breakfast), a fine scenic route. Other routes lead north and west to the Mexican border. No official crossing point.

Transport Buses from Huehuetenango to San Juan Ixcoy, Soloma, Santa Eulalia, San Mateo Ixtatán (US$3) and Barillas (US$3.50) leave at 0930, 1000, 2330 and midnight, very crowded, be early and get your name high up on the list as passengers are called in order. The bus returns to Huehuetenango from San Mateo (at least 5 hours) at 0200, 0300, 0700, 1100 and 1330, but it is advised to take 2 days over the trip. Solomarita buses (1 Av and 2 C) run as far as Soloma, at 0500 and 1300. Concepcionita at 1100, 1300, 1530 also to Soloma. 5 kilometres beyond the turn off to Todos Santos Cuchumatán (see below) the road becomes rough, narrow and steep.

Todos Santos Cuchumatán

To get to **Todos Santos**, you must ascend the front range of the **Cuchumatanes** mountains above Chiantla. At the top, in 15 kilometres there is a *mirador* at about 3,300 metres, a short distance to the left of the road with a stupendous view to the south. In good visibility, you can see most of the volcanoes from Tacané on the Mexican border to Acatenango overlooking Antigua. There are nine small pyramids inscribed with verses of the poet Juan Diégez Olarerri with a garden and monument to peace in the centre. This commemorates the end of the civil war in December 1996 and construction was poignantly being completed by the army in 1999 at a spot overlooking where some of the worst tragedies took place. The new paved road continues over bleak moorland to Paquix where the road divides, and the paving ceased in 1999. The road to the north continues to Soloma (see above). The other to the west goes through Aldea Chiabel, noted for its outhouses, more obvious than the small dwellings they serve. The road crosses a pass at 3,394 metres before a difficult long descent to Todos Santos, about 50 kilometres from Huehuetenango. This road should not be attempted in a saloon car.

The village of Todos Santos is very interesting. It consists of one long, two-kilometre street down a valley, hemmed in by 3,800 metre mountains. Some of Guatemala's best weaving is done there, and fine *huipiles* may be bought in the cooperative on the main street (cash and travellers' cheques exchanged) and direct from the makers. There are also embroidered cuffs and collars for men's shirts, men's red trousers, and colourful crocheted bags made by the men. The Saturday-Sunday market is fascinating (best Saturday); also Wednesday. A museum (US$1 entrance) in the main plaza has a collection of antiques, farm tools and (poorly) stuffed animals. The attendant is pleased to explain everything. Proceeds go to the city park fund. A Spanish Language School, Proyecto Lingüístico de Español, is one block from the Parque Central. US$115 per week, food rather basic; you can also learn Mam, the local dialect. The school is part of La Hermandad Educativa non-profit language study organization with a school in Quetzaltenango and offices in the USA (452, Mansou WA 98831, T/F800-9639889) and Europe (Odensegade 4B, gaarden, 8000 Arhus C, Denmark, T861-82624, F861-30886, and Hammerstr 3, 90482 Nüremberg, Germany, T911-5441005, F911-5441006). Nuevo Amanecer is another school, started by Benito Ramírez to provide equal opportunities for the female members of the community; US$100 a week including food, fanily lodging, sauna, activities, films.

Altitude: 2,481m, hence strong sun during the day and cold at night
Colour map 4, grid B2

Excursions From Todos Santos, one can hike south to **San Juan Atitán**, five hours (more interesting costumes; market Thursday) and from there the highway at San Sebastián or San Rafael, one day's walk. F *Hospedaje San Diego*, basic, friendly, clean, food US$1.15. Also, walk southeast to **Santiago Chimaltenango** (seven hours, stay in school, ask at Municipalidad), then to San Pedro Necta, and on to the Pan-American Highway for bus back to Huehuetenango.

The highest point of the Cuchumatanes, 3,837 metres is to the northeast of Todos Santos and can be reached from the village of Tzichem on the road to Concepción

Huista. The hike takes about five hours and is best done in the late afternoon, spending the night near the top on a plateau at about 3,700 metres, convenient for camping (wood but no water). A compass is essential in case of mist. A 1:50,000 map is available at the Casa Andinista in Antigua, or at the IGN in Guatemala City.

It is also possible to walk northwest from Chiantla to Todos Santos Cuchumatanes, 13 hours, or better, two days, staying overnight at El Potrillo in the barn owned by Rigoberto Alva. This route crosses one of the highest parts of the Cordillera at over 3,500 metres. Alternatively, cycle the 40 kilometres gravel road, steep in places but rewarding. If you camp, secure your belongings.

Sleeping **F** *Hospedaje Casa Familiar*, up the hill, close to central park, hard beds, friendly family of Santiaga Mendoza Pablo, hot shower and sauna extra (about US$1), breakfast, dinner US$2.50, delicious banana bread, spectacular view, popular and recommended. Santiaga's sister-in-law, Nicolasa Jerónimo Ramírez, owns the **Tienda Maribe** further up the hill and rents rooms, **F**, friendly. Both women make and sell *típicas* and give weaving lessons, US$1 per hour: other families offer basic accommodation. **F** *Hospedaje La Paz*, friendly but fleas and cold, enclosed parking, shared showers. **F** *Hotelito Todos Santos*, above Parque Central, hot water, expanding 1999. **F** *Mam*, just below *Casa Familiar*, friendly, clean, hot water, great view of valley, good value. **F** *Las Ruinas*, up the street from *Casa Familiar*, 4 large rooms, reasonable beds, great view from rooftop bar. *Hospedaje Tres Olguitas*, very basic, dark, hot showers US$0.40, cheap meals, require a couple of hours notice.

Eating *Comedor Katy*, near *Casa Familiar*, good food, will prepare vegetarian meals on request, good value. *Tzolkin*, on main street and *Ixcanac*, opposite, good food. *Cuchumatán*, nearby, good for a drink and food. *Comedor* in market.

Festivals **1 November**, characterized by a horse race in which riders race between 2 points, having a drink at each turn until they fall off. The festival begins on 21 October.

Shopping A fair selection of old woven items can be bought from a small house behind the church and from a few other shops on, or just off, the main road. Good selection of local items at **Cooperativa Estrella de Occidente**, on main street just below church, each item is marked with the name of the member who benefits from the sale. **Casa Mendoza**, a little further uphill from *Casa Familiar*, sells trousers, shirts, *huipiles*, bags and jackets, all made to measure, also has sauna, rents rooms (**F**), ask in street for Telesforo Mendoza's daughter, Isabela, who will take you there; she also cooks meals, US$1.10.

Transport Bus to **Huehuetenango**, 3-4 hours, crowded on Monday and Friday, 6 buses between 0500 and 0630, others until 1230 or 1300. The drive is spectacular, but much of the lower land has been overgrazed and there is much soil erosion. If you do not have much luggage you can walk the 16 km uphill to Tres Caminos, the junction, where you can pick up the buses from Soloma. For petrol, ask at *El Molino*.

Jacaltenango
Much pride is taken in marimba playing, eg at football matches

The road from Todos Santos continues northwest through Concepción Huista (where the women wear towels as shawls) to Jacaltenango (bus from Todos Santos at 1600, bus to Huehuetenango at 0230 and 0300, may be others, also pick-ups). In this area Jacalteco is spoken; the *feria titular* is 29 January to 3 February, with a firework jamboree (mostly at ground and eye level) and a community dance. The hat maker in Canton Pilar supplies the hats for Todos Santos, he welcomes viewers and will make a hat to your specifications (but if you want a typical Todos Santos leather *cincho*, you must get it there).

Beyond Jacaltenango, the road goes north to Nentón (two *hospedajes*, very basic) and then on to Gracias a Dios and the Mexican border near Tziscao, from where there is a road and buses to Hidalgo and Comitán. So far as we are aware this is not an official crossing point. **NB** Check on safety in this region before visiting especially in the light of recent problems in the border area with Chiapas.

The Pan-American Highway runs west from Huehuetenango, swinging gently from one side of a gorge to the other, reaching the Guatemalan border post at **La Mesilla**.

This is the Pan-American Highway route to Mexico, the most scenic (certainly in Guatemala), faster and cooler than the coastal roads which are preferred by heavy transport.

Guatemalan immigration Open 0800-1200, 1400-1800. You may be able to pass through out of hours for a US$0.50 surcharge.

There is a tourist office (**Inguat**) in the Guatemalan immigration building.

The Mexican border post is in Ciudad Cuauhtémoc (just a few buildings, not a town) which is about 4 km from the Guatemalan frontier at La Mesilla. There are pick-ups during the day US$0.65 per person.

Entering Guatemala A tourist card for Guatemala can be obtained at the border, normally available for 30 days (although you may be given 90 days, if you request it) renewable in Guatemala City. See under **Guatemala – Essentials** for those who need visas. It is advisable to obtain a visa in advance, that is to say from Comitán. You should pay US$1 or equivalent in quetzales to enter Guatemala, and the border is open until 1800; beware of extra charges and bribery. There is sometimes a US$1 charge at customs for **not** searching your luggage. If unsure, request a receipt, and if asked if you are doubting his word, confess you are a writer and interested in official documents.

Crossing by private vehicle Some charges are posted, or printed on the documentation. Read the small print, ask for receipts and watch out for overcharging. Full details under **Getting around – car** in **Essentials**.

Mexican consulates Mexican visas are available at the border, but better at *Farmacia El Cid* in Huehuetenango for US$1, which saves time at the border. See also under Quetzaltenango, **Embassies & consulates**.

Sleeping & eating At the first gas station, 7 km from La Mesilla, is **E** *Reposo La Gasolinera*, with hot shower, cheaper without, clean, good breakfast in restaurant (other meals, US$1.75, poor), ample parking. Recommended. **F** *Mirasol*, insanitary, no running water, front rooms reasonable. **F** *Mily's*, hot water, with bath, good views. *Restaurant Yamy*, opens 0700, good breakfast, popular. In **La Democracia**, 14 km from La Mesilla, is an unsigned *mesón*, 1 block north of the market, basic, clean, **F** (under US$3).

Exchange Rates are not usually favourable at the border in either currency. You can try Banco Quetzal in La Mesilla, Banco del Café, 300m from border (good rates), or haggle in the street, but it is probably better to change a minimum amount and go for more favourable rates in Huehuetenango, Quetzaltenango or Guatemala City. Bus drivers may give you a better deal than money changers, no harm in trying!

Transport Buses from La Mesilla to Huehuetenango US$2 (1st class – foreigners tend to be overcharged – 2nd class US$1). Express buses run by El Cóndor and Velásquez, who have the better service, go to Guatemala City (US$5, 6 hours). Do not buy a ticket at the border until a bus leaves as some wait while others come and go. If you miss the last bus to Huehuetenango, you may be able to negotiate a ride out of La Mesilla. If not, there are rooms at the border and a few kilometres beyond; the border officials are helpful with accommodation. From Guatemala City, 19 C, 2-01, Zona 1, at 0400, 0900, 1000 and 1100. Change at Los Encuentros for Lake Atitlán and Chichicastenango, and at Chimaltenango or San Lucas for Antigua. When changing buses at the border, note that Mexican buses are more spacious for luggage; the Guatemalan ones often put large bags on the roof, so keep valuables, breakables, etc in your hand luggage. Also be prepared to push for a seat.

Cuatro Caminos to Talismán and Tecún Umán

Salcajá The old route of the Pan-American Highway runs west from Cuatro Caminos through Quetzaltenango to Tapachula, in Mexico. Five kilometres from San Cristóbal it reaches the small *ladino* town of **Salcajá**, where jaspé skirt material has been woven since 1861, well worth a visit. Yarn is tied and dyed, then untied and wraps stretched around telephone poles along the road or along the riverside. Many small home weavers will sell the lengths – five or eight *varas* – depending on whether the skirt is to be wrapped or pleated. The finest, of imported yarn, cost US$40. Market, Tuesday, mostly fruit and vegetables; it is early, as in all country towns. The church of San Jacinto behind the market is 16th century and also worth a visit.

Sleeping & eating There are 2 hotels in town: **D** *La Mansión de Don Hilario*, 3 Av, 3-21, Zona 2, T7689569, next door to *Cafesama* restaurant, which is good. **F** *Salcajá*, 3 Av final, Zona 1, T7689594, restaurant. Excellent unnamed bakery on third street up the hill parallel to main street where buses pass in town centre. Try *caldo de frutas*, a highly alcoholic, but clandestine drink, "when it's well made it's sweet and doesn't hit you until you try to stand up". It is not openly sold. There is also *rompopo*, made with eggs.

Quetzaltenango

Population: over
125,000
Altitude: 2,335m
Colour map 4, grid C2

Quetzaltenango (commonly known as Xela – pronounced 'shella' – 14½ kilometres southwest of Cuatro Caminos, is the most important city in western Guatemala. The climate is decidedly cool and damp, particularly November to April, and there is no heating anywhere. Set among a group of high mountains and volcanoes, one of which, Santiaguito, the lower cone of Santa María (which can be easily climbed, see Box), destroyed the city in 1902 and is still active. It is a modern city, but with narrow colonial-looking streets and a magnificent plaza (between 11 and 12 Av and 4 and 7 C).

Sights Especially interesting is the stately but quaint **Teatro Municipal** (14 Av and 1 C). There is a modern gothic-style church, the **Sagrado Corazón**, on the Parque Juárez near the market; other churches include **San Juan de Dios** on 14 Av and **La Transfiguración**, from which there is a good view. The **cathedral** is a large modern building with a 17th-century façade, grey stone and marble ornamentation and a beautiful Virgen del Rosario chapel on the north side of the nave. The **Museo de Historia Natural** on the south side of the Parque Central, has a delightful collection of historical documents, precolumbian pottery, stuffed birds, marimbas, and many other items. ■ *Monday-Friday, 0900-1800, Saturday 0800-1600 (closed in December).* There is also the **Museo de Arte**, 12 Av y 7 C, in the Casa de la Cultura, interesting collection of contemporary Guatemalan art with special exhibitions and a strange collection of stuffed animals, and the unique **Museo del Ferrocarril** Nacional de los Altos (see Box).

Excursions Many places of interest around on roads north to Huehuetenango, west to San Marcos and Mexico, south to Ocós and Champerico. According to folklore, on the Llanos de Urbina near **Olintepeque**, an Indian town six kilometres north from Quetzaltenango (on a road parallel to the main road), the greatest battle of the conquest was fought, and Alvarado slew King Tecún Umán in single combat. When Tecún Umán was struck, a quetzal is said to have flown out of his chest. The river is still known as Xequizel, the river of blood. Market, Tuesday, with an unusual emphasis on animals; *fiestas*, June 20-25. The local idol, San Pascual Baillón, has its own little church. Frequent buses from Quetzaltenango, US$0.12.

Eight kilometres to the northeast is **San Andrés Xecul**, a small village in beautiful surroundings and a very colourful church with a yellow frontage and extraordinary figurines (some claim that the church is the oldest in Central America and is often

Ferrocarril Nacional de los Altos

An extraordinary electric railway was built by Krupp and AEG of Germany between 1925 and 1930, to connect Quetzaltenango with San Felipe Retalhuleu. At that time, road connections were poor and San Felipe gave access via the main international railway to the ports and the capital.

The route chosen was through Zunil and down the gorge in a series of curves, bridges and tunnels beside Santa María volcano. A large power station was built at Santa María de Jesús. At the time it was the steepest railway gradient in the world. Each carriage and freight car had its own power unit and services began enthusiastically in March 1930. It was a success from the start.

Considerable storm damage was done to the track and 2 bridges in September 1933 and the idiosyncratic President Ubico refused to allow the necessary straightforward repairs to be made. Eventually the rails were taken up and the assets auctioned off. The route of the line can still be seen in places and much of it, including a tunnel, has been incorporated into the main road to Retalhuleu. The main station is now the military zone on 4 C in Zona 3.

The FNLA museum, 7 C/12 Av (entrance US$0.10) has an exceptional historic record of the railway, not to be missed. Open Monday-Friday 0800-1200, 1400-1800.

used in national tourist leaflets). Birds nest in the beam holes of the church roof and walls. There is also an attractive chapel, up the cobbled street, similarly painted. There are bright murals all round the plaza. Rituals can be observed at the Altar 'Maya'. Small but attractive market, Thursday. Direct buses to Quetzaltenango, US$0.25. Beyond San Andrés the road climbs 18 kilometres to San Carlos Sija, at 2,642 metres, with wide views. A climb through conifers for another 10 kilometres to **Cumbre del Aire**, with grand views of volcanoes in one direction, and of Cuchumatanes mountains in the other. Another 25 kilometres is the junction with the Pan-American Highway.

To the south of Xela there are hot steam baths at Los Vahos, reached by a dirt road to the right (three kilometres) on the outskirts of town on the road to Almolonga; a taxi will take you there and back with a one hour wait for US$1.50. Six kilometres southeast is **Almolonga**, which is noted for its fine 16th-century church (may be locked) and beautiful costumes, especially skirts, which are hard to buy. There is also a very interesting vegetable market, market days Wednesday and Saturday. *Fiesta* 28-30 June. Good swimming pool (entrance, US$0.25). About one kilometre further on are the thermal baths of Cirilo Flores (US$0.50 for large pool, US$1 to soak for an hour, hot, soothing water but heavily used – frequently cleaned) and El Recreo (entrance, US$0.30); bus from Quetzaltenango, US$0.15. It is a good three to four-hour walk back over El Baúl; ask in the village. El Baúl itself is a hill to the east of the city, reached by winding road, or direct trail to the top where there is a cross (visible from the city), a monument to Tecún Umán.

At Easter, 12-18 September and Christmas, rooms need to be booked well in advance.

Sleeping
All addresses are Zona 1 unless stated.

A *Pensión Bonifaz*, 4 C, 10-50, T7614241, F7612850 (not a *pensión* but an excellent hotel), good restaurant, clean, comfortable, US cable TV in all rooms, pool (noisy at times), central heating but lower rooms are warmer than upper rooms, quiet, (good for taking afternoon coffee and cakes). **B** *Villa Real Plaza*, 4 C, 12-22, T/F7616780, dignified colonial building nicely converted, restaurant has good vegetarian food, good value.

B *Del Campo*, Km 224 Carretera a Cantel, T7611165, F7610074, at city limits (4 km) at turn-off to Retalhuleu, good meals (*El Trigal*, European and Chinese). Recommended. **B** *Modelo*, 14 Av A, 2-31, T7612529, friendly, hot showers, good restaurant (4 course meal US$3) and breakfast from 0715, safe parking; also **D** *Anexo Hotel Modelo*, 14 Av A, 3-22, T7612606, good value.

C *Casa del Viajero*, 8 Av, 9-17, T7610743, with bath, hot water, limited but good restaurant, English-speaking manager, parking (US$0.30 extra), fax service. **C** *Casa Florencia*, 12 Av 3-61, T7612326, clean, cable TV, parking, good breakfast.

D *Casa Suiza*, 14 Av A, 2-36, T7630242, with bath, breakfast US$1.50, pleasant but run down. **D** *Centroamericana Inn*, Blvd Minerva 14-09, Zona 3, T7630261. **D** *Gran Hotel Americano*, 14 Av, 3-47, T7612118, good, friendly, room telephones, restaurant, breakfast recommended, TV, good value but noisy. **D** *Kiktem-Ja*, 13 Av, 7-18, T7614304, good location, colonial-style rooms, all with bath, hot water, open fires, car parking inside gates. Recommended. **D** *Río Azul*, 2 C, 12-15, T7630654, all rooms with bath, clean, comfortable, friendly, good location, secure but a bit tatty, owner an Internet freak.

E *Casa Kaehler*, 13 Av, 3-33, T7612091, very nice, clean, hot water all day, some rooms very cold, a bit creaky but OK. **E** *Los Alpes*, Diagonal 3, 31-04, Zona 3, T7635721, Swiss-owned, private bath. Recommended. **E** *Pensión Altense*, 9 C, 8-48, T7612811, with bath (cheaper without), new part recommended, hot water extra, restaurant, parking, secure. **E** *Pensión Andina*, 8 Av, 6-07, T7614012, hot water morning only, friendly, clean, restaurant, good value. **E** *Casa Iximulew*, 15 Av 4-59, with breakfast, also apartments minimum 4 days, restaurant next door *El Rincón de los Antojitos* under same ownership.

Quetzaltenango

0 metres 200
0 yards 218

■ **Sleeping**
1 Casa Iximulew & El Rincón de los Antojitos
2 Casa Kaehler & Radar 99
3 Casa Suiza
4 Kiktem-Ja
5 Modelo
6 Pensión Bonifaz
7 Río Azul

F *Pensión El Quijote*, 10 C 9-19, T7635228, hot water, clean, helpful, good views.
E *Pensión Horiana*, 14 C, 0-07, hot water, restaurant attached, run down, overpriced.
F *Radar 99*, 13 Av near C 4, with bath and hot water (advise the previous night for the morning), cheaper without bath, friendly, not too clean, use of kitchen, padlock useful, will arrange parking in guarded car park opposite. **F** *Casa Argentina*, Diagonal 12, 8-37, hot water, cooking facilities, clean, friendly. **F** *San Rafael*, 7 C 15-36, next to *Blue Angel*, hot showers, good value. Recommended.

F *Pensión Emperador*, 15 C 0-18, clean, no hot water. **F** *Pensión San Nicolás*, Av 12, 3-16, very basic, dirty, friendly, sunny patio, parking. **F** *Quetzalteca*, 12 Av 3-06, basic, clean, cold at night, icy water if there is any.

Kopetín, 14 Av, 3-31, friendly, good, meat and seafood dishes, about US$5.50 per meal. *El* **Eating**
Maruc, 23 Av A, 1-16, good, medium-priced, barbecued meat, dancing. Recommended.
Royal París, 14 Av A, 3-06, T7611943, French owners Bruno and Suzanne, small but reasonably priced, good food, excellent choice, including vegetarian, cheap snacks and soups, main course US$5-8, *table d'hôte* US$2.50, chocolate crêpes, nice atmosphere, live music at

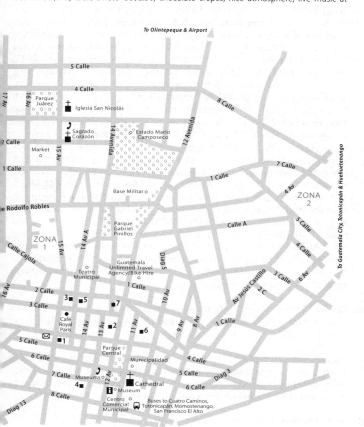

To Olintepeque & Airport

5 Calle

4 Calle

8 Calle

17 Av · 16 Av
Parque Juárez
Iglesia San Nicolás

Sagrado Corazón
14 Avenida
Estado Mario Camposeco
12 Avenida

2 Calle
Market · 15 Av

1 Calle

7 Calle

1 Calle

Base Militar

4 Av
ZONA 2

Calle Rodolfo Robles

5 Calle

Parque Gabriel Pinillos

Calle A

4 Calle

ZONA 1
Calle Cajola
15 Av · 14 Av A

Diag 5

Guatemala Unlimited Travel Agency/Bike Hire

1 Calle

3 Calle

6 Av

Av Jesús Castillo
2 C

Teatro Municipal

16 Av

2 Calle
3 Calle

3 · 5
7

9 Av · 8 Av

1 Calle

Café Royal París
14 Av · 13 Av · 2
11 Av · 6

5 Calle
1

Parque Central

6 Calle

Municipalidad

4 Calle

7 Calle
Museums
12 C · 2 Av

5 Calle
Diag 3

8 Calle
4

Cathedral
Museum

6 Calle

Diag 13

Centro Comercial Municipal

Buses to Cuatro Caminos, Totonicapán, Momostenango, San Francisco El Alto

To Guatemala City, Totonicapán & Huehuetenango

To Retalhuleu & Fuentes Georginas

Guatemala

weekends. Recommended. *El Rincón de los Antojitos*, 15 Av y 5 C (French/Guatemalan owned, Thierry y María Roquet), vegetarian and local cuisine, good food, US$4-5 main course, closed Sunday, see also **Travel Agents** below. *Shanghai*, 4 C, 12-22, Chinese, reasonable prices. *Woon Kooc*, 4 C 13-28, Zona 3, very good Chinese, friendly service, large portions reasonably priced. Recommended. *Pizza Ricca*, 14 Av, 2-42, good, value, friendly staff, mixed reports. *Pizza Bambino*, 14 Av y 4 C, Zona 3, good prices, popular with gringos, excellent vegetarian pizza. *Giuseppe's Gourmet Pizzas*, Edif Santa Rita, 15 Av, 3-68, good pizzas, friendly service. *Pizza Cardinali*, 14 Av, 3-41, good food, owned by Benny, a NY Italian, large pizzas. Recommended. *Arturo's*, 14 Av A, 3-09, good for meat, wide menu, bar facilities, nice atmosphere. *La Rueda*, 4 C, 28-40, Zona 3, 100m from Templo Minerva, expensive steakhouse. *Pocholo's*, 7 Av, 10-17, Zona 5, international and Spanish. *Panchoy*, 0 C 8-81, Zona 9, expensive. *Albamar*, 4 C 13-84, Zona 3, 12 Av 7-18, Zona 1 and other locations, good meals, nice atmosphere, good service. *El Deli Crepe*, 14 Av, 3-15, good tacos, *almuerzo* US$1.50, great milkshakes, crepes OK, reasonable prices. *Ut'z Hua*, Av 12 y C 3, typical food, very good, filling, inexpensive. *El Chaparral*, 1 C y 14 Av, Zona 3, for good grills, good atmosphere. *Café Baviera* (often called Bavaria), 5 C, 13-14, nice atmosphere, good cheap meals and praised for excellent pies and coffee, good for breakfasts, also at 14 Av A-80, opposite Teatro Municipal, also email centre. *Café Berna*, 16 Av, 3-35, Zona 3, good breakfasts, excellent sandwiches, cheesecake, open until 2000, expensive. *La Vienesa*, 9 Av entre 4 y 5 C, bakery/coffee shop, popular with locals, nice place to study local scene. *La Esperanza*, Diagonal 11, good food in evenings, with or without meat, good local information. *Los Balcones*, 7 C, 10-67, next to the cathedral, small, good, classical music. *Café y Chocolate La Luna*, 8 Av, 4-11, good cheap snacks, also very good chocolates, pleasant atmosphere in a colonial house, good meeting place, open till 2100. *Café Armadillo Pie*, 4 C, 22-15, Zona 3, imported Zurich chocolates and marzipan for sale, good pies and coffee, play dominoes, nice place. *Blue Angel Video Café*, 7 C, 15-22, Zona 1, great salads, light meals, good selection of movies Monday-Saturday 1415-2300, Sunday 1500-2300. *Taverna Alemana*, C Rodolfo Robles, 24 Av, away from the centre but worth it, typical German food, run by Guatemalans, variety of imported beers, great giant subs for US$5. *Van Gogh*, 12 Av, 17 C, decorated in Van Gogh style, good. *La Taberna de Don Rodrigo*, 14 Av entre 1 y 2 C, warm and cosy bar, reasonable food, draught beer in pint glasses. *Aladino's Bar and Restaurant*, 20 Av, 0-66 Zona 3, T7631608, Mexican bar, good selection of drinks, excellent food, good music, not expensive. *Salón Bar Tecún*, Pasaje Enríquez, off plaza 12 Av/5 C, bar, local food, video. *Los Antojitos*, 9C, 11-05, good food, draught beer, inexpensive. *Xelapán*, several locations, good cakes and bread, including wholemeal. *Helados La Americana*, 14 Av, 4-41, Zona 1, best ice cream. *Pan y Pasteles*, 4 C, 26-19, Zona 3, excellent bakery, only open Tuesday and Friday, 0900-1430. Recommended. The *comedor* opposite Galgos office is recommended for good, filling breakfast before a journey. *Enanos*, 5 C next to Parque Central, good cheap breakfast. *Brazil*, 13 Av 7-38, family-run, friendly.

Entertainment **Cinemas** *Cadore*, 13 Av and 7 C, *Roma*, 14 Av A and Calle A. *Alpino*, Plaza Ciani, 24 Av y 4 C, Zona 3. *Paraíso*, 14 Av A 1-10, interesting films; *Polanco*, in shopping centre 14 Av/4 C. Cost US$0.85-US$1.50. See also *Blue Angel Video Café*.

Theatre *Teatro Municipal*, 14 Av/1 C, main season May-November, theatre, opera etc, tickets about US$7. *Green House Café-Teatro*, or *Casa Verde*, 12 Av, 1-40, T7630271, daily programme of live music, poetry, dance, theatre etc, board games, cheap international calls and fax, useful bulletin board, café/restaurant, bar, best meeting place in town.

Festivals **9-17 September** and Holy Week (very interesting).

Shopping For local items try the markets of which there are 4: main market at **Templo de Minerva** at Western edge of town (take local bus, US$0.04), has craft section; at the southeast corner of **Parque Centro América** (central park) is a shopping centre with craft stalls on the upper levels, food, clothes, etc below. Another market at 2 C y 16 Av, Zona 3, south of Parque Benito Juárez. *Típica Chivita*, Centro Comercial Municipal, 2nd level, makes up locally produced woollen blankets into jackets. *Xekijel*, 7 C, 10/11 Av, T7614734, just off plaza, same side of road as tourist office, very good for textile lengths and *artesanía*. *Talabartería Quetgo*, C Rodolfo Robles, 15-53, excellent selection, good starting prices. Every first Sunday of the month, there is an *artesanía* market in Parque Central, with a marimba band playing in the morning. Of the markets around Quetzaltenango, the more interesting are at Zunil, San Andrés Xecul and San Francisco el Alto. For food shopping, in the **Mont Blanc** commercial centre, *El Paiz*, 4 C y 19 Av, Zona 3. Good shops, boutiques and food in El Portal commercial centre, 13 Av, 5-38. *Mérida* supermarket in the *mercado*, Av 15, C 1, Zona 3.

Bookshops *Bellas Letras*, 3 C, 12-31, T7634680, new and second-hand books in several languages, maps etc. *Vrisa*, 15 Av, 3-64, T7613237, has a good range of English language second-hand books, paperbacks and magazines, coffee shop and cycle hire. Recommended.

Photography Good quality development at Konica, 15 Av opposite Post Office. Kodak, Fuji etc each have several shops around town.

Sports **Climbing**: for rock climbing on neighbouring volcanoes, contact Miguel Morales, 4 C, Diag 3-67, T7562105 (home), 7614673 (office). For general mountain climbing: *Asociación Quezalteca de Andinismo*, trekking and volcano climbing, meetings at 5 C, 8-43 on Tuesday 2030, good Spanish and some experience very useful. **Tennis**: *Club Tenís Quezalteco*, 4 C, 18-50, Zona 3, T7612356, for information and temporary membership.

Transport **Local Bicycle hire**: *Xela Sin Límites* travel agency, 12 Av, 1 C, T/F7616043, US$6 per day, US$30 per week, deposit required.

    Air To Guatemala City Inter at 0900 and 1520 daily, US$40 plus tax, 1 way.

    Buses To **Guatemala City**, Galgos, C Rodolfo Robles 17-43, T7612248, Zona 3, 1st class buses, 7 a day from 0330-1645 (US$4, 4 hours, will carry bicycles – several adverse comments on Galgos services to Guatemala City 1998); Marquensita average a day (office in the capital 21 C, 1-56, Zona 1). Líneas América to Guatemala City, 6 a day from 7 Av, 3-33 Zona 2, T7614587. Transportes Alamo has at least 5 daily from 14 A 3-60, Zona 3, T7612964. For **Antigua**, change at Chimaltenango (Galgos, US$3 to Chimaltenango 0800, 1000). To **Huehuetenango** 0500 and 1530, US$1.65. From Quetzaltenango you can get to three border crossings: La Mesilla via Huehuetenango (if you cannot get a regular bus catch a chicken bus from behind the market, see map, plenty of them and not too crowded early in the morning); Talismán bridge and Tecún Umán (frequent buses from there to Tapachula), buses run all day from Minerva terminal, but you will probably have to change buses in Malacatán. Regular buses to **Cuatro Caminos** US$0.40 (where buses for Guatemala City and Huehuetenango stop on the highway), **Totonicapán**, 1 hour (US$0.35), **San Francisco El Alto** (US$0.35), **Momostenango** (0600, US$0.55) and **Retalhuleu**, 1½ hours (US$0.90). Also many 2nd class buses to many parts of the country from Zona 3 market by Parque Minerva (13 Av y 4 Calle A), eg Transportes Velásquez to **Huehuetenango**, US$1, 2 hours; to **Malacatán**, 5 hours, US$2; to **Los Encuentros**, US$2; to **Chichicastenango**, Transportes Velóz, US$1, 2½ hours; to **Panajachel**, Transportes Morales, US$2, 2½ hours; to **Zunil**, US$0.30, 40 minutes; also to **La Mesilla** at 0800. Bus to town from 2nd class terminal, No 3 from just below Templo de Minerva through the market.

Directory **Banks** Many banks on the central plaza. *Banco Occidente*, 12 Av, 5-12, on west side, Mon-Fri 0900-1900, Sat 0930-1400. *Banco Inmobiliario*, northwest corner. *Banco Industrial*, eastside, corner 5 C, Visa ATM. *Banco Quetzal*, Av 14/C 4, good rates for TCs; *G & T*, 14 Av, 3-17. Many other banks do Visa but for Mastercard, go to *Banco Continental*, 2nd floor of the Montblanc commercial building, 4 C, 19 Av, Zona 3 (also Visa); many banks are open 0900-1800 and on Sat morning.

    Communications Post and Telegraph Office: 15 Av y 4 C, Telephone (Telgua) 13 Av between 6 and 7 C, Zona 1, and 15 Av y 3 C, Zona 3, near Mercado La Democracia. The Tourist Service Centre (CEDEM) on C Rodolfo Robles 17-23 will send a fax cheaper than Telgua. You can also receive phone calls here. Other places to try are *Maya Communications*, Pasaje Enríquez above *Bar Tecún*, open 0800-0100, also email, which is interlinked with offices in Antigua and Panajachel, T/F7612832. *Green House Café*, see under Theatre. *Speed Calls*, behind the Post Office. *Internet Café*, 1 C Callejón 16, 1-20,

Guatemala

Volcanoes and views

To reach the **Santa María volcano** (3,772 metres) take the bus to Llano del Piñal from the Central bus station (every 30 minutes or when full from the Shell station on Av 9; last bus back from Llano del Piñal leaves at 1830; taxi about US$5). Get off at the crossroads and follow the dirt road towards the right side of the volcano until it sweeps up to the right (about 40 minutes), where you should take the footpath on the left (marked for some distance); bear right at the saddle where another path comes in from the left – look carefully, it is easily missed. A rough 5½-hour climb (1,500 metres – take plenty of water) but worth it for the superb views of the Pacific and to watch the still active crater, **Santiaguito** (2,488 metres), on the Pacific side. Do not attempt to climb this cone, several people were killed in 1990 when overtaken by an eruption (see also page 704). There are frequent clouds of poisonous gas. The volcano can also be reached from Retalhuleu (see page 705) by bus to Palajunoz, from where it is also a 4½-hour climb. It is possible to camp at the summit, or on the saddle west of the summit, but cold and windy. Early morning is the best time for views, and the dawn can be `magic'. Santa María is popular with picnickers on Sunday. You can arrange a guide in Llano del Piñal for about US$6 (eg Alfonso, who lives in the last house on the right before the road turns upward on to the foot of Santa María). From Quetzaltenango, the cost is about US$30 per person including transport and guide. There is a good view from the **Siete Orejas volcano** (inactive, 3,370 metres) 10 kilometres northwest of Santa María.

T7611436, open 0900-1700, internet, fax; another at 4 C 15-23, 2 doors from Post Office. Check around for the best rates.

Cultural centres Alianza Francesa de Quetzaltenango, 15 Av, 3-64, T7614076, runs French courses including one-to-one tuition, many cultural events (exhibitions, films on Thur evening, lectures, etc).

Embassies & consulates Consulate: Mexican, 21 Av 8-64, Zona 3, T7675542/5, Mon-Fri 0900-1300, take photocopies of passport and some nationalities have to show copy of international credit card.

Hospitals & medical services Dr Oscar Armando de León A at the hospital is an English speaking doctor, 9 C, 10-41, T7612956. Dr Luis Méndez, 1 C 23, Zona 3. Also speaks English.

Language schools There are many schools, most of which offer individual tuition, accommodation with families, extra-curricular activities and excursions. Mayan languages are also offered by some. Several schools fund community development projects and students are invited to participate with voluntary work. Extra-curricular activities are generally better organized at the larger schools (despite the factory atmosphere). Prices start from US$100 per week including accommodation but rise in Jun-Aug to US$120-150. The following have been recommended by students: **English Club and International Language School**, 3 C, 15-16, Apdo Postal 145, F7632198. Harry Danvers is an expert on indigenous culture, worth a visit. **Proyecto Lingüístico Quezalteco de Español**, 5 C, 2-40, T/F7631061, plq@c.net.gt. See also under Todos Santos Cuchumatán for US and European offices. For information also write to National Registration Center for Study Abroad, 823 North 2nd St, PO Box 1393, Milwaukee, W1 53201, USA. **Casa de Español Xelahú**, Callejón 15, Diagonal 13-02, T7619954, F7615953, office@casaxelaju.com, USA contact: 2206, Falcon Hill Drive, Austin TX78745, T512-4166991, F512-4168965. **Spanish School Juan Sisay**, 15 Av, 8-38, Apartado Postal 392, T/F7631684. **Instituto Central América (ICA)**, 1 C, 16-93, T7631871, in USA: RR Box 101, Stanton, Nebraska, 68779 T402-4392943. Internet access for students' use (for a fee). **Centro de Estudios de Español Pop Wuj**, 1 C, 17-72, 5 C, 2-40, T/F7618286. **Desarrollo del Pueblo**, 19 Av 0-34, Zona 3, T/F7616754, Apartado Postal 41, in UK, Hannah Roberts, 48 Thorncliffe Rd, Oxford OX2 7BB, T01865-552653. **Ulew Tinimit**, 8 Av 3-30, PO Box 346, T/F7631713. **Academia Latinoamericana Mayense** (ALM), 15 Av, 6-75, PO Box 375 and 376, T7612707. **Proyecto Lingüístico de Santa María**, 14 Av A, 1-26, Apartado Postal 230, T7612570, F7618281. **Utatlán**, 12 Av, 4-32, PO Box 239, T7630446, possibility of voluntary work with under-privileged children. **Centro del Lenguaje América Latina**, 19 Av, 3-63, Zona 3, T7616416. **Minerva Spanish School**, 24 Av, 4-39. **Guatemalensis**, 19 Av, 2-41. **Kie-Balam**, Diagonal 12 4-46, T7611636; US contact: M M Weese, 894 Patricia Drive, Elgin, IU 60120, T847-8882514. Also recommended is **Q'anil, Encuentro de Expresión Cultural**, 15 Av, 6-24, Zona 3, small, non-profit collective, also teaches traditional music. **La Paz**, Diagonal 11 7-38, T/F7612159.

INEPAS, 15 Av, 5 C, information at *Rincón de los Antojitos*, also linked to a primary school founded by the Roquets in a Maya village. *Artes Latinas*, 10 Av C-09, T/F7612717, E cafenet.xele@quetzal.net. See also *AmeriSpan* on page 40.

Laundry *Minimax*, 14 Av C-47, T7612952, 0730-1930, US$2.15, wash and dry. *Lavandería Pronto*, 7 C, 13-25, Zona 1, good cheap service. *Lavandería El Centro*, 15 Av, 3-51, Zona 1, US$2 wash and dry, very good service.

Tour companies & travel agents *SAB Agencia de Viajes*, 1 C, 12-35, T7616402, good for cheap flights. Thierry Roquet at *El Rincón de los Antojitos* restaurant arranges trips to volcanoes, hot springs, markets, cross country treks, etc. Recommended. A guide, José, advertises in Post Office, cafés, friendly Spanish teacher, speaks English, can take you to Santa María Volcano, US$8 per person, Laguna Chicabal, US$7 per person, or hot springs, usually at weekends.

Tourist offices *Inguat*, 7 C, 11-35, southwest corner of the Plaza, T7614931. Mon-Fri, 0800-1300, 1400-1700, free maps of city.

Useful addresses Hairdresser: *Sala de Belleza Anny*, good haircut US$6, 13 Av, 4-60, Zona 3, Plaza Monterrey. Ask for Anny. **Insurance:** *G & T* motoring insurance from *Seguros Occidental* behind Banco del Café, which is on main plaza. **Mechanic:** *Taller Enderezad*, corner of 8 Av and 3 C, Zona 1. Recommended for car repairs. Also *Don Abdullio* at 6 C, 5-48, Zona 2. **Volunteer work:** *SCDRYS*, Sociedad Civil para Desarrollo Replicable y Sostenible, Diagonal 11, 7-17 (1 block from *Blue Angel Video Café*) for social work opportunities in the area and Quiché (ask for Guillermo Díaz).

Quetzaltenango to Champerico

Via Retalhuleu the 53-kilometres link between the old Pan-American Highway and Pacific Highway, is paved all the way. The first town (11 kilometres) is **Cantel**, which has the largest textile factory in the country. Market, Sunday; *fiestas*, 12-18 August (main day 15) and a passion play at Easter.

Nine kilometres from Quetzaltenango is Zunil, picturesquely located in the canyon of Río Samalá. Market, Monday, Friday, small and colourful but swamped if two busloads of tourists come in (beware pickpockets); *fiesta*, 22-26 November (main day 25), and a very colourful Holy Week. On the Saturday there is a very slow procession through the village, followed by a performance of Christ's life in the plaza outside the church, lots of comedy. No market that Monday when the inhabitants go to the cemetery and pray for their dead. Striking church, inside and out. The local sacred idol is San Simón, a life size dummy, dressed differently at different times, for example in ski wear: hat, scarf, gloves and sunglasses, or in a black suit and wide-brimmed hat, complete with cigar; the statue is moved from time to time to different houses. Enquire locally for the present location. A small charge is usually made or a donation expected. Behind the church is a cooperative (*Santa Ana*) which sells beautiful *huipiles*, and shirt and skirt materials.

Zunil

Zunil Pico, rises to 3,542 metres to the southeast of the town. On its slopes are the thermal baths of **Fuentes Georginas**, ■ *Monday-Saturday 0800-1700, Sunday 0800-1600, US$1.45*; E *Turicentro Fuentes Georginas*, eight bungalows (a bit run down) with two double beds, cold shower, fireplace with wood, no electricity after 2100, candles provided, barbecue grills for guests' use near baths. Reasonably priced restaurant set into the hillside overlooking the Fuentes. After heavy rains in late 1998, there was a significant rockfall into the pool which damaged the basin and demolished the restaurant. By early 1999 the Fuentes and restaurant were restored but the former elegant statue has not been replaced. Ask to see the photos of the damage. Present (1999) temperatures are about 55°C, curiously increased after higher rainfall, but there is considerable fluctuation. There are steam vents in the slopes above the Fuentes, worth a 45 minutes hike up the hill. The path is in good condition, but keep left to avoid a cul-de-sac. Fuentes Georginas can be reached either by walking the eight kilometres, uphill to south of Zunil (300 metres ascent; take right fork after four kilometres, robbery has occurred here), by pickup truck (US$5.50), or hitch a ride. Alternatively, take the bus from Quetzaltenango to Mazatenango, but get out at the sign to Fuentes Georginas, or ask for advice in Zunil.

Taxi from Quetzaltenango is about US$11. The road, with spectacular views down the valley and across to Volcán Santa María, was paved in 1998, but was damaged by the rains in several places which are quite dangerous. The thermal baths of Aguas Amargas are also on Zunil mountain, below Fuentes Georginas; they are reached by a road heading east before Santa María de Jesús.

The road descends through Santa María de Jesús (large hydro-electric station) to bypass **San Felipe**, at 760 metres, 35 kilometres from Zunil. Tropical jungle fruits. Beyond, three kilometres, is **San Martín**, with a branch road to Mazatenango. Just before San Felipe is a turn to the right for El Palmar. The river here flows directly down from the active Santiaguito, and a recent eruption combined with heavy rains led to a pyroclastic flow which wiped out the small town and left an extraordinary legacy. The river, which changed its course, now flows directly through the centre of the church. Heavy erosion since leaves the west front and the altar separated by a 30 metre deep ravine. Upstream, most properties are now abandoned. One exception is Finca El Palmar where there is a plaque to the four climbers killed on the mountain in 1990. They left from here to climb to the crater (see Box page 679).

Mazatenango
Population: 37,850
Altitude: 380m

18 kilometres from San Martín, Mazatenango is the chief town of the Costa Grande zone. It is not especially attractive though the Parque Central is very pleasant with many fine shade trees. The Pacific Highway now bypasses the town. There is a huge festival in the last week of February, when hotels are very full and double their prices. At that time, beware of children carrying (and throwing) bags of flour. There is a cinema.

Sleeping C *Alba*, 7 C, 0-26, Zona 2, T8720264, OK. **D** *San Pablo*, Pacific Highway Km 153 in San Bernardino, with bath, fan, cable TV, restaurant alongside. **E** *Roma*, 3 C 5-30, T8720139, quiet street in pleasant area, very nice. **E** *La Gran Tasca*, 7 Av, 4-53, T8720316, with bath, fan, cable TV, friendly owners, good value. Recommended. **E** *Recreo*, Av La Libertad 8-27, T8720435, friendly family, close to main plaza but noisy. **F** *Sarah*, by the old railway station, with bath. **F** *Santa Bárbara*, bottom of 6 Av facing railway station, clean, nice. **F** *Chinchilla*, 4 C, 5-17, beside church on Parque Central, clean, friendly, cafetería attached. **F** *Gloria*, 5 C, 1-13, ½ block from Texaco station, quiet side street, clean, decent. **F** *Costa Rica*, 1 Av, 2 C near the petrol stations.

Eating *Maxim's*, 6 Av, 9-23, extensive *churrasco* and Chinese menus, reasonable prices, spotless, interesting range of Chinese porcelain for sale. Highly recommended. *Pagoda Dorada*, 9 C, 6-17, average Chinese, locally popular, inexpensive. *Pizza Cardinale*, 1 Av, 10 C, good pizzas, take away service. *La Tabla*, 1 Av, steakhouse near bus stations. *Yogen Früz*, 6 Av, 9-33, fresh fruit yogurts a speciality. *Holanda Helados*, Parque Central, huge choice of ice creams. *Croissants Pastelería*, Parque Central, excellent pastries, juice etc.

Transport Buses They leave frequently from petrol stations to **Guatemala City**, US$1.50; to the border at **Tecún Umán** US$1.50.

Directory Banks *Banco de Los Trabajadores*, 7 C, 3-18, Zona 1. *Banco Occidente*, 6 Av, 8 C (Visa). *Banco Industrial*, 7 C, 2-52 (TCs). *Bancor*, 1 C, 1 Av (Visa and Mastercard). *Bancafé*, 1 C, 1 Av, Zona 2 (TCs). **Communications** *Telgua* on the Pacific Highway at eastern entrance to town.

Seven kilometres west of Mazatenango is **Cuyotenango** (C *Posada del Sol*, T8720166, bungalows, a/c, hot water, pool, parking, restaurant, quiet, clean, friendly), where a dirt road goes 65 kilometres down to the coast, at **El Tulate**. There is a white sand bar with a lagoon behind.

Retalhuleu

Southwest 11 kilometres from San Martín is **Retalhuleu**, capital of the Department of the same name with a fine *Palacio del Gobierno*. It serves a large number of coffee and sugar estates. **Museo de Arqueología y Etnología**, next to the *Palacio*, small but interesting collection and a permanent exhibition of photos of old Retalhuleu, entry US$1.45. Don't miss the old railway station, a museum in itself with first and second class waiting rooms and timetables showing trains three days a week to Guatemala City. A 1992 calendar gathers dust while many wagons rust on the tracks outside. You can look at it all from the *Cab Bus Café* on a renovated part of the platform. *Fiesta*, 6-12 December.

Population: 42,000
Altitude: 240m
Retalhuleu is normally referred to as 'Reu', both in conversation and on bus signs
Colour map 4, grid C2

Excursions

One of the best ancient sites to visit outside El Petén is **Abaj Takalik**, about 10 kilometres north of the Pacific Highway near El Asintal on the Río Nil. The side road through coffee fincas is paved through El Asintal to the site, thought to date from 800 BC and occupied until 900 AD. At its height, the settlement comprised four cities covering nine square kilometres, only a fraction of which has been excavated and even less opened to the public. In the very well-presented part that you can see, the main temple buildings are mostly up to 12 metres high suggesting an early date before techniques were available to build Tikal-sized structures. Olmec style figures abound, human and animal, frogs facing east for fertility and birth, jaguar and crocodile facing west towards darkness and the afterlife. A ball court in an early 'T' design has been found. There is a small museum and a collection of threatened indigenous animals. It is scrupulously maintained and well worth a visit. Entrance US$3.50, nationals US$0.30, guide included (Genaro López recommended). To get there drive or get a bus to El Asintal and walk the pleasant four kilometres to the site entrance. Take water and refreshments.

Sleeping

Out of town B *Costa Real*, on Pacific Highway, Km 182.5, T7712402, F7712412, motel style with rooms circling pools, a/c, hot water, TV, telephone in rooms, restaurant, busy at weekends. **B** *La Colonia*, 1½ km to the north at Km 178, T7710054, a/c, recreation area, pool, good food. Recommended. **C** *Siboney*, 5 km northwest of Reu in San Sebastián, Km 179, T7710149, F7710711, with bath, bungalow style round large pool, excellent restaurant, try *caldo de mariscos* US$6, *paella* for 2 US$11. *Hostal de San Martín*, San Martín Tzapotitlán, 3 km north of San Sebastián, Km 180.5, a recreational complex owned by IRTRA, Instituto de Recreación de los Trabajadores Privados, with hotel complex, Parque Acuático Xocomil (a watersports park). Though private, you may be able to visit, for information call T7712673 or 2890268 (Guatemala). **In town: B** *Posada de Don José*, 5 C, 3-67, T7710180, F7711179, full service hotel, a/c and fan, TV, telephone, very good restaurant, Sunday buffet 1200-1500, live music most evenings. Recommended. **D** *Astor*, 5 C, 4-60, T7710475, T7712562, colonial style round delightful courtyard, a/c, hot water, TV, telephone, parking, restaurant credit cards. Recommended. **D** *Modelo*, 5 C, 4-53, T7710256, with bath, fan, OK. **F** *Hilman*, 7 Av 7-99, fan, clean, parking, basic but acceptable. **F** *Pacífico*, 7 Av, 9-29, opposite Mercado San Nicolás, dismal, last resort only.

Eating

La Luna, 5 C, 4-97, on Parque Central, good *típico* meals: breakfast US$2, lunch and dinner US$3, also Chinese menu, good. *El Volován*, on Parque Central, delicious cakes, pies and ice creams. *Stivi's Café*, 5 Av, 2 C, good snacks, salads, milk shakes, better than average coffee, modern, comfortable, pleasant atmosphere. *Pollo Llanero*, 7 Av, 8-39, clean, good, inexpensive. *El Patio*, 5 C/4 Av, OK. *Comedor Mary*, opposite *Hotel Hilman*.

Transport

Air Inter office in *Posada de Don José*, daily flights to Guatemala at 0700, US$35, plus tax, one way. **Bus** Services along Pacific Highway to Mexico (Talismán and Tecún Umán) and Guatemala City stop at Reu. Bus station at 7 Av/10 C.

Directory

Banks *Banco del Agro*. TCs. *Banco Industrial*. TCs, Visa. *Banco Occidente*. Mastercard. *Banco Inmobiliario*, Mastercard. **Communications** *Telgua*, 5 C 4-18, Mon-Fri 0800-2000, Sat to 1800, Sun to 1200. **Embassies & consulates** Consulate: Mexican 5 C/3 Av.

Guatemala

Champerico 43 kilometres southwest of Retalhuleu by a paved road, Champerico was once the
Population: 4,500 third most important port in the country, but is little used now. Good black sand
Colour map 4, grid C2 beach but there is a strong undercurrent; good fishing. There is a municipal fresh
water swimming pool US$0.50. Mosquitoes, day and night.

Sleeping D *Posada del Mar*, on outskirts of town, Km 222, T7737104. E *El Submarino*, at
beach end of 3 Av, T7737237, cheerful rooms with comfortable beds and modern plumbing,
TV, good restaurant overlooking beach. F *Miramar*, 2 C, Av Coatepeque, T7737231, nice restaurant with dark wood bar, Spanish owners, good. F *Martita*, opposite *Miramar*, with bath,
cheaper without, fan, restaurant. F *Hospedaje Buenos Aires*, 3 Av, 4 C, clean, neat rooms in
nice clapboard house with balcony, bit noisy from traffic. F *Hospedaje Recinos*, 7 C, Av
Coatepeque, clean but small dark rooms, basic.

Eating *Alcatraz*, next to *El Submarino*, good. *Frutilandia*, 3 Av opposite market, juices,
liquados, ice cream. Other good restaurants on the beach.

Transport Buses To Quetzaltenango direct 0400, 0600 and 0800. Later, change at Reu.
Every 30 minutes to **Retalhuleu**. Direct bus to **Guatemala City**, 0245, 0545, 1030, 4-5 hours.

Directory Communications Post Office: 1 C, just off 3 Av. **Telgua**: 2 C, 3 Av, beside Palacio
Municipal.

Quetzaltenango west to Mexico

15 kilometres to **San Juan Ostuncalco** (*Altitude*: 2,530 metres), a pleasant, prosperous town with a big white church, noted for good weekly market on Sunday and
beautiful sashes worn by men. *Fiesta*, Virgen de la Candelaria, 29 January-2 February. See below for the road south to the Pacific town of Ocós. The road, which is
paved, switchbacks 37 kilometres down valleys and over pine-clad mountains to a
plateau looking over the valley in which are San Pedro and San Marcos, also known
as La Unión. **San Marcos** (*Altitude*: 2,350 metres) is one kilometre or so beyond San
Pedro. **San Pedro** (full name San Pedro Sacatepéquez, same name as the town near
Guatemala City) has a huge market Thursday. Its Sunday market is less interesting.
There is an interesting Palacio Municipal (known as the Palacio Maya) built in 1926,
with a wooden clocktower. The Indian women wear golden-purple skirts.

  Tajumulco volcano, 4,220 metres (the highest in Central America), can be
reached by taking the road from San Marcos to San Sebastián; after the latter, several
kilometres on is the summit of a pass at which a junction to the right goes to Tacaná,
and to the left is the start of the ascent of Tajumulco, about five hours climb. Once
you have reached the ridge on Tajumulco, turn right along the top of it; there are two
peaks, the higher is on the right. The one on the left (4,100 metres) is used for sha-
manistic rituals; people are not very friendly, so do not climb alone. The last bus
back from Tajumulco village leaves about 1500 so you need to start out from San
Marcos very early, 0200 bus going to Tacaná recommended, very slow road, 20 kilometres to Tuchán takes two hours, no accommodation available on the way. Ask in
the village of Tuchán for Juan Pérez y Pérez, a guide who lives at the start of the
climb, US$5 per person. **Tacaná** volcano may be climbed from Sibinal village.

  About 15 kilometres west of San Marcos the road begins its descent from 2,500
metres to the lowlands. In 53 kilometres to **Malacatán** it drops to 366 metres. This
was one of the toughest stretches in Central America, but now the surface is paved. It
is a tiring ride with continuous bends, but the scenery is attractive.

Sleeping & At **San Juan Ostuncalco**: F *Ciprés Inn*, 6 Av, 1-29, T7616174, clean, hot water, good atmo-
eating sphere, TV, good restaurant, traditional blue wooden building, converted private house,
modern bathrooms. Highly recommended. F *El Embajador*, 7 C, 1 Av, good views. *Ricafé* for
burgers and sandwiches, aquarium. At **San Marcos**: D *Fairmont*, 10 C 8-74, T7604893, hot

water, parking. **D** *Siesta*, 9 Av 7-77, T7601441, restaurant. **E-F** *Maya*, negotiate price, shower, hot water. **E** *Pérez*, 9 C, 2-25, T7601007, with good dining room, meals US$2. At **San Pedro**: All under US$3: *Bagod*, 5 Av 8-29, T7605366, noisy. *Bethalonia*, 3 blocks north of main plaza. *El Valle*, simple but clean. *Pensión Victoria*, 4C and 9 Av, basic but clean, rooms around a central courtyard, pleasant owner. **Restaurants**: *La Cueva de Los Faraones*, 5 C, 1-11, a real Italian menu, chef Sr Franco Manzini, moderate prices. Recommended. *Brasilia*, 7 Av, 4-19, excellent typical breakfast for US$0.85. At **Malacatán**: **D** *La Estancia*, 3 C, 3-43, T7769382, a/c, restaurant, parking. **F** *América*, lunch, US$1, good. **F** *Pensión Santa Lucía*, 5 C, 5-25, Zona 1, T7769415. Several other hotels and *hospedajes*, under US$3.

The international bridge over the Río Suchiate at **Talismán** into Mexico is 18 kilometres west of Malacatán. Beyond the bridge the road goes on to Tapachula.

Guatemalan immigration Normally open 24 hours. It is a 200 metre walk between the 2 border posts.

Frontier with Mexico – Talismán/Tapachula

NB We have received reports of armed robberies at the border day and night, for example in the toilets.

Mexican consulate There is a service at the border and at Malacatán (closed at 1300).

Crossing by private vehicle If entering by car, especially a rented car, be prepared for red tape, miscellaneous charges, vehicle fumigation and frustration. See **Essentials**. There are lots of pushy children around, employing one of them for US$2-3 could smooth progress.

Sleeping There is a *hospedaje* at the border but better accommodation nearby (see above) or in Mexico.

Exchange Money changers offer the same (reasonable) rates on both sides of the border. There is no bank on the Guatemalan side.

Transport From the border to Quetzaltenango, it is best to go via Retalhuleu (take Galgos bus from the border), but you can go by bus to Malacatán, then bus (or taxi US$5) to San Marcos, 1½ hours, lovely scenery, walk up hill to Parque Central, ask for Galgos bus stop or catch a van, US$0.70 per person plus US$0.70 for bags on top, to Quetzaltenango. Beware of overcharging on buses from the border to Quetzaltenango. Bus Talismán-Guatemala City, US$4, Galgos 6 a day, 5 hours because of checkpoints; if there is no direct bus, you have to go to Malacatán for buses to Guatemala City (which may go via Tecún Umán).
  This border is not used much by heavy transport. Hitchhikers will find Tecún Umán better. There are also more direct buses from Tecún Umán to the capital than from Talismán.
  Travelling by bus to Mexico is quicker from Quetzaltenango than from San Marcos. Most traffic seems to go via Coatepeque and not via San Marcos; the former road is longer but is reported very good. From Quetzaltenango, there are frequent buses to Talismán via San Marcos or Coatepeque, and probably more via Coatepeque to Ciudad Tecún Umán; buses from Xela marked 'Talismán' usually involve a change in Malacatán, 40 minutes from border (US$0.30 by bus from shelter at back of Malacatán bus station). From San Pedro, frequent local buses from 0430 to 1630 to Malacatán, from where colectivos, often crowded, will get you to the border. Or take bus from Quetzaltenango to Retalhuleu, 1½ hours, US$0.55, then another to the border, 2 hours, US$1.85.

The road to the coastal plain from San Juan Ostuncalco (see page 706) is the most attractive of all the routes down from the highlands, paved but not busy, bypassing most of the small towns through quickly changing scenery as you lose height. After San Juan, go south for one and a half kilometres to **Concepción Chiquirichapa**, with a bright blue and yellow church, which is one of the wealthiest villages in the country. It has a small market early every Thursday morning. *Fiesta* 5-9 December.

San Martín
Sacatepéquez Five and a half kilometres beyond is **San Martín** (sometimes known as Chile Verde, famous for its hot chillies; this village appears in Miguel Angel Asturias' *Mulata de Tal*), in a windy, cold gash in the mountains. *Huipiles* and shirts from the cottage up behind the church. Accommodation next door to the Centro de Salud (ask at the Centro), US$0.50. Food in *comedor* opposite church, US$0.20. Indians speak a dialect of Mam not understood by other Maya tribes, having been separated from them during the Quiché invasion of the Guatemalan highlands. The men wear very striking costumes. Market, Sunday. *Fiesta* 7-12 November (main day 11). Ceremonies of initiation held on 2 May at nearby **Laguna Chicabal**, in the crater of a volcano. The walk to the lake from San Martín takes about two hours, ask any campesino for the path to Laguna Chicabal. It is possible to camp at the lake. The last bus to Quetzaltenango leaves at 1900. It is often cloudy at Las Nubes (naturall) and everything gets noticeably greener.

Coatepeque By **Colomba** (basic *hospedaje*) you are in the lowlands. From Colomba a road
Population: 13,657 branches south (28 kilometres) to Retalhuleu: the main road runs 21 kilometres
Altitude: 700m west from Colomba to **Coatepeque** on the Pacific Highway; one of the richest coffee zones in the country; also maize, sugar-cane, bananas and cattle. There is a bright, modern church in the leafy Plaza Central. *Fiesta*, 11-19 March.

Sleeping **A** *Virginia*, at Km 220, T/F7751801, hot water, pool, restaurant. **D** *Villa Real*, 6 C, 6-57, T7751308, F7751939, friendly, comfortable, restaurant, cable TV, a/c, good value. **D** *Baechli*, 6 C, 5-35, T7751483, with bath, parking. **E** *Europa*, 6 C, 4-01, T7751860, in front of the plaza, with bath, parking. **F** *Posada Santander*, 6 C, 6-43, T7753122, shared bath, basic, but OK. **E** *Mansión Residencial*, 0 Av, 11-49, Zona 2, T7752018. Many restaurants around the plaza.

Transport **Buses** Bus from Quetzaltenango, US$0.40 (buses to/from the capital as for Talismán).

Directory **Banks** *Banco Continental*, *BAM*, *Bancafé* and several others.

The paved Pacific Highway goes to **Tecún Umán**, 34 kilometres west, on the Mexican frontier, separated by the Río Suchiate from the Mexican town of Ciudad Hidalgo.

Frontier with **Guatemalan immigration** The 1 km bridge over the river separates the 2 border posts.
Mexico – Pedestrians pay US$0.15, cycle taxis cost US$1, toll for cars. For a fee, boys will help you with
Tecún your luggage. Open normally 24 hours.
Umán/Ciudad
Hidalgo **Mexican consulates** See Malacatán and Quetzaltenango.

Sleeping **D** *Pirámide*, 3 Av 4-46, restaurant, parking. **E** *Maxcel*, 3 Av, 1 C, Zona 2. **F** *Lourdes*, 1 Av A, Zona 1.

Exchange Banco de Guatemala, 1 Av entre 4 y 5 C, Zona 2, and other banks will not cash pesos. Money changers on the street will. Reasonable rates reported.

Transport Buses run from the Mexican side of the border to Tapachula, 30 minutes, cheap (beware of overcharging). The bus to Guatemala City costs US$4, run by Fortaleza, 4 direct buses daily, 5 hours, frequent slower buses via Retalhuleu and Mazatenango. Colectivo from Coatepeque, US$0.50. See also under the Talismán crossing.

Ocós, a small port now closed to shipping, is served by a 22-kilometre road south from Tecún Umán. Across the river from Ocós is **Tilapa**, a small resort; buses from Coatepeque and ferries from Ocós (**F** *Pensión Teddy*, friendly). The swimming is good, but both here and at Ocós there are sharks, so stay close to the shore.

Background

The land

A lowland ribbon, nowhere more than 50 kilometres wide, runs the whole length of the Pacific shore. Cotton, sugar, bananas and maize are the chief crops of this lowland, particularly in the Department of Escuintla. There is some stock raising as well. Summer rain is heavy and the lowland carries scrub forest.

From this plain the highlands rise sharply to heights of between 2,500 and 3,000 metres and stretch some 240 kilometres to the north before sinking into the northern lowlands. A string of volcanoes juts boldly above the southern highlands along the Pacific. There are intermont basins at from 1,500 to 2,500 metres in this volcanic area. Most of the people of Guatemala live in these basins, drained by short rivers into the Pacific and by longer ones into the Atlantic. One basin west of the capital has no apparent outlet and here, ringed by volcanoes, is the splendid Lake Atitlán. The southern highlands are covered with lush vegetation over a volcanic subsoil. This clears away in the central highlands, exposing the crystalline rock of the east-west running ranges. This area is lower but more rugged, with sharp-faced ridges and deep ravines modifying into gentle slopes and occasional valley lowlands as it loses height and approaches the Caribbean coastal levels and the flatlands of El Petén.

The lower slopes of these highlands, from about 600 to 1,500 metres, are planted with coffee. Coffee plantations make almost a complete belt around them. Above 1,500 metres is given over to wheat and the main subsistence crops of maize and beans. Deforestation is becoming a serious problem. Where rainfall is low there are savannas, where water for irrigation is now drawn from wells and these areas are being reclaimed for pasture and fruit growing.

Two large rivers flow down to the Caribbean Gulf of Honduras from the highlands: one is the Río Motagua, 400 kilometres long, rising among the southern volcanoes; the other, further north, is the Río Polochic, 298 kilometres long, which drains into Lake Izabal and the Bay of Amatique. There are large areas of lowland in the lower reaches of both rivers, which are navigable for considerable distances; this was the great banana zone.

To the northwest, bordering on Belize and Mexico, in the peninsula of Yucatán, lies the low, undulating tableland of El Petén (36,300 square kilometres). In some parts there is natural grassland, with woods and streams, suitable for cattle, but large areas are covered with dense hardwood forest. Since the 1970s large-scale tree-felling has reduced this tropical rain forest by some 40 percent, especially in the south and east. However, in the north, which now forms Guatemala's share of the Maya Biosphere Reserve (with Mexico and Belize), the forest is protected, but illegal logging still takes place. Deep in the tangled rain forest lie the ruins of Maya cities such as Tikal and Uaxactún. In the Department of Petén, almost one-third of the national territory, there are only 250,000 people.

Climate Climate, dependent upon altitude, varies greatly. Most of the population lives at between 900 and 2,500 metres, where the climate is healthy and of an even springlike warmth – warm days and cool nights. The pronounced rainy season in the highlands is from May to October; the dry from November to April.

History

For early history see the introductory chapter to Central America. Cochineal and indigo were the great exports until 1857, when both were wiped out by competition from synthetic dyes. The vacuum was filled by cacao, followed by coffee and bananas, and essential oils.

Only coffee of the Bourbon variety is planted below 600 metres, and until 1906, when bananas were first planted there, the low-lying *tierra caliente* had been used mostly for cane and cattle raising. The first plantations of the United Fruit Company were at the mouth of the Motagua, near Puerto Barrios, then little more than a village. Blacks from Jamaica were brought in to work them. The plantations expanded until they covered most of the *tierra caliente* in the northeast – along the lower Motagua and around Lake Izabal.

In the 1930s, however, the plantations were struck by disease and the Company began planting bananas in the Pacific lowlands; they are railed across country to the Caribbean ports. There are still substantial plantations at Bananera, 58 kilometres inland from Puerto Barrios, though some of the old banana land is used for cotton and *abacá* (manila hemp).

Social reform Jorge Ubico, an efficient but brutal dictator who came to power in 1931, was deposed in 1944. After some confusion, Juan José Arévalo was elected President and set out to accomplish a social revolution, paying particular attention to education and labour problems. He survived several conspiracies and finished his term of six years. Jacobo Arbenz became President in 1950, and the pace of reform was quickened. His Agrarian Reform Law, dividing large estates expropriated without adequate compensation among the numerous landless peasantry, aroused opposition from landowners.

Military rule In June 1954, Colonel Carlos Castillo Armas, backed by interested parties and with the encouragement of the United States, led a successful insurrection and became President. For the next three decades the army and its right-wing supporters suppressed left-wing efforts, both constitutional and violent, to restore the gains made under Arévalo and Arbenz; many thousands of people, mostly leftists but also many Indians, were killed during this period.

Return of democracy In August 1983 General Oscar Mejía Victores took power. He permitted a Constituent Assembly to be elected in 1984, which drew up a new constitution and worked out a timetable for a return to democracy. Presidential elections, held in December 1985, were won by Vinicio Cerezo Arévalo of the Christian Democrat party (DC), who took office in January 1986. In the 1990 elections the Christian Democrats fared badly, their candidate failing to qualify for run-off elections between Jorge Serrano Elías, the eventual winner, of the Solidarity Action Movement (MAS) and Jorge Carpio of the National Centrist Union (UCN).

Civil unrest By 1993 when President Serrano's government reached mid-term, the country was in disarray. Political, social and economic policies pursued by the government had alienated nearly everybody and violence erupted on the streets led by a wave of student riots. The Christian Democrats and the UCN centrists withdrew their support in Congress, leaving the government without a majority. Amid growing civil unrest, President Serrano suspended the constitution, dissolved Congress and the Supreme Court and imposed press censorship, with what appeared to be military support for his auto-coup. International and domestic condemnation for his action was immediate and most foreign aid was frozen. After only a few days, Serrano was ousted by a combination of military, business and opposition leaders and a return to constitutional rule was promised. Congress approved a successor to Serrano immediately, electing as president Ramiro de León Carpio, who had previously been the human rights ombudsman. This spectacular choice led to much optimism, which proved short-lived. Although progress was made in talks between the government and the Guatemalan National Revolutionary Unity (URNG), assassinations, kidnapping and human rights violations continued. Some communities, displaying no faith in the security and justice systems, took the law into their hands to deal with criminals. Land invasions also continued and strikes in the public and private sectors continued in 1994 and early 1995. In this climate, the public's distaste at corrupt congressional deputies and ineffectual government was not diminished. The president seemed powerless to restore any confidence because Congress deliberately failed to approve bills on constitutional, police, or tax reform, and other laws. The reform of election procedures and political parties had been called for by a referendum in 1994, which obliged Congressional elections to be called. The result gave a majority of seats to the Guatemalan Republican Front (FRG), led by ex-president Efraín Ríos Montt. Voter turnout was under 20 percent of the electorate. Despite an alliance of four parties against the FRG's control of Congress, Ríos Montt was elected to the presidency of Congress for 1994-96.

Ríos Montt's candidate in the 1995 presidential election, Alfonso Portillo, lost by a slim margin to Alvaro Arzú of the National Advancement Party (PAN). Although backed by the business élite, the army and the urban middle class, Arzú proposed to increase social spending, curtail tax evasion, combat crime and bring a speedy conclusion to peace negotiations with the URNG guerrillas.

Towards peace

One of the earliest moves made by President Serrano was to speed up a process of talks between the government and the URNG, which began in Oslo in March 1990. The sides, including the military, met in Mexico City in April 1991 to discuss such topics as democratization and human rights, a reduced role for the military, the rights of indigenous people, the resettlement of refugees and agrarian reform. Progress was slow and several rounds of talks were held with little achieved. The URNG remained active, but in late 1993 negotiations recommenced, leading to a Global Human Rights accord signed between the government and rebels on 29 March 1994. Further talks and the setting up of a Civil Society Assembly (to deliberate on the displaced and victims of war, a truth commission and other issues) raised hopes, but by March 1995 no solution to the civil war had been found. The main stumbling block was the issue of the rights of indigenous people; while the government and URNG could not reach agreement, indigenous groups were excluded from the talks. A related problem, land ownership, also had to be addressed by the Peace Commission. After UN Secretary General Boutros Boutros Ghali expressed the frustration of many in late-1994, talks were given new impetus and a timetable for decisions, leading to an acccord by August 1995, was drawn up with the aid of the UN's Guatemala mission (MINUGUA) and the Norwegian government. The timetable proved over-ambitious, but, on taking office, President Arzú committed himself to signing a peace accord. In February 1996 he met the URNG leadership, who called a ceasefire in March. Arzú immediately ordered the military to suspend anti-guerrilla operations. Subsequent negotiations had to resolve issues such as social and agrarian reform, constitutional reform, the reintegration of guerrillas into civilian and political life, the future role of the military and the question of an amnesty for those on each side accused of human rights violations. In October, after intense discussions and some compromises, the URNG agreed to sign a bilateral ceasefire. On 29 December 1996 a peace treaty was signed, ending 36 years of armed conflict. An amnesty was agreed which would limit the scope of the Commission for Historical Clarification and prevent it naming names in its investigations of human rights abuses. The 3,000 URNG guerrilla troops congregated in six special camps, ready for demobilization in March 1997 when a 60-day disarmament process began, supervised by the UN. Although the demobilization was completed successfully, difficulties remained over human rights in the peace process. Nothing emphasized this more than the bludgeoning to death of Bishop Juan Gerardi Conedra, the ecclesiastical coordinator for the Project for the Recuperation of Historical Memory in April 1998. Two days before his murder the Project released *Guatemala Nunca Más* (Never Again), a report detailing 150,000 deaths and 50,000 disappearances in the civil conflict (50,000 and 10,000 more respectively than other estimates). 80 percent of the human rights violations, the report said, were caused by the military. At the same time, the Commission for Historical Clarification was undertaking its own investigation, with wide support from almost all sectors, but facing reluctance from the military to release information.

In the run-up to elections in November 1999, a referendum on constitutional reforms resulting from the peace accords was held on 16 May. Among the issues were greater recognition for indigenous languages, judicial changes to benefit the indigenous population and limits on the power of the armed forces. Although the legislative assembly had approved these issues, many elements were rejected by the urban, *ladino* voters, whose majority outnumbered the votes of the rural population. This led to a growing sense of frustration over the slow progress in the peace accords and over the hardline efforts to prevent the establishment of responsibility for human rights violations in the civil war. Nevertheless, in March 1999, President Clinton on an official visit apologised for the United States' part in the violent counter-insurgency campaign after documents were declassified for the Commission for Historical Clarification.

Culture

People About half the total population are classed as Amerindian. (Estimates of the Amerindian population vary, from 40 percent to 65 percent.) Over 40 percent are *ladino*, while five percent are white, two percent black and 3.9 percent other mixed race or Chinese. UN statistics show that 87 percent of the population live in poverty and 72 percent can not afford a minimum diet. Some 65 percent of the people live at elevations above 1,000 metres in 30 percent of the total territory; only 35 percent live at lower elevations in 70 percent of the total territory.

NB The word *ladino*, used all over Central America but most commonly in Guatemala, applies to any person with a 'Latin' culture, speaking Spanish and wearing normal Western clothes, though he or she may be pure Amerindian by descent. The opposite of *ladino* is *indigena*; the definition is cultural, not racial.

The indigenous people of Guatemala are mainly of Maya descent. There are 22 recognized language groups of the Guatemalan Maya, with 100 or more dialects. The largest of the 22 indigenous groups are Quiche, Kekchi and Mam. A brief description of their culture follows.

When the Spaniards arrived from Mexico City in 1523 they found little precious metal: only some silver at Huehuetenango. Those who stayed settled in the intermont basins of the southern highlands around Antigua and Guatemala City and intermarried with the groups of native subsistence farmers living there. This was the basis of the present *mestizo* population living in the cities and towns as well as in all parts of the southern highlands and in the flatlands along the Pacific coast; the indigenous population is still at its most dense in the western highlands and Alta Verapaz. They form two distinct cultures: the almost self-supporting indigenous system in the highlands, and the *ladino* commercial economy in the lowlands.

The scenery of the Indian regions west of the capital is superb and full of colour. In the towns and villages are colonial churches, often with splendid interiors. The coming of the Spaniards transformed outer lives: they sing old Spanish songs, and their religion is a compound of image-worshipping paganism and the outward forms of Catholicism, but their inner natures remain largely untouched.

Their markets and *fiestas* are of outstanding interest. Festivals are a riot of noise, a confusion of processions, usually carrying saints, and the whole punctuated by grand firework displays and masked dancers. The chief *fiesta* is always for a town's particular patron saint, but all the main Catholic festivals and Christmas are celebrated to some extent everywhere.

Costume & Indian dress is unique and attractive, little changed from the time the Spaniards arrived: the
dress colourful head-dresses, *huipiles* (tunics) and skirts of the women, the often richly patterned sashes and kerchiefs, the hatbands and tassels of the men. It varies greatly, often from village to village. Unfortunately a new outfit is costly, the Indians are poor, and denims are cheap. While men are adopting western dress in many villages, women are slower to change. As a result of the increase in employment opportunities and the problems of land distribution (see below), many Indians are now moving from the highlands to the *ladino* lowland areas; other Indians come to the southern plains as seasonal labourers whilst retaining their costumes, languages and customs and returning to the highlands each year to tend their own crops.

Education 50 percent of the population aged 25 and over have had no formal schooling and a further 22 percent failed to complete primary education.

Religion There is no official religion but about 70 percent consider themselves Roman Catholic. The other 30 percent are Protestant, mostly affiliated to evangelical churches, which have been very active in the country in the past 25 years.

The Economy

Structure of production

The equitable distribution of occupied land is a pressing problem. US Aid statistics show that 68 percent of the cultivable land is in the hands of two percent of the landowners, 20 percent in the hands of 22 percent, and 10 percent in the hands of 78 percent, these figures corresponding to the large, medium and small landowners. A quarter of the land held by the small owners was sub-let to peasants who owned none at all. There were 531,636 farms according to the 1979 census, of which 288,083 (54 percent) were of less than 1.4 hectares, 180,385 (34 percent) were of under seven hectares, while 482 (less than one percent) were of more than 900 hectares. Between 1955 and 1982, 665,000 hectares were redistributed (compared with 884,000 between 1952 and 1954), but it was estimated that in 1982 there were 420,000 landless agricultural workers. A peaceful movement of *campesinos* (farm labourers) was formed in 1986 to speed land distribution.

In international trade the accent is still heavily on agriculture, which accounts for over two thirds of total exports. Coffee is the largest export item, followed by sugar, but bananas, vegetables, sesame and cardamom are also important crops. There has been an attempt to diversify agricultural exports with tobacco, fruit and ornamental plants, and beef exports are increasing.

The industrial sector has been growing steadily; the main activities, apart from food and drink production, include rubber, textiles, paper and pharmaceuticals. Chemicals, furniture, petroleum products, electrical components and building materials are also produced. The encouragement of *maquila* industries in the mid-1980s attracted foreign investment, much of it from the Far East, and created low-paid jobs for about 80,000 Guatemalans, mostly in garment manufacturing. In 1994, *maquila* exports were the third largest item in Guatemala's foreign sales (US$147mn to USA alone). At the same time, though, 60 factories moved to Mexico to be within the NAFTA bloc, with a loss of 20,000 Guatemalan jobs. The decline was forecast to continue.

Oil has been discovered at Las Tortugas and Rubelsanto in the Department of Alta Verapaz and in the northern Petén in a basin known as Paso Caballos. The Rubelsanto find is estimated to have proven and probable reserves of 27.3 million barrels. Production in 1996 was running at around 20,000 b/d. A pipeline transports oil from Rubelsanto to the port of Santo Tomás de Castilla. Several new wells are under development in El Petén and Guatemala is nearly self-sufficient. Several foreign oil companies are interested in exploration in Guatemala. Offshore exploration has so far been unsuccessful. There are three oil refineries. In order to lessen imports of petroleum, five hydroelectricity projects have been developed including Aguacapa (90 Mw) and Chixoy (300 Mw). A 120 Mw coal power plant is under construction on the Pacific coast. The first coal facility in Central America, it was due for completion in 1999 at a cost of US$170mn.

Recent Trends

Guatemala's poor growth record in the first half of the 1980s was attributable to the world recession bringing low agricultural commodity prices, particularly for coffee, and political instability both at home and in neighbouring Central American countries. The return to democracy and economic restructuring brought confidence and higher rates of growth as inflows of foreign funds were renewed. Other factors improving the balance of payments included moderate imports, rising exports, a rebound in tourism and selective debt rescheduling arrangements. An attempt at economic liberalization in 1989, involving the floating of the exchange rate, was reined in in 1990. The Government reintroduced control over the rate after it fell sharply, causing a surge in inflation. Measures were announced to reduce liquidity and curb the fiscal deficit by raising tax income, although two previous efforts to increase taxes were followed by military coup attempts and had to be diluted.

The Government which took office in January 1991 sought an agreement with the IMF to reduce the fiscal deficit and inflation and stabilize the exchange rate. Efforts were also made to refinance the external debt owed to official international financial institutions. Inflation was cut from 41.1 percent in 1990 to 10.1 percent in 1992 and has remained at around that level ever since.

Gdp rose by 3.2 percent in 1991 and 4.8 percent in 1992. Growth slowed to four percent in 1993 and 1994 as investment was restricted after the insecurity of the Serrano *auto-coup*. Growth did not translate into higher investment in agriculture or industry. Nor did it produce improvements in under- or unemployment, land use or raise standards of living. High interest rates attracted capital inflows and international reserves increased from US$19mn in 1990 to US$786mn by end-1994. A 15-month standby arrangement was signed with the IMF in December 1992 but had to be renegotiated by the de León Carpio government. A new agreement was signed in late 1993 and much of the administration's economic planning was tied to IMF structural adjustment.

The credit and investment picture improved in 1995, led by multilateral lending to the private sector in areas such as tourism, agroindustry and energy. In 1996, confidence improved as talks progressed with the URNG for peace and social and agrarian reform but there was a slowdown in investment reflected in slower import demand and gdp grew by only 3.1 percent.

The Government estimates it needs US$2.6bn to fulfill its commitments agreed in the peace accords. While about US$1.9bn is to be provided by international lending institutions and donors, the balance has to come from taxes. The Government has pledged to combat poverty and inequality by increasing social spending, with a doubling of health and education expenditure over four years. Funds are also needed to reform the judiciary, the police and the army and provide aid for returning refugees. Privatization is now a priority with 95 percent of the state telecommunications company Telgua, originally to be sold in 1997, delayed until October 1998 by legal challenges. In the previous month, a Spanish-led consortium bought the Guatemala Electricity Company (EEGSA). The state-run railway system was taken over in 1997 by Railroad Development of the USA, which reopened a section of the Caribbean line to freight in April 1999. The entire route to the Caribbean ports was due to be operational by end-1999, with extension to the Pacific to follow.

Communications There are 18,000 kilometres of roads, 16 percent of which are paved. A railway links the Caribbean seaboard with the Pacific, running from Puerto Barrios up the Motagua valley to Guatemala City and on to the port of San José. From Santa María a branch line runs west through Mazatenango to the port of Champerico and the Mexican frontier. With the closure in 1995 to passengers of the line Guatemala City – Puerto Barrios, there are only freight services on Guatemala's railways. There are 867 kilometres of public service railways and 290 kilometres of plantation lines.

Government

Guatemala is a Republic with a single legislative house with 80 seats. The Head of State and of government is the President. The country is administratively divided into 22 Departments. The Governor of each is appointed by the President, whose term is for five years. The latest constitution was dated May 1985.

Conservation

The quetzal, a rare bird of the Trogon family, is the national emblem. A stuffed specimen is perched on the national coat of arms in the Presidential Palace's ceremonial hall and others are at the Natural History Museums in Guatemala City, Quetzaltenango, the *Camino Real Hotel* in Guatemala City and in the Historical Exhibit below the National Library. (Live ones may be seen, if you are very lucky, in the Biotopo on the Guatemala City-Cobán road, or in heavily forested highlands.)

Conservation and National Parks

Cecon (Centro de Estudios Conservacionistas) and Inguat (addresses under **Tourist Information**, Guatemala City) are setting up Conservation Areas (Biotopos) for the protection of Guatemalan wildlife (the quetzal, the manatee, the jaguar, et cetera). Several other national parks (some including Maya archaeological sites) and forest reserves have been set up or are planned. The main ones are given in the text. Those interested should see Thor Janson's books *Animales de Centroamérica en Peligro, Maya Nature* and *The Quetzal* (in English) available at Editorial Piedra Santa bookstores in Guatemala City and Antigua.

Belize

Belize

Essentials

Belize, formerly known as British Honduras, borders on Mexico and Guatemala, and has a land area of about 8,867 square miles, including numerous small islands known as Cayes. Its greatest length (north-south) is 174 miles and its greatest width (east-west) is 68 miles. Within this small territory the landscape varies from mountainous forests with abundant wildlife, fertile foothills where sugar, rice, cattle and fruit trees are cultivated, swampy coastlands and beautiful beaches on the Cayes. The reefs and cayes form a 150-mile barrier reef with crystal clear water for diving and snorkelling and are a major tourist attraction.

Planning your trip

Many travellers are dismayed by the state of **Belize City** and hassling by residents, but the authorities are working hard to clean it up and present a better face to tourists. Special police have been introduced and crime is much less nowadays, but you are still likely to be offered drugs on the streets. It is possible to avoid Belize City all together, but it is worth spending a day or two having a look around and getting a feel for the old town. Generally, the longer people stay, the better they like it. The tiny capital, **Belmopan**, is an excursion from Belize City, there is not much to see and very few places to stay, even government workers prefer to commute from Belize City.

Where to go

The **northern cayes** are the main recipients of tourism to Belize. Pleasant resorts and budget places to stay attract a wide range of travellers wishing to sample the delights of a Caribbean island. The atmosphere is very laid back but there are lots of watersports for the active, including some spectacular diving or snorkelling on the barrier reef. **Ambergris Caye** and **Caye Caulker** are the two most developed cayes, from where you can take excursions to the smaller cayes and marine parks.

The Northern Highway leads from Belize City to the Mexican border through some of the most productive farm land in the country. There is still plenty of room for wildlife, however, and several sanctuaries, including the **Community Baboon Sanctuary**, for black howler monkeys, the **Crooked Tree Lagoons and Wildlife Sanctuary**, for birds, and the 9,000-hectare **Shipstern Nature Reserve** incorporating hardwood forests, lagoons and savannah. There are also the archaeological remains of **Altun Ha**, which was once a major Maya ceremonial site and a trading post between the Caribbean and the interior, and **Lamanai**, one of Belize's largest archaeological sites with a 112-foot temple, the tallest known preclassic Maya structure. **Orange Walk**, the country's second city, is in the north. A very mixed race city, getting its wealth from agriculture, you can find Mennonites, Creoles, Maya and other Central Americans.

The Western Highway leads from Belize City to **San Ignacio** and the Guatemalan border, also past many nature reserves and wildlife sanctuaries where you can find eco-resorts, basic lodges and working farms offering accommodation. The **Mountain Pine Ridge** area offers great hiking, amid spectacular forests, rivers, rapids, waterfalls and caves. San Ignacio itself has a pleasant climate and is in a beautiful setting in wooded hills straddling the Macal River. Most people spend some time here before moving on to Guatemala and it is noted as one of the friendliest areas in the country. There are several Maya sites, notably **Xunantunich**, with its plazas, temples, ball court and 'castillo', and **Caracol**, from the late classic period, where the Sky Palace pyramid reaches a height of 138 feet.

The Southern Highway runs through sparsely populated countryside dotted with Indian settlements. It is much wetter here, but the coast is being developed for tourism and new hotels and lodges are being built, providing lots of choice for all budgets. You can also stay at guest houses in Indian villages as part of a community tourism project. Offshore cayes are reached by boat from **Dangriga** or Mango Creek, several of which are private or have very small settlements and offer seclusion, relaxation, lovely beaches and fabulous water. Near Punta Gorda are the ruins of **Lubaantun**, a late Maya ceremonial site.

When to go Shade temperature is not often over 90°F (32°C) on the coast, even in the hotter months of February to May (the 'dry season', but see below). Inland, in the west, day temperatures can exceed 100°F (38°C), but the nights are cooler. Between November and February there are cold spells during which the temperature at Belize City may fall to 55°F (13°C). Humidity is

Belize

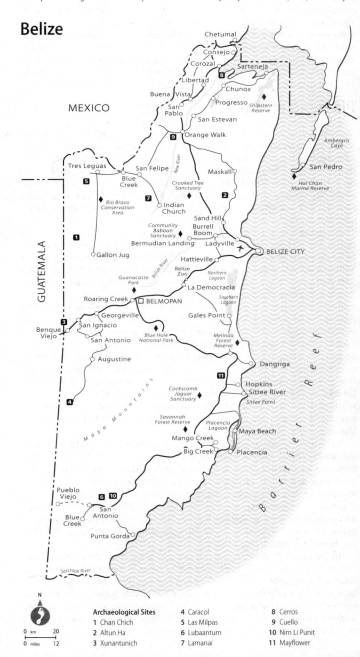

MEXICO

Chetumal
Consejo
Corozal
Sarteneja
Libertad
8
Buena Vista
Chunox
San Pablo
Progresso
Shipstern Reserve
San Estevan
9 Orange Walk

GUATEMALA

Tres Leguas
San Felipe
Maskall
5
Blue Creek
Crooked Tree Sanctuary
2
San Pedro
Hol Chan Marine Reserve
Ambergris Caye
Rio Bravo Conservation Area
7
Indian Church
Sand Hill
1
Community Baboon Sanctuary
Burrell Boom
Bermudian Landing
Ladyville
Gallon Jug
Hattieville
BELIZE CITY
Guanacaste Park
Belize Zoo
Northern Lagoon
La Democracia
Roaring Creek
BELMOPAN
Southern Lagoon
Georgeville
Gales Point
3
San Ignacio
Benque Viejo
San Antonio
Blue Hole National Park
Melinda Forest Reserve
Augustine
Dangriga
11
Hopkins
Cockscomb Jaguar Sanctuary
Sittee River
Sittee Point
4
Savannah Forest Reserve
Placencia Lagoon
Maya Beach
Mango Creek
Big Creek
Placencia
Pueblo Viejo
6 **10**
Blue Creek
San Antonio
Punta Gorda
Sarstoon River

Maya Mountains

Barrier Reef

Belize

N

0 km 20
0 miles 12

Archaeological Sites
1 Chan Chich
2 Altun Ha
3 Xunantunich
4 Caracol
5 Las Milpas
6 Lubaantum
7 Lamanai
8 Cerros
9 Cuello
10 Nim Li Punit
11 Mayflower

New River
Belize River

normally high, making it 'sticky' most of the time in the lowlands.

There are sharp annual variations of rainfall, there is even an occasional drought, but the average at Belize City is 65 inches, with about 50 inches in the north and a great increase to 170 inches in the south. Generally, the driest months are April and May; in June and July there are heavy showers followed by blue skies; September and October tend to be overcast and there are lots of insects. Hurricanes can threaten the country from June to November, but they are infrequent. An efficient warning system has been established and there are hurricane shelters in most towns and large villages. Hurricane Preparedness instructions are issued annually.

Clothing The business dress for men is a short-sleeved cotton or poplin shirt or *guayabera* (ties not often worn) and trousers of some tropical weight material. Formal wear may include ties and jackets, but long-sleeved embroidered *guayaberas* are commoner. Women should not wear shorts in the cities and towns; acceptable only on the cayes and at resorts.

What to take

Nature conservation Conservation is now a high priority, with nature reserves sponsored by the Belize Audubon Society, the Government and various international agencies. 'Nature tourism' is Belize's fastest growing industry. By 1992 18 national parks and reserves had been established, including: Half Moon Caye, Cockscomb Basin Wildlife Sanctuary (the world's only jaguar reserve), Crooked Tree Wildlife Sanctuary (swamp forests and lagoons with wildfowl), Community Baboon Sanctuary, Blue Hole National Park, Guanacaste Park, Society Hall Nature Reserve (a research area with Maya presence), Bladen Nature Reserve (watershed and primary forest), Hol Chan Marine Reserve (reef eco-system), Rio Bravo Conservation Area (managed by the Programme for Belize, 1 King Street, Belize City, T02-75616/7, or John Burton, Old Mission Hall, Sibton Green, Saxmundham, Suffolk, IP17 2JY), the Shipstern Nature Reserve (butterfly breeding, forest, lagoons, mammals and birds: contact PO Box 1694, Belize City, T08-22149 via BCL Radio phone, or International Tropical Conservation Foundation, Box 31, CH-2074 Marin-Ne, Switzerland). Five Blue Lakes National Park, based on an unusually deep karst lagoon in Cayo District off the Hummingbird Highway was designated in April 1991. On 8 December 1991 the government created three new forest reserves and national parks: the Vaca Forest Reserve (52,000 acres), Chiquibul National Park (containing the Maya ruins of Caracol, 265,894 acres), both in Cayo District, and Laughing Bird Caye National Park (off Placencia). The first eight listed are managed by the Belize Audubon Society, 12 Fort Street, Belize City (PO Box 1001), T02-34988, F02-34985. Glovers Reef was declared a marine reserve in 1993. Caye Caulker also now has a Marine Reserve at the north end of the caye.

Special interest travel

Belize Enterprise for Sustained Technology (BEST) is a non-profit organization committed to the sustainable development of Belize's disadvantaged communities and community-based ecotourism, for example Gales Point and Hopkins Village; PO Box 35, Forest Drive, Belmopan, T08-23043, F08-22563.

A wildlife protection Act was introduced in 1982, which forbids the sale, exchange or dealings in wildlife, or parts thereof, for profit; the import, export, hunting or collection of wildlife is not allowed without a permit; only those doing scientific research or for educational purposes are eligible for exporting or collecting permits. Also prohibited are removing or exporting black coral, picking orchids, exporting turtle or turtle products, and spear fishing in certain areas or while wearing scuba gear.

On 1 June 1996 a National Protected Areas Trust Fund (PACT) was established to provide finance for the 'protection, conservation and enhancement of the natural and cultural treasures of Belize'. Funds for PACT will come from a BZ$7.50 Conservation Fee paid by all foreign visitors on departure by air, land and sea, and from 20 percent of revenues derived from protected areas entrance fees, cruise ship passenger fees, et cetera. **NB** Visitors pay only one PACT tax every 30 days, so if you go to Tikal, for example, then leave from Belize airport, show your receipt in order not to pay twice.

Bird watchers are recommended to take Petersen's *Field Guide to Mexican Birds*.

Fishing The rivers abound with tarpon and snook. The sea provides game fish such as sailfish, marlin, wahoo, barracuda and tuna. On the flats, the most exciting fish for light tackle – the bonefish – are found in great abundance. Seasons are given below. In addition to the restrictions on turtle and coral extraction noted above, **Nature Conservation**, the following regulations apply: no person may take, buy or sell crawfish (lobster) between 15 February and 14 July, shrimp from 15 April to 14 August, or conch between 1 July and 30 September.

Fishing seasons: Billfish: blue marlin, all year (best November-March); white marlin, November-May; sailfish, March-May. Oceanic: yellowfin tuna, all year; blackfin tuna, all year; bonito, all year; wahoo, November-February; sharks, all year. Reef: kingfish, March-June; barracuda, all year; jackfish, all year; mackerel, all year; grouper, all year; snapper, all year; permit, all year; bonefish, November-April; tarpon, June-August. River: tarpon, February-August; snook, February-August; snapper, year round.

Operators In Belize City: *Blackline Marine*, PO Box 332, Mile 2, Western Highway, T44155, F31975; *Sea Masters Company Ltd*, PO Box 59, T33185, F02-62028; *Caribbean Charter Services*, PO Box 752, Mile 5, Northern Highway, T45814 (have guarded car and boat park), fishing, diving and sightseeing trips to the Cayes. *Belize River Lodge*, PO Box 459, T02-52002, F02-52298, excellent reputation.

Diving The shores are protected by the longest barrier reef in the Western Hemisphere. Lighthouse Reef, the outermost of the three north-south reef systems, offers pristine dive sites in addition to the incredible Blue Hole, a sinkhole exceeding 400 feet. Massive stalagmites and stalactites are found along overhangs down the sheer vertical walls of the Blue Hole. This outer reef lies beyond the access of most land-based diving resorts and even beyond most fishermen, so the marine life is undisturbed. An ideal way to visit this reef is on a liveaboard dive boat. An exciting marine phenomenon takes place during the full moon each January in the waters around Belize when thousands of the Nassau groupers gather to spawn at Glory Caye on Turneffe Reef.

Old wrecks and other underwater treasures are protected by law and cannot be removed. Spear fishing, as a sport, is discouraged in the interests of conservation. The beautiful coral formation is a great attraction for scuba diving, with canyons, coves, overhangs, ledges and walls. There are endless possibilities for underwater photography: schools of fishes amid the hard and soft coral, sponges and fans. Boats can only be hired for diving, fishing or sightseeing if they are licensed for the specific purpose by the government. This is intended to ensure that tourists travel on safe, reliable vessels and also to prevent the proliferation of self-appointed guides. Try to see that the boat which is taking you to see the reef does not damage this attraction by dropping its anchor on, or in any other way destroying, the coral. The coral reefs around the northerly, most touristy cayes are dying. There are decreasing numbers of small fishes as a necessary part of the coral lifecycle in more easily accessible reefs, including the underwater parks.

Archaeological conservation The protection of the Mayan heritage of Belize is also high on the agenda. Excavation continues on several sites, supported by overseas countries and universities. In 1997, the European Union agreed to provide funding for the Maya Archaeological Site Development Programme (MASDP), specifically directed towards protection, promotion and exhibition of various sites in Belize including Lubaantun, Nim Li Punit, Lamanai and Caracol. 10% of the funds will be contributed by the Belize government. For information, contact MASDP at the Archaeology Department, T08-22106.

Finding out more The Belize Tourist Board, as well as its office in Belize City (Level 2, Central Bank Building, Gabourel Lane, PO Box 325, T02-77213/73255, F02-77490, btbb@btl.net, www.belizenet. com, www.travelbelize.org), also has offices in the **USA**, 15 Penn Plaza, 415 Seventh Avenue, 18th Floor, New York, NY 10001, T800-6240686, 212-2688798, F212-6953018; **Canada**, Belize High Commission, 273 Patricia Avenue, Ottawa, K1Y V6C, T613-7227187; **Germany**, Belize Tourist Board/WICRG, Lomenstr-28, 2000 Hamburg 70, T49-40-6958846, F49-40-3800051; **UK**, c/o Belize High Commission (see **Representation Overseas** above).

Before you travel

Documents All nationalities need passports, as well as sufficient funds and, officially, an onward ticket, although this is rarely requested for stays of 30 days. Visas are usually not required from nationals of all the countries of EC, some Commonwealth countries, for example Australia, New Zealand, most Caribbean states, USA, Canada, Leichtenstein, Mexico, Norway, Finland, Panama, Sweden, Turkey, Uruguay, Venezuela. Citizens of India, Austria and Switzerland do need a visa. There is a Belizean Consulate in Chetumal, Mexico, at Avenida Alvaro Obregón 226A, T24908, US$25. Visas may not be purchased at the border. Free transit visas are available at borders (for 24 hours). It is possible that a visa may not be required if you have an onward ticket, but check all details at a Consulate before arriving at the border. Those going to other countries after leaving Belize should get any necessary visas in their home country. Visitors are initially granted 30 days' stay in Belize; this may be extended every 30 days for US$12.50 up to six months at the Immigration Office, Government Complex, Mahogany Street, Belize City, T02-24620 (to the west of the city, near Central American Boulevard). At the end of six months, visitors must leave the country for at least 24 hours. Visitors must not engage in any type of employment, paid or unpaid, without first securing a

Getting in

Belize

Belize embassies and consulates

Canada (changes frequently), 1080 Cote Beaver Hill, Suite 1720, Montréal, Québec, H2Z 1S8, T514-8714741.
UK, High Commission, 22 Harcourt House, 19 Cavendish Square, London W1M 9AD, T0171-4999728; F0171-4914139.
USA, 415 Seventh Avenue, New York, NY 10001, T800-6240686, F212-6953018.

work permit from the Department of Labour; if caught, the penalty for both the employer and the employee is severe. Travellers should note that the border guards seem to have complete power to refuse entry to people whose looks they do not like. There have also been reports that tourists carrying less than US$30 for each day of intended stay have been refused entry. Cyclists should get a passport stamp to indicate an 'imported' bicycle.

Customs Clothing and articles for personal use are allowed in without payment of duty, but a deposit may be required to cover the duty payable on typewriters, dictaphones, cameras and radios. The duty, if claimed, is refunded when the visitor leaves the country. Import allowances are: 200 cigarettes or half a pound of tobacco; 20 fluid ounces of alcohol; one bottle of perfume. Visitors can take in an unspecified amount of other currencies (charges were brought in 1993 against two people who brought in an excessive amount of US dollars, later dropped, maximum amount may now be set). No fruit or vegetables may be brought into Belize; searches are very thorough. Firearms may be imported only with prior arrangements. Pets must have proof of rabies inoculations and a vet's certificate of good health. CB radios are held by customs until a licence is obtained from Belize Communications Ltd.

Money

Currency The monetary unit is the Belizean dollar, stabilized at BZ$2=US$1. Currency notes (Monetary Authority of Belize) are issued in the denominations of 100, 50, 20, 10, 5, 2 and 1 dollars, and coinage of 1 dollar, 50, 25, 10, 5 and 1 cent is in use. Notes marked Government of Belize, or Government of British Honduras, are only redeemable at a bank; all notes should be marked **Central Bank** of Belize. The American expressions Quarter (25c), Dime (10c) and Nickel (5c) are common, although 25c is sometimes referred to as a shilling. US dollars are accepted everywhere. **NB** A common cause for complaint or misunderstanding is uncertainty about which currency you are paying in; make sure it is always clear from the start whether you are being charged in US or Belizean dollars.

Exchange See under **Banks**, Belize City. For Western Union, T275924. Good rates for Mexican pesos in Belize. Best rates of exchange at the borders.

Cost of living The cost of living is high because of the heavy reliance on imports and extra duties. This applies especially to food, car hire, driving. In addition, licences are required to provide many services, which involve payment. Budget travellers also find exploring the interior difficult because public transport is limited and car hire is beyond the means of many. VAT of 15 percent is charged on all services, but should **not** be charged in addition to the seven percent hotel tax.

Getting there

Air From Miami, American Airlines and Taca have daily flights; flights from Europe (for example British Airways from London) or Canada connect with Taca. From Houston, Continental and Taca daily, but too early for similar connections with European flights. Taca flies from Los Angeles daily. Continental flies from Orange County (Monday-Saturday). Also daily direct flights to Guatemala City, San Pedro Sula, San Salvador (all Taca). Connections with San José, Panama City and Tegncigalpa are via San Salvador. Taca, Maya Island Air and Tropic Air all fly daily from Flores, Guatemala, to Belize City. Caribbean Air flies from Roatán, Honduras, on Saturday. Aero Caribe flies from Campeche, Cancún, Chetumal and Mérida daily. Isleña from San Pedro Swa (daily), La Ceiba (daily), Roatán (daily).

Boat For boat services to/from Honduras and Guatemala, see under Dangriga, Placencia, Mango Creek and Punta Gorda. The only boat from Guatemala goes to Punta Gorda; from Puerto Cortés, Honduras, boats go to Dangriga, Mango Creek and Placencia. Obtain all necessary exit stamps and visas before sailing. See under each town for details. American Canadian Caribbean Line has a Ship *MV Caribbean Prince* which visits cayes and mainland Belize, 75 passengers, well organized, excellent food.

Touching down

Departure tax Departure tax of US$15 on leaving from the international airport, but not for transit passengers who have spent less than 24 hours in the country. There is also a security screening charge of US$1.25.

PACT tax All visitors must pay the BZ$7.50 PACT tax on departure; see page 721.

Safety Apart from taking certain precautions in Belize City, the visitor should feel at no personal risk anywhere in Belize. The authorities are keen to prevent the illegal use of drugs. The penalties for possession of marijuana are six months in prison or a US$3,000 fine, minimum.

Tipping In restaurants, 10 percent of the bill; porters in hotels US$2; chambermaids US$0.50 per day. Taxi drivers are not tipped.

Where to stay

All hotels are subject to 7 percent government tax (on room rate only). **Camping** No tent sites. Camping on the beaches, in forest reserves, or in any other public place is not allowed. **NB** Butane gas in trailer/coleman stove size storage bottles is available in Belize.

Getting around

Bus Public transport between most towns is by bus, trucks carry passengers to many isolated destinations, although they are no longer allowed to carry passengers to places served by buses. Enquire at market place in Belize City. By law, buses are not allowed to carry standing passengers; some companies are stricter than others. Most buses are ex-US school buses, small seats, limited legroom. There are a few ex-Greyhounds. All bus companies sell seats in advance. Most buses have no luggage compartments so bags which do not fit on the luggage rack are stacked at the back of the bus. Get a seat at the back to keep an eye on your gear; rough handling is more of a threat than theft.

Touching down

Official time *Official time is six hours behind GMT.*

Hours of business *Retail shops are open 0800-1200, 1300-1600 and Friday 1900-2100, with a half day from 1200 on Wednesday. Small shops open additionally most late afternoons and evenings, and some on Sunday 0800-1000. Government and commercial office hours are 0800-1200 and 1300-1600 Monday to Friday.*

IDD 501. Equal tones with long pause mean it is ringing. Equal tones with either equal pause or short equal pauses indicate it is engaged.

Voltage *110/220 volts single phase, 60 cycles for domestic supply. Some hotels use 12 volt generators.*

Weights and measures *Imperial and US standard weights and measures. The US gallon is used for gasoline and motor oil.*

Motoring Motorists should carry their own driving licence and certificate of vehicle ownership. Third party insurance is mandatory, and can be purchased at any border (BZ$25 a week, BZ$50 a month, cars and motorbikes are the same, cover up to BZ$20,000 from the Insurance Corporation of Belize). Border offices are open Monday-Friday 0500-1700, Saturday 0600-1600, closed Sunday. Also offices in every district. Valid International Driving Licences are accepted in place of Belize driving permits. Fuel costs BZ$4.82 (regular) or BZ$4.98 (super) for a US gallon but can be more in remote areas. Unleaded gasoline is now available in Belize.

Traffic drives on the right. When making a left turn, it is the driver's responsibility to ensure clearance of both oncoming traffic and vehicles behind; generally, drivers pull over to the far right, allow traffic from behind to pass, then make the left turn. Many accidents are caused by failure to observe this procedure. All major roads have been, or are being, improved, but they are still poor in many areas, particularly when it rains.

Selling cars Sellers of cars must pay duty (if the buyer pays it, he may be able to bargain with the customs official). The easiest type of vehicle to sell is either a pick-up or a four-door sedan. Smaller more economical cars are becoming more popular. Prices are quite good particularly in Orange Walk (ask taxi drivers in Belize City). Also, O Perez & Sons, at their grocery store, 59 West Canal Street, Belize City, T02-73439, may be able to help or refer you on to Norm, who sells cars for people at 10 percent commission (recommended for fast sale). The Belikin bridge over Haulover Creek on west side of town is a prime site for buying and selling cars. At parking lot here you pay a small fee only if you sell your car. *Freetown Auto World and Club*, 150 Freetown Road, T02-30405, also buys and sells. If all else fails try selling car for spare parts, Santos Díaz and Sons, CA Boulevard, T02-24545/6.

Car hire Only 1 car rental company will release registration papers to enable cars to enter Guatemala or Mexico (Crystal—see below). Without obtaining them at the time of hire it is impossible to take hire cars across national frontiers. It is best to take a scheduled tour to Tikal or Flores in Guatemala, if intending to return to Belize, because the road is in a poor state and because entry through military checkpoints is quicker. Car hire cost is high in Belize owing to heavy wear and tear on the vehicles. You can expect to pay between US$65 for a Suzuki Samuri to US$125 for an Isuzu Trooper per day. Cautious driving is advised in Belize as road conditions, while improving steadily, are generally poor except for the Northern and Western Highways and there is no street lighting in rural areas. When driving in the Mountain Pine Ridge area it is prudent to check carefully on road conditions at the entry gate; good maps are essential. Emory King's *Drivers Guide to Belize* is helpful when driving to the more remote areas.

Maya Island Air (see **Airline offices**, Belize City) flies daily to each of the main towns and offers charter rates to all local airstrips of which there are 25; only twin-engined planes are used and their safety record is good. Tropic Air flies to most places too. Other companies have charters from Belize City to outlying districts: Belize Aero Company, T02-44021; Cari Bee Air Service, flies mainly to the Cayes, also scheduled service to San Pedro, T04-44253; Javier Flying Services, T02-45332; National Charters, T02-45332.

(margin) **Car/Car hire**

(margin) Belize

(margin) **Air**

Hitchhiking Hitchhiking can be difficult as there is little traffic.

Keeping in touch

Language English is the official language, but Spanish is widely spoken. Belize Broadcasting Network (BBN) devotes about 40 percent of its air-time to the Spanish language. A Low German dialect is spoken by the Mennonite settlers, and Mayan languages and Garifuna are spoken by ethnic groups.

Postal services Airmail postage to UK eight days. US$0.38 for a letter, US$0.20 for a postcard; US$0.50 for letter to European continent; US$0.30 for a letter to USA, US$0.15 for a post card; US$0.30 postcard, US$0.50 letter to Australia, takes two to three weeks. Parcels: US$3.50 per half-kilo to Europe, US$0.38 per half-kilo to USA. The service to Europe and USA has been praised, but sea mail is not reliable. Belize postage stamps are very attractive. Mail may be sent to any local post office, c/o General Delivery.

Telephone services All towns have a telephone office and in most villages visitors can use the community phone. Payphones are being improved and cardphones are fairly commonplace in Belize City and elsewhere. There is a direct-dialling system between the major towns and to Mexico and USA. Local calls cost US$0.25 for three minutes, US$0.12 for each extra minute within the city, US$0.15-0.55 depending on zone. Belize Telecommunications Ltd (known as BTL), Church Street, Belize City, open 0800-1800 Monday-Saturday, 0800-1200 Sunday and holidays, has an international telephone, telegraph and telex service. To make an international call from Belize costs far less than from neighbouring countries. US$3 per minute to UK and Europe (a deposit of US$15 required on all international calls); US$1.60 to North, Central and South America and the Caribbean; US$4 to all other countries. Collect calls to USA, Canada, Australia and UK only.·For the international operator, dial 115. International telex US$1.60 per minute to USA, US$3 to Europe, US$4 elsewhere; telegram US$0.16 per word to USA, US$0.30 to Europe, US$0.40 elsewhere. AT&T's USA Direct, UK Direct, Hong Kong Direct must have AT&T card and ID. BT Chargecard service to the UK is available. Fax US$4.80 to North, Central and South America and the Caribbean, US$9 to Europe, US$12 elsewhere, plus US$2.50 service charge.

Many establishments have direct dial numbers using radio or cellular phones. Belize Communications, Belmopan (Rick and Sue Simpson), is a telephone and fax service used by many establishments not yet reached by direct phone line: T08-23180, F08-23235. Those on the service, who will be contacted by Belize Communications by radio, include the US Embassy, CARE, Maya Island Air, Guanacaste Park, The Blue Hole, Cockscomb, Shipstern Nature Reserve, Chaa Creek, Ix Chel Farm, Mountain Equestrian Trails, Maya Mountain Lodge, duPlooy's, Banana Bank Ranch, Warrie Head, Belize Audubon Society.

Media **Newspapers** Belize: *Belize Times* (PUP supported), *Reporter* (weekly); *Amandala*; monthlies *Belize Today*, and *Belize Review*; bi-monthly *Belize Currents*.

Belize First, quarterly in the USA, has articles on travel, life, news and history in the country: Equator Travel Publications Inc, 280 Beaverdam Road, Candler, NC 28715, USA, F704-6671717 (US$27 a year in Belize, USA, Canada, Mexico, US$37 elsewhere); *Belize Online* www.belize.wm. Also recommended online information is *Belize Report* at www.belizereport.com.

Food and drink

Different cuisines Seafood is abundant, fresh and reasonably cheap; beef is plentiful. Presentation varies: vegetables are not always served with a meat course. For the cheapest meals, order rice. It will come with beans and (as often as not) banana or plantain, or chicken, vegetables or even a blending of beef with coconut milk. Better restaurants have a selection of Mexican dishes; there are also many Chinese restaurants, not always good and sometimes overpriced.

Drink Belikin beer is the local brew, average cost US$1.75 a bottle; many brands of local rum available. The local liqueur is called *nanche*, made from crabou fruit; it is very sweet. All imported food and drink is expensive. Rainwater is commonly served as drinking water. See **Fishing**, page 722, with regard to the closed season for certain seafoods: do not order these items during these periods unless you are certain they have been legally caught.

Holidays and festivals

1 January: New Year's Day; February: San Pedro Carnival, Ambergris Caye; 9 March: Baron Bliss Day; 14-18 March: San José Succotz Fiesta; Good Friday and Saturday; Easter Monday; 21 April: Queen's birthday; 1 May: Labour Day: 3-4 May: Cashew Festival (Crooked Tree); 17 May: Coconut Festival (Caye Caulker); 24 May: Commonwealth Day; 29 June: San Pedro Day; 18-19 July: Benque Viejo Fiesta; 10 September: St George's Caye Day; 21 September: Belize Independence Day; 12 October: Pan American Day (Corozal and Orange Walk); 19 November: Garifuna Settlement Day; 25 December: Christmas Day; 26 December: Boxing Day.

NB Most services throughout the country close down Good Friday to Easter Monday: banks close at 1130 on the Thursday, buses run limited services Holy Saturday to Easter Monday, and boats to the Cayes are available. St George's Caye Day celebrations in September start two or three days in advance and require a lot of energy.

Health

Those taking common precautions find the climate pleasant and healthy. Malaria is reportedly under control, but once again precautions against the disease are essential. Also use mosquito repellent. Dengue fever exists in Belize. Inoculation against yellow fever and tetanus is advisable but not obligatory. No case of either has been reported in years.

Medical facilities Out-patients' medical attention is free of charge. Myo' On Clinic Ltd, 40 Eve Street, Belize City, T02-45616, has been recommended, it charges reasonably for its services. Nearby is the Pathology Lab, 17 Eve Street, recommended. Also recommended are Belize Medical Associates, next to the new city hospital, and Dr Lizama, Handyside Street, consultation US$17.50. The British High Commission in Belmopan, T22146/7 has a list of recommended doctors and dentists.

Belize

Belmopan and Belize City

Belmopan, the capital, suffers from being created for political rather than economic reasons, and apart from some interesting buildings, it has little to offer the visitor. The real centre of the country remains Belize City which, while typical of the main cities of Central America – considerable historical interest, all the main services, good communications to everywhere else, and a certain amount of street crime, is quite Caribbean in appearance.

Belmopan

Population: 6,490
Phone code: 08
Colour map 4, grid B3

Belmopan has been described as 'a disaster for the budget traveller'.

Belmopan is the capital; the seat of government was moved there from Belize City in August 1970. It is 50 miles inland to the west, near the junction of the Western Highway and the Hummingbird Highway to Dangriga (Stann Creek Town), very scenic. It has a National Assembly building (which is open to the public), two blocks of government offices (which are copies of Mayan architecture), police headquarters, a public works department, a hospital, over 700 houses for civil servants, a non-governmental residential district to encourage expansion, and a market. It was projected to have a population of 40,000, so far there are only a fraction of that. Many government workers still commute from Belize City. **The Department of Archaeology** in the government plaza has a vault containing specimens of the country's artefacts, as there is no museum to house them. The city can be seen in less than an hour. A recent addition is the civic centre. The Western Highway from Belize City is now good (one-hour drive), continuing to San Ignacio, and there is an airfield (for charter services only).

Excursions Nearby are Belize Zoo and Guanacaste Park both well worth a visit (as Belmopan's accommodation is so expensive it may be better to take an early bus to either from Belize City rather than go from the capital). See **Western Belize**, below.

Sleeping **L-AL** *Belmopan Convention*, 2 Bliss Parade, T22130, F23066 (opposite bus stop and market), a/c, hot water, swimming pool, restaurant, bars. **A** *Bull Frog*, 23/25 Half Moon Ave, T22111, a/c, good, reasonably priced, laundry (these 2 are a 15-minute walk east of the market through the Parliament complex). **C** *El Rey Inn*, 23 Moho St, T23438, big room with fan, hot and cold water, basic, clean, friendly, restaurant, laundry on request, central.

Eating *Caladium*, next to market, limited fare, moderately priced, small portions, and *El Rey*, see above; there are several *comedores* at the back of the market, and *International Café* near the market, recommended. Also a couple of bakeries nearby. Local food is sold by vendors, 2 stands in front sell ice cream (closed Saturday and Sunday), fruit and vegetable market open daily, limited produce available Sunday. Shops close 1200-1400. No cafés open Sunday.

Transport **Buses** To **San Ignacio**, 1 hour, US$1, frequent service by Batty and Novelo from 0730-2100. To **Belize City**, 1 hour, US$1.50 frequent service by Batty, Z line and others. To **Dangriga**, **Mango Creek** and **Punta Gorda**, see under those towns. To **Orange Walk** and **Corozal** take an early bus to Belize City and change.

Directory **Banks** *Barclays Bank International* (0800-1300, Mon-Fri, and 1500-1800 Fri). ATM, Visa transactions, no commission (but see Belize City, below). **Embassies & consulates** *British High Commission*, North Ring Rd, next to the Governor's residence (PO Box 91, T22146/7, F22761). Officially 'visits' Belize City, 11 Marks St, T45108, Mon, 0900-1100. The commission has a list of recommended doctors and dentists. *El Salvador*, 2 Ave Rio Grande, visa on the spot valid 1 month for 90-day stay, 1 photo, US$38 cash, better to get it in Guatemala, maps available (PO Box 215, T/F23404). *Costa Rica*, 2 Sapodilla St, T22725, F22731. *Panama*, 79 Unity Blvd, T22714 (Embassy, for Consulate see Belize City). Venezuelan Consul General, 18/20 Unity Blvd, T22384.

Belize City

Belize City is the old capital and chief town. Most of the houses are built of wood, often of charming design, with galvanized iron roofs; they stand for the most part on piles about seven feet above the ground, which is often swampy and flooded. There are vast water butts outside many houses, with pipes leading to the domestic supply. Ground-floor rooms are used as kitchens, or for storage. A sewerage system has been installed, and the water is reported safe to drink, though bottled water may be a wise precaution. Belize City hotels and tourist board are keen to develop the city. It has been improved over recent years with the canal being cleaned. There are plans to develop the sea front from the centre towards the *Fiesta Inn*. The introduction of tourist police has had a marked effect on crime levels. Just under a quarter of the total population live here, with the African strain predominating. Humidity is high, but the summer heat is tempered by the northeast trades.

Hurricane Hattie swept a 10-foot tidal wave into the town on 31 October 1961, and caused much damage and loss of life. In 1978, Hurricane Greta caused extensive damage. Belize escaped Hurricane Mitch in 1998 as it turned south and hit Honduras and the Bay Islands.

Population: 52,670
Phone code: 02 (unless otherwise indicated)
Colour map 4, grid B4

Sights

Haulover Creek divides the city; the swing bridge across the river is opened, if required, at 0530 and 1730 daily to let boats pass. Among the commonest craft are sandlighters, whose lateen sails can be seen off Belize City. Three canals further divide the city. The main commercial area is either side of the swing bridge, although most of the shops are on the south side, many being located on Regent and Albert streets. The area around **Battlefield** (formerly Central) **Park** is always busy, but it is no distance to Southern Foreshore with its views of the rivermouth, harbour and out to sea. At the southern end of Regent Street, the **Anglican Cathedral** (St John's) and **Government House** nearby are interesting; both were built in the early 19th century. In the days before the foundation of the Crown Colony the kings of the Mosquito Coast were crowned in the Cathedral, built with bricks brought from England as ships' ballast. In the Cathedral (not always open), note the 19th century memorial plaques which give a harrowing account of early death from 'country fever' (yellow fever) and other tropical diseases. The **museum** in Government House is open Monday-Friday, 0830-1200, 1300-1630, entry US$2.50. It contains some interesting pictures of colonial times, displays of furniture and silver and glassware, as well as a display showing fishing techniques and model boats.

On the north side of the swing bridge, turn left up North Front Street for some of the cheaper hotels and the A & R Station, from which boats leave for the Cayes. Turn right for the Post Office and roads which lead to **Marine Parade** (also with sea views). Opposite the Post Office is the new **Marine Terminal** and **Museum** housed in a colonial building, the former fire station. It features a mangrove exhibition, reef exhibition and aquarium, entry US$3. At the junction of Cork Street at Marine Parade is the *Radisson Fort George* whose Club Wing, a copper-coloured glass tower, is a considerable landmark. **Memorial Park** on Marine Parade has a small obelisk, two cannon, concrete benches, and is peppered with the holes of landcrabs. The small park by the **Fort George Lighthouse** has a children's play area and is a popular meeting place.

Coming in by sea, after passing the barrier reef, Belize City is approached by a narrow, tortuous channel. This and the chain of mangrove cayes give shelter to what would otherwise be an open roadstead.

Belize is the nearest adequate port to the State of Quintana Roo (Mexico), and re-exports mahogany from that area. It also handles substantial container traffic for Yucatán.

Security

Tourist police patrol the city centre to prevent attacks on tourists, give safety advice, etc. They wear greenish uniforms and have, since their introduction in August 1995, greatly reduced crime in the city. Their presence in other areas, eg San Pedro, is steadily increasing.

Watch out for conmen, some in uniform, who would like to disappear with your money. Do not trust the many self-appointed 'guides' who also sell hotel rooms, boat trips to the Cayes, drugs, etc. Local advice is not even to say "no"; just shake your head and wag your finger if approached by a stranger. Street money changers are not to be trusted either. It is wise to avoid small, narrow side streets and stick to major thoroughfares, although even on main streets you can be victim to unprovoked threats and racial abuse. A common sense attitude is needed and a careful watch on your possessions is recommended. No jewellery or watches should be worn. Travel by taxi (US$2.50 flat rate) is advisable particularly at night and in the rain. Areas which are best avoided at night (because they are frequented by crack users) are near Pinks and Bride's Alleys opposite Tourist Office, on the Southern Foreshore and the area bounded by the Southside Canal, Haulover Creek and Collet Canal (where the bus stations are).

Cars should only be left in guarded carparks. For a tip, the security officer at the *Fiesta Inn* will look after your car for a few days while you go to the Cayes.

Sleeping
■ *on maps*
Price codes:
see inside front cover

LL-L *Fiesta Inn and Marina*, Newtown Barracks (PO Box 1758), T32670, F34322, on sea front (but not central), marina facilities, a/c, good food and service in restaurant and bar (a/c with sea views, expensive), good business facilities, informal snack bar near the dock is lively at night, nice pool and children's play area. **LL-AL** *Belize Biltmore Plaza*, Mile 3 Northern Highway, T32302, F32301, Best Western, comfortable rooms, a/c, restaurant (nice atmosphere, a/c, good selection), excellent English pub-style bar (but karaoke in bar most evenings), pool, conference facilities, a long way from town (US$3.50 or more by taxi). **LL-A** *Bellevue*, 5 Southern Foreshore (T77051, F73253, fins@btl.net), a/c, private bath, good laundry service, restaurant (nice atmosphere, good lunches with live music, steaks), leafy courtyard pool, nice bar with live music Friday and Saturday nights, good entertainment, recommended. **L** *Radisson Fort George*, 2 Marine Parade, PO Box 321, T33333, F73820, radexec@btl.net, in 3 wings (Club Wing, Colonial Section and former *Holiday Inn Villa*), each with excellent rooms, a/c, helpful staff, reservations should be made, safe parking, good restaurant, good pool (non-residents may use pool for US$10), recommended. **L-A** *Chateau Caribbean*, 6 Marine Parade, by Fort George, T30800, F30900, chateaucar@btl.net, main building is a beautiful well-maintained colonial building, a/c, with good bar, restaurant (excellent Chinese and seafood, sea view, good service) and discotheque, parking. **L** *The Great House*, 13 Cork St, T33400, F33444, greathouse@btl.net, opposite *Radisson*, large colonial-style house, all 6 rooms have a/c and private balcony, good restaurant below.

A *Alicia's Guest House*, corner Dean St and Chapel Lane, T75082, with a/c, some with fan, fruit and tea/coffee included, owner Anselmo Ortiz (Alicia, his daughter) friendly and helpful. **A** *Bakadeer Inn*, 74 Cleghorn St, T31286, F31963, private bath, breakfast US$4, a/c, TV, fridge, friendly, recommended. **A** *Colton House*, 9 Cork St, T44666, F30451, E coltonhse@btl.net, named after owners, delightful 1928 colonial style home, private bath, some a/c, overhead fans, large rooms, friendly, helpful, quiet. **A** *Four Fort Street* (address as name), T30116, F78808, fortst@btl.net, full breakfast included, 6 rooms, all with 4-poster beds and shared bath, charming, excellent restaurant, recommended.

B *El Centro*, 4 Bishop St, T72413, a/c, restaurant, good value. **B** *Glenthorne Manor*, 27 Barrack Rd, T44212, with or without bath, colonial-style, safe, getting run down, meals available, overpriced. **B** *Mopan*, 55 Regent St, T77351, hotelmopan@btl.net, with bath, breakfast, a/c, in historic house, has restaurant and bar (owner Jean Shaw), nice but pricey, helpful with information, transport arrangements. **B** *Royal Orchid*, 153 New Rd and Douglas Jones St, T32783, F32789, a/c, with bar, restaurant, laundry service, Chinese, not central.

C *Freddie's*, 86 Eve St, T44396, with shower and toilet, fan, hot water, clean, very nice, secure, very small. **C** *Isabel Guest House*, 3 Albert St, above Matus Store, PO Box 362, T73139, 3 double rooms, 1 huge triple room, quiet except when nearby disco operating at weekends, private shower, clean, friendly, safe, Spanish spoken, highly recommended. **C** *Orchidia*, Regent St, clean, safe. **C** *Sea Side Guest House*, 3 Prince St, T78339, friends@btl.net, **E** per person in bunk room, lots of rules but popular, very clean, pleasant verandah, owned by Quaker Group.

Belize City

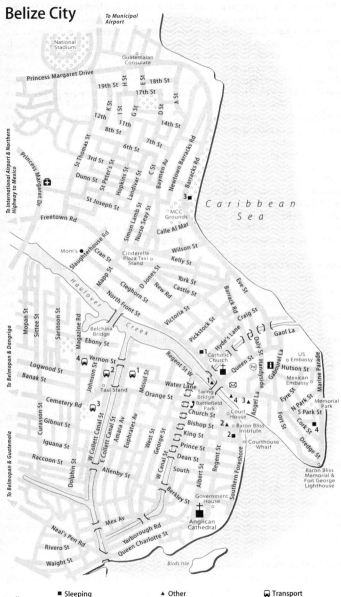

To Municipal
Airport

National
Stadium

Guatemalan
Consulate

Princess Margaret Drive

19th St
18th St
17th St
H St
E St
K St
G St
D St
A St
12th
11th
14th St
8th St
7th St
6th St

To International Airport & Northern
Highway to Mexico

Princess Margaret Dr

St Thomas St
3rd St
St Peter's St
Hopkins St
Dunn St
Landivar St
C St
Baymen Av
Newtown Barracks Rd
Barracks Rd

St Joseph St

Freetown Rd

Simon Lamb St
Nurse Seay St

MCC
Grounds

Calle Al Mar

*C a r i b b e a n
S e a*

Mom's

Slaughterhouse Rd
Cran St
Mapp St

Cinderella
Plaza Taxi
Stand

Wilson St
Kelly St

Cleghorn St
D Jones St
New Rd

York St
Castle St

Eve St

North Front St

Victoria St

Pickstock St

Barrack Rd
Craig St

H a u l o v e r

Mopan St
Sittee St
Sarstoon St
Magazine Rd

Belchina
Bridge

Ebony St

C r e e k

Regent St W

Hyde's Lane

Daly St

Gaol La

To Belmopan & Dangriga

Logwood St
Banak St

Johnson St

Vernon St

Mosul St

Water Lane

Orange St

Catholic
Church

Queen St

Pol

Handyside

Gabriel La

US
Embassy

Hutson St

Mexican
Embassy

Marine Parade

Taxi Stand

Cemetery Rd

W Collett Canal St
E Collett Canal St
Amara Av
Euphrates Av

Swing
Bridge

Battlefield
Park

Church St

Court
House

Angel La

Eye St

N Park St

S Park St

Memorial
Park

To Belmopan & Guatemala

Curasson St
Gibnut St
Iguana St
Raccoon St
Dolphin St

West St
George St

Bishop St
King St
Prince St
Dean St

Baron Bliss
Institute

Courthouse
Wharf

Fort St

Cork St
Dredge St

Allenby St

W Canal St
Berkley St

Albert St
Regent St

South
Albert St

Southern Foreshore

Baron Bliss
Memorial &
Fort George
Lighthouse

Neal's Pen Rd
Rivero St

Mex Av

Yarborough Rd
Queen Charlotte St

Government
House

Anglican
Cathedral

Waight St

Birds Isle

N

Not to scale

■ Sleeping	▲ Other	🚌 Transport
1 Area of Cheaper Hotels	1 A & R Station, Boats to Cayes	1 Batty Bus
2 Bellevue	2 Brodie's Department Store	2 James Bus
3 Fiesta Inn	3 Honduran Consulate	3 Novello's Bus
4 Radisson Fort George	4 Marine Terminal & Museum	4 Venus Bus & Z-Line

D *Belize River Lodge*, Ladyville, PO Box 459 Belize City, T52002, F52298, 10 minutes from airport on Belize River, excellent accommodation, food and fishing (from lodge or cruises), also scuba facilities, numerous packages. **D** *Bon Aventure*, 122 North Front St, T44248, **E** in dormitory, purified water available, a bit run down, not very clean, but one of the best cheap options in Belize City, Malaysian Chinese owners helpful and friendly, secure, Spanish spoken, laundry service, good meals at reasonable prices; opposite are **D** *Mira Rio*, 59 North Front St, service criticised, rooms OK but small, shared hot shower, fan, toilet, clean, covered verandah overlooking Haulover Creek, Spanish spoken, good food, noisy bar opposite. **D** *Downtown Guest House*, 5 Eve St, T30951, small rooms, hot shower, towel, soap; secure, friendly, clean, noisy but recommended. **D** *North Front Street Guest House*, T77595, 1 block north of Post Office, 15-minute walk from Batty bus station, 124 North Front St, no hot water, fan, book exchange, TV, friendly, laundry, good information, keep windows closed at night and be sure to lock your door.

Eating

It can be difficult to find places to eat between 1500 and 1800.

Four Fort Street (at that address), near Memorial Park, nice atmosphere, sit out on the verandah, desserts a speciality, recommended (see **Sleeping**). *Macy's*, 18 Bishop St, T73419, recommended for well-prepared local game, Creole cooking, different fixed menu daily, charming host. *Mango*, 164 Newtown Barracks Rd, T45020 (a short taxi ride from major hotels), considered by many as best restaurant in the city, varied menu. *DIT's*, 50 King St, good, cheap. *Big Daddy's*, Church St opposite BTL office, good cheap food. *Mar's*, 118 North Front St, clean, pleasant, family cooking, reasonable prices, good. *Marlin*, 11 Regent St West, overlooking Belize River, T73913, varied menu, good seafood.

Chinese *New Chon Saan*, 55 Euphrates Av, T72709, best Chinese in town, pleasant atmosphere (taxi ride), takeaway. *Hong Kong*, 50 Queen St, reasonably priced, dirty, smelly, rats. *Canton*, New Rd, large portions, good. *China Garden*, 46 Regent St, lunch specials. *Shek Kei*, 80 Freetown Rd, good. *Ding Ho*, North Front St, good, try their 'special' dishes. *Yin Kee*, 64 Freetown Rd. *Taiwan*, 93 Cemetery Rd.

Sea Rock, 190 Newtown Barracks Road, good Indian food. *Pizza Pronto*, Barrack Rd, very good pizzas, inexpensive. *Pop 'n' Taco*, Regent St, good sweet and sour chicken, cheap, friendly service. *Edward Quan Fried Chicken*, New Rd, takeaway, good. *H & L Burgers*, 4 locations. *Playboy*, 11 King St, good sandwiches. *Blue Bird*, Albert St, cheap fruit juices, specialities, modest, clean, reasonable. *Tropicana*, Queen St, green building on corner next to *Hong Kong*, good set menu lunch. *Judith's Pastries*, south end of Queen St, good cakes, pastries. *Babb's*, Queen and Eve Sts, good pastries, meat pies, juices, friendly. *De-Lites*, opposite Brodies Department Store, quick, tasty snacks. *Flores Fruit*, north end of Barrack Rd, tamal lunch US$1, good juices.

Night life

Bars Best and safest bars are found at major hotels, *Fort George*, *Biltmore Plaza*, *Bellevue* and *Four Fort Street*. If you want a little local charm **Lindbergh's Landing**, 164A Newtown Rd (next to *Mango*) is fun, open air with sea view, big Latin dance evening on Sunday. Lots of bars some with juke boxes and poolrooms. *Privateer*, Mile 4½ on Northern Highway, on seafront, expensive drinks but you can sit outside. Try the local drink, anise and peppermint, known as 'A and P'; also the powerful 'Old Belizeno' rum. The local beer, Belikin, is good, as is the 'stout', strong and free of gas. Guinness is also served, but is expensive.

Clubs and discos *Hard Rock*, corner of Queen/Handyside Sts, good dance floor, a/c; the bigger hotels, eg *Bellevue*, *Fiesta*, have good discos. *Lumba Yaard*, 1 mile out of town along Northern Highway, recommended.

Shopping

Handicrafts, woodcarvings, straw items, are all good buys. The Belize Chamber of Commerce has opened a Belize crafts sales room on Fort Street, opposite *Four Fort Street* restaurant, to be a showcase and promote crafts people from all over Belize, come here first. *Nile*, 49 Eve St, Middle East. *Go Tees*, 23 Regent St, T74082, excellent selection of T-shirts (printed on premises), arts and crafts from Belize, Guatemala and Mexico: jewellery, silver, wood carvings, clothes, paintings, etc; also has a branch at Belize Zoo, good zoo T-shirts and cuddly animals. Zericote (or Xericote) wood carvings can be bought in Belize City, for example at *Brodies Department Store* (Central Park end of Regent Street), which also sells postcards, the *Fort George Hotel*, the small gift shop at *Four Fort Street*, or from Egbert Peyrefitte, 11a Cemetery Road. Such wood carvings are the best buy, but to find a carver rather than buy the tourist fare in shops, ask a taxi driver. (At the Art Centre, near Government House, the wood sculpture of Charles Gabb, who introduced carving into Belize, can be seen.) Wood carvers sell their work in front of the main hotels. The market is by the junction of North Front Street and Fort Street. *Ro-Macs*, 27 Albert St, excellent supermarket includes wide selection of imported foods and wines. *Thrift Center*, 2 Church St, good food store. The whole city closes down on Sunday except for a few shops open on Sunday morning, eg Brodies in the centre of town. Banks and many shops are closed on Wednesday afternoons.

Bookshops *Book Centre*, 2 Church St, above Thrift Center, very good, has second-hand books and back issues of US magazines. *Belize Bookshop*, Regent St (opposite *Mopan Hotel*), ask at counter for 'racy' British greetings cards. *Angelus Press*, 10 Queen St, excellent selection of stationery supplies, books, cards, etc. *The Book Shop*, 126 Freetown Rd, new and second-hand books, also exchange books.

Transport

Local Car hire: Budget PO Box 863, 771 Bella Vista (near International Airport, can pick up and drop off car at airport, office almost opposite *Biltmore Plaza Hotel*), T32435, good service, well-maintained vehicles, good deals (Suzukis and Isuzu Troopers); **Crystal**, Mile 1.5 Northern Highway, T31600, Jay Crofton, helpful, cheapest deals in town, but not always most reliable, wide selection of vehicles including 30-seater bus, will release insurance papers for car entry to Guatemala and Mexico, he also buys second-hand cars but at a poor price; **Pancho's**, 5747 Lizarraga Ave, T45554; **National**, International Airport, T31586 (Cherokee Chiefs); **Avis**, at *Fort George Hotel*, T78637, airport T52385, largest fleet, well-maintained, Daihatsus and Isuzu Troopers. **Smith & Sons**, 125 Cemetery Rd, T73779 (less reliable than in the past); **Gilly's**, 31 Regent St, T77613; **Lewis**, 23 Cemetery Rd, T74461. CDW ranges from US$10 to US$20 per day. **Safari**, 11a Cork St, beside *Radisson Fort George Hotel*, T30268, F35395, Isuzu Troopers.

Taxis: have green licence plates (drivers must also have identification card); within Belize, US$2.50 for 1 person; for 2 or more passengers, US$1.75 per person. International Airport to Belize centre, US$15; municipal airport to centre, US$7.50. (**NB** If you check several hotels, you may be charged for each ride.) There is a taxi stand on Central Park, opposite Barclays, another on the corner of Collet Canal Street and Cemetery Road. Outside Belize City, US$1.75 per mile, regardless of number of passengers. Belize City to the resorts in Cayo District approximately US$100-125, 1-4 people (ask for Edgar August or Martin at *Radisson Fort George* desk, they are reliable and can do guided tours around Belize). Best to ask price of the ride before setting off. No meters, so beware of overcharging and make sure fare is quoted in BZ$. No tips necessary. If you have a complaint, take the licence plate and report to the Taxi Union.

Air There is a 10-mile tarmac road to the Phillip Southwest Goldson International Airport; modern check-in facilities, toilets, restaurant, bank (open 0830-1100 and 1330-1630, not Sunday), viewing deck and duty-free shop, a/c. No facilities on Arrivals side. Taxi fare US$15; make sure your taxi is legitimate. Any bus going up the Northern Highway passes the airport junction (US$0.75), then 1$\frac{1}{2}$ mile walk. Taxi from junction to airport US$2.50. There is a shuttle to Cayo (San Ignacio, to any hotel in town or *Eva's bar*) from the airport at 1400 and 1630, US$25 1 way.

There is a municipal airstrip for local flights, 15 minutes out of town, taxi, US$7.50, no bus service. Services to San Pedro, Caye Chapel, Caye Caulker with Tropic Air and Maya Island Air, flights every 30 minutes, 0700 to 1630. Flights to and from the islands can be taken from the International Airport and companies link their flights to meet or leave international departures; add approximately US$12 each way to the price to/from municipal airport.

Services also to Corozal (Tropic Air), half an hour. Big Creek, San Ignacio, Placencia, Dangriga, Punta Gorda, with Maya Island Air and Tropic Air.

Buses Within the city the fare is US$0.50. There are bus services to the main towns. To **Chetumal** (see Mexico, **Yucatán Peninsula**), about 15 daily each way, several express Batty Buses from 0600 stopping at Orange Walk and Corozal only, US$8.50, 3 hours. Slower buses taking up to 4 hours including crossing, US$7.50, with 2 companies: Batty Bus, 54 East Collet Canal Street, T74924, F78991, and Venus, Magazine Road, T73354. If taking a bus from Chetumal which will arrive in Belize City after dark, decide on a hotel and go there by taxi. Batty Bus to **Belmopan** and **San Ignacio**, express bus 0900, US$3, with refreshments and video, ordinary bus, Monday-Saturday frequent 0600 to 1900, Sunday 0630 to 1700. Novelo's run until 2000. The 0600, 0630 and 1015 buses connect at the border with services to Flores, Guatemala. To San Ignacio, Benque Viejo and the Guatemalan border via Belmopan, Novelo's, West Collet Canal, T77372 (can store luggage US$0.50), US$1.25 to Belmopan, US$3 to Benque, US$2.50 to San Ignacio, hourly Monday-Saturday, 1100 to 1900. The last possible bus connection to Flores leaves the border at 1600, but it is better to get an earlier bus to arrive in daylight. Several Batty buses leave for **Melchor de Mencos**, from 0600 to 1030. To **Flores, Guatemala**, minibuses leave the A & R Station on Front Street at 0500, make reservation the previous day. To **Dangriga**, via Belmopan and the Hummingbird Highway. Z-line (T73937), from Venus bus station, daily, 0800, 1000, 1100, 1500, 1600, plus Monday 0600, US$5; to Dangriga via Coastal Highway (unsurfaced), Richies Busline, East Collet Canal Street, 1430, on to Placencia, 4½ hours, US$7.50. James Bus Line, Pound Yard Bridge (Collet Canal), unreliable, slow, 9-12 hours, to **Punta Gorda** via Dangriga, Cockscomb Basin Wildlife Sanctuary and Mango Creek, daily 0800 and 1500, US$11. **NB** The bus stations are in an unsafe area of town. If taking a bus early in the morning, try to stay near the bus station as you will find it difficult to find a taxi before about 0530, and walking through this part of town in darkness with luggage is dangerous. If arriving at in the late evening, you should be able to find a taxi, eg Batty Bus Station to centre, US$2.50. During the day, since it is not far from the bus terminals to the centre, or to the boat dock for the Cayes, don't be given the run-around by taxi drivers.

Shipping For boats to the Cayes and other places in Belize, see under destinations.

Directory **Airline offices** Local: *Tropic Air*, Belize City T02-45671, San Pedro 02-62012/62117/62029, F06-22338. *Maya Island Air*, 6 Fort St, PO Box 458, Belize City T02-31362, municipal airport 02-2336, International 02-52336, San Pedro 02-62611, F02-30585/30031. **International:** *Taca* (Belize Global Travel), 41 Albert St (T02-77363/77185, F75213), International T02-52163, F02-52453, also *British Airways*, T77363, International T02-52060/52458. *American*, Valencia Building, T02-32522/3/4 and *Continental Airlines*, 32 Albert St, T02-78309/78463/78223, International 02-52263/52488. *Aerovías*, in *Mopan Hotel*, 55 Regent St, T02-75383/75445/6, F75383, for Flores/Guatemala.

Banks All banks have facilities to arrange cash advance on Visa card. The *Belize Bank* is particularly efficient and modern, US$0.50 commission on Amex cheques but a big charge for cash against Visa and Mastercharge; also *Barclays Bank International*, with some country branches, slightly better rates, 2% commission, no charge for Visa/Mastercharge, only ATMs in the country for foreign-issued Visa cards. *Atlantic Bank*, 6 Albert St, or 16 New Rd (the latter in a safe area), quick efficient service, small charge for Visa/Mastercharge, smaller queues than Belize Bank or Barclays. *Bank of Nova Scotia*. Banking hrs: Mon-Thur 0800-1300, Fri 0800-1200 and 1300-1630. It is easy to have money telexed to Belize City. Guatemalan quetzales are very easy to obtain at the borders, less easy in Belize City. *American Express*, good exchange rates at *Belize Global Travel Services*, 41 Albert St (T77185/77363/4). Money changers at Batty Bus terminal just before departure of bus to Chetumal (the only place to change Mexican pesos except at the border). *Khan's*, inside the Marine Terminal, will change currency, travellers' cheques and give cash advances. Some shops change without commission.

Communications **Post Office:** letters, Queen St and North Front St, 0800-1700 (1630 Fri); parcels, beside main Post Office, these must be wrapped in brown paper, sold by the yard in large stationery shop around the corner in Queen St. Letters held for 1 month. Beautiful stamps sold. **International telecommunications:** telegraph, telephone, telex services, Belizean Telecommunications Ltd, 1 Church St just off Central Park, 0800-1800, 0800-1200 on Sun. Also public fax service and booths for credit card and charge calls to USA, UK. Also **internet** service US$3 1½ hours, only 1 computer. *Khan's*,

An adventurers dream. Belize is a peaceful, English-speaking paradise only 2 hours from the US. With a diversity of adventure opportunities unmatched by any other country, the people of Belize have protected 40% of the country as parks and reserves. Belize is on the Caribbean coast nestled between Mexico and Guatemala and offers an intriguing mix of tropical forests rich with wildlife, majestic 3,675 foot mountains, mysterious Maya temples, and diving and fishing experiences beyond compare. In a single day you can go from tropical forest to the longest barrier reef in the Western Hemisphere. And the people are as warm and friendly as the climate.
Discover Belize.
And let the adventures begin.

Contact the Belize Tourism Board (from the UK) at **00 501-2-31913** or (the US) at **1-800-624-0686** or visit us at our website:
www.travelbelize.org/kayaking

inside the Marine terminal, has an email service.

Cultural centres *Baron Bliss Institute*, public library, temporary exhibitions; has 1 Stela and 2 large discs from Caracol on display. *Audubon Society*: see under Nature Conservation in the Introduction. *The Image Factory*, 91 Front St, has exhibitions of contemporary art, open Mon-Fri 0900-1800.

Embassies & consulates See also under Belmopan. *Mexican* Embassy, 20 Park St, T30193/4, open 0900-1230, Mon-Fri, documents returned 1530-1630; if going to Mexico and requiring a visa, get it here, not at the border, tourist card given on the spot, note that long queues are normal, arrive early, get visa the afternoon before departure. *Honduras*, 91 North Front St, T45889. *Costa Rica*, 8-18th St, T44796. *Panama* Consulate, 5481 Princess Margaret Drive, T34282. *Guatemala Embassy*, 1 St John St, Belize City, T33314, F35140. *Guatemala* Consulate, 6A Saint Matthew St, near municipal airstrip, T33150, open 0900-1300, will not issue visas or tourist cards here and tell you to leave it till you reach San José Succotz (see page 762). *Jamaica*, 26 Corner Hyde's Lane and New Rd, T45926, F23312. *US* Embassy, 29 Gabourel Lane, T77161/2, consulate is on Hutson St, round corner from embassy's entrance on Gabourel Lane, consulate open 0800-1000 for visitor visas, library 0830-1200, 1330-1630 Mon-Fri, but am only on Wed. *Canada*, 83 North Front St, T31060. *Belgium*, Marcelo Ltd, Queen St, T45769. *The Netherlands*, 14 Central American Blvd, T73612. *France*, 9 Barrack Rd, T32708. *German* Honorary Consul, 123 Albert St, T73343. *Denmark*, 13 Southern Foreshore, T72172. *Norway*, 1 King St, T77031, F77062. *Sweden*, 13 Queen St, T77234. *Italy*, 18 Albert St, T78449. *Israel*, 4 Albert and Bishop St, T73991/73150, F30750.

Laundry *Central American Coin-Op Laundry*, junction Barrack Rd and Freetown Rd, wash US$3.50, dryer US$1.50, powder US$0.50, self-service.

Places of worship There are an Anglican Cathedral, a Catholic Cathedral, a Methodist and a Presbyterian church. The Baptist Church is on Queen St.

Tour companies & travel agents Tours: *S and L Guided Tours*, 91 North Front St, T77593, F77594, recommended group travel (minimum 4 persons for most tours, 2 persons to Tikal). *Native Guide Systems*, 2 Water Lane, T75819, F74007, PO Box 1045, individual and group tours. A great many others both inside and outside Belize. Tourist Bureau has a full list. If booking tours in

Belize

Belize from abroad it is advisable to check prices and services offered with a reputable tour operator in Belize first.

Tourist offices *Belize Tourist Board*, Level 2, Central Bank Building, Gabourel Lane, PO Box 325, T77213, F77490, from Uk T00 501 2 31913, USA T1-800-624-0686, btbb@btl.net (open 0800-1200, 1300-1700 Mon-Thur, and till 1630 Fri), provides complete bus schedule (care, may be out of date) with a map of Belize City, as well as list of hotels and their prices. Also has *Mexico and Central American Handbook* for sale and a list of recommended taxi guides and tour operators, and free publications on the country and its Maya ruins, practical and informative. Excellent maps of the country for US$3 (postage extra). The jail building right in front of the Central Bank is being developed into a Museum of Belize City, where the BTB will have an information office. *Belize Tourism Industry Association* (private sector body for hotels, tour companies, etc), 10 North Park St, T75717, F78710, brochures and information on all members throughout Belize. Enquire for all details of all Belize tour operators. Suggested reading is *Hey Dad, this is Belize*, by Emory King, a collection of anecdotes, or more seriously, *Warlords and Maize Men, a guide to the Mayan Sites of Belize*, Association for Belize Archaeology, available in bookshops. Maps (US$3), books on Belizean fauna etc available at Angelus Press, Queen St. Above the Post office is the Survey Office selling maps, 2-sheet, 1:250,000 US$10, dated, or more basic map US$2 (open Mon-Thur 0830-1200, 1300-1600, but 1530 on Fri).

Caribbean Charter Services, Mile 5 North Highway, PO Box 752. Belize City, T30404, F33711, is a tourist information centre and agency for airline flight tickets, boat charters, inland resorts and other facilities, Bulletin Board Service, owned by Ms Ruha'mah Stadtlander.

The Northern Cayes

Belize City

The cayes off the coast are most attractive, relaxing, slow and very 'Caribbean'. An excellent place for all forms of diving and sea fishing. They are popular destinations, especially from February to May and in August. Ask around (for example, the skippers of the boats to Caye Caulker or Chapel) for information on staying with families on the smaller, lesser populated cayes.

There are 212 square miles of cayes. **St George's Caye**, *nine miles northeast of Belize, was once the capital and was the scene of the battle in 1798 which established British possession. The larger ones are Turneffe Island and Ambergris and Caulker Cayes. Fishermen live on some cayes, coconuts are grown on others, but many are uninhabited swamps. The smaller cayes do not have much shade, so be careful if you go bathing on them. Sandflies infest some cayes (for example Caulker), the sandfly season is December to beginning of February; mosquito season June, July, sometimes October.*

Getting there Travel by boat to and between the islands is becoming increasingly regulated and the new licensing requirements will probably drive the cheaper boats out of business. In general, it is easier to arrange travel between the islands once there, than from Belize City. Most boats to Caye Caulker (and some to Ambergris Caye) now leave from the new Marine Terminal opposite the Post Office between 0900 and 1700; fare to Caye Caulker US$7.50. Others (*Triple J* at 0900, *Andrea* at 1500) leave from Courthouse Wharf; *Seascape* departs from outside Bellevue Hotel at 1600.

St George's Caye On St George's Caye: **AL** *Cottage Colony*, PO Box 428, Belize City, T02-77051, F02-73253, colonial-style cabañas with dive facilities, price varies according to season, easy access from Belize City. **L** *St George's Island Lodge and Cabañas*, T02-12121, sgl.belize@btl.net, PO Box 625, Belize City, in USA, T1-800-6786871, eight rooms and six thatched cottages over the water, prices include two dives, all meals, transfer from international airport. Specialist diving resort including advanced and Nitrox certification. Boat fare is US$15, day trips are possible.

Caye Chapel Caye Chapel is free of sandflies and mosquitoes and there are several beaches, cleaned daily. Forty minutes by boat from Belize City, US$7.50. The *Pyramid Island*

Resort owns the island (**A**, credit cards not accepted); it has an excellent beach and dive courses (PADI). Be careful if you hire a boat for a day to visit Caye Chapel: the boatmen enjoy the bar on the island and your return journey can be unreasonably exciting. Also, there are very few fish now round this caye. There is a landing strip used by local airlines, which stop flights between Belize and San Pedro on request.

Long Caye is now being taken over by a private corporation.

Long Caye

The Cayes

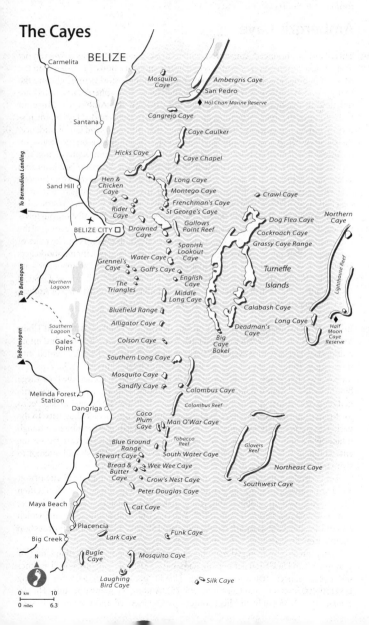

Moonlight Shadows Lodge, **Middle Long Caye**, T08-22587, still being developed. *Ricardo's Beach Huts*, Blue Field Range (59 North Front Street, PO Box 55, Belize City, T02-44970), recommended, charming and knowledgeable host, rustic, authentic fish camp feel, overnight camps to **Rendez-vous Caye, English Caye** and **Sargeants Caye** can be arranged with Ricardo, excellent food, snorkelling. *Spanish Bay Resort*, PO Box 35, Belize City, T02-77288, also under development, dive facilities. *The Wave*, **Gallows Point Caye** (9 Regent Street, Belize City, T02-73054), six rooms, watersports facilities and diving.

Ambergris Caye

Population: 3,000
Phone code: 026
Colour map 4, grid B4

This island (pronounced Am*bergris*), with its town of **San Pedro**, has grown rapidly over the last couple of years, with over 50 hotels and guest houses registered on the island. Buildings are still restricted to no more than three storeys in height and the many wooden structures retain an authentic village atmosphere. New hotels are opening all the time. **Tourist information** office in the **Ambergris Museum** (T2298) opposite *Fido's*. The museum is new and has excellent displays on the history of the town and the caye. It should be noted that, although sand is in abundance, there are few beach areas around San Pedro town. The emphasis is on snorkelling on the nearby barrier reef and Hol Chan Marine Park, as well as the fine scuba diving, sailing, fishing and board sailing. The main boat jetties are on the east (Caribbean Sea) side of San Pedro, but the yacht harbour is increasingly moving to the west (lagoon) side where a new marina will shortly be completed. In fact it can be dangerous to swim near San Pedro as there have been serious accidents with boats. Boats are restricted to about five miles per hour within the line of red buoys about 25 yards offshore but this is not always adhered to. There is a 'safe' beach in front of the park, just to the south of the Government dock. A short distance to the north and south of San Pedro lie miles of deserted beach front, where picnic barbecues are popular for day-tripping snorkellers and birders who have visited nearby small cayes hoping to glimpse flamingoes or scarlet ibis. If you go north you have to cross a small inlet with hand pulled ferry, US$0.50 for foreigners. The British Ordnance Survey has published a Tourist Map of Ambergris Caye, scale 1:50,000, with a plan of **San Pedro**, 1:5,000.

Excursions

Just south of Ambergris Caye, and not far from Caye Caulker, is the **Hol Chan Marine Park**, an underwater natural park. The office (with reef displays and information on Bacalar Chico National Park) is on Caribeña St, T2247. Divided into three zones, zone A is the reef, where fishing is prohibited. Entry US$2.50. Zone B is the seagrass beds, where fishing can only be done with a special licence; the Boca Ciega blue hole is here. Zone C is mangroves where fishing also requires a licence. Only certified scuba divers may dive in the reserve. Contact the Reserve Manager in San Pedro for further information. Several boatmen in San Pedro offer snorkelling trips to the park, US$20 (not including entry fee), two hours. Fish feeding is prohibited although it takes place at Shark-Ray Alley, where about 15 sharks and 15 rays are fed for the entertainment of 60 tourists. Only very experienced snorkellers should attempt to swim in the cutting between the reef and the open sea; seek advice on the tides.

San Pedro is well known for its diving. Long canyons containing plenty of soft and hard coral formations start around 50-60 feet and go down to 120 feet. Often these have grown into hollow tubes which make for interesting diving. Tackle Box, Esmeralda, Cypress, M & Ms and Tres Cocos are only some of the dive sites which abound in the area. Visability is usually over 150 feet. There is a recompression chamber in San Pedro.

Tours can also be arranged from here to visit many places on the mainland (for example Altun Ha US$60 per person; Lamanai US$125 per person) as well as other water experiences (catamaran sailing US$40 per person, deep sea fishing US$150-400, manatee and Coco Solo US$75). Among the many operators *Hustler Tours*, T02-62538 (Billy and his brothers are experienced and very helpful) are recommended. Day cruises to Caye Caulker and barrier reef on the island trader *MV Winnie Estelle* is good value at US$45 per person to include snacks and soft drinks. Other day snorkelling trips from US$25 to Caye Caulker with stops at Sting Ray Alley and coral gardens. Snorkel rental US$5, discount through tour group.

In San Pedro LL *Belize Yacht Club*, PO Box 1, T2777, F2768, all rooms are suites with fully-furnished kitchens, bar and restaurant, pool, docking facilities. **LL-L** *Paradise Villas*, condominiums alongside *Paradise Resort*, owners let villas when not occupied, T3077, F3831, a/c, the collection of 20 villas around a small (and not always very clean pool) are well equipped and convenient. **LL-AL** *Ramon's Village Resort*, T2071/2213, F2214, or USA 601-649-1990, F601-425-2411 (PO Drawer 4407, Laurel, MS 39441), agree on which currency you are paying in, 61 rooms, a diving and beach resort, all meals and all diving, highly recommended even for non-divers (fishing, swimming, boating, snorkelling), very efficient, comfortable rooms, pool with beach club atmosphere. **L** *Mayan Princess*, T2778, F2784, centre of village on seafront, clean, comfortable. **L-AL** *Paradise Resort Hotel*, T2083, F2232, wide selection of rooms and villas, good location, villas better value, cheaper summer rates, all watersports.

    AL *Rock's Inn Apartments*, T2326, F2358, good value and service. **AL** *San Pedro Holiday Hotel*, PO Box 1140, Belize City, T2014/2103, F2295, 16 rooms in good central location, fun atmosphere with good facilities, reasonable value. **AL** *Sun Breeze*, T2347/2191/2345, F2346, near airport, Mexican style building, a/c, comfortable, all facilities, good dive shop, recommended. **AL-B** *Coral Beach*, T2013, F2001, central location, slightly run down but good local feel and excellent watersports facilities including dive boat charter, tours for fishing and scuba available. **AL** *Changes in Latitudes*, T/F2986, latitudes@btl.net, next to *Yacht Club*, new, breakfast included, Canadian owner. **AL-A** *Spindrift*, T2018, F2251, 24 rooms, 4 apartments, unattractive block but central location, good bar and restaurant, popular meeting place, trips up the Belize River, a/c, comfortable. **AL-B** *Barrier Reef*, T2075, F2719, handsome wooden house in centre, a/c, pool. **A** *Lily's*, rooms with sea view, some with a/c, others with fan, clean, T2059.

    B *Casa Blanca*, San Pedro town, T2630. **B** *Conch Shell Inn*, facing sea, some rooms with kitchenette, T2062. **B** *Hide Away Lodge*, PO Box 484, Belize City, T2141/2269, good value but a bit run down. **B** *Martha's* (**D** in low season), PO Box 27, San Pedro, T2054, F2589, good value, recommended. **B** *San Pedrano*, San Pedro, T2054/2093, clean and good value.

    C *Thomas*, airy rooms, fan, bath (tub, not shower), drinking water, clean, friendly.

    D *Rubie's*, San Pedro Town on the beach, fan, private bath, good views, beach cabaña, central, recommended as best value in town, T2063/2434.

Just outside San Pedro LL *Caribbean Villas*, T2715, F2885, 10 units, homely, attractive development, bird-watching tower. **LL** Coco Caye Villa, book in USA T212-982-5809, F212-982-6750, ggsharp@interport.net, just to the north of San Pedro in private development, pool, beach, good value for 6 people. **LL** *Mata Chica Resort*, 4 miles north, T/F02-3012, matachica@btl.net, European owned and managed, beautiful and styish stucco and thatched cabañas on a lovely beach, fantastic restaurant, *Mambo*. **LL** *Journey's End*, PO Box 13, San Pedro, T2173, F2028, jscott@btl.net, 4.5 miles north, excellent resort facilities including diving, resort club theme, but overpriced. **LL-L** *Captain Morgan's Retreat*, 3 miles north of town, T2567, F2616, access by boat, thatched roofed cabañas with private facilities, pool, dock, secluded, recommended. **LL-L** *El Pescador*, on Punta Arena beach 3 miles north, PO Box 793, Belize City, T/F2398, access by boat, specialist fishing lodge with good reputation, a/c, good food and service. **LL-AL** *Victoria House*, PO Box 22, San Pedro, T2067/2240, F2429, (USA (800) 247-5159, T404-373-0068, F404-373-3885, info@victoriahouse.com, including meals, 1 mile from town, 3 different types of room, excellent facilities, good dive shop and watersports, windsurfing US$15 per hour, highly recommended. **L-AL** *Playador*, near Belize Yacht Club, T2870, F2871, 20 rooms, cabañas on the beach. **AL** *Capricorn Resort*, 3 miles north of town, T2809, F021-2091, capricorn@btl.net, wooden cabins on beach with great restaurant.

Sleeping
■ *on maps*
Price codes:
see inside front cover

Belize

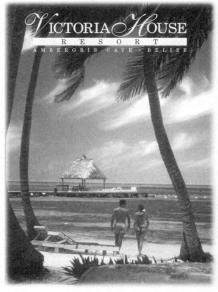

El Patio, south of town, beyond Belize Yacht Club, good, inexpensive Mexican-style food, live **Eating** music in evenings. *Rasta Pasta*, at *Sunbreeze Hotel*, south end of Front St, great spicey food ● *on maps* and barbecues. *Elvi's Kitchen*, popular, upmarket, live music and roof built around flamboyant tree, can be very busy, won international award 1996; 1 block north is *Ambergris Delight*, pleasant, inexpensive, clean; *Lily's Restaurant*, best seafood in town, friendly, good breakfast, excellent value but quite basic. *Alijua*, in San Pedro, Croatian owned, good food, also rents suites with kitchen, US$100 for 4 persons. *Jade Garden Restaurant*, Chinese, sweet and sour everything, drinks expensive. *Estel's* on the beach, good food and 1940s-50s music. *Celi's*, behind *Holiday Hotel*, good seafood, recommended. *La Parrilla*, opposite *Holiday Hotel*, small, Tex-Mex, quite good. *Little Italy*, at *Spindrift Hotel*, popular but expensive. *Fido's Courtyard*, towards north end of Front Street, lively bar-restaurant often with live music, good lunch and dinner. For those staying in villas, contact Denny 'The Bun Man', for fresh coffee, orange juice, and excellent cinnamon buns. He will deliver in time for breakfast, T3490.

Big Daddy's Disco, open evenings but gets cranked up at midnight. *Tarzan Disco*, nearby **Bars** on Front St, good atmosphere; For entertainment, try 'Chicken Drop' in Pier Lounge at *Spindthrift Hotel*, you bet US$1 on which square the chicken may leave its droppings on.

Diving: instruction to PADI open water widely available, from US$350-400 at Amigos del **Sports** Mar, divemaster Grant Crimmins, opposite *Lily's*; freelance instructor Lynne Stevens can be contacted through *Marinos* restaurant. Blue Hole (Chris Allnatt, in centre of town, good for advice, information and trips), T/F2982, bluehole@btl.net and Amigos del Mar (opposite *Lily's*) have been repeatedly recommended. Harte Lemmle, a Canadian, who sometimes works for Reef Divers, can be contacted at *Seychelle Guesthouse*, T3817 and is also recommended. Check diving shop's recent safety record before diving. **Sea kayaking** with expert guide, Elito Arceo, T3221 or 014-6043, office just north of airport. **Snorkelling** trips on the *Winnie Estelle*, a 40-foot motor cruiser with large deck area, US$55 day trip, open bar, snacks. Daniel Núñez, T3214, does trips to the Maya sites on the north of the caye in the new Bacalar Chico National Park.

Rocks Supermarket has good range of supplies. There are many gift shops in the centre of **Shopping** town. Try *Fidos* which has *Sunsation Gift Shop*, *Belizean Arts* (paintings and prints by local artists), *Amber Jewelry* and *Realty Café*. Wave runners (US$50 per hour), hobie cats (US$25 per hour) and parasailing (US$40) can be hired here.

Air Tropic Air (T2012) and Maya Island Air (T2345) have flights to/from both Belize City air- **Transport** ports, many daily. Maya Island Air also flies to Caye Caulker, while both airlines fly to Corozal, several daily flights.

Sea More interesting than going by air are the boats. To Belize City US$10-15 depending on boat. *Andrea* from San Pedro at 0700, returning from Courthouse Wharf at 1500. *Seascape* at 0800, returning from *Bellevue Hotel* at 1600. *Triple J* at 1500, returning from Courthouse Wharf at 0900; several other regular departures. All these call at Caye Caulker (and Caye Chapel and St George's Caye on request). Many regular boats between Caye Caulker and Ambergris Caye, US$7.50. Shuttle boats to hotels north of town, many from Fido's Dock.

Vehicle rental: golf carts US$10 per hour, make sure battery is fully charged before hiring; gives quick access to southern, quieter end. Bicycles US$5 per hour, try negotiating for long-term rates, good way to get around.

NB One cannot in practice walk north along the beach from San Pedro to Xcalak, Mexico.

Banks *Atlantic Bank* and *Bank of Belize*, open Mon-Thur 0800-1300, Fri 0800-1630. Small **Directory** denominations of US currency in regular use. **Travel Agencies** *Travel and Tour Belize* in town helpful, T2031. They can arrange charter flights to Corozal, with a request stop at Sarteneja (for the Shipstern Butterfly Farm see page 751). Another recommended travel agency is Amigo Travel on Front St, T2180.

Caye Caulker

Phone code: 022

If swimming in the 'cut', beware of fishing and powerboats using it as a route from the ocean to the west side; several serious accidents have occurred.

A lobster-fishing island (closed season 15 February-14 July), used to be relatively unspoilt, but the number of tourists is now increasing. The houses are of wood, the majority built on stilts. Some services are reported to have deteriorated, rubbish is appearing everywhere and theft and unpleasantness by some mainlanders who go to the caye with tourists; on the other hand the islanders are friendly. The atmosphere seems to be much more relaxed out of the high tourist season; nevertheless, women should take care if alone at night. A Marine Reserve has been established at the north end of the caye. There are no beaches as the coast is largely mangrove forest, but you can swim at the channel ('cut' or 'split', formed by a recent hurricane) or off one of the many piers. A reef museum has opened with enlarged photos of reef fish, free for school parties, tourists are asked for a US$2 donation to help expansion. There are only 10 vehicles on the island, one of which is used solely to transport Belikin beer. Sandflies are ferocious in season (December-February), take trousers and a good repellent. Make sure you fix prices before going on trips or hiring equipment, and clarify whether you are talking US$ or BZ$. Do not pay the night before.

A walk south along the shore takes you to the new airstrip, a gash across the island, and to mangroves where the rare Black Catbird (*Melanoptila glabirostris*) can be seen and its sweet song heard. In this area there are lots of mosquitoes. A campaign to make the Black Catbird's habitat and the associated reef a Nature Reserve (called Siwa-Ban, after the catbird's Maya name) can be contacted at *Galería Hicaco* (Ellen McCrea, near *Tropical Paradise*), or 143 Anderson, San Francisco, California.

Excursions **Reef trips** (see also under **Sleeping**) Prices are regulated: Manatees US$27.50; San Pedro, Hol Chan and Shark Alley US$17.50. Both are all day trips. They seem to be cheaper from Caye Caulker than Ambergris Caye. It is almost impossible to arrange boat trips the evening before; just wander down the main street at 1000, ask around for names of boat men, and you can not fail. Hol Chan gets very crowded and the earlier you get there the better. Try to ascertain that the boat operator is reliable. Anyone taking trips must be approved by the Tour Guide Association and should have a licence to prove it. In late 1997, several guides were arrested for operating without licences. Insist on evidence your guide is licenced to encourage high standards and for your own safety. Try to go with a group of five to seven people, larger numbers are less enjoyable. We have received reports of theft of valuables left on board while snorkelling and even of swimmers being left in the water while the boat man went off to pick up another group. Protect against sunburn on reef trips, even while snorkelling.

Reef trip operators Neno Rosado (T2302) has been approved by the association and is reliable and knowledgeable. Mervin, a local man, is reliable for snorkelling trips, he will also take you to Belize City. Driftwood Snorkelling, T2011, on the front by the *Miramar Hotel*, good snorkelling and diving trips and information. Carlos Tours, T2093, Carlos is a very good guide, leaves from *Cindy's Café*. Also recommended are Ras Creek, 'a big man with a big heart', in his boat, US$12.50 including lunch; Alfonso Rosardo, a Mexican, reef trips for up to 6 people, 5-6 hours, sometimes offers meals at his house afterwards; Obdulio Lulu (a man) at *Tom's Hotel* goes to Hol Chan and San Pedro for a full day (if he catches a barracuda on the return, he will barbecue it at the hotel for US$0.75); Raoul and Charles, also from *Tom's Hotel*, US$12.50; also Harrison (ask around for him, he goes to see manatees, then to a small island to see the coral reef, US$25, recommended). Lobster fishing and diving for conch is also possible. 'Island Sun', near the 'cutting', local husband and American wife, very conscientious; day tours to reef, plus snorkel hire (1000-1400); day tour to San Pedro and Hol Chan, plus snorkel hire, plus entry fee for reserve, recommended. Capt Jim Novelo, of *Sunrise* boat, does trips to Hol Chan and San Pedro, 1000-1600, and snorkelling excursions to the Turneffe Islands, Half Moon Caye, Bird Sanctuary and Blue Hole, 0630-1700, every Tuesday, December-April, July-August, or on request, US$67.50 including lunch and drinks, T2195, F2239. A sailing boat also goes to Hol Chan, but the trip takes a long time, leaving only a short while for snorkelling, departs 1000, US$12 for a day. Mask, snorkel and fins for US$2.50, cheapest (for instance at the post office, or *Sammie's Pastry Shop*). Benji, owner of a small sailboat and Joe Joe, his Rasta captain, will take you to Placencia or the Cayes, fun.

The cheapest end of town is the south, but it is a long way from the 'cutting' for swimming or snorkelling. A map which can be bought on arrival lists virtually everything on the island. Camping on the beach is forbidden.

Sleeping

B *Tropical Paradise*, T2124, F2225 (PO Box 1206 Belize City), cabins, rooms from **D**, hot showers, clean, not very comfortable, restaurant (see below), good excursions. **B** *CB's*, further south than *Tropical Paradise*, T2176, with bath, clean, 12 beds, no advance bookings, good, small beds, restaurant. **B** *Rainbow*, on the beach, T2123, 10 small bungalows, with shower, rooms also, **C**, hot water, good. Beach houses can also be rented for US$50-150 a month. **B** *Anchorage*, near *Ignacio's*, new 2-storey building, comfortable, tiled rooms with private bathrooms, pleasant atmosphere, friendly family, breakfast and drinks served under shade on the beach.

C *Edith's*, rooms with bath or private chalet, recommended, hot water, fan. **C** *Shirley's Guest House*, T2145, south end of village, very relaxing, recommended. **C** *Tree Tops*, T2008, F2115, clean, spacious rooms, comfortable beds, beach views, German spoken, powerful fan, cable TV, friendly, good value, recommended. **C** *Vega's Far Inn* rents 7 rooms, all doubles, T2142, with ceiling fan and fresh linen, flush toilets and showers (limited hot water) shared with camping ground, which is guarded, has drinking water, hot water, clean toilets, barbecue, can rent out camping gear (camping costs US$6 per person, overpriced).

D *Tropical Star*, T2196, small rooms, smelly recycled shower water, basic, but reasonable for the caye. **D** *Deisy's*, T2150, with shower, toilet and fan, reductions for longer stays, will store valuables, clean, friendly, safe, cheaper rooms downstairs, cash travellers' cheques, rooms with communal bathroom not good value, hot water. **D** *Ignacio Beach Cabins*, T2212 (PO Box 1169, Belize City), small huts or hammocks just outside town, for double room, **C** for a hut for 3-4, quiet, clean, recommended, toilet and shower facilities in private cabins only, cheap lobster tails and free coconuts (Ignacio runs reef trips and he has equipment, he is principally a lobster fisherman). **D** *Marin*, T44307, (also private hut) with bath, clean, helpful, recommended (the proprietor, John Marin, will take you out for a snorkelling trip on the reef). **D-E** *Mira Mar*, T44307, 2nd floor rooms best, clean showers, recommended, bargain if staying longer, helpful owner Melvin Badillo. **D** *Barbara's Guest House*, near north end, T2025, Canadian-run, good budget rooms, also safe hammock spaces, **E**, in thatched cabin.

E *Sandy Lane*, T2217, 1 block back from main street, bungalow-type accommodation, clean, shared toilet and hot showers, run by Rico and Elma Novelo, recommended. **E-D** *Tom's*, T2102, with shared bath and fan, up to **C** in cabin with 3 beds, basic, clean, cold water, long walk from beach, laundry service US$5, safe deposit, barbecue. Tom's boat trips go to various destinations, including Hol Chan and coral gardens, and to Belize City. In all accommodation take precautions against theft.

Tropical Paradise for excellent seafood, varied menu, slightly more expensive than others (also the only place selling ice cream). *The Sandbox*, run by American couple, one of the Caye's social centres, good chocolate cake, ice cream, recommended. Cakes and pastries can be bought at houses displaying the sign, recommended are *Deisy's*, *Jessie's* (open 0830-1300, 1500-1700), and a very good one near the telephone exchange office. *Glenda's*, near *Hotel Marin*, try the delicious lobster, or chicken 'Burritos', chicken, vegetables, chile and sauce wrapped in a tortilla for US$0.50, also good breakfast with cinnamon rolls, closed evenings; also good for 'Burritos', *Rainbow*, on waterfront near channel, good value, beautiful view. *Popeye's*, on shore, excellent pizzas. *Claudette*, next to Fishermen's Wharf, US$1.25, delicious. *Marin's*, good seafood in evening, cable TV, expensive but worth it. *Martínez*, good seafood, good prices. *Paradise Burgers*, near the Split, also fish sandwiches. *Cindy's*, on main street, good coffee, fresh yoghurt, good breakfasts. *Sid's*, good fish, large portions,

Eating

good fresh juices. *Chans Garden*, Chinese, try the chop suey, not cheap. *Ocean Side*, nice seafood, big portions, good atmosphere, cable TV, on expensive side. *Little Kitchen*, fish and French fries US$4, occasionally lobster, good. *I & I Bar*, mellow, laid back, good view from upper deck, pricey. Many private houses serve food. Buy lobster or fish from the cooperative and cook up at the barbecue on the beach; beer is sold by the crate at the wholesaler on the dock by the generator; ice for sale at *Tropical Paradise*.

Sports **Watersports** **Windsurfing**: equipment hire from Orlando, US$10 per hour, poor quality, bring your own or go to San Pedro. **Canoes**: for hire from Salvador, at painted house behind *Marin's* restaurant, US$10 a day. **Sea kayaks**: from Ellen at *Galería Hicaco*, US$12.50 for half day, also next to *Ignacio Beach Cabins* at US$15 half day, better kayaks. Go **fishing** with Rolly Rosardo, four hours, US$45, up to five people, equipment, fresh bait and instruction provided. **Diving**: Frenchie's Diving Service, T2234, charges US$330 for a four-day PADI course, friendly and effective, two-tank dive US$60, also advanced PADI instruction. Day excursion diving Blue Hole, et cetera, US$65, snorkellers welcome. Also recommended for excellent instruction are *Caye Caulker School of Scuba* (T2292). Many **sailing** trips available for US$18 per person (stops for snorkelling too). Ask Chocolate for all-day trips to the manatee reserve in the south of Belize. It may be possible to hire a boat for 6-8 people to Chetumal.

Shopping There are at least four small 'markets' on the island where a variety of food can be bought; prices are 20-50 percent higher than the mainland. Bookstore on opposite side of island to ferries has many different magazines, including *Time* and *Newsweek*.

Transport **On the island** You can rent golf carts, US$5 per hour, popular, the locals rent them to take the family for a drive.

Air Maya Island Air flies to/from Belize City, Corozal and San Pedro, several daily. Flying is recommended if you have a connection to make.

Sea Boats leave from the Marine Terminal on North Front Street (see above), for Caye Caulker, between 0900-1700, returning 0630-1600, daily, US$12.50, buy tickets in advance from desk inside Marine Terminal, 45 minutes one way (can be 'exciting' if it's rough). The Caye Caulker Water Taxi Association regulates schedules and fares; the office on Caye Caulker is opposite BTL. Recommended boats: Emilio Novelo's *Ocean Star* (good, cheaper than others); Chocolate's *Soledad* ('Chocolate' is white, over 70 years old and has a white moustache). Boats from San Pedro en route to Belize City 0700-0800, US$12.50. *Triple J* (see above, San Pedro) boat, recommended, daily service, from Ambergris Caye 0700, 45 minutes, US$12.50. To get to Flores or Chetumal buy onward tickets at any travel agency on the caye and take the boat at 0800.

Directory **Banks** Rates for changing cash and TCs are reasonable. *Atlantic Bank* (Visa advances available US$5 commission) and many places for exchange. Gift shops will charge a commission. **Communications** International telephone and fax connections available on Caye Caulker (telephone exchange is open 0900-1230, 1400-1630; cardphone outside office can be used for international calls. Collect calls possible at least to North America at no charge. Fax number at telephone exchange is 501-22-2239). **Travel agencies** *Dolphin Bay Travel*, PO Box 374, Belize City, T/F2214, is highly recommended and can arrange domestic and international flights as well as local excursions.

English Caye 12 miles off Belize City, English Caye is beautiful, with no facilities; take a day trip only. It is part of the reef so you can snorkel right off the beach. *Sunrise Travel*, Belize City, T72051/ 32670, can help arrange a trip, book in advance.

Turneffe Islands

The islands are one of Belize's three atolls. On **Big Caye Bokel** is *Turneffe Islands Lodge*, PO Box 480, Belize City, which can accommodate 16 guests for week-long fishing and scuba packages. *Turneffe Flats*, 56 Eve Street, Belize City, T02-45634, in a lovely location, also offers week-long packages, for fishing and scuba; it can take 12 guests, but is to be expanded. *Blackbird Caye Resort*, c/o Blackbird Caye Co, 11a Cork Street, Belize, T02-32772, F02-34449, Manager, Kent Leslie, weekly packages arranged, is an ecologically-oriented resort on this 4,000 acre island used by the Oceanic Society and is a potential site for a Biosphere Reserve underwater project. Reservations in the USA, T713-6581142, F713-6580379. Diving or fishing packages available, no bar, take your own alcohol. On Calabash Caye, *Coral Cay Conservation* in conjunction with University College of Belize has a marine studies programme. For information contact CCC in the UK, T0171-4986248, F0181-7739656.

Lighthouse Reef

Lighthouse Reef is the outermost of the three north-south reef systems off Belize, some 45 miles to the east of Belize City. There are two cayes of interest, Half Moon Caye (on which the lighthouse stands) and 12 miles to the north, the caye in which Blue Hole is found. **Half Moon Caye** is the site of the **Red-Footed Booby Sanctuary**, a national reserve. Besides the booby, which is unusual in that almost all the individuals have the white colour phase (normally they are dull brown), magnificent frigate birds nest on the island. The seabirds nest on the western side, which has dense vegetation (the eastern side is covered mainly in coconut palms). Of the 98 other bird species recorded on Half Moon Caye, 77 are migrants. Iguana, the wish willy (smaller than the iguana) and the *anolis allisoni* lizard inhabit the caye, and hawksbill and loggerhead turtles lay their eggs on the beaches. The Belize Audubon Society, 12 Fort Street, maintains the sanctuary; there is a lookout tower and trail. The lighthouse on the caye gives fine views of the reef. It was first built in 1820: the present steel tower was added to the brick base in 1931 and now the light is solar powered. Around sunset you can watch the boobies from the lookout as they return from fishing. They land beside their waiting mates at the rate of about 50 a minute. They seem totally unbothered by humans.

There are no facilities; take all food, drink and fuel. On arrival you must register with the warden near the lighthouse (the warden will provide maps and tell you where you can camp).

It is possible to stay on one of the private islands in the reef, 12 kilometres from the Blue Hole, all inclusive one week stays, contact PO Box 1435, Dundee, Fla, USA, T1-800-4233114, F1-813-4392118 (USA).

In Lighthouse Reef is the **Blue Hole**, recently declared a National Monument, an almost circular sinkhole, 1,000 feet across and with depths exceeding 400 feet. The crater was most likely formed by a meteor, thousands of years ago. It was studied by Jacques Cousteau in 1984. Stalagmites and stalactites can be found in the underwater cave. Entry to the Blue Hole is US$4. Scuba diving is outstanding at Lighthouse Reef, including two walls which descend almost vertically from 30-40 feet to several thousand.

Excursions Frenchie, of *Frenchie's Diving*, runs regular trips from Caye Caulker to **Half Moon Caye** and the **Blue Hole**, US$65 for snorkellers, more for divers. To charter a motor boat in Belize City costs about US$50 per person if 10 people are going (six hours' journey). Organized trips can be booked through any dive shop in San Pedro. Bill Hinkis, in San Pedro Town, Ambergris Caye, offers three-day sailing cruises to Lighthouse Reef for US$150 (you provide food, ice and fuel). Bill and his boat *Yanira* can be found beside the lagoon off Back Street, just north of the football field. Out Island Divers, San Pedro, do various two to three day trips. Other sailing vessels charge US$150-250 per day. Speed boats charge US$190 per person for a day-trip including lunch and three dives, recommended. The main dive in the Blue Hole is very deep, at least 130 feet (almost 50 metres); the hole itself is 480 feet deep. Check your own qualifications as the dive operator probably will not. It is well worth doing if you are qualified. Keep an eye on your computer or dive charts if doing subsequent dives.

For southern cayes, see under **Southern Belize**.

Belize City

Northern Belize

North Belize is notable for its agricultural productivity, sugar, fruit, market gardening, providing much of Belize's food. There are some notable wildlife sanctuaries and nature reserves, and a fair share of the country's countless Maya sites, many recently found and yet to be fully explored.

Belize City to Mexican border

Two main roads penetrate the country from Belize City: one to the north and another to the west. The Northern Highway is very patched up as it leaves Belize City until it divides into the New Alignment, which is well paved to the Mexican border, and the Old Northern Highway (narrow, paved, in reasonable condition).

Bermudian Landing/ Community Baboon Sanctuary

15 miles out of Belize City there is a turning left to **Bermudian Landing** (12 miles on a rough road from the turn off). The village was once a transfer point for timber floated down the Belize River and now a small Creole village. Here there is a local wildlife museum (sponsored by the World Wildlife Fund) and the **Community Baboon Sanctuary** nearby, with black howler monkeys, locally called baboons. Trails have been made in and around the reserve, which encompasses eight villages, all of whose inhabitants collaborate to protect the howlers' habitat. Check with the Sanctuary warden if you wish to visit. Boats can be hired from the warden for river trips to see monkeys and birds. Booklet (US$3, excellent) from the Audubon Society, 12 Fort Street, Belize City. A guided walk costs US$6 per person. The warden will also arrange accommodation locally and may allow overnight parking at the site for a small donation, T44405. Many freelance guides seek business from arriving vehicles, but it is better to get a licensed guide from the visitor's centre.

Sleeping **At Bermudian Landing** **A-C** *Jungle Drift Lodge*, 400 yards from museum, cabañas have been built by John and Madeline Estephan of the tour company, Jungle Drift (PO Box 1442, Belize City, T01-49578, F02-78160, jungled@btl.net, www.belizemallcom/jungled), screened windows, fans, cheaper with shared bath, discounts for students, travellers' cheques, Visa, Mastercard accepted, camping US$5 per person, bring tent, river tours US$20 per person recommended, transport from Belize City in pick up, US$40, 1-4 people, on request, breakfast, lunch and dinner, US$2.50-7.50; canoe rentals in Burrell Boom for trips on Belize River to see birds, howler monkeys, manatee, hicatee.

Transport Bus from Belize City, Mcfadzean Bus from corner of Amara Ave and Cemetery Road, 1215, 1715 Monday-Friday; 1200, 1400 Saturday; Rancho Bus (Pook's Bus) from Batty Bus terminal on Mosul Street, 1700 Monday-Friday, 1300 Saturday, check details, US$1.50-2, 1 hour. A day trip is very difficult by public transport so it is best to stay the night.

Crooked Tree

The Northern Highway continues to **Sand Hill** where a dusty or muddy three mile road turns off to the northwest to the **Crooked Tree Lagoons and Wildlife Sanctuary**, set up in 1984, an exceptionally rich area for birds. The network of lagoons and swamps attracts many migrating birds and the dry season, October-May, is a good time to visit. You may see the endangered jabiru stork, the largest flying bird in the Western Hemisphere, five feet tall with a wingspan of 11-12 feet, which nests here, as well as herons, ducks, vultures, kites, ospreys, hawks, sand pipers, kingfishers, gulls, terns, egrets and swallows. In the forest you can also see and hear howler monkeys. Other animals include coatimundi, crocodiles, iguanas and turtles. Glenn Crawford is a very good guide as is Sam Tillet (see **Sleeping** below). The turn off to the Sanctuary can be hard to find as the sign is difficult to spot, especially if coming from the south. The intersection is 22 miles from Orange Walk and 32 miles from Belize City. There is another sign further south indicating the Sanctuary but this does not lead to the Wildlife Sanctuary, just the park boundary. The mango and cashew trees in the village of Crooked Tree are said to be 100 years old. Birdwatching is best in the early morning, but, as buses do not leave Belize City early, for a day trip take an early Corozal bus, get off at the main road (about one and a quarter hours from Belize City) and hitch to the Sanctuary. The village is tiny and quaint, occupied mostly by Creoles. Boats and guides can be hired for approximately US$70 per boat (maximum four people). It may be worth bargaining as competition is high. Trips include a visit to an unexcavated Mayan site. Lots of birds can be seen, especially near the lagoon. It is easy to get a lift, and someone is usually willing to take visitors back to the main road for a small charge. Entry is US$4 (Belizeans US$1); you must register at the visitor's centre, drinks are on sale, but take food. There is a helpful, friendly warden, Steve, who will let you sleep on the porch of the visitors' centre.

Sleeping

A *Bird's Eye View Lodge*, T02-32040, 02-57027, F02-24869, birdseye@btl.net, www.belize. net.com/birdseye.html (owned by the Gillett family; in USA New York T/F718-8450749), single and double rooms, shower, fan, also bunk accommodation, US$10, camping US$5, meals available, boat trips, horseriding, canoe rental, nature tours with licensed guide, ask for information at the Audubon Society (address above). **A** *Paradise Inn*, run by the Crawfords, cabins with hot showers, restaurant, is well maintained and friendly, T02-44333, boat trips, fishing, horse riding and tours available.

B-C *Sam Tillet's Hotel*, T021-12026, in centre of village, wood and thatch cabin, tiny restaurant, great trips. Cabins may be rented at US$33 for a night, up to 4 people. Camping and cheap rooms (house of Rev Rhayburn, **E**, recommended, meals available) can also be arranged if you ask.

Transport

Buses from Belize City with JEX and Batty, former 1035 and others, latter 1600; return from Crooked Tree at 0600-0700, sometimes later. Batty Bus also on Sunday, leaves Belize City 0900, retunrs 1600.

Altun Ha

North of Sand Hill the road forks, the quicker route heading direct to Orange Walk, the older road looping north then northwest.

The Maya remains of **Altun Ha**, 31 miles north of Belize City and two miles off the old Northern Highway, are worth a visit, entrance US$1.50 (insect repellent necessary); they are open 0900-1700. Since there is so little transport on this road, hitching is not recommended, best to go in a private vehicle or a tour group. Vehicles leave Belize City for **Maskall** village, eight miles north of Altun Ha, several days a week, but same-day return is not possible. With warden's permission, vehicle overnight parking is permitted free, but there is no accommodation in nearby villages. Tourist Board booklets on the ruins are out of print now. Altun Ha was a major ceremonial centre in the Classic Period (250-900 AD) and a trading station linking the Caribbean coast with Maya centres in the interior. The site consists of two central plazas surrounded by 13 partially excavated pyramids and temples. What the visitor sees now is composite, not how the site would have been at any one time in the past. Nearby is a large reservoir, now called Rockstone Road ('Altun Ha' is a rough translation of the modern name). The largest piece of worked Maya jade ever found, a head of the Sun God Kinich Ahau weighing nine and a half pounds, was found here, in the main temple (B-4) in 1968. It is now in a bank vault in Belize City.

Sleeping Just north of Maskall is **LL *Maruba Resort***, T03-22199 also USA 713-719-2031, a hotel, restaurant and spa, all rooms different, some a/c, German spoken, good birdwatching, including storks in the nearby swamp; has caged animals and birds.

Orange Walk

The New Alignment runs to (66 miles) Orange Walk, centre of a district where about 17,000 Creoles, Mennonites and Maya Indians get their living from timber, sugar planting and general agriculture.

Population: 19,000
Phone code: 03
Colour map 4, grid B3

Orange Walk is an agricultural centre and the country's second city. A toll bridge (BZ$0.25 for motorbikes, BZ$0.80 for cars) now spans the New River a few miles south of the town at Tower Hill. Spanish is the predominant language. It is a centre for refugees from other parts of Central America, while Mennonites from the surrounding colonies also use it as their marketing and supply town. There are some pleasant wooden buildings on the streets leading off Queen Victoria Avenue, which is the main road through town. The clock tower, town hall and Park, on this street at the heart of the city, is where the Belize City-Mexico border buses stop. Also on this street, which is dusty in dry weather, are some concrete buildings such as 'Big Pink', otherwise known as *Mi Amor Hotel*, Chinese restaurants, shoe shops, electrical goods sellers and purveyors of reggae music. The other public buildings are beside the football pitch, while the Catholic cathedral and school are towards the river from the Park (take Church Street out of the Park). The only battle fought on Belizean soil took place here, during the Yucatecan Race Wars (1840-60s); the Maya leader, Marcus Canul was shot in the fighting (1872). A new market was opened in 1996, overlooking New River, well organized, good food stalls, interesting architecture.

Sleeping **C** *Chula Vista*, Trial Farm, T22227, at gas station (closed) just north of town, safe, clean, helpful owner, but overpriced. **C** *d'Victoria*, 40 Belize Rd (Main St), T22518, a/c, shower, hot water, parking, quite comfortable, pool, but somewhat run down. **C** *St Christopher's*, 10 Main St, opened 1997, beautiful clean rooms and bathrooms, highly recommended. **D** *Camie's Hotel and Restaurant*, on Park at Queen Victoria Ave, T22661, with bath and fan, hot rooms, spartan but OK, offstreet parking. **B-D** *Mi Amor*, 19 Belize-Corozal Rd, T22031, with shared bath, with bath and fan, or with a/c, nice, clean, restaurant. **E** *Jane's*, 2 Baker's St, T22473 (extension on Market Lane), large house in pleasant location but smelly. **E** *La Nueva Ola*, 73 Otro Benque Rd, T22104, large car park, run down, probably the cheapest. Neither of these is recommended. Parking for vehicles is very limited at hotels.

Eating The majority of restaurants in town are Chinese, eg *Hong Kong II*, next to *Mi Amor*. *Golden Gate*, Baker's St, Chinese specialities, cheap. *King Fu*, Baker's St, excellent Chinese, filling, US$5. *Julie's*, near police station, good, inexpensive creole cooking; similarly at *Juanita's*, 8 Santa Ana St (take road beside Shell station), open 0600 for breakfast and all meals. Most restaurants and bars are open on Sunday. Many good bars eg *San Martín*. On Clarke St behind hospital is *The Diner*, main road, centre, good meals for US$3, very friendly, taxi US$4 or walk.

Transport Bus Station is on street beside the fire station, on the main road. All Chetumal buses pass Orange Walk Town (hourly); Belize-Orange Walk, US$3. Corozal-Orange Walk, US$1.50, 50 minutes. For Lamanai take bus to Indian Church (Monday, Wednesday, Friday 1600).

Directory **Banks** *Scotia Bank* on Park, BZ$1 commission/transaction. *Belize Bank* on Main St (down Park St from Park, turn left); same hrs as Belize City (see page 734). Shell Station will change TCs.

A road heads west from Orange Walk, then turns south, parallel first to the Mexican border, then the Guatemalan (where it becomes unmade). Along this road are several archaeological sites: **Cuello** is four miles west on San Antonio road, behind Cuello Distillery (ask there for permission to visit); taxi about US$3.50. Site dates back to 1000 BC; although it has yielded important discoveries in the study of Maya and pre-Maya cultures, there is little for the layman to appreciate and no facilities for visitors. At **Yo Creek**, the road divides, north to San Antonio, and south, through miles of cane fields and tiny farming settlements parallel to the Mexican border as far as **San Felipe** (20 miles via San Lazaro, Trinidad and August Pine Ridge). At August Pine Ridge there is a daily bus to Orange Walk at 1000. You can camp at the house of Narciso Novelo, T03-33019, relaxing place to stay. At San Felipe, a branch leads southeast to Indian Church (35 miles from Orange Walk, one hour driving on improved, white marl road, passable all year, four-wheel drive needed when wet). Another road heads west to Blue Creek Village (see below).

Lamanai

Near **Indian Church**, one of Belize's largest archaeological sites, **Lamanai** stretches along the west side of New River Lagoon 22 miles by river south of Orange Walk. While the earliest buildings were erected about 700 BC, culminating in the completion of the 112-foot major temple, N10-43, about 100 BC (the tallest known preclassic, Maya structure), there is evidence the site was occupied from 1500 BC. With the Spanish and British sites mentioned below, and the present day refugee village nearby, Lamanai has a very long history. The Maya site has been partially cleared, but covers a large area so a guide is recommended. The views from temple N10-43, dedicated to Chac, are superb; look for the Yin-Yang-like symbol below the throne on one of the other main temples, which also has a 12-foot tall mask overlooking its plaza. Visitors can wander freely along narrow trails and climb the stairways.

At nearby Indian Church a Spanish mission was built over one of the Maya temples in 1580; the British established a sugar mill here last century; remains of both buildings can still be seen. Note the huge flywheel engulfed by a strangler fig. The archaeological reserve is jungle again and howler monkeys can be seen (with luck) in the trees. There are many birds, and mosquitoes (wear trousers, take repellent) in the wet season, but the best way to see birds is to reach Lamanai by boat. The earlier you go the better.

The community phone for information on Indian Church, including buses, is 03-23369.

At Indian Church AL *Lamanai Outpost Lodge*, Colin and Ellen Howells, T/F233578, lamanai@btl.net, a short walk from Lamanai ruins, overlooking New River Lagoon, package deals available, day tours, 28 foot pontoon boat, canoes, thatched wooden cabins with bath and fan, hot water, electricity, restaurant, still expanding. A resident archaeologist and a naturalist run field study courses here. Nazario Ku, the site caretaker, permits camping or hammocks at his house, opposite path to Lamanai ruins, good value for backpackers. **Sleeping**

Boats Herminio and Antonio Novelo run boat trips from Orange Walk, T03-22293, F03-22201, PO Box 95, 20 Lovers Lane, 5 passengers per boat, US$30 per person including lunch, 1½-2 hours to Lamanai. **Transport**

For transport to Lamanai, see Orange Walk, **Buses**. **Transport**

West of San Felipe is Blue Creek (10 miles), largest of the trim Mennonite settlements. Many of the inhabitants of these close-knit villages arrived in 1959, members of a Canadian colony which had migrated to Chihuahua to escape encroaching modernity; they preserve their Low German dialect, are exempt from military service, and their industry now supplies the country with most of its poultry, eggs and vegetables. Some settlements, such as Neustadt in the west, have been abandoned because of threats by drug smugglers in the early 1990s. In 1998 Belize and Mexico signed an agreement to build an international bridge from Blue Creek across the **Blue Creek** river to La Unión, together with a river port close to the bridge. It is not known when work will start.

A large area to the south along the **Rio Bravo** has been set aside as a conservation area (see **Nature Conservation**). Within this Conservation Area, there is a study and accommodation centre near the Mayan site of **Las Milpas, AL** *Rio Bravo Field Station*, three cabañas, spacious, comfortable, with a thatched roof overhanging a large wooden deck. For more information call T03-30011, or contact the Programme for Belize in Belize City (T02-75616). To reach the site, go six miles west from Blue Creek to Tres Leguas, then follow the signs south towards the Rio Bravo Escarpment. The site of Las Milpas is at present being excavated by a team from the University of Texas and Boston University, USA. A good road can be followed 35 miles south to Gallon Jug, where **Chan Chich, LL** with meals or without, a jungle tourism lodge has been built around a Maya ruin, recommended, PO Box 37, Belize City, T02-75634, F02-76961 (flights to Chan Chich from Belize City, 0900 Monday, Wednesday and Friday, US$98 return, and can be chartered from elsewhere). Another road has recently been cut south through Tambos to the main road between Belmopan and San Ignacio; travel in this region is strictly a dry weather affair. Phone before setting out for *Chan Chich* for reservations and information on the roads.

Northeast of Orange Walk

From Orange Walk a road crosses New River and runs six miles northeast to **San Estevan**. San Estevan can also be reached either by a poor road going north from Carmelita (the junction of the Old and New Alignments of the Northern Highway, seven miles south of Orange Walk), or by a road heading southeast from the Northern Highway between San José and San Pablo. These two towns, some 10 miles north of Orange Walk, merge into one another; the turning, unsigned on the right is before San Pablo proper. Drive four miles on a rough road through sugar cane field to a T-junction; turn right and after three miles you come to a hand-cranked ferry across the New River (fare anything from nothing to US$1.50, operates 0600-2200). If going to Progresso and Sarteneja, after the ferry turn left up the hill to the police station, where the road bears right. Follow this road straight through San Estevan. The Maya ruins near San Estevan have reportedly been 'flattened' to a large extent and are not very impressive. Ten miles from San Estevan is a road junction: straight on is **Progresso**, a village picturesquely located on the lagoon of the same name. The right turn, signposted, runs off to the Mennonite village of Little Belize and continues (in poor condition) to **Chunox**, a village with many Maya houses of pole construction. In the dry season it is possible to drive from Chunox to the Maya site of Cerros (see below).

Sarteneja The main road continues east, in improved state, over swampy land to Sarteneja (40 miles from Orange Walk; one-hour drive, only impassable in the very wet), a small fishing and boat-building settlement founded by Yucatán refugees in 19th century. There are many remains of an extensive Maya city scattered throughout the village. The main catch is lobster and conch. On Easter Sunday there is a regatta, with all types of boat racing, dancing and music; very popular. There is also windsurfing.

Sleeping Recommended accommodation at *Fernando's Guest House*, on seafront near centre, T04-32085; *Sayab Cabañas*, by water tower, with thatched cabins and private bath; **D** *Diani's*, on the seashore, restaurant. Houses can be rented for longer stays.

Transport Sarteneja can be reached by **boat** from Corozal in 30 minutes, but only private charters, so very expensive (compared with 3 hours by road). **Bus** from Belize City with Venus, 1200, and Perez, 1300 (from the gas station on North Front St). No buses Sunday.

Shipstern Nature Reserve

Three miles before Sarteneja is the visitors' centre for the Reserve, which covers 9,000 hectares of this northeast tip of Belize. Hardwood forests, saline lagoon systems and wide belts of savannah shelter a wide range of mammals (all the fauna found elsewhere in Belize, except monkeys), reptiles and 200 species of birds. Of the mammals you are most likely to see coatis and foxes. Also, there are mounds of Maya houses and fields everywhere. The remotest forest, south of the lagoon, is not accessible to short-term visitors. There is a botanical trail leading into the forest with trees labelled with Latin and local Yucatec Maya names; a booklet is available. At the visitor's centre is the **Butterfly Breeding Centre**, ■ *0900-1200, 1300-1600 except Christmas and Easter, US$5 including excellent guided tour.* (Choose a sunny day for a visit if possible; on dull days the butterflies hide themselves in the foliage.) Mosquito repellent is essential. There is dormitory accommodation at the visitors' centre, rather poor, US$10 per person. A day trip by private car is possible from Sarteneja or Orange Walk.

North of Orange Walk

One mile from the Northern Highway, in San José and San Pablo, is the archaeological site of **Nohmul**, a ceremonial centre whose main acropolis dominates the surrounding cane fields (the name means 'Great Mound'). Permission to visit the site must be obtained from Sr Estevan Itzab, whose house is opposite the water tower.

The Northern Highway continues to Corozal (96 miles from Belize City), formerly the centre of the sugar industry, now with a special zone for the clothing industry and garments exports. It is a mixture of modern concrete commercial buildings and Caribbean clapboard seafront houses on stilts. Much of the old town was destroyed by Hurricane Janet in 1955. Like Orange Walk Town it is economically depressed; there has been a greater dependence on marijuana as a result. Corozal is much the safer place. It has been open to the sea with a pleasant waterfront where the market is held. There is no beach but you can swim in the sea and lie on the grass. Fishermen return to Sarteneja from Corozal pm, you can bargain for a ride.

Corozal
Population: 8,020
Phone code: 04
Colour map 4, grid B3

Excursion A road leads seven miles northeast to **Consejo**, a seaside fishing village on Chetumal Bay; taxi about US$10.

Sleeping A-C *Tony's*, South End, T22055, F22829, with a/c, clean, comfortable units in landscaped grounds, recommended, but restaurant overpriced. D *Caribbean Village Resort*, South End, PO Box 55, T22045, F23414, hot water, US$5 camping, US$12 trailer park, recommended, restaurant. D *Nestor's*, 123, 5th Ave South, T22354, with bath and fan, OK, refrescos available, good food. Next door to *Nestor's* E *Papa's Guest House*, good value. E *Capri*, 14 Fourth Ave, on the seafront, T22042, somewhat run down but OK for a night or two, with or without private bath, towels and soap provided but no mirror, bar and dance hall downstairs. E *Maya*, South End, T22082, hot water, quieter than *Nestor's* food good, meal US$5. Pleasant, clean guest house, **E**, to the north of town, on east side of main street, no name but look for sign which reads: *rooms/comfortable and clean*, next to used car dealer, very friendly, fan, good value.

Camping *Caribbean Motel and Trailer Park*, see above, camping possible but not very safe (US$4 per person), shaded sites, restaurant.

Eating *Club Campesino*, decent bar, good fried chicken after 1800. *Skytop*, 5th Ave South, friendly, good food, excellent breakfast, recommended, good view from roof. *Gongora's Pastry*, south west corner of main square, hot pizza pieces US$1-1.50, cakes and drinks. *Border*, 6th Ave South, friendly Chinese, good food, cheap. *Newtown Chinese*, 7th Ave, just north of the gas station on the other side of the main road, large portions, good quality, from US$3, slow service. *Rexo*, North 5th St, Chinese. Also Chinese: *Bumpers* (recommended), *King of Kings*; *Hong Kong*.

Transport Air Maya Island Air, 3 flights daily from Belize City via Caye Caulker and San Pedro (Ambergris Caye); Tropic Air daily from San Pedro. Airstrip 3 metres south, taxi US$1.50. **Buses** There are 15 buses a day from Belize City by Venus Bus, Magazine Road, and Batty Bus, 54 East Collet Canal, normal buses 3 hours, US$4, express buses 2½-3 hours, US$5. Both continue to Chetumal where they terminate at the market, 1 kilometre from the Mexican bus terminal, but they pass the terminal; ask the driver to let you off there; because of the frequency, there is no need to take a colectivo to the Mexican border unless travelling at unusual hours (US$2.50). The increased frequency of buses to Chetumal and the number of money changers cater for Belizeans shopping cheaply in Mexico, very popular, book early. For those coming from Mexico who are more interested in Tikal than Belize, it is possible to make the journey border to border in a day, with a change of bus, to Novelo's, in Belize City. Timetables change frequently, so check at the time of travel. There are also tourist minibuses which avoid Belize City.

Directory Banks *Bank of Nova Scotia*, *Atlantic Bank* (charges US$2.50 for Visa cash advances) and *Belize Bank* (does not accept Mexican pesos, charges US$7.50 for Visa cash advances), open same hrs as Belize City. For exchange also ask at the bus station (see page 734).

Six miles northeast of Corozal, to the right of the road to Chetumal, is **4 Miles Lagoon**, about a quarter of a mile off the road (buses will drop you there). Clean swimming, better than Corozal bay, some food and drinks available; it is often crowded at weekends.

Cerros & Santa Rita Across the bay to the south of Corozal stand the mounds of **Cerros**, once an active Maya trading port whose central area was reached by canal. Some of the site is flooded but one pyramid, 69 feet high with stucco masks on its walls, has been partially excavated. Boat from Corozal, walk around bay (boat needed to cross mouth of the New River) or dry-season vehicular trail from Progresso and Chunox (see above). More easily accessible are the ruins of **Santa Rita**, only a mile out on the Northern Highway, opposite the Coca Cola plant; once a powerful and cosmopolitan city, and still occupied when the Spaniards arrived in Belize, the site's post-classic murals and buildings have long been destroyed; only 50 feet tall Structure seven remains standing, entry US$1.

Frontier with Mexico Eight miles north beyond Corozal is the Mexican frontier at **Santa Elena**, where a bridge across the Río Hondo connects with Chetumal, seven miles into Mexico. The border can be very busy and therefore slow especially at holiday times when chartered coaches bring shoppers to Mexico.

Belizean immigration Border crossing formalities are relatively relaxed. The border is open 24 hours a day. Exit tax by PACT, see page 721.

Crossing by private vehicle If driving to Belize, third party insurance is obligatory. It can be purchased from the building opposite the immigration post.

Mexican Immigration Mexican tourist cards for 30 days are available at the border. To extend the tourist card beyond 30 days, go to immigration in Cancún. The Mexican Embassy is in Belize City if you need a visa.

Exchange Money changers are on the Belize side of the border. You can buy pesos at good rates with US and Belizean currency. Rates for Belizean dollars in Mexico will be lower. Coming from Mexico, it is best to get rid of pesos at the border. Compare rates at the small bank near the frontier with the street changers on the Belizean side. The shops by the border will also change money.

Transport   The Northern Highway is in good condition. Driving time to the capital 3 hours. There are frequent buses from Corozal to Belize City, see under Corozal. All northbound buses from Belize City go to Chetumal: Batty in am, Venus in pm up to 1900. Contact Henry Menzies in Corozal, T04-23415, who runs taxis into Chetumal for about US$25, quick and efficient way to get through to the border. If leaving Mexico, he will collect you in Chetumal.

Western Belize

Belize City

West Belize, from Belmopan to the Guatemalan border, has some spectacular natural sights, exciting rivers and, in the Mountain Pine Ridge area, some of the best limestone scenery in Central America, notably waterfalls and caves. There are many Maya sites.

Belize City to San Ignacio

The Western Highway leaves Belize City past the cemetery, where burial vaults stand elevated above the boggy ground, and runs through palmetto scrub and savannah landscapes created by 19th century timber cutting. At Mile 16 is **Hattieville**, originally a temporary settlement for the homeless after hurricane Hattie in 1961. It has become a permanent town of some 2,500 people and is also home to the new Belize prison with its many juvenile offenders. From here, an all-weather road runs north to **Burrell Boom** (Texaco station) and the Northern Highway, a convenient bypass for motorists wishing to avoid Belize City. The Highway roughly parallels the Sibun River, once a major trading artery where mahogany logs were floated down to the coast in the rainy season; the placename 'Boom' recalls spots where chains were stretched across rivers to catch the logs.

The small but excellent **Belize Zoo**, at Mile 28.5, see yellow sign. Wonderful collection of local species (originally gathered for a wildlife film), lovingly cared-for and displayed in wire-mesh enclosures amid native trees and shady vegetation, including jaguar and smaller cats, pacas (called 'gibnuts' in Belize), snakes, monkeys, parrots, crocodile, tapir ('mountain cow'), peccary ('wari') and much more. Recommended, even for those who hate zoos; ■ *T08-13004, open daily 0900-1600, US$7.50.* Get there early to avoid coach parties' arrival. All buses from Belize City along the Western Highway pass the zoo, one hour. Tours by enthusiastic guides; T-shirts and postcards sold for fundraising. Nearest restaurant 45 minutes' walk away at La Democracia, only cold drinks and snacks sold at the zoo.

Belize Zoo

The highway gently climbs toward the foothills of the Maya Mountains through stands of Caribbean pine. Look out for the foothill known as the 'Sleeping Giant', seen in profile south of the highway when heading west. Between the Zoo and *JB's* (see below) the coastal road to Dangriga heads south.

Sleeping   L *Jaguar Paw Jungle Lodge*, on curve of Caves Branch River on road south at Mile 31, enquiries T02-35395, with 3 meals, opened 1996. Possible basic lodging at the Education Centre at Belize Zoo, ask at the reception, take a torch.

At Mile 31.5 the Wildlife Sanctuary is sponsored by the Belize Center for Environmental Studies (PO Box 666, Belize City, T02-45545) and Rainforest Action Information Network (RAIN, PO Box 4418, Seattle, Washington 98104, T206-3247163). It contains 1,070 acres of tropical forest and savannah between the Highway and the

Monkey Bay Wildlife Sanctuary

Sibun River (great swimming and canoeing). Birds are abundant and there is a good chance of seeing mammals. Pedro, the caretaker, can be hired for guided tours of the trails. Dormitory accommodation US$7.50 per person, or you can camp on wooden platform with thatched roof for US$5, swim in the river, showers available, take meals with family for US$4 (it is planned to provide cooking facilites in the future). Nearby at Mile 33 is *JB's*, a bar and restaurant 'in the middle of nowhere', a popular stopping place decorated with the insignia of the British soldiers who have passed through, good food, reasonably priced.

Guanacaste Park Forty seven miles from Belize City, a minor road runs two miles north to B *Banana Bank Ranch*, resort accommodation, with meals, horseriding, birding, river trips, et cetera, T/F08-12020, PO Box 48, Belmopan, bbl@pobox.com. A mile further on is the highway junction for Belmopan and Dangriga. At the confluence of the Belize River and Roaring Creek here is the 50-acre Guanacaste Park, a national park protecting a parcel of rainforest and a huge 100-year-old guanacaste (tubroos) tree, which shelters a wide collection of epiphytes including orchids. Many mammals (jaguarundi, kinkajou, agouti, et cetera) and up to 100 species of birds may be seen from the three miles of nature trails cut along the river. This is a particularly attractive swimming and picnicking spot at which to break the journey to Guatemala. It has a visitors' centre, where luggage can be left. Entrance US$2.50. Take an early morning bus from Belize City, see the park in a couple of hours, then pick up a bus going to San Ignacio or Dangriga.

Roaring Creek
Population: 1,000 Soon after the junction is Roaring Creek, once a thriving town but now rather overshadowed by the nearby capital. Five hundred yards from the Texaco station on the main road, follow the oasis sign for free overnight parking. Six miles beyond the turning to the capital is **AL** *Warrie Head Lodge*, Ontario, T08-23826 or for reservations T02-77257, F02-75213 (PO Box 244, Belize City), bzadventur@btl.net, a working farm offering accommodation. They cater mainly for groups but it is well kept, homely and a lovely spot for river swimming. Just before the *Warrie Head*, at Teakettle, there is a turning south along a dirt road for five miles to Pook's Hill Reserve and **AL** *Pook's Hill Lodge*, PO Box 14, Belmopan, T08-12017, F08-23361 a 300-acre private nature reserve on Roaring Creek, run by Ray and Vicki Snaddon, six cabañas, horses, rafting, birdwatching et cetera.

Baking Pot, Georgeville & Spanish lookout The Highway now becomes narrower and curves through increasingly lush countryside. At Mile 60 is **A** *Caesar's Place*, four rooms with bath, clean riverside campground with security, four full hookups for RVs, with showers and bathroom facilities, restaurant and bar, good general store, swimming, musicians welcome to play with 'in-house' group, highly recommended, T09-22341 (PO Box 48, San Ignacio, under same ownership as *Black Rock* – see below). The important but unimpressive **Baking Pot** archaeological site is just beyond the bridge over Barton Creek (Mile 64); two more miles brings us to **Georgeville** (another Mennonite community; try the ice cream and cheese), from where a gravel road runs south into the Mountain Pine Ridge Forest Reserve (see below). The highway passes the turnoff at Norland for **Spanish Lookout**, a Mennonite settlement area six miles north (*B & F Restaurant*, Centre Road, by Farmers Trading Centre, clean, excellent value); ask in San Ignacio if you are interested in visiting this area. Climbing up a forested valley the road reaches Santa Elena, linked by the substantial Hawkesworth suspension bridge to its twin town of San Ignacio. (At the bridge is Belize's first set of traffic lights; the bridge is only one vehicle's width.)

San Ignacio

Seventy two miles from Belize City and 10 miles from the border, San Ignacio (locally called Cayo) is the capital of Cayo District and western Belize's largest town, an agricultural centre serving the citrus, cattle and peanut farms of the area, and a good base for excursions into the Mountain Pine Ridge and western Belize. It stands amid attractive wooded hills at 200-500 feet, with a good climate, and is a nice town to rest in after Guatemala. The town is on the eastern branch of the Old, or Belize River, known as the Macal. The river journey of 121 miles from Belize, broken by many rapids, needs considerable ingenuity to negotiate the numerous 'runs'. More Spanish is spoken than English in San Ignacio.

Population: 11,315 including Santa Elena
Phone code: 09
Colour map: 4, grid B3

Tours
Local taxis which offer tours of Mountain Pine Ridge (described below) in the wet season probably won't get very far; also, taking a tour to Xunantunich (also described below) is not really necessary. Canoe trips up the Macal River are well worthwhile. They take about three hours upstream, half that on return, guides point out iguanas in the trees and bats asleep on the rock walls. Ask at *Eva's Bar* (T22267) for information on canoe trips with Tony, bird and wildlife watching, US$12.50 per person, two to three people, visiting medicinal plant research farm (US$5 extra), small rapids, et cetera, 0830-1600, good value; or with Bob, who does jungle river trips, US$30 for two people in a canoe, all-day tour. Highly recommended. Bob is very helpful and will organize tours for you but you may end up with an indifferent guide, make sure you tell him exactly what you want. Tours to Tikal can also be arranged. *Westland Tours* charge US$40 per person for tour to Caracol including Río Frío Cave, Río On pools and García sisters gift shop, 12 hours; cheaper to hire a car if with a group, difficult to get lost. Another trip is to Barton Creek Cave, one and a half-hour drive followed by a three and a half-hour canoe trip in the cave; cost is US$20 per person minimum three people. Hiring a canoe to go upstream without a guide is not recommended unless you are highly proficient as there are class two

BELIZE

San Ignacio

N
Not to scale

■ **Sleeping**
1 Belmoral
2 Central &
  Farmers Emporium
3 Hi-Et
4 Princesa
5 San Ignacio

rapids one hour from San Ignacio. A recommended guide is Ramón Silva from *International Archaeological Tours*, West St, next to Martha's Guest House, T23991, iatours@btl.net, who arrange tours throughout Belize and in the Petén. Also recommended are *David's Adventure Tours*, near main bus stop, T23674, visits to Barton's Creek Cave or guided canoe trips along the Macal River.

Excursions A short walk from San Ignacio (800 metres from *Hotel San Ignacio*) is **Cahal Pech**, a Maya site and nature reserve on a wooded hill overlooking the town. A Visitor's Centre was opened in 1997. A museum is being built on site. Admission US$2.50, open daily. The man who sells tickets will lend you a guidebook written by some of the archaeologists who worked on the site; it is now out of print so must be returned.

Four miles west of San Ignacio on a good road is Bullet Tree Falls on the western branch of the Belize River, here in its upper course known as the Mopan River; a pleasant cascade amid relaxing surroundings.

Twelve miles north of San Ignacio, near Bullet Tree Falls, is **El Pilar Archaeological Reserve for Maya Flora and Fauna**, an archaeological site which straddles the border with Guatemala. Although it is a large site (about 38 hectares), much of it has been left intentionally uncleared so that selected architectural features are exposed within the rainforest. The preserved rainforest here is home to hundreds of species of birds and animals. There are five trails, three archaeological, two nature, the longest of which is a mile and a half long. There are more than a dozen pyramids and 25 identified plazas. Unusually for Maya cities in this region, there is an abundance of water (streams and falls). Take the Bullet Tree Road north of San Ignacio, cross the Mopan River Bridge and follow the signs to El Pilar. The Reserve is seven miles from Bullet Tree on an all-weather limestone road. It can be reached by vehicle, horse or mountain bike (hiking is only recommended for the experienced; carry lots of water). The caretakers, who live at the south end of the site in a modern green-roofed house, are happy to show visitors around. The Cayo Tour Guides Association works in association with the Belize River Archaeological Settlement Survey (BRASS) and can take visitors. See also *Trails of El Pilar: A Guide to the El Pilar Archaeological Reserve for Maya Flora and Fauna* (published 1996).

About 10 miles south of San Ignacio, above the river and adjacent to the Chaa Creek Cottages at Ix Chel Farm (see below), is the unusual **Rainforest Medicine Trail**, established as a place for study and preservation of native medicinal plants by Dr Rosita Arvigo, an American disciple of Mayan healer Eligio Panti of San Antonio in the Mountain Pine Ridge (he died 1996, aged 103), call T23870 to arrange a visit (only necessary for groups). From the turn off on the Benque road it is a pleasant four-mile walk to Ix Chel; lifts are often possible. The plants are labelled in four languages. Visits can be arranged by calling 08-23180; self-guided tour with field guide, US$6.75 per person, guided tours with local guide, US$5.75 per person, group tours with the director by arrangement (Belizeans free). Dr Arvigo sells selections of herbs (the jungle salve, US$5, has been found effective against mosquito bites) and a book on medicinal plants used by the Maya (US$8, US$2 postage and packing, from General Delivery, San Ignacio, Cayo District).

At nearby Tipu are the remains of one of the few old Spanish mission churches established in Belize.

Sleeping
■ *on maps*
Price codes:
see inside front cover

In centre of town Up the hill, as you turn left on the San Ignacio side of the suspension bridge, is **AL-B** *San Ignacio*, 18 Buena Vista Rd, T22034/22125, F22134, sanighot@btl.net, on road to Benque Viejo, with bath, a/c or fan, hot water, clean, helpful staff, swimming pool, excellent restaurant, visited by the Queen in 1994, highly recommended. **B** *Plaza*, 4a Burns Ave, T23332, a/c, cheaper without, with bath, parking. **C-D** *Venus*, 29 Burns Ave, with or without bath, fan, clean, hot water, free coffee and fruit, thin walls, noisy, Saturday market and bus station behind hotel, recommended. **C-D** *Piache*, 18 Buena Vista Rd, around the bend in the road from *San Ignacio*, PO Box 54, T22032/22109, with or without bath, cold water, basic, overpriced, bar in pm, also tour agent. **D** *Martha's Guest House*, 10 West St,

T22276, comfortable rooms with balcony, lounge area, good restaurant, friendly, clean, kitchen facilities, the family also runs August Laundromat. **D** *New Belmoral*, 17 Burns Ave, T22024, with shower, cable TV, hot water, fan or a/c, a bit noisy (clean and friendly). **D** *Tropicool*, Burns Ave, shared bath, fan, clean. **D** *Princesa*, Burns Ave and King St, with bath, clean, helpful, secure, manager Mathew Galvez. **E** *Central*, 24 Burns Ave, T22253, clean, secure, fans, shared hot showers, book exchange, friendly, verandah with hammocks, uncomfortable beds but recommended, no restaurant but eat at *Eva's Bar* next door. **E** *Hi-Et*, 12 West St, T22828, noisy, fans, low partition walls, not very clean, but nice balcony, friendly, helpful, family run, clothes washing permitted, no meals, use of kitchen possible. **E** *Imperial*, Burns Ave, basic, noisy, shared bath, dirty, but popular. **F** *Mrs Espat's*, up the hill from *Hi-Et*, rooms next door to small shop and house. **NB** San Ignacio has a lively disco on Friday and Saturday, some hotels may be noisy.

In Santa Elena **D** *Snooty Fox*, 64 George Price Ave, overlooking Macal River, rooms and apartments, some with bath, others shared bath, good value canoe rental.

Camping *Mida's*, ½ mile from town, near river, go down Burns Ave, turn right down unpaved road after wooden church, after 200 yards turn left, campground is 300 yards on right, US$15 per car and 2 people including electricity, cabins available at US$20, hot showers, electricity, water, restaurant, owner Maria, very helpful, good value, also organize trips to Tikal. ½ mile further is *Cosmos* camping, US$2.50 per person for tents, washing and cooking facilities, cabins **E**, run by friendly Belizean family, good breakfasts, canoe and bikes for hire, good.

West of San Ignacio: *Mopan River Resort*, T32047, F33272, mrr@best.com, www.MopanRiverResort.com, Belize's first all-inclusive, luxury resort on the river, opposite Benque Viejo, accessible only by boat, 12 thatched cabañas in coconut grove with verandas, minimum stay 7 nights, includes airport transfers, meals, drinks, daily tours plus Tikal and Caracol, tax and service, rates from US$680 per person per week, open November-June, contact Pamella S Picon, Manager, for advance booking. **AL-A** *Nabitunich Cottages* (Rudi and Margaret Juan), turn off the Benque road 1½ miles beyond Chial, offers spectacular views of Xunantunich and another, unexcavated Maya ruin, jungle trails, excellent birdwatching, with fields going down to beautiful Macal river on working farm, own transport recommended, excursions not arranged, very homely if slightly basic, T09-32309, F09-32096, rudyjuan@btl.net, or c/o Benque Viejo Post Office. You may camp here, US$6 per person. **C-D** *Clarissa's Falls*, on Mopan River, down signed track on the Benque Road, owned by Chena Galvez, thatched cottages on riverbank by a set of rapids, also bunkhouse with hammocks or beds, US$7.50 per person, camping space and hookups for RVs, rafting, kayaking and tubing available, wonderful food in the restaurants.

South of San Ignacio **L** *Chaa Creek Cottages*, on the Macal River, 5 miles upstream from San Ignacio, including breakfast, lunch US$9, dinner US$16.50, discounts June-October, set on a working farm in pleasant countryside, highly recommended. Electricity in the restaurant/bar area only; cabins have oil lamps. You can swim or canoe in the river. Trips on the river, to Xunantunich, to Tikal, to Mountain Pine Ridge, to Caracol, nature walks, horse riding and jungle safaris organized by Chaa Creek Inland Expeditions; also joint vacations arranged with *Rum Point Inn*, Placencia. Latest project is blue morpho butterfly breeding centre. If coming by road, turn off the Benque road at Chial, 6 miles from San Ignacio; hotel will collect you by boat from San Ignacio (US$25 for 4), or from international airport (US$125); reservations PO Box 53, San Ignacio, T22037, F22501, chaacreek@btl.net, or hotel office at 56 Burns Ave, San Ignacio. **L** *duPlooys'*, turn left on the road to Benque on same road for Chaa Creek, then follow signs (including one steep hill), on the Macal River, T23101, F23301, duplooys@pobox.com, including all meals in jungle lodge, bar with deck overlooking trees and river. New **Belize Botanic Gardens** on 50 acres of rolling hills next to lodge with hundreds of orchids, dozens of named tree species, with ponds and lots of birds. Ken duPlooy or expert guide Phillip Mai lead daily tours. Run by Ken and Judy du Plooy formerly of Charleston, South Carolina. Good food, recommended. **L** *Ek Tun*, 10-minute walk before

Black Rock but across the river, owned by the Darts, a Colorado couple, 2 4-person cabins, good food, cellular T0912002, in USA 303-442-6150, ektunbz@btl.net, or check for space through *Eva's Bar*. **AL-B** *Black Rock Lodge*, on the Macal River, road sometimes requires four-wheel drive depending on weather, 6 stone and thatch cabañas, solar-powered electricity and hot water, hiking, riding, canoeing, birdwatching, excursions, breakfast US$7, lunch US$8, dinner US$15; Caesar Sherrard, PO Box 48, San Ignacio, Cayo, T22341/23296, F23449, blackrock@btl. net, www.belizenet.com/blackrock.html (see also *Caesar's Place*, above). **AL** *Windy Hill Cottages*, on Graceland Ranch 2 miles west off highway, T22017, F23080, 14 cottage units, all with bath, dining room, small pool, nature trails, horse riding and river trips can be arranged, expensive. **B** *Cahal Pech Cottages*, $\frac{1}{2}$ mile south of town centre just past the Visitor Centre for the ruins, open log cabins, bath and hot water, friendly, good meals, will arrange trips (not to be confused with *Cahal Pech Cabins* nearby). **C** *Parrot Nest*, T23702, parrot@btl.net, near village of Bullet Tree Falls, 3 miles from San Ignacio (taxi US$5), small but comfortable tree houses in beautiful grounds by the river, breakfast and dinner included, canoeing, birdwatching, horse riding available. Also near Bullet Tree Falls is a restaurant, **Terry's**, limited menu but good food.

East of San Ignacio **AL-B** *Maya Mountain Lodge* (Bart and Suzi Mickler), $\frac{3}{4}$ mile from San Ignacio at 9 Cristo Rey Rd in Santa Elena (taxi from town US$2.50, bus US$0.25), welcoming, special weekly and monthly rates and for families, restaurant, excursions are more expensive than arranging one in town, 10% service charge added to total bill, T22164, F22029, PO Box 46, San Ignacio, laundry, postal service, self-guided nature trail. Swimming, hiking, riding, canoeing, fishing can be arranged. Explore Belize Tours in the region and beyond; also 'Parrot's Perch' social and educational area with resident naturalist and ornithologist. Edgar is a good taxi driver/guide. *Mountain Equestrian Trails*, Mile 8, Mountain Pine Ridge Rd (from Georgeville), Central Farm PO, Cayo District, T23310, F23361, T08-23180 for reservations, 08-22149 for office, reservations in USA T941-488-0522, F941-488-3953 or 1-800-838-3913, offers $\frac{1}{2}$-day, full-day and 4-day adventure tours on horseback in western Belize, 'Turf' and 'Turf and Surf' packages, and other expeditions, excellent guides and staff; birdwatching tours in and around the reserve; accommodation in 4 *cabañas* doubles with bath, no electricity, hot water, mosquito nets, good food in *cantina*, *Chiclero Nature Trails*, tents under rainforest canopy are a new development, US$499 for 4 nights, including meals, trip to Caracol, birdwatching, caving etc; highly recommended (owners Jim and Marguerite Bevis, in conjunction with neighbouring landowners, have set up a biosphere reserve, incorporating nearby Salvadorean refugees). **LL-AL** *Blancaneaux Lodge*, Mountain Pine Ridge Rd, Central Farm, PO Box B, Cayo District, T/F23878, once the mountain retreat of Francis Ford Coppola and his family, now villas and cabañas, full amenities, overlooking river, private air strip. **AL** *Five Sisters Lodge*, $2\frac{1}{2}$ miles beyond *Blancaneaux Lodge*, T/F21005, fivesis@btl.net, rustic cottages lit by oil lamps, great views, recommended, good value restaurant. **AL** *Pine Ridge Lodge*, on road to Augustine, just past turning to Hidden Valley Falls, T23310, F22267, cabañas in the pinewoods, including breakfast.

Eating
● *on maps*

Running W, in the *San Ignacio Hotel*, is one of the best restaurants in town; *Maxim's*, Bullet Tree Rd and Far West St, Chinese, good service, cheap, very good food, popular with locals, noisy TV at the bar. *Serendib*, 27 Burns Ave, good food and good value, Sri Lankan owners, good, tasty Indian-style food, open 1030-1500, 1830-1100, closed Sunday. *Eva's Bar*, 22 Burns Ave, T22267, good, helpful, local dishes, bike rental, email and internet facilities, tours. *Yesteryear*, next door, good breakfast, better value than *Eva's*. Good bakery on West Street, behind *Eva's*. *The Sand Castle*, take a right turn off King St to river, the open air restaurant is at the back of the building, music, good food and prices. *Belize Chinese*, below *Jaguar Hotel*, good Chinese and Italian, good breakfasts, cheap. *Café Maya*, Burns Ave, owned by Mel and Eric Barber, very good. *HL Burgers*, Burns Ave, good food. *Martha's Kitchen*, below *Martha's Guest House*, very good breakfasts and Belizean dishes, good information. *Doña Elvira Espat* serves good meals at her house (including breakfast), advance notice required, good, friendly with good local information (no sign, corner of Galvez Street and Bullet Tree Road). Her daughter *Elvira Quiróz*, is also an excellent cook, meals served in her home: 6 Far West

Street, T22556, advance notice required, vegetarian available, reasonable prices.

On a hill, with TV station, beside the road to Benque Viejo before the edge of town is *Cahal Pech* tavern, serving cheap drinks and meals, with music and dancing at weekends, the place to be, live bands are broadcast on TV and radio all over Belize, good views. On a hill across the track from the tavern is Cahal Pech archaeological site (see above). The *Blue Angel* on Burns Ave is popular with the younger crowd, very dark, fun, live bands, dancing, small admission charge.

Riding: *Easy Rider*, Bullet Tree Rd, T23310, full day tours for US$40 including lunch.   **Sports**

Black Rock Gift Shop, near *Eva's*, linked to *Black Rock Lodge*, luggage can be left here if   **Shopping** canoeing from Black Rock to San Ignacio, large selection of arts and crafts, workshop. Fruit and vegetable market every Saturday am.

Buses To **Belize City**: Batty Bus departs 1300, 1400, 1500 and 1600; early morning buses   **Transport** from the border stop at the bridge in front of the police station and from the bus terminal at 0500, 0600 and 0700. Later morning trips go from Benque Viejo at parking area behind Burns Avenue, US$2.50, 3½ hours. A 1000 or 1100 bus will connect with the 1500 bus to Chetumal. Novelo, starts at 0400 and runs on the hour until about 1200. To **Belmopan**, 1 hour, US$1. **Taxi**: to Guatemalan border, about US$5 (colectivo US$2.50, bus US$0.75), to Xunantunich US$20, to Belize City US$75, to Tikal US$100. **Minibuses**: also run to Tikal, US$20 per person return, making a day trip possible. Ask taxi drivers for information. Organized tours cost about US$60.

Banks *Belize Bank* offers full service, TCs, Visa and Mastercard cash advances. *Atlantic Bank*, Burns   **Directory** Ave also does cash advances. Both change US$5 commission for cash advances. *Eva's Bar* changes TCs at a very good rates. Changers in the town square give better rates of exchange for dollars cash and TCs than you can get at the border with Guatemala. The best place to change dollars into quetzales is in Guatemala. **Communications** Post Office: above the police station, reliable parcel service. **NB** All shops and businesses close 1700-1900. **Telecommunications**: *BTL* office at further end of Burns Ave, opposite *Venus Hotel*, long distance calls and fax service. **Internet**: *Eva's Bar*.

Xunantunich

At Xunantunich ('Maiden of the Rock'), now freed from heavy bush, there are Classic Maya remains in beautiful surroundings; the heart of the city was three plazas aligned on a north-south axis, lined with many temples, the remains of a ball court, and surmounted by the 'Castillo'; at 130 feet this was thought to be the highest man made structure in Belize until recent measurement of the Sky Palace at Caracol; the impressive view takes in jungle, the lowlands of the Petén and the blue flanks of the Maya Mountains. Maya graffiti can still be seen on the wall of Structure A-16; friezes on the Castillo, some restored in modern plaster, represent astronomical symbols. Extensive excavations took place in 1959-60 but only limited restoration work has been undertaken. A leaflet on the area is available from the Archaeological Dept for US$0.15. About one and a half miles further north are the ruins of Actuncan, probably a satellite of Xunantunich; both sites show evidence of earthquake damage.

Xunantunich is open 0800-1700, entry US$2.50 and, apart from a small refreshment stand, no facilities for visitors, but a new museum is now being built, helpful guides at the site, bring own refreshments; beware of robbery on the road up to the ruins, government employees accompany visitors up the hill (try hitching back to the ferry with tourists travelling by car). It is in any case an extremely hot walk up the hill on the white, limestone road with little or no shade. Start early! You can swim in the river after visiting the ruins. Just east of the ferry, Magaña's Art Centre and the Xunantunich Women's Group sell locally made crafts and clothing in a shop on a street off the highway.

Access To reach Xunantunich hitch, or take a 0800-0830, or 0900-0930 bus from San Ignacio towards the border to the village of San José Succotz (7 miles, US$0.75), where a hand-operated ferry takes visitors and their cars across the Mopan River (0800-1700, free weekdays, US$0.50 at weekends); there is then a 20-minute walk uphill on dirt road (even motorcyclists may find the track impossible after rain). Return buses to San Ignacio pass at about lunchtime.

San José Here is a large Yucatec Maya village below Xunantunich where Spanish is the first
Succotz language and a few inhabitants preserve the old Maya customs of their ancestral village (San José in the Petén); the colourful fiestas of St Joseph and the Holy Cross are celebrated on 19 March and on a variable date in early May respectively each year. There is a Guatemalan Consulate on the Western Highway, opposite the Xununtunich ferry (see **Frontier with Guatemala**, below).

Mountain Pine Ridge

Colour map 4, grid B3 Mountain Pine Ridge is a Forest Reserve (59,000 hectares) covering the northwest portion of the Maya Mountains. The undulating country is well-watered and covered in largely undisturbed temperate pine and gallery forest; in the valleys are lush hardwood forests filled with orchids, bromeliads and butterflies. The enjoyable river scenery, high waterfalls, numerous limestone caves and shady picnic sites attract about 50 visitors per day during the dry season: a popular excursion despite the rough roads. Hitching is difficult but not impossible. Try contacting the Forestry Conservation Officer, T09-23280, who may be able to help. Two reasonable roads lead into the reserve: from Georgeville to the north and up from Santa Elena via Cristo Rey; these meet near **San Antonio**, a Mopan Maya village with many thatched-roof houses and the nearby Pacbitun archaeological site (where stelae and musical instruments have been unearthed). At San Antonio, the García Sisters have their workshop, museum, shop where they sell carvings in local slate and guest house (**D**). You can sample Maya food and learn about use of medicinal plants; this is a regular stop on tours to the Mountain Pine Ridge. A donation of US$0.50 is requested; US$12.50 is charged to take photos of the sisters at work. Two buses a day from San Ignacio, 1000 and 1430, from market area, but check times of return buses before leaving San Ignacio.

On the Mountain Pine Ridge Road from Georgeville, one mile from the junction near San Antonio, is *Green Hills* and the **Belize Butterfly House**, opened 1997 by Jan Meerman and Tineke Boomsma, a fine collection of butterflies in a natural environment. There is an associated botanical collection which provides foodplants for the butterflies. A fascinating place for the enthusiast. ■ *0900-1600, from Christmas to Easter, US$2.50, outside this period and for further information, contact: Belize Tropical Forest Studies, PO Box 208, Belmopan, T923310, F823361.*

The main forest road meanders along rocky spurs, from which unexpected and often breathtaking views emerge of jungle far below and streams plunging hundreds of feet over red-rock canyons; a lookout point has been provided to view the impressive **Hidden Valley Falls** (said to be over 1,000 feet high (often shrouded in fog October-January); on a clear day it is said you can see Belmopan from the viewpoint. There is a picnic area and small shops here. It is quite a long way from the main road and is probably not worth the detour if time is short particularly in the dry season when the flow is restricted. On many heights stand forestry observation towers: bushfires are a constant threat in the dry season. Eighteen miles into the reserve the road crosses the **Río On**. Here, where the river tumbles in inviting pools over huge granite boulders, is one of Belize's most beautiful picnic and swimming spots. The rocks from little water slides are good for children. The rocks can be slippery and, in the wet season, bathing is not possible.

Five miles further is **Augustine** (also called Douglas D'Silva, or **Douglas Forest Station**), the main forest station (*Population*: 170) where there is a shop, accommodation in two houses (bookable through the Forestry Dept in Belmopan, the area Forestry Office is in San Antonio) and a camping ground, US$1, no mattresses (see rangers for all information on the area). Keep your receipt, a guard checks it on the way out of Mountain Pine Ridge. A mile beyond Augustine is a cluster of caves in rich rainforest; the entrance to the **Rio Frio Cave** (in fact a tunnel) is over 65 feet high; many spectacular rock formations and sandy beaches where the river flows out. Trees in the parking area and along the Cuevas Gemelas nature trail, which starts one hour from the Rio Frio cave, are labelled. A beautiful excursion; highly recommended. In the Mountain Pine Ridge note the frequent changes of colour of the soil and look out for the fascinating insect life. If lucky you may see deer.

Forestry roads continue south further into the mountains, reaching **San Luis** (six miles), the only other inhabited camp in the area (*Population*: 100, post office, sawmill and forest station), and continuing on over the granite uplands of the Vaca Plateau into the **Chiquibul Forest Reserve** (186,000 hectares).

The four forest reserves which cover the Maya Mountains are the responsibility of the Forestry Department, who have only about 20 rangers to patrol 400,000 hectares of heavily-forested land. A hunting ban prohibits the carrying of firearms. Legislation, however, allows for controlled logging; all attempts to have some areas declared National Parks or biosphere reserves have so far been unsuccessful.

NB At the driest time of year, normally February to May, that is when the Mountain Pine Ridge is reasonably accessible, there is an ever-present danger of fire. Open fires are strictly prohibited and you are asked to be as careful as possible.

Caracol

About 24 miles south-southwest of Augustine, Caracol (about one hour by four-wheel drive) is a rediscovered Maya city; the area is now a National Monument Reservation. Caracol was established about 300 BC and continued well into the Late Classic period; glyphs record a victorious war against Tikal. Why Caracol was built in such a poorly-watered region is not known, but Maya engineers showed great ingenuity in constructing reservoirs and terracing the fields. The Sky Palace ('Caana') pyramid climbs 138 feet above the site, which is being excavated by members of the University of Central Florida. Excavations take place February-May but there are year-round caretakers who will show you around. Admission US$15. Currently very knowledgeable guides escort groups around the site twice daily and a new information centre is being built. As the site is largely unprotected you are free to walk and examine parts of the buildings which would be closed to visitors or well protected. For this reason unescorted visitors are not welcome. Best to obtain an officially authorized permit to visit the site from the Forestry Office in San Antonio. Throughout this largely unknown region are vast cave systems stretching west into Guatemala, but there are absolutely no facilities and none of the caves is open to the casual traveller. The only months in which a trip by road to Caracol can be guaranteed are April and May, but the road has been improved and with four-wheel drive is passable for much of the year. The road is interesting as you pass many chiclero trees in the rainforest, it crosses over a river and then immediately climbs the Mountain Pine Ridge, the difference is very pronounced. A number of places in San Ignacio, and Mountain Equestrian Trails (see above), offer horseback tours to Caracol, US$185.

Mountain Pine Ridge has no public transport. Apart from tours, hiring a mountain bike (from **Transport** *Eva's Bar*), a vehicle or a taxi are the only alternatives. Everything is well signposted. The private pick-ups which go into San Ignacio from Augustine are usually packed, so hitching is impossible. Taxis charge US$88 for five people. Roads are passable but rough between January and May, but after June they are marginal and are impossible in the wet (September-November); essential to seek local advice at this time.

Nine miles up-river from San Ignacio on a good road is the tranquil town of **Benque**   **Benque Viejo**

Viejo del Carmen, near the Guatemalan frontier. *Population*: 3,312, many of whom are Maya Mopan Indians. There are police and military barracks near the border.

There are caves nearby, open 0800-1600, ask locals to show you the road, near the hydroplant.

Sleeping E *Maya*, 11 George St, T09-32116, and **E** *Okis*, George St, T09-32006, opposite the bus station, are the least bad. There is a green hotel, **F**, good, on left side of main road to Guatemala. The hotels on the Guatemalan side are much cheaper than Belize so if on a tight budget try to cross the border even late in the afternoon. From Benque to the border is a 20-minute walk, 1.6 kilometres.

Eating Meals at *Riverside Restaurant*, on main square; *Restaurant Los Angeles*, Church St; *Hawaii*, on main street, recommended; or at one of picturesque huts.

Transport Road Novelo's run many daily buses from Belize City to **Benque Viejo**, US$3, 0330-1100; frequent buses from San Ignacio to Benque Viejo, taxi US$10, or colectivo from central square, US$2 (or US$2 to Melchor de Mencos in Guatemala, 30 minutes). Note that not all buses go through the frontier to Melchor de Mencos but turn round near the border and return to Benque Viejo. Get off the bus and walk the short distance to the frontier post. All buses that do cross stop at the border (contrary to what the taxi drivers might tell you).

Frontier with Guatemala

Belizean immigration Border hours are 0800-1200 and 1400-1700. Everyone leaving Belize has to pay the PACT exit tax (see page 721).

Guatemalan consulate Opposite the ferry in San José Succotz, open Monday-Friday 0900-1300; visas for those who need them easily arranged. Most nationalities can obtain a tourist card (sometimes a visa) at the border.

Exchange You will get better rates purchasing quetzals at the border than anywhere before Puerto Barrios or Guatemala City. Compare rates at the **Banco de Guatemala** with the money changers. Check what you receive and do not accept damaged notes.

Transport From Benque Viejo to Melchor de Mencos, by taxi US$1.50, by colectivo US$0.50. For bus services, see under Benque Viejo.

On the Guatemalan side someone will carry the luggage to **Melchor de Mencos** (see **Guatemala, Section 3, El Petén**), where there is a landing strip (flights to Flores). There is also a road (very rough) on to Santa Elena, for Flores (a bus leaves the border for Flores at 1330, US$2.65, or several daily buses from Melchor de Mencos, 3½ hours, US$2.65, leave Belize City at 0600, 0630 or 1015 to make a connection to Flores); unless you take a tourist minibus, it is only possible to get to Tikal by bus by asking the driver of the border-Flores bus to let you off at the road junction (El Cruce), where you can get a connecting bus to Tikal (see same section of Guatemala chapter). See that section also, **Flores Travel Agents** for direct minibus services between Flores/Santa Elena and Belize City.

Southern Belize and the Southern Cayes

Belize City

Southern Belize is the remotest part of the country, sparsely populated but with many Indian settlements akin to those across the border in Guatemala. Maya ruins abound and nature reserves are increasing in numbers. Roads are poor, not helped by the wetter climate. However, access to the attractive coast is improving.

Belize City to Punta Gorda

About two miles beyond the Belize Zoo on the Western Highway a good dirt road runs southeast to **Gales Point**, a charming fishing village of 300 on a peninsula at the south end of Manatee Lagoon, 15 miles north of Dangriga. The villagers are keen to preserve their natural resources and there are a lot of the endangered manatee and hawksbill turtles. Boat tours of the lagoon are recommended. Turn off the highway at **La Democracia** (signed Manatee Road) and head east, then southeast, around Cumberland Hill, to join the Gales Point-Melinda road about three miles south of Gales Point (La Democracia to the junction 23.2 miles). At **Melinda Forest Station** the turnoff is signed Belize New Road. The government has upgraded the road as a short cut to Dangriga, bypassing Belmopan and it is now the quickest route, called the Coastal Highway. Day and overnight excursions of a wide variety, from US$30 per boat holding six to eight people, contact Kevin Andrewin of Manatee Tour Guides Association on arrival. Community phone, T02-12031, minimum 48 hours notice is advisable, ask for Alice or Josephine. Gales Point can be reached by inland waterways from Belize City, but boat services have largely been superceded by buses. At least two daily Z-line buses between Belize City and Dangriga use the coastal road.

Gales Point

Sleeping LL *Manatee Lodge*, resort fishing camp, 7-day all-inclusive package; T77593, US res: T800-7827238. The Gales Point Bed and Breakfast Association arranges basic accommodation, **E**, no indoor plumbing, meals available, contact Hortence Welch on arrival.

Along the Hummingbird Highway

The narrow Hummingbird Highway branches off the Western Highway 48 miles west of Belize City, passes Belmopan and branches 52 miles southeast to Dangriga. Its surface is newly paved. It climbs through rich tropical hardwood forest until reaching Mile 13, where a track leads off to **St Herman's Cave**; the path passes through shady ferns until descending in steps to the cave entrance. You can walk for more than a mile underground: torch and spare batteries essential. There is a four-kilometre trail to a campsite from the visitors' centre.

Two miles further on is the Blue Hole National Park, an azure blue swimming hole fringed with vines and ferns, fed by a stream which comes from St Herman's Cave and re-enters another 100 feet away. Entry to the Park is US$4, there is a Visitor Centre at the entrance on the road. This is typical karst limestone country with sinkholes, caves and underground streams. The water appearing here is deliciously cool after a long journey underground to disappear into the top of a large underwater cavern. Eventually this joins the Sibun River which enters the sea just south of Belize City. There is a rough two and a half mile trail, through low secondary forest, between St Herman's Cave and the Blue Hole, good walking shoes required. A sign on the roadway warns visitors against thieves; lock your car and leave someone on

Blue Hole National Park

guard if possible when swimming. An armed guard and more wardens have been hired to prevent further theft and assaults.

Sleeping AL-A *Caves Branch Jungle Lodge*, ½ mile past St Herman's Cave, T/F08-22800, radio T08-23180 at lodge, caves@pobox.com, PO Box 356, Belmopan, reached along ½-mile track, signed on the left, any bus between Belmopan and Dangriga will stop, secluded spot on banks of Caves Branch River, great trips through caves, 7-mile underground float, guided jungle trips. Comfortable cabañas with private baths or **D** pp in the bunkhouse, camping US$5 per person, good, clean, shared bathrooms, delicious meals served buffet style.

The peaks of the mountains continue to dominate the south side of the highway until about Mile 30, when the valley of the Stann Creek begins to widen out into Belize's most productive agricultural area. Large citrus groves stretch along the highway: grapefruit, bananas and Valencia oranges, which are processed into canned juices and concentrates at centres like Pomona (Mile 40). The drive to Dangriga from Belmopan can take from two to two and a half hours, depending on road conditions.

Canoeing or tubing trips can be organized from Over-the-Top Camp on the Hummingbird Highway (try Kingfisher in Placencia) down the Indian Creek, visiting Caves five, four, three and then Daylight Cave and Darknight Cave. Vehicle support is brought round to meet you on the Coastal Highway near Democracia.

Turn east at Mile 32 for four miles along a gravel road to **Tamandua**, a wildlife sanctuary in **Five Blue Lakes National Park**. Follow the track opposite *Over the Top* restaurant, turning right and crossing the stream for Tamandua, then another two miles or straight on and following the signs for the National Park, 1½ miles, where there is camping. For further information on Five Blue Lakes National Park contact Friends of 5 Blues, PO Box 111, Belmopan, T08-12005, or the warden, Lee Wengrzyn, a local dairy farmer, or Augustus Palacio (see below).

Sleeping **On the Hummingbird Highway** At Mile 31, **E** *Palacios Mountain Retreat*, Augustus Palacio, St Martha, Hummingbird Highway, Cayo District, good for relaxing, *cabañas*, friendly, helpful, family atmosphere, safe, good local food; swimming in river, tours to waterfall in forest, caves and lagoon, Five Blue Lakes National Park; beware sandflies.

Dangriga

Population: 10,000
Phone code: 05
Colour map 4, grid B4

The chief town of the Stann Creek District, has a population of largely Black Caribs (Garifunas, always ask before taking photographs). It is on the seashore, with the usual Belizean aspect of wooden houses elevated on piles, and is a cheerful and busily commercial place. The river which meets the sea here, North Stann Creek is alive with flotillas of boats and fishermen. There are several gas stations, a good hospital and an airfield with regular flights. The beach has been considerably cleaned up and extended, being particularly nice at the *Pelican Beach Hotel*, where it is raked and cleaned daily. Palm trees have been planted by *Pal's Guest House* where the beach has been enlarged. Dangriga (until recently called Stann Creek) means 'standing waters' in Garifuna.

Sleeping **L-AL** *Pelican Beach*, outside town (PO Box 14), on the beach north of town, T22044, F22570, bzhotels@btl.net, with private bath, hot water and a/c, verandah, pier with hammocks, 20 rooms, excellent restaurant, bar, games lounge, gift shop, tours arranged, helpful (taxi from town US$2.50, or 15-minute walk from North Stann Creek). **AL** *Bonefish*, Mahogany St, T22165, on seafront on outskirts of town, a/c, colour TV with US cable, hot water, takes Visa, good restaurant. **B** *Pal's Guest House*, 868A Magoon St, Dangriga, T22095, 10 units on beach, all with balconies, sea views, bath, fan, cable TV, cheaper rooms in main building, Dangriga Dive Centre, T23262, runs from next door, Derek Jones arranges fabulous trips to the cayes (see also Hangman's Caye below).
D *Riverside*, 5 Commerce St, T22168, F22296, clean, shared bathroom, nice common

area. **D** *Rio Mar*, 977 Southern Foreshore, sea views, cheaper rooms not recommended, friendly, good, music piped into all rooms, you will hear your neighbour's even if yours is turned off. **D** *Sofie's Hotel & Restaurant*, Chatuye St, unimpressive but pleasant. **E** *Bluefield Lodge*, 6 Bluefield Rd, T22742, bright new hotel, owner Louise Belisle very nice, spotless, comfortable beds, very helpful, secure, highly recommended. **E** *Catalina*, 37 Cedar St, T22390, very small, dirty but friendly, store luggage. **E** *New Central*, 119 Commerce St, T22008, shared cold shower, fans, thin walls, cramped but reasonably safe and friendly. **E** *Cameleon*, fan and shared bath, clean, nice balconies. Also you can stay in private homes (basic), eg Miss Caroline's.

Riviera Bar/Restaurant, good meals, clean. *Starlight* near *Cameleon*, towards bridge, Chinese, cheapish, good. *Ritchie's Dinette*, on main street north of Police Station, creole and Spanish food, cheap, simple, large portions, popular for breakfast, bakeries. *Sunrise*, similar. *Pola's Kitchen*, 25a Tubroose St, near *Pal's Guest House*, excellent breakfasts, cheap, clean, good atmosphere. *Ricky's*, good reasonable local food. *King Burger* (not the international chain) do good breakfasts, lunches and takeaways. *Riverside Café*, south bank of river, just east of main road, nicer inside than it looks, good breakfast, good service and food, best place to get information on boats to Tobacco Caye. *Comedor Elizabeth*, good local food.   **Eating**

Listen for local music 'Punta Rock', a unique Garifuna/African based Carib sound, now popular throughout Belize. *Local Motion Disco*, next to *Cameleon*, open weekends, Punta rock, reggae, live music. *Riviera Club*, between bridge and Bank of Nova Scotia, popular nightclub at weekends (see **Eating** above). *Kennedy's Club*, ¼ mile north of the Police Station, good atmosphere. A local band, the *Turtles*, maintain a Punta museum in town. Studios can be visited. Homemade instruments are a Garifuna speciality, especially drums.   **Entertainment**

18-19 November, *Garifuna*, or *Settlement Day*, re-enacting the landing of the Black Caribs in 1823, fleeing a failed rebellion in Honduras. Dancing all night and next day; very popular. Booking is advisable for accommodation. Private homes rent rooms, though. At this time, boats from Puerto Barrios to Punta Gorda (see below) tend to be full, but launches take passengers for US$10 per person.   **Festivals**

Air Maya Island Air and Tropic Air from Belize City several daily, also from Punta Gorda via Placencia. Tickets from Rodney at the airstrip (T22294), or at *Pelican Beach Hotel*.   **Transport**

Buses From **Belize City**, Z-Line, Magazine Street, several daily from 0800, plus 0600 Monday, returning daily from 0530, US$5, 4½ hours (buy ticket in advance to reserve numbered seat, the bus stops at the Blue Hole National Park); also via Coastal Highway, 2 hours, Ritchies Busline, US$5. 5 buses Monday-Saturday, to **Punta Gorda**, 1400 on Sunday, 4-5 hours, US$6.50 (very crowded), stops at Independence, near Mango Creek. Bus to **Placencia** daily at 1200 direct, 1630 (Z-Line and Ritchies) via Hopkins and Sittee River, US$4 (schedules change often, as do bus companies); to **Belmopan**, 2½ hours, US$3. The Z-Line bus terminal is at the road junction at the south end of town. Buses run daily to Gales Point at 0830 from Ritchie's Buses on the main street.

Sea A fast skiff leaves 0900 (be there at 0800) on Saturday for Puerto Cortés, Honduras, US$50; departs from north bank of river by bridge, T23227, ask for Carlos. Crossing takes 3 hours and can be dangerous in rough weather. Check in advance procedures for exit formalities, if PACT exit tax has to be paid and you will have to pay to enter Honduras. You can hire a boat for around US$25 per person in a party to Belize City, enquire locally.

Banks *Bank of Nova Scotia. Barclays Bank International* (Mastercard and Visa). *Belize Bank* (Visa cash advances). Same hours as Belize City (see page 721). Change TCs at Z-Line bus station, good rates, or at the large hardware store north of the main bridge. **Tour companies & travel agents** *Treasured Travels*, 64 Commerce St, T22578, is very helpful, run by Diane; *Pelican Beach Hotel* runs tours to Cockscombe Basin, Gales Point and citrus factories. *Rosado's Tours*, T22119/22020, 35 Lemon St. *Rodney* at the airstrip also runs tours, T22294.   **Directory**

Cayes near Dangriga

Tobacco Caye 35 minutes by speedboat from Dangriga (US$15), this tiny island, quite heavily populated, has lots of local flavour and fishing camp charm. It is becoming a little commercialized, but still has an authentic feel. It sits right on the reef; you can snorkel from the beach although there are no large schools of fish. No sandflies on the beach; snorkelling equipment for rent. Boats go daily, enquire at *Riverside Café*, Dangriga, Captain Buck or Anthony charge US$12-15 per person. **Diving**: *Second Nature Divers*, English-owned, good guides and equipment, recommended spot to visit is sharks cave, Martin can be contacted via *Island Camps* (see below).

Sleeping **AL** *Ocean's Edge Fishing Lodge*, full board, 6 cabins on stilts joined by elevated walkways, run by Raymond and Brenda Lee, excellent food, diving and fishing can be arranged, USA T713-894-0548. **C** *Reefs End Lodge*, PO Box 10, Dangriga, basic, small rooms, excellent host and food, boat transfer on request from Dangriga. **C** *Hotel Larnas*, T05-22571/2, USA T909-9434556, has its own fishing pier, snorkelling equipment hire $10 per day, good Caribbean-style food, mosquito net, shared shower, recommended. **C** *Island Camps*, PO Box 174 (51 Regent St, Belize City, T02-72109), owner Mark Bradley will pick up guests in Dangriga, A-frame huts and campground US$5 per person a night, meals on request, reef excursions, friendly, good value, recommended. **D** *La Gaviota*, next to *Ocean's Edge*, rather basic, communal facilities. There is no electricity on the island.

Hangman's Caye There is a new dive resort on this tiny, private island; six attractive cabañas with balcony over the sea, private bath, restaurant and bar.

South Water Caye South Water Caye, the focus of a new marine reserve, is a lovely palm-fringed tropical island, with beautiful beaches, particularly at the south end.

Sleeping Part of the caye is taken up by *Blue Marlin Lodge*, PO Box 21, Dangriga, T05-22243, F05-22296, marlin@btl.net, an excellent dive lodge offering various packages; small sandy island with snorkelling off the beach; good accommodation and food; runs tours. *Frangipani House* and *Osprey's Nest* are 2 comfortable cottages owned by the *Pelican Beach Hotel*, available for rent; the *Hotel* also has **Pelican University**, which is ideal for groups as it houses 10-22 at US$60 per person per day including 3 meals (details from *Pelican Beach Hotel* as above). **Leslie Cottages**, 5 units, T05-22119, F23152, izebelize@aol.com, US contact T800-5485843 or 508-6551461.

South of Dangriga

The Southern Highway connects Dangriga with Punta Gorda in the south. It is a wide, flat, dirt road: dusty in the dry season, muddy in the wet but being paved with international funding. Public transport is limited and may be suspended after heavy rain. Hitching possible, but little traffic. Six miles inland from Dangriga the road branches from the Hummingbird Highway and heads south through mixed tropical forests and palmettos and pines along the fringes of the Maya Mountains. West of the road, about five miles from the junction with the Hummingbird Highway, a track leads to **Mayflower**, a Mayan ruin. Work has begun on opening it up and they say it will be the biggest archaeological site in southern Belize.

Hopkins 15 miles from Dangriga a minor road forks off four miles east to the Garifuna fishing village of Hopkins. Watch out for sandflies when the weather is calm. The villagers throw household slops into the sea and garbage on the beach.

Sleeping South of Hopkins, just north of Sittee River, is **L-AL** *Jaguar Reef Lodge*, T/F212041, postal address Hopkins General Delivery, Stann Creek District, 14 thatched cabañas and central lodge on sandy beach, diving, snorkelling, kayaking, C-Breathe Center, non-divers can go down to 25 feet with special breathing equipment, mountain bikes, birdwatching and wildlife excursions. **B** *Hopkins Inn*, T05-37013, hopkinsinn@btl.net, white cabins with private bathroom on beach south of centre, very clean and friendly, German spoken. For longer stays, ask for **B** *Seaside Garden*, T05-22889, owner Barry Swan, a lovely 2-room cabin, minimum 3-night stay. **B-D** *Seagull's Nest*, T05-37015, south of the centre, rooms and bunks in wooden house or in new concrete house with kitchenettes, fan, all clean and well-run. **C-D** *Tipple Tree Beya*, tipple@btl.net, English/American-run, rooms in new wooden house just before *Sandy Beach Lodge*, camping US$4.50 per person, self-contained house available. **D-E** *Caribbean View*, at north end of village, basic rooms, shared bath. **D-E** *Sandy Beach Lodge*, T05-37006, a women's cooperative, run by 10 women who work in shifts, arrive before 1900 or they will have gone home, 9 beachside rooms and large restaurant, 20-minute walk south of village, quiet, safe, friendly, clean. **E** *Swinging Armadillos*, T05-37016, on the pier, 5 rooms, outdoor shower, seafood restaurant, bar, usually the best in the village.

Eating *Over The Waves* has good food. *Ronnie's Kitchen*, turquoise house on stilts north of the police station (follow the road left from the bus stop), excellent food, friendly service, open 0630-2100, lunch includes burritos and chicken US$3-5, Ronnie also runs a library and gives good local advice.

Transport Buses From Dangriga, Z-Line and Ritchies around 1200 and 1630.

Cockscomb Basin Wildlife Sanctuary

Four miles further on, the Southern Highway crosses the Sittee River at the small village of **Kendal** (ruins nearby); one mile beyond (20 miles from Dangriga) is the new village of **Maya Centre** (or Center) from where a bad seven-mile track winds west through Cabbage Haul Gap to the **Cockscomb Basin Wildlife Sanctuary** (41,457 hectares), the world's first jaguar sanctuary. This was created out of the Cockscomb Basin Forest Reserve in 1986 to protect the country's highest recorded density of jaguars (*Panthera onca*) and their smaller cousins, the puma ('red tiger'), the endangered ocelot, the diurnal jaguarundi, and the exquisite margay. Many other mammals share the heavily-forested reserve, including coatis, collared peccaries, agoutis, anteaters, Baird's tapirs, and tayras (a small weasel-like animal). There are red-eyed tree frogs, boas, iguanas and fer-de-lances, and over 290 species of birds, including king vultures and great curassows. The Sanctuary is a good place for relaxing, listening to birds (scarlet macaws can be seen), showering under waterfalls, et cetera. This unique reserve is sponsored by the government, the Audubon Society, the World Wildlife Fund and private firms like the Jaguar car company; donations are very welcome.

Entry US$5, Belizeans US$1.25. Park HQ is at the former settlement of Quam Bank (whose **Admission** milpa-farming inhabitants founded Maya Centre outside the reserve); here there is an informative visitors' centre. Three miles of jungle trails spread out from the visitors' centre, but walkers are unlikely to see any of the big cats. Note that the guards leave for the day at 1600. You will see birds, frogs, lizards and snakes. Longer hikes can be planned with the staff; it is an arduous 4-5 day return climb to Victoria Peak (3,675 feet) and should not be undertaken casually. There is virtually no path, a guide is essential; February-May best for the climb. The best guides to the Reserve live in Maya Centre, contact Julio Saqui, of Julio's Cultural Tours, T05-12020, he runs the village shop and can look after any extra luggage. At *Greg's Bar*, on the main road in the middle of the village, you can contact Greg Sho, a very experienced river and mountain guide who can also arrange kayak trips.

There is usually space on arrival, but to guarantee accommodation, travellers can contact the **Sleeping** Belize Audubon Society, 12 Fort Street, Belize City, T02-34985, Dangriga T05-22044 (*Pelican Beach Hotel*), or write to Ernesto Saqui, PO Box 90, Dangriga. **D** *Nu'uk Che'il Cottages*, Maya

Centre, T05-12021, simple thatched rooms in a garden next to the forest, take the botanical trail and learn about Maya medicine from Aurora Saqui; Ernesto, her husband, can arrange transport to the Reserve Headquarters for US$12.50 one way. At the Park HQ there is a picnic area and camping area (US$1.50); there are new purpose-built cabins, **C**, and dormitories, **E** per person. Potable water is available, also earth toilets, but you must bring your own food, other drinks, matches, torch, sheet sleeping bag, eating utensils and mosquito repellent; nearest shop is at Maya Centre.

Transport Can be booked at the time of reservation, or locals will drive you from Maya Centre, other-wise it is a 6-mile, uphill walk from Maya Centre to the reserve. All buses going south from Dangriga go through Maya Centre, 40 minutes, US$2.50-3; and north from Placencia, return bus at 0700, 0900, etc to Dangriga (allow 2 hours for the walk down to Maya Centre). If walk-ing, leave all unneeded gear in Dangriga in view of the uphill stretch from Maya Centre, or you can leave luggage at Julio's little store in Maya Centre for US$0.50 per day. A taxi from Dangriga will cost about US$50, it is not difficult to hitch back. The rainy season here extends from June to January.

Sittee River Village
Colour map 4, grid B4

Turning east towards the Caribbean just before Kendal a road leads down the Sittee River to **Sittee River Village** and **Possum Point** Biological Station.

Sleeping LL *Lillpat Sittee River Resort*, PO Box 136, Dangriga, T/F05-12019, lillpat@btl.net, 4 a/c rooms on the Sittee River, pool, restaurant, bar, very convenient for Cockscomb, birdwatching and fishing. The Biological Station has a **D**, 16-room hotel, restaurant, specializes in student package tours from the USA and discourages casual guests. **E-F** per person *Glover's Guest House*, T08-22505, 5 rooms, on river bank, restau-rant, camping, jungle river trips, run by Lomont-Cabral family and starting point for boat to their *North East Caye* (see below). **B-E** *Toucan Sittee*, 400 yards down river from *Glovers*, T37039, run by Neville Collins, lovely setting, rooms with screens and fans, hot water, or fully-equipped riverside apartments, great meals around US$6, grow most of their fruit and veg, also over 50 medicinal plants. **F** *Isolene's*, family house, Isolene cooks good meals in restaurant opposite. **B** *Bocatura Bank*, T05-22006, cottages, restaurant.

Glover's Reef Glover's Reef, about 45 miles offshore, is an atoll with beautiful diving and a Marine Reserve since 1993. The reef here is pristine, and the cayes are unspoilt.

Sleeping *Manta Reef Resort*, Glover's Reef Atoll, PO Box 215, 3 Eyre St, Belize City, T02-31895/32767, F02-32764; 9 individual cabins with full facilities, in perfect desert island setting, 1 week packages available only, reservations essential; excellent diving and fishing, good food, highly recommended (E6 photo lab available). On 9-acre **North East Caye** is

Glover's Atoll Resort (Gilbert and Marsha-Jo Lomont and Becky and Breeze Cabral, PO Box 563, Belize City, T01-48351/05-12016, F08-23505/23235, glovers@btl.net, www. belizemall. com/ gloversatoll, no reservations needed). There are 8 cabins with wood burning stoves, US$99-149 per person per week + 7 percent room tax. Camping US$80 per person a week (including trip out and back). Occasional rice and seafood meals, bring food, some groceries and drinking water available. A new beach has been created by Hurricane Mitch, and the resort also comprises Lomont Caye and Cabral Caye which have beaches, both of 1 acre and within swimming distance. Boats for hire, with or without guide, also canoes, rowboats, windsurfer; full PADI/NAUI dive centre, snorkel and scuba rental, tank of air for shore dive US$14; boat dive includes air and gear US$36; no diving alone, certified divers must do tune-up dive, US$20, 4-day NAUI certification course US$295. Fly fishing with Breeze as guide, US$75 per ½ day. Families welcome. Contact the Lomonts in advance to obtain a full breakdown of all services and costs. Best to bring everything you will need including food, torch, soap, candles, sun screen, toilet paper, alcoholic and/or soft drinks, allowing for possible supply shortages or bad weather when boats stop running. Facilities are simple, don't expect luxury and guests are invited to help out occasionally.

Transport To North East Caye, 4 daily Z-Line buses (T05-22160) from Dangriga to Sittee River and go to the *Glover's Guest House* at Sittee River Village (see above). Also 2 daily buses from Placencia. Alternatively, take any bus going south to the Sittee junction and take a ride to the guest house. If you get lost, phone ahead for help. At 0800 Sunday a sailing boat leaves for the Reef 5 hours, US$20 per person one way (price included in accommodation package), returns Saturday. At other times, charter a boat (skiff or sailing boat, US$200 one way, up to 8 people, diesel sloop US$350, up to 30 people).

Further down the Southern Highway watch for signs to hotels (nothing official, look   Maya Beach
carefully). Nine miles leads to Riverside, then down a spit of land to **Maya Beach**.

Sleeping AL *Green Parrot Beach Houses*, T/F06-22488, greenparot@btl.net, beach houses on stilts, all with sea view, sleep up to 5, kitchen, open air restaurant and bar, highly recommended. **AL** *Singing Sands Inn*, T/F06-22243, run by Bruce Larkin and Sally Steeds, 6 thatched cabins with bathrooms, hot water, fans, ocean view, snorkelling in front of the resort at False Cay, diving instruction with Sally, windsurfing, canoe and mountain bike hire, fishing, tours arranged, restaurant and bar on the beach. **AL** *Tropical Lodge*, T06-22077, full board, camping **F**, hot showers, own dock and diving facilities, run by Ted and Peggy Williams, remote, good place to relax, or enjoy the Caribbean, US reservations T813-6395717.

The road continues south to **Seine Bight**, becoming rougher, with sand mixed into mud, four-wheel drive advisable, huge holes appear and fill up with water in wet season. **LL** *Rum Point Inn*, T06-23239, F06-23240 (in USA T504-4650769, F4640325), full board, delightful cabins, owned by an American entomologist, good food, dive shop. **B** *Hotel Seine Bight*, T06-23536, mikepam@btl.net, small, very good restaurant, run by English couple Pamela and Mike. Several new, higher and lower priced places to stay. For an entertaining evening with dinner contact Lola Delgado, who runs *Lola's Café and Art Gallery*, sign at south end of village. Lola and her husband Edward are both accomplished artists and her vivid paintings of village scenes are in great demand yet still at good prices. Visit the *Kulcha Shack* restaurant, gift shop, bar with dancing, run by Dewey, promoting Garifuna culture and traditions. Five miles further is Placencia.

Placencia

Placencia (also spelt Placentia), is a little resort 30 miles south of Dangriga, at the end   *Phone code: 06*
of a long spit of land reached by bus. There are no streets, just a network of concrete   *Colour map 4, grid B3*
footpaths and wooden houses under the palms. No riding of bicycles or motorbikes on footpaths or you face a fine of BZ$25. Electricity and lighting on the main path have been installed. Although the village is rather dirty, the atmosphere has been described as good, laid back, with lots of Jamaican music. **Big Creek**, on the

mainland opposite Placencia, is three miles from Mango Creek (see below). Fresh water is now piped from Mango Creek and is of good quality.

Excursions Trips can be made to the coral reef, 16 kilometres off-shore. Day trips including snorkelling, lunch, from US$25 per person; scuba diving also available, ask for Bryan Young. Prices are from about US$65 for two dives (gear extra). Ellis, of Kingfisher/Belize Adventures, has been recommended as knowledgeable and pleasant local guide, T06-23104/23204, good for land-based tours, while Jimmy Westby (lives behind *Flamboyant Bar*) is good for water excursions, snorkelling day trip including lunch to Laughing Bird Cay, six to 12 people, US$20 per person, kayaking tours, two to seven days, US$100 for two including camping gear and food. There are day tours by kayak or boat to Monkey River and **Monkey River Town**, south along the coast, you can see howler monkeys, toucans, manatees, iguanas, cost US$115 including guiding for five to six people. The town can be reached by a rough road, but not recommended in wet weather. The road ends on north side of river and the town is on the south side, so call over for transport. There is accommodation. Trips up river can also be arranged here with locals but kayaking is best organized in Placencia. Dave Dial, *Monkey River Magic*, T06-23204, runs good tours, usually leaves 0700 daily, US$40. José Oh can be contacted at *Turtle Inn* for tours including hiking, birdwatching, et cetera, recommended. Also recommended is Dave Vernon of *Deb and Dave's Last Resort*, an excellent tour guide; he also rents kayaks and good mountain bikes.

Sleeping **AL** *Serenity Resort*, just north of *Rum Point Inn*, itself just north of the airstrip, T23232, F23231, serenity@btl.net, good beach, well run, good bar and restaurant. **AL** *Turtle Inn*, on beach close to airstrip, just south of *Kitty's*, T23244, F23245, turtleinn@btl.net, includes delicious breakfast, thatched cabañas, dive shop, a little basic for price but friendly, restful. **AL** *Ranguana Lodge*, T23112, wooden cabins on the ocean, very clean. **A** *Trade Winds Cottages*, South Point, T23122, F23201, Mrs Janice Leslie, cabins and rooms in a spacious private plot on the south beach. **A** *Coconut Cottage*, T/F23234, on beach halfway down the village, beautiful, private cabins, very well run.

That rooms may be hard to find in pm, eg after arrival of the bus from Dangriga.

B *Barracuda and Jaguar Inn*, T23330, F23250, wende@btl.net, in the village, comfortable cabins with deck, including good breakfast, good restaurant, English/Canadian run. **B-D** *Seaspray*, T/F23148, seaspray@btl.net, cheaper in low season, very nice, good value, bar.

C *Paradise Vacation Resort*, full board or single meals available, clean, creole cooking, run by Dalton Eiley and Jim Lee, they offer reef fishing, snorkelling, excursions to the jungle, Pine Ridge, Mayan ruins and into the mountains. If arriving by air at Big Creek, first contact Hubert Eiley, T23118, who will arrange for a boat to take you to Placencia. **C** *Sonny's Resort*, T23103, cabins on the ocean, good restaurant (see below). **C** *Deb and Dave's Last Resort*, on the road, T23207, F23117, debanddave@btl.net, very good budget rooms with shared bathroom, hot water, kayak and bike rental.

D *Conrad and Lydia's Rooms*, T/F23117, 5 double room with shared toilet and shower, situated on a quiet part of the beach, with excellent breakfast, good other meals, excellent coconut bread, recommended, Conrad is a boat owner, ask for his prices. *Kitty's Place*, just south of the airstrip, about 1 mile north of the beginning of the village, T23227, F23226, kittys@btl.net, beach apartment **B**, weekly rates cheaper, rooms **D** with hot showers, very good restaurant with buffet Friday and Saturday evenings. **D** *Lucille's Rooms*, run by Lucille and her family, private bath, clean rooms, good beds, fans, good value, meals by arrangement.

E *Julia's Budget Hotel*, T23185, no private bath, stuffy and hot, central, friendly, reliable wakeup call for bus. Mr Clive rents 2 houses, **F** per person per day, also camping; George Cabral has a 2-bed apartment to rent in town, T23130. Camping on the beach or under the coconut palms. The bus stop outside Kingfisher office is a good place to start looking for rooms, lots of budget accommodation nearby. Usually several houses to rent, US$75-150 per week, try *Ted's Houses*, T23172, just past the market and near where the buses stop.

Belize

La Petite Maison, T23172, near *Ted's Houses*, gourmet French cuisine during winter season, expensive but worth it. *The Galley*, good fish and shellfish (depending on the day's catch), try the seaweed punch, information on fishing and snorkelling, slow service, recommended. *Flamboyant Restaurant and Bar*, a bit of cool luxury and excellent food, popular and good place for meeting local guides, catch them early before they get drunk. *Sunrise*, good, reasonably-priced food. *Tentacles*, thatch roof, nice balcony, good music. *Merlene's*, on south shore, one of the best, opens early for good breakfast, also has apartment for rent. *Sonny's Resort Restaurant*, excellent fish and seafood. *Daisy's*, has good, homemade ice cream. *Dockside Bar*, good music, dancing at weekends. *Chili's*, good hamburgers and American-style breakfasts with potatoes. *Omar's Fast Food*, fish, meat, burgers, *burritos*, good cheap breakfasts. At least 5 shops (fresh fruit and vegetables supplied to *The Market*, opens 0800-1200, 1500-1800, Sunday 0800-1200, closed Thursday, changes travellers' cheques and cash, a video-cassette movie theatre, 4 bars, the fishing co-operative, open Monday-Saturday, am, sells fish cheaply, also ice, and supplies the town's electricity.

Eating

Air Placencia has its own airstrip. Maya Island Air and Tropic Air fly several times a day Belize City (international and municipal), also Dangriga, Punta Gorda.

Transport

 Buses From Dangriga at 1200 direct, or 1630 via Hopkins and Sittee River, US$4, 3½ hours, return at 0530 and 0600, connecting with 0900 bus to Belize City. From Belize City via Coastal Highway and Dangriga, 4 hours, US$7.50, Ritchies Busline. Times and operators change constantly.

 Boats Regular service Mango Creek-Placencia, *Hokey Pokey*, 0830 and 1430; return 1000 and 1600, US$10 return; meets Dangriga and Punta Gorda buses. *Kingfisher* (see **Excursions**) sails to Puerto Cortés, Honduras, Saturday 0900, US$50.

Banks *Atlantic Bank* near the gas station at the south point is open Mon-Fri. **Communications** There is a *BTL* office in the centre where you can make international calls and receive and send fax messages. Payphones here and at the gas station. **Post Office:** open Mon-Fri 0800-1200, 1330-1600. **Useful services** There is a police station. Visa extensions obtainable in Mango Creek.

Directory

Little Water Caye is privately owned and about 17 miles southeast of Placencia, just short of the edge of the Barrier Reef where the sea floor drops to over 1,000 metres. The lagoon is good for fly fishing and snorkelling, with good diving sites nearby. The German owners, Karl Kohlbecker and Andreas Wüstefeld have established *Little Water Caye Resort* with accommodation and facilities for nine guests in three cabañas, full board US$400 for three days, two nights for two, US$750 for seven days, six nights including transport from Placencia. For more information, T/F06-12019 or T49-211-1649612, F49-211-1649613, Düsseldorf, Germany.

Little Water Caye

Ranguana Caye is private, leased from the Government, and reached from Placencia. Reservations through the Resort's Office in Placencia near *Sea Spray Hotel*, T/F06-23112, open Monday-Saturday, 0800-1830, accepts major credit cards or ask at BTL for Jean on the Caye. Getting there costs US$75 for up to four people. A room sleeps three, **B**, with bathroom and fan. Camping possible, **F** per person, bathrooms and barbecue pits provided but bring food. Kayaks US$30 per day. Divers must bring their own scuba equipment.

Ranguana Caye

At the southernmost end of the Belize Barrier Reef are the Sapodilla Cayes. Tours are arranged from Guatemala (for example see under Río Dulce-El Tortugal Resort) or can be made from Placencia. There are settlements on a few of the Cays including Hunting Caye.

Sapodilla Cayes

Mango Creek is a banana exporting port, 30 miles (40 by road) south of Dangriga. The road through the Stann Creek Valley to Mango Creek is to be surfaced following the granting of an IDB loan in 1998. Mayan community groups opposed the project on ecological grounds.

Mango Creek
Colour map 4, grid B4

Sleeping and eating **C** *Hello I Hotel* (at Independence) run by Antonio Zabaneh at the shop where the Z-Line bus stops, clean, comfortable, helpful. **D** *Ursella's Guest House*, 6 rooms. **F** Hotel above *People's Restaurant*, clean, basic, ask to borrow a fan and lamp, at night you can listen to 'the sounds of the whole Belizean Zoo on the wooden floor, walls and ceiling', shower is a bucket of water in a cabin, 'don't use too much soap or you'll have to go back to the house for a refill' (Harry Balthussen), restaurant basic also; food better at the white house with green shutters behind it (book 2 hours in advance if possible). *Goyo's Inn/Restaurant Independence* (no accommodation), family-owned, good food.

Transport **Buses** Belize City-Mango Creek, Z-Line, or the less regular James Bus Service, from Pound Yard Bridge, US$8.50; bus Mango Creek-Belmopan, US$6.50. There is an **airport** at **Independence**, nearby. **Sea** Motorized canoe from Mango Creek to **Puerto Cortés**, Honduras, irregular; ask Antonio Zabaneh at his store, T06-22011, who knows when boats will arrive, US$50 one way, 7-9 hours (rubber protective sheeting is provided, hang on to it, usually not enough to go round, nor lifejackets, but you will still get wet unless wearing waterproofs, or just a swimming costume on hot days; it can be dangerous in rough weather). Remember to get an exit stamp, preferably in Belize City, but normally obtainable at the police station in Mango Creek, not Placencia (the US$10 departure tax demanded here is not official). See Placencia **Transport** for Mango Creek-Placencia boats.

Directory **Banks** *Barclays Bank* is open Fri only 0900-1200.

The turnoff from the Southern Highway for Mango Creek, Independence and Big Creek comes 15 miles after the Riversdale turnoff, running four miles east through the **Savannah Forest Reserve** to the swampy coast opposite Placencia. The Highway itself continues through forest and limestone outcrops, as the foothills of the mountains press in on the west. About 35 miles beyond the junction, 10½ miles north of the T-junction for Punta Gorda, half a mile west of the road, is the **Nim Li Punit** archaeological site; unrestored, partially cleared, Nim Li Punit ('Big Hat') was only discovered in 1974; a score of stelae, 15-20 feet tall, were unearthed, dated 700-800 AD. A ball court, several groups of buildings and plazas, only southernmost group open to visitors. Worth visiting. Signed trail from the highway.

A short distance beyond, the highway passes **Big Falls**, where there are hot springs; here you can swim, camp or sling a hammock, but first seek permission of the landowner, Mr Peter Alaman, who runs the general store on the highway and has a guest house, **D**. **E** per person *Xaiha*, co-operatively owned cabins on the bank of the Rio Grand, bunks and private rooms. This is a popular weekend picnicking spot and a pleasant place to break the journey south. Four miles from Big Falls, the Highway reaches a T-junction (Shell station), the road to San Antonio branches right (west), the main road turns sharp left and runs down through another forest reserve for 13 miles to Punta Gorda. The road is paved between Big Falls and Punta Gorda, the rest of the Southern Highway is being paved in stages.

Punta Gorda

Population: 4,000
Phone code: 07
Colour map 4, grid B3

Rainfall in this region is exceptionally heavy, over 170 inches annually, and the vegetation suitably luxuriant.

The capital of Toledo District, is the last town of any size in Belize, a marketing centre and fishing port with a varied ethnic makeup: Creoles, Kekchi, Mopan, Chinese, East Indians, et cetera, descendants of the many races brought here over the years as labourers in ill-fated settlement attempts. At **Toledo**, three miles north, can be seen the remains of the sugar cane settlement founded by Confederacy refugees after the Civil War. he coast, about 100 feet above sea level, is fringed with coconut palms. Punta Gorda is a pleasant, breezy, quiet place; the seafront is clean (once you get away from Front Street, where it is smelly with fish and rotting vegetables) and enjoyable, but swimming is not recommended. The Voice of America has a tall antenna complex on the edge of town. On Main Street is a pretty park with a new clock tower, and the bus terminus, while on the parallel Front Street are the civic centre, a new market hall and post office/government office. Most of the (little) activity takes place around the pier. Market days Wednesday and Saturday.

AL *Traveller's Inn*, near Z-Line bus terminal, including breakfast, bath, a/c, restaurant, bar, clinical atmosphere, information on tours and services. **C** *Punta Caliente*, 108 José María Nuñez St, T22561, double or king size, excellent value, very good restaurant. **C** *Tate's Guest House*, 34 José María Nuñez St, T22196, a/c, cheaper without, clean, hot water, bathroom, TV, parking, frienldy, Mr Tate is the Postmaster, Mrs Tate is a teacher so breakfast has to be before 0730, laundry service. **D** *Circle C*, 1 block from bus terminal, OK. **D** *Goyo's*, facing clocktower, new, bath, clean, cable TV. **D** *Nature's Way Guest House*, 65 Front St, T22119 (PO Box 75), thfec@btl.net, clean, good breakfast, will arrange accommodation in Maya villages (Guesthouse Program), ecologically- aware tours, fishing, sailing, has van, camping gear and trimaran for rent, recommended. **D** *Pallavi*, 19 Main St, T22414, recently enlarged, tidy, balcony, clean, friendly. **D** *St Charles Inn*, 23 King St, T22149, with or without bath, spacious rooms, fan, cable TV, good. **E** *Mahung's Hotel*, corner North and Main St, T22044, cockroaches, reasonable, also rents mountain bikes, US$10 per day. **E** *Wahima*, T22542, on waterfront, clean and safe, owner Max is local school teacher, friendly and informative. **F** per person *Airport Hotel*, quiet, OK, communal bathrooms, clean, spartan. You can flag down the 0500 bus to Belize in front of *Wahima* or *Pallavi*, buy ticket the night before. Sony's Laundry Service near airstrip.

Sleeping
■ *on maps*
Price codes:
see inside front cover

Kowloon, 41 Front St, good food. *Lucille's Kitchen*, Main St next to Texaco, friendly, good, cheap meals, open until about 2200, but if she's not there, 'just holler'. *Fishermans Inn*, Front St, run by Americans Darcy and Billy, good food and conversation, excellent breakfasts with free coffee refills. Good Garifuna restaurant at the *Punta Caliente Hotel* at south end of town (see above). *Morning Glory Café*, Front Street, good breakfasts and good seafood. *El Café*, North Street, 2 blocks west of *Lucille's*, best coffee in town, good breakfasts and is the first to open. Bakery selling excellent 'sticky buns' near *Wahima*. *Honeycomb* bar on Front St, especially good around Garifuna Day when spontaneous music, singing and dancing bursts forth.

Eating
● *on maps*

Air Daily flights with Maya Island Air and Tropic Air from Dangriga, Placencia, Belize City (both airports). Tickets at Alistair King's (at Texaco station) and Bob Pennell's hardware store on Main Street. Advance reservations essential.

Transport

Buses From Belize, 9 hours (longer in heavy rain), US$11, Z-Line, Monday to Saturday 0500, 0800, 1200 and 1500, Sunday 0500, 1000 and 1500, ticket can be bought day before, beautiful but rough ride; Z-Line bus to Belize City 0500, 0900, 1200 stopping at Mango Creek, Dangriga and Belmopan (schedules change on holidays). Z-Line terminal is at very south end of José María Núñez Street; lobby of *Traveller's Inn* serves as ticket office. James Bus line to Belize City Tuesday, Friday, 1100, after ferry from Puerto Barrios arrives, also 0600 Sunday; departs from government buildings near ferry dock. To **San Antonio** from square, see below for schedules; buses to **San Pedro Columbia** and San José Wednesday and Saturday 1200, return Wednesday and Saturday am. Buses are usually delayed in the wet season.

Banks *Belize Bank*, at one end of the park (a/c, a cool haven), will change excess BZ$ for US$ on production of passport and ticket out of the country. They do not change Quetzales and charge US$7.50 for advancing cash against Visa card. You can change BZ$ for Quetzales at the Customs in Punta Gorda and Puerto Barrios, but don't expect a good rate. **Tourist offices** *Toledo Visitors Information Center*, also called 'Dem Dats Doin', in booth by pier, PO Box 73, T22470, Alfredo and Yvonne Villoria, information on travel, tours, guiding, accommodation with Indian families (Homestay Program), message service, book exchange, for the whole of Toledo district, free. *Tourist Information Centre*, Front St, T22834, F22835, open Mon-Fri, 0830-1200, 1300-1800, Sat 0800-1200, flight reservations worldwide, hotels, tours, boat trips to Honduras.

Directory

belize

Boats to Guatemala

Belizean immigration Exit stamps for people and vehicles can be obtained at the Customs House next to the pier on Front Street. Be there at least 1 hour before departure, or 2 hours if loading a motorcycle. PACT exit tax payable, see page 721.

Guatemalan consulate If you need a visa it must be obtained in Belize City. Tourist cards are available in Puerto Barrios.

Exchange There are money changers at both ends of the crossing, but it is better to wait until in Guatemala before buying quetzals. Neither side changes travellers' cheques. Try to get rid of any BZ$ in Belize.

Transport Boats Small, fast skiffs leave from the main dock in front of the immigration office every day at 0830-0900, also usually one at 1600, returning 1300-1400. Almost all go directly to Puerto Barrios, US$12.50, though they sometimes call at Livingston, US$10. There are also services to Izabal and Río Dulce (Guatemala) and Honduras. No need to book in advance though preferable to ensure space. Check with Paco's, 3 Clemente Street, T07-22246, or Requena's, T07-22070, 12 Front Street.

NB Officials in Livingston do not have the authority to issue vehicle permits to anything other than water craft. Beware however of unsafe, unseaworthy craft. The weather can be treacherous, and you and your luggage will certainly get wet.

San Pedro Columbia

Inland from Punta Gorda there are several interesting villages in the foothills of the Maya Mountains. Take the main road as far as the Dump, the road junction (so named because they dumped soil there when clearing land for rice paddies) with the Southern Highway. Take the road to San Antonio. After nearly two miles is a branch to **San Pedro Columbia**, a Kekchi village. (Kekchi is a sub-tribe of Maya speaking a distinct language.) The Maya and Kekchi women wear picturesque costumes, including Guatemalan huipiles. There are many religious celebrations, at their most intense (mixed with general gaiety) on San Luis Rey day (5 August).

Sleeping C-D, with Alfredo and Yvonne Villaria, *Dem Dats Doin'* (see Punta Gorda, **Tourist offices**). **E** *Guest House*, dormitory. You can buy drinks and get breakfast at the large, yellow stone house.

Four kilometres beyond the village, up some very steep, rocky hills, is Fallen Stones Butterfly Ranch, owned by an English man, leave messages at Texaco gas station, T07-22126, not only butterfly farm exporting pupae but also hotel, **L** including tax, service and breakfast, jungle tours, laundry, airport transfers.

Lubaantun

Beyond San Pedro, continuing left around the church, then right and downhill to the new concrete bridge, then left for a mile, is the trail to the Maya remains of Lubaantun ('Fallen Stones'), the major ceremonial site of southern Belize. It was last excavated by a Cambridge University team in 1970 and found to date from the 8th-9th centuries, late in the Maya culture and therefore unique. A series of terraced plazas surrounded by temples and palaces ascend along a ridge from south to north; the buildings were constructed with unusual precision and some of the original lime-mortar facings can still be discerned. Excavation revealed some interesting material: whistle figurines, iron pyrite mirrors, obsidian knives, conch shells from Wild Cane Caye, et cetera. The site is little-visited and, according to latest reports, could be better maintained. Opening hours are 0800-1600 daily; a caretaker will point out things of interest. Refreshments should be taken; dubious local food at a hut nearby. Toilets provided. This whole region is a network of hilltop sites, mostly unexcavated and unrecognizable to the layman.

Blue Creek

Blue Creek is another attractive Indian village with a marked trail to Blue Creek caves (caretaker is guide, US$12.50 per person, Maya drawings in middle of cave) through forest and along rock strewn creeks. Good swimming nearby but choose a spot away from the strong current. Turn off three miles before San Antonio at *Roy's Cool Spot* (good restaurant; daily truck and all buses pass here). Halfway to Blue Creek is **E** per person *Roots and Herbs*, a couple of simple cabins with mosquito nets, Pablo is an excellent guide, good food. Turn left at *Jim's Pool Room* in Manfredi Village, then continue about five miles. Blue Creek is 35 minutes by bicycle from San Antonio. Very basic accommodation at the house at the beginning of the trail to the caves.

Close to the Guatemalan border is one of the most interesting Maya cities, Pusilhá, which is only accessible by boat. Many stelae were found here dating from 573 to 731 AD; carvings are similar to those at Quiriguá, Guatemala. Rare features are a walled-in ball court and the abutments remaining from a bridge which once spanned the Moho River. Swimming in the rivers is safe and refreshing. There are plenty of logging trails and hunters' tracks penetrating the southern faces of the Maya Mountains, but if hiking in the forest do not go alone. **Pusilhá**

San Antonio (21 miles from Punta Gorda) was founded by refugees from San Luis in Guatemala in the late 19th century. Nearby there are Maya ruins of mainly scientific interest. Community phone for checking buses and other information, T07-22144. **San Antonio**

Sleeping and eating **D** *Bol's Hilltop Hotel*, showers, toilets, meals extra, clean; meals also from *Theodora*, next to hotel, and *Clara*, next to hotel and Theodora, both with advance notice: local specialities are *jippy jappa/kula*, from a local plant, and chicken *caldo*.

Shopping Eight stores: *Lucio Cho* sells cold beer and soda and has the local post office; *Matildo Salam* is building a hotel above his shop; medical centre in the village. Crafts such as basketry made from *jippy jappa* and embroidery can be found in this area.

Transport Bus from Punta Gorda, US$1.50, 1-1½ hours, Monday, Wednesday, Friday, Saturday 1230, from west side of Central Park, also 1200 on Wednesday and Saturday, continuing to Santa Cruz, Santa Elena and Pueblo Viejo (1 hour from San Antonio). Alternatively, hire a pick-up van in Dangriga, or get a ride in a truck from the market or rice co-operative's mill in Punta Gorda (one leaves early pm); or go to the road junction at Dump, where the northern branch goes to Independence/Mango Creek, the other to San Antonio, 6 miles, either hitch or walk. Bus from San Antonio to **Punta Gorda** Monday, Wednesday, Friday, Saturday 0530 also 0500 Wednesday and Saturday (having left Pueblo Viejo at 0400); if going to **Dangriga**, take the 0500, get out at Dump to catch 0530 Z-Line bus going north. This area is full of places to explore and it is well worth hiring a vehicle.

Transport can sometimes be arranged from Pueblo Viejo along a rough road to Jalacté (also reached by trail from Blue Creek and Aguacate), from where it is a 30-minute hike to Santa Cruz del Petén (often muddy trail). From here trucks can be caught to San Luis on the highway near Poptún. There is no Guatemalan government presence at this border; entry stamps cannot be obtained. **NB** Although locals cross to shop in Guatemala, it is strictly illegal to cross this border. Guatemalan maps are inaccurate. **Crossing into Guatemala**

Neil McAllister writes: An interesting alternative from Punta Gorda is to stay in Indian villages. Two schemes exist; one is run by villagers as a non-competitive co-operative. **San Miguel**, **San José (Hawaii)**, **Laguna**, and **Santa Cruz** are isolated villages beyond Dump towards San Ignacio. **Barranco** is a Garifuna village south of Punta Gorda, accessible by boat or poor road. These have joined together and have developed a visitor scheme which benefits the villages. Each village has built a well appointed guest house, simple, but clean, with sheets, towels, mosquito nets, oil lamps, ablutions block, and total of eight bunks in two four-bunk rooms. Visitors stay here, but eat in the villagers' houses on strict rotation, so each household gains equal income and only has to put up with intruding foreigners for short periods.

They have their privacy, and so do you.

Village children and many men speak English. Many expressed fears for what the arrival of power (and television) will do to their culture, and are keen to protect their heritage. Dancing and music were previously banned by the Church, but the Indians have relearned old dances from elderly villagers and are buying and learning instruments to put on evening entertainments. Home-made excursions are arranged, these vary from four-hours' trek through local forest, looking at medicinal plants, and explaining agriculture (very interesting) as well as seeing very out-of-the-way sights like caves and creeks (take boots, even in dry season). The village tour could be skipped, as it is easy to walk around and chat to people, although by doing this freelance, you deprive the 'guide' of income.

This experience does not come cheap: one night for two people, with a forest tour and two meals came to almost US$50 but all profits go direct to the villages, with no outsiders as middlemen. Dormitory accommodation costs US$9 per person. All villagers share equally in the venture, so there is no resentment, or pressure from competing households, and gross profits from the Guest House are ploughed back into the villages' infrastructure, schools et cetera. The scheme is co-ordinated by Chet Smith at *Nature's Way Guest House*, Punta Gorda, who donates assistance and booking facilities for the scheme. You may have to arrange your own transport, or a vehicle can be hired. Hitching not recommended, as some villages are remote, and may have one car a day visiting. Enquire also at the Toledo Information Centre in Punta Gorda. Local attractions include San Antonio waterfall, 30-minute walk from San Antonio towards Santa Cruz; caves at San José (Hawaii); Uxbenka ruins and caves two and a half-hour walk from San Antonio (turn off right just before Santa Cruz), commanding view from ruins; Santa Cruz waterfalls, 10 minutes beyond the village, deep and cold. For Uxbenka and Santa Cruz, take Chun's bus on Wednesday and Saturday at 1300 from San Antonio and arrange return time. Do not take Cho's bus, it does not return.

Agricultural 'roads' push down to the southern border with Guatemala along the Sarstoon (Sarstún) River but there is little permanent settlement. At **Barranco**, the only coastal hamlet south of Punta Gorda, there is a village guest house. A bad track leads to Barranco through Laguna and Santa Theresa (turn off left before Dump), or through Blue Creek and San Lucas, or go by boat. Information can be had at *Nature's Way*, Punta Gorda.

Background

The land

The coastlands are low and swampy with much mangrove, many salt and fresh water lagoons and some sandy beaches. In the north the land is low and flat, but in the southwest there is a heavily forested mountain massif with a general elevation of between 2,000 and 3,000 feet. In the eastern part are the Maya Mountains, not yet wholly explored, and the Cockscomb Range which rises to a height of 3,675 feet at Victoria Peak. To the west are some 250 square miles of the Mountain Pine Ridge, with large open spaces and some of the best scenery in the country.

From 10 to 40 miles off the coast an almost continuous, 150-mile line of reefs and cayes (often spelt cays, meaning islands, pronounced 'keys') provides shelter from the Caribbean and forms the longest coral reef in the Western Hemisphere (the fifth-longest barrier reef in the world). Most of the cayes are quite tiny, but some have been developed as tourist resorts. Many have beautiful sandy beaches with clear, clean water, where swimming and diving are excellent. (However, on the windward side of inhabited islands, domestic sewage is washed back on to the beaches, and some beaches are affected by tar.)

The most fertile areas of the country are in the northern foothills of the Maya Mountains: citrus fruit is grown in the Stann Creek valley, while in the valley of the Mopan, or upper Belize River, cattle raising and mixed farming are successful. The northern area of the country has long proved suitable for sugar cane production. In the south bananas and mangoes are cultivated. The lower valley of the Belize River is a rice-growing area as well as being used for mixed farming and citrus cultivation.

History

Throughout the country, especially in the forests of the centre and south, are many ruins of the Classic Maya Period, which flourished here and in neighbouring Guatemala from the fourth to the ninth century and then somewhat mysteriously (most probably because of drought) emigrated to Yucatán. It has been estimated that the population then was 10 times what it is now.

The first settlers were English with their black slaves from Jamaica who came about 1640 to cut logwood, then the source of textile dyes. The British Government made no claim to the territory but tried to secure the protection of the wood-cutters by treaties with Spain. Even after 1798, when a strong Spanish force was decisively beaten off at St George's Caye, the British Government still failed to claim the territory, though the settlers maintained that it had now become British by conquest.

When they achieved independence from Spain in 1821, both Guatemala and Mexico laid claim to sovereignty over Belize as successors to Spain, but these claims were rejected by Britain. Long before 1821, in defiance of Spain, the British settlers had established themselves as far south as the river Sarstoon, the present southern boundary. Independent Guatemala claimed that these settlers were trespassing and that Belize was a province of the new republic. By the middle of the 19th century Guatemalan fears of an attack by the United States led to a *rapprochement* with Britain. In 1859, a Convention was signed by which Guatemala recognized the boundaries of Belize while, by Article 7, the United Kingdom undertook to contribute to the cost of a road from Guatemala City to the sea 'near the settlement of Belize'; an undertaking which was never carried out.

Heartened by what it considered a final solution of the dispute, Great Britain declared Belize, still officially a settlement, a Colony in 1862, and a Crown Colony nine years later. Mexico, by treaty, renounced any claims it had on Belize in 1893, but Guatemala, which never ratified the 1859 agreement, renewed its claims periodically.

Belize became independent on 21 September 1981, following a United Nations declaration   **Independence** to that effect. Guatemala refused to recognize the independent state, but in 1986, President Cerezo of Guatemala announced an intention to drop his country's claim to Belize. A British military force was maintained in Belize from independence until 1993, when the British government announced that the defence of Belize would be handed over to the government on 1 January 1994 and that it would reduce the 1,200-strong garrison to about 100 soldiers who would organize jungle warfare training facilities. The last British troops were withdrawn in 1994 and finance was sought for the expansion of the Belize Defence Force. Belize was admitted into the OAS in 1991 following negotiations between Belize, Guatemala and Britain. As part of Guatemala's recognition of Belize as an independent nation (ratified by Congress in 1992) Britain will recompense Guatemala by providing financial and technical assistance to construct road, pipeline and port facilities that will guarantee Guatemala access to the Atlantic.

Elections Mr George Price, of the People's United Party (PUP), who had been re-elected continuously as Prime Minister since internal self-government was instituted in 1964, was defeated by Mr Manuel Esquivel, of the United Democratic Party (UDP), in general elections held in December 1984 (the first since independence), but was returned as Prime Minister in 1989. The National Alliance for Belizean Rights (NABR) was created in 1992 by a defector from the UDP. General elections were held early, in 1993, and contrary to forecasts, the PUP was defeated. The UDP, in alliance with the NABR, won 16 of the 29 seats, many by a very narrow margin, and Mr Esquivel took office as Prime Minister with the additional portfolios of Finance and Defence. In the months following the elections, a corruption scandal rocked Belizean politics. Several PUP members, including the former Foreign Minister were arrested on charges of offering bribes to two UDP members of the House of Representatives to persuade them to cross the floor. They were later acquitted.

Mr Price retired from the PUP party leadership in 1996, aged 77, after 40 years in the post. He was succeeded by Mr Said Musa, a lawyer. In 1997 the PUP had a spectacular success in the municipal elections, winning all seven Town Boards for the first time ever, reversing the position since 1994 when the UDP won them all. It continued its electoral success in 1998 in the August general election, when it won an unprecedented 26 of the 29 seats in the House of Representatives. The UDP won the other three, but Mr Esquirel lost his seat. The new government moved quickly to carry out its election promises. A review of the tax system was announced, the loss-making Broadcasting Corporation of Belize was privatized, logging licences to Malaysian companies were to be reviewed and allegations of corruption in state institutions under the former government were to be investigated. A 14-member Political Reform Commission was set up at the beginning of 1999 to look at Belize's system of governance and make recommendations on how to achieve greater democracy.

Hurricane Mitch in 1998 brought flooding and wind damage, but Belize escaped the full force of the storm. A large-scale evacuation of coastal areas moved about 60,000 people to the interior. High tides and heavy rain flooded the cayes, but tourist facilities were back to normal by the winter season.

Culture

People About 30 percent of the population are predominantly black, of mixed ancestry, the so-called Creoles, a term widely used in the Caribbean. They predominate in Belize City and along the coast, and on the navigable rivers. 44 percent of the population are mestizo; 11 percent are Maya Indians, who predominate in the north between the Hondo and New rivers and in the extreme south and west. About seven percent of the population are Garifuna (Black Caribs), descendants of the Black Caribs deported from St Vincent in 1797; they have a distinct language, and can be found in the villages and towns along the southern coast. They are good linguists, many speaking Mayan languages as well as Spanish and 'Creole' English. They also brought their culture and customs from the West Indies, including religious practices and ceremonies, for example Yankanu (John Canoe) dancing at Christmas time. The remainder are of unmixed European ancestry (the majority

Mennonites, who speak a German dialect, and are friendly and helpful) and a rapidly growing group of North Americans. The Mennonites fall into two groups, generally speaking: the most rigorous, in the Shipyard area on The New River, and the more 'integrated' in the west, Cayo district, who produce much of Belize's poultry, dairy goods and corn. The newest Mennonite settlements are east of Progresso Lagoon in the northeast. There are also East Indian and Chinese immigrants and their descendants.

English is the official language, although for some 180,000 the *lingua franca* is 'Creole' English. Spanish is the *lingua franca* for about 130,000 people. Spanish is widely spoken in the northern and western areas. In addition, it is estimated that 22,000 people speak Mayan languages, 15,000 Garifuna and 3,000 speak German. Free elementary education is available to all, and all the towns have secondary schools.

Language & education

The economy

Belize's central problem is how to become self-sufficient in food: imports of food are still some 20% of the total imports. Necessity is forcing the people to grow food for themselves and this is gathering pace. One difficulty is that the territory is seriously under-populated and much skilled labour emigrates. Three immigrant Mennonite communities have already increased farm production, and new legislation provides for the development of lands not utilized by private landowners.

Structure of production

This is still the most important sector of the Belizean economy, directly or indirectly employing more than half the population, and bringing in 65% of the country's total foreign exchange earnings. The main export crops, in order of importance, are sugar, citrus and bananas. Maize, beans, cocoa and rice are grown, and attempts are also being made to increase the cattle herd. Poultry, eggs and honey production grew significantly during the 1980s.

Timber is extracted during the first six months of the year. Forest products were for a long time the country's most important export, but their relative importance has fallen. The government has encouraged the establishment of a veneer plant to increase the domestic value added in wood product exports. There were local protests in 1995-96 against the granting of logging licences; 17 concessions totalling 555,000 acres were granted in the Toledo district, some of which overlapped with Maya reserves. In 1999, the new PUP government revoked a logging licence after the Malaysian company was found to have contravened the conditions of the licence. Marine products (for example shrimp and conch) are around 11% of exports, though some of the traditional grounds have been overfished and restrictions necessary for conservation are enforced.

There is also some light industry and manufacturing (dominated by sugar refining and citrus processing) now contributes about 14% of gdp. The value of clothing exports has risen to 10% of domestic exports (excluding re-exports), making garments the fifth most important export item in 1998. Oil was discovered, near the Mexican border, in 1981; the search for oil is being intensified on and off shore.

With the emergence of ecotourism and natural history-based travel as a major expansion market within the travel industry, the Belize government is encouraging the development of tourism facilities and services. Tourism in Belize is the second largest foreign revenue earner, behind agriculture, with tourist arrivals rising by 10% in 1998 to 160,696.

The 1995 Banks and Financial Institutions Act brought the regulation and supervision of the financial sector in line with Caricom requirements. New or amended legislation is pending on offshore banking and ship registration following a 1994 report by a British Government adviser, which recommended 'more regulation and supervision and rather less free enterprise'. Some 10,000 International Business Companies (IBCs) have been registered in Belize under 1990 legislation, while the open marine register numbers about 300 ships.

The slowing down of economic growth at the beginning of the 1980s was attributable to

Recent trends

decline in the sugar industry and pressures on Belize's international accounts. Prudent financial policies in the mid-1980s led to the elimination of external debt arrears and the increase of foreign exchange reserves. In 1985-94 gdp grew at an average of 7.9% a year, with positive, though slower rates of growth recorded since then, and by end-1996 official reserves stood at US$56.1mn, the highest level for six years.

The departure of the British army garrison meant the loss of US$30mn to the Belize economy and the rise in gdp slowed from 6% in financial year 1992/93 to 3.8% in 1993/94. The decline in fiscal receipts led the Government to raise taxes and curb public sector pay rises (which led to strikes and demonstrations). A 1995 IMF mission highlighted the sluggish economy, the scarcity of domestic savings and high unemployment, with the large government deficit worsening the balance of payments. The election of a PUP government in August 1998 brought a serious drive to clean up the fiscal accounts, eliminate waste and corruption in state institutions and reform the tax system. By 1999 an operating budget surplus was forecast but borrowing for capital projects was expected to result in an overall deficit of less than 4% of gdp. The 15% VAT was replaced by a sales tax of 8%, with small businesses exempt, but 12% is charged on sales of petroleum products, alcohol and tobacco.

Communications

Formerly the only means of inland communication were the rivers, with sea links between the coastal towns and settlements. The Belize River can be navigated by light motor boats, with enclosed propellers, to near the Guatemalan border in most seasons of the year, but this route is no longer used commercially because of the many rapids. The Hondo River and the New River are both navigable for small boats for 100 miles or so. Although boats continue to serve the sugar industry in the north, the use of waterborne transport is much diminished.

Some 1,721 miles of roads, of which 20% are paved, connect the eight towns and many villages in the country. Many of the dirt roads are of high quality, smooth and well-maintained, but in outlying areas others are impassable in the wet season. There are road links with Chetumal, the Mexican border town, and the Guatemalan border town of Melchor de Mencos. The main roads are the Northern Highway (from the Mexican border at Santa Elena to Belize City via Orange Walk), the Western Highway (from Belize City to the Guatemalan border at Benque Viejo del Carmen via San Ignacio), the Hummingbird Highway (from the Western Highway at Belmopan to Dangriga on the coast), the new Coastal Highway (from La Democracia on the Western Highway also to Dangriga) and the Southern Highway (from the Hummingbird Highway six miles west of Dangriga to Punta Gorda further down the coast).

The road system has been upgraded in the interests of tourism and further improvements are planned. There are no railways in Belize.

Government

Belize is a constitutional monarchy; the British monarch is the chief of state, represented by a Governor-General, who is a Belizean. The head of government is the Prime Minister. There is a National Assembly, with a House of Representatives of 29 members (not including the Speaker) elected by universal adult suffrage, and a Senate of eight: five appointed by the advice of the Prime Minister, two on the advice of the Leader of the Opposition, one by the Governor-General after consultation. General elections are held at intervals of not more than five years.

El Salvador

6

El Salvador

Essentials

Planning your trip

El Salvador is the smallest, most densely populated and most integrated of the Central America republics. Its intermont basins are a good deal lower than those of Guatemala, rising to little more than 600 metres at the capital, San Salvador. Across this upland and surmounting it run two more or less parallel rows of volcanoes, 14 of which are over 900 metres. The highest are Santa Ana (2,365 metres), San Vicente (2,182 metres), San Miguel (2,130 metres), and San Salvador (1,893 metres). One important result of this volcanic activity is that the highlands are covered with a deep layer of ash and lava which forms a porous soil ideal for coffee planting.

San Salvador is a cosmopolitan city with a variety of architectural styles. Its history has been dogged by earthquakes, the last being in 1986. The city centre is always busy and is not safe at night, so newcomers are best advised to head to the western areas around Boulevard de los Héroes, with its shopping malls and restaurants, and the residential districts of Escalón and the Zona Rosa. If the city is not to your taste, the Pacific coast is only a short drive away and **La Libertad** is a good place from which to start exploring the Balsam coast and the surfing beaches.

Throughout the country volcanoes dominate the landscape and the scenery is one of El Salvador's main attractions. Even close to the capital, **Parque Balboa** affords fine views through the dramatic Puerta del Diablo (the Devil's Door). Below the park is **Panchimalco**, an old village with a growing handicarft industry. **Cerro Verde National Park**, just west of San Salvador is a popular excursion for its prospect over Izalco and Santa Ana volcanoes and the beautiful Lago de Coatepeque. Also a short distance west of the capital are the country's main archaeological sites, **San Andrés** and the unique **Joya de Cerén**, where a Maya settlement has been preserved under volcanic ash, no grand temples and sculptures, just dwellings and everyday objects. Also in this part of the country is the site of Tazumal. The main city of the west is **Santa Ana**, but there are other towns and villages which can be visited on the various routes that lead to Guatemala. There are very few pockets of undisturbed land, mainly because El Salvador is farmed intensively. On the border with Guatemala and Honduras is **Montecristo**, a remnant of cloud forest administered jointly by the three countries, while another such survivor is **El Imposible**, which, as its name suggests, is not easy to get to.

North of San Salvador, near the Honduran border, is the town of **La Palma**, where handicrafts of brightly-painted wood and other styles are made. Also north, but heading more to the east is **Suchitoto**, one of the best-preserved colonial towns. In eastern El Salvador are the cities of **San Vicente** and **San Miguel** and the port of La Unión/Cutuco. There are many small traditional towns here, too, and those interested in the recent civil war can visit **Ciudad Segundo Montes**, north of San Miguel, where refugees have been repatriated close to the guerrillas' former headquarters of **Perquín**. The beaches of the **Costa del Sol** are definitely worth a stop for their long stretches of sand and estuaries. The **Gulf of Fonseca**, too, has islands with secluded beaches which you can explore. In some parts of the country the infrastructure for tourism is quite rudimentary, but in others (such as in the capital, in the places of interest nearby and some of the beach resorts), it is well-developed. As it is a small country, many facilities are designed for people driving from San Salvador for the day or weekend, but the independent traveller should not be put off as there is an efficient bus network and one of the few remaining passenger trains in Central America (San Salvador to Metapán, via Aguilares and Texistepeque).

The rainy season for the whole country is May to October, sometimes stretching into April and November. September and October can be very wet, but not every year. Highest temperatures and humidity will be found on the coast and in the lowlands, with the heat at its greatest in March to May. The coolest months are December to February. Resorts inland and especially on the coast are busiest at weekends and holiday times.

Business is active all year round, except in August, which is the holiday season. Christmas and Easter periods should also be avoided by business visitors. Business is centralized in the capital, but it is as well to visit Santa Ana and San Miguel.

Finding out more Local information can be got from the Corporación Salvadoreña de Turismo (Corsatur), Boulevard del Hipódromo 508, Col San Benito, San Salvador, T2430427, F2787310. Other sources of information: *Discover El Salvador* is a hotel book with tourist information available from Leonor Alvarenga de Castellanos, 1a C pte Condominio Montemaria, Edif A#2B, T/F503-2980127. See also *Useful Websites* under **Further reading** below.

Before you travel

Getting in **Documents** Every visitor must have a valid passport. No visas or tourist cards are required for nationals of the following countries staying 30 days: Argentina, Austria, Belgium, Chile, Colombia, Denmark, Finland, France, Germany, Iceland, Ireland, Israel, Italy, Japan, Liechtenstein, Luxembourg, Netherlands, Norway, Panama, Paraguay, South Korea, Spain, Sweden, Switzerland, United Kingdom, Costa Rica, Guatemala, Honduras, Nicaragua. All other nationalities require a visa, which costs US$30 in advance for a 30-day stay, or a tourist card which can be obtained at the frontier for US$10, payable in dollars. Overstaying the limit on a tourist card can result in fines of US$3-7 a month. A visa application form should be requested from your nearest Salvadorean embassy/consulate that will detail the requirements and cost. Evidence of your travel plans may be requested. Allow two weeks for processing. A few nationalities, including Cuba, require a visa with prior authorization. Immigration officials can authorize up to 90 days stay in the country, extensions may be permitted on application to Migración, Centro de Gobierno (see under San Salvador). Multiple entry visas are only permitted to US citizens.

Special arrangements can be made for business visitors, journalists, those wishing to study in El Salvador, residency/work permits et cetera requiring authenticated documents to support the application, for example photographs, police good conduct reports, certificates of good

El Salvador

El Salvador embassies and consulates

Belgium, *Av de Tervuren 171, 2nd Flr, 1150 Brussels, T7330485.*

Canada, *151 Bloor St, West Suite 320, Toronto, M5S 1S4, Ontario, T416-9750812, also 209 Kent St, Ottawa, K2P 1Z8, T613-2382939; 1080 Beaver Hall, Bureau 1064, Montréal, Quebec, T514-8616515.*

France, *12 rue Galilée, 75116 Paris, T331-47239803.*

Germany, *Adenaueralle 238, D-53113 Bonn 1, T228-49549913.*

Italy, *Via Gualtiero Castellini 13, scala B int, 3, 00197 Roma, T396-8066605.*

Japan, *Kowa 38, Building 803, Nishi Azabu, Ch, Japan 106, T403-34994461.*

Spain, *Calle Serrano 114, 2°Edif Izquierda, 28006 Madrid, T311-5658002.*

UK, *Tennyson House, 159 Great Portland St, London W1N 5FD, T0171 436 8282, visa information line T0891 444 580.*

USA, *embassy: 2308 Calif St NW, Washington DC, 20008, T202-3876511; consulates at 1212 North Broadway Av, Suite 100, Santa Ana, CA 92701, T714-5423246, 46 Park Ave, 2nd floor, New York, NY10016, T212-8893608, 870 Market St, Suite 508, San Fransisco, CA, T415-7817924, and 300 Biscayne Blvd Way, Suite 1020, Miami, FL 33131, T305-3718850 (others in Los Angeles, New Orleans, Chicago, Houston, Dallas and Boston)*

health, with varying charges up to US$100. Business visas can be arranged in 48 hours.

Always check at a Salvadorean consulate for changes to these rules.

Journalists should register on arrival with the Secretaría Nacional de Comunicaciones (SENCO), T2710058, office near the Casa Presidencial.

Customs All personal luggage is allowed in free. Also allowed: 50 cigars or 200 cigarettes, and two litres of liquor, two used cameras or a video recorder, one tape machine, one portable computer or typewriter and new goods up to US$500 in value (best to have receipts). There are no restrictions on the import of foreign currency; up to the amount imported and declared may be exported. The import and export of local currency is limited to 200 colones, although at land borders you may bring in more. All animal products are prohibited from importation, with the exception of boned, sterilized and hermetically sealed meat products. Fruits are inspected carefully and destroyed if necessary. Hide, skins and woollen goods will be fumigated against disease. Animals must be free of parasites, fully inoculated and have a veterinary certificate and import permit. **NB** If electing to go through the 'Nothing to Declare' channel at the airport, you must not be carrying more than three bags.

Money

Currency The unit is the colón (¢), divided into 100 centavos. Banknotes of 5, 10, 25, 50 and 100 colones are used, and there are nickel coins for one colón, and for fractional amounts. The colón is often called a peso. Black market trading is done in the street, but *casas de cambio* may give better rates. If arriving by air, change money at the airport for convenience. Do not find yourself in the countryside without cash: travellers' cheques

Prices in El Salvador are sometimes quoted in US dollars. Make sure which currency is being used.

and credit cards are of no use outside cities. See under San Salvador, **Banks**, regarding exchange of travellers' cheques. Most hotels and lodging places accept US$ cash and many, except the smallest, accept credit cards. Branches of *Pollo Campero* (fastfood) in San Salvador, San Miguel and Santa Ana accept US$ cash at a rate slightly worse than the bank rate, open 0700-2100 daily. Always have some cash dollars available for emergencies, but do not advertise to anyone that you are carrying dollars in cash. Credit cards are accepted in most upscale establishments. Transactions are subject to five percent commission and are charged at the official rate. There are international Visa ATMs in El Salvador, but none for Mastercard. For cash advances on Visa or Mastercard, go to **Aval-Visa** or certain banks in San Salvador, see page 805. **NB** Dollars can be bought easily in San Salvador and you should exchange all remaining colones into dollars before leaving the country for Guatemala or Honduras, where colones may only be changed at international bus terminals at unfavourable rates. For tipping, US dollar bills have more prestige than local currency, even at lower value.

Getting there

Air **From Europe** To Miami with any transatlantic carrier, thence to San Salvador with American or Taca. Iberia flies from Barcelona and Madrid via Miami, where you change planes.

From the USA Apart from Miami other cities with flights to San Salvador are: Atlanta (Delta, American), Greenville/Spartanburg Hartford (Delta), Houston (American, Continental, Taca), New Orleans (American, Taca), Los Angeles (United, Taca), San Francisco (Taca, United), New York (Continental, Taca), Washington (Taca, Continental). **From Canada** Toronto (Lacsa).

From Central America From Belize City (Taca), Guatemala City (Copa, Taca, Aviateca, Lacsa), Managua (Aviateca, Copa, Taca), Mexico City (Aviateca, Taca), Panama City (Taca, Copa), Roatán (Taca), San José (Taca, Lacsa, Copa), San Pedro Sula (Taca), Tegucigalpa (Taca). See **Introduction and Hints** for the Visit Central America Programme air pass.

From South America From various Colombian cities, including Bogotá, Caracas, Guayaquil, Quito, Lima and Santiago (Chile) with Lacsa via San José or Copa via Panama City.

From the Caribbean From Havana (Lacsa). Several other islands are connected through Panama City for example Kingston (Copa), Port-au-Prince (Copa), San Juan (Copa or Lacsa), or through Miami.

Touching down

Airport tax There is a 13 percent tax on international air tickets bought in El Salvador. There is also an airport tax of US$24.70 (215 colonies, dollars accepted), if staying more than six hours. MCO tickets can be bought.

Border taxes Border formalities tend to be relatively brief, although thorough searches are common. There is an entry and an exit tax of about US$0.65 (¢5). These taxes are payable only at the 'colecturía' office at borders; do not pay any other official.

Conduct Because tourism infrastructure is rebuilding, visitors may need some patience. They should also expect curiosity towards tourists of an unkempt appearance. Some rudeness has been reported, as has unwarranted attention towards women, but most El Salvadoreans are friendly and eager to practice English. El Salvadoreans are not used to the custom of foreigners spending long hours writing and talking in a café. San Salvador has few places where foreigners gather (so far). Better for this are La Libertad, Zunzal and recognized tourist areas.

Safety The legacy of many years of civil war is still visible in certain areas. In addition, poverty abounds. Peace has left many ex-combatants armed but unemployed, which, together with the enforced return from the USA of Salvadorean gang members, has led to the unenviable distinction of El Salvador having the worst levels of violent crime on the continent. Robbery at gunpoint is common, especially in the countryside and of people in cars. Since March 1996, the army and the civil police (PNC) have been patrolling the highways in an effort to reduce

Touching down

Official time *Time in El Salvador is six hours behind GMT.*
Hours of business *0800-1200 and 1400-1730 Monday to Friday; 0800-1200 Saturday. Banks in San Salvador 0900-1700 Monday to Friday, 0900-1200 Saturday; different hours for other towns given in text. Government offices: 0800-1600 Monday to Friday.*
IDD *503. Equal tones with long pauses means it is ringing. Equal tones with equal pauses indicate it is engaged.*
Voltage *110 volts, 60 cycles, AC (plugs are American, two flat pin style). Supply is far from stable; mains supply alarm clocks will not work and important electrical equipment should have surge protectors.*
Weights and measures *The **metric system** is used alongside certain local units such as the vara (836 millimetres, 32.9 inches), manzana (7,000 square metres, or 1.67 acres), the libra (0.454 kilograms, about one English pound), and the quintal of 100 libras. Some US weights and measures are also used. US gallons are used for gasoline and quarts for oil.*

crime. Do not stop for lone gunmen dressed in military-looking uniforms. Vehicle theft is very common. If renting a car, buy a steering lock. Visitors to San Salvador should seek advice on where is not safe inside and outside the city.

Foreigners are prohibited from participating in politics by Salvadorean law. Stay clear of any student rallies. It is wise not to camp out. Be prepared for police checks and possibly body searches on buses (the officers are polite, if respected).

You are strongly advised to register with your embassy if staying for more than just a few days. Carry your Embassy's phone number with you. The British consulate, for example, advises on local legal procedures, lawyers, English-speaking doctors, help with money transfers and with contacting banks or relatives, and will make local hospital visits. The consulate cannot give free legal advice, supply money or obtain employment or accommodation. The services it does provide are only for those who have registered. Other consulates may provide the same services, but you should find out in advance what your own country's diplomatic procedures are.

Tipping In up-market restaurants: 10 percent, in others, give small change. Nothing for taxi-drivers except when hired for the day; airport porters, *boinas rojas*, US$1 per bag; haircut US$0.20, not obligatory.

Where to stay

Hotels Do not check into the first hotel you come to: if you have the time, shop around. There are new places opening all the time.

Getting around

Train Passenger rail services exist in some rural areas.

Bus Transport is difficult for the budget traveller, as many of the cheaper buses do not have space for luggage. It is better to arrive from Guatemala or Honduras by Pullman or luxury bus, which have good luggage security. Bus services are good and cover most areas every 15-30 minutes, although buses themselves are usually crowded and their drivers are not always very careful. The best time to travel by bus is 0900-1500; avoid Friday and Sunday pm. The buses are always brightly painted, particularly so around San Miguel. Bags on bus seats will be charged as passengers. Roof racks are rare.

Car At the border, after producing a driving licence and proof of ownership, you are given a *comprobante de ingreso* (which has to be stamped by immigration, customs and quarantine) costing 100 colones to stay for 60 days. You receive a receipt, vehicle permit and vehicle check document. Under no circumstances may the 60 days be extended, even though the driver may have been granted 90 days in the country. Other fees for bringing a car in amount to 50 colones. A few kilometres from the border the *comprobante* will be checked. Leaving the country, a *comprobante de ingreso*, must be stamped again and, if not intending to return, your permit must be surrendered; total cost 15 colones. Do not overstay your permitted time if you do not wish to be fined. Leaving the country for a few days in order to return for a new permit is not recommended as customs officials are wise to this and may demand bribes. To bring a vehicle in permanently involves a complex procedure costing thousands of dollars. A good map, both of republic and of capital, can be obtained from Texaco or Esso, or from the Tourist Institute. Petrol costs per US gallon US$2.25 (*sin plomo, leadfree*), US$2.25 (super), US$2 (regular), US$1.30 (diesel). Roads are generally good throughout the country, but look out for crops being dried at the roadside or in central reservations. Take care of buses, which travel very fast, and other forms of bad driving.

Insurance: compulsory third party programme in El Salvador (can be arranged at the border, enquire first at consulates). Under the 1996 seat-belt law, you must wear one: fine for not doing so is US$34. The fine for driving intoxicated is US$55. Do not attempt to bribe officials.

Selling a vehicle is possible, older (that is cheaper) and diesel cars/vans preferred. You need a good lawyer (ask at your embassy for guidance), visits to the Ministerio de Hacienda (Finance Ministry) and Aduana (Customs) required and you must find a buyer. There are dealers on the outskirts of San Salvador towards Santa Ana. A time consuming process.

Hitchhiking　Hitchhiking is comparatively easy.

Keeping in touch

Language　Spanish, but English is widely understood in business circles. Spanish should be used for letters, catalogues et cetera.

Postal services　Air mail to and from Europe can take up to one month, but normally about 15 days, US$0.35; from the USA, one week. Certified packets to Europe cost US$9.40, good service; swifter, but more expensive is EMS (US$23 to Europe). Courier services are much quicker, but cost more. The correct address for any letter to the capital is 'San Salvador, El Salvador, Central America'. The main post office is at the Centro de Gobierno.

Telephone services　ANTEL, the state telecommunications company, was privatized in 1998 and was split into CTE (Corporación de Telecomunicaciones de El Salvador) for the terrestrial phone network, and

Emergency numbers:
Police 121
(In San Salvador) Fire
Service 2712227
Red Cross 2225155
Hospital 2254481
Maternity 2210128

Intelsa for cellular services. The market has been opened up to competition and a number companies operate. T114 for information (English spoken) and details on new phone numbers in San Salvador. The charge for a local telephone call is 75 centavos for three minutes. New phones are being introduced, some which accept cards, others which accept all coins. To make international calls from private phones, each company has its own access code: Salnet 147 + 0 + codes, El Salvador Telecom dial 156, CTE Antel dial 155, Telefónica dial 144; the companies are competitive on rates especially to the USA, look for the adverts in the *Diario de Hoy* and *Prensa Gráfica*. A private call, fax or telex to Europe costs US$5 per minute (if made from private telephones or CTE). To the USA, the rate depends on which part of the country you are calling. Cheap rate for calls to Europe starts at 2400, to the USA at 2000. Calls made from hotels are more expensive. Direct dialling is available to Europe, three minutes, minimum, USA (US$1.30 per minute) and other parts of the world. For collect calls to USA, Mexico and Central America, dial 113 from any public phone, 120 from a private phone. No collect calls to Europe (except to Spain), Australia or Asia. For long-distance calls within El Salvador, T110 for enquiries, national collect calls and to leave messages (*citas*) at CTE; international long-distance 119; US Sprint operator 191; MCI operator 195; AT&T 8001785 (bilingual service).

Public fax and telex at CTE. British business travellers can use the telex system at the Embassy.

Newspapers In San Salvador: *Diario de Hoy* (right wing) and *La Prensa Gráfica* (centre) every **Media**
morning, including Sunday; both have the most complete listings of cultural events in San
Salvador. *Co Latino* is a left wing newspaper. *El Mundo* in the afternoons, except Sunday.
Relatively new is *La Noticia*, weekly, popular. There are provincial newspapers in Santa Ana,
San Miguel (for example *Periódico de Oriente*, weekly) and elsewhere. *Tendencias* is a leftish
monthly magazine. US newspapers and magazines available at leading hotels and **The
Bookshop**, Galerías, Paseo Escalón, San Salvador. British newspapers can be read at the
British Club.

Radio There are 80 radio stations: one is government owned, several are owned by
churches.

Television There are four commercial television stations, all with national coverage, and one
government-run station with two channels. There are three cable channels, all with CNN
news, et cetera. All luxury and first class hotels and some guesthouses in San Salvador have
cable for guests.

Food and drink

Try *pupusas*, stuffed *tortillas* made of corn or ricemeal, in several varieties, including **Local cuisines**
chicharrón, pork; *queso*, cheese; *revueltas*, typical, tasty and cheap. They are sold at many street
stalls, and are better there than at restaurants, but beware stomach infection. On Saturday
and Sunday nights people congregate in *pupuserías*. *Pavo* (turkey) is common and good, as
are the red beans (*frijoles*). *Tortillas* in El Salvador are smaller, but thicker than in neighbouring
countries. A *boca* is an appetizer, a small dish of yucca, avocado or chorizo, served with a drink
before a meal. Do not eat in restaurants whose menus do not give prices; you will very likely
be overcharged. Apart from San Salvador, restaurants tend to close early, around 2000.

Coffee makes an excellent souvenir and is good value. Beers: *Suprema* is stronger than **Drink**
Pilsener, while *Golden Light* is a reduced alcohol beer.

Shopping

Turtle products, live and stuffed birds, live orchids and cacti, reptile skin handicrafts are sold
on the streets of the capital, despite being prohibited by law. The División Medio Ambiente of
PNC is helpful if you wish to complain: 5 Calle Poniente entre 77 y 79 Avenida Norte, Col
Escalón, San Salvador.

Holidays and festivals

The usual ones are 1 January, Holy Week (three days, government 10 days), 1 May, 10 May,
Corpus Christi (half day), first week of August, 15 September, 2 and 5 November (half day), 24
December (half day) and Christmas Day. Government offices are also closed on religious
holidays. Little business in Easter Week, the first week of August, and the Christmas-New Year
period. Banks are closed for balance 29, 30 June and 30, 31 December.
   Look in the newspapers for details of regional fiestas, rodeos and other fairs. There are
many artesan fairs, for example at San Sebastián and San Vicente, which are worth a visit but
which go largely unnoticed in the capital.

Health

The gastro-enteritic diseases are most common. Visitors should take care over what they eat **Health/disease**
during the first few weeks, and should drink *agua cristal* (bottled water). Specifics against **risks**
malaria should be taken if a night is spent on the coast, especially in the east of the country.
Cases of dengue have been reported, even in the capital city. The San Salvador milk supply is
good, and piped water is relatively pure. For diarrhoea, mild dysentry and parasitic infections

get *Intestinomicina* tablets from any chemist or large supermarket. For amoebic dysentry take *Nor-Ameb Forte* tablets. Also effective for stomach ailments are *Yodocclorina* tablets available at chemists and supermarkets.

Further reading

For information about investment and export, see '*El Salvador is Your Best Buy*,'from FUSADES, Boulevard Santa Elena, Urbanización Santa Elena, Antiguo Cuscatlán, La Libertad, El Salvador (off the road to Santa Tecla, Pan American Highway, to southwest of the capital) T2783386, F2783354 (in USA Vip Sal No 1313, PO Box 02-5364, Miami, FL 33102-5364, T1-800-7888144). *Rincón Mágico de El Salvador* and *El Salvador Prehistórico*, both available at Banco Agrícola Comercial, Paseo Escalón 3635, San Salvador (US$72). The El Salvador Iguana Foundation (a private project in aid of the environment) publishes an illustrated book on the country, tourism and business, US$15, in English and Spanish; Alex Salaverino, Apartado Postal 121 Calle G, San Salvador, T8861524 (cellular), F2793276. *Amor de Jade*, by Walter Raudales, to be published in English too, is a novel based on the life of El Salvador's Mata Hari (now ex-comandante Joaquín Villalobos'wife). See also the novels of Manlio Argueta, *Un día en la vida* (1980) and *Cuzcatlán, donde bate la mar del sur* (1986), both about peasants during El Salvador's conflict.

Useful websites: For information on El Salvadorean political and social issues, see Center for Investigation of El Salvadorean Public Opinion (CIOPS) at www.utec.edu.sv (in Spanish). The website www.buscaniguas.com.sv gives access to lots of useful information, as does *El Diario de Hoy* at www.elsalvador.com (look in Otros Sitios for tourist information). Leftist newspaper *Co Latino* at www.colatino.com. *La Prensa Gráfica* newspaper at www.gbm.net/la_prensa_grafica. *Telemovil* has information of activating cellphones in El Salvador (chip US$7). www.telemovil.com. For advice on the next hurricane season go to www.huracan.net.

San Salvador

San Salvador

A city which has suffered from natural and man-made disasters from which it has not had the ability to recover. Probably not a place to stay for long, but the best point to start from to see the many attractions of El Salvador.

San Salvador, the capital, is in an intermont basin on the Río Acelhuate, with a ring of mountains round it. The valley is known as 'Valle de las Hamacas' because of its frequent seismic activity. It is a predominently modern city, but founded on one of the earliest European cities in the Americas. San Salvador was first established by Gonzalo, brother of the *conquistador* Pedro de Alvarado in 1525. The settlement was named in honour of Christ the Saviour who, Pedro believed, had saved him from death in his first attempt to conquer the peoples of Cuscutlán, as the region wasknown. In 1528 the town was moved to a site near present-day Suchitoto and 20 years later was relocated to its present site. Over the next three centuries it developed into the capital of the province of San Salvador. The city has been destroyed by earthquakes 14 times since 1575, the last being in 1986. Nowadays the buildings are designed to withstand seismic shocks.

Population
Central city: 800,000
Including outlying
suburbs:
2.3m (estimated);
Altitude: 680m
Colour map 4, grid C3

Ins and outs

The international airport (SAL) is at Comalapa, 46 kilometres southeast of San Salvador towards Costa del Sol beach, reached by a 4-lane, toll highway which is to be lit all the way. Some domestic flights use the old airport at Ilopango, 13 kilometres east of the capital. Most international buses arrive at the Puerto Bus terminal, Alameda Juan Pablo II y 19 Avenida Norte, although luxury services and Tica Bus have their own terminals. Domestic bus lines use terminals at the east, south and west ends of the city. Full details are given under **Buses Long Distance** below.

Getting there

The main focal points of the city are the historical centre, the commercial district around Bou-levard de los Héroes and the residential and commercial districts of Escalón and Zona Rosa further west. City buses and taxis are needed to get between the three (see **Local transport**, below).

Getting around

Four broad streets meet at the centre: Avenida Cuscatlán and its continuation Avenida España run south to north, Calle Delgado and its continuation Calle Arce from east to west. This principle is retained throughout: all the *avenidas* run north to south and the *calles* east to west. The even-numbered *avenidas* are east of the central *avenidas*, odd numbers west; north of the central *calles*, they are dubbed Norte, south of the central *calles* Sur. The even-numbered *calles* are south of the two central *calles*, the odd numbers north. East of the central *avenidas* they are dubbed Oriente, west of the central *avenidas* Poniente. Although it sounds complicated, this system is really very straightforward, and can be grasped quickly.

The *climate* is semi-tropical and healthy, the water-supply relatively pure. Days are often hot, especially in the dry season, but the temperature drops in the late afternoon and nights are usually pleasantly mild. Since it is in a hollow, the city has a very bad smog problem, caused mainly by traffic pollution.

Sights

A number of important buildings are near the main intersection. On the east side of Avenida Cuscatlán is the **Plaza Barrios**, the heart of the city. A fine equestrian statue looks west towards the renaissance-style **Palacio Nacional** (1904-11). To the north is the **new cathedral**, which was left unfinished for several years after Archbishop Romero suspended its construction (to use the money to alleviate poverty). Work was resumed in 1990 and completion was due in 1999, the last consecration of a cathedral in the millennium. To the east of the Plaza Barrios, on Calle Delgado, is the **Teatro Nacional** (the interior has been magnificently restored). If you walk along 2 Calle Oriente you come on the right to the **Parque Libertad**: in its centre is a flamboyant monument to Liberty looking east towards the rebuilt church of El Rosario where José Matías Delgado, father of the independence movement, lies buried. The **Palacio Arquiepiscopal** is next door. Not far away to the southeast (on 10 Avenida Sur) is another rebuilt church, **La Merced**, from whose bell-tower went out Father Delgado's tocsin call to independence in 1811.

Across Calle Delgado, opposite the theatre, is **Plaza Morazán**, with a monument to General Morazán. Calle Arce runs west to the **Hospital Rosales**, in its own gardens. On the way to the Hospital is the great church of **El Sagrado Corazón de Jesus**, which is well worth a visit, don't miss the stained glass windows. Turn left (south) here and you come after one block to the **Parque Bolívar**, with the national printing office to the south and the Department of Health to the north. Four streets north of Calle Arce is the Alameda Juan Pablo II, on which stands **Parque Infantil**, in which is the Palacio de los Deportes. One block west is the **Centro de Gobierno**, with many official buildings. New offices are under construction further west between 17 and 19 Avs Norte.

The north side of Parque Bolívar is Calle Rubén Darío (2 Calle Poniente), which becomes Alameda Roosevelt, then Paseo General Escalón as it runs through the commercial and residential districts west of the centre. Heading west this boulevard

San Salvador west

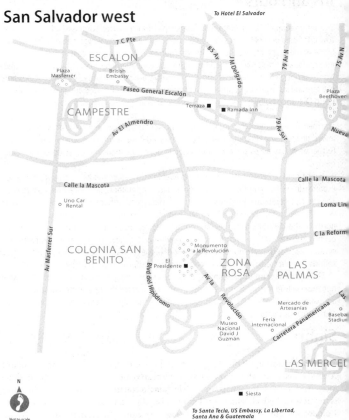

To Hotel El Salvador

7 C Pte

ESCALON

85 Av N · JM Delgado · 79 Av N · 75 Av N

Plaza Masferrer

British Embassy

Plaza Beethoven

Paseo General Escalón

CAMPESTRE

Terraza ■ · ■ Ramada Inn

Av El Almendro

79 N 15 Av

Nueva

Calle la Mascota

Calle la Mascota

Uno Car Rental

Loma Lin

Av Masferrer Sur

C la Reform

COLONIA SAN BENITO

Monumento a la Revolución

El Presidente ■

ZONA ROSA

LAS PALMAS

Blvd del Hipódromo

Av la Revolución

Mercado de Artesanias

Carretera Panamericana

Feria Internacional

Baseba Stadiu

Museo Nacional David J Guzmán

LAS MERCEI

Related map
A Overlap with
San Salvador East,
page 794

N

Not to scale

■ Siesta

To Santa Tecla, US Embassy, La Libertad,
Santa Ana & Guatemala

first passes **Parque Cuscutlán**. A major junction is with 49 Avenida: to the south this avenue soon passes the national stadium, **Estadio Olímpico Flor Blanca**, before becoming the main highway to the international airport. To the north, 49 Avenida crosses Alameda Juan Pablo II. Beyond this junction it changes name to **Boulevard de los Héroes**, on which are the fashionable shopping centres, Metrocentro and the newer Metrosur, the *Camino Real* hotel, some of the city's better restaurants and a glut of fast food places, a busy area at all times, especially at night. At the Shell station by Metrocentro, mariachis and other musicians gather each evening, waiting to be hired; others wander around the restaurants, playing to the diners.

Continuing west along Alameda Roosevelt, the next landmark is the **Monumento Al Salvador del Mundo**, a statue of Jesus standing on the Earth atop a column, in the middle of the Plaza Las Américas. From this junction the Carretera Panamericana heads southwest to Santa Tecla. Straight ahead is **Paseo General Escalón**, Parque Beethoven and an area with many restaurants, shops and the Colonia Escalón residential district. Another important residential and entertainment region is the **Zona Rosa** and **Colonia San Benito**, reached either from the Carretera Panamericana, or from Escalón. In this leafy suburb, some of the most elegant restaurants and the *Hotel Presidente* are found.

Worth visiting is the **Maria Auxiliadora Church**, situated in Barrio San Miguelito. This multi-coloured marble temple is one of the city's landmarks,

displaying a Venetian clock tower. There is a spectacular view of the city from the bell-tower.

Museums

Museo Nacional David J Guzmán, opposite Feria Internacional on Avenida de la Revolución y Carretera a Santa Tecla, has been under reconstruction for several years (1999); the only operating archaeological museums until the new museum has been built are at Joya de Cerén and Tazumal (see pages 817 and 821). **Museo de Historia Nacional**, see below. **Museo de Ciencias Físicas Stephen Hawking**, Av Reforma 179, Col San Benito, sections on astronomy, ecology, electronics and bio-chemistry. ■ *admission Monday-Friday by appointment only T2233027, Saturday open to the public 1000-1600*. **Museo Militar de las Fuerzas Armadas** behind the presidential palace of San Jacinto at the former Cuartel El Zapote, collection of exhibits of weapons, uniforms and decorations of the armed forces, also weapons captured from FMLN guerrillas.

San Salvador east

Related maps
A Overlap with San Salvador West, page 792
B San Salvador centre, page 796

N

Not to scale

To Airport & Planes de Renderos

■ **Sleeping**
1 Alameda
2 Camino Real
3 Casa Grande
4 Florida's

5 Happy House
6 San Carlos
7 Ximena's Guest House

Excursions

A good **sightseeing tour** of from two to three hours by car starts along Avenida Cuscatlán: it includes the Zoo (which though small, is quiet and attractive ■ *T2700728, Tuesday-Sunday 0900-1600, US$0.60, buses 2 – zoo, and 12 from centre*) and, 550 metres from the zoo, **Saburo Hirao Park and Museum of Natural History,** beautiful Japanese gardens and small, interesting museum(■ *Col Nicaragua, US$0.65, bus 2 – zoo, or 12, Wednesday-Sunday 0900-1600, parking in the grounds US$0.65*). You pass the Casa Presidencial and go on up to the new residential district in the mountain range of **Planes de Renderos**. This place is crowned by the beautiful **Parque Balboa** (good view of city from El Mirador at the foot of the Park). Parque Balboa is a Turicentro, with cycle paths, playground, gardens, et cetera ■ *daily 0800-1800.* From the park a scenic road runs to the summit of **Cerro Chulo**, from which the view, seen through the Puerta del Diablo (Devil's Door), is even better. The Puerta consists of two enormous nearly vertical rocks which frame a magnificent view of the San Vicente volcano. The rocks are very steep but the sides can be climbed for an even better view. A little beyond the car park and drinks stands

at the Puerta is a path climbing up a further summit, from which there are 360° views: to the coast, Lago Ilopango, the capital and volcanoes, including San Salvador, Izalco and Cerro Verde and San Vicente.

There are local buses to Parque Balboa (12, US$0.20 from eastern side of Mercado Central, and 17, from same location to the Mirador), and to Puerta del Diablo (No 12-MC marked 'Mil Cumbres') about every hour. There are reports that mugging is increasingly common at Cerro Chulo; it is unsafe to make the trip alone, and do not be there after dark. At the foot of Cerro Chulo is Panchimalco (see below); the road to Panchimalco and the coast branches off the road to Parque Balboa at the village of Los Planes, some kilometres before the park.

The Teleférico on Cerro San Jacinto overlooking the city and Lago de Ilopango has good views, cafeterías and a children's funfair. Highly recommended. ■*T293-0546/5711, F2930478. Open daily, but best on weekdays, Reached by bus 9 from centre, US$3 return.* **Family Park**, en route to the airport has a nice nature park and trails, discount on pool and drinks. From Terminal Sur take microbus 113(San Luis Talpa) which stops near airport.

Essentials

Check *Guía Activa* Yellow Pages for local telephone numbers, their office is at *Hotel Camino Real* (see below), T2438500.

The city centre is dangerous after dark, but Boulevard de los Héroes, the Zona Rosa and Escalón are relatively safe. At night, though, take taxis even for short distances, including on Boulevard de los Héroes, especially the stretch east of the Esso gas station (known as 'Little America' – lots of crime). Tourist police now patrol Zona Rosa and Puerto de la Libertad on

San Salvador centre

Not to scale

■ **Sleeping**
1 American Guest House
2 Custodio

3 León
4 Nuevo Panamericano
5 Ritz Continental

El Salvador

bicycles day and night; there are plans to extend this to other areas. Consult them if in trouble, only use the emergency number 121 in very serious cases. In general robberies, particularly on crowded city buses, have increased: pickpocketing and bag-slashing are common. In the downtown markets, don't carry cameras, don't wear watches or jewellery and don't flash dollars around. In fact, women are advised not to wear expensive jewellery anywhere; they are also advised to carry a whistle at night, to attract attention in case of assault. If accosted on the street with the word 'Colon', keep walking. Drivers, especially women, should take care at night at traffic junctions where windows should be kept closed (if the glass is tinted, so much the better).

L *Camino Real*, Blvd de los Héroes, T2601333/3888, F2605660, camino@sal.gbm.net (a Westin hotel), completely renovated, smart, formal atmosphere (popular with business visitors), Avis car hire, Taca desk, shop selling souvenirs, postcards, US papers and magazines, also has special deals for weekends and Easter with access to Club Bahia del Sol, 2 young children free with parents. **L** *Hotel El Salvador* (formerly *Sheraton*), T2635444, F2632583, hotelsal@es.com.sv, 11 C Poniente y 89 Av Norte on the slopes of the volcano in Colonia Escalón, outdoor pool, renovated, very pleasant, friendly, security guard on every floor. **L** *Presidente Marriot*, T2434444, F2434912, hydhp@es.com.sv/sansalvador.marriot@salnet.net, Av La Revolución, San Benito, pool, garden, very pleasant, good buffets some nights, excellent service but expensive. *Holiday Inn*, Blvd Santa Elena, T2477000, F2477070, arteproy@ejje.com, luxury 5-star service and prices. **LL** *Princess*, T2984545, F2984742, 5-star with character, President Clinton stayed there once.

AL *Best Western*, T2790377, F2433732, on Autopista Sur, off Pan-American Highway, west of the city, very friendly, restaurant. **AL** *Terraza*, T2630044, F2233223, 85 Av Sur and C Padre Aguilar, 4-star, cable TV, hot water, English spoken, pool, weekly rates available. **AL** *Alameda*, T2600299, F2603011, 43 Av Sur and Alameda Roosevelt, good service, tour information, parking, TV. **AL** *Jesusalén*, C del Mirador 5005, Col Escalón, T2791491, F2791488, pool, restaurant, cable TV, private parking. **AL** *Mediterráneo Plaza*, 15 C Poniente 4319, Escalón, T2634592, F2634612, a/c, cable TV, pool, garden, good. **AL** *Novo Apart Hotel*, T2602288, F2605053, informacion@novoapart-hotel.com, 61 Av Norte 4617 (in cul-de-sac), rooms with bath and kitchen, mini swimming pool, garden, pleasant, US$900 per month. **AL** *Ramada Inn*, T2630033, F2634099, 85 Av Sur and J J Cañas, just off Paseo Escalón, TV, pool, bar, restaurant. **AL** *Suky Aparto-Hotel*, Paseo Escalón, Edif Alpine 5262, T2794009, F2794208. **AL** *Monark*, Cerro Verde Pte, 500 metres from US embassy, T/F2892703, pool, jacuzzi, restaurant, a/c, cable TV. **A** *Austria*, T2240791, F2783105, 1 C Poniente 3843 (between 73 and 75 Av), small, quiet, family atmosphere, English and German-speaking owner, price includes coffee and toast, convenient. Also **A** *Casa Austria*, C Jucuaran, pl G No 1, Santa Elena, 400 metres from US Embassy, hard to find (turn left Blvd Knights of Malta), buses 34, 44, T2783612, F2783105, renovated, clean, popular with business travellers, includes breakfast, good service, parking. **A** *Casa Blanca*, 89 Av Norte 719, T2241830, F2784466, with continental

Sleeping

Prices are without meals unless otherwise stated. In the downtown area, some hotels lock doors very early. Value added tax (IVA) added to bills at major hotels. This tax (13 percent) is not included in our classifications.

■ *on maps
Price codes:
see inside front cover*

El Salvador

(Map of San Salvador showing Parque Centenario, Alameda Juan Pablo Segundo, 5 Calle Ote, 3 Calle Ote, 1 Calle Ote, Mercado Cuartel, Calle Delgado, Parque Libertad, El Rosario, Director General of Police, with avenues 4 Av Nte, 6 Av Nte, 8 Av Nte, 10 Av Nte, 12 Av Nte, 4 Av Sur, 6 Av Sur, 8 Av Sur, 10 Av Sur, 12 Av Sur) breakfast, new, cable TV, with bath, clean, good. **A** *Escalón Plaza*, 89 Av Norte 1416, Col Escalón, T2637480, F2637464, elegant, a/c, cable TV, good value, limited parking. **A** *Hacienda Santa Fé*, C La Ceiba 254, Col Escalón, T/F2984069, a/c, cable TV, bath, phone, includes breakfast, takes credit cards. **A** *Posada Los Abetos*, C Los Abetos 15, Col San Francisco T/F2243260, near the Zona Rosa and the Carretera Panamericana, includes breakfast, quiet, TV, cafetería, discount with this *Handbook*, English, French and German spoken by owner Jill Lacaya. **A** *Myers Guest House*, Av Masferrer, 7a C Pte Bis 5350, T2646725 E hotmyers@quik.elsv.com, bus 52 from terminal, good service plus internet service, recommended.

B *Casa Grande*, C Los Sisimiles y Av Bernal, Col Miramonte, T2747450, F2747471, discount for longer stay, pleasant. **B** *Internacional Puerto Bus*, Alameda Juan Pablo II y 19 Av Norte, at Puerto Bus terminal, T2211000, F2222138, a/c, TV, wake-up service, etc. **B** *Townhouse* Bed and Breakfast, 3 C Poniente 4409, Col Escalón, between Avs 85-87 Norte, T2230247, discount for groups and long stay, very nice, parking, English-speaking owner. **B** *Villa Antigua*, C Mirador 4420, 1 block from *Hotel El Salvador*, T/F2452763, small, colonial-style, includes continental breakfast, reservations required, limited parking. **B** *Casa de Huéspedes Maya*, Pasaje Leo 6E, Ciudad Satélite, T/F2744438, with bath, pool, restaurant, nice patio.

Non-luxury hotels not in the centre **B** *Good Luck*, Av Los Sisimiles 2943, Col Miramonte (turn left at *Camino Real* and go uphill 200 metres), T2601655, F2260476, TV, shower, **C** without a/c, hot water, bright but simple, restaurant, secure parking. **C** *Florida's*, T2602540, F2602654, Pasaje Los Almendros 115, off Blvd de los Héroes, all rooms with bath, fan, laundry service, secure, proprietor speaks English, good value, recommended (near *Camino Real*: popular with journalists). **C** *Grecia Real* Av Sisimiles 2922, Col Miramontes, T261*577, F2601820, with good Greek restaurant, recommended. **C** *Happy House*, Av Sisimiles 2951, Col Miramonte, T2266892, F2266866, good, friendly, often full, parking, restaurant, good breakfast. **C** *International Guest House*, 35 Av Norte 9 Bis, T2267343, towards University, near Cine Variedades, friendly, with bath, good. **D** *Casa Clementina*, Av Morazán y Av Washington 34, Col Libertad, T2255962, very friendly, clean, pleasant, garden. **D** *Occidental*, 49 Av Norte 171, T2237715, renovated building, parking, popular with local business visitors, good. **D** *Ximena's Guest House*, T2602481, F2602427, C San Salvador 202-A, Colonia Centroamérica (René and Lisa Carmona), **C** with cable TV, a variety of rooms, **E** per person in 4-bed dormitory, discounts for long stay, clean, pleasant, cable TV in lobby, kitchen, fresh banana bread and carrot cake daily, breakfast US$1.75, other meals if ordered in advance, conveniently located, but not easy to find (it's roughly behind the Esso station on Blvd de los Héroes, take C Gabriela Mistral from Blvd de los Héroes).

Downtown hotels **NB** If staying in the older downtown area, note that there are few places open to eat after 1830. Restaurants are open late in the western sections of the city. **B** *Ritz Continental*, T2220063, F2229842, 7 Av Sur 219, pool, a/c, big rooms, friendly, quiet, good restaurant, charm of a somewhat run down luxury hotel. **C** *American Guest House*, T2710224, F2713667, 17 Av Norte No 119 entre C Arce y 1 C Poniente, 3 blocks from Puerto Bus, with bath (cheaper without), hot water, fan, helpful, will store luggage, accepts credit cards, discounts for groups, weekly rates, *Cafetería La Amistad*, parking nearby, good. **C** *Family Guest Home*, T2221902, F2212349, 1 C Poniente Bis 925, safe inside (don't walk alone outside late at night), clean, friendly, helpful, expensive meals available, convenient for Puerto Bus (but advise owner if you have an early start), but overpriced and they may overcharge you if you arrive late. **D** *Centro*, 9 Av Sur 410, T2715045, a bit box-like, checkout 0900, TV, phone, friendly, washing facilities, clean, safe, recommended. **D** *San Carlos*, T2228975, C Concepción 121, with bath, early morning call (extra charge), doors locked 2400, cold drinks available, good, resident cockroaches but otherwise clean, Tica bus leaves from outside (ticket reservations in lobby office hours), owner arranges evening tours of the city US$6 per person (don't go into town any other way at night). The following **C-D** hotels can be found in the area round the Universidad Nacional, buses 44 and 30B: *El Torogoz*, Reparto Santa Fe, 35 Av Norte 7B, T2251656, eltorogoz@vianet.com.sv; *Oasis*, Pasaje Santa, Marta 1, zone 9, oasis@es.com.sv; *El izote*, Av izalco, Av 4 No40, T/F2746459; *Internatinal Guest House*, 35 Av Norte, No9 bis, T/F2267343, eltorogoz@vianet.com.sv; *Posada San Jose*, Av A 141, T/F2262100, posadasj@latinmail.com; *Alezas Guest House*, 37 Ave Norte y Las Rosas 24, T/F2251422; *Casa de Huespedes Santa Fe*, 35 Av Norte 14, T2255891; *Villa Antigua*, Las Orquídeas 941, T2260551.

E *Custodio*, T2225503, 10 Av Sur 109, basic, clean, safe, and friendly. **E** *Hospedaje Izalco*, T2222613, C Concepción 666, parking, most rooms with bath, TV lobby, dangerous area after dark. **E** *Imperial*, T2225159, C Concepción 659, serves reasonable meals and has car park, more expensive with toilet and shower. **E** *Nuevo Panamericano*, 8 Av Sur 113, T/F2222959, . with cold shower, safe, closes early (but knock on the door), will do laundry, meals from US$2 and parking space, recommended. **E** *Pensión Rex*, 10 Av north 213, with bath, quiet, safe, run by Sra Rosalinda, recommended. **E** *Roma*, Blvd Venezuela near Terminal de Occidente, good but front rooms noisy. **E** *Yucatán*, C Concepción, shared bath, safe, with parking. **E-F** *León*, T2220951, C Delgado 621, friendly, poor water supply, safe, parking.

F *Hospedaje El Turista*, 1C y 12 Av Norte 210, fan, clean, quiet, dingy, little privacy, does laundry. **F** *Hospedaje España*, 12 Av Norte, No 123, fan, clean, bright, good value. Many cheap *hospedajes* near Terminal de Oriente, dubious safety, not recommended for single women, avoid *La Avenida*. 3 doors along Concepción is **F** *Emperador*, with bath, friendly, good value, clean, laundry facilities on roof, recommended.

On the Paseo General Escalón *Diligencia*, 83 Av Sur, for good steaks, and *El Bodegón*, 77 Av Norte, proprietor Spanish, both excellent. *La Mar*, 75 Av Sur, seafoods, and *Siete Mares*, T2243031, good seafood. *Asia* moderately priced Chinese. *La Fonda del Sol*, No 4920, opposite Villas Españolas shopping centre, Italian, popular with business set, good value, highly recommended. *La Pampa Argentina*, highly recommended for steaks, popular. *Quecos*, opposite Plaza Alegre, Mexican, good variety. *Las Carnitas*, Parque Beethoven, good beef, reasonable prices, less pretentious and costly than similar places. *Rancho Alegre*, Parque Beethoven, good choice of food, relatively cheap, travellers' meeting place, closed Sunday, also at Metrosur, south of Metrocentro, where there is a whole group of different restaurants sharing the same space. *La Fuente*, Leonel Fuentes, 83 Av Norte y 9 C Poniente, Escalón, local food, family-oriented with play park for children, open noon-2100 (T2633188). *Pizzería Capri*, 85 Sur y J J Cañas, 1 block south of Paseo Escalón. *Pastelería Suiza/Salón de Té Lucerna*, 85 Sur y Paseo Escalón 4363. *Le Bavarois* for cakes, in same block as *Mister Donut* and *Biggest*, between 85 and 87. *Beto's Escalón*, Pasaje Dordelly 4352 between 85 and 87 Av Norte (above Paseo Escalón), best seafood in the city, also Italian, great service, parking, recommended. *Sports Bar and Grill*, lower level Villavicencio Plaza, Paseo Escalón y 99 Av Norte, 1 block below Redondel Masferrer, 1100-2400 Monday-Thursday, 1100-0200 Friday-Saturday, 1100-2200 Sunday, good varied menu, popular, English-speaking owner, friendly staff, trendy, TV screens, American-football theme. *Tacos* and *pupusas* at Redondel Masferrer, good view over the city, lively atmosphere, mariachis. In Colonia Escalón, *Rosal*, 93 Av Norte y C El Mirador, near *Hotel El Salvador*, Italian, good. *Kamakura*, 93 Av Norte 617, T2231274, Japanese, expensive, good.

Eating
● *on maps*

In the **Metrocentro area** on Boulevard de los Héroes there are many restaurants, including US and US-style fast food places. *Neskazarra*, C Sierra Verde 3008, Col Miramonte, T2268936, Basque, moderately priced, good. *Pueblo Viejo*, in Metrosur, T2985318, open 1100-2000, popular for lunch, local and steak dishes, including *parrillada*, and seafood. *La Casa del Gran Buffet*, between *Camino Real* and Esso, T2258401, all you can eat, lunch and dinner US$9. *Felipe's*, 27 C Poniente off Blvd de los Héroes, popular Mexican, good value. Behind *Camino Real* is a row of restaurants on C Lamatepec: *Hola Beto's*, No 22, T2268621, seafood; *Caminito Real*, No 19, local food, popular, good value, tasty; *Comida Lo Nuestro/Taco Taco*, local food, simple; *Hang Ly*, good Chinese, cheap; *Asia*, also Chinese, good portions, reasonable prices. Restaurant at *Hotel Good Luck* (see above) does good lunch specials, Chinese. *Tabasco*, Gabriela Mistral y Centroamérica, just up from Esso station on Blvd de los Héroes, Mexican, open 1200-2200. *Que Taco*, Av Pasco, Col Miramonte, good Mexican. *La Taberna del Viejo*, C Gabriela Mistral/Av 4 de Mayo 104, *pupusas* a speciality, good service. *Ipanema Grill*, Antigua C San Antonio Abad 1, T2744887, Brazilian chef, good. *La Ventana-El Café*, C San Antonio Abad 2335, T2256893, opposite Centro Comercial San Luis, about 500 metres up from Cine Variedades, European-style, international food, popular with foreigners; open 0800-2400, 0900-2300 Sunday, US and European newspapers, recommended. *El Trapiche*, Av Bernal 587, Col Yumuri, T2604663, Colombian and South American dishes, recommended.

Restaurants in the **Zona Rosa**, Boulevard Hipódromo, San Benito, are generally very good, but expensive. These include: *La Ola*, very good meals and moderately priced; *L'Opera*, C La Reforma 222, T/F2237284, French, good lunch specials, expensive; *Osteria dei Cualtro Galti*, C La Reforma 232, T2231625, Italian, good but expensive; *München*, German; *Paradise*, corner of Reforma, T2244201 for steak and lobster, excellent food and service (*Pizza Hut* next door), another branch on Blvd de los Héroes (all popular); *Basilea/Schaffer's*, nice garden atmosphere and small shopping centre, restaurant and excellent cakes (from *Shaw's Bakery* next door; see also **Coffee shops** below). *Dynasty*, No 738-B, known for best Chinese food in city, but not cheap. Next door is *Madeira*, No 738, T2983451, pleasant atmosphere, international, expensive. Also in San Benito, *Dallas*, T2793551, 79 Av Sur 48, for steaks and seafood, very good, exaggerated service, prices from moderate to expensive, another branch on Autopista Sur (bus 44). Nearby, in Col La Mascota, *El Cortijo Español*, 79 Av Sur y Pasaje A, Spanish. *Texas Meats*, C La Mascota, good for steaks. *Tre Fratelli*, Boulevard Hipódromo 307, moderate and popular.

Others include *China Palace*, Alameda Roosevelt 2731, excellent value (oldest Chinese restaurant in San Salvador); *Pupusería Margot*, opposite Estado Mayor on the road to Santa Tecla, good.

Vegetarian restaurants *La Zanahoria*, C Arce 1144, T2222952. *Govinda's*, 51 Av Norte 147, Col Flor Blanca, T232468, take bus 44 (a bit hard to find, but worth it). *Kalpataru*, Av Masferrer 127, 100 metres north of Redondel Masferrer, T2792306, open 2230, full restaurant service and lunch buffet, nice atmosphere. *El Tao*, 21 Av Norte, C 27 y C 29 Poniente, and Centro de Gobierno, 19 C Poniente, and 19 Av Norte, Col Layco. *Todo Natural*, 39 Av Norte 934, T2259918, near Cine Variedades, good, meals US$2-4, also has rooms **D** per person. *Koradi*, 9 Av Sur y 4 C Poniente. *Arbol de Vida*, 21 Av Norte y Arce.

Branches of fast-food restaurants may be found in many parts of town: *Pizza Hut, Sir Pizza*, good pizzas and pasta, *Toto's Pizza. MacDonalds* and *Biggest* (hamburgers), *Wendy*, Blvd de los Héroes and Paseo Escalón, *Pollo Campero* (fried chicken), *Mr Donut* (US-style breakfasts, pastries, sandwiches, soups, salad, fresh juice, newspapers) at Metrocentro, Paseo Escalón, and elsewhere, open 0700-2000 daily. *Pops* and *Holanda* (ice cream parlours), several outlets throughout town, recommended.

Cafés There are numerous *cafeterías* serving cheap traditional meals such as *tamales, pupusas, frijoles*, rice with vegetables, etc. Often these places can be found around the major hotels, catering for guests who find the hotel meals overpriced. *Café Don Alberto*, C Arce and 15 Av Sur, good and cheap. *Actoteatro*, 1 C Poniente (between 15 and 13 Av north, near *American Guest House*), good atmosphere, patio, music, clown shows and theatre at weekends 1900, good buffet lunch, cheap, central, recommended. *Café de Don Pedro*, Roosevelt y Alameda, next to Esso filling station, good range of food, mariachi groups, open all night another branch in Chiltiapan, near Plaza Merliot Mall, also 24 hour. *Bandidos*, Blvd Hipódromo 131, snacks, drinks, live music Thursday-Saturday, cover US$3, opens 1900. *Café Teatro*, attached to the Teatro Nacional, serves very good lunches, good value (see also *La Ventana* above and **Nightclubs** below).

Comedores Good, cheap *comedores* in Occidente bus terminal. Food markets in various parts of the city have stalls selling cheap food. Gourmet and delicatessen fare at *Señor Tenedor*, Plaza Jardín, Av Olímpica 3544, opposite Ciné Deluxe, 0900-2200, nearest thing to an American deli, good value, breakfast buffet, good choice of salads and sandwiches. *Pronto Gourmet*, lunch counter service, good value. *Kreef Deli*, in Metrosur near Pueblo Viejo, German style, and in Paseo Escalón 77 Av Sur 3945, T2238063. *Comida a la Vista*, buffet *comedores* around centre, clean, cheap.

Coffee shops *Shaw's* (good coffee and chocolates), Paseo Escalón 1 block west of Plaza Beethoven, Zona Rosa (see above) and at Metrocentro, also sell US magazines and greetings cards. *Victoria*, bakery, good for pastries.

Bars *Las Antorchitas*, Blvd de los Héroes, good local orchestra with a dance floor, French and English spoken, cover charge US$1.20. *La Luna*, C Berlín 228, off Blvd de los Héroes, Urb Buenos Aires 3, T225-4987/5054, good mixture of music, different themes each night, shows start 2100-2130, matched well by mixed arty clientèle, very popular, reasonably-priced drinks and snacks, cover charge US$2.30, closed Sunday and Monday, but open for lunch Monday-Friday, 1200-1500, set menu about US$2.50, no cover except Friday Salsa nights, US$6, take taxi late at night. *Club 'M'*, C José Martí 7, San Benito, T2239321, trendy. *Sinatra's Bar*, Centro Comercial Loma Linda, T2245736, piano-bar, expensive. *Villa Fiesta*, Blvd de los Héroes opposite Hospital Bloom, live music, popular, US$6 cover, good. See also *British Club*, and **Nightclubs**, below.

Bars & nightclubs

Clubs *Club Salvadoreño* admits foreigners, owns a fine Country Club on Lago Ilopango called Corinto (with a golf course, green fee US$23), cabins for rent US$30 per day (not holidays), and has a seaside branch at Km 43 on the coast road, near La Libertad, much frequented during the dry season, November to April; T/F2251634, Lic Oscar Paloma, Monday-Friday 0800-1200, 1330-1600. The *Automobile Club of El Salvador* has a chalet for bathing at La Libertad. See also *Atami Beach Club* under La Libertad, page 813. *Club Náutico*, at the Estero de Jaltepeque, famous for its boat races across the mud flats at low tide. *Lips*, Paseo General Escalon 5146, men's club with dancing girls, billiards, casino under construction March 1999.

Nightclubs All leading hotels have their own nightclub. All discos have ladies' night on Wednesday and Thursday when women enter free and get a discount on drinks; go in a group. Zona Rosa, Colonia San Benito, has many bars/discos/open-air cafés in a 5-block area, well-lit, crowded Friday-Saturday night (discos' cover charge is US$7), take bus 306 from near Esso/Texaco/Mundo Feliz on Boulevard de los Héroes before 2000, taxi thereafter. *Mario's* on Blvd Hipódromo, Zona Rosa, with good live music; *Papasitos*, Blvd Los Próceres (Autopista Sur), near *Dallas* restaurant and Cuscatlán tower, popular up-market nightspot, T2735770. *Lapsus*, Paseo Escalón, lively. *Santa Fe*, Av Masferrer Sur 26, T2986217, also lively. *Café Teatro*, by National Theatre, Tuesday-Saturday, jazz on Tuesday, various music other nights. *La Luna*, C Berlín 228, Urb Buenos Aires 3, 2 blocks from Blvd de los Héroes, see under **Bars**, above. *Villa Fiesta*, Blvd de los Héroes Norte, T2262143 for reservation Friday-Saturday, restaurant/bar, Monday-Wednesday Latin music (Grupo Fiesta), Thursday Rumba Seis, Friday-Saturday Latin music with guest bands (cover US$11). *Liverpool*, Blvd Constitución, Col Escalón, good live rock, Tuesday-Saturday (see also *British Club*, below, Friday pm rock). Marimba concerts Saturday and Sunday 1700-2100 at *La Tortuga Feliz*, 4a C Pte 1-5 Santa Tecla; not so happy turtle served in the speciality soup. Check *La Prensa Gráfica* and *El Diario de Hoy*.

Many cinemas, including *Presidente*, near *Hotel Presidente* in Col San Benito. *Colonial*, Col La Sultana, near entrance to the UCA. *Variedades*, C San Antonio Abad. *Beethoven*, Plaza Beethoven, Paseo Escalón. Best quality cinemas cost US$2, films in English with Spanish subtitles. The *Masferrer* 5-screen complex, Redondel Masferrer at end of Paseo Escalón, charges US$3.50, screenings 1500-2100, take bus 52 or taxi late at night. Similarly *Multiplex*, in Galerías Esalón Mall. 'Arthouse' films are shown at *La Luna* (see **Bars**) on Tuesday 1800, free, *Cine Presidente* and *Cine Caribe*, Plaza Las Américas, see press for details. Alliance Française arranges film seasons, T2238084. Ballet and plays at the *Teatro Nacional de Bellas Artes*, and music or plays at the Teatro Cámera. Folk music in *Café Teatro*, in the Teatro Nacional.

Entertainment

During Holy Week, and the fortnight preceding 6 August, are held the celebrations of *El* **Festivals**

El Salvador

Salvador del Mundo. As a climax colourful floats wind up the Campo de Marte (the park encompasssing the Parque Infantil and Palacio de Deportes; 9 Calle Poniente and Avenida España). On 5th August, an ancient image of the Saviour is borne before the large procession: there are church services on the 6th, Feast of the Transfiguration. On **12 December**, Day of the Indian, there are processions honouring the Virgin of Guadalupe in El Salvador (take bus 101 to the Basílica de Guadalupe, on the edge of the city on the Carretera a Santa Tecla, to see colourful processions.)

Shopping *Mercado Cuartel*, crafts market, 8 Av Norte, 1 C Oriente, a few blocks east of the Teatro Nacional, rebuilt after a disastrous fire in 1995. Towels (Hilasal brand) may be bought here with various Maya designs. Good market in the centre on Calle Arce between 2 Avenida Sur and 7 Avenida Sur. Crafts may also be bought at the *Mercado Nacional de Artesanías*, opposite the Estado Mayor on the road to Santa Tecla (buses 101A, B or C, 42B, 79, 34, 30B), at prices similar to the Mercado Cuartel, but better than Metrocentro or elsewhere in San Salvador; most stalls have similar items, open 0800-1800 daily. *Tienda Artesanías La Cosecha*, in Casa Cultural La Mazorca, C San Antonio Abad 1447, T/F2265219, 100 metres north of entrance to university, on left, good prices, large selection (bus 30B, 26, 44). *Acogipiri*, handicapped and women's project, ceramics retail and wholesale, Gabriela Mistral 4, Pasaje 11, No 563, Col Centroamérica, T2267854, F2265269, Eileen Girón Batres (speaks English), eilgiro@es.com.sv. Custom-made handicrafts (pottery, wood, jewellery, jade), antiques at *Pedro Portillo*, Antigua C San Antonio Abad, Urb Lisboa, Casa 3, p 2, T2844753 in advance. *El Arbol de Dios*, La Mascota y Av Masferrer, T2246200, arts & crafts store, restaurant, museum and garden, operated by famed local artist Fernando Llort from La Palma, open Monday-Saturday 1000-2200; *La Cosecha*, centro Cultural La Mazoroca, San Antonio Abad 1447, T2265219, exhibitions and workshop producing T-shirts, posters etc relating to Civil War, also wholesale prices. *Hipe Europa*, on Carretera Santa Tecla, behind Esso gas station, huge variety, open till 2300 Monday-Saturday, Sunday 2000, buses 101, 42, 42b, 79, 30b.

Metrocentro, the large shopping precinct with adequate parking on the Blvd de los Héroes, northwest of the city centre, contains 2 of best known department stores, *Siman* and *Swartz*, together with boutiques, gift shops and a small supermarket. An extension has some 35 further shops, including *El Rosal*, 8a Etapa, Local 278, wide variety of local handicrafts. It is accompanied by another shopping complex, *Metrosur*, to the south, which has fewer shops (0900-2000 Monday-Saturday, 0900-1900 Sunday). Another shopping centre, *Villas Españolas*, is on the Paseo Escalón, 1 block south of the Redondel Masferrer; it is rather more exclusive, with expensive boutiques, several impressive furniture stores, and a minimarket specializing in tinned food from around the world. The supermarket *La Tapachulteca* is on Redondel Masferrer itself. There is another called *Feria Rosa* opposite the Foreign Ministry on the road to Santa Tecla (Pan-American Highway), which is by no means fully occupied; similarly the *Plaza Merliot* in Merliot suburb. Also *Plaza San Benito*, San Benito, with *La Despensa de Don Juan*, best supermarket in the city. Paseo Escalón has a wide variety of boutiques and gift shops in all price ranges. Prices in shopping centres are much higher than in the centre of town. There are also some exclusive shops in the Zona Rosa. *El Sol* and *Europa* are 2 major supermarkets in Plaza Beethoven, Paseo Gen Escalón and Av 75 Norte.

Towels can also be bought in the centre at *Hula Hula*, 2 blocks east of the Cathedral, where there are also street traders. For modern art and antiques try *Galería Rosenthal*, Centro Comercial El Manantial, C Reforma 232, San Benito, run by Pietro Yanelli, T2240158, speaks Italian, some English, helpful. *Viejos Tiempos*, 3 C Poniente entre 9 y 11 Av Norte, Centro, T2226203, Jorge Antonio Sibrian, antiques, frames, odd articles, recommended. Visa and Mastercard are increasingly accepted in shops. Several small galleries and antique shops around Escalón (side streets north of Paseo Escalón); nice gallery/antique store *Sol y Luna*, 7a C Pte, Polish-Salvadorean-owned.

Bookshops At the Universidad de El Salvador (UES) and the Universidad Centroamericana (UCA). *Cervantes*, 9 Av Sur 114 in the Centre and Edif El Paseo No 3, Paseo Escalón. *Bautista* (T2222457), 10 C Poniente 124, religious bookshop. *Cultura Católica*, opposite Teatro

Nacional. *El Arabe* (T2223922) 4 Av Norte. *Clásicos Roxsil* (T2281212), 6 Av Sur 1-6, Santa Tecla. *Editorial Piedra Santa*, 1 C Poniente, 21 Av Norte 1204, T2222147 (bus 29). *Etc Ediciones* in Basilea Shopping Centre, San Benito. *The Book Shop*, Galerías, Local 357, Paseo Gral Escalón at 71 Av Norte (5 blocks from Salvador del Mundo, buses 16, 52), books and magazines in English, good prices, owners Alejandro and Carol Morales speak English, also at Metrocentro 8a Etapa, Local 274, also branches in Guatemala City and San Pedro Sula. *Eutopia*, Av La Capilla 258, San Benito, new and used books, good prices. Regular book fairs at the Teatro Nacional. Some English books at *Librería Cultural Salvadoreña* (T245443) in Metrosur. Others at *Librería Quixaje*, C Arce, and a few at *Shaw's* chocolate shops. American magazines and secondhand books at *La Revista*, Hipódroma 235, Zona Rosa, large selection. Magazines and newspapers in English can be bought at leading hotels (eg *Miami Herald* at *Hotel Presidente*, 1 day old, US$2.25, also *Camino Real*); many shops sell US magazines.

Hairdressing *Pino di Roma*, Colonia San Benito, for ladies, high standards, latest styles, US$10 cut, shampoo and blow-dry. Many unisex parlours all over the city, US$3-US$5.

Tobacco For those interested in cigars: *Timber Box* in *Hotel El Salvador*, T2985444, fine cigars and other tobaccos, accessories, open Monday-Friday 0930-1230, 1330-1900, Saturday 0930-1230, Lic Edward Neuwald Meza.

Sports For all sporting events, check *La Prensa Gráfica* and *El Diario de Hoy*. **Baseball**: on the field opposite Mercado Nacional de Artesanías, Tuesday-Friday 1700, Cuban and US coaches, local teams, admission US$1.25. **Bowling**: at Bolerama Jardín and Club Salvadoreño. **Motor racing**: at new El Jabalí autodrome on lava fields near Quetzaltepeque. **Mountain Bikes**: at *Bike Doctor Racing*, Centro Comercial Juan Pablo II 313A, Blvd San Antonio Abad, T/F2255657. **Rollerskating rink**: Av La Reforma, 100 metres from international school and Spanish Embassy, open daily, large, ample parking, skate rental, bus 30B. **Soccer**: is played on Sunday and Thursday according to programme at the Cuscatlán and Flor Blanca Stadiums. **Tennis/squash**: *Raquet Club Complex*, opposite Hotel El Salvador has 6 tennis courts and 6 squash courts. **Watersport equipment**: *Amphibious*, Centro Comercial Plaza San Benito, C La Reforma 114, local 1-16, T/F3353261, owner Robert Rotherham (and 2 sons), surfboard rental US$15 per day, kayak rental, windsurf lessons, excursions arranged, also deep sea fishing US$180 up to 6 people, English spoken, equipment for sale; also has mountain bike rental.

Transport **Local Bus**: city buses are either blue and white for normal services, or red and white for special services, *preferenciales*. Most routes have both normal and special buses. Fares are ¢1.50 (US$0.18) for normal services, more expensive after 1800; ¢2 (US$0.23) for special services. Most run 0500-2000, after which use taxis. Route 101 buses to/from Santa Tecla are blue and white for either class of service. Some useful routes: 29 from Terminal de Oriente to Metrocentro via downtown; 30 Mercado Central to Metrocentro; 30B from Mundo Feliz (100 metres up from Esso station on Boulevard de los Héroes) to Escalón, 79 Avenida Norte, Zona Rosa (San Benito), Alameda Roosevelt and back to Metrocentro along 49 Avenida; 34 San Benito-Mercado de Artesanías-Terminal de Occidente-Mercado Central-Terminal Oriente; 52 'Paseo' Parque Infantil-Metrocentro-Plaza Las Américas-Paseo Escalón-Plaza Masferrer; 52 'Hotel' Parque Infantil-Metrocentro-*Hotel El Salvador*-Plaza Masferrer. Most buses stop running at 2100.

Car hire: local insurance (about US$10-15 per day plus a deductible US$1,000 deposit) is mandatory and 13 percent IVA applies: rentals from **Avis**, 43 Av Sur 137 (T2242623, F2246272, airport 3399268), also at leading hotels (*Camino Real* 2239103, *El Salvador* 2242710) can rent in advance from abroad. **Uno**, member of Affinity International, Edif Sunset Plaza, Av Masferrer Sur y C Mascota, Col Maquilishuat (bus 101D), T2794127, F2794128, 24-hour emergency service, cellular 2981122, unidad 11988, unorent@gbm.net, www.unorentacar.com/uno, English and French spoken by owner, Xavier Deprez, best prices and service, airport office, office in San Miguel, 24-hour emergency service, cellular phone in vehicles, free transfer from airport, excursions arranged, **Budget**, Cond Balam

El Salvador

Quitzé, 89 Av Sur y Escalón (T2985187, Airport 3399186); **Hertz**, Av Los Andes behind *Hotel Camino Real* (T2268099, Airport 3399481); **Horus**, Cond Balam Quitzé 29, Escalón, T2985858, F2980500; **Tropic Car Rental**, Av Olímpica 3597, Escalón, T2237947, F2793236 (runs tours, has four-wheel drive vehicle, good service). *Colon Renta Autos*, T/F2741410, will collect at hotel, no English spoken. *Sandoval & Co*, T2354405, sub compact late model cars from US$10 per day, English spoken; *Euro Rent-a-Car*, T2355232, near university area, daily rates from US$10; *Granados*, T2749779, has four-wheel drive; *Universal*, 73 Av Norte 239, Col Escalón, T2794767, English spoken.

Taxis: plenty (all yellow), none has a meter, ask fare before getting in. Fares: local journeys 3-4 kilometres US$6 by day, US$6-US$7 at night. On longer trips, negotiate, about US$12 per hour or US$75 for a 6-7 hour day. Few drivers speak English. They will charge more in the rain. More expensive taxis may be hired from: Acontaxis (T2701176/8), Cobra (T2792258), Dos Pinos (T2211285/1286, 2222321), Acomet (T2765136). Taxis Acacya specializes in services to the airport (see below). For airport/beach trips call *Transportes Rapalo*, T2251079, quick service.

Car repairs: Carlos Granicio, San Jacinto, Colonia Harrison T2706830 for general car repairs. Julio Henríquez, *Auto-Inter*, 10 Av Sur 1-7, Santa Tecla, T2288433, 0800-1600 Monday-Friday, speaks English, or contact through René Carmona at *Ximena's Guest House*. *Taller Mundar*, owned by English-speaking José Mungia, Pasaje Carolina Lote #15, Col Paraíso de la Escalón. Be aware that spare parts are hard to come by in El Salvador.

Insurance: Francisco Ernesto Paz, Asesor (for El Salvador and Central American companies), Boulevard de los Héroes, Pasaje Los Angeles 151 (turn right at *Toto's Pizza*), T2257491.

Car papers: Ministerio de Hacienda, 'Tres Torres', turn left on Boulevard de los Héroes 300 metres past Texaco station.

Air The international airport (SAL) at Comalapa is 46 kilometres southeast from San Salvador towards Costa del Sol beach, reached by a 4-lane toll highway (to be lit all the way). Acacya minibus to airport, from 3 Calle Poniente y 19 Avenida Norte (San Salvador T2714937/4938, Airport 3399271/9282), 0600, 0700, 1000, 1400 (be there 15 minutes before), US$3 one-way. (Leave from airport when full, on right as you go out, but unreliable.) Acacya also has a taxi service, US$16, the same as other radio taxi companies; ordinary taxis charge US$18, US$25 at night. A luxury bus service runs to 2 hotels for US$8.50, known as Aerobuses, T2239206, and leaving the airport 4 times a day. Taxi to La Libertad beach US$20-30; to Costa del Sol US$8-10. Airport carpark US$1.25 initial charge, plus US$1.25 per hour. The prices in the gift shops at the airport are exorbitant; there is a post office, a tourist office, two exchange desks, including Banco Hipotecario (open daily 0700-1900) and duty-free shopping for departures and arrivals.

The old airport is at Ilopango, 13 kilometres east of the city. It is primarily used by the air force. However, small planes fly from Ilopango to San Miguel (30 minutes, good), Usulután, Santa Rosa de Lima, San Francisco Gotera and La Unión; tickets from the civilian traffic offices (TAES, Taxis Aéreos El Salvador, T2950363 or T/F2950330, in San Miguel Sra de Domínguez T6613954, or Gutiérrez Flying Service). Linea Aérea Salvadoreña, LASA (T2431015, F2432540) runs a daily service to San Miguel at 0630 and 1630, returning at 0715 and 1715 for US$35 return plus tax. This airline also connects both San Miguel and Ilopango with the international airport at Comalapa. Also charter flights are easily arranged. For private aviation, tours, lessons, air taxis, *Club Salvador de Aviacion Civil y Reserva*, T2950821.

Trains San Salvador-Sonsonate-Metapán, through coffee plantations.

Buses Long distance: domestic services go from Terminal de Occidente, off Boulevard Venezuela, T2233784 (take city buses 4, 7C, 27, 44 or 34); Terminal de Oriente, end of Avenida Peralta in Centro Urb Lourdes (take city buses 29 from Metrocentro, 42 from Alameda, or 4, 7 Calle), very crowded with buses and passengers, keep your eyes open for the bus you want; and Terminal Sur, San Marcos, Zona Franca, about 9 kilometres from the city (take city bus 26 from Universidad Nacional area or Avenida España downtown, take taxi to city after 1830). Routes and fares are given under destinations.

International Buses Standard service to Guatemala: a confederation of buses (Pezzarossi, Taca, Transesmer, Melva, Vencedora, Daniel Express and Centro América) operate to Guatemala City more or less hourly (5½ hours) from the Puerto Bus terminal at Alameda Juan Pablo II y 19 Avenida Norte; T2223224, T/F2222138; you can walk there from city centre, but not advisable with luggage; take bus 101D from Metrocentro, or bus 29, 52 to 21 Avenida Norte, 2 blocks south of terminal (city buses don't permit heavy luggage). The terminal has a *casa de cambio*, good rates, open daily, a restaurant (overpriced) and a hotel, alternatively stay at *American Guest House*, 5 minutes' walk or US$3 by taxi with luggage (see above). There are 16 departures daily 0330-1600 Monday-Saturday, 12 on Sunday, and the fare is US$8, 5 hours.

Luxury service to Guatemala: King Quality, Condominio Balam Quitzé, Paseo Escalón y 89 Avenida, T2433633, F2237616 (or Pullmantur Paseo Escalón, Centro Comercial Porteño No 4, T2794176, F2233718), runs a daily service at 0630 and 1530 from *Hotel Presidente*, to Guatemala City for US$27.50 (US$49.50 return), luxury service, with a/c, film, drinks and meals; also to Tegucigalpa 0700, US$45 return. *Hotel Princess* has a luxury shuttle on microbus to Guatemala City US$30 o/w. Tica Bus (from address below, but calls at Puerto Bus) runs to Guatemala at 0530, US$9 one way. Reserve all Tica Bus services in advance. Also from Terminal de Occidente, El Cóndor goes to **Talismán**, Mexico, via Sonsonate, La Hachadura and Escuintla, US$12, 0330, 9½ hours, also 0700-0800 to Guatemala City, compared with Galgos on the same route from Puerto Bus, 1030 and 0300, 9 hours, better service, US$10.30. If you want to go direct to Mexico with no stopover in Guatemala, call T2605864/2605865, F2625200, they will arrange 1st class air conditioned bus to Tapachula with one change in Guatemala City, passport formalities done on bus.

To Tegucigalpa: through Pullman services: Cruceros del Golfo from Puerto Bus, T2222158, 0600 and 1600 daily, US$18, 7 hours, arrive early; Ticabus from *Hotel San Carlos*, C Concepción 121, T2224808, US$15, leaves 0500, ticket office opens 0430, change buses in Honduras, direct to Managua. King Quality departs at 0600, US$25. Alternatively, take local services from Terminal de Oriente Ruta 306 to Santa Rosa de Lima, 4 hours, US$2.20, less time by express US$2.50, then Ruta 346 to the border at El Amatillo, 30 minutes, US$0.40, last bus to border 1730; see Honduras chapter for onward transport.

To countries further south: Ticabus to Managua US$35, San José US$50, Panama City US$75. King Quality to Managua, departs from Puerto Terminal daily at 0530, US$40, air conditioned 1st class service.

Airline offices *Grupo Taca*, (Taca,Aviateca, Lacsa, Copa and Nica), main office 1st floor, Centro Comercial, Galerias Escalon, between 71 & 73 Av Norte,(buses 52, 30B, 16). 0800-1730 Mon-Fri, luggage claims (airport) T3399060, airport office T3399155, 24-hr switchboard T2985055 (Taca)/5088 (Aviateca)/1322 (Lacsa)/9129 (Copa), F2233757 (all airlines). *Mexicana*, Centro Profesional Presidente, Edif B, Local 3, T2433633, F2433634. *American*, Edif La Centroamericana, Alameda Roosevelt 3107, p 4, T2980629, F2980762, open 0800-1730, 0800-1130 on Sat (also at Redondel Masferrer, 800 metres west of *British Club*, end Paseo Escalón, bus 52 Paseo, 0800-1800 Mon-Sat). *United*, Galerías Escalón, Local 14, 71 Av Norte y Paseo Gen Escalón, Col Escalón, T2985503, F2985536. *Continental*, Edif Torre Roble, p 9, Blvd de los Héroes, T2603263, F2611668. *Iberia*, Centro Comercial Plaza Jardín, local C, Carretera a Santa Tecla, T2232600, F2238463. *Air France*, Blvd El Hipódromo No 645, T2638192. *Lufthansa*, 87 Av Norte, FountainBlue Plaza, Col Escalón, T2632850. *KLM*, Centro Comercial La Mascota, local 10, Carretera a Santa Tecla y C La Mascota, T2230757, F2230248. *British Airways*, 43 Av Norte 216, T2609933, F2606576. *Aerolíneas Argentinas*, Alameda Roosevelt 3006, T2605450. *Alitalia*, 55 Av Sur entre Avs Olimpica y Roosevelt, T2981855. *KLM*, Av De los Andes 2956, Local 4, 2nd Flr, Col Miramonte, T2640604. *Japan Airlines*, Edif Edim-Lama, Blvd Del Hipódromo 645, T2638192, F2643416.

Directory

Banks Most banks (except Cuscatlán, see below) open 0900-1700 Mon-Fri, 0900-1200 Sat; *casas de cambio* keep the same hrs but most close 1300-1400 for lunch. Changing dollars cash is not a problem. The banks have branches in all the shopping malls and in large hotels such as *Princess*, *Radisson* (open daily till 1900). *Banco Agrícola Comercial de El Salvador*, Paseo Escalón 3635, T2791033, F2243948, good for remittances from abroad, English spoken. *Banco Salvadoreño*, C Rubén Darío 1236, good rates for TCs and Visa card advances. International department of *Banco Cuscatlán* is in Santa Tecla (bus 101D), international currencies may be cashed here, 0900-1300, 1345-1600 Mon-Fri, 0900-1200

Sat. The branch at *Hotel El Salvador* is open 0900-2000 Mon-Fri, 0900-1200 Sat. There are *casas de cambio* throughout the city, offering prices that differ by no more than a few centavos. TCs may be changed at *casas de cambio* (several opposite Parque Infantil on Alameda Juan Pablo Segundo between 9 and 10 Avs Norte) with passport and one other form of photograpic ID. TCs in European currency may be cashed at banks and the American Express and Aval Visa offices. Never change money with the street changers in Parque Infantil, in front of the *casas de cambio*. Quetzales, Mexican pesos and lempiras may be changed at *Casa de Cambio El Quetzal*, Alameda Juan Pablo Segundo y 19 Av Norte (Puerto Bus terminal), 0800-1700 Mon-Fri, 0800-1200 Sat. Dollars may be bought freely at *casas de cambio* and on the black market, with little variation in price. Accounts in dollars may be opened at **Citibank**, Edif SISA, 2nd Flr near El Salvador del Mundo.

Aval-Visa, Av Olímpica y 55 Av Norte (in Centro Comercial, behind Credomatic), does cash advances on Visa, T2793077. In emergency, for Visa International or Mastercard, T2245100; Visa TCs can only be changed by Visa cardholders. Visa ATMs can be found at Aval card 24-hr machines, the majority at Esso and Shell service stations (eg Esso Blvd los Héroes), but also at Metrocentro, 8th floor food court, and Centro de Servicio, Av Olímpica. See also pages 78-79 in the yellow pages. *Western Union* for money transfers, c/o Banco Salvadoreño branches, T2252503 (48 other branches throughout the country, look out for the black and yellow sign), head office Almeda Roosevelt y 43 Av Sur 2273-B, T2791611, Mon-Fri 0800-1700, Sat 0800-1200, take passport and photographic ID to claim funds in colones (30 mins from USA/Canada, 2-3 hrs from Europe). *American Express* is at *El Salvador Travel Service*, Carretera Panamericana y C Mascota (by Shell Station, bus 42 and 101), T2793844, F2230035; to change TCs, get them stamped at the Amex desk then go upstairs round the back to Banco del Comercio, open 0900-1700, to get the cash; must take passport. Amex loss or theft, T2230177. When making purchases with credit cards, identity may be asked for, as well as an address in El Salvador.

Conventions: El Salvador is considered a world convention destination as a result of the efforts of San Salvador Convention & Visitors Bureau, accredited by the 3 major international associations of convention organizations, IACVB, MDI and ASAE. For pre-convention info pack, contact *Buro de Convenciones y Visitantes de la ciudad de San Salvador*, Torre VIP, Hotel El Salvador suite 354, T263-2635/2636, F2632637. **International Industrial Fair**: Since 1960, the halls of Feria Internacional de El Salvador (FIES) hold numerous exhibits with the latest technology from industrial countries. During the 2nd week of Nov in each even numbered year, the most important trade fair in Central America and the Caribbean takes place. For calendar of trade fairs, contact *Feria Internacional de El Salvador*, Av Revolucion 222, Col San Benito, T2430244, F2433161, fies@es.com.sv. The feria complex can be reached via bus 34 and 30B towards Santa Tecla or Ciudad Merlot.

Communications Post Office: central Post Office at the Centro de Gobierno with EMS, T2714018, super-fast service: branches at Almacenes Siman (Centro), Librería Hispanoamérica, Centro Comercial Gigante (Col Escalón), Metrocentro, with EMS, Mercado Local No 3, Mercado Modelo, 1st floor above PHL stationer on Plaza Morazán, Av Olímpica y 57 Av Norte, next to *Super Selectos* (behind *Casa de Regalos*, owned by Canadian Moe Heft, who repairs watches and is helpful, T2235944, open 0830-1700 and Sat am). Good service to Europe. Open Mon-Fri 0730-1700, Sat 0730-1200. Lista de Correos, Mon-Fri 0800-1200, 1430-1700, good service for mail collection. **Fax service:** CTE Centro, C Rubén Darío y 3 Av Norte, charge by the min, Guatemala US$0.92, USA US$2.35. More expensive at CTE Metrocentro. Many courier services throughout the city. *DHL*, 43 Av Norte 228, T2790411, F2232441. *Gigante Express*, C Rubén Darío 1003, T2224969, F2224809. *León Express*, Alameda Roosevelt entre 49 y 51 Av Sur, No 2613, T2243005, F2243660, has *casa de cambio*. *International Bonded Couriers*, 1 C Poniente y 63 Av Norte, Escalón, Edif Comercial A&M 15, T2790347, F2791814. *UPS*, C El Progreso 3139, Col Roma, T/F2453844/5. **Telephones:** CTE/Antel at the Centro de Gobierno, Metrocentro (open 0700-1930, 1830 for fax), and other locations. See Telephone services, page 788. New French phone boxes have cropped up all over the city, card only, available at fast food stores such as *Pollo Campero*, direct dialling to anywhere in the world, also collect calls. **Email:** *Cyber Café Enlínea*, Av Río Lempa y C Marmara No 18, Col Jardines de Guadalupe, about 6 kilometres from downtown behind Universidad José S Cañas, a little below *Hotel Siesta*, buses 5, 27, 42, 44, 101-C, T2430673, www.cybercafé.com.sv and www.enlinea.com.sv, US$3.45 per hr, good food. *Quik Internet*, Av Masferrer Nte, Calle El Mirador y Av Rep Fed de Alemania, Block 162B, Col Escalón, T2647001. *Cybercentro*, 25 Av Norte No 583, T2250588. *Cafe Internet Ejje.com*, in Metrocentro 2nd level, also at Galerías Escalón, Paseo Escalón between 71 and 73 Avs, both open Mon-Sat 0900-2000, Sun 1000-1800. *Genesis*, Hotel El Salvador, T2645437.

Cultural centres *British Club*, Paseo Escalón 4714, p2, Aptdo postal (06) 3078, opposite Farmacia Paseo, T2236004, F2240420, open Mon-Sat 1700-midnight, Sun 1300-2100, has bar (with imported British beer, US$2.50-US$3.50), restaurant open to non-resident visitors (great fish and chips, US$4.50), British newspapers, an English language library, darts (open night on Wed), live music Fri (cover US$3.50 for non-members), snooker and a small swimming pool (temporary visitor's cards if introduced by a member, monthly membership US$20, but free for non-resident visitors up to 2 months with use of pool and tennis courts). *American Society*, T2241330, Chester Stemp, 0800-1600 Mon-Fri, at International School, or Pastor Don Dawson, T2235505 (Union Church), or Donald Lee, cultural activities, open only to US citizens and their spouses and children, emergency assistance for US citizens. Family membership US$20 per year, single US$14. *El Centro Español*, off the Paseo Escalón, is open to non-members, has 2 pools (one for children), tennis courts, weight training room and aerobics salon. *Club Arabe*, C Mirador, 3 blocks above *Hotel El Salvador*, open to members' guests, swimming pool, sauna, tennis, bar. *EL Centro Cultural*, Pasaje Senda Florida Sur, behind Edif Sisa, Carretera Santa Tecla, near Salvador del Mundo, T2791868, Mon-Fri 0800-1800, Sat 0800-1200, art exhibitions, monthly shows.

Embassies & consulates Embassies: *Guatemalan*, 15 Av Norte 135 y C Arce (0900-1200), T2222903/2712225, F2213019, visas issued within 24 hrs. *Honduran*, 37 Av Sur 530, Col Flor Blanca, T2712139, F2212248, Mon-Fri 0900-1200, 1300-1500. *Nicaraguan*, 71 Av Norte y 1 C Poniente 164, Col Escalón, T2237729, F2237201, Mon-Fri 0800-1300, 1500-1700. *Belizean*, Condominio Médico, local 5, p2, Blvd Tutunichapa, Urb la Esperanza, T2263588, F2263682. *Mexican*, Pasaje 12 y C Circunvalación, San Benito, behind *Hotel Presidente*, T2981079, Mon-Fri 0800-1100. *Panamanian*, Alameda Roosevelt y 55 Av Norte 2838, T2980884, F2980773. *Costa Rican*, Edif La Centroamericana, p3, Alameda Roosevelt 3107, T2790303. *US*, Blvd Santa Elena, Antiguo Cuscutlán, Unit 3116, T2784444, F2786011, outside the city, reached by bus 101A, open Mon-Fri 0800-1600. *Canadian Honorary Consulate*, Av Las Palmas III, Col San Benito, T2794659. *British*, Edif Inter Inversiones, Paseo Gen Escalón 4828, PO Box 1591, T2981763, F2983328, has British newspapers (British citizens are requested to register here), open Mon-Fri 0800-1300. *German*, 77 Av Norte y 7 C Poniente 3972, T2236140, F2983368. *French*, 1 C Poniente 3718, Col Escalón, T2794018. *Swiss*, *Pastelería Lucerna*, 85 Av Sur y Paseo Escalón 4363, T2793047. *Norwegian Consulate*, 73 Av Norte, Escalón, 100 metres north of Paseo Escalón, near Galerías. *Finnish*, C Circunvalación y Av de la Revolución, Ap 3B, Col San Benito, T2791912. *Italian*, Av La Reforma 154, Col San Benito, T2237325. *Israeli*, 85 Av Norte 614, Col Escalón, T223-9221/8770.

Hospitals & medical services Dentist: *USAM Dental Clinic*, 19 Av Norte between 1 C Pte and Juan Pablo II, near Puerto Bus Terminal, bus 101D and 30A from Metrocentro, opens 0800, go early for emergency treatment. **Doctors:** *Medicentro*, 27 Av Norte is a good place to find doctors in most specialist fields in the afternoon mostly after 1500. *Dr Jorge Panameno*, T2259928, 24-hour beeper 2981122, unit 90069, English-speaking, makes house calls at night for about US$35. **Hospitals:** *Hospital de la Mujer*, entre 81 y 83 Av Sur y C Juan José Cañas, Col Escalón (south of Paseo), bus 52 Paseo, T2238955, F2791441. *Hospital Pro-Familia*, 25 Av Norte 483, 11 blocks east of Metrocentro, T225-6100/4771, clinics and 24-hr emergency, reasonable prices; *Hospital Baldwin*, 37 Av Norte 297 y Prolongación C Arce, near Metro Sur, T2985131, emergency, excellent; if short of cash or in emergency, public *Hospital Rosales*, 25 Av Norte y 3 C Poniente, long waits. *Clínicas Médicas*, 25 Av Norte 640 (bus 3, 9, 44 centro from Universidad Nacional), T/F2255233/2250277. **NB** If you contract a serious stomach or gastro problem, the doctor will send you for tests, which will cost US$5-6 **Optitians:** *Optica Ianuzzelli*, C Arce, Centro, between 11 and 13 Av Sur, T2710182, free eye test.

Libraries The library of the UCA, Universidad Centro Americana José S Cañas, Autopista Sur, the road to the airport, is said to be the most complete collection in the capital. *Centro Cultural Salvadoreño*, Av Los Sisimiles, Metrocentro Norte, T2269103, 0800-1100, 1400-1700, English library, excellent. *Intercambios Culturales de El Salvador*, 67 Av Sur 228, Col Roma, T2451488, F2243084, extensive Spanish and English reference library, local artistic exhibitions, computer school. US information library at *American Chamber of Commerce*, 87 Av Norte 720, apto A, Col Escalón, Aptdo Postal (05) 9, Sr Carlos Chacón, speaks English, helpful.

Language schools Spanish: *Escuela de Idiomas Salvador Miranda*, PO Box 3274, Correo Centro de Gobierno, T2221352, F2222849, US$125-150 per week including board. *Cihuatan Spanish Language Institute* (Ximena's), C San Salvador 202-B, San Salvador, Col Centro América (near *Hotel Camino Real*), T503-2602481, René or Lisa Carmona, F2602427, or Lisa Carmona F2241330 daytime; rates are US$125 per week including board at *Ximena's Guesthouse* in the city or nearby farm, *Lisa's Inn*, 17 kilometres from the capital between Apopa and Guazapa (buses San Salvador-Aguilares stop at the farm). *Superior de Idiomas Cambridge*, Av La Capilla 226 Col San Benito, T/F2641253, E esi@ejje.com, good teachers, also sometimes require native speakers of English and other languages to teach.

Places of worship *Anglican Centre (St John's Episcopal Church)*, 63 Av Sur and Av Olímpica, services on Sun, 0900 in English, 1000 in Spanish. *American Union Church*, C 4, off C La Mascota, T2235505, has services in English on Sun at 0930, and also has a gift shop (local crafts and textiles) and an English paperback library with a wide selection, free (both open Wed and Sat 0900-1200, 1400-1700); take bus 101D. *Chapel in San Benito*, Av La Capilla, English mass Sun 1600, US embassy T2784444 0830-1530 for information. *Lutheran*, C 5 de Noviembre y 8 Av Norte 242, T2266010, German and English spoken. *Synagogue* (conservative), Rabino Gustavo Kraselnik, Blvd El Hipódromo, No 626, casa 1, Col San Benito, Hebrew services Fri 1830, Sat 0745, most members speak English.

Tour companies & travel agents Numerous Tourist agents, including: *El Salvador Travel Service*, Centro Comercial La Mascota, see *American Express* under **Banks**. *U Travel*, Av Revolución, Col San Benito, T2430566. For bus tours for groups (US$45-US$60 per day per person): *Amor Tours*, 73 Av Sur, Col Escalón, local 21 Edif Olimpic Plaza, T2235130, F2790363, 20 years' experience, expensive. *Set Tours*, Av Olímpica 3597, T2793236, F2793235. *Pullmantur*, in *Hotel El Presidente*, T2794166, F2237316, besides luxury bus service to Guatemala (see above), offers excellent package tours to Antigua. *Dive Pacific*, 79 Av Sur 135, Col Escalón, T2238304, F2232774, Rodolfo González, PADI instructor, excellent but expensive, English spoken, for diving off the Pacific coast at Playa Los Cóbanos, fishing tours, and dives in lakes Coatepeque and Ilopango. *El Salvador Divers*, 3 C Poniente 5020A, Col Escalón, T/F2230961, owner speaks English and German. *Oceánica*, diving school, Centro Comercial Campestre (frente al Club Campestre), Paseo Gral Escalón (cellular) T8876488 all hours, English spoken. *Magic Tours*, Galería Rosa 5, San Benito, T2793536, local and Central America, contact Ana Lucía Flores. *Jaguar Tours*, Hotel Siesta, near Col San Benito, T2788968, F2788973, for horse riding tours. *El Salvador Tours*, Villa Española Shopping Centre, Local 3, Paseo Escalón, approx 95 Av Norte, T/F2643110, saltours@es.com.sv, recommended for Punta Mango surf trips; *Paseo Travel* Paseo Escalón 5035, T2636214, paseo.travel@ejje.com; *Linda Travel*, 67 Av Sur 144 Escalón, T2982714, F2245634, lindtrvl@vianet.com.sv; *Network Travel*, Ciudad Merliot, in front of plaza Merliot, T2889478/2889549, turavnet@sal.gbm.net, Guatemalan package tour specialists; *Promotur*, T2220062, Sun-only excursions in microbuses, recommended. *Travellers Assistance Plan International*, 37 Av Sur 531, Col Flor Blanca, T2712168, cellphone 8854307, offers medical insurance, life and vehicle insurance for all Central America for those staying long periods. *Donald Lee*, Central America manager for The Spanish Connection, www.spanishconnection.com, offers assistance to business travellers with information on El Salvador, Guatemala and Costa Rica, will also advise travellers on where to find honest services in the region, T2635841/8955179, F2433575, Donlee@spanishconnection.com.

Tourist offices *Corporación Salvadoreña de Turismo*, Blvd del Hipódromo 508, Col San Benito, T2437835, F2430427, mturismo@ejje.com (*Corsatur*): take bus 34 from centre, or 30B from Mundo Feliz or Salvador del Mundo; walk 4 blocks uphill from roundabout. The tourist office at the international airport is open 0800-1630 Mon-Fri, T3399454, English spoken by Sr Nelson Sánchez. Good information on buses, turicentros, archaeological sites, beaches, national parks, etc. Texaco and Esso also sell good **maps** at some of their respective service stations. The best maps of the city and country (US$3 and $2 respectively) are available from the *Instituto Geográfico Nacional*, Av Juan Bertis No 79, Ciudad Delgado. See also **Tourist Information**, page 784.

Useful addresses Ambulance/rescue: (Comandos de Salvamento), T2220817/2211310. **Red Cross:** Av Henry Dunat y 17 Av Norte, T2241330, emergency 24-hr T2225155, co-ordinates aid for 50,000 Salvadoreans displaced by Hurrican Mitch. **Immigration department:** in the Ministry of Interior Building, Centro de Gobierno, T2212111, open Mon-Fri 0800-1600. They will consider sympathetically extending tourist visas, but be prepared with photos and plenty of patience. **Complaints:** Director General of Police, 6 C Oriente, T2714422. Also at *Unidad Metropolitana Nacional Civil*, I C Poniente and 13 Av Norte. **Police:** emergency T121, 123, or 2281156, no coin needed from new coin phones. In San Salvador, metropolitan police respond to tourist complaints. **For women visitors:** *Instituto de Estudios de la Mujer*, Cemujer, Blvd María Cristina 144, T/F2265466, Spanish only (Raquel Cano, T/F2215486, works with Cemujer; her husband is helpful with information). American Women's Association, Patricia Arias T2733204 for information, cultural and social events for English-speaking women, US$4.60 per year. *La Luna*, see above, is owned by women and has access to many women's organizations; ask for Beatriz, who speaks English and French; it is a safe place for women to go alone or in a group; office at C Berlín y 4 de Mayo, look for 'Ropero' sign, open daytime, T2255054 (tell them Pato sent you). At *Ximena's Guest House* (see **Sleeping**) ask for Norwegian Lena, resident, who speaks 7 languages. *Conamus Women's Center*, Florida Pasaje las Palmeras 130, T2602671, open business hrs Mon-Sat, Marina Navarro is very helpful. *Centro Internacional de Solidaridad (CIS)*, Blvd Universitario 4, next to Cine Reforma, T2262623 (PO Box 1801, New York, NY 10159, T212-2291290, F212-6457280), for language classes, brigade work, FMLN programmes and schools. *Instituto para la Rescate Ancestral Indígena Salvadoreña (RAIS)*, Av Santiago 20, Col San Mateo, has programmes for local aid to Indian communities and the Nahual language and customs.

Those interested in serious development and export of arts and crafts should contact Salvador Monterrosa at Europe Union NGO Prodesar, Pasaje Los Pinos 241, Col Escalón T2632400, F2635350, prodesar@gbm.net. UCA University Simeon Cañas, T2733503, English language programme, always need certified English teachers, pay US$9 per hr. Also qualified teachers at university level often needed at The American University, T2433527, speak to Dr Gavidia.

Around San Salvador

Many places can be visited in a day from San Salvador by car or by frequent bus services. These include trips to Panchimalco and Lago de Ilopango; to the crater of San Salvador volcano (see Santa Tecla, below); and to the volcano of Izalco (1,910 metres) and the nearby park of Atecosol, and Cerro Verde (see page 817); or to Lago de Coatepeque (lunch at *Hotel del Lago* or *Torre Molinos*) and to Cerro Verde in 90 minutes; to the garden park of Ichanmichen (see Zacatecoluca, page 837); Sihuatehuacán (page 819) and the pyramid of Tazumal (page 821). At weekends the coast around La Libertad (see below) is very popular. Bus 495 from the Terminal del Occidente goes to the seaside resort of Costa del Sol (see page 837).

The Mountaineering Club of the University of San Salvador sponsors day hikes every Sunday morning. Transportation from downtown San Salvador is provided. See local papers on Saturday for details. The club is extremely friendly and the excursions are strongly recommended.

Panchimalco
14½ km south by a paved road

Around it live the Pancho Indians, descendants of the original Pipil tribes; a few have retained more or less their old traditions and dress. Streets of large cobbles, with low adobe houses, thread their way among huge boulders at the foot of Cerro Chulo (see also page 795). A very fine baroque colonial church, Santa Cruz, has a white façade with statues of eight saints. Inside are splendid woodcarvings and wooden columns, altars, ceilings and benches. Note especially the octagonal ceiling above the main altar, painted a silvery blue. There is a bell incised with the cypher and titles of the Holy Roman Emperor Charles V, and the cemetery is said to be colourful. An ancient ceiba tree shades the market place (disappointing market). The **Centro de Arte y Cultura Tonatiuh**, gallery, museum and shop, Calle Principal 14 bis, T28088-36/27, has a good atmosphere, fair prices and supports local youth projects, ask for the painter, Eddie Alberto Orantes. The *fiesta* of Santa Cruz de Roma is held on 12-14 September, with music and traditional dances; on 3 May (or the second Sunday of the month) there is the procession of Las Palmas. Bus 17 from Mercado Central at 12 Calle Poniente, San Salvador, every 45 minutes, US$0.30, 45 minutes, or minibus from near Mercado Central, very crowded but quicker (30 minutes), and cheaper (US$0.35).

Lago de Ilopango

A four-lane highway, the Boulevard del Ejército, runs east for 14½ kilometres from San Salvador to Ilopango airport, beyond which is Lago de Ilopango, 15 kilometres by eight, in the crater of an old volcano, well worth a visit. Pre-Conquest Indians used to propitiate the harvest gods by drowning four virgins here each year. There are a number of lakeside cafés and bathing clubs, some of which hire dug-outs by the hour. The cafés are busy in the dry season (try *Teresa's* for fish dishes), but often closed in the middle of the year. *Hotel Vista del Lago*, T2270208, three kilometres from Apulo turn off on Highway, is on a hill top. Private chalets make access to the lake difficult, except at clubs and the Turicentro Apulo. Bus 15, marked Apulo, runs

El Salvador

Gringos in El Salvador and Guatemala – a short history
(A personal view by Donald T Lee)

In the late 1960s, thousands of young wanderers, I among them, went "on the road" (using the South American Handbook, of course), emulating the 1950s Beat Generation, inspired by writers like Jack Kerouac and William Burroughs. Both generations of travellers were in search of adventure and, in the times before faxes, call-back services and email, it was a golden age. We arrived, and we kept on arriving, some for only a short visit, some still going strong today, running successful businesses and raising grandchildren. In El Salvador, scores of ex-pats stayed in guesthouses like Casa Clarke in the then laid-back capital. They taught English during the week (no certificates were needed in those days, as long as you were a native speaker), then headed for the pristine Pacific beaches of La Libertad less than an hour's drive away. News of the lifestyle spread on the gringo-graph up north, inspiring thousands of visitors to El Salvador between 1969 and 1979. The flow dried up during the civil war that escalated after 1980. Many El Salvadoreans, both wealthy and poor, fled north, legally or illegally, to the USA and Canada (now El Hermano Lejano, still numbering some 1.2 million, remits an average of US$3 million daily to families back home). The ex-pats who stayed lived a kind of barricaded life, often staying in La Libertad, looking out for one another, unable to do anything regarding the conflict. Besides, most of us were not politically motivated and never will be. The Peace Accord was signed in 1992, ushering in a new era of reconstruction. Locals began travelling again and research and development began for receptive tourism in a climate of intense competition between the Central American republics. The El Salvadorean American Society was revived in 1993 and now has more than 200 active members and the British Club, with many ex-pat US members, provides a social and cultural centre. There are also foreign NGOs, the US Peace Corps and other international services to increase the ex-pat numbers.

In Guatemala, a number of 'gringo-friendly', ex-pat 'ghettos' existed, in the wealthier areas of Guatemala City, in Antigua, in Panajachel on Lago Atitlán, and at Río Dulce on the Caribbean coast, where yachts docked at the marinas. Scores of ex-pats also deserted the country during the worst days of the Guatemalan conflict in the early to mid-1980s. A different type of 'grifter and grafter' began arriving in Guatemala City in the mid-1980s, bringing a shadier colour to the downtown drinking spots. With the return to democracy in the late 1980s, early 1990s, tourism picked up. Antigua became more and more crowded as its Spanish-student population grew. Panajachel became a commercial centre for exporters of traditional weavings and Chichicastenango market seemed to get busier and larger each week. Quetzaltenango developed as an alternative Spanish school centre, gearing itself more to those who wanted to practice their Spanish with locals, rather than in Antigua's or Panajachel's bars and clubs. These changes encouraged many ex-pats to head for El Salvador, Honduras or elsewhere, preferring to move on, sort of fade away, or (in cases of illness or economic necessity) move back with extreme reluctance to North America or Northern Europe.

Now that Guatemala has its own peace agreement, Central Americans are entering an era of upscale tourism, trade and commerce. Means of rapid communications proliferate and emergency funds can be transferred to a traveller who has been 'caught short' in less than two hours. A far cry from when I once waited in southern Mexico in the late 1960s for a bank transfer via Laredo, Texas: three weeks later and some 13 pounds lighter, down to my last peso, I finally received my money.

from the bus stop on Parque Hula Hula to the lake (via the airport), 70 minutes, US$0.30. Entrance to the Turicentro camping site costs US$0.60; bungalow US$3.45; parking US$0.60; plenty of hammock hanging opportunities; showers and swimming facilities, all rather dirty. The water is reported to be polluted in parts near the shore and it is busy at weekends. The eastern shore is less polluted and is reached from Cojutepeque.

Also known as Nueva San Salvador, 13 kilometres west of the capital by the Pan-American Highway, the town is 240 metres higher and much cooler, in a coffee-growing district.

Sleeping D *Hotel Monte Verde*, on the main road towards Los Chorros, T2281263. F *Hospedaje San Antonio*, 4 Av Poniente, 2 blocks south of Plaza, and an unnamed **F** *Hospedaje*, C Daniel Hernández y 6 Av, 3 blocks from Parque San Martín, green door, good, safe, will store luggage. **F** *Posada La Libertad*, La Libertad, Av Melvin Jones No 4-1, 3 blocks south of Parque, T2284071, with bath, will store lugggage.

Eating *Restaurant La Tortuga Feliz*, 4 C Poniente 1-5, marimba music, garden, pleasant setting, good local food. *Comedor y Pupusería Tikal*, 2 C, half block west of 1 Av Sur, pleasant, clean, cheap.

Buses 101 and 101-A, B and D, leave 3 Avenida Norte, near the junction with Calle Rubén Darío, San Salvador, every 10 minutes for Santa Tecla (US$0.20).

This consists of a large massif with an impressive crater, one and a half kilometres wide and 543 metres deep known as **El Boquerón**, and a significant 1,960 metres peak about two kilometres to the east, called **El Picacho**, which dominates the capital. A rough road goes north from one block east of Plaza Central in Santa Tecla which climbs up and passes between the two features. A walk clockwise round the crater takes about two hours; the first half is easy, the second half rough. Take care not to fall from the ridge. The views are magnificent, if somewhat spoilt by TV and radio towers and litter. The inner slopes of the crater are covered with trees, and at the bottom is a smaller cone left by the eruption of 1917. The path down into the crater starts at the westernmost of a row of antennae studding the rim, 45 minutes down (don't miss the turn straight down after 10 minutes at an inconspicuous junction with a big, upright slab of rock 20 metres below), one hour up. Near the summit is La Laguna botanical garden. You can follow the road north and then turn right through extensive coffee plantations and forest to reach the summit of **El Picacho**. This also makes an excellent climb from the Escalón suburb of San Salvador, in the early morning preferably, taking about three to four hours return trip (take a guide).

El Salvador

Transport Ruta 103 buses at 0800, 1100 and 1400, returning at 0930, 1230 and 1530, leave from 4 Avenida Norte y Calle Hernando for El Boquerón (US$0.30), or pick-ups from the Parque Central; from the end of the busline you must walk 45 minutes to the crater, but you can drive to within 50 metres.

At Los Chorros, in a natural gorge six kilometres northwest of Santa Tecla, there is a beautiful landscaping of four pools below some waterfalls. The first pool is shallow, and bathers can stand under the cascades, but there is good swimming in the other three. ■ *US$0.60. Car park fee: US$0.60.* There is a trailer park at Los Chorros, with restaurant and showers and a hotel D *Monte Sinai*, T2266623. Bus 77 or 79 from 11 Av Sur y C Rubén Darío in San Salvador.

La Libertad and the Pacific Coast

Just before Santa Tecla is reached, a branch road turns south for 24 kilometres to La Libertad, 34 kilometres from San Salvador and just 25 minutes from the airport. It is a fishing port and, in the dry season, a popular seaside resort. The pier is worth seeing for the fish market awnings and, when the fleet is in, the boats hauled up out of the water along its length. On the seafront are several hotels, lodgings and restaurants. At a small plaza, by the *Punta Roca* restaurant, the road curves left down to the point, for views of La Libertad bay and along the coast. The cemetery by the beach has tombstones curiously painted in the national colours, blue and white. The

La Libertad is very crowded at weekends and holidays. Service can be off hand. Do not stay out alone late at night

Population: 22,800
Colour map 4, grid C3

market street is two streets inland from the seafront.

The coast east and west has good fishing and surf bathing (El Zunzal beach is the surfers' favourite, see below). Watch out for undercurrents and sharks. The beaches are black volcanic sand (which can be very hot); they are dirty but the surf is magnificent (watch your belongings). Surf season is November-April. There are also swimming pools, admission US$0.15. La Libertad is laid back and not very clean, none of the hotels has hot water and there are no ATM machines.

The Costa del Bálsamo (the Balsam Coast), between La Libertad and Acajutla (see below), is a historical name, but on the steep slopes of the departments of Sonsonate and La Libertad, scattered balsam trees are still tapped. The pain-relieving balsam, once a large export, has almost disappeared. Bus along the coast to Sonsonate at 0600 and 1300, about four hours.

Sleeping **In La Libertad** Turning right from 4 Calle Poniente at the *Punta Roca* restaurant, the following are on the road to the point: **A** *La Posada de Don Lito*, T3353166, and beside it **B** *La Hacienda de Don Rodrigo*, older hotel with character, OK. Next to *Don Lito* is **C** *Rick*, T3353033, with bath, clean, friendly, restaurant, good value. Signed behind *Rick's* is *El Retiro Familiar*, with café. **C-D** *Puerto Bello*, 2 C Poniente, on the main avenue, with bath, run-down, small rooms. By the park at 4 C Poniente are **C** *Rancho Blanco*, cheaper without a/c, cheaper still without bath, 4 rooms, pool, garden. **D** *La Posada Familiar* on opposite corner, **F** without bath, popular with surfers and backpackers, basic, meals, clean, good value, hammocks, parking. Next door is *La Paz*, budget accommodation. Nearby is **E** *Pensión Amor y Paz*, very basic, small rooms, no ventilation, dirty, friendly owner. **E** *Nuevo Amanecer*, 1 C Poniente No 24-1, safe, clean. *Bar Gringo* on the beach front lets rooms, so does the *Miramar* restaurant (negotiable).

At Playa Conchalío **B-C** *Conchalío*, T3353194, large, nice, but no a/c, good restaurant, pool, and **C** *Los Arcos*, T3353490, better value, a/c, TV, 300 metres from beach, safe, quiet, with pool, garden and restaurant.

Eating Seafood is good in the town, especially at *Punta Roca* (American-owned, Robert Rotherham), try the shrimp soup, T/F3353261, open 0800-2000, or 2300 weekends, safe, English-spoken, daughter-in-law Erika offers advice for women travellers, see *Amphibious*, under San Salvador **Watersports**. Opposite *La Posada de Don Lito* is *Rancho Mar El Delfín*. By 4 C Poniente: *El Nuevo Altamar* for good seafood and *El Viejo Altamar*. *Sagrado Corazón de Jesus*, 1 Av Norte, good value, large helpings, try their *pupusas de queso*. *Pupusería*, specializes in snacks, recommended. *Los Mariscos*, good, reasonable prices, popular, closed Monday. Cheap restaurants near the pier; also cheap food in the market. *La Fonda Española*, *Los Amigos* and *Sandra* are also in this area (Playa La Paz).

Transport **Local Bus**: No 102 from San Salvador leaves from 4 Calle Poniente, between 13 and 15 Avenida Sur, 1 hour via Santa Tecla, US$0.45. To Zacatecoluca at 0500, 1230 and 1530. La Libertad's bus terminal is on 2 Calle Oriente, east of the pier. **Taxi**: US$15-20 one way, US$30 return, negotiate. There is also a minivan service that will take groups on tour anywhere in the country, contact Robert Rotherham T3353261. **Car repairs**: good workshop on 7 Avenida Sur, Francisco is helpful, good quality work, you can sleep in vehicle while the job is done.

La Libertad is at Km 34 from San Salvador. Continuing west from the port, at Km 36 is Playa Conchalío, quieter than La Libertad. At Km 38 are the **D** *Cabañas Don Chepe* at the start of the **Playa El Majahual**, at the other end of which is **D** *Hospedaje El Pacífico*, a surfers' hotel. This beach does not have a safe reputation, nor is it clean. Other cheaper hotels include **F** *Hospedaje Surfers-Inn*, very basic but friendly, run by Marta, who serves meals. Bus 80 from La Libertad.

Zunzal, Km 42, is the best surfing beach in this area and where the Club Salvadoreño and the Automobile Club have their beach premises. *El Bosque Club*, T3353011, day cabins only, closes 1800. Many local houses for rent. At Km 49.5 is the *Atami Beach Club*, T2239000, with large pool, private beach, expensive restaurant, two bars, gardens, a beautiful place. In the grounds of *Atami* is a private 'rancho' (kitchen, two bedrooms, small pool, hammocks, 150 metres from private beach, cooking, safe, US$100 for maximum four). Access to *Club Atami* for US and other non-Central American passport-holders US$8, including cabaña for changing. A short distance beyond, Km 51, is El Zonte and the *Turicentro Bocana*.

At Km 64, turn inland to the large village of **Jicalapa**, on high rockland overlooking the ocean. There is a magnificent festival here on St Ursula's day (21 October). Jicalapa is three kilometres beyond Teotepeque. The Carretera Litoral continues for a further 40 kilometres or so to Acajutla past rocky bays and remote black sand beaches and through tunnels. Take great care with the sea if you bathe along this coast.

At the east end of La Libertad is Playa La Paz, two kilometres beyond which is **Playa Obispo**. (**A** *El Malecón de Don Lito*, T3353201; **D** *Rancho Blanco*, T3353584; on the beach several good value seafood restaurants, for example *Mariscos Freddy* and *La Marea*. Nearby is *Motel Siboney*, good.) Opposite the motel there is a trail up the Río San Antonio, one kilometre to the waterfall Salto San Antonio (50 metres) and two kilometres to the Salto y Cueva Los Mangos (60 metres). Bus 287 from La Libertad to the San Antonio quarry will get you there. One kilometre further east is Playa Las Flores with excellent seafood restaurant *La Dolce Vita*, 200 metres east of the Shell gas station, T3353592, also *La Curva de Don José*, T3353436, recommended. About one kilometre east of La Curva, on the right towards San Diego is the *Fisherman's Club* (T3353272), with pool, tennis courts and a good restaurant. Entry US$6. Good beach but beware of rip tide, only advisable for surfers.

Eight kilometres from La Libertad, on a turn off from the Carretera Litoral, is **Playa San Diego**, nice but deserted: *Río Mar Club*, T2227879; *Mad Mike's Bed & Breakfast*, run by surfer Miguel Johnson, private beach facing property, short and longer term accommodation. Bus for San Diego beach, from Calle 2 Oriente in La Libertad, US$1, 30 minutes. The Carretera Litoral heads east, but inland, to join the airport highway by San Luis Talpa; it then continues to Zacatecoluca. At the point near El Zonte, near Km 51 on the main road, is *Rosa's*, east of the river, three basic rooms with fan, separate toilet, cold showers, **F** for room, US$1 for hammock space, very helpful, excellent meals (US$2-3), very quiet during the week, beautiful beach with fine sunsets.

Western El Salvador

Some very interesting natural features and beautiful countryside. The trip to Cerro Verde and Izalco is a 'must'. Santa Ana is an important coffee-growing centre and the city is worth a visit.

Routes to Guatemala

The route from the capital south to La Libertad and along the coast to the port of Acajutla, has already been given. A quicker route to Acajutla goes west on the Pan-American highway through Santa Tecla, past Los Chorros and then in three and a half kilometres, bears left to Sonsonate and south to the port. There are four roads which cross into Guatemala, through La Hachadura (see under Sonsonate, page 816, San Cristóbal (via the Pan-American Highway, page 821), Las Chinamas (see under Santa Ana, page 823) and Anguiatú (beyond Metapán, page 824).

Izalco
Population: 43,000

From the junction with the Pan-American Highway, route CA 8 (heavy lorry traffic) runs west, past Armenia, to the town of Izalco at the foot of Izalco volcano (eight kilometres from Sonsonate, bus 53C, US$0.10). The town of Izalco and Izalco volcano are not directly connected by road. A paved road branches off the highway 14 kilometres before the turning for Izalco town (about 22 kilometres from Sonsonate) and goes up towards Cerro Verde and Lago de Coatepeque (see below). The town has resulted from the gradual merging of the *ladino* village of Dolores Izalco and the Indian village of Asunción Izalco (**F** *Hospedaje San Rafael*, next to the church on the Central Park, very basic, no shower, dirty, noisy, motorcycle workshop, but safe and friendly, no alternative). **Festivals**, 8 to 15 August and during the Feast of St John the Baptist from 17 to 24 June.

Near Izalco, at the edge of town, is the spacious swimming pool of Atecozol, in the middle of a beautiful park with a restaurant (renovated 1999, Turicentro, admission US$0.60, parking US$0.60, bungalow US$3.45). The park is shaded by huge mahogany trees, palms, aromatic balsam trees and *amates*. There is a battlemented tower; a monument to Tlaloc, god of rain; another to Atlacatl, the Indian who, on this spot, shot the arrow which lamed the *conquistador* Pedro de Alvarado; and a statue to the toad found jumping on the spot where water was found.

Caluco Just south of Izalco, a few kilometres off the main road to San Salvador is **Caluco** which has a colonial church and a ruined Dominican church, bus 432 from Sonsonate. Two kilometres from Caluco are Las Victorias Falls on the Río Chiquihuat, with two caves above the falls. On the same road out of Caluco is the meeting of hot and cold streams at Los Encuentros to form the Río Shuteca/Aguas Calientes. Five kilometres southeast of the town is La Chapina pool and springs on the farm of the same name.

Sonsonate

Population: 120,000.
Altitude: 225 metres
Colour map 4, grid C3

64 kilometres from the capital, Sonsonate, produces sugar, tobacco, rice, tropical fruits, hides and balsam. It is in the chief cattle-raising region. The city was founded in 1552 and is now hot, dirty and crowded. The beautiful El Pilar church (1723) is strongly reminiscent of the church of El Pilar in San Vicente. The Cathedral has many of the cupolas (the largest covered with white porcelain) which serve as a protection against earthquakes. The old church of San Antonio del Monte (completed 1861), one kilometre from the city, draws pilgrims from afar (*fiesta* 22-26 August). There is a small railway museum, look for the locomotive at the entrance to the city on the highway from San Salvador, Km 65. An important market is held each Sunday. The market outside the church is quite well-organized. In the northern outskirts of the city there is a waterfall on the Río Sensunapán. Legend has it that an Indian princess drowned there, and on the anniversary of her death a gold casket appears below the falls. The main annual event is *Feria de Candelaria* in February.

Excursions CA 8 northwest to Ahuachapán (see page 822), 40 kilometres all paved, spectacular scenery, frequent buses from Sonsonate, No 285, US$0.50, two hours: the road goes through the Indian village of **Nahuizalco**. The older women still wear the *refajo* (a doubled length of cloth of tie-dyed threads worn over a wrap-round skirt), and various crafts are still carried on, although use of the Indian language is dying out. The night market has preHispanic food on sale. *Fiestas* 19-25 June, religious festival, music, *Danza de los Historiantes* (see **The Music of the Region** at the beginning of the book) and art exhibitions; 24-25 December, music and *Danza de los Pastores*. (Bus 53 from Sonsonate, US$0.10). Beyond is **Jauyúa** (just off the main road), with Los Chorros de la Calera two kilometres north (bus 205 from Sonsonate), **E** *Hotel El Típico*, 1 C Oriente 1-2.

Apaneca, see under Ahuachapán, is also passed.

In the Sonsonate district are a number of waterfalls and other sites of natural beauty: to the west, near the village of **Santo Domingo de Guzmán** (bus 246 from Sonsonate) are the falls of El Escuco (two kilometres north), Tepechapa (one and a half kilometres further) and La Quebrada (further still up the Río Tepechapa), all within walking distance of Santo Domingo and each other. Walk through the town, then follow the river. Several spots to swim. Festival in Santo Domingo, 24-25 December, with music and dancing. From **San Pedro Puxtla** (bus 246; modern church built on the remains of a 18th century edifice) you can visit the Tequendama Falls on the Río Sihuapán. Bus 219 goes to **Cuisnahuat** (18th century baroque church, *fiesta*, 23-29 November, San Judas), from where it is two kilometres south to the Río Apancoyo, or four kilometres north to **Peñón El Escalón** (covered in balsam trees) and El Istucal Cave, at the foot of the Escalón hill, where Indian rites are celebrated in November.

B-C *Agape*, at Km 63 on outskirts of the town in the Asociación Agape complex, converted convent, gardens, suites and rooms, a/c or fan, safe parking, good restaurant, cable TV, recommended. Ask Father Flavian Mucci, the director of the Association, to show you round. **B** *Plaza* 9 Oriente, Barrio del Angel, T4516627, F4516745, a/c rooms, good restaurant, pool, recommended.

E *Castro*, on main street 3 blocks from Parque, with bath, fan, good, safe, friendly, some rooms with bed and hammock. **E** *Hospedaje Veracruz*, Av Rafael Campo, T4510616, very noisy, unfriendly, not recommended. **E** *Orbe*, 4 C Oriente y 2 Av Sur, T4511416, parking, good restaurant.

F *El Brasil*, 4 Av Norte, basic, clean and friendly. **F** *Hospedaje Blue River*, near bus station, with bath, large, clean rooms. *Florida*, beside bus terminal, fan, basic, manager speaks English.

My Mom's at *Agape*, highly recommended. *Nuevo Hilary*, Av Rafael Campos No 1-3, local and Chinese food, generous servings, moderate prices. *Caften Teto*, nearby, clean, friendly, good servings.

Trains The train up to the mountains and Metapán passes here about 1030-1100; see museum above.

Buses No 248 to Santa Ana, US$1 along CA 12 north, 39 kilometres, a beautiful journey through high, cool coffee country, with volcanoes in view; to Ahuachapán, 2 hours, slow, best to go early in the day; San Salvador to Sonsonate by No 205, US$0.80, 80 minutes, very frequent. There is also a bus from San Salvador along the coast at 0600 and 1300, beautiful ride. Take care at the bus terminal and on rural routes (eg in Nahuizalco area).

Airline offices *Taca*, T4510694.

Route CA 12 goes southwest from Sonsonate to Acajutla, Salvador's main port serving the western and central areas, 85 kilometres from San Salvador (the port is eight kilometres south of the Coastal Highway). It handles about 40 percent of the coffee exports and is a popular seaside resort during the summer (good surfing, though beaches are dirty, suffering from occasional oil spills).

Sleeping **C** *Kilo 2*, at San Julián just outside town, T4523192. **C** *Miramar*, with bath and fan, clean, reasonable restaurant/bar. *Lara*, by beach, with bath and fan, clean, car parking. **E** *Pensión Gato Negro*, opposite Belinda store, run by Japanese couple, with good restaurant, varied food, generous portions, meals US$1 to US$1.50. There are 2 motels, **D**, on the outskirts of town.

Eating *Pizza y Restaurante Perla del Mar* serves good shakes and food at reasonable prices. There are good seafood restaurants in Barrio La Peña.

Buses 207 from Occidente terminal, San Salvador, US$2.80, or 252 from Sonsonate US$0.30. 58 kilometres from Santa Ana.

Route CA 2 turns off CA 12 about four kilometres north of Acajutla, 16 kilometres

Sleeping
■ *on maps*
Price codes:
see inside front cover

Eating

Transport

Directory

Acajutla
Population: 36,000
Colour map 4, grid C3

El Salvador

south of Sonsonate, and runs 43 kilometres west to the Guatemalan frontier point of **La Hachadura**.

The coastline here is mainly black sand with few public facilities. Some turtles use this area and it is worth enquiring if you can visit a conservation unit.

Frontier with Guatemala – La Hachadura-Pedro de Alvarado The border is at the bridge over the Río Paz, with a filling station and a few shops nearby.

Salvadorean immigration The immigration facilities are on either side of the bridge; a relaxed crossing.

Crossing by private vehicle The border crossing is quite straightforward but a private vehicle requires a lot of paperwork (about 2 hours).

Sleeping In La Hachadura **F** *El Viajero*, fans, safe, clean, good value.

Transport To **San Salvador**, Terminal de Occidente, No 498, 3 hours; to **Ahuachapán**, by market, No 503, US$0.75, 50 minutes.

Barra de Santiago & Los Cóbanos The beaches northwest of Acajutla at Metalío (safe for camping, but no formal place to stay) and **Barra de Santiago** are recommended. At Barra de Santiago, 30 kilometres west of Acajutla, the beach is across a beautiful lagoon. A bird sanctuary is being developed on the estuary; nearby is a turtle farm and museum. René Carmona of *Ximena's* in San Salvador rents rooms at a rancho here (**B** per person per day, clean, safe, including gas stove, maid service, guardian has motor launch for excursions, US$12 per hour, US$75 per day, closed May-June); transport can be provided from the capital with advance notice (address under San Salvador **Sleeping**, reservation required). There are government plans to develop the Isla del Cajete nearby into a tourist complex, to attract Guatemalans. Also recommended is Salinitas, scenic, peaceful but too many rocks for safe bathing; a modern tourist complex here contains cabins, restaurants, gardens, pool, and a zoo. **Los Cóbanos** (14 kilometres south of Acajutla, bus from Sonsonate) has seen some improvement. Two hotels: **D** *Sol y Mar*, T4510137, weekends only; **E** *Mar de Plata*, at Punta Remedios, 24 cabins, T4513914. *Dive Pacific* (see San Salvador, **Tour companies**) has a guesthouse for clients. Abraham Ríos runs deep-sea fishing charters, US$180 per day, four people, English spoken, enquire locally. Fishermen arrange boat trips, negotiate a price.

Reserva Nacional Bosque El Imposible So called because of the difficulty of getting into it, this 'impossibility' has also helped to preserve some of the last vestiges of El Salvador's flora and fauna on the rocky slopes and forests of the coastal Cordillera de Apaneca. Among the mammals are puma, ocelot, agouti and ant bear; birds include black crested eagle, white hawk and other birds of prey, black and white owl, and woodpeckers; there is also a great variety of reptiles, amphibians and insects, the greatest diversity in the country. There are eight different strata of forest, with over 300 species of tree identified. The park, of 3,130 hectares, is managed by the Centro de Recursos Naturales (CEREN) and the Servicio de Parques Nacionales y Vida Silvestre (SPNVS), under the auspices of the Ministerio de Agricultura y Ganadería. The park is maintained by Salvanatura and US Peace Corps volunteers: contact Dora Eugenia Coen/Communications, Pasaje Istmania 315 (77-79 Av Norte), Col Escalón, San Salvador, T/F2233620, T2633111, messages 2234225. Access (suitable only for four-wheel drive or hiking) is from the road to La Hachadura, either from the turnoff by the archaeological site of **Cara Sucia** (12 kilometres before La Hachadura), or by two routes leading to San Francisco Menéndez. Cara Sucia is being excavated; it is an Olmec site.

Santa Tecla to Santa Ana

The Pan-American Highway, good dual carriageway road, parallels the old Pan-American Highway, bypassing Santa Ana. The road, with turnoffs for Sonsonate and Ahuachapán, carries on to San Cristóbal on the Guatemalan frontier.

15 kilometres from Santa Tecla, seven kilometres from the junction with the Sonsonate road, there is a junction to the right. This road forks immediately, right to Quezaltepeque, left (at *Joya de Cerén* café) to **San Juan Opico**. After a few kilometres on the San Juan road, you cross the railway by the Kimberley-Clark factory; at the railway is *Restaurante Estación Sitio del Niño* (seafood, steak, local dishes, in an old station, open from 0730 Tuesday-Sunday, horseriding tours to San Andrés, see below, contact *Jaguar Tours* in San Salvador, US$60-70 per day per person including lunch and a/c transport). After a girder bridge across a river is a grain store, beside which is **Joya de Cerén** (32 kilometres from the capital). This is a major archaeological site, not for spectacular temples, but because this is the only known site where ordinary Mayan houses have been preserved having been buried by the ash from the nearby Laguna Caldera volcano about 600 AD. Buildings and construction methods can be clearly seen; a painted book and household objects have been found. All the structures are covered with protective roofing. The site has a small but good museum, café, toilets and car park, entrance US$3 (El Salvador and Central American nationals US$0.80), parking charge US$0.60. Children offer replicas for sale. Bus from San Salvador No 108, Terminal de Occidente, to San Juan, US$0.45, one hour.

There is an excavated archaeological site at **San Andrés**, half-way between Santa Tecla and Coatepeque on the estate of the same name. (Its full name is La Campana de San Andrés.) A group of low structures stand in the valley (Structure 5, the furthest from the entrance, is closed because of erosion). There are good views of the nearby hills. Colonial era ruins (C 1700) about one kilometre away are being excavated and a five-kilometre walkway now connects San Andrés, the colonial ruins and Joya de Cerén. The site is open 0900-1700, Tuesday-Sunday, US$3; it is popular for weekend picnics, otherwise it is quiet. There is a café. It is at Km 32.5 on the Pan-American Highway, just after the Hilasal towel factory (bus 201 from Terminal de Occidente, US$0.80).

Lago de Coatepeque

At El Congo, some 13 kilometres before Santa Ana a short branch road leads (left) to Lago de Coatepeque, a favourite weekend resort with good sailing and fishing near the foot of Santa Ana volcano. The surroundings are exceptionally beautiful. Many weekend homes line the north and east shore, making access to the water difficult, but there are public *balnearios*: *Casa Blanca* and *Recreativa El Jordán*, US$0.05 per person, parking US$0.25. There are two islands in the lake, Anteojo close to the hotels and Teopán on the far side from the hotels (private, with nature reserve, archaeological excavations and hiking trails, permission from owners for ferry across and hiking, weekdays only; no access at weekends). Launches charge US$5.75-8.60 per person for lake trips, depending on the size of the group, or about US$15 for two hours (negotiate with the owners). Cerro Verde is easily reached in 90 minutes by good roads through impressive scenery (see below). *Fiesta*, Santo Niño de Atocha, 25-29 June.

B *Del Lago*, T4469511, San Salvador T2791143, F2245875, manager Lic Lucio Bastillo speaks English and German, pool, old (cheaper) and new rooms, good beds, nice setting, beautiful lakeside view, good restaurant (try the crab soup), very busy on Sunday, will change dollars, recommended, midweek specials. **B** *Torremolinos*, T4469437, F4411859, in Santa Ana C J Mariano Méndez Poniente 33, T4404836, F4404130, pool, good rooms (a couple with hot showers), restaurant, bar, good service, boating excursions, pool, popular at weekends with music, lively. **D** *Amacuilco*, 300 metres from CTE/Antel, very helpful manager (Sandra), 6 rooms (but avoid those which overlook the kitchen), reductions for weekly and monthly stays, art gallery, offers marimba classes and Spanish and Nahuat lessons, all meals available, live music Friday and Saturday night, pool, good view, secure, recommended, boat excursions on lake, tours arranged from US$30-40 per day (US$100 d per week includes breakfast and dinner); in Santa Ana, contact through *Almacén Silueta*, Av Independencia Sur 11 b, 1 block from *Pollo Campero*, T4410608, Amita Gutiérrez; **F** basic, dirty rooms next to *Torremolinos*, towards the CTE/Antel office, unfriendly; also **F**, in white house across the street from *Amacuilco*, friendly. Plenty of *comedores*.

Transport **Buses** From Santa Ana, hourly bus 220 'El Lago' to the lake, US$0.40; from San Salvador, bus 201 to El Congo (bridge at Km 50) on Pan American Highway, US$1, then pick up the 220 bus to the lake, US$0.45. Other buses to Guatemala may also stop at El Congo, check. Taxi from Santa Ana US$10.

Directory **Communications** *CTE/Antel*, 50m from *Torremolinos*, good phone service, helpful, local and long distance, cash only, can arrange for messages to be left here (US$0.60).

Cerro Verde and Izalco Volcano

From El Congo another road runs south, above the east shore of Lago Coatepeque. When you reach the summit, a paved road branches right, climbing above the south end of the lake to **Cerro Verde** (2,030 metres) with its fine views of the **Izalco volcano** (1,910 metres). The road up to Cerro Verde is lined with beautiful flowers. A 30-minute walk, including a nature trail, around the Cerro Verde National Park leads to a series of miradores with views of Lago Coatepeque and Santa Ana volcano, with Finca San Blas at its foot. There is an orchid garden. Cerro Verde can be very busy at weekends. For the best view of Izalco go in the morning, but in the afternoon clouds around the cone can be enchanting.

Izalco was known as the "Lighthouse of the Pacific" because of the regularity of the fiery explosions.

The volcano, as can be seen from the lack of vegetation, is recent. Historical records show that activity began in the 17th century as a sulphurous smoke vent, but in February 1770, violent eruptions formed a cone which was in more or less constant activity until 1957. There was a small eruption in 1966 through a blowhole on the southeast slope evidenced by two 1,000 metres lava flows. Since that time, it was been quiescent.

To climb Izalco: a path leads off the road (signposted) just below the car park on Cerro Verde. In 20-30 minutes descend to the saddle between Cerro Verde and Izalco, then 1-1½ hours up (steep, but manageable); three hours from base, go in a group, thieves congregate at the base. Beware of falling rocks when climbing. A spectacular view from the top. For a quick descent, find a rivulet of soft volcanic sand and half-slide, half-walk down in 15 minutes, then 45 minutes to one hour back up the saddle. This 'cinder running' needs care, strong shoes and a thought for those below. You are probably also aiding erosion.

Try to ensure that low cloud is not expected before planning to go.

NB Well-dressed, bilingual thieves operate around Cerro Verde and Izalco. Don't give personal details (for example itinerary, room number) to smart, English-speaking strangers and refuse offers of assistance, meals, et cetera. If driving to Cerro Verde, take care late afternoon/evening as assaults have been reported. PNC (police) can arrange escorts for small groups on Izalco; do not go alone.

Sleeping & services The fine **A-B** *Hotel Montaña* (T2712434, F2221208, or reserve through Corsatur in San Salvador) at the top of Cerro Verde was originally built so that the international set could watch Izalco in eruption; unfortunately, the eruptions stopped just as the hotel was completed. Room prices vary according to view and which meals are taken; from Monday-Thursday room price is **C** without meals (better anyway to pay for meals separately); very comfy rooms with views of Izalco volcano or forest, huge fireplaces, but no wood available for fires, and can be cold at night; relaxing. There is a restaurant and café; food is good, at fairly reasonable prices. Non-residents pay US$0.60 to enter hotel. To enter the Cerro Verde park costs US$0.60 (has to be paid before you can reach the hotel), car park (US$0.60). There are cabañas for rent, **D** at weekends, **E** in the week without water, and camping (tent or motor-home) is permitted, good (ask the warden if you need basics for preparing meals).

The junction 8 kilometres from the top of Cerro Verde can be reached by the Santa **Transport** Ana-Sonsonate bus, No 248 (US$1), leaving Santa Ana at 0600 and 1530 with several others in between, 2 hours (return 1300, 1530, 1700). It can also be caught at El Congo (ask around for accommodation if you are stuck here), or, in the other direction, from the highway out-side Izalco town; from the junction, hitch up to the National Park and hotel (no problem, especially at weekends). 3 buses daily go up to Cerro Verde: two buses from El Congo arrive at the park at 0630 and 1700-1730, one from Santa Ana arrives at 1230 (dep Santa Ana 1030). On Saturday and Sunday morning there are direct buses from Santa Ana to Cerro Verde car park. Check carefully the times of the buses leaving Cerro Verde in the afternoon.

Three quarters of the way to Cerro Verde, a track branches off to the right to Finca San Blas (also can be reached on foot from Cerro Verde car park, 20 minutes). From there it is 30 minutes down to the saddle and a one and a half hours walk straight up the very impressive **Santa Ana volcano**, 2,365 metres, the highest point in El Salvador apart from two points on the Honduran frontier. There are four craters inside one another; the newest crater has a lake and fuming columns of sulphur clouds. You can walk around the edge and down on to the ledge formed by the third crater (beware of the fumes). Spectacular views, but it can be hazy in the dry season. A rough map is available at reception in *Hotel Montaña*.

Santa Ana

Santa Ana, 55 kilometres from San Salvador and capital of its Department, is the sec-ond largest city in the country. The intermont basin in which it lies on the northeast slopes of Santa Ana volcano is exceptionally fertile. Coffee is the great crop, with sugar-cane a good second. The city, named Santa Ana La Grande by Fray Bernardino Villapando in 1567, is the business centre of western El Salvador. There are some fine buildings, the neo-gothic **cathedral**, and several other churches, espe-cially El Calvario, in neo-classical style. Of special interest is the classical **Teatro Nacional** on the north side of the plaza, originally completed in 1910, now being restored and one of the finest in Central America. A guide (small charge) will show you round on weekdays. A donation from the Organization of American States is being used to replace the seating. *Fiesta* 1-26 July, Fiestas Julias.

Population: 400,000
Altitude: 776m
Colour map 4, grid C3

On the west of the town is the El Trapiche swimming pool. Microbus 51 El Molina **Excursions** from the centre of Santa Ana goes to **Turicentro Sihuatehuacán**, on city outskirts; US$0.75 admission to pools, café and park, same price for parking. Renovation was scheduled for 1999. José Luis Estrada formerly of ISTU in Atiquizaya (see page 822) works at the Turicentro Wednesday to Sunday, 0800-1500.

B-C *Internacional*, 25 C Poniente y 10 Av Sur, T4400810, with bath, restaurant in same build- **Sleeping** ing, safe parking for motorcycles, TV, not the most conventional of hotels. **B-C** *Sahara*, 3 C Poniente y 10 Av Sur, T/F4478865, good service.

D *Roosevelt*, 8 Av, Sur y 5 C Poniente, T4411702, rooms with bath and cold water, choose between noisy monkeys at the front, cockroaches in back rooms, meals available when full, free parking. **D** *La Libertad*, near cathedral, 4 C Oriente 2, T4412358, with bath, good value, friendly, clean, helpful, will change dollars, safe car park across the street US$2 for 24 hours.

E *Colonial*, 8 Av Norte 2, clean, helpful, good breakfasts for less than US$1, a little noisy, not recommended for single women. **E** *Livingston*, 10 Av Sur, 29, T4411801, with bath, cheaper without, cheap and clean. **E** *Pensión Lux*, on Parque Colón, Av JM Delgado No 57, T4403383, large rooms. **E** *Monterrey*, 10 Av Sur, 9-11, T4412758, without bathroom. *Venecia*, 11 C Poniente between 14 and 16 Av Sur, T4411534.

F *Hospedaje San Miguel*, Av J Matías Delgado 26, T4413465, cheaper without bath, basic, clean, car park. **F** *hospedajes* south of Parque Colón. **F** *Hospedaje Tikal*, 10 Av Sur y C 9, clean, quiet, large rooms, free chilled drinking water.

Eating *Kiyomi*, 4 Av Sur between 3 and 5C, good food and service, clean, reasonable prices. *Los Horcones*, on main plaza next to church, like a jungle lodge inside, good cheap meals. *Parrillada Texana*, Av Independencia Sur, good grilled chicken, garlic bread and salads, good value. *Kyjau*, C Libertad near park, Chinese, large portions. *Talitunal*, 5 Av Sur 6, vegetarian, open 0900-1900, closed Sunday, attractive, good lunch, owner is a doctor and expert on medicinal plants. *Kikos*, Av Independencia Sur, near 5 C, good chicken and pizza. *Veras Pizza*, Av Independencia Sur, good salad bar. *Pollo Campero*, Av Independencia Sur, accepts US dollars. *Pupusería Memita*, 25 C Poniente, recommended for fresh *pupusas* made to order. It is cheaper and usually good value to eat in *comedores*, or at the market in front of the cathedral. There are also food stalls on the side of the plaza. Look for excellent pineapples in season. Everything closes at about 1900.

Entertainment 2 dance clubs on 15 Calle Poniente near 4 Avenida Sur, good music Wednesday-Saturday, dinner served. *El Gato*, Av Independencia Sur 24, theatrical co-operative, T4476264 for programme, coffee house atmosphere.

Transport **Buses** No 201 from Terminal del Occidente, San Salvador, US$0.60, 1 hour, every 10-15 minutes, 0400-1830. To La Libertad, take 'autopista' route bus to San Salvador and change buses

Santa Ana

in Nueva San Salvador. Buses (Melva, Pezzarossi and others) leave frequently from 25 Calle Poniente y 8 Avenida Sur (T4403606) for Guatemala City, full fare as from San Salvador, 4-4½ hours including border stops. Alternatively there are local buses to the border for US$0.45; they leave from the market. Frequent buses to Metapán and frontier at Anguiatú.

Banks Banks will change dollars cash and TCs. *Banco Salvadoreño*, English spoken. Large supermarket near Parque Libertad open 0800-2300 has bank inside for exchange. Black market around the banks (called Wall St by the locals!). **Communications** Post Office: 7 C y 2 Av Sur. **Laundry** *Lavandería Solución*, 7C Poniente 29, wash and dry US$2.50 per load, ironing service, recommended. **Useful addresses** Police: emergency T121. **Tour companies & travel agents** Agency at 4 Av Norte y 2 C Poniente, T4477269, for flight reservations.

Directory

The border with Guatemala is 30 kilometres from Santa Ana along the paved Pan-American Highway at **San Cristóbal** (**F** *Hotel El Paso*, basic, friendly).

This is the Carretera Panamericana crossing to Guatemala taken by the international buses and much heavy traffic. There is an Inguat office on the Guatemalan side.

Frontier with Guatemala – San Cristóbal

Salvadorean immigration The border is open from 0600-2000. Some inconsistency has been reported about fees charged but, in general, expect standard procedures.

Transport To Santa Ana, No 236, US$0.60, 1½ hours, 0400-1800.

Texistepeque, 17 kilometres north of Santa Ana on the road to Metapán, has an 18th century baroque church, with *fiestas* on 23-27 December and 15 January. The town is on the San Salvador-Sonsonate-Metapán railway, on which there are passenger services. A railway runs eastwards along the south bank of the Río Lempa to Aguilares on Troncal del Norte (San Salvador – Cerrón Grande reservoir – El Poy, on the border with Honduras, see next section). A passenger service operates every day leaving Aguilares at 0700, returning 1400, 54 kilometres through unspoiled countryside, US$0.55 one way. The old passenger carriages have been refurbished. About seven kilometres east is the starting point for river trips on the Río Lempa (contact Carolina Nixon at Corsatur; her company, *Ríos Tropicales* has equipment rental, T/F2232351 San Salvador).

Texistepeque

16 kilometres from Santa Ana, on the road to Ahuachapán is Chalchuapa (). President Barrios of Guatemala was killed in battle here in 1885, when trying to reunite Central America by force. There is some good colonial-style domestic building; the church of Santiago Apóstol is particularly striking, almost the only one in El Salvador which shows strong indigenous influences (restored 1997-98). (*Fiestas* 18-21 July, Santiago Apóstol, and 12-16 August, San Roque.) See the small but picturesque lake, and the **Tazumal** ruin next to the cemetery in Chalchuapa, built about AD 980 by the Pipil Indians but with its 14-step pyramid now, alas, restored in concrete. The site has been occupied since 5000 BC and in the **Museo Regional de Chalchuapa** are the artefacts found in the mud under the lake. There are very interesting bowls used for burning incense, intricately decorated with animal designs. Some of the exhibits of the Museo de Arqueología in San Salvador, damaged in the 1996 earthquake, are temporarily on show here. The ruin is only five minutes' walk from the main road ■ *0900-1200 and 1300-1700, closed on Monday, US$3.* Near the ruins is a souvenir shop, *Tienda Tazumal* (selling good reproductions and jewellery, dollars accepted or changed) run by Elida Vides de Jaime, 11 Avenida Sur 31, T4440803, on the main road. Elida's husband can act as a guide to Tazumal and other nearby ruins, helpful, speaks some English. Bus No 236 from Santa Ana, 30 minutes, US$0.25.

Chalchuapa
Population: 34,865
Altitude: 640m

Sleeping & eating **E** *Gloria*, Av 2 de Abril, T4440131. A new hotel is under construction. Opposite the entrance to the ruins is *Manhattan Bar and Grill*, 7 Av Sur y 5 C Oriente 32, T4440074, has

El Salvador

disco 7 days a week, good service, clean, helpful. Also *5 Calles* by entrance to ruins. *Acajutla*, 7 C Oriente 9, T4440511, high quality seafood, popular, not cheap, accepts credit cards.

Embassies & consulates Guatemalan consul in Chalchuapa, Av Club de Leones Norte, between Primero and C Ramón Flores, unmarked blue house, knock for attention.

The road continues 12 kilometres west to **Atiquizaya**, a small, quiet town with one *hospedaje* (**F**), several good *pupuserías* (1600-2100) and *Restaurante Atiquizaya*, one kilometre at intersection with main highway to Ahuachapán, good. Also at the intersection a sculptor in metal exhibits and sells his work (Km 89). There is a *turicentro* six kilometres west at hot springs (park, camping, turn off road to Ahuachapán at Finca La Labor, Km 94, seven kilometres on dirt road); at Cataratas del Río Malacachupán is a 50 metres waterfall into a lagoon, very beautiful, one kilometre hike to get there. Nearby is Volcán Chingo on the Guatemalan border. For a local guide, contact José Luis Estrada, who speaks English, T4441672 (not Sunday) and who arranges long-term accommodation (**E-F**) in the area, English teachers welcome (will trade lessons Spanish-English). Camping is possible. **Transport** There are frequent buses to the river from the central park in Atiquizaya; buses 202 and 456 from Terminal Occidente in San Salvador, two hours, US$0.90. From Santa Ana, 45 minutes, US$0.40. All Ahuachapán buses stop in the central parque.

Ahuachapán

Population: 80,000
Altitude: 785m
Colour map 4, grid C3

The capital of its Department, is 35 kilometres from Santa Ana. It is a quiet town with low and simple houses, but an important distribution centre. Coffee is the great product. Like many places in the area, it draws the mineral water for its bath-house from some hot springs near the falls of Malacatiupán, nearby. You can bathe in the river above the falls, and camp in the vicinity. The falls are over 70 metres high and steam impressively, especially in the early morning. Downstream, where the hot water merges with the cold of the Río Frío, steam rises everywhere. This can be reached by bus (hourly most of the day) or four-wheel drive along a five kilometre dirt road from Atiquizaya (see above), or the same distance north of Ahuachapán. Pick-ups can be hired with driver for US$9 per day. Power is generated from the falls of Atehuezián on the Río Molino, which cascade prettily down the mountain-side. See also the *ausoles*: geysers of boiling mud with plumes of steam and strong whiffs of sulphur. The ground is warm to the touch. The *ausoles* are used for generating electricity; only the smallest remains uncovered by drums and pipes. One can take a bus from Ahuachapán to El Barro, take a taxi or walk the five kilometres to the area. Permission to visit the power station can be obtained from the barracks on the hill overlooking the town as the site is guarded by the Army.

Sleeping **B** *Casa Blanca*, 2 Av Norte y Gerardo Barrios, T/F4432505, 2 rooms a/c, clean, good, recommended (owner's husband is a doctor, Dr Escapini). **B-C** *El Parador*, Km 103, 1½ kilometres west of town, hotel and restaurant, a/c, good service, motel-style, relaxing, helpful owner, Sr Nasser, recommended. Buses to border stop outside, T/F4430331, T4431637. **E** *San José*, 6 C Poniente, opposite the park, with bath, clean, friendly, parking. **F** *Hospedaje Granada*, 3 blocks down from plaza by market, shared bath, clean. **F** *Hospedaje Milagro*, clean, basic, near bus station.

Eating One can get good meals at *Restaurant El Paseo*, *Restaurant Tanya* and *El Parador*. Good and inexpensive meals at *Mixta's Restaurante*. *Pastelería María*, good cakes and biscuits. *Super Selectos* supermarket in Centro Comercial at entrance to town.

Transport **Buses** Ahuachapán is 100 kilometres from the capital by bus 202 from San Salvador (US$0.90), every 20 minutes 0430-1830, 0400-1600 to the capital, 2 hours via Santa Ana. Microbuses to border in front of Almacén northwest corner of parque, US$0.45, 25 minutes, slower buses same price. Frequent buses and minivans to the border at Km 117, Las Chinamas.

This is an indigenous town, 15 kilometres northeast of Ahuachapán. There are large, interesting colonial ruins at the entrance to town open 0900-1600, look for guard, or visit Casa de la Cultura office, *Concultura*, some 3,000 metres on main street north, interesting photos on display same hours, closed 1230-1330. The town is near the northern entrance of El Imposible National Park; access by hiking or four-wheel drive in the dry season, with permit only. There are no lodgings in town. *Café Tacuba*, 500 metres above Casa de la Cultura, serves excellent food, fresh vegetables, inexpensive (Lydia de González, daughter Mónica and US husband speak English), 0800-1600. The town is worth a visit, especially for the scenic ride through coffee plantations en route. Buses, US$0.60, 45 minutes, rough road, leave the terminal in Ahuachapán every 30 minutes, 0500-1530, return 1630-1700, via Ataco.

Tacuba

A road runs northwest through the treeless Llano del Espino, with its small lake, and across the Río Paz into Guatemala.

This is a busy crossing as it is the fastest road link from San Salvador (117 kilometres from Las Chinamas) to Guatemala City, 121 kilometres (via the Santa Ana bypass, then to Ahuachapán and on to the border). The road to the border is being widened and repaved for its entire length, except where it passes through Chalchuapa at Km 78 and Ahuachapan at Km 100.

Frontier with Guatemala – Las Chinamas-Valle Nuevo

Salvadorean immigration A straightforward crossing: quick service if your papers are ready.

Crossing by private vehicle If driving with non-Central American licence plates, expect about 45 minutes for formalities; hire a *tramite* (young boy) to hustle your papers through, US$2-3. Your vehicle will probably be searched by anti-narcotics officers (DOAN); do not refuse as your papers will be checked again 300 metres into El Salvador. PNC (police) are courteous and efficient.

Exchange Coming from Guatemala, cash your quetzales at the border, check what you are given. Change money with the women in front of the ex-ISTU office next to Aduana, they are honest. Good quetzal-dollar rate, cash only.

Transport 300 metres above immigration, frequent buses to Ahuachapán, No 265, US$0.45, 25 minutes. Change there to No 202 to San Salvador. Between 0800 and 1400 you may try for a space on one of the international pullmans, negotiate with drivers' aide, about US$3.50 to capital.

Between Ahuachapán and Sonsonate is Apaneca, founded by Pedro de Alvarado in 1543 (. It is 90 kilometres from San Salvador, 29 kilometres from Las Chinamas, with a colonial centre, one of the oldest parochial churches in the country, a traditional parque and a municipal market selling fruit, flowers and handicrafts. Other local industries include coffee, flowers for export and typical furniture. There are two small lakes nearby to the north, Laguna Verde and Laguna Las Ninfas, whose crater-like walls are profusely covered in tropical forest. This is the Cordillera de Apaneca, part of the narrow highland belt running southeast of Ahuachapán. The lakes are popular with tourists. It is possible to swim in the former, but the latter is too shallow and reedy. There is also a beautiful natural pool called the Balneario de Azumpa. (Accommodation at Apaneca, **A** *Cabañas de Apaneca*, T2790099, F4522536; *Apaneca Tennis Club*; also two restaurants, *La Casona* and *La Casa de Mi Abuela*.) Local buses run some distance away, leaving one with a fairly long walk. Laguna Verde can be reached by walking from Apaneca to Cantón Palo Verde and Hoyo de Cuajuste, then a further kilometre from where the road ends. East of Apaneca

Apaneca
Population: 12,000
Altitude: 1,450m, the highest town in the country
Average temperature: 18°C

is the Cascada del Río Cauta (take bus 216 from Ahuachapán towards Jujutla, alight three kilometres after the turn-off to Apaneca, then walk along trail for 300 metres).

Nine kilometres west of Ahuachapán near the village of **Los Toles** are the Tehuasilla falls, where the Río El Molino falls 60 metres (take bus 293 from Ahuachapán to Los Toles, then walk one kilometre, or go by car).

Metapán
Population: 51,800
32 km N of Santa Ana

Metapán is about 10 kilometres northeast of Lago de Güija. Its colonial baroque cathedral of San Pedro is one of the very few to have survived in the country (it was completed by 1743). The altarpieces have some very good silver work (the silver is from local mines) and the façade is splendid. (*Fiesta patronal*, San Pedro Apóstol, 25-29 June.) Lots of easy walks with good views towards Lago de Metapán and, further on, Lago de Güija. There are many lime kilns and a huge cement plant.

Sleeping **B** *San José*, Carretera Internacional Km 113, near bus station, T4420556/0320, a/c, quiet, cable TV, safe parking, good, restaurant on ground floor (Sra García, the manager, will help with transport to Montecristo). **F** *Ferrocarril*, west end of town. **F** *Hospedaje Central*, 2 Av Norte y C 15 de Septiembre, with bath, clean friendly, popular.

Eating *Rincón del Pelón*, best in town, helpful, friendly. *Comedor Carmencita*, 2 Av Norte, clean, popular, basic meals but cheap.

Buses From Santa Ana No 235, US$0.80, 1 hour. If driving San Salvador-Metapán, a new bypass skirts Santa Ana.

Montecristo National Nature Reserve

If planning to walk in the hills near Metapán, seek local advice and do not walk alone.

A mountain track from Metapán gives access to El Salvador's last remaining cloud forest. There is an abundance of protected wildlife. This now forms part of El Trifinio, or the International Biosphere 'La Fraternidad', administered jointly by Guatemala, Honduras and El Salvador. Near the top of Cerro Montecristo (2,418 metres), which is the point where the three frontiers meet, there is an orchid garden, with over 100 species (best time to see them in flower is early Spring), an orchard and a camping ground in the forest. The views are stunning as is the change of flora and fauna with the altitude. For information, contact Sr Randolfo Cabezas, Secretary international relations, area Metapán, coordinator on El Trifinio with EU, T4420278, Spanish only.

It is 20 kilometres from Metapán to the park. It takes 1½-2 hours to go up, less to return. The trails to the summit take 1½ hours. Park employees escort visitors, best Monday-Friday; admission is paid 5 kilometres before the park, US$1.25 per person, plus US$3 for vehicle. Four-wheel drive is necessary in the wet season (mid-May to mid-October). Camping is permitted. To hire four-wheel drive and driver costs US$45 return, 7 hours; eg Sr Francisco Xavier Monterosa, C 15 de Septiembre Casa 40, T4420373, c/o Isaac Monterosa.

A good paved road runs from Metapán to the Guatemalan frontier at **Anguiatú**. Three and a half kilometres out of Metapán on this road is a hotel, **E** *Montecristo*, with seven rooms.

Frontier with Guatemala – Anguiatú

This is normally a quiet border crossing except when there are special events at Esquipulas in Guatemala.

Salvadorean immigration The usual requirements apply; relaxed crossing.

Exchange Good rates reported.

Transport To Santa Ana, No 235A, US$0.80, 1¾ hours. To Metapán 40 minutes, US$0.25.

This is the best route from San Salvador to northwest Guatemala, Tikal and Belize but there is an alternative through Honduras (see under El Poy, page 827). There is a road of sorts from Metapán to El Poy and 2 buses a day, 4 hours, US$1.80, through attractive countryside.

On the Guatemalan border, the lake, 16 kilometres by eight, is very beautiful and dotted with small islands, but it is not easy to reach. A new dam at the lake's outlet generates electricity for the western part of the country. It is possible to walk round parts of the lake, but there is no proper track and fences reach down to the water's edge. Ask permission to enter the hiking trails; vehicle access is difficult. Boat trip to **Isla Tipa**, once a sacred Maya site, may be arranged through *Amacuilco Guest House* at Lago de Coatepeque. Ask directions to the Cerro de Figuras where there are interesting rock drawings. Special excursions may be available through *Jaguar Tours* in San Salvador. The border with Guatemala passes through the lake so there is the chance that you may have to account for your presence there. Carry a copy of your passport and entry stamp in case you are questioned. Bus 235 from Santa Ana, US$0.55, one hour. **Lago de Güija**

Northern El Salvador

San Salvador

The route from San Salvador to Western Honduras passes through the delightful handicraft centre of La Palma.

There was much guerrilla and counter-insurgency activity in the northern areas, but there is now freedom of movement. The Troncal del Norte (Ruta CA 4) is paved throughout; the first 12 kilometres, due north to Apopa are autopista, thereafter it is being reconstructed (1999). It is 2½ hours by car from San Salvador to La Palma, then 11 kilometres to the border at El Poy. **Routes to western Honduras**

Warning Most, if not all, the mines laid during the Civil War have been cleared. However, if you are visiting the remoter areas, especially on foot, seek local advice.

A friendly town with a good market and a new shopping centre. It is the junction with a good road to Quezaltepeque (12 kilometres). Bus 38B from San Salvador to Apopa, US$0.15. **Apopa**
Population: 20,000

A paved road runs east from Apopa to Tonacatepeque, an attractive small town on a high plateau. It has a small textile industry and is in an agricultural setting. There has been some archaeological exploration of the town's original site, five kilometres away. A paved road from Tonacatepeque runs 13 kilometres south to the Pan-American Highway, some five kilometres from the capital. In the other direction, a dry-weather road runs north to Suchitoto (see next section). **Tonacatepeque**

Three kilometres beyond Apopa, on CA 4 Km 17, is a finca belonging to the owners of *Ximena's Guest House* in San Salvador. It is being developed as an ecological centre with accommodation, restaurant and language school. *Restaurante Coma y Punto* serves local meals (it is planned to serve mostly natural foods, vegetarian meals with own-grown produce). *Lisa's Inn* will accommodate students in the Spanish language school, and a hotel is to be built higher up the hill. Visitors will be able to relax, or help on the finca. It is planned to run tours to Suchitoto, the Cerrón Grande lake for watersports and to Guazapa volcano, which played a prominent part in the civil war. For information, contact René Carmona at *Ximena's* (address under San Salvador **Sleeping**). Any bus from Terminal de Oriente to Aguilares passes the entrance, US$0.25.

21 kilometres from Apopa is **Aguilares**, four kilometres beyond which are the ruins of **Cihuatán**. The name means 'place of women' and it was presided over by female royalty. Entry only with permission from the watchman.

Chalatenango
Population: 30,000
Altitude: 450m
Colour map 4, grid C3

The highway passes the western extremity of the Cerrón Grande reservoir. A branch to the right skirts the northern side of the reservoir to Chalatenango, capital of the department of the same name. Rural Chalatenango is mainly agricultural with many remote villages and many non-governmental organizations working in the area. Chalatenango , 55 kilometres from San Salvador, is a delightful little town with annual fairs and *fiesta* on 24 June and 1-2 November. It is the centre of an important region of traditional livestock farms. Good market and several craft shops for example *Artesanías Chalateca*, for bags, hammocks et cetera.

Take special care here if you walk in the countryside: areas off the main road may be mined. Local residents usually (but not always) know which places are safe.

Sleeping and eating Two *hospedajes*: **F** *El Nuevo Amanecer*, basic, good views of the Cathedral from the 2nd floor; 1 unnamed, **F**. *La Peña*, steaks and seafood, live music at night.

Transport Bus 125 from Oriente terminal, San Salvador, US$1.10, 2½ hours.

La Palma

Population: 14,770
Altitude: 1,100m
Colour map 4, grid C3

The main road continues north through Tejutla (beautiful views at Km 72) to La Palma (84 kilometres from San Salvador). A charming village set in pine clad mountains, and well worth a visit. It is famous for its local crafts, particularly the brightly painted wood carvings and hand-embroidered tapestries. Also produced are handicrafts in clay, metal, cane and seeds. There are a number of workshops in La Palma where the craftsmen can be seen at work and purchases made. Information on the town and surrounding area can be obtained from the Casa de Cultura (Concultura). *Fiesta*: mid or late February, Dulce Nombre de María.

Sleeping & eating
AL *Entre Pinos*, 3 kilometres north of La Palma, reservations (San Salvador)T2701151/7, 1st-class resort complex, a/c, pool, cable TV, sauna. **B-C** *Hotel La Palma y Restaurante de la Montaña*, T335-9012/9202, book ahead for weekends and holidays, 6 large rooms, clean, with bath, friendly, restaurant limited menu but good, beautiful gardens, ceramics workshop, ample parking, recommended. Owner is Lic Salvador Zepeda; there is a room for let **F** behind the store where the bus heading south stops, army cots, basic bath, not cheap but you have little choice. Ask around for a room (**E-F**), but not after dark. *La Terraza Cafetería*, 2 blocks from church on road to El Poy, upstairs, open daily 0800-1900, good typical food, cheap, T3359015. *El Poyeton*, 1 block down hill from *La Terraza*, 50 metres on left, local food, also has basic rooms. *La Estancia*, next to Gallery Alfredo Linares (see below), on C Principal, open 0800-2000, good menu, bulletin board, T/F3359049. *Del Pueblo*, C Principal 70, owner María Adela friendly, good basic menu, also incorporates *Artesanías El Yute*.

Shopping
Handicrafts *Cooperativa La Semilla de Dios*, Plaza San Antonio, T3359098, F3359010, the original cooperative founded by Fernando Llort in 1971, huge selection of crafts and paintings, helpful, if unable to go to La Palma, visit *El Arbol de Dios*, end C La Mascota at Av Masferrer Sur, Col Maquilishuat, galleries and *tiendas*, concerts, cultural events, restaurant, garden, T2246200/2791537, F2791538, tours in English, German or Spanish, managers María José Llort and Karl Hoffman. *Barrotienda* in *Hotel La Palma*. *Palma City*, C Principal behind church, T3359135, Sra Alicia Mata, very helpful with finding objects, whether she stocks them or not, wood, ceramics, *telas*, etc. *Gallery Alfredo Linares*, T3359049 (Sr Linares' house), well-known artist whose paintings sell for US$18-75, open daily 0900-1700, friendly, recommended.(Ask in pharmacy if gallery is unattended). *Taller La Campina*, Marta Morena Solís, T3359029, good handicrafts, good prices (phone in advance). *Cerámica San Silvestre*, T3359202, opposite *Hotel La Palma*, wholesale/retail, good. *Artesanías El Típico*, Blanca Sola de Pineda, C Principal, T3359210, good. *Artesanías El Tecomate*, Carlos Alfredo Mancía, T3359068, F3359208, also good work in wood. (The products are also sold in San Salvador, but are much more expensive, eg at *Artesanías La Palma*, Av Sisimiles 2911, Col Miramonte, T2269948.)

Buses From San Salvador, Terminal de Oriente, to La Palma, No 119, US$1.25, 3 hours, last return leaves at 1630. **Transport**

Six kilometres north of La Palma is the picturesque village of San Ignacio, which has two or three small *talleres* producing handicrafts. 20 minutes by bus, US$0.10 each way. Also near La Palma there is a river reached by rough road (14 kilometres), beautiful, and the summit of Miramundo, about 2,000 metres, with trails and wilderness. Be prepared to hike. Ask in *Hotel La Palma* for a guide (recommended). Most areas are accessible by four-wheel drive.

Western Honduran Border

The road continues north to the frontier at **El Poy**, for western Honduras, **D** *Hotel Cayahuanca*, Km 93.5, T3359464, friendly, good but expensive restaurant.

At Citalá, one kilometre off the highway just before El Poy, is a small, basic hotel, *El Trifinio*. The town itself is unexciting. From Citalá an adventurous road goes to Metapán (see page 824). Three to four buses daily take three hours for the 40 kilometres, rough but beautiful. If driving, use four-wheel drive. There is much reforestation under way in the area.

The crossing is straightforward in both directions but it is best to arrive early in the day. At holiday times it is busy. The border posts are 100 metres apart. **Frontier with Honduras – El Poy**

Exchange Bargain with money changers at the border for the best rate for lempiras. They are unwilling to offer rates better than 1 colón = 1 lempira. Cash dollars and travellers' cheques can be changed in banks in Nuevo Ocotepeque.

Transport To San Salvador, Terminal de Oriente, No 119, US$1.35, 3-4 hours, often crowded, hourly, last bus from the capital 1600. The same bus to La Palma US$0.15, 30 minutes.

This route is used from El Salvador to northwest Guatemala, crossing this border then into Guatemala at Agua Caliente, 45 minutes by car. However, roads are better through Anguiatú with only one frontier to cross. This is a good route for Copán and San Pedro Sula (7 hours by car San Salvador-Copán, including 45 minutes at border).

Eastern El Salvador

An agricultural zone, the north of which was fiercely disputed between the army and guerrillas. Among the attractions are lakes, volcanoes, beaches and the towns of the Lempa Valley.

There are two roads to the port of La Unión/Cutuco on the Gulf of Fonseca: (i) the Pan-American Highway, 185 kilometres mostly in bad condition, through Cojutepeque and San Miguel (see below); (ii) the Coastal Highway, also paved, running through Santo Tomás, Olocuilta, Zacatecoluca, and Usulután (see page 836). **Routes to La Unión/Cutuco**

Pan-American Highway

The road is dual carriageway out of the city, but becomes single carriageway for several kilometres either side of Cojutepeque. These sections are twisty, rough and seem to induce some very bad driving. There is also a great deal of litter along the roadside; look beyond it for fine views. A short branch road (about two kilometres beyond Ilopango airport) leads off right to the west shores of Lago de Ilopango. A little further on another road branches off to the lake's north shore.

Suchitot & Cerrón Grande At San Martín, 18 kilometres from the capital, a paved road heads north to Suchitoto (*Population*: 30,000) 25 kilometres away on the southern shore of the Embalse Cerrón Grande, also known as Lago de Suchitlán. Suchitoto was founded by either the Pipíl or Yaqui Indians and there are archaeological sites in the area. It is a pleasant, small, colonial town with attractive balconied houses and an interesting, restored church. There is a splendid view from the church tower. Arts and cultural festivals take place every February and there is a small museum, **Casa Museo de Alejandro Cotto,** for more information, call Sr Cotto ■ *T2840040 open 0830-1600 daily, US$3, guided tour in Spanish.* The local cigar factory can be visited. Local specialities include *salporitas* (made of corn meal) and *chachamachas.* Try the local *pupusas* in the market and at the corner near CTE/Antel. Boat excursions across to remote areas in neighbouring Chalatenango available, ask around, negotiate prices.

Sleeping and eating B-C *La Posada de Suchitlán*, Final 4C Poniente, T/F3351164, Swedish-run (Arne and Elinor Dahl) reservation required (in San Salvador F2602427, René Carmona or Donald Lee), colonial style, excellent hotel and restaurant, nice view. **F** *Hostal El Viajero*, at entrance to town, very basic. *Café El Obraje*, clean, reasonably priced. *Pupusería Vista al Lago*, Av 15 de Septiembre 89, good food.

Boat trips go to lakeside villages associated with the FMLN in the recent civil war. 12 kilometres away, on the road to Aguilares, a Parque de la Reconciliación is being developed at the foot of Guazapa volcano (contact Cedro in San Salvador, T2280812, cedro@euromaya.com). Also, three kilometres along this road is Aguacayo with a large church, heavily damaged in the war. Buses to Aguilares, three a day, poor road.

A road runs east from Suchitoto to Ilobasco (see below), passing Cinquera, whose villagers returned home in February 1991 after six years displacement, and Tejutepeque.

Cojutepeque
Population: 31,300

The capital of Cuscatlán Department, 34 kilometres from San Salvador is the first town on the Pan-American Highway. Lago de Ilopango is to the southwest. Good weekly market. The town is famous for cigars, smoked sausages and tongues, and its annual fair on 29 August has fruits and sweets, saddlery, leather goods, pottery and headwear on sale from neighbouring villages, and sisal hammocks, ropes, bags and hats from the small factories of Cacaopera (Department of Morazán). There is also a sugar cane festival on 12-20 January. That part of town on the Pan-American Highway is full of foodstalls and people selling goods to passengers on the many passing buses.

Excursions Cerro de las Pavas, a conical hill near Cojutepeque, dominates **Lago de Ilopango** and gives splendid views of wide valleys and tall mountains. Its shrine of Our Lady of Fátima draws many pilgrims. There are religious ceremonies on May 13.

Sleeping & eating E *Motel Edén*, with shower. **E** *Hospedaje Viajero*, 1 block east of *Turista* (also hourly rentals). **E** *Turista*, 5 C Oriente 130, beware of extra charges. *Comedor Toyita*, good value. *Comedor Familiar*, good.

Buses No 113 from Oriente terminal in San Salvador, US$0.55; buses leave from here on the corner of the plaza 2 blocks from the main plaza.

Ilobasco
Population 48,100

From **San Rafael Cedros**, six kilometres east of Cojutepeque, a 16-kilometre paved road north to Ilobasco has a branch road east to Sensuntepeque at about Km 13. Many of **Ilobasco's** population are workers in clay; its decorated pottery is now mass-produced and has lost much of its charm, but it is worth shopping around; try

Hermanos López at entrance to town; also José y Víctor Antino Herrera, Avenida Carlos Bonilla 61, T3322324, look for *Kiko* sign, fine miniatures for sale. The area around, devoted to cattle, coffee, sugar and indigo, is exceptionally beautiful. Annual fair: 29 September. An all-weather road leads from Ilobasco to the great dam and hydroelectric station of Cinco de Noviembre at the Chorrera del Guayabo, on the Río Lempa. Bus 111 from Terminal de Oriente US$0.80, one and a half hours. Another road with fine views leads to the Cerrón Grande dam and hydroelectric plant; good excursion by bus or truck. One can climb the hill with the CTE/Antel repeater on top for a view of the whole lake created by the dam.

Sleeping Hotel in Ilobasco, **D** *La Casona*, C Bernardo Perdomo y 3 Av Sur, T3322388, F3322050, recommended. *Hotel Ilobasco*, on road to hospital, has the town's ony real restaurant.

Sensuntepeque, 35 kilometres east of Ilobasco, is a pleasant town at 900 metres, in the hills south of the Lempa valley. It is the capital of Cabañas Department, once a great source of indigo. There are some interesting ceremonies during its fair on 4 December, the day of its patroness, Santa Bárbara. It can be reached from the Pan-American Highway from near San Vicente.**E** *Hospedaje Jandy*. **E** *Hospedaje Oriental*.

Sensuntepeque
Population: 45,000
Colour map 4, grid C4

From Sensuntepeque, the conventional way east is to head back to the Pan-American Highway by bus and continue to San Miguel. It is possible, however, to alight at Dolores (no accommodation), take a truck at dawn to the Río Lempa, cross in a small boat to San Juan, then walk three hours to **San Gerardo**, from where one bus at 1100 goes daily to Ciudad Barrios (see below). This area was badly damaged during the war. Most roads are appalling and water and electricity are often cut.

Four kilometres from the turning to Ilobasco, further south along the Pan-American Highway at **Santo Domingo** (Km 44 from San Salvador) a paved road leads in five kilometres to **San Sebastián** where colourfully patterned cloth hammocks and bedspreads are made. You can watch them being woven on complex looms of wood and string, and can buy from the loom. Behind *Funeraria Durán* there is a weaving workshop. Sr Durán will take you past the caskets to see the weavers. The Casa de Cultura, about 50 metres from the plaza, will direct visitors to weaving centres and give information on handicrafts. Before buying, check prices and beware overcharging. Market on Monday. The 110 bus from the Oriente terminal runs from San Salvador to San Sebastián (one and a half hours, US$0.80). There are also buses from Cojutepeque.

San Vicente

61 kilometres from the capital, San Vicente lies a little southeast of the Highway on the Río Alcahuapa, at the foot of the double-peaked **San Vicente volcano** (or **Chinchontepec**), with very fine views of the Jiboa valley as it is approached. The city was founded in 1635. Its pride and gem is El Pilar (1762-69), the most original church in the country. It was here that the Indian chief, **Anastasio Aquino**, took the crown from the statue of San José and crowned himself King of the Nonualcos during the Indian rebellion of 1832. El Pilar stands on a small square one and a half blocks south of the Parque Central. On the latter is the cathedral, whose nave is draped with golden curtains. In the middle of the main plaza is a tall, open-work clock tower, quite a landmark when descending the hill into the city. Three blocks east of the main plaza is the *tempisque* tree under which the city's foundation charter was drawn up. The tree was decreed a National Monument on 26 April 1984. There is an extensive market area a few blocks west of the centre and hammock sellers can be found on nearby streets. An army barracks takes up an entire block in the centre. A small war museum opened in 1996-97; ask the FMLN office here or in San Salvador. San Vicente has a lovely setting and is a peaceful place to spend a night or two. Carnival day: 1 November.

Although all street signs have names, it seems that numbers are preferred.

Population: 56,800
Colour map 4, grid C4

El Salvador

Excursions Three kilometres southeast of the town is the Balneario **Amapulapa**, a Turicentro. There are three pools at different levels in a wooded setting. US$0.60 entry and US$0.60 parking charges. Unfortunately the site has a bad litter problem and a reputation for petty crime. Women should not walk there alone. Reached by buses 158, 177 and 193 from San Vicente bus station, US$0.10. **Laguna de Apastepeque**, near San Vicente off the Pan-American Highway, is small but picturesque. The Turicentro at the lake costs US$0.60 to enter and to park. Take bus 156 from San Vicente, or 499 from San Salvador. Ask in San Vicente for guides for climbing the volcano.

Sleeping **D** *Central Park*, on Parque Central, T3330383, with bath, TV, a/c, phone, good, clean, cheaper with fan, cheaper still without TV, café downstairs. **D** *Villas Españolas*, ½ block from main square, smart, good value, parking. **E** *Casa Romero*, after the bridge, 1st turning on the left, no sign, clean, good meals. **F** *Casa de Huéspedes Germán y Marlon*, T3330140 1 block from plaza, shared bath, 1 bed and 1 hammock in each room, very clean and friendly. **F** *Casa de Huéspedes El Turista*, Indalecio Miranda y Av María de los Angeles, well kept, fan, good.

Eating *Taiwan*, Parque Central. *La Casona*, on same plaza as El Pilar church. *Comedor Rivoli*, Av María de los Angeles Miranda, clean, good breakfast and lunches. *Comedor La Cabaña*, just

San Vicente

To Pan American Highway & San Salvador

Esso

Texaco

Justo Aguilar · Antonio Ruiz

5 C Pte · 5 C Ote/Domingo Santos

Centro Judicial

Cambio León

F A Figueroa/3 C Pte · Dr A J Cañas

Tempisque Tree

Clock Tower · Cathedral

Lic Hernán Miranda

Alcaldía · Zorra Tree · Daniel Díaz

Bus to Apasteque · Army Barracks · Procuraduría para la Defensa de los Derechos Humanos

Ahorromet · Gobernación · 1 de Julio 1823

European Commission

Lic Basilio Meriño · Alberto de Merino

El Pilar

Indalecio Miranda · Juan C Segovia

N

| 0 | metres | 150 |
| 0 | yards | 164 |

■ **Sleeping**
1 Casa de Huéspedes Germán y Marlon
2 Central Park
3 Villas Españolas

● **Eating**
1 Comedor La Cabaña
2 Comedor Rivoli
3 La Casona
4 Pops
5 Salón de Té María
6 Taiwan

off main plaza. *Casablanca*, good shrimp, steaks, and you can swim in their pool for US$1.15. *Chentino's Pizza*, good fruit juices. *Salón de Té María*, opposite barracks, café, cakes and snacks. *Pops*, next to Banco Hipotecario on main plaza, ice cream. *La Nevería*, close to bus station, good ice cream.

Bus 116 from Oriente terminal, San Salvador, US$0.90, 1½ hours, every 10 minutes or so. **Transport** Returning to the capital, catch bus at bus station (Avenida Victoriano Rodríguez y Juan Crisóstomo Segovia), or outside the Cathedral, or on the road out of town. To **Zacatecoluca**, No 177, US$0.40 from bus station. Buses to some local destinations leave from the street that goes west-east through the market (eg No 156 to **Apasteque**). You have to take 2 buses to get to **San Miguel** (see below), 1st to the Pan-American Highway (a few kilometres), where there is a bus and food stop, then another on to San Miguel, US$1.30 total.

Banks *Banco Hipotecario* on main plaza, exchange counter at side, 'leave guns and mobile phones **Directory** with the guard, please'. *Casa de Cambio León*, C Dr Antonio J Cañas, off northeast corner of main plaza. **Communications** Post Office: in Gobernación, which is 2 Av Norte y C 1 de Julio 1823. **Telephones:** CTE/Antel, 2 Av Norte/Av Canónigo Raimundo Lazo, southeast of plaza.

The Highway (in reasonable condition after San Vicente) used to cross the Río Lempa by the 411 metre-long Cuscatlán suspension bridge (destroyed by guerrillas in 1983). It now crosses an emergency bridge.

10 kilometres south of the Pan-American Highway is **Berlín**, known for its quality **Berlín** coffee plantations. *Hotel Berlines* and *Villa Hermosa*, both **E**. (Take care if driving in this area, especially after 1300.)

From Berlín there is a road round the north of Volcán de Tecapa to **Santiago de María**, which itself is on a road between the Pan-American and coastal highways (**E** *Villa Hermosa*, 3 Av Norte 4, T6630146; bus 309 from Terminal del Oriente, two and a half hours, US$1.15). Half way is Alegría from which you can visit the **Laguna de Alegría** in the crater of the volcano, fed by both hot and cold springs. (The volcano last erupted in 1878.) The lake level is low during the day but rises at 1600 each afternoon. Local guides charge US$12 per day.

San Miguel

136 kilometres from San Salvador, the capital of its Department was founded in 1530 *Population: 380,000* as a military fortress by Don Luis de Moscoso at the foot of the volcanoes of **San** *approximately* **Miguel**: **Chaparrastique**, which erupted in 1976, and **Chinameca**. San Miguel is the *Colour map 4, grid C4* third largest city in El Salvador, with one of the fastest-growing economies in Central America and has some very pleasant plazas and a bare 18th century cathedral. The city's theatre dates from 1909, but from the 1960s it was used for various purposes other than the arts. Some silver and gold are mined. It is an important distribution centre. The arid climate all year round makes the region ideal for growing maize, beans, cotton and sisal. *Fiesta* of the Virgen de la Paz: 3rd Saturday in November.

A new Metrocentro shopping centre has opened southeast of the centre. The Turicentro of Altos de la Cueva is one kilometre north; take town bus 60, admission, car parking US$0.60; swimming pools, gardens, restaurants, sports facilities, bungalows for rent US$3.45, busy at weekends. There is a charming church with statues and fountains in its gardens about 16 kilometres away at Chinameca. **Excursions**: Aqua Park, Pan-American Highway at Km 156 towards La Unión, T6611864, 35 metre high chutes, unique in Central America, playground, good restaurant, recommended. **El Capulín** natural pools at the village of **Moncagua**, the waters run from pumice-stone caves and are said to be medicinal. Take bus towards Ciudad Barrios.

Sleeping

Very few in centre, most on the entrance roads

A *Trópico Inn*, Av Roosevelt Sur 303, T6611800, F6611399, clean, comfortable, reasonable restaurant, swimming pool, garden. **B** *El Mandarín*, Av Roosevelt N, T6690918, a/c, pool, good Chinese restaurant. **C** *Motel Milián*, Panamericana Km 136, T6611970, pool, good value, recommended, good restaurant. **D** *China House*, Panamericana Km 137, T6695029, clean, friendly. **D** *Greco*, 10 C Poniente 305, T6611411, fan, good food and service, often full weekdays. **D** *Hispanoamericano*, 6 Av Norte y 8 C Oriente, T6611202, with toilet and

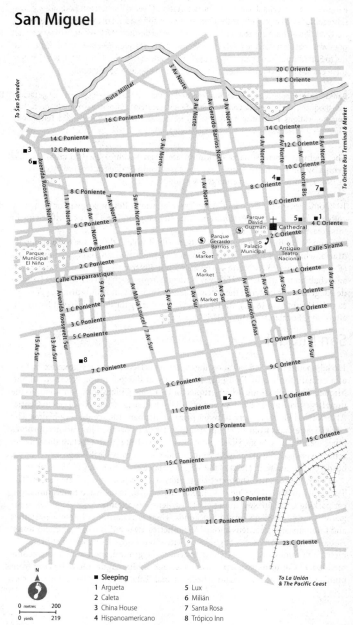

San Miguel

■ Sleeping

1 Argueta
2 Caleta
3 China House
4 Hispanoamericano
5 Lux
6 Milián
7 Santa Rosa
8 Trópico Inn

0 metres 200
0 yards 219

shower, parking. **E** *Santa Rosa*, 8 Av Norte y 6 C, good. **E-F** *Caleta*, 3 Av Sur 601, T6613233, basic, inexpensive, ample parking, fan, popular with local business travellers.

Plenty of cheap places near the bus station, eg **E** *Hospedaje Argueta*, 4 C Oriente y 6-8 Av. **E** *San Rafael*, 6 C Oriente y 10 Av Norte, T6614113, with bath, clean, fan, parking. **E** *Anexo La Terminal*, opposite bus station, good breakfast. **F** *Migueleña*, 4 C Oriente No 610, very basic but good value, clean, large rooms, towels, bath, fan. **F** *Pension Lux*, 4 C Oriente, 6 Av, reasonable.

La Puerta del Sol, 3 Av Sur, 4 C Poniente, good variety. *El Gran Tejano*, 4 C Poniente, near cathedral, great steaks. *Chetino's Pizzería*, 5 C Poniente, near Centro Médico. *Bati Club Carlitos*, 12 Av Norte. There are branches of *Pollo Campero*, all accept dollars, and a *Burger King* and a *Wendy's* for fast food lovers, and a good *Pizza Hut* 2 blocks north of the cathedral. Try *bocadillos de totopostes*, maize balls with either chilli or cheese; also *tustacos*, which are like small tortillas with sugar or honey. Both are delicious and traditional in San Miguel. South towards El Cuco at Km 142.5 is the *La Pema* restaurant, an interesting octagonal structure with the Chaparrastique volcano framed in one of the rear sections, popular, seafood specialities, moderate prices, open 1100-1700, closed Monday, T6676055. All buses to El Cuco and to Usulatán will stop there if requested.

Eating

All San Salvador supermarkets have branches here.

Shopping

Local Car rental: Uno, Av Roosevelt Sur y C Chaparrastique 701, T6617618, emergency 2981122, unidad 51390.

Air Airport 5 kilometres south of the centre, taxi US$4. Regular daily flights to the capital, see under San Salvador.

Transport

Buses No 301 from Oriente terminal, San Salvador (US$2.50, every 30 minutes from 0500 to 1630, 2½ hours). There are also 3 comfortable, express buses daily, US$5, 2 hours. There are frequent buses to the Honduran border at El Amatillo, US$1.

Airline offices *Taca*, Condominio San Benito, opposite *Hotel Trópico Inn*, Av Roosevelt, T6611477. **Banks** Local banks. Open: 0830-1200, 1430-1800. *Banco Cuscatlán* will change TCs, but you must produce receipt of purchase, otherwise, TCs are difficult to change. *Casa de Cambio Lego*, 2 C Poniente, overlooking market. **Useful addresses** Police: emergency T121.

Directory

From San Miguel a paved road runs south to the Pacific Highway. Go south along it for 12 kilometres, where a dirt road leads to Playa El Cuco (see page 838). Bus 320 from San Miguel, US$1. The climate in this area is good. A mainly paved, reasonable road goes to San Jorge and Usulatán: leave the Pan-American Highway five kilometres west of San Miguel. The road goes through hills and coffee plantations with superb views of San Miguel volcano. The volcano can be climbed from **Placita** on the road to San Jorge, about four hours up. Ask at Placita for information, a guide costs about US$5.

To the northwest are the Indian ruins of **Quelapa** (bus 99, US$0.50), but there is not much to see. From Quelapa a road continues north to **Ciudad Barrios**.

The capital of Morazán Department can be reached from the Oriente terminal in San Salvador, or from San Miguel (bus 328). Foreigners are not usually allowed beyond here on Route 7 to the Honduran border. Two places to stay: **F** *Hospedaje San Francisco*, Av Morazán 29, T6640066, nice garden and hammocks; *Motel Arco Iris*, next door. Beyond San Francisco, the road runs to Jocaitique (there is a bus) from where an unpaved road climbs into the mountains through pine forests to Sabanetas, near the Honduran border. Accommodation at both Jocaitique and Sabanetas.

San Francisco Gotera

22 kilometres northeast of San Francisco is **Corinto** with two rock overhangs which show faint evidence of precolumbian wall paintings. They are 20 minutes north of

Corinto

the village on foot, just east of the path to the Cantón Coretito. The caves are open seven days a week; take an early bus, No 327 from San Miguel, US$1.

Ciudad Segundo Montes Eight kilometres north of San Francisco Gotera is **Ciudad Segundo Montes**, a group of villages housing 8,500 repatriated Salvadoran refugees (the community is named after one of the six Jesuit priests murdered in November 1989). If you would like to visit this welcoming, energetic place, ask for the Ciudad Segundo Montes (CSM) office in San Salvador at the UCA university, or in San Francisco Gotera (T6640033). When you get to CSM, ask to be let off at San Luis and go to the Oficina de Recepción. You will be put up in a communal dormitory; meals in *comedores* cost US$1; there is a bath house (spring-fed showers). Free tours of the community are given and there is beautiful hiking.

14 kilometres north of San Francisco is **Delicias de la Concepción**, where fine decorated hammocks and ceramics are made; good prices, helpful, worth a visit. Buses every 20 minutes from San Francisco.

Perquín
Population: 5,000
Altitude: 1,200m
Colour map 4, grid C4

Further along this road is Perquín 205 kilometres from San Salvador (), which was the guerrilla's 'Capital'. This was the scene of much military activity. War damage is still clearly visible around the town, but all is now peaceful. Thousands who fled the fighting in the 1980s are now returning and rebuilding. There is a very interesting museum, open Tuesday-Sunday 0830-1600, entrance US$1.20, guided tours in Spanish. *Fiesta* 1-5 October. The scenery is beautiful. Nearby villages such as Arambala and El Mozote can be visited. At the latter is a memorial to a massacre in 1981. Five kilometres west of Perquin is **Arambala** which is slowly reconstructing. Locals will give you a tour of the town and church, destroyed by fire in the 1980s and being rebuilt. Here too massacres took place in the 1980s. Near Perquín, turn off two kilometres south, are the park and trails of **Cerro Pelón**. Nearby is El Llano del Muerto, a tourist area of naturally heated pools and wells. North of Perquín straddling the new border with Honduras is one of the few unpolluted rivers in the country. Contraband activity here means frequent military patrols; always carry a copy of your passport. The people of Morazán are more reserved with strangers than in the rest of El Salvador; it is best not to travel alone, or else arrange an escorted tour from FMLN in San Salvador. If travelling on your own, four-wheel drive or pickup rental is advised.

Sleeping B *Hotel Perquín Lenca*, 2 kilometres south of town, below Cerro El Gigante, cabins, excellent restaurant. **E** pp *Casa de huéspedes Gigante*, 1 kilometre south downhill from the centre (look for sign), CTE Perquín T6615077 ext 246, 4 beds per room, clean, cold showers, friendly, meals served, power turned off at 2100.

Transport Bus San Miguel-Perquín, No 332B, US$1.50, 2¾ hours. Bus from Terminal Oriente in San Salvador takes 6 hours, very crowded, luggage a hindrance. Bus or truck from Ciudad Segundo Montes. Transport back to CSM or San Miguel may be difficult in the afternoons.

Frontier with Honduras – Perquín

The Honduran border has been moved, by treaty, to within three kilometres north of Perquín; this area has been the subject of disputes and definition problems for many decades. It was one of the basic causes of the 'football war' of 1969 (see reference in the introduction to the Honduras chapter) and there were military confrontations between El Salvador and Honduras in early 1997. There is a border crossing five kilometres past the frontier and the route to Marcala and La Esperanza, Honduras, is open. There is a bus service from Marcala to San Miguel, five hours, US$3.50, using this route, but the road may be impassable after heavy rains.

It is another 42 kilometres from San Miguel to the port of La Unión/Cutuco. Shortly before it gets there the Pan-American Highway turns north for 33 kilometres to the Goascarán bridge at **El Amatillo** on the border with Honduras.

To save time when travelling eastwards from San Miguel, take the Ruta Militar northeast through Santa Rosa de Lima to the Goascarán bridge at El Amatillo, a total of 58 kilometres.

Santa Rosa is a charming little place with a wonderful colonial church, set in the hills. There are gold and silver mines. Market on Wednesday. A curiously large number of pharmacies and shoe shops. The FMLN office here has details about the Codelum project, a refugee camp in Monte Barrios, very interesting. *Fiesta* 22-31 August.

Santa Rosa de Lima
Population: 27,300

Sleeping & eating F *Florida*, Ruta Militar, helpful, fairly clean, basic, 3 parking spaces (arrive early). **F** *Hospedaje Gómez*, basic, hammocks, fan, clean. **F** *Hospedaje Mundial*, near market, rooms OK, with fan, basic, friendly, lots of parking space. **F** *Recreo*, 2 blocks from town centre, friendly, fan, noisy, basic. *El Tejano*, behind main church, friendly. Many *comedores*, most popular is *Chayito*, 'buffet', on Ruta Militar, and *Comedor Leyla*, next to bus stop, is good. *Martina*, near the bridge, good food including *sopa de apretadores* at US$7. Unnamed *comedor* on the Pan-American Highway, good and cheap.

Buses To the Honduran border every 15 minutes, US$0.50. Direct buses also to San Salvador, No 306, US$3 from 0400 until 1400, 3½ hours.

Banks *Banco de Comercio* will change TCs, also *Servicambio* near the church.

The bridge over the Río Goascarán is the border, with El Amatillo on both sides.

Frontier with Honduras – El Amatillo

Salvadorean immigration The border closes at 1700 and may close for 2 hours at lunchtime. This is a very busy crossing, but is easy for those going on foot.

Crossing by private vehicle You will be hounded by *tramitadores* offering to help. Accepting one will make it easier to get through but try to choose carefully and monitor progress. Procedures are detailed in **Essentials, Motoring**. Car searches are thorough at this crossing.

Sleeping Near the border there are 2 *hospedajes*, both basic, **F** *Anita* with *comedor* and *Dos Hermanos*.

Exchange There are many money changers, accepting all Central American currencies and travellers' cheques, but beware of short-changing on Nicaraguan and Costa Rican currencies. Good rates for colones to lempiras.

Transport To San Miguel, No 330, US$1.50, 1 hour 40 minutes. See also Santa Rosa de Lima.

La Unión/Cutuco

The port of La Unión/Cutuco (*Population*: 43,000), on the Gulf of Fonseca, handles half the country's trade.

Colour map 4, grid C4

To **Conchagua** to see one of the few old colonial churches in the country. The church was begun in 1693, after the original Conchagua had been moved to its present site after repeated attacks on the island settlements by the English. *Fiestas patronales* 18-21 January and 24 July. (Good bus service from La Unión, No 382, US$0.10.) **Volcán Conchagua** (1,243 metres) can also be climbed and is a hard walk, particularly near the top where stout clothing is useful against the vegetation. About four hours up and two hours down. You will be rewarded by superb views over San Miguel volcano to the west and the Gulf of Fonseca which is bordered by El Salvador, Honduras and Nicaragua (where the Cosigüina volcano is prominent) to the east.

Excursions

You can take an early morning boat to the Salvadorean islands in the Gulf of

Fonseca. These include Isla Zacatillo (about one hour), Isla Conchagüita and the largest **Isla Meanguera** (about four kilometres by seven kilometres) which takes about two and a half hours. Meanguera has attractive small secluded beaches with good bathing, for example Marahual, fringed with palm trees. You must obtain permission and may have to leave your passport. The customs will check your luggage. Take your own provisions, although there is excellent seafood, lobster, shark steaks, etc, available from fishermen. There are no official *hospedajes*, but locals will allow you to camp and may offer a room (better to arrange in La Unión before you arrive). Launches leave La Unión between 0900 and 1200, back very early, 0200 Monday and Friday from Marahual beach, cost US$1. For information of excursions to the islands, contact Carolina Nixon through Corsatur in San Salvador, otherwise go to *Hotel El Pelícano* and enquire. Lots of local boatmen offer trips; negotiate a price.

You can reach El Tamarindo on the mainland coast (see below) from La Unión, bus 383, US$0.50. Also from La Unión, the ruins of Los Llanitos can be visited.

Sleeping **C** *Centroamérica*, 4C Oriente, 1-3 Av, T6644029, with fan, more with a/c, noisy. **E** *El Pelícano*, Final C Principal El Hüisquil, T6644649, 20 rooms. **E** *San Carlos*, opposite railway station, good meals available. **F** *Hospedaje El Dorado*, 1 block from plaza, shared bath, nice rooms with fan, some with bath, very clean, recommended. Opposite *Hospedaje Annex Santa Marta*, a bit further away from plaza is **E** *San Francisco*, T6644159, clean, friendly, some rooms with hammocks and fan, safe parking, noisy, but OK. **F** *Hospedaje Annex Santa Marta*, with shower and fan, not bad.

Eating *La Patia*, for fish. *Comedores Gallego* and *Rosita*, recommended. *Comedor Tere*, Av Gen Menéndez 2.2, fairly good. *Amanecer Marino*, beautiful view of the bay. Bottled water is impossible to find, but *agua helada* from clean sources is sold (US$0.05 a bag).

Transport **Bus** Terminal is at 3 Calle Poniente (block 3); to San Salvador, No 304, US$2, 4 hours, many daily, direct or via San Miguel, one passes the harbour at 0300. (No 320 to San Miguel US$0.45). Bus to Honduran border at El Amatillo, No 353, US$1.65.

Boats It may be possible to take a cargo boat to Costa Rica; ask the captains in Cutuco. Outboards cross most days from La Unión to Potosí (Nicaragua), weather permitting. You must get your exit permission in La Unión. Make arrangements 1 day ahead, and check at customs office. There is reportedly a boat to Honduras, but it is easier to go by land.

Directory **Banks** Exchange at *Cafetín Brisas del Mar*, 3 Av Norte y 3 C Oriente. *Banco Agrícola Comercial* for US$ cash and TCs. Black market sometimes in centre. **Useful addresses** Customs: 3 Av Norte 3.9. **Immigration:** at 3 C Oriente 2.8.

Coastal Highway

This is the second road route, running through the southern cotton lands. It begins on a four-lane motorway to Comalapa airport. The first place of any importance after leaving the capital is (13 kilometres) **Santo Tomás**. There are Indian ruins at **Cushululitán**, a short distance north.

Beyond, a new road to the east, rising to 1,000 metres, runs south of Lago de Ilopango to join the Pan-American Highway beyond Cojutepeque.

10 kilometres on from Santo Tomás is **Olocuilta**, an old town with a colourful market on Sunday under a great tree. Good church. Both Santo Tomás and Olocuilta can be reached by bus 133 from San Salvador.

The highway to the airport crosses the Carretera Litoral (CA 2) near the towns of San Luis Talpa and Comalapa. The coastal highway goes east, through Rosario de la Paz, across the Río Jiboa and on to Zacatecoluca.

Costa del Sol

Just after Rosario, a branch road to the south leads to La Herradura (Bus No 153 from Terminal del Sur to La Herradura, US$0.90, one and a half hours) and the Playa Costa del Sol on the Pacific, being developed as a tourist resort. Before La Herradura is a small supermarket on the left. The beach is on a narrow peninsula, the length of which are private houses which prevent access to the sand until you reach the Turicentro (0800-1800). Here cabañas can be rented for the day, or for 24 hours (not suitable for sleeping), admission and car parking US$0.80 each, US$1.60 overnight (camping and cabaña rental may be refused). It is crowded at weekends and on holidays. Vehicle camping possible on the beach. There are extensive sandy beaches; the sea has a mild undertow, go carefully until you are sure.

Sleeping

Some luxury hotels: **LL** *Bahía del Sol Marina & Yacht Club*, 104 villas with luxury fittings, docking for boats, T2785222/6661, F2785252, bahia@salnet.net. **LL** *Pacific Paradise*, T2712606, F8870545, rooms and bungalows, overpriced. **L** *Tesoro Beach*, T3340600, F2791287, apartment style rooms, swimming pool, 9-hole golf course, also overpriced. **A** *Izalco Cabaña Club*, T3340616, F2240363, good value, 30 rooms, pool, seafood a speciality. **D** *Miny Hotel y Restaurant Mila*, Km 66 opposite police station, very friendly, owner Marcos speaks English, clean, simple, fan, pool, good food, beach access. Take bus 495 from Terminal Sur, San Salvador; buses are very crowded at weekends, but the resort is quiet during the week. Cheaper accommodation can be found 1 kilometre east on the next beach, Los Blancos, and also in La Herradura, eg **E** *La Sirena*, by the bus terminal, 10 rooms, fan, restaurant.

Tasajera island

At the southeast end of the Costa del Sol road, near the *Pacific Paradise* hotel, a ferry (US$1.75) leaves for Tasajera island in the Estero de Jaltepeque (tidal lagoon). For boat excursions, take Costa del Sol bus to the last stop and negotiate with local boatmen. To hire a boat for the day costs US$75 (per boat), including pilot, great trip into the lagoon, the mangroves, dolphin watching and up the Río Lempa. There is interesting wildlife on the island. **L** *Suites Jaltepeque*, resort with suites and rooms, a/c, pool, private beach, special mid-week rates, T/F2233151, suitesjaltepeque@salnet.net.

Between Rosario de la Paz and Zacatecoluca, a road branches north to the small towns of **San Pedro Nonualco** and **Santa María Ostuma** (with an interesting colonial church and a famous *fiesta* on 2 February); both are worth visiting, but not easy to get to. Bus 135 from Terminal del Sur goes to San Pedro. If you get off this bus at the turn off to San Sebastián Arriba, you can walk to the **Peñón del Tacuazín** (or del Indio Aquino), 480 metres above sea level, which is four and a half kilometres north of Santiago Nonualco. A cave at its summit was used as a refuge by Anastasio Aquino (see page 829), before his execution in April 1833.

Zacatecoluca

Population: 81,000
Altitude: 201m
Colour map 4, grid C4

The capital of La Paz Department is 56 kilometres from San Salvador by road and 19 kilometres south of San Vicente. Good place to buy hammocks, eg nylon 'doubles', US$13. José Simeón Cañas, who abolished slavery in Central America, was born here. There is a cathedral in the Moorish style, and an excellent art gallery.

Sleeping **D** *El Litoral*, on the main road Km 56. **E** *Hospedaje Viroleño*. **F** *Hospedajes América* and *Popular* clean. **F** *Hospedaje Primavera*, clean, friendly, fan. *Comedor Margoth* (beware high charging).

Buses Bus 133 from Sur terminal, San Salvador. Direct bus to La Libertad 1540, US$0.65, or take San Salvador bus and change at Comalapa, 2 hours.

Ichanmichen

Near the town is the garden park and Turicentro of Ichanmichen ('the place of the little fish'). It is crossed by canals and decorated with natural spring pools where you can swim. It is very hot but there is plenty of shade. Admission and car parking each

El Salvador

US$0.75, bungalow rental US$4; take bus 90 from Zacatecoluca.

Between Km 69 and 70, turn south for **Centro Recreativo Las Ruedas**, T3930865, or take Usulután bus from Terminal Sur, San Salvador, 1½ hours. Entry to the centre costs US$0.90.

Both the road and a railway cross the wide Río Lempa by the Puente de Oro (Golden Bridge) at **San Marcos**. (The road bridge has been destroyed; cars use the railway bridge.) Off the main road near here is **La Nueva Esperanza** where there is a community that has returned from Nicaragua, dormitories to sleep and a good place to go and help if you have a few days to spare. 20 kilometres beyond the bridge, a branch road (right) leads to tiny **Puerto El Triunfo** on the Bahía de Jiquilisco, with a large shrimp-freezing plant (**E** *Hotel/Restaurant Jardín*). Boats can be hired to take you to the islands in the Bahía de Jiquilisco, which are being developed with holiday homes, but are very beautiful.

Usulután
Colour map 4, grid C4

About 110 kilometres from the capital is Usulután (*Population*: 69,000), capital of its Department (90 metres above sea level); large, dirty, unsafe, a useful transit point only. Bus 302 from San Salvador, US$1.40.

Sleeping **E** *España*, on main plaza, T6620378, recommended. Nice patio, restaurant, bar and discotheque. several others in same price range.

Playa El Espino

Playa El Espino can be reached from Usulután, by slow bus from Usulután or car (four-wheel drive) or pickup; it is very remote but lovely. A luxury resort complex is under construction, but there is no other lodging.

The Coastal Highway goes direct from Usulután to La Unión/Cutuco.

Laguna El Jocotal

Beyond Usulután, two roads go northeast to San Miguel, the first from 10 kilometres along at El Tránsito, the second a further five kilometres east, which keeps to the low ground south and east of San Miguel volcano. Two kilometres beyond this turning on the Carretera Litoral is a short road to the right leading to Laguna El Jocotal, a national nature reserve supported by the World Wildlife Fund, which can be visited, enquire at the entrance. You will see more if you hire a boat. It has an abundance of birds and snakes.

Playa El Cuco
Cases of malaria have been reported from El Cuco

12 kilometres from the junction for San Miguel there is a turn to the right leading in seven kilometres to Playa El Cuco, a popular beach with several places to stay (**F**), near the bus station (bus 320 to San Miguel, US$0.45, one hour last bus 1600). The main beach is liable to get crowded and dirty at weekends and holidays, but is deserted mid-week (single women should take care here). Locals warn against walking along the beach after sunset.

Sleeping **D** *Cucolindo*, 1 kilometre along the coast, cabin for 4, basic, cold water, mosquitos. *Posada*, cold showers, parking US$6. **E** *Palmera*, with or without bath, impersonal and no direct beach access. **D** *Los Leones Marinos*, T6199015, with bath, clean and tidy. Nearby is the **B** *Trópico Club*, T6611288, with several cabins, run by the *Trópico Inn* in San Miguel which can provide information. **F** *El Rancho*, hammocks only, in cane shacks, basic, friendly, shower from bucket drawn from well. Another popular beach, **El Tamarindo**, is reached by another right turn off the road to La Unión, *cabañas* for rent (**AL** *Playa Negra*, T6611726, F6612513. **A** *Torola Club*, run by *Izalco Club* at Costa del Sol, T6644516, F2240363, recommended. Also **C** *Las Tunas*), and basic *pensión*. In Tamarindo you can stay at the Workers' Recreational Centre, but first obtain a permit from the Ministry of Labour, 2 Avenida Sur 516, San Salvador. Entry is usually only granted to those related to members and smartly dressed ones at that.

Transport Boat from El Tamarindo across the bay leads to a short cut to La Unión; bus from La Unión 20 minutes.

Background

The land

The total area of El Salvador is 21,041 square kilometres. Guatemala is to the west, Honduras to the north and east, and the Pacific coastline to the south is approximately 321 kilometres long.

Lowlands lie to the north and south of the high backbone. In the south, on the Pacific coast, the lowlands of Guatemala are confined to just east of Acajutla; beyond are lava promontories till we reach another 30-kilometre belt of lowlands where the 325 kilometres long Río Lempa flows into the sea. The northern lowlands are in the wide depression along the course of the Río Lempa, buttressed south by the highlands of El Salvador and north by the basalt cliffs edging the highlands of Honduras. The highest point in El Salvador, Cerro El Pital (2,730 metres) is part of the mountain range bordering on Honduras. After 160 kilometres the Lempa cuts through the southern uplands to reach the Pacific; the depression is prolonged southeast till it reaches the Gulf of Fonseca.

El Salvador is located on the southwest coast of the Central American Isthmus on the Pacific Ocean. As the only country in the region lacking access to the Caribbean Sea it does not posses the flora associated with that particular coastal zone. El Salvador nevertheless has a wide variety of colourful, tropical vegetation; for example over 200 species of orchid grow all over the country. As a result of excessive forest cutting and therefore the destruction of their habitats, many of the animals (such as jaguars and crested eagles) once found in the highlands of the country have diminished at an alarming rate. In response to this problem several nature reserves have been set up in areas where flora and fauna can be found in their most unspoilt states. Among these nature reserves are the Cerro Verde, Deininger Park, El Imposible Woods, El Jocatal Lagoon and the Montecristo Cloud Forest.

Climate

El Salvador is fortunate in that its temperatures are not excessively high. Along the coast and in the lowlands it is certainly hot and humid, but the average for San Salvador is 28°C with a range of only about 3°. March, April and May are the hottest months; December, January and February the coolest. There is one rainy season, from May to October, with April and November being transitional periods; there are only light rains for the rest of the year: the average is about 1,830 millimetres. Occasionally, in September or October, there is a spell of continuously rainy weather, the *temporal*, which may last from two or three days to as many weeks. The pleasantest months are from November to January. From time to time the water shortage can become acute.

History

When Spanish expeditions arrived in El Salvador from Guatemala and Nicaragua, they found it relatively densely populated by several Indian groups, of whom the most populous were the Pipiles. By 1550, the Spaniards had occupied the country, many living in existing Indian villages and towns. The settlers cultivated cocoa in the volcanic highlands and balsam along the coast, and introduced cattle to roam the grasslands freely. Towards the end of the 16th century, indigo became the big export crop: production was controlled by the Spaniards, and Indians provided the workforce, many suffering illness as a result. A period of regional turmoil accompanied El Salvador's declaration of independence from the newly-autonomous political body of Central America in 1839: Indian attempts to regain their traditional land rights were put down by force.

Coffee emerged as an important cash crop in the second half of the 19th century, bringing with it improvements in transport facilities and the final abolition of Indian communal lands.

The land question was a fundamental cause of the peasant uprising of 1932, which was brutally crushed by the dictator General Maximiliano Hernández Martínez. Following his overthrow in 1944, the military did not relinquish power: a series of military coups kept them in control, and they protected the interests of the landowning oligarchy.

1980s Civil War The most recent military coup, in October 1979, led to the formation of a civilian-military junta which promised far-reaching reforms. When the reforms were not carried out, the opposition unified forming a broad coalition, the Frente Democrático Revolucionario, which adopted a military wing, the Farabundo Martí National Liberation Front (FMLN) in 1980. Later the same year, the Christian Democrat, Ing José Napoleón Duarte was named as President of the Junta. At about the same time, political tension reached the proportions of civil war.

Duarte was elected to the post of President in 1984, following a short administration headed by Dr Alvaro Magaña. Duarte's periods of power were characterized by a partly-successful attempt at land reform, the nationalization of foreign trade and the banking system, and violence. In addition to deaths in combat, 40,000 civilians were killed between 1979 and 1984, mostly by right-wing death squads. Among the casualties was Archbishop Oscar Romero, who was shot while saying mass in March 1980. Nothing came of meetings between Duarte's government and the FMLN, aimed at seeking a peace agreement.

The war continued in stalemate until 1989, by which time an estimated 70,000 had been killed. The Christian Democrats' inability to end the war, reverse the economic decline or rebuild after the 1986 earthquake, combined with their reputation for corruption, caused a resurgence of support for the right-wing National Republican Alliance (ARENA). An FMLN offer to participate in presidential elections, dependent on certain conditions, was not accepted, and the ARENA candidate, Lic Alfredo Cristiani, won the presidency comfortably in March 1989, taking office in June.

Peace talks again failed to produce results, and in November 1989, the FMLN guerrillas staged their most ambitious offensive ever, which paralysed the capital and caused a violent backlash from government forces. FMLN-government negotiations resumed with UN mediation following the offensive, but the two sides could not reach agreement about the purging of the Armed Forces, which had become the most wealthy institution in the country after 10 years of US support.

Peace negotiations Although El Salvador's most left-wing political party, the Unión Democrática Nacionalista, agreed to participate in municipal elections in 1991, the FMLN remained outside the electoral process, and the civil war continued unresolved. Talks were held in Venezuela and Mexico after initial agreement was reached in April on reforms to the electoral and judicial systems, but further progress was stalled over the restructuring of the armed forces and disarming the guerrillas. There were hopes that human rights would improve after the establishment in June 1991 of a UN Security Council human rights observer commission (ONUSAL), charged with verifying compliance with the human rights agreement signed by the Government and the FMLN in Geneva in April 1990. Finally, after considerable UN assistance, the FMLN and the Government signed a peace accord in New York in January 1992 and a formal ceasefire began in February. A detailed schedule throughout 1992 was established to demobilize the FMLN, dismantle five armed forces elite battalions and initiate land requests by ex-combatants from both sides. The demobilization process was reported as completed in December 1992, formally concluding the civil war. The US agreed at this point to 'forgive' a substantial portion of the US$2bn international debt of El Salvador. In March 1993, the United Nations Truth Commission published its investigation of human rights abuses during the civil war. Five days later, the legislature approved a general amnesty for all those involved in criminal activities in the war. This included those named in the Truth Commission report. The Cristiani government was slow to implement not only the constitutional reforms proposed by the Truth Commission, but also the process of land reform and the establishment of the National Civilian Police (PNC). By 1995, when Cristiani's successor had taken office, the old national police force was demobilized, but the PNC suffered from a lack of resources for its proper establishment. In fact, the budget for the implementation of the final peace accords was deficient and El Salvador had to ask the UN for financial assistance.

1994 elections & after

Presidential and congressional elections on 20 March 1994 failed to give an outright majority to any presidential candidate. The two main contenders, Armando Calderón Sol of Arena and Rubén Zamora, of a coalition of the FMLN, Democratic Convergence and the National Revolutionary Movement, faced a run-off election on 24 April, which Calderón Sol won. Besides his government's difficulties with the final stages of the peace accord, his first months in office were marked by rises in the cost of living, increases in crime, strikes and protests, and occupations of the Legislature by ex-combatants. The government's failure to solve these problems continued into 1996, with the United Nations adding its weight to criticisms, especially of the lack of progress on implementing the social projects designed to reintegrate civil war combatants into civilian life. This contributed to the electorate's sense of disillusion, exacerbated by considerable realignment of the country's political parties. The congressional and mayoral elections of March 1997 highlighted these issues further. Only 41 percent of the electorate bothered to vote. In the National Assembly, Arena won 29 seats, FMLN increased its tally to 28 seats, the National Conciliation Party (PCN) won 11, the Christian Democrats (PDC) nine and minority parties seven seats. FMLN managed to run neck-and-neck with Arena until within a year of the March 1999 presidential elections. The party's inability to select a presidential candidate, however, caused it to lose ground rapidly, so much so that in the poll Arena's candidate, Fransisco Flores won with sufficient votes to avoid a second ballot. Since less than 40 percent of the electorate voted, Flores could not claim a clear mandate in the face of such a huge rejection of the political system. Most interpreted the abstention as a lack of faith in any party's ability to solve the twin problems of poverty and crime.

Culture

The population is far more homogeneous than that of Guatemala. The reason for this is that El Salvador lay comparatively isolated from the main stream of conquest, and had no precious metals to act as magnets for the Spaniards. The small number of Spanish settlers intermarried with those Indians who survived the plagues brought from Europe, to form a group of mestizos. There were only about half a million people as late as 1879. With the introduction of coffee, the population grew quickly and the new prosperity fertilized the whole economy, but internal pressure of population has led to the occupation of all the available land. Several hundred thousand Salvadoreans have emigrated to neighbouring republics because of the shortage of land and the concentration of land ownership, and more lately because of the civil war.

People

Of the total population, some 10 percent are regarded as ethnic Indians, although the traditional Indian culture has almost completely vanished. Other estimates put the percentage of pure Indians as low as five percent. The Lenca and the Pipil, the two surviving indigenous groups, are predominantly peasant farmers. Only one percent are of unmixed white ancestry, the rest are mestizos.

With a population of 280 to the square kilometre, El Salvador is the most densely populated country on the American mainland. Health and sanitation outside the capital and some of the main towns leave much to be desired, and progress was very limited in the 1980s and early 1990s because of the violence.

Education & religion

Education is free if given by the government, and nominally obligatory. There are 43 universities, three national and the others private or church-affiliated. There is also a National School of Agriculture. The most famous are the government-financed Universidad Nacional and the Jesuit-run Universidad Centroamericana (UCA). Roman Catholicism is the prevailing religion.

··

 Handicrafts of El Salvador

The artists' village of La Palma, in a pine-covered valley under Miramundo mountain, is 84 kilometres north of the capital, 10 kilometres south of the Honduran frontier. Here, in 1971, the artist Fernando Llort "planted a seed", known as the copinol (a species of the locust tree) from which sprang the first artists' cooperative, now called La Semilla de Dios (Seed of God). The copinol seed is firm and round; on it the artisans base a spiritual motif that emanates from their land and soul. The town and its craftspeople are now famous for their work in wood, including exotically carved cofres (adorned wooden chests), and traditional Christmas muñecas de barro (clay dolls) and ornamental angels. Wood carvings, other crafts and the designs of the original paintings by Llort are produced and exported from La Palma to the rest of El Salvador and thence worldwide. In 1971 the area was almost exclusively agricultural; today 75 percent of the population of La Palma and neighbouring San Ignacio are engaged directly or indirectly in producing handicrafts. The painter Alfredo Linares (born 1957 in Santa Ana, arrived in La Palma 1981 after studying in Guatemala and Florence) has a gallery in La Palma, employing and assisting local artists. His paintings and miniatures are marketed abroad, yet you will often find him working in the family pharmacy next to the gallery. Many of La Palma's images are displayed on the famous Hilasal towels. If you

cannot get to La Palma, visit the shop/gallery/workshop of Fernando Llort in San Salvador, Arbol de Dios.

20 kilometres from the capital is the indigenous town of Panchimalco, where weaving on the loom and other traditional crafts are being revived. Many nahaut traditions, customs, dances and the language survived here as the original Indians hid from the Spanish conquistadores in the valley beneath the Puerta del Diablo (now in Parque Balboa). In 1996 the painter Eddie Alberto Orantes, and his family opened the Centro de Arte y Cultura Tunatiuh, named after a nahuat deity who is depicted as a human face rising as a sun over a pyramid. The project employs local youths (from broken homes, or former addicts) in the production of weavings, paintings and ceramics.

In the mountains of western El Salvador, villages in the coffee zone, such as Nahuizalco, specialize in weaving henequen, bamboo and reed into table mats and in wicker furniture. There are also local artists like Maya sculptor Ahtzic Selis, who works with clay and jade. East of the capital, at Ilobasco (60 kilometres), many ceramic workshops produce items including the famous sorpresas, miniature figures enclosed in an egg shell. In the capital, there are crafts markets in which to bargain for pieces, while throughout the country outlets range from the elegant to the rustic. Everywhere artists and artisans welcome visitors into their workshops.

··

The economy

Structure of production   Agriculture is the dominant sector of the economy, accounting for three quarters of export earnings. Coffee and sugar are the most important crops, but attempts have been made at diversification and now soya, shrimp, sesame, vegetables, tropical flowers and ornamental plants are being promoted as foreign exchange earners. The sector was badly affected by drought in 1994-95 and 1997, followed by the El Niño phenomenon at end of 1997 and into 1998 when excessive rainfall hit El Salvador's Pacific coastline. The drought cut production of basic grains, cotton and hemp, and pasture for cattle (average weight and milk yields were greatly reduced) while the rains damaged the coffee and sugar crops. Further damage was inflicted on the sector, especially the east of the country, by Hurricane Mitch in 1998. By early 1999 it was clear that coffee exports were 50 percent lower than the previous season. Not only had there been crop damage, but low world prices were contributing to the drop in sales. In June 1999 President Flores announced measures to reactivate the flagging rural economy.

Land ownership has been unevenly distributed with a few wealthy families owning most of the land, while the majority of agricultural workers merely lived at subsistence level. This led to serious political and social instability despite attempts at agrarian reform by successive governments, including a determined one involving cooperatives in 1980. The Arena Government put an end to the formation of cooperatives and encouraged existing cooperatives to divide into individual farms. In 1992 the Government and the FMLN agreed a Land Transfer Programme (PTT) designed to distribute 166,000 hectares of land to about 48,000 Salvadoreans at a cost of US$143mn. The plan was beset by problems with implementation and acquisition of land which caused serious delays in the distribution of land to potential beneficiaries.

The most important industries are food processing and petroleum products: others include textiles, pharmaceuticals, shoes, furniture, chemicals and fertilizers, cosmetics, construction materials, cement (and asbestos cement), drink processing, rubber goods. Maquila factories have grown rapidly in recent years, particularly garment assemblers, providing an estimated 20,000 jobs. Exports of manufactured goods, mostly to other Central American countries, account for some 33 percent of foreign exchange earnings, although the economic slow-down throughout Central America after Hurricane Mitch reduced El Salvador's export potential.

There are small deposits of various minerals: gold, silver, copper, iron ore, sulphur, mercury, lead, zinc, salt and lime, but only limited amounts of gold, silver and limestone are produced. There is a gold and silver mine at San Cristóbal in the Department of Morazán. In 1975 a geothermal power plant came into operation at Ahuachapán, with capacity of 30 mw. The plant was expanded by 60 mw in 1978. Hydraulic resources are also being exploited as a means of generating power and saving oil import costs, but the intention of closing thermal plants has been thwarted by the poor condition of the infrastructure and disruption during the civil war. Electricity has been in short supply since 1991, first as a result of extensive sabotage, then as a result of a lack of rain to fill the hydroelectricity lakes. With electricity demand growing at six percent a year, new investment for the sector from Japan and the Inter American Development Bank announced in 1996 was much needed.

Recent trends The country's agricultural and industrial production, and consequently its exporting capability, were severely curtailed by political unrest. In 1986 further economic and social damage was caused by an earthquake; damage to housing and government property alone was estimated at US$311mn, while the total, including destruction and disruption of businesses was put at US$2bn. El Salvador was heavily dependent upon aid from the USA to finance its budget. Total US assistance was estimated at over US$4bn in the 1980s. The government which took office in 1989 outlined a national rescue plan, which was not fully implemented, and attempted, unsuccessfully, to put order into public finances, reduce inflation and encourage exports. However, the lack of foreign exchange reserves remained a serious constraint and El Salvador was declared ineligible for World Bank lending after arrears exceeded limits.

By 1990 progress was becoming evident as inflation eased, gdp grew slightly and the fiscal deficit was reduced. The privatization of banks and other state-run enterprises got under way, the trade deficit was lowered by an 18 percent increase in exports, private savings rose and so did foreign exchange reserves. International creditors praised the Government's economic stabilization efforts, with the IMF, the World Bank and the InterAmerican Development Bank all committing finance during 1990 and 1991. The Consultative Group for El Salvador (22 donor countries and 15 international and regional organizations) agreed in 1992 to provide about US$800mn to support the National Reconstruction Plan (PNR), a five-year, US$1.4bn project to alleviate poverty and consolidate peace. Foreign aid and loans in 1993 helped to boost private investment and stabilize the colón against the US dollar. Other positive factors were growth in construction and services as rebuilding and rehabilitation of infrastructure after the civil war progressed, overall gdp growth and a fall in inflation. Cristiani's administration also reduced the foreign debt and cut the fiscal deficit.

President Calderón Sol continued his predecessor's policies of aiming for growth and low inflation. Inflation was successfully contained with the result that 1999's target (2.5-4.5 percent) was the lowest since the 1960s. At the same time, though, tight monetary control limited demand. Consequently gdp growth fell from around six percent in both 1994 and

1995 to 3.5 percent in 1998. In mid-1996, the president announced measures to stimulate investment in production, promote jobs and increase social spending, since no progress had been made in alleviating poverty. After much dissent, the sale of the state telecommunications company, Antel, was launched at end of 1997 and completed in 1998. The power supply sector was also privatized, with electricity generation to follow. Savings were promoted by the launching of private pension funds in 1998. El Salvador was the first Central American country to introduce the scheme. In the first month of his term, June 1999, President Flores outlined his economic priorities as reducing the fiscal deficit, which stood at 3 percent of gdp, through some reorganization of the tax system and controls on government spending by a public sector wage freeze. Help for the agricultural sector would be complemented by road-building and efforts to stem violence in rural areas and to cut smuggling. For most Salvadoreans raising living standards was of paramount importance.

Government

Legislative power is vested in a unicameral Legislative Assembly, which has 84 seats and is elected for a three-year term. The head of state and government is the president, who holds office for five years. The country is divided into 14 departments.

Communications

There are 562 kilometres of railway; rural passenger services run in the northwest of the country: San Salsavador to Metapán and Aguilares to Texistepeque. In 1995 the road length was 12,320 kilometres, of which 14 percent was paved.

El Salvador

Honduras

7

Honduras

Essentials

Planning your trip

Honduras is larger than all the other Central American republics except Nicaragua, but has a smaller population than El Salvador, less than a fifth its size. Bordered by Nicaragua, Guatemala, and El Salvador, it has a narrow Pacific coastal strip, 124 kilometres long, on the Gulf of Fonseca, but its northern coast on the Caribbean is some 640 kilometres long.

Where to go

Hurricane Mitch deluged Honduras in October 1998 with torrential rain which caused great loss of life and major damage to almost all parts of the country. News reports have painted a bleak picture, even up to August 1999, but visitors considering including Honduras in their itinerary should in no way be deterred. It is possible to visit all the main tourist areas of the country and many parts which lie off the beaten track. Road travel was running without hindrance (but not without detours) just a few weeks after the storm hit and the situation has continued to improve. The tourist industry, which is one area in which swift positive returns for the country can be seen, is fully open for business and is desperate for visitors to return.

The capital and administrative centre of Honduras is **Tegucigalpa**, which has an older part with some colonial buildings and a newer section where many modern hotels, shops and businesses are located. Across the Río Choluteca is Tegucigalpa's twin city, **Comayagüela**, where the markets and bus termini are to be found. Around the capital are many colonial villages, old mining towns, handicraft centres and good hiking areas, including La Tigra national park.

A good paved highway runs north from Tegucigalpa to the second city, and main business centre of the country, **San Pedro Sula**. The road passes the old colonial capital of Comayagua and beautiful Lago Yojoa. North of San Pedro Sula is the **North Coast**, which has a number of centres for the visitor. The main port is **Puerto Cortés**, to the west of which is Omoa, an increasingly popular beach and fishing village with an old fort, from where an overland route enters Guatemala. East of Puerto Cortés is **Tela**, a more established resort, then **La Ceiba**, a good place for visiting nearby national parks (eg Pico Bonito and Cuero y Salado) and for getting to the Bay Islands, and **Trujillo**, once the capital of the country on a wide bay. In addition to the parks already mentioned, there are several areas set aside as wildlife refuges on the Caribbean.

The **Bay Islands**, Utila, Roatán and Guanaja, plus the smaller Hog Islands, are one of Honduras' main tourist destinations. The largely English-speaking islands curve northeast from the coast. They have good beaches and Guanaja was, until Hurricane Mitch stopped overhead, covered with pine trees. It is now recovering fast. The other islands were hardly affected at all. But it is for their underwater environment that Utila and Roatán are best known. There is wonderful diving here and Utila is certainly the cheapest dive centre in the Caribbean.

West of San Pedro Sula, near the frontier with Guatemala, is Honduras' premier Maya archaeological site, **Copán**, where new discoveries are still being made, and some fine Maya art can be seen. Nearby is the recently-opened site of El Puente. In the west are quiet colonial towns such as **Gracias** and **Santa Bárbara**, opal mines, Lenca Indian communities and the Mount Celaque National Park. There is lots of good hiking, for instance in the vicinity of **Santa Rosa de Copán**, a good way to explore the more traditional parts of the country.

Honduras's short **Pacific** coast on the Gulf of Fonseca is little visited, other than on the routes to Nicaragua and El Salvador. The main town in the region is Choluteca and, in the gulf, is the town of Amapala on the extinct volcanic Isla del Tigre. Another route to Nicaragua is that **east of the capital** through the town of Danlí, which passes the Panamerican Agricultural School at Zamorano and the old mining town of Yuscarán.

Northeast of Tegucigalpa is Olancho, an agricultural and cattle-raising area, which leads eventually to the Caribbean coast at **Trujillo**. Juticalpa and Catacamas are the main towns here and the mountains of the district have cloudforest, hiking trails and conservation areas. Beyond Olancho is **Mosquitia**, forested, swampy and almost uninhabited. Efforts are being made to preserve this relatively untouched area and to promote sustainable development

Honduras

among the Miskito and Pesch Indians who live there. Ecotourism initiatives in some of the communities on the coast and inland have been set up and these make for adventurous and rewarding travel. The main ways of getting around are by boat, small plane or on foot.

When to go   The Caribbean coast is wet all year round, but the heaviest rain falls from September to February. The dry season inland is November to April, December and January being the coolest months, April and May the hottest. Some of the central highland areas enjoy a delightful climate, with a freshness which makes a pleasant contrast to the humidity and heat of the lowland zones. In Tegucigalpa lowest average temperatures are 14°C in January and February, and the highest 30°C April-May. The cooler season in San Pedro Sula is November to February, but the rest of the year is very hot.

Finding out more   The **Ministerio Hondureño de Turismo** has its main office at Edificio Europa, Avenida Ramón E Cruz y Calle República de México, Colonia San Carlos, Tegucigalpa, T2383974/2224002, F2382102. There is also an office at Toncontín airport and regional tourist offices (see also under Tegucigalpa, page 862). *HONDURAS tips*, published by *COPAN tips*, edited by John Dupuis in San Pedro Sula, Apartado Postal 2699, Edif Rivera y Cía, p 7, of 705, 3 C 6 Av 50, T/F5529557, hondurastips@ honduras.com. www.hondurastips.honduras.com, is a weighty quarterly publication full of interesting and useful tourist information, in English and Spanish, free (available in Tegucigalpa from Ministerio Hondureño de Turismo). The website www.honduras.com, has lots of information, including latest news. Another site, www.in-honduras.com, gives access to Honduran newspapers, travel information, news and other useful material. Also try www.netsys.hn/.

Maps   The **Instituto Geográfico Nacional** produces two 1:1,000,000 maps (1995) of the country, one a tourist map including city maps of Tegucigalpa, San Pedro Sula and La Ceiba, and the other with a good road network although it does not show all the roads. Both maps widely available in bookshops in major cities and some hotels. There is also a Texaco road map (1992).

Before you travel

Getting in   **Documents**   A visa is not required, nor tourist card, for nationals of all west European countries, USA, Canada, Australia, New Zealand, Japan, Argentina, Chile, Guatemala, Costa Rica, Nicaragua, El Salvador, Panama and Uruguay. Citizens of other countries need either a tourist card which can be bought from Honduran consulates for US$2-3, occasionally less, or a visa, and they should enquire at a Honduran consulate in advance to see which they need. The price of a visa seems to vary per nationality, and according to where bought. It is imperative to check entry requirements in advance at a consulate. Two-day transit visas costing US$5, for any travellers it seems, are given at the El Florido border for visiting Copán, but you must leave at the same point and your right of return to Guatemala is not guaranteed, especially if your Guatemalan visa is valid for one journey only.

Visitors from all countries who do not need a visa may stay for 30 days, although visitors from Germany, Japan and Chile are allowed 90 days. Some travellers, regardless of nationality, have reported 90 day permits given in airport immigrations. Make sure border officials fill in your entry papers correctly and in accordance with your wishes. Extensions of 30 days are easy to obtain (up to a maximum of six months' stay, cost US$5). There are immigration offices for extensions at Tela, La Ceiba, San Pedro Sula, Santa Rosa de Copán, Siguatepeque, La Paz and Comayagua, and all are more helpful than the Tegucigalpa office. A valid International Certificate of Vaccination against smallpox is required only from visitors coming from the Indian subcontinent, Indonesia and the countries of southern Africa. A ticket out of the country is necessary for air travellers (if coming from USA, you won't be allowed on the plane without one); onward tickets must be bought outside the country. (It is not impossible to cash in the return half of the ticket in Honduras, but there is no guarantee and plenty of time is needed.) Proof of adequate funds is sometimes asked for at land borders.

Customs   There are no Customs duties on personal effects. 200 cigarettes or 100 cigars, or half a kilogram of tobacco, and two quarts of spirit are allowed in free.

Honduran embassies and consulates

Belgium (also the Netherlands and Luxembourg), Avenue des Gaulois 8, 1040 Brussels, T322-7340000, F322-7352626
Canada, 151 Slater Street, Suite 805-A, Ottawa, Ontario K1P 5H3, T613-2338900, F613-2320193
France, 8 Rue Crevaux, 75116 Paris, T47558645, F47558648
Germany, Ubierstrasse-1, D-53173 Bonn, T228-356394, F228-351981
Italy, Gian Battista de Vico 40, Interno 8, Roma, T06-3207236, F06-3207973
Japan, 38 Kowa Bldg, 8F No 802, 12-24 Nishi

Azabu 4, Chome Minato Ku, Tokyo 106, T03-34091150, F03-34090305
Mexico, Alfonso Reyes 220, Colonia Condesa, México, DF, T2115747, F2115425
Spain, Calle Rosario Pino 6, Cuarto Piso A, Madrid 28020, T341-5790251, F341-5721319
Sweden, Sturegatan 12, 114, 36 Stockholm, T6653231, F6650917
UK, 115 Gloucester Place, London W1H 3PJ, T0171-4864880, F0171-4864550
USA, 3007 Tilden Street NW, Pod 4M, Washington, DC 20008, T202-9667702, F202-9669751.

Money

Currency The unit is a lempira. It is divided into 100 centavos. There are nickel coins of 5, 10, 20, and 50 centavos. Bank notes are for 1, 2, 5, 10, 20, 50 and 100 lempiras. Any amount of any currency can be taken in or out.

Credit cards Mastercard and Visa are accepted in major hotels and most restaurants in cities and larger towns. Cash advances from Credomatic, Boulevard Morazán, Tegucigalpa, and branches of Banco Atlántida, Aval Card and Honducard throughout the country. Credomatic represents American Express and issues and services Amex credit cards. Cash advances using Mastercard costs US$10 in banks. Acceptance of credit cards in Honduras is patchy and commissions can be as high as six percent. It is advisable therefore to have available travellers' cheques and US$ in cash as well.

Money may be changed at the free rate in banks, but a street market offers rates which are usually higher than the official rate.

Getting there

Air There are no direct flights to **Tegucigalpa** from Europe, but connecting flights can be made via Miami, then American Airlines or Taca, or Guatemala City (with KLM or Iberia), then Taca. To Tegucigalpa from New York and Miami with American Airlines; from Houston with Continental. Taca flies daily from Guatemala City, Mexico City and San Salvador; Lacsa fly to Tegucigalpa from San José; other Central American cities have connecting flights.

Iberia flies to **San Pedro Sula** via Miami from Madrid and Barcelona five days a week. American Airlines fly daily from Chicago and Miami; also from Miami, Taca and Iberia. Continental flies from Houston daily; Taca daily from Los Angeles, Houston, New Orleans, New York. Lacsa flies from San José to San Pedro Sula direct; Taca flies from Belize City, Guatemala City and San Salvador. Copa flies from Guatemala City, San Juan (Puerto Rico) and Panama City to San Pedro Sula. Isleña flies from Belize City.

Taca flies to **La Ceiba** from San Salvador. Isleña flies from Belize City daily and Grand Cayman Island twice a week to La Ceiba. See Roatán, page 916 for flights to the island.

Boat The *MV Regal Voyager* is a 112-cabin cruise line which sails from Puerto Cortés, Wednesday, 1800, arriving in Brownsville, Texas, Saturday, 0700, returning Sunday 1800, getting in to Puerto Cortés Wednesday, 0600, from US$80 per person, gym, restaurants, cinema, jacuzzi, sauna, casino, duty-free shop. In Tegucigalpa T2385055, F2390666, in San Pedro Sula T5575840, F5533519, in Puerto Cortés T5550045, F5531322.

Touching down

Border hours Note that the border offices close at 1700, not 1800 as in most other countries; there is an extra fee charged after that time.

Clothing Western; suits optional for most businessmen; on the north coast, which is much hotter and damper, dress is less formal. Laundering is undertaken by most hotels.

Cost of living Honduras is not expensive for the visitor (two people travelling together can expect to pay US$40 per person per day), but prices for services offered to tourists can fluctuate a lot. Before bargaining over a few dollars, or insisting on prices quoted as a guide in this Handbook, put the price offered in perspective with the exchange rate and with prices offered elsewhere. In this way, you can avoid antagonism.

Entry & departure taxes **Air** There is an airport departure tax of US$25 (not charged if in transit less than nine hours). There is a 10 percent tax on all tickets sold for domestic journeys, and a 10 percent tax on airline tickets for international journeys.

Land Taxes are charged on entry and exit at land borders, but the amount charged varies from border to border, despite notices asking you to denounce corruption. Entry is 20 lempiras (or US$2) and exit is 10 lempiras. Double is charged on Sunday. If officials make an excess charge for entry or exit, ask for a receipt. Do not attempt to enter Honduras at an unmanned border crossing. When it is discovered that you have no entry stamp you will either be fined US$60, or escorted to the border and you have to pay the guard's food and lodging (you may be able to defray some of this cost by spending a night in jail). It is advisable always to carry means of identification, because spot-checks have increased.

Tipping Normally 10 percent of bill.

Getting around

Road Buses tend to start early in the day; however, some night buses run between major urban centres. Try to avoid bus journeys after dark as there are many more accidents and occasional robberies. Hitchhiking is relatively easy. If hiring a car, make sure it has the correct papers, and emergency triangles which are required by law. The main arteries are in excellent condition, but off the main roads standards decline rapidly. Children fill in holes with grit in the hope of receiving a tip.

Motoring Regular gasoline/petrol costs US$1.45 per US gallon on the north coast, US$1.50 in the central region and US$1.52 in remote regions such as the Mosquitia. Super costs US$1.50, US$1.52 and US$1.55 respectively. Unleaded petrol is available everywhere. Diesel costs US$1 and kerosene is US$0.90. Fuel pumps often display price per half gallon.

On entering with a car (from El Salvador at least), customs give a 30-day permit for the vehicle, but transit police only give eight days entry. This must be renewed in Tegucigalpa (anywhere else authorization is valid for only one department). Charges for motorists appear to be: on entry, US$14 in total for a vehicle with two passengers, including provisional permission from the police to drive in Honduras, US$1 (official minimum) for car papers, fumigation and baggage inspection; on exit, US$2.30 in total. Motorcyclists face similar charges. These charges are changing all the time and differ significantly from one border post to another (up to US$40 sometimes). They are also substantially increased on Saturday, Sunday and holidays and by bribery. You will have to pass through Migración, Registro, Tránsito, Cuarentena, Administración, Secretaría and then a police vehicle check. At each stage you will be asked for money, for which you will not always get a receipt. No fresh food is allowed to cross the border. On arriving or leaving with a vehicle there are so many checks that it pays to hire a *tramitador* to steer you to the correct officials in the correct order (US$1-2 for the guide).

There are frequent police searches on entry or exit from towns and villages. Only stop if signalled to do so. Be alert if there are policemen around, they will try to spot an infraction of

Touching down

Official time *Six hours behind GMT.*
Hours of business *Monday to Friday:*
0900-1200; 1400-1800 Saturday: 0800-1200,
and some open in the afternoon. Banks in
Tegucigalpa 0900-1500; 0800-1100 only
along the north coast on Saturday. In San
Pedro Sula and along the north coast most
places open and close half an hour earlier in
the morning and afternoon than in
Tegucigalpa. Post Offices: Monday-Friday
0700-2000, Saturday 0800-1200.
IDD *504. Long equal tones with long pauses*
means it is ringing. Short tones with short

pauses indicate engaged.
Voltage *Generally 110 volts but,*
increasingly, 220 volts is being installed.
US-type flat-pin plugs.
   NB *Honduras has two electric power*
producers but accidents and water shortages
sometimes lead to power cuts.
Weights and measures *The metric system*
of weights is official and should be used, but
the libra (pound) is still often used for meat,
fish etc. Land is measured in varas (838
millimetres) and manzanas (0.7 hectares).

---

the laws to collect a fine, for example parking on the wrong side of the road, stopping with your wheels beyond the line at a 'Stop' sign, seat belt violations. You can be fined if you do not have two reflecting triangles and a fire extinguisher in your car. Your licence will be taken until the fine is paid; on-the-spot fines are not legal, but are common. Try to go to a police station.

Air   There are airstrips in the larger and smaller towns. Airlines which make internal flights are: Isleña, Sosa and Caribbean Air. Details are given in the text.

Bicycles   Bicycles are regarded as vehicles but are not officially subject to entrance taxes. Bicycle repair shops are difficult to find, and parts for anything other than mountain bikes may be very hard to come by. Some buses and most local flights will take bicycles. Most main roads have smooth shoulders and most traffic respects cyclists. It is common for cars to blow their horn to signal their approach.

Keeping in touch

Language   Spanish, but English is spoken in the north, in the Bay Islands, by West Indian settlers on the Caribbean coast, and is understood in most of the big business houses. Trade literature and correspondence should be in Spanish.

Postal services   Air Mail takes four to seven days to Europe and the same for New York. Letters up to 20 grams cost US$0.40 to all parts of the world. Small packages 500 grams-1 kilogram, US$3 to USA or Europe; sea mail to Europe US$3 up to five kilograms, US$4.50 up to 10 kilograms, takes several months. Note that this service is not available in Guatemala, so it might be convenient to send things from Tegucigalpa or San Pedro Sula main Post Offices.

Telephone services   Hondutel provides international telephone, fax and telex services from stations throughout the country. Telephone service between Honduras and Europe costs about US$4.81 per minute; calls to USA US$2.70 per minute. Collect calls to North America, Central America and some European countries (not possible to Netherlands, Australia, Switzerland or Israel) can be made from Hondutel office in Tegucigalpa. Fax charges are per page, plus 12 percent tax, to North America US$1.80, to Europe US$1.80, to South America and the Caribbean US$2, to the rest of the world US$3. To receive a fax at Hondutel costs one lempira per page.
   Email   Details of cafés and other places offering email and internet services to travellers are given in the text.

Media   **Newspapers**   The principal newspapers in Tegucigalpa are *El Heraldo, La Tribuna* and *El Periódico*. In San Pedro Sula: *El Tiempo, El Nuevo Día* and *La Prensa* (circulation about 45,000). English weekly paper: *Honduras This Week*, Edificio Berna Exitos 204, Col Rubén Darío, Apartado Postal 1312,

Tegucigalpa, T2315821, F2322300, hontweek@hondutel.hn, www.marrder.com/htw/, available at limited locations throughout the country, comes out on Saturday, costs US$0.35.

Television There are six television channels and 167 broadcasting stations. Cable TV is available in every large town.

Food and drink

Different cuisines Cheapest meals are the *comida corriente* or (sometimes better prepared and dearer) the *comida típica*; these usually contain some of the following: beans, rice, meat, avocado, egg, cabbage salad, cheese, *plátanos*, potatoes or yucca, and always tortillas. Make sure that pork is properly cooked. *Carne asada* is charcoal roasted and served with grated cabbage between tortillas, good, though rarely sanitarily prepared. *Tajadas* are crisp, fried *plátano* chips topped with grated cabbage and sometimes meat; *nacatamales* are ground, dry maize mixed with meat and seasoning, boiled in banana leaves. *Baleadas* are soft flour tortillas filled with beans and various combinations of butter, egg, cheese and cabbage. *Pupusas* are thick corn tortillas filled with chicharrón (pork sausage), or cheese, served as snacks with beer. *Tapado* is a stew with meat or fish (especially on the north coast), plantain, yucca and coconut milk. *Pinchos* are meat, poultry, or shrimp kebabs. *Sopa de mondongo* (tripe soup) is very common.

Cheap fish is best found on the beaches at Trujillo and Cedeño. While on the north coast, look for *pan de coco* (coconut bread) made by *garífuna* (Black Carib) women and *sopa de camarones* prepared with coconut milk and lemon juice.

Drink Soft drinks are called *refrescos*, or *frescos* (the name also given to fresh fruit blended with water, check that bottled water is used as tap water is unsafe); *licuados* are fruit blended with milk. Bottled drinking water is readily available in most places. Orange juice, usually sweetened, is available in paper cartons everywhere. *Horchata* is morro seeds, rice water and cinnamon. Coffee is thick and sweet. There are five main brands of beer, Port Royal Export, Imperial, Polar, Nacional and Salva Vida (good, more malty than the other four). Local rum is cheap, try Flor de Cana white, or amber seven years old.

Shopping

The best articles are those in wood. Straw items are also highly recommended. Leather is cheaper than in El Salvador and Nicaragua, but not as cheap as in Colombia. The coffee is good. Note that film can be expensive, but Konica film can be bought for US$4 to US$5 for 36 exposures, for example at Laboratorio Villatoro, stores in major towns. For bulk purchases (say 50 rolls) try their head office on Calle Peatonal, Jardín de Italia, Tegucigalpa.

Sales tax is 12 percent, often only charged if you ask for a receipt; 15 percent on alcohol and tobacco. There is also a four percent extra tax on hotel rooms.

Holidays and festivals

Most of the feast days of the Roman Catholic religion and also 1 January: New Year's Day; 14 April: Day of the Americas; Holy Week: Thursday, Friday, and Saturday, before Easter Sunday; 1 May: Labour Day; 15 September: Independence Day; 3 October: Francisco Morazán; 12 October: Columbus' arrival in America; 21 October: Army Day.

Health

Health/disease risks Dysentery and stomach parasites are common and malaria is endemic in coastal regions, where a prophylactic regime should be undertaken and mosquito nets carried. Inoculate against typhoid and tetanus. There is cholera, so eating on the street or at market stalls can not be recommended. Drinking water is definitely not safe; drink bottled water which is available amost everywhere. Ice and juices are usually made with purified water. Otherwise boil or sterilize water. Salads and raw vegetables are risky. There are hospitals at Tegucigalpa and all the larger towns.

Tegucigalpa

The capital and nearby excursions to old mining settlements in the forested mountains: a great contrast between the functional modern city and some of the oldest villages in the country.

The city stands in an intermont basin at between 950 and 1,100 metres above sea level. It was founded as a mining camp in 1578: the miners found their first gold where the north end of the Soberanía bridge now is. The name means 'silver hill' in the original Indian tongue. It did not become the capital until 1880. On three sides it is surrounded by sharp, high peaks. It comprises two former towns: Comayagüela and Tegucigalpa built at the foot and up the slopes of El Picacho. A steeply banked river, the Choluteca, divides the two towns, now united administratively as the Distrito Central. Tegucigalpa has not been subjected to any disaster by fire or earthquake (but see below), being off the main earthquake fault line, so retains many traditional features. Many of the stuccoed houses, with a single heavily barred entrance leading to a central patio, are attractively coloured. However, the old low skyline of the city has now been punctuated by several modern tall buildings. Its altitude gives it a reliable climate: temperate during the rainy season from May to November; warm, with cool nights, in March and April, and cool and dry, with very cool nights, in December to February. The annual mean temperature is about 74°F (23°C).

Population: 800,000
Altitude: 1,000m
Colour map 4, grid C4

The Carretera del Sur (Southern Highway), which brings in travellers from the south and from Toncontín Airport, runs through Comayagüela into Tegucigalpa. It goes past the obelisk set up to commemorate 100 years of Central American independence, and the Escuela Nacional de Bellas Artes, with a decorated Mayan corridor and temporary exhibitions of contemporary paintings and crafts.

The torrential rains of Hurricane Mitch in October 1998 had a devastating effect on the Distrito Central. The Río Choluteca burst its banks, flooding the lower levels of the city, washing away bridges and destroying homes and businesses. In addition, the rain loosened the soil on the steep hillsides on which several neighbourhoods were built, causing them to collapse with great loss of life. Traffic was badly disrupted while the bridges were down. In 1999 the city's electricity distribution network was being renewed and there were daily power cuts.

Ins and outs

The international airport, Toncontín, is six and a half kilometres south of the centre. The airport is in a narrow valley creating difficult landing conditions: early morning fog or bad weather can close the airport. There is no central bus station. Bus companies have their offices scattered throughout Comayagüela. On arrival, unless staying at a hotel close to the company's depot, it is advisable to take a taxi to your lodging until you have acquainted yourself with the city.

Getting there

The Tegucigalpa section of the city uses both names and numbers for streets, but names are now used more commonly. In Comayagüela, streets disgnated by number are the norm. Addresses tend not to be very precise, especially in the colonias around Boulevard Morazán east and south of the centre of Tegucigalpa. There are buses and taxis for city transport. **NB** Generally speaking, Tegucigalpa is cleaner and safer (especially at night) than Comayagüela. If you have anything stolen, report it to Dirección de Investigación Criminal (DIC), 5 Avenida, 7-8 Calle (next to Edificio Palermo), T2374799.

Getting around

Sights

Crossing the river from Comayagüela by the colonial Mallol bridge, on the left is the

Nicaragua

old **Casa Presidencial** (1919, now the Museo Presidencial, the new one is a modern building on Boulevard Juan Pablo II in Colonia Lomas del Mayab). Calle Bolívar runs through the area containing the Congress building and the former site of the University, founded in 1847. The site is now the **Galería Nacional de Arte**, with a permanent art exhibition (see **Museums** below). In Colonia Palmira, Tegucigalpa, is the Boulevard Morazán, with shopping and business complexes, embassies, banks, restaurants, cafeterías, bars, et cetera. You can get a fine view of the city from the **Monumento a La Paz** on Juana Laínez hill, near the Estadio Nacional (National Stadium). ■ *Open till 1700.*

The backdrop to Tegucigalpa is the summit of **El Picacho** with the Cristo del Picacho statue looming up to the north (see **Excursions**, below), although it is hard to see during spring because of smog. From Plaza Morazán go up 7 Avenida and the Calle de la Leona to **Parque La Leona**, a handsome small park with a railed walk overlooking the city. Higher still is the reservoir in El Picacho, also known as the **United Nations Park**, which can be reached by a special bus from the number 9 bus stop, behind Los Dolores church (in front of Farmacia Santa Bárbara), Sunday only, US$0.15; alternatively, take a bus to El Piligüin or Corralitos (daily) at 0600 from the north side of Parque Herrera in front of the Teatro Nacional Manuel Bonilla.

Tegucigalpa

To Barrio el Chile & Alternative Route to North

COMAYAGÜELA

N

Not to scale

Calle Bolívar leads to the main square, Plaza Morazán (commonly known as Parque Central). On the eastern side of the square are the **Palacio del Distrito Central**, and the domed and double-towered **Cathedral** built in the late 18th century. See the beautiful gilt colonial altarpiece, the fine examples of Spanish colonial art, the cloisters and, in Holy Week, the ceremony of the Descent from the Cross.

Avenida Miguel Paz Barahona, running through the northern side of the square, is a key avenue. On it to the east is the church of **San Francisco**, with its clangorous bells, and (on 3 Calle, called Avenida Cervantes) the old **Spanish Mint** (1770), now the national printing works. If, from Plaza Morazán, we go along Avenida Miguel Paz Barahona westwards towards the river, by turning right along 5 Avenida (Calle Los Dolores) we come to the 18th century church of **Virgen de los Dolores**. Two blocks north and three blocks west of the church is Parque Concordia with good copies of Maya sculpture and temples.

Back on Avenida Miguel Paz Barahona and further west are the **Teatro Nacional Manuel Bonilla**, with a rather grand interior (1915) and, across the square, the beautiful old church of **El Calvario**. Built in elegant colonial style, El Calvario's roof is supported by 14 pillars. It contains images of the Virgen de la Soledad, San Juan and the archangels San Miguel and San Rafael. On Easter Friday processions start and end here. Crossing the bridge of 12 de Julio (quite near the theatre) one can visit Comayagüela's market of San Isidro.

Museums

On Calle Bolívar, next to Congress, in a beautifully restored building (1654) adjoining the church in Plaza La Merced, is the **Galería Nacional de Arte**, housing a very fine collection of Honduran modern and colonial art, also prehistoric rock carvings and preColombian ceramics (some remarkable pieces). There are useful descriptions of exhibits, and explanations of the mythology embodied in the prehistoric and preColombian art (in Spanish only but a brochure in English and Spanish is in preparation). ■ *Tuesday-Saturday 1000-1700, Sunday 1000-1400, US$5, bookshop and cafetería.* **Museo de la Historia Republicana Villa Roy**, former site of the **Museo Nacional**, in 1936 home of a former President, Julio Lozano, was restored, reconstructed and reopened in 1997. There are seven main rooms presenting Honduras' history from independence in 1821 to 1963, as well as supporting cultural presentations and temporary exhibits. It is situated on a hilltop one block above the beautiful Parque Concordia on Calle Morelos 3A. ■ *0900-1630, closed Sunday, US$1.50.* In the Edificio del Banco Central, 12 Calle entre 5 y 6 Avenida, Comayagüela, is the **Pinacoteca Arturo H Medrano**, with a collection of approximately 500 works by five Honduran artists and, in the same building, the **Museo Numismático**, with a collection of coins and banknotes from Honduras and around the world. ■ *Monday-Friday, 0900-1200, 1300-1600*. **Museo de la República de Honduras** (formerly the **Museo Histórico**), in the former Presidencial Palace, better on the 19th century than the 20th, visitors can see the President's office and the Salón Azul state room. ■ *0830-1630, Monday-Saturday, US$1.20, reduced for Central Americans, children and students.*

Sleeping

There is a 4% tax on hotel bills, plus 12% sales tax; check if it is included in the price.

■ *on maps Price codes: see inside front cover*

Seven large new hotels are under construction, including *Camino Real* and *Crowne Plaza*. Opened in 1999 is **LL** *Princess*, Col Alameda, T2205081, 180 rooms, all facilities. **In Tegucigalpa**: **LL** *Honduras Maya*, Av República de Chile, Colonia Palmira, T2323191, F2327629, cheaper if you are a resident of Honduras, rooms and apartments, casino, swimming pool US$3.50, bars (the main bar is relaxed and you get appetizers with every alcoholic drink, US TV channels), cafeterías (*Black Jack's Snack Bar, Cafetería 2000*), restaurant (*El Candelero*), conference hall and convention facilities for 1,000, view over the city from uppermost rooms. **L** *Plaza San Martín*, on Plaza San Martín (near *Honduras Maya*), Colonia Palmira, T2328267, F2311366, good cafetería, nice bar, great views of the city from the top terrace. **AL** *Alameda*, Blvd Suyapa (some distance from centre), T2326902, F2326932, comfortable, pool, restaurant *Le Chalet* (T2326920). **AL** *Paseo Miramontes*, Calle Paseo Miramontes, Col Miramontes, T2328179/2391855, a/c, modern, cable TV, including breakfast, parking. **AL** *Humuya Inn Guest House*, Colonia Humuya 1150, 5 minutes from airport, T2392206, F2395099, humuyain@david.intertel.hn, rooms and service apartments, US owner, recommended. **A** *Suites La Aurora*, Apart-Hotel, Av Luis Bográn 1519, Colonia Tepeyac, T2329891, F2320188, rooms with kitchenette, cable TV, excellent restaurant, swimming pool, helpful staff. **A-B** *Rosemarie Bed & Breakfast*, Col Elvel, 5 C, behind Tiendas Carrión, T2325766, F2391134, a/c, bath, cable TV, phone, free local calls, comfortable, continental breakfast, safe. At El Hatillo, on the hill north of Tegucigalpa is the comfortable mountain inn *Gloriales*, beautiful setting and fine views of La Tigra forest, T2224950, lovely rooms, fine cuisine, reservations essential; also the new *La Estancia Country Resort*, Corralitos, with restaurant, T2118651, F2118653. *Downtown*: **AL-B** *Excelsior*, Av Cervantes 1515, T2372638, with bath, hot water, a/c, restaurant, refurbished 1998. **A** *Plaza*, on Av Paz Barahona, in front of Post Office (T2372111, F2372119), good, *Papagayo* restaurant good for breakfast and set lunch. **AL** *La Ronda*, Av Máximo Jérez entre Corleto y Las Damas, 5 blocks from cathedral, T2378151/55, F2371454, a/c, TV, restaurant, cafetería (*Rondalla*) and nightclub. **AL** *Prado*, Av Cervantes y H Mutute, T2370121, F2371454, *La Posada* restaurant.

B *Istmania*, 5 Av (Los Dolores), 7-8 C (T2371638/39, F2371446) near Church of Los Dolores, *Versalles* restaurant. **C** *MacArthur*, Av Lempira entre del Telégrafo y Los Dolores, T2375906, F2380294, a/c, TV, private bath, cheaper without a/c. Recommended. **D** *Nuevo Boston*, Av Jérez No 321, T2379411, good beds, spotless, cable TV, hot water, central. Repeatedly recommended. Good value, no credit cards, rooms on street side noisy, friendly, free coffee, mineral water and cookies in lounge, stores luggage, well run. **C-D** *Krystal*, Máximo Jérez y S Mendieta, T2378804, F2378976, TV, a/c, good rooms, not very welcoming, parking, restaurant for 1,000 (special events only), rooftop bar with good view.

F *Fortuna*, 5 Av, Peatonal Dolores beside Los Dolores church, without bath, blanket, towel, soap or toilet paper (more expensive with bath), good, clean, friendly, basic, stores luggage; there are several other cheap hotels in this area. **D** *Granada 1*, Av Gutemberg 1401, Barrio Guanacaste (hot water on 2nd floor only), good, clean, safe, TV lounge, table tennis, T2222654. **D** *Granada 2 and 3*, on the street leading uphill (to Barrio Casamate) from northeast corner of Parque Finlay, T2377079 (fax service for guests 2384438), better beds, hot water in all rooms, safe parking, both can be noisy from passing traffic so try to get a room away from the street. Recommended. Popular with Peace Corps. **E** *Marichal*, Los Dolores y Colón (T2370069) (ask for a back room), noisy, clean, centrally located. **E** *Nan Kin*, Av Gutemberg, Barrio Guanacaste, opposite San Miguel gas station, T2380291/2380271, F2380299, clean, friendly, safe, hot water, huge cheap Chinese meals, clothes washing service, good value.

F *Iberia*, Peatonal Los Dolores, T2379267, hot showers, clean, friendly, refurbished, stores luggage, cheaper without fan.

F *Hospedaje Sureño*, next door but one to *Fortuna*, friendly, safe, shared bath, room to dry laundry. **F** *Tegucigalpa*, Av Gutemberg 1645, basic but OK.

Comayagüela Convenient for buses to the north and west and there are many cheap *pensiones* and rooms. It is noisier and dirtier than Tegucigalpa, and many establishments are unsuitable for travellers. If you are carrying luggage, take a taxi. **C-D** *Centenario*, 6 Av, 9-10 C, T2221050, safe parking. Recommended. **D-E** *Real de Oro*, Av Cabañas, 11 and 12 C, clean, friendly. **D-E** *Palace*, 8-9 Av, 12 C, T2376660, new. **E** *Condesa Inn*, 7 Av, 12 C, clean, hot shower, a/c, TV, cafetería, very friendly, a bargain. Recommended. **E** *Ismary*, 4-5 Av, 5 C, T2381393, with bath, new. **E** *San Pedro*, 9 C, 6 Av, with bath, **F** without or with private cold shower, popular, restaurant. **E-F** *Hotel Richard No 1*, 4 C, 6-7 Av, 'laundry' on roof. **F** *California*, 6 Av, 22-23 C, private bath, friendly, close to Mi Esperanza bus station for Nicaragua. **F** *Colonial*, 6 y 7 Av, 6 C, No 617, T2375785, with bath, hot water, clean, secure (but unsafe area), front desk unhelpful, otherwise good service and value, restaurant next door (serves breakfast). **F** *Hotelito West*, 10 C, 6-7 Av, towels and soap, hot water all day, very friendly, change travellers' cheques. Recommended. **F** *Ticamaya*, 6 Av, 8 C, soap, towels and clean sheets daily, quiet, friendly, restaurant. **G** *Hotelito Latino*, 6 Av, 8 C, very basic, friendly, safe, cafetería.

Eating

Latin American *Taco Loco*, Paseo Rep Argentina behind Blvd Morazán, Mexican fast food. *José y Pepe's*, Av República de Panamá, excellent steaks, good service, good value. Warmly recommended.

International food In all the best top hotels. *Alondra*, Av Rep de Chile on east side of Honduras Maya, fine, expensive. *Casa María*, Av Ramón E Cruz, Col Los Castaños, 1 block off Blvd Morazán, good food and atmosphere. *El Pórtico*, near Blvd Morazán, T2367099, good food but don't be in a hurry. *Rojo, Verde y Ajo*, 1 Av B, Col Pamira, good food, reasonable price, closed Sunday. *Tony's Mar*, Blvd Juan Pablo II y Av Uruguay, Col Tepeyac, T2399379, seafood, good, simple, New Orleans style, US$8 per person.

Chinese *China Food*, 2 blocks before the easternmost bridges on Blvd Morazán, ½ block to the right, good value. *Cam Fong*, 1 block off Blvd Morazán on Av Ramón E Cruz. *Pekín*, 3 C, No 525, Barrio San Rafael, 1 block west of Av Rep de Chile and Hotel Maya. *Miraura*, Blvd Morazán and in the pedestrian street in the centre. *Palacio Real*, Col Tepeyac, 1 block off Blvd Juan Pablo II and Burger King. *Waimin*, Centro Comercial Unicentro, Blvd Suyapa, 1 block from Col Elvel. *Taiwan*, round corner from Hotels Granada 2 and 3, on Av Máximo Jérez, huge portions, good value. *Mei-Mei*, Pasaje Midence Soto, central. Recommended. *Ley-Hsen*, Pasaje Fiallos Soto. There are several good Chinese restaurants on C del Telégrafo in centre, enormous helpings at reasonable prices. **Japanese**: *Daymio*, on Plaza Benito Juárez, Col Palmira. *Suchi Bar* in the Bakery Center, 1 Av B, Col Palmira.

Meat *El Arriero*, Av República de Chile, near Honduras Maya, very good steaks, also seafood, expensive. *El Patio 2*, easternmost end of Blvd Morazán, excellent traditional food and kebabs, good service and atmosphere, good value for the hungry. Recommended. *Jack's Steak House*, same street, also burgers and American style sandwiches. *La Hacienda*, Blvd Morazán, the largest restaurant in the city. *El Ganadero*, C La Isla, behind the Congress building, steaks, chicken, seafood, good. *El Trapiche*, Blvd Suyapa, opposite National University, colonial ranch atmosphere, good steaks, expensive. Recommended. *El Corral*, Col Alameda, in front of Hotel Princess. *El Charrua*, Av Rep de Chile, Col Palmira.

Italian and Pizzerías *Roma*, Av Santa Sede, C Las Acacias 1601, 1 block off Av Rep de Chile, Col Palmira, the oldest Italian restaurant in the city, good pizzas and other food. *El Padrino*, 1

A meal in a good restaurant costs between US$6-11; for hotel restaurants, see above. Most places are closed on Sunday.

● *on maps*

Honduras

block off Blvd Morazán, Col Montecarlo behind Popeye's, very good for pizzas and other dishes. *Tito*, ½ block off Blvd Morazán on Aj Juan Lindo, good pizzas. *Tre Fratelli*, 1 Av B, Col Palmira.

Spanish *El Gachupín*,off Blvd Morazán, Col El Castaño Sur, first class, Mediterranean-style, garden setting.

Cafeterías *Bar Mediterráneo*, C S Mendieta entre Máximo Jérez y Colón, delicious goat meat, and cheap set meals. *Duncan Maya*, Av C Colón 618 opposite central Pizza Hut, good and cheap. *'Stacolosa*!, Paseo de Panamá y Paseo Argentina off Av Rep de Chile, Col Palmira, is a good cheap eating place, classical music and friendly owner, open 0700-1900. *Café y Librería Paradiso*, Av Paz Barahona 1351, excellent coffee and snacks, good library, paintings, prints and photos to enjoy, newspapers and magazines on sale, good meeting place. *Don Pepe's Terraza*, Av Colón 530, upstairs, T2221084, downtown, cheap, live music, but typical Honduran atmosphere. Recommended. *Al Natural*, C Hipólito Matute y Av Miguel Cervantes, some vegetarian, some meat dishes, huge fresh fruit juices, antiques, caged birds, nice garden atmosphere. *Brik Brak*, C Peatonal just off the Parque Central, open 24 hours. Recommended. *Chomy's Café*, Centro Comercial Asfura, Av Cervantes and two branches in Col San Carlos (C Ramón Rosa and C San Carlos), good quiches, desserts, coffee, tea. *Cafetería Típico Cubano*, Parque Finlay, open 0700-1800 (1200 Sunday), good breakfast, good service.

Others For Garifuna food, try *Yurumey*, Av JM Gálvez. Centro Comercial Multiplaza in Colonia Lomas del Mayab has a large food court with many different outlets. Several *Burger Kings*, *Pizza Huts*,one near Parque Central (with good salad bar), *McDonalds*, *Wendys*, *Popeyes* and *Pollos Camperos* all over the city. *Super Donuts*, Peatonal, Blvd Morazón, good for filling buffet breakfasts (not just doughnuts!), popular with locals. *La Gran Muralla*, opposite Hotel Nan Kin (see above), good cheap food, very friendly. Recommended. *Veracruz* C del Telégrafo entre M Jérez y Colón, near Hotels Boston and Fortuna, good breakfast, closed Sunday. Unnamed restaurant at C del Telégrafo 1314, just off M Jérez, good value breakfast, lunch and dinner. *Basilio's*, repostería y panadería, C Peatonal entre Los Dolores y S Mendieta, good cakes, breads and pastries. *Sirias*, next door to Hotel Granada 3, best place to eat in the immediate neighbourhood. *Pastelería Francesa*, opposite French embassy. Recommended. *Salman's* bakeries, several outlets in the centre, good bread and pastries.

In Comayagüela *Cafetería Nueva Macao*, 4 Av No 437, large portions, Chinese. *Comedor Tulin*, 4 Av entre 4 y 5 C, good breakfasts. *Bienvenidos a Golosinas*, 6 Av, round corner from Hotel Colonial, friendly, basic meals, beer.

Entertainment and shopping

Entertainment In front of the Universidad Nacional on Blvd Suyapa is La Peña, where every Friday at 2100 there is live music, singing and dancing, entrance US$1.40. All the top hotels have nice bars. Blvd Morazán has plenty of choice in night life including Taco Taco, a nice bar, sometimes with live Mariachi music; next door Tequila, a popular drinking place only open at weekends; Iguana Rana Bar is very popular with locals and visitors; similarly Confettis disco. Blvd Juan Pablo II has discos with various types of music. TGI Friday's in Multiplaza, Col Lomas del Mayab. La Puerta del Alcalá, 3½ blocks down from Taca office on Blvd Morazán, Col Castaño Sur, pleasant open setting.

Cinemas Plazas 1 to 5 in Centro Comercial Plaza Miraflores on Blvd Miraflores; Regis, Real and Opera at Centro Comercial Centroamérica, Blvd Miraflores (all have good US films). Multiplaza, Col Lomas del Mayab, has 6 cinemas. In city centre, double cinemas Lido Palace, and Variedades. Tauro and Aries, 200 metres up Av Gutemberg leading from Parque Finlay to Colonia Reforma (same street as Hotels Granada 2 and 3), tickets US$1.65.

Shopping **Bookshops** *Metromedia*, Edif Casa Real, Av San Carlos, behind Centro Comercial Los Castaños, Blvd Morazán, English books, both new and second-hand, for sale or exchange (small fee for exchange), wide selection of US magazines. *Shakespeare's Books*, Av Paz Barahona 1120, near C Las Damas, has a large selection of second-hand English-language books, US owner also runs Tobacco Road Tavern on the same premises, email and internet available. *Librería Paradiso* (see under Cafetería listing above). For books in Spanish on Honduras and Central America, *Editorial Guaymuras*, Av Miguel Cervantes 1055. Good book and news stand, and maps in Hotel Honduras Maya. Second-hand bookstalls in Mercado San Isidro (6 Av y 2 C, Comayagüela), good value.

Markets Mercado San Isidro, 6 Av at 1 C, Comayagüela, many things for sale, fascinating but filthy, do not buy food here. Saturday is busiest day. Mercado de Artesanías, 3 Av, 15 C next to Parque El Soldado (the market was swept away by the Mitch floods, but was being rebuilt in 1999; traders had stalls on the street outside). Good supermarkets: Sucasa, in Blvd Morazón, Más y Menos, in Av de la Paz. Chinese supermarket on C Salvador, one block south of Peatonal, near the post office in the centre, open till 2000.

Photography *Kodak* on Parque Central and Blvd Morazán for excellent, professional standard development of slides. *Fuji* in front of the Cathedral and on Blvd Morazán.

Souvenir shops *Candú*, opposite Hotel Maya, and in Av Rep de Chile. Also in Valle de Angeles, see **Excursions**. The best hotels all have souvenir shops.

Transport

Buses: cost US$0.08-US$0.12, stops are official but unmarked. **Local**
Car hire: Avis, T2320088 or 2339548, *Edif Palmira* and airport; **Molinari**, T2375335 or 2331307, 1 Av 2 C Comayagüela and airport; **Budget**, T2359528-31, 2336927, Blvd Suyapa and airport; **Hertz**, Centro Comercial Villa Real, Col Palmira, T2390772, airport 2343784. **Maya**, Av Rep de Chile 202, Col Palmira, T2320682.
Car repairs: Metal Mecánica, 1 block south of Av de los Próceres, Colonia Lara. Volkswagen dealer near Parque Concordia, good for repairs.
Taxis: about US$1.40-US$2 per person (no reduction for sharing, but bargaining possible), never pay what they say first; more after 2200, but cheaper (US$0.25) on designated routes eg Miraflores to centre.

Motorists leaving Tegucigalpa for San Pedro Sula or Olancho can avoid the congestion of **Getting out of** Comayagüela market by driving north down to Barrio Abajo, crossing the river to Barrio El Chile **Tegucigalpa** and taking the motorway up the mountainside, to turn right to Olancho, or left to rejoin the northern outlet to San Pedro Sula (at the 2nd intersection, turn right for the old, winding route, go straight on for the new, fast route). A peripheral highway is being built around the city.

Toncontín airport opens at 0530. Check-in at least 2 hours before departure; snacks, souvenir **Air** shops, several duty free stores. Buses to airport from Comayagüela, on 4 Av between 6 and 7 C, or from Av Máximo Jérez in downtown Tegucigalpa; into town US$0.06-0.19, 20 minutes from left-hand side outside the airport; yellow cabs, US$4, smaller colectivo taxis, US$2 or more. Agree taxi fare at the airport.

To **San Pedro Sula** on Northern Highway, 4 hours (7 companies include Sáenz, Centro **Buses** Comercial Perisur, Blvd Unión Europea, T2334229, El Rey, 6 Av, 9 C, Comayagüela, T2378584, Hedmán Alas, 11 Av, 13-14 C, Comayagüela, T2377143, Norteños, 3 blocks up from Mamachepa market, T2370706, and a new company: Viajes Nacionales (Viana) Servicio Ejecutivo Clase Oro, terminal on Blvd de Las Fuerzas Armadas by Gasolinera Esso, El Prado, next to Toyota, T2254235). Saenz and Hedmán Alas both have a highly recommended luxury service (book in advance), with a/c, film, snacks and refreshments, 3 hours 15 minutes. To **Tela** and **La Ceiba**, Traliasa, 8 C 6 y 7 Av, Comayagüela, T2373647. Also Etrusca to Tela and La Ceiba, T2200137. Mi Esperanza, 6 Av, 23 or 26 C, Comayagüela, T2252863, to **Choluteca**, To **Trujillo**, Cotraibal, 7 Av 10-11 C, Comayagüela. To **La Esperanza**, Empresa Joelito, 4 C, No

834, Comayagüela. To **Comayagua**, Transportes Catrachos, Col Torocagua, Blvd del Norte, Comayagüela. To **Valle de Angeles** and **Santa Lucía**, from stop on Av La Paz (near filling station opposite hospital). To **Juticalpa** and **Catacamas**, Empresa Aurora, 8 C, 6-7 Av, Comayagüela, T2373647. For **Danlí** and **El Paraíso**, for the Nicaraguan border at Los Manos, see under those towns in **East of Tegucigalpa**.

For travellers leaving Tegucigalpa, take the Tiloarque bus on Av Máximo Jérez, by C Palace, and alight in Comayagüela at Cine Centenario (Av 6) for nearby Empresa Aurora buses (**for Olancho**) and El Rey buses (for San Pedro Sula or **Olancho**); 3 blocks northwest is Cine Lux, near which are Empresas Unidas and Maribel (8 Av, 11-12 C, T2373032) for **Siguatepeque**. Tiloarque bus continues to Mi Esperanza bus terminal (for Choluteca and Nicaraguan frontier). Take a 'Carrizal' or 'Santa Fe' bus from Tegucigalpa for the hill ascending Belén (9 C) for Hedmán Alas buses to San Pedro Sula and for Comayagua buses (to town centre, cheaper but slower than main line buses to San Pedro Sula which drop passengers on main road, a taxi ride away from the centre). By the Mamachepa market is the Norteños bus line for San Pedro Sula; also nearby are buses for **Nacaome** and **El Amatillo** frontier with El Salvador.

International buses: Tica Bus, 16 C, 5-6 Av, Comayagüela, T2387040, 2200579, 2200581, office opens 0730, to Managua 0900 (US$20, 9 hours), San José (US$35), San Salvador (US$15), Guatemala City (US$25) and Panama (US$60) daily. Make sure you reserve several days ahead, you have to go to the office to reserve (taxi from centre US$2). Alternatively to **Nicaragua**, take Mi Esperanza bus to San Marcos de Colón, then taxi or local bus to El Espino on border. To San Marcos, 4 a day from 0730, and direct to frontier at 0400, US$2.50, 5 hours (0730 is the latest one that will get you into Nicaragua the same day). Or Mi Esperanza bus to Río Guasaule frontier, several daily, 4 hours, US$2. To **San Salvador**, Cruceros del Golfo, Barrio Guacerique, Blvd Comunidad Económica Europea, Comayagüela, T2337415, US$18, at 0600 and 1300, 6 hours travelling, 1 hour or more at border, connections to Guatemala and Mexico; direct bus to border at El Amatillo, US$2.50, 3 hours, several daily; alternatively from San Pedro Sula via Nueva Ocotepeque and El Poy. To San Salvador and **Guatemala**, King Quality luxury service from Cruceros del Golfo terminal, 0600 and 1300. Alternatively, to Guatemala go to San Pedro Sula and take Escobar, Impala or Congolón to Nueva Ocotepeque and the frontier at Agua Caliente, or take the route via Copán (see page 928).

Directory

Airline offices For national flights: *Isleña airlines*, Galerías La Paz, Av de la Paz, at Toncontín airport 2331130. *Caribbean Air* at the airport, T2331906. **International carriers**: *Grupo Taca*, Blvd Morazán y Av Ramón E Cruz, T2390148 or airport 2335756. *Iberia*, Ed Palmira, opposite Honduras Maya, T2327760, also *American* in this building, p 1, T2321414 (airport 2339680), F2321380. *KLM*, Ed Ciicsa, Av Rep de Chile y Av Rep de Panamá, Col Palmira, T2326410. *Lufthansa*, Edif Plaza del Sol, No 2326, Av de la Paz, T2367560, F2367580. *Air France* Galerías La Paz, Av de la Paz, T2370216. *Alitalia*, Av de la Paz, T2366082. *British Airways*, Edif Sempe, Blvd Comunidad Económica Europea, T2253916. *Continental*, Av República de Chile, Col Palmira, T2200999. *Copa*, Edif Plaza del Sol, Av de la Paz. *Japan Airlines*, Edif Midence Soto, p 12, in front of Parque Central, T2379914.

Banks All banks have several branches throughout the city; we list the main offices. Branch offices are unlikely to change TCs, only US dollars cash. *Lloyds Bank*, Av Ramón E Cruz, off Blvd Morazán and Av de la Paz, take any San Felipe bus (Rivera y Cía), get out above US Embassy, walk back, turn left and bank is 300 metres on right. Open 0900-1500, closed Sat, Sterling and Canadian dollars changed. *Banco Atlántida*, 5 C in front of Plaza Morazán (may agree to change money on Sat up to 1200). *Banco de Honduras (Citibank)*, Blvd Suyapa. *Bancahorro*, 5 C in front of Plaza Morazán. *Bancahsa*, 5 C (Av Colón) in the centre. *Banexpo*, Av Rep de Chile, Col Palmira. *Banco de Occidente*, 3 C (Cervantes) y 6 Av (S Mendieta) in the centre. *Banco del País*, Calle Peotonal in the centre, changes TCs. Visa and Mastercard cash advances (no commission) and TCs at *Credomatic de Honduras*, Blvd Morazán, and at *Honducard*, Av de la Paz y Ramón E Cruz and at *Aval Card*, Blvd Morazán. Also at branches of *Banco Ficensa, Futuro, Banco Atlántida, Banexpo, Banco del País, Ficohsa, Banhcresa*,and *Banco de Occidente*. Credomatic is the American Express agent. Banks are allowed to trade at the current market rate (see Currency in Essentials), but there is a street market along the C Peotonal off the Parque

Central, opposite the Post Office and elsewhere. Exchange can be difficult on Sat, try *Coin*, a casa de cambio on Av de la Paz inside Supermercado Más y Menos, same rates as banks, no commission, Mon-Fri 0830-1730, Sat 0900-1200, changes TCs but will photocopy cheques and passport; another branch of Coin on C Peatonal, good rates. Recommended.

Communications Post Office: Av Paz Barahona/C del Telégrafo, Lista de Correos (Poste Restante) mail held for 1 month, US$0.20 per letter. Mail boxes in main supermarkets. Books should be packed separately from clothes etc when sending packages. The Post Office will send and receive faxes. **Telecommunications:** Hondutel, C del Telégrafo y Av Colón, has several direct AT&T lines to USA, no waiting. Phone, fax and telegrams; open 24 hrs for phone services only. Also at 6 Av, 7-8C, Comayagüela, with post office. **Email:** *Café Cyberplace*, Barrio La Plazuela, Av Cervantes, opposite Souvenirs Maya, T2205200, open 0900-1900, US$2 for 30 mins. *Café Don Harry*, Av Rep de Chile 525, Edif Galerías TCB, T2206174, pipo1@sigmanet.hn. *Multinet*, 1 Av B, Galerías Maya, Col Palmira, T2323181, 0800-2100, US$4.45 per hr, also at Mall Multiplaza, local 114, Blvd Juan Pablo II, Col Lomas del Mayab, adae@usa.net. *Galaxy*, Plaza Cristadel, C H Matute 1228 entre M Jérez y Colón, central, 0830-1900 Mon-Sat. Shakespeare's Books (see under **Bookshops**).

Cultural centres *Alianza Francesa*, Colonia Lomas del Guijarro, cultural events Fri afternoon, French films Tues 1930, T2391529. *Centro Cultural Alemán*, 8 Av, C La Fuente, German newspapers to read, cultural events, T2371555. *Instituto Hondureño de Cultura Interamericana* (IHCI), C Real de Comayagüela has an English library and cultural events, T2377539.

Embassies & consulates *El Salvador*, Colonia San Carlos No 219, 1 block from Blvd Morazán, T2368045, 2367344, F2360436, friendly. *Guatemala*, Col Las Minitas 4 C, Casa 2421, T2329704/5018, F2328469, Mon-Fri, 0900-1300, take photo, visa given on the spot, US$10. *Nicaragua*, Colonia Lomas del Tepeyac, Av Choluteca 1130, bloque M-1 (T2329025, F2311412), 0800-1200, US$25, visa issued same day, but can take up to 2 days, has to be used within 4 weeks of issue; for Nicaraguan embassy, take Alameda bus from street behind Congress building (from Parque Merced descend towards river, but don't cross bridge, instead turn left behind Congress and ask for bus stop on right-hand side), alight before Planificación de Familia and climb street on left beside Planificación. *Costa Rica*, Colonia El Triángulo, 1a C, frente a casa 3451, T2321768, F2321876, bus to Lomas del Guijarro to last stop, then walk up on your left for 300 metres. *Mexico*, Av República de México, Paseo República de Brasil 2402, Col Palmira, T2326471, F2314719, opens 0900, visa takes 24 hrs. *Panama* (T2395508, F2328147, p 2) and *Colombia*, T2321709, F2328133, p 4 (Embassy 2325131), both in Ed Palmira, opposite Honduras Maya. *Belize Consulate*, in Hotel Honduras Maya, T2390134.

    Argentina, Col Rubén Darío 417, T2323376. *Brazil*, Colonia La Reforma, Casa 1309, T2366310. *Chile*, Ed Interamericana, p 6, Blvd Morazán, T2322114. *Ecuador*, Av Juan Lindo 122, Col Palmira, T2365980. *Peru*, C La Reforma 2618, Col La Reforma, T2210596. *Venezuela*, Col Rubén Darío 2116, T2321879.

    USA, Av La Paz (0800-1700, Mon-Fri, take any bus from north side of Parque Central in direction 'San Felipe', T2369320/29, F2369037). *Canada*, Ed Comercial Los Castaños, p 6, Blvd Morazán, T2314538, F2315793. *Japan*, Colonia San Carlos, entre 4 y 5 C, 2 blocks off Blvd Morazán and Av de la Paz, T2366829, behind Los Castaños Shopping Mall.

    UK, Ed Palmira, p 3, opposite Hotel Honduras Maya (Apdo Postal 290, T2320612/18, F2325429). *Germany*, Ed Paysen, p 3, Blvd Morazán, T2323161, F2329518. *Finnish Consulate*, Edif Próceres, Av Los Próceres, T2369655, F2366740. *France*, Colonia Palmira, 3 C, Av Juan Lindo, T2366432, F2368051. *Spain*, Col Matamoros 801, T2366589, near Av de la Paz and US Embassy. *Italy*, Av Principal 2602, Col Reforma, T2366391, F2365659. *Netherlands Consulate*, Edif Barahona, Col Alameda, next to INA, T2315007, F2315009. *Spain*, Col Matamoros, C Santander 801, T2366875, F2368682. *Swedish Consulate*, Av Altiplano, Retorno Borneo 2758, Colonia Miramontes, T/F2324935.

Hospitals & medical services Dentist: *Dra Rosa María Cardillo de Boquín*, Ed Los Jarros, Sala 206, Blvd Morazán, T2310583. Recommended. *Dr Roberto Ayala*, DDS, C Alfonso XIII 3644, Col Lomas de Guijarro, T2322407. Pharmacy: *Farmacia Rosna*, in pedestrian mall off Parque Central, T2370605, English spoken. Recommended. *Regis Palmira*, Ed Ciicsa, Av República de Panamá, Col Palmira. *El Castaño*, Blvd Morazán. Private hospitals: Hospital y Clínica Viera, 5 C, 11 y 12 Av, Tegucigalpa, T2377136. Hospital la Policlínica SA 3 Av, 7 y 8 C, Comayagüela, T2373503. Centro Médico Hondureño, 3 Av, 3 C, Barrio La Granja, Comayagüela, T2336028.

Laundry *Mi Lavandería*, opposite Repostería Calle Real, 3 C, 2 Av, Comayagüela, T2376573, Mon-Sat 0700-1800, Sun and holidays 0800-1700. Recommended. *Lavandería Super Jet*, Av Gutemberg, about

300 metres east of Hotel Granada, US$0.20 per kilo. Recommended. *La Cisne*, 1602 C La Fuente/Av Las Delicias, US$2.50 up to 5 kg, same day service. Recommended. *Lavandería Italiana*, Barrio Guadalupe, 4 blocks west of Av Rep de Chile 300 block.

Places of worship Churches: Episcopal Anglican (Col Florencia, take Suyapa bus) and Union Church, Colonia Lomas del Guijarro, with services in English. Catholic mass in English at the chapel of Instituto San Francisco at 1000 every Sun.

Tour companies & travel agents *Trek Honduras*, Ed Midence Soto 218, T2390743, F2375776, downtown, tours of the city, Bay Islands, Copán, San Pedro Sula, Valle de Angeles and Santa Lucía. *Mundirama*, Edif Ciicsa, Av Rep de Panamá, Col Palmira. *Explore Honduras Tour Service*, Ed Medcast, 2nd level, Blvd Morazán, T2397694, F2369800, Copán and Bay Islands. *La Moskitia Ecoaventuras*, PO Box 3577, Tegucigalpa, T/F2379398, for trips to Mosquitia. *Centro Americana de Turismo*, west end of Blvd Morazán before the bridges, Tegucigalpa, specializing in Honduras. *Gloria Tours* across from north side of Parque Central in Casa Colonial, information centre and tour operator. *Alambra Travel*, Av Rep de Chile, by parking area of Hotel Honduras Maya, good service.

Tourist offices *Ministerio Hondureño de Turismo*, Edif Europa, Av Ramón E Cruz y C Rep de México, p 3, above Lloyds Bank (see **Banks** for how to get there), Col San Carlos, T2383974/2224002, F2382102, also at Toncontín airport. Open 0830-1530, provides lists of hotels and sells posters, postcards (cheaper than elsewhere) and slides. Information on cultural events around the country from Teatro Manuel Bonilla, better than at regional tourist offices. El Mundo Maya, a private tourist information centre, behind the cathedral next to the Parque Central, T2222946. For information on **National Parks**, see page 958.

Useful addresses **Immigration:** Dirección Gen de Migración, Av Máximo Jérez, next to Hotel Ronda, Tegucigalpa. **Peace Corps:** opposite Edif Ciicsa, on Av República de Chile, up hill past Hotel Honduras Maya. The volunteers are a good source of information.

Short excursions from Tegucigalpa

Suyapa Southeast of Tegucigalpa is Suyapa, a village with a big church which attracts pilgrims to its wooden figure of the Virgin, a tiny image about eight centimetres high set into the altar. 1-4 February is a fiesta, during which they hold a televised 'alborada' with singers, music, fireworks et cetera, from 2000-2400 on the second evening. Take a bus to the University or to Suyapa from 'La Isla', one block northwest of the city stadium.

Santa Lucía
Population: 4,230
Altitude: 1,400-1,600m

Northeast of Suyapa, on the way to Valle de Angeles take a right turn off to visit the quaint old mining village of Santa Lucía , perched precariously on a steep mountainside overlooking the wide valley with Tegucigalpa below. The town has a beautiful colonial church with a Christ given by King Philip II of Spain in 1592; there is a festival in the second and third weeks of January. There is a charming legend of the Black Christ which the authorities ordered to be taken down to Tegucigalpa when Santa Lucía lost its former importance as a mining centre. Every step it was carried away from Santa Lucía it became heavier. When impossible to carry it further, they turned round and by the time they were back to Santa Lucía, it was as light as a feather. The town is lively with parties on Saturday night. There are souvenir shops in the town, including *Cerámicas Ucles* just past the lagoon, second street on left, and another ceramics shop at the entrance on your right. There are good walks up the mountain on various trails; fine views of Tegucigalpa from above.

A good circuit is to descend east from the mountain towards San Juan del Rancho through lovely landscapes on a good dirt road, then connect with the paved road to El Zamorano. From there continue either to El Zamorano, or return to Tegucigalpa (see below for opposite direction).

Eating One small *comedor* next to the plaza/terrace of the municipality, but on Sunday there is more food available on the streets; also Czech restaurant *Miluka* serving Czech and Honduran food. Recommended.

Transport Bus to Santa Lucía from Mercado San Pablo, hourly service, US$0.30, past the statue of Simón Bolívar by the Esso station, Av de los Próceres, Tegucigalpa.

About a 30-minute drive from Tegucigalpa, **Valle de Angeles** is on a plain below **Monte San Juan**, of which **Cerro El Picacho**, 2,270 metres (at the top is a zoo of mostly indigenous animals, open Thursday-Sunday, US$0.25), is the highest point, and **Cerro La Tigra**. It is surrounded by pine forests and the climate stays cool the year round. There are old mines, many walks possible in the forests, picnic areas, swimming pool, crowded on Sunday. Hospital de los Adventistas, in the valley, a modern clinic, sells vegetables and handicrafts; there are many handicraft shops in town, good for leather goods, items in wood, hats and so on. A visit to the pavilion of arts and crafts organized by the national Asociación de Artesanías is recommended.

Valle de Angeles
Population: 6,635
Altitude: 1,310m

The 22-kilometre road between the capital and Valle de Angeles was damaged in 20 places by Hurricane Mitch.

Sleeping and services *Centro Turístico La Florida* at Km 20, T7662121, has hotel, restaurant and sports facilities, horse riding, swimming pool, day entry US$2.30, zoo, open all year, big development. Opposite is the Dutch-owned restaurant *Las Tejas*. **D** pp *Los Tres Pinos* Bed & Breakfast Inn, Casa 907, Barrio El Edén, Carretera a San Juancito, T7662879, English spoken, with bath, hot water, laundry facilities, horse rental, airport pick-up, excursions. Recommended. **D** *Hotel y Restaurante Posada del Angel*, service indifferent, moderate prices. *Rudy's Café and Grill*, 1 block north of Parque Central, T7662628, rudys@hondutel.hn, kmotz@hondudata.com, and next door *La Casa de las Abuelas*, wine bar, café, library, satellite TV, video, email, fax and phone service, tourist information and art gallery. *Restaurante Turístico de Valle de Angeles*, on top of hill overlooking town, also good. *Restaurant Papagayo* for typical dishes. *Comedor La Abejita*. Several others.

Tegucigalpa environs

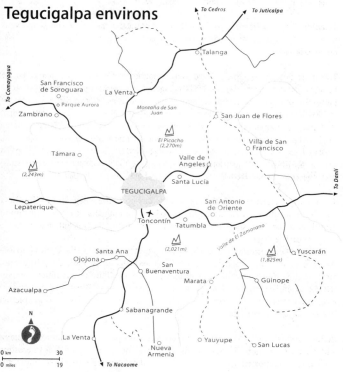

Continue to San Juan de Flores (also called Cantarranas) and San Juancito, an old mining town. From here you can climb the La Tigra cloud forest and even walk along the top before descending to El Hatillo and then to Tegucigalpa.

La Tigra There are bracing climbs to the heights of Picacho in the **La Tigra National Park**
National Park cloud forest. Sunday morning early is a good time but weekdays are quieter. Go first to the *Amitigra* office, Edificio Italia, 6th floor, about 3 blocks southwest of Amex office in Av República de Panamá; helpful. Book a visit here in advance. Single hikers must have a guide. There are two approach routes: go to El Piligüin for the Jutiapa entrance, from where you can start hiking, or to *Gloriales Inn*, in El Hatillo (see below, **Sleeping**). You can also walk, it is 24 kilometres from Tegucigalpa to the Jutiapa entrance. Then hike to the visitors' centre of La Tigra at El Rosario (10 kilometres, 3 hours, easy hiking, superb). Alternatively, go to **San Juancito** (**F** *Hotelito San Juan*, six rooms with shared bathroom, grocery store next door also sells fuel, drinks and can prepare *comida corriente*, same owners, T7662237), above which is the National Park (well worth a visit, a stiff, one-hour uphill walk to El Rosario visitor centre, park offices and six trails ranging from 30 minutes to eight hours, US$10 entry, bring insect repellent). A recommended hike is the Sendero La Esperanza, which leads to the road; turn right then take the Sendero Bosque Nublado on your left. The whole circuit takes about one hour 20 minutes. A few quetzal birds survive here. Do not leave paths when walking as there are precipitous drops (get advice about personal safety before setting out, robberies have occurred). In the rainy season (June, July, October-November) there is a spectacular 100 metres waterfall (Cascada de la Gloria) which falls on a vast igneous rock.

From Parque Herrera buses throughout the day go to the village of **El Piligüin**; a delightful 40-minute walk down the pineclad mountainside leads to El Chimbo (meals at *pulpería* or shop, ask anyone the way), then take bus either to Valle de Angeles or Tegucigalpa.

At Km 24 on Zamorano road, climb the highest peak through the Uyuca rain forest, information from Escuela Agrícola Panamericana in the **Valle del Zamorano**, or from their office near the Edificio Italia, Colonia Palmira (see Amitigra, above) T2332717, in Tegucigalpa. The school has rooms for visitors. Visits to the school are organized by some tour operators. On the northwest flank of Uyuca is the picturesque village of **Tatumbla**.

Ojojona A 30-minute drive, 24 kilometres south of Tegucigalpa, is Ojojona, another quaint
Population: 6,670 old village; turn right down Southern Highway. The village's pottery is interesting
Altitude: 1,400m (but selection reported to be poor). *La Casona del Pueblo* offers the best handicrafts

in town, including fine and rustic ceramics. *Fiesta* 18-20 January. There are two well preserved colonial churches in Ojojona (notice the fine paintings), plus two more in nearby Santa Ana which is passed on the way from Tegucigalpa. Ojojona is completely unspoiled.

Sleeping F *Posada Joxone*, comfortable. *Comedor*.

Transport Bus every 15-30 minutes from C 4, Av 6, Comayagüela, near San Isidro market, US$0.40, 1 hour. From same location, buses go west to **Lepaterique** ('place of the jaguar'), another colonial village, over an hour's drive through rugged, forested terrain. Distant view of Pacific on fine days from heights above village.

Sabanagrande

Just off the main highway 40 kilometres south of the capital is Sabanagrande, with an interesting colonial church (1809, Nuestra Señora del Rosario 'Apa Kun Ka', the place of water for washing); *fiesta* La Virgen de Candelaria, 1-11 February. This typical colonial town with cobbled streets is a good day trip from Tegucigalpa. At 1,000 metres it has a mild climate, beautiful scenery with pleasant walks, including views to the Pacific and the Gulf of Fonseca. The town is famous for its *rosquillas* (a type of biscuit). A US Peace Corps worker was helping to develop tourism in the town in 1999.

North of Tegucigalpa

Taking the Olancho road, you come to **Talanga** with post office and Hondutel near the market on the main road. (From the Parque Central an unpaved road south leads to the Tegucigalpa-Danlí road making a triangular route possible back to the capital.) Just beyond Talanga, an unpaved road turns north to Cedros and Minas de Oro, 66 kilometres. After 41 kilometres, take the small road to your left; at Km 58 is the turn off to Esquías (eight kilometres away). The last part of the road to Minas de Oro is in poor condition, high clearance recommended.

North of Tegucigalpa

Cedros, one of Honduras' earliest settlements, dates from Pedro de Alvarado's mining operations of 1536. It is an outstanding colonial mining town, with cobbled streets, perched high on an eminence, amid forests. The festival of El Señor del Buen Fin takes place in the first two weeks of January. Buses to Talanga, Cedros and San Ignacio: Reynita de San Ignacio in Mercado Zonal Belén, Comayagüela, T2240066.

Minas de Oro

Population: 6,000
Altitude: 1,060m

On a forested tableland, Minas de Oro is a centre for walking in attractive hill country. It is a picturesque old mining town. There is a fine view from Cerro Grande which overlooks the town, and a more interesting hike up Cerro El Piñón about three kilometres north towards Victoria. Poor road Minas de Oro to Victoria 18 kilometres, on to Sulaco (bus service) with connections from

Honduras

Sulaco to Yorito, Yoro and San Pedro Sula and to Cedros. Several buses daily Sulaco-Yoro.

Sleeping and eating Several *pensiones*, including F *Hotelito Girón* and *Los Pinares* (meals US$1). *Comedor El Rodeo*, or eat at Doña Gloria's house, good, large helpings, US$0.80.

Transport Buses 4-hour bus ride with Transportes Victoria, 10 Av 11 C Barrio Belén, Comayagüela at 1300, returning from Minas de Oro at 0400 daily (US$1.90).

To the west of Minas de Oro it is three kilometres to Malcotal and a further four kilometres to Minas de San Antonio both surrounded by hills, mostly stripped of trees (high clearance vehicle, four-wheel drive in wet, recommended between Minas de Oro and San Antonio). There is a fine two-hour forested walk over to **Esquías** (good comedor, *Tita's*, accommodation available in private houses, ask at *Tita's*) with a fine church with one of the most fascinating colonial façades in Honduras, extravagant palm motifs, floating angels and, at the apex, a bishop with hands outstretched in blessing. There is a monument in the plaza to a local hero, the American Harold Brosious, 1881-1950, who arrived in Malcotal in 1908 to prospect for gold. He founded a school there (closed since his death), for the children of local illiterate peasants. As Brosious' fame as a teacher spread, pupils arrived from throughout Honduras and neighbouring countries. Daily bus services Esquías-Tegucigalpa and Esquías-Comayagua.

10 kilometres east of Minas de Oro is San José del Potrero beyond which is **Sulaco**. Above Sulaco is the Montaña de la Flor region where there are settlements of Xicaque Indians. They are also to be found in the lowlands around Victoria where they sell their handicrafts.

Tegucigalpa to San Pedro Sula

On or near the country's main road route are the former capital of Comayagua, Lago Yojoa and some beautiful scenery with Lenca Indian communities.

Támara The Northern Highway between Tegucigalpa and San Pedro Sula leaves the capital and enters the vast intermont basin of Támara. A turning at Támara village leads to San Matías waterfall, a delightful area for walking in cool forested mountains.

Sleeping 500 metres southwest of the toll station near the Balneario San Francisco is F *Hotel Posada Don Willy*, with bath (electric shower), clean, quiet, fan, excellent value.

Zambrano The road climbs to the lovely forested heights to **Parque Aventuras** at Km 33, open at weekends, good food, swimming pools, horses, bikes, then to **Zambrano** at Km 34 (*Altitude*: 1,450 metres) and **Parque Aurora** at Km 36, midway between Tegucigalpa and Comayagua, about 50 kilometres from the capital. It has a small zoo, nice swimming pools and picnic area among pine-covered hills, a lake with rowing boats (hire US$1 per hour), a snack bar and lovely scenery. Good birdwatching. This spot would be perfect for camping and for caravans, which need to avoid the narrow streets and congestion of Tegucigalpa (camping US$0.50 per person, admission US$0.70, food supplies nearby). Zambrano village is west of the highway; there is not a lot there but once off the main road it is very peaceful with a lovely climate all year round and lots of pine trees. Good walking in the area with waterfalls 100 metres high.

Sleeping A-C *Casitas Primavera*, Barrio La Primavera (Zambrano), 1,600 metres west of main road, cosy, rustic houses, lovely setting, sleep 6 (arrangements can be made for 1 or 2 people, **E**), T8986625 weekends, T2392328 weekdays. **L-A** *Caserío Valuz*, T8986625 (Zambrano), T2392328 (Tegucigalpa), 15 rooms with bath, 5 with chimneys 12 with balconies, 1, 2 and 3-night packages including all meals, also 3 rooms for backpackers, **E**, with use of kitchen, volunteer work in exchange for room and board possible, a great place to relax, hike, read, paint; it is 1½ kilometres from the highway, 20 minutes' walk on the road to Catarata Escondida.

Eating *Comedor La Estancia*, on the main road, very good *comida corriente*, very good bread. Dippsa fuel station has a restaurant.

Transport From the capital take any bus going north to Comayagua, Siguatepeque, La Paz.

Before descending to the Comayagua valley the Northern Highway reaches another forested mountainous escarpment. A track leads off to the right (ask for directions), with about 30 minutes climb on foot to a tableland and natural fortress of **Tenampua** where Indians put up their last resistance to the *conquistadores*, even after the death of Lempira. It has an interesting wall and entrance portal.

Soon after the Tenampua turning, a short road runs west, through Villa San Antonio, to La Paz, capital of its Department in the western part of the Comayagua valley. From the new church of the Virgen del Perpetuo Socorro, on the hill, there is a fine view of the town, the Palmerola airfield, and the Comayagua Valley. The town has all paved roads, a soccer stadium and many public services thanks to ex-president Córdoba who lives there. The Casa de la Cultura in the centre has an attractive exhibit of Lenca handicrafts, open daily.

La Paz
Population: 19,900
Altitude: 690m
Colour map 4, grid C4

Excursions A paved road runs southwest from La Paz to Marcala (see page 936, frequent minibuses two hours, US$1). Two kilometres off this road lies **San Pedro de Tutule** (*Altitude*: 1,400 metres), the marketplace for the Indians of **Guajiquiro** (one of the few pure Indian communities in Honduras, several kilometres south of Tutule). Market: Sunday morning and Thursday. (**F** *Hospedaje Valestia*, good, basic, *comedor* opposite.)

Five kilometres north of La Paz, on the paved road to Comayagua, is **Ajuterique**, which has a fine colonial church, worth a visit.

Sleeping and eating All **F** *Pensión San Francisco* (quite nice). *Ali*, friendly, 5 rooms, bath, hot water, eat at *Ali's Restaurant*, food and lodging excellent. *Rico Lunch*, near church, good and friendly.

Transport Buses from Comayagua, Cotrapal (opposite Iglesia La Merced), every hour from 0600, US$0.40, passing Ajuterique and Lejamaní; frequent minibus Comayagua-La Paz, 35 minutes, US$0.50. Lila bus from the capital, from opposite Hispano cinema in Comayagüela. Colectivo taxi from main north-south highway to La Paz, US$2. In La Paz all buses leave from boulevard crossroads, look for the statue of the soldier. Minibus to Marcala, 3 daily, 0530, 0630, 0800, 1½ hours, US$1.50.

Directory Banks *Bancahsa, Banco Atlántida, Banadesa*.

Comayagua

Comayagua is a colonial town in the rich Comayagua plain, one and a half hours' drive (93.5 kilometres) north from the capital. It was founded on 7 December 1537 as Villa Santa María de Comayagua, on the site of an Indian village by Alonzo de

Population: 59,535
Altitude: 550m
Colour map 4, grid C4

Honduras

Cáceres. On 3 September 1543, it was designated the Seat of the Audiencia de los Confines by King Felipe II of Spain. President Marco Aurelio Soto transferred the capital to Tegucigalpa in 1880.

Sights There are several old colonial buildings: the former University, the first in Central America, founded in 1632, closed in 1842 (it was located in the Casa Cural, Bishop's Palace, where the bishops have lived since 1558); the churches of La Merced (1550-58) and La Caridad (1730); San Francisco (1574); San Sebastián (1575). San Juan de Dios (1590, destroyed by earthquake in 1750), the church where the Inquisition sat, is now the site of the Santa Teresa Hospital. El Carmen was built in 1785. The most interesting building is the Cathedral in the Central Park, with its square plain tower and its decorated façade with sculpted figures of the saints, which contains some of the finest examples of colonial art in Honduras (closed 1300-1500). The clock in the tower was originally made over 800 years ago in Spain; it was given to Comayagua by Felipe II in 1582. At first it was in La Merced when that was the Cathedral, but moved to the new Cathedral in 1715. There are two colonial plazas shaded by trees and shrubs. A stone portal and a portion of the façade of Casa Real (the viceroy's residence) survives. It was built 1739-41, but was damaged by an earthquake in 1750 and destroyed by tremors in 1856. The army still uses a quaint old fortress built when Comayagua was the capital. There is a lively market area.

Museums
In mid-1999 only the Cathedral was open to visitors. Otherwise, much rebuilding going on.

There are two museums: the ecclesiastical museum, half a block north of Cathedral (■ *daily 0930-1200, 1400-1700, US$0.60)* and the **Museo de Arqueología** (housed in the former Palacio de Gobernación, one block south of Cathedral at the corner of 6 Calle and 1 Avenida NO, ■ *Wednesday-Friday 0800-1600, Saturday, Sunday 0900-1200, 1300-1600, US$1.70)*. The latter is small scale but fascinating, with six rooms each devoted to a different period. Much of the collection comes from digs in the El Cajón region, 47 kilometres north of Comayagua, before the area was flooded for the hydroelectricity project.

Excursions To the coffee town of **La Libertad** (■ *hourly bus, two hours, US$0.75)*, several *hospedajes* and *comedores*; a friendly place. Before La Libertad is **Jamalteca** (one and a half hours by bus US$0.50), from where it is a 40-minute walk to a large, deep pool into which drops a 10-metre waterfall surrounded by lush vegetation. Here you can swim, picnic or camp, but it is on private property and a pass must be obtained from the owner (ask at Supermercado Carol in Comayagua). Best to avoid weekends, when the owners' friends are there.

The **Parque Nacional Montaña de Comayagua** is only 13 kilometres from Comayagua, reached from the villages of San José de la Mora (four-wheel drive necessary) or San Jerónimo and Río Negro (usually passable in 2WD). Contact Fundación Ecosimco at 0 Calle y 1 Avenida NO in Comayagua for further information. The mountain, 2,407 metres, has about 6,000 hectares of cloud forest and is a major watershed for the area.

Sleeping
■ *on maps*
Price codes:
see inside front cover

D *Norymax*, C Central y 3 Av SO, Barrio Torondón, T7721210, a/c, cheaper rooms also, all with bath, hot water, car park. **E** *América Inn*, 2 Av y 1 C NO, T7720360, F7720009, a/c, hot water, private bath, TV, cheaper with fan. **E** *Emperador*, C Central y 4 Av SO, Barrio Torondón, T7720332, good, a/c, cable TV, cheaper with fan. **E** *Imperial*, 3 Av SO, Barrio Torondón, opposite *Norymax*, T7720215, with bath and fan, clean, friendly, good value, parking. **E** *Libertad*, south side of Parque Central, nice courtyard, much choice of room size, clean apart from the toilets, cold water shower outside, helpful, good restaurant 2 doors away. **E** *Motel Puma*, off the same Blvd, garage parking, hot water, with bath (catering for short-stay clientèle). **E** *Quan*, 8 C NO, 3 y 4 Av, T7720070, excellent, with private bath, popular. **F** *Honduras*, 2 Av NO, 1 C, clean, friendly, some rooms with bath. **F** *Luxemburgo*, 4 Av NO y 2 C, laundry facilities, good value, rooms at front are noisy.

Plenty of places at under US$3 pp, eg *Hospedajes Tío Luís* and *Miramar*, 1 C NO y 1 Av

NO, *Hospedajes Galaxia* and *Primavera* 2 C NO y 1 Av NO by Texaco station on Panamericana by bus stop, *Hospedaje Terminal*, 2 C NO y 3 Av NO, all basic, not very clean but cheap.

Hein Wong on Parque Central, Chinese and international food, good, a/c, reasonable prices. *Flipper*, 1 Av NO y 6 C, ice cream, tacos, etc. *Juanis Burger Shop*, 1 Av NO, 5 C, near southwest corner of Parque Central, friendly, good food, OK. *Las Palmeras*, south side of Parque Central, good breakfasts, open 0800, good portions. *Fruty Tacos*, 4 C NO, just off southwest corner of Parque Central, good snacks and licuados. Good unnamed *comedor* 2 doors west of *Hospedaje Terminal*, clean, good breakfast. In the Centro Turístico Comayagua is a restaurant, bar, disco, and swimming pool; good for cooling off and relaxing; C del Estadio Hispano, Barrio Arriba.

Eating
Parque Central is surrounded by restaurants and fast food establishments.

Cinema Valladolid, at north end of 2 Av.

Entertainment

Air The US military base at Palmerola, 8 kilometres from Comayagua, was designated a commercial national and international airport in 1993, to operate initially as a cargo export/import facility and later to take passenger traffic.

Buses To **Tegucigalpa**, US$1.10, every 45 minutes, 2 hours (Hmnos Cruz, Comayagua, T7720850); to **Siguatepeque**, US$0.55 with Transpinares. To **San Pedro Sula**, US$1.50, 3 hours, either catch a bus on the highway (very crowded) or go to Siguatepeque and change buses there. Incoming buses to Comayagua drop you on the main road outside town. From here you can walk or taxi into town. Buses depart from Torocagua: colectivo from C Salvador y Cervantes in town, **Car rental**: **Amigo**, on the road to Tegucigalpa and San Pedro Sula, T7720371.

Transport

Banks Only *Bancahsa* near Parque Central changes TCs, but others for cash: *Banco Atlántida*, *Banco de Occidente*, *Bancahorro*, *Banco Sogerín*, *Banhcafé*, *Ficensa*, *Banadesa*, *Bamer* and *Banffaa*. **Hospitals & medical services** Dentist: *Dr José de Jesús Berlioz*, next to Colegio León Alvarado, T7720054. **Tour companies & travel agents** *Cramer Tours* in Pasaje Arias. *Rolando Barahona*, Av Central. *Inversiones Karice's*, 4 Av NO, very friendly and helpful. **Useful addresses** Immigration: Migración is at 6 C NO, 1 Av, good place to get visas renewed, friendly.

Directory

Honduras

The Northern Highway crosses the Comayagua plain, part of the gap in the mountains which stretches from the Gulf of Fonseca to the Ulúa lowlands. 32 kilometres northwest of Comayagua is Siguatepeque, a town set in forested highlands with a cool climate. It is the site of the Escuela Nacional de Ciencias Forestales (which is worth a visit) and, being exactly half-way between Tegucigalpa and San Pedro Sula (128 kilometres), a collection point for the produce of Intibucá, Comayagua and Lempira departments. The Cerro and Bosque de Calanterique, behind the Evangelical Hospital, is 45 minutes' walk from town centre. The Parque Central is pleasant, shaded by tall trees with the church of San Pablo on the north side and the cinema, *Hotel Versalles* and *Boarding House Central* on the east side; Hondutel and the Post Office are on the south side.

Siguatepeque
Population: 39,165
Altitude: 1,150m
Colour map 4, grid C4

Sleeping D *Zari*, T7732015, hot water, cable TV, own generator, parking. E *Boarding House Central*, Parque Central, T7732108, simple, but very good value, beware of the dog which bites. E *Internacional Gómez*, 21 de Junio, T7732868, with bath, F without, hot water, clean, use of kitchen on request, parking. F *Mi Hotel*, 1 kilometre from highway on road into town, with bath, parking, restaurant. F *Versalles*, on Parque Central, excellent, restaurant.

Eating *Pizzería Venezia*, one on main street, another on highway south to Tegucigalpa, excellent pizzas (owner from Venice), also serves good sandwiches and fruit drinks. *Pollos Kike*, next door, pleasant setting for fried chicken addicts; *Juanci's*, also on main street, American-style hamburgers, good steaks and snacks, open until 2300. *Bicos*, southwest corner of Parque Central, nice snack bar/patisserie. *Supermercado Food* has a good snack bar inside. *Cafetería Colonial*, 4 Av SE (just behind the church), good pastries and coffee, outside seating. On the Northern Highway there are several restaurants: 3 kilometres north,

Restaurante y Cafetería (with supermarket). *Granja d'Elia*, open all day, lots of vegetables, meat too, buffet, all you can eat US$2.50, French chef, not to be missed, veg from own market garden and breads on sale outside. *Nuevo* and *Antiguo Bethania*, quite a long way out of town, good, abundant, inexpensive meals.

Shopping A good leatherworker is Celestino Alberto Díaz, Barrio San Antonio, Casa 53, 2 C NE, 6 Av NE. 1 block north of Celestino's is a good shoemaker, leather shoes made for US$25.

Transport Bus to **San Pedro Sula**, from the west end of town every 35 minutes, US$1.35. **Tegucigalpa** with Empresas Unidas or Maribel, from west plaza, south of market, US$1.50, 3 hours. Alternatively take a taxi, US$0.50, 2 kilometres to the highway intersection and catch a Tegucigalpa-San Pedro Sula bus which passes every 30 minutes; to **Comayagua**, Transpinares, US$0.50, 45 minutes; to **La Esperanza** buses leave from near *Boarding House Central*, 1st departure 0530, several daily, taxi from town centre US$0.50.

Directory Banks *Bancahsa, Banco Atlántida, Banco de Occidente, Banco Sogerin.*

From Siguatepeque, a beautiful paved road goes through lovely forested mountainous country, southwest via **Jesús de Otoro** (two basic *hospedajes* and Balneario San Juan de Quelala, US$0.30 entry, *cafetería* and picnic sites) to La Esperanza (see page 935).

From Siguatepeque the Highway goes over the enormous forested escarpment of the continental divide, before descending towards Lago Yojoa. Just south of **Taulabé** on the highway are the caves of Taulabé, with stalactites and bats (illuminated and with guides, open daily). 16 kilometres south of the lake and just north of Taulabé is the turnoff northwest of a paved road to Santa Bárbara (see page 919).

Lago Yojoa
Colour map 4, grid C4

81 kilometres south of San Pedro Sula, 635 metres above sea level, 22½ kilometres long and 10 kilometres wide, the lake is splendidly set among mountains. Changes in the water level may affect the lake's appearance. To the west rise the Montañas de Santa Bárbara; to the east the **Parque Nacional Montaña Cerro Azul-Meámbar**. Pumas, jaguars and other animals live in the forests and pine-clad slopes. It also has a great many waterfalls, the cloud forest forming part of the reservoir of the Lago Yojoa basin. The 50 square kilometre park is 30 kilometres north of Siguatepeque and its highest point is 2,047 metres. To get to any of the entry points (Meámbar, Jardines, Bacadia, Monte Verde or San Isidro), four-wheel drive is necessary. A local ecological group, Ecolago, has marked out the area and is to offer guided tours of the park. Contact Enrique Campos at *Motel Agua Azul*. Ecolago has guides who are expert in identifying regional birds; at least 373 species have been identified around the lake. At one time the lake was full of bass, but overfishing and pollution decimated the fish stocks. Efforts are being made to clean up the lake and limited fishing is again possible. For more information, contact Proyecto Humuya, Atrás Iglesia Betel, 21 de Agosto (T7732426) Siguatepeque, or Proyecto de Desarrollo Río Yure, San Isidro, Cortés, Apartado 1149, Tegucigalpa. The Northern Highway follows the eastern margin to the lake's southern tip at **Pito Solo**, where sailing boats and motor boats can be hired. On the northern shore of Lago Yojoa is a complex of precolumbian, settlements called **Los Naranjos** which are believed to have had a population of several thousand. It is considered to be the country's second most important archaeological zone spanning the period from 1000 BC to 1000 AD, and including two ballcourts. The site is being developed for tourism by the Institute of Anthropology and History. From the lake it is about 37 kilometres down to the hot Ulúa lowlands. (Bus to Lake from San Pedro Sula, US$1, one and a half hours; bus from Lake to Tegucigalpa with Hedmán-Alas, US$3, 3-5 hours, 185 kilometres. Damage to the Northern Highway north of the lake during Hirricane Mitch forced transport to make a detour on the more westerly route through Río Lindo. This did not cause undue delay.)

Sleeping and eating L *Gualiqueme*, luxurious cottage at edge of lake, originally built for executives of the Rosario mine, now a hotel, 4 bedrooms in main house, 2 in annex, daily, weekly, monthly rental, weekend packages include ferry and fishing boat, for information contact Richard Joint at Honduyate, T2332648, F2392324. **A-C** *Brisas del Lago*, T5534884, F5533341, large hotel, good restaurant but overpriced, launches for hire. **B** *Finca Las Glorias*, T5660461, F5660553, bath, a/c, hot water, TV, bar, good restaurant, pool, great views. **C-D** *Motel Agua Azul* (at north end of lake, about 3 kilometres west from junction at Km 166), T9917244, simple, clean cabins for 2 or more persons, meals for non-residents, but food and service in restaurant is poor, beautiful gardens, manager speaks English, swimming pool, fishing, horseriding and boating, launches for hire, mosquito coils. Recommended (except when loud karaoke is in full swing). **C** *Los Remos*, T5578054, has cabins and camping facilities at Pito Solo, at the south end of the lake, and rooms in **E** range, clean, beautiful setting, good food, nice for breakfasts, no beach but swimming pool, boat trips, parking US$3. *Only Bass*, 500 metres from *Motel Agua Azul* serves fresh fish from lake. Highly recommended. *Comedores* on the road beside the lake serve the fish (bass) that is caught there (*Restaurant Margoth*, 1 kilometre north of *Los Remos*. Recommended.) Roadside stalls near Peña Blanca sell fruit. Buses between Tegucigalpa and San Pedro stop to let passengers off at *Los Remos*, and at Peña Blanca, 5 kilometres from the turning for *Agua Azul*. At Peña Blanca on north side of Lake are **F** *Hotel Maranata*, clean, near bus stop, friendly, and *Comedor El Cruce*, very good home cooking. *Brisas del Canal*, local food. Recommended, but small portions. *Panadería Yoja*, one block from *Hotel Maranata*, good juices and pastries.

A paved road skirts the lake's northern shore for 12 kilometres via Peña Blanca. One unpaved road heads southwest to **El Mochito**, Honduras' most important mining centre. A bus from 2 Avenida in San Pedro Sula goes to Las Vegas-El Mochito mine where there is a cheap *pensión* (**F**) and walks along the west side of Lago Yojoa. Buses will generally stop anywhere along east side of lake. Another unpaved road heads north from the northern shore, through Río Lindo, to **Caracol** on the Northern Highway. This road gives access to the Pulhapanzak waterfall, with some unexcavated ceremonial mounds adjacent, and to Ojo de Agua, a pretty bathing spot near Caracol.

The impressive waterfall at **Pulhapanzak** is on the Río Lindo; by car it's a one and a half hours' drive from San Pedro, longer by bus. There is a bus from Peña Blanca every two hours to the falls, or take a Mochito or Cañaveral bus from San Pedro Sula from the bus station near the railway (hourly 0500-1700) and alight at the sign to the falls, at the village of Santa Buena Ventura, US$0.95. Alternatively stay on the bus to Cañaveral (take identification because there is a power plant here), and walk back along the Río Lindo, two hours past interesting rock formations and small falls. There is swimming in terrace-like pools about 20 minutes' walk from Pulhapanzak (for a small tip boys will show off their diving skills). The waterfall (42 metres) is beautiful in, or just after the rainy season, and in sunshine there is a rainbow at the falls. There is a picnic area and a small *cafetería* (or there is a good *comedor* 15 minutes' walk away down in the village), but the site does get crowded at weekends and holidays; there is a small admission charge (US$1). The caretaker allows camping for US$0.85. Recommended. There are two rooms available (under US$3) and a hotel is planned. Leave early for this trip. Last return bus leaves at 1630 during the week.

10 kilometres north of the lake on the Northern Highway is the turn-off for the village of **Santa Cruz de Yojoa** (**F** *Hospedaje Paraíso*, with bath, clean, fan, friendly), and at 24 kilometres is the **El Cajón** hydroelectric project (to visit the dam, apply at least 10 days in advance: T2222177, or in writing to Oficina de Relaciones Públicas de la ENEE, 1 Avenida, Edif Valle-Aguiluz, Comayagüela, DC). El Cajón hydroelectric dam (226 metres high) has formed a 94-square kilometre lake, which lies between the departments of Cortés, Yoro and Comayagua. The dam is 22 kilometres from Santa Cruz de Yojoa.

Honduras

At Km 46, south of San Pedro Sula, there is a paved road leading east through banana plantations to Santa Rita, thence either east to Yoro, or north to Progreso and Tela, thus enabling travellers between Tegucigalpa and the north coast greatly to shorten their route by avoiding San Pedro Sula. Shortly before San Pedro Sula, the road divides and becomes a toll road. The toll road's surface is poor in places.

San Pedro Sula

Population: 500,000
Altitude: 60-150m
Colour map 4, grid B2

San Pedro Sula, 58 kilometres south of Puerto Cortés by road and railway, 265 kilometres from Tegucigalpa, the second largest city in Honduras, is a centre for the banana, coffee, sugar and timber trades, a focal distributing point for northern and western Honduras with good road links, and the most industrialized centre in the country. Its business community is mainly of Arab origin. It is considered the fastest growing city between Mexico and Panama.

The city was founded by Pedro de Alvarado on 27 June 1536. The large neo-colonial-style cathedral, started in 1949, was completed many years later. San Pedro Sula is situated in the lush and fertile valley of the Ulúa (Sula) River, beneath the forested slopes of the Merendón mountains and, though pleasant in the cooler season from November to February, reaches very high temperatures in the rest of the year with considerable humidity levels. It is, nevertheless, a green city, clean and the traffic is not too bad.

The higher and cooler suburb of Bella Vista with its fine views over the city affords relief from the intense heat of the town centre. The cafetería and foyer swimming pool of *Hotel Sula* provide a cool haven for visitors.

Ins & outs **Getting there** San Pedro Sula is a more important international gateway than Tegucigalpa. Its airport, Ramón Villeda Morales (SAP) is 17 kilometres from the city centre. There is no bus station; companies have their own terminals, mostly in the southwest part of the city.

Getting around The city is divided into four quadrants: noreste (northeast, NE), noroeste (northwest, NO), sudeste (southeast, SE) and sudoeste (southwest, SO), where most of the hotels are located. There are buses, minibuses and taxis for getting around town.

Museums **Museo de Antropología e Historia**, 3 Avenida, 4 Calle NO, with displays of the cultures that once inhabited the Ulúa valley, up to Spanish colonization, and, on the first floor, local history since colonization; ■ *open Tuesday-Sunday 1000-1600, US$0.40, gift shop (handicrafts, books etc)*. Museum café in adjacent garden with fine stela, good set lunch. **Museo Jorge Milla Oviedo**, 3 Avenida 9 Calle NE, Barrio Las Acacias, T5525060, run by the foundation which cares for the Cuero y Salado Wildlife reserve (see page 892).

Exhibitions **Expocentro**, Avenida Junior, off Boulevard to Puerto Cortés, temporary exhibitions, conferences and fairs.

Excursions One can take a taxi up the mountain behind the city for US$2-2.50; good view, and interesting vegetation on the way up. Lake Ticamaya, near Choloma, is worth visiting between June and December.

The flooding that accompanied Hurricane Mitch all but wiped out the banana plantations in the Ulúa valley east and north of San Pedro Sula. At the time of writing it is not known how long it will take for the local economy of towns like La Lima to recover.

Sleeping
■ *on maps*
Price codes:
see inside front cover

LL *Camino Real Inter-Continental*, T5530000/7050, F5522626, sanpedrosula@interconti. com, Blvd del Sur at Centro Comercial Multiplaza, new. **LL** *Hotel y Club Copantl*, Col Los Arcos, Blvd del Sur, T5530900/5567108, F5567890, Copantl2@simon.intertel.hs, corporate rates available, Olympic sized pool, tennis courts, gym, sauna, disco, casino (the only one in town, foreigners only, take passport), car and travel agencies. Other luxury hotels are **LL** *Princess*, Av Circunvalación SO, T5506141, **LL** *Los Próceres*, Av de los Próceres 17 y 18 Av No, T5574457; a *Holiday Inn* is due to open in 1999. **AL** *Gran Hotel Sula*, 1 C, 3 y 4 Av, on north side of Parque Central, T5529999, F5577000, pool, restaurant (upstairs, very good, grills recommended, reasonably priced) and café (for authentic North American breakfast, view of pool), also good, 24-hour service. **AL** *St Anthony*, 3 Av 13 C No 13 SO, T5580744/5504868, F5581019, rooms and suites all with balcony, a/c, phone, cable TV, pool, pool bar, jacuzzi, gym.

AL *Honduras Plaza*, 6 C 4 Av NO, T5532424, F5532140, a/c, restaurant/bar, cable TV, own generator, parking, in respectable area but overpriced. **AL** *Suites Delvalle*, Apart-hotel, 6 Av 11C NO, T5520134, F5520137, fcastro@globalnet.hn, big, comfortable rooms with cooker, fridge, cable TV, coffee machine in hall, buns provided for breakfast, good. **AL** *Hotel-Suites Los Andes*, Av Circunvalación 84, T5534425, F5571945, restaurant, café, jacuzzi, 40-channel

San Pedro Sula

■ Sleeping	
1 Acrópolis	4 Brisas del Occidente
2 Ambassador	5 Camino Real
3 Bolívar	6 Ejecutivo
	7 Gran Hotel Sula
	8 Honduras Plaza
	9 Los Próceres
	10 Montecristo
	11 Palace Internacional

12 París	**🚌 Transport**
13 Plaza Cristal	1 Hedmán Atlas
14 Saint Anthony	2 El Rey
15 San José	3 Impala
16 San Juan	4 Citul
17 San Pedro	5 Toritos y Copanecos
18 Suites Delvalle	6 Atlántico
19 Suites Los Andes	7 Gama & Casasola

cable TV, bilingual secretarial service, garden, parking, own generator. **AL** *Plaza Cristal Suites Hotel*, 10 Av 1-2 C NO, T5508302, F5507227, phone, cable TV, bank, travel agency. **AL** *Aparthotel Almendral*, Av Circunvalación, Colonia Trejo, behind *Wendy's*, T5524289, F5566476, a/c, cable TV, kitchenette.

A-B *Palace Internacional*, 3 C 8 Av SO, Barrio El Benque, T5507974, F5500969, hipalace@simon.intertel.hn, a/c, helpful staff, internet service, parking, pool, bar, restaurant OK. **B** *Ejecutivo*, 2 C 10 Av SO, T5533218, F5525868, a/c, cable TV, café/bar, phone, own generator.

C *Acrópolis*, 3 C 2 y 3 Av SE, T/F5572121, a/c, cable TV, parking, café, comfortable, friendly, good value. **C** *Ambassador*, 5 Av 7 C SO, T5576824, F5575860. **C** *Bolívar*, 2 C 2 Av NO, T5524218, F5534823, recently redecorated (but not all rooms), a/c, TV, own generator, pool, restaurant, OK but reception unhelpful. **C** *Gran Hotel Conquistador*, 2 C 7 y 8 Av SO, opposite *Cine Tropicana*, T5527605, F5529290. **C** *Gran Hotel San Pedro*, 3 C 2 Av SO, T5501513, F5532655, private bath, a/c, **E** with fan, popular, clean, good value, rooms overlooking street are noisy, stores luggage, self-service restaurant next door (*Bio's Café*) with book exchange. **C** *Manhattan*, 7 Av 3-4 C SO, T5502316, a/c, a bit run down. **D** *Palmira 1*, 6 C 6 y 7 Av SO, T5533674, clean, convenient, large parking area. **D** *Terraza*, 6 Av 4-5 C SO, T5503108, F5574798, dining room dark, friendly staff, **E** without a/c. **D** *Colombia*, 3 C 5 y 6 Av SO, T5533118, a/c or fan.

E *El Nilo*, 3 C 2 Av SO, T5534689, nice rooms, friendly. **E** *La Siesta*, 7 C 2 Av SE, T5522650, F5580243, private bath, a/c or fan, double or twin beds, clean, but noisy.

F *Brisas del Occidente*, 5 Av 6-7 C SO, T5522309, 5-storey building, fan, some rooms without window, laundry facilities, friendly, grubby. **F** *Montecristo*, 2 Av 7 C Southeast, T5571370, noisy, not very clean, fan, safe. **F** *París*, 3 Av 3 C SO, near *El Nilo* and bus station for Puerto Cortés, shared bath, poor water supply, clean but noisy. **F** *San José*, 6 Av 5 y 6 C SO, T5571208, friendly, clean, safe, cheap and cheerful. **F-G** *San Juan*, 6 C 6 Av SO, T5531488, modern building, very noisy, clean, helpful, good value. **F** *Parador*, 6 C 1 Av SE, safe, good value. **F** cheap hotels between bus terminals and downtown market, often dirty and noisy.

Eating
● *on maps*

International In all the top hotels. *Don Udo's*, Blvd Los Próceres, restaurant and café-bar, T5533106, Dutch owner, big international menu, good wine list, Sunday brunch 1000-1400. *Pamplona*, on plaza, opposite *Gran Hotel Sula*, pleasant décor, good food, strong coffee, excellent service. *Alejandro's*, Av Circunvalación SO.

Meat *Pat's Steakhouse*, Av Circunvalación SO, very good. *La Espuela*, Av Circunvalación, 16 Av 7 C NO, good grilled meats. Recommended. *Las Tejas*, 9 C 16 y 17 Av, Av Circunvalación, good steaks and fine seafood, as also at nearby sister restaurant *La Tejana*, 16 Av 19 C SO, Barrio Suyapa, T5575276. **Seafood** *Gamba Tropic*, 5 Av 4-5 C SO, delicious seafood, good wine, medium prices, a/c. Recommended. *Chef Mariano*, 16 Av 9-10 C SO, Barrio Suyapa, T5525492, Garífuna management and specialities, especially seafood, Honduran and international cuisine, attentive service, a/c, not cheap but good value, open daily for lunch and dinner.

Chinese *Copa de Oro*, 2 Av 2 y 3 C SO, extensive Chinese and western menu, a/c, pleasant. Recommended. *Shanghai*, 4 Av, C Peatonal, good Chinese, popular on Sunday, a/c. *Sim Kon*, 17 Av 6 C NO, Av Circunvalación, Chinese. *La Fortuna*, 2 C 7 Av NO, big menu of Chinese and international, Chinese food very good, not expensive, smart, good service, a/c.

Mexican *Bar El Hijo del Cuervo*, 13 C 7-8 Av NO, Barrio Los Andes, authentic Mexican cuisine, informal setting of *champas* in tropical garden with fountain, à la carte menu, tacos, quesadillas etc.

Fast Food *Pollo Campero* on Av Circunvalación SO. Many branches of *Popeye's* for greasy chicken, *Pizza Hut*, *Wendy's*, *McDonalds*, *Little Caesars*, *Church's Chicken* and *Burger King*, also *Taos* for ice-cream. *TGI Friday's*, Blvd Los Próceres, 1 block from Av Circunvalación, 1st branch of US chain in Honduras, new, smart, a/c.

Spanish *La Huerta de España*, 21 Av 2 C SO, Barrio Rio de Piedras, 4 blocks west of Av Circunvalación, supposedly best Spanish cuisine in town, open daily until 2300.

Italian *Italia y Más*, 1 C 8 Av NO, genuine Italian food, pizza, homemade ice cream, very good.

Cafés *Café del Campo*, 5 C 10 Av NO, best coffee in town, 20 varieties, good à la carte breakfasts, big sandwiches, fish and prawn specialities US$6-8, bartender is cocktail specialist, smart, a/c, good service, very nice. *Café Skandia*, ground floor, *Gran Hotel Sula*, open 24 hours, best place for late night dinners and early breakfasts, good club sandwiches etc, good service. *Café Nani*, 6 Av 1-2 C SO, very good pastelería. *Café Venecia*, 6 Av 4-5 C, good juices, cheap. *Bio's Café*, next to *Gran Hotel San Pedro*, good, also book exchange with good selection of books in English. *Espresso Americano*, 2 branches, in C Peatonal, 4 Av, off southwest corner of Parque Central, and in Megaplaza shopping mall, closed Sunday, great coffee, cookies.

Bars *Mango's*, 16 Av 8-9 C SO, Barrio Suyapa, open 1900 onwards, open terrace, pool tables, dance floor, rock music, snacks. *Frogs Sports Bar*, Blvd Los Próceres, just above *Don Udo's*, 3 different bars, a/c, pool tables, 2nd-storey open deck overlooking their own beach volleyball court, giant TV screens showing US sports, snack bar, disco at weekends (karaoki), open 1700 until late, happy hour 1800-1900.

Bars & nightclubs

Nightclubs (with shows) *Cherrie's*, Bulevar Circunvalación entre 1 y 2 C NE, open 2000-0200, popular.

Discotheques *Henry's*, *Confetis*, both on Av Circunvalación NO; more exclusive is *El Quijote*, 11 C 3-4 Av SO, Barrio Lempira, cover charge.

Cinemas There are 8 cinemas, a/c, look in local press for details.

Entertainment

Theatre *The Círculo Teatral Sampedrano* stages occasional amateur productions (see below, **Cultural centres**). The *Proyecto Teatral Futuro*, formed in 1995, is a semi-professional company presenting contemporary theatre of Latin American countries and translations of European playwrights (ranging from Molière to Ionesco), as well as ballet, children's theatre, and workshops. Offices and studio-theatre at 4 C 3-4 Av NO, Edif INMOSA, 3rd Flr, T5523074, contact the project's artistic director, Oscar Zelaya, for news of current activities.

The city's main festival, *Feria Juniana*, is in the last days of **June**.

Festivals

Bookshops *Librería Editorial Guaymuras*, 10 Av 7 C NO, wide range of Hispanic authors, including their own publications. *La Casa del Libro*, 1 C 5-6 Av SO, comprehensive selection of Spanish and English language books, good for children's books and games, microfiche information, central, just off Parque Central. *Librería Atenea*, Edif Trejo Merlo, 1 C 7 Av SO, wide choice of Latin American, US and British fiction, philosophy, economics etc; *Librería Cultura*, 1 C 6-7 Av SO, cheap paperbacks, Latin American classics.

Shopping

Food *Gourmet Foods*, Blvd Los Próceres, between *Don Udo's* and *Frogs*, delicatessen, lots of expensive goodies eg French and Dutch cheeses, caviar, smoked salmon, Italian sausages, French champagne etc, T5533106 (home delivery).

Handicrafts Large artesan market, Mercado Guamilito Artesanía, 6 C 7-8 Av NO, typical Honduran handicrafts at good prices (bargain), but mostly imported goods from Guatemala and Ecuador, also good for fruit and vegetables. *Honduras Souvenirs*, C Peatonal No 7, mahogany woodcraft. The *Museum Gift Shop*, has lots of cheap *artesanía* gifts, basketwork, pottery etc, open during museum visiting hours. For fine leatherwork, *Latino's Leather*, 7 C 12-13 Av SO, superb bags, belts, briefcases etc. *Danilo's Pura Piel*, factory and shop 18 Av B/9 C SO. *La Maison du Cuir*, Av Circunvalación opposite *Los Andes* supermarket. *Lesanddra*

Honduras

Leather at Megaplaza Shopping Mall. The *IMAPRO Handicraft School* in El Progreso has a retail outlet at 1 C 4-5 Av SE, well worth visiting, fixed prices, good value, good mahogany carvings. For fine art and handicrafts, *MAHCHI Art Gallery* has no rival, exuberant paintings, ceramic vases, beautiful *artesanía*.

Transport   **Local** Local buses cost US$0.10, smaller minibuses cost US$0.20. **Car rentals**: Avis, 1 C, 6 Av NE, T5530888; Blitz, *Hotel Sula* and airport (T5522405 or 6683171); Budget, 1C 7av NO, T5522295,airport T6683179; Maya Eco Tours, 3 Av NO, 7-8 C and airport (T5522670 or 6683168); Molinari, *Hotel Sula* and airport (T5532639 or 6686178); Toyota, 3 Av 5 y 6 C NO, T5572666 or airport 6683174. Rental of a four-wheel drive car costs US$85 per day includes tax and insurance after bargaining, good discounts for long rental. **Car repairs**: Invanal, 13 C, 5 y 6 Av Northeast, T5527083, excellent service from Sr Víctor Mora. **Bike repairs**: there are few shops for parts. One with some imported parts is *Dibisa* on 3 Av y 11 C SO. **Motoring**: if coming from the south, and wishing to avoid the city centre when heading for La Lima or El Progreso, follow signs to the airport. **Taxi**: ask the price 1st and bargain if necessary. Parque Central to Av Circunvalación costs about US$1.50, to *Hotel Copantl* US$4.

Air A taxi to the airport costs US$7.75-9.25 per person, but bargain hard. No hotels near the airport. Yellow airport taxis cost US$13. Buses and colectivos do not go to the airport terminal itself; you have to walk the final 1 kilometre from the La Lima road (bus to this point, US$0.10). Tourist office, duty free, Global One phones, Bancahsa for Visa and Amex Tcs (two other banks don't change TCs – money changers give a good rate for dollars and will exchange lempiras into dollars), restaurant on 2nd floor. Flights to Tegucigalpa (35 minutes), La Ceiba, Utila and to Roatán. See **Essentials** for international flights.

Train Enquire to see if services on the Tela-Puerto Cortés line are continuing to San Pedro Sula.

Buses To **Tegucigalpa**, 4-4½ hours, 250 kilometres by paved road, main bus services with comfortable coaches and terminals in the town centre are: Hedman Alas, 8-9 Av NO, 3 C, T5531361, 0630 to 1730 (US$6), which is good, no meals, TV movies; Transportes Sáenz, 8 Av 5-6 C SO, T5534969, better buses, meals, US$8; El Rey, Av 7, C 5 y 6, T5534264, or Express 10 Av 8-9 C, Barrio Paz Barahona, T5578355; Transportes Norteños, 6 C 6-7 Av, T5522145, last bus at 1900; Viana, Av Circunvalación, 200 metres southwest of *Wendy's*, T569261. The road to **Puerto Cortés** is paved; a pleasant 45-minute journey down the lush river valley, buses to Puerto Cortés (Empresa Impala, 2 Av, 4-5 C SO No 23, T5533111, several each hour, or Citul, 6 Av, 7-8 C), to **Omoa** (3 C East from 0600), east to **La Lima, El Progreso, Tela** and **La Ceiba** (Tupsa and Catisa, 2 Av SO, 5-6 C, hourly on the hour, US$2.50, 2½-3 hours) with a change of bus in El Progreso. To **Trujillo**, 3 per day, a/c, US$5, 6 hours, comfortable, Cotraibal departs from 1 Av, 7-8 C SE.

Buses run south to **Lago Yojoa** and Tegucigalpa, and southwest to **Santa Rosa** and then through the Department of Ocotepeque with its magnificent mountain scenery to the **Guatemalan border** (US$3.40 to the border by bus). Congolón and Torito/Copanecos serve **Nueva Ocotepeque** and **Agua Caliente** on the Guatemalan border on alternate days, Congolón dep 2400, Torito 2400 and early morning and early afternoon; Congolón, 8 Av 10 C SO, T5531174, Torito, 11 C 7 Av SO, T5573691, one block apart; to **Santa Rosa de Copán**, with connections at La Entrada for **Copán**, Empresa Toritos y Copanecos (T5534930) leaving from 6-7 Av 11 C SO, every 45 minutes, 0330-1700, US$2 to Santa Rosa. Direct bus to Santa Rosa US$2.50, 4 daily. Take these buses to La Entrada, 2 hours, US$1.30, or US$1.45 on the fast bus, for connection to **Copán**. Road paved all the way. Direct bus to Copán with Casasola-Cheny Express, 3 a day, or Gama Express (T5522861/6) at 0700 and 1930, both from 6 C 6-7 Av, by *Hotel Palmira*, 3 hours in comfortable, fast buses, see under Copán for details.

Directory   **Airline offices** *Grupo Taca*13 Av NO esq norte de la Circunvalación, Barrio Los Andes, T5570525, airport T6683333. *Copa*, Bajos de Hotel Sula 1 C, T5505583, airport 6686776. *Iberia*, Edif Quiroz p 2, T5501604/4609, airport T6683216/9. *Isleña*, Edif Trejo Merlo, 1 C 7 Av SO, T5528322, airport T6683181. *Sosa*, 8 Av 1-2 C SO, Edif Roman, T5506548, airport 6683128. *American*, Ed Firenze, Barrio Los Andes, 16 Av, 2-3 C, T5580524, airport T6683241. *Continental*, Plaza Versalles, Av Circunvalación, T5574141, airport T6683208.

Banks *Banco Atlántida*, on Parque Central, changes TCs at good rates. *Lloyds Bank* at 4 Av SO 26, between 3 y 4 C. *Banco de Honduras (Citibank)*. *Bancahorro*, has a beautiful mural in its head office, 5 Av, 4 C SO. *Bancahsa*, 5 Av, 6-7 C SO, changes TCs. *Banco Continental*, 3 Av, 3-5 C SO No 7. *Banffaa*, *Banco de Occidente*, 6 Av, 2-3 C SO. *Bancomer*, 4 C, 3-4 Av NO. *Banhcafé*, 1 C, 1 Av SE and all other local banks. *Amex* is at *Credomatic*, 5 Av y 2 C NO, also for Visa and Mastercard. These 2 also at *Aval Card*, 14 Av NO y Circunvalación, and *Honducard*, 5 Av y 2 C NO. Good rates at *Lempira Cambios*, 4 C and 3 Av SO for cash and TCs; also at *Casa de Cambio DICORP*, Centro Comercial Galerías, 1 C 15 Av NO, Blvd Morazán, open Mon-Fri 0900-1600. A host of dealers buy dollars in Parque Central and the pedestrian mall.

Communications Post Office: 3 Av SO between 9-10 C. **Telephone:** Hondutel, 4 C 4 Av SO. Collect calls can be made from lobby of *Gran Hotel Sula*. **Email:** Internet Café in Multiplaza centre, T5506077/5503388, US$5 per hr.

Cultural centres *Centro Cultural Sampedrano*, 3 C, 4 Av NO No 20, T5533911, USIS-funded library, cultural events, occasional concerts, art exhibitions and theatrical productions. *Alianza Francesa*, on 23 Av 3-4 C SO, T5524359/5531178, has a library, French films on Wed, and cultural events on Fri.

Embassies & consulates *Belize*, Km 5 Blvd del Norte, Col los Castaños, T5510124, 5510707, F5511740. *Guatemala*, 8 C 5-6 Av NO, No 38, T/F5533560. *Nicaragua*, Col Trejo, 23 Av A entre 11 C B y 11 C C No 145, T/F5503394. *Costa Rica*, Hotel St Anthony, T5580744, F5581019. *El Salvador*, Edif Rivera y Cía, p 7, local 704, 5 y 6 Av 3 C, T/F5534604. *Mexico*, 2 C 20 Av SO 201, Barrio Río de Piedras, T5532604, F5523293. *UK*, 13 Av 10-12 C SO, Suyapa No 62, T5572046, F5529764. *France*, Col Zerón, 9 Av 10 C 927, T5574187. *Germany*, 6 Av NO, Av Circunvalación, T5531244, F5531868. *Spain*, 2 Av 3-4 C NO 318, Edif Agencias Panamericanas, T5580708, F5571680. *Italy*, Edif La Constancia, p 3, 5 Av 1-2 C NO, T5523672, F5523932. *Netherlands*, 15 Av 7-8 C NE, Plaza Venecia, Local 10, T5571815, F5529724.

Hospitals & medical services Dentist: *Clínicas Dentales Especializadas*, Ed María Antonia, 3a C entre 8 y 9 Av NO, apartamento L-1, Barrio Guamilito, T5580464.

Laundry *Lavandería Almich*, 9-10 Av, 5 C SO No 29, Barrio El Benque. *Excelsior*, 14-15 Av Blvd Morazán. *Rodgers*, 4a C, 15-16 Av SO, No 114. *Lava Facil*, 7 Av, 5 C NO, US$1.50 per load.

Tour companies & travel agents *Explore Honduras*, Edif Paseo del Sol, 1 C 2 Av NO, T5526242, F5526239, interesting 1-day and overnight tours with a/c bus, to Copán from US$55, Lake Yojoa and Pulhapanzak waterfall, to Lancetillo Botanical Park, Omoa, all around US$65 including guided tour, entrance fees, lunch. *Maya Tropic Tours* in lobby of *Gran Hotel Sula*, T/F5578830, mayatt@netsy.hn, run by helpful Jorge Molamphy and his wife. *Cosmos*, 3 y 4 C 10 Av NO, Centro Comercial Mónaco, local 24, T5527270, F5578790, very helpful and efficient. *Mesoamérica Travel*, Edif Picadelli, local 206, 1 y 3 Av 11 C SO, PO Box 637, T5570332, F5576886, www.mesoamerica-travel.com, individual and group tours arranged; also here, *Fundación Patuca*, info@mesoamerica-travel.com. Several other agencies. **Private tour operator:** *Javier Pinel*, PO Box 2754, T/F5574056, local and regional tours, also offers bed and breakfast.

Tourist offices *Sectur*, Edif Inmosa, 4C, NO, 3-4 Av, T5523023/95, and at airport, road maps US$2.25 but no other maps. **Immigration**: Calle Peatonal, just off Parque Central, or at the airport.

20 kilometres west of San Pedro Sula, the cloud forest national park is managed by **Cusuco** Fundación Ecológica Hector Rodrigo Pastor Fasquelle (HRPF), 7 Avenida, 1 Calle **National Park** NO, San Pedro Sula, T5521014/5596598, F5576620. Also contact Cohdefor, 10 Avenida, 5 Calle NO, Barrio Guamilito, San Pedro Sula, T553-4959/2929, or Cambio CA, who run tours. In the 1950s this area was exploited for lumber but was declared a protected area in 1959 when the Venezuelan ecologist, Geraldo Budowski reported that the pine trees here were the highest in Central America. Cutting was stopped and the lumber company abandoned the site. The area includes tropical rainforest and cloud forest with all the associated flora and fauna. It includes **Cerro Jilinco**, 2,242 metres and **Cerro San Ildefonso**, 2,228 metres. HRPF produces a bird checklist. Quetzals can be seen here. There are four trails, ranging from 30 minutes to two days. They use old logging roads, traversing forested ridges with good views. Entrance to the park is US$10 which includes a guided trip; you cannot go on

Honduras

☞ *Hike from Buenos Aires to Tegucigalpita*

This route to the coast follows a mule trail around the northeast side of the Cusuco National Park. The scenery is superb and you see a good range of wildlife.

From Buenos Aires walk east along an unpaved track to Bañaderos. A smaller track branches left just before you enter Bañaderos and immediately twists its way down, with frequent switchbacks, to a river in the valley below the road. It takes about an hour to reach the river, from where the path is fairly straightforward. Heading northeast, the trail climbs steeply away from the river before dropping again to another village (2 hours), where there is a small shop selling drinks.

From the village the path climbs to the pass (four to five hours). Much of the ascent is steep and water sources are scarce. There are some flat areas to camp as you approach the

pass. After the pass head north to the village of Esperanza. Signs that you are nearing the village are clear as you begin to enter small coffee plantations, among the heavily forested slopes. On this side of the pass water sources are plentiful. Esperanza has two shops and it is possible to camp on the village football field.

It is about 4 hours, almost all downhill, from Esperanza to the coast road. There are no more water sources and temperatures can be very high. Where the path meets the road there is a well-stocked shop. From there it is a 30-minute walk on a tarmac road to Tegucigalpita (hospedaje). The bus terminal is on this road, just past the turning for the village.

Mike and Pauline Truman

your own. Permission from HRPF is required to walk through the Park to Tegucigalpita on the coast. There is a visitors' centre but bring your own food. You cannot stay or camp in the park, but camping is possible outside. Access by dirt road from Cofradía (*Cafetería Negro*, one block northwest of plaza, good food), on the road to Santa Rosa de Copán, then to **Buenos Aires**: two hours by car from San Pedro Sula, four-wheel drive recommended; bus San Pedro Sula-Cofradía, one hour, US$0.15, from 5 Avenida, 11 Calle SO (buses drop you at the turnoff, one kilometre from town); pick-up Cofradía-Buenos Aires one and a half hours, US$1.75, best on Monday at 1400 (wait at the small shop on outskirts of town on Buenos Aires road); the park is 12 kilometres from Buenos Aires. Ask in Buenos Aires for Carlos Alvaréngez-López who offers lodging and food half-way to the park, very friendly, camping possible US$3 per person. No hotels in the village but you can stay in the small house owned by the Park authorities (many cockroaches). Two *comedores* in town, *Comedor Tucán*, good.

The North Coast

Honduras' Caribbean coast has a mixture of banana-exporting ports, historic towns (in particular Trujillo), beach resorts, and Garífuna villages. There is Pico Bonito national park, other wildlife refuges, and the overland 'Jungle Trail' to Guatemala.

Puerto Cortés to Guatemala

Puerto Cortés

Population: 65,000
Colour map 4, grid B4

Puerto Cortés, on a large bay backed by Laguna de Alvarado, is 58 kilometres by road and rail from San Pedro Sula, 333 from Tegucigalpa, and only two days' voyage from New Orleans. Most of Honduran trade passes through it and it is now the most important port in Central America. The climate is hot, tempered by sea breezes;

many beautiful palm-fringed beaches nearby; rainfall, 2,921 millimetres. Ferocious mosquitoes in this area, especially during the rainy season. It has a small oil refinery, and a free zone. The Central Park contains many fine trees with a huge Indian poplar in the centre providing an extensive canopy. The tree was planted as a sapling in 1941. The park was remodelled in 1996/97 with new flowerbeds, fountain and bronze statues.

Excursions West to **Tulián**, along the bay, for picnics and very good freshwater bathing. Mini-buses departing from the Esso petrol station in the centre (US$0.35 each way) ply along the tropical shoreline past Tulián west to the 'laid-back' village of Omoa (or three hours' walk, 15 kilometres from Puerto Cortés) with its popular beach (see below).

Tours from Puerto Cortés to Copán to visit the Maya ruins and tourist parties at the Ustaris Hacienda can be arranged with travel agents.

Beaches Buses from Puerto Cortés go east to beaches of coconut palms at **Travesía**, **Baja Mar**, and others, which are beautiful, and unspoilt. Café at Travesía, and at Baja Mar. The best stretch of beach is between the two villages, but the width of sand is narrow even at low tide. The black fishing communities are very friendly. Beware of sunburn, and mosquitoes at dusk.

Sleeping **AL** *Playa*, 4 kilometres west at Cienaguita, T6650453, F6652287, hotel complex, directly on beach, cable TV, good fish dishes in restaurant. **B** *Costa Azul*, Playa El Faro, T6652260, F6652262, restaurant, disco-bar, billiards, table tennis, pool, horse riding, volley ball, good value. **C** *International Mr Ggeerr*, 9 C, 2 Av E, T6650444, F6650750, no hot water, very clean, a/c, bar, video, satellite TV, recommended. No restaurant. **C** *El Centro*, 3 Av 3-4 C, T6651160, bath, a/c, hot water, cable TV, 14 rooms by mid-1997, parking, garden, café, pleasant, well-furnished (building in progress 1998). **C** *Hotel-restaurante Costa Mar*, Playas de la Coca Cola, T6651367, new, pleasant. **E** *Frontera del Caribe*, Playas de Camaguey, calle a Travesía, T6655001, very friendly, quiet, safe, on beach, restaurant on 1st floor, open, airy, good food, 7 rooms on 2nd floor, private bath, cold water, linen changed daily, fan, recommended. **F** *Formosa*, 3 Av 2 C E, with bath (some without), no towel, but soap and toilet paper provided, clean, fan, good value, friendly Chinese owner. **F** *Colón*, 3 Av 2 C O, opposite *Hotel Puerto Limón* in clapboard building, clean, safe, basic.

Eating *Pekin*, 2 Av 6-7 C, Chinese, a/c, excellent, good service, a bit pricey but recommended. Supermercado *Pekin* next door. On same block *Matt's*, a/c, nice bar, good food, not expensive, and *La Cabaña* bar and restaurant. *Burger Boy's*, 2 Av 8 C, lively, popular with local teenagers. *Kasike's Restaurant-Bar-Peña*, 3 Av y 9 C and *Carnitas Tapadera*, grills, same

Puerto Cortés centre

block. *Café Consulado*, 2 Av 8 C, very pleasant, nice snacks, fish, prawn dishes, a/c, bar. Recommended. Next door to *Candiles*, 2 Av, 7-8 C, good grills, reasonable prices, open-air seating. *Repostería Ilusión*, 4 C E opposite Parque, pastries, bread (turtle, crocodile loaves), coffee, nice for breakfast. *Repostería y Pastelería Plata*, corner of 3 Av and 2 C E, near Parque Central, good bread and pastries, excellent cheap *almuerzo*, buffet-style, kids' playroom. Recommended. Also at 3 Av 3 C and, 2 Av y 4-5 C, opposite Parque. *El Zaguán*, 2 Av 5-6 C, closed Sunday, popular with locals, good for refreshments, cheap. *Comedor Piloto*, 2 Av 1-2 C, open 0700-1800, closed Sunday, new, clean, satellite TV, fans, good value and service, popular.

Festivals In **August**, including '*Noche Veneciana*' on third Saturday.

Shopping There is a souvenir shop in the Aduana administration building (opposite Hondutel), *Marthita's*. The market in the town centre is quite interesting, 3 C entre 2 y 3 Av.

Transport **Trains** The railway station is near the harbour entrance. There are 2 trains a week (Friday and Sunday) to *Tela*, 0700, 4 hours, US$1, 1,067 metres gauge. Timetables change.

Buses Bus service at least hourly to San Pedro Sula, US$0.75, 45 minutes, Citul (4 Av entre 3 y 4 C) and Impala (4 Av y 3 C, T2550606). Citul from San Pedro Sula arrives in Puerto Cortés at 2 Av y 5 C, on Parque. Bus to Omoa and Tegucigalpita from 3 C entre 2 y 3 Av, old school bus, loud music, very full, guard your belongings.

Sea To Guatemala A boat leaves from Omoa for Lívingston, no fixed schedule, US$25 per person. Irregular boats also leave for Puerto Barrios. Ask at *Fisherman's Hut*, Omoa, for Sr Juan Ramón Menjivar (phone line pending). In Puerto Cortés information from Ocean Travel at 3 Av, 2 blocks west of plaza. **To Belize** Boats to Belize leave from beside the bridge over the lagoon (Barra La Laguna), buy tickets at wooden shack facing *Kokito* bar just before bridge. A launch leaves Puerto Cortés, for Mango Creek, Belize, US$50, 7 hours, no fixed schedule; can be dangerous in rough weather. A fast skiff sails usually Wednesday and Saturday to Dangriga and/or Placencia, US$50, about 3 hours. Remember to get your exit stamp.

Once a week the 73 foot yacht *Osprey* sails from Puerto Cortés to Utila, German/American crew, 2 days passage, all inclusive US$46, ask at Restaurant *El Delfin*. There are occasionally other boats **to the Bay Islands**, but none scheduled. It is possible to visit the harbour on Sunday morning, ask at the gate. Most boats wait until they have sufficient cargo before they set sail. Price is around US$10.

Directory **Banks** *Banco de Comercio* cashes TCs. *Banco de Occidente*, 3 Av 4 C E, cashes Amex TCs, accepts Visa/Mastercard. *Bancahsa*, 2 Av, 2 C. All banks open Mon-Fri 0800-1700, Sat 0830-1130. Banks along 2 Av E, include *Sogerín*, *Bamer*, *Atlántida* (2 Av, 3-4 C, unhelpful), *Bancomer*, *Bancahsa*. **Communications** Telephone: Hondutel, at dock entrance, Gate 6, includes fax and AT&T. Direct to USA. **Post Office:** next door to Hondutel. **Health** *Policlínica*, 3 Av just past 1 C, open 24 hrs. **Places of worship** Protestant Church: Anglican/Episcopal. **Security** Avoid 4 C between 1 and 2 Av, lots of bars, drunks, beggars. The area on 1 Av opposite the dockyards should also be avoided, lots of prostitution, drunks, unpleasant by day, dangerous at night. **Tour companies & travel agents** *Bahía Travel/Maya Rent-a-Car*, 3 Av, 3 C, T6653064, F2551123. *Ocean Travel*, Plaza Eng, 3 Av 2 C, T6650913. *Irema*, 2 Av 3-4 C, T66551506, F6650978. **Useful addresses** Immigration: the Immigration Office is on 3 Av, 5 C (it is not noted for its efficiency, exit stamps cost US$2.50-US$5, depending on the official). If entering Puerto Cortés by boat, go to Immigration immediately (don't be persuaded by the boat captain to fill in your tourist card on the boat). Passports are sometimes collected at the dock and you must go later to Immigration to get them; US$1 entry fee, make sure that you have the stamp. This is the only official payment; if asked for more, demand a receipt.

Omoa

Population: 2,500
Colour map 4, grid B4

Omoa , 15 kilometres from Puerto Cortés has an 18th century castle, Fortaleza de San Fernando, now renovated and worth a visit. Entrance US$0.85, tickets on sale at gate, guides available, open Tuesday-Sunday 0800-1700. There is a Visitors' Centre (closed for renovation early 1997) and a small interesting museum. During the week Omoa is a quiet, friendly fishing village, but at weekends it is overwhelmed by Hondurans from

San Pedro and the place gets littered. Roli and Berni (Swiss) run tours of Honduras and Guatemala and to the *cayos* (a handful of small islands, one and a half hours by boat), good snorkelling. Near Omoa are two waterfalls (Los Chorros), with lovely walks to each, and good hiking in attractive scenery both along the coast and inland.

At Omoa you can stay at **C** *Bahía de Omoa*, T6589076, on beach, with bath, a/c, English, German and Dutch spoken, use of washing machine, comfortable and clean, owner Heinz has motor launch for fishing or scuba diving and catamaran, sleeps 4, US$3,000 per week. **B** *Prado Mar Lodge*, Barrio Motrique (San Pedro Sula) T5532880, behind beach, cabins with bath, fridge. **D** *Gemini B*, on main access road to beach, bath, fan, cafetería, parking, lawn, new, comfortable. **E-F** *Tatiana*, on beach, with bath. **F** *Hospedaje Champa Julita*, on beach, friendly, fan, basic, run down. **F** *Roli and Berni's Place*, T/F6589082, yaxpactours@www.lemaco.hn, 300 metres from beach, T6589082, clean rooms with private bath and hot water, more planned, good information here of the region, email, fax and phone service, bikes and kayaks for guests' use, games, garden, campground. Recommended. Also on the road to the beach is *Hospedaje Puerto Grande*, but rooms are boxlike and sanitation unspeakable. **F** the *tienda* where the bus stops has cheap, basic rooms, shared bathroom, OK. **F** *Hospedaje El Centro* is in the centre of the village. The alternatives are going back to Puerto Cortés or going back 3 kilometres to Chivana, where there is the **A** *Acantilados del Caribe* (*Caribbean Cliff Marine Club*), on the road to Omoa from Puerto Cortés, **AL** at weekends, restaurant, good food, bar, discotheque, supermarket, small nature reserve with hiking and riding trails, beach, speed boats, nice atmosphere (PO Box 23, Puerto Cortés; T/F6651403; in USA T1-800-3274149, F305-4448987).

Sleeping

Restaurants include *Cayuquitos*, on beachfront, good value meals all day; *La Macarela*, northwest end of beach, good food, owner Silvia speaks English, good view; *El Delfín; Wahoo*, good seafood. *Virginia*, 200 metres on left of pier, small, friendly, good seafood; *Fisherman's Hut*, 200 metres to right of pier, new, clean, good food, seafood, recommended.

Eating

Services In Omoa, the bank takes Visa, Mastercard and TCs. There are offices for immigration, post and Hondutel. **Useful addresses** Immigration: *Migración* has an office on the main Rd opposite Texaco.

Directory

The coastal road heads southwest from Omoa towards the Guatemalan border at Corinto, where it stops. About eight kilometres from Omoa is a nice stretch of beach

North Western coast

at the mouth of the Río Coto, with the very pleasant **D** *Río Coto Hotel-Restaurant*, a/c, pool, good. 15 kilometres southwest of Omoa (Km 30½, Carretera de Puerto Cortés a Cuyamel) at **Pueblo Nuevo** on the banks of the Río Coco, is **A** *EcoRancho*, a dairy *hacienda* owned by César López. It is a beautiful ranch at the foot of the Omoa mountain range with luxury accommodation, fine family cooking, hiking, riding, bird and butterfly watching, swimming, fishing, learning to milk a cow. Also **B** cabins in two mountain sites, one at Esmeralda (500 metres), the other at Río Coco (1,000 metres), both organic coffee and cardamom plantations, camping also available, equipment provided. Tour packages arranged to include Ranguana Cay (Belize), Río Dulce (Guatemala) and other lodges. Contact the manager, Rafael Aguilera at PO Box 130, San Pedro Sula, T/F5566156, T5568780. Continuing along the coast road you come to a Garífuna village, **Mazca** (or Masca), where Doña Lydia has built bamboo and palm-thatched cabins on stilts beside her house behind the beach, under US$3, warm family atmosphere, good Garífuna cooking. A few *champas* on the beach provide fish meals and cold drinks.

Frontier with Guatemala

Honduran immigration Before leaving for the frontier, obtain your exit stamp from the Oficina de Migración in Puerto Cortés (see under Puerto Cortés **Shipping**), or Omoa.

Entering Honduras You must have a Guatemalan exit stamp in your passport before crossing the frontier and obtain an entry stamp in Puerto Cortés as soon as possible. Any custom formalities will take place there. You may be asked for an entry tax, ask for a receipt (see **Documents**, page 848).

Guatemalan Consulate See San Pedro Sula.

Transport Buses leave Puerto Cortés for Omoa and **Corinto** on the frontier every hour or so (Línea Costeños, Ruta 3 or 4).

The crossing to Guatemala, which used only to be possible on foot and by boat, has been greatly simplified now more buses run and bridges have been built over the Río Motagua. A road connecting Puerto Cortés and Puerto Barrios (Guatemala), with a new bridge over the river, was due for completion in 1999, but the storm of 1998 did cause some delays. The present route is: take a bus to Corinto (as above), or, from Omoa, take a bus to Tegucigalpita (30 kilometres) and from there a bus or pick-up to Corinto (20 kilometres). The road goes through **Cuyamelito** where there is *Hospedaje Monte Cristo*, behind the bridge, under US$3. From Corinto a pick-up goes 10 kilometres to the suspension bridge at the frontier (a new concrete bridge is being built 800 metres upriver). Across the bridge, in Guatemala, is Finca Arizona, from where there is an hourly bus to Puerto Barrios. From Cuyamelito, it is still possible to go overland: it is a two kilometre walk to the wharf from where a dug out takes you through the swamps to the border, US$1.50, first one at 0600, no controls. Another boat, US$2.50, on the Guatemalan side (Río Tinto) takes you to the Barra de Motagua and on to Finca la Inca banana plantation where you have to wait for a bus or hitch to Puerto Barrios. Take protection against the sun and mosquitoes. In the rainy season be prepared for delays and wear suitable footwear.

Tela to Trujillo

Tela

Population: 67,890
Colour map 4, grid B4

Tela, some 50 kilometres to the east, is reached from San Pedro Sula (bus service via El Progreso, watch out for thieves on bus, padlocks are no deterrent, stay with your bags at all times). Tela used to be an important banana port before the pier was partly destroyed by fire. It is pleasantly laid out, with a sandy beach. Tela Viejo to the east is the original city; Tela Nuevo is the residential area built for the executives of the American banana and farming company which established itself in the city. Old and new Tela are joined by two bridges. There is a pleasant walk along the beach east to

Prolansate

The **Fundación Para la Protección de Lancetilla, Punta Sal y Texiguat (Prolansate)** is a non-governmental, apolitical, non-profit organization based in Tela. Originally set up by Peace Corps volunteers, it is now operated by local personnel and is involved in environmental programmes to protect and educate in conjunction with community development and ecotourism. It is currently managing four protected areas: Parque Nacional 'Jeannette Kawas' (Punta Sal), Jardín Botánico Lancetilla, Refugio de Vida Silvestre Texiguat, Refugio de Vida Silvestre Punta Izopo. There are plans to extend the area of the national park (see map), named after a former Treasurer and President of Prolansate who was assassinated in 1995, but there are complications with the location of several Garífuna villages. The Prolansate Visitors' Centre is at Calle 9 Avenida 2-3 Northeast, T4482035. They organize trips to Punta Sal, Punta Izopo and Lancetilla, with expert guides, as well as providing information about other national parks, wildlife refuges and bird sanctuaries.

Ensenada (a café and not much else) and Triunfo, or west to San Juan (see **Excursions**; also see **Security**, below).

A **Garífuna Museum** opened in 1996 at the river end of Calle 8 (also known as J Calle del Valle, its original name), PO Box 127, T4482244. It is an interesting and colourful introduction to Garífuna history and culture, with special emphasis on the contribution made by Honduran and Belizean Garífunas to contemporary music in the form of the frenetic rhythms of Punta, a blend of rock and roll, Afro-Caribbean and Spanish influences, originally a ritual dance. Also here is the art gallery of the Tela Artists Association, exhibiting many local artists. The museum shop sells *artesanía* and oil paintings. ■ *open until 2100. US$0.40.*

Excursions

Jardín Botánico at **Lancetilla** (established 1926), five kilometres inland; open Monday-Friday, 0730-1530; Saturday, Sunday and holidays 0830-1600, admission US$5. The garden was founded as a plant research station by United Fruit Co, then from 1975 was run by Cohdefor, but is now managed by Prolansate. Over 1,000 varieties of plants and over 200 bird species have been identified. It has fruit trees from every continent, the most extensive collection of Asiatic fruit trees in the Western Hemisphere, orchid garden, plantations of mahogany and teak alongside a 1,200-hectare virgin tropical rainforest. Guided tours recommended. Ask for a good guided tour at the Cohdefor office. *Hospedaje* (E *Turicentro Lancetilla*, T4482007, a/c) and *comedor*, full at weekends. No camping allowed. Either take employees' bus from town centre at 0700, or take a taxi from Tela, US$1.55, but there are few in the park for the return journey in the afternoon, so organize collection in advance. Be warned, there are many mosquitoes. Good maps available in English or Spanish US$0.30.

Local buses and trucks from the corner just east of the market go east to the Black Carib village of **Triunfo de la Cruz**, site of the first Spanish settlement on the mainland, in a beautiful bay, in which a sea battle between Cristóbal de Olid and Francisco de Las Casas (two of Cortés' lieutenants) was fought in 1524. Bus to Triunfo de la Cruz, US$0.40 (about five kilometres, if no return bus, walk to main road where buses pass). A *Caribbean Coral Inn*, T4482942, with bath, fan. F *Hotel El Triunfo*, with bath or D furnished apartments. Cheap houses and *cabañas* for rent in Triunfo de la Cruz. Beyond Triunfo de la Cruz is an interesting coastal area including the cape, **Punta Izopo** (one and a half-hour walk along the beach, take water) and the mouth of the Río León. This and the immediate hinterland was declared a National Wildlife Refuge in 1992. For information contact Prolansate. To get right into the forest and enjoy wildlife, it is best to take an organized tour.

Honduras

The area west of Tela is being developed for tourism, with investment in infrastructure (roads, bridges) and hotels and resorts. The Carib villages of **Tornabé** and **San Juan** (four kilometres west of *Villas Telamar*), are worth a visit, beautiful food (fish cooked in coconut oil). In Tornabé (taxi US$3) there are eight bungalows for rent, some a/c, some fan, hot water, at **A** *The Last Resort*, with breakfast, T/F4482545 run by the Pacheco family, a great place to relax, full board available, good restaurant.

Further northwest, along palm-fringed beaches and blue lagoons, is **Punta Sal**, a lovely place. To get there you need a motor boat or take a bus (three a day) to Tornabé and hitch a ride 12 kilometres, or take the crab truck at 1300 for US$0.40 (back at 1700), on to **Miami**, a small, all-thatched fishing village (two hours' walk along beach from Tornabé), beer on ice available, and walk the remaining 10 kilometres along the beach. There are also pick-ups from Punta Sal to Miami, contact Prolansate for information. The direct route from Tela along the coast may be impassable (sand and water) to passenger cars though you can leave your car in Tornabé safely in the hands of locals for a few lempiras, and walk from there. *Garifuna Tours* (address below), Tela, run tours for US$10, food extra. Alternatively, take a motorized *cayuco* from Tela to **Río Tinto** beyond Punta Sal, and explore from there. This area is now a 80,000 hectare National Park (see map), contact Prolansate for information. It includes forest, mangroves, wetlands and lagoons. Once inhabited only by Garífuna, the area has recently suffered from immigration of cattle farmers who have cleared the forest, causing erosion, and from a palm oil extraction plant on the Río San Alejo, which has dumped waste in the river

Parque Nacional Jeannette Kawas (Punta Sal)

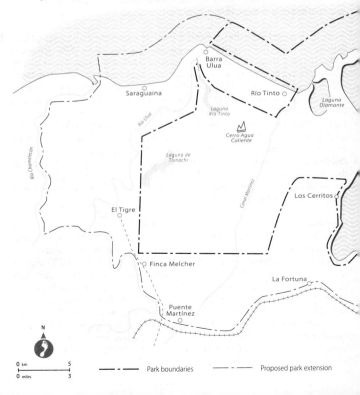

and contaminated the lagoons. Conservation and environmental protection programmes are now under way.

There is a small hotel in Río Tinto, two *comedores* and accommodation is also available in private houses. From Río Tinto it is possible to walk west along the beach to Puerto Cortés; it is about 20 kilometres from Río Tinto to Baja Mar (4-5 hours' walk), from where buses run to Puerto Cortés. This would be quicker than taking buses Tela-Progreso-San Pedro Sula-Puerto Cortés, but not quicker than the train. *Cayucos* arrive in Tela early morning for shopping, returning to Río Tinto between 1000 and 1200, very good value.

See Security below, regarding walking in and around Tela.

A *Sherwood*, T4482416, on waterfront, some cheaper rooms, a/c, TV, hot water, upper rooms have balconies and are airy, new pool, new (1997) annex, English speaking helpful owner, Travellers' cheques or credit cards accepted, staff friendly and honest, restaurant busy at weekends. **A** *Villas Telamar*, T4482196, F4482984, a complex of wooden bungalows, set on a palm-fringed beach, price for rooms, villas from **AL**, restaurant, bar, golf club, swimming pool, conference centre, redeveloped 1996. **C** *Apart-Hotel Ejecutivos*, 8 C 3 Av NE, T4481076, a/c, hot water, TV, 8 rooms with kitchenette. **B** *César Mariscos*, T4482083, on beach, new, a/c, large rooms, restaurant. **B** *Maya Vista*, T/F4481497, at top of hill, steep flight of steps starting opposite *Preluna*, Canadian-owned, French and English spoken, bath, a/c, hot water, bar, restaurant, delicious French-Canadian cuisine, fantastic views. **C** *Presidente*, on central park, T4482821, F4482992, good restaurant and pleasant bar. **C** *Bahía Azul*, 11 C, 6 Av NE, T4482381 with a/c or fan, on western end of beach, avoid rooms on road side, good restaurant overlooking the sea, fine location. **C** *Bertha's*, 8 C, 9 Av NE, near bus terminal, new brick building, with bath, a/c, cheaper with fan, clean. Recommended. **C** *Nuevo Puerto Rico*, T4482413, on the waterfront, lovely situation but exposed in June-December wet season, a/c or fan, small rooms, fridge, balcony, TV, poor service, run down, large restaurant.

D *Sinai*, 6 Av 6 C, previously Av Honduras, T4482661, 3 blocks south of Parque Central, with bath and a/c, **E** without. **D** *Tela*, 9 C, 3-4 Av NE, T4482150, clean, airy, fans, hot water, will do laundry, with restaurant, but meagre breakfast, otherwise very good. **C** *Tía Carmen*, 8 C 5 Av, next to Bancahorro, T4481476, a/c, hot water, TV, comfortable, well-furnished rooms, friendly, efficient, excellent restaurant. **E** *Mar Azul*, 11 C, 5 Av NE, T4482313, with fan and bath, charming helpful owner. **E** *Minihotel La Posada del Sol*, 8 C 3 Av NE, opposite *Ejecutivos*, T44821211, with bath, **F** without, clean, laundry facilities, nice garden, bookshop on ground floor sells US magazines. **E-F** *Mi Casa es Su Casa*, 6 Av 10-11 C, bed and breakfast, private house, sign outside, friendly, family atmosphere. **E** *Mundo Unido*, Colonia 4 de Enero, dirección San Juan, 5 minutes out of town by bus or taxi (US$1), French owned, helpful, cabins, mosquito nets, hammock space, cooking

Sleeping
During Easter week, the town is packed; room rates double and advance booking is essential.

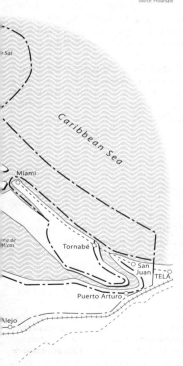
Source: Prolansate

Honduras

facilities, horse riding US$25-30 per day (not for the inexperienced), recommended. **F** *Playa*, 11 C, 3-4 Av NE, basic, bedbugs. **F** *Preluna*, 9 C, 7-8 Av Northeast, opposite bus terminal, delightful clapboard building, restaurant, quiet but reported deteriorating. **F** *Boarding House Sara*, 11 C, 6 Av behind the restaurant *Tiburón Playa*, T4482370, basic, with bath, or without, poor sanitation, has 3 good cabins priced according to number of occupants, popular with backpackers, friendly, noisy especially at weekends from all night discos.

Out of town, 3 kilometres on highway to La Ceiba, *El Retiro*, set back from the road by a small river, attractive setting, camping in vehicle allowed.

Eating

The best eating in Tela is in the hotel restaurants.

Luces del Norte, of Doña Mercedes, 11 C, 2 Av NE, towards beach from Parque Central, next to *Hotel Puerto Rico*, delicious seafood and good typical breakfasts, very popular, also good information and book exchange. *César's* (also hotel, see above), on the beach, serves good seafood, open from 0700, very good breakfast menu. Also *Sherwood's*, see above, good food, attractive, popular, enjoy the view from the terrace, also opens 0700 and serves excellent breakfast. *Los Angeles*, 9 C, 2 Av NE, Chinese, run by Hong Kong owners, large helpings, good. *Vista Maya*, in hotel (see above), run by Québécois Pierre, fine cuisine. *Tuty's Café*, 9 C NE near Parque Central, excellent fruit drinks and good cheap lunch specials, very slow service, take a book. *Comedor Acuario*, near *Boarding House Sara*, local food, cheap. Recommended. *Bahía Azul* (see hotel above), excellent cheap meals. *Pizzería El Bambino*, 11 C, 50 metres from new bridge, good pasta, pizza, open-air eating on terrace, nice children's playground. *Garífuna*, at river end of 8 C, with *champas* at river's edge, typical garífuna fare, conch soup, *tapado* (fish stew with coconut and yuca). *Merendero Tía Carmen*, at the hotel, good food, Honduran specialities, good *almuerzo*. *Casa Azul*, Barrio El Centro, Italian restaurant and bar, French Canadian owners, helpful, comfortable, good. *El Magnate*, 11 C 1 Av NE, close to old bridge, à la carte menu, pork chops speciality, open until midnight, good, disco Friday, Saturday, Sunday. *Alexandro's*, pedestrian mall, international menu, popular, often crowded, seafood specialities. Also on pedestrian mall are *La Cueva*, smart, big menu includes steak, chicken, seafood, pricey. *La Cascada*, next door, modest *comedor* in clapboard shack, cheap, home cooking, good, open early until late.

In Tela Nueva, all along the boulevard, *Los Pinchos*, shish-kebab speciality, meat and seafood, very good, nice patio, soothing music, closed Monday. *Marabú*, excellent, also rooms to rent, **C**. *Cafetería La Oso*, offshoot of *Hotel Tía Carmen's Merendero*. *Repostería y Baleadas Tía Carmen*, across the boulevard, same excellent Honduran specialities, very good. *Estancia Victoria*, new, elegant restaurant/bar, a/c, not cheap, good, international menu.

Entertainment **Cinema** 9 C, US$0.40-0.60.

Festivals *Fiesta*: *San Antonio* in June.

Transport **Local Bicycle**: hire from Garífuna Tours, 9 C y Parque Central (see below).

Trains The railway service to Puerto Cortés runs 2 days a week, 4 hours, Friday, Sunday, 1300, US$1. Check locally for exact schedule, can be daily in high season.

Buses Catisa or Tupsa lines from San Pedro Sula to **El Progreso** (US$0.50) where you must change to go on to **Tela** (3 hours in all) and **La Ceiba** (last bus at 1900). On Catisa bus ask to be let off at the petrol station on the main road, then take a taxi to the beach, US$0.50. Bus from Tela to **El Progreso** every 30 minutes, US$1; to **La Ceiba**, 2½ hours, US$1. Direct to **Tegucigalpa**, Traliasa, 1 a day from *Hotel Los Arcos*, US$4.50, same bus to **La Ceiba** (this service avoids San Pedro Sula); to **Copán**, leave by 0700 via El Progreso and San Pedro Sula to arrive same day.

Directory **Banks** *Banco Atlántida* (with ATM), *Bancahsa*, 9 C 3 Av, Visa and Mastercard, *Banadesa*, *Bancahorro*, 8 C 5 Av, changes TCs. *Casa de Cambio La Teleña*, 4 Av, 9 C NE for US$, TCs and cash. Exchange dealers on street outside Post Office. **Communications** Hondutel and Post Office: both on 4 Av NE. Fax service and collect calls to Europe available and easy at Hondutel. **Hospitals & medical services** *Centro Médico CEMEC*, 8 Av 7 C NE, open 24 hrs, X-rays, operating theatre, smart, well-equipped, T/F4482456. **Laundry** *El Centro*, 4 Av 9 C, US$2 wash and dry. *Lavandería San José*, 1 block northeast of market. *Lavandería Banegas*, Pasaje Centenario, 3 C 1 Av. **Security** Through 1998,

Tela was suffering a law and order crisis. Robberies on the beach may occur day or night and on the streets at night. Muggings and rape also reported. Walking around in company provides no protection. Check carefully before making tours on your own. **Tour companies & travel agents** *Garífuna Tours*, southwest corner of Parque Central, T4481069, F4482904, garifuna@hondutel.hn, knowledgeable and helpful, day trips to Punta Sal (US$15) and Punta Izopo (US$11), good value, also mountain bike hire, US$4.60 per day, email service. *Barana Tours*, 30 metres south of Parque Central, T4481173, good personal service, English spoken, good value trips. *Galaxia Travel Agency*, 9 C 1 Av Northeast, near river, T4482152, F4482082, for reservations and confirmations of national and international flights. **Useful addresses** Immigration: *Migración* is at the corner of 3 Av and 8 C.

La Ceiba

100 kilometres east of Tela, known as 'Ceibita La Bella', the capital of Atlántida Department, it stands on the narrow coastal plain between the Caribbean and the rugged Nombre de Dios mountain range, crowned by the spectacular Pico Bonito (2,435 metres). It was once the country's busiest port but trade has now passed to Puerto Cortés and Puerto Castilla. There is still some activity mainly to serve the Bay Islands; La Ceiba is the usual starting point for visits to the Bay Islands. The climate is hot, but tempered by sea winds. The main plaza is worth walking around; it has statues of various famous Hondurans including Lempira and two ponds with alligators or turtles basking in one of them; also a tourist information kiosk. There are some white sand beaches and good river bathing (for example Venado, three kilometres up the Río Cangrejal) out of town, but the beaches near the dock are not recommended (for details see under **Excursions** below). There is a Garífuna community by the beach at the end of Calle 1E.

Population: 80,160
Colour map 4, grid B4

A **butterfly and insect museum** has a collection of 5,000 butterflies and 1,000 other insects at Colonia El Sauce, Segunda etapa Casa G-12. You get a 25-minute video in both Spanish and English and Robert and Myriam Lehman guide visitors

Honduras

La Ceiba

Caribbean Sea

Quay

o Customs

o Immigration

Parque Manuel Bonilla

Email o
Email o

Av Valle · Av Cabañas · Av Morazán · Av Colón

Av La República
Av San Isidro
Av Atlántida
Av 14 de Julio
Av Ramón Rosa
Av La Bastilla

1 Calle
4 Calle
5 Calle
6 Calle
7 Calle
8 Calle
9 Calle
10 Calle

■ 1
Lafitte Travel Agency

■ 4

Market ■ 2

Fundación Cuero y Salado

■ 3   5 ■

o Cinema

Parque Central
o TACA
o Isleña & Sosa

✝ Cathedral

To Bus Station & West

Boulevard 15 de Septiembre

To East

N

Not to scale

■ **Sleeping**
1 Ceiba & Iberia
2 Colonial

3 Gran Hotel París
4 Italia

5 Príncipe

expertly through the mysteries of lepidopterae. Interesting for all ages. Hand-painted butterfly T-shirts for sale. ■ *T4422874, rlehman@gbm.hn, Monday-Saturday 0800-1200, 1400-1700, closed Wednesday afternoon, US$1.30, student reductions.*

There is also a **Butterfly Farm** 12 kilometres west of La Ceiba (large sign). ■ *0800-1630 daily, entry US$6.*

Excursions **Jutiapa**, a small, dusty town with a pretty little colonial church. Contact United Brands office in La Ceiba (off main plaza) to visit a local pineapple plantation. Two interesting Garífuna villages near La Ceiba are **Corozal** at Km 209½ (with beach Playas de Sambrano, and **B** *Hotel Villa Rhina*, T4432517, F4433558, with pool and restaurant near the turn off from the main road) and **Sambo Creek** (also nice beaches and simple hotel-restaurant **E** *Hermanos Avila*, clean, food OK. *La Champa* restaurant, seafood Garífuna style, bar, delightful location. Recommended).

Near the towns of Esparta and El Porvenir thousands of crabs come out of the sea in July and August and travel long distances inland. Catarata El Bejuco, seven kilometres along the old dirt road to Olanchito (11 kilometres from La Ceiba): follow a path signposted to Balneario Los Lobos to the waterfall about one kilometre up the river through the jungle. Good swimming from a pebbly beach where the river broadens. Along this road is El Naranjo near which is the *Omega Adventure Lodge* with rooms **E** and *cabañas*. Rafting and kayaking on the Río Cangrejal, varied holidays arranged. Information: Apartado 923, La Ceiba, T4410384, Ext 14, F4430700, Udo Wittemann. See page 892.

20 kilometres down the old road to Olanchito is Yaruca, reached by bus; good views of Pico Bonita. **Eco-Zona Río María**, five kilometres along the Trujillo highway, signposted path up to the foothills of the Cordillera Nombre de Dios, a beautiful walk through the lush countryside of a protected area. Just beyond Río María is Balneario Los Chorros (signposted) a series of small waterfalls through giant boulders into a deep rock pool. Great for swimming. Refreshments nearby. Upstream there is some beautiful scenery and you can continue walking through the forest and in the river, where there are more pools. Another bathing place, Agua Azul with restaurant is a short distance away.

Beaches White sand beaches in and near La Ceiba include: Playa Miramar (dirty, not recommended), La Barra (better), Perú (across the Río Cangrejal at Km 205½, better still, quiet except weekends, deserted tourist complex, restaurant, access by road to Tocoa, 10 kilometres, then signposted side road one and a half kilometres, or along the beach six kilometres from La Ceiba), La Encenada (close to Corozal). The beaches near the fishing villages of Río Esteban and Balfate are very special and are near Cayos Cochinos (Hog Islands) where the snorkelling and diving is spectacular. The Hog Islands (see page 901) can be reached by *cayuco* from **Nuevo Armenia**, a nondescript Garífuna village connected by road to Jutiapa: **E** *Chichi*, three small rooms, fan, mosquito net, clean, friendly, good food available. Bus from La Ceiba at 1100 US$0.75, two and a half hours. At the bus stop is the office of the man who arranges boat trips to Hog Islands, US$10, trips start at 0700, you may see dolphins, quite an experience. Take whatever you need with you as there is almost nothing on the smaller cays. However, the Garífuna are going to and fro all the time.

NB Many bridges on the roads leading to La Ceiba were washed away by Hurricane Mitch, principally over the Ríos Bonito and Aguán. A Bailey bridge was erected over the Río Bonito in February 1999 and access to the east was not being disrupted. The city itself was badly affected, but all services were back to normal by mid-1999.

Sleeping
Electricity is irregular, have candles/torches at the ready.

B *La Quinta*, exit carretera La Ceiba-Tela, opposite Club de Golf, T4430223, F4430226, restaurant, laundry, cable TV, swimming pool, immaculate, good value. **A** *Siesta VIP*, Blvd 15 de Septiembre, next to Banco Central, T4430968, F4430974, phone, TV, room service, bar, restaurant, airport pick-up. **A** *Tesla's Guest House*, T/F4433893, C Montecristo 212, Col El Naranjal, opposite Hospital La Fé, 5 rooms, private bathrooms, hot water, a/c, pool, phone, minibar, barbecue, laundry, friendly family owners speak English, German, French and Spanish, airport collection. **B-C** *Partenon Beach*, T/F4430434, Greek-owned, family apartments, new annex with very nice rooms, cable TV, English speaking desk staff, swimming pool, expensive but excellent restaurant, home made pasta, lovely salad bar. Highly recommended. **B** *Colonial*, Av 14 de Julio, entre 6a y 7a C, T4431953/4, F4431955, a/c, sauna, jacuzzi, cable TV, rooftop bar, restaurant with varied menu, nice atmosphere, tourist office, tours available. **B** *Gran Hotel París*, Parque Central, T/F4432391, some rooms cheaper, a/c, own generator, faded, swimming pool, parking. **C** *Ceiba*, Av San Isidro, 5 C, T4432737, with fan or a/c and bath, restaurant and bar, uncomfortable, but good breakfast. Next door to *Ceiba* is **C** *Iberia*, T4430401, a/c, window without screen. Recommended. **C** *Italia*, four doors from the *Colonial*, on Av 14 de Julio, T4430150, clean, a/c, good restaurant with reasonable prices, parking in interior courtyard. **C** *Posada Don Giuseppe*, Av San Isidro at 13 C, T/F4422812, bath, a/c, hot water, **E** with fan, TV, bar, restaurant, comfortable. **C** *Paraíso*, C 4 E, Barrio La Isla, T4433535, bath, a/c, hot water, TV, restaurant, 4 blocks from beach, bar, restaurant.

D *Príncipe*, 7 C between Av 14 de Julio and Av San Isidro, T4430516, cheaper with fan and shared bath, bar/restaurant, TV. **D** *San Carlos*, Av San Isidro, 5 y 6 C, rooms are clean with fan, colourful cafetería, and its own bakery, good breakfasts, where Bay Islanders assemble Tuesday mornings for boat trip to Utila. **D-E** *El Conquistador*, Av La República, T4432851, cheaper with fan, shared bath, safe, clean, TV. **C-D** *Gran Hotel Libano*, at bus terminal, T4432102, good, restaurant, a/c or fan, bath. **D-E** *Tropical*, Av Atlántida between 4 y 5 C, T4422565, with bathroom, fan, basic, small rooms noisy, cold drinks and water sold in foyer. **E** *Florencia*, Av 14 de Julio, some a/c, TV, clean, bath, friendly, dark rooms but recommended. **D** *Granada*, Av Atlántida, 5-6 C, T4432451, bath, a/c, clean, safe, cheaper with fan. **E** *Rotterdam Beach*, 1 C, Barrio La Isla, T4400321, on the beach, with bath, fan, clean, friendly, pleasant garden, good value. Recommended. Next door is **E** *Amsterdam 2001*, T4422292, run by Dutchman Jan (Don Juan), good for backpackers, dormitory beds or rooms, with laundry, *Dutch Corner Café* for great breakfasts. **E** *El Caribe*, 5 C between Av San Isidro and Av Atlántida, T4431857, with bath, friendly, run down, cockroaches. **F** *La Isla*, 4 C between 11 and 12 Av, T4432835, nice traditional clapboard house with bath, nice rooms, fans but beware of bugs. On Av 14 de Julio **F** *Real* (at corner of 6 C), cold shower and need to ask for water to be turned on, small rooms, better rooms on upper floor, fan. **F** *Las 5 Rosas*, C 8 near Av Le Bastilla, opposite Esso, clean, simple rooms, bath, fan, laundry, good value.

Many cheap hotels on Av La República, beside railway line leading from central plaza to pier, eg *Arias*, *Los Angeles*, but most of them are dirty, noisy, short stay places. This area is unsafe at night.

Camping At the airport for US$0.20. You may sleep in your vehicle but no tent camping. Hotel at airport entrance **F** *El Cique*, basic but convenient.

Eating

Ricardo's, Av 14 de Julio, 10 C, very good seafood and steaks, garden setting and a/c tables. Recommended. *Palace*, 9 C, Av 14 de Julio, large Chinese menu, seafood, churrasco. Recommended. *La Carreta*, 4 C, 2 Av E, Barrio Potrerito (near Parque Manuel Bonilla), good value, charcoal-broiled meat, about US$17 for 2, try *anafre*, a bean and cheese dish. Recommended. *Toto's*, Av San Isidro, 17 C, good pizzería. *Las Dos Fronteras*, Av San Isidro, 13 C, good Mexican and American food, open 0700-2200, another branch at Plaza del Sol Shopping Centre, good food, limited choice. *Cafetería Mi Delicia*, Av San Isidro, 11 C, good food at low prices, plentiful breakfasts, family atmosphere. *Cri Cri Burger*, Av 14 de Julio, 3 C, facing attractive Parque Bonilla good fast food, several branches in town. Recommended. *Masapán*, 7 C Av San Isidro-Av República, self-service, varied, well-prepared choice of dishes, fruit juices, good coffee, open 0630-2200. Recommended. *Café El Pastel*, Av San Isidro with 6 C, good cheap breakfasts, set lunches, snacks, open 0700-2100. *El Canadiense*, Parque Manuel Bonilla, north end of Av 14 de Julio, western food, steaks etc, busy bar, open 0800-2300, closed Sunday, book exchange, operates Harry's Horseback Riding trips to Pico Bonito, 6 hours, US$25, expat guide, food provided. *La Plancha*, C 9, Av la Bastilla, behind Esso, T4432304, a/c, *churrasquería*. *Café le Jardin*, Av La Bastilla, 7-8 C, Barrio La Isla, owners

Honduras

Michel (chef) and Lisette (la patronne), outstanding French cuisine, good value wine, open lunch and dinner Monday-Saturday. Highly recommended. *Pizza Hut*, on main plaza, good salad bar, large restaurant, US$2.25 lunchtime special, pizza, salad, drink, playground. *Toñita*, opposite *Hotel Partenon*, good seafood, pleasant atmosphere. *Cobel*, 7 C, opposite *Príncipe*, good breakfasts, excellent set lunches, very popular with locals, closes 1730. Recommended. *Paty's*, Av 14 de Julio between 6 and 7 C, milkshakes, wheatgerm, cereals, donuts, etc, purified water, clean. Opposite is an excellent pastry shop. There are two more *Paty's* at 8 C E and at the bus terminal. There are several good fish restaurants at end of C 1 E, *El Pescado* and *Brisas de la Naturaleza* and *La Barra*, overlooking the river, good prawn soup, music and dancing in bar from 2100, very pleasant garden setting. *La Chavelita*, end of 4 C E, overlooking Río Cangrejal, open daily, lunch and dinner, seafood, popular. *Expatriates Bar & Grill & Cigar Emporium*, at Final de C 12, above Refricón, 3 blocks south, 3 blocks east of Parque Central, open 1600-2400, closed Wednesday, Canadian owned, very expat atmosphere, US TV and newspapers, sports shown, barbecue and Mexican food, US$2-5 a meal. *Deutsch-Australian Club*, beach end of Av 14 de Julio, run by German retired to Honduras after living in Australia, German food and seafood, busy bar, open 1200 until very late.

Entertainment **Cinema** 8 C y Av San Isidro in Plaza Tropical commercial centre, new, comfortable, digital Dolby stereo.

Discotheques *Leonardo's. D'Lido. Buho's*, 1 C, Thursday, Friday, Saturday 2000-0400, disco free with dinner Thursday; several others along 1 C. *Safari, Golding Rock, La Kosta, La Concha; Santé's*, reasonable prices.

Festivals *San Isidro*, La Ceiba's patron saint, is on **15 May**. The celebrations continue for two weeks, ending 28 May, the highlight being the international carnival on the third Saturday in May, when La Ceiba dons party dress and dances all night to the Afro-Caribbean rhythms of the country's Garífuna bands.

Shopping *El Regalito*, good quality souvenirs at reasonable prices in small passage by large Carrión store. *T Boot*, store for hiking boots, C 1, east of Av San Isidro, T4432499.

La Ceiba & the coast

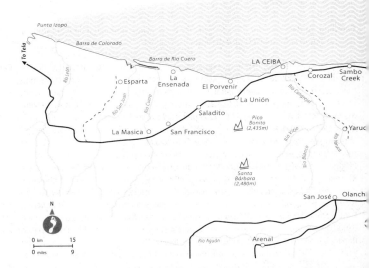

Local Car rental: Molinari in *Hotel París* on Parque Central, T/F4430055. **Maya** **Transport**
Rent-a-Car, *Hotel La Quinta*, T4433071, F4430226; **Dino's Rent-a-Car**, *Hotel Partenon Beach*,
T4430404, F4430434.

Air Golosón (LCE), 9.7 kilometres out of town. See **Getting there**, in **Essentials**, for
international services. For full details of flights to Bay Islands, see next section. Isleña
(T4430179/4412521 airport), flies to San Pedro Sula, Trujillo, Puerto Lempira, Roatán,
Guanaja; Taca and Lacsa fly to Tegucigalpa and San Pedro Sula. Sosa flies to Ahuas, Puerto
Lempira, San Pedro Sula, Roatán and Utila. Caribbean Air flies to San Pedro Sula and Roatán.
At weekends there are some charter flights which may be better than the scheduled flights.
Taxi to town US$4 per person or walk 200 metres to the main road and share for US$1 with
other passengers, also buses from bus station near *Cric Cric Burger* at end 3 Av, US$0.15. Inter-
city buses (eg from Tela) pass by the entrance.

Buses Taxi from centre to bus terminal, which is a little way west of town (follow Blvd 15
de Septiembre), costs US$0.75 per person, or there are buses from Parque Central. Most
buses leave from here. Traliasa and Etrusca bus service to **Tegucigalpa** via Tela US$6, avoid-
ing San Pedro Sula (US$1 to Tela, 2 hours); also hourly service to **San Pedro Sula**, US$2 (3-4
hours). To **Trujillo**, 3 hours *directo*, 4½ hours *local* (very slow), every 1½ hours or so, US$3;
daily bus La Ceiba-Trujillo-Santa Rosa de Aguán; to **Olanchito**, US$1, 3 hours; also regular
buses to Sonaguera, Tocoa, Balfate, Isletas, San Esteban and other regional locations.

Sea *M/V Tropical* sails daily (except in bad weather) to the Bay Islands (see next section
for full details) from the new dock (Muelle de Cabotaje), 6 kilometres outside town. Take taxi,
US$2-3 per person, if sharing with 4 people (but make sure if the price quoted is per person
or total), bus will only take you part of the way, inconvenient 1½ hours walk from there, some
assaults reported early morning.

Banks *Bancahsa*, 9 C, Av San Isidro and *Bancomer*, Parque Central, both cash TCs. Open 0830-1130, **Directory**
1330-1600; Sat 0800-1200. *Banco Atlántida*, Av 14 de Julio, has ATM that accepts Visa and they will
cash TCs at good rates. Cash advances on Visa and Mastercard from *Credomatic* on Av San Isidro
opposite *Hotel Iberia*; also American Express. *Honducard*, Av San Isidro for Visa, next to *Farmacia
Aurora*. Better rates for US$ cash from *cambistas* in the lounges of the bigger hotels (and at travel
agency next door to *Hotel Príncipe*). *Master Cambio*, Av San Isidro opposite *Hotel Iberia*. **Money
Exchange**, at back of Supermercado Los
Almendros, 7 C Av San Isidro with Av 14 de Julio,
open daily 0800-1200, 1400-1800, T4432720,
good rates for US$ cash and TCs.

Communications Post Office: Av Morazán,
13 C O. *Hondutel* for international telephone calls
is at 2 Av, 5 y 6 C E.

Hospitals & medical services Doctor: *Dr
Gerardo Meradiaga*, Edif Rodríguez García, Ap No
4, Blvd 15 de Septiembre, general practitioner,
speaks English. *Dr Siegfried Seibt*, Centro Médico,
1 C and Av San Isidro, speaks German. **Hospital:**
Vincente D'Antoni, Av Morazán, T4432264,
private, competent, well equipped. Private room
and doctor's fees about US$40 per day for
in-patients.

Tour companies *EuroHonduras*, in foyer of
Hotel Italia, or Hospital Eurohonduras,
T/F4430933, eurohonduras@caribe.hn, local
tours (also Mosquitia), river trips, kayaking, good
value, information, German, French, Spanish and
English spoken. Highly recommended. Also
guest house, see above. *Laffite*, Av San Isidro
between 5 y 6 C, T4430115, F4430354, helpful
and informative. *Tourist Options*, *Hotel Caribbean
King*, T4400265, F4430859, touristoptions@
caribe.hn, good value tours. *Pedal and Paddle*,

Av 14 de Julio, T4432762, rafting possible all year. *Caribbean Travel Agency*, run by Ann Crichton, Av San Isidro, Edif Hermanos Kawas, Apdo Postal 66, T4431360/1, F4431360, helpful, shares office with *Ríos Honduras* (affiliate of Rocky Mountain Outdoor Center, Howard, Colorado, USA), T4430780, rios@hondurashn.com, offering whitewater rafting, trips on the Río Cangrejal, spectacular, reservations 1 day in advance. *Junglas Tropicales Oscar Pérez*, T/F4433757, PO Box 471, informative guide, 3-day rafting trip on Río Sico, also whitewater rafting US$50 per person, exciting, entertaining day, other tours available. Highly recommended. *Omega Tours*, write to Udo Wittemann, Correos Nacional, Apdo 923, La Ceiba, T4410384 ext 14, runs rafting and kayaking trips and jungle hikes, and own hotel 8 hours upstream on the River Cangrejal (see page 888). Other tour companies offering whitewater rafting on the Río Cangrejal (class II, III and IV rapids) include *Tropical River Rafting and Tropical Jungle Tours*, Av Paz Barahona entre 1 y 2 C, Zona Viva Roterdam, T4433757, jungle@laceiba.com, 4 hours down the rapids with expert guide, US$50. *La Mosquitia Eco Aventuras*, Av 14 de Julio at Parque Manuel Bonilla, T/F4420104, mosquitia@tropicohn.com, Jorge Satavero, very knowledgeable, enthusiastic and flexible. Recommended. *La Ceiba Ecotours*, Av San Isidro, 1st block, 50 metres from beach, T/F4434207, hiking and riding in Pico Bonito national park, visits to other nearby reserves, whitewater rafting, trips to La Mosquitia. Several other agencies. With plenty of choice, make enquiries to find a tour that suits your needs and to verify credentials.

National Parks

Pico Bonito   The **Pico Bonito** national park (674 square kilometres) is the largest of the 11 parks designated in 1987. It has deep tropical hardwood forests which shelter, among other things, jaguars and three species of monkey, deep canyons and tumbling streams and waterfalls (including Las Gemelas which fall vertically some 200 metres). Development of the park by Curla (Centro Universitario Regional del Litoral Atlántico) continues under the supervision of Cohdefor, the forestry office. Curla has a *campamento* with accommodation under construction for visiting scientists, but you can camp. The camp is five kilometres (one and a half hours' walk) on a good path from **Armenia Bonito** to the west of La Ceiba, frequent buses from Parque Manuel Bonilla by the Ruta 1 de Mayo urban bus, one hour. Visitors can take the path to the Río Bonito with some spectacular river scenery. Swimming possible in deep rock pools. A route is being created around the foothills and there are a few interesting trails in the forest. Guide recommended: Oscar Zelaya, a forest inspector appointed by Curla, who can be contacted in Armenia Bonito. Pico Bonito itself (2,435 metres) has been climbed infrequently, it takes at least nine days. The preferred route is along the Río Bonito, starting from near the *campamento*, and from there up a ridge which climbs all the way to the summit. Expertise in rock climbing is not necessary, but several steep pitches do require a rope for safety; good physical condition is a necessity. Poisonous snakes, including the fer-de-lance (*barba amarilla*) will probably be encountered *en route*.

For further information on the Park contact Cohdefor at their local office six kilometres out of town along the Carretera La Ceiba-Tela, T4431033, where the project director is Sr Allan Herrera. Maps are being prepared by Curla but not yet available. Take care if you enter the forest: tracks are not yet developed, a compass is advisable. Tour companies in La Ceiba arrange trips to the Park. A day trip, horse riding through the Park can be arranged through Harry's at *Bar El Canadiense*, 14 de Julio, near Parque Manuel Bonilla. Trip includes food and guide, US$25. Recommended.

Cuero y Salado   37 kilometres west of La Ceiba between the Cuero and Salado rivers, near the coast, is the **Cuero y Salado Wildlife Reserve**, which has a great variety of flora and fauna, with a large population of local and migratory birds. It extends for 13,225 hectares of swamp and forest. The reserve is managed by the Fundación Cuero y Salado (Fucsa) – Refugio de Vida Silvestre, one block north and three blocks west of Parque Central (see map) to the left of the Standard Fruit Company, La Ceiba, T/F504-4430329, Apartado Postal 674, which was formed in 1987. The Foundation is open to volunteers, preferably who speak English and Spanish. Part of the programme is to teach environmental education at two rural schools. Travel agencies in La Ceiba run tours there, but Fucsa arranges visits and owns the only accommodation in the reserve. Before going to the Reserve, check with Fucsa in La Ceiba. Although the office only has basic information, they are helpful and there are displays and books about the flora and fauna to be found in the park. A charge of about US$10 is made to enter the reserve, which you can pay at Fucsa, keep the receipt, plus US$5 per person for accommodation. A guide and kayak for a one-hour trip costs about US$10. Boat-men charge about US$20 for a two-hour trip or US$40 for five hours (6-7 persons maximum) US$6 to US$7 for the guide. To get there independently, take a bus to **La Unión** (every hour, 0600 until 1500 from La Ceiba terminus, US$0.30, one and a half hours, ask to get off at the railway line, *ferrocarril*, or Km 17), an interesting jour-ney through pineapple fields. There are several ways of getting into the park from La Unión. Walking takes one and a half hours (avoid midday sun), take water. Groups usually take a *motocarro*, a dilapidated train which also transportes the coconut crop – there is no fixed timetable – but if you're lucky enough to catch it, it costs US$12, payable at the Park office, 15 minutes' journey. From near Doña Tina's house (meals available), take a *burra*, a flat-bed railcar propelled by two men with poles (a great way to see the countryside) to the community on the banks of the Río Salado (nine kilometres, one hour, US$8 each way). Here is Fucsa's administration centre, with photos, charts, maps, radio and a two-room visitors house, sleeping four in basic bunks, electricity from 1800-2100. No mosquito nets (so avoid September and October if you can). Don't wear open footwear as snakes and yellow scorpions can be found here. The refuge is becoming increasingly popular, so book lodging in advance. There is space for tents. Meals cost extra and are served by Doña Estela Cáceres (refried beans, egg, tortillas, etc) in her main family room, with pigs, chick-ens and children wandering in and out. Give her prior notice. It is worth bringing your own provisions too, especially drinking water.

Nilmo, a knowledgeable biologist who acts as a guide, takes morning and evening boat trips for those staying overnight, either through the canal dug by Standard Fruit, parallel to the beach, between the palms and the mangroves, or down to the Salado lagoon. Five kayaks are available for visitors' use. The early morning is the best time for views of the Pico Bonito national park, for birdlife and for howler monkeys. Also in the reserve are spider and capuchin monkeys, iguanas, jaguar, tapirs, crocodiles, manatee, hummingbirds, toucans, ospreys, eagles, and vultures. A five-hour trip will take you to Barra de Colorado where the manatees are. Ask to see the garden where local people are taught to grow food without burning the forest. The beach along the edge of the reserve is 28 kilometres long, with a strip of the sea also protected by Fucsa. Fishing is possible, and camping at Salado Barra but you need a permit for both. There are extensive coconut groves along the coast owned by Standard Fruit Co. Although it is possible to go to the Salado and hire a villager and his boat, a qualified guide will show you much more. It is essential to bring a hat and sun lotion with you.

To return to La Unión, it is another *burra* ride or a two-hour walk along the railway, little shade; then, either wait for a La Ceiba bus, last one at 1500, or ask for the short cut through grapefruit groves, 20 minutes, which leads to the main La Ceiba-Tela road on which there are many more buses back to town, 20 minutes, US$0.40.

La Ceiba to Trujillo

A paved road runs from La Ceiba to Trujillo (see below) and Puerto Castilla. At Savá, the bridge over the Río Aguán was washed away by Mitch, but traffic is passing through here without difficulties (August 1999). Like the Ulúa, the Aguán valley was flooded extensively by Mitch. The La Ceiba-Trujillo road meets the road heading southwest to Olanchito and Yoro, newly paved to Olanchito and a good gravel surface thereafter, which involves a river cross-ing (for continuation to El Progreso, see page 898). It is possible to go La Ceiba-Jaruca-San José-Olanchito, but Yaruca-San José is no more than a mule track.

Tocoa
Colour map 4, grid B5

Between Savá and Trujillo is the rapidly-growing town of Tocoa, also in the Aguán valley. The Catholic church is the modern design of a Peace Corps Volunteer. It is not known which services are open after Mitch.

Sleeping *La Esperanza*, T4443371. *Victoria*, T4443031. *Jamil*, T4443562, all in Barrio El Centro. *La Confianza*, T4443304, Barrio Abajo. **E** *San Patricio*, Barrio El Centro, T4443401, with bath, a/c, cheaper without, TV. **F** *Hotelito Rosgil*, near bus station, with bath but water problems.

Eating *Rigo*, Barrio El Centro, good Italian food and pizzas. *Gran Vía*, on east side of park. Good *comedor* opposite the bus station.

Entertainment Cinema Cine Maya.

Transport Bus Several buses daily to La Ceiba US$2.50, and to Trujillo, US$1.

Directory Banks *Banadesa, Banffaa, Bancahsa, Banco Atlántida, Banco Sogerín*.

Trujillo

Population: 45,000
Colour map 4, grid B5

Ninety kilometres from Savá, was a port and former capital. The population includes a rapidly expanding North American community. This quiet town with a pleasant atmosphere was founded in 1525 (the oldest in Honduras) by Juan de Medina; Hernán Cortés arrived there after his famous march overland from Yucatán in pursuit of his usurping lieutenant, Olid. It was near here that William

Trujillo & the coast

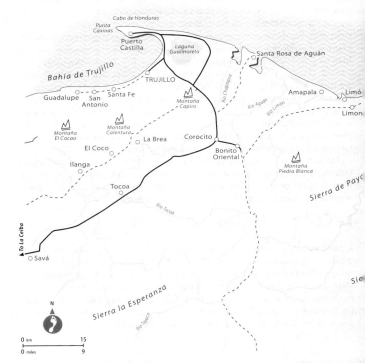

Walker (see under **Nicaragua**) was shot in 1860 (a commemorative stone marks the spot in the rear garden of the hospital, one block east of the Parque Central); the old cemetery where he is buried (near *Hotel Trujillo*) is interesting, giving an idea of where early residents came from. It is rather overgrown, with collapsed and open tombs. **Fortaleza Santa Bárbara**, a ruined Spanish fortress overlooking the Bay, is worth a visit, entrance US$1. Most of the relics found there have been moved to the museum of Rufino Galán (see below) but there are a few rusty muskets and cannon balls. The beach is clean and the water is calm and shallow, safe for children.

The **Parque Nacional Capiro y Calentura** can be reached by walking (or taking a taxi) up the hill past the *Villa Brinkley Hotel*. The road to the summit is in poor condition from the entrance of the park and can be driven only with four-wheel drive. It takes 4-6 hours to walk it and on a clear day you can see Roatán. There used to be a secret military tracking station at the top but this is now a Hondutel relay installation and there are no longer any restrictions on access. The walk is best done very early in the morning and there are lots of forest sounds of birds and monkeys. Insect repellent needed if you pause. As with all walking in this area, it is best to go in a group to avoid attacks. The park is run by the Fundación Capiro Calentura Guaimoreto (Fucagua), which has a temporary office first left after *Hotel Mar de Plata*, a couple of doors before the cinema, open Monday-Friday. They have information on all the reserves in the area and also on hiking and tours. Until a new office is built in the park, entry tickets must be bought here before going to Capiro y Calentura. They are opening up new trails, improving old ones and organizing guided tours through parts of the forest. The hike along the Sendero de la Culebrina uses the remnants of a colonial stone road used to transport gold from the mines in the Valle de Aguán. It

Excursions

Honduras

runs along the Río Mojagua and leads to **Cuyamel**, 37 kilometres from Trujillo, just off the road to Sonaguera. Half way up the Cerro de las Cuevas, seven kilometres beyond Cuyamel, are impressive caves showing vestiges of occupation by preColumbian Pech Indians.

Fucagua also administers the **Refugio de Vida Silvestre, Laguna de Guaimoreto (RVSLG)**, northeast of Trujillo, where there is a bird island (Isla de los Pájaros), monkeys and good fishing. To visit, either arrange a trip with Fucagua, a tour agency such as Turtle Tours, or take a bus from Trujillo towards Puerto Castilla, alight just after the bridge which crosses the lagoon, then walk away from the lagoon for about 200 metres to a dirt track on the left. Follow this and cross a low bridge and on the left is the house of a man who rents dugout canoes. The Isla de los Pájaros is about three kilometres up the lagoon, a bit too far for a dugout. Another alternative is to go down to the wharf in Trujillo and ask for Reinardo, who runs the local fishermen's co-op. He hires out motorized canoes and launches (price depends on the number of passengers and length of trip). There are no roads, paths or facilities in the area.

Twenty minutes' walk from Trujillo plaza (follow on road beyond *Hotel Trujillo*) is the **Museo y Piscina Rufino Galán Cáceres** which has a swimming pool filled from the Río Cristales with changing rooms and picnic facilities. Close by, the wreckage of a US C-80 aircraft which crashed in 1985 forms part of Sr Galán's museum; inside the museum is more information and memorabilia about the accident. The rest of the collection is a mass of curios, but with some very interesting objects. ■ *US$1, US$0.50 for swim.*

West of Trujillo, just past the football field on the Santa Fe road is the Río Grande, which has lovely pools and waterfalls for river bathing, best during rainy season. Take the path on far side of river, after about 10 minutes cut down to the rocks and follow the river upstream along the boulders.

Two kilometres along the road is **C** *Campamento*, T4344244, round thatched bar, good food, and 10 rooms, lovely setting, mountain backdrop, on unspoilt beach, showers, palm trees, shade, basic but clean, ask about camping, two unfortunate chained monkeys. There are interesting villages of Black Caribs (Garífuna) west of Trujillo. The road is rough, often impassable in wet weather, jeeps needed even in dry season. **Santa Fe**, 10 kilometres west of Trujillo (US$0.30 by bus, leaves when full, get there by 0800 for seat), is a friendly place with several good Garífuna restaurants for example *Comedor Caballero* (also known as *Pete's Place*, good for lunch, huge portions, lobster, vegetarian food, highly recommended) and *Las Brisas de Santa Fe*, on the endless white sandy beach. The bus service continues to San Antonio (good restaurant behind the beach) and Guadalupe. Walk in the morning along the beach to Santa Fe and then get a bus back to Trujillo, taking plenty of water and sun block. This stretch of beach is outstanding, but watch out for *marea roja*, a sea organism which colours the water pink and can give irritating skin rashes to bathers. Also, be warned, there have been attacks on the beach and local people consider this walk unsafe. Best to go in a large group.

Beaches
Before setting out ask which beaches are safe.

Good beaches are on the peninsula and around the Trujillo Bay. Take a bus from near the Parque Central towards Puerto Castilla and ask the driver to let you off at the path about one kilometre beyond the bridge over the lagoon. The other beaches around Puerto Castilla are separated by mangroves, are littered and have sandflies. Other sandy beaches can be reached by taking any bus from the Parque Central one and a half kilometres, to the side road leading to the landing strip and *Bahía Bar-Restaurant*; the white sand stretches for many kilometres northwards. The beaches in town tend to be dirty, but do not be tempted to walk westwards towards Santa Fe to find a cleaner stretch of sand. It is not safe and tourists have been assaulted and robbed. Women should not walk on the beach alone, day or night.

Sleeping
■ *on maps*
Price codes: see inside front cover

A *Christopher Columbus Beach Resort*, T4344966, F4344971, 51 rooms and suites (**L-AL**), a/c, cable TV, swimming pool, restaurant, watersports, tennis, painted bright turquoise, outside town along the beach, drive across airstrip; the other side of the airstrip at road turnoff is **B** *Trujillo Bay*, T/F4344732, 25 a/c rooms with cable TV, includes continental breakfast, tasty cooking at their in-house restaurant *Schooners*, laundry. **C** *Villa Brinkley* (known locally as Miss Peggy's), T4344444, F4344000, on the mountain overlooking the bay, swimming pool, good view, large rooms, wooden furniture in Maya style, big bathrooms, sunken baths, fan, cheaper rooms in annex, full of character and friendly, motorbike rental, restaurant good though for evening meal only (in USA T412-7912273, Rd 3, Parker, PA16049). **C** *Colonial*, T4344001, F4344878, with bath, on plaza, *hacienda* style, restaurant (*El Bucanero*, see below), a/c, safe and clean, recently refurbished. **C** *O'Glynn*, T4344592, smart, clean, good rooms and bathrooms, a/c, TV, fridge in some rooms.

E *Albert's Place*, T4344431, 2 blocks south of Parque Central, red brick house, beautifully restored, nice garden, good value, English spoken. **F** *Coco Pando*, Barrio Cristales, T4344748, behind beach, Garífuna-owned, clean, bright airy rooms, restaurant serving typical Garífuna dishes, runs popular weekend disco nearby. **E-F** *Catracho*, 3 blocks south of church, then a block east, T4344438, basic, clean, noisy, no water at night, wooden cabins facing a garden, camping space US$1.50, parking. **D** *Emperador*, T4344446, with bath and fan, small, dark rooms, rather depressing. **E** *Mar de Plata*, up street west, T4344458, upstairs rooms best, with bath, fan, friendly and helpful, beautiful view from roof. **D** *Trujillo*, T4344202, up the hill from the market, fan, clean sheets daily, rooms with shower and toilet, TV, good value. Recommended, but ask for a corner room, cockroaches in ground floor rooms, nice breeze. **F** *Buenos Aires* opposite *Catracho*, T4344431, monthly rates available, pleasant, clean, peaceful, but cabins damp and many mosquitos, organizes tours to national park.

In the village of Silin, on main road southeast of Trujillo, is **B** *Resort y Spa Agua Caliente Silin*, T4344249, F4344248, cabañas with cable TV, pool, thermal waters, restaurant, massage given by Pech Indian, Lastenia Hernández, very relaxing.

Eating

Don't miss the coconut bread, speciality of the Garífuna.

El Bucanero, on main plaza, a/c, video, good *desayuno típico* for US$2. *Galaxia*, 1 block west of plaza, good seafood at reasonable prices, popular with locals. *Oasis*, opposite Bancahsa, outdoor seating, Canadian owned, good meeting place, information board, good food, bar, English books for sale, book exchange, local tours. *Granada*, in the centre, good Garífuna dishes, seafood and standard meals, great *sopa de camarones*. Recommended. Breakfasts and snacks, also bar, friendly service, good value. *Nice and Ease*, sells ice cream and cakes. Nearby is *Pantry*, Garífuna cooking and standard menu, cheap pizzas, a/c. *Don Perignon*, uphill from *Pantry*, some Spanish dishes, good local food, cheap.

On the beach there used to be a row of thatched bars, *champas*, with hammocks, toilets, showers and shade. Most of them closed after Hurricane Mitch. *Bahía Bar-Restaurant*, T4344770, on the beach by the landing strip next to *Christopher Columbus*, popular with ex-pats, also Hondurans at weekends, good vegetarian food, showers, toilets.

Entertainment

Nightlife Barrio Cristales, weekends only, Punta music, lively atmosphere. Recommended. Hand made tambore drums and turtle shells, conch horn, dancing is a challenge. The **cinema** shows US current releases.

Festivals

San Juan Bautista in June, with participation from surrounding Garífuna (Black Carib) settlements.

Shopping

Garí-Arte Souvenir, T4344207, in the centre of Barrio Cristales, is highly recommended for authentic Garífuna souvenirs. Owned by Ricardo Lacayo and open 7 days a week. *Tienda Souvenir Artesanía* next to *Hotel Emperador*, handicrafts, hand-painted toys. Three supermarkets in the centre.

Transport

Air Trujillo has an airstrip east of town near the beach hotels. Isleña flies daily to La Ceiba to connect with onward Isleña flights to San Pedro Sula and Tegucigalpa. Booking office at *Christopher Columbus Resort*, T4344966.

Buses The town can be reached by bus from San Pedro Sula, Tela and La Ceiba by a paved road through Savá, Tocoa and Corocito. From La Ceiba it is 3 hours by direct bus, 4 hours by *local*. 3 direct Cotraibal buses in early morning from Trujillo, buses every 1½ hours, 6 hours, US$5. Bus from **Tegucigalpa** (Comayagüela) with Cotraibal, 7 Av between 10 and 11 C, US$6, 9 hours; some buses to the capital go via La Unión, which is not as safe a route as via San Pedro Sula. To **San Pedro Sula**, 5 daily 0200-0800, US$5. Public transport also to San Esteban and Juticalpa (from in front of church at 0400, but check locally, arriving 1130, US$5.20 – see page 946). Bus to **Santa Fe** at 0930, US$0.40, leaves from outside *Glenny's Super Tienda*; to **Santa Rosa de Aguán** and **Limón** daily.

Sea Cargo boats leave for ports in Mosquitia (ask all captains at the dock, wait up to 3 days, see page 950), the Bay Islands (very difficult) and Honduran ports to the west. Enquire at the jetty.

Directory

Banks *Banco Atlántida* on Parque Central and *Bancahsa*, both cash US$, TCs and handles Visa. *Banco de Occidente* also handles Mastercard and Western Union. **Communications** Post Office and Hondutel: (F4344200) 1 block up from church. **Hospitals & medical services** Hospital on main road east off square towards La Ceiba. **Language schools** Two schools: Centro Internacional de Idiomas, Belinda Linton, Apdo Postal 71, Trujillo, T/F4344777 (Spanish and Garífuna courses, culture, music and dance, branch in La Ceiba), and Ixbalanque, T4344461, F6514432 (branch in Copán, see below), US$125 per week for 4 hrs per day instruction, staying with locals is possible. **Libraries** Library in middle of square. **Laundry** Next to *Disco Orfaz*, wash and dry US$2.50. **Tour companies & travel agents** *Turtle Tours* at *Hotel Villa Brinkley* (address above – agency at *Oasis Café*), run trips to Río Plátano, 6 days, 5 nights US$400, also to beaches, jungle hikes, etc. Guided tours by motorbike, 7-17 days with back-up vehicle. Bike rental US$35 per day. Very helpful even if you want to travel independently to Mosquitia, German, English, Spanish spoken, T/F4344431. Several other enterprises organize tours to Capiro y Calentura, Guaimoreto and the *Hacienda Tumbador Crocodile Reserve*, privately owned, accessible only by 4WD and with guide, US$5 entry, eg *Oasis*, *Gringo's Bar*. *Gringo's* also advertises trips to Tumbador followed by visit to beach near Puerto Castilla and lunch. **Useful addresses** Immigration: *Migración* has an office opposite *Mar de Plata*.

Puerto Castilla There is a meat-packing station and active shrimping centre. Puerto Castilla is one of the two containerized ports of the Honduran Caribbean coast, mainly exports including bananas, grapefruit and palm oil. There is a naval base and helicopter station. Near the village, a large crucifix marks the spot where Columbus reputedly conducted the first mass on American soil in 1502. (Restaurant *Brisas de Caribe*, good.)

Santa Rosa de Aguán is an interesting coastal town of 7,000 hospitable English and Spanish-speaking inhabitants some 40 kilometres from Trujillo, one of the largest Garífuna communities. The spreading settlement lies at the mouth of the Río Aguán, the greater part on the east of the bay. It suffered great loss of life and property in Hurricane Mitch. Check on conditions before going there. Bus from Trujillo from Parque Central Monday-Saturday. Also bus service from La Ceiba. If driving from Trujillo, turn left at Km 343, 20 kilometres along the highway, where a good gravel road runs another 20 kilometres to Santa Rosa. From where the road ends at the west bank, take a canoe ferry across to the east side. White sand beach stretches all the way to Limón (see page 952), the thundering surf is an impressive sight. Take drinking water, insect repellent, mosquito coils and high factor sun screen.

El Progreso to Olanchito

El Progreso This important but unattractive agricultural and commercial centre (no longer just a
Population: 106,550 banana town) on the Río Ulúa, is 30 minutes' drive on the paved highway southeast
Colour map 4, grid B4 of San Pedro Sula en route to Tela. Following Huricane Mitch, check which services are open.

Sleeping D *Gran Hotel Las Vegas*, 2 Av, 11 C N, T6664667, smart, a/c, good restaurant called *La Copa Dorada*. **D** *Municipal*, 1 Av, 7-8 C N, T6664061, with a/c and bath, clean. **E** *Plaza Victoria*, 2 Av, 5-6 C S, T6662150, opposite Migración, with bath, cheap laundry, pool, good. **F** *Emperador*, 2 Av, 4-5 C S, 8 blocks west of bus terminal, attractive, with bath, cheaper without. **E** *Honduras*, 2 Av 3 C, T6664264, in front of Banco Atlántida, with bath, run down, meals US$1.25. **F** *La Casa Blanca*, 4 C, 2 Av N, traditional white and yellow clapboard house with covered balcony, quiet but beware of giant cockroaches.

Eating *Comida Buffet América*, 2 Av N, ½ block east of market, open 0700 to 1500, good vegetarian food. *Elite*, 1 Av, 4-5 C N, mixed reports. *Mr Kike* (pronounced Keekeh) on the ground floor of the *Hotel Municipal* building, a/c, good. *Red Dragon Pub*, 4 C, 1-2 Av N, owned by an Englishman, Steve, good source of local information, good bar and restaurant. *Los Tarros*, on San Pedro Sula road just before bridge, good but not cheap. *La Parrilla*, next to gasolinera on road to Santa Rita, good steaks and international food, a/c.

Festivals Fiesta: *La Virgen de Las Mercedes*, third week of **September**. Visit the Santa Isabel handicraft centre, where women are taught wood carving.

Shopping Good artesanía, *Imapro*, T2664700, on the road to Tela.

Transport *Transportes Ulúa*, (18 C y 6 Av, Barrio Villa Adela, Comayagüela, T2381827) 4 daily, a/c; in El Progreso, 5 Av y Blvd, T6663270.

Directory Banks About a dozen different banks in town. **Tour companies & travel agents** *Agencia de Viajes El Progreso*, 2 Av 3-4 C N, T6664101.

Five kilometres south of El Progreso is the Santuario Señor de Esquipulas in the village of Arena Blanca where there is a festival on 13 January in honour of the Black Christ of Esquipulas. The temple has baroque and modern architecture, with trees and gardens.

The highway is paved 25 kilometres south of El Progreso to Santa Rita; if you continue towards the San Pedro Sula-Tegucigalpa highway, you avoid San Pedro Sula when travelling from the north coast to the capital. 10 kilometres south of El Progreso on the paved highway to Santa Rita, at the village of Las Minas, is El Chorro (one kilometre off the highway), a charming waterfall and natural swimming pool. A rugged hike can be made into the mountains and on to El Negrito from here.

Parque Nacional Pico Pijol The park is 32 kilometres from **Morazán**, Yoro, a town 41 kilometres from Progreso (bus from Progreso or Santa Rita). In Morazán are *Hospedaje El Corazón Sagrado*, several restaurants and a disco. The lower slopes of Pico Pijol have been heavily farmed, but the top is primary cloud forest, home to many quetzales. Access by vehicle is possible as far as Subirana. A guide is needed from there to Tegucigalpita (large cave nearby) and access is difficult, with no infrastructure. Another trail to the summit (2,282 metres) starts at **Nueva Esperanza** village (bus from Morazán, Parque Central); ask for the correct trail. The first day is tough, the second tougher: the first is all uphill with no shade, the second requires a lot of clearing with a machete. At the summit is a tree with a guest register. Take a compass and a topographical map. Also in the park is the waterfall at **Las Piratas**; take a bus from Morazán to Los Murillos and then walk to El Ocotillo. Ask for Las Piratas. Further up the river are some beautiful, deep pools.

The highway is also paved from Santa Rita to Yoro, a prosperous little town of ranchers and farmers, in pleasant surroundings with mountains to the north, east and south. The **Parque Nacional Montaña de Yoro** is eight kilometres to the southeast (access from Marale), comprising 257 square kilometres of cloud forest, home to the Tolupanes indigenous people, also known as Xicaques. The Asociación Ecológica Amigos de la Montaña de Yoro has an office in the Parque Central in Yoro.

Yoro
Colour map 4, grid B4

Sleeping E *Nelson*, comfortable rooms with bath, fan, modern, good restaurant/bar and nice outdoor swimming pool on 3rd floor, bar/disco on roof with marvellous views. Warmly recommended. **E-F** *Palacio*, on main street, restaurant, nice, all rooms with bath and fan. **F** *Anibal*, corner of Parque Central, restaurant, excellent value, private or shared bath, clean, pleasant, wide balcony.

Eating Best restaurants in hotels, several *comedores* along main street.

Transport Hourly bus service to El Progreso, several daily to Sulaco.

Directory Banks *Banco Atlántida* on Parque Central. **Communications** Post Office and Hondutel 1 block from Parque Central.

From Yoro a dirt road continues to Olanchito via **Jocón**, through attractive country (**F** *Hospedaje*, clean, basic and other accommodation, ask around) as the road snakes along the pine-forested slopes of Montaña Piedra Blanca and Montaña de la Bellota, with fine views of the surrounding valleys and distant mountain ranges. Buses from Yoro to Olanchito go as far as Río Aguán, US$1.50, which is a bit too deep to ford. Cross the river in an ox cart or giant inner tube with waterproof floor pushed across by wading drivers, US$0.35, then get on another, waiting bus to Olanchito, US$1. The road then runs parallel to the river through lush cattle and farming country.

Olanchito
Population: 12,200
Colour map 4, grid B5

A prosperous but hot town (called La Ciudad Cívica) in the Agúan valley in the hills to the southeast of La Ceiba. The town was founded, according to tradition, by a few stragglers who escaped from the destruction of Olancho el Viejo, between Juticalpa and Catacamas, then a wealthy town. They brought with them the crown made of hides which the image of the Virgin still wears in the church of Olanchito. There is a natural bathing spot, Balneario El Higueral.

Sleeping **D** *Hotel Olanchito*, Barrio Arriba, C La Palma, T4466385, a/c, under same management is **E** *Valle Aguán y Chabelito*, 1 block north of Parque Central, T446-6718/6546, single rooms, with a/c, double rooms with fan, all rooms with cable TV, best in town, with best restaurant. **F** *Colonial*, C del Presidio, good value, bath, fan, cheaper with shared bath, restaurant, parking. Opposite is **E** *Olimpic*, bath, a/c, TV.

Eating *La Ronda*, best in town, Chinese and international, main dishes US$4. Recommended. *Comedor Doña Luisa* in front of Radio Station and 3 blocks south of Park. *Bar/restaurant Uchapa*, *Helados Castillo*.

Entertainment Cinema *Cine Gardel*.

Festivals Second week of **September**, *Semana Cívica*.

Transport Buses from **La Ceiba**, 2½ hours, US$1 via Jutiapa and Savá (Cotol 7 times a day; Cotrail); to **Trujillo**, 3 hours, US$3.75 via Savá and Tocoa (Cotol); to Yoro 0430 daily, 5 hours.

Directory Banks *Bancahsa* changes TCs. *Bancahorro*. *Sogerín*. *Atlántida*. *Importadora Rosita* has better exchange rates.

Santa Rita to Olanchito

The Bay Islands

Tegucigalpa

Warm Caribbean waters with excellent diving, white sand beaches, tropical sunsets are some of the attractions. The culture is very un-Latin American: English is widely spoken and there are still Black Carib descendants of those deported from St Vincent in 1797.

Hog Islands

The Hog Islands (Cayos Cochinos), with lovely primeval hardwood forests, are 17 kilometres northeast of La Ceiba (two small islands and 13 palm-fringed cays). **Cochino Grande** is the larger island, rising to 143 metres, **Cochino Pequeño** the smaller. Both have lush tropical vegetation and fewer biting insects than the Bay Islands. There are Garífuna fishing villages of palm-thatched huts at Chachauate on Lower Monitor Cay, and East End Village on Cochino Grande. Transport to the Hog Islands can be sought on the supply *cayuco* from Nuevo Armenia (see page 888), or by chartering a boat from Utila. There is a small, dirt airstrip. Dugout canoes are the local form of transport. The islands are privately owned and access to most of the cays is limited, being occupied only by caretakers. The Cayos Cochinos and surrounding waters are now a National Marine Reserve and rangers are being trained. Spear fishing, nets and traps are not allowed, although line fishing is permitted.

Plantation Beach Resort on Grande, rustic cabins, on hillside, hot water, fans, diving offshore, yacht moorings, good steep walk up to lighthouse for view over cays to mainland, music festival end-July, local bands and dancers, they charge US$30 for the trip from La Ceiba, T/F4420974, in USA T800-6283723, VHF 12, pbr@hondurashn.com, www.clearlight.com/vmoe/ dive/planta.htm, Apdo Postal 114, La Ceiba. At Chachauate, stay with fishing family or rent thatched hut (US$6) and a garifuna woman will cook for you. Small restaurant but bring own drinking water. A few small *tiendas* sell beer and sodas. Short wade to *Pelican Bar*, run by Al, opens on demand. This island is free of mosquitoes and sandflies. Bring snorkel equipment, kayaks can be hired. **Cayo Timón** (also known as North Sand Cay) can be visited from Utila, 1¼ hours by boat; you can rent the cay, **E** pp, minimum 6, 8 is comfortable, A-frame, Polynesian style, do overnight diving trips or combine with Eurohonduras river trips (see La Ceiba, **Travel agents**), very basic, quiet, peaceful, contact Henrik and Susan Jensen at the *Green House*, Utila, or phone Roy and Brenda at *Thompson's Bakery*, Utila, T4253112, for information.

Sleeping

Cayos Cochinos/ Hog Islands

Cochino Grande

Cochino Pequeño

North West Cay

North East Cay

Lower Monitor

Timón

Coral Reefs

Pelon

Sandy Cays

N

0 km   2
0 miles 1.2

Bay Islands

The **Bay Islands** (Islas de la Bahía) lie in an arc which curves northeast away from a point 32 kilometres north of La Ceiba. The three main islands are **Utila**, **Roatán**, and **Guanaja**. At the eastern end of Roatán are three small ones: **Morat, Santa Elena**, and **Barbareta**; there are other islets and 52 cays. The traditional industry is fishing, mostly shellfish, with fleets based at French Harbour. Boat-building is a dying industry. Tourism is now a major source of income, particularly because of scuba diving attractions. There are English-speaking blacks who constitute the majority of

Population: 60,000

Honduras

the population, particularly on Roatán. Utila has a population which is about half black and half white, the latter of British stock descended mainly from settlers from Grand Cayman who arrived in 1830. Latin Hondurans have been moving to the islands from the mainland in recent years. Columbus anchored here in 1502, on his fourth voyage. In the 18th century the islands were bases for English, French and Dutch buccaneers. They were in British hands for over a century but were finally ceded to Honduras in 1859. The government schools teach in Spanish, and the population is bi-lingual. The islands are very beautiful, but beware of the strong sun (the locals bathe in T-shirts) and sand flies and other insects.

The underwater environment is rich and extensive; reefs surround the islands, often within swimming distance of the shore. Caves and caverns are a common feature, with a wide variety of sponges and the best collection of pillar coral in the Caribbean. Several parts have been proposed as marine reserves by the Asociación Hondureña de Ecología: the Santuario Marino de Utila, Parque Nacional Marino Barbareta and Parque Nacional Marino Guanaja. Turtle Harbour, Utila, and Sandy Bay/West End, Roatán are now Marine Parks and the latter has permanent mooring buoys at the popular dive sites. The Bay Islands have their own conservation association (see under **Roatán**, below). We strongly recommend snorkellers and divers not to touch or stand on the coral reefs; any contact, even the turbulence from a fin, will kill the delicate organisms.

Utila

41 sq km
Population: 2,400
Colour map 4, grid B4

The island only 32 kilometres from La Ceiba, is low lying, with only two hills, Pumpkin, and the smaller Stewarts with an aerial. The latter is nearer the town, which is known locally as **East Harbour**. The first inhabitants were Paya Indians and there is some archaeological evidence of their culture. Later the island was used by pirates; Henry Morgan is reputed to have hidden booty in the caves. The population now is descended from Black Caribs and white Cayman Islanders with a recent influx from mainland Honduras. Independence Day (15 September) festivities, including boxing and climbing greased poles, reported worth staying for.

Excursions You can hike to **Pumpkin Hill** (about four kilometres down the lane by Bancahsa, bikes recommended) where there are some freshwater caves and a beach nearby (watch out for sharp coral). It can be very muddy after rain. It is also possible to walk on a trail from the airfield to **Big Bight** and the iron shore on the east coast, about two kilometres, exploring tidal pools; nice views and beach but it is rocky so wear sandals. An interesting way of visiting the north coast is to hire a canoe (or kayak

Utila

from Gunter's) and paddle from the lagoon past the *Blue Bayou* through the mangroves and the canal (about 2-3 hours); look out for a rare sighting of a crocodile, a huge one was killed in 1995; take snorkelling gear and explore the reef offshore if the sea is not too rough. Canoe hire US$10 per day. Trails to the north coast are only passable in the dry months (April-September), through the swamp and past the dead forest, best to hire a local child to show you the way.

Utila is the cheapest and least developed of the islands to visit; there are no big resorts, although a couple of small, lodge-style, upmarket places have opened, otherwise there is rather simpler accommodation. Sunbathing and swimming are not particularly good, but there is a swimming hole near the airport. At the left-hand end of the airstrip (from the town) is one of the best places for coral and quantity of fish. Jack Neal Beach has white sand with good snorkelling and swimming; development is now starting. Snorkelling is also good off the shore by the *Blue Bayou* restaurant, a 20-minute walk from town, but you will be charged US$1 for use of the facilities. There are hammocks and a jetty, which is the only place to get away from the terrible sandflies. Look out for the American, Dick (with a beard and a parrot on his shoulder), who takes four-hour snorkelling trips for US$10. *Laguna Beach Resort* is on the other side of the lagoon.

A 20-minutes motorboat ride from East Harbour are the Cays, a chain of small islands populated by fisherfolk off the southwest coast of Utila known as the Cayitos de Utila. **Jewel Cay** and **Pigeon Cay** are connected by a bridge and are inhabited by a fishing community which reportedly settled there to get away from the sandflies on Utila. There is a basic hotel, *Vicky's*, a few restaurants, a Saturday night disco, a dive shop run by Jan, and little else. The Cays are occasionally used by Utila dive shops as a surface interval between dives. **Diamond Cay** is privately owned, there are a few rooms in cabins for rent (**E**), and tents, a bar, restaurant, fish barbecue and snorkel gear for hire. **Water Cay** is one of the few places where you can camp, sling a hammock or, in emergency, sleep in, or under, the house of the caretaker; take food and fresh water, or rent the caretaker's canoe and get supplies from Jewel Cay. The caretaker collects a US$1.25 per person fee for landing and the same for a hammock. There are no facilities, but Jan from the Cays can bring you breakfast if you order it the day before. It is a coconut island with 'white holes' (sandy areas with wonderful hot bathing in the afternoon). The best snorkelling is off the south shore, a short walk from the beach, shallow water all around. To hire a *dory* (big motorized canoe) costs US$5 per person; many boatmen go and will collect you in the evening, recommended. You may also be able to go out with a diving party and be picked up in the afternoon or persuade a boatman to take you to one of the remoter cays. *Gunter's Dive Shop* runs water taxis to the cays for US$10, also Roy at the *Green House Book Exchange*, US$6.50, plus hammock hire US$1.

The Cays

Utila Reef Resort, USA T1-800-2639876, Utila T/F4253254, on south coast, Lower Lagoon, by *Pretty Bush* dive site, accommodation for 10, US$865 per person 8-day package includes 3 meals, 3 boat dives a day, unlimited shore diving, 2 double beds in each room, a/c. **L-AL** *Laguna Beach Resort*, T/F4253239, in USA, Utila Tours Inc, T1-800-66-UTILA 318-8930013, F318-8935024, lodge with bungalows each with own jetty, 6-day package includes meals and diving US$750-800, non-diver US$600-650, fishing offered, can accommodate maximum 40, on point opposite *Blue Bayou*. **AL** *Utila Lodge*, T4253143, F4253209, usually booked through US agent T1-800-2828932, an all-wooden building with decks and balconies, harbour view, a/c, 8 rooms, clean and modern, meals only when they have guests, dive shop (*Bay Islands College of Diving*) on site. **C** *Sharky's Reef Cabins*, the Point, T4253212, a/c, cable TV, porch over lagoon, fans. Cheaper hotels are along Main St or just off it.

D *Hotel Utila*, T4253340, on water next to *Lodge*, cheaper rooms downstairs, very clean, 24-hour water and power, fan, nice view, secure. **D** *Palm Villa*, cabins for 4, cooking facilities, good value, run by Willis Bodden. **D** *Mango Inn*, T4253335, with bath, cheaper without, fan,

Sleeping
■ on maps
Price codes:
see inside front cover

Honduras

spotless, helpful, roof terrace, reduction for students with *Utila Dive Centre*, good restaurant and coffee bar. Recommended. **D-E** *Bay View*, T4253114, 100 metres from *Utila Lodge*, with or without bath, private pier, family run. **D-E** *Harbour View*, T4253159, F4253359, right on water, *Parrot's Dive* on site, cheaper rooms with shared bathrooms upstairs, rooms with private bath downstairs, hot water, own generator, cleaning done only on arrival, TV, fans, run by Roger and Maimee. **D-E** *Laguna del Mar*, opposite and owned by *Trudy's*, T4253103, terrace, very clean, fans, mosquito nets, diving offered with *Underwater Vision*. **E** *Celena*, main street, T4253228, with bath, clean, fan, Visa and Mastercard accepted. Recommended. **E** *Countryside*, T4253216, 10 minutes' walk out of town, shared bath, rooms and apartments, quiet, clean, friendly, fan, porch, ask in town for Woody and Annie. **E** *Cross Creek* (see also **Diving** below), clean basic rooms, bathrooms, for divers on courses, cheaper than for non-divers. **E** *Margaritaville*, at very end of the village, T4253366, very clean, big rooms with 2 double beds, private bathroom, friendly, but no water or electricity at night. **E** *Spencer*, Main St, T4253162. **F** *Tropical*, Mammie Lane, 15 double rooms, kitchen, fans, has own water supply and generator, safe. **E** *Trudy's*, T/F4253103, 5 minutes from airport, with and without bath, very clean, comfortable. Recommended. *Underwater Vision* dive shop on site. **E-F** *Coopers Inn*, T4253184, cheaper if you dive with *Captain Morgan's*, very clean and friendly, Danish cook. Recommended. **F** *Blue Bayou*, 25 minutes out of town, 1 hour walk from airfield, very basic, insanitary, bad sand flies, good place to hire a bike, snacks and drinks available, restaurant only in high season, hammocks on the beach US$1, free to guests, take torch for night-time. **F** *Sea Side*, pleasant, clean, near *Gunter's*, meals available. **F** *Monkey Tail Inn*, noisy, T4253155, wooden building, fan, bring mosquito net, you may share your room with bats, water all the time. Cheap and very basic rooms at **F** *Blueberry Hill* T4253141, and houses for rent, lots of signs along the road. **F** *Loma Vista*, beyond *Bucket of Blood Bar*, T4253243, clean, fan, shared bath, very friendly, washes clothes cheaply. **F** *Delaney's*, good value, good small restaurant. **F** *Lizzie*, clean, comfortable, fan, shared facilities, friendly, no power from 0000-0600.

Eating

Menus are often limited by the supply boat, on Tuesday restaurants have everything, by the weekend some drinks run out.

Bahía del Mar by airport, burgers, pizzas, etc, hammock and camping space on little pier. *Sharky's Reef*, near airport, open Wednesday-Sunday 1800-2100, good portions, well prepared, try steamed shark steak and their vodka sours. *Captain Roy's*, also by airport, good, especially for breakfast, good prices but slow. *Mermaid's Corner*, breakfast from 0700, huge pizza (US$6) and pasta, about US$2.50-3 main course, good value but nothing special, no alcohol. *Sea Side* (see above under **Sleeping**) offers good fish but very slow service; *Island Café*, daily specials, good, up on covered verandah, at both these restaurants you order inside and help yourself to drinks from fridge then wait for food to be brought out to you. *Garden Rose*, opposite *Utila Lodge*, good food, reasonable prices. *Joyas*, 150 metres from *Gunter's*, home cooking, pleasant, cheap. *Jade Seahorse*, open 0700-2300, opposite *Bucket of Blood*, excellent *licuados*, good food. *Manhattan* good, average prices. *Sidewalk Café*, good food and breakfasts, helpful, bicycles for hire. *Delaney's Island Kitchen*, open 1730-2200 for pizza, lasagne and veg dishes, Danish cook, good specials nightly. *Las Delicias*, open 1700-2400, shark steak and local food, limited menu, music, lively bar each night. *Myrtle's*, open 1000-2330, by far the quickest lunch in town, delicious *comida corriente* served by Terricina, opposite casino, locals' hangout. *Pandy's Place* for typical food and TV. *7 Seas*, open 0630-2200, breakfast, fish, burgers, slow service. *Tropical Sunset*, open 0800-2200, fish, burgers, lobster, ice cream. *Reef Bar & Grill*, open Tuesday-Saturday 0630-1100, 1700-2300 for breakfast on the balcony, sunset drinks, also Sunday barbecue 1200-1500. *Ormas*, simple but good food, excellent coconut bread, also serves beer. *Thompsons Bakery*, open 0600-1200, best place for breakfast, very informal, friendly, good cakes, lots of information. Good yogurt, cakes, bottled water at *Henderson's* store. *Green Ribbon* store has cakes and sandwiches to order. *Selly's*, very good food, closed to regular custom but Selly will cook if you get a group of 6 minimum, great kingfish, also rooms available. *Bundu Café*, in same building as *Green House Book Exchange*, excellent food, quiche, salads, sandwiches, juices and other drinks, run by friendly couple Steve and Fran. Recommended. "Quite a social centre".

Bars *Bucket of Blood*, owned by Mr Woods, a mine of information on the history of Utila and the Cays. *Reef Bar*, *Dory Bar*, *Las Delicias*, and *Casino* are lively (Saturday night), as is *Captain Roy's*, next to the airport; *Bahía del Mar*, bar with pier, swimming. *Sea Breaker*, thatched bar, on waterfront behind *Orma's*, open Tuesday, Friday, Saturday, 1730-2300, happy hour 1730-1900, jugs of cocktails, popular. *Club 07*, opens Thursday and Saturday, free rum 2200-2300, good dancing. *Barracuda*, at the end of town, good drinks.

Diving: there are several dive sites along the south coast, where permanent moorings have **Sports** been established to minimize damage to the coral reef. Although the reef is colourful and varied, there are not a lot of fish and lobster have almost disappeared. The dive sites are close to shore at about 20 metres depth but they are all boat dives. Diving off the north coast is more spectacular, with drop-offs, canyons and caves. Fish are more numerous, helped by the establishment of the *Turtle Harbour Marine Reserve and Wildlife Refuge*.

Utila is essentially a dive training centre. It is very popular; you can learn to dive here cheaper than anywhere else in the Caribbean, particularly if you include low living expenses. It is best to do a course of some sort, students come first for places on boats and fun divers have to fit in. However, Utila has a reputation for poor safety and there have been too many accidents requiring emergency treatment in the recompression chamber on Roatán. Choose an instructor who may be bossy but fun, with small classes and who cares about safety, follow the rules on alcohol/drug abuse and pay particular attention to the dive tables. There is a rapid turnover of instructors; many stay only a season to earn money to continue their travels and some have a lax attitude towards diving regulations. Check that equipment looks new and well-maintained. Boats vary, you may find it difficult to climb into a dory if there are waves. Not all boats have oxygen on board. Dive insurance at US$2 per day for fundivers, US$6 for students (advanced, or open water), US$20 for divemasters is compulsory and is available from the BICA office: it covers air ambulance to Roatán and the recompression chamber. Treat any cuts from the coral seriously, they do not heal easily possibly because the water is polluted in some areas.

Honduras

From time to time all the dive shops agree to fix prices. A PADI Open Water course costs US$130-US$150 (includes US$14 for certificate) with 6 dives, an Advanced course costs US$120-US$150 with 5 dives. Credit cards, if accepted, are 8 percent extra. Competition is fierce with over 15 dive shops looking for business, so you can pick and choose. Once qualified, fun dives are US$30 for 2 tanks, US$125 for 10 tanks. Most schools offer instruction in English or German; French and Spanish are usually available somewhere, while tuition handbooks are provided in numerous languages including Japanese. A variety of courses is available up to instructor level. If planning to do a diving course, it is helpful but not essential to take passport-sized photographs with you for the PADI certificate. *Cross Creek*, run by Ronald Janssen, T4253134, F4253234, scooper@hondutel.hn, www.ccreek.com, 2 boats, maximum 8 people per instructor, 2-3 instructors, new equipment, 8 kayaks for hire (US$10 per day), accommodation on site for students, 18 rooms. *Gunter's* dive school, T/F4253350, is based at *Sea Side Inn*, contact George or Roland, the instructor, Pascal Floss, is experienced, has been on the island a long time and is recommended as the best person for finding fish and other aquatic life on the reef. *Utila Watersports*, run by Troy Bodden; quality of instructors varies. Troy also hires out snorkel gear, photographic and video equipment and takes boat trips, T/F4253239. Chris Phillips from the *Utila Dive Centre*, T4253326, F4253327, very professional courses, well-maintained equipment, recommended, sometimes takes divers to north coast in fast dory, recommended but no shade, surface interval on cays. *Bay Islands College of Diving*, T4253143, on main street close to Hondutel tower, 5 star PADI facility, experienced and well qualified staff, good boats ranging from 50 foot for large parties to skiff for smaller ones, environmentally sound. *Paradise Divers*, on the seafront behind Hendersons supermarket, relaxed and friendly, www.todomundo.com/paradisedivers. *Captain Morgan's*. T/F4253161, has been recommended for small classes, good equipment, friendly staff.

Shopping **Arts and crafts**: Gunter Kordovsky is a painter and sculptor with a gallery at his house, good map of Utila, paintings, cards, wood carving.

Transport **Local** Bike hire is about US$2-2.50 a day, US$12.50 a week, next to Casino (beware dogs, especially if cycling alone).

Air Sosa has scheduled flights to La Ceiba, US$16.50, 3 times a day Monday-Saturday. Caribbean Air, T/F2451466, has scheduled flights to Roatán on Saturday. Always reserve flights and make onward reservations in advance. The dirt airstrip begins and ends in the sea; there is no terminal building, just a few benches under a tree; get there 15 minutes before flight. Local transport between airport and hotels, or walk.

Sea *MV Tropical* from **La Ceiba** to Utila scheduled service, T2451796, US$10, buy tickets on the day, a/c, videos, comfortable, fast (1 hour), recommended, Monday-Friday 1000, return 1130. Be at the landing stage 30 minutes before sailing. *MV Starfish* (mainly cargo but some passengers) goes from Utila to **La Ceiba** once or twice a week 0500 (be early or sleep on board previous night) returning from La Ceiba 1200, US$5 each way (information from *Green Ribbon* store). There are irregular boats to **Puerto Cortés**, times posted in main street, 7 hours, US$7.50, ask at public dock.

Boats from Utila to Roatán can be chartered for about US$70. Occasional freight boats, eg *Utila Tom*, take passengers from Utila to Roatán. It's a 3-hour journey between the two islands and you and your possessions are liable to get soaked.

Directory **Banks** Dollars are accepted on the island, have some with you for diving courses. Banks (*Bancahsa* and *Banco Atlántida*) open 0800-1130, 1330-1600 Mon-Fri, 0800-1130 Sat. Bancahsa changes dollars and gives cash against a Visa card, but not Mastercard. *Henderson's Supermarket* changes US$ cash at a better rate than the banks. *Thompson's Bakery* will change dollars and TCs. Ronald Janssen at *Cross Creek Divers* does Amex, Visa and Mastercard advances plus 8%, other establishments do the same.

Communications There is a **post office** at the pier opposite *Captain Morgan's Dive Centre* (0830-1200, 1400-1700 Mon-Fri, 0830-1130 Sat) and a **Hondutel** (0700-1700 Mon-Fri, 0700-1100 Sat) office near *Utila Lodge*. The main service is reported as unreliable. Hondutel sends (and receives) faxes,

F4253106, North America US$1.80, Europe US$2.25, South America and Caribbean US$2, rest of world US$3 per page plus 7% tax. Ronald Janssen also runs Intertel, an international phone (no fax) service: North America US$4 per min, Europe US$7.50 (2 mins minimum), Mexico and Central America US$2, South America US$7, elsewhere US$8.50; incoming fax US$1, no sending faxes. Also email and computer centre. Email also 50m up from *Thompson's Bakery*, on main street, first floor.

Places of worship Churches: 7th Day Adventist, Baptist, Church of God, Methodist (with a charming wooden church built in 1870).

Tour companies & travel agents Contact Henrik and Susan Jensen at the Green House, T4253335, for tours to Timón, one of the Hog Cays; they also run boat trips to Jack Neal beach 5 kilometres from town with white sand, blue bathing hole, excellent snorkelling, also restaurant, *Zanzibar*, for lunch and snacks, bungalows planned, 4 boats a day, US$3 return. They also run a book exchange. Shelby McNab runs *Robinson Crusoe Tours* and takes visitors on half-day tours around the island (US$10 per person) explaining his theory that Daniel Defoe based his famous book on Robinson Crusoe on Utila (not Alexander Selkirk off Chile), fascinating.

Useful information Electricity: goes off between 2400 and 0600. **Local Newspaper:** *Utila Times*, in English, published monthly, excellent source of local information, 6 month subscription US$20, single copy US$1 from Utila Times, Utila, Bay Islands, Honduras, CA. The **BICA Visitor Centre** in front of *Mermaid's Restaurant* has information on Honduran national reserves and sells Utila T-shirts. Marion Howell is the current President of BICA. Donations welcomed for conservation efforts. **Water:** frequent problems. On dry days and when there is no breeze sandflies are most active. Coconut oil, baby oil or Avon 'Skin-so-Soft' helps to ward them off. Take insect repellent. 'Off', sold at *Henderson's* supermarket is good for after dark biters.

Roatán

Roatán is the largest of the islands. It has a paved road running from West End through to French Harbour, almost to Oak Ridge, continuing unpaved to Punta Gorda and Wilkes Point; there are other, unmade roads. Renting a car or scooter gives access to many places that public transport does not reach. The capital of the department, **Coxen Hole**, or Roatán City, is on the southwest shore. Besides being the seat of the local government, it has immigration, customs and the law courts. There is a Post Office, supermarket, several handicraft shops, photo shops, banks, travel agents and various stores. Buses leave from outside the supermarket. It is a scruffy little town with not much of tourist interest but some souvenir shops are opening. There is a bookshop: *Casi Todo II*. You can find cheap lodgings and all public transport fans out from here. If taxis are shared, they are *colectivos* and charge the same as buses.

127 sq km
Population: 10,245
Colour map 4, grid B5

At **Sandy Bay** are the **Carambola Botanical Gardens**. For details contact Bill or Irma Brady, T4451117 (■ *0700-1700 daily, US$3, guided tours or nature trails, well worth a visit*). The gardens were begun in 1985 and contain many flowering plants, ferns and varieties of trees; a 20-minute walk from the garden goes to the top of Monte Carambola past the Iguana Wall, a breeding ground for iguanas and parrots. There is a visitor centre and gift shop and plans to locate a tourist campground above the gardens. The Roatán Museum is at *Anthony's Key Resort*, Sandy Bay. It displays the history of the islands and has a collection of artefacts, ■ *0900-1500, closed Wednesday. There is also a bird sanctuary at Sandy Bay, entrance US$5.*

Sandy Bay

Transport From Coxen Hole to Sandy Bay is a two-hour walk, or a US$1 bus ride, hourly 0600-1700; taxi drivers will try to charge much more. The per person fare from Coxen Hole is US$1. If you take a private taxi, *privado*, you should negotiate the price in advance. The official rate from the airport to Sandy Bay/West End is US$8 per taxi regardless of the number of passengers.

A further five minutes by road beyond Sandy Bay, this is a growing community near the west tip of the island and the most popular place to stay. There are numerous good foreign and local restaurants with an abundance of pizza/pasta places, as well

West End

Honduras

as hotels, cabañas and rooms to rent. It is a stiff walk from Coxen Hole over the hills (three hours) to West End, or take the bus on the paved road for US$0.80, 20 minutes, they run until 1700 or later to meet the boat from the mainland. You can take a small motor boat from *Foster and Vivian's Restaurant* for a 10-minute ride to West Bay (0900-2100, US$1.10 each way, more at night), or walk along the beach, 45 minutes.

West Bay **West Bay** is a beautiful, clean, beach with excellent snorkelling on the reef, particularly at the west end, where the reef is only 10-20 metres off shore and the water is shallow right up to where the wall drops off at 50-75 metres out and scuba diving begins. There are a couple of jetties where you can escape the sandflies which lurk in the powdery white sand, worst in the afternoon. Take your own food and drinks, and insect repellent. Developers have recently discovered the delights of West Bay and the atmosphere is changing fast. Apartments, hotels, bars and restaurants are springing up. A variety of luxury cabins and homes are available for daily, weekly and monthly rental. Watch out for jellyfish in the shallow water at certain times of the year. A taxi from the airport to West Bay costs US$15, check the vehicle can withstand the dirt road.

French **French Harbour**, on the south coast, with its shrimping and lobster fleet, is the main
Harbour fishing port of Roatán. There is no beach. There are two seafood packing plants: Mariscos Agua Azul and Mariscos Hybour. The road passes *Coleman's* (*Midway*) *Bakery*, where you can buy freshly-baked products. The bay is protected by the reef and small cays which provide safe anchorage. *French Harbour Yacht Club* and Romeos Marina (at Brick Bay) offer services for visiting yachts. Several charter yachts are based here. There are a few cheap, clean places to stay, expensive hotels and dive resorts. Eldon's Supermarket is open daily and has a range of US imported food. *Gios Restaurant* and *Casa Romeos* serve top quality seafood.

Across the The main road goes across the mountain ridge along the island with side roads to
island Jonesville, Punta Gorda and Oak Ridge. You can take a bus on this route to see the island's hilly interior, with beautiful views from coast to coast. Alternatively, hire a small four-wheel drive, which is almost as cheap if shared between four people, and allows you to explore the dirt roads and empty bays along the island's northern tip. **Jonesville** is known for its mangrove canal, which is best reached by hiring a taxi boat in Oak Ridge. **Oak Ridge**, situated on a cay (US$0.40 crossing in a dory from the bus stop), is built around a deep inlet on the south coast. It is a charming little fishing port, with rows of dwellings on stilts built on the water's edge (bus Coxen Hole-Oak Ridge, one hour depending on passengers, US$1.10). Numerous boatmen will meet you at the dock offering mangrove tours. Make sure they take you to the Jonesville mangroves: turn right out of the harbour. The mangrove tunnel is a 40

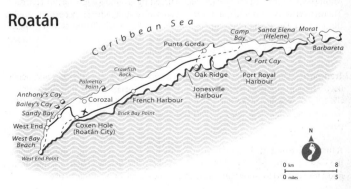

Roatán

minute dory boat tour of the mangroves. There is a clear canal at the end of the tunnel which is recommended for snorkelling, US$10-12 per boat. As well as its hotels, there is a grocery store and a couple of good restaurants.

In **Punta Gorda** on the north coast, the oldest established community on Roatán, Black Caribs retain their own language, music, dance, food, crafts and religion. Carib Week, 8-12 April, is a good time to experience their customs. Bus from Coxen Hole costs US$1. There are also boat tours which include Punta Gorda (and the mangrove tunnel, US$25 per person with Averyll at *Librería Casi Todo* in West End, T4451255). There is a bar/restaurant serving local food. The paved road ends at the turning for Punta Gorda and from here the road is rough and sometimes too muddy for vehicles to get through. **Marble Hill Farms** is down a small track to the left on the north coast, where you can buy a variety of tropical jams, jellies and spices. The gardens have been landscaped over many years by Lisa and Brian Blancher and their produce is all home grown. Lisa also creates batik and tie dye clothing not on sale anywhere else. Open Monday-Saturday, 0900-1700. Beyond here the road deteriorates but leads to Diamond Rock, Camp Bay (five kilometres from the paved road) and Paya Beach. **Camp Bay** has a nice beach but parts of it have been closed off. It is a long swim to the reef. New resorts and timeshare developments are being built along this stretch of coast.

Hire a boat to **Port Royal**, famous in the annals of buccaneering but now just a community of private houses; old British gun emplacements on Fort Cay, one kilometre off-shore. No bus from Port Royal to Oak Ridge, and it's a tough three-hour walk. The **Port Royal Park and Wildlife Refuge** is the largest highland reserve on Roatán, protecting pines and endemic species of flora and fauna, threatened by hunting, the pet trade and habitat destruction. At present it lacks facilities or management and is relatively inaccessible (contact Bay Islands Conservation Association for information). There are also several archaeological sites of the Payan inhabitants.

In glass-bottomed yacht of Dennis, at *Belvedere's Lodge* on the headland at Halfmoon Bay, T4451171, with snorkelling trips to secluded bays beyond Antony's Key. He also takes charters and sunset cruises all along the coast. Horseriding available from *Keifitos* or *Jimmy's* in West End. *Sea Toye*, a 57 foot yacht based in French Harbour, owned by Capt Clay Douglass, known as 'Blue', charter day sail or longer (for example three days Cayos Cochinos), NAUI, YMCA instructor, own tanks, compressor and weights, bring own dive equipment, eight-day charter US$895, in USA T800-4325828 or 708-6585828, Jerry and Sherry Bresnakan. Alex does day trips to Punta Gorda and 2/3 day trips in his sailboat *Adventure Girl*. His boat is moored at Ocean Divers dock, contact here or at Tyll's. Far Tortugas charters, trimaran *Genesis*, does sailing trips with snorkelling and reef drag (snorkellers towed behind slow moving boat), US$45 per day, US$25 per half day, contact *Casi Todo*, West End, T4451347. Fishing arranged through Eddie, contact at *Cindy's* next to Ocean Divers, West End, small dory, local expert, good results, US$ 30 per hour, but prices can vary. Alternatively, go fishing in style from French Harbour, Hot Rods sports fisher, US$500 per day charter, T4451862. See *Casi Todo* for the *Jimni* fishing tours, half and full day. Fishing trips also available on *Flame*, contact Darson or Bernadette, T4451616, US$ 20 per hour. They also do trips to Cayos Cochinos (diving available), Utila and island tours, US$ 250 per boat. Kayak rentals and tours from Seablades, contact Alex at *Casi Todo,* three to seven day kayak tours, US$150-250. Day and half day rental US$ 20-12 (with instruction), kayaks available at Tyll's. *Genesis* used as support boat for 2-7 day trips around Roatán US$175-1,250, ask for Sally or T4430780 in La Ceiba. From *Rick's American Café*, Casablanca charters on yacht *Defiance III*, sunset cruises, party trips, full day snorkelling, also can be arranged through *Casi Todo*. At West Bay beach is a glass bottomed boat, *Caribbean Reef Explorer*, US$20 per one and a half hours, unfortunately includes fish feeding, which

Punta Gorda to Camp Bay

Excursions

Honduras

upsets the reef ecological balance. Glass bottom boat and three person submarine toursfrom the dock at Half Moon Bay, US$25 per person. You can also do day trips to the mainland, whitewater rafting on the Río Cangrejal with Rios Honduras is US$125 per day round trip with lunch, T4430780, 4431361, or contact *Casi Todo*. Mopeds, bikes, island tours: Captain Van's Rentals, West End; also from Ole Rentavan, T4451819.

Sleeping **At West End** **AL** *Lost Paradise*, T4451306, F4451388, paradise@simon.intertel.hn, rooms and cabins, most people on packages, diving, nice jetty for sunset watching. **A-B** *Georphi's Tropical Hideaway*, T4451794, F4451205, individual cabins, 2 bedrooms, kitchens, coffee shop under trees with excellent cookies and pancakes, open all day. **A-B** *Half Moon Bay*, T4451075, F4451213, USA T813-9351700, F813-9331977, bungalows and cabins with bath, restaurant with excellent seafood. **A-D** *Sunset Inn*, T4451925, oceandivers@globalnet.hn, **D** rooms above *Ocean Divers* dive shop, shared bathroom, **A-C** in main hotel, private bath, some with kitchen and up to 5 beds, some with a/c, hot water, friendly, recommended, good discounts with diving in low season, Italian seafood restaurant. **AL-B** *Coconut Tree* (owner Vincent Bush), across the road from Half Moon Bay, T4451648, private cabins (3 double beds), a/c, kitchen, balcony, hot water, fan, fridge, clean, friendly, discounts in low season. **A-B** *Pura Vida*, T/F4451141, a/c, cheaper with fan, hot water, restaurant/bar/pizzeria open all day. **A-B** *Dolphin*, opposite Halfmoon Bay, hot water, fan, some a/c, kitchens. **A-B** *Posada Arco Iris*, apartments in Halfmoon Bay, kitchen, hot water, fan, large balcony, friendly owners. **A-B** *Mermaid Beach*, T4451335, mbc@gte.net, clean, quiet, with bath, fan or a/c, dive shop next door (see below).

B *Seagrape Plantation*, T4451428, cabins with 2 beds, bathroom, hot water, family atmosphere, friendly, Visa accepted, nice location on rocky promontory but no beach, snorkelling, full service restaurant and bar, inclusive packages available. **B** *Trish's Wish*, F4451205, Canadian owned, various sizes, cabin and apartments with kitchen, behind *West End Divers*, on hillside, clean. Recommended. Lower rate for long term. **B** *Hillside Garden Cabins*, on the hill above *Lost Paradise* cabins with hot water, fan, quiet, friendly and helpful owner, Ornic. **B-C** *Casa Calico*, F4451946, F4451171, pbs@globalnet.hn, PO Box 135, Roatán, comfortable, cable TV, videos, rooms and apartments, fan, 2 rooms with a/c, garden, huge balconies, apartments sleep 4 or more with kitchen, hot water, noisy in morning, owned by Frances Collins, friendly, helpful. **B-C** *Foster's Cabins* and rooms, bit crowded and noisy. **B-C** *Sea Breeze*, T4451717, nice rooms, hot water, baths, a/c optional at US$5 per night, suites and studios available with kitchens, windsurfers and kayaks for rent. **B-C** *Keifitos Plantation Resort*, bungalows on hillside above beach, beautiful setting, short walk from village, mosquitoes, bar, good breakfasts to 1300, champagne breakfasts Sunday, horses for rent with guide, friendly owners, very quiet, very clean. Recommended. **B-D** *Roberts-Hill*, T4451176, basic rooms with bath and fan, 2-storey cabaña and new cabins on the beach next to *Keifitos*. **C** *Burke's* cottages, east end of village past Half Moon Bay, T4451252, private bath and kitchen, **D** without, cold water. **C** *Pinocchio's*, owner Patricia, 4 double rooms behind *Sea View Restaurant*, follow *Stanley's* signs, good restaurant. **C-D** *Anderson's*, T4555365, basic rooms, shared bath, clean, fan, lower rates for longer stays, behind *Chris' Tienda*.

D *Bamboo Hut*, T4555365, cabins, shared bathroom, central, next door to *Ocean Divers*, also laundry US$4 per load. **D** *Belvedere's* cabins on beach behind *Chris's Tienda*, T4451171, private bath, restaurant serving steaks, seafood, pasta and salad. **D** *Delzie* has a nice private room, ask at *Chris' Tienda*. **D-E** *Chillies*, in Half Moon Bay, double rooms and dormitory, clean, fully equipped kitchen, lounge, big balcony, camping and hammocks available, excellent value. **F** *Dora Miller* (no sign), 2 houses behind *Jimmy's*, washing facilities, no fan, no mosquito nets, basic, noisy, friendly. **F** *Jimmy's Lodge*, hammocks or communal rooms, extremely basic, smelly, ground floor room has crabs at night, very friendly, cheap meals, snorkelling gear and horseriding available, it is very cheap to string a hammock here, but very exposed and tin roof, you'll be bitten by sandflies, hosepipe as a shower. **E-F** *Sam's*, end of Miller Av, double rooms and dormitory, some fans, island style dinners. Other **E-F** places to stay include *Hotel Suárez, Yoly's, Kenny's* (also camping, under US$3), all basic but friendly,

Roatán - West End

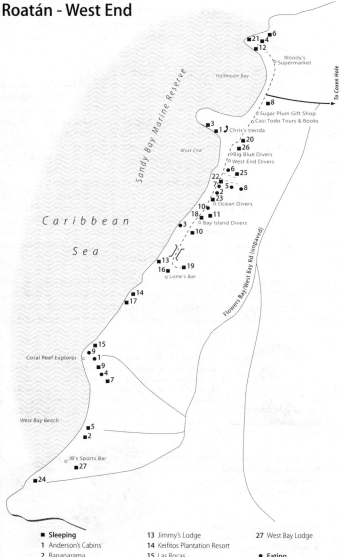

Woody's Supermarket

Halfmoon Bay

■ 21 ■ 4 ■ 6
■ 12

To Coxen Hole

■ 8

Sandy Bay Marine Reserve

○ Sugar Plum Gift Shop
○ Casi Todo Tours & Books

■ 3
■ 1 ♪ Chris's tienda

West End

■ 20
■ 26
○ Big Blue Divers
○ West End Divers

■ 6 ■ 25
22 ■
7 ■ ● 5 ● 8
● 2
■ 23
○ Ocean Divers

10 ●
18 ■ ■ 11
● 3
○ Bay Island Divers

■ 10

C a r i b b e a n

S e a

■ 13
■ 16 ■ 19
○ Lone's Bar

Flowers Bay/West Bay Rd (unpaved)

■ 14
■ 17

■ 15
● 9
● 1
○ Coral Reef Explorer
■ 9
● 4 ● 7

West Bay Beach

■ 5
■ 2

○ JB's Sports Bar
■ 27

■ 24

N
Not to scale

■ Sleeping	13 Jimmy's Lodge	27 West Bay Lodge
1 Anderson's Cabins	14 Keifitos Plantation Resort	
2 Bananarama	15 Las Rocas	● Eating
3 Belvedere's Cabins & Glass Bottom Boat	16 Mermaid Beach & Native Sons Water Sports	1 Café del Mar
4 Burkes Cabins	17 Robert's Hill Cabins	2 Cindy's Island Food & Fishing Trips
5 Cabaña Roatana	18 Robert's Hill	3 Foster's Bar & Restaurant
6 Casa Calico	19 Sam's	4 Neptuno Seafood Grill
7 Coconut Tree 2	20 Sea Breeze	5 Pinnochios & Rooms
8 Coconut Tree Cabins & Supermarket	21 Seagrape Plantation Resort	6 Pura Vida
9 Foster's Beach House	22 Suárez	7 Seaview
10 Foster's Cabins	23 Sunset Inn (above Ocean Divers)	8 Stanley's Island
11 Georphi's Tropical Hideaway	24 Tabayana Beach Resort	9 The Bite on the Beach
12 Half Moon Bay Cabins & Restaurant	25 Trish's Wish Apartments	10 Tropico Italiano
	26 Valerie's Dormitory	

water and electricity not guaranteed, take insect repellent; *Valerie's*, dormitory accommodation, communal central area with cooker and fridge, private rooms **D**, hospitable, but watch your belongings, reports of theft, overpriced; At Gibson Bight, on the road to West End, are *Alexander's Cabins*, T4451501.

At West Bay L-AL *Sea Pearl*, F445-1205/1214, double storey apartments on the beach, a/c, hot water, tiled kitchen, handmade furniture, nicely decorated. **L-AL** *Casa Carnival* (USA) T913-3857755, large luxury house on beach, 2 bedrooms with bath, TV, a/c, long term rates available. **L-B** *Las Rocas*, T4451841, duplex cabañas next to *Bite on the Beach*, very close together, hot water, balcony, smaller cabins sleep 3, larger ones sleep 6, free boat transport to West End and back. **AL** *Tabayana Resort*, at far end of beach, T4451904, upmarket, lovely location, expensive restaurant, no alcohol permitted, outdoor freshwater showers US$1.50. **AL** *Fosters*, new rooms, a/c, hot water in the 'beach house', T4451124. **AL** *Cabaña Roatana*, T4451271, in the USA T1-888-6269531, comfortable beachfront rooms with half kitchen, a/c, hot water, beach towels, some snorkelling gear, café open 1100-1600 for sandwiches, beer, snacks. Recommended. **AL-A** *Coconut Tree 2*, T4451648, luxury cabins with hot water, a/c, balcony on the beach. **B** *Bananarama*, just behind *Cabaña Roatana*, F4451271, banarama@globalnet.hn, with bath, hot water, fan, PADI dive courses available, German-owned, good value. **B** *West Bay Lodge*, behind *JB's*, follow sandy path, 2 minutes' walk, F4451471, westbaylodge@globalnet.hn, cabins with hot water and fan, owners Reiner and Maren, she is a qualified masseuse, good breakfast included.

At Sandy Bay AL *Anthony's Key Resort*, T445-1003/1274, F4451140, in USA T305-6661997, 800-2273483, F305-6662292, closes for 2 weeks in October, glorious situation, accommodation in small wooden cabins, launch and diving facilities (only open to resident guests), the owner, Julio Galindo, is very serious about helping the environment and

local community, the resort's own cay, Bailey's, has a small wildlife reserve (parrots, cockatoo, toucan, monkeys, agoutis, turtles), it has a museum of some archaeological and colonial history, natural history laboratory, A-V lecture hall (entry for non-guests US$2); it also has a dolphin enclosure in a natural pool, guests can swim or dive with the dolphins, expensive, closed Wednesday (in the 1996 storms, 7 dolphins escaped but remain around the islands and occasionally approach dive boats). **A** pp *Oceanside Inn*, T504-4451552, F4451532, full board, clean, comfortable, friendly owners Joseph and Jenny, nice deck with view of bay, superb restaurant, diving packages offered, but no beach nearby, otherwise recommended. **B-C** *Caribbean Seashore Bed & Breakfast*, new, on the beach at West Sandy Bay, hot water, private bath, cooking facilities, friendly management, T4451123.

At French Harbour L-A *Fantasy Island Beach Resort*, T4555222, F4451268, 80 rooms, a/c, on a 15-acre cay, man-made beach, pool, diving and many other watersports, tennis, conference facilities, mixed reports. **AL** *Casa Romeo's* , T4555518, comfortable rooms with views over the bay, transport to beach, ask about scuba diving packages, excellent restaurant good for seafood.**AL** *Coco View Resort*, T4555011, F4451416, in USA 1-800-2828932, good shore diving, on lagoon. **A-B** *French Harbour Yacht Club*, T4451478, F4451459, cable TV in every room, suites available, nice location, view over yacht harbour, small pool, dive packages, expensive but good food (especially lunch). **A-C** *Buccaneer*, T4555032, F4555845 (Tegucigalpa T2369003, F2369800, San Pedro Sula T5526242, F5526239), dive packages, mixed reports on hotel. **B** *The Faro Inn*, T4551536, above *Gios* seafood restaurant, TV, phone, a/c, large rooms, including continental breakfast. **D** *Harbour View*, a/c, private bathroom, opposite *Romeo's*. **E** *Britos*, with fan, very good value. **E** *Dixon's Plaza*, past the *Buccaneer*, good. **E** *Hotelito*, sometimes no water, in the village. **E** *Hotelito Joe*, rooms with fan and private bath, clean restaurant downstairs serving local dishes. **E** *Isabel*, comfortable, restaurant, free transport to airport.

At Brick Bay AL *Caribbean Sailing Club*, modern hotel, with breakfast. **C** *Palm Tree Resort*, T4451986, cabins with bath, homecooking island style, quiet, diveshop, wall diving with boat available.

At Mount Pleasant A-B *Executivo Inn*, on road to French Harbour opposite electricity plant, T4555020, F4555658, nice rooms, a/c, hot water, TV, pool, no beach.

At Oak Ridge L *Reef House Resort*, T4352297, F4352142, in USA 1-800-3288897, F210-3417942, PO Box 40331, San Antonio Texas 78229, including meals, various packages, includes diving, wooden cabins with seaview balconies, seaside bar, private natural pool, dock facilities, good snorkelling from the shore. **E** *San José Hotel*, with bath (2 rooms), cheaper without (3 rooms), clean, pleasant, good value, water shortages, good food, English-speaking owner, Louise Solórzano. *BJ's Backyard Restaurant*, at the harbour, island cooking, fishburgers, smoked foods, reasonable prices. There is a *pizzería* and, next door, a supermarket. *Pirate's Hideaway*, at Calabash Bay, east of Oak Ridge, seafood, friendly owner.

At Port Royal L *Roatán Lodge*, accommodation in cabins, hosts Brian and Lisa Blancher provide scuba diving and snorkelling expeditions.

At Punta Gorda L-A *Henry's Cove*, T4352180, 5527183, secluded retreat on hill, a/c, pool, cabins sleep 6, or rooms, seafood restaurant; rooms to rent with local families. *Ben's Restaurant*, on coast road south out of village, has nice cabins to rent, **B**, T4451916, dive shop (US$35 per dive), limited equipment, disorganized, wooden deck over sea, local food, bar, friendly, safe parking.

At Paya Bay AL *Paya Bay Beach Club and Restaurant*, T/F4352139, cabins, private bath, hot water, wonderful ocean and beach views, owned by Mervin and Lurlene McNab, beautiful restaurant, seafood US$5-10, beach bar and showers, open breakfast, lunch, dinner, homemade soursop juice, remote, long rough drive but worth it.

At Coxen Hole C *Airport View* (**D** without bath or a/c), T4451074. **C** *Cay View*, C Principal, T4451222, F4451179, a/c, bath, TV, phone, laundry, restaurant, bar, overlooks water, overpriced. *Osgood Key*, cabins, maximum 8 people, bar, restaurant, taxi boat at end of road near *Cay View*, T2451541. **C-E** *Mom*, on main road into Coxen Hole, above pharmacy, next to hospital, private or shared bath, modern, clean, a/c, TV. **E** *El Paso*, T4451367, next door to *Cay View*, shared bath, restaurant. **F** *Naomi Allen*, near the bus depot, fan, clean, good. Many of the cheaper hotels in the **F** range have water shortages.

Eating **West End** *Half Moon Bay* restaurant, nice location to sit on terrace overlooking sea, more expensive than most, dishes between US$6-US$15, but excellent food, service can be very slow. *Foster and Vivian's Restaurant* is on a jetty, good atmosphere for pre-dinner drinks, reggae music, basic meals, no sandflies, great sundeck, Thursday is band/dance/party night, also rooms to rent, **B**, T4451008. *Sea View Restaurant*, Italian chef/manager, extensive menu, pasta, fish, chicken, pizza, good salads. *Deja Blue*, Asian and Middle East specialities, good location, salad buffet, expensive but worth it. *Tony's Pizzeria*, in the *Sunset Inn*, fresh fish, good. *Pura Vida*, Italian, restaurant and pizzeria next to *West End Divers*, good atmosphere. *Lighthouse*, on the point next to *Belvedere's*, local dishes, good coffee and breakfasts, fried chicken and seafood. *The Cool Lizard*, Mermaid Beach, seafood, vegetarian and chicken, homemade bread, salads, nice atmosphere, good. *Rudy's*, has good pancakes and cookies for breakfast, sandwich combos, good atmosphere but pricey, open all day. *Stanley's*, up hill about 50 metres north of *Sunset Inn*, small sign up path, island cooking, menu changes daily, evening meal only, at 1900, cheap, good food, try their coconut dinner, friendly. *Pinocchio's*, along same path, excellent pasta, great stir fry and delicious salads, run by Patricia and Howard. *Belvedere's*, on water, nice setting, tasty Italian food, open 1900-2100. Recommended. *Cindy's*, next to *Sunset Inn*, local family lunches and breakfast in garden, fish caught same morning, also lobster and king crab. Recommended. *Coconut Tree*, entrance to West End, supermarket, food not special, bar shows sport, football games etc. *Woods Supermarket*, cheap hot dogs and *baleadas* at lunch between 1100 and 1300, good. *Punta del Ovest* music village, exotic, clay oven pizzas, 200 metres along path behind *Bamboo Hut*. *Bahia Azul* on the beach, chicken, fish and pasta, popular Friday nights. *Coral Reef*, Mexican and seafood, good tacos, good prices. *Cannibal Café*, in the *Seabreeze*, excellent Mexican food, large helpings, good value. *Velva's Place*, at the far end of Halfmoon Bay, island style seafood and chicken dishes, try the conch soup, good prices. *Tyll's Kitchen*, in Tyll's Dive Shop, now open for breakfast, happy hour for rum and beer goes on all day. *Keifito's Hangout*, good breakfasts, champagne on Sunday, reasonable prices. *Tartines and Chocolate*, French bakery/patisserie in Half Moon Bay, good bread and pastries. *Online Café*, Starbucks coffee, bagels, light meals and refreshments etc, email service. *Rick's American Café*, Sandy Bay, tree top bar, shows all sports events, best steaks on Roatán, US$10. Recommended. Some children sell tasty doughnuts and cinnamon rolls. The *pastelito* boy sells vegetarian pastry puffs for L2 each and oranges for L1.

West Bay *The Bite on the Beach*, open Wednesday-Saturday and Sunday brunch, huge deck in gorgeous position on the point over West Bay, excellent, fresh food and great fruit punch, owned by Gene and Dian. Recommended. *Neptuno Seafood Grill*, between *Fosters* and *Coconut Tree 2*, seafood, paella, BBQ crab, extensive bar, open daily for lunch and dinner, will arrange sea trips and car rentals, more expensive than the *Bite*. *West Bay Lodge* serves a good breakfast on a nice balcony overlooking sea. Recommended.

Coxen Hole *Comedor Ray Monty*, very cheap, set meal US$1.50 but avoid the meat, fish good. *Gloria's*, good local food, reasonable prices, TV, popular with locals. *Qué Tal Café*, good, export quality coffee, herbal teas, sandwiches and pastries, shares space with bookstore, on road to West End. *El Punto*, bar with one basic dish, very cheap. *HB Warren*, large well-stocked supermarket (best place on island for fresh fruit) with cafetería, mainly lunch and snacks, open 0700-1800. Pizza stand opposite *Warren's*, slices US$1.50. *El Paso*, next to the *Cay View*, good seafood soup. *Pizza Rey*, opposite Warren's, pizza slices. *Hibiscus Sweet Shop*, homemade fruit pies, cakes and biscuits. There is a good seafood restaurant on Osgood Cay a few minutes by free water taxi from wharf.

French Harbour *French Harbour Yacht Club*, daily specials, pizza, salads, sandwiches, usually very good. *Romeo's*, (Romeo is Honduran-Italian), good seafood, and continental cuisine. *Gios*, seafood, king crab a speciality. *Tres Flores*, on the hill, good views, Mexican specialities, they will pick up groups from West End T2450007. *Iguana Grill*, international cuisine, suckling pig. There is a *taquería* close to Bancahsa on the main road, good tacos, burritos and hamburgers.

Discotheques Informal ones which come alive about midnight, play mostly reggae, salsa, *punta* and some rock. *Harbour View*, Coxen Hole, Thursday-Sunday nights, late, US$0.50 entrance, very local, usually no problem with visitors but avoid local disputes, hot and atmospheric. *Al's*, Barrio Las Fuertes, before French Harbour, closed Saturday night, salsa and plenty of punta. *Bolongas*, French Harbour, weekends, late, US$1 entrance, more upmarket, modern building, sometimes live Honduran bands and classy stripshow. *Foster's*, the late night hotspot in West End, dance music Thursday night as well as band nights. *Bahía Azul*, Friday is party night, DJ, dancing. *Lone's Bar*, Mermaid Beach, nightly BBQ, reggae music. | **Entertainment**

Supermarkets Best to buy food, insect repellent in Coxen Hole. *Coconut Tree* at West End expensive. *Woods* is cheaper; in French Harbour, *Eldon* is also expensive. *Ezekiel*, West End, opposite church, fruit and vegetables, selection varies. | **Shopping**

Local Newspaper *Coconut Telegraph*, 6 issues per year, in English, good information on Roatán and the Bay Islands. Subscriptions: Central America and USA US$25 per year, Canada US$30, elsewhere US$35 from Coconut Telegraph, Cooper Building, Suite 301, Coxen Hotel, Roatán, T4451660, F4451659.

Diving: the establishment of the *Sandy Bay/West End Marine Park* along 4.2 kilometres of coast from Lawson Rock around the southwest tip to Key Hole has encouraged the return of large numbers of fish in that area and there are several interesting dive sites. Lobsters are still rare, but large grouper are now common and interested in divers. Mooring buoys must be used, anchoring and spear fishing are not allowed. If the sea is rough off West End try diving around French Harbour (or vice versa) where the cays provide some protection. There are more mangroves on this side, which attract fish. Flowers Bay on the south side has some spectacular wall dives, but not many fish, and it is calm during the 'Northers' which blow in December-February. Few people dive the east end except the liveaboards (Bay Islands Aggressor, The Aggressor Fleet, Romeo Tower, French Harbour, T4451518, F4451645, or in the USA. PO Drawer K, Morgan City, LA 70881-000K, T504-3852416, F504-3840817 or 800-3482628 in USA or Canada) and people on camping trips to Pigeon Cay, so it is relatively unspoilt. Because fishing is allowed to the east, tropical fish are scarce and the reef is damaged in places. Apart from expecting some stormy days in December-February, you can also expect stinging hydroids in the top few feet of water around March-April which bother people who are sensitive to stings. Symptoms are itching while swimming, mostly over weed, usually on parts of the body covered by the swimsuit: vinegar is the local remedy. Divers are usually unaffected as they go below the hydroids. | **Sports**

As on Utila, the dive operators concentrate on instruction but prices vary (since December 1994 the municipal government has set minimum prices) and there is more on offer; not everyone teaches only PADI courses. Prices for courses and diving vary with the season. In low season good deals abound. Open Water US$225, Advanced US$160, fun dives US$30, or cheaper if you take a package, snorkel rental US$20 per day. Despite the huge number of dive students, Roatán has a good safety record but it still pays to shop around and find an instructor you feel confident with at a dive shop which is well organized with well-maintained equipment. As in other 'adventure' sports the cheapest is not always the best. Dive insurance is US$2 per day, and is sometimes included in the course price. If you do not have dive insurance and need their services, the hyperbaric chamber charges a minimum of US$800. They also treat other diving related problems for a minimum fee. The chamber will not accept insurance from people who have dived outside the sports diving safety limits (maximum depth 130 feet/39 metres).

West End *Ocean Divers* at *Sunset Inn*. Recommended, T/F4451925, oceandivers@globalnet.hn run by Conor Megan and Phil Stevens with emphasis on safety and fun, good equipment, multilingual instructors, PADI courses, BSAC, the only shop with nitrox instruction, fast boats, also rooms and restaurant, dive/accommodation packages available. *Sueño del Mar Divers*, good, inexpensive, American-style operation, they tend to dive the sites closest to home, T4451717. *West End Divers*, Italian owned, competant bilingual instructors, PADI Dive Centre. *Tyll's Dive*, multilingual instructors, PADI, SSI courses, good boats, accommodation also available. *Native Son's Water Sports*, next to *Mermaid* cabins, run by Alvin, local instructor, PADI and PDSI courses and fun dives. *Aquarius Divers*, PADI courses, fun dives, excursions to the south walls in conjunction with Scuba Romance dive shop, Brick Bay. **At West Bay Beach**: *Bananarama*, in centre of beach, next to *Cabana Roatana*, small, friendly, run by young German family, boat and shore diving. **At Gibson Bight**: *The Last Resort*, T4451838, F4451848, lastresort@globalnet.hn, in USA T305-8932436, mostly packages from the USA. **At Sandy Bay**: *Anthony's Key Resort*, mostly hotel package diving, also swim and dive with dolphins, see above. **At Dixon Cove**: *Scuba Romance*, new shop and equipment, large diesel boat and compressor, diving the south wall and the reef at Mary's Place, overnight trips to Barbareta, 6 dives, US$80, sleeping on the boat, work with *Palm Cove Resort*, cabin style accommodation, home cooking.

Transport **Local Car rental**: Sandy Bay Rent-A-Car, US$42 per day all inclusive, jeep rental, T4451710, F4451711, agency also in West End outside *Sunset Inn*; **Toyota**, opposite airport, have pickups, US$46, four-wheel drive, US$65, Starlets US$35 per day, also 12-seater bus, US$56 per day, T4451166; **Avis**, T4451568, Las Samurais and Coronas; **Roatan Rentals**, West End, range of vehicles, pickups and vans for rent; **Captain Van**, West End, vans, also mopeds and bicycles, **Ole**, T4451819, vans for hire.

Air If travelling to or from the mainland, check fares available on the day of travel, it may be cheaper to fly than to go by sea. US$2 entry tax is charged on arrival. The airport is 20 minutes' walk from Coxen Hole, or you can catch a taxi from *outside* the airport for US$1.50. There is a hotel reservation desk in the airport, T4451930. Change in Coxen Hole for taxis to West End. US$1 per person for *colectivos*. If you take a taxi from the airport they charge US$8 per taxi; if you pick one up on the main road you may be able to bargain down to US$5. Caribbean Air, Isleña, Sosa fly from **La Ceiba** several times a day, US$23 one way (fewer on Sunday); flights also to and from **Tegucigalpa**, US$60, via **San Pedro Sula** (Caribbean Air and Isleña), US$50, frequency varies according to season. From **Utila** on Saturday with Caribbean Air. No other direct flights to other islands, you have to go via La Ceiba (to Utila US$38.50, to Guanaja US$51). Always buy your ticket in advance (none on sale at airport), reservations are not always honoured. From the USA, Taca flies on Saturday from **Houston**, on Sunday from Miami. From Central America, daily flights from **Belize City** (Isleña, Caribbean Air), Saturday from **San Salvador** (Taca). Airlines: Taca, at airport T4451387; Isleña, airport T4451550; Sosa, airport T4451154. *Casi Todo* sells all inter-Honduras and Caribbean air tickets, same price as airlines.

Sea *M/V Tropical* sails from La Ceiba to Coxen Hole, Roatán, fast (2 hours, longer if rough), comfortable, a/c, videos, US$11 one way from the Nuevo Muelle de Cabotaje 6 kilometres from town (taxi US$1.50 per person): Monday 0500, return 0730, depart La Ceiba again 1530; Tuesday-Friday Roatán-La Ceiba 0700, La Ceiba-Roatán 1530; Saturday Roatán-La Ceiba 0700, La Ceiba-Roatán 1100, return 1400; Sunday La Ceiba-Roatán 0700, return 1530. Times frequently change, check in good time before travelling, T4555056. No sailings in bad weather. At times the crossing can be rough, sea-sick pills available at ticket counter. Irregular boats from Puerto Cortés and Utila. Cruise ships visit from time to time, mostly visiting Tabayana Resort on West Bay.

Directory **Banks** *Banco Atlántida, Bancahsa, Banco Sogerín* and *Banffaa* in Coxen Hole, there is also a

Credomatic office where you can get a cash advance on your Visa/Mastercard, upstairs, before *Cay View Hotel* on the main street; 5 banks in French Harbour; *Bancahsa* in Oak Ridge, T2452210, Mastercard for cash advances. No banks in West End. No exchange facilities at the airport. Dollars and lempiras can be used interchangeably for most services. **Communications** Post Office: in Coxen Hole, stamps not always available, bring them with you or try *Librería Casi Todo* in West End. **Telecommunications:** very expensive, you will be charged as soon as a call connects with the satellite, whether or not the call goes through. Hondutel in Coxen Hole, fax is often broken. *Supertienda Chris*, West End, T/F4451171, 1 min to Europe US$10, USA, Canada $5. Both *Librería Casi Todo* and *Rudy's Cabins* in West End have a fax, US$10 per page to Europe, US$5 to USA. *Rudy's* charge US$2 a min to receive phone calls. Send or receive email, Online Café and the Sunset Inn. *The Lucky Lemp*, opposite Qué Tal coffee shop, main street Coxen Hole, phone, fax and email services. *Paradise Computer*, Coxen Hole, 10 minutes' walk down road to West End. **Hospitals & medical services** Ambulance and **Hyperbaric Chamber:** Anthony's Key with full medical service. Local hospital, Ticket Mouth Rd, Coxen Hole, T4451499. **Dentist:** upstairs in the Cooper building for emergency treatment, but better to go to La Ceiba or San Pedro Sula. **Doctor:** Dr Jackie Bush has a clinic in Coxen Hole, no appointment necessary, for blood or stool tests etc.

Tour companies & travel agents Airport travel agency at the airport, has information on hotels, will make bookings, no commission. *Bay Islands Tour and Travel Center*, in Coxen Hole (Suite 208, Cooper Building, T4451585, 4451146) and French Harbour. *Tropical Travel*, in *Hotel Cay View*, T4451146. *Columbia Tours*, Barrio El Centro, T4451160, good prices for international travel, very helpful. *Casi Todo I* in West End or *Casi Todo 2* in Coxen Hole can arrange tours, locally and on the mainland, including fishing, kayaking, island tours, trips to Barbareta and Copán. Local and international air tickets also sold here as well as new and second-hand books, open Mon-Sat, 0900-1630 (see above **Excursions**). Carlos Hinds, T4451446, has a van for trips, reasonable and dependable. **Tourist offices** Bay Islands Conservation Association, Edif Cooper, C Principal, Coxen Hole, T4451424, Charles George; Farley Smith, an American volunteer, is extremely helpful. BICA manages the Sandy Bay/West End Marine Reserve and has lots of information about the reef and its conservation. Excellent map of the island at about 1:50,000 supplied by Antonio E Rosales, T4451559. Local information maps also from *Librería Casi Todo*, West End.

Barbareta Island

East of Roatán, the island is a private nature reserve, where hiking trails have been laid out and there are beaches, good diving and sport fishing. The adjacent Pigeon Cays are ideal for snorkelling, shallow scuba, picnics. There are stone artefacts on the island, and you can hike in the hills to caves which may have been inhabited by Paya Indians. The island was once owned by the descendants of Henry Morgan. The island, plus its neighbours Santa Elena and Morat, are part of the proposed Barbareta National Marine Park.

Reservations are required for all visitors, contact the **LL** *Barbareta Beach Club*, PO Box 63, La Ceiba, T4451255, no phone, VHF 88A. Accommodation including meals in lodge or beach bungalows, restaurant, bar, tours, sports, horses included, charter flights from La Ceiba or Roatán US$72 per person, minimum two people, or charter boat from Roatán US$36 per person, minimum two people, all one way only. One-day walking tours with guide, lunch, snorkelling, US$35. Divers should bring their own equipment, but tanks, weights, guide and boat are available, US$25 one tank, US$40 two tanks. Bonefishing with guide and boat, US$150 full day, deep sea fishing US$300 half-day, US$550 full day. Also hobie cat, windsurfing, kayaks, mountain bikes for rent. In the USA: 7105 Mobile Street, Suite 17, Fair Hope, Alabama 36532, T205-9908948, F205-9281659.

Averyll from *Casi Todo*, West End, Roatán, can arrange sailing tours, charter flights and accommodation, **A-B**, T4451347, F4451946.

Honduras

Guanaja

56 sq km
Population: 5,000
Colour maps 4, grid B5

Columbus called **Guanaja**, the easternmost of the group, the Island of Pines, and the tree was abundant until Hurricane Mitch swept most of them away. Since then, a great replanting effort has commenced and, until the new pines have grown, there are a great many flowering and fruiting plants thriving on the island. The island was declared a forest reserve in 1961, and is now designated a national marine park also. Good (but sweaty) clambering on the island gives splendid views of the jungle and the sea. Several attractive waterfalls. The first English settler was Robert Haylock, who arrived in 1856 with a land title to part of the island, two cays which now form the main settlement of Bonacca and some of the Mosquito coast. He was followed in 1866 by John Kirkconnell, who purchased Hog Cay, where the Haylocks raised pigs away from the sandflies. These two families became sailors, boat builders and land-owners, and form the basis of the present population. Much of Guanaja town, locally known as **Bonacca** (*Population: 2,000*), covering a small cay off the coast, is built on stilts above sea water, with boardwalks and concrete pathways, hence its nick-name: the 'Venice of Honduras'. There are three other small villages: **Mangrove Bight**, **Savannah Bight** and **North East Bight** on the main island. There are Indian graves around Savannah Bight. Bathing is made somewhat unpleasant by the many sandflies. These and mosquitoes cannot be escaped on the island, all the beaches are infected (coconut oil, baby oil or any oily sun tan lotion will help to ward off sandflies). The cays are better, including Guanaja town. South West Cay is specially recommended.

Sleeping   **LL** *Bayman Bay Club*, beautiful location, see the sunset from the tree house deck, T4534191, F4534179, in USA 1-800-5241823, F954-3702276 and **LL** *Posada del Sol*, on an outlying cay, T6683348, T/F6683347, posada@netsys.hn, in USA T561-624 3483/3225, 800-6423483, both include meals launch trips, diving, fitness studio, 1st class, the latter has a good underwater photographic and video facility for divers.
AL *Club Guanaja Este*, full board, many aquatic activities, and horseriding and hiking, reservations and information PO Box 40541, Cincinnati, Ohio 45240 or travel agents. **L** *Bahía Resort*, full board, bungalows, pool, disco, bar, Italian restaurant, T/F4534212. **B** *Alexander*, T4534326, 20 rooms, or US$100 in 3-bed, 3-bathroom apartment, diving and fishing resort, packages: US$98 per person includes 3 dives a day, US$110 per person includes bone fishing and trawling, US$85 per person includes snorkelling and hiking, all with 3 meals a day and lodging. **C** *El Rosario*, T4534240, with bath and a/c, nice. **B-C** *Miller* (cheaper without a/c or bath), TV, restaurant, T4554327. **C-D** *Harry Carter*, T4554303, ask for a fan, clean. **E** *Miss Melba*, 3 rooms in boarding house, run by friendly, talkative lady (born 1914) with lots of interesting stories and island information, shared bathroom, cold water, great porch and gardens just before *Hotel Alexander* sign on left, house with flowers. *Casa Sobre El Mar*, on Bound Cay, T4534269 (2231095 in Tegucigalpa), offers all-inclusive packages. *Day Inn*, hotel and restaurant.

Guanaja

Harbour Light, through *Mountain View* discotheque, good food reasonably priced for the **Eating**
island. *The Nest*, T4534290, good eating in the evening. *Glenda's*, good standard meals for
under US$1, small sandwiches. *Fifi Café*, named after the hurricane which wiped out most of
the houses in 1974, popular local hangout.

Sports Diving and Sailing: the most famous dive site off Guanaja is the wreck of the *Jado* **Entertainment**
Trader, sunk in 1987 in about 30 metres on a flat bottom surrounded by some large coral pin-
nacles which rise to about 15 metres. Large black groupers and moray eels live here, as does
a large shy jewfish and many other fish and crustaceans. *Jado Divers*, beside *Melba's*, US$26
for 2 dives, run by Matthew, American. Preston Borden will take snorkellers out for US$25 per
boat load (4-6 people), larger parties can be accommodated with larger boat, or for custom
excursions, very flexible, T4534326. *SV Railovy*, T504-4534135, F504-4534274, is a 40' yacht
running local cruises and excursion packages; also sailing, diving and snorkelling services,
and PADI courses. Ask for Hans on VHF radio channel 70.

Air The airport is on Guanaja but you have to get a water taxi from there to wherever you are **Transport**
staying; there are no roads or cars; Sosa and Isleña (T4534208) fly daily from La Ceiba, 30 minutes. Other non-scheduled flights available.

Sea The *Suyapa* sails between Guanaja, La Ceiba and Puerto Cortés. The *Miss Sheila* also
does the same run and goes on to George Town (Grand Cayman). Cable Doly Zapata,
Guanaja, for monthly sailing dates to Grand Cayman (US$75 one way). Irregular sailings from
Guanaja to Trujillo, 5 hours. Irregular but frequent sailings in lobster boats for next to nothing
to Puerto Lempira in Caratasco Lagoon, Mosquitia, or more likely, only as far as the Río
Plátano (see page 953).

Banks *Bancahsa, Banco Atlántida.* **Directory**

Copán and Western Honduras

*Honduras' major Maya attraction is close to the Guatemalan border; it is a lovely site,
with a pleasant town nearby. This whole area has many interesting towns and villages,
most in delightful hilly surroundings, often producing handicrafts. Some of these places
have a colonial history, some are Lenca Indian communities.*

Santa Bárbara

The Western Highway runs from San Pedro Sula southwest along the Río *Population: 23,000*
Chamelecón to Canoa (58 kilometres, from where there is a paved road south to *Altitude: 290m*
Santa Bárbara, a further 53 kilometres) and Santa Rosa de Copán; it goes on to the *Colour map 4, grid C4*
border with Guatemala and El Salvador. Santa Bárbara is 32 kilometres west of Lago
Yojoa, 221 kilometres from Tegucigalpa, in hot lowlands. Panama hats and other
goods of *junco* palm are made in this, one of the nicest main towns in Honduras
although it has little of architectural or historical interest compared with, for example, Gracias, Ojojona or Yuscarán. It is surrounded by high mountains (for example
Cerro Guatemalilla), hills, forests and rivers. The majority of the population is
fair-skinned (some red-heads) and the people are very lively. Santa Bárbara is a
good base for visiting the villages in the department of the same name (see below). In
the vicinity the ruined colonial city of **Tencoa** has recently been rediscovered. The
paved road goes on to join the Northern Highway south of Lago Yojoa.

Excursions Between Santa Bárbara and Lago Yojoa is the **Parque Nacional de Santa Bárbara** which contains the country's second highest peak, Montaña de Santa Bárbara, 2,744 metres. The rock is principally limestone with many subterranean caves (see also below). There is little tourist development as yet, only one trail has been laid out and a guide can be found in Los Andes, a village above Peña Blanca and Las Vegas. Best time to visit is the dry season, January-June. For more information contact Asociación Ecológica Corazón Verde, at the Palacio Municipal, Santa Bárbara. There is a Cohdefor office just below the market (look for the sign board) but they are not helpful.

The Department of Santa Bárbara is called the 'Cuna de los Artesanos', with over 10,000 manufacturers of handicrafts. The main products come from the small *junco* palm, for example fine hats, baskets, et cetera. The principal towns for *junco* items are **La Arada**, 25 minutes from Santa Bárbara on the road to San Nicolás (see below), then branching off south, and Ceguaca, on a side road off the road to Tegucigalpa. Flowers and dolls from corn husks are made in Nueva Celilac (also below). *Mezcal* is used to make carpets, rugs and hammocks, it is easy to find in towns such as **Ilama** (*Population*: 7,000) on the road to San Pedro Sula, with one of the best

Western Honduras

small colonial churches in Honduras (no accommodation). *Tule* is used to make *petates* (rugs) and purses.

In the Department of Santa Bárbara is an area known as **El Resumidero**, in which are the Quezapaya mountain, and six others over 1,400 metres, and a number of caves (Pencaligüe, Los Platanares, El Quiscamote, and others). From Santa Bárbara, go to El Níspero and thence to El Quiscamote; or go to San Vicente Centenario (thermal springs nearby), and on to San Nicolás, Atima, Berlín, and La Unión, all of which have thermal waters, fossils, petrified wood and evidence of volcanic activity.

San Nicolás is 20 kilometres from Santa Bárbara on a paved road; it was founded on 20 February 1840 after the disappearance of Viejo Celilac, near Cerro Capire. In the centre of town is the big tree called 'Anacahuite' (in Lenca, place of reunion), planted in 1927. There is a nice Catholic church; other points of interest, La Peña, Las Cuevas del Masical (you will probably not find them on your own, a local guide will take you to the caves for a fee), Quebrada Arriba and El Violín. You can drive to the ruined church of Viejo Celilac and on to Nueva Celilac, high on the mountain, a pleasant little town with a Vía Crucis procession on Good Friday.

North of Santa Bárbara is **Colinas**, reached by bus from San Pedro Sula (from near Avenida Los Leones). The village is picturesque, with a basic *pensíon* (under US$3), near the church; excellent set meals from *Chinita* near the gas station. Climb the mountain with El Gringo Guillermo (Bill Walton) to Laguna Colorada, US$3 (a long drive through coffee *fincas*); he plans to build tourist cabins.

C-E *Boarding House Moderno*, Barrio Arriba, T6432203, rooms with fan better value than with a/c, with hot shower, quiet, parking. Recommended. **C-E** *Gran Hotel Colonial*, 1½ blocks from Parque Central, T6432665, fans in all rooms, some with a/c, cold water, sparsely furnished, friendly, clean, good view from roof. Recommended. *Santa Marta*, on La Independencia, basic, noisy. **F** *Hospedaje Rodríguez*, with bath, dark, clean, friendly, helpful, walls don't meet the ceiling, noisy. **F** *Rosileí*, clean, pleasant, *comedor* attached. **F** *Ruth*, C La Libertad, T6432632, rooms without windows, fan. — **Sleeping**

Pizzería Don Juan, Av Independencia, very good pizzas. *Comedor Everest*, by bus stop on Parque Central, friendly, good *comida corriente*. *Comedor Norma*, family food, friendly. *Las Tejas*, near Rodríguez, friendly, good pizzería. *Doña Ana*, 1 block above Parque Central, door and window frames painted black, no sign, restaurant in her dining room, crammed with bric-a-brac, no menu, no choice, set meal of meat, rice, beans, bananas, plentiful and good but boring. *El Brasero*, half block below Parque Central, extensive menu of meat, chicken, fish, Chinese dishes, good food, well-prepared. Recommended. *Repostería Charle's*, on Parque Central, excellent cakes, pastries, about the only place open for breakfast. *Helados Arco Iris*; *Cafetería Repostería Betty's*, both also on Parque Central. On main street, *McPollo*, clean, smart, good, and the delightfully named *Comedor Remembranzas del Verde*, good, cheap *comida corriente*. — **Eating**

Cinema *Galaxia*. — **Entertainment**

Buses to **Tegucigalpa**, 0700 and 1400 daily, weekends 0900, US$3, 4½ hours with Transportes Junqueños (passing remote villages in beautiful mountain scenery); from **San Pedro Sula**, 2 hours, US$1.90, 7 a day between 0500 and 1630. Bus to San Rafael at 1200, 4 hours. Onward bus to Gracias leaves next day. — **Transport**

Banks *Banco Atlántida, Bancafé, Banco Sogerín, Banco de Occidente* and *Banadesa*. — **Directory**

The road from San Pedro Sula towards Guatemala runs southwest through Sula (*Sula Inn*, motel style 500 metres east of La Entrada, at La Maduna junction) to La Entrada (115 kilometres from San Pedro), where it forks left for Santa Rosa (see below) and right for an attractive 60 kilometres road through deep green scenery to Copán. The regular bus is recommended rather than the dangerous minibus service. The road is paved throughout and in good condition. — **Routes**

La Entrada A hot, dusty town. Banco Sogerín will cash travellers' cheques.

> **Sleeping C-E** *San Carlos*, at junction to Copan Ruinas, T8985228, a/c, modern, cable TV, bar, swimming pool, restaurant (T/F6612187), excellent value. **E** *Central*, by Shell station, with 2 beds, **F** with 1, either with bath, fans, cold water, OK. **F** *Hospedaje Copaneco*, 1 Av No 228, T8985181, Barrio El Progreso, on road to San Pedro Sula. Opposite is **F** *Hotel Gran Bazar*, basic, **E** with bath. *Hospedaje Alexandra*, on the main road, T8985075. *Hotel Tegucigalpa*, opposite Shell station, on main road, T8985046. **F** *Hospedaje María*, good, limited food. **F** *Hospedaje Golosino Yessi*, parking, small rooms, OK. Eat in the market or at the bus station (to west, on Santa Rosa road), or at *Comedor Isis*, excellent. Plenty of other good restaurants.

El Puente El Puente, now a National Archaeological Park, is reached by taking a turn-off, 4.5 kilometres west from La Entrada on the Copán road, then turn right on a well-sign-posted, paved road six kilometres to the Visitors' Centre. It is near the confluence of the Chamelecón and Chinamito rivers and is thought to have been a regional centre between 600 and 900 AD. There are over 200 structures, many of which have been excavated and mapped since 1984 by the Honduran Institute of Anthropology and History together with the Japanese Overseas Cooperation Volunteers. Several have been cleared and partially restored, including a 12 metres high pyramid; there are also stelae. The visitors' centre has a *cafetería* and a souvenir shop. There is a museum of anthropology, well worth a visit and an introduction to Copán. ■ *0800-1600, US$5, US$1.50 for Central Americans. You are not allowed to camp at the site, but ask the locals nearby. Getting there:* From **La Entrada** the cheapest transport is by truck. From **Copán** ask about a truck by *Hotel Paty* and negotiate for the 60 kilometres, 1 hour ride, about US$25 for 2 includes 1½ hours at the site and a stop at **Las Lagunas** to see the roosting cattle egrets (recommended).

A few kilometres beyond La Entrada is the small town of **La Florida** (*Population*: 24,100, primitive accommodation). The owner of the gas station here will advise archaeologists about the many Maya ruins between La Florida and Copán. There are a number of hilltop stelae between the border and Copán.

Copán

Colour map 4, grid C3 The magnificent Maya ruins of Copán are 395 kilometres by road from Tegucigalpa or 172 from San Pedro Sula, and one kilometre from the pleasant village, called Copán Ruinas. There is a signposted path beside the road from the village of Copán to the ruins, passing two stelae en route (one kilometre, no need to take a minibus). It is advisable to get to the ruins as early as possible, or late in the day (though it takes a full day to see them properly). There are several tame scarlet macaws (caged at night). They love shirt buttons.

Admission Entry to ruins and Las Sepulturas US$10 (US$2.50 for Central Americans), open 0800-1600, admission valid for 1 day. Guided tours available all year (recommended, US$20 for 2 hours); recommended is Antonio Ríos, T8983414, owner of restaurant/shop opposite the ruins. Photographs of the excavation work and a maquette of the site are located in a small exhibition room at the ruins' Visitors' Centre. There is a tourist office in the Parque Arqueológico, next to the bookshop, with local and country maps, and a Spanish/English guide book for the ruins, which is rather generalized. Useful recent books are: *Scribes, Warriors and Kings: City of Copán*, by William and Barbara Fash (1991), and History Carved in Stone, a guide to Copán by William Fash and Ricardo Agarcía (third edition, 1998, US$3), published locally and available at the site. (See also general account of Maya history in the Horizons to this book.) Luggage can be left for no charge (clean toilets here, too). There is a cafetería by the entrance to the ruins, and also a handicrafts shop.

The **Copán Museum** on the town square has good explanations in Spanish of the **Museums**
Maya Empire and stelae. There is a good selection of artefacts and a burial site. It is a
good idea to visit the museum before the ruins. ■ *Monday-Saturday, 0800-1200,
1300-1600, US$2.*

The magnificent **Museum of Mayan Sculpture**, opened in 1996, next to the Visitor's Centre, is an impressive and huge two storey museum and sculpture park
which houses the newly excavated carvings. In the middle of the museum is an open

Copán archaeological site

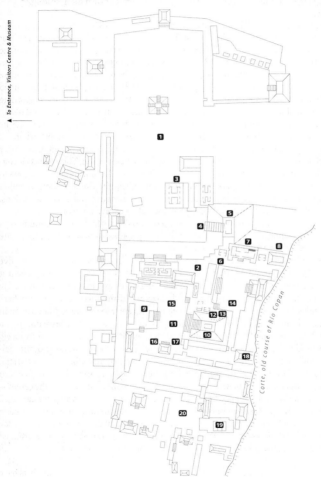

N

Not to scale

1	Main Plaza with Stelae	9	Structure 13	14	East Court/Plaza de los
2	Acropolis	10	Structure 16		Jaguares
3	Ball Court	11	Altar Q	15	Plaza Occidental
4	Hieroglyphic Stairway	12	Rosalila Building	16	Altar I
5	Structure 26		(within Structure 16)	17	Altar H
6	Council House, Temple 22A	13	Hunal Building	18	Temple 18
7	Temple of Meditation/		(beneath Rosalila)	19	Structure 32
	Temple 22		& Tomb of Founder	20	Zona Residencial
8	House of Knives				

air courtyard with a full size reproduction of the Rosalila temple, found intact buried under Temple 16 with its original paint and carvings (see below). A reproduction of the doorway to Temple 16 is on the upper floor. The new museum houses the original stelae to prevent weather damage, while copies will be placed on site. Over 2,000 other objects found at Copán are also in the museum. It is essential to visit the museum before the ruins. Good explanations in Spanish and English. The exit leads to the ruins via the nature trail. ■ *US$5, ticket from main ticket office, not at the museum.* The building has a structural problem, which has closed the entrance (through a serpent's head) and one part of the exhibition. Earthquakes in July 1999 forced the complete closure of the museum; it was not known for how long.

The ruins When Stephens and Catherwood examined the ruins in 1839, they were engulfed in jungle. In the 1930s the Carnegie Institute cleared the ground and rebuilt the Great Stairway, and since then they have been maintained by the Government. Some of the most complex carvings are found on the 21 stelae, or three metre columns of stones on which the passage of time was originally believed to be recorded. Under many of the stelae was a vault; some have been excavated. The stelae are deeply incised and carved with faces, figures and animals. They are royal portraits with inscriptions recording deeds and lineage of those portrayed as well as dates of birth, marriage(s) and death. (Some of the finest examples of sculpture in the round from Copán are now in the British Museum or at Boston.) Ball courts were revealed during excavation, and one of them has been fully restored. The Hieroglyphic Stairway leads up a pyramid; the upper level supported a temple. Its other sides are still under excavation. The Stairway is covered for protection, but a good view can be gained from the foot and there is access to the top via the adjacent plaza. After Hurricane Mitch, the Rosalila temple, within Temple 16, was opened to the public, as were other previously restricted excavations, in an effort to attact more visitors. Much fascinating excavation work is in progress, stacks of labelled carved stones under shelters, and the site looks like becoming even more interesting as new buildings are revealed. The most atmospheric buildings are those still half-buried under roots and soil.

The last stela was set up in Copán between AD 800 and 820, after less than five centuries of civilized existence. The nearby river has been diverted to prevent it encroaching on the site when in flood. One kilometre beyond the main ruins, along the road to San Pedro Sula, is an area called **Las Sepulturas**, a residential area where ceramics dating back to 1000 BC have been found; entry to this site included in main Copán ticket. Exhibits from the site are on display in the Copán Museum. It is a delightful site, beautifully excavated and well-maintained, peaceful and in lovely surroundings. Also near the ruins is a nature trail (called **Sendero Natural**) through the jungle to the minor ball court; take mosquito repellent if you intend to stand still. The trail takes 30 minutes. After 1600 is the best time to see animals on the Sendero Natural, open until 1700. About four kilometres from the main centre is the ceremonial site known as **Los Sapos** (the toads), a pre-classic site with early stone carvings. The sapo was a Mayan symbol of fertility. East of the main ruins, near Los Sapos is a stone, Estela 12, which lines up with another, Estela 10 on the other side of the valley at sunrise and sunset on 12 April annually. Horse rides to Los Sapos can be arranged with guides at main Visitors' Centre at Copán for US$25, 3-4 hours.

Excursions There are many caves around Copán to visit, in some of which, Mayan artifacts have been found. Ask locally. Also, here and in the neighbouring part of Guatemala, are a few remaining Chorti Indian villages, interesting to visit, particularly on 1 November, Día de Los Muertos, when there are family and communal ceremonies for the Dead.

To **Agua Caliente**, 20 kilometres from Copán, thermal springs, reached by a road through villages and beautiful scenery. 45 minutes by vehicle, pick-ups go sometimes for about US$17, shared between passengers. Tours are run by *Tunkul, Vamos a Ver and Tres Locos* (the last two in conjunction, four-hour evening trip US$5 per person). Cross the river and follow the trail up to the springs but only swim in the river where the very hot water has mixed with the cold. Changing facilities and toilets in the park, open 0800-1700, US$1.10 entrance fee, take all food and water.

Nine kilometres from Copán is **Santa Rita**, a small, colonial town on the Copán River with cobblestones and red roofs (*Hospedaje Santa Rita* and unnamed restaurant recommended, off main road next to Esso, speciality tajadas, huge portions, outdoors, floor covered in pine needles, cheap). A lovely four-hour walk goes upstream (expect to get wet feet, take swimsuit) to El Rubí, a boulder and waterfall, and beyond to a small rock canyon, more waterfalls, and return through the countryside with lovely views of the valley and town. Outside Santa Rita, 11 kilometres from Copán Ruinas, is **A** *Hacienda El Jaral*, formerly a working farm, now a hotel with a cluster of duplex cottages on a broad, tropical flower lined lawn, with a pool, good horses to hire or for guided tours, mountain hiking nearby and a lake where egrets return most of the year in the evening to spend the night, in October-May up to 3,000 have been seen there; included on several tour programmes, owned by the Bueso family, T5524457, F5524891. Recommended. Also has a petrol/gas station.

AL *Posada Real de Copán*, on hill overlooking Copán, T6514480, F6514497, operated by Biltmore, in the Best Western chain, full service major hotel, restaurant, too far from town to walk. **AL-C** *Marina*, on the Plaza occupying almost an entire block, T6514070-2, F6514477, hmarinac@netsys.hn, www.hotelmarinacopan.hn, swimming pool, sauna, restaurant, bar, live marimba music at weekends, also caters for tour groups, large rooms with TV, suites, very tasteful and spacious, friendly, nice atmosphere. Recommended. **A** *Plaza Copán*, on Parque Central, T6514508, F6514039, h copan@hondutel.hn, 20 a/c rooms, hot water, TV, pool, cafetería, email service for guests. **A-B** *Madrugada*, T6514092, F5578830, take street from southeast corner of Parque, go down steps and turn right, by the river, unprepossessing

Sleeping
Generally hotels are expensive here compared with other places in Honduras.

Copán

with thanks to John Dupuis , Honduras Tips

To Hot Springs

To Guatemala

To Copán Archaeological Park

Souvenirs Maya Mundo

Clinic

Palacio Municipal

Parque Central

Market

Museum

Cathedral

Lavandería Justo a Tiempo

Copán Net

Galería de Arte Machi

N

Not to scale

■ **Sleeping**	10 Marina Copán	2 Carnitas Nia Lola
1 Acrópolis Maya	11 Paty	3 Comedor Isabel
2 Brisas de Copán	12 Plaza Copán	4 El Sesteo
3 California	13 Popol Nah	5 La Llama del Bosque
4 Camino Maya & Elisa's Café	14 Via Via	6 Los Gauchos
5 La Casa del Café & Iguana Azul	15 Yaragua	7 Típicos El Rancho
6 La Posada	16 Yaxpac	8 Tres Locos
7 Los Gemelos		9 Tunkul
8 Los Jaguares	● **Eating**	10 Vamos de Ver
9 Madrugada	1 Bar Macanudo	

exterior but nice colonial-style interior, 15 rooms (upstairs best). **A-B** *Camino Maya*, corner of main plaza, T6514646, F6514517, hcmaya@david.intertel.hn, with bath, good restaurant, rooms bright and airy, cable TV, fans, rooms on courtyard quieter than street, English spoken, nice patio garden with parrot, balcony on some upstairs rooms. **B** *Acrópolis Maya*, opposite, and under same ownership as, Brisas de Copán, T6514634, F6514118, large rooms, a/c, TV, with bath, hot water, parking, accepts credit cards, new. **B** *Los Jaguares* on Plaza opposite Marina, T6514451/4075, 9 rooms, with bath, TV, a/c, hot water, friendly staff, locked parking, no restaurant. **B** *La Casa de Café*, 4½ blocks west of Plaza, T6514620, F6514623, casadecafe@mayanet.hn, www.todomundo.com/casadecafe, renovated colonial home, with breakfast, coffee all day, library, good information, lovely designed garden, beautiful views, friendly and interesting hosts, English spoken, very popular so best to reserve in advance, tours arranged through Xupi Tours, protected parking. Recommended. **C** *La Posada*, north of Parque Central, being remodelled 1999, private bath, hot water, fan, basic old rooms **F**. **C-D** *Yaragua*, ½ block east of the Plaza, T6514464, F6514050, with bath, hot water, safe, clean, friendly.

D *Bella Vista*, on hill by former police barracks, T6514502, clean, safe but poorly situated, good value. **C** *Hotelito Brisas de Copán*, T6514118, terrace, modern rooms with bath, hot water, quiet, limited parking. Recommended. **D** *Popul Nah*, on street off southeast corner of Plaza, T6514095, fan, hot shower, safe parking, very clean, but cockroaches, hospitable. Recommended. **D** *Paty*, T6514021, F6514109, under the same ownership as one of the minibus companies, fan, bath, no meals, good value. Recommended, lots of parking. **D** *Café ViaVia Copán*, next to Tunkul, T6514652, part of a worldwide Belgian network of cafés (Joken Tours), breakfast US$2.75, special price for students with card and for stays over a week, hot water, good beds, bar. **E** *California*, opposite Los Gemelos, with Bar Tres Locos, run by chatty American, nice rooms with original décor, good beds, fan, laundry, book exchange, nice lawn, good cooking, a bit expensive (evening meal), good place for backpackers and women travelling alone. **E** *Hotelito Yaxpac*, opposite *Típicos El Rancho*, 1 block north of Parque Central, T6514025, 4 rooms with bath, cold water, nice view of countryside from balcony. **E** *La Siesta*, 2 blocks west of main plaza on street that is plaza's northern edge, with bath, cheaper without, clean, fan, laundry facilities on roof. **F** *Honduras*, T6514082, dark, only for the desperate. **F** *Hospedaje Los Gemelos*, one block down from Banco Occidente, T6514077, F6514315, maricela@hondutel.hn, without bath, clean, fans, good value, best place for backpackers, friendly, pleasant patio, good for single women, also laundry facilties, email, internet, phone and fax service. Recommended. **E-F** *Hostel Iguana Azul*, next to La Casa de Café and under same ownership, T/F6514632, www.todomundo.com/iguanaazul, dormitory style bunk beds in 2 rooms, shared bath, also 3 more private double rooms, hot water, simple, clean, comfortable, common area with TV, books, magazines, travel guides (including the Handbook), maps, garden, fans, safe box, English spoken. **F** *Posada del Viajero*, on road into town from the border, T6514638, some rooms with bath, cheaper without, cold shower, meals served, relaxing.

Camping Free camping by the Texaco station next to the ruins, no facilities. Also some houses will accommodate cheaply, enquire (eg house opposite *Popul Nah*).

Eating *Llama del Bosque*, 2 blocks west of Plaza, open for breakfast, lunch and dinner, bar, pleasant, recommended, large portions of reasonable food, try their carnitas típicas, touristy, long waits common because of popularity, meals about US$5.50, soup US$2.25. *Tunkul*, opposite Llama del Bosque, good food includes vegetarian meals, large portions, not cheap, happy hour 2000-2100, always loud music, large outdoor patio, nice for relaxing breakfast, helpful. Recommended. Next door is *Café ViaVia Copán* (see above), cultural events as well as food, bar, lodging. *Comedor Isabel*, next to Llama del Bosque, typical comedor atmosphere, green walls, slow service, relatively clean, average food, dinner US$2.50. *Café Cinema Vamos a Ver*, 1 block from Plaza, Dutch owned, Dutch cheese, lots of vegetables, good sandwiches and snacks, complete dinner US$5, shows films at 1900, US$1, pleasant, good value, open 0700-2200. Recommended. *Elisa's* at

Camino Maya, excellent food at reasonable prices, pleasant, good service. Recommended. *El Sesteo*, next to Hotel Paty, typical lunch US$3, dinner US$3-4.50, non-descript atmosphere. *Típicos El Rancho*, 1 block west of bridge to ruins, good and cheap, open-air restaurant, friendly, delicious tacos, turritos, licuados etc. Recommended. *Chuspi'p Pollo*, opposite Hotel La Siesta, typical comedor, ugly, hangout for beer-drinking cowboys, fried chicken, sometimes open until 0130. *Tres Locos* for New York style pizza and bar, simple menu, good breakfasts, almost opposite Los Gemelos. *Los Gauchos*, Uruguayan grilled specialities, expensive but good quality meats, renovated house, open 1000-2200. *Carnitas Nía Lola*, 2 blocks south of Parque Central, at end of road, nice view over river and valley, popular meeting place, open 0700-2200, see 'la fragua' bellows and brazier, comida típica, inexpensive, busy bar, relaxed atmosphere. *Comedor El Jacal*, opposite El Sesteo, typical food, recommended for decent budget meal, breakfast, lunch and dinner, cable TV, can arrange rented rooms. *Café Welchez* in Hotel Marina Copán, good cakes but expensive and coffee 'unpredictable'. *Bar Macanudo*, on same street as Copán Net, next block, loud and popular, good for drinks.

Transport

Air 1 to 3-day trip from Guatemala City to Copán can be arranged by air (40 minutes' flight to a finca airstrip, then bus, 25 minutes), US$180 includes guide for 1 day, hotel accommodation extra. Try Jungle Flying (also charter flights between Tikal and Copán), Av Hincapié, 18 C, Zona 13, Guatemala City, T2604920, 2604917, F2314995, or many other agencies.

Buses Direct buses from San Pedro Sula in front of *Hotel Palmira*, to Copán Ruinas, *Gama Express*, T6614421, 0700 and 1930, returns from Copán 0600 and 1500, *Cheny Express*, 1400, returns 0700, tickets in Copán from Souvenirs *Maya Mundo* next to *Los Gemelos*, both comfortable, reclining seats, efficient, good value, highly recommended. Express minibus service to San Pedro Sula, airport and Tela from *Hotel Paty*, US$11, and to La Ceiba US$18.50. Numerous small boys greet you on arrival to carry bags or offer directions for a small fee. There are regular slow buses (Copanecos or Torito lines) from San Pedro Sula to La Entrada, US$1.50 (2½ hours), 0345-1700; from La Entrada to Copán, US$1.85 by bus (2 hours), from 0500 every 45 minutes (or when full) till 1630, stops at entrance to ruins. If going by bus from San Pedro Sula, and returning, it is impossible to see Copán in 1 day. Three early morning buses from Copán to Santa Rosa, 3½ hours, US$2. Buses from Copán to La Entrada for connecting buses going north or south, 0400-1700.

Motoring There is a Texaco filling station by the ruins. Note that the main bridge into town was badly damaged by Hurricane Mitch and can no longer take vehicles. It is, however, possible to drive by an alternative route into Copán Ruinas. A huge landslide wrecked a part of the road between Santa Rita and Copán, but a detour was soon in operation.

Directory

Banks TCs (poor rate) may be changed at the *Banco de Occidente* on plaza (0800-1200, 1400-1600, Mon-Fri, 0800-1100 Sat, very crowded on Sat), *Banco Atlántida*, *Banhcreser*, next to Atlántida, all three take Visa, but no ATM. Guatemalan currency can be changed at Copán; it is possible to change quetzales near where buses leave for the border or Gabriela shop next to Camino Maya Hotel, which also accepts Amex TCs. **Communications** Post Office: next to museum, open Mon-Fri 0800-1200, 1400-1700, Sat 0800-1200, beautiful stamps available; stamps also sold at corner shop opposite. Telephone: phone calls can be made from the office of Hondutel 0800 to 2100. Email: *Copán Net*, one block southwest of Parque Central, copannet@hondutel.hn, open 0800-2100 (but Sat morning is for local children), 2 lempiras/minute. Also at *Hotel Los Gemelos*, see above, same rates for internet, plus charges to send and receive email, phone and fax service. **Language schools** *Ixbalanque*, T/F6514432, ixbalan@gbm.hn, one to one teaching plus board and lodging with local family, US$125 for 1 week, 4 hrs teaching a day. **Laundry** *Lavandería Justo a Tiempo*, one block south, half block west from main plaza, same day service. **Tour companies & travel agents** *Go Native Tours*, T/F6514432, same number for Ixbalanque language school (see above). *MC Tours*, in *Hotel Marina*, T6514453, mctour@netsys.hn local and countrywide tours. Horses for hire (but look around and bargain). You will probably be approached with offers of horse hire: a good way of getting to nearby attractions. Horse riding to Los Sapos and Las Sepulturas, US$10 for 3 hrs. Several birdwatching tours, contact Jorge Barraza, a local guide, or a tour operator such as *Xukpi Tours*, T6514435. **Useful addresses** Immigration: office in Palacio Municipal.

Frontier with
Guatemala
*There are many money
changers but for US$
or TCs, change in
Copán, better rates.*

Honduran immigration The Honduran immigration office is at El Florido on the border and you get stamps there. They charge entry and exit fees (see **Documents** page 850) ask for a receipt for any 'extra' charges.

Leaving Honduras by private vehicle If leaving with a vehicle, you need 3 stamps on your strip from Migración US$, Tránsito (where they take your Proviso Provisional), and Aduana (where they take you Pase Fronterizo document and cancel the stamp in your passport).

Guatemalan consulate For visas, either San Pedro Sula or Tegucigalpa. Guatemalan tourist cards are available at the border.

Transport Pick-up trucks run all day until 1700 every day between Copán Ruinas and the border, 30 minutes, connecting with buses to Guatemalan destinations, erratic service. The cost should be about US$2.50. Bargain for a fair price. There is also a bus which charges US$0.80, schedule unknown. There is a direct minibus service Copán-Antigua Guatemala run by *Monarcas Travel* at Los Gemelos, Copán, US$45, 1500 daily, pick up from hotels (in Antigua 7 Av Norte No 15A, T/78324779, geotours@gua.net, leaves 0400).

Just to visit Copán, those needing visas can obtain a 72-hour exit pass at the border but you must recross at the same border post before expiry.

To enter (or return to) Guatemala an alternative route is via Santa Rosa de Copán and Nueva Ocotepeque (see below and Guatemala chapter for transit into Guatemala).

Santa Rosa de Copán

153 kilometres by road from San Pedro Sula, Santa Rosa is the centre of a rich agricultural and cattle-raising area. The town is set in some of the best scenery in Honduras; the weather is remarkably fine. Much maize and tobacco is grown in the area. The Flor de Copán traditional hand-rolling cigar factory next to the *Hotel Elvir* may give tours, ask for the production manager; large selection of cigars for sale, well worth a visit. Santa Rosa is a colonial town with cobbled streets. Originally known as Los Llanos, it was made a municipality in 1812 and became capital of the department of Copán when it was split off from Gracias (now Lempira). The central plaza and church are perched on a hilltop. There is a quieter parque at C Real Centenario y 6 Av SO, which is fenced, a nice place to relax. The main market is at 1 C and 3 Av NE, not much of note except the leather goods. Farmers' markets are held daily in Barrio Santa Teresa, take 4 C SE past 5 Av SE, and at 4 C SE and 5 Av SE on Sunday 0500 to 1000. The bus station is, unfortunately, at the bottom of the hill but there is a bus. The town holds a festival to Santa Rosa de Lima from 21 to 31 August. The Tobacco Queen is crowned at the end of the week.

There are buses from Santa Rosa west to the small town of **Dulce Nombre de Copán** (US$0.55). There are rooms available next to the Hondutel office. Hikers can continue west through mountains to stay at the primitive village of **San Agustín** (buses and pick-ups from Santa Rosa), take hammock or sleeping bag, continuing next day through Mirasol you reach the Ruinas road at El Jaral. Now you are 11 kilometres east of Copán ruins (see Copán **Excursions** above).

Numerous daily buses go through **Cucuyagua** (40 minutes, US$0.60, Restaurant *Brisas de Copán*, on side street, ask, good, clean), scenic river, good swimming and camping on its banks and **San Pedro de Copán**, an attractive village and an entry point into the Parque Nacional Celaque; to **Corquín**, *altitude*: 850 metres (US$0.75, two hours), two good *pensiones*, one **F** with a charming garden, recommended. From here take a bus, six a day (also one bus a day from Santa Rosa de Copán) or a rough, dusty, one and a half-hours ride in a pick-up truck (US$0.75) to **Belén Gualcho**, a Lenca village, 1,500 metres up in mountains, a good base to explore the

surrounding mountains and valleys, especially north towards Monte Celaque. Belén
Gualcho is perched on a mountainside, with two colonial churches, one architecturally fine with three domes and a fine colonnaded façade with twin bell towers, the
other rustic. There is an interesting Sunday market from 0500, over by 1000. There
are numerous short walks from town in most directions, all affording postcard-type
views. You can walk two hours to waterfalls (90 metres drop). Head for El Paraíso
then ask for directions. Everyone knows where they are.

Sleeping and eating Hotels fill up quickly on Saturday as traders arrive for the Sunday market. **In Belén Gualcho** All under US$3: **F** *Hotelito El Carmen* (2 blocks east down from the
church in the plaza), friendly, clean, good views. Recommended. **F** *Hotel Belén*.
F *Hospedaje Doña Carolina*; electricity goes off at 2130 so take a torch and candle. Films are
shown every evening at 1930, ask anyone, US$0.10. *Comedor Mery*, 1 block northwest of
plaza, good food in a welcoming family atmosphere. *Las Haciendas*, also good. 2 more
comedores on south side of plaza and east side on corner with store.

Transport To Santa Rosa daily at 0430 (Sunday at 0930). To Gracias from main plaza at
0400, 0500, 1330.

A mule trail connects Belén Gualcho with **San Manuel de Colohuete** (*Altitude*:
1,500 metres), which has a magnificent colonial church whose façade is sculpted
with figures of saints. Buses to San Manuel from Gracias at 1300, four hours, and
usually a pickup returning in the evening. There are no hotels so you must ask villagers about places to stay. There is an equally fine colonial church 30 minutes by
four-wheel drive vehicle to the southwest at **San Sebastián Colosuca** (*Altitude*:
1,550 metres). The village has a mild climate (two *hospedajes*; or try Don Rubilio;
food at Doña Clementina García or Doña Alicia Molina). The *feria de San Sebastián*

Santa Rosa de Copán centre

With thanks to Michael J Grey

■ Sleeping	3 Continental	10 Hospedaje Santa Rosa
1 Blanca Nieves	4 Copán	11 Hospedaje Suyapa
2 Castillo	5 Elvir	12 Maya Central
	6 Hospedaje Calle Real	13 Rosario
	7 Hospedaje Maya	
	8 Hospedaje San Pedro	**● Eating**
	9 Hospedaje Santa	1 Chiky's
	Eduviges	2 El Rodeo

3 Flamingo
4 Las Haciendas
5 Las Haciendas II
6 On Fu
7 París
8 Pizza Pizza
9 Rincón Colonial
10 Well

☞ *Walking from San Miguel Colohuete to Belén Gualcho*

There is a well-defined, well-used and therefore easy to follow mule trail linking these two villages. Maps are not essential as there are communities at many points along the way where advice can be sought. A map of the area is available from the Lenca Cultural Centre in Gracias.

The path leading away from the village leaves from opposite the pulpería and comedor where the bus drops you, heading west and downhill into a valley. The path is used by four-wheel drive vehicles and continues to San Sebastián. Just after the community of San José, after passing the last house, the path to Belén branches off. A small path leaves the four-wheel drive track and climbs steeply up to your right and more northwest.

One hour: just after Peña Blanca, the path direction becomes unclear after it crosses an area of white chalky rocks. There are several other paths here. The main path heads north and steeply downhill at this point.

Two hours: there is water all the year round in the Quebrada de Rogán.

Three hours: all year round water in Río Gualmite, a short descent. After is a longish, steep ascent.

Four hours: just after this point, the path branches on a large flat grassy area. Both paths lead to Belén Gualcho. The one to the

left drops and crosses the river and then you are faced with a long, arduous and very steep ascent. We would recommend taking the path to the right, which exits to the far right of a grassy area by three small houses.

Five hours: the path climbs as it skirts around the Cerro Capitán. Just after passing the steepest part of the Cerro Capitán, a small landslide forces the path into a descent almost to the river. From here only 20 metres above the river, you can walk steeply down off the path to the river bank where there is the most perfect camp site. Flat, sandy soil in some shade on the edge of a coffee plantation and two metres from the river.

Six hours: from the camping site there is a long, continuous climb before dropping down sharply to cross the river. It is possible, but difficult to cross the river at the point the path meets it. Take a small path off to the right just before the river, which leads to a suspension bridge. From the river it is a long climb, not especially steep, but continuous, to Belén Gualcho. It is situated between two small peaks that can be seen clearly after crossing the river. There are increasing numbers of houses after crossing the river and the odd pulpería where you can buy refrescos or food.

Mike and Pauline Truman

---

is on 20 January. No alcohol may be sold in the village and there are no soldiers here. An hour's walk away is the Cueva del Diablo; six kilometres away is Cerro El Alta with a lagoon at the top. From San Sebastián, a mule trail goes via the heights of Agua Fría to reach the route near the frontier at Tomalá.

Alternatively, one can walk five hours east from San Manuel to **La Campa** (very nice colonial church); for non-walkers there is a daily bus San Manuel-La Campa-Gracias. Irregular transport on the 18 kilometres dirt road to Gracias. There is a *hospedaje* in La Campa, ask at Hondutel. Red pottery is made there. San Matías is the patron saint, *fiesta*: 23-24 February, well worth visiting, thousands celebrate the mostly indigenous traditions.

A paved road runs east from Santa Rosa to San Juan de Opoa, where it turns southeast towards Gracias. At Km 25 from Santa Risa to Gracias is *Las Tres Jotas* (the 3 'J's) run by the Alvarenga family (T6620530, Sr Joel Alvarenga, padre), a tobacco plantation with swimming pools, hot water tubs and a manmade lake in a beautiful setting. There is live marimba music, a nice restaurant and drinks. Entry at week-ends about US$1 to use all facilities. Good walking and views of the Río Higuito; ask about camping. From Santa Rosa there is a two-hour, 0630 and 0730, US$1 bus ride to **Lepaera** (a few hundred inhabitants, very basic *hospedaje*, under US$3, opposite market, and *comedores*, the best one adjoins the market) perched on a lovely moun-tainside east of San Juan de Opoa (also reached from Gracias). One can scale the peak (Cerro Puca, 2,234 metres, stiff climb, start early morning for day trip) or descend on foot by an old mule trail heading back to Santa Rosa (four and a half hours), crossing the river on a swingbridge (*hamaca*), then hitchhiking.

C *Elvir*, C Real Centenario SO, 3 Av SO, T6620103, overpriced, safe, clean, quiet, all rooms have own bath, TV, hot water, drinking water, good but pricey meals in cafetería or restaurant. Recommended. **D** pp *Mayaland*, T6620233, F6620805, opposite bus station, parking, restaurant, cable TV. **D-E** *Continental*, 2 C NO y 2-3 Av, T6620801/2, on 2nd floor, musty, with bath, hot water, fan, cable TV, friendly management. **E** *Copán*, 1 C 3 Av, T6620265, with bath, hot water, **F** without, cell-like rooms but clean, safe, hot water in morning. **E** *Hospedaje Santa Eduviges*, 2 Av NO y 1 C NO, good beds, clean, pleasant, good value but some rooms damp. **E** *Maya Central* (not to be confused with *Hospedaje Maya*), 1 C NO y 3 Av NO, T6620073, with bath, cold shower, pleasant. **E** *Rosario*, 3 Av NE No 139, T6620211, cold water, with bath, **F** without. **F** *Blanca Nieves*, 3 Av NE, Barrio Mercedes, T6621312, new, clean, safe, with bath and hot water, cheaper without, good value, laundry facilities. **F** *Castillo*, next door to *Maya Central*, T6620368, new, clean. **F** (under US$3): *Hospedaje Calle Real*, Real Centenario y 6 Av NE, clean, quiet, friendly, best of the cheaper places but sometimes water failures. *Hospedaje Maya*, 1 C NE y 3-4 Av, noisy, not clean, only for the desperate, car park. *Hospedaje Santa Rosa*, 3 Av NE No 42, Barrio Mercedes, T6621421, basic, clean, safe, cold water, laundry facilities, welcoming. *Hospedaje San Pedro*, 2 C NE, basic, dirty, OK at night, noisy by day. *Hospedaje Suyapa*, 2 C NE, basic, noisy in the day, OK at night.

Sleeping
■ *on maps*
Price codes:
see inside front cover

Flamingo, 1 Av SE, off main plaza, T6620654, relatively expensive but good pasta and chop suey, popular with locals. *Las Haciendas*, 1 Av SE, varied menu, filling *comida corriente*. Recommended. *Las Haciendas II*, 1 C SO, smaller, more intimate, same menu. *Rincón Colonial*, 1 Av SE, typical local cuisine, good, less expensive than its neighbours. *Paris*, C Real Centanario, ½ block from Parque Central, expensive but very good food, sit in nice garden. *El Rodeo*, 1 Av SE, good menu, specializes in steaks, nice atmosphere (if you don't mind animal skins on the walls), pricey. *Pizza Pizza*, Real Centenario 5 Av NE, 4½ blocks from main plaza, one of the best in town, good pizza and pasta, pleasant surroundings in old colonial house, great coffee, best meeting place, US owned, good source of information. Recommended. *Chikys*, 1 C SO y 1 Av SO, Mexican, good food, atmosphere, music and beer. Recommended. *On Fu*, 1 Av SO, near *Chikys*, 2nd floor, Chinese and local dishes, large servings, good vegetables, attentive service. *Well*, 3 C SE, Chinese, a/c, huge portions, good value and service. There is a good *comedor* at the bus terminal, *Merendera El Campesino*. On the *carretera La Gran Villa*, some of the tastiest meats and meals in Santa Rosa, run by Garifuna family. Recommended.

Eating
● *on maps*

Discotheques *Glamour*, *Tropical's* (one block from *Hotel Copán*).

Entertainment

Buses from Santa Rosa to **Tegucigalpa** (lovely scenery, lush pine forests, colonial villages), Toritos, leaves at 0400 from terminal, Monday-Saturday, 0400 and 1000 Sunday, US$5, 7-8 hours. To **Gracias** Transportes Lempira, 0745, 0915, 1130, 1345, 1515, 2 hours, US$1.50 (road paved). To **San Pedro Sula**, US$2, 4 hours, every 45 minutes from 0400-1730, express service daily 2½ hours, US$2.70 (Empresa Torito), bus to **La Entrada**, 1 hour, US$0.50. To **Copán Ruinas**, 4 hours for 100 kilometres on good road, US$2, several direct daily (eg Etumi at 1130, 1215, 1345), but you may have to change at La Entrada. South on paved road to **Nueva Ocotepeque** 6 daily, US$1.50, 2½ hours. There you change buses for Guatemala (1 hour to border, US$1, bus leaves hourly until 1700). Local 'El Urbano' bus to centre from bus station (on Carretera Internacional, 2 kilometres below town, opposite *Hotel Mayaland*), US$0.35; taxi US$0.50. If coming from the Guatemalan border at Nueva Ocotepeque, the bus will stop at the end of town near Av Centenario (main street).

Transport

Banks *Banco de Occidente* (best exchange rates) and *Atlántida*, both on main plaza. Atlántida has Visa ATM, maximum withdrawal US$30. *Banadesa*, and 2 branches of *Bancahsa* (fast service) on C Real Centenario (Occidente and Bancahsa change TCs). **Hospitals & medical services** *Clínica Médica Las Gemas*, 2 Av NO, near Hotel Elvir, T6661428, run by Dr Soheil Rajabian (speaks English among other languages), first class attention. **Dentist:** *Dr Ricardo Reyes*, 3 Av 349, Barrio Santa Teresa, T6620007. **Tour companies & travel agents** *Lenca Land Trails*, at *Hotel Elvir*, T6620805, F6620103, run by Max Elvir,

Directory

organizes cultural tours of the Lenca mountain villages in western Honduras, excellent source of information about the region. **Guide:** Ask at *Flor de Copán* cigar factory for *José Pineda* who runs tours to tobacco plantations at weekends, informative, only 30 minutes from town, lovely countryside. **Useful addresses** *Immigration*, Av Alvaro Contreras y 2 C NO, helpful, extensions available.

Gracias

Population: 19,380
Altitude: 765m
Colour map 4, grid C4

The main road continues to Gracias, 50 kilometres from Santa Rosa, the largest town on this road. It is one of the oldest and most historic settlements in the country, dominated by the highest mountains in Honduras, Montañas de Celaque, Puca and Opulaca. It is a charming, friendly town and both the town and surrounding countryside are worth a visit.

racias was the centre from which Francisco de Montejo, thrice Governor of Honduras, put down the great Indian revolt of 1537-38. Alonzo de Cáceres, his lieutenant, besieging Lempira the Indian leader in his impregnable mountain-top fortress at Cerquín, finally lured him out under a flag of truce, ambushed him and treacherously killed him. When the Audiencia de los Confines was formed in 1544 Gracias became for a time the administrative centre of Central America.

Sights

There are three colonial churches, San Sebastián, Las Mercedes, San Marcos (a fourth, Santa Lucía, is southwest of Gracias), and a restored fort, with two fine Spanish cannon, on a hill immediately west of centre, five minutes' walk. The fort, **El Castillo San Cristóbal**, has been well restored, and at the foot of the northern ramparts is the tomb of Juan Lindo, President of Honduras 1847-1852, who introduced free education through a system of state schools.

Excursions

Some six kilometres from Gracias along the road to Esperanza (side road signposted), swim in hot, communal thermal pools in the forest, Balneario Aguas Termales (one hour by a path, one hour 20 minutes by the road). To find the path, walk two kilometres beyond the bridge over Río Arcagual to a second bridge before which turn right by a white house. Climb the hill and walk 55 metres along the top where a left hand path leads to the pools, entry US$1.50, open daily 0600-2000, rental of towels, hammock, inner tube, restaurant/bar, recommended. Good place to barbecue.

18 kilometres away is La Campa (see page 930). From Gracias buses go through coffee plantations to San Rafael (makeshift accommodation) from where one can hitch to El Níspero (*pensión*) and catch a bus to Santa Bárbara. Also on the road to San Rafael, a short detour leads to **La Iguala**, a tiny village attractively set between two rivers, magnificent colonial church. Irregular transport from/to Gracias.

It takes at least a whole day to climb from Gracias to the summit of **Monte Celaque** (2,849 metres, the highest point in Honduras). Most people allow two days to enjoy the trip. The trail begins from behind the visitors' centre of the Celaque National Park (1,400 metres) which is eight kilometres from Gracias, two hours' walk. There are several intersections, best to ask at each. Entry fee US$2.50 plus US$1 per night. The first five and a half kilometres can be driven in a standard car, the rest only with four-wheel drive. Transport can be arranged through the Lenca Centre at US$5 per person, minimum three people, worth it. Armando Mondragon, at Texaco station, T8984002, does trips, including lunch. At the centre there are seven beds, shower and cooking facilities, US$1, drinks available, well-maintained. There is another cabin nearby with 10 beds. Take a torch and sleeping bag. Behind the centre is a trail going down to the river where a crystal clear pool and waterfall make for wonderful bathing. Ask the guide the exact way or pay US$6 for the guide. There is a warden, Miguel, living nearby (he can supply food and beer but safer to take supplies from Gracias), but contact Cohdefor in Gracias before leaving for full information. The Lenca Centre has maps of area and hires out camping gear. There are a number of international volunteers working on the project. Division Chief

Enrique is exceedingly helpful and friendly. There is a trail all the way to the summit (trees are marked with ribbons) which takes at least six hours: the first three hours are easy to a campsite at 2,000 metres (campamento Don Tomás) where there is small hut (locked, key at the centre), the rest of the way is steep. There is another camping site, *Campamento Naranjo*, with water, at about 2,500 metres. Between these two sites, it is particularly steep and in cloud forest. Look out for spider monkeys. Above 2,600 metres quetzals have been seen. Many hikers don't bother with the summit as it is forested and enclosed, four hours down to the visitor centre. Don't forget good hiking boots, warm clothing, insect repellent, and given the dense forest and possibility of heavy cloud, a compass is recommended for safety. Also, beware of snakes. There are plans to extend the trail westward from the summit to Belén Gualcho (see above) and to create a nature trail near the visitors' centre.

Visiting the other peaks around Gracias is more complicated but interesting. Information, maps which you can photocopy, camping gear, guided tours can be found at the Lenca Cultural Centre.

Sleeping

D-E *Posada de Don Juan*, C Principal opposite Banco de Occidente, T6561020, F6561247, good beds, great hot showers, nice big towels, laundry, some rooms have TV, parking. **D** Los

Gracias

To Santa Rosa de Copán

Texaco

Email

5

Cohdefor

Las Mercedes

1

Palacio Municipal

Cohdefor

Market

4

Parque Central

3

2

Castillo San Cristóbal

3 5

San Marcos

1

4

Río Arcagual

To La Esperanza

2

San Sebastián

To Santa Lucía & Celaque | To La Campa

N

Not to scale

Path to Aguas Termales ▼

■ **Sleeping**	4 Posada de Don Juan	2 El Señorial
1 Erick	5 San Antonio	3 Guancascos & Centro
2 Iris		Cultural Los Lencas
3 La Posada del	● **Eating**	4 La Fonda
Rosario	1 Alameda	5 Rancho de Lily

Honduras

Lencas Cultural Centre at *Guancascos* rents 3 furnished rooms in **La Posada del Rosario**, west end of Hondutel road, T6561219, F6561234, old colonial house, family atmosphere, bath, hot water, also rents 2-room cabin at **Villa Verde** adjacent to Monte Celaque Visitors' Centre. **E Colonial**, 1 block south of *Erick*, T6561238, with bath, fan, bar, restaurant, very good. **F Iris**, 3 blocks south of Plaza, 1 block west, opposite San Sebastián church, T6561086, clean, cold water, closes at 2200, disco Saturday. **F San Antonio**, no sign, main street, 2 blocks from Texaco station, T6561071, clean, pleasant, friendly, good. **E Erick**, same street as bus office, T6561066, with bath, cheaper without (cold shower), TV, comfortable beds, fresh, bright, clean, good value, no laundry facilities, stores luggage, and shop open daily with trekker food, very convenient. Recommended. **F Herrera**, shared bath, noisy, basic. **F Hospedaje Corazón de Jesús**, on main street by market, clean, OK. **F Hospedaje El Milagro**, north side of market, basic.

Eating *Guancascos* and popular cultural centre **Los Lencas**, on Parque Central in front of church, T6561219 (reported to be relocating to *Posada del Rosario*), owned by Dutch lady, good variety of local and international food, also vegetarian, excellent breakfast, purified water used in fruit juices, recommended, music, exhibition of Lenca pottery, tourist information centre, also book swap and good local maps for walking. **Alameda**, 3 blocks west of *La Fonda*, white house, no sign, open 1100-2200 for lunch and dinner, excellent cooking, meat, fish, some vegetarian dishes, salads, main courses US$3-4, *comida corriente* US$2, elegant setting, dining room faces wild garden with fruit trees, not to be missed, under same management is **La Fonda**, 2 blocks south of Parque Central, good food, good value, attractively decorated. Recommended. **El Señorial**, main street, simple meals and snacks, once house of Dr Juan Lindo. **Comedor Graciano** and **Pollo Gracianito** on main street, good value. **Rancho de Lily**, 3 blocks west of Hondutel, good value, rustic cabin, bar service, good snacks. For breakfast, *comedores* near the market, or, better, the restaurant at *Hotel Iris* (good *comida corriente* too) or *Guancascos*.

Transport To **La Esperanza** a mail car goes Tuesday, Thursday, Saturday, 0400, or take bus to Erandique, 1315, get off at San Juan from where bus goes to La Esperanza the next day, or hitch, or rides can be taken on pick-up trucks for US$1.50 (dep 0700 or earlier from south end of main street on highway). The road is much improved as far as San Juan. You can easily find a pick-up this far, 1½ hours, US$0.90. Thereafter it is all-weather and can be rough. There is a bus service from Gracias to **Santa Rosa de Copán**, US$1, from 0530, 6 times a day, 1½ hours; beautiful journey through majestic scenery, the road is paved. Daily bus service to **Lepaera** 1400, 1½ hours, US$0.85; daily bus to **San Manuel de Colohuete** at 1300. Cotral bus ticket office is 1 block north of Parque Central. Torito bus, a few metres from the main terminal, has buses to the Guatemalan frontier at Agua Caliente, one at 1000, change buses at Nueva Ocotepeque.

Directory **Banks** *Banco de Occidente*. **Communications** Hondutel and Post Office: 1 block south of Parque Central, closes 1100 on Sat. **Cultural centres** Music lessons including marimba, flute etc available, Ramón Alvarenga, 2 blocks west of the parque central on the same side as Iglesia San Marcos. **Tour companies & travel agents** *Guancascos' Tourist Centre*, on Parque Central arranges tours and expeditions to Monte Celaque Parque Nacional, local villages and other attractions.

Southwest from Gracias, up in the Celaque mountains is Belén Gualcho. Also Corquín, San Pedro de Copán and Cucuyagua on or just off the highway between Santa Rosa and Nueva Ocotepeque (see page 928).

Gracias to Erandique

After Gracias, the road runs 52 kilometres to **San Juan del Caite** (two *hospedajes*, *Lempira* and *Sánchez*, two restaurants nearby, helpful people and Peace Corps workers). From here a dirt road runs 26 kilometres south to **Erandique** (*Population*: 10,000), founded in 1560. Set high in pine-clad mountains not far from the border with El Salvador, Erandique is a friendly town, and very beautiful. Lempira was born nearby, and was killed a few kilometres away. The third weekend in January is the local *fiesta* of San

Sebastián. Best time to visit is at the weekend. Market days are Friday and Sunday. Each of the three *barrios* has a nice colonial church. There is one basic *hospedaje*, G, run by the elderly Doña Bárbara in the main street and one simple *Comedor Inestroza* which can serve you eggs, beans and tortillas; no electricity, torch essential. For the visitor there are lakes, rivers, waterfalls, springs and bathing ponds; you need to ask around. Camping is possible outside town by the small lagoon. Nearby is **San Antonio** where fine opals (not cut gems, but stones encased in rock) are mined and may be purchased. The many hamlets in the surrounding mountains are reached by roads that have been resurfaced or recently built. The landscapes are magnificent.

Transport There are minibuses to Erandique from bridge on road to La Esperanza 1100 daily, although most people go by truck from Gracias (there is sometimes a van service as far as San Juan) or La Esperanza (change trucks at San Juan intersection, very dusty). Return minibus to Gracias at 0500 daily, which connects with the bus to La Esperanza in San Juan. Trucks leave Erandique 0700 daily, but sometimes earlier, and sometimes a 2nd one leaves around 0800 for Gracias, otherwise be prepared for a long wait for a pick-up.

There are several roads radiating from Erandique, including one to **Mapulaca** and the frontier with El Salvador (no migración or aduana or bridge here, at the Río Lempa), a road to San Andrés and another to Piraera (all passable with a car).

Beyond San Juan del Caite the main, but still rough and stony, road winds through beautiful mountain pine forests 43 kilometres to La Esperanza. From there the road continues in good condition 98 kilometres to Siguatepeque. Capital of Intibucá Department, La Esperanza is an old colonial town in a pleasant valley. It has an attractive church in front of the park. There is a grotto carved out of the mountainside west of the town centre, a site of religious festivals. Good views. Market: Thursday and Sunday, at which Lenca Indians from nearby villages sell wares and food but no handicrafts. Nearby is **Yaramanguila**, an Indian village. The area is excellent for walking in forested hills, with lakes and waterfalls. In December-January it is very cold. You can hike to **Cerro de Ojos**, a hill to the northwest and visible from La Esperanza. It is forested with a clearing on top littered with many cylindrical holes. No one knows how they were formed, a strange phenomenon. The turning to this hill is on the La Esperanza to San Juan road. Ask for directions.

La Esperanza
Altitude: 1,485m
Colour map 4, grid C4

Sleeping There are simple but pleasant *pensiones*, eg **E** *Hotel Solis*, T8982080, 1 block east of market, bath and hot water, restaurant. Recommended. **F** *El Rey*, in Barrio La Morera, T8982078, clean, friendly. **F** *Hotel Mina*, T8982071, good beds, clean, very friendly, 1 block south of east side of market, food available. **F** *Hotel y Comedor San Antonio*. **F** *La Esperanza*, T8982068, with bath, cheaper without, warm water, clean, TV, friendly, good meals. **F** *Rosario*, basic, on road to Siguatepeque. **F** *Mejía Batres*, ½ block from Parque Central, with bath, clean, friendly, excellent value.

Eating *Restaurant Magus*, 1 block east of Plaza, 'good food in a formica video bar atmosphere'. Unnamed restaurant in front of Iglesia de la Esperanza, very good *comida corriente*, worth it. *Lucky's*, excellent meat dishes as well as hamburgers. *Pizza Venezia*, on edge of town towards Marcala, good Italian dishes. *Café El Ecológico*, corner of Parque Central, home-made cakes and pastries, fruit drinks, delicious home-made jams.

Festivals The third week in **July** is the *Festival de la Papa*. **8 December** is the fiesta of the *Virgen de la Concepción*.

Transport Buses from La Esperanza to **Tegucigalpa** several daily (Cobramil, also to San Pedro Sula, and Joelito, 4 hours, US$2.60), to **Siguatepeque** 0700, 0900, last at 1000, US$1.20, 2 hours; bus, La Esperanza, Siguatepeque, Comayagua at 0600; buses also go from La Esperanza to the Salvadorean border; bus stops by market. Hourly minibuses to

Yaramanguila, 30 minutes. Daily bus to **Marcala** 2 hours at 1230 (but check), US$0.80 (truck, US$1.20, 2¼ hours). Daily minibus service to San Juan, dep between 1030-1200 from a parking space mid-way between the two bus stops, 2½ hours, pick-ups also do this journey, very crowded; for Erandique, alight at Erandique turn off, 1 kilometre before San Juan and wait for truck to pass (*comedor* plus basic *hospedaje* at intersection). If going to Gracias, stay on the La Eseranza-San Juan bus until the end of the line where a pick-up collects passengers 15 minutes or so later, 1 hour San Juan-Gracias.

Directory Banks *Banco de Occidente, Banco Atlántida* and *Banadesa.*

Marcala
Population: 10,770
Altitude: 1,300m
Colour map 4, grid C4

An unpaved road of 35 kilometres, runs from La Esperanza southeast to Marcala, Department of La Paz (a paved road goes to La Paz). The Marcala region is one of the finest coffee-producing areas of Honduras. Visit 'Comarca' at the entrance to town to get a good idea of how coffee is processed. *Semana Santa* is celebrated with a large procession through main street. *Fiesta* in honour of San Miguel Arcángel, last week of September. No immigration office.

Excursions During the hotter months, March to May for example, a cooler climate can be found in the highlands of La Paz, pleasant temperatures during the day and cold (depending on altitude) at night. Marcala is a good base from which to visit Yarula, Santa Elena, Opatoro, San José and Guajiquiro (see page 867). In the immediate vicinity of Marcala is **Balneario El Manzanal**, three kilometres on the road to La Esperanza; it has a restaurant, two swimming pools and a boating lake, open Saturday and Sunday only. For panoramic views high above Marcala, follow this hike (one hour). Head north past *Hotel Medina*, turn right (east) after the hotel and follow the road up into hills. After two kilometres the road branches. Take the left branch and immediately on the left is a football field. A small path leaves from this field on the west side taking you through a small area of pine trees then out onto a ridge for excellent views. The track continues down from the ridge back to town, passing an unusual cemetery on a hill.

Estanzuela is an area next to a small village of the same name. It is regarded as a favourite spot to visit at weekends. It is a large grassy area next to a river, a dam has been built to provide an area for bathing, excellent camping (no food or drinks sold here). Best visited in the rainy season as the river is higher and the area greener. Take the road to La Esperanza from the Marcala to La Paz road. After 20 minutes (by car) take a right hand turning to Estanzuela. It is a one-hour walk from the turnoff passing the village of Estanzuela to the area.

There are caves nearby on Musula mountain, the Cueva de las Animas in Guamizales and Cueva de El Gigante and El León near La Estanzuela with a high waterfall close by. Other waterfalls are El Chiflador, 67 metres high, Las Golondrinas, La Chorrera and Santa Rosita. Transport goes to La Florida where there is good walking to the village of **Opatoro** and climbing Cerro Guajiquiro. Between Opatoro and Guajiquiro is the **Reserva Las Trancas**, a heavily-forested mountain where quetzales have been seen.

Yarula and **Santa Elena** are two tiny municipalities, the latter about 40 kilometres from Marcala, with beautiful views (bus Marcala-Santa Elena 1230 returns 0500 next day, two hours 45 minutes, enquire at Gámez bus office opposite market; truck daily 0830 returns from Santa Elena at 1300). Sometimes meals are available at *comedores* in Yarula and Santa Elena. The dirt road from Marcala gradually deteriorates, the last 20 kilometres being terrible, high clearance essential, four-wheel drive recommended. In **La Cueva Pintada**, south of Santa Elena, there are precolumbian cave paintings ('*pinturas rupestres*') of snakes, men and dogs; ask for a guide in Santa Elena. Ask also in this village about the 'Danza de los Negritos', performed at the annual fiesta of Santiago, 24-25 March, in front of the church. A special performance may be organized, the dancers wearing their old, wooden masks, if suitable payment is offered.

Hiking around San José

Hike 1 From San José, head northwest down through Limón. Take a small path to the left towards some high ground, a large area covered with pine above some rocky escarpments, about one hour from the centre of San José. A 30-minute trail runs along the outer edge of the high ground with many vantage points overlooking the forest, canyons and mountains. There are many paths which lead down into valleys and canyons below, and a couple of small communities.

Hike 2 Five kilometres from San José is a turnoff called Cerro Bueno (ask locally for directions), with a few houses and a comedor. Explore the terrain to the south, where there are valleys, canyons and waterfalls. Ask for the path to Portillo Norte and Sapotal. Sapotal is a small community in an attractive valley from where you can continue via Aguacatal and Grandeo back to the main La Paz-Marcala road. There are many small villages in this fertile area and almost no tourists.

Mike and Pauline Truman

The village of **San José** (*Altitude*: 1,700 metres) is a Lenca Indian community where the climate can be cool and windy even in the hottest months. The scenery is superb. Good hill walking (see box for two examples; there are many others; also rivers for swimming). Frequent pick-ups from Marcala, and two daily minibuses at about 0815 and 0900; from San José to Marcala minibuses depart at 0615 and 0645, one hour, US$1. There is a good *comedor* 500 metres before plaza on main road, clean and cheap. (**F** unnamed hotel, run by British man, Nayo, or Nigel Potter, basic but comfortable and clean, with meals, he also takes groups to stay in Lenca villages, US$5 per person plus US$10 per person for accommodation in a village; ask for the house of Doña Gloria, or of Profe Vinda or of Nayo or Ruth. At least one of these will be present to meet visitors. Nayo knows most of the local pathways. Good camping 10 minutes' walk away. Write to Nigel J Potter at San José, Marcala, Depto La Paz, CP15201, Honduras.)

Sleeping **E** *Medina*, on main road through town, T8981866, the most comfortable, clean, modern with bath, cafetería, free purified water. Highly recommended. **F** *Hospedaje Edgar*, main street, beginning of town, clean, basic, no sheets (under US$3). **F** *Hospedaje Jairo*, with bath, 2 blocks east of main square. **F** *Hotel-Comedor Rosita* at end of main street, opposite *Darwin*.

Eating *El Mirador*, on entering town by petrol station, nice views from verandah, good food. Recommended. *Darwin*, on main street in centre, cheap breakfasts from 0700. Recommended. *Riviera Linda*, opposite *Hotel Medina*, pleasant atmosphere, spacious, a little pricey but good food. *Jarito*, opposite market entrance, good. *Café Express*, beside Esso, good breakfast and *comida corrida*. Recommended.

Entertainment **Discotheque** *Geminis*.

Transport Buses to **Tegucigalpa** 0500 and 1000 daily via La Paz, 4 hours (bus from Tegucigalpa at 0800 and 1400, Empresa Lila, 4-5 Av, 7 C, No 418 Comayagüela, opposite Hispano cinema); bus to **La Paz** only, 0700, 2 hours, US$1; several minibuses a day, 1½ hours, US$1.50. Bus also from Comayagua. Pick-up truck to **San José** at around 1000 from market, ask for drivers, Don Santos, Torencio, or Gustavo. Bus to **La Esperanza** at about 0830, unreliable, check with driver, Don Pincho, at the supermarket next to where the bus is parked (same street as *Hotel Medina*), 1½-2 hours, otherwise hitching possible, going rate US$1.20. Bus to **San Miguel**, El Salvador, Transportes Wendy Patricia, 0500, 1200, 7 hours, US$3.50, office half block southeast of market.

Directory **Banks** *Banco de Occidente*, *Banhcafé*, and *Banco Sogerín*.

Frontier with El Salvador South of Marcala the road crosses into El Salvador, three kilometres before Perquín (see page 834). There have been several confrontations with the Honduran military in the area but the border dispute has been settled by treaty. Ask locally for security conditions but more travellers are reporting no problems in crossing. There are buses from Marcala to San Miguel, El Salvador, and from Perquín to the frontier in the early morning. The rustic border crossing office is about five kilometres inside Honduras. The road is not shown on some Honduran maps.

Nueva Ocotepeque

Colour map 4, grid C3 There is an old colonial church, La Vieja (or La Antigua) between Nueva Ocotepeque and the border; it is in the village of Antigua Ocotepeque, founded in the 1540s, but destroyed by a flood from Cerro El Pital in 1934.

National Parks The **Guisayote Biological Reserve** protects 35 square kilometres of cloud forest, about 50 percent virgin, reached from the Carretera Occidental. Access is from El Portillo, the name of the pass on the main road north. There are trails and good hiking. El Portillo to El Sillón, the park's southern entrance, 3-5 hours. Twice daily *buseta* from El Sillón to Ocotepque. **El Pital**, three kilometres east of Nueva Ocotepeque, but two kilometres vertically above the town, 2,730 metres; the third highest point in Honduras with several square kilometres of cloud forest. The park has not been developed for tourism.

The **Montecristo National Park** forms part of the Trifinio/La Fraternidad project, administered jointly by Honduras, Guatemala and El Salvador. The park is quite remote from the Honduran side, 2-3 days to the summit, but there are easy-to-follow trails. Access is best from Metapán in El Salvador. From the lookout point at the peak you can see about 90 percent of El Salvador and 20 percent of Honduras on a clear day. The natural resources office, for information, is opposite Texaco, two blocks from *Hotel y Comedor Congolón* at south end of town. Raymond J Sabella of the US Peace Corps has written a very thorough description of the natural and historical attractions of the Department, including hikes, waterfalls and caves.

Sleeping **In Nueva Ocotepeque C-D** *Sandoval*, opposite Hondutel, T6533098, F6533408, rooms and suites, breakfast included, private bath, hot water, cable TV, mini-bar, phone, room service, restaurant attached, good value. **D** *Maya Chortis*, Barrio San José, 4 C 3 Av NE, T6533377, nice rooms with bath, double beds, hot water, fan, TV, mini-bar, phone, room service, quieter rooms at back, including breakfast, good restaurant, good value. **D** *Santander*, clean, good restaurant. **E-F** *San Antonio*, 1 C, 3 Av, T6533072, small rooms but OK. **F** *Gran*, with bath, cold water, pleasant, clean, single beds only, about 250 metres from town at the junction of the roads for El Salvador and Guatemala, just north of town, at Sinuapa. **F** *Hotel y Comedor Congolón*, also bus agency, shared bath, very noisy in morning. **F** *Hospedaje del Viajero*, on plaza. **F** *Hotelito San Juan*, pleasant and cheap. **F** *Hotelito Turista*, half block from San José bus terminal. **F** *Ocotepeque*, by Transportes Toritos, clean but noisy.

Eating Best at *Sandoval* and *Don Chepe* at *Maya Chortis*, excellent food, main courses US$4-6, small wine lists, good value. Recommended. *Merendera Ruth*, Parque Central, and *Comedor Nora*, 2 C NE, just off Parque Central, both offer cheap *comida corriente*, preferable to *comedores* around bus terminal.

Transport Transportes Escobar daily service Tegucigalpa-Nueva Ocotepeque/Agua Caliente, via La Entrada and Santa Rosa de Copán (12 Av entre 8 y 9 C, Barrio Concepción, Comayagüela, T2374897; *Hotel Sandoval*, T6533098, Nueva Ocotepeque). From Nueva Ocotepeque, buses to San Pedro Sula stop at La Entrada (US$1.70), 1st at 0030, for connections to Copán. There are splendid mountain views. From San Pedro Sula there are regular buses via Santa Rosa south (6 hours, US$4.50); road is well paved.

Banks Banco del Occidente will change TCs.

You can cross into Guatemala at Agua Caliente, 16 kilometres from Nueva Ocotepeque. There are three banks (open 0800-1700, Saturday 0800-1500), a tourist office on the Honduran side, the *Comedor Hermanos Ramírez* for food, and one *hospedaje* (bargain).

Honduran immigration All formalities completed at the border, open 0700-1800. There is an army of money changers outside the Honduran Migración building, keep lempiras for exit stamp and minibus ride Agua Caliente-Atulapa.

Guatemalan consulate The nearest Guatemalan consulate is in San Pedro Sula.

Transport There are several buses a day from San Pedro Sula to Agua Caliente, 1st at 0300 (eg Congolón, Toritos) US$4.45, 6-7 hours. Buses from Nueva Ocotepeque to Agua Caliente every 30 minutes from 0630, US$0.60. Money changers get on the bus between Nueva Ocotepeque and the border, good rates for US$ cash. Minibuses go to Esquipulas, US$0.25, with connections to destinations in Guatemala.

Directory

Frontier with Guatemala
This can be a busy crossing but is quicker, cheaper (less graft) and more efficient than the crossing at El Florido.

From Tegucigalpa to the Pacific

From the capital to the Gulf of Fonseca, with volcanic islands and Honduras' Pacific ports, San Lorenzo and Amapala. Also, the Pan-American Highway routes to El Salvador and Nicaragua, the latter through the hot plain of Choluteca.

Tegucigalpa to Goascarán

A paved road runs south from the capital through fine scenery. Many sections were damaged by Hurricane Mitch. Beyond Sabanagrande (see page 865) is **Pespire**, a picturesque colonial village with a beautiful church, San Francisco, with triple domes. Pespire produces small, delicious mangoes. At **Jícaro Galán** (92 kilometres. *Population*: 3,000) the road joins the Pan-American Highway, which in one direction heads west through **Nacaome** (*Population*: 4,475), where there is a colonial church, to the border with El Salvador at **Goascarán** (*Population*: 2,190). At Jícaro Galán, international buses, for example Ticabus, from San Salvador, Tegucigalpa and Managua meet and exchange passengers.

Sleeping There are hotels of a sort at Goascarán; **Nacaome**: **D** *Perpetuo Socorro*, Barrio el Centro, T8954453, a/c, TV. **F** *Intercontinental* in centre, basic, tap and bucket shower, friendly. **F** *Suyapa*, basic, cheap; and **Jícaro Galán**: **C** *Oasis Colonial*, T8812220, hotel, nice rooms, good restaurant and pool, in hot sticky area, and an unnamed, basic guesthouse. Restaurants at all these places.

The Santa Clara bridge over the Río Goascarán is the border with El Salvador. El Amatillo appears to be on both sides of the border.

Frontier with El Salvador

Honduran immigration The border closes at 1700. Try to avoid lunchtime when there may be a 2-hour break. This border is very relaxed.

Crossing by private vehicle Expect to be besieged by *tramitadores* touting for your business. They wear a black and white uniform of sorts with name badges and carry an identity card issued by the border station. Pick any one you like the look of, they can be as young as 12, but will take the strain out of the 3-4 hour border crossing. Expect to pay about US$25 to the various officials on both sides, not all of whom will offer to give you a receipt.

Salvadorean consulate See Choluteca.

Sleeping 2 cheap *hospedajes*, *San Andrés* and *Los Arcos* on the Honduran side.

Exchange Moderate rates of exchange from money changers.

Transport Bus Tegucigalpa-El Amatillo, hourly, US$1.50, 4 hours. El Amatillo-Choluteca, US$1, 3 hours, every 30 minutes, microbuses.

A temporary pass can be purchased on the Honduran side for US$1.50 for a visit to the Salvadorean **El Amatillo**, for an hour or so. Many Hondurans cross to purchase household goods and clothes.

San Lorenzo
Population: 21,025
Colour map 4, grid C4

In the other direction from Jícaro Galán, the Pan-American Highway goes south to the Pacific coast (46 kilometres) at San Lorenzo, on the shores of the Gulf of Fonseca, a dirty town. The climate on the Pacific litoral is very hot. The shrimp farms on this part of the coast were largely washed away in the 1998 storm.

Sleeping **D** *Miramar*, Barrio Plaza Marina, T8812038/39, 26 rooms, 4 a/c, good restaurant, overpriced, in rough dockside area, best not to walk there. Also **E** *Paramount*, and **E-F** *Perla del Pacífico*, fan, bath, comfortable, clean, friendly, central, charming, new block. Recommended.

Eating *Restaurant-Bar Henecán*, on Parque Central, a/c, good food and service, not cheap but worth it. Recommended. *Restaurant and Disco Don Paco*, main street.

Transport Frequent service of small *busitos* from Tegucigalpa to San Lorenzo (US$1) and to Choluteca (US$1.50).

Directory Banks *Bancahorro* (changes US$ cash and TCs), *Banco de Occidente*, and *Banco Atlántida* (no exchange); Chinese grocery gives good rates for US$ cash.

Amapala
Population: 7,925
Colour map 4, grid C4

The Pacific port of Amapala, on Isla del Tigre, has been replaced by Puerto de Henecán in San Lorenzo, reached by a 3.5-kilometre road which leaves the Pan-American Highway on the eastern edge of San Lorenzo. The **Isla del Tigre** is yet another place reputed to be the hiding-place of pirate treasure. In the 16th century it was visited by a number of adventurers, such as Sir Francis Drake. Amapala was capital of Honduras for a brief period in 1876, when Marco Aurelio Soto was president. Amapala has a naval base, but otherwise it is 'a charming, decaying backwater'. Fishermen will take you, but not by motor launch, to San Lorenzo for a small fee: the trip takes half a day. It is possible to charter boats to La Unión in El Salvador. The deep-sea fishing in the gulf is good. The 750 metres extinct volcano, Amapala, on the island has a road to the summit, where there is a US army unit and a DEA contingent. You can walk round the island in half a day.

Sleeping **B** *Hotel Villas Playa Negra*, Aldea Playa Negra, T8988534, 8988580, 7 rooms with a/c, 7 with fan, pool, beach, restaurant poor value, very isolated, lovely setting. **F** *Pensión Internacional* on the harbour, very basic, otherwise only local accommodation of low standard. Ask for Doña Marianita, who rents the 1st floor of her house, **F** *Al Mar*, above Playa Grande, fan, scorpions, lovely view of mountains and sunset.

Eating *Restaurant-Bar Miramar* by the harbour, overlooking the sea, pleasant, very friendly, good meals, hamburgers and boquitas, and you can hang your hammock. Several clean *comedores* in the new Mercado Municipal.

Transport A 31-kilometre road leaves the Pan-American Highway 2 kilometres west of San Lorenzo, signed to Coyolito. It passes through scrub and mangrove swamps before crossing a causeway to a hilly island, around which it winds to the jetty at **Coyolito** (no *hospedajes* but a *comedor* and *refrescarías*). Motorized launches ply between Coyolito and Amapala, US$0.35 per person when launch is full (about 10 passengers), about US$4 to hire a launch (but you will probably have to pay for the return as well). First boat leaves Amapala at 0700 to connect with first Coyolito-San Lorenzo bus at 0800; next bus from Coyolito at 0900.

Directory **Banks** *Banco El Ahorro Hondureño*. **Hospitals & medical services** Dentist: *Oscar Gutiérrez*, T8988117.

The Pan-American Highway runs southeast from San Lorenzo past Choluteca and San Marcos de Colón to the Nicaraguan border at El Espino, on the Río Negro. The Pan-American Highway's total length in Honduras is 151 kilometres: 40 kilometres Goascarán-Jícaro Galán, 111 kilometres Jícaro Galán-El Espino.

Choluteca

Choluteca, 34 kilometres from San Lorenzo in the plain of Choluteca, expanding rapidly. Coffee, cotton and cattle are the local industries. The town was one of the earliest foundations in Honduras (1535) and still has a colonial centre. The church of **La Merced** (1643) is being renovated and was to have been reconsecrated before the end of the 1990s. The Casa de la Cultura and Biblioteca Municipal are in the colonial house of José Cecilio del Valle on the corner of the Parque Central. The social centre of San José Obrero is at 3 Calle SO; handicrafts can be bought there. Look out for carved wood, especially chairs. A fine steel suspension bridge crosses the broad river at the entrance into Choluteca from the north (it was built in 1937). The climate is very hot; there is much poverty here.

Population: 87,889
Colour map 4, grid C4

The city was heavily damaged by floods during Hurricane Mitch. The suspension bridge still stands, but both banks of the Río Choluteca suffered massive destruction.

Excursions 40 kilometres from Choluteca over a paved road (deteriorates after Punta Ratón turn-off) leads to **Cedeño** beach. A lovely though primitive spot, with clean sand stretching for miles and often thundering surf (**NB** the beach shelves sharply); avoid public holiday and weekend crowds. Take a good insect repellent. Spectacular views and sunsets over the Gulf of Fonseca south to Nicaragua and west to El Salvador, with the volcanic islands in the bay. *Getting there:* Hourly bus from Choluteca, US$0.60 (1½ hours).

A turn off leads from the Choluteca-Cedeño road to Ratón beach, much more pleasant than Cedeño, bus from Choluteca 1130, returns next morning.

Sleeping **C** *La Fuente*, Carretera Panamericana, past the bridge, T8820253/63, F8820273, with bath. Recommended. Swimming pool, a/c, meals. 1 block away is **D** *Centroamérica*, T8823525, F8822900, a/c, good restaurant, bar, pool, good value; opposite is *Restaurant Conquistador*, a bit pricey, but changes money for customers. **D** *Camino Real*, road to Guasaule, T8820610, F2822860, swimming pool, good steaks in restaurant. Recommended. **D-E** *Pierre*, Av Valle y C Williams, T8820676, with bath (ants in the taps), a/c or fan, TV, free protected parking, cafetería has good breakfasts, very central, credit cards accepted. Recommended. **E** *Brabazola*, Barrio Cabañas, T8825535, a/c, comfy beds, TV, good. **E** *Pacífico*, near Mi Esperanza terminal, outside the city, clean, cool rooms, fan, hammocks, quiet, safe parking, fresh drinking water, breakfast US$1.50. **F** *Hibueras*, Av Bojórquez, Barrio El Centro,

T8820512, with bath and fan, clean, purified water, *comedor* attached, good value. **F** *San Carlos*, Paz Barahona 757, Barrio El Centro, with shower, fan, very clean, pleasant. **F** *Santa Rosa*, 3 C NO, in the centre, just west of market, T8820355, some with bath, pleasant patio, laundry facilities, clean, friendly. Recommended.

Tourism project east of Choluteca, at El Corpus, **D** pp *Escuela de Español Mina Clavo Rico*, El Corpus, Choluteca 51103, T/F8873501, US$90 per week, full board, living with local families, language classes (US$4 per hour), riding, craft lessons, work on farms, excursions.

Eating *El Conquistador*, on Panamericana, opposite *La Fuente*, steaks etc, outdoor seating, good. Recommended. *Frosty*, on main street, owned by *Hotel Pierre*, good food and juices. Recommended. *Alondra*, Parque Central, old colonial house, open Friday-Sunday only. *Comedor Central*, opposite side of Parque, *comida corriente* daily specials, *licuados*, sandwiches, good for breakfast. Local specialities are the drinks *posole* and *horchata de morro*.

Festivals The local feast day, of the *Virgen de la Concepción*, **8 December** begins a week of festivities, followed by the *Festival del Sur*, 'Ferisur', which attracts many visitors from Tegucigalpa.

Shopping *Mercado Municipal*, 7 Av SO, 3 C SO, on outskirts.

Transport Buses to El Espino (Nicaraguan border) from Choluteca, US$1.15, 1 hour, 1st at 0700, last at 1400. Also frequent minibuses to El Amatillo (El Salvador border) via San Lorenzo, US$1, from bus stop at bridge. Buses to Choluteca from Tegucigalpa with Mi Esperanza, Bonanza and El Dandy; Bonanza continue to San Marcos and depart Tegucigalpa hourly from 0530, 4 hours to Choluteca, US$1.90. The municipal bus terminal is about 10 blocks from the new municipal market, about 8 blocks from Cathedral/Parque Central; Mi Esperanza has its own terminal 1 block from municipal terminal. **Motoring**: the Texaco service station is just before the bridge.

Directory **Banks** *Banco de Honduras*, *Banco Atlántida* (Visa ATM), *Banco El Ahorro Hondureño*, *Banco del Comercio*, *Banco del País*, *Bamer*, *Banco Sogerín*, *BANFFAA*, *Banco de Occidente*, Blvd Choluteca, open 0800-1630, and on Sat 0830-1130 or 1200. Only *Banco de Comercio* changes TCs. Can be difficult to exchange money in Choluteca. **Communications** Post Office: 0800-1700, 0800-1200 on Sat, US$0.15 per letter for poste restante. **Telephone:** collect calls to Spain, Italy, USA only. **Embassies & consulates** The *El Salvadorean Consulate* is to south of town, fast and friendly, open 0800-1500 daily. **Tour companies & travel agents** *Agencia de Viajes Tropical*, Edif Rivera y Compañía, T8822831/2.

San Marcos de Colón
Population: 9,570

Beyond Choluteca is a long climb to San Marcos, 915 metres in the hills. This clean, tidy town is peaceful and beautifully cool.

Sleeping **E** *Colonial*, friendly, clean, erratic water supply. **F** *Hotelito Mi Esperanza*, 1 block west of Banco Atlántida, near the bus terminal, T2813062, 17 rooms, nice, clean, friendly, cold showers. **F** *Hospedaje Flores*, friendly, clean, cell-like rooms, washing facilities, breakfast and typical dinner, good, exchange.

Eating *Restaurante Bonanza*, near main plaza, clean, good food, friendly service. *Parrillada Candilejas*, good food, children's play area; also *Taquería Bonanza*, 2 blocks from Pan-American highway on road to centre, Mexican specialities, clean, inexpensive.

Transport Bus from Choluteca throughout the day, US$0.75, 1½ hours; buses from Tegucigalpa, Mi Esperanza, 6 Av 23 or 26 C, Comayagüela and Bonanza, 5 a day from 0530, US$2, 4 hours.

10 kilometres beyond San Marcos the road enters Nicaragua at **El Espino** (*Altitude*: 890 metres).

Honduran immigration Immigration is 100 metres from the border, open 0800-1600 (till 1630 on Nicaraguan side). Beware of taxis offering to take you to the border after 1600.

Nicaraguan consulate In Tegucigalpa.

Exchange Exchange is easy at this crossing for dollars, córdobas, Costa Rican colones and Salvadorean colones but the rate for buying córdobas is better on the Nicaraguan side. Duty free shop on the Nicaraguan side.

Transport Taxis/minibuses run from Choluteca and San Marcos to the border. From San Marcos they only leave when totally full, US$1, US$0.50 for locals. To Tegucigalpa, there is a direct bus through Choluteca with Empresa Esperanza, 4 hours.

There is another route from Choluteca to Nicaragua through **El Triunfo** to the border at the bridge over the Río Guasaule. This route is preferred by the international buses, the road is in good condition, apart from those sections damaged by Hurricane Mitch. The bridge across the river was washed away, but when the water is low vehicles drive across while small boats ferry foot passengers. Check conditions in the wet season. It may be worth choosing one of the many 'helpers' to steer you to the correct officials. Fix price beforehand.

Procedures as for El Espino except:
Honduran immigration Open 0800-1600. On Tica Bus, passengers' passports are collected by an official as the bus enters Honduras. Entry tax is paid to the official, who returns passports after sniffer dogs have checked the bus for drugs. No other customs checks.

Exchange There is a bank, but lots of money changers offer rates slightly worse than in the capital. Watch out for children who try to distract you while changing money.

Transport Bus Choluteca-Guasaule, US$1, 45 minutes.

East of Tegucigalpa

The alternative route to Nicaragua, through Danlí and Las Manos: off this road is a detour to old mining centres in the hills.

Tegucigalpa to Nicaragua

A good paved road runs east from Tegucigalpa to Danlí, 92 kilometres away, in the Department of El Paraíso (gas at Km 28, Km 50, Danlí and El Paraíso). There are no signs when leaving Tegucigalpa so ask often. Some 40 kilometres along, in the Zamorano valley (see page 864), is the Escuela Agrícola Panamericana run for all students of the Americas with US help: it has a fine collection of tropical flowers (visits should be booked in advance at the office in Tegucigalpa).

San Antonio de Oriente

At **Zamorano** (Km 29) turn off up a narrow winding road for about six kilometres to the picturesque old mining village of **San Antonio del Oriente**, much favoured by Honduran painters such as Velásquez (it has a beautiful church).

Huw Clough and Kate Hennessy describe the hike to San Antonio del Oriente: At Zamorano the bus will drop you off a few 100 metres before the road junction to San Antonio, from where a small path on the left goes through some trees for 10 minutes before joining the main dirt road. From here on up it is a winding, rocky route through tall, thin pine woods, rising quickly for an impressive view of the broad, flat valley. After about 40 minutes the main road turns sharply to the right, while a smaller track continues in roughly the same direction along the left-hand slope of a mountain. If you go to the right this leads to San Antonio del Oriente after a fairly long climb for an hour. If it is sunny, the path is dusty and glaring and there is little shade in the middle of the day. But reaching the village is a fine reward: red-tiled roofs and white plastered walls clinging to the hillside, with a very quaint little church overlooking the valley. There is one *pulpería*. From here, a steep, 15-minute climb over the ridge leads to San Antonio del Occidente, an even simpler, smaller village (also with one tiny *pulpería*). A much shorter (about 30 minutes) walk from San Antonio del Occidente down the other side of the mountain comes back to the junction mentioned above. The hike can be done in reverse, which is probably easier. It is little problem to hitch back to Tegucigalpa. *Getting there:* Direct bus to San Antonio del Oriente from Tegucigalpa at 0630, return trip 0400, US$1.75.

Güinope From Zamorano, a road goes to Güinope, a pretty, white, dusty town with a church (1820) whose façade is charming. The town is famed for its oranges and jam; try the orange wine 'La Trilla', matured in oak barrels, US$2.50 per bottle. Good walking in the area. *Fiesta*, Festival de la Naranja, at the end of March.

Sleeping F *Merlin*, with bath, clean, good value. *Comedor Lilian*, down side street; snack bar next to bus office on Parque Central.

Transport Bus from Tegucigalpa, mercado Jacaleapa, 1st at 0730, 1st from Güinope at 0515, frequent service. Some buses to Güinope continue south to San Lucas and San Antonio de Flores.

Yuscarán At Km 47½, a paved road branches south to Yuscarán, in rolling pineland country.
Population 9,270 The climate here is semi-tropical. Yuscarán was an important mining centre in colo-
Altitude: 1,070m nial days and is a picturesque, typically Spanish colonial village, with cobbled streets
Colour map 4, grid C4 and houses on a steep hillside. Ask to see the museum near the town plaza, you have to ask around to find the person who has the key, antiques and photographs displayed in a restored mansion which belonged to a mining family. There is a Casa de Cultura in the former Casa Fortín, open Monday-Saturday. The Yuscarán distilleries, one in the centre, the other on the outskirts, are considered by many to produce the best *aguardiente* in Honduras (tours possible). Cardomom plantations are being developed here. The Montserrat mountain which looms over Yuscarán is riddled with mines. The old Guavias mine is close to Yuscarán, some four kilometres along the road to Agua Fría. About 10 kilometres further along this road, a narrow, winding road climbs steeply through pine woods to the summit of *Pico Montserrat* (1,891 metres), with fine views all around. The summit of Montserrat is the **Reserva Biológica de Yuscarán**.

Sleeping D-E hotel, owned by Dutchman Freek de Haan and his Honduran wife and daughter, T892-7213/7228; private or dormitory rooms, beautiful views of Nicaraguan mountains in the distance. **F** *Hotel Carol*, 6 modern rooms with bath and hot water, annex to owner's fine colonial house, safe, family atmosphere, good value. *Cafetería Colonial*, opposite Banco de Occidente, which changes cash and travellers' cheques, excellent *desayuno típico* and *comida corriente*.

Transport Frequent buses to Zamorano and Tegucigalpa; from the capital buses leave from Mercado Jacaleapa. For information, ask anyone in the Parque Central in Yuscarán.

Danlí, 102 kilometres from Tegucigalpa, is noted for sugar and coffee production, a large meat-packing company (Orinsa), and is a centre of the tobacco industry. There are four cigar factories; visit the Honduras-América SA factory (right-hand side of Ciné Aladino) and purchase export quality cigars at good prices (open Monday-Friday, 0800-1200, 1300-1700, Saturday 0800-1200), or Placencia Tabacos, on the road to Tegucigalpa to see cigar-making, better prices than at Santa Rosa.

Danlí
Population: 30,000
Altitude: 760m
Colour map 4, grid C5

Sleeping Centro Turístico Granada with **C-D** *Gran Hotel Granada*, T8832499, F8832774, bar, cable TV, accepts Visa, restaurant and swimming pool, locals pay half price of non-nationals. Recommended. **E** *La Esperanza*, Gabriela Mistral, T8832106, next to Esso station, bath, hot water, fan (**D** with a/c), TV, drinking water, friendly, good car parking. **F** *Apolo*, El Canal, T8832177, next to Shell station, with bath, clean, basic. **F** *Danlí*, C El Canal, opposite *Apolo*, without bath, good. **F** *Eben Ezer*, 3½ blocks north of Shell station, T8832655, basic, hot showers. **F** *Las Vegas*, next to bus terminal, noisy, restaurant, washing facilities, parking. **F** *Regis*, 3 blocks north of Plaza Central, with bath, car park, basic.

Eating *Pepylu's*, very good; *Rancho Típico* near *Hotel Danlí*, excellent. *Pizzería Picolino*, 2 blocks southwest of Parque Central, good pizzas, pleasant atmosphere. *McBeth's*, snackbar, good ice cream; *Nan-kin 2*, Chinese. *Rodeo*, good food and service. *El Gaucho* and *España*, in the centre of town, are good. *El Paraíso de las Hamburguesas*, cheap, good, owner very friendly. *Comedor Claudio*, good *comida corriente*, good information from locals.

Festivals Its *fiesta* lasts all of the third week of August (*Fiesta del Maíz*, with cultural and sporting events, all-night street party on the Saturday); it is very crowded with people from Tegucigalpa.

Transport Buses From **Tegucigalpa**, US$2, from Blvd Miraflores near Mercado Jacaleapa (from left hand side of market as you face it), Colonia Kennedy, Tegucigalpa, hourly, 2 hours, arrive 1½ hours before you intend to leave, long slow queues for tickets (take 'Kennedy' bus from C La Isla near the football stadium in central Tegucigalpa, or taxi, US$1.20, to Mercado Jacaleapa). Express bus from Colonia Kennedy, 0830, 1230, and 1700, US$2.

Directory Banks *Banco Atlántida* changes TCs without problems. Cash on Visa card, maximum US$50. Other banks as well. **Hospitals & medical services** Dentist: *Dr Juan Castillo*, Barrio El Centro, T8832083.

One road continues east from Danlí to Santa María (several buses daily), crossing a mountain range with panoramic views. From Danlí to the north is Cerro San Cristóbal and the beautiful Lago San Julián.

Another paved road goes south 18 kilometres to El Paraíso, from which a connecting paved road, 12 kilometres, links with the Nicaraguan road network at Las Manos/Ocotal. El Paraíso is a picturesque town in an area producing coffee, bananas and rice.

El Paraíso
Population: 27,291
Colour map 4, grid M5

Sleeping E-F *5a Av Hotel y Restaurant*, 5 Av y 10 C, T8934298, with bath, hot water, parking, restaurant specializes in Mexican-American food. **F** *Lendy's*, Barrio Nuevo Carmelo, by bus station, T8934461, clean, friendly, prepares food. There are others, but better to stay in Danlí.

Eating *Comedor Edith*, on a small square on main road, after Parque Central towards border, US$0.85 for a meal.

Transport Minibuses run from Danlí terminal to El Paraíso, frequent (0600 to 1740), US$0.40, 30 minutes, don't believe taxi drivers who say there are no minibuses. Emtra Oriente, Av 6, C 6-7, runs 4 times a day from Tegucigalpa to **El Paraíso**, 2½ hours, US$1.50;

buses from El Paraíso to **Las Manos**, about every 90 minutes, US$0.35, 30 minutes, or taxi US$4, many people willing to share, 15 minutes bumpy ride.

Directory Banks *Bancahsa, Banco Atlántida, Banadesa, Banhcafé, Banco Sogerín.*

Frontier with Nicaragua

This is recommended as the best of the three routes from Tegucigalpa to Nicaragua.

Honduran immigration Border at **Las Manos** open 0800-1600.

Crossing by private vehicle Whether entering or leaving Honduras, you will find *tramitadores* will help you through the paperwork, and are recommended. Total costs are about US$25 and the receipts may not quite tally with what you have paid.

Exchange Buy and sell your córdobas in Nicaragua.

Transport Direct bus Las Manos to Tegucigalpa, 0930, US$2.

Tegucigalpa

Northeast of Tegucigalpa

Through the agricultural and cattle lands of Olancho a road runs to Trujillo on the Caribbean coast. Reachable only by air or sea is Honduras' Mosquitia coast with rivers and swamps, coastal lagoons, tropical forests and very few people.

Tegucigalpa to Limón

The Carretera de Olancho runs from the capital through Guaimaca (hotel, **F**, on plaza above restaurant *Las Cascadas*, good value, clean, friendly) and San Diego (restaurant *El Arriero*), to **Campamento**, 127 kilometres, a small, friendly village surrounded by pine forests (*Hotelito Granada* and *Hospedaje Santos*), and on to the Río Guayape, 143 kilometres. By the river crossing at **Los Limones** is an unpaved road north to **La Unión**, through beautiful forests and lush green countryside. F *Hospedaje San Carlos*, good vegetarian food; *Hotel La Muralla, Hotel Karol* and several *comedores* in La Unión. 14 kilometres north is the **Refugio de Vida Silvestre La Muralla-Los Higuerales**, where quetzales and emerald toucanettes can be seen in March-May in the cloud forest. The Park comprises the three peaks of La Muralla, 1,981 metres, Las Parras, 2,064 metres and Los Higuerales, 1,985 metres. Park entrance fee US$1. Cohdefor has an office on the main plaza for information, closed weekends. You are now required to take a guide with you on the trail. Cost is US$4, arrange in La Unión. The four trails range from one kilometre to 10 kilometres and are recommended. Two campsites in the forest (contact Cohdefor on T/F2221027 for prior arrangements), or there is accommodation for 1-2 at the visitors' centre. When camping you may hear jaguars 'screaming' in the night. Buses from Comayagüela to La Unión, daily, take four hours. (If driving from San Pedro Sula, take the road east through Yoro and Mangulile; from La Ceiba, take the Savá-Olanchito road and turn south 13 kilometres before Olanchito.) To get to the Park, hire a truck from La Unión for about US$18. Little traffic so difficult to hitchhike.

Juticalpa

Population: 74,000
Altitude: 420m
Colour map 4, grid C5

The main road continues another 50 kilometres from Los Limones to Juticalpa (capital of Olancho department), in a rich agricultural area, herding cattle and growing cereals and sugar-cane. Airfield. There is a paved road northeast through the cattle land of Catacamas, continuing to just beyond Dulce Nombre de Culmi. The road from Juticalpa to Trujillo on the coast is described below.

Sleeping **E** *Antúñez*, 1 C NO y 1 Av NO, a block west of Parque Central, T8852250, with bath, **F** without, friendly, clean, also annex in same street. **E** *Las Vegas*, 1 Av NE, T8852700, central, ½ block north of Parque, cafetería, clean, friendly. **F** *El Paso*, 1 Av NE y 6 C NO, 6 blocks south of Parque (on way to highway), T8852311, quiet, clean, bath, fan, laundry facilities. Highly recommended. **F** *Familiar*, 1 C NO between Parque and Antúñez, with bath, clean. Basic but recommended. **F** *Fuente*, 5 minutes from bus station on left side of main road to town centre, basic but rooms are large and clean. **F** *Regis*, 1 C NO, balcony, good value.

Eating *El Centro*, 2 C NO; *Dirro's Pizzería* on Parque Central. *Asia*, Chinese food, also on Parque Central. *Casa Blanca*, 1 C SE, quite smart with a good cheap menu, good paella. *El Rancho*, 2 Av NE specializes in meat dishes, wide menu, pleasant. Others offering barbecued meats in same area are *El Rodeo* and *La Galera*, 2 Av NE, specializes in *pinchos*. *Comedor Any*, 1 Av NO, good value, friendly. *El Tablado*, 1 Av NE entre 3 y 4 C NO, good fish, bar. *Tropical Juices*, Blvd de los Poetas, good fruit juices. *Helados Frosty*, near Parque Central, ice creams etc. From 0600 Saturday the market in Parque Central has good selection of food, fruit, vegetables and souvenirs, said to be best outdoor market in Olancho.

Transport Bus station is on 1 Av NE, 1 kilometre southeast of Parque Central, taxis US$0.50. Hourly to **Tegucigalpa** from 0330 to 1800; bus to **San Esteban** from opposite Aurora bus terminal at 0800, 6 hours, US$2.25. Bus to **Trujillo** dep 0400, 9 hours, US$5.20. Bus to **Tocoa** at 0500.

Directory Banks Local banks: *Bancahsa* (the only one that will change TCs, with insistence), *Banco Atlántida, Bancahorro, Banco de los Trabajadores, Banco de Occidente, Banco Sogerín, Banhcafé*. **Communications** Post Office: 2 blocks north from Parque Central, opposite Shell station. **Telephones:** *Hondutel* on main St, 1 block from Parque Central.

Catacamas

Catacamas, 210 kilometres from Tegucigalpa, is in the Río Guayape valley, at the foot of the Agalta Mountains in the Department of Olancho. The town was established by the Spaniards, the colonial church dates from the early 18th century. It is an agricultural and cattle-raising district with the National School of Agriculture (ENA) in town. Ask if you can visit their agricultural demonstration plots in the Guayape valley, five kilometres south of the town. El Sembrador school, which offers room and board, is also south of the town towards San Pedro and is run by North Americans. It is more or less self contained with its own farms and electricity generators. The Río Guayape (named after an Indian dress, *guayapis*) is famous for the gold nuggets found in it. During the hot months, the banks near the bridge are a popular bathing place, at Paso del Burro on the way to San Pedro Catacamas. Catacamas received a boost in the 1980s when the US built a military base in El Aguacate, 20 kilometres to the northeast, later used by the Nicaraguan 'Contras'. *Fiesta* St Francis of Assisi, 4 October.

Altitude: 400m
Colour map 4, grid C5

Honduras

Patada de burro

From February to May you can taste the vino de coyol, extracted from a palm (a hole is made at the top of the trunk and the sap which flows out is drunk neat). With sugar added it ferments and becomes alcoholic (chicha), so strong it is called patada de burro (mule kick).

Hiking in the mountains behind Catacamas is very beautiful. From Murmullo there are trails to coffee farms. Four kilometres east of Catacamas is the Río Talgua with interesting caves in which significant precolumbian remains have been found. The area and caves are worth a visit. Hiking to El Boquerón, stop off at the main road near Punuare, 17 kilometres west of Catacamas, and walk up Río Olancho, which has nice limestone cliffs and a pretty river canyon. Through much of the canyon the stream flows underground. **Excursions**

E *Central*, in Barrio El Centro, T8994276, with bath, cheaper without, big mango tree in front. **Sleeping**

E *Juan Carlos*, Barrio José Trinidad Reyes, T8994212, good restaurant. Recommended. **E** *La Colina*, T8994488, with bath, hot water, fan, TV, parking. **F** *Rápalo*, Barrio San Sebastián, T8994348. **F** *Las Brisas*, Barrio El Campo, T8994560. **F** *Catacamas*, Blvd Las Acacias, T8994082.

Eating *Continental*, chicken dishes, pizza, US beer. *Asia*, Chinese. *Comedor Ejecutivo*, buffet style meals US$2, local craft decorations. *As de Oro*, good beef dishes, Wild West décor.

Entertainment **Cinema** *Cine Maya*, Barrio El Centro.

Discotheque *Fernandos*. *Extasis*. *Montefresco*, outside town towards Tegucigalpa, pool (US$1.20), live music 2 evenings a week.

Transport Buses **Tegucigalpa** to Juticalpa/Catacamas, Empresa Aurora, 8 C 6-7 Av, Comayagüela, T2373647, hourly 0400-1700, 3¼ hours US$2 to Juticalpa, 4 hours US$2.75 to Catacamas. Juticalpa-Catacamas, 40 minutes, US$0.60. Bus Catacamas-**Dulce Nombre de Culmí** (see below), 3 hours, US$1.35, several daily.

Eastern Honduras

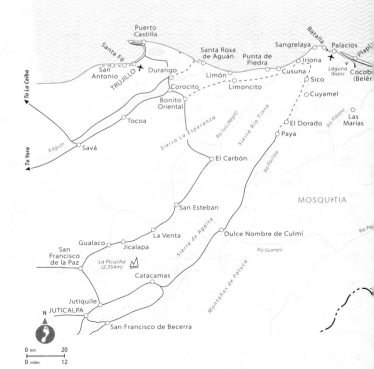

Banks *Banco El Ahorro Hondureño, Banco Atlántida, Banco de Occidente, Banco Sogerín*, all in **Directory**
Barrio El Centro. **Hospitals & medical services** Dentist: *Elvia Ayala Lobo*, T8994129.

Beyond Catacamas, a rough road continues northeast up the Río Tinto valley to
Dulce Nombre de Culmí, **F** *Hospedaje Tania*, very basic, on the main street, several
comedores on the main plaza. Further on is **Paya** where the road becomes a mule
track but in 3-4 days in the dry season a route can be made over the divide (Cerro de
Will) and down the Río Paulaya to Mosquitia (see next section). Local police say that
there is a path in the dry season from Dulce Nombre to San Esteban (about 30
kilometres).

Juticalpa to Trujillo

There is a fine scenic road from Juticalpa to Trujillo. From Juticalpa head northeast
and turn left where the paved road ends, to **San Francisco de la Paz** (several
hospedajes, **F**). Beyond San Francisco is **Gualaco**, which has an interesting colonial
church. **F** *Calle Real*, near Parque Central, basic, friendly, will store luggage.

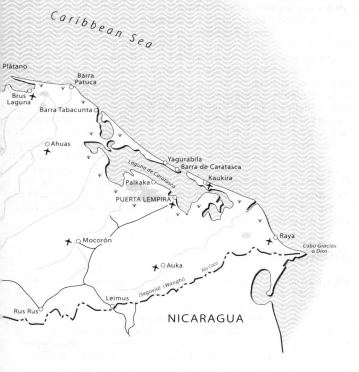

F *Hotelito Central*, similar; both under US$3. Other places to stay. *Comedor Sharon* is one of several places to eat. Several buses a day to Juticalpa and to the north Coast (Tocoa and Trujillo).

San Esteban Twenty three kilometres from Gualaco is San Esteban. On the way you pass Agalta mountain and some of the highest points in Honduras, and the waterfalls on the Río Babilonia. San Esteban has a lurid recent history. For 10 years from 1987 there was a violent family dispute between the Najeras and the Turcios, which engulfed the whole community. 80 people were killed before a truce was agreed in 1997 which has so far held. There is a military detachment here primarily to supervise the ceasefire. If it sounds like the 'Wild West', remember that electricity arrived here only in 1994 and the telephone in 1997.

Sleeping **F** *Hotel San Esteban*, very friendly, clean. **F** *Centro*, very clean, nice family, best. **F** *Hotel Hernández*, cheapest. 3 nice *comedores* nearby.

After San Esteban the road continues to **Bonito Oriental** (via El Carbón, a mahogany collection point with Paya Indian communities in the vicinity). There are four hotels here. The final 38 kilometres from Bonito Oriental to Trujillo are paved, through Corocito. There are many dirt roads between San Francisco and Trujillo. If driving, ask directions if in any doubt. Fuel is available in each big village but there is none between San Esteban and Bonito Oriental.

Parque Nacional Sierra de Agalta Between the roads Juticalpa-Gualaco-San Esteban and Juticalpa-Catacamas- Dulce Nombre de Culmí lies the cloudforest of the Parque Nacional Sierra de Agalta, extending over 1,200 hectares and reaching a height of 2,590 metres at Monte de Babilonia, a massif with a number of interesting mountains. Several different ecosystems have been found with a wide variety of fauna and flora: 200 species of birds have been identified so far. There are several points of entry. Contact Cohdefor in Juticalpa, Culmí, Gualaco, San Esteban or Catacamas for information on access, maps, guides, mules and lodging. There is no infrastructure in the park, but a base camp is being built. A good trail leads to La Picucha mountain (2,354 metres). Access is from El Pacayal, 750 metres, a short distance towards San Esteban from Gualaco, bus at 0700 which goes on to Tocoa. There are two campsites on the trail, the first at 1,060 metres is just short of *La Chorrera* waterfall which has a colony of white collared swifts that nest in the cave behind the falls. 4-6 hours above is the second campsite, 1,900 metres. The final section is mainly dwarf forest with low undergrowth on the summit. There is a good viewpoint one kilometre beyond, the site of two abandoned radio towers. The terrain is too difficult (and there is no trail) on southeast to Catacamas. There is much wildlife to be seen, hiking time two days.

From Gualaco there are other trails into Mount Babilonia with spectacular views over Olancho and Mosquitia; from La Venta you can visit the double waterfall of the Río Babilonia, another track from the east side skirts the flank of Montaña de Malacate. To the west of Gualaco, there is an area of limestone with some fine active and dry caves. Enquire in Gualaco for possibilities.

Mosquitia

This is the name given to the region in the far northeast of the country, which is forested, swampy and almost uninhabited, but well worth visiting. The western boundary of Mosquitia is Cabo Camarón near Palacios and the mouth of the Río Sico. Apart from the one road that stretches 100 kilometres from Puerto Lempira to Leimus and a further 100 kilometres to Ahuasbila, both on the Río Coco, there are no roads in the Honduran Mosquitia. Many places can only be reached by plane, boat or on foot. Malaria is endemic in this area; take anti-malaria precautions.

Mopawi (Mosquitia Pawisa) is the best source of information and provides the main means of access to communities in Mosquitia for travellers. It is a non-profitmaking, non-sectarian organization dedicated to the development of the region and the conservation of the biodiversity of its flora and fauna. The head office is in Puerto Lempira, T8987460, and there are offices in Tegucigalpa (Residencias Tres Caminos, 4b, lote 67, Aptdo 2175, T2358659/2399234, mopawi@optinet.hn), and in La Ceiba (Av La República, media cuadra del muelle viejo, Aptdo 776, T/F4430553/0295). It has offices in Sico, Champas, Las Marías, Batalla/Belén/Cocobila, Ahuas, Wampusirpe, Krausirpe, Ebi, Tipi, Mocorón and Sui. Mopawi is concerned with the protection of natural and human resources throughout Mosquitia and Gracias a Dios. Among its many programmes is the conservation of marine turtles and the green iguana. In Mosquitia the Reserva Biosfera Río Plátano is destined to be joined with the Reserva Antropológica Tawakha and the Reserva Nacional Patuca which, together with Mosquitia Nicaragüense, will constitute one of the largest forest reserves north of the Amazon. This will not happen until Tawakha and Patuca receive congressional decree. **NB** Mosquitia was very badly affected by Hurricane Mitch, but by mid-1999 it was perfectly possible to visit the region. The Río Patuca, however, should not be visited by travellers on their own because of tension between the Tawakha, colonizers and cattle ranchers and gold prospectors. If you wish to visit this area go with an organized tour. In fact, it is best to go with a guide anywhere in the region, especially if you do not speak Spanish. Having said that, few Miskitos or Pesch speak Spanish.

Tour companies & travel agents

La Moskitia Ecoaventuras, address under La Ceiba, Tour companies and travel agents, see page 892, Jorge Satavero. He has no contact address in Tegucigalpa, but the Instituto Hondureño de Turismo will be able to find him if he is the city. He specializes in tours and expeditions in Mosquitia. *Mesoamerica Travel* and Fundación Patuca (Hauke Hoops), see under San Pedro Sula Tour companies & travel agents (page 877) also specialize in travel in this region. Mesoamerica is the only company to run tours to the Zona Arriba of the Río Patuca (5 or 10 days). See also under San Pedro Sula, La Ceiba and Trujillo.

Transport

Air From **Tegucigalpa**: Setco flies Tuesday and Thursday to Mocorón and Puerto Lempira, US$64 one way, US$120 return, T2331711/2; agent in Mocorón is Charly (who also has a restaurant), and in Puerto Lempira the wife of Federico, the local mechanic. Alas de Socorro fly to Ahuas, T2337025. This company charters planes for US$565, but per person it is US$60 one way to Ahuas.

From **La Ceiba**: Isleña flies daily except Sunday to Palacios. Isleña and Sosa fly daily except Sunday to Puerto Lempira and Sosa flies Monday, Wednesday, Friday to Brus Laguna and Ahuas. SAMi flies to various villages from Puerto Lempira, eg Ahuas, Brus Laguna, Belén. There are expensive express flights to places like Auka, Raya, Kaukira. Alas de Socorro operates from Ahuas to collect sick people from villages to take them to Ahuas hospital, contact the Moravian church (in Puerto Lempira Reverend Stanley Goff, otherwise local pastors will help).

Sea Coastal vessels leave irregularly from La Ceiba to Brus Laguna and Puerto Lempira and back (2-3 day journey), carrying passengers and cargo. Information is available from the Mopawi office in La Ceiba, or at the pier itself. Essential equipment: torch. From Trujillo, ask at the dock on the east part of the beach, wait 1½-3 days, take sleeping bag (not recommended for women, especially single women: all-male crews). Fare Trujillo-Palacios US$4.50, Brus Laguna US$6.80; sometimes boats go to Puerto Lempira.

Palacios

Palacios, situated on a lagoon near Cabo Camarón, is the the main access point for travellers to Mosquitia. It has few mosquitoes; cannons are relics of an old English fort.

You can cross the lagoon by cayuco (US$0.50) from Palacios to the Black Carib village of **Batalla**, from which it is 112 kilometres west along beach to Limón (see below). It is easy to get boats from Palacios to Plaplaya (on Lago Ibans, the next lagoon east), Raísta (US$15) and Cocobila/Belén. Trips down the Río Plátano are possible, boats have to be arranged through Felix Marmol. Trips can go as far as Las Marías (see below).

Sleeping There is a hotel at the airport (**E**), good, but meals at the airport are poor value. Room for US$3 with Felix Marmol, everyone calls him Don Félix, who has information on boats to lagoons and meals for US$2. **D** *Río Tinto Lodge*, T/F2374793, Don Felix has recently opened this ecotourist hotel, 10 rooms, bath, purified water, all woodwork locally made, beautiful view of Laguna Bacalar, guided tours of Río Plátano Biosphere Reserve, nearby is the World Wildlife Fund's Turtle Conservation Project, also a butterfly farm and a botanical garden. A 7-room hospedaje has been built by Trek de Honduras, accommodation for 14 guests, electricity, filtered water, restaurant, 5-day tours (including fishing expeditions) arranged out of La Ceiba; T2381944/5, Trek de Honduras, or USA 1-800-6549915, Trek International. Alternatively, you can go independently, at considerably less cost, and ask around for somewhere to stay, eg the local teacher may let you sleep at the school. There are a few shops in town.

Transport Air There are flights direct to Palacios from La Ceiba six days a week (see above), US$25 one way. A US$10 fee for entering Mosquitia was introduced at Palacios airport in 1995. **Boat** Two boats, the *Margarita* and the *Sheena Dee* sail irregularly from La Ceiba to Palacios; also fishing boats from Trujillo.

Sico One can take a picturesque cayuco trip from Palacios or Plaplaya up the Río Sico for US$50 for a hired trip or about US$6 if you can get a lift on a cargo *cayuco* to Sico village (contact Mr Carlos Mejía who speaks perfect English and has basic rooms to rent, **F**, his wife Ofelia sells meals for US$2, also possible food and meals with David Jones, who runs the store). At Sico the remains of a railway built in the late 1920s by a banana company can be seen, including the pillars of a bridge over the river. This was abandoned after disastrous floods in the 1930s. There is no public electricity or piped water in Sico but two schools, a health centre and alligators in the river. A strenuous 32 kilometres walk from Sico may be made (only in dry months from March to May) up forested Río Paulaya Valley to stay with Mundo Jones, whose father mined gold here for 60 years and on eventually to Dulce Nombre de Culmí (see above).

There is a gruelling beach route out of Mosquitia from Palacios/Batalla, but this is not recommended in the wake of Hurricane Mitch and in view of the inadvisability of walking alone on empty beaches. If you wish to leave Mosquitia overland, the best possibility would be to try to get a boat to **Icoteya** on the Río Sico. From Icoteya the Río Sico is navigable downstream to Sico village past the farms of Los Fales, Los Naranjos and Los Andes. Cayucos can be hired, though expensive.

From Icoteya there are two buses daily to Tocoa through Limoncito (for Limón on the coast) and Francia. There are buses from La Ceiba and Trujillo to Limoncito and Limón. At **Limón** there is a fine, clean beach, with lovely swimming; accommodation is available at *Hospedaje Martínez* (also serves meals) and there is a friendly *comedor*, *Bar-Restaurant Kerolyn*. This is a Spanish-speaking Garífuna community. Two buses a day Trujillo-Limón, first at 0830; from Limón, several buses daily to Tocoa and La Ceiba.

Mosquito-free **Cocobila** (Belén), picturesquely situated on a sandspit between the ocean and huge, sweetwater Ibans Lagoon. Excellent meals (US$2) with Miss Erlinda, but be sure to order in advance; ask at the Mopawi office about accommodation. Boats go to **Plaplaya** at the mouth of the Río Sico (bad mosquitoes and 'niguas' which burrow into the soles of your feet), or walk the distance in over two hours along the beach. Room and meals with Doña Evritt de Woods at Plaplaya. Accommodation here is very basic (US$3, no toilet facility). After Plaplaya is the village of **Raísta**, where there is a butterfly farm, which breeds species to export. For

US$3, Ed will give explanations. Accommodation (US$3) is in rooms in a large house in a fenced-off compound; river water for washing, toilet hut, laundry area. There is a restaurant near the landing stage (Eddy Boden and his wife).

Transport Boats to La Ceiba, or up the Río Sico to Sico. A boat leaves Plaplaya at 0600 for the 0730 plane out of Palacios. For the same plane a boat leaves Raísta at 0400 (boatman Umberto Marmol). Plátano village at the mouth of the Río Plátano can be reached by lobster boat from Guanaja or by the supply ships from La Ceiba to Brus Laguna (in all cases cayucos take passengers from ship to shore); Plátano-Brus Laguna, 1½ hours, US$2.50 (plus 45 minutes-1 hour on foot between the westernmost edge of the lagoon, Barra, and Plátano), Plátano-La Ceiba, US$25.

The **Reserve** was established by the UN and the Honduran government in 1980 to protect the outstanding natural and cultural resources of the Río Plátano valley and environs. The tropical jungles that still cloak the landscape here shelter a number of endangered birds, mammals, and fish, among them scarlet macaws and harpy eagles, jaguars and tapirs, and the cuyamel, a prized food fish going extinct throughout Honduras. In addition, there are a number of archaeological sites about which little is known, and the fabled lost White City of the Maya is said to be hidden somewhere in the thick jungles of the Plátano headwaters.

Río Plátano Reserve

Miskito and Pech Indians living along the lower Plátano cultivate yuca, bananas, rice, corn, and beans, as well as hunting and fishing. The upper (southern) portion of the Plátano watershed was virgin jungle until quite recently, but is being quickly populated by *mestizo* immigrants from the poverty-stricken south of Honduras. These new residents are cutting down the forest to plant crops, hunting wildlife mercilessly, and using homemade dynamite in a very destructive form of fishing. The government's intention in 1995 officially to allow settlers into the Sico and Paulaya valleys, on the western edge of the reserve, was roundly criticized. It was feared that the agrarian reform programme would lead to the desertification of Río Plátano. Given the pressure the Reserve is under, it is recommended to visit it sooner rather than later.

Transport To get there, you can fly or take one of the boats that periodically leave from La Ceiba and Trujillo to either Palacios, Cocobila/Belén or Barra Río Plátano, the main villages in the vicinity of the river mouth. Expect to pay perhaps US$25 for passage from La Ceiba or US$5 from Trujillo. A boat from Palacios to Cocobila/Belén cost US$3 per person, US$20 for the whole boat, 45 minutes. From Belén to the Biosphere headquarters in Kuri is a 45-minute walk or 10-minute ride (US$2). The staff and locals are friendly and the staff or the teacher (of the few who can speak Spanish) can probably put you up for the night. They can also help you contract with a *tuk-tuk* (motorized dug-out canoe) to carry you upriver as far as Las Marías, the cost is about US$80 per person return and takes 6-8 hours (3-4 downstream). Daily boat rental costs about US$20.

A Miskito-Pesch village that is the limit of upstream settlement. There is a hospital in Las Marías where you may be able to stay (chocolate and hand woven bags for sale to make money for the community), but usually you are assigned accommodation in the village: 3-4 *hospedajes* (family houses, US$3), also serving meals, US$2. Each *hospedaje* has a map in several languages explaining local routes and attractions. No drinks for sale, purify your water. The journey upstream to Las Marías, although beautiful, can become very tedious and painful on the back and backside. On arrival in Las Marías, arrange return at once. Birdwatching can provide diversion; there are three species of toucan, tanagers, herons, kingfishers, vultures, hawk eagles, oropendolas. If lucky you may see crocodiles or iguanas.

Las Marías

An alternative route to Las Marías is by boat across Ibans Lagoon, 45 minutes by *tuk-tuk*, then six and a half hours' walk through jungle ('semi-path', hot, mosquitoes, take lots of water and insect repellent, and wear good hiking boots that don't mind getting wet). In Belén, ask for Rosendo Mejía or Sergio to act as a guide. Bargain hard for a rate (about US$12.50 per person) and pay separately for the boat trip. Make sure you are paying for one way only.

Once in Las Marías, it is possible to arrange at El Comité de Ecoturismo for guides (US$5) or trips upstream in a *pipante*. This is a shallow dugout canoe manoeuvered with poles (*palancas*) and paddles (*canaletes*): remarkably graceful. Each pipante can carry up to two passengers and their gear, plus three villagers who pole it upstream. The cost per day to rent pipante and crew is about US$12.50 per person (negotiable, you must provide all food, for crew as well). Among the sights are precolumbian rock carvings, some involve a two-day trip. It is also possible to take an excursion into the forest for four, or eight hours. The walk (or run, it's taken very briskly) is an interesting way to see neotropical jungle, but do not expect to see much wildlife. High prices are charged for everything in Las Marías, but remember that it is their only source of income. On your return, if not on an organized tour, use the radio in Kuri to call Palacios for a boat to fetch you in Belén and don't forget to reserve a flight out of Palacios if you need one. On any trip take drinking water, or water purifiers, food, insect repellent, sun protection for boat journeys, candles and camping gear.

The rainy season is from June-December: it is harder to advance upriver then.

Brus Laguna
Colour map 4, grid C5

It is a 15-minute scenic flight from Puerto Lempira (see below) above Caratasca Lagoon and grassy, pine-covered savannas to **Ahuas**, one hour walk from the Patuca River (fabled for gold). There is a hospital here, as well as four missions, but poor accommodation, not much else besides. **F** Hospedaje y Comedor Suyapa, basic, no electricity, meals, US$1.25; mosquito repellent and coils absolutely essential here. Irregular cayucos sail down to **Brus Laguna** for US$2.50, at one mouth of the Patuca River, or US$12.50 (15-minutes) scenic flight in the mission plane. The airstrip is four kilometres from village, take a lift for US$1. There is a disco at the riverside to the left of the bridge. Plague of mosquitoes for all but five months of the year (winter and spring). Two tiny hilly islands near the entrance to the wide lagoon were hideouts where pirates once lurked.

Sleeping and eating George Goff rents rooms (good but basic, limited electricity, **F**) and his wife Elga cooks tasty meals for US$2, he speaks English and will also help with mission-plane flights. Behind his house is a hospedaje being built by the 'Medio-Francés', Colindre (who speaks English, German, French, 'Scandinavian' and Spanish); he operates tours on the Brus Laguna and Río Plátano (can pick up people in La Ceiba if requested). Food and lodging only to those on tour with him. Write to him: Sr Colindre, Brus Laguna, Gracias a Dios, Honduras. Meals generally to be ordered in advance, try *Hospedaje Cruz* or Doña Norma, Doña Aurora or Doña Gladys.

Puerto Lempira

Colour map 4, grid C4

Puerto Lempira is on the large Caratasca Lagoon. In Puerto Lempira is the main office of Mopawi (see above). The airstrip is only five minutes' walk from town.

Regular *tuk-tuks* (motorized canoes) cross the lagoon to Kaukira, US$1.20 (a nice place, but no hotels or anything), Yagurabila and Palkaka. The *tuk-tuks* leave Kaukira daily, except Sunday, at 0500, returning during the morning. In the afternoon the lagoon is usually too rough to cross.

Sleeping
D *Gran Hotel Flores*, some rooms with bath. Recommended. *Villas Caratascas*, huts with bath, restaurant, disco. **F** *Pensión Moderno* (good, friendly, electricity 1800-2230), and inferior **F** *Pensión Santa Teresita*, Barrio El Centro, T8987434.

Eating
La Mosquitia, Centro Comercial Segovia in main street, breakfasts and cheap fish. *Glorieta*, left of landing bridge, fish, lagoon breezes. *Delmy*, 3 blocks north of main street, chicken and

other dishes, noisy. *Doña Aida*, north side of main road to landing bridge, fresh orange juice. *Quinto Patio*, good breakfasts.

Discotheque *Hampu*, by landing bridge.

Airline offices *SAM*, T8987491. *Sosa*, T8987467. **Banks** *Banco Nacional de Desarrollo Agrícola* changes dollars at poor rates, bad reputation.

Inland by road from Puerto Lempira are **Mocorón** (*Charly's* restaurant, see above, rooms available **F** per person) and **Rus Rus** which may be visited with difficulty (there is no public transport but any vehicle will give a lift); a beautiful, quiet village (accommodation at Friends of America hospital's house; meals from Capi's next door, ask Friends about transport out). A branch off this road leads southeast to **Leimus** on the Río Coco and the frontier with Nicaragua. Ask for Evaristo López (at whose house you can get breakfast) who can arrange transport to Leimus, most days, 3-4 hours for about US$3.50. He is also knowledgeable about area safety.

Honduran immigration If you wish to cross here, obtain your exit stamp in Puerto Lempira. The Office of *Migración* is open until 1100, Monday-Friday. This office is reported as very helpful and a good source of information.

For further details see the section on the Nicaraguan Mosquitia under **The Caribbean Coast**.

Background

The land

Much of the country is mountainous: a rough plateau covered with volcanic ash and lava in the south, rising to peaks such as Cerro de las Minas in the Celaque range (2,849 metres), but with some intermont basins at between 900 and 1,800 metres. The volcanic detritus disappears to the north, revealing saw-toothed ranges which approach the coast at an angle; the one in the extreme northwest, along the border with Guatemala, disappears under the sea and shows itself again in the Bay Islands. At most places in the north there is only a narrow shelf of lowland between the sea and the sharp upthrust of the mountains, but along two rivers: the Aguán in the northeast, and the Ulúa in the northwest, long fingers of marshy lowland stretch inland between the ranges. The Ulúa lowland is

Honduras national parks

National parks

1 Capiro y Calentura
2 Celaque
3 Cerro Azul Meambar
4 Cuero y Salado

5 El Cusuco
6 La Fraternidad
7 La Muralla
8 La Tigra

particularly important; it is about 40 kilometres wide and stretches southwards for 100 kilometres. From its southern limit a deep gash continues across the highland to the Gulf of Fonseca, on the Pacific. The distance between the Caribbean and the Pacific along this trough is 280 kilometres; the altitude at the divide between the Río Comayagua, running into the Ulúa and the Caribbean, and the streams flowing into the Pacific, is only 950 metres. In this trough lies Comayagua, the old colonial capital. The lowlands along the Gulf of Fonseca are narrower than they are along the Caribbean; there is no major thrust inland as along the Ulúa.

The prevailing winds are from the east, and the Caribbean coast has a high rainfall and is covered with deep tropical forest. The intermont basins, the valleys, and the slopes sheltered from the prevailing winds bear oak and pine down to as low as 600 metres. Timber is almost the only fuel available. In the drier areas, north and south of Tegucigalpa, there are extensive treeless savannas.

The Spaniards, arriving in the early 16th century, found groups of Indians of the Maya and other cultures. Pushing east from Guatemala City they came upon silver in the

southeast, and in 1578 founded Tegucigalpa near the mines. The yield was comparatively poor, but enough to attract a thin stream of immigrants. Settlement during the ensuing century was mostly along the trail from Guatemala City: at Gracias, La Esperanza, Comayagua and the department of Santa Bárbara, where the largest white population is found. Gradually these settlements spread over the south and west, and this, with the north coast, is where the bulk of the population lives today. The Spaniards and their descendants ignored the northern littoral and the Ulúa lowlands, but during the 19th century US companies, depending largely on black workers from the British West Indies and Belize, developed the northern lowlands as a great banana-growing area. Today the largest concentration of population per square kilometre is in the Department of Cortés, which extends northwards from Lago Yojoa towards the Caribbean; it includes the major portion of the river basins of Ulúa and Chamelecón, also known as the Sula valley: the most important agricultural area in the country, with San Pedro Sula as its commercial centre and Puerto Cortés as its seaport. The Atlantic littoral consumes two-thirds of the country's imports, and ships the bananas which are the country's major export.

Even today, land under some form of cultivation is only 18 percent of the total, while meadows and pastures make up 14 percent of total land use. Rugged terrain makes large areas unsuitable for any kind of agriculture. Nevertheless, there are undeveloped agricultural potentials in the flat and almost unpopulated lands of the coastal plain east of Tela to Trujillo and Puerto Castilla, in the Aguán valley southward and in the region northeast of Juticalpa. The area further to the northeast, known as the Mosquitia plain, is largely unexploited and little is known of its potential.

Climate Rain is frequent on the Caribbean littoral during the whole year; the heaviest occurs from September to February inclusive. In Tegucigalpa the dry season is normally from November to April inclusive. The coolest months are December and January, but this is when heavy rains fall on the north coast, which may impede travel. The driest months for this area are April and May, though very hot. However, weather predictions in this area have become more difficult in recent years, whether because of the *El Niño* phenomenon or for other reasons. Rain, when it comes, is usually heavy, but of short duration. You will get plenty of sunshine everywhere.

National Parks The National Parks office, Conama, is next to the Instituto Nacional Agrario in Tegucigalpa, chaotic but friendly, a good source of information. Cohdefor, the national forestry agency is also much involved with the parks, they have an office at 10 Avenida 4 Calle NO, San Pedro Sula, T2534959. The parks system has been in existence legally since a congressional decree was passed in 1987. Natural Reserves continue to be established and all support and interest is most welcome. Parks in existence are La Tigra, outside Tegucigalpa (see page 863), and the Biosphere of the Río Plátano (see page 953). Under development since 1987 are Monte Celaque (see page 932), Cusuco (see page 877), Punta Sal (see page 884), Capiro y Calentura (see page 895), Cerro Azul-Meámbar (see page 870), Montaña de Yoro (see page 899) and Pico Bonito (page 892) these parks have visitors' centres, hiking trails and primitive camping), and the following have been designated national parks by the government: Montecristo-Trifinio (see page 938), Cerro Azul (Copán), Santa Bárbara (see page 919), Pico Pijol (Yoro, see page 899), Agalta (Olancho – page 950) and Montaña de Comayagua (see page 868). Wildlife Refuges covered in the text are Punto Izopo (page 883), Cuero y Salado (page 892), Las Trancas (page 936) and La Muralla-Los Higuerales (page 946). For information on protected areas in the Bay Islands, see page 901.

History

For Honduras' early history, see the introductory chapter to Central America. Honduras was largely neglected by Spain and its colonists, who concentrated on their trading partners further north or south. The resulting disparity in levels of development between Honduras and its regional neighbours caused problems after independence in 1821. Harsh partisan battles among provincial leaders resulted in the collapse of the Central American

Federation in 1838. The national hero, General Francisco Morazán was a leader in unsuccessful attempts to maintain the Federation and the restoration of Central American unity was the main aim of foreign policy until 1922.

Honduras has had a succession of military and civilian rulers and there have been 300 internal rebellions, civil wars and changes of government since independence, most of them in the 20th century. Political instability in the past led to a lack of investment in economic infrastructure and sociopolitical integration, making Honduras one of the poorest countries in the Western Hemisphere. It earned its nickname of the 'Banana Republic' in the first part of the 20th century following the founding of a company in 1899 by the Vaccaro brothers of New Orleans which eventually became the Standard Fruit Company and which was to make bananas the major export crop of Honduras. The United Fruit Company of Boston was also founded in 1899 and in 1929 was merged with the Cuyamel Fruit Company of Samuel Zemurray, who controlled the largest fruit interests in Honduras. United Fruit (UFCo), known as El Pulpo (the octopus), emerged as a major political influence in the region with strong links with several dictatorships.

Banana Republic

The 1929 Great Depression caused great hardship in the export-oriented economies of the region and in Honduras it brought the rise of another authoritarian régime. Tiburcio Cariás Andino was elected in 1932 but through his ties with foreign companies and other neighbouring dictators he was able to hold on to power until renewed turbulence began in 1948 and he voluntarily withdrew from power in 1949. The two political parties, the Liberals and the Nationals, came under the control of provincial military leaders and after two more authoritarian Nationalist governments and a general strike in 1954 by radical labour unions on the north coast, young military reformists staged a palace coup in 1955. They installed a provisional junta and allowed elections for a constituent assembly in 1957. The assembly was led by the Liberal Party, which appointed Dr Ramón Villeda Morales as President, and transformed itself into a national legislature for six years. A newly created military academy graduated its first class in 1960 and the armed forces began to professionalize its leadership in conjunction with the civilian economic establishment. Conservative officers, nervous of a Cuban-style revolution, preempted elections in 1963 in a bloody coup which deposed Dr Villeda, exiled Liberal Party members and took control of the national police, which they organized into special security forces.

In 1969, Honduras and El Salvador were drawn into a bizarre episode known as the 'Football War', which took its name from its origin in a disputed decision in the third qualifying round of the World Cup. Its root cause, however, was the social tension aroused by migrating workers from overcrowded El Salvador to Honduras. In 13 days, 2,000 people were killed before a ceasefire was arranged by the Organization of American States. A peace treaty was not signed, though, until 1980, and the dispute provoked Honduras to withdraw from the Central American Common Market (CACM), which helped to hasten its demise.

Football War

The armed forces, led chiefly by General López Arellano and his protegés in the National Party, dominated government until 1982. López initiated land reform, but despite liberal policies, his régime was brought down in the mid-1970s by corruption scandals involving misuse of hurricane aid funds and bribes from the United Brands Company. His successors increased the size and power of the security forces and created the largest air force in Central America, while slowly preparing for a return to civilian rule. A constituent assembly was elected in 1980 and general elections held in 1981. A constitution was promulgated in 1982 and President Roberto Suazo Córdoba, of the Liberal Party, assumed power. During this period, Honduras cooperated closely with the USA on political and military issues, particularly in moves to isolate Nicaragua's left wing government, and became host to some 12,000 right wing Nicaraguan contra rebels. It was less willing to take a similar stand against the FMLN left wing guerrillas in El Salvador for fear of renewing border tensions. In 1986 the first peaceful transfer of power between civilian presidents for 30 years took place when José Azcona del Hoyo (Liberal) won the elections. Close relations with the USA were

Transition to democracy

Decline of the Military

The Honduran armed forces were at their most powerful in the 1980s, when with US support in the attempt to destabilize the Sandinista régime in Nicaragua, their numbers rose to about 25,000. Since then they have seen their political and economic power eroded and their size cut to around 7,000 with the loss of compulsory military service. They have lost control of key enterprises, such as the telecommunications monopoly, the merchant marine and the state migration authority. Their allocation from the state budget has also been cut. President Reina also curbed military influence in government and started to bring those responsible to task for human rights abuses.

In 1994 the military-controlled security force, the DNI, was officially dismantled and a new Directorate for Criminal Investigations (DIC) began operations in 1995. In 1996 an ad hoc commission was set up to oversee the creation of a new Civilian National Police (PNC) to replace the discredited, military-controlled Public Security Forces (FUSEP) of 6,500 men and draw up new public security legislation. The process was completed in May 1998.

The disgruntled armed forces were further dismayed with the indictment by a civilian court in 1995 of 11 military officers accused of human rights violations in the 1980s including a case when six students were kidnapped and tortured. The order highlighted the role of the USA and Argentina in training the Honduran military intelligence unit, the Battalion 3-16, in the 1980s. As clandestine cemeteries were discovered, the military denied there were any human rights violations. In a show of force, the Commander in Chief, Gen Luis Alonso Discua, sent armoured cars into Tegucigalpa as a warning to the Government, saying he did not trust the justice system. Gen Discua was the first commander of the B3-16 and there was an outcry from international human rights groups when he was appointed in 1996 to Honduras' delegation on the UN Security Council. The Committee of Relatives of the Detained and Disappeared (COFADEH) also took legal action against high-ranking army officers to uncover human rights abuses by the B3-16 and allegations were made against General Discua and the subsequent armed forces chief, General Mario Hung Pacheco. Several bombs exploded in key political locations which were suspected to have been planted by disaffected elements in the army and there were also suspicions that the military was a factor behind the rising crime wave of kidnappings and bank robberies.

In the first year of President Flores' term the military lost legal impunity and the civilian authorities were given the right to audit the armed forces' budget and investigate military businesses. The post of commander-in-chief was unanimously abolished by congress in a draft consitutional amendment in September 1998 and, in January 1999, the constitution was changed to recognize the president as commander-in-chief. Flores excercised his right in this role in August 1999 when he sacked several leading officers who were believed to have disobeyed the civilian defence minister and to have been fomenting unrest in the ranks.

maintained in the 1980s, Honduras had the largest Peace Corps Mission in the world, non-governmental and international voluntary agencies proliferated and the government became increasingly dependent upon US aid to finance its budget.

In 1989, general elections were won by the right wing Rafael Leonardo Callejas Romero of the National Party, which won a 14-seat majority in the National Assembly. Under the terms of the Central American Peace Plan, the contra forces were demobilized and disarmed by June 1990. The Honduran armed forces have come under greater pressure for reform as a result of US and domestic criticism of human rights abuses. An Ad Hoc Commission, set up by President Callejas, published a report in April 1993 recommending a series of institutional reforms in the judiciary and security services, including the resolution by the Supreme Court of all cases of jurisdictional conflict between civilian and military courts. This and other measures led to some, but not complete improvement in the respect for human rights.

In the campaign leading up to the 1993 general elections, the Liberal candidate, Carlos Roberto Reina Idiáquez, pledged to provide every citizen 'techo, trabajo, tierra y tortilla' (roof, work, land and food), arguing for a more socially-conscious face to the economic adjustment programme inaugurated by President Callejas. Reina duly won the elections with a 53.4 percent majority over his National Party rival, Oswaldo Ramos Soto. Although many of his economic policies were unpopular and he was unable to alleviate widespread poverty in the short term, President Reina received approval for his handling of the military and investigations of human rights abuses (see box).

The 1997 presidential elections were again won by the Liberal candidate, Carlos Flores Facusse, with 53 percent of the vote over the National Party candidate, Nora Gúnera de Melgar, who received 42 percent. Carlos Flores had the support of the business community, who believed he would control public spending and reduce the government deficit in line with IMF targets, but he also campaigned against economic austerity and in favour of bridging the gap between rich and poor. The passage of Hurricane Mitch over Honduras in October 1998 forced the Flores administration to refocus all its attention on rebuilding the country at all levels, social, economic and infrastructural. The president set up a 'reconstruction cabinet' to oversee the mammoth task.

Liberal government since 1993

Culture

There are few pure Indians (an estimated seven percent of the total population), and fewer of pure Spanish and other European ancestry. The two largest concentrations of Indians are 1) the Chortis from Santa Rosa de Copán westwards to the border with Guatemala; the Lencas in the departments of Lempira, Intibucá and, above all, in the highlands of La Paz. 2) There are about 45,000 Miskito Indians who live on the Caribbean coast, as well as several communities of Garífunas (black Caribs). The population is 90 percent *mestizo*. Some 53 percent are peasants or agricultural labourers, with a low standard of living.

People

Education is compulsory, but not all the rural children go to school. 33 percent of the population over the age of 10 have no formal schooling. The National University is based in Tegucigalpa though it also has departments in Comayagua, San Pedro Sula and La Ceiba. Also in Tegucigalpa are the Universidad José Cecilio del Valle, the Universidad Católica (with campuses in San Pedro Sula and Choluteca), the Universidad Tecnológica Centro Americana and the Universidad Pedagógica Nacional; there is also the Universidad de San Pedro Sula, the Universidad Pedagógica Francisco Morazán and the Universidad Tecnológica Centroamericana. The majority of the population is Catholic, but there is complete freedom of religion.

Religion & education

The economy

Honduras has traditionally been the poorest economy in Central America with one of the lowest income rates per head in all Latin America although the war in Nicaragua depressed income levels there below even those of Honduras. The distribution of land continues to be a pressing problem, with an estimated 170,000 farming families lacking sufficient land for subsistence agriculture. New legislation in 1992 was designed to encourage private enterprise, making it easier to sell land and prompting large landholdings, leaving campesinos with only small parcels of land. Unemployment (and under-employment) is about 40 percent of the working population, owing to low investment, and poor harvests and labour disputes in the agricultural sector. After decades of low inflation when the currency was fixed, the 1990s have been a severe shock to the population and real incomes have fallen sharply as the effects of economic liberalization have been felt. It is estimated that 80 percent of the population live in poverty and the minimum wage has not kept pace with inflation.

Over half of the population lives by the land: coffee, bananas and shrimp are the main

Structure of production

Honduras

export crops and Honduras is the world's fourth largest exporter of bananas. Cotton, once important, is now far less so. Tobacco, maize, beans, rice and sugar are grown mostly for domestic use but small quantities are sometimes exported. Cigars have a good international reputation. Cattle raising is important and exports of both meat and livestock are growing. Timber is a major export; controversy over the development of forestry reserves in the Department of Olancho has laid the future expansion of the industry open to doubt.

Honduras has considerable reserves of silver, gold, lead, zinc, tin, iron, copper, coal and antimony, but only lead and zinc and small quantities of gold and silver are mined and exported. Japanese agencies are assisting in further exploration for lead and zinc deposits. Considerable offshore exploration for petroleum is in progress. There is an oil refinery at Puerto Cortés and another at San Lorenzo on the Pacific and exports of petroleum derivatives are becoming significant. The US$600mn hydroelectric scheme at El Cajón was constructed to reduce the country's oil bill. The Government has begun the process of privatizing the energy sector.

Local industries are small, turning out a wide range of consumer goods, besides being engaged in the processing of timber and agricultural products. The more important products are furniture, textiles, footwear, chemicals, cement and rubber. Maquila industries in the northern cities of San Pedro Sula, Choloma and Villanueva, in Comayagua and elsewhere grew rapidly in the 1980s but stagnated in the mid-1990s. Several companies relocated in 1995-96 to other countries and Honduras was criticized for labour abuses, low pay and poor conditions in the sector. Maquiladoras account for 20 percent of total exports. Most are in clothing, but there are others processing wood and a variety of goods, employing about 38,000 people.

Recent trends Honduras' total external debt amounted to some US$4bn in 1999, and under normal conditions about a third of foreign exchange receipts are spent on debt servicing (see below). From 1982 the government held negotiations to reschedule its debt with commercial banks but failed to sign any agreement. Arrears mounted and in 1989 the negotiating committee disbanded to allow banks individually to recover their debts as best they could. In 1990 a new economic package was introduced with emergency spending cuts and revenue raising measures designed to reduce the fiscal deficit. The lempira was allowed to float freely against the US dollar in a legalization of the black market rate where the currency had been trading at L4=US$1 compared with the official rate since 1926 of L2=US$1. President Callejas thereby attempted a rapprochement with the international financial community; Honduras had previously been declared ineligible to borrow from the IMF, the World Bank and the Inter-American Development Bank (IDB), while US aid had been cut by 30 percent. Negotiations with the multilateral agencies led to the clearing of arrears and new loans to support the economic programme.

The effect of structural adjustment measures on the population, however, were not favourable: unemployment rose, inflation soared and poverty grew, causing considerable social problems. By 1992 inflation was down to 8.8 percent and gdp rose by 4.6 percent although structural adjustment remained unpopular. Inflation began to creep up in 1993 and by 1994 the new President faced a deteriorating economy. Gdp fell by 1.5 percent while inflation rose to 21.7 percent. Not only had the foreign debt risen and targets not been met in the last year of Callejas' term, but also the foreign lending institutions' loss of confidence in Honduras made it difficult for Reina to fund social programmes. Renegotiation of external debt was only possible to a limited extent as over half was owed to multilateral lending agencies, principally the IDB and the World Bank. In 1995 gdp growth improved but inflation remained high and monetary policy had to be tightened with higher lending rates.

In 1996 the Government approved a 25 percent increase in the minimum wage, but this was immediately wiped out by a 30 percent rise in the price of basic foodstuffs. Strikes in the public sector to demand further wage rises, no job cuts and price controls put pressure on the Government, which was already struggling to meet the targets of its IMF economic programme. The Government increased social spending in 1997 in the face of rising crime, labour unrest and widespread poverty, despite jeopardizing its IMF programme and potential future debt forgiveness if budget deficit targets were missed. In April 1998 the IMF refused to approve a letter of intent because of a failure to meet fiscal deficit targets. President Flores introduced an austerity package in the same month, raising VAT, putting four percent tax on tourist services and bringing in other tax changes. At the same time efforts were made to reduce the impact of higher VAT on the poor.

Honduras' entire economic framework was shattered by Hurricane Mitch. According to early estimates 70 percent of economic output was lost, with the main export crops largely destroyed (bananas, shrimp), or prevented from reaching ports by road damage (coffee). There was also major destruction of power and water services, housing and businesses. Joblessness, especially in the agricultural sector, increased greatly. Although immediate reconstruction was of paramount importance, long-term plans to take into consideration agricultural methods, land clearance and reforestation and environmental controls were assessed in order to prevent a recurrence of a disaster on such a scale. Preliminary estimates of US$2bn to rebuild the country may well prove conservative. To bring in funds, the government proposed to accelerate the privatization of state concerns such as Hondutel and ENEE, the electricity company. The main source of finance, however, would have to be the international community and Honduras received commitments to aid from many quarters, including the USA, the Paris Club group of creditor nations, the World Bank and IADB. The IMF, in March 1999, agreed a three-year structural adjustment package which included US$215mn of support. There was however, considerable debate after Mitch about awarding Honduras full debt-relief, but multilateral and bilateral creditors did not in the main write off the country's debts, preferring instead to offer moratoria on repayments.

Government

Honduras is a multi party republic. The Legislature consists of a single 128-seat Chamber. Deputies are elected by a proportional vote. Executive authority rests with a President, directly elected for four years. No President may serve two terms in succession. The National Assembly elects members of the Supreme Court, which, together with the Court of Appeal, Justices of the Peace and lesser tribunals, constitute the judiciary. The Constitution was revised by a Constituent Assembly elected in April 1980. The country is divided into 18 departments, each with an administrative centre, and further subdivided into 297 municipalities.

Communications

The railways are in the north. In 1993 the Tela Railroad Company closed its entire operation along the Atlantic coast, while the Ferrocarril Nacional de Honduras has since downgraded its one remaining passenger service between Tela and Puerto Cortés to a twice-weekly ferrobus.

A light aeroplane is the only way of getting to La Mosquitia, but the road system in the rest of the country has improved rapidly in recent years and Honduras probably has the best roads in Central America. Total road length is now 15,100 kilometres, of which 3,020 kilometres are paved, almost 10,000 kilometres are all-weather roads and the remainder are passable in the dry season. The main paved roads are the Northern Highway linking Tegucigalpa, San Pedro Sula and Puerto Cortés; the road west from Puerto Cortés along the north coast, through Omoa, to the Guatemalan frontier; the highway from Tegucigalpa to Olancho, passing through Juticalpa and Catacamas; the Pan-American Highway in the southwest between El Salvador and Nicaragua, and the Southern Highway which runs to it from Tegucigalpa; the north Coast Highway joining San Pedro Sula with Progreso, Tela, La Ceiba and Trujillo; from Progreso a paved road runs south through Santa Rita to join the San Pedro Sula-Tegucigalpa highway 44 kilometres south of San Pedro; there is also a paved road from Santa Rita to Yoro; the Western Highway links San Pedro Sula with Santa

Rosa de Copán, Nueva Ocotepeque and the Guatemalan and Salvadorean frontiers, with a branch from La Entrada to Copán ruins; the road from Santa Rosa de Copán to Gracias is also paved, as are the Carretera de Santa Bárbara and on to the Western Highway (Carretera del Occidente), from Lago Yojoa to Santa Bárbara, and the stretches from La Paz to Marcala in the Department of La Paz and Siguatepeque to La Esperanza; the road linking Choluteca on the Pan-American Highway with the Nicaraguan frontier at Guasaule; the Eastern Highway linking Tegucigalpa, Danlí, El Paraíso and Las Manos (Nicaraguan frontier); the road from Tegucigalpa to Santa Lucía and Valle de Angeles; some of the road along the island of Roatán. Travel is still by foot and mule in many areas. Tegucigalpa, La Ceiba, San Pedro Sula and Roatán all have international airports. More details in the text above. **NB** The road network, paved and unpaved, is recovering fast after the ravages of Hurricane Mitch. All major routes were open soon after the storm and transport is flowing freely.

Nicaragua

8

Nicaragua

Essentials

Planning your trip

Nicaragua is the largest Central American republic. The lowlands which stretch inland from **Where to go**
the Caribbean coast are largely unpopulated. Almost all the people and all the economic
activity are concentrated in the west and south: in the highlands, around the two great lakes
(Managua and Nicaragua) and below the volcanic chain which runs parallel to the Pacific
shore. The country is at the junction of three continental plates and earthquakes and volcanic
eruptions are a constant reminder of this. Dramatic evidence can be seen in the capital,
Managua, whose centre was destroyed by an earthquake in 1972. The old cathedral stands
open to the skies, preserved as a museum, and other sites in the former centre are
monuments to this aspect of Nicaragua's natural history and to its recent civil war. The capital
is now a rapidly changing place, with new construction, symbolized in the startling new
cathedral. Within easy reach are the Pacific beaches of Pochomil and Masachapa, busy at
weekends and holidays, but quiet otherwise.

The capital stands on the southern shore of Lake Managua. Two routes head round the
lake and continue **to Honduras**. The first goes through the highlands in which are the towns
of Matagalpa, Jinotega and Estelí. These are agricultural areas, with excursions possible to
rural communities and good walking country. The other main route north, taken by the
international buses, goes south of Lake Managua to the former colonial capital, **León**, a city of
old houses, beautiful churches and some captivating festivals (eg Holy Week and the
Immaculate Conception, 7-8 December). It is also the birthplace of one of Latin America's
greatest poets, Rubén Darío. From here you can go to the Pacific beach of Poneloya, to
Chinandega and on to Nicaragua's northernmost volcano, Cosigüina, now a national park, or
make for the frontier post at El Guasaule.

Southeast of Managua is **Masaya**, a major centre for handicrafts, with several villages
nearby whose artesans specialize in different products. The smoking volcano of Santiago, in
the Masaya group, looms close by and the crater lake of Apoyo is only a short distance away.
The road continues to **Granada**, Nicaragua's other major colonial city, on the shores of Lake
Nicaragua. Here, too, are some fine Spanish buildings, with the added attraction of 354 islands
in the lake for boat trips and nature watching. Also accessible from Granada is Isla Zapatera,
an old volcano and precolumbian site. Ometepe island is a special place, with its two
volcanoes, forested slopes, indigenous petroglyphs and welcoming inhabitants. It can be
reached from Granada, but more easily from the lakeside town of San Jorge. In the southeast
corner of Lake Nicaragua is San Carlos at the outlet of the **Río San Juan**, which flows along
the Costa Rican border to San Juan del Norte through some of Central America's most
unspoilt forest. The potential for nature tourism here is enormous. A short sail away from San
Carlos is the Solentiname archipelago, a group of forested islands which are home to a
community of artists. The town of San Juan del Sur is on Nicaragua's southern Pacific coast,
where the sunsets are fabulous. Neighbouring beaches are best reached by boat and close by
is the country's most important turtle nesting ground at La Flor.

The main ports on the **Caribbean** are Bluefields and Puerto Cabezas. The former is the
more visited of the two and from Managua you either fly, or go by bus and boat. Out to sea are
the two small Corn Islands, fringed with coral and popular for surfing and bathing.

The dry season runs from December to May, and the wettest months are usually June and **When to go**
October. Best time for a business visit: from March to June, but December and January are the
pleasantest months.

Tourist information The Institute of Tourism, PO Box 122, Managua, **Finding out**
T505-2222962/2281337, F2281187, has a wide range of brochures and information packs. **more**
The office open to the public is on the north corner of the building, first floor. Website
www.intur.gob.ni. In the **USA**, PO Box 140357, Miami, FL 33114-0357, T305-8600747,

Nicaragua

Nicaraguan embassies and consulates

Belgium, 55 Avenue de Wolvendael, 1180 Brussels, T02-3756500, F02-3757188.
Canada, 130 Albert Street, suite 407, Ottawa, Ontario KIP 5G4, T613-2349361-2, F613-2387666.
France, 34 Avenue Buaeaud, 75116 Paris, T1-44059042, F1-44059242.
Germany, Konstantinstrasse 41, D-53179 Bonn, T228-352787, F354001.
Israel, Touro 17, Jerusalem, Israel 94102, T2-256997.
Italy, Via Brescia 16, sala 1, int 7, 00198 Roma, T6-8413471, F8411695.
Japan, Kowa Bldg 38, RM 903, 4-1-24, Nishi-Azabu, Minato-Ku, Tokyo 106, T3-4990400, F4993800.
Mexico, Payo de Rivera 120, Lomas de

Chapultepec, CP 11000, T540-56256, F5206960.
Spain, Paseo de la Castellana 127, 1 B, 28046 Madrid, T1-5555510, F5555737.
Sweden, Sandhamnsgatan 40, 6TR, 11528 Stockholm, T8-6671857, F8-6624160.
UK, Vicarage House, 58-60 Kensington Church Street, London W8 4DB, T0171-9382373, F0171-9370952.
USA, 820, 2nd Avenue, 8th floor, suite 802, New York, NY 10017, T212-9831981, F212-9895528; 8370 West Flagler Street, suite 220, Miami, FL 33144, T305-2200214, F2208794; 870 Market Street, suite 1050, San Francisco, CA94102, T415-7656821, F7656826.

F8600746. In **Spain**, Apartado Correos 10,998, 28080 Madrid. At Managua airport, T2331539. Local information service, T112. Another website with useful information is www.consuladodenicaragua.com.

Work opportunities Volunteer work in Nicaragua is not as common after the 1990 elections as it was during the Sandinista years. Foreigners now work in environmental brigades supporting the FSLN, construction projects, agricultural co-operatives and environmental organizations. Certain skills are in demand, as elsewhere in the developing world; to discover the current situation, contact non-governmental organizations in your home country (for example Nicaraguan Network, 1247 East Street, SE, Washington, DC 20003, T202-5449355, F5449360, or PO Box 4496, Fresno, CA 93744, T209-2260477, in the USA), twin town/sister-city organizations and national solidarity campaigns (NSC/ENN Brigades, 129 Seven Sisters Road, London N7 7QG, T0171-2729619; Dutch Nicaragua Komitee, Aptdo Postal 1922, Managua). Casa Danesa, T2678126, F2786684 (Managua), may be able to help Scandinavians, and others, to find volunteer work, usually for three months, but shorter may be acceptable.

Before you travel

Getting in **Documents** Visitors must have a passport with six months validity (at least), and may have to show an onward ticket and proof of at least US$200 (or equivalent in córdobas) in cash or cheques for a stay of more than a week in the country. **NB** Credit cards are becoming gradually more widely used in Nicaragua, so may be accepted instead of cash. No visa is required by nationals of most western countries do not except former USSR countries and some Latin American countries. Nationals of the following countries do not need a visa: Guatemala, El Salvador, Honduras, Chile, Bolivia, Argentina, Uruguay, USA, Belgium, Denmark, Finland, Greece, Hungary, Ireland, Liechtenstein, Luxembourg, Netherlands, Norway, Poland, Spain, Sweden, Switzerland or the United Kingdom for a 90-day stay.

Visa rules are changing frequently, check before you travel. Citizens of all other countries need a visa, which can be bought before arriving at the border, is valid for arrival within 30 days, and for a stay of up to 30 days, it costs US$25; two passport photographs are required. A full 30-day visa can be bought at the border, but it is best to get your visa in advance. Visas take less than two hours to process in the embassies in Guatemala City and Tegucigalpa, but have been known to take 48 hours elsewhere. When consultation with Managua is required (the countries to which this applies include India, the Arab countries, Cuba, the People's

Republic of China and Hong Kong), it takes longer. Extensions can be obtained at the Dirección de Migración y Extranjería in Managua: arrive at the office before 0830. From the small office on the righthand side, you must obtain the *formulario* (three córdobas). Then queue at the *caja* in the large hall to pay US$25 or 150 córdobas for your extension. This can take hours. In the meantime you can complete forms. With the receipt of payment you queue at the window on the right. With luck you will receive the extension stamp for midday; at any event you should get it the same day. Another possibility is to leave the country for at least 72 hours and re-enter on a new visa. Commercial travellers should carry a document from their firm accrediting them as such.

An onward air ticket can be cashed if not used, especially if issued by a large company, but bus tickets are sometimes difficult to encash. It is reported, however, that the Nicaraguan Embassy in a neighbouring country is empowered to authorize entry without the outward ticket, if the traveller has enough money to buy the ticket. Also, if you have a visa to visit another Central American country, you are unlikely to be asked to show an outward ticket. This applies to all Central American countries: be two visas ahead!

Duty free and export restrictions Duty-free import of half a kilogram of tobacco products, three litres of alcoholic drinks and one large bottle (or three small bottles) of perfume is permitted.

Money

Currency The unit is the córdoba oro (C$), divided into 100 centavos. It was introduced in July 1990, at a par with the US dollar. The córdoba oro was devalued to 5 = US$1 in March 1991 and the old córdoba was withdrawn from circulation on 30 April 1991; a further devaluation in January 1993 set the dollar at six córdobas oro, to be followed by continuous mini-devaluations. The exchange rate at the end of May 1999 was 11.35 córdobas oro = US$1. Notes in circulation are for 1, 5, 10 and 25 centavos, 1, 5, 10, 20, 50 and 100 córdobas oro. Coins in circulation are 20 and 50 centavos and 1 and 5 córdobas oro (replacing notes of these values). Try to avoid obtaining the larger notes, as no-one ever has enough change (but see **Banks** under Managua). The import and export of foreign and local currencies are unrestricted. Visa and Mastercard are accepted in nearly all restaurants and hotels, and in many shops. This applies to a lesser extent to Amex, Cred-o-Matic and Diners Club. Don't rely exclusively on credit cards.

Changing travellers' cheques is difficult outside Managua; while the situation is improving, it is best to carry US dollar notes and sufficient local currency away from the bigger towns.

Getting there

Air

From Europe Take any transatlantic flight to Miami and connect to American, Nica, Lacsa, Iberia; or Taca via San Salvador; or Lacsa via San José. Iberia to Managua five times a week from Barcelona and Madrid via Miami (connections from other European cities).

From USA See above for Miami. Continental flies from Houston daily. Los Angeles, Taca, via San Salvador, or Lacsa via San José. Detroit and Nashville, American Airlines daily. San Francisco, Continental daily via Houston. New York, Taca, Aviateca and Lacsa. From other North American cities, make connections in Miami, or with Taca in San Salvador, or Aviateca in Guatemala City.

From Latin America From **Guatemala City**, Copa, Taca, Aviateca; from **Mexico City**, Aviateca; **Panama City**, Copa; **San José**, Copa, Lacsa; **San Salvador**, Copa, Aviateca, Taca; **San Juan** and **Santo Domingo**, Copa. Otherwise make connections in San José, San Salvador or Panama City. All flight tickets purchased by non-residents must be paid in US dollars.

Touching down

Cost of living

Nicaragua is not an expensive country as far as hotel accommodation is concerned, and public transport is fairly cheap. For food, as a rough guide, a *comida corriente* costs about US$1.40 (meals in restaurants US$6-13, breakfasts US$2.50-3.50). However, on the islands or in out of the way places where supplies have to be brought in by boat or air, you should expect to pay more.

Clothing Dress is informal; business men often shed jackets and wear sports shirts, but shorts are never worn. The wearing of trousers is perfectly OK for women.

Entry & exit taxes The cost of entry overland is US$7 (possibly paid in córdobas), plus a US$1 municipal tax (at Sapoá on the Costa Rican border, at least), plus an extra US$2 on Saturday, Sunday and holidays. Exit tax for foreigners is US$2 in dollars cash, US$5 on Saturday, Sunday and holidays. If in the slightest doubt about charges, insist on being given a receipt and go to the Immigration Department in Managua to verify the charge. Motorists should see under **Motoring** below.

All arriving passengers by air pay an entry tax of US$5, while departing passengers must pay an airport tax of US$20, payable in US dollars. All passengers have to pay a sales tax of US$5 on all tickets issued in and paid for in Nicaragua; a transport tax of one percent on all tickets issued in Nicaragua to any destination.

Safety Visitors to Nicaragua must carry their passports (or a photocopy) with them at all times. There are police checkpoints on roads and in outlying districts; the police search for firearms. They may inspect luggage on entering and leaving Nicaragua. Do not photograph any military personnel or installations.

Pickpocketing and bagslashing occurs in Managua in crowded places, and on buses throughout the country. Apart from Managua at night, most places are generally safe. Reports of robberies and assaults in Northern Nicaragua indicate that care should be taken in this area, enquire about conditions before going, especially if proposing to leave the beaten track.

Sports Baseball is the national game, more important than soccer, and the best building in many towns is the baseball stadium. The season runs from November to the end of April.

Tipping US$0.50 per bag for porters; no tip for taxi drivers.

Getting around

Air Domestic flights should always be reconfirmed immediately on arrival for return. There is a 20-pound hand luggage limit. Stowed luggage 30 pounds free, maximum 100 pounds. Domestic departure tax is 10 córdobas.

La Costeña operates internal air services to San Carlos, Nueva Güinea, Siuna, Rosita, Bonanza, Puerto Cabezas, Waspám, Bluefields and Corn Islands (see text for details).

Bus Local buses are the cheapest in Central America, but are crowded. Baggage that is loaded on to the roof or in the luggage compartment may be charged for, usually at half the rate for passengers or a flat fee of US$0.50.

Motoring Motorists and motorcyclists must pay US$30 in cash on arrival at the border (cyclists pay US$2, and up to US$9 at weekends, though this tends to vary from one customs post to the next). Several cyclists have said that you should take a 'proof of purchase' of your cycle or suggest typing out a phoney 'cycle ownership' document to help at border crossings. Motorists also pay the same entry tax as other overland arrivals (see above). Do not lose the receipts, they have to be produced when you leave; without them you will have to pay again. Vehicles not cleared by 1630 are held at customs overnight. Up to four hours of formalities are possible when entering Nicaragua with a vehicle. On leaving, motorists pay five córdobas, as well as the usual exit tax. For procedures at each border, see the relevant sections of text. Make sure you get all the correct stamps on arrival, or you will encounter all sorts of problems once inside the country. Low octane gasoline costs US$1.60 per litre; diesel, US$1.35. Unleaded petrol is widely available, US$1.70 super, US$1.55 regular. Service stations close at 1700-1800.

Touching down

Official time 6 hours behind GMT.
Hours of business 0800-1200, 1430-1730 or 1800. Banks: 0830-1200, 1400-1600, but 0830-1130 on Saturday. Government offices are not normally open on Saturday in Managua, or in the afternoon anywhere.
IDD 505. Equal tones with long pauses indicate it is ringing. Equal tones with equal pauses means engaged.
Voltage 110 volts AC, 60 cycles.
Weights and measures The metric system

is official, but in domestic trade local terms are in use; for example, the medio, which equals a peck (2 dry gallons), and the fanega, of 24 medios. These are not used in foreign trade. The principal local weight is the arroba=25 pounds (lbs) and the quintal of 101.417 English pounds. Random variety of other measures in use include US gallon for petrol, US quart and pint for liquids; vara (33 inches) for short distances and the pound for certain weights.

For motorcyclists, the wearing of crash helmets is compulsory. Beware when driving at night, many cars have no lights. Your car may be broken into if unattended and not in a secure place. In general, major roads are not in very good shape.

Hitchhiking Hitchhiking is widely accepted, but not easy because so many people do it and there is little traffic, offer to pay ('pedir un ride').

Keeping in touch

Language A basic knowledge of Spanish is essential for independent travel in Nicaragua. On the Atlantic coast English is widely spoken, but in the rest of the country only at expensive hotels, tour companies and airline offices.

Postal services Airmail to Europe takes two to four weeks (letter rate five córdobas); from Europe seven to 10 days; to USA four córdobas (three córdobas to Miami); to Australia six córdobas.

Telephone services Telegraph and telephone lines are owned by the Empresa Nicaragüense de Telecomunicaciones (Enitel), formerly known as Telcor. Automatic national and international telephone calls are possible from any private or public phone. Card phones were introduced in 1994.

Phone numbers in Nicaragua have seven digits. Outside Managua each town has a three-figure prefix, followed by four digits: León 311, Masaya 522, Granada 552, Bluefields 822, Corinto 342, Chinandega 341, Jinotepe 412, Rivas 453, Ometepe Moyogalpa 459, Ometepe Altagracia 552, San Juan del Sur 458, San Jorge 453, Boaco 842, Diriamba 422, La Boquita 552, San Marcos 432, Juigalpa 812, Santo Tomás 819, Estelí 713, Matagalpa 612, Jinotega 632, Somoto 722, Ocotal 732, Puerto Cabezas 282, Corn Island 285, San Carlos 283. If you are phoning from inside the prefix zone you dial the seven digits, but if you are dialling a different zone you put 0 in front, for example to dial a Managua number from Masaya would be 0266-8689. The international code for Nicaragua is 505, followed by a seven-digit number.

International or national calls can be made at any Enitel office, ■ 0700-2200. All phone calls can be paid for in córdobas. Rates: US$10 for three minutes to USA, US$11.50 to Europe. You may have to wait a long time for a line, except for early in the morning on weekdays. You have to say in advance how long you want to talk for. Person to person calls are charged extra. Collect calls to the USA are easy ('a pagarse allá'), also possible to Europe. For SPRINT, dial 171; AT&T 174 and MCI 166. To connect to phone services in Germany dial 169, Belgium 172, Canada 168, Spain 162, Netherlands 177, UK 175. International Fax services are available in all major cities, US$4.50 per page to Europe. See under Managua **Telecommunications** for Enitel's excellent telephone directory.

Media **Newspapers** All published in Managua, but many widely available in the country: Dailies: La Prensa, centre, the country's best, especially for coverage of happenings outside of Managua;

El Nuevo Diario, centre-left and sensationalist; *La Tribuna*, right-leaning, short on news. Weeklies: *El Seminario*, left-leaning, well-written; *7 Días*, pro-Government; *Tiempo del Mundo*, owned by Rev Moon, good coverage of South America, not much on Nicaragua. Monthlies: *Nicanews*, English language, centre-right and not much in-depth reporting (www.nicanews.com.ni not updated frequently); *El País*, pro-Government, good features, well-written.

Food and drink

Restaurants Fifteen percent tax is added to all restaurant bills and 10% service is added or expected as a tip. **NB** The *Colectivo de Soja* encourages the use of soya as an alternative source of protein; vegetarian restaurants of this chain are in Masaya, Managua, Granada, San Juan del Sur and Estelí. Some Nicaraguan 'pizzas' are not much like the real thing, and the coffee can be terrible.

Different cuisines Try *nacatamales*, cornflower dumplings stuffed with meat and vegetables, boiled in banana leaves, an excellent value meal; or *Gallo Pinto*, a tasty dish of rice and beans. Fizzy drinks are known as 'gaseosas' in Nicaragua as in neighbouring countries. Fresh drinks are 'refrescos'.

Holidays and festivals

1 January: New Year's Day; **March or April:** Thursday of Holy Week and Good Friday; **1 May:** Labour Day; **19 July:** Revolution of 1979; **14 September:** Battle of San Jacinto; **15 September:** Independence Day; **2 November:** All Souls' Day (Día de los Muertos); **7 and 8 December:** Immaculate Conception (Purísima); **25 December:** Christmas Day.

Businesses, shops and restaurants all close for most of Holy Week; many companies also close down during the Christmas-New Year period. Holidays which fall on a Sunday are taken the following Monday. Local holidays are given under the towns.

Health

Take the usual tropical precautions about food and drink. Tap water is not recommended for drinking generally and avoid uncooked vegetables and peeled fruit. Intestinal parasites abound; if requiring treatment, take a stool sample to a Government laboratory before going to a doctor.

Malaria Malaria risk exists especially in the wet season; take regular prophylaxis. **Dengue fever** is also present, including in Managua; avoid being bitten by mosquitoes.

Nicaragua

Managua

Managua, the nation's capital and commercial centre since 1858, is on the southern shores of Lake Managua (Lago Xolotlán), at an altitude of between 40 and 150 metres. It is 45 kilometres from the Pacific, but 148 kilometres from the main port, Corinto, though a new port, Puerto Sandino (formerly Puerto Somoza), is only 70 kilometres away. Managua was destroyed by an earthquake in March 1931, and part of it swept by fire five years later; it was completely rebuilt as an up-to-date capital and commercial city, but the centre was again completely destroyed, apart from a few modern buildings, by another earthquake in December 1972. There was further severe damage during the Revolution of 1978-79. Flooding as a result of Hurricane Mitch in October 1998 caused some loss of lakeside areas, but the city was largely unaffected.

Population: 864,201
Colour map 4, grid C5

Since 1997, the old centre has become a garden monument. Despite seismologists warnings (Managua is built over 14 seismic faults, one of which runs directly through the old centre), some important buildings are being built, including a new presidential palace, between the ruins of the old Cathedral and the lake front (the epicentre in 1972). Two areas now lay claim to being the heart of Managua and both have brand new multilevel shopping centres. The older of the two is based on the Hotel Interconti-nental, with a new shopping and cinema complex, complete with a US-style 'food court', and nearby Plaza España, which has the country's best supermarket and numerous shops, banks, travel agents, tour companies and nearly every airline office in the country. The other heart of Managua is based on the Carretera a Masaya, from the new Cathedral to Camino de Oriente. This stretch of four-lane highway includes the Rotunda Rubén Darío, the Metrocentro shopping complex, numerous restaurants, the financial centre of the country (Edificio Banic) and the cinema, disco and offices of Camino de Oriente.

Ins & outs

Getting there   The airport is 12 km east of the city, near the lake. Buses and taxis run to the city. International bus services arrive at their own terminals in different parts of the city (addresses are given below, **Transport, International buses**). Some, such as Tica, Cruceros del Golfo, Panaline and Nicabus, are in Barrio Martha Quezada, where most of the cheap hotels are to be found. Provincial bus services have 3 main arrival/departure points (see **Transport, Bus**, below). City buses and taxis serve the provincial terminals.

Getting around   Directions are given according to landmarks; in place of cardinal points, the following are used: Al Lago (north), Arriba (east), Al Sur (south), Abajo (west). (This applies to the whole country; even where there are street names or numbers, Nicaraguans give direction by landmarks.) Some landmarks are places which no longer exist (eg *Lacmiel* restaurant), so it may take a bit of time to find your way around. Budget travellers tend to congregate in the Barrio Martha Quezada, which is just west and within walking distance of the *Hotel Intercontinental*. It is also within walking distance of Plaza España. The Carretera a Masaya area is some distance from the old centre and Martha Quezada, so to get there, or to the provincial bus terminals, some form of city transport will have to be taken. Buses are cheap but crowded. Their routes can be hard to fathom; some of the main ones are given under **Transport, Local Bus**, below. Taxis have either red number plates (licensed) or blue (pirates); the former are theoretically safer. Taxi-sharing in Managua is common, so don't be surprised if the driver stops to pick someone up on roughly the same route. For more details, see **Tansport, Local** and **Security**, below.

Sights

In the old centre of Managua, one can still see examples of colonial architecture in the **Palacio Nacional de la Cultura** (previously the Palacio de los Héroes de la Revolución), which has been beautifully restored and has permanent and temporary exhibits in the Nicaraguan National Gallery, the **Museo Nacional** and the National Library. A 20-minute introductory guided tour is included in the US$1 admission, available in French and English, ■ *Daily 0800-1700.*

The atmosphere of an old and sad cathedral in ruins, accentuated at night when concerts are performed with moody lighting and a host of bats.

The old **Cathedral** is now open as a museum. It has been tastefully restored; only the roof of narrow steel girders, glass and the side window support bars were added to keep it standing. Check the *Guía Fácil* for schedules. ■ *Entry from 0900, US$1.* **Centro Cultural Managua**, behind the Palacio Nacional de Cultura, has a good selection of before and after photos of quake-struck Managua in 1972. There are some antique and craft shops and art exhibits in galleries downstairs. Upstairs, to the right and to the far end, is the office of *Guía Fácil*, the most comprehensive guide to what's happening in Managua. These buildings are situated on the **Parque Central** and provide a striking contrast with the modern **Teatro Rubén Darío** on the lake shore (good plays and musical events; also Sala Experimental. ■ *Entry US$1.50 to US$3.50 depending on show*). There are usually temporary exhibitions in the theatre so, in the day, ask at the window to view the exhibit and you can probably look at the auditorium as well. The **Parque de la Paz**, just southeast of the Parque Central, is part of the rebuilding programme for the old centre. It is very popular at weekends, both during the day and in the evenings. There are free concerts every Sunday night. The park is a graveyard for weapons and a few dozen truckloads of AK-47s are buried there, some of which can be seen sticking out of the cement.

Three blocks south of the Parque Central are the offices of the presidency and the

Managua

■ **Sleeping**	● **Eating**	
1 Estrella	1 Los Gauchos	2 Barrio Linda Vista
2 Fiedler	2 Sandy's	3 CST
3 Intercontinental		4 Las Piedrecitas
4 Palace	🚍 **Transport**	5 Nuevo Diario
	1 Sirca Bus	6 7 Sur

N

0 km   1
0 miles   0.6

Nicaragua

Nicaraguan parliament, which includes the city's only high-rise building, once the Banco de América, now the offices of the congressmen and women (diputados).

A significant landmark is the *Hotel Intercontinental*, designed a little like a Maya pyramid, which is about a dozen blocks south of the old Cathedral (not too far to walk). Its entrance is on Avenida Bolívar and in front of it is the new Plaza Inter shopping centre with cinemas, restaurants and shops. The Bolívar-Buitrago junction, at the northwest corner of Plaza Inter, is on a number of important bus routes.

Parque Nacional de la Loma de Tiscapa can be reached from behind the hotel by an access road for the military which the public may use. ■ *1200-1630 daily.* Tell the guards that you want to visit the park and they should let you in. Follow the road to the top where the giant black statue of Sandino stands. This is the finest view of the city and of the Laguna de Tiscapa. Since the 1996 change in government it has not been well-maintained, but the spot has much historical significance. It is the site of the former presidential palace, Sandino was assassinated here, and underneath the park facing the laguna (now blocked by a fence) are the torture chambers of the Somoza regime.

To the west of the *Intercontinental* is the **Barrio Martha Quezada**. This district (see **Ins & outs** above) is a mixture of quite well-to-do housing side by side with poorer dwellings. South again, through the Bolonia district, is **Plaza España** by the Rotondo El Güengüense roundabout. Plaza España is reached either by continuing over the hill above the *Intercontinental* and branching right at the big junction, or by going south on Williams Romero, the Avenida at the west edge of Barrio Martha Quezada (bus 118).

A new **Cathedral** has been inaugurated (1993), 500 metres south of the Laguna de Tiscapa. It was designed by a Mexican architect, Ricardo Legoretto; comments on the exterior range from "strikingly beautiful" to "sacrilegious". The interior, which is mostly unadorned concrete, has been described as "post-nuclear, with an altar resembling a futuristic UN Security Council meeting room". Many visitors are fascinated by the Sangre de Cristo room, where a lifesize, bleeding Christ is encased in a glass and steel dome, illuminated by a domed roof with hundreds of holes for the sun to filter through. At night, the dome sparkles with the glow of lightbulbs in the holes. Access, for pedestrians only, is from the Metrocentro junction.

Sketch / Main Streets Only

Carretera Norte

Pista Portezuelo

Sabana Grande

Blvd Buenos Aires

Mercado Iván
o Montenegro

To Airport, Hotels Camino
Real & Las Mercedes

To Plaza El Mayoreo Bus Station

From Metrocentro, around which much new construction is taking place, the Carretera a Masaya passes through Altamira district (restaurants, a few hotels, internet cafés, Sirca bus) to the financial centre, the Semáforas de la Centroamérica and Camino de Oriente.

The **Iglesia Santa María de los Angeles**, Barrio Riguero (east of Metrocentro, south of Pista de la Municipalidad), was the initial setting for the 'misa revolucionaria', a Catholic/secular mass, interesting wall paintings. The mass is now celebrated only on special occasions and not necessarily at this church.

Nicaragua

Excursions

There are several volcanic-crater lakes in the environs of Managua, some of which have become centres of residential development, and also have swimming, boating, fishing and picnicking facilities for the public. Among the more attractive of these lakes is **Laguna de Xiloá**, situated about 16 kilometres from Managua just off the new road to Léon. At Xiloá there is a private aquatic club (El Náutico); small restaurants and hotels; boats can be rented; bathing possible on the narrow beach (with caves, drownings have occurred). On Saturday and Sunday, the only days when buses run, Xiloá gets very crowded, but it is quiet during the week, when you must walk there. You can camp there. Take bus 113 to Las Piedrecitas for bus to Xiloá, Saturday and Sunday only (US$0.35); admission US$1.60 for cars, US$0.30 for pedestrians. Other lakes within a 45-minute drive of Managua are the Laguna de Masaya and Laguna de Apoyo (see page 1003 and 1004), situated respectively at Kms 35 and 15 on the Masaya road.

The **Huellas de Acahualinca** are Managua's only site of archaeological interest. These are prehistoric (6,000-year-old) animal and human footprints which have been preserved in tufa, located close to the old centre of town, near the lakeshore at the end of the south Highway. There is still some debate as to the origin and purpose of the footprints. There is also a small, interesting museum which exhibits a variety of prehistoric artefacts. Entry US$1, all explanations in Spanish. Taxi or car recommended, not a nice neighbourhood. Buses 102, 12 or 6 pass the site, look out for a concrete tower and a huge stone slab by a small red footbridge. There are no signs. By road, take the street that leads west (abajo) from the old centre and continue to the big building of López Richardson International Inc. Turn right (al Lago) immediately before López Richardson; the pavement becomes a dirt road and, just after it does, on the right is the museum.

A 10-kilometre drive down Carretera Sur – this is the Pan-American Highway – through the residential section of Las Piedrecitas passes the US Ambassador's residence to **Laguna de Asososca**, another small lake (the city's reservoir) in the wooded crater of an old volcano. Piedrecitas Park is to one side of the lake: there is a beautiful three and a half kilometre ride, playgrounds for children, a café, and splendid view of Lake Managua, two smaller lakes – Asososca and Xiloá – and of Momotombo volcano. Beyond again is the little **Laguna de Nejapa** (medicinal waters). The Pan-American Highway to Costa Rica passes through **Casa Colorada** (hotel), 26 kilometres from Managua, at 900 metres, with commanding views of both the Pacific and of Lake Managua, and a delightful climate (but no trees because of poisonous gases from Santiago volcano, see page 1002).

Thirty kilometres from Managua is the village of Mateare, a pleasant fishing and agricultural town with some of the finest lake fish in Lake Managua (eat at your own risk). The lake is much cleaner here than on the Managua side and the fishermen will take you to the little volcanic island of **Momotombito**. The best time of year to visit is during the rainy season, with the island green and the swell on the lake small. The boat ride in the dry season can be alarming and you may get very wet. Price about US$60 for the day. There are other small islands in the shadow of the smoking Momotombo volcano which peers over the lake from the mainland shore. Momotombito is a nature reserve, and has much bird and reptile life and a legendary family of albino crocodiles. There is a small military outpost on the calm side of the island. Stop there to check in if you wish to hike on the islands. Bring drinks or food as gifts for the (non-uniformed) guards, who are very friendly and usually quite bored. They might take you hiking for a small fee (make an offer) to see what is left of many precolumbian idols, most of which have been robbed, though one can be seen in the Museo Nacional. The guards know of others still on the island. As Momotombito is the best place in Nicaragua for snake lovers, a guard and his machete is indeed a highly recommended asset for hiking around the island.

Essentials
Sleeping

Try to choose a central hotel (ie near *Intercontinental* or Plaza España) since transport to the outskirts is so difficult. There are two good hotels close to the airport, **LL** *Camino Real* (*Princess Reforma*), Km 9½ Carretera Norte, Apdo Postal C118, T2631381, F2631380, 2 km from terminal, shuttle bus to the airport free, superb, beautiful gardens, new conference hall, English spoken, restaurant, live music. **AL** *Las Mercedes*, Km 11 Carretera Norte, T2631011/28, F2631082/3, under new ownership (1999), excellent food, but expensive, charming open-air restaurant, pleasant hotel, opposite airport (4 minutes' walk), often means eating and swimming in a mist of jet fuel, 3 swimming pools, beware mosquitoes after dark, tennis court, barber shop, all rooms have cable TV, a/c, bath, fridge, phone, local phone calls can be made here when airport office is shut, 2 tame red macaws accept food, snowy white owls in trees at night; the outdoor café is the best place to kill time near the airport.

LL *Princess*, Km 4½ Carretera a Masaya, T2705045, brand new, a/c, cable TV, hot water, 2 telephones in every room, laundry service, restaurant, bar, internet service, secretary service, friendly front desk, centrally located, some rooms with view of lake. **L** *Intercontinental*, 'El Inter', 101 Octava C SO, T2286991, 2283530/9, F2285208/2283087, PO Box 3278, some rooms small for the price, slow service, sauna, use of swimming pool for non-residents on Sunday, US$10, bookshop, handicraft shop, buffet, breakfast and lunch (see below), Visa cards accepted, do not take photographs in vicinity, as the area behind is the HQ of the armed forces. **L-AL** *Mansión Teodolinda*, Bolonia, T2281050, F2224908, hotel@teodolinda.com.ni, a/c, private bath with hot water, kitchenette with refrigerator, cable TV, telephone, pool, bar, restaurant, laundry service, very clean, often full with business people, good location. **L-AL** *Las Colinas*, Las Colinas, Embajada de España 3 C al lago, T2760035/2760162, a/c, with bath, hot water, cable TV, bar, restaurant, pool, secure parking, far from centre (no taxis or buses).

AL *King's Palace*, Km 5 Carretera a Masaya, T2774548, F2782456, a/c, hot water, cable TV, internet, poor value but good location. **AL-A** *Hostal Real*, Bolonia, opposite German Embassy, T2668133/2681438, private bath with hot water, breakfast included, internet, cable TV, interesting and unique airy rooms decorated with antiques and art, "the most

15% tax is added to hotel bills. The Government stipulates a small additional charge for rooms with a telephone (whether used or not).

■ *on maps Price codes: see inside front cover*

Barrio Martha Quezada

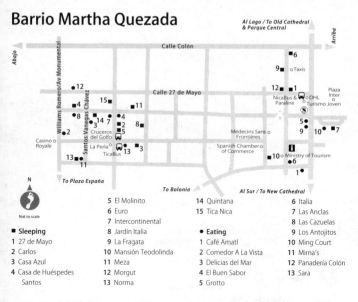

N
Not to scale

■ **Sleeping**
1 27 de Mayo
2 Carlos
3 Casa Azul
4 Casa de Huéspedes
  Santos
5 El Molinito
6 Euro
7 Intercontinental
8 Jardín Italia
9 La Fragata
10 Mansión Teodolinda
11 Meza
12 Morgut
13 Norma
14 Quintana
15 Tica Nica

● **Eating**
1 Café Amatl
2 Comedor A La Vista
3 Delicias del Mar
4 El Buen Sabor
5 Grotto
6 Italia
7 Las Anclas
8 Las Cazuelas
9 Los Antojitos
10 Ming Court
11 Mirna's
12 Panadería Colón
13 Sara

Nicaragua

beautiful hotel interior in Nicaragua", very clean, very well booked so reserve in advance, centrally located. Highly recommended. **A** *Casa Verde*, Bello Horizonte, Iglesia Pío X, 1 C arriba, 5 C al sur, T2493845, new, a/c, cable TV, gym, laundry service, restaurant, hair salon, owned by famous Sandinista revolutionary Tomás Borge, clean, friendly. At Km 8.5 on Carretera Sur is **A** *César*, T2652760/2888, great value, often fully booked, call ahead, Swiss-run, garden, safe, very good food, garage, swimming pool for children. **A** *Estancia La Casona* Bolonia, Canal 2, 1 C al lago, ½ C abajo, T2661685, F2665677, bneret@ibw.com.ni, includes breakfast, private bath with hot water, a/c, cable TV, telephone, laundry service, bar, secure parking, monthy rates available. **A** *Estrella*, Semáforos de Rubenia 2CN, T2897213, 2897010/3, F2897104, a/c, swimming pool, with breakfast, long way from centre, book in advance as it's very popular. **A** *La Posada del Angel*, Rotunda El Güegüense (Plaza España), 2 C abajo, 1 C al lago, 1 C abajo, 1 C a lago, T/F2661347, private bath with hot water, cable TV, a/c, mini-bar, telephone, laundry service, recommended. **A** *Ticomo* at Km 8½, Carretera Sur, T265-1427/1273, F2651529, has parking facilities, rents apartments, a/c, with maid service and kitchenette, breakfast extra, overpriced, lovely gardens with lots of birds, rooms smelly and in need of refurbishment. **A-B** *Europeo*, Bolonia, Canal 2, 75 metros abajo, T/F2685999, a/c, private bath, hot water, cable TV, includes continental breakfast, restaurant, bar, fax, secure parking, laundry service, internet, very clean, interesting furnishings, each room unique, very friendly and helpful staff, hotel proceeds go to a drug rehabilitation programme, quiet but central location, highly recommended.

B *Colón*, Km 4½ Carretera a Masaya, del Lacmiel 2 C arriba, T2782490, near Sirca bus terminal, with bath and a/c, **C** with fan, cable TV, secure, clean, good restaurant. At Km 3.5 on Carretera Sur is **B** *D'Lido*, from match factory 2½ blocks south, T2666145, F2664560, restaurant not recommended, use of swimming pool by non-residents, US$1. **B** *El Hotelito*, Parque El Carmen, 1 C al norte o de Montoya, 2 C arriba y 1 C al Sur, T2662751, F2662756, a/c, pleasant, convenient, has an interesting collection of contemporary Nicaraguan paintings. **B** *Euro del Intercontinental* 2 C al Lago, 1 C abajo, T2222292, a/c or fan, TV, bath, breakfast extra,

Altamira

To Metrocentro & Hotel Princess

Ex-Lacmiel   La Fonda   Colón
● o Coyotes ■
Domino's Pizza ●   Casa del ● ● Martín Fierro
Pomodoro
La Cocina de   Alianza o
Doña Haydée ●   Francesa
Optica   o Mi Oficina Internet
Matamoros o   o
Mexican   Casa del Café
Embassy
■ Kings
Palace
✉
Distribuidora o
Vicky
Coconut Grove Plaza
& Cyber Café
Bongo   o
● 🚌 Sirca Bus

o Shell

o BANIC 💲 Forex

o Banco del Café

o La Colonia
Semáforas de la
Centroamérica   Pista Portezuelo

N

Camino
de Oriente o
Not to scale   *To Masaya & Granada*

Carretera a Masaya

water and coffee available all day. **B** *La Fragata*, Estatua Simón Bolívar 1 C al oeste, 50 varas al sur, a block west of the *Intercontinental*, T2224179, F2224133, remodelled, good value, includes full breakfast, good restaurant, new beds, hot showers (not electric), cable TV, a/c, central, recommended. **B** *Las Cabañas*, near Plaza 19 de Julio, good, helpful, with pool and decent restaurant next door. **B** *Montserrat*, Bolonia, de la Central de los Pipito 1 C al lago, medio arriba, T2668074, F2665060, bath, a/c, cable TV, takes credit cards, breakfast extra. **B** *Morgut*, 1 block west of *Intercontinental*, T2223340, F2223543, a/c, hot water, cable TV, laundry. Opposite is **D** *Casa de Huéspedes 27 de Mayo*, T2281263, with bath and fan, no breakfast.

C *Casa de Fiedler*, 8 C Sur-Oeste 1320 (west of Barrio Martha Quezada – from CST 2 blocks south and 1½ blocks west), T2666622, with bath and a/c or fan, comfortable, soft mattresses, clean, friendly, popular, accepts travellers' cheques, cold Victoria beer sold, good breakfasts, coffee all day, has interesting collection of precolumbian ceramics. **C** *Casa San Juan*, C Esperanza 560, T2783220, F2670419, shared bath and private bath, clean, owner's family sleeps in, safe, excellent breakfasts for US$3, friendly, good value. Highly recommended. **D** *Casa de Huéspedes Castillo*, Casa del Obrero 1 C arriba, 1½ al Sur, 2 blocks from Ticabus, also known as *Casa Ramiro*, with bath, fan, some with a/c, clean, quiet, safe.

Many hotels west of *Intercontinental Hotel* in the Barrio Martha Quezada and near the Cine Dorado (now called *Casino Royale*, but still ask for 'Cine Dorado'). To get from *Intercontinental Hotel* to the Cine Dorado, walk west for 10 minutes to a main north-south road, Av Williams Romero, Cine Dorado is just south. *Most hotels here have very thin walls and are therefore noisy.*

E pp *Jardín de Italia*, Ticabus 1 C arriba, ½ al lago, T2227967, some rooms with a/c more expensive, with bath, no breakfast. Recommended. **E** *El Pueblo*, 3 blocks north, 2 blocks E from *Intercontinental*, simple, old house, big rooms, private bath, friendly. **E** *Hospedaje Carlos*, ½ block north of Ticabus, rooms on left at the back better than on right, cold shower, fan, a/c extra, good value, clean, *Comedor El Ancla* on opposite corner. **E** *Hospedaje Quintana*, from Ticabus, 1 block north, then ½ a block west, rooms with fan, shared shower (cold), laundry, clean, good value, family-run. Recommended for longer stays. **E** *Gabruina*, T2682169, 1 block south of Ticabus, friendly.

F *Pensión Norma*, shared rooms, basic, popular but poor beds (*Comedor Mirna's* nearby). **F** *Hospedaje Meza*, from Ticabus 1 block north, 1 east, OK, laundry facilities, TV. **F** *El Dorado*, turn left out of Ticabus station, clean, small rooms of varying standard, key deposit charged. **F** *Hospedaje Tica Nica*, 1½ blocks north of Ticabus, with or without bath, noisy, use of kitchen. **F** pp *Sultana*, at the Ticabus terminal, dormitory accommodation, friendly, clean, fan, handy if you have an early bus, otherwise noisy from 0500 and overpriced. The owners of *Hospedaje Mangaia* often wait at Ticabus, free transfer to and from terminal, 1 block south then about 5 towards Plaza España, turn left in C Gabriel Cardinal Cabrera, 2nd house on right, No 930, T2680480/2668867 (Optica Nicaragüense). In the same block as Ticabus is *Casa Azul*, which is popular but pushy. **F** *El Molinito*, ½ block from Ticabus, meals available, good value, basic, clean, hot in the day. **F** *Casa de Huéspedes Santos*, from Ticabus, 1 block north, 1½ west, with bath but washbasins outside, no soap, towel or toilet paper, clean, bright, basic, good value, spacious courtyard with hammocks, friendly, serves meals, including breakfasts and snacks.

Children tout for hotels in Barrio Martha Quezada, especially at Ticabus; they say places are full when they aren't, claim commission even when they haven't directed you, and so on.

Eating

The *Hotel Intercontinental* serves enormous breakfasts (0600-1100) for US$8 (plus 15% tax and service charge), and an excellent lunch between 1200 and 1500, US$12 for as much as you want, open to non-residents (best to dress smartly); major credit cards accepted. *Hotel Las Mercedes* also serves a good US$12 buffet lunch on weekdays. ● *on maps*

New restaurants in Managua are opening all the time, other established ones are moving to new areas. The following list is by food type with a focus on the 3 main areas for the visitor. Inexpensive meals are US$2-4, mid-priced US$5-8 and expensive US$9 and upwards for a full meal.

Nicaragua

European *Hotel César*, Km 8½ Carretera Sur, T2652760, expensive and good, try duck in orange sauce, best place for those craving real Euro-food, cheeses, wines, etc. *Las Delicias del Bosque*, Colegio Centroamericana 5 Km al sur, T08830071, restaurant for the Nicaraguan power brokers, lovely setting in hills, good food, Wednesday-Saturday only, expensive. *Kameleón*, Colonial Los Robles, T2772700, mid-priced, interesting varied menu, Swiss owners, recommended.

Spanish *El Mesón Español*, Mansión Teodolinda 3 C al sur, very good, expensive, either totally empty or completely full with high level government employees. *El Mesón Express*, Plaza Inter food court, budget version of above, good paella for US$3.30, cup of wine US$1, good value, but overlit noisy location. *Rincón Español*, Iglesia El Carmen, 2 C al lago, 1 C abajo, mid-priced, good.

French *Bistro Parisien*, Camino de Oriente, opposite Alhambra theatres, T2787213, mid-priced good salads, big Quiche Lorraine for US$4 that can feed 3, excellent café espresso. *La Marseillaise*, C Principal Los Robles, T2770224, closed Sunday, daily specials, good wine list, very expensive and tasty.

Greek *Acrópolis*, Colonia Los Robles, Plaza El Sol, 2 C al sur, 5 C arriba, T2774361, new, mid-priced, mixed reports. *Souvlaki's* opposite *Casa del Café*, new, cheap, good pizza, slow friendly service, recommended.

Italian *La Casa del Pomodoro*, de Lacmiel 100 metros arriba, new. *Grotto*, across the street from Plaza Inter, expensive, mixed reports, power lunches. *Italia*, Bolonia next to Institute of Tourism, Managua's best Italian food, mid-priced, try seafood pizza or octopus in garlic butter, also excellent soups and pastas, highly recommended. *Michelangelo*, Rotonda Metrocentro, 1 C al sur, ½ abajo, expensive pastas and pizzas, bar, cocktails, fast efficient service, popular with expat community. *Pasta Fresca*, del Sandy Carretera a Masaya 2 C arriba, mid-priced, excellent fresh pasta, great bread, good service, highly recommended. *Pizza Valenti*, Colonial Los Robles, best cheap pizza, US$4.50. *Pizza House*, 1 block north of *Pizza Valenti*, more expensive pizza, but better cheese and service.

Middle Eastern *El Mediterráneo*, Km 5 Carretera a Masaya, next to *Kings Palace Hotel*, good humus, shawarma, mid-priced.

Steak Houses For the best value, *Las Brasas*, behind Cinema 1 & 2, Camino Oriente, good cheap Nicaraguan fare, traditional, outdoors, great atmosphere, sea bass US$5.50, churrasco steak US$5, best deal to drink rum with friends, half bottle comes with bowl of ice, limes, a coke and 2 plates of food, US$9.50. *El Churrasco*, Rotonda El Güegüense (Plaza España), expensive and very good beef dishes. *Harry's Grill Argentino*, frente a los semáforos del Super de la Centroamérica, T2702382, very expensive Argentine dishes with imported beef, very good. *Los Gauchos*, Carretera a Masaya Km 3.5, very famous, very overpriced, locals eat elsewhere. *Martín Fierro*, de Lacmiel 1 C arriba, best steak, Argentine grill, excellent. *La Plancha*, various locations, T2782999 for nearest one, good value, very generous portions, good beef, very popular, one Nicaraguan serving often can feed two foreigners, recommended.

Central American *Los Antojitos*, opposite *Intercontinental*, interesting photos of Managua pre-earthquake, good food and good portions, and garden (open at 1200). *La Cocina de Doña Haydée*, frente a Pastelería Aurami, Planes de Altamira, T2706100, mid-priced, once a popular family kitchen eatery that has gone upscale, traditional Nicaraguan food at higher prices than elsewhere, very popular with foreign residents, good. *El Cartel*, across Carretera a Masaya from Metrocentro, T2772619, expensive traditional fare, dance floor, nice setting, popular with Miami crowd. *Guayacán*, Km 11½ Carretera a Masaya, T2799638, grilled beef, closed Mondays. *Rincón Salvadoreño*, Bolonia, Rotonda El Güegüense, 1 C al lago, 1 C arriba, *pupusas*, *tamales* and *quesadillas*, very cheap, simple and good. *Topkapi*, Camino de Oriente, across from Alhambra cinema, pizza (US$2.50), tacos, Nicaraguan food, inexpensive, good people watching, outdoor seating, recommended. *La Fonda*, de Lacmiel 1 C al este, opposite *Casa del Pomodoro*, good, try *quesadilla suprema*, also has vegetarian.

Mexican *La Hora del Taco*, Sandy's Carretera a Masaya 1 C arriba, T2770949, mid-priced traditional Mexican fair, good, nice setting outside at back. *Jalapeño's*, Rotonda Metrocentro, 1 C abajo, ½ al sur, T2786341, mid-priced trendy California-style Mexican restaurant, good *tacos*, *tortilla* soup. *María Bonita*, Altamira, de la Vicky 1½ C abajo, T2704326, mid to expensive, closed Monday, wildly popular on weekend nights with a noisy, happy crowd, good food and service, fun, recommended. *Tacos al Pastor*, Carretera a Masaya across from Camino de Oriente, T2782650, budget to mid-priced, also *burritos* and *enchiladas*, popular with young crowd.

Cuban *Bongo*, Carretera a Masaya across from Colegio Teresiano, mid-priced, food not special but good cocktails, upper class crowd.

Chinese *China de Asia*, de Lacmiel 1 C arriba, ½ al sur, Taiwanese specialties, mid-priced, good. *Rincón Chino*, Km 4½ Carretera Norte, T2440155, cheap, popular, traditional fare. *Ming Court*, in front of *Intercontinental*, very good, expensive, elegant, try the shark soup.

Japanese *Bonsai*, in Colonia Los Robles, T2787017, sushi, sachemi, closed Mondays. *La Estrella de Oriente*, across from *Mansión Teodolinda*, expensive, maki sushi, crab, salmon, nice cosy decor, embassy crowd.

Sea Food *Arrecife*, Camino de Oriente, T2780898, mid-priced, good location for people watching, crab salad, *shrimps alla romana*, closed Tuesdays. At Km 6½ on Carretera Sur is *The Lobster's Inn*, very good. *Las Lugo*, Carretera a Masaya Km 4.5, best seafood, expensive but worth it, octopus US$13, lobster US$17, sea bass US$11.

Fast Food *La Ballena que Cayó del Cielo*, next to Camino de Oriente, T2773055, cheap to mid-price, Nicaragua's best hamburgers, good grilled chicken, salsa and merengue videos. *La Crema Batida*, Camino de Oriente, T2772517, cheap, North American style foods with many ice cream combinations, family crowd. *Famous Burger and Fries*, Carretera a Masaya across from Colegio Teresiano, cheap and greasy. *McDonald's*, Plaza España, the clown shows his face in Nicaragua for the first time since the revolution. *Sandy's* is the poor local version of MacDonald's, one on Carretera a Masaya, Km 4, and 2 other branches. *Subway*, Carretera a Masaya across from Colegio Teresiano, also inside many mini-markets at Texaco gas stations, cheap North American chain, nothing special.

In the *Intercontinental*/**Plaza España** /**Barrio Martha Quezada area**: *Taco's*, Av Williams Romero on corner with and opposite road to *Pensión Norma*, tacos and natural *refrescos*. *Comedor Sara*, next to Ticabus, cheap, popular with gringos, serves breakfast, has noticeboard. *Eskimo* ice cream, on C 27 de Mayo before ex-Cine Cabrera. Near *Santos*, *China Bien Bien*, on 27 de Mayo, 1 block south and 1 block abajo from CST, T669045, excellent fast food, Chinese. *Delicias del Mar*, ½ block from *Santos* on Santos Vargas Chávez, reported good. *Las Anclas*, 1 block from *Casa Santos*, good seafood. *Mirnas*, near *Pensión Norma*, open 0700-1500, good breakfasts and *comidas*. *Comedor a la Vista*, opposite *Casino Royale* (Cine Dorado), popular.

Bakeries *Colón*, 27 de Mayo, 1 block behind *Casa de Huéspedes Santos*, popular, good value. *Tonalli*, Bolonia, 1 block west and 1½ north from *Hotel Mansión Teodolinda*, fresh breads, pastries, quiches, excellent large pretzels on Friday. *Alemania*, Bolonia, 2 blocks north of Institute of Tourism, OK. *Baguette*, Planes de Altamira, good, off Carretera a Masaya at Km 4½, just behind *Sorbet Inn* ice cream shop, also good. *Aurami*, Planes de Altamira, off Carretera a Masaya at Km 5, ½ block west, best in Managua.

Cafés *Casa del Café*, Altamira, popular with foreigners, nice building, small bookshop, pricey, good cake, not so good expresso. *La Bodeguita del Centro*, in front left corner of Centro Cultural Managua, Cuban-owned, great food, Cuban coffee, bohemian crowd, nice atmosphere, concerts Friday night. Recommended.

Bars *Bar Chaman*, Colonial Los Robles, US$2 entrance, young, wild crowd, no room to breath, rock and roll and old disco on tape, lots of dancing and sweating, great fun. *La Ruta Maya*, de Montoya 150 metres east, entrance US$5. *El Parnaso*, Metrocentro 1 block south, very hip crowd, bookshop open during Colonia Centro América, opposite Shell, fun crowd who fill big dance floor and dance non-stop, no entrance fee, live music, ranchera, salsa, merengue. *Café Amatl*, Bolonia, terminally hip crowd, bookshop open during the day, lunch US$1.50, nice outdoor setting, good crêpes at night, good live music, Brazilian, reggae, folk. Recommended. *La Cavanga*, trendy new bar next to the Centro Cultural Managua.

Bars & nightlife

Nicaragua

Discotheques *Zima*, Camino de Oriente, T2670123, the largest disco in Central America. *La Cabaña* in the *Intercontinental* and the *Piano Bar* across the street, the latter is a cultural experience. *Cat's Club*, at the edge of the Martha Quezada district, good dance music.

Entertainment and shopping

Entertainment *Guía Fácil* is the most comprehensive guide to films, theatre, dance, restaurants, art exhibits and what's on in Managua. Highly recommended. US$1.20. Can be found at the Centro Cultural Managua, La Colonia Supermarket in Plaza España and at the Ministry of Tourism.

Ballet Ballet Tepenahuatl, folkloric dances in the ruins of the *Gran Hotel*.

Cinemas *Cinemateca Nacional*, Parque Central south corner, US$2, best movies in Managua, Monday-Friday 1830, 2000, Saturday, Sunday 1600, 1800, 2000. *Alianza Francesa*, Altamira, 1 block north of Mexican embassy, Friday 1900, free, French films, art exhibits during the day. *Cinema 1 & 2*, Camino de Oriente, US films, Spanish subtitles, US$3. *Alhambra 1, 2 & 3*, Camino de Oriente, US films, Spanish subtitles, US$3, bring sweater for polar a/c. *Plaza Inter*, 4 screens, American films, subtitles in Spanish, buy tickets in advance for weekend nights.

Festivals Santo Domingo is the patron saint of Managua. His festival is held at El Malecón from **1 to 10 August**: church ceremonies, horse racing, bull-fights, cock-fights, a lively carnival; proceeds to the General Hospital. **1 August** (half day) and **10 August** are local holidays.

Shopping The best place to buy handicrafts, and just about anything else, is the *Mercado Ricardo Huembes* (also called Mercado Central). *Artesanía* from all parts of the country at the northeast end of the parking lot. Some handicrafts (goldwork, embroidery, etc) are available in the refurbished Metrocentro, in the new Plaza Inter and in Centro Comercial Managua (good general shopping here). For Mercado Huembes, on Pista Portezuelo, buses 110 or 119. A smart shop selling Nicaraguan arts and crafts is *Takesa*, del *Intercontinental* 2 C al sur, ½ abajo, Edif Bolívar 203, T2683301, high quality and high prices. *Mi Pueblo* at Km 9.5 on Carretera Sur, T08825650, sells handicrafts, plants and also has a good restaurant. Postcards for sale at Tourist Office, Ministry of Culture, Mercado Huembes and *Intercontinental Hotel* (several times more expensive); also at Tarjetas Gordión. Most ordinary shops are in private houses without signs. Almacenes Internacionales (formerly Dollartienda, and Diplotienda), opposite *Los Gauchos* restaurant on Carretera a Masaya, offers Western-style goods, take your passport, accepts dollars and travellers' cheques if to value of purchase. There is an a/c supermarket on Plaza España. For chocolate, *Chocolatería Gorbea*, Calle Principal Los Robles, Pizza House 50 metros al sur, T2784091.

Mercado Oriental is not recommended, black market goods and criminals.

Bookshops *Editorial Vanguardia* in the Centro Antonio Valdivieso, C José Martí, near *Mirador Tiscapa* (also sells records), and at the Centro Comercial Managua; see *Amatl Libro Café* above. Many bookshops sell maps, postcards, badges, stickers and other tourist items. Small selection at the Centro Sandinista de Trabajadores, Ho Chi Minh Way.

Sports **Baseball**: between Plaza de España and Plaza 19 de Julio on Sunday mornings (the national game), a good seat US$0.20. Also there are basketball, cockfighting and bullfighting (but no kill), swimming, sailing, tennis, golf.

Transport

Local **Bus**: service in Managua costs US$0.13 approximately. City buses run every 10 minutes 0530-1800, every 15 minutes 1800-2200, when last services begin their routes; buses are frequent but it is difficult to fathom their routes. Beware of pickpockets on the crowded urban buses, particularly those on tourist routes. The principal bus routes are: 101 from Las Brisas, passing CST, *Intercontinental Hotel*, Mercado Oriental, then on to Mercados San Miguel and Mayoreo; 103 from 7 Sur to Mercado Lewites, Plaza 19 de Julio, Metrocentro, Mercado San Miguel and Villa Libertad; 109 from Teatro Darío to the Bolívar/Buitrago junction just before *Intercontinental*, turns east, then southeast to Mercado Huembes/bus station; 110 runs from

Buses can be very full, though not always so.

7 Sur to Villa San Jacinto passing *en route* Mercado Lewites, Plaza 19 de Julio, Metrocentro, Mercado Huembes/bus station and Mercado San Miguel; 113 from Ciudad Sandino, Las Piedrecitas, CST, *Intercontinental*, to Mercado Oriental; 116 runs east-west below *Intercontinental*, on Buitrago, also passing CST; 118 takes a similar route but turns south on Williams Romero to Plaza España, thence to Israel Lewites bus station; 119 runs from Plaza España to Mercado Huembes/bus station via Plaza 19 de Julio; 123 runs from Mercado Lewites via 7 Sur and Linda Vista to near Palacio Nacional de Cultura, and Nuevo Diario.

Car hire: Avis, by Centro Comercial Nejapa, T2650112/2331624. **Budget**, Barrio Altagracia, Estatua Montoya 1 C al sur 1 C al oeste, T2666226/2667419. **Hertz** at the airport, *Hotel Intercontinental* (T2222320), or Edif Caribe Motors, Km 4 Carretera Sur, T2668399, F2668400. **Leo's** southwest side of Rotunda Güegüense, T2663719. Rates are US$30 per day Group A to US$65 per day Group G (all a/c), unlimited mileage, US$10 per day accident protection, tax not included, discounts for 2 weeks or more. Given the poor public transport and the decentralized layout of Managua, you may find that renting a car is the best way to get around. Alternatively, hire a taxi for journeys out of Managua, about US$10 per hour from an office opposite *Hotel Intercontinental*, T2223469 (opens 0930). **Renault garage**: Km 6 Carretera Norte, in front of Coca Cola; efficient spare parts service.

Taxis: can be flagged down along the street. They also cruise the bus stations looking for arriving passengers, but it is cheaper to get a taxi on the street nearby. There is a taxi stand just below *Hotel Morgut*, west of *Intercontinental*. Taxis are the best method of transport for foreigners in Managua; bargain the fare before entering (fares range from US$0.80-US$1 for a short trip, US$1.50-US$2.5 across town, US$5 to airport). Fares are always per person, not per car. **NB** It may be handy to have the telephone number of your hotel with you. Street names and numbers are not universal in the city and the taxi driver may not know your destination, make sure you know the co-ordinates of your destination if it is a private residence. If heading for Barrio Martha Quezada, ask for the *Hotel Intercontinental* if you do not know your exact destination. Recommended radio taxis (for early flights or late night transport) are Coop 25 de Febrero, T2225218/4728, or Coop 2 de Agosto, T2631512/1838, get price quote on the phone, normally 30% more expensive.

Air César Augusto Sandino (MGA), modernized 1997. Take any bus marked 'Tipitapa' from Mercado Huembes, Mercado San Miguel or Mercado Oriental (near Victoria brewery), US$0.16. Alternatively, take a taxi for no more than US$7. Be early for international flights since formalities are slow and thorough and can take 2 hours. X-ray machines reported safe for film. Two duty free shops, café, toilets through immigration; some departing passengers (eg on Aviateca and Nica flights) are offered free coffee, juice and a *pastel* in the departure hall. Internal flights to eg Bluefields and the Corn Islands are given in the text below. You are not allowed to stay overnight in the airport. There is a bank at the airport which closes at 1600 and it is difficult to obtain local currency elsewhere at the airport.

Long distance

Nicaragua

Bus The bus station by the Mercado Roberto Huembes (Mercado Central), on Pista Portezuelo (see map), is for **Rivas**, **Granada**, **Masaya**, **San Juan del Sur** and **Sapoá**. Take bus 109, which starts from Parque Central and runs below the *Hotel Intercontinental*, or bus 119. For full details, see under destinations. For **León**, **Corinto** and **Pacific Coast** and **Chinandega**, the terminal is beside Mercado Israel Lewites, Pista de la Municipalidad, on southwest side of city. To get from the 1st bus station to the 2nd, take bus 110, or take bus 109, then change at *Intercontinental* to bus 118. It is probably simpler to take a taxi, US$3. Buses to **Estelí**, **Matagalpa**, **Somoto**, **Las Manos**, **San Carlos**, **Boaco**, **Juigalpa** and **Rama** leave from the terminal at Plaza Mayoreo, on Pista Sabana Grande and Pista de Mayoreo, in the east of the city, take the 101 bus which stops at the terminal.

Buses tend to be very full; children scramble on board first, grab seats and 'sell' them to passengers. Possible (and safer) to sit on your luggage than put it on the roof. You may have to pay extra for your baggage. Cotran, T2897820; Cotlántico, T2800036; AMSA, T2652138.

International buses: *Ticabus* to San José three times daily, US$10 single, 10-11 hours; also to Panama (US$35), Tegucigalpa (0500, US$20), San Salvador (0500, US$31) and Guatemala

City (0500, US$39), terminal is in Barrio Martha Quezada (old Cine Dorado, 2 cuadras arriba, west of *Hotel Intercontinental*, T2223031/6094, T/F2222096); passengers can stay overnight at the terminal for US$6 per person – see **Sleeping**, above. When departing Managua you must check in 1 hour in advance, with passport and ticket. On the opposite corner is *Cruceros del Golfo*, T2281454, F2223065, office open Monday-Saturday 0900-1300, 1400-1800, Sunday 1000-1700, Managua to San Salvador 0430 daily, book 1 week in advance, US$35 (next day connection to Guatemala City; check if service goes via Tegucigalpa). *Sirca Express* leaves 0500 daily to San José, US$10, 13 hours (you can stop anywhere in Costa Rica, but same price); Sirca office and terminal in Altamira, del Distribuidora Vicky 2 C al sur, T2673833/2775726. *Transnica* express to San José, office and terminal at Rotonda Santo Domingo, 150 metres east, opposite Ramac, departs Managua 0700 and 1000 daily, US$12 1 way, a/c, TV, video, snacks, toilet, T2782090, F2786014. *NicaBus*, also runs to San José, US$10 one way, office del Cine Cabrera 3 C arriba, T2281373/1383 (next to DHL, just west of *Intercontinental*). *Panaline* is at the same location, charging US$35 to Panama City. A cheaper way of travelling to San José is to take a bus Managua-Rivas, then colectivo to border and another between the border posts, then take local bus to San José; takes 15 hours altogether, cost about US$8. Similarly, taking local buses to Tegucigalpa will cost you about US$5. International buses are always booked-up many days in advance and tickets will not be sold until all passport/visa documentation is complete. Look in *El Nuevo Diario* Sección 2, 'Servicios', for buses running to San Salvador, Tegucigalpa, Guatemala City and Mexico.

Directory

Airline offices Around Plaza España: *Aeroflot* (T2663588), *Air France* (T2662612), *American Airlines*, T2663900, *Aviateca*, *Lacsa*, *Nica*, *Taca* (T2663136), *British Airways* in the same office, *Iberia* (T2664440), *Japan Airlines* (T2662588), *KLM* (T2668052, 300m east), *LanChile* (T2667011), *LTU*, Rotonda Güegüense, 2½ C arriba, T2667734. *Alitalia*, de Los Pipitos 1½ C abajo, T2667031. *Continental* (T2703403), Carretera a Masaya Km 4. *Copa*, 1 C abajo de Sorbet Inn, Carretera a Masaya, T2675438. *Mayan World Airlines*, Pancasán 3 etapa, No 39, T2783257. *La Costeña* (for the Atlantic coast), at the airport, T2631281/1228. Foreigners may pay in dollars or córdobas for internal flight tickets, but dollars only for international tickets.

Banks *Banco Nicaragüense del Interior y Comercio* at Plaza España changes bank notes only, similarly *Banexpo*. *Banco Centroamericano* and *Banco de América Central*, Plaza España, both change TCs at 5% commission. *Casas de cambio: Multicambios*, across Av Monumental from Plaza España, Mon-Fri 0830-1700, Sat 0800-1200, for US$ cash and TCs, 2% commission. *Forex*, on the lower ground floor of the Banic building, Carretera a Masaya, US$ cash into córdobas or vice-versa, Mon-Fri 0830-1230, 1330-1700, Sat 0830-1200. It is advisable to change money in Managua as it is difficult elsewhere, though getting easier. Present TC receipts in banks when changing them. Córdoba cash advances on Visa, Mastercard and Visa at *Cred-o-matic*, Camino de Oriente on Carretera a Masaya, Mon-Fri 0800-1645, Sat 0800-1200. *BanPro*, Carretera a Masaya, nearer Metrocentro and Subway sandwich shop, also advances cash on Visa at 2½% commission, open Mon-Fri 0830-1630, Sat 0830-1300. Banks on Plaza España advertise Visa but do not have facilities to advance cash to foreigners. Money changers on the street (*coyotes*) during business hours are legitimate and their rates differ little from banks. After 1800 and on Sun they are usually tricksters. Several hang out at the road junction in Altamira by restaurants *La Fonda* and *Casa del Pomodoro*. On Sun you can change money at *Intercontinental* and *Pinolero* cambio, Iglesia Carmen 1 block south, open daily, long queues. US dollars accepted everywhere, change given in córdobas. Any note larger than US$5 or 50 córdobas will present a change problem, especially for taxis, unless you are in a restaurant, hotel or supermarket.

Communications General Post Office: 3 blocks west of Palacio Nacional and Cathedral, 0700-1600 (closed Sat pm). Wide selection of beautiful stamps. Poste Restante (Lista de Correos) keeps mail for 45 days, US$0.20 per letter. There is another Post Office in the Centro Comercial Managua. **Telecommunications:** Enitel, same building as Post Office. Mercado Roberto Huembes (Eduardo Contreras), on bus route 109 from *Hotel Intercontinental*, open 0700-2230. The Enitel office in Altamira sells an excellent phone directory for US$6 which is also the best tourist guide. For sending faxes, use the Enitel office in the Palace of Communications downtown (4 pages to USA US$4). **Email and internet:** *Mi Oficina*, Altamira opposite *Casa de Café*, T2704517, jtoledo@mioficina.com.ni, Mon-Fri

0800-2000, Sat-Sun 0900-1800, US$3.50 per hr, no coffee. *Cyber-Café*, de la Distribuidora Vicky 1 C al oeste y 2 C al sur, Plaza Coconut Grove, T2788526, servicio@cybercafe.com.ni, Mon-Sat 0900-2200, US$3 per hr, serves coffee. *Hotel Camino Real*, business centre, US$15 per hr.

Cultural centres Lending library, *Casa Ben Linder*, 3 blocks south 1½ blocks east of Estatua Monseñor Lezcano, also good book exchange, T2664373. *Alianza Francesa*, in Altamira near Mexican Embassy, films on Fri evenings, friendly.

Embassies & consulates *Panamanian*, Consulate, Colonia Mantica, el Cuartel General de Bomberos, 1 C abajo, casa 93, T/F2668633, open 0830-1300, visa on the spot, valid 3 months for a 30-day stay, US$10, maps and information on the Canal. *Costa Rican*, Montoya 11/2 Sts east, C 27 de Mayo, T2663986, F2663955, open 0900-1500. *Honduran* Consulate, Km 12.5 Carretera a Masaya, T2798231, F2798228, open Mon-Fri, 0830-1530 (bus 118 from *Hotel Intercontinental*), Embassy, Planes de Altamira 64, T2670184, F2670183. *Guatemalan*, just after Km 11 on Masaya Rd, T2799609, F2799610, fast service, 0900-1200 only. *Mexican*, from Km 4.5 on Carreta a Masaya, take the 2nd St on the left and it's at the 1st crossroads on your right, in Altamira, T2775886, F1782886. *Venezuelan*, Km 10.5 Carreterea a Masaya, T2760267, F2678327.

USA, Km 4½ Carretera del Sur (T2666010, F2663865), open 0730-0900. *Canadian Consul*, costado este de Casa Nazaret, 1 Carriba, C El Nogal No 25, T2680433, F2681985, open Mon-Thur 0900-1200.

British, El Reparto, 'Los Robles', Primera Etapa, Entrada Principal de la Carretera a Masaya, Cuarta Casa a la mano derecha, T2780014, F2784083, Apdo Aéreo 169, open 0900-1200. *French*, Iglesia El Carmen 1½ abajo, T2226210, F2281057, open 0800-1600; *Dutch*, del Canal 2 1 cuadra al norte, 1 cuadra al oeste, Apdo 3534, T2666175, F2660364, open 0800-1600. *Swiss*, Restaurante Marseillaise 2 C al lago, Apdo Postal 166, T2773235, F2785263. *Swedish*, from Plaza España, 1 block west (Abajo), 2 blocks to the lake, ½ block west (Abajo), Apdo Postal 2307, T2660085, F2666778, open 0800-1200. *Danish* Consulate General, Rotonda El Güegüense 1 C abajo, 2 C al lago, ½ C abajo, T2680250, F2668095, open 0800-1400. *Finnish*, Hospital Militar 1 St North, 1½ west, T2667947/2663415, open 0800-1200, 1300-1500. *German*, 200m north of Plaza España (towards lake), T2663917/8, F2667667, open Mon-Fri 0900-1200; *Italian*, Rotonda El Güegüense 1 C al lago, T2666486, F2663987, open 0900-1200.

Hospitals & medical services Hospitals: are generally crowded and queues very long. Recommended are *Hospital Bautista*, T2497070/7277, F2497327, *Hospital Militar Escuela Alejandro Dávila Bolaños*, T2222172, F2222391 (go south from *Intercontinental* and take 2nd turn on left), and *Hospital Alemán-Nicaragüense HNA*, from Siemens on Km 6 of Carretera Norte, 3 blocks south, operated with German aid, mostly Nicaraguan staff, make an appointment by phone in advance. Private clinics are an alternative, eg *Policlínica Nicaragüense*, consultation US$30. *Med-Lab*, 300m south of Plaza España, is recommended for tests on stool samples, the director speaks English. *Dr César Zepeda Monterrey* speaks English, American-trained. *Dr Sergio López*, Clínica SA Helena, Monte de los Olivos, Los Robles, T2787228, good but speaks Spanish only.

Language classes Spanish classes: and thorough introduction to Nicaragua: *Casa Nicaragüense de Español*, Km 11.5 Carretera Sur; accommodation with families. *Universidad Centroamericana* has Spanish courses which are cheaper, but with larger classes.

Security Returnees from the USA are introducing new skills learned in American inner cities. The best thing (if you are worried) is to avoid the city buses altogether, and if you find yourself in a very poor neighbourhood take the next taxi. Never walk at night unless you are in a good area or shopping centre zone. Taxis are cheap and friendly, use them (for added security, take a radio taxi – see above). Long distance buses are fine, but be careful in the market when you arrive to take the bus, try for a window seat and then relax. Nicaraguan people are among the friendliest in the world and paranoia will not serve you. Arriving in Managua at night is not a problem, but have your hotel chosen in advance and go directly in a taxi to your hotel. The Mercado Oriental (do not be confused with the Camino de Oriente which is very safe and fun) and its barrio Ciudad Jardín should be avoided at all costs, assaults in the day and night time. Roberto Huembes (Mercado Central) has the best crafts section outside of the Masaya market and is safe. The Barrio Martha Quezada is much safer than it used to be; a nightwatchman cycles around until 0500 blowing a whistle.

Managua is one of the safest cities in Latin America, but there are thieves and some gangs in the very poor areas.

Tour companies & travel agents *Tours Nicaragua*, del Hotel Intercontinental 2 cuadras al sur, ½ cuadra abajo, Edif Bolívar, Bolonia, T/F2666663, cel 088-41712, nicatour@nic.gbm.net, www.nvmundo.com/toursnicaragua. Tours to all parts of the country in vans with a/c, boats, small

Nicaragua

plane and 4x4, English, German, French, Italian, Russian speaking guides, cultural and historical tours of Granada and León, bird watching and/or hiking, archaeological tours led by expert on Río San Juan and Solentiname Islands, Isla de Ometepe, Isla Zapatera, Pacific surfing, snorkelling in Corn Island, cigar and coffee plantation tours, climbing in cloud forests and complete volcanic tours, excursions to Indio Maíz, Los Guatusos wildlife reserves, prices based on group size, also Spanish classes at Laguna de Apoyo, hotel reservations, contact Ninoska García, helpful, plenty of free advice. *Schuvar Tours*, Plaza España Edif Bamer No 4, T2663588, contact Mercedes. *Momotombo Tours*, Ciudad Jardín, casa F-35, contact Enrique. *Atlántida*, Plaza España, one block east, ½ block north, T266-4050/8721/4160, contact Francis or Lisette. *Aeromundo*, east corner of Plaza España, T266-8725/3408, contact Esmeralda. *Viajes Globo*, Bolonia, Edif Policlínica, T266-4515/9742, contact María José. *Turismo Joven*, Calle 27 de Mayo, del Cine Cabrera 3 C al este, T2222619-21, F2222143, turjoven@munditel.com.ni (same block as Nica Bus and Panaline), travel agency and representative for international student identity cards, affiliated to Youth Hostel Association. *Otec*, Hospital Militar 1 C al lago, ½ abajo, T2681583/2668613.

Tourist offices *Institute of Tourism* (Instituto Nicaragüense de Turismo – Intur), 1 block west of *Hotel Intercontinental*, enter by side door, Apdo Postal 122, T2222962/3333 or 2281337, F2281187. Airport T2331539. Information service T112. Closed Sat. Standard information available, including on all types of transport in the country. Maps of Managua dated 1993, and whole country on reverse, US$2. They will help with finding accommodation with families, with full board. Information on national parks and conservation should be obtained from *Sistema Nacional de Areas Protegidas* (Sinap), at Ministerio de Medio Ambiente y Recursos Naturales (Marena), Km 12.5 Carretera Norte, T2632617/9. *Guía Fácil*, the Managua listings magazine, can be reached on T/F2281289, www.guiafacil.com.ni. Another Managua website is www.managua-net.com.ni (in Spanish).

Useful addresses Customs: Km 5 Carretera del Norte, bus No 108. **Immigration:** near Ciudad Jardín, Antiguo Edif del Seguro Social, bus 101, 108, open 0800-1600, T2443989/3960/2292.

Pacific beaches

There are several beaches on the Pacific coast, about an hour's drive from Managua. The nearest are **Pochomil** and **Masachapa** (54 kilometres from Managua, side by side, bus service from terminal in Israel Lewites market every 35 minutes, US$1 to Pochomil) and **Casares** (69 kilometres from Managua, dirty, thorns on beach; two restaurants). A few kilometres from Casares is **La Boquita**, visited by turtles from August to November. Otherwise, La Boquita beach is to be avoided, frequent muggings and unreliable tap water supplies. Because of their proximity to the capital, these are very popular during the season (January-April) and tend to be somewhat crowded. Out of season, except at weekends, Pochomil is deserted (don't sleep on the beach, mosquitoes will eat you alive); it is cleaner the further south you go, but there are strong waves and rocks here, so swim with care. It is being developed as a tourist centre with hotels and restaurants. Few hotels at present, **A** *Ticomo Mar*, just south of the presidential beach house on the nicest part of Pochomil beach, a/c and bath, best hotel in the region apart from *Montelimar* (see below), but still poor value; **B** *Baja Mar*, with a/c, **C** without, basic, not worth the money; **D** *Alta Mar*, new. Masachapa is cheaper but dirtier; hotels on beach, **F** (but *Terraza* not recommended); **D** *Hotel Summer* on the main street to the beach, restaurant, fair; **F** *Hotel Rex*, very basic. Very slow bus journey from Managua. Near Pochomil and Masachapa is the *Montelimar* resort, built by the Sandinistas, now owned by Spain's Barceló group. It is expensive (**L** all inclusive) and becoming popular with package tours. It has a broad, unspoilt sandy beach ideal for bathing and surfing; 202 apartments in bungalows, a/c, minibar, cable TV, bathroom, "largest swimming pool in Central America", two smaller ones, fine restaurant, several bars, disco, fitness centre, shops, laundry, tennis, casino (US$50 per person for use of all facilities for the day, six hours, including buffet lunch). The nearest public transport is three kilometres away at Masachapa, taxi from Managua US$30 (70 kilometres), or hire a car. Reservations (Managua) T2284132/33/37/45, F2284146.

A visit to the broad, sandy **El Velero** beach (turn off at Km 60 on the old road to León and then follow signs) is recommended despite the US$3.50 entrance charge and poor road. All facilities controlled by the INSSBI, for the benefit of state employees, and at weekends is fully booked for weeks in advance. You may be able to rent a cabin (**E** for two) in the week, pay extra for sheet and pillows. You can eat in the restaurant (*Pirata Cojo*, not cheap), at the INSSBI cafetería (bring your own utensils, buy meal ticket in advance, or take your own food). However, the beach itself is beautiful, and the sea is ideal for both surfing and swimming. **El Tránsito** is a beautiful, undeveloped Pacific beach; bus from Managua at 1200, 1315, 1500 (from Terminal Lewites), return at 0600 or 0700, US$0.70. Good cheap meals from Sra Pérez on the beach (possible accommodation); *Restaurant Yolanda*, beach flats for four to six people normally available mid-week at north end (Centro Vacacional de Trabajadores, good value).

Managua to Honduras

Managua

There are three border crossings to Honduras, the Pan-American Highway gives access to each. After leaving Lake Managua, the road goes through hilly country, with various types of agriculture, mining and pines. A detour through Matagalpa and Jinotega enters good walking country. Estelí, a major centre, has, like many other places, evidence of Revolution damage.

The Pan-American Highway runs from Managua to Honduras (214 kilometres) and is paved the whole way. Also paved is the branch road to Matagalpa and Jinotega. The border crossing with Honduras on the Pan-American Highway is through Somoto to El Espino (see below).

The first stretch of 21 kilometres to Tipitapa is along the southern edge of Lake Managua. **Tipitapa**, to the southeast of the lake about two and a half kilometres away from the shore, on the other side of the Highway, was a tourist resort with hot sulphur baths and a casino. Some of the buildings are in ruins, but the resort has been reopened and you can swim in clean water in the baths. There is a colourful market, and a *fiesta* of El Señor de Esquipulas on 13-16 January. Swimming in El Trapice park, US$0.50.

Tipitapa
Colour map 4, grid C5

Nicaragua

Sleeping There is a *Hospedaje (Lazo)* at the main road junction.

Eating *Salón Silvia*, unpretentious. Slightly cheaper, but good, is the a/c restaurant attached to the thermal baths. *Entre Ríos*, helpful, looks like the best in town.

Buses From **Managua**, Plaza Mayoreo, via La Fanisa, Waspan, La Subasta, Aeropuerto and Zona Franca, every 10 minutes 0530-2100, 45 minutes, US$0.25. Bus to **Estelí**, US$1.40, pick up on the carretera coming from Managua, every 30 minutes, 0455-1755. Bus to **Masaya**, US$0.35, every 20 minutes 0500-1900, 1 hour, change there for Granada.

The Pan-American Highway goes north through Tipitapa to Sébaco, 105 kilometres. Fourteen kilometres before reaching Sébaco is **Ciudad Darío** (off the main road, turning to the west), where the poet Rubén Darío was born; you can see the house, which is maintained as a museum. There is an arts festival for the week of his birthday, 18 January. **F** *Hospedaje El*, one and a half blocks before the bridge on left, basic, friendly. Cheap good food from *Comedor Crismar* on Plaza Central.

In **Sébaco** there is **D** *Motel El Valle*, on the highway one kilometre towards Ciudad Darío, with restaurant, clean, fan, shower, quiet, patio with pool, English and Italian spoken. East of the highway is **Esquipula**, 100 kilometres from Managua, two and a half hours by bus, a good place for hiking, fishing, riding. **F** *Hotel Oscar Morales*, clean, shower, friendly.

Sébaco and the area around it was badly affected by Hurricane Mitch. Sébaco itself was damaged almost beyond repair.

Matagalpa

Population: 95,270
Altitude: 678m
Phone code: 061
Colour map 4, grid C5

From Sébaco a 24-kilometre branch road leads (right) to **Matagalpa**, in the best walking country in Nicaragua. Matagalpa has an old church, but it is about the only colonial style building left; the town has developed rapidly in recent years. It was badly damaged in the Revolution, but is undergoing reconstruction, regaining much of its original character. The birthplace of Carlos Fonseca is now a museum (closed for some time), one block east of the more southerly of the two main plazas; in the northerly square (with the Cathedral) is a Galería de los Héroes y Mártires (closed 1999). The Centro Popular de la Cultura is two and a half blocks north, four blocks east from the northeast corner of the Cathedral plaza. The town has a very erratic water supply. The main occupation is coffee planting and there are cattle ranges; the chief industry is the Nestlé powdered-milk plant. A 32-kilometre road runs from Matagalpa to the Tuma valley.

Sleeping
Many places shut their
doors by 2200-2300.

C *Selva Negra*, at 1,200 metres, 10 kilometres on road to Jinotega at Km 139½, T6123883, F2658342 (in Managua), cabins, **B**, more comfortable, good, as is the expensive restaurant (reserve in advance at weekends by telegram), good starting point for walks, private rainforest reserve, with 10 different paths (visitors US$2.50 for which credit is given in the

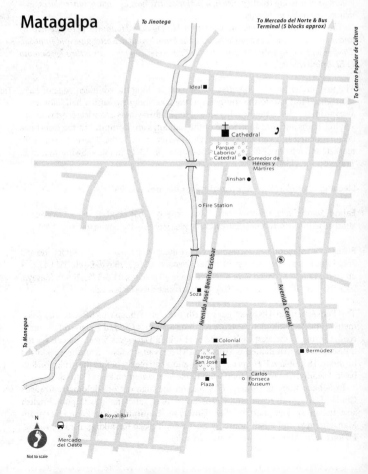

Matagalpa

restaurant), ask hotel for free map. **D** *Ideal*, Tienda Rosalinda ½ C al oeste, T6122483, with bath, **E** without, better rooms are upstairs, beware overcharging, good but expensive restaurant, disco on Saturday.

E *Bermúdez*, east of northeast corner of Parque San José, T6123439, with bath, **F** without, poor, run down, good car parking, helpful, meals; ½ block west is **E** *Hospedaje Matagalpa*, T6123834, with bath, **F** without, clean, light and airy. **F** *Hospedaje Colonial*, on Parque San José, basic; on the other side of this plaza **F** *Hospedaje Plaza*, small rooms with thin walls and peepholes, poor beds, mosquitoes, no sign, basic. **F** *Soza del Río*, with bath, nice patio, good value, opposite river, basic.

Eating

Jinshan, 1 block south of Parque Laborio, Chinese, good. *Lanchería Marcia*, opposite fire station, good value lunch. *Chepi*, Parque San José, large portions, excellent value, popular. *Comedor Sabita* northwest corner of Parque San José, family-run, good breakfasts and lunch. *Comedor Colonial*, north side of same plaza, good in the evening. *Rotisería La Casona*, Av José Benito Escobar, good economical chicken.

Festivals

24 September, *Día de La Merced*, is a local holiday.

Shopping

Mercado del Norte, close to northern highway (filthy); Mercado del Oeste, unfriendly *comedor*, swarms of flies and mosquitoes, is 2 blocks west of *Royal Bar*. Look for fine black pottery made in a local co-operative.

Transport

Buses Terminal Sur, by Mercado del Oeste for destinations north, south and west including Managua, Estelí and Jinotega: every 30 minutes to/from **Managua**, 127 kilometres, take 2½ hours, US$1.40. From **Tipitapa**, 2 hours. To **Jinotega**, from Terminal del Sur, US$1, every 30 minutes, 1½ hours, 0545-1745; to **Estelí**, every 30 minutes, 0520-1720, 2 hours, US$1. Terminal Norte, by Mercado del Norte, is for all other destinations. Taxi between terminals US$0.50. One bus a day to **León**, 0600, US$3 (luggage US$1); check which terminal in advance.

Directory

Banks Money changers near the Cathedral offer 'interesting' rates.

Jinotega

Population: 20,000
Altitude: 1,004m
Phone code: 063
Colour map 4, grid C5

There is a badly deteriorated 34-kilometre highway from Matagalpa to **Jinotega**, a pleasant, friendly town. There are famous images the in church, if not open, ask around. The Somoza jail has been converted into a youth centre. Several banks near the main plaza. There is a beautiful hike from behind the cemetery to the cross above the city, 90 minutes round trip, a steep climb. Excellent coffee grown here and in Matagalpa. Road (18 kilometres) to El Tuma power station; another to Estelí, through La Concordia, unpaved, picturesque, but very little transport from La Concordia to Estelí.

Sleeping **E** *Primavera*, 4 blocks north of Esso service station, T6322400. **F** *Hotel y Soda La Tica*, next to bus station, motel-type, beware of overcharging in the restaurant. **F** *Tito*, ½ block from plaza, clean, food.

Transport Buses from Managua via Matagalpa, 0630, 0800, 0930, 1100, 1230, 4 hours, US$2.70. From Matagalpa via Selva Negra, every 45 minutes 0545-1745, 2 hours, US$1.

From Jinotega an 80-kilometre, unpaved road goes to the main highway at Condega, 51 kilometres from the Honduran border (see below). This road passes through **San Rafael del Norte** (**F** *Hospedaje Rocío*, shared bath, reasonable, good food). There are some good murals in the local church, and a chapel on the hill behind, at Tepeyak, built as a spiritual retreat; very interesting recent history, involved in Sandinista struggle. Trucks from Jinotega market to San Rafael del Norte at 0700, 0800 and 0900, thereafter regular buses; trucks to Estelí at 0700, US$1, three hours. The road passes through another picturesque village, **Yalí**.

The 134-kilometre section from Sébaco (see above) to the border at El Espino is

Nicaragua

through sharp hills with steep climbs and descents, but reasonably well banked and smooth.

A reasonable road leads off the Pan-American Highway 10 kilometres northwest of Sébaco, near **San Isidro** (F *Camposinos*), to join the Pacific Highway near León (110 kilometres). This is an attractive alternative route to Managua through the Chinandega cotton growing area, past the spectacular chain of volcanoes running west from Lake Managua, and through León. (Bus Estelí-San Isidro, every 30 minutes, two hours, US$0.50, San Isidro-León, every 30 minutes, three to four hours, US$1.50.) On this road, 12 kilometres north of the intersection with the Chinandega-León road, is **San Jacinto**; 200 metres to the west of the road is a field of steaming, bubbling mud holes, worth visiting. You should approach carefully, the ground may give and scald your legs, but follow other footmarks for safety. A fast camera shutter will catch the mud in the air. After San Isidro, the Pan-American Highway goes through **La Trinidad** (*Cafetería Los Coquitos*, good value meals) before reaching Estelí.

Estelí

Population: 71,550
Altitude: 606m
Colour map 4, grid C5

This is a rapidly developing departmental capital (heavily damaged during the Revolution of 1978-79, and some of the damage still remains). It is the site of prehistoric carved stone figures (in a park in front of the tourist information office). Worth visiting are the **Casa de Cultura** (fiestas, meetings, exhibitions) and **Galería de los Héroes y Mártires** next door, opposite fire station (mementoes and photographs of those killed defending the Revolution, sad but interesting, wonderful paintings on the outside walls). Leave a donation as they are desperate for funds to maintain the museum. For the Salvadorean co-operative, take Avenida Bolívar/Calle Principal from Cathedral Plaza towards the bus station; some crafts, café with posters all over the walls, good. The Ministry of Health Information Centre, on Gran Vía Bolívar, four blocks from Plaza, is involved with projects to revive traditional medicine and healing; it offers advice on a wide range of herbal remedies. Also ask at the Reforma Agraria Office (above Banco de América) if you wish to see any local farming co-operatives. The Amnlae women's centre has social and educational projects which are interesting to visit and which may welcome volunteers. There is a children's playground in the main plaza, very lively on Sunday evenings.

Sleeping
■ *on maps*
Price codes:
see inside front cover

C *Moderno*, T7132378, east corner of Cathedral, 2½ blocks south, hot water, clean, friendly. Recommended. **D** *El Mesón*, Av Bolívar, 1 block north of Cathedral and plaza, T7132655, with shower, fan, clean, restaurant, TV, changes travellers' cheques. Recommended. **D** *Nicarao*, 1½ blocks south of main plaza, Av Bolívar/C Principal, with shower (cheaper without), restaurant, leafy patio, closes at 2200. Recommended.

E *Barlop*, 5 blocks north of main square, T7132486, 12 rooms, 6 of which are good, 6 basic, former have showers, good, friendly. **E** *Mariela*, behind bus station, clean, safe, washing facilities, very small rooms, parking inside gates, basic. **F** *Galo*, Nicaragua y Central, clean, friendly. **F** *Hospedaje El Chepito*, 4 blocks north of bus terminal, quiet, clean, friendly. **F** *Hospedaje San Francisco*, 1 block further north. **F** *Hospedaje Ignacio*, 8 C Sur y Central, near *San Francisco*, with bath, pleasant, nice garden, laundry facilities.

● *on maps*

China Garden, on main plaza, good food, friendly waiters, but a bit like a hangar. *Café Palermo*, 1 block west of C Principal, south of main plaza, very good food. *El Mesero*, off C Principal, 3 blocks north of bus station, popular and very good despite appearance. About 3 blocks north of park on Av Bolívar is *Panadería España*, good but pricey. *Las Brisas*, northwest corner of plaza, good Chinese and local. *El Porchesito*, on main street 5 blocks from bus station, good, cheap, try *tostones jalapeños* and *jugo de guayaba*. *Soda La Confianza*, 1 block south of Parque Central, cheap, good food.

Bars *Villa Vieja*, ½ block north of Parque Central on Av Bolívar, good atmosphere, live music at weekends.

Estelí

To Somoto & Honduras

Río Estelí

Gran Vía Bolívar

■1

●3

Markets ○

■3

2● ☩
Park ☐☐☐ Cathedral
☐☐☐
Galería de los ○ ○ Fire Station
Héroes y
Mártires ○ Casa de ♪ Calle Perú
Cultura

Amnlae
Women's
Centre ○

■5

⑨ 4■

○ El Salvador Cooperative
Ministry of Health
○ Information Centre

Calle Principal

Carretera Panamericana

●1

✚

🚌 ○ Markets

2■

Gran Vía Bolívar

To Managua

■ Sleeping	● Eating
1 Barlop	1 El Mesero
2 Mariela	2 Las Brisas
3 Mesón	3 Panadería
4 Moderno	España
5 Nicarao	

N
▲
Not to scale

Shopping

Two small markets, 1 north, 1 south of Parque Central. Big supermarket, *Supermercado Económico*, on C Principal.

Transport

Buses leave from the market south of Parque Central; walk down Av Bolívar/C Principal, 20 minutes, or take a *camioneta*. Through buses drop passengers at the turn-off to Parque Central, 1 kilometre from bus terminal. To/from **Managua**, US$1.40, 3 hours 25 minutes, half-hourly service, express 2 hours 45 minutes, US$1.85. For **León**, take any bus going on the main road east towards Managua and change at San Isidro, 30 minutes, US$0.50; from here buses wait by the roadside to continue south to León (see above). There is a daily minibus to **León** at 0645 (0545 Monday). For Honduras change at Somoto (for El Espino crossing), frequent service from Estelí between 0530 and 1720, US$0.90, 1 hour 40 minutes, and shuttle service from there, 45 minutes, US$0.50. Or change at Ocotal (for Las Manos crossing) hourly, 1½ hours, US$1 express, but go before 0800 to cross the border before lunch. 'Express' buses originating in Managua leave Estelí for Ocotal at 0755 and 1910.

Directory

Banks *Banpro*, Parque Central, Visa cash advance, US$3 commission, efficient. *Agencia de Viajes Tisey* in *Hotel Mesón* changes TCs at the official rate; many street changers, for cash only, on Av Bolívar. **Communications** Email: *Computer Soluciones*, 1 block south, 1 block east of Cenac, US$10 per hr. **Language schools** *Cenac*, Centro Nicaragüense de Aprendizaje y Cultura, Apdo 40, Estelí, T7132025, 2 offices: Texaco 5 cuadras al Este, ½ cuadra al Sur, and De los Bancos 1 cuadra al Sur, ½ cuadra al Este, frente a Farmacia San Sebastián: Spanish classes, living with a family, full board, travelling to countryside, meetings and seminars, opportunities to work on community projects, cost US$100 per week. Also teaches English to Nicaraguans and others and welcomes volunteer tutors. Cenac is run by women, but is separate from the Movimiento de Mujeres, *Casa Nora Artonga*, Apdo 72, Esteli, which also occupies one of the Cenac buildings and offers classes. Also *Casa de Familias*, Costado Noreste del Hospital, 1 cuadra al Carretera, US$100 per week. *Los Pipitos-Sacuanjoche Escuela de Español*, del Teatro Nancy ½ al sur, Apdo 80, T7132154, F7132240, sacuanjoche@ibw.com.ni, all profits go to disabled children and their families, excursions to local co-operatives, political parties, social projects, nature reserve (see below) are part of the course, staying with families, US$120-170

Nicaragua

per week, flexible, co-ordinator is German Katharina Pförtner. **Tour companies & travel agents** Travel agency *Tisey*, Apdo Postal No 63, T7133099, F7134029. Tours of cigar and coffee plantations available through *Tours Nicaragua* in Managua.

Miraflor

altitude 800-1,500m
area 5,675 ha

Miraflor is a Reserva Natural northeast of Estelí, but in the Department of Jinotega. It has a wide range of flora and fauna (including the quetzal) and the Laguna de Miraflor. The Unión de Cooperativas Agropecuarias Héroes y Mártires de Miraflor, which operates in the reserve and is in charge of environmental protection, has a tourism project. This has been stepped up after the damage caused by Hurricane Mitch, with wooden huts, basic facilities, meals, horse hire (US$2 for 2 hours), guided walks, US$20 per person. Contact Porfirio Zepeda (speaks English), T/F7132971, miraflor@ibw.com.ni (address: contiguo a Talleres del Mingob, Estelí), or Katharina Pförtner (see *Los Pipitos-Sacuanjoche*, above) and Gene Hinz, T7134041. Recommended for a visit to see rural life, beautiful area for riding.

Bathing

Near Estelí at Puente La Sirena, 200 metres off the road to Condega, or Salto Estanzuela, five kilometres south of Estelí, a waterfall of 25 metres, with a deep pool at the bottom, surrounded by trees and flowers (including orchids – only worth it in the rainy season), at least five kilometres off the Managua road, four-wheel drive recommended. Take the dirt road, starting 500 metres south of Estelí on Pan-American Highway, through San Nicolás. Since there are no signs, it is worth hiring a guide.

El Sauce

A very poor but spectacular gravel road from Estelí runs to El Sauce, 45 kilometres (see page 999); after 20 kilometres an equally rough road branches north to Achuapa. North of **Achuapa**, an unmade road continues through **San Juan de Limay** (one *hospedaje*), an *artesanía*, and marble town, and **Pueblo Nuevo** (two basic *hospedajes*), near which is an archaeological site. From here the road goes on to join the Pan-American Highway a few kilometres east of Somoto.

Condega

Population: 8,531
Altitude: 550m

After Estelí, the Highway goes to **Condega**, a quiet town producing agricultural goods, mostly beans and corn. It was once an Indian village where pottery was made and the name Condega means 'pottery makers'. The museum in the Casa de la Cultura on the main plaza exhibits Indian pottery and other artefacts. ■ *Monday-Friday 0800-1200, 1400-1700, Saturday 0800-1200.*

Sleeping F *Hospedaje Framar*, on main plaza next to Casa de Cultura, T7522393, 14 very clean and pleasant rooms, under US$3 pp, cold showers, shared facilities, nice garden, very quiet, safe, friendly, owner speaks English, excellent value. Recommended.

Eating About 6 very cheap places including *Comedor Rosa Amelia Peralta*, 1 block north off main plaza, *Linda Vista*, 6 blocks southwest of main plaza. No banks, a few mini-supermarkets.

Somoto

Population: 15,000

Continuing along the highway you get to Somoto, nice town, lovely setting, centre of pitch-pine industry. F *Baghal*, clean, friendly, helpful. Recommended. F *Internacional*, 1 block from central plaza, clean and basic. F *Panamericano*, on main plaza, but new section being built will be more expensive, landlord helpful, speaks English, quiet. Recommend ed. F *Pensión Marina*, shared shower, under US$3. *Victoria*, serves good food. *Chinatlan*, good.

Just before reaching Somoto there is a road junction at **Yalagüina** (F *Hospedaje*, with restaurant, at intersection). Twenty kilometres beyond Somoto is **El Espino**, which is five kilometres from the Honduran border at La Playa.

Frontier with Honduras – El Espino

Nicaraguan immigration The Nicaraguan passport control and customs are in the ruined customs house, 100 metres from the Honduran border. The Nicaraguan side is open 0900-1300 and 1400-1700.

Crossing by private vehicle Motorists leaving Nicaragua should enquire in Somoto if an exit permit has to be obtained there or at El Espino. This also applies to cyclists.

Services There is a duty free shop and a food bar on the Nicaraguan side but several cafés on the Honduran side. No money changers on Nicaraguan side but locals will oblige, even with lempiras. There is nowhere to stay in El Espino.

Transport Minibuses run between Somoto and the border US$0.40 plus US$0.40 per bag, and at least 2 buses daily Somoto-Estelí 0610 and 1410 which continue to Managua, US$2.15, 5 hours; Managua-Somoto 0700 and 1400, 3¾ hours, US$3. On the Honduran side, taxis go between the border and where Mi Esperanza bus stops, when totally full, ie 9-10 people, US$1 for foreigners, less for locals. On the Nicaraguan side taxis wait to take you to Somoto, they will probably try to overcharge, pay no more than US$8.

A road turns off right (18 kilometres) to **Ocotal**, a clean, cool, whitewashed town on a sandy plain (well worth a visit). It is near the Honduran border, to which a road runs north (bus marked Las Manos), wonderful scenery. Close by, at **San Albino**, there are many gold mines and gold is washed in the Río Coco (bus only from Ciudad Sandino – formerly Jícaro, 50 kilometres from Ocotal).

Ocotal
Population: 30,000
Altitude: 600m
Colour map 4, grid C5

Sleeping At Ocotal E *Hotel Restaurant Mirador*, opposite bus station, clean, friendly, with bath. **F** *El Portal*, no sign, some new rooms, shared bath, clean, reasonable. Recommended. **F** *Pensión Centroamericana*, not as dirty as most others, but unfriendly. **F** *Pensión Wilson*, good, friendly. **F** *La Esquinita*, main street. **F** *Hospedaje El Castillo*, basic, quiet, close to bus, candles provided for blackouts. *Segovia*, 1 block north of plaza on C Central, cheap, basic, OK. There is a pleasant hotel near the border, 8 kilometres north of Ocotal, called *Las Colinas*, pool, safe car park, bar, information.

Eating Several on the main plaza including *Llamada del Bosque*, good *comida corriente*.

Buses The bus station is on the highway, 1 kilometre south of town centre, 15-20 minutes walk from Parque Central. Bus (or truck) Ocotal-Somoto, US$0.40; Ocotal-Estelí, 1000 and others, US$0.80, 2 hours, beautiful views; Ocotal-Managua, 0850 and 1530, US$2.85; Managua-Ocotal, 0500 and 1615, 5 hours.

Banks *Banco Banic* (near the plaza) will change TCs. The Shell petrol station changes US$ cash.

The Las Manos/Ocotal crossing is at 1,200 metres and quite cool. This is recommended as the best route from Tegucigalpa to Managua.

Frontier with Honduras – Las Manos/ Ocotal

Nicaraguan immigration Open 0800-1200, 1300-1600. All those arriving must fill in an immigration card, then present their luggage to the customs authorities and obtain a receipt, and present these to the immigration authorities with passport and entry fees. Leaving the country, fill out a card, pay the tax and get your passport stamped.

Crossing by private vehicle After completing immigration procedures, go to Tránsito to pay for the vehicle permit, obtain clearance from Revisión, and get your vehicle permit from Aduana (customs). Travellers advise that if it is busy, go first to Aduana and get your number in the queue – if necessary shout at the clerks until they give you one. On leaving the country, complete the immigration requirements, then go to Tránsito to have the vehicle checked, and to Aduana to have the vehicle stamp in the passport cancelled. Surrender the vehicle permit at Aduana and take another form back to Tránsito; this will be stamped, signed and finally handed over at the exit gate.

Exchange Money changers operate on both sides offering córdobas at a little better than

Nicaragua

the street market rate in Nicaragua – if they have them. Rates for cash and travellers' cheques are better in Estelí.

Transport Bus from 4 blocks north of main plaza in Ocotal, US$0.40, otherwise take a truck or hitch. Beware of taxis: agree the fare before getting in. See above for onward buses.

NB The highlands of Madriz and Nueva Segovia departments suffered heavily during Hurricane Mitch. The main roads are open and through traffic to Honduras is not affected (1999), but if going to outlying areas, make enquiries on conditions in advance.

Managua to Corinto

The route from the capital through Pacific lowlands to the Gulf of Fonseca runs beside a chain of volcanoes, from Momotombo on Lake Managua to Cosigüina overlooking the Gulf. The city of León has been deeply involved in Nicaragua's history since colonial times. On the Pacific coast are the beaches at Poneloya and the major port of Corinto.

The first city of note along the highway is León, 88 kilometres from Managua. The Pacific Highway between Managua and Corinto (140 kilometres) follows the shore of Lake Managua and goes on to Chinandega; it has been continued to Corinto and to the Honduran border. The old, paved road to León crosses the Sierra de Managua, offering fine views of the lake (it is no longer than the Pacific Highway, but is in good condition).

About 60 kilometres down the new road to León lies the village of **La Paz Centro**. (**F** *Hospedaje El Caminante*, close to Highway, basic, friendly, cheap. **F** *Hospedaje El Buen Gusto*, friendly, fairly clean, basic. Several truck stop restaurants. Much handmade pottery here, good range and very cheap, ask to see the potters' ovens and production of bricks; try the local speciality *quesillo*, cream cheese served ready-to-eat in plastic bags, all along the highway.) Frequent bus service from Managua, Terminal Lewites, every 30 minutes. It is from here that one can gain access to the volcano **Momotombo**, which dominates the Managua skyline from the west. It is also possible to camp on the lakeside here in full view of the volcano.

You have to have a permit from Empresa Nacional de Luz y Fuerza in Managua to climb Momotombo from the south; they have built a geothermal power station on the volcano's slopes; alternatively, ask police in León Viejo for a permit (very difficult to get). We understand no permit is required to climb the volcano from the north.

At the volcano's foot lies **León Viejo**, which was destroyed by earthquake and volcanic eruption on 31 December 1609 and is now being excavated (very interesting). It was in the Cathedral here that Pedrarias and his wife were buried (see **Early, Post-Conquest History** in Introduction to Central America). Archaeological excavations have revealed the Cathedral, the Convento de la Merced, the Casa del Gobernador and other foundations of buildings. The ruins can be reached by bus from Managua to La Paz Centro (0830), then another to León Viejo. Walk one kilometre to the ruins where lots of guides offer their services for free. Take a return bus at 1400.

León

Population: 123,865
Colour map 4, grid C5

León was founded by Hernández de Córdoba in 1524 at León Viejo, 32 kilometres from its present site (see above). The city moved to its present site in 1610. It was the capital from its foundation until Managua replaced it in 1858; it is still the 'intellectual' capital, with a university (founded 1804), religious colleges, the largest cathedral in Central America, and several colonial churches. It is said that Managua became the capital, although at the time it was only an Indian settlement, because it was half-way between violently Liberal León and equally violently Conservative Granada.

The city has a traditional air, its colonial charm unmatched elsewhere in Nicaragua, except perhaps Granada: narrow streets, roofs tiled in red, low adobe houses and time-worn buildings everywhere. The old Plaza de Armas, in front of the Cathedral, is now Parque Jérez, but is usually referred to as Parque Central; it contains a statue of General Jérez, a mid-19th century Liberal leader. One block south and one block west of the Parque is the **Teatro Municipal**, whose grand frontage hides a rather poor interior, in need of funds for restoration.

The **Cathedral**, Basílica de la Asunción, begun in 1746 and not completed for 100 years, is an enormous building. Legend has it that the plans for the cathedrals of Lima, Peru and León were switched by mistake. It has a famous shrine, 145 centimetres high, covered by white topazes from India given by Philip II of Spain, which is kept in a safe in the vestry, and the bishop holds the key; a very fine ivory Christ; the consecrated Altar of Sacrifices and the Choir of Córdoba; the great Christ of Esquipulas, a colonial work in bronze whose cross is of very fine silver; and statues of the 12 Apostles. At the foot of one of these statues is the tomb of Rubén Darío, the 19th-century Nicaraguan poet, and one of the greatest in Latin America, guarded by a sorrowing lion. All the entrances to the Cathedral are guarded by lions.

Sights

León has the finest colonial churches in Nicaragua, more than 12 in all, and they are the city's most significant attraction. **La Recolección**, with a beautiful baroque Mexican façade, built in 1786, has a neoclassical interior with mahogany woodwork. **La Merced**, built in 1615, one of the oldest in León, also has fine woodwork inside and a newly restored exterior (1999). La Merced was burned by pirates in 1685 and is notable for its seven different altars. **San Felipe** was built at the end of the 16th century for the religious services of the black and mulatto population of the city, rebuilt in the 18th century in a manner true to its original form, a mixture of baroque and neoclassical. During the same period **El Calvario** was constructed, and is notable for its neoclassical façade attributed to the growing French influence in Spain at the time. The Convent and Church of **San Francisco** is the oldest convent with a church in León and was founded in 1639. It still carries two plateresque altars from Spain and its original pillars. In 1830, after the expulsion of the Franciscans from Nicaragua, it was used by various civic organizations and is now a gallery, entrance US$1.50. **Iglesia de San Nicolás de Laborío**, founded in 1618 for the local Indian population, is the most modest of the León churches, constructed of wood and tiles over adobe walls with an unostentatious façade and a simple altar, ten metres high. The celebration for San Nicolás is 10 September. **Iglesia NS Pilar de de Zaragoza** was built from 1884 to 1934 and is unique for its two octagonal turrets and arched doorway with tower above. There is a pleasant walk south across the bridge, past the church of Guadalupe, to the cemetery.

Churches
To see their interiors or attend mass, one must plan to visit in the morning from 0700-0900, or in the afternoon from 1600-1800, though hours vary.

The western end of the city is the oldest, and here is the oldest of all the churches: the parish church of San Juan Bautista in **Subtiava** (1530, local literature dates the current district at 1681 and the church at 1700). Las Casas, the Apostle of the Indies, preached here on several occasions. It has a fine façade, the best colonial altar in the country and an interesting representation of the sun ('El Sol'), carved in wood in mid-nave on the ceiling. The church has been beautifully reconstructed. The roof was rebuilt, under the supervision of the 'Comisión 500 años'. Near the Subtiava church are a small Comunidad Indígena Sutiaba, with an anthropological and historical museum (■ *US$1*), and the ruins of the parish churches of Vera Cruz and Santiago, both crumbling and unapproachable. Also in the suburb of Subtiava is the **Casa de Cultura** with interesting murals. (It's about a dozen blocks from the Parque Central to Subtiava.)

Nicaragua

Museums The house of Rubén Darío, the famous 'Four Corners' in Calle Rubén Darío, is now the **Museo-Archivo Rubén Darío**. It has an interesting collection of personal possessions, photographs, portraits and a library with a wide range of books of poetry in Spanish, English and French. Darío died in 1916 in another house in the northwest sector marked with a plaque. The poet who lived in Darío's house after his death, Alfonso Cortés, and who died there, mad, in 1969, has a museum-archive on C

León

Nicaragua

■ **Sleeping**
1 América
2 Avenida
3 Colonial
4 Europa
5 Hotelito Calle Real
6 Yenín

● **Eating**
1 Café El Sesteo
2 Capricornio
3 Casa Vieja
4 Eskimo
5 Hong Kong
6 Lacmiel
7 Las Ruinas
8 Oasis
9 Pizza Caliente
10 Rinconcito Flor de Sacuanjoche

N

0 metres (approx) 150
0 yards (approx) 164

Rubén Darío, opposite the Parque Rubén Darío. ■ *Tuesday-Saturday 0900-1200, 1400-1700, Sunday 0900-1200, entry and guided tour free but donation requested (US$1)*. A plaque marks the spot in the centre of the city where the first President Somoza was assassinated in 1956 by poet Rigoberto López Pérez.

1978-79 Revolution León was the centre of heavy fighting during the 1978-79 Revolution. There are many monuments from that time in the city (descriptions of León's fight against the Somoza régime can be found in *Fire from the Mountain: The Making of a Sandinista* by Omar Cabezas). Visitors can see **El Fortín**, the ruined last stronghold of the Somocista national guard (a commemorative march goes there each July, from the Cathedral, go west about 10 blocks, then south, best in early morning, great views of town and several volcanoes); **El Veinte Uno**, the national guard's 21st garrison, also ruined, and scene of an important battle in April 1979, with the jail around the corner converted into a garden with a statue to El Combatiente Desconocido (the unknown warrior) (three blocks south of cathedral); **statue of Luisa Amanda Espinoza**, the first woman member of the FSLN to die (in 1970), after whom the women's organization (AMNLAE) is named (seven to eight blocks north of market behind Cathedral, in Barrio San Felipe); two blocks west of La Merced church is the **Centro Popular de la Cultura** (frequent exhibitions and events, the only place in León to see live folk concerts, schedule on the front door). Across the street from the north side of the Cathedral is an interesting mural covering the history from precolumbian times to the Sandinista revolution, completed in 1990. It surrounds a commemorative park, the **Mausoleo Héroes y Mártires**. There is also the **Galería Héroes y Mártires** at Calle 1 NO entre Avenidas 1 y 2, which sells handicrafts and houses the twinning office with New Haven (USA).

To Chinandega

To Chinandega

New Market

6 Calle NE

3 Calle NE

2 Calle NE

Carretera Circunvalación

To Managua

To Managua

▲ **Other**
1 Casa de Gobierno
2 Mausoleo Héroes y Mártires
3 Parque Jérez/ Parque Central

Nicaragua

Sleeping
■ *on maps*
Price codes:
see inside front cover

B *Austria*, de la catedral 1 C al sur, ½ abajo, T3111206, new, central, hot water, a/c, cable TV, clean, secure parking, often full, breakfast US$3. Recommended. **B** *Colonial*, del UNAN 50 metros al norte, 2½ blocks north of Parque Central, T3112279, F3113125, pleasant, fine old building and patio but small rooms and in need of refurbishment, a/c, **C**

with fan, bath (**D** without), good views from upstairs, front rooms with balcony can be noisy from disco opposite at weekends, restaurant (breakfast US$3, other meals US$4). **B** *Europa*, 3 C NE, 4 Av, 2 blocks south of railway station, T3116040, F3112577, with bath and a/c, **D** with fan, cold water, brusque service, comfortable patios with bar and shade, coffee available, restaurant expensive, limited parking inside, guard will watch vehicles parked on street. **B** *Gran*, from bus terminal ½ block south, T3111327, with bath, a/c, clean, safe parking, breakfast US$4, other meals US$5, new, book ahead.

D *América*, Av Santiago Argüello, 2 blocks east of cathedral, with bath and fan, clean, good value, nice patio, a bit run down, friendly, nice garden, breakfast US$2, other meals US$3, cold drinks, convenient location, also secure garage nearby. **D** *Avenida*, near Mercado San Juan, **F** without bath, family run, fan, cable TV, good food US$1-2, friendly, laundry facilities, popular. **D** *Primavera*, on exit road to Chinandega, T3114216, with bath and a/c, **E** with fan, helpful and friendly, secure parking, breakfast US$1.50, other meals US$3. **E** *Monte Cristo*, 4 blocks beyond *Hotel Avenida*, on same street, English spoken, bath and fan, laundry service, meals on request, good.

F pp *La Posada del Doctor*, Parque San Juan 20 metros abajo, T3114343, F3115986, new, shared bath, fan, clean, some rooms with bunks, good value, very nice. **F** pp *Hotelito Calle Real*, C Rubén Darío opposite San Francisco, T3111120, with bath and fan, has *comedor*. **F** *Telica*, with shower, fan, noisy, cockroaches, breakfast, 4 blocks north of railway station, not recommended. **F** *Yenín*, Av Cdte Pedro Aráuz, opened 1997, pleasant, garden, good value.

Eating

Many restaurants are closed all day Sunday.

El Sesteo, next to Cathedral, on Parque Central, renovated, very good place for food and people watching. *Italian Pizza*, behind *El Sesteo*, good, mid-priced, family atmosphere. In the centre *Pizza Caliente* has 3 branches. *La Casa Vieja*, 1½ blocks north of San Francisco church, pleasant bar, good quality snacks, good value. Highly recommended. *El Barcito*, northwest of Parque Central, popular, soft drinks, milk shakes, slow service. *El Oasis*, C 5 and Av Central, good value, limited menu, popular. *Central*, C 4 Norte, good *comida corriente*. *Comedor Las Paiz*, behind the market, good lunch buffet, includes 1 litre of fruit juice for 20 córdobas. *Capricornio*, C 2 NO, near Central University, good *comida corriente*, interesting atmosphere. Across the street is *Rinconcito Flor de Sacuanjoche*, vegetarian meals, meat dishes, lunch and breakfast, good. *Lacmiel*, 5 blocks south of Cathedral, good food, live music, open air. Recommended. *El Rincón Azul*, C Central Rubén Darío, about 1½ blocks west of Parque Jérez, an excellent bar, very cheap, also a local art gallery, open 1500-2400. Recommended. *Casa Popular de Cultura*, 1 block north of plaza central, 2½ blocks abajo, sandwiches and hamburgers, nice atmosphere, find out what's going on. *Ruinas*, 1 block west of Telcor on Rubén Darío, friendly, live music at weekends. Chinese restaurant *Hong Kong*, 1 C NO, ½ block north of Parque, T3116572, popular with locals. *Eskimo* ice cream parlour, C Rubén Darío at the back of San Francisco. *Los Pescaditos*, near Subtiava church, excellent for fish at reasonable prices. Recommended. Also in Subtiava, *Caperas*, good Nicaraguan food, inexpensive. On the Carretera Circunvalación, *Caña Brava*, the best food in town, try their 'pollo deshuesado' (boneless chicken). *Montezerino*, Km 91 on the bypass, T3112638, outdoor, good meat and fish, pleasant.

Bars

Bar El Alamo, 1 block north of Plaza, good atmosphere, cheap draft beer.

Entertainment

Cinemas Two in centre. **Discos** Like all Nicaraguans, the Leoneses love to dance; all dancing is to taped music played at full volume. *Discoteca Dilectus*, at south entrance to city, upscale crowd, a/c, parking, US$5 entrance, drinks and food expensive, Wednesday-Sunday. *Discoteca Nueva Túnel*, at exit to Carretera a Chinandega, US$2 cover. *Video Luna*, across the street from *Hotel Colonial*, entrance US$1, Saturday and Sunday nights only. Also next to La Merced park is a small disco upstairs, in a brown wooden house, unsigned and unnamed, but very popular.

Festivals

The Holy Week ceremonies are outstanding, as are the festivities on **7 December**, *Día de la Concepción*; much singing, dancing, fireworks and festive crowds. Throughout December, Santa Lucía is celebrated in Subtiava; there are processions, religious and cultural events, sports and Pepe Cabezón (a giant head on legs) accompanies La Gigantona (an impossibly tall princess) through the city. **20 June** (*Liberation by Sandinistas*), **24 September**; **1 November** (*All Saints' Day*).

The old market (dirty) is in the centre, and the new market is at the bus terminal, 5-6 blocks east of the old railway station, which itself is now Mercado San Juan, not touristy, good local atmosphere. Good supermarket, *La Unión*, on C 1 Norte, one block north of central market. Bookshop *Libro Centro Don Quijote*, next to *Hotelito Calle Real*, has secondhand books, a few in English.

Local Taxis around town charge US$0.50. **Buses** From bus station at new market: **Managua-León**, 2 hours 15 minutes, US$1.25, every 30 minutes, US$1.35 express, 1 hour 20 minutes, frequent but check if it goes to the León bus terminal or the Shell station on the Managua highway. Colectivo, US$5. Bus to **Chinandega** (1¼ hrs, US$0.50) and **Corinto** (US$0.85) half-hourly between 0430 and 1800. For **Estelí**, daily express minibus at 0500 and 1500, or take a bus to **San Isidro** (every 30 minutes), 2½ hours, US$1.50, then catch a bus going north from Managua or Matagalpa. To **Matagalpa** direct, at 0445 and 1400, US$2.80, but cheaper to take a bus to San Isidro and catch one of the many buses there from Estelí to Matagalpa, US$0.80. To border with Honduras take a bus from the market to Chinandega, and from there another bus to Somotillo. The Tica Bus (T3316153) to El Salvador stops at the Shell Station on the Managua side of town sometime between 0630 and 0730 daily. Pick-up from bus terminal to centre US$0.20.

Bus to **El Sauce**, 72 kilometres, where there is a large 19th century church (burnt down in 1997), and a riotous fair in February (**F** *Hospedaje Diana*, clean, basic. *Viajero*, noisy, fan, friendly, good food. *Restaurant Mi Rancho* and others) via **Malpaisillo** (unnamed *hospedaje* at village entrance, 4 rooms, basic, **F**). Buses from El Sauce: to León, frequent, 2½-3 hours, US$1.40; to Honduran border 0500 daily, 2 hours, US$1.60. Four daily trucks between El Sauce and Estelí, on a very rough road.

Banks Most of the country's banks are represented in the blocks north of the cathedral. *Bancentro*, C 1 NE entre Central y 1 E will change TCs, 3% commission. *Banpro* changes dollars cash. *Interbank* is behind *El Sesteo*. **Communications** Post Office is opposite a Recolección church. **Telephone:** Enitel (Telcor), Parque Central, opposite Cathedral. Phone calls abroad possible. Small Enitel office on Darío, on road to Subtiava, about 10 blocks from main plaza, open till 2200. **Tourist Offices** 2 C Norte y 2 Av NO, brochures in Spanish, helpful staff but little information available. A good, multilingual guide and/or Spanish teacher, Mauricio Avellán Solórzano, de Farmacia Norma 2½ C al este, T3112809, red gate, very friendly and helpful; any hotel will contact him.

There is a bumpy 21-kilometre road from León that leads through sweeping ranch land to two very tranquil beach communities, Poneloya and Las Peñitas. Both contain long stretches of beautiful sandy beaches and a mixture of humble houses and rich vacation homes. Most of the coast has big waves and strong currents (swim here with great caution): the south end of Las Peñitas and Puerto Mántica, at the north end of Poneloya, are the best for swimming, good surfing in between, but no boards available to rent. The sun is very strong here, not much shade and the locals are very relaxed and friendly. During the week you will have the beaches to yourself, on weekends young people and families come from León and in Semana Santa it is packed. It is possible to rent four-wheel motorbikes at the *pulpería* at the intersection of the road to Las Peñitas and Poneloya, called *Licorería Estela de los Mares* (US$10 per hour, you must also show driving licence, sign a release form and pay a US$10 deposit).

Sleeping & eating C *Suyapa Beach*, in Las Peñitas, T317390, F3116257 (León), best in region, a/c, **D** with fan, some rooms with ocean view and nice breeze upstairs (ask), all with private bath, very clean, swimming pool and outdoor beach shower, group discounts, restaurant is OK, mid-priced with great view. Hotel owner/bull rancher Roberto Reyes is very helpful. Recommended. **D** *Posada de Poneloya*, opposite Lacayo, cabinas with bath, a/c or fan, car park. **E** *Lacayo*, great location, dusty rooms, restaurant has good *repochetas*, basic, meals, bats in the roof and beware of insects at night, bring coils. *Restaurante Cáceres*, good *comida corriente*. *La Peña del Tigre*, good but expensive fish restaurant down the road, huge portions, friendly, open air, nice views – it is near a tall rock on the beach where bathing is dangerous and prohibited.

Transport Take bus 101 from León's Terminal Interurbana, or the central market west to the bus stop near Subtiava church on Calle Darío, then walk 3 minutes to Terminal Poneloya outside the market, from where a small bus leaves every hour or so for Las Peñitas (US$0.45) at the south end of Poneloya beach. Taxi from León costs around US$6.

Chinandega
Population: 97,387
Colour map 4, grid C4

Chinandega is one of the hottest and driest towns in Nicaragua, and is about 35 kilometres beyond León. This is one of the main cotton-growing districts, and also grows bananas and sugar cane. Horse-drawn cabs for hire. Good market by the bus terminal. Local holiday: 26 July.

Sleeping A *Los Volcanes*, Km 129 Carretera a Chinandega, at entrance to city, T3411000, new, hot water, a/c, cable TV, telephone, bar, restaurant, clean, good service. Recommended. **B** *Cosigüina*, T3413636, F3413689, in city centre, just south of Banco Nacional, expensive, a/c, cable TV. **C-D** *Glomar* (shower extra), safe, may be closed Sunday evening, owner (Filio) will change dollars, but mistrusts foreigners, his son is friendly, good food, cold beer. **F** *Pensión Cortés*, south of Parque Central, basic. **F** *Chinandega*, basic, fan, shared bath, decent.

Eating *Corona de Oro*, Chinese, 1½ blocks east of Parque Central, expensive. *Central Palace*, same street. *Italian Pizza*, Iglesia San Antonio 175 varas este, good. *Caprax Pizza*, 1 block east of Parque Central.

Buses From **Managua**, by road, 3 hours 15 minutes, US$1.95. From **León**, 1 hour 15 minutes, US$0.50. From Chinandega, buses leave from near the new market at southeast edge of town for **Corinto**, **León**, **Managua** and **Somotillo**. Bus to the Honduran border 1¾ hours, US$0.80. Buses for **Potosí**, **El Viejo** and **Puerto Morazán** leave from the Mercadito at northwest of town. A local bus connects Terminal, Mercado and Mercadito.

Communications Post Office and telephones: in Enitel building opposite *Caprax Pizza*.

Not far away, near **Chichigalpa**, is Ingenio San Antonio, the largest sugar mill in Nicaragua, with a railway between the town and the mill (six kilometres, five trains a day each way, 7 May-November, passengers taken, US$0.10; also bus US$0.30). While there are no official tours of the installations, you can apply at gate (portón) 14 to be shown around. On the edge of Chichigalpa itself is the Flor de Caña distillery; on leaving you will recognize the picture on all the labels, a palm-shaded railway leading towards Chichigalpa with volcanoes in the background. Enitel in Chichigalpa: from Texaco on the main road take second street on left, then first on right. ■ *0800-1200, 1400-1700*.

A road runs northeast to Puerto Morazán. This passes through the village of El Viejo (US$0.20 by bus from Chinandega, five kilometres) where there is an old church. (Restaurant: *El Retoño*, on main street, north of market; bars close to market.) **Puerto Morazán** (hotel), 26 kilometres from Chinandega (buses, eight a day, one and a half hours, US$0.40), is a poor, muddy village with reed huts on a navigable river running into the Gulf of Fonseca. From Chinandega there are four buses a day to **Potosí**, at least three hours, US$1.20. *Comedor Adela*, 24-hour service, cheap. You can sling your hammock at the *comedor* 150 metres past immigration for US$0.50. Ask Héctor for permission to stay in the fishing co-operative. The fishermen are very friendly. The passenger ferry from Potosí to La Unión (El Salvador) has been suspended, but there is an open boat from La Unión ad hoc. Ask around.

It is a four-hour hike to the cone of **Cosigüina** volcano. On 23 January 1835, one of the biggest eruptions in history blew off most of the cone, reducing it from 3,000 metres to its present height of 800 metres. There are beautiful views from the cone over the islands belonging to Honduras and El Salvador. There is plenty of wildlife in the area, including poisonous snakes, so take a machete. The path is overgrown and very difficult to follow, you may need a guide. There are pleasant black sand beaches; the sea, although the colour of *café con leche*, is clean. In the centre of the village are warm thermal springs in which the population relaxes each afternoon. The volcano and the surrounding dry tropical forest are a Reserva Natural, administered by Marena (the Ministry of the Environment and Natural Resources) in Managua.

From Chinandega a paved road, badly in need of repair in its middle section, goes to the Honduran border on the **Río Guasaule** near **Somotillo** (E *Las Vegas*, small rooms, fan, none too clean, restaurant; *Hospedaje/Bar El Panamericano*), where it is continued by a better road to Choluteca, Honduras. Bus from Chinandega, one hour 45 minutes, US$1.25.

NB Most of the bridges on the Highway in León and Chinandega departments and all between Chinandega and the border, and the border bridge itself, were washed away by Hurricane Mitch. As early as December 1998, traffic was flowing freely between Managua and Guasaule, with vehicles making detours where necessary.

Nicaraguan immigration The distance between the border posts is 500 metres. There are no colectivos, so you must walk, take one of the tricycles with parasol, or hitch a lift. Vehicles drive through the water. Foot passengers are ferried across the river in small boats while the bridge is out. The international buses use this crossing. The procedure when leaving Nicaragua (on Ticabus, at least) is that an official takes all passports from passengers as soon as the bus leaves Chinandega and he fills out all the immigration forms. He also collects the exit tax. At the border, the official with the passports and documents disappears and passengers alight from the bus to await his return and be called by name to re-embark. This takes about 45-60 minutes. Once back on the bus, a Honduran official takes your passport and you go through Honduran procedures.

Frontier with Honduras – Guasaule

Exchange Money changers offer the same rates for córdobas to lempiras as on the Hinduran side. There is a recommended bank beside immigration, *Banco de Crédito Centroamericano*, good rates, no commission (will accept photocopy of passport if yours is being checked by immigration).

Transport Buses run every 30 minutes from the border to Chinandega, US$0.80. Express bus to Managua, Mercado Lewites terminal at 0500 and 1545, 3½ hours, US$2.85 via Somotillo and León. From Managua to Río Guasaule at 1810.

Jiquilillo beach, 42 kilometres from Chinandega, is reached by a mostly-paved road branching off the El Viejo-Potosí road. It lies on a long peninsula; small restaurants (for example *Fany*) and lodgings.

Twenty one kilometres from Chinandega, Corinto is the main port of entry, and the only port at which vessels of any considerable size can berth. About 60 percent of the country's commerce passes through it. The town itself is on a sandy island, Punto Icaco, connected with the mainland by long railway and road bridges. There are beautiful old wooden buildings with verandahs, especially by the port. (Entry to the port is barred to all except those with a permit.) On the Corinto-Chinandega road is Paseo Cavallo beach (*Restaurante Buen Vecino*). The sea is treacherous, people drown here every year.

Corinto
Population: 30,000
Colour map 4, grid C4

There are no facilities in Corinto's barrier islands, but they are beautiful with crashing surf on one side, calm and warm swimming water on the other. The journey can be negotiated with any fisherman, but there are two who are particularly

Nicaragua

trustworthy and reliable, named Isidro and Lester. They can be reserved in advance through their aunt, Guadalupe Hernández, who lives next to the Alcoholics Anonymous building in Corinto, T3422490. Tell her you want to visit Castañones, US$10 each way, pre-arrange departure and pickup times. Bring anything you might need with you to the island. A *panga* can be rented for the whole day for US$40 so you can explore the numerous islands and mangroves. Lots of birdlife but also lots of sand flies, bring repellent (see Bay Islands section, Honduras, for suggestions).

Sleeping **D** *Central*, in front of Port Buildings, clean, a/c. **F** *Hospedaje Luvy*, fan, dirty bathrooms, 2 blocks from plaza.

Eating *Meléndez*, on main plaza, good but pricey. *El Imperial*, evenings only; cheapest meals in market, but not recommended.

Managua to Granada

From Lake Managua to Lake Nicaragua, with more volcanoes in view: Santiago is near Masaya, a centre for handicrafts in a tobacco-growing zone; Mombacho is near Granada, a richly historical city; Concepción is a perfect cone rising out of Isla Ometepe, one of a number of islands that can be visited by boat on Lake Nicaragua.

The main route is by a 61 kilometres paved road with a fast bus service through Masaya.

Santiago Volcano The entrance to **Volcán Masaya National Park** is at Km 23. The Masaya volcano was called by the indigenous Chorotega people Popogatepe, or 'mountain that burns'. The Chorotegas believed that eruptions were a sign of anger from the goddess of fire, Chacitutique, and to appease her they made sacrifices to the lava pit, which often included children and young women. Father Francisco de Bobadilla planted a cross on the summit of Masaya in the 16th century to exorcize the 'Boca del Infierno'; the cross visible today commemorates the event. Many Spanish chroniclers visited the crater, including Oviedo in 1529 and Blas de Castillo in 1538, who descended into it in search of gold! Volcán Nindirí last erupted in 1670, Volcán Masaya burst forth in 1772 and again in 1852, forming the Santiago crater between the two peaks; this in turn erupted in 1932, 1946, 1959 and 1965 before collapsing in 1985, and the resulting pall of sulphurous smoke made the soil in a broad belt to the Pacific uncultivable. Ninety years ago German engineers Schomberg and Scharfenberg, attempting to produce sulphuric acid from the volcano's emissions,

The volcanic chain

drilled into an unexpected 400 metre-wide lava tube, resulting in explosions and landslides; no one has attempted anything similar since. Remains of these old installations can still be seen; consult the *guardabosques* for information.

The National Park of Volcán Masaya was created in 1979 and is the country's oldest. It covers an area of 54 kilometres and contains 20 kilometres of trails leading to and around two volcanoes, five craters and one lake. The Visitor's Centre is 1.5 kilometres in from the entrance (called the *Centro de Interpretación Ambiental*). Shortly after is a beautiful area with toilets, picnic facilities and barbecues (*asadores*) for the use of visitors. Camping is possible here but no facilities after the Visitor's Centre closes. Next door is a good science museum, entrance free. From here a short path leads up to Cerro El Comalito, good views of Mombacho, the lakes and the extraordinary volcanic landscapes of the Park; longer trails continue to Lake Masaya and the San Fernando crater. Because of the potential danger involved, visits to the fumaroles at Comalito require special authorization from rangers, who warn that they may have to place this area off-limits if visitors are injured touching or throwing the surrounding rocks. The paved road (20-25 kph speed limit) continues south across the 1670 lava flow to the twin crests of Masaya and Nindirí, which actually consist of five craters (Santiago – still emitting sulphurous gases, San Fernando, San Juan, Nindirí and San Pedro). There is parking and a recreation area here. Park rangers will escort groups of no more than five down a path leading to several lava caverns, visitors are not allowed to touch the fragile walls or roofs of these caves. Park guides and *guardabosques* are very knowledgeable about the area's history and early indigenous inhabitants. The park is a wonderful excursion but take something to drink, a hat and robust footware if planning much walking. Entrance US$4 per person (bus passengers alight at Km 23 on the Managua-Masaya route, or easy to hitchhike from either place, especially on Sunday). ■ *The Park is open 0900-1700, Tuesday-Friday, and until 1900 on Saturday and Sunday.* Soft drinks, bottled water and sometimes fresh coconut water are available at the summit of Santiago crater.

Masaya

Twenty nine kilometres southeast of Managua, Masaya is the centre of a rich agricultural area, growing many crops including tobacco. Small **Laguna de Masaya** (at the foot of Masaya volcano, water too polluted for swimming but an attractive and tranquil view from the town) and Santiago volcano are near the town. Interesting Indian handicrafts are sold in the market and a gorgeous *fiesta* is held on 30 September, for its patron, San Jerónimo (Indian dances and local costumes). There is a new Centro de Artesanías (closed Sunday), near the former hospital and overlooking Laguna de Masaya, but the choice is not as wide as the market. The old 19th century market which was ruined during the revolution has been restored and is now referred to as the 'new' market. The market is safe, clean, with parking, very popular with Nicaraguans, excellent hammocks, nice leather work, colourful woven rugs used as wall hangings, wicker furniture. The market used for the last 20 years is now called the 'old' market; it is crowded, dirty, claustrophobic and not recommended. Masaya is also the centre for Nicaraguan rocking chairs, which can be purchased in kit form, packed for taking by air. The Co-operativa Teófilo Alemán has a good selection at around US$35. The best place for Indian craft work is **Monimbo** (visit the church of San Sebastián here), and 15 minutes

Population: 88,971
Colour map 5, grid A1

Nicaragua

from Masaya is **Villa Nindirí**, which has a rich museum and an old church with some even older images. There are horse-drawn carriages, some very pretty and well-kept. **Statue of Sandino**. The town suffered severely in the Revolution of 1978-79. Visit the Museo de Héroes y Mártires. ■ *Monday-Friday*. Another museum is that of Camilo Ortega, which has interesting exhibits on recent history; 45 minutes' walk from central plaza, ask directions.

Excursions Just outside Masaya, on the road from Managua, is an old fortress, **Coyotepe**, also called La Fortillera, ■ *US$0.50*. It was once a torture centre, and is now deserted, eerie, "with a Marie Celeste feel to it" (take a torch, or offer a volunteer US$1-2 to show you around). Near the Masaya Lake, south of the town, there are caves with prehistoric figures on the walls; ask around for a guide.

Niquinohomo is Sandino's birthplace, and the house where he lived from the age of 12 with his father is opposite the church in the main plaza. There used to be a museum here but the exhibits have now been transferred to Managua.

San Juan de Oriente is a charming colonial village with an interesting school of pottery (products are for sale). Nearly 80 percent of the inhabitants are engaged in the ceramic arts. Ask to see Doña Silvia at the entrance to the village, she will take you to see her workshop during working hours. It is a short walk to neighbouring Catarina (famous for ornamental plants), and a one kilometre walk or drive uphill to El Mirador, with a wonderful view of **Laguna de Apoyo** (Granada and Volcán Mombacho in the distance on a clear day) which is very clean, quiet during week but busy at weekends. Entrance fee US$0.20. **Sleeping** on lake shore; **B-C** *Narome*, T8839093, very clean, great views and setting, restaurant, jacuzzi. Get out of the bus at Km 38 on Managua-Granada road, walk one and a half hours or hitch, easy at weekends. There is a language school, *Apoyo Intensive Spanish School 'Proyecto Ecológico'*, T2784800 ext 11670, groups of four, five hours tuition a day. Five-day programme, US$195, US$230 for a week including accommodation and food (vegetarians catered for) or US$750 per month, family stays available. Money from the nonprofit school goes towards educational, ecological and employment projects in the local community. Good birdwatching and walking in the dry forest. Transport from Managua, if arranged in advance, costs US$25, otherwise it's a 35-minute walk from the rim of the crater at Valle de Apoyo, to which buses run from the main road.

Sleeping
■ *on maps*
Price codes:
see inside front cover

C *Motel Cailagua* (Km 29.5, Carretera a Granada, T5224435), about 2 kilometres from Masaya, with bath and a/c, **D** with bath and fan, large rooms, clean, good, very friendly, meals available (but breakfast only by arrangement), reasonably priced, parking inside gates. Recommended. **D** *Monte Carlo*, 1½ blocks from *Regis* on same side, small rooms, clean, friendly, bar, restaurant serves good burgers. **E** *Regis*, Sergio Delgado (main street), T5222300, shared bath, fan, clean, breakfast (other meals if ordered), fruit juices, helpful owner. Recommended. **F** *Masayita*, 2 blocks west of central park, clean, basic. *Pensiones* are hard to find, and dirty when you've found them (eg *Rex*, avoid).

Eating *Nuevo Bar Chegris*, ½ block south around corner from *Regis*, very good food in huge portions, excellent *comida corriente* for US$2.50, nice garden. Recommended. *Alegría*, C Real San Geronimo, ½ block north of Parque Central, good, clean, comfortable, not expensive, good pizzas. *La Jarochita*, near park, Mexican, excellent, mid-priced, try chicken *enchilada* in *mole* sauce. *Pochil*, near park, good food, ask for vegetarian dishes. *Cafetín Verdí*, in central park, good atmosphere, snacks, ice cream. *Panadería Corazón de Oro*, 2-3 blocks towards highway from the church, excellent cheese bread (*pan de queso*), US$0.50 a loaf. There are 2 *Fuentes de Soda* near the northeast corner of the Parque Central, both good, and 5 blocks north of the Parque Central is a small park with a Pepsi stand that sells excellent fresh 'Tutti-Frutti' fruit juice.

Transport Buses depart from the terminal near the market. To **Managua** every 15 minutes, US$0.35; to **Granada** every 20 minutes, US$0.25, to **Jinotepe** via Niquinohomo, Masatepe, San Marcos and Diriamba every 20 minutes. There is also a bus service to **Tisma**.

Banks *Banco Americano* on Parque Central changes TCs and cash at good rates. Street changers around market and plaza. **Communications** Post Office: on Parque Central. **Email:** *Satel Cia Ltda*, Curaçao 1 abajo, T5225550, US$10 per hr, also has maps and tourist information. Also opposite main post office (entrance not on Parque Central). **Hospitals & medical services** Doctors: *Dr Freddy Cárdenas Ortega*, near bus terminal, recommended gynaecologist. *Dr Gerardo Sánchez*, next to town hall, speaks some English. **Tourist offices** On main highway in the block between the 2 main roads into Masaya; helpful, mostly Spanish spoken, but some English 'if you look baffled'.

Directory

Granada

Another 19 kilometres by road is Granada, on Lake Nicaragua. It is the third city of the republic and was founded by Hernández de Córdoba in 1524 at the foot of Mombacho volcano. The rich city was three times attacked by British and French pirates coming up the San Juan and Escalante rivers, and much of old Granada was burnt by filibuster William Walker in 1856, but it still has many beautiful buildings and has faithfully preserved its Castilian traditions.

Population: 71,783
Colour map 5, grid A1

The centre of the city, some distance from the lake, is the **Parque Central**, with many trees and food stalls in its park, civic buildings, the *Hotel Alhambra* and the Cathedral around its edge. The **Cathedral**, rebuilt in neoclassical style, is simpler in design and ornamentation than the church of **La Merced**, which was built in 1781-83, half-destroyed in the civil wars of 1854 and restored in 1862. Its interior is painted in pastel shades, predominantly green and blue. It has some unusual features and interesting lighting. Continuing away from the centre, beyond La Merced, is the church of **Jalteva** (or Xalteva), which faces a pleasant park with formal ponds. Not far from Jalteva is **La Pólvora**, an old fortress that has been partially restored and opened to the public. Donations accepted by the caretaker, nice rooftop with church and volcano view east from the turrets. Also nearby is **Museo de las Arenas**, in a restored fortress. If one heads towards the Managua bus terminal from Jalteva, the **Hospital** is passed. Built in 1886, it is now in very poor shape. The chapel of **María Auxiliadora**, where Las Casas, Apostle of the Indies, often preached, is hung with Indian lace and needlework. ■ *Church open to public at 1600.*

Sights
To view the interiors of Granada's churches you must time your visit from 0600-0800, or from 1500-1700.

From the Parque Central, in the opposite direction to La Merced, is the fortress-church of **San Francisco** with wonderful sculptures. Next door is the **Museo del Convento de San Francisco**, originally a convent (1524), then a Spanish garrison, William Walker's garrison, a university and lastly an institute; the cloister surrounds about three dozen tall palms. Restoration is now complete and it is the country's most interesting precolumbian museum, housing 28 sculptures from Isla Zapatera in the lake. They date from AD800-1200, note especially the double sculptures of standing or seated figures bearing huge animal masks, or doubles, on their heads and shoulders ('El Lagarto', 'La Tortuga', jaguars, etc). ■ *The museum is open 0800-1800; US$1 entrance.* The Museo del Convento de San Francisco also contains several galleries with changing exhibits of Nicaraguan art, a snack bar and the local branch office of the Nicaraguan Institute of Tourism.

A road runs from the Parque Central to Plaza España by the dock on the lake; the church of **Guadalupe** is on this road. **Casa de los Tres Mundos** is the international foundation that has restored and runs **La Casa de Los Leones**, a beautiful colonial house, with art exhibits and concerts, check bulletin board for events. From Plaza España it is a short distance to the **Complejo Turístico** (■ *US$0.12*), a large area with restaurants and bars (see below), paths and benches. The lake beach is popular, having been cleaned up and built into a nice, if often windy park; marimba bands stroll the beach and play a song for you for a small charge.

Horse drawn carriages are for hire and are used here, as in Masaya, as taxis by the locals. The drivers are also very happy to take foreigners around the city, US$4.50 for half an hour, US$9 for one hour. You can see most of the city's sites in a half-hour rental, but if you want to enter the fort, churches and museum, one hour is recommended. A nice walk, or carriage ride, starts from La Pólvora and continues down Calle Real, past La Capilla María Auxiliadora, La Jalteva, La Merced to Parque Central. From the Cathedral you can then continue to La Virgen de Guadalupe and to the lake front along the Calle la Calzada.

Sleeping

There is a shortage of hotels and restaurants in Granada (do not arrive after 2100 at the latest).

■ *on maps Price codes: see inside front cover*

A-C *Alhambra*, Parque Central, T5526316/5524486-9, F5522035, pleasant, comfortable rooms with bath, large restaurant, good breakfasts, high prices, terrace is nice place for a beer overlooking Plaza Central, often has good, live music, parked cars guarded by nightwatchman.

B *Granada*, C La Calzada (opposite Guadalupe church), T5522178, F5524128, a/c, cable TV, electric showers, poor beds, restaurant for all meals (overpriced), café, disco, bar, lovely view from front balcony but rather faded. **B** *Another Night in Paradise*, next to *Granada*, new (open in late 1999), T5527113, bath, fan, Italian, English and French spoken. **B** *Valencia*, opposite Supermercado Lacayo on C Real, T/F5524828, guaita@tmx.com.ni, with a/c, cable TV, bath, **D** with fan, no TV and shared bath, nice rooms with generous use of cedar and guanacaste wood, friendly and helpful owner Alfredo, excellent beds, charming restaurant

Granada

Parque Sandino 🚌 3

San Francisco & Museo del Convento

Av Arellano

Casa de los Leones & Mi Café
Email
3 ■ Calle la Calz

🚌 1

Atravezada
Palacio de Cultura ○ 🚌 3 1 Plaza Central
Casa Pellas ○ Cathedral Av Caimito
○ Alcaldía

Hospital ○

La Merced

La Jalteva

Email

Av Vega

La Pólvora ○

Market

🚌 2

N
Not to scale

To Nandaime   *To Puerto Asese*

■ **Sleeping**
1 Alhambra   3 Pensión Vargas
2 Granada & Another
   Night in Paradise

🚌 **Buses**
1 Buses to Managua
2 Buses to Rivas
3 Minibuses to Managua

Nicaragua

with US$3 breakfast and lunch and US$7-23 dinners, bar, very clean, central, recommended.

C *Casa Colonial*, half block west of *Mi Café* on C Arsenal, T5527107, new, very quiet but central location, 250-year old house with two gardens, private bath and fan, cable TV upon request, clean, good value, recommended. **C** *Posada Don Alfredo*, from La Merced 1 block to the north, T/F5524455, charlyst@tmx.com.ni, new, with bath, **D** without, 165-year-old house with much of original flavour, high ceilings, dark rooms, English and German spoken by friendly, helpful owner Alfred, clean, good location, kayaks and bicycles for rent US$12 and US$10 per day respectively, gigantic German breakfast for US$7.

D *Italiano*, La Calzada, T/F5527047, next to Iglesia Guadalupe, Italian owned, with bath and fan, nice patio, restaurant and bar, good value.

E *Hospedaje Esfinge*, opposite market, rooms with character, patio with washing facilities, friendly, clean, motorcycle parking in lobby, safe, laundry. Recommended. **E** *La Calzada*, C La Calzada near Guadalupe church, huge rooms with bath, fan, clean, friendly, great breakfasts. **F** *Central*, C la Calzada, friendly, clean, laundry facilities, popular, no mosquito nets, good restaurant. **F** *Pensión Vargas*, C La Calzada, basic, very nice people (pity about the condition of their animals), sun-heated shower, clean, nice garden.

Lago de Nicaragua

Dock

Plaza de España

El Ancla

Guadalupe

Complejo o Turístico

To Puerto Asese

To Puerto Asese

Eating
● *on maps*

Mi Café, in the La Casa de Los Leones, T5522800, very good, great outdoor and indoor setting, Granada's best salads (washed in chlorinated water), great espresso, omelettes, beef dishes; also sea bass, shrimp, pastas, large selection of fresh fruit drinks, open 0730-2200, closed Wednesday, concerts every Friday night, entrance US$1.50; owner, Don Mariano, is a historian who loves to talk (in French or Spanish) about Granada. *Pizza Hot*, next to *Hotel Alhambra*, good mid-priced pizza, nice setting. *Mediterráneo*, C Caimito, T5526764, open 0800-2300 everyday, lovely colonial house, quiet garden setting, expensive and popular with foreigners, Spanish owners and menu, very good seafood (paella not so good). *El Ancla*, opposite *Hotel Granada*, family run, clean, great Big Mac, good. *El Volcán*, 1 block south of La Merced, run by Danielo, friendly, good *brochetas*, breakfasts, plans for future accommodation. *Eskimo's*, C La Calzada, good ice cream; between *El Ancla* and *Eskimo's* is a cheap, good chicken place. *Tasa Blanca*, near market, friendly, good percolated coffee. Cheap food at the friendly *Café Astoria*, near plaza central. *Soyanica*, near Plaza Central, vegetarian, grotty, food nothing special. *Las Portales*, Plaza Central, opposite Enitel, simple, good. *Cafetín Amigo*, near Cathedral towards lake, good food, good value. *Comida Típica*, 1 block back to plaza from *Pensión Vargas*, cheap and good. Good breakfasts at the market.

The street that runs behind the *Hotel Alhambra*, C Atravezada, has, or is close to, most of Granada's nightlife, restaurants,

Nicaragua

market, etc. On this street, next to the cinema, is the very popular *Flamingo*, an inexpensive canteen with cheap beer and a very diverse clientele, particularly at night. Upstairs is *Charley's Disco Bar*, more upscale with dancing and popular with international crowd. Also along Atravezada are: *El Túnel*, inexpensive good bar with snacks, dark interior, popular for secretive liaisons; *El Prix*, ice cream, fried chicken, beer, snacks, inexpensive; *Dragón Dorado*, upstairs in the tourist complex, mid-priced Cantonese fare, attentive service, mediocre food. *Bullpen*, from Los Cocos, 1 block east, very cheap drinks and good soups. Near the Shell station, *Tito Bar*, good local place, with inexpensive typical Nicaraguan food, also *La Colina del Sur*, excellent lake fish and avocado salad, expensive but worth it, recommended. Just before the Complejo Turístico, *Caribbean Blue*, reggae music, Thursday-Sunday.

In the **Complejo Turístico** are many places for dancing and eating (it can be a miserable place at beginning of rainy season because of flying insect life). For meals, recommended are *El Cubano*, mid-priced bar and restaurant with Nica and Cuban food, and *La Terrazza La Playa*, mid-priced, great *cerdo asado* and *guapote filete*. Recommended for dancing and drinking are *El Bamboo*, young crowd, current music, occasional live acts, pool tables, and *César*, open Friday and Saturday only, very popular, inexpensive bar, merengue and salsa music. *Cocibolca* restaurant on Isla Cocibolca is reached by launch.

Entertainment **Cinema** One block behind *Hotel Alhambra*, good, modern, two screens.

Festivals **Holy Week**: *Assumption of the Virgin*, **14-30 August**; and Christmas (masked and costumed mummers).

Shopping **Market** (large green building in the centre) is dark, dirty and packed; lots of stalls on the streets outside, also horse cab rank and taxis. Main shopping street runs north-south, west of plaza. *Supermercado Lacayo*, C Real opposite *Hotel Valencia*. Next to the outdoor market is *Supermercado Pali*; *Almacén Internacional* near *Hotel Alhambra*.

Transport **Buses** leave from an area 200 metres beyond the market behind the *Hospedaje Esfinge*, except those going to/from Managua, which leave from a 'fenced lot uptown' (see map); buses to the capital every 20 minutes. Two companies run fast minibuses to **Managua**, US$0.80, 1 hour (these do not stop in Masaya but will stop at the junction); from Parque Sandino every 20 minutes, or from Casa Pellas every 15 minutes. Another bus service from the capital leaves from **La Piñata**, opposite Universidad Centroamericana (UCA) every 2 hours after 1000, US$1, no a/c but seat guaranteed. Return buses to Managua on Sunday are very crowded (being first in the queue is no guarantee of boarding). Bus to **Masaya**, US$0.30, half an hour. Bus to **Nandaime**, every 20 minutes, US$0.50. To **Rivas** 8 a day 0610-1810 (timings erratic), 1½ hours, US$1. It's often quicker to take a bus to Nandaime and then another on from there. Sirca Bus from Managua via Granada to **San José** from corner, 1 block from plaza on road to market, booking ahead essential, office is at Sr Cabezas, **Camas y Colchones Sant Ana**, 1½ blocks from plaza on road to market. Tica from Managua via Granada to San José, agency at Av Arellano, Hospital San Juan de Dios, ½ C al sur, T5524301.

Directory **Banks** *Banco de Centro América* on Parque Central and *Banco Centro* (1 block west of plaza) will change TCs, for better rates change TCs and cash dollars on the street. **Communications** Telephones: Enitel on corner northeast of Parque Central, by Casa de los Leones, open until 2200. One page fax to UK US$5, to USA US$3.40. **Email:** *Computer Internet Service*, from Casa Pellas 75m west, T5522544, F5523061, US$7 per hr. Other places beside Cathedral, US$5.50 per hr; on Atravezada 1 block south of San Francisco, US$3.50 per hr; from Casa Pellas 1 block south, ½ block west, US$5.50 per hr. **Language school** *Casa Xalteva*, C Real Xalteva 103, T/F5522436, casaxal@ibw.com.ni, small Spanish classes, 1 week to several months, homestays arranged, voluntary work with children, recommended. *GLSN*, C Real Xalteva, 6½ blocks west of Parque Central, 1 block from Jalteva church, US$55 per week, or US$85 with accommodation, 4 hrs tuition per day. Recommended. **Tour companies & travel agents** *Auxiliadora Travel Agent*, Iglesia La Merced 1 C al oeste, C Real Xalteva, Apdo 180, T2983304, most helpful and efficient. *Oro Travel*, Convento San Francisco ½ C al norte, T5524568, owner Pascal speaks French, English and German, friendly, helpful, good tours of Mombacho volcano reserve. *Viajes Griffith*, C Real No 414, T5524358, F5526262, English spoken.

Lake Nicaragua

The 'Gran Lago de Nicaragua' or Lago Cocibolca, 148 kilometres long by 55 kilometres at its widest (8,264 square kilometres), is a freshwater lake abounding in salt-water fish, which swim up the Río San Juan from the sea and later return. The lake shark, seen regularly on the east side of Isla Ometepe, is a rare fresh water variety in the bull shark family (*carcharhinus nicaragüensis*). Terrapins can be seen sunning themselves on the rocks and there are many interesting birds. The lake has three major archipelagos, which make up over 400 islands, and the largest lake island in the world, Ometepe. Created by a massive eruption of Volcán Mombacho 3,000 years ago, Las Isletas Archipelago, which is just southeast of Granada, accounts for 354 of them, most of which are inhabited and covered with lush vegetation. The **Zapatera Archipelago** is the most significant precolumbian site in Nicaragua and a national reserve. Tours are available, guided by an archaeologist from *Tours Nicaragua* in Managua, a rough one hour journey from Las Isletas in a fast boat. In the southeastern part of the lake is the Solentiname Archipelago (see below).

Colour map 5, grid A1/2

A *Nicarao Lake Resort* on the island of La Ceiba, T2281316, includes all meals, a/c, good beds, part-time generator, precious setting, lake perch in restaurant. *Santa Clara*, a furnished house with 3 bedrooms, US$200 per weekend.

Sleeping

Boats The islands can be visited either by hired boats or motor launches, from the Complejo Turístico (see above), at US$20 per hour for the whole boat, or from the restaurant at the end of the road beyond the Complejo Turístico, US$50 per hour for 6 in a motor launch, or US$10 per hour for 2 in a rowing boat. Another option is to take the morning bus (or taxi US$3.50) from Granada to **Puerto Asese**, 3 kilometres further south, a tranquil town at the base of the Asese peninsula at the head of the Ensenada de Asese. (Pleasant *Restaurante Asese*, T4592269, on the lake, good value, fish specialities.) Boats can be hired for US$10-12 per hour for 2 people. Trips to various lake destinations (Zapatera, El Muerto, the Solentiname Islands, Río San Juan) can be arranged in the yacht *Pacífico*, up to 15 people on day trips, 8 for overnight voyages, lunch included, recommended for a group (information and reservations in Granada, T459-4305/2269). See San Jorge, below, for the most frequently-used service.

Transport

Ometepe

The largest freshwater island in the world, Ometepe, has two volcanoes, one of them, **Concepción**, a perfect cone rising to 1,610 metres. The other is **Volcán Maderas**, 1,394 metres. There are two villages on the island, on either side of Volcán Concepción: **Moyogalpa** (*Population*: 4,500) and **Alta Gracia**, which are connected by bus. Moyogalpa has the atmosphere of a tourist port and lacks the charm of Alta Gracia and the other smaller villages here. Ometepe has the kindest people in Nicaragua, partly because the revolution and civil war were never waged here. There are many indigenous petroglyphs, a school of precolumbian-style ceramics and some large basalt statues, similar to those housed in the San Francisco museum in Granada, standing unprotected in Alta Gracia's central park. In Moyogalpa, change money in the two biggest grocery stores, one opposite *Hotel Colonial*, or in hotels. Peculiar to the town are the huge trees with (modest) houses underneath. From Moyogalpa you can hire a bicycle and ride to Punta Jesús María, 4-5 kilometres south, well-signposted from the road just before Esquipulas, where there is a nice beach, swimming, small café.

Population: 32,000
Colour map 5, grid A1

A new museum has opened in Alta Gracia, half a block from the central park, entrance US$1, guide in Spanish. Ask for the birdwatching place about three kilometres from Alta Gracia; birds fly in the late afternoon to nest on offshore islands. The wharf is about two kilometres from the town, there is a pick-up that meets the boats. You can stroll to the base of **Volcán Concepción** for good views of the lake and the company of many birds and howler monkeys (*congos*). To climb the volcano, leave

Nicaragua

from Cuatro Cuadros, two kilometres from Alta Gracia, and make for a cinder gully between forested slopes and a lava flow. There are several fincas on the lower part of the volcano. The ascent takes about five hours (take water). Alpine vegetation, the crater radiating heat and the howler monkeys are attractions. Very steep near summit. You can get a guide by asking near the pier, worthwhile as visibility is often restricted by clouds and it is easy to get lost, especially in the final stages (US$25 per group). Eduardo Ortiz and his son, José, of Cuatro Cuadros, will guide. Also Borman Gómez, meets boats from San Jorge, house is two blocks east, half a block south of the dock (ask for Casa Familia Gilberto Arcia), US$3.60 per person, speaks English. There is an alternative route up Volcán Concepción from behind the church in Moyogalpa. Again, a guide is recommended because of route finding in jungle sections (machete useful) and cloud, eight hours up, camping possible near the top. South of Volcán Concepción is Charco Verde lagoon and a waterfall worth visiting.

Around the island
Between Alta Gracia and **Balgües** (small basic *hospedaje*) is **Santo Domingo** with a wide grey sand beach. There is a small place to eat at the north end of the beach.

For **Volcán Maderas**, take an early bus (0430 or 0530) from Alta Gracia to Balgües (or stay overnight there), ask for *Hacienda Magdalena* (20 minutes walk), go up through banana plantations and forest to the top, beautiful lagoon in the crater, four to five hours up (can be very muddy, strong boots recommended). There is an entrance fee of US$1.75 to climb Maderas. This is one of the country's two finest Pacific basin cloud forests. Hear the howler monkeys all the way up. On the southwest flank of Volcán Maderas is Salto San Ramón, a 110-metre waterfall. In several locations on the island are Indian petroglyphs, the best being near *Hacienda Magdalena*. The climb to the summit of Volcán Maderas is not technical, but a guide may be helpful. Guides can be found at the coffee co-operative in Balgües, *Hacienda Magdalena*, or at *Hotel Ometepetl* in Moyogalpa, ask for Antonio. Take water on all hikes and climbs. Accommodation: **F** at the *Hacienda Magdalena*, a working co-operative farm, hammock space US$1, good meals around US$2, friendly, basic, very popular with travellers. You can work in exchange for lodging, one month minimum. Camping possible.

Sleeping
Alta Gracia **E** *Central*, on main street to Moyogalpa, attractive courtyard and dining room, good friendly service, with bath, nice patio, cabañas in garden, recommended. **F** *Castillo*, on

Isla de Ometepe

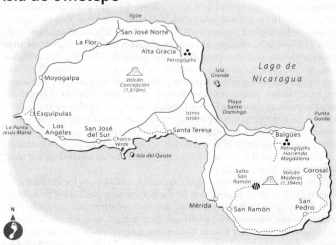

same road, friendly, water problems, good food, slow service, owner Ramón Castillo is 'an uncappable fount of information' and can organize trips to rock carvings on the volcano, US$4 per person or US$12 for a group guide. *Las Cabañas*, close to Playa Santa Domingo, new. In **Moyogalpa** C *Ometepetl*, on main street from dock, T4594276, F4594132, bath, a/c, rooms dirty, friendly, poor food, best rental cars on the island. **C-E** *Cari*, ½ block from pier, T4594263, F4594283, best location, poor service, some a/c, restaurant. **F** *El Colonial*, on main street from dock, with bath, clean, balcony, good food, recommended. **F** *Pensión Aly*, opposite Shell, clean, uncomfortable beds, helpful, poor value and service in restaurant. **F** per person *Asyl*, close to jetty, with restaurant. **F** *El Pirata*, on the east side of town, T4594262. **G** *Pension Jade*, good atmosphere, friendly, water problems, meals available good value. *Los Ranchitos*, on same street as telephone company, excellent food, reasonable prices, 2 branches, both good, new rooms in **E** range in 1998. Highly recommended. In **Santo Domingo** **C-F** *Villa Paraíso*,in cabañas with bath and fan or in lodge without bath, Austrian owner, German spoken, clean, lake view, friendly, peaceful, lovely setting, best food on the island (but won't permit you to bring own food to hotel), good birdwatching. Highly recommended. **D** *Istian*, south of *Villa Paraíso*, across the beach, reservations through *Ometepetl*, new, simple, clean, fan, bath, views to both volcanoes, friendly, recommended. **F** *Pensión Santo Domingo*, comfortable.

Boat The best access route to the island is from San Jorge on the lake's southwest shore (see below) to Moyogalpa. Cars are transported. Five boats a day Monday-Saturday, 2 boats on Sunday; the best boat, *La Señora del Lago*, leaves 1100 from San Jorge and returns 1300 from Moyogalpa, US$1.50 each way, 1 hour. Early morning boats are cheaper at US$1 (they have no bar). Those prone to seasickness should buy *Nausil* from farmacia before trip, the lake can have very big wind swells. Express buses from Mercado Huembes bus terminal in Managua to San Jorge at 0830 and 1500 (2 hours, US$1.60) meet ferries to Moyogalpa. Return from San Jorge to Managua 0745 and 1445, connecting with 0600/0630 and 1230/1330 ferries from Moyogalpa.

Launches sail from Granada to Alta Gracia Monday, Thursday and Saturday, 1200 and 1600, ticket office open 0900. Five hours to Alta Gracia, US$1. Boats leave Alta Gracia for Granada on Wednesday, Friday and Sunday. Everything left on deck will get wet; as it can be very crowded, a good spot for sleeping is on the cabin roof. Snacks and soft drinks sold on board. A cargo boat at 1100 from Alta Gracia takes passengers, 4 hours. Ticket office in Granada is at the dock; ENAP T5522745.

Bus on the island, 3 a day from Moyogalpa to Alta Gracia (45 mins-1 hr, US$0.50) and Balgües (1 hr, US$0.75) and return; none on Sunday.

Tours and tourist information There is a new tourist office, up the hill from the harbour in Moyogalpa, which offers good information, tours, horseriding, bus timetables, etc. Write to: Fundación Entre Volcanes, de la Gasolinera Esso 1 C y ½ al Sur, Moyogalpa, Ometepe, Nicaragua. Local guides can be found at Ecotur Ometepe, T/F4594118. *Ometepe Tours*, in Moyogalpa, del BND ½ al lago, T4594105, sells a useful booklet with maps and information, also in San Jorge, contiguo al muelle, T4534779. *Tours Nicaragua* in Managua offer guided tours of archaeological sites and volcano climbs.

Transport

Directory

Nicaragua

Solentiname Islands

One hour by fast boat, two or more by public boat from San Carlos (see below), is the 36-island archipelago of Solentiname. These sparsely-populated islands are covered with humid tropical forest, home to many birds and a unique school of painting and balsa wood sculptures.

San Fernando Island, C *Hotel Isla Solentiname*, with meals, safe, pretty grounds, acceptable but basic (you wash in the lake). Alternatively, you can stay in private homes, basic but very clean. Apart from the hotel, there is no electricity on the island, so take a torch. The diet is somewhat limited but there is lots of fresh fruit. Ask for Julio Pineda or his sister Rosa, one of the local artists. Many locals carve and paint balsa wood figures.

Colour map 5, grid A2

Isla La Venada, named for its plentiful population of deer, is also home to artists, in particular the house of Rodolpho Arellano who lives on the south side of the island. He is one of the region's best painters and his wife, daughters and grandson all paint tropical scenes and welcome visitors to see and purchase their works. On the north side of the island is a series of semi-submerged caves with some of the best examples of petroglyphs from the precolumbian Guatuso tribe.

Isla El Padre is inhabited only by howler monkeys, even though it is privately owned. Circling the island by boat can usually locate them in the trees.

Isla Mancarrón The largest in the chain, with the highest elevation at 250 metres, Mancarrón is where the famous revolutionary/poet/sculptor/Catholic priest/Minister of Culture, Ernesto Cardenal, made his name by founding a primitivist school of painting, poetry and sculpture, and even decorating the local parish church in naive art. The church is closed and no mass is said (1998). There is a monument to the Sandinista flag outside the church. Hiking is possible on the island where many parrots and Moctezuma Oropendolas make their home. The island's hotel of the same name is part of the local folklore as its founder Alejandro Guevara was a hero of the Sandinista revolution and his widow Nubia and her brother Peter now look after the place.

Sleeping **L** *Refugio Mancarrón*, up the hill from the dock and church, T2603345 (Managua), 5522059 (Solentiname), includes 3 meals per day, clean airy rooms with screened windows, mosquito netting, generated power at night, ping-pong, rocky beach, great bird watching, meals are traditional Nicaraguan fare with fruit juices, bar, purified water, hiking on Mancarrón led by the always fun Peter (in Spanish only, US$10 for 4), also to other islands and Los Guatusos in boat, highly recommended.

Transport Private transfers from San Carlos to Solentiname 1-1½ hours, US$55-85 per boat. The public boat goes Tuesday and Friday only at 1100 from San Carlos, 0300 from Mancarrón, 3½ hours, US$2.15. Although expensive by Nicaraguan standards, a package arranged in Managua including all transport and full board is the best bet.

Los Guatusos **Wildlife Reserve** *500 sq km area of wetland, rain forest and gallery forest* Known as the cradle of wildlife for Lake Nicaragua, it is home to many exotic and varied species of bird life and reptiles. It is heavily populated by monkeys, especially howlers. The reserve is crossed by three rivers, Guacalito, Zapote and (most popular for boat touring) Papaturro. It is essential to be at the park for sunrise to see a quality and quantity of wildlife that is astonishing. After 1030 the river often becomes busier with immigration traffic of labourers heading to Costa Rica. There is a public boat San Carlos-Papaturro daily except Sunday at 1100 and 1400, US$1, but return schedule not known, 1½ hours. It is only 30 minutes to one hour from Mancarrón into the reserve. Your name and passport number may have to be given to the police post at Papaturro. Tours can be booked with Managua tour operators, or at the *Hotel Mancarrón* in Solentiname. Cost US$85-125 per boat for 5-6 hours.

Southern shore

San Jorge *Colour map 5, grid A1* On Sunday in summer, San Jorge is very lively with music, baseball, swimming and lots of excursion buses. **D** *Mar Dulce*, 300 metres south of dock, bath, TV, parking. **F** *Nicarao*, left off the Rivas-San Jorge road, a short distance from the dock, basic meals, friendly.

From San Jorge a road runs through Rivas (frequent bus service, US$0.30, half an hour) to the port of San Juan del Sur or onwards along the west coast of the lake to Sapoá and the Costa Rican border. Another road runs parallel to the eastern side of the lake through San Lorenzo, Juigalpa, Acoyapa, San Bartolo and down to the shore where about 45 kilometres north of San Carlos is **San Miguelito** (*Population*: 8,000), a small fishing village where the boats call between San Carlos and Granada.

Vendors with drinks and food board the boats. **D** *Cocibolca*, at the end of the jetty, T5526107, F5526104, colonial style, ask for a room with balcony, hard beds, riding arranged by the owner, Franklin.

Río San Juan

The Río San Juan, running through deep jungles, drains Lake Nicaragua from the eastern end into the Caribbean at San Juan del Norte. At over 190 kilometres in length with more than 17 tributaries, it runs the length of the southern border of the Indio Maíz Biological Reserve and makes the most natural connection between the Atlantic and Pacific Oceans. This great river has played an integral part in Nicaragua's colonial and post-colonial history and is one of the most accessible of the country's many pristine nature-viewing areas. First sailed by the Spanish in 1525, the complete length of the river was not navigated until 24 June 1539, the day of San Juan Bautista, hence its name. In colonial times it was a vital link between the Spanish Caribbean and the port of Granada. After three attacks by Caribbean pirates on Granada, the Spanish built a fortress at El Castillo in 1675. Twice the English tried to take the fort in the 18th century, failing the first time at the hands of the teenaged Nicaraguan national heroine, Rafaela Herrera, and succeeding with Lord (then Captain) Nelson, who lost an eye in the battle, but later had to withdraw owing to tropical diseases. In the 19th century the filibuster William Walker used the San Juan to take Granada, and when expelled by the combined Central American forces escaped back down the river. Later it became the site of many aborted canal projects, one of which was abandoned after a kilometre had been dredged. Today it is a most rewarding boat journey for anyone with an interest in ecology.

Colour map 5, grid A2

San Carlos

San Carlos is the capital of the Río San Juan department and the jumping off point for excursions to Solentiname (see above), Río Frío to Costa Rica and the Río San Juan itself, with the two great nature reserves of Los Guatusos (see above) and Indio Maíz (see below). Launches ply down the river irregularly from the lakeside. Much of the town was destroyed by fire in 1984, but much rebuilding has been done. In the wet it is a very muddy place. At San Carlos are the ruins of a fortress built for defence against pirates.

Population: 15-20,000
Colour map 5, grid A2

All hotels are basic, with bugs, rats etc. One possibility is **B** *Cabinas Leyka*, Policia Nacional 2 C al oeste, T2830354, with bath, a/c, **D** with fan, balcony with view of the lake, serves breakfast; another is **F** *Hospedaje Peña*, near central plaza, unhelpful. **F** *Casa de Protocolo*, top of town on park opposite church, clean, nets, private bath. *Restaurante Río San Juan*, good meals, room for rent, **F**, dirty, noisy. Also **F** *Hotelito San Carlos*, by jetty, with fan, basic, breakfast US$1.25, and *Yuri*, nice room, cheap, friendly. Several *comedores* including **F** *Félix Dining Room*, 2 plastic tables on the main street but good meal for US$1.50. *Bar-restaurant Kaoma*, Río San Carlos, fresh fish caught by the owner. Recommended. *Oasis*, by the lake. *Bar Miralago*, by the lake, painted pink and purple, good grilled meat and salad, but fearsome mosquitoes in the evening. If your hotel has no running water, there is a bath house by the pier.

Sleeping & eating

Air La Costeña flies from Managua Monday-Saturday, US$61 return, sit on right side on way to San Carlos for breathtaking flight over Ometepe's 2 volcanoes. Taxi airstrip to dock US$1. **Buses** There is a daily bus from Mercado El Mayoreo, Managua, at 0530 to San Carlos, via San Miguelito, 9 hours, US$4.75; return to Managua at 0800, 8 hours, and 0200 on Tuesday and Friday, 7½ hours. The section between Acoyapa and San Carlos, 4 hours, has been described as 'hellish'. **Lake** Boat services from Granada to San Carlos go on Monday and Thursday, at 1500 via San Miguelito, and at 1600 via Altagracia. Both cost US$2.60 and each journey lasts 12 hours (Enap in Granada, T5522745). Boats can be hired to explore the shores of the lake south of the Solentiname Islands.

Transport

Nicaragua

San Carlos to **San Juan del Norte** departs Tuesday at 0600, journey takes 10 or more hours, US$13 one way. Return from San Juan del Norte to San Carlos is on Thursday at 0400, 12 or more hours. This trip may not be passable at the end of the dry season (April/May) if water levels are low. Private transportation for the river is best arranged in advance in Managua with tour operators there. Travel time to San Juan del Norte in private boat with 65 or larger motor are: 1¾ hours San Carlos to El Castillo; 20 minutes El Castillo to Río Bartola; 2¼ hours Bartola to Río Sarapiquí; 2 hours Sarapiquí to San Juan del Norte. Non-stop journey takes 6½ hours, average cost for boat and driver is US$900-1,200 round-trip. Group tours with *Tours Nicaragua* in Managua of the river, complete with private boat transfers and tours, lodging, bilingual guide and food for 1 week at US$1,000 per person with a minimum of 5 travellers.

Directory **Banks** No exchange for TCs, only cash with street changers.

Frontier with Costa Rica – San Carlos to Los Chiles This has now become a frequented crossing point between Nicaragua and Costa Rica and is normally quick and hassle free. There is a track of sorts from the south side of the Río San Juan, but most travellers go by boat up the Río Frío.

Nicaraguan immigration Border is now open 7 days a week 0800-1600. Exit stamps must be obtained in San Carlos Monday-Friday only. Check with the police in advance for the latest position.

Transport There are launches from San Carlos to Los Chiles, US$3.50, 1½ hours. Several launches a day, the first normally leaving at 1000. If you get on last at San Carlos, you will be first off at Los Chiles for the Costa Rican *migración* which closes at 1200 for lunch. **NB** The entire Nicaragua-Costa Rica border along the Río San Juan is ill-defined and the subject of inter-government debate.

El Castillo Some 60 kilometres down river is El Castillo, built around the restored ruins of the 18th-century Spanish fort called La Fortaleza de la Inmaculada Concepción. The old fort has a good history museum inside where the entrance fee of US$1 is collected (well-presented, closes 1200 for lunch). It was here that Nelson did battle with the Spanish forces (see above). Great views of the river in both directions from the fortress. The town is on a wide bend in the river where some shallow but tricky rapids run the whole width. Horseriding possible, about US$6 per hour.

Sleeping **C** *Albergue El Castillo*, T2492508, new but oddly designed, shared bath. **E** *Richardson*, with bath, excellent breakfasts, crayfish cooked to order (reserve by 1600 for evening meal), very good value. **F** *Hospedaje Manantial*, on left of main street as you leave the boat, none too clean, no view, basic, breakfast US$1.50, lunch US$2. **F** *Hospedaje Aurora*, basic, but kindly owners, veranda with rocking chair overlooking river, serves food.

Eating *Bar Cofalito*, on the jetty, crayfish on menu, good view but poor quality. Better value is the *soda* facing the quay. *Doña Amelia*, good meals also on the wharf, very clean, cheap. *Naranjano*, good food.

Transport There are about 4 daily boats from San Carlos to El Castillo, schedules seem to change frequently (5 hours), US$1.50. Other boats do the trip but without fixed schedules. If planning to continue on from El Castillo, it can only be done by prior arrangement in San Carlos or Managua, though you may find a ride downstream with patience and a wad of cash.

Indio Maíz Biological Reserve A few kilometres downstream is the Río Bartola and the beginning of the Indio Maíz Biological Reserve, 3,000 square kilometres of mostly primary rain forest and home to over 600 species of birds, 300 species of reptiles and 200 species of mammals including many big cats and howler, white face and spider monkeys. Camping is possible: ask the lone park ranger where you may camp, his guard house is across the Río Bartola from the *Refugio Bartola* lodge.

Sleeping B pp *Refugio Baratola*, including 3 meals (**C** without food), fruit juices, simple rooms with solid beds, ask for mosquito netting, excellent meals cooked by one of Managua's finest chefs, recommended crayfish (*camarones del río*), *cerdo a la plancha*, purified water, very clean. Pet spider monkey at lodge, Daniela, loves men and bites women. *Refugio Bartola* is also a research station and training ground for young Nicaraguan biologists; it has a labyrinth of well mapped trails behind the lodge in the reserve. The hotel guide is very knowledgeable, but speaks only Spanish, he will also take you down the Río Bartola in canoe, great wildlife viewing, birding, and so on. "Fantastic." Make all transport arrangements with care.

The river past Bartola becomes more beautiful and unpopulated. Here the Costa Rican border reaches to the south bank of the river, and while the Costa Rican side is partially deforested and populated, the Nicaraguan side containing the Indio Maíz Reserve is almost entirely intact. Many turtles, birds and crocodiles can be seen in this section of the river. Two hours minimum down river is the Río Sarapiquí and immigration check points for both Costa Rica and Nicaragua.

There is a simple, friendly, Nicaraguan-owned, lodge on the Sarapiquí called *Paraíso de la Frontera* or Doña Adilia's place, **D** per person, shared bath, fan, she also has a small store to buy supplies. If coming from the Río San Juan to Río Sarapiquí you will need to check in with the Costa Rican guard station to spend the night, or even if you just want to pick up something at the store. If continuing down the river without stopping you only need to check in at the Nicaraguan station on the Río San Juan. The guards there will let you use their bathroom.

Past the Sarapiquí, the San Juan branches north and both sides of the river become part of Nicaragua again (and heavily forested) as the Río Colorado heads into Costa Rica. Two hours or so later, the San Juan drains into the Caribbean via a series of magnificent forest-wrapped lagoons. The Río Indio must be taken to reach the isolated, but surprisingly affluent village of San Juan del Norte.

San Juan del Norte

One of the wettest places on the American continent at over 5,000 millimetres of rain per year, San Juan del Norte is also one of the most beautiful, with primary rain forest, lagoons, rivers and the Caribbean Sea. It is settled by a gregarious, small population (estimated at 650), though it was once a boom town in the 19th century, when the American industrialist Cornelius Vanderbilt was running his steamship line between New York and San Francisco. Then called Greytown, San Juan del Norte was the pickup point for the steamship journey to the Pacific via the Río San Juan, Lake Nicaragua to La Virgen and then by mule overland to San Juan del Sur. This service was quite popular during the 'gold rush' of San Francisco and Mark Twain made the crossing as a young man from San Francisco to New York. He recounted the journey in his book *Travels with Mr Brown*. This town remained in its location on the Bahía San Juan del Norte (actually a coastal lagoon) until the 1980s, when fighting caused its population to flee. Re-established in its current location on the Río Indio, the village is separated from the Caribbean Sea by a dense wedge of rain forest, 400 metres wide, on the east bank of the Río Indio. The population is a mix of Miskito, Creole and Hispanic. There is no land route from here to Bluefields.

Due to its proximity to Limón, Costa Rica, colones are the standard currency here as all the food and supplies are more easily bought there than in San Carlos. In Sarapiquí and San Juan del Norte, córdobas, colones and dollars are all accepted, with change normally given in colones.

Colour map 5, grid A2

Nicaragua

E pp *Hotel Virgin Paradise* (or Melvin's Place), on the river, ceiling fan, private bath, clean, bring coils or mosquito netting, owner Melvin speaks English and is very helpful, bar, restaurant, night-time generated power, gazebo on the river with TV, bottled water for sale, highly recommended.

Sleeping

Eating The food in San Juan del Norte is simple, fresh lobster if in season, if not the fried snook is recommended. Other seafood is fresh. ***Doña Ester's Place***, just down the river from Melvin's Place, is the town's restaurant, though others to open soon, average dish costs US$3. Drinks in town consist of Costa Rican beer, Nicaraguan rum and Coca-Cola.

Entertainment **Discos** There are two discos which are full of festive locals on weekend nights. Dancing is to reggae as well as salsa, rap and merengue. If staying at Melvin's Place (and Melvin is in town) he will take you to the disco at night to make sure you have a good time and make it back home. It is a short walk to either one, but a ride in his *super-panga* is not to be missed; if offered, hold on tight.

Excursions If coming in your own boat (chartered), a trip further down the Río Indio is recommended, abundant wildlife, virgin forest and Rama Indians (please respect their culture and privacy). A visit to the ruins of old Greytown is also interesting, with a well marked trail that leads through various cemeteries buried in the forest and to the town centre where only foundations and the church bell remain. Swimming is best in the Blue Lagoon, though the Caribbean is also accessible, but with many sharks. If coming on the public boat from San Carlos, Melvin can arrange tours with one of his *pangas*.

Frontier with Costa Rica – Greytown This area of the Caribbean coast is a narcotics zone, with drugs being landed from San Andrés (Colombia). Before attempting to cross, seek information on general safety.

Nicaraguan immigration There is no official immigration in San Juan del Norte, although travellers have reported being able to get stamps from the authorities here that were accepted when checked elsewhere. Otherwise you must go to Bluefields or to one of the posts up the Río San Juan. Equally take advice on what to do on arrival in Costa Rica.

Transport You can go by boat from San Juan del Norte to Barra del Colorado in Costa Rica, ask about fishing boats and canoes.

Managua

Managua to Costa Rica

The Pan-American Highway to the Costa Rican border passes through agricultural land, with branches inland to Granada and to the Pacific coast. A useful stopping place is Rivas: from here to the border, Lake Nicaragua and Volcán Concepción are to be seen. For sunsets, go to San Juan del Sur.

The Pan-American Highway, in good condition, has bus services all the way to San José de Costa Rica (148 kilometres). The road runs into the Sierra de Managua, reaching 900 metres at Casa Colorada, 26 kilometres from Managua. Further on, at El Crucero (a cool and pleasant place), a paved branch road goes through the Sierra south to the Pacific bathing beaches of Pochomil and Masachapa (see page 986).

Diriamba
Population: 26,500
Altitude: 760m
Colour map 5, grid A1

The Highway continues through the beautiful scenery of the Sierras to **Diriamba**, 42 kilometres from Managua in a coffee-growing district. In the centre of the town is the **Museo Ecológico de Trópico Seco**, with displays of local flora and fauna including coffee and turtles. There is also a section on volcanoes. ■ *Tuesday-Saturday 0800-1200, 1400-1700, Sunday 0800-1200, T4222129, entry US$1.* Its great *fiesta* is on 20 January. There is a 32-kilometre dirt road direct to Masachapa (no buses). Five kilometres north of Diriamba a paved road branches off the highway to Managua and runs east through San Marcos, Masatepe (famous for wooden and rattan furniture) and Niquinohomo to Catarina and Masaya.

Sleeping and eating **E** *Diriangén*, with bath, parking. Good fish at restaurant *2 de Junio*. Before Diriamba on the Carretera Sur, just after the turning to Masatepe at Las Esquinas, is **El Patio de Don Pedro**, mostly Mexican food, mid-priced, nice decor, sleepy service.

Five kilometres beyond Diriamba is Jinotepe, capital of the coffee-growing district of Carazo. It has a fine neo-classical church with modern stained glass windows from Irún, in Spain. The *fiesta* in honour of St James the Greater is on 24-26 July. 5 July is celebrated here as 'liberation day'.

Jinotepe
Population: 17,600
Altitude: 760m

Sleeping **C** *Jinotepe*, T412-2978/2947, modern, 3-storey building 1 block north and 1 block west of Parque Central, comfortable, with bath and fan, dance floor, fine restaurant, good service. **F** *Hospedaje San Carlos*, no sign, ask around for it.

Eating *Pizza Danny's* is very good, 50 metres north of municipal building (try their *especial*, small but delicious, US$7).

Buses For Managua leave from the terminal in the northeast corner of town, every 20 minutes, US$0.55; to Nandaime every 30 minutes, US$0.35; to Diriamba-Masaya every 20 minutes.

Banks Black market for dollars in Parque Central.

La Concepción is a small, industrious village in the highlands, very typical of this part of Nicaragua, where no travellers go. The area is rich in pineapple, pitaya, coffee, mandarins and oranges and the people welcoming. Access is by bus from Jinotepe, every 20 minutes, US$0.50, or from Managua's Roberto Huembes terminal, every half an hour, US$0.75. Accommodation can be found at the house of Jacinto Caldero, an old barber who lives next to the Banco del Café on the Carretera (**E** with full board, **F** without). Don Jacinto also shows visitors around on foot for US$20 per day to meet the local people (including the blind guitarist and songwriter Santiago), farms and countryside.

From **Nandaime**, 21 kilometres from Jinotepe, altitude 130 metres, a paved road runs north to Granada (bus US$0.50). Nandaime has two interesting churches, El Calvario and La Parroquia (1859-72). The annual *fiesta* is 24-27 July, with masked dancers. Unnamed *hospedaje*, **E**, and restaurant *La Cabaña*, good local dishes, a favourite with truck drivers.

Rivas

About 45 kilometres beyond Nandaime (US$0.40 by bus) is Rivas. The Costa Rican national hero, the drummer Juan Santamaría, sacrificed his life here in 1856 when setting fire to a building captured by the filibuster William Walker and his men. On the town's Parque Central is a lovely old church (in need of repair). In the dome of the Basilica, see the fresco of the sea battle against the ships of Protestantism and Communism. The Parque has some old, arcaded buildings on one side, but also some new buildings. Rivas is a good stopping place if in transit by land through Nicaragua. The bus station, adjacent to the market, is on the northwest edge of town about eight blocks from the main highway. The road from the lake port of San Jorge joins this road at Rivas; 11 kilometres beyond Rivas, at La Virgen on the shore of Lake Nicaragua, it branches south to San Juan del Sur.

Population: 34,000
Colour map 5, grid A1

C *Cacique Nicarao*, 2 blocks west of Parque Central, next to the cinema (3 blocks south and 2 east from bus terminal), T4533234, F4533120, with a/c, cheaper with fan, comfortable, slow service, shower, cold water, best in town, clean, well-equipped, good restaurant, Visa accepted, secure parking. Recommended.

Sleeping

Nicaragua

E *Pensión Primavera*, small rooms but clean, shared bath, friendly, basic.

F *El Coco*, on Pan-American Highway near where bus from frontier stops, noisy, basic, small rooms, shower, interesting bar, *comedor* with vegetarian food, nice garden. **F** *Hospedaje Delicia*, on main Managua-border road, basic and dirty, friendly. **F** *Hospedaje Internacional*, where the Sirca bus stops, near the Texaco station, good breakfast. Several on Highway, **E** *Hospedaje Lidia*, near Texaco, clean, noisy, family-run. (At the Texaco station, Lenín, who speaks English, is very helpful.)

Eating *Restaurant Chop Suey*, in the arcade in Parque Central. *Rinconcito Salvadoreño*, in the middle of the Parque Central, open air, charming. *Comedor Lucy*, on street leaving Parque Central at corner opposite Banco de Nicaragua, '*comidas corrientes y vegetarianos*'. *Restaurant El Ranchito*, near *Hotel El Coco*, friendly, serves delicious chicken and *churrasco*.

Transport **Buses** To the frontier **Sapoá/Peñas Blancas**: every hour or so: 0645, 0730 and 1100, good for connections for buses to San José (US$0.60, 1 hour); taxis available, about US$15 from bus terminal, add US$2 from town centre, or a place in a colectivo, US$3. Alternatively, try to get on the Sirca bus which stops at the Sirca office about 0800, Monday, Wednesday, Friday and Saturday. (**NB** Tica bus stops in Rivas, but only to let people off.) Trucks on this section are generous with hitchhikers and are useful for continuing through the gap between customs and beyond. Bus to **Managua**, from 0400 (last one 1700), 2½ hours, US$1.40; taxi, US$40. Several daily buses to **Granada**; it may be quicker to take the Managua bus and change at Nandaime. Frequent bus to **San Jorge** on Lake Nicaragua, US$0.20 (taxi to San Jorge, US$1.50).

Directory **Banks** Black market near market, good rates. **Communications** Entel is 3 blocks south of Parque Central, or 7 blocks south and 3 blocks east from bus terminal. **Tour companies & travel agents** *Turnicarao*, 1 block south from Plaza, T4534157, F4533371, arranges local tours, good place to send faxes.

A few kilometres before Rivas, coming from Nandaime, is a road to the left to Potosí, a quiet village with *Comedor Soda Helen*, one block from the Parque Central; meals are available in the evening if you request them.

Between Nandaime and Rivas are various turnings south which lead eventually to the Pacific coast (all are rough, high clearance better than four-wheel drive). One of these turnings, 89 kilometres from Managua if going via Diriamba and Jinotepe (61 kilometres from Peñas Blancas), just south of the Río Ochomogo bridge, is signposted **Refugio de Vida Silvestre Río Escalante Chacocente**. This reserve, 4,800 hectares of forest and beach, is the second most important turtle nesting site in the country and one of the biggest tracts of tropical dry forest in the Pacific basin. The forest is full of mammal, reptile and bird life and the beach is very long and empty. Bring your own hammock and shade. The road to the coast (45 kilometres, dirt, rough) goes to Las Salinas. Turn right here to **Astillero**, which has a fishing co-operative, and continue to the reserve. You will probably have to ask directions to the reserve several times and cross a number of rivers, the last of which is very wide (it can't be crossed after rain without a very strong four-wheel drive, lots of speed and bravado). Camping is safe and you can buy fish from the co-op. At **Chacocente**, there is a Marena office, a government-sponsored turtle sanctuary (the only signs after Astillero say 'authorized personnel only'; don't be put off, they welcome visitors, but ask for directions). The Marena wardens protect newly-hatched turtles and help them make it to the sea (a magnificent sight during November and December). Unfortunately, new-laid turtle eggs are considered to have aphrodisiac properties and are used as a dietary supplement by the locals. Marena is virtually powerless to prevent egg theft, although for two months a year the place is protected by armed military personnel. The Marena personnel are friendly and helpful (ask about similar projects around the country); entry US$0.70.

San Juan del Sur

San Juan del Sur is 28 kilometres from Rivas via the Pan-American Highway, 93 kilometres from Granada. The road from the Pan-American Highway is in good condition. There is a direct dirt road from Rivas, good only when dry, going through beautiful countryside. It has a beautiful bay with a sandy beach and some rocky caves reached by walking round the point opposite the harbour. Sunsets at San Juan del Sur have to be seen to be believed. The town beach is dirty, so it is best to take a boat to others, such as Playa del Coco and Playa del Tamarindo, 15 kilometres away on the poor road to Ostional; and Marsella, five kilometres north of San Juan where there is a kiosk on the beach. The surfing on these and nearby beaches is good. At weekends and on holidays, especially at *Semana Santa*, San Juan is busy, but otherwise the beaches are quiet during the week. It is best not to wander on the beaches after dark and at low tide there may be stingrays, but the officials at the Customs Office can tell you the tide times.

Refugio de Vida Silvestre La Flor, covers 800 hectares of tropical dry forest, mangroves, estuary and beach. A beautiful, sweeping cove with light tan sand and many trees, it is the most important and heavily-visited beach by nesting sea turtles (season August to November). Armed guards protect the turtle arrivals during high season and the rangers are very happy to explain the turtle's reproductive habits (in Spanish). Arrivals are at times in the thousands and usually for a period of 3 days. Many birds live in the protected mangroves at the south end of the beach. Entrance costs US$1.70 and can be made by four-wheel drive or on foot. Exit for the dirt path south is 200 metres before the entrance to San Juan del Sur, 21 kilometres from the highway, several rivers must be crossed, most with solid bottoms. Camping is provided (one tent only) during the turtle arrivals, US$6 per night, first come, first served. Bring hammock and mosquito netting, insects are vicious at dusk.

Population: 4,750
Colour map 5, grid A1

Sleeping

Note that hotel prices in San Juan del Sur double for Semana Santa and Christmas/New Year.

A *Casablanca*, opposite *Bar Timon*, T/F4582135, a/c, cable TV, private bath, restored house, clean, friendly, laundry service, secure parking, transfers to San Jorge or Peñas Blancas US$25 per person, in front of beach, recommended. **B** *Aramara Lodge*, new, de la Cabañita 1 block north, T4582259 (San Juan), T2661719 (Managua), aguzman@uam.edu.ni, **A** at weekends, includes breakfast, a/c, cable TV, pool, traditional house, very cute with balconies and living room, friendly, 1 block from beach, recommended. **B** *Royal Chateau*, from the church 2 blocks north, cheaper without a/c, **C** single with fan, cable TV, clean, secure parking, pool, bar and restaurant, breakfast US$2.50, other meals to order, 4 blocks from beach. **B** *Villa Renata*, behind the church to the left, T4582568, marked by small wooden sign, 5 rooms, includes breakfast, fan, private bath, very clean, prices are negotiable at low season, lovely wooden house with hardwood floors, well decorated with ample windows and light, English spoken, 4 blocks from beach.

C *Joxi*, T4582348, friendly, clean, a/c, bath, bunk beds, Danish run, restaurant, bar, sailing trips on the boat *Pelican Eyes* can be arranged here.

E *Buengusto*, very basic but very friendly, helpful, good fish restaurant, on seafront. **E** *Hospedaje Casa No 28*, 40 metres from beach, near minibus stop for Rivas, shared showers, mosquitoes (ask owner for coils), kitchen and laundry facilities, clean, friendly owners, good. On same street as *Joxi* is **E** *Estrella*, on Pacific, with meals, balconies overlooking the sea, partitioned walls, shower, take mosquito net and towel, clean, popular. **E** *Guest House Elizabeth*, opposite bus terminal, T4582270, clean, fan, friendly and helpful owner, has tied up monkey. **E** *Irazú*, 1 block from beach, some rooms with bath, very run down.

F *Gallo de Oro*, 500 metres north of town, very basic but friendly and cheapest around, nice setting at end of beach. **F** *Hospedaje Juliet*, from the church 1 block north, T4582333, dark clean rooms, ask for fan, some with bath, others without, basic, soft beds, breakfast US$1.50, family-run, 4 blocks from beach. **F** *Hospedaje La Fogata*, clean, friendly, family run, good food. Recommended.

Camping Customs Office may give permission for camping and to park motor-caravans and trailers on the wharves if you ask them nicely. Motor-caravans and trailers may also be parked on Marsella beach: coming south, turn right on entering San Juan, by shrimp-packing plant.

Eating *El Camarón de Oro*, from the market 1½ blocks north, Spanish, seafood, good service, mid-priced, recommended. *Las Lugo*, from Correos 1 block east, expensive seafood, fresh fish, despite being by the sea nothing like as good as its sister restaurant in Managua. *O Sole Mio*, from *Hotel Casablanca* 500 metres north, best Italian, mid-priced, pizza and pasta, recommended. *Salón Siria*, good. *Soya*, vegetarian and meat dishes, fruit, *refrescos*, *chorizo de soya*, good, cheap and friendly, also has a room to rent (**F**). Good *panadería* 1 block from beach. Good cafés along the beach for breakfast and drinks; the beach front restaurants all serve good fish (about US$4 a meal), eg *Timon Bar*, *gambas*, lobster (US$9) and prawns are specialities, most popular place in town, mediocre food, worst service. *Marie Bar*, opposite, excellent food, English and German spoken, excursions to La Flor and fishing. Breakfast and lunch in market, eg *Comedor Zapata*. *Comedor Angelita* serves very good fish dishes.

Sports **Surfing:** The coast north and south of San Juan del Sur is among the best in Central America for surfing, all access is by boat or long treks in 4WD. The country's most accomplished, knowledgeable surfer and surf guide, Sergio Calderón, known to all in town as 'Chelo', lives in San Juan del Sur and owns the *Action Surf Shop*, from Las Cabiñitas 75 metres south, T4582441, surf clothing, wax and beach toys for sale, surf boards from 6'0" to 7'2" for rent, US$2 hour or US$10 per day, same rates for boogie boards, also rents bicycles. Chelo (who speaks only Spanish and 'surf English') knows all the best spots on the south Pacific Coast and will take you surfing for US$20 per day, plus boat costs. Normal boat costs US$25 per hour plus gasoline. Also planning a surf school in the near future, ask.

Transport **Buses** Minibus from **Rivas** Market, regular, crowded, 55 minutes, US$0.60. Direct bus **Managua**, Mercado Huembes, at 1600, 1700, return from San Juan 0500, 0600, 3½ hours, US$2.60.

Directory **Banks** There is no bank, hotels *Casablanca* and *Joxi* and some shops, like *Pulpería Sánchez*, will change money. **Communications** Post Office: 150m left (south) along the seafront from the main junction. Email: *Casa Joxi* has internet services, US$12 per hour. **Health** The dispensary, where you have to pay for medicines, has good service. **Laundry** Most of the mid to upper-priced hotels will do laundry for their guests on request. Near *Soya Restaurant* (ask there), hand wash, line dry.

Frontier with Costa Rica – Peñas Blancas This is the only road crossing between the two countries. There are two duty free shops (not worth bothering with), *Hospedaje El Mesón* with restaurant and several *comedores* on the Nicaraguan side.

Nicaraguan immigration ■ *0800-1200 and 1300-1745*. When entering the country, you show your passport at the border but the Nicaraguan Migración is at *Sapoá*, 4 kilometres into Nicaragua, to which you can take a minibus (they go when full) or taxi, US$0.70 pp. International bus passengers have to disembark and queue for immigration to stamp passport. Then you must unload your baggage and wait in a line for the customs official to arrive. You will then be asked to open your bags, the official will give them a cursory glance and then you reload. Passports and tickets will be checked again back on the bus. For travellers not on a bus, there are plenty of small helpers on hand. Allow 45 minutes to complete the formalities.

Crossing by private vehicle Entering: after you have been through Migración, find an inspector who will fill out the preliminary form to be taken to Aduana. At the Vehículo Entrando window, the vehicle permit is typed up and the vehicle stamp is put in your passport. Next, go to Tránsito to pay for the car permit. Finally, ask the inspector again to give the final check.

Leaving: First pay your exit tax at an office at the end of the control station, receipt given. Then come back for your exit stamp, and complete the Tarjeta de Control Migratorio.

Motorists must then go to Aduana to cancel vehicle papers: exit details are typed on to the vehicle permit and the stamp in your passport is cancelled. Find the inspector in Aduana who has to check the details and stamp your permit. If you fail to do this you will not be allowed to leave the country – you will be sent back to Sapoá by the officials at the final Nicaraguan checkpoint. Note that there is no fuel going into Nicaragua until Rivas, 37 kilometres.

Exchange Same rates on either side, but the bank on the Nicaraguan side offers better rates than the money changers.

Transport There is an hourly bus service from Sapoá to Rivas from 0730-1630, US$0.70, 1 hour. The last bus Rivas–Managua is at 1630, US$1.40, 2½ hours. There can be long waits when the international buses are passing through. A good time to cross, if you are going independently, is around 0900, before the buses arrive.

The Caribbean Coast

Managua

Nicaragua's eastern tropical lowlands are very different from the rest of the country: there is heavy rainfall between May and December; the economy is based on timber, fishing and mining. The people are mostly Miskito Indians, but with much African influence. English is widely spoken. To reach the Caribbean port of Bluefields, from where you can go to the Corn Islands, you either have to fly or take the famous 'Bluefields Express' down river.

NB In Nicaragua, the Caribbean coast is almost always referred to as the Atlantic coast.

The area, together with about half the coastal area of Honduras, was never colonized by Spain. From 1687 to 1894 it was a British Protectorate known as the Miskito Kingdom. It was populated then, as now, by Miskito Indians, whose numbers are estimated at 75,000. There are two other Indian groups, the Sumu (5,000) and the Rama, of whom only a few hundred remain, near Bluefields. Also near Bluefields are a number of Garifuna communities. Today's strong African influence has its roots in the black labourers brought in by the British to work the plantations and in Jamaican immigration. The Afro-Nicaraguan people call themselves creoles (*criollos*). The largest number of inhabitants of this zone are Spanish-speaking *mestizos*. The Sandinista revolution, like most other political developments in the Spanish-speaking part of Nicaragua, was met with mistrust. Although the first Sandinista junta recognized the indigenous peoples' rights to organize themselves and choose their own leaders, many of the programmes initiated in the region failed to encompass the social, agricultural and cultural traditions of eastern Nicaragua. Relations deteriorated and many Indians engaged in fighting for self-determination. About half the Miskito population fled as refugees to Honduras, but most returned after 1985 when a greater understanding grew between the Sandinista Government and the people of the east Coast. The Autonomous Atlantic Region was given the status of a self-governing region in 1987; it is divided into Región Autonomista Atlántico Norte (RAAN) and Región Autonomista Atlántico Sur (RAAS).

At **San Benito**, 35 kilometres from Managua on the Pan-American Highway going north, the Atlantic Highway branches east, paved all the way to Rama on the Río Escondido, or Bluefields River. Shortly after Teustepe, a paved road goes northeast to Boaco. A turn-off, unpaved, goes to **Santa Lucía**, a village inside a crater, with a women's handicraft shop. There is also a co-operative here with an organic farming programme (information from Unag in Matagalpa). *Casa de Soya*, good food, **From Managua to Rama**

Nicaragua

friendly owners, single room for rent, basic, **F**. Good views from nearby mountains. Two trucks a day from Boaco, US$1, one bus a day to/from Managua. **Boaco** (*Population*: 15,000), 84 kilometres from Managua, has a nice square with good views of the surrounding countryside. **E** *Hotel Sobalvarro*, on the plaza, is good. **F** *Hotel Boaco*, at the entrance to the town, basic. Its specialities are white cheese and cream. From Boaco, unpaved roads go north to Muy Muy and Matagalpa, and south to Comoapa (*Population*: 4,000). Bus Managua-Boaco every 40 minutes from Plaza Mayoreo, two hours 10 minutes, US$1.50.

Juigalpa

Population: 30,000
139 km from Managua
Buses every 30 mins,
US$1.85, 2½ hrs
Colour map 5, grid A1

The Atlantic Highway continues through Juigalpa. A pleasant town with one of the best museums in Nicaragua, with a collection of idols resembling those at San Agustín, Colombia. Small zoo in the valley below town. The bus terminal is in the town centre near the market, up the hill. Banks on main plaza accept US$ only, no travellers' cheques.

Sleeping   D *Hotel La Quinta*, on main road at the east end of town, a/c or fan, bath, clean, friendly, restaurant has good food and a fine view of surrounding mountains. **E** *Hospedaje Rubio*, on main road going north, clean, friendly, with bath (**F** without), TV, laundry. **F** *Hospedaje Central*, basic and noisy, just about OK. *Hospedaje Angelita* next door, a bit more expensive, better; the hospedaje in *Comedor San Martín* is unfriendly; better is *Presillas* (Km 269), unnamed, beside *Comedor González*; all **F** per person.

A gravel road goes to La Libertad, a goldmining town at 600 metres (*Population*: 4,000, *hospedaje*), and on to Santo Domingo. From Juigalpa a road goes direct to the shore of Lake Nicaragua at Puerto Díaz. From here pick-ups will go to the monastery of **San Juan de las Aguas** for about US$1.20 per person if four passengers (Pedro Córtez recommended, Oswaldo Melón not so). The guide will show you the path through swamps to the monastery (two to three kilometres) which was founded in 1689. It's a little neglected, but has several wooden statues. The monks are very friendly and will let you stay the night if you ask. Take your own food and leave a donation. Ask to see the cave/tunnel complex that was used when the monks hid from besieging Indians (Vincent van Es, Enschede, Netherlands).

Twenty five kilometres south of Juigalpa an unpaved road turns off to **Acoyapa** (seven kilometres. *Population*: 5,000, *hospedaje*), El Morrito, San Miguelito and San Carlos on Lake Nicaragua (see page 1013).

The main road goes east to **Santo Tomás** (*Population*: 10,000, several *hospedajes*) and smaller villages (including La Gateada, turn-off to **Nuevo Güinea**, centre of cacao production, connected by air from Managua via San Carlos on Friday with La Costeña, T2850160), to **Cara de Mono** (*hospedaje*), on the Río Mico, and finally to **Rama** (*Population*: 35,000), 290 kilometres from Managua. The town was badly hit by Hurricane Joan in October 1988 when the river rose 16 metres above normal height. It is now poor and dirty. *Hospedaje Ramada Inn* seems to be the best; *El Viajero* is quite good; Hotels *Amy* and *Johanna* both **E**, neither has showers, *Amy* cleaner and quieter, near main jetty. Good cheap food at *Comedor Torres*. Buses Managua-Rama from Plaza El Mayoreo, express at 2230 daily, US$4.35, normal hourly 0300-1100, US$3.90, 7-9 hours,. Bus Juigalpa to Rama every hour 0430 to 1800, four and a half hours, US$1.30, terrible road even though paved (Coatlántico T2631559).

Rama to Bluefields

On the 'Bluefields Express', the ferry from Rama to Bluefields, some 200 people, assorted animals and goods crowd the deck. The journey passes through the sparsely populated eastern half of Nicaragua. The river is wide and fast flowing, passing land that is mostly cultivated, with the occasional poor farmer's dwelling. After the devastation of Hurricane Joan in 1988, some reconstruction has taken place although much of the population has not returned from the capital.

Take a bus from Plaza El Mayoreo, Managua, to Rama (see above), and then catch the ferry, US$3.50, 5 hours. The schedule appears to be express boat Tuesday, Thursday, Saturday, Sunday at 1700 from Rama, 0500 from Bluefields; ordinary boat Monday, Wednesday, Friday in the early morning from Rama, between 1100 and 1300 from Bluefields. Food and soft drinks are sold on the ferry. **Transport**

Alternative services are run by Brooks-Hamilton (Managua), T2496953, Bluefields T08222875, Tuesday, Thursday, Sunday 2400 from bus station at De La Siemens 2 cuadras al lago, Km 3 Carretera Norte, Managua (city buses 109, 112, 120, 123), boat leaves Rama 0600, return from Bluefields same day 0630, bus 0930, US$15.50 Managua-Bluefields. Also from Plaza El Mayoreo daily at 2300, arriving Rama 0500 and Bluefields 0600, returning 1530, Rama 0900, Managua 1530, US$10.45, T2801812 or 08222930. Fast boats, *pangas*, can be hired for US$12-15 Rama–Bluefields, taking 1½ hours, or hitch on a fishing boat.

Bluefields

Bluefields, the most important of Nicaragua's three Caribbean ports, gets its name from the Dutch pirate Abraham Blaauwveld. It stands on a lagoon behind the bluff at the mouth of the Bluefields River (Río Escondido), which is navigable as far as Rama (96 kilometres). In May there is a week-long local festival, Mayo-Ya!, with elements of the British Maypole tradition and local music, poetry and dancing. *Fiesta*, 30 September for San Jerónimo. Bananas, cabinet woods, frozen fish, shrimps and lobsters were the main exports until the hurricane in 1988. *Population: 35,000* *Colour map 5, grid A2*

Tragically, in October 1988, Hurricane Joan destroyed virtually all of Bluefields, but the rebirth is well underway. Information on the region can be found at the Cidca office. Local bands practise above the Ivan Dixon Cultural Centre, beside the library. There are several bars, a couple of reggae clubs, *comedores* and restaurants (two with a/c), and an Almacén Internacional. Prices are about the same as in Managua, but the atmosphere has become tense and grasping, with many 'guides' offering their services and leading visitors to buy things at inflated prices. Be prepared for frequent power and water cuts.

B *South Atlantic*, near central square, next to Enitel, run by Fanny and Hubert Chambers (native language English), with bath, safe, a/c, cable TV, fridge, clean, friendly, excellent food, *South Atlantic II*, new annex in the main street. **B** *Tía Irene*, Barrio Pointeen, T/F8222143, a/c, with bath, clean, owner Carol Biden speaks English and French and is helpful, excursions offered to surrounding areas, highly recommended. *Caribbean*, bath, a/c, near centre of town, good cook (Angela), friendly. Recommended. **C** per person *Costa Sur*, **E** *El Dorado*, may offer floor space to late arrivals. **E** *Hollywood*, has its own well and generator, friendly, restaurant, clean, will change travellers' cheques. **E** *Marda Maus*, one of the nicer places in its price range with bath and fan, dark, not too clean, no restaurant, soft drinks available, near market. **F** *Airport*, above *Costeña* office at airport, clean, friendly. **F** *Claudia*, clean, comfortable, cable TV, room on street side best. **F** *Cueto*, opposite *Hollywood,* with bath, but no running water, basic. *Café Central*, good value meals, provides accommodation, has colour TV. *Restaurant Flottante*, built over the water at the end of the main street, average prices, slow service, great view. Everywhere can be full if you arrive late, or are last off the ferry. **Sleeping & eating**

Air The airport is 3 kilometres from the city centre; either walk 30 minutes or take a taxi jeep that waits by the runway. **La Costeña** flies to Bluefields (T8222750), from Managua, US$66 return, 4 times daily (3 on Monday Managua-Bluefields, 3 on Sunday Bluefields-Managua). On Monday, Wednesday and Friday, La Costeña flies to Bluefields via Puerto Cabezas. Daily flights to/from Corn Islands (see below). Managua office of the airline is in the domestic terminal at the airport (T2631228). Bring passport, it is sometimes asked for in the departure lounge. There is a customs check on return to Managua. **NB** Flights rarely leave on time, and sometimes leave early. **Transport**

Sea El Bluff is a small island with a village harbour, some oil tanks and a small, dirty beach. It is accessible by *panga* (speedboat) from the wharf at the market. When the *panga* is full, pay your

Nicaragua

fare, no more than US$1.70. Watch out for Richard Hooker who works on the *pangas*, he allegedly makes up stories about needing money for medicines, and overcharges for boat fares. **Hotel**: **E** *El Bluff*, with bath, cheaper without, fan, limited water, friendly, restaurant, pleasant.

From the main wharf small boats leave irregularly for villages on the coast and Laguna de Perlas, such as Tasbapounie (*hospedaje* run by Mr Leonard Richard Brent); food may be scarce in all settlements. A boat leaves daily 0800-0900 to **Laguna de Perlas** (Pearl Lagoon), 80 kilometres north of Bluefields 3-6 hours, US$4.35. The lagoon itself is some 50 kilometres long with mostly Creole villages round its shores, eg Pearl Lagoon, Haulover, Brown Bank, La Fe, Orinoco, Marshall Point and San Vicente. Raitipura and Kakabila are Indian villages. In Raitipura there is a Danish housing project (run by Mogens Vibe). He takes on volunteers (minimum 1 week), recommended. At the village of Pearl Lagoon there is a hostel, *Miss Ingrid's*, very friendly, stay with the entertaining family. Larger vessels may be available for transport to Puerto Cabezas, but there is no transport south of Bluefields.

On outlying areas of the Región Autonomista Atlántico Sur, Cindy Gersony of Sarasota, Florida, writes: **Río Kurinwás** area: it might occasionally be possible to get a boat to the town of **Tortuguero** (also called Nuevo Amanecer) some distance up the the Kurinwás River. The Kurinwás is a fascinating, largely uninhabited jungle area, where it is possible to see monkeys and much other wildlife. Tortuguero (about a six-hour speedboat ride from Bluefields, several days by regular boat) is a *mestizo* town of about 1,000. It will really give you a taste of the frontier.

Río Grande area: The Río Grande is the next river north of the Kurinwás, connected to the Pearl Lagoon by the Top-Lock Canal. At its mouth are five interesting villages: the four Miskito communities of Kara, Karawala, Sandy Bay Sirpi, and Walpa, and the Creole village of La Barra. **Sandy Bay Sirpi** is situated on both the river and the Caribbean, and has a nice beach. Travelling upriver, the Río Grande is a noticeable contrast to the Río Kurinwás; it is much more settled, dotted with farms and cattle grazing. Quite a bit upriver (also about a six-hour speedboat ride from Bluefields, several days by regular boat), the traveller will come to the *mestizo* town of **La Cruz de Río Grande** (*Population*: about 1,700). It was founded about 1922 by Chinese traders to serve workers from a banana plantation (now defunct) further upriver. La Cruz has a very pretty church, and there are resident expatriate (US) priests of the Capuchin order in the town. The adventurous can walk between La Cruz and Tortuguero: each way takes about 10 hours in the dry season, 12 in the rainy. **NB** There was partial damage from Hurricane Mitch on the Río Grande, eg at Karawala and La Cruz de Río Grande.

Corn Islands

Colour map 5, grid A2   The Corn Islands, in the Caribbean opposite Bluefields, are two small beautiful islands fringed with white coral and slender coconut trees, though sadly many on the larger island were blown down by the 1988 hurricane. The smaller island, **Little Corn**, escaped serious damage; it can be visited by boat from the larger island, **Big Corn**, jaunty one hour ride by *panga*. The larger is a popular Nicaraguan holiday resort; its surfing and bathing facilities make it ideal for tourists (best months March and April). The nicest beaches are Long Bay and Brik Bay. The islands are also for relaxation (take lots of books and suntan lotion). Everything is naturally more expensive than on the mainland. If you climb the mountain, wear long trousers, as there are many ticks. The language of the islands is English. The islanders are very friendly but petty thievery has been reported, even clothes stolen off a washing line. The local coconut oil industry has been devastated by Hurricane Joan, but lobsters provide much prosperity. On Little Corn Island there is no electricity, no phones, just pristine white sand beaches and some of the Caribbean's finest undisturbed coral reefs. An Italian resort is planned, so visit now.

Sleeping   **B** *El Paraíso Club Cabinas*, Briggs Bay, T2855111, with bath, porch with hammock, clean, bar, restaurant, horses, bicycles and snorkelling gear for rent, noisy part of the island but popular, recommended. **C** *Bayside Hotel*, some rooms with a/c, oceanfront on the best snorkelling reef on the island, service slow, suffered hurricane damage in 1996, a bit run down. **C** *Panorama*, close to beach, clean, simple, private bath. **D** *Hospedaje Miramar* is recommended, serves meals. **D** *Hospedaje Playa Coco*, also serves meals. **E** *Brisas del Mar*, Playa Coco, basic, loud disco in same building, good breakfast, restaurant. **E** *Casa Blanca* (actually blue), at Playa Coco, Miss Florence's house, running water, noisy. The chief problem in all the hotels is rats, which may not be dangerous, but neither are they pleasant. Electric power 1400-2400 only, failures are not uncommon.

On **Little Corn Island A3** *Casa Iguana*, on a 3 ha bluff overlooking the sea, US owned, friendly, helpful, 2 cabins with bath, sleeps 2-3, simple, can be booked through *Tours Nicaragua* in Managua.

Sevva's Place, 500 metres past *Bayside Hotel*, T2855058, seafood, chicken, fine location, good food, mid-priced, highly recommended. *Fisherman's Cave*, next to dock, popular, mid-priced, average food. *Comedor Lissie*, good hearty meal US$2. *Comedor Blackstone*. *Mini Café*. Ice cream parlour. Several bars and reggae clubs. *Dugout de la Tonia* has the cheapest beer and good *punta* music. Ask around for where meals are available; the restaurants serve mainly chicken and chop suey, but in private houses you can find much better fare. Try fresh coconut bread (from family stores, a must), banana porridge and sorrel drink (red, and ginger-flavoured). There is occasionally a shortage of bottled water. Main market area is near Will Bowers Wharf and is a cheap place to eat. Dollars are widely used. Since the price of everything is generally high and there is no bank, take the cash you need with you.

Eating

Swimming: the best beach for swimming is Long Beach on Long Bay; walk across the island from Playa Coco. For **fishing** (barracuda, etc), contact Ernie Jenkie (about US$5 per hour). It is possible to **dive** off the Corn Islands although the equipment "looks like leftovers from the Second World War". The reef is good, however, and dives are very cheap.

Sports

Air La Costeña flies from Managua and Bluefields to the Corn Islands, daily at 0630 and 1400 from Managua, 0700 and 1535 from Corn Islands (0845 and 1535 on Sunday), US$85 return. The same advice on passport and customs applies as under Bluefields. Air services are suspended from time to time because of the poor state of the runway on Big Corn. Book well in advance and book return immediately on arrival.

Transport

Sea Passenger-carrying cargo boats leave Bluefields for the Corn Islands from the docks of Copesnica, north of town, around a small bay and past the ruined church: Wednesday, Friday, Sunday 0700-1000, return Thursday, Sunday, Tuesday, US$4.35 one way. The water around Bluefields is dirty, muddy brown, soon becoming a clear, sparkling blue. There is usually a boat from Bluefields (the *Lynx Express*), via El Bluff, on Wednesday at 0830, 4 hours, but there is no guarantee. Boats back to Bluefields leave from Will Bowers Wharf; tickets available in advance from nearby office. You may be able to find a lobster, or other fishing boat that will take you but make sure the boat is properly equipped and seaworthy. Check with the Capitanía in Bluefields, or in El Bluff and with anyone else you can find who has information. Trips take 5-8 hours. A boat leaves most days from the dock in Briggs Bay for Little Corn Island, ask around on arrival as schedules change. To hire a boat, go to the dock and ask around, normal charge US$40 one way, US$80 for the *panga* for a full day.

Banks The only bank on the island is *Caley Dagnall*, between the airstrip and the dock.

Directory

Puerto Cabezas

Puerto Cabezas is the capital of the RAAN, the northern Atlantic Coast autonomous region, and it has a distinctly different atmosphere from Bluefields; it is principally a large Miskito village. Puerto Cabezas can offer an excellent introduction to the Miskito

Population: about 30,000
Colour map 4, grid C6

part of the country. You can arrange to stay in small Miskito villages, for example near Haulover, a few hours by boat south of Puerto Cabezas. There are significant minorities of *mestizos* (referred to on the Coast as *españoles* or the Spanish) and Creoles, many of whom came to 'Port' by way of Las Minas (see below). Spanish is a second language for most residents, although most speak it well (at least those who live in Puerto itself); many speak at least some English, and for some, it is their native language. The local name for Puerto Cabezas is Bilwi, although the name is of Sumo origin. The Miskitos conquered the Sumos to obtain the town sometime in the last century.

There are two main roads, the only paved streets, which run parallel to each other and to the sea. At the southern end of the town (the airport is at the northern end) is the port area; a walk along the pier at sunset is highly recommended. The main market occupies the central part of town. Travellers' cheques can be changed by Augusto Chow, ask for 'El Chino'.

Beaches There is a beach in the town limits, but it is reputed to be dirty. A clean, and lovely, beach, Poza Verde, can be found several kilometres north of town: it has white sand, calm water and sandflies. Take the road out of town for about 15 minutes and turn right on the track marked *SW Tuapi* (*SW* stands for *switch*); follow it for a few kilometers to the sea. You can also walk six kilometres along the beach from Puerto Cabezas, or take a taxi (US$30 for three hours, with bargaining, the track is very bad).

Sleeping **Hospedaje E** *Cayos Miskitos*, 2 blocks east of the plaza, good, comfortable rooms with bath, clean, friendly, breakfast by arrangement in advance only. **E** *El Viajante*, also clean, central, very friendly, basic wooden rooms with fan, singles only, shared baths, *comedor* serves good breakfast to its guests. **E** *Ricardo Pérez*, friendly, clean, all room have windows, meals available.

Eating The 3 best restaurants are the *Atlántico*, *Jumbo*, which serves Chinese food and is close to the sea, and *Pizzería Mercedita*, near the harbour, very good, expensive. Recommended. Wide liquor selection, good service. *El Zaire*, popular, with TV, food and service disappointing. There are also numerous *comedores*. Prices are much higher than elsewhere in Nicaragua because almost everything has to be brought in by air.

Transport **Air** The airstrip is 3 kilometres from the town. From the airport, it is possible to get a taxi that will charge US$1 to any point in Puerto (it is also possible to walk). La Costeña (T2631281) flies daily from Managua in small (20 seats) planes. On Monday, Wednesday, Friday, La Costeña flies from Managua via Siuna, Bonanza, Rosita and Bluefields. Cancellations are not infrequent, best to make reservation and pay just before plane leaves. Bring your passport: there are 'immigration' checks by the police in Puerto, and sometimes in the waiting lounge in Managua; also, there is a customs check when returning from the Coast by air to Managua.

Road It is not possible to rent a vehicle or bicycle in Puerto, but arrangements for a car and driver can be made with a taxi driver or others (ask a taxi or at your *hospedaje*). Public bus service is available between Puerto and Waspám (see below) and from Matagalpa (14 hours). Furthermore, Puerto is connected by road to Managua; however, this 559-kilometre trip should only be attempted in the dry season (early January to mid-May) in a four-wheel drive vehicle. With luck, it will take only 2-3 days (the road, almost all of it unpaved, is not bad from Managua to Siuna, but becomes very difficult after that); do not drive at night. **NB** If you drive back from Puerto to Managua, take the road out of town and turn left at the sign, *SW Wawa*. Check on the road conditions after Hurricane Mitch in the highlands around Matagalpa on this route.

Directory **Hospitals & medical services** Hospital: located on the outskirts of Puerto, on the road leading out of town.

Waspám and the Coco River

The Coco River (called the *Wanghi* in Miskito) is the heart of Miskito country. Waspám is often referred to as 'the capital of the Río Coco'. There is a road from Puerto to Waspám; during the dry season, the 130-kilometre trip should take about three hours by four-wheel drive vehicle, several hours longer by public bus (leaves Puerto 0700, Monday-Saturday, with luck returns from Waspám 1200). The bus can be boarded at several points in Puerto along the road leading out of town, cost is US$5 to go to Waspám. This trip will take you through the pine forests, red earth, and plains north of Puerto towards the Coco River (the border with Honduras), and you will pass through two Miskito villages, Sisin and Santa Marta. Hitching rides is possible, if you cannot get all the way to Waspám, make sure you are left at Sisin, Santa Marta or La Tranquera. Give rides to, or take lifts from the military. Never travel at night.

Spanish spelling Waspán
Population: about 2,500

NB This area of Nicaragua was the worst hit by Hurricane Mitch. Many Miskito communities along the Coco River vanished. Make thorough enquiries in advance before travelling to this region.

Las Minas

This area comprises the gold mining towns of Siuna, La Rosita and Bonanza, and is part of the RAAN (Northern Atlantic Coast Autonomous Region), but is significantly inland from the Coast. Las Minas is a somewhat depressed region since the demise of the mines (Bonanza has the only working mine of the three towns, although Siuna's still employs some people), but the atmosphere is very much frontierish. A Canadian company has bought the mines in Siuna and Bonanza.

Colour map 4, grid C5/6

Siuna is the largest town, and all three are predominatly *mestizo*, with a Creole minority; the surrounding rural areas have a significant Sumo population as well as some Miskitos.

Siuna
Colour map 4, grid C5

Sleeping & eating **E** *Chino*, the best and most expensive. **F** *Troysa*, clean. **F** *Costeño*, 100 metres east of airstrip, basic. In Barrio La Luz there is a hotel above a billiard hall. A recommended place to eat is either of the 2 *comedores* called **Desnuque**, 1 in the market, and the other on a hill near the baseball stadium and airstrip, the latter has good pizza as well as typical Nicaraguan food. **Comedor Siuna**, opposite *Hotel Costeño*, has good *comida corriente*. In **Rosita**, a recommended place to eat is **Comedor Jassy**, near the entrance of town on the Siuna side; there is an **hospedaje**, **E**, no name, near the market (noisy, but basically clean).

Transport **Air** La Costeña flies from the capital to Siuna direct daily, also Monday, Wednesday, Friday, on the flight to Bluefields via Siuna, Rosita, Bonanza and Puerto Cabezas, reservations in Siuna, T2632142/2143.

There are 2 road links from Managua, one through Matagalpa and Waslala (which may still be suffering from Mitch damage), the other through Boaco, Muy Muy, Matiguás and Río Blanco; the 330-kilometre drive is very scenic (and takes about 7 hours by four-wheel drive vehicle in the dry season); however, check on the security situation before starting out. There is a bank in Siuna. There are also bus links. **La Rosita** is 70 kilometres east of Siuna, and it is also possible to drive on through to Puerto Cabezas, although the road is in very poor shape.

Routes
Do not drive after dark

Parque Nacional Saslaya

Created in 1971, Saslaya was the first national park in Nicaragua, located within the Bosawás Biosphere Reserve which contains the largest tropical cloud forest in Central America. Development is now underway to encourage local communities to get involved in ecotourism as an incentive to preserve the area's rich natural and cultural

Colour map 4, grid C5

heritage. One of these projects is the Proyecto Ecoturístico Rosa Grande, supported by Nature Conservancy and the Peace Corps. The community of **Rosa Grande**, 25 kilometres from Siuna, is near an area of virgin forest with trails, waterfalls on the river Labú and lots of wildlife including monkeys and large cats. One path leads to a lookout with a view over the Cerro Saslaya; another, circular path to the northwest goes to the Rancho Alegre falls. Guides can be hired for US$5.50 a day. Excursions for two or more days cost only US$13 per person for guide, food and camping equipment.

Sleeping & eating G *BOSAWAS field station*, on the river Labú, has hammocks, clean but simple, locally produced and cooked food about US$1.25. In Rosa Grande a meal at *Comedor Melania* costs about US$1.

Information Contact Don Trinidad at the *comedor* on arrival in Santa Rosa. In Siuna you can contact the office of the Proyecto Bosawás, 200 metres east of the airstrip. ■ *Monday-Friday, 0800-1700*. Groups of 5 or more must reserve in advance, contact the Amigos de Saslaya, c/o Proyecto Bosawás, Siuna, RAAN, by post or telegram. Large groups are not encouraged.

Transport **Bus** Daily from Siuna market at 0500 and 0730, sometimes another at 1100, US$2.25.

Background

The land

There are three well-marked regions: (1) A large triangular-shaped central mountain land whose apex rests almost on the southern border with Costa Rica; the prevailing moisture-laden northeast winds drench its eastern slopes, which are deeply forested with oak and pine on the drier, cooler heights. (2) A wide belt of eastern lowland through which a number of rivers flow from the mountains into the Atlantic. (3) The belt of lowland which runs from the Gulf of Fonseca, on the Pacific, to the Costa Rican border south of Lake Nicaragua. Out of it, to the east, rise the lava cliffs of the mountains to a height of 1,500-2,100 metres. Peninsulas of high land jut out here and there into the lowland, which is generally from 65 to 80 kilometres wide along the Pacific, but is at its narrowest, 20 kilometres, between La Virgen on Lake Nicaragua and San Juan del Sur.

Lakes

In the plain are the two largest sheets of water in Central America and 10 crater lakes. The capital, Managua, is on the shores of Lake Managua (Xolotlán), 52 kilometres long, 15 to 25 wide, and 39 metres above sea-level. Its maximum depth is only 30 metres. The Río Tipitapa drains it into Lake Nicaragua, 148 kilometres long, about 55 kilometres at its widest, and 32 metres above the sea; Granada is on its shores. The 190-kilometre Río San Juan drains both lakes into the Caribbean and is one of 96 principle rivers in the country. The longest is the Río Coco, on the border with Honduras, at 680 kilometres.

Volcanoes

Lying at the intersection of three continental plates, Nicaragua has a very unstable, changing landscape. Through the Pacific basin runs a row of 28 major volcanoes, six which have been active within the 20th century. The northernmost is Cosigüina, overlooking the Gulf of Fonseca, at 800 metres with a lake in its crater. Its final eruption was in 1835. Northeast of Chinandega begins the Maribios volcanic chain, with Chonco (1,105 metres) and the country's highest, the cone of San Cristóbal (1,745 metres), which recommenced erupting in 1971 after a long period of inactivity. This volcano's lava discharge was used as a lighthouse by Pacific pirates in a very destructive raid on the colonial capital of León in 1685. Just south rises Volcán Casita which is notable for its pine forest, the southernmost of its kind in the American continent's northern hemisphere. A side of Casita collapsed during the torrential rains of Hurricane Mitch (1998), burying numerous villages in Posoltega and killing many hundreds of people. Further south, just before León, is the very active Telica (1,061 metres) with eruptions occurring every five years, and the extinct cones of little Santa Clara and Orata (836 metres), which is believed to be the oldest in the chain. Just south of León is one of the youngest volcanoes on the planet, Cerro Negro, which was born in 1850 and has risen from sea level to 450 metres in this short period. Its most recent eruptions occurred in 1992 and 1995 and it frequently coats León in a thick black soup. Volcán Pilas is formed of various craters, the highest of which rises 1,001 metres and contains one active crater known as El Hoyo which last erupted in 1954. Other extinct cones lie between Pilas and the majestic Momotombo (1,300 metres), which overlooks the shores of Lake Managua and last erupted in 1905, though a geothermal plant utilizes its energy daily. The chain ends with little Momotombito, which forms an island in Lake Managua. Managua's volcanoes are all extinct and six contain crater lakes. The Dirianes volcanic chain begins just north of Masaya with the complex of the same name, including the smoking, lava-filled Santiago crater and four extinct craters and a lagoon. Masaya is the only volcano on the American continent with a consistent lava pool. The last eruptions occurred in 1965 and 1979 and after a nine year period of calm began to smoke heavily again in 1995 with an eruption expected soon. South between Masaya and Granada is the extinct Apoyo, which died very violently 2,000 years ago, leaving the deep blue Laguna de Apoyo, six kilometres in diameter. Along the shores of Lake Nicaragua and shadowing Granada is Volcán Mombacho (1,345 metres), wrapped in cloud forest. This father of Las

Isletas had a major structural collapse in 1570, wiping out an indigenous village at its base. The volcanoes of Lake Managua include the Isla de Zapatera (600 metres), a national park and precolumbian site, and the final two in the Nicaraguan chain, which make up the stunning Isla de Ometepe: the symmetrical and active cone of Concepción (1,610 metres), which last erupted in 1956, and the cloud forest covered Maderas (1,394 metres), which holds a lake in its summit.

Climate The wet, warm winds off the Caribbean pour heavy rain on the Atlantic coastal zone, especially in the southern basin of the Río San Juan, with more than six metres annually. While the dry season on the Atlantic coast is only short and not wholly dry, the Pacific dry season, or summer (November to April), becomes very dusty, especially when the winds begin to blow in February. There is a wide range of climates. According to altitude, average annual temperatures vary between 15° and 35°C. Midday temperatures at Managua range from 30° to 36°C, but readings of 38° are not uncommon from March to May, or of 40° in January and February in the west. It can get quite cold, especially after rain, in the Caribbean lowlands. Maximum daily humidity ranges from 90 to 100 percent.

History

Nicaragua was at the crossroads between northern and southern prehispanic cultures and there is evidence of human habitation dating back 30,000 years. In Managua, near the crater lake of Acahualinca, are some well-preserved human and animal footprints of what appears to be a mass flight from a volcanic eruption 6,000 years ago. The best understood cultures are the Chorotegas, who came from Mexico around 800 AD, and the Nicaraos from the same region, who partially displaced the Chorotegas in the Pacific basin around 1200 AD. The Nicaraos set up a very successful society which traded with people from Mexico to Peru. The more primitive Chorotegas (Nahua speakers) remained in the areas not occupied by the Nicarao (Nahuat speakers), though some were pushed down into Guanacaste and the complete relationship between the two has yet to be fully explained. The most interesting precolumbian remains are the many petroglyphs left by unnamed pre-Chorotega cultures, and the Chorotegas' own large basalt figures found in and around Lake Nicaragua, in particular on the islands of Zapatera and Ometepe. Nicaragua is rich in ceramic history, with 3,000 years of continuous occupation being found in some areas. The Ramas and Sumos, of South American lowland origin, populated the eastern seaboard regions, but are almost extinct today. Other precolumbian cultures of note were the mountain Matagalpa people, thought to be related to the Lenca, the strangely primitive, understudied Chontales who inhabited the eastern side of the two lakes and, in the area that is now León, the Subtiava people who are perhaps from Baja California in Mexico.

Christopher Columbus arrived on the Caribbean shores of Nicaragua in 1502 on his fourth and final voyage. The Spanish explorer Gil González Dávila arrived in 1522 overland from Panama and, searching for the wealthiest chief of all, arrived on the western shores of Lake Nicaragua to meet the famous Nicarao chief, Nicaragua. The 16th-century Spanish chroniclers described the Nicarao's land as the most fertile and productive they had ever seen in the Americas. The chief Nicaragua and Dávila engaged in long philosophical conversations conducted through a translator and eventually the great chief agreed to accept Christianity. After the conversion to Christianity of more than 19,000 people, Dávila was chased out of Nicaragua by the fierce Chorotega chieftain, Diriangen, whose troops decimated Dávila's small force. In 1524 a stronger army was sent and the populace was overcome by Francisco Hernández de Córdoba. Granada and León were founded on the shores of Lake Nicaragua and Lake Managua respectively. In 1570 both colonies were put under the jurisdiction of Guatemala.

The local administrative centre was not rich Granada, with its profitable crops of sugar, cocoa, and indigo, but impoverished León, then barely able to subsist on its crops of maize, beans and rice. This reversal of the Spanish policy of choosing the most successful settlement as capital was due to the ease with which León could be reached from the Pacific. In 1858 Managua was chosen as a new capital as a compromise, following violent rivalry between Granada and León.

For more on Nicaragua's early history, see the introductory chapter to Central America. The country became an independent state in 1838.

The famous (or infamous) filibustering expedition of William Walker is often referred to in the text. William Walker (1824-60) was born in Nashville, Tennessee, graduated at the University in 1838, studied medicine at Edinburgh and Heidelberg, was granted his MD in 1843, and then studied law and was called to the bar. On 5 October 1853, he sailed with a filibustering force to conquer Mexican territory, declared Lower California and Sonora an independent republic and was then driven out. In May 1855, with 56 followers armed with a new type of rifle, he sailed for Nicaragua, where Liberal Party leaders had invited him to help them in their struggle against the Conservatives. In October he seized a steamer on Lake Nicaragua belonging to the Accessory Transit Company, an American corporation controlled by Cornelius Vanderbilt. He was then able to surprise and capture Granada and make himself master of Nicaragua as Commander of the Forces. Two officials decided to use him to get control of the Transit Company; it was seized and handed over to his friends. A new government was formed and in June 1856 Walker was elected President. On 22 September, to gain support from the southern states in America he suspended the Nicaraguan laws against slavery. His Government was formally recognized by the USA that year. A coalition of Central American states, backed by Cornelius Vanderbilt, fought against him, but he was able to hold his own until May 1857, when he surrendered to the US Navy to avoid capture. In November 1857, he sailed from Mobile with another expedition, but soon after landing near Greytown, Nicaragua, he was arrested and returned to the USA. In 1860 he sailed again from Mobile and landed in Honduras. There he was taken prisoner by Captain Salmon, of the British Navy, and handed over to the Honduran authorities, who tried and executed him on 12 September 1860. Walker's own book, *The War in Nicaragua*, is a fascinating document.

Walker's expedition

In 1909, US Marines assisted Nicaraguan Conservative leaders in an uprising to overthrow the Liberal president, José Santos Zelaya. In 1911 the USA pledged help in securing a loan to be guaranteed through the control of Nicaraguan customs by an American board. In 1912 the United States sent marines into Nicaragua to enforce the control. Apart from short intervals, they stayed there until 1933. During the last five years of occupation, nationalists under General Augusto César Sandino waged a relentless guerrilla war against the US Marines. American forces were finally withdrawn in 1933, when President Franklin Roosevelt announced the 'Good Neighbour' policy, pledging non-intervention. An American-trained force, the Nicaraguan National Guard, was left behind, commanded by Anastasio Somoza García. Somoza's men assassinated General Sandino in February 1934 and Somoza himself took over the presidency in 1936. From 1932, with brief intervals, Nicaraguan affairs were dominated by General Anastasio Somoza until he was assassinated in 1956. His two sons both served a presidential term and the younger, General Anastasio Somoza Debayle, dominated the country from 1963 until his deposition in 1979; he was later assassinated in Paraguay.

US involvement

The 1978-79 revolution against the Somoza Government by the Sandinista guerrilla organization (loosely allied to a broad opposition movement) resulted in extensive damage and many casualties (estimated at over 30,000) in certain parts of the country, especially in Managua, Estelí, León, Masaya, Chinandega and Corinto. After heavy fighting General Somoza resigned on 17 July 1979, and the Government was taken over by a Junta representing the Sandinista guerrillas and their civilian allies. Real power was exercised by nine Sandinista *comandantes* whose chief short-term aim was reconstruction. A 47-member Council of State formally came into being in May 1980; supporters of the Frente Sandinista de Liberación Nacional had a majority. Elections were held on 4 November 1984 for an augmented National Constituent Assembly with 96 seats; the Sandinista Liberation Front won 61 seats, and Daniel Ortega Saavedra, who had headed the Junta, was elected president. The Democratic Conservatives won 14 seats, the

1978-79 revolution

Independent Liberals nine seats and the Popular Social Christians six (the Socialists, Communists and Marxists/Leninists won two seats each). The failure of the Sandinista Government to meet the demands of a right-wing group, the Democratic Co-ordinating Board (CDN), led to this coalition boycotting the elections and to the US administration condemning the poll as a 'sham'.

The Sandinistas Despite substantial official and private US support, anti-Sandinista guerrillas (the 'contras') could boast no significant success in their war against the Government. In 1988, the Sandinistas and the contras met for the first time to discuss the implementation of the Central American Peace Plan drawn up by President Oscar Arias Sánchez of Costa Rica, and signed in August 1987. To comply with the Plan, the Nicaraguan Government made a number of political concessions. By 1989 the contras, lacking funds and with diminished numbers, following a stream of desertions, appeared to be a spent force; some participated in general elections held on 25 February 1990. The Sandinista Government brought major improvements in health and education, but the demands of the war against the contras and a complete US trade embargo did great damage to the economy as a whole. The electorate's desire for a higher standard of living was reflected in the outcome of the elections, when the US-supported candidate of the free market National Opposition Union (UNO), Sra Violeta Chamorro, won 55.2 percent of the vote, compared with 40.8 percent for President Ortega. The 14-party alliance, UNO, won 52 seats in the National Assembly, the FSLN 38 and the Social Christian Party one seat. Sra Chamorro, widow of the proprietor of *La Prensa*, who was murdered by General Somoza's forces in 1978, took office on 25 April 1990. The USA was under considerable pressure to provide substantial aid for the alliance it created and promoted, but of the US$300m promised for 1990 by the US Congress, only half had been distributed by May 1991. President Chamorro's refusal to dismiss the Sandinista, General Humberto Ortega, from his post as head of the armed forces (EPS), and to drop the Nicaraguan case against the USA at the International Court of Justice, were said to be hindrances to more rapid disbursement. (The Court in The Hague found the USA guilty in 1986 of crimes against Nicaragua in mining its harbours.)

The lack of foreign financial assistance prevented any quick rebuilding of the economy. The Government's scant resources did not permit it to give the disarmed contra forces the land and services that had been promised to them. Demilitarized Sandinistas and landless peasants also pressed for land in 1991, with a consequent rise in tension. Factions of the two groups rearmed, to be known as recontras and recompas; there were many bloody conflicts. Divisions within the UNO coalition, particularly between supporters of President Chamorro and those of vice-president Virgilio Godoy, added to the country's difficulties. Austerity measures introduced in early 1991, including a devaluation of the new córdoba oro, strained the relationship between the administration, Sandinista politicians and the National Workers' Front (FNT), the so-called 'concertación', a pact which the private sector refused to sign. Pacts signed in January 1992 between Government, recontras and recompas failed to stop occasional heavy fighting over the next two years. In 1994, however, a series of bilateral meetings between previously entrenched parties and ceasefires announced by the EPS and the main recontra group, FN 3-80 (Northern Front 3-80) contributed to a disarmament accord proposed by archbishop Miguel Obando y Bravo between the Government and FN 3-80.

The achievement of a more peaceful state of affairs, if not reconciliation, did not remove other political tensions. After the UNO coalition realigned itself into new political groupings and returned to the National Assembly following a boycott in 1993, the FSLN began to fall apart in 1994. By early 1995, the Sandinistas had become irrevocably split between the orthodox wing, led by Daniel Ortega, and the Sandinista Renewal Movement (MRS), led by Sergio Ramírez. The MRS accused the orthodox wing of betraying Sandinista principles by forming pacts with the technocrats and neoliberals of the Government. The MRS was itself accused of opportunism. Linked to this was considerable manoeuvring over UNO-inspired constitutional reform. The National Assembly approved 67 amendments of the constitution, among which were the strengthening of the legislative branch of government at the expense of the executive, and the prohibition of relatives of the president from seeking that office. President Chamorro denied the validity of the reforms, but the National Assembly unilaterally adopted them in February 1995.

In 1995 the National Assembly approved legislation governing the 20 October 1996 presidential elections. The frontrunner was Arnoldo Alemán, former mayor of Managua, of the Liberal alliance. His main opponent was Daniel Ortega of the FSLN, who regarded Alemán's policies as a return to Somoza-style government. After reviewing the vote count because of allegations of fraud, the Supreme Electoral Council (CSE) announced on 8 November that Arnoldo Alemán had won 51 percent of the vote compared with 37.7 percent for Daniel Ortega and the rest divided among the other 21 candidates. The FSLN appealed and called for new elections in Managua and Matagalpa but this was rejected. The OAS declared the elections fair but flawed. Ortega announced he would respect the legality but not the legitimacy of the Government of Alemán, whose position was weakened by his Liberal Alliance failing to win an outright majority in the National Assembly.

The 1996 elections

The Sandinistas have maintained pressure on the Alemán government, with strikes, protests and intermittent negotiations. A deal was reached in 1997 on compensation for properties expropriated under the Sandinista government, involving 1,293 claims by foreigners. The agreement avoided a suspension of US aid and the USA gave Nicaragua a year to sort out property rights involving US citizens.

Political machinations continue to create uncertainty, not just between parties, but within parties themselves. The Sandinistas' divisions were sharpened in 1998 by accusations against Daniel Ortega by his stepdaughter, Zoilamérica Narváez Murillo, that he had sexually abused her in her youth. Narváez and a colleague, Henry Petrie, belonged to a dissident faction of the FSLN which was expelled from the party at the time of the accusations. Both Ortega's wife and Narváez' brother said the charges were false. The inability to make economic advances also remains a major problem and international and domestic observers point out that over 70 percent of Nicaraguan families live below the poverty line. In 1998 two meteorological events caused even greater hardship for parts of the country: the drought (and related fires) from the El Niño phenomenon and, much more costly in terms of lives lost and property destroyed, the floods and storm damage from Hurricane Mitch.

Political & economic uncertainty

Culture

Population density is low: 38.1 persons to the square kilometre, compared with El Salvador's 269. Nine in 10 of the people of Nicaragua live and work in the lowland between the Pacific and the western shores of Lake Nicaragua, the southwestern shore of Lake Managua, and the southwestern sides of the row of volcanoes. It is only in later years that settlers have taken to coffee-growing and cattle-rearing in the highlands at Matagalpa and Jinotega. Elsewhere, the highlands, save for an occasional mining camp, are very thinly settled.

People

The densely forested eastern lowlands fronting the Caribbean were neglected, because of the heavy rainfall and their consequent unhealthiness, until the British settled several colonies of Jamaicans in the 18th century at Bluefields and San Juan del Norte (Greytown). But early this century the United Fruit Company of America (now United Brands) opened banana plantations inland from Puerto Cabezas, worked by blacks from Jamaica. Other companies followed suit along the coast, but the bananas were later attacked by Panama disease and exports today are small. Along the Mosquito coast there are still English-speaking communities of African, or mixed African and indigenous, descent. Besides the *mestizo* intermixtures of Spanish and Indian (69 percent), there are pure blacks (nine percent), pure Indians (five percent) and mixtures of the two (mostly along the Atlantic coast). A small proportion is of unmixed Spanish and European descent. For a brief survey of the people of eastern Nicaragua, see the introductory paragraphs of **The Caribbean Coast**.

Religion & Roman Catholicism is the prevailing religion, but there are Episcopal, Baptist, Methodist
education and other Protestant churches. Illiteracy was reduced by a determined campaign of the
Sandinista government in the 1980s. Higher education at the Universidad Nacional
Autónoma de Nicaragua at León, with three faculties at Managua, and the private Jesuit
Universidad Centroamericana (UCA) at Managua is good. There are two, separate
Universidades Nacionales Autónomas de Nicaragua (UNAN).

The economy

Structure of The World Bank classes Nicaragua among the world's poorest countries and its per capita
production income is the lowest in Latin America. The economy is based on agriculture, which
contributes almost 35 percent of gdp. The principal export items are coffee, sugar, beef,
seafood and bananas. The Government has encouraged a diversification of exports, and
exports of tobacco and other agricultural products have gained in importance. After being
hampered in the early 1990s by violence and lack of credit, the agricultural sector has failed
to recover because of adverse weather conditions, low prices and mounting debts owed
by farmers to state development banks. In 1997 a rural debt relief programme was
announced, whereby farmers could either pay off their debts immediately and escape
interest and penalty charges, or have the debt cut by half and repay it over 10 years with
interest. First El Niño, then Hurricane Mitch inflicted further blows to agriculture in 1998,
the coffee crop being particularly hard hit by the October storm.

Main industries are food processing (sugar, meat, shrimps), textiles, wood, chemical and
mineral products. Mineral resources are scarce but there are gold deposits producing
about 42,000 troy ounces a year. Copper and silver are also mined.

Recent trends Since the late 1970s gdp has fallen, starting with a decline of 29 percent in 1979. In
1981-90 it fell by an annual average of 2.4 percent, with only one year of positive growth. In
the same period per capita income fell by an average of 5.6 percent a year. The collapse
was caused by guerrilla insurgency, the US trade embargo, fluctuations in Central American
Common Market trade, floods, drought and changing commodity prices. Growth has
usually been led by agriculture when weather, international prices and political conditions
have been favourable.

Inflation has been a problem since the 1972 earthquake; it rose to 84 percent in 1979 as
a result of the civil war, moderating to an average of 30 percent in 1980-84. As an effect of
insurgency requiring heavy budget spending on defence and other difficulties, the rate
climbed rapidly to an estimated 24,000 percent in 1988, while the public sector deficit rose
to 27 percent of gnp. In 1988 a new currency was introduced as part of an anti-inflation
package which realigned prices of the dollar and basic goods, but neither this nor
subsequent economic packages succeeded in eliminating inflation over the next decade.

Nicaragua has long been dependent upon foreign aid. It averaged US$600m a year in
1980-89, of which the USSR is believed to have granted nearly half. The EEC and Canada
were the other major donors. Nicaragua's foreign debt, including arrears, amounted to
some US$12bn (1990), but reduced foreign exchange earnings since the mid-1980s (partly
because of the US blockade) made it impossible for the Government to service any debt
other than that owed to multilateral institutions and the Paris Club debtor countries. In
March 1995 Nicaragua asked the Paris Club to write off US$1.2bn of debt prior to seeking
major restructuring terms on commercial bank and other debts. The aim was to reduce its
debts to under US$3bn and its debt service to US$120m a year. In 1996 Russia agreed to
write off 90 percent of Nicaragua's bilateral debt of US$3.4bn and to restructure the
remainder over 15 years. Germany also agreed to forgo 80 percent of bilateral debt, while
also granting DM250m in aid for infrastructure and signing an investment protection
agreement. By end-1996 debt forgone programmes had cut the total government debt to
US$3.8bn.

In 1990 the US-supported Government of Pres Violeta Chamorro took office amid great
optimism that the economy could be revived on the back of renewed trade with the USA.
Trade sanctions were lifted and the US Congress was asked to provide US$300m in aid

immediately, to be followed by a further US$200m. Other countries were also asked for US$100m. These funds were to be used to resume debt service to the IMF and multilateral development agencies, for economic restructuring, for agricultural, oil and medical supplies, to rebuild bridges, schools, roads and hospitals and repatriate and resettle the contra rebel forces and other refugees. However, by mid-1991 disbursements had been insufficient to help the administration out of its extremely straightened circumstances. Emergency measures, including the introduction of another new currency, the córdoba oro, failed to stabilize the economy. With the old and new currencies in circulation side-by-side, a shortfall in foreign aid and a consequent lack of economic progress, confidence in each currency collapsed. By 1992, however, progress was apparent in some areas as slow growth resumed and inflation fell to only 3.9 percent. The trend was reversed in 1993 owing to deep austerity and political instability; gdp fell and inflation rose to 28.3 percent. In 1994, gdp growth returned, but gdp per capita continued to decline. In the five years to 1994 it had fallen by 48 percent.

Some sectors, for example energy, tourism and gold mining, benefited from foreign investment in the mid-1990s and the seafood industry showed marked improvement. Overall, though, progress was hampered by the farm crisis, the large trade deficit, a lack of reserves and the demands on resources of what foreign debt was being repaid.

President Alemán promised to continue the structural adjustment programme of the Chamorro government and to create 100,000 jobs a year by reactivating agriculture, tourism and attracting foreign investment. The reduction of poverty and the promotion of growth were to be given high priority, while further debt relief was being sought. In 2000, Nicaragua will be a candidate for debt relief under the new highly indebted poor country (HIPC) initiative, provided it has an IMF agreement in place. External debt totalled around US$6bn in 1998, three times the size of gdp. Nicaragua's entire economic outlook was radically altered, however, by Hurricane Mitch (October 1998). With reconstruction forced to the top of the agenda and a new focus given to the issue of debt relief, there were signs in early 1999 that not only were financial resources being targeted at areas of greatest need, but also that a political unity not seen for many years was emerging.

Government

A new Constitution was approved by the 92-member National Constituent Assembly in 1986 and signed into effect on 9 January 1987. Legislative power is vested in a unicameral, directly elected National Assembly of 92 representatives, each with an alternate representative, with a six-year term. In addition, unelected presidential and vice presidential candidates become representatives and alternates respectively if they receive a certain percentage of the votes. Executive power is vested in the President, assisted by a Vice President and an appointed Cabinet. The Presidential term is five years. **Constitution**

The main Pacific **ports** are Corinto, San Juan del Sur and Puerto Sandino. The two main Atlantic ports are Puerto Cabezas and Bluefields. The **roads** have been greatly extended and improved. The Pan-American Highway, from the Honduran border to the borders of Costa Rica (384 kilometres), is paved the whole way and so is the shorter international road to the Honduran frontier via Chinandega. The road between Managua and Rama (for Bluefields) is paved, but is not in good condition. There are now 17,146 kilometres of road, of which 10 percent are paved. Until 1 January 1994, there was one operational **railway**, the Ferrocarril del Pacífico, 349 kilometres long, single track, with a gauge of 1.067 metres. On that date all railway services were suspended and the tracks were torn up, although the stations were preserved. One private line remains and a railway museum is being put together. See also **Getting around** and **Further reading** in **Essentials**. **Communications**

Costa Rica

9

Costa Rica

Essentials

Planning your trip

Costa Rica is the smallest but two – El Salvador and Belize – of the Central American republics and only Panama and Belize have fewer inhabitants. It is known throughout Latin America as the continent's purest democracy and in November 1989, celebrated its centenary of democracy. The Army was abolished in 1949, though it should be stressed that there is a very efficient-looking khaki-clad Civil Guard. Costa Rica has the highest standard of living in Central America, the second lowest birth rate (after Panama) and the greatest degree of economic and social advance. Tourism is well-developed, particularly nature tourism, attracted by the many national parks and biological reserves protecting a variety of ecosystems.

Where to go

San José, the capital, is the main entry point, but unless you particularly like capital cities, you only need spend a couple of days there, visiting museums and other sights and organizing things prior to visiting the rest of the country. Costa Rica's main attractions are its countryside, nature and wildlife, rather than its towns, several of which have lost their colonial buildings in earthquakes and are now mostly modern.

Northeast of San José are the volcanoes of **Irazú** and **Turrialba**, both of which can be visited. The area around them is a popular area for birdwatching, with the cloud forest of the **Tapantí National Park** attracting many species including the quetzal. It is also a prime site for whitewater rafting on the Reventazón and Pacuare rivers. Several comfortable lodges cater for nature tourism and offer guided tours.

West of San José the PanAmerican Highway runs through the **Meseta Central** to the Nicaraguan border, initially past several agricultural towns and villages which make pleasant weekend excursions for the residents of the capital. The Poás volcano smokes and geysers eject great columns of steam, but the National Park is open to visitors and trails are marked. The most spectacular of Costa Rica's volcanoes is **Arenal**, which you would not want to climb because it is still active. A perfect cone, it is everyone's idea of what a volcano should look like, best watched at night when the red hot larva can be seen spewing out of the top and rolling down the mountain side, accompanied by impressive sound effects. Not to be missed. Arenal stands at the head of a very picturesque lake of the same name, where you can fish or windsurf.

South of Lake Arenal, but best reached from the coastal port city of Puntarenas, is the most visited forest reserve, **Monteverde**. This private, 10,500-hectare, cloud forest reserve offers a limited network of trails to a limited number of visitors a day in order to protect the resplendant quetzal and other endangered birds and over 100 species of mammals (six endangered cats), reptiles and amphibians. Other private reserves have been established alongside Monteverde, which are also well worth a visit.

The northwest of the country is drier and the province of **Guanacaste** is cattle country with its own distinctive music and dance. National parks in this area protect dry tropical forest, while on the Pacific beaches turtles lurch up the sand to lay their eggs, watched by wardens to prevent egg stealing. The **Nicoya peninsula** is also hot, with miles of white sand beaches. Resort hotels are springing up all along the coast, but despite the construction work transport links are still poor so there remain huge areas of unspoilt beaches where accommodation is more rustic.

The main town on the Caribbean coast is **Puerto Limón**, where the weather is hot and humid. From here up to the Nicaraguan border there are few settlements and transport is via a network of canals. The vegetation is lowland tropical rain forest and much of the area is protected by the **Tortuguero National Park**, where turtles nest. Several lodges offer all-inclusive packages with guided tours of the waterways and the wildlife, but it is possible to travel independently, stay in family-run cabins and hire your own guide. From Puerto Limón down to the Panamanian border there are beaches, tropical rain forest and a variety of places to stay, connected by a good road to the frontier.

The southern Pacific coast of Costa Rica comprises some lovely beaches in beautiful surroundings. A few places have been overdeveloped and building continues, but several areas are protected or still remote enough not to be crowded. The PanAmerican Highway runs inland from San José to Panama through some really spectacular mountain scenery. The country's highest mountain is here: **Chirripó Grande** at 3,820 metres. Lodges offer birdwatching and guided tours in the Cordillera de Talamanca, where the Chirripó National Park and the neighbouring La Amistad International Park protect the largest area of virgin forest in the country with the greatest biological diversity. In the extreme south around the Golfo Dulce and the **Peninsula de Osa** there are more conservation areas of tropical wet forest, with swamps and empty beaches.

When to go Altitude, as elsewhere in Central America, determines the climate, but the *tierra templada* and the *tierra fría* start at about 300 metres lower on the Pacific than on the Atlantic side. The Pacific side is the drier, with patches of savanna among the deciduous forest; the Atlantic side has heavy rainfall, 300 days a year of it, and is covered far up the slopes with tropical forest: about 31 percent of Costa Rica is forested (half forested in 1950).

The climate varies from the heat and humidity of the Caribbean and Atlantic lowlands to warm temperate on the Meseta Central and chilly temperate at the greater heights. On the Cordillera Talamanca, the average temperature is below 16°C. There are dry and wet seasons: on the Pacific side there is a well-defined wet season from May to November with a little decrease during the July-August *'veranillo'*. The Atlantic side has no specific dry season but

Costa Rica & national parks

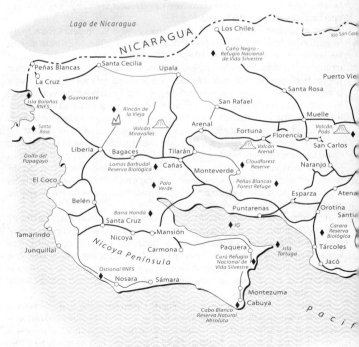

0 km 50
0 miles 30

National Parks
RNFS Refugio Nacional de Fauna Silvestre
IG   Islas Guayabo, Negritos & de los Pájaros Reservas Biológicas

there is less rainfall between March and September. Between May and November, the rainfall in the Meseta Central averages 1,950 millimetres and roads are often bogged down. The hottest months are March and April. Between December and February is the best time to visit. However, for the visitor, rain is part of the enchantment of the tropics and apart from the infrequent cyclonic storms, most of the rain is in short, sharp downpours.

Tourists particularly enjoy the many well-kept and well-guarded national parks and nature reserves which protect some samples of the extraordinarily varied Costa Rican ecosystems. Some of the last patches of dry tropical forest, for instance, can be found in the Santa Rosa National Park, and other parks protect the unique cloud forest.

Nature tourism

The **Servicio de Parques Nacionales** (SPN, Avenida 8, Calle 25, open Monday-Friday, 0800-1600, write in advance to Apartado 10094, or T2334070, 2334246, 2334118) in San José administers the National Park system. For information and permits to visit and/or camp in the Parks apply to **Fundación de Parques Nacionales** (FPN), 300 metres north and 150 metres east of Santa Teresita Church, Barrio Escalante, Calle 23, Avenida 15, San José, T2572239, open Monday-Friday 0800-1700, Saturday 0800-1200. Most permits can be obtained at park entrances. To contact park personnel by radio link or make accommodation reservations, T2334160, but good Spanish is a help (bilingual operators at National Parks can be reached by dialing 192). If you make reservations at their San José office, make sure they have made them direct with the park and that you have clear references on the confirmation to avoid

difficulties on arrival. If you want to work as a volunteer in the parks, contact Stanley Arquedas of the SPN, mornings only. An alternative is to go to AVSO, Calle 17-19, Avenida 2, 75 metres east of Museo Nacional, T2225085, San José.

On 15 April 1996 a standard entrance fee of US$6 for all National Parks was introduced. Manuel Antonio, Guayabo, Cabo Blanco and Braulio Carrillo (Quebrada González ranger station) are closed Monday. Cabo Blanco is also closed Tuesday.

Bird watchers and butterfly lovers have long flocked to Costa Rica to see some of the 850 or so species of birds (the whole of the United States counts only about 800 species) and untold varieties of butterflies. All of these can best be seen in the parks, together with monkeys, deer, coyotes, armadillos, anteaters, turtles, coatis, raccoons, snakes, wild pigs, and, more rarely, wild cats and tapirs. Good field guides are Petersen, *Birds of Mexico and Central America* and *Birds of North America*; Stiles/Skutch, *Guide to the Birds of Costa Rica*; Ridgely, *Birds of Panama*; Golden Guide, *Birds of North America*; Daniel H Janzen, *Costa Rican Natural History*; Philip J de Vries, *Butterflies of Costa Rica*; *Birds of the Rainforest-Costa Rica*, published by FUNDECOR and USAID; *Biodiversity of Costa Rica*, published by INBio.

Nature guides can be found at The Bookshop in San José, and there is also available an illustrated book, *The National Parks of Costa Rica*, by Mario A Boza (1986), which gives a good impression of what the different parks are like. Also available is *Areas de conservación y sus parques nacionales* by the Asociación Ecologista de Vida Silvestre (1998), T/F2230851.

Although the National Parks and other privately owned reserves are a main tourist attraction, many are in remote areas and not easy to get to on public transport; buses or coaches that do go tend to stay for a short time only. There is a growing tendency for tour companies to dominate the National Park 'market' to the exclusion of other public transport. For those on tight budgets, try making up a party with others and sharing taxis or hiring a car. Descriptions of the individual parks, and how to get there, will be found in the text.

The Audubon Society holds an Eco-Tourism Seminar on Wednesday at 1830 at the Friends' Peace Center, Calle 15 y Avenida 8, San José. A National Park slide show with 164 slides on the National Park system, with a period for questions and answers, is held on Monday, Wednesday, Saturday, at 1000-1130 at Cine Variedades, Calle 5, Avenida 1-Central, 50 metres north of Plaza de la Cultura, US$3.

Watersports The rivers of Costa Rica have proved to be highly popular for **white water rafting**, kayaking and canoeing, both for the thrill of the rapids and the wildlife interest of the quieter sections. The seven most commonly run rivers are the Reventazón (and the Pascua section of it), Pacuare, Corobicí, Sarapiquí and El General. You can do a daytrip but to reach the big class IV rapids you usually have to take two to three days. The Reventazón is perhaps the most accessible but the Pacuare has been recommended as a more beautiful experience. The Corobicí is slow and popular with bird watchers. Ríos Tropicales (see San José Travel Agencies, page 1070) has been recommended for its guides and its equipment. **NB** Heavy rain may cause cancellations, so you need flexibility in your plans. Offshore, **snorkelling** and **scuba diving** are offered by several hotels, but you have to pick your spot carefully. Anywhere near a river will suffer from poor visibility and the coral reef has died in many places because of agricultural pollutants washed downstream. Generally, on the Caribbean side you can see wrecks and coral reefs, particularly in the southeast towards the Panamanian border, while on the Pacific side you see large pelagics and sportfish. Liveaboard dive boats head for the islands of Caño and Isla del Coco. Divers are not permitted in National Parks or reserves, nor within 500 metres of the protected sea turtle zone north of Tortuguero National Park. **Windsurfing** is good along the Pacific coast and on Lake Arenal, particularly the west end. Lots of hotels have equipment for hire and operators in San José will know where the best conditions prevail at any time. Be careful of obstacles in the water along rocky coastlines and near river mouths. **Surfing** is also popular off the Pacific beaches, attracting professionals who follow storm surges along the coast. **Sport fishing** is done off either coast and at different times of the year. Snook and tarpon are caught in the Caribbean, the largest snook being found in September and October, mostly north of Limón (where there are several fishing lodges), but also towards Panama. In the Pacific bill fishing is well-developed.

Association **football** (soccer) is the national sport (played every Sunday at 1100, September to May, at the Saprissa Stadium). There are **golf courses** around the country, see under San José. There is **sea-bathing** on both Atlantic and Pacific coasts (see text). The Meseta is good country for **riding**; horses can be hired by arrangement directly with owners. Most fiestas end with **bullfighting** in the squares, an innocuous but amusing set-to with no horses used. Bullfights are held in San José during the Christmas period. There is no kill and spectators are permitted to enter the ring to chase, and be chased by, the bull.

Other amusements

The information offices of the **Instituto Costarricense de Turismo** are on Avenida 4, Calle 5-7, 11th floor, ICT building, San José (T2231733/8423, toll free 800-0123456), open 0800-1600 Monday to Friday. All tourist information is given here. Take complaints about hotel overcharging to the Instituto. For more details, see page 1072.

Finding out more

There are a number of Web sites on Costa Rica; recommended is Costa Rica's Travelnet at http://centralamerica.com, which contains general information, maps, descriptions of national parks, photographs, butterflies, selected hotels, car rental, airlines and schedules, tours and packages. Also useful is www.info.co.cr/which has lots of links, including to Costa Rican newspapers.

Before you travel

Documents A passport is required. For visits of up to 90 days the following do not need visas: nationals of most Western European countries, the USA, Canada, Israel, Japan, Romania, Hungary, Poland, Argentina, Uruguay, Panama, Paraguay and South Korea. The following also do not need a visa, but visits are limited to 30 days: citizens of Australia, New Zealand, Iceland, Monaco, most East European countries, South Africa, Taiwan, Singapore, most Middle Eastern countries, most Caribbean countries and most Central and South America countries, including Brazil, Mexico, Ecuador, Guyana, Guatemala, El Salvador and Honduras. Notwithstanding this, some travellers report that 90 days may be allowed for nationals of some of these countries. All other nationalities need a visa, costing US$25, valid for only 30 days (this includes Italy, Greece, Nicaragua, Peru, Dominican Republic, CIS, India, Indonesia, Egypt, Turkey). Make absolutely sure that you get an entry stamp in your passport and insist even if border officials tell you otherwise. Failure to have a stamp can lead to numerous problems on departure. Some nationalities have to have a tourist card, US$2 on entry.

Getting in

After requesting an extension, when departing Costa Rica you will have to pay a US$38 departure tax (the same as Costa Ricans or residents). If you overstay the 30 (or 90) day permitted period, you must report to Immigration before leaving the country. A fine of US$2 per month will be charged, you will be given five days to leave the country and will have to pay the departure tax. For longer stays ask for a Prórroga de Turismo at Migración in San José. For this you need three passport photos, an airline or bus ticket out of the country and proof of funds (for example travellers' cheques); you can apply for an extension of one or two months, 300 colones per month. The paperwork takes three days. If you leave the country, you must wait 72 hours before returning, but it may be cheaper and easier to do this and get a new 30-day entry. Travel agents can arrange all extension and exit formalities for a small fee.

An onward ticket (a bus ticket, which can be bought at the border immigration office or sometimes from the driver on Tica international buses, a transatlantic ticket or an MCO will sometimes do) is asked for, but can be refunded in San José with a loss of about US$3 on a US$20 ticket. Cashing in an air ticket is difficult because you may be asked to produce another ticket out of the country. Also, tourists may have to show at least US$300 in cash or travellers' cheques before being granted entry (especially if you have no onward ticket). Always carry a passport, or photocopy, for presentation at spot-checks. Failure to do so may mean imprisonment.

Customs Half a kilo of manufactured tobacco and three litres of liquor are allowed in duty-free. Any amount of foreign or local currency may be taken in or out.

Warnings Those arriving by air from Colombia can expect to have their persons and baggage carefully searched because of the drug traffic in the area. In Costa Rica, particularly on the Atlantic coast, do not get involved with drugs: many dealers are undercover police agents.

There has been much illegal immigration into Costa Rica: this explains why Migración officials sometimes grill visitors in their hotels.

Money

Currency The unit is the colón, formerly sub-divided into 100 céntimos. Old coins in use are for 50 centavos and 1, 2, 5, 10 and 20 colones. In 1995 new, golden coloured, smaller coins were minted for 5, 10, 25, 50 and 100 colones. Public telephones use 5, 10 and 20 colón coins. Paper money in use: 50, 100, 500, 1,000, 2,000, 5,000 and 10,000 colones.

Banks Exchange of US dollars (etc) must be effected in a bank, and for bank drafts and transfers commission may be charged (set by the banks themselves). Most tourist and first class hotels will change dollars for guests only, the same applies in restaurants and shops if you buy something. Hardly anyone will change damaged US dollar notes. A legal parallel (street) market has existed since February 1992. It is almost impossible to exchange any other major currency in Costa Rica. Every major bank issues Visa/Mastercard, including Credomatic. Most banks (for example Banco Nacional, Banco de San José) will process cash advances on Visa/Mastercard. ATMs which will accept international Visa and/or Mastercard are available at most banks, shopping malls and San José airport. However, travellers report that Visa is more acceptable than Mastercard in Costa Rica.

Credit cards Credomatic handles all credit card billings; they will not accept a credit card charge that does not have the imprint of the borrower's card plus an original signature. This is the result of fraud, but it makes it difficult to book tours or accommodation over the phone. For card loss or theft, Amex T2330044, Visa T2232211, Mastercard T2532155.

Touching down

Hours of business 0800 or 0830 to 1100 or 1130 and 1300 to 1700 or 1730 (1600, government offices), Monday to Friday, and 0800 to 1100 on Saturday. Shops: 0800 to 1200, 1300 to 1800 Monday to Saturday.
IDD 506. Equal tones with long pauses means it is ringing. Equal tones with equal pauses indicates engaged.
Official time Standard time is six hours behind Greenwich Mean Time.
Voltage 110, 60 cycles, AC (US flat-pin plugs).
Weights and measures For Customs the metric system of weights and measures is compulsory. Traders use a variety of weights and measures, including English ones and the old Spanish ones.

Getting there

Air

From Europe Direct scheduled flights from Amsterdam (Martinair), Frankfurt (Condor) and London (British Airways). Iberia flies from Barcelona and Madrid but you have to change planes in Miami. Most European cities connect with the British Airways flight from Gatwick on Sunday, or through US cities – Miami, Houston, Dallas – with American Airlines or Continental. There are charter flights in season from several European cities.

From North America Atlanta (Delta), Baltimore (Delta), Boston (American Airlines), Chicago (Continental), Dallas (American Airlines, Aviateca), Houston (Continental), Los Angeles (Lacsa, United), Miami (Lacsa, American, Martinair, Iberia), New Orleans (Lacsa), New York (Lacsa, United), Orlando (Lacsa), San Francisco (United, Taca), Tampa (Condor), Toronto (Lacsa), Washington DC (United).

From South America Bogotá (Lacsa, SAM), Cali (SAM), Caracas (Lacsa), Cartagena (SAM), Guayaquil (Lacsa), Lima (Lacsa), Quito (Lacsa), Santiago (Lacsa).

From Central America Cancún (Lacsa), David, Panama (Aeroparlas), Guatemala City (United, Lacsa, Aviateca, Copa), La Ceiba (Lacsa), Managua (Copa, Lacsa), Mexico City (Lacsa, Mexicana, United), Panama City (Taca, Copa, Lacsa), San Pedro Sula (Lacsa), San Salvador (Copa, Lacsa, Taca), Tegucigalpa (Lacsa).

From the Caribbean Havana (Cubana, Lacsa), San Andrés (SAM), San Juan (Lacsa, Copa), Santo Domingo (Copa).

Touching down

Departure tax

There is an airport departure tax for tourists of US$17, payable in colones or dollars (travellers' cheques not accepted). There is a five percent tax on airline tickets purchased in the country. On arrival and departure at land frontiers, 75 colones (US$0.30) has to be paid.
  NB Exit taxes, by air or land, and legislation regarding visa extensions, are subject to frequent change and travellers should check these details as near to the time of travelling as possible.

Safety

Look after your belongings in hotels (use the safe), hired cars and on beaches. Theft is on the increase and we have received reports of violent robberies in those dangerous parts of San José mentioned in the **Warning**, page 1056.

Tipping

A 10 percent service charge is automatically added to restaurant and hotel bills, as well as 15 percent sales tax. Tip porters, hairdressers and cloakroom attendants. Taxis and cinema usherettes, nil.

Where to stay

A 13 percent sales tax plus 3.39 percent tourism tax (total 16.39 percent) are added to the basic price of hotel rooms. A deposit is recommended at the more expensive hotels in San José, especially in the high season, December-April, to guarantee reservations. If you arrive late at night, even a guaranteed reservation may not be honoured.

The Costa Rica Bed & Breakfast Group includes 50 Bed & Breakfast inns and small hotels around the country in its membership. They can be contacted through the president, Debbi McMurray, Apartado 493-1000, San José, T2234168, F2234157.

Getting around

Roads & motoring

Driving in Costa Rica allows for much flexibility of travel, with certain precautions. Main roads are not always obvious, road signs in remote areas are scarce and driving after dark is not recommended. Use your mile counter to help you find the right road. Speed limits are low (80 kmph, 100 kmph on some roads) and there are rigorous radar speed traps, especially at the entry to towns and on the Pan-American Highway. If caught, you may have your number plate confiscated and have to pay a court fine (+30 percent tax) to get it back. Do not attempt to pay an on-the-spot fine (see below). Unpaved roads are slow going, so leave plenty of time for your trip, 20 kmph may be your maximum speed. Many of the nature parks are in remote areas and four-wheel drive may well be needed, certainly a car with high clearance is recommended; in the wet season some roads will be impassable. Check that bridges are not down. Always ask locals or bus drivers what the state of the road is before embarking on a journey, but do not assume that if the buses are running, a car can get through too.

Beware of policemen trying to charge on-the-spot fines. Fines in Costa Rica may only validly be paid at official stations in San José and major towns. If you pay a fine immediately, you still run the risk of getting reported and having to pay when you leave the country.

It is illegal to ride in a car or taxi without wearing seatbelts. Motorcyclists must wear crash helmets.

Tourists who come by car or motorcycle pay US$10 road tax and can keep their cars for an initial period of 90 days. This can be extended for a total period of six months, for about US$10 per extra month, at the Instituto Costarricense de Turismo, or at the Customs office, Avenida 3, Calle 14, if you take your passport, car entry permit, and a piece of stamped paper (*papel sellado*) obtainable at any bookshop. If you intend to drive in the country for more than three months, you are required to apply for a Costa Rican Driver's Licence at Avenida 18, Calle 5, San José. Cars are fumigated on entry: exterior US$3; interior US$1.40. It is now mandatory for foreign drivers to buy insurance stamps on entry; US$17.75 for one month (US$8 for motorcycles), US$27.70 for two months, US$37.65 for three months. If you have an accident, contact Policía de Tránsito, San José T2268436 or 2272189.

If you want to travel on from Costa Rica without your car, you should leave it in the customs warehouse at Calle Blancos in San José. A customs agent is recommended unless you want to spend several weeks learning the system. Recommended, at a reasonable price, is Camilo Lacayo SA (Apartado 54-1300 San José, T2553174), located 100m west and 25m south of the Calle Blancos *Aduanas*. Boris Barrantes León is helpful and speaks English. The requisite papers are called *guías*: either for up to two months or up to a year (US$100 for the latter). Charges at the warehouse depend on the value of the car, for example a 1970 VW microbus valued at US$3,500 cost US$1 per day. A complete inventory of the vehicle and contents is made when leaving the car. Recovering the car is a lengthy procedure of several days. You have to visit the Central Bank to certify that you have not requested dollars for the price of the car, that is, you have not sold it. The customs agency you first dealt with should guide you through this for no extra charge. The *aduanas* will either escort you to the frontier or you can buy another three months' insurance and have the car stamped back into your passport. This requires a visit to Central Customs (orange building, Avenida 1, Calle 14). Be sure to tell the Customs Agency that you want to reinsure the car when depositing it, doing this should save some paperwork and time. The whole operation needs time and patience.

Car hire firms are not covered by tourist regulations and many complaints have been made **Car hire**
to the authorities concerning their operations. If hiring a car, be very cautious. Most leases do
not allow the use of a normal car off paved roads. Always make sure the spare tyre is in good
order, as holes are frequent. You can have tyres fixed at any garage for about US$3 in 30
minutes. Tyres without rims are confiscated and burnt by the Customs. Hired cars bear special
number plates and are easily identified. Be particularly careful not to leave valuables in a hired
car, which is a sitting target. If you can, reserve your vehicle in advance, especially if there is a
particular type you want. Costa Rica's web site has been recommended for advance
reservations. Check your vehicle carefully as the rental company will try to claim for the
smallest of 'damages'. International driver's licence and credit card generally required.
(Discounts available during 'green season', May-November.) Insurance costs US$10-17 per
day extra; deductible is between US$750 and US$1,500, depending on company, some will
charge extra to waive deductible, eg Budget, US$2.50 a day; basic prices: smallest car US$38
per day includes unlimited mileage or US$228 per week; jeep costs US$54 per day, US$324
per week, includes unlimited mileage. Four-wheel drive are very popular and in limited
supply, you may have to reserve a week in advance. Cash deposits or credit card charges
range from US$600 to US$1,000, so check you have sufficient credit. You can often obtain
lower rentals by making reservations before arrival with the major companies. If you plan to
drop off a hired car, check with several firms for their charges: Elegante, Ada and National
appear to have the lowest drop-off fees. Insurance will not cover broken windscreens (unless
you are involved in an accident), driving on unsurfaced roads or damaged tyres. If you have
an accident always call the traffic police and rental car company. Licence plates will
automatically be removed. Do not move your car until the police arrive. Never bribe traffic
police, ask them to issue a ticket. Some traffic police will tell you to return to San José, or
another place, trying to get you to bribe them to avoid interrupting your trip. Always report
any demands for money to the tourism authorities.

An Enduro is best for seeing all the country. Keep clear of taxis and buses who will pay no **Motorcycle**
attention to you. Wearing a helmet is obligatory, renters provide simple ones without front **rental**
glass. You will need strong dark glasses. The paved roads offer frequent surprises, deep holes,
rivers and landslides over the road, planks of bridges in a rotten state. You need good
rainwear even in the dry season. However, you have increased mobility and speed on dirt
roads and riding is very enjoyable outside the San José area due to low traffic.

Car parts are very expensive because of high import tax. If the parts are needed for leaving **Spares**
the country you can order them from abroad yourself and avoid the tax but it takes time. Ask
Sr Marcheno in the Aduana de Vehículos, Avenida 3, Calle 10, Spanish required. It is best not to
try and sell your car here as the import tax is 70 percent. Spares are available for Japanese
makes in San José. San José is also the best place to get Land Rover spares. Try Oswaldo von
Breymann, Avenida 7, Casa 27, Calle 5-7, T212274, San José, for motorcycle spares (BMW and
MZ); he is a good mechanic. Yamaha dealer, Lutz Hermanos y Cía Ltda, Calle 1 between
Avenida 5 and 7, San José, T2553566, F2330658. Motorcycle spares, including BMW, Avenida 7
between Calle 1 and 3, T2352173.

Main fuel stations have regular (unleaded) US$0.48 (109 colones) and diesel US$0.34 (77.30 **Fuel**
colones) per litre; super gasoline (unleaded) is available throughout the country, US$0.51
(114.60 colones). Leaded fuel is unavailable.

Road tolls vary between US$0.30 and US$1. The following are 60 colones, San José-San José **Road tolls**
airport; San José-Santa Ana; San José-Cartago. 120 colones, San José airport-San Ramón. 200
colones, San José-Guápiles. San José-Cartago, San José-Santa Ana and San Ramón-airport
have automatic machines accepting 5, 10, 20 colón coins.

Airports There are domestic airports or airstrips, with scheduled services, at Barra Colorado, **Air**
Carrillo, Coto 47, Fortuna, Golfito, Liberia, Nosara Beach, Palmar, Puerto Jiménez, Punta Islita,
Quepos, Tamarindo, Tambor, Tortuguero, with Sansa or Travelair. For details see page 1066.

Cycling John Gilchrist tells us that cycling is easier in Costa Rica than elsewhere in Central America; there is less heavy traffic and it is generally 'cyclist friendly'. However, paving is thin and soon deteriorates; look out for cracks and potholes, which bring traffic to a crawl. Unsurfaced roads are horrible on a bicycle. The prevailing wind is from the northeast, so if making an extensive tour, travelling in the direction of Panama-Nicaragua is slightly more favourable. Be prepared for a lot of rain. It is perfectly possible to travel light, without tent, sleeping bag or cooking equipment. Particularly bad for cyclists is the Nicoya Peninsula; a mountain bike is recommended for the terrain and the poor road state.

Recommended reading for all users: *Baker's The Essential Road Guide to Costa Rica*, with detailed strip maps, kilometre by kilometre road logs, motoring information plus San José map and Bus Guide (130 pages: Bill Baker, Apartado 1185-1011, San José, T/F2201415). Cycle shop: *El Mundo de Ciclismo*, Paseo Colón, Calle 26, San José, good stock of newest bicycle parts; Tecnillantas, Avenida 10, San Martín, has cycle tyres (also motorcycle and car tyres).

Hitchhiking Hitchhiking is easy and safe by day in the week. There is not much traffic off the main roads.

Keeping in touch

Postal services Mail by sea from the UK takes from two to three months and 10 to 14 days by airmail. Airmail letters to Europe cost 90 colones, postcards 70 colones; to North/South America, letters 70 colones, 55 colones for postcards; to Australia, Africa and Asia, letters 70 colones, postcards 65 colones. 'Expreso' letters, 55 colones extra, several days quicker to USA and North Europe. Registered mail, 150 colones. All parcels sent out of the country by foreigners must be taken open to the post office for clearance. *Lista de Correos*, charges 50 colones per letter and will keep letters for four weeks. The contents of incoming parcels will be the subject of plenty of paperwork, and probably high duties. You normally have to come back the next day.

Telephone services Long-distance telephone services are run by the Instituto Costarricense de Electricidad (ICE) and by Cía Radiográfica Internacional de Costa Rica (RACSA). Local cables, though, are sent from the main post office in San José, Avenida 1-3, Calle 2. Rates at the RACSA Telecommunications Centre, Avenida 5, Calle 1, San José, to USA are US$1.45 per minute (reduced rate 1900-2200 and all day Saturday/Sunday, US$1.09 per minute), to Europe, Caribbean, South America, US$2.50 per minute (US$2), plus 13 percent sales tax, open 0700-2200. Internet access US$2 per hour. Phone cards are available for long distance calls at US$10 and US$20. Phone cards with 'Personal Identification Numbers' can be used for direct dialling from a private phone which is cheaper than rates from a public phone or RACSA office. Calls abroad can be made from phone booths; collect calls abroad may be made from special booths in the telephone office, Avenida 5, Calle 1, San José, or from any booth nationwide if you dial 116 for connection with the international operator. Collect calls can be made from any public phone. Phone cards from the following countries are accepted: Brazil, Canada, France, Holland, Denmark, Hong Kong, Italy, Japan, South Korea, UK and USA. A call to USA; US$1.60 per minute Monday-Friday 0700-1900, US$1.20 per minute Monday-Friday 1900-2200, US$0.65 per minute Monday-Friday 2200-0700 and weekends. Call to UK, Europe, Canada; US$2.50 per minute Monday-Friday 0700-1900, US$2 per minute Monday-Friday 1900-2200, US$1.25 per minute Monday-Friday 2200-0700 and weekends. All rates subject to 13 percent sales tax. Country Direct dialling codes are (all prefix 0800): MCI -012-2222, AT&T 0114-114, Sprint -013-0123, Italy -039-1039, Germany -049-1049, Switzerland -041-1184, Belgium -032-1032, Britain -044-1044, Canada -015-1161, France -033-1033, Worldcom -014-4444, Denmark -045-1045, Spain -034-1034, Finland -358-1358, Holland -031-1111, Japan -081-1081, New Zealand -064-1064. Public telex booth at Radiográfica SA, Avenida 5, Calle 1 (telex CR 1050); the telex must show your name and Tel no or address for them to advise you; also public Fax service, to receive, 100 colones (F+506-223-1609 or +506-233-7932); to send, US$3 per page to Europe, US$2.42 night rate (CRI; US$2.80 ICE), US$1.93 per page to USA, US$1.45 night rate.

Media **Newspapers** The best San José morning papers are *La Nación* (www.nacion.co.cr) and *La*

República; there is also *Al Día*. *La Prensa Libre* is a good evening paper. *Libertad*, weekly newspaper (socialist). *El Debate* is another good weekly. Three weekly news magazines are: *Rumbo* (political), *Triunfo* and *Perfil* (popular). *La Gazette* is the official government weekly paper. *Tico Times* (http://ticotimes.co.cr/ Friday, subscriptions Dept 717, PO Box 025216, Miami FL 33102-5216, or Apdo 4632-1000 San José, T2581558, F2336378, ttcirc@sol.racsa.co.cr) and *Costa Rica Today* (free in better hotels and restaurants, subscriptions Ediciones 2000 SA, Acc No 117, PO Box 025216, Miami FL 33102) in English (look in the classifieds for Spanish classes). The former is better for news and classifieds (also publishes annual *Exploring Costa Rica*), the latter has weekly features of interest to travellers, for example hotels under US$10 in San José or railway news. *Central America Weekly* in English, Spanish, German and Italian. *The Latin America*, US$1, has travel information, bed and breakfast places, local airline schedules, useful, Apartado 661, Alajuela, T4419263, F4410222. *Adventures in Costa Rica* (Starflame Productions, PO Box 508, Jackson, CA 95642) is a monthly newsletter on travel in, and the affairs of Costa Rica (US$48 for 12 issues).

Television Six local TV stations, many MW/FM radio stations throughout the country (new radio station 'Welcome Radio' is in English, Spanish and German, 800 Khz AM). Local Voz de América (VOA) station. Many hotels and private homes receive one of the four TV stations offering direct, live, 24-hour TV from the USA (Canal 19, Supercanal, Cable Color and Master TV-channels 56, 58, 60. All US cable TV can be received in San José on the two cable stations).

Food and drink

Sales tax of 13 percent plus 10 percent service charge added to restaurant bills. *Sodas* (small restaurants) serve local food, which is worth trying. Very common is *casado*, a cheap lunch which includes rice, beans, stewed beef or fish, fried plantain and cabbage. *Olla de carne* is a soup of beef, plantain, corn, yuca, *ñampi* and *chayote* (local vegetables). *Sopa negra* is made with black beans, and comes with a poached egg in it; *picadillo* is another meat and vegetable stew. Snacks are popular: *gallos* (filled tortillas), *tortas* (containing meat and vegetables), *arreglados* (bread filled with the same) and *empanadas*. *Pan de yuca* is a speciality, available from stalls in San José centre. For breakfast, try *gallo pinto* (rice and beans) with *natilla* (a slightly sour cream). Best ice cream can be found in *Pops* shops. *Schmidt* bakeries are highly recommended; they also serve coffee. Also *La Selecta* bakeries. In general, eating out in Costa Rica is more expensive than elsewhere in Central America.

Local cuisine

There are many types of cold drink, made either from fresh fruit, or milk drinks with fruit (*batidos*) or cereal flour whisked with ice cubes. Drinks are often sugared well beyond North American tastes. The fruits range from the familiar to the exotic; others include *cebada* (barley flour), *pinolillo* (roasted corn), *horchata* (rice flour with cinnamon), *chan*, 'perhaps the most unusual, looking like mouldy frogspawn and tasting of penicillin' (Michael J Brisco). All these drinks cost the same as, or less than, bottled fizzy products. Excellent coffee. Local beers are Bavaria, Bremen, Pilsen, Imperial and Tropical (which is low alcohol).

Drink

Shopping

Best buys are wooden items, ceramics and leather handicrafts. **NB** Many wooden handicrafts are made of rainforest hardwoods and deforestation is a critical problem. Coffee should have 'puro' on the packet or it may have additives.

What to buy

Holidays and festivals

1 January: New Year's Day; 19 March: St Joseph; Easter: three days; 11 April: Battle of Rivas; 1 May: Labour Day; June: Corpus Christi; 29 June: St Peter and St Paul; 25 July: Guanacaste Day; 2 August: Virgin of Los Angeles; 15 August: Mothers' Day; 15 September: Independence Day; 12 October: Columbus Day; 8 December: Conception of the Virgin; 25 December: Christmas Day; 28-31 December: San José only.

NB During Holy Week, nearly everyone is on holiday. Everywhere is shut on Thursday, Friday, many shops on Saturday, and Sunday, and most of the previous week as well (in San José and Cartago only a small percentage of businesses and services close Monday-Wednesday and Saturday of Holy Week; almost all transport stops on Good Friday only, with limited transport on Thursday).

Health

Health/disease risks Drinking water is safe in all major towns; elsewhere it should be boiled. Water purification tablets et cetera hard to find but Tratagua, SA, Apartado 141-2050, Montes de Oca will make up Superdor (a chlorine based product) for you, two drops for each litre of water, at a nominal cost. Intestinal disorders are prevalent in the lowlands although Chagas disease is now rare. Malaria is on the increase; malaria prophylaxis is advised for visitors to the lowlands, especially near the Nicaraguan border; in Costa Rica it is available only from the Ministerio de Salud in San José (free), or at the Nicaraguan border. Dengue fever has been recorded in Liberia and Puntarenas. Uncooked foods should not be eaten. The standards of health and hygiene are among the best in Latin America. Ice cream, milk, et cetera are safe. See also notes on snakebite and mosquitoes under Corcovado National Park, page 1147.

San José

The capital stands in a broad, fertile valley which produces coffee and sugar-cane. It was founded in 1737 but frequent earthquakes have destroyed most of the colonial buildings and the modern replacements are not very inspiring. The climate is excellent, though the evenings can be chilly. The lowest and highest temperatures run from 15° to 26°C. Slight earthquake shocks are frequent. Rainy season: May to November. Other months are dry.

Ins & outs

The international airport is 16 kilometres from the centre along a good motorway. A taxi costs US$10 but there are also very efficient buses running every 10 minutes. Long distance buses have their terminals scattered all round town, see map, but connections are good with other Central American capitals and within Costa Rica.

Getting there

Buses run in and out of the city centre to outlying districts, so it is not difficult to come in to town if you choose a hotel in a quiet suburb. There is also a circular route all round town in each direction. Taxis can be ordered by phone or hailed in the street; they are red and should have meters. Traffic is congested, so you are not recommended to drive in the city centre, but car hire is good for trips out of town.

Getting around
Few buildings have numbers, so find out the nearest cross-street when getting directions (200m means two blocks, etc).

Streets cross one another at right-angles. Avenidas run east-west; the Calles north-south. The three main streets are Avenida Central, Avenida 2 and the intersecting Calle Central: the business centre is here. The best shops are along Avenida Central. Avenidas to the north of Avenida Central are given odd numbers; those to the south even numbers. Calles to the west of Calle Central are even-numbered; those to the east odd-numbered. The Instituto Costarricense de Turismo has an excellent map of the city, marking all the important sights and business houses.

It is best not to take a car into San José between 0700 and 2000; traffic is very heavy although new traffic laws have freed up the flow. Watch out for no parking zones or you will get towed away. Many of the narrow streets are heavily polluted with exhaust fumes. Seven blocks of the Avenida Central, from Banco Central running east to Plaza de la Cultura, are closed to traffic. Many people prefer to stay in the suburbs or in Heredia to escape the pollution.

Sights

Many of the most interesting public buildings are near the intersection of Avenida Central and Calle Central. The **Teatro Nacional** (1897): marble staircases, statuary, frescoes and foyer decorated in gold with Venetian plate mirrors, is just off Avenida Central, on Calle 3. It has a good coffee bar. ■ *Sightseeing visits, Monday-Saturday 0900-1700, US$2.* Nearby is **Plaza de la Cultura**, Avenida Central, Calle 3-5. Along Calle Central is **Parque Central**, with a bandstand in the middle among trees (bands play at 1100 on second Sunday of each month). To the east of the park is the **Cathedral**; to the north is the **Raventos theatre**; to the south are the **Rex Theatre** and a branch of the Banco Nacional. North of Avenida Central, on Calle 2, is the **Unión Club**, the principal social centre of the country. Opposite it is the **General Post and Telegraph Office**. The **Museo Nacional**, with a good collection of precolumbian antiquities, is in the reconstructed Vista Buena barracks, east from the Plaza de la Cultura along Avenida Central. Facing it is the **Plaza de la Democracia**, constructed to mark the November 1989 centenary of Costa Rican democracy. The **Palacio Nacional** (Avenida Central, Calle 15) is where the Legislative Assembly meets; any visitor can attend the debates, sessions start normally at 1600.

The attractive Paseo Colón continues the Avenida Central west to the former **La**

Population: 968,367 metropolitan area
Provincial population: 1,220,412
Altitude: 1,150m
Colour map 5, grid B2

Sabana airport (now developed as a sports centre, which is worth visiting) with a colonial-style building with frescoes of Costa Rican life in the Salón Dorado, see **Museo de Arte Costarricense** below. Further west is La Sabana, which has the **Estadio Nacional**, seating 20,000 spectators at (mainly) football matches, basketball, volleyball and tennis courts, a running track, lake and swimming pool.

Museums
Student cards give reductions in most museums.

Museo Nacional, Calle 17, Avenida Central and 2, very interesting, archaeology, anthropology, national history, some gold, ex-President Arias' Nobel Peace Prize, information in Spanish and English, replicas of precolumbian jewellery may be bought at reasonable prices. ■ *Tuesday-Sunday, 0900-1630, US$3.20, children free.* **Museo de Oro** in the Plaza de la Cultura complex with art museums adjoining the Teatro Nacional, Avenida Central, Calle 3-5, excellent, electronic system, Inform, costs US$2.25, mark the display numbers and the equipment tells you about the display in the language selected (Spanish or English), complete tour takes 40 minutes (deposit all bags at entrance). ■ *T2230528/4233, ext 282, Tuesday-Sunday, 1000-1630, US$3.70, US$1.50 with student card.* **Museo de Arte Costarricense** at the end of Paseo Colón, Calle 42, in La Sabana park in the old airport building, small but interesting display of paintings and sculptures. ■ *T2227155/7247, Tuesday-Sunday, 1000-1630, Sunday free, US$1.50, US$1 for students.* In the INS building, Avenida 7, Calle 9-13, is the **Museo del Jade Fidel Tristan** on the 11th floor, with jade carvings, pottery, sculpture et cetera, interesting, explained in Spanish and English, a 'must', and a beautiful view over the city ■ *Monday-Friday, 0830-1630, US$1.90.* **Museo de Ciencias Naturales**, Colegio La Salle, ■ *T2321306, Monday-Saturday 0800-1600, Sunday 0900-1700, US$1, (in the grounds of the Ministry of Agriculture; take 'Estadio Sabana' bus from Avenida 2, Calle 1 to the gate).* **Museo de**

San José main streets & districts

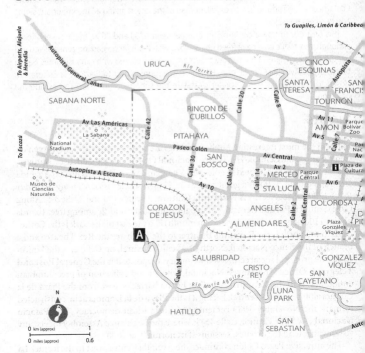

Entomología, in basement of School of Music building of the University of Costa Rica in San Pedro, many beautiful insects, only museum of its kind in Central America. ■ *T2255555, ext 318, Monday-Friday 1300-1700, to check times, entry US$1.50.* **Museo de Criminología,** Avenida 8, Calle 17-19, display of forensic medicine and various grisly exhibits, ■ *Monday-Friday 0700-1630, free.* **Museo de Arte Contemporáneo y Diseño**, Avenida 3, Calle 15-17, in the old liquor factory next to the Biblioteca Nacional, now the Centro Nacional de la Cultura ■ *T2577202/9370, Tuesday-Friday 1000-1700, Saturday 1000-1600, US$2.* **Museo Dr Rafael Angel Calderón Guardia**, Barrio Escalante, Avenida 11 y Calle 25-27, memorial to former president and sociology museum. ■ *T2251218, Monday-Saturday 0900-1700, US$0.70.* **Museo Filatélico y Numismático**, in General Post Office, second floor. ■ *Monday-Friday 0800-1600, free.* **Scientific and Cultural Centre (Museo del Niño** in old prison), Calle 4, Avenida 9, history and culture for children. ■ *T2237003, Tuesday-Friday 0800-1600, Saturday-Sunday 1000-1700, US$2, children US$1.*

Parks & zoos

Two blocks north of the Museo Nacional is **Parque Nacional**, with a grandiloquent bronze monument representing the five Central American republics ousting the filibuster William Walker (see Nicaraguan chapter) and the abolition of slavery in Central America. There is also a statue donated by the Sandinista Government of Nicaragua to the people of Costa Rica. To the north of the park is the **Biblioteca Nacional**.

Still further north is **Parque Bolívar**, now turned into a recreation area, small charge for entry, with zoo (see below). Along Avenida 3, to the west of Parque Nacional, are the four gardens of the remodelled **Parque Morazán**, with another bandstand at the centre. A little to the northeast, **Parque España**, cool, quiet, and intimate, has for neighbours the **Casa Amarilla** (Yellow House), seat of the Ministry of Foreign Affairs, and the **Edificio Metálico**, which houses several of the main schools. In the park opposite the church of La Merced is a huge carved granite ball brought from the archaeological site at Palmar Norte. There are others at the entrance to the Museo de Ciencias Naturales.

Simón Bolívar National Zoo and Botanical Gardens in Parque Simón Bolívar (Avenida 11, just east of Calle 7); Go down Calle 11 about three blocks from Avenida 7. Remodelled and much improved, with all native plants numbered and listed in a brochure; animals' cages are small. Sloths can be seen in the trees. ■ *Monday-Friday 1000-1530, Saturday-Sunday 0900-1700, US$3.70, also restaurant and souvenir shop.* **Serpentarium**, Avenida 1, Calle 9-11, T2254210, worth a visit especially if you are going to the National Parks or the jungle. Good variety of snakes and other reptiles. Staff helpful if you speak Spanish. ■ *Entrance adults US$3, children US$0.75, open Monday-Sunday 0900-1800.* **Mundo Sumergido Aquarium**, San Francisco de

CALLE BLANCOS

GUADALUPE

UNION JARDIN

Calle 1

To San Isidro de Coronado

To Sabanilla

Autopista

MIRAFLORES

LOMAS ESCALANTE
Av 13

VASQUEZ DENT

University of Costa Rica Entomology Museum

Calle 33

Av Central

To Cartago

Calle 29

LOS YOSES

JARDIN

MONTE ALEGRE

Autopista Estado de Israel

CALDERON MUÑOZ

UJARRAS

SAN DIMAS

Aduana Postal
Zapote (for postal packets)

QUESADA DURAN

Plaza de Toros

To Curridabat

GLORIA

To Desamparados

Ríos (400m east, 200m north of Y-shaped roundabout to San Francisco). ■ *Monday-Saturday 1000-2000.*

Excursions

San José is a good centre for excursions into the beautiful Meseta Central. The excursions to the Orosí valley and volcano of Irazú are given under Cartago. Poás volcano (described on page 1080) can be visited from Alajuela. Enquire first about the likely weather when planning a visit to Poás or Irazú. To reach Barva take a bus to San José de la Montaña (see page 1117). A road runs northeast of San José to (11 kilometres) **San Isidro de Coronado**, a popular summer resort (bus from Terminal Coronado, Avenida 7, Calle Central and 1). Those interested in medical research can visit the **Instituto Clodomiro Picado** snake farm, T2290335, open Monday-Friday 0800-1600 (snake feeding, Friday only 1400, Spanish only), take Dulce Nombre de Coronado bus from Avenida 3, Calle 3-5, 30 minutes, or San Antonio Coronado bus

San José centre

■ Sleeping
1 Al Alóki
2 Ambassador
3 Amstel Amon
4 Aurola Holiday Inn
5 Barceló Amon
6 Britannia
7 Casa Verde
8 Corobicí

9 Del Rey
10 Don Carlos
11 Dunn Inn
12 Edelweiss
13 Gran Hotel Costa Rica
14 Hemingway
15 Joluva
16 Kekoldi

to end of line and walk 200 metres downhill. They also sell snake-bite serum. The road goes on through fine countryside to **Las Nubes** (32 kilometres), a country village which commands a great view of Irazú. **San Antonio de Escazú** hosts the National Oxcart Drivers' Day (Día del Boyero) festival, the second weekend in March, with festivities culminating on the Sunday in a colourful oxcart parade from the school to the centre, accompanied by typical *payasos*. Open air dancing in the evening to a marimba.

Acua Mania water park, just off airport highway at traffic lights, 600 metres south of *Hotel Herradura*, San Antonio de Belén road. ■ *0900-1900 Monday-Friday, 0900-2200 Saturday-Sunday.* **Parque de Diversiones**, two kilometres west of Hospital México, has a 'Pueblo Antiguo' theme park next to it depicting Costa Rica of 1880-1930, with areas of the city, the country and the coast. ■ *US$7.* Held at the theme park is a *Vivencias Costarricenses* show, Wednesday-Sunday, 1000-1400, US$35 includes show, lunch, transport, guide and taxes; *Noches Costarricences*

Theme parks

17 La Amistad	**2** Heredia buses	**10** Terminal Caribe (Sixaola)
18 Morazán	**3** Liberia buses	**11** Terminal Cartago
19 Santo Tomás	**4** Panaline Bus	**12** Terminal Coca Cola
20 Vesuvio	**5** Sirca Bus	**13** Terminal Los Santos
21 Villa Tournon	**6** Tica Bus	**14** Terminal Puntarenas
	7 Transnica Bus	**15** Terminal Turrialba
🚌 Bus Stations	**8** Terminal Alfaro	
1 Alajuela & airport buses	**9** Terminal Atlántico Norte	

Costa Rica

show, Saturday-Sunday, 1800-2100, US$35 includes show, dinner, transport, guide and taxes.

Butterfly farms   Just outside **Guácima**, 35 minutes west of San José, 20 minutes south of Alajuela, is a Butterfly Farm, dedicated to rearing and exporting over 70 species of butterfly. The farm is believed to be the second largest in the world (the largest is in Taiwan). It was created by Joris Brinckerhoff, a former Peace Corp volunteer, and his wife in 1990. Guides are most informative but you may be disappointed if there are not many butterflies in the enclosure when you visit. The shop is full of overpriced T-shirts. ■ *T4380115, daily, 0900-1700, US$14 adults, US$7 students, US$7 children under 12, one and a half-hour guided tours, every two hours. Bus for La Guácima Monday-Saturday from Avenida 1, Calle 20-22, 1100 and 1400, return 1515, one hour, US$0.40, at last stop walk 300m from school south to butterfly sign (also minibuses, US$5). From Alajuela take bus marked 'La Guácima abajo', one block south, one block west of Tikal supermarket, 0620, 0900, 1100, 1300, 40 minutes, returns 0945, 1145, 1345, 1545, 1745.* Another butterfly farm is **Spirogyra**, 100m east, 150m south of Centro Comercial El Pueblo (near *Hotel Villa Tournon*), ■ , *T2222937, daily, 0800-1600, printed guide in English, last guided tour 1530, US$6 for tourists, U$$3 students, take 'Calle Blancos' bus from Calle 3 and Avenida 5 to El Pueblo.*

Essentials

Warning   Pickpockets, grab and run thieves, and muggings are on the increase in San José, especially in the centre, in the market, at the Coca Cola bus station, in the Barrios of Cuba, Cristo Rey, México, 15 de Setiembre and León XIII. Keep away from these areas at night and on Sunday, when few people are around. Also be careful on buses; leave nothing unattended. Street gangs, known as *chapulines*, are mostly made up of minors. The US embassy has produced a booklet *Helpful Hints For United States Citizens In Costa Rica*, available at the *Tico Times* office, some hotels and the US embassy. You must carry your passport (or a photocopy) with you at all times and make sure your papers are in order. A tourist helpline operated by tourist police has bilingual operators, 24 hours (call free 800-0123456).

Sleeping

Central   **LL** *Aurola Holiday Inn*, C 5, Av 5, pool, T2337233, F2222621, mainly business clientèle, casino (smallest wager US$4, free drinks if you play), good view of city, go to 16th floor and walk up emergency stairs.

L-AL *Balmoral*, C 7, Av Central, T2225022, F2217826, unimaginative but comfortable commercial hotel, café/restaurant slow service but good food. **L-AL** *del Rey*, Av 1, C 9, on busy corner in restored pink and white building, looks like iced cake, nice single, double, triple rooms, standard or deluxe, suites, children under 12 free, free city tour on a/c bus, walls a bit thin, restaurant, casino, Apdo 6241-1000, T2217272/2573130, F2210096.

AL *Europa*, C Central, Av 3, T2221222, F2214609, pleasant, comfortable rooms, cable TV, pool, central, good for business visitors, suites available, prior reservation recommended, rooms on street side can be noisy, good restaurant. **AL** *Fleur de Lys*, C13, Av 2-6, T2231206, F2573637, fleurdelys@sol.racsa.co.cr, mansion house, good restaurant, bar, recommended. **AL** *Gran Hotel Costa Rica*, C 3, Av 2, T2214000, F2213501, all right for 1 night stopover, food adequate, breakfast from 0400, buffet US$7, English-speaking staff, ground floor casino, noisy. **AL-A** *Doña Inés*, C 11, Av 2-6, PO Box 1754-1002, T2227443, F2235426, edelweis@sol.racsa.co.cr, clean, quiet, safe, Italian-run. **AL-A** *La Gran Vía*, C 3, Av Central, T2227737, F2227205, comfortable, helpful, good value. **AL-A** *Costa Rica Morazán*, C 7, Av 1, T2224622, F2333329, book in advance, rooms vary, some **B**, recommended by some, casino, parking, airport shuttle. **AL-A** *Presidente*, C 7, Av Central, T2223022, F2211205, extensively refurbished 1994/95. **AL-A** *Royal Dutch*, C 4, Av Central-2, T2221066, F2332927, suites, restaurant, recommended.

A *Best Western San José Downtown*, Av 7, C 6-8, T2554766, 1-800-5281234, F2554613, bath, TV, a/c, includes breakfast, rustic rooms, free coffee and bananas all day, pool, sauna, parking, recommended. **A** *La Mansión*, C9, Av 10, T2220423, F2227947, mansion@sol.racsa.co.cr, nice house, some noisy rooms, good restaurant. **A** *Mesón del Angel*, C20, Av3-3B, T2221997, F2232781, near Coca-Cola terminal, recommended.

B *Ara Macao*, Barrio California, 50m south of *Pizza Hut*, 5 minutes from centre, T2332742, includes breakfast, small, quiet. **B** *Classic B&B*, C20, Av 3, T2234316, F2573123, near Coca-Cola terminal, nice decor, TV, recommended. **B** *Diana's Inn*, C 5, Av 3, Parque Morazán, near *Holiday Inn*, an old building formerly used by the president, now restored, includes breakfast and taxes, discounts available, a/c, TV, hot water, noisy, luggage storage, safety box, T2236542, F2330493. **B** *Doral*, C 6-8, T2330665, F2334827, bath, TV, central, clean, helpful staff, soft mattresses, a bit noisy, restaurant. **B** *Galilea*, Av Central, C 13, T2336925, friendly, hot showers, back rooms quiet, rooms on C 3 have nice view of Plaza Democracia and Museo Nacional, run by Dutch lady, English and German also spoken. **B** *La Gema*, Av 12, C 9-11, T2572524, F2221074, bath, TV, pleasant, friendly. **B** *Park*, C 2, Av 4, T2216944, clean with bar. **B** *Plaza*, C 2, Av Central, T2225533, F2222614, TV, phone, bar, restaurant. **B** *Royal Garden*, C Central, Av 2, T2570023, F2571517, central, casino, Chinese restaurant, Dim Sum for breakfast. **B-C** *Aranjuez*, C 19, Av 11-13, T2561825, F2233528, shared or private bathroom, splendid breakfast, free coffee all day, hairdriers, friendly English speaking staff, clean, well-kept, nice gardens, bag store, recommended, Apdo 457-2070. **B-C** *Chalet Bavaria B&B*, C 19 y Av2-6, T2228597, for travellers, German-run, free laundry, airport pick-up, parking, hot water, cable TV, recommended.

C *Belmondo*, C 20, Av 9, T2229624, T2570816, 20 refurbished rooms, clean, includes breakfast, tiny pool. **C** *Brunelles's* bed and breakfast, T2351561, Bo Fletcher, Tibas, pick-up available. **C** *Casa Las Mercedes*, 700m west of Colegio Sión, Los Colegios district of Moravia, T2359280, book in advance, breakfast US$4, quiet, clean, good food, good base for extended stays (eg language students). **C** *Centroamericano*, Av 2, C 6-8, private bath, clean small rooms, very helpful, will arrange accommodation in other towns, free shuttle (Monday-Friday) to airport, laundry facilities, recommended. **C** *Diplomat*, C6, Av 2, T2218133, with bath, restaurant/bar. **C** *Fortuna*, Av 6, C 2 y 4, T2235344, quiet, helpful, recommended. **C** *Pensión de la Cuesta*, Av 1, C 11-15, T2552896, 4 rooms with shared bath, includes breakfast.

D *Bellavista*, Av Central, C 19/21, T2230095, breakfast included, friendly and helpful, with bath, clean, opposite *Dennies* restaurant. **D** *Bienvenido*, C 10, Av 1-3, T2332161, very clean, hot shower, good restaurant, near centre and airport bus, best hotel near Coca Cola bus station. **D** *Boston*, C Central, Av 8, T2210563, with or without bath, good, very friendly, but noisy, will store luggage. **D** *Capital*, Av 3-5, C 4, T/F2218583, remodelled, cable TV, bath, fan. **D-E** *Pensión Continental*, same address, T2331731, avoid small rooms downstairs, hot water, clean, friendly, laundry, helpful, coffee available, no meals except for breakfast, recommended. **D** *Berlín*, Av 8, C 2, clean, safe, quiet, fans, central, but seen better days. **D** *Cocorí*, C 16, Av 3, T2330081/2332188, with bath, hot water, by bus to Peñas Blancas, parking. **D** *Compostela*, C 6, Av 3-5, T2571514, bath, friendly, small rooms, family-run, quiet, door locked at 2300, recommended. **D** *Johnson*, C 8, Av Central, T2237633, friendly, clean, restaurant and bar, good value, popular with Peace Corps and cockroaches, recommended but can be noisy. **D** *San José*, C 14, Av 5, with shower, clean, friendly, near bus station. **D** *Príncipe*, Av 6, C Central-2, T2227983, with bath, top rooms best, quiet, friendly.

E *Aurora*, Av 4, C 8, T2221463, with bath, **F** without, good value, hot shower, nylon sheets and plastic mattress covers, sweaty, very noisy nightclub nearby (till 0500), rooms on 2nd floor are the least noisy, mixed reports, *Soda Aladino* next door is very good. **E** *Casa Ridgeway*, Centro de Amigos para la Paz, C 15, Av 6-8, T/F2336168, 1-4 beds in room, shared bath, use of kitchen, friendly, laundry possible. **E-F** *Gran Imperial*, C 8, Av 1-Central, T2227899, mixed reports, small rooms, thin walls, clean, sometimes noisy, limited hot showers, new laundry downstairs, more expensive than laundromat, restaurant with good prices, best to reserve, locked luggage store, good for meeting other travellers, notice board, TV. **E** *Crucero*, C4, Av 7-9, T2333124, basic but clean. **E** *Marlyn*, C 4, Av 7-9, T2333212, more with bath, hot showers, safe, will store luggage, parking for motorcycles (just). **E** *Generaleño*, Av 2, C 8-10, T2337877, with bath, cold water, good value. **E** *Oak Harbour Inn*, Av 3, C18-20,

Costa Rica

T2560041, laundry, with breakfast. **E** *Roma*, C 14, Av Central-1, T2232179, uphill from Alajuela bus station, clean, safe, good value but windowless rooms, stores luggage. **E-F** *Rialto*, Av 5, C 2, 1 block from Correos, shared bath, hot water, safe, friendly but can be very noisy.

F *Nuevo Rialto*, Av 1, C 6-8, popular but leave valuables with office, noisy rooms at front, recommended. **F** *Residencial Balboa*, Av 10, C 6, safe, cold shower, thin walls, basic, cheap; diagonally opposite *Gran Imperial* is **F** *Valencia*, C 8, Av 1, clean, friendly, noisy.

Barrio Amón **LL-L** *Barceló Amón Plaza*, Av 11, C 3b, in Barrio Amón, T2570191, F2570284, very helpful, clean, 75 rooms, plus suites new pink building, casino, restaurant, snack bar, underground parking.

AL *Britannia*, C 3, Av 11, T2236667, F2236411, britania@sol.racsa.co.cr, 1910 Spanish style restored mansion, high standard, antique furniture, very good service, excellent restaurant, worth the money. **AL** *Casa Morazán*, C7, Av 7, T2574187, F2574175, good restaurant, a/c, cable TV. **AL** *La Casa Verde de Amón*, C 7, Av 9, Barrio Amón, T2230969, casaverd@sol.racsa.co.cr, small, renovated old house, deluxe, good breakfast, helpful. **AL-A** *Don Carlos*, C 9, Av 7-9, T2216707, F2550828, hotel@doncarlos.co.cr, 36 rooms, interesting traditional building, much artwork and statuary, sundeck, free coffee, Annemarie's giftshop good selection, credit cards accepted, airport shuttle, tours arranged. **AL-A** *Dunn Inn*, Barrio Amón, C 5, Av 11, Apdo 6241-1000, T2223232/3426, F2214596, includes breakfast and local phone calls, *Rincón Tropical* restaurant. **AL-A** *Santo Tomás*, Av 7, C 3-5, T2550448, F2223950, hotelst@sol.racsa.co.cr, central, full payment requested in advance, credit cards accepted with 7% fee, several languages spoken, attractive décor, noisy. **AL-A** *Taylor's Inn*, Av 13, C 3-3b, T2574333, F2211475, taylor@catours.co.cr, with breakfast, old house nicely restored.

B *Hemingway Inn*, Av 9, C 9, T/F2211804, hemingway@ametisol.com, central, Spanish style, includes breakfast, patio and tropical garden. **B** *Hotel Rey Amón*, Av 7, C9, T2333819, parking, with bath, cable TV, breakfast. **B** *Joluva*, C 3b, Av 9-11, T2237961, F2577668, joluva@sol.racsa.co.cr, with breakfast, old house, friendly, safe, good laundry service, good value. **B** *Kekoldi*, Av 9, C 3b, T2233244, F2575476, kekoldi@sol.racsa.co.cr, old house imaginatively refurbished, colourful, 14 big rooms with bath, helpful, snacks and bar service, some traffic noise. **C** *Cinco Hormigas*, C15, Av 9-11, T/F2578581, cincohormigasrojas@crtimes.com, nice decor, small house, recommended.

Barrio Otoya **AL** *Al Alóki*, C 13, Av 9, T2231598, F2212533, john@aloki.com, US-owned, elegant 19th century restored mansion, antique furnishings, only 7 rooms, 20-seat restaurant recommended, book in advance, bar, patio, very pleasant, no credit cards, front doors locked at 2300. **AL** *D' Raya Vida*, bed and breakfast villa run by Michael Long, take Av 9 to C 17 (corner of emergency room of Hospital Calderón Guaria, turn left to end of street, then left on Av 11 (dead-end street, 50 metres) then right 100 metres to black gate, includes airport transfers, 4 double rooms, children by prior arrangement, meals available, wonderful garden, T2234168, F2234157, draya@yellowweb.co.cr. **AL-A** *Vesuvio*, Av 11, C 13-15, T2217586, F2218325, info@hotelvesuvio.com, includes breakfast, 20 rooms, private bath, secure parking, very quiet, comfortable, email, good restaurant, show your *Handbook* for 20 percent discount.

B *Edelweiss*, Av 9, C 13-15, 100m east of Condovac offices, T2219702, F2221241, edelweis@sol.racsa.co.cr, English, German and Spanish spoken, clean, comfortable, native hardwood furniture and carved doors, pleasant courtyard bar, helpful, friendly, recommended. **B** *La Amistad*, Av 11, C 15, T2580021, F2211409, Cell3812793, wolfgang@sol.racsa.co.cr, with breakfast, remodelled 1999, very popular, good value, with bath, TV, fan, net café, German owned.

Barrio Tournón **LL-L** *Radisson Europa San José*, T2573257, F2213976, modern, well-equipped, beautiful, gym, pools, bars, restaurant, café, conference facilities, church, casino, fine views.

AL *Villa Tournon*, T2336622, F2225211, attractive, excellent service, landscaped garden, pool, rooms facing the street are noisy from traffic a few minutes walk from El Pueblo (see **Shopping**).

On, or just off, Paseo Colón are **LL-L** *Quality Hotel Centro Colón*, near the Centro Colón building, off Paseo Colón, Av 3, C 38, T2572580, F2572582, luxury hotel.

AL *Parque del Lago*, T2578787, F2331617, Av 2, C 40, east side of La Sabana, airport courtesy van, breakfast buffet included. **AL** *Rosa del Paseo*, Paseo Colón, C 28-30, T2573213, F2232776, beautifully-restored mansion, breakfast included. **AL** *Ambassador*, C 26, Paseo Colón, T2218155, F2553396, central, modern, casino, bar, restaurant, coffee shop, cable TV, phone in rooms, travel agency, restaurants and cinemas opposite, cheaper to take your own taxi on the street, front rooms noisy from traffic, back rooms fine, nice suite. **AL** *Grano de Oro*, C 30, Av 2, T2553322, F2212782, granoro@sol.racsa.co.cr, converted 19th century mansion, 35 rooms and suites, beautiful terrace gardens, friendly, tasteful, good value.

B *Petit Victoria*, C 26, 50m from Paseo Colón, T2331812, F2225272, bath, minibar, cable TV, kitchen, convenient, breakfast included.

C *Cacts*, Av 3 bis, C 28-30, near *Pizza Hut* Paseo Colón, T2212928, F2218616, safe, good service, breakfast included, TV, friendly, recommended. **C** *Ritmo del Caribe*, Paseo Colón y C 32, T2212928, F2218616, ritmo_del_caribe@compuserve.com, simple, good, front rooms noisy, free airport shuttle, good value.

LL-L *Costa Rica Marriott*, near Juan Santamaría airport, 700m west of Firestone, San Antonio de Belén, T2980000, F2980011, 246 rooms, 2 pools, restaurants, golf, tennis. **LL-L** *Meliá Cariari*, near airport, T2390022, F2392803, pool, tennis, 18 hole golf course, celebrity hotel. **LL-L** *Herradura Resort and Convention Center*, near the airport, *Sakura* Japanese restaurant, pool, T2390033, F2392292, hherradu@sol.racsa.co.cr.

L-AL *San José Palacio*, near airport, T2202034, F2202036, part of the Barceló chain, all rooms a/c, fridge, cable TV, 1 executive floor, 5 normal floors, pool, spa, squash, tennis, sauna, casino, convention centre, caters for European tours, café, piano bar, restaurant, but out of town and few shops etc nearby.

AL *Irazú*, La Uruca, next to San José 2000 shopping centre, T2324811, F2324685, rates negotiable off-season, rooms without a/c, children under 12 free, casino, conference facilities, pool, tennis, sauna, recommended, transport downtown, hotel will organize excursions and visits, good pavement café, mixed reports.

In the area of **Los Yoses, San Pedro,** University of Costa Rica are: **AL** *Milvia*, 4 kilometres west of downtown in San Pedro, 250m northwest of De Muñoz y Nane shopping centre, T2254543, F2257801, arrractive boutique hotel, converted wooden mansion once the home of a 1930s revolutionary, personal service. **AL** *D'Galahi*, behind University of Costa Rica, San Pedro, pool, nice rooms and apartments, T2341743. **AL** *Don Fadrique*, Los Yoses, C37, Av 8, T2258186, F2249746, fadrique@sol.rasca.co.cr, nice hotel with restaurant, breakfast. **AL** *Le Bergerac*, C 35 Los Yoses, T2347850, F2259103, with continental breakfast, French atmosphere, fan, TV, restaurant, bar.

B *Tres Arcos*, Av 10, C 37-39, no 3773, Los Yoses, T2250271, Canadian-owned, close to restaurants, buses, nice area, includes breakfast.

C *Mr Tucker's Inn*, Los Yoses, T2537911 (in Canada 905-5625591), includes breakfast, some rooms with bath, comfortable, recommended, Mr Tucker has microbus for airport transfers, day trips, etc.

Apartotels (with kitchen, etc) can be cheaper for longer stays, weekly or monthly rates. **A** *Apartotel Los Yoses*, T2250033, Los Yoses, passably clean, comfortable beds, fridge and stove functional, tiny pool, attractive and secure area with supermarket, laundromat and restaurants nearby. **C** *Apartamentos Scotland*, C 27, Av 1, weekly or monthly for furnished apartments, T2230833, F2575317, scotland@sol.racsa.co.cr; also in San Pedro, near the University is **Casa Agua Buena**, rooms for US$150-250 per month, weekly rate also, common kitchen, telephone, TV, washing machine, comfortable, quiet, call Richard (Rick) Stern, T/F2342411, or write to Apdo 366-2200, Coronado, Costa Rica.

L *Corobicí*, Sabana Norte, T2328122, F2315834, Japanese-owned, casino, conference facilities, pool and fitness centre, rainforest and jungle tours (by *Río Colorado Lodge* office in hotel).

L-AL *Torremolinos*, C 40, Av 5 bis, T2225266, F2553167, LanChile office, bar, restaurant, pool, sauna, 200m from Sabana, near Yoahan commercial centre, free transport into town.
AL-A *Tennis Club*, Sábana Sur, Apdo 4964, T2321266, F2323867, 2-star, 20 minutes from centre, a/c, shower, TV, swimming pool, tennis courts, snack bar, restaurant, recommended.
AL *Apartotel Cristina*, Sabana Norte, T2311618, F2202096, aparcrit@sol.racsa.co.cr, new, pool, garage parking, coin laundry, a/c. **AL** *Apartotel El Sesteo*, Sabana Sur, 200m south of McDonalds, T2961805, sesteo@sol.racsa.co.cr, pool, new. **AL** *Apartotel La Sabana*, Sabana Norte, T2202422, F2317386, lasfromana@sol.racsa.co.cr, pool, sauna, parking, a/c.

Western suburbs Around **Escazú** and **Santa Ana** are **LL-L** *Camino Real* Próspero Fernández Highway, Multiplaza Mall, Escazú, T2897000, F2898998, 261 rooms, golf course and luxury spa, international business hotel poor location on city margin. **LL-L** *Tara Resort Hotel*, San Antonio de Escazú, T2286992, F2289651, taraspa@sol.racsa.co.cr, beautiful mansion, includes breakfast and transport, suites, conference facilities, recommended restaurant, pool, beautiful views, climb nearby Pico Blanco mountain. **LL-L** *San Gildar*, San Rafael de Escazú, T2898843, F2286454, pentacor@sol.racsa.co.cr, luxury.

AL *Posada Canal Grande*, Santa Ana, near airport, T2284101, F2825733, pool, peaceful area. **AL** *Posada El Quijote*, Bello Horizonte de Escazú, Apdo 1127-1250, T2898401, F2898729, renovated colonial house with modern art collection, with bath, hot water, cable TV, breakfast included, gardens, 15 minutes from centre, 15 minutes from airport, airport pickup available (in USA Dept 239-SJO, PO Box 025216, Miami, FL 33102-5216, T800-5706750, ext 8401). **AL** *La Casa de las Tías*, 100m south of Centro Comercial El Cruce, San Rafael de Escazú, T2895517, F2897353, with breakfast, 5 rooms with bath, fan, airport pickup. **AL** *Pine Tree Inn*, Trejos Montealegre Escazú, T2897405, F2282180, 15 rooms with bath, cable TV, pool. **AL-A** *Amstel Escazú*, T2897681, F2820620, 14 rooms, 2 suites, pool, parking. **AL-A** *Tapezco Inn*, 50m south of San Miguel church, Escazú, T2281084, F2897026, with breakfast, pool, sauna, jacuzzi. **AL-A** *Villa Escazú Bed and Breakfast*, 1 kilometre southwest of Escazú, near bus route, 4 rooms with private or shared bathroom, large gardens and patio, T/F2289566, ask for Inéz or Mary Ann. **AL-A** *Bonaire*, Escazú, English-speaking bed and breakfast, nice, friendly, T2280866.

A *Pico Blanco Inn*, San Antonio de Escazú, T2281908, F2895189, all rooms with balconies and views of Central Valley, several cottages, English owner, restaurant with English pub, Costa Rican flavour, pool, airport pickup can be requested, recommended.

C *Linda Vista Lodge Bed and Breakfast*, Escazú, cosy rooms, spectacular views.

Apartotels LL *Apartotel Villa de Rio*, San Rafael de Escazú, T2898833, F2898627, cable TV and VCR, gymnasium, pool, transportation to city centre.

Pensiones are **D** *Astoria*, Av 7, No 749, T2212174, but rooms vary, cockroaches, hot showers, uncomfortable beds, thin walls, noisy. **D** *Musoc*, C 16, Av 3-5, T2229437, with or without private bath, very clean, hot water, luggage stored, will do laundry, friendly, near (and somewhat noisy) bus stations, but recommended.

E *Araica*, Av 2 No 1125, T2225233, without bath, clean, dark, thin walls, friendly. **E** *Reforma Hilton*, C 11, No 105, with bath, T2219705, restaurant. **E** *Superfamiliar*, Av 2, C 9-11, shared bath. **E** *Moreno*, C 12, Av 6-8, T2217136, with bath. **E** *América*, Av 7, C 4, T2214116, clean, large rooms, good value. **E** *Otoya*, C 1, Av 3-5, T2213925, clean, friendly, luggage store, hot water, English spoken, use of phone, recommended.

F *Americana*, C 2, Av 2, without bath, large rooms, friendly, luggage store, laundry facilities. **F** *Boruca*, C 14, Av 1-3, Coca Cola market, T2230016, without bath, hot water, laundry service, popular with Peace Corps. **F** *Corobici*, Av 1, C 10-12, cold shared showers, run down, like a men's boarding house. **F** *Managua*, C 8, Av 1-3, small rooms, basic, hard beds, cold shared showers, clean and cheap, safe, helpful, will wash clothes, recommended.

Tica Bus terminal **E** *Avenida Segunda*, Av 2, C 9-11, T2220260, price varies, friendly, stores luggage. **F** *Salamanca*, Av 2, C 9-11, cold water, adequate. **F** *Tica Linda*, Av 2, No 553 (tiny sign),

T2330528, friendly, noisy, some beds uncomfortable, fairly clean, little privacy, cheap laundry, good information, will store luggage, good place to receive international phone calls, 'gringo' place, often full, next door is the *Esmeralda Mariachi Palace*, Av 2, C 5-7, large restaurant/bar with live bands playing requests, which operates all night except Sunday. There are several hotels in **F** range near the various markets, such as the *Comerciante* annex, C 10, Av 3-5, quite clean; *España*, Av 3-5, C 8, run by a Spanish family. Cheaper hotels usually have only wooden partitions for walls, so they are noisy. Also, they often rent only by the hour. **NB** Hotels in the red light district, C 6, Av 1-5, near Mercado Central, charge on average US$10 with toilet and shower for a night. **NB also** It is difficult to find cheap hotels with parking, but next to *Ribadavia*, C Central, Av 7-9, is a 24-hour parking lot. There are a couple of cheap *parqueos* on C 9 Av 1-3 with cheap hotels in the vicinity.

Toruma Youth Hostel, the only official YHA member in Costa Rica, T2244085, Av Central, C 31-33, 95 beds, restaurant, clean, hot water not always available, crowded but safe, lockable compartments in each room, **E** per person including breakfast, **D** for those who do not hold ISIC or YHA membership; music, free for guests, on Friday and Saturday nights; a good place for meeting other travellers to arrange group travel. You can leave bags there safely for US$0.50 per day. Youth hostel information: Recaj, PO Box 10227, 1000 San José. Discounts at affiliated hotels and lodges (see text) are available if reservations are made through Recaj. **Youth Hostel**

For B-and-B accommodation in San José and Costa Rica contact *Costa Rica Bed and Breakfast Group*, c/o Michael Long, Apdo 493-1000, San José, or at *D'Raya Vida*, T2234168, F2234157 (see above); also Pat Bliss, *Park Place*, Escazú, T/F2289200, corpfaxi@sol.racsa.co.cr. They have over 30 inns and hotels in their directory. **B** *Diana's Inn*, Av 3, C 5, 1 block from *Aurora Holiday Inn*, T2236542, F2330495, dianas@sol.racsa.co.cr, helpful, friendly, small breakfast, noisy. **Bed & breakfast**

Belén, in San Antonio de Belén, 2 kilometres west of intersection at Cariari and San Antonio, 5 kilometres from airport, turn off Highway 1 on to Route 111, turn right at soccer field then 1st left for 1 kilometre, T2390421, F2391316, US$10 per day, American-owned, shade, hot showers, laundry, friendly, recommended, good bus service to San José. **Trailer Park**

Sixteen kilometres east of San José near Tres Ríos, 1 kilometre south of Pan-American Highway, turn off signed to Istaru Campo Escuela, 1st *finca* on the right is *Para Las Orejas*, where you can camp, bathrooms available, T/F2799752, back-packing Spanish goats for hikers, goats' milk. **Camping**

Eating

Apart from the hotels, the best ones are the *Bastille*, French type (limited choice), on Paseo Colón. *La Hacienda Steak House*, C 7, Av Central-2, expensive but good, upstairs is a good Mexican *taquería*. *La Estancia* in El Pueblo, typical Costa Rican steakhouse, be sure to use the garlic sauce, recommended. *La Tranquera* (parking space) on the highway to Cartago at Curridabat, 6-8 kilometres east of San José, serves good steaks and other foods (orchestra for dancing at weekends). *Los Ranchos* Steak House, Sabana Norte near *Hotel Corobicí*, reliable, good food. *Casa de Matute Gómez*, mansion built in 1930, famous landmark in Barrio González Lehmann; on north side of old La Sabana airport on Av 3 and about C 50 are 2 good restaurants, *El Chicote* (country-style; good grills) and *El Molino*. *Los Anonos*, in Escazú area, grills. Also *La Flecha*, Centro Colón Building, Paseo Colón, superb. *Lobster Inn*, Paseo Colón, C 24, T2238594, seafood, large choice, expensive. *La Cocina de Leña*, El Pueblo, seafood, excellent menu, upmarket, pricey. *Marbella*, Centro Comercial de la C Real, San Pedro de Montes de Oca, T2249452, fish, packed on Sunday, very good. *La Casa de los Mariscos*, Los Yoses. *Italiano*, Carretera a Sabanilla, 1 block north of Av Central; *Machu Picchu*, C 32, Av 1-3, good, recommended. *Peruveana*, also C 32, Av 1-3, reasonable prices. *Al Andalus*, Av 7 y 9 C, T2576556, Spanish, Costa Rican and international, nice atmosphere, reasonable. *Goya*, Av 1, C 5-7, Spanish food. *Casa de España*, in Bank of America, C 1, good lunches. *Masia de*

Costa Rica

Triquell, Edif Casa España, Sabana Norte, T2963528, Catalan, warmly recommended, closed Sunday. *Tomy's Ribs*, Av 6, C 11-13, good barbecued beef and pork. *Antojitos*, on Paseo Colón, on Pavas Highway west of Sabana and in Centro Comercial Cocorí (road to suburb of San Pedro), serves excellent Mexican food at moderate prices. *El Balcón de Europa*, C 9, Av Central-1, Italian, great atmosphere, popular, but some dishes rather small and tasteless. *Pizzería Finisterre*, next door, similar menu, good pizzas, recommended, but cheaper if slightly less posh. *Pizza Metro*, Av 2, C 5-7, good Italian, small and cosy, not cheap, recommended. *Pasta Factory*, Av 1, C 7, excellent Italian, recommended. *San Remo*, C 2, Av 3-5, also Italian, local food too, *menú del día*, recommended, friendly service, good value, frequently recommended (closed Sunday). *Café Mundo*, Av 9, C 13-15, opposite *Hotel Edelweiss*, old mansion tastefully restored, good salads, pasta etc. *La Esquina del Café*, Av 9, C 3b, speciality coffee roasters but also good restaurant, souvenir shop, live music twice a month, daily 0900-2200. *La Esmeralda*, Av 2, C 7, reasonably priced, clean, good local dishes, live Costa Rican music in the evenings, recommended. *Morazán*, C 9, Av 3, facing Parque Morazán, not touristy, popular with locals, friendly, excellent breakfast, delicious blackberry juice.

Chinese   *Fortuna*, Av 6, C 2-4; *Kaw Wah*, Av 2, C 5-7, recommended. *Kuang Chaou*, C 11, Av Central-2. *Lung Mun*, Av 1, C 5-7, reasonably priced. *Tin Jo*, C 11, Av 6-8, T217605, good Chinese and other Asian dishes. *Wing On*, Av 7, C 13-15, good, cheap. Also recommended, *Fu Lu Su*, C 7, Av 2, Chinese, Korean, very good. *Tin Hao*, Av 10, C 4, T2211163, good. *Corona de Oro*, Av 3, round the corner from the Post Office, good and cheap. and *Kam King*, Av 10, C 19-21. *Jardín Jade*, Av 4, C 4-6, good value.

Vegetarian   *Don Sol*, Av 7b No 1347, excellent 3 course lunch US$1.60, run by integral yoga society (open only for lunch). *Vishnu*, Av 1, C 1-3, good quality, cheap and good *plato del día*, try their soya cheese sandwiches and ice cream, sells good wholemeal bread, also on C 14, Av 2, open daily, 0800-2000. *El Edén*, Av 5, C Central, same food and prices as *Vishnu*. *La Mazorca*, in San Pedro, near University of Costa Rica (Rodrigo Facio site), vegetarian and health foods. *La Nutrisoda*, Edif Las Arcadas, open 1100 to 1800, homemade natural ice cream; *Laxmi*, Av 8, C 8. *Macrobiótica*, C 11, Av 6-8, health shop selling good bread. *Naturama Uno*, Av 1, opposite Omni building, cheap. *Shakti*, Av 8, C 13, excellent. *Soda Vegetariana*, next to Librería Italiana. *Musab de San José*, 75 metres north of municipalidad de Montes de Oca, San Pedro, T2241163, excellent.

Fast food   *Churrería Manolo*, Av Central, C Central-2 (new restaurant upstairs), and another branch on Av Central, good sandwiches and hot chocolate. *Comedor* beneath 'Dorado' sign, C 8, Av 4-6, very cheap. *Pollo Obay*, Av 10, 6 C, good fried chicken. *Pollo Tico*, Av 1, C 10-12, variety of meals with good dishes around US$1, popular, open 24 hours. *La Fánega*, in San Pedro, for excellent hamburgers, folk music some nights. *La Geishita*, C Central, Av 14, cheap *casado*. *Las Condes*, C 11, Av Central-1, inexpensive. *Lido Bar*, C 2, Av 3, for *casado*. *Orléans*, also in San Pedro, serves crêpes. *Pastel de Pollo*, C 2, Av 6-8, excellent pies. *Pizza Hut*, C 4, Av Central-2, also several other branches, open Sunday, good value pasta and salad, popular, queues to get in, recommended. *Salón París*, Av 3, C 1-3, recommended. *Soda Amón*, C 7, Av 7-9, good, cheap *casados*. *Soda Coliseo*, Av 3, C 10-12, next to Alajuela bus station, recommended. *Soda La Casita*, Av 1, C Central, clean, breakfast US$1.25. *Soda La Luz*, Av Central, C 33, good filling meals, cheap. *Soda Magaly*, Av Central, C 23, near Youth Hostel, good, cheap. *Soda Maly*, Av 4, C 2-4, Chinese and tico, good. *Soda Nini*, Av 3, C 2-4, cheap. *Soda Poás*, Av 7, C 3-5, good value. *Soda Puntarenas*, C 12, Av 7-9, good for light meals and breakfast, open 0500-2200. *Soda El Parque*, C 2, Av 4-6, good wholesome meals around US$3, clean. *Soda Brenes*, Av 10, C Central-2, simple, delicious *olla de carne*, big portions, cheap. *La Vasconia*, Av 2, C 5, restaurant and soda bar, good breakfast. *The Sandwich*, good all-night soda, 1 block north of Ticabus station.

Autoservicios do not charge tax and service and represent best value; they also sell beer: *Corona de Oro*, Av 3, C 2-4 (next to *Nini*) excellent, and *Kings*, Av 1, C 1-3, opposite Cine Omni. Food bars in restaurants in the Mercado Central (C 6-8) are good for breakfast and lunch, but none of them is open in the evening, high standards of sanitation. Try *Soda Flor de Costa Rica*, entrada Noroeste, pabellón de las flores, very good and cheap meals, very clean, open 0700-1800, T2217881. At lunchtime cheaper restaurants offer a set meal called a *casado*, US$1.50-2.50, which is good value; eg in the snack bars in the *Galería* complex, Av Central-2, C 5-7. Try *Chichorronera Nacional*, Av 1, C 10-12, very popular, or *Popular*, Av 3, C 6-8, good *casado*. *El Merendero*, Av 6, C 0-2, cheap local food, popular with Ticos.

Helados Rena, C 8, Av Central, excellent. Also *Helados Boni*, C Central, Av 6-8, home-made ice cream. *Pops*, near Banco Central, and other outlets, for ice cream (excellent). *Heladería Italiano*, excellent ice cream. Also for ice cream *Holanda*, Av Central, C Central and other outlets in San José, great ice cream. *Spoon*, Av Central, C 5-7, good coffee and pastries, gives 10% ISTC discount. *Fudge*, Centro Comercial Los Lagos, Escazú, coffee and pastries. *El ABC*, Av Central, C 9-11, self-service, good, clean, cheap. *La Selecta* bakeries recommended. *Le Croissant*, Av Central, C 33, good French bakery. *Café del Teatro*, in foyer of National Theatre, reasonably priced, belle époque interior, popular meeting place for poets and writers, pleasant for a snack. At the bus station women sell *panbon* and delicious coconut pies.

Ice cream, confectionery, etc

Bars and Nightlife

Good places to have a drink include *Josephine's*, Av 9, C 2-4, T2564396, 2572269, striptease, expensive; and *El Cuartel de la Boca del Monte*, Av 1, C 21-23, live music at weekends, popular, recommended, 60's atmosphere, entrance US$5.40 but worth it. *Chelle's*, Av 0, C 9, excellent bar. *Las Abejas*, C 1, gay disco. *Las Rosas*, C 1, Av Central, bars on 3 floors, good. *Nashville South*, C 5, Av 1-3, popular. *Beatles*, C 9, Av Central, good music, popular with ex-pats. *Centro Comercial El Pueblo* has restaurants, bars and 2 discos.

Bars

Grill La Orquídea at the *Hotel Balmoral*. *Les Moustaches* in Centro Colón, Paseo Colón, C 38, expensive. Many restaurants and bars with varying styles of music at El Pueblo centre on road to San Francisco (take 'Calle Blancos' bus from C 1, Av 5-7, alight 500m after river); also 3 discos here, *Cocoloco*, *Infinito* (US$2.90, not crowded) and *La Plaza* (very luxurious, US$2.90, great discothèque). Discos in the centre: *Kamakiri*, on the way to Tibas; *Top One* (US rock music); *La Rueda* (for the over 30's); *Bikini Club*, C 7, Av 0-1, topless dancing, cheap. Other nice, less expensive dance spots downtown: *El Túnel del Tiempo*, *Talamanca* and *Disco Salsa 54* (do not wear shorts, they will not let you in); *La Torre*, C 7, Av Central-Av 1, popular gay disco. Also *Montecarlo*, corner of C 2, Av 4 (Parque Central); *El Cuartel de la Boca del Monte*, see under **Bars**. Nightspots west of C 8 are in the red light district. Some hotels have **casinos** with Black Jack and a sort of roulette shooting an arrow on a revolving wheel. No entrance fee, no formal dress required. Some nightspots do not appreciate long haired men. You can buy chips with colones or dollars from the croupier and once you start to play, the drinks and cigarettes are free. The casino at the *Gran Hotel Costa Rica* has been recommended.

Nightclubs

Entertainment and shopping

Cinemas Many excellent modern cinemas showing latest releases. *Sala Garbo*, Av 2, C 28. *Cinemateca* at the UCR's Abelardo Bonilla auditorium (university), San Pedro, shows good films at 1700 and 1900 daily. Prices, US$2.50-US$3. See *La Nación* for films and times. See also under **National parks**, page 1042.

Entertainment

Theatres All are closed on Monday. *Teatro Nacional*, Av 2, C 3-5 (recommended for the productions, the architecture and the bar/café), US$1.15 for guided tour, behind it is La Plaza de la Cultura, a large complex. *Teatro Carpa*, outdoor, alternative; plays, films, C 9, opposite Parque Morazán. *Teatro Tiempo* (also called Sala Arlequín), C 13, Av 2-Central. *Compañía Nacional de Teatro*. *Teatro Melico Salazar* on Parque Central for popular, folkloric shows every Tuesday, T2214952. *Teatro del Angel*, Av Central, C 13-15. 3 modern dance companies. All good.

Festivals **28 to 31 December**. Festivities last from 18 December to 5 January, with dances, horse shows and much confetti-throwing in the crowded streets. The annual El Tope horse parade starts at noon on 26 December and travels along the principal avenues of San José. A carnival starts next day at about 1700 in the same area. Fairs, firework displays and bull running (anyone can take part!) at El Zapote, frequent buses from the centre. Also parades during Easter week in the streets.

Shopping Market on Av Central, C 6-8, open 0630-1800 (Sunday 0630-1200), good leather suitcases and wood. Mercado Borbón, Av 3-5, 8-10, fruit and vegetables in abundance. More and more *artesanía* shops are opening, eg **Mercanapi** (a cooperative, cheaper than most, C 11, Av 1) and **Mercado Nacional de Artesanía** (C 11, Av 4), and others on Av Central, C 1-3. *La Casona*, a market of small *artesanía* shops, C Central, Av Central-1, is interesting, lots of little stalls. For jade, try **Brazil Gems**, Parque Morazán. In Moravia (8 kilometres from centre) *El Caballo Blanco*, T2356797, workshops alongside, and **HHH** are good for leather work. The leather rocking chairs (which dismantle for export) found in some *artesanía* shops are sometimes cheaper in Sarchí. **Amir Galería de Arte**, Av Central, C 1-3, Edif Galería Nacional for local paintings (will send paintings abroad promptly). Coffee is good value and has an excellent flavour (although the best quality is exported). **Automercados** are good supermarkets in several locations (eg C 3, Av 3). Generally, shopping is cheaper in the centre than in the suburbs. At the international airport on the 2nd floor, above Continental airlines ticket counter, you can buy cut orchids which are approved by the USDA and Canadian Department of Agriculture, T4877086.

El Pueblo, near the *Villa Tournon Hotel*, is an area of shops, bars, restaurants and discos, built in a traditional *'pueblo'* style. Another big new shopping centre is at San Pedro, on the eastern ring road. Also *Multiplaza Mall*, near *Camino Real*, Escazú, excellent shops, lots of cinemas.

Bookshops *The Bookshop*, Av 11, C 3-5, in Casa Amón, ½ block west of *Hotel Amstel Amón* in Barrio Amón (T2227619), good selection of English language books (double US prices), buys second-hand books, but no exchange, very good range, some English, art gallery, café, open 0900-1800. *Universal*, Av Central, C Central-1, T2224038, for Spanish books and maps. *Lehmann*, Av Central, C 3, F2336270, maps (large-scale topo maps not always in stock), Spanish, a few English books and magazines. *7th Street Books*, C 7, Av Central-Av 1, T2232240, F2234128, wide variety of new and used books in English including *Footprint Handbooks*, book exchange, open Monday-Saturday 0900-1800, Sunday 1000-1800. *Librería Italiana*, C 3, Av Central-1, English, French, Italian books, German magazines. *Staufer*, near Centro Cultural, Los Yoses, also in Centro Comercial San José 2000 and Plaza del Sol shopping mall in Curridabat, English and German books. *Mora Books*, Av 1, C 3-5, in Omni building above *Pizza Hut*, large selection of used books, reasonable prices. *Librería Vlate* book exchange, Av 6, C 3-5, has large choice of Spanish books and a few in English. *Gambit*, Av 3, C 5-7, Los Yoses, T2830603, used books, English, French, German. *Librería Internacional*, Barrio Dent, 400m west of Taco Bell in San Pedro, T2836965, English, German and Spanish titles at about 20% over US prices, special order service. *Jiménez*, C Central, Av 3-5, excellent for maps of San José and the country. *Casa de las Revistas*, C 5, Av 1-3, foreign papers, magazines, books and local publications, postcards. *Periódicos Americanos*, in the Yaohan Shopping Centre, Sabana Norte, T2214664, best selection of magazines and some books. *Kiosko La Catedral*, opposite Parque Central, sells American magazines, newspapers from several countries, including *Financial Times*, books, postcards and gifts; Candy shop next to *Gran Hotel Costa Rica* has good selection of magazines and newspapers in English, German etc.

Photography One-hour colour processing available at all *IFSA* (Kodak) branches, poor reports received. Fuji processing in 1 hour at *Universal* stores. *Taller de Equipos Fotográficos*, 120m east of kiosk Parque Morazán, Av 3, C 3-5, 2nd floor, T2231146 (Canon repairs – authorized workshop); *Tecfot*, Av 7, C Central, T2211438, repairs all types of cameras, good service, reasonable rates. Film prices are well above those of Europe. *Video Camera Rentals*, Av 7, behind *Aurola Holiday Inn*, T2570232, US$29 per day, US$168 per week for Panasonic

'Palmcorders'. *Warning*: The X-ray machine at Juan Santamaría airport is not filmsafe, regardless of what the airport security guards try to make you believe.

Bungee jumping: after Rafael Iglesias Bridge (Río Colorado), continue on Pan-American   **Sport**
Highway 1½ kilometres, turn right at *Salón Los Alfaro*, down track to Puente Colorado. *Tropical Bungee* operate 0800-1400 Saturday and Sunday, available weekdays for groups of 5 or more, US$45 1st jump, T2336455; full moon and water dips on request. *Geoventuras Bike Tours* run tours from San José, Tuesday, Thursday, and Saturday, 0800, return about 1700, US$85 including lunch, T2212053. **Golf**: *Costa Rica Country Club* (San Rafael de Escazú), 9 holes; *Hotel Meliá Cariari Country Club* (near San José), 18 holes. *Los Reyes Country Club* (near Alajuela), 9 holes. *Hotel Tango Mar Beach Resort* (Playa Tambor), 9 holes. *Hotel Meliá Playa Conchal* (Playa Conchal), 18 holes. **Swimming pools**: the best is at Ojo de Agua, 5 minutes from the airport, 15 minutes from San José. It is open until 1700; direct bus from Parque Carrillo, Av 2, C 20-22, US$0.25 or take bus to Alajuela via San Antonio de Belén. There is also a pool in La Sabana (at west end of Paseo Colón), entrance US$3, open 1200-1400, about 2 kilometres from the city centre. Open air pool at Plaza González Víquez (southeast section of city).

Transport

Buses: bus fares in **San José**: large buses: US$0.10, small: US$0.15 from the centre outwards.   **Local**
Hand baggage in reasonable quantities is not charged, but no trunks of any kind are taken. A cheap tour of San José can be made on the bus marked 'periférico' from Paseo Colón in front of the Cine Colón, a 45-minute circle of the city. A smaller circle is made by the 'Sabana/Cementerio' bus, pick it up at the Parque Morazán or on Av 3; a 'Cementerio/Sabana' bus does the route in reverse.

Car rentals: Most local agencies are to the north of Paseo Colón. **Budget**, C 30, Paseo Colón, T2233284, open Monday-Saturday, 0800-1900, Sunday, 0800-1800, also at international airport, T4414444, open Monday-Sunday, 0600-2100, and at *Hotel Cariari*; **Avis**, Sabana Norte, T2329922; **Dollar**, C Central, Av 9, T2333339, good rates; **Hertz**, C 38, Paseo Colón, T2211818/2235959, F2211949; **Meir**, good rates for four-wheel drive but check insurance, C 11, Av 14, T2574666; **Adobe**, T2215425, F2219286, adobe@centralamerica.com, in North America T1-800-8261134, in Spain Oky de Costa Rica, 101761.2005@compuserve.com, Japanese cars and four-wheel drive, drop-off at the beach if you fly Travelair, flexible insurance, drivers aged 18-21 accepted with US$1,500 on credit card; **National**, C 36, Av 7, T2334044, easy to get on to autopista for Alajuela; and many local ones (**Elegante**, C 10 Av 13-15, T2210066, F2215761, PO Box 30-1005, San José, cars, jeeps, vans, minimum age 23, has branches throughout the country, mixed reports). Various companies at airport, including **Ada**, T2337733, F2335555, AutosADA@sol.racsa.co.cr, www.icr.co.cr/ada, cars and jeeps, similar prices to Adobe; **Santos**, T4413044; **Hertz**, T4410097. Never leave anything in a hired car, always use car parks in San José, never leave your car on the street, even in daylight. Car parking costs US$1.25 per hour, worth it when so many cars are broken into. Regular reports of robbery in the National Parks.

Car repairs: at *Repuestos Tiribí SA*, Desamparados, 50m south of Puente Tiribí, Swiss-owned, helpful, T2591098.

Motorcycle rental: from **Heat Renta Moto**, Edif Ofomeco, p 7, 2 Av, 11 y 13 C, T2216671, F2213786, with offices in other tourist centres, for motorcycles, scooters, mountain motorbikes, US$30-35 per day, US$5-7 per hour, deposit US$500; **Moto Rental SA**, Thilo Pfleiderer, Paseo Colón 26, T2327850, Suzuki Enduro for US$200 pw unlimited mileage, deposit US$500 or credit card (see also **Motoring**, page 1046).

Motorcycle repairs: *Taller Daytona 500*, in Pavas, 200m east of US Embassy, T/F2201726, run by Roberto Dachner, who speaks Spanish, English and Hebrew. *Harleymania*, in Pavas, T/F2201726, F2353953, repairs to all makes of motorcycle.

Costa Rica

Cycle Repairs: *Cyclo Quiros*, Apartado 1366, Pavas, 300m west of US Embassy, the brothers Quiros have been repairing bikes for 20 years, good place for general info and repairs, highly recommended.

Taxis: minimum fare US$0.63 for 1st kilometre, US$0.32 additional kilometre, 20% extra 2200-0500. Waiting time US$3.15 per hour. To order a taxi, T2545847, 2359966. Taxis are red and should have electronic meters (called 'Marías'). Short journeys in the city are around US$2-3, bargain if you feel the price is too high. For journeys over 12 kilometres price should be negotiated between driver and passenger. Look in the classified adverts of the *Tico Times* for car and driver hire.

Long distance   **Air**   The Juan Santamaría international airport (SJO) is at El Coco, 16 kilometres from San José by motorway (5 kilometres from Alajuela). Airport information, 24 hours, T4432622. The Sansa terminal for domestic flights is next to the main terminal. There is another terminal about 1 kilometre west of the main terminal used by charter flights and private planes. Bus from Av 2, C 10-12, or Av 2, C 12-14, every 10 minutes from 0500-2100, US$0.50 (good service, plenty of luggage space), or by Alajuela bus via the motorway from C 14, Av 5-7. Taxi to and from airport, US$12-13 (can be less if ordered in advance), US$15 at night; Sansa runs a free bus service to the airport for its passengers. Taxis run all night from the main square to the airport and for early flights, you can reserve a taxi from any San José hotel the night before. All taxi companies run a 24-hour service. During the holiday period (December-January), Juan Santamaría airport allows only ticketed passengers into the main terminal at peak times of 0600-0830, 1100-1400. Bank at the airport open 0800-1600; at other times try car rental desks, the restaurant cash desk or money changers at the entrance. ITMs at the airport accept international Visa and Mastercard. ICT has a helpful tourist office in the main terminal for maps, information and hotel reservations (but be careful you are not paying too much if you take this service). There is also a booth near the exit. X-ray machines reported unsafe for film (see **Photography** above). There is a hotel at the airport, **AL** *Hampton Inn*, T4430043, F4429523 (toll free within Costa Rica 800-HAMPTON), courtesy pick-up to both terminals (see **Alajuela Sleeping**). Services at the airport are generally inadequate.

Travelair and light aircraft use the Tobias Bolaños airport (SYQ) at Pavas, about 8 kilometres west of San José.

Internal flights: Sansa (next to the main terminal at Juan Santamaría airport) and **Travelair** (from Tobias Bolaños) operate internal flights throughout the country. Sansa check-in is at office on Paseo Colón, C 24, 2 hours before departure (free bus to and from airport). Check schedules on 2219414 or 2333258, F2552176. Sansa airport office T4418035/4411401. For Travelair reservations, T2961102, 2963408, F2200413. If you made reservations before arriving in Costa Rica, confirm and collect tickets as soon as possible after arrival. Book ahead, especially for the beaches. In February and March, planes can be fully booked 3 weeks ahead. On all internal scheduled and charter flights there is a baggage allowance of 12 kilograms/25 pounds. Oversized items such as surfboards, bicycles etc are charged US$15 if there is room in the cargo hold.

From San José you can fly to Barra del Colorado, Coto 47, Golfito, Jacó, Liberia, Nosara, Palmar Sur, Puerto Jiménez, Punta Islita, Quepos, Sámara, Tamarindo, Tambor, Tortuguero.

Charter flights: Veasa, T2321010, F2327934, long-established, at Pavas; Alfa Romeo Aéreo Taxi, at Pavas, T2964344, and Puerto Jiménez, T7355178, Capitán Alvaro Ramírez. Helisa (Helicópteros Internacionales) operate helicopter sightseeing flights to Monteverde etc, T2229212, F2223875.

Long distance buses   There are services to most towns, see text for details of times, prices etc. Check before leaving where the bus stops at your destination, some routes do not go to the centre of towns, leaving passengers some distance away. Up to date timetables can be obtained from the Instituto Costarricense de Turismo (Infotur), Av 10, C 3 No 868, T2234481. Alternatively a free leaflet *Hop on the Bus*, giving times but no prices, is distributed by Ecole Travel and KitCom and published on the internet, updated every 2 months, www.yellowweb.co.cr/crbuses.html. Bus stations are scattered around town (see map): **Alajuela** (including airport) from Av 2, C 10-14 during the day, from Av 2, C 2 after 2400. **Cahuita, Limón, Manzanillo, Puerto Viejo de Talamanca, Sixaola** from Terminal Caribe (Guapileños, Caribeños, Sixaola); **Jacó, Carará, Quepos, Manuel Antonio, Uvita** from Terminal Coca Cola; **Cañas, San Isidro de El General** (2 companies, Musoc and Tuasur), **Santa Cruz** (½ block west), **Peñas Blancas** (100m north) from outside Terminal Coca Cola; **Cartago** from Terminal Cartago during the day, after 2030 from *Gran Hotel Costa Rica*, Av 2, C 3-5; **Ciudad Quesada (San Carlos), Fortuna, Guápiles** (Braulio Carrillo), **Los Chiles, Caño Negro, Monteverde** (outside terminal), **Puerto Jiménez** (outside terminal), **Puerto Viejo Sarapiquí, Tilarán** (½ block north) from Terminal Atlántico Norte; **Playa del Coco, Liberia** from C 14, Av 1-3; **Golfito, Nicoya, Nosara, Palmar Norte, Paso Canoas, Sámara, San Vito, Tamarindo** from Terminal Alfaro; **Heredia** from Terminal Heredia or a minibus from Av 2, C 10-12; **Irazú volcano** from Av 2, C 1-3, opposite *Gran Hotel Costa Rica*; **Poás volcano** from Av 2, C 12-14; **Puntarenas** from Terminal Puntarenas; **Santa María de Dota** from Terminal Los Santos; **Turrialba** from Terminal Turrialba.

International buses It is important to check how far in advance you must book tickets for international buses; in December-January, buses are often booked 2 weeks ahead, while at other times of the year outside holiday seasons, there is no need to book at all.

Sirca (250 metres norte Hospital San Juan de Dios, T2569072, open Sunday-Friday, 0800-1700, Saturday 0800-1200) has a new service with video and a/c to Managua.

Ticabus terminal is at C 9-11, Av 4 (T2218954), office open Monday-Sunday 0600-2200, book before Saturday for Monday buses. It is here that all refund claims have to be made (have to be collected in person). Ticabus to **Guatemala City**, 0600, 0730, 60 hours, US$35, with overnight stay in **Managua** and **San Salvador**. To **Tegucigalpa**, 0600, 0730, 48 hours, overnight stay in Managua. To Managua, US$15, 11 hours including 1 hour at Costa Rican side of border and another 2 hours on Nicaraguan side while they search your bags for drugs. The Ticabus journey from San José to **Panama City** leaves at 0600, 0730, 2200 daily, US$20 one-way, 20 hours (book at least 3 days in advance), check if you are interested. To get a Panamanian tourist card one must buy a return ticket. **NB** The Ticabus from Panama City tends to arrive early, even at 0300, and you are left on the street. There is a 24-hour café nearby if you wish to avoid the expense of a hotel.

Transnica, C22, Av 3-5, T2210953, runs new buses with TV, video, a/c, snacks, toilet, to **Managua** daily at 0530 and 0900, US$12 one way. Before departure have your ticket confirmed on arrival at the terminal; when buying and confirming your ticket, you must show your passport. When boarding the bus you are given an immigration form.

Nicabus at Gran Terminal del Caribe, T2564248, to Managua 0600 and 0830, US$12.50 one way, US$20 return.

Panaline goes to Panama City daily at 1400 from C 16, Av 5, T2551205, US$22 one way, US$41 return, reduction for students, arrives 0700. TV/video, a/c, payment by Visa/Mastercard accepted.

To **David**, from Terminal Alfaro, US$18 (buses daily at 0730 and 1200, 9 hours); book in advance. They are modern, comfortable buses, although there is not much room for long legs, but they have the advantage of covering a scenic journey in daylight. A bus to **Changuinola** via the Sixaola-Guabito border post leaves San José at 1000 daily, 8 hours, US$8, from opposite Terminal Alfaro, T5561432 for information, best to arrive 1 hour before departure; the bus goes via Siquirres and is the quickest route to **Limón**.

Directory

Airline offices Addresses (and telephone numbers) of major airlines: *Copa*, Av 5, C 1 (2226640, 2226650). *SAM*, Paseo Colón, C 38-40, Edif Centro Colón, p 2 (233-3066). *Lacsa*, Av 5, C 1 (2960909). *Sansa*, Paseo Colón, C 24 (2219414, see **Internal flights** below). *Taca*, Av 3, C 40 (2221790). *Nica*, T2554949. *Mexicana*, C 5, Av 7-9 (2576334), Mexican Tourist Card available here. *Saeta*, C 13, Av 11, T2235648. *Varig*, Av 5, C 3-5 (2570094). *Servivensa*, Edif Centro Colón, p 2, Paseo Colón, C 38-40 (2571441). *TWA*, Paseo Colón, C 34-36 (2214638), F2230226. *Continental*, Oficentro La Virgen No 2,

200m south, 300m east and 50m north of American Embassy, Pavas (2964911, 2330266). *British Airways*, C 13, Av 13, Edif Teral II, No 1314, T2235648. *Delta*, Paseo Colón, C 40, Edif San Jorge (2572433). *Iberia*, Paseo Colón, C 40 (2278266). *KLM*, Sabana Sur, behind Contoralaría General Building (2204112). *Lufthansa*, C 5, Av 7-9 (2217444). *Air France*, Condominio Vista Real, p 1, 50m west and 10m north of POP's, Curridabat, T2800069. *Swiss Air*, C Central, Av 1-3 (2216613). *Singapore Airlines*, Av 1, C 3-5 (2553555). *Lloyd Aéreo Boliviano*, Av 2, C 2-4, upstairs (2551530). *American*, opposite *Hotel Corobicí*, Sabana Este (2571266). *Aviateca*, Av 3, C 40 (2338390, 2554949). *Alitalia*, C 38, Av 3, Centro Comercial Los Alcazares (2226138). *Aeroperlas*, 150m east of *Hampton Inn*, Juan Santamaría airport, T4400093. *Aeroperú*, Av 5, C 1-3 (2237033, 2285842). *LTU International Airways* (German charter airline), Condominio da Vinci, Oficina No 6, Barrio Dent, T2349292. *Condor Airlines* (German charter airline), C 5, Av 7-9, T2217444. *Aero Costa Rica* (to Miami and Orlando), 200m north of Fuente de la Hispanidad, San Pedro (2962020 for reservations). *United Airlines*, Sabana Sur, behind Contoralaría General Building, T2204844 (at airport). *Korean Air*, Edif Alde, p 1, C 1, Av Central-1 (2221332). *Travelair*, T2327883, 2963408, F2200413 (see **Internal Flights** below).

Banks Opening times: Mon-Fri, 0900-1500. *Banco Nacional* (see page 1044), head office, Av 3, C 2-4, will change TCs into dollars but you pay a commission, accepts Visa credit cards as do most of the bigger banks in San José and other major towns; another branch in INS building, C 11, Av 7-9, long queues to change TCs. *Banco de Costa Rica*, Av Central, C 4, changes TCs, open 1030-1700, long queues, 3% commission. *Banco de San José*, C Central, Av 3-5, commission 2.5%. Money can be sent through Banco de San José or Banco de Costa Rica at 4% commission. Credit card holders can obtain cash advances from Banco de San José (Visa, Mastercard) and Credomatic Los Yoses in colones (Mastercard ATM) and Banco Popular y Desarrollo (Visa ATM). minimum cash advance: US$50 equivalent. ATMs which will accept international Visa/Mastercard are available at most banks, shopping malls and San José airport. *Banco Crédito Agrícola de Cartago*, 9 branches, also makes advances on Visa, no commission, no limits. *Scotiabank*, C Central, Av 2, Visa cash advances, charges 0.49% commission on currency exchange. For emergencies, eg loss of card, Mastercard/Visa T2570155, Amex T001-800-5282121, Diners Club T2572351 (Mon-Fri), T2577878 (Sat-Sun). Banks may charge whatever commission they please on TCs (no commission on US$ cash) and other services: shop around for the best deal. The best exchange rates for Amex TCs can be found at American Express (see **Travel agents** below). *Banco Mercantil*, Av 1, C Central-2, has safe deposit lockers for US$15 per month. A legal 'parallel' market has existed since Feb 1992, the centre for which is the corner of Av 2, C 2, also all around the *Banco Central* (beware fake notes, in particular US$100 notes), up to 10% better rates, will even accept TCs. Take all the usual precautions. *Hermanos Villalobos Money Exchange*, recommended, better rate for cash than TCs; Ed Schyfter, C 2, Av 1-Av Central, p 2, behind Banco Central. Most hotels will change dollars (cash or TCs) into colones, but only for guests; hotels cannot sell dollars, however.

Communications Post Office: C 2, Av 1-3, open for sale of stamps Mon-Fri, 0700-1700, Sat-Sun 0700-1800 (outside these hours stamps may be bought from the lottery seller who sits under the big tree opposite the Post Office entrance). Stamp vending machine in main Post Office. Post Office charges 50 colones for receiving letters (*Lista de Correos*, open Mon-Fri 0800-1700, quick service). Couriers: *DHL*, Paseo Colón, C 30-32, T2231423. *Jet Ex* (Federal Express agent), on Pavas road, T2316610, F2311488. *UPS*, Av 3, C 30-32, T2577447, F2575343. **Telephone and cable services:** faxes and internal telegrams from main Post Office. Fax or cable abroad from RACSA, Av 5, C 1, T2232720, F2231609, 0730-2100, charges per page, also receives for US$1, unlimited pages, internet access and email, US$3 per hr (see **Essentials**). *ICE, Instituto Costarricense de Electricidad*, Av 2, C 1, has a fax service, also phone calls here (phone card only), open 0700-2200, 3 mins call to UK US$10, friendly service (cheaper than Radiográfica, but check). Some shops offer fax service. Collect telephone calls can be made from any public telephone. English speaking operators are available. See also under **Essentials**. Email: *KitCom*, 3rd level Edif Ferencz, C 3 y Av 3, T2580303, F2580606, send and receive email, fax, voice mail, kitcom@yellowweb.co.cr, US$2 for 30 minutes, free coffee, Mon-Fri 0830-2000, Sat 0930-1700, has bus information. *Cyber Café*, 2 Av between ICE and *Gran Hotel Costa Rica* in Las Arcadas, 0700-1900 daily, T2333310, F2333430, cybercafe@searchcostarica.com, popular. Another at Plaza San Pedro No 7, 50m west of Banco Popular, T2247295, F2247382, open 24 hrs, www.internetcafecr.com.

Cultural centres Centro Cultural Costarricense Norteamericano, C 37, Av 1-5, Los Yoses, T2259433, good films, plays, art exhibitions and English-language library, open to 1930, free. *Alianza Franco Costarricense*, Av 7, C 5, French newspapers, French films every Wed evening, friendly.

Embassies & consulates *Nicaraguan*, Av Central, C 25-27, opposite *Pizza Hut*, T2222373, 2333479, 2338747, Mon-Fri, 0830-1200, US$25, dollars only, passport photo, 24-hr wait for visa or sometimes less. *Panamanian*, C 38, Av 7 (275m north of Centro Colón building, Paseo Colón area), T2253401, tough about onward ticket, open 0900-1400, you need a photograph and photocopy of your passport, visa costs US$10 cash and takes up to 24 hrs, if they tell you to come back after 1300 to collect your visa, be there at 1245. *Honduran*, Del Itan, 300 Este y 200 Nte, T2349502. *Salvadorean*, C 30, Paseo Colón-Av 1, Casa 53, T2249034, receives documents 0900-1300, returns them 1430-1500. *Guatemalan*, De la *Pizza Hut* en Plaza del Sol, Curridabat, 50m east, 100m north, 50m east, Casa No 3, T2832555, F2832556, open Mon-Fri, 0900-1300, visa given on the spot, US$10 in some cases (dollars only, see Guatemala **Information for travellers**). *Mexican*, Consulate, Av 7, C 13-15, T2570633, 2214448, Mon-Fri 0830-1200 to receive documents, returns them 1500-1600. *Argentine*, 400m south of *MacDonalds*, Curridabat, T2216869, 2346270, 0800-1530, Mon-Fri. *Brazilian*, C 20-22, Av 2, T2575484, T2331092. *Chilean*, Los Yoses, 50m Este, 225m Oriente del Automercado, T2244243. *Colombian*, Barrio Dent, de Taco Bell San Pedro 150m Oeste, casa mano derecha, T2836861, F2836818. (Mon-Fri 0900-1200), issues free tourist cards for Colombia, but onward ticket must be shown and sometimes 2 photos provided. *Ecuadorean*, Sabana Sur, Colegio Médicos 100m east, 125m southwest, T2321503, 2311899, open Mon-Fri 0800-1100, 1200-1400. *Paraguayan*, T2539487. *Peruvian*, Los Yoses, 200m Sur, 50m Oriente del Automercado, T2259145. *Uruguayan*, Los Yoses, Av 14, C 35-37, T2349909. *Venezuelan*, Los Yoses, de la 5ta entrada, 100m south, 50m west, consulate open Mon-Fri 0900-1230, T2255813, 2258810, visa issued same day, US$30, helpful. *US*, Consulate and Embassy (T2203939, 0800-1630 Mon-Fri, T2203127 after hours and weekends), in the western suburb of Pavas, opposite Centro Comercial, open Mon-Fri, 0800-1630 (0800-1000 only for visa applications), catch a ruta 14 bus to Pavas Zona 1 from Av 1 and C 18. *Canadian*, Building 5 (3rd floor) of Oficentro Ejecutivo La Sabana, Sabana Sur, T2964149, F2964270. *Japanese*, Rohrmoser, de la Nunciatura 400m Oriente y 100m Norte, T2321255. *South Korean*, Rohrmoser, 200m Oriente y 100m Sur Entrada Blvd de Rohrmoser, T2203160. *Israeli* C 2, Av 2-4, Edif Parque Central, p 5, T2216444, 2216011. *British*, Centro Colón, p 11, end of Paseo Colón with C 38 (Apdo 815-1007), T2215566. *German*, Rohrmoser, 200m Norte y 75m Este de la casa de Oscar Arias, T2325533, open Mon-Fri, 0900-1200. *Swiss*, Paseo Colón, Centro Colón, p 10, C 34/36, T2330052, open Mon-Fri, 0900-1200. *French*, Curridabat, 200m south, 25m west of Indoor Club, T2250733. *Belgian*, Av 3, C 35-37, T2256633. *Dutch*, Oficentro Ejecutivo La Sabana, Sabana Sur, Mon-Fri 0900-1200, T2961490. *Italian*, Los Yoses, Av 10, C 33-35, T2246574. *Spanish*, Paseo Colón, C 32, T2221933. *Norwegian*, Centro Colón, 10th Flr, T2571414. *Polish*, T2251481. *Russian*, T2721021.

Hospitals & medical services Dentists: *Clínica Dental Dr Francisco Cordero Guilarte*, T2323645, Sabana Oriente, opposite Colegio La Salle, take bus marked Sabana Estadio. *Dra Fresia Hidalgo*, Uned Building, San Pedro, 1400-1800, English spoken, reasonable prices, recommended, T2342840. *Dr Otto J Ramírez González*, C 14, Av Central, Noreste Hospital San Juan de Dios, Edif Maro, T2334576, speaks only Spanish. *Fernando Baldioceda* and *Silvia Oreamuno*, 225m north of Paseo Colón on the street which intersects at the Toyota dealership: both speak English. *Alfonso Villalobos Aguilar*, Edif Herdocía, p 2, Av 3, C 2-4, T2225709. Doctor: *Dr Jorge Quesada Vargas*, *Clínica Internacional*, Av 14, C 3-5, speaks German. Consultations: *ILPES*, 50m sur de la Mucap Los Yoses, hotline for emergencies, information on where to go, covers AIDS etc, English and Spanish speakers, T2833374, or 2832532, Mon-Fri 1300-1800. Hospitals: Social Security Hospitals have good reputations (free to social security members, few members of staff speak English), free ambulance service run by volunteers: Dr Calderón Guardia (T2224133), San Juan de Dios (T2220166), México (T2326122). The *Clínica Bíblica* C 1, Av 14, 24-hr pharmacy (T2236422) and *Americana* Av 14, C Central-1 (T2221010), have been recommended. both offer 24-hr emergency service at reasonable charges and have staff who speak English. better than the large hospitals, where queues are long. Inoculations: Bíblica will arrange TB vaccinations, prepares Spanish summaries of treatment, medication, etc, accepts credit cards, and has emergencies it cannot handle. Yellow fever inoculation, *Ministerio de Salud* (Av 4, C 16), Dpto de Enfermedades Epidémicos, Dr Rodrígo Jiménez Monge, or at his private clinic, C 5, Av 4, T2216658. Free malaria pills also from Ministerio de Salud, from information desk in office to left of ministry. Although the Ministerio de Salud does not have a stock of gamma globulin (Hepatitis A), they will inject it free if you buy it in a pharmacy. Dermatologist: *Dr Elias Bonilla Dib*, C Central, Av 7-9, T2212025. Red Cross Ambulance, T2215818.

Language schools The number of schools has increased rapidly. Listed below are just a selection recommended by our readers. Generally, schools offer tuition in groups of 2-5 over 2-4 weeks. Lectures, films, outings and social occasions are usually included and accommodation with families is encouraged. Many schools are linked to the university and can offer credits towards a US course. Rates, including lodging, are around US$1,000 a month. *Instituto Universal de Idiomas*, Av 2, C 9, T2570441,

F2239917, stresses conversational Spanish. *Costa Rican Language Academy*, Av Central, C 25-27, Apdo 336-2070 Sabanilla, Montes de Oca, T2338938, 2338914, F2338670, run by Aída Chávez, offers Latin American music and dancing as well as language study and accommodation with local families. *Academia Latinoamericana de Español*, Aptdo 1280, 2050 San Pedro, Montes de Oca, T2249917, F2258125, recommended. the *British Institute (Instituto Británico)* in Los Yoses, teaches English and Spanish, T2349054, F2531894, antonio@yellowweb.co.cr, Apdo 8184, 1000 San José. *Intensa*, C 33, Av 5-7, Barrio Escalante, PO Box 8110-1000, T2246353, 2256009, F2534337. *Instituto de Lenguaje Pura Vida*, T2370387, F2606269, Apdo 890-3000, Heredia, in USA T714-5340125, F5341201, airport pick-up, 5 days', 7 days' accommodation with local family, 2 meals a day, cultural activities, US$330 but can be less if they need to fill spaces. *Central American Institute for International Affairs*, Apdo 10302, San José, T2338571, F2215238, conversation Spanish courses. *Comunicare*, Apdo 1383-2050, San José, T/F2244473, offers language study (staying with families), volunteer work, and cultural activities. *Intercultura Costa Rica*, Apdo 1952-3000, Heredia, T2608480, F2609243, info@ spanish-intercultura.com, intensive courses with excursions to beaches, volcanoes, etc, homestays available. *AmeriSpan*, PO Box 40513, Philadelphia, PA 19106-0513, T800-8796640 (USA and Canada), 215-9854522 (elsewhere), F215-9854524, info@amerispan.com, has affiliated schools in San José, Escazú, Alajuela and Heredia. *Academia Tica*, PO Box 1294-2100, T2290013, F2927186, www.arweb.com/actica/. *Instituto de Español Costa Rica*, Apartado 1405-2100 Guadalupe, T/F2834733, iespcr@sol.racsa.co.cr, English, French and German spoken.

Laundry Washing and dry cleaning at Centro Comercial San José 2000, 0730-2000, US$3.75 for large load. *Sixaola*, branches throughout San José, US$3.50 a load, 2 hrs dry cleaning available, expensive. *Martinizing*, US franchise, at Curridabat, Sabana Oriente (by new ring road) and Escazú, recommended. *Lavandería Costa Rica*, Av 3, C 19-21, US$5 for a large load. below *Hotel Gran Imperial*, US$3 to wash, US$3 to dry, quick and very friendly. *Lavandería*, C 8, Av Central-1, T2582303. Several on C Central, Av 10-12. *Lavandería Alemana*, C19, Av 2-6, cheap, recommended.

Libraries *Biblioteca Nacional* (opposite Parque Nacional, has art and photography exhibitions), open Mon-Fri 0830-1630. *Universidad de Costa Rica*, in San Pedro suburb.

Places of worship Protestant, in English: *The Good Shepherd*, Sun 0830, Av 4, C 3-5, T2221560 (Anglican). *Union Church*, Moravia, T2356709, services 1000. free bus service from downtown hotels. times and locations given in Fri *Tico Times*. *International Baptist Church*, in San Pedro, 150m north from ex-Banco Anglo Costarricense corner, on San Pedro or Periférico bus route, T2537911 for information or to contact Pastor Dr Tom Hill, prayer line T2440569, English services at 0900 on Sun, Spanish services 1800, Sun school at 1100, nursery provided, Chinese services at 1100 on Sun. Bible study on Wed evenings, T2342943 for information. *Escazú Christian Fellowship* (Country Day School campus), Sun 1730, T2315444. *Victory Christian Centre* (from Hermanos Monge Gas Station, 200m south, 100m east, 200m south, Santa Ana, free shuttle bus, T2408571, Sun 1000). **Roman Catholic** services in English at *Herradura* Hotel, 1600 every Sun. *Centro de los Amigos para la Paz*, Quaker, English books, US periodicals, information, T2210302.

It is much cheaper to take tours aimed at the local rather than the foreign tourist market.

Tour companies & travel agents *Swiss Travel Service*, in *Hotel Corobicí*, T2314055, PO Box 7-1970, F2313030, with branches in *Hotels Sheraton, Irazú, Cariari, Amstel Amon* and *Balmoral*, large agency, good guides, much cruise business, warmly recommended. *Viajes Alrededor del Mundo*, T2236011, at the *Holiday Inn*, Eduardo Ureña is recommended for finding cheap flights to South America. *Tam Travel Corporation*, 4 branches, one in *San José Palacio Hotel*, open 7 days a week, PO Box 1864, 24-hr

Costa Rica

answering service T222-2642/2732, F2216465. *LA Tours*, PO Box 492-1007, Centro Colón, T2214501, F2245828, Kathia Vargas extremely helpful in rearranging flights and reservations. *Aviatica*, C 1, Av 1, T2227461, helpful for airline tickets. *Agencia Super Viajes*, American Express representative, Oficientro Ejecutivo La Sabana, Edif #1 Sabana, Apdo PO Box 3985, T2200400. *COOPRENA* (National Eco-Agricultural Cooperative Network of Costa Rica), is a group supporting small farmers, it offers tours of mangroves, rainforests, farms, beaches, etc, US$35 per day (accommodation and food included), contact Leilo Solano, Apdo 6939-1000, San José, T259-3401/8442, F2599430, for more details. *Aventuras Naturales*, Av Central, C 33-35, T2253939, offers white water rafting. Those specializing in naturalist tours include: *Costa Rica Expeditions*, Av 3, C Central/2, upmarket wildlife adventures include white water rafting (US$89 for 1-day trip on Río Pacuare, includes lunch and transport, good, other rivers from US$69-85) etc, they own *Tortuga Lodge, Corcovado Lodge Tent Camp, Monteverde Lodge* and *Costa Rica White Water*. PO Box 6941-1000, T2570766/2220333, F2571665, costaric@expeditions.co.cr. www.expeditions.co.cr. staffed 365 days a year, 0530-2100, also answering service, highly recommended, good range of postcards in their souvenir shop next door. *Horizontes*, C 28, Av 1-3, T2222022, F2554513, horizont@sol.racsa.co.cr, high standards, educational and special interest, advice given and arrangements made for groups and individuals. *Ríos Tropicales*, Paseo Colón, next to Mercedes Benz, PO Box 472, 1200 San José, T2336455, F2554354, specialists in white water rafting and kayaking, good selection and careful to assess your abilities, good food, excellent guides, US$250 for 2-day trip on Río Pacuare, waterfalls, rapids, including camping and food. *Sarapiquí Aguas Bravas*, T2922072, F2294837, white water rafting on various rivers. *Costa Rica Sun Tours* 'Eco-Center' offers reservations and Sansa ticketing for adventure or nature lovers, regular departures for Arenal, Monteverde, Corcovado, Tortuguero and Manuel Antonio, Av 4, C 36, T2553418, 2553518, F2554410, www.crsuntours.com, tours can often be arranged at very short notice, warmly recommended. *Ecole Travel*, C 7, Av Central-Av 1, T2232240, F2234128, ecolecr@sol.racsa.co.cr, Chilean-Dutch, tours to Tortuguero, Corcovado etc and tailor-made excursions off the beaten track. *Typical Tours*, p 2-3, Las Arcadas, next to the *Gran Hotel Costa Rica*, PO Box 623-1007, T2338486 24 hrs, F2338474, city tours, volcano tours, nature reserves, rafting, cruising. *Braun Eco Tourism*, Av 8-10, C Central (in *Hotel Ritz*), T2331731, F2228849, basic but beautiful tours to out of the way places, recommended, but tour guides need to improve their biology. *Exotur*, T2275169, F2272180, Nella Fiorentini, very helpful, recommended. *Green Tropical Tours*, C 1, Av 5-7, T/F2552859, tours to Guayabo National Monument, Los Juncos, Cloud Forest etc.

Arena Tours, Av 7, C 13-15, tours to Tortuguero, US$74, includes boat transport, food, accommodation, 1 night. *Jungle Lodge*, T2330133, F2330778, to Tortuguero channels, 3 days, 2 nights, includes transport from San José via Siquirres to Puerto Hamburgo, very good wildlife. Day tours to the Gulf of Nicoya with transport from San José including: luxury yacht cruise on the *Fantasia* (T2550791) to Tortuga Island, Wed, Sat, Sun, from San José US$65 including lunch. *Calypso Island Cruise* Wed, Fri, Sun, US$69 including lunch, T2333617. *Bay Island Cruises* to Tortuga Island (T2965551, F2965095). *Blue Sea Cruises*, T2337274, to Tortuga Island. *Cruceros del Sur*, T2201679, F2202103, PO Box 1198-1200, Pavas, San José, offers cruises to Curú Wildlife Refuge and Tortuga Island, US$79. *Costa Sol Cruises*, Wed, Fri, Sat, Sun, US$70 including breakfast and lunch, visits beach near Tambor. *Seaventures Yacht*, 2-night packages, floating hotel visits Cabo Blanco Nature Reserve in Gulf of Nicoya (T2200722). *Aerolíneas Turísticos de América*, T2321125, F2325802, run charter flights around central Costa Rica from Tobias Bolaños airport, US$65 per person per hr, minimum 4 persons. *Armo Tours*, C1, Av Central-1, T2572620, F2571389, armotour@sol.racsa.co.cr, highly recommended for national tours, service, German, English, French, Italian spoken. *The Costa Rica Company*, Terra Nova, Apartado 11666-100, T2577317, F2577348, mcastro@nacion.co.cr, tree-top canopy tours in the rain forest.

Tourist offices *Instituto Costarricense de Turismo*, information office: p 11, ICT building, Av 4 C 5-7, T223-1733/8423, toll free 800-012-3456, open Mon-Fri 0800-1600. Also at Juan Santamaría airport (very helpful, will check hotels for you) and at borders. Road maps of Costa Rica, San José and the metropolitan area and public transport timetables available. **Infotur** computerized hotel reservation and information system at Av 10, C 3, T2234481, check whether there is a commission (reports of 20%) before making a booking. *Otec, youth and student travel office*, extremely helpful, C 3, Av 1-3, Edif Ferenz, T2560633/2570633, F2332321, apdo 323-1002 San José, special discounts, for ISTC and FIYTO members, has discount booklet for shops, hotels, restaurants, museums, cinemas, theatres, tourist attractions and more, excellent for travel arrangements, special student airfares to Latin America, US, Europe, bus and car rental arrangements, good tours of Costa Rica. The *Instituto Geográfico*, Av 20, C 9-11 at Ministry of Public Works and Transport, supplies very good topographical maps for walkers, 0730-1200 (which can be bought, at higher prices, at Librerías Universal and Lehmann). *American Express* office has good, free maps of San José. New up-to-date maps are available at most bookstores. Recommended city map published by Jitan, US$3.

Useful addresses Immigration: on the airport highway, opposite Hospital México. you need to go here for exit visas, extensions, etc. If they are busy, you could queue all day. To get there, take bus 10 or 10A Uruca, marked 'México', then cross over highway at the bridge and walk 200m along highway. Better to find a travel agent who can obtain what you need for a fee, say US$5. Make sure you get a receipt if you give up your passport. **Judiciary:** thefts should be reported in San José to Recepción de Denuncias, Organismo de Investigación Judicial, C19, Av 6-8, T2550122.

Useful phone numbers Emergency: **Police:** T117. **Fire:** T118. **Police, Fire, Red Cross** (bilingual operators): T911.

The Meseta Central

Hilly and fertile, the temperate climate makes this a major coffee growing area. Fairly heavily populated, with picturesque and prosperous towns, each with a unique church, built in the shadow of volcanoes.

The Meseta central: east

Cartago

*Population: 30,000
Altitude: 1,439m
22½ km from San José
on a toll road
(US$0.75)*

Cartago stands at the foot of the Irazú volcanic peak and is encircled by mountains. It was founded in 1563 and was the capital until 1823. The town is small, though the neighbourhood is densely populated. Earthquakes destroyed it in 1841 and 1910, and it has been severely shaken on other occasions. That is why there are no old buildings, though some have been rebuilt in colonial style.

Sights The most interesting church is the **Basílica de Nuestra Señora de Los Angeles**, the Patroness of Costa Rica, rebuilt 1926 in Byzantine style; it houses **La Negrita**, under 15 centimetres high, an Indian image of the Virgin which draws pilgrims from all over Central America because of great healing powers attributed to it. In the Basilica is an extraordinary collection of very finely-made silver and gold images, no larger than three centimetres high, of various parts of the human anatomy, presumably offered in the hope of being healed. Worth seeing is the old parish church (**La Parroquia**), ruined by the 1910 earthquake and now converted into a delightful garden retreat with flowers, fish and humming birds. There is an impressive procession on Good Friday.

Excursions **Aguas Calientes** is four kilometres southeast of Cartago and 90 metres lower. Its *balneario* (warm water swimming pool) is a good place for picnics. Four kilometres from Cartago on the road to Paraíso is the **Jardín Lankester orchid garden** (run by the University of Costa Rica, T5519877), 10 minutes' walk from the main road (ask bus driver to let you out at Campo Ayala, Cartago-Paraíso bus, departs every 30 minutes from south side of central park in Cartago, 15 minutes), taxi from Cartago, US$3; the best display is in April. Although off the beaten track, the gardens are definitely worth a visit; open 0800-1500 daily except Christmas, Easter and New Year, US$3.10. One kilometre further on is Parque Doña Ana (La Expresión), a lake with picnic area, basketball courts, exercise track and bird watching, open 0900-1700, US$0.50. Get off bus at Cementerio in Paraíso and walk one kilometre south. At Paraíso, *Restaurant Continental* is recommended.

Ujarrás (ruins of a colonial church and village) is six and a half kilometres east of Cartago by a road from Paraíso and is on the shores of the artificial Lago Cachi. There is an hourly bus from Paraíso. Legend has it that in 1666, English pirates, including the youthful Henry Morgan, were seen off by the citizens of Ujarrás aided by the Virgin. The event is now celebrated each 16 April when the saint is carried in procession from Paraíso to the ruined church.

Another road runs southeast from Paraíso through a beautiful valley to the small town of **Orosi**, in the enchanting Orosi valley, down which flows the tumultuous Reventazón. Here are magnificent views of the valley, a 17th century mission with colonial treasures (closed on Monday), and just outside the town two *balnearios* (bathing, US$1.60) and restaurants serving good meals at fair prices. The *miradores* of Ujarrás and Orosi both offer excellent views of the Reventazón valley. **B** *Los Angeles B&B*, Av 4, C14-16, T/F5510957, clean, nice rooms. **C** *Hotel Río*, T5333128, F5333057, 2 pools, dirty. **F** per person *Montaña Linda*, from bus stop cross the football field, turn left and after 2 blocks turn right, hotel at end of road, near hot springs, T5333640, cabins, double rooms and dormitory, hot showers, share kitchen, bicycle hire, camping or hammock US$2, owner Marco runs tourist information. *Getting there:* Bus from Cartago, from southwest corner of ruined church, hourly 0800-2200, 40 minutes, or microbus 1330, 1530, every 45 minutes on Sunday, US$0.30.

A beautiful one-day drive is a circular route from Cartago to Orosi, then opposite Orosi, on the other side of the Reventazón, to **Palomo**, **D** *Río Palomo*, cabins, pool, laundry facilities, good restaurant. Continue round the Presa de Cachi to **Cachi** where there is a dam with artificial lake (very popular with residents of San José, Charrarra buses from one block north of Cartago ruins, several daily). The Charrarra tourist complex, with a good campsite, good restaurant, swimming pool, boat rides on the Orosi River and walks, can be reached by direct bus on Sunday, otherwise 30-minute walk from Ujarrás. The road goes on round the north side of the lake to Ujarrás, then back to Cartago. From the dam, a dirt road continues down the valley 15 kilometres to Tucurrique (**C** *Los Rápidos*, pleasant cabins, restaurant, good birding and horseriding, owner rents rafts with guide for US$100 per day, English and German spoken). It is here where white water rafting begins. A start has been made to pave the road.

Sleeping

E *Casa Blanca* in Barrio Asís, 2 kilometres from centre, easy walk, not very clean, no sheets, hot water, clean towels, noisy all night. **F** *El Rey*, C 5, Av 6-8, very dirty. **F** *Familiar Las Arcadas*, at railway station (rents rooms hourly late into the night). **F** *Venecia*, cold water. **F** rooms to rent in private house, Armando Cortéz, 350 Sur de Las Ruinas, T5511316.

Eating

Salón París, very good food. *City Garden*, Av 4, C 2-4. *Puerta del Sol*, in front of the Basilica. *Pizza Hut*, opposite La Parroquia ruins. *Auto 88*, east of public market, meal US$2-3, cafetería style, beer drinking room adjoining dining room. Restaurants, among other places, are closed on the Thursday and Friday of Holy Week, so take your own food.

Festivals

The *feast day* is **2 August**, when the image is carried in procession to other churches in Cartago and there are celebrations throughout Costa Rica.

Costa Rica

Shopping **Bookshop** *Librería Cartago*, C 1, Av 2-4. **Market** There is a market facing the train station.

Transport From **San José** buses from Terminal Cartago every 10 minutes, 0500-2400, 45 minutes, return 0445-2300, on Friday-Saturday also 2400-0500, hourly, after 2030 buses leave from *Gran Hotel Costa Rica*, Av 2, C 3-5.

Directory **Banks** *Banco Fincomer* changes TCs quickly with 1% commission. **Communications** Post Office: the main post office is at C 1, Av 2-4, near the park.

Volcán Irazú

Colour map 5, grid B2 Forty kilometres from Cartago is the crater of Irazú (3,432 metres). Irazú crater is a half-mile cube dug out of the earth, and all around is desolate grey sand, with little wildlife other than the ubiquitous Volcano Junco, a bird like a dunnock, and the few plants which survive in this desert. The phrase 'it's like the surface of the moon' describes Irazú quite well. The clouds come down early, obscuring the view, but if you can get there early (no entrance gate) it is wonderful to see the sun shining on the mountain and the clouds in the valley.

Admission There is a small museum. National Park rules forbid visitors to walk around the crater: on the north side is a 'Prohibido pasar' sign, which should not be passed. The only permitted walk is on the southerly side, which ends before the high crest. ■ *0800-1530 most of the year; from 1 December-30 April 0800-1700 on Friday, Saturday, Sunday, normal hours other days, US$6.*

Sleeping & On the way up are the **D** *Hotel Montana* (not very helpful, no keys to rooms), **E** *Hotel Irazú*,
eating T2530827, and 10 kilometres further on, the **D** *Bar-Restaurant Linda Vista*, has rooms, one of the highest restaurants in Central America at about 3,000 metres; near Rancho Redondo, west of Volcán Irazú, is **AL-A** *Hacienda San Miguel*, T2295058, F2291097, includes breakfast, restaurant, pool, horseriding, jacuzzi, steam bath, lake, magnificent views, continental divide passes through property, Pacific and Caribbean slope birds to be seen.

Transport A yellow 'school' express bus run by Buses Metropoli SA T2720651, runs from San José Saturday, Sunday and holidays, 0800 from *Gran Hotel Costa Rica*, stops at Cartago ruins 0830 to pick up more passengers, returns 1215 with lunch stop at *Restaurant Linda Vista* (whose every internal surface is covered with business cards, bank notes, etc), US$6. A public bus leaves 0730 on Saturday from the same place, Av 2, C 3, in front of the hotel. Taxi from Cartago is US$24 return (it is very difficult to get taxis to return for you in the morning if you have stayed at the crater overnight). A taxi tour from Orosi costs US$10 per person, minimum 3 people, and stops at various places on the return journey, eg Cachi dam and Ujarrás ruins. Beware of theft from hired cars. Overnight parking US$3. Since it can be difficult to find a decent hotel in Cartago, it may be easier to take one of the guided tours leaving from San José, about US$30; tours to Irazú and Orosi valley US$28-30. Horse riding tour, 5½ hours includes lunch, transport from San José, T2552011, US$70. It is possible to get a bus from Cartago to Tierra Blanca (US$0.33) and hitch a ride in a pick-up truck. Alternatively you can take a bus from Cartago to Sanatorio. Ask the driver to drop you at the crossroads just outside Tierra Blanca. From there you walk to the summit, 16 kilometres. 1½ kilometres from the crater a road leads to Laguna Verde; the road is paved, but steep beyond the Laguna. If driving from San José, take the turn-off at the *Ferretería San Nicolás* in Taras, which goes directly to Irazú, avoiding Cartago. On Saturday and Monday a bus goes from Cartago to San Juan, 12 kilometres from the summit (0630 and 1300); **E** *Hotel Gran Irazú*, comfortable, clean.

Tapantí Twelve kilometres beyond Orosi is the **Refugio Nacional de Fauna Silvestre**
National Park **Tapantí**, run by the Forest Service, on the headwaters of the Reventazón. It is a
From June to 5,113-hectare reserve of mainly cloud forest and pre-montaine humid forest with
November-December 211 species of birds recorded, including the quetzal which nests in late spring and
it rains every can be found on the western slopes near the entry point. Jaguar and ocelot are found
afternoon.

Irazú: clouds and views

"Stupendous views: you look down on mountain tops, clouds, light aircraft. Wear good shoes and a hat, the sun is strong. Those with sensitive skins should consider face cream if the sulphur fumes are heavy. By 1300 (sometimes by even 0900 or 1000) clouds have enveloped the lower peaks and are beginning to close in on Irazú."

J Douglas Porteous

"In the afternoon the mountain top is buried in fog and mist or drizzle, but the ride up in the mist can be magical, for the mountainside is half-displaced in time. There are new jeeps and tractors, but the herds of cattle are small, the fields are quilt-work, handcarts and oxcarts are to be seen under the fretworked porches of well-kept frame houses. The land is fertile, the pace is slow, the air is clean. It is a very attractive mixture of old and new. Irazú is a strange mountain, well worth the ride up."

Mike Marlowe

in the reserve as well as monkeys, orchids and ferns. There are picnic areas, a nature centre with slide shows (ask to see them) and good swimming in the dry season (November-June), and trout fishing (1 April to 31 October). ■ *Open daily 0800-1600, US$6.* The **B** *Kiri Lodge* is 1½ kilometres from the entrance (T2842024, beeper T2252500, San José T2578064, F2578065, good trails, excellent lodging and food, peaceful, very friendly), or the guards may let you camp on or near the parking lot at the entrance. *Getting there:* To get there take 0600 bus from Cartago to Orosi which goes to Puricil by 0700, then walk (5 kilometres), or take any other Cartago-Orosi bus to Río Macho and walk 9 kilometres to the refuge, or take a taxi from Orosi (ask for Julio who, for US$7 round trip, will take 6 passengers), or San José, US$50.

Turrialba

Turrialba (57 kilometres from San José), on the old railway between Cartago and Puerto Limón. The railway ran down to Limón on a narrow ledge poised between mountains on the left and the river on the right but no longer operates. The Centro Agronómico Tropical de Investigación y Enseñanza (CATIE) covers more than 2,000 acres of this ecologically diverse zone (with many fine coffee farms), has one of the largest tropical fruit collections in the world and houses an important library on tropical agriculture; visitors welcome. Past CATIE on the south side of the river, a large sugar mill can be seen, a conspicuous landmark. This is in Atirro which is also the centre for macadamia nuts.

Population: 20,000
Altitude: 646m
Colour map 5, grid B2

Costa Rica

Excursions The **Turrialba volcano** may be visited from Cartago by a bus from Calle 4 y Avenida 6 to the village of San Gerardo, or from Turrialba to Santa Cruz. Unpaved roads from these two villages meet at *Finca La Central*, on the saddle between Irazú and Turrialba.

Many white water rafting companies are based in Turrialba, offering trips to the Reventazón and Pacuare rivers. By contacting the guides in Turrialba you can save about 30 percent on a trip booked in San José, provided they are not already contracted. Guides include Tico, at *Tico's River Adventures*; Ronald Bottger, *Serendipity Adventures*, T5560462, recommended. New tourist information centre, Info-cen-tur, opposite Parque Central above restaurant *Nuevo Hong Kong*, English spoken. The rafting is excellent; the Pascua section of the Reventazón can be class five at rainy times. Pacuare is more beautiful (and more expensive).

Two kilometres from Finca La Central (see above) **AL** per person *Volcán Turrialba Lodge*, T/F2734335. Accessible only by four-wheel drive but the lodge can arrange transport. Six rooms with bath, trails and natural thermal pools, one hour by horseback to crater edge. Southeast of Turrialba beyond La Suiza is **L** *Albergue de Montaña Rancho Naturalista*,

Sleeping

price per person includes gourmet meals, with bath, horse riding, guided tours, transfers from San José and airport, 10 rooms, reservations essential, write PO Box 364-1002 San José, T2677138, 7-14 night programmes organized for birdwatchers and naturalists. Fourteen kilometres southeast of Turrialba, 2 kilometres before La Suiza, 1 kilometre from main road at Hacienda Atirro, **LL-L** *Casa Turire*, 12 luxury rooms with bath, 4 suites, cable TV, phone, restaurant, pool, tennis, library, games room, in the middle of a 1,620-hectare sugar/coffee/macadamia nut plantation, putting green and driving range, virgin rainforest nearby, trails, horses, bike rental, lots of excursions, T5311111, F5311075, CasaTurire@centralamerica.com. **AL** *Wagelia*, Av 4, Entrada de Turrialba (T5561566), with bath, 18 rooms, some a/c, restaurant, best, annex just outside town, beautiful gardens, pool, bar, highly recommended. **C** *Turrialtico*, on road to Limón, on top of hill with extensive views, clean, private bath, comfortable, friendly. In a row facing the railway station are: **E** per person *Interamericano*, Av 1, T5560142, with bath, clean, popular, parking, safe for motorbikes. **F** per person *Central*, T5560170, with bath, restaurant, basic. *Clen* and *Chamango*. **F** *Pensión Primavera*, 1 block away.

Eating   *Restaurant Nuevo Hong Kong*, good, reasonable prices. *Pizzería Julián*, on the square. *Las Palmeras*, alongside railway track, nice bar, good music. *Soda Burbuja*, local dishes very good value. *La Garza*, on main square, cheap, local good food.

Transport   Buses run from San José every hour 0500-2200 from Terminal Turrialba, C 13, Av 6-8, 1½ hours; from Cartago, 1 hour, US$0.60, runs until about 2200.

Moravia del Chirripó   From Turrialba you can get to the village of Moravia del Chirripó, east of Turrialba, where guides and horses can be hired for an excursion into the jungled, trackless area of the Talamanca Indians, where there are legends of lost goldfields (bus from Turrialba takes four hours, only certain in dry season; in wet season go to Grano de Oro, from where it's a one hour walk. No accommodation in Moravia, stay put at *pulpería* in Grano de Oro). Trips can be arranged to the **Cabecar Indian Reserve** of Alto Pacuare, also east of Turrialba; the reserve is a two and a half-hour hike from Río Vereh, and is good for serious naturalists and hikers; T *Jadetour* 2349905, Flor de Lys Rojas.

Guayabo   About 19 kilometres north of Turrialba, near Guayabo, an Indian ceremonial centre has been excavated and there are clear signs of its paved streets and stone-lined water channels. The archaeological site, 217 hectares, four kilometres from the town of Guayabo, is now a National Monument, and dates from the period AD 1000 to 1400. From Guayabo it is a one and a half hour walk to the site. There are excellent walks in the park, plenty of birds and wildlife to be seen. ■ *Open daily except Monday, 0800-1500, US$6, local guide available, water, toilets, no food.* **D** *Albergue y Restaurant La Calzada*, T5560465, 5566091 to leave message, best to make a reservation. *Getting there:* From Turrialba, there are buses at 1100 (returning 1250) and 1710 (returning 1750) and, on Sunday, at 0900, return 1700 (check times, if you miss it it is quite difficult to hitch as there is little traffic), US$0.45 to Guayabo. If you cannot get a bus all the way to Guayabo, several buses each day pass the turn-off to Guayabo, the town is a 2-hour walk uphill (taxi US$10, easy to hitch back).

Further north along this road (one and a half hours' drive) is Santa Cruz, from which the Turrialba volcano can be reached (see above). Costa Rica Expeditions and other tour operators offer day trips to Guayabo for about US$65 per person (minimum four persons).

Going northeast from Turrialba, the main road follows the Río Reventazón down to Siquirres (see page 1119). On this road is Pavones with **D** *Albergue Mirador Pochotel*, T5560111. Following the old railway down the valley, you come in 10 kilometres to **Peralta**, formerly a station and now more of a ghost village with a couple of sleepy bars. The old station is derelict but is the start of an interesting walk east down the track, through two tunnels full of large bats and past one of the landslides that closed the line in 1991. You can eventually reach Laguna Bonilla where there are boats for hire. The walk and return takes four to five hours, requires good footwear and you may see tiny red and blue poison dart frogs. One of the local farmers used to send milk to San José by train, now makes a good cheese.

The Meseta central: west

The Pan-American Highway runs initially through the Meseta Central from San José to the Nicaraguan border, 332 kilometres, completely paved and good. From San José it leads past the airport, bypassing Alajuela and a number of smaller towns mentioned below, to San Ramón before descending to Esparza on the coastal plain.

A paved road and a railway run from the capital to the two other main towns of the Meseta: Heredia and Alajuela.

Heredia

The capital of its province, 10 kilometres from San José, is a great coffee and cattle centre. The town is mostly new and only the main square has a colonial atmosphere in its architecture. The main church was built in 1797. There is a statue to the poet Aquileo Echeverría (1866-1909). The School of Marine Biology at the Universidad Nacional campus has a **Museo Zoológica Marina**, check opening times. Heredia is a convenient and pleasant place to stay, away from the pollution of San José but close to the capital and the airport, with good public transport.

Population: 30,000
Altitude: 1,200m

One of the largest coffee 'beneficios' is La Meseta; the bus from Heredia to Santa Bárbara will drop you at the gate and you can ask for a guided tour. There is also a coffee tour from San José to Café Britt's coffee farm near Barva de Heredia where you can see the processing factory, tasting room and multimedia presentation of the story of coffee. You can arrange to be picked up at various points in San José, US$20,

Excursions

Costa Rica

Meseta central west

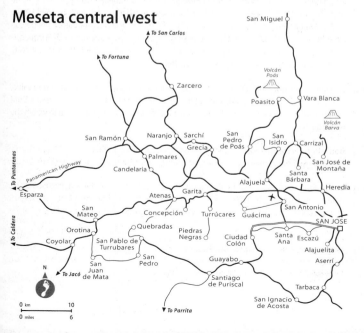

tours in high season 0900, 1100 and 1500, two hours, in low season at 0900 and 1100, T2602748, F2381848 for details, www.cafebritt.com (take 'Barva' bus from 200m north of main square to stop after 'El Castillo').

Above Heredia is the historic town of **Barva**, on the slope of the Barva volcano; frequent buses to/from Heredia. *Los Jardines Bed and Breakfast*, T2601904. At Barva the Huetar Gallery is recommended for arts, crafts and delicious food. There is also a **Museo de Cultura Popular**, 500m east of the Salón Comunal de Santa Lucía de Barva. Beyond Barva is **Santa Bárbara**, good seafood at the *Banco de los Mariscos* on the north side of the central plaza.

Five kilometres west of Heredia is **San Joaquín de Flores**, a small town in a rural setting with views of the Barva and Poás volcanoes.

Sleeping **LL** *Rosa Blanca Country Inn*, de luxe suites, restaurant and bar for guests only, 1.6 kilo-metres from Santa Bárbara de Heredia, Apdo Postal 41-30-09, T2699392, F2699555.

AL *Bougainvillea de Santo Domingo*, includes breakfast, excellent service, pool, recom-mended, T2441414, F2441313, spectacular mountain setting, free shuttle bus to San José. **AL** *Hotel Valladolid*, C7, Av7, T2602905, new luxury hotel with restaurant, jacuzzi, sauna, a/c, fridge, microwave, nice views. **A-B** *Apartotel Vargas*, 8 large, well-furnished apart-ments with cooking facilities, hot water, laundry facilities, TV, enclosed patio with garage and nightwatchman, English speaking staff, Sr Vargas will collect you from airport, recom-mended, 800m north of Colegio Santa Cecilia and San Francisco Church, Apdo 510-3000, Heredia, T2378526, 2381810, F2604698. **A** *América*, C 0, Av 2-4, just off central park, T2609292, F2609293 pick-up service from international airport. **A** *La Posada de la Montaña Bed and Breakfast* (*Heredia Mountain Inn*) at San Isidro de Heredia, T2688096 (USA T417-6372066) includes breakfast, 2 nights minimum, some rooms with kitchenette, suites, airport or San José pickup.

B *San Jerónimo Lodge*, T2923612, F2923243, 50-acre reserve, 20 minutes from San José on Guápiles road, 800m east of church at San Jerónimo de Moravia, horse riding, hiking, bik-ing. **B** *Hotel Villa Zurquí*, just off Limón highway at San Luís de Santo Domingo, 5 minutes from entrance to Braulio Carrillo National Park, 6 rooms with private or shared bathroom, including breakfast, T2688856. **C** *Hotel Heredia*, C6, Av3-5, T2380880, quiet, laundry, some shared rooms. **D** *Las Flores*, Av 10, C 12-14, T3823418, with bath, clean, quiet, opened 1998.

F *Colonial*, C 4-6, Av 4, clean, friendly, parking for motorcycles in restaurant. **F** per person *Herediana*, C 6, T2373217, friendly, safe parking, restaurant, recommended. **F** *El Parqueo*, C 4, Av 6-8, T2375258, T2382882, opposite central market, friendly; and **F** *El Verano*, C 4, Av 6, T2382882, run down, basic, both close to bus terminal.

Eating *La Nueva Floresta*, south side of main square, Chinese, balcony, large portions, good value, recommended. Pastry shop, *Pastelería Snoopy*, ½ block west of main square, good. *Café Azzurra*, great ice cream, cakes, shakes, capuchino, on main plaza, great place to watch the world go by.

Shopping **Bookshop** *Book Swappers*, diagonal to *MacDonalds*, run by Jill Chalfont and Frank García, new and used books, newspapers, CDs, postcards, open Monday-Saturday 0930-1900.

Transport **Buses** From **San José** from Heredia terminals, buses every 10 minutes daily, 0500-0015, then every 30 minutes to 0400, 25 minutes, US$0.30, or minibus from Av 2, C 10-12, every 15 minutes 0600-2000. Return buses from Av 4, C Central. Local buses leave from Av 8, C 2-4, by market.

Directory **Language schools** *Intercultura Costa Rica*, in Heredia, T/F2722234, mail address Apdo 487, Alajuela, small intensive classes. *Centro Panamericana de Idiomas*, in San Joaquín de Flores, PO Box 151-3007, T2656866, F2656213, accommodation with local families.

Alajuela

Alajuela, capital of its province, is a midsummer resort for people from the capital, but easy to do as a day trip. It is famous for its flowers and its market days (Saturday market is good value for food); an interesting craft cooperative produces pictures in relief metalwork. The unusual church of La Agonía in the east part of town has murals done from life. The national hero, Juan Santamaría, the drummer who fired the building at Rivas (Nicaragua) in which Walker's filibusters were entrenched in 1856, is commemorated by a monument. The **Museo Histórico Juan Santamaría** tells the story of this war, confusingly ■ *Tuesday-Sunday 1000-1700*. Alajuela Souvenir and Gift Center next door. Three kilometres outside the town is the **Ojo de Agua** swimming pool and sauna in beautiful surroundings: a popular bathing and boating resort. ■ *US$1.20 per person, plus US$0.80 per vehicle*. The gushing spring which feeds the pool also supplies water for Puntarenas. At Río Segunda de Alajuela is **Amigo de las Aves**, an experimental bird breeding farm hoping to reintroduce native macaws back into the wild; contact owners, Richard and Margo Frisius (T4412658), to arrange a visit.

Population: 49,568
Altitude: 952m
Colour map 5, grid B2

L *Hotel Club Martino*, opposite zoo, T4338382, F4339052, martino@sol.racsa.co.cr, luxury, excellent Italian restaurant, large pool, gym, squash & tennis courts etc. **AL-A** *Hampton Inn*, airport hotel, 2 kilometres east of Juan Santamaría, 100 rooms, double glazing, a/c, pool, bar, casino, no restaurant, fast food places nearby, discounts for children and senior citizens, T4430043, F4429532, hampton@sol.racsa.co.cr. **A** *Alajuela*, C 2, Av Central-2, T4416595, new rooms with TV and phone, **C** with shower, clean, friendly, free coffee, the only one appropriate for women travellers (best to book in advance). **A** *Buena Vista*, above the city with an all-round view, T4428595, F4428701, 25 rooms with bath, TV, pool, restaurant. **A** *La Rosa de America*, in Barrio San José, T4332741, pool, restaurant, fan, hot water, recommended. **A** *Posada Aeropuerto B&B*, T4417569, behind Juan Santamaría airport on road to Ojo de Agua, free transport from airport, some rooms with private bath, useful for early flights. **B** *Hotel 1915*, C2, Av5-7, T4410465. **B** *Apartotel El Erizo*, Av C, C18-20, T4404825, parking, laundry, apartments. **B** *Paraíso Tropical*, T4414882, cabins with tiled floors, with bath, hot water, airport shuttle, nice gardens. **B** *Islands Inn*, 500m east of central park, T4420573, owned by David and Erika Quesada, 8 rooms with bath, breakfast included. **B** *Tuetal Lodge*, 3 kilometres north of Alajuela, T4421804, tuetal@sol.racsa.co.cr, cabins surrounded by 5 acres of gardens, some with kitchenette, pool, restaurant, also treehouses, camping area, plans to open a hostal. **C** *Pensión Alajuela*, T4416251, bath, hot water, fan, parking for US$5. **C** *La Guaria Inn*, Av2, C1-3, T4419573, private accommodation, use of kitchen, own bathroom. **C** *Casa de Huéspedes*, Av2, C3-5, T4421515, yzv@yahoo.com, private house with communal kitchen, rooms with fan, fridge, shared bath.

D *Villa Real*, Av3, C 1, T4414022, simple, clean, shared bath, use of kitchen. **D** per person *Villa Tourist Inn*, near stadium, T4420692, parking. **D** *Charlie's Albergue*, a couple of streets from parque, T/F4410115, need to bargain. **F** *El Americano*, at Turrúcares, T4877192, with bath. **F** *El Real*, C 8, Av 1-Central, not recommended, short stay only, opposite bus terminal.

Mango Verde hostel, 50m west of Museo Juan Santamaría, T4416330, F4426257. See also hotels near airport, given under San José.

Five kilometres north of Alajuela **LL** *Villas Xandari*, a coffee finca overlooking the Central Valley, T4432020, F4424847, hotel@xandari.com, USA T805-6847879, F805-6844295, 16 private villas, health restaurant, organic gardens, many facilities.

Near **Carrizal** (on the road to San Miguel), which can be reached by bus from Alajuela, is **E** *La Rana Holandesa*, T/F4830816, a bed and breakfast run by John and Vicky Dekker, from Holland; they have 2 large, bright, clean rooms with separate entrance, lovely gardens, wonderful view over central valley, warmly recommended, for US$70 plus fuel, John Dekker will drive you anywhere in his four-wheel drive, free airport pickup, T/F4830816, 150m Noroeste Esquina Los Pérez, Carrizal de Alajuela.

Sleeping

Costa Rica

El Cencerro, on Parque Central, good meat, especially steaks, good service, nice view over

Eating

park from the terrace. *Pizza Hut*, central. *La Jarra*, near Alajuela hotel, good cheap meals in pleasant surroundings. *La Sirenita*, nothing special but OK.

Transport **Buses** From San José Av 2, C 10-14, every 5 minutes 0400-2200 to airport and Alajuela, 30 minutes, every 10 minutes 2200-2400, hourly after 2400 from Av 2, C 2, US$0.33. To Sarchí from Av Central, C 8, 0500-2200, US$0.50, 1½ hours.

Volcán Poás

Make sure you arrive at the volcano before the clouds. Clouds often hang low over the crater after 1000 permitting little to be seen.

From Alajuela two paved roads run to the 2,708-metre volcano Poás, 57 kilometres by road from San José, either through San Pedro de Poás and Fraijanes, or along the road to San Miguel, turning to Poás at the restaurant on the bend in the road just before you get to Vara Blanca. In the **National Park of Poás** (5,317 hectares), the still-smoking volcano is set in beautiful tropical forest. The park has abundant birdlife and has the only true dwarf cloudforest in Costa Rica. Trails are well marked. The crater is one and a half kilometres across (said to be the second largest in the world). In another area geysers may throw steam 600 metres or so. Just before the viewing point there is a path off the road leading to a still, forest-fringed lake in another crater, 30 minutes return. Another path is an alternative route back to the Visitors' Centre, 30 minutes' walk.

Admission Entrance to Park, US$6. The Park gates are open 0800-1600 daily (1 hour later Friday, Saturday, Sunday, 1 December-30 April), but if you wish to get in earlier you can leave your car/taxi at the gates and walk the 3 kilometres up the hill. The main crater is 1 kilometre along a road from the car park. There is a visitors' centre by the car park, with explanations of the recent changes in the structure, an insect museum on the 2nd floor (■ *0800-1600, daily, adults US$2.50, teens US$1.50, under 10s US$0.50*), and a good café next door, and toilets further along the road to the crater. The volcano is very crowded on Sunday, go in the week if possible.

Sleeping You cannot camp in the Park but there are several places advertising cabins on the road up to Poás; take food and water. If you get stuck in Poás ask the Peace Corps volunteer for help in finding somewhere to sleep. **AL** *La Providencia Mountain Lodge*, near Poás NP (2 kilometres from green entrance gate to volcano, unpaved road), private reserve, beautiful horse-riding tour US$25-30 including lunch, T (San José) 2322498, F2312204; At San Pedro de Poás there is an interesting bar, *La Vía*, with cheap food, free snacks and good music. Further on look for **AL** *Poás Volcano Lodge*, 200m from Vara Blanca junction on road to Poasito, at *El Cortijo* farm, sign on gate, farm road 1 kilometre to house, T4822194, English-owned, includes breakfast, dinner, good wholesome food, rooms in converted buildings with bath, or in farmhouse with shared bath, some rooms cheaper, jungle trail, good walking, 25 minutes to volcano by car, 1½ hours from San José, T/F4822513, PO Box 5723-1000, San José, or in UK T01420-549205, poasvl@sol.racsa.co.cr, www.arweb.com/poas. **A** *La Laguna del Lagarto Lodge*, T (San José) 2898163, F2895295, private reserve, German-run, restaurant, boat trips, horse riding, canoeing. **B** *Albergue Ecológico Los Cipreses*, Barrio San José de los Angeles de Grecia, 1 kilometre from Poás, 11 kilometres from Grecia, T4445723, F4944650, 2 cabins, camping available. **C** *Lagunillas Lodge*, T4485506, farmhouse, simple, horses, private atmosphere, nice views. **D** *Country Club Monte del Mago*, about 40 kilometres away at Carrillo de Poás, T6612410, with bath, swimming pool, restaurant, sometimes no food or water. **Campsite**: trailer park nearby, with hookups: the *Inca*.

Transport The volcano can be reached by car from San José. A taxi for 6 hours with a side trip will cost about US$50-60. There is a daily excursion bus from the main square of Alajuela right up to the crater, leaving at 0900, connecting with 0830 bus from San José (from Av 2, C 12-14); be there early for a seat, if full before 0900 the bus will leave, although extra buses run if necessary, the area gets very crowded, US$4 return, T2372449 or 2225325 for information. The bus waits at the top with ample time to see everything (clouds permitting), returning at 1400-1430. Daily bus Alajuela-Poasito 1200 (US$1). From **Poasito** hitch a lift as it is a

10-kilometre walk. Other options include taking a 0600 or 1600 bus from Alajuela to **San Pedro de Poás**, hitch/taxi to Poasito and stay overnight there, hiking or hitching up the mountain next morning; taking a 0500 bus from Alajuela to Poasito which arrives 2 hours before the Park gates open.

From **Vara Blanca** the road continues north round the east side of the volcano through Cinchona and Cariblanco (voluntary toll/lottery US$0.20 for road construction). The road is twisty, winding through lush forest, waterfalls down to the lowlands at **San Miguel**. Here the road splits, leading either northeast to Puerto Viejo de Sarapiquí (see below) or northwest to **Venecia** (three and a half hours, US$2.50 by bus from San José), interesting church; one hotel, **F**, clean, friendly; *Restaurant El Parque*, near church, good local food. Nearby is **Ciudad Cutris**, precolumbian tumuli. A good road goes to within two kilometres of Cutris, from there walk or take four-wheel drive vehicle; get a permit to visit from the local *finca* owner. West of Venecia is Aguas Zarcas, another road junction. Just beyond, on the road to San Carlos, is **LL-AL** *El Tucano Country Club*, 90 rooms and suites, pleasant, hot springs of iron and sulphur, swimming pool, jacuzzi, sauna, casino, tennis, mini golf, horse riding, restaurant, T4603152, F4601692, from here it is only eight kilometres to San Carlos (see page 1084). About 40 kilometres north of Aguas Zarcas is **Boca Tapada** on the Río San Carlos in the jungle and not far from its junction with the Río San Juan and the Nicaraguan border. Here there is the **A** *La Laguna del Lagarto Lodge*, T2898163/5295, 12 rooms with bath, six with shared bath, friendly, good for watching animals, 500 hectares of forest, boat trips down Río San Carlos to Río San Juan.

Ten kilometres northeast of San Miguel is La Virgen, where *Rancho Leona* is located **La Virgen** near the Río Sarapiquí. Good for kayaking, T7106312 for two-night packages, US$75, equipment and guides included, very basic accommodation and expensive but good home cooked dishes at the ranch and nightly frog concerts. Take the Río Frío bus from San José and ask to get off at *Rancho Leona*, the 1600 bus goes through the Braulio Carrillo National Park and ends at *Rancho Leona*, three and a half hours. Also at La Virgin is Juan Carlos, a recommended guide for rafting (class one, two and three possible on the Río Sarapiquí) from US$25 per person, T7611148. (See page 1117 for Puerto Viejo de Sarapiquí.)

Sleeping **AL** *La Quinta de Sarapiquí Lodge*, on Sardinal River (Bajos de Chilamate), family-run lodge, 6 rooms with bath and fan, T/F7611052. At Chilamate, 15 kilometres further on, is the **B** per person *Albergue Ecológico Islas del Río*, includes meals, 5 rooms with private bathroom, 3 rooms with shared bathroom, Río Sarapiquí trips arranged, T2330366 in San José, 7106898, T7666574 (affiliated to the Youth Hostel network). **E** *Rancho Leona*, T/F7611019, rleona@sol.racsa.co.cr, basic dormitories, free for kayak renters.

The road from Alajuela to San Carlos (see page 1084) passes through several of the **Grecia** Meseta Central towns, with good paved roads to others. Much of this region is devoted to coffee growing and the hills are covered with green coffee bushes, interspersed with other plants for shade, often shrouded in cloud and rain. Eighteen kilometres northwest from Alajuela, Grecia is in a major pineapple-growing area and has an interesting church, made entirely of metal to replace a wooden one. The **Museo Regional de Grecia** is in the Casa de la Cultura. ■ *Monday-Friday, 0900-1700, free.* A short distance along the road to Alajuela is *El Mundo de los Serpientes*, a snake farm with over 30 species, open 0800-1600, US$11, reductions for biology students, information T/F4943700.

Sleeping **D** *Cabaña Los Cipreses. Posada de Grecia*, bed and breakfast, T4445354. *Complejo Trailer y Cabinas Los Trapiches.* **G** *Pensión Quirós*, with bath.

A few kilometres further is Sarchí, where you can visit the factory that produces the **Sarchí** traditional painted ox-carts, which are almost a national emblem. The three main *artesanías* are together, either side of the road and selling hand-made furniture, cowhide rocking chairs and wooden products as well as the ox-carts, which come in all sizes. Look out for the bus shelters, painted in the style of the carts. The pink church in Sarchí is especially attractive at sunset. Also **Valle de Mariposas** (next to Mercado de Artesanías), 40 species of butterflies, including Morphos (■ *T4544196, 0900-1700 daily, US$6*). Travel agents in San José charge US$20 or more, often combining Sarchí with a trip to Poás volcano.

Sleeping B *Villa Sarchí Lodge*, T/F4544006, 11 rooms, restaurant, owned by Ramon Rodrigues. **D** *Cabinas Daniel Zamora*, T4544596, with bath, fan, hot water, very clean. **E** *Cabinas Sarchí*, T4544425, with bath, opposite Banco Nacional, you may have to call owner if unattended.

Transport Express bus from San José, C 16, Av 1-3, 1215, 1730 and 1755, Monday-Friday, returning 0530, 0615, 1345, Saturday 1200, 1½ hours. Tuansa buses every 30 minutes, 0500-2200 from Alajuela bus station, 1½ hours.

Naranjo
Colour map M5B2

The road continues on through Naranjo (Roberto Kopper offers balloon tours, about 30 minutes, 300 metres, T4500318). On the Panamericana, one kilometre west of the turnoff for Naranjo is **A** *Rancho Mirador*, T4511302, F4511301, good value cabañas, good restaurant with local food, a spectacular view of coffee fincas and San José in the distance, owner Rick Vargas who was formerly a stunt pilot in the USA.

Zarcero

Twenty five kilometres from Naranjo Zarcero is notable for its topiary. There are frequent bus services from San José/Alajuela through Naranjo to San Carlos (Ciudad Quesada) and buses stop in Zarcero in the main plaza, which is the highlight of the place. The bushes are clipped into the shapes of arches leading up to the white church with twin towers, animals, people dancing, a helicopter, baskets, many designs like Henry Moore sculptures, also a small grotto. The interior of the church is entirely of wood, even the pillars, painted cream and pale grey with patterns in blue, brown, green and pink; cartouches, emblems and paintings.

Sleeping and eating C *Don Beto*, by the church, T/F4633137, with bath, very friendly, clean. *Soda/Restaurant El Jardín*, on 1st floor, overlooks the plaza with good view of topiary, local lunches and breakfasts. The town is also known for cheese and fruit preserves.

San Ramón

Just after Llano Bonito, before reaching Zarcero, a turning left goes to **San Ramón**, 76 kilometres from San José. A clean town with an attractive Parque Central. Street market Saturday mornings. The **Museo de San Ramón**, Frente de Parque, records the history and culture of the local community ■*Tuesday-Friday, 1300-1700*. Good walking for example to the northwest, take the bus to La Paz and get off at the bridge over the Río Barranca. Also you can visit the coffee processing plant (in season) at the Cooperativa de Café in San Ramón.

Sleeping E *Hotel Nuevo Jardín*, with bath, hot water. **F** *El Viajero*, basic, clean, communal bathroom, TV in lounge. **F** *Washington*, dirty, unfriendly, not recommended. There are local families who offer room and board, try Sra Miriam Bamfi, T4456331 or Sra María del Carmen Ulate, T4456007, Spanish speaking only. **On the San Ramón to La Fortuna road**: heading north, is **L-AL** *Hotel Villa Blanca*, 800 hectares of primary cloud forest, naturalist hikes, T6611600, vilablan@sol.racsa.co.cr; also **AL** *Valle Escondido Lodge*, at San Lorenzo on same road, comfortable rooms with private bath, set in 400 acres of primary forest, riding, bird watching, T2310906, F2329591. **B-D** *La Posada B&B*, T/F4457359, hoteles@sol.racsa.co.cr, 400m north of the cathedral, parking, 12 decent rooms, shared bath. **E** *Gran Hotel*, T4456363, 100m south of the cathedral and 350m east, simple rooms, ok.

Eating *Restaurant Tropical*. Excellent ice cream parlour near the northwest corner of the Parque.

Transport Buses run to surrounding villages and towns. To San José every 45 minutes between 0800-2100.

Seven kilometres southeast of San Ramón is **Palmares** (one hotel), which has a pretty central park with lovely tall trees, in which are said to be five sloths. Eight paths radiate from the bandstand. On the side of the park opposite the stone church is the municipal market.

After Palmares you can either pick up the Pan-American Highway, or continue south to Atenas, which is on the road from San José to San Mateo, leading on to Esparza and the Pacific coast. This road to the coast is well-used and in good condition. The church and main plaza in Atenas lie on an earthquake fault. There is a Library on the plaza, which also serves as the office for the bus company, Cooptransatenas, T4465767. Many daily buses to San José, either direct or via Alajuela, US$0.60. Local speciality, *toronja rellena*, a sweet filled grapefruit. Atenas is reputed to have the best climate in the world, with stable temperatures of between 17 and 32° C the year round (plus rain of course).

Atenas
Colour map 5, grid B2

Sleeping **AL** *El Cafetal Inn*, T4465785, cafetal@cafetal.com, out of town in St Eulalia, 4.7 kilometres towards Grecia, private house, nice setting, large pool, 10 nice rooms with hot water, recommended. **B** *Ana's Place*, includes breakfast, private bathroom, special weekly/monthly rates, T4465019. **C** *Villa Tranquilidad*, T4465460, 6 rooms, Canadian owned, quiet, welcoming, hard to find, phone for reservations/directions.

Atenas to Alajuela

Driving from Atenas towards Alajuela, you pass *Fiesta de la Maíz* soda/restaurant by a green church on the side of the road, where they sell only products made of maize, you can try spoonfuls before you buy. Open weekends only, very busy, a stopping place for weekenders on their way to Jacó Beach. Nearby is the Enchanted Forest, popular with children. Also the Zooave, between Atenas and Alajuela in La Garita de Alajuela, Canadian owner, over 100 species of native birds and 25 exotic species, toucans, parrots, black swans, eagles, also all four monkeys as well as other mammals and reptiles. Now recognized as a Wildlife Rescue Centre, Zooave has been successful in breeding endangered birds ■ *T4338989, open daily, 0900-1700, US$8.70.*

La Garita de Alajuela

Costa Rica

Sleeping **AL** *Chatelle Country Resort*, T4877081, F4877095, 6 rooms with bath, some rooms with kitchenette, TV, spacious, comfortable beds, beautiful gardens, good restaurant, pool, weekly/monthly rates, airport pickup available at no extra charge, opposite the *Chatelle Country Resort* is an orchid nursery with a marvellous variety of blooms, run as a hobby by an enthusiastic English-speaking optometrist, who will give you a guided tour for US$3.50. At the Alajuela, La Garita, San Pedro de Poás fork is **AL** *Las Orquídeas Inn*, T4339346, F4339740, orchid@sol.racsa.co.cr, 12 rooms with bath, 4 rooms shared bath, no children under 13 accepted, pick up from airport 10 minutes away, pool. **A** *Río Real*, T/F4877022, includes breakfast, pool, restaurant, bar.

Eating *Mi Quinta*, good food, swimming pools, sports facilities also available for a small charge. The area is quiet and agricultural with fields of sugar cane and cattle pastures; pleasant walking to places of interest.

Aserrí to San Pablo de Turrubares

Ten kilometres south of San José is **Aserrí**, a village with a beautiful white church, where on Friday and Saturday evenings, street bands play from 2000, followed by marimbas. Extremely popular among locals, the dancing is fabulous. *Chicharrones* and *tortillas* to eat, plus liquor. Further along the same road is *Mirador Ram Luna*, a restaurant with a fine panoramic view. At the end of the black-top road is **San Ignacio de Acosta**, again with a good church containing life-size Nativity figures. Buses from San José (Calle 8, Avenida 12-14 in front of the Baptist church) via Aserrí hourly from 0500-2230, return 0430-2100, one hour. The unpaved road continues to **Santiago de Puriscal**, which was the epicentre for many earthquakes in 1990, the church is now closed as a result. Excellent views from the town and the road. From here it is possible to take a dirt road to the Pacific coast, joining the coastal road near Parrita (see page 1132). Alternatively, take the road to **San Pablo de Turrubares** (a soccer field, a church, a *soda* and a bar), from where you can either head west for Orotina, via an unpaved road through San Pedro and San Juan de Mata, or for Atenas via Quebradas, then east to Escobal, next stop on railway, then four-wheel drive necessary to Atenas.

A road has been built from San José west to Ciudad Colón by-passing Escazú and Santa Ana (**AL** *Hotel Posada Canal Grande*, T2824089/4101/4103, F2825733, Apdo 84-6150), which will eventually pass San Pedro de Turrubares going to Orotina, with the aim of replacing the Pan-American Highway to the coast.

San José

The Central Northwest

The northern lowlands stretching to the Nicaraguan border. In the eastern foothills of the Cordillera de Tilarán is Lago Arenal, beneath the highly active Volcán Arenal. The rivers provide fine opportunities for seeing wildlife.

San Carlos
Colour map 5, grid B2

Also known as **Ciudad Quesada, San Carlos** lies 48 kilometres from the Pan-American Highway and can be reached by a road which branches off the highway near Naranjo. At the foot of the mountains it is the main town of the lowland cattle and farming region and is a hub of communications. The market (*centro comercial*) is near the Parque Central. There is a large, efficient Social Security Hospital on the north side of town on the road to Florencia, better to come here for first aid treatment rather than to local village doctors.

Sleeping D *El Retiro*, T4600403, with bath, clean and comfortable. **E** *Balneario Carlos*, T4601822, cottages with cooking facilities, with bath, swimming pool. **E** *Conquistador*, with bath. **E** *La Central*, T4600301, with bath, restaurant. Several basic *pensiones* around corner from Banco Popular, all **F**, eg *Diana*. **F** *La Terminal*, T4602158, at bus station. Breakfast served in the market; 3-4 Chinese restaurants in town. Eight kilometres from town is *El Tucano*, see page 1066.

Transport Direct bus from Terminal Atlántico Norte, San José, 2¼ hours, hourly, from 0645-1815, US$2.20, return 0645-1815. From San Carlos buses go northwest to Tilarán via Fortuna and Arenal (0630 and 1400), other buses go to Fortuna through El Tanque (5 daily, 1 hour), San Rafael de Guatuso and Upala, north to Los Chiles (3 hours, US$2.10), northeast to towns on the Río San Carlos and Río Sarapiquí, including Puerto Viejo de Sarapiquí, and east to the Río Frío district.

San Carlos to Los Chiles

From San Carlos a paved road runs northwest to **Florencia** (service station). At Platanar de San Carlos, at Hacienda Platanar is **AL** *Hotel La Garza* (eight kilometres from Florencia, T4755222, F4755015), bungalows with bath and fan, overlooking river, guided tours, boat trips, fishing, 750 acres of forest and cattle ranch. At a junction the route to the north leads 13 kilometres to **Muelle San Carlos**. **AL** *Country Club Tilajari Hotel Resort*, T/F4601083 (T2284603 F2284004, San José) 48 luxurious rooms, four suites, a/c, tennis, three pools, sauna, bar and restaurant, horses, boat trips and other excursions organized, 29 kilometres to Arenal, recommended.

Los Chiles
Colour map 5, grid A2

A further 74 kilometres north through flat land where orange plantations have replaced forest, leads to Los Chiles near the Nicaraguan border. From here you can arrange boat/fishing trips up the slow-moving Río Frío, through dense tropical vegetation into the **Caño Negro Wildlife Refuge** and Caño Negro Lake, to see alligators, turtles, monkeys, a wide variety of birdlife, fish and fauna. Ask about guides at the *Restaurant Los Petates*, varied menu, good portions, cheap, friendly or *Restaurant El Parque*, good home cooking. A four-hour tour with Esteban, recommended. Oscar and Enrique also recommended, cost about US$50. Alternatively, *Aventuras Arenal* in Fortuna run trips to Caño Negro (see below). It is cheaper to get a boat from Los Chiles to the Park rather than taking a tour from elsewhere and convenient if you are going on to Nicaragua, though there are not always boats available. Call the park administration, T4601301, for reservations for food and lodging; boat to the Park Tuesday and Thursday, 0730. You can see much of the wildlife without going into the Park.

Sleeping B *Caño Negro Lagoon Lodge*, 17 kilometres south of Los Chiles on a rough dirt road, four-wheel drive only, rustic rooms, T4600124. **C** *Cabinas Eco-directa*, T4711197, new, restaurant, 8 rooms with bath, hot water. **D** *Cabinas Jaribú*, T/F4711055, hot water, fan. **C** *Guajipal Lodge*, T4711242, with breakfast, bath, cold water, tours arranged. **F** *Carolina*, small rooms but very clean, friendly. **F** *Central*, basic, mosquito nets, small rooms, camping available, and tours for US$30 for 5 people; some restaurants. **F** *Onassis*, by main plaza, clean but no fan.

This crossing point is now open to foreigners but there is no road link, and San Carlos on the Nicaraguan side is remote from the rest of that country.

Frontier with Nicaragua – Los Chiles

Sleeping and eating F *Hotel Central*, cheaper without bath, no fan, friendly, good value. Restaurant *Los Petates*, good food, check the bill. Supermarket *El Chileno* is unfriendly and overcharges.

Costa Rican immigration All formalities are in Los Chiles which is a few kilometres short of the border. The office is close to the river and leaving procedures are normally straightforward. There is a bank nearby. If entering Costa Rica, officials can be more difficult, mainly because they are sensitive about the many Nicaraguan immigrants wishing to enter the country. They usually close for lunch at 1200.

Transport Air Sansa has flights San José-Los Chiles on Tuesday, Thursday, Sunday. **Boat** A regular launch goes down the Río Frío across the Río San Juan to San Carlos, 1500, 1-2 hours, US$3.50. There are other launches if demand is sufficient. You can follow the track north to the San Juan River and then find a ferry to cross, but enquire before trying this route. **Bus** Going into Costa Rica, there are direct buses to San José daily, 0500, 1500, 5 hours, from San José Terminal Atlántico Norte to Los Chiles at 0530, 1530, 217 kilometres, alternatively take a bus to Ciudad Quesada San Carlos from where there are good services.

See under **Nicaragua – San Carlos** and **San Juan del Norte/Greytown** for details on the Río San Juan border.

The road running west from the junction in Florencia (paved, good) leads to Fortuna, from where you can explore the Arenal region.

Fortuna
Population: 4,500
Altitude: 254m
Colour map 5, grid A2

Sleeping AL *Bosques de Chachagua*, at Chachagua on road to San Ramón, about 12 kilometres southeast of Fortuna, individual suites, rainforest, riding, tours to Caño Negro, contact Vesa Tours, T2390328, F2934206. **AL** *Las Cabañitas*, 4 kilometres east of La Fortuna, 30

Costa Rica

cabins with private baths, 2 pools, observatory for viewing Arenal volcano, restaurant, highly recommended. T479-9400/9343, F4799408, cabanita@sol.racsa.co.cr. **B** *Albergue Ecoturístico La Catarata*, 2 kilometres from town, rough road, T4799522, F4799178, reservations essential, co-operative, organic garden, homemade soaps and shampoos, good fresh food, butterfly farm, taxi US$2, hot water, laundry, all meals. 100 metres away is **B** *Cerro Chato*, with bath, hot water, breakfast, 2 rooms, helpful, Miguel Zamora, T4799494/9404, Cell 2849280, F4799575, PO Box 1927-1000, San José. **B** *Cabañas de Montaña de Fuego*, between La Fortuna and Tabacón, includes breakfast, 3 cabins with private baths, T/F4799106. **B** *Rancho El Corcovado*, pool, clean, overlooks river and wildlife. **B** *Villa Fortuna*, T/F4799139, fans or a/c, private bath, hot water, small fridge, nice pool. **B-C** *San Bosco*, T4799050, all rooms with private bath, quiet, signs on main road, clean, friendly, nice gardens with terrace and view of the volcano, recommended. **C** *Cabinas Rossi*, T47990232, cabrossi@sol.racsa.co.cr, 1 kilometre towards the volcano, with breakfast, friendly owner, hot water, fan, watch the volcano from the garden, horses rented, good value. **D** *Cabinas La Amistad*, T4799364, clean, friendly, hot water, hard beds. **E** *Cabinas Carmela*, O Av y O C, very central, hot showers, arranges tours. **D** *Las Colinas*, private bath, good views, pleasant. **F** per person *Albergue Burio*, includes continental breakfast, private bath, T4799076, F4799010, 8 rooms with bath, try to get an inside cabin, others noisy, Arenal volcano trips, fishing arranged, motorbikes welcome, camping in garden, affiliated to the Youth Hostel network. **E** *Cabinas Jerry*, T4799063, cabins with bath, hot water, mixed reports. **E** *Cabinas Sissy*, 100m south and 100m west of church, T4799356/9256, bath, hot water, clean, ask if they will do laundry, will store luggage. **E** *Centro Recreación* Volcán Arenal, 50m south of church, private accommodation, simple rooms, breakfast, owned by local dentist, nice garden with amusing pets. **E** *Cabinas Las Flores*, 2 kilometres on road to Volcano, T4799307, friendly, clean. **F** per person *Cabina Las Tejas*, private bath, bike rental, tours to Arenal and hot springs, US$7. **F** *Posada Inn*, shared bath, fan, use of kitchen, nice owners. **F** per person *Cabinas Charlie*, T4799454, run by Charlie and María Rodríguez, take good care of their guests, clean, friendly, English spoken, hot water, fan, use of kitchen, night tours to volcano US$7. **F** *Cabinas Christina*, clean, hot water. **F** *Cabinas Aduana*, hot water, tours to volcano.

Eating *Las Chicaritas*, near bridge, nice setting, breakfast from 0600, cheap, recommended. *Choza de Laurel*, behind the church, self-service US$1.50-US$4.50, typical food, friendly. *Rancho Cascada*, on corner of Parque with high conical thatched roof, good bocas, films shown in evenings. *Soda del Río*, good, safe, friendly, some rooms. *El Jardín*, good place to watch the world go by, *menu del dia* US$2.25. *Nene*, good food, pleasant service, not expensive. *El Jinete*, at busstop, good food, friendly, good value. *La Vaca Muca*, a bit out of the village on the way to Tabacón. Public phone with international access.

Transport Buses There are daily buses at 0615, 0840, 1130, from Terminal Atlántico Norte, San José, 4½ hours, via San Carlos, US$2.50, return at 1245, 1445; 6 buses a day from San Carlos, 1 hour, US$1, 4 different routes. Two buses a day to Tilarán, 0800 (connecting bus Tilarán-Puntarenas 1300) and 1700 US$2.90, 4 hours.

Directory Banks Banco Nacional de Costa Rica will change travellers' cheques, US$1 commission. **Tour companies & travel agents** Several include *Aventuras Arenal*, La Fortuna, T4799133, Rodrigo Salazar: *Caño Negro Tours*, US$40-50; Arenal lake sunset trip US$40-50, fishing US$27 per hour, Cerro Chato tour, US$25.

About six kilometres uphill south of Fortuna are the 70-metre **Río Fortuna Waterfalls**, up a pleasant road through yuca and papaya plantations with places to buy drinks along the way. Admission US$1.25. You can bathe there but it is safer 50 metres downstream. You can walk or drive, but four-wheel drive is necessary, or bicycle hire US$2 per hour (hard work), or you can hire a horse for the day at around US$14. White water rafting available. Take care when climbing down to falls, it is steep and slippery, take shoes with a good tread and swimming clothes. Two to three hours' climb above the falls is the crater lake of Cerro Chato. The top (1100 metres) is reached through mixed tropical/cloud forest, with a good view (if you are lucky) but beware of snakes on the path. A guide, if you need one, US$9.

Volcán Arenal

From Fortuna the road travels north around the base of the 1,633-metre volcano Arenal to the manmade **Lago Arenal** and hydroelectric dam. The volcano has been continuously active since July 1968, when an eruption killed 78 people and more or less destroyed three villages including Tabacón which was situated above the Balneario. It is a classic cone shape of the Stromboli type characterized by explosions sending hot grey clouds of sulphurous gases which can descend the slopes at an alarming speed. There are also lava streams, mainly on the west side. The most recent major activity was in May 1998. Although the side facing Fortuna is green, the side facing the lake is grey and barren, with lava flows clearly visible. There are three active craters and several fumaroles which spew out red hot lava and steam. The activity is particularly impressive at night, accompanied by rumbles, crashes and intermittent roars (rather like someone moving furniture upstairs) to wake you up. If you are visiting in the rainy season you will not see much as the volcano is obscured by clouds and rain and there can be bad weather for weeks. Some operators will charge less if you don't see anything. All year round, there are usually clouds and rain in the afternoons. However, if you can hire a taxi for a trip at about 0400-0500, the sky is often clearer then. On no account try to walk up the volcano beyond the level of the vegetation; some of those who have tried have not returned alive. However, there is good hiking on the lower slopes from Fortuna. Recommended guides are Carlos and Didier.

Colour map 5, grid B2

Some say there is greater volcanic activity around full moon.

The volcano is a national park, entry US$6. There are many chalets and tourist facilities round the attractive lake, but not many people. The Park office has water. Bathing in the warm water from quiet shady beaches is possible. Taxi from Fortuna to Tabacón US$4.50.

Admission

Thermal baths Ten kilometres northwest of Fortuna is *Balneario Tabacón*, a thermal pool with three bars, restaurant, (■ *1000-2200 daily, closed if there is a serious eruption*). The water is hot and stimulating: there are a number of pools at descending heights and different temperatures, waterslides, a waterfall to sit under, et cetera. The food is good and the fruit drinks thirst quenching. The entrance fee seems to vary up to as much as US$14 but cheaper after 1800 (US$13). The resort is very popular with evening coach tours from San José. There are cheaper hot springs across the road for US$5. Better are the hot waters about four kilometres further along the road at Quebrada Cedeña, clean and safe, no sign but look for local parked cars.

Swim after dark when you can see the lava coming down the volcano, a spectacular sight, not to be missed.

Also near Fortuna are the Cavernas del Venado, limestone caves that can be visited. Tours from Fortuna with all necessary equipment, US$20. Buses from San Carlos en route to Tilarán daily, return transport to Fortuna at 2200.

4 kilometres after El Tabacón a left turn on to a gravel road (sign 1 kilometre Parqueo) leads eventually to the **AL-B** *Arenal Observatory Lodge* (PO Box 1195, 1250 Escazú, Costa Rica, T2573273, F2553529 (Costa Rica Sun Tours) or T2552011 (Eco-Center), Observatory@centralamerica.com, four-wheel drive recommended along this 9-kilometre stretch (taxi-jeep from Fortuna, US$12). The Observatory was built in 1987 as a research station and now has 24 rooms in separate blocks, basic cabins with bunk beds and bath, a dining room/lodge, and newer rooms with queen size bed (some with views of volcano), double, or triple, private bathroom, hot water showers, price per person, includes taxes and meals, depending on size of group, children under 3 free, 3-10 half price; 1-day tour from San José US$69; spectacular views of volcano across valley of Río Agua Caliente and of Lake Arenal, good walking, riding and bird watching in the area, fishing with guide on the lake US$100 for

Sleeping

Costa Rica

2 people. Also offers trips to Caño Negro with experienced naturalist, and hiking to Monteverde. On the north side of the lake about 2 kilometres off the paved road from Fortuna (four-wheel drive required) is the more comfortable **L-AL** *Arenal Lodge*, meals extra, good food, 6 rooms with bath, 12 junior suites, cheaper rooms have no views, 5 chalet duplexes on ridge above lodge, great views, T (San José) 2283189, F2286798, viewing deck, fishing trips arranged on the lake. **AL** *Arenal Vista Lodge*, 25 rooms with bath, arranges boat trips, riding and hiking, T2201712, F2323321. **A** *Cabañas Arenal Paraíso*, 7.5 kilometres from Fortuna, T/F4799006, 12 nice houses with bath, fridge, nice terrace views of the volcano. **L** *Tabacón Resort Hotel*, 12 kilometres on right, T2561500, tabacon@sol.racsa.co.cr, overpriced luxury hotel. **AL** *Linda Vista del Norte Lodge*, near *Arenal Vista Lodge*, T4799263, nice views, horse riding tours, hot water, recommended. **C** *Mirador Los Lagos*, T4799126, 8 cabins with volcano view, 8 tents, sleep 4, **C**, camping areas, day visits US$2.75, excellent food and spectacular views of the volcano over the lake with a campsite US$2.75 per night, with good facilities and small café. There are three marked footpaths towards the lava fields and lakes through the forest. About 4 kilometres from Fortuna on the road to Lake Arenal, turn at sign on left side of the road 'Bienvenidos a Junglas y Senderos Los Lagos'. Site is 2 kilometres uphill, very steep, good facilities, **F** per person, tours to hot springs at night. This is one of the best places to watch the volcanic activity at night. **C** *La Catarata Ecotourist Lodge*, 2 kilometres west of La Fortuna on road to volcano, 6 cabins, bathroom, one of 3 lodges run by community association and supported by WWF Canada and CIDA Canada. 6 kilometres from Arenal is **C** *Hospedaje La Ceiba*, overlooking Lake Arenal, good, helpful, great panoramic views, good breakfast. **Camping**: is possible on edge of lake, no services but good view of volcano at night, 500m past Park entrance on road to *Arenal Observatory Lodge*, take dirt road to right, 500m to lake where locals also camp.

Directory **Tour companies & travel agents** There are several tour agencies offering night tours to Arenal volcano and thermal baths, a typical 4-hour tour costs US$25pp for volcano view, balneario or river hot waters, entry to park to see the lava, soft drinks and transport, hotel pickup, sometimes at 0300-0400 to be sure you see the lava. *Celin's*, in front of *Hotel Fortuna*, is recommended, runs day and night tours to the volcano, including boat on the lake and baths. The entry fee to the baths may not be included in your tour price, check. You leave Fortuna at about 1815 and return by 2200.

The south side of the lake is very difficult to drive, with many fords; it is possible to get a boat from the dam across the lake to Río Chiquito then hike to Monteverde, or a more direct route is to hike up the Río Malanga.

Fortuna to Monteverde

There is a road round the north of the lake, mostly paved, which leads to Tilarán. If driving yourself, you can get from Fortuna to Monteverde via Tilarán in a day, but set out in good time to avoid driving after dark. The lakeside road is frequently impassable because of fallen bridges and landslides (check before setting out), and the last 10 kilometres just before Arenal village are rough although passable with high clearance vehicles all year (partly paved but in bad condition). A good café for a meal and drink is *Toad Hall* between Fortuna and Arenal, friendly, US owned, souvenir shop, good value. An alternative route is to take the road from Fortuna to **San Rafael de Guatuso**, which runs parallel but further north. There is a 'voluntary' toll of US$1 between Jicarito and San Rafael for reconstruction work on this road. You can come back to the lake either by turning off before San Rafael through Venado (where there are caves), or from San Rafael itself, where there are a couple of basic hotels. Both roads are unpaved and very slow, 20 kmph maximum speed in a car, but go through lovely countryside with beautiful views, especially when you approach the lake.

Three kilometres from Colonia Río Celeste near San Rafael de Guatuso is the **B** *Magil Forest Lodge*, set in 800 acres on the foothills of the 1,916-metre volcano **Tenorio** (now a national park, 10,000 hectares). The *Lodge*, includes meals, has 10 rooms with private bath. If you continue along the road from San Rafael northwest towards the Nicaraguan border you come to **Upala** (airport, Sansa flights Tuesday, Thursday, Sunday) and Caño Negro. There is now a direct bus from San José to Upala (from Av 5, C 14 at 1445, four hours, US$2.80), where there are the *Hotel Rigo*, *Hotel Upala*, T4700169, *Pensión Isabella*, **F** *Pensión Buena Vista*, basic, food available. Nearby is **AL** *Los Ceibos Lodge*, **B** without meals, T2280054, private reserve, riding US$6 per hour, tours to Caño Negro, Río Celeste and Volcán Tenorio.

The San Rafael-Arenal road joins the lakeside road just north of Arenal town; no signs if driving from Arenal to San Rafael, it is just a track. If you turn left about four kilometres out of San Rafael before the river, four-wheel drive necessary, you come to the Guatuso Indian villages of Tonjibe, Margarita and El Sol.

Arenal

Arenal is a pleasant little town, 20 kilometres along the lake from the volcano, with wonderful views. Four kilometres east of the town is **Arenal Botanical Gardens**, opened in 1993, with many flowers, birds, butterflies, a delightful place (still under development) ■ *T6955266 ext 273, F6955387, 0900-1600 (closed October), US$3.50*. Luis Diego Murillo, T6955008, operates sightseeing tours around the lake and the volcano.

Sleeping AL *Marina club Hotel*, T4799178, situated on the lake, pool, horses, windsurfing and canoeing. **AL** *Joya Sureña*, T6944057, F6944059, joysur@solracsa.co.cr, 28 rooms, working cattle farm, riding, gym, sauna, pool. **AL** *Los Héroes*, on road from Arenal Volcano to Nuevo Arenal, T2846315, Swiss-style, pool, horses, rooms with lake view more expensive. Ten kilometres from Arenal towards Tilarán, **A** *Hotel Pequeña Helvecia*, Swiss-owned, clean, pool, good food. Two kilometres west of the gardens is **B** *Villa Decary*, T/F3833012, decary@yellowweb.co.cr, 5 rooms and a bungalow for rent. **B** *Chalet Nicolás*, T6944041, bed and breakfast (a speciality), run by retired Americans, hot water, friendly, recommended. Two kilometres from the centre towards Tilarán. **D-E** *Cabinas Rodríguez*, clean, friendly. There is also a campsite on Lago Coter, north of Lake Arenal. The **AL-C** *Lago Coter Eco-Lodge*, is popular with birdwatchers, 19 rooms in main building with shared bathrooms rather grim, or 16 brighter cabins with private bath and newer furniture, family-style meals, bar, pool table, games, lots of tours, watch out for snakes on roads and paths, canopy tour with platforms in the forest, T2575075, F2577065 in San José.

Eating *Pizzería e Ristorante Tramonti*, T6955266, ext 282, for Italian cuisine, good.

Sport Fishing: several places rent fishing tackle, but if you want a boat, guide and full package try *Rainbow Bass Fishing Safaris*, run by Dave Myers, US$200 a day for 2 anglers, fishing licence US$30 for 2 months, PO Box 7758-1000, San José, T2292550, 222834, F2357662. **Windsurfing**: the *Tilawa Windsurfing Center* is on the west side of the lake, which is the best side for windsurfing; mornings are best, particularly December-January, equipment for rent.

Transport Frequent buses to Tilarán, Fortuna, 1 a day to San Rafael.

Directory Tour companies & travel agents Several include *Aventuras Arenal*, La Fortuna, T4799133, Rodrigo Salazar: *Caño Negro Tours*, US$40-50; Arenal lake sunset trip US$40-50, fishing US$27 per hour, Cerro Chato tour, US$25.

Tilarán

Colour map 5, grid B2

From Arenal, the lakeside road is good, paved, with fine views, 25 kilometres to Tilarán. Tilarán is a modern town. Tourist office half a block from plaza, on right side of church. Cata Tours have a branch office in Tilarán, T6955953, offering several excursions and pickup from Cañas-Liberia area hotels.

Sleeping A *Mystica Resort*, T3821499, F6955387, barbara_moglia@quorum.nacion.co.cr, hillside cabins overlooking Arenal lake, windsurfing equipment rental. **A** *Rock River Lodge* on the road skirting the lake, T/F6955644, rokriver@sol.racsa.co.cr, 6 rooms with bathroom, restaurant. **B** *Cabinas Naralit*, T6955393, south of church, clean, new buildings. **B** *The Spot Tourist Center*, Tilarán, 16 rooms with bath, restaurant, fishing, horses, day trips, T6955711, F6955579. **D** *Puerto San Luis Lake Resort*, T6955797, 15 rooms with private bathroom, refrigerator, TV and fan, restaurant, boat rentals, fishing equipment, windsurf boards, trips to Arenal volcano and lake, T6955950. Nearby, **C** *Bahía Azul*, T6955750, with breakfast, fan refrigerator, TV. **D** *Cabinas El Sueño*, T6955347, rooms around central patio, hot water, quiet, friendly, recommended. **D** *Cabinas Mary*, T6955479, with bath, small pleasant rooms upstairs recommended. **D** *Hotel Guadalupe*, T6955943, 8 nice rooms with bath, recommended. **E** *Surf* (Youth Hostel), small, clean, very friendly. **E** *Tilarán*, T6955043, round the corner from the bus terminal, with hot shower, cheaper without, clean, friendly, restaurant. **E** *Central*, T6955363, with shared bath (more with), noisy. The office of the *Albergue La Casona del Lago* (affiliated to the Youth Hostel network), on the left hand corner (with public phone) of 1st main junction as you come into town from the lake, has windsurfing equipment, very helpful.

Transport Buses Direct bus from San José, 4 daily, 4 hours, from ½ block north or Terminal Atlántico Norte, buy ticket at terminal, and 4 daily buses from Cañas. Two daily buses to San Carlos via Fortuna at 0700 and 1230. To Fortuna, 3 hours, US$2.90. Daily bus to Santa Elena (for Monteverde), 1230, 2½ hours, US$1.65, return 0700 daily. Tilarán-Puntarenas 0600, 1300, 3 hours, US$3. If you get the 1230 bus Tilarán-Liberia you can get from there to the Nicaraguan border before it closes.

To get to Monteverde (two to three hours, four-wheel drive recommended), go through the town until you come to a T-junction opposite a green house, go left and follow paved road to Quebrada Grande. As you enter Quebrada Grande, take the unpaved road to the left before the church, it is very rough. At Dos de Tilarán is a sign: 30 kilometres to Monteverde, follow this road to Cabeceras. There the road forks, take either the left, longer route via Nubes, or right, down dale and uphill, both poor, to Santa Elena (nine kilometres) and thence to Monteverde.

The Northwest

The route of the Pan-American Highway passes near the cloud forest of Monteverde in the Cordillera de Tilarán, the marshes of the Palo Verde National Park, the active Volcán Rincón and the dry tropical forest of the Santa Rosa National Park on the Pacific coast as it crosses the great cattle haciendas of Guanacaste.

The Pan-American Highway from San José descends from the Meseta Central to **Esparza**, an attractive town with a turbulent early history, as it was repeatedly sacked by pirates in the 17th century, belying its peaceful aspect today. **E** *Hotel Castanuelas*, T6355105, a/c, quiet, cooler alternative to Puntarenas; **F** per person *Pensión Córdoba*, clean and modern.

The stretch of the Highway between San Ramón and Esparza (34 kilometres) includes the sharp fall of 800 metres from the Meseta Central. (Beware of fog on this stretch if driving or cycling.) Beyond Esparza there is the *Bar/Restaurant Mirador Enis*, a popular stopping place for tour buses et al, service station opposite, fruit stalls nearby, before a left turn at **Barranca** for Puntarenas, 15 kilometres. In Barranca there is **D** *Hotel Río Mar*, with bath, restaurant, good. If going from San José to Monteverde, it is possible to change buses in Barranca, rather than going all the way to Puntarenas, if you leave the capital before 1230.

Puntarenas

Puntarenas is on a five-kilometre spit of land thrusting out into Nicoya Gulf and enclosing the Estero lagoon. This is a run-down neglected town typical of small tropical ports. There are, however, plans for a face-lift. It is hot (mean temperature 27° C), the beaches are dirty, and are crowded on Sunday. There is a public swimming pool on the end of the point (US$1 entrance), very hot. Good surfing off the headland. Across the gulf are the mountains of the Nicoya Peninsula. In the gulf are several islands, the Islas Negritos, to which there are passenger launches. The chief products around Puntarenas are bananas, rice, cattle, and coconuts. Puntarenas is being replaced as the country's main Pacific port by Caldera.

Population: 50,000
Colour map 5, grid B2

Museum of Marine History and the City of Puntarenas, in the Cultural Centre by the main church and tourist office. ■ *Monday-Friday 0830-1200, 1300-1630 daily, US$1.80.*

Sights

Crossing to Nicoya Peninsula see page 1105.

Excursions

Isla San Lucas was a prison island, but a luxury resort has now been built. You may visit its beautiful beaches on Sunday. Launch leaves Puntarenas Sunday 0900; returns 1500, US$1.50.

Isla Jesuita, in Gulf of Nicoya has an hotel: *Hotel Isla Jesuita*, lodge and cottages, hammocks reached by hotel's boat or public launch from Puntarenas. Package rates from San José, also arrangements can be made in the USA T800-3279408.

Isla Gitana, 13 kilometres southwest of Puntarenas has two rustic cabins, **A** per person including meals, tropical paradise island, white sand beach, lots of wildlife, swimming pool, kayaking, windsurfing. The lodge can arrange speed boat transfers from Puntarenas or meet the Puntarenas-Paquera launch. Contact Linda Ruegg, T6612994.

On the old San José-Puntarenas railway, near the new port of Caldera, is **Mata de Limón**, which has a beach. It is on a lagoon surrounded by mangroves, peaceful. Bus from Puntarenas market every hour (marked to Caldera). **Sleeping**: **E** *Casablanca*, Av 14, C 2-4, T2222921, full board available, or cabins. **E** *Manglares*, near former train stop, reasonable, good restaurant. Excellent bar/restaurant next to railway booking office. South of the village (care when crossing wooden bridge at night, missing planks!) there are several basic places to stay, **F**, but acceptable: *Viña del Mar*, *Villas Fanny*, *Villas América*. Good fishing nearby.

AL *Complejo Turístico Yadrán*, Av 4, C35-37, T6612662, luxury, pool, etc. **A** *Las Brisas*, on the waterfront, Paseo Los Turistas Al Final, with bath, good restaurant, swimmimg pool, T6614140, but reservations reported not honoured. **A-B** *Tioga*, Barrio El Carmen, T6610271, beachfront and C 17, with bath, hot water, includes continental breakfast, swimming pool, friendly, very good indeed, but make sure you know what you are being charged. **A** *Porto Bello*, Av Central, C 68-70, next door, with bath, a/c, pool, quiet, clean, gardens, excellent food, helpful Italian owner, T6611322. *Yacht Club*, T6610784, at Cocal, caters for members of foreign yacht clubs. Others are **C** *Chorotega*, C 3, Av 3, T6610998, with bath and fan, **D** without, although price list disagrees with what they actually charge, clean, central (1 block east of river). **C** *Cabinas Midey*, C13, Av 2-4, T/F6611553, also apartment for up to 6, US$8 per person. **C** *La Punta*, Av 2, C 6-8, T6610696, 1 block from car ferry, with bath, friendly, clean, hot water, restaurant, secure parking, pool, American-owned, big rooms. **D** *Cabinas El Jorón*, C 25, 7 blocks from ferry, T6610467, roomy, fridge, a/c, restaurant, recommended. **D** *Las Hamacas* on waterfront, T6610398, nice rooms but noisy. **D** *Viking*, C 32, Av 2, new, on the beach. **D** *Gran Imperial*, 500m from station on road to town, T6610579, friendly, hot water, private bath. **E** *Ayi Con*, C 2, Av 1-3, T6610164, a little noisy but clean. **E** *Cayuga*, C 4, Av Central, with shower, a/c, restaurant, dirty, run down. **E** *Río*, Av 3, C Central-2, T6610331, near market, Chinese owners, with shower, basic and noisy, but friendly. **E** *Cabezas*, Av 1, C 2-4, T6611045, with fan, cheaper without, basic, clean, very good value, recommended.

Sleeping
Thieves abound on the beach.

F *Miramar*, also near market, fan, good deal. F *Monte Mar*, opposite *El Fela Bar*, clean, small rooms, thin walls, shared bath. *Cabinas Thelma*, very good, friendly (ask at *Holman Bar*, C 7). Many *cabinas* on Av 2. Apartments for rent from Jacob Puister, Contigua Casino, Central, p 2, T6610246, US$37 for 2 weeks. Accommodation difficult to find December-April, especially at weekends.

At Roble, 18 kilometres east of Puntarenas, on the coast L *Caribbean Village Fiesta*, T6630808, F6631516, all-inclusive, 174 rooms with bath, a/c, cable TV, 3 pools, boat rentals, restaurants, tennis, casino. B *Villa del Roble*, by the sea, T6630447, 5 rooms, quiet, small pool, charming. B *Casa San Francisco*, T6630148, near regional hospital, run by 2 Canadian ladies, with breakfast, pool, friendly, clean, laundry facilities, helpful, recommended.

At San Isidro de Puntarenas D *Cabinas Orlando*, with bath and kitchen. *San Isidro Hotel and Club* has a Youth Hostel, east, T2332244, F2216822.

Eating Next to *Hotel Tioga* is *Aloha Restaurant* (pushy waiters). *Mariscos Kahite Blanco*, C 17, near launch, excellent seafood. *Kahite Negro*, next door, good local food. *Casa de Mariscos*, C 7, Paseo de los Turistas, good seafood, reasonable prices. A number of Chinese restaurants on the main street (eg *Mandarín*, good value). Good food from market stalls, eg *sopa de carne*. *Fonda Brisas del Pacífico*, near wharf, good value *casado*. *Soda Vanessa*, Av 1, clean, cheap, good breakfast for under US$1. There is a lively nightlife in the cheaper bars. On the beach, *Miramare*, C 17-19, good but expensive; nearby, C 19-21, is *Bierstube*, good for sandwiches, hamburgers, but beware overcharging. Recommended bars: *Pier 14*, near wharf, good pizza and hamburgers made by Captain Ed from Mobile (Alabama) and his wife. *Yate Bar*, friendly, English-speaking owner. *El Fela* bar, opposite Banco Anglo Costarricense, clean, cool, a must for women just to see the toilet decor. **At Roble** *María Vargas*, bar and restaurant, friendly, good food, reasonable prices.

Festivals *Fiesta de la Virgen del Mar*, **Saturday closest to 16 July**, carnival and regatta of decorated fishing boats and yachts.

Shopping Market, shops and banks on Calle Central, opposite end to beach.

Transport **Buses** Bus terminal for San José is at Av 4, C 2-4. Buses every 40 minutes 0415-1900 to San José, 2 hours, US$2.50. Buses from San José leave from Terminal Puntarenas, 0600-1900. Daily bus to Santa Elena for Monteverde, see page 1093. Buses south to Quepos from main bus station, 0500, 1100 and 1300 (high season) via Jacó, US$2.70, 4 hours, return 0430, 1030, 1500. To Liberia with Empresa Arata daily 1730, return 0830, 2½ hours, US$1.50, also many buses passing through Puntarenas pick up passengers for Liberia. Good café at bus terminal where you can await your bus. Tourist information office has up to date bus timetables.

Directory **Banks** *Banco Nacional* changes TCs, but painfully slow service. **Communications** Post Office: near church on C 5, beach side, hard to find. **Telecommunications:** ICE and Radiográfica, Av C, C 2-4. **Tour companies & travel agents** *Turisol Travel Agency*, C 1, Av 3, T6611212. For boat excursions (sailing or motor boats) from Puntarenas call Cath Mercer T2321020 at ASICS tours in San José. See under San José **Travel agents** for cruises in the Gulf of Nicoya.

Monteverde

To visit the Monteverde Cloud Forest Reserve, follow the Pan-American Highway northwest to Km 149, turning right just before the Río Lagarto. Continue for about 40 kilometres on mostly gravel road (allow two and a half hours) to Santa Elena. Parts of the road are quite good, but in wet weather four-wheel drive is recommended for the rough parts. Check that your car rental agreement allows you to visit Monteverde. A 33 kilometre shorter route is to take the Pipasa/Sardinal turn-off from the Pan-American Highway. At the park in Sardinal turn left, then go via Guacimal to the Monteverde road. The bus from Puntarenas goes via Km 149.

Santa Elena is a charmless place two and a half kilometres before Monteverde village, but it is cheaper here than staying nearer to the Reserve. Next to the clinic is a Serpentarium, open daily 0700-1600, US$5. Banco Nacional, open 0900-1500, will change travellers' cheques with commission and advance cash against Visa.

Santa Elena

Sleeping **B** *Finca Valverde*, 300m east of Banco Nacional, T6455157, with bath, nice gardens for birdwatching, bar, restaurant. **B** *Sunset Hotel*, 1½ kilometres on road to Tilarán, T6613558, on top of hill, nice location, friendly, clean, warm showers, good breakfast, German spoken. **C** *Arco Iris*, 100m north of Banco Nacional, with bath, restaurant, horses for rent, plenty of parking, T6455067, F6455022, arcoiris@sol.racsa.co.cr. **C** and up *Bed and Breakfast Marbella*, 10m east of National Bank, T6455298, owned by Carmen Acosta and Pablo Comancho, rooms without and with bath, without and with breakfast, warm, spacious, comfortable, hospitable, recommended, hot water. **C** *Monte Los Olivos Ecotourist Lodge*, 6 kilometres north of Santa Elena on road to Quebrada Grande, 4 cabins with private bathroom, 5 with shared bathroom, one of 3 lodges run by community association and supported by WWF Canada and CIDA Canada. **C** *Mirador Lodge San Gerardo*, T6455087, 6 kilometres north of Santa Elena, dirt road, May-November you probably need a horse, cabins with bath or dormitory accommodation (**E**), restaurant, own private rain forest park for birdwatching nearby. **D** *Cabinas Tucán*, T6455017, bargain for lower price in off season, with bath in nice rooms, or **E** in basic cabins with shower (supposedly hot), friendly management, good breakfast and restaurant recommended but closed Sunday lunch. **E** *Pensión Santa Elena*, T6455298, cheaper for YHA members, clean, good food, vegetarians catered for, unlimited free coffee (**C** includes 3 meals). **F** *Canopy Tour Base Camp*, clean, friendly, electric hot shower, free transport to Monteverde for guests, riding on healthy horse, US$5 per hour, food average, but good *casado*. **F** *El Colibrí*, clean, friendly, timber built with balconies. **F** *Hospedaje el Banco*, family-run, friendly, hot shower, clean, good information, English spoken, good breakfast. **F** *Pensión Cabinas Marín*, 500m uphill past the Agricultural College, spacious rooms, room 8 has a nice view, good breakfasts, friendly. **E** *Pensión El Sueño* (The Dream), very friendly, hot shower, small but nice rooms, clean, pricey meals, car park, run by Rafa Trejos who does horseback trips into the mountains to see quetzals, etc, US$35. *Chunches*, good Expresso bar and snacks, used books, magazines, laundromat, opposite *Pensión Santa Elena*.

Transport **Buses** Bus from Puntarenas, Terminal Empresarios Unidos, daily at 1415, 2½-4 hours, returns 0600, US$2.20, this bus arrives in time to catch a bus to Puerto Quepos for Manuel Antonio (the company has one new bus and one old bus, take the new, safer in many respects). See Monteverde **Transport**, below, for buses from San José. For an alternative route to Santa Elena from Arenal, see pages 1087-1090. Buses to Tilarán daily at 1130 and 1630, 2½ hours, US$1.65.

Monteverde

The settlement at **Monteverde** was founded by American Quakers in the 1950s; it is strung out along the road without any centre. It is essentially a group of dairy farms and a cheese factory run by a cooperative, which you can tour. Excellent cheeses of various types can be bought, also fresh milk, ice cream and *cajeta* (a butterscotch spread) are sold. The Quakers have an English Library at Monteverde.

The **Monteverde Butterfly Garden** is beautifully presented large garden. They are mainly concerned with breeding and research and do not export ■*open daily, 0930-1600, US$5 including guided tour, best time for a visit 1100-1300*. Near the Butterfly Garden is *Finca Ecológica*, , bird lists, good birding and wildlife in this transitional zone between cloud and tropical dry forest, guides available. ■ *0700-1700 daily, US$5, free map.*

From Monteverde to the Reserve is a minimum 45 minutes' walk uphill, about four kilometres, but there are lovely views looking towards the sea and the Nicoya peninsula, particularly in the evening (when you are coming down and can appreciate them). A new **Skywalk** has been constructed half way between Santa Elena and the Park, five suspension bridges through the cloud forest are linked, the highest being 42 metres above the ground. ■*Open daily 0700-1600, US$8, student US$6, child US$4, for information T6455238, skywalk@sol.racsa.co.cr.*

Orchid Garden, with about 400 species collected by Gabriel Barboza. ■ *T64555010, open daily 0800-1700.* The garden is 100 metres behind the *Hotel Sapo Dorado.*

Just before the Field Station is the **Hummingbird Gallery**, where masses of different hummingbirds can be seen darting around a glade, visiting feeding dispensers filled with sugared water. ■ *0930-1700.* Outside the entrance is a small shop/photo gallery which sells pictures and gifts. Slide shows daily at 1630 (three times a week sometimes), US$3.70, T6611259 (photos by Michael and Patricia Fogden). There is also a slide show at *Hotel Belmar, The Hidden Rainforest,* by Bobby Maxson, 1930 daily except Friday.

Sleeping **L** *Monteverde Lodge,* T800-6334734 toll free in USA, T6455057 locally, F6455126, or book through Costa Rica Expeditions, T2220333, recommended, restaurant, jacuzzi, daily slide shows 1815. **AL** *Sapo Dorado,* just before *Hotel de Montaña,* 10 suites with fireplace, good but expensive restaurant open 0700-2100, T6455010, F6455180. **AL** *Fonda Vela,* T6455125,

Monteverde

◀ *To Santa Elena Cloud Forest Reserve and Tilarán*

SANTA ELENA

▲ *To San José*

Serpentarium
Health Clinic

Heliconia

Monteverde
Lodge

Pensión
Manakin

De Montaña
Monteverde

Belmar
Conservation League

Quebrada Sucia

Butterfly
Garden

El Bosque &
Restaurant ■

MONTEVERDE

Casem

Service
Station

Stella's Bakery

Bajo Tigre Trail

Cheese
Factory

Río Guacimal

Pensión
Flor Mar ■

Fonda Vela

N

0 metres 250
0 yards 273

F6455119 (or San José T2231083, F2571416), FondaVela@centralamerica.com, private bathroom, hot water, 25 rooms and suites in 7 cabins, nearest to Reserve, 25 minutes' walk, on a 14-hectare farm with forest and trail system, good birding, some camping, horses for hire, excellent restaurant (open to public), bar, TV room, art gallery. **AL** *El Establo*, next to *Heliconia*, T/F6455110, 19 carpeted rooms with private bathroom, restaurant, 50-hectare farm with 50% cloud forest, own nature guide, good birdwatching, riding stables, 35 horses, family-run, transport available, very accommodating, recommended. **AL** per person *San Luis Biological Station and Ecolodge*, T/F6455277, on 65 hectares of farmland and cloud forest in the San Luis Valley, adjoining Monteverde Cloud Forest, 5 cabins, horse riding, swimming in river and other options. **AL** *Cloud Forest Lodge*, 300 metres north of *Sapo Dorado*, T6455058, F6455168, 12 rooms with bath, restaurant, beautiful views (Canopy Tours, T2552463/6455243, offer tours of 5 platforms, connected by steel cables, to explore the forest canopy, US$40 per person, at *Cloud Forest Lodge*). **AL** *Heliconia*, T6455109, F6455205, 100 metres before *Hotel de Montaña*, private bathroom, restaurant, very comfortable, excellent food, warmly recommended. **AL** *Hotel de Moñtana Monteverde*, T6455046, F6455320, in San José T2337078, F2226184, EP, just before service station on right, comfortable, recommended, set meals, good, wholesome food, sauna, jacuzzi, horses for hire, good views of Nicoya, excellent birdwatching on 6-hectare reserve, transport from San José available. **AL-A** *Belmar*, T6455201, F6455135, Belmar@centralamerica. com, 300 metres from service station, Swiss chalet-style, beautiful views of Nicoya, restaurant, good, transport from San José available.

A *Villa Verde*, 2 kilometres before reserve, rooms with hot showers, others with shared

Santa Elena

bath, cabins with kitchenette, includes good meals, restaurant, clean, nice, excellent views, T6455025, F6455115. **B-D** *El Bosque*, next to restaurant of same name, 21 rooms, T/F6455129, hot showers, comfortable, clean, lovely rooms with fine views, safe parking. **C** *Pensión Manakin*, just before *Hotel de Moñtana*, turn right, drive 75m, T6455080, 6 cabins with bath or **F** with shared bath, 10% discount for students with ID, meals available (US$3-4), clean, friendly, good food. Youth Hostel annex, **E** per person with breakfast, or full board, if not busy can arrange to use kitchen facilities, 800m off the main road at Cerro Plano, will collect you from bus station if you have reservation, transport to Reserve or Santa Elena, US$2 per person. Gary Diller, an American guide, highly recommended, rents rooms in his house, **D**, T6455045, late afternoon, early evening. **D** *Monteverde Inn*, T6455156, turnoff 100m before *Hotel de Montaña*, private bathroom, full board, good mattresses. **E** per person *Pensión Flor Mar*, T6455009, F6455088, between Monteverde and Reserve, full board, or **E** with breakfast in dormitory, helpful, hot shower, luggage stored, owned by Marvin Rockwell, one of the original Quaker settlers (he is a mine of information), small area for camping.

Johnny's Pizza, on main road between Santa Elena and Monteverde, wood oven-cooked pizzas, café, souvenir shop.

Eating

Costa Rica

Restaurant El Bosque, next to Casem Shop, good food, clean, open from 0630; between Gas Station and El Bosque, *La Cascada* and *Cerro Verde*. *Stella's Bakery*, opposite Service Station, has good granola and cakes.

Shopping Casem, a cooperative gift shop, is located just outside Monteverde on the road to the Reserve next to *El Bosque* restaurant. It sells embroidered shirts, T-shirts, wooden and woven articles and baskets.

Transport **Buses** Direct bus, Monteverde Express, runs from Calle 12, 125m north of Avenida 7, just outside Terminal Atlántico Norte, San José (3½ hours, US$5) daily at 0630 and 1430. Leaves from *Hotel Villa Verde* also at 0630, 1430. Calls at Santa Elena. Be early. Check times in advance, Saturday bus does not always run in low season, T6455032 in Santa Elena, T2223854 in San José for information. Be aware that this service is not 'express', it stops to pick up passengers all along the route, and is not a comfortable ride. Alternatively, get the bus to Puntarenas and change there for Santa Elena, see above. **Taxis** available between Santa Elena and Monteverde, US$6.85, and between Monteverde and the Reserve, US$5.75 (hunt around for good prices). Not so easy to find a taxi for return trip, best to arrange beforehand. Road toll at Monteverde US$0.60. There is a service station, open Monday-Saturday 0700-1800, Sunday 0700-1200. **Horses** Several places rent horses; look for signs between Santa Elena and Monteverde or ask at your hotel.

Directory **Art Gallery** *Galería Extasis*, 250m south of *La Cascada*, exhibits sculptures by the Costa Rican artist, Marco Tulio Brenes. **Language schools** A branch of the *Centro Panamericano de Idiomas*, in Heredia, has opened, T6455026, accommodation with local families.

Monteverde Cloud Forest Reserve

The best months are January to May, especially February, March and April.

The 10,500-hectare, private Monteverde Reserve (owned and managed by the non-profit research and educational association, the Tropical Science Centre) is mainly primary cloud forest. It contains over 400 species of birds (including the resplendant quetzal, best seen between January and May, which are the dry months, especially near the start of the Nuboso trail, three-wattled bellbird and bare-necked umbrellabird), over 100 species of mammals (including monkeys, baird's tapir and six endangered cats: jaguar, jaguarundi, margay, ocelot, tigrillo and puma), reptiles, amphibians (including the golden toad, now thought to be extinct not having been seen since 1989). The reserve includes an estimated 2,500 species of plants and more than 6,000 species of insects. The entrance is at 1,500 metres, but the maximum altitude in the reserve is over 1,800 metres. Mean temperature is between 16° and 18°C and average annual rainfall is 3,000 millimetres. The weather changes quickly and wind and humidity often make the air feel cooler. The trails are in good condition and there are easy, short and interesting walks for those who do not want to hike all day. Trail walks take from two hours to all day or more. Sendero Brillante and others may be restricted. The Bajo Tigre trail (US$3.50) takes one and a half hours, parking available with notice (T6455003) a guide can be arranged, no horses allowed on trail, open 0800-1600. There is a trail northwards to the Arenal volcano but not recommended as very overgrown. Free maps of the reserve at the entrance and an excellent Nature Trail Guide. Follow the rules, sign the register, indicating where you are going in case you get lost, stay on the paths, leave nothing behind, take no fauna or flora out, no radios or tape recorders allowed.

Admission The Reserve entrance is at the field station, 45 minutes' walk from the settlement at Monteverde. The total number of visitors to the Reserve at any one time is 250 (100 in high season), but be there before 0700 to make sure of getting in during high season (hotels will book you a place for the following day). Tour buses come in from San José every day and be warned that travellers have told us there is little chance of seeing much wildlife. Entrance fee US$8 (students with ID half-price) valid for multiple entry during the day, can not be purchased in advance; 3-day pass 20% discount. Reserve office open 0700-1630 daily; the park opens at 0600 and closes at 1700. Shelter facilities throughout the Reserve cost US$3.50 plus key deposit of US$5, bring sleeping bag and flashlight. You can make your own meals. Dormitory-style accommodation for up to 30 people at entrance, *Albergue Reserva Biológica de Monteverde*, T6612655, US$20 full board only. Reservations required for all Reserve accommodation (usually booked up by groups). A small shop at the office sells various checklists, postcards, slides, gifts and excellent T-shirts, the proceeds of which help towards the conservation project.

Donations to the Reserve can be made at the Reserve office or Tropical Science Centre (Apdo 8-3870, 100 San José, T2252649 or 2533308, F2534963) at El Higuerón, 100m Sur y 125m Este, Barrio La Granja, San Pedro, or the Monteverde Conservation League (Apdo 10165, 1000 San José, T6612953), open 0830-1600, opposite Monteverde service station. Donations are welcomed for purchasing additional land and for maintaining and improving the existing Reserve area. If you are interested in volunteer work, from non-skilled trail maintenance to skilled scientific assistance work, surveying, teaching or studying on a tropical biology programme, contact the Conservation League, at the address above. The Conservation League is working with schools in the area on education regarding conservation, forests, etc. **Donations**

Recommended equipment includes binoculars (750s-1040s), good camera with 400-1,000 ASA film, insect repellent, sweater and light rainwear. Rubber boots are a must for the longer walks, at all times of year but especially in the rainy season, and can be rented at the park office for US$0.80 or at hotels. **Equipment**

Natural History walks with biologist guides, every morning and afternoon, 3-4 hours, US$12 (children half price); reserve in advance at the office or at your hotel. If you use a private (non-Reserve) guide you must pay his entrance fee. An experienced and recommended guide is Gary Diller (Apdo 10165, 1000 San José, T6455045); he specializes in birds. There are six others operating, of varying specialization and experience. Tomás Guindon offers a night tour in the Reserve, 1900, T6611008, US$13. A guide is recommended if you want to see wildlife since the untrained eye misses a lot. **Guides**

Adjoining the Monteverde Cloud Forest is the **International Children's Rainforest** (*El Bosque Eterno de los Niños*), established in 1988 after an initiative by Swedish schoolchildren to save forests. Currently at 13,000 hectares, the land is bought and maintained with children's donations and the aim is to expand to include a further 5,500 hectares. There are plans to bring school groups to the forest, but there are no trails open to the public although the 'Jaguar Canyon' will be opening soon (1998). Entrance US$5, students US$2.

Reserva Sendero Tranquilo, a private property near the Monteverde Cheese Factory arranges entrance reservations and guiding with owner David Lowther, or Julie Kraft, T6612952. Entry restricted to 12 people at any one time.

Monteverde Music Festival, classical and jazz concerts between December and March at sunset, at *Hotel Fonda Vela* (T6455125 for information), local and foreign musicians, entry US$9, T6612950; schedules and transportation from hotels.

An alternative trail network is in the **Finca Ecológica**, two kilometres southwest of Santa Elena, open 0700-1600. The trails are flat and there is good birdwatching and wildlife, US$3 entrance.

Santa Elena Cloud Forest Reserve

One kilometre along the road from Santa Elena to Tilarán, a five kilometre track is signposted to the **Reserve**, managed by the **Centro Ecológico Bosque Nuboso de Monteverde**. It is 83 percent primary cloudforest and the rest 17-year-old secondary forest at an elevation of 1,700 metres, bordered by the Monteverde Cloud Forest Reserve and the Arenal Forest Reserve. There is an eight kilometre path network and

Costa Rica

several lookouts where you can see and hear the Arenal volcano. The 'canopy tour' is recommended, you climb inside a hollow strangler fig tree then cross between two platforms along aerial runways 30 metres up, good views of orchids and bromeliads, then down a 30-metre hanging rope at the end. There are generally fewer visitors here than at Monteverde. The Centro Ecológico Bosque Nuboso is administered by the local community and profits go to five local schools. It was set up by the Costa Rican government in 1989 with collaboration from Canada. The rangers are very friendly and enthusiastic. There is a small information centre where rubber boots can be hired and a small café open at weekends. Hand-painted T-shirts for sale. Entrance US$8, students US$4, opens 0700-1600, T/F6455236 for information. It is a long, steep hike from the village, alternatively hire a taxi, carload US$6.50.

Continuing on the Pan-American

Forty three kilometres north of Barranca on the Pan-American Highway is the turn off for **Las Juntas**. This road is an alternative to route to Monteverde for those driving from the Tempisque ferry or Guanacaste; a third of it is paved. After Las Juntas, is the Abangares mining ecomuseum at **La Sierra de Abangares**, 0600-1800 daily, US$1.80.

Forty seven kilometres north of Barranca a left turn goes to the Tempisque ferry and after about six kilometres a road off to the right at San Joaquín leads to the **A** per person *Hacienda Solimar Lodge*, a 1,300-hectare cattle farm with over half dry tropical virgin forest bordering Palo Verde National Park near Porozal in the lower Tempisque River basin. The freshwater Madrigal estuary on the property is one of the most important areas for waterbirds in Costa Rica, surrounded by gallery forest (only guests staying at the Hacienda can visit). Recommended for serious birdwatchers. Reservations essential, T6690281 or contact Birdwatch, Apdo 6951, 1005 San José, T2284768, F2281573, eight rooms with private or shared bathroom, includes meals, minimum two nights, transport available on request, local guide, horseriding.

Cañas   Sixty seven kilometres north of Barranca is **Cañas**. Six buses daily, 0830-1645, also 1815 Friday, Sunday, return buses 0400-1350, two more on Sunday, three and a half hours, from just outside Coca Cola terminal, Calle 16, Avenida 3-5, San José. Buses to Tilarán, Nuevo Arenal, past the volcano and on to San Carlos. The turn off for Tilarán is at the filling station, no signs. For a description of this route in reverse see pages 1084-1090. Five buses a day to Tilarán, from the park, 30 minutes, US$0,50, minibus US$1.

Sleeping and services   D *Cañas*, C 2, Av 1, T6690039, with bath, clean, pleasant. **E** *El Corral*, C 4, Av Central, T6691467, with bath. **E** *Gran*, with bath and fan, grubby. **F** *Guillén*, C Central, Av 2; also *Luz* and others; *Restaurant Panchitos* on main square is good and inexpensive. Good Chinese restaurants, eg *Central*, on main square, in centre of Cañas. 4 kilometres north of Cañas is a hotel, **AL** *La Pacífica*, on Pan-American Highway, T6690266, F6690555, Swiss-run, with good restaurant, cottages, cabins, pool, and rafting down the Río Bebedero to Palo Verde. The property extends to 2,000 hectares, of which half is a cattle farm and half dry, tropical forest. You can have a guided tour of the farm (US$10) and there is an extensive library on dry, tropical forests. **B** *Nuevo Hotel Cañas*, T6691294, 10 nice rooms, pool. **C** *Capazuri B&B*, T/F6690580, 2.5 kilometres north of Cañas, also good camping US$3 per person. **F** *Cabinas Corobicí*, near San Jose bus terminal, car park, T6690241, 11 good rooms with bath. The restaurant *Rincón Corobicí*, next to *La Pacífica*, clean and pleasant, has a small zoo and offers rafting down Río Corobicí, T6690544. If you turn north off the Panamerican Highway just after Corobicí, you will eventually come (58 kilometres) to Upala (see page 1089). After 34 kilometres you reach **Bijagua de Upala**, between the volcanoes Tenorio and Miravalles. The **C** *Bijagua Heliconias Ecotourist Lodge* is here, 6 cabins with private bathroom, one of 3 lodges run by community association and supported by WWF Canada and CIDA Canada.

Transport Bus The bus station is 500 metres north of the centre, where all buses depart from except for those to San José, which leave from the terminal 300m west of Parque Central. To San José: Transporte Cañas, T6690145, 8 daily from 0400, 3 hours. To Liberia 10 daily from 0530. To Tilarán, 6 daily from 0600; to Puntarenas 8 daily from 0600.

Directory Tour companies & travel agents Two local tour agencies are *Safaris Corobicí* (US$35 per person for 2 hr rafting, US$60 ½-day, T/F6692091, F6691091) and *Transporte Palo Verde* (F6690544), run by Jay Thomas Connerly and Gregg Dean, offering bird watching, boat trips down the Corobicí, no white water but lots of wildlife, and Río Bebedero to Palo Verde, bicycling and other trips. Safaris Corobicí is 4 km past Cañas on the Pan-American Highway, 25m before the entrance to Centro Ecológico La Pacífica; Transporte Palo Verde is in *Hotel El Corral* in Cañas on the Pan-American Highway. *CATA Tours*, T2962133, rafting tours and full-day tours to Palo Verde National Park.

On the Nicoya Peninsula, is the **Palo Verde National Park**, over 5,700 hectares of marshes with many water birds. Indeed, in the Laguna, over 50,000 birds are considered resident. Research Station, operated by OTS, T2405033, has accommodation facilities, ordinary visitors US$40 with meals, student researchers, US$22, senior researchers, US$32. Day visits with lunch, US$15, minimum six persons. Make advance reservations. Turn off the Pan-American Highway at **Bagaces**, half way between Cañas and Liberia, no public transport. The Palo Verde Administration offices are in Bagaces, next to service station, T6711062. Camping and possible lodging in park. Two ranger stations, Palo Verde and Catalina. Check roads in wet season. Fantastic views from limestone cliffs. Estación Biológica is a research station run by the OET. They organize natural history walks and basic accommodation. Information and reservations T (San José) 2406696, reservas@offseason.ots.ac.cr.

Palo Verde National Park

If you turn north at Bagaces on Route 164 and drive through **Guayabo** (E *Las Brisas*, bath, hot water, fans), to Km 30, you get to *Parador Las Nubes del Miravalles*, T6711011 ext 280, home cooking for breakfast, lunch and dinner, tent and mattress rental, horse rental, good hiking to **Miravalles volcano** and waterfalls, very friendly and hospitable people on working *finca*, from here you can take a boat up the Río Pizote to Lake Nicaragua.

Guanacaste Province

The Pan-American Highway runs for 125 kilometres from Cañas to the Nicaraguan border. It passes through the low hills of **Guanacaste Province**, which includes the Peninsula of Nicoya and the lowlands at the head of the gulf. The Province, with its capital at Liberia, has a distinctive people, way of life, flora and fauna. The smallholdings of the highlands give way here to large *haciendas* and great cattle estates. Maize, rice, cotton, beans and fruit are other products, and there is manganese at Playa Real. The rivers teem with fish; there are all kinds of wildlife in the uplands.

The people are open, hospitable, fond of the pleasures of life: music, dancing (the Punto Guanacasteco has been officially declared the typical national dance), and merry-making (cattle and jollity often go together). There are many *fiestas* in January and February in the various towns and villages, which are well worth seeing. Rainfall is moderate: 1,000 to 2,000 millimetres a year, there is a long dry season which makes irrigation important, but the lowlands are deep in mud during the rainy season.

Liberia

Liberia is a neat, clean, cattle town with a triangular, rather unattractive church in the most modern style and a small meticulous market (119 kilometres from Esparza, 79 from Peñas Blancas). A well paved branch road leads southwest into the Nicoya

Population: 40,000
Colour map 5, grid A1

Peninsula. There is a tourist information centre, three blocks south of the plaza on Calle 1, look for signs on the main road, helpful, English spoken, leave donation as the centre is not formally funded (information however is not always accurate). In the same building is the **Museo del Sabanero** (Cowboy Museum), a poorly presented display of artefacts. ■ *Both museum and tourist centre are open 0800-1200, 1300-1600 Monday-Saturday, US$0.45.*

Sleeping **AL** *Las Espuelas*, 2 kilometres south, good, a/c, satellite TV, swimming pool, round trip bus service from San José, day tour to San Antonio cattle ranch, US$60, American Express accepted (T6660144, F2253987; reservations, San José, T2934544, F2934839). **AL** *Best Western El Sitio*, just off highway on road to Nicoya, T6661211, htlsitio@sol.racsa.co.cr, bath, a/c, good. **B** *Boyeros*, on Pan-American Highway, T6660722, F6662529, pool, bath, restaurant. **B** *La Siesta*, C 4, Av 4-6, T6660678, with bath, clean, swimming pool, helpful owner who speaks English. **B** *Hostal Ciudad Blanca*, from Gobernación 200m south, 150m east, T6663962, 12 nice but dirty rooms, a/c, hot water, phone, TV, restaurant/bar, parking, rooster wake up call. **B** *Bramadero Motel*, not all rooms have bath, open air restaurant and bar but somewhat noisy, swimming pool, Guanacaste Tours located here, T6660371. **B** *Hotel del Aserradero*, Interamerican y Av3, T6661939, 16 nice rooms with bath. **C** *Guanacaste*, 4 blocks from plaza towards Pan-American Highway, 25 west of Pulmitan bus station, friendly, clean, cold water, restaurant, safe parking, money exchange, Ticabus agency, transfers and tours, camping area, English spoken, group discount, 15% student discount, recommended, also has affiliated youth hostel annex, **D-E** to share 6-bedded room with own bath, T6660085, F6662287, htlguana@sol.racsa.co.cr.

D *Intercontinental*, new, good. **E** *Liberia*, 50m from main square, T6660181, with bath, **E** with shared bath, fans, clean, friendly, good information board and restaurant, laundry facilities, recommended. **E** *Hospedaje El Dorado*, contact *Hotel La Siesta*, C 4, Av 4-6, for booking, clean, fan. **E** *Anita*, C 4 y Av 8, T6661285, with bath, laundry facilities, clean, café and

Liberia

■ Sleeping	3 La Posada del Tope	6 Margarita
1 Boyeros	4 La Siesta	7 Motel Bramadero &
2 El Sitio	5 Liberia	Guanacaste Tours

To San José

0 metres 100
0 yards 109

shop, good. **E** *La Casona*, 300m south of Parque Central, T/F6662971, rooms for up to 5 peo-ple, shared bath, hot water, washing facilities, rooms facing street get very hot, owner José Alberto Chavarría has 2-person tent to rent, US$5 per day. **E** *La Ronda* (about 2 kilometres south on the Highway, T6660417), with bath, restaurant. **E** *Margarita*, on La Inmaculada/Central, variously reported as "nice old house" and "filthy, not recommended". **E** *Los Sagitarios*, 5 blocks east and 1 block north from bus station, T6660950, with bath, run by Dutchman and Costa Rican, breakfast and dinner available, friendly. **E** *Motel Delfín*, 5 kilo-metres north of Liberia on the Pan-American Highway, with bath, run down, large swim-ming pool. **E** *Hotel Daysita*, Av 5, C11-13, T6660197, restaurant, pool, quiet, not central. **F** *Posada del Tope*, C Central, 3 blocks south from cathedral, T6661313, cold shower, laundry facilities, clean, friendly, helpful, parking. **F** *Pensión Golfito*, 1 block northeast of square, basic, clean, noisy, unfriendly, no fan.

Chinese *Cantón*, very good; *Chop Suey*, C Central, big helpings, try the chop suey. *Shan Ghai*. *Hong Kong*, 1½ blocks east of church, Chinese, cheap and cheerful. *Copa de Oro*, next to *Hotel Liberia*, Chinese, huge dishes, good value. **Eating**

Others *Pronto Pizzeria*, C 1, Av 2-4, good food (not just pizzas) in a charming colonial house. *Pizzería da Beppe*, Av 0, C 10, genuine clay oven. On the west side of the Plaza is *Soda Las Tinajas*, which specializes in *refrescos*. *Jardín de Azúcar*, just off plaza, self service, good variety and tasty; also in the bus station. *El Bramadero*, Interamerican, Av C-1, popular, mid price range, breakfast from 0630. *Panymiel*, Av Central, C 8-10, good value. *Jauja*, Av C, C10, pizza and pasta. *Cafe Ole*, Av C, C4-6, nice café with seats outside, closed Sunday.

Papers/books *Mini Galería Fulvia*, in arcade at C Central-Av 3, sells *Tico Times*, English papers and books, English spoken, helpful. **Shopping**

Car rental *Sol* and *Toyota* car rental agencies (see map) offer same prices and allow you to leave the vehicle at San José airport for US$50. **Transport**

Air The Tomás Guardia International Airport at Liberia (LIR) was reopened in 1992, revamped in 1995 and renamed Daniel Oduber Quirós Airport, after the former President who came from Guanacaste. The new runway can handle large jets and charter flights, and direct daily flights to Miami. Lacsa, T6660306; Sansa, T2219414; Travelair, T2327883.

Buses The station for Cañas and San José is at Calle 12, Avenida 3-5; regular Pulmitan de Liberia buses Liberia-San José, hourly between 0400 and 0800, every 2 hours 1000-2000, 4 hours, US$2.70 (Cañas US$0.85), you can buy the ticket the day before from the office (blue house) diagonally opposite bus terminal. Buses from San José from C 14, Av 1-3, 0600-2000. Terminal for local buses in Liberia C 12, Av 7-9. CNT bus Liberia-Peñas Blancas, US$1.25, 1st bus at 0530, several daily, usually very crowded at 0900 and 1200, 1½ hours. Libe-ria-Filadelfia-Santa Cruz-Nicoya, 14 a day between 0500-2030, 2 hours, US$1.80, T6800111, Empresa Esquivel Liberia-Nicoya, 4 daily; to Playa Panamá and Playa Hermosa 5 daily. To Playa de Coco 7 daily, US$0.80, 45 minutes. To Puntarenas, Empresa Arata, 5 a day, 2½ hours, return 1730, as well as through buses which stop en route. Nine a day to La Cruz and the Nic-araguan border. **NB** Not all through buses come into town but they all do stop at the main crossroads on the Pan-American highway.

Banks *Banco Popular* and *Bancrecer* both have Visa ATMs. *Banco de Costa Rica* on main St *Credomatic*, Av Central, Mastercard ATM. For money exchange, try *Casa de Cambio* on C 2 or ask around, eg *Restaurant Chun San*, behind the Cathedral. **Hospital & medical services** Social security hospital is quite good. **Tour companies & travel agents** *Puntonorte Travel Agency*, T6660363. *Tiquicia Travel*, in Hotel Guanacaste, T6664485. *Viajes Colón*, opposite *Hotel Sitio*, T6662363. **Tourist Information:** C1, Av 6, T6661606, open Mon-Sat 0800-1200, 1330-1700. A recommended guide for the nearby National Parks is *Alejandro Vargas Rodríguez* who lives in front of the Cruz Roja, T6661889. **Directory**

Rincón de la Vieja National Park This National Park (14,084 hectares, northeast of Liberia) was created to preserve the area around the Volcán Rincón de la Vieja, including dry tropical forest and various geothermal curiosities: mudpots, hot sulphur springs, hot springs of various other kinds. The ridge of which the volcano is the highest peak can be seen from a wide area around Liberia; it is often shrouded in clouds. The area is cool at night and subjected to strong, gusty winds and violent rains; in the day it can be very hot, although always windy. These fluctuations mark all of the continental divide, of which the ridge is a part. From time to time the volcano erupts, tossing rocks and lava down its slopes. The last eruption was in November 1995. In the park are lots of birds including toucans, parrots, and also howler monkeys, armadillos and coatis. There are also lots of ticks and other biting insects. Horses can be rented from the park. The climb to the volcano requires camping near the top (need a tent), or at the warden's station, in order to ascend early in the morning before the clouds come in.

There are two ways into the park: the southern route, which has less traffic, goes from Puente La Victoria and leads, in about 25 kilometres, to the Santa María sector, closest to the hot springs. In this part, you can stay for US$2.50 per person in an old, spacious, refurbished *hacienda* two kilometres inside the park. Bring your own food and bedding, or camp. From the old *hacienda* you can hike eight kilometres to the boiling mudpots (Las Pailas) and come back in the same day; the sulphur springs are on a different trail and only one hour away. The northern route turns right off the Pan-American Highway five kilometres northwest of Liberia, through Curubandé (no public transport on this route). Beyond Curubandé, you cross the private property of Hacienda Lodge Guachipelin, US$1.80 to cross.

Admission Entrance to park US$6. Camping costs US$1.70. To get there: a taxi costs US$20-30 one way from Liberia. The *Hotel Guanacaste*, will arrange transport for US$15, minimum 6 passengers, depart 0700, 1 hour to entrance, return 1700, take food and drink. You can also hitch, most tourist vehicles will pick you up. If you take your own transport you will need four-wheel drive, although during the dry season a vehicle with high clearance is adequate.

Sleeping B *Hacienda Lodge Guachipelin*, T4422848, F4421910, meals available, 10 rooms, camping US$1.70 but no fires, naturalist guides, riding, hot springs, sulphur springs, mud pools, waterfalls (transport from Liberia arranged, US$16 per person round trip). **F** *Miravieja Lodge*, T6622004, Giovanni Murillo, rustic lodge in citrus groves, meals, transport and tours available. Also *Buena Vista Lodge*, T6956147, pickup arranged from Liberia. If you stay at the farm, **B** *Albergue Rincón de la Vieja* (affiliated to the Youth Hostel network) T/F6955553, includes food, pool, camping US$5, call the proprietor, Alvaro Wiessel, who will pick you up in Liberia. Also packages including transport from San José. The *Albergue* is on the edge of the Park, there are horses for rent, guides, tours. From there it is 3¼ hours to the volcano, 30 minutes to Las Pailas, 45 minutes to the thermal springs, Azufrales, 2¼ hours to the Hidden Waterfalls.

Twenty kilometres north of Liberia is Costa Rica's first commercial ostrich farm, blueneck and black breeds; T2286646/2315068, Javnai Menahen for information on tours.

Twenty three kilometres north of Liberia, turn off northeast to Quebrada Grande, four kilometres from which is **B** *Santa Clara Lodge*, T6660473, F6660475, four rooms shared bath, one room with bath, cattle farm, riding, dry forest.

Santa Rosa National Park Thirty seven kilometres north of Liberia, about half-way to the Nicaraguan border, is the **Santa Rosa National Park** (37,118 hectares). Together with the Murciélago Annex, which lies north of the developed park, it preserves some of the last dry tropical forests in Costa Rica, and shelters abundant and relatively easy-to-see wildlife. They are also attempting to reforest some of the cattle ranches of the area (helped by the fact that cattle have not been profitable in recent years). During the dry season, the animals depend on the water holes, and are thus easy to find (except at the end of the season when the holes dry up). The tracks in the Park are wide with little shade; one hiker reports seeing more four-wheel drive vehicles than animals. In the park is the Santa Rosa Hacienda (Casona), at the start of the nature trail and close to the camp. The nature trail will give you a good idea of the wildlife in the Park in about two hours. At the Casona, the patriots repelled the invasion of the filibuster Walker, who had entrenched himself in the main building. A **Museo Histórico de Santa Rosa** in the Casona is open daily 0800-1500. Look for the T-shirts in the gift shop.

Admission Entry US$6; camping US$2.15 per person.

Sleeping There is a pleasant campground at Administration, about 7 kilometres from the entrance with giant strangler figs that shade your tent from the stupendously hot sun, and very adequate sanitary facilities, picnic tables, and so forth for US$1.40 per night. There is a small *comedor* for meals (breakfast 0600-0630, lunch 1100-1200, evening 1700-1800, good) and drinks near the camp ground but recommended to bring some of your own supplies; a tent is useful: essential in the wet season. You can rent tents in Liberia for US$5 per day with a US$100 deposit; ask at the tourist information centre. You may be able to sleep on the verandah of one of the scientists' houses. Bring a mosquito net and insect repellent. If the water is not running, ask at Administration. Take care, there are plenty of poisonous snakes.

Transport Santa Rosa National Park is easy of access as it lies west of the Pan-American Highway, about 1 hour north of Liberia. Any bus going to Peñas Blancas (from Liberia) on the Nicaraguan border will drop you right at the entrance at a cost of US$0.70, 40 minutes. Last bus returns to Liberia at about 1800.

Michael Tesch and Leone Thiele of Cape Paterson, Australia, write "**Playa Naranjo** (12 kilometres, three hours' walk or more or use four-wheel drive) and **Playa Nancite** (about the same distance from the entrance) are major nesting sites of Leatherback and Olive Ridley sea turtles. The main nesting season is between August and October (although stragglers are seen up to January regularly) when flotillas of up to 10,000 Ridley turtles arrive at night on the seven kilometres long Playa Nancite. Females clumsily lurch up the beach, scoop out a two-foot hole, deposit and bury an average of 100 ping-pong-ball sized eggs before returning exhausted to the sea" (see also **Ostional**, page 1112). Playa Nancite is a restricted access beach; you need a written permit to stay there free, otherwise, US$1 per day to camp, or US$1.50 in dormitories. Permits from SPN in San José, and the Park Administration building at Santa Rosa. Make sure you have permission before going, rangers may otherwise give you a hard time. Research has been done in the Playa Nancite area on howler monkeys, coatis and the complex interrelation between the fauna and the forest. No horses are available to rent. Playa Naranjo has good camping, drinking water and a barbecue. The beach is unspoilt and quiet and very good for surfing. Travellers frequently tell us that it is one of the most attractive beaches in the country.

The last town before the border is **La Cruz**, with a bank (terribly slow service for exchange of cash or travellers' cheques) and hotels.

La Cruz
Colour map 5, grid A1

Sleeping A *Colinas del Norte*, ecological lodge 5 minutes after La Cruz on Pan American Highway, Km 300, T6799132, rustic rooms with bath, transport available. **AL** *Ecoplaya Beach Resort*, T6799380, F2894536, well-maintained with nice restaurant. Sixteen kilometres east of La Cruz is **A** per person *Hotel Hacienda Los Inocentes*, on slopes of volcano Orosi, includes meals, 11 rooms with bath, pool, horses, forest trails and guides, T2655484 or 6799190. **C** *Hostal de Julia*, 400m east of Parque Central, T/F6799084, new, parking, with bath, fan. **C** *Amalia's Inn*, 100m south of Parque Central, T/F6799181, nice views, pool, recommended. West of La Cruz, on Bahías Salinas looking over to Isla Bolaños, is *La Salinas Trailer Park y Cabinas*, drinking water, showers, toilets, tennis, barbecue, fishing boats and horses to rent, 1 kilometre beach, T2336912, 2282447, 2280690, PO Box 449-1007, San José. **E** *Cabinas Santa Rita*, T6799062, nice, clean, secure, on main road, 200m from bus terminal, recommended.

Eating *Soda Estadio*, good, cheap. *Restaurant Mirador*, at the end of the only paved street, has superb views. *Ehecatl*, good fish and rice, also has lovely views over the bay. At nearby Ciruelas de Miramar, there is a good restaurant. *Palenque Garabito*; try their fried yucca.

Isla Bolaños is a 25-hectare National Wildlife Refuge to protect the nesting sites of the brown pelican, frigatebird and American oystercatcher. The island is covered with dry forest and you can only walk round the island at low tide. No camping allowed. The incoming tidal surge is very dangerous, be off the island before the tide comes in.

The border with Nicaragua is at **Peñas Blancas**.

Frontier with Nicaragua – Peñas Blancas

Immigration Office hours 0800-1800 (Nicaragua 0800-1200 and 1300-1745). On leaving Costa Rica you have to go to Migración to surrender your passport to be stamped and to give in your immigration form. At another window you pay 75 colones for another stamp and to get your passport back. Trolley pullers charge US$0.50 to carry bags between these posts, a short distance. Visa stamps, US$25, are given at the border, but officials may try to send you back to Rivas. Across the border, passports are inspected on the Nicaraguan side, then you must take the minibus to Sapoá, where entry formalities are carried out, 4 kilometres away (US$0.65). Crossing to Nicaragua may be a slow process; if you arrive when a Tica, Sirca or other international bus is passing through this is especially true (at least 3 hours). If you have no outward ticket for Costa Rica, and are challenged, you can buy a cheap bus ticket back to Nicaragua at the border (valid for 1 year).

There is a duty free shop, a good bar and restaurant adjoining the Costa Rican immigration offices; a good free map of Costa Rica is available from the tourist office at the border (the desk opposite the counter where one pays entry tax).

Crossing by private vehicle Entering Costa Rica by car, first pay your entrance stamp, then go to Aduana Permiso de Vehículo for your vehicle permit (state how long you want); at the Seguro Obligatorio window purchase insurance. Your vehicle is then briefly inspected before you can depart. Fumigation is free. Leaving by car, just hand over the printed vehicle permit you were given on arrival. For documents and other requirements, see **Essentials – Documents**.

Exchange There is a bank (in *aduana*, usually changes cash, does not change travellers' cheques, open 0800-1200, 1300-1600) and a black market (good rates if you shop around; 'España' changes travellers' cheques at fair rates).

Transport There are several express or ordinary buses a day from/to San José, 100m north of Coca Cola terminal, 4 hours or 6 hours, US$5, only the earliest (at 0430 and 0500) from San José will get you to the border before it closes. Bus from the frontier to Liberia, US$1.25, 1½ hours. Only a few buses from La Cruz, US$0.60, taxi costs US$4-5.

The Nicoya Peninsula

Fringed by white sand beaches, hilly and hot. Few towns and poor roads; a few large hotel resorts are increasingly taking over what were isolated coves; small reserves to protect wildlife and the geological formations of Barra Honda.

The Nicoya Peninsula can be reached by road via Liberia (bus Liberia-Nicoya, see page 1101); or you can take the Pan-American Highway to a point 62 kilometres beyond Puntarenas, at a sign to **Río Tempisque ferry**. After crossing on this ferry (hourly 0630-2030, car US$2.40, bicycle or motorbike US$1, pedestrians US$0.20, queues of up to one hour on Sunday) you can drive to Nicoya. Just across the river is **AL** *Hotel Rancho Humo*, T San José 2552463, boat trips on Ríos Tempisque and Bebedero, visits to Palo Verde and Barra Honda national parks. (At La Mansión junction there is a good restaurant, *Tony Zecca Ristorante Il Nonno*, sandwiches and steaks, reasonable prices, menu in six languages, interesting international visitor's book to sign, open Sunday.) An 800-metre bridge is to be built across the river five kilometres north of the present ferry.

A third route is to take the **Salinero car ferry** from Puntarenas across the Gulf of Nicoya to Playa Naranjo, US$1.55 per person, US$3.35 for motorcycle or bicycle, US$8.50 per car, one and a half hours, crossings at 0300, 0700, 1050, 1450, 1900, returns 0510, 0850, 1250, 1700, 2100, weather permitting, T6611069 for exact times. Snacks and drinks sold on the ferry. The ferry dock is about one kilometre from Puntarenas bus station, local buses run between the two. Buses meet the ferry for Nicoya (through Carmona, 40 kilometres unpaved, 30 kilometres paved road, crowded, noisy, frequently break down, US$1.25, two and a quarter hours), Sámara (US$1.30), Coyote, Bejuco and Jicaral.

A fourth route is to take the launch from Puntarenas to **Paquera** (one and a half hours, US$1.25 or 3.25 first class, 0500, 1230, 1700, does not run in bad weather, has toilets, drinks and snacks). On arrival, get on the bus (which waits for the ferry) as quickly as possible (to Cóbano two to three hours, US$1.25, bad road, to Montezuma US$2.60, one and a half hours at least), pay on the bus, or get a taxi. Launch Paquera-Puntarenas (T6612830) at 0800, 1430 and 2030; tickets are sold only when the incoming boat has docked. In Puntarenas this boat docks in the canal north of the city centre; it is a 10-minute walk due south to the bus terminal for San José.

Also, from Puntarenas to Paquera, *Hotel Playa Tambor* (see below) runs a vehicle ferry (hotel buses get priority), Naviera-Tambor SA, leaving Puntarenas 0415, 0845, 1230, 1730, leaving Paquera 0600, 1030, 1430 and 1915. A bus to Tambor will be waiting at Paquera on your arrival. Also ferry from Puntarenas docks at 0415, 0845, 1230, 1600, 1930, return 0600, 1030, 1415, 1800, 2115 with bus connecting at Paquera for Cóbano. All the beaches on the Nicoya Peninsula are accessible by road in the dry season. Most places can be reached by bus from Nicoya. **Paquera** is a small village 20 kilometres along the coast from Playa Naranjo towards the main tourist areas. There are a few shops and some lodgings, for example *Cabinas Rosita* on the inland side of the village. It is separated from the quay by a kilometre or so, where apart from a good soda, one restaurant and a public telephone, there are no facilities. There is no bus connection between Playa Naranjo and Paquera and the road is reported as barely driveable. Montezuma (popular) can be reached in four hours from Puntarenas if you get the early launch.

Nicoya, on the Peninsula, is a pleasant little town distinguished by possessing the country's second-oldest church. The main square is leafy, with occasional concerts. Use the telephones on the square for international calls.

Nicoya
Colour map 5, grid B2

Sleeping **B** *Curime*, T6855238, F6855530, with bath, TV, pool, volleyball, restaurant.

B *Cabinas Rio Tempisque*, T6866650, on main road to Santa Cruz, pool, a/c, bath, hot water, fridge. **D** *Jenny*, with bath, T6855050, a/c, towels and soap, TV, spotless, recommended. **D** *Las Tinajas*, near central plaza, T6855081 with bath, modern, clean, good value. **E** *Chorotega*, T6855245, with bath (**F** without), very good, clean, quiet, clothes washing facilities (good Chinese *soda* opposite). **E** *Pensión Venecia*, opposite old church, on square, T6855325, good value, recommended. **E/F** *Cabinas Loma Bonita*, behind hospital, T6855269, fans, bar, shaded parking. **F** *La Elegancia*, on square, with bath.

Eating A good restaurant is *Chop Suey* (Chinese). *Daniela*, breakfast, lunches, coffee, refrescos, good. *Teyo*, near *Hotel Jenny*, good, quick service. Opposite *Chorotega* is *Soda El Triángulo*, good juices and snacks, friendly Hong Kong owners. *Café de Blita*, 2 kilometres outside Nicoya towards Sámara, good.

Transport Bus from San José, 8 daily from Terminal Alfaro, 6 hours; from Liberia hourly 0500-1900; from Santa Cruz hourly 0630-2130. To Playa Naranjo at 0500 and 1300, US$1.45, 2¼ hours.

Directory Banks Banks on the main square charge commission and are very slow, but the a/c is welcome. Try *Soda El Triángulo*, above.

Nineteen kilometres northeast of Nicoya and 12 kilometres southeast of Santa Cruz,

Nicoya Peninsula

To Nicaragua

Bagaces

Liberia

Santa Ana

Reserva Biológica Lomas Barbudal

Refugio Nacional de Fauna Silvestre Dr Rafael Lucas Rodríguez Caballero

Playa Hermosa

Playa del Coco

Sardinal

Filadelfia

Rio Tempisque

Playa el Ocotal

Belén

Playa Pan de Azúcar

Gua

Playa Flamingo & Brasilito

Santa Cruz

Nicoya

Huacas

Refugio Nacional de Vida Silvestre Tamarindo

27 de Abril

Bel

Isla Capitán

Tamarindo

Playa Avellana

Playa Junquillal

Junquillal

Refugio Nacional de Fauna Silvestre de Ostional

Nosa

Playa Azul

Ostional

Playa Nosara

N

0 metres 10
0 yards 6

is **Guaitil**, where local artisans specialize in reproductions of indigenous Chorotegan pottery. They use the same methods used by Indians long ago, with minimal or no use of a wheel and no artificial paints. Ceramics are displayed at the local *pulpería*, or outside houses. At **San Vicente**, two kilometres southeast of Guaitil, local craftsmen work and sell their pottery at a new building in the centre.

Beaches on the Nicoya Peninsula

Generally, even in high season, you will be able to find a beautiful beach which is uncrowded. There are so many of them, just walk until you find what you want. You will see plenty of wildlife along the way, monkeys, iguanas and squirrels as well as many birds. There can be dangerous undertows on exposed beaches; the safest bathing is from those beaches where there is a protective headland, such as at Playa Panamá in the north. Beaches are described here working round the peninsula from where the car ferry docks in the Gulf.

At Playa Naranjo there are several expensive eating places by the ferry landing, also a gas station.

Playa Naranjo

Sleeping **B** *Oasis del Pacífico* (**D** in rainy season), T/F6611555, a/c, old building on beach,

clean, quiet, pool, good restaurant, free transport from ferry, recommended. **C** *El Paso*, T/F6612610, with bath, **D** without, cold water, clean, pool. **C** *Playas Naranjo*, 200m from ferry, T/F6613877. **E** *Cabinas Maquinay*, 1.3 kilometres towards Jicaral, T3827261, restaurant, disco, pool, tennis court, recommended. *Disco Bar Restaurante Maquinay*, past *El Paso*, T6611763, has a couple of rooms, **E** with shower, insects, Belgian-run, disco on Sunday.

North of Playa Tambor is the **Curú National Wildlife Refuge**. Only 84 hectares, but five different habitats exist here with 110 species of birds. Access is through private land, T661-2392/6392 in advance and ask for Doña Julieta.

Tambor   Tambor, 15 kilometres from Paquera, is a small village with a dark sand beach, some shops and restaurants. The beach is beautiful: 14 kilometres long, rolling surf, one and a half hours on a boneshaking road from ferry; cruise ships from Puntarenas come here. However, part of the beach has been absorbed by the large and controversial *Playa Tambor Beach Resort*. Built around a cattle farm by the Barceló group, of Spain, the resort is alleged to have encroached on the public beach and drained a swamp which was a wildfowl habitat. A second stage is planned at Punta Piedra Amarilla, with a 500-ship yacht marina, villas and a total of 1,100 rooms.

Sleeping   **L** *Hotel Barceló Playa Tambor*, includes meals, 5-star, all amenities, tennis, pool, exercise room, TV, entertainment, bus from Montezuma stops outside gate, most people arrive by plane to the airstrip or by resort bus, T6830303, F6830304, tambor@sol.racsa.co.cr, Apdo Postal 771-1150, La Uruca, San José. **L** *Tango Mar*, T2899328, tangomar@sol.racsa.co.cr, 3 kilometres from Tambor, all services including golf course and its own spectacular waterfall. **L** *Tambor Tropical*, T6830011, 3 kilometres from Tambor airstrip, full services. At Tambor, **C** *Dos Lagartos*, T/F6830236, cheap, clean, good value. On the beach, **D** *Cabinas Cristina*, with bath, T6830028, cheaper without, good food; **D** *Cabinas del Bosque*, T6830039, clean. **E** *Hotel Hermosa Playa*, basic but clean, shared bath, restaurant. Follow signs on main road as you enter town. *Bahía Ballena Yacht Club*, 15 minutes' walk from Tambor, open in the high season only, friendly, free English book exchange, weekly traditional dances, good restaurant/bar, excellent place if you are looking for a crew position on a yacht June to August, many US craft here at that time. In the village, there is a shop with public phones, a supermarket, agency for bicycle hire, and a good American-owned restaurant on the jetty. Take a torch for returning to hotel at night.

Cóbano, near Montezuma, can be reached by bus from Paquera ferry terminal, and buses for Tambor, Cóbano and Montezuma meet the launches from Puntarenas (there is an airstrip with flights from San José). All roads out of Cóbano, north, west and south, require four-wheel drive. Cóbano has a petrol/gas station.

Montezuma

Colour map 5, grid B2   From Cóbano it is a three-minute ride by taxi (or hitch) to Montezuma, a very popular small village on the sea (hence noisy and not too clean). It has become very touristy and, in busy periods, hotels fill up every day, so check in early. Although it does get crowded, there are some wonderful beaches, many are rocky, with strong waves making it difficult to swim, but very scenic. There are beautiful walks along the beach, sometimes sandy, sometimes rocky, always lined with trees. There is a tourist information centre, Monte Aventuras, which is very helpful and often knows which hotel has space; ask here first before looking around (ask for Jaime or Rebeca). The once popular *Cabinas Karen* are now closed. Doña Karen died of cancer in October 1994. Prior to her death, she donated her land to the National Parks in memory of her late husband; it is called **Reserva Absoluta Olaf Wessberg**, not open to the public. Cabinas Karen now houses park guards.

Excursions   Monte Aventuras centre hires bicycles, US$11 per day and organizes tours, for example to Tortuga Island (one hour away), white sand, palms, whole day with lunch and snorkelling, US$30; Sunset Cruise, US$17; four-day, three-night Ecotour to Curú, Arenal, Cano Negro and Barra Honda, US$180 per person including transport, accommodation, breakfast, guides, minimum six.

Close to the village, 20 minutes up the Montezuma River, is a beautiful, huge waterfall with a big, natural swimming pool (it's beyond a smaller waterfall). Intrepid walkers can carry on up to further waterfalls but it is very dangerous and fatal accidents have been reported. Six kilometres north of Montezuma is another waterfall with a pool right by the beach; the walk there passes Playa Cocal (huge, flat, sandy), and Playa Cocalito, where Sr Vásquez lives in a house with Cocalito written on the balcony and sells coconuts and mangoes in season. Horses for hire from the hotels, but carefully inspect that the horses are fit and not overworked, for the sake of the horses. Luis Angel hires horses for experienced or inexperienced riders, US$20 to waterfall, four hours, along beach. Roger is good and takes care of his horses, contact him at the little white house opposite the grocery store. You can change money at this store.

Sleeping **AL** *El Jardín*, with bath, fan, ocean view, T/F6420074. **A** *Los Horizontes*, on road to Cóbano, T/F6420534, language school, restaurant, pool, hot water, highly recommended. **AL** *El Sano Banano*, T6420068, elbanano@sol.racsa.co.cr, on the beach, with bath, fridge. **B-C** *Mangos*, 20 cabins, T/F6420259, clean, new. **B** *Los Caballos*, 3 kilometres from Montezuma on road to Cóbano, T6420124, naturelc@sol.racsa.co.cr, 8 rooms with bath, pool, outdoor restaurant, ocean views, gardens, 5 minutes from beach, horses a speciality. **B** *Amor de Mar*, T6420262, lovely garden, breakfast and snacks available, clean, friendly, away from town, recommended. **C** *Cabinas El Pargo Feliz*, T6420064, has cabins with bath, and serves good food in a calm atmosphere. **C** *La Cascada*, near the river, past *Lucy's*, on the road to Cabuya, T6420057, with bath, fan, clothes washing facilities, restaurant. **C** *La Aurora*, run by Kenneth (German) and Angela (Costa Rican) Kock, 8 rooms with bath, fan, mosquito net, breakfast room, garden, hammocks, T/F6420051, also boat trips for fishing or snorkelling, overpriced. **B-D** *Alfaro*, prices vary according to demand, beware overcharging, rents tents (US$7 for 2), poor facilities but clean tents and mattresses.

D *Cabinas Mar y Cielo*, T6420261, with restaurant, good food, popular, has cabins for up to 8. **D** *Casa Blanca*, 3 rooms, fans, kitchen facilities, German-owned. **D** *Mochila Inn*, between *El Jardín* and Cóbano, T6420030, cabins, clean, family-run, shared bath, hot water, use of family kitchen, keep food in your room away from marauding animals. **D** *Cabinas Las Rocas*, 20 minutes south of Montezuma, good but quite expensive meals, small, seashore setting, isolated; 5 kilometres south is **D** *Fernando Morales Cabins*; see also Cabuya below (these places usually have space when other places are full). **D** *Montezuma Pacific*, bath, hot water, a/c, T6420204. **D** *Hermanos y Hermanas de la Madre Tierra*, 2 kilometres from village, camping F, American-run, higher up and cooler at night than on beach, vegan food, small portions, nice walks. **D** *Montezuma*, T6420058, next to *Mary Cielo*, **E** in off season, with breakfast, balcony, private shower (cold) and fan, cheaper with shared bath, ask for sea view, large rooms (but some have cracked white asbestos wall covering), clean, restaurant (adds 23% tax and service), small book exchange. **E** *Pensión Tucán*, T6420194, very clean, wood-panelled rooms, shared shower and toilet, fan, mosquito net on window, you may cook food, good value, recommended. **E** *Lucy*, opposite *Alfaro*, T6420273, without bath, fan, mosquitoes, laundry facilities, sea views, friendly, follow road around the beach to the south, recommended. **E** *Pensión Arenas*, on the beach, T6420308, run by Doña Meca, basic but OK, without bath, with fan, friendly, cool, clean, also camping, but noisy cockerels at dawn. A Danish family (ask for Inge and Jacob) lives a few kilometres outside village and rents out rooms, good food, free horses.

Camping *Rincón de los Mono*, 500m along the beach from the centre of Montezuma, T6430048, clean, well organized, lockers for rent, many monkeys.

Eating *El Chico*, popular beach hangout. *El Pargo Feliz*, nice terrace. *Soda Las Gemelas*, simple local food. *Soda El Caracol*, fish from US$4. *Los Mangos*, Italian food. *Lucy*, fresh fish and seafood. Next door to the *Cabinas Karen* (see above) there is *El Sano Banano*, a health food restaurant, good vegetarian food, large helpings, daily change of menu, milkshakes, fresh fruit and yoghurt, owned by Dutch/Americans, at night they show movies free if you spend over US$1.50 on food or US$1.25 per person. *Burrito Bandido*, recommended for good Mexican burritos, good value, big helpings. The *Soda La Frescura*, by the *tienda* is good value, good breakfast, delicious shrimp and snapper and lobster *casado* for around US$3. *El Jardín*, opposite *Tucán*, vegetarian, good fruit juices. *Pizzería*, next to *Hotel Montezuma*, self-service, good. Fruit and vegetable cars come to Montezuma.

Shopping   *Made in Costa Rica* souvenir shop, next to *Hotel Montezuma*, is good; a percentage of the profits goes to an ecological fund, including clearing up the beach; also has book exchange.

Transport   **Buses** Montezuma-**Paquera** daily at 0530, 1000, 1400 tickets available in advance from tourist information centre; be at bus stop in centre in good time as the bus fills up quickly, US$2.60, 2 hours. Bus connects with boats to Puntarenas. Bus to **Cabo Blanco**, Wednesday-Sunday 0800, 0900, 1000, US$6, book in Aventuras Montezuma. **Taxi** Montezuma-**Cóbano** US$3.50; taxi Paquera-Montezuma US$12.

Cabo Blanco Reserve   Eleven kilometres from Montezuma is the Cabo Blanco Reserve (1,172 hectares). Marine birds include frigate birds, pelicans and redfooted boobies. There are also monkeys, anteaters, kinkajou and collared peccary. Bathing in the sea or under small waterfall. ■ *0800-1600 (closed Monday, Tuesday, entry US$6), jeep/taxi from Montezuma US$4.50-5, first at 0700, returns 1600.* Six kilometres from the entrance is beautiful Playa Balsitas, where there are lots of pelicans and howler monkeys.

At **Cabuya**, two kilometres from Cabo Blanco Reserve (**D** *El Ancla de Oro*), the sea can be cloudy after rough weather. Cabuya Island can be visited on foot at low tide. On the road west out of Cabuya, *Cafetería El Coyote* specializes in local and Caribbean dishes, owners Wilfred and Jenny. This road goes beyond Cabuya to the attractive little village of **Mal País** on the west coast of the peninsula. The coast here is virtually unspoilt with long white beaches, creeks and natural pools, just a few facilities, including a camping place. Bus Montezuma-Cabuya US$1. Alternatively, fly San José-Tambor and take transport from there.

Sleeping   Three hundred metres from the Reserve entrance is **F** *El Palenque*, camping, restaurant, American run, friendly, recommended. **A** *Celaje*, T/F6420374, on beach, very good Italian restaurant, pool, with bath, hot water, good. **B** *Cabo Blanco*, T4434432, 10 rooms with bath, with breakfast, fan or a/c, pool. In Cabuya village: **D** *Cabinas y Restaurante El Ancla de Oro* (also some at **E**), T6420023, F6420025, some cabins with bath, others shared bathroom, seafood restaurant, lobster dinners US$10, filling breakfasts, owned by Alex Villalobos, horses US$20 per day with local guide, mountain bike rental, transport from Paquera launch available. *El Delfín* restaurant at crossroads, friendly, good value local food. At **Mal País**, **AL** *Star Mountain Eco-Resort*, T6420024, with breakfast, horseriding, owners Laura and Bill Clay, will meet visitors at Tambor, Cóbano or Montezuma airstrips. **C** *Cabinas Mar Azul*, run by Jeannette Stewart, camping possible, T6420298, delicious fried fish, shrimp, lobster. Also a pleasant motel, **D** *Cabañas Bosque Mar*, T6400074, clean, large rooms, hot water shower, attractive grounds, good restaurant on beach nearby, 3 kilometres to Cabo Blanco Reserve. Continuing north along the coast, the next beach is **Playa Santa Teresa** with **A** *Trópico Latino Lodge*, T/F6420062, Tropico@centralamerica.com, bamboo-decorated rooms, restaurant, pool, Italian run, good value, the manager is a keen surfer and can give you information on the best spots. **AL-C** *Mal País Surf Camp*, T/F6400061, restaurant, pool, also camping **F** per person. **AL** *Milarepa*, on beach, T6400023, milarepa@mail.ticonet.co.cr, nice bamboo bungalows, open-air bathroom. **D** *Cabinas Playa Santa Teresa*, T6400137, 150m from beach, surfboard rental, horses, German-run. **F** *Cabinas/Camping Zeneida's*, on the beach.

Sámara
Colour map 5, grid B2
The beach at **Sámara**, 37 kilometres from Nicoya on a paved road, is recommended as probably the safest major bathing beach in Costa Rica. The litter problem is being

tackled with litter bins, warning signs, refuse collection and bottle banks on **Playa Carrillo** which is five kilometres away at the south end of the beach. Both places have airstrips served by scheduled services from San José.

Sleeping and eating L *Guanamar Beach Resort*, on hill at end of Playa Carrillo, T/F6560054, hheradu@sol.racsa.co.cr, beautiful view from bar, pool, satellite TV, horseriding, sport fishing. **AL-A** *Las Brisas del Pacífico*, bungalows with a/c, or hotel rooms with fan, T6560250, labrisa@sol.racsa.co.cr, hotel part on hill, beautiful grounds, direct access to beach, pool, expensive restaurant, German-owned. **AL** *Isla Chora*, tourist complex with 10 bungalows and 4 fully-equipped apartments, a/c, pool, T6560174, F6560173. **A** *Mirador de Sámara Aparthotel*, T6560044, F6560046, owned by German Max Mahlich, 6 apartments each sleep 5, information on tours and boat trips, some run by Max, restaurant. **A** *Hotel Fénix*, on beach, fans, hot water, pool, friendly, T6560158, F6560162, confenix@sol.racsa.co.cr. **B** *Giada*, T6560132, imagine@sol.racsa.co.cr, 250m from beach, hot water, nice decor. **B** *Casa del Mar*, T6560264, restaurant, pool. **B** *Marbella*, T6560121, F6560122, German-run, beautiful grounds, pool, good service, about 300m from beach, recommended. **C** *Belvedere*, German-owned, small rooms, but very clean. **C** *Cabinas Bellavista*, horses for rent. **C-D** *Cabinas Cecilia*, excellent food. **C** *Latino*, T/F6560043, new, 10 large rooms with bath, fan. **C-D** *Casa Valera*, T6560511, on beach with communal kitchen, also 2 houses.

  D *Cabinas Cantamar*, T6560284, cafe, art gallery, simple rooms on the beach. **D** *Cabinas Arenas*, comfortable, cheaper for longer stays, good restaurant opposite, pleasant bar next door. **D** *Cabinas Yoice*, with bath, kitchen, friendly. **E** *Guesthouse Pericos*, helpful, shared kitchen, luggage store. **E** *Mirador*, opposite Marbella, German-owned, bargain price off-season, use of kitchen. **E** *Cabinas Atenas*, near bus stop, rooms upstairs with fan best. **E** *Cabinas Los Almendros*, on beach, restaurant, disco Saturday. **E** *Cabinas Punto*, Sámara. **E** *Doña Marta*, on beach, with bath, not too clean, camping allowed in garden US$0.75; next door is *Camping Coco*, clean, with showers, lights in trees, good for hammocks, US$2.50, recommended, occasionally noisy, good restaurant behind; *Restaurant Mirador*, best seafood in town. *Panadería* close to centre and police station, Italian owned, good *pan integral* and coffee, good information including map of town and details of accommodation. There is another good restaurant on the beach with a fishing boat outside; *Bar El Ancla*, in front of *Doña Marta*, good, local food; *Bar La Góndola*, in centre of village.

Transport Air Sansa operates daily flights to Playa Sámara (PLD) from San José via Punta Islita; Travelair to Playa Carrillo via Tambor, daily. **Buses** From Nicoya, 45 kilometres, US$1.15, 1½ hours, 0800, 1500, 1600, return 0530, 0630, 0730, 1330, 1630. Express bus from Terminal Alfaro, San José daily at 1230, return Monday-Saturday 0345, Sunday 1300, 6 hours. It is not possible to go from Sámara along the coast to Montezuma, except in four-wheel drive vehicle; not enough traffic for hitching.

North of Sámara is Nosara, with two beaches, Guiones, which is safe for swimming, and Peladas; a colony of expatriates has formed the Nosara Civic Association, to protect its wildlife and forests, and prevent exploitation.

Nosara
Colour map 5, grid B2

Sleeping AL *Hotel Playa de Nosara*, T6820121, run down; excellent restaurant, *Olga's Bar*, on beach nearby. **B** *Rancho Suizo Lodge*, T6820057, F6820055, Swiss-owned, bungalows, restaurant, credit cards accepted, whirlpool, hiking, riding, bird and turtle-watching. **B** *Villa Taype*, T6820188, 2 pools, tennis, restaurant, bar. **D** *Casa Río Nosara*, T6820117, rancho style house with cabins and nice garden, clean, friendly, camping, canoe tours and horseriding arranged, German owners. **E** *Cabinas Agnell*, T6820142, with bath, good value, garage next door rents bikes. **B** *Estancia Nosara*, T6820178, estancia@nosara.com, rooms and a condominium. Twelve kilometres south of Nosara is **A** *Villaggio*, at Punta Guiones de Garza, T6860784, an upmarket yet simply furnished beach hotel with vacation ownership plan, 30 bungalows, international restaurant, club house, bars, pool, disco, good packages arranged in San José, T2332476, F2224073. **F** *Cabinas Chorotega*, T6820129, 8 simple, clean rooms, shared or own bath.

Transport Buses daily from Nicoya to Nosara, Garza, Guiones daily from main station, 1300, return 0600, US$2, 2 hours, 65 kilometres; from San José daily from Terminal Alfaro at 0600, 6 hours, return 1245, and 5 flights a week from San José.

North of Nosara is **Playa Ostional** where Olive Ridley turtles lay their eggs in July-November and where a coastal strip is now protected by the **Refugio Nacional de Fauna Silvestre de Ostional**. The turtles arrive for nesting at high tide. The villagers are allowed to harvest the eggs in a designated area of the beach, the rest are protected and monitored. Outside the egg laying period it is exceptionally quiet. There is very basic accommodation in cabins next to the village shop in Ostional eg **F** per person *Cabinas Ostional*, with bath, clean, friendly; *Cabinas Guacamaya*, with bath, clean, good food on request. You can camp on the beach. One kilometre south of *Cabinas Guacamaya* is a good restaurant, *Mirador de los Tortugueros*, coffee and pancakes recommended, good atmosphere. *Getting there:* There is one bus a day at 0500 to Santa Cruz and Liberia, returns at 1230 from Santa Cruz, 3 hours, US$1.75, very dusty. Four-wheel drive needed in rainy season if coming from Sámara.

Playa Junquillal A number of beaches are reached by unpaved roads from the Nicoya-Liberia road. They can be reached by bus from the Liberia bus station. Playa Junquillal is one of the cleanest beaches in Costa Rica and still very empty. It is completely off the beaten track and has almost no tourist facilities.

Sleeping AL *Hotel Antumalal*, with bath, pool, T6530425. **AL** *Villa Serena*, with meals, T6530430, German owners, helpful. **B** *Hibiscus*, T/F6530437, garden, 50m to beach, German-run. **C** *Castillo Divertido*, T6530428, German-run, ocean views in some rooms, bath, recommended. **D** *El Manglar*, overlooking mangroves, run by Italian couple, Los Claudios, tastefully designed, shared bathroom, good showers, double mosquito netting everywhere, kitchen upstairs, Claudio has a boat for excursions, US$8 per hour. **D** *Guacamaya Lodge*, T/F6530431, nice location with pool, ocean views, Swiss cuisine. **C-D** *Junquillal*, T6530432, cabins, nice, friendly, good food. **F** *Camping Los Malinches*, near *Hotel Hibiscus* on main road, nice location, clean bathroom.
  North of Junquillal and south of Avellana is **A-AL** *Iguanazul*, T6530123, 1-800-9483770, 24 different sizes of cabins on a cliff, hot water, fan or a/c, pool, restaurant, bar, great sunsets, sport fishing on 27-foot *Marlin Genie*, close to good surfing.

Transport Bus from Liberia to Santa Cruz (on the Nicoya road), then bus at 1000 or 1415 from Guillermo Sánchez store to Paraíso (US$0.80), from where it is a 4-kilometre walk to Playa Junquillal, or take a car from one of the *cantinas* (road in bad shape).

Playa Tamarindo
Good surfing at north end.

Another good beach is Playa Tamarindo, 70 kilometres southeast of Liberia. Road to Tamarindo is paved but for the last few kilometres. The beach is becoming popular, particularly December-January. It is advisable not to leave valuables unattended (even in hotels). There is a small, expensive, mini-market. Tours to see leatherback turtles are arranged through hotels, US$15 per person with guide. Cheaper tours than through hotels from *TAM Tours*, in commercial centre opposite *Tamarindo Diria Hotel*.

Sleeping L-A *Best Western Vista Villas*, T6530114, F6530115, tamvv@sol.racsa.co.cr, condo-hotel, 7 luxury villas with extra sofa bed, sleep 4, a/c, verandah, safe box, kitchen, 100m from *Johan's Bakery*, internet access for guests, secure surfboard storage, owners are keen surfers. **AL** *El Jardín de Edén*, T/F6530111, includes breakfast, 150m from beach on hill, 18 rooms with fan and a/c, jacuzzi, 2 pools, 2 apartments. **AL** *Tamarindo Diria*, with bath, T/F6530031, full range of services, good restaurants, house parrots, expensive tours offered with good guide. **L** *Capitán Suizo*, T6530075, F6530292, 8 villas, 22 rooms with patio or balcony, pool, restaurant, kayaking, scuba diving, surfing, sport fishing available, riding on hotel's own horses, Swiss management, a/c. **AL** *Tropicana*, T/F6530261, pool, bath, hot water. **AL** *El Milagro*, T6540042, F6530050, 32 decent rooms with bath, expensive. **AL** *Finca Monte Fresco*, 2½ kilometres from Tamarindo, T6530241, F6530243, very good, fully-equipped cabins, breakfast, pool, German, English, Spanish spoken, riding, sailing trips on *Samonique III* yacht, recommended. **AL** *Pasa Tiempo*, T6530096, F6530275, nice complex at the beach with pool, bar, restaurant, garden. **A** *Pueblo Dorado*, T6530008, 22 rooms, a/c, pool. **A** *La Reserva*, a few kilometres before Tamarindo, T/F6544182, a/c, good facilities, pool, Italian run, disco. **A-B** *Cabinas Hotel Zullymar*, T6530140, recommended, rooms with a/c and cheaper cabins, good beach bar. **B** *Pozo Azul*, T6530280, cabins, a/c, cheaper in low season, cooking facilities, clean, good, swimming pool. **B-C** *Cabinas Marielos*, T6530141, with bath, clean, use of kitchen. **D-E** *Rodamar*, 50 metres from *Tamarindo Vista*, no a/c or fan, no mosquito nets, but clean, helpful, use of kitchen, shared bath. **F** per person *Dolly's*, basic, some rooms with bath, bars on balcony, unfriendly, key deposit only returned after room inspection, lots of rules and regulations. Camping nearby, a cheap place to sling a hammock or rent a tent but thefts reported.

Eating *Fiesta del Mar*, large thatched open barn, good food, good value. *Stellas*, very good, try dorado with mango cream, recommended. *Johan's Bakery*, good breakfasts from 0600, exceptional pastries and pizzas. *Coconut Café*, pizzas, pastries and best fish on beach. Check the *sodas* for good breakfasts and cheap evening meals. *Pedro's*, buy drinks from bar over road, eat the freshest fish in town. *El Cocodrilo*, French food, nice garden, open 0600. *Milagro*, buffet breakfast from 0700, fish & seafood. *Frutas Tropicales*, snacks and breakfast. *Arco Iris*, cheap vegetarian.

Transport Air Several daily flights to Tamarindo (TNO) with Sansa and Travelair from San José which connect with international arrivals. Daily flight from Fortuna with Sansa. **Buses** From Santa Cruz, 2030 daily. Tamarindo to Santa Cruz bus 0645, US$1.25. Express bus from San José daily from Terminal Alfaro, 1530, return 0600 Monday-Saturday, 0600, 1230 Sunday, 5½ hours. Bus back to San José, can be booked through *Hotel Tamarindo Diria*, US$5.

The beaches go on for many kilometres. North of Playa Tamarindo is Playa Grande and the **Refugio Nacional de Vida Silvestre de Tamarindo** (also known as Parque Nacional Marinas las Baulas de Guanacaste), which surrounds the hotels. **Playa Grande**

Sleeping A *Hotel Las Tortugas*, 11 rooms with bathroom, pool, restaurant, meals included, T6530423, nela@cool.co.cr, giant leatherback turtle nesting ground November-March. Tours arranged, guides cost about US$6 per person, with a boat, US$12. **AL** *Villa Baula*, right behind beach, T6530494, hotelvb@sol.racsa.co.cr, bungalows with bath, fans, guided walks September-February to see leatherback turtles. **AL-A** *Cantarana*, T6530486, postmaster@unicaribbean.com, well-maintained complex at the mangrove with garden, excellent kitchen, 500m from beach, kayak rental, recommended. **F** *Cabinas/Restaurante Playa Grande*, 500m before beach, 8 cabins with bath and kitchen, also camping.

Playa Flamingo has white sand but has been aggressively developed and polluted. **Playa Flamingo**

Sleeping LL *Flamingo Marina Resort*, next to the sportfishing marina, with meals, T2901858, F23118158, hotflam@sol.racsa.co.cr. **LL** *The Presidential Suites* (T680-06200444), **B** *Villas Flamingo*, T6800960. **AL** *Centro Vacacional Playa Bahía Flamingo*, T6800976. **LL** *Club Flamingo*, T2338056. *Flamingo Beach Condo Rentals* and **LL** *Club Playa Flamingo*, T6800620. **L** *Fantasías Flamingo*, T6544350, flamingo@sol.racsa.co.cr, luxury hotel. **AL** *Mariner Inn*, T6544081, F6544024, 12 new rooms with bath, a/c. Free camping on the beach.

At **Playa Potrero** (black sand) **B** *Cabinas Bahía Esmeralda*, T6544480, Italian restaurant, garden, pool, hot water, roof ventilator. **D** *Hotel Bahía Potrero*, T/6544183, bar, pool, 10 rooms with bath. **B** *Cabinas Isolina* T6544333, 250m from beach, nice garden, roof ventilator. **E** *Cabinas Mayra*, T6544213, on beach, friendly, camping.

Playa Conchal, a beautiful 3-kilometre beach full of shells, now dominated by the

LL *Meliá Playa Conchal*, T6544123, F6544181, 5-star resort, 308 suites, 18-hole golf course, largest swimming pool in Central America, tennis courts, conference centre, casino.

Playa Brasilito: several unattractive hotels/cabinas along the road. **C** *Ojos Azules*, T/F6544346, run by Swiss couple, 14 cabins, good breakfasts with homebaked bread, good value. **D** *Al Odisea*, *cabinas*, hot water, helpful owner, Marc, T6544125, *Bar Marisquería* attached, excellent food, reasonable prices, fresh juices recommended; *Hospedaje Olga*, comfortable, horses, but parrot talks to the geese at dawn. Restaurant *La Boca de la Iguana*, on beach, good value.

Playa Pan de Azúcar: **AL** *Hotel Sugar Beach*, T6544242, F6544239, 10 rooms, 6 with a/c, 50m from beach, fishing trips and horseriding available, 7 kilometres north of Playa Flamingo.

Playa Ocotal: a particularly nice beach, good diving facilities, **LL-AL** *El Ocotal Resort Hotel*, T6700323, F6700083, elocotal@sol.racsa.co.cr, rooms, suites and bungalows, PADI dive shop on beach, sport fishing, surfing, tennis, 3 pools, car hire, excursions. **A** *Villa Casa Blanca*, 10 rooms, T6700448, with breakfast, friendly and informative, family atmosphere, small pool.

Transport Bus from San José to Flamingo, Brasilito and Potrero, daily from ½ block west of Terminal Coca Cola, 0800, 1000, 6 hours, return 0900, 1400. From Santa Cruz daily 0630, 1500, return 0900, 1700, 64 kilometres to Potrero.

Playa del Coco

Popular is Playa del Coco in an attractive islet-scattered bay hemmed in by rocky headlands, the best beaches are to the south; to reach it one should leave the bus at Comunidad (road paved). There are bars, restaurants and one or two motels along the sandy beach; all activities concentrate on the beach and fishing. Snorkelling and diving are nothing special, but for a diving expedition to the Islas Murciélagos contact *Mario Vargas Expeditions*, PO Box 6398-1000, Playa del Coco, T2232811, F2231916. Be wary of excursion to secluded Playa Verde, accessible by boat only, as some boatmen collaborate with thieves and reap the rewards later.

Sleeping A-B *Rancho Armadillo Inn*, just south of main road to Playa del Coco, 5 rooms, a/c, T6700108, F6700441. **A-B** *Villas Flores*, T6700269, 1 suite with a/c, 8 rooms with fan, spearfishing, sportfishing, and diving arranged. **AL** *Hotel Coco Verde*, T6700494. **AL** *La Puerta del Sol*, T6700195, nice complex with tennis, gym etc. **A** *Pato Loco Inn*, T/F6700145, parking, very clean rooms. **B** *Coco Palms*, T6700367, central, german-run, large pool, parking. **B** *Vista del Mar*, T/F6700753, on beach, quiet. **B** *Flor de Itabo*, T6700011, F6700003, a/c rooms, 5 bungalows, good restaurant and bar with really cold beer, pool, horse-riding, excursions, specialists in big-game fishing. **C** *Villa del Sol*, T/F506-6700085, Canadian owned (Quebec), pool, clean, friendly, safe, big garden with parrots, recommended. **D** *Luna Tica*, T6700279, also has a dormitory (friendly, clean), both usually full at weekends. **D** *Cabinas Playa del Coco*, T6700110, F6700167, with bath and cockroaches but good reasonable restaurant.

Eating *Cocos*, cheaper seafood than others. *Beach Club Zebra*, nice views, good seafood. *Playa del Coco*, popular, open 0600. *San Francisco Treats*, good lasagne, ice cream, closed Wednesday. *Papagayo*, good seafood.

Transport Bus from San José from C 14, Av 1-3, 0800, 1400, 5 hours, return 0800, 1400 US$4.50. 3-4 buses daily from Liberia 0530-1630, return 0700-1800 (Arata company).

Playa Hermosa

This is one of the nicest resorts but accommodation is expensive (road paved). Walking either to the left or the right you can find isolated beaches with crystal-clear water.

Sleeping LL *Malinche Real*, T6700033, F6700300, luxury villas with 2 guest houses, with bath, TV, pools, several restaurants, jacuzzi, sauna, conference facilities. **L** *Costa Smeralda*, on adjacent beach (Playa Buena), T6700044, F6700379, Spanish style 68-room resort, many facilities. **A** *El Velero*, beachfront, T6700036, nice rooms, fan, pool, clean, good reasonably priced restaurant. **B** *Villa del Sueño*, T6700026, Canadian owned, pool, good restaurant. **B** *Playa Hermosa Cabinas*, run by an American couple, T6720046, clean, good reasonably-priced food; also cheaper cabins (**F** per person). **D** *Ecotours and Lodge*, 50m south of Aquasport, T6700458. **E** *Cabinas Vallejos*, T3857714, 70m from *Playa Hermosa Cabins*, 7 rooms, friendly owner hoping to expand hotel, helpful; 3 small restaurants on the beach. **AL** *Condovac La Costa*, T6700388/2212264, F2214619, luxury bungalows, a/c, more expensive are the suites with kitchenettes, TV, a/c, lots of hot water, arranges scuba-diving etc, good beach access, good restaurants and bars. **B** *Condo Hotel Costa Alegre*, T6700218. **L** *Complejo Turístico Los Corales*, T6700255. cheaper places at the other end of the beach. **AL** *La Finsterra*, T/F6700293, pool, sailing tours. **AL** *Playa Hermosa Inn*, T/F6720063, on beach, parking, safe. **AL** *Sol Playa Hermosa*, T (San José) 2570607, ugly concrete building, but 54 rooms with ocean views. **E** *El Cenizaro*, T6720186, 8 rooms on beach with bath, cold water.

Transport Bus from Liberia, Empresa Esquivel, 0730, 1130, 1530, 1730, 1900, return 0500, 0600, 1000, 1600, 1700, US$0.80.

Playa de Panamá (road paved) is a rather unattractive place with a dirty beach, a few basic fish restaurants and a *pulpería*. **Playa de Panamá**

The big Papagayo tourist complex near Playa Panama started in 1993, but is taking ages to complete.

Sleeping **D** *Los Bananos*, cabins, restaurant and bar, with bath, friendly, English spoken, good hiking, swimming, horseriding can be arranged, recommended (address is Apdo 137, Liberia, Guanacaste). **D** *Cabinas Vallejo*, with bath; camping possible on beach; *Jardín del Mar* with good facilities, restaurant, tents for hire.

Buy food inland in Santa Cruz, northwest of Nicoya. Santa Cruz is known as Costa Rica's National Folklore City because of its colourful *fiestas*, dancing and regional food. January is the month for the *fiesta* dedicated to Santo Cristo de Esquipulas, when it can be difficult to find accommodation. There is also a rodeo fiesta in January. **Santa Cruz**

Sleeping and eating **D** *La Pampa*, T6800586, close to parque, good. **D** *Diria*, T6800080, bath, restaurant. **D** *Plaza*, T6800169, next to bus station, friendly owner, restaurant. **E** *Hospedaje Avellanas*, comfortable rooms, friendly atmosphere, fan, good value. **E** *Pensión Isabel*, behind the church, bath, hot water. *Coopetortilla* is an excellent place to eat.

Transport Bus San José-Santa Cruz, 9 daily, 0700-1800, 4½ hours, US$5, C 20, Av 1-3, ½ block west of Terminal Coca Cola, return 0300-1700; bus Santa Cruz-Tamarindo, 2030, return 0645, US$1, also to Playa Flamingo and nearby beaches, 0630, 1500, return 0900, 1700, 64 kilometres; Santa Cruz-Liberia every hour, US$1, 0530-1930; Santa Cruz-Nicoya hourly 0630-2130, US$0.35; taxi Santa Cruz-Nicoya, US$10.50 for 2 people.

Small park in the north of the Nicoya Peninsula (2,295 hectares). No permit required, entry US$6. Created to protect some caves (in particular Terciopelo) on a *mesa* and small remainders of dry tropical forest at the *mesa's* foot. First go to Nicoya, from where there are several buses a day to **Quebrada Honda** (first bus 1030, last bus returns for Nicoya 1630, giving you only two hours in the park); this settlement one hour's walk away from the park. Alternatively, get a lift. The road to the park, after the yellow national park sign, on the main road, is three kilometres paved then six kilometres good gravel. The park office is at **Barra Honda**, at the foot of the *mesa*, and there are two different trails to the top; two hours' hiking. Also noteworthy are the *cascadas*, bizarre limestone fountains built by sedimentation on a seasonal riverbed. You'll need a guide to get here, as the trails are hopelessly muddled by cowpaths; arrange in advance for the visit to the cave. A full visit requires harnesses, ropes and guides, US$33 for three guides, US$11 per person for equipment. Avoid coming in the rainy season (May to November), but the dry season is exceedingly hot in the **Barra Honda National Park** open fields. Bring your own food from Nicoya. Turinsa operates a Saturday tour from San José to the Barra Honda caves, T2219185, US$90 includes breakfast and lunch. Las Delicias Ecotourism Project, owned and operated by local community at park entrance, T6855580, three bungalows, comfortable accommodation, camping, **F**, Costa Rican meals at reasonable prices, guided tours available.

San José

From San José to the Atlantic Coast

Initially dominated by active volcanoes and mountainous rain forest, the land falls away to the flat Caribbean lowlands, sparsely populated, with major tropical rain forest national parks at Tortuguero and Barra del Colorado, where canals and rivers are the means of communication.

There are two routes from San José to Puerto Limón on the Atlantic coast. The main road goes over the Cordillera Central through the Braulio Carrillo National Park down to Guápiles and Siquirres. This new road is prone to fog and can be dangerous. The old road follows the route of the railway to Cartago, south of Irazú volcano to Turrialba and Siquirres.

Twelve kilometres from San José on the main highway, 150 metres east of Zurquí gas station, is **A-B** *Villa Zurquí*, T2688856, F2685084, also houses with kitchen, nice gardens, nice if you have a car and don't want to stay in the city.

Braulio Carrillo National Park

This large park was created to protect the high rain forest north of San José from the impact of the new San José-Guápiles-Puerto Limón highway. It extends for 44,099 hectares with five different types of forest (entry US$6). Wildlife includes many species of birds, jaguar, ocelot and Baird's tapir. Various travel agencies offer naturalist tours, approximately US$65 from San José. San José to Guápiles and Puerto Limón buses go through the park. There are two main centres on the highway: Zurquí just after the toll station, coming from San José, before the tunnel; it has services and the 250-metre Los Jilqueros trail to the river. The Quebrada González centre is 23 kilometres beyond the Zurquí centre, just over the Río Sucio at the Guápiles end. It has a new administration building open 0800-1530, closed Monday. There are trails here: Las Palmas, 1.6 kilometres (needs rubber boots); across the road are El Ceibo, one kilometre, circular, and Botarrama, entry two kilometres from Quebra da González (El Ceibo and Botarrama are to be joined). Good birdwatching. The views down the Río Patria canyon are impressive.

Beyond Quebrada González (1½ kilometres) is *Los Heliconios* butterfly garden with insect museum and frogs, entry US$6, 20-minute trail and others of 1-2 hours in Reserva Turística El Tapir which adjoins it (separate entry US$6).

An aerial tram (*teleférico*) takes visitors 35 metres up into the rainforest, interesting to see the vegetation of the canopy but best to be there early to see birds (tram hours 0600-1530, except Monday 0900-1530, tourist buses arrive 0800); 90 minutes' ride costs US$47.50 (including guided nature walk, children half price, children under five not allowed); T San José 2575961, F2576053; office, Rainforest Aerial Tram, Avenida 7, Calle 7, behind *Aurola Holiday Inn*, has bus service from San José around 0800 daily, US$17.50 with pickups at most major hotels. Guarded car park for private vehicles. Restaurant for breakfast and lunch US$7.50. It can be difficult to get reservations during the high season. It is beyond the park, 5.3 kilometres from the Río Sucio bridge, before Guápiles.

Costa Rica

The national park also includes Barva Volcano, 2,906 metres. The latter is only   **Volcán Barva**
accessible from Heredia, there is no entrance from the new highway; bus from market Monday-Friday at 0630, 1100, 1600, return 0730, 1300, 1700, Saturday 0630, 1100, 1600, Sunday 1100, 1600, return one hour later, walk six kilometres to park entrance then four kilometres to lagoon.

From **San José de la Montaña** it is four hours' walk to Sacramento but some buses (about four a day) continue towards Sacramento halving the walk time (otherwise walk, hitchhike, or arrange a ride with the park director). Taxi Heredia-Sacramento, US$7. Ranger station and camping site nearby, from which three kilometres of easy climb to the top. Good views; park entry US$6, no permit needed here. Jungle Trails (T2553486) offers day trips from San José to Barva Volcano. Easter Week is a good choice. The park is widely known among (illegal) birdcatchers. Be careful when leaving your car, regular reports of theft from rental cars.

Sleeping   In **San José de la Montaña**   All with beautiful views across the Meseta Central: **AL** *El Pórtico*, T2606000, F2606002, cosy, clean, pool, sauna, good food, recommended. **A** *Hotel Chalet Tirol*, 3 kilometres north of *Castillo Country Club*, bath, beautiful views, T2677070, tours to *Dundee Ranch Hotel* at Cascajal. **D** *Cabinas Las Ardillas*, T2602172, all with bath. **D** *El Cypresal*, T2374466, sauna, pool, rustic, heavily booked weekends. **In Sacramento B** *Volcán Barva Lodge*, cabin with kitchen sleeps 4, more cabins being built, T2283197. **D** *Sacramento Lodge*, T3810367, local cuisine, horses, rustic room with bath.

Further on, at the *Soda Gallo Pinto* is the **Bosque Lluvioso** 170-hectare private reserve, ■ *T2240819, 0700-1700*. It is at Km 56 on Guápiles highway (Rancho Redondo), 170 hectares, visitors' centre, restaurant, trails in primary and secondary forest, entry US$15.

See page 1118 for *Rara Avis*, northeast of Braulio Carrillo.

Thirteen kilometres before Guápiles is the turn off at Santa Clara to Puerto Viejo de Sarapiqui. At the junction is *Robertos Rancho*, a good, popular roadside restaurant, T7104609.

Puerto Viejo de Sarapiquí

Puerto Viejo de Sarapiquí is 20 kilometres beyond La Virgen (see page 1081) and   *Colour map 5, grid A2*
some 40 kilometres north of the San José-Limón highway. It was once an important port on the Río Sarapiquí. Launches can be taken via the Río Colorado to the Canales de Tortuguero and there is reported to be a cargo boat once a week to Barra del Colorado (no facilities, bring own food, hammock, sleeping bag) (see pages 1122-1125), and on to Moín, about 10 kilometres by road from Puerto Limón. There is good fishing on the Río Sarapiquí.

In the neighbourhood is the **Organization for Tropical Studies** station at **La Selva Biological Station** on the Río Sarapiquí. To visit, phone in advance to book, T7101515. Visitors are provided with maps of the superb primary rain forest. ■ *Guided natural history walk with bilingual naturalists from 0800-1130 or 1330-1600, US$20 per person*. There are different styles of accommodation, including dormitories; overnight rates reduced for a senior researcher, student researcher (letter of introduction required and prior arrangement) book well in advance. High rates for tourists help to support the scientists. Try to avoid the rainy season. To get there by car from San José, take the highway through the Braulio Carrillo National Park (Route 32) and then take Route 4, which turns off near Santa Clara to Puerto Viejo 13 kilometres before Guápiles; it bypasses Río Frío and goes via Las Horquetas (see below). Alternatively, drive via San Miguel and Le Virgen, and through Puerto Viejo: park at the suspension bridge then walk. There is also a private reserve bordering the Braulio Carrillo National Park called *La Danta Salvaje* (The Wild Tapir), 410 hectares of primary rain forest, small limited treks arranged with meals, US$190

The Río San Juan is wholly in Nicaragua, so you technically have to cross the border and then back into Costa Rica. This will cost US$5 and you will need passport/Visa.

per person, for information T/F7500012. Buses run from Puerto Viejo.

The river flows into the San Juan, which forms the northern border of Costa Rica. River trips on the Sarapiquí and on the Río Sucio are beautiful (US$15 for two hours); contact William Rojas in Puerto Viejo (T7666260) for trips on the Río Sarapiquí or to Barra del Colorado and Tortuguero, or ask for the Lao brothers who will advise you. The cost of a launch to Tortuguero is about US$150, but you may be able to find a place on a boat for US$40 or even less. The whole trip takes about five hours.

Sleeping **A** *El Bambú*, opposite park, T7666005, F7666132, in centre, bath, fan, TV, including breakfast, very nice. **D** *Mi Lindo Sarapiquí* by Park, 6 rooms with bath, fan, hot water, restaurant, T7666074. **F** *Cabinas Monteverde*, T7666236, with bath, but reported dirty. Hotels *El Antiguo* (T7666205) and *Santa Marta*, both **G**; *pensiones Las Brisas* and *Hospedaje Gonar*, (T7666196) both **F**, latter above hardware store (*ferretería*), not signed, clean, spacious, fan, *Pip's* restaurant, good. Good food by the river near cargo boat wharf, nice view from the veranda.

Nearby is **AL** *Selva Verde Lodge*: on 600 acres of virgin rainforest reserve, 40 double rooms, 5 bungalows for 4, caters mainly for tour groups, T7666800 (Lodge), T7666277 (reservations), travel@holbrooktravel.com, extensive library, evening lectures by biologists, excellent for birdwatchers and naturalists with extensive trail system, rafting, canoeing and riding through property; tours with biologists organized. It is next to the Sarapiquí Conservation Learning Center, community library and resource centre for environmental protection. Across the river from the OTS station is the **B** *Sarapiquí Ecolodge*, 4 rooms, shared bathroom, price per person includes meals, **D** without food, lodging, birdwatching, river trips, horseriding, T7666122 (daytime only), F2368762. Near La Selva Biological Station is **B** *El Gavilán Lodge*, T2349507, F2536556, gavilan@sol.racsa.co.cr, includes breakfast, set in gardens by the river pier, good restaurant, good jungle paths, riding and river tours, 10 rooms private bath, 10 rooms shared bath, special group and student/reseacher rates, day trips and overnight trips from San José.

Transport From **San José** 6 daily from Terminal Atlántico del Norte, 1½ hours through Braulio Carrillo NP, or 4 hours through Heredia, 3 daily. From **Ciudad Quesada** daily from Parada Municipal at 0500, 1730, return 5 a day, 3 hours.

Seventeen kilometres south of Puerto Viejo, near **Las Horquetas de Sarapiquí**, is *Rara Avis*, rustic lodges in a 1,500 acre forest reserve owned by ecologist Amos Bien. This admirable experiment in educating visitors about rainforest conservation takes small groups on guided tours (rubber boots provided), led by biologists. You must be prepared for rough and muddy trails, lots of insects but great birdwatching. In San José T/F2564876, in Horquetas T7643131. (Affiliated to the Youth Hostel network.) The road from the Limón Highway to Puerto Viejo is now paved, the turn off is near Santa Clara, 13 kilometres west of Guápiles, it bypasses Río Frío and goes via Las Horquetas.

Also part of *Rara Avis Lodge* are **LL** *Waterfall Lodge*, includes meals, private bath. **A** *Albergue El Plástico*, 3 kilometres before *Waterfall Lodge*, rustic with shared bath, minimum 2 nights, book well in advance.

Guápiles Guápiles, one hour from San José (bus US$1.45), is the centre of the Río Frío banana
Colour map 5, grid B2 region.

Sleeping and eating **A** *Casa Río Blanco*, take first right before the Río Blanco bridge and follow signpost for 1.1 kilometre, T/F3820957, with breakfast, accommodates 12 guests, run by North Americans interested in biology and the environment, vegetarian food. **A** *Happy Rana Lodge* (just before Guápiles on same side road), T3851167, F7106309, cabins in rainforest, transportation from San José with 24 hours notice, take first right before Río Blanco bridge, 3 kilometres along gravel road. Both are recommended. **C** *Cabinas Car*, 50m west of the church, T7100035, 10 rooms with fan. **C** *Centro Turístico Río Blanco*, on main road, T7107857, with bath, fan, recommended. **E** *Cabinas Irdama*, T7107034, with bath, TV. **E** *Keng Wa* (opposite Bank) and **E** *As de Oros*, in Centro Commercial El Carao, T7106663, with bath; all **F**: *Hugo Sánchez Cheng*, *Cariari* and *Alfaro*, with bath, above noisy bar; *Hospedaje Guápiles*, good, T7106179. Restaurant *Los Guapes* good Chinese. Before reaching Guápiles, 800m off the highway at the Río Corinto is *Morpho Lodge*, good for hiking, river swimming, cooking facilities.

The new highway runs alongside a railway to Guácimo. Costa Flores offer guided tours of the world's largest flower farm, US$15 per person, T2201311. **B** *Rio Palmas*, 1 kilometre past Earth School, 30 rooms, private bathroom, pool, restaurant, T7600305, F7600296, the 200-hectare property includes ornamental plant farm and rainforest. **Guácimo**

It is another 25 kilometres from Guácimo to Siquirres, a clean, friendly town and junction for roads and former railways. **Siquirres**
Colour map 5, grid B2

Sleeping **D** *Centro Turístico Pacuare*, T7686482, renovated, large pool. **D** *Don Quito*, 3.3 kilometres towards Siquirres, T7688533, pleasant, good restaurant. In the **E** range: *Wilson*, *Cocal*, *Idamar*, *Las Brisbas* and *Vidal*. Also *Cabinas Pacaya*, on the main road. **F** *Alcema*, 50m east of market, T7688157, some dark rooms, with fan, clean, shared bath.

Transport Buses leave San José from just outside Terminal Atlántico Norte, 0630 then hourly 0830-1800, return 0530-1900, 100 kilometres. The road Siquirres-Puerto Limón is paved.

Twenty eight kilometres beyond Siquirres is **Matina**, a small place on the railway but off the highway. It is a short distance from the Caribbean where there is a privately owned reserve accessible by canal from Matina, the **Reserva para la Naturaleza Pacuare**, about 30 kilometres north of Puerto Limón. Run by Englishman, John Denham, it has a six-kilometre stretch of leatherback turtle nesting beach, protected and guarded by the Reserve. Volunteers patrol the beach in May and June, measuring and tagging the turtles, US$50 per person per week, includes good meals and accommodation. For volunteer working, contact Carlos Fernández, Corporación de Abogados, Avenida 8-10, Calle 19, No 837, San José, T2330508 or 2330451, F2212820.

Puerto Limón

Puerto Limón, on a palm-fringed shore backed by mountains, is the country's most important port. It was built on the site of an ancient Indian village, Cariari, where Columbus landed on his fourth and last voyage. It is very humid and it rains nearly every day. Much of the population is black but there is also a large Chinese contingent, involved mainly in restaurants, food stores and hotels; they even have their own part of the cemetery. *Population: 56,525*
Colour map 5, grid C3

The seafront promenade and the **Parque Vargas** next to it are popular places for social gatherings, especially in the evening. In Parque Vargas is a botanical display, a shrine to sailors and fishermen and a bandstand. However, the park is in rather poor condition and the Hoffman's two-toed sloths which used to live in its trees seem to have disappeared. The **Museo Etnohistórico de Limón**, Calle 2, Avenida 2, features material relating to Columbus' arrival in Limón. ■ *Monday-Friday, 0900-1200, 1300-1600*. The nightlife is good, particularly for Caribbean music and dancing. Some 2.8 million bunches of bananas are exported each year. New docks were recently completed. **Sights**

Excursions **Moín**, six and a half kilometres north of Puerto Limón, has docks for tankers, container and ro-ro ships, and is also the departure point for barges to Barra del Colorado (eight hours). Moín has a pleasant beach, buses run every 40 minutes from 0600-1740, 30 minutes, US$0.10. Boats run from Moín to Tortuguero (see below) and may be hired at the dockside. Go early for a good bargain. A severe earthquake struck the Caribbean coast of Costa Rica and Panama in April 1991 which raised land and caused the Tortuguero canals (see below) around Matina to dry up. Japdeva has carried out dredging work but boats for Tortuguero River now also depart from Hamburgo de Siquirres on the Río Reventazón. Boats still run from Barra del Colorado to Tortuguero.

Sleeping

Beware of theft at night, and remember it is a port as well as a tourist town; there are a lot of drunks roaming the streets.

In Puerto Limón C *Acón*, C 3, Av 3, T7581010, with bath, a/c, clean, safe, good restaurant, a bit run down, popular discotheque *Aquarius*. **C** *Tete*, Av 3, C 4-5, T7581122, with bath, fan. **D** *Park*, Av 3, C 1-2, T7980555, sea facing rooms quiet and cool, recently renovated, restaurant good. **D** *El Paraíso*, Av 4, C 2-3, next to Methodist church, small clean rooms, fan, basic. **D** *International*, Av 5, C 2-3, T7580545, with bath, a/c, Chinese owner, reasonable. **D** *Continental*, Av 5, C 2-3, T7980532, 24 good rooms with a/c. **E** *King*, Av 2, next to PO on main square, T7581033, with bath and fan, very clean. **E** *Caribe*, Av 2, C 1-3, T7580138. **E** *Hotel Los Angeles*, Av 3, C 4-5, T7582068. **E** *Miami*, Av 2, C 4-5, T7580490, back rooms quieter, a/c, Chinese food in restaurant. **E** *Ng*, C 3, Av 5, T7582134, cheaper rooms without bath, fan extra charge, basic, untidy, friendly, laundry. **E** *Linda Vista*, Parque Vargas, basic, friendly, noisy. **E** *Palmeras*, Av 2, C 3. **E** *Cariari* Av 3, C 2. **E** *Hotel Wilson*, Av 3, C 4-5, T7585028, basic, OK. **E-F** *Palace*, near market, small, helpful, fan, safe, chairs on balcony. **F** *Hong Kong*, on main street, clean but noisy. **F** *Pensión El Sauce*, 1 block from main square, rats. **F** *Pensión Hotel Costa Rica*, 1½ blocks east of central park, small rooms, noisy. **F** *Venus*, Av 5 near Lincoln, beach view, rats, spiders, beds 'like medical plank beds', avoid. **F** *Balmoral*, near market, basic. **F** *Pensión Los Angeles*, Av 7,

Puerto Limón

To Portete & Moín

Avenida 8

Avenida 7

Avenida 6

Avenida 5

Calle 5

Calle 4

Calle 3

Radio Casino

Avenida 4

2

5

Paseo Juan Santamaría

Avenida 3

Calle 7

Calle 6

1

Gobernación

2

Calle 2

Calle 1

Parque Vargas

3 Market & Plaza

1

Museo Etnohistórico

Avenida 2

4

Baseball Park

Avenida 1

Customs

Breakwater

To San José

Calle 8

Calle 9

Muelle Nacional

To Airport & Cahuita

Swimming Pool

N

0 metres 150

0 yards 164

■ **Sleeping**
1 Acón
2 Costa Rica

3 Los Angeles
4 Miami
5 Park

🚌 **Transport**
1 Bus to San José
2 Bus to Cahuita

C 6-7, with bath, cheap, noisy, mosquitoes, probably of ill repute. **F** *Pensión El Cano*, next to *Pensión Los Angeles*, fan, friendly, clean, share showers, OK.

At **Playa Bonita** **AL** *Matama*, T7581123, F7584499, recently refurbished, bath, a/c, restaurant, tennis, pool, boats for rent to Tortuguero. **A-B** *Apartotel Cocorí*, T/F7582930, with bath, hot water, some with a/c, pool, restaurant popular with locals, boat trips to Tortuguero arranged. **C** *Cabinas Playa Bonita*, T/F7983090, with bath, fan or a/c, 200m from ocean.

In nearby **Portete** **AL** *Maribú Caribe*, T7584543, F7583541, 3½ kilometres out of Limón, bungalow accommodation, swimming pool. **C** *Cabinas Getsemaní*, T7581123, cabins, bath, a/c, restaurant, pleasant.

In **Moín** **B** *Moín Caribe*, T7581112, uphill from where the bus from Puerto Limón stops, friendly, nice, clean, good place to stay before Tortuguero, good value. **C** *Moín Club*, T7582436, F7581112, walking distance of Moín port, 15 rooms.

Several Chinese restaurants eg *Samkirson*, C 3, Av 3-4, good value. *La Fuente*, cheap. *Palacio Encantador*, 50m east of Stadium, good. *Park Hotel*, Av 3, C 1-2, does good meals, US$2.25. *Restaurant La Chucheca* serves good *comidas* and breakfast. *Springfield*, serves good, Caribbean-style meals, recommended, also has disco. *La Hacienda*, for steaks, cheap. *Soda/Restaurant Mares*, on market square, open 0700-1400, good food. *Soda/Restaurant Roxie*, opposite hospital, some way out of town, good value *casado*. *Doña Toda*, good, near market. *Harbour Restaurant*, good value meal of the day. *Mönpik* for good ice cream (the biggest supermarket in town). *Milk Bar La Negra Mendoza* at the central market has good milk shakes and snacks. *Casados* in market in the day, outside it at night, good, cheap food. Try *pan bon*, spicy bread from Creole recipe, sold near bus stop for San José. Cheap food at the corners of the Central Park and at *Familia Torres*, Av 5, ½ block from *Hotel Ng*, very good value. *Diplo's Bar*, cheap Limón food, try the soup. *Marisquería El Cevichito*, Av 2, C 3-4, nice fish, *ceviche*. *Brisas del Caribe*, Av 2, C 1, cheap noodles, meat, seafood. *Antillta*, C 6, Av 4-5, Caribbean rice and beans, meat.

Eating
A place to eat is harder to find than a nightclub.

Fiesta: in **October**, very crowded and expensive.

Festivals

Swimming: Japdeva, the harbour authority, has a 25-metre pool open to the public for a small fee in the harbour area.

Sport

Air Travelair and Sansa from the capital. Keep luggage to a minimum or you will be charged for excess baggage.

Buses Town bus service is irregular and crowded. Service from **San José** with CoopeLimón, T2237811 and Caribeño, every hour, 0500-1900, daily, return from the street between central plaza and Parque Vargas (ignore the old signs for the departure point), US$2.90, 162 kilometres, 2½-4 hours. To **Cartago**, US$2. Bus to **Cahuita** from Radio Casino, 0500, 0800, 1000, 1300, 1600, 1800, US$0.80, 1 hour, continues to Puerto Viejo and Sixaola. To **Manzanillo**, from Av 4, C 3-4, at 0600, 1430, returning 1130, 1900, 1½ hours, US$1.50. To **Moín** from C 4, Av 4, every 30 minutes between 0600-2200. To **Siquirres/Guápiles**, 13 daily, 8 direct.

Transport

Banks *Banco Nacional*, Av 2, C 3, open Mon-Fri, 0830-1545. *Banco de Costa Rica*, Av 2, C 1, open Mon-Fri 0900-1400. **Communications** Post Office: opposite central market. **Telephones:** *ICE* for international calls at Av 2, C 5-6 and at C 3, Av 4-5, open Mon-Thurs, 0800-1700, Fri 0800-1600. **Hospitals & medical services** *Red Cross*, C 3, Av 1-2, T7580125. Hospital on the road to Moín, T7583549. **Places of worship** Protestant Church: Baptist, with services in English.

Directory

The Atlantic Coast

The Río San Juan forms the border between Costa Rica and Nicaragua; the frontier is not in mid-river but on the Costa Rican bank. English is spoken widely along the coast. Between Puerto Limón and the Río San Juan is a long stretch of coastline with various settlements linked by a canal system which follows the coast.

Tortuguero National Park

Tortuguero is a 18,947-hectare National Park protecting the Atlantic green turtle egg-laying grounds and the Caribbean lowland rain forest inland. The turtles lay their eggs at night from June to August (the eggs start hatching in the second week of September), but before going to watch, contact the National Park administration (they have some basic but good guide books of the area for sale) for instructions, otherwise you may disturb the protected turtles (take a torch if going at night). Unfortunately people still eat turtle eggs and meat, even though they are protected. It is depressing to see the nests robbed by morning. No permission is needed to enter the park, but to visit the turtles you must pay US$6 park entrance fee and US$5 each for a guide, no matter how many you are. Guides (authorized ones only, with ID card) will let you watch one turtle laying eggs, although you may have to wait an hour; be patient. Do not swim at Tortuguero because of the sharks.

A Visitor Centre has information on the Park and the turtles and a gift shop. There is a 1.4 kilometre well-marked trail with trees named, recommended. Also the Caribbean Conservation Corporation has opened a natural history museum in the village of Tortuguero, very informative. ■ *1000-1200, 1400-1730, entrance free*. Park rangers are friendly and make trips into the jungle waterways; particularly recommended for viewing tropical rain forest wildlife (birds, alligators, tapirs, jaguars, ocelots, peccaries, anteaters, manatees, sloths, monkeys, gars); their trips are quite short, about US$2 per person for three to four hours' trip. Take insect repellent against the ferocious mosquitoes, ticks and chiggers.

Tours You can hire a canoe and guide for about US$3 per hour per person, minimum 4, excellent way to see wildlife including crocodiles, ask for Damma. Johnny Velázquez: US$3.55 per person per hour for tours of canals in a motor boat, US$30 per hour in fishing boat on the sea, maximum 2, gear and bait included, US$10 per hour night tour. Alberto: US$2.25 per hour per person if he goes with you in a canoe, or US$1.25 if you go alone, he lives next to *Hotel Mayscar*. Rubén: lives in the last house before you get to the National Park office, sign on pathway, recommended for 4-hour tour at dusk and in the dark. Chico: lives behind *Sabina's Cabinas*, US$2 per hour, recommended local guide, will take you anywhere in his motor boat. Ernesto: born in Tortuguero, 15 years experience as a guide, contact him at *Tropical Lodge* or through his mother, who owns *Sabina's Cabinas*. Rafael: a biologist, recommended, speaks Spanish and English (his wife speaks French), lives ½ kilometre behind Park Rangers' office, ask rangers for directions, he also rents canoes. There are several boats for rent from Tortuguero, ask at the *pulpería*.

Sleeping At the Southern end of the Park is Parismina, where you can stay at the **L** *Tarpon Lodge*, T2357766, includes meals, boat and guide; there is also a cheap *pensión*, **F**, basic, fan, bargain. Further north is the settlement of Tortuguero itself. There are several hotels: **Río Parismina Lodge**, T2226633 (USA toll free 800-3385688, F512-8293770), luxury, fishing packages from US$999. **L** *Tortuga Lodge*, price per person includes meals, T (San José) 2570766, F2571665, comfortable accommodation, but rooms 1-6 are dark and lack fresh air, excellent food (owner Costa Rican Expeditions, packages available from San José, better value than staying there independently though you may still be charged extra for everything, 2 minutes' boat ride from village, US$8). **L** *Ilan Ilan*, price per person includes meals,

T2552031, clean, cold showers, friendly, English-speaking owner. **L** *Jungle Lodge*, price per person includes meals, T2330133, F2220568, 3-day, 2-night package tours with transport from San José. **L** *Caribbean Magic Eco-Lodge*, T2565363, includes meals and boat trips, rustic cabins; *Pachira Lodge*, T3822239, in San José: T2567080, F2231119, 5 minutes from Park, 3 day/2 night package includes transport, food, tours with bilingual guide, US$239, highly recommended. **AL** *Laguna Lodge*, T2253740, F2838031, 20 rooms with bath and fan, restaurant, bar, beautiful gardens, tour packages available from San José, includes unlimited boat trips. **AL** *Mawamba Lodge*, T2237490, F2225463, mawamba@sol.racsa.co.cr, price per person includes meals, comfortable, fans, restaurant, canal and egg-laying turtles in front of property. **B** *Manatí Lodge*, 8 rooms with bath, T3830330. **E** *Cabinas Miss Junie*, T7100523, fan, bath, next to restaurant. **F** *Sabina's Cabinas*, friendly, small, basic rooms, but next to beach. **D** *Tropical Lodge*, on the river, 6 basic huts with bath and fan. **D** *Cabinas Tortuguero*, nice garden, good food, hot water, hammocks. **D** *Mery Scar*, T7106716, Nicaraguan-owned, fans, safe, cheap food clean, basic. There are many cheap cabañas in the **E-F** range, the boatmen or villagers will help you find them.

Thirty kilometres north of Tortuguero is **AL** *Samay Laguna*, T2847047, PO Box 12767-1000, San José, tours offered, transport by seaplane possible.

Six kilometres north of Tortuguero is the **Caño Palma Biological Station**, administered by the Canadian Organization for Tropical Education and Rainforest Conservation (in Canada T905-6832116), basic rooms, **B** per person, includes meals, pickup from Sansa flights to Barra del Colorado can be arranged; a good place for serious naturalists or just for unwinding, accommodation for up to 16 in wooden cabin, freshwater well for drinking and washing. Don't dally on arrival if you want cheap accommodation. You can sometimes camp at the National Park office for US$2.50.

Rainforest Concern (27 Landsdowne Crescent, London W11 2NS, T0171-2292093, F2214094, rainforest@gn.apc.org) runs a lodge in the *Pacuare Nature Reserve* on the Tortuguero Canal. In San José, Av 8-10, C 19 No 837, T2330451, F2212820, fdezlaw@sol.racsa.co.cr. Tours and volunteer work available, minimum stay one week.

Good food is limited: *Miss Junie's* good local dishes, reservation necessary. *Miriam's*, at soccer field, very good Caribbean food. *Olger's Bar*, seafood, expensive. *The Vine*, expensive Italian. *Tropical Lodge*, good, cheap food. *El Dolar*, small menu, good *casado*. **Eating**

Tío Leo's, Saturday night is dancing night, happy, enjoyable, great dancing, but a notorious surplus of men. Disco near *Sabina's Cabinas*. **Nightlife**

The Jungle Shop specializes in handicrafts. **Shopping**

Boats A regular boat leaves Moín at 0900, US$25, 4 hours, returning about 1400, check the times which frequently change. Tickets sold once boat is under way. You can bargain at Moín for a boat to take you to Tortuguero and bring you back 3-4 days later, at around US$50-60 provided a party of 6 can be arranged. *Viajes Laura*, T7582410, highly recommended, daily service, open return US$50 if phoned direct, more through travel agencies, pick up from hotel, will store luggage, lunch provided, excellent for pointing out wildlife on the way. It is also possible to take a bus from Siquirres to Freeman (unpaved road), a Del Monte banana plantation, from where unscheduled boats go to Tortuguero; ask around at the bank of the Río Pacuare, or call the public phone office in Tortuguero (T7106716, open 0730-2000) and ask for Johnny Velázquez to come and pick you up, US$57, maximum 4 passengers, 4 hours. Sometimes heavy rains block the canals, preventing passage there or back. Contact Willis Rankin (Apdo 1055, Limón, T7981556) an excellent captain who will negotiate rampaging rivers. All river boats for the major lodges (see below) leave from **Hamburgo** or **Freeman**. If excursion boats have a spare seat you may be allowed on. Generally it is getting more difficult to 'do it yourself', but it is still possible, ask around the boat owners in Moín. Official tours and tourist guides with accommodation included are now normal, bargain for a good price. A 2-day, 1-night trip from Puerto Limón with basic accommodation, turtle watching trip and transport (no food) costs about US$65 per person, T2256220. **Road** A local municipality **Transport**

commenced extending a road from Guápiles to Tortuguero and cut a track of 2 kilometres within the National Park without permits or permission. An outcry from conservation groups and other authorities stopped the roadbuilding. You can take a bus from Guápiles to **Cariari** on the Río Tortuguero and take a boat from there, 9½ hours, US$15 return, to Tortuguero, or a boat from Puerto Viejo de Sarapiquí to Barra del Colorado and from there to Tortuguero (see below). Caño Blanco Marina runs a daily bus-boat service San José-Tortuguero at 0700, US$50 return, T2569444 (San José), T7100523 (Tortuguero), from 2 Av, 1-3 C, San José. **Air** Flights daily from San José with Sansa and Travelair to Tortuguero, and to Parismina, Monday, Wednesday, Friday, Sunday, or charter.

Directory **Tour companies & travel agents** Tours from San José include transport, meals, 2 nights lodging, guide and boat trips for US$219-252 per person (double occupancy). The main tours are *Mawamba Boats*, T2225463, 2237490, F2554039, minimum 2 people, 3 days/2 nights, daily, private launch so you can stop en route, with launch tour of National Park included, accommodation at *Mawamba Lodge*, PO Box 10050 San José, you can return to San José by charter flight (US$344 per person) or take the Río San Juan-Río Sarapiquí trip from Puerto Viejo de Sarapiquí (5 hours, US$347 per person based on 2 people); then bus back to San José or stay at *Selva Verde Lodge*; *Miss Caribe* and *Miss America* boats, T2330155 operate Tues, Fri, Sun, 2-night/ 3-day packages using *Jungla Lodge*; *Colorado Prince* boat, 3-day/2-night package, Tues, Fri, Sun US$200, using *Ilan Ilan Lodge*, T2553031. *Tortuga Lodge* and *Laguna Lodge* also offer similar packages. *Parismina Tarpon Rancho* (PO Box 10560-1000, San José, F2221760) offers tours of Tortuguero, Braulio Carrillo National Park and fishing trips. OTEC (see page 1072) runs 3-day/ 2-night tours for US$180, with small student discount, a trip to see the turtles in Jul-Sep costs extra. Tours from Puerto Viejo de Sarapiquí, including boat trip to Tortuguero, meals, 2 nights lodging, guide and transport to San José cost US$275-400 per person (double occupancy).

Barra del Colorado

The canals pass many small settlements, and for many of them the barge is their only means of communication. The canals are part artificial, part natural; they were originally narrow lagoons running parallel to the sea, separated from it by ¾ kilometre of land. Now all the lagoons are linked, and it is possible to sail as far as **Barra del Colorado**, in the extreme northeast of Costa Rica, 25 kilometres beyond Tortuguero. The town is divided by the river, the main part being on the northern bank. There is a plan to link the Parque Nacional Tortuguero with the **Refugio Nacional de Fauna Silvestre Barra del Colorado** into a continuous National Park area. The area is world famous for fishing.

Sleeping **AL** *Río Colorado Lodge*, T2324063, F2315987, price per person includes 3 meals and fishing with guide, for serious fishermen, night-vision scopes, reservations recommended. **AL** *Casa Mar*, T4412820, with bath. **AL** *Silver King Lodge*, T (San José) 2880849 (toll free in USA 1-800-8473474), price per person, deluxe sports fishing hotel, 5-night packages includes flights, meals, rooms with bath, fan, hot water. **B** *Isla de Pesca*, T2392405, with bath. **C** *Tarponland Lodge*, T7106917, cabins, run by Guillermo Cunningham, very knowledgeable and helpful. *Tropical Tarpon Lodge*, T San José 2252336, with bath. If you have a tent you may be able to camp at *Soda La Fiesta*. Lots of mosquitoes.

Transport **Air** Flight San José-Barra del Colorado daily with Sansa. **Boat** From Barra to Tortuguero takes 1 hour and costs US$28.50. A motorized canoe can take 8 people and costs up to US$50, 2 hours. Try and arrive in a group as boats are infrequent.

Frontier with Nicaragua – Barra del Colorado Once across the Río Colorado (which in fact is the south arm of the Río San Juan delta), you can walk to Nicaragua (see under Nicaragua, San Juan del Norte) along the coast, but it is a long 30-kilometre beach walk, take food and lots of water. Most hikers overnight en route. Seek advice before setting out.

Costa Rican immigration This is not a regular border crossing and there are no formal facilities on the Costa Rican side. Do not leave for Nicaragua by boat or on foot without

Soda Kukula, great breakfast, fresh bread, German owner. *Soda Sedentario*, very good breakfasts, yoghurt and fruits. *Momma Mia Pizza*, good, sit outside. *Típico*, very friendly service, good breakfasts, reggae music. *Marisquería*, at Puerto Vargas Park entrance, Italian, jovial host, also has rooms. *Cabinas Algebra* on the Black Beach has a good restaurant and the bar is away from the crowds, recommended. *Salón Vaz*, lively at weekends with reggae music and Rastas, popular with travellers and locals, main gathering point, safe for lone women. *La Soda BBQ Grill*, good fish dishes around US$6.50. *Cha Cha Cha* (formerly *La Fiesta Italiana*), very good Italian, pasta from US$4. *Pizzería El Cactus*, good food, service.

Bus service direct from San José from Terminal del Caribe Sixaola, 0600, 1530, return 0730, 0930, 1100, 1630, US$4, T2578129, Transp Mepá, 4 hours, US$4.50, and from Puerto Limón, in front of Radio Casino, 0500, 0800, 1000, 1300, 1600, 1800, return 0630, 0730, 1100, 1300, 1600, 1800, 2000, 1 hour, US$0.80, T7581572, both continuing on paved road to Bribri, 2 basic *residencias*, and on to Sixaola on the Panamanian border (US$1, 2 hours). The bus drops you at the crossing of the 2 main roads in Cahuita. **Taxi** Puerto Limón-Cahuita, US$20. **Transport**

Banks Money exchange is difficult except occasionally for cash dollars (Cahuita Tours (see below) changes US$ and TCs). Take plenty of colones from Limón. Nearest bank is in Bribri (20 km). Several places accept credit cards. **Tours and rentals** Tony Mora runs glass-bottomed boats over the coral reef. Snorkelling equipment for hire. Also horses can be hired, but ensure they are in good shape. Bicycles can be hired for about US$7 per day and you can cycle to Puerto Viejo and the Panamanian border through some beautiful scenery. *Cahuita Tours*, T7580232, F7580082, excursions by jeep and glass-bottomed boat, bike, diving and snorkelling equipment rental. **Useful information** Cahuita Tours (see above) also houses the post office and international telephone service (ICE). The National Park services have warned against muggings in the park at night, if walking the path take a torch. There have also been some rapes. Some of the jungle has been cleared for safety. Also beware of theft on the beach, and drug pushers who may be undercover police. **Directory**

Puerto Viejo

The beaches at Puerto Viejo de Talamanca, 19 kilometres southeast of Cahuita, are also worth a visit (be alert for thieves). They are quiet during the week, busy at weekends, good surfing. The black beach is the best for safe swimming. There is a public telephone in the Chinaman store in Puerto Viejo, the only one in the area. You need to bring towels, insect repellent and a torch. Bicycles can be rented for US$6 per day but not good quality. There is a small, English book exchange, ask for directions. The *Asociación Talamanqueña de Ecoturismo y Conservación* provides tourist information, sells locally made crafts and T-shirts, guide service, rainforest hikes, snorkelling and fishing trips. Tours cost US$15 (half-day), or US$22 (full day), T/F7500188, 7500191. It is possible to walk along the beach from Puerto Viejo to Cahuita in one day (22 kilometres, five hours) but not recommended. There is a channel to cross (Home Creek) and reports of tourists being robbed. *Colour map 5, grid B3*

AL *El Pizote Lodge*, cabin with bath, **B**, rooms with shared bath, T7500088. **B** *La Perla Negra*, T7500111, F7500114, pool, restaurant. **C** *Maritza*, T7500003, in cabins, with bath, clean, highly recommended. **D**, shared bathroom, clean, friendly, English spoken, a map in the bar shows all the hotels and *cabinas* in the area. **C** *Coco Loco Lodge*, T/F7500281, quiet, garden, nice wooden house. **D** *Cabinas Yucca*, T7500285, nice beach garden, parking, German-run. **D** *Casa Máximo*, with breakfast, basic rooms. **D** *Cabinas Chimuri*, T/F7583844, north edge of town, thatched huts with balconies from which you can observe the wildlife, horseriding. **D** *Jacaranda*, T7500069, some rooms with bath, restaurant. **D** *Escape Caribeño Bungalows*, 500m along road to Punta Ura, German management, communal kitchen, free morning coffee, well-furnished cottages with TV, fully equipped. **D** *Pura Vida*, T7500002, Swiss run, friendly, very clean, hammocks, recommended. **D** *Cabinas Grant*, large rooms, clean, fan, shower, parking, restaurant, nice patio. **D** *Cabinas Casa Verde*, T7500015, F7500047, comfortable rooms, nets, fan, shared bath, hot water, nice gardens, helpful owner. **E** *Hotel Puerto Viejo*, nice balconies, Mexican food, good breakfasts, popular **Sleeping**

with surfers. **E** *Talamanca*, 400m from centre, clean, fan, helpful owner, use of kitchen. **E** *Cabañas Joli*, 250m from bus stop, clean, basic, fan, OK. **E** *Samasati Lodge & Retreat Center*, T2241870, samasati@samasati.com, half way between Cahuita and Puerto Viejo, beautiful mountain location, vegetarian restaurant, meditation courses, reservation recommended. **F** *Cabinas Manuel León*, with bath, T7580854. **F** *Kiskadee*, T7500075, small jungle lodge with 2 dormitories, kitchen available, American-run, about 200m from football field, from where it is signposted, recommended, take torch and rubber boots. **F** *Cabinas Salsa Brava*, popular with surfers. *Cabinas Black Sands*, a bamboo, laurel wood and thatch cabin of Bri-Bri Indian design T5561132.

Eating *Café Pizzería Coral*, good breakfasts, good main meals, not cheap, recommended. *Cramba*, excellent pizzas. *Garden Restaurant*, opens 1700, good food, highly recommended. *El Parquecito*, facing sea, nice breezy atmosphere, specializes in fish and seafood (evenings only). *Green Garden*, clean, nice pastries, food from Trinidad, Californian style, very expensive. *Johnny's Place*, Chinese food, large portions, specialities of the day recommended. *Soda Tamara*, open 0600-2100, local good quality homemade snacks. *Soda Miss Zami*, good food, good value. *Stanford's Disco*, lively nightlife. *Bambú*, nearby, good food. *Bar Sandborn*, recommended for an evening beer. *Taberna Popo*, lively bar-disco, live music some nights, Carib and rock. *Amimodo*, good restaurant near beach, excellent Italian. *Pizzería Caraocean*, good home made bread, pasta etc. *Marcos Pizzería*, closed Tuesday. *Celeste*, good Belgian-French food, closed Tuesday. *Salsa Brava*, Spanish food, closed Sunday.

Transport Daily bus from San José from Terminal Sixaola, 0600, 1530, return 0700, 0900, 1600, 4½ hours, US$4.65; from Limón daily from Radio Casino, 0500, 0800, 1000, 1300, 1600, 1800, return 0600, 1230, 1300, 1500, 1600, 2000, 1½ hours; 30 minutes from Cahuita, US$0.45.

Directory **Communications Email:** from the Mail Office, US$2 to send, US$1 to receive, altecmail@sol.racsa.co.cr.

Beaches

There are a number of popular beaches southeast along the road from Puerto Viejo. At about four kilometres is **Playa Cocles** which has some of the best surfing on this coast. Two kilometres further on is **Playa Chiquita** with many places to stay. Beyond this is **Punta Uva** from where you can visit the **Hitoy Cerere Biological Reserve**. Another five kilometres to **Manzanillo**, followed by white sand beaches and rocky headlands to **Punta Mona** and the **Gandoca-Manzanillo Wildlife Refuge**, where, among other projects, marine scientists are studying ways of protecting the giant leatherback turtle. For more information, contact ANAI, T2246090. Volunteer work may be possible.

Sleeping **At Playa Cocles D** *Cabinas Surf Point*; **F** *Cabinas y Soda Garibaldi*. **At Playa Chiquita LL** *Villas del Caribe*, 2 floor apartments with kitchen, living room, bath, T2332200. **AL** *Punta Cocles*, recommended, 60 nice cabins, a/c, pool, forest trails, car rentals, boat trips, guides, horse riding, mountain bikes, transport from San José available, T San José 2348055, F2348033. **AL** *Playa Chiquita Lodge*, 11 rooms with private bathroom, French restaurant and bar, 500m from beach, naturalist guides available, T2336613, F2237479. **AL** *Hotel Kasha*, 3 bungalows with bath and fan, open-air gym, jacuzzi and restaurant, T2846908, F2322056. **A** *Miraflores Lodge and Restaurant*, T2332822, 10 rooms, a/c, breakfast included, with bath, fan, beautiful gardens, lots of wildlife, English and French spoken, boating tours to Monkey point. **A** *Yare*, T2845921, with kitchenette, fan, hot water, restaurant. **B** *La Isla Inn*, 50m from beach, with bath, fan, breakfast available. **D** *Tío Lou Cabins*, T2273517. **At Playa Uva AL** *Shawandha Lodge*, T7500037, shawanda@sol.racsa.co.cr, large complex in rain forest, bungalows, expensive. **AL** *Almonds and Corals Tent Camp*, T2722024, tents with bath and hot water on platforms in the forest, pool, restaurant, trips arranged to Punta Mona, snorkelling (equipment rental), bike hire. **A** *La Costa de Papito*, 3 bungalows managed by Eddie Ryan, fan, with bath. **A** *Cariblue Bungalows*, T7500057, cariblue@sol.racsa.co.cr, nice complex with garden. **E** *Selvin Cabins* and restaurant, *Walaba Travellers Hostel*, with room and dormitory accommodation. **At Manzanillo AL** *Hotel Las Palmas*, cabins, 60 ocean view rooms, pool, snorkelling, rainforest, tours, transport from San José, Wednesday, Friday, Sunday, US$30 return, US$20 one way, T/F2553939. **E** *Cabinas/Restaurant Maxi*, basic, nice rooms. **C** *Cabinas Pangea*, behind Aquamor, 2 nice rooms with bath, also house on beach with kitchen. **E** *Cabinas Las Veraneas*, T7542298, rooms with shared bath.

Express bus to Manzanillo from Terminal Sixaola, San José, daily, 1600, return 0630. From Limón daily 0600, 1430, return 1130, 1900, 1½ hours. **Transport**

Take road from Cahuita to Hotel Creek where one road (dirt) goes to Puerto Viejo **Bribri** and another (paved) to Bribri, one of the villages at the foot of the Talamanca range, which has been declared an Indian Reserve. Halfway between Hotel Creek and Puerto Viejo is *Violeta's Pulpería*. From Limón, Aerovías Talamaqueñas Indígenas fly cheaply to **Amubri** in the Reserve (there is a *Casa de Huéspedes* run by nuns in Amubri). Villages such as Bribri, Chase, Bratsi, Shiroles and San José Cabécar can be reached by bus from Cahuita. Several buses daily to Bribri from Limón. (For a good introduction to the Talamanca mountains, read *Mamita Yunai* by Fallas, or *What Happen* by Palmer.)

Continuing south from Bribri is **Sixaola**, on the border with Panama. **Frontier with Panama – Sixaola**

Costa Rican immigration The border is open 0700-1700. Remember to advance watches by 1 hour on entering Panama.

In both countries, the local greeting in this area is 'OK?'. This means, 'good morning, how are you', 'I'm not going to attack you', 'can I help you?' If you don't want a chat, simply answer 'all right'.

Sleeping Just before the bridge: **E** *Cabinas Sánchez*, with bath. **E** *Imperio*, 8 simple cabins with ventilator, shared bath. **E** *Nuevo Hotel Siquirreño*, opposite Cabinas Sánchez on other side of railway, with bath, simple. **F** *Central*, Chinese run with good restaurant, and **F** *Pensión Doris*.

Exchange There are no banks in Sixaola, but it may be possible to change money in one of the shops before the bridge, eg *Soda Central*, but rates, especially to the US dollar are very poor. Shops near the border in Panama will accept colones but shops in Changuinola and beyond do not.

Transport A narrow-gauge railway runs to Almirante (Panama) from Guabito, on the Panamanian side.

If crossing to Panama take the earliest bus possible to Sixaola (see Panama, **The North-Western Caribbean Coast**, page 1226). Direct San José-Sixaola bus from Terminal del Caribe Sixaola, Autotransportes Mepe (T2210524), 5 hours, US$6.30, 0600, 1530, plus 0800 on Saturday, return 0500, 0730, 0930, 1430; also 6 daily from Puerto Limón (Radio Casino), 4 hours. It is cheaper to take the bus from Sixaola to Puerto Limón then another from Limón to San José rather than the through service.

San José

The South Pacific Coast

At the foot of the cordillera, the narrow lowlands are cattle ranches or planted to African palm. Beaches, particularly those in the Manuel Antonio National Park, are a major attraction.

From Esparza on the Pan-American Highway a road runs 21 kilometres southeast to **San Mateo** (from where a road runs northeast to Atenas – see Meseta Central section). Just before San Mateo, at Higuito de San Mateo, is *Las Candelillas*, a 26-hectare farm and reforestation project with fruit trees and sugar-cane. There is a camping area with showers, pool and riding, T4289157, 4288434. **A** *El Rancho Oropéndola*, is at San Mateo, cabins with private bath or rooms with shared bath, rustic and peaceful, pool, nature trails, T/F4288600.

From San Mateo a road runs south to **Orotina**, which used to be an important road/rail junction on the route San José-Puntarenas (**C** *Cabinas Kalim*, near plaza, T4288082). Orotina excursion: Finca Los Angeles, T2245828, offers one-day nature tour on horseback US$65 through the mountains to the beach. Near Orotina, beyond the village of Coopebarre, is the Iguana Park, where you can watch, eat or buy (as pets) the reptiles. Five-kilometre trails, gift shop (US$15 entry, US$10 for guided tour, open 0800-1600).

Cascajal West of Orotina the road forks, northwest to the port of Caldera, southwest to the Pacific Coast at Tárcoles. Along the Caldera road is Cascajal.

Sleeping **L** *Dundee Ranch Hotel*, a working ranch, has 11 rooms with private bathroom, a/c, pool and restaurant, T4288776. **A** *Hacienda Doña Marta* is a 260-hectare working ranch and dairy farm with 6 cabinas, pool, bar and restaurant for guests, horseriding, next to Carara Biological Reserve, see below, reservations and information from *Finca Rosa Blanca Country Inn*, PO Box 23, Santa Bárbara de Heredia, T4828126.

The coastal road continues through Jacó, Quepos, Playa Dominical and thence inland to San Isidro de El General. The road is paved as far as Parrita (after Jacó) and is generally good with few pot holes. Thereafter it is a good, but dusty, gravel road (difficult for motorbikes because of loose gravel), paved in villages, until Paquita, just before Quepos. Here the road deteriorates and paving is poor. After Quepos the road is still unpaved to Dominical, a hard ride, and although from Dominical the road inland through Barú to San Isidro is paved, landslides can make this section hazardous. Check the state of the roads and bridges before setting out to San Isidro if driving yourself and do not assume that if the buses are getting through, cars can too. High clearance is needed if a bridge is down. In the dry season motorists can do a round trip in a day starting from San José.

Carara Between Orotina and Jacó, just after the Río Tárcoles bridge (where crocodiles may
Biological be spotted in the river and scarlet macaws may be seen flying out of the forest into the
Reserve sunset just before dusk, 1700-1730), is the Carara Biological Reserve, 4,700 hectares with abundant wildlife. Scarlet macaws, which are using artificial nest boxes to help the birds reproduce in safety from poachers and predators, are best seen around 0630 or 1700. A good place to look for them is near the Río Tárcoles bridge, but take care: thefts and robberies reported in this area. Also to be seen in the Reserve are white-faced monkeys, coatis and crocodiles.

There is a 30-40 minute circular path starting by the office, approximately 1,300 metres; trails have been improved with funds from British Embassy. ■ *0700-1600, US$6*. San José travel agencies offer tours. If going by car, leave nothing of value in the car park.

Next to Carara is La Catarata, a private reserve with a 200(?)metre waterfall with natural pools for bathing; take the gravel road up the hill beside *Hotel Villa Lapas*: five kilometres to entrance, two and a half kilometre hike to falls and pools. ■ *information T2364140, 0800-1500, December 15-April 15, US$7.50. There are signs on the main road.*

Sleeping **AL** *Hotel Villa Lapas*, next to the reserve (from Río Tarcolitos, turn left and go 500m), reservations T6370232, F6370227, with bath, pool, good restaurant, good birdwatching, easy access to mouth of Río Tárcoles, riding, guided tours to Carara, recommended, animals come close to the hotel at night. At **Playa Tárcoles**: **C** *Cabinas Carara*, basic, 16 cabins with bath, small, simple restaurant, pool, superb birdwatching at mouth of Río Tárcoles about 5 kilometres along this road, T/F6370178. Three kilometres from Tárcoles is *El Tico*, a good seafood restaurant. **AL-A** *Tarcol Lodge*, basic rooms with shared bath, over-priced, on south bank of mouth of Río Tárcoles, high tide surrounds lodge on 3 sides, low tide uncovers mud flats attracting thousands of birds, packages include transport, meals and tours, 5 bedrooms, 2 bathrooms, Apdo 364-1002, San José, T/F2848045, same management as *Albergue de Montaña Rancho Naturalista*, near Turrialba. Further south is **Punta Leona** with **LL** *Hotel Leona Mar*, T2312868, 750 acres, spacious rooms with bath, a/c, cable TV, kitchen, access to Punta Leona Club pools. South of Punta Leona is **L** *Villa Caletas*, French owned, 8 rooms, 20 bungalows, with amazing views, spectacular sunsets, lush gardens, pool, restaurant, boat and nature tours, T2573653, F2222059.

Fifteen kilometres from Carara is Jacó Beach, a large stretch of sandy beach, rather noisy and commercial, popular with surfers and weekenders from San José. Be careful of the rip tides all along this coast.   **Jacó**

Sleeping **L** *Hotel Villas Jacó Princess*, villas with kitchenette, a/c, T6433064, F6433010. **AL** *Best Western Jacó Beach Resort*, T6431000, F6433246 (or San José 2201441, or 1-800-5281234 in North America), a/c, TV, minibar, hot water, tennis, volley ball, restaurant and coffee shop, helpful staff, good service, recently upgraded. **AL** *Copacabana*, Apdo 15, Jacó, T/F6433131, Canadian-owned, on beach, attractive, clean, tours and sporting activities arranged, rooms quiet, fans, hot showers, suites for 4 with kitchenettes available, pool, bar with TV and live music, boutique, restaurant, car rentals, credit cards accepted, recommended. **AL** *Jacó Fiesta*, T6433147, F6433148, bath, cable TV, phone, refrigerator, rooms hold 4/5 people, 4 pools, tennis, restaurant, highly recommended. English, German, French spoken. **AL** *Paraíso del Sol*, T6433250, 2 types of room, pool and children's pool, recommended. **A** *Pochote Grande*, T6433236, near beach, pool, German-run. **A** *Club de Mar*, T6433194, bath, fans, south end of beach, some rooms have separate living room and kitchenette. **B** *Cabinas Tangeri*, T6433001, modern, attractive landscaping, pool, excellent value for groups. **B** *Zabamar*, T6433174, F6433175, large rooms, pool, American owners, helpful, small restaurant, reservations recommended. **C** *Coral*, T6433067, on beach south of town, 2 pools, hammocks, German owned, restaurant, warmly recommended. **D** *Cabinas Heredia*, with bath, and **D** *Cabinas Las Brisas*, T6433087, attractive grounds, on beach, but run down. Other hotels and many *cabinas*, including **C** *Cabinas Las Palmas*, T6433005, with bath and fan, cold water, clean. **C** *Cabinas Gipsy Italiano*, T/F6433448, near beach, with bath, hot water. **D** *El Jardín*, on beach, with bath, no hot water but clean, friendly, pool. **D** *Bohío*, near beach, private bath, cold water, fan, swimming pool. **D** *Sol y Luna Cabinas*, Italian run, large rooms with bath, clean, fan, mosquito nets, restaurant. **D** *Cabinas La Cometa*, T/F6433615, central, with fan, shared bath, hot water, very clean. *Camping El Hicaco* and *Restaurant Los Hicacos* both down same access to the beach.

Eating *La Hacienda*, good bar and snacks. *Jacó Rock Café*, good food, good value; *Jacó Bell*, Mexican fast food. *Sunrise Grill*, breakfast from 0700, closed Wednesday. *La Fragata*, pasta, fish. *La Ostra*, fish, breakfast.

Transport **Air** Travelair operates daily flights to San José (Pavas). **Buses** From Coca Cola bus station, opposite Plaza Jacó-Complex, next to *Pizza Hut*, sales T6433135, San José, 0730 and 1530 daily, returning 0500, 1100, 1500, 2½-3 hours, US$2.

Costa Rica

Jacó to Puerto Quepos

From Jacó the road (with many potholes) runs along the coast giving lovely views of the ocean, several turnoffs to beaches along the way, including **Playa Hermosa**, **Esterillos Este** and **Playa Palma**, near Parrita.

Sleeping At **Playa Hermosa** **AL** *Hotel Terrazas del Pacífico*, T6433222, with bath, phone, cable TV, good surfing. **A** *David*, T6433737, F6433736, resort with fully-equipped gym. **B** *Villa Hermosa* (ex-*Cabinas Villa Ballena*), T6433373, taycole@sol.racsa.co.cr, on beach nice pool, a/c, kitchen. **C** *Vista Hermosa*, T6433422, on beach, pool, simple rooms. **E** *Rancho Grande*, T6433529, large wooden house with communal kitchen, popular with surfers.

At **Esterillos Este** **AL** *Hotel El Delfín*, T7799246, swimming pool, all rooms with breezy balcony, secluded, clean, recommended, good restaurant, considered by many one of the most delightful beach hotels in Costa Rica. **B-C** *Auberge du Pelican*, F7799236, safe, French restaurant.

At **Playa Palma** **C** *Rooms Maldonado*, T2861116, rooms with bath, cold water, kitchen. **E** *Rooms/Restaurant Alex*, 2.6 kilometres south, with bath, fan, recommended. **F** *Las Brisas*, simple rooms near beach. **E** *Hotel Memo*, with bath, **F** *Hotel El Nopal*, and **F** *Cabinas Calevo*, with bath, clean, parking.

At **Playa Palo Seco** **AL** *La Isla*, T7799016, bar, pool, horse and canoe trips, hot water, a/c. **B** *Beso del Viento* bed and breakfast, Playa Palo Seco, 5 kilometres, T7799674, swimming pool, Canadian owners.

After Parrita the gravel road travels through palm plantations and the landscape is flat, becoming rather tedious after a few kilometres of palm trees. Many of the plantation villages along the way are worth seeing for their two-storey, balconied houses laid out around a central football pitch. On bridges along this road, the carriageway narrows to single track; take care especially at night.

Puerto Quepos

Colour map 5, grid B2

Built by United Brands as a banana exporting port the town is now run down. The banana plantations were overwhelmed by Panama disease in the early 1950s and have been replaced by 8,200 hectares of African Palm for oil. Mechanization was cut back when it was realized that tractors were damaging the roots of the palm trees and now oxen or mules pull carts along the rows, while tractors pulling several wagons load up at the ends of the rows. South of Quepos the coast has been developed for tourism, with numerous hotels built along the beach inevitably spoiling an attractive stretch of jungle clad coastline sweeping steeply down to the sea. Quepos is now important as a service town for local and foreign tourists. It is also cheaper to stay here than on the beach and there are many restaurants, bars and shops.

Sleeping
Difficult to find accommodation on Saturday, December-April and when local schools are on holiday.

AL *Rancho Casa Grande*, 5 kilometres inland close to airstrip, lovely yellow *casitas* in gardens, pool, a/c, jacuzzi, local agent for Travelair flights, near airport, T7771903, F7771575. **AL-A** *Hotel Sirena*, T/F7770528, new hotel with restaurant, pool, 14 quite good rooms with private bathroom, a/c. **A** *Kamuk*, central, T7770379, F7770258, shower, TV, a/c, ocean view, bar and restaurant at street level with large screen videos. **B** *Itzamaná*, T7770351, cross bridge on way out of Quepos, turn half left at telephone box, continue past stop sign and along dog-leg in road, follow road to left where it peters out, hotel about 30m back on right, bath, cold water, clean, fan, friendly, good value, free bus to Manuel Antonio. **D** *El Parque*, T7770063, on waterfront road, friendly, clean, a bit run down but good value, private bath, fan. **E-F** *Mar y Luna*, T7770394, with or without bath, quiet, clean, very friendly. **D** *Viña del Mar*, T/F7771968, with bath, fan, pool, restaurant. **E** *Majestic*, T7770294, noisy, shared bath, on the same street as Banco de Costa Rica. **F** *Hospedaje La Macha*, with fan, basic, noisy, little privacy, next to Post Office and soccer field behind bus station. **F** *Cabinas Kali*, 200m northeast of bus station, T7771491, nice rooms, family run, clean, friendly, safe but noisy. **F** *Sánchez*, 100 metres west of football pitch, T7770491, without bath, OK. On the road which leads to Manuel Antonio but still in town are **C** *Hotel Quepos*, T7770274, with bath, **D** without, simple, recommended. **C** *Villas Mar y Sol*, T7770307, F7770562, good bakery next door. **C** *Cabinas Mar-Su* in Boca Vieja district, no signs, about 300m before bridge entering town, large, clean, comfortable cabins, fan, bathroom, a/c extra, car park. **D** *Doña Alicia*, beside football pitch, big cabin with bath, friendly, quiet, parking, can wash clothes. **D** *Cabinas Mary*, T7770218, by football pitch behind bus station, clean, friendly, OK. **B-D** *Ceciliano*, T7770192 with bath, family run, quiet, small rooms, hot. **D** *Mavio*, with bath, recommended. **D** *Hotel Malinche*, T7770093, cafetería, parking, 12 quite good rooms with private bathroom, fan. **D** *Cabinas El Cisne & Sensación Tropical*, 75m north of Catholic church and football pitch, T7770719, safe, family-run, secure parking, bigger rooms on left, recommended.

Eating

In town is the *Iris* restaurant and *Arco Iris* discotheque both T7770449. *Isabel*, good breakfast choice, bulletin board, helpful staff, good food. *Restaurant El Turista* has good, cheap fruit juices. *El Gran Escape*, central, good food, good value, recommended. *La Boca Nueva*, on sea front, pleasant outside bar with reasonably priced meals, giant outdoor chess set. *Soda La Marquesa*, very good, popular, cheap *casados*, lots of other dishes, good for breakfast. *Soda La Coquita*, next to *Hotel Melissa*, very good value. *Dos Locos*, Mexican food, good iced coffee. *Soda Nido* and *Restaurant Ana*, cheap *casados*. *Soda Nahomi*, good sandwiches, near park, next to laundry, *Lavanderías de Costa Rica*. *Soda El Kiosko* on seafront, near *Hotel Kamuk*, good juices, fish dishes, international cuisine, popular. *Pan Aldas*, bakery, same road as bus station, Italian run, good. *George's American Bar and Grill*, on road to Manuel Antonio, 1 block from sea, on corner, breakfast, lunch, dinner, popular with travellers and English-speaking residents, T7770186. *Café Milagro*, towards Manuel Antonio, best expresso, cakes, pies, Cuban cigars, souvenirs, freshly roasted coffee for sale; another branch on the waterfront in town. *Alfredo's Italian Deli*, opposite *Dos Locos*, excellent pasta, cheeses, bread and meats. There are other restaurants further along the coast towards Manuel Antonio.

Shopping

The municipal market is at the bus station, buy fruit and bread here as the *Super Mas* supermarket is not well stocked. *La Buena Nota*, souvenir shop, also sells some English language newspapers etc, a good place to seek local information, run by Anita Myketuk and Donald Milton, who has initiated a lifesaving programme and publicity on rip tides, T7770345.

Transport

Air There are several daily flights from San José, with Sansa (international connections) and Travelair. Book in advance. In Quepos the Sansa office is under *Hotel Quepos*, T7770161. Hustler Tours also run flights.

Buses There are 3 direct buses a day from the capital, from Terminal Coca Cola, 0600, 1200, 1800, return 0600, 1200, 1700, book a day in advance, 3½ hours, US$4; a local bus, 6 daily, US$3.50, takes 5-6 hours, leaving the main road at Parrita to wind its way through the mountains and rural settlements, crowded, uncomfortable, you could walk faster at times. From **Quepos** there are buses northwest along the coast to **Puntarenas**, 3½ hours, 0430, 1030, and 1500, return 0500, 1100, 1430, US$2.10. Two daily buses via Dominical to **San Isidro de El General**, 0500 and 1330, 3½ hours, US$2.50, connections can be made there to get to the Panamanian border, return 0700, 1330.

Taxis: congregate at the junction of the coastal road and the park, by the road to Manuel Antonio. Minibuses meet flights at the airport.

Motorbike hire: Pico Rent-a-Bike, opposite *Hotel Malinche* 200m from beach, T7770125, several models from US$25 per day. See also information at *Restaurant Isabel*.

Taximar **boat** from Quepos to Dominical, Isla del Caño and Bahía Drake: leaves Quepos dock Tuesday, Thursday, Saturday, Sunday 0700 for *Hotel Punta Dominical*, then to Isla del Caño or Bahía Drake, T7711903.

Directory

Banks *Banco Popular* has ATM for Visa. The best place to exchange TCs or US$ cash is at

Distribuidora Puerto Quepos, opposite Banco de Costa Rica, open 0900-1700, no paperwork, no commission, all done in 2 mins, same rate as banks. Visa card is the preferred credit card in this area, Mastercard can attract a 6% added commission. **Communications** The Post Office is on the walkway by the football pitch, open 0800-1700. **Language schools** *Escuela D'Amore*, in a great setting overlooking the ocean, half way between Quepos and the National Park, T7771143, live with local families. *Escuela del Pacífico*, 2 km from town, T7770805, www.escueladelpacifico.com, US$350 per week including lodging in owners' hotel, good classes. **Laundry** *Lavanderías de Costa Rica*, near the football pitch, good. **Tour companies & travel agents** Opposite the football pitch is a travel agency, *Amigos del Río*, tours, good guides. *Blue Marlin*, with tours, information, next to *Hotel Quepos*. **Useful addresses** Immigration is on the same street as the Banco de Costa Rica. **Police:** T7770196.

Manuel Antonio National Park

Seven kilometres south of Quepos along a paved road the park is 683 hectares of swamps and beaches with a rich variety of fauna and flora. Plenty of birds, snakes, lizards, monkeys and sloths can be seen. The forest grows right down to three beautiful, but frequently crowded beaches: **Espadilla Sur**, **Manuel Antonio** and **Puerto Escondido**, and iguanas and white-faced monkeys often come down on to the sand. Hiking is good in the park. A 45-minute trail, steep in places, runs round the Punta Catedral between Espadilla Sur and Manuel Antonio beaches. The walk to Puerto Escondido, where there is a blow hole, takes about 50 minutes. The map sold at the entrance shows a walk up to a *mirador*, which has good views of the coastline, worth taking. The entrance to the park is reached by crossing a tidal river (plastic shoes recommended, it is sometimes very high or alternatively, a boat will take you across the river for US$0.55), open 0700-1600, closed Monday, US$6. Early and late are the best times to see the wildlife. Breakfast and other meals available from stalls just before the river, where cars can be parked and minded for US$1 by the stallholders. Basic toilets and picnic tables by the beaches, cold water showers at Manuel Antonio and Espadilla Sur beaches. Keep clear of the manzanilla trees and do not eat their poisonous apples. You are not supposed to feed the monkeys but people do, which means that they can be a nuisance, congregating around picnic tables expecting to be fed and rummaging through bags if given the chance. Leave no litter and take nothing out of the park, not even sea shells. Overdevelopment outside the park and overuse within has led to problems of how to manage the park with inadequate funds. In 1992 the National Park Service (SPN) threatened to close it and a number of tour operators removed it from their itineraries. The beaches in the park are safer than those outside, but rip tides are dangerous all along the coast. Look for local safety literature. Beaches slope steeply and the force of the waves can be too strong for children. Watch out for logs and other debris in the water. Sea Kayaking, T7770574, Ríos Tropicales, 50m north of Manuel Antonio School, one-day or multi-day tours, includes transport, also mountain biking, equipment and professional guides, Kelly and John have been recommended.

Sleeping

There are hotels all along the road from Quepos to Manuel Antonio, many shut in the low season. In high season, best to book ahead. The area is full to bursting at weekends with many locals camping on the beach.

Nearest the park is **D** *Hotel Manuel Antonio*, T7777237, restaurant, good breakfast, camping possible nearby, ask in the restaurant. On a side road just before the park is **E** per person *Costa Linda*, T7770304, double rooms or **F** per person in 6-bedded room, with cooking facilities, fan, water shortage, T7770304, watch out for racoons raiding the outdoor kitchen in the night, good breakfasts, dinner rather pricey. **AL** *Hotel Villabosque*, 50m from beach, 150m from National Park, 10 rooms with a/c, private bathroom, includes breakfast, T/F7770463. **A** *Cabinas Espadilla*, T7770416, fan (not very effective), water shortages, clean, 10 minutes' walk from beach. **B-C** *Vela Bar*, T7770413, Apdo 13 Quepos, large rooms with bath, fans, safes, very good restaurant, fishing and other trips, also has a fully-equipped house to rent. Further along is *Soda El Grano de Oro*, basic rooms at back, see Betty. Heading towards Quepos, on the main road, is *Bar del Mar*, T7770543, which rents surfboards, sells drinks and light meals and has a collection of English novels to read in the bar. Just off the road 25m further on, in a small lay-by, are the restaurants *Mar y Sombra*, T7770003, good *casado especial* and jumbo shrimps with shady tables on the beach, sun-loungers for hire and *Amor y Mar*, T7770510, a souvenir shop, **D** *Caycosta*, and *Cabinas Ramírez*, T7770003, with bath, food and bar, hammocks and camping free, guests can help with cooking in exchange. **B** *Cabinas Los Almendros*, cheaper for longer stays, private bath, fan, clean, quiet, reasonable restaurant, T7770225.

Proceeding along the main road towards Quepos, you come to *Cabinas Pisces*, T7770294/0046, and **AL** *Karahé*, on private road, T7770170, F7770152, includes breakfast, cabins on a steep hillside with lovely view, sleep 3/4, recommended, fridge, bath, a/c or fan, good restaurant, swimming pool across the road, access to beach, can walk to park along the beach. **AL** *Costa Verde*, near beach, apartments for 2-3 people, with kitchenette and bath, 2-bedroom villas available, T7770584, F7770560, well-appointed, recommended. **AL** *Villa Nina*, unmistakable bubblegum pink, T7771628, F7771497, short walk to beach, 8 rooms, fully screened, bath, small pool, microwave ovens and fridges for hire, pleasant, friendly. **B-D** *La Arboleda*, T7770414, cabins on hillside leading down to beach sleep 2/3, bath, fan, good recommended, Uruguayan restaurant, 8-hectare wood, beware snakes, crabs and monkeys in the yard at night. Three minutes from *Arboleda* is **L-A** *Nature's Beachfront Apartotel*, T7771473, F7771475, suites and studios, apdo 376, Quepos 6350. **LL** *El Salto*, T7770130, F4412938, Apdo 119, Quepos, MAP in cabins with bath sleeping up to 4, includes taxes and eco-tour of own Reserve with waterfalls, 4 kilometres of trails, horses, lovely peaceful setting on hill, open air restaurant and bar, gardens, pool. **LL-A** *Eclipse*, Apdo 11-6350, Quepos, T/F7770408, F7771738, USA T760-7536827, F760-7532227, or villatucan@sand.net, Costa Rican/French run, Mediterranean feel, standard rooms, junior suites or houses, 3 pools, very helpful, good service, a/c, fan, hot water, recommended as 'best in the region', restaurant, *Jardin Gourmet*, T7771728, delicious food, worth the price. Nearby are the cabins of *John and Mavis Beisanz*, T2491507, also expensive but very good; further on same side road, **AL** *Divisamar*, T7770371, pool, restaurant, a/c. *Barba Roja* restaurant, popular, not cheap, grilled tuna good, art gallery and gift shop, boat charter T7770424; **A** *Los Mogotes*, T7771043, F7770582, includes breakfast, 8 rooms, pool and restaurant (home of the singer late Jim Croce). **L** *Villas Nicolás*, T7770481, F7770451, nicolas@sol.racsa.co.cr, 10 rooms, 10 suites with kitchenette, pool. **AL** *Byblos*, T7770411, F7770009, low season, **LL** high season MAP, all in bungalows, sleep 1-4, French restaurant, pool, cruise in *Byblos I* boat 0800-1500, US$50 per person includes drink and sandwiches. **AL** *Villas El Parque*, 5 kilometres from Quepos, T7770096, F7770538, large suites, attractive pool, restaurant with Mexican and South American choices. **LL** *Sí Como No*, environmental resort, T7770777, F7771093, sicomono@sol.racsa.co.cr, 5 kilometres from Quepos, 16-hectare reserve, hotel, restaurant, pool, small shopping centre and 7 villas with 2 bedrooms will sleep 6, a/c, kitchenette. **AL** *Hotel Casablanca*, T/F7770253, cblanca@sol.racsa.co.cr, smart, lovely view, German-owned, friendly, all facilities, pool, recommended, on corner of road to **LL** *Mariposa*, T7770456, F7770050, also fine position, villas 250m above beach, include breakfast, dinner, taxes and service, no credit cards, no guests under 15, bar (book meals in advance), pool (US$1 for non-residents). **LL** *El Parador*, 2 kilometres from the road on Punta Quepos, half way between Quepos and the Park, T7771414, F7771437 (**AL** low season), 55 rooms, new all facility hotel, stunning views of the ocean, in style of Spanish parador, helicopter landing pad. **L** *Makanda by the Sea*, T7770442, F7771032, makanda@sol.racsa.co.cr, 1 kilometre down from main road, 6 villas and studios. **LL** *Tule Mar*, 3 kilometres south of Quepos, T7770580, F7771579, with breakfast, 14 octagonal 2 bedroom bungalows with domed roof lights, pool, snack bar, own beach. **AL** *Villa Oso*, T7770233, spectacular sea views; off the main road away from the sea, **A** *El Lirio*, T7770403, including breakfast and taxes, small, very comfortable; close to Quepos, **AL-A** *Plinio*, T7770055, on hillside, 13 rooms, restaurant, bar, pool, recommended. **C** *Cabinas Pedro Miguel*, opposite, T7770035. Take a torch when walking on roads at night; there are snakes, some poisonous. Take all precautions against mosquitoes, even in daytime. **AL-A** *Hotel California*, (1.5 km turn off left, T7771234, F7771062, hotelcal@sol.racsa.co.cr): swimming pool, private reserve (75 hectares), 22 pleasant rooms with private bathroom (hot water), TV, safe, fan or a/c. **AL** *Kekoldi Beach Hotel*, Villa La Roca, 4.2 km right, T7771349, kekoldi@sol.racsa.co.cr (or through hotel in San José), 20 minutes from beach, 5 rooms with fridge, good views.

Transport There are 3 express buses a day (see Quepos), direct from **San José**, 4 hours, US$5. At weekends buy ticket day before, bus fills to standing room only very quickly. Return tickets are sold on main road between the few sodas, get them in advance, bus gets crowded in Quepos. Roads back to San José on Sunday evening are packed. A regular bus service runs 6 times a day (roughly half-hourly in high season) from beside **Quepos** market, starting at 0545, last bus back at 1700, US$0.35. Taxi from Quepos, shared, US$0.65 per person. Minibuses meet flights from San José to the airport at Quepos (see above), US$2.25.

Puerto Quepos to Dominical

Playa Matapalo Thirty kilometres southeast from Quepos towards Dominical along the unpaved coastal road ('carretera Costanera') is Playa Matapalo, a huge, beautiful sandy beach recommended for surfing and relaxing.

> **Sleeping AL** *Coicota Lodge*, near Savegre, T/F01-3026781, edi.luety@bluewin.ch, farm close to the river, rafting, walking trails. **C** *Bar y Cabinas El Coquito del Pacífico*, comfortable cabins with bath, palm gardens, good breakfast, Swiss owned, recommended (T Braun Ecoturismo in San José T2331731, F2228849). *Restaurant La Piedra Buena*, T/F7713015, has basic accommodation, beach access, also Swiss owned. Good restaurant, *Julio's*, also rooms to rent.

Dominical
Colour map 5, grid B2
Twelve kilometres further is Dominical, at the mouth of the Río Barú, where the road turns inland to San Isidro de El General. This road is very steep and has some unpaved sections, from a few metres to a few kilometres. Dominical has become very popular with surfers, hotel prices soar in high season and most hotels are next to noisy bars, preventing sleep at night.

> **Sleeping AL** *Villas Río Mar Hotel and Resort*, T7870052, 500m from beach, 40 bungalows with bath, fridge and fan, pool, jacuzzi, tennis court, riding, all inclusive. **AL** *Escaleras Inn*, 2 guest rooms, with breakfast, T7715247. **A** *Hacienda Barú*, T7870003, F7870004, 344-hectare reserve, cabins with private bath, hiking, riding. **B** *Cabinas Nayarit*, T7870033, beach front cabins, bath, hot water. **B** *Hotel Pacífico Edge*, 4 large cabins with views of ocean and rainforest, T7711903 (Selvamar reservation service). **B** *Hotel Diuwak*, T/F2238195, 400m from San Clemente Bar bus stop. **C** *Cabinas Bejuco*, 300m from beach, T/F7711903, new cabins with bathtubs, peaceful. **D-C** *Albergue Willdale*, T7870023, fan and bath, bikes, boat trips, fishing and horses available. **D** *Posada del Sol*, 100m from beach, owned by Mariela Badilla, local historian, fascinating, 4 rooms, bath, fan, patio with hammocks, also 2-bedroom apartment with kitchen for US$100 per week, highly recommended. PO Box 126-8000, San Isidro de El General. **D-E** *Cabinas El Coco*, with or without bath, negotiate price, reported dirty, unfriendly, noisy. **E** *Cabinas Roca Verde*, T7870036, friendly, fan, restaurant, recommended. **E** *Cabinas Costa Brava*, south of the village, restaurant, basic but friendly.
>
> Four kilometres south is **Punta Dominical** (no transport) **AL** *Cabinas Punta Dominical*, T7711903, restaurant, fishing, riding, good value for seekers of solitude. **B** per person *Finca Brian y Milena*, near Dominical, 400m above ocean, T7711903 (for reservations), cabins with bath, including meals, forest, waterfall, horses. 4 kilometres south of Dominical, **B** *Bella Vista Lodge*, great view, good large meals, owned by 'Woody Dycer', local character (American), organizes trips, T7711903 (Selva Mar reservation service). There are also houses to rent, contact Cassandra T/F7870062. **D-E** *Cabinas San Clemente*, T7870026, on beach, clean, with or without a/c, friendly, US owned, restaurant, **E** per person, rooms over bar, shared bath, fan; *Gringo Place*, bar/restaurant under same ownership, good.

> **Transport** Bus Quepos-Dominical 0500, 1330, 3½ hours; Dominical-San Isidro, 4 buses a day, 1st 0645, 1 hour; last bus from San Isidro to Dominical 1600; bus Dominical-Quepos 0700, 1330; to San José, 7 hours.

Uvita Eighteen kilometres south of Dominical is the village of Uvita. In the area you can walk, swim in a waterfall in the forest or at the beach, take a boat trip, watch seabirds. The road south from Uvita was badly affected by the 1996 hurricane, but is being repaved as far as Ciudad Cortés, and access to the beaches of Playa Ballena and Playa Bahía is getting easier with consequent development of the area and the construction of *cabinas*.

Sleeping **E** *Cabinas Uvita*, 100 metres left, 4 very simple *cabinas* with private bathroom, sleep 3. **D** *Cabinas Los Laureles*, 200 metres turn off left, nice location, 3 *cabinas* with private bathroom, simple and quite good. **D** *Cabinas Coco Tico*, 250 metres left, information c/o Pulpería, 6 clean *cabinas*, sleep 3, with private bathroom. **D** *Cabinas/Camping Hegalva*, before Bahía left, red sign, private house with garden, 2 quite good *cabinas* with private bathroom, camping US$2 per person. **D** *Cabinas Punta Uvita*, left opposite *Restaurant Los Almendros*, 2 pleasant *cabinas* with private bathroom. **E** *Cabinas/Soda El Ranchito*, on the right, 2 quite simple, older *cabinas* with private bathroom. **B** *Cabinas El Chamán*, nice location, 2 kilometres south on the beach, 8 simple *cabinas* with private bathroom, camping US$4 per person. **C** *El Chamán*, German owner, very friendly, nice beach, isolated. *Cabinas Hegalva*, rooms with hot shower, meals, camping.

Transport Bus San José to Uvita from Terminal Coca Cola, Monday-Friday 1500, Saturday-Sunday 0500, 1500, return Monday-Friday, 0530, Saturday-Sunday 0530, 1300, 7 hours. From San Isidro daily 0800, 1600, return 0600, 1400.

You can hire boats to take you out to Isla Ballena, part of Ballena Parque Nacional Marino, wonderful views looking back to the mainland. Be careful of the surf, do not attempt to swim ashore on to the island. **Ballena Parque Nacional Marino**

Sleeping **A** *Cabinas Ballena* and **C** *Rocaparadiso*, both 6 kilometres south of Uvita in front of Ballena Parque Nacional Marino, T2204263 for information.

Further down the road to Palmar Norte is **Las Ventanas de Osa Wildlife Refuge**, 36-hectare, private reserve and lodge built by the late Fred Ross; five-night packages including transport, meals, guided tours, US$900 per person, T USA 1-800-5617751, Costa Rica 2365926/2847780. New on **Playa Tortuga: AL** *Hotel Villas Gaia*, T/F office 2569996, dionec@sol.racsa.co.cr, new complex, about 200m to the beach, swimming pool and restaurant (Swiss and international kitchen, vegetarian dishes) with ocean view, diving school, horses, 12 large bungalows with private bathroom (hot water), fan and terrace.

San José to the Panama border

Through the mountains, past El Chirripó, the highest peak, dropping down along the valley of the Río de El General to the tropical lowlands of the Pacific coast and the Panama border.

The Pan-American Highway to the Panama border runs 352 kilometres from San José (lots of potholes, frequent rockslides during rainy season, roadworks and poor conditions, be careful driving, don't drive at night), first to Cartago (toll road, US$0.30), and southwards over the mountains between Cartago and San Isidro de El General (124 kilometres). This is a spectacular journey. The climate is ideal for orchids. At Cartago begins the ascent of **Cerro Buena Vista** (3,490 metres), a climb of almost 2,050 metres to the continental divide, a little lower than the peak; the highest point of the road is 3,335 metres at Km 89. At this height there is an interesting *páramo* ecosystem. Those unaccustomed to high altitude should beware of mountain sickness brought on by a too rapid ascent, see **Health Information**, page 49. For 16 kilometres it follows the crest of the Talamanca ridge, with views, on clear days, of the Pacific 50 kilometres away, and even of the Atlantic, over 80 kilometres away.

Santa María de Dota At Km 51 from San José, a side road leads off the Pan-American Highway to the peaceful and very pleasant mountain village of Santa María de Dota (1,460 metres). Santa María is quiet, and beautifully situated; it is in a good area for walking, and eight kilometres away is a small lake where many waterbirds nest. From Santa María one can hike (10 hours) to the Pacific coast of the Puerto Quepos district, or go by road (three hours in a four-wheel drive vehicle).

Sleeping & eating **AL** per person *Albergue de Montaña Chacón*, including all meals and horses, good cabins, simple meals, T7711732, good chance of seeing quetzales on the property (short trail map available), and there is trout fishing in the Río Savegre. **D** *Cecilia's Cabinas*, Apartado 805 1 (San José), T5411233, run by Ana Cecilia Ureña, 4 cabins, rustic, clean, hot showers, bedding if required, common area for cooking, relaxing, quiet, nice views, 15 minutes' walk from town centre, parking, very friendly. **F** *Hospedaje Fonda Marieuse*, T5411176, shared bath, clean, basic, very friendly, run by an elderly lady, Doña Elsie, recommended. **E** *Hotel and Restaurant Dota*, near square, without bath; *Soda Gómez*, next to bus station, large portions, cheap.

At **San Marcos de Tarrazú**, 10 km west of Santa María, bus 15 minutes, US$0.25: **F** *Marilú*, restaurant. **E** *Continental*, with bath. **F** *Zacateca*, with bath. *Bar y Pulpería La Cueva*, good, has bunkhouse, T/F5411278. *Finca El Edén*, near **Copey de Dota**, 10 kilometres east from Santa María, no phone but T5411299 to leave message, 2 cabins, riding, treks into the mountains. Also in Copey is **B** *El Toucanet Lodge*, T5411435, with breakfast, 6 units, family run, with bath, hot water, restaurant, pleasant climate, many country attractions.

At **San Gerardo de Dota: AL** *Trogón Lodge*, T2237490, F2225463, 10 rooms with private bathroom.

Transport Bus from San José to Santa María via San Marcos, US$2.10, 2½ hours, 5 daily from Av 16, C 19-21, Terminal Los Santos.

Genesis II Four and a half kilometres east of Km 58 (Cañón church) is **Genesis II**, a 40-hectare cloudforest reserve at 2,360 metres.

Sleeping Available at **AL-B** *Genesis II Lodge*, rooms with shared bath, for birders and naturalists, T3810739, F5510070, genesis@yellowweb.co.cr, www.yellowweb.co.cr/genesis, and www.hotels.co.cr/genesis/volunt.html for volunteers; transport available from San José. There is also a student volunteer programme: write to Steve and Paula Friedman, Apartado 655, 7050 Cartago, or SJO 2031, 1601 NW 97th Ave, Unit C-101, PO Box 025216, Miami FL33102-5216. Conditions are basic, the climate can be cold and damp and rooms are heated with electric heaters and hot water bottles on request, hot showers. The plant and animal life make it a worthwhile stopover; full details of the work involved are set out in the information sent with the application form. Vegetarians catered for.

Km 62 At Km 62 on the Pan-American Highway is the **AL** *Albergue de Montaña Tapantí*, also called *Hotel Tapantí*, T2320436, Spanish-owned, 10 quite good, large rooms, sleep 5, private bathrooms, hot water, some with balcony, restaurant with fireplace, beautiful location, one hour to San José, one-night packages including transport and guided trips available.

Km 70 At Km 70: **B** pp *Finca El Mirador de Quetzales*, T3818456, 43 hectare forest property at 2,650 metres, Eddie Serrano or one of his sons will show visitors quetzales and other endemic species of the highlands (Jorge, Oscar and Carlos are recommended guides), two new cabins with wonderful view and private bath, 7 basic cabins sleep 4, shared bathroom (ask for plenty of blankets), including breakfast, dinner and guided hike.

At Km 71 is another *Finca Quetzal*. **Km 71**

At **Km 78**: *Casa Refugio de Ojo de Agua*, a historic pioneer home with picnic tables in front of the house. **Km 78**

The highest point is at Km 89.5 (temperatures below zero at night). At **Km 95**: **E** *Hotel and Restaurant Georgina*, at almost 3,300m, basic, clean, friendly, good food (used by southbound Tracopa buses), good birdwatching, ask owners for directions for a nice walk to see quetzales. **Km 89.5**

At **Km 107** at **División** turn off and follow the signs for the four kilometres to the **Reserva Privada Avalón**, where there are more than 60 species of birds recorded. Accommodation, **B**, **E** for bunk bed, camping possible, food at reasonable cost, guides and horses available. Volunteers accepted. Contact Scott Miller, Apartado 846, San Isidro de El General, T/F7717226. They may be able to meet you at the main road with a horse to take your luggage. Taxi from San Isidro US$20. **Km 107**

The road then drops down into San Isidro (in a fertile valley in the centre of a coffee and cattle district. The town is growing fast. The **Museo Regional de Pérez Zeledón** is in the old marketplace, now the Complejo Cultural, Calle 2. ■ *Monday-Friday, 0800-1200, 1330-1630, free*. Seven kilometres north of San Isidro is the **Centro Biológico Las Quebradas**, with 750 hectares, trails, dormitory accommodation for researchers. ■ *T7714131, 0800-1400 Tuesday-Friday, 0800-1500 Saturday-Sunday, closed October*.

San Isidro de El General
Population: 41,513
702m
Colour map 5, grid B2

Sleeping **AL-A** *Del Sur*, T771-3033/3039, F7710527, 6 kilometres south of town, with bath, comfortable, swimming pool, tennis, good restaurant. **B** *Talari Mountain Lodge*, 10 minutes from San Isidro, 8-hectare farm, T7710341, with bath, rustic. **E** *Amaneli*, close to San José buses, with restaurant. **D-E** *Hotel Chirripó*, south side of Parque Central, T7710529, private or shared bath, near bus office, clean, very good restaurant, free covered parking, good, recommended. **E** *Iguazú*, modern. **E** *Manhattan*, T7710606, with bath. **F** *El Jardín*, good value, small, laundry facilities, and good restaurant (especially the breakfast), recommended. **F** *Hotel Balboa* in the centre, bath, recommended. **F** *Pensión Jerusalem*, friendly, clean. On the road towards San Gerardo de Rivas, about 4 kilometres from San Isidro, *Centro Turístico de Praderea*, T7710918, wonderful views, botanical garden, hiking trails. 6 kilometres. **E** *Hotel/Restaurant Amanelli*, T7710352, 41 quite good rooms with private bathroom, fan, some noisy. **F** *Cabinas /Restaurant El Descanso*, T7711866, simple restaurant, horses US$3.50 per hour, 8 simple, small, but acceptable *cabinas* with shared bathroom. **F** per person *Restaurant/Hotel Roca Dura*, nice, small restaurant, 7 *cabinas*, sleep 4, simple and quite good, shared bathroom. **F** *Cabinas San Gerardo*, 8 very simple *cabinas*, small, but clean, shared bathroom. **D-E** *Cabinas/Restaurant Elimar*, swimming pool, simple restaurant, 4 quite good *cabinas* with private bathroom (hot water). **F** per person *Cabinas Mary*, T7300187, 15 simple rooms. **F** per person *Cabinas El Buen Amigo*, T7300188, 9 *cabinas* with fan, quiet, simple and quite good. **E-F** per person *Hotel/Cabinas Casa Amarilla*, 300m east of bus station, T7866251, 19 rooms, very basic, but acceptable. *Rancho La Botija*, T7711401, 3823052, restaurant, pool, hiking, open 0900 at weekends, restaurant open daily.

Eating *Astoria*, north side of square. *Restaurant Wu Fu* is good, *Hong Kong*, across the park from *Hotel Chirripó*, reasonable prices. *Restaurant El Tenedor*, good food, not expensive, friendly, big pizzas, recommended. *Soda Mönpik*, good hamburgers, *batidos*, ice cream, north side of Parque Central. *Soda Katty*, by bus station, good reasonable food. Other *sodas* in the indoor market. *Panadería El Tío Marcos*, south side of Parque, very good bakery. *Café del Teatro*, small snack bar, helpful owner is planning to open a tourist office; paintings for sale and plays in Spanish every month or so. Ask in advance for early (0400) breakfast if climbing Chirripó.

Transport Bus terminal at Avenida 6, C Central-2 at the back of the new market and adjacent streets. To and from **San José** (just outside Terminal Coca Cola), hourly service 0530-1700, US$3.30, 3 hours (buses to the capital leave from the Interamericana, C 2-4). However, Tracopa buses coming from San José, going south go from C 3/Pan-American Highway, behind church, to **Palmar Norte**, US$2.25; **Paso Canoas**, 0830-1545, 1930 (direct), 2100; **David** (Panama) direct, 1000 and 1500; **Golfito** direct at 1800; **Puerto Jiménez**, 0900 and 1500. Waiting room but no reservations or tickets sold.

Chirripó National Park

From San Isidro de El General one can go to the highest mountain in Costa Rica, **Cerro Chirripó Grande** (3,820 metres) in the middle of the **Chirripó National Park** (50,150 hectares), including a considerable portion of cloud forest (entry US$6, crowded in season, make reservations in Oficina de los Parques Nacionales in San Isidro, T7713155). Splendid views from the mountaintops; interesting alpine environment on the high plateau, with lakes of glacial origin and very diverse flora and fauna. The Chirripó National Park and the neighbouring **La Amistad International Park** (193,929 hectares), established in 1982, extend along the Cordillera de Talamanca to the Panamanian border and comprise the largest area of virgin forest in the country with the greatest biological diversity.

Sleeping At entrance to La Amistad Park there is **AL** *Monte Amou Lodge*, T2656149, with bath, guided walks with naturalists, electricity is generated to 2200; and a chalet lodge on a coffee plantation, **A** per person *La Amistad*, all inclusive, good hiking, excellent guide, recommended rooms and food, contact owner Roberto Montero, c/o Tropical Rainbow Tours, T2338228, F2554636, San José.

Transport At San Isidro de El General, get food and take the 0500 Pueblo Nuevo bus from northwest corner of Parque Central, or the 1400 from the new bus station to San Gerardo de Rivas (US$1.05, 1½ hour, return at 0700 and 1600) which passes the entrance to the Park. Highly interesting trip up the Río Chirripó valley.

San Gerardo de Rivas

San Gerardo de Rivas is situated in a cool, pleasant landscape at the confluence of two rivers. Horses can be rented. There is a hot spring near San Gerardo: before crossing the new concrete bridge turn left to 'Herradura' for 10 minutes then look for the sign after Parqueo Las Rosas; go down to the suspension bridge, cross the river and continue for 10 minutes to the house where you pay, entrance US$1.

Sleeping **F** *Marín*, basic but friendly and good value, good *comedor*. Sr Francisco Elizondo Badilla (the local 'champion' climber) and his family have a small cabin, **F** per person *Cabinas El Descanso*, with 7 bunks, bathroom, hearty meals available, recommended, phone town administrator for information on availability, T7711866, gas stove for hire, horses for rent and guide services offered, recommended. Along the road beyond the Rangers office, bear right over a bridge and *El Descanso* is on the left. You can stay at the small hotel opposite the football pitch called **F** *Roca Dura*, built on a huge boulder, hot showers, good *comedor*, nice view, shop next door, ½ kilometre out of village, friendly owners. You can camp at or near the park office, in San Gerardo near the bus stop. Check in first and pay US$0.30. **E** *Cabinas/Restaurant Elimar*, swimming pool, simple restaurant, 4 quite good *cabinas* with private

Climbing the Chirripó peaks

If you wish to climb the mountains, you may obtain information from the SPN office in San José (see **National Parks**). Start in the early morning for the eight to ten hours' hike, US$6 entry for each day spent in the park, plus US$2.40 shelter fee per night, maximum 40 persons in park at any one time. The Park entrance is about two and a half hours' walk from San Gerardo. Book accommodation in advance in San José, otherwise pay and obtain permit at the Park office in San Gerardo. You may be told the Refugio is fully booked, but this is not always the case when you get there. The shelter, where the horses will take you, consists of two good, but cold huts, Refugios Base Crestones. They are two hours from the top at 3,400 metres where there normally is a park ranger. Hang up food or the mice will get it. Bring your own gas

stove, which can be hired from Posada El Descanso or the shop near Cabinas Chirripó. Two peaks can be reached from these huts, **Crestones**, 45 minutes, and **Ventisqueres**, one and a half hours. There is another shelter, Refugio LlanoBonito (2,500 metres), simple but clean, wooden floor, two levels to sleep on, no door but wind protection, drinking water, toilet, about four hours' walk from San Gerardo, three hours' walk on to Refugios Base Crestones. Plan for at least two nights on the mountain, and bring warm sleeping bags and waterproof clothing. It can be hot in the daytime, though. In the rainy season trails up the plateau are uncomfortably slippery and muddy, and fog obscures the views. These are stiff walks, but no technical climbing is called for. Time your descent to catch the afternoon bus back to San Isidro.

bathroom, hot water. **F** *Cabinas San Gerardo*, 8 very simple *cabinas*, small, but clean, shared bathroom.

Continuing southeast along the highway, at Km 142 is **B** *Huerta de Buena Salud*, pool, good for bed and breakfast. **Km 142**

At Km 197 (from San José) is Buenos Aires, with **F** *Cabinas Mary*, 500m from centre, **Buenos Aires** T7300187, quiet clean. **F** *Cabinas La Redonda Familiares*, close to the Pan-American Highway. **F** *Cabinas El Buen Amigo*, T7300188, 9 *cabinas* with fan, quiet, simple and quite good. Next door is *Soda Refresquería El Parque*, good *casados*. *Flor de la Sabana*, good restaurant, good value. The section of the highway running alongside the Río Grande de Térraba is prone to landslides which can cut it off for days.

At Palmar Norte (Km 257) a paved road leads to Ciudad Cortés and from there you **Palmar Norte** can follow a new road along the coast northwest to Dominical (see page 1136).

Sleeping **D** cabin **E** rooms *Hotel y Cabinas Casa Amarilla*, T7866251, 300m east of bus station, with fan, rooms at back quieter, rooms over restaurant noisy but cheaper. **C** *Cabinas Tico-Alemán*, Interamericana left, T7866232, 25 *cabinas* with private bathroom. **E** *Cabinas/Restaurant Wah-Lok*, Interamericana left, 12 *cabinas* with private bathroom. **F** *Hotel Xinia*, 150m east from bus station, 26 rooms, very simple, but acceptable, shared bathroom.

Transport Express bus to Palmar Norte from Terminal Alfaro, San José, 7 daily 0600-1800, 5 hours, 5 buses return to the capital 0445-1300.

At Palmar Sur (gas station), 99 kilometres from the Panamanian border, a banana **Palmar Sur** plantation has stone spheres, one and a half metres in diameter and accurate within five millimetres, which can also be seen in other places in Costa Rica. They are of preColumbian Indian manufacture, but their use is a matter of conjecture; among recent theories are that they were made to represent the planets of the solar system, or that they were border markers. Flights daily with Sansa and Travelair San José-Palmar Sur. From Palmar a bus goes to Sierpe, from where a boat sails to Bahía Drake (page 1149).

San Vito

Colour map 5, grid B3 Near the border is the town of San Vito, built by Italian immigrants among denuded hills; it is a prosperous but undistinguished town. The road from Paso Real to San Vito is now paved and has lovely views. There is a new bridge over the Río Térraba just after the Paso Real junction.

Excursions On the road from San Vito to Ciudad Neilly at **Las Cruces** there are the **Wilson Botanical Gardens**, T7733278, owned by the Organization for Tropical Studies, six kilometres from San Vito. It consists of 145 hectares of tropical plants, orchids, other epiphytes, and tropical trees. ■ *US$6, good self guide booklet for the principal trail US$2.20.* Many birdwatchers come here. It is possible to spend the night here if you arrange first with the Organization of Tropical Studies in San José, T2406696 (cost around US$64 per person double occupancy a night with food, senior researchers US$32, day visits with lunch US$18 per person). OTS welcomes any donations; Organization for Tropical Studies, Box 90630, Durham NC 27708-0630 USA. On the same road is *Finca Cántaros*, specializing in local arts and crafts, owned by Gail Hewson Gómez. Worth a look even if you don't buy anything.

Sleeping & **F** *Hotel Pitier*, ½ kilometre out of town on road to Sabalito, new, clean, with bath. *Las Mirlas*
eating in same location and price range but more attractive; and **D** *El Ceibo*, in new part with bath and hot water, **E** in old part, T7733025, good restaurant. **E** *Cabinas Las Huacas*, T7733115, 13 acceptable *cabinas* with private bathroom, hot water, TV. **F** *Hotel Jardín*, opposite hospital, 3 simple *cabinas* with private bathroom. **F** *Cabinas Firenze*, T7733741, 6 simple *cabinas*, sleep 5, with private bathroom. There are also 2 good Italian restaurants in San Vito, *Lilianas* and *Mama Mías*, genuine Italian cuisine, reasonable prices. *Jimar* off central plaza is OK. *Soda El Jardín* opposite hospital, cheap, friendly, good. Hotels also in the nearby village of Cañas Gordas on the frontier with Panama (no crossing).

Transport **Bus** Direct buses San José to San Vito, 4 daily, 0545-1445, from Terminal Alfaro, C 14, Av 5; direct bus San Vito-San José 0530, 6 hours, *corriente* buses take 8 hours. Alternative route, not all paved, via Ciudad Neily (see below); from San Vito to Las Cruces at 0530 and 0700; sit on the right to admire the wonderful scenery; return buses pass Las Cruces at 1510.

Frontier with The road from San Vito to Ciudad Neily is paved and in good condition. From San
Panama - Vito a good gravel road, paved in places, runs via **Sabalito** to the Panama border at
Sabalito Río Sereno. There are through buses Sabalito-San José. See Panama chapter, page 1221 for details of this frontier crossing.

Golfito

Thirty one kilometres north of the border a road (26 kilometres) branches south at Río Claro (several *pensiones* and a fuel station) to Golfito, the former banana port. Golfito is a six kilometres long linear settlement between the gulf (Golfo Dulce) and steep forested hills. Entering the town from the south are a group of hotels leading in two kilometres or so to the town centre of painted buildings with saloon bars, open fronted restaurants and cheap accommodation. Nearby is the dilapidated *'muellecito'* used by the ferries to Puerto Jiménez and water taxis. A further kilometre north are the container port facilities and the Standard Fruit local HQ though many of the banana plantations have been turned over to oil palm and other crops. However, the port is now active with container traffic. Beyond the port is the airstrip and another set of hotels. Golfito became a free port in 1990, which has become popular with shoppers and at weekends it is difficult to get a hotel room. You must obtain a permit the previous day if you wish to shop there (passport required). There is an ICT Tourist Office, T7750496.

The **Refugio Nacional de Fauna Silvestre Golfito** has been created in the steep forested hills overlooking Golfito, originally to protect Golfito's watershed. It is rich in rare and medicinal plants and has abundant fauna. There are some excellent hikes in the Refuge. It is supervised by the University of Costa Rica and they have a field office in Golfito.

Also, 30 minutes by water taxi from Golfito, you can visit **Casa Orquídeas**, a family owned botanical garden with a large collection of herbs, orchids and local flowers and trees, T7355062 for information.

To the north of Golfito is a new conservation area of tropical wet forest, **Piedras Blancas National Park**. The area was being exploited for wood products, but was purchased in 1994 with help from the Austrian government and private interests, notably Michael Schnitzler, the classical violinist. All logging has now ceased and efforts are devoted to a research centre and ecotourism. This is concentrated in an area designated **Esquinas National Park**. Near the village of **La Gamba** a tourist lodge has been built: LL*Esquinas Rainforest Lodge*, T2930780, 3807468, F2932632, gasguis@sol.racsa.co.cr, full board, private baths, verandas overlooking the forest, tours, all profits to the local community. La Gamba is six kilometres along a dirt road from Golfito, or four kilometres from Villa Briceño on the Pan-American Highway between Piedras Blancas and Río Claro.

Near airport **A** *Sierra*, T7750666, F7750087, 72 rooms, a/c, pool, restaurant. **B** *Golfo Azul*, with bath and a/c, T7750871, good restaurant.

Sleeping

In the **'banana town'**, **E** *Cabinas Evelyn*, with fan and bath. **E** *Cabinas Princesa del Golfo* and *Casa Blanca Lodge*, T7750124, 5 rooms, both in fine frame houses with beautiful gardens. **F** *Cabinas Marlin*, small neat rooms, fan, hot water, friendly.

In the main town to the **south** *Del Cerro*, Edif Wachong, T7750006, F7750551, 20 rooms, private bathroom, laundry services, fishing boat rentals. **B** *Las Gaviotas*, 18 rooms, with excellent restaurant on waterfront, with bath, a/c, T7750062, F7750544. **D** *Costa Rica Surf*, T7750034, also one cheap, single room, friendly. **D** *El Gran Ceibo*, next to *Gaviotas*, T7750403, small pool, a/c. **D** *Mar y Luna*, T7750192, 8 rooms, with bath, fan, restaurant on stilts above the sea. **D** *Koktsur*, T7750327, cabins with private bath. **E** *Golfito*, T7750047, with bath, run down. **E** *Delfina*, shared bath, fan, car park, friendly, owner speaks English, basic, rooms on street noisy. **D** *Cabinas Miramar*, T7550169, fan. **F** *El Uno*, above restaurant of same name, basic, friendly. Seven kilometres before Golfito, **D** *La Purruja Lodge*, T7751054, 5 cabins with bath, plus camping US$2 per tent.

La Dama del Delfín Restaurant, new restaurant downtown, breakfast from 0700, snacks (hamburger, sandwiches, spaghetti), homemade bakery, closed for dinner and Sunday. *Cubana*, near Post Office, good food, try the *batidos*. *Luis Brenes*, opposite Texaco, good simple food, good meeting place. *Soda Pavas*, in front of parque central, cheap, also have rooms in the hills, **E**. Many eating places near centre.

Eating

Air Daily flights San José-Golfito, with Sansa and Travelair, some via Coto 47 or Puerto Jiménez. Runway is all-weather, tight landing between trees; 2 kilometres from town, taxi US$0.50. **Buses** From **San José** 0700, 1500 daily from Terminal Alfaro, return 0500, 1300, US$6, 8 hours; from San Isidro de El General, take 0730 bus to Río Claro and wait for bus coming from Ciudad Neily. Bus Golfito-**Paso Canoas**, US$1.25, hourly from outside *Soda Pavo*, 1¼ hours. **Sea** Asociación de Boteros, water taxis in and around Golfito, opposite ICE building, T7750712, to Cacao Beach, Punta Zancudo, Punta Encanto or to order, US$20 per hour up to 5 persons.

Transport

Banks *Banco Nacional* near muelle, open Mon-Fri 0830-1535.

Directory

Golfito beaches

About six kilometres (one and a half hour walk) north round the bay from Golfito is the **Playa de Cacao**. A taxi boat from Golfito will take you there for US$2.50, or you can drive (if it hasn't rained too heavily) along an inland road, starting at the left of the police station in Golfito, and left again a few kilometres later.

Sleeping **B** *Cabinas Playa Cacao*, T/F2564850, T (San José) 2211169, isabel@sol.racsa.co.cr, huts with small kitchen, private bathroom, hot water. **B** *Cabinas Palmas*, 6 cabins, US-owned, friendly, clean, shower and toilet, directly on beach, 5 minutes north of Golfito by water taxi, T7750375 (leave message, Spanish only). Next to *Cabinas Palmas*, good, cheap restaurant, *Siete Mares*. Also at Playa de Cacao is the *Zamia Biological Station*, arrange with Sr Odette at Travelair office in Golfito, maximum 4 persons, student exchanges.

Beyond Playa de Cacao is **Playa San Josecito** and the **AL** *Golfo Dulce Lodge*, T7750373, F7750573, cabins with bath and hot water, guided hikes and trips, Swiss-owned.

30-45 minutes by boat northwest of Golfito, at **Playa Cativo**, is Michael Medill's **LL** *Rainbow Adventures*, *cabinas*, includes all meals, snacks, beer and soft drinks, transport, private beach with no other hotels, jungle tours, tours of the gulf, fishing, snorkelling, bordered by National Park, Apdo 63, Golfito, T/F7750220, in USA, 5875 northwest Kaiser Rd, Portland, Oregon 97229, T503-6907750, F503-6907735 for reservations.

At beautiful **Playa Zancudo**, about 15 kilometres by sea south of Golfito (US$1.75 by colectivo ferry at 0600, 1200, return 0500, 1300), you can stay in cabins at **AL** *Roy Ventura*, with a/c, organizes fishing trips. **B** *Casa Tranquilidad B&B*, T7750449, F7750373, large house with terrace, 4 nice rooms with private bathroom, hot water, with breakfast. **B** *Los Cocos*, T/F7760012, loscocos@sol.racsa.co.cr, Apdo 88, Golfito, 10 good, small houses at the ocean with private bathroom, hot water, mosquito net, fan, kitchenette, refrigerator, veranda. **C** *Los Ultimos Paraísos*, T7760050, with bath, fan, mosquito nets, hammocks or **C-D** *Sol y Mar*, run by Rick and Lori, T7760014, F7760015, solymar@zancudo.com, 4 screened cabins, hot water, fan, 3-storey rental house, US$450-550, 50m from ocean, bar/restaurant, meals 0700-2000, home baked bread, great fruit shakes, volleyball with lights for evening play, badminton, paddleball, boogie boards, library. To get there contact staff of Yacht Club at the entrance of Golfito and ask to radiophone to Zancudo, 7750056, well recommended. **E** *Pensión Fin del Mundo*, over *Restaurant Tranquilo*, 6 simple rooms with fan, mosquito net, clean, shared bathroom. English book exchange at *Tienda Buen Precio*.

South of Golfito, at **Punta Banco** is **AL** *Tiskita Jungle Lodge*, T2336890, F2554410, tiskita@sol.racsa.co.cr, a 162-hectare property including a fruit farm, with excellent birdwatching, 14 cabins overlooking ocean, owned by Peter Aspinall, c/o Sun Tours, Apdo 1195-1250 Escazú. Overlooks beach, cool breezes, waterfall, jungle pools, trails through virgin forest. All-inclusive package tours from San José including roundtrip air transport. *Tiskita* can be combined with *Corcovado Tent Lodge Camp* at Carate, Osa Peninsula. *Casa Punta Banco*, managed by Malcolm Miles, is a jungle home in 265 acres of forest, you're on your own for US$700 per week, T7750131. Day trips offered by boat to Sirena Ranger Station in Corcovado National Park.

Near Punta Banco at **Pavones** is **B** *Pavones Surf Lodge*, includes meals, 2 cabins with bath, 6 rooms with shared bath, T2222224, F2222271 in San José. Also at Pavones is **C** *Cabinas La Ponderosa*, owned by 2 surfers, large cabins, fan, with bath, fishing diving etc, T USA-407-7837184. The beach is rocky, but good surfing.

Transport A bus leaves Golfito for Pavones at 1400, and from Pavones to Golfito at 0500, 3 hours, US$2.50. A spit of land continues south to Punta Burica with no roads and only one or two villages. The crest of the peninsula is the boundary with Panama.

Osa Peninsula

Across the gulf from Golfito is the **Osa Peninsula**.

Puerto Jiménez

Puerto Jiménez has the feel of a frontier town, perhaps because of the gold prospec- Population: 2,500
tors seeking riches in several mineral areas on the peninsula. In fact, most miners
were cleared from the Corcovado National Park area in 1985, though there are still
some licenced operations and a few pirate panners who enter the park illegally.
There are gold mines near **Carate** (see below) on the Pacific coast and elsewhere on
the Peninsula.

Near Puerto Jiménez is **Dos Brazos**; ask for the road which goes uphill beyond
town, to see the local gold mines. Several buses a day to Dos Brazos, last bus back at
1530 (often late); taxi US$7.25.

Puerto Jiménez is popular with foreigners for its laid-back, sometimes lively
atmosphere, its reasonable beaches nearby and, of course, the beautiful National
Park on the other side of the peninsula. A particular charm of Puerto Jiménez is its
relative freedom from road traffic. There are good local walks to the jungle (you will
see monkeys and many birds) and to the beach and mangroves. You can also walk
towards Carate, branch to the right and in four kilometres there are good views of
the peninsula. A topographical map is a big help, obtainable from Instituto
Geográfico in San José. There is an ICE tourist office on the main street in town open
Monday-Friday 0800-1530.

In **Puerto Jiménez B** *Agua Luna*, facing pier, T7355034, new rooms with bath, good res- **Sleeping**
taurant. **B** *Doña Leta's Bungalows*, close to airstrip, T/F7355180, cabins in gardens adjoining beach, large rooms with bath, clean, comfortable, kitchenette, fridge, fan,
recommended. **C** *Manglares*, with bath and fan, clean, small, cold showers, café, bar,
friendly, T7355002, F7355121, Ramón can arrange tours to Corcovado, mangrove gardens
attract many species of birds. **D** *Cabinas Puerto Jiménez*, on the gulf shore, T7355090,
F7355215, big rooms, friendly, good value. **F** *Cabinas Marcelina*, T7355007, F7355045, with
bath, clean, friendly, nice front yard. **E** *Hotel Restaurant Choza del Maglán*, cabins in garden. **E** *Cabinas Oro Verde*, T7355241, run by Silvia Duirós Rodríguez, clean, comfortable,
with bath, fan. **F** *Cabinas Brisas del Mar*, T7355012, with bath. **F** *Cabinas Tomson*, 50m
from the centre, with bath, fan, clean. **F** per person *Pensión Quintero*, T7355078, clean,
good value, will store luggage, ask here for Fernando Quintero, who rents horses and has a
boat for up to 6 passengers, good value, he is also a guide, recommended.

At **Dos Brazos**, **D** *Corcovado Ecology Lodge*, T7751422, F7355045, friendly, rainforest
tours US$25 per day, 5 simple, somewhat dark rooms, shared bathroom. **D** *Sr and Sra Talí*,
T7751422, have rooms, include breakfast, clean, shared bath, laundry facilities, jungle tours,
riding, good food, recommended.

Five kilometres from Rincón, on the road to Puerto Jiménez, at the northeast side of the
neck of the peninsula, is **F** per person *Profecto Boscoso*, a naturalists' camp where visitors
can stay in camp beds, 3 meals US$3.65, information from Fundación Neotrópica, C 20, Av 3 y
5, San José, T2330003, ask for Walter Rodríguez, who is developing ecotourism facilities. Five
kilometres from Puerto Jiménez is **A** *Playa Preciosa Lodge*, T7355005, 4 cabins, good swimming and surfing.

At the tip of the Peninsula, 18 kilometres south of Puerto Jiménez, at **Cabo Matapalo**, is
L *Bosque del Cabo Wilderness Lodge*, includes meals, T/F7355206 (or T2224547 San José),
for ecotourists, 30-minute taxi jeep ride from Puerto Jiménez, 7 bungalows with ocean view.
L *Lapa Ríos Wilderness Resort*, T7355130, F7355179, includes meals, 14 luxury
palm-thatched bungalows on private 400-hectare reserve (80% virgin forest, owners Karen
and John Lewis), camping trips, boats can be arranged from Golfito. **L** *Hacienda Bahía
Esmeralda*, T3818521, F7355045, nice location, view over Golfo Dulce, 3 rooms with bathroom, 3 luxury cottages.

Costa Rica

Eating *Restaurant El Paraíso*, typical food, cheap. *Carolina's Restaurant*, highly recommended for fish. *Jocette*, opposite *Carolina's*, good meeting place. *El Rancho*, good pizzas and bar with music to 0100.

Transport **Air** There are daily flights between Puerto Jiménez and Golfito with Travelair and both Sansa and Travelair from San José, for information T7355017 or 7750607. **Buses** Note: a café at the bus terminal opens at 0430 when you can get a cheap but reasonable breakfast. From **San José**; just outside Terminal Atlántico Norte (C 12, Av 7-9), there are 2 buses daily to Puerto Jiménez at 0600 and 1200 via San Isidro, US$7, 10 hours, return 0500 and 1100, T7712550. There are also buses from San Isidro, leaving from *Soda Frutera del Sol* at 0930 and 1500 daily, next to Castrol on Pan-American Highway, US$3, returns at 0330 and 1100, 6 hours. To reach Puerto Jiménez from the Pan-American Highway (70 kilometres), turn right at the restaurant about 30 kilometres south of Palmar Sur; the road is newly paved to Rincón, thereafter best tackled with four-wheel drive as a few rivers have to be forded (high clearance essential). They are working on bridges. Bus Puerto Jiménez-Ciudad Neily 0500 and 1400, 3½ hours, US$2.50. There is a police checkpoint 47 kilometres from the Pan-American Highway. Trucks, called 'taxis' run daily between Puerto Jiménez and La Palma (several, 1 hour, US$1.50); from the small settlement of La Palma an all-weather road goes to Rincón. **Sea** Two boats leave from Golfito Muelle to Puerto Jiménez at 1100, US$2.50, 1½ hours, return 0600, or you can charter a taxi boat for about US$60, up to 8 passengers. Alternatively,

Southern Costa Rica & the Osa Peninsula

if you want to visit the western side of the peninsula, take taxi or bus from Palmar Nte to Sierpe (30 minutes) and ask for a boat going down the river. This may take some time because boats are heavily laden with the locals' shopping. It is a 2-hour boat trip down river and across the sea to Agujitas (see below), a small village near the **Marenco** Biological Station (information, PO Box 4025, San José, T2211594 or 2339101), 3 and 4-night packages available, US$575-690 per person, with transport from San José (8 hours by vehicle and boat, less by plane and boat).

Corcovado National Park

The **Park**, including the **Isla del Caño** (200 hectares), comprises over 54,000 hectares. It consists largely of tropical rainforests, and includes swamps, miles of empty beaches, and some cleared areas now growing back. It is located at the western end of the Osa Peninsula, on the Pacific Ocean. If short of time and/or money, the simplest way to the park is to take the pick-up truck from outside *Carolina's Restaurant* in Puerto Jiménez to **Playa Carate**, most days at 0600 and 1400, two and a half hours, US$4 one way, returning at 0800 and 1600, ask in advance about departure (Cirilo Espinoza, T7355075, or Ricardo González, T7355068, for four-wheel drive jeep taxi). It may be possible to book a flight with the Servicio de Parques Nacionales (SPN) in Puerto Jiménez, or take a private flight to Carate or La Sirena in the Park for

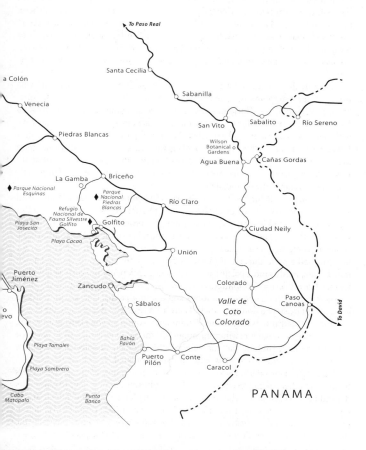

Peninsula de Osa – rain, snakes and mosquitoes

*Avoid the rainy season. Bring umbrellas (not raincoats, too hot), because it will rain, unless you are hiking, in which case you may prefer to get wet. Shelters can be found here and there, so only mosquito netting is indispensable. Bring all your food if you haven't arranged otherwise; food can only be obtained at Puerto Jiménez and Agujitas in the whole peninsula, and lodging likewise. The cleared areas (mostly outside the park, or along the beach) can be devastatingly hot. Chiggers (coloradillas) and horseflies infest the horse pastures and can be a nuisance, similarly, sandflies on the beaches; bring spray-on insect repellent. Another suggestion is vitamin B1 pills (called thiamine, or 'tiamina'). Mosquitoes are supposed to detest the smell and leave you alone but see **Health**. Get the Instituto Geográfico maps, scale 1:50,000. Remember finally that, as in any tropical forest, you may find some unfriendly wildlife, like snakes (fer-de-lance and bushmaster snakes may attack without provocation), and herds of peccaries. You should find the most suitable method for keeping your feet dry and protecting your ankles; for some, rubber boots are the thing, for others light footwear which dries quickly.*

US$36 per person, ask for Captain Alvaro Ramírez of Alfa Romeo Aéreo Taxi service at the airstrip, T7355178, F7355112. The SPN office in Puerto Jiménez is near the airport, open daily 0830-1200, 1300-1700, T7355036, ask for Carlos Quintero; they will give permits for entering the park (US$6 for up to four days) and will book accommodation at **La Sirena** in dormitories, maximum 20 people, **F** for bed (reservation essential), take sheets/sleeping bag, camping **F**, no reservation needed, three meals available. Bring mosquito netting. There is occasional trouble between gold prospectors and the park guards. If it is dangerous for visitors you will not be allowed into those parts.

At **Carate** there is a dirt airstrip and a store, run by Gilberto Morales and his wife Roxana (they rent rooms, but often full of gold miners, they also have a tent for hire, but take sleeping bag). Thirty minutes' walk west along the beach is **L** *Corcovado Lodge*, with 20 walk-in tents with two campbeds each, in a beautiful coconut grove with hammocks overlooking the beach; to be sure of space book through Costa Rica Expeditions in San José (see under **Travel agents**). Clean showers and toilets; good food, take a flashlight. Behind the camp is a trail into the jungle with a wonderful view of the bay from a clearing; many birds to be seen, plus monkeys and frogs. The whole place is highly recommended.

Five minutes' walk further down the beach is **La Leona** park wardens' station and entrance to the park. To go beyond here costs US$6 per day, whether you are walking to La Sirena (18 kilometres, six hours, along the beach, tough in the sun), or just visiting for the day. Lodging is available at La Leona, **F**, maximum 12 people in basic rooms or camping, meals available, book in high season through SPN; horses for hire. Beyond here to the end of **Playa Madrigal** is another two to two and a half hours' walk, partly sandy, partly rocky, with some rock pools and rusty shipwrecks looking like modern art sculptures. The shore rises very steeply into the jungle which grows thickly with mangroves, almonds and coconut palms. Check with wardens about high tide so you don't get stuck. There are a couple of rivers along the beach, the first Río Madrigal, is only about 15 minutes beyond La Leona (lovely and cool, clear and deep enough for swimming about 200 metres upstream, a good place for spotting wildlife). The best place for seeing wildlife, though, is La Sirena, where there are paths inland and the terrain is flatter and more isolated.

You can head inland from Sirena on a trail past three conveniently spaced shelters to **Los Patos** after passing several rivers full of reptiles (20 kilometres, six to nine hours depending on conditions). The wooden house is the Ranger Station with electricity and TV, with four beds available at US$1.75 per night, meals possible if you do not bring your own food. Its balcony is a great observation point for birds especially the redheaded woodpecker. From Los Patos you can carry on to the park border, then,

crisscrossing the Río Rincón to **La Palma** (small hostal), a settlement near the opposite side of the Peninsula (13 kilometres, six more hours); from which there are several
'taxis' making the one-hour trip to Puerto Jiménez (see above). An offshoot of this trail
will lead you to a raffia swamp that rings the **Corcovado Lagoon**. The lagoon is only
accessible by boat, but there are no regular trips. Caymans and alligators survive here,
sheltered from the hunters. Horses can be rented cheaply at Sirena.

From Sirena you can walk north along the coast to the shelter at **Llorona** (adequate; plenty of water, waterfalls, in fact), from which there is a trail to the interior
with another shelter at the end. From Llorona you can proceed north through a forest trail and then along the beach to the station at **San Pedrillo** on the edge of the
park. You can stay here, camping or under roof, and eat with the rangers, who love
company. From San Pedrillo you can take the park boat (not cheap) to Isla del Caño,
a lovely park outpost with two men (see under Puerto Quepos for Taximar boat service from Quepos and Dominical to Isla del Caño or Bahía Drake).

You will find both hiking boots and sandals useful if you are walking any distance
in the Park.

On round the coast is *Casa Corcovado Jungle Lodge*, outside the Park in the forest,
but with 500 metres of beach more or less opposite Isla del Caño, seven bungalows,
many facilities, packages from two nights full board with boat transport (two hours)
from Sierpe US$357, T2563181, F2567409, www.casacorcovado.com.

Continue north to the village of Agujitas, outside the park. Frequent trips with the
park boat from San Pedrillo to Agujitas.   **Agujitas**

Sleeping L *Marenco   Beach   &   Rainforest   Lodge*,   T2581919,   F2551346,
marenco@sol.racsa.co.cr, private reserve (500 hectares), lodge on hill, 8 rustic rooms with
private bathroom, fan, terrace with ocean view package: 4 days/3 nights from San José
including flight US$575. **B** per person *Cabinas Sir Francis Drake*, with bath, meals,
T7712436. **A** per person *Playa Cocalito Lodge*, Punta Agujitas, 7 cabins, full board, restaurant serving organically-grown fruit and vegetables, horseriding, trips to Corcovado National
Park, T/F7866150. **D-E** *Cecilia's Lodge*, bunk beds in dormitory with shower or rooms in the
house, full board, camping possible, Cecilia rents horses, takes you riding, visit to Isla del
Caño or Marenco possible, will arrange return transport to Sierpe, nice landscape, friendly
family, recommended. *Cabinas Jinete de Osa*, contact Isa, on beach, clean, friendly,
T2733116.

There are new tourist facilities at **Bahía Drake**, close to Isla del Caño.   **Bahía Drake**
In March 1579, Sir Francis Drake careened his ship on Playa Colorada in Bahía
Drake; a plaque commemorating the 400th anniversary of the event was erected in
Agujitas.

Sleeping L *Aguila de Osa Inn*, includes meals, suites **LL** including meals, fishing, hiking,
canoeing and horse riding available, T2962190, F2327722. **AL** per person *La Paloma Jungle
Lodge*, includes meals, T2390954, radio phone 2392801, 6 cabins with bath, guided tours
with resident biologist. **A** per person *Drake Bay Wilderness Camp*, with meals, cabins, tents
available, pleasant family atmosphere, canoeing, ocean fishing, trips to Corcovado, Isla del
Cano, horse riding facilities, large reductions for children, recommended, T7712436, charter
flights available. **A** *Albergue Jinetes de Osa*, T San José 2333333 = beeper, 5 rooms with
shared bathroom, sleep 3, and 4 new double rooms with private bathroom. **A** *Río Sierpe
Lodge*, T2845595, F7866291, new lodge at the river, 11 simple rooms, sleep 3, with private
bathroom. **A** *Cocalito Lodge*, T/F7866150, 8 simple *cabinas* with private bathroom. *Hotel El
Caballito de Mar*, 7 rooms, owned by Rob Messenger, scuba diving trips to Isla de Cano
sport fishing and jungle trips, T2315028.

From Agujitas you can get a boat (road under construction) to **Sierpe** on the Río
Sierpe (see above; boat from Sierpe to Bahía Drake, one and a half hours, US$60

Costa Rica

return/boat). Sierpe is connected by bus with the town of Palmar Sur (flights from San José, see above) on the Pan-American Highway.

Isla del Coco A thickly-wooded island and National Park of 24 square kilometres, 320 kilometres off the Peninsula of Osa on the submarine Cocos Ridge which extends some 1400 kilometres southwest to the Galápagos Islands. It has a two-man outpost. Contact Costa Rica Expeditions for reasonably priced tours; also Otec in San José, see page 1072. Arrangements for reaching it by chartered boat can be made in Puntarenas, after a permit has been obtained from the Government, or you can take a scuba diving cruise on the *Okeanos Agressor*, 10 days, two sailings a month, T2320572 ext 60 (in USA: PO Drawer K, Morgan City, LA 70381, T504-3852416, F504-3840817). It was at one time a refuge for pirates, who are supposed to have buried great treasure there, though none has been found by the 500 expeditions which have sought it. The offshore waters are a fisherman's paradise.

Ciudad Neily, Paso Canoas & Panama border At **Ciudad Neily**, about 18 kilometres from the border, are the F*Motel Rancho*, T7833201, with bath. E *Hotel Musuco*, T7833048, with bath, F without, fan, good, clean, quiet. E *Cabinas Heyleen*, T7833080, 9 simple *cabinas* with private bathroom, fan. D *Centro Turístico Neily*, T7833301, 41 *cabinas*, sleep 5, with private bathroom, fan. D *Cabinas Helga*, T7833146, 13 *cabinas*, sleep 4, with private bathroom. D *Cabinas Andrea*, T7833784, 18 clean *cabinas* with private bathroom, fan, TV. Ten kilometres from the border is the E *Camino Real*, with restaurant, where it is possible to camp. Here and there on the road *cantinas* sell local food. Daily bus to San José, Tracopa, from main square, US$8, seven hours (on Sunday buses from the border are full by the time they reach Ciudad Neily). The road goes (plenty of buses, 20 minutes, US$0.35) to **Paso Canoas** on the Panamanian border. Colectivo to border US$1.10, very quick.

Frontier with Panama – Paso Canoas

At Paso Canoas shops sell luxury items brought from Panama at prices considerably lower than those of Costa Rica (for example sunglasses, stereo equipment, kitchen utensils, etc).

Immigration Border open 0600-1100, 1300-1700, 1800-2100 Costa Rica time. Remember Costa Rica is 1 hour behind Panama. For information on entering Panama, see **Entry requirements** on page 1161; for entry procedures see **Panamanian immigration**, page 1222.

Customs No fruit or vegetables can be taken into Panama.

Crossing by private vehicle Those motoring north can get insurance cover at the border for US$17 ensuring public liability and property damage.

Sleeping E *Azteca*, T7322217. F *Cabinas Interamericano*, with bath and fan, some rooms with a/c, very good value. F *Hotel Don Alberto*, 9 acceptable rooms with fan, shared bathroom. F *Pensión El Paso*, OK rooms with shower. F *Cabinas Jiménez*, 18 quite good *cabinas* with private bathroom, fan. F *Pensión Tania*, T7322199, 15 simple rooms, sleep 3, with private bathroom, fan. F *Cabinas Velice*, T7322302, 10 older, simple *cabinas*, sleep 5, with private bathroom, fan. F *El Descanso*, T7322261, on the Panama border.

Exchange Banks either side of border close at 1600 local time. The bank on the Costa Rican side gives a slightly better dollar rate for colones. No difficulty in getting rid of surplus colones with money changers.

Transport Bus San José-Paso Canoas, US$9, 8 hours from Terminal Alfaro at 0500, 1300, 1630, 1800, return 0430, 0730, 1500 (T2237685). Care: not all buses go to the border. International buses that reach the border after closing time wait there till the following day.

Background

The land

Costa Rica lies between Nicaragua and Panama, with coastlines on both the Caribbean (212 kilometres) and the Pacific (1,016 kilometres). The distance between sea and sea is from 119 to 282 kilometres. A low, thin line of hills between Lake Nicaragua and the Pacific is prolonged into northern Costa Rica with several volcanoes (including the active volcano, Arenal), broadening and rising into high and rugged mountains and volcanoes in the centre and south. The highest peak, Chirripó Grande, southeast of the capital, reaches 3,820 metres. Within these highlands are certain structural depressions; one of them, the Meseta Central, is of paramount importance. To the southwest this basin is rimmed by the comb of the Cordillera; at the foot of its slopes, inside the basin, are the present capital, San José, and the old capital, Cartago. Northeast of these cities about 30 kilometres away, four volcano cones rise from a massive common pedestal. From northwest to southeast these are Poás (2,704 metres), Barva (2,906 metres), Irazú (3,432 metres), and Turrialba (3,339 metres). Irazú and Poás are intermittently active. Between the Cordillera and the volcanoes is the Meseta Central: an area of 5,200 square kilometres at an altitude of between 900 and 1,800 metres, where two-thirds of the population live. The northeastern part of the basin is drained by the Reventazón through turbulent gorges into the Caribbean; the Río Grande de Tárcoles drains the western part of it into the Pacific.

There are lowlands on both coasts. The Nicaraguan lowland along the Río San Juan is continued into Costa Rica, wide and sparsely inhabited as far as Puerto Limón. A great deal of this land, particularly near the coast, is swampy; southeast of Puerto Limón the swamps continue as far as Panama in a narrow belt of lowland between sea and mountain.

The Gulf of Nicoya, on the Pacific side, thrusts some 65 kilometres inland; its waters separate the mountains of the mainland from the 900 metre high mountains of the narrow Nicoya Peninsula. From a little to the south of the mouth of the Río Grande de Tárcoles, a lowland savanna stretches northwest past the port of Puntarenas and along the whole northeastern shore of the Gulf towards Nicaragua.

Below the Río Grande de Tárcoles the savanna is pinched out by mountains, but there are other banana-growing lowlands to the south. Small quantities of African palm and cacao are now being grown in these lowlands. In the far south there are swampy lowlands again at the base of the Peninsula of Osa and between the Golfo Dulce and the borders of Panama. Here there are 12,000 hectares planted to bananas. The Río General which flows into the Río Grande de Térraba, runs through a southern structural depression almost as large as the Meseta Central.

History

During his last voyage in September 1502, Columbus landed on the shores of what is now Costa Rica. Rumours of vast gold treasures (which never materialized) led to the name of Costa Rica (the Rich Coast). The Spaniards settled in the Meseta Central, where there were some thousands of sedentary Indian farmers (whose numbers were soon greatly diminished by the diseases brought by the settlers). Cartago was founded in 1563 by Juan Vásquez de Coronado, but there was no expansion until 145 years later, when a small number left Cartago for the valleys of Aserrí and Escazú. They founded Heredia in 1717, and San José in 1737. Alajuela, not far from San José, was founded in 1782. The settlers were growing in numbers (many farmers emigrated from northern Spain) but were still poor and raising subsistence crops only.

Spanish settlement

Independence from Spain was declared in 1821 whereupon Costa Rica, with the rest of Central America, immediately became part of Mexico. This led to a civil war, during which, two years later, the capital was moved from Cartago to San José. After independence, the

Independence & coffee

Costa Rica

government sought anxiously for some product which could be exported and taxed for revenue. It was found in coffee, introduced from Cuba in 1808, which Costa Rica was the first of the Central American countries to grow. The Government offered free land to coffee growers, thus building up a peasant landowning class. In 1825 there was a trickle of exports, carried on mule-back to the ports. By 1846 there were ox-cart roads to Puntarenas. By 1850 there was a large flow of coffee to overseas markets: it was greatly increased by the opening of a railway from San José and Cartago to Puerto Limón along the valley of the Reventazón in 1890.

From 1850, coffee prosperity began to affect the country profoundly: the birth rate grew, land for coffee was free, and the peasant settlements started spreading, first down the Río Reventazón as far as Turrialba; then up the slopes of the volcanoes, then down the new railway from San José to the old Pacific port of Puntarenas.

Banana industry Bananas were first introduced in 1878; Costa Rica was the first Central American republic to grow them and is now the second largest exporter in the world. Labour was brought in from Jamaica to clear the forest and work the plantations. The industry grew and in 1913, the peak year, the Caribbean coastlands provided 11 million bunches for export, but the spread of disease lowered the exports progressively. The United Fruit Company then turned its attentions to the Pacific litoral especially in the south around the port of Golfito. However, although some of the Caribbean plantations were turned over to cacao, *abacá* (Manilla hemp) and African palm, the region has regained its ascendancy over the Pacific litoral as a banana producer. By the end of the century over 50,000 hectares were planted to bananas, mostly in the Atlantic lowlands.

In the 1990s Chiquita, Dole and del Monte, the multinational fruit producers, came under international pressure over labour rights on their plantations. Two European campaign groups targeted working conditions in Costa Rica where, despite constitutional guarantees of union freedom, there was a poor record of labour rights abuse. Only 10 percent of Costa Rica's 50,000 banana workers were represented by unions. The rest preferred to join the less political *solidarista* associations, which provide cheap loans and promote savings, and avoid being blacklisted or harassed. Del Monte agreed in 1998 to talk to the unions after a decade of silence, while Chiquita declared its workers were free to choose trade union representation.

Democratic government Costa Rica's long tradition of democracy begain in 1889 and has continued to the present day with only a few lapses. In 1917 the elected president Alfredo González, was ousted by Federico Tinoco, who held power until 1919, when a counter revolution and subsequent elections brought Julio Acosta to the presidency. Democratic and orderly government followed until the campaign of 1948 when violent protests and a general strike surrounded disputed results. A month of fighting broke out after the Legislative Assembly annulled the elections, leading to the abolition of the constitution and a junta being installed, led by José Figueres Ferrer. In 1949 a constituent assembly drew up a new constitution and abolished the army. The junta stepped down and Otilio Ulate Blanco, one of the candidates of the previous year, was inaugurated. In 1952, Figueres, a socialist, founded the Partido de Liberación Nacional (PLN), and was elected President in 1953. He dominated politics for the next two decades, serving as President in 1953-58 and 1970-74. The PLN introduced social welfare programmes and nationalization policies, while the intervening conservative governments encouraged private enterprise. The PLN was again in power from 1974-78 (Daniel Oduber Quirós) 1982-86 (Luis Alberto Monge), 1986-90 (Oscar Arias Sánchez) and 1994-98 (José María Figueres).

President Arias drew up proposals for a peace pact in Central America and concentrated greatly on foreign policy initiatives. Efforts were made to expel Nicaraguan contras resident in Costa Rica and the country's official proclamation of neutrality, made in 1983, was reinforced. The Central American Peace Plan, signed by the five Central American presidents in Guatemala in 1987, earned Arias the Nobel Peace Prize, although progress in implementing its recommendations was slow.

In the 1990 general elections, **Rafael Angel Calderón Fournier**, a conservative lawyer and candidate for the Social Christian Unity Party (PUSC), won a narrow victory with 51 percent of the vote, over the candidate of the PLN. Calderón, the son of a former president who was one of the candidates in the 1948 disputed elections, had previously stood for election in 1982 and 1986. The President's popularity slumped as the effects of his economic policies were felt on people's living standards, while his Government was brought into disrepute by allegations of corruption and links with narcotraffickers.

In the February 1994 elections another former president's son was elected by a narrow margin. **José María Figueres**, 39, of the PLN, won 49.6 percent of the vote, 2.2 points ahead of his PUSC rival. In the Legislature, the PLN won 29 seats and the PUSC 25, while smaller parties won the remaining seats. The election was won on economic policies. Figueres argued against neo-liberal policies, claiming he would renegotiate agreements with the IMF and the World Bank, but in his first year of office, a third Structural Adjustment Programme (backed by the international agencies and drawn up by the previous administration) was approved. A subsequent National Development Plan and a Plan to Fight Poverty contained a wide range of measures designed to promote economic stability and improve the quality of life for many sectors of society. While the plans were partly responding to the protests that followed the approval of the Adjustment Programme, many of their proposals were at variance with the Programme's policies.

PLN government, 1994-98

   Labour strife increased in 1995-96 as tax increases and price rises cut into earnings. The granting of work permits to 50,000 Nicaraguan manual labourers was highly unpopular in the face of rising Costa Rican unemployment. Crime increased, particularly in San José, Limón and on the Caribbean coast, and the number of tourists arriving fell. The Government's popularity plummetted and the President was judged the least popular in recent history. There were allegations of corruption, links to narco traffickers and money laundering, with involvement by legislators and the judiciary.

Elections were held on Sunday 1 February 1998 and they were won by the PUSC candidate, **Miguel Angel Rodríguez**, with 46.6 percent of the vote, two percent ahead of the PLN candidate. Thirty percent of voters abstained. The new president took office on 8 May 1998, promising to make women, the young and the poor a priority for his government.

1998 elections

Culture

In all provinces save Limón over 98 percent are whites and *mestizos* but in Limón 33.2 percent are blacks and 3.1 percent indigenous Indians, of whom only 5,000 survive in the whole country. There are three groups, the Bribri (3,500), Boruca (1,000) and Guatuso. Although officially protected, the living conditions of the indigenous Indians are very poor. In 1992 Costa Rica became the first Central American country to ratify the International Labour Oranganization treaty on indigenous populations and tribes. However, even in Limón the percentage of blacks is falling: it was 57.1 in 1927. Many of them speak Jamaican English as their native tongue. Much of the Caribbean coastland, more especially in the north, remains unoccupied. On the Pacific coastlands a white minority owns the land on the *hacienda* system rejected in the uplands. About 46 percent of the people are *mestizos*. The population has risen sharply in the mountainous Peninsula of Nicoya, which is an important source of coffee, maize, rice and beans.

People

   Contact with the rural population is easy: the people are friendly and enjoy talking. (The national adjective, *costarricense*, is rather a mouthful: the universal short form is '*tico/a*'.)

The economy

The country's economy is based on the export of coffee, bananas, meat, sugar and cocoa. The Meseta Central with its volcanic soil is the coffee-growing area: here too are grown staple crops: beans, maize, potatoes and sugar cane, and the dairy farming is both efficient and lucrative. Diversification of exports has been successful, with non-traditional crops now

Structure of production

accounting for about 60 percent of revenues. The fluctuations in coffee prices, and therefore exports, has prompted some producers to turn to other crops. Costa Rica remains the second largest banana exporter in the world with production dominated by US multinational companies. The country's timber industry is very small and its resources have yet to be commercially utilized although deforestation has occurred at an alarming rate.

High growth in the industrial sector has led to considerable economic diversification, and manufacturing accounts for about 19 percent of gdp, compared with 17 percent in the case of agriculture. Industry is largely concerned with food processing but there is also some production of chemicals (including fertilizers, also exported), plastics, tyres, et cetera. Current major industrial projects include aluminium processing, a petrochemical plant at Moín, and a tuna fish processing plant at Golfito. The port of Caldera on the Pacific coast has been improved and manufacturing for export is being encouraged. A US microprocessor assembly plant near San José is expected to earn more than bananas and coffee in exports and rival income from tourism.

There are small deposits of manganese, mercury, gold and silver, but only the last two are worked. Deposits of iron ore are estimated at 400 million tons and sulphur deposits at 11 million tons. Considerable bauxite deposits have been found but have not yet been developed. In 1980, the Arenal hydroelectric plant was opened and there are projects to develop the Corobicí and other hydroelectric complexes. Oil companies are interested in offshore concessions in the Pacific. There is an oil refinery at Puerto Limón.

Tourism is now a major industry and is the main source of foreign exchange revenue generating US$661mn in 1995, from 760,000 tourists. Numbers rose to about 1.2 million in 1998 and 1999. The construction of hotels has soared and although most new businesses in the 1980s were small-scale eco-lodges of less than 50 rooms, in the 1990s the Government has allowed foreign investors to build some huge resorts for mass tourism in a controversial reversal of previous policy. Land prices have soared, driven up by foreign, mainly US, purchasers. The latest megaproject is the Gulf Papagayo Project, taking in several beaches in Guanacaste, expected to be the largest leisure city in Central America with some 20,000 rooms. In the first phase 6,900 rooms will be built, including 2,000 hotel rooms, 50 luxury villas, 400 family villas and 700 apartments, with shopping centres, golf course and other facilities. Conservation groups have criticized the development because of its environmental impact, the proximity of national parks and reserves, and the destruction of ecosystems.

Recent trends Despite several IMF-supported austerity programmes, the Costa Rican economy still suffers from large public sector deficits, partly because of a high level of government spending on social welfare. The country amassed a large foreign debt, which, including accumulated arrears, amounted in 1989 to US$5bn and was one of the highest per capita in the developing world. In the late 1980s, Costa Rica turned to the IMF and the World Bank for help in adjusting its economy and was one of the first countries to take advantage of a US-sponsored, debt reduction proposal. An agreement was negotiated with commercial bank creditors in 1989-90, to be supported by funds from official creditors. The economic programme was hugely unpopular as spending cuts in health, social security and education increased poverty and unemployment, leading to strikes and protests. In 1991-92 economic growth picked up, inflation declined and unemployment fell. Many new jobs were created in tourism, with 54 new hotels being built in 1992. By the end of 1994 total debt had fallen to just over US$3bn.

In that year a third structural adjustment loan was signed with the IMF against considerable local opposition. The new government was under pressure to reduce poverty (17.25 percent of the population) and, at the same time, limit the budget deficit which, was equivalent to eight percent of gdp in 1994, and cut inflation, which accelerated to 20 percent in the same year. President Figueres intended that an increased rate of devaluation of the colón and tax reform should help reduce the balance of payments deficit, maintain gdp growth at a little below its 1994 level of five percent and prevent depletion of international reserves.

In 1995 legislation was approved to liberalize the banking system, support privatization

The tourism debate

A debate over development of tourism in Costa Rica raged in 1993-94 (and continues) with the Government in favour of developing mass tourism along the beaches of Nicoya and Guanacaste Provinces. Ecotourism lobbyists argued hotly that small scale tourism was more beneficial for conservation purposes, supported by many tour agents, who pointed out that at present, ecotourists spend an average of 15 days in the country, spending freely on local services, while holidaymakers to resorts average five days and spend almost nothing. One particular project at Tambor sparked heated criticism, when Barceló, the Spanish developers of a 400-room hotel on the beach, infringed several laws and regulations (see Tambor, page 1108). The incident dented Costa Rica's ecotourism reputation. Growth of hotels has been spectacular in the 1990s and although most have been of less than 50 rooms, there are now several large resorts along the beaches, which, like Tambor, damage habitats and the ecology and more are planned (see also page 1154).

and end state monopolies in insurance, hydrocarbons and telecommunications. Labour unions opposed many of the economic measures and the layoff of 8,000 public sector workers. There were many strikes, including an extended protest by teachers. The effort of keeping the fiscal deficit under control (3.5 percent of gdp in 1995) prompted congress to approve the Economic Guarantees bill in 1996 after five years of debate. This legislation limits the deficit to one percent of gdp, sets up a special authority to oversee state spending, grants greater autonomy to the central bank and allows Congress more control over national budgets. Implementation was delayed until 1999, allowing another round of elections in the interim. In the meantime gdp grew less than one percent in 1996, inflation was nearly 15 percent and the fiscal deficit reached 5.5 percent of gdp. 1997 and 1998 were little better, with a public sector deficit of over four percent of gdp.

Government

Costa Rica is a unitary multiparty republic with one legislative house, the Legislative Assembly of 57 deputies, elected by proportional representation for four years. Executive authority is in the hands of the President, elected for the same term by popular vote. Men and women over 18 have the right to vote. Voting is secret, direct and free. Judicial power is exercised by the Supreme Court of Justice.

Communications

Costa Rica has a total of 35,600 kilometres of roads of which 17 percent are paved. The Pan-American Highway runs the length of the country, from the Nicaraguan to the Panamanian borders. A highway has been built from Orotina to Caldera, a new port on the Gulf of Nicoya which has replaced Puntarenas as the principal Pacific port, and a highway is being built from Orotina to Ciudad Colón. Another road has been completed from San José via Guápiles and Siquirres to Puerto Limón. Also a road was completed in 1993 from Orotina to Playas de Jacó to improve access to the Pacific beaches. This has still to be extended to Parrita, Quepos and Ciudad Cortés. All four-lane roads into San José are toll roads, US$0.75; some toll roads outside San José are US$0.35.

There used to be 1,286 kilometres of railways, all of 1.067 metres gauge. These are now closed. Unfortunately the spectacular line from San José to Puerto Limón suffered major damage from landslides in 1991.

Panama

10

Panama

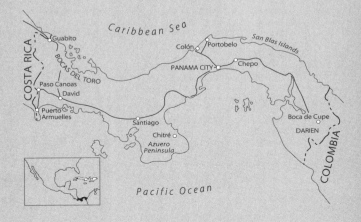

Essentials

Planning your trip

The S-shaped isthmus of Panama, 80 kilometres at its narrowest and no more than 193 kilometres at its widest, is one of the great cross-roads of the world. Its destiny has been entirely shaped by this junction. To it Panama owes its national existence, the make-up of its population and their distribution: two-fifths of the people are concentrated in the two cities which control the entry and exit of the canal. The Canal Area, formerly the US Canal Zone, has been returned to Panamanian jurisdiction; this long process began in 1964, when Panama secured the right to fly its flag in the Zone alongside that of the USA, and is due for completion when Panama assumes full authority for the Canal at noon on 31 December 1999.

Where to go

The capital, **Panama City**, is at the Pacific end of the Panama Canal, which divides the country but links the Caribbean Sea with the Pacific Ocean. The first city, to the east, was sacked by the pirate, Henry Morgan, and the old section, or Casco Viejo, of this one dates from 1673. It is being restored and becoming quite a tourist attraction. The modern city is spread around the Bahía de Panamá with its banks and high rise buildings overlooked by the Parque Natural Metropolitano, a unique national park within the limits of the capital city. Panamá is best known for the **Canal**, built at a cost of 20,000 lives for the benefit of commercial and strategic interests. Opened in 1914 by the USA, the 10-mile-wide corridor finally reverts to Panamanian ownership on 31 December 1999. The Canal is surprisingly beautiful, consisting of a river-fed lake, Lago Gatún, 26 metres above sea level, reached by a series of locks on the Pacific and Caribbean sides which raise and lower 30 ships a day. Within the lake is Barro Colorado island, now a biological reserve, to which the animals fled and were stranded when the basin was flooded. At the Caribbean end of the Canal is **Colón**, the country's major port for container and other shipping, with the second largest free zone in the world, for dedicated shoppers. East along the coast is **Portobelo**, once the site of fortified warehouses containing gold and silver brought from Peru to be shipped to Spain. Off the coast of Colón lie 365 islands which make up the **San Blas archipelago**, of which about 50 are inhabited by the Kuna Indians, who have complete internal autonomy. However, the islands can be visited and hotels and lodges are being opened to cater for growing tourist interest.

From Panama City to Costa Rica the **Pan-American Highway** runs through a variety of agricultural zones, Pacific beaches, colonial towns and mountain landscapes. Open pastures and savannas give way to sugar and other plantations as you approach **David**, the hot and humid third city of the Republic. It is an attractive colonial and modern city with good communications and an ideal base from which to reach the mountain resort of **Boquete** and explore the cooler Chiriquí Highlands and the Volcán Barú, where there is good hiking. North of the Cordillera Central are the Caribbean lowlands where bananas are grown in vast quantities and offshore are the islands of **Bocas del Toro** and the **Isla Bastimentos National Marine Park** where turtles come to nest. These islands are worth a visit if you enjoy snorkelling or diving, beaches, birdwatching and other wildlife.

Darién in the east is the most inhospitable part of Panamá. There are no roads through the jungle to link Panamá with Colombia, but the fit and adventurous are often tempted to have a go at crossing the border on foot and by boat. However, armed insurgents from Colombia are currently active in the area and it is extremely dangerous, so it would be sensible to postpone this expedition for some time.

When to go

Rainfall along the Caribbean side of the central Cordillera is much heavier, averaging about 4,000 millimetres during the course of the year, than on the Pacific slope, where the average is about 1,700 millimetres, but both areas are marked by pronounced seasonal variation. Temperatures, however, do not vary much. At lower altitudes, year-round, daytime temperatures are usually 30°-32°C (85°-90°F), dropping at night to (70°-72°F). Above 500 metres, temperatures are palpably lower, making the highland towns attractive spots to visit.

Panama

Rainfall begins to taper off sometime in December, and the months of January, February, March and sometimes April constitute the dry season or *verano* (summer). Rainfall on the Pacific side is scarce or absent altogether, though on the Atlantic side one may expect a downpour 365 days a year. This is the period of school vacations and family holidays. In March or April the rains return, and the season known in Panama as the *invierno* (winter) begins, although temperatures remain in the high 20's and low 30's°C (high 80's and low 90's°F). Even in the rainy season, however, the downpours, though very heavy, usually last only an hour or two, and almost always come in mid-afternoon.

The result is deep tropical forest along the Caribbean coast, on the northern slopes, in Darién and in the higher elevations of Chiriquí. On the Pacific coast the tropical forest gives way to semi-deciduous trees and, in the vast expanses cleared for grazing, savanna between the sea and the mountains.

The rate of deforestation in Panama has accelerated in the 1980s and early 1990s. Although more of the country is forested than any other Central American republic except Belize, the loss of forest in 1990 was estimated at 220,000 acres, against felling of up to 154,000 acres per year between 1985 and 1989. The government reported a slowing of deforestation during 1993-95, but in early 1996 estimated it was continuing at 2,200 acres (100 hectares) a year. Deforestation is affecting the pattern of rainfall upon which depend not only the birds (over 800 species), animals, insects and plants, but also the Panama Canal. A further threat to the Canal is silting as a result of soil erosion.

What to take **Clothing** Lightweight tropical type clothes for men, light cotton or linen dresses or trousers for women. Because of the heat, raincoats are useless except the lightest plastic variety. Umbrellas are more practical. You need warm clothing at night in the highlands.

Special interest travel **Nature tourism** With a relatively small population and much rugged terrain, Panama has a lot of remote, relatively unexploited areas, many of which have been declared National Parks, Wildlife Refuges and Forest Reserves. Most can be visited without hindrance or charge, that is, if you can get there. Transport can be very difficult and facilities non-existent; the largest, Darién NP, is a good example. Many of these protected places are mentioned in the text. For more information, contact Asociación Nacional de Conservación de la Naturaleza (**ACON** – see under Panama City – **Useful addresses**, page 1188).

Watersports With almost exactly 2,000 kilometres of coastline split between the Pacific and the Caribbean, and situated at the northern end of one of the wettest areas of the world, Panama has an awful lot of water in and around it. The potential for watersports is great, most of which remains unexploited. There are, however, some opportunities. **Diving** is the best locally developed sport and is very varied. The Caribbean coral reefs are similar to those of Belize and Honduras except that they extend southeast for 100 kilometres along from the Costa Rica border and then from Colón 300 kilometres to the border with Colombia. For information on these areas, see under Bocas del Toro, Portobelo and the San Blas Islands. The Pacific has quite different eco-systems owing to the much greater tidal ranges, differing water temperature and density et cetera. Because of easier accessibility, diving is better developed. Places to go include Taboga, the Pearl Islands, Iguana Island and Coiba National Park. A third, and perhaps unique experience, is diving in the lakes of the Panama Canal, mainly to visit wrecks and submerged villages. **Snorkelling** is popular in the less remote of the places mentioned under diving; equipment can be hired in most of the resorts. **White water rafting** and other forms of river running are limited at present to the Chiriquí river system near David and the Chagres National Park area north of Panama City.

Finding out more See under Panama City for address of IPAT, Instituto Panameño de Turismo. In USA: Laura Haayen, 1110 Brickell Avenue, Suite 103, Miami, FL 33131, T305-5792001, F5790910.

Before you travel

Documents   Visitors must have a passport, and in most cases a tourist card (issued for 30
days and renewable for another 60 in the Immigration Office, Panama City, or in David,
addresses in text above) or a visa (issued for 30 days, extendable to 90 days in Panama).
Tourist cards are available at borders, from Panamanian consulates, Ticabus or airlines. To
enter Panama you must have an onward flight ticket, travel agent confirmation of same, or be
able to demonstrate that you have sufficient funds to cover your stay and departure (US$500,
or US$150 for Costa Ricans, US$1,000 for Dominicans). 'Sufficient funds' do not have to be in
cash; valid credit cards and travellers' cheques accepted, even notice of wire transfer awaiting
you in Panama City. Recent travellers report these are asked for on the land frontier with Costa
Rica and at Puerto Obaldía (Darién); generally officers are not very strict unless they fear you
may be destitute. Once in Panama, you cannot get a refund for an onward flight ticket unless
you have another exit ticket. Copa tickets can be refunded at any office in any country (in the
currency of that country), but it can take five days to get your money back in Panama
compared with two days in San José, Costa Rica. If not entering Panama at the main entry
points (Tocumen airport, Paso Canoas), expect more complicated arrangements.

Neither visas nor tourist cards are required by nationals of Austria, Chile, Costa Rica, El
Salvador, Finland, Germany, Honduras, Spain, Switzerland and the UK. US citizens may enter
on a tourist card obtained at port of entry.

Citizens of the following countries need a visa which is free: the Netherlands, Norway,
Denmark, Colombia and Mexico. Before visiting Panama it is advisable to enquire at a
Panamanian consulate whether you need a visa stamped in your passport, or whether a
tourist card will suffice.

A visa costing the local equivalent of US$10 must be obtained by all other nationals. These
can be purchased with minimum delay by citizens of countries, not named above, in Central
and South America, the EU, the Caribbean Islands, Australia, New Zealand, Canada, Japan,
Israel, Dominican Republic and some others. However, visas for citizens of many African,
Eastern European and Asian countries require authorization from Panama, which takes 3-5
days (this includes Hong Kong, India, Poland, the former Soviet republics, and also Cuba and
South Africa).

30-day tourist cards can be renewed twice for a total of a further 60 days. The necessary
documents must all be obtained in advance: a photo-ID card (*carné*), to be surrendered when
you return for an exit visa, will be issued, allow 1-2 hours for this. Requirements are two
passport photos, a ticket out of the country or proof of sufficient funds, a brief letter
explaining why you wish to extend your stay, a letter from a permanent resident accepting
legal and financial responsibility for you during your extra days in Panama, and two
photocopies of the name page and the entry stamp page of your passport. All papers must
be presented at *Prórrogas* in the immigration office and a fee of US$11 paid for each 30 day
extension before the photo ID card is issued. There are similar requirements for renewing a
visa but include two photocopies of the original visa. Tourists who stay more than 30 days will
require an exit visa.

Exit visas   Visitors who have been in Panama for more than 30 days must have an exit
permit stamped in their passports before leaving. A *paz y salvo* slip must be obtained from
the Ministerio de Hacienda y Tesoro by filling in a simple form, US$1. Present this with the ID
card issued when you renewed your tourist card or visa to the 'permiso de salida' window in
the Inmigración y Naturalización for the exit stamp. Both have expiration dates, so plan
accordingly. It is best to visit the government office early in the day. There are fines and
time-wasting hassle if you miss the expiry dates. For where to go, see **Useful addresses**,
under Panama City and David.

Customs   Even if you only change planes in Panama you must have the necessary papers for
the airport officials. The Panamanian Customs are strict; drugs without a doctor's prescription
are confiscated.

Panama embassies and consulates

Canada, 130 Albert St. Suite No.300 Ottawa, ON. Kip 5G4, T2367177, F2365775.
France, 145, avenue de Suffren, Paris 75015, T47832332, F45.67.99.43.
Germany, Lutzowstrasse 1, 53173 Bonn, T228-361036, F228-363558
Greece, AKTI MIAOYLI 23, Athens, T4133180.
Italy, Viale Regina Margherita No.239, Cuarto Piso, Interno 11, 00198 Roma, T44252173/44265436, F44265443.
Israel, Hei Be 'iyar No.210 Tercer Piso, Aptdo 3, Kikar Hamedina, Apartado Postal 21260, Tel Aviv, T3-260849, F3-6910045.

Portugal, R. Pedro Sintra, 15, Lisbon 1400, T301 9046, F301 9063
Spain, Raimundo Férnandez Villaverde, 26, Madrid 28071, T577 50 83.
USA, 2862 McGill Terrace NW, Washington D.C. 20008, T202 483-1407.
UK, 48 Park Street, London W1Y 3PD, T0171-4934646, F0171-4934333
There are embassies/consulates in most other European countries, many US cities, throughout the Americas, and selected countries elsewhere. These can be found on www.mire.gob.pa/embajada.html.

Duty free and export restrictions Cameras, binoculars, et cetera, 500 cigarettes or 500 grams of tobacco and three bottles of alcoholic drinks for personal use are taken in free. **NB** Passengers leaving Panama by land are *not* entitled to any duty-free goods, which are delivered only to ships and aircraft.

Money

Currency The unit of currency in Panama is the Balboa (B/.), but Panama is one of the few countries in the world which issues no paper money; US banknotes are used exclusively. There are 'silver' coins of 50c (called a *peso*), 25c (called *cinco reales* or *cuara*, from US 'quarter'), 10c (called a *real*) and copper of 1c. All coins are used interchangeably with US equivalents, which are the same in size and composition. US coins and notes are legal tender in Panama. There is great reluctance in Panama to accept US$50 and US$100 dollar notes because of counterfeiting. Do not be offended if asked to produce ID and sign a register when spending them. Easier to use US$20, 10, 5 and 1 notes. You can take in or out any amount of foreign or Panamanian currency. If travelling north remember that US dollar notes, especially smaller denominations, are useful in all Central American countries and may be difficult to obtain in the other republics. Having a supply of US$5 and US$1 notes greatly facilitates border crossings and traffic problems in Central America where 'fees' and 'instant fines' can become exorbitant if you only have a US$20 note.

ATMs Visa ATMs are available at branches of Telered (T001-800-1110016 if card is lost or stolen). Mastercard/Cirrus ATMs are available at Caja de Ahorros offices and others in the Pronto system (Mastercard emergency number, T001-800-3077309). See under **Banks**, Panama City, for other ATMs and for credit card phone numbers. For Western Union, T2691055.

Getting there

Air **From Europe** No direct services. Connecting flights go to Miami, then by American or Copa to Panama City. Iberia from Madrid via Miami. From Frankfurt, Paris, Madrid and London, there is a connection via Bogotá with Avianca and SAM.

From USA Direct flights from Atlanta (American, Delta), Dallas (American), Houston (Continental), Los Angeles (Continental), Miami (American, Copa, Iberia), New York (American, Continental or Lassa, change planes in San José), Orlando (American), Savannah (Delta). Eva Airways has a flight from Los Angeles which originates in Taipei. For other US cities, connections are made in Miami or Houston.

From Central America Flights from Guatemala City (Copa), Managna (Lacsa), San José (Copa, Lacsa, Taca), San Salvador (Copa, Taca). There are no direct flights to Tegucigalpa, only Lacsa with connection in San José or Taca in San Salvador, but Copa flies direct to San Pedro

Sula. **From Mexico** Mexico City (Copa, LAB, Mexicana), Cancún (LAB), or connection via San José. **From South America** Lots of flights from Colombia with Copa (Barranquilla, Bogotá, Cartagena, Cali, Medellín) and SAM (Bogotá). **NB** One-way tickets are not available from Colombia to Panama, on SAM, or Copa, but a refund on an unused return portion is possible, less 17 percent taxes, on SAM. LAB from Santa Cruz (Bolivia). From Guayaquil and Quito, Continental, Ecuatoriana and Copa. Copa from Santiago de Chile and Lima. From Caracas, Mexicana, Copa and Aeropostal. **From the Caribbean** Copa has flights from Havana, Kingston, Montego Bay, Port-au-Prince, San Juan and Santo Domingo.

Sea The Panama Canal is on the itineraries of some shipping services from Europe and the USA which take passengers. It is also possible to travel by sea to/from Colombia. See page 1203 for connections with San Blas.

    There are about two boats a week from Colón for San Andrés Island, Colombia, from which there are connections with Cartagena; the *Johnny Walker* takes 30 hours, but the service is very irregular and travellers have sometimes waited over a week in vain. There are (contraband) boats from Coco Solo, Colón, to the Guajira Peninsula, Colombia. Three-day journey, uncomfortable, and entirely at your own risk; captains of these boats are reluctant to carry travellers (and you may have to wait days for a sailing – the customs officials will let you sleep in the wind-shadow of their office, will watch your luggage and let you use the sanitary facilities). A passenger travelling in a contraband boat had some problems in the DAS office about getting an entrance stamp: they wanted official papers from the boat's captain showing that he brought him in. You have to bargain for your fare on these boats. Accommodation is a little primitive.

Touching down

Airport tax An airport exit tax of US$20 has to be paid by all passengers (cash only). There is a US$4 tax on every US$100 on air tickets purchased in Panama.

Cost of living Prices are somewhat higher than in the rest of Central America, although food costs much the same as in Costa Rica. The annual average increase in consumer prices fluctuates in line with US trends.

Tipping In restaurants: 10 percent of bill. Porters, 15 cents per item, but US$1 would be expected for assistance at the airport. Cloakroom, 25 cents. Hairdressers, 25 cents. Cinema usherettes, nothing. Taxi drivers don't expect tips, but see **Taxis** under Panama City.

Getting around

Air Aeroperlas, the local airline which operates most domestic flights, is safe and reasonable, but service is basic. A paid ticket is required to confirm reservations, as locals tend to make reservations they neither use nor cancel. Flights reported fully-booked in advance very often have seats available; show up 1-2 hours early and register on Lista de Espera. Booking through travel agents recommended. Ticket counter and security personnel are sometimes poorly trained.

    There are local flights to most parts of Panama by the airlines Ansa, Aeroperlas, Parsa, Transpasa, Chitreana and Aerotaxi. On all internal flights passengers must present their identity documents, declare their own weight, in pounds (not kilos or stone, and have their luggage weighed. As excess baggage charges are frequent, ask if it is cheaper to ship excess as air freight (*carga*) on the same flight.

Bus Some of the long distance buses are small 'mini' buses, normally modern and comfortable but more large modern a/c buses are being introduced. They are more expensive than elsewhere in Central America, but nevertheless good value and recommended. Slower 'regular' buses run in country areas. 'Express' buses with a/c operate between Panama City and Colón and to David and the frontier with Costa Rica.

Panama

Touching down

Hours of business *Government departments, 0800-1200, 1230-1630 (Monday to Friday). Banks: open and close at different times, but are usually open all morning, often on Saturday. Shops and most private enterprises: 0700 or 0800-1200 and 1400-1800 or 1900 every day, including Saturday.*

Business interests are concentrated in Panama City and Colón.

IDD *507. Equal tones with long pause mean it is ringing. Double ring repeated regularly indicates it is engaged.*
Official time *GMT minus five hours (Eastern Standard Time).*
Voltage *US-style 110 volt, 60 Hz AC throughout the country. 220 volt is occasionally available in homes and hotels.*
Weights and measures *Both metric and the US system are used.*

Roads There are now about 9,700 kilometres of roads, of which 3,100 kilometres are paved. Road building is complicated by the extraordinary number of bridges and the large amount of grading required. The road running from Colón to Panama City is the only fully paved one crossing the isthmus, but another excellent and very scenic road crosses the isthmus from Gualaca in Chiriquí to the town of Chiriquí Grande in Bocas del Toro, crossing atop the spectacular, Swedish-built Fortuna hydroelectric dam (see **Buses** under **Transport**, page 1225). The Pan-American Highway, usually called the Interamericana in Panama, runs east from Panama City to Chepo and into the province of Darién, and west to the Costa Rican border. It is paved throughout (paving in the east ends at the Panamá/Darién provincial border) and is being improved. There is a modern toll road between Panama City and La Chorrera, and the section between David and La Concepción is being converted into a modern, four-lane divided highway. New highways are being built around Panama City to ease grid lock traffic congestion. A Corredor Sur toll highway will run from Tocumen to Paitilla, partly over a causeway in the Bay of Panama. Parts opened June 1999, the remainder due for completion end-1999. A Corredor Norte runs north of the city and joins the Transístmica to Colón; the latter is being widened to four lanes.

Speed limit on the Pan-American Highway is 90 kilometres per hour (but 60 is more realistic when planning a day's driving); the toll stretch (US$0.60) between Chame and Panama City has a 100 kilometres per hour limit. Observe 40 kilometres per hour speed zones in villages. Most streets have no lighting, many hotel signs are unlit, so try to be at your destination before dusk (about 1830 January, 1800 July). Even driving at night in Panama City is unadvisable. Right turn against a red light is legal in cities if no vehicles are approaching from the left. If charged with a traffic violation, you should receive a document stipulating the infraction; fines to be paid to Dirección Nacional de Tránsito y Transporte Terrestre (Departamento de Infracciones Menores, Panama City, T2625687). In general, Panamanian highway police are helpful and approachable, but some Spanish is an advantage. If you *have* committed an infraction, accept the ticket and pay it later. Fines are less than in Europe or the USA. If you are sure an unscrupulous minor traffic policeman is harassing you, speak English and insist firmly but courteously that you be given a ticket or released. A sample of harassment is to be asked to produce the driver's manual or the fire extinguisher, both mandatory, neither usually in the car. It is not recommended, or necessary to offer cash.

Car Hire Companies are listed under Panama City, **Transport**. Rental cars are not allowed out of the country; they are marked by special license plates. Rates vary from company to company and from model to model: on average they start at US$24 per day for a small saloon to US$65 for four-wheel drive jeep, free mileage, insurance US$8 per day, five percent tax, US$500 deposit (can be paid by credit card), minimum age 23, home driver's licence acceptable. In general four-wheel drives must be booked five days in advance. If planning to rent from an international company, consult it before leaving home. Sometimes very good deals are available that cannot be made at the Panama office.

Motoring Coming in by road from Costa Rica, passengers and vehicle (car or motorcycle) are given 30 days at the frontier. US$1 is payable for fumigation, US$3 for minibus. Exit calls for four papers which cost US$4.20 (obtainable, as are extensions for entry permits, from Customs in Paitilla airport). Taking a car with Panamanian plates to Costa Rica requires a permit from the Traffic Police (*Tránsito*) obtainable on presentation of the ownership certificate and a document from the Judicial Police (*PTJ*), indicating that the vehicle has not been reported stolen. A travel agency, for example Chadwick's in Balboa, will arrange this for you, for US$30. Super grade gasoline (called *super*) costs about US$1.90 per US gallon (3.78 litres); unleaded is available in larger towns. Low octane (*regular* or *normal*) costs about US$1.80; diesel about US$1.30. Station attendants do not expect tips. For motorcyclists, note that a crash helmet must be worn. **NB** You may not take dogs into Panama by car, though they may be flown or shipped in if they have general health and rabies certificates; dogs and cats have to spend 40 days in quarantine after entry.

NB It used to be virtually impossible for a tourist to sell a car in Panama unless it could be shown (with help from the Consulate) that the money was needed for a fare home. Recent reports suggest that the whole procedure is now a lot easier. The vendor needs a document stating that the car has been sold, obtainable from a notary/lawyer. It is a great help if you have arranged for the Panamanian Embassy in San José (or elsewhere) to issue a Factura Consular from which the stated value of the car is used to calculate the import taxes payable. Taxes have to be paid by the buyer and if the title of the car is still in the seller's name, the buyer needs a similar document to be able to arrange all the paperwork at the Aduana/Customs. You have to authorize the buyer to pay the taxes for you by means of this document. A helpful address, both for finding potential buyers, and for the paperwork, is: Fernie and Co Shipping Agency, Sr Pérez, Panama City, English spoken. Another helpful office with English-speaking staff is in the same building as the Diablo Heights supermarket (in the street across the railway from the main entry of Marcos A Gelabert airport, the former Albrook air base), which deals with license plates, transfer of titles. A great many US service personnel used this facility. There is a bulletin board outside. Your embassy will give you advice. At present, Japanese second-hand cars are the most popular.

Taking a vehicle to Colombia, Venezuela or Ecuador is not easy or cheap. The best advice is to shop around the agencies in Panama City or Colón to see what is available when you want to go. Both local and international lines take vehicles, and sometimes passengers, but schedules and prices are very variable. To **Colombia**, agents include: Sudamericana de Vapores, T2293844, Cristóbal-Buenaventura; Boyd Steamship Corporation, T2636311, Balboa-Buenaventura or Guayaquil. To Barranquilla: Vicente Simones, Colón T1951262, beeper 270-0000, code 700283, will arrange all paperwork for US$25: car passage US$800, motorcycle US$50, plus US$50 per passenger, no accommodation on ship other than hammock space, take food and drink for a week (even though voyage should be three days). To Cartagena, Captain Newball, Edificio Los Cristales, Piso 3, Calle 38 y Avenida Cuba, Panama City. On the same route Central American Lines sail once a week, agent in Panama, Colón T4412880, Panama City 2361036. Also, Geminís Shipping Co SA, Apdo Postal No 3016, Zona Libre de Colón, Rep de Panamá, T441-6269/6959, F4416571. Mr Ricardo Gil was helpful and reliable. Another agent, Barwil, next door to Citibank in Colón, T4415533 (Colón), 2637755 (Panama City), will arrange shipments to Colombia (Cartagena) and elsewhere in Latin America. If sending luggage separately, make enquiries at Tocumen airport, for example Tampa, T2384439.

One alternative is to try to ship on one of the small freighters that occasionally depart from Coco Solo Wharf in Colón for Turbo in Colombia, which allow you to travel with your car. Obviously there is a considerable element of risk involved (suspect cargo, crews and seaworthiness), though the financial cost is lower than on a regular line.

Some small freighters go only to intermediate ports such as San Andrés, and it is then necessary to get another freighter to Cartagena. Navieras Mitchell ship cars regularly to San Andrés and Barranquilla. Office at Coco Solo Wharf, T4416942. You may have to wait up to a week in San Andrés to make the onward connection. From Colón to San Andrés takes two days and from San Andrés to Cartagena takes three days. There are two boats plying

Shipping a vehicle

Panama

regularly between Colón (Pier 3) and San Andrés that are big enough for vans, but there is no schedule; they leave when they finish loading. There are also two regular boats between San Andrés and Cartagena; each stays in port about 15 days, but it can be longer. Shipping companies on San Andrés know that they have a monopoly, so take care when dealing with them and do not believe all they tell you.

You can complete all formalities yourself if you wish. There is no need to hire a freight forwarder (US$70-90 per day) or a customs broker. The best way to ship a vehicle is in a 6m x 2.20m x 2.28m container, US$900, large enough for a four-wheel drive or VW Combi, but open-top containers are available for higher vehicles. First find a shipping company (for example Seabord Marine LDT, Agent: Sea Cargo SA, Panama). Get your copy of the Bill of Loading, which must say under domestic routing instructions: *Esta mercancía (carro) no tiene fines de lucro. Para uso personal.* Make four copies of the Bill of Loading, car registration documents, passport page with personal identification and the page with the Panama Customs and Immigration stamp. With these and US$20 in US$1 bills go to the Ministerio Público, Policia Técnica Judicial, Secretaría General and ask for an export letter: Decreto Ejecutivo No 10 de Enero de 1963 (office hours 0800-1200, 1300-1600). Take this next to the Ministario de Hacienda y Tesoro, Dirección de Aduanas, Sección Control de Vehículos, where you get another letter allowing you to enter the port in Colón and put the car in the container. Arrange with your shipping company which day this should be done. Container freight is at Manzanillo International Terminal, CCFS, T4300455 (Lucía Jeff speaks English). CCFS handling charge about US$150. They will drive the car into the container and secure it. Make sure the container and seal numbers are put on the Bill of Loading. Next day take all paperwork again to Hacienda so that the car can be cleared from your passport. Deliver the stamped Bill of Loading and port paperwork to the shipping company. 24 hours after the ship sails, pick up the original Bill of Loading from the shipping company, get their counterpart's address in Cartagena and buy a one-way air ticket by showing Copa the Bill of Loading.

Customs formalities at the Colombian end will take 1-3 days to clear (customs officials do not work at weekends). Cartagena is the best port because it is privately run, more secure and more efficient. Go first to customs: DIAN, Manga CL27 A 24-83, Diagonal DIAN, Jefe División de Servicio al Comercio Exterior Ciudad. Here you will receive, free of charge, the necessary documents to enter the port (takes about 24 hours). Go to your shipping agent while this is being done, with all your paperwork, get the Bill of Loading stamped and ask for a freight release letter, clearing to unload the container, the name of the port (there are two) and pier and the name of the operating company who moves the container, cuts the seal and unloads the car. Then go to the port with the documents to arrange a time for unloading, cost about US$150. Next day go again to DIAN and get an appointment with a DIAN inspector in the port. He will inspect the car and stamp it into your passport. Then go back to DIAN to get the paperwork signed before returning to the port to get a final letter of disembarkation and drive away.

To **Ecuador**: Weekly (sometimes more often) sailings with combined services of P&O, Nedlloyd, Hapaglloyd, about US$900 for a six-metre container. Shipping to Guayaquil from Panama's new container port of Manzanillo, next to Colón, is the best choice, preferable to Colombia or Venezuela. TNE (Transportes Navieros Ecuatorianos, T2692022) ship vehicles to Guayaquil; agent in Cristóbal, Agencia Continental SA, T4451818. Another agent recommended in Cristóbal: Wilford & McKay, in front of *La Fortuna* restaurant, two blocks from the bus station, contact Sr Rosas or María del Carmen, T4450461. Customs agents cost US$60 in Colón, US$120 in Guayaquil; 12 days from starting arrangements in Panama to leaving Guayaquil docks. Seek advice on paperwork from the Ecuadorean consul in Panama. Barwil (Panama City T2637755, Colón 4415533) will ship vehicles to Arica, **Chile**. Recommended.

It is also possible to ship a vehicle to **Venezuela**, from Cristóbal usually to La Guaira, but Puerto Cabello is possible. Agents include: Cia Transatlántica España, T2696300, to La Guaira. Also Barwil Agencies (see above). Also Vencaribe (a Venezuelan line), agent in Cristóbal: Associated Steamship, T2521258 (Panamá), T4450461 (Cristóbal). There are several agencies in Colón/Cristóbal across the street from the Chase Manhattan Bank and next door to the YMCA building. Formalities before leaving can be completed through a travel agency – recommended is Continental Travel Agency, at the *Hotel Continental*, T2636162 – Rosina Wong was very helpful. In Venezuela there are customs complications (without carnet) and this route is not really recommended.

Warning: If you are not using a container, the contents of your vehicle are shipped at your own risk – generally considered to be a high one! Anything loose, tools, seat belts, et cetera, is liable to disappear, or to be swapped for an inferior replacement (for example spare tyre). One reader who escaped theft had chained two padlocked, wooden boxes to the car seats. Theft is particularly prevalent on the Colombia route.

Most people ship their vehicles from Panama to South America by sea but some find air-freighting much more convenient. Generally it is faster and avoids many of the unpleasant customs hassles, but is more expensive. Prices vary considerably. The major carriers, if they permit it on a regular commercial flight, tend to charge more than the cargo lines and independents. Prices and availability change from month to month depending on the demand by regular commercial shippers. You are generally not allowed to accompany the vehicle. For Copa Cargo, T2384414, Tocumen airport, talk to Otto Littman. Varig will ship vehicles to Brazil (Rio), Buenos Aires or Santiago de Chile.

Air-freighting a vehicle

Taking a motorcycle from Panama to Colombia can only be done on a cargo flight. Drain oil and gasoline, and remove the battery before loading; the bike goes in with just an inch to spare so you must expect a scratch or two. Insist on loading the bike yourself. Having bought your passenger ticket, and checked your bike in at the carrier's office, go to customs at the airport with your entry permit and freight papers, and pay US$4.20 to have the stamp cancelled in your passport. You may have to take your airway bill to the Colombian Consulate for stamping three hours before flight time. Allow two days in Panama. Retrieving the bike in Colombia, although costing very little (US$10 approximately), will take from 0900 to 1630 for paperwork (or up to two days if there are any peculiarities in your documents).

Keeping in touch

Spanish, but English is widely understood. The older generation of West Indian immigrants speaks Wari-Wari, a dialect of English incomprehensible to other English speakers, but is the origin of much Panamanian Spanish slang. Indians in rural areas use their own languages, though many are bilingual.

Language

Great care should be taken to address all mail as 'Panama' or 'RP' (Republic of Panama). Mail addressed to the 'Panama Canal Zone' is likely to be returned to sender. Air mail takes 3-10 days, sea mail 3-5 weeks from Britain. Rates (examples) for air mail (up to 15 grams) are as follows: Central, North and South America and Caribbean, 35c; Europe, 45c up to 10 grams, 5c for every extra five grams; Africa, Asia, Oceania, 60c. Parcels to Europe can only be sent from the post office in the El Dorado shopping centre in Panama City (bus from Calle 12 to Tumba Muerto).

Postal services

Post offices, marked with blue and yellow signs, are the only places permitted to sell stamps.

The radio station at Gatún is open to commercial traffic; such messages are handled through the Government telegraph offices. The telegraph and cable companies are given under the towns in which they operate. **Telex** is available at the airport, the cable companies and many hotels. Rate for a three-minute call to Britain is US$14.40, and US$4.80 for each minute more. **Telephone** calls can be made between the UK and Panama any time, day or night. Collect calls are permitted to Italy, Spain, Sweden, UK, all of North America, Israel, Japan and some others, three minutes minimum, rates are higher than direct, especially to USA, dial 106, the international operator. Cost of direct dialled calls, per minute or fraction: Central America US$1.04 (1700-2159 US$0.80, 2200-0659 US$0.72); USA US$1.12 (1700-1859 US$0.96, 1900-0659 US$0.72); Mexico, Canada US$2 (1700-0659 US$1.60); Caribbean US$1.60-2.40 depending on country (US$1.60 to some countries 1700-0759); South America US$2 (1700-0759, US$1.60); West Europe US$2.40; Japan US$3; elsewhere US$3.20 (1700-0659

Telephone services

US$3), all plus US$1 tax per call. Lowest rates apply Sunday all day. For AT & T dial 109. For SPRINT (collect calls only) T115 and MCI T108. BT Chargecard calls to the UK can be made through the local operator. Intercontinental contact by satellite is laid on by the Pan-American Earth Satellite Station. The local company is Intercomsa. For email and internet there are several cyber cafés, see Panama City, **Communications**.

Media   **Newspapers**   *La Prensa* is the major local daily newspaper, others are *La Estrella de Panamá*, *El Universal de Panamá*, *El Panamá América*, and two tabloids, *Crítica Libre* and *El Siglo*. *Colón News* (weekly – Spanish and English). In English is the biweekly *Panama News*. The international edition of the *Miami Herald* is printed in Panama, and many other US newspapers are widely available in the capital.

Food and drink

Local cuisines   In Panama City the range of food available is very broad with a profusion of restaurants and well-stocked supermarkets. In the interior tastes are simpler and available ingredients less varied. Because country people do not traditionally use ovens, most food is boiled or fried in vegetable oil (usually soybean oil). Virtually any restaurant will have a meal of the day, *la comida corriente*: a serving of meat, chicken or fish, white rice and a salad, a dish of boiled beans, or both, garnished with a *tajada* (slice) of fried ripe plantain. It will cost about US$2 in the towns, perhaps more in the city, less in villages. A bowl of *sopa de carne* (beef broth with vegetables) or *de pescado* (country chowder) is usually available as a first course for US$0.50. Breakfast normally consists of eggs, or a small beefsteak or slice of liver fried with onions and tomatoes, bread and butter and some combination of *frituras* (see below).

The staple of Panamanian food is white rice, grown not in paddies but on dry land, and usually served at every meal, often with the addition of chicken, shrimp, vegetables, et cetera. Meat is usually fried (*frita*) or braised (*guisada*), rarely grilled except in the better restaurants. Beef is common, but grass fed and rather tough, though low in fat content. Pork, chicken and (excellent) fish are usually to be preferred.

The national dish is *sancocho de gallina*, a stew of chicken, yuca, *ñame* (dasheen), plantain, cut-up pieces of corn on the cob, potatoes, onions and strongly flavoured with *culantro*, an aromatic leaf similar in flavour to coriander (*cilantro*). *Ropa vieja* ('old clothes') is beef boiled or steamed until it can be shredded, then sautéed with onions, garlic, tomatoes and green or red peppers, often served with yellow rice (coloured with *achiote*). Piquant *ceviche*, eaten as a first course or a snack with cold beer, is usually raw corvina or shellfish seasoned with tiny red and yellow peppers, thin slices of onion and marinated in lime juice; it is served very cold with crackers (beware of the bite). A speciality of the Caribbean coast is *sao*, pigs' feet pickled with lime and hot peppers. Also try *arroz con coco*, coconut rice, or the same with *tití*, tiny shrimp; also *fufú*, a fish chowder with coconut milk. *Mondongo* is the stewed tripe dish called *menudo* in Mexico; the Panamanian version is less spicy, but very well seasoned.

For special occasions and whenever the new, young corn has been harvested (February and August), certain traditional corn dishes are prepared. Look for *serén*, a golden corn soup flavoured with *culantro* and mild peppers, or a sweeter version called *pesada* (or just *pesá*), with brown sugar and milk added; *tamales*, a thick cake of corn-meal mush filled with spiced chicken or pork wrapped in *bijao* leaves and steamed; *bollo*, similar, shaped like an ear of corn, without the meat filling; *bollo de coco*, flavoured with coconut and either salt or sugar, steamed in coconut-palm or sugar-cane leaves.

Frituras are eaten at breakfast, as a snack or as a cheap, filling lunch: they include *carimañola*, a cigar-shaped cake of mashed yuca, filled with seasoned, chopped pork and fried golden brown; *tortillas* or *almojábanas* of corn-meal dough fried to a golden yellow; *patacones* (called *tostones* in Central America), slices of unripe green plantain fried till partially softened, flattened and refried until golden; *totorrones* or *turulitas*, fat, sweet cakes of corn batter with juicy kernels of young corn mixed in, fried dark brown; plus *bolitas de carne*, mildly spiced meatballs, *salchichas*, small sausages, *chicharrones*, pieces of pork rind with a thin strip of meat, deep fried; *tasajo*, smoked lean beef; *hojaldras* or *arepas*, thin cakes of wheat flour batter, leavened with baking powder and fried; *empanadas*, pastry-dough triangles filled with meat, chicken, cheese or sweetened fruit. Prices for these will normally be quoted by the *real* (multiples of US$0.05).

Sweets Most *panaderías* sell good pastries: in Panama City most of the European standards are available; in the country, try *empanadas* (see above), *orejas*, *costillas* or *ma'mellena* ('fills me up more', sweet bread-pudding with raisins); *dulces*, of coconut, pineapple, et cetera, are cakes or pastries, not sweets/candies as elsewhere (the latter are *confites*). In restaurants, as well as the ubiquitous *flan*, try *plátano a la tentación*, ripe plantain simmered with brown cane sugar, cinnamon and raisins, *sopa a la borracha*, a rich sponge cake macerated in rum, garnished with raisins and prunes marinated in sherry, *arroz con cacao*, chocolate rice pudding, *buñuelos de viento*, a puffy fritter served with syrup (called *sopaipillas* further north), and *sopa de gloria*, sponge cake soaked in cooked cream mixture with rum added. Local ice creams are safe; try the fresh fruit flavours such as *guanábana* (soursop), mango, pineapple, et cetera. Among the items sold at the roadside you may see bottles stopped with a corncob, filled with *nance*, a strong-flavoured, yellow-green fruit packed with water and allowed to ripen and ferment slightly; *pifá/pixbae*, a bright orange fruit which, when boiled, tastes much like sweet potato (two or three will see you though to your next meal); *níspero*, the tasty, acidic yellow fruit of the chicle tree.

Drink There are dozens of sweetened fruit drinks found everywhere in the country, making excellent use of the many delicious tropical and temperate fruits grown here: *naranja* (orange), *maracuyá* (passion fruit), *guayabo*, *zarzamora* (raspberry), *guanábana*, et cetera. The generic term is *chicha dulce* which also includes drinks made with rice or corn. Most common carbonated canned drinks are available. Panamanian beer tends to be low in alcohol, *Panamá* and *Soberana* the most popular locally. Foreign beers, some imported, others locally brewed, include *Löwenbrau* and *Guinness*. *Chicha fuerte* is the alcoholic form of corn or rice drink fomented with sugar, brewed mostly in the countryside. Sample with care. The local rum, for example *Carta Vieja*, is not bad. *Seco*, a harsh brand of 'white lightening' made from the juice of sugar cane, brand name *Herrerano*, deserves considerable respect.

Holidays and festivals

Holidays 1 January: New Year's Day; 9 January: Martyrs' Day; Shrove Tuesday: Carnival. Good Friday; 1 May: Labour Day (Republic); 15 August: Panama City only (O); 1 November: National Anthem Day (O); 2 November: All Souls (O); 3 November: Independence Day; 4 November: Flag Day (O); 5 November: Independence Day (Colón only); 10 November: First Call of Independence; 28 November: Independence from Spain; 8 December: Mothers' Day; 25 December: Christmas Day.

O=Official holiday, when banks and government offices close. On the rest – national holidays – business offices close too. Occasional others are added at short notice.

School holidays are December-March when holiday areas are busy; make reservations in advance.

Festivals The *fiestas* in the towns are well worth seeing. That of Panama City at Carnival time, held on the four days before Shrove Tuesday, is the best (book hotels and car hire in advance at this time). During carnival women who can afford it wear the *pollera* dress, with its 'infinity of diminutive gathers and its sweeping skirt finely embroidered', a shawl folded across the shoulders, velvet slippers, tinkling pearl and polished fish-scale hair ornaments (called *tembleques* from their quivering motion) in spirited shapes and colours. The men wear a *montuno* outfit: round straw hats, embroidered blouses and trousers sometimes to below the knee only, and carry the *chácara*, or small purse.

At the Holy Week ceremonies at Villa de Los Santos the farces and acrobatics of the big devils – with their debates and trials in which the main devil accuses and an angel defends the soul – the dance of the 'dirty little devils' and the dancing drama of the Montezumas are all notable. The ceremonies at Pesé (near Chitré) are famous all over Panama. For other festivals in this region, see under the **Azuero Peninsula**, page 1207. At Portobelo, near Colón, there is a procession of little boats in the canals of the city. See under Portobelo for the *Congos*, page 1200.

There are, too, the folk-tunes and dances. The music is cheerful, combining the rhythms of Africa with the melodic tones and dance-steps of Andalusia, to which certain characteristics of the Indian pentatonic scale have been added. The *tamborito* is the national dance. Couples dance separately and the song – which is sung by the women only, just as the song part of the *mejorana* or *socavón* is exclusively for male voices – is accompanied by the clapping of the audience and three kinds of regional drums. The *mejorana* is danced to the music of native guitars and in the interior are often heard the laments known as the *gallo* (rooster), *gallina* (hen), *zapatero* (shoemaker), or *mesano*. Two other dances commonly seen at *fiestas* are the *punto*, with its promenades and foot tapping, and the *cumbia*, of African origin, in which the dancers carry lighted candles and strut high.

Bullfights are an important part of rural fairs, as are rodeo events. The bulls are not killed in Panama.

The Ngöbe-Bugle (Guaymí) Indians of Chiriquí province meet around 12 February to transact tribal business, hold feasts and compete for brides by tossing balsa logs at one another; those unhurt in this contest, known as Las Balserías, are viewed as heroes and are said to be regarded as promising suitors.

Health

Health/disease risks   No particular precautions are necessary. Water in Panama City and Colón is safe to drink. In smaller towns, it is best to drink boiled or bottled water to avoid minor problems caused by indifferently maintained municipal distribution systems. Yellow fever vaccination is recommended before visiting Darién. Malaria prophylaxis for that area is highly recommended. It is currently very difficult to obtain chloroquine in Panama; stock up before arrival. In fact, stock up with all medicines, they are very costly in Panama. Tampons are available in larger towns at the same price as in the UK. Hospital treatment is also expensive; insurance underwritten by a US company would be of great help.

Further reading

History   For the history of the Canal, see David McCullough's *The Path Between the Seas*. For the era of military rule, John Dinges, *Our Man in Panamá*. Graham Greene's *Getting to Know the General* (Torrijos) is subjective and, as such, is not historically reliable, but is worth reading. John Le Carré's recent *Tailor of Panamá* is a cynical but entertaining view of Panama City society. Manuel Noriega has written *America's Prisoner* (Random House).

For ornithologists, Robert S Ridgely's and John Gwynn's *The Birds of Panama*, Princeton University, describes 929 species and is richly illustrated. The Spanish edition has both English and Spanish names in the text.

Panama City

Panama City is a curious blend of old Spain, American progress, and the bazaar atmosphere of the east. It has a polyglot population unrivalled in any other Latin American city. For the sober minded, the palm-shaded beaches, the islands of the Bay and the encircling hills constitute a large part of its charm. The cabarets and night life (very enterprising) are an attraction to those so inclined. The city has been expanding since 1979, with new developments along the southern end of the Canal and skyscrapers springing up around the Bahía de Panamá.

The City, capital of the Republic, was founded on its present site in 1673 after Morgan had sacked the old town, now known as Panamá Viejo, six and a half kilometres to the east. Most of Panama City is modern; the old quarter of the city (the Casco Viejo) – the part that Spain fortified so massively just as the era of widespread piracy was coming to an end – lies at the tip of a peninsula; both it and Panamá Viejo are being extensively restored.

Ins & outs

For flights see **Essentials, Getting there**. Tocumen international airport is 27 kilometres from the city centre and there are taxis and buses for getting into Panama City as well as car hire. The bus journey should take one hour but can take up to three in the rush hour, see Air, page 1185. The city is well served by international buses from Central American countries, via Costa Rica down the Panamerican highway, into the centre of town.

Getting there
Colour map 6, grid A2

The old part of the city, Casco Viejo, can easily be toured on foot. There are old, usually crowded buses for getting to other districts, very cheap, or reasonable taxis which charge on a zone system and can be shared if you wish to economize. At night, radio taxis are preferable. Taxis can also be hired by the hour for a city tour.

Getting around

Security Panamanians are generally friendly and helpful. Accustomed to foreigners, they are casual about tourists. However, as in any large city with many poor people, certain areas can be dangerous after dark and reasonable precautions should be taken at all times. Attacks have been reported in the Casco Viejo and Panamá Viejo, Marañón (around the market), San Miguelito (on the way in from Tocumen airport) and Calidonia can be dangerous; never walk there at night and take care in daylight, too. For this reason, be careful when booking into a hotel or *pensión* between Calles 9 and 30, ie west of Plaza Herrera (where most of the cheap ones are to be found). Poor districts like Curundú and Hollywood are also best avoided. Probably the safest area for visitors to stay is Bella Vista. Taxis are the safest way to travel around the city, and drivers will give you good advice on where not to go. If concerned, lock the doors of the taxi. See **Taxis** under **Transport**, below.

Tourist Police have now appeared in the downtown areas of the city, recognizable by their broad armbands. They are proving helpful for safety and for answering questions.

El Chorrillo, the area west from Plaza Santa Ana to Ancón Hill, was largely destroyed in Operation Just Cause; it was a dangerous area so if you wish to visit it show a genuine interest in the district's recent history. We have received recent reports of muggings here.

Population The metropolitan area has a population of over 600,000 (585,000 at 1990 census). Adjacent to the city, but constituting a separate administrative district, is the town of San Miguelito, once a squatter community, now a residential area for 300,000 people of limited means. Every available square inch of hillside is built upon here. A hospital is being built for the town. In the province of Panamá, there are 1.2 million people.

NB Some of the street names have recently been changed, which may make finding your way around a little difficult. The locals are likely still to refer to the streets by their old names, so if in doubt ask. Also, because there is no postal delivery to homes or businesses, few buildings display their numbers, so try to find out the nearest cross street.

Sights

Casco Viejo Most of the interesting sights and the budget hotels are in the Casco Viejo (the 'Old Compound', also known as the Casco Colonial or San Felipe), which occupies the narrow peninsula east of Calle 11. In 1992 local authorities began reviving some of the area's past glory by painting many of the post-colonial houses in soft pastels and their decorations and beautiful wrought-iron railings in relief; new shops and restaurants are being installed in restored buildings in an attempt to make the Casco Viejo a tourist attraction. At the walled tip of the peninsula is the picturesque **Plaza de Francia**, with its red poinciana trees and obelisk topped by a cockerel (symbol of the Gallic nation), which has a document with 5,000 signatures buried beneath it. Twelve large narrative plaques and many statues recall the French Canal's construction history and personalities; the work of Cuban doctor Carlos Finlay in establishing the cause of yellow fever is commemorated on one tablet. Facing the plaza is the French Embassy, housed in a pleasant early 20th century building. Built flush under the old seawalls around the plaza are *Las Bóvedas* (The Vaults), the thick-walled colonial dungeons where prisoners in tiny barred cells were immersed up to their necks during high tides. Nine 'vaults' were restored by IPAT in 1982 and converted into art galleries and a handicraft centre. The French restaurant *Las Bóvedas* occupies another two 'vaults' next to the former Palacio de Justicia (partly burned during Operation Just Cause and now housing the National Institute of Culture).

Steps lead up from the Plaza Francia to the promenade (**Paseo de Las Bóvedas**) which runs along the top of the defensive walls surrounding the peninsula on three sides. This is a popular place for an evening stroll; it is ablaze with bougainvillea and affords good views of the Bahía de Panamá, the Sierra Majé on the Panamá/Darién provincial border (on a clear day), Calzada Amador (known during the Canal Zone era as the Causeway) and the islands beyond (see under Fuerte Amador, page 1191).

Two blocks northwest of the Plaza (Avenida A and Calle 3) are the restored ruins of the impressive **Church and Convent of Santo Domingo** (1673, but destroyed by fires in 1737 and 1756), both with paired columns and brick inlaying on their façades. The famous 15 metre-long flat arch (*arco chato*) which formed the base of

Panama City orientation

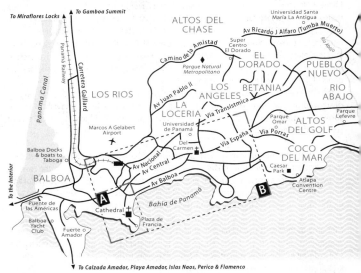

Related maps
A Casco Viejo,
page 1174
B Main streets,
page 1178

the choir was built entirely of bricks and mortar with no internal support. When the great debate as to where the Canal should be built was going on, a Nicaraguan postage stamp showing a volcano, with all its implications of earthquakes, and the stability of this arch – a supposed proof of no earthquakes – are said to have played a large part in determining the choice in Panama's favour. A chapel on the site has been converted into the interesting **Museo de Arte Colonial Religioso**, whose treasures include a precious golden altar, a delicate snail staircase, silver relics and wooden sculptures from as far away as Lima and México, 19th century engravings of the city, and the skeleton of a woman found by archaeologists during excavation of the Church. ■ *T2282897. Open Monday-Friday 0900-1600.* Behind Santo Domingo, across Avenida Central, the neoclassical **Teatro Nacional** (850-seat capacity) opened in 1908 with Verdi's *Aida* being performed in what was then considered the state of the art in acoustics. French-influenced sculptures and friezes enliven the façade, while Roberto Lewis' paintings depicting the birth of the nation adorn the theatre's dome. The ballerina, Dame Margot Fonteyn, who married a member of the prominent Arias family and was a long-time resident of Panama until her death in 1991, danced at the theatre's reinauguration, after many years of restoration, in 1974. ■ *Free entry during normal working hours after asking permission of the security guard.*

Diagonally opposite the Teatro Nacional (Avenida B and Calle 3) is the peaceful **Plaza Bolívar**, with a statue of the Liberator, draped in robes, standing below a large vulture, surrounded by plaques of his deeds. Facing the square are the faded *Hotel Colonial*, the **Church of San Felipe Neri** (interesting but open only on 26 May), and many 19th century houses still displaying roofs of red clay tiles bearing the stamp 'Marseilles 1880'. On the east side stand **San Francisco Church** (colonial but 'modified' in 1917 and modernized in 1983) and the **San Francisco Convent** (1678), largest of all the religious buildings, which was restored by Peruvian architect Leonardo Villanueva. The Bolivarian Congress of June 1826, at which Bolívar proposed a United States of South America, was held in the Chapter Room of the Convent; here also the 1904 Constitution was drafted. This northern wing was dedicated as the **Instituto Bolívar** in 1956; its wood panelling, embossed leather benches and paintings (restored in part by the government of Ecuador) may be viewed with an

Colón

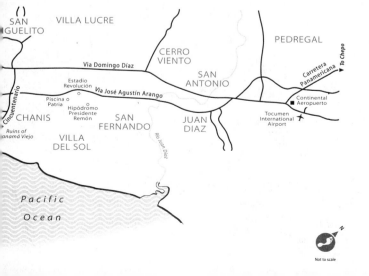

Panamá

authorized guide from the Bolivarian Society, T2622947.

Another long block west of Plaza Bolívar, and one block north on the seafront (Avenida Alfaro) between Calles 5 y 6, is the **Palacio Presidencial**, the most impressive building in the city, built as an opulent residence in 1673 for successive colonial auditors and governors, enlarged and restored under President Belisario Porras in 1922. Graceful patios and mother-of-pearl decorated columns give a Moorish flavour, and murals by Lewis adorn the official reception salons. The incumbent president, who commutes daily from his private house in Altos del Golf, has restricted access to the street in front of the Palacio, but visitors who ask permission at the guard office are allowed to approach the gate and view the courtyard from the outside. Exterior photography is allowed. Porras introduced two white Darién herons during one of his presidential terms and a number of their descendants are always to be seen around the fountain of the Moorish patio, leading to the popular nickname of the residence: *Palacio de las Garzas* or Palace of the Herons. A few blocks west, Avenida Alfaro begins to curve north around the waterfront to the colourful **Central Market**, Mercado San Felipe (see **Shopping**, below) and the wharves where fishermen land their catches, coastal vessels anchor (a 15 metre tidal range allows beaching for maintenance) and cargo boats leave for Colombia (Muelle Inglés).

Two blocks south of the Presidential Palace is the heart of the old town, the **Plaza Catedral** or **Independencia**, with busts of the Republic's founders and surrounding public buildings. On the west is the **Cathedral** (1688-1794), its twin towers, domes and classical façade encrusted with mother-of-pearl; three of the tower bells were brought from Old Panamá Cathedral. To the right of the main altar is a subterranean passage which leads to other *conventos* and the sea. On the southwest corner with Calle 7 is the neoclassical **Palacio Municipal** (City Hall), on the first floor of which is the **Museo de Historia de Panamá** (see **Museums**, below). The former Post Office next door, originally built in 1875 as the Grand Hotel ("the largest edifice of that kind between San Francisco and Cape Horn" according to a contemporary newspaper), is the city's best example of French architecture. It became de Lesseps' headquarters during Canal excavations in the 1880s and was sold back to Panamá in 1912; it has been entirely gutted and converted into a **Museum of the Panama**

Panama City: Casco Viejo

Canal (Museo del Canal Interoceáno). ■ *Entrance US$2*. The east side of the Plaza is dominated by the former **Archbishop's Palace**, which was later occupied by a university and subsequently by a shelter for runaway youth (now closed), and the *Central Hotel* (1884), once the most luxurious in Central America (interior Palm Garden, restaurants, barber shop, 100 rooms with private baths, wooden staircase imported from New York) and the centre of Panamá's social life for decades; today it is very decrepit but still retains echoes of its former elegance.

There are a number of other interesting religious structures within two or three blocks of the Cathedral but the most-visited is the church of **San José** (Avenida A y Calle 8, one block west and south of the Plaza Catedral) with its famous Altar de Oro, a massive baroque altar carved from mahogany and according to common belief veneered with gold. This was one of the few treasures saved from Henry Morgan's attack on Old Panamá in 1671 and there are different versions of how it was concealed from the buccaneers (whitewashed by the priest, covered in mud by nuns, even a remark attributed to Morgan hinting that he was not deceived!). A beautiful organ, an 18th century original pulpit with a painting by an unknown artist on its tiny roof and several smaller carved wooden altars, can also be seen. Two blocks further west along Avenida Central is the church of **La Merced**, burnt in 1963 and now completely restored. It was near here that the landward gate of the fortified city stood. A block to the south down Calle 9 is **Plaza Herrera**; the French influence is evident in the windows and flower-filled cast-iron balconies of the green and light pink houses and *pensiones*. Behind Plaza Herrera are the ruins of the 'Tiger's Hand Bulwark', where the defensive wall ended and the landward side moat began. The strongpoint held a 50-man military post and 13 cannon, and was demolished in 1856 as the town expanded westwards but restored again in 1983. Portions of the moat can still be detected.

Avenida Central & Calidonia

From Calle 10 onwards the Avenida Central, Panama City's main commercial street, enters the 'mainland' and begins to curve northwest then sweeps northeast almost parallel with the shore through the whole town, changing its name to Vía España – the municipality has installed signs reading 'Avenida Central España' along a transitional section – on its course northeast to Tocumen Airport. At its crossing with Calle B is the small Plaza Santa Ana with a colonial church (1764), a favourite place for political meetings; the plaza has many restaurants and is a good place at which to catch buses to all parts of the city. Nearby, running towards the Central Market between Avenida Central and Calle B (officially known as Carrera de Chiriquí), is an exotic, narrow alley called **Salsipuedes** – 'Get out if you can' – where crowded stalls sell everything from fruit to old books to medicinal plants; 78 percent of the street's residents in 1892 were Chinese merchants but the city's Chinatown (*Barrio Chino*) is now largely confined to nearby Calle Juan Mendoza and adjacent Calle B with a typical Chinese archway at the entrance, several good Chinese restaurants and general shops.

The neighbourhood is safe enough during the day (watch for pickpockets in the throng) but don't linger late at night, best to leave before 1930

The next section of Avenida Central was recently converted into a pedestrian precinct, called El Peatonal, with trees and decorations, a/c department stores, and wandering street vendors. **Plaza 5 de Mayo** (at Calle 22 Este) is another busy bus stop from which buses leave for the Canal. In the centre of the Plaza is an obelisk honouring firemen who died in a gunpowder magazine explosion on the site in May 1914. Housed in the old railway station (1913-46) here is the now closed **Museo Antropológico Reina Torres de Araúz** (see **Museums**, below), formerly called the Museum of Panamanian Man, almost opposite the Plaza de Lesseps. This area is the southern fringe of the **Calidonia** district, where live the descendants of the British West Indian blacks brought in to build the railway and the Canal. Calidonia is a labyrinth of tightly-packed wooden structures, exotic and unassimilated, where outsiders should exercise extreme caution.

La Exposición

Calle 23 Este leads east from the Plaza down to the broad Avenida Balboa along the waterfront. The sprawling Santo Tomás Hospital is here (Calle 36); facing it on a semi-circular promontory jutting out from this promenade (another popular jogging stretch) is a great monument to Vasco Núñez de Balboa (1924), who stands sword and cross aloft as when he strode into the Pacific on 1 October 1513. The statue stands on a white marble globe poised on the shoulders of a supporting group representing the four races of Man. To the east a pleasant park area is being developed. A short distance up the esplanade are the British ambassador's residence and the US Embassy. Two more pleasant plazas, Porras and Arias, can be found behind the Santo Tomás Hospital across Avenida 3 Sur (Justo Arosemena). This central part of the city is known as **La Exposición** because of the international exhibition held here in 1916 to celebrate the building of the Canal. Further north, as Avenida Balboa begins to curve around the other end of the Bay of Panama to Punta Paitilla and the former domestic airport, is **Bella Vista**, once a very pleasant residential district (many private homes now converted to business use) undergoing a renaissance and site of some of the best hotels in our **B** and **C** ranges. It includes the neighbourhood of Perejil ('Parsley'), originally called Perry Hill. Bordering this on the north, where Vía España passes the Iglesia del Carmen, is **El Cangrejo** ('the crab') apartment and restaurant district, with many upmarket stores and boutiques. The University City is on the Transisthmian Highway making student demonstrations a frequent cause of traffic jams. Opposite the campus is the Social Security Hospital. All these areas are evidence of Panama City's sensational growth since the post-war economic boom and the spread of the centre eastwards; the attractive residential suburb of Punta Paitilla was an empty hill where hunting was practised as recently as the 1960s.

Museums

Museo Afro-Antillano, Justo Arosemena y Calle 24, one block east of Plaza 5 de Mayo, T2621668, illustrated history of Panamá's West Indian community and their work on the Canal, small library. ■ *Tuesday-Saturday 0900-1600, Sunday 1500-1800, US$0.50.* **Museo de Arte Colonial Religioso** (Santo Domingo Convent, see above); **Museo Antropológico Reina Torres de Araúz**, Avenida Central at south side of Plaza 5 de Mayo, T2624138, five salons (partly looted during Operation Just Cause) exhibiting Panamanian history, anthropology and archaeology, rare collection of pre-Columbian gold objects and ceramics (Profesora Torres de Araúz was a renowned anthropologist and founder of the museum, died 1982); closed in 1998. **Museo de Historia de Panamá**, in the Palacio Municipal on Plaza Catedral (see above), T2286231/2628089, the nation's history since European landfall, and includes highlights of the treaty between Panama and the USA which led to the construction of the Canal. ■ *Open Monday-Friday 0800-1600, US$0.50.* **Museo de Ciencias Naturales**, Avenida Cuba y Calle 30, T2250645, good sections on geology, palaeontology, entomology and marine biology. ■ *Tuesday-Saturday 0900-1600, Sunday 0900-1300, US$0.50.* **Museo de Arte Contemporáneo**, Avenida de los Mártires (Ancón), entrance on Avenida San Blás, T2628012, in former Masonic Lodge (1936), permanent exhibition of national and international modern paintings and sculptures with special exhibitions from time to time; marquetry, silkscreen and engraving workshops, library of contemporary visual art open to students, entry free but donations welcomed (privately owned). ■ *Open Monday-Friday 0900-1600, Saturday 0900-1200.* **Museo Casa del Banco Nacional**, Avenida Cuba y Calle 34, T2250640, large numismatic and stamp collection and history of banking from the 19th century, old postal and telephone items and historic photos, not widely-known but worth a visit. ■ *Open Monday-Friday 0800-1200, 1330-1600, Saturday 0830-1300.* **Museum of the Independence Soldier**, Paseo de las Bóvedas near the Plaza de Francia, T2281905, small, even less well-known museum dedicated to mementos and souvenirs of Panama's independence from Colombia in 1903, interesting for the history buff. ■ *Open Monday-Friday 0800-1600, US$0.25.* **Museo Postal**, Filatélico y Telegráfico, Avenida Central, opposite Don Bosco church, T2252803, stamp collections, ducuments, equipment, maps, photos et cetera. ■ *Open Monday-Friday 0900-1600*. **Mi Pueblito**, north side of Avenida de los Mártires, east of the entrance to Quarry Heights is a nostalgic replica of a mid-19th century Panamanian village of the Central Provinces. Around the plaza with its fountain are the church, rectory with its internal patio, grocery store, telegraph office, *talabartería* (saddlery), *trapiche* (sugar-cane press), very nicely portrayed. ■ *Small admission charge, open to 2200 (on a busy road so best to take a taxi)*.

Parks

The 265-hectare **Parque Natural Metropolitano** is located between Avenida Juan Pablo II and the Camino de la Amistad, west of El Cangrejo along the Río Curundú. Office ■ *open Tuesday-Sunday 0900-1600. Park open 0730-1800*. As well as a *mirador* (150 metres) with a splendid view over the city and a glimpse of the Canal, there are two interpretive walking trails from which tití monkeys, agoutis, coatis, white-tailed deer, sloths, turtles and up to 200 species of birds may be glimpsed (go early morning for best viewing); green iguanas sun themselves on every available branch. The Smithsonian Institution has installed a unique crane for studying the little-known fauna in the canopy of this remnant of tropical semi-deciduous lowland forest. The Visitor's Centre (T2325516) on Avenida Juan Pablo II runs guided one-hour tours and holds regular slide shows. No Inrenare permit is required for this recommended, easy excursion. Bus, marked 'Tumba Muerto', from Avenida Central, and ask to be dropped at the Depósito. Park is signposted from here, otherwise make for the crane and the tree covered hill.

Claimed to be the only natural forest within the limits of a Latin American metropolitan capital

Essentials
Sleeping

LL *Marriott Panamá*, C 52 y Ricardo Arias, Bella Vista, T2109100, F2109110, complete luxury. **LL** *Miramar Intercontinental*, Av Balboa y Av Federico Boyd, T2141000, F2234891, tallest building in the Republic, sea view, marina, pools, spa, restaurants, etc. **LL** *Caesar Park*, Vía Israel and C 77, T2700477, F2260116, near the sea and the Atlapa convention centre, restaurant, pool, health spa, etc. **LL-L** *Best Western Central Park*, Vía España, La Cresta, T2233100, F2239630, beswescp@pty.com. **L** *El Panamá*, Vía España, at Vía Venetto (C 55), T2695000, F2236080, former *Hilton*, tropical Art Deco style, vast rooms, good swimming pool, 'bags of charm'. **L** *Radisson Royal Panama*, World Trade Centre, T2653636, F2653550, pool, spa, business centre, computer services, piano bar, reading room. **L** *Country Inn*, Av Miguel Brostella, El Dorado, T2635404, F2646082, pool, *Friday's* restaurant.

AL *Golden Tulip Costa del Sol*, Vía España y Federico Boyd, PO Box 8572, Zona 5, T2237111, F2236636, www.costadelsol-pma.com, 242 junior suites, kitchenettes, launderettes on all 7 floors, pool, 2 saunas, tennis, business centre, rooftop bar, restaurant and pizzería, shopping arcade with Indian restaurant, tour agency on site for excursions, airport transfer US$8. **AL** *Plaza Paitilla Inn* (former *Holiday Inn*), Punta Paitilla, T2691122, F2231470, weekend cheap rates available, restaurant, café, nightclub, swimming pool. **AL** *Riande Continental*, Vía España y C Ricardo Arias, T2639999, F2694559, in the business district, pool, nightclubs, restaurants (see also **Eating**), but noisy till 2230 from organ music (a Wurlitzer), undergoing major expansion. **AL** *Granada*, Av Eusebio A Morales, T2644900, F2640930, also with casino, pool, restaurant. **AL** *El Ejecutivo*, C Aquilino de la Guardia at C 52, T2643333, F2691944, pool, a bit shabby. **AL** *Riande Continental Aeropuerto*, near Tocumen airport (10 minutes), T2203333, F2205017, a/c (reductions for more than 1 night), clean, free transport to airport, good breakfasts, pool (loud music all day), tennis, casino. **A** *Aramo*, Vía Brasil y Abel Bravo, a/c, restaurant, T2690174, F2692406. **A** *Costa del Sol*, Vía España y Av Federico Boyd, T2237111, F2236636, costasol@sinfo.net, rooftop restaurant and

There is a 10 percent tax on all hotel prices. Most hotels are a/c.

■ *on maps*
Price codes:
see inside front cover

pool, kitchenettes in all rooms, washers and dryers on all floors, jogging area, will arrange trips.

Many mid-range hotels on Calle 30 Este. **B** *Europa*, Vía España y C 42, T2636911, F2636749, opposite former Teatro Bella Vista, another casino hotel, restaurants and pool. Recommended. **B** *Gran Hotel Soloy*, Av Perú y C 30, T2271133, F2270884. **B** *Veracruz*, Av Perú y C 30, T2273022, F2273789, with breakfast, very good restaurant, clean, good, but rooms at front noisy. **B** *Costa Inn*, Av Perú y C 39, T2271522, F2251281, a/c, hot water, TV, pool, use of fridge, safe parking, shabby, restaurant noisy and smokey. **B** *Roma*, Av Justo Arosemena y C 33, T2273844, F2273711, restaurant with Italian emphasis, rooftop pool.

C *Acapulco*, C 30 Este y Av Perú, T2253832, a/c, clean, comfortable, TV, private bath, excellent restaurant, safe parking, conveniently located. Recommended. **C** *Andino*, C 35 off Av Perú, T2251162 (formerly *Hotel Lux*), completely renovated, large rooms, TV, phones, fridge, a/c, private baths, hot water, restaurant (just OK, but cheap), family-run, quiet street. Highly recommended. **C** *California*, Vía España y C 43, T2637844, with bath, a/c, TV, restaurant, friendly, safe. **C** *Caribe*, Av Perú, T2250404, F2273115, a/c. **C** *Centroamericano*, Av Justo Arosemena y Av Ecuador, T2274555, very clean, good reading lights, TV. **C** *Covadonga*, C 29 entre Av Perú y Av Cuba, next to *Residencia Turístico Volcán*, a/c, cable TV, pool on roof, next door is a clean restaurant of same name. **C-D** *Dos Mares*, C 30 entre Perú y Cuba, T2276150, a/c, bath, hot water, pool on roof, good restaurant, TV, phone. Recommended. **C** *Montreal*, Vía España near *Restaurant Lesseps*, T2634422, shower, toilet, a/c, TV, phone, takes credit cards, rooms on street noisy, safe car park. **C** *Riazor*, C 16, near *Ideal*, T2280777, a/c with bath, hot water, good value, cheap restaurant downstairs next to the

Panama City main streets

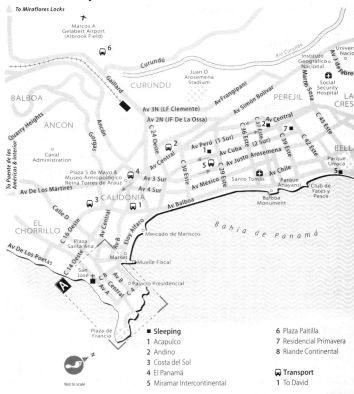

■ **Sleeping**	6 Plaza Paitilla
1 Acapulco	7 Residencial Primavera
2 Andino	8 Riande Continental
3 Costa del Sol	
4 El Panamá	🚌 **Transport**
5 Miramar Intercontinental	1 To David

Not to scale

Ticabus office, therefore well placed as you arrive late from Costa Rica on the bus, but also much noise from buses.

D *Bella Vista*, Via España y C 42, a/c, cable TV, private bath, safe deposit. Recommended. **D** *Discovery*, Av Ecuador, T2251140, clean, fairly quiet, safe parking, good value. **D** *Colón*, C 12, Ote and Calle B, T2288506, with shower (cheaper without), a/c, erratic water supply. **D** *Caracas*, C 12 on Plaza Santa Ana, large, clean rooms, friendly, fans, beware rooms with outside windows, hot showers. **D** *Central*, Plaza Catedral, T2628044/96, with bath, **E** shared bath, fan, very spacious foyer, faded colonial charm – ie run down, safe motorcycle parking, reasonably priced, rooms on plaza have balcony, you can bargain if staying more than a week, very good value. **D** *Ideal*, C 17 just off Av Central, T2622400, a/c (cold), shared hot shower, pool, cable TV, good location, between Plazas Santa Ana y 5 de Mayo, safe, west-bound buses from airport pass outside, for buses to airport go to Avenida B, 1 block south of Avenida Central. **D** *Las Tablas*, Av Perú y C 29 Este, between *Hotels Soloy* and *Caribe*, with bath, **E** without, cold water, fan, safe, quiet except for rooms overlooking street (opposite is *El Machetazo* supermarket, food for cheap meals, but crowded). **D** *Residencia Turístico Volcán*, C 29, between Avs Perú y Cuba, T2255263, opposite Migración, next to Museo de Ciencias Naturales, fan, a/c extra, with shower, friendly, safe, clean.

Cheaper accommodation can be found in *pensiones*: **E** *Colón*, Av Central, C 30, T2288510, without bath, clean, but noisy in the front room. **E** *Foyo*, Santa Bárbara 8-25, T2628023, cheap restaurant downstairs, similar to **E-F** *Herrera*, Plaza Herrera y C 9, T2288994, variety of prices, some with a/c, TV and fridge, bars on main door, restaurant. **E** *Panamá*, C 6 No 8-40, T2226490, clean. **E** *Las Palmeras*, Av Cuba between C 38-39, T2250811, with shower (more with toilet as well), safe, clean, quiet. **E** *Mi Posada*, C 12 y Av Central (Plaza Santa Ana), basic, mixed reports. **E** *Rivera*, Av C 11 Ote, 8-14, off Av A, pleasant and friendly, but noisy (monthly rates available). **E** *Pensión Panamericana*, Plaza Herrera, Casco Viejo, dark rooms, balcony rooms good value. **E** *Pensión Universal*, Av Central 8-16, behind Cathedral, T2282796, shared bath, fan. **E** *Residencial Primavera*, Av Cuba y C 42, on edge of Bella Vista, 1 block east of Av España, T2251195, with bath and fan, quiet residential area. Recommended. **E** *Tropical*, C de San Blas No 8-18, 2½ blocks from Post Office, T2227034, clean. **E** *Sevilla*, Av Justo Arosemena 46-40, T2272436, with bath and a/c, cheaper without, good. **F** *Santa Ana*, overlooking Plaza Santa Ana, helpful; many (unlisted here) on Av México.

Apartments for rent at **AL** *Suites Ambassador*, C, D, in centre of El Cangrejo district, T2637274, F2647872, well-furnished rooms, pool, gym. **AL** *Tower House Suites*, C 51 No 36, Bella Vista, T2692244, F2692869, centre of commercial district. **A** *Apartotel Las Vegas*, C 55 (Via Veneto) y C Eusebio A Morales, T2645033, F2230047. Recommended. Good restaurant on the patio. **B** *Apartotel Plaza*, Av Batista opposite University campus, T2645033, F2642256, and others. All have kitchenette, colour and cable TV, some with pool. Daily, weekly and monthly rates are available.

2 To Colón
3 Ticabus & Hotel Ideal
4 Panaline & Hotel Internacional
5 Padafront & Colón
6 To the Interior (Under construction 1999)

On the way to the airport are 'love motels', 'push buttons', with drive-in garages. For US$10-15 you have a nice room and shower and a few hours' relaxation, even with noble intentions. If your time is up a bell rings and you have to return to your car. You wait while they count the towels, then they open the garage.

NB Electricity and water cuts are frequent in Panama City, though usually very brief. Most better-class hotels have generators and large cisterns.

Camping There are no official sites but it is possible to camp on some beaches or, if in great need (they agree, but don't like it much) in the Balboa Yacht Club car park. It is also possible to camp in the Hipódromo grounds (11 kilometres east of the city, on Vía España) but there are no facilities; this is allowed if you are waiting to ship your vehicle out of the country. Also possible, by previous arrangement, at La Patria swimming pool nearby, and at the Chorrera (La Herradura) and La Siesta beaches on the Pan-American Highway. Camping Gaz is available at *Ferretería Tam SA*, Av B, No 54; at *Super 99* grocery stores, cheap.

Eating

Eating
● *on maps*

As a cosmopolitan city, there is a wide range of restaurants, many of good quality in all styles and price ranges. There are good restaurants in most of the more expensive hotels, eg *Rendezvous*, at the *Riande Continental*, is good value, open 24 hours, superb Sunday brunch from 1030-1500 US$9.50.

Local, Panamanian *El Trapiche*, Vía Argentina 10, many dishes including *empanadas* – meat filled fritters, and *mondongo* – seasoned tripe, also in Panamá Viejo, T2215241, similar food with traditional music and dance programmes, call for information. *Las Tinajas*, on C 51, near *Ejecutivo Hotel*, T2637890, Panamanian food and traditional entertainment most evenings at 2100, craft shop. Recommended. *Bohío Turístico*, Vía Cincuentenario, Panamá Viejo, on seafront, open air, palm thatched building (*bohío*). *Jimmy's*, Paseo Cincuentenario just beyond Atlapa Centre, T2261096, good grills, seafood, fast food and fish, served under a thatched roof, very popular, also on Av Samuel Lewis opposite *Hotel Riande Continental*, a/c, self service, good for breakfast and lunch.

Grills *Los Años Locos*, opposite *Caesar Park Hotel*, T2266966, Argentine *parrillada* steakhouse, good value. *Gauchos Steak House*, C Uruguay y C 48, choose your own steak, learn the names of the cuts, say you will salt your own, good. *Martín Fierro*, C Eusebio A Morales, T2641927, meat, seafood. *La Tablita*, Transisthmian Highway, Los Angeles district, T2601458, good steaks, reasonable.

Chinese *Lung Fung*, Transisthmian Highway and Los Angeles, very popular with Chinese residents for Saturday and Sunday, Cantonese-style brunch, very good food and value. *Madame Chang*, C 48 off Aquilino de la Guardia, elegant, good food, pricey, erratic service. *Rey Kung*, Vía España y C 46, opposite *Hotel Central Park*, T2690956, very reasonable, dim sum breakfast, lunch, good food. *Manhattan*, Vía España, Edif Domino, clean, reasonable, Chinese. *Kwang Chow*, in the Salsipuedes area of Av Balboa, sells Tsingtao beer. Recommended. *Gran China*, Av Balboa, between C 26 y 27, Chinese, good value. *Palacio Imperial*, C 17 near Ticabus office, Chinese, good and cheap. *Kalua*, close to the *Hotel El Panamá*, very good Chinese, reasonable prices. *Tang*, Calle A y Cenbule, off Plaza Santa Ana, cheap, friendly, recommended.

Swiss *El Rincón Suizo*, C Eusebio A Morales, T2638310, charming mountain hut atmosphere, good Swiss rösti, *raclette, fondue*, chef Willy Diggleman. *1985*, same street, larger than *El Rincón* but same management.

French *Calypso*, Vía España y C 46, La Cresta, T2230749, French restaurant and bar. *La Cocotte*, C Uruguay 138, T2138250, in former private house, excellent food, expensive, Hillary Clinton slipped out of the embassy to eat here. *Las Bóvedas*, in converted dungeons at seaward end of Casco Viejo, T2288068, good French food, expensive, art galleries adjoining, live jazz Thursday-Saturday (best to take a taxi there). *Casco Viejo*, C 50, Mansión Dante, excellent food, interesting decor, closed Sunday. Expensive but recommended. *Dali*, Av Samuel Lewis y Santa Rita, Daliesque décor, also Italian food. *Le Bistrot*, Centro Comercial La

Florida, C 53, good, expensive (under same ownership is *Siete Mares*, next to *El Cortijo*, see below).

Indian *Calcutta*, Av Federico Boyd; *Paladar Hindú*, Calle A Navarro, authentic Indian, inexpensive, Karaoke bar.

Japanese & Korean *Ginza Teppenyaki*, C Eusebio A Morales, opposite *Hotel Granada*, lobster, seafood, imported beef, diners surround the chef at his grill. *Benihana*, C 60, Obarrio, favoured by Japanese locals. *Oriental Palace*, Av Samuel Lewis No 15, just down from *Continental Hotel*, T2235744, Korean, Japanese and Chinese food, 1st class, sushi bar, 4 floors of dining rooms. *Korea House*, C 52, block north of Vía España opposite Cine Aries, Japanese, sushi bar, Korean. *Club Fuji*, Vía Brazil, C 32, Obarrio, 1 of the best Japanese in town. *Matsuei*, Av Eusebio A Morales A-12, Japanese, excellent, pricey.

Italian *Athen's*, C San Miguel, Obarrio (also C Ricardo Arias), excellent pizza also Greek and near-Eastern food, noisy, young people, very good. *Caffé Pomodoro*, Av Eusebio A Morales, north of C 55, in patio of *Apartotel Las Vegas,* garden setting, also a/c, North Italian pasta and sauces, informal, moderately priced. *Nápoli*, C 57, Obarrio, 1½ blocks south of Vía España, big, family-style, good Italian, pizzas with real Italian dough. *Las Américas*, Av 1 Sur, C 57/58, 1 block south of Vía España, T2234676, elegant, good cellar.

Spanish *Manolo*, Vía Argentina, sidewalk terrace, a favourite for politicians and young people in evenings and Sunday am, beer from the tap served with *tapas, churros* (doughnut-like fried cakes) a speciality, also on Vía Venetto y C Eusebio A Morales, tables or counter, same menu, prices and service. *Angel*, Vía Argentina 68, T2636411, seafood, imported mussels, eel, *bacalao* (cod). *El Mesón del Prado*, Edif Alcalá, Tumba Muerto, T2609466, informal, tables and counter, bar, seafood, snacks, moderate prices. *Marbella*, Av Balboa y C 39, seafood *cazuela de mariscos, paella,* good but not cheap. *El Cortijo*, between Eusebio A Morales and Vía Argentina on Calle D, T2696386. *Del Prado*, Vía Argentina, T2642645, busy at lunchtime, full meals, sandwiches, open late. *Café Balear*, C Colombia 17, north of Parque Urracá, T2692415, extensive menu, colonial style town house.

Mexican *La Mejicanita*, Av Justo Arosemena y C 50, La Florida shopping centre, good. *México Lindo* 1900, Av Balboa y C Uruguay, T2654743, bay view, nice décor, trendy live music evenings, Mexican beer and margaritas, check hours.

Vegetarian *Mireya* C Ricardo Arango y C Ricardo Arias, near *Continental Hotel*, T2691876, health food bakery, good value. Recommended. Also at Calle 39 y Av Balboa, Bella Vista. *Mi Salud*, C 31 y Av México 3-30, owned by dietary specialist Carlos Raúl Moreno, open Monday-Saturday 0700-1900. *Govinda's*, C 47, No 24, Marbella, many specialities.

Other restaurants *Centolla's Place*, Vía España, Río Abajo, T2217056, Caribbean seafood, catering to Antillean community, friendly, cheap, worth a taxi ride. Recommended. *La Fregata*, Av Samuel Lewis, Obarrio, good food, medium priced. *La Casa del Marisco* (seafood) on Av Balboa, is open-air. *La Marina*, in the Club de Peces y Yates on Av Balboa near US embassy, excellent food, moderate to expensive, where local notables enjoy lunch with their mistresses. *La Cascada*, Av Balboa y C 25, beef, pork, seafood, enormous helpings, open air, 'doggy bags' given, fake waterfall, lifesize animal décor in concrete ('OTT Disneyland'), good service, credit cards not accepted, menus in charming English to takeaway, closed Sunday. Highly recommended. The same management runs *Las Costillitas* on Vía Argentina, same menu (which takes 30 minutes to read), same reasonable prices, open Sunday. *TGI Friday's*, C 49 y Av Aquilino de la Guardia, near Lloyds Bank, T2694199, huge US franchise operation, good food, hordes of young people, recommended to call ahead for waiting list. *Mango's Pub & Grill*, C Uruguay 1-24, T2694856, US style bar and food, many imported beers, best hamburger south of Houston, live music Tuesday and Saturday, recommended for lunch and evening. *Riazor*, C 16, 15-105, T2282541, just as it was 40-50 years ago, cheap local food served with style. Recommended. Take a taxi at night. *Pavo Real*, C 51, just west of C Ricardo Arias, Campo Alegre, up-scale English pub with restaurant, darts, good food, ex-pat hangout, journalist's refuge during 'Just Cause', open 1200-2400, Monday-Tuesday, till 0330 Wednesday-Saturday, live music from 2200, closed Sunday. *Niko's Café*, Vía España near El Rey supermarket, T2640136, also El Dorado Shopping Centre, T2600022, very good, cheap, self-service, also at Paitilla airport. *La Victoria*, next to Minimercado Teresa on Av Central, open 1100-2300, very cheap (US$1 a meal) with juke box and a/c. Recommended. Also recommended is unnamed restaurant opposite, very popular with locals.

Cafés and fast food *Krispy*, *McDonald's*, *Frutilandia*, *Dairy Queen*, *Hardee's*, *Burger King*, *Kentucky Fried Chicken*, *Pizza Pizza* and *Don Lee* all have their branches. *La Viña*, corner C 6 Ote and Av A, behind Post Office, good, cheap. Also *La Esquina*, Av A y C 12 Ote. *La Conquista*, Calle J, up Av Central. *La Cresta* (good food from US$1), Vía España and C 45. *A & P* on Av Central opposite the National Museum, good. *Markany*, Av Cuba y Av Ecuador, good snacks. *Café Coca Cola*, Av Central and Plaza Santa Ana, pleasant, friendly, reasonably priced – US$3 for set lunch. *Café Jaime*, corner of C 12 and Av Central, for good *chichas* (natural drinks). *Café Central*, Av Central, between C 28 and 29, Calidonia, basic and cheap food, OK. There are good pavement cafés along Avenida Balboa. *Dulcería Panadería La Gran Vida*, Av Central 11-64 (between C11 y 12), good chicha juice, good cheap ice cream, good empanadas and cakes. Recommended.

Night life   **Cabarets and discotheques**   *Hotel Riande Continental*; *Josephine's*, C 50 y Av Uruguay, El Cangrejo, cover charge US$20, continuous show 2100-0400 daily except Sunday. *Le Palace*, C 52, opposite *Hotel El Ejecutivo*, T2691844, no cover, shows from 2030 nightly. *Oasis*, Vía Brasil. **Recommended discos**: *Bacchus*, Vía España and Elvira Méndez. *Magic*, C 50 diagonal a C Uruguay. *Cubares*, next door. *Capo's*, Vía Cincuentenario. *Las Molas*, entrance to Chase Manhattan Bank, Vía España, Los Angeles district, small band, rural decor, drinks US$1.50. *Unicornio*, C 50 y R Arias 23 is nightclub with discothèque and gambling; reasonable prices, will admit foreigners for US$3 a week. *La Parrillita*, Av 11 de Octubre in Hato Pintado district, is a restaurant/disco in a railway carriage. *Fonda Antioqueña*, Panamá Viejo, T2211268, Colombian restaurant, bar, disco, daily 24 hours. *La Chiva Parrandera* as an open sided bus that tours the hot-spots 2000-2330, T2633144, F2646764 for information, US$20 per person.

Casinos   More than 20, some in main hotels. State-managed and profits intended for charitable public institutions; most offer black jack, baccarat, poker, roulette and slot machines (*traganikles*). Winnings are tax-free and paid without deductions. The *National Lottery* is solemnly drawn (televised) each Wednesday and Sunday at 1300 in Plaza de la Lotería between Avs Perú y Cuba; 4-digit tickets, called *billetes* or *pedazos*, cost US$1, a win pays up to US$2,000; 'chance' tickets, with only 2 digits cost US$0.25, and pay up to US$14.

Live music clubs   *Nottingham*, Fernández de Córdoba, Vista Hermosa, T2610314, live salsa at weekends, no cover charge, restaurant. *Vino's Bar*, C 51 y Colombia, Bella Vista, T2640520, live salsa at weekends, cover charge, restaurant. *Hotels Granada* and *Soloy* (*Bar Maitai*, T2271133) are recommended for live Latin music at weekends. *Giorgio's*, 1 block south of Vía Porras. *Café El Aleph*, Vía Argentina north of Vía España, T2642844, coffee house atmosphere, snacks and full meals, Internet facilities, occasional art shows, live jazz at weekends, phone for programme. *Café Gardel*, Vía Argentina, T2693710, small restaurant, tiny bar, perfect intimate atmosphere for live jazz.

Entertainment and shopping

Entertainment   **Theatres and cinemas**   There are occasional official presentations and concerts held at the **Teatro Nacional** (folklore sessions every other Sunday, check dates; monthly National Ballet performances when not on tour). The **Anayansi Theatre** in the Atlapa Convention Centre, Vía Israel, San Francisco, has a 3000-seat capacity, good acoustics, regular recitals and concerts. **Balboa Theatre** near Steven's Circle and Post Office in Balboa, with folkloric groups and jazz concerts sponsored by National Institute of Culture. **Guild Theatre** in the Canal Area at Ancón mounts amateur productions mainly in English. *La Prensa* gives full listings of cultural events. The usual a/c **cinemas** (US$2.50 except Balboa cinema near Steven's Circle, US$2); by law all foreign films must be subtitled in Spanish. Newspapers publish daily programming (*cartelera*). **Cine Universitario** in the National University, T2642737, US$1.50 for general public, shows international and classic movies, daily (not holidays) at 1700, 1900 and 2100.

Festivals   On Independence Day, **3 November**, practically the whole city seems to march in a parade lasting about 3½ hours, based in the old part of the city. Colourful, noisy, spectacular. Another parade takes place the following day. Carnival activities include a parade on Shrove

Tuesday and have become more elaborate and interesting than in former years. The munici-pality has also instituted an annual Christmas parade, in which the growing displacement by US-style Christmas traditions of the Latin American emphasis on the Nacimiento and the Three Kings is much in evidence.

Shopping

Duty-free imported luxuries of all kinds are an attraction at the *Zona Libre* in Colón (purchases sealed and delivered to Tocumen airport), but Panama City is a booming fashion and mer-chandise centre where bargains are not hard to find; anything from crystal to cashmere may often be cheaper than at point of origin.

The smartest shops are along C 50 (Av 4 Sur) in Campo Alegre, and Vía España in Bella Vista and El Cangrejo, but Avenida Central is cheaper and the best and most popular place for clothing (not great quality), hi-fi and photographic equipment, perfumes, curios, souve-nir T-shirts and Asian handicrafts. Colombian emeralds and pearls may also be purchased at reasonable prices from many establishments.

Traditional Panamanian *artesanía* includes *molas* (embroidered blouse fronts made by Kuna Indians, eg Emma Vence, T2618009); straw, leather and ceramic items; the *pollera* cir-cular dress, the *montuno* shirts (embroidered), the *chácara* (a popular bag or purse), the *chaquira* necklace made by Ngöbe-Buglé (Guaymí) Indians, and jewellery. Indigenous Darién carvings of jungle birds and animals from cocobolo wood or *tagua* nut make interest-ing souvenirs (from US$10 up to US$250 for the best, museum-quality pieces); *Colecciones*, Vía Italia opposite *Hotel Plaza Paitilla Inn*, has a wide selection. Plenty of straw articles avail-able, including baskets, bags, traditional masks and Panama hats (US$150 for the best qual-ity); try *Flory Salzman* (not cheap) on Vía Venetto near *El Panamá Hotel*, nearby *Inovación*, or *Indutípica*, Av A y C 8 Ote (opposite San José Church) for reproductions of pre-Columbian ceramics and jewellery, necklaces, Kuna *molas* (prices starting from US$2.50) from the Darién and Ngöbi-Buglé dresses from Bocas del Toro. The *Gran Morrison* department store chain (best-supplied is in Paitilla, also at *Hotel Continental* and on Vía España near C 51 Este) have good-quality handicraft sections, as well as postcards and books in English. Another good selection is at *Artesanías Nacionales* in Panamá Viejo, one of several Indian co-ops selling direct from open-air outlets, eg in the Canal Area at Balboa and along the road to Miraflores Locks at Corozal (every day if not raining). The Tourist Office has a full list of *artesanía* shops available, including those in the main hotels. *Reprosa*, Av Samuel Lewis y C 54 (T2690457) features a unique collection of pre-Columbian gold artefacts reproduced in sterling silver vermeil; David and Norma Dickson make excellent reproductions for sale (Panamá Guacas, T2666176). Of the various commercial centres, with banking, entertainment and parking facilities, the largest is *El Dorado Mall and Shopping Centre*, in the Tumba Muerto district at Av Ricardo Franco y C 71 (shops open Monday-Saturday 0900-1900, Sunday 1500-1900; cin-ema, plenty of restaurants and playgrounds). Similar are: *Plaza New York*, C 50, which has several travel agencies and a well-known disco; *Plaza California*, near *El Dorado*; and *Bal Harbour*, Vía Italia near Punta Paitilla (Monday-Saturday 0900-1900, Sunday 1100-1900); the *Balboa Mall* on Av Balboa is the newest but is closed on Sunday. The *Supermercado El Rey* on Vía España just east of *Hotel Continental*, at *El Dorado*, and other locations, *Super 99*, *Farmacias Arrocha*, *Casa de la Carne* (expensive) and *Machetazo*, also a department store (on Av Central, Calidonia) are said to be the best of the city's supermarkets. Army-Navy store on Avenida Central near Plaza 5 de Mayo sells camping and hiking equipment. Similarly *Army Force*, east end pedestrianized section of Av Central, west of Plaza 5 de Mayo.

The central market *Mercado San Felipe*, close to the docks and Palacio Presidencial, is the place for fresh produce (pigs, ducks, poultry, geese, etc) as well as parrots and pets. Most interesting part of the Market is the chaotic shopping area along C 13 and the waterfront (Terraplen), the best place to buy second-hand jungle and military supplies (eg powerful insect repellents, machetes, webbing, cooking equipment, etc) for a trek into the forested interior. The nearby fish market is clean and prices are the best in town. Another bazaar-like shopping area lines Vía España as it passes through Calidonia beyond the Plaza 5 de Mayo; as has been said, this *barrio* is for the adventurous by day and definitely dangerous at night.

Bargain hard as prices are extremely competitive

Bookshops *Librería Argosy*, Vía Argentina north of Vía España, El Cangrejo, T2235344, very good selection in English, Spanish and French, sell tickets for musical and cultural events. Recommended. *Gran Morrison* department stores around the city stock books, travel guides and many magazines in English; many Spanish and English magazines also at branches of *Farmacias Arrocha, Super 99* and *Gago* supermarkets/drugstores. *National University Bookshop*, on campus between Av Manuel Espinosa Batista and Vía Simón Bolívar, T2233155, for excellent range of specialized books on Panamá, national authors, social sciences and history, open Monday-Friday 0800-1600, closed weekends. Highly recommended. (The campus *Simón Bolívar Library* has extensive Panamanian material, only for matriculated students but visitors engaged in special research can obtain a temporary permit from the Director, Monday-Friday 0800-2000, Saturday 0900-1300.) Near the University is *La Garza* bookshop, Av José de Fábrega y C 47, good supply of Latin American literature (Spanish only). The *Smithsonian Tropical Research Institute Public Library*, Edif Topper, Av de los Mártires (opposite National Assembly), has best English-language scientific library in Panamá, open Monday-Friday 0800-1600. International edition of the *Miami Herald* printed locally on *La Prensa*'s presses, widely available at news-stands and hotels, as are leading US papers and magazines.

Photographic *Foto Enodi* and *Foto Decor*, Vía Porras, Kodak slides developed in a day. Many other places for developing and equipment. In some places you will get a free film. Camera repairs at *Relojería*, watch shop, on C Medusin, off Av Central in Calidonia.

Sports **Bathing**: Piscina Patria (the Olympic pool), take San Pedro or Juan Díaz bus, US$0.15. Piscina Adán Gordón, between Av Cuba and Av Justo Arosemena, near C 31, 0900-1200, 1300-1700 (except weekends to 1700 only). Admission US$0.50 (take identification), but beards and long hair frowned on (women must wear bathing caps); take a padlock for clothes locker. **Beaches**: many beaches within $1\frac{1}{2}$ hours' drive of the city. Fort Kobbe beach (US$7.50 admission, with vouchers given for drinks and hotdogs, bus from Canal Area bus station US$0.75, 30 minutes) and Naos beach (US$1, Amador bus from same station, US$0.30, then 2 kilometre walk along Causeway) have been recommended. Veracruz beach is not recommended as it is both dirty and dangerous (all are dangerous at night). **Cockfights**: at the *Club Gallístico*, Vía España near junction with Vía Cincuentenario, T2215652, most Sundays, same bus as for race track, but get out at crossing with C 150. **Golf**: *Panama Golf Club*, T2667777; *Coronado Beach Golf Club* (open to tourists who get guest cards at Coronado office on C 50). Similarly at *Fort Amador Golf Club* tourists can play, green fees and rented clubs US$20 for the day. A spectacular view of the canal and the city. **Horse races**: (pari-mutuel betting) are held Saturday, Sunday and holidays at the Presidente Remón track (bus to Juan Díaz, entry from US$0.50-2.50).

Transport

Local **Bus**: the traditional small buses known as *chivas*, consisting of locally made wooden bodies grafted onto truck chassis, have all but disappeared, though occasionally may be seen on the street. Most buses in urban areas are second-hand US school buses painted in fanciful designs, but otherwise in poor condition (the small buses going into Balboa are at least 40 years old); blaring radios have recently been prohibited. During a downpour, windows are slammed shut and the temperature inside rises even further. Most out-bound (east) buses travel along Avenida Perú, through Bella Vista, before fanning out to their various destinations. In-bound (west) buses travel along Vía España and Av Central through the Calidonia shopping district. Basic fare US$0.15, usually paid to the driver upon descending; if there is a fare box, deposit upon entering. To stop at the next authorized stop, call out '*parada*' to the driver.

Car rental: at the airport (**Hertz**, T2384081; **Avis**, T2384069; **National**, T2384144; also **International**, T2384404; **Budget** and **Dollar**). Other offices in El Cangrejo: **Avis**, Vía Venetto, T2640722; **International**, Vía Venetto, T2644540; **Barriga**, Edif Wonaga 1 B, Calle D, T2690221; **Gold**, C 55, T2641711; **Hertz**, *Hotel Marriott*, T2264077 ext 6202, C 50, T2636966, El Cangrejo T2636511; **Budget**, T2638777; **Discount**, T2236111; **Dollar**, T2697555. **Bicycles**: *Almacén The Bike*, C 50 opposite Telemetro, good selection of cycle parts.

Taxis: service generally good, but can be scarce during peak hours; voluntary sharing is common, but not recommended after dark. Most newer taxis have a/c, look for closed windows when hailing. If taxi already has a passenger, the driver will ask your destination to see if it coincides with the other passenger's. If you do not wish to share, waggle your index finger or say "No, gracias". If you are in a taxi and the driver stops for additional passengers, you may refuse politely. Zone system: US$0.75 for 1 passenger within 1 zone, US$0.25 for each additional zone. Additional passengers US$0.25 each regardless of zones; sharing passengers each pay full fare. Panamanians rarely tip, but foreigners should add US$0.25 or US$0.50 to the fare. Hourly hire, recommended for touring dubious areas, US$7 per hour, US$8 with a/c. Radio taxis summoned by telephone highly recommended. Listed in yellow pages under 'Taxis'. Add US$0.40 to fare for pick-up. Taxis earn enough to provide adequate vehicles; feel free to reject unsavoury-looking, battered, old cars. 'Tourist taxis' at major hotels (aged, large American cars with 'SET' number plates) have a separate rate structure: they are more expensive than those you can flag down on the street. Agree on fares in advance, or arrange through the hotel *conserje*.

Traffic system: several major downtown arteries become 1-way during weekday rush hours, eg Av 4 Sur/C 50, 1-way heading west 0600-0900, east 1600-1900. The Puente de las Américas can be used only to go into or out of town depending on time and day, mostly weekends; these directions are not always clearly signed.

Air Tocumen (airport code PTY), 27 kilometres. Taxi fares about US$20, but if you want to share, drivers will try to find other passengers. A full cab should be US$8 per person. A regular taxi charges US$12 to or from Panama City to the airport; on arrival, leave the terminal area and walk 300 metres to the traffic circle where there is a bus shelter, safe but hot during the day. For about US$3 (should only be US$1.20) driver takes you by Panamá Viejo, just off the main airport road. Buses to airport are marked 'España-Tocumen', 1 hour, US$0.35, but if going at a busy time, eg in the morning rush hour, allow 90 minutes to 3 hours. From airport to city, walk out of the terminal and across the main road to the bus shelter. There is a 24-hour left-luggage office near the Budget car rental desk for US$1 per article per day (worth it, since theft in the departure lounge is common). The tourist office at the airport remains open to meet late flight arrivals. There are duty-free shops at the airport with a wide selection and good prices. Most facilities are found in upper level departure area (Banco Nacional de Panamá, Cable & Wireless office for international phone, fax and internet access); car rental is downstairs at arrivals.

Long distance

The domestic airport has been moved from Paitilla to the former US air force base, Albrook Field, and is now called the Marcos A Gelabert airport. Charter flights go to many Darién outposts. Sample hourly rates for private hire: Twin Otter 20 passenger, US$630; Rodolfo Causadias of Transpasa (T2260842) is an experienced pilot for photographic work. There is also an active Aero-Club.

Trains Station on Carretera Gaillard. The only passenger service is on Sunday as far as Summit or Colón. For information, T2527720.

Intercity buses A new central bus terminal (*piquera*) built in El Chorrillo was boycotted by operators and passengers who considered the neighbourhood dangerous. A temporary terminal has opened in Curundú, opposite Inrenare office. Unfortunately there are no city buses and the area is unsafe so a taxi is essential. Most long-distance buses (except for Chiriquí and Colón) leave from here. A new bus terminal was being built in 1999, due for completion end-year, in Albrook, near the domestic airport.

Unlike urban versions, most long-distance buses are fairly modern and in good condition, usually a/c on long hauls. Ask if a/c on next bus out is functioning: if not, you may choose to wait for the 1 after. Buses going west to the Interior tend to be well booked up, so make sure you reserve in advance: for the midnight express to David, early on the day of departure (only).

Buses to **David** leave *piquera* at west end of Av Balboa hourly 0700-1300, then 1½ hourly till 1900, US$10.60. Express at 2400 (5½-6 hours), 15-minute rest stop at Santiago, fare US$15. Buses on this route have improved since the start-up of a new service from Panama

City to David and the frontier with Costa Rica, Padafront, C 33 just north of Av Justo Arosemena. T2274210, cost to frontier US$12, 7-8 hours, to David US$10.60, 6-7 hours, to La Concepción US$11. 10 departures daily with a 30-minute meal stop in Santiago or Aguadulce; more frequent departures at peak weekends; express, 5-6 hours, US$5 extra, at 2300, 2400. Best to purchase tickets the night before.

Buses to **Colón** leave from Avenida Perú, C 30, near *Hotel Veracruz*, opposite *Hotel Soloy*; express buses every 20 minutes 0500-1900, less frequent at weekends, US$1.75-2.25, under 2 hours.

Orange buses to all **Canal Area** destinations (Balboa, Miraflores, Paraíso, Kobbe, etc) leave from SACA terminal near Plaza 5 de Mayo; from the Plaza, walk past the National Assembly tower and turn left.

International buses: buses going north to Central America tend to be well booked up, so make sure you reserve a seat in advance and never later than the night before departure. Ticabus, with office by *Hotel Ideal*, C 17 Ote, T262-2084/6275, run a/c buses to **San José**, daily 1000, arrives 0400, US$20 1-way (but check times and prices which are for ever changing); also to **Managua** daily, US$35; this service now runs as far as **Guatemala City**, US$91 (4 days, overnight in Managua and El Salvador, US$75), leaves 1100. A/c rarely works. (Tickets are refundable; they pay on the same day, minus 15 percent.) Panaline to San José from *Hotel Internacional* in the Plaza 5 de Mayo leaves daily at 1300. The buses have a/c, TV/videos and drinks and are reported more comfortable than Ticabus, US$22. Whichever route you choose (international bus, Padafront Panama City-Paso Canaos then change to Tracopa for San José, or Panama City-David, David-frontier, then change to Costa Rican buses), it should be possible to go between the 2 capitals in under 24 hours. Ticabus and Panaline do not stop in David but take passengers at the border at 1800 and 1900 respectively.

Directory

Airline offices *Copa*, Av Justo Arosemena y C 39, T2275000, F2271952 for reservations, airport T2384053. *Aeroperlas*, Paitilla Airport, T2694555, F2694564. *Parsa*, Paitilla Airport, T2263803, F2263422. *Ansa*, Paitilla Airport, T2267891, F2264070. *Nica*, Vía España y C 52, Ed Ogawa, T2644144, F2694855. *Aviateca*, Suite Montecarlo p 6, T2232992, F2232993. *Lacsa*, Av Justo Arosemena 31-44, T2250193 for reservations, airport T2384116. *Taca*, Calle B, Suites Montecarlo, p 6, El Cangrejo, T269-6214/6066 for reservations, airport T2384015. *SAM*, Calle MM Icaza No 12, Edif Grobman, T2691222 for reservations, airport T2384096. *Avianca*, T2235225. *Avensa*, Calle MM Icaza, T2649906, F2639022. *American*, C 50, Plaza New York, T2696022 for reservations, airport T2384140, F2690830. *British Airways* at Lacsa (above). *Continental*, Av Balboa y Av 4, Ed No 17, T2639177. *United*, T2698555. *Iberia*, Av Balboa y C 45, T2273671 reservations, airport T2384163, F2272070. *KLM*, Urb Obarrio y C 53E, T2233747 for reservations, airport T2384025, F2646358. *Lufthansa*, Agencias Continental, C 50, Ed Fidanque, p 1, T2691549, F2638641. *Cubana*, T2272122. *Aerolíneas Argentinas*, T2693815. *LAB*, T2636433. *LanChile*, T2260133. *Varig*, Calle MM Icaza, T2647666 for reservations, airport T2384501, F2638179. *AeroPerú*, T2696970.

Banks See also **Money** in **Essentials**. The *Chase Manhattan Bank* (US$0.65 commission on each TC), Visa advances. *Citibank* has plenty of ATMs for cash withdrawals for its own debit or credit cardholders, also Visa cash advances. *Lloyds Bank*, C Aquilino de la Guardia y C 48, Bella Vista, T2636277, 2638693 for foreign exchange, offers good rates for sterling (the only bank which will change sterling cash, and only if its sterling limit has not been exhausted). *Bank of America*, Av José de la Cruz Herrera, C 53 Este, no commission on own TCs, US$0.10 tax. Thomas Cook TCs exchangeable at *Banco Sudameris* and *Algemene Bank Nederland*. Deutschmarks exchanged at *Deutsch-Südamerikanische Bank*. Panamanian banks' hours vary, but many open 0800-1500 Mon-Fri, 0800-1200 Sat. Try to avoid 15th and last working day of the month, paydays. *Banco General* takes American Express, Bank of America and Thomas Cook TCs. Also *Banco del Istmo*, C 50, open Mon-Fri 0800-1530, Sat 0900-1200, changes TCs. You can buy Amex TCs at *Banco Mercantil del Istmo* on Vía España (they also give cash advances on Mastercard). *American Express*, C 50 y 59, Mon-Fri 0830-1600, does not exchange TCs, clients' mail only. International Service Center, T001-800-1110006. ATMs for withdrawals from foreign bank accounts (as opposed to advances on a credit card), using bank cards with Visa symbol: *Banco General* at Av Central y 4 Sur (Balboa), and at *Banco Continental* near hotel of same name. Visa T2640988; Mastercard T2635221; Diners T2638195. Possible to change South American currencies (poor rates) at

Panacambios, ground floor, Plaza Regency, behind *Adam's Store*, Vía España, near the Banco Nacional de Panamá and opposite *Hotel Riande Continental* (it also has postage stamps for collectors).

Communications Post Office: there is no postal delivery in Panama. Recipients either have a post office box (*apartado*), or receive mail via General Delivery/Poste Restante (*Entrega General*). The new main post office is at the west end of Av Balboa at Av B, opposite the Mercado de Mariscos (new seafood market), open Mon-Fri 0700-1745, Sat 0700-1645; 'Poste Restante' items held for a month. Official name and zone must be included in the address: Main Post Office = 'Zona 1, Central, Av Balboa opposite Mercado de Mariscos'; C 30 East/Av Balboa = 'Zona 5, La Exposición'; El Dorado Shopping Centre, Tumba Muerto = 'Zona 6A, El Dorado'; Vía España, Bella Vista (in front of Piex store) = 'Zona 7, Bella Vista'. Parcels sent 'poste restante' are delivered either to Encomiendas Postales Transístmicas at the El Dorado Centro Comercial or the main Post Office if there is no duty to pay on the goods; if not they are delivered to the nearest post office. Post Office operates a courier system called EMS to most Central and South American countries, Europe, US and some Asian countries. Packages up to 20 kg: 2 to 3 days to USA (500g documents to Miami US$13); 3 to 4 days Europe US$20; Asia US$25. Also private courier services, eg *United Parcel Services*, Edif Fina, C 49, El Cangrejo, ½ kg to London or Paris, 3-4 days, US$30; *Jet Express* (*Federal Express*), Edif Helga, Vía España y Av 4 Sur/C 50, ½ kg to Miami, 2 days, US$19. Panamá issues highly-regarded stamps; foreigners may open a 'philatelic account' and order stamps, 1st-day covers, commemorative issues, etc, provided a minimum US$20 in account: Dirección de Filatelía, Dirección de Correos y Telégrafos, Apdo 3421, Panamá 1 (Vía España, Calidonia, opposite Don Bosco Church).

Telecommunications: Cable & Wireless has its main office in Vía España, on the ground floor of Banco Nacional building. It offers excellent but expensive international telephone, telex, fax and modem (use Bell 212A type) facilities. Collect calls to 21 countries, dial 106. Public payphones take 5, 10 and sometimes 25 cent coins. Phone cards are available in denominations of US$3, 5, 10, 20 and US$50, for local, national and international calls. For cost of international calls, see **Essentials**. Local calls in Panama City, US$0.10 per 3 mins, US$0.05 for each additional min; within the country, US$0.15 per min.

Email: plushest is *Internet Café*, C 76 y Av 5 B South (C quinta-B Sur), diagonally opposite *Hotel Caesar Park*, San Francisco, T2701052/3, cruiser@inter-cafe.com, open Tues-Sat 1130-2300, Sun 1300-2300, 12 stations US$3 per hr until 1700, then US$4 (US$10 monthly rate), food and bar; more central is *Cibercafé*, C Eusebio A Morales, 2 doors west of Vía Venetto, El Cangrejo, T2651257, ciber2@sinfo.net, Mon-Fri 1000-2200, Sat till 2230, 9 stations US$3 per hr, light food, no bar; in Los Tucanos Shopping Center, Blvd El Dorado, *CyberCentro Panamá*, T2363290, ccp@mail.pty.com, or ccp@mail.ccp.pty.com, www.ccp.pty.com, Mon-Thur 1000-2200, Fri-Sat till 2300, Sun 1200-2000, last Sat of month 'all-night surfing', 9 stations, no smoking, US$4 per hr, 30 mins minimum, 'frequent surfer' plan. Ciber Café Morales y Torre de Alba US$2.50 per hr.

Cultural centres *Alianza Francesa*, C 49, Bellavista, T2642737, film each Wed at 2000.

Embassies & consulates *Costa Rican*, C Gilberto Ortega 7, Edif Miramar, T2642980 (open 0800-1330). *Nicaraguan*, Av Federico Boyd y C 50, T2230981 (0900-1300, 1500-1800). *Salvadorean*, Vía España, Edif Citibank, p 4, T2233020 (0900-1300). *Guatemalan*, C Abel Bravo y C 57, Bella Vista, Edif Torre Cancún, Apt 14A, T2693475, F2231922, 0800-1300. *Honduran*, Av Justo Arosemena y C 31, Edif Tapia, p 2, T2258200 (0900-1400). *Mexican*, Edif Bank of America, p 5, C 50 y 53, T2635021 (0830-1300). *Venezuelan*, Edif Banco Unión, Av Samuel Lewis, T2691014 (0830-1230), visa takes 24 hrs. *Colombian*, MM Icaza 12, Edif Grobman, p 6, PO Box 4407 (Zona 5), T2649266, open 0800-1300, the *Ecuadorean* embassy is housed in the same building, T2642654. *Chilean* C Elvira Mendez y Vía España, T2238333.

US, Av Balboa y 40, Edif Macondo, p 3, T2271777, F2271964, PO Box 6959 (Zona 5) (0800-1700). Consulate in new Miramar building, C 39 y Av Balboa, ground floor (hotel and restaurant in same building). *Canadian*, Calle MM Icaza, Edif Aeroperú, p 5, T2647014 (0800-1100). *British*, Torre Swiss Bank, C 53, Zona 1, T2690866, F507-2690866, Apdo 889 (0800-1200). *French*, Plaza Francia, T2287835 (0830-1230). *German*, Edif Bank of America, C 50 y 53, T2637733 (0900-1200). *Netherlands*, Altos de Algemene Bank, Calle MM Icaza, 4, T2647257 (0830-1300, 1400-1630). *Swedish*, Vía José Agustín Arango y Juan Díaz, T2335883 (0900-1200, 1400-1600). *Swiss*, Av Samuel Lewis y C Gerardo Ortega, Edif Banco Central Cancellería, p 4, T2649731, PO Box 499 (Zona 9A), open 0845-1145. *Italian*, C 1, Parque Lefevre 42, T2263111, open 0900-1200. *Danish*, C Ricardo Arias, Edif Ritz Plaza, p 2, T2635872, open 0800-1200, 1330-1630. *Spanish*, Plaza Porras, entre Av Cuba y Av Perú, C 33A, T2275122 (0900-1300). *Norwegian*, Av Justo Arosemena y C 35, T2258217 (0900-1300, 1400-1630). *Finnish*, Carretera Transístmica, C 85, T2363000. *Japanese*, C 50 y 61, Edif Don Camilo, T2636155 (0830-1200, 1400-1700). *Israeli Embassy*, Edif Grobman, Calle MM Icaza, p 5, PO Box 6357, T264-8022/8257.

Hospitals & medical services Dentist: Dr Daniel Wong, *Clínica Dental Marbella*, Edif Alfil (ground floor), near Centro Comercial Marbella, T2638998. Dr D Lindo, T2238383, very good but fix price before treatment. *Balboa Dental Clinic*, El Prado, Balboa, T2280338, good, fair price. **Hospitals:** the *US Gorgas Army Community Hospital* (see map) has closed and US medical facilities have moved to the Howard Air Force Base, across the Puente de Las Américas. The private clinics charge high prices; normally visitors are treated at either the *Clínica San Fernando* (T2292004) or the *Clínica Paitilla* (T2696060), both have hospital annexes. For inoculations buy vaccine at a chemist, who will recommend a clinic; plenty in La Exposición around Parque Belisario Porras.

Laundry *Lavamático Lavarápido*, C 7 Central No 7-45, ½ block from Plaza Independencia, Mon-Sat 0800-2000, Sun 0900-1400, US$0.75 with hot water, US$0.60 cold, soap and drying extra. Many around Plaza Catedral; wash and dry US$2.

Places of worship Services in English at *St John's Episcopalian*, Avs 12 de Octubre y La Paz, Betania, Sun 0700. *Baptist*, C Balboa 914, La Boca, Sun 1100 and 1900. *Methodist*, Av Central y C 16 Este, Sun 0900. *Kol Shearith Israel Synagogue*, Av Cuba y C 36, services Fri 2000, Sat 1100. *Baha'i Temple*, Mile 8 on Transístmica Highway (Ojo de Agua district), Baha'i HQ for all of Latin America, modern, white domed, worth seeing for its architecture (open daily 1000-1800, Sun service 1000), taxi round trip for US$8 with an hour to see the temple can be arranged.

Tour companies & travel agents *Viajes Panamá SA*, C 52, Av Federico Boyd, Edif Costa del Sol, T2230644 or 2230630, English spoken. *Viajes Riande*, east side of *Hotel Riande Continental*, C Ricardo Arias, T2694569, English spoken, very helpful. *Tropic Tours*, Edif Comosa near *El Panamá Hotel*, well organized trips, multilingual. *Eco-Tours de Panamá*, Ricardo Arias 7 (near *Hotel Continental*), T2633077, F2633089, PO Box 465, 0800-1700 Mon-Sat, a wide variety of trips, from relaxing cultural excursions to the San Blas islands, to high altitude forest hikes, bilingual guides. Highly recommended. *Viajes Airemar*, C 52 y Ricardo Arias 21, T223-5395/5336. Highly recommended for flights to South American destinations. *Viajes Marsal*, C 50 y Manuel M Icaza, near Banco Iberoamericano, T223-5321/5447/9851, helpful, efficient, English spoken. *5 Continentes*, Av Principal La Alameda, Edif Plaza San Marcos, T2608447/9, helpful with shipping a car. Recommended. *Rapid Travel*, C 53, El Cangrejo, Edif Las Margaritas, T2646638, F2646371. *Chadwick's* and *Starlite*, see page 1190. *Sun Line Tours*, C Eusebio A Morales, Edif Estela, local 2, El Cangrejo, Apdo Postal 2323, Zona 9A, Panama, T2696620/2638451, F2237609, for Panama Canal Transits (US$99, recommended) and trips to Contadora. *Viajes Arco Iris*, Av Justo Arosemena y C 45, Bella Vista, Edif Dollar, T2273318, F2273386, for full range of local tours. *Viajes Ira Clase*, at *Hotel Costa del Sol*, Vía Espana y Federico Boyd, tours and excursions. *Continental SA*, Av 7 y Vía España, T2635531, in *Riande Continental* building, friendly, good. Mrs Vicky Turner (American) of *Panamá Adentro* (Inside Panama) conducts city, beach tours for 1-3 people, half-day US$50, full-day US$100, in her own car, or up to 6 people in a/c minibus, full-day US$200, T2648855.

Tourist office Tourist Bureau: information office of the *Instituto Panameño de Turismo (IPAT)*, in the Atlapa Convention Centre, Vía Israel opposite *Hotel Caesar Park*, Apdo 4421, Panamá 5. Office open 0900 to 1600; issues good list of hotels, *pensiones*, motels and restaurants, and issues a free *Focus on Panama* guide (available at all major hotels, and airport); T226-7000/2861, F2262544, ask for 'información', helpful, English spoken. *Getting to Know Panama*, by Michèle Labrut, published by Focus Publications (Apdo 6-3287, El Dorado, Panamá 6A, RP, F2250466, US$12), has been recommended as very informative. Best **maps** (based on US government topographic maps) from *Instituto Geográfico Nacional Tommy Guardia (IGNTG)*, on Vía Simón Bolívar, opposite the National University (footbridge nearby, fortunately), take Transístmica or Tumba Muerto bus: physical map of the country in 2 sheets, US$4 each; Panama City map in many sheets, US$4 per sheet (travellers will only need 3 or so). At the back of the Panama Canal Commission telephone books are good maps of the Canal Area, Panama City and Colón.

Useful addresses Conservation: Asociación Nacional de Conservación de la Naturaleza (ANCON), C Alberto Navarro, El Cangrejo (Apdo 1387, Panamá 1), T2648100, F2641836 for comprehensive information on the country's natural attractions and environmental matters. **Customs:** for renewal of permits and obtaining exit papers for vehicles at Paitilla airport. **Immigration:** Migración y Naturalización, Av Cuba (2 Sur) y C 29, T2258925; visa extensions and exit permits issued Mon-Fri 0800-1530. **Ministerio de Hacienda y Tesoro:** Av Perú/C 36, T2274879, for tax compliance certificate (*paz y salvo*) required for exit visa (*permiso de salida*).

Nearby excursions
Panamá Viejo

A visit is recommended to the ruins of Panamá Viejo, six and a half kilometres northeast along the coast.

A wander among the ruins still gives an idea of the site's former glory, although many of the structures have been worn by time, fungus and the sea. The narrow King's Bridge (1620) at the north end of the town's limits is a good starting point; it marked the beginning of the three trails across the Isthmus and took seven years to build. Walking south brings the visitor to Convento de San José, where the Golden Altar originally stood (see above, Panama City); it was spared by the great fire that swept the town during Morgan's attack (which side started it is still debated). Several blocks further south is the main Plaza, where the square stone tower of the Cathedral (1535, 1580) is a prominent feature. In the immediate vicinity are the Cabildo, with imposing arches and columns, the remnants of Convento de Santo Domingo, the Bishop's Residence, and the Slave Market (or House of the Genovese), whose gaol-like structure was the hub of the American slave trade; there were about 4,000 African slaves in 1610, valued at about 300 pesos apiece! Beyond the plazas to the south, on a rocky eminence overlooking the bay, stand the Royal Houses, the administrative stronghold including the Quartermaster's House, the Court and Chancellery, the Real Audiencia and the Governor's Residence.

Further west along the Pacific strand are the dungeons, kitchens and meat market (now almost obliterated by the sea); a store and refreshment stands cluster here on the south side of the plaza, and handicrafts from the Darién are sold along the beach. Across Calle de la Carrera stands another great complex of religious convents: La Concepción (1598) and the Compañía de Jesús (1621). These too were outside the area destroyed by the 1671 fire but are today little more than rubble. Only a wall remains of the Franciscan Hospital de San Juan de Dios, once a huge structure encompassing wards, courtyards and a church. Another block west can be seen part of the Convento de San Francisco and its gardens, facing the rocky beach. 100 metres west is the beautiful Convento de La Merced, where Pizarro, Almagro and their men attended Mass on the morning they sailed on their final and momentous expedition to Perú; Morgan stored his plunder here until it could be counted, divided up and sent back to the Atlantic side. At the western limit of Panamá Viejo stands La Navidad Fort (1658). Its purpose was merely to defend the Matadero (Slaughterhouse) Bridge across the Río Agarroba but its 50-man garrison and half-dozen cannon were no match for the determined force of privateers; the bridge is also known as Morgan's Bridge because it was here that the attack began.

The whole area (unfenced, free entry) is attractively landscaped, with plenty of benches to rest on, and floodlit at night. Late afternoon when the sun is low is an especially nice time to visit, although at least two hours should be allowed to appreciate the site fully. The main ruins are police patrolled and reasonably safe. Take care, though, between the King's Bridge and the ruins; if arriving at this north entrance by taxi, it is prudent to pause at the bridge then continue in the taxi the one kilometre to San José, where the main ruins begin. Dame Margot Fonteyn, the ballerina, is buried alongside her husband Roberto Arías Guardia in the Jardín de la Paz cemetery behind Panamá Viejo. IPAT has a handicrafts store (*Artesanía Nacional*) at the ruins, although prices are rather expensive. It also organizes free folklore events and local dance displays on six Saturdays in the dry season (*verano*), which are worth seeing. The Tourist Office in Panama City (T2267000) has full schedules and can supply professional guides if required. Taxi from the centre, US$1.80; buses from Vía España or Avenida Balboa, US$0.20. Panamá Viejo also makes a good excursion for passengers with time to kill at nearby Tocumen Airport; taxis can be as much as US$5 but still reasonable, especially if this is all one will have the chance to see of

☞ *Henry Morgan and the sack of 'Golden Panama'*

Panamá Viejo was the original site of Panama City, founded by Pedro Arias de Avila (often called 'Pedrarias') on 15 August 1519 as a storage point for Peruvian gold until it could be loaded onto mules and transported across the Isthmus, initially to Venta de Cruces and Fort San Lorenzo, later along the Camino Real to Nombre de Dios and Portobelo for shipment to Spain. The town became the centre of the New World, gold mines in Veraguas and Darién contributed two tons of gold a year, and many expeditions to North, Central and South America were launched from here. Panamá was recognized as a town in 1521 and granted a coat of arms. By 1570 a quarter of its 500 residents were extremely wealthy, and the town could boast a grand cathedral, a dozen religious institutions, a hospital, lavish public buildings, huge warehouses and a thriving slave market. No

enemy had ever penetrated as far as 'Golden Panama', not even Francis Drake, so the shock was all the greater when Henry Morgan and his 1,200 men, after a gruelling nine-day overland trek from San Lorenzo, fell upon the town on 28 January 1671 and captured it after a three-hour battle. They took 600 prisoners for ransom, looted for three weeks and took away a fortune in gold, silver and gemstones valued at £70,000, which required 195 mules to transport it back to the Caribbean. (With this Morgan bought respectability: he was knighted and appointed Governor of Jamaica, where he died in 1688.) After the attack, the population was transferred to the present-day Casco Viejo section of Panama City, which could be enclosed by walls and defended on both landward and seaward sides.

Panamá. Alternatively, take any bus marked Vía España, get off at Vía Cincuentenario, then take a bus to Panamá Viejo, total cost US$0.45.

Balboa

Balboa Yacht Club has a notice board with cheap crewing (no experience necessary) trips to Ecuador and the Galapagos. Usual price is US$5 a day for food; seven days' journey to Ecuador.

Colur map 6, grid A2

Balboa docks are about three and a quarter kilometres from Panama City, an average of 10 minutes by taxi.

Balboa stands attractively between the Canal quays and Ancón Hill, which lies between it and Panama City. It has been described as an efficient, planned, sterilized town, a typical American answer to the wilfulness and riot of the tropics.

The Canal administration building (with fine murals on the ground floor) and a few official residences are on Balboa Heights. At the foot of Balboa Heights is Balboa, with a small park, a reflecting pool and marble shaft commemorating Goethals, and a long parkway flanked with royal palms known as the Prado. At its eastern end is a theatre, a service centre building, post office and bank. Farther along Balboa Road is a large YMCA (no lodging).

Directory **Banks** *Citibank. Chase Manhattan Bank.* **Communications** Post Office: Av Balboa and El Prado. Telecommunications: INTEL; Tropical Radio & Telegraph Co Public Telex booth. **Tour companies & travel agents** *Chadwick's*, in YMCA building, T2722741/2286329. *Starlite Travel*, in former Balboa railway station opposite Canal Administration building, T2326401, T2326448, both excellent, English spoken.

Ancón

Ancón curves round the hill of the same name north and east and merges into Panama City. It has picturesque views of the palm-fringed shore. The name has also been applied to the district, including the village of Balboa, created when the area reverted to Panama.

The following walk takes in the sights of Ancón: walk to the top of the hill in the morning for views of the city, Balboa and the Canal (conveniences and water fountain at the top – you may have to climb part of the radio tower to see anything); the entrance is on Avenida de los Mártires (formerly Avenida de Julio and briefly

Avenida Presidente Kennedy). Return to Avenida de los Mártires and take a clockwise route around the hill, bearing right onto Balboa Road (Avenida Estado de Jamaica), passing Chase Manhattan and Citibank, until you reach Stevens Circle where Kuna Indians sell *molas*. Here are the Post Office and a cafetería. Then walk down the Prado lined with royal palms to the Goethals Memorial and up the steps to the Administration Building to see the recently-restored murals of the Construction of the Canal (entrance free, identity must be shown to the guards). Follow Heights Road until it becomes Gorgas Road. You will pass the headquarters of the Smithsonian Tropical Research Institute (where applications to visit Barro Colorado Island are made) and, among trees and flowers, the former Gorgas Army Community Hospital. Gorgas Road leads back to Avenida de los Mártires, but look out for the sign to the **Museo de Arte Contemporáneo** (see **Museums** above), before Avenida de los Mártires. Two libraries are open to the public: that of the Smithsonian Tropical Research Institute in the Canal Area, opposite Plaza 5 de Mayo, and that of the Panama Canal College, underneath the Bridge of the Americas. **NB** Take care on Ancón Hill, robberies sometimes occur.

At the foot of Ancón Hill the Instituto Nacional stands on the four-lane Avenida de los Mártires.

Fuerte Amador

Before the Puente de las Américas is a long peninsula into the Pacific on which is Fuerte Amador, formerly the HQ of the Panamanian Defence Force, seized by US forces in 1989 and returned to Panama in 1994. Beyond Fuerte Amador are the formerly fortified islands of Naos, Perico and Flamenco, linked by the four kilometre causeway (**Calzada Amador**) built of rubble excavated from the Canal. To cross the causeway costs US$0.25. There are many interesting buildings in this area bearing the marks of the conflict and some attractive lawns and parkland. The Calzada is used by joggers and cyclists (bikes for hire at the causeway entrance, US$1.50-2 per hour); it has fine views of the Puente de las Américas and ships lined up to enter the Canal. *Mi Ranchito*, the charming, simple, outdoor restaurant, T2284909, at the far end of the Calzada, is highly recommended in the evening for seeing the skyline and passing ships, as well as good traditional food and drink (cheap). There are small charges for entry and for swimming at Solidaridad beach on Naos (crowded weekends but not recommended – water polluted). Here there is a small marine park with local marine life displayed. At Punta Culebra on Naos is the new **Marine Exhibition Center** of the Smithsonian Tropical Research Institute, interesting aquaria and exhibitions on marine fauna. Open Tuesday-Friday 1300-1700, Saturday-Sunday 1000-1700, T2276022 ext 2366. There are two small restaurants on the next island, Perico, and the promise (with luck) of a cold beer. Flamenco, the last of the islands, is headquarters for the National Maritime Service and is closed to the public. The causeway and islands have been declared a 'tourism zone'.

Taboga Island

There is a launch service to Taboga Island, about 20 kilometres offshore. The island is a favourite year-round resort; its pineapples and mangoes have a high reputation and its church is one of the oldest in the western hemisphere (admission to beach at *Hotel Taboga*, US$6, redeemable in 'funny money' to buy food and drink, good swimming, covered picnic huts extra). There are other good places to swim around the island, but the south side of the island is rocky and sharks regularly visit.

The trip out to Taboga is very interesting, passing the naval installations at the Pacific end of the Canal, the great bridge linking the Americas, tuna boats and shrimp fishers in for supplies, visiting yachts from all over the world at the Balboa Yacht Club, and the Calzada Amador. Part of the route follows the channel of the Canal, with its busy traffic. Taboga itself, with a promontory rising to 488 metres, is

Panama

carpeted with flowers at certain seasons. There are few cars in the meandering, helter-skelter streets, and only one footpath as a road.

The first Spanish settlement was in 1515, two years after Balboa's discovery of the Pacific. It was from here that Pizarro set out for Peru in 1524. For two centuries it was a stronghold of the pirates who preyed on the traffic to Panama. Because it has a deep-water, sheltered anchorage, it was during colonial times the terminal point for ships coming up the west coast of South America. El Morro, at low tide joined to Taboga, is at high tide an island; it was once owned by the Pacific Steam Navigation Company, whose ships sailed from there. For a fine view, walk through the town and up to the top of Cerro Turco, the hill with a cross at the summit (285 metres), to the right of the radar station (there is a shady short cut, ask locals). When surveying the view, don't miss the pelican rookery on the back side of the island; it is an easy walk down. Further south is Cerro Vigía (307 metres), the highest point, a two-hour hike from the central plaza; wear ankle boots and take mosquito repellent. Another trail runs west along the north coast, about one hour, pleasant beaches. The southern coast of Taboga and all of neighbouring Isla Uraba are wildlife reserves; permit from Inrenare required, office near *Hotel Taboga*. All items are expensive on the island. Bring cash: there is no bank on the island.

Sleeping **A** *Taboga*, T2502122, F2230116, Apdo 550357, Paitilla, Panamá, 300 metres east of wharf, a/c, TV, restaurant, café, beach, tropical birds. **C** *Chu*, on main St, 200 metres left of wharf, T2502036, wooden colonial style, thin walls, shared bath, beautiful views, own beach, terrace restaurant serving traditional fish and chicken dishes. You may be able to find locals to stay with, ask around.

Transport **Boats** Taboga is reached in 1-1½ hours from Pier 17-18 in Balboa (check the times in advance – T2284348 office, or 2325395 pier); taxi Bella Vista-Pier 18, US$3-4 per person. There are 2 boats daily during the week (0830 and 1500 or 1700 Thursday) and 3 boats on Saturday, Sunday and holidays (0830, 1130 and 1600). Return boats at 1000 and 1630 or 1830 - Thursday; 1000, 1430 and 1700 at weekends. From November to January there are 3 boats daily. Return fare US$7. You can charter a boat for US$120 per day including fishing. Ask for Sam at the Balboa Yacht Club.

Pearl Islands

Colour map 6, grid A2

It is a longer trip by launch, some 75 kilometres, to the **Pearl Islands**, visited mostly by sea anglers for the Pacific mackerel, red snapper, corvina, sailfish, marlin, and other species which teem in the waters around. High mountains rise from the sea, but there is a little fishing village on a shelf of land at the water's edge. There was much pearl fishing in colonial days. **Contadora**, one of the smallest Pearl Islands, has become quite famous since its name became associated with a Central American peace initiative. It was also where the Shah of Iran was exiled, in a house called Puntalara, after the Iranian Revolution. Contadora is popular with Canadian, Spanish and Italian holidaymakers and is becoming crowded, built up and consequently not as peaceful as it once was. Lack of drinking water is now harming the tourist development. Beautiful beaches with crystal-clear water. Good skin-diving and sailing, three-hour boat trip. Beware the sharks.

Sleeping & Contadora has *Hotel de Villas*, T2504030, and the very luxurious chalet complex
eating **L** *Contadora Resort and Casino*, same ownership as *El Panamá*, nice location on beach, but reported run down, T2504033, F2504000, in Panama City, T2695966, F2694721. *Gallo Nero*, run by German couple, Gerald and Sabine, restaurant with good seafood especially lobster, pizza and pasta, by runway, reasonable prices. *Michael's*, opposite *Gallo Nero*, good pizzas, ice cream. *Fonda Sagitario*, nearby, café, cheap; also a supermarket and a duty free shop.

Air Return air ticket to **Contadora** from Paitilla, US$45 by Aeroperlas, T2694555 (extra flights at weekends, 15 minutes, crowded). Paitilla-**San Miguel**, US$35 return, twice weekly. Mountain bike hire US$5 per hour, by entrance to *Caesar Park*.

Tour companies & travel agents 1-day trip to Contadora on Sun, US$50 per person includes food and drinks. 3 day package tour, US$150 for 2. Recommended. Argonaut Steamship Agency, C 55 No 7-82, Panama City, T2643459, runs launch cruises.

Cerro Azul

About 40 kilometres east of Panama City is Cerro Azul, a cooler highland area abutting Chagres National Park. At 850 metres elevation, the area has been developed as a weekend cottage resort. It is best visited by private car.

A *Hostal Casa de Campo*, T2700018, F2260336, casacamp@sinfo.net, formerly private residence, all rooms with bath, hot water, pool, jacuzzi, massage, scenic walks, holistic health activities, interesting flora, fauna, birding, lovely dining room, seniors, groups welcome. *Cabañas 4x4*, T2266206, F2267616, rustic cabins in forest setting, electricity 1800-2000 only. **B** *Mesón Tía Toya*, at El Castillo, T2325806, friendly country restaurant with nice porch for dining, also has good cottages for daily rental.

The Canal, Colón and the San Blas Islands

The Canal

The Panama Canal consists of an artificial, river-fed lake, Lago Gatún, 26 metres above sea-level, across which ships sail after having been raised from sea-level by the series of locks on either the Atlantic or the Pacific approach. They are then lowered by the locks on the opposite side. As the crow flies the distance across the isthmus is 55 kilometres. From shore to shore the Canal is 67½ kilometres, or 82 kilometres (44.08 nautical miles) from deep water to deep water. It has been widened to 150 metres in most places. The trip normally takes eight or nine hours for the 30 ships a day passing through. On the Atlantic side there is a normal variation of 30 centimetres between high and low tides, and on the Pacific of about 380 centimetres, rising sometimes to 640 centimetres.

From the Pacific, the Canal channel goes beneath the Puente de las Américas and passes the port of Balboa. The waterway has to rise 16½ metres to the Lago **Miraflores**. The first stage of the process is the Miraflores Locks, one and a half kilometres before the lake. A taxi to the Locks from the city, US$10. At the far end of the Lake, ships are raised another nine and a half metres by the single-step Pedro Miguel Locks, after which the 13 kilometres Gaillard, or Culebra Cut is entered, a narrow rock defile leading to Lago Gatún. Opposite Miraflores Locks, there is a swing bridge. Gaillard Cut can be seen from Contractor's Hill, on the west side, reached by car (no buses) by turning right three kilometres past Puente de las Américas, passing Cocolí, then turning as signed. The road beyond Cocolí goes on to Posa, where there are good views of the Locks, the cut and former Canal Zone buildings.

Barro Colorado

The largest section of the Canal is in Lago Gatún, the Canal's passage through which is 37 kilometres. In the lake is **Barro Colorado** island, to which the animals fled as the basin slowly filled. It is now a biological reserve for scientific research. Visits can be arranged with the Smithsonian Institute in Ancón, US$22 including boat, audio-visual display and lunch; take a Gamboa Summit bus from next to Plaza 5 de Mayo (0600 and 0615) to the Dredging Division dock at Gamboa (US$0.65), from where the boat leaves. Trips go on Tuesday and Saturday only for 15 people. Make arrangements with the Institute in Ancón, preferably the previous week to see if a space is available (the tours are booked up many months in advance). Individuals may be able to join a tour party. The excursion is highly recommended for seeing wildlife, especially monkeys. Visitors without permits will be turned away on arrival. For longer stays, write to the Director, Smithsonian Tropical Research Institute, Box 2072, Balboa, Panamá. Administration, T2276022; hours 0800-1145, 1315-1515. Tours also arranged by *Eco-Tours*, Panama City, T2633077, F2633089: Barro Colorado island is only seen from the water, but tourists walk a nature trail on the Gigante Peninsula, which is also part of the national park.

Gatún Locks

10 kilometres southwest of Colón are the Gatún Locks (*Esclusas de Gatún*) and their neat attendant town. The observation point here (open 1000-1630) is perhaps the best spot in the Canal Area for photographing the passage of ships. (Bus from Colón to Gatún Locks US$0.75.) The most magnificent of the Canal's locks, Gatún integrates all three lock 'steps' on the Atlantic side, raising or lowering ships to the 26 metres level of the Lake in one operation. The flights are in duplicate to allow ships to be passed in opposite directions simultaneously. Passage of the Locks takes about one hour. The road forks after crossing the Lock: the left-hand branch crosses the Chagres River by bridge just downstream from the graceful Gatún Dam, which was the largest earth dam in the world when constructed in 1906. Enough water must be impounded in the reservoir during the rainy season to operate the locks throughout the 3-4 month dry season, since a single ship's transit can use up to 50 million gallons. (A high level reservoir, Lago Alajuela, formerly Madden Lake, feeds the lake and maintains its level; see below.) Opposite the power plant is the *Tarpon Club* (T443-5316/5216 – owned by the same family as the posh *Tropic Star Lodge* in Piñas), a fishing club which has a very nice restaurant, disco and bar; good place to rent boats for a cruise around the Lake. A short distance further south is an attractive lakeside picnic area and small boat launching area. The partly-paved road goes on down the lake to Escobal and Cuipo through lovely scenery (good birding); no hotels in Cuipo but plenty of buses to/from Colón (US$1.60, two hours; US$0.25 to the Locks).

Tours Most people are surprised by the Canal. Few foresee that the scenery is so beautiful, and it is interesting to observe the mechanics of the passage. *Eco-Tours de Panamá* (telephone and fax numbers under Panama City **Travel Agencies**) offer a day-long full transit through the canal on a luxury yacht for US$109. *Agencia Giscomes*, T2640111, also offers trips through the canal every second and fourth Saturday (or Sunday) of the month, leaves at 0730. Also *Mia Travel*, T2638044, do a complete yacht transit of the Canal every Friday and Saturday, provided they have 20 passengers, cost US$99 adult, US$79 children. It takes eight hours with lunch and snacks included. Partial boat trips are also offered on the canal, through Miraflores locks as far as Pedro Miguel locks. *Argo Tours*, T228-6069/4348, F228-1234, pcanal@panama.phoenix.com (www.bigditch.com), Balboa, offer half transits every Saturday from pier 17, Balboa, 0730, US$45, children under 12 US$25, refreshments and snacks on sale, and once a month (usually the second Saturday), a full transit including breakfast, lunch, open bar, bus back from Cristóbal, US$90, children US$70 (MV *Islamorada* arrives at the Caribbean side about 1800). Highly recommended. Enquire at any travel agent. Otherwise since the Panama City-Colón train is not running (except to Summit on Sunday, US$2 return), travellers should take a bus to the Miraflores Locks (open 0900-1700, best between 0900-1000 for photos and 1430-1800 for viewing only) to see shipping. Try to find out when large boats, particularly cruise liners, are in transit. The viewing gallery and a good brochure are free. A detailed model of the canal, formerly in the Department of Transport at Ancón, has been moved here and there is also an eight minute free slide show given throughout the day, with explanations in Spanish and English. About 250 metres past the entrance to the Locks is a road (left) to the filtration plant and observatory, behind which is a picnic area and viewing point. Orange bus from Panama City to Miraflores Locks leaves from the bus station next to Plaza 5 de Mayo (direction Paraíso), 20 minutes, US$0.35. Ask driver to let you off at the stop for 'Esclusas de Miraflores', from where it's a 10-minute walk to the Locks. Taxi to the Locks, US$10 per hour. Another good way to see the Panama Canal area is to rent a car, or, if you have done well at the casinos, by air: Aerotours, T2628710, fly Piper J3 Cub trips, 30 minutes US$60 per person, full coast to coast, two hours, US$200.

The very best way to see the Canal is by boat: it is possible to traverse the canal as a linehandler (no experience necessary) on a yacht; the journey takes two days. Note that more boats pass the canal from north to south than the other way around. Yachts are allowed into the canal on Tuesday and Thursday only. The yacht owners need four-line handlers. Go to the Panama Canal Yacht Club in Colón, or the Yacht Clubs in Cristóbal (downstairs from the building next to the Wharf), or in Balboa a couple of days before, and ask people hanging around the bar. The Balboa Club offers a good daily lunch special; good place to watch canal traffic. 50 metres right of the Club is a small white booth which has a list of boat departures for the next day; ask here if you can go to the dock and take the motor boat which shuttles out to yachts preparing for passage. Ask to speak to captains from the launch and see if they'll let you 'transit'. At Cristóbal you can approach the boats directly at their moorings. They have to book their passage through the canal 48 hours in advance and are subject to a hefty fine if they default through lack of line handlers. However, don't expect too much, there may be many others with the same idea – see bulletin board at Balboa Club – and at times less than one private boat a week goes through the Canal. Some say that May-June and November-December are the best times to try.

Lago Alajuela

It is a two-hour drive through picturesque jungle to Lago Alajuela (formerly Madden Lake, east of the Canal). The lake, used to generate electricity as well

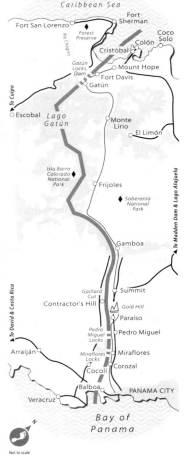

Panama Canal

as to maintain the level of Lago Gatún, covers 50 kilometres and is incorporated within the Chagres National Park. The drive runs from Balboa along the Gaillard Highway and near the Canal. Beyond Fort Clayton there is a fine view of the Miraflores and Pedro Miguel locks. Beyond Pedro Miguel town a road branches off to the left to Summit (Las Cumbres), where there are experimental gardens containing tropical plants from all over the world (closed Monday) and a good, small zoo containing native wildlife. In Las Cumbres the restaurant *La Hacienda* serves native dishes. (The trip to Summit may be made by train on Sunday or buses marked Gamboa, every 1-1½ hours, from bus station next to Plaza 5 de Mayo, US$0.45, one and a half hour journey; the Paraíso bus will also take you to the Miraflores and Pedro Miguel locks.) The road to Lago Alajuela (37 kilometres) crosses the Las Cruces trail (an old cannon marks the spot), and beyond is deep jungle. If walking the trail, take machete and compass. Halfway along the Las Cruces trail (one and a quarter hours) a gravel track, the Plantation Road, turns left, emerging after one and a quarter hours more on the Gamboa Highway one and a half kilometres north of Summit. A large area of rain forest between Lago Gatún and Lago Alajuela has been set aside as **Parque Nacional Soberanía** (trails for walking). The Park has an information centre at the Summit Garden. A novel place to stay in the region is the C *Cabañas Flotantes* in the Chagres River, thatched cabins moored between Lago Alajuela and the Canal. For further information call *Panama Paradise*, T2699860.

Colón and Cristóbal

Landfall on the Caribbean side for the passage of the Canal is made at the twin cities of Cristóbal and Colón, the one merging into the other almost imperceptibly and both built on Manzanillo Island at the entrance of the Canal; the island has now been connected with the mainland. Colón was founded in 1852 as the terminus of the railway across the isthmus; Cristóbal came into being as the port of entry for the supplies used in building the Canal.

At **Cristóbal** ships usually dock at Pier No 9, five minutes from the shops of Colón. Vehicles are always waiting at the docks for those who want to visit Colón and other places.

Sights

Population: 122,500
Colour map 6, grid A2

Colón was originally called Aspinwall, after one of the founders of the transisthmian railway. The French-influenced **Cathedral** at Calle 5 y Avenida Herrera has an attractive altar and good stained glass windows. ■ *1400-1745 daily*. The *Washington Hotel*, on the seafront at the north end of the town, is the most historic structure and is worth a look. The original wooden hotel was built in 1850 for employees of the Railroad Company; President Taft ordered a new fireproof hotel be built in 1912 and the old one was later razed. Although remodelled a number of times, today's building, with its broad verandahs, waving palms, splendid chandelier, plush carpets and casino, still conjures up a past age; the a/c cafetería provides an excellent view of ships waiting to enter the Canal. Next door is the **Casa de Lesseps**, home of the Suez Canal's chief engineer during the 1880s (not open to the public). Across from the *Washington* is the Old Stone Episcopal Church, built in 1865 for the railway workers; it was then the only Protestant church in Colombia (of which Panamá was a province). Running north through the centre of Colón is the palm-lined Avenida Central, with many statues (including one of Columbus and the Indian Girl, a gift from the Empress of France); the public market is at the corner of Calle 11 but holds little of interest. Front Street (Avenida del Frente), facing the Bahía de Limón, has many old wooden buildings with wide verandahs. This is the main commercial street and is quite active but has lost its past splendour; the famous Bazar Francés closed in 1990, the curio shops are unnoteworthy and the railway station stands virtually deserted except for the movement of a few freight trains. Nevertheless, there is talk of declaring the whole of Colón a Free Zone, the authorities are moving to give the city new housing and employment (residential estates like 'Rainbow City' and

'Puerto Escondido' are being extended on the landward side to relocate entire neighbourhoods of slums), and the demands on Cristóbal's busy port facilities (200 million tons of cargo a year) continue to increase. It is to be hoped that if these plans are realized, Colón may become a pleasant place again.

The main reason to come to Colón is to shop at the present **Zona Libre** (Free Zone), the second-largest in the world, an extensive compound of international stores and warehouses established in 1949 and surrounded by a Berlin-like wall. Businessmen and tourists from all over Latin America come here to place orders for the (mostly bulk) merchandise on offer, or to arrange duty-free importation of bulk goods for re-export to neighbouring countries after packaging. Individual items can be bought at some stores, which theoretically must be mailed out of the country or sent in-bond to Tocumen airport before you leave (allow a day for delivery and check-in two hours early to pick up the goods). Bargain hard for good prices, but most items are almost as competitively priced in Panama City. Several banks provide exchange facilities. ■ *A passport or official ID must be shown to gain entry to the Zone, which is open Monday-Friday 0800-1700 (a few places retail on Saturday am, but not many). If with your own car, pay a minder US$1 to watch it while in the Zone, very necessary.*

The 30-minute beach drive around Colón's perimeter is pleasant and cool in the evening; despite the slums at the south end there are some nice homes along the east shore of the peninsula. Permission from the Port Authority security officer is required to enter the port area, where agents for all the world's great shipping lines are located in colonial Caribbean-style buildings dating from 1914. Almost lost in a forest of containers is the *Cristóbal Yacht Club* (T4415881), whose open-air restaurant and historically decorated bar offer very good food (seafood and Chinese); this is the place to enquire about sailing boat charters to the San Blas Islands or shorter trips aboard visiting yachts.

Excursions A well-paved road branches off the Transisthmus Highway at Sabanitas, 10 kilometres east of Colón, and runs northeast along the coast for 34 kilometres to the historic Spanish garrison port of Portobelo (see below), founded in 1519 on the protected bay in which Columbus sought shelter in 1502. The rocky Costa Arriba is very attractive, with a number of lovely white-sand beaches (crowded at weekends). María Chiquita (14 kilometres) has a bathing pavilion, toilets, bar and restaurant managed by the government tourist bureau; a local speciality is *sao*, Jamaican-style pig's feet pickled with lime and chillies, sold from roadside stalls. Three kilometres further on is Playa Langosta, also with swimming facilities, bar and restaurant. There are plenty of small restaurants along this road serving fresh seafood. A group of people can rent a coastal boat at Puerto Pilón (US$100-150 a day) for an adventurous ride to Portobelo, seas are often rough, take precautions. In Buenavista, just before entering Portobelo, a cannon marks the spot where Henry Morgan landed for his devastating 15-day sack of the town in 1668.

Warning Do not go to the city alone. Mugging, even in daylight, is a real threat in both Colón and Cristóbal. We have received repeated warnings of robbery in Colón, often within five minutes of arrival. The two main streets and some of the connecting ones are guarded by police officers; you are strongly recommended not to leave their range of sight. One traveller recommends having a few dollars handy, so that "muggers are less likely to strip you for more".

Sleeping **AL** *Washington*, Av del Frente Final, T4419662, art deco style, guarded enclave, clean, good restaurant, good view of ships entering the canal, there is also a small casino. **B** *Carlton*, C 10 y Av Meléndez, T4450744, is the next best hotel. **C** *Andros*, Av Herrera, between C 9 y 10, T441-0477/7923, modern, clean, fan or a/c, bath, TV, good restaurant, cafetería. **C** *Sotelo*, C 10 y 11 con Av Guerrero, T4417542, also has a casino. **D** *Pensión Plaza*, Av Central, T4413216, is clean, cheap. **E** *Pensión Acrópolis*, Av Amador Guerrero y C 11, opposite *Sotelo*, T4411456, shared bath. If destitute try the Salvation Army.

Eating See above for *Cristóbal Yacht Club*. *VIP Club*, C 11 y Av del Frente, T4413563, popular with visiting businessmen and port officials. *Panamá* and *Antonio*, both Av Herrera y C 11, unremarkable but decent. **For Caribbean food**: *Restaurant Teresa*, Av Amador Guerrero y C 12.
La Cabaña, Av Central y C 8. *Hotels Washington, Carlton* and *Andros* have good restaurants.
YMCA restaurant, Av Bolívar between C 11 y 12, mostly Chinese menu, comparatively expensive. Several fast food outlets, eg *KFC*, Paseo Centenario near C 7.

Entertainment **Cinemas** *Teatro Lido*, across from YMCA on Bolívar, and *Teatro Rex*, C 5 and Av Central.

Sports **Clubs**: golf (18 holes) at *Brazos Brook Country Club*. *Rotary Club*, weekly lunches.

Transport **Local Taxis**: tariffs vary but not expensive, US$5-7 per hour, US$50-80 per day. Car rental
and taxis on Front Street facing C 11; most drivers speak some English and can advise on
'no-go' areas. Avis has 2 offices.
  Air Former US France Field AFB has replaced Colón's old airstrip as the busy local airport,
on mainland east of city, taxi under US$1 but bargain. Aeroperlas has many flights daily Mon-
day-Friday to Panama City; US$50 return. The above flights are hectic with Free Zone execu-
tives, no reservation system so allow plenty of time or plan to stay the night in Colón.
  Buses Bus station on Front Street and C 12. Express (a/c) US$2.25, and regular buses,
US$1.75, daily to **Panama City** every 20 minutes, less frequent at weekends, about 2 hours.
Hourly to **Portobelo** daily, US$2, 1 hour.
  Sea Shipping a vehicle: to South America, see page 1165.

Directory **Banks** *Chase Manhattan Bank. Citibank. Banco Nacional de Panamá. Caja de Ahorros. Lloyds Bank*
agency in Colón Free Zone, at Av Santa Isabel y C 14, T4452177. Open 0800-1300, Mon to Fri.
Communications Post Office: in Cristóbal Administration Building, on corner of Av Bolívar and C 9.

West of Colón

From Colón the Caribbean **Costa Abajo**, stretching west of the Canal, can also be
visited. The road leaves Colón through new housing developments (on the left is the
modern city of Margarita) and runs 10 kilometres southwest to the Gatún Locks (see
under **The Canal** above).

  The north road branch at Gatún follows Limón Bay through a well-preserved forest reserve to Fort Sherman, running beside the remnants of the French Canal excavations (most of their work on the Atlantic side is now below the Lake while the
Pacific excavations were incorporated into the US construction). Fort Sherman is
heavily-forested military property and a guard at the gate may issue you with a pass;
since it is also the US Army's Jungle and Guerrilla Warfare Training Center it is
advisable not to court any unpleasant surprises by leaving the road, which is gravel
and well signposted (no public transport) for the 10 kilometres to Fuerte San
Lorenzo.

Fuerte San Lorenzo

Colour map 6, grid A2 Perched on a cliff-top promontory overlooking the mouth of the Río Chagres with
great views of the coast, San Lorenzo is one of the oldest and best-preserved Spanish
fortifications in the Americas. Construction had begun the year before Drake
launched a 23-ship attack on the post (1596) and proceeded up the Chagres in an
unsuccessful attempt to reach Panama City. Morgan fought a bloody 11-day battle
to take the fort as a prelude to his decisive swoop on Panamá Viejo in 1671. Although
new defences were then built, they were unable to prevent British Admiral Edward
Vernon's successful attack in 1740 (one of Vernon's cannon with the GR monogram
can still be seen). Engineer Hernández then spent seven years strengthening the garrison (1760-67), but the threat to San Lorenzo gradually receded as Spanish galleons

were diverted to the Cape Horn route and the era of the freebooters approached its end. The last Royalist soldiers left the fort in 1821 as Colombia declared its independence from Spain. The earliest artillery sheds can be seen on the lower cliff level but most of the bulwarks, arched stone rooms and lines of cannon are 18th century. The site recently underwent an extensive UNESCO renovation programme and is well worth a visit. There is a picnic area and a tiny beach is accessible by a steep path down the cliff. Take insect repellent.

There is no crossing of the Chagres at San Lorenzo; to continue down the **Costa Abajo** one must return to the Gatún Dam and take the gravel road along the west side of the river, which winds its way through pristine forest to the coastal village of Piña and its kilometre-long beach. The road runs west along a steep and rocky shore punctured by many small coves to Nuevo Chagres and Palmas Bellas, quiet fishing resorts in coconut palm groves, but with few facilities. Four-wheel drive is required to continue to Río Indio and Miguel de la Borda, where the road comes to an end. The villages beyond, including historic Río Belén where one of Columbus' ships was abandoned in 1502, remain accessible only by sea.

East of Colón
Portobelo

'Beautiful Port' was the northern terminus of the Camino Real, where Peruvian trea- *Population: 5,850* sure carried on mule trains across the Isthmus from Panama City was stored in forti- *Colour map 6, grid A2* fied warehouses until the periodic arrival of the Spanish Armada, the famed Fairs where the wealth of the New World was exchanged for goods and supplies from Europe. So much material changed hands that the 1637 Fair (described by Englishman Thomas Gage) took 30 days for the loading and unloading to be completed. In the Royal **Contaduría** or Customs House bars of gold and silver were piled up like firewood. Such riches could hardly fail to attract foreign corsairs; Portobelo was one of Francis Drake's favourite targets but also his downfall; he died here of dysentery in 1596 and was buried in a lead-lined coffin in the bay off Isla Drake. By the beginning of the 17th century several *castillos* (Santiago, San Gerónimo and San Fernando) had been built of coral stone quarried nearby to protect the harbour. Attacks continued, however, until in 1740 the treasure fleets were rerouted around the Horn and the Portobelo Fairs ended. The fortifications were rebuilt after Vernon's attack in 1744 but they were no longer seriously challenged, leaving the fortresses visible today. The largest, the aptly-named 'Iron Castle', was largely dismantled during Canal construction (its stones form the breakwaters at the north entrance to the Canal), but there are many other interesting ruined fortresses, walls, rows of cannon and remains of the town's 120 houses and public buildings to be seen standing along the foreshore amid the present-day village. (Note that Fuerte San Lorenzo and the nearby beach of La Huerta can only be reached by boat.) The Contaduría (1630) was recently restored, with similar plans in place for the Plaza, Hospital Chapel and the Fernández House.

In **San Felipe Church** (1776) is the 17th century, cocobolo-wood statue of the Black Christ, about whose origin there are many legends. One tells of how it was found by fishermen floating in the sea during an epidemic of cholera in the town. It was brought ashore and immediately the epidemic began to wane. Another says that the life-size image was on its way to Cartagena when the ship put in to Portobelo to buy supplies; after being thwarted five times by contrary weather to leave port, the crew decided the statue wished to remain in Panamá, it was thrown overboard, floated ashore and was rescued by the locals.

D *Aquatic Park*, on road towards Colón, dormitory accommodation, expensive. **D** *Divers* **Sleeping** *Haven*, friendly, US owner, safe parking, somewhat run down.

Eating   *El Hostal del Rey*, corner of central park, good meals and value. *Restaurant-Bar Los Cañones*, T4482032. *La Torre*, T4482039, on main road 2 kilometres before the town, good food; a number of small *fondas* serving coconut rice with fresh shrimps, Caribbean food (spicy) with octopus or fish, or *fufú* (fish soup cooked with coconut milk and vegetables).

Festivals   The Black Christ's miraculous reputation is celebrated each **21 October**, when purple-clad pilgrims come from all over the country and the statue is paraded through the town at 1800 on a flower and candle-covered platform carried by 80 men (who take three steps forward and two steps back to musical accompaniment); feasting and dancing till dawn follow the solemn procession.

Other *fiestas* in the Portobelo region (for example New Year's Eve, Carnival, Patron Saint's Day, **20 March**) are opportunities to experience the *Congos*. Unlike the dance of the same name found elsewhere on the Caribbean coast, the *Congo* here is the name given both to the main, male participants and a slowly enfolding ritual which lasts from the *Día de los Reyes*, 6 January (Epiphany) to Easter. Among the various explanations of its symbolism are elements of the people's original African religions, their capture into slavery, their conversion to Catholicism and mockery of the colonial Spaniards. Members of the audience are often 'imprisoned' in a makeshift palisade and have to pay a 'ransom' to be freed.

Transport   **Bus**   Buses from Colón, every hour from 0700 from the bus station on Front Street y Calle 13, 1 hour, US$2; María Chiquita, 40 minutes, US$0.80. Portobelo can be visited from Panama City in a day without going into Colón by taking an early bus as far as the Sabanitas turnoff (US$1) and waiting for a Colón-Portobelo service (US$1).

Directory   **Tourist office**   IPAT now has an office in Portobelo (T4482060) and can provide guides, schedules of *Congos* and other performances, and comprehensive information about the many local points of interest, including the surrounding 4,850-hectare Portobelo National Park, scuba diving sites (superb) and renting a boat to visit secluded beaches nearby.

Isla Grande

Colour map 6, grid A2   A narrow gravel road (being extended by the US military but four-wheel drive recommended at present, limited bus service) continues on northeast from Portobelo to Isla Grande, Nombre de Dios (25 kilometres) and Palenque. Scuba diving offered at several places along the road. It passes through Garrote and La Guaira (**D** *Cabañas Montecarlo*, T4412054), from where *pangas* can be hired (US$1) at the car park to cross to Isla Grande, a favourite with international visitors because of its relaxed lifestyle, fishing, scuba diving and snorkelling, windsurfing and dazzling white palm-fringed beaches. The island's 300 black inhabitants make a living from fishing and coconut cultivation, and a powerful French-built lighthouse crowns the small island's northern point. There are a number of colourful African-tinged festivals held here throughout the year, particularly on 24 June, 16 July and the pre-Lenten Carnival with *Congos*.

Sleeping &   Popular on holidays and dry season weekends, make reservations in advance, prices often dou-
eating   ble during high season. **A** *Isla Grande*, T2643046, F2640646, bungalows scattered along an excellent sandy beach; boat, snorkel and jet ski hire, restaurant, minizoo (toucans, crocodiles, monkeys, etc), reduced tariffs on weekdays. Recommended. **B** *Posada Villa Ensueño*, T268-2926/1445, good café/bar. **B** *La Cholita*, similar prices. **B** *Candy Rose*. **C** *Cabañas Jackson*, T4416472, many huts/bungalows available. **C** *Posada Guayaco*. All hotels have bars and simple restaurants, *Candy Rose* serves drinks with a special octopus cooked in coconut milk.

Nombre de Dios

Colour map 6, grid A2   The beautiful, deserted mainland beaches continue as the 'road' heads east to Nombre de Dios. The historic town (1520) near the present village was once the thriving trading port which first hosted the famed Fairs, located at the end of the stone-paved Camino Real from the capital. By the 1550s more than half the trade between Spain and its colonies was passing through its lightly-defended harbour, but in 1594 the decision was made to move operations to the more-sheltered site of Portobelo. The Camino Real was diverted and Nombre de Dios was already dying when Drake captured and burnt it two years later, so that William Dampier could describe the site some years later as "only a name ... everything is covered by the Jungle with no sign that it was ever populated". Excavations have taken place, revealing the Spanish town, parts of the Camino Real, a broken cannon and other objects (most now in the National Museum). The modern village has few facilities (no hotel), but a beautiful beach can be enjoyed by those few who get this far. A *cayuco* (US$3 per person, 12 minutes) can be taken to Playa Damas, an unusual beach where alternating patches of red and white sand resemble a chess board; the beach is owned by an amateur ecologist who has built some rustic huts and a campsite (*Costa El Oro*, T2635955) on a small island here, he also offers expert guidance on local fishing and diving spots.

The track staggers on as far as Cuango, a few kilometres east of **Palenque**, another unspoilt hamlet with a good beach where very rudimentary huts are being built for visitors. Locals eagerly await the road's eventual extension through a succession of seaside villages to the Golfo de San Blas opposite El Porvenir, the capital of the Kunas' self-governed *comarca* of Kuna Yala (Kuna Earth). If a good road is built, tropical fishing villages like Miramar and Palmira, with their welcoming people, white-sand beaches, offshore reefs and crystal-clear waters will become accessible for tourism.

Camino Real

Although little of the Camino Real remains, its two branches from Madden Lake/Lago Alajuela across the mountains to Nombre de Dios (30 kilometres) and Portobelo can still be hiked. The trail starts at the old manganese mining zone (Mina 1, on the dirt road that runs from the Transístmica to a little way up the Río Boquerón). Buses run occasionally from the Transístmica to Salamanca, roughly where the Río Boquerón empties into Madden Lake. The trail follows the Río Boquerón up to the continental divide and the Río Nombre de Dios down the northern watershed to the coast near the present-day town. This historic trek is easy for anyone with reasonable fitness, as one can drive to entry and exit points. Guides are not really necessary, the rivers are beautiful (and carry little water in the dry season) and the jungle almost untouched; the trail is straightforward and rises only to 330 metres at the divide. Allow about three days for the Boquerón-Nombre de Dios trek. The trail to Portobelo branches off the above at the Río Diablo or Río Longue. After you leave the Boquerón you will need to navigate by compass. The Diablo takes the trekker higher into the divide (700 metres) than the Longue (the route the treasure-laden mules followed, 350 metres) and the terrain is more broken; both lead to the Río Cascajal (higher reaches are strewn with large boulders), which descends to the Caribbean. The highest point in the region, Cerro Brujo (979 metres), is passed *en route*. There are jaguars in this forested refuge, but they are unlikely to present any danger to hikers. The Cascajal reaches the road about one kilometre east of Portobelo. The Boquerón-Portobelo hike is more demanding than the other and takes four days maximum, a good machete is essential, solitude is guaranteed for at least two days.

To the south and east of the Camino Real are the rivers of the Chagres system which flow into Lago Alajuela. Some of these are now being exploited for rafting. Check with tourist agencies in Panama City.

San Blas Islands

Colour map 6, grid A2 *An interesting trip can be made to the San Blas (or Las Mulatas) archipelago, which has 365 islands ranging in size from tiny ones with a few coconut palms to islands on which hundreds of Kuna Indians live. About 50 are inhabited. The islands, off the Caribbean coast east of Colón, vary in distance from the shore from 100 metres to several kilometres and are strung out along the coast for over 200 kilometres from the Gulf of San Blas to the Colombian border.*

The Kuna (Cuna, or Tule) are the most sophisticated and politically organized of the country's three major groups. They run the San Blas Territory virtually on their own terms, with internal autonomy and, uniquely among Panama's Indians, send their representative to the National Assembly. Each community is presided over by a *sáhila* (or chief). The Kuna have their own language, but Spanish is widely spoken. The women wear gold nose and ear-rings, and costumes with unique designs based on local themes, geometric patterns, stylized fauna and flora, and pictorial representations of current events or political propaganda. They are outside the Panamanian tax zone and have negotiated a treaty perpetuating their long-standing trade with small craft from Colombia. Many men work on the mainland, but live on the islands.

Photographers need plenty of cash, as the set price for a Kuna to pose is US$1 per photo. *Molas* (decorative handsewn appliqué for blouse fronts) cost upwards of US$10 each (also obtainable in many Panama City and Colón shops). You can also try the San Blas perfume, Kantule, similarly available in city shops.

There are about 20 airstrips in the San Blas Islands and province, but most are 'larger' than the islands or places on which they are built. They include: El Porvenir, Cartí, Río Sidra, Río Azúcar, Narganá, Corazón, Río Tigre, Playón Chico, Tupile, Tikankiki, Ailigandi, Achutupu (also known as Uaguitupu), Mamitupu, Ogobsucum, Ustupu, Mansucum, Mulatupu, Tubuala, Calidonia, Puerto Obaldía. You can be dropped off at any island or village and discuss your return with the pilot. It is probably not a wise idea since most of the islands may have nice-looking beaches, but no drinking water or food.

Sleeping Any travel agent in Panama can book a San Blas tour. One of the agents which will handle bookings is *Chadwicks*, see **Balboa** above. A 1-night stay in the vicinity of El Porvenir costs US$120 including food and lodging at the *Hotel Hanay Kantule* (also spelt *Anai Katule*) on Wichibwala, T2200746. You have to get up early for the return flight. Other hotels in the Porvenir area include *C San Blas*, T262-1606/5410, on Nalunega Island, price includes breakfast, lunch, lobster dinner and 2 excursions, owner Sr Burgos meets incoming flights every morning and boats to Cartagena pick up passengers from here. *Residencial Turístico Yeri*, T2623402. The *Hanay Kantule* charges US$55 per person a night, all others US$27, including food. For the *Hanay*, ask for Israel Fernández on arrival at El Porvenir.

Hotels and lodges are being opened on the islands off the Caribbean coast. These include, from west to east: *Sugtupu Hotel* in the Cartí-Sugtupu community (from the coast of Cartí a road runs inland to the Pan-American Highway at **El Llano** – see page 1227). **A** *Kuanidup*, some 7 huts on the island, good food, lovely beaches, no electricity, bathrooms in the centre of the island. At Narganá there is a basic hotel, **F**, and 1 restaurant, *El Caprichito*, good crab dishes. **L** *Kwadule*, near Corazón de Jesús and Narganá, owned by the Noveys, very nice restaurant/bar over the reef, some cabins built over the water, with bath. A short canoe ride from Narganá is Isla Tigre, a very traditional island. Further east again, reached from Playón Chico, is the **LL** *Iskardup Ecoresort* (T2696017, F2691604), with cabins, bar, restaurant, solar power, package tours include trips to mainland and 'junjogging'(!). In the Ailigandi community is *La Palmera* hotel, restaurant and bar. Another recommended trip is to *Dolphin Lodge*, owned by a Kuna Indian family on the island of Uaguitupu, US$139 including air fare, meals and overnight stay (bookings through *Eco-Tours*, T2633077, F2633089). These last 2 are about half way along the coast between El Porvenir and the Colombian border. **C** hotel next to airport, very good food.

IPAT lists the following *fiestas* in the San Blas islands: **February**, anniversary of the *Tule Revolution*, at Playón Chico, Tupile, Ailigandi and Ustupu. **19 March**, *fiesta patronal* on Narganá. **8 July**, anniversary of *Inakiña* on Mulatupo. **29-31 July**, *fiesta patronal* on Fulipe. **20 August**, *Charles Robinson anniversary* on Narganá. **3 September**, anniversary of *Nele-Kantule* on Ustupo. **11 September**, anniversary of *Yabilikiña* on Tuwala. All involve dances, games, meals and speeches and are traditional, except those on Narganá, which have a stronger western element (but also typical dancing and food).

Air 3 companies fly from Panamá City. The most popular destination is El Porvenir (other airports are listed above), on the north side of the Golfo de San Blas, where tourists are picked up by boat to go to a neighbouring island, about 20 minutes ride. 1-way fares to the islands are US$27 to El Porvenir and US$42 to Puerto Obaldía. All other airport fares are scaled in between (price includes a 5 percent sales tax). You must take your passport because every month or so a hijack attempt to Colombia is made. All flights leave between 0600 and 0630, Monday-Saturday, returning 0800-0830. Evening and Sunday flights must be booked privately. Baggage over 15 kilograms is charged at US$0.25 per lb – ie wear your heavy stuff.

Sea There are occasional boats to the San Blas islands from Colón, but there is no scheduled service and the trip can be rough. One ship that goes from time to time is the *Almirante*, try to find the captain, Figueres Cooper, who charges US$30 for the trip. The port captain's office at Coco Solo may have information on boat departures, T4415231 or 4451055, although most boats are 'not keen on being landed with potentially stranded gringos'. Alternatively, go to Portobelo (see above) and try for a boat from there, 9 hours to El Porvenir, every other day, US$17.

There are two sailing boats regularly taking passengers from Cartagena, *Colombia*, to San Blas and back. Frequency depends on the number of people who sign up. Journey time 2 days to reach the San Blas islands, 2 more to Porvenir for the airport and immigration, US$185 one way, safer than many cargo boats. Reservations in Cartagena at *Hotel Chalet Swizo*, chalet@col3.telecom.com.co. For general information, www.salelawrence.com/sailing.htm, or contact Sr Burgos at *Hotel San Blas*.

The 'Interior'

Cross the Puente de las Américas for the most densely-populated rural quarter of the country, a Panama that is in great contrast to the cosmopolitan capital and the Canal: colonial towns, a variety of agricultural zones, traditional crafts and music, Pacific beaches and beautiful mountain landscapes with some good walking. The Pan-American Highway traverses this region, known generally to Panamanians as 'El Interior' (though the term can refer to any area outside the capital), en route to Costa Rica.

Panama City to Costa Rica

The Pan-American Highway, also known as the Interamericana, runs westwards from Panama City through Concepción to the Costa Rican border (489 kilometres), and is well graded and completely paved. A main branch road turns south from Divisa to Chitre, Los Santos and Las Tablas (see below, **Azuero Peninsula**). Leaving Panama City, the Pan-American Highway crosses the **Puente de las Américas** over the Canal at the Pacific entrance. The bridge was built between 1958 and 1962 by the USA to replace the ferry crossing. It is 1,653 metres long and with the road surface 117 metres above the seaway, more than high enough to allow all ships to pass under it. It has three lanes, a four-lane approach from Panama City and a pedestrian pavement all the way (muggings have occurred on the bridge in broad daylight, so be careful!). Lane changes are frequent during busy hours and vaguely indicated. Be observant. It is the only way for vehicles to cross the canal. Buses run to a *mirador* on the far side of the bridge from the city.

Where the road west crosses the savannas, there are open pastures and fields where clumps of beautiful trees, including mangoes and palms, alternate with grass. In the west, acacia and teak plantings are often seen. Watch for typical 'living fences', whose posts sprout in the humid climate. New growth is periodically harvested for additional posts.

La Chorrera

Population: 37,000
Colour map 6, grid A2

The first place you reach, 13 kilometres from Panama City, is the small town of **Arraiján** (*Population*: 6,600). Another 21 kilometres by four-lane highway (toll US$0.50) takes you to La Chorrera; an interesting store, *Artes de las Américas*, has items in wood, et cetera. A branch road (right) leads one and a half kilometres to El Chorro, the waterfall from which the town takes its name. On 20 kilometres, among hills, is the old town of Capira; good food next to Shell station run by Chinese. Just west of Capira is a sign indicating the turn-off to Lídice, four kilometres north of the Highway. At the foot of Cerro Trinidad, which local tradition calls 'the end of the Andes', the town was the home of Czech immigrants who, in 1945, succeeded in having the name changed from Potero to commemorate Lidice in their homeland, which had suffered so heavily in the Second World War.

The Highway passes through the orange groves of Campana (where a 10-kilometre road climbs to **Altos de Campana National Park**; several trails, rangers will advise; lodging at ranger station is possible, five kilometres up the road), and then twists down to Río Sajalices (bathing) and the low-level plains. Good views on the road to the summit of Cerro Campana. 10 kilometres up a side road, two kilometres before the village of Chicá is a colony of retired North Americans, who appreciate visitors.

Sleeping
D *Tropical*, pink and green building on Panamericana, with fan, bath. Recommended.
D *Hospedaje Lamas*, on side street just right of *Tropical*, a/c or fan, clean, big rooms, TV. Recommended.

San Carlos and beaches

Colour map 6, grid A2

At Bejuco, five kilometres east of Chame, there is a turn off for Punta Chame, at the end of a 28-kilometre peninsula, with a white-sand beach, a few houses, and a hotel/restaurant. At low tide the sand is alive with legions of small pink crabs. From here there is a splendid view northeast to Taboga Island and the entrance to the Canal in the distance. Food is prepared by the beach and there are several bars. A pick-up runs between the highway and the beach, US$1.

Beyond Chame are two beaches: **Nueva Gorgona** where the beach is about 3-4 kilometres long, waves increase in size from west to east, and there is a well-stocked grocery store. The other is **Playa Coronado**, the most popular in Panama, even so it is rarely crowded. Homeowners from Playa Coronado have installed a checkpoint at the turning, unaffiliated with the police station opposite. Be polite, but do not be deterred from using the public beach.

Sleeping & eating
B *Gorgona Hayes*, T2237775, with pleasant pool, fountain, tennis court, restaurant, good.
B *Cabañas de Playa Gorgona*, T2692433, cheaper, with kitchenettes, barbecue grills, pool, shade, hammocks, on the ocean, prices rise at weekend. Camping possible on Palmar Beach, **F**. Restaurant *El Prado*, on the beach.

Opposite the turning to Playa Coronado is a road inland to Las Lajas and on into the hills and **Lagunas del Valle**, about one hour from the Highway. **B** *Hostal Chiquito*, a 160-hectare farm with eight guest rooms, two double rooms in separate units, meals included, riding, hiking, lake swimming, electricity evenings only, transport provided from Panama City, information T2364632 (Panama City).

10 kilometres beyond Playa Coronado is the town of **San Carlos**, near the sea; good river and sea-bathing (beware jelly fish and do not bathe in the estuarine lake). Not many restaurants in San Carlos, but there are plenty of food shops.

Beyond San Carlos is the Río Mar beach, with the **A** *Río Mar*, T2230192, which has a good seafood restaurant. *Getting there*: Bus Panama City-San Carlos, frequent from 0615, US$3.50, San Carlos-David, US$10.

El Valle

Five kilometres on, a road (right) leads after a few kilometres to a climb through fine scenery to the summit of Los Llanitos (792 metres), and then down 200 metres to a mountain-rimmed plateau (7 by 5½ kilometres) on which is comparatively cool **El Valle**, a small summer resort; direct bus from Panama City US$3.50, or US$1 from San Carlos. Four kilometres before El Valle is a parking spot with fine views of the village, waterfall nearby. Soapstone carvings of animals, straw birds, painted gourds (*totumas*), carved wood tableware, pottery and *molas* are sold in the famous Sunday market, which is very popular with Panamanians and tourists. There is also a colourful flower market. The orchid nursery has a small zoo and Panama's best-known petroglyphs can be seen near the town. This is one of many good walks in the vicinity (ask directions); another is to the cross in the hills to the west of town.

Gold coloured frogs can be seen in the area, and there are trees with square-shaped trunks, near Hotel Campestre.

Sleeping

B *Hotel Campestre*, T9936146/2219602, F2264069, lunch from US$6. **B** *Cabañas Las Mozas*, T9936071, offers *Cocina Arabe*. **B** *Cabañas Potosí*, T9936181. **D** *El Greco Motel*, C Central, T9936149. **E** *Pensión Niña Dalia*, no towels or soap, will look after bags; private houses nearby rent rooms, **F** with meals; accommodation hard to find at weekends.

The town has no real centre; everyone cycles.

We leave Panamá Province at La Ermita and enter Coclé, whose large tracts of semi-arid land are used for cattle raising.

Santa Clara and Antón

Santa Clara, with its famous beach, 115 kilometres from Panama City, is the usual target for motorists with *cabañas* at the beach, fishing, launches for hire, and riding. The beach is about 20 minutes walk from the Pan-American Highway.

Sleeping

There are *cabañas* to rent, the principal centre is **Cabañas Las Sirenas**, T2325841, F2325842, **AL** per day for 5 people, **L** for 7 (minimum 2 nights), in an attractive landscaped environment. 100 metres from the Highway on the north side is *XS Memories*, T9933096, 12 full service RV hookups in a gated compound, also 3 hotel rooms, sports bar and restaurant.

About 13 kilometres beyond is **Antón** (*Population*: 5,100): it has a special local type of *manjar blanco*. There is a crucifix here which is reputed to be miraculous. **D** *Hotel Rivera*, with bath and a/c, cheaper without bath, a/c or fan, clean, Km 131, T9972245. Across the Pan-American Highway is **E** *Pensión/Restaurant Panamá*, friendly, clean, safe, a/c. **E** *Chung*, on Highway, moderately-priced food.

Penonomé

On 20 kilometres is the capital of Coclé: Penonomé, an old town even when the Spaniards arrived. An advanced culture here, revealed by archaeologists, was overwhelmed by volcanic eruption (things found are in Panama City, in the American

Population: 10,715
Colour map 6, grid A1

Museum of Natural History in New York, and in the **Museo Conte de Penonomé** here, ■ *T9978490, Tuesday-Saturday 0900-1230, 1330-1600, Sunday 0830-1300*). There is a local university and the Mercado de Artesanato on the Highway is worth a visit. There is a delightful central plaza with the air of a tiny provincial capital of times past. The town is frequently the lunch stop for motorists making the whole-day trip from Panama City to the western border.

Sleeping & eating

C-D *Dos Continentes*, Av Juan D Arosemena, T9972325, with shower, a/c, pool, restaurant. **E** *Pensión Dos Reales*, C Juan Vásquez, basic, mosquitos, noisy. **E** *Pensión Los Pinos*, on left of Highway to Panama City, with bath and fan (**D** with a/c). **E** *Res El País*, with bath, C Juan Arosemena near church and Parque, no sign but look for black lanterns on wall, good value. Also, good basic restaurant, *Cielo Mar*, will let you sling a hammock free. *Mac Aro*, on Juan Arosomena, good for light meals, takeaway, English spoken.

Just under one kilometre north of Penonomé is Balneario Las Mendozas, on street of the same name, an excellent river pool for bathing in deep water. Further up the Río Zaratí, also known as the Santa María, is La Angostura where the river dives down a canyon; dirt access road usually suitable for ordinary cars. There are copper and gold mining activities in this area and further north beyond La Pintada, where a new 35-kilometre road has been built to Coclecito on the Caribbean side of the Continental Divide. The operating mining company is also involved in conservation work including reforestation near La Angostura. Northeast of Penonomé is Churuquita Grande (camping possible near river with waterfall and swimming hole); Feria de la Naranja last weekend of January, inauguration and dancing on Saturday, big day on Sunday which includes a colourful parade and huge displays of fruit. Further inland, an excellent purpose-built lodge for walkers and ecotourists has been opened: **AL** *Posada del Cerro La Vieja*, Apdo 543 Estafeta 9A Carrasquilla, Panama City, local address, Chiguirí Arriba, Coclé, T2234553, F2644858; it offers guided treks on foot or mule, including through the mountains to El Valle, or across the isthmus to the Atlantic coast, the final stage by dugout.

24 kilometres west of Penonomé is El Caño, and three and a half kilometres from the main road is the **Parque Arqueológico del Caño** with a small museum, some excavations (several human skeletons found in the burial site), and standing stones. ■*T9624183. Tuesday-Friday 0900-1600, Saturday-Sunday 1030-1300, closed Monday. US$1*).

A further seven kilometres along the Pan-American Highway is **Natá** (*Population*: 5,150), one of the oldest towns in Panama and the Americas (1520). The early colonists fought constant Indian attacks led by Urracá. The Iglesia de Santiago Apóstol (1522) is impressive, with some interesting wood carvings. It is sadly run-down now; donations gratefully received for restoration work in progress. Around the plaza are other colonial buildings.

Aguadulce

Population: 14,800
Colour map 6, grid B1

10 kilometres beyond we enter the sugar area and come to Aguadulce, a prosperous supply centre (bus from Panamá, US$6); local pottery for sale; cane fields, tomato-processing plants and *salinas* nearby.

Sleeping

C *El Interamericano*, on Pan-American Highway, T9974363, with bath, a/c, TV, balcony, clean rooms, swimming pool. **D** per person *Pensión Sarita*, T9974437, and others (it may be possible to sleep by the fire station).

17 kilometres beyond Aguadulce, just after the large Santa Rosa sugar plantation, a road leads off right to the mountain spa of **Calobre** (31 kilometres); the hot springs are, however, a good hour's drive away, on a very rough road; grand mountain scenery. (Bus Panama City-Aguadulce, US$5.)

Azuero Peninsula

Six kilometres after the Calobre turnoff is the crossroads town of **Divisa**, 214 kilometres from the capital. (The town itself is one kilometre north of the Highway.) From here a major paved road branches off south into the **Azuero Peninsula**, one of the earliest parts of Panama to be settled. Despite recent road paving in the south and east, many of the peninsula's small towns are still remote and preserve much of their 400-year-old colonial traditions, costumes and substantial white churches.

Festivals Most towns of any size on the Peninsula have annual Carnivals (the four days before Ash Wednesday) but Las Tablas' is especially picturesque and popular with visitors; accommodation is in short supply at this time throughout the region.

Chitré

After passing through **Parita** (*Population*: 6,600), whose church dates from 1556, our road reaches the cattle centre of Chitré (37 kilometres), capital of Herrera Province and the best base for exploration. The Cathedral (1578) is imposing and beautifully preserved. The small **Museo de Herrera**, on Calle Manuel Correa, has interesting historical exhibits. ■ *Tuesday-Saturday 0830-1200, 1300-1600; Sunday 0900-1200, US$0.35*. The town is known primarily for its red clay pottery, especially roofing and floor tiles which are exported, and for its woven mats and carpets. The IPAT tourist office is in the Ministerio de Comercio e Industria building on the main road out to Los Santos; very friendly but no English spoken, details on the Peninsula's many festivals and points of interest. ■ *Monday-Friday, 0830-1200, 1245-1630*.

Population: 34,400
Colour map 6, grid B1

Excursions There are some nice beaches close to Chitré served by local buses (20 minutes, US$0.90); for example Playas Monagre and El Rompio and at Punta Agallito, where many migratory birds congregate and are studied at the Humboldt Ecological Station. Along the swampy coast just to the north is the 8,000-hectare **Sarigua National Park**, established in 1984 to preserve the distinctive tropical desert and mangrove margins of the Bahía de Parita; ancient artefacts have been unearthed within the park's boundaries; the pre-Columbian site of Monegrillo is considered very significant but there is little for the non-specialist to appreciate.

Two kilometres west of Chitré is **La Arena**, the centre for Panamanian pottery. The Christmas festivities here, 22-25 December, are worth seeing, with music, dancing, bull running in the *plaza de toros* and cock fights (popular all over Panamá). Tourist agencies in Panama City can arrange whirlwind shopping tours to La Arena. Bus from Chitré; five minutes, US$0.30, taxi US$1.50.

Sleeping **D** *El Prado*, Av Herrera 4260, opposite Cathedral, T9964620, clean and modern, quiet, well run, a/c, parking, upstairs restaurant. Recommended. **D-E** *Santa Rita*, C Manuel Correa y Av Herrera, T9964610, near main plaza, clean, large rooms, modern, cheaper rooms have fans and cold water, restaurant, good value. **E** *Pensión Central*, next to *El Prado*, with bath, clean and friendly, comfortable but noisy and overpriced. Plenty of eating places near the Plaza and in the *mercado* (beside the Cathedral). **E** *Pensión Colombia*, C Manuel Correa near museum (3 blocks from Plaza), T9961856, fans and private baths, good budget value.

Festivals *Fiesta de San Juan Bautista*, **24** June; the district's founding (1848) is celebrated with colourful parades and historical events each 19 October.

Transport **Buses** Chitré is the transport hub of the peninsula but has no central bus terminal; most buses leave from different points around the Cathedral. To **Panama City** (250 kilometres), regular departures by several companies, 4 hours, US$7.25. To **Divisa**, 30 minutes, US$1.30;

same fare and time to **Las Tablas** (buses leave when full). To **Tonosí**, 3 hours, US$4.15; to **Santiago**, 1½ hours, US$2.50. Daily flights (except Sunday) to the capital with Chitreana de Aviación, US$27.50 – these also serve Los Santos, Guararé and Las Tablas; taxi to the small airport US$1.50 (maximum).

Los Santos

Population: 9,000
Colour map 6, grid B2

Los Santos, only four kilometres across the Río La Villa from Chitré in Los Santos province, is an old, charming town with a fine 18th century church (San Anastacio) containing many images. The first call for Independence came from here; the interesting **Museo de la Nacionalidad** on the Plaza Bolívar is in the lovely house where the Declaration was signed on 10 November 1821, entrance charge US$0.25.

Sleeping   **C** *La Villa de Los Santos*, T9968201, a/c caravans, with swimming pool and good restaurant. **E** *Pensión Deportiva*, no single rooms, private showers.

Festivals   The four-day Feast of Corpus Christi (40 days after Easter) is celebrated in Los Santos with one of the country's most famous and popular festivals, medieval dances, skits and costumes galore, a glorious distillation of the Peninsula's uniquely-strong Spanish roots and well worth attending. The *Feria de Azuero* is held at the end of April (variable date). 'Little Devil' (*diablito*) and other masks featuring prominently in these *fiestas* are the local handicraft speciality and may be purchased from many stalls or workshops around town (also in Parita).

The main road continues 22 kilometres southeast through agricultural country to the tiny town of **Guararé** (*Population*: 700), notable only for its folkloric museum, the **Museo Manuel Zárate** two blocks behind the church, T9962535, where examples of Azuero's many traditional costumes, masks and crafts are exhibited in a turn-of-the-century house. There is also a wealth of traditional dance, music and singing contests during the annual National Festival of *La Mejorana* (24 September). Two hotels: *Eida* and *Guararé*.

Las Tablas

Population: 22,140
Colour map 6, grid B2

Las Tablas (six kilometres further) is capital of Los Santos province and the Peninsula's second-largest city, 67 kilometres from the Divisa turnoff. The central **Iglesia de Santa Librada** with its gold-leaf altar and majestic carvings is one of the finest churches in this part of Panamá and is now a National Historic Monument. Lacking other outstanding points of interest (except perhaps **El Pausilipo**, former home of thrice-President Porras – known to Panamanians as 'the great man' – and in the process of being turned into a museum), Las Tablas is nevertheless widely-known for its *Fiesta de Santa Librada* and incorporated *Fiesta de la Pollera*. The *pollera* is a ruffled, intricately-embroidered in a single colour, off-the-shoulder dress based on colonial fashions and now the national costume of Panamá; *polleras* are made in a number of villages near Las Tablas (for example La Tiza, El Cocal, San José), the most beautiful coming from Santo Domingo (five kilometres east); another high-quality manufacturing centre is La Enea, a small village close to Guararé.

Excursions The lovely and unspoilt beach of El Uverito is about 10 kilometres to the east of town but has no public transport; taxi US$4.50. A paved road also runs to the port of Mensabé.

Sleeping &   **C** *Oria*, Vía Santo Domingo, T9946315, out of town. **D** *Piamonte*, Av Belisario Porras, T9946372, **eating**   a/c only. **E** *Pensión Mariela*, opposite, basic, run down. **E** *Pensión Marta*, dirty, unfriendly, noisy and overpriced. Some eating places around the church but not a lot of variety.

Festivals   *Fiesta de la Pollera* (19-23 July).

Buses To **Panama City**, several daily, 4½ hours, US$7; to **Santo Domingo**, 10 minutes, US$0.40; to **Tonosí**, 2½ hours, US$4.25. Last bus from Los Santos to Las Tablas at 1800.

South of Las Tablas

Smaller, badly-paved roads fan out from Las Tablas to the beaches along the south coast and the small hill villages in the interior. A circular tour around the eastern mountain range can be done by continuing south to Pocrí and Pedasí (42 kilometres), then west to Tonosí, all with their ancient churches and lack of spectacular sights, but typical of the Azuero Peninsula. Another 57-kilometre paved road runs directly over the hills from Las Tablas to Tonosí, good as far as the small tropical village of Flores.

Pedasí

A peaceful colonial town, the municipal library, near the church (in front of a service *Colour map 6, grid B2* station) has many old volumes. Beautiful empty beaches (beware dangerous cross-currents when swimming) and crystal-clear seas are three kilometres away. The local festival is *Patronales de San Pablo* (29 June). Most things hereabouts, it seems, are run by the Moscoso clan, including a charming wildfowl reserve near the beach, with storks and herons. Offshore between Pocrí and Pedasí is **Isla Iguana**, a wildlife sanctuary protecting the island's birdlife, reptiles and forest; the IPAT office in Chitré can arrange a tour with knowledgeable naturalist René Chan who lives locally. **C** *Pensión Moscoso*, T9952203, with shower, TV, a/c (**E** without), clean, good, friendly, meals arranged by owner at nearby bar. Another cabin-style hotel at the entrance to town. *Turístico JR's*, T9952176, owner was head chef at *Hotel El Panamá*, Swiss/French dishes. Recommended. *Getting there:* From Las Tablas leave when full, US$2.65, 1½ hours, bumpy trip.

Playa Venado

The road onwards is quite good as far as **Cañas** (no hotel), running near the Pacific coast for a short distance, with a string of lovely coves and sandy beaches accessible by rough tracks. 10 kilometres before Cañas, a small sign points to the black-sand beach of **Playa Venado**, a surfer's paradise down a long dirt road (being improved); can be busy at weekends.

A branch road from Tonosí goes a few kilometres further south to Cambutal; little reason to detour here as the beaches are a long way out and difficult to get to. The main inland road turns back north following the Río Tonosí, crosses a saddle between the two mountain ranges occupying the centre of the Peninsula (picturesque views of forested Cerro Quema, 950 metres), and arrives at **Macaracas**, another attractive but unremarkable colonial town, from where two paved roads return to Los Santos and Chitré (35 kilometres).

Tonosí has the **D** *Pensión Boamy*, with a/c, **E** with bath, a restaurant, gas station, **Sleeping at** pharmacy and a few basic shops; there are *cabañas* for rent (**E** per person), plenty of **Playa Venado** idyllic camping spots and a small basic restaurant.

One bus a day to Playa Venado from Las Tablas at 1300, about 2 hours, US$3.20, return at **Transport** 0700. No direct bus Pedasí-Tonosí; Pedasí-Cañas at 1500, US$1 (returns 0700); Cañas-Tonosí 1 a day. Tonosí-Las Tablas, 4 a day between 0700 and 1300, US$2, 1½ hours, leave when full; a milk truck leaves Tonosí at 0700 for Chitré, via Cañas, Puerto Venado, Pedasí and Las Tablas, takes passengers, returns 1230. Bus Tonosí-Chitré via Macaracas, 4 a day before 1100, 3 hours, US$4, mostly good, paved road. Hitching is very difficult in this area.

Ocú

Population: 2,750
Colour map 6, grid B1

About 45 kilometres west of Chitré is Ocú, another old colonial town, whose inhabitants celebrate quite a few notable *fiestas* throughout the year with traditional dress, music, masks and dancing, for example San Sebastián, the district's patron saint, costumed folklore groups, 19-24 January; the *Festival del Manito* at the Assumption (15 August). Straight from medieval Spain, and well-worth witnessing, are the festivities of *El Matrimonio Campesino*, *El Penitente de la Otra Vida* and *El Duelo del Tamarindo*. IPAT tourist offices (Panama City, David, Santiago, Chitré) are best informed about dates and details. Ocú is also known for its woven hats, which are cheaper than elsewhere in Panamá. **E** *Posada San Sebastián*, on the plaza, fans, clean bathrooms, patio, charming. *Getting there:* Ocú can be reached directly from the Pan-American Highway (19 kilometres) by a paved turnoff south just past the Río Conaca bridge (11 kilometres west of Divisa); *colectivos* run from here for US$0.80. Alternatively, a mostly gravel road runs west from Parita along the Río Parita valley, giving good views of the fertile agricultural landscapes of the northern Peninsula. Several buses a day from Chitré, 1 hour, US$1.75, and buses on to Panama City, US$7. For those with limited time, a representative glimpse of the countryside and villages could be had by taking a bus from Chitré to Pesé, Los Pozos or Las Minas, all in the foothills of the western range, and then another to Ocú; staying the night and taking another bus on to Santiago to return to the Panama City-David highway.

The central mountains effectively cut off the western side of the Pensinsula from the more developed eastern half. Only one road down from the Highway, a gruelling gravel/dirt ribbon which staggers from near Santiago as far south as the village of Arenas (80 kilometres) before giving up in the face of the surrounding scrubby mountain slopes. Eastward from here the Peninsula reaches its highest point at Cerro Hoya (1,559 metres); no roads penetrate either to the coast or into the mountains, ensuring solitude for the **Cerro Hoya National Park**, which protects most of the southwest tip.

Santiago to David

Santiago

Population: 32,560
Colour map 6, grid B1

The road from the junction at Divisa to Santiago, the next town, 37 kilometres, runs across the Province of Veraguas, the only one which has seaboards on both oceans. It is very dry in the summer. Santiago, capital of the Province, is well inland; one of the oldest towns in the country, in a grain-growing area. Very good – and cheap – *chácaras*, macramé bags adopted by male peasants from the Indians as a convenient carryall for lunch, a file for sharpening the machete, and other necessities in the fields, are sold in the market here. Santiago is the mid-point rest stop for cross-country buses. 18 kilometres north is **San Francisco**; it has a wonderful old church with wooden images, altar pieces and pulpit. Adjacent to the church is a swimming pool.

Sleeping **In Santiago** **C** *Gran David*, on Pan-American Highway, T9984510, a/c, TV, cheaper with black and white TV, **E** with fan, all rooms have bath, clean, pool, good inexpensive restaurant. Recommended. **C** *Piramidal* on Pan-Am Highway, T9984483, a/c, TV, shower, clean, quiet, good pool. Recommended. **C** *Roselas Apartotel*, Vía San Francisco, T9987269, apartments with kitchen, a/c, hot water, clean, friendly, safe parking for motorcycles. **D** *Santiago*, C 2 near the Cathedral, T9984824, clean, with a/c, TV and shower, cheaper with shared bath. Recommended.
Pensiones on Av Central: **E** *Jigoneva*, No 2038, basic, friendly. **E** *Central*, next door, basic, all rooms with shower, Chinese owner. *Continental*, next door, friendly, basic, shared bath. Swimming pool near town centre.

Transport Buses from Penonomé, US$4, from Aguadulce, US$2.50; Panama City-David buses stop outside *Hotel Piramidal*; bus to David from here US$7; to Panama City US$7.

West of Santiago is the turn-off to **La Atalaya**, site of a major pilgrimage and festival in honour of a miraculous statue of Christ, and home of the Instituto Jesús Nazareno, an important agricultural school for rural boys (open to visitors on Sunday). Further on is La Mesa, with a beautiful, white colonial church. The old, bad road through **Soná** (43 kilometres. *Population*: 5,000) in a deep fertile valley to **Guabalá**, near Remedios the country's largest stock-raising centre, has been replaced by a direct paved highway from Santiago to Guabalá. This saves a couple of hours. From Guabalá to David is 92 kilometres.

About 17 kilometres west of Guabalá is **Las Lajas**, take turn-off at San Félix. Las Lajas has good, wide beaches (no facilities, two bars, costly shade for cars – shark-infested waters and strong waves). To get there take a bus from David to the turn off (US$2.50), then walk three kilometres to the town, from where it is 10 kilometres to the beach (taxis only, US$5).

38 kilometres west of Las Lajas is a turning left to Horconcitos and 13 kilometres further beyond, on a dirt road, is the tiny fishing village of Boca Chica. From there you can cross in a few minutes to the island of Boca Brava US$1 per person, in the **Golfo de Chiriquí National Maritime Park**. On the island is *Restaurante Boca Brava*, with **D** cabins, **E** cane huts and **F** per person camping. Abundant fauna, interesting flora, snorkelling on the nearby rocks, German owners, (radio) T7743117, code 8731.

About 10 kilometres east of David is the small town of **Chiriquí**. A new paved road through Gualaca leads north to the mountains and over the divide to Chiriquí Grande, see page 1224.

David

David, capital of Chiriquí Province (*Population*: 368,023), a hot and humid city, rich in timber, coffee, cacao, sugar, rice, bananas and cattle, is the third city of the Republic. It was founded in colonial times as San José de David and has kept its traditions intact while modernizing itself. 24-hour Shell station at Avenida Cincuentenario y Calle C, Nte; there are now plenty of service stations on the Pan-American Highway.

Population: 102,400
Colour map 6, grid B1

Sights The attractive town has a fine central plaza, Parque Cervantes, with the colonial style Iglesia de San José on its west side. The bell tower in Barrio Bolívar was built separately as a defence against Indian attacks. Palacio Municipal, opposite *Hotel Nacional* on Avenida and Calle Central.

Museums **Museo José de Obaldía**, Calle 8 Este, No 5067 y Calle A, Nte, four blocks from Plaza, historical and art museum in house of the founder of Chiriquí province. ■ *Tuesday-Saturday 0900-1600, US$0.25.*

Excursions A few kilometres north of David on the Boquete road is *Balneario Majagua*, where you can swim in a river under a waterfall; cold drinks for sale. There is another bathing place on the right 10 kilometres further on. Take a Dolega or Boquete bus and ask the driver to let you out. About two kilometres along the main road to the border is the *Casco Viejo* rum factory, free tour and something to take away with you. Also visit the *Conservas de Antaño* (Old Fashioned Preserves) company in the Buenos Aires section across the suspension bridge. They produce excellent jams (strawberry, passion fruit, raspberry, mango, pineapple et cetera) and are the only asparagus growers in the country shipping daily to restaurants in Panama City. It is a family owned business, very friendly, T7201539.

Sleeping **A** *Nacional*, C Central, T7752221, clean rooms, good restaurant, small gaming room, major renovations in 1997 unfortunately replacing its former charm with modern services. **B** *Fiesta*, on Pan-American Highway, T7755454, good pool (US$2 for non-residents). **D** *Iris* on Parque Cervantes T7752251, with bath and fan (a/c more). Recommended. **D** *Saval*, Calle D, Nte between Cincuentenario y Av 1 Este, T7753543, a/c, small restaurant, clean and friendly. **E** *Pensión Clark*, Av Francisco Clark, T7743452, bath, north of bus terminal. **E-F** *Pensión Costa Rica*, Av 5 Este, Calle A, Sur, T7751241, variety of rooms, some with shower, a/c, or small, noisier rooms, toilet and fan, basic, clean, safe, and friendly, good value. **E** per person *Pensión Fanita*, Manuel J Posa between C 5 y 6, with bath and a/c, cheaper without a/c, not clean noisy, hourly rentals. *Pensión y Restaurante Canton*, C Central, Av 4-6 Este, opposite supermarket, fan, good beds, but run down and security not good. **F** *Pensión Rocío No 2*, with shower, big rooms with partition walls, good value restaurant. Most cheap hotels are on Av 5 Este.

Eating *Las Cacerolas*, Av Obaldía behind Super Barú, just off Pan-American Highway, self-service, clean, fresh Panamanian dishes all day, a/c, cheap. Highly recommended. *Mariscos Daiquirí*, Av Central, Calle C Sur, fish and seafood, not cheap, but good. *Jimar*, corner of Calle C Nte and Av Bolívar, good steaks. *Las Vegas*, Av Obaldía, opposite *Hotel Nacional*, steaks and pastas. *Parrillada El Portal*, Calle A Sur, Av 5 Este, good. *Don Pan*, opposite *Pensión Costa Rica*, excellent shop/café with sandwiches, cakes. *Restaurant Bar Bon Jour*, just outside town towards Boquete, very pleasant, steaks and pizzas good. *El Steak House*, Pan-American Highway west of Av Obaldía, good Chinese, moderate prices. Many around central plaza (*Parque*, *Don Pedro*, *Pollo Riko*, all a/c). *Oasis*, 2 blocks west of Parque, good, reasonable prices. *Café Don Dicky*, Calle C Nte near Av Domingo Díaz, better than it looks, Pizza House round corner. *América* in bus station, 0500-2400, others opposite and of varying quality in municipal market, Av Obaldía, near Av 3 de Noviembre, 4 blocks north of plaza.

David

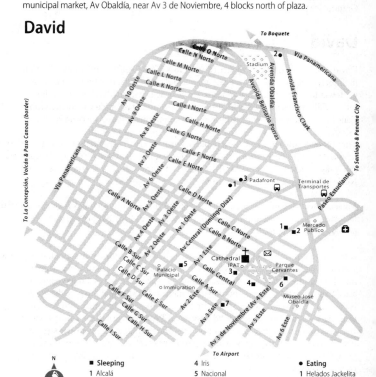

Sleeping
1 Alcalá
2 Avenida
3 Castilla

4 Iris
5 Nacional
6 Occidental & Multi-Café
7 Panama Rey

Eating
1 Helados Jackelita
2 La Cacerola
3 Palacio Oriental

Not to scale

Cinema *Plaza* cinema, by Parque Cervantes. **Discotheque** *Metropolitan*, plays salsa. **Entertainment**

Major week-long international fair and fiesta in **mid-March**. **Festivals**

Local Bus: urban buses US$0.20; taxis US$0.65 in city. **Car hire**: Budget, T7755597; **Hertz**, **Transport**
T7756828; **Mike's**, T7754963; **Fecar**, T7753246, reasonable. If wishing to rent a four-wheel
drive vehicle for Volcán Barú, do so in David.

 Air Several Aeroperlas flights a day from Panama City, US$55 1-way. Also to Bocas del
Toro and Changuinola, both US$22.50 1-way. New frequent service to San José, Costa Rica,
about US$90; enquire at Aeroperlas desk in Panama City.

 Buses The main bus terminal is at Av 2 Este, 1 block north of Av Obaldía. All companies
use this except Padafront, whose terminal is nearby at Av 2 Este y Av Obaldía. To **Panama
City** regular buses US$10.60, express US$15, 6 hours, 10 daily with Padafront, good service.
To Paso Canoas (border with Costa Rica), US$1.50, 1½ hours, every 15 minutes 0500-1830.
Direct to San José with Tracopa, 0830 daily, US$12, 8 hours, with stop in San Isidro. Boarding
Tracopa buses here can be chaotic as tickets are only sold once the bus has arrived, and then
people start clamouring for seats immediately. An alternative way to Panama City is to Santi-
ago and then to Panama City. Regular bus to **Boquete** from bus station (US$1.40) 1 hour. To
Volcán, 1½ hours, US$2.30, every 15 minutes, 0700-1800; **Chiriquí Grande**, 3 hours, US$7,
1½ hourly intervals 0630-1600. To **Cerro Punto**, 2¼ hours, US$3.

Banks *Citibank* on Plaza, only Citibank TCs. *Banco del Istmo*, Av 2 Este between Calle B Nte and C **Directory**
Central, for Visa cash advances and changes Bank of America TCs. *Banco Nacional de Panamá*,
0800-1330 (generally very convenient, but officious guards have been known to turn away
neatly-dressed travellers wearing shorts), changes Amex TCs, 1% commission plus US$0.10 tax per
cheque. *Banco General*, 1 block from main plaza, changes TCs, 1% commission, Visa ATM. *Caja de
Ahorro* (Caja Pronto), for Mastercard and Amex TCs. **Communications** Post Office: Calle C Nte, 1
block from Parque Cervantes. **Telecommunications:** Intel, Calle C Nte, telex and long-distance
telephone, open daily 0900-2030. **Internet** *Sinfonet*, Av Domingo Diaz y Calle E Norte, US$2 per
hour. *Electrónica Nacional*, Av Obaldía, opposite *Domino's Pizza*, US$1.50 per hour. **Cyber café** Av
Belisario Parrio, near bus terminal, 6 PCs, US$5 per hour. Recommended. **Embassies &
consulates** Costa Rican Consulate: Av 2 Ote entre Calles D y G, diagonal a la Provedora Barú,
T7741923. Consul is Juan Flores Badilla. **Laundry** *Cisne Blanca*, Av 3 Este, Mon-Sat 0700-1900.
Laundry next to *Pensión Costa Rica*, US$2 a load, wash and dry. **Tourist office** Beside the church, in
the blue building, T7754120, not much information, Mon-Fri 0830-1630. Sr Oscar Renán Ortega, owner
of *Viajes 4 Tours*, Vía Belisario Porras, T7751397, F7754652, specializes in local information. **Useful
addresses** Immigration office: Calle E Sur between Avs 3 y 4 Ote, T7741332/7754515. **Ministerio de
Hacienda y Tesoro:** Calle C Nte, 1 block from Parque Cervantes, near the Post Office.

Chiriquí Highlands

*The area around Boquete, Volcán Barú and the Cerros Punta and Totuma to the west
constitute the Tierras Altas de Chiriquí. This zone enjoys a spring-like climate the year
round: the mingling of Atlantic and Pacific winds creates an atmospheric oddity called
the bajareque (literally 'falling down'), a fine mist or moisture always in the air, especially at higher altitudes where cloud forest dominates. This, combined with the black
volcanic soil, creates highly fertile conditions.*

Boquete

A well-paved road climbs gently north from David into the cool highlands to the east   *Phone code: 507*
of Volcán Barú, passing (in 10 kilometres) a waterfall with a swimming hole at its   *Colour map 6, grid B1*
base, open-air restaurant/bar and space for wild camping. It passes through Dolega
(swimming pool, notable for its carnival four days before Ash Wednesday) before
reaching (35 kilometres) the popular mountain resort of Boquete, at 1,060 metres,

in the valley of the Río Caldera, with the slopes of the Volcán Barú to the west. Around is a beautiful panorama of coffee plantations, orange groves, strawberry fields, and gardens which grow the finest flowers and vegetables in the country. The town has many attractions: good lodging and facilities, fishing, riding, and mountain climbing, and not too expensive. Prettier than the main plaza is Parque de las Madres, with fountains, flower beds, a monument to motherhood and a children's playground. The fairground east of the river is the site for the *Feria de las Flores y el Café*, held each year mid-January. A Feria de las Orquídeas is held in April, which is interesting with many varieties of local and exotic orchids, as well as other flowers. The cemetery is worth a visit (see map). There is a panoramic view from the 'Bienvenidos a Boquete' arch at the *Coffee Bean Restaurant* (see below).

Sleeping

Accommodation is difficult to find during the Feria.

AL *La Montaña y El Valle*, Jaramillo Arriba, opposite *El Explorador Cafetería*, T/F7202211, montana@chiriqui.com. 2½ kilometres from San Juan Bautista church in Boquete (pass church, turn right at fork, cross river, turn left at intersection, then follow signs), 3 deluxe cottages in 2½ hectares (with kitchen, hot water, spacious), fine views, gourmet takeaway kitchen, also camping US$7 for 2. **AL** *Panamonte*, T7201327/4, with bath, some with kitchen, dinner costs US$13.50 and is highly recommended, popular, garden boasts over 200 varieties of orchid, very attractive surroundings, run by the Collins family (Swedish/American), horse hire US$3 per hour, guides available (ask about hot springs, Los Pozos de Caldera, see **Excursions** below, and Finca Lérida, see under Volcán Barú below; other excursions also available, such as the Río Monte Ecological Tour, ask for maps of the area). **B** *Villa Lorena Cabañas*, T7201848, US$50 per day for 4 people. **C** *Fundadores*, T7201298, restaurant, beautiful place with stream running through. **C** *Pensión Topáz*, T7201005, opened 1996, with bath (1 room without bath **D**), garden with view of Volcán Barú, pool, good breakfasts, run by Schöb family (artist/anthropologist), tours arranged. **C** *Rebequet*, T7201365, excellent rooms around a garden, with bath, TV and fridge, kitchen and eating area for guests' use, popular. Recommended. **D** *Pensión Marilós*, Av A Este y C 6 Sur, T7201380, opposite *Rebequet*, with bath (1 single **E** without bath), hot water, English spoken, very clean and well run, motorcycle parking. Recommended. Often full but will permit sharing, tours also organized, will store bags. **D** *Pensión Virginia*, main plaza, English-speaking owner, very friendly, has small restaurant.

Eating

Coffee Bean/Grano de Café, T7201624, a café on road 3 kilometres south of town, fantastic views, good snacks, book exchange, formerly had a lioness, T-shirts still available, very friendly, English-speaking owner. *Chinese Food*, yes that's its name, on Parque Central, cheap and good. On Av Central, south of the central park, Parque D Médica, *Pizzería La Volcánica*, ½ block from main plaza, good pizzas and pasta at reasonable prices. Opposite is *La Conquista*, delicious trout. Also on this side of the road are *Casona Mexicana*, for Mexican food, and *Lourdes*, outside terrace, friendly, good value. *Mary* and *Túnel* on plaza, *Rocío*, ½ block away, good value. Excellent patisserie on Avenida 11 de Abril, close to the church; on same avenue is *Pub Café*, nice atmosphere. *Pastelería Alemana*, south of the arch at the entrance to town, delicious coffee and pastries.

45 minutes' walk from Boquete (past *Hotel Panamonte*) is a new restaurant *El Explorador*, beautiful location, picnic area, children's playground, hammocks etc, entrance to area, US$1, but free to restaurant (excellent local food, breakfast and dinner).

Sports

River rafting: next to *Lourdes* restaurant, across from parque Domingo Merica, T7201505, F7201506, rafting@panama-rafting.com, bilingual father-and-son team Héctor and Iann Sánchez of *Chiriquí River Rafting*, offer 4-hour Class III and IV trips with modern equipment on Río Chiriquí from Caldera, near Boquete, to Gualaca on Fortuna-Chiriquí Grande highway, April-December, US$90 per person, and also can arrange lodging, transport to starting-point or vehicle delivery to landing point. During dry season, December-April, they arrange trips on Río Chiriquí Viejo (Class III/IV Technical) parallel to Costa Rican border from Breñón, near Río Sereno, to Paso Canoas. Panama office T2365218, hsanchez@panama.c-com.net; in Boquete T7202112. Recommended. Also *Panama River Rafting*, Sr Graciano Cruz, speaks English, T7741230, offers shorter trips, US$75 per person. **Hiking**: *Tierras Altas*, Av A Ote,

Boquete

To CEFATI Restaurant & David

■ Sleeping

1 Cabañas Villa Lorena
2 Fundadores
3 Panamonte
4 Pensión Marilos
5 Pensión Topáz
6 Pensión Virginia
7 Rebequet

● Eating

1 Casona Mexicana
2 La Conquista
3 Lourdes
4 Pizzería La Volcánica
5 Rocío

T7201342, arranges guided tours to Volcán Baru, Cerro Punta etc and can give advice on where to stay overnight. Also arranges rafting.

Directory **Laundry** *Econopronto*, Av Central, 50m from church, closed Sun and lunchtimes. *Lavomático Benny*, just south of church, very friendly, US$1 to wash. **Useful services** *Colabanco* changes TCs with a commission of US$1 per cheque. On the main street, Av 11 de Abril, or Fundadores, are Banco Nacional (cashes TCs, as will the cooperative opposite the bank on the plaza), *farmacia*, cinema, *Dejud* supermarket; on Av A Este are the post office, market and church of San Juan Bautista.

Hikes & excursions To the summit of **Volcán Barú** (3,475 metres), 21 kilometres west of Boquete, the first seven kilometres is paved, but the rest of the track is very rough, bumpy and steep for which four-wheel drive is necessary (there are no service stations en route). The paved road, sometimes lined with aromatic pines, goes through coffee groves, mainly tended by Ngöbe-Buglé (Guaymí) Indians, most numerous in the area during the year-end harvest season. Shortly after the end of the paved road you come to the entrance to the national park. There is a small Inrenare (National Resources Institute) office here, not always manned, and there is also an office on the southern outskirts of town, near the Colegio Franciscano, at which information is available. The track winds up from the office through impressive, tall cloud forest, thick with hanging creepers, lichen and bromeliads. The steep cuttings are carpeted with a glorious array of ferns and colourful flowers; many birds can be seen, including bee hummingbirds and wild turkeys, also squirrels. The perfume from the flowers, especially in the wet season when there are many more blooms, is magnificent.

As the road rises, increasingly steeply, wonderful views appear, of the Boquete valley, the Río Caldera running through a steep gorge, and the misty plain beyond stretching to the sea (best seen in the early morning with the rising sun behind). About three-quarters of the way up there is a crater on the left, with a sign leading to a mirador, about a 15 minutes' walk.

At the summit the jungle is replaced by a forest of TV and radio aerials, in fenced-off enclosures. A short path leads to a small cross and a trigonometric point,

Boquete environs

Based on Map by Ing I Ordóñez

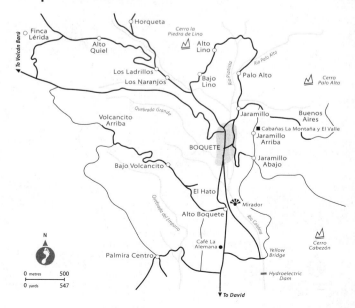

from which there are the best views all around, of dusty craters and the valley of Volcán, Bambito and Cerro Punta below. The barren, dusty slopes contrast spectacularly with the dark green forest, with wisps of mist and cloud clinging to the treetops. Sometimes horizontal rainbows can be seen in the haze, formed in the *bajareque* drizzle. There are many mini-craters around the main summit, with dwarf vegetation, lichens and orchids.

There is a makeshift campsite in a small grove of bushes on the left of the road before the final summit. From the cross there is a path down to the main crater where there is also plenty of flat ground for camping (local hikers say it is safer in groups). There is no running water – take plenty for the climb as well as for camping. Previous campers have badly littered the camping area and the graffiti is appalling. Take back everything you bring with you. After about 1100 you will probably have the place to yourself; it is very quiet and atmospheric. You may be able to stay in one of the manned TV properties, ask for advice from *Tierras Altas* (see under **Sports** above). The path that leads down from the cross branches right towards Volcán (no water on this path until you are out of the woods, at least two and a half hours).

In a suitable vehicle it takes about two hours to the top (depending on the weather), or from the park office, 4½-6 hours hike up, three hours down. A guide to the summit is not necessary, but Gonzalo Miranda (T6376023) and Generoso Rodríguez, neither trained guides, but both very knowledgeable and willing, take visitors to the summit, and to other sites, fix a price beforehand. T7201165 (the Rodriguez's home, they speak some English) or 7201261, his office, or leave a message with Sr Frank, who speaks good English, at *Pensión Marilós*. 'Zona Urbana' minibuses go virtually to the end of the asphalt. Vehicles belonging to Intel, the cable and telephone companies, often go up to the summit. They are not allowed to take passengers officially, but drivers may give you a lift if you start walking from their office in Boquete before 0800. They are also very friendly and like a chat. A taxi to the end of the paved road costs US$4. Hiking from the summit back to Boquete takes six hours.

The managers of the *Hotel Panamonte* in Boquete own the *Finca Lérida*, on the slopes of Barú volcano, ask at the hotel's front desk if you would like to visit. There are many trails in the cloud forest where quetzales have been seen and bell birds heard. Entrance to the Finca costs US$1.50 per person. 'Zona Urbana' minibuses run to the Finca.

Other attractions include: *Café Ruiz*, on the northern edge of Boquete, a small factory known for its premium-grade roasted coffees. They welcome visitors for a free guided tour (Don José Ruiz speaks English), explaining the whole process from harvesting to hand selecting only the best beans and vacuum packing the product, T720-1392/1432. Los Ladrillos, a few kilometres further up the Caldera valley, is a small area of basalt cliffs with octagonal fingers of rock in clusters, similar to Northern Ireland's Giant's Causeway. Beyond is Horqueta, a picturesque hillside area of coffee groves, with a roadside waterfall and banks of pink impatiens; beautiful views to the south.

27 kilometres north of the Pan-American Highway (15 kilometres from Boquete) is a turn off east to Caldera (14 kilometres), from where a 25-30 minute walk leads to **Los Pozos de Caldera**, a well-known series of hot springs said to be good for rheumatism sufferers. No facilities, they are on land belonging to the Collins family (*Hotel Panamonte* in Boquete), who ask only that visitors and campers leave the area clean and litter-free. There are six buses a day from David to Caldera, four a day from Boquete to Caldera, and there are pick-ups from the main road to the village. River rafting trips on the Chiriquí start from Caldera (see **Sports**, above).

A recommended half-day walk is across the suspension bridge in Boquete, then take a righthand fork winding steeply uphill. After about 30 minutes the paved road gives way to gravel; keep going to a crossroads (10 minutes) where you take the righthand fork, heading due south. (For a view of the Pacific continue straight on from the crossroads for five minutes.) The righthand fork continues with the river on your right and sweeping hillsides to your left. Eventually you rejoin the main road, turning right along an avenue lined with pine trees. The road winds down and across a big yellow bridge by a dam. After an exposed, flat stretch you meet the main road into Boquete from David; from here it is 30 minutes back to town and a well-deserved stop at the *Grano de Café*.

West of David After David, a dirt road turns off to the left to **Las Palmas**, a pleasant orange-growing village which welcomes tourists. Just before the village is a waterfall where a single column of water falls into a pool, delightful for swimming and camping.

The Pan-American Highway, undergoing widening to a modern divided highway, goes through cattle land from David 26 kilometres west to **La Concepción** (*Population*: 11,900), often called Bugaba, which is the name of the district, by the locals. It is an important agricultural shipping point also widely-known for its hand-made saddles. There are several fair hotels (for example *Rico*, C 2 Ote and the Highway; and *Caribe*, Av 1 Sur), but better accommodation in Volcán, Cerro Punta or David; a local *fiesta*, La Candelaria, is held at the end of January. *Lee Chang Hermanos* stores recommended for food, supplies, auto parts. Fill up before going to Volcán if lead-free petrol required.

Transport 10 buses daily to Panama City via David with Padafront, US$11, 7 hours; terminal beside Delta petrol station next to *El Sótano* restaurant, east of Volcán intersection on Pan-American Highway, T7704485. Local buses depart from the main plaza, called 'El Parque', old fashioned and picturesque, every 20 minutes to Volcán (US$1.65), David (US$0.50), and Paso Canoas (US$0.75).

Western Highlands

La Concepción is the gateway to the western section of the **Tierras Altas** (Highlands) **of Chiriquí**, an area bounded on the north by the Cordillera and on the west by the Costa Rican border, a prosperous agricultural region known for vegetables, flowers, superb coffees, and the Brown Swiss and Holstein dairy herds that thrive in the cool highland pastures. Less tourist-oriented than Boquete, the area is a bird-watchers' mecca and popular with residents of Panama City wishing to cool off for a few days. It has a wide variety of accommodation. Daytime temperatures are spring-like; evenings and nights chilly. Some days can be rather windy in the dry season. Mornings are especially clear and beautiful year-round. Travellers entering Panama from the north should consider a visit before pushing on to Panama City, 500 kilometres on.

La Concepción to Volcán

There is a very good paved road north from Concepción, rising 1,600 metres in 32 kilometres to Volcán. From Cuesta de Piedra, a turning to the right will take you to the canyons of the Macho de Monte, a rather small river which has worn very deep and narrow gorges. Further on, on the left, is the Mirador Alan Her, with good views from the purpose-built tower (US$0.10 unless you've bought something in the snackbar) to the sea, and on a clear day, the Punto Burica peninsula which marks the Panamá-Costa Rica frontier. On sale are very good local cheeses, especially the mozzarella. Near Volcán, excellent wood carvings at *Artes Cruz*; Don Cruz speaks English, will make charming souvenirs to order; they will be ready on your return trip.

Volcán

Colour map 5, grid B3 A rapidly growing farming town, with nurseries growing ferns for export, the *Café Volcán Barú* plant, and a small factory owned by the Swiss Bérard family producing excellent European-style sausages, pickled and smoked meats, including Panamanian *tasajo* (smoked jerky). San Benito school is noted for hardwood furniture, woodcarvings using *cocobolo* (a rare hardwood) and hand-painted ceramics sold for the benefit of the school; Bro Ælred will let you browse through his warehouse full of English books from the now-closed Canal Zone libraries and take away what you will; also visit *Cerámica Beija-Flor* run by local women who market their own wares. Southwest of town is the **Las Lagunas de Volcán** nature reserve with two beautiful lakes; abundant aquatic and other birdlife, high vehicles or four-wheel drive required in wet season. La Fuente park (signed from the main road) has playing fields and a spring-fed swimming hole (source of Río Gariché) excellent for children (US$0.25). Volcán is a good jumping-off place for the 6-12 hour ascent of the Volcán Barú. Climbers frequently climb the west side, camp overnight at the summit, and descend to Boquete in the morning. See details under Boquete. Guides can be arranged in Volcán; climbers do get lost; time lost from a wrong turning on the track can result in being caught in an inhospitable spot at nightfall.

Festival

The local *fiesta*, the *Feria de las Tierras Altas*, is held in *La Fuente* Park on the second weekend of December, rodeo, dancing, crafts fair and many attractions.

Sleeping

Price categories shown for cottages are for 1 or 2 persons, but most accommodate larger groups for the same price or slightly more.

A *Altozano*, Caizán Rd 2 kilometres from sign on main road, T7714076, charming new cottages for 1-6 people on secluded farm, full kitchen and bath, good hot water, fireplaces, good views, American owner Sr David will recommend guides, arrange tours, climbs of Cerro Punta or Volcán Barú, provide information in Spanish, English, French. Recommended. **A** *Las Huacas*, main street at west end of town, T7714363, nice cottages, hot water, clubhouse, elaborate gardens, interesting aviaries, English spoken. **A** *Cabañas Dr Esquivel*, T7714770, several large houses in a compound on the road behind *Supermercado Bérard*, friendly. **C** *Don Tavo*, main street, T7714258, new, private baths, hot water, restaurant, clean, friendly. Recommended. **C** *Dos Ríos*, T7714271, older wooden building (upper floor rooms quieter), restaurant, bar (Sr Goyo speaks English), garden with stream, private baths, hot water unreliable. **C** *Cabañas Reina*, signed from main road, T7714338, self-contained units with a kitchen in lawn setting. **C** *Valle la Luna*, signed from main road, T7714225, older cabins. **D** *Motel California*, on main street, T7714272, friendly Croatian owner speaks English, clean private baths, hot water, larger units for up to 7, US$45, restaurant, bar, quiet, good. **D** *Cabañas Señorial*, main street at entrance to town, T7714239, basic, OK. **E** *El Oasis*, behind restaurant, C La Fuente, T7714644, bar can be noisy. **E** *Cabañas Morales*, Nueva California, T7714435.

Eating

Plenty of cheap eating places, including *pizzerías*; good fish brought from coast daily, *Marisquería El Pacífico*, main road east of main intersection. Recommended. *Lorena*, tables on porch.

Night life

Discos Weekend discos at *Eruption* and *Kalahari*, rustic, good places to meet local youth.

Directory

Banks *Banco Nacional* and *Banco de Istmo*, Mon-Fri 0800-1500, Sat 0800-1200, both change dollar TCs. **Communications** Ironmongers/hardware store *Ferremax*, main road opposite police station, sends and receives international fax (7714461), 0700-1200, 1400-1800, US$1.50 per page plus telephone charge, and ferremax@pananet.com, US$2 per message; English spoken. **Laundry** *Lavamático Volcán*, main road opposite *Jardín Alegría* dancehall. Service only US$2.50, wash, dry and fold, reliable, Doña Miriam will have washing ready when promised.

The road divides at the police station in Volcán; the right branch continues north to Bambito and Cerro Punta (22 kilometres), following the Chiriquí Viejo river valley up the northwest foothills of Volcán Barú. Cross the dry plain of *Los Llanos de Volcán*, with coffee farms in the hill to the west. Just beyond *Paso Ancho* is the moderately priced *La Hacienda Restaurant*, T7714152, fresh trout, barbecued chicken. Recommended. At tiny **Bambito** is the luxurious **AL** *Hotel Bambito*, T7714265, F7714207, indoor pool, spa, conference room, good but expensive restaurant, with a view of a looming cliff, tennis courts, motor-scooter rental, horse-riding, mini-golf – the lot! Very good bargains can be negotiated here in the off-season. Across the road is

Truchapan, a trout farm supplying the hotel and the *Hotel Panamá* in Panama City. Visits are free, trout is US$2.65 per lb. Many roadside stands sell fresh vegetables and *chicha,* a fruit drink made from wild raspberries or fresh strawberries in season.

Cerro Punta

Altitude: 2,130m At the end of the road (buses from David via La Concepción and Volcán, two and a quarter hours, US$3.25), is Cerro Punta, in a beautiful valley which is the heart of a vegetables and flower-growing zone, and a region of dairy and racehorse farms. It is sometimes called 'Little Switzerland' because of its Alpine-style houses and the influence of Swiss and former-Yugoslav settlers; there is a settlement called Nueva Suiza just south of town. The countryside, full of orchids and rainbows, is beautiful, though economic pressures push the fields ever higher up the hillsides at the cost of the wooded areas. Many fine walks in the crisp mountain air. Continue through Cerro Punta to follow the main street as it curves to the left. Haras Cerro Punta (topiary initials clipped in the hedge) and Haras Carinthia (name visible on stable roof) are well known thoroughbred farms who will usually receive visitors and show them round. Further on is the small bridge at Bajo Grande; the right fork will lead to *Respingo,* where there is a small forest ranger station. Here, as well as at the end of the paved road – where the Fernández brothers, for a negotiated price will arrange to meet and guide you at the edge of the **Volcán Barú National Park** – quetzales can be seen in the early morning.

Continuing along this road is the starting point of the eight hours' hike (minimum), mostly downhill after an initial climb, to Boquete (the track is clear in places and there are a few signs showing the direction and time – ambitious – to Boquete); the last part is down the Río Caldera canyon. It is easier in the dry season, December-April. Don't hike alone, take a machete and sufficient provisions for two days in case of mishap, wear ankle boots, and notify someone before leaving and on arrival. This hike is also recommended for bird watching. **Parque la Amistad** is another park, 6.8 kilometres from the centre of Cerro Punta (signposted at road junction), the last section to the park office for four-wheel drive only. (Four-wheel drive taxis are available in town; drivers will arrange to park your car in a safe place; negotiate hourly price: US$8 per hour for two passengers is official.) It has been open since 1991, with two trails, good for bird watching, including quetzales (US$2 per person). Nature buffs should also visit Los Quetzales reserve inside Parque La Amistad. See **Sleeping**.

Sleeping **AL** *Cabañas Los Quetzales,* T7712182, F7712226, at Guadalupe, a true forest hideaway, 3 self-contained cabins, baths, hot water, no electricity, on a spectacular cloud forest reserve at 2,020 metres, inside Parque La Amistad, nearly 100 bird species, including quetzales, visible from porches, streams, trout hatchery, primeval forest, four-wheel drive only, bit of a hike from parking area, but worth it, owner Carlos Alfaro, fluent English, can arrange transport or daily cook. **C** *Hotel Cerro Punta,* T7712020, with 8 simple rooms and a quite good restaurant, just before the turning to La Amistad. **C** *Hotel Los Quetzales,* T7712182, F7712226, Guadalupe, 10 basic rooms with baths, same owners as *Cabañas Los Quetzales,* sauna, restaurant, conference room, *pizzería.*

Volcán to the From the fork at the police station in Volcán, the left branch loops 48 very scenic
frontier kilometres west, climbing over the Cerro Pando, and passing through beautiful cattle country and coffee plantations on a well paved, little travelled, winding road to the Costa Rican frontier. Los Pozos, an area of small thermal pools, beside a rushing river, is a good campsite, but only accessible by four-wheel drive vehicles and hard to find as the turn-off from Volcán-Río Sereno road is unmarked. Enquire at *Panadería Mollek* (good expresso, pastries), opposite police station in Volcán. Sr Juan Mollek has a farm at Los Pozos and can provide information. At Río Colorado, 15 kilometres from Volcán, *Beneficio Café Durán,* a coffee processing plant whose delicious aroma of fermenting pulp and drying beans will announce its proximity

from kilometres away, is hospitable to visitors. At Santa Clara, 25 kilometres from Volcán, is the *Finca Hartmann*, 1,300-1,800 metres, where the US Smithsonian Tropical Research Institute maintains a biological research station devoted to ecological studies. Enter the unmarked drive 50 metres west of petrol station, next to a green house with 'Ab Santa Clara #2' sign and proceed one kilometre on a dirt road. Latest (1997) bird-watching checklist compiled by researchers lists 277 species observable on the densely wooded coffee and cattle farm which borders *La Amistad International Park* to the north. Biologists and the Hartmann family welcome visitors and have information in Spanish and English. The Hartmanns (who are also excellent auto mechanics) have a comfortable wooden cabin available in the woods one kilometre beyond the end of the dirt road (**AL** no electricity but with bath and hot water).

Frontier with Costa Rica – Río Sereno

The village of **Río Sereno** has the air of a cowboy town. The Panamanian businesses are around the plaza (including Banco Nacional – will change travellers' cheques), and the Costa Rican businesses along a street right on the border. Approaching the village from Volcán, large installations from the era of military government, now abandoned, are visible on the right. At the *alto* stop sign, the bus station is just to the right. Follow the main street left along the plaza (public telephone) to where it ends at a steep road crossing diagonally. This is the border with Costa Rica, otherwise unmarked. Numerous vendors' stalls, especially Sunday during coffee harvest (October-December or January), when Indian workers and families shop. It is safe to park (and lock) your vehicle in the open area of *Almacén Universal*. Costa Rican shops, selling leather goods, a few crafts, clothing, gladly accept US$ at current rates. Do not miss the upper floor of *Super Universal* and *Supermercado Xenia*. If entering Panama, sell colones here; it will be much more difficult at Volcán or David and rates will be worse in Panama City.

D *Hotel Los Andes*, good. Several good eating places. *Bar Universal* recommended for fried chicken with plantain chips (family atmosphere during the day, more raucous Saturday pm and on pay day during the coffee harvest). Sr Eli has a new, unnamed restaurant at the top end of the Costa Rican street, good food, friendly and helpful. **Sleeping & eating**

This is a minor international crossing post, recommended because the area is prettier and cooler than Paso Canoas (see below), but only for those using public transport, private vehicles cannot complete formalities here, and Panamanian tourist cards are not available. Customs and immigration officials at Río Sereno are unconcerned about local pedestrians or small purchases crossing in either direction. **Crossing to Costa Rica**

Immigration and customs are in the wooden police station visible on the hill north of the main Panamanian street. Departing travellers who have been in Panama for over 30 days should see **Essentials**, for details on exit permits. Those entering Panama with a visa, or from countries which require neither visa nor tourist card, will be admitted; those requiring a tourist card and US citizens without a visa will be directed to Paso Canoas. **Panamanian immigration**

The office is in a new white building at Río Sereno, open 0800-1600 Costa Rican time, Sunday till 1400. Departing travellers who have overstayed their 90-day permit will be directed to Paso Canoas for the required tax payments and fines. **Costa Rica immigration**

There is a frequent bus service dawn to dusk from David to Río Sereno, 3 hours, US$4, via La Concepción, Volcán, Santa Clara; several minibuses daily Río Sereno-Paso Canoas, 2½ hours, US$2.50. On the Costa Rican side bus from San Vito via Sabalito (see page 1142) to the border. **Transport**

Río Sereno to Paso Canoas A recently-paved, winding road runs 50 kilometres south along the Panama side of the border to Paso Canoas, about one and a half hours by car, 2-2½ by bus. If questioned at the Breñón frontier station (unlikely), travellers who could not enter at Río Sereno should explain that they are en route to Paso Canoas to complete formalities, which is permissible. At Km 41, an impressive cascade over 100 metres high pours over a cliff on the left of the Río Chiriquí Viejo below. For information on **white water rafting** on the Rio Chiriquí Viejo from Breñón during the dry season, see Boquete, **Sports**, above. There is a good view of the river valley at Km 47, with Volcán Barú visible to the northeast.

Frontier with Costa Rica – Paso Canoas

30 kilometres west of La Concepción on the Pan-American Highway is Paso Canoas, the principal port of entry between Costa Rica and Panama. At Jacú there is a secondary checkpoint, where most often only cars and buses heading east from the border are checked. Have passport, tourist card, vehicle permit, driver's licence handy in case they are asked for (usually hassle-free).

Paso Canoas is a busy border town, with many shops and outdoor stalls. Many good eating places, especially open-front restaurants opposite Costa Rican customs. Informally crossing back and forth among shops and business areas is easy, but travellers intending to leave one country for the other must submit to formalities before proceeding.

Panamanian immigration Panamanian customs are open 24 hours – remember Panama is 1 hour ahead of Costa Rica. However, the Costa Rican side is open 0700-1200, 1400-1800, 1900-2200 Panama time. After checking in at Entrada, buy a tourist card from the IPAT tourist office (open 0800-2300) around the corner of the building to the left. Then return to Entrada for entry stamp. All relatively quick and painless, unless an international bus has arrived just before you. Free maps of Panama available at IPAT.

Sleeping **E** *Palace*, clean bathroom, basic. There is a reasonable restaurant at the border.

Exchange Money changers on the Panamanian side will change colones into dollars at a good rate; the Banco Nacional de Panama cashes travellers' cheques, also has Visa ATM.

Transport Buses to Panama City via La Concepción and David with Padafront, T7276642, 10 daily every 1½-2 hours, from terminal on northeast corner of main intersection. Reservations recommended; first leg from border to David unlikely to be full, but onward to Panama City may be booked up (they require reserved tickets to be paid for the previous day, but will hold seats for travellers arriving same day from Costa Rica; explain when reserving). Fare to Panama City, US$12; express 2300, 2400 US$17. Regular buses run to David for US$1.50, 1½ hours.

Puerto Armuelles

*1990 population: 12,975
Colour map 5, grid B3*

Due south of Paso Canoas, on a good paved road, is **Puerto Armuelles**, the port through which all the bananas grown in the area used to be exported before strikes forced producers to send their bananas by road to the Caribbean coast for shipping. Puerto Armuelles on the Pacific and Almirante and Chiriquí Grande (Bocas del Toro) are the only ports in Panama outside the Canal area at which ocean-going vessels habitually call and anchor in deep water close inshore. For information on visiting banana plantations, consult Chiriquí Land Company (Chirilanco), the local subsidiary of Chiquita Brands. Beyond the church and supermarket, opposite the golf course, in the smaller of two buildings is the management office (*gerencia*) – no scheduled tours, but the staff will give good advice.

Sleeping **C** *Kokos Place*, T7707049. **E** *Pensión Trébol*, 1 block from waterfront. Plenty of cheap eating places, eg *Enrique's*, Chinese, good. *Club Social*, on water, ask any taxi, chicken and rice dishes.

Trains Chiriquí Railway: passenger service Puerto Armuelles-Progreso (half way to Paso **Transport** Canoas), twice a day each way, 2 hours, US$1. There is also a 'Finca Train', 4 decrepit, converted banana trucks, leaving at 1500 for the banana *fincas*, returning, by a different route, at 1800. No charge for passengers. Minibuses also leave all day for the *fincas*.

Buses from David via Concepción and Paso Canoas, every 15 minutes 0500-2000, 2½ hours, US$3.

The Northwestern Caribbean Coast

Panama City

Different again, Panama's Caribbean, banana-growing region has historical links with Columbus' 4th voyage and with black slaves imported to work the plantations. Ports of varying age and activity lie on the Laguna de Chiriquí, all linked by ferry. Here is an alternative land route to Costa Rica. This region is subject to very heavy rainfall from daily afternoon downpours to violent tropical storms. Normally, only from January to March is there much respite.

Laguna de Chiriquí to Costa Rica

Across the Cordillera from David, on the Caribbean side, is the important banana growing region which extends from **Almirante** northwest across the border to Costa Rica. In the 1940-50 period, disease virtually wiped out the business and plantations were converted to *abacá* and cacao. Resistant strains of banana were developed and have now all but replaced *abacá* and cacao. Thriving banana plantations are throughout this area on the mainland, many owned by Cobanat (Cooperativa Bananera del Atlántico), who export through Chiquirí Land Company, a subsidiary of Chiquita Brands (formerly United Fruit Company) or Dole, subsidiary of Standard Brands. Bananas are exported to Europe from Almirante, where, if you must, there are places to stay, **B** *Cocomo-on-the-Sea*, seafront, T7579259, breakfast included, good plumbing, simple and clean, home cooked meals, German-American owners, limited Spanish. **D-E** *San Francisco*, a/c or fan, small dark rooms, overpriced. **D-E** *Hong Kong*, with fan, or more expensive with a/c, restaurant. **E** *Albergue Bahía*, T7789211, clean, friendly owner, will store belongings. **E** *Pensión Colón*, basic nice rooms, friendly owner.

Isla Colón and Bocas del Toro

Across the bay are a number of islands, the most important of which is Isla Colón, *Colour map 5, grid B3* which used to be a major banana producer, but this did not revive with the mainland plantations. Its main sources of income now are fishing and tourism, centred on **Bocas del Toro** on the southeast tip of the island. Bocas del Toro deserves a visit (*Fiesta del Mar* end September/early October): peaceful, quiet, English spoken by most of the black population. The protected bay offers all forms of watersport and diving, beautiful sunrises and sunsets, and, on land, tropical birds, butterflies, red frogs and other wildlife. Do not go to deserted stretches of beach alone. Excursions can be made to the islands of the archipelago (Bastimentos – see below, Carenero, Solarte), to Isla del Cisne, a bird sanctuary, and to the beautiful Islas Zapatillas, for beaches and fishing. At **Bastimentos** is a National Marine Park: on this island and on Isla Colón are turtle nesting grounds, whose protection is being improved. Tours of the Marine Park cost US$75 per boat (0900-1600); entry to the park is US$10 extra. There is snorkelling and a lunch stop. Colón also has a cave of long-beaked white bats, which fly out at dusk (tour US$10, plus US$5 for lunch on beach). You can walk to the cave, a pleasant day there and back, but ask locals for directions and advice on safety. On Bastimentos it's a 30-minute walk to northern beaches with soft off-white sand and strong undertow; ask directions, take food and drink, or ask if anywhere is open selling meals. Note that many of the names relate to Columbus' landfall here on his fourth voyage in October 1502 (Carenero was where he careened his ships, Bastimentos where he took on supplies, et cetera). The area has a rich buccaneering past, too.

Between Almirante and the Costa Rica border is **Changuinola** with an airstrip.

50 kilometres to the southeast of Almirante is **Chiriquí Grande** which has a road connection with the rest of the country (see below) but none to Almirante. There are understood to be plans for one but nothing has been done. (See below for all **Transport** details.)

A devastating earthquake struck northwest Panamá and southeast Costa Rica on 21 April 1991. An island in the bay which sank during the earthquake now shows as a patch of shallow turquoise water.

Sleeping **At Bocas del Toro** **C-D** *Las Brisas*, on the sea (formerly *Botel Thomas*), T7579428, F7579257, Apdo 5, Bocas del Toro, wooden building on stilts, with bath and fan, restaurant, bicycle, snorkel and canoe hire, good but cockroaches and thin walls. Ask for recommended guide Baillo. **D** *Bahía*, T7579626, building formerly the HQ of the United Fruit Company, nice cafetería, laundry. **D** *Sagitarius*, 1 block from main street, T7579578, new 1997, with bath, fan, clean, good. **E** *Hospedaje Heike*, on main square, 2 rooms. Highly recommended. **F** per person *Hospedaje Heidi*, on main street, northwest corner of central plaza, good restaurant on ground floor, front rooms airy, pleasant, nice view, back rooms above kitchen less good.

At Bastimentos **E** *Pensión Bastimentos*, friendly, fan, hot water, shared bathroom, restaurant – seafood speciality, laundry service, tours. *Calypso Club*, breakfast US$2.50, dinners from US$3.50, room and hammocks for rent, boat trips to the National Marine Park arranged. Rooms may also be arranged through Gabriel.

At Changuinola **D** *Changuinola*, T7588681, near airport. **D** *Carol*, T7588731, 100 metres from bus station, with bath, a/c, restaurant next door same ownership. Restaurant *El Caribe*, near airport. Recommended. Also nightclubs (*54* best), cinema and theatre.

At Chiriquí Grande **D** *Pensión Emperador*, T7579656, overlooking wharf, clean, friendly, balcony. **E** *Hotel Buena Vista*, does breakfasts, friendly, shared bath, nice. **F** per person *Osiris*, fan, basic but OK, awful food. **E** *Pensión Guillerma*, both are further away from the port's 24-hour generator so may be quieter, basic, shared bath (latter has noisy bar downstairs), take a flashlight, power only from 1800-2400. **E** *Hotel Fuente*, with bath, 1 block from waterfront next to *panadería*, friendly, clean, best in town, no sign, just ask.

Eating **At Bocas del Toro** *Las Delicias*, good food (also has rooms above, T7579318). *El Lorito Don Chico*, on main St, popular, cafetería-style, good dishes and cakes, inexpensive, bar by public dock very active, especially at weekends. *Red Lobster*, opposite *Las Brisas*, same owners, small, very friendly, good food and cheap. *Todo Tropical*, opposite police station, good seafood, American owned, you are invited to draw on the walls. *Pomodoro*, on C 3, good Italian, great atmosphere and music, reasonably priced. *Rápido Sub*, good sandwiches. *Le Pirate* bar has an information stand on the main street.

At Chiriquí Grande *Mama Gina*, next to ferry dock, good. *Dallys*, popular, to right of wharf, and *Café*, also good.

Sports **Diving**: there are several places in the Bocas del Toro archipelago popular for diving. On Isla Colón, **AL** *Mangrove Inn Eco-Dive Resort*, T/F7579594, restaurant, office in Bocas del Toro,

C 3 (Mangrove Roots Shop), with several good locations near the resort for scuba diving and for snorkelling in the clear waters around Mangrove Point. Their dive shop, *Turtle Divers*, has equipment for sale and rent and arranges courses and excursions. They also have underwater photo equipment. Also in Bocas del Toro town is *Bocas Dive Shop*, C 3, similar services, 2 dives US$40. 3 neighbouring islands are also visited. **Snorkelling** gear can be hired (eg from *Las Brisas* hotel, *Le Pirate* bar), US$5 a day.

Air Bocas del Toro and Changuinola can be reached by Aeroperlas from Paitilla Airport (US$42-47 1-way) and David. To David, 0800 Monday-Friday. Fare Changuinola-Bocas del Toro, US$8 1-way. **Transport**

Trains The banana railways provide links between Guabito on the Costa Rican frontier, Changuinola and Almirante. No passenger trains although passage can be negotiated with officials. Schedules and fares should be checked with the Chiriquí Land Company, Almirante T7583215.

Buses There is a road from Changuinola to Almirante (buses every 30 minutes till 2000, 30 minutes, US$1). Bus to San José leaves Changuinola 1000 daily US$8, 6-7 hours, one stop for refreshments in Limón, but many police checks (this bus may not always run).

From Chiriquí Grande in Bocas del Toro there is a spectacular road over the mountains, mostly paved but some rough stretches and some earthquake damage under repair, passing through virgin rain forest, the Cricamola Indian Reservation and the Fortuna hydroelectric plant, to Gualaca and finally Chiriquí on the Pan-American Highway east of David (the turn off is 10 kilometres east of David, just after the Río Chiriquí bridge). Bus to David from Chiriquí Grande hourly to 1700 daily, 3 hours, US$7. Bus Panama City to Changuinola via Chiriquí Grande, ferry to Almirante, then road, departs Panama City from C 30 between Hotels *Dos Mares* and *Soloy* at 0500, not on Monday; leaves Changuinola from *Tropicana* restaurant opposite Banco Nacional, 0645, 19 hours, US$22.

Boat Water taxis from Almirante to Bocas del Toro daily from 0700 till 1430, except Wednesday, 30 minutes minimum, US$3, leave when full. Water taxi Bocas del Toro direct to Chiriquí Grande, US$10, and from Almirante to Chiriquí Grande, frequent, 1½hours, US$10.

Vehicle ferry ('Palanga') from Almirante to Chiriquí daily (except Monday) at 0800, US$40 per car, and US$4 per adult, 5 hours if lucky; ferry Chiriquí Grande-Almirante daily (except Monday), 1330. The car ferry calls at Bocas del Toro Friday and Sunday at 0900 and, on the return trip, at 1700 back to Almirante.

To Bocas del Toro by canoe with outboard motor, US$10, or US$15 for 2. Hire boats or water taxis in Bocas del Toro to Bastimentos and the other islands. Boat to Bastimentos US$2 per person one-way, ask around *Le Pirate* bar and arrange time to be picked up. If hiring a boat, try to arrange it the day before, US$5 per hour not including petrol, 4 hours minimum, can take 5 people. If going on to Costa Rica from Bocas, get the first water taxi for connections at Sixaola. There is reported to be a ferry between Bocas del Toro and Colón at the weekends, US$22, but we await full information.

Bicycle hire US$7.50 per day from *Las Brisas*; shop on main street, Isla Colón, southwest corner of plaza, charges US$15 per day, new bikes; another place just north of government building charges US$10, nearly new, in all cases check bikes carefully. **Moped** hire at south end of main street, US$30 per day, also check machines carefully.

Banks *Banco Nacional de Panamá*, Av F, between C 1/C 2, Bocas del Toro, open Mon-Fri 0800-1500, Sat 0900-1200. At Changuinola: *Banco del Istmo*, open till 1500 weekdays, 1200 Sats, changes Amex Tcs ad cash advances on Visa and Mastercard. **Directory**

At the continental divide (Km 56 from Pan-American Highway) there is a good restaurant, *Mary's*, buses stop here. On the southern side of the Fortuna Reserve is **B** *Finca La Suiza*, T7743117, Quadrifoglio, David F7744030, owned by a Swiss couple, Herbert Brüllmann and Monika Kohler, excellent for birdwatching on forest trails, very good food, comfortable accommodation with bath and hot water, breakfast US$3.50, dinner US$8.50. To get there from Gualaca: pass the sign to Los Planes

(16.4 kilometres) and the turning to Chiriquicito; 300 metres after this junction is the sign for the Fortuna Reserve, one kilometre beyond the sign is the gate to the *Finca* on the right. From Chiriquí Grande, the entrance is one kilometre on the David side of *Restaurant Mary*. There are basic rest stops with views of both oceans 20.5 and 22.5 kilometres south of the continental divide. There is a 10-metre waterfall three kilometres south of the divide. Going north from the continental divide to Chiriquí Grande is a cyclist's delight – good road, spectacular views, little traffic and downhill all the way.

Frontier with Costa Rica – Guabito

Panamanian immigration

The border at Sixaola-Guabito is open 0800-1800 Panama time. Advance clocks 1 hour entering Panama. Formalities for entry/exit for each country are performed at either end of the banana train bridge which crosses the frontier. Just a short walk over the bridge; onward ticket may not be asked for on the Costa Rican side.

Entering Panama If you need a visa or tourist card, best to obtain it in San José. Entry charge normally US$0.75 (receipt given) although if you already have a visa you may not be charged, 30 days given if you already have a visa, 5 days' entry card if not, US$2 (extensions at Changuinola airport immigration, opens 0830 – 5 passport photos, photographer nearby charges US$7 for 6).

Sleeping

No accommodation in **Guabito**, but if seeking cheap accommodation, cross the border as early as possible in order to get as far as Almirante (US$1 by bus).

Exchange

It is difficult to change colones to dollars in Guabito. If not returning to Costa Rica, try to use up all colones before crossing the border. Also in Guabito, have only small denomination US dollar bills to hand, US$50 notes unlikely to be accepted.

Transport

The bus from Changuinola to the frontier and back is marked 'Las Tablas', US$0.75, 30 minutes (every hour until 1700), or colectivo taxi, US$1.25 per person (private taxi US$10). Bus to San José, Costa Rica, at 1000 and 1600, US$8, 6-7 hours, 1 stop for refreshments, but many police checks, also to Puerto Viejo, US$6.

Darién and how to get to Colombia

East of Chepo is known as Darién, which is over a third of the area of Panama and almost undeveloped. Most villages are accessible only by air or river and on foot.

At the end of 1992, Panama and Colombia revealed a plan to build a road through the Darién Gap which includes environmental protection. Construction of a previous project had been halted in the 1970s by a lawsuit filed by US environmental groups who feared deforestation, soil erosion, endangerment of indigenous groups and the threat of foot-and-mouth disease reaching the USA. Of course, the more people who walk the Darién Gap, the greater the pressure for building a road link. The Darién Gap road linking Panama with Colombia will not be open for many years, though, so the usual way of getting to Colombia is by sea or air. It is possible to go overland, but the journey is in fact more expensive than going by air and considerably more dangerous.

The Pan-American Highway ends at Yaviza; from there, if you want to cross by land to South America, it's on foot through the jungles of Darién. Alternative routes to Colombia are also given.

By land

The Pan-American Highway runs east 60 kilometres from Panama City to the sizeable town of **Chepo**. There are no hotels or *pensiones* in Chepo, but if you are stuck there, ask at the fire station, they will be able to find a place for you. There is a document check in Chepo and at one or two other places. From Chepo the Highway has been completed as far as **Yaviza** (225 kilometres); it is gravel from Chepo until the last 30 kilometres which are of earth (often impassable in the rainy season).

From **El Llano**, 18 kilometres east of Chepo, a road goes north to the Caribbean coast. After 27 kilometres it passes the *Nusagandi Nature Lodge* in the Pemansky Nature Park. The Lodge is in Kuna (Cuna) territory, in an area of mostly primary forest. Visits can be arranged through Centro de Aventuras, Parque Urracá, Panama City, T2258946, F2276477. The coast is reached at Cartí, 20 kilometres from Nusagandi. From here there is access to the San Blas Archipelago.

35 kilometres east of Chepo it crosses the new Lago Bayano dam by bridge (the land to the north of the Highway as far as Cañazas is the **Reserva Indígena del Bayano**). Lago Bayano dam supplies a significant amount of Panama's electricity, and has been a source of friction with the Kuna Indians who occupy the land around the lake and especially above in the catchment area. However, it is hoped that the new autonomous *Comarca*, created in 1996, will confirm the Indian title to the land and set up conservation measures.

From bus terminal in Panama City, buses leave every 2 hours 0630-1430 for **Pacora**, US$0.80, **Buses** Chepo, US$1.60, **Cañitas**, 4 hours, US$3.10, **Arretí**, 6 hours, US$9, **Metetí** and **Canglón**, 8 hours, US$11.20. Beyond, to **Yaviza**, in the dry season only, January-April, US$15, 10 hours minimum. Plenty of pick-ups run on the last stretch to Yaviza, eg about 3 hours from Metetí to Yaviza.

The main villages (Yaviza, Púcuro, Paya and Cristales) have electricity, radios and **The land route** cassette decks, canned food is available in Yaviza, Pinogana, Unión de Chocó, Púcuro and Paya (but no gasoline), only the Emberá-Wunan (also spelt Wunaan) of the Chocó and Kuna women retain traditional dress. Organized jungle tours to Kuna Indians, Emberá-Wunan Indians and the Río Bayano costing from US$65 to over US$300 can be purchased through *Mar Go Tours*, Apdo 473, Balboa.

The bus service from Panama City (see above) has its problems, the road is bad and may be washed out after rains. Find out before you leave how far you can get. Alternatively there is an irregular boat to Yaviza, about once a week, US$12 including meals, leaving from the harbour by the market in the old city, information from Muelle Fiscal, Calle 13 next to the Mercado Público. The only sleeping accommodation is the deck (take a hammock) and there is one primitive toilet for about 120 people. The advertised travel time is 16 hours, but it can take as much as two days.

Another possibility is to fly to La Palma (see page 1234) and take the much shorter **Yaviza/El Real** boat trip to Yaviza, or direct to El Real (three a week, US$68 return), which is about 10 kilometres from Yaviza. There is only one hotel at **Yaviza** (**E** *Tres Américas*, pay in *Casa Indira* shop next door, take mosquito coils – nowhere to hang a net, basic, noisy, meals available but not very sanitary); there is a TB clinic and a hospital. Crossing the river in Yaviza costs US$0.25. From Yaviza it is an easy 1-2 hours' walk to **Pinogana** (small and primitive), where you have to cross the Río Tuira by dugout, US$1 per person. From Pinogana you can walk on, keeping the river to your left to Vista Alegre (three hours), recross the river and walk a further 30 minutes to **Unión de Chocó** (some provisions and you can hammock overnight; you can sleep in the village hall but use a net to protect against *vinchucas* – Chagas disease). One kilometre up-river is Yape, on the tributary of the same name, then 3-4 hours walking to Boca de Cupe. Alternatively you can go by motor dugout from Pinogana to Boca de

··

Cautions and general notes on crossing the Darién gap

In planning your trip by land or along the coast to Colombia, remember there are strict rules on entry into Colombia and you must aim for either Turbo or Buenaventura to obtain your entry stamp. Failure to do this will almost certainly involve you in significant fines, accusations of illegal entry, or worse in Colombia. Also, do not enter Darién without first obtaining full details of which areas to avoid because of the activities of drug traffickers, bandits and guerrilla groups, mostly from Colombia, but operating on both sides of the border. **Latest information (mid-1999) is that armed Colombian insurgents, hostile to travellers including tourists, regularly cross into Panamanian territory. Additional Panamanian forces have been sent into the area and the situation is dangerous. If information has not improved before you set out to cross Darién by land either way, you are advised not to go**.

The New Tribes Mission, after the kidnap of three missionaries, has withdrawn its staff from the area and therefore one of a traveller's main sources of assistance has disappeared.

1   The best time to go is in the dry months (January-mid April); in the wet season (from May) it is only recommended for the hardy. Even when totally covered in mosquito repellent you will get bitten and you run the risk of dengue fever.

2   Travel with a reliable companion or two.

3   Talk to knowledgeable locals for the best advice. Hire at least one Indian guide, but do it through the village corregidor, whose involvement may add to the reliability of the guides he selects. (Budget up to US$8 per day for the guide and his food. Negotiate with the chief, but do not begrudge the cost.)

4   Travel light and move fast. The journey as described below takes about 7 days to Turbo.

5   Maps of the Darién area can be purchased from the Ministerio de Obras Públicas, Instituto Geográfico Nacional Tommy Guardia, in Panama City (US$4, reported to contain serious mistakes). Information is also available from Asociación de Conservación de la Naturaleza, Calle Alberto Navarro, El Cangrejo (Apartado 1387), Panamá City, T2648100, F2641836.

··

Cupe (about US$65 per boat). Or you can take a boat from Yaviza to **El Real** (US$10), where there is a very basic place to stay, *El Nazareno*, for US$10 a night. Directly opposite there is a lady who will prepare meals if given notice. From there take a motor dugout to Boca de Cupe, about US$15-20 per person, 5 hours (if possible, take a banana dugout, otherwise bargain hard on boats). A boat all the way to Paya costs about US$35 per person for groups of 4-5. Boats from El Real are not very frequent and may only go as far as Unión de Chocó or Pinogana. A jeep track runs from El Real to Pinogana. There are various other combinations of going on foot or by boat, prices for boat trips vary widely, so negotiate. They tend to be lower going downstream than up. It is wise to make payment always on arrival.

Boca de Cupe
Colour map 6, grid A3

Stay the night at Boca de Cupe with a family; food and cold beer on sale here (last possibility if you are going through to Colombia); *Restaurant Nena* (blue building near landing dock) meals US$2, good information. You can go with Emberá-Wunan Indians to Unión de Chocó, stay one or two days with them and share some food (they won't charge for lodging). The Emberá-Wunan are very friendly and shy, better not to take pictures. In Boca de Cupe get your exit stamp (though you may be told to get it at Púcuro) and keep your eye on your luggage. Lodging in Boca de Cupe for US$12.50 with Antonio (son of María who helped many hikers crossing Darién, but who died in 1989). Don Ramón will prepare meals for US$2 and let you sleep on his floor. From Boca de Cupe to Púcuro, dugout, US$20-50, to Paya (if river level high enough) US$80. The section Boca de Cupe-Púcuro is possible on foot (see Bradt Publications' *Backpacking in Central America*).

Púcuro   Púcuro is a Kuna Indian village and it is customary to ask the chief's permission to stay (he will ask to see your passport – immigration here, if arriving from Colombia, can be very officious). The women wear colourful ornamented *molas* and gold rings through their noses. There is a small shop selling tinned meats, salted biscuits et cetera. Visitors usually stay in the assembly house. People show little interest in travellers there; stop with your luggage. From Púcuro you can walk through lush jungle to Paya, six hours (guide costs US$20, not really necessary, do not pay in advance), which was the capital of the Kuna Empire. From Púcuro to Paya there are four river crossings. The path is clear after the first kilometre.

In Paya you may be able to stay in the assembly house at the village, but it is mandatory to go two kilometres away eastwards to the barracks. You can stay there, US$2.50 per person, recommended (passport check, baggage search and, on entry into Panama at least, all gear is treated with a chemical which eats plastic and ruins leather – wash it off as soon as possible), and for US$2-2.50 you will get meals. The Kuna Indians in Paya are more friendly than in Púcuro. From Paya there are two routes.

Paya
Colour map 6, grid A3

Route 1

From Paya, the next step is a 4-6 hours' walk to **Palo de las Letras**, the frontier stone, where you enter Los Katios, one of Colombia's National Parks (see below). The path is not difficult, but frequently blocked up to the frontier. From there you go down until you reach the left bank of the Río Tulé (in three hours, no water between these points), you follow it downstream, which involves seven crossings (at the third crossing the trail almost disappears, so walk along the river bed – if possible – to the next crossing). If any of these watercourses are dry, watch out for snakes. About 30 minutes after leaving this river you cross a small creek; 45 minutes further on is the abandoned camp of the Montadero, near where the Tulé and Pailón rivers meet to form the Río Cacarica. Cross the Cacarica and follow the trail to the MA (Ministerio del Medio Ambiente – Colombian National Parks) abandoned rangers' hut at **Cristales** (seven hours from Palo de las Letras). Guides Paya-Cristales (they work in a rota and always go in pairs), US$55-200. Guides carry a gun and a small bag of provisions. They travel very fast and barely give you time to stop for a drink. If you insist on walking beyond Montadero, a machete, compass and fishing gear (or extra food) are essential; the path is so overgrown that it is easier, when the river is low, to walk and swim down it (Cristales is on the left bank, so perhaps it would be better to stick to this side). Occasional dugout to **Bijao** (or Viajado), two hours, for around US$120 per boat. There is no village nearby, so arrive prepared. It is possible to walk to Bijao down the right (west) bank of the Río Cacarica (heavy going). From the bend to the east of the river the path improves and it is one hour to Bijao. At Bijao ask for the IRENARE station, where you can eat and sleep (floor space, or camp). At the end of 1998 guerrillas seized Bihao, killing several people and driving out others, so it is unclear what facilities are available now. From Bijao a motor dugout used to run to **Travesía** (also called Puerto América) for US$40 per person (2-5 hours), from where motorboats go to Turbo for US$10 (in scheduled boat – if it stops; if not it'll cost you about US$250 to hire a boat). Travesía has some accommodation and provisions but has been reported as expensive and anti-gringo. Once again, there is a walking route south to Limón (two hours) and east to La Tapa (half an hour). A cargo boat may be caught from here to Turbo (price unknown). One *residencial* and a shop in Travesía. The last section from Travesía down the Atrato goes through an area full of birdlife, humming birds, kingfishers, herons, et cetera, and 'screamers', about the size of turkeys and believed to be unique to the Atrato valley. The river enters the Great Atrato swamp and thence to the Bahía de Colombia. Turbo is on the opposite coast.

On arrival in Turbo, you must go to the DAS office (Security Police) at Postadero Naval, north along Cra 13 near airport (open 0800-1630), to get your entrance stamp. If you fail to do this, you will have to wait until Cartagena, or elsewhere, and then explain yourself in great detail to DAS and quite likely be fined. If you arrive at the weekend and the DAS is closed, make sure you obtain a letter or document from the police in Turbo that states when you arrived in Colombia. The problems with this route are mostly on the Colombian side, where route finding is difficult, the undergrowth very difficult to get through, and the terrain steep. Any rain adds greatly to the difficulties, though equally, when the water is low, boats need more pole assistance, and the cost increases.

If you are coming into Panama from Colombia by these routes, and you have difficulty in obtaining entry stamps at Púcuro or Boca de Cupe, obtain a document from an official en route stating when you arrived in Panama. This may be equally hard to get. Then go to the Oficina Nacional de Migración in Panama City (who may send you to the port immigration) and explain the problem. One traveller reports hearing of several arrests of travellers caught without their entry stamp. Many of these 'illegals' stay arrested for weeks. It may help to be able to prove that you have sufficient money to cover your stay in Panama.

The **Katios National Park** (*Warning*: entry by motorized vehicle is prohibited), extending in Colombia to the Panamanian border, can be visited with mules from the MA headquarters in Sautatá (rangers may offer free accommodation, very friendly). In the park is the Tilupo waterfall, 125 metres high; the water cascades down a series of rock staircases, surrounded by orchids and fantastic plants. Also in the park are the Alto de la Guillermina, a mountain behind which is a strange forest

Darién

of palms called 'mil pesos', and the Ciénagas de Tumaradó, with red monkeys, waterfowl and alligators.

Route 2

The second route is a strenuous hike up the Río Paya valley through dense jungle (machete country) for about 16 hours to the last point on the Paya (fill up with water), then a further three hours to the continental divide where you cross into Colombia. Down through easier country (3-4 hours) brings you to **Unguía** (**F** *Residencias Viajero*, with bath; **F** *Doña Julia*, also with bath; several basic restaurants) where motor boats are available to take you down the Río Tarena, out into the Gulf of Urabá, across to Turbo. This trip should not be taken without a guide, though you may be lucky and find an Indian, or a group of Indians making the journey and willing to take you along. They will appreciate a gift when you arrive in Unguía. Hazards include blood-sucking ticks, the inevitable mosquitoes and, above all, thirst.

There are many other possible routes from Panama crossing the land frontier used by locals. Most involve river systems and are affected by water levels. There are few tracks and no reliable maps. We have heard of successful crossings using the Ríos Salaqui and Balsas, and a land route Jaqué-Jurado-Riosucio. Good guides and serious planning are essential.

Health advice

Dr Richard Dawood, author of *Travellers' Health: How to Stay Healthy Abroad*, and photographer Anthony Dawton, crossed the Darién Gap at the end of the wet season (November). We are pleased to include Dr Dawood's health recommendations for such a journey.

Acclimatization to a hot climate usually **Heat** takes around three weeks. It is more difficult in humid climates than in dry ones, since sweat cannot evaporate easily, and when high humidity persists through the night as well, the body has no respite. (In desert conditions, where the temperature falls at night, adaptation is much easier.) Requirements for salt and water increase dramatically under such conditions. We had to drink 12 litres per day to keep pace with our own fluid loss on some parts of the trip.

We were travelling under extreme conditions, but it is important to remember that the human thirst sensation is not an accurate guide to true fluid requirements. In hot countries it is always essential to drink beyond the point of thirst quenching, and to drink sufficient water to ensure that the urine is consistently pale in colour.

Salt losses also need to be replaced. Deficiency of salt, water, or both, is referred to as heat exhaustion; lethargy, fatigue and headache are typical features, eventually leading to coma and death. Prevention is the best approach, and we used the pre-salted water regime pioneered by Colonel Jim Adam and followed by the British Army; salt is added to all fluids, one quarter of a level teaspoon (approximately one gram) per pint – to produce a solution that is just below the taste threshold. Salt tablets, however, are poorly absorbed, irritate the stomach and may cause vomiting; plenty of pre-salted fluid should be the rule for anyone spending much time outdoors in the tropics. (Salted biscuits are recommended by Darién travellers.)

Sun Overcast conditions in the tropics can be misleading. The sun's rays can be fierce, and it is important to make sure that all exposed skin is constantly protected with a high factor sun screen – preferably waterproof for humid conditions. This was especially important while we were travelling by canoe. A hat was also essential.

Food & water Diarrhoea can be annoying enough in a luxurious holiday resort with comfortable sanitary facilities. The inconvenience under jungle conditions would have been more than trivial, however, with the added problem of coping with further fluid loss and dehydration.

Much caution was therefore needed with food hygiene. We carried our own supplies, which we prepared carefully ourselves: rather uninspiring camping fare, such as canned tuna fish, sardines, pasta, dried soup, biscuits and dried fruit. In the villages, oranges, bananas and coconuts were available. The freshly baked bread was safe, and so would have been the rice.

We purified our water with two percent tincture of iodine carried in a small plastic dropping bottle, four drops to each litre – more when the water is very turbid – wait 20 minutes before drinking. This method is safe and effective, and is the only suitable technique for such conditions. (Another suggestion from Peter Ovenden is a water purifying pump based on a ceramic filter. There are several on the market, Peter used a Katadyn. It takes about a minute to purify a litre of water. When the water is cloudy, for example after rain, water pumps are less effective and harder work. Take purification tablets as back-up – Ed.) It is also worth travelling with a suitable antidiarrhoeal medication such as Arret.

Malaria Chloroquine resistant malaria is present in the Darién area, so appropriate antimalarial medication is essential. We took Paludrine, two tablets daily, and chloroquine, two tablets weekly. Free advice on antimalarial medication for all destinations is available from the Malaria Reference Laboratory, T0891-600350 in the UK. An insect repellent is also essential, and so are precautions to avoid insect bites.

Insects Beside malaria and yellow fever, other insect-borne diseases such as dengue fever and leishmaniasis may pose a risk. The old fashioned mosquito net is ideal if you have to sleep outdoors, or in a room that is not mosquito-proof. Mosquito nets for hammocks are widely available in Latin America. An insecticide spray is valuable for clearing your room of flying insects before you go to sleep, and mosquito coils that burn through the night giving off an insecticidal vapour, are also valuable.

Ticks It is said that ticks should be removed by holding a lighted cigarette close to them, and we had an opportunity to put this old remedy to the test. We duly unwrapped a pack of American duty-frees that we had preserved carefully in plastic just for such a purpose, as our Indian guides looked on in amazement, incredulous that we should use these prized items for such a lowly purpose. The British Army expedition to Darién in 1972 carried 60,000 cigarettes among its supplies, and one wonders if they were for this purpose! The cigarette method didn't work, but caused much amusement. (Further discussion with the experts indicates that the currently favoured method is to ease the tick's head gently away from the skin with tweezers.) New advice from Dr Hollins of Stockbridge, England is that cigarettes are definitely a no-no since it roasts the tick but leaves the mouthpiece in the skin. In the jungle, this could lead to a dangerous tropical ulcer. Ticks breathe through small openings in the skin. Smoothing with oil or vaseline will kill the tick and release the mouthparts. So too will alcohols. When removing, don't pull straight – the best way to break off the head – but gently and firmly twist to left or right while pulling to dislodge the barbs. Use tweezers, as close to the tiny head as possible.

A yellow fever vaccination certificate is required from all travellers arriving from infected areas, and vaccination is advised for personal protection. **Vaccinations**

Immunization against hepatitis A (see **Health information** in the Horizons) and typhoid are strongly advised.

Attacks by dogs are relatively common: the new rabies vaccine is safe and effective, and carrying a machete for the extra purpose of discouraging animals is advised.

In addition, all travellers should be protected against tetanus, diptheria and polio.

You can get some food along the way, but take enough for at least five days. Do take, though, a torch/flashlight, and a bottle of rum (or similar!) and useful items for those who give help and information. A compass can save your life in the remoter sections if you are without a guide – getting lost is the greatest danger according to the rangers. It is highly recommended to travel in the dry season only, when there is no mud and fewer mosquitoes. A hammock can be very useful. If you have time, bargains can be found, but as pointed out above, costs of guides and water transport are steadily increasing. Buying pesos in Panama is recommended as changing dollars when you enter Colombia will be at poor rates. You will need small denomination dollar notes on the trip.

Taking a motorcycle through Darién is not an endeavour to be undertaken lightly, and cannot be recommended. The late Ed Culberson (who, in 1986 after two unsuccessful attempts, was the first to accomplish the feat) wrote: "Dry season passage is comparatively easy on foot and even with a bicycle. But it simply cannot be done with a standard sized motorcycle unless helped by Indians at a heavy cost in dollars ... It is a very strenuous, dangerous adventure, often underestimated by motorcyclists, some of whom have come to untimely ends in the jungle." Culberson's account of his journey (in the October 1986 issue of *Rider* and in a book, *Obsessions Die Hard*, published 1991 by Teakwood Press, 160 Fiesta Drive, Kissimmee, Fla, USA, 34743, T407-3487330) makes harrowing reading, not least his encounter with an emotionally unstable police official in Bijao; the 46-kilometre 'ride' from Púcuro to Palo de las Letras took six days with the help of six Indians (at US$8 a day each). Two riders were caught in an early start of rains in 1991 and barely escaped with their machines.

Not to be outdone, crossing by bicycle has been successfully completed.

By sea

Boats leave, irregularly, from the Coco Solo wharf in Colón (minibus from Calle 12, 15 minutes, US$0.80, taxi US$4) for Puerto Obaldía, via the San Blas Islands. These are small boats and give a rough ride in bad weather, cost around US$30 per person, take your own food, water and shade; with stops, 2-4 days. There are flights with Ansa (T226-7891/6881) and Transpasa (T226-0932/0843) at 0600-0630 from Panama City to Puerto Obaldía daily except Sunday for US$44 single (book well in advance). There are also flights with Aerotaxi and Saansa. Puerto Obaldía is a few kilometres from the Colombian border. There are *expresos* (speedboats) from Puerto Obaldía (after clearing Customs) to Capurganá, and then another on to Acandí (**F** *Hotel Central*, clean, safe; **F** *Hotel Pilar*, safe). From Acandí you can go on to Turbo, on the Gulf of Urabá, no fixed schedule (you cannot get to Turbo in the

Puerto Obaldía

same day; take shade and drinks and be prepared for seasickness). From Turbo, Medellín can be reached by road. Walk from Puerto Obaldía to Zapzurro, just beyond the frontier, for a dugout to Turbo, US$15, where you must get your Colombia entry stamp. It seems that most of the boats leaving Puerto Obaldía for Colombian ports are contraband boats. One traveller obtained an unnecessary visa (free) from the Colombian consul in Puerto Obaldía which proved to be useful in Colombia where soldiers and police took it to be an entry stamp.

Sleeping There is a good *pensión* in Puerto Obaldía: **E** *Residencia Cande*, nice and clean, which also serves very good meals for US$1.50, book in advance for meals.

Directory **Useful services** Also in Puerto Obaldía are shops, Colombian consulate, Panamanian immigration, but nowhere to change TCs until well into Colombia (not Turbo); changing cash is possible. (**NB** Arriving in Puerto Obaldía you have to pass through the military control for baggage search, immigration – proof of funds and onward ticket asked for - and malaria control.)

Capurganá Alternatively one can get from Puerto Obaldía to Acandí on the Colombian side of
(Colombia) the border, either by walking nine hours or by hiring a dugout or a launch to Capurganá (US$8), thence another launch at 0715, 1 hour, US$3. Several hotels in Capurganá, **B** *Calypso*, with a Medellín number for reservations, 094-2503921, **D** *Naútico*, **E** *Uvita*, clean, safe, **E** *Al Mar*. There are cheaper *pensiones* and you can camp near the beach. Good snorkelling. There is a Panamanian consul in Capurganá (Roberto) that issues Panamanian visas. There are Twin Otter flights to Medellín. To walk to Capurganá takes four hours, guide recommended (they charge US$10); first go to La Miel (two hours), then to Zapzurro (20 minutes), where there are shops and cabins for rent, then 1-1½ hours to Capurganá. Most of the time the path follows the coast, but there are some hills to cross (which are hot – take drinking water). From Acandí a daily boat is scheduled to go at 0800 to Turbo (US$15, three hours). Take pesos, if possible, to these Colombian places, the rate of exchange for dollars is poor.

On the Pacific side, there is another possible route to Colombia. Although not quick, it is relatively straightforward (spoken Spanish is essential). Take a bus from Panama (Plaza 5 de Mayo) to **Metetí**, 50 kilometres from Yaviza (**E** *Hospedaje Feliz*, basic 'box' rooms), the junction for transport to **Puerto Quimba**, where boats can be taken to La Palma. Alternatively, take a bus to **Santa Fe**, which is 100 kilometres short of Yaviza and off to the south, a rough but scenic 6-8 hours (US$8, three a day, check times). In Santa Fe it is possible to camp near the police post (no *pensiones*). Then hitch a ride on a truck (scarce), or walk two hours to the Río Sabanas at Puerto Lardo (11 kilometres) where you must take a dugout or launch to La Palma, or hire one (US$5, two hours; also reached by boat from Yaviza, US$3, eight hours – bank changes travellers' cheques in La Palma). **La Palma** is the capital of Darién; it has one *pensión* (friendly, English-speaking owners, **F**, with cooking and laundry facilities, or see if you can stay with the *guardia*). There are daily Aeroperlas flights from Panama City to La Palma, US$31, and to Jaqué, US$37 three days a week; also to Yaviza three days a week, but check with the airline Parsa, T226-3883/3803. They have an office at the domestic airport in Panama City. It is not clear if you can get a plane from La Palma to Jaqué, but there are boats. **Jaqué** is on the Pacific coast, near Puerto Piña, 50 kilometres north of the Colombian border. At **Bahía Piña** is the *Tropic Star Lodge*, T2645549, where a luxury fishing holiday may be enjoyed on the sea and in the jungle for over US$1,000 a week. (Information from *Hotel El Panamá*.) Bahía Piña has a 700-metre runway, used mainly by the expensive fishing resort.

Alternatively, at the Muelle Fiscal in Panama City (next to the main waterfront market, near Calle 13), ask for a passenger boat going to Jaqué. The journey takes 18 hours, is cramped and passengers cook food themselves, but costs only US$12. Jaqué (*Population*: 1,000) is only reached by sea or air (the airstrip is used mostly by the wealthy who come for sport fishing); there are small stores with few fruit and vegetables, a good *comedor*, one *hospedaje*, **F** *Hospedaje Chavela*, clean, basic, friendly (but it is easy to find accommodation with local families), and camping is possible anywhere on the beautiful four-kilometre beach. The guard post is open every day and gives exit stamps. Canoes from Jaqué go to Juradó (US$20, four and a half hours) or Bahía Solano (US$45, 160 kilometres, with two overnight stops) in Chocó. The first night is spent in Juradó (where the boat's captain may put you up and the local military commander may search you out of curiosity). There are flights from Juradó to Turbo, but it is possible to get 'stuck' in Juradó for several days. Bahía Solano is a deep-sea fishing resort with an airport and *residencias*. Flights from Bahía Solano go to Quibdó, connecting to Cali, or Medellín (all flights have to be booked in advance; the town is popular with Colombian tourists). On this journey, you sail past the lush, mountainous Pacific coast of Darién and Chocó, with its beautiful coves and beaches, and you will see a great variety of marine life.

NB It is not easy to get a passage to any of the larger Colombian ports as the main shipping lines rarely take passengers. Those that do are booked up well in advance. The Agencias Panamá company, Muelle 18, Balboa, represents Delta Line and accepts passengers to Buenaventura. Anyone interested in using the Delta Line ships should book a passage before arriving in Panama. The only easy way of getting to Colombia is to fly (see **Essentials**).

Shipping agencies do not have the authority to charge passages. Many travellers think they can travel as crew on cargo lines, but this is not possible because Panamanian law requires all crew taken on in Panama to be Panamanian nationals.

Colombia officially demands an exit ticket from the country. If you travel by air the tickets should be bought outside Panama and Colombia, which have taxes on all international air tickets. If you buy air tickets from IATA companies, they can be refunded. Copa tickets can be refunded in Cartagena (Calle Santos de Piedra 3466 – takes four days), Barranquilla – two days - Cali or Medellín. Refunds in pesos only. Copa office in Panama City, Avenida Justo Arosemena y Calle 39, T2275000.

Background

The land

Panama is most easily visualized as a horizontal S, with the 767-kilometre Caribbean coastline on the north and the 1,234-kilometre Pacific coast on the south and lying between 7° north and 10° north of the Equator. The Canal, which runs southeast-northwest, bisects the country from east to west; the mountains that run along the isthmus divide the country from north to south. About half the population lives in Panama City, on the east side of the Canal at its southern terminus. Most of the rural population lives in the quarter of the country south of the mountains and west of the Canal.

At the border with Costa Rica there are several inactive volcanic cones, the boldest of which is the Volcán Barú, 3,475 metres high and the highest point in the country. The sharp-sided Cordillera de Talamanca continues southeast at a general altitude of about 900 metres, but subsides suddenly southwest of Panama City. The next range, the San Blas, rises east of Colón (the city at the north end of the Canal) and runs into Colombia; its highest peak is Tacarcuna, at 1,875 metres. A third range rises from the Pacific littoral in the southeast; it runs along the Pacific coast of Colombia as the Serranía de Baudó.

Good fortune decreed a gap between the Talamanca and San Blas ranges in which the divide is no more than 87 metres high. The ranges are so placed that there is a gap, through which the Canal runs, from northwest to southeast. To reach the Pacific from the Atlantic we must travel eastwards, and at dawn in much of the country the sun rises over the Pacific.

History

The history of Panama is the history of its pass-route; its fate was determined on that day in 1513 when Balboa first glimpsed the Pacific (see the History to the Central America section). Panama City was of paramount importance for the Spaniards: it was the focus of conquering expeditions northwards and southwards along the Pacific coasts. All trade to and from these Pacific countries passed across the isthmus. As part of Colombia and its predecessors, Panama was traditionally considered part of South America until recent years, when it has more and more been classed as a Central American republic. The distinction has political significance as international economic integration increases in importance.

The Camino Real Panama City was founded in 1519 after a trail had been discovered between it and the Caribbean. The Camino Real (the Royal Road) ran from Panama City to Nombre de Dios until it was re-routed to Portobelo. An alternative route was used later for bulkier, less valuable merchandise, a road built from Panama City to Las Cruces, now swallowed up by Gatún Lake. It ran near Gamboa on the Culebra Cut, and traces of it can still be seen. Las Cruces was on the Chagres River, which was navigable to the Caribbean, particularly during the rainy season.

Intruders were early attracted by the wealth passing over the Camino Real. Sir Francis Drake attacked Nombre de Dios, and in 1573 his men penetrated inland to Vera Cruz, further up the Chagres River on the Camino Real, plundering the town. Spain countered later attacks by building strongholds and forts to protect the route: among others San Felipe at the entrances to Portobelo and San Lorenzo at the mouth of the Chagres. Spanish galleons, loaded with treasure and escorted against attack, left Portobelo once a year. They returned with European goods which were sold at great fairs held at Portobelo, Cartagena and Veracruz. There was feverish activity for several weeks as the galleons were loaded and unloaded. It was a favourite time for attack by enemies, especially those with political as well as pecuniary motives. Perhaps the most famous was the attack by Henry Morgan in 1671. He captured the fort of San Lorenzo and pushed up the Chagres River to Las Cruces. From there he descended upon Panama City, which he looted and burnt. A month later Morgan returned to the Caribbean with 195 mules loaded with booty. Panama City was rebuilt on a new site, at the base of Ancón hill, and fortified. With Britain and Spain at war, attacks reached their climax in Admiral Vernon's capture of Portobelo in 1739 and the fort of San Lorenzo the next year. Spain abandoned the route in 1746 and began trading round Cape Horn. San Lorenzo was rebuilt: it is still there, tidied up and landscaped by the US Army.

In 1821, Gran Colombia won independence from Spain. Panama, in an event celebrated annually on 28 November, declared its own independence and promptly joined Bolívar's Gran Colombia federation. Though known as the 'Sovereign State' of Panama it remained, even after the federation disintegrated, a province of Colombia.

Some 30 years after independence, streams of men were once more moving up the Chagres and down to Panama City: the forty-niners on their way to the newly discovered gold fields of California. Many perished on this 'road to hell', as it was called, and the gold rush brought into being a railway across the isthmus. The Panama Railroad from Colón (then only two streets) to Panama City took four years to build, with great loss of life. The first train was run on 26 November 1853. The railway was an enormous financial success until the re-routing of the Pacific Steam Navigation Company's ships round Cape Horn in 1867 and the opening of the first US transcontinental railroad in 1869 reduced its traffic. Having been out of operation for several years, plans were announced in 1998 to refurbish the line and recommence services.

The Panama Railroad

Ferdinand de Lesseps, builder of the Suez Canal, arrived in Panama in 1881, and decided to build a sea-level canal along the Chagres River and the Río Grande. Work started in 1882. One of the diggers in 1886 and 1887 was the painter Gauguin, aged 39. About 30 kilometres had been dug before the Company crashed in 1893, defeated by extravagance and tropical diseases (22,000 people died) and also by the engineering difficulties inherent in the construction of the Canal. Eventually the Colombian government authorized the Company to sell all its rights and properties to the United States, but the Colombian Senate rejected the treaty, and the inhabitants of Panama, encouraged by the States, declared their independence on 3 November 1903. The United States intervened and, in spite of protests by Colombia, recognized the new republic. Colombia did not accept the severance until 1921.

Building of the canal

Immediately following its independence, Panama, represented in Washington by the controversial Frenchman, Philippe Bunau-Varilla, signed a treaty granting to the USA 'in perpetuity' a 10-mile-wide corridor across the isthmus over which the USA would exercise authority 'as if it were sovereign'. Bunau-Varilla, an official of the bankrupt French canal company, presented the revolutionary junta with the *fait accompli* of a signed treaty. The history of Panama then became that of two nations, with the Canal Zone governor, also a retired US general, responsible only to the President of the USA.

Before beginning the task of building the Canal the United States performed one of the greatest sanitary operations in history: the clearance from the area of the more malignant tropical diseases. The name of the physician William Crawford Gorgas will always be associated with this, as will that of the engineer George Washington Goethals with the actual building of the Canal. On 15 August 1914, the first full passage was made, by the ship *Ancón*.

During this period and until the military seized power in 1968, a small, commercially-orientated oligarchy dominated Panamanian politics, although presidential successions were not always smooth and peaceful.

As a result of bitter resentment, the USA ended Panama's protectorate status in 1939 with a treaty which limited US rights of intervention. However, the disparity in living standards

1939 Treaty with USA

continued to provoke anti-US feeling, culminating in riots that began on 9 January 1964 (the day is commemorated annually as Martyrs' Day) and the suspension of diplomatic relations for some months.

In 1968 Arnulfo Arias Madrid was elected president for the third time, having been ousted twice previously. After only 10 days in office he was forcibly removed by the National Guard which installed a provisional junta. Brigadier General Omar Torrijos Herrera ultimately became Commander of the National Guard and principal power in the junta, dominating Panamanian politics for the next 13 years. Gradually, the theoretically civilian National Guard was converted into a full-scale army and renamed the Panama Defence Forces. Constitutional government was restored in 1972 after elections for a 505-member National Assembly of Community Representatives, which revised the 1946 constitution, elected Demetrio Basilio Lakas Bahas as president, and vested temporary extraordinary executive powers in General Torrijos for six years. Torrijos' rule was characterized by his pragmatic nationalism; he carried out limited agrarian reform and nationalized major industries, yet satisfied business interests; he had close links with left wing movements in Cuba, El Salvador and Nicaragua, yet reached agreement with the USA to restore sovereignty over the canal zone to Panama and to close US military bases. In 1978 elections for a new National Assembly were held and the new representatives elected Arístedes Royo Sánchez president of the country. General Torrijos resigned as Chief of Government but retained the powerful post of Commander of the National Guard until his death in a small plane air-crash in 1981. There followed several years of rapid governmental changes as tension rose between presidents and National Guard leaders.

General Noriega's Administration

Following an election in May 1984, Nicolás Ardito Barletta was inaugurated in October for a six-year term, though the fairness of the elections was widely questioned. He was removed from office by military pressure in September 1985 as he attempted to assert some civilian control and was replaced by Eric Arturo Delvalle. Sr Delvalle's attempts to reduce military influence in government, by then concentrated principally in the hands of General Manuel Antonio Noriega Moreno, led to his own removal by General Noriega in February 1988. Manuel Solís Palma was named president in his place.

With the economy reeling and banks closed as a result of US economic sanctions, the campaign leading up to the election of May 1989 saw the growing influence of a movement called the *Civilista* Crusade, led by upper and middle-class figures. When their coalition candidate, Guillermo Endara Galimany, triumphed over Noriega's candidate, Carlos Duque Jaén, the election was annulled by the military.

General Noriega appointed Francisco Rodríguez as provisional President in September. However, in December, General Noriega formally assumed power as Head of State, which provoked a US military invasion (Operation 'Just Cause') on 20 December to overthrow him. He finally surrendered in mid-January, having taken refuge in the Papal Nunciature on Christmas Eve, and was taken to the USA for trial on charges of drugs trafficking and other corruption offences. Sr Endara was installed as President. The Panamanian Defence Forces were immediately remodelled into a new Public Force whose largest component is the civilian National Police, with a compulsory retirement after 25 years' service. More than 150 senior officers were dismissed and many were arrested.

After 'Just Cause'

After the overthrow of General Noriega's administration, the US Senate approved a US$1bn aid package including US$480mn in direct assistance to provide liquidity and get the economy moving again. A further US$540mn aid package was requested from the USA, Japan, Taiwan and the EEC to enable Panama to help clear its US$610mn arrears with multilateral creditors and support the Panamanian banking system, but inevitably there were delays and little progress was made until 1991. The USA put Panama under considerable pressure to sign a Treaty of Mutual Legal Assistance, which would limit bank secrecy and enable investigation into suspected drug traffickers' bank accounts. Higher levels of crime and drugs trafficking led to the Government passing a law to create the Technical Judicial Police (PTJ) to pursue criminals. Charges of corruption at the highest level were made by Panamanians and US officials and President Endara was further weakened by allegations that his law firm had been involved with companies owned by drugs traffickers.

Though the economy grew under President Endara, street crime also increased. There were continuing social problems and pro-military elements failed in a coup attempt and isolated bombings.

Fears that violence would disrupt the 1994 elections were unfounded. In the presence of 2,000 local and international observers, polling was largely incident-free and open, receiving praise world-wide. The winner of the presidency with less than a third of the popular vote was Ernesto Pérez Balladares of the Partido Revolucionario Democrático (PRD), whose campaign harked back to the record of the party's founder, Omar Torrijos, successfully avoiding any links with its more recent leader, Noriega. The PRD also won a narrow majority in the Legislative Assembly. In second place was the widow of thrice-elected and thrice-deposed president Arnulfo Arias, Mireya Moscoso de Gruber of the Partido Arnulfista, supported by Endara, and third was the lawyer, Salsa star and actor, Rubén Blades, whose party Papa Egoró ('Mother Earth') won six seats in the legislature on its first electoral outing. Pérez Balladares, who appointed a cabinet containing members of opposition parties as well as from the PRD, gave priority in his campaign to tackling the problem of social inequality, unemployment, deteriorating education and rising crime which had characterized the end of Endara's term. In January 1995, it was announced by the government that a coup against Pérez Balladares had been foiled. All sides in the Assembly hastened to support the government and pledge their commitment to democracy. **1994 elections & after**

In the following months, many of the government's policies, such as changes in labour law, new tax legislation and a proposed amnesty for human rights offenders during the Noriega regime, proved controversial. The president regretted the slow progress in tackling crime; he also had to admit, in mid-1996, that his election campaign had received funds from the Cali drugs cartel. His assertion that he was ignorant of this at the time was largely accepted. There was also a growing recognition throughout 1997 and into 1998 that the banking sector was successfully eradicating money-laundering and was adopting internationally approved standards.

The President's economic policies proved an electoral failure when the 1999 general elections brought Mireyra Moscoso to the presidency with 45 percent of the vote. Her rival, Martín Torrijos, son of Omar, leader of the PRD coalition, won 38 percent. Moscoso's campaign called for more measures to cut poverty. She is the first female Panamanian head of state.

The former Canal Zone was a ribbon of territory under US control extending eight kilometres on either side of the Canal and including the cities of Cristóbal and Balboa. The price paid by the United States Government to Panama for construction rights was US$10mn. The French company received US$40mn for its rights and properties and US$25mn were given to Colombia in compensation. The total cost at completion was US$387mn. Panama long ago rejected the perpetuity clause of the original Canal Treaty. In April 1978 a new treaty was ratified and on 1 October 1979 the Canal Zone, now known officially as the Canal Area, including the ports of Cristóbal and Balboa, the Canal dry docks and the trans-isthmus railway, was formally restored to Panamanian sovereignty. The US Southern Command moved to Miami in 1997 and by the end of 1999, the few remaining bases will close. **Canal area**

Though polls indicated that many Panamanians supported retention of US military bases, largely because of their employment of civilians and direct governmental expenditures in Panama (about US$350mn a year in 1995 and 1996), vocal minorities demanded their departure. Until the final transfer of ownership on 31 December 1999 the Canal administration is in the hands of the Comisión del Canal, on which Panama now has four out of nine seats. An Inter-Oceanic Regional Authority (ARI), headed by ex-president Ardito Barletta, has been created by Panama to manage the disposition of real estate handed over by the USA during and after the transition. The Canal Administrator (CEO) and

95 percent of Canal employees are now Panamanian.

According to 1996 figures, about 13,700 ships passed through the Panama Canal annually, providing US$105mn for the Panamanian government (out of total Canal revenues of US$486mn). For several years, the possibility of widening the Canal, or even building a new one, has been under study. A report in 1993 estimated that the Canal would reach maximum shipping capacity in 2025, but re-evaluation led to a modernization programme, due for completion in 2005. This includes the widening of the Gaillard Cut, upgrading of the locks and a 20 percent increase in the capacity for shipping. If demand rises as quickly as expected, even the current programme will be insufficient. Immediate problems include the inability of the existing locks to handle large ships, the inadequacy of the purpose-built lakes to supply enough water for the operation of the locks (made worse by silting as a result of deforestation and, in 1998, by drought caused by El Niño) and the scale of fees charged to ships and small vessels in transit.

Culture

People   The population is mostly of mixed descent but there are communities of Indians, blacks and a few Asians. Most of the rural population live in the six provinces on the Pacific side, west of the Canal. There is only one rural population centre of any importance on the Caribbean: in Bocas del Toro, in the extreme northwest. Of the 60 Indian tribes who inhabited the isthmus at the time of the Spanish conquest, only three have survived in any number: the Kunas (also spelt Cunas, frequently so in Colombia) of the San Blas Islands (50,000), the Guaymíes, who prefer to be called Ngöbe-Buglé, of the western provinces (80,000), and the Emberá-Wunan, formerly known as Chocóes of Darién (10,000). These, and a few others, such as the Teribes, account for six percent of the total population. Indian opposition to the opening of copper mines at Cerro Colorado (see **Economy** below) and demonstrations supporting greater autonomy for Indians in the area characterized 1996, but were inconclusive. However, an administrative enclave, the Comarca, providing for some Ngöbe-Buglé home rule, has been created.

In Bocas de Toro half the population speaks Spanish, half speaks English.

Numbers of African slaves escaped from their Spanish owners during the 16th century. They set up free communities in the Darién jungles and their Spanish-speaking descendants, known as *cimarrones*, can still be seen there and in the Pearl Islands. The majority of Panama's blacks, often bilingual, are descended from English-speaking West Indians, brought in for the building of the railway in 1850, and later of the Canal. There are also a number of East Indians and Chinese, a few of whom, especially in the older generations tend to cling to their own languages and customs.

Education   Education is compulsory from the age of six to 15. About 92 percent of children attend elementary school. English is the compulsory second language in secondary schools. There are several universities, including the mammoth **Nacional**, with 55,000 students, the **Tecnológica**, with 13,000, the important catholic **Santa María La Antigua** (5,000 students), and eight small, private ones.

Religion   Panama's Constitution makes Roman Catholicism the official religion of the country, but guarantees freedom of practice to all others. As with neighbouring countries, evangelical churches have been active in recent years. A mosque has recently been built in David, the third city of the Republic.

The economy

Structure of   Panama's economy has traditionally been founded on income derived from services
production   rendered to visitors, taking advantage of its geographical position, its banking centre, and Canal employees and US military personnel spending money in the Republic. However, this

contribution is lessening proportionately with the departure of the US military and canal personnel, and as the country seeks to develop new sources of income: tourism, industry, copper.

Apart from the Canal (see above), the other traditional mainstay of the Panamanian economy is agriculture, which contributes about 10% of gdp. Agrarian reform brought the post-1968 governments much support from tenant-farmers and squatters, but has been discontinued and settlements (*asentamientos*) formed by the Torrijos government are in decline. 44% of the land is classified as forested, but deforestation has been occurring at an alarming rate (see above, **Climate**, page 1159), principally because of pressures from increasing unemployment and a rising population, as people move into isolated areas. The leading agricultural export crop is bananas, a large proportion of which are marketed by the Chiriquí Land Company (Chirilanco), a subsidiary of the transnational Chiquita Brands, and most of the rest purchased and exported by Dole, a subsidiary of Standard Brands. The upheavals in the world banana market, including EU constraints on imports from Central America, have led to a large decline in exports. Shrimp is another major export, having grown to about the same value as bananas and competing strongly with Ecuador and Honduras for the US market. Raw sugar is also an important export item, while lesser amounts of coffee and hides and skins are sold abroad. Coffee production is increasing rapidly in Chiriquí Province.

The main industry is food processing and there are textile and clothing concerns and cement, chemicals, plastics and other light industries. Petroleum products, made from imported crude, are the only industrial export. The lowering of import tariffs in 1993, as a part of trade liberalization measures, contributed to a decline in manufacturing output. At the same time, the IMF has encouraged the state to privatize many of the industries it controls. Many companies, including power and telecommunications, have been sold to the private sector.

Vast deposits of copper have been found in Panama. The mine at Cerro Colorado, if fully developed, could be one of the largest in the world as its reserves are said to exceed one billion tonnes. However, a 25-year concession granted to a Canadian company is vigorously opposed by the Ngöbe-Buglé indigenous group. There is also copper at Petaquilla, Cerro Chorcha and Río Pinto. Proven copper reserves are six billion tonnes and export revenues are forecast at US$500mn a year by the next century (if Cerro Colorado and Petaquilla are fully developed). Large coal deposits have been found at Río Indio. The country also has gold and silver deposits. So far no oil has been discovered, but exploration is taking place. The country's mining code is being revised to speed up approval of mining concessions and encourage foreign investment.

One of the most dynamic sectors of the economy is banking. Since 1970 offshore banks have increased from 20 in number to 115 with the establishment of liberal conditions and the abolition of currency controls. In the mid-1980s, total assets amounted to over US$40bn, while deposits were around US$35bn. However, in 1987-88, political uncertainties severely affected the international banking centre. Loss of confidence led many banks to close their offices and move to other offshore centres such as the Bahamas or the Cayman Islands, the level of assets declined, and deposits fell to US$5bn by 1990. In 1990 the new government amended banking regulations to reduce money laundering and legislation to end banking secrecy was approved by the Legislative Assembly in July 1991. By 1993, the financial sector was flourishing again, boosted by the relaxation of restrictions on financial services throughout Latin America. Although deposits were affected by the Mexican crisis in 1995, declining by 13% to US$20bn, they have risen again since then.

Following a rapid accumulation of foreign debt by the public sector in the late 1970s and early 1980s, the debt service burden became intolerable. Panama received assistance after 1983 from the IMF and the World Bank in support of its fiscal and structural adjustment programme, while commercial banks rescheduled existing loans and provided new money on easier terms. As a result of the 1988 financial crisis, Panama fell into arrears to all its creditors; consequently, capital inflows were halted; the IMF declared Panama ineligible to

Recent trends

borrow and the World Bank cut off loan disbursements. Moreover, the US economic blockade which began in 1988 directly caused a 16% fall in gdp that year, followed by a 12% fall the next. In 1990 the economy recovered slightly from its very low base, principally because of a 20% increase in commercial activity in the Colón Free Zone, but delays in reaching agreements with external creditors over the repayment of US$2.7bn of arrears postponed economic recovery. In 1992 Panama succeeded in paying US$646mn in arrears to multilateral and governmental creditors, making it eligible for new credits for the first time in four years. Until then it had relied heavily on US aid, which amounted to US$985mn since President Endara took office in 1990, of which US$451mn were donations. In 1996 Panama signed a debt reduction and refinancing agreement with commercial banks, covering US$2bn of principal and US$1.5bn of interest arrears equivalent to about 30% of Panama's total bank debt.

The adoption of neoliberal economic policies brought rising discontent as spending cuts caused job losses. Strikes and demonstrations became commonplace and poverty increased. The economic plan announced at the outset of Pérez Balladares' term gave priority to reducing poverty by 50%, though it achieved little. According to local statistics in 1997, one third of the population lives below the poverty line, over 10% in extreme poverty (according to the World Bank, wealth distribution is among "the most unequal in the hemisphere"). Support for the government's emphasis on social development was given by the IADB, which approved a US$1.5bn loan over five years. The inflation rate, just over one percent, is among the lowest in the world. Contributing factors are the use of the US dollar, which limits the domestic money supply, slow economic growth in recent years and high unemployment, which keeps wages low and leaves the majority of the population with little purchasing power.

Government

Constitutional reforms were adopted by referendum in April 1983. Legislative power is vested in a unicameral, 72-member Legislative Assembly which is elected by universal adult suffrage for a term of five years (and whose elections are hotly contested, in part because a five-year term yields members total compensation of US$600,000 each). Executive power is held by the President, assisted by two Vice Presidents and an appointed Cabinet. Panama is divided into nine provinces and two autonomous Indian reservations. Provincial governors are appointed by the central authorities. Each province is divided into several districts. The magistrates (*alcaldes*) of the larger districts, who combine both executive and judicial functions, are elected, others appointed. They in turn appoint subordinate authorities (*corregidores*) in the towns and villages.

Footnotes

11

Footnotes

11

Travellers' letters

We are very grateful to all travellers who have written to us, either by post or increasingly by email, over the last year. Alex and Tamar, (Mex, Gua, Els, Hon, Nic, Pan); Daniel Acquah, London SW19, England (Pan, Col); Eyal Alkopher, Ramat Gan, Israel (Mex); Laura Allen, (Gua); Lone Bak, Denmark (Mex, Gua, Cos); Anna Balaguer, Bray, England (Mex); Arik Barzilay, Israel (Mex, Gua, Hon, Cos); Anders , Marianne Berntsen, Tysse, Norway (Mex, Gua); Friederike Blum, Braunau, Austria (Gua); Carsten Bogs, (Gua); Karen Bonniot, Firminy, France (Cos, Mex, Gua); Claire Boobbyer, Westerham, England (Mex, Gua, Cos); Karin Breistein, Norway (Gua); Simon Burchell, Haselmere, England (Mex); Simon Burchill, Haslemere, England (Mex); James Byrne, (Mex); Mary Ray Cate, Sante Fe, NM, USA (Mex); Millaine Cornish, London SW19, England (Pan, Col); Nicholas Couis, Maylands, South Australia (Gua); Nick Couis, Maylands, Australia (Mex); Nicholas Covis, (Gua, Bel); J L Cox, Teddington, England (Mex).

Kathy Dale, Aboyne, Scotland (Mex); Jacqueline Dammers, Utrecht, The Netherlands (Bel, Hon, Nic, Cos, Pan); Jack Davis, La Luz, NM, USA (Mex); Ben Diamond, London, England (Nic); Martin Dilig, Berlin, Germany (Mex, Bel, Gua, Hon); Andy Dodd, London, England (Hon, Gua); Hanno Doenz, Schruns, Austria (Mex, Bel, Gua); Gwithian Doswell, Oxford, England (Nic); Doris Dresel, Sasbach, Germany (Gua); Klaus Dressel, (Gua); Tracie Eagles, London, England (Hon, Gua); Matthias Fehrenbach, Immenstaad, (Cos, Pan); Andre Fournier, (Cos); Andre Fournier, (Mex, Cos); Patrick Georget, (Cos); Michael Glaeser, (Col, Pan); Sam Gordon, (Nic); Yvon Grenier, Rouyn-Noranda, Canada (Mex, Gua, Hon, Cos); Micheal J Grey, Berea, USA (Hon); Erik Hage, Olsvik, Norway (Cos, Nic); Brooke Harlowe, Selinsgrove, PA, USA (Pan); Deborah Heap, (Gua); Art and Barb Hess, (Mex); Alan Hickey, (Mex, Gua, Hon, Nic); Elise Holland, Mill Valley, CA, USA (Gua); Lucas Houben, (Gua, Hon, Nic, Cos, Pan, Hints); Alastair Humphreys, Edinburgh, Scotland (Mex, Gua, Bel, Els, Cos, Pan).

Georgina Iliff, London, England (Els, Hon, Gua, Pan, Cos, Nic, Ecu); Bill Irwin, New York, NY, USA (Gua); Alban Johnson, Hobart, Tasmania (Mex); Ben Kane, Ireland (Mex); Ben Kane, Budleigh Salterton, England (Hon, Nic, Cos, Pan); Ikuo Kato, Tokyo, Japan (Mex, Hon, Nic, Cos, Pan, Bel); Christina , Buster Kennett, UK (Mex); Adam Kent, Gainesville, FL, USA (Mex); Annick , Phillipp Kroenberg, Switzerland (Gua, Bel, Els, Nic, Pan, Cos); Pieter Kroese, Utrecht, The Netherlands (Bel, Hon, Nic, Cos, Pan); Joel Simeon Kurzman, San Francisco, CA, USA (Mex, Gua, Hon, Nic, Cos, Pan); Karin Lammersen, Stuttgart, Germany (Gua, Mex); Pascal Le Colletter, Banos, Ecuador (Ecu, Hon); Christina Lesseis, Toronto, Canada (Gua); Gerlinde Leyrer, Stuttgart, Germany (Mex); Iben Lindemark, Copenhagen, Denmark (Gua, Hon, Nic); Charles Locher, Richmond, CA, USA (Mex); Ute , Rudolf Lohn, Hamburg, Germany (Mex, Gua, Pan); Ulf Lund, Oslo, Norway (Cos); Eric Malfit, Tournon, France (Mex, Hon, Nic, Cos, Pan); Brigit Marent, Schruns, Austria (Mex, Bel, Gua); Catherine Marren, Exeter, England (Bel); Claude (The Yak) Marthaler, Geneva, Switzerland (Mex, Gua, Hon, Nic, Cos, Pan); Patrick McCrea, (Gua); Catherine McFarlane, Edinburgh, Scotland (Mex, Hon); Francisco Mejia, El Monte, CA, USA (Els); Grant Miller, Imperial Beach, USA (Cos, Els); Catherine Montague, Sidcup, England (Ecu, Pan, Cos, Nic, Hon, Gua, Bel, Mex); Martin Morgan, Leicester, England (Mex); Lennie Mosaic, Dallas, TX, USA (Mex).

Paul Neumann, Portland, USA (Cos); Sergio Oesch, (Hon); Jordi Palou, Decatur, USA (Mex); Majorie Powell, Puebla, Mexico (Cos); Marjorie Powell, (Mex, Gua, Hon, Nic); Prof John W Price, Gainesville, FL, USA (Pan, Cos); Klaus Reuter, Munich, Germany (Mex); David Richards, Aboyne, Scotland (Mex); Sarah Ringler, (Mex); David Rosemeyer, (Gua); Jeff Rothman, (Mex); Steve Scott, Blackpool, England (Mex, Bel, Gua); Steve Scott, Blackpool, UK (Mex, Gua, Hon, Nic, Cos); Jerome Scully, Cabanas, El Salvador (Els, Mex, Gua); Philippe Slama, Pully, Switzerland (Mex, Gua, Hon, Nic, Cos); Kurt Sollinger, Vienna, Austria (Mex); Thomas Seier Sorensen, Copenhagen, Denmark (Mex, Gua, Els, Hon); Veronita Spalinger, Oaxaca, Mexico (Mex, Gua); Mindy Spar, (Gua); Lee Stanley, Sequim, WA, USA (Pan); Christian Stäubli, Liestal, Switzerland

(Mex); Dr W B Stern, Basel, Switzerland (Cos); Martin Suter, Zurich, Switzerland (Cos); Catherine Tomlinson, London, England (Mex, Gua, Bel); Jorge Valle-Aguiluz, Zambrano, Honduras (Hon); Freya van den Bossche, Vinderhoute, Belgium (Mex); Clive Walker, San Jose, Costa Rica (Hon); Liz Walton, England (Mex, Bel, Gua); Liz Walton, Budleigh Salterton, England (Hon, Nic, Cos, Pan); Paul H White, Sabanagrande, Honduras (Hon); Ueli Wuthrich, Bern, Switzerland (Cos); and Irene Zeilinger, (Mex).

Climatic tables

The following tables have been very kindly furnished by Mr R K Headland. Each weather station is given with its altitude in metres (m). Temperatures (Centigrade) are given as averages for each month; the first line is the maximum and the second the minimum. The third line is the average number of wet days encountered in each month.

	Jan	Feb	Mar	Apr	May	Jun	Jul	Aug	Sep	Oct	Nov	Dec
Acapulco, Mexico	29	31	31	31	32	32	32	32	31	31	31	31
3m	21	21	21	22	23	24	24	24	24	23	22	21
	0	0	0	0	2	9	7	7	12	6	1	0
Guatemala City	23	25	27	28	29	27	26	26	26	24	23	22
1,490m	11	12	14	14	16	16	16	16	16	15	14	13
	2	2	2	5	8	20	17	16	17	13	6	2
Havana	26	27	28	29	30	31	31	32	31	29	27	26
49m	18	18	19	21	22	23	24	24	24	23	21	19
	6	4	4	4	7	10	9	10	11	11	7	6
Managua,	30	30	30	32	32	31	31	31	31	31	30	30
Nicaragua	23	24	26	28	27	26	26	25	26	24	24	24
46m	0	0	0	0	6	12	11	12	15	16	4	1
Mérida, Mexico	28	29	32	33	34	33	33	33	32	31	29	28
22m	17	17	19	21	22	23	23	23	23	22	19	18
	4	2	1	2	5	10	11	12	13	7	3	3
Mexico City	19	21	24	25	26	24	23	23	23	21	20	19
2,309m	6	6	8	11	12	13	12	12	12	10	8	6
	2	1	2	6	9	14	19	18	17	8	3	2
Monterrey,	22	24	29	31	33	32	33	30	27	22	18	
Mexico	9	11	14	17	20	22	22	22	21	18	13	10
538m	3	3	3	4	4	4	4	3	8	5	4	4
Panama City	31	31	32	32	31	30	31	30	30	30	29	30
36m	21	21	22	23	23	23	23	23	23	22	22	23
	4	2	1	6	15	16	15	15	15	16	18	12
San José	24	24	26	27	27	27	26	26	27	26	25	24
Costa Rica	14	14	15	16	16	16	16	16	16	15	15	15
1,172m	1	0	1	4	17	20	18	19	20	22	14	4
San Salvador	30	31	32	32	31	30	30	30	29	29	29	29
700m	16	16	17	19	19	19	18	18	19	18	17	16
	0	3	2	5	12	20	21	20	18	14	4	1
Tegucigalpa	25	27	29	30	30	28	28	28	29	27	26	25
Honduras	14	14	15	16	18	19	17	17	17	17	16	15
935m	4	2	1	3	14	18	10	10	17	16	8	4

Sources: H.M.S.O. Meteorological Reports   K.L.M. Climatic Data Publication

Footnotes

Advertisers

Shorts

Special interest pieces on and about the region

Index

Note: grid references to the colour maps are shown in *italics* after place names. So Acapulco *M3C3* can be found on Map3, grid C3

footnotes

Map Index

Will you help us?

We try as hard as we can to make each Footprint Handbook as up-to-date and accurate as possible but, of course, things always change. Many people write to us - with corrections, new information, or simply comments. If you want to let us know about an experience or adventure - hair-raising or mundane, good or bad, exciting or boring or simply something rather special - we would be delighted to hear from you. Please give us as precise information as possible, quoting the edition number (youÆll find it on the front cover) and page number of the Handbook you are using. Your help will be greatly appreciated, especially by other travellers. In return we will send you details about our special guidebook offer.

> *Write to Elizabeth Taylor*
> *Footprint Handbooks*
> *6 Riverside Court*
> *Lower Bristol Road*
> *Bath BA2 3DZ*
> *England*
> *or email info@footprintbooks.com*

Complete listing

Latin America
Argentina Handbook 1st
1 900949 10 5 £11.99
Bolivia Handbook 1st
1 900949 09 1 £11.99
Bolivia Handbook 2nd
1 900949 49 0 £12.99
Brazil Handbook 1st
0 900751 84 3 £12.99
Brazil Handbook 2nd
1 900949 50 4 £13.99
Caribbean Islands Handbook 2000
1 900949 40 7 £14.99
Chile Handbook 2nd
1 900949 28 8 £11.99
Colombia Handbook 1st
1 900949 11 3 £10.99
Cuba Handbook 1st
1 900949 12 1 £10.99
Cuba Handbook 2nd
1 900949 54 7 £10.99
Ecuador & Galápagos Handbook 2nd
1 900949 29 6 £11.99
Mexico Handbook 1st
1 900949 53 9 £13.99
Mexico & Central America Handbook 2000
1 900949 39 3 £15.99
Peru Handbook 2nd
1 900949 31 8 £11.99
South American Handbook 2000
1 900949 38 5 £19.99
Venezuela Handbook 1st
1 900949 13 X £10.99
Venezuela Handbook 2nd
1 900949 58 X £11.99

Africa
East Africa Handbook 2000
1 900949 42 3 £14.99
Morocco Handbook 2nd
1 900949 35 0 £11.99
Namibia Handbook 2nd
1 900949 30 X £10.99
South Africa Handbook 2000
1 900949 43 1 £14.99
Tunisia Handbook 2nd
1 900949 34 2 £10.99
Zimbabwe Handbook 1st
0 900751 93 2 £11.99

Wexas
Traveller's Handbook
0 905802 08 X £14.99
Traveller's Healthbook
0 905802 09 8 £9.99

Asia
Cambodia Handbook 2nd
1 900949 47 4 £9.99
Goa Handbook 1st
1 900949 17 2 £9.99
Goa Handbook 2nd
1 900949 45 8 £9.99
India Handbook 2000
1 900949 41 5 £15.99
Indonesia Handbook 2nd
1 900949 15 6 £14.99
Indonesia Handbook 3rd
1 900949 51 2 £15.99
Laos Handbook 2nd
1 900949 46 6 £9.99
Malaysia & Singapore Handbook 2nd
1 900949 16 4 £12.99
Malaysia Handbook 3rd
1 900949 52 0 £12.99
Myanmar (Burma) Handbook 1st
0 900751 87 8 £9.99
Nepal Handbook 2nd
1 900949 44 X £11.99
Pakistan Handbook 2nd
1 900949 37 7 £12.99
Singapore Handbook 1st
1 900949 19 9 £9.99
Sri Lanka Handbook 2nd
1 900949 18 0 £11.99
Sumatra Handbook 1st
1 900949 59 8 £9.99
Thailand Handbook 2nd
1 900949 32 6 £12.99
Tibet Handbook 2nd
1 900949 33 4 £12.99
Vietnam Handbook 2nd
1 900949 36 9 £10.99

Europe
Andalucía Handbook 2nd
1 900949 27 X £9.99
Ireland Handbook 1st
1 900949 55 5 £11.99
Scotland Handbook 1st
1 900949 56 3 £10.99

Middle East
Egypt Handbook 2nd
1 900949 20 2 £12.99
Israel Handbook 2nd
1 900949 48 2 £12.99
Jordan, Syria & Lebanon Handbook 1st
1 900949 14 8 £12.99

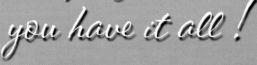

Metro system Mexico City

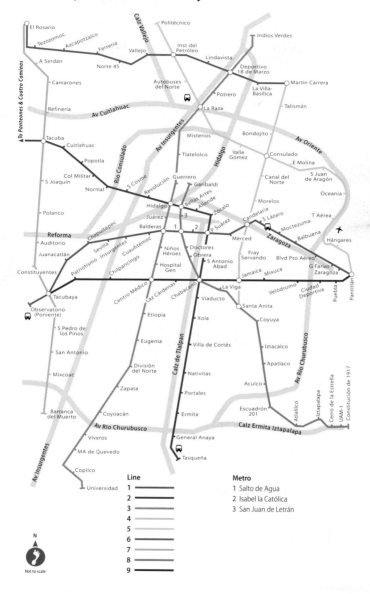

Line
1
2
3
4
5
6
7
8
9

Metro
1 Salto de Agua
2 Isabel la Católica
3 San Juan de Letrán

N
Not to scale

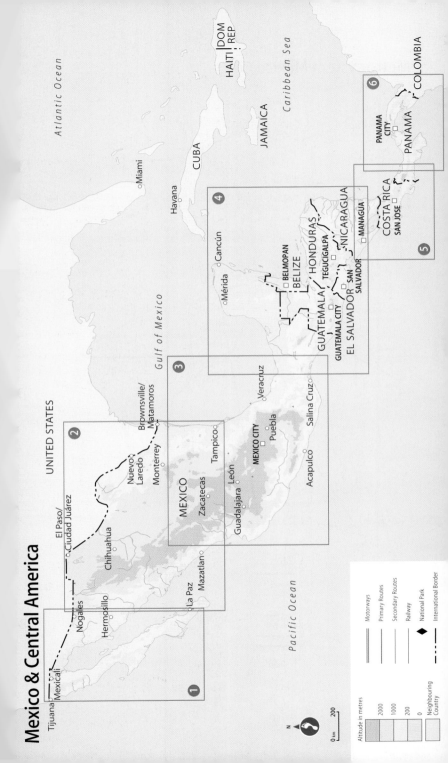

Mexico & Central America

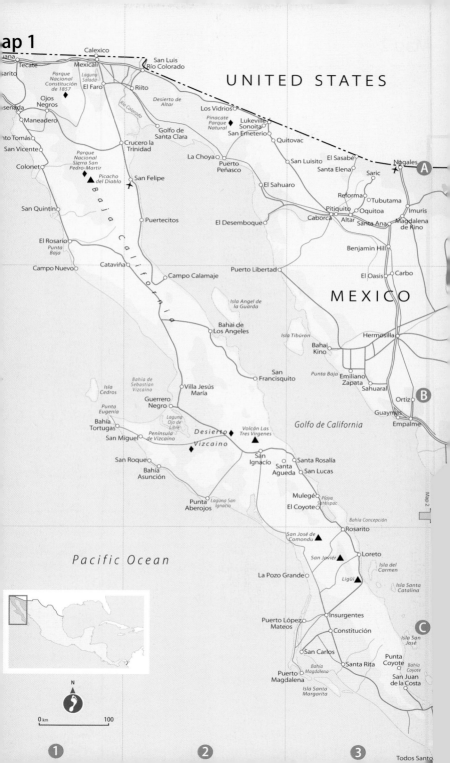

UNITED STATES

Ciudad Acuña

Boquillas
del Carmen   Morelos
Piedritas   El Milagro   Los Picos

Piedras Negras   Eagle Pass
El Guaje   Río Sabinas   Allende
Nueva Rosita
Palau
El Rivas   Melchor   Sabinas
Muzquiz

Nuevo Laredo   Laredo
Anahuac

Lampazos
de Naranjo
ra Mojada   Monclova
Cuatrociénegas   Castaños
La Víbora   de Carranza   Sabinas   Nueva
Guimbalete   Hidalgo   Ciudad
Tanque Nuevo   Guerrero   Roma
Ciudad Miguel
Alemán
Reynosa   McAllen
Tlahualilo   General   Brownsville
de   Hidalgo   Treviño   Río Bravo   Matamoros
Zaragoza   San Nicolás   Valle
San Pedro   García Caves   Dl Garzas   Hermoso
mez Palacio   Matamoros   Saltillo   Santa   Monterrey   China   Santa
orreón   Arteaga   Teresa
Parras   General   Agua   Guadalupe
de la   Cepeda   Nueva   Allende
Fuente   Montemorelos
Map 3   San
Linares   Fernando
uan Aldama   Concepción   de Presas
uel Auza   Est Camacho   del Oro   San   San Carlos   La Carbonera
Roberto
San Tiburcio   Nuevo
res   Padilla   La Pesca
ía   Río Grande   Presa de las
Real de   Ciudad   Adjuntas
Catorce   Victoria   Soto la
brerete   Jamauve   Marina
resnillo de   Matehuala
lez Echeverría   La Cruz
Santo Domingo   Gómez
Jérez de   Farías
araiso   García   Zacatecas   Tula   Ciudad   La Cruz
Salinas   Guadalupe   Moctezuma   Huizache   Mante   Manuel
Luis   Santo Domingo   Antiguo
Villanueva   Moya   Moreles   Ciudad
uejucar   Ciudad   Madero
del Maíz   Tampico
San Luis   Río   Ciudad   Panuco
Potosí   Verde   Cárdenas   Valles   Tamuín
Rayón

4   5   6

N

0 km   100

A

B

C

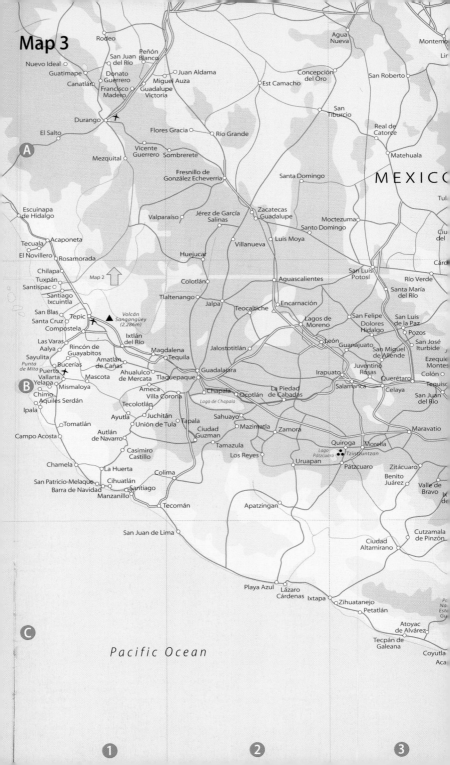

Map 4

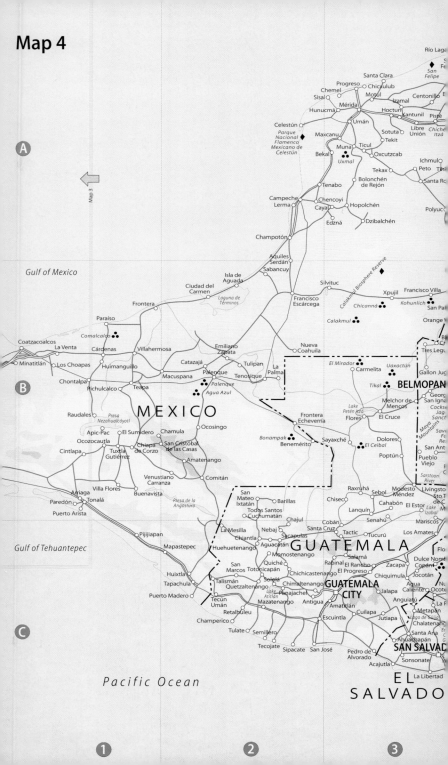

Gulf of Mexico

Río Lagar
Santa Clara
San
Felipe
Chicxulub
Progreso
Chemel
Motul
Sisal
Izamal
Centonillo
Hunucmá
Mérida
Hoctum
Kantunil
Pisté
Celestún
Umán
Libre
Union
Chichi
Itzá
Sotuta
Parque
Nacional
Flamenco
Mexicano de
Celestún
Maxcanu
Muna
Tekit
Ticul
Oxcutzcab
Bekal
Uxmal
Ichmul
Tekax
Peto
Tih
Bolonchén
de Rejón
Santa Ro
Tenabo
Campeche
Chencoyi
Hopolchén
Lerma
Cayal
Polyuc
Edzná
Dzibalchén
Champotón

Aquiles
Serdán
Sabancuy
Silvituc
Calakmul Biosphere Reserve
Xpujil
Francisco Villa
Isla de
Aguada
San Pal
Ciudad del
Carmen
Laguna de
Términos
Francisco
Escárcega
Chicanná
Kohunlich
Frontera
Orange
Paraíso
Calakmul
Bl
Cc
Comalcalco
Nueva
Coahuila
Coatzacoalcos
Tres Legu
La Venta
Cárdenas
Villahermosa
Emiliano
Zapata
El Mirador
Uaxactun
Gallon Ju
Minatitlán
Los Choapas
Huimanguillo
Catazajá
Tulipan
Carmelita
Chontalpa
Macuspana
Palenque
La
Palma
Tikal
BELMOPAN
Pichulcalco
Teapa
Tenosique
Palenque
Georg
San Ign
Melchor de
Mencos
Raudales
Agua Azul
Cocks
Jag
Sanct
Presa
Nezahualcóyotl
MEXICO
Frontera
Echeverría
Lake
Petén Itza
El Cruce
Flores
Apic-Pac
El Sumidero
Chamula
Ocosingo
Maya
Mountains
Save
Fc
Re
Ocozocautla
Bonampak
Sayaxché
Dolores
Cintlapa
Tuxtla
Gutiérrez
Chiapa
de Corzo
San Cristóbal
de las Casas
Benemérito
El Ceibal
San Ant
Amatenango
Poptún
Pueblo
Viejo
Arriaga
Villa Flores
Venustiano
Carranza
Comitán
Sarstoon
River
Livingsto
Paredón
Tonalá
Buenavista
San
Mateo
Ixtatán
Barillas
Raxruhá
Sebol
Modesto
Méndez
Sto T
de
Puerto Arista
Presa de la
Angostura
Chisec
Cahabón
El Estor
Izabal
Pijijiapan
Todos Santos
Cuchumatán
Lanquín
Senahú
Mariscos
La Mesilla
Nebaj
Chajul
Santa Cruz
Tactic
Tucurú
Los Amates
Mapastepec
Huehuetenango
Chiantla
Aguacatán
Sacapulas
Cobán
GUATEMALA
Dulce Nom
Huixtla
San
Marcos
Momostenango
Salamá
Zacapa
Copán
Tapachula
Talismán
Totonicapán
Rabinal
El Rancho
Chiquimula
Jocotán
Quetzaltenango
Quiché
Chichicastenango
El Progreso
Ocote
Puerto Madero
Tecún
Umán
Sololá
Chimaltenango
GUATEMALA
CITY
Jalapa
Agua
Caliente
La P
Mazatenango
Pinajachel
Lake
Atitlán
Antigua
Anguiatú
Retalhuleu
Amatitlán
Cuilapa
Jutiapa
Metapán
Champerico
Escuintla
Lago de Guija
Chalatenan
Tulate
Semillero
Santa Ana
Ahuachapán
SAN SALVAD
Tecojate
Sipacate
San José
Pedro de
Alvarado
Sonsonate
Acajutla
La Libertad
EL
SALVADO

Gulf of Tehuantepec

Pacific Ocean

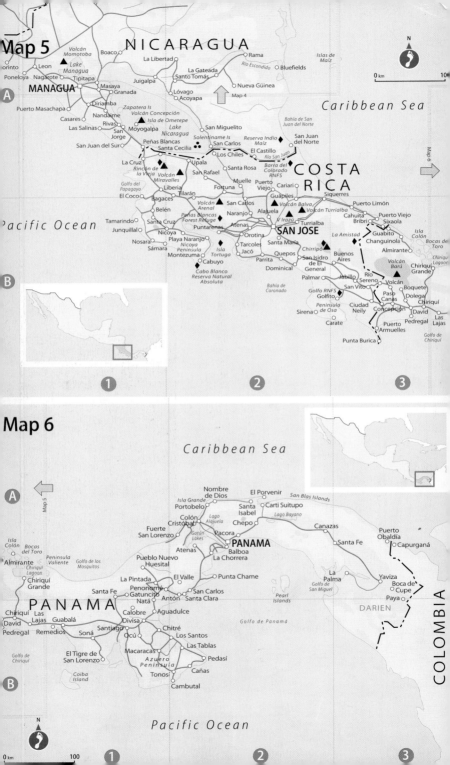